WHO WAS WHO

VOLUME IX

1991–1995

WHO'S WHO

*An annual biographical dictionary
first published in 1849*

WHO WAS WHO

Published by
A & C BLACK

WHO WAS WHO

1991–1995

A COMPANION TO

WHO'S WHO

CONTAINING THE BIOGRAPHIES
OF THOSE WHO DIED DURING
THE PERIOD 1991–1995

A & C BLACK
LONDON

FIRST PUBLISHED 1996
BY A & C BLACK (PUBLISHERS) LIMITED
35 BEDFORD ROW LONDON WC1R 4JH

COPYRIGHT © 1996 A & C BLACK (PUBLISHERS) LTD

ISBN 0 7136 4496 6

Entries from Who Was Who may not be reproduced, in any form whatsoever, without the written permission of the publishers.

The publishers make no representation, express or implied, with regard to the accuracy of the information contained in this book and cannot accept any legal responsibility for any errors or omissions that may take place.

Typeset by Clowes Computer Composition, printed and bound in Great Britain by William Clowes Ltd, Beccles and London

PREFACE

This, the ninth volume of biographies removed from *Who's Who* on account of death, contains the entries of those who died between 1991 and 1995. Those whose deaths were not notified until after this volume went to press are listed as Addenda at the beginning of the biographical section.

The entries are as they last appeared in *Who's Who*, with the date of death added and in some cases further information, such as posthumous publications. It has not always been possible to ascertain the exact date of death, and the editors will welcome such information for inclusion in the next edition of this volume.

This volume is the first to cover a five-year period rather than a decade – an innovation made in response to demand that additions to the *Who Was Who* series should appear more frequently. Its publication coincides with that of the CD-Rom *Who's Who 1897–1996: one hundred years of biography*, which comprises *Who Was Who* volumes I–IX and *Who's Who 1996*. It is hoped that this application of new technology to *Who Was Who* will open up areas of interest and research to historians and general users alike.

CONTENTS

ABBREVIATIONS USED IN THIS BOOK

Some of the designatory letters in this list are used merely for economy of space and do not necessarily imply any professional or other qualification.

A

AA Anti-aircraft; Automobile Association; Architectural Association; Augustinians of the Assumption
AAA Amateur Athletic Association; American Accounting Association
AAAL American Academy of Arts and Letters
AA&QMG Assistant Adjutant and Quartermaster-General
AAAS American Association for the Advancement of Science
AAC Army Air Corps
AACCA Associate, Association of Certified and Corporate Accountants (*now see* ACCA)
AACE Association for Adult and Continuing Education
AAF Auxiliary Air Force (*now see* RAux AF)
AAFCE Allied Air Forces in Central Europe
AAG Assistant Adjutant-General
AAI Associate, Chartered Auctioneers' and Estate Agents' Institute (*now* (after amalgamation) *see* ARICS)
AAIL American Academy and Institute of Arts and Letters (*now see* AAAL)
AAM Association of Assistant Mistresses in Secondary Schools
AAMC Australian Army Medical Corps (*now see* RAAMC)
A&AEE Aeroplane and Armament Experimental Establishment
A and SH Argyll and Sutherland Highlanders
AAPS Aquatic and Atmospheric Physical Sciences
AAS American Astronomical Society
AASA Associate, Australian Society of Accountants (*now see* FCPA)
AASC Australian Army Service Corps
AATSE Australian Academy of Technological Sciences and Engineering
AAUQ Associate in Accountancy, University of Queensland
AB Bachelor of Arts (US); able-bodied seaman; airborne
ABA Amateur Boxing Association; Antiquarian Booksellers' Association; American Bar Association
ABC Australian Broadcasting Commission; American Broadcasting Companies; Amateur Boxing Club
ABCA Army Bureau of Current Affairs
ABCC Association of British Chambers of Commerce
ABCFM American Board of Commissioners for Foreign Missions
ABI Association of British Insurers
ABIA Associate, Bankers' Institute of Australasia
ABINZ Associate, Bankers' Institute of New Zealand
ABIS Association of Burglary Insurance Surveyors
ABM Advisory Board of Ministry
ABNM American Board of Nuclear Medicine
ABP Associated British Ports
Abp Archbishop
ABPsS Associate, British Psychological Society (*now see* AFBPsS)
ABRC Advisory Board for the Research Councils
ABS Associate, Building Societies' Institute (*now see* ACBSI)
ABSA Association for Business Sponsorship of the Arts
ABSI Associate, Boot and Shoe Institution
ABSM Associate, Birmingham and Midland Institute School of Music
ABTA Association of British Travel Agents
ABTAPL Association of British Theological and Philosophical Libraries
AC Companion, Order of Australia; *Ante Christum* (before Christ)
ACA Associate, Institute of Chartered Accountants
Acad. Academy
ACARD Advisory Council for Applied Research and Development
ACAS Advisory, Conciliation and Arbitration Service; Assistant Chief of the Air Staff
ACBSI Associate, Chartered Building Societies Institute
ACC Association of County Councils; Anglican Consultative Council
ACCA Associate, Chartered Association of Certified Accountants

ACCEL American College of Cardiology Extended Learning
ACCM Advisory Council for the Church's Ministry (*now see* ABM)
ACCS Associate, Corporation of Secretaries (*formerly* of Certified Secretaries)
ACDP Australian Committee of Directors and Principals
ACDS Assistant Chief of Defence Staff
ACE Association of Consulting Engineers; Member, Association of Conference Executives
ACF Army Cadet Force
ACFA Army Cadet Force Association
ACFAS Association Canadienne-Française pour l'avancement des sciences
ACFHE Association of Colleges for Further and Higher Education
ACG Assistant Chaplain-General
ACGI Associate, City and Guilds of London Institute
ACGS Assistant Chief of the General Staff
ACIArb Associate, Chartered Institute of Arbitrators
ACIB Associate, Chartered Institute of Bankers
ACII Associate, Chartered Insurance Institute
ACIS Associate, Institute of Chartered Secretaries and Administrators (*formerly* Chartered Institute of Secretaries)
ACIT Associate, Chartered Institute of Transport
ACLS American Council of Learned Societies
ACM Association of Computing Machinery
ACMA Associate, Chartered Institute of Management Accountants (*formerly* Institute of Cost and Management Accountants)
ACNS Assistant Chief of Naval Staff
ACommA Associate, Society of Commercial Accountants (*now see* ASCA)
ACORD Advisory Committee on Research and Development
ACOS Assistant Chief of Staff
ACOST Advisory Council on Science and Technology
ACP Association of Clinical Pathologists; Associate, College of Preceptors; African/Caribbean/Pacific
ACPO Association of Chief Police Officers
ACRE Action with Rural Communities in England
ACS American Chemical Society; Additional Curates Society
ACSEA Allied Command South East Asia
ACSM Associate, Camborne School of Mines
ACT Australian Capital Territory; Australian College of Theology; Associate, College of Technology; Association of Corporate Treasurers
ACTT Association of Cinematograph, Television and Allied Technicians
ACTU Australian Council of Trade Unions
ACU Association of Commonwealth Universities
ACWA Associate, Institute of Cost and Works Accountants (*now see* ACMA)
AD Dame of the Order of Australia; *Anno Domini* (in the year of the Lord); Air Defence
aD ausser Dienst
ADAS Agricultural Development and Advisory Service
ADB Asian Development Bank; Associate of the Drama Board (Education)
ADB/F African Development Bank/Fund
ADC Aide-de-camp
ADCM Archbishop of Canterbury's Diploma in Church Music
AD Corps Army Dental Corps (*now* RADC)
ADC(P) Personal Aide-de-camp to HM The Queen
ADEME Assistant Director Electrical and Mechanical Engineering
Ad eund *Ad eundem gradum*; and *see under* aeg
ADFManc Art and Design Fellow, Manchester
ADFW Assistant Director of Fortifications and Works
ADGB Air Defence of Great Britain
ADGMS Assistant Director-General of Medical Services
ADH Assistant Director of Hygiene
Adjt Adjutant
ADJAG Assistant Deputy Judge Advocate General
ADK Order of Ahli Darjah Kinabalu

Adm.	Admiral
ADMS	Assistant Director of Medical Services
ADOS	Assistant Director of Ordnance Services
ADP	Automatic Data Processing
ADPA	Associate Diploma of Public Administration
ADS&T	Assistant Director of Supplies and Transport
Adv.	Advisory; Advocate
ADVS	Assistant Director of Veterinary Services
ADWE&M	Assistant Director of Works, Electrical and Mechanical
AE	Air Efficiency Award
AEA	Atomic Energy Authority; Air Efficiency Award (*now see* AE)
AEAF	Allied Expeditionary Air Force
AEC	Agriculture Executive Council; Army Educational Corps (*now see* RAEC); Atomic Energy Commission
AECMA	Association Européenne des Constructeurs de Matériel Aérospatial
AEE	Atomic Energy Establishment
AEEU	Amalgamated Engineering and Electrical Union
AEF	Amalgamated Union of Engineering and Foundry Workers (*later* AEU, *now see* AEEU); American Expeditionary Forces
aeg	*ad eundem gradum* (to the same degree—of the admission of a graduate of one university to the same degree at another without examination)
AEGIS	Aid for the Elderly in Government Institutions
AEI	Associated Electrical Industries
AEM	Air Efficiency Medal
AER	Army Emergency Reserve
AERE	Atomic Energy Research Establishment (Harwell)
Æt., Ætat.	*Ætatis* (aged)
AEU	Amalgamated Engineering Union (*now see* AEEU)
AF	Admiral of the Fleet
AFA	Amateur Football Alliance
AFAIAA	Associate Fellow, American Institute of Aeronautics and Astronautics
AFASIC	Association for All Speech Impaired Children
AFB	Air Force Base
AFBPsS	Associate Fellow, British Psychological Society
AFC	Air Force Cross; Association Football Club
AfC	Association for Colleges
AFCAI	Associate Fellow, Canadian Aeronautical Institute
AFCEA	Armed Forces Communications and Electronics Association
AFCENT	Allied Forces in Central Europe
AFD	Doctor of Fine Arts (US)
AFDS	Air Fighting Development Squadron
AFHQ	Allied Force Headquarters
AFI	American Film Institute
AFIA	Associate, Federal Institute of Accountants (Australia)
AFIAP	Artiste, Fédération Internationale de l'Art Photographique
AFIAS	Associate Fellow, Institute of Aeronautical Sciences (US) (*now see* AFAIAA)
AFICD	Associate Fellow, Institute of Civil Defence
AFIMA	Associate Fellow, Institute of Mathematics and its Applications
AFM	Air Force Medal
AFNORTH	Allied Forces in Northern Europe
AFOM	Associate, Faculty of Occupational Medicine
AFRAeS	Associate Fellow, Royal Aeronautical Society (*now see* MRAeS)
AFRC	Agricultural and Food Research Council (*now see* BBSRC)
AFV	Armoured Fighting Vehicles
AG	Attorney-General
AGAC	American Guild of Authors and Composers
AGARD	Advisory Group for Aerospace Research and Development
AGC	Adjutant General's Corps
AGH	Australian General Hospital
AGI	Artistes Graphiques Internationaux; Associate, Institute of Certificated Grocers
AGR	Advanced Gas-cooled Reactor
AGRA	Army Group Royal Artillery; Association of Genealogists and Record Agents
AGSM	Associate, Guildhall School of Music and Drama; Australian Graduate School of Management
AHA	Area Health Authority; American Hospitals Association; Associate, Institute of Health Service Administrators (*now see* AHSM)
AHA(T)	Area Health Authority (Teaching)
AHQ	Army Headquarters
AHSM	Associate, Institute of Health Services Management
AH-WC	Associate, Heriot-Watt College, Edinburgh

ai	*ad interim*
AIA	Associate, Institute of Actuaries; American Institute of Architects; Association of International Artists
AIAA	American Institute of Aeronautics and Astronautics
AIAgrE	Associate, Institution of Agricultural Engineers
AIAL	Associate Member, International Institute of Arts and Letters
AIArb	Associate, Institute of Arbitrators (*now see* ACIArb)
AIAS	Associate Surveyor Member, Incorporated Association of Architects and Surveyors
AIB	Associate, Institute of Bankers (*now see* ACIB)
AIBD	Associate, Institute of British Decorators
AIBP	Associate, Institute of British Photographers
AIBScot	Associate, Institute of Bankers in Scotland
AIC	Agricultural Improvement Council; Associate of the Institute of Chemistry (*later* ARIC, MRIC; *now see* MRSC)
AICA	Associate Member, Commonwealth Institute of Accountants; Association Internationale des Critiques d'Art
AICC	All-India Congress Committee
AICE	Associate, Institution of Civil Engineers
AIChE	American Institute of Chemical Engineers
AICPA	American Institute of Certified Public Accountants
AICS	Associate, Institute of Chartered Shipbrokers
AICTA	Associate, Imperial College of Tropical Agriculture
AID	Agency for International Development (USA)
AIDS	Acquired Immunity Deficiency Syndrome
AIE	Associate, Institute of Education
AIEE	Associate, Institution of Electrical Engineers
AIF	Australian Imperial Forces
AIG	Adjutant-Inspector-General
AIH	Associate, Institute of Housing
AIHort	Associate, Institute of Horticulture
AIIA	Associate, Insurance Institute of America; Associate, Indian Institute of Architects
AIIMR	Associate, Institute of Investment Management and Research
AIInfSc	Associate, Institute of Information Scientists
AIIRA	Associate, International Industrial Relations Association
AIL	Associate, Institute of Linguists
AILA	Associate, Institute of Landscape Architects (*now see* ALI)
AILocoE	Associate, Institute of Locomotive Engineers
AIM	Associate, Institution of Metallurgists (*now see* MIM); Australian Institute of Management
AIMarE	Associate, Institute of Marine Engineers
AIMC	Associate, Institute of Management Consultants
AIME	American Institute of Mechanical Engineers
AIMgt	Associate, Institute of Management
AIMSW	Associate, Institute of Medical Social Workers
AInstM	Associate Member, Institute of Marketing
AInstP	Associate, Institute of Physics
AInstPI	Associate, Institute of Patentees and Inventors
AIP	Association of Independent Producers
AIPR	Associate, Institute of Public Relations
AIProdE	Associate, Institution of Production Engineers
AIQS	Associate Member, Institute of Quantity Surveyors
AIRTE	Associate, Institute of Road Transport Engineers
AIRTO	Association of Independent Research and Technology Organizations
AIS	Associate, Institute of Statisticians (*later* MIS)
AISA	Associate, Incorporated Secretaries' Association
AIStructE	Associate, Institution of Structural Engineers
AITI	Associate, Institute of Translators and Interpreters
AITP	Associate, Institute of Town Planners, India
AJAG	Assistant Judge Advocate General
AJEX	Association of Jewish Ex-Service Men and Women
AK	Knight, Order of Australia; Alaska
AKC	Associate, King's College London
AL	Alabama
ALA	Associate, Library Association; Association of London Authorities
Ala	Alabama (US)
ALAA	Associate, Library Association of Australia
ALAI	Associate, Library Association of Ireland
ALAM	Associate, London Academy of Music and Dramatic Art
ALCD	Associate, London College of Divinity
ALCM	Associate, London College of Music
ALCS	Authors Lending and Copyright Society
ALFSEA	Allied Land Forces South-East Asia
ALI	Argyll Light Infantry; Associate, Landscape Institute
ALICE	Autistic and Language Impaired Children's Education
ALLC	Association for Literary and Linguistic Computing
ALP	Australian Labor Party

ALPSP	Association of Learned and Professional Society Publishers
ALS	Associate, Linnean Society
Alta	Alberta
ALVA	Association of Leading Visitor Attractions
AM	Albert Medal; Member, Order of Australia; Master of Arts (US); Alpes Maritimes
AMA	Association of Metropolitan Authorities; Assistant Masters Association (later AMMA, *now see* ATL); Associate, Museums Association; Australian Medical Association
AMARC	Associated Marine and Related Charities
Amb.	Ambulance; Ambassador
AMBDA	Associate Member, British Dyslexia Association
AMBIM	Associate Member, British Institute of Management (*now see* AIMgt)
AMBritIRE	Associate Member, British Institution of Radio Engineers (*now see* AMIERE)
AMC	Association of Municipal Corporations
AMCST	Associate, Manchester College of Science and Technology
AMCT	Associate, Manchester College of Technology
AME	Association of Municipal Engineers
AMEME	Association of Mining Electrical and Mechanical Engineers
AMet	Associate of Metallurgy
AMF	Australian Military Forces
AMGOT	Allied Military Government of Occupied Territory
AMIAE	Associate Member, Institution of Automobile Engineers
AMIAgrE	Associate Member, Institution of Agricultural Engineers
AMIBF	Associate Member, Institute of British Foundrymen
AMICE	Associate Member, Institution of Civil Engineers (*now see* MICE)
AMIChemE	Associate Member, Institution of Chemical Engineers
AMIE(Aust)	Associate Member, Institution of Engineers, Australia
AMIED	Associate Member, Institution of Engineering Designers
AMIEE	Associate Member, Institution of Electrical Engineers (*now see* MIEE)
AMIE(Ind)	Associate Member, Institution of Engineers, India
AMIERE	Associate Member, Institution of Electronic and Radio Engineers
AMIH	Associate Member, Institute of Housing
AMIMechE	Associate Member, Institution of Mechanical Engineers (*now see* MIMechE)
AMIMinE	Associate Member, Institution of Mining Engineers
AMIMM	Associate Member, Institution of Mining and Metallurgy
AMInstBE	Associate Member, Institution of British Engineers
AMInstCE	Associate Member, Institution of Civil Engineers (*now see* MICE)
AmInstEE	American Institute of Electrical Engineers
AMInstR	Associate Member, Institute of Refrigeration
AMInstT	Associate Member, Institute of Transport (*now see* ACIT)
AMInstTA	Associate Member, Institute of Traffic Administration
AMINucE	Associate Member, Institution of Nuclear Engineers
AMIRSE	Associate Member, Institute of Railway Signalling Engineers
AMIStructE	Associate Member, Institution of Structural Engineers
AMMA	Assistant Masters & Mistresses Association (*now see* ATL)
AMN	Ahli Mangku Negara (Malaysia)
AMP	Advanced Management Program; Air Member for Personnel
AMRINA	Associate Member, Royal Institution of Naval Architects
AMS	Assistant Military Secretary; Army Medical Services
AMSO	Air Member for Supply and Organisation
AMTE	Admiralty Marine Technology Establishment
AMTRI	Advanced Manufacturing Technology Research Institute
ANA	Associate National Academician (America)
ANAF	Arab Non-Arab Friendship
Anat.	Anatomy; Anatomical
ANC	African National Congress
ANECInst	Associate, NE Coast Institution of Engineers and Shipbuilders
ANGAU	Australian New Guinea Administrative Unit
Anon.	Anonymously
ANU	Australian National University
ANZAAS	Australian and New Zealand Association for the Advancement of Science
Anzac	Australian and New Zealand Army Corps
AO	Officer, Order of Australia; Air Officer
AOA	Air Officer in charge of Administration

AOC	Air Officer Commanding
AOC-in-C	Air Officer Commanding-in-Chief
AOD	Army Ordnance Department
AOER	Army Officers Emergency Reserve
APA	American Psychiatric Association
APACS	Association of Payment and Clearing Systems
APCK	Association for Promoting Christian Knowledge, Church of Ireland
APD	Army Pay Department
APEX	Association of Professional, Executive, Clerical and Computer Staff
APHA	American Public Health Association
APIS	Army Photographic Intelligence Service
APM	Assistant Provost Marshal
APMI	Associate, Pensions Management Institute
APR	Accredited Public Relations Practitioner
APS	Aborigines Protection Society; American Physical Society
APsSI	Associate, Psychological Society of Ireland
APSW	Association of Psychiatric Social Workers
APT&C	Administrative, Professional, Technical and Clerical
APTC	Army Physical Training Corps
AQ	Administration and Quartering
AQMG	Assistant Quartermaster-General
AR	Associated Rediffusion (Television); Arkansas
ARA	Associate, Royal Academy
ARACI	Associate, Royal Australian Chemical Institute
ARAD	Associate, Royal Academy of Dancing
ARAeS	Associate, Royal Aeronautical Society
ARAgS	Associate, Royal Agricultural Societies (*ie* of England, Scotland and Wales)
ARAIA	Associate, Royal Australian Institute of Architects
ARAM	Associate, Royal Academy of Music
ARAS	Associate, Royal Astronomical Society
ARBA	Associate, Royal Society of British Artists
ARBC	Associate, Royal British Colonial Society of Artists
ARBS	Associate, Royal Society of British Sculptors
ARC	Architects' Registration Council; Agricultural Research Council (later AFRC); Aeronautical Research Council
ARCA	Associate, Royal College of Art; Associate, Royal Canadian Academy
ARCamA	Associate, Royal Cambrian Academy of Art
ARCE	Academical Rank of Civil Engineer
ARCIC	Anglican-Roman Catholic International Commission
ARCM	Associate, Royal College of Music
ARCO	Associate, Royal College of Organists
ARCO(CHM)	Associate, Royal College of Organists with Diploma in Choir Training
ARCPsych	Associate Member, Royal College of Psychiatrists
ARCS	Associate, Royal College of Science
ARCST	Associate, Royal College of Science and Technology (Glasgow)
ARCUK	Architects' Registration Council of the United Kingdom
ARCVS	Associate, Royal College of Veterinary Surgeons
ARE	Associate, Royal Society of Painter-Printmakers (*formerly* of Painter-Etchers and Engravers); Arab Republic of Egypt; Admiralty Research Establishment
AREINZ	Associate, Real Estate Institute, New Zealand
ARELS	Association of Recognised English Language Schools
ARIAS	Associate, Royal Incorporation of Architects in Scotland
ARIBA	Associate, Royal Institute of British Architects (*now see* RIBA)
ARIC	Associate, Royal Institute of Chemistry (later MRIC; *now see* MRSC)
ARICS	Professional Associate, Royal Institution of Chartered Surveyors
ARINA	Associate, Royal Institution of Naval Architects
Ark	Arkansas (US)
ARLT	Association for the Reform of Latin Teaching
ARMS	Associate, Royal Society of Miniature Painters
ARP	Air Raid Precautions
ARPS	Associate, Royal Photographic Society
ARR	Association of Radiation Research
ARRC	Associate, Royal Red Cross
ARSA	Associate, Royal Scottish Academy
ARSC	Association of Recorded Sound Collections
ARSCM	Associate, Royal School of Church Music
ARSM	Associate, Royal School of Mines
ARTC	Associate, Royal Technical College (Glasgow) (*now see* ARCST)
ARVIA	Associate, Royal Victoria Institute of Architects
ARWA	Associate, Royal West of England Academy
ARWS	Associate, Royal Society of Painters in Water-Colours
AS	Anglo-Saxon

ASA	Associate Member, Society of Actuaries; Associate of Society of Actuaries (US); Australian Society of Accountants; Army Sailing Association; Advertising Standards Authority
ASAA	Associate, Society of Incorporated Accountants and Auditors
ASAI	Associate, Society of Architectural Illustrators
ASAM	Associate, Society of Art Masters
AS&TS of SA	Associated Scientific and Technical Societies of South Africa
ASBAH	Association for Spina Bifida and Hydrocephalus
ASC	Administrative Staff College, Henley
ASCA	Associate, Society of Company and Commercial Accountants
ASCAB	Armed Services Consultant Approval Board
ASCAP	American Society of Composers, Authors and Publishers
ASCE	American Society of Civil Engineers
ASCHB	Association for Study of Conservation of Historic Buildings
AScW	Association of Scientific Workers (*now see* ASTMS)
ASD	Armament Supply Department
ASE	Amalgamated Society of Engineers (later AUEW, then AEU; *now see* AEEU); Association for Science Education
ASEAN	Association of South East Asian Nations
ASH	Action on Smoking and Health
ASIAD	Associate, Society of Industrial Artists and Designers
ASIA(Ed)	Associate, Society of Industrial Artists (Education)
ASLE	American Society of Lubrication Engineers
ASLEF	Associated Society of Locomotive Engineers and Firemen
ASLIB or Aslib	Association for Information Management (*formerly* Association of Special Libraries and Information Bureaux)
ASM	Association of Senior Members
ASME	American Society of Mechanical Engineers; Association for the Study of Medical Education
ASO	Air Staff Officer
ASSC	Accounting Standards Steering Committee
ASSET	Association of Supervisory Staffs, Executives and Technicians (*now see* ASTMS)
AssocISI	Associate, Iron and Steel Institute
AssocMCT	Associateship of Manchester College of Technology
AssocMIAeE	Associate Member, Institution of Aeronautical Engineers
AssocRINA	Associate, Royal Institution of Naval Architects
AssocSc	Associate in Science
Asst	Assistant
ASTA	Association of Short Circuit Testing Authorities
ASTC	Administrative Service Training Course
ASTMS	Association of Scientific, Technical and Managerial Staffs (now part of MSF)
ASVU	Army Security Vetting Unit
ASWDU	Air Sea Warfare Development Unit
ASWE	Admiralty Surface Weapons Establishment
ATA	Air Transport Auxiliary
ATAE	Association of Tutors in Adult Education
ATAF	Allied Tactical Air Force
ATC	Air Training Corps; Art Teacher's Certificate
ATCDE	Association of Teachers in Colleges and Departments of Education (*now see* NATFHE)
ATCL	Associate, Trinity College of Music, London
ATD	Art Teacher's Diploma
ATI	Associate, Textile Institute
ATII	Associate Member, Chartered Institute (*formerly* Incorporated Institute, then Institute) of Taxation
ATL	Association of Teachers and Lecturers
ato	Ammunition Technical Officer
ATPL (A)or(H)	Airline Transport Pilot's Licence (Aeroplanes), or (Helicopters)
ATS	Auxiliary Territorial Service (*now see* WRAC)
ATTI	Association of Teachers in Technical Institutions (*now see* NATFHE)
ATV	Association TeleVision
AUA	American Urological Association
AUCAS	Association of University Clinical Academic Staff
AUEW	Amalgamated Union of Engineering Workers (later AEU, *now see* AEEU)
AUS	Army of the United States
AUT	Association of University Teachers
AVCC	Australian Vice-Chancellors' Committee
AVCM	Associate, Victoria College of Music
AVD	Army Veterinary Department
AVLA	Audio Visual Language Association
AVR	Army Volunteer Reserve
AWA	Anglian Water Authority
AWO	Association of Water Officers (*now see* IWO)
AWRE	Atomic Weapons Research Establishment

aws	Graduate of Air Warfare Course
AZ	Arizona

B

b	born; brother
BA	Bachelor of Arts
BAA	British Airports Authority
BAAB	British Amateur Athletic Board
BAAL	British Association for Applied Linguistics
BAAS	British Association for the Advancement of Science
BAB	British Airways Board
BAC	British Aircraft Corporation
BACM	British Association of Colliery Management
BACUP	British Association of Cancer United Patients
BAe	British Aerospace
BAED	Bachelor of Arts in Environmental Design
B&FBS	British and Foreign Bible Society
BAFO	British Air Forces of Occupation
BAFPA	British Association of Fitness Promotion Agencies
BAFTA	British Academy of Film and Television Arts
BAG	Business Art Galleries
BAgrSc	Bachelor of Agricultural Science
BAI	*Baccalarius in Arte Ingeniaria* (Bachelor of Engineering)
BAIE	British Association of Industrial Editors
BALPA	British Air Line Pilots' Association
BAO	Bachelor of Art of Obstetrics
BAOMS	British Association of Oral and Maxillo-Facial Surgeons
BAOR	British Army of the Rhine (formerly *on* the Rhine)
BAOS	British Association of Oral Surgeons (*now see* BAOMS)
BAppSc(MT)	Bachelor of Applied Science (Medical Technology)
BARB	Broadcasters' Audience Research Board
BARC	British Automobile Racing Club
BArch	Bachelor of Architecture
Bart	Baronet
BAS	Bachelor in Agricultural Science
BASc	Bachelor of Applied Science
BASCA	British Academy of Songwriters, Composers and Authors
BASEEFA	British Approvals Service for Electrical Equipment in Flammable Atmospheres
BASW	British Association of Social Workers
Batt.	Battery
BBA	British Bankers' Association; Bachelor of Business Administration
BB&CIRly	Bombay, Baroda and Central India Railway
BBB of C	British Boxing Board of Control
BBC	British Broadcasting Corporation
BBFC	British Board of Film Classification
BBM	Bintang Bakti Masharakat (Public Service Star) (Singapore)
BBS	Bachelor of Business Studies
BBSRC	Biotechnology and Biosciences Research Council
BC	Before Christ; British Columbia; Borough Council
BCAR	British Civil Airworthiness Requirements
BCC	British Council of Churches (*now see* CCBI)
BCE	Bachelor of Civil Engineering; Before the Christian Era
BCh or BChir	Bachelor of Surgery
BChD	Bachelor of Dental Surgery
BCIA	British Clothing Industries Association
BCL	Bachelor of Civil Law
BCMF	British Ceramic Manufacturers' Federation
BCMS	Bible Churchmen's Missionary Society
BCOF	British Commonwealth Occupation Force
BCom or BComm	Bachelor of Commerce
BComSc	Bachelor of Commercial Science
BCPC	British Crop Protection Council
BCS	Bengal Civil Service; British Computer Society
BCSA	British Constructional Steelwork Association
BCURA	British Coal Utilization Research Association
BCYC	British Corinthian Yacht Club
BD	Bachelor of Divinity
Bd	Board
BDA	British Dental Association; British Deaf Association; British Dyslexia Association
Bde	Brigade
BDQ	Bachelor of Divinity Qualifying
BDS	Bachelor of Dental Surgery
BDSc	Bachelor of Dental Science
BE	Bachelor of Engineering; British Element

BEA	British East Africa; British European Airways; British Epilepsy Association
BEAMA	Federation of British Electrotechnical and Allied Manufacturers' Associations (formerly British Electrical and Allied Manufacturers' Association)
BE&A	Bachelor of Engineering and Architecture (Malta)
BEAS	British Educational Administration Society
BEC	Business Education Council (now see BTEC)
BEc	Bachelor of Economics
BECTU	Broadcasting, Entertainment, Cinematograph and Theatre Union
BEd	Bachelor of Education
Beds	Bedfordshire
BEE	Bachelor of Electrical Engineering
BEF	British Expeditionary Force; British Equestrian Federation
BEM	British Empire Medal
BEMAS	British Education Management and Administration Society
BEME	Brigade Electrical and Mechanical Engineer
BEng	Bachelor of Engineering
BEO	Base Engineer Officer
Berks	Berkshire
BESO	British Executive Service Overseas
BEVA	British Equine Veterinary Association
BFI	British Film Institute
BFMIRA	British Food Manufacturing Industries Research Association
BFPO	British Forces Post Office
BFSS	British Field Sports Society
BFWG	British Federation of Women Graduates
BGS	Brigadier General Staff
BHA	British Hospitality Association
Bhd	Berhad
BHF	British Heart Foundation
BHRA	British Hydromechanics Research Association
BHRCA	British Hotels, Restaurants and Caterers' Association (now see BHA)
BHS	British Horse Society
BI	British Invisibles
BIBA	British Insurance Brokers' Association (now see BIIBA)
BIBRA	British Industrial Biological Research Association
BICC	British Insulated Callender's Cables
BICERA	British Internal Combustion Engine Research Association (now see BICERI)
BICERI	British Internal Combustion Engine Research Institute
BICSc	British Institute of Cleaning Science
BIEC	British Invisible Exports Council (now see BI)
BIEE	British Institute of Energy Economics
BIF	British Industries Fair
BIFU	Banking Insurance and Finance Union
BIIBA	British Insurance & Investment Brokers' Association
BIM	British Institute of Management
BIR	British Institute of Radiology
BIS	Bank for International Settlements
BISF	British Iron and Steel Federation
BISFA	British Industrial and Scientific Film Association
BISPA	British Independent Steel Producers Association
BISRA	British Iron and Steel Research Association
BITC	Business in the Community
BJ	Bachelor of Journalism
BJSM	British Joint Services Mission
BKSTS	British Kinematograph, Sound and Television Society
BL	Bachelor of Law; British Library
BLA	British Liberation Army
BLDSA	British Long Distance Swimming Association
BLE	Brotherhood of Locomotive Engineers; Bachelor of Land Economy
BLegS	Bachelor of Legal Studies
BLESMA	British Limbless Ex-Servicemen's Association
BLitt	Bachelor of Letters
BM	British Museum; Bachelor of Medicine; Brigade Major; British Monomark
BMA	British Medical Association
BMedSci	Bachelor of Medical Science
BMEO	British Middle East Office
BMet	Bachelor of Metallurgy
BMEWS	Ballistic Missile Early Warning System
BMG	British Military Government
BMH	British Military Hospital
BMilSc	Bachelor of Military Science
BMJ	British Medical Journal
BMM	British Military Mission
BMR	Bureau of Mineral Resources
BMRA	Brigade Major Royal Artillery
Bn	Battalion
BNAF	British North Africa Force
BNC	Brasenose College
BNEC	British National Export Council
BNF	British National Formulary
BNFL	British Nuclear Fuels Ltd
BNOC	British National Oil Corporation; British National Opera Company
BNP	Banque Nationale de Paris
BNSC	British National Space Centre
BNSc	Bachelor of Nursing Science
BOAC	British Overseas Airways Corporation
BomCS	Bombay Civil Service
BomSC	Bombay Staff Corps
BoT	Board of Trade
Bot.	Botany; Botanical
BOTB	British Overseas Trade Board
BOU	British Ornithologists' Union
Bp	Bishop
BPA	British Paediatric Association
BPG	Broadcasting Press Guild
BPharm	Bachelor of Pharmacy
BPIF	British Printing Industries Federation
BPMF	British Postgraduate Medical Federation
BPsS	British Psychological Society
BR	British Rail
Br.	Branch
BRA	Brigadier Royal Artillery; British Rheumatism & Arthritis Association
BRB	British Railways Board
BRCS	British Red Cross Society
BRE	Building Research Establishment
Brig.	Brigadier
BritIRE	British Institution of Radio Engineers (now see IERE)
BRNC	Britannia Royal Naval College
BRS	British Road Services
BRurSc	Bachelor of Rural Science
BS	Bachelor of Surgery; Bachelor of Science; British Standard
BSA	Bachelor of Scientific Agriculture; Birmingham Small Arms; Building Societies' Association
BSAA	British South American Airways
BSAP	British South Africa Police
BSC	British Steel Corporation; Bengal Staff Corps
BSc	Bachelor of Science
BScA, BScAgr	Bachelor of Science in Agriculture
BSc(Dent)	Bachelor of Science in Dentistry
BSc (Est. Man.)	Bachelor of Science in Estate Management
BScN	Bachelor of Science in Nursing
BScSoc	Bachelor of Social Sciences
BSE	Bachelor of Science in Engineering (US)
BSES	British Schools Exploring Society
BSF	British Salonica Force
BSFA	British Science Fiction Association
BSI	British Standards Institution
BSIA	British Security Industry Association
BSJA	British Show Jumping Association
BSME	Bachelor of Science in Mechanical Engineering; British Society of Magazine Editors
BSN	Bachelor of Science in Nursing
BSNS	Bachelor of Naval Science
BSocSc	Bachelor of Social Science
BSRA	British Ship Research Association
BSS	Bachelor of Science (Social Science)
BST	Bachelor of Sacred Theology
BSurv	Bachelor of Surveying
BT	Bachelor of Teaching; British Telecommunications
Bt	Baronet; Brevet
BTA	British Tourist Authority (formerly British Travel Association)
BTC	British Transport Commission
BTCV	British Trust for Conservation Volunteers
BTDB	British Transport Docks Board (now see ABP)
BTEC	Business and Technology (formerly Technician) Education Council
BTh	Bachelor of Theology
BTP	Bachelor of Town Planning
Btss	Baroness
Bty	Battery
BUAS	British Universities Association of Slavists
Bucks	Buckinghamshire
BUGB	Baptist Union of Great Britain
BUPA	British United Provident Association
BURA	British Urban Regeneration Association
BV	Besloten Vennootschap
BVA	British Veterinary Association
BVetMed	Bachelor of Veterinary Medicine
BVI	British Virgin Islands
BVM	Blessed Virgin Mary

BVMS	Bachelor of Veterinary Medicine and Surgery
BVSc	Bachelor of Veterinary Science
BWI	British West Indies
BWM	British War Medal

C

C	Conservative: 100
c	child; cousin; *circa* (about)
CA	Central America; County Alderman; Chartered Accountant (Scotland and Canada); California
CAA	Civil Aviation Authority
CAABU	Council for the Advancement of Arab and British Understanding
CAAV	(Member of) Central Association of Agricultural Valuers
CAB	Citizens' Advice Bureau; Centre for Agricultural and Biosciences (*formerly* Commonwealth Agricultural Bureau)
CACTM	Central Advisory Council of Training for the Ministry (later ACCM; *now see* ABM)
CAER	Conservative Action for Electoral Reform
CAFOD	Catholic Fund for Overseas Development
CALE	Canadian Army Liaison Executive
Calif	California (US)
CAM	Communications, Advertising and Marketing
Cambs	Cambridgeshire
CAMC	Canadian Army Medical Corps
CAMRA	Campaign for Real Ale
CAMS	Certificate of Advanced Musical Study
CAMW	Central Association for Mental Welfare
C&G	City and Guilds of London Institute
Cantab	*Cantabrigiensis* (of Cambridge)
Cantuar	*Cantuariensis* (of Canterbury)
CARD	Campaign against Racial Discrimination
CARE	Cottage and Rural Enterprises
CARICOM	Caribbean Community
CARIFTA	Caribbean Free Trade Area (*now see* CARICOM)
CAS	Chief of the Air Staff
CASI	Canadian Aeronautics and Space Institute
CAT	College of Advanced Technology; Countryside Around Towns
CATE	Council for the Accreditation of Teacher Education
Cav.	Cavalry
CAWU	Clerical and Administrative Workers' Union (later APEX)
CB	Companion, Order of the Bath; County Borough
CBC	County Borough Council
CBCO	Central Board for Conscientious Objectors
CBE	Commander, Order of the British Empire
CBI	Confederation of British Industry
CBIM	Companion, British Institute of Management (*now see* CIMgt)
CBiol	Chartered Biologist
CBNS	Commander British Navy Staff
CBS	Columbia Broadcasting System; Confraternity of the Blessed Sacrament
CBSA	Clay Bird Shooting Association
CBSI	Chartered Building Societies Institute (*now see* CIB)
CBSO	City of Birmingham Symphony Orchestra
CC	Companion, Order of Canada; City Council; County Council; Cricket Club; Cycling Club; County Court
CCAB	Consultative Committee of Accountancy Bodies
CCAHC	Central Council for Agricultural and Horticultural Co-operation
CCBE	Commission Consultative des Barreaux de la Communauté Européenne
CCBI	Council of Churches for Britain and Ireland
CCC	Corpus Christi College; Central Criminal Court; County Cricket Club
CCE	Chartered Civil Engineer
CCF	Combined Cadet Force
CCFM	Combined Cadet Forces Medal
CCG	Control Commission Germany
CCH	Cacique's Crown of Honour, Order of Service of Guyana
CChem	Chartered Chemist
CCHMS	Central Committee for Hospital Medical Services
CCIA	Commission of Churches on International Affairs
CCIS	Command Control Information System
CCJ	Council of Christians and Jews
CCPR	Central Council of Physical Recreation
CCRA	Commander Corps of Royal Artillery
CCRE	Commander Corps of Royal Engineers
CCREME	Commander Corps of Royal Electrical and Mechanical Engineers
CCRSigs	Commander Corps of Royal Signals

CCS	Casualty Clearing Station; Ceylon Civil Service; Countryside Commission for Scotland
CCSU	Council of Civil Service Unions
CCTA	Commission de Coopération Technique pour l'Afrique
CCTS	Combat Crew Training Squadron
CD	Canadian Forces Decoration; Commander, Order of Distinction (Jamaica); Civil Defence; Compact Disc
CDA	Co-operative Development Agency
CDEE	Chemical Defence Experimental Establishment
CDipAF	Certified Diploma in Accounting and Finance
Cdo	Commando
CDRA	Committee of Directors of Research Associations
Cdre	Commodore
CDS	Chief of the Defence Staff
CDU	Christlich-Demokratische Union
CE	Civil Engineer
CEA	Central Electricity Authority
CEC	Commission of the European Communities
CECD	Confédération Européenne du Commerce de Détail
CECG	Consumers in European Community Group
CEDEP	Centre Européen d'Education Permanente
CEE	Communauté Economique Européenne
CEED	Centre for Economic and Environmental Development
CEF	Canadian Expeditionary Force
CEFIC	Conseil Européen des Fédérations de l'Industrie Chimique
CEGB	Central Electricity Generating Board
CEI	Council of Engineering Institutions
CEIR	Corporation for Economic and Industrial Research
CEM	Council of European Municipalities (*now see* CEMR)
CEMA	Council for the Encouragement of Music and Arts
CEMR	Council of European Municipalities and Regions
CEMS	Church of England Men's Society
CEN	Comité Européen de Normalisation
CENELEC	European Committee for Electrotechnical Standardization
CEng	Chartered Engineer
Cento	Central Treaty Organisation
CEPT	Conférence Européenne des Postes et des Télécommunications
CERL	Central Electricity Research Laboratories
CERN	Organisation (*formerly* Centre) Européenne pour la Recherche Nucléaire
CERT	Charities Effectiveness Review Trust
Cert Ed	Certificate of Education
CertITP	Certificate of International Teachers' Program (Harvard)
CEST	Centre for Exploitation of Science and Technology
CET	Council for Educational Technology
CETS	Church of England Temperance Society
CF	Chaplain to the Forces
CFA	Canadian Field Artillery
CFE	Central Fighter Establishment
CFM	Cadet Forces Medal
CFR	Commander, Order of the Federal Republic of Nigeria
CFS	Central Flying School
CGA	Community of the Glorious Ascension; Country Gentlemen's Association
CGeol	Chartered Geologist
CGH	Order of the Golden Heart of Kenya (1st class)
CGIA	Insignia Award of City and Guilds of London Institute (*now see* FCGI)
CGLI	City and Guilds of London Institute (*now see* C&G)
CGM	Conspicuous Gallantry Medal
CGRM	Commandant-General Royal Marines
CGS	Chief of the General Staff
CH	Companion of Honour
Chanc.	Chancellor; Chancery
Chap.	Chaplain
ChapStJ	Chaplain, Order of St John of Jerusalem (*now see* ChStJ)
CHAR	Campaign for the Homeless and Rootless
CHB	Companion of Honour of Barbados
ChB	Bachelor of Surgery
CHC	Community Health Council
Ch.Ch.	Christ Church
Ch.Coll.	Christ's College
CHE	Campaign for Homosexual Equality
ChLJ	Chaplain, Order of St Lazarus of Jerusalem
CHM	Chevalier of Honour and Merit (Haiti)
(CHM)	*See under* ARCO(CHM), FRCO(CHM)
ChM	Master of Surgery
Chm.	Chairman or Chairwoman
CHN	Community of the Holy Name
CHSC	Central Health Services Council
ChStJ	Chaplain, Most Venerable Order of the Hospital of St John of Jerusalem
CI	Imperial Order of the Crown of India; Channel Islands

CIA	Chemical Industries Association; Central Intelligence Agency
CIAD	Central Institute of Art and Design
CIAgrE	Companion, Institution of Agricultural Engineers
CIAL	Corresponding Member of the International Institute of Arts and Letters
CIArb	Chartered Institute of Arbitrators
CIB	Chartered Institute of Bankers
CIBS	Chartered Institution of Building Services (*now see* CIBSE)
CIBSE	Chartered Institution of Building Services Engineers
CIC	Chemical Institute of Canada
CICB	Criminal Injuries Compensation Board
CICHE	Committee for International Co-operation in Higher Education
CICI	Confederation of Information Communication Industries
CID	Criminal Investigation Department
CIDEC	Conseil International pour le Développement du Cuivre
CIE	Companion, Order of the Indian Empire; Confédération Internationale des Étudiants
CIEx	Companion, Institute of Export
CIFRS	Comité International de la Rayonne et des Fibres Synthétiques
CIGasE	Companion, Institution of Gas Engineers
CIGRE	Conférence Internationale des Grands Réseaux Electriques
CIGS	Chief of the Imperial General Staff (*now see* CGS)
CIIA	Canadian Institute of International Affairs
CIL	*Corpus inscriptionum latinarum*
CIM	China Inland Mission
CIMA	Chartered Institute of Management Accountants
CIMarE	Companion, Institute of Marine Engineers
CIMEMME	Companion, Institution of Mining Electrical and Mining Mechanical Engineers
CIMgt	Companion, Institute of Management
CIMGTechE	Companion, Institution of Mechanical and General Technician Engineers
C-in-C	Commander-in-Chief
CINCHAN	Allied Commander-in-Chief Channel
CIOB	Chartered Institute of Building
CIPD	Companion, Institute of Personnel and Development
CIPFA	Chartered Institute of Public Finance and Accountancy
CIPL	Comité International Permanent des Linguistes
CIPM	Companion, Institute of Personnel Management (*now see* CIPD)
CIR	Commission on Industrial Relations
CIRES	Co-operative Institute for Research in Environmental Sciences
CIRIA	Construction Industry Research and Information Association
CIRP	Collège Internationale pour Recherche et Production
CIS	Institute of Chartered Secretaries and Administrators (*formerly* Chartered Institute of Secretaries); Command Control Communications and Information Systems; Commonwealth of Independent States
CISAC	Confédération Internationale des Sociétés d'Auteurs et Compositeurs; Centre for International Security and Arms Control
CIT	Chartered Institute of Transport; California Institute of Technology
CITB	Construction Industry Training Board
CIU	Club and Institute Union
CIV	City Imperial Volunteers
CJ	Chief Justice
CJC	Companions of Jesus Christ
CJM	Congregation of Jesus and Mary (Eudist Fathers)
CL	Commander, Order of Leopold
cl	*cum laude*
Cl.	Class
CLA	Country Landowners' Association
CLIC	Cancer and Leukemia in Children
CLIP	Common Law Institute of Intellectual Property
CLit	Companion of Literature (Royal Society of Literature Award)
CLJ	Commander, Order of St Lazarus of Jerusalem
CLP	Constituency Labour Party
CLRAE	Congress (*formerly* Conference) of Local and Regional Authorities of Europe
CLY	City of London Yeomanry
CM	Member, Order of Canada; Congregation of the Mission (Vincentians); Master in Surgery; Certificated Master; Canadian Militia
CMA	Canadian Medical Association; Cost and Management Accountant (NZ)
CMAC	Catholic Marriage Advisory Council

CMath	Chartered Mathematician
CMB	Central Midwives' Board
CMet	Chartered Meteorologist
CMF	Commonwealth Military Forces; Central Mediterranean Force
CMG	Companion, Order of St Michael and St George
CMLJ	Commander of Merit, Order of St Lazarus of Jerusalem
CMM	Commander, Order of Military Merit (Canada)
CMO	Chief Medical Officer
CMP	Corps of Military Police (*now see* CRMP)
CMS	Church Mission (*formerly* Church Missionary) Society; Certificate in Management Studies
CMT	Chaconia Medal of Trinidad
CNAA	Council for National Academic Awards
CND	Campaign for Nuclear Disarmament
CNI	Companion, Nautical Institute
CNO	Chief of Naval Operations
CNR	Canadian National Railways
CNRS	Centre National de la Recherche Scientifique
CO	Commanding Officer; Commonwealth Office (after Aug. 1966) (*now see* FCO); Colonial Office (before Aug. 1966); Conscientious Objector; Colorado
Co.	County; Company
C of E	Church of England
C of S	Chief of Staff; Church of Scotland
Coal.L or Co.L	Coalition Liberal
Coal.U or Co.U	Coalition Unionist
CODEST	Committee for the Development of European Science and Technology
COHSE	Confederation of Health Service Employees
COI	Central Office of Information
CoID	Council of Industrial Design (*now* Design Council)
Col	Colonel
Coll.	College; Collegiate
Colo	Colorado (US)
Col.-Sergt	Colour-Sergeant
Com	Communist
Comd	Command
Comdg	Commanding
Comdr	Commander
Comdt	Commandant
COMEC	Council of the Military Education Committees of the Universities of the UK
COMET	Committee for Middle East Trade
Commn	Commission
Commnd	Commissioned
CompAMEME	Companion, Association of Mining Electrical and Mechanical Engineers
CompICE	Companion, Institution of Civil Engineers
CompIEE	Companion, Institution of Electrical Engineers
CompIERE	Companion, Institution of Electronic and Radio Engineers
CompIGasE	Companion, Institution of Gas Engineers
CompIMechE	Companion, Institution of Mechanical Engineers
CompIWES	Companion, Institution of Water Engineers and Scientists
CompOR	Companion, Operational Research Society
CompTI	Companion of the Textile Institute
Comr	Commissioner
Comy-Gen.	Commissary-General
CON	Commander, Order of the Niger
Conn	Connecticut (US)
Const.	Constitutional
Co-op.	Co-operative
COPA	Comité des Organisations Professionels Agricoles de la CEE
COPEC	Conference of Politics, Economics and Christianity
COPUS	Committee on the Public Understanding of Science
Corp.	Corporation; Corporal
Corresp. Mem.	Corresponding Member
COS	Chief of Staff; Charity Organization Society
COSA	Colliery Officials and Staffs Association
CoSIRA	Council for Small Industries in Rural Areas
COSLA	Convention of Scottish Local Authorities
COSPAR	Committee on Space Research
COSSAC	Chief of Staff to Supreme Allied Commander
COTC	Canadian Officers' Training Corps
CP	Central Provinces; Cape Province; Congregation of the Passion
CPA	Commonwealth Parliamentary Association; Chartered Patent Agent; Certified Public Accountant (Canada) (*now see* CA)
CPAG	Child Poverty Action Group
CPAS	Church Pastoral Aid Society
CPC	Conservative Political Centre

CPEng	Chartered Professional Engineer (of Institution of Engineers of Australia)
CPhys	Chartered Physicist
CPL	Chief Personnel and Logistics
CPM	Colonial Police Medal
CPR	Canadian Pacific Railway
CPRE	Council for the Protection of Rural England
CPRW	Campaign for the Protection of Rural Wales
CPS	Crown Prosecution Service
CPSA	Civil and Public Services Association
CPSU	Communist Party of the Soviet Union
CPsychol	Chartered Psychologist
CPU	Commonwealth Press Union
CQSW	Certificate of Qualification in Social Work
CR	Community of the Resurrection
cr	created or creation
CRA	Commandor, Royal Artillery
CRAC	Careers Research and Advisory Centre
CRAeS	Companion, Royal Aeronautical Society
CRAG	Clinical Resources and Audit Group
CRASC	Commander, Royal Army Service Corps
CRC	Cancer Research Campaign; Community Relations Council
CRCP(C)	Certificant, Royal College of Physicians of Canada
CRE	Commander, Royal Engineers; Commission for Racial Equality; Commercial Relations and Exports
Cres.	Crescent
CRMP	Corps of Royal Military Police
CRNCM	Companion, Royal Northern College of Music
CRO	Commonwealth Relations Office (now see FCO)
CS	Civil Service; Clerk to the Signet
CSA	Confederate States of America
CSAB	Civil Service Appeal Board
CSB	Bachelor of Christian Science
CSC	Conspicuous Service Cross; Congregation of the Holy Cross
CSCA	Civil Service Clerical Association (now see CPSA)
CSCE	Conference on Security and Co-operation in Europe
CSD	Civil Service Department; Co-operative Secretaries Diploma; Chartered Society of Designers
CSDE	Central Servicing Development Establishment
CSEU	Confederation of Shipbuilding and Engineering Unions
CSG	Companion, Order of the Star of Ghana; Company of the Servants of God
CSI	Companion, Order of the Star of India
CSIR	Commonwealth Council for Scientific and Industrial Research (now see CSIRO)
CSIRO	Commonwealth Scientific and Industrial Research Organization (Australia)
CSO	Chief Scientific Officer; Chief Signal Officer; Chief Staff Officer; Central Statistical Office
CSP	Chartered Society of Physiotherapists; Civil Service of Pakistan
CSS	Companion, Star of Sàrawak; Council for Science and Society
CSSB	Civil Service Selection Board
CSSp	Holy Ghost Father
CSSR	Congregation of the Most Holy Redeemer (Redemptorist Order)
CStat	Chartered Statistician
CSTI	Council of Science and Technology Institutes
CStJ	Commander, Most Venerable Order of the Hospital of St John of Jerusalem
CSU	Christlich-Soziale Union in Bayern
CSV	Community Service Volunteers
CSW	Certificate in Social Work
CT	Connecticut
CTA	Chaplain Territorial Army
CTB	College of Teachers of the Blind
CTC	Cyclists' Touring Club; Commando Training Centre; City Training College
CText	Chartered Textile Technologist
CTR(Harwell)	Controlled Thermonuclear Research
CU	Cambridge University
CUAC	Cambridge University Athletic Club
CUAFC	Cambridge University Association Football Club
CUBC	Cambridge University Boat Club
CUCC	Cambridge University Cricket Club
CUF	Common University Fund
CUHC	Cambridge University Hockey Club
CUMS	Cambridge University Musical Society
CUNY	City University of New York
CUP	Cambridge University Press
CURUFC	Cambridge University Rugby Union Football Club
CV	Cross of Valour (Canada)
CVCP	Committee of Vice-Chancellors and Principals of the Universities of the United Kingdom
CVO	Commander, Royal Victorian Order
CVS	Council for Voluntary Service

CVSNA	Council of Voluntary Service National Association
CWA	Crime Writers Association
CWGC	Commonwealth War Graves Commission
CWS	Co-operative Wholesale Society
CWU	Communication Workers Union

D

D	Duke
d	died; daughter
DA	Dame of St Andrew, Order of Barbados; Diploma in Anaesthesia; Diploma in Art
DAA&QMG	Deputy Assistant Adjutant and Quartermaster-General
DAAG	Deputy Assistant Adjutant-General
DA&QMG	Deputy Adjutant and Quartermaster-General
DAC	Development Assistance Committee; Diocesan Advisory Committee
DACG	Deputy Assistant Chaplain-General
DAD	Deputy Assistant Director
DAdmin	Doctor of Administration
DADMS	Deputy Assistant Director of Medical Services
DADOS	Deputy Assistant Director of Ordnance Services
DADQ	Deputy Assistant Director of Quartering
DADST	Deputy Assistant Director of Supplies and Transport
DAG	Deputy Adjutant-General
DAgr	Doctor of Agriculture
DAgrFor	Doctor of Agriculture and Forestry
DAMS	Deputy Assistant Military Secretary
D&AD	Designers and Art Directors Association
DAppSc	Doctor of Applied Science
DAQMG	Deputy Assistant Quartermaster-General
DArch	Doctor of Architecture
DArt	Doctor of Art
DArts	Doctor of Arts
DASc	Doctor in Agricultural Sciences
DATA	Draughtsmen's and Allied Technicians' Association (later AUEW(TASS))
DATEC	Art and Design Committee, Technician Education Council
DBA	Doctor of Business Administration
DBE	Dame Commander, Order of the British Empire
DC	District Council; District of Columbia (US)
DCAe	Diploma of College of Aeronautics
DCAS	Deputy Chief of the Air Staff
DCB	Dame Commander, Order of the Bath
DCC	Diploma of Chelsea College
DCCH	Diploma in Community Child Health
DCDS	Deputy Chief of Defence Staff
DCE	Diploma of a College of Education
DCG	Deputy Chaplain-General
DCGRM	Department of the Commandant General Royal Marines
DCGS	Deputy Chief of the General Staff
DCh	Doctor of Surgery
DCH	Diploma in Child Health
DCIGS	Deputy Chief of the Imperial General Staff (now see DCGS)
DCL	Doctor of Civil Law
DCLI	Duke of Cornwall's Light Infantry
DCLJ	Dame Commander, Order of St Lazarus of Jerusalem
DCM	Distinguished Conduct Medal
DCMG	Dame Commander, Order of St Michael and St George
DCMHE	Diploma of Contents and Methods in Health Education
DCnL	Doctor of Canon Law
DCO	Duke of Cambridge's Own
DComm	Doctor of Commerce
DCP	Diploma in Clinical Pathology; Diploma in Conservation of Paintings
DCS	Deputy Chief of Staff; Doctor of Commercial Sciences
DCSO	Deputy Chief Scientific Officer
DCT	Doctor of Christian Theology
DCVO	Dame Commander, Royal Victorian Order
DD	Doctor of Divinity
DDes	Doctor of Design
DDGAMS	Deputy Director General, Army Medical Services
DDH	Diploma in Dental Health
DDL	Deputy Director of Labour
DDME	Deputy Director of Mechanical Engineering
DDMI	Deputy Director of Military Intelligence
DDMO	Deputy Director of Military Operations
DDMS	Deputy Director of Medical Services
DDMT	Deputy Director of Military Training
DDNI	Deputy Director of Naval Intelligence
DDO	Diploma in Dental Orthopaedics
DDOS	Deputy Director of Ordnance Services
DDPH	Diploma in Dental Public Health

DDPR	Deputy Director of Public Relations
DDPS	Deputy Director of Personal Services
DDR	Deutsche Demokratische Republik
DDRA	Deputy Director Royal Artillery
DDS	Doctor of Dental Surgery; Director of Dental Services
DDSc	Doctor of Dental Science
DDSD	Deputy Director Staff Duties
DDSM	Defense Distinguished Service Medal
DDST	Deputy Director of Supplies and Transport
DDWE&M	Deputy Director of Works, Electrical and Mechanical
DE	Doctor of Engineering; Delaware
DEA	Department of Economic Affairs
decd	deceased
DEconSc	Doctor of Economic Science
DEd	Doctor of Education
Del	Delaware (US)
Deleg.	Delegate
DEME	Directorate of Electrical and Mechanical Engineering
DEMS	Defensively Equipped Merchant Ships
(DemU)	Democratic Unionist
DenD	Docteur en Droit
DEng	Doctor of Engineering
DenM	Docteur en Médicine
DEOVR	Duke of Edinburgh's Own Volunteer Rifles
DEP	Department of Employment and Productivity; European Progressive Democrats
Dep.	Deputy
DERA	Defence Evaluation and Research Agency
DES	Department of Education and Science (now see DFE)
DèsL	Docteur ès lettres
DèS or DèsSc	Docteur ès sciences
DesRCA	Designer of the Royal College of Art
DFA	Doctor of Fine Arts
DFAS	Decorative and Fine Art Society
DFC	Distinguished Flying Cross
DFE	Department for Education
DFH	Diploma of Faraday House
DFLS	Day Fighter Leaders' School
DFM	Distinguished Flying Medal
DG	Director General; Dragoon Guards
DGAA	Distressed Gentlefolks Aid Association
DGAMS	Director-General Army Medical Services
DGEME	Director General Electrical and Mechanical Engineering
DGLP(A)	Director General Logistic Policy (Army)
DGMS	Director-General of Medical Services
DGMT	Director-General of Military Training
DGMW	Director-General of Military Works
DGNPS	Director-General of Naval Personal Services
DGP	Director-General of Personnel
DGPS	Director-General of Personal Services
DGS	Diploma in Graduate Studies
DGStJ	Dame of Grace, Order of St John of Jerusalem (now see DStJ)
DGU	Doctor of Griffith University
DH	Doctor of Humanities
DHA	District Health Authority
Dhc	Doctor honoris causa
DHEW	Department of Health Education and Welfare (US)
DHL	Doctor of Humane Letters; Doctor of Hebrew Literature
DHM	Dean Hole Medal
DHMSA	Diploma in the History of Medicine (Society of Apothecaries)
DHQ	District Headquarters
DHSS	Department of Health and Social Security (now see DoH and DSS)
DHum	Doctor of Humanities
DHumLit	Doctor of Humane Letters
DIAS	Dublin Institute of Advanced Sciences
DIC	Diploma of the Imperial College
DICTA	Diploma of Imperial College of Tropical Agriculture
DIG	Deputy Inspector-General
DIH	Diploma in Industrial Health
DIMP	Darjah Indera Mahkota Pahang
DIntLaw	Diploma in International Law
Dio.	Diocese
DipAA	Diploma in Applied Art
DipAD	Diploma in Art and Design
DipAe	Diploma in Aeronautics
DipArch	Diploma in Architecture
DipASE	Diploma in Advanced Study of Education, College of Preceptors
DipAvMed	Diploma of Aviation Medicine, Royal College of Physicians
DipBA	Diploma in Business Administration
DipBS	Diploma in Fine Art, Byam Shaw School

DipCAM	Diploma in Communications, Advertising and Marketing of CAM Foundation
DipCC	Diploma of the Central College
DipCD	Diploma in Civic Design
DipCE	Diploma in Civil Engineering
DipEcon	Diploma in Economics
DipEd	Diploma in Education
DipEE	Diploma in Electrical Engineering
DipEl	Diploma in Electronics
DipESL	Diploma in English as a Second Language
DipEth	Diploma in Ethnology
DipFD	Diploma in Funeral Directing
DipFE	Diploma in Further Education
DipGSM	Diploma in Music, Guildhall School of Music and Drama
DipHA	Diploma in Hospital Administration
DipHSM	Diploma in Health Services Management
DipHum	Diploma in Humanities
DipLA	Diploma in Landscape Architecture
DipLib	Diploma of Librarianship
DipM	Diploma in Marketing
DipN	Diploma in Nursing
DipNEC	Diploma of Northampton Engineering College (now City University)
DipPA	Diploma of Practitioners in Advertising (now see DipCAM)
DipPSA	Diploma in Public Service Administration
DipREM	Diploma in Rural Estate Management
DipSMS	Diploma in School Management Studies
DipSoc	Diploma in Sociology
DipTA	Diploma in Tropical Agriculture
DipT&CP	Diploma in Town and Country Planning
DipTh	Diploma in Theology
DipTMHA	Diploma in Training and Further Education of Mentally Handicapped Adults
DipTP	Diploma in Town Planning
DipTPT	Diploma in Theory and Practice of Teaching
DIS	Diploma in Industrial Studies
DistTP	Distinction in Town Planning
DIur	Doctor of Law
Div.	Division; Divorced
Div.Test	Divinity Testimonium (of Trinity College, Dublin)
DJAG	Deputy Judge Advocate General
DJPD	Dato Jasa Purba Di-Raja Negeri Sembilan (Malaysia)
DJStJ	Dame of Justice, Order of St John of Jerusalem (now see DStJ)
DJur	Doctor Juris (Doctor of Law)
DK	Most Esteemed Family Order (Brunei)
DL	Deputy Lieutenant
DLC	Diploma of Loughborough College
DLES	Doctor of Letters in Economic Studies
DLI	Durham Light Infantry
DLit or DLitt	Doctor of Literature; Doctor of Letters
DLittS	Doctor of Sacred Letters
DLJ	Dame of Grace, Order of St Lazarus of Jerusalem
DLO	Diploma in Laryngology and Otology
DM	Doctor of Medicine
DMA	Diploma in Municipal Administration
DMD	Doctor of Medical Dentistry (Australia)
DME	Director of Mechanical Engineering
DMet	Doctor of Metallurgy
DMI	Director of Military Intelligence
DMin	Doctor of Ministry
DMiss	Doctor of Missiology
DMJ	Diploma in Medical Jurisprudence
DMJ(Path)	Diploma in Medical Jurisprudence (Pathology)
DMLJ	Dame of Merit, Order of St Lazarus of Jerusalem
DMO	Director of Military Operations
DMR	Diploma in Medical Radiology
DMRD	Diploma in Medical Radiological Diagnosis
DMRE	Diploma in Medical Radiology and Electrology
DMRT	Diploma in Medical Radio-Therapy
DMS	Director of Medical Services; Decoration for Meritorious Service (South Africa); Diploma in Management Studies
DMSc	Doctor of Medical Science
DMSSB	Direct Mail Services Standards Board
DMT	Director of Military Training
DMus	Doctor of Music
DN	Diploma in Nursing
DNB	Dictionary of National Biography
DNE	Director of Naval Equipment
DNI	Director of Naval Intelligence
DO	Diploma in Ophthalmology
DOAE	Defence Operational Analysis Establishment
DObstRCOG	Diploma of Royal College of Obstetricians and Gynaecologists (now see DRCOG)
DOC	District Officer Commanding

DocEng	Doctor of Engineering
DoE	Department of the Environment
DoH	Department of Health
DoI	Department of Industry
DOL	Doctor of Oriental Learning
Dom.	*Dominus* (Lord)
DOMS	Diploma in Ophthalmic Medicine and Surgery
DOR	Director of Operational Requirements
DOrthRCS	Diploma in Orthodontics, Royal College of Surgeons
DOS	Director of Ordnance Services; Doctor of Ocular Science
Dow.	Dowager
DP	Data Processing
DPA	Diploma in Public Administration; Discharged Prisoners' Aid
DPD	Diploma in Public Dentistry
DPEc	Doctor of Political Economy
DPed	Doctor of Pedagogy
DPH	Diploma in Public Health
DPh or	
DPhil	Doctor of Philosophy
DPharm	Doctor of Pharmacy
DPhilMed	Diploma in Philosophy of Medicine
DPhysMed	Diploma in Physical Medicine
DPLG	Diplômé par le Gouvernement
DPM	Diploma in Psychological Medicine
DPMS	Dato Paduka Mahkota Selangor (Malaysia)
DPP	Director of Public Prosecutions
DPR	Director of Public Relations
DPS	Director of Postal Services; Director of Personal Services; Doctor of Public Service
DPSA	Diploma in Public and Social Administration
DPSE	Diploma in Professional Studies in Education
DPsych	Doctor of Psychology
DQMG	Deputy Quartermaster-General
Dr	Doctor
DRA	Defence Research Agency (*now see* DERA)
DRAC	Director Royal Armoured Corps
DRC	Diploma of Royal College of Science and Technology, Glasgow
DRCOG	Diploma of Royal College of Obstetricians and Gynaecologists
DRD	Diploma in Restorative Dentistry
Dr ing	Doctor of Engineering
Dr jur	Doctor of Laws
DrŒcPol	*Doctor Œconomiæ Politicæ* (Doctor of Political Economy)
Dr rer. nat.	Doctor of Natural Science
Dr rer. pol.	Doctor of Political Science
DRS	Diploma in Religious Studies
DRSAMD	Diploma of the Royal Scottish Academy of Music and Drama
DS	Directing Staff; Doctor of Science
DSA	Diploma in Social Administration
DSAC	Defence Scientific Advisory Council
DSAO	Diplomatic Service Administration Office
DSC	Distinguished Service Cross
DSc	Doctor of Science
DScA	Docteur en sciences agricoles
DSCHE	Diploma of the Scottish Council for Health Education
DScMil	Doctor of Military Science
DScPol	Doctor of Political Sciences
DSc (SocSci)	Doctor of Science in Social Science
DSD	Director Staff Duties
DSF	Director Special Forces
DSIR	Department of Scientific and Industrial Research (later SRC; then SERC)
DSL	Doctor of Sacred Letters
DSLJ	Dato Seri Laila Jasa (Brunei)
DSM	Distinguished Service Medal
DSNB	Dato Setia Negara Brunei
DSNS	Dato Setia Negeri Sembilan (Malaysia)
DSO	Companion of the Distinguished Service Order
DSocSc	Doctor of Social Science
DSP	Director of Selection of Personnel; Docteur en sciences politiques (Montreal)
dsp	*decessit sine prole* (died without issue)
DSS	Department of Social Security; Doctor of Sacred Scripture
Dss	Deaconess
DSSc	Doctor of Social Science
DST	Director of Supplies and Transport
DStJ	Dame of Grace, Most Venerable Order of the Hospital of St John of Jerusalem; Dame of Justice, Most Venerable Order of the Hospital of St John of Jerusalem
DTA	Diploma in Tropical Agriculture
DTD	Dekoratie voor Trouwe Dienst (Decoration for Devoted Service)

DTech	Doctor of Technology
DTH	Diploma in Tropical Hygiene
DTh or	
DTheol	Doctor of Theology
DThPT	Diploma in Theory and Practice of Teaching
DTI	Department of Trade and Industry
DTM&H	Diploma in Tropical Medicine and Hygiene
DU	Honorary Doctor of the University
Dunelm	*Dunelmensis* (of Durham)
DUniv	Honorary Doctor of the University
DUP	Democratic Unionist Party; Docteur de l'Université de Paris
DVA	Diploma of Veterinary Anaesthesia
DVH	Diploma in Veterinary Hygiene
DVLA	Driver and Vehicle Licensing Authority
DVLC	Driver and Vehicle Licensing Centre
DVM	Doctor of Veterinary Medicine
DVMS or	
DVM&S	Doctor of Veterinary Medicine and Surgery
DVR	Diploma in Veterinary Radiology
DVSc	Doctor of Veterinary Science
DVSM	Diploma in Veterinary State Medicine

E

E	East; Earl; England
e	eldest
EAA	Edinburgh Architectural Association
EACR	European Association for Cancer Research
EAGA	Energy Action Grants Agency
EAHY	European Architectural Heritage Year
EAP	East Africa Protectorate
EAW	Electrical Association for Women
EBC	English Benedictine Congregation
Ebor	*Eboracensis* (of York)
EBRD	European Bank for Reconstruction and Development
EBU	European Broadcasting Union
EC	Etoile du Courage (Canada); European Community; European Commission; Emergency Commission
ECA	Economic Co-operation Administration; Economic Commission for Africa
ECAFE	Economic Commission for Asia and the Far East (*now see* ESCAP)
ECCTIS	Education Courses and Credit Transfer Information Systems
ECE	Economic Commission for Europe
ECGD	Export Credits Guarantee Department
ECLA	Economic Commission for Latin America
ECLAC	United Nations Economic Commission for Latin America and the Caribbean
ECOVAST	European Council for the Village and Small Town
ECSC	European Coal and Steel Community
ECU	English Church Union
ED	Efficiency Decoration; Doctor of Engineering (US); European Democrat
ed	edited
EdB	Bachelor of Education
EDC	Economic Development Committee
EdD	Doctor of Education
EDF	European Development Fund
EDG	European Democratic Group; Employment Department Group
Edin.	Edinburgh
Edn	Edition
EDP	Executive Development Programme
Educ	Educated
Educn	Education
EEC	European Economic Community (*now see* EC); Commission of the European Communities
EEF	Engineering Employers' Federation; Egyptian Expeditionary Force
EEIBA	Electrical and Electronic Industries Benevolent Association
EETPU	Electrical Electronic Telecommunication & Plumbing Union (*now see* AEEU)
EETS	Early English Text Society
EFCE	European Federation of Chemical Engineering
EFTA	European Free Trade Association
eh	ehrenhalber (honorary)
EI	East Indian; East Indies
EIA	Engineering Industries Association
EIB	European Investment Bank
EICS	East India Company's Service
E-in-C	Engineer-in-Chief
EIS	Educational Institute of Scotland
EISCAT	European Incoherent Scatter Association
EIU	Economist Intelligence Unit

ELBS	English Language Book Society
ELSE	European Life Science Editors
ELT	English Language Teaching
EM	Edward Medal; Earl Marshal
EMBL	European Molecular Biology Laboratory
EMBO	European Molecular Biology Organisation
EMP	Electro Magnetic Pulse; Executive Management Program Diploma
EMS	Emergency Medical Service
Enc.Brit.	Encylopaedia Britannica
Eng.	England
Engr	Engineer
ENO	English National Opera
ENSA	Entertainments National Service Association
ENT	Ear Nose and Throat
EO	Executive Officer
EOC	Equal Opportunities Commission
EOPH	Examined Officer of Public Health
EORTC	European Organisation for Research on Treatment of Cancer
EP	European Parliament
EPP	European People's Party
EPSRC	Engineering and Physical Sciences Research Council
er	elder
ER	Eastern Region (BR)
ERA	Electrical Research Association
ERC	Electronics Research Council
ERD	Emergency Reserve Decoration (Army)
ESA	European Space Agency
ESCAP	Economic and Social Commission for Asia and the Pacific
ESF	European Science Foundn
ESL	English as a Second Language
ESNS	Educational Sub-Normal Serious
ESRC	Economic and Social Research Council; Electricity Supply Research Council
ESRO	European Space Research Organization (*now see* ESA)
ESTA	European Sciences and Technology Assembly
ESU	English-Speaking Union
ETA	Engineering Training Authority
ETH	Eidgenössische Technische Hochschule
ETUC	European Trade Union Confederation
ETUCE	European Trade Union Committee for Education
EU	European Union
EUDISED	European Documentation and Information Service for Education
Euratom	European Atomic Energy Community
EurChem	European Chemist
Eur Ing	European Engineer
EUROM	European Federation for Optics and Precision Mechanics
EUW	European Union of Women
eV	eingetragener Verein
Ext	Extinct

F

FA	Football Association
FAA	Fellow, Australian Academy of Science; Fleet Air Arm
FAAAI	Fellow, American Association for Artificial Intelligence
FAAAS	Fellow, American Association for the Advancement of Science
FAAO	Fellow, American Academy of Optometry
FAAP	Fellow, American Academy of Pediatrics
FAARM	Fellow, American Academy of Reproductive Medicine
FAAV	Fellow, Central Association of Agricultural Valuers
FAAVCT	Fellow, American Academy of Veterinary and Comparative Toxicology
FABE	Fellow, Association of Building Engineers
FACC	Fellow, American College of Cardiology
FACCA	Fellow, Association of Certified and Corporate Accountants (*now see* FCCA)
FACCP	Fellow, American College of Chest Physicians
FACD	Fellow, American College of Dentistry
FACDS	Fellow, Australian College of Dental Surgeons (*now see* FRACDS)
FACE	Fellow, Australian College of Education
FACerS	Fellow, American Ceramic Society
FACI	Fellow, Australian Chemical Institute (*now see* FRACI)
FACMA	Fellow, Australian College of Medical Administrators (*now see* FRACMA)
FACMG	Fellow, American College of Medicinal Genetics
FACOG	Fellow, American College of Obstetricians and Gynæcologists
FACOM	Fellow, Australian College of Occupational Medicine

FACP	Fellow, American College of Physicians
FACR	Fellow, American College of Radiology
FACRM	Fellow, Australian College of Rehabilitation Medicine
FACS	Fellow, American College of Surgeons
FACVT	Fellow, American College of Veterinary Toxicology (*now see* FAAVCT)
FADM	Fellow, Academy of Dental Materials
FAeSI	Fellow, Aeronautical Society of India
FAFPHM	Fellow, Australian Faculty of Public Health Medicine
FAGO	Fellowship in Australia in Obstetrics and Gynaecology
FAGS	Fellow, American Geographical Society
FAHA	Fellow, Australian Academy of the Humanities
FAI	Fellow, Chartered Auctioneers' and Estate Agents' Institute (*now* (after amalgamation) *see* FRICS); Fédération Aéronautique Internationale
FAIA	Fellow, American Institute of Architects
FAIAA	Fellow, American Institute of Aeronautics and Astronautics
FAIAS	Fellow, Australian Institute of Agricultural Science
FAIB	Fellow, Australian Institute of Bankers
FAIBiol	Fellow, Australian Institute of Biology
FAICD	Fellow, Australian Institute of Company Directors
FAIE	Fellow, Australian Institute of Energy
FAIEx	Fellow, Australian Institute of Export
FAIFST	Fellow, Australian Institute of Food Science and Technology
FAII	Fellow, Australian Insurance Institute
FAIM	Fellow, Australian Institute of Management
FAIP	Fellow, Australian Institute of Physics
FAMA	Fellow, Australian Medical Association
FAMI	Fellow, Australian Marketing Institute
FAmNucSoc	Fellow, American Nuclear Society
FAMS	Fellow, Ancient Monuments Society
F and GP	Finance and General Purposes
FANY	First Aid Nursing Yeomanry
FANZCA	Fellow, Australian and New Zealand College of Anaesthetists
FANZCP	Fellow, Australian and New Zealand College of Psychiatrists (*now see* FRANZCP)
FAO	Food and Agriculture Organization of the United Nations
FAOrthA	Fellow, Australian Orthopaedic Association
FAPA	Fellow, American Psychiatric Association
FAPHA	Fellow, American Public Health Association
FAPI	Fellow, Australian Planning Institute (*now see* FRAPI)
FAPM	Fellow, Association of Project Managers
FAPS	Fellow, American Phytopathological Society
FArborA	Fellow, Aboricultural Association
FARE	Federation of Alcoholic Rehabilitation Establishments
FARELF	Far East Land Forces
FAS	Fellow, Antiquarian Society; Fellow, Nigerian Academy of Science; Funding Agency for Schools
FASA	Fellow, Australian Society of Accountants (*now see* FCPA)
FASc	Fellow, Indian Academy of Sciences
fasc.	fascicule
FASCE	Fellow, American Society of Civil Engineers
FASI	Fellow, Architects' and Surveyors' Institute
FASME	Fellow, American Society of Mechanical Engineers
FASPOG	Fellow, Australian Society for Psychosomatic Obstetrics and Gynaecology
FASSA	Fellow, Academy of the Social Sciences in Australia
FAusIMM	Fellow, Australasian Institute of Mining and Metallurgy
FAustCOG	Fellow, Australian College of Obstetricians and Gynæcologists (*now see* FRACOG)
FBA	Fellow, British Academy; Federation of British Artists
FBCO	Fellow, British College of Optometrists (*formerly of* Ophthalmic Opticians (Optometrists)) (*now see* FCOptom)
FBCS	Fellow, British Computer Society
FBEC(S)	Fellow, Business Education Council (Scotland)
FBES	Fellow, Biological Engineering Society
FBHA	Fellow, British Hospitality Association
FBHI	Fellow, British Horological Institute
FBHS	Fellow, British Horse Society
FBI	Federation of British Industries (*now see* CBI); Federal Bureau of Investigation
FBIA	Fellow, Bankers' Institute of Australasia (*now see* FAIB)
FBIAT	Fellow, British Institute of Architectural Technicians
FBIBA	Fellow, British Insurance Brokers' Association (*now see* FBIIBA)
FBID	Fellow, British Institute of Interior Design
FBIIBA	Fellow, British Insurance and Investment Brokers' Association
FBIM	Fellow, British Institute of Management (*now see* FIMgt)
FBINZ	Fellow, Bankers' Institute of New Zealand

FBIPP	Fellow, British Institute of Professional Photography
FBIRA	Fellow, British Institute of Regulatory Affairs
FBIS	Fellow, British Interplanetary Society
FBKS	Fellow, British Kinematograph Society (*now see* FBKSTS)
FBKSTS	Fellow, British Kinematograph, Sound and Television Society
FBOA	Fellow, British Optical Association
FBOU	Fellow, British Ornithologists' Union
FBPICS	Fellow, British Production and Inventory Control Society
FBPsS	Fellow, British Psychological Society
FBritIRE	Fellow, British Institution of Radio Engineers (later FIERE)
FBS	Fellow, Building Societies Institute (later FCBSI; *now see* FCIB)
FBSI	Fellow, Boot and Shoe Institution (*now see* FCFI)
FBSM	Fellow, Birmingham School of Music
FC	Football Club
FCA	Fellow, Institute of Chartered Accountants; Fellow, Institute of Chartered Accountants in Australia; Fellow, New Zealand Society of Accountants; Federation of Canadian Artists
FCAI	Fellow, New Zealand Institute of Cost Accountants; Fellow, Canadian Aeronautical Institute (*now see* FCASI)
FCAM	Fellow, CAM Foundation
FCAnaes	Fellow, College of Anaesthetists (*now see* FRCA)
FCASI	Fellow, Canadian Aeronautics and Space Institute
FCBSI	Fellow, Chartered Building Societies Institute (*now see* FCIB)
FCCA	Fellow, Chartered Association of Certified Accountants
FCCEA	Fellow, Commonwealth Council for Educational Administration
FCCS	Fellow, Corporation of Secretaries (*formerly of* Certified Secretaries)
FCCT	Fellow, Canadian College of Teachers
FCEC	Federation of Civil Engineering Contractors
FCFI	Fellow, Clothing and Footwear Institute
FCGI	Fellow, City and Guilds of London Institute
FCGP	Fellow, College of General Practitioners (*now see* FRCGP)
FCH	Fellow, Coopers Hill College
FChS	Fellow, Society of Chiropodists
FCI	Fellow, Institute of Commerce
FCIA	Fellow, Corporation of Insurance Agents
FCIArb	Fellow, Chartered Institute of Arbitrators
FCIB	Fellow, Corporation of Insurance Brokers; Fellow, Chartered Institute of Bankers
FCIBS	Fellow, Chartered Institution of Building Services (*now see* FCIBSE); Fellow, Chartered Institute of Bankers in Scotland
FCIBSE	Fellow, Chartered Institution of Building Services Engineers
FCIC	Fellow, Chemical Institute of Canada (*formerly* Canadian Institute of Chemistry)
FCIH	Fellow, Chartered Institute of Housing
FCII	Fellow, Chartered Insurance Institute
FCIJ	Fellow, Chartered Institute of Journalists
FCILA	Fellow, Chartered Institute of Loss Adjusters
FCIM	Fellow, Chartered Institute of Marketing; Fellow, Institute of Corporate Managers (Australia)
FCIOB	Fellow, Chartered Institute of Building
FCIPA	Fellow, Chartered Institute of Patent Agents (*now see* CPA)
FCIPS	Fellow, Chartered Institute of Purchasing and Supply
FCIS	Fellow, Institute of Chartered Secretaries and Administrators (*formerly* Chartered Institute of Secretaries)
FCISA	Fellow, Chartered Institute of Secretaries and Administrators (Australia)
FCIT	Fellow, Chartered Institute of Transport
FCIWEM	Fellow, Chartered Institution of Water and Environmental Management
FCM	Faculty of Community Medicine
FCMA	Fellow, Chartered Institute of Management Accountants (*formerly* Institute of Cost and Management Accountants)
FCMSA	Fellow, College of Medicine of South Africa
FCNA	Fellow, College of Nursing, Australia
FCO	Foreign and Commonwealth Office
FCOG(SA)	Fellow, South African College of Obstetrics and Gynæcology
FCollH	Fellow, College of Handicraft
FCollP	Fellow, College of Preceptors
FCommA	Fellow, Society of Commercial Accountants (*now see* FSCA)
FCOphth	Fellow, College of Ophthalmologists (*now see* FRCOphth)
FCOptom	Fellow, College of Optometrists
FCP	Fellow, College of Preceptors
FCPA	Fellow, Australian Society of Certified Practising Accountants
FCPath	Fellow, College of Pathologists (*now see* FRCPath)
FCPS	Fellow, College of Physicians and Surgeons
FCP(SoAf)	Fellow, College of Physicians, South Africa
FCPSO(SoAf)	Fellow, College of Physicians and Surgeons and Obstetricians, South Africa
FCPS (Pak)	Fellow, College of Physicians and Surgeons of Pakistan
FCRA	Fellow, College of Radiologists of Australia (*now see* FRACR)
FCS	Federation of Conservative Students
FCS or **FChemSoc**	Fellow, Chemical Society (now absorbed into Royal Society of Chemistry)
FCSD	Fellow, Chartered Society of Designers
FCSHK	Fellow, College of Surgeons of Hong Kong
FCSLT	Fellow, College of Speech and Language Therapists
FCSP	Fellow, Chartered Society of Physiotherapy
FCSSA or **FCS(SoAf)**	Fellow, College of Surgeons, South Africa
FCSSL	Fellow, College of Surgeons of Sri Lanka
FCST	Fellow, College of Speech Therapists (*now see* FCSLT)
FCT	Federal Capital Territory (*now see* ACT); Fellow, Association of Corporate Treasurers
FCTB	Fellow, College of Teachers of the Blind
FCU	Fighter Control Unit
FCWA	Fellow, Institute of Costs and Works Accountants (*now see* FCMA)
FDA	Association of First Division Civil Servants
FDF	Food and Drink Federation
FDI	Fédération Dentaire Internationale
FDP	Freie Demokratische Partei
FDS	Fellow in Dental Surgery
FDSRCPSGlas	Fellow in Dental Surgery, Royal College of Physicians and Surgeons of Glasgow
FDSRCS or **FDS RCS**	Fellow in Dental Surgery, Royal College of Surgeons of England
FDSRCSE	Fellow in Dental Surgery, Royal College of Surgeons of Edinburgh
FE	Far East
FEAF	Far East Air Force
FEANI	Fédération Européenne d'Associations Nationales d'Ingénieurs
FEBS	Federation of European Biochemical Societies
FECI	Fellow, Institute of Employment Consultants
FEE	Fédération des Expertes Comptables Européens
FEF	Far East Fleet
FEFC or **FEFCE**	Further Education Funding Council for England
FEI	Fédération Equestre Internationale
FEIDCT	Fellow, Educational Institute of Design Craft and Technology
FEIS	Fellow, Educational Institute of Scotland
FELCO	Federation of English Language Course Opportunities
FEng	Fellow, Royal Academy (*formerly* Fellowship) of Engineering
FES	Fellow, Entomological Society; Fellow, Ethnological Society
FESC	Fellow, European Society of Cardiology
FF	Fianna Fáil; Field Force
FFA	Fellow, Faculty of Actuaries (in Scotland); Fellow, Institute of Financial Accountants
FFAEM	Fellow, Faculty of Accident and Emergency Medicine
FFARACS	Fellow, Faculty of Anaesthetists, Royal Australasian College of Surgeons (*now see* FANZCA)
FFARCS	Fellow, Faculty of Anaesthetists, Royal College of Surgeons of England (*now see* FRCA)
FFARCSI	Fellow, Faculty of Anaesthetists, Royal College of Surgeons in Ireland
FFAS	Fellow, Faculty of Architects and Surveyors, London (*now see* FASI)
FFA(SA)	Fellow, Faculty of Anaesthetists (South Africa)
FFB	Fellow, Faculty of Building
FFCM	Fellow, Faculty of Community Medicine (*now see* FFPHM)
FFCMI	Fellow, Faculty of Community Medicine of Ireland
FFDRCSI	Fellow, Faculty of Dentistry, Royal College of Surgeons in Ireland
FFF	Free French Forces
FFFP	Fellow, Faculty of Family Planning of the Royal College of Obstetricians and Gynaecologists
FFHC	Freedom from Hunger Campaign
FFHom	Fellow, Faculty of Homœopathy
FFI	French Forces of the Interior; Finance for Industry
FFOM	Fellow, Faculty of Occupational Medicine
FFOMI	Fellow, Faculty of Occupational Medicine of Ireland

FFPath, RCPI	Fellow, Faculty of Pathologists of the Royal College of Physicians of Ireland
FFPHM	Fellow, Faculty of Public Health Medicine
FFPHMI	Fellow, Faculty of Public Health Medicine of Ireland
FFPM	Fellow, Faculty of Pharmaceutical Medicine
FFPS	Fauna and Flora Preservation Society
FFR	Fellow, Faculty of Radiologists (*now see* FRCR)
FG	Fine Gael
FGA	Fellow, Gemmological Association
FGCL	Fellow, Goldsmiths' College, London
FGCM	Fellow, Guild of Church Musicians
FGDS	Fédération de la Gauche Démocratique et Socialiste
FGGE	Fellow, Guild of Glass Engineers
FGI	Fellow, Institute of Certificated Grocers
FGS	Fellow, Geological Society
FGSM	Fellow, Guildhall School of Music and Drama
FGSM(MT)	Fellow, Guildhall School of Music and Drama (Music Therapy)
FHA	Fellow, Institute of Health Service Administrators (*formerly* Hospital Administrators; *now see* FHSM)
FHAS	Fellow, Highland and Agricultural Society of Scotland
FHCIMA	Fellow, Hotel Catering and Institutional Management Association
FHFS	Fellow, Human Factors Society
FHKIE	Fellow, Hong Kong Institution of Engineers
FHMAAAS	Foreign Honorary Member, American Academy of Arts and Sciences
FHS	Fellow, Heraldry Society; Forces Help Society and Lord Roberts Workshops
FHSA	Family Health Services Authority
FHSM	Fellow, Institute of Health Services Management
FH-WC	Fellow, Heriot-Watt College (*now* University), Edinburgh
FIA	Fellow, Institute of Actuaries
FIAA	Fellow, Institute of Actuaries of Australia
FIAAS	Fellow, Institute of Australian Agricultural Science
FIAA&S	Fellow, Incorporated Association of Architects and Surveyors
FIAgrE	Fellow, Institution of Agricultural Engineers
FIAgrM	Fellow, Institute of Agricultural Management
FIAI	Fellow, Institute of Industrial and Commercial Accountants
FIAL	Fellow, International Institute of Arts and Letters
FIAM	Fellow, International Academy of Management
FIAP	Fellow, Institution of Analysts and Programmers
FIArb	Fellow, Institute of Arbitrators (*now see* FCIArb)
FIArbA	Fellow, Institute of Arbitrators of Australia
FIAS	Fellow, Institute of Aeronautical Sciences (US) (*now see* FAIAA)
FIASc	Fellow, Indian Academy of Sciences
FIAWS	Fellow, International Academy of Wood Sciences
FIB	Fellow, Institute of Bankers (*now see* FCIB)
FIBA	Fellow, Institute of Business Administration, Australia (*now see* FCIM)
FIBD	Fellow, Institute of British Decorators
FIBiol	Fellow, Institute of Biology
FIBiotech	Fellow, Institute for Biotechnical Studies
FIBMS	Fellow, Institute of Biomedical Sciences
FIBP	Fellow, Institute of British Photographers
FIBScot	Fellow, Institute of Bankers in Scotland (*now see* FCIBS)
FIC	Fellow, Institute of Chemistry (*now see* FRIC, FRSC); Fellow, Imperial College, London
FICA	Fellow, Commonwealth Institute of Accountants; Fellow, Institute of Chartered Accountants in England and Wales (*now see* FCA)
FICAI	Fellow, Institute of Chartered Accountants in Ireland
FICD	Fellow, Institute of Civil Defence (*now see* FICDDS); Fellow, Indian College of Dentists; Fellow, International College of Dentists
FICDDS	Fellow, Institute of Civil Defence and Disaster Studies
FICE	Fellow, Institution of Civil Engineers
FICeram	Fellow, Institute of Ceramics (*now see* FIM)
FICFM	Fellow, Institute of Charity Fundraising Managers
FICFor	Fellow, Institute of Chartered Foresters
FIChemE	Fellow, Institution of Chemical Engineers
FICI	Fellow, Institute of Chemistry of Ireland; Fellow, International Colonial Institute
FICM	Fellow, Institute of Credit Management
FICMA	Fellow, Institute of Cost and Management Accountants
FICorrST	Fellow, Institution of Corrosion Science and Technology
FICS	Fellow, Institute of Chartered Shipbrokers; Fellow, International College of Surgeons
FICT	Fellow, Institute of Concrete Technologists
FICW	Fellow, Institute of Clerks of Works of Great Britain
FIDA	Fellow, Institute of Directors, Australia
FIDCA	Fellow, Industrial Design Council of Australia
FIDE	Fédération Internationale des Echecs; Fellow, Institute of Design Engineers; Fédération Internationale pour le Droit Européen
FIDEM	Fédération Internationale de la Médaille
FIEAust	Fellow, Institution of Engineers, Australia
FIEC	Fellow, Institute of Employment Consultants
FIED	Fellow, Institution of Engineering Designers
FIEE	Fellow, Institution of Electrical Engineers
FIEEE	Fellow, Institute of Electrical and Electronics Engineers (NY)
FIEHK	Fellow, Institution of Engineering, Hong Kong
FIElecIE	Fellow, Institution of Electronic Incorporated Engineers (*now see* FIEIE)
FIEI	Fellow, Institution of Engineering Inspection (*now see* FIQA); Fellow, Institution of Engineers of Ireland
FIEIE	Fellow, Institution of Electronics and Electrical Incorporated Engineers
FIEJ	Fédération Internationale des Editeurs de Journaux et Publications
FIERE	Fellow, Institution of Electronic and Radio Engineers (*now see* FIEE)
FIES	Fellow, Illuminating Engineering Society (later FIllumES; *now see* FCIBSE); Fellow, Institution of Engineers and Shipbuilders, Scotland
FIET	Fédération Internationale des Employés, Techniciens et Cadres
FIEx	Fellow, Institute of Export
FIExpE	Fellow, Institute of Explosives Engineers
FIFA	Fédération Internationale de Football Association
FIFF	Fellow, Institute of Freight Forwarders
FIFireE	Fellow, Institution of Fire Engineers
FIFM	Fellow, Institute of Fisheries Management
FIFor	Fellow, Institute of Foresters (*now see* FICFor)
FIFST	Fellow, Institute of Food Science and Technology
FIGasE	Fellow, Institution of Gas Engineers
FIGCM	Fellow, Incorporated Guild of Church Musicians
FIGD	Fellow, Institute of Grocery Distribution
FIGO	International Federation of Gynaecology and Obstetrics
FIH	Fellow, Institute of Housing (*now see* FCIH); Fellow, Institute of the Horse
FIHE	Fellow, Institute of Health Education
FIHM	Fellow, Institute of Housing Managers (later FIH; *now see* FCIH)
FIHort	Fellow, Institute of Horticulture
FIHospE	Fellow, Institute of Hospital Engineering
FIHT	Fellow, Institution of Highways and Transportation
FIHVE	Fellow, Institution of Heating & Ventilating Engineers (later FCIBS and MCIBS; *now see* FCIBSE)
FIIA	Fellow, Institute of Industrial Administration (later CBIM and FBIM); Fellow, Institute of Internal Auditors
FIIB	Fellow, International Institute of Biotechnology
FIIC	Fellow, International Institute for Conservation of Historic and Artistic Works
FIIDA	Fellow, International Interior Design Association
FIIM	Fellow, Institution of Industrial Managers
FIInfSc	Fellow, Institute of Information Scientists
FIInst	Fellow, Imperial Institute
FIIP	Fellow, Institute of Incorporated Photographers (*now see* FBIPP)
FIIPC	Fellow, India International Photographic Council
FIIPE	Fellow, Indian Institution of Production Engineers
FIL	Fellow, Institute of Linguists
FILA	Fellow, Institute of Landscape Architects (*now see* FLI)
FILDM	Fellow, Institute of Logistics and Distribution Management (*now see* FILog)
FilDr	Doctor of Philosophy
Fil.Hed.	Filosofie Hedersdoktor
FILLM	Fédération Internationale des Langues et Littératures Modernes
FIllumES	Fellow, Illuminating Engineering Society (*now see* FCIBSE)
FILog	Fellow, Institute of Logistics
FIM	Fellow, Institute of Materials (*formerly* Institution of Metallurgists, then Institute of Metals)
FIMA	Fellow, Institute of Mathematics and its Applications
FIMarE	Fellow, Institute of Marine Engineers
FIMatM	Fellow, Institute of Materials Management (*now see* FILog)
FIMBRA	Financial Intermediaries, Managers and Brokers Regulatory Association
FIMC	Fellow, Institute of Management Consultants
FIMCB	Fellow, International Management Centre from Buckingham
FIMechE	Fellow, Institution of Mechanical Engineers
FIMfgE	Fellow, Institution of Manufacturing Engineers (*now see* FIEE)

FIMFT	Fellow, Institute of Maxillo-facial Technology
FIMgt	Fellow, Institute of Management
FIMGTechE	Fellow, Institution of Mechanical and General Technician Engineers
FIMH	Fellow, Institute of Materials Handling (later FIMatM); Fellow, Institute of Military History
FIMI	Fellow, Institute of the Motor Industry
FIMinE	Fellow, Institution of Mining Engineers
FIMIT	Fellow, Institute of Musical Instrument Technology
FIMLS	Fellow, Institute of Medical Laboratory Sciences (now see FIBMS)
FIMLT	Fellow, Institute of Medical Laboratory Technology (later FIMLS)
FIMM	Fellow, Institution of Mining and Metallurgy
FIMMA	Fellow, Institute of Metals and Materials Australasia
FIMS	Fellow, Institute of Mathematical Statistics
FIMT	Fellow, Institute of the Motor Trade (now see FIMI)
FIMTA	Fellow, Institute of Municipal Treasurers and Accountants (now see IPFA)
FIMunE	Fellow, Institution of Municipal Engineers (now amalgamated with Institution of Civil Engineers)
FIN	Fellow, Institute of Navigation (now see FRIN)
FINA	Fédération Internationale de Natation Amateur
FInstAM	Fellow, Institute of Administrative Management
FInstArb(NZ)	Fellow, Institute of Arbitrators of New Zealand
FInstB	Fellow, Institution of Buyers
FInstBiol	Fellow, Institute of Biology (now see FIBiol)
FInstD	Fellow, Institute of Directors
FInstE	Fellow, Institute of Energy
FInstEnvSci	Fellow, Institute of Environmental Sciences
FInstF	Fellow, Institute of Fuel (now see FInstE)
FInstFF	Fellow, Institute of Freight Forwarders Ltd (now see FIFF)
FInstHE	Fellow, Institution of Highways Engineers (now see FIHT)
FInstLEx	Fellow, Institute of Legal Executives
FInstM	Fellow, Institute of Meat; Fellow, Institute of Marketing (now see FCIM)
FInstMC	Fellow, Institute of Measurement and Control
FInstMSM	Fellow, Institute of Marketing and Sales Management (later FInstM; now see FCIM)
FInstMet	Fellow, Institute of Metals (later part of Metals Society; now see FIM)
FInstNDT	Fellow, Institute of Non-Destructive Testing
FInstP	Fellow, Institute of Physics
FInstPet	Fellow, Institute of Petroleum
FInstPI	Fellow, Institute of Patentees and Inventors
FInstPS	Fellow, Institute of Purchasing and Supply (now see FCIPS)
FInstSM	Fellow, Institute of Sales Management (now see FInstSMM)
FInstSMM	Fellow, Institute of Sales and Marketing Management
FInstW	Fellow, Institute of Welding (now see FWeldI)
FINucE	Fellow, Institution of Nuclear Engineers
FIOA	Fellow, Institute of Acoustics
FIOB	Fellow, Institute of Building (now see FCIOB)
FIOH	Fellow, Institute of Occupational Hygiene
FIOM	Fellow, Institute of Office Management (now see FIAM)
FIOP	Fellow, Institute of Printing
FIOSH	Fellow, Institute of Occupational Safety and Health
FIP	Fellow, Australian Institute of Petroleum
FIPA	Fellow, Institute of Practitioners in Advertising
FIPD	Fellow, Institute of Personnel and Development
FIPDM	Fellow, Institute of Physical Distribution Management (later FILDM)
FIPENZ	Fellow, Institution of Professional Engineers, New Zealand
FIPG	Fellow, Institute of Professional Goldsmiths
FIPHE	Fellow, Institution of Public Health Engineers (now see FIWEM)
FIPlantE	Fellow, Institute of Plant Engineers (now see FIIM)
FIPM	Fellow, Institute of Personnel Management (now see FIPD)
FIPR	Fellow, Institute of Public Relations
FIProdE	Fellow, Institution of Production Engineers (later FIMfgE; now see FIEE)
FIQ	Fellow, Institute of Quarrying
FIQA	Fellow, Institute of Quality Assurance
FIQS	Fellow, Institute of Quantity Surveyors
FIRA	Furniture Industry Research Association
FIRA(Ind)	Fellow, Institute of Railway Auditors and Accountants (India)
FIRE(Aust)	Fellow, Institution of Radio Engineers (Australia) (now see FIREE(Aust))
FIREE(Aust)	Fellow, Institution of Radio and Electronics Engineers (Australia)
FIRI	Fellow, Institution of the Rubber Industry (later FPRI)
FIRM	Fellow, Institute of Risk Management
FIRSE	Fellow, Institute of Railway Signalling Engineers
FIRTE	Fellow, Institute of Road Transport Engineers
FIS	Fellow, Institute of Statisticians
FISA	Fellow, Incorporated Secretaries' Association; Fédération Internationale des Sociétés d'Aviron
FISE	Fellow, Institution of Sales Engineers; Fellow, Institution of Sanitary Engineers
FISITA	Fédération Internationale des Sociétés d'Ingénieurs des Techniques de l'Automobile
FISM	Fellow, Institute of Supervisory Managers
FISOB	Fellow, Incorporated Society of Organ Builders
FISP	Fédération Internationale des Sociétés de Philosophie
FIST	Fellow, Institute of Science Technology
FISTC	Fellow, Institute of Scientific and Technical Communicators
FISTD	Fellow, Imperial Society of Teachers of Dancing
FIStructE	Fellow, Institution of Structural Engineers
FISW	Fellow, Institute of Social Work
FITD	Fellow, Institute of Training and Development (now see FIPD)
FITE	Fellow, Institution of Electrical and Electronics Technician Engineers
FIW	Fellow, Welding Institute (now see FWeldI)
FIWE	Fellow, Institution of Water Engineers (later FIWES; then FIWEM; now see FCIWEM)
FIWEM	Fellow, Institution of Water and Environmental Management (now see FCIWEM)
FIWES	Fellow, Institution of Water Engineers and Scientists (later FIWEM; now see FCIWEM)
FIWM	Fellow, Institution of Works Managers (now see FIIM)
FIWPC	Fellow, Institution of Water Pollution Control (later FIWEM; now see FCIWEM)
FIWSc	Fellow, Institute of Wood Science
FIWSP	Fellow, Institute of Work Study Practitioners (now see FMS)
FJI	Fellow, Institute of Journalists (now see FCIJ)
FJIE	Fellow, Junior Institution of Engineers (now see CIMGTechE)
FKC	Fellow, King's College London
FKCHMS	Fellow, King's College Hospital Medical School
FL	Florida
FLA	Fellow, Library Association
Fla	Florida (US)
FLAA	Fellow, Library Association of Australia
FLAI	Fellow, Library Association of Ireland
FLAS	Fellow, Chartered Land Agents' Society (now (after amalgamation) see FRICS)
FLCM	Fellow, London College of Music
FLHS	Fellow, London Historical Society
FLI	Fellow, Landscape Institute
FLIA	Fellow, Life Insurance Association
FLS	Fellow, Linnean Society
Flt	Flight
FM	Field-Marshal
FMA	Fellow, Museums Association
FMAAT	Fellow Member, Association of Accounting Technicians
FMANZ	Fellow, Medical Association of New Zealand
FMES	Fellow, Minerals Engineering Society
FMF	Fiji Military Forces
FMI	Foundation for Manufacturing and Industry
FMS	Federated Malay States; Fellow, Medical Society; Fellow, Institute of Management Services
FMSA	Fellow, Mineralogical Society of America
FNA	Fellow, Indian National Science Academy
FNAEA	Fellow, National Association of Estate Agents
FNCO	Fleet Naval Constructor Officer
FNECInst	Fellow, North East Coast Institution of Engineers and Shipbuilders
FNI	Fellow, Nautical Institute; Fellow, National Institute of Sciences in India (now see FNA)
FNIA	Fellow, Nigerian Institute of Architects
FNM	Free National Movement
FNZEI	Fellow, New Zealand Educational Institute
FNZIA	Fellow, New Zealand Institute of Architects
FNZIAS	Fellow, New Zealand Institute of Agricultural Science
FNZIC	Fellow, New Zealand Institute of Chemistry
FNZIE	Fellow, New Zealand Institution of Engineers (now see FIPENZ)
FNZIM	Fellow, New Zealand Institute of Management
FNZPsS	Fellow, New Zealand Psychological Society
FO	Foreign Office (now see FCO); Field Officer; Flying Officer
FODA	Fellow, Overseas Doctors' Association
FODC	Franciscan Order of the Divine Compassion
FOIC	Flag Officer in charge
FOMI	Faculty of Occupational Medicine of Ireland
FONA	Flag Officer, Naval Aviation
FONAC	Flag Officer Naval Air Command

FOR	Fellowship of Operational Research
For.	Foreign
FOREST	Freedom Organisation for the Right to Enjoy Smoking Tobacco
FOX	Futures and Options Exchange
FPA	Family Planning Association
FPC	Family Practitioner Committee (*now see* FHSA)
FPEA	Fellow, Physical Education Association
FPHM	Faculty of Public Health Medicine
FPhS	Fellow, Philosophical Society of England
FPI	Fellow, Plastics Institute (later FPRI)
FPIA	Fellow, Plastics Institute of Australia
FPMI	Fellow, Pensions Management Institute
FPRI	Fellow, Plastics and Rubber Institute (*now see* FIM)
FPS	Fellow, Pharmaceutical Society (*now see* FRPharmS); Fauna Preservation Society (*now see* FFPS)
FPhysS	Fellow, Physical Society
f r	fuori ruole
FRA	Fellow, Royal Academy
FRACDS	Fellow, Royal Australian College of Dental Surgeons
FRACGP	Fellow, Royal Australian College of General Practitioners
FRACI	Fellow, Royal Australian Chemical Institute
FRACMA	Fellow, Royal Australian College of Medical Administrators
FRACO	Fellow, Royal Australian College of Ophthalmologists
FRACOG	Fellow, Royal Australian College of Obstetricians and Gynaecologists
FRACP	Fellow, Royal Australasian College of Physicians
FRACR	Fellow, Royal Australasian College of Radiologists
FRACS	Fellow, Royal Australasian College of Surgeons
FRAD	Fellow, Royal Academy of Dancing
FRAeS	Fellow, Royal Aeronautical Society
FRAgS	Fellow, Royal Agricultural Societies (*ie* of England, Scotland and Wales)
FRAHS	Fellow, Royal Australian Historical Society
FRAI	Fellow, Royal Anthropological Institute of Great Britain & Ireland
FRAIA	Fellow, Royal Australian Institute of Architects
FRAIB	Fellow, Royal Australian Institute of Building
FRAIC	Fellow, Royal Architectural Institute of Canada
FRAIPA	Fellow, Royal Australian Institute of Public Administration
FRAM	Fellow, Royal Academy of Music
FRAME	Fund for the Replacement of Animals in Medical Experiments
FRANZCP	Fellow, Royal Australian and New Zealand College of Psychiatrists
FRAPI	Fellow, Royal Australian Planning Institute
FRAS	Fellow, Royal Astronomical Society; Fellow, Royal Asiatic Society
FRASB	Fellow, Royal Asiatic Society of Bengal
FRASE	Fellow, Royal Agricultural Society of England
FRBS	Fellow, Royal Society of British Sculptors; Fellow, Royal Botanic Society
FRCA	Fellow, Royal College of Art; Fellow, Royal College of Anaesthetists
FRCCO	Fellow, Royal Canadian College of Organists
FRCD(Can.)	Fellow, Royal College of Dentists of Canada
FRCGP	Fellow, Royal College of General Practitioners
FRCM	Fellow, Royal College of Music
FRCN	Fellow, Royal College of Nursing
FRCO	Fellow, Royal College of Organists
FRCO(CHM)	Fellow, Royal College of Organists with Diploma in Choir Training
FRCOG	Fellow, Royal College of Obstetricians and Gynaecologists
FRCOphth	Fellow, Royal College of Ophthalmologists
FRCP	Fellow, Royal College of Physicians, London
FRCPA	Fellow, Royal College of Pathologists of Australasia
FRCP&S (Canada)	Fellow, Royal College of Physicians and Surgeons of Canada
FRCPath	Fellow, Royal College of Pathologists
FRCP(C)	Fellow, Royal College of Physicians of Canada
FRCPE or FRCPEd	Fellow, Royal College of Physicians, Edinburgh
FRCPGlas	Fellow, Royal College of Physicians and Surgeons of Glasgow
FRCPI	Fellow, Royal College of Physicians of Ireland
FRCPSGlas	Hon. Fellow, Royal College of Physicians and Surgeons of Glasgow
FRCPsych	Fellow, Royal College of Psychiatrists
FRCR	Fellow, Royal College of Radiologists
FRCS	Fellow, Royal College of Surgeons of England
FRCSCan	Fellow, Royal College of Surgeons of Canada
FRCSE or FRCSEd	Fellow, Royal College of Surgeons of Edinburgh
FRCSGlas	Fellow, Royal College of Physicians and Surgeons of Glasgow
FRCSI	Fellow, Royal College of Surgeons in Ireland
FRCSoc	Fellow, Royal Commonwealth Society
FRCUS	Fellow, Royal College of University Surgeons (Denmark)
FRCVS	Fellow, Royal College of Veterinary Surgeons
FREconS	Fellow, Royal Economic Society
FREI	Fellow, Real Estate Institute (Australia)
FRES	Fellow, Royal Entomological Society of London
FRFPSG	Fellow, Royal Faculty of Physicians and Surgeons, Glasgow (*now see* FRCPGlas)
FRG	Federal Republic of Germany
FRGS	Fellow, Royal Geographical Society
FRGSA	Fellow, Royal Geographical Society of Australasia
FRHistS	Fellow, Royal Historical Society
FRHS	Fellow, Royal Horticultural Society (*now see* MRHS)
FRHSV	Fellow, Royal Historical Society of Victoria
FRIAS	Fellow, Royal Incorporation of Architects of Scotland; Royal Institute for the Advancement of Science
FRIBA	Fellow, Royal Institute of British Architects (*and see* RIBA)
FRIC	Fellow, Royal Institute of Chemistry (*now see* FRSC)
FRICS	Fellow, Royal Institution of Chartered Surveyors
FRIH	Fellow, Royal Institute of Horticulture (NZ)
FRIN	Fellow, Royal Institute of Navigation
FRINA	Fellow, Royal Institution of Naval Architects
FRIPA	Fellow, Royal Institute of Public Administration (the Institute no longer has Fellows)
FRIPHH	Fellow, Royal Institute of Public Health and Hygiene
FRMCM	Fellow, Royal Manchester College of Music
FRMedSoc	Fellow, Royal Medical Society
FRMetS	Fellow, Royal Meteorological Society
FRMIA	Fellow, Retail Management Institute of Australia
FRMS	Fellow, Royal Microscopical Society
FRNCM	Fellow, Royal Northern College of Music
FRNS	Fellow, Royal Numismatic Society
FRPharmS	Fellow, Royal Pharmaceutical Society
FRPS	Fellow, Royal Photographic Society
FRPSL	Fellow, Royal Philatelic Society, London
FRS	Fellow, Royal Society
FRSA	Fellow, Royal Society of Arts
FRSAI	Fellow, Royal Society of Antiquaries of Ireland
FRSAMD	Fellow, Royal Scottish Academy of Music and Drama
FRSanI	Fellow, Royal Sanitary Institute (*now see* FRSH)
FRSC	Fellow, Royal Society of Canada; Fellow, Royal Society of Chemistry
FRS(Can)	Fellow, Royal Society of Canada (used when a person is also a Fellow of the Royal Society of Chemistry)
FRSCM	Hon. Fellow, Royal School of Church Music
FRSC (UK)	Fellow, Royal Society of Chemistry (used when a person is also a Fellow of the Royal Society of Canada)
FRSE	Fellow, Royal Society of Edinburgh
FRSGS	Fellow, Royal Scottish Geographical Society
FRSH	Fellow, Royal Society for the Promotion of Health
FRSL	Fellow, Royal Society of Literature
FRSM or FRSocMed	Fellow, Royal Society of Medicine
FRSNZ	Fellow, Royal Society of New Zealand
FRSSAf	Fellow, Royal Society of South Africa
FRST	Fellow, Royal Society of Teachers
FRSTM&H	Fellow, Royal Society of Tropical Medicine and Hygiene
FRTPI	Fellow, Royal Town Planning Institute
FRTS	Fellow, Royal Television Society
FRVA	Fellow, Rating and Valuation Association (*now see* IRRV)
FRVC	Fellow, Royal Veterinary College
FRVIA	Fellow, Royal Victorian Institute of Architects
FRZSScot	Fellow, Royal Zoological Society of Scotland
FS	Field Security
fs	Graduate, Royal Air Force Staff College
FSA	Fellow, Society of Antiquaries
FSAA	Fellow, Society of Incorporated Accountants and Auditors
FSAE	Fellow, Society of Automotive Engineers; Fellow, Society of Art Education
FSAI	Fellow, Society of Architectural Illustrators
FSAIEE	Fellow, South African Institute of Electrical Engineers
FSAM	Fellow, Society of Art Masters
FSArc	Fellow, Society of Architects (merged with the RIBA 1952)
FSaRS	Fellow, Safety and Reliability Society
FSAScot	Fellow, Society of Antiquaries of Scotland
FSASM	Fellow, South Australian School of Mines
FSBI	Fellow, Savings Banks Institute
fsc	Foreign Staff College
FSCA	Fellow, Society of Company and Commercial Accountants
FScotvec	Fellow, Scottish Vocational Education Council

FSCRE	Fellow, Scottish Council for Research in Education
FSDC	Fellow, Society of Dyers and Colourists
FSE	Fellow, Society of Engineers
FSG	Fellow, Society of Genealogists
FSGT	Fellow, Society of Glass Technology
FSI	Fellow, Chartered Surveyors' Institution (*now see* FRICS); Fellow, Securities Institute
FSIAD	Fellow, Society of Industrial Artists and Designers (*now see* FCSD)
FSLAET	Fellow, Society of Licensed Aircraft Engineers and Technologists
FSLCOG	Fellow, Sri Lankan College of Obstetrics and Gynaecology
FSLTC	Fellow, Society of Leather Technologists and Chemists
FSMA	Fellow, Incorporated Sales Managers' Association (later FInstMSM, then FInstM)
FSMC	Freeman of the Spectacle-Makers' Company
FSME	Fellow, Society of Manufacturing Engineers
FSMPTE	Fellow, Society of Motion Picture and Television Engineers (USA)
FSNAD	Fellow, Society of Numismatic Artists and Designers
FSNAME	Fellow, American Society of Naval Architects and Marine Engineers
FSRHE	Fellow, Society for Research into Higher Education
FSRP	Fellow, Society for Radiological Protection
FSS	Fellow, Royal Statistical Society
FSTD	Fellow, Society of Typographic Designers
FSVA	Fellow, Incorporated Society of Valuers and Auctioneers
FT	Financial Times
FTAT	Furniture, Timber and Allied Trades Union
FTC	Flying Training Command; Full Technological Certificate, City and Guilds of London Institute
FTCD	Fellow, Trinity College, Dublin
FTCL	Fellow, Trinity College of Music, London
FTI	Fellow, Textile Institute
FTII	Fellow, Chartered Institute (*formerly* Incorporated Institute, then Institute) of Taxation
FTMA	Fellow, Telecommunications Managers Association
FTP	Fellow, Thames Polytechnic
FTS	Fellow, Australian Academy of Technological Sciences and Engineering; Flying Training School; Fellow, Tourism Society
FTSC	Fellow, Tonic Sol-fa College
FUCUA	Federation of University Conservative and Unionist Associations (*now see* FCS)
FUMIST	Fellow, University of Manchester Institute of Science and Technology
FVRDE	Fighting Vehicles Research and Development Establishment
FWAAS	Fellow, World Academy of Arts and Sciences
FWACP	Fellow, West African College of Physicians
FWCMD	Fellow, Welsh College of Music and Drama
FWeldI	Fellow, Welding Institute
FWSOM	Fellow, Institute of Practitioners in Work Study, Organisation and Method (*now see* FMS)
FZS	Fellow, Zoological Society
FZSScot	Fellow, Zoological Society of Scotland (*now see* FRZSScot)

G

GA	Geologists' Association; Gaelic Athletic (Club); Georgia
Ga	Georgia (US)
GAI	Guild of Architectural Ironmongers
GAP	Gap Activity Projects
GAPAN	Guild of Air Pilots and Air Navigators
GATT	General Agreement on Tariffs and Trade (*now* World Trade Organisation)
GB	Great Britain
GBA	Governing Bodies Association
GBE	Knight or Dame Grand Cross, Order of the British Empire
GBGSA	Governing Bodies of Girls' Schools Association (*formerly* Association of Governing Bodies of Girls' Public Schools)
GBSM	Graduate of Birmingham and Midland Institute School of Music
GC	George Cross
GCB	Knight or Dame Grand Cross, Order of the Bath
GCBS	General Council of British Shipping
GCCC	Gonville and Caius College, Cambridge
GCFR	Grand Commander, Order of the Federal Republic of Nigeria
GCH	Knight Grand Cross, Hanoverian Order
GCHQ	Government Communications Headquarters

GCIE	Knight Grand Commander, Order of the Indian Empire
GCLJ	Grand Cross, St Lazarus of Jerusalem
GCLM	Grand Commander, Order of the Legion of Merit of Rhodesia
GCM	Gold Crown of Merit (Barbados)
GCMG	Knight or Dame Grand Cross, Order of St Michael and St George
GCON	Grand Cross, Order of the Niger
GCSE	General Certificate of Secondary Education
GCSG	Knight Grand Cross, Order of St Gregory the Great
GCSI	Knight Grand Commander, Order of the Star of India
GCSJ	Knight Grand Cross of Justice, Order of St John of Jerusalem (Knights Hospitaller)
GCSL	Grand Cross, Order of St Lucia
GCStJ	Bailiff or Dame Grand Cross, Most Venerable Order of the Hospital of St John of Jerusalem
GCVO	Knight or Dame Grand Cross, Royal Victorian Order
gd	grand-daughter
GDBA	Guide Dogs for the Blind Association
GDC	General Dental Council
Gdns	Gardens
GDR	German Democratic Republic
Gen.	General
Ges.	Gesellschaft
GFD	Geophysical Fluid Dynamics
GFS	Girls' Friendly Society
ggd	great-grand-daughter
ggs	great-grandson
GGSM	Graduate in Music, Guildhall School of Music and Drama
GHQ	General Headquarters
Gib.	Gibraltar
GIMechE	Graduate, Institution of Mechanical Engineers
GL	Grand Lodge
GLAA	Greater London Arts Association (*now see* GLAB)
GLAB	Greater London Arts Board
GLC	Greater London Council
Glos	Gloucestershire
GM	George Medal; Grand Medal (Ghana)
GMB	(Union for) General, Municipal, Boilermakers
GMBATU	General, Municipal, Boilermakers and Allied Trades Union (*now see* GMB)
GmbH	Gesellschaft mit beschränkter Haftung
GMC	General Medical Council; Guild of Memorial Craftsmen; General Management Course (Henley)
GMIE	Grand Master, Order of the Indian Empire
GMSI	Grand Master, Order of the Star of India
GMWU	General and Municipal Workers' Union (later GMBATU; *now see* GMB)
GNC	General Nursing Council
GOC	General Officer Commanding
GOC-in-C	General Officer Commanding-in-Chief
GOE	General Ordination Examination
Gov.	Governor
Govt	Government
GP	General Practitioner; Grand Prix
GPDST	Girls' Public Day School Trust
GPMU	Graphical, Paper and Media Union
GPO	General Post Office
GQG	Grand Quartier Général
GR	General Reconaissance
Gr.	Greek
GRSM	Graduate of the Royal Schools of Music
GS	General Staff; Grammar School
gs	grandson
GSA	Girls' Schools Association
GSM	General Service Medal; (Member of) Guildhall School of Music and Drama
GSMD	Guildhall School of Music and Drama
GSO	General Staff Officer
GTCL	Graduate, Trinity College of Music
GTS	General Theological Seminary (New York)
GUI	Golfing Union of Ireland
GWR	Great Western Railway

H

HA	Historical Association; Health Authority
HAA	Heavy Anti-Aircraft
HAC	Honourable Artillery Company
HACAS	Housing Association Consultancy and Advisory Service
Hants	Hampshire
HARCVS	Honorary Associate, Royal College of Veterinary Surgeons
Harv.	Harvard
HAT	Housing Action Trust

HBM	His (or Her) Britannic Majesty (Majesty's); Humming Bird Gold Medal (Trinidad)
hc	*honoris causa* (honorary)
HCEG	Honourable Company of Edinburgh Golfers
HCF	Honorary Chaplain to the Forces
HCIMA	Hotel, Catering and Institutional Management Association
HCO	Higher Clerical Officer
HCSC	Higher Command and Staff Course
HDA	Hawkesbury Diploma in Agriculture (Australia)
HDD	Higher Dental Diploma
HDFA	Higher Diploma in Fine Art
HDipEd	Higher Diploma in Education
HE	His (or Her) Excellency; His Eminence
HEA	Health Education Authority
HEC	Ecole des Hautes Etudes Commerciales; Higher Education Corporation
HEFCE	Higher Education Funding Council for England
HEFCW	Higher Education Funding Council for Wales
HEH	His (or Her) Exalted Highness
HEIC	Honourable East India Company
HEICS	Honourable East India Company's Service
Heir-pres.	Heir-presumptive
HEO	Higher Executive Officer
HEQC	Higher Education Quality Council
Herts	Hertfordshire
HFARA	Honorary Foreign Associate of the Royal Academy
HFEA	Human Fertilisation and Embryology Authority
HFRA	Honorary Foreign Member of the Royal Academy
HG	Home Guard
HGTAC	Home Grown Timber Advisory Committee
HH	His (or Her) Highness; His Holiness; Member, Hesketh Hubbard Art Society
HHA	Historic Houses Association
HHD	Doctor of Humanities (US)
HI	Hawaii
HIH	His (or Her) Imperial Highness
HIM	His (or Her) Imperial Majesty
HJ	Hilal-e-Jurat (Pakistan)
HKIA	Hong Kong Institute of Architects
HKIPM	Hong Kong Institute of Personnel Management
HLD	Doctor of Humane Letters
HLI	Highland Light Infantry
HM	His (or Her) Majesty, or Majesty's
HMA	Head Masters' Association
HMAS	His (or Her) Majesty's Australian Ship
HMC	Headmasters' Conference; Hospital Management Committee
HMCIC	His (or Her) Majesty's Chief Inspector of Constabulary
HMCS	His (or Her) Majesty's Canadian Ship
HMHS	His (or Her) Majesty's Hospital Ship
HMI	His (or Her) Majesty's Inspector
HMIED	Honorary Member, Institute of Engineering Designers
HMMTB	His (or Her) Majesty's Motor Torpedo Boat
HMOCS	His (or Her) Majesty's Overseas Civil Service
HMS	His (or Her) Majesty's Ship
HMSO	His (or Her) Majesty's Stationery Office
HNC	Higher National Certificate
HND	Higher National Diploma
H of C	House of Commons
H of L	House of Lords
Hon.	Honourable; Honorary
HPk	Hilal-e-Pakistan
HQ	Headquarters
HQA	Hilali-Quaid-i-Azam (Pakistan)
HRCA	Honorary Royal Cambrian Academician
HRGI	Honorary Member, The Royal Glasgow Institute of the Fine Arts
HRH	His (or Her) Royal Highness
HRHA	Honorary Member, Royal Hibernian Academy
HRI	Honorary Member, Royal Institute of Painters in Water Colours
HROI	Honorary Member, Royal Institute of Oil Painters
HRSA	Honorary Member, Royal Scottish Academy
HRSW	Honorary Member, Royal Scottish Water Colour Society
HSC	Health and Safety Commission
HSE	Health and Safety Executive
HSH	His (or Her) Serene Highness
Hum.	Humanity, Humanities (Classics)
Hunts	Huntingdonshire
HVCert	Health Visitor's Certificate
Hy	Heavy

I

I	Island; Ireland
IA	Indian Army; Iowa
Ia	Iowa (US)
IAAF	International Amateur Athletic Federation
IAC	Indian Armoured Corps; Institute of Amateur Cinematographers
IACP	International Association of Chiefs of Police
IADB	Inter American Development Bank
IADR	International Association for Dental Research
IAEA	International Atomic Energy Agency
IAF	Indian Air Force; Indian Auxiliary Force
IAHM	Incorporated Association of Headmasters
IAM	Institute of Advanced Motorists; Institute of Aviation Medicine
IAMAS	International Association of Meteorology and Atmospheric Sciences
IAMC	Indian Army Medical Corps
IAMTACT	Institute of Advanced Machine Tool and Control Technology
IAO	Incorporated Association of Organists
IAOC	Indian Army Ordnance Corps
IAPS	Incorporated Association of Preparatory Schools
IAPSO	International Association for the Physical Sciences of the Oceans
IARO	Indian Army Reserve of Officers
IAS	Indian Administrative Service; Institute for Advanced Studies; International Academy of Science
IASC	International Arctic Science Committee
IASS	International Association for Scandinavian Studies
IATA	International Air Transport Association
IATUL	International Association of Technological University Libraries
IAU	International Astronomical Union
IAWPRC	International Association on Water Pollution Research and Control
ib. or ibid.	*ibidem* (in the same place)
IBA	Independent Broadcasting Authority; International Bar Association
IBCA	International Braille Chess Association
IBG	Institute of British Geographers (*now see* RGS)
IBRD	International Bank for Reconstruction and Development (World Bank)
IBRO	International Bank Research Organisation; International Brain Research Organisation
IBTE	Institution of British Telecommunications Engineers
i/c	in charge; in command
ICA	Institute of Contemporary Arts; Institute of Chartered Accountants in England and Wales (*now see* ICAEW)
ICAA	Invalid Children's Aid Association
ICAEW	Institute of Chartered Accountants in England and Wales
ICAI	Institute of Chartered Accountants in Ireland
ICAO	International Civil Aviation Organization
ICBP	International Council for Bird Preservation
ICBS	Irish Christian Brothers' School
ICC	International Chamber of Commerce
ICCROM	International Centre for Conservation at Rome
ICD	*Iuris Canonici Doctor* (Doctor of Canon Law); Independence Commemorative Decoration (Rhodesia)
ICE	Institution of Civil Engineers
ICED	International Council for Educational Development
ICEF	International Federation of Chemical, Energy and General Workers' Unions
Icel.	Icelandic
ICES	International Council for the Exploration of the Sea
ICF	International Federation of Chemical and General Workers' Unions (*now see* ICEF)
ICFC	Industrial and Commercial Finance Corporation (later part of Investors in Industry)
ICFTU	International Confederation of Free Trade Unions
ICHCA	International Cargo Handling Co-ordination Association
IChemE	Institution of Chemical Engineers
ICI	Imperial Chemical Industries
ICJ	International Commission of Jurists
ICL	International Computers Ltd
ICM	International Confederation of Midwives
ICMA	Institute of Cost and Management Accountants (*now see* CIMA)
ICME	International Commission for Mathematical Education
ICOM	International Council of Museums
ICOMOS	International Council of Monuments and Sites
ICorrST	Institution of Corrosion Science and Technology
ICPO	International Criminal Police Organization (Interpol)
ICRC	International Committee of the Red Cross
ICRF	Imperial Cancer Research Fund
ICS	Indian Civil Service
ICSA	Institute of Chartered Secretaries and Administrators

ICSD	International Council for Scientific Development
ICSID	International Council of Societies of Industrial Design; International Centre for Settlement of Investment Disputes
ICSS	International Committee for the Sociology of Sport
ICSTIS	Independent Committee for Supervision of Telephone Information Services
ICSTM	Imperial College of Science, Technology and Medicine, London
ICSU	International Council of Scientific Unions
ICT	International Computers and Tabulators Ltd (*now see* ICL)
ID	Independence Decoration (Rhodesia); Idaho
Id	Idaho (US)
IDA	International Development Association
IDB	Internal Drainage Board; Industrial Development Board
IDC	Imperial Defence College (*now see* RCDS); Inter-Diocesan Certificate
idc	completed a course at, or served for a year on the Staff of, the Imperial Defence College (*now see* rcds)
IDRC	International Development Research Centre
IDS	Institute of Development Studies; Industry Department for Scotland
IEA	Institute of Economic Affairs
IEC	International Electrotechnical Commission
IEE	Institution of Electrical Engineers
IEEE	Institute of Electrical and Electronics Engineers (NY)
IEEIE	Institution of Electrical and Electronics Incorporated Engineers (*now see* IEIE)
IEETE	Institution of Electrical and Electronics Technician Engineers (later IEEIE; *now see* IEIE)
IEI	Institution of Engineers of Ireland
IEIE	Institution of Electronics and Electrical Incorporated Engineers
IEME	Inspectorate of Electrical and Mechanical Engineering
IEng	Incorporated Engineer
IERE	Institution of Electronic and Radio Engineers
IES	Indian Educational Service; Institution of Engineers and Shipbuilders in Scotland; International Electron Paramagnetic Resonance Society
IExpE	Institute of Explosives Engineers
IFAC	International Federation of Automatic Control
IFAD	International Fund for Agricultural Development (UNO)
IFAW	International Fund for Animal Welfare
IFBWW	International Federation of Building Woodworkers
IFC	International Finance Corporation
IFIAS	International Federation of Institutes of Advanced Study
IFIP	International Federation for Information Processing
IFL	International Friendship League
IFLA	International Federation of Library Associations
IFORS	International Federation of Operational Research Societies
IFPI	International Federation of the Phonographic Industry
IFRA	World Press Research Association
IFS	Irish Free State; Indian Forest Service
IG	Instructor in Gunnery
IGasE	Institution of Gas Engineers
IGPP	Institute of Geophysics and Planetary Physics
IGS	Independent Grammar School
IGU	International Geographical Union; International Gas Union
IHA	Institute of Health Service Administrators
IHospE	Institute of Hospital Engineering
IHSM	Institute of Health Services Management
IHVE	Institution of Heating and Ventilating Engineers (later CIBS)
IIExE	Institution of Incorporated Executive Engineers
IILS	International Institute for Labour Studies
IIM	Institution of Industrial Managers
IIMR	Institute of Investment Management and Research
IIMT	International Institute for the Management of Technology
IInfSc	Institute of Information Scientists
IIS	International Institute of Sociology
IISI	International Iron and Steel Institute
IISS	International Institute of Strategic Studies
IIT	Indian Institute of Technology
IL	Illinois
ILA	International Law Association
ILEA	Inner London Education Authority
ILEC	Inner London Education Committee
Ill	Illinois (US)
ILO	International Labour Office; International Labour Organisation
ILP	Independent Labour Party
ILR	Independent Local Radio; International Labour Review

IM	Individual Merit
IMA	International Music Association; Institute of Mathematics and its Applications
IMCB	International Management Centre from Buckingham
IMCO	Inter-Governmental Maritime Consultative Organization (*now see* IMO)
IME	Institute of Medical Ethics
IMEA	Incorporated Municipal Electrical Association
IMechE	Institution of Mechanical Engineers
IMechIE	Institution of Mechanical Incorporated Engineers
IMEDE	Institut pour l'Etude des Méthodes de Direction de l'Entreprise
IMF	International Monetary Fund
IMGTechE	Institution of Mechanical and General Technician Engineers
IMinE	Institution of Mining Engineers
IMM	Institution of Mining and Metallurgy
IMMLEP	Immunology of Leprosy
IMMTS	Indian Mercantile Marine Training Ship
IMO	International Maritime Organization
Imp.	Imperial
IMRO	Investment Management Regulatory Organisation
IMS	Indian Medical Service; Institute of Management Services; International Military Staff
IMTA	Institute of Municipal Treasurers and Accountants (*now see* CIPFA)
IMU	International Mathematical Union
IMunE	Institution of Municipal Engineers (now amalgamated with Institution of Civil Engineers)
IN	Indian Navy; Indiana
INASFMH	International Sports Association for People with Mental Handicap
Inc.	Incorporated
INCA	International Newspaper Colour Association
Incog.	Incognito
Ind.	Independent; Indiana (US)
Inf.	Infantry
INFORM	Information Network Focus on New Religious Movements
INSA	Indian National Science Academy
INSEA	International Society for Education through Art
INSEAD or Insead	Institut Européen d'Administration des Affaires
Insp.	Inspector
Inst.	Institute
InstBE	Institution of British Engineers
Instn	Institution
InstSMM	Institute of Sales and Marketing Management
InstT	Institute of Transport (*now see* CIT)
INTELSAT	International Telecommunications Satellite Organisation
IOB	Institute of Banking (*now see* CIOB)
IOC	International Olympic Committee; Intergovernmental Oceanographic Commission
IOCD	International Organisation for Chemical Science in Development
IODE	Imperial Order of the Daughters of the Empire
I of M	Isle of Man
IOGT	International Order of Good Templars
IOM	Isle of Man; Indian Order of Merit
IOOF	Independent Order of Odd-fellows
IOP	Institute of Painters in Oil Colours
IOTA	(Fellow of) Institute of Transport Administration
IoW	Isle of Wight
IPA	International Publishers' Association
IPCS	Institution of Professional Civil Servants
IPFA	Member or Associate, Chartered Institute of Public Finance and Accountancy
IPHE	Institution of Public Health Engineers (*now see* IWEM)
IPI	International Press Institute; Institute of Patentees and Inventors
IPlantE	Institution of Plant Engineers (*now see* IIM)
IPM	Institute of Personnel Management
IPPA	Independent Programme Producers' Association
IPPF	International Planned Parenthood Federation
IPPR	Institute for Public Policy Research
IPPS	Institute of Physics and The Physical Society
IProdE	Institution of Production Engineers (later Institution of Manufacturing Engineering; *now see* IEE)
IPS	Indian Police Service; Indian Political Service; Institute of Purchasing and Supply
IPU	Inter-Parliamentary Union
IRA	Irish Republican Army
IRAD	Institute for Research on Animal Diseases
IRC	Industrial Reorganization Corporation; Interdisciplinary Research Centre
IRCAM	Institute for Research and Co-ordination in Acoustics and Music

IRCert	Industrial Relations Certificate
IREE(Aust)	Institution of Radio and Electronics Engineers (Australia)
IRI	Institution of the Rubber Industry (*now see* PRI)
IRO	International Refugee Organization
IRPA	International Radiation Protection Association
IRRV	(Fellow/Member of) Institute of Revenues, Rating and Valuation
IRTE	Institute of Road Transport Engineers
IS	International Society of Sculptors, Painters and Gravers
Is	Island(s)
ISBA	Incorporated Society of British Advertisers
ISC	Imperial Service College, Haileybury; Indian Staff Corps
ISCM	International Society for Contemporary Music
ISCO	Independent Schools Careers Organisation
ISE	Indian Service of Engineers
ISI	International Statistical Institute
ISIS	Independent Schools Information Service
ISJC	Independent Schools Joint Council
ISM	Incorporated Society of Musicians
ISMAR	International Society of Magnetic Resonance
ISME	International Society for Musical Education
ISMRC	Inter-Services Metallurgical Research Council
ISO	Imperial Service Order; International Organization for Standardization
ISSA	International Social Security Association
ISSTIP	International Society for Study of Tension in Performance
ISTC	Iron and Steel Trades Confederation; Institute of Scientific and Technical Communicators
ISTD	Imperial Society of Teachers of Dancing
IStructE	Institution of Structural Engineers
IT	Information Technology; Indian Territory (US)
It. or Ital.	Italian
ITA	Independent Television Authority (later IBA)
ITAB	Information Technology Advisory Board
ITB	Industry Training Board
ITC	International Trade Centre; Independent Television Commission
ITCA	Independent Television Association (*formerly* Independent Television Companies Association Ltd)
ITDG	Intermediate Technology Development Group
ITEME	Institution of Technician Engineers in Mechanical Engineering
ITF	International Transport Workers' Federation
ITN	Independent Television News
ITO	International Trade Organization
ITU	International Telecommunication Union
ITV	Independent Television
ITVA	International Television Association
IUA	International Union of Architects
IUB	International Union of Biochemistry (*now see* IUBMB)
IUBMB	International Union of Biochemistry and Molecular Biology
IUC	Inter-University Council for Higher Education Overseas (*now see* IUPC)
IUCN	World Conservation Union (*formerly* International Union for the Conservation of Nature and Natural Resources)
IUCW	International Union for Child Welfare
IUGS	International Union of Geological Sciences
IUHPS	International Union of the History and Philosophy of Science
IULA	International Union of Local Authorities
IUP	Association of Independent Unionist Peers
IUPAC	International Union of Pure and Applied Chemistry
IUPAP	International Union of Pure and Applied Physics
IUPC	Inter-University and Polytechnic Council for Higher Education Overseas
IUPS	International Union of Physiological Sciences
IUTAM	International Union of Theoretical and Applied Mechanics
IVF	In-vitro Fertilisation
IVS	International Voluntary Service
IWA	Inland Waterways Association
IWEM	Institution of Water and Environmental Management
IWES	Institution of Water Engineers and Scientists (*now see* IWEM)
IWGC	Imperial War Graves Commission (*now see* CWGC)
IWM	Institution of Works Managers (*now see* IIM)
IWO	Institution of Water Officers
IWPC	Institute of Water Pollution Control (*now see* IWEM)
IWS	International Wool Secretariat
IWSA	International Water Supply Association
IWSOM	Institute of Practitioners in Work Study Organisation and Methods (*now see* IMS)
IWSP	Institute of Work Study Practitioners (*now see* IMS)

IY	Imperial Yeomanry
IYRU	International Yacht Racing Union
IZ	I Zingari

J

JA	Judge Advocate
JACT	Joint Association of Classical Teachers
JAG	Judge Advocate General
Jas	James
JCB	*Juris Canonici* (or *Civilis*) *Baccalaureus* (Bachelor of Canon (or Civil) Law)
JCR	Junior Common Room
JCS	Journal of the Chemical Society
JCD	*Juris Canonici* (or *Civilis*) *Doctor* (Doctor of Canon (or Civil) Law)
JCI	Junior Chamber International
JCL	*Juris Canonici* (or *Civilis*) *Licentiatus* (Licentiate in Canon (or Civil) Law)
JCO	Joint Consultative Organisation (of AFRC, MAFF, and Department of Agriculture and Fisheries for Scotland)
JD	Doctor of Jurisprudence
jd	*jure dignitatis* (by virtue of status)
JDipMA	Joint Diploma in Management Accounting Services
JG	Junior Grade
JInstE	Junior Institution of Engineers (*now see* IMGTechE)
jl(s)	journal(s)
JMB	Joint Matriculation Board
JMN	Johan Mangku Negara (Malaysia)
JMOTS	Joint Maritime Operational Training Staff
Jno. or Joh.	John
JP	Justice of the Peace
Jr	Junior
jsc	qualified at a Junior Staff Course, or the equivalent, 1942–46
JSD	Doctor of Juristic Science
JSDC	Joint Service Defence College
jsdc	completed a course at Joint Service Defence College
JSLS	Joint Services Liaison Staff
JSM	Johan Setia Mahkota (Malaysia)
JSPS	Japan Society for the Promotion of Science
JSSC	Joint Services Staff College
jssc	completed a course at Joint Services Staff College
jt, jtly	joint, jointly
JUD	*Juris Utriusque Doctor* (Doctor of Both Laws (Canon and Civil))
Jun.	Junior
Jun.Opt.	Junior Optime
JWS or jws	Joint Warfare Staff

K

KA	Knight of St Andrew, Order of Barbados
Kans	Kansas (US)
KAR	King's African Rifles
KBE	Knight Commander, Order of the British Empire
KC	King's Counsel
KCB	Knight Commander, Order of the Bath
KCC	Commander, Order of the Crown, Belgium and Congo Free State
KCH	King's College Hospital; Knight Commander, Hanoverian Order
KCHS	Knight Commander, Order of the Holy Sepulchre
KCIE	Knight Commander, Order of the Indian Empire
KCL	King's College London
KCLJ	Knight Commander, Order of St Lazarus of Jerusalem
KCMG	Knight Commander, Order of St Michael and St George
KCSA	Knight Commander, Military Order of the Collar of St Agatha of Paternò
KCSG	Knight Commander, Order of St Gregory the Great
KCSHS	Knight Commander with Star, Order of the Holy Sepulchre
KCSI	Knight Commander, Order of the Star of India
KCSJ	Knight Commander, Order of St John of Jerusalem (Knights Hospitaller)
KCSS	Knight Commander, Order of St Silvester
KCVO	Knight Commander, Royal Victorian Order
KCVSA	King's Commendation for Valuable Services in the Air
KDG	King's Dragoon Guards
KEH	King Edward's Horse
KEO	King Edward's Own
KG	Knight, Order of the Garter
KGCSS	Knight Grand Cross, Order of St Silvester

KGStJ	Knight of Grace, Order of St John of Jerusalem (*now see* KStJ)
KH	Knight, Hanoverian Order
KHC	Hon. Chaplain to the King
KHDS	Hon. Dental Surgeon to the King
KHNS	Hon. Nursing Sister to the King
KHP	Hon. Physician to the King
KHS	Hon. Surgeon to the King; Knight, Order of the Holy Sepulchre
K-i-H	Kaisar-i-Hind
KJStJ	Knight of Justice, Order of St John of Jerusalem (*now see* KStJ)
KLJ	Knight, Order of St Lazarus of Jerusalem
KM	Knight of Malta
KORR	King's Own Royal Regiment
KOSB	King's Own Scottish Borderers
KOYLI	King's Own Yorkshire Light Infantry
KP	Knight, Order of St Patrick
KPM	King's Police Medal
KRRC	King's Royal Rifle Corps
KS	King's Scholar; Kansas
KSC	Knight of St Columba
KSG	Knight, Order of St Gregory the Great
KSJ	Knight, Order of St John of Jerusalem (Knights Hospitaller)
KSLI	King's Shropshire Light Infantry
KSS	Knight, Order of St Silvester
KStJ	Knight, Most Venerable Order of the Hospital of St John of Jerusalem
KStJ(A)	Associate Knight of Justice, Most Venerable Order of the Hospital of St John of Jerusalem
KT	Knight, Order of the Thistle
Kt	Knight
KY	Kentucky
Ky	Kentucky (US)

L

L	Liberal
LA	Los Angeles; Library Association; Literate in Arts; Liverpool Academy; Louisiana
La	Louisiana (US)
LAA	Light Anti-Aircraft
Lab	Labour
LAC	London Athletic Club
LACSAB	Local Authorities Conditions of Service Advisory Board
LAE	London Association of Engineers
LAMDA	London Academy of Music and Dramatic Art
LAMSAC	Local Authorities' Management Services and Computer Committee
LAMTPI	Legal Associate Member, Town Planning Institute (*now see* LMRTPI)
L-Corp. or **Lance-Corp.**	Lance-Corporal
Lancs	Lancashire
LAPADA	London & Provincial Antique Dealers' Association
LARSP	Language Assessment, Remediation and Screening Procedure
Lautro	Life Assurance and Unit Trust Regulatory Organisation
LBC	London Broadcasting Company
LBHI	Licentiate, British Horological Institute
LC	Cross of Leo
LCAD	London Certificate in Art and Design (University of London)
LCC	London County Council (later GLC)
LCh	Licentiate in Surgery
LCJ	Lord Chief Justice
LCL	Licentiate of Canon Law
LCP	Licentiate, College of Preceptors
LCSP	London and Counties Society of Physiologists
LCST	Licentiate, College of Speech Therapists
LD	Liberal and Democratic; Licentiate in Divinity
LDDC	London Docklands Development Corporation
LDiv	Licentiate in Divinity
LDS	Licentiate in Dental Surgery
LDV	Local Defence Volunteers
LEA	Local Education Authority
LEDU	Local Enterprise Development Unit
LEP	Local Ecumenical Project
LEPRA	British Leprosy Relief Association
LèsL	Licencié ès lettres
LG	Lady Companion, Order of the Garter
LGSM	Licentiate, Guildhall School of Music and Drama
LGTB	Local Government Training Board
LH	Light Horse

LHD	*Literarum Humaniorum Doctor* (Doctor of Literature)
LHSM	Licentiate, Institute of Health Services Management
LI	Light Infantry; Long Island
LIBA	Lloyd's Insurance Brokers' Association
Lib Dem	Liberal Democrat
LIBER	Ligue des Bibliothèques Européennes de Recherche
LicMed	Licentiate in Medicine
Lieut	Lieutenant
LIFFE	London International Financial Futures and Options Exchange
Lincs	Lincolnshire
LIOB	Licentiate, Institute of Building
Lit.	Literature; Literary
LitD	Doctor of Literature; Doctor of Letters
Lit.Hum.	*Literae Humaniores* (Classics)
LittD	Doctor of Literature; Doctor of Letters
LJ	Lord Justice
LLA	Lady Literate in Arts
LLB	Bachelor of Laws
LLCM	Licentiate, London College of Music
LLD	Doctor of Laws
LLL	Licentiate in Laws
LLM	Master of Laws
LM	Licentiate in Midwifery
LMBC	Lady Margaret Boat Club
LMC	Local Medical Committee
LMCC	Licentiate, Medical Council of Canada
LMed	Licentiate in Medicine
LMH	Lady Margaret Hall, Oxford
LMR	London Midland Region (BR)
LMS	London, Midland and Scottish Railway; London Missionary Society
LMSSA	Licentiate in Medicine and Surgery, Society of Apothecaries
LMRTPI	Legal Member, Royal Town Planning Institute
LNat	Liberal National
LNER	London and North Eastern Railway
LOB	Location of Offices Bureau
L of C	Library of Congress; Lines of Communication
LP	Limited Partnership
LPH	Licentiate in Philosophy
LPO	London Philharmonic Orchestra
LPTB	London Passenger Transport Board (later LTE; *now see* LRT)
LRAD	Licentiate, Royal Academy of Dancing
LRAM	Licentiate, Royal Academy of Music
LRCP	Licentiate, Royal College of Physicians, London
LRCPE	Licentiate, Royal College of Physicians, Edinburgh
LRCPI	Licentiate, Royal College of Physicians of Ireland
LRCPSGlas	Licentiate, Royal College of Physicians and Surgeons of Glasgow
LRCS	Licentiate, Royal College of Surgeons of England
LRCSE	Licentiate, Royal College of Surgeons, Edinburgh
LRCSI	Licentiate, Royal College of Surgeons in Ireland
LRFPS(G)	Licentiate, Royal Faculty of Physicians and Surgeons, Glasgow (*now see* LRCPSGlas)
LRIBA	Licentiate, Royal Institute of British Architects (*now see* RIBA)
LRPS	Licentiate, Royal Photographic Society
LRT	London Regional Transport
LSA	Licentiate, Society of Apothecaries; Licence in Agricultural Sciences
LSE	London School of Economics and Political Science
LSHTM	London School of Hygiene and Tropical Medicine
LSO	London Symphony Orchestra
Lt	Lieutenant; Light
LT	London Transport (*now see* LRT); Licentiate in Teaching
LTA	Lawn Tennis Association
LTB	London Transport Board (later LTE; *now see* LRT)
LTCL	Licentiate of Trinity College of Music, London
Lt Col	Lieutenant Colonel
LTE	London Transport Executive (*now see* LRT)
Lt Gen.	Lieutenant General
LTh	Licentiate in Theology
LU	Liberal Unionist
LUOTC	London University Officers' Training Corps
LVO	Lieutenant, Royal Victorian Order (*formerly* MVO (Fourth Class))
LWT	London Weekend Television
LXX	Septuagint

M

M	Marquess; Member; Monsieur
m	married
MA	Master of Arts; Military Assistant; Massachusetts

MAA Manufacturers' Agents Association of Great Britain
MAAF Mediterranean Allied Air Forces
MAAT Member, Association of Accounting Technicians
MACE Member, Australian College of Education; Member, Association of Conference Executives
MACI Member, American Concrete Institute
MACM Member, Association of Computing Machines
MACS Member, American Chemical Society
MADO Member, Association of Dispensing Opticians
MAE Member, Academia Europaea
MAEE Marine Aircraft Experimental Establishment
MAF Ministry of Agriculture and Fisheries
MAFF Ministry of Agriculture, Fisheries and Food
MAI *Magister in Arte Ingeniaria* (Master of Engineering)
MAIAA Member, American Institute of Aeronautics and Astronautics
MAICE Member, American Institute of Consulting Engineers
MAIChE Member, American Institute of Chemical Engineers
Maj. Gen. Major General
MALD Master of Arts in Law and Diplomacy
Man Manitoba (Canada)
M&A Mergers and Acquisitions
MAO Master of Obstetric Art
MAOT Member, Association of Occupational Therapists
MAOU Member, American Ornithologists' Union
MAP Ministry of Aircraft Production
MAPsS Member, Australian Psychological Society
MARAC Member, Australasian Register of Agricultural Consultants
MArch Master of Architecture
Marq. Marquess
MASAE Member, American Society of Agricultural Engineers
MASC Member, Australian Society of Calligraphers
MASc Master of Applied Science
MASCE Member, American Society of Civil Engineers
MASME Member, American Society of Mechanical Engineers
Mass Massachusetts (US)
MATh Master of Arts in Theology
Math. Mathematics; Mathematical
MATSA Managerial Administrative Technical Staff Association
MAusIMM Member, Australasian Institute of Mining and Metallurgy
MB Medal of Bravery (Canada); Bachelor of Medicine
MBA Master of Business Administration
MBASW Member, British Association of Social Workers
MBC Metropolitan/Municipal Borough Council
MBCS Member, British Computer Society
MBE Member, Order of the British Empire
MBES Member, Biological Engineering Society
MBFR Mutual and Balanced Force Reductions (negotiations)
MBHI Member, British Horological Institute
MBIFD Member, British Institute of Funeral Directors
MBIM Member, British Institute of Management (*now see* MIMgt)
MBKS Member, British Kinematograph Society (*now see* MBKSTS)
MBKSTS Member, British Kinematograph, Sound and Television Society
MBOU Member, British Ornithologists' Union
MBPICS Member, British Production and Inventory Control Society
MBritIRE Member, British Institution of Radio Engineers (later MIERE; *now see* MIEE)
MBS Member, Building Societies Institute (*now see* MCBSI)
MBSc Master of Business Science
MC Military Cross; Missionaries of Charity
MCAM Member, CAM Foundation
MCB Master in Clinical Biochemistry
MCBSI Member, Chartered Building Societies Institute
MCC Marylebone Cricket Club; Metropolitan County Council
MCCDRCS Member in Clinical Community Dentistry, Royal College of Surgeons
MCD Master of Civic Design
MCE Master of Civil Engineering
MCFP Member, College of Family Physicians (Canada)
MCh or
MChir Master in Surgery
MChE Master of Chemical Engineering
MChemA Master in Chemical Analysis
MChOrth Master of Orthopaedic Surgery
MCIBS Member, Chartered Institution of Building Services (*now see* MCIBSE)
MCIBSE Member, Chartered Institution of Building Services Engineers
MCIH Member, Chartered Institute of Housing
MCIM Member, Chartered Institute of Marketing
MCIOB Member, Chartered Institute of Building

M.CIRP Member, International Institution for Production Engineering Research
MCIS Member, Institute of Chartered Secretaries and Administrators
MCIT Member, Chartered Institute of Transport
MCIWEM Member, Chartered Institution of Water and Environmental Management
MCL Master in Civil Law
MCMES Member, Civil and Mechanical Engineers' Society
MCom Master of Commerce
MConsE Member, Association of Consulting Engineers
MConsEI Member, Association of Consulting Engineers of Ireland
MCOphth Member, College of Ophthalmologists (*now see* MRCOphth)
MCP Member of Colonial Parliament; Master of City Planning (US)
MCPA Member, College of Pathologists of Australia (*now see* MRCPA)
MCPath Member, College of Pathologists (*now see* MRCPath)
MCPP Member, College of Pharmacy Practice
MCPS Member, College of Physicians and Surgeons
MCS Madras Civil Service; Malayan Civil Service
MCSD Member, Chartered Society of Designers
MCSEE Member, Canadian Society of Electrical Engineers
MCSP Member, Chartered Society of Physiotherapy
MCST Member, College of Speech Therapists
MCT Member, Association of Corporate Treasurers
MD Doctor of Medicine; Military District; Maryland
Md Maryland (US)
MDC Metropolitan District Council
MDes Master of Design
MDS Master of Dental Surgery
MDSc Master of Dental Science
Me Maine (US)
ME Mining Engineer; Middle East; Master of Engineering; Maine
MEAF Middle East Air Force
MEC Member of Executive Council; Middle East Command
MEc Master of Economics
MECAS Middle East Centre for Arab Studies
Mech. Mechanics; Mechanical
MECI Member, Institute of Employment Consultants
Med. Medical
MEd Master of Education
MEF Middle East Force
MEIC Member, Engineering Institute of Canada
MELF Middle East Land Forces
Mencap Royal Society for Mentally Handicapped Children and Adults
MEng Master of Engineering
MEO Marine Engineering Officer
MEP Member of the European Parliament
MESc Master of Engineering Science
MetR Metropolitan Railway
MetSoc Metals Society (formed by amalgamation of Institute of Metals and Iron and Steel Institute; now merged with Institution of Metallurgists to form Institute of Metals)
MEXE Military Engineering Experimental Establishment
MF Master of Forestry
MFA Master of Fine Arts
MFC Mastership in Food Control
MFCM Member, Faculty of Community Medicine (*now see* MFPHM)
MFGB Miners' Federation of Great Britain (*now see* NUM)
MFH Master of Foxhounds
MFHom Member, Faculty of Homœopathy
MFOM Member, Faculty of Occupational Medicine
MFPaed Member, Faculty of Paediatrics, Royal College of Physicians of Ireland
MFPHM Member, Faculty of Public Health Medicine
MGA Major General in charge of Administration
MGC Machine Gun Corps
MGDSRCS Member in General Dental Surgery, Royal College of Surgeons
MGGS Major General, General Staff
MGI Member, Institute of Certificated Grocers
MGO Master General of the Ordnance; Master of Gynaecology and Obstetrics
Mgr Monsignor
MHA Member of House of Assembly
MHCIMA Member, Hotel Catering and Institutional Management Association
MHK Member of the House of Keys
MHort (RHS) Master of Horticulture, Royal Horticultural Society
MHR Member of the House of Representatives
MHRA Modern Humanities Research Association

MHRF	Mental Health Research Fund
MHSM	Member, Institute of Health Services Management
MI	Military Intelligence; Michigan
MIAeE	Member, Institute of Aeronautical Engineers
MIAgrE	Member, Institution of Agricultural Engineers
MIAM	Member, Institute of Administrative Management
MIAS	Member, Institute of Aeronautical Science (US) (now see MAIAA)
MIBC	Member, Institute of Business Counsellors
MIBF	Member, Institute of British Foundrymen
MIBiol	Member, Institute of Biology
MIBritE	Member, Institution of British Engineers
MIB(Scot)	Member, Institute of Bankers in Scotland
MICE	Member, Institution of Civil Engineers
MICEI	Member, Institution of Civil Engineers of Ireland
MICFor	Member, Institute of Chartered Foresters
Mich	Michigan (US)
MIChemE	Member, Institution of Chemical Engineers
MICM	Member, Institution of Credit Management
MICorrST	Member, Institution of Corrosion Science and Technology
MICS	Member, Institute of Chartered Shipbrokers
MIDPM	Member, Institute of Data Processing Management
MIE(Aust)	Member, Institution of Engineers, Australia
MIED	Member, Institution of Engineering Designers
MIEE	Member, Institution of Electrical Engineers
MIEEE	Member, Institute of Electrical and Electronics Engineers (NY)
MIEEM	Member, Institute of Ecology and Environmental Management
MIEI	Member, Institution of Engineering Inspection
MIEIE	Member, Institution of Electronics and Electrical Incorporated Engineers
MIE(Ind)	Member, Institution of Engineers, India
MIEnvSc	Member, Institute of Environmental Science
MIERE	Member, Institution of Electronic and Radio Engineers (now see MIEE)
MIES	Member, Institution of Engineers and Shipbuilders, Scotland
MIET	Member, Institute of Engineers and Technicians
MIEx	Member, Institute of Export
MIExpE	Member, Institute of Explosives Engineers
MIFA	Member, Institute of Field Archaeologists
MIFF	Member, Institute of Freight Forwarders
MIFireE	Member, Institution of Fire Engineers
MIFM	Member, Institute of Fisheries Management
MIFor	Member, Institute of Foresters (now see MICFor)
MIGasE	Member, Institution of Gas Engineers
MIGeol	Member, Institution of Geologists
MIH	Member, Institute of Housing (now see MCIH)
MIHM	Member, Institute of Housing Managers (later MIH)
MIHort	Member, Institute of Horticulture
MIHT	Member, Institution of Highways and Transportation
MIHVE	Member, Institution of Heating and Ventilating Engineers (later MCIBS)
MIIA	Member, Institute of Industrial Administration (later FBIM)
MIIM	Member, Institution of Industrial Managers
MIInfSc	Member, Institute of Information Sciences
MIL	Member, Institute of Linguists
Mil.	Military
MILGA	Member, Institute of Local Government Administrators
MILocoE	Member, Institution of Locomotive Engineers
MIM	Member, Institute of Metals (formerly Institution of Metallurgists)
MIMarE	Member, Institute of Marine Engineers
MIMC	Member, Institute of Management Consultants
MIMechE	Member, Institution of Mechanical Engineers
MIMEMME	Member, Institution of Mining Electrical & Mining Mechanical Engineers
MIMgt	Member, Institute of Management
MIMGTechE	Member, Institution of Mechanical and General Technician Engineers
MIMI	Member, Institute of the Motor Industry
MIMinE	Member, Institution of Mining Engineers
MIMM	Member, Institution of Mining and Metallurgy
MIMunE	Member, Institution of Municipal Engineers (now amalgamated with Institution of Civil Engineers)
MIN	Member, Institute of Navigation (now see MRIN)
Min.	Ministry
Minn	Minnesota (US)
MInstAM	Member, Institute of Administrative Management
MInstBE	Member, Institution of British Engineers
MInstCE	Member, Institution of Civil Engineers (now see FICE)
MInstD	Member, Institute of Directors
MInstE	Member, Institute of Energy
MInstEnvSci	Member, Institute of Environmental Sciences
MInstF	Member, Institute of Fuel (now see MInstE)
MInstHE	Member, Institution of Highway Engineers (now see MIHT)
MInstM	Member, Institute of Marketing (now see MCIM)
MInstMC	Member, Institute of Measurement and Control
MInstME	Member, Institution of Mining Engineers
MInstMet	Member, Institute of Metals (later part of Metals Society, now see MIM)
MInstP	Member, Institute of Physics
MInstPet	Member, Institute of Petroleum
MInstPI	Member, Institute of Patentees and Inventors
MInstPkg	Member, Institute of Packaging
MInstPS	Member, Institute of Purchasing and Supply
MInstR	Member, Institute of Refrigeration
MInstRA	Member, Institute of Registered Architects
MInstT	Member, Institute of Transport (now see MCIT)
MInstTM	Member, Institute of Travel Managers in Industry and Commerce
MInstW	Member, Institute of Welding (now see MWeldI)
MInstWM	Member, Institute of Wastes Management
MINucE	Member, Institution of Nuclear Engineers
MIOA	Member, Institute of Acoustics
MIOB	Member, Institute of Building (now see MCIOB)
MIOM	Member, Institute of Office Management (now see MIAM)
MIOSH	Member, Institution of Occupational Safety and Health
MIPA	Member, Institute of Practitioners in Advertising
MIPD	Member, Institute of Personnel and Development
MIPlantE	Member, Institution of Plant Engineers (now see MIIM)
MIPM	Member, Institute of Personnel Management (now see MIPD)
MIPR	Member, Institute of Public Relations
MIProdE	Member, Institution of Production Engineers (now see MIEE)
MIQ	Member, Institute of Quarrying
MIQA	Member, Institute of Quality Assurance
MIRE	Member, Institution of Radio Engineers (later MIERE)
MIREE(Aust)	Member, Institution of Radio and Electronics Engineers (Australia)
MIRO	Mineral Industry Research Organisation
MIRT	Member, Institute of Reprographic Technicians
MIRTE	Member, Institute of Road Transport Engineers
MIS	Member, Institute of Statisticians
MISI	Member, Iron and Steel Institute (later part of Metals Society)
MIS(India)	Member, Institution of Surveyors of India
Miss	Mississippi (US)
MIStructE	Member, Institution of Structural Engineers
MIT	Massachusetts Institute of Technology
MITA	Member, Industrial Transport Association
MITD	Member, Institute of Training and Development (now see MIPD)
MITE	Member, Institution of Electrical and Electronics Technician Engineers
MITI	Member, Institute of Translation & Interpreting
MITT	Member, Institute of Travel and Tourism
MIWE	Member, Institution of Water Engineers (later MIWES; then MIWEM; now see MCIWEM)
MIWEM	Member, Institution of Water and Environmental Management (now see MCIWEM)
MIWES	Member, Institution of Water Engineers and Scientists (later MIWEM; now see MCIWEM)
MIWM	Member, Institution of Works Managers (now see MIIM)
MIWPC	Member, Institute of Water Pollution Control (later MIWEM; now see MCIWEM)
MIWSP	Member, Institute of Work Study Practitioners (now see MMS)
MJA	Medical Journalists Association
MJI	Member, Institute of Journalists
MJIE	Member, Junior Institution of Engineers (now see MIGTechE)
MJS	Member, Japan Society
MJur	Magister Juris (Master of Law)
ML	Licentiate in Medicine; Master of Laws
MLA	Member of Legislative Assembly; Modern Language Association; Master in Landscape Architecture
MLC	Member of Legislative Council
MLCOM	Member, London College of Osteopathic Medicine
MLitt	Master of Letters
Mlle	Mademoiselle
MLM	Member, Order of the Legion of Merit (Rhodesia)
MLO	Military Liaison Officer
MLR	Modern Language Review
MM	Military Medal; Merchant Marine
MMA	Metropolitan Museum of Art
MMB	Milk Marketing Board
MMD	Movement for Multi-Party Democracy
MME	Master of Mining Engineering

Mme	Madame
MMechE	Master of Mechanical Engineering
MMet	Master of Metallurgy
MMGI	Member, Mining, Geological and Metallurgical Institute of India
MMin	Master of Ministry
MMM	Member, Order of Military Merit (Canada)
MMS	Member, Institute of Management Services
MMSA	Master of Midwifery, Society of Apothecaries
MN	Merchant Navy; Minnesota
MNAS	Member, National Academy of Sciences (US)
MNECInst	Member, North East Coast Institution of Engineers and Shipbuilders
MNI	Member, Nautical Institute
MNSE	Member, Nigerian Society of Engineers
MNZIS	Member, New Zealand Institute of Surveyors
MNZPI	Member, New Zealand Planning Institute
MO	Medical Officer; Military Operations; Missouri
Mo	Missouri (US)
MoD	Ministry of Defence
Mods	Moderations (Oxford)
MOF	Ministry of Food
MOH	Medical Officer(s) of Health
MOI	Ministry of Information
MOMI	Museum of the Moving Image
Mon	Monmouthshire
Mont	Montana (US); Montgomeryshire
MOP	Ministry of Power
MOrthRCS	Member in Orthodontics, Royal College of Surgeons
MoS	Ministry of Supply
Most Rev.	Most Reverend
MoT	Ministry of Transport
MOV	Member, Order of Volta (Ghana)
MP	Member of Parliament
MPA	Master of Public Administration; Member, Parliamentary Assembly, Northern Ireland
MPBW	Ministry of Public Building and Works
MPH	Master of Public Health
MPhil	Master of Philosophy
MPIA	Master of Public and International Affairs
MPMI	Member, Property Management Institute
MPO	Management and Personnel Office
MPP	Member, Provincial Parliament
MPRISA	Member, Public Relations Institute of South Africa
MPS	Member, Pharmaceutical Society (*now see* MRPharmS)
MR	Master of the Rolls; Municipal Reform
MRAC	Member, Royal Agricultural College
MRACP	Member, Royal Australasian College of Physicians
MRACS	Member, Royal Australasian College of Surgeons
MRAeS	Member, Royal Aeronautical Society
MRAIC	Member, Royal Architectural Institute of Canada
MRAS	Member, Royal Asiatic Society
MRC	Medical Research Council
MRCA	Multi-Role Combat Aircraft
MRCGP	Member, Royal College of General Practitioners
MRC-LMB	Medical Research Council Laboratory of Molecular Biology
MRCOG	Member, Royal College of Obstetricians and Gynaecologists
MRCOphth	Member, Royal College of Ophthalmologists
MRCP	Member, Royal College of Physicians, London
MRCPA	Member, Royal College of Pathologists of Australia
MRCPath	Member, Royal College of Pathologists
MRCPE	Member, Royal College of Physicians, Edinburgh
MRCPGlas	Member, Royal College of Physicians and Surgeons of Glasgow
MRCPI	Member, Royal College of Physicians of Ireland
MRCPsych	Member, Royal College of Psychiatrists
MRCS	Member, Royal College of Surgeons of England
MRCSE	Member, Royal College of Surgeons of Edinburgh
MRCSI	Member, Royal College of Surgeons in Ireland
MRCVS	Member, Royal College of Veterinary Surgeons
MRE	Master of Religious Education
MRES or	
MREmpS	Member, Royal Empire Society
MRHS	Member, Royal Horticultural Society
MRI	Member, Royal Institution
MRIA	Member, Royal Irish Academy
MRIAI	Member, Royal Institute of the Architects of Ireland
MRIC	Member, Royal Institute of Chemistry (*now see* MRSC)
MRIN	Member, Royal Institute of Navigation
MRINA	Member, Royal Institution of Naval Architects
MRPharmS	Member, Royal Pharmaceutical Society
MRSanI	Member, Royal Sanitary Institute (*now see* MRSH)
MRSC	Member, Royal Society of Chemistry
MRSH	Member, Royal Society for the Promotion of Health
MRSL	Member, Order of the Republic of Sierra Leone

MRSM or	
MRSocMed	Member, Royal Society of Medicine
MRST	Member, Royal Society of Teachers
MRTPI	Member, Royal Town Planning Institute
MRurSc	Master of Rural Science
MRUSI	Member, Royal United Service Institution
MRVA	Member, Rating and Valuation Association
MS	Master of Surgery; Master of Science (US); Mississippi
MS, MSS	Manuscript, Manuscripts
MSA	Master of Science, Agriculture (US); Mineralogical Society of America
MSAAIE	Member, Southern African Association of Industrial Editors
MSAE	Member, Society of Automotive Engineeers (US)
MSAICE	Member, South African Institution of Civil Engineers
MSAInstMM	Member, South African Institute of Mining and Metallurgy
MS&R	Merchant Shipbuilding and Repairs
MSAutE	Member, Society of Automobile Engineers
MSC	Manpower Services Commission; Missionaries of the Sacred Heart; Madras Staff Corps
MSc	Master of Science
MScD	Master of Dental Science
MSD	Meritorious Service Decoration (Fiji)
MSE	Master of Science in Engineering (US)
MSF	(Union for) Manufacturing, Science, Finance
MSH	Master of Stag Hounds
MSI	Member, Securities Institute
MSIAD	Member, Society of Industrial Artists and Designers (*now see* MCSD)
MSINZ	Member, Surveyors' Institute of New Zealand
MSIT	Member, Society of Instrument Technology (*now see* MInstMC)
MSM	Meritorious Service Medal; Madras Sappers and Miners
MSN	Master of Science in Nursing
MSocIS	Member, Société des Ingénieurs et Scientifiques de France
MSocSc	Master of Social Sciences
MSocWork	Master of Social Work
MSR	Member, Society of Radiographers
MSt	Master of Studies
MSTD	Member, Society of Typographic Designers
MT	Mechanical Transport; Montana
Mt	Mount, Mountain
MTA	Music Trades Association
MTAI	Member, Institute of Travel Agents
MTB	Motor Torpedo Boat
MTCA	Ministry of Transport and Civil Aviation
MTD	Midwife Teachers' Diploma
MTech	Master of Technology
MTEFL	Master in the Teaching of English as a Foreign or Second Language
MTh	Master of Theology
MTIRA	Machine Tool Industry Research Association (*now see* AMTRI)
MTPI	Member, Town Planning Institute (*now see* MRTPI)
MTS	Master of Theological Studies
MUniv	Honorary Master of the University
MusB	Bachelor of Music
MusD	Doctor of Music
MusM	Master of Music
MV	Merchant Vessel, Motor Vessel (naval)
MVEE	Military Vehicles and Engineering Establishment
MVO	Member, Royal Victorian Order
MVSc	Master of Veterinary Science
MW	Master of Wine
MWA	Mystery Writers of America
MWeldI	Member, Welding Institute
MWSOM	Member, Institute of Practitioners in Work Study Organisation and Methods (*now see* MMS)

N

N	Nationalist; Navigating Duties; North
n	nephew
NA	National Academician (America)
NAACP	National Association for the Advancement of Colored People
NAAFI	Navy, Army and Air Force Institutes
NAAS	National Agricultural Advisory Service
NAB	National Advisory Body for Public Sector Higher Education
NABC	National Association of Boys' Clubs
NAC	National Agriculture Centre
NACAB	National Association of Citizens' Advice Bureaux
NACCB	National Accreditation Council for Certification Bodies

NACETT	National Advisory Council for Education and Training
NACF	National Art-Collections Fund
NACRO	National Association for the Care and Resettlement of Offenders
NADFAS	National Association of Decorative and Fine Arts Societies
NAE	National Academy of Engineering
NAEW	Nato Airborn Early Warning
NAHA	National Association of Health Authorities (now see NAHAT)
NAHAT	National Association of Health Authorities and Trusts
NALGO or Nalgo	National and Local Government Officers' Association
NAMAS	National Measurement and Accreditation Service
NAMCW	National Association for Maternal and Child Welfare
NAMH	MIND (National Association for Mental Health)
NAMMA	NATO MRCA Management Agency
NAPT	National Association for the Prevention of Tuberculosis
NARM	National Association of Recording Merchandisers (US)
NAS	National Academy of Sciences
NASA	National Aeronautics and Space Administration (US)
NASDIM	National Association of Security Dealers and Investment Managers (later FIMBRA)
NAS/UWT	National Association of Schoolmasters/Union of Women Teachers
NATCS	National Air Traffic Control Services (now see NATS)
NATFHE	National Association of Teachers in Further and Higher Education (combining ATCDE and ATTI)
NATLAS	National Testing Laboratory Accreditation Scheme
NATO	North Atlantic Treaty Organisation
NATS	National Air Traffic Services
Nat. Sci.	Natural Sciences
NATSOPA	National Society of Operative Printers, Graphical and Media Personnel (formerly of Operative Printers and Assistants)
NAYC	Youth Clubs UK (formerly National Association of Youth Clubs)
NB	New Brunswick; Nebraska
NBA	North British Academy
NBC	National Book Council (later NBL); National Broadcasting Company (US)
NBL	National Book League
NBPI	National Board for Prices and Incomes
NC	National Certificate; North Carolina (US)
NCA	National Certificate of Agriculture
NCARB	National Council of Architectural Registration Boards
NCB	National Coal Board
NCC	National Computing Centre; Nature Conservancy Council (now see NCCE); National Consumer Council
NCCE	Nature Conservancy Council for England (English Nature)
NCCI	National Committee for Commonwealth Immigrants
NCCL	National Council for Civil Liberties
NCD	National Capital District, Papua New Guinea
NCDAD	National Council for Diplomas in Art and Design
NCET	National Council for Educational Technology
NCH	National Children's Homes
NCLC	National Council of Labour Colleges
NCOPF	National Council for One Parent Families
NCSE	National Council for Special Education
NCSS	National Council of Social Service
NCTA	National Community Television Association (US)
NCTJ	National Council for the Training of Journalists
NCU	National Cyclists' Union
NCVCCO	National Council of Voluntary Child Care Organisations
NCVO	National Council for Voluntary Organisations
NCVQ	National Council for Vocational Qualifications
ND	North Dakota
NDA	National Diploma in Agriculture
NDak	North Dakota (US)
ndc	National Defence College
NDD	National Diploma in Dairying; National Diploma in Design
NDH	National Diploma in Horticulture
NDIC	National Defence Industries Council
NDP	New Democratic Party
NDTA	National Defense Transportation Association (US)
NE	North-east
NEAB	Northern Examinations and Assessment Board
NEAC	New English Art Club
NEAF	Near East Air Force
NEARELF	Near East Land Forces
NEB	National Enterprise Board
Neb	Nebraska (US)
NEBSS	National Examinations Board for Supervisory Studies
NEC	National Executive Committee
NECCTA	National Education Closed Circuit Television Association
NECInst	North East Coast Institution of Engineers and Shipbuilders
NEDC	National Economic Development Council; North East Development Council
NEDO	National Economic Development Office
NEH	National Endowment for the Humanities
NEL	National Engineering Laboratory
NERC	Natural Environment Research Council
Nev	Nevada (US)
New M	New Mexico (US)
NFC	National Freight Consortium (formerly Corporation, then Company)
NFCG	National Federation of Consumer Groups
NFER	National Foundation for Educational Research
NFHA	National Federation of Housing Associations
NFMS	National Federation of Music Societies
NFS	National Fire Service
NFSH	National Federation of Spiritual Healers
NFT	National Film Theatre
NFU	National Farmers' Union
NFWI	National Federation of Women's Institutes
NGO	Non-Governmental Organisation(s)
NGTE	National Gas Turbine Establishment
NH	New Hampshire (US)
NHBC	National House-Building Council
NHS	National Health Service
NI	Northern Ireland; Native Infantry
NIAB	National Institute of Agricultural Botany
NIACRO	Northern Ireland Association for the Care and Resettlement of Offenders
NIAE	National Institute of Agricultural Engineering
NIAID	National Institute of Allergy and Infectious Diseases
NICEC	National Institute for Careers Education and Counselling
NICG	Nationalised Industries Chairmen's Group
NICS	Northern Ireland Civil Service
NID	Naval Intelligence Division; National Institute for the Deaf; Northern Ireland District; National Institute of Design (India)
NIESR	National Institute of Economic and Social Research
NIH	National Institutes of Health (US)
NIHCA	Northern Ireland Hotels and Caterers Association
NII	Nuclear Installations Inspectorate
NILP	Northern Ireland Labour Party
NIMR	National Institute for Medical Research
NISTRO	Northern Ireland Science and Technology Regional Organisation
NJ	New Jersey (US)
NL	National Liberal; No Liability
NLCS	North London Collegiate School
NLF	National Liberal Federation
NLYL	National League of Young Liberals
NM	New Mexico
NMR	Nuclear Magnetic Resonance
NNMA	Nigerian National Merit Award
NNOM	Nigerian National Order of Merit
Northants	Northamptonshire
NOTB	National Ophthalmic Treatment Board
Notts	Nottinghamshire
NP	Notary Public
NPA	Newspaper Publishers' Association
NPFA	National Playing Fields Association
NPk	Nishan-e-Pakistan
NPL	National Physical Laboratory
NRA	National Rifle Association; National Recovery Administration (US); National Rivers Authority
NRAO	National Radio Astronomy Observatory
NRCC	National Research Council of Canada
NRD	National Registered Designer
NRDC	National Research Development Corporation
NRPB	National Radiological Protection Board
NRR	Northern Rhodesia Regiment
NS	Nova Scotia; New Style in the Calendar (in Great Britain since 1752); National Society; National Service
ns	Graduate of Royal Naval Staff College, Greenwich
NSA	National Skating Association
NSAIV	Distinguished Order of Shaheed Ali (Maldives)
NSF	National Science Foundation (US)
NSM	Non-Stipendiary Minister
NSMHC	National Society for Mentally Handicapped Children (now see Mencap)
NSPCC	National Society for Prevention of Cruelty to Children
NSQT	National Society for Quality through Teamwork
NSRA	National Small-bore Rifle Association
N/SSF	Novice, Society of St Francis
NSTC	Nova Scotia Technical College

NSW	New South Wales
NT	New Testament; Northern Territory (Australia); National Theatre (*now see* RNT); National Trust
NT&SA	National Trust & Savings Association
NTDA	National Trade Development Association
NTUC	National Trades Union Congress
NUAAW	National Union of Agricultural and Allied Workers
NUBE	National Union of Bank Employees (*now see* BIFU)
NUFLAT	National Union of Footwear Leather and Allied Trades (*now see* NUKFAT)
NUGMW	National Union of General and Municipal Workers (later GMBATU)
NUHKW	National Union of Hosiery and Knitwear Workers (*now see* NUKFAT)
NUI	National University of Ireland
NUJ	National Union of Journalists
NUJMB	Northern Universities Joint Matriculation Board
NUKFAT	National Union of Knitwear, Footwear and Apparel Trades
NUM	National Union of Mineworkers
NUMAST	National Union of Marine, Aviation and Shipping Transport Officers
NUPE	National Union of Public Employees
NUR	National Union of Railwaymen (*now see* RMT)
NUS	National Union of Students
NUT	National Union of Teachers
NUTG	National Union of Townswomen's Guilds
NUTN	National Union of Trained Nurses
NUU	New University of Ulster
NV	Nevada
NVQ	National Vocational Qualification
NW	North-west
NWC	National Water Council
NWFP	North-West Frontier Province
NWP	North-Western Province
NWT	North-Western Territories
NY	New York
NYC	New York City
NYO	National Youth Orchestra
NZ	New Zealand
NZEF	New Zealand Expeditionary Force
NZIA	New Zealand Institute of Architects
NZRSA	New Zealand Retired Services Association

O

O	Ohio (US)
o	only
OA	Officier d'Académie
OAM	Medal of the Order of Australia
O & E	Operations and Engineers (US)
O & M	organisation and method
O & O	Oriental and Occidental Steamship Co.
OAS	Organisation of American States; On Active Service
OASC	Officer Aircrew Selection Centre
OAU	Organisation for African Unity
OB	Order of Barbados
ob	*obiit* (died)
OBE	Officer, Order of the British Empire
OBI	Order of British India
OC	Officer, Order of Canada (equivalent to former award SM)
OC or o/c	Officer Commanding
oc	only child
OCA	Old Comrades Association
OCC	Order of the Caribbean Community
OCDS or ocds Can	Overseas College of Defence Studies (Canada)
OCF	Officiating Chaplain to the Forces
OCS	Officer Candidates School
OCSS	Oxford and Cambridge Shakespeare Society
OCTU	Officer Cadet Training Unit
OCU	Operational Conversion Unit
OD	Officer, Order of Distinction (Jamaica)
ODA	Overseas Development Administration
ODI	Overseas Development Institute
ODM	Ministry of Overseas Development
ODSM	Order of Diplomatic Service Merit (Lesotho)
OE	Order of Excellence (Guyana)
OEA	Overseas Education Association
OECD	Organization for Economic Co-operation and Development
OED	Oxford English Dictionary
OEEC	Organization for European Economic Co-operation (*now see* OECD)
OF	Order of the Founder, Salvation Army

OFEMA	Office Française d'Exportation de Matériel Aéronautique
OFFER	Office of Electricity Regulation
OFM	Order of Friars Minor (Franciscans)
OFMCap	Order of Friars Minor Capuchin (Franciscans)
OFMConv	Order of Friars Minor Conventual (Franciscans)
OFR	Order of the Federal Republic of Nigeria
OFS	Orange Free State
OFSTED	Office for Standards in Education
OFT	Office of Fair Trading
Oftel	Office of Telecommunications
OGS	Oratory of the Good Shepherd
OH	Ohio
OHMS	On His (or Her) Majesty's Service
O i/c	Officer in charge
OJ	Order of Jamaica
OK	Oklahoma
OL	Officer, Order of Leopold; Order of the Leopard (Lesotho)
OLJ	Officer, Order of St Lazarus of Jerusalem
OLM	Officer, Legion of Merit (Rhodesia)
OM	Order of Merit
OMCS	Office of the Minister for the Civil Service
OMI	Oblate of Mary Immaculate
OMM	Officer, Order of Military Merit (Canada)
ON	Order of the Nation (Jamaica)
OND	Ordinary National Diploma
Ont	Ontario
ONZ	Order of New Zealand
OO	Order of Ontario
OON	Officer, Order of the Niger
OP	*Ordinis Praedicatorum* (of the Order of Preachers (Dominican)); Observation Post
OPCON	Operational Control
OPCS	Office of Population Censuses and Surveys
OPSS	Office of Public Service and Science
OQ	Officer, National Order of Quebec
OR	Order of Rorima (Guyana); Operational Research; Oregon
ORC	Orange River Colony
Ore	Oregon (US)
ORGALIME	Organisme de Liaison des Industries Métalliques Européennes
ORL	Otorhinolaryngology
ORS	Operational Research Society
ORSA	Operations Research Society of America
ORSL	Order of the Republic of Sierra Leone
ORT	Organization for Rehabilitation through Training
ORTF	Office de la Radiodiffusion et Télévision Française
os	only son
OSA	Order of St Augustine (Augustinian); Ontario Society of Artists
OSB	Order of St Benedict (Benedictine)
osc	Graduate of Overseas Staff College
OSFC	Franciscan (Capuchin) Order
O/Sig	Ordinary Signalman
OSNC	Orient Steam Navigation Co.
osp	*obiit sine prole* (died without issue)
OSRD	Office of Scientific Research and Development
OSS	Office of Strategic Services
OST	Office of Science and Technology
OStJ	Officer, Most Venerable Order of the Hospital of St John of Jerusalem
OSUK	Ophthalmological Society of the United Kingdom
OT	Old Testament
OTC	Officers' Training Corps
OTL	Officer, Order of Toussaint L'Ouverture (Haiti)
OTU	Operational Training Unit
OTWSA	Ou-Testamentiese Werkgemeenskap in Suider-Afrika
OU	Oxford University; Open University
OUAC	Oxford University Athletic Club
OUAFC	Oxford University Association Football Club
OUBC	Oxford University Boat Club
OUCC	Oxford University Cricket Club
OUDS	Oxford University Dramatic Society
OUP	Oxford University Press; Official Unionist Party
OURC	Oxford University Rifle Club
OURFC	Oxford University Rugby Football Club
OURT	Order of the United Republic of Tanzania
Oxon	Oxfordshire; *Oxoniensis* (of Oxford)

P

PA	Pakistan Army; Personal Assistant; Pennsylvania
Pa	Pennsylvania (US)
PAA	President, Australian Academy of Science

pac	passed the final examination of the Advanced Class, The Military College of Science
PACE	Protestant and Catholic Encounter
PAg	Professional Agronomist
P&O	Peninsular and Oriental Steamship Co.
P&OSNCo.	Peninsular and Oriental Steam Navigation Co.
PAO	Prince Albert's Own
PASI	Professional Associate, Chartered Surveyors' Institution (now see ARICS)
PBS	Public Broadcasting Service
PC	Privy Counsellor; Police Constable; Perpetual Curate; Peace Commissioner (Ireland); Progressive Conservative (Canada)
pc	per centum (in the hundred)
PCC	Parochial Church Council
PCE	Postgraduate Certificate of Education
PCEF	Polytechnic and Colleges Employers' Forum
PCFC	Polytechnics and Colleges Funding Council
PCL	Polytechnic of Central London
PCMO	Principal Colonial Medical Officer
PdD	Doctor of Pedagogy (US)
PDG	Président Directeur Général
PDR	People's Democratic Republic
PDRA	post doctoral research assistant
PDSA	People's Dispensary for Sick Animals
PDTC	Professional Dancer's Training Course Diploma
PE	Procurement Executive
PEI	Prince Edward Island
PEN	Poets, Playwrights, Editors, Essayists, Novelists (Club)
PEng	Registered Professional Engineer (Canada); Member, Society of Professional Engineers
Penn	Pennsylvania
PEP	Political and Economic Planning (now see PSI)
PER	Professional and Executive Recruitment
PEST	Pressure for Economic and Social Toryism
PETRAS	Polytechnic Educational Technology Resources Advisory Service
PF	Procurator-Fiscal
PFA	Professional Footballers' Association
pfc	Graduate of RAF Flying College
PFE	Program for Executives
PGA	Professional Golfers' Association
PGCE	Post Graduate Certificate of Education
PH	Presidential Order of Honour (Botswana)
PHAB	Physically Handicapped & Able-bodied
PhB	Bachelor of Philosophy
PhC	Pharmaceutical Chemist
PhD	Doctor of Philosophy
Phil.	Philology, Philological; Philosophy, Philosophical
PhL	Licentiate of Philosophy
PHLS	Public Health Laboratory Service
PhM	Master of Philosophy (USA)
PhmB	Bachelor of Pharmacy
Phys.	Physical
PIA	Personal Investment Authority
PIARC	Permanent International Association of Road Congresses
PIB	Prices and Incomes Board (later NBPI)
PICAO	Provisional International Civil Aviation Organization (now ICAO)
pinx.	pinxit (he painted it)
PIRA	Paper Industries Research Association
PITCOM	Parliamentary Information Technology Committee
PJG	Pingat Jasa Gemilang (Singapore)
PJK	Pingkat Jasa Kebaktian (Malaysia)
Pl.	Place; Plural
PLA	Port of London Authority
PLC or plc	public limited company
Plen.	Plenipotentiary
PLI	President, Landscape Institute
PLP	Parliamentary Labour Party; Progressive Liberal Party (Bahamas)
PMA	Personal Military Assistant
PMC	Personnel Management Centre
PMD	Program for Management Development
PMG	Postmaster-General
PMN	Panglima Mangku Negara (Malaysia)
PMO	Principal Medical Officer
PMRAFNS	Princess Mary's Royal Air Force Nursing Service
PMS	Presidential Order of Meritorious Service (Botswana); President, Miniature Society
PNBS	Panglima Negara Bintang Sarawak
PNEU	Parents' National Educational Union
PNG	Papua New Guinea
PNP	People's National Party
PO	Post Office
POB	Presidential Order of Botswana
POMEF	Political Office Middle East Force
Pop.	Population
POUNC	Post Office Users' National Council
POW	Prisoner of War; Prince of Wales's
PP	Parish Priest; Past President
pp	pages
PPA	Periodical Publishers Association
PPARC	Particle Physics and Astronomy Research Council
PPCLI	Princess Patricia's Canadian Light Infantry
PPE	Philosophy, Politics and Economics
PPInstHE	Past President, Institution of Highway Engineers
PPIStructE	Past President, Institution of Structural Engineers
PPITB	Printing and Publishing Industry Training Board
PPP	Private Patients Plan
PPRA	Past President, Royal Academy
PPRBA	Past President, Royal Society of British Artists
PPRBS	Past President, Royal Society of British Sculptors
PPRE	Past President, Royal Society of Painter-Printmakers (formerly of Painter-Etchers and Engravers)
PPRIBA	Past President, Royal Institute of British Architects
PPROI	Past President, Royal Institute of Oil Painters
PPRP	Past President, Royal Society of Portrait Painters
PPRTPI	Past President, Royal Town Planning Institute
PPRWA	Past President, Royal Watercolour Association
PPS	Parliamentary Private Secretary
PPSIAD	Past President, Society of Industrial Artists and Designers
PQ	Province of Quebec
PR	Public Relations; Parti républicain
PRA	President, Royal Academy
PRBS	President, Royal Society of British Sculptors
PRCS	President, Royal College of Surgeons
PRE	President, Royal Society of Painter-Printmakers (formerly of Painter-Etchers and Engravers)
Preb.	Prebendary
PrEng.	Professional Engineer
Pres.	President
PRHA	President, Royal Hibernian Academy
PRI	President, Royal Institute of Painters in Water Colours; Plastics and Rubber Institute
PRIA	President, Royal Irish Academy
PRIAS	President, Royal Incorporation of Architects in Scotland
Prin.	Principal
PRISA	Public Relations Institute of South Africa
PRO	Public Relations Officer; Public Records Office
Proc.	Proctor; Proceedings
Prof.	Professor; Professional
PROI	President, Royal Institute of Oil Painters
PRO NED	Promotion of Non-Executive Directors
PRORM	Pay and Records Office, Royal Marines
Pro tem.	Pro tempore (for the time being)
Prov.	Provost; Provincial
Prox.	Proximo (next)
Prox.acc.	Proxime accessit (next in order of merit to the winner)
PRS	President, Royal Society; Performing Right Society Ltd
PRSA	President, Royal Scottish Academy
PRSE	President, Royal Society of Edinburgh
PRSH	President, Royal Society for the Promotion of Health
PRSW	President, Royal Scottish Water Colour Society
PRUAA	President, Royal Ulster Academy of Arts
PRWA	President, Royal West of England Academy
PRWS	President, Royal Society of Painters in Water Colours
PS	Pastel Society; Paddle Steamer
ps	passed School of Instruction (of Officers)
PSA	Property Services Agency; Petty Sessions Area
psa	Graduate of RAF Staff College
psc	Graduate of Staff College († indicates Graduate of Senior Wing Staff College)
PSD	Petty Sessional Division; Social Democratic Party (Portugal)
PSGB	Pharmaceutical Society of Great Britain (now see RPSGB)
PSI	Policy Studies Institute
PSIAD	President, Society of Industrial Artists and Designers
PSM	Panglima Setia Mahkota (Malaysia)
psm	Certificate of Royal Military School of Music
PSMA	President, Society of Marine Artists
PSNC	Pacific Steam Navigation Co.
PSO	Principal Scientific Officer; Personal Staff Officer
PSOE	Partido Socialista Obrero Español
PSSC	Personal Social Services Council
PTA	Passenger Transport Authority; Parent-Teacher Association
PTE	Passenger Transport Executive
Pte	Private
ptsc	passed Technical Staff College
Pty	Proprietary
PUP	People's United Party
PVSM	Param Vishishc Seva Medal (India)

PWD	Public Works Department
PWE	Political Welfare Executive
PWO	Prince of Wales's Own
PWR	Pressurized Water Reactor

Q

Q	Queen; Quartering
QAIMNS	Queen Alexandra's Imperial Military Nursing Service
QALAS	Qualified Associate, Chartered Land Agents' Society (*now* after amalgamation) *see* ARICS)
QARANC	Queen Alexandra's Royal Army Nursing Corps
QARNNS	Queen Alexandra's Royal Naval Nursing Service
QBD	Queen's Bench Division
QC	Queen's Counsel
QCVSA	Queen's Commendation for Valuable Service in the Air
QEH	Queen Elizabeth Hall
QEO	Queen Elizabeth's Own
QFSM	Queen's Fire Service Medal for Distinguished Service
QGM	Queen's Gallantry Medal
QHC	Honorary Chaplain to the Queen
QHDS	Honorary Dental Surgeon to the Queen
QHNS	Honorary Nursing Sister to the Queen
QHP	Honorary Physician to the Queen
QHS	Honorary Surgeon to the Queen
Qld	Queensland
Qly	Quarterly
QMAAC	Queen Mary's Army Auxiliary Corps
QMC	Queen Mary College, London (*now see* QMW)
QMG	Quartermaster-General
QMW	Queen Mary and Westfield College, London
QO	Qualified Officer
QOOH	Queen's Own Oxfordshire Hussars
Q(ops)	Quartering (operations)
QOY	Queen's Own Yeomanry
QPM	Queen's Police Medal
Qr	Quarter
QRIH	Queen's Royal Irish Hussars
QRV	Qualified Valuer, Real Estate Institute of New South Wales
QS	Quarter Sessions; Quantity Surveying
qs	RAF graduates of the Military or Naval Staff College
QSM	Queen's Service Medal (NZ)
QSO	Queen's Service Order (NZ)
QUB	Queen's University, Belfast
qv	*quod vide* (which see)
qwi	Qualified Weapons Instructor

R

(R)	Reserve
RA	Royal Academician; Royal (Regiment of) Artillery
RAA	Regional Arts Association
RAAF	Royal Australian Air Force
RAAMC	Royal Australian Army Medical Corps
RABI	Royal Agricultural Benevolent Institution
RAC	Royal Automobile Club; Royal Agricultural College; Royal Armoured Corps
RACDS	Royal Australian College of Dental Surgeons
RACGP	Royal Australian College of General Practitioners
RAChD	Royal Army Chaplains' Department
RACI	Royal Australian Chemical Institute
RACO	Royal Australian College of Ophthalmologists
RACOG	Royal Australian College of Obstetricians and Gynaecologists
RACP	Royal Australasian College of Physicians
RACS	Royal Australasian College of Surgeons; Royal Arsenal Co-operative Society
RADA	Royal Academy of Dramatic Art
RADAR	Royal Association for Disability and Rehabilitation
RADC	Royal Army Dental Corps
RADIUS	Religious Drama Society of Great Britain
RAE	Royal Australian Engineers; Royal Aerospace Establishment (*formerly* Royal Aircraft Establishment)
RAEC	Royal Army Educational Corps
RAeS	Royal Aeronautical Society
RAF	Royal Air Force
RAFA	Royal Air Force Association
RAFO	Reserve of Air Force Officers (*now see* RAFRO)
RAFRO	Royal Air Force Reserve of Officers
RAFVR	Royal Air Force Volunteer Reserve
RAI	Royal Anthropological Institute of Great Britain & Ireland; Radio Audizioni Italiane

RAIA	Royal Australian Institute of Architects
RAIC	Royal Architectural Institute of Canada
RAM	(Member of) Royal Academy of Music
RAMC	Royal Army Medical Corps
RAN	Royal Australian Navy
R&D	Research and Development
RANR	Royal Australian Naval Reserve
RANVR	Royal Australian Naval Volunteer Reserve
RAOC	Royal Army Ordnance Corps
RAPC	Royal Army Pay Corps
RARDE	Royal Armament Research and Development Establishment
RARO	Regular Army Reserve of Officers
RAS	Royal Astronomical Society; Royal Asiatic Society; Recruitment and Assessment Services
RASC	Royal Army Service Corps (*now see* RCT)
RASE	Royal Agricultural Society of England
RAuxAF	Royal Auxiliary Air Force
RAVC	Royal Army Veterinary Corps
RB	Rifle Brigade
RBA	Member, Royal Society of British Artists
RBC	Royal British Colonial Society of Artists
RBK&C	Royal Borough of Kensington and Chelsea
RBL	Royal British Legion
RBS	Royal Society of British Sculptors
RBSA	(Member of) Royal Birmingham Society of Artists
RBY	Royal Bucks Yeomanry
RC	Roman Catholic
RCA	Member, Royal Canadian Academy of Arts; Royal College of Art; (Member of) Royal Cambrian Academy
RCAC	Royal Canadian Armoured Corps
RCAF	Royal Canadian Air Force
RCamA	Member, Royal Cambrian Academy
RCAS	Royal Central Asian Society (*now see* RSAA)
RCDS	Royal College of Defence Studies
rcds	completed a course at, or served for a year on the Staff of, the Royal College of Defence Studies
RCGP	Royal College of General Practitioners
RCHA	Royal Canadian Horse Artillery
RCHM	Royal Commission on Historical Monuments
RCM	(Member of) Royal College of Music
RCN	Royal Canadian Navy; Royal College of Nursing
RCNC	Royal Corps of Naval Constructors
RCNR	Royal Canadian Naval Reserve
RCNVR	Royal Canadian Naval Volunteer Reserve
RCO	Royal College of Organists
RCOG	Royal College of Obstetricians and Gynaecologists
RCP	Royal College of Physicians, London
RCPath	Royal College of Pathologists
RCPE or RCPEd	Royal College of Physicians, Edinburgh
RCPI	Royal College of Physicians of Ireland
RCPSG	Royal College of Physicians and Surgeons of Glasgow
RCPsych	Royal College of Psychiatrists
RCR	Royal College of Radiologists
RCS	Royal College of Surgeons of England; Royal Corps of Signals; Royal College of Science
RCSE or RCSEd	Royal College of Surgeons of Edinburgh
RCSI	Royal College of Surgeons in Ireland
RCT	Royal Corps of Transport
RCVS	Royal College of Veterinary Surgeons
RD	Rural Dean; Royal Naval and Royal Marine Forces Reserve Decoration
Rd	Road
RDA	Royal Defence Academy
RDC	Rural District Council
RDF	Royal Dublin Fusiliers
RDI	Royal Designer for Industry (Royal Society of Arts)
RDS	Royal Dublin Society
RE	Royal Engineers; Fellow, Royal Society of Painter-Printmakers (*formerly* of Painter-Etchers and Engravers); Religious Education
REACH	Retired Executives Action Clearing House
react	Research Education and Aid for Children with potentially Terminal illness
Rear Adm.	Rear Admiral
REconS	Royal Economic Society
Regt	Regiment
REME	Royal Electrical and Mechanical Engineers
REngDes	Registered Engineering Designer
REOWS	Royal Engineers Officers' Widows' Society
REPC	Regional Economic Planning Council
RERO	Royal Engineers Reserve of Officers
RES	Royal Empire Society (*now* Royal Commonwealth Society)
Res.	Resigned; Reserve; Resident; Research
RETI	Association of Traditional Industrial Regions

Rev.	Reverend; Review
RFA	Royal Field Artillery
RFC	Royal Flying Corps (*now* RAF); Rugby Football Club
RFD	Reserve Force Decoration
RFH	Royal Festival Hall
RFN	Registered Fever Nurse
RFPS(G)	Royal Faculty of Physicians and Surgeons, Glasgow (*now see* RCPSG)
RFR	Rassemblement des Français pour la République
RFU	Rugby Football Union
RGA	Royal Garrison Artillery
RGI	Royal Glasgow Institute of the Fine Arts
RGJ	Royal Green Jackets
RGN	Registered General Nurse
RGS	Royal Geographical Society
RGSA	Royal Geographical Society of Australasia
RHA	Royal Hibernian Academy; Royal Horse Artillery; Regional Health Authority
RHAS	Royal Highland and Agricultural Society of Scotland
RHB	Regional Hospital Board
RHBNC	Royal Holloway and Bedford New College, London
RHC	Royal Holloway College, London (*now see* RHBNC)
RHF	Royal Highland Fusiliers
RHG	Royal Horse Guards
RHistS	Royal Historical Society
RHQ	Regional Headquarters
RHR	Royal Highland Regiment
RHS	Royal Horticultural Society; Royal Humane Society
RHV	Royal Health Visitor
RI	(Member of) Royal Institute of Painters in Water Colours; Rhode Island
RIA	Royal Irish Academy
RIAI	Royal Institute of the Architects of Ireland
RIAM	Royal Irish Academy of Music
RIAS	Royal Incorporation of Architects in Scotland
RIASC	Royal Indian Army Service Corps
RIBA	(Member of) Royal Institute of British Architects
RIBI	Rotary International in Great Britain and Ireland
RIC	Royal Irish Constabulary; Royal Institute of Chemistry (*now see* RSC)
RICS	Royal Institution of Chartered Surveyors
RIE	Royal Indian Engineering (College)
RIF	Royal Inniskilling Fusiliers
RIIA	Royal Institute of International Affairs
RILEM	Réunion internationale des laboratoires d'essais et de recherches sur les matériaux et les constructions
RIM	Royal Indian Marines
RIN	Royal Indian Navy
RINA	Royal Institution of Naval Architects
RINVR	Royal Indian Naval Volunteer Reserve
RIPA	Royal Institute of Public Administration
RIPH&H	Royal Institute of Public Health and Hygiene
RIrF	Royal Irish Fusiliers
RLC	Royal Logistic Corps
RLSS	Royal Life Saving Society
RM	Royal Marines; Resident Magistrate; Registered Midwife
RMA	Royal Marine Artillery; Royal Military Academy Sandhurst (*now* incorporating Royal Military Academy, Woolwich)
RMB	Rural Mail Base
RMC	Royal Military College Sandhurst (*now see* RMA)
RMCM	(Member of) Royal Manchester College of Music
RMCS	Royal Military College of Science
RMedSoc	Royal Medical Society, Edinburgh
RMetS	Royal Meteorological Society
RMFVR	Royal Marine Forces Volunteer Reserve
RMIT	Royal Melbourne Institute of Technology
RMLI	Royal Marine Light Infantry
RMN	Registered Mental Nurse
RMO	Resident Medical Officer(s)
RMP	Royal Military Police
RMPA	Royal Medico-Psychological Association
RMS	Royal Microscopical Society; Royal Mail Steamer; Royal Society of Miniature Painters
RMT	Rail, Maritime and Transport Union
RN	Royal Navy; Royal Naval; Registered Nurse
RNAS	Royal Naval Air Service
RNAY	Royal Naval Aircraft Yard
RNC	Royal Naval College
RNCM	(Member of) Royal Northern College of Music
RNEC	Royal Naval Engineering College
RNIB	Royal National Institute for the Blind
RNID	Royal National Institute for Deaf People (*formerly* Royal National Institute for the Deaf)
RNLI	Royal National Life-boat Institution
RNLO	Royal Naval Liaison Officer
RNR	Royal Naval Reserve
RNS	Royal Numismatic Society
RNSA	Royal Naval Sailing Association
RNSC	Royal Naval Staff College
RNT	Registered Nurse Tutor; Royal National Theatre
RNTNEH	Royal National Throat, Nose and Ear Hospital
RNUR	Régie Nationale des Usines Renault
RNVR	Royal Naval Volunteer Reserve
RNVSR	Royal Naval Volunteer Supplementary Reserve
RNXS	Royal Naval Auxiliary Service
RNZAC	Royal New Zealand Armoured Corps
RNZAF	Royal New Zealand Air Force
RNZIR	Royal New Zealand Infantry Regiment
RNZN	Royal New Zealand Navy
RNZNVR	Royal New Zealand Naval Volunteer Reserve
ROC	Royal Observer Corps
ROF	Royal Ordnance Factories
R of O	Reserve of Officers
ROI	Member, Royal Institute of Oil Painters
RoSPA	Royal Society for the Prevention of Accidents
(Rot.)	Rotunda Hospital, Dublin (after degree)
RP	Member, Royal Society of Portrait Painters
RPC	Royal Pioneer Corps
RPE	Rocket Propulsion Establishment
RPMS	Royal Postgraduate Medical School
RPO	Royal Philharmonic Orchestra
RPR	Rassemblement pour la République
RPS	Royal Photographic Society
RPSGB	Royal Pharmaceutical Society of Great Britain
RRC	Royal Red Cross
RRE	Royal Radar Establishment (*now see* RSRE)
RRF	Royal Regiment of Fusiliers
RRS	Royal Research Ship
RSA	Royal Scottish Academician; Royal Society of Arts; Republic of South Africa
RSAA	Royal Society for Asian Affairs
RSAF	Royal Small Arms Factory
RSAI	Royal Society of Antiquaries of Ireland
RSAMD	Royal Scottish Academy of Music and Drama
RSanI	Royal Sanitary Institute (*now see* RSH)
RSAS	Royal Surgical Aid Society
RSC	Royal Society of Canada; Royal Society of Chemistry; Royal Shakespeare Company
RSCM	Royal School of Church Music
RSCN	Registered Sick Children's Nurse
RSE	Royal Society of Edinburgh
RSF	Royal Scots Fusiliers
RSFSR	Russian Soviet Federated Socialist Republic
RSGS	Royal Scottish Geographical Society
RSH	Royal Society for the Promotion of Health
RSL	Royal Society of Literature; Returned Services League of Australia
RSM	Royal School of Mines
RSM or RSocMed	Royal Society of Medicine
RSMA	Royal Society of Marine Artists
RSME	Royal School of Military Engineering
RSMHCA	Royal Society for Mentally Handicapped Children and Adults (*see* Mencap)
RSNC	Royal Society for Nature Conservation
RSO	Rural Sub-Office; Railway Sub-Office; Resident Surgical Officer
RSPB	Royal Society for Protection of Birds
RSPCA	Royal Society for Prevention of Cruelty to Animals
RSRE	Royal Signals and Radar Establishment
RSSAf	Royal Society of South Africa
RSSAILA	Returned Sailors, Soldiers and Airmen's Imperial League of Australia (*now see* RSL)
RSSPCC	Royal Scottish Society for Prevention of Cruelty to Children
RSTM&H	Royal Society of Tropical Medicine and Hygiene
RSUA	Royal Society of Ulster Architects
RSV	Revised Standard Version
RSW	Member, Royal Scottish Society of Painters in Water Colours
RTE	Radio Telefis Eireann
Rt Hon.	Right Honourable
RTL	Radio-Télévision Luxembourg
RTO	Railway Transport Officer
RTPI	Royal Town Planning Institute
RTR	Royal Tank Regiment
Rt Rev.	Right Reverend
RTS	Religious Tract Society; Royal Toxophilite Society; Royal Television Society
RTYC	Royal Thames Yacht Club
RU	Rugby Union
RUC	Royal Ulster Constabulary
RUI	Royal University of Ireland
RUKBA	Royal United Kingdom Beneficent Association
RUR	Royal Ulster Regiment

RURAL	Society for the Responsible Use of Resources in Agriculture & on the Land
RUSI	Royal United Services Institute for Defence Studies (*formerly* Royal United Service Institution)
RVC	Royal Veterinary College
RWA or	
RWEA	(Member of) Royal West of England Academy
RWAFF	Royal West African Frontier Force
RWF	Royal Welch Fusiliers
RWS	(Member of) Royal Society of Painters in Water Colours
RYA	Royal Yachting Association
RYS	Royal Yacht Squadron
RZSScot	Royal Zoological Society of Scotland

S

(S)	(in Navy) Paymaster; Scotland
S	Succeeded; South; Saint
s	son
SA	South Australia; South Africa; Société Anonyme
SAAF	South African Air Force
SABC	South African Broadcasting Corporation
SAC	Scientific Advisory Committee
sac	qualified at small arms technical long course
SACEUR	Supreme Allied Commander Europe
SACIF	sociedad anónima commercial industrial financiera
SACLANT	Supreme Allied Commander Atlantic
SACRO	Scottish Association for the Care and Resettlement of Offenders
SACSEA	Supreme Allied Command, SE Asia
SA de CV	sociedad anónima de capital variable
SADF	Sudanese Auxiliary Defence Force
SADG	Société des Architectes Diplômés par le Gouvernement
SAE	Society of Automobile Engineers (US)
SAMC	South African Medical Corps
SARL	Société à Responsabilité Limitée
Sarum	Salisbury
SAS	Special Air Service
Sask	Saskatchewan
SASO	Senior Air Staff Officer
SAT	Senior Member, Association of Accounting Technicians
SATB	Soprano, Alto, Tenor, Bass
SATRO	Science and Technology Regional Organisation
SB	Bachelor of Science (US)
SBAA	Sovereign Base Areas Administration
SBAC	Society of British Aerospace Companies (*formerly* Society of British Aircraft Constructors)
SBS	Special Boat Service
SBStJ	Serving Brother, Most Venerable Order of the Hospital of St John of Jerusalem
SC	Star of Courage (Canada); Senior Counsel; South Carolina (US)
sc	student at the Staff College
SCA	Society of Catholic Apostolate (Pallottine Fathers); Société en Commandité par Actions
SCAA	School Curriculum and Assessment Authority
SCAO	Senior Civil Affairs Officer
SCAPA	Society for Checking the Abuses of Public Advertising
SCAR	Scientific Committee for Antarctic Research
ScD	Doctor of Science
SCDC	Schools Curriculum Development Committee
SCF	Senior Chaplain to the Forces; Save the Children Fund
Sch.	School
SCI	Society of Chemical Industry
SCIS	Scottish Council of Independent Schools
SCL	Student in Civil Law
SCM	State Certified Midwife; Student Christian Movement
SCONUL	Standing Conference of National and University Libraries
Scot.	Scotland
ScotBIC	Scottish Business in the Community
SCOTMEG	Scottish Management Efficiency Group
SCOTVEC	Scottish Vocational Education Council
SD	Staff Duties; South Dakota
SDA	Social Democratic Alliance; Scottish Diploma in Agriculture; Scottish Development Agency
SDak	South Dakota (US)
SDB	Salesian of Don Bosco
SDF	Sudan Defence Force; Social Democratic Federation
SDI	Strategic Defence Initiative
SDLP	Social Democratic and Labour Party
SDP	Social Democratic Party
SE	South-east
SEAC	South-East Asia Command
SEALF	South-East Asia Land Forces

SEATO	South-East Asia Treaty Organization
SEC	Security Exchange Commission
Sec.	Secretary
SED	Scottish Education Department
SEE	Society of Environmental Engineers
SEFI	European Society for Engineering Education
SEN	State Enrolled Nurse
SEPM	Society of Economic Palaeontologists and Mineralogists
SERC	Science and Engineering Research Council (*now see* EPSRC and PPARC)
SERT	Society of Electronic and Radio Technicians (*now see* IEIE)
SESO	Senior Equipment Staff Officer
SFA	Securities and Futures Authority
SFInstE	Senior Fellow, Institute of Energy
SFInstF	Senior Fellow, Institute of Fuel (*now see* SFInstE)
SFTA	Society of Film and Television Arts (*now see* BAFTA)
SFTCD	Senior Fellow, Trinity College Dublin
SG	Solicitor-General
SGA	Member, Society of Graphic Art
SGBI	Schoolmistresses' and Governesses' Benevolent Institution
Sgt	Sergeant
SHA	Secondary Heads Association; Special Health Authority
SHAC	London Housing Aid Centre
SHAEF	Supreme Headquarters, Allied Expeditionary Force
SH&MA	Scottish Horse and Motormen's Association
SHAPE	Supreme Headquarters, Allied Powers, Europe
SHEFC	Scottish Higher Education Funding Council
SHHD	Scottish Home and Health Department
SIAD	Society of Industrial Artists and Designers (*now see* CSD)
SIAM	Society of Industrial and Applied Mathematics (US)
SIB	Shipbuilding Industry Board; Securities and Investments Board
SICOT	Société Internationale de Chirurgie Orthopédique et de Traumatologie
SID	Society for International Development
SIESO	Society of Industrial and Emergency Services Officers
SIMA	Scientific Instrument Manufacturers' Association of Great Britain
SIME	Security Intelligence Middle East
SIMG	*Societas Internationalis Medicinae Generalis*
SinDrs	Doctor of Chinese
SIROT	Société Internationale pour Recherche en Orthopédie et Traumatologie
SIS	Secret Intelligence Service
SITA	Société Internationale de Télécommunications Aéronautiques
SITPRO	Simpler Trade Procedures Board (*formerly* Simplification of International Trade Procedures)
SJ	Society of Jesus (Jesuits)
SJAB	St John Ambulance Brigade
SJD	Doctor of Juristic Science
SJJ	Setia Jubli Perak Tuanku Ja'afar
SL	Serjeant-at-Law; Sociedad Limitada
SLA	Special Libraries Association
SLAC	Stanford Linear Accelerator Centre
SLAET	Society of Licensed Aircraft Engineers and Technologists
SLAS	Society for Latin-American Studies
SLD	Social and Liberal Democrats
SLP	Scottish Labour Party
SM	Medal of Service (Canada) (*now see* OC); Master of Science; Officer qualified for Submarine Duties
SMA	Society of Marine Artists (*now see* RSMA)
SMB	Setia Mahkota Brunei
SME	School of Military Engineering (*now see* RSME)
SMHO	Sovereign Military Hospitaller Order (Malta)
SMIEE	Senior Member, Institute of Electrical and Electronics Engineers (New York)
SMIRE	Senior Member, Institute of Radio Engineers (New York)
SMMT	Society of Motor Manufacturers and Traders Ltd
SMN	Seri Maharaja Mangku Negara (Malaysia)
SMO	Senior Medical Officer; Sovereign Military Order
SMP	Senior Managers' Program
SMPTE	Society of Motion Picture and Television Engineers (US)
SMRTB	Ship and Marine Requirements Technology Board
SNAME	Society of Naval Architects and Marine Engineers (US)
SNCF	Société Nationale des Chemins de Fer Français
SND	Sisters of Notre Dame
SNH	Scottish Natural Heritage
SNP	Scottish National Party
SNTS	Society for New Testament Studies

SO	Staff Officer; Scientific Officer; Symphony Orchestra
SOAS	School of Oriental and African Studies
Soc.	Society
Soc & Lib Dem	Social and Liberal Democrats (*now see* Lib Dem)
SocCE(France)	Société des Ingénieurs Civils de France
SODEPAX	Committee on Society, Development and Peace
SOE	Special Operations Executive
SOGAT	Society of Graphical and Allied Trades (*now see* GPMU)
SOLACE or	
Solace	Society of Local Authority Chief Executives
SOLT	Society of London Theatre
SOM	Society of Occupational Medicine
SOSc	Society of Ordained Scientists
SOTS	Society for Old Testament Study
sowc	Senior Officers' War Course
SP	Self-Propelled (Anti-Tank Regiment)
sp	*sine prole* (without issue)
SpA	Società per Azioni
SPAB	Society for the Protection of Ancient Buildings
SPARKS	Sport Aiding Medical Research for Children
SPCA	Society for the Prevention of Cruelty to Animals
SPCK	Society for Promoting Christian Knowledge
SPCM	Darjah Seri Paduka Cura Si Manja Kini (Malaysia)
SPD	Salisbury Plain District; Sozialdemokratische Partei Deutschlands
SPDK	Seri Panglima Darjal Kinabalu
SPG	Society for the Propagation of the Gospel (*now see* USPG)
SPk	Sitara-e-Pakistan
SPMB	Seri Paduka Makhota Brunei
SPMK	Darjah Kebasaran Seri Paduka Mahkota Kelantan (Malaysia)
SPMO	Senior Principal Medical Officer
SPNC	Society for the Promotion of Nature Conservation (*now see* RSNC)
SPNM	Society for the Promotion of New Music
SPR	Society for Psychical Research
SPRC	Society for Prevention and Relief of Cancer
sprl	société de personnes à responsabilité limitée
SPSO	Senior Principal Scientific Officer
SPTL	Society of Public Teachers of Law
SPUC	Society for the Protection of the Unborn Child
Sq.	Square
sq	staff qualified
SQA	Sitara-i-Quaid-i-Azam (Pakistan)
Sqdn or **Sqn**	Squadron
SR	Special Reserve; Southern Railway; Southern Region (BR)
SRC	Science Research Council (later SERC); Students' Representative Council
SRCh	State Registered Chiropodist
SRHE	Society for Research into Higher Education
SRIS	Science Reference Information Service
SRN	State Registered Nurse
SRNA	Shipbuilders and Repairers National Association
SRO	Supplementary Reserve of Officers; Self-Regulatory Organisation
SRP	State Registered Physiotherapist
SRY	Sherwood Rangers Yeomanry
SS	Saints; Straits Settlements; Steamship
SSA	Society of Scottish Artists
SSAC	Social Security Advisory Committee
SSAFA or	
SS&AFA	Soldiers', Sailors', and Airmen's Families Association
SSBN	Nuclear Submarine, Ballistic
SSC	Solicitor before Supreme Court (Scotland); Sculptors Society of Canada; *Societas Sanctae Crucis* (Society of the Holy Cross); Short Service Commission
SSEB	South of Scotland Electricity Board
SSEES	School of Slavonic and East European Studies
SSF	Society of St Francis
SSJE	Society of St John the Evangelist
SSM	Society of the Sacred Mission; Seri Setia Mahkota (Malaysia)
SSO	Senior Supply Officer; Senior Scientific Officer
SSRC	Social Science Research Council (*now see* ESRC)
SSSI	Sites of Special Scientific Interest
SSStJ	Serving Sister, Most Venerable Order of the Hospital of St John of Jerusalem
St	Street; Saint
STA	Sail Training Association
STB	*Sacrae Theologiae Baccalaureus* (Bachelor of Sacred Theology)
STC	Senior Training Corps
STD	*Sacrae Theologiae Doctor* (Doctor of Sacred Theology)
STh	Scholar in Theology

Stip.	Stipend; Stipendiary
STL	*Sacrae Theologiae Lector* (Reader or a Professor of Sacred Theology)
STM	*Sacrae Theologiae Magister* (Master of Sacred Theology)
STP	*Sacrae Theologiae Professor* (Professor of Divinity, old form of DD)
STRIVE	Society for Preservation of Rural Industries and Village Enterprises
STSO	Senior Technical Staff Officer
STV	Scottish Television
Subst.	Substantive
SUNY	State University of New York
Supp. Res.	Supplementary Reserve (of Officers)
Supt	Superintendent
Surg.	Surgeon
Surv.	Surviving
SW	South-west
SWET	Society of West End Theatre (*now see* SOLT)
SWIA	Society of Wildlife Artists
SWPA	South West Pacific Area
SWRB	Sadler's Wells Royal Ballet
Syd.	Sydney

T

T	Telephone; Territorial
TA	Telegraphic Address; Territorial Army
TAA	Territorial Army Association
TAF	Tactical Air Force
T&AFA	Territorial and Auxiliary Forces Association
T&AVR	Territorial and Army Volunteer Reserve
TANS	Territorial Army Nursing Service
TANU	Tanganyika African National Union
TARO	Territorial Army Reserve of Officers
TAS	Torpedo and Anti Submarine Course
TASS	Technical, Administrative and Supervisory Section of AUEW (now part of MSF)
TAVRA or	Territorial Auxiliary and Volunteer Reserve
TA&VRA	Association
TC	Order of the Trinity Cross (Trinidad and Tobago)
TCCB	Test and County Cricket Board
TCD	Trinity College, Dublin (University of Dublin, Trinity College)
TCF	Temporary Chaplain to the Forces
TCPA	Town and Country Planning Association
TD	Territorial Efficiency Decoration; Efficiency Decoration (T&AVR) (since April 1967); Teachta Dala (Member of the Dáil, Eire)
TDD	Tubercular Diseases Diploma
TE	Technical Engineer
TEAC	Technical Educational Advisory Council
TEC	Technician Education Council (*now see* BTEC); Training and Enterprise Council
Tech(CEI)	Technician
TEFL	Teaching English as a Foreign Language
TEFLA	Teaching English as a Foreign Language to Adults
TEM	Territorial Efficiency Medal
TEMA	Telecommunication Engineering and Manufacturing Association
Temp.	Temperature; Temporary
TEng(CEI)	Technician Engineer (*now see* IEng)
Tenn	Tennessee (US)
TeolD	Doctor of Theology
TES	Times Educational Supplement
TESL	Teaching English as a Second Language
TESOL	Teaching English to Speakers of other Languages
TET	Teacher of Electrotherapy
Tex	Texas (US)
TF	Territorial Force
TFR	Territorial Force Reserve
TFTS	Tactical Fighter Training Squadron
TGEW	Timber Growers England and Wales Ltd
TGO	Timber Growers' Organisation (*now see* TGEW)
TGWU	Transport and General Workers' Union
ThD	Doctor of Theology
THED	Transvaal Higher Education Diploma
THELEP	Therapy of Leprosy
THES	Times Higher Education Supplement
ThL	Theological Licentiate
ThSchol	Scholar in Theology
TIMS	The Institute of Management Sciences
TLS	Times Literary Supplement
TMMG	Teacher of Massage and Medical Gymnastics
TN	Tennessee
TNC	Theatres National Committee
TOSD	Tertiary Order of St Dominic

TP	Transvaal Province
TPI	Town Planning Institute (*now see* RTPI)
Trans.	Translation; Translated
Transf.	Transferred
TRC	Thames Rowing Club
TRE	Telecommunications Research Establishment (later RRE)
TRH	Their Royal Highnesses
TRIC	Television and Radio Industries Club
Trin.	Trinity
TRRL	Transport and Road Research Laboratory
TS	Training Ship
TSB	Trustee Savings Bank
tsc	passed a Territorial Army Course in Staff Duties
TSD	Tertiary of St Dominic
TSSA	Transport Salaried Staffs' Association
TUC	Trades Union Congress
TULV	Trade Unions for a Labour Victory
TUS	Trade Union Side
TV	Television
TVEI	Technical and Vocational Education Initiative
TWA	Thames Water Authority
TX	Texas
TYC	Thames Yacht Club (*now see* RTYC)

U

U	Unionist
u	uncle
UAE	United Arab Emirates
UAR	United Arab Republic
UAU	Universities Athletic Union
UBC	University of British Columbia
UBI	Understanding British Industry
UC	University College
UCAS	Universities and Colleges Admissions Service
UCCA	Universities Central Council on Admissions
UCCF	Universities and Colleges Christian Fellowship of Evangelical Unions
UCET	Universities Council for Education of Teachers
UCH	University College Hospital (London)
UCL	University College London
UCLA	University of California at Los Angeles
UCLES	University of Cambridge Local Examinations Syndicate
UCMSM	University College and Middlesex School of Medicine
UCNS	Universities' Council for Non-academic Staff
UCNW	University College of North Wales
UCRN	University College of Rhodesia and Nyasaland
UCS	University College School
UCSD	University of California at San Diego
UCW	University College of Wales; Union of Communication Workers (*now see* CWU)
UDC	Urban District Council; Urban Development Corporation
UDF	Union Defence Force; Union démocratique française
UDR	Ulster Defence Regiment; Union des Démocrates pour la Vème République (*now see* RPR)
UDSR	Union Démocratique et Socialiste de la Résistance
UE	United Empire Loyalist (Canada)
UEA	University of East Anglia
UED	University Education Diploma
UEFA	Union of European Football Associations
UF	United Free Church
UFAW	Universities Federation for Animal Welfare
UFC	Universities' Funding Council
UGC	University Grants Committee (later UFC)
UIAA	Union Internationale des Associations d'Alpinisme
UICC	Union Internationale contre le Cancer
UIE	Union Internationale des Etudiants
UISPP	Union Internationale des Sciences Préhistoriques et Protohistoriques
UITP	International Union of Public Transport
UJD	*Utriusque Juris Doctor* (Doctor of both Laws, Doctor of Canon and Civil Law)
UK	United Kingdom
UKAC	United Kingdom Automation Council
UKAEA	United Kingdom Atomic Energy Authority
UKCC	United Kingdom Central Council for Nursing, Midwifery and Health Visiting
UKCIS	United Kingdom Chemical Information Service
UKERNA	United Kingdom Education and Research Networking Association
UKIAS	United Kingdom Immigrants' Advisory Service
UKISC	United Kingdom Industrial Space Committee
UKLF	United Kingdom Land Forces
UKMF(L)	United Kingdom Military Forces (Land)

UKMIS	United Kingdom Mission
UKOOA	United Kingdom Offshore Operators Association
UKPIA	United Kingdom Petroleum Industry Association Ltd
UKSLS	United Kingdom Services Liaison Staff
ULCI	Union of Lancashire and Cheshire Institutes
ULPS	Union of Liberal and Progressive Synagogues
UMDS	United Medical and Dental Schools
UMIST	University of Manchester Institute of Science and Technology
UN	United Nations
UNA	United Nations Association
UNCAST	United Nations Conference on the Applications of Science and Technology
UNCIO	United Nations Conference on International Organisation
UNCITRAL	United Nations Commission on International Trade Law
UNCSTD	United Nations Conference on Science and Technology for Development
UNCTAD or Unctad	United Nations Commission for Trade and Development
UNDP	United Nations Development Programme
UNDRO	United Nations Disaster Relief Organisation
UNECA	United Nations Economic Commission for Asia
UNEP	United Nations Environment Programme
UNESCO or Unesco	United Nations Educational, Scientific and Cultural Organisation
UNFAO	United Nations Food and Agriculture Organisation
UNFICYP	United Nations Force in Cyprus
UNHCR	United Nations High Commissioner for Refugees
UNICE	Union des Industries de la Communauté Européenne
UNICEF or Unicef	United Nations Children's Fund (*formerly* United Nations International Children's Emergency Fund)
UNIDO	United Nations Industrial Development Organisation
UNIDROIT	Institut International pour l'Unification du Droit Privé
UNIFEM	United Nations Development Fund for Women
UNIFIL	United Nations Interim Force in Lebanon
UNIPEDE	Union Internationale des Producteurs et Distributeurs d'Energie Electrique
UNISIST	Universal System for Information in Science and Technology
UNITAR	United Nations Institute of Training and Research
Univ.	University
UNO	United Nations Organization
UNRRA	United Nations Relief and Rehabilitation Administration
UNRWA	United Nations Relief and Works Agency
UNSCOB	United Nations Special Commission on the Balkans
UP	United Provinces; Uttar Pradesh; United Presbyterian
UPGC	University and Polytechnic Grants Committee
UPNI	Unionist Party of Northern Ireland
UPU	Universal Postal Union
UPUP	Ulster Popular Unionist Party
URC	United Reformed Church
URSI	Union Radio-Scientifique Internationale
US	United States
USA	United States of America
USAAF	United States Army Air Force
USAF	United States Air Force
USAID	United States Agency for International Development
USAR	United States Army Reserve
USC	University of Southern California
USDAW	Union of Shop Distributive and Allied Workers
USM	Unlisted Securities Market
USMA	United States Military Academy
USN	United States Navy
USNR	United States Naval Reserve
USPG	United Society for the Propagation of the Gospel
USPHS	United States Public Health Service
USPS	United States Postal Service
USR	Universities' Statistical Record
USS	United States Ship
USSR	Union of Soviet Socialist Republics
USVI	United States Virgin Islands
UT	Utah
UTC	University Training Corps
UU	Ulster Unionist
UUUC	United Ulster Unionist Coalition
UUUP	United Ulster Unionist Party
UWCC	University of Wales College of Cardiff
UWE	University of the West of England
UWIST	University of Wales Institute of Science and Technology
UWT	Union of Women Teachers

V

V	Five (Roman numerals); Version; Vicar; Viscount; Vice
v	*versus* (against)
v or **vid.**	*vide* (see)
VA	Virginia
Va	Virginia (US)
VAD	Voluntary Aid Detachment
V&A	Victoria and Albert
VAT	Value Added Tax
VC	Victoria Cross; Voluntary Controlled
VCAS	Vice Chief of the Air Staff
VCDS	Vice Chief of the Defence Staff
VCGS	Vice Chief of the General Staff
VCNS	Vice Chief of the Naval Staff
VD	Royal Naval Volunteer Reserve Officers' Decoration (*now* VRD); Volunteer Officers' Decoration; Victorian Decoration
VDC	Volunteer Defence Corps
Ven.	Venerable
Vet.	Veterinary
VG	Vicar-General
VHS	Hon. Surgeon to Viceroy of India
VIC	Victoria Institute of Colleges
Vice Adm.	Vice Admiral
Visc.	Viscount
VM	Victory Medal
VMH	Victoria Medal of Honour (Royal Horticultural Society)
Vol.	Volume; Volunteers
VP	Vice-President
VPP	Volunteer Political Party
VPRP	Vice-President, Royal Society of Portrait Painters
VQMG	Vice-Quartermaster-General
VR	*Victoria Regina* (Queen Victoria); Volunteer Reserve
VRD	Royal Naval Volunteer Reserve Officers' Decoration
VSO	Voluntary Service Overseas
VT	Vermont
Vt	Vermont (US)
VUP	Vanguard Unionist Party

W

W	West
WA	Western Australia; Washington
WAAF	Women's Auxiliary Air Force (later WRAF)
WAOS	Welsh Agricultural Organisations Society
Wash	Washington State (US)
WCC	World Council of Churches
W/Cdr	Wing Commander
WCMD	Welsh College of Music and Drama
WDA	Welsh Development Agency
WEA	Workers' Educational Association; Royal West of England Academy
WES/PNEU	Worldwide Education Service of Parents' National Educational Union
WEU	Western European Union
WFSW	World Federation of Scientific Workers
WFTU	World Federation of Trade Unions
WhF	Whitworth Fellow
WHO	World Health Organization
WhSch	Whitworth Scholar
WI	West Indies; Women's Institute; Wisconsin

Wilts	Wiltshire
WIPO	World Intellectual Property Organization
Wis	Wisconsin (US)
Wits	Witwatersrand
WJEC	Welsh Joint Education Committee
WLA	Women's Land Army
WLD	Women Liberal Democrats
WLF	Women's Liberal Federation
Wm	William
WMO	World Meteorological Organization
WNO	Welsh National Opera
WO	War Office; Warrant Officer
Worcs	Worcestershire
WOSB	War Office Selection Board
WR	West Riding; Western Region (BR)
WRAC	Women's Royal Army Corps
WRAF	Women's Royal Air Force
WRNS	Women's Royal Naval Service
WRVS	Women's Royal Voluntary Service
WS	Writer to the Signet
WSAVA	World Small Animal Veterinary Association
WSPA	World Society for the Protection of Animals
WSPU	Women's Social and Political Union
WUS	World University Service
WV	West Virginia
WVa	West Virginia (US)
WVS	Women's Voluntary Services (*now see* WRVS)
WWF	World Wide Fund for Nature (*formerly* World Wildlife Fund)
WY	Wyoming
Wyo	Wyoming (US)

X

X	Ten (Roman numerals)
XO	Executive Officer

Y

y	youngest
YC	Young Conservative
YCNAC	Young Conservatives National Advisory Committee
Yeo.	Yeomanry
YES	Youth Enterprise Scheme
YHA	Youth Hostels Association
YMCA	Young Men's Christian Association
YOI	Young Offenders Institute
Yorks	Yorkshire
YPTES	Young People's Trust for Endangered Species
yr	younger
yrs	years
YTS	Youth Training Scheme
YVFF	Young Volunteer Force Foundation
YWCA	Young Women's Christian Association

Z

ZANU	Zimbabwe African National Union
ZAPU	Zimbabwe African People's Union

ADDENDA I

The following biographies are of those whose deaths occurred before 31 December 1990, but were not reported until after the volume of *Who Was Who* covering the years 1981–1990 had been published.

ARCHER, Sir Clyde Vernon Harcourt, Kt 1962; Judge of the Court of Appeal, Bahamas, 1971–75; *b* 12 Nov. 1904; *s* of Clarence V. E. Archer; *m* 1939, Jeanette Williams (*née* Ware); one *d*; *m* 1957, Isabella Fergusson (*née* d'Oliveira). *Educ:* Harrison Coll., Barbados; Cambridge Univ. Barrister-at-law, Gray's Inn; Clerk to the Attorney-General, Barbados, 1930; Police Magistrate Barbados, 1935; Judge, Bridgetown Petty Debt Court, 1938; Legal Draftsman, 1944, Solicitor-General, 1953, Puisne Judge, 1954, Trinidad and Tobago; Chief Justice of the Windward Islands and Leeward Islands, 1958; a Federal Justice, WI, 1958–62. *Publication:* (jointly) revised edition of the Laws of Barbados, 1944. *Address:* 40 Graeme Hall Terrace, Christchurch, Barbados.

Died 31 Jan. 1989.

ATKINS, Henry St J., DSc; President, University College, Cork, 1954–63, retired; *b* 19 March 1896; *s* of Patrick Atkins and Agnes Egan, Cork; *m* 1929, Agnes E. O'Regan, MB, BCh (*d* 1960); one *s* one *d*. *Educ:* Christian Brothers, North Monastery, Cork; University Coll., Cork. BSc (Math. Science) 1915; post-grad. scholar, MSc 1923. Prof. of Pure Maths, University Coll., Cork, 1936–54; Registrar, 1943–54. Hon. DSc 1955. MRIA 1957. *Recreations:* golf, fishing. *Address:* Knockrea Park, Cork. *T:* Cork 32448. *Clubs:* National University of Ireland; Cork City and County (Cork). *Died 12 Oct. 1987.*

BARBOUR, Walworth; US Ambassador to Israel, 1961–73; *b* 4 June 1908; *s* of Samuel Lewis Barbour and Clara Hammond; unmarried. *Educ:* Harvard Coll., USA. Vice Consul, Naples, 1932; Athens, 1933; Baghdad, 1936; Sofia, 1939; Dip. Sec., Cairo, 1941; Athens, 1944; Dept of State, Washington, 1945–49; Minister, Moscow, 1949–51; Dept of State, Washington, 1951–55; Deputy Asst Sec. of State for European Affairs, 1954–55; American Minister, London, 1955–61. Hon. Fellow, Weizmann Inst. of Sci., 1970. Hon. PhD: Tel Aviv, 1971; Hebrew Univ. of Jerusalem, 1972; Hon. LLD Dropsie, Pa, 1973. *Recreation:* golf. *Clubs:* Swinley Forest (Surrey); Chevy Chase (Md, USA). *Died 21 July 1982.*

BODEN, Edward Arthur; retired; Agent-General for Saskatchewan, Canada, 1973–78; *b* 13 Nov. 1911; *s* of English and Welsh parents; *m* 1939, Helen Harriet Saunders; one *s* one *d*. *Educ:* Cutknife, Saskatchewan, Canada. Born and raised on a Saskatchewan farm and actively farmed until 1949, retaining interest in farm until 1973. Royal Canadian Mounted Police, 1937–39. Saskatchewan Wheat Pool and Canadian Fedn of Agriculture, 1939–73; held several active positions in these organisations and retired, as 1st Vice-Pres., 1973; in this field acted on various provincial and national govtl bds and cttees; Advr to Saskatchewan Dept of Industry and Commerce, 1977–78; Policy Advr, Dept of Agriculture, and Co-ordinator of Sask's 75th Anniv. Celebration for Agricl features 1980, 1979–81; with others, rep. Canada at internat. agricultural confs in different parts of the world. Sen. Counsellor, Provincial Sen. Citizens' Council, 1982–. *Recreations:* boxing,

hunting. *Address:* Box 988, Battleford, Saskatchewan S0M 0E0, Canada. *Died 14 Sept. 1990.*

BOWMAN, Sir George, 2nd Bt *cr* 1961, of Killingworth, Northumberland; *b* 2 July 1923; *s* of Sir James Bowman, 1st Bt, KBE, and of Jean, *d* of Henry Brook, Ashington, Northumberland; *S* father, 1978; *m* 1960, Olive (*née* Case); three *d. Heir:* none. *Address:* Parkside, Killingworth Drive, Newcastle upon Tyne NE12 0ES.

Died 1990 (ext).

BROCKHOFF, Sir Jack (Stuart), Kt 1979; company director; *b* 11 March 1908; *s* of late Frederick Douglas Brockhoff and Lola Landon Brockhoff; *m* 1st, 1935; 2nd, 1980, Ursula Edith. *Educ:* Wesley Coll., Vic. Retired 1973 as Chairman and Managing Director: Brockhoff's Biscuits Pty Ltd; Arnott-Brockhoff-Guest Pty Ltd; Dir, Arnotts Ltd; Chm. of Dirs, Jack Brockhoff Foundn. *Recreations:* golf, bowls, fishing. *Address:* 113 Beach Road, Sandringham, Vic 3191, Australia. *T:* 5989227. *Clubs:* Woodlands Golf, Victoria Golf, Sandringham, Sandringham Yacht, Royal Automobile of Victoria, Victoria Racing, Victoria Amateur Turf.

Died 3 Sept. 1984.

BROUMAS, Nikolaos; retired General; Hon. Deputy Chief, Hellenic Armed Forces; Ambassador of Greece to the Court of St James's, 1972–74; *b* 22 Aug. 1916; *s* of Taxiarches and Kostia Broumas; *m* 1945, Claire Pendelis; two *d. Educ:* Greek Military Academy. US Infantry Coll., 1947–48; Greek Staff Coll., 1952; Greek Nat. Defence Coll., 1954. Co. Comdr, Greece, 1940–41, Western Desert, 1942–43 and Italy, 1944; Co. and Bn Comdr, Greek Guerrilla War, 1946–49; Liaison Officer, Allied Comd Far East, Korean War, 1951; Dep. Nat. Rep. to NATO Mil. Cttee, 1959–61; Dep. Chief of Greek Armed Forces, 1969–72. Kt Comdr, Orders of George I and of the Phoenix. (Greek) Gold Medal for Valour (4 times); Military Cross (twice); Medal for Distinguished Services (twice); Medal of Greek Italian War; Medal of Middle East War; UN Medal of Korean War, 1951; US Bronze Star Medal with oak leaf cluster, 1951. *Recreation:* hunting. *Address:* 5 Argyrokastrou Street, Papagos, Athens, Greece. *Deceased.*

BROWN, Brig. Athol Earle McDonald, CMG 1964; OBE 1956; *b* 2 Jan. 1905; *s* of W. J. C. G. and Alice Catherine Brown, Armidale, NSW; *m* 1929, Millicent Alice Heesh, Sydney; two *s* one *d. Educ:* Armidale Sch., NSW; Royal Australian Naval Coll.; Sydney Univ. Served War of 1939–45: Royal Australian Artillery, AIF, Middle East and New Guinea; Director, War Graves Services, AIF, 1944–46; Lt-Col, 1944; Brigadier, 1946. Secretary-General: Imperial War Graves Commn, 1946–60; Commonwealth-Japanese Jt Cttee, 1956–69; Dir and Sec.-Gen., Commonwealth War Graves Commn, Pacific Region, 1960–69. *Recreations:* golf, bowls, motoring. *Address:* 351 Belmore Road, North Balwyn, Victoria

WHO WAS WHO 1991–1995

3104, Australia. *T:* 8577544. *Clubs:* Royal Automobile of Victoria, Masonic (Melbourne).

Died 5 Aug. 1987.

BYRNE, Sir Clarence (Askew), Kt 1969; OBE 1964; DSC 1945; company director, mining, insurance and construction, Queensland; *b* 17 Jan. 1903; *s* of George Patrick Byrne, Brisbane, Qld, and Elizabeth Emma Askew, Dalby, Qld; *m* 1928, Nellie Ann Millicent Jones; one *s* one *d. Educ:* Brisbane Technical Coll. Mining develt and exploration, 1925–30; oil exploration, Roma, Qld, 1930–40. Served War, 1940–46 (DSC, Amer. Bronze Star Medal): Lt-Comdr; CO, HMAS Warrego, 1944–45. Pres., Qld Chamber of Mines, 1961–70; Exec. Dir, Conzinc Riotinto of Australia Ltd (Resident, Qld, 1957–68); formerly: Chm., Qld Alumina Ltd; Director: Thiess Holdings Ltd; Walkers Ltd. Former Mem., Aust. Mining Industries Council, Canberra. *Recreations:* fishing, ocean cruising. *Address:* Culverston, Dingle Avenue, Caloundra, Qld 4551, Australia. *T:* (74) 911228. *Clubs:* United Service, Queensland (Brisbane).

Died 30 April 1987.

CARR, Rear-Adm. Lawrence George, CB 1971; DSC 1954; Chief of Naval Staff, New Zealand, and Member of the Defence Council, 1969–72; management consultant; *b* 31 Jan. 1920; *s* of late George Henry Carr and Susan Elizabeth Carr; unmarried. *Educ:* Wellington Technical Coll., NZ; Victoria Coll., Univ. of New Zealand. Served War: entered RNZNVR, 1941; commissioned, 1942; on loan to RN, in HM Destroyers in N Atlantic, Medit., W African Coast, English Channel, 1941–44; HMNZS Achilles in Pacific Theatre and NZ, 1945–46; permanent Commn, RNZN, 1946; qual. as communications specialist, 1947; served in: British Medit. Fleet, 1948; RNZN, 1949–72: various appts; in command HMNZS Kaniere, in Korea, 1953–54 (DSC); Comdr Dec. 1953; Exec. Officer, HMNZS Philomel, 1954–55; jssc 1956; Deputy Chief of Naval Personnel, 1957–59; qual. Sen. Officers War Coll., Greenwich, 1959–60; Captain June 1960; in command HMNZS: Philomel, 1960–62; Taranaki, 1962–64; idc 1965; Commodore, Auckland, 1966–68; Chief of Naval Personnel, Second Naval Mem., NZ Naval Bd, 1968–69. Nat. Parly Cand., Nov. 1972; Chm., Nat. Party, Pakuranga Electorate, 1976–82. Exec. Dir, Laura Fergusson Trust for Disabled Persons (Auckland), 1982–85. Mem. Bd, Spirit of Adventure Trust, 1972–; Patron, Coastguard (NZ); Vice-Patron, Co. of Master Mariners, NZ. *Recreations:* golf, fishing, shooting, sailing, tennis, chess. *Address:* Unit 75 Remuera Gardens, 57 Richard Farrell Avenue, Remuera, Auckland, New Zealand. *Clubs:* Wellington, Royal New Zealand Yacht Squadron, Auckland Racing.

Died 9 Sept. 1990.

CHERENKOV, Prof. Pavel Alexeevich; Soviet physicist; Member of the Institute of Physics, Academy of Sciences of the USSR; *b* 28 July 1904. *Educ:* Voronezh State Univ., Voronezh, USSR. Discovered the Cherenkov Effect, 1934. Corresp. Mem., 1964–70, Academician, 1970–, USSR Acad. of Scis. Awarded Stalin Prize, 1946; Nobel Prize for Physics (joint), 1958. *Address:* Academy of Sciences of the USSR, Leninsky Prospekt 14, Moscow V-71, USSR. *Died 6 Jan. 1990.*

CHERMONT, Jayme Sloan, Hon. KCVO 1968; Brazilian Ambassador to the Court of St James's, 1966–68, retired; *b* 5 April 1903; *s* of Ambassador E. L. Chermont and Mrs Helen Mary Chermont; *m* 1928, Zaíde Alvim de Mello Franco Chermont (decd); no *c. Educ:* Law Sch., Rio de Janeiro Univ. Entered Brazilian Foreign Office, 1928; served in Washington, 1930–32; Rio de Janeiro, 1932–37; London, 1937; transf. to Brazil, 1938; 1st Sec., 1941; Buenos Aires, 1943–45; transf. to Brazil, 1945; Counsellor, Brussels, 1948–50; Minister Counsellor, London (periodically Chargé d'Affaires), 1950–53;

various appts, Brazilian FO, 1953–57; Consul-Gen., New York, 1957–60; Ambassador to Haiti, 1960–61; Head of Political and Cultural Depts, Brazil, 1961; Sec.-Gen., FO, 1962–63; Ambassador to Netherlands, 1963–66. Headed Brazilian Delegn to UN Gen. Assembly, 1962. Orders from many foreign countries. *Recreations:* golf, chess, bridge, stamps, coins, books. *Address:* Rua Siqueira Campos no 7–7, Copacabana, Rio de Janeiro, Brasil. *Clubs:* Jockey, Country, Itanhangá Golf (Rio).

Died 15 Oct. 1983.

CHRISTENSEN, Eric Herbert, CMG 1968; Chairman, Victrose Holdings (Channel Islands) Ltd, since 1985; Director: Seagull Cold Stores, since 1980; Gambia Oil Company Ltd, since 1985; *b* 29 Oct. 1923; *s* of George Vilhelm Christensen and Rose Fleury; *m* 1951, Diana, *d* of Rev. Joseph Dixon-Baker; four *s* three *d.* Teacher, St Augustine's Sec. Sch., Bathurst, 1941–43; Military Service, W African Air Corps (RAF), Bathurst, 1944–45; Clerk, The Secretariat, Bathurst, 1946–47; Head of Chancery, then Vice-Consul, French Consulate, Bathurst, 1947–60; acted as Consul on several occasions; Attaché, Senegalese Consulate-Gen., Bathurst, 1961–65, acted as Consul-Gen. on several occasions; Asst Sec. (Ext. Affairs), Gambia Govt, 1965; Principal Asst Sec., Prime Minister's Office, Bathurst, 1966–67; Sec.-Gen., President's Office, Perm. Sec., Min. of External Affairs, and Sec. to the Cabinet, The Gambia, 1967–78; also Hd, Public Service, 1967–78. Foreign decorations include: Grand Officer, Order of the Brilliant Star of China (Taiwan), 1966; Officer, Order of Merit of Islamic Republic of Mauritania, 1967; Knight Commander's Cross, Badge and Star, Order of Merit of Federal Republic of Germany, 1968; Order of Republic of Nigeria, 1970; Grand Officer, National Order of Republic of The Gambia, 1970; Order of Diplomatic Merit, Republic of Korea, 1970, and also those from Egypt, Republic of Guinea and Republic of Liberia; Comdr, Nat. Order of the Lion, Senegal, 1972; Chevalier de la Légion d'Honneur, 1975. *Recreations:* reading, photography, philately, chess.

Died 30 July 1990.

CLUSKEY, Frank; TD (Lab) for Dublin South, since 1987; *b* April 1930; *m* Eileen Gillespie (decd); one *s* two *d. Educ:* St Vincent's Sch., Glasnevin; Harvard Univ., USA. A Branch Sec., Workers' Union of Ireland, 1954–68; Member, Dublin City Council, 1960–63; Lord Mayor of Dublin, 1968–69. TD (Lab) Dublin S Central, 1965–81 and 1982–83; Member: Cttee of Public Accounts and Cttee of Procedure, 1965–69 and 1970–73; Parly Sec. to Min. of Social Welfare, 1973–77; former Labour Opposition Front Bench Spokesman on Justice, Social Welfare, and Labour; Leader of the Labour Party, Ireland, 1977–81; Minister for Trade and Commerce, 1982–83. Mem., European Parlt, 1981–82. *Address:* 1 Glasnevin Park, Dublin 11, Ireland. *Died 7 May 1989.*

CRAIGIE, John Hubert, OC 1967; FRS 1952; *b* 8 Dec. 1887; *s* of John Yorston Craigie and Elizabeth Mary Pollock; *m* 1926, Miriam Louise, *d* of Allen R. Morash and Clara Louise (*née* Smith). *Educ:* Harvard Univ. (AB); University of Minnesota (MSc); University of Manitoba (PhD). Dalhousie Univ., 1914. Served European War, 1914–18, Canadian Expeditionary Force, 1915–18; Indian Army, 1918–20. Canada Dept of Agriculture: Plant Pathologist, 1925–27; Senior Plant Pathologist, 1927–28; Officer-in-Charge (of Laboratory), Dominion Laboratory of Plant Pathology, Winnipeg, 1928–45; Associate Dir, Science Service, Canada Dept of Agriculture, Ottawa, 1945–52; retired 1952. Hon. DSc: University of British Columbia, 1946; University of Manitoba, 1959; Hon. LLD: University of Saskatchewan, 1948; Dalhousie Univ.,

1951. *Publications:* papers in scientific journals. *Address:* 950 Bank Street, Ottawa, Ontario K1S 5G6, Canada.
Died 26 Feb. 1989.

DAVIS, Hon. Sir Maurice, Kt 1975; OBE 1953; QC 1965; Chief Justice of the West Indies Associated States Supreme Court, and of Supreme Court of Grenada, 1975–80; *b* St Kitts, 30 April 1912; *m* Kathleen; one *s* five *d.* Mem. Legislature, St Kitts, 1944–57; Mem., Exec. Council, St Kitts; Dep. Pres., Gen. Legislative Council, and Mem., Fed. Exec. Council, Leeward Is. Pres., St Kitts Bar Assoc., 1968–75. *Recreations:* cricket, football. *Address:* PO Box 31, Basseterre, St Kitts, West Indies.
Died 23 Oct. 1988.

DYMOND, Charles Edward, CBE 1967; JP; HM Diplomatic Service, retired; *b* 15 Oct. 1916; *s* of Charles George Dymond and Dora Kate Dymond (*née* Gillingham); *m* 1945, Dorothy Jean Peaker; two *s* two *d.* *Educ:* Tiverton Grammar Sch.; Exeter Univ. BSc (Econ) London. Royal Artillery, 1939–46; BoT Regional Div., 1946; Trade Commn Service, 1951; Trade Comr, Johannesburg, 1951; Cape Town, 1955; Nairobi, 1957; Sen. Trade Comr, Lagos, 1963–64; Counsellor (Commercial), Lagos, 1965–66; Counsellor i/c, British High Commn, Auckland, 1967–73; Comr for Pitcairn Islands, 1970–72; Consul-General, Perth, 1973–76. JP Western Australia, 1980. *Address:* PO Box 15, Sawyers Valley, WA 6074, Australia.   *Died 17 Jan. 1985.*

EASTWOOD, (George) Granville, OBE 1973; General Secretary, Printing and Kindred Trades Federation, 1958–73; *b* 26 June 1906; *s* of George and Anne Eastwood; *m* 1st, 1934, Margaret Lambert (*d* 1967); no *c*; 2nd, 1971, Elizabeth Gore Underwood (*d* 1981). *Educ:* Burnley. Compositor, Burnley, 1927; Asst Sec., Printing and Kindred Trades Fedn, 1943–58; Workpeople's Sec., HMSO Deptl Whitley Council, 1958–73; Joint Secretary: Printing and Allied Trades Jt Industrial Council, 1958–66; Jt Bd for Nat. Newspaper Industry, 1965–67. Member: Council, Printing Industry's Research Assoc., 1958–73; City and Guilds of London Inst., 1958–73; Council, Inst. of Printing, 1961–76; ILO Printing Conf., Geneva, 1963; Econ. Develt Cttee for Printing and Publishing, 1966–72; Printing and Publishing Industry Trng Bd, 1968–74; Industrial Arbitration Bd, 1973–76; Editorial Adv. Bd, Ind. Relns Digest, 1973–; DHSS Community Health Council, 1974–76; Advisory, Conciliation and Arbitration Service Panel, 1976–80; toured USA and Europe with EDC Jt Mission, 1968. Governor: Chelsea Sch. of Art, 1963–71; Nat. Heart Hosp., Brompton Hosp. and London Chest Hosp., 1969–76. *Publications:* George Isaacs, 1952; Harold Laski, 1977. *Recreations:* reading, gardening. *Address:* 16 The Vineries, Enfield, Mddx EN1 3DQ. *T:* 081-363 2502.   *Died 14 April 1989.*

ERKIN, Feridun Cemal, Hon. GBE 1967; Minister of Foreign Affairs, Turkey, 1962–65; *b* 1899; *m* Madame Mukaddes Feridun Erkin (*d* 1955). *Educ:* Galatasaray Lyceum, Istanbul; Faculty of Law, University of Paris. First Sec., London, 1928–29; Chief of Section, Ankara, 1930–33; Counsellor and Chargé d'Affaires, Berlin, 1934–35; Consul-Gen., Beirut, 1935–37; Dir-Gen., Econ. Dept, Min. of Foreign Affairs, 1937; Dir-Gen., Polit. Dept, 1939; Asst Sec.-Gen., 1942; Deleg, UN Conf. San Francisco, 1945; Sec.-Gen. of Min., 1945; Chm. Turkish Delegn, final session of League of Nations, 1946; Ambassador to Italy, 1947–48; to USA, 1948–55; to Spain, 1955–57; to France, 1957–60; to the Court of St James's, 1960–62. Lately Senator. Turkish Governor to Internat. Banks, 1954; Mem. Internat. Diplomatic Academy, 1949–; Mem. Inst. of France, 1959–. Grand Cross of several foreign Orders, including Grand Cross of the Legion of Honour of France. *Publications:* The Turkish-Soviet relations and the Problem of the Straits,

1968 (French and Turkish edns); articles in daily papers and journals. *Recreation:* classical music. *Address:* Ayaspaşa, Sarayarkasi Sok 24/9, Istanbul, Turkey.
Died 21 June 1980.

ESPINOSA, Dr Augusto; Senator of the Republic of Colombia, 1958–74 and 1978; *b* 5 June 1919; *m* 1944, Myriam de Espinosa; three *s.* *Educ:* Universidad Nacional, Colombia (Dr in Law and Pol Scis, 1942). Manager, Banco de Bogotá, Bucaramanga, 1943–46; Gen. Manager, Agriculture, Industrial and Mining Credit Bank, 1959–61. Deputy and Pres., Deptl Assembly of Santander, 1943; Councillor and Pres. of Council of Bucaramanga, 1945–47; Mem., House of Representatives, 1947–51 and 1974–78; Minister of Agriculture, 1958–59; Pres. of Senate, 1963–64; Ambassador to UN and Perm. Colombian Rep., UN, 1970–73; Ambassador to UK, 1982–84. Pres., First Commn of the Senate, 1982. Grand Cross, Order of Merit, France, 1964. *Publications:* El Pensamiento Económico y Político en Colombia (The Economic and Political Thought in Colombia), 1942; essays and articles in leading Colombian newspapers and magazines. *Recreations:* reading, writing; fond of dogs. *Clubs:* Jockey, Country (Bogotá, Colombia).   *Deceased.*

FARRELL, James; Procurator Fiscal, South Strathclyde, Dumfries and Galloway (formerly Lanarkshire) at Airdrie, 1955–75; Solicitor; *s* of Thomas Farrell and Margaret Farrell (*née* Quigley); *m* 1952, Margaret Clare O'Brien; one *s* three *d.* *Educ:* Our Lady's High Sch., Motherwell; St Patrick's Coll., Armagh, N Ireland; Glasgow Univ. (BL). In private practice as a solicitor, prior to joining Procurator Fiscal Service of the Crown. In latter capacity, Prosecutor for the Crown in the Sheriff Court, leading evidence at inquiries, there, into circumstances of death, particularly in suspicious, sudden and unexplained circumstances, fatal accidents, and where the public interest generally is involved; precognition and preparation of cases for High Court of Justiciary, and investigation relating to estates where the Crown may have to intervene as Ultimus Haeres, etc. *Recreations:* golf, bridge, gardening, photography, motoring, walking. *Address:* Clairville, 4 Belleisle Avenue, Uddingston, Glasgow G71 7AP. *T:* Uddingston (01698) 813385. *Club:* St Mungo's Academy FP Centenary (Glasgow).
Died 18 May 1985.

FLAVELLE, Sir (Joseph) David (Ellsworth), 3rd Bt *cr* 1917; *b* 9 Nov. 1921; *s* of Sir (Joseph) Ellsworth Flavelle, 2nd Bt, and of Muriel, *d* of William Norman McEachren; *S* father, 1977; *m* 1942, Muriel Barbara, *d* of Reginald Morton; three *d.* *Address:* Waterlot, 1420 Watersedge Road, Clarkson, Ontario L5J 1A4, Canada.
Died 27 Feb. 1985 (ext).

FORREST, Sir James (Alexander), Kt 1967; FAA; Chairman: Chase NBA Group Ltd, 1969–80; Alcoa of Australia Ltd, 1970–78; Director, National Bank of Australasia Ltd, 1950–78 (Chairman, 1959–78); Director, Australian Consolidated Industries Ltd, 1950–77 (Chairman, 1953–77); *b* 10 March 1905; *s* of John and Mary Gray Forrest; *m* 1939, Mary Christina (*née* Armit); three *s.* *Educ:* Caulfield Grammar Sch.; Melbourne Univ. RAAF and Dept Aircraft Production, 1942–45. Partner, Hedderwick Fookes & Alston, Solicitors, 1933–70, Consultant, 1970–73; Dir, Australian Mutual Provident Society, 1961–77 (Dir, 1945–, Chm., 1955–77, Victoria Branch Bd); Dir, Western Mining Corp. Ltd, 1970–77. Member: Victoria Law Foundn, 1969–75; Council, Royal Children's Hosp. Research Foundn, 1960–78; Scotch Coll. Council, 1959–71; Council, Monash Univ., 1961–71; Council, Boy Scouts Assoc. of Aust., 1949–73; Aust. Scout Educn and Trng Foundn, 1976–; Board, Art Foundn of Victoria, 1977–80. FAA (by Special Election) 1977. Hon. LLD Monash, 1979. *Recreations:* golf, fishing.

Address: 11 Russell Street, Toorak, Victoria 3142, Australia. *T:* 20–5227. *Clubs:* Melbourne, Australian (Melbourne); Union (Sydney).

Died 26 Sept. 1990.

FRASER, Alexander Macdonald, AO 1981; PhD; FAIM, FTS; Director, Queensland Institute of Technology, 1966–81, Life Fellow 1981; *b* 11 March 1921; *s* of late John Macdonald Fraser and of Esther Katie Fraser; *m* 1951, Rita Isabel Thomason; one *s*. *Educ:* Church of England Grammar Sch., Brisbane; Univ. of Queensland (BE); Imperial Coll. of Science and Technology, Univ. of London (DIC, PhD). MIE(Aust). Military service, 1942–45 (despatches, New Guinea, 1944). Engineer: British Malayan Petroleum Co., 1947–50; Irrigation and Water Supply Commission, Qld, 1951–54 and 1957–65; Research, Imperial Coll. of Science and Technology, 1954–57. *Recreation:* golf. *Address:* 3 Wynyard Street, Indooroopilly, Qld 4068, Australia. *T:* 3707945. *Club:* Indooroopilly Golf (Brisbane).

Died 27 Feb. 1987.

FULLER-ACLAND-HOOD, Sir (Alexander) William; *see* Hood.

GILKISON, Sir Alan (Fleming), Kt 1980; CBE 1972; Chairman: J. E. Watson & Co. Ltd, Invercargill, New Zealand, 1958–81; Southland Frozen Meat & P.E. Co. Ltd, 1959–82; *b* 4 Nov. 1909; *s* of John Gilkison and Margaret Gilkison (*née* Thomson); *m* 1950, Noeline Cramond; two *s*. *Educ:* Southland Boys' High School; Timaru Boys' High School. Started work with J. E. Watson & Co. Ltd, 1930; General Manager, 1958–75. Director and Deputy Chairman, Air New Zealand, 1961–75; Chairman, NZ National Airways Corp., 1967–75. *Address:* PO Box 208, Wanaka, New Zealand. *T:* Wanaka 7597. *Clubs:* Invercargill, Wellington (NZ).

Died 13 Jan. 1990.

GRANT, George; *b* 11 Oct. 1924; *m* 1948, Adeline (*née* Conroy), Morpeth; one *s* four *d*. *Educ:* Netherton Council Sch.; WEA. Member Bedlingtonshire UDC, 1959–70 (Chm. for two years). Member: Labour Party, 1947–; NUM (Chm., 1963–70). MP (Lab) Morpeth, 1970–83; PPS to Minister of Agriculture, 1974–76. *Recreations:* sport, gardening. *Address:* 4 Ringway, Choppington, Northumberland. *Clubs:* Working Men's, in the Bedlington and Ashington area.

Died 27 March 1984.

GUÐMUNDSSON, Guðmundur I., Comdr with Star, Order of the Falcon, 1957; Hon. KBE; Ambassador of Iceland to Belgium, 1977–79, and concurrently to Luxembourg, NATO and EEC; *b* 17 July 1909; *m* 1942, Rósa Ingólfsdóttir; four *s*. *Educ:* Reykjavík Grammar Sch.; Univ. of Iceland. Grad. in Law 1934. Practised as Solicitor and Barrister from 1934; Barrister to Supreme Court, 1939; Sheriff and Magistrate, 1945–56. Mem. Central Cttee, Social Democratic Party, 1940–65, Vice-Chm. of Party, 1954–65; Member of Althing (Parlt), 1942–65; Minister of Foreign Affairs, 1956–65; Minister of Finance, 1958–59; Chm., Icelandic Delegn to UN Conf. on Law of the Sea, Geneva, 1958 and 1960; Mem. and Chm. of Board of Dirs, Fishery Bank in Reykjavík, 1957–65; Ambassador of Iceland: to UK, 1965–71, and concurrently to the Netherlands, Portugal and Spain; to United States, 1971–73, and concurrently to Argentina, Brazil, Canada, Mexico and Cuba; to Sweden, 1973–77 and concurrently to Finland, Austria and Yugoslavia. Establishment of Republic Medal, 1944. Grand Cross, Order of: White Rose (Finland); North Star (Sweden); Orange-Nassau (Netherlands); Chêne (Luxembourg); Southern Cross (Brazil); St Olav (Norway); Phoenix (Greece). *Address:* Solvallagata 8, 101 Reykjavik, Iceland.

Died 19 Dec. 1987.

GUJADHUR, Hon. Sir Radhamohun, Kt 1976; CMG 1973; solicitor; Chairman, Consortium Cinematographique Maurice Ltée; Director, Trianon Estates Ltd; Managing Director of companies; *b* Curepipe Road, Mauritius, 1909; *m*; eight *c*. *Educ:* Church of England Aided Sch., Curepipe; Curepipe De la Salle Sch., Port Louis; Royal Coll., Curepipe; St Xavier Coll., Calcutta. Mem., Municipal Council, 1943–47; Dep. Mayor, Port Louis, 1947; Mem. (nominated), Town Council, Curepipe, 1957–60 (Chm., 1963). MLA, Bon-Accord/Flacq, 1967–82; Dep. Speaker of Legislative Assembly, Mauritius, 1968–69, 1974–82. *Address:* Port Louis, Mauritius. *Club:* Mauritius Turf (Steward, 1970; Chm. 1974).

Died 12 Aug. 1988.

HAMILTON, Francis Hugh; Sheriff of North Strathclyde, since 1984; *b* 3 Dec. 1927; *s* of late Hugh Hamilton and Mary Catherine (*née* Gallagher); *m* 1968, Angela Haffey; one *d*. *Educ:* Notre Dame Convent, Glasgow; St Aloysius' Coll., Glasgow; Univ. of Glasgow (BL 1948). Nat. Service, 1948–50; commnd RASC. Admitted Solicitor, 1951; Town Clerk's Office, Glasgow, 1952–53; in private practice, 1953–84; Sen. Partner, Hamilton & Co., Solicitors, Glasgow, 1967–84; Temp. Sheriff, 1980; Floating Sheriff, 1984–. Pres., Glasgow Bar Assoc., 1963–64; Mem. Council, Law Soc. of Scotland, 1975–84. *Recreations:* music, playing the piano rather badly and bridge very badly. *Address:* 4 Park Quadrant, Glasgow G3 6BS. *T:* 041–332 2265. *Died 8 Nov. 1989.*

HARDINGE, Sir Robert Arnold, 7th Bt *cr* 1801; *b* 19 Dec. 1914; *s* of Sir Robert Hardinge, 6th Bt and Emma Vera, *d* of Charles Arnold; *S* father, 1973. *Heir:* kinsman 6th Viscount Hardinge [*b* 25 Aug. 1956; *m* 1985, Julie Therese Sillett; two *d*, and one step *s*]. *Died Feb. 1986.*

HAWKEY, Rt Rev. Ernest Eric; *b* 1 June 1909; *s* of Richard and Beatrice Hawkey; *m* 1943, Patricia Spark. *Educ:* Trinity Grammar Sch., Sydney, NSW. Deacon, 1933; priest, 1936; Curate: St Alban's, Ultimo, 1933–34; St Paul, Burwood, 1934–40; Priest-in-charge, Kandos, 1940–46, Rector, 1946–47; Australian Board of Missions: Actg Organising Sec., 1947–50; Organising Sec., 1950–68; Canon Residentiary, Brisbane, 1962–68; Bishop of Carpentaria, 1968–74. *Recreations:* music, gardening. *Address:* 2/12 Wellington Street, Clayfield, Queensland 4011, Australia. *T:* 2622108. *Died 25 July 1986.*

HICKS, Sir John (Richard), Kt 1964; FBA 1942; Fellow of All Souls College, Oxford, since 1952; *b* 8 April 1904; *s* of late Edward Hicks, Leamington Spa; *m* 1935, Ursula K. Webb (*d* 1985). *Educ:* Clifton Coll.; Balliol Coll., Oxford. Lectr, London Sch. of Economics, 1926–35; Fellow of Gonville and Caius Coll., Cambridge, 1935–38; Hon. Fellow, 1971; Prof. of Political Economy, University of Manchester, 1938–46; Official Fellow of Nuffield Coll., Oxford, 1946–52; Drummond Prof. of Political Economy, University of Oxford, 1952–65. Member: Revenue Allocation Commn, Nigeria, 1950; Royal Commn on the Taxation of Profits and Income, 1951. Hon. Fellow, LSE, 1969. (Jtly) Nobel Prize for Economics, 1972. *Publications:* The Theory of Wages, 1932, revised edn 1963; Value and Capital, 1939; (with U. K. Hicks and L. Rostas) The Taxation of War Wealth, 1941; The Social Framework, 1942, 4th edn 1971; (with U. K. Hicks) Standards of Local Expenditure, 1943; (with U. K. Hicks and C. E. V. Leser) The Problem of Valuation for Rating, 1944; (with U. K. Hicks) The Incidence of Local Rates in Great Britain, 1945; The Problem of Budgeting Reform, 1948; A Contribution to the Theory of the Trade Cycle, 1950; (with U. K. Hicks) Report on Finance and Taxation in Jamaica, 1955; A Revision of Demand Theory, 1956; Essays in World Economics, 1960; Capital and Growth, 1965; Critical Essays in Monetary Theory, 1967; A Theory of Economic History, 1969; Capital and Time, 1973; The

Crisis in Keynesian Economics, 1974; Economic Perspectives, 1977; Causality in Economics, 1979; Collected Papers, 3 vols, 1981–83; A Market Theory of Money, 1989. *Address:* Porch House, Blockley, Glos.
Died 20 May 1989.

HILEY, Sir Thomas (Alfred), KBE 1966; Chartered Accountant, Australia, since 1932; *b* 25 Nov. 1905; *s* of William Hiley and Maria (*née* Savage); *m* 1929, Marjory Joyce (*née* Jarrott) (*d* 1972); two *s. Educ:* Brisbane Grammar Sch.; University of Qld. State Public Service, 1921; Public Accountancy, 1923; in practice (Public Accountant), 1925. MLA, Qld Parliament, 1944–66: for Logan, 1944–50; for Coorparoo, 1950–60; for Chatsworth, 1960–66; Dep. Leader of Opposition, 1950; Treasurer of Qld and Minister for Housing, 1957; Treasurer, 1963; Deputy Premier of Qld, 1965; retired, 1966. Pres., Inst. of Chartered Accts in Aust., 1946–47. Hon. MCom University of Qld, 1960. *Recreations:* shooting, fishing, cricket. *Address:* Illawong, 39 The Esplanade, Tewantin, Qld 4565, Australia. *T:* (71) 497175. *Club:* Queensland (Brisbane). *Died 6 Nov. 1990.*

HOMANS, Prof. George Caspar; Professor of Sociology, Harvard University, 1953–81, then Emeritus; *b* 11 Aug. 1910; *s* of Robert Homans and Abigail (*née* Adams); *m* 1941, Nancy Parshall Cooper; one *s* two *d. Educ:* St Paul's Sch., Concord, New Hampshire; Harvard Univ. (AB). Harvard University: Junior Fellow, 1934–39; Instructor in Sociology, 1939–41; Associate Professor of Sociology, 1946–53. Simon Vis. Prof., Univ. of Manchester, 1953; Prof. of Social Theory, Univ. of Cambridge, 1955–56; Vis. Prof., Univ. of Kent, 1967. Overseas Fellow, Churchill Coll., Cambridge, 1972. Pres., American Sociological Assoc., 1963–64; Mem., Nat. Acad. of Sciences, USA, 1972. Officer, US Naval Reserve (Lieut-Commander), 1941–45. *Publications:* Massachusetts on the Sea, 1930; An Introduction to Pareto, 1934; Fatigue of Workers, 1941; English Villagers of the 13th Century, 1941; The Human Group, 1950; Marriage, Authority and Final Causes, 1955; Social Behaviour, 1961, rev. edn 1974; Sentiments and Activities, 1962, rev. edn 1988; The Nature of Social Science, 1967; Coming to my Senses (autobiog.), 1984; Certainties and Doubts, 1987; The Witch Hazel (poems), 1988. *Recreations:* forestry, sailing. *Address:* 11 Francis Avenue, Cambridge, Mass 02138, USA. *T:* (617) 5474737. *Club:* Tavern (Boston, USA).
Died 29 May 1989.

HOOD, Sir William Acland, 8th Bt *cr* 1806 and 6th Bt *cr* 1809; *b* 5 March 1901; *s* of William Fuller-Acland-Hood (*d* 1933) and Elizabeth (*d* 1966), *d* of M. Kirkpatrick, Salt Lake City, USA; *S* to baronetcies of kinsman, 2nd Baron St Audries, 1971; *m* 1925, Mary (*d* 1990), *d* of late Augustus Edward Jessup, Philadelphia; one *d* (one *s* decd). *Educ:* Wellington; RMA Woolwich; Univ. of California (MA). Naturalized American citizen, 1926. Formerly Lieutenant RE. Professor, Los Angeles City College, retired. *Heir:* none. *Address:* HC02–Box 577, 29 Palms, California 92277, USA. *T:* (619) 3679345.
Died 6 Feb. 1990 (ext).

HUSAIN, Abul Basher M.; *see* Mahmud Husain.

INCE, Wesley Armstrong, CMG 1968; solicitor and company director; *b* 27 Nov. 1893; *s* of John and Christina Ince, Melbourne; *m* 1919, Elsie Maud Ince, *d* of William H. Smith, Melbourne; two *d. Educ:* Wesley Coll., Melbourne; Melbourne Univ. Admitted practice Barrister and Solicitor, 1917; Partner, Arthur Robinson & Co., 1919–67. Chairman: Claude Neon Industries Ltd, 1932–70; Rheem Australia Ltd, 1937–67; Petroleum Refineries (Aust.) Ltd, 1952–61; Director: International Harvester Co. of Australia Pty Ltd, 1945–74; Hoyts Theatres Ltd, 1934–76; Dulux Australia Ltd, 1945–74.

Foundn Mem. Council, Inst. of Public Affairs, 1942; Foundn Mem., Australian-American Assoc., 1941 (Federal Pres., 1962–63, 1965–67). *Recreations:* golf, bowls, swimming. *Address:* 372 Glenferrie Road, Malvern, Vic 3144, Australia. *T:* 20 9516. *Clubs:* Athenæum (Melbourne); Royal Melbourne Golf, Melbourne Cricket.
Died 26 Nov. 1990.

JAMES, John Anthony, CMG 1973; FRACS; Visiting Neurosurgeon, Wellington Hospital Board, Wellington, NZ, 1965–77; retired 1978; *b* 2 April 1913; *s* of Herbert L. James and Gladys E. Paton; *m* 1941, Millicent Ward, Australia; three *s* one *d. Educ:* Melbourne Church of England Grammar Sch.; Melbourne Univ. (MB, BS). Served War: Surgeon-Lieut, RANR, 1940–43. Neurosurgeon, Neurosurgical Unit, Dunedin Hosp., 1947–52; Dir, Neurosurgical Unit, Otago Univ.; Sen. Lectr in Neurosurgery, Otago Univ., 1951–64. *Publications:* contribs to surgical jls. *Address:* 136 Vipond Road, Whangaparaoa, New Zealand. *Club:* Wellington (Wellington, NZ). *Died 19 June 1987.*

JOHNSON, Sir Robin Eliot, 7th Bt *cr* 1818, of Bath; *b* 1929; *s* of Major Percy Eliot Johnson (*d* 1962) (*g g s* of 2nd Bt) and Molly, *d* of James Payn; *S* kinsman, Sir Victor Philipse Hill Johnson, 6th Bt, 1986; *m* 1954, Barbara Alfreda, *d* of late Alfred T. Brown; one *s* two *d. Educ:* St John's College, Johannesburg. *Heir:* *s* Patrick Eliot Johnson, *b* 1955. *Died July 1989.*

KENYON, Clifford, CBE 1966; JP; farmer; *b* 11 Aug. 1896; *m* 1922, Doris Muriel Lewis, Herne Hill, London; three *s* two *d. Educ:* Brighton Grove Coll., Manchester; Manchester Univ. Joined Labour Party, 1922; Mem. Rawtenstall Council, 1923; Mayor, 1938–42; resigned from Council, 1945. MP (Lab) Chorley Div. of Lancs, 1945–70. JP Lancs, 1941. *Died 29 April 1979.*

KING, Joseph, OBE 1971; JP; Group Industrial Relations Advisor, Smith and Nephew Associated Cos Ltd, 1978–82; *b* 28 Nov. 1914; *s* of John King, coal miner, and Catherine King (*née* Thompson); *m* 1939, Lily King (*née* Pendlebury); one *s* five *d. Educ:* St James' RC Sch., Atherton, Lancashire. Left school at age of 14 and commenced work in cotton mill, 1929. Took active part in Union of Textile and Allied Workers from early years in industry. Elected, 1949: Labour Councillor, Tyldesley; Trades Union Organiser; Dist Sec., NE Lancs. Gen. Sec., Nat. Union of Textile and Allied Workers, 1962–75; Jt Gen. Sec., Amalgamated Textile Workers' Union, 1974; Mem., TUC Gen. Council, 1972–75; Member, many cttees in Textile Industry. Industrial Advr ACAS NW Reg., 1975–78. Created Accrington Pakistan Friendship Association, 1961 (Pres.). Dir, Castle Cards Ltd, Preston, 1984–85. JP Accrington, 1955. *Recreations:* pleasure in domestic work in the home and family and in trade union and political field. *Address:* 44 Southwood Drive, Baxenden, Accrington, Lancs. *T:* Accrington (0254) 394551. *Died 21 Sept. 1989.*

KING, Michael; business consultant in private practice, since 1984; *b* 31 Aug. 1934; *s* of Mac and Jessie King; *m* 1960, Teresa Benjamin; one *s* one *d. Educ:* Buckhurst Hill School; London Univ. (BA). Buyer, Ford Motor Co., 1958–64; Purchasing Manager, Servicing Manager, Hotpoint, 1964–68; Dir and Div. Man. Dir, Lake & Elliot, 1968–72; Chief Exec., Heatrae-Sadia International, 1972–84; Chief Exec., E Anglian RHA, 1985–88. Freeman, City of London; Liveryman, Coopers' Co. *Recreations:* tennis, skiing, music, antiques, computers. *Address:* Moat Cottage, Pleshey, Essex CM3 1HG. *T:* Chelmsford (0245) 37202. *Club:* Institute of Directors.
Died 23 Jan. 1990.

KOHOBAN-WICKREME, Alfred Silva, CVO 1954; Member, Ceylon Civil Service; Secretary to the Cabinet,

1968–70; *b* 2 Nov. 1914; *s* of D. S. Kohoban-Wickreme; *m* 1941, Mona Estelle, *d* of P. R. Krisnaratne. *Educ:* Trinity Coll., Kandy; University Coll., Colombo. BA (Hons) London, 1935. Cadet, Ceylon Civil Service, 1938; served as Magistrate, District Judge, Asst Govt Agent etc, until 1948; Chief Admin. Officer, Ceylon Govt Rly, 1948; Asst Sec., Min. of Home Affairs, 1951; attached to Ceylon High Commissioner's Office in UK, May-July, 1953; Dir of Social Services and Commissioner for Workmen's Compensation, Ceylon, 1953; Conservator of Forests, Ceylon, 1958; Port Commissioner, Ceylon, 1959; Postmaster General and Dir of Telecommunications, Dec. 1962; Permanent Sec., Ministry of: Local Govt and Home Affairs, April 1964; Cultural Affairs and Social Services, June 1964; Ministry of Communications, 1965. Organised the Queen's Tour in Ceylon, April 1954 (CVO). *Recreations:* sports activities, particularly Rugby football, tennis and cricket. *Address:* 6 Kalinga Place, Jawatta Road, Colombo 5, Sri Lanka. *T:* (residence) 86385.

Died 7 Aug. 1989.

LANDA, Hon. Abram, CMG 1968; LLB; Notary Public; Agent-General for New South Wales in London, 1965–70; *b* 10 Nov. 1902; *s* of late D. Landa, Belfast; *m* 1930, Perla (*d* 1976), *d* of late L. Levy; one *s* one *d*. *Educ:* Christian Brothers' Coll., Waverley, NSW; University of Sydney. Solicitor, 1927–. MLA for Bondi, NSW, 1930–32 and 1941–65; Minister for Labour and Industry, 1953–56; Minister for Housing and Co-operative Societies, 1956–65; Minister for Housing, NSW, 1956–65. Past Member Senate, University of Sydney; Past Trustee, NSW Public Library. *Recreations:* swimming, bowls. *Address:* 22 Coolong Road, Vaucluse, NSW, Australia. *Club:* Tattersall's (Sydney). *Died 22 Sept. 1989.*

LEBETER, Fred; Keeper, Department of Transport and Mining, Science Museum, 1953–67, retired; *b* 27 Dec. 1903; *e s* of Arthur Lebeter, Mining Engineer, and Lucy Wilson; *m* 1926, Sybil Leah, *o d* of Henry Ward; (one *d* decd). *Educ:* Rotherham and Bridgnorth Gram. Schs; Birmingham Univ. BSc 1925; MSc (Research on Classification of British Coals) 1926. Manager, Magnesite Mines and Works, Salem, S India, 1926–31; Lecturer in Mining, Heanor Mining Sch., 1931–33; Sen. Lectr in Mining, Chesterfield Tech. Coll., 1933–37; Asst Keeper, Science Museum, 1937–39; Dep. Chief Mining Supplies Officer, Min. of Fuel and Power, 1939–47; Asst Keeper, Science Museum, 1947–49, Dep. Keeper, 1949–53. Consultant on Mine Ventilation and Underground Transport, 1931–; Mem. Council Nat. Assoc. of Colliery Managers (Midland Br.), 1935–37; Adviser to Coal Commission, Germany, on Mining Supplies, 1944; UK rep. to European Coal Organisation, 1945–47; United Kingdom delegate to European Coal Organisation, Paris, 1946. Mem., Industrial Cttee, National Museum of Wales, 1959–67. *Publications:* contributor of many technical articles to Colliery Engineering, Mine and Quarry Engineering, historical articles in Zeitschrift für Kunst und Kultur im Bergbau, etc. *Recreations:* sport, gardening. *Address:* 6 Bay House, Pelham Road, Seaford, E Sussex BN25 1EP. *T:* Seaford (0323) 894751.

Died 5 Dec. 1988.

LEO, Dame Sister Mary, DBE 1973 (MBE 1963); Member of the Sisters of Mercy, Auckland; *b* 3 April 1896; *née* Kathleen Agnes Niccol; *d* of Henry Malcolm Niccol and Agnes Teresa (*née* Cannell). *Educ:* Auckland Teachers' Coll., Auckland Univ.; Trinity Coll., London (LTCL). Specialised in vocal training. Entered Order of Sisters of Mercy, 1923; a singing teacher for over 40 years; pupils who gained international success included Dame Kiri Te Kanawa, DBE, Heather Begg, Mina Foley and Malvina

Major. Biography in preparation. *Address:* St Mary's Convent, PO Box 47025, Ponsonby, Auckland 1, New Zealand. *Died 5 May 1989.*

LOOKER, Sir Cecil (Thomas), Kt 1969; Chairman, Australian United Corporation Ltd; Principal Partner, Ian Potter & Co., Sharebrokers, 1967–76 (Partner, 1953); Director of various other companies; *b* 11 April 1913; *s* of Edward William and Martha Looker; *m* 1941, Jean Leslyn Withington; one *s* two *d*. *Educ:* Fort Street Boys' High Sch., Sydney; Sydney Univ. (BA). Apptd to Commonwealth Public Service, 1937; Private Sec. to Prime Minister (Rt Hon. later Sir Robert Menzies), 1939–41. War of 1939–45: RANVR, 1942–45. Resigned Commonwealth Public Service, 1946, and joined Ian Potter & Co. Chm., Stock Exchange of Melbourne, 1966–72 (Mem. 1962–78); Pres., Australian Associated Stock Exchanges, 1968–71. Apptd by Dept of Territories as Dir of Papua and New Guinea Development Bank, 1966. Chairman: Exec. Cttee, Duke of Edinburgh's Third Commonwealth Study Conf., Aust., 1966–68; Aust. Adv. Cttee, Duke of Edinburgh's Fifth Study Conf., Canada, 1980. *Recreation:* farming. *Address:* 26 Tormey Street, North Balwyn, Victoria 3104, Australia. *T:* 857–9316. *Clubs:* Australian, Royal Automobile Club of Victoria (Melbourne) (President). *Died 19 Sept. 1988.*

LUCKHOO, Hon. Sir Joseph (Alexander), Kt 1963; Judge, Belize Court of Appeal, since 1987; *b* 8 June 1917; *e s* of late Joseph Alexander Luckhoo, KC and Irene Luckhoo; *g s* of Moses Luckhoo, official interpreter to the Courts; *m* 1964, Leila Patricia Singh; three *s* one *d*. *Educ:* Queen's Coll., British Guiana; University Coll., London (BSc 1939). Barrister, Middle Temple, 1944; practised at Bar, British Guiana. Crown Counsel, British Guiana, 1949; Legal Draftsman, 1953; acted as Solicitor Gen., British Guiana, 1952, 1954 and 1955; Puisne Judge, British Guiana, 1956; Acting Chief Justice, 1959; Chief Justice, 1960–66; Chief Justice, Guyana, 1966; Judge, Court of Appeal, Jamaica, 1967–76; Acting Pres., Court of Appeal, Jamaica, 1972, 1973, and 1974–76; Reserve Judge, 1978–81, Judge, 1981–82, President, 1982–87, Bahamas Court of Appeal; Judge of Ct of Appeal, Turks and Caicos, 1979, Pres., 1982–87. Chairman: Judicial Service Commission, 1961–66; Law Reform Cttee, Jamaica, 1973–76. *Publications:* Editor: Law Reports of British Guiana, 1956–58; British Guiana section of West Indian Reports, 1958–61, Jamaica section, 1970–72; Dominion Report Service (Canada), 1977–87. *Recreation:* watching sport. *Address:* 31 Aldenham Crescent, Don Mills, North York, Ontario M3A 1S3, Canada.

Died 4 Feb. 1990.

McCAW, Hon. Sir Kenneth (Malcolm), Kt 1975; QC (Australia) 1972; Attorney-General of New South Wales, 1965–75, retired; *b* 8 Oct. 1907; *s* of Mark Malcolm and Jessie Alice McCaw; *m* 1968, Valma Marjorie Cherlin (*née* Stackpool); two *s* one *d*. *Educ:* matriculated evening college. Left school, 1919; farm and saw-mill hand; clerk, commercial offices and law office, 1922–28; articled law clerk, 1928–33; admitted Solicitor and founded city law firm, 1933; Attorney, Solicitor and Proctor, NSW Supreme Court, until 1965; admitted to NSW Bar, 1965. Councillor, NSW Law Soc., 1945–48. MLA (L) for Lane Cove, NSW, 1947–75, retired. *Publication:* People Versus Power, 1978. *Recreations:* swimming, walking, Braille reading, music, elocution. *Address:* Woodrow House, Charlish Lane, Lane Cove, NSW 2066, Australia. *T:* (2) 4271900. *Clubs:* Sydney, Lane Cove Businessmen's, (Charter Mem.) Lane Cove Lions (all Sydney/Metropolitan). *Died 13 Sept. 1989.*

McSHINE, Hon. Sir Arthur Hugh, TC; Kt 1969; Chief Justice of Trinidad and Tobago, 1968–71; Acting Governor-General, Trinidad and Tobago, 1972; *b* 11 May

1906; *s* of Arthur Hutton McShine, CBE; *m* Dorothy Mary Vanier; one *s* one *d. Educ:* Queen's Royal Coll., Trinidad. Called to Bar, Middle Temple, 1931; practised at Trinidad Bar for eleven years; Magistrate, 1942; Senior Magistrate, 1950; Puisne Judge, 1953; Justice of Appeal, 1962. Acting Governor-Gen., Trinidad and Tobago, 1970. *Recreations:* music, chess (Pres., Caribbean Chess Fedn and Trinidad Chess Assoc.), flying (holder of private pilot's licence). *Address:* 6 River Road, Maraval, Port-of-Spain, Trinidad. *Clubs:* Trinidad and Tobago Turf, Trinidad and Tobago Yacht. *Died 10 June 1983.*

MAHMUD HUSAIN, Syed Abul Basher; Chief Justice of Bangladesh, 1975–78; *b* 1 Feb. 1916; *s* of late Syed Abdul Mutakabbir Abul Hasan, eminent scholar; *m* 1936, Sufia Begum; three *s* five *d. Educ:* Shaistagonj High Sch.; M. C. Coll., Sylhet; Dacca Univ. (BA, BL). Pleader, Judge's Court, Dacca, 1940–42; Hon. Supt, Darul-Ulum Govt-aided Sen., Madrassa, Dacca, 1937–42; Additional Govt Pleader, Habiganj, 1943–48; Advocate, Dacca High Ct Bar, 1948–51; Attorney, Fed. Ct of Pakistan, 1951, Advocate, 1953, Sen. Advocate, Supreme Ct of Pakistan, 1958; Asst Govt Pleader, High Ct of E Pakistan, 1952–56; Sen. Govt Pleader, 1956–65; Actg Advocate-Gen., E Pakistan for some time; Judge: High Ct of E Pakistan, 1965; High Ct of Bangladesh, 1972; Appellate Div. of High Ct of Bangladesh, Aug. 1972; Appellate Div. of Supreme Ct of Bangladesh, Dec. 1972. Mem. Bar Council, High Ct, Dacca, 1958–66; Chm., Enrolment Cttee, E Pakistan Bar Council, 1966–69; played important role in Muslim League and Pakistan Movement. Member: Coll. Rover Crew, 1933–34; Dacca Univ. OTC, 1935–39; Local Bd, Habiganj, 1944–50; Councillor: Assam Provincial Muslim League, 1944–47; All India Muslim League, 1945–47; All Pakistan Muslim League, 1947–55; Member: Constituent Assembly of Pakistan, 1949–54; Commonwealth Parly Assoc., 1950–54; Inter-Parly Union, 1950–54; Pakistan Tea Bd, 1951–54; Exec. Council, Univ. of Dacca, 1952–54; Local Adv. Cttee, East Bengal Rlwy, 1952–54; Dir, Pakistan Refugees Rehabilitation Finance Corp., 1953–54. Leader of Hajj Delegn of Bangladesh, 1975; attended Internat. Islamic Conf., London, 1976 (Chm., Third Session). *Address:* 56/1 Shah Saheb Lane, Narinda, Dhaka, Bangladesh. *T:* 238986.

Died 2 Aug. 1982.

MAJITHIA, Sir Surendra Singh, Kt 1946; industrialist; *b* 4 March 1895; *s* of late Hon. Sardar Bahadur Dr Sir Sundar Singh Majithia, CIE, DOL; *m* 1921, Lady Balbir Kaur (*d* 1977), *d* of late General Hazura Singh, Patiala. *Educ:* Khalsa Collegiate High Sch.; Khalsa Coll., Amritsar. Chairman, Saraya Sugar Mills Ltd, Sardarnagar; Senior Managing Partner, Saraya Surkhi Mill, Sardarnagar; Dir, Punjab & Sind Bank Ltd, Amritsar. Member: Khalsa College Council, Amritsar; Akal College Council, Gursagar; UP Fruit Development Board, Lucknow. President, Chairman, etc, of many educational foundations and social activities. Past member, various Advisory and Consultative Cttees. Chairman, Lady Parsan Kaur Charitable Trust (Educnl Soc.), Sardarnagar; Patron: Wrestling Federation of India; UP Badminton Assoc.; Life Mem., Internal Soc. of Krishna Consciousness; Hon. Mem., Mark Twain Soc., USA; Member, Garden Advisory Cttee, Gorakhpur. Hon. DLitt Gorakhpur, 1970. *Address:* PO Sardarnagar, Dist Gorakhpur, Uttar Pradesh, India. *Clubs:* Gorakhpur, Nepal (Gorakhpur).

Died 28 May 1983.

MALIK, Bidhubhusan; *b* 11 Jan. 1895; *s* of Raibahadur Chandrasekhar Malik, Chief Judge, Benares State; *m* 1916, Leelabati, *d* of Saratkumar Mitra, Calcutta; two *s. Educ:* Central Hindu Coll., Benares (graduated, 1917); Ewing Christian Coll. (MA in Economics, 1919); Allahabad Univ. (LLB 1919); LLD (*hc*) Saugur Univ.

Vakil, Allahabad High Court, 1919; started practice in the civil courts in Benares; left for England in Sept. 1922; called to Bar, Lincoln's Inn, 1923; joined Allahabad High Court Bar, 1924; Member of Judicial Cttee of Benares State, 1941; Special Counsel for Income Tax Dept, 1943; Judge, Allahabad High Court, 1944; Chief Justice, High Court, Allahabad, Dec. 1947; thereafter Chief Justice, UP, 26 July 1948–1955, excepting 3 March-1 May 1949, when acted as Governor, Uttar Pradesh. Commissioner for Linguistic Minorities in India, 1957–62. Member: Constitutional Commission for the Federation of Malaya, 1956–57; Air Transport Council of India, 1955–62; National Integration Commn, India. Constitutional Adviser to Mr Jomo Kenyatta and the Kenya African National Union, Lancaster House Conference, London, 1961–62; Constitutional Expert for Republic of Congo appointed by UNO, Aug.-Oct. 1962; Constitutional Adviser to Kenya Government, Kenya Independence Conference, Lancaster House, Sept.-Oct. 1963; Adviser, Mauritius Constitutional Conference, London, Sept.-Nov. 1965. Vice-Chancellor, Calcutta Univ., 1962–68 (Life-Mem. Senate); President: Jagat Taran Educn Soc., 1924–; Jagat Taran Degree Coll., 1924–; Jagat Taran Inter Coll., 1924–; Jagat Taran Golden Jubilee Eng. Med. Sch. and Hindi Med. Primary Sch., 1924–; Harijan Ashram Degree Coll., Allahabad, 1968–. Former Mem. Council, Ewing Christian Coll. (Pres., Old Boys' Assoc., 1976–). Founder Mem., Lions Club, Allahabad, 1959–60; Rotary Club: Pres., Allahabad; Mem., Allahabad and Calcutta. Founder President: Golf Club, Allahabad, 1949–55; Allahabad Badminton Assoc., 1949–55. *Address:* 23 Muir Road, Allahabad, India. *Died 19 April 1981.*

MARTELL, Edward Drewett; Chairman of The Freedom Group, 1953; *b* 2 March 1909; *e s* of E. E. Martell and Ethel Horwood; *m* 1932, Ethel Maud Beverley; one *s. Educ:* St George's Sch., Harpenden. In coal trade, 1926–28, then entered journalism. Formerly: News Editor, World's Press News; Gen. Manager, The Saturday Review; Managing Editor, Burke's Peerage and Burke Publishing Co.; Sports staff of The Star. Served War of 1939–45, with RAC (Capt.). On demobilisation established own bookselling and publishing company. Mem. LCC, 1946–49; contested (L) Rotherhithe, 1946, and N Hendon, 1950; East Ham (Ind.), 1957; SE Bristol (Nat. Fellowship C), 1963. Dep. Chm., Liberal Central Assoc., 1950–51; Trustee, Winston Churchill Birthday Trust, 1954. Founded: Free Press Soc., 1955; People's League for the Defence of Freedom, 1956 (first Chm.); Anti-Socialist Front, 1958; National Fellowship (co-founder), 1962; New Daily (also Editor), 1960. *Publications:* (with R. G. Burnett) The Devil's Camera, 1932; (with R. G. Burnett) The Smith Slayer, 1940; The Menace of Nationalisation, 1952; The Menace of the Trade Unions, 1957; Need the Bell Toll?, 1958; (with Ewan Butler) Murder of the News-Chronicle and the Star, 1960; Wit and Wisdom-Old and New, 1961; A Book of Solutions, 1962. *Recreations:* lawn tennis; Sherlock Holmes and Father Brown. *Address:* BM Box 2044, WC1. *Died 3 April 1989.*

MARTIN, James Arthur, CMG 1970; FASA; company director; *b* 25 July 1903; *s* of late Arthur Higgins Martin and Gertrude, *d* of George Tippins. *Educ:* Stawell and Essendon High Schools, Victoria; Melbourne Univ. FASA 1924. Joined The Myer Emporium Ltd, Melbourne, 1918; The Myer Emporium (SA) Ltd, Adelaide, 1928, Man. Dir 1936, Chm. and Man. Dir, 1956–68, retd; Dir, Myer (Melbourne) Ltd, department store, 1936–68, retd. *Recreations:* gardening, walking, motoring. *Address:* 17 Hawkers Road, Medindie, SA 5081, Australia. *T:* Adelaide 442535. *Clubs:* South Australian Cricket, South Australian Jockey (Adelaide). *Died 17 March 1989.*

MARY LEO, Sister; *see* Leo, Dame Sister Mary.

MICHALOPOULOS, André, CBE 1937 (OBE 1919); FRSA; Professor Emeritus of Classical Literatures and Civilizations, since 1964, Professor 1957–64, Fairleigh-Dickinson University; *b* 1897; *m* 1st, 1924, Aspasia Eliasco; one *s* two *d*; 2nd, 1964, Countess Eleanor von Etzdorf. *Educ:* St Paul's Sch., London; Oriel Coll., Oxford (Scholar; BA 1st Cl. Hons Litt Hum., 1920; MA 1927). Priv. Sec. to Eleutherios Venizelos, Prime Minister of Greece, 1917 and 1921–24; Mem. Greek Delegation, Lausanne Peace Conference, 1922–23; Civil Governor of Lemnos, Imbros, Tenedos, and Samothrace, 1918–19; Governor of Corfu and adjacent islands, 1924–25; left public service for business, 1925; Managing Dir of Athens-Piraeus Water Co.; dir of several banking, industrial, and commercial corps in Athens; Pres. of the Anglo-Hellenic League, Athens, 1935–45; broadcast nightly English news commentary from Athens during Greco-Italian War, 1940–41; joined Greek forces in Crete, April 1941; Gen. Sec. of Nat. Cttee of Greeks of Egypt for resistance, May 1941; followed Greek Govt to S Africa, Aug. 1941; Mem. Greek Cabinet (Minister of Information in London, Washington and Cairo), Sept. 1941–May 1943. Lectured and broadcast extensively in S Africa, Great Britain, USA, Canada, 1941–43; Minister Plenipotentiary for Greece i/c information in America, 1945–46; Special Adviser on American Affairs to Royal Greek Embassy in Washington, 1950–67; Mem., Supreme Educnl Council of Greek Orthodox Archdiocese in N and S America, 1962–70. Visiting Professor, Kansas City University, 1949. Participated, as Chm. or panel-mem., in Invitation to Learning programme, Columbia Broadcasting System, 1947–65; Master of Ceremonies and political and literary commentator on weekly Hellenic Television Hour, New York, 1955–56. Broadcast to Greece on Voice of America programme, 1950–55. Participated in annual American Foreign Policy Conf., Colgate Univ., 1951–61; lectured and broadcast in the 48 States of USA and in Canada. FRSA 1936; Mem. Academy of American Poets, 1956; Mem. Poetry Society of America, 1957. Fellow, Ancient Monuments Soc. (London), 1958. Hon. LittD Westminster Coll., Utah. Archon, Order of St Andrew; Grand Protonotary of Oecumenical Patriarchate of Constantinople, 1967. Commander, Order of George I (Greece) with swords, 1941; Commander, Order of the Phœnix (Greece), 1936; Chevalier, Legion of Honour (France), 1934; Commander, Order of Orange Nassau (Netherlands), 1939. *Publications:* Homer, an interpretative study of the Iliad and Odyssey, 1965; Greek Fire: a collection of broadcasts, articles and addresses, 1943; two collections of Verse 1923 and 1928; contribs to Encyclopedia Americana and Funk & Wagnall's Reference Encyclopaedia; chapters and articles in Greek, English, Scottish, American, Canadian, Egyptian, French, and South African books, reviews and newspapers; weekly book reviews for King Features Syndicate (USA), 1959–75. *Address:* The Normandy, 1120 North Shore Drive, Apt 1103, St Petersburg, Florida 33701, USA. *T:* (813) 8236352. *Deceased.*

MILLIGAN, Veronica Jean Kathleen; Senior Partner, Civlec Advisory Industrial Development Services, industrial consultants, since 1966; *b* 11 March 1926; *d* of Gilbert John O'Neill and Jennie Kathleen Robertson; *m* 1945, Francis Sutherland Milligan; one *s* (and one *s* decd). *Educ:* Pontypridd Intermediate Grammar Sch.; University Coll., Cardiff (BA Wales, DipEd); (evenings) Polytechnic of Wales (HNC Elec. and Endorsements, Dip. Management Studies). CEng, MIEE; MBIM. Sch. teacher, Glam Educn Authority, 1948–51; Grad. Trainee/Senior Elec. Engr, Electricity Supply Industry, 1952–65. Manpower Adviser/Consultant to Manpower and Productivity Services, Dept of Employment (on secondment), 1969–73; Chm. and Dir, RTR Engineering

Ltd, 1982–86; Dir, Vantage Engrg & Maintenance Ltd, 1985–87. Pres., Women's Engrg Soc., 1977–79; Chm., E Wales Area, IEE, 1976–77 and Mem. Council, 1976–78. Member: Gwent AHA, 1976–88; Gwent FPC, 1985–; National Water Council, 1977–80; Industrial Tribunals Panel, 1977–83; Commn on Energy and Environment, 1978–; Management Adv. Panel for Craftsmen, DHSS, 1979–88; Nat. Staff Cttee for Works Staff, DHSS, 1981–82; Rent Assessment Panel, 1981–; Monitoring Cttee, Nat. Financial Incentive Scheme for NHS Maintenance Depts, 1982–88. *Publications:* short papers in learned jls. *Recreations:* industrial careers advice to schools, industrial history, landscaping, walking. *Address:* Park Cottage, Rhiwderin, Newport, Gwent NP1 9RP. *T:* Newport (0633) 893557, Pontypool (0495) 762311.

Died 3 Sept. 1989.

MORGAN, Sir Ernest (Dunstan), ORSL; KBE 1971 (OBE 1951; MBE 1940); JP; DCL; *b* 17 Nov. 1896; *s* of Thomas William Morgan and Susan Barnett; *m* 1st, 1918, Elizabeth Mary Agnes Collier; one *d*; 2nd, 1972, Monica Fredericka Davies; one *s* three *d*. *Educ:* Zion Day School, Freetown; Methodist Boys' High School, Freetown. Government Dispenser, 1914–20; Druggist, 1917. MHR Sierra Leone, 1956–61; Member: Freetown City Council, 1938–44; Fourah Bay Coll. Council, 1950–54; Chairman: Blind Welfare Soc., 1946–52; Public Service Commn, 1948–52. JP Sierra Leone, 1952. *Recreation:* tennis. *Address:* 15 Syke Street, Freetown, Sierra Leone. *T:* Freetown 23155 and 22366. *Club:* Freetown Dinner.

Died 9 Dec. 1979.

MORI, Haruki; Adviser to Japanese Foreign Office, since 1975; *b* 1911; *m* 1940, Tsutako Masaki; four *s. Educ:* Univ. of Tokyo. Ministry of Foreign Affairs, served USA and Philippines, 1935–41; Head of Economic Section, Dept of Political Affairs, 1950–53; Counsellor, Italy, 1953–55, Asian Affairs Bureau, 1955–56; Private Sec. to Prime Minister, 1956–57; Dep. Dir-Gen., Economic Affairs Bureau, 1957; Dir-Gen., American Affairs Bureau, 1957–60; Minister Plenipotentiary to UK, 1960–63, to France, 1963–64; Ambassador to OECD, 1964–67; Dep. Vice-Minister for Foreign Affairs, 1967–70; Vice-Minister for Foreign Affairs, 1970–72; Japanese Ambassador to the Court of St James's, 1972–75. *Recreation:* golf. *Address:* c/o Ministry of Foreign Affairs, Tokyo, Japan.

Died 18 Aug. 1988.

NAIRN, Air Vice-Marshal Kenneth Gordon, CB 1945; chartered accountant; *b* 9 Nov. 1898; *m* 1920, Mary Fleming Martin; two *s* one *d. Educ:* George Watson's Coll., Edinburgh; Univ. of Manitoba. Lived in Edinburgh till 1911; proceeded to Canada; service in Strathcona Horse and transferred to RFC 1916–19; Pilot, rank Lt; moved to Vancouver from Winnipeg, 1921. Hon. Wing Commander of 111 Aux. Squadron RCAF 1933; Active Service, 1939–45; on Air Council as Air Mem. Accounts and Finance till Oct. 1944, then Special Adviser to Minister for Air on Finance. Hon. ADC for Province of BC to the Governor-General, Viscount Alexander, 1947. Norwegian Cross of Liberation, 1948. *Recreations:* golf, fishing, yachting. *Address:* 1611 Drummond Drive, Vancouver, BC V6T 1B7, Canada. *T:* 2241500. *Clubs:* Royal Air Force; Vancouver, Royal Vancouver Yacht (Vancouver).

Died 29 Oct. 1988.

NARAIN, Sir Sathi, KBE 1980 (MBE 1971); Managing Director, Narain Construction Co. Ltd, since 1945; *b* 26 Sept. 1919; *s* of Suramma and Appalsamy Narain; *m* 1969, Hannah Shakuntla (*née* Pratap); three *s. Educ:* Suva, Fiji. Government apprentice carpenter, 1933–44; Man. Dir, Narain Construction Co. Ltd, 1945–, and of subsidiary companies (hotels, land development, road development, shipping), 1950–; Director: Burns Philps South Sea Co. Ltd; Queensland Insurance Co. Ltd. Suva City Councillor,

1956–59; Member of Parliament, 1963–67. Mem., CPA, 1970. Hon. Architect, Fiji Assoc. of Architects, 1983. *Recreations:* golf, bowling. *Address:* (business) Narain Construction Co. Ltd, Box 1288, Suva, Fiji. *T:* 381086; (residence) 20 Narain Place, Tamavua, Suva, Fiji. *T:* 381027. *Clubs:* Defence, Royal Yacht, Fiji (Suva, Fiji); Tattersall (Sydney, Aust.).   *Died 20 Oct. 1989.*

NICCOL, Kathleen Agnes; *see* Leo, Dame Sister Mary.

NICHOL, Muriel Edith; JP; *b* 1893; *e d* of Richard Collingham Wallhead, late MP Merthyr Tydfil, and Ellen (*née* Staines); *m* James Nichol, MA; one *s*. Counsellor, Welwyn Garden City UDC, 1937–45 (Chm. 1943–44); formerly Dep. Chm., Welwyn Magistrates' Court. MP (Lab) North Bradford, 1945–50; Mem. Parly Delegation to India, Jan.-Feb. 1946; Mem., Curtis Cttee (Home Office) on Care of Children, 1945–46. JP Herts, 1944. *Recreations:* local government, social welfare, education.
       Died 1983.

NOAD, Sir Kenneth (Beeson), Kt 1970; Consulting Physician, 1931–84; Patron, Australian Postgraduate Federation in Medicine (President, 1966–84); *b* 25 March 1900; *s* of James Beeson and Mary Jane Noad; *m* 1935, Eileen Mary Ryan; no *c. Educ:* Maitland, NSW; Sydney University. MB, ChM 1924, MD 1953, Sydney; MRCP 1929; FRCP 1948; Foundn FRACP 1938 (PRACP 1962–64). Hon FACP 1964; Hon. FRCPE 1968. Served War of 1939–45, Palestine, Egypt, Greece, Crete, New Guinea; Lt-Col Comdr Medical Div. of an Australian General Hospital. Dir, Northcott Neurological Centre, 1958–84. Pres., Medico-Legal Soc. of NSW, 1964–68. Hon. DLitt and Hon. AM Singapore. *Publications:* papers in Brain, Med. Jl of Australia. *Recreations:* walking, music. *Address:* 22 Billyard Avenue, Elizabeth Bay, NSW 2011, Australia. *Clubs:* Australian (Sydney); Royal Sydney Golf.   *Died 24 May 1987.*

PARARAJASINGAM, Sir Sangarapillai, Kt 1955; Senator, Ceylon, 1954–59; Chairman, Board of Directors, Colonial Motors Ltd, 1961–74; former Member, Board of Trustees, Ceylon Social Service League; *b* 25 June 1896; *s* of late W. Sangarapillai, social worker and philanthropist; *m* 1916, Padmavati, *d* of Sir Ponnambalam Arunachalam; one *s* one *d. Educ:* St Thomas' Coll., Mt Lavinia. Past President, Board of Directors, Manipay Hindu Coll. (Manager, 1929–61); Past President, Ceylon Poultry Club; Member, National Savings Cttee; Past Chairman, Board Governors, Ceylon Inst. of Scientific and Industrial Research. Formerly Chairman: Board of Directors, Agricultural and Industrial Credit Corporation of Ceylon; Education Cttee, Ceylon Social Service League; Low Country Products Assoc., 1943–44 and 1944–45; Ceylon Coconut Board; Coconut Commn; Past Member: Textile Tribunal; Land Advisory Cttee; Ceylon Tea Propaganda Board; Coconut Research Scheme; Radio Advisory Board; Excise Advisory Cttee; Central Board of Agriculture; Income Tax Board of Review; Rice Advisory Board; Services Standing Wages Board; Board for Approval of Credit Agencies; Commn on Broadcasting; Past President Vivekananda Society; Rotary Club of Colombo; Governor, Rotary Internat. District 320, 1951–52; formerly Trustee and Hon. Treasurer, Ceylon Society of Arts; formerly Manager, all Schools managed by Ceylon Social Service League. JP Ceylon 1923. Travelled widely in the UK, Europe, USA, India, Far East. Coronation Medals, 1937 and 1953. *Recreations:* gardening, agriculture, farming. *Address:* No 50 Pathmalaya, Flower Road, Colombo 7, Sri Lanka. *T:* 23159.   *Died 5 July 1983.*

PARKER, A(gnes) Miller, RE; Artist and Wood-engraver; *b* Irvine, Ayrshire, 25 March 1895; *d* of William McCall and Agnes Mitchell Parker; *m* 1918, William McCance, Artist (marr. diss. 1963, and she legally assumed maiden name); no *c. Educ:* Glasgow School of Art (Diploma, Haldane Scholar). Instructress, Glasgow School of Art, 1918–20; Art Mistress, Maltmans Green School, Gerrards Cross, 1920–28; Art Mistress, Clapham High School and Training Coll., 1928–30; Walter Brewster Prize, 1st International Exhibition of Engraving and Lithography, Chicago, 1929; Wood-engraver to Gregynog Press, Newtown, Montgomeryshire, 1930–33. *Publications:* Chief Illustrated Editions; Esopes Fables by Caxton, 1931; Daisy Matthews and three other tales by Rhys Davies, 1932; XXI Welsh Gypsy Folk-Tales, collected by John Sampson, 1933; The House with the Apricot by H. E. Bates, 1933; Forest Giant-translated from the French by J. H. Ross (Colonel T. E. Lawrence), 1935; Through the Woods by H. E. Bates, 1936; Down the River by H. E. Bates, 1937; Gray's Elegy written in a Country Church-yard (Limited Editions Club of NY), 1938; Richard II-Shakespeare (Limited Editions Club of NY), 1940; A Shropshire Lad by A. E. Housman, 1940; The Return of the Native by Thomas Hardy (Limited Editions Club of NY), 1942; Essays in Russet by Herbert Furst, 1944; Spring of the Year by Richard Jefferies, 1946; The Life of the Fields, 1947, Field and Hedgerow, 1948, The Open Air, 1948, The Old House at Coate, 1948, by Richard Jefferies; Animals Under the Rainbow by Aloysius Roche, 1952; The Faerie Queene by Edmund Spenser, vols I and II, 1953; Lucifer by J. C. Powys, 1956; Tess of the D'Urbervilles, 1956, and Far From the Madding Crowd, 1958, by Thomas Hardy (New York); The Tragedies of Shakespeare (New York), 1959; The Mayor of Casterbridge by Thomas Hardy (Limited Editions Club of NY), 1964; Poems of Shakespeare (Limited Editions Club of NY), 1967; Jude the Obscure by Thomas Hardy (Limited Editions Club of NY), 1969. *Recreations:* fishing and cats.   *Died 13 Nov. 1980.*

PATTINSON, Hon. Sir Baden, KBE 1962; LLB; Member, legal firm Pattinson, McLaughlin & Reid Smith; *b* 22 Dec. 1899; *m* 1926, Florence, *d* of T. A. Doman. Mayor of Maitland, 1928–30, and 1933; Mayor of Glenelg, 1944–47; MHA, South Australia: for Yorke Peninsula, 1930–38; for Glenelg, 1947–65; Minister of Education, SA, 1953–65. *Recreations:* horse riding, reading. *Address:* 12 Maturin Road, Glenelg, Adelaide, SA 5045, Australia.
       Died 17 Dec. 1978.

PIXLEY, Norman Stewart, CMG 1970; MBE 1941; VRD 1927; retired company director; Dean of the Consular Corps of Queensland, 1965–72; Hon. Consul for the Netherlands, 1948–72; *b* Brisbane, 3 May 1898; 2nd *s* of Arthur and Florence Pixley; *m* 1931, Grace Josephine, *d* of Arthur and Grace Spencer; twin *s* one *d. Educ:* Bowen House Sch.; Brisbane Grammar School. Served in RANR, 1913–46; Comdr, RANR, retd. Councillor, National Trust of Queensland; Pres., Qld Lawn Tennis Assoc., 1948–52; Pres., Brisbane Chamber of Commerce, 1952–53; Leader of Aust. Delegn to British Commonwealth Chambers of Commerce Conf., 1951; founded Qld Div. of Navy League, 1953 (Pres. until 1969). FRHistSoc Qld 1965 (Pres. 1968–83). Kt, Order of Orange Nassau, 1964. *Publications:* papers on Australian history in Jl of Royal Hist. Soc. Qld, etc. *Recreations:* tennis, yachting, golf. *Address:* 1/16 Dovercourt Road, Toowong, Queensland 4066, Australia. *T:* 701150. *Clubs:* Queensland, United Service, Indooroopilly Golf (Qld).
       Died 4 Jan. 1989.

PRASADA, Krishna, CIE 1943; JP; ICS retired; Director-General, Posts and Telegraphs, New Delhi, 1945–53; *b* 4 Aug. 1894; *s* of Pandit Het Ram, CIE; *m* 1911, Bishan Devi (*d* 1950); three *s. Educ:* Bareilly; New Coll., Oxford. Joined ICS 1921; Joint Magistrate and subsequently a District Magistrate in UP; services borrowed by Government of India in 1934, when he was appointed as

Postmaster-General; led Government of India deputations to International Tele-communications Conference, Cairo, 1938, Buenos Aires, 1952, and to International Postal Congress, Paris, 1947; retired, 1954. Director, Rotary International, 1961–63. *Recreation:* tennis (Oxford Tennis Blue (1921) and played for India in the Davis Cup in 1927 and 1932; won All India Tennis Championships).*Address:* D/152, East of Kailash, New Delhi 24, 65 India.
Died 1982.

READE, Sir Clyde Nixon, 12th Bt *cr* 1661; *b* 8 Sept. 1906; *s* of Sir George Reade, 10th Bt and Carrie (*d* 1953), *d* of Nathan Nixon, USA; *S* brother, Sir John Reade, 11th Bt, 1958; *m* 1st, 1930, Trilby (*d* 1958), *d* of Charles McCarthy; 2nd, 1960, Alice Martha (marr. diss. 1968), *y d* of Joseph Asher, USA. A Royal Arch Mason.*Heir: kinsman* Kenneth Ray Reade [*b* 23 March 1926; *m* 1944, Doreen D. Vinsant; three *d*].
Died 1982.

RICHARDSON, Sir Egerton (Rudolf), OJ 1975; Kt 1968; CMG 1959; Permanent Representative of Jamaica to the United Nations, New York, 1981–84; *b* 15 Aug. 1912; *s* of James Neil Richardson and Doris Adel (*née* Burton); *m* Vera May Barrow (*d* 1966); one *s* one *d. Educ:* Calabar High School, Kingston, Jamaica; Balliol Coll., Oxford. Entered Civil Service, 1933; Secretary Land Policy Co-ordinating Committee, 1943–53; Permanent Sec., Min. of Agric. and Lands, 1953–54; Under-Sec. Finance, 1954–56; on secondment, CO, London, 1953–54; Financial Secretary, Jamaica, 1956–62; Ambassador: and Permanent Representative at UN, 1962–67; to USA, 1967–72; to Mexico, 1967–75; Permanent Sec., Min. of the Public Service, 1973–75. *Recreations:* swimming, golf, astronomy. *Address:* c/o Ministry of Foreign Affairs, 85 Knutsford Boulevard, Kingston 5, Jamaica.
Died 8 Oct. 1988.

ROCHETA, Manuel Farrajota; Military Order of Christ of Portugal; Hon. GCVO 1955; Ambassador for Portugal in Madrid, 1968–74, retired; *b* 6 Aug. 1906; *s* of Manuel and Rosa Rocheta; *m* 1933, Maria Luiza Belmarco Rocheta; one *d. Educ:* Lisbon University. Entered Diplomatic Service, 1931; Assistant Consul Hamburg, 1934; Consul Copenhagen, 1935–39; First Sec. and Chargé d'Affaires *ai*, Bucarest, 1943–45; First Sec. and Chargé d'Affaires *ai*, Dublin, 1945; First Secretary, Washington, 1946, Counsellor, 1947, Minister-Counsellor, 1950 (Chargé d'Affaires, 1 Nov. 1946–31 March 1947 and 11 Feb. 1950–6 June 1950); Asst Dir-Gen. of Political Dept, Foreign Affairs Ministry, Lisbon, 1951; Minister-Plen. and Dir-Gen. of Political Dept, Foreign Ministry, Lisbon, 1954; Minister in Bonn, 1956, Ambassador, 1956–58; Ambassador: to Rio de Janeiro, 1958–61; to the Court of St James's, 1961–68. Doctor in Law, Univ. of Bahia, Brazil. Grand Cross of several foreign orders.*Recreations:* walking, swimming. *Address:* c/o Ministry of Foreign Affairs, Lisbon, Portugal. *Died 21 Jan. 1989.*

ROSS, Norman Stilliard; Assistant Under-Secretary of State, Fire Department, Home Office, 1976–79; *b* 10 April 1919; *s* of late James Ross and Mary Jane Elizabeth Ross; *m* 1946, Sarah Cahill; one *s* two *d. Educ:* Solihull Sch., Warwickshire; Birmingham Univ. (BA). Served in local govt, City of Birmingham, 1935–39. War service, Army, RAMC and RAOC, in France, Belgium, Kenya, Ceylon, Burma and India, 1939–46 (despatches, France and Belgium, 1940). Asst Principal, Min. of Fuel and Power, 1949; Home Office, 1950–79; Asst Private Sec. to Sec. of State, 1950–52; Principal, 1952; Asst Sec., 1963; Asst Under-Sec. of State, 1976. *Recreations:* walking, music, reading. *Address:* 27 Detillens Lane, Limpsfield, Oxted, Surrey RH8 0DH. *T:* Oxted (0883) 712579.
Died 29 Dec. 1990.

RYBURN, Rev. Hubert James, CMG 1959; MA (Oxon and NZ), BD (Union); *b* 19 April 1897; *s* of Very Rev. Robert Middelton Ryburn and Anna Jane Steadman; *m* 1st, 1931, Jocelyn Maud Dunlop (*d* 1980), *d* of Prof. F. W. Dunlop; two *s* two *d*; 2nd, 1981, Isabella Paterson May. *Educ:* Otago University; Oxford University; Union Theological Seminary, NY. Rhodes Scholar, 1921–24. Ordained a minister of the Presbyterian Church of New Zealand, 1926; Minister: Bay of Islands, 1926–29; St Andrews', Dunedin, 1929–41; Master of Knox College, Dunedin, 1941–63. Member: Council of Otago University, 1946–71, Pro-Chancellor, 1954–55, Chancellor, 1955–70; Senate of Univ. of NZ, 1948–61. Hon. LLD (Otago). *Publication:* Te Hemara, James Hamlin, 1980. *Recreation:* fishing. *Address:* 15 Cornwall Street, Dunedin, New Zealand. *T:* 42–032. *Died 30 June 1988.*

SAN VINCENZO FERRERI, 8th Marquis of; **Alfio Testaferrata Ghâxaq** (Marquis Testaferrata); *b* 1911; *s* of Daniel Testaferrata Bonici Ghâxaq and Agnese (*d* 1941), *d* of Baroncino Nicola Galea di San Marciano; *S* father, 1945. *Educ:* Stonyhurst College, Blackburn; University Coll., Oxford. Member: Cttee of Privileges of Maltese Nobility, 1948–65; Royal Numismatic Society, 1962–85; Société suisse de Numismatique, 1962–85. Hereditary Knight of the Holy Roman Empire; Patrician of Rome, Messina, and Citta di Castello. *Address:* 29 Villegaignon Street, Mdina, Malta, GC. *T:* 674139. *Club:* Casino Maltese (Valletta). *Died 8 Jan. 1988.*

SEWELL, Sir (John) Allan, Kt 1977; ISO 1968; company director; *b* 23 July 1915; *s* of George Allan Sewell and Francis Doris Sewell; *m* 1st, 1939, Thelma Edith Buchholz (*d* 1965); one *s* one *d*; 2nd, 1978, Yoko Fukano, *d* of I. Fukano, Kyoto, Japan. *Educ:* Brisbane Grammar Sch. Dir of Local Govt, 1948–60; Under Treasurer of Qld, 1960–70; Auditor-General of Qld, 1970–78; Chm., State Govt Insurance Office, Qld, 1979–81. *Recreation:* game fishing. *Address:* 63 Ryans Road, St Lucia, Brisbane, Qld 4067, Australia. *Clubs:* Queensland (Brisbane); Cairns Game Fishing (Cairns); Moreton Bay Game Fishing (Brisbane).
Died 22 Aug. 1988.

SHOLL, Hon. Sir Reginald (Richard), Kt 1962; MA, BCL, Oxon; MA Melbourne; QC; retired Judge; former legal consultant and company director, Melbourne and Queensland; *b* 8 Oct. 1902; *e s* of late Reginald Frank and Alice Maud Sholl (*née* Mumby), Melbourne; *m* 1st, 1927, Hazel Ethel (*d* 1962), *yr d* of late Alfred L. and Fanny Bradshaw, Melbourne; two *s* two *d*; 2nd, 1964, Anna Campbell, *widow* of Alister Bruce McLean, Melbourne, and *e d* of late Campbell Colin and Edith Carpenter, Indiana, USA. *Educ:* Melbourne Church of England Grammar Sch.; Trinity Coll., Univ. of Melbourne; New Coll., Oxford. 1st Cl. Final Hons and exhibn, Sch. of Classical Philology, and Wyselaskie Schol. in Classical and Comparative Philology and Logic, Melbourne Univ., 1922; Rhodes Schol., Victoria, 1924; 1st Cl. Final Hons, School of Jurisprudence, Oxford, 1926, Bar Finals, London, 1926 and BCL, Oxford, 1927; Official Law Fellow, Brasenose Coll., Oxford, 1927. Called to Bar, Middle Temple, 1927; journalist, London, 1927; Tutor in Classics, Melbourne Univ., 1928–29; Lectr in law, 1928–38; Barrister, Melbourne, 1929–49; admitted to Bars of NSW and Tasmania, 1935. Served Aust. Army, 1940–44; Capt. retd. Chm. various Commonwealth Bds of Inquiry into Army contracts, 1941–42; KC Vic. and Tas., 1947, NSW 1948; Justice of the Supreme Court of Victoria, 1950–66; Australian Consul-Gen. in New York, 1966–69; Chm., Western Australian Parly Salaries Tribunal, 1971–77. Consultant: to Russell, Kennedy & Cook, solicitors, Melbourne, 1969–79; to Bell, Bell and Fradgley, solicitors, Qld, 1979–82; Dir, Nat. Trustees Executors and Agency Co. of Australasia Ltd, 1969–79,

Vice-Chm., 1976–79, Consultant, 1979–85; Chm., Sperry Rand Corp. (Australia), 1969–74, and Mem. Internat. Adv. Bd, Sperry Rand Corp. (USA), 1971–74. Pres. ESU (Vic. Br.) 1961–66; Fed. Chm., ESU in Aust., 1961–63, 1969–73; Trustee, Northcote Trust Fund, 1978–; Member: Aust. Bd of Trustees, Northcote Children's Emigration Fund for Aust., 1950–78; Bd, US Educnl Foundn in Aust., 1961–64; Archbishop-in-Council, Dio. Melbourne, 1958–66, 1969–79; Advocate of Diocese of Melbourne, 1969–79; Mem. Councils: Trinity Coll., Melbourne, 1939–66; C of E Grammar Sch., Melbourne, 1960–66; Peninsula Sch., Mt Eliza, 1960–63; Toorak Coll., 1969–71; C of E Girls' Grammar Sch., Melbourne, 1969–75; Aust. Adv. Council of Elders, 1983–; Hon. Life Mem., Nat. Gall. of Vic., 1975 (Trustee, 1950–63, Dep. Chm. 1958). Pres. Somers Area, Boy Scouts Assoc. (Vic. Br.), 1955–64, 1972–76; Member: State Exec. Boy Scouts Assoc., 1958–66, (Vice-Pres., 1964–66); Nat. Council Australian Boy Scouts Assoc., 1959–69, 1975–; Cttee, Overseas Service Bureau (Australia), 1970–71; Foundn Dir, Winston Churchill Memorial Trust in Australia, 1965–66, Dep. Nat. Chm., 1969–75, Dep. Nat. Pres., 1975–81; Chm., Nat. Fellowship Cttee, 1965–66, 1969–75; Mem., Victoria Cttee, Duke of Edinburgh's Award in Australia, 1964–66; Chairman, Vict. Supreme Court Rules Cttee, 1960–66; Chm., Royal Commn, Western Australia Inquiry into the airline system, 1974–75. Stawell Orator, 1970; Fellow, Trinity Coll., Melbourne, 1981. *Publications:* contrib. to legal periodicals. *Recreations:* golf, bowls, sailing, gardening; formerly football (Melbourne Univ. blue) and lacrosse (Oxford half-blue). *Address:* 6/7 Britannia Avenue, Broadbeach, Qld 4218, Australia. *Clubs:* Melbourne, Australian (Melbourne); Queensland (Brisbane); Melbourne Cricket (1918–), Surfers Paradise Bridge (Qld). *Died 7 Aug. 1988.*

SHORT, Rev. John, MA (Edinburgh); PhD (Edinburgh); Hon. DD (St Andrews); Minister of St George's United Church, Toronto, Canada, 1951–64; *b* Berwickshire, 27 March 1896; *m* 1st; one *s* one *d*; 2nd, 1939, Anneliese, 2nd *d* of Dr C. J. F. Bechler, Danzig; two *s. Educ:* Edinburgh University. Trained for a business career but attracted by religious convictions to the Christian ministry; began to study for same just before the war of 1914–18; joined army and served for 3 years and 6 months; commenced studies at Edinburgh; graduated MA. First class honours in Philosophy; awarded John Edward Baxter Scholarship in Philosophy for 3 years; received University Diploma in Education and Medal; trained for Teacher's Certificate; awarded Doctorate in Philosophy for a thesis on the Philosophic Character of English XIVth Century Mysticism; medallist in class of Moral Philosophy, and in Metaphysics; Prizeman in Psychology; trained in Scottish Congregational College for Ministry under Principal T. Hywel Hughes, DLitt, DD. Called to Bathgate Evangelical Union Congregational Church, 1924; Minister of Lyndhurst Road Congregational Church, Hampstead, 1930–37. Minister of Richmond Hill Congregational Church, Bournemouth, 1937–51; Chairman of the Congregational Union of England and Wales, 1949–50. Mason: 3° Home Lodge Amity, Poole, Dorset, 18° Downend Chapter Rose Croix, Gloucester, 1953; affiliated Ashlar Lodge, 247 GRC, Toronto, 1952; 32° Moore Sovereign Consistory, Hamilton, Ont, 1964; 33° Supreme Council A&ASR, Dominion of Canada (Hon. Inspector Gen.), 1967. DD (hc): St Andrews Univ., 1950; McMaster Univ., Hamilton, Ontario, 1964. *Publications:* Can I Find Faith?, 1937; All Things are Yours (book of sermons), 1939; The Interpreter's Bible Exposition of I Corinthians; Triumphant Believing, 1952. *Recreations:* gardening, reading, and travel. *Address:* 162 Coldstream Avenue, Toronto, Ont M5N 1X9, Canada. *T:* (416) 4898614. *Died 7 Jan. 1989.*

SHUTE, John Lawson, CMG 1970; OBE 1959; Member: Council of Egg Marketing Authorities of Australia, 1970–79; Egg Marketing Board of New South Wales, 1970–79; Director, Arthur Yates & Co. Pty Ltd, 1970–80; *b* Mudgee, NSW, 31 Jan. 1901; *s* of John and Marion Shute, Mudgee; *m* 1937, Constance W. M., *d* of J. Douglas; two *s. Educ:* Parramatta High Sch. Asst Sec., Primary Producers' Union, NSW, 1923–33, Gen.-Sec., 1933–42; Sec., Federated Co-operative Bacon Factories, 1927–42; Member: NSW Dairy Products Bd, 1934–46; Commonwealth Air Beef Panel, 1962; Dir, Commonwealth Dairy Produce Equalisation Cttee, 1941–46; 1st Sec. Aust. Dairy Farmers' Fedn, 1942; Mem. Exec. and Asst Sec., Empire Producers' Conf., 1938; Mem. Special Dairy Industry Cttee apptd by Commonwealth Govt, 1942; Dep. Controller, Meat Supplies, NSW, 1942–46. Chairman: Aust. Meat Bd, 1946–70; Aust. Cttee of Animal Production, 1947–70; Aust. Cattle and Beef Research Cttee, 1960–66; Belmont-Brian Pastures Res. Cttee, 1962–76; Aust. Meat Research Cttee, 1966–70; Aust. Frozen Cargo Shippers' Cttee, 1967–70; Member: Export Development Council, 1958–66; Overseas Trade Publicity Cttee, 1955–70; Australia Japan Business Co-operation Cttee, 1962–70; Industry Co-operative Programme, FAO, 1973–78 Cttee, Working Gp on Integrated Meat Develt, 1975–78); NSW Rural Reconstruction Bd, 1942–71. Life Mem., Rural Youth Orgn of NSW, 1961. Life Mem., Australia-Britain Soc., 1979; Hon. Life Mem., Australian Veterinary Assoc., 1970–. Freedom, City of London, 1951; Mem., Worshipful Co. of Butchers, 1950. *Recreations:* Rugby Union (former Internat. rep.), cricket. *Address:* 5/2 Woonona Avenue, Wahroonga, NSW 2076, Australia. *Clubs:* Commercial Travellers' (NSW); Eastwood Rugby Union (NSW). *Deceased.*

SIEVE, James Ezekiel Balfour, PhD; FCA; *b* 31 July 1922; *s* of Isaac and Rachel Sieve; *m* 1953, Yvonne Manley; two *s. Educ:* London Sch. of Economics. BSc Econ, PhD. With Urwick Orr & Partners, 1950–54; Aquascutum & Associated Cos Ltd, 1954–68, Finance Dir, 1957–68; Metal Box Ltd, 1968, Finance Dir, 1970–80; Hacker Young, Chartered Accountants, 1981–. Governor, Home Farm Trust (residential care of mentally handicapped), 1974–; Member: Tax Reform Cttee, 1975–; Nat. Freight Co. (formerly Nat. Freight Corp.), 1977–. *Publication:* Income Redistribution and the Welfare State (with Adrian Webb), 1971. *Recreation:* relaxing with family. *Address:* 56 Hampstead Lane, NW3 7JP. *Died 11 Jan. 1983.*

SINGHANIA, Sir Padampat, Kt 1943; President of the JK Organisation, India; *b* 1905; *s* of late Lala Kamlapat Singhania; *m* Srimati Anusiya Devi; four *s* one *d. Educ:* home. A pioneer of cotton, rayon, nylon, jute, woollen textiles, sugar, aluminium, steel and engineering, plastic, strawboard, paper, chemicals, oil industries, shipping, cement, tyres and tubes, dry cell batteries, banking; Patron, large number of social, educational, political, and literary institutions. Founder of the Merchants' Chamber of UP; ex-Pres. of Federation of Indian Chambers of Commerce and Industry; ex-Pres., Employers' Assoc. of Northern India; Member 1st Indian Parliament, 1947–52, and many government and semi-govt bodies; formerly Chairman, Board of Governors, IIT Kanpur. Dr of Letters, Kanpur Univ., 1968. *Recreations:* riding, music, buildings, studies. *Address:* Kamla Tower, Kanpur 208001, India. *TA:* Laljuggi, Kanpur. *T:* 69854, 51147 and 62988. *Telex* KP215. *Died 18 Nov. 1979.*

SINHA, 3rd Baron *cr* 1919, of Raipur; **Sudhindro Prosanno Sinha;** Chairman and Managing Director, MacNeill and Barry Ltd, Calcutta; *b* 29 Oct. 1920; *s* of Aroon Kumar, 2nd Baron Sinha (*s* of Satyendra Prasanna, 1st Baron

Sinha, the first Indian to be created a peer) and Nirupama, yr d of Rai Bahadur Lalit Mohan Chatterjee; S father, 1967; m 1945, Madhabi, d of late Monoranjan Chatterjee, Calcutta; one s two d (and one s decd). Educ: Bryanston School, Blandford. Heir: s Hon. Susanta Prasanna Sinha [b 1953; m 1972, Patricia Orchard; one d (and one s one d decd]. Address: 7 Lord Sinha Road, Calcutta, India.

Died 6 Jan. 1989.

SMITH, Ralph Emeric Kasope T.; see Taylor-Smith.

SOYSA, Sir Warusahennedige Abraham Bastian, (Sir Bennet Soysa), Kt 1954; CBE 1953 (MBE 1950); JP; formerly Mayor of Kandy, Sri Lanka. Address: 30/8 Sangaraja Mawatha, Kandy, Sri Lanka.

Died 20 Oct. 1981.

SPANN, Keith, CB 1980; CVO 1977; Secretary, Premier's Department, Queensland, 1978–82, retired; b 8 Nov. 1922; s of late G. F. A. Spann; m 1946, Marjorie, d of W. R. Golding, CMG, MBE; three s. Educ: State High School, Gympie. Joined Queensland Public Service, 1938; Dept of Auditor-Gen., 1948–61; Sec. to Cabinet, 1961–64; Asst Under Sec., Premier's Dept, 1964–70, Under Sec., 1970–78. Recreations: fishing, golf, woodworking, gemmology. Address: 2 Quaver Court, Bridgeman Downs, Queensland 4035, Australia.   *Died 15 Jan. 1990.*

SPRIGGS, Leslie, JP; b 22 April 1910; British; m 1931, Elfrida Mary Brindle Parkinson. Educ: Council Sch.; Trade Union Adult Schools. TU Scholarship to Belgium, 1951. Merchant Service, then Railwayman until 1958. Formerly: President, NW (NUR) District Council, Political Section, 1954; Vice-President, Industrial Section, 1955. Served as Auditor to Lancs and Cheshire Region of the Labour Party. Formerly Lecturer, National Council of Labour Colleges on Industrial Law, Economics, Foreign Affairs, Local Government, Trade Union History. MP (Lab) St Helens, June 1958–1983; Member Parliamentary Groups: Employment, Environment, Health, Industry, Transport, and Trade, incl. aviation, shipping, textiles, clothing and footwear. JP N Fylde, 1955. Recreations: Rugby League, athletics, water polo, soccer, bowls, gardening. Address: 38 Knowle Avenue, Cleveleys, Lancs FY5 3PP. T: Cleveleys (0253) 852746.

Died 22 May 1990.

STRAUSS, Hon. Jacobus Gideon Nel, QC (South Africa) 1944; Leader of the South African United Party, 1950–56; MP for Germiston District 1932–57; b Calvinia, CP, 17 Dec. 1900; s of late H. J. Strauss; m 1928, Joy Carpenter; two s two d (and one s decd). Educ: Calvinia High Sch.; Univ. of Cape Town; Univ. of South Africa. Private Sec. to the Prime Minister (General J. C. Smuts), 1923–24; practice at Johannesburg Bar, 1926–53; Minister of Agriculture and Forestry in Smuts Cabinet, 1944; succeeded Field Marshal J. C. Smuts as Leader of the Opposition, 1950. Recreations: riding, mountaineering, golf. Address: PO Box 67398, Bryanston, Transvaal, 2021, South Africa. Clubs: Rand, Royal Johannesburg Golf (Johannesburg).   *Died 7 March 1990.*

TAYLOR-SMITH, Prof. Ralph Emeric Kasope; Professor of Chemistry, Fourah Bay College, University of Sierra Leone, 1980–84 (formerly Associate Professor, on leave, as Ambassador of Sierra Leone to Peking, 1971–74; High Commissioner in London for Sierra Leone, and Ambassador to Norway, Sweden and Denmark, 1974–78); b 24 Sept. 1924; m 1953, Sarian Dorothea; five s. Educ: CMS Grammar Sch., Sierra Leone; Univ. of London (BSc (2nd Cl. Hons Upper Div.); PhD (Org. Chem.)). CChem, FRSC. Analytical chemist, 1954; Demonstrator, Woolwich Polytechnic, 1956–59; Lectr, Fourah Bay Coll., Sierra Leone, 1959–62 and 1963; post-doctoral Fellow, Weizmann Inst. of Sci., 1962–63; Research Associate, Princeton Univ., 1965–69; Fourah Bay College: Sen.

Lectr, 1965; Dean, Faculty of Pure and Applied Sci., 1967; Associate Prof., 1968 and 1969. Visiting Prof., Kalamazoo Coll., Mich, 1969. Service in academic and public cttees, including: Mem. Council, Fourah Bay Coll., 1963–65 and 1967–69; Mem., Senate, 1967–69, and Court, 1967–69, Univ. of Sierra Leone; Mem., Student Welfare Cttee, 1967–69; Univ. Rep., Sierra Leone Govt Schol. Cttee, 1965–68; Mem., Bd of Educn, 1970. Pres., Teaching Staff Assoc., Fourah Bay Coll., 1971. Chm., Sierra Leone Petroleum Refining Co., 1970. Delegate or observer to academic confs, 1958–69, incl. those of W African Science Assoc., and Commonwealth Univ. Conf., Sydney, Aust., 1968. Fellow, Thames Polytechnic, 1975; FRSA 1979. Publications: papers to learned jls, especially on investigations on plants of West Africa. Recreations: tennis, swimming. Address: c/o Department of Chemistry, Fourah Bay College, University of Sierra Leone, Private Mail Bag, Freetown, Sierra Leone.

Died 29 Jan. 1987.

TESTAFERRATA, Marquis; see San Vincenzo Ferreri, Marquis of.

WEBB, Lt-Gen. Sir Richard (James Holden), KBE 1974 (CBE 1970; MBE 1952); CB 1972; b 21 Dec. 1919; s of late George Robert Holden Webb and Jessie Muriel Hair; m 1950, Barbara, d of Richard Griffin; one s one d. Educ: Nelson Coll., NZ; Royal Military Coll., Duntroon (Aust.); Staff Coll., Haifa; US Artillery School, Oklahoma; Joint Services Staff Coll., Latimer; Imperial Defence Coll. Commissioned NZ Army 1941. Served War, with Divisional Artillery, 2nd NZ Expeditionary Force, in Middle East and Italy, 1942–45, and Korea, 1950–51 (despatches twice). Quartermaster-Gen., NZ Army, 1967; Dep. Chief of Gen. Staff, NZ Army, 1969–70; Chief of Gen. Staff, NZ Army, 1970–71; Chief of Defence Staff, NZ, 1971–76. Chm., Local Govt Commn, 1978–85. Comdr, Legion of Merit (US), 1971. Address: Pahangahanga, Waimate North, RD1 Ohaeawai, Bay of Islands, New Zealand. Club: Wellington (Wellington, NZ).   *Died 24 Jan. 1990.*

WEDEGA, Dame Alice, DBE 1982 (MBE 1962); retired; b 20 Aug. 1905; d of Wedega Gamahari and Emma. Educ: Kwato Mission School, Milne Bay, PNG; trained in domestic arts, bookbinding, teaching and nursing. Missionary and teacher among head-hunting tribes of SE Papua during 1930s; first Papuan woman to attend internat. conf., Unesco/Pan Pacific, NZ, 1952; first Papuan Girl Guide Comr, 1956; welfare worker with Agric. Dept, helping village women upgrade land and crops, 1958; developed Ahioma Trng Centre, Milne Bay, for village women to learn domestic arts and child care, 1960–68; Mem., Legislative Council, 1961 (first Papuan woman); sent by Govt to assist women in Bougainville during copper mining dispute, 1969–70; as worker with Moral Re-Armament visited and lectured in Asia and Europe, incl. N Ireland, Sweden, Lapland; attended MRA internat. confs in Ceylon, India, Switzerland, Australia and PNG. Publication: Listen My Country (autobiog.), 1981. Recreation: swimming. Address: K.B. Mission, Box 32, Alotau, Milne Bay Province, Papua New Guinea.

Died 3 Dec. 1987.

WICKREME, Alfred Silva K.; see Kohoban-Wickreme.

WILSON, Maj.-Gen. Arthur Gillespie, CBE 1955; DSO 1946; b 29 Sept. 1900; s of late Charles Wilson, originally of Glasgow, Scotland; m 1st, 1927, Edna D. L. Gibson (d 1940); no c; 2nd, 1953, Shirley H. Cruickshank, d of late Colin Campbell, Queenscliff, Victoria, Australia; no c. Educ: North Sydney Boys' High School, NSW, Australia; Royal Military College, Duntroon, Australia. Commissioned Aust. Staff Corps, 1921; served India with various British and IA Artillery Units, 1924; commanded

Royal Aust. Artillery, Thursday Island, 1926–28; Staff College, Quetta, 1935–36; GSO3, AHQ, 1938; continued to serve in various appts at AHQ until joined AIF, 1940; GSO1 HQ AIF UK and then Assistant Mil. Liaison Officer, Australian High Commissioner's Office, UK, until 1943, when returned to Australia; served with AIF New Guinea Philippines and Borneo, 1943–45; DDSD(o) Land Headquarters, 1944–45; commanded British Commonwealth Base BCOF Japan, 1946–47; served various appts AHQ and HQ Eastern Command, 1947–52; Aust. Army Rep., UK, 1953–54; GOC, Central Command, Australia, 1954–57; retired 1957. *Address:* Leahurst Cottage, Crafers, South Australia 5152, Australia. *Club:* Naval, Military and Air Force (Adelaide).

Died 15 Feb. 1982.

WILSON, Stanley Livingstone, CMG 1966; DSO 1943; Visiting Surgeon, Dunedin Hospital, 1937–66, Hon. Consulting Surgeon, Dunedin Hospital, since 1966; *b* 17 April 1905; *s* of Robert and Elizabeth Wilson; *m* 1930, Isabel, *d* of William Kirkland; two *s* one *d. Educ:* Dannevirke High School; University of Otago. Univ. Entrance Schol., 1923; MB, ChB 1928; FRCS 1932; FRACS 1937. Resident Surgeon, Dunedin Hosp., Royal Northern and St Mary's Hosps, London, 1929–37. NZ Medical Corps, Middle East; Solomons, 1940–44; OC 2 NZ Casualty Clearing Station, Pacific, 1943–44. President, Otago BMA, 1948; Council, RACS 1951–63 (President, 1961–62). Examiner in Surgery, Univ. of Otago, 1952–65; Court of Examiners, RACS, 1948–60; Mem., Otago Hosp. Bd, 1965–74. Hon. Fellow, American Coll. of Surgeons, 1963. Hon. DSc Otago, 1975. *Recreation:* golf. *Address:* 27 Burwood Avenue, Dunedin, NW1, New Zealand. *T:* 741061. *Club:* Dunedin (Dunedin).

Died 2 June 1990.

ADDENDA II

The following biographies are of those whose deaths occurred between 1991 and 1995 but were not reported until after the main part of this volume had gone to press.

ADAMS-SCHNEIDER, Rt Hon. Sir Lancelot (Raymond), KCMG 1984; PC 1980; Ambassador of New Zealand to the United States, 1982–85; *b* Wellington, NZ, 11 Nov. 1919; *s* of A. A. Adams; *m* 1945, Shirley Lois, *d* of L. A. Brunton; two *s* one *d*. *Educ:* Mt Albert Grammar School. Served War of 1939–45, NZ Medical Corps. Formerly Gen. Manager of department store, Taumarunui; Mem. Borough Council and Pres., Chamber of Commerce, Taumarunui; Exec. Member, NZ Retailers' Fedn. Vice-Chm. of Nat. Party in Waitomo electorate; Mem. S Auckland Div. Exec.; MP (Nat.) for Hamilton, 1959–69, for Waikato, 1969–81; Minister of Broadcasting, and Assistant to Minister of Customs, 1969; Minister of Customs, Asst Minister of Industries and Commerce, 1969–72; Minister of Health, Social Security and Social Welfare, Feb.-Nov. 1972; Opposition Spokesman on Health and Social Welfare, 1972–75, and on Industry, Commerce and Customs, 1974–75; Minister of Trade and Industry, 1975–81. *Address:* 6 Kimberley Way, Khandallah, Wellington 4, New Zealand.
Died 3 Sept. 1995.

ANDERTON, James, CBE 1966 (OBE 1956); CEng, MIMinE; *b* 3 Nov. 1904; *s* of Richard and Rebecca Anderton; *m* 1st, 1931, Margaret Asbridge (*d* 1945); no *c*; 2nd, 1949, Lucy Mackie; no *c*. *Educ:* Wigan and District Mining and Technical Coll. Manager of various collieries. On nationalisation of mining industry in 1947 became Asst Agent for a group of collieries in St Helens, Lancs; later made Prod. Man., St Helens Area, N Western Div.; Area Gen. Man., St Helens Area, 1949; Dep. Chm., Scottish Div., NCB, 1958. Chm., North Western Div., NCB, 1961–67. Gullick Ltd, Wigan: Dir, 1967–70; Mining Consultant, 1970–81. Hon. FIMinE, 1967. Medal, Instn of Mining Engineers, 1965; Alfried Krupp von Bohlen und Halbach Prize for Energy Research, 1979. *Recreation:* golf. *Address:* The Knoll, Mere Road, Newton-le-Willows, Merseyside WA12 0BJ. *T:* Newton-le-Willows (019252) 5901.
Died 28 July 1994.

BROUN, Sir Lionel John Law, 12th Bt, *cr* 1686; *b* 25 April 1927; *o s* of Sir (James) Lionel Broun, 11th Bt and Georgie, *y d* of late Henry Law, Sydney, NSW; *S* father 1962. *Heir: c* William Windsor Broun [*b* 11 July 1917; *m* 1952, D'Hrie King, NSW; two *d*]. *Address:* 23 Clanalpine Street, Mosman, NSW 2088, Australia.
Died 10 Aug. 1995.

BROWN, Lt-Col Sir Charles Frederick Richmond, 4th Bt *cr* 1863; TD; DL; *b* 6 Dec. 1902; *er s* of Frederick Richmond Brown (*d* 1933; 2nd *s* of 2nd Bt); *S* uncle, 1944; *m* 1st, 1933, Audrey (marr. diss., 1948), 2nd *d* of late Col Hon. Everard Baring, CVO, CBE, and late Lady Ulrica Baring; one *s* two *d*; 2nd, 1951, Hon. Gwendolen Carlis Meysey-Thomson (marr. diss. 1969; she *d* 1989), *y d* of 1st (and last) Baron Knaresborough; 3rd, 1969, Pauline (*d* 1994), *widow* of Edward Hildyard, Middleton Hall, Pickering, Yorks. *Educ:* Eton. Joined Welsh Guards, 1921; Captain 1932; retired with a gratuity, 1936; joined 5th Bn Green Howards, Territorial Army, as a Major,

March 1939; Lieut-Colonel comdg 7th Bn Green Howards, July 1939, and proceeded to France with 7th Bn, April 1940. DL, North Riding of County of York, 1962. Hon. Alderman, after 27 years' service, of N Riding and N Yorks CC. *Heir: s* George Francis Richmond Brown [*b* 3 Feb. 1938; *m* 1978, Philippa Jane, *d* of late E. J. Wilcox; two *s*]. *Recreations:* ornithology, growing species rhododendrons, country pursuits. *Address:* Wranghams, Middleton, Pickering, N Yorks YO18 8NX. *Clubs:* Cavalry and Guards, Pratt's; Yorkshire (York).
Died 9 July 1995.

CASS, Sir John (Patrick), Kt 1978; OBE 1960; Director: Farmers and Graziers Co-operative Co., since 1962; The Land Newspaper Ltd, since 1964; Queensland Country Life Newspaper, since 1977; *b* 7 May 1909; *s* of Phillip and Florence Cass; *m* 1932, Velma Mostyn; two *s*. *Educ:* Christian Brothers College, Young, NSW. Gen. Pres., Farmers and Settlers Assoc. of NSW, 1954–59; Senior Vice-Pres., Aust. NFU, 1960–70; Chm., NSW Wheat Research Cttee, 1954–72; Mem., Aust. Wheat Board, 1952–77, Chm., 1972–77. Agricultural Man of the Year in Australia, 1977. *Address:* Stoney Ridge, Crowther, NSW 2692, Australia. *Clubs:* Royal Automobile of Australia, Royal Automobile of Victoria.
Died 2 Aug. 1995.

CATER, Douglass; writer and educator in USA, since 1968; President, Washington College, Chestertown, Maryland, 1982–90; Founding Fellow, and Trustee since 1982, Aspen Institute (Director, Programme on Communications and Society, 1970–76); *b* Montgomery, Ala, 24 Aug. 1923; *s* of Silas D. Cater and Nancy Chesnutt; *m* 1950, Libby Anderson; two *s* two *d*. *Educ:* Philip Exeter Acad. (grad.); Harvard Univ. (AB, MA). Served War, 1943–45, with OSS. Washington Editor, The Reporter (Magazine), 1950–63; Nat. Affairs Editor, 1963–64; Special Assistant: to Sec. of Army, 1951; to the President of the United States, 1964–68. Vice-Chm., The Observer, 1976–81. Consultant to Dir, Mutual Security Agency, 1952. Visiting Professor, 1959–: Princeton Univ.; Weslyan Univ., Middletown, Conn; Stanford Univ., etc. Guggenheim Fellow, 1955; Eisenhower Exchange Fellow, 1957; George Polk Meml Award, 1961; NY Newspaper Guild, Page One Award, 1961. Mem., Delta Sigma Chi. *Publications:* (with Marquis Childs) Ethics in a Business Society, 1953; The Fourth Branch of Government, 1959; Power in Washington, 1963; Dana: the irrelevant man, 1970. *Address:* 2411 E Cloverdale Park, Montgomery, AL 36106, USA.
Died 15 Sept. 1995.

DAVIES, (William Michael) Neil; Member, Inner London Education Authority, 1980–86 (Chairman, 1982–83); *b* 5 Feb. 1931; *s* of William Henry Davies and Hilda Mary (*née* Fielding); *m* 1955, Myra Blanch Clair Smalley (marr. diss. 1981); two *s* one *d*; *m* 1983, Elizabeth Ann Virgin, textile artist, lecturer and author. *Educ:* Neath Technical Coll.; Fircroft Coll.; Birmingham Univ. Probation Officer, Birmingham, Monmouthshire and Somerset, 1962–76; Principal Child Care Adviser, Lambeth Bor. Council,

1976–82. Member: Taunton Bor. Council, 1968–74; London Bor. of Bexley, 1978–82. Greater London Council: Mem. for Woolwich W, 1980–86; Vice-Chm., Public Services and Fire Bde Cttee, 1980–86; Chm., Thames Barrier Sub Cttee, Educn Cttee, and London Youth Cttee, 1980–86; Vice-Chm., Greater London Trng Bd, and Sports Sub Cttee, 1980–86; Mem., Staff Cttee, Arts and Recreation Cttee, Transport Cttee, and Entertainments Licensing Cttee, 1980–86. Member, National Joint Councils: Fire Bde, 1980–86; Probation Service, 1980–86; Local Authority Bldg Trades, 1980–86. Member: Thames Water Authority, 1980–84; NEC, National Assoc. of Maternal and Child Welfare, 1980–86. Contested (Lab) Ripon, 1979. Founder: Avalon Athletic League, 1966; Westwood Athletic League, 1967. Alcalde, San Antonio, Texas, 1985. *Recreations:* sport (athletics coach), music, cooking, walking, crafts. *Address:* 1 Wingrad House, Jubilee Street, E1 3BJ. *T:* 0171–790 1093. *Clubs:* London Welsh Association, Rugby.
Died 30 April 1995.

DILLON, Sir Max, Kt 1979; *b* 30 June 1913; *s* of Cyril and Phoebe Dillon; *m* 1940, Estelle Mary Jones; one *s* one *d*. *Educ:* Wesley Coll., Melbourne; Melbourne Univ. (Faculty of Commerce). FCPA (AASA (Sen.) 1939); ACIS 1940; FAIM 1947. General Manager, Cable Makers Australia Pty Ltd, 1957–70; Dep. Man. Dir, Metal Manufactures Ltd Gp, 1970–75. President: Aust. Council of Employer Fedns, 1967–69; Associated Chambers of Manufactures, 1974–77; Confedn of Aust. Industry, 1977–80; Chairman: Nat. Employers Policy Cttee, 1971–73 and 1975–78; Central Industrial Secretariat Council, 1972–77; Productivity Promotion Council, 1971–74; Member: Nat. Labour Adv. Council, 1966–72; Nat. Labour Consultative Council, 1977–80; Exec. Cttee, Aust. Manufacturing Council, 1978–80. *Recreations:* golf, swimming. *Address:* 33 Church Street, Pymble, NSW 2073, Australia. *T:* (02) 443160. *Clubs:* Australian, Elanora Country (Sydney).
Died 28 Oct. 1995.

DIVER, Hon. Sir Leslie Charles, Kt 1975; President, Legislative Council, Western Australia, 1960–74; Member, Legislative Council (Country Party) for Central Province, Western Australia, 1952–74; *b* Perth, Australia, 4 Nov. 1899; *s* of late J. W. Diver; *m* 1st, 1922, Emma J. (decd), *d* of late F. Blakiston; one *s* two *d*; 2nd, 1971, Mrs Thelma May Evans (decd). Farmer and grazier. Chairman: Kellerberrin Road Bd, 1940, 1942–46; Hon. Royal Commn on Retailing of Motor Spirits, 1956. Chm., Sixth Aust. Area Conf., Commonwealth Parly Assoc., 1961; Rep. WA Parlt, Town Planning Adv. Cttee. Warden, State War Meml, 1967–68. *Publication:* From Plough to Politics (autobiog.). *Recreations:* bowls, Australian rules football. *Address:* Dryandra Hostel, Leake Street, Kellerberrin, WA 6410, Australia. *Clubs:* Eastern Districts (Kellerberrin); Manning Memorial Bowling. *Died 4 Aug. 1995.*

EVANS, David Philip, CBE 1968; MSc, PhD; FRSC; Principal, Glamorgan Polytechnic, Treforest, Pontypridd, Glam, 1970–72; *b* 28 Feb. 1908; *s* of D. C. and J. Evans, Port Talbot, Glam; *m* 1938, Vura Helena (*née* Harcombe); one *s*. *Educ:* Port Talbot County Grammar Sch.; University Coll., Cardiff (Fellow, 1981). Lectr in Chemistry, Cardiff Technical Coll., 1934–44; Principal: Bridgend Technical Coll., Glam, 1944–52; Glamorgan Coll. of Technology, Treforest, 1952–70. Hon. Fellow, Polytechnic of Wales, 1984. *Publications:* numerous papers in various chemical jls. *Recreations:* gardening, music. *Address:* Tree Tops, St Bride's Road, Ewenny Cross, Ewenny, Bridgend, Mid Glam CF35 5RG. *T:* Bridgend (01656) 661354.
Died 19 Sept. 1995.

FAIRBAIRN, Hon. Sir David Eric, KBE 1977; DFC 1944; Australian Ambassador to the Netherlands, 1977–80; grazier, 1939–71; *b* 3 March 1917; *s* of Clive Prell Fairbairn and Marjorie Rose (*née* Jowett); *m* 1945, Ruth Antill (*née* Robertson); three *d*. *Educ:* Geelong Grammar Sch.; Cambridge Univ. (MA). Served RAAF, 1940–45, England and New Guinea. MP (L) Farrer, NSW, 1949–75; Minister: for Air, 1962–64; for Nat. Develt, 1964–69; for Educn and Science, March-Aug. 1971; for Defence, 1971–72. *Recreations:* golf, gardening. *Address:* 18 Yarralumla Bay, 51 Musgrave Street, Yarralumla, ACT 2600, Australia. *T:* (6) 2814659. *Clubs:* Melbourne (Melbourne); Commonwealth (Canberra); Royal Canberra Golf. *Died 1 June 1994.*

FRYBERG, Sir Abraham, Kt 1968; MBE 1941; retired; *b* 26 May 1901; *s* of Henry and Rose Fryberg; *m* 1939, Vivian Greensil Barnard; one *s*. *Educ:* Wesley Coll., Melbourne; Queen's Coll., University of Melbourne. MB, BS (Melbourne) 1928; DPH, DTM (Sydney) 1936; Hon. MD (Qld); Hon. FACMA. Served with 9 Australian Div. (Tobruk, Alamein), 1940–45. Resident Med. Officer, then Registrar, Brisbane Hosp. and Brisbane Children's Hosp., 1929–33; GP, Hughenden, 1934; Health Officer, Qld Health Dept, 1936–46 (except for war service); Dep. Dir-Gen., 1946, Dir-Gen. of Health and Medical Services, Qld, 1947–67, retired. Hon. Col, RAAMC Northern Comd, 1962–67. SBStJ 1958. *Recreation:* racing. *Address:* 19 Dublin Street, Clayfield, Qld 4011, Australia. *T:* (7) 32622549. *Club:* United Service (Brisbane).
Died 13 Oct. 1993.

GOOD, Tan Sri Donal Bernard Waters, CMG 1962; JMN (Malaysia), 1965; PSM (Malaysia), 1970; Commissioner of Law Revision, Malaysia, 1963; *b* 13 April 1907; *er s* of William John and Kathleen Mary Good; *m* 1930, Kathryn, *er d* of Frank Lucas Stanley and Helena Kathleen Stanley, Dublin; one *s* one *d*. *Educ:* The High Sch., Dublin; Trinity Coll., Dublin (Scholar and Moderator in Classics, 1927–29; MA 1932; LLB 1933). Barrister, King's Inns, Dublin (Benchers' Prizeman), 1935; Barrister, Gray's Inn, 1948. Resident Magistrate, Kenya, 1940–45; Malayan Planning Unit, 1945; Crown Counsel, Malayan Union, 1946–48; Legal Adviser: Negri Sembilan and Malacca, 1948–49; Johore, 1949–50; Legal Draftsman, Sierra Leone, 1951–52; Legal Adviser, Selangor, 1952; Senior Federal Counsel, Federation of Malaya, 1952–55; Actg Solicitor-Gen., 1953 and 1955; Actg Judge of Supreme Court, 1953; Judge of Supreme Court, 1955–59; Judge of the Court of Appeal, Federation of Malaya, 1959–62. Chm. Detainees Review Commn, 1955–60; Pres., Industrial Court, 1956–57; Chm. Detained Persons Advisory Board, 1960. Coronation Medal, 1953. *Address:* Cullum Welch Court, Morden College, SE3 0PW.
Died 19 Oct. 1993.

GRIFFITHS, Prof. John William Roger, FEng; Professor of Electronics, Department of Electronic and Electrical Engineering, Loughborough University of Technology, 1967–84, then Emeritus; *b* 27 Nov. 1921; *s* of Samuel William Henry Griffiths and Alice Griffiths; *m* 1945, Pauline Edyth Griffiths (*née* Marston); one *s*. *Educ:* Waterloo Grammar Sch.; Bristol Univ. BSc 1949, PhD 1958. FEng 1991, FIEE; FIOA. Served War, HM Forces, 1939–46. Scientific Civil Service, 1949–55; Lectr, then Sen. Lectr, Birmingham Univ., 1955–67; Loughborough University of Technology: Head of Dept of Electronic and Electrical Engrg, 1968–80; Dean of Engineering, 1972–75; Sen. Pro-Vice-Chancellor, 1978–80. Vis. Prof., Inst. of Radio Physics, Calcutta, 1963–65. Mem., Govt Adv. Panel on Satellite TV Standards, 1983. *Publications:* Signal Processing in Underwater Acoustics, 1972; many papers in learned jls. *Recreations:* sport, gardening. *Address:* 80 Rectory Road, Wanlip, Leicestershire LE7 4PL. *T:* Leicester (0116) 267 6336. *Died 4 May 1995.*

GUNN, Bunty Moffat, CBE 1993 (OBE 1981); JP; Chairman, Lanarkshire Health Board, 1981–93 (Member,

1973–81); *b* 4 Sept. 1923; *d* of William M. and Dolina Johnston; *m* 1946, Hugh McVane Houston Gunn; three *s* one *d*. *Educ:* Grange School for Girls; Grangemouth High School. DSCHE 1980. Councillor: Lanark CC, 1970–73; Strathclyde Regional Council, 1973–82; Chairman, Scottish Council for Health Education, 1974–80. Vice-Pres., Royal British Legion, CS&W Branch, 1978–. JP City of Glasgow 1972. *Recreations:* grandchildren, golf, theatre, music. *Address:* 198 Dukes Road, Burnside, Rutherglen, Glasgow G73 5AA. *T:* 0141–647 8258. *Club:* Cathkin Braes Golf (Strathclyde).

Died July 1994.

HARTY, Most Rev. Michael; Bishop (RC) of Killaloe, since 1967; *b* Feb. 1922; *s* of Patrick Harty, Lismore, Toomevara, Co. Tipperary, Ireland. *Educ:* St Flannan's Coll., Ennis, Ire.; St Patrick's Coll., Maynooth, Ire.; University Coll., Galway. Priest, 1946; Prof., St Flannan's Coll., Ennis, 1948; Dean, St Patrick's Coll., Maynooth, 1949, 1955–67; Asst Priest, dio. Los Angeles, 1954. BA, BD, LCL, DD (Hon.); HDiplEduc. *Address:* Westbourne, Ennis, Co. Clare, Ireland. *T:* (065) 28638.

Died 8 Aug. 1994.

HODGKINSON, Rev. Canon Arthur Edward; Retired Priest-in-Charge of St Ebba's, Eyemouth, Diocese of Edinburgh, 1982–86; *b* 29 Oct. 1913; *s* of Arthur and Rose Hodgkinson. *Educ:* Glasgow High School; Edinburgh Theol College. LTh Durham 1942. Deacon, 1939; priest, 1940. Curate, St George's, Maryhill, Glasgow, 1939–43; Choir Chaplain, 1943, and Precentor of St Ninian's Cath., Perth, 1944–47; Curate-in-Charge, St Finnian's, Lochgelly, 1947–52, and Rector, 1952–54; Rector, Holy Trinity, Motherwell, 1954–65; Provost of St Andrew's Cathedral, Aberdeen, 1965–78; Area Sec., Dioceses of Monmouth, Llandaff, Swansea and Brecon, and St Davids, USPG, 1978–82. Commissary to Bp of St John's, 1961–78; Mem., Anglican Consultative Council, 1971–77; Canon of St Mary's Cath., Glasgow, 1963–65. Hon. Canon of Christ Church Cathedral, Connecticut, 1965–78; Hon. Canon of Aberdeen, 1981. *Recreations:* motoring, travel. *Address:* 36 Forbes Road, Edinburgh EH10 4ED.   *Died 19 April 1995.*

JAMES, Dr David William Francis, OBE 1989; Chief Executive, British Ceramic Research Ltd (formerly British Ceramic Research Association), 1982–91 (Director of Research, 1978–82); *b* 29 March 1929; *s* of Thomas M. and Margaret A. James, Merthyr Tydfil; *m* 1953, Elaine Maureen, *d* of Thomas and Gladys Hewett, Swansea; two *d*. *Educ:* Cyfarthfa Castle Sch., Merthyr Tydfil; Univ. of Wales (BSc); Univ. of London (PhD). FICeram 1985; FIM 1991; LRPS 1993. Research Asst, Inst. of Cancer Research, Royal Marsden Hosp., 1950–54; Flying Officer, RAF, 1954–56; Research Officer, Imperial Chemical Industries (later Mond Div.), 1956–60; Lectr and Sen. Lectr, UC North Wales, Bangor, 1960–71; Dep. Principal, Glamorgan Polytechnic, 1971–72; Principal and Director, Polytechnic of Wales, 1972–78. Council for National Academic Awards: Mem., 1976–82; Mem., Cttee for Research, 1976–83; Mem., Cttee on Entry Qualifications, 1976–79; Mem., Cttee for Academic Policy, 1979–80; Mem., Gen. Cttee, 1979–83; Chm., Sub-Cttee on College Research Degrees, 1981–85 (Mem., Working Party on Res. Policy, 1982–84); Mem., Cttee for Instns, 1982–86; Mem., Research Adv. Cttee, 1985–87; Mem., Credit Accumulation and Transfer System Adv. Bd, 1986–87. Member: WJEC Techn. Educn Cttee, 1972–78, Techn. Examns Cttee and Management Adv. Cttee, 1972–75; SRC Polytechnics Cttee, 1975–78; Mid-Glamorgan Further Educn Cttee, 1974–78; F and GP Cttee, CDRA, 1983–86 (Vice-Chm., 1985–86); Exec. Cttee, AIRTO, 1986–91 (Pres., 1987–88); Council, CBI, 1986–88. Pres., Inst. of Ceramics, 1989–90 (Mem. Council, 1988–93;

Mem., Editl Bd, 1985–93); Vice Pres., Inst. of Materials, 1992–93. Member: Court, Univ. of Wales; Court, UWIST, 1972–78; Court, Univ. of Surrey, 1978–91; Governor, WestminsterColl., 1983–88. *Publications:* research papers in various jls; several patents. *Recreations:* photography, reading, church work. *Address:* Fairways, Birchall, Leek, Staffs ST13 5RD. *T:* Leek (01538) 373311.

Died 17 Nov. 1995.

KELLETT, Alfred Henry, CBE 1965; Chairman, South Western Areas, National Coal Board, 1967–69, retired; *b* 2 Aug. 1904; British; *m* 1934, Astrid Elizabeth (*née* Hunter); one *s* three *d*. *Educ:* Rossall Sch.; Sidney Sussex Coll., Cambridge; Univ. of Birmingham. Man. Dir, Washington Coal Co. Ltd, 1940–47; Area Gen. Man., NCB Durham Div., 1950–59; Dep. Chm., Durham Div., 1960; Chm., South Western Div., NCB, 1961–67. CStJ. *Recreation:* travel. *Address:* Pent House, Benenden, Cranbrook, Kent TN17 4EH.

Died 11 Sept. 1995.

LING, Arthur George, FRIBA; PPRTPI; architect and town planner in practice with Arthur Ling and Associates; *b* 20 Sept. 1913; *s* of George Frederick Ling and Elsie Emily (*née* Wisbey); *m* 1939, Marjorie Tall; one *s* three *d*. *Educ:* Christ's Hospital; University College, London (Bartlett School of Architecture). BA (Architecture), London. Architect in office of E. Maxwell Fry and Walter Gropius, 1937–39; Structural Engineer with Corporation of City of London (air raid shelters and War debris clearance), 1939–41; Member town planning team responsible for preparation of County of London Plan, 1943, under direction of J. H. Forshaw and Sir Patrick Abercrombie, 1941–45; Chief Planning Officer, London County Council, 1945–55; Head of Department of Town Planning, University College, London Univ., 1947–48; Sen. Lecturer in Town Planning, 1948–55; City Architect and Planning Officer, Coventry, 1955–64; Prof. and Head of Dept of Architecture and Civic Planning, Univ. of Nottingham, 1964–69, Special Prof. of Environmental Design, 1969–72. Visiting Professor: University of Santiago, Chile, 1963; Univ. of NSW, Australia, 1969; Chancellor Lectures, Univ. of Wellington, NZ, 1969. Joint Architect for Development Plan for University of Warwick. Cons. Architect Planner, Runcorn New Town Corporation. UN (Habitat) Project Manager, Physical Perspective Plan 1981–2000, Libyan Jamahiriya, 1977–80. Former Chairman, Board of Chief Officers, Midlands Housing Consortium; Past Vice-Pres., RIBA; President: RTPI, 1968–69; Commonwealth Assoc. of Planners, 1968–76. Mem., Sports Council, 1968–71; Vice-Chm., E Midlands Sports Council, 1968–76. Pres., Heckington Village Trust, 1974–84. RIBA Dist. in Town Planning, 1956; Silver Medallist (Essay), 1937; Hunt Bursary, 1939. Fellow University College, London, 1967. *Publications:* Urban and Regional Planning and Development in the Commonwealth, 1988; contrib. to professional journals on architecture and town planning. *Address:* The Old Barn, 11 Luke's Close, Helmdon, Northants NN13 5UQ.

Died 20 Dec. 1995.

LOUGHEAD, Peter, DPhil; Under Secretary, Coal Division, Department of Trade and Industry, since 1994; *b* 26 Aug. 1950; *s* of Arnold George Loughead and Dora Loughead; *m* 1st, 1975, Kristien Wynants (marr. diss. 1989); 2nd, 1993, Virginia Pasqua Dias. *Educ:* Liverpool Inst.; Lincoln Coll., Oxford (MA, DPhil). Admin Trainee, Dept of Prices and Consumer Protection, 1975; Principal, DoI, 1980; on secondment as First Sec., UK Rep., Brussels, 1982; Asst Sec., DTI, 1985–92; HM Treasury, 1992; Under Sec., Coal Review Team, 1992–93, Coal Privatisation Unit, 1993–94, DTI. *Recreation:* Everton FC. *Address:* Department of Trade and Industry, 1 Palace Street, SW1E 5HE.   *Died 24 Oct. 1995.*

McKAY, Archibald Charles; Sheriff of Glasgow and Strathkelvin, 1979–95; *b* 18 Oct. 1929; *s* of Patrick McKay and Catherine (*née* McKinlay); *m* 1956, Ernestine Maria Tobia; one *s* three *d*. *Educ:* Knocknacarry, Co. Antrim; St Aloysius' Coll., Glasgow; Glasgow Univ. (MA, LLB 1954). National Service commn, 1955–56. Started practice in Glasgow as solicitor, 1957; estabd own firm of solicitors, 1961; apptd to the Bench, 1978. Pres., Glasgow Bar Assoc., 1967–68. *Recreations:* flying, motor cycling, amateur radio, tennis. *Address:* 96 Springkell Avenue, Pollokshields, Glasgow G41 4EL. *T:* 0141–427 1525.
Died 2 Oct. 1995.

MAIN, Frank Fiddes, CB 1965; FRCPEd; Chief Medical Officer, Ministry of Health and Social Services, Northern Ireland, 1954–68, retired; *b* 9 June 1905; *s* of Frank and Mary Main, Edinburgh; *m* 1931, Minnie Roberta Paton; two *s* two *d*. *Educ:* Daniel Stewart's Coll., Edinburgh; Edinburgh Univ. MB, ChB 1927; DPH 1931; MRCPEd 1954; FRCPEd 1956. Medical Officer of Health, Perth, 1937–48; Senior Administrative Medical Officer, Eastern Regional Hosp. Bd (Scotland), 1948–54. Crown Mem., Gen. Med. Council, 1956–69. QHP 1956–59. *Recreation:* golf. *Address:* Balnacarron, 116 Hepburn Gardens, St Andrews, Fife KY16 9LT.
Died 10 June 1994.

MAYOH, Raymond Blanchflower; Under Secretary, Department of Health and Social Security, 1979–83, retired; *b* 11 Nov. 1925; *s* of Charles and Isabella Mayoh; *m* 1956, Daphne Yvonne Bayliss; one *s* one *d* (and one *s* decd). *Educ:* Colwyn Bay County Sch.; University College of North Wales. Assistant Principal, Ministry of Pensions, 1950; Principal, Ministry of Health, 1955; Assistant Secretary, 1965. *Recreations:* gardening, bird watching. *Address:* 20 Willingale Way, Thorpe Bay, Southend-on-Sea, Essex SS1 3SL. *T:* Southend (01702) 586650.
Died 28 Dec. 1995.

MITCHELL, Dr James Clyde, FBA 1990; Emeritus Fellow, Nuffield College, Oxford, 1985 (Official Fellow, 1973–85); *b* 21 June 1918; *s* of George Shellard Mitchell and Rosina Kate Jones; *m* 1st, 1942, Edna Masken (*d* 1962); three *s* one *d*; 2nd, 1964, Hilary Flegg (*d* 1976); one step *d*; 3rd, 1987, Jean Edwards. *Educ:* Univ. of Natal (BA(Soc. Sci)); Univ. of Oxford (MA; DPhil 1950); Univ. of Manchester (MA). Served War, Air Navigator, SAAF, 1942–45. Rhodes-Livingstone Institute, Northern Rhodesia: Asst Anthropologist, 1945–50; Sen. Sociologist, 1950–52; Dir, 1952–55; Prof. of African Studies and Sociology, UC of Rhodesia and Nyasaland, 1955–65; Prof. of Urban Studies, Univ. of Manchester, 1966–73. Rivers Meml Medal, for distinguished fieldwork, RAI, 1964. *Publications:* The Yao Village, 1956, 3rd edn 1971; The Kalela Dance, 1957; (ed) Social Networks in Urban Situations, 1969, 2nd edn 1971; (ed with J. Boissevain) Network Analysis: studies in interaction, 1973; (ed) Numerical Techniques in Social Anthropology, 1980; Cities, Society and Social Perception, 1987; contrib. sociol and anthropol jls. *Recreations:* bird-watching, gardening. *Address:* 25 Staunton Road, Headington, Oxford OX3 7TJ. *T:* Oxford (01865) 62539.
Died 15 Nov. 1995.

OSMAN, Sir (Abdool) Raman (Mahomed), GCMG 1973; CBE 1963; Governor-General of Mauritius, 1972–77; *b* 29 Aug. 1902, of Mauritian parents; unmarried. *Educ:* Royal College, Mauritius; Inns of Court, London. District Magistrate, Mauritius, 1930–38; Additional Substitute Procureur and Advocate General, 1938–50; Actg Procureur and Advocate-General, 1950–51; Actg Chief Justice, Apr.-Nov. 1958; Puisne Judge, Supreme Court of Mauritius, 1950–59, Sen. Puisne Judge, 1959–60, retired. Hon. DCL Mauritius, 1975. *Address:* Le Goulet Terrace, Tombeau Bay, Mauritius. *Club:* Port Louis Gymkhana.
Died 16 Nov. 1992.

SCHNEIDER, Rt Hon. Sir Lancelot Raymond A.; *see* Adams-Schneider.

A

AARVOLD, His Honour Sir Carl (Douglas), Kt 1968; OBE 1945; TD 1950; DL; Recorder of London, 1964–75; *b* 7 June 1907; *s* of late O. P. and J. M. Aarvold, West Hartlepool, County Durham; *m* 1934, Noeline Etrenne Hill, Denton Park, Yorks; three *s*. *Educ:* Durham Sch.; Emmanuel College, Cambridge (Hon. Fellow, 1976). Called to the Bar, Inner Temple, 1932; North Eastern Circuit. Master of the Bench, Inner Temple, 1959. Recorder of Pontefract, 1951–54; a Judge of the Mayor's and City of London Court, 1954–59; Common Serjeant, City of London, 1959–64; Chm., City of London QS, 1969–71. Chm., Inner London Probation Cttee, 1965–75; Pres., Central Council of Probation Cttees, 1968–75; Chm., Home Sec.'s Adv. Bd on Restricted Patients, 1978–81. Chairman: RAC, 1978–81; Statutory Cttee, Pharmaceutical Soc., 1981–86. DL Surrey, 1973. Hon. LLD Dalhousie, 1962; Hon. DCL Durham, 1965. Pres., Lawn Tennis Assoc., 1962–81. *Recreations:* golf, tennis, gardening. *Address:* The Coach House, Crabtree Lane, Westhumble, Dorking, Surrey. *T:* Dorking (0306) 882771. *Died 17 March 1991.*

ABBOTT, Anthony Cecil, MC 1945; RDI 1972; RIBA; Senior Designer, BBC Television, since 1962 (Designer, 1954–62); *b* 21 Aug. 1921; *s* of Col Albert Leigh Abbott, MC, and Alice Elizabeth Abbott. *Educ:* Dulwich Coll.; Architectural Assoc. (AADip Hons). Served Army, 1939–45 (Captain). AA, 1946–51; Architects' Dept, LCC; private practice, designing new Kuwait, 1952–54. *Work for television includes: opera:* Billy Budd, 1966; Rigoletto, La Bohème, Faust, 1968; Otello, 1969; *drama:* Horror of Darkness, 1964; Brothers Karamazov, Poet Game, 1965; The Idiot, Somerset Maugham, 1984, Out of the Unknown, Ross, 1966; Richard II, Beyond the Sunrise, 1968; Rembrandt, Vortex, 1969; St Joan, The Tempest, 1970; Traitor, The General's Day, Sextet, 1971; Oh Fat White Woman, The Grievance, The Merchant of Venice, Lady Windermere's Fan, 1972; Caucasian Chalk Circle, Loyalties, Secrets, An Imaginative Woman (film), Twelfth Night, 1973; The Applecart, Forget-Me-Not-Lane, Savages, 1974; A Story to Frighten the Children (film), Look Back in Anger, 1975; 84 Charing Cross Road, A Picture of Dorian Gray, Abide with Me (film), Rogue Male (film), 1976; Heartbreak House, She Fell Amongst Thieves (film), 1977; Beaux Stratagem, Richard II, Julius Caesar, 1978; Crime and Punishment, 1979; Dr Jekyll and Mr Hyde, The Crucible, The Fatal Spring, 1980; Timon of Athens, Little Eyolf, Baal, 1981; Accounts, 1982; Shibear–Going Home; A Fellow by the Name of (film); Mr Pye (film), 1985; *theatre work includes:* Hotel in Amsterdam, Time Present, This Story is Yours, Look Back in Anger, 1968; Fidelio (opera), The Marquise, So What About Love, 1969; The Entertainer, 1974; The Exorcism, 1975; Julius Caesar (opera), 1984. Awards: Guild of TV Directors and Producers: Designer of the Year, for The Idiot, 1984, Billy Budd, 1966; Pye Colour Award: Best Colour Prodn, for Otello, 1969; Soc. of Film and TV Arts: Designer of the Year, for Vortex, Rembrandt, 1970. *Recreations:* gardening, music, travel. *Address:* 116 Marine Parade, Kemp Town, Brighton, Sussex BN2 1DD. *Died 10 March 1992.*

ABDELA, His Honour Jack Samuel Ronald, TD 1948; QC 1966; a Circuit Judge, Central Criminal Court (formerly Deputy Chairman, Inner London Quarter Sessions), 1970–86; *b* 9 Oct. 1913; *s* of Joseph and Dorothy Abdela, Manchester; *m* 1942, Enid Hope Russell, *y d* of Edgar Dodd Russell, London; one *s* (and one *s* decd). *Educ:* Manchester Gram. Sch.; Milton Sch., Bulawayo; Fitzwilliam House, Cambridge (MA). Called to the Bar, Gray's Inn, 1935. 2nd Lieut, Lancashire Fusiliers (TA), 1938; Lieut-Col, Comdt 55 Div. Battle School, 1943; 7th Bn Royal Welch Fusiliers, NW Europe, 1944–46; Major, Inns of Court Regt (TA), 1946–52. Liveryman, Worshipful Company of Painter-Stainers. *Recreations:* swimming, tennis, gardening. *Address:* Tall Trees Cottage, Shipton-under-Wychwood, Oxfordshire OX7 6DB. *Club:* Savage. *Died 14 May 1994.*

ABEL SMITH, Col Sir Henry, KCMG 1961; KCVO 1950; DSO 1945; DL; late Royal Horse Guards; Governor of Queensland, 1958–66; Administrator, Australian Commonwealth, during part of 1965; *b* 8 March 1900; *er s* of late Francis Abel Smith and Madeline St Maur, *d* of late Rev. Henry Seymour; *m* 1931, Lady May Cambridge, *o surv. c* of Earl of Athlone, KG, GCB, GCMG, GCVO, DSO, PC, FRS (*d* 1957), and Princess Alice, Countess of Athlone, VA, GCVO, GBE (*d* 1981); one *s* two *d*. *Educ:* RMC, Sandhurst. Entered RHG, 1919; Capt. 1930; Major, 1934; Temp. Lieut-Col 1941; Lieut-Col 1944; Acting Colonel, Corps of Household Cavalry, 1946; retired, 1950. ADC to Earl of Athlone, Governor-General of S Africa, 1928–31. DL Berks 1953. KStJ 1958. Hon. LLD Univ. of Queensland, 1962. Hon. Air Cdre, RAAF, 1966. *Recreations:* hunting, shooting, fishing, polo. *Address:* Barton Lodge, Winkfield, Windsor, Berks SL4 4RL. *T:* Winkfield Row (0344) 882632. *Club:* Turf.
Died 24 Jan. 1993.

ABELL, Sir Anthony (Foster), KCMG 1952 (CMG 1950); Gentleman Usher of the Blue Rod, in the Order of St Michael and St George, 1972–79; *b* 11 Dec. 1906; 2nd *s* of late G. F. Abell, JP, Foxcote Manor, Andoversford, Glos; unmarried. *Educ:* Repton; Magdalen Coll., Oxford. Joined Colonial Admin. Service, Nigeria, 1929. Resident, Oyo Province, Nigeria, 1949; Governor and C-in-C, Sarawak, 1950–59; High Commissioner, Brunei, 1950–58. Family Order of Brunei (First Class), 1954. *Address:* Gavel House, Wherwell, Andover, Hants SP11 7JH. *Clubs:* MCC, Royal Over-Seas League, United Oxford & Cambridge University. *Died 8 Oct. 1994.*

ABELL, Charles, OBE 1948; CEng; Consultant, British Airways Overseas Division, 1974–77; *b* 1 Dec. 1910; *s* of late Major George Henry Abell and Muriel Abell (*née* Griesbach); *m* 1st, 1939, Beryl Anne Boyce (*d* 1973); one *s*; 2nd, 1976, M. A. Newbery. *Educ:* Sherborne Sch. Imperial Airways, 1934–39; BOAC, 1939–74: Manager No 3 Line, 1946–51; Dep. Operations Dir (Engineering), 1951–55; Chief Engineer, 1955–68; Engineering Dir, 1968–74; Board Mem., 1972–74; Chm., British Airways Engine Overhaul Ltd, 1972–74. Hon. FRAeS (Vice-Pres., 1972–74; Pres., 1976–77); Hon. FSLAET (Pres. 1973–74). British Silver Medal for Aeronautics, RAeS, 1957. *Recreation:* sailing. *Address:* Five Oaks, Woodlands Road West, Virginia Water, Surrey GU25 4PL. *T:* Wentworth (0344) 2560. *Clubs:* Cruising Association; Royal Lymington Yacht. *Died 17 July 1992.*

ABERCROMBIE, Prof. David, FBA 1991; Professor of Phonetics, Edinburgh University, 1964–80, then Emeritus

Professor; *b* 19 Dec. 1909; *e s* of Lascelles Abercrombie, FBA, and Catherine Abercrombie; *m* 1944, Mary, *d* of Eugene and Mary Marble, Carmel, Calif; no *c. Educ:* Leeds Grammar Sch.; Leeds Univ.; University Coll., London; Sorbonne. Asst Lectr in English, LSE, 1934–38; Dir of Studies, Inst. of English Studies, Athens, 1938–40; Lectr in English: Cairo Univ., 1940–45; LSE, 1945–47; Lectr in Phonetics, Leeds Univ., 1947–48; Edinburgh Univ.: Lectr in Phonetics, 1948–51; Sen. Lectr, 1951–57; Reader, 1957–63. Lectr in Linguistics and Phonetics, Glasgow Univ., 1980–81. *Publications:* Isaac Pitman: a Pioneer in the Scientific Study of Language, 1937; Problems and Principles in Language Study, 1956; English Phonetic Texts, 1964; Studies in Phonetics and Linguistics, 1965; Elements of General Phonetics, 1967; Fifty Years in Phonetics: selected papers, 1991. *Address:* 13 Grosvenor Crescent, Edinburgh EH12 5EL. *T:* 031–337 4864.
Died 4 July 1992.

ABERCROMBIE, Robert James, CMG 1964; General Manager, Bank of New South Wales, 1962–64, retired; *b* 9 July 1898; *s* of P. M. Abercrombie, Whitburn, Scotland; *m* 1924, Dorothy, *d* of H. F. Oldham; two *d. Educ:* Sydney Grammar School; Scotch Coll., Melbourne. Chairman, Consultative Council of Export Payments Insurance Corporation, 1958–64; Chairman, Australian Bankers' Assoc., 1964. *Recreation:* golf. *Address:* 1 Hillside Avenue, Vaucluse, NSW 2030, Australia. *Club:* Union (Sydney).
Died 9 Jan. 1992.

ABRAHAMS, Allan Rose, CMG 1962; *b* 29 Nov. 1908; *s* of late Mr and Mrs Frank Abrahams; *m* 1948, Norma Adeline Neita; one *s* two *d. Educ:* Jamaica College, Jamaica. Joined Civil Service, 1927; Permanent Secretary, Ministry of Communications and Works, Jamaica, 1955–64, retired. *Recreation:* gardening. *Address:* 20 Widcombe Road, Kingston 6, Jamaica. *T:* 78214. *Club:* Kingston (Kingston, Jamaica).
Died 16 Nov. 1991.

ABRAMS, Mark Alexander, PhD; Director of Research Unit, Age Concern, 1976–85; *b* 27 April 1906; *s* of Abram Abrams and Anne (*née* Jackson); *m* 1st, 1931, Una Strugnell (marr. diss. 1951); one *s* one *d*; 2nd, 1951, Jean Bird; one *d. Educ:* Latymer Sch., Edmonton; London Sch. of Economics, Univ. of London. Fellow, Brookings Institute, Washington, DC, 1931–33; Research Department, London Press Exchange, 1933–39; BBC Overseas Dept, 1939–41; Psychological Warfare Board and SHAEF, 1941–46; Man. Dir, then Chm., Research Services Ltd, 1946–70; Dir, Survey Res. Unit, SSRC, 1970–76. Vice-Pres., PSI, 1978– (Mem. Council, 1978–82); Member: Metrication Bd, 1969–79; Exec. Council, Austrian Soc. for Social Sci. Res.; Business Educn Council, 1974–77. *Publications:* Condition of the British People, 1911–1946, 1947; Social Surveys and Social Action, 1951; Beyond Three Score and Ten, 1980; People in Their Sixties, 1983. *Recreation:* listening to music. *Address:* 12 Pelham Square, Brighton, East Sussex BN1 4ET. *T:* Brighton (0273) 684537. *Club:* Civil Service.
Died 25 Sept. 1994.

ABRAMSON, Sidney, CMG 1979; retired from Department of Trade (Under Secretary, 1972–81); *b* 14 Sept. 1921; *s* of Jacob and Rebecca Abramson; *m* 1st, 1946, Lerine Freedman (marr. diss. 1958); two *s*; 2nd, 1960, Violet Ellen Eatly. *Educ:* Emanuel Sch., London; Queen's Coll., Oxford. Joined Civil Service, 1948; served Board of Trade, later Dept of Trade, 1950–81, including delegns to OEEC and EFTA, and GATT Secretariat. *Recreations:* music, gardening, writing. *Address:* 26 Arlington, N12 7JR. *T:* 081–445 1264.
Died 16 July 1994.

ABU BAKAR, Datuk Jamaluddin, PNBS 1977; JMN 1967 (AMN 1965); High Commissioner for Malaysia in United Kingdom and Ambassador to Ireland, 1986–88; *b* Seremban, 19 May 1929; *m* Datin Rahmah Jamaluddin; one *s* two *d. Educ:* Univ. of Malaya (BA Hons History); LSE (Internat. Relns). Min. of For. Affairs, Malaya, 1957; Second Sec., Bangkok, 1958; Consul, Songkhla, 1961; First Sec., Cairo, 1963; Prin. Asst Sec., Min. of For. Affairs, 1966; Counsellor, Washington, 1969; Dep. Sec.-Gen. (Gen. Affairs), Min. of For. Affairs, Apr. 1971; Sec.-Gen., Min. of Culture, Youth and Sports, Nov. 1971; Sec.-Gen., Min. of Nat. Unity, 1973; Ambassador to Kuwait, 1974; High Comr to India, Feb. 1978; seconded to Bintulu Develt Authy, Sarawak, Oct. 1978; Ambassador to Tokyo, 1981. *Recreation:* sports, including golf and tennis. *Address:* c/o Ministry of Foreign Affairs, Wismaputra, Kuala Lumpur, Malaysia.
Died 12 Feb. 1992.

ACKLAND, Rodney; playwright; *b* 18 May 1908; *m* 1952, Mab (*d* 1972), *d* of Frederick Lonsdale. First play, Improper People, Arts, 1929; Marionella, Players, 1930; Dance With No Music, Arts and Embassy, 1931; Strange Orchestra, Embassy and St Martin's, 1932; Ballerina, adapted from Lady Eleanor Smith's novel, Gaiety, 1933; Birthday, Cambridge, 1934; The Old Ladies, adapted from Sir Hugh Walpole's novel, New and St Martin's, 1935; After October, Criterion and Aldwych, 1936; Plot Twenty-One, Embassy, 1936; The White Guard, adapted from the Russian play by Michael Bulgakov, Phœnix, 1938; Remembrance of Things Past, Globe, 1938; Sixth Floor, adapted from the French play by Alfred Gehri, St James's, 1939; The Dark River, Whitehall, 1943; Crime and Punishment, adapted from Dostoevsky, New, 1946; (with Robert G. Newton) Cupid and Mars, Arts, 1947; Diary of a Scoundrel, based on a comedy by Ostrovsky, Arts, 1949; Before the Party, adapted from Somerset Maugham's short story, St Martin's, 1949, revived, Queen's and Apollo, 1980; The Pink Room, Lyric, Hammersmith, 1952; A Dead Secret, Piccadilly, 1957; adapted Farewell, Farewell, Eugene, Garrick, 1959; Smithereens, Theatre Royal, Windsor, 1985; adapted Ostrovsky's Too Clever By Half, Old Vic, 1988. *Publications:* Improper People; Dance With No Music, 1933; Strange Orchestra; The Old Ladies; Birthday; After October; Crime and Punishment, 1948; Cupid and Mars; Diary of a Scoundrel, 1948; Before the Party; Farewell, Farewell, Eugene; The Celluloid Mistress (autobiography); The Other Palace; Dark River, 1972. *Address:* c/o Eric Glass Ltd, 28 Berkeley Square, W1X 6HD.
Died 6 Dec. 1991.

ACKROYD, Sir John (Robert Whyte), 2nd Bt *cr* 1956, of Dewsbury, West Riding of Yorkshire; *b* 2 March 1932; *s* of Sir Cuthbert Lowell Ackroyd, 1st Bt, and Joyce Wallace (*d* 1979), *d* of Robert Whyte; *S* father, 1973; *m* 1956, Jennifer Eileen MacLeod, *d* of H. G. S. Bishop; two *s* two *d. Educ:* Bradfield Coll.; Worcester Coll., Oxford (BA 1955, MA 1958). Commissioned RA, 1951; Sword of Honour, Mons Officer Cadet Sch., 1951; served in Jordan, 1951–52. Oxford Univ., 1952; Steward, OUDS, 1954. Underwriting Mem. of Lloyd's, 1959–; Engineer Planning & Resources Ltd, 1968–75. Mem. Gen. Council, Victoria League for Commonwealth Friendship, 1973; Hon. Sec., The Pilgrims of GB, 1966; Hon. Sec., RCM, 1986–91 (Mem. Council, 1981–91; FRCM 1988); Vice-Pres., Bromley Symphony Orch., 1979. Vice Dir, Dystonia Soc., 1994–. Patron, London and Internat. Sch. of Acting, 1983–. Mem. Court, City Univ., 1989–. Church Warden: St Mary-le-Bow, Cheapside, 1973–87; The Church of All Hallows, 1973–87. FZS 1970 (Mem. Council, 1987–90); FRSA 1989. Freeman of the City of London; Liveryman Carpenters' Co. *Publication:* (ed) Jordan, 1978 (to commemorate Silver Jubilee of HM King Hussein of Jordan). *Recreations:* music, theatre. *Heir: s* Timothy Robert Whyte Ackroyd, *b* 7 Oct. 1958. *Address:* The Malt

House, Old Alresford, Hants SO24 9DU. *Clubs:* Garrick; (Life Mem.) Union Society (Oxford).
Died 30 Aug. 1995.

ACLAND, Brig. Peter Bevil Edward, OBE 1945; MC 1941; TD; Vice-Lord-Lieutenant of Devon, 1962–78; *b* 9 July 1902; *yr s* of late Col Alfred Dyke Acland, CBE, TD and Hon. Beatrice, *d* of Rt Hon. W. H. Smith and 1st Viscountess Hambledon; *m* 1927, Bridget Susan Barnett (served ME, 1940–43; despatches), *d* of late Canon H. Barnett; two *s*. *Educ:* Eton; Christ Church, Oxford. Sudan Political Service, 1924–40. Served War of 1939–45: Abyssinia, Western Desert, Ægean (wounded, despatches). Comd Royal Devon Yeomanry, 1947–51, Hon. Col, 1953; Chairman, Devon AEC, 1948–58; Member, National Parks Commission, 1953–60; Chairman, Devon T&AFA, 1960. DL Devon, 1948; High Sheriff for Devon, 1961; JP 1962. 4th Class Order of the Nile; Greek War Cross. *Address:* Little Court, Feniton, Honiton, Devon EX14 0BE.
Died 9 Jan. 1993.

ACTON, Antony; *see* Acton, W. A.

ACTON, Sir Harold (Mario Mitchell), Kt 1974; CBE 1965; author; *b* 5 July 1904; *s* of Arthur Mario Acton and Hortense Mitchell, La Pietra, Florence. *Educ:* Eton Coll.; Christ Church, Oxford (BA). FRSL. Lectr in English Literature, National University of Peking and Peking Normal College, 1933–35; lived for seven years in Peking, devoting much time to Chinese Classical Theatre. Served in RAF during War of 1939–45, chiefly in Far East. Hon. DLitt New York Univ., 1973. Grand Officer, Republic of Italy; Kt of the Constantinian Order. *Publications:* Aquarium, 1923; An Indian Ass, 1925; Five Saints and an Appendix, 1927; Humdrum, 1928; Cornelian, 1928; This Chaos, 1930; The Last Medici, 1932, new edn 1958; (in collab.) Modern Chinese Poetry, 1936; (in collab.) Famous Chinese Plays, 1937; Peonies and Ponies, 1941; Glue and Lacquer, 1941 (Four Cautionary Tales, 1947, reprint of former); Memoirs of an Aesthete, 1948; Prince Isidore, 1950; The Bourbons of Naples, 1956; The Last Bourbons of Naples, 1961; Florence (an essay), 1961; Old Lamps for New, 1965; More Memoirs of an Aesthete, 1970; Tit for Tat, 1972; Tuscan Villas, 1973, repr. as The Villas of Tuscany, 1984; Nancy Mitford: a memoir, 1975; (in collab.) The Peach Blossom Fan, 1976; The Pazzi Conspiracy, 1979; The Soul's Gymnasium (short stories), 1982; Three Extraordinary Ambassadors, 1984; (in collab.) Florence, a traveller's companion, 1986. *Recreations:* jettatura, hunting the Philistines. *Address:* La Pietra, Florence, Italy. *T:* 474448. *Club:* Savile.
Died 27 Feb. 1994.

ACTON, (William) Antony; *b* 8 April 1904; *o s* of late William Walter Acton, Wolverton Hall, Pershore, Worcs; *m* 1932, Joan, *o c* of late Hon. Francis Geoffrey Pearson; one *d*. *Educ:* Eton; Trinity College, Cambridge. HM Treasury, 1939–45; Managing Director, Lazard Bros & Co. Ltd, 1945–53; Director: The National Bank Ltd, 1945–70 (Chm., 1964–70); Bank of London and South America Ltd, 1953–70; Standard Bank Ltd, 1953–70; Ottoman Bank, 1953–58; Bank of London and Montreal Ltd., 1959–64; Bank of West Africa Ltd, 1954–70; Bank of Ireland, 1966–70; National Commercial Bank of Scotland, 1967–70; National and Commercial Banking Group Ltd, 1969–70; The Whitehall Trust, 1945–70. High Sheriff, County of London, 1955. *Recreation:* travelling. *Address:* Poste Restante, Corfu, Greece. *T:* Corfu (661) 91236. *Club:* White's.
Died 3 March 1993.

ADAM, (David Stuart) Gordon; Director, Barclays Bank UK, 1977–87; Chairman, International Trust Group Ltd, 1983–89 (Director, 1982–93); *b* 21 Dec. 1927; *o s* of late James Adam, RCNC and Florence (*née* Kilpatrick); *m* 1965, Rosanne, *er d* of late William Watson of Ardlamont;

two *s* one *d*. *Educ:* Upper Canada College; Queen's Univ., Belfast (LLB); Trinity Hall, Cambridge (MA, LLM); AMP, Harvard Business Sch. Called to the Bar, Gray's Inn, 1951 (scholar and exhibnr). War Office, 1952–53; joined Barclays Bank, 1954; Southern and Central Africa, 1956–57; Local Dir, 1959, Gen. Man., 1968; Dep. Chm., Barclays Bank Trust Co., 1977–82; Chm., Barclays Internat. Devlt Fund, 1985–87; Dir, various cos in Barclays' Group. Indep. Dir, Henry Ansbacher Ltd, 1989–. Mem. Council, CBI, 1972–77. Chairman: Council, Wycombe Abbey Sch., 1981–91; Girls Education Co., 1981–91 (Dir, 1977–). Trustee, Combined Trusts Scholarship Trust, 1987–. *Address:* Mulberry Hill, Wendover, Bucks HP22 6NQ. *T:* Wendover (01296) 623200. *Clubs:* Boodle's, Kandahar.
Died 27 Dec. 1995.

ADAM, Robert Wilson, (Robin); Deputy Chairman, General Accident, since 1987 (Director, since 1980); *b* 21 May 1923; *s* of R. R. W. Adam; *m* 1957, Marion Nancy Scott. *Educ:* Fettes, Edinburgh. Royal Scots, 1942; commnd RIASC, 1942; served in India and Burma (Major). Chartered Accountant, 1950. Joined British Petroleum Co. Ltd, 1950; Pres., BP North America Inc., New York, 1969–72; Director: BP Canada, 1969–84 (Chm., 1981); BP Trading Ltd, 1973–75; The Standard Oil Co. (Sohio), 1972–76 and 1978–83; a Man. Dir, 1975–83, and Dep. Chm. 1981–83, British Petroleum Co. plc; Chairman: MEPC, 1984–88 (Dir, 1982–88); London & Scottish Marine Oil, 1985–88; Director: Motherwell Bridge Holdings Ltd, 1984–; Royal Bank of Canada, 1984–88; TRW Inc., 1986–. Lay Mem., Stock Exchange Council, 1983–85. Mem., British N America Cttee, 1980–88; Trustee, Foundn for Canadian Studies, 1975–80. *Address:* 25 Onslow Square, SW7 3NJ. *Clubs:* Brooks's, MCC; Berkshire Golf.
Died 27 May 1993.

ADAMS, Surg. Rear-Adm. Maurice Henry, CB 1965; MB, BCh, DOMS; *b* 16 July 1908; *s* of Henry Adams and Dorothea (*née* Whitehouse); *m* 1938, Kathleen Mary (*née* Hardy); one *s* two *d*. *Educ:* Campbell Coll.; Queen's University, Belfast. MB, BCh, 1930. RN Medical Service, 1933; HMS Cornwall, 1934; HMS Barham, 1936; Central Air Medical Board, 1940; HMS Activity, 1942; RN Hospital, Haslar, 1944; Med. Dept, Admiralty, 1946; RN Hospital: Malta, 1950; Chatham, 1952; MO i/c Trincomalee, 1957; Med. Dept, Admiralty, 1958; Medical Officer-in-Charge, Royal Naval Hosp., Malta, 1963; QHS, 1963–66; retd 1966. *Recreations:* sailing, golf. *Address:* Canberra, Rock, Cornwall PL27 6LF.
Died 21 May 1992.

ADAMS, Richard John Moreton G.; *see* Goold-Adams.

ADAMSON, Rt Rev. Mgr Canon Thomas; Residential Hospital Chaplain, Lourdes Hospital, Liverpool; Provost Emeritus, Liverpool Metropolitan Cathedral; *b* 30 Sept. 1901; *s* of George and Teresa Adamson, Alston Lane, near Preston. *Educ:* St Edward's College, Liverpool; Upholland College; Oscott College, Birmingham; Gregorian University, Rome. Ordained priest, 1926; Beda College, Rome, 1926–28; Private Secretary to Archbishop of Liverpool, 1928–45; Parish Priest of St Clare's, Liverpool, 1945–88; Canon, Liverpool Metropolitan Cathedral 1950, Provost 1981–88. Privy Chamberlain to Pope Pius XI, 1932; Domestic Prelate to Pope Pius XII, 1955; Vicar General to Archbishops of Liverpool, 1955–65; Protonotary Apostolic to the Pope. *Address:* Lourdes Hospital, Greenbank Road, Liverpool L18 1HQ.
Died 21 April 1991.

ADDISON, 3rd Viscount *cr* 1945, of Stallingborough; **Michael Addison;** Baron Addison 1937; *b* 12 April 1914; 2nd *s* of 1st Viscount Addison, KG, PC, MD, FRCS, and Isobel McKinnon (*d* 1934), *d* of late Archibald Gray; *S* brother, 1976; *m* 1936, Kathleen Amy, *d* of Rt Rev. and Rt Hon. J. W. C. Wand, KCVO, PC, and Amy Agnes Wiggins; one *s* two *d*. *Educ:* Hele's School, Exeter; Balliol Coll., Oxford. BA (PPE) 1935, MA 1965. Min. of Labour, 1935; War Damage Commission, 1940. Served RAFVR, 1941–45, FO Intell. Branch. War Damage Commn and Central Land Bd, 1945–51; Min. of Supply/Aviation, 1951–63; HM Treasury, 1963–65; Sen. Lectr, Polytechnic of Central London (School of Management Studies), 1965–76; retired, 1976. Member: Royal Inst. of Public Administration; Assoc. of Teachers of Management. *Recreation:* gardening. *Heir: s* Hon. William Matthew Wand Addison [*b* 13 June 1945; *m* 1970, Joanna Mary, *e d* of late J. I. C. Dickinson; one *s* two *d*]. *Address:* Old Stables, Maplehurst, Horsham, West Sussex RH13 6RD. *T:* Lower Beeding (0403) 891298. *Club:* Oxford Union Society. *Died 23 March 1992.*

ADDISON, Prof. Cyril Clifford, PhD, DSc (Dunelm); FRS 1970; FInstP, FRSC; Professor of Inorganic Chemistry, University of Nottingham, 1960–78, Dean of Faculty of Pure Science, 1968–71, Leverhulme Emeritus Fellow, 1978; *b* 28 Nov. 1913; *s* of late Edward Thomas Addison and Olive Clifford; *m* 1939, Marjorie Whineray Thompson; one *s* one *d*. *Educ:* Workington and Millom Grammar Schools, Cumberland; University of Durham (Hatfield College). Scientific Officer, British Launderers' Research Assoc., 1936–38; Lectr, Harris Inst., Preston, 1938–39; Ministry of Supply, Chemical Inspection Dept, 1939–45; Chemical Defence Research Estab., 1945; Univ. of Nottingham: Lectr, 1946; Reader in Inorganic Chemistry, 1952. Lectures: Corday-Morgan, E Africa, 1969; Liversidge, 1976. Dist. Vis. Prof., Auburn Univ., Alabama, 1979–80. Member: Chemical Soc. Council, 1954–57 (Pres. 1976–77); Inst. of Chemistry Council, 1948–51 and 1962–65 (Vice-Pres., 1965–67). Hon. DSc: Dunelm, 1977; Warwick, 1979. *Publications:* The Chemistry of the Liquid Alkali Metals, 1984; numerous papers in Jl Chemical Soc., Trans Faraday Soc., etc. *Recreations:* mountain walking, gardening. *Address:* Department of Chemistry, The University, Nottingham NG7 2RD. *T:* Nottingham (0602) 515151.
Died 1 April 1994.

ADDISON, Sir William (Wilkinson), Kt 1974; JP; DL; Chairman of Council, The Magistrates' Association, 1970–76; *b* Mitton, WR Yorks, 4 April 1905; *s* of Joseph Addison, Bashall Eaves; *m* 1929, Phoebe, *d* of Robert Dean, Rimington, WR Yorks. Verderer of Epping Forest, 1957–84. Chm., Epping Petty Sessions, 1955–76, combined Epping and Ongar Petty Sessions, 1968–76; Magistrates' Association: Mem. Council, 1959–76; Dep. Chm. of Council, 1966–70; Chm., Treatment of Offenders Cttee, 1961–68; Chm. Exec. Cttee, 1968–75. Member: Hill Hall Prison Board of Visitors, 1955–70; Chelmsford Prison, 1958–77; Bullwood Hall Borstal, 1962–76; Home Sec.'s Adv. Council on Probation and After-Care, 1964–67; Lord Chancellor's Adv. Council on Trng of Magistrates, 1964–73; Magistrates' Courts Rule Cttee, 1968–74; Council, Commonwealth Magistrates Assoc., 1970–75; Assessor to Deptl Cttee on Liquor Licensing, 1971. Member: Court, Univ. of Essex, 1965–; Adv. Council, Univ. of Cambridge Inst. of Criminology, 1972–78; Vice-Pres., 1980, Pres., 1985–, Assoc. of Genealogists and Records Agents; Mem. Council, Essex Archaeol Soc., 1949–71 (Pres., 1964–67); Vice-Pres., Council for the Protection of Rural England (Essex), 1984–; Pres. or Chm. of several bodies connected with local history and the preservation of antiquities in Essex, inc. Victoria County History and Friends of Essex Churches. JP 1949, DL 1973, Essex. FSA 1965; FRHistS 1965. *Publications:* Epping Forest, 1945; The English Country Parson, 1947; Essex Heyday, 1949; Suffolk, 1950; Worthy Dr Fuller, 1951; English Spas, 1951; Audley

End, 1953; English Fairs and Markets, 1953; Thames Estuary, 1953; In the Steps of Charles Dickens, 1955; Wanstead Park, 1973; Essex Worthies, 1973; Portrait of Epping Forest, 1977; Understanding English Place-Names, 1978; Understanding English Surnames, 1978; The Old Roads of England, 1980; Local Styles of the English Parish Church, 1982; Farmhouses in the English Landscape, 1986; Epping Forest: figures in a landscape, 1991. *Recreation:* exploring the English countryside for evidence of local history. *Address:* Ravensmere, Epping, Essex. *T:* Epping (0378) 73439.
Died 1 Nov. 1992.

ADEBO, Simeon Olaosebikan, Chief; The Okanlomo of Itoko and Egbaland, CFR 1979; CMG 1959; Chancellor, University of Lagos, Nigeria, 1984–92; *b* 5 Oct. 1913; *s* of late Chief Adebo, the Okanlomo of Itoko, Abeokuta; *m* 1941, Regina Abimbola, *d* of Chief D. A. Majekodunmi, Abeokuta; three *s* one *d*. *Educ:* St Peter's Sch., Ake, Abeokuta; Abeokuta Grammar Sch.; King's Coll., Lagos, Nigeria. BA Hons (London) 1939; LLB Hons (London) 1946. Called to Bar, Gray's Inn, 1949. Accountant in trg, Nigerian Rly, 1933; Admin. Officer Cadet, Nigerian Govt, 1942; Asst Fin. Sec. to Govt of Nigeria, 1954; Western Nigeria: Admin. Officer, Class I, 1955; Perm. Sec., Min. of Finance, 1957; Perm. Sec. to Treasury and Head of Civil Service, 1958; Head of Civil Service and Chief Secretary to Government, 1961; Permanent Representative of Nigeria at UN and Comr-Gen. for Economic Affairs, 1962–67; UN Under-Secretary-General and Exec. Dir of UNITAR, 1968–72. Chancellor, Univ. of Ife, 1982–84. Mem., Constituent Assembly on draft constitution of Nigeria, 1977. Chairman: Nat. Universities Commn of Nigeria, 1975–77; Bd of Govs, Nat. Inst. for Policy and Strategic Studies, 1979–82. Mem., Soc. for Internat. Develt. Hon. LLD: Western Michigan, 1963; Nigeria, 1965; Fordham, 1966; Lincoln, 1966; Beaver Coll., 1966; Ife, 1968; Ibadan, 1969; Columbia, 1971; Ahmadu Bello, 1973; Open Univ., 1975; Lagos, 1978; Hon. DCL, Union Coll., 1965. *Publications:* (with Sir Sydney Phillipson) Report on the Nigerianisation of the Nigerian Civil Service, 1953; Our Unforgettable Years, 1984; Our International Years, 1988. *Recreation:* swimming. *Address:* Abimbola Lodge, Ibara, PO Box 139, Abeokuta, Nigeria. *Clubs:* Commonwealth Trust; Nigeria Society (Lagos); Abeokuta (Nigeria).
Died 30 Sept. 1994.

ADELSTEIN, Abraham Manie, MD; FRCP, FFPHM; Visiting Professor, London School of Hygiene and Tropical Medicine, 1981–84, retired 1985; *b* 28 March 1916; *s* of Nathan Adelstein and Rosa Cohen; *m* 1942, Cynthia Gladys Miller; one *s* one *d*. *Educ:* Univ. of Witwatersrand. MB, ChB, MD. FRCP 1977. Health Officer (res. and medical statistics), SA Railways, 1947–61; Sen. Lectr, Univ. of Manchester, 1961–67; OPCS, 1967–81 (SPMO and Chief Medical Statistician, 1975–81). Donald Reid Medal, LSHTM, 1979; Bisset Hawkins Medal, RCP, 1982. *Publications:* Thesis on Accident Proneness, 1950; papers in scientific jls on the distribution and aetiology of various diseases (diseases of heart, nervous system, respiratory system, cancer, accidents) and of methods of collecting, analysing and publishing national statistics. *Address:* 21 Dunstan Road, NW11 8AG. *T:* 081–455 9983.
Died 18 Oct. 1992.

ADEMOLA, Rt Hon. Sir Adetokunbo (Adegboyega), GCON 1972; CFR 1963; KBE 1963; Kt 1957; PC 1963; Chancellor, University of Nigeria, since 1975; *b* 1 Feb. 1906; *e s* of late Sir Ladapo Ademola, Alake of Abeokuta, KBE, CMG; *m* 1939, Kofoworola, *yr d* of late Eric Olawolu Moore, CBE; three *s* two *d*. *Educ:* King's Coll., Lagos, Nigeria; Selwyn Coll., Cambridge. Attached to

Attorney-General's Chambers, Lagos, Nigeria, 1934–35; Assistant Secretary, Secretariat, Southern Provinces, Nigeria, 1935–36; private law practice, Nigeria, 1936–39; Magistrate, Nigeria, 1939; served on commn for Revision of Courts Legislation, Nigeria, 1948; served on commn to enquire into Enugu (Nigeria) disturbances, 1949; Puisne Judge, Nigeria, 1949; Chief Justice, Western Region, Nigeria, 1955–58; Chief Justice of Nigeria, 1958–72. Deputy Chm., United Bank for Africa, 1972–74. Hon. Bencher, Middle Temple, 1959. Chairman: Commonwealth Foundn, 1978; Adv. Cttee on Conventions and Regulations of the ILO (Mem., 1962); Member: Internat. Commn of Jurists, 1961 (later Hon. Mem.); Internat. Olympic Cttee, 1963. Hon. LLD Ahmadu Bello, Nigeria, 1962; Hon. DSc Benin, 1972. *Recreations:* golf, horse racing. *Address:* The Close, Adetokunbo Ademola Street, Victoria Island, Lagos, Nigeria. *T:* (1) 52219. *Clubs:* Island, Metropolitan, Yoruba Tennis (Lagos); Ibadan Recreation, Ibadan (Ibadan).

Died 29 Jan. 1993.

ADIE, Jack Jesson, CMG 1962; BA (Oxon); *b* 1 May 1913; *s* of late P. J. Adie; *m* 1940, Patricia McLoughlin (decd); one *s* two *d*. *Educ:* Shrewsbury Sch.; Magdalen Coll., Oxford. Entered Colonial Administrative Service, 1938; served in Zanzibar, 1938–48 (on military service, 1940–42 in Kenya Regt, KAR, and Occupied Territory Administration): posts included Private Sec. to The Sultan, Private Sec. to British Resident and Sen. Asst Sec.; seconded to Colonial Office, 1949–51, as Principal; Asst Sec., Kenya, 1951; Sec. for Educn and Labour, Kenya, 1952; Sec. for Educn, Labour and Lands, Kenya, 1954; acted as Minister for Educn, Labour and Lands, Kenya, Sept. 1955–Feb. 1956; Chief Sec., Barbados, 1957; Perm. Sec. for Forest Development, Game and Fisheries, Kenya, April-Dec. 1958; for Agriculture, Animal Husbandry and Water Resources, and Chm. African Land Development Bd, Dec. 1958–July 1959; for Housing, and Chm. Central Housing Bd, Nov. 1959–April 1960; for Housing, Common Services, Probation and Approved Schools, April 1960–April 1961; for Labour and Housing, 1961–62; acted as Minister for Labour and Housing, Jan.-April 1962; Perm. Sec. for Labour, 1962–63; retd from HMOCS, Jan 1964; Temp. Principal, Min. of Overseas Develt, 1964–69. Brilliant Star of Zanzibar, 4th class, 1947. *Address:* 3 Braemar, Kersfield Road, Putney, SW15 3HG. *Died 27 March 1992.*

ADLEY, Robert James; MP (C) Christchurch, since 1983 (Bristol North East, 1970–74; Christchurch and Lymington, 1974–83); *b* 2 March 1935; *s* of Harry and Marie Adley; *m* 1961, Jane Elizabeth Pople; two *s*. *Educ:* Falconbury; Uppingham. Lived and worked in Malaya, Singapore, Thailand; established Pearl & Dean (Thailand) Ltd, 1956; Sales Director, May Fair Hotel, 1960–64; Director: William Jacks plc, 1984–; Home Rouxl Ltd, 1990–92; Marketing Consultant, Scott's Hospitality Ltd. Chairman: Select Cttee on Transport, 1992–; Cons. Transport Cttee, 1991–92; All Party Publishing Gp; British-United Arab Emirates All Party Gp; Chairman, Parliamentary Groups: British-Jordanian; British-ASEAN; British-Chinese; British-Hungarian; British-Paraguay; British-Spanish; British-Syrian; British-Thai; Mem., Chairmen's Panel. Pres., Western Area Young Conservatives, 1972. Member: Nat. Council, British Hospitality Assoc.; Railway Correspondence and Travel Soc.; Cttee, National Railway Museum; Founder and First Chm., Brunel Soc.; Trustee, Brunel Engineering Centre Trust; Exec. Mem., SS Great Britain Project. *Publications:* Hotels, the Case for Aid, 1966; One Man, No Vote, 1976; A Policy for Tourism, 1977; British Steam in Cameracolour 1962–68, 1979; Take It or Leave It, 1980; In Search of Steam, 1981; The Call of Steam, 1982; To China for Steam, 1983; All Change Hong Kong, 1984; In Praise of Steam, 1985; Wheels, 1987; Covering my Tracks, 1988; Tunnel Vision, 1988; Out of Steam, 1990. *Recreations:* railway photography, railway enthusiast. *Address:* House of Commons, SW1A 0AA. *T:* 071–219 4438. *Club:* Carlton. *Died 13 May 1993.*

ADRIAN, 2nd Baron, *cr* 1955, of Cambridge; **Richard Hume Adrian,** DL; MD; FRCP 1987; FRS 1977; Professor of Cell Physiology, University of Cambridge, 1978–92; Master of Pembroke College, 1981–92; Vice-Chancellor, University of Cambridge, 1985–87; *b* 16 Oct. 1927; *o s* of 1st Baron Adrian, OM, FRS, FRCP, and Hester Agnes (DBE 1965) (*d* 1966), *o d* of late Hume C. and Dame Ellen Pinsent, DBE, Birmingham; *S* father, 1977; *m* 1967, Lucy Caroe, MA, PhD. *Educ:* Swarthmore High Sch., USA; Westminster Sch.; Trinity Coll., Cambridge (MA). MB, BChir Cantab. UCH, 1951; National Service, RAMC, 1952–54; Univ. of Cambridge: G. H. Lewes Student, Physiol Lab., 1954; Univ. Demonstr, 1956; Fellow, Corpus Christi Coll., 1956–60; Univ. Lectr, 1961; Reader in Exptl Biophysics, 1968; Fellow of Churchill Coll., 1961–81, Hon. Fellow 1985; Hon. Fellow, Darwin Coll., 1987. Mem., British Library Bd, 1987–93; Trustee: British Museum, 1979–93; British Museum (Nat. Hist.), 1984–88; Mem. Council, Royal Soc., 1984. For. Mem., Amer. Philosophical Soc. Prime Warden, Goldsmiths' Co., 1990–91. DL Cambs, 1993. Docteur *hc* Poitiers, 1975. *Publications:* articles in Jl of Physiol. *Recreations:* sailing, skiing. *Address:* Frostlake Cottage, Malting Lane, Newnham, Cambridge CB3 9HF. *T:* Cambridge (01223) 63410; Umgeni, Cley, Holt, Norfolk NR25 7RY. *T:* Cley (01263) 740597.

Died 4 April 1995 (ext).

ADSHEAD, Mary; *b* 15 Feb. 1904; *m* 1929, Stephen Bone (*d* 1958); two *s* one *d*. Trained at Slade School under Prof. Henry Tonks. Mural paintings in public and private buildings; illustrations, designs for GPO stamps. Chief works: murals in: restaurant at Luton Hoo; St Peter's Church, Vauxhall Estate, Luton; Civic Centre, Plymouth; Town Hall, Totnes; Commonwealth Inst.; Messrs Costain & Sons; The Post House, Leicester; Beatson Mural, Beatson Walk Underpass, Rotherhithe, 1982 (mosaic mural depicting the return of the Fighting Temeraire to Rotherhithe; media used were: mosaics, high fired tiles; cast iron mould for cannon and aluminium strip framework for ships; also various screeds; work carried out for Southwark Council in conjunction with Land Use Consultants); exhibn of easel pictures, Sally Hunter Gall., 1986; exhibn of watercolours, Sally Hunter Gall., 1989. *Recreations:* swimming, travel (visited by car France and Italy, by air Western Canada, USA, Turkey, Portugal, Austria, Russia and Sweden). *Died 3 Sept. 1995.*

AGNEW, Sir Anthony Stuart; *see* Agnew, Sir J. A. S.

AGNEW, Major Sir (George) Keith, 5th Bt *cr* 1895, of Great Stanhope Street, London; TD 1951; *b* 25 Nov. 1918; 2nd *s* of Major Sir John Stuart Agnew, 3rd Bt, TD, DL, and Kathleen (*d* 1971), *d* of late I. W. H. White; *S* brother, 1993; *m* 1948, Anne Merete Louise, *yr d* of Baron Johann Schaffalitzky de Muckadell, Fyn, Denmark; two *s*. *Educ:* Rugby; Trinity Coll., Cambridge. Commnd TA, 1937; active service, 1939–46; retd 1957. JP Suffolk, 1949–88. *Heir: s* John Keith Agnew, *b* 19 Dec. 1950. *Address:* Blackthorpe Farm, Rougham, Bury St Edmunds IP30 9JG. *Died 12 April 1994.*

AGNEW, Sir Godfrey; *see* Agnew, Sir W. G.

AGNEW, Sir (John) Anthony Stuart, 4th Bt, *cr* 1895, of Great Stanhope Street, London; *b* 25 July 1914; *s* of Sir John Stuart Agnew, 3rd Bt, TD, DL, and Kathleen (*d* 1971), *d* of late I. W. H. White, Leeds; *S* father, 1957. *Educ:* privately in Switzerland. *Heir: b* Major George Keith Agnew, TD [*b* 25 Nov. 1918; *m* 1948, Anne Merete

Louise, *yr d* of Baron Johann Schaffalitzky de Muckadell, Fyn, Denmark; two *s*]. *Address:* c/o Blackthorpe Farm, Rougham, Bury St Edmunds, Suffolk.

Died 6 Feb. 1993.

AGNEW, Sir Keith; *see* Agnew, Sir G. K.

AGNEW, Sir (William) Godfrey, KCVO 1965 (CVO 1953); CB 1975; Chairman, Lady Clare Ltd, 1970–87 (Director, 1948–87); Vice-Chairman, Sun Life Assurance Society plc, 1983–84 (Director, 1974–84); Director, Sun Life Properties Ltd, 1980–84; *b* 11 Oct. 1913; *o s* of late Lennox Edelsten Agnew and Elsie Blyth (*née* Nott), Tunbridge Wells; *m* 1st, 1939, Ruth Mary (*d* 1962), *e d* of late Charles J. H. O'H. Moore, CVO, MC, and late Lady Dorothie Moore; three *s* three *d;* 2nd, 1965, Lady (Nancy Veronica) Tyrwhitt, *widow* of Adm. Sir St John Reginald Joseph Tyrwhitt, 2nd Bt, KCB, DSO, DSC; two step *s* one step *d. Educ:* Tonbridge. Solicitor, 1935; entered Public Trustee Office, 1936. Served RA and Surrey and Sussex Yeomanry, 1939–46; Major, 1945. Senior Clerk, Privy Council Office, 1946–51; Clerk of the Privy Council, 1953–74 (Deputy Clerk, 1951–53); Dep. Sec., Cabinet Office, 1972–74. Director: Seaway Shipping Agencies Ltd, 1971–80; Seaway Holdings Ltd, 1971–80; Artagen Properties Ltd, 1976–80. Chairman, Sembal Trust, 1967–73. Mem., Bd of Hon. Tutors, Council of Legal Educn, Univ. of WI, 1973–; Consultant: CEI, 1974–79; University Coll., Cardiff, 1982–84; Univ. of Wales Inst. of Science and Technol., 1982–84. Hon. FIMechE, 1968; Hon. FIMunE, 1974; Hon. FCIBSE (formerly Hon. FCIBS), 1975; Hon. FICE, 1984. *Clubs:* Army and Navy; Swinley Forest Golf; Rye Golf.

Died 10 Dec. 1995.

AH-CHUEN, Sir Moi Lin Jean (Etienne), Kt 1980; Minister of Local Government, Mauritius, 1969–76; Chairman: Chue Wing & Co. Ltd, since 1977; The Mauritius Union Assurance Co. Ltd, since 1977; *b* 22 Feb. 1911; *s* of Jean Georges Ah-Chuen and Li Choi; *m* 1929, Jeanne Hau Man Mui; five *s* six *d. Educ:* De La Salle School, Mauritius. Mem., Mauritius Legislative Assembly, 1948–76. Founder (Chm. and Man. Dir), ABC Store (Chue Wing & Co. Ltd), 1931–68; Dir, Chinese Daily News, 1942–. Alternately Pres. and Vice-Pres., Chinese Chamber of Commerce, 1942–64. Chairman: Union Shipping Ltd; ABC Motors Co. Chm., Chinese Nat. Coll. Pres., Chinese Cultural Centre, 1968–; mem. or past mem., various other social and charitable organisations. *Recreations:* bridge, travelling, sports. *Address:* 5 Reverend Lebrun Street, Rose Hill, Mauritius. *T:* 43804. *Clubs:* Mauritius Turf, Chinese Traders (Mauritius).

Died 23 Oct. 1992.

AILSA, 7th Marquess of, *cr* 1831; **Archibald David Kennedy,** OBE 1968; Baron Kennedy, 1452; Earl of Cassillis, 1509; Baron Ailsa (UK), 1806; *b* 3 Dec. 1925; *s* of 6th Marquess of Ailsa and Gertrude Millicent (*d* 1957), *d* of Gervas Weir Cooper, Wordwell Hall, Bury St Edmunds; *S* father 1957; *m* 1954, Mary, 7th *c* of John Burn, Amble; two *s* one *d. Educ:* Nautical Coll., Pangbourne. Scots Guards, 1943–47; Royal Northumberland Fusiliers, 1950–52. National Trust for Scotland, 1953–56. Territorial Army, 1958–68; Hon. Col, Ayr and Renfrew Battalion ACF, 1980–90. Patron, Isle of Man Railway Soc., 1978–; Chm., Scottish Assoc. of Boys Clubs, 1978–82. Chm., Anglo-Somali Soc., 1987–90. *Recreations:* walking, motoring, modelling, sailing. *Heir: s* Earl of Cassillis [*b* 13 Sept. 1956; *m* 1979, Dawn Leslie Anne Keen (marr. diss. 1989); two *d*]. *Address:* Cassillis, Maybole, Ayrshire KA19 7JN. *Clubs:* Carlton; New (Edinburgh). *Died 7 April 1994.*

AINLEY, Sir (Alfred) John, Kt 1957; MC 1940; Chief Justice, Kenya, 1963–68; retired; Chairman of Industrial Tribunals, 1972–76; *b* 10 May 1906; *o s* of late Rev. A. Ainley, Cockermouth, Cumberland; *m* 1935, Mona Sybil Wood (*d* 1981); one *s* two *d. Educ:* St Bees Sch.; Corpus Christi Coll., Oxford. Called to Bar, 1928; Magistrate, Gold Coast, 1935; Crown Counsel (Gold Coast), 1936; Puisne Judge, Uganda, 1946–55; Chief Justice of Eastern Region, Nigeria, 1955–59; Combined Judiciary of Sarawak, N Borneo and Brunei, 1959–62. Served War of 1939–45, West African Forces, E Africa and Burma. *Address:* Horrock Wood, Watermillock, Penrith, Cumbria CA11 0JJ. *Died 19 Jan. 1992.*

AIREY OF ABINGDON, Baroness *cr* 1979 (Life Peer), of Abingdon in the County of Oxford; **Diana Josceline Barbara Neave Airey;** *b* 7 July 1919; *d* of late Thomas A. W. Giffard, MBE, JP, and Angela Erskine Giffard (*née* Trollope); assumed by deed poll, 1979, the surname of Airey; *m* 1942, Airey Middleton Sheffield Neave, DSO, OBE, MC (assassinated, March 1979), MP Abingdon; two *s* one *d. Educ:* privately and abroad. Quartermaster, RAF Hospital, 1939; later with Foreign Office (PWE) and Polish Ministry of Information, London. Then, in politics with her husband. Member: N Atlantic Assembly, 1983–84; Select Cttee on Eur. Communities (Sub-Cttee F), 1986–87. Trustee: Nat. Heritage Meml Fund, 1980–88; Imperial War Mus., 1984–90; Dorney Wood Trust, 1980–; Stansted Park Foundn, 1983–. Freedom, City of London, 1980. *Recreations:* reading, theatre, opera. *Address:* House of Lords, SW1. *Died 27 Nov. 1992.*

AISHER, Sir Owen (Arthur), Kt 1981; Founder Member, Marley Ltd, 1934, Chairman, 1945–82, then Life President, Marley plc; *b* 28 May 1900; *s* of late Owen Aisher, Branksome Park, Poole; *m* 1921, Ann Allingham (*d* 1989); two *s* two *d.* Mem. Court of Paviors. Pres., RYA, 1970–75; had many successes in off-shore racing, inc. Fastnet Race, 1951; was elected Yachtsman of the Year, 1958. *Recreations:* sailing, fishing, shooting. *Address:* Faygate, South Godstone, Surrey RH9 8JD. *Clubs:* Reform, City Livery, Royal Thames Yacht, Royal Ocean Racing (Adm. 1969–75); Ranelagh Sailing; Little Ship (Pres.); Royal Southern Yacht (Hamble); Royal Yacht Squadron, Royal London Yacht, Island Sailing (Adm.) (Cowes); Bembridge Sailing; Royal Motor Yacht (Poole); New York Yacht, Seawanhaka Corinthian Yacht (USA); Royal St George Yacht (Eire); Royal Cape Yacht (South Africa).

Died 26 Sept. 1993.

AITKEN, Prof. John Thomas; Professor of Anatomy, University of London at University College, 1965–80, then Emeritus; *b* 16 May 1913; *s* of David and Helen Aitken; *m* 1941, Doreen Violet Whitaker; two *s* two *d. Educ:* High School, Glasgow; Grammar School, Hull; Glasgow University. MB, ChB 1936, MD 1950. University College, London, 1940–80. *Publications:* Manual of Human Anatomy (in collab.); Essential Anatomy (in collab.); papers on regeneration of nerves and muscles, in various jls. *Recreation:* gardening. *Address:* Woodpeckers Cottage, Sway Road, Brockenhurst, Hants SO42 7RX. *T:* Lymington (0590) 22493. *Died 2 Feb. 1992.*

ALBU, Austen Harry, BSc (Eng); FCGI, CEng; *b* London, 21 Sept. 1903; *s* of Ferdinand and Beatrice Rachel Albu; *m* 1st, 1929, Rose (*d* 1956), *d* of Simon Marks, Newcastle; two *s*; 2nd, 1958, Dr Marie Jahoda, CBE. *Educ:* Tonbridge School; City and Guilds College (Imperial College of Science and Technology). Works Manager, Aladdin Industries, Greenford, 1930–46; Dep. Pres., Govtl Sub-Commn, CCG, 1946–47; Dep. Dir, British Institute of Management, Feb.-Nov. 1948. MP (Lab) Edmonton, 1948–Feb. 1974; Minister of State, Dept of Economic Affairs, 1965–67. Fellow, Imp. Coll. of Science and Technology. DUniv Surrey, 1966. *Address:* 17 The Crescent, Keymer, West Sussex BN6 8RB.

Died 23 Nov. 1994.

ALDAM, Jeffery Heaton, CBE 1980; MC 1945; County Education Officer, Hampshire, 1973–83, retired; *b* 11 Nov. 1922; *s* of William and Clara Ellen Aldam; *m* 1950, Editha Hilary Mary (*née* Preece); two *s* two *d. Educ:* Chesterfield Grammar Sch.; Trinity Coll., Cambridge (MA); Harvard Univ. (AM). Served 13th/18th Royal Hussars (QMO), 1942–45. Admin. Asst, Asst Educn Officer, then Sen. Asst Educn Officer, Norfolk CC, 1949–56; Dep. County Educn Officer, NR Yorks CC, 1957–62; Chief Educn Officer, East Suffolk CC, 1962–71; County Educn Officer, (former) Hampshire CC, 1972–73. Mem., Court and Council, Univ. of Southampton, 1972–. *Recreations:* reading, walking, gardening. *Address:* 18 Lynford Way, Weeke, Winchester SO22 6BW. *T:* Winchester (0962) 853594.   *Died 30 Oct. 1993.*

ALDINGTON, Sir Geoffrey (William), KBE 1965 (OBE 1946); CMG 1958; HM Diplomatic Service, retired; *b* 1 June 1907; *s* of late Henry William Aldington; *m* 1932, Roberta Finch; two *d. Educ:* City of London School; Magdalen Coll., Oxford. Student Interpreter, China Consular Service, 1929; Vice-Consul (Grade II), China, 1931; Vice-Consul, Peking, 1931–33; Private Secretary to HM Minister, Peking, 1933–35; Foreign Office, 1936–37; Acting Consul, Chungking, 1937–39; Consul, Tsingtao, 1939–41; seconded to Min. of Information, 1943–45; Actg Consul-Gen., Hankow, 1945–46; Suptg Consul, Shanghai, 1946–47; Foreign Office, 1947–50; Political Adviser to Hong Kong Govt, 1950–53; Consul-Gen. Zagreb, Yugoslavia, 1954–56; Consul-General at Philadelphia, Pa, USA, 1956–61; HM Ambassador to Luxembourg, 1961–66; also Consul-General, Luxembourg, 1962–66. *Recreations:* riding, reading. *Address:* Rustlings, 4 Tudor Close, Barnmeadow Lane, Great Bookham, Surrey KT23 3DP. *T:* Bookham (0372) 54088. *Clubs:* Hong Kong (Hong Kong); Racquet (Philadelphia, USA).
                                        Died 19 Feb. 1992.

ALDOUS, Alan Harold; Director, Sixth Form Studies, Longsands School, later Longsands Community College, St Neots, 1976–88; retired; *b* 14 Nov. 1923; *o s* of George Arthur and Agnes Bertha Aldous; *m*; one *s* one *d. Educ:* Ilford County High Sch. for Boys; Jesus Coll., Oxford (MA). Royal Signals and Royal West African Frontier Force, 1943–46. Oxford Univ., 1942 and 1946–49; Asst Master, St Dunstan's Coll., Catford, 1949–54; Asst Master, Merchant Taylors' Sch., Crosby, 1954–59; Headmaster, King's Sch., Pontefract, 1959–70; Headmaster, Leeds Grammar Sch., 1970–75. *Recreations:* music, reading, the countryside. *Address:* Casterbridge, Madeley Court, Hemingford Grey, Huntingdon, Cambs PE18 9DF. *T:* St Ives (0480) 66153.   *Died 24 Feb. 1992.*

ALDRED, Cyril, FRSE 1978; *b* 19 Feb. 1914; 3rd *s* of late Frederick Aldred and Lilian Ethel (*née* Underwood); *m* 1938, Jessie Kennedy Morton; one *d. Educ:* Sloane Sch.; King's Coll. and Courtauld Art Inst., Univ. of London (BA). Asst Keeper, Royal Scottish Museum, 1937; Scottish Educn Dept, 1939. Served War, RAF (Signals), 1942–46. Associate Curator, Dept of Egyptian Art, Metropolitan Museum of Art, New York, 1955–56; Keeper, Dept of Art and Archaeology, Royal Scottish Museum, Edinburgh, 1961–74. Mem. Cttee, Egypt Exploration Soc., 1959–76. *Publications:* The Development of Ancient Egyptian Art, 1952; The Egyptians, 1961, 3rd edn 1987; Egypt to the End of the Old Kingdom, 1965; Akhenaten, a New Study, 1968; Jewels of the Pharaohs, 1971; Akhenaten and Nefertiti, 1973; Tutankhamun, Craftsmanship in Gold in the Reign of the King, 1979; Egyptian Art in the Days of the Pharaohs, 1980; Akhenaten, King of Egypt, 1988; scripts for BBC programmes, Tutankhamun's Egypt, 1972, etc; chapters in: History of Technology; Cambridge Ancient History (3rd edn); Egypte (Univers des Formes); numerous articles on Ancient Egyptian art and archaeology

in scientific periodicals. *Address:* 4a Polwarth Terrace, Edinburgh EH11 1NE. *T:* 031–229 2845.
                                        Died 23 June 1991.

ALDRIDGE, Michael William ffolliott; actor; *b* 9 Sept. 1920; *s* of Dr Frederick James Aldridge and Kathleen M. M. Aldridge; *m* 1947, Kirsteen Rowntree; three *d. Educ:* Watford Grammar Sch.; Gresham's Sch., Holt, Norfolk. Served RAF, 1940–46 (Flight-Lieut). First professional appearance in French without Tears, Palace Theatre, Watford, 1939; in rep. at Bristol, Blackpool, Sunderland, Sheffield, Bradford and Amersham, 1939–40; first London appearance in This Way to the Tomb, Garrick, 1946; toured with Arts Council Midland Theatre Co., 1946–48; title rôle in Othello, Nottingham, 1948, Embassy, 1949; with Birmingham Rep., 1949; Old Vic Co. at New Theatre, 1949–50: Love's Labour's Lost, She Stoops to Conquer, The Miser, Hamlet; with Arts Council Midland Theatre Co., 1950; Bristol Old Vic, 1951–52: title rôle in Macbeth, Two Gentlemen of Verona, Of Mice and Men; Chichester Festival, 1966–69, 1971–72. London appearances include: Escapade, St James's, Strand, 1953–54; Salad Days, Vaudeville, 1954; Free As Air, Savoy, 1957; Moon for the Misbegotten, Arts, 1960; Vanity Fair, Queen's, 1962; The Fighting Cock, Duke of York's, 1966; Heartbreak House, Lyric, 1967; The Cocktail Party, Wyndham's, Haymarket, 1968; The Magistrate, Cambridge, 1969; Bequest to the Nation, Haymarket, 1970; Reunion in Vienna, Piccadilly, 1972; Absurd Person Singular, Criterion, 1973; The Tempest, RSC at The Other Place, 1974; Jeeves, Her Majesty's, 1975; Lies, Albery, 1975; The Bed before Yesterday, Lyric, 1976; Rosmersholm, Haymarket, 1977; The Old Country, Queen's, 1978; Bedroom Farce, Nat. Theatre at The Prince of Wales, 1978; The Last of Mrs Cheyney, Cambridge, 1980; Noises Off, Lyric, Hammersmith and Savoy, 1982; The Biko Inquest, Riverside, 1984; Relatively Speaking, Greenwich, 1986. *Films* include, 1946–: Nothing Venture; Bank Holiday Luck; The North Sea Bus; Murder in the Cathedral; A Life for Ruth; Chimes at Midnight; The Public Eye; Bullshot; Turtle Diary; Mussolini; Clockwise; Murder by the Book; Shanghai Surprise. *Television* plays and serials include: The Man in Room 17; Happy and Glorious; Bleak House; Sense and Sensibility; Fall of Eagles; Love for Lydia; Tinker, Tailor, Soldier, Spy; Love in a Cold Climate; Voyage Round My Father; Spy Ship; Reilly; Under the Hammer; Charlie; Charters and Caldicote; Last of the Summer Wine; The Understanding; Game, Set and Match; Chronicles of Narnia; Countdown to War; Stanley and the Women. *Recreation:* sailing. *Address:* 11 Crooms Hill, Greenwich, SE10 8ER.
                                        Died 10 Jan. 1994.

ALEXANDER OF POTTERHILL, Baron *cr* 1974 (Life Peer), of Paisley; **William Picken Alexander,** Kt 1961; LHD, PhD, MEd, MA, BSc; FBPsS; General Secretary, Association of Education Committees (England, Wales, Northern Ireland, Isle of Man and Channel Islands), 1945–77; *b* 13 Dec. 1905; *y s* of Thomas and Joan Alexander; *m* 1933, Mary Cochrane McLauchlan (marr. diss. 1949); *m* 1949, Joan Mary, *d* of Robert and Margaret Williamson; one *s* (and one *s* decd). *Educ:* Paisley Grammar School; Glasgow Univ. Schoolmaster in Scotland, 1929–31; Asst Lectr in Education, Glasgow Univ., 1931–32; Rockefeller Research Fellow, 1932–33; Deputy Director of Education, Walthamstow, 1934–35; Director of Education, Margate, 1935–39; Sheffield, 1939–44. Joint Sec. to Management Panel of Burnham Committees and Associated Committees negotiating salaries of teachers, 1945–73. Hon. DLitt Leeds, 1977. *Publications:* Intelligence, Concrete and Abstract, 1935; The Educational Needs of Democracy, 1940; A Performance Scale for the Measurement of Technical Ability, 1947; A Parents' Guide to the Education Act,

1944, 1947; Education in England, 1953; Towards a new Education Act, 1969, etc. *Recreations:* golf, contract bridge. *Address:* 3 Moor Park Gardens, Pembroke Road, Northwood, Middlesex HA6 2LF. *T:* Northwood (0923) 821003. *Club:* Moor Park Golf (Herts).

Died 8 Sept. 1993.

ALEXANDER, Sir Alexander Sandor, (Sir Alex), Kt 1974; Senior Managing Director, Lehman Brothers International (Europe) (formerly Lehman Brothers International Ltd), since 1992; Chairman, J. Lyons and Company, 1979–89; Vice-Chairman, 1982–88, Deputy Chairman, 1988–89, Allied-Lyons plc; *b* 21 Nov. 1916; *m* 1946, Margaret Irma Vogel; two *s* two *d. Educ:* Charles Univ., Prague. Dir, 1954–69, Man. Dir and Chief Exec., 1967–69, Chm. 1969, Ross Group Ltd; Chm., Imperial Foods Ltd, 1969–79; Dir, Imperial Group Ltd (formerly Imperial Tobacco Group Ltd), 1969–79; Man. Dir, Shearson Lehman Hutton Internat. Inc., later Lehman Brothers Internat. Ltd, 1989–92. Director: National Westminster Bank Ltd, South East Region, 1973–84; Ransomes, Sims & Jefferies plc, 1974–83; Alfred McAlpine, 1978–94; Unigate, 1978–89; Tate & Lyle, 1978–89; Arbor Acres Farms, USA, 1985–91; London Wall Holdings, 1986–; Hiram Walker-Gooderham and Worts, Canada, 1987–89; Dep. Chm., British United Trawlers, 1969–81. President: Processors and Growers Research Orgn, 1978–82; British Food Export Council, 1973–76; Member: Eastern Gas Bd, 1963–72; Agric. Econ. Develt Cttee, 1974–78; Governor: British Nutrition Foundn, 1975–79; Royal Ballet, 1985–; Dir, Royal Opera House, Covent Garden, 1987–; Chairman: Royal Opera House Trust, 1987–91; Theatre Royal (Norwich) Trust Ltd, 1969–84; Trustee, 1975–89, Vice Chm., 1978–89, Glyndebourne Arts Trust; Member: National Theatre Develt Council, 1984–; Court, UEA, 1963–; Trustee: Charities Aid Foundn, 1979–86; Thrombosis Res. Inst., 1988–; Friend of RCP, 1982–. FIMgt; FRSA. High Sheriff, Norfolk, 1976. *Recreations:* tennis, shooting, painting, opera, ballet. *Address:* Lehman Brothers International (Europe), One Broadgate, EC2M 7HA. *T:* (office) 071-601 0011. *Died 25 July 1994.*

ALEXANDER, Rear-Adm. Robert Love, CB 1964; DSO 1943; DSC 1944; *b* 29 April 1913; *o s* of Captain R. L. Alexander, Edinburgh; *m* 1936, Margaret Elizabeth, *o d* of late George Conrad Spring and Mrs Maurice House; one *s* three *d* (and one *d* decd). *Educ:* Merchiston Castle; Royal Naval College, Dartmouth. Joined RNC, 1927; Cadet HMS Repulse, 1930; Midshipman HMS Kent, 1931–33; Sub-Lieut, qualified in submarines, 1935. Served throughout War of 1939–45 in submarines: first command HMS H32, 1940; later commands: HMS Proteus, 1942; HMS Truculent, 1942–44; HMS Tuna, 1945. Second in command and in temp. command HMS Glory, Korean War, 1951–52; in command First Destroyer Squadron, 1957; Imperial Defence College, 1959; in command HMS Forth and 1st Submarine Squadron, 1960; Captain Submarines and Minesweepers, Mediterranean, and NATO Commander Submarines, Mediterranean, HMS Narvik, 1960–62; Vice Naval Deputy to the Supreme Allied Commander Europe, 1962–65. Lieut 1936; Comdr 1946; Capt. 1952; Rear-Adm. 1962; retd, 1965. *Address:* Tythe Barn, South Harting, Petersfield, Hants GU31 5PY. *T:* Harting (073085) 505. *Died 24 April 1993.*

ALFORD, Ven. John Richard; Archdeacon of Halifax, 1972–84, then Emeritus; *b* 21 June 1919; *s* of Walter John and Gertrude Ellen Alford. *Educ:* Fitzwilliam House, Cambridge (History Tripos Pts 1 and 2, BA 1941, MA 1947); Cuddesdon College, Oxford. Deacon 1943, priest 1944, Wakefield; Curate, St Paul, King Cross, Halifax, 1943–47; Curate, Wakefield Cathedral, 1947–50; Tutor, Wells Theological College, 1950–56; Priest Vicar, Wells

Cathedral, 1950–56; Vice-Principal, The Queen's College, Birmingham, 1956–67; Exam. Chaplain to Bp of Kimberley and Kuruman, 1961–65; Domestic Chaplain, Director of Ordinands, and Exam. Chaplain to Bp of Chester, 1967–72; Vicar of Shotwick, Chester, 1967–72; Hon. Canon of Chester Cathedral, 1969–72, Emeritus, 1972; Canon Residentiary of Wakefield Cathedral, 1972–84, Emeritus 1985–; Examining Chaplain to Bp of Wakefield, 1972–84. Mem., General Synod of C of E, 1980–84; Vice-Pres., CEMS, 1980–86. *Recreations:* music, walking. *Address:* College of St Barnabas, Blackberry Lane, Lingfield, Surrey RH7 6NQ. *T:* Lingfield (01342) 870829. *Club:* Royal Over-Seas League.

Died 27 Feb. 1995.

ALFVÉN, Prof. Hannes Olof Gösta, PhD; Emeritus Professor of Plasma Physics, Royal Institute of Technology, Stockholm; *b* Sweden, 30 May 1908; *s* of Johannes Alfvén and Anna-Clara Romanus; *m* 1935, Kerstin Erikson, *d* of Rolf E. and Maria Uddenberg; one *s* four *d. Educ:* Univ. of Uppsala (PhD 1934). Prof. of Theory of Electricity, 1940–45, of Electronics, 1945–63, and of Plasma Physics, 1963–73, Royal Inst. of Technology, Stockholm. Prof. (part-time), Univ. of California at San Diego, 1967–89. Pres., Pugwash Confs on Science and World Affairs, 1967–72; Member: Bd of Dirs, Swedish Atomic Energy Co., 1956–68; Science Adv. Council of Swedish Govt, 1961–67. Member: Swedish Acad. of Sciences; several foreign acads incl. Royal Society, London, 1980, Acad. of Sciences of the USSR, Nat. Acad. of Sciences, Washington, DC. Hon. DSc Oxon. 1977. Awarded Gold Medal of Royal Astronomical Soc. (Gt Britain), 1967; Nobel Prize for Physics, 1970; Lomonosov Medal, 1971; Franklin Medal, 1971; Dirac Medal, 1994. *Publications:* Cosmical Electrodynamics, 1948; On the Origin of the Solar System, 1956; Cosmical Electrodynamics: Fundamental Principles (jointly), 1963; World-Antiworlds (Eng. trans.), 1966; (as Olof Johannesson) The Tale of the Big Computer (Eng. trans.), 1968; Atom, Man and the Universe (Eng. trans.), 1969; (with Kerstin Alfvén) M70–Living on the Third Planet, 1971; (with G. Arrhenius) Evolution of the Solar System NASA SP-345, 1976; Cosmic Plasma, 1981; papers in physics and astrophysics. *Address:* c/o Division of Plasma Physics, Alfvén Laboratory, Royal Institute of Technology, 100 44 Stockholm, Sweden.

Died 2 April 1995.

ALLAN, Sir Colin (Hamilton), KCMG 1977 (CMG 1968); OBE 1959; FRAI 1950; Her Majesty's Overseas Civil Service, retired; *b* 23 Oct. 1921; *yr s* of late John Calder Allan, Cambridge, NZ; *m* 1955, Betty Dorothy, *e d* of late A. C. Evans, Brisbane, Australia; three *s. Educ:* Hamilton High Sch., NZ; College House, Canterbury Univ., NZ; Magdalene College, Cambridge. Military Service, NZ, 1942–44. Cadet, Colonial Admin. Service, British Solomon Is, 1945; District Comr, Western Solomons, 1946; District Comr, Malaita, 1950; Special Lands Comr, 1953; Sen. Asst Sec., Western Pacific High Commn, 1957; Asst Resident Comr, New Hebrides, 1959, British Resident Comr, 1966–73; Governor and C-in-C, Seychelles, and Comr, British Indian Ocean Territory, 1973–76; Governor, Solomon Is, and High Comr for Western Pacific, 1976–78. Delegate: Seychelles Constitutional Conf., 1975, 1976; Solomon Is Constitutional Conf., 1977. Vis. Fellow, Research Sch. of Pacific Studies, Australian Nat. Univ., 1979; Visiting Lecturer: Law Sch., Auckland Univ., 1981–89; Univ. of NSW, Sydney, 1988; Univ. of Otago, 1989. Chm., Ranfurly Library Service, NZ, 1985–93; Member: Leprosy Trust Bd (NZ), 1980–91; NZ Adv. Council, Province of Melanesia, 1982–92. Commandeur, l'Ordre Nationale du Mérite (France), 1966. *Publications:* Land Tenure in the British Solomon Islands Protectorate, 1958; Solomons Safari, 1989; papers on colonial administration. *Recreations:* malacology, collecting, reading The Times. *Address:* Glen Rowan, 17 Sale Street, Howick, Auckland, New Zealand.

Died 5 March 1993.

ALLAN, Gordon Buchanan, TD 1950; BA; CA; *b* 11 Aug. 1914; *s* of late Alexander Buchanan Allan, MIMechE, and Irene Lilian Allan, Glasgow; *m* 1971, Gwenda Jervis Davies, *d* of late John William and Elizabeth Davies, Porthcawl, Glam. *Educ:* Glasgow Academy; High Sch. of Glasgow; Glasgow Univ. Mem., Inst. of Chartered Accountants of Scotland, 1937. Commissioned into Royal Signals (TA), 1938. Served War of 1939–45, DAAG, GHQ, India, 1945, Major. Director: George Outram & Co. Ltd, 1960–75 (Dep. Man. Dir and Financial Dir, 1970–75); Holmes McDougall Ltd, 1966–72. Mem. Press Council, 1969–74. Vice-Pres., Scottish Daily Newspaper Soc., 1970, Pres. 1971–73; Dir, Glasgow Chamber of Commerce, 1971–75. Member: UK Newsprint Users' Cttee, 1972–75; Council, CBI, 1972–74; Finance Cttee, RIIA, 1975–77; Merchants' House of Glasgow, 1975–. Mem. Bd, Bield Housing Assoc. Ltd, 1978–; Trustee, Bield Housing Trust, 1975–. Governor, The Queen's College, Glasgow, 1976–89. *Recreations:* music, golf. *Address:* 3 Winchester Court, Glasgow G12 0JN. *T:* 041–334 2353. *Club:* Royal Scottish Automobile (Glasgow). *Died 12 Feb. 1994.*

ALLAN, John Gray, CBE 1975; Legal Adviser and Solicitor to the Crown Estate Commissioners, 1961–77; *b* 10 Nov. 1915; *s* of late John Allan, CB, LLD, FSA, FBA, and Ida Mary (*née* Law). *Educ:* Charterhouse; Oriel College, Oxford. Called to Bar, Middle Temple, 1940. War Service, 1940–46: The Black Watch, GSO2 (War Office and Allied Land Headquarters, Melbourne), 1942–46. Legal Branch, Min. of Agriculture, Fisheries and Food, 1946–57; Deputy Legal Adviser, Crown Estate Office, 1957. *Recreations:* golf, bridge. *Address:* 5 Rheidol Terrace, N1 8NT. *T:* 071–226 7616. *Club:* Boodle's.

Died 25 June 1994.

ALLARD, Sir Gordon (Laidlaw), Kt 1981; President, Royal Victorian Eye and Ear Hospital, 1964–80; *b* 7 Aug. 1909; *s* of G. Allard; *m* 1935, Phyllis Rosemary, (Cherry), Singleton; one *s* . *Educ:* Scotch Coll., Melbourne. FCA; FCA (NZ). Joined Flack & Flack, later Price Waterhouse & Co., 1927; Partner, and a Sen. Partner, in Australia and NZ, 1942–74. Chm., AMI-Toyota Ltd, 1976–85 (Dir, 1975–86). Mem., Gen. Council, Inst. of Chartered Accountants in Australia, 1962–70 (Victorian Chm., 1962–64). *Recreations:* golf, bowls, gardening. *Address:* 4 St Martins Close, Kooyong, Vic 3144, Australia. *Clubs:* Melbourne, Australian (Melbourne); Royal Melbourne Golf, Frankston Golf. *Died 15 Oct. 1994.*

ALLEN, Rear-Adm. Sir David, KCVO 1991; CBE 1985; Defence Services Secretary, 1988–91; Chief Naval Supply and Secretariat Officer, 1988–91; retired; Independent Inspector, Lord Chancellor's Panel, since 1992; *b* 14 June 1933; *s* of late A. V. Allen and G. M. Allen; *m* 1962, Margaret Gwendolin Todd; two *s*. *Educ:* Hutcheson's Grammar School, Glasgow; BRNC Dartmouth. Joined RN 1949; Supply Officer, HMS Fife, 1970–72; MoD, 1973–75; Fleet Supply Officer, Staff of C-in-C Fleet, 1975–77; Sec. to Chief of Staff, Fleet, 1977–78; Sec. to Controller of the Navy, 1978–81; Chief Staff Officer (Personnel), Naval Air Comd, 1981–82; Sec. to Chief of Naval Staff and First Sea Lord, 1982–85; HMS Cochrane in Comd and Flag Captain to FO Scotland and NI, 1985–87; Staff of Chief of Defence Staff, 1987–88. Dir, Avalon NHS Trust, 1993–. *Recreations:* family and friends, reading, gardening, beef cattle and sheep breeding, shooting, fishing, house maintenance. *Club:* Farmers'.

Died 13 Jan. 1995.

ALLEN, Rev. Canon Derek William; Vicar of St Saviour and St Peter's, Eastbourne, since 1976; Prebendary of Heathfield, Chichester Cathedral, since 1984; *b* 2 Nov. 1925. *Educ:* Eastbourne College; Oriel College, Oxford. Deacon, 1952; priest, 1953; Curate of Christ the Saviour, Ealing, 1952–54; Tutor, 1954–56, Chaplain, 1956–60, St Stephen's House, Oxford; Asst Chaplain, Pembroke College, Oxford, 1955–60; Sub-Warden, King's College Hostel and Lecturer in Theology, King's College, London, 1960–62; Principal, St Stephen's House, Oxford, 1962–74; Warden: Community of St Mary the Virgin, Wantage, 1966–80; Community of Servants of the Cross, Lindfield, 1981–. Examining Chaplain to Bp of Chichester, 1980–. Mem. Gen. Synod, Church of England, 1985–. *Publications:* articles in: Theology, Church Quarterly Review, Internat. Rev. of Missions, Lambeth Essays on Unity, Sobornost. *Recreations:* music, poetry, bridge. *Address:* The Vicarage, Spencer Road, Eastbourne, Sussex BN21 4PA. *T:* Eastbourne (0323) 22317. *Club:* Athenæum. *Died 22 Jan. 1991.*

ALLEN, (Harold) Norman (Gwynne), CBE 1965; FEng 1979; retired 1977; *b* 30 April 1912; *yr s* of Harold Gwynne Allen and Hilda Margaret Allen (*née* Langley), Bedford; *m* 1938, Marjorie Ellen (*née* Brown); one *s* three *d*. *Educ:* Westminster Sch.; Trinity Coll., Cambridge (BA 1933; MA 1936). FICE, FIMechE, FRINA, FIMarE, FIEE. Engrg trng, John Samuel White & Co. Ltd, Cowes, John Brown & Co. Ltd, Clydebank, and in Merchant Navy, 1933–37; W. H. Allen Sons & Co. Ltd, Bedford: progressive staff appts, 1937–43; Dir 1943–77; Techn. Dir 1945–52; Jt Man. Dir 1952–; Dep. Chm. 1962–70; Chm. 1970–77; Amalgamated Power Engrg Ltd, Bedford: Techn. Dir 1968–70; Dep. Chm. 1970–77. Belliss & Morcom Ltd, Birmingham, 1968–77. Mem. Bedfordshire CC, 1947–50. Mem. Council: British Internal Combustion Engrg Res. Assoc., 1952–60 (Chm. 1953–54); British Hydromechanics Res. Assoc., 1947–59; IMechE, 1952–70 (Vice-Pres. 1959–65, Pres. 1965); Mem. Adv. Cttee, Nat. Engrg Lab., 1971–73 (Mem. Steering Cttee 1962–68); Mem. British Transport Commn Res. Adv. Council, 1958–60; Vice-Chm. of Council, Mander Coll., Bedford, 1958–74; Governor, Coll. of Aeronautics, Cranfield, 1955–69 (Vice-Chm. 1962–69); Charter Pro-Chancellor, Cranfield Inst. of Technology, 1969–75; Mem. Bd, Council of Engrg Instns, 1964–66; Mem. Exec. Bd, BSI, 1970–76. Provost, Buffalo Hunt of Manitoba, 1960. Dir, Son et Lumière, Woburn Abbey, 1957. Hon. DSc Bath, 1967; Hon. DSc Cranfield, 1977. *Publications:* papers in jls of IMarE, S African IMechE, Engrg Inst. Canada, IMechE. *Recreations:* gardening (MRHS), countryside (Mem. Nat. Trust), magic (Mem. Magic Circle). *Address:* 15 Mullings Court, Dollar Street, Cirencester, Glos GL7 2AW.

Died 6 Dec. 1995.

ALLEN, Sir Peter (Christopher), Kt 1967; MA, BSc (Oxon); Director, 1951–63, Chairman, 1968–71, ICI Ltd (a Deputy Chairman, 1963–68); Advisory Director, New Perspective Fund, 1973–85; *b* Ashstead, Surrey, 8 Sept. 1905; *s* of late Sir Ernest King Allen and Florence Mary (*née* Gellatly); *m* 1st, 1931, Violet Sylvester Wingate-Saul (*d* 1951); two *d;* 2nd, 1952, Consuelo Maria Linares Rivas (*d* 1991). *Educ:* Harrow; Trinity Coll., Oxford (Hon. Fellow 1969). Joined Brunner, Mond & Co., Ltd, 1928; Chm., Plastics Div. of ICI Ltd, 1948–51 (Man. Dir, 1942–48); Pres. and Chm., ICI of Canada Ltd, 1961–68; Dir, British Nylon Spinners Ltd, 1954–58; Pres., Canadian Industries Ltd, 1959–62, Chm., 1962–68; Director: Royal Trust Co., Canada, 1961–64; Bank of Montreal, 1968–75; BICC, 1971–81. Vice-President: Inst. of Manpower Studies, 1968–76; Manufacturing Chemists' Assoc., USA, 1961–62 (Dir, 1959–62); Member and Vice-Chairman: Council of Assoc. of Brit. Chem. Manufacturers, 1963–65; Bd of Dirs, Société de Chimie Industrielle, 1968; President:

Plastics Inst., 1950–52; Brit. Plastics Fedn, 1963–65; Univ. of Manchester Inst. of Sci. and Technology, 1968–71; Vice-Pres., British Assoc. for Commercial and Industrial Educn, 1969–; Mem. of Council, CBI, 1965–67. Chm., BNEC, 1970–71 (Mem., 1964–67); Chm., Cttee for Exports to Canada, 1964–67); Mem., British Overseas Trade Bd, 1972–75. Governor, Nat. Coll. of Rubber Technology, 1964–68; Member: Court, British Shippers' Council, 1968–70; Export Council for Europe, 1962–65; Overseas Development Inst. Council, 1963–64; Iron and Steel Holding and Realisation Agency, 1963–67; NEDC for Chemical Industry, 1964–67; Commonwealth Export Council, 1964–67; Industrial Policy Group, 1969–71. Pres., Transport Trust, 1967–88. FBIM 1968; FInstD 1969; FRGS 1980. Hon. Member: Chemical Industries Assoc., 1968– (Pres., 1965–67; Mem. Council, 1967–68); Canadian Chemical Producers' Assoc., 1962–. Chm., Anglo-Spanish Soc., 1973–80. Trustee, Civic Trust, 1970–76. Governor, Harrow School, 1969–82. Freeman, City of London, 1978. Knight Grand Cross, Spanish Order of Civil Merit, 1981. *Publications:* The Railways of the Isle of Wight, 1928; Locomotives of Many Lands, 1954; On the Old Lines, 1957; (with P. B. Whitehouse) Narrow Gauge Railways of Europe, 1959; (with R. A. Wheeler) Steam on the Sierra, 1960; (with P. B. Whitehouse) Round the World on the Narrow Gauge, 1966; (with Consuelo Allen) The Curve of Earth's Shoulder, 1966; (with A. B. MacLeod) Rails in the Isle of Wight, 1967; Famous Fairways, 1968; Play the Best Courses, 1973, 2nd edn 1988; (with P. B. Whitehouse) Narrow Gauge the World Over, 1976; The 91 Before Lindbergh, 1985; The Sunley Book of Royal Golf, 1989. *Recreations:* foreign travel, railways, golf, writing. *Address:* Telham Hill House, near Battle, E Sussex TN33 0SN. *Clubs:* Carlton; Royal and Ancient, Royal Cinque Ports, Rye, Royal St George's; Oxford and Cambridge Golfing Soc.; Augusta National (Ga, USA); Pine Valley (NJ, USA).

Died 24 Jan. 1993.

ALLEN, Rowland Lancelot, CB 1968; Principal Assistant Treasury Solicitor, 1963–69, retired; *b* 17 Feb. 1908; *s* of Rowland Allen and Maud Annie Allen (*née* Bacon); *m* 1934, Elizabeth Ethel (*née* Lewis) (*d* 1982); two *s* one *d*. *Educ:* Eton College. Called to the Bar, Inner Temple, 1931; Public Trustee Office, 1934; Treasury Solicitor's Dept, 1940; Foreign Compensation Commission, 1950–53; Treasury Solicitor's Dept, 1953. *Recreation:* golf. *Address:* 12 Raeburn Court, St John's Hill, Woking, Surrey GU21 1QW. *T:* Woking (0483) 724326.

Died 3 Jan. 1992.

ALLEN, Walter Ernest, author and literary journalist; *b* Birmingham, 23 Feb. 1911; 4th *s* of Charles Henry Allen and Annie Maria Thomas; *m* 1944, Peggy Yorke, 3rd *d* of Guy Lionel Joy and Dorothy Yorke Maundrell, Calne, Wilts; two *s* two *d*. *Educ:* King Edward's Grammar School, Aston, Birmingham; Birmingham University. Assistant Master, King Edward's Grammar School, Aston, Birmingham, 1934; Visiting Lecturer in English, State University of Iowa, USA, 1935; Features Editor, Cater's News Agency, Birmingham, 1935–37; Assistant Technical Officer, Wrought Light Alloys Development Assoc., 1943–45. Asst Literary Editor, New Statesman, 1959–60, Literary Editor, 1960–61. Margaret Pilcher Vis. Prof. of English, Coe Coll., Iowa, 1955–56; Visiting Professor of English: Vassar College, New York, 1963–64; Univ. of Kansas, 1967; Univ. of Washington, 1967; Prof. of English, New Univ. of Ulster, 1967–73; Berg Prof. of English, New York Univ., 1970–71; Vis. Prof. of English, Dalhousie Univ., Halifax, NS, 1973–74; C. P. Miles Prof. of English, Virginia Polytechnic Inst. and State Univ., 1974–75. FRSL. *Publications:* novels: Innocence is Drowned, 1938; Blind Man's Ditch, 1939; Living Space, 1940; Rogue Elephant, 1946; Dead Man Over All, 1950;

All in a Lifetime, 1959; Get Out Early, 1986; Accosting Profiles, 1989; *topography:* The Black Country, 1946; *literary criticism:* Writers on Writing, 1948; Arnold Bennett, 1948; Reading a Novel, 1949; The English Novel: a Short Critical History, 1954; Six Great Novelists, 1955; Tradition and Dream, 1964; George Eliot, 1964; The Urgent West: an Introduction to the Idea of the United States, 1969; Transatlantic Crossing: American visitors to Britain and British visitors to America in the nineteenth century, 1971; The Short Story in English, 1981; As I Walked Down New Grub Street, 1981. *Address:* 4B Alwyne Road, N1 2HH. *T:* 0171–226 7085.

Died 28 Feb. 1995.

ALLENBY, Rt Rev. (David Howard) Nicholas, SSM; Assistant Bishop, Diocese of Worcester, 1968–91; *b* 28 Jan. 1909; *s* of late William Allenby; unmarried. *Educ:* Kelham Theological College. MA (Lambeth), 1957. SSM 1933; deacon, 1934; priest, 1935. Curate of St Jude, West Derby, Liverpool, 1934–36; Tutor, Kelham Theological College and Public Preacher, Diocese of Southwell, 1936–44; Rector of Averham with Kelham, 1944–57; Mem., Southwell RDC, 1944–52; Proctor in Convocation, Southwell, 1950–57; Editor of Diocesan News and Southwell Review, 1950–55; Hon. Canon of Southwell, 1953–57, Canon Emeritus, 1957–62; Personal Chaplain to Bishop of Southwell, 1954–57; Rural Dean of Newark, 1955–57; Provincial of Society of Sacred Mission in Australia, 1957–62; Commissary, Melanesia, 1958–62; Warden of Community of Holy Name, City and Diocese of Melbourne, 1961–62; Bishop of Kuching, 1962–68; Commissary, Kuching, 1969. Chaplain, St Oswald's Almshouses, Worcester, 1973–84. *Publication:* Pray with the Church, 1937 (jointly). *Recreations:* reading, painting. *Address:* Loughton, Sir John Reid Unit, The Hospice of Our Lady and St John, Manor Farm, Willen, Milton Keynes MK15 9AB. *Clubs:* Commonwealth Trust, Royal Over-Seas League. *Died 28 Feb. 1995.*

ALLERTON, 3rd Baron, *cr* 1902, of Chapel Allerton; **George William Lawies Jackson;** Squadron-Leader Auxiliary Air Force, retired; late Lieutenant Coldstream Guards; *b* 23 July 1903; *s* of 2nd Baron and Katherine Louisa (*d* 1956), *y d* of W. W. Wickham, JP, Chestnut Grove, Boston Spa; *S* father, 1925; *m* 1st, 1926, Joyce (who obtained a divorce, 1934; she *d* 1953), *o c* of late J. R. Hatfeild, Thorp Arch Hall, Yorks; (one *s* decd); 2nd, 1934, Mrs Hope Aline Whitelaw (marr. diss. 1947; she *d* 1987); 3rd, 1947, Anne (*d* 1989), *er d* of late James Montagu, Skippetts, nr Basingstoke; (one *d* decd). *Educ:* Eton; RMC, Sandhurst. *Recreations:* shooting, golf. *Heir:* none. *Address:* Loddington House, Leicestershire LE7 9XE. *T:* Belton (057286) 220. *Clubs:* White's, Turf, Pratt's. *Died 1 July 1991 (ext).*

ALLISON, Charles Ralph, MA; Secretary, Lord Kitchener National Memorial Fund, 1968–83; Headmaster of Brentwood School, 1945–65; *b* 26 May 1903; *s* of Harry A. Allison, FCA, and Gertrude Wolfsberger; *m* 1930, Winifred Rita, *d* of A. C. Williams; two *s* one *d*. *Educ:* Caterham Sch.; University Coll., London; St Catharine's College, Cambridge (Exhibitioner). Assistant Master, Worksop College, 1928; Malvern College, 1929–36; English Tutor, Stowe School, 1936–38; Headmaster of Reigate Grammar School, 1938–40, and Alleyn's School, 1940–45. Formerly Mem. Cttee, Headmasters' Conf. (Vice-Chm. 1965). Governor: Sidney Perry Foundation (Chm., 1961–87; Pres., 1987; Jt Pres., 1988); Lindisfarne Coll., Ruabon, 1954–81; Brentwood Sch., 1970–85; Stowe Sch., 1965–80. Vice-Chm., Commonwealth Youth Exchange Cttee, 1970–72; Vice-Pres., Eastern Region, UNA, 1965–83. Mem., Nat. Commn for UNESCO, 1954–65 (UK Delegate to Gen. Confs, 1958 and 1960). Member: Cttee, Governing Bodies' Assoc., 1972–79,

1980–83; Essex Education Cttee, 1967–74. Reader in the Parish of: St Mary's, Great Warley, 1967–83; St Alban, Tattenhall, 1985–. *Address:* Groom's Cottage, Chester Road, Tattenhall, Cheshire CH3 9AH. *T:* Tattenhall (0829) 70827. *Club:* East India, Devonshire, Sports and Public Schools.   *Died 25 Dec. 1991.*

ALLISON, Rt Rev. Sherard Falkner, MA, DD, LLD; *b* 19 Jan. 1907; *s* of Rev. W. S. Allison; *m* 1936, Ruth Hills; one *s* two *d* (and one *s* decd). *Educ:* Dean Close School, Cheltenham; Jesus Coll., Cambridge (Scholar); Ridley Hall, Cambridge. 1st Cl. Classical Tripos, Parts I and II; 2nd Class Theological Tripos, Part I and Jeremie Septuagint Prize. Curate of St James', Tunbridge Wells, 1931–34; Chaplain of Ridley Hall, Cambridge, and Examining Chaplain to Bishop of Bradford, 1934–36; Vicar of Rodbourne Cheney, Swindon, 1936–40; Vicar of Erith, 1940–45; Principal of Ridley Hall, Cambridge, 1945–50; Bishop of Chelmsford, 1951–61; Bishop of Winchester, and Prelate of the Most Noble Order of the Garter, 1961–74. Examining Chaplain to Bishop of Rochester, 1945, and to Bishop of Ely, 1947; Select Preacher: Univ. of Cambridge, 1946, 1955, 1962; Univ. of Oxford, 1953–55, 1963; Proctor in Convocation, Diocese of Ely, 1949. Hon. Fellow, Jesus College, Cambridge, 1963. DD Lambeth, 1951; Hon. DD: Occidental Coll., Los Angeles, 1959; Wycliffe Coll., Toronto, 1959; Hon. STD Church Divinity Sch. of the Pacific, 1959; Hon. LLD: Sheffield, 1960; Southampton, 1974. *Publication:* The Christian Life, 1938 (joint). *Recreations:* sailing, water-colour sketching, bird watching, gardening. *Address:* Winton Lodge, Alde Lane, Aldeburgh, Suffolk IP15 5DZ. *T:* Aldeburgh (0728) 452485.   *Died 31 May 1993.*

ALLSEBROOK, Peter Winder, CBE 1986; DL; Chairman, TNT (UK) Ltd, since 1973; UK Chairman, Truckline Ferries (Poole) Ltd, since 1973; Deputy Chairman, Freightliners Ltd, 1979–88; Director, TNT Ltd, since 1973; *b* 4 Nov. 1917; *s* of late Wilton Allsebrook, JP, Skegby Hall, Notts, and Charlotte Allsebrook; *m* 1948, Elizabeth (*née* Rissik); two *s* two *d* (and one *s* decd). *Educ:* Fettes College; Caen Univ.; Oxford Univ. FCIT. Enlisted RN, 1939; transf. by War Office to Army; commissioned Sherwood Foresters, 1940; captured Tobruk; POW, Italy, 1940; escaped 1941; crossed lines, Cassino, 1942; despatches 1944 (Europe); demobilised Lt-Col, 1946. Man. Dir, Sagit Trust Co., 1950–65; Dir, A. H. Moody Ltd (Queen's Award for Industry, 1978); Poole Harbour Comr; Past Pres., Dorset Chamber of Commerce and Industry; Chm., Trng and Enterprise Council for Dorset. Trustee, Salisbury Cathedral Spire Trust; Chm., Dorset, Royal Jubilee and Prince's Trusts; Mem., numerous County and charity organisations. Dorset: DL 1986; High Sheriff, 1990–91. CBIM; FRSA. *Recreation:* sailing. *Address:* Milton Mill, West Milton, Bridport, Dorset DT6 3SN. *T:* Powerstock (030885) 432 and 391. *Clubs:* Carlton, Oriental; Achilles; Royal Naval Sailing Association, RM Yacht.   *Died 14 March 1991.*

ALPHAND, Hervé Jean-Charles; Grand Officier, Légion d'Honneur, 1968; *b* 31 May 1907; *s* of Charles Hervé and Jeanne Alphand; *m* 1930, Claude Rober-Raynaud; *m* 1958, Nicole Merenda (*d* 1979). *Educ:* Lycée Janson de Sailly; Ecole des Sciences Politiques. Inspector of Finances and Dir Dept of Treaties, Min. of Commerce, 1937–38; Financial Attaché to Embassy, Washington, 1940–41; Dir of Economic Affairs for French National Cttee in London, 1941–44; Director-General, Economic, Financial and Technical Affairs, Min. of Foreign Affairs, 1945; French Ambassador to OEEC; French Dep. to Atlantic Council, 1950, and Mem. NATO Perm. Council, 1952–54; Ambassador: to UN, 1955–56; to USA, 1956–65; Secretary-General, Min. of Foreign Affairs, France,

1965–73. *Publication:* L'étonnement d'être, journal de 1939 à 1973, 1978. *Address:* 122 rue de Grenelle, 75007 Paris, France.   *Died 13 Jan. 1994.*

ALSTEAD, Stanley, CBE 1960; MD, FRCP; Professor Emeritus, Regius Chair of Materia Medica, University of Glasgow; formerly Senior Visiting Physician, Stobhill Hospital, Glasgow; *b* 6 June 1905; *s* of late Robert Alstead, OBE, sometime MP, and Anne Alstead; *m* 1st, 1932, Nora (*d* 1980), 2nd *d* of late M. W. and Nell Sowden; one *s*; 2nd, 1982, Dr Jessie, (Janet), McAlpine Pope. *Educ:* Wigan Grammar Sch.; Liverpool Univ. MD Liverpool (N. E. Roberts Prize); FRCP; FRCPGlas; FRCPE; FRSE. Held various appts in north of England; appointed Pollok Lecturer in Pharmacology, Univ. of Glasgow, 1932, and became interested in clinical aspects of subject; Cons. Physician, Highlands and Islands, based Inverness, 1947; Regius Prof. of Materia Medica and Therapeutics, Univ. of Glasgow, 1948–70. Hon. Prof., Univ. of East Africa (Makerere University Coll.) and Hon. Physician to Kenyatta Nat. Hosp., Nairobi, Kenya, 1965–66. Served War of 1939–45, in RAMC as medical specialist to 5 CCS in Tunisia and Sicily, and in Belgium and Egypt as Officer in Charge of Med. Div. 67 Gen. Hosp. and 63 Gen. Hosp. with rank of Lt-Col (despatches). Pres. RFPSG (later RCPSGlas), 1956–58 (Hon. Fellow, 1979). Member: British Pharmacopœia Commn, 1953–57; Standing Jt Cttee on Classification of Proprietary Preparations; Commn on Spiritual Healing (General Assembly of Church of Scotland). Jt Editor, Textbook of Medical Treatment. *Publications:* papers in med. jls on results of original research in clinical pharmacology. *Recreations:* gardening, music (violin), reading poetry. *Address:* Glenholme, Glen Road, Dunblane, Perthshire FK15 0DJ. *T:* Dunblane (0786) 822466. *Club:* College (Glasgow).
                                        Died 4 April 1992.

ALSTON, (Arthur) Rex; freelance broadcaster and journalist with The Daily Telegraph, retired 1988; BBC commentator, 1943–61; *b* 2 July 1901; *e s* of late Arthur Fawssett Alston, Suffragan Bishop of Middleton, and Mary Isabel Alston; *m* 1st, 1932, Elspeth (*d* 1985), *d* of late Sir Stewart Stockman and Lady Stockman; one *s* one *d*; 2nd, 1986, Joan, *widow* of T. C. A. Wilson, dental surgeon. *Educ:* Trent College; Clare College, Cambridge. Assistant Master, Bedford School, 1924–41; joined BBC, Jan. 1942. *Publications:* Taking the Air, 1950; Over to Rex Alston, 1953; Test Commentary, 1956; Watching Cricket, 1962. *Recreations:* golf, gardening. *Address:* Garlands, Ewhurst, Cranleigh, Surrey GU6 7QA. *T:* Cranleigh (0483) 277315. *Clubs:* East India, Devonshire, Sports and Public Schools, MCC.
                                        Died 8 Sept. 1994.

AMBROSE, James Walter Davy; Judge, Supreme Court of Singapore, 1958–68; *b* 5 Dec. 1909; *s* of Samuel Ambrose; *m* 1945, Theresa Kamala Ambrose; no *c. Educ:* Free Sch., Penang; Oxford Univ. Asst Official Assignee, Singapore, 1936; Police Magistrate and Asst District Judge, Malacca, 1940; Registrar, Superior Court, Malacca, 1945; Dep. Public Prosecutor, 1946; Sen. Asst Registrar, Supreme Courts of Ipoh, Penang, and Kuala Lumpur, 1947–52; President, Sessions Court, Penang, 1953; Acting District Judge and First Magistrate, Singapore, 1955; Official Assignee, Public Trustee, and Comr of Estate Duties, Singapore 1957. *Address:* Block 10B, Apartment 04–06, Braddell Hill, Singapore 2057.
                                        Died 28 Oct. 1992.

AMHERST, 5th Earl, *cr* 1826; **Jeffery John Archer Amherst,** MC 1918; Baron Amherst of Montreal, 1788; Viscount Holmesdale, 1826; Major, late Coldstream Guards; Manager, External Affairs, BEA, 1946; Director of Associated Companies, 1946–66, retired; Hon. Commission as Wing Commander, Royal Air Force, 1942;

b 13 Dec. 1896; *e s* of 4th Earl and Hon. Eleanor Clementina St Aubyn (*d* 1960), *d* of 1st Baron St Levan; *S* father, 1927. *Educ:* Eton; RMC Sandhurst. Served European War, 1914–18, with Coldstream Guards (MC); placed on RARO, 1921; recalled, 1940; served Middle East, 1940–44. Reportorial Staff, New York Morning World, 1923–29; Commercial Air Pilot and General Manager, Air Line Company, 1929–39; Asst Air Adviser to British Railways, 1945–46. *Publication:* Wandering Abroad (autobiog.), 1976. *Heir:* none. *Clubs:* Cavalry and Guards, Travellers', Pratt's, Garrick.

Died 4 March 1993 (ext).

AMIS, Sir Kingsley, Kt 1990; CBE 1981; author; *b* 16 April 1922; *o c* of William Robert and Rosa Amis; *m* 1st, 1948, Hilary Ann (marr. diss. 1965), *d* of Leonard Sidney and Margery Bardwell; two *s* one *d*; 2nd, 1965, Elizabeth Jane Howard (marr. diss. 1983). *Educ:* City of London School; St John's, Oxford (Hon. Fellow, 1976). Served in Army, 1942–45. Lectr in English, University Coll. of Swansea, 1949–61 (Hon. Fellow, 1985); Fellow of Peterhouse, Cambridge, 1961–63. Cholmondeley Award, 1990. *Publications: novels:* Lucky Jim, 1954 (Somerset Maugham Prize, 1955; filmed, 1957); That Uncertain Feeling, 1955 (filmed as Only Two Can Play, 1962); I Like it Here, 1958; Take a Girl Like You, 1960; One Fat Englishman, 1963; (with Robert Conquest) The Egyptologists, 1965; The Anti-Death League, 1966; (as Robert Markham) Colonel Sun, 1968; I Want it Now, 1968; The Green Man, 1969; Girl, 20, 1971; The Riverside Villas Murder, 1973; Ending Up, 1974; The Alteration, 1976; Jake's Thing, 1978; Russian Hide-and-Seek, 1980; Stanley and the Women, 1984; The Old Devils (Booker Prize), 1986 (adapted for stage, 1989); The Crime of the Century, 1987; Difficulties with Girls, 1988; The Folks that Live on the Hill, 1990; We Are All Guilty, 1991; The Russian Girl, 1992; You Can't Do Both, 1994; The Biographer's Moustache, 1995; *short stories:* My Enemy's Enemy, 1962; Collected Short Stories, 1980, enlarged edn, 1987; Mr Barrett's Secret and Other Stories, 1993; *verse:* A Frame of Mind, 1953; A Case of Samples, 1956; A Look Round the Estate, 1967; Collected Poems 1944–1979, 1979; *belles-lettres:* New Maps of Hell, 1960; The James Bond Dossier, 1965; (as William Tanner) The Book of Bond, or Every Man His Own 007, 1966; What Became of Jane Austen?, 1970; *non-fiction:* On Drink, 1972; Rudyard Kipling and his World, 1975; Every Day Drinking, 1983; How's Your Glass?, 1984; (with J. Cochrane) Great British Songbook, 1986; Memoirs, 1991; *edited:* G. K. Chesterton selected stories, 1972; Tennyson, 1972; Harold's Years, 1977; The New Oxford Book of Light Verse, 1978; The Faber Popular Reciter, 1978; The Golden Age of Science Fiction, 1981; The Amis Anthology, 1988; The Crime of the Century, 1989; The Amis Collection, 1990; The Amis Story Anthology, 1992. *Recreations:* music, thrillers, television. *Address:* c/o Jonathan Clowes, Iron Bridge House, Bridge Approach, NW1 8BD. *Club:* Garrick. *Died 22 Oct. 1995.*

AMRITANAND, Rt Rev. Joseph; Bishop of Calcutta, 1970–82; *b* Amritsar, Punjab, India, 17 Feb. 1917; *m* 1943, Catherine Phillips; one *s* one *d*. *Educ:* District Board School, Toba Tek Singh, Punjab; Forman Christian Coll., Lahore; Punjab Univ. (BA); Bishop's College, Calcutta; Wycliffe Hall, Oxford. Deacon 1941, priest 1943; Missionary-in-charge of CMS Mission Field, Gojra, 1946–48; Bishop of Assam, 1949–62; Bishop of Lucknow, 1962–70; translated, after inauguration of Church of North India, Nov. 1970; first Bishop of Durgapur, 1972–74. *Recreations:* reading, bird watching, visiting, helping anyone in need on the road, intercessional ministering. *Address:* 182 Civil Lines, Bareilly, UP 243001, India.

Died 27 Nov. 1994.

ANDERSON, Carl David, PhD; Professor of Physics, California Institute of Technology, 1930–76, then Emeritus; Chairman, Division of Physics, Mathematics and Astronomy, 1962–70; *b* 3 Sept. 1905; *s* of Carl David Anderson and Emma Adolfina Ajaxson; *m* 1946, Lorraine Bergman; two *s*. *Educ:* California Institute of Technology. BS 1927, PhD 1930. War activities on projects, 1941–45; Presidential Certificate of Merit, 1945. Conducted research on X-rays, gamma rays, cosmic rays, elementary particles, etc. Member: Nat. Acad. of Sciences; Amer. Philosoph. Soc.; Amer. Acad. of Arts and Sciences. Gold Medal, Amer. Inst., City of NY, 1935; Nobel Prize in Physics, 1936; Elliott Cresson Medal of the Franklin Inst., 1937; John Ericsson Medal of Amer. Soc. of Swedish Engineers, 1960, etc. Hon. degrees. *Address:* California Institute of Technology, Pasadena, Calif 91109, USA.

Died 11 Jan. 1991.

ANDERSON, David Colville, VRD 1947, and Clasp, 1958; QC (Scotland) 1957; *b* 8 Sept. 1916; *yr s* of late J. L. Anderson of Pittormie, Fife, solicitor and farmer, and late Etta Colville; *m* 1948, Juliet, *yr d* of Hon. Lord Hill Watson, MC, LLD; two *s* one *d*. *Educ:* Trinity Coll., Glenalmond; Pembroke Coll., Oxford; Edinburgh Univ. BA (Hons) Oxford 1938; LLB (Distinction) 1946. Thow Scholar, Maclagan Prizeman, Dalgety Prizeman, Edinburgh Univ. Lecturer in Scots Law, Edinburgh Univ., 1947–60; Advocate, 1946; Standing Junior Counsel to Ministry of Works, 1954–55, and to War Office, 1955–57. Contested (C) Coatbridge and Airdrie, 1955, and East Dunbartonshire, 1959; MP (C) Dumfries, Dec. 1963–Sept. 1964. Solicitor-General for Scotland, 1960–64; Vice-Chairman, Commissioners of Northern Lighthouses, 1963–64; Hon. Sheriff-Substitute, Lothians and Peebles, 1965–; Chm., Industrial Tribunals (Scotland), 1971–72; Chief Reporter for Public Inquiries and Under Sec., Scottish Office, 1972–74. Joined RNVR, 1935. In VIII awarded Ashburton Shield, Bisley, 1933 (Trinity Coll., Glenalmond; schools event); Inter-Services XX at Bisley, 1936–38. Served War of 1939–45 in destroyers (despatches); Lieut 1940; Egerton Prizeman in Naval Gunnery, 1943; Flotilla Gunnery Officer, Rosyth Escort Force, 1943–45; led special operation N Norway, 1945; Lt-Comdr 1948. King Haakon VII Liberty Medal, 1946. *Relevant Play:* The Case of David Anderson QC by John Hale (Manchester, and Traverse Theatre, Edinburgh, 1980; Lyric Studio Hammersmith, 1981). *Address:* 8 Arboretum Road, Edinburgh EH3 5PD. *T:* 0131–552 3003. *Club:* New (Edinburgh). *Died 31 Dec. 1995.*

ANDERSON, Dame Frances Margaret, (Dame Judith Anderson), AC 1991; DBE 1960; actress; *b* Adelaide, South Australia, 10 Feb. 1898; *d* of James Anderson Anderson and Jessie Saltmarsh; *m* 1937, Prof. B. H. Lehman (marr. diss. 1939); *m* 1946, Luther Greene (marr. diss. 1950). *Educ:* Norwood High Sch., South Australia. Started Theatre with Julius Knight; toured Australia and America, 1918; played in: The Dove, 1925; Behold the Bridegroom, 1927; Strange Interlude, 1930; Mourning becomes Electra, 1931; Come of Age, 1934; The Old Maid, 1935; Hamlet, 1936; Macbeth (London), 1937; Family Portrait, 1939; Three Sisters, 1942; Medea (New York, 1947–48; toured America, 1948–49; Paris Internat. Drama Festival, 1955); The Seagull, Edin. Fest., 1960, Sept. at Old Vic; The Oresteia, 1966; Hamlet, 1970. *Films:* Rebecca, Edge of Darkness, Laura, King's Row, Spectre of the Rose, The Red House, Pursued, Tycoon, Cat on a Hot Tin Roof, Macbeth, Don't Bother to Knock, A Man Called Horse, Star Trek III; TV: The Chinese Prime Minister, 1974. *Recreation:* gardening.

Died 3 Jan. 1992.

ANDERSON, Prof. Sir (James) Norman (Dalrymple), Kt 1975; OBE (mil.) 1945 (MBE 1943); LLD; FBA 1970;

QC 1974; Professor of Oriental Laws in the University of London, 1954–75, then Emeritus Professor; Director of the Institute of Advanced Legal Studies in the University of London, 1959–76; *b* 29 Sept. 1908; *s* of late William Dalrymple Anderson; *m* 1933, Patricia Hope, *d* of A. Stock Givan; one *s* and two *d* decd. *Educ:* St Lawrence Coll., Ramsgate; Trinity Coll., Cambridge (Senior Scholar). 1st Class, Law Tripos Parts I and II (distinction in Part I); BA 1930; 1st Class LLB 1931; MA 1934. Called to the Bar, Gray's Inn, 1965. Missionary, Egypt General Mission, 1932; served War of 1939–45 in Army as Arab Liaison Officer, Libyan Arab Force, 1940; Sec. for Sanusi Affairs, Civil Affairs Branch, GHQ, MEF, 1941; Sec. for Arab Affairs, 1943; Political Sec., 1943; Chief Sec. (Col), 1944; Lectr in Islamic Law, Sch. of Oriental and African Studies, 1947; Reader in Oriental Laws in Univ. of London, 1951–53; Hd of Dept of Law, SOAS, 1953–71, then Hon. Fellow, SOAS; Dean of Faculty of Laws, Univ. of London, 1965–69. President, Soc. of Public Teachers of Law, 1968–69. Chm. UK Nat. Cttee of Comparative Law, 1957–59; Vice-Chm. Internat. African Law Assoc.; Visiting Professor: Princeton Univ. and New York Univ. Law Sch., 1958; Harvard Law Sch., 1966. Conducted survey of application of Islamic Law in British African possessions for Colonial Office, 1950–51. President: BCMS, 1963–86; CPAS, 1974–86; Scripture Union, 1975–80; Victoria Inst., 1978–85; Lawyers' Christian Fellowship, 1987–89. First Chairman, House of Laity in Gen. Synod of Church of England, 1970–79 (Mem., 1970–80; Mem. former Church Assembly, 1965–70); Anglican delegate to the World Council of Churches. Hon. DD St Andrews, 1974; Hon. LittD Wheaton Coll., 1980. Libyan Order of Istiqlal, Class II, 1959. *Publications:* Al-'Aql wa'l Iman (in Arabic), 1939; Islamic Law in Africa, 1954; Islamic Law in the Modern World, 1959; Into the World: The Need and Limits of Christian Involvement, 1968; Christianity: the witness of history, 1969; Christianity and Comparative Religion, 1970; Morality, Law and Grace (Forwood Lectures), 1972; A Lawyer among the Theologians, 1973; Law Reform in the Muslim World, 1976; Issues of Life and Death, 1976; Liberty, Law and Justice (Hamlyn Lectures), 1978; The Mystery of the Incarnation (Bishop John Prideaux Lectures), 1978; The Law of God and the Love of God, 1980; God's Word for God's World, 1981; The Teaching of Jesus, 1983; Christianity and World Religions: the challenge of pluralism, 1984; Jesus Christ: the witness of history, 1984; An Adopted Son (autobiog.), 1986; Freedom Under Law, 1987; Islam in the Modern World: a Christian perspective, 1990; Editor: The World's Religions, 1950, 4th edn 1975; Changing Law in Developing Countries, 1963; Family Law in Asia and Africa, 1968; numerous articles in periodicals. *Address:* 9 Larchfield, Gough Way, Cambridge CB3 9LR. *T:* Cambridge (01223) 358778. *Club:* Athenæum.   *Died 2 Dec. 1994.*

ANDERSON, Dame Judith; *see* Anderson, Dame F. M.

ANDERSON, Sir Kenneth, KBE 1962 (CBE 1946); CB 1955; *b* 5 June 1906; *s* of Walter Anderson, Exmouth; *m* 1932, Helen Veronica Grose (*d* 1986); one *s* one *d. Educ:* Swindon Secondary Sch.; Wadham Coll., Oxford (MA). Entered India Office, 1928; Asst Sec., 1942; Dep. Financial Adviser to British Military Governor, Germany, 1947–48; Imperial Defence Coll., 1949; Under-Sec., HM Treasury, 1950–51; Dep. Director-General, 1954–66 and Comptroller and Accountant-General, 1952–66, GPO. Officer, Order of Orange-Nassau, 1947. *Address:* 7 Milton Close, N2 0QH. *T:* 081–455 8701. *Club:* United Oxford & Cambridge University.   *Died 28 Sept. 1992.*

ANDERSON, Lindsay (Gordon); film and theatre director; *b* 17 April 1923; 2nd *s* of late Maj.-Gen. A. V. Anderson and Estelle Bell Sleigh. *Educ:* Cheltenham Coll.; Wadham

Coll., Oxford. Associate Artistic Director, Royal Court Theatre, 1969–75. Governor, British Film Institute, 1969–70. *Films include:* Wakefield Express, 1953; Thursday's Children (with Guy Brenton), 1954; O Dreamland, 1954; Every Day Except Christmas, 1957; This Sporting Life, 1963; The White Bus, 1966; Raz, Dwa, Trzy (The Singing Lesson), for Warsaw Documentary Studio, 1967; If . . . ., 1968 (Grand Prix, Cannes Fest., 1969); O Lucky Man!, 1973 (Film Critics' Guild award for best film of 1973); In Celebration, 1974; Britannia Hospital, 1982; If You Were There . . . , 1985; The Whales of August, 1988; Glory! Glory!, 1989; Is That All There Is? (Special Jury Prize, Florence, 1992). *Productions in theatre:* The Waiting of Lester Abbs, 1957; The Long and the Short and the Tall; Progress to the Park; Jazzetry; Serjeant Musgrave's Dance, 1959; The Lily White Boys; Billy Liar; Trials by Logue, 1960; The Fire-Raisers, 1961; The Diary of a Madman, 1963; Andorra, 1964; Julius Caesar, 1964; The Cherry Orchard, 1966, 1983; first Polish production of Inadmissible Evidence (Nie Do Obrony), Warsaw, 1966; In Celebration, 1969; The Contractor, 1969; Home (also NY), 1970; The Changing Room, 1973; The Farm, 1974; Life Class, 1974; What the Butler Saw, 1975; The Sea Gull, 1975; The Bed Before Yesterday, 1975; The Kingfisher, 1977 (NY, 1978); Alice's Boys, 1978; Early Days, 1980; Hamlet, 1981; The Holly and the Ivy, NY, 1982; The Playboy of the Western World, 1984; In Celebration, NY, 1984; Hamlet, Washington, DC, 1985; Holiday, 1987; The March on Russia, 1989; Jubilee, 1990; The Fishing Trip, 1991; Stages, 1992. *Video plays:* Home, 1971; Look Back in Anger, NY, 1980. *Television play:* The Old Crowd, 1979. Editor, film quarterly, Sequence, 1947–51. *Publications:* Making a Film, 1952; About John Ford, 1981; contrib. to Declaration, 1957. *Address:* 9 Stirling Mansions, Canfield Gardens, NW6 3JT.   *Died 30 Aug. 1994.*

ANDERSON, Marian, (Mrs Orpheus H. Fisher); American contralto; *b* Philadelphia, Pa, 27 Feb. 1897; *m* 1943, Orpheus H. Fisher (*d* 1985). *Educ:* Philadelphia; New York; Chicago; and in Europe. MusD Howard Univ., 1938. Singing career began in 1924; 1st prize at Lewisohn Stadium competition, New York, 1925; made numerous tours in the United States, Europe, Japan, Israel, India, Pakistan, Korea, etc; Ulrica in Verdi's The Masked Ball, Metropolitan Opera House, New York, 1955. US Delegate to UN, 1958. Made many recordings. Numerous American and other hon. doctorates; Bok Award, 1940; Litteris et Artibus Medal, Sweden, 1952; Yukusho Medal, Japan, 1953; Gimbel Award, 1958; Gold Medal, US Inst. of Arts and Sciences, 1958; US Presidential Medal of Freedom, 1963; Congressional Gold Medal, 1978. Finnish decoration, 1940. *Publication:* My Lord, What a Morning, 1957.   *Died 8 April 1993.*

ANDERSON, Sir Norman; *see* Anderson, Sir J. N. D.

ANDERSON, Walter Charles, CBE 1968; solicitor; General Secretary, National and Local Government Officers Association, 1957–73; Member, Independent Broadcasting Authority, 1973–78; *b* 3 Dec. 1910; *s* of William Walter John Anderson and Mary Theresa McLoughlin; *m* 1941, Doris Jessie Deacon; two *s. Educ:* Bootle Grammar Sch. and Wigan Grammar Sch.; Liverpool Univ. (LLB). Articled Clerk, J. W. Wall & Co., Solicitors, Bootle, Liverpool, 1930–33; Asst Solicitor, Bootle, 1933–34; Dep. Town Clerk, Heywood, 1934–37; Asst Solicitor, Nalgo, 1937–41; Royal Air Force, 1941–45; Legal Officer, Nalgo, 1945–50; Dep. Gen. Sec., Nalgo, 1950–57. Mem., Gen. Council of TUC, 1965–73. Member: Fulton Cttee on Civil Service Recruitment, Structure, Management and Training, 1966–68; Nat. Insurance Adv. Cttee, 1970–74; Industrial Injuries Adv. Council, 1970–74;

Nat. Inst. of Econ. and Social Res., 1970–76; Royal Commn on Civil Liability and Compensation for Personal Injury, 1973–78; Industrial Arbitration Bd, Workpeople's Rep., 1972. *Publication:* Simonds' Local Government Superannuation Act, 1937 (rev. and ed), 1947. *Recreations:* sport, gardening. *Address:* 1 The Comyns, Bushey, Watford WD2 1HN. *T:* 0181–950 3708.
Died 1 March 1995.

ANDREWS, Air Cdre Charles Beresford Eaton B.; *see* Burt-Andrews.

ANDREWS, Lt-Col Harold Marcus E.; *see* Ervine-Andrews.

ANFINSEN, Dr Christian Boehmer; Professor of Biology, Johns Hopkins University, since 1982; *b* Monessen, Pa, 26 March 1916; *s* of Christian Boehmer Anfinsen and Sophie (*née* Rasmussen); *m* 1941, Florence Bernice Kenenger (marr. diss. 1978); one *s* two *d*; *m* 1979, Libby Esther Shulman. *Educ:* Swarthmore Coll. (BA); Univ. of Pennsylvania (MS); Harvard (PhD). Amer.-Scand. Foundn Fellow, Carlsberg Lab., Copenhagen, 1939; Sen. Cancer Res. Fellow, Nobel Inst. Medicine, Stockholm, 1947; Asst Prof. of Biological Chemistry, Harvard Medical Sch., 1948–50; Head of Lab. of Cellular Physiology and Metabolism, Nat. Heart Inst., Bethesda, Md, 1950–62; Prof. of Biochemistry, Harvard Med. Sch., 1962–63; Head of Lab. of Chem. Biol., Nat. Inst. of Arthritis, Metabolism and Digestive Diseases, Bethesda, 1963–82. Rockefeller Fellow, 1954–55; Guggenheim Fellow, Weizmann Inst., Rehovot, Israel, 1958. Mem., Bd of Governors, Weizmann Inst., Rehovot, 1960–. Member: Amer. Soc. of Biol Chemists (Pres., 1971–72); Amer. Acad. of Arts and Scis; Nat. Acad. of Scis; Royal Danish Acad.; Washington Acad. of Scis; Fedn Amer. Scientists (Vice-Chm., 1958–59, and 1974–75); Pontifical Acad., 1980. Hon. DSc: Swarthmore, 1965; Georgetown, 1967; Pennsylvania, 1973; NY Med. Coll., Gustavus Adolphus Coll., 1975; Brandeis, 1977; Providence Coll., 1978; Hon. MD Naples, 1982. (Jtly) Nobel Prize for Chemistry, 1972. *Publication:* The Molecular Basis of Evolution, 1959. *Address:* Department of Biology, Johns Hopkins University, Baltimore, MD 21218, USA.
Died 14 May 1995.

ANSELL, Sir Michael Picton, Kt 1968; CBE 1951; DSO 1944; DL; First President/Chairman, British Equestrian Federation, 1972–76; Show Director, Royal International Horse Show, and Horse of the Year Show, 1949–75; *b* 26 March 1905; *s* of Lieut-Col G. K. Ansell and K. Cross; *m* 1st, 1936, Victoria Jacintha Fleetwood Fuller (*d* 1969); two *s* one *d;* 2nd, 1970, Eileen (*née* Stanton) (*d* 1971), *widow* of Maj.-Gen. Roger Evans, CB, MC. *Educ:* Wellington; RMC Sandhurst. Gazetted 5th Royal Inniskilling Dragoon Guards, 1924, Col, 1957–62. War of 1939–45: Lieut-Col to command 1st Lothian & Border Yeo., 1940 (severely wounded and prisoner, 1940); discharged disabled, 1944. Chairman: British Show Jumping Assoc., 1945–64, 1970–71 (Pres., 1964–66); (first) British Horse Soc. Council, 1963–72 (Hon. Dir, British Horse Soc., 1952–73). Yeoman, Worshipful Co. of Saddlers, 1963; Freeman: Worshipful Co. of Farriers, 1962; Worshipful Co. of Loriners, 1962. Mem. Council, St Dunstan's, 1958– (a Vice-Pres., 1970, Vice-Chm., 1975–77, Pres., 1977–86). DL 1966, High Sheriff 1967, Devon. Chevalier, Order of Leopold, Belgium, 1932; Commander's Cross, Order of Merit, German Federal Republic, 1975; Olympic Order, Silver, IOC, 1977. *Publications:* Soldier On (autobiog.), 1973; Riding High, 1974; Leopard, the Story of My Horse, 1980. *Recreations:* show jumping (International, 1931–39), polo International, fishing, gardening. *Address:* c/o Lloyds Bank, Bideford, Devon EX39 2AD.
Died 17 Feb. 1994.

ANSON, Malcolm Allinson; Chairman: Imperial Group Ltd, 1980–81; Wessex Water Authority, 1982–87; *b* 23 April 1924; *s* of Sir Wilfrid Anson, MBE, MC, and Olive Anson (*née* Bourne); *m* 1st, 1950, Alison Lothian (marr. diss. 1992), *d* of late Sir Arthur Lothian, KCIE, CSI; three *s* one *d;* 2nd, 1992, Elizabeth Joan Twiston-Davies, JP, *d* of late Brig. C. G. Maude, DSO, OBE, MC and *widow* of Capt C. E. Twiston-Davies. *Educ:* Winchester; Trinity College, Oxford (MA). War Service, Royal Horse Artillery, 1943–46. Joined Imperial Tobacco Co. (of GB & Ireland) Ltd, 1948; Dir, 1968; Dep. Chm., Imperial Gp Ltd, 1979–80. Director: Bristol Waterworks Co., 1981–82; Nat. Westminster Bank, 1981–85; Local Dir, Coutts & Co., 1989–. Chairman: Bristol Assoc. of Youth Clubs, 1963–71; Endeavour Training, 1969–76; Bristol Cancer Help Centre, 1983–91; Avon Enterprise Fund, 1984–90. Dir, Oxford Univ. Business Summer Sch., 1966; Chm., Careers Adv. Bd, Bristol Univ., 1971–91; Vice-Chm., Clifton Coll. Council, 1978–; Dir, Ullswater Outward Bound Mountain Sch., 1971–83. High Sheriff of Avon, 1977–78. Master, Society of Merchant Venturers, Bristol, 1979–80. *Recreations:* ski-ing, sailing, shooting, golf. *Address:* Drax House, Tilshead, Salisbury, Wilts SP3 4SJ. *T:* Shrewton (0980) 620473. *Club:* Cavalry and Guards.
Died 13 Aug. 1992.

ANSTEY, Sidney Herbert; HM Diplomatic Service, retired; Consul-General, Atlanta, 1968–70; *b* 4 June 1910; *m* 1937, Winifred Mary Gray; three *s* one *d.* Foreign Office, 1940–49; Vice-Consul, Nantes, 1950; First Sec. and Consul, Port-au-Prince, 1951; Belgrade, 1952; Vienna, 1953; Dep. Finance Officer, Foreign Office, 1957; First Sec., Paris, 1960, Counsellor, 1963; Consul, Bilbao, 1965; Consul-Gen., Bilbao, 1966. *Address:* 17 Hambledon Hill, Epsom, Surrey. *T:* Epsom (03727) 25989.
Died 5 Sept. 1991.

ANTCLIFFE, Kenneth Arthur; Director of Education, City of Liverpool, 1975–89; *b* 1923; *m* 1st, Constance; four *d;* 2nd, Susan. *Educ:* Mexborough Grammar Sch.; Reading Univ. Served with Irish Fusiliers. *Recreations:* reading, writing, walking, bird watching, gardening, bridge. *Address:* 56 Alderley Road, Hoylake, Wirral L47 2BA.
Died 2 Jan. 1992.

ANTHONY, Sir Mobolaji B.; *see* Bank-Anthony.

ANTROBUS, Sir Philip Coutts, 7th Bt, *cr* 1815, of Antrobus, Cheshire; *b* 10 April 1908; *s* of late Geoffrey Edward Antrobus and Mary Atherstone, *d* of Hilton Barber, JP, Halesowen, Cradock, Cape Province; *S* cousin, 1968; *m* 1st, 1937, Dorothy Margaret Mary (*d* 1973), *d* of late Rev. W. G. Davis; two *s* one *d;* 2nd, 1975, Doris Primrose (*d* 1986), *widow* of Ralph Dawkins; 3rd, 1990, Esmé Florence Bayes, *widow* of Frank Mawer. Served War, 1939–45 (POW). *Heir: s* Edward Philip Antrobus [*b* 28 Sept. 1938; *m* 1966, Janet (*d* 1990), *d* of Philip Sceales; one *s* two *d*]. *Address:* West Amesbury House, West Amesbury, near Salisbury, Wilts SP4 7BH. *T:* Amesbury (01980) 623860.
Died 1 Aug. 1995.

APPLETON, Rt Rev. George, CMG 1972; MBE 1946; *b* 20 Feb. 1902; *s* of Thomas George and Lily Appleton; *m* 1929, Marjorie Alice (*d* 1980), *d* of Charles Samuel Barrett; one *s* two *d. Educ:* County Boys' School, Maidenhead; Selwyn Coll., Cambridge; St Augustine's Coll., Canterbury. BA Cantab 1924 (2nd Cl. Math. Trip. pt 1, 1st Cl. Theological Trip. pt I); MA 1929. Deacon, 1925; priest, 1926; Curate, Stepney Parish Church, 1925–27; Missionary in charge SPG Mission, Irrawaddy Delta, 1927–33; Warden, Coll. of Holy Cross, Rangoon, 1933–41; Archdeacon of Rangoon, 1943–46; Director of Public Relations, Government of Burma, 1943–46; Vicar of Headstone, 1947–50; Sec., Conf. of Brit. Missionary Societies, 1950–57; Rector of St Botolph, Aldgate,

1957–62; Archdeacon of London and Canon of St Paul's Cathedral, 1962–63; Archbishop of Perth and Metropolitan of W Australia, 1963–69; Archbishop in Jerusalem and Metropolitan, 1969–74. Buber-Rosenzweig Medal, Council of Christians and Jews, 1975. *Publications:* John's Witness to Jesus, 1955; In His Name, 1956; Glad Encounter, 1959; On the Eightfold Path, 1961; Daily Prayer and Praise, 1962; Acts of Devotion, 1963; One Man's Prayers, 1967; Journey for a Soul, 1974; Jerusalem Prayers, 1974; The Word is the Seed, 1976; The Way of a Disciple, 1979; The Practice of Prayer, 1980; Glimpses of Faith, 1982; Praying with the Bible, 1982; Prayers from a Troubled Heart, 1983; The Quiet Heart, 1983; (ed) The Oxford Book of Prayer, 1985; Hour of Glory, 1985; Entry into Life, 1985; The Heart of the Bible, 1986; Understanding the Psalms, 1987; 100 Personal Prayers for Today, 1988; Prayer in a Troubled World, 1988; Paul the Interpreter, 1989; Unfinished—a critical autobiography, 1990. *Address:* 5 James Street, Oxford OX4 1ET.
Died 28 Aug. 1993.

ARBUTHNOT, Sir John (Sinclair-Wemyss), 1st Bt *cr* 1964, of Kittybrewster, Aberdeen; MBE 1944; TD 1951; *b* 11 Feb. 1912; *s* of late Major K. W. Arbuthnot, the Seaforth Highlanders; *m* 1943, Margaret Jean, *yr d* of late Alexander G. Duff; two *s* three *d. Educ:* Eton; Trinity Coll., Cambridge. MA Hons in Nat. Sciences. Served throughout War of 1939–45, in RA, Major (wounded); Dep. Inspector of Shell, 1942–45; hon. pac 1944. Contested (C): Don Valley Div. of Yorks, 1935; Dunbartonshire, 1945. MP (C) Dover Div. of Kent, 1950–64; PPS to Parly Sec., Min. of Pensions, 1952–53, to Minister of Pensions, 1953–56, and to Minister of Health, 1956–57; a Chm. of Committees and a Temporary Chm. of the House, 1958–64; Parliamentary Chm., Dock & Harbour Authorities Assoc., 1962–64; Mem., Public Accounts Cttee, 1955–64; Member Parliamentary Delegations: to the Iron and Steel Community, 1955; to West Africa, 1956; to USA, 1957; to The West Indies, 1958; to Zanzibar, Mauritius and Madagascar, 1961; Leader of Parliamentary Delegation to Bulgaria, 1963. Second Church Estates Comr, 1962–64; Church Comr for England and Mem., Bd of Governors, 1962–77 (Dep Chm., Assets Cttee, 1966–77); Mem., Church Assembly and Gen. Synod of Church of England, 1955–75 (Panel of Chairmen, 1970–72); Trustee, Lambeth Palace Library, 1964–77; Chm., Archbp of Canterbury's Commn to inquire into the organisation of the Church by dioceses in London and the SE of England, 1965–67. Member: Crathorne Cttee on Sunday Observance, 1961–64; Hodson Commn on Synodical Government for the Church of England, 1964–66; Standing Cttee, Ross Inst., 1951–62. A Vice Pres., Trustee Savings Banks Assoc., 1962–76; in business in tea industry concerned with India, Ceylon and the Cameroons, 1934–74; Chairman: Estates & Agency Holdings Ltd, 1955–70; Folkestone and District Water Co., 1974–87; Joint Hon. Sec. Assoc. of British Chambers of Commerce, 1953–59. *Recreation:* gardening. *Heir: s* William Reierson Arbuthnot, *b* 2 Sept. 1950. *Address:* Poulton Manor, Ash, Canterbury, Kent CT3 2HW. *T:* Ash (0304) 812516. *Clubs:* Carlton, Commonwealth Trust.
Died 13 June 1992.

ARCHER, Frank Joseph, RE 1960 (ARE 1940); RWS 1976 (ARWS 1972); Head of School of Fine Art, Kingston Polytechnic, Kingston upon Thames (formerly Kingston College of Art), 1962–73, retired; *b* 30 June 1912; *s* of Joseph and Alberta Archer; *m* 1939, Celia Cole (*d* 1990); one *s* one *d. Educ:* Eastbourne Grammar Sch.; Eastbourne Sch. of Art; Royal Coll. of Art. ARCA 1937; Rome Scholar, Engraving, 1938; British Sch. at Rome, 1938. Paintings bought by numerous local authorities and private collectors. *Address:* Flat 1, Stony Down, 8 Milnthorpe

Road, Eastbourne, East Sussex BN20 7NN. *T:* Eastbourne (01323) 723381.
Died 31 March 1995.

ARDWICK, Baron *cr* 1970 (Life Peer), of Barnes; **John Cowburn Beavan;** Member of European Parliament, 1975–79; *b* 29 April 1910; *s* of late Silas Morgan Beavan and Alderman Emily Beavan, JP; *m* 1934, Gladys (*née* Jones); one *d*; one *s* by Anne Symonds. *Educ:* Manchester Grammar Sch. Blackpool Times, 1927; Evening Chronicle, Manchester, 1928; Manchester Evening News, 1930; London staff, Manchester Evening News, 1933; News Editor, Manchester Evening News, Manchester, 1936; Asst Editor, Londoner's Diary, Evening Standard, and leader writer, 1940; News Editor and Chief Sub, Observer, 1942; Editor, Manchester Evening News, 1943; Dir, Manchester Guardian and Evening News Ltd, 1943–55; London Editor, Manchester Guardian, 1946–55; Asst Dir, Nuffield Foundation, 1955–60; Editor, Daily Herald, 1960–62; Political Adviser to the Daily Mirror Group, 1962–76. Mem. Editorial Bd, The Political Quarterly, 1978–; Chm., Press Freedom Cttee, Commonwealth Press Union, 1980–; Hon. Sec., British Cttee, Internat. Press Inst., 1972–76. Chm., Industrial Sponsors, 1975–92. Chm., Back Benchers' Co-ordinating Cttee, 1986–93. A Pres., European Movement, 1989. *Address:* 10 Chester Close, SW13 0JE. *T:* 081–789 3490. *Club:* Garrick.
Died 18 Aug. 1994.

ARIAS, Dame Margot Fonteyn de, (Dame Margot Fonteyn), DBE 1956 (CBE 1951); Prima Ballerina Assoluta; President of the Royal Academy of Dancing, since 1954; Chancellor of Durham University, since 1982; *b* 18 May 1919; *m* 1955, Roberto E. Arias (*d* 1989). Hon. degrees: LittD Leeds; DMus London, Oxon and Durham; LLD Cantab; DLitt Manchester; LLD Edinburgh. Benjamin Franklin Medal, RSA, 1974; Internat. Artist Award, Philippines, 1976; Hamburg Internat. Shakespeare Prize, 1977. Order of Finnish Lion, 1960; Order of Estacio de Sa, Brazil, 1973; Chevalier, Order of Merit of Duarte, Sanchez and Mella, Dominican Republic, 1975. *Publications:* Margot Fonteyn (autobiog.), 1975, rev. edn 1989; A Dancer's World, 1978; The Magic of Dance, 1980 (BBC series, 1979); Pavlova Impressions, 1984; Swan Lake—as told by Margot Fonteyn, USA 1989. *Address:* c/o Royal Opera House, Covent Garden, WC2.
Died 21 Feb. 1991.

ARLOTT, (Leslie Thomas) John, OBE 1970; wine and general writer, The Guardian; topographer; broadcaster; *b* Basingstoke, 25 Feb. 1914; *s* of late William John and Nellie Jenvey Arlott; *m* 1st, 1940, Dawn Rees; one *s* (and one *s* decd); 2nd, 1959, Valerie France (*d* 1976); one *s* (one *d* decd); 3rd, 1977, Patricia Hoare. *Educ:* Queen Mary's Sch., Basingstoke. Clerk in Mental Hospital, 1930–34; Police (Detective, eventually Sergeant), 1934–45; Producer, BBC, 1945–50; General Instructor, BBC Staff Training School, 1951–53. Contested (L) Epping Division, 1955 and 1959. President: Cricketers' Assoc., 1968–; Hampshire Schools Cricket Assoc., 1966–80. Hon. MA Southampton, 1973. Sports Journalist of 1979 (British Press Award); Sports Personality of 1980 (Soc. of Authors' Pye Radio Award); Sports Presenter of the Year, 1980 (TV and Radio Industries Club Award). DUniv. Open, 1981. *Publications:* (with G. R. Hamilton) Landmarks, 1943; Of Period and Place (poems), 1944; Clausentum (poems), 1945; First Time In America (anthology), 1949; Concerning Cricket, 1949; How to Watch Cricket, 1949, new edn 1983; Maurice Tate, 1951; Concerning Soccer, 1952; (ed) Cricket (Pleasures of Life series), 1953; The Picture of Cricket, 1955; English Cheeses of the South and West, 1956; Jubilee History of Cricket, 1965; Vintage Summer, 1967; (with Sir Neville Cardus) The Noblest Game, 1969; Fred: portrait of a fast bowler, 1971; The Ashes, 1972; Island Camera: the Isles of Scilly in the photography of the Gibson family, 1973, repr. 1983; The Snuff Shop, 1974; (ed) The Oxford Companion to Sports and Games, 1975; (with Christopher Fielden) Burgundy, Vines and Wines, 1976; Krug: House of Champagne, 1977; (with Patrick Eagar) An Eye for Cricket, 1979; Jack Hobbs: a profile of The Master, 1981; A Word From Arlott (ed David Rayvern Allen), 1983; (ed) Wine, 1984; Arlott on Cricket, 1984; (with Patrick Eagar) Botham, 1985; (with Mike Brearley) Arlott in Conversation with Mike Brearley, 1986; John Arlott's 100 Greatest Batsmen, 1986; Arlott on Wine, 1986; The Essential John Arlott, 1989; Basingstoke Boy, 1990. *Recreations:* watching cricket, drinking wine, talking, sleeping, collecting aquatints, engraved glass, and wine artefacts. *Address:* c/o The Guardian, 119 Farringdon Road, EC1R 3ER. *Clubs:* National Liberal, MCC (Hon. Life Mem., 1980); Master's; Forty; Somerset County Cricket (Hon. Life Mem., 1982), Hampshire County Cricket (Hon. Life Mem., 1984).

Died 14 Dec. 1991.

ARMSTRONG, Rt Rev. John, CB 1962; OBE 1942; Assistant Bishop in the Diocese of Exeter, 1969–88; *b* 4 Oct. 1905; *y s* of late John George and Emily Armstrong; *m* 1942, Diana Gwladys Prowse (*d* 1989), 2nd *d* of Admiral Sir Geoffrey Layton, GBE, KCB, KCMG, DSO and *widow* of Lieut Geoffrey Vernon Prowse; one step *s*. *Educ:* Durham School; St Francis Coll., Nundah, Brisbane, Qld. LTh, 2nd Class Hons, Australian College of Theology, 1932. Ordained deacon, 1932, priest, 1933; Mem. Community of Ascension, Goulburn, 1932–33; Curate, St Martin, Scarborough, 1933–35; Chaplain RN, HMS Victory, 1935; Courageous, 1936–39; 6th Destroyer Flotilla, 1939–41 (despatches 1940); RM Div., 1941–43; Commando Group, 1943–45; HMS Nelson, 1945; Sen. Naval Chaplain, Germany, 1946–48; Excellent, 1948–50; RM Barracks, Portsmouth, 1950–53; Indomitable, 1953; RN Rhine Sqdn, 1953–54; HMS Vanguard, 1954; Tyne, 1954; HM Dockyard, Malta, and Asst to Chaplain of the Fleet, Mediterranean, 1955–57; HMS Bermuda, 1957–59; RM Barracks, Portsmouth, 1959–60; Chaplain of the Fleet and Archdeacon of the Royal Navy, 1960–63; Bishop of Bermuda, 1963–68; Vicar of Yarcombe, Honiton, 1969–73. QHC, 1958–63. Life Mem., Guild of Freemen of City of London. *Address:* c/o Lady Riches, 34 Cheriton Road, Winchester SO22 5AY.

Died 30 Dec. 1992.

ARMSTRONG, Sir Thomas Henry Wait, Kt 1958; MA, DMus; FRCM; Hon. FRCO, Hon. RAM; Principal, Royal Academy of Music, 1955–68; Organist of Christ Church, Oxford, 1933–55; Student of Christ Church, 1939–55, Student Emeritus, 1955, Hon. Student, 1981; Choragus of the University and University Lecturer in Music, 1937–54; Conductor of the Oxford Bach Choir and the Oxford Orchestral Society; Musical Director of the Balliol Concerts; *b* 15 June 1898; *o s* of Amos E. Armstrong, Peterborough, Northants; *m* 1926, Hester (*d* 1982), 2nd *d* of late Rev. W. H. Draper; one *s* one *d*. *Educ:* Choir Sch., Chapel Royal, St James's; King's Sch., Peterborough; Keble Coll., Oxford (Hon. Fellow, 1955); Royal Coll. of Music. Served RA, BEF, France, 1917–19. Organist, Thorney Abbey, 1914; Sub-organist, Peterborough Cathedral, 1915; Organ Scholar, Keble Coll., Oxford, 1916; Sub-organist, Manchester Cathedral, 1922; Organist, St Peter's, Eaton Square, 1923; Organist of Exeter Cathedral, 1928. Cramb Lectr in Music, Univ. of Glasgow, 1949. A Dir, Royal Opera House, 1958–69. Former Chm., Fedn of Music Socs; Chairman: Musicians Benevolent Fund, 1963; Royal Philharmonic Soc., 1964–68; former Mem., Vic-Wells and Sadler's Wells Bd of Govs; Pres., ISM, 1946 and 1961. Sen. Music Advr to Delius Trust, 1961–; Trustee, Countess of Munster Musical Trust. Many broadcasts to schools and on musical subjects;

on juries of many internat. competitions and examined in many universities. Hon. FTCL. Hon. DMus: Edinburgh; Royal Univ. of Brazil, 1963. *Compositions:* various, the larger ones remain unpublished. *Publications:* include choral music, songs and church music, together with many occasional writings on music. *Address:* 1 East Street, Olney, Bucks MK46 4AP. *Club:* Garrick.

Died 26 June 1994.

ARNOLD, Vere Arbuthnot, CBE 1970; MC 1945; TD 1953; JP; DL; Chairman, Ross T. Smyth & Co. Ltd, 1957–80; *b* 23 May 1902; *s* of Rev. H. A. Arnold, Wolsingham Rectory, Co. Durham; *m* 1928, Joan Kathleen (*d* 1993), *d* of C. J. Tully, Wairarapa, NZ; one *s* one *d*. *Educ:* Haileybury Coll.; Jesus Coll., Cambridge (BA). Ross T. Smyth & Co. Ltd, 1924, Director, 1931. Pres., Liverpool Corn Trade Association, 1947–48 and 1951–52. Chm., Runcorn Develt Corp., 1964–74. Served War of 1939–45 as Major (MC, TD). JP County of Chester, 1949; High Sheriff, Cheshire, 1958; DL Cheshire, 1969. *Recreations:* shooting, fishing. *Address:* Ardmore, Great Barrow, near Chester CH3 7JM. *T:* Tarvin (0829) 40257.

Died 15 April 1994.

ARRAU, Claudio; concert pianist; *b* Chillan, Chile, 6 Feb. 1903; American citizen, 1979; *m* 1937, Ruth Schneider (*d* 1989); one *s* one *d* (and one *s* decd). Gave first recital at Santiago at age of 5; musical education in Europe financed by Chilean Govt; studied at Stern Konservatorie Berlin, under Martin Krause; won Liszt Prize 1919, 1920 (not awarded in 45 years), Schulhoff prize, Ibach prize, 1917, and, in 1927, first place in Geneva International Piano Competition; appeared in US, Canada, England, France, Holland, Italy, Germany, Scandinavia, Russia, South America, Mexico, Cuba, Hawaii, South Africa, Australia, Israel, Japan, NZ, Iceland, Hong Kong, Singapore, Ceylon, New Delhi and Bombay. Chile named many more than a dozen streets in his honour throughout the country. Cycle performances included: all keyboard works of Bach in 12 recitals, Berlin, 1935; all Beethoven Sonatas, 8 recitals, Berlin, Buenos Aires, Santiago, NY and London; all Beethoven Sonatas, Diabelli Variations (first BBC broadcast from London, 1952), all Beethoven, NY Season, 1953–54, 1962; renowned also for Chopin, Schumann, Brahms, Liszt, Debussy. Decorations from France, Germany, Mexico, Chile, Italy; International UNESCO Music Prize, 1983. *Address:* c/o ICM Artists Ltd, 40 West 57 Street, New York, NY 10019, USA.

Died 9 June 1991.

ARROWSMITH, Sir Edwin (Porter), KCMG 1959 (CMG 1950); *b* 23 May 1909; *s* of late Edwin Arrowsmith and of Kathleen Eggleston Arrowsmith (*née* Porter); *m* 1936, Clondagh, *e d* of late Dr W. G. Connor; two *d*. *Educ:* Cheltenham Coll.; Trinity Coll., Oxford (MA). Assistant District Commissioner, Bechuanaland Protectorate, 1932; in various District posts, Bechuanaland Protectorate, 1933–38; Commissioner, Turks and Caicos Islands, BWI, 1940–46; Administrator, Dominica, BWI, 1946–52; Resident Commissioner, Basutoland, 1952–56; Governor and Commander-in-Chief, Falkland Islands, 1957–64, and High Commissioner, British Antarctic Territory, 1962–64; Dir of Overseas Services Resettlement Bureau, 1965–79. Mem. Council, St Dunstan's, 1965–. Vice-Pres., Royal Commonwealth Soc. for the Blind, 1985– (Chm., 1970–85). Vice-Pres., Freshwater Biol Assoc., 1984– (Pres., 1977–83). *Recreation:* flyfishing. *Address:* 25 Rivermead Court, SW6 3RU. *T:* 071–736 4757. *Clubs:* Flyfishers', Hurlingham, Commonwealth Trust.

Died 10 July 1992.

ARTHINGTON-DAVY, Humphrey Augustine, LVO 1977; OBE 1965; HM Diplomatic Service, retired; High Commissioner to Tonga, 1973–80, and Western Samoa, 1973–77; *b* 1920. *Educ:* Eastbourne Coll.; Trinity Coll.,

Cambridge. Indian Army, 1941; Indian Political Service, 1946; Civil Service of Pakistan, 1947; CRO, 1958; British Representative in the Maldives, 1960; Deputy High Commissioner: Botswana, 1966; Mauritius, 1968; Tonga, 1970. *Recreation:* travel. *Address:* c/o Grindlays Bank, 13 St James's Square, SW1; PO Box 56, Nuku' Alofa, Tonga, South Pacific. *Club:* Naval and Military.
Died 29 May 1993.

ARTHUR, Rt Rev. Robert Gordon; *b* 17 Aug. 1909; *s* of George Thomas Arthur and Mary Arthur; *m* Marie Olive Cavell Wheen; two *s* two *d. Educ:* Launceston and Devonport High Schs, Tasmania; Queen's Coll., Univ. of Melbourne. MA (Hons) 1932. Deacon, 1949; priest, 1949; Rector of: Berridale, NSW, 1950–53; St John's, Canberra, ACT, 1953–60; Wagga Wagga, NSW, 1960–61; Archdeacon of Canberra, 1953–60; Asst Bp of Canberra and Goulburn, 1956–61; Bishop of Grafton, NSW, 1961–73; Rector of St Philip's, Canberra, 1973–74; Priest-in-charge of Bratton, Wilts, 1975–78, and Rural Dean of Heytesbury, 1976–78; Hon. Asst Bishop of Sheffield, 1978–80. *Address:* 4 Berry Street, Downer, Canberra, ACT 2602, Australia. *Died 9 June 1992.*

ASHBROOK, 10th Viscount, *cr* 1751 (Ire.); **Desmond Llowarch Edward Flower,** KCVO 1977; MBE 1945; DL; Baron Castle Durrow, 1733; Member of Council of Duchy of Lancaster, 1957–77; *b* 9 July 1905; *o s* of 9th Viscount and Gladys, *d* of Gen. Sir George Wentworth A. Higginson, GCB, GCVO; *S* father, 1936; *m* 1934, Elizabeth, *er d* of Capt. John Egerton-Warburton and Hon. Mrs Waters; two *s* one *d. Educ:* Eton; Balliol Coll., Oxford (BA 1927). Served War of 1939–45, RA. Formerly a Chartered Accountant. JP, 1946–67, DL 1949, Vice-Lieutenant, 1961–67, Cheshire. *Heir: s* Hon. Michael Llowarch Warburton Flower [*b* 9 Dec. 1935; *m* 1971, Zoë Mary Engleheart; two *s* one *d*]. *Address:* Woodlands, Arley, Northwich, Cheshire CW9 6LZ.
Died 5 Dec. 1995.

ASHBURTON, 6th Baron, *cr* 1835; **Alexander Francis St Vincent Baring,** KG 1969; KCVO 1961; JP; DL; Lord Lieutenant and Custos Rotulorum, Hampshire and Isle of Wight, 1960–73 (Vice-Lieutenant, 1951–60); High Steward of Winchester, 1967–78; Receiver-General to the Duchy of Cornwall, 1961–74; *b* 7 April 1898; *o s* of 5th Baron and Hon. Mabel Edith Hood (*d* 1904), *d* of 4th Viscount Hood; *S* father, 1938; *m* 1924, Hon. Doris Mary Thérèse Harcourt (*d* 1981), *e d* of 1st Viscount Harcourt; two *s. Educ:* Eton; Royal Military Coll. Lieut The Greys, 1917–23; Flt-Lt AAF, 1939, retd as Group Captain, 1944. Director: Baring Brothers & Co. Ltd, 1962–68 (Managing Director, 1928–62); Alliance Assurance, 1932–68; Pressed Steel Co. Ltd, 1944–66; Mem. London Cttee, Hongkong & Shanghai Banking Corp., 1935–39. Treasurer, King Edward VII Hospital Fund for London, 1955–64, Governor, 1971–76; Trustee: King George's Jubilee Trust, 1949–68; Chantrey Bequest, 1963–81; St Cross Hospital of Noble Poverty, Winchester, 1961–81. Chm., Hampshire and IoW Police Authy, 1961–71. President: Hampshire and IoW Territorial Assoc., 1960–67 (Mem., 1951–60); Eastern Wessex Territorial Assoc., 1968–70. CC 1945, CA 1955, JP 1951, DL 1973, Hants. KStJ 1960. *Heir: s* Hon. Sir John Francis Harcourt Baring, KCVO [*b* 2 Nov. 1928; *m* 1st, 1955, Susan Mary Renwick (marr. diss. 1984), *e d* of 1st Baron Renwick, KBE, and Mrs John Ormiston; two *s* two *d*; 2nd, 1987, Mrs Sarah Crewe, *d* of late J. G. Spencer Churchill]. *Address:* Itchen Stoke House, Alresford, Hants SO24 0QU. *T:* Alresford (0962) 2479.
Died 12 June 1991.

ASHBY, Baron *cr* 1973 (Life Peer), of Brandon, Suffolk; **Eric Ashby,** Kt 1956; FRS 1963; DSc London, MA Cantab; DIC; Chancellor, Queen's University, Belfast, 1970–83; Fellow of Clare College, Cambridge, 1958, Life Fellow 1975; *b* 24 Aug. 1904; *s* of Herbert Charles Ashby, Bromley, Kent, and Helena Chater; *m* 1931, Elizabeth Helen Farries, Castle-Douglas, Scotland; two *s. Educ:* City of London Sch.; Imperial Coll. of Science, Univ. of London; Univ. of Chicago. Demonstrator at Imperial Coll., 1926–29; Commonwealth Fund Fellow in Univ. of Chicago and Desert Laboratory of Carnegie Institution, 1929–31; Lectr, Imperial Coll. of Science, 1931–35; Reader in Botany, Bristol Univ., 1935–37; Prof. of Botany, Univ. of Sydney, Australia, 1938–46; Harrison Prof. of Botany and Dir of Botanical Labs, Univ. of Manchester, 1946–50; Pres. and Vice-Chancellor, Queen's Univ., Belfast, 1950–59; Master of Clare College, Cambridge, 1959–75; Vice-Chancellor, Univ. of Cambridge, 1967–69. Chm., Aust. National Research Council, 1940–42; Chm., Professorial Board, Univ. of Sydney, 1942–44; Mem., Power Alcohol Committee of Enquiry, 1940–41; conducted enquiry for Prime Minister into enlistment of scientific resources in war, 1942; Trustee, Aust. Museum, 1942–46; Dir, Scientific Liaison Bureau, 1942–43; Counsellor and Chargé d'Affaires at Australian Legation, Moscow, USSR, 1945–46; Chairman: Scientific Grants Cttee, DSIR, 1955–56; Postgraduate Grants Cttee, DSIR, 1956–60; Northern Ireland Adv. Council for Education, 1953–58; Adult Education Cttee, 1953–54; Commn for Post-Secondary and Higher Educn in Nigeria, 1959–61; Cttee of Award of Commonwealth Fund, 1963–69 (Member, 1956–61); Royal Commn on Environmental Pollution, 1970–73; Working Party on Pollution Control in connection with UN conf. on the Environment, Stockholm, June 1972. Member: Advisory Council on Scientific Policy, 1950–53; Nuffield Provincial Hospitals Trust, 1951–59; Advisory Council on Scientific and Industrial Research, 1954–60; Univ. Grants Cttee, 1959–67; Commonwealth Scholarship Commn, 1960–69; Council of Royal Soc., 1964–65; Governing Body, Sch. of Oriental and African Studies, Univ. of London, 1965–70; Vice-Chm. Assoc. of Univs of Brit. Commonwealth, 1959–61; Pres., Brit. Assoc. for the Advancement of Science, 1963. Walgreen Prof., Michigan, 1975–77; Lectures: Godkin, Harvard Univ., 1964; Whidden, McMaster Univ., 1970; Bernal, Royal Soc., 1971; Prof-at-large, Cornell Univ., 1967–72; Trustee: Ciba Foundation, 1966–79; British Museum, 1969–77; Fellow: Imperial Coll. of Science; Davenport Coll., Yale Univ.; Hon. Fellow, Clare Hall, Cambridge; Hon. FRSE; Hon. FRIC. Hon. Foreign Mem., Amer. Acad. of Arts and Sciences. Hon. LLD: St Andrews; Aberdeen; Belfast; Rand; London; Wales; Columbia; Chicago; Michigan; Windsor; Western Australia; Manchester; Johns Hopkins; Liverpool; Hon. ScD Dublin; Hon. DSc: NUI; Univ. of Nigeria; Southampton; Hon. DLitt: W Ont; Sydney; Hon. DPhil Tech. Univ., Berlin; Hon. DCL East Anglia; Hon. DHL: Yale; Utah. Jephcott Medal, RSM, 1976. Order of Andrés Bello, first class, Venezuela, 1974. *Publications:* Environment and Plant Development, translated from German, 1931; German-English Botanical Terminology (with Elizabeth Helen Ashby), 1938; Food Shipment from Australia in Wartime; Challenge to Education, 1946; Scientist in Russia, 1947 (German trans., 1950); Technology and the Academics, 1958 (Japanese trans., 1963; Spanish trans, 1970); Community of Universities, 1963; African Universities and Western Tradition, 1964 (French trans. 1964); (with Mary Anderson) Universities: British, Indian, African, 1966 (Spanish trans. 1972); Masters and Scholars, 1970; (with Mary Anderson) The Rise of the Student Estate, 1970; Any Person, Any Study, 1971; (with Mary Anderson) Portrait of Haldane, 1974; Reconciling Man with the Environment, 1978 (Spanish trans. 1981); (with Mary Anderson) The Politics of Clean Air, 1981. *Recreation:* chamber music. *Address:* 22 Eltisley Avenue, Cambridge CB3 9JG.
Died 22 Oct. 1992.

ASHCROFT, Dame Edith Margaret Emily, (Dame Peggy Ashcroft), DBE 1956 (CBE 1951); actress; Director, Royal Shakespeare Company, since 1968; *b* 22 Dec. 1907; *d* of William Worsley Ashcroft and Violet Maud Bernheim; *m* 1st, 1929, Rupert Hart-Davis (marr. diss.; he was knighted, 1967); 2nd, 1934, Theodore Komisarjevsky (marr. diss.); 3rd, 1940, Jeremy Hutchinson, QC, later Lord Hutchinson of Lullington (marr. diss. 1966); one *s* one *d. Educ:* Woodford Sch., Croydon; Central Sch. of Dramatic Art. Member of the Arts Council, 1962–64. Ashcroft Theatre, Croydon, named in her honour, 1962. First appeared as Margaret in Dear Brutus, Birmingham Repertory Theatre, 1926; parts included: Bessie in One Day More, Everyman, Eve in When Adam Delved, Wyndham's, 1927; Mary Bruin in The Land of Heart's Desire, Hester in The Silver Cord, 1928; Constance Neville in She Stoops to Conquer, Naomi in Jew Süss, 1929; Desdemona in Othello with Paul Robeson, 1930; Fanny in Sea Fever, 1931; Cleopatra, Imogen, Rosalind, etc, at Old Vic and Sadler's Wells, 1932; Juliet in Romeo and Juliet, New, 1935; Nina in The Seagull, New, 1936; Portia, Lady Teazle, and, Irina in Three Sisters, Queen's, 1937–38; Yeliena in White Guard and Viola, Phoenix, 1938–39; Cecily Cardew in The Importance of Being Earnest, 1939–40, and Dinah in Cousin Muriel, 1940, both at Globe; revival of Importance of Being Earnest, Phoenix, 1942; Catherine in The Dark River, Whitehall, 1943; Ophelia, Titania, Duchess of Malfi, Haymarket Repertory Season, 1944–45; Evelyn Holt in Edward my Son, His Majesty's, 1947; Catherine Sloper in The Heiress, Haymarket, 1949; Beatrice and Cordelia, Memorial Theatre, Stratford-on-Avon, 1950; Viola, Electra and Mistress Page, Old Vic, 1950–51; Hester Collyer in The Deep Blue Sea, Duchess, 1952; Cleopatra, Stratford-on-Avon and Princes, 1953; title-rôle, Hedda Gabler, Lyric, Hammersmith and Westminster, 1954; Beatrice in Much Ado About Nothing, Stratford Festival Company, 1955 (London, provinces and continental tour); Miss Madrigal in The Chalk Garden, Haymarket, 1956; Shen Te in The Good Woman of Setzuan, Royal Court, 1956; Rosalind, Imogen, Cymbeline, Stratford-on-Avon, 1957; Julia Rajk in Shadow of Heroes, Piccadilly, 1958; Stratford-on-Avon Season, 1960: Katharina in The Taming of the Shrew; Paulina in The Winter's Tale; The Hollow Crown, Aldwych, 1961; title rôle in The Duchess of Malfi, Aldwych, 1961; Emilia in Othello, Stratford-on-Avon, 1961, also Madame Ranevskaya in The Cherry Orchard, subseq. Aldwych; Margaret of Anjou in Henry VI and Margaret in Edward IV, also Margaret in Richard III, Stratford-on-Avon, 1963, Aldwych, 1964; Mme Arkadina in The Seagull, Queen's, 1964; Mother in Days in the Trees, Aldwych, 1966; Mrs Alving in Ghosts, 1967; A Delicate Balance, Aldwych, 1969; Beth in Landscape, Aldwych, 1969; Katharine of Aragon in Henry VIII, Stratford-on-Avon, 1969; The Plebeians Rehearse the Uprising, Aldwych, 1970; The Lovers of Viorne, Royal Court, 1971 (Evening Standard Best Actress Award, 1972); All Over, Aldwych, 1972; Lloyd George Knew My Father, Savoy, 1972; Beth in Landscape, Flora in A Slight Ache, Ashcroft Theatre, foreign tour and Aldwych, 1973; The Hollow Crown, tour in US, 1973; John Gabriel Borkman, National, 1975; Happy Days, National, 1975, 1977; Old World, Aldwych, 1976; Watch on the Rhine, Edinburgh Fest. and National, 1980; Family Views, National, 1981; All's Well that Ends Well, Stratford-on-Avon, 1981, Barbican, 1982. Entered films 1933; subsequent films include: The Wandering Jew, The Thirty-nine Steps, The Nun's Story (played Mother Mathilde), Hullabaloo over Georgie and Bonnie's Pictures, 1979; Passage to India, 1985 (Oscar award; BAFTA Award); Madame Sousatzka, 1988; She's Been Away, 1989 (Venice Film Fest. Award); Queen Victoria for BBC Radio, 1973; television: series include: Queen Mary in

Edward and Mrs Simpson, ITV, 1978; The Jewel in the Crown, Granada, 1984 (BAFTA Award); A Perfect Spy, 1987; plays include: Caught on a Train, BBC2, 1980 (BAFTA Award); Cream in My Coffee, LWT, 1980. Special Award, British Theatre Assoc., 1982; Special Award, BAFTA, 1990. Olivier Special Award, SWET, 1991. Hon. DLitt: Oxford, 1961; Leicester, 1964; Warwick, 1974; Bristol, Reading, 1986; Hon. DLit London, 1965; Hon LittD Cantab, 1972; DUniv Open, 1986. Hon. Fellow, St Hugh's College, Oxford, 1964. King's Gold Medal, Norway, 1955; Comdr, Order of St Olav, Norway, 1976. *Address:* Flat 14, 9–11 Belsize Grove, NW3. *Died 14 June 1991.*

ASHCROFT, Dame Peggy; *see* Ashcroft, Dame E. M. E.

ASHFORD, (Albert) Reginald, CMG 1962; Assistant Secretary, Board of Customs and Excise, 1952–73; *b* 30 June 1914; *s* of Ernest and Ethel Ashford; *m* 1946, Mary Anne Ross Davidson (*d* 1990); one *s. Educ:* Ealing Grammar Sch.; London Sch. of Economics (BSc Econ). Entered Civil Service, 1931 as Clerical Officer, MoT; Exec. Officer, Customs and Excise, 1934; Private Sec. to Chm. of Bd, 1943–46; Principal, 1946; UK Delegate: to internat. confs on reduction of barriers to trade, incl. GATT, Geneva, 1947, Havana, 1947–48, Annecy, 1949, Torquay, 1950, and intermediate meetings (sometime Chm., wkg parties); to Econ. Commn for Europe, 1948–56 (TIR Convention, 1949); to UNESCO, Florence, 1950 (Chm., Drafting Cttee of Internat. Convention on Importation of Educnl, Scientific and Cultural Materials); to Customs Co-operation Council, Brussels, 1953–60 (Chm., Perm. Tech. Cttee, 1954, and Finance Cttee, 1958–59). European Tariff discussions and European Free Trade Area Agreement, Brussels, Paris, Stockholm, 1953–60; transferred by choice to home div., 1960. Vice Chm., Bucks Assoc. for Blind, 1979–81. *Address:* 4 Tithe Green, Rustington, West Sussex BN16 3QX. *T:* Rustington (01903) 776545. *Died 20 Sept. 1995.*

ASHLEY, Maurice Percy, CBE 1978; *b* 4 Sept. 1907; *s* of Sir Percy Ashley, KBE, and Doris Ashley (*née* Hayman); *m* 1st, 1935, Phyllis Mary Griffiths (*d* 1987); one *s* one *d*; 2nd, 1988, Patricia Ann Entract. *Educ:* St Paul's Sch., London; New Coll., Oxford (History Scholar). 1st Class Hons Modern History; DPhil Oxon; DLitt Oxon, 1979. Historical Research Asst to Sir Winston Churchill, 1929–33; Editorial Staff, The Manchester Guardian, 1933–37; Editorial Staff, The Times, 1937–39; Editor, Britain Today, 1939–40; Deputy Editor, The Listener, 1946–58, Editor, 1958–67; Research Fellow, Loughborough Univ. of Technology, 1968–70. Pres. Cromwell Association, 1961–77. Served in Army, 1940–45 (Major, Intelligence Corps). *Publications include:* Financial and Commercial Policy under the Cromwellian Protectorate, 1934, 2nd edn 1962; Oliver Cromwell, 1937; Marlborough, 1939; Louis XIV and the Greatness of France, 1946; John Wildman: Plotter and Postmaster, 1947; Mr President, 1948; England in the Seventeenth Century, 1952, rev. edn, 1978; Cromwell's Generals, 1954; The Greatness of Oliver Cromwell, 1957, rev. edn 1967; Oliver Cromwell and the Puritan Revolution, 1958; Great Britain to 1688, 1961; The Stuarts in Love, 1963; Life in Stuart England, 1964; The Glorious Revolution of 1688, 1966, new edn 1968; Churchill as Historian, 1968; A Golden Century, 1598–1715, 1969; (ed) Cromwell: great lives observed, 1969; Charles II: the man and the statesman, 1971; Oliver Cromwell and his World, 1972; The Life and Times of King John, 1972; The Life and Times of King William I, 1973; A History of Europe 1648–1815, 1973; The Age of Absolutism 1648–1775, 1974; A Concise History of the English Civil War, 1975, rev. edn 1990; Rupert of the Rhine, 1976; General Monck, 1977; James II, 1978; The House of

Stuart, 1980; The People of England: a short social and economic history, 1982; Charles I and Oliver Cromwell, 1987; The Battle of Naseby and the Fall of Charles I, 1992. *Recreations:* bridge, gardening. *Address:* 2 Elm Court, Cholmeley Park, N6 5EJ. *T:* 0181–340 3659. *Club:* Reform.

Died 26 Sept. 1994.

ASHTON, Rev. Canon Patrick Thomas, LVO 1963; Chaplain to the Queen, 1955–86; *b* 27 July 1916; *s* of Lieut-Col S. E. Ashton, OBE; *m* 1942, Mavis St Clair Brown, New Zealand; three *d* (one *s* decd). *Educ:* Stowe; Christ Church, Oxford (MA); Westcott House, Cambridge. Served War of 1939–45 as Captain, Oxfordshire Yeomanry. Curate, St Martin-in-the-Fields, 1947–51; Rector of All Saints, Clifton, Beds, 1951–55; Rector of Sandringham with West Newton and Appleton, and Domestic Chaplain to the Queen, 1955–70; Rector: Sandringham Gp of Eight Parishes, 1963–70; Swanborough Team of Parishes, 1970–73; Priest-in-charge of Avebury with Winterbourne Monkton and Berwick Bassett, 1974–77; Rector, Upper Kennet team of Parishes, 1975–77; a Canon of Salisbury Cathedral, 1975; Rural Dean of Marlborough, 1976–77. *Address:* Field Cottage, Bottlesford, Pewsey, Wilts SN9 6LU. *T:* Woodborough (0672) 851340.

Died 2 April 1994.

ASHTON HILL, Norman, MBE (mil.) 1945; TD; Consultant, Ashton Hill Bond, Solicitors and Commissioners for Oaths, 1981 (Principal Partner, 1948–81); *b* 1 March 1918; *s* of Sydney and Marguerite Ashton Hill, Bewdley, Worcs; *m* 1971, Ireina Hilda Marie; one *s* two *d* by former *m*. *Educ:* Uppingham Sch.; Birmingham Univ. (LLB Hons). Served War, 1939–45: commnd 2nd Lieut TA, 1939; BEF, BLA, BAOR; Staff Coll. (psc); mentioned in despatches; NW Europe War Crimes, 1945–46; Hon. Lt-Col, Royal Warwickshire Regt. Enrolled Gibraltar Bar, 1971. Chm., Radio Trent Ltd, 1973–79; Dir, 1971–78, Vice-Chm., 1972–78, Bonser Engrg Ltd. Director: Lunn Poly (formerly Sir Henry Lunn Ltd) (Vice-Chm., 1954–68); Eagle Aviation Ltd, and Cunard Eagle Airways Ltd and Group, 1952–68; North Midland Construction Plc, 1971–85; Morgan Housing Co. Ltd and Group, 1962–81; Derby Music Finance Ltd, 1978–84; Cooper & Roe Ltd, 1979–80. Chairman: Air Transport Cttee, ABCC, 1958–82 (a Vice-Pres. ABCC, 1977–88); Air Transp. Cttee, ICC UK (formerly British National Chamber of Internat. Chamber of Commerce), 1970–88; Air Transport Users Cttee, 1980–82 (Mem., 1976–82; Dep. Chm., 1978–79; Hon. Consultant, 1982–86); Fedn of Air Transport Users Representatives in the Economic Community, 1982–86 (Hon. Pres., 1987); Rapporteur to Internat. Foundn of Airline Passengers Assoc., 1986–. CRAeS 1980. NSPCC: Hon. Vice-Pres., and formerly Hon. Gen. and Cases Sec., Nottingham Br.; Mem. Central Exec. Cttee, 1955–80, Vice-Chm., 1974–80; Hon. Vice-Pres. Hon. Vice-Consul for Norway, Notts, 1955–80. Assistant, Glaziers Co., 1978–87. FRSA. Kt (1st Cl.), Order of St Olav, Norway, 1972. *Recreations:* gardening, shooting, humanities. *Address:* Apartado 435, Estepona, Málaga 29680, Spain. *T:* (34) 52–793719. *Club:* Royal Aero.

Died 10 Oct. 1991.

ASHWORTH, Brig. John Blackwood, CBE 1962; DSO 1944; retired 1965; *b* 7 Dec. 1910; *s* of Lieut-Col H. S. Ashworth (killed in action, 1917), Royal Sussex Regt, and late Mrs E. M. Ashworth; *m* 1944, Eileen Patricia, *d* of late Major H. L. Gifford (Royal Ulster Rifles) and of Lady Gooch; one *d*. *Educ:* Wellington Coll.; RMC, Sandhurst. Commissioned Royal Sussex Regt, 1930; Instructor RMC, 1938; War of 1939–45 (despatches twice); OC Training Centre, 1942; OC 1/5 Queen's Royal Regt (wounded, DSO), 1944; GSO1, War Office, 1944; OC 4/5 Royal Sussex, 1945; OC 1st Royal Sussex, 1946; GSO1, Brit.

Middle East Office, 1947; AMS War Office, 1948; OC 1st Royal Sussex, 1951; Comdt Joint Sch. of Chemical Warfare, 1954; Commander 133rd Inf. Bde (TA), 1957; Director of Military Training, War Office, 1959–62; Inspector of Boys' Training, War Office, 1962–65. ADC to the Queen, 1961–65. Col, Royal Sussex Regt, 1963–66; Dep. Col, The Queen's Regt (Royal Sussex), 1967–68. DL Sussex 1972–83. OStJ 1950. Grand Officer, Order of House of Orange, 1967. *Address:* 16 Castlegate, New Brook Street, Ilkley, W Yorks LS29 8DF. *T:* Ilkley (0943) 602404.

Died 3 April 1994.

ASHWORTH, Prof. William; Professor of Economic and Social History, 1958–82, Dean of Faculty of Social Sciences, 1968–70, and Pro-Vice-Chancellor, 1975–78, University of Bristol; *b* 11 March 1920; *s* of Harold and Alice Ashworth; unmarried. *Educ:* Todmorden Grammar Sch.; London Sch. of Economics and Political Science. Served 1941–45, RAPC and REME. BSc (Econ.) 1946; PhD 1950. Research Assistant, London Sch. of Economics and Political Science, 1946–47; on staff of Cabinet Office (Historical Section), 1947–48; Assistant Lecturer and Lecturer in Economic History, London Sch. of Economics and Political Science, 1948–55; Reader in Economic History in the Univ. of London, 1955–58. *Publications:* A Short History of the International Economy, 1952 (revised 1962, 1975, 1987); Contracts and Finance (History of the Second World War: UK Civil Series), 1953; The Genesis of Modern British Town Planning, 1954; An Economic History of England, 1870–1939, 1960; History of the British Coal Industry: the nationalized industry 1946–1982, 1986; The State in Business 1945 to the mid-1980s, 1991; contributor to: London, Aspects of Change, ed by Centre for Urban Studies, 1964; Victoria County History of Essex, 1966; The Study of Economic History, ed N. B. Harte, 1971. Articles and reviews in Economic History Review and other jls. *Address:* 31 Calton Gardens, Bath BA2 4QG. *T:* Bath (0225) 426888.

Died 19 March 1991.

ASIMOV, Prof. Isaac, PhD; Professor of Biochemistry, University of Boston, since 1979; author; *b* 2 Jan. 1920; *s* of Judah Asimov and Anna Rachel (*née* Berman); *m* 1st, 1942, Gertrude Blugerman (marr. diss. 1973); one *s* one *d*; 2nd, 1973, Dr Janet Jeppson. *Educ:* Columbia Univ. (BS 1939, MA 1941, PhD 1948, all in chemistry). Joined Faculty of Boston Univ. Sch. of Medicine, 1949; retd from academic labors, 1958, but retained title. First professional sale of short story, 1938; first book published, 1950; 400th book published, 1988. *Publications:* over 400 books, including: I, Robot, 1950; The Human Body, 1963; Asimov's Guide to Shakespeare, 1970; Asimov's Guide to Science, 1972; Murder at the ABA, 1976; The Collapsing Universe, 1977; In Memory Yet Green (autobiog., vol. 1), 1979; A Choice of Catastrophes, 1979; In Joy Still Felt (autobiog., vol. 2), 1980; In the Beginning, 1981; Foundation's Edge, 1982; The Robots of Dawn, 1983; Asimov's New Guide to Science, 1984; Asimov's Guide to Halley's Comet, 1985; Robots and Empire, 1985. *Recreation:* a man's work is his play: my recreation is writing. *Address:* 10 West 66th Street, New York, NY 10023, USA. *T:* 212–362–1564.

Died 6 April 1992.

ASKWITH, Hon. Betty Ellen, FRSL; *b* 26 June 1909; *o d* of 1st and last Baron Askwith, KCB, KC, and Lady Askwith, CBE; *m* 1950, Keith Miller Jones (*d* 1978). *Educ:* Lycée Français, London; North Foreland Lodge, Broadstairs. *Publications:* First Poems, 1928; If This Be Error, 1932; Poems, 1933; Green Corn, 1933; Erinna, 1937; Keats, 1940; The Admiral's Daughters, 1947; A Broken Engagement, 1950; The Blossoming Tree, 1954; The Tangled Web, 1960; A Step Out of Time, 1966; Lady Dilke, 1969; Two Victorian Families, 1971; The

Lytteltons, 1975; A Victorian Young Lady, 1978; Piety and Wit: Harriet Countess Granville 1785–1862, 1982; Crimean Courtship, 1985; with Theodora Benson: Lobster Quadrille, 1930; Seven Basketfuls, 1932; Foreigners, 1935; Muddling Through, 1936; How to Be Famous, 1937; *translations:* The Tailor's Cake, 1947; A Hard Winter, 1947; Meeting, 1950. *Recreation:* reading Victorian novels. *Address:* 9/105 Onslow Square, SW7 RLU. *T:* 0171–589 7126. *Died 10 April 1995.*

ASPREY, Algernon; independent artist and designer; *b* 2 June 1912; *s* of George Kenneth Asprey and Charlotte Esta Asprey; *m* 1939, Beatrice (*née* Bryant); one *s* one *d* (and one *d* decd). *Educ:* Bowden House Prep. Sch., Seaford; Charterhouse; Sch. of Art, Regent Street Polytechnic, London. Served War, 1940–46: commnd Scots Guards, Captain. Joined Asprey of Bond Street, 1933; with Aspreys, 1946–71, when own business, Algernon Asprey, formed; re-appointed Dir, Asprey & Co. Ltd, 1979–81; Chm., Algernon Asprey (Furnishing) Ltd, 1971–81. Chairman: Purchase Tax Cttee in post war years to disbandment; Guards Club, 1960–65. Pres., Bond Street Assoc., 1968–81 (Chm., 1965–68). Mem. Cttee, Friends of Royal Acad. Prime Warden, Worshipful Co. of Goldsmiths, 1977–78; Hon. Mem., Interior Decorators and Designers Assoc., 1983–. *Recreations:* painting, sailing, golf. *Address:* Magnolia Cottage, Upper House Lane, Shamley Green, Surrey GU5 0SX. *T:* Cranleigh (0483) 271502. *Club:* Cavalry and Guards (Hon. Mem.). *Died 27 May 1991.*

ASTIN, Prof. Alan Edgar, OBE 1989; Professor of Ancient History, Queen's University of Belfast, since 1967; Chairman, Arts Council of Northern Ireland, since 1986; *b* 14 June 1930; *s* of Harold William Astin and Winifred Clara Astin; *m* 1955, June Doris Bowring; two *s. Educ:* Kingston Grammar Sch., Kingston-on-Thames; Worcester Coll., Oxford Univ. (MA). Queen's University of Belfast: Asst Lectr, 1954–57; Lectr, 1957–67; Dean, Faculty of Arts, 1971–75; Dean, Faculty of Theology, 1985–90; Pro-Vice-Chancellor, 1975–79. Vis. Prof., Yale Univ., 1966. Mem., Inst. for Advanced Study, Princeton, NJ, 1964–65, 1975, 1983–84. Chm., Govt Wkg Pty to advise on Management of Schs in NI, 1979 (Astin Report). Vice Pres., Roman Soc., 1977. MRIA 1973. *Publications:* The Lex Annalis before Sulla, 1958; Scipio Aemilianus, 1967; Cato the Censor, 1978; (ed jtly) 2nd edn Cambridge Ancient History, Vol. VII(I), 1984, Vol. VII(II), 1989, Vol. VIII, 1989; articles in learned jls. *Recreations:* the arts generally, with special interest in opera and ballet. *Address:* Queen's University of Belfast, Belfast BT7 1NN. *T:* Belfast (0232) 245133. *Died 3 June 1991.*

ASTLEY, Sir Francis Jacob Dugdale, 6th Bt, *cr* 1821, of Everleigh, Wiltshire; Head of Classics Department, The Atlantic College, St Donat's Castle, Glamorgan, 1962–69, retired; *b* 26 Oct. 1908; *s* of Rev. Anthony Aylmer Astley (6th *s* of 2nd Bt) and 2nd wife, Margaret Lily (*d* 1948), 2nd *d* of Rev. Francis Harcourt Gooch; *S* kinsman 1943; *m* 1934, Brita Margareta Josefina, *d* of late Karl Nyström, Stockholm; one *d. Educ:* Marlborough; Trinity Coll., Oxford. Lectr in Classics, Cairo Univ., 1936–40; Field Security Officer, Captain, 1940–46; Sen. Lectr, University Coll. of Ghana, 1948–61. *Heir:* none. *Address:* Heath Mount, Rake, Liss, Hants GU33 7PG.
Died 25 March 1994 (ext).

ATKINSON, Colin Ronald Michael, CBE 1989; Principal, Millfield Schools, Somerset, 1986–90 (Headmaster, Millfield School, 1971–86, Acting Headmaster, 1969–70, Governor since 1977); Chairman, HTV West, since 1988; *b* 23 July 1931; *s* of R. and E. Atkinson; *m* 1957, Shirley Angus; two *s* one *d. Educ:* Hummersknott, Darlington, Co. Durham; Durham Univ. (BA); Queen's Univ., Belfast (BA); Loughborough Coll. of Educn. MEd Univ. of Bath,

1977. Served 5th Fusiliers (Northumberland) in Kenya, 1954–56. The Friends' School, Great Ayton, 1956–58; Haughton School, Darlington, 1958–60; Millfield, 1960–. West of England Hockey and Chief Divl coach, 1965–69; Founder and former Member: Nat. Hockey Coaching Cttee; Nat. Cricket Coaching Cttee, 1967–71; Chm., Phys. Educn Cttee of Schools Council, 1974–79; former Minister for Sport and Recreation's Nominee for SW Council for Sport and Recreation. Chairman: Hillside Property Co. Ltd, 1982–; Edington School Ltd, 1974–; Shapwick Senior School Ltd, 1984–; Dir, Millfield School, 1977–; Vice-Chm., HTV Group, 1988–91. Member: TCCB (Chm., Discipline Cttee, 1981–87; Chm., Marketing Cttee, 1987–); Cricket Council of UK. President: Somerset CCC; Somerset Schools Cricket Assoc.; Somerset Old Players' Assoc. *Publications:* An Experiment in Closed Circuit TV at Millfield School, 1970; various articles. *Recreations:* County Representation in various sports; Captain Somerset CCC XI, 1965–67 and County Hockey XI, 1963–65; latterly a bad golfer. *Address:* The Barn, 1 Bove Town, Glastonbury, Somerset. *Clubs:* East India, MCC, Free Foresters, I Zingari. *Died 25 June 1991.*

ATKINSON, Leslie, CMG 1965; OBE 1961; Managing Director, Leslie Atkinson Pty Ltd, 1960; Member of Export Development Council, Sydney, 1959; *b* 11 Jan. 1913; *s* of J. Atkinson; *m* 1935, Ellen, *d* of J. Kinsey; one *s* one *d. Educ:* Wollongong Technical Sch. Controller, Nock and Kirby Ltd, 1943–49, Associate Dir, 1949–53; Dir and General Manager, Carr and Elliott, 1953–59. Pres., Sydney Junior Chamber of Commerce, 1946–47; Vice-Pres. and Hon. Treasurer, Sydney Chamber of Commerce, 1949–53 (Pres., 1953–54, 1957–58); Vice-Pres., Associated Chambers of Commerce of the Commonwealth of Australia, 1956–57 (Pres., 1964–65). Mem. of Standing Cttee, NSW Methodist Conference, 1957–62. *Address:* 47 Woniora Road, Hurstville, NSW 2220, Australia. *Died 4 Jan. 1994.*

ATKINSON, Prof. Richard John Copland, CBE 1979; MA; FSA 1946; Professor of Archaeology, University College, Cardiff, 1958–83, then Emeritus; *b* 22 Jan. 1920; *e s* of Roland Cecil Atkinson and Alice Noel Herbert Atkinson (*née* Wright); *m* 1st, 1942, Hester Renée Marguerite Cobb (*d* 1981); three *s*; 2nd, 1981, Judith Marion O'Kelly. *Educ:* Sherborne School; Magdalen College, Oxford. Asst Keeper, Department of Antiquities, Ashmolean Museum, Oxford, 1944–49; Lectr in Prehistoric Archæology, Univ. of Edinburgh, 1949–58; Dep. Principal, UC Cardiff, 1970–74. Member: Ancient Monuments Board for Wales, 1959–86; Cttee of Enquiry into Arrangements for Protection of Field Monuments, 1966–68; Science-Based Archaeology Cttee, SRC, 1977–81 (UGC Assessor, SERC, 1981–86); Royal Commission: on Ancient and Historical Monuments in Wales, 1963–86 (Chm., 1984–86); on Historical Monuments (England), 1968–86 (acting Chm., 1984); UGC, 1973–82 (Vice Chm., 1976–77; Chm., Arts Sub-cttee, 1978–82). Vice-President: Prehistoric Society, 1963–67; Council for British Archæology, 1970–73 (Hon. Sec., 1964–70); Dir, BBC Silbury Hill project, 1967–70; Chm., York Minster Excavation Cttee, 1975–86. *Publications:* Field Archæology, 1946; Stonehenge, 1956; Stonehenge and Avebury, 1959; Archæology, History and Science, 1960; Stonehenge and Neighbouring Monuments, 1979; The Prehistoric Temples of Stonehenge and Avebury, 1980; articles in archæological journals. *Recreation:* reading. *Address:* Warren House, Mountain Road, Pentyrch, Cardiff CF4 8QP.
Died 10 Oct. 1994.

ATKINSON, William Christopher; Stevenson Professor of Hispanic Studies in University of Glasgow, 1932–72; Director, Institute of Latin-American Studies, 1966–72; *b*

Belfast, 9 Aug. 1902; *s* of Robert Joseph Atkinson; *m* 1928, Evelyn Lucy (*d* 1990), *d* of C. F. Wakefield, Hampstead; one *s* three *d*. *Educ:* Univs of Belfast and Madrid. Lectr in Spanish at Armstrong Coll., Newcastle upon Tyne, 1926–32. Hon. Sec., Modern Humanities Research Assoc., 1929–36; Head of Spanish and Portuguese sections, Foreign Research and Press Service of Royal Institute of International Affairs, 1939–43; Visiting British Council Lecturer to Latin America, 1946, 1960, 1971; Hon. Prof. National Univ. of Colombia, 1946; Chm. 1st Scottish cultural delegation to USSR, 1954; Carnegie Research Fellow visiting US Univs, 1955; Member, Hispanic Society of America, 1955 (Corresp. Mem., 1937); Rockefeller Fellow visiting Latin-American Univs, 1957; Visiting Prof. of Portuguese Studies, University Coll. of Rhodesia and Nyasaland, 1963. Commander, Order of Prince Henry the Navigator, Portugal, 1972. *Publications:* Spain, A Brief History, 1934; The Lusiads of Camoens, 1952; The Remarkable Life of Don Diego, 1958; A History of Spain and Portugal, 1960; The Conquest of New Granada, 1961; The Happy Captive, 1977; contributions to Encyclopædia Britannica, learned periodicals and reviews, and to composite works on Spanish and Portuguese studies. *Recreations:* travel, tramping. *Address:* 361 Albert Drive, Glasgow G41 5PH. *T:* 041–427 6173.   *Died 19 Sept. 1992.*

ATTLEE, 2nd Earl, *cr* 1955; **Martin Richard Attlee;** Viscount Prestwood, 1955; Chairman, Keith Wilden Public Relations Ltd; *b* 10 Aug. 1927; *o s* of 1st Earl Attlee, KG, OM, CH, PC, FRS, and Violet Helen (*d* 1964), *d* of H. E. Millar; *S* father, 1967; *m* 1st, 1955, Anne Barbara (marr. diss. 1988), *er d* of late James Henderson, CBE, Bath, Somerset; one *s* one *d*; 2nd, 1988, Margaret Deane Gouriet, *o d* of late Geoffrey George Gouriet, CBE, Hampton Court, Surrey. *Educ:* Millfield Coll.; Southampton University Coll. (later Southampton Univ.). MIPR 1964. Served in Merchant Navy, 1945–50. Active Mem. Hon. Artillery Company, 1951–55. Asst PRO, Southern Region, British Rail, 1970–76. Founder Mem., SDP, 1981; SDP spokesman on transport (excluding aviation) and on maritime affairs, House of Lords, 1984–89; SDP Dep. Whip, House of Lords, 1988–89. Mem., H of L All Party Defence Study Gp. Contested (SDP) Hampshire Central, European Parlt, Dec. 1988. Pres., Nat. Assoc. Industries for the Blind and Disabled Inc. *Publication:* Bluff Your Way in PR, 1971. *Recreations:* writing, DIY. *Heir: s* Viscount Prestwood, *b* 3 Oct. 1956. *Address:* 1 Cadet Way, Church Crookham, Aldershot, Hants GU13 0UG. *T:* Aldershot (0252) 628007. *Clubs:* Pathfinders', Press.   *Died 27 July 1991.*

ATTWELL, Rt Rev. Arthur Henry; Assistant Bishop of Blackburn, since 1988; *b* 5 Aug. 1920; *s* of Henry John and Kate Attwell; *m* 1982, Muriel Isobel Hesson. *Educ:* various state schools; Leeds Univ. (BA 1941); College of the Resurrection, Mirfield. BD 1947, MTh 1958, MA 1972 all London. Deacon 1943, priest 1944; Curate of St George, Wolverton, 1943–45; Curate of Wigan, 1945–51; Sub-warden of St Paul's Coll., Grahamstown, S Africa, 1951–52; Dean of Kimberley, S Africa, 1952–60; Rector of Workington, Cumberland, 1960–72; Hon. Canon of Carlisle, 1964–72, 1978–83; Rural Dean of Cockermouth and Workington, 1960–72; Canon Residentiary of Carlisle Cathedral, 1972–78; Vicar of St John's, Windermere, 1978–82; Archdeacon of Westmorland and Furness, 1978–83; Dir, Carlisle Diocesan Training Inst., 1978–83; Bishop of Sodor and Man, 1983–88. Proctor in Convocation, 1965–82; Exam. Chaplain to Bishop of Carlisle, 1972–83. *Recreation:* travel. *Address:* 60 Emesgate Lane, Silverdale, Lancs LA5 0RN. *T:* Silverdale (0524) 701008.   *Died 2 March 1991.*

AUBREY-FLETCHER, Sir John (Henry Lancelot), 7th Bt *cr* 1782, of Clea Hall, Cumberland; a Recorder of the Crown Court, 1972–74; Metropolitan Magistrate, 1959–71; *b* 22 Aug. 1912; *s* of Major Sir Henry Aubrey-Fletcher, 6th Bt, CVO, DSO, and Mary Augusta (*d* 1963), *e d* of Rev. R. W. Chilton; *S* father, 1969; *m* 1939, Diana Fynvola, *d* of Lieut-Col Arthur Egerton (killed in action, 1915), Coldstream Guards, and late Mrs Robert Bruce; one *s* (one *d* decd). *Educ:* Eton; New Coll., Oxford. Called to Bar, 1937. Served War of 1939–45, Grenadier Guards, reaching rank of temp. Lieut-Col and leaving Army with rank of Hon. Major. Dep. Chm., Bucks Quarter Sessions, 1959–71. High Sheriff, Bucks, 1961. *Heir: s* Henry Egerton Aubrey-Fletcher [*b* 27 Nov. 1945; *m* 1976, Roberta Sara, *d* of late Major Robert Buchanan, Blackpark Cottage, Evanton, Ross-shire, and of Mrs Ogden White; three *s*]. *Address:* The Gate House, Chilton, Aylesbury, Bucks HP18 9LR. *T:* Long Crendon (0844) 347.
     Died 19 June 1992.

AUERBACH, Charlotte, PhD, DSc; FRS 1957; FRSE; Professor of Genetics in the University of Edinburgh (Institute of Animal Genetics), 1967, Emeritus 1969 (Lecturer, 1947–57; Reader, 1957–67); *b* 14 May 1899. *Educ:* Edinburgh Univ. (PhD, DSc). Did pioneering work on the chemical induction of mutations. Hon. Mem., Genetics Soc., Japan, 1966; Foreign Mem., Kongelige Danske Videnskabernes Selskab, 1968; Foreign Associate, Nat. Acad. of Sciences, USA, 1970. Hon. Dr: Leiden, 1975; Bloomington, Indiana, 1985; Hon. ScD: Dublin, 1977; Cambridge, 1977. Darwin Medal, Royal Soc., 1976. *Publications:* Genetics in the Atomic Age, 1956; The Science of Genetics, 1961; Mutation Pt 1–Methods, 1962; Heredity, 1965; Mutation Research, 1976; papers in various genetical journals. *Address:* Tyne Lodge, 131 Grange Loan, Edinburgh EH9 2HB.
     Died 17 March 1994.

AUGER, Pierre Victor; Grand Croix, Legion of Honour; Director-General European Space Research Organisation (ESRO), 1962–67, retired; Professor, Faculty of Sciences, University of Paris, 1937–69; *b* 14 May 1899; *s* of Victor E. Auger, Prof., Univ. of Paris, and Eugénie Blanchet; *m* 1921, Suzanne Motteau; two *d*. *Educ:* Ecole Normale Supérieure, Paris; Univ. of Paris. Université de Paris (Faculté des Sciences): Asst, 1927; Chef de Travaux, 1932; Maître de Conférences, 1937; Research Associate, Univ. of Chicago, 1941–43; Head of Physics Div., joint Anglo-Canadian research project on atomic energy, 1942–44; Dir of Higher Education, Min. of Education, France, 1945–48; Mem. Exec. Board of UNESCO, 1946–48; Membre du comité de l'Energie Atomique, France, 1946–48; Dir, Natural Sciences Dept, UNESCO, 1948–59; Special Consultant, UNO and UNESCO, 1959–60; Chm., French Cttee on Space Research, 1960–62. Mem., French Academy of Sciences, 1977. Feltrinelli International Prize, 1961; Kalinga Internat. Prize, 1972; Gaede-Langmuir Award, 1979. FRSA. *Publications:* Rayons cosmiques, 1941; L'Homme microscopique, 1952; Current Trends in Scientific Research, 1961; scientific papers on physics (X-rays, neutrons, cosmic rays), 1923–; papers on philosophy of science, 1949–. *Address:* 12 rue Emile Faguet, 75014 Paris, France. *T:* 45409634.   *Died 24 Dec. 1993.*

AUGUSTINE, Fennis Lincoln; High Commissioner for Grenada in London, 1979–84; *b* 22 April 1932; *s* of late Mr Augustine and of Festina Joseph; *m* 1973, Oforiwa Augustine; one *s* one *d*. *Educ:* London Univ. (LLB); Ruskin Coll., Oxford (Labour Studies). Called to the Bar, Inner Temple, 1972. *Recreations:* cricket, music. *Address:* c/o Augustine & Augustine Chambers, Lucas Street, St George's, Grenada.   *Died 23 Dec. 1993.*

AUSTIN, Prof. Lloyd James, FBA 1968; Emeritus Fellow of Jesus College, Cambridge; Emeritus Drapers Professor of French, University of Cambridge; *b* 4 Nov. 1915; *s* of late J. W. A. Austin and Mrs J. E. Austin (*née* Tymms), Melbourne, Australia; *m* 1939, Jeanne Françoise Guérin, Rouen, France; three *s* one *d. Educ:* Melbourne Church of England Grammar Sch.; Univ. of Melbourne; Univ. of Paris. French Government Scholar, Paris, 1937–40; Lecturer in French, Univ. of Melbourne, 1940–42. Active Service as Lieut (Special Branch) RANVR, SW Pacific area, 1942–45. Lecturer in French, Univ. of Melbourne, 1945–47; Lecturer in French, Univ. of St Andrews, 1947–51; Research work in Paris, 1951–55; Fellow of Jesus Coll., Cambridge, 1955–56, 1961–80; Professor of Modern French Literature, Univ. of Manchester, 1956–61; Lecturer in French, Univ. of Cambridge, 1961–66, Reader, 1966–67, Drapers Prof. of French, 1967–80; Librarian, Jesus Coll., Cambridge, 1965–68, 1972–73. Hon. Sen. Res. Fellow, Inst. of Romance Studies, Univ. of London, 1990. Herbert F. Johnson Visiting Prof., Inst. for Research in the Humanities, Univ. of Wisconsin, 1962–63; Mem., Editorial Bd, French Studies, 1964–80, Gen. Editor, 1967–80, Mem. Adv. Bd, 1980–; Pres., Assoc. Internat. des Etudes Françaises, 1969–72 (Vice-Pres., 1966–69). Hon. FAHA 1985; Hon. Member: Soc. for French Studies, 1980–; Société d'Histoire Littéraire de la France, 1980; Mem., Acad. Royale de Langue et de Littérature Françaises de Belgique, 1980. Docteur *hc* Paris-Sorbonne, 1973. Prix Henri Mondor, Acad. française, 1981; Prix internat. des amitiés françaises, Soc. des Poètes français, 1982. Chevalier de l'Ordre des Arts et des Lettres, 1971; Officier de l'Ordre National du Mérite, 1976. *Publications:* Paul Bourget, 1940; (ed) Paul Valéry: Le Cimetière marin, 1954; L'Univers poétique de Baudelaire, 1956; (ed with E. Vinaver and G. Rees) Studies in Modern French Literature, presented to P. Mansell-Jones, 1961; (ed with H. Mondor) Les Gossips de Mallarmé, 1962; (ed with H. Mondor) Stéphane Mallarmé: Correspondance (1871–1898), 11 vols, 1965–85; (ed) Baudelaire: L'Art romantique, 1968; (contrib.) The Symbolist Movement in the Literature of European Languages, 1982; Poetic Principles and Practice, 1987; (ed) Mallarmé: Poésies, 1989; Essais sur Mallarmé; contrib. to French Studies, Modern Languages, Modern Language Review, Forum for Modern Language Studies, Bulletin of the John Rylands Library, Mercure de France, Nouvelle Revue Française, Revue des Sciences Humaines, Revue d'Histoire littéraire de la France, Revue de littérature comparée, Romanic Review, Studi francesi, Synthèses, Revue de l'Université de Bruxelles, L'Esprit créateur, Comparative Literature Studies, Wingspread Lectures in the Humanities, Encyclopædia Britannica, Yale French Studies, Meanjin Quarterly, Australian Jl for French Studies, AUMLA, Quadrant, etc. *Recreations:* watching cricket, tennis, looking at pictures, listening to music, travel. *Address:* 2 Park Lodge, Park Terrace, Cambridge CB1 1JJ. *T:* Cambridge (01223) 359630; Jesus College, Cambridge.   *Died 30 Dec. 1994.*

AUSTIN, Sir Michael (Trescawen), 5th Bt *cr* 1894, of Red Hill, Castleford, W Riding; General Commissioner of Inland Revenue, 1965–86; *b* 27 Aug. 1927; *s* of Sir William Ronald Austin, 4th Bt and Dorothy Mary (*d* 1957), *d* of L. A. Bidwell, FRCS; *S* father, 1989; *m* 1951, Bridget Dorothea Patricia, *d* of late Francis Farrell; three *d. Educ:* Downside. Served War of 1939–45 with RNVR. MFH for 10 years. *Heir: b* Anthony Leonard Austin [*b* 30 Sept. 1930; *m* 1st, 1956, Mary Annette (marr. diss. 1966), *d* of Richard Kelly; two *s* one *d*; 2nd, 1967, Aileen

Morrison Hall, *d* of William Hall Stewart; one *d*]. *Address:* Goldburn, Okehampton, Devon EX20 3BD.
         Died 3 Aug. 1995.

AXWORTHY, Geoffrey (John); Artistic Director of Sherman Theatre, University College, Cardiff, 1970–88, retired; *b* Plymouth, 10 Aug. 1923; *s* of William Henry Axworthy and Gladys Elizabeth Kingcombe; *m* 1st, 1951, Irene Dickinson (*d* 1976); two *s* one *d*; 2nd, 1977, Caroline Griffiths; one *s* one *d. Educ:* Exeter Coll., Oxford (MA). On staff of: Univ. of Baghdad, 1951–56; Univ. of Ibadan, Nigeria, 1956–67 (founded Travelling Theatre, 1961; first Director, Sch. of Drama, 1962–67); Principal, Central School of Speech and Drama, London, 1967–70. *Address:* 22 The Walk, West Grove, Cardiff CF2 3AF. *T:* Cardiff (0222) 490696.   *Died 16 April 1992.*

AYKROYD, Sir Cecil William, 2nd Bt, *cr* 1929, of Birstwith Hall, Hampsthwaite, co. York; *b* 23 April 1905; *e s* of Sir Frederic Alfred Aykroyd, 1st Bt, Strathallan Castle, Perthshire, and Fairlight Hall, near Hastings, and late Lily May, *e d* of Sir James Roberts, 1st Bt, LLD; *S* father 1949; unmarried. *Educ:* Charterhouse; Jesus Coll., Cambridge. BA 1926. Dir, Nat. Provincial Bank Ltd, 1958–69 (Dir Bradford and District Bd, 1946–69). *Recreations:* fishing, shooting. *Heir: nephew* James Alexander Frederic Aykroyd [*b* 6 Sept. 1943; *m* 1973, Jennifer, *d* of Frederick William Marshall; two *d*]. *Address:* Birstwith Hall, near Harrogate, North Yorks HG3 2JW. *T:* Harrogate (0423) 770250.   *Died 23 June 1993.*

AYLESTONE, Baron *cr* 1967 (Life Peer); **Herbert William Bowden,** CH 1975; CBE 1953; PC 1962; Chairman, Independent Broadcasting Authority (formerly Independent Television Authority), 1967–75; *b* 20 Jan. 1905; *m* 1st, 1928, Louisa Grace (decd), *d* of William Brown, Cardiff; one *d*; 2nd, 1993, Vicki Clayton. RAF, 1941–45. Leicester City Council, 1938–45. MP (Lab) S Leicester, 1945–50, S-W Div. of Leicester, 1950–67; PPS to Postmaster-Gen., 1947–49; Asst Govt Whip, 1949–50; a Lord Comr of the Treasury, 1950–51; Dep. Chief Opposition Whip, 1951–55; Chief Opposition Whip, 1955–64; Lord Pres. of the Council and Leader of the House of Commons, 1964–66; Secretary of State for Commonwealth Affairs, 1966–67; joined SDP, 1981; Dep. Speaker, House of Lords, 1984–92; joined Lib. Dems, 1992. Gold Medal, RTS, 1975. *Address:* c/o House of Lords, SW1A 0PW.   *Died 30 April 1994.*

AYLING, Air Vice-Marshal Richard Cecil, CB 1965; CBE 1961 (OBE 1948); Adjudicator, Immigration Appeals, 1970–88; *b* 7 June 1916; *s* of A. C. Ayling, LDS, Norwood, London; *m* 1st, 1941, Patricia Doreen Wright (*d* 1966); one *s* one *d*; 2nd, 1971, Virginia, *d* of Col Frank Davis, Northwood; two *d. Educ:* Dulwich Coll. No 3(F) Sqdn, 1936–39; served RNZAF, 1940–43; Comd No 51 Sqdn (Bomber Comd), 1944; Station Comdr, Bomber Comd, 1944–45; Staff Coll., 1945; Staff of Central Bomber Estabt, 1946–48; Air Staff (Plans) Far East, 1948–50; Air Min. (OR1 and Dep. Dir Policy Air Staff), 1951–54; Station Comdr, Bomber Comd, 1954–58; Asst Chief of Defence Staff, Min. of Defence, 1958–59; Dir of Organisation (Estabts), Air Min., 1960–61; SASO, Flying Training Command, 1962–65; Min. of Defence, 1965–66; AOA, RAF Air Support (formerly Transport) Comd, 1966–69; retd, 1969. *Recreations:* ski-ing, sailing, gardening. *Address:* Buckler's Spring, Buckler's Hard, Beaulieu, Hants SO42 7XA. *T:* Buckler's Hard (01590) 616204. *Club:* Royal Lymington Yacht.
         Died 27 June 1995.

B

BABER, Ernest George, CBE 1987; Judge of the Supreme Court of Hong Kong, 1973–86; *b* 18 July 1924; *s* of late Walter Averette Baber and Kate Marion (*née* Pratt); *m* 1960, Dr Flora Marion, *y d* of late Dr Raymond Bisset Smith and Mrs Jean Gemmell Bisset Smith (*née* Howie); one *s* two *d*. *Educ:* Brentwood; Emmanuel Coll., Cambridge (MA, LLM). Served RN, 1942–47 (Lieut (S)). Called to Bar, Lincoln's Inn, 1951. Resident Magistrate, Uganda, 1954–62; Magistrate and President of Tenancy Tribunal, Hong Kong, 1962; Senior Magistrate, 1963–67; District Judge, 1967–73. *Recreations:* children, music, walking. *Address:* 18 Cumnor Hill, Oxford OX2 9HA. *Club:* Hong Kong (Hong Kong).
Died 7 Jan. 1994.

BACK, Kathleen, (Mrs J. H. Back); *see* Harrison, Kathleen.

BACKHOUSE, Jonathan; retired; *b* 16 March 1907; 2nd *s* of late Lt-Col Miles Roland Charles Backhouse, DSO, TD, and Olive Backhouse; *m* 1934, Alice Joan Woodroffe (*d* 1984); two *s* one *d*. *Educ:* RNC Dartmouth. Served War of 1939–45, Royal Artillery. Merchant Bank, 1924–28; Stock Exchange, 1928–50; Merchant Bank, 1950–70. *Recreations:* shooting, etc. *Address:* Breewood Hall, Great Horkesley, Colchester, Essex CO6 4BW. *T:* Colchester (0206) 271260. *Club:* Royal Thames Yacht.
Died 7 Dec. 1993.

BACON, Baroness *cr* 1970 (Life Peer), of Leeds and Normanton; **Alice Martha Bacon,** CBE 1953; PC 1966; DL; *b* 10 Sept. 1909; *d* of late County Councillor Benjamin Bacon, miner. *Educ:* elementary schs, Normanton, Yorks; Normanton Girls' High Sch.; Stockwell Training Coll.; external student of London Univ. Subsequently schoolmistress. MP (Lab) NE Leeds, 1945–55, SE Leeds, 1955–70; Minister of State: Home Office, 1964–67; Dept of Educn and Science, 1967–70. Mem. National Executive Cttee of Labour Party, 1941–70; Chm., Labour Party, 1950–51. DL W Yorkshire, 1974. Hon. LLD Leeds, 1972. *Address:* 53 Snydale Road, Normanton, West Yorks WF6 1NY. *T:* Wakefield (0924) 893229.
Died 24 March 1993.

BACON, Francis; artist; *b* Dublin, 28 Oct. 1909; English parents. Self-taught. Exhibited furniture and rugs of his own design, Queensbury Mews studio; began painting, 1929; destroyed nearly all earlier works, 1941–44; rep. GB with Ben Nicholson and Lucian Freud, 27th Venice Biennale, 1954. *One-man exhibitions:* Hanover Gall., London, 1949, 1950, 1951, 1952, 1954, 1957, 1959; Durlacher Bros, NY 1953; ICA, 1955; Galerie Rive Droite, Paris, 1957; Galleria Galatea, Turin, 1958, 1970; Marlborough Fine Art, London, 1960, 1963, 1965, 1967, 1983, 1985, 1989; Tate Gall., 1962 (retrospective) (travelled to Mannheim, Turin, Zürich, Amsterdam, 1962), 1985 (retrospective) (travelled to Stuttgart, Berlin, 1985–86); Solomon R. Guggenheim Mus., NY, 1963 (retrospective) (travelled to Chicago, Houston, 1963); Kunstverein, Hamburg, 1965 (retrospective) (travelled to Stockholm, Dublin, 1965); Galerie Maeght, Paris, 1966, 1984, (Lelong Gall.) 1987; Oberes Schloss, Siegen, 1967; Marlborough Gall., NY, 1968, 1980, 1984, 1987, 1990; Grand Palais, Paris, 1971 (retrospective) (travelled to Düsseldorf, 1972); Metrop. Mus. of Art, NY, 1975; Marlborough Gall., Zürich, 1975; Musée Cantini,

Marseilles, 1976; Galerie Claude Bernard, Paris, 1977; Mus. de Arte Moderno, Mexico, 1977 (travelled to Caracas, 1977–78); Fundación Juan March, Madrid, 1977 (travelled to Barcelona, 1978); Nat. Mus. of Modern Art, Tokyo, 1983 (retrospective) (travelled to Kyoto, Nagoya, 1983); Galerie Beyeler, Basle, 1987; Central Hall of Artists, Moscow, 1988; Marlborough Gall., Tokyo, 1988–89; Hirshhorn Mus., Washington, 1989–90 (retrospective) (travelled to LA, NY, 1990); Tate Gall., Liverpool, 1990–91. *Important works include:* Three Studies for Figures at the Base of a Crucifixion, 1944; Figure in a Landscape, Fig. Study II, 1945–46; Painting, 1946; Head I, 1948; Two Figures, 1953; Study after Velasquez's Portrait of Pope Innocent X, 1953; Man in Blue, 1954; Study for a Portrait of Van Gogh, 1957; Three Studies for a Crucifixion, 1962; Three Figures in a Room, 1964; Crucifixion, 1965; Triptych inspired by T.S. Eliot's poem, Sweeney Agonistes, 1967; Portrait of Isabel Rawsthorne Standing in a Street in Soho, 1967; Triptych, 1971, 1972, 1973, 1974; Landscape, 1978; Jet of Water, 1978; Triptych inspired by the Oresteia of Aeschylus, 1981; Study of the Human Body, 1982; Study for Self Portrait—Triptych, 1985–86; Second Version of Triptych 1944, 1988. Paintings acquired by major museum collections throughout the world. Rubens Prize, 1967; Painting Prize, Carnegie Inst., Pittsburgh, 1967. *Address:* c/o Marlborough Fine Art, 6 Albemarle Street, W1X 4BY.
Died 28 April 1992.

BACON, Francis Thomas, OBE 1967; FRS 1973; FEng 1976; consultant on fuel cells, retired; *b* 21 Dec. 1904; 2nd *s* of T. W. Bacon, Ramsden Hall, Billericay; *m* 1934, Barbara Winifred, *y d* of G. K. Papillon, Manor House, Barrasford; one *s* one *d* (and one *s* decd). *Educ:* Eton Coll.; Trinity Coll., Cambridge. CEng, MIMechE 1947. With C. A. Parsons & Co. Ltd, Newcastle-on-Tyne, 1925–40 (i/c production of silvered glass reflectors, 1935–39); experimental work on hydrogen/oxygen fuel cell at King's Coll., London, for Merz & McLellan, 1940–41; Temp. Expmtl Officer at HM Anti-Submarine Experimental Estbt, Fairlie, 1941–46; expmtl work on hydrogen/oxygen fuel cell at Cambridge Univ., 1946–56 (for ERA); Consultant to: NRDC on fuel cells at Marshall of Cambridge Ltd, 1956–62; Energy Conversion Ltd, Basingstoke, 1962–71; Fuel Cells Ltd, AERE, 1971–72; Johnson Matthey PLC, 1984–. British Assoc. Lecture, 1971; Bruno Breyer Meml Lecture and Medal, Royal Aust. Chem. Inst., 1976. S. G. Brown Award and Medal, Royal Soc., 1965; British Silver Medal, RAeS, 1969; Churchill Gold Medal, Soc. of Engineers, 1972; Melchett Medal, Inst. of Fuel, 1972; Vittorio de Nora Diamond Shamrock Award and Prize, Electrochemical Soc. Inc., 1978; (first) Sir William Grove Meml Medal, Royal Instn, 1991. Hon. FSE 1972. Hon. DSc Newcastle upon Tyne, 1980. *Publications:* chapter 5 in Fuel Cells (ed G. J. Young), 1960; chapter 4 in Fuel Cells (ed W. Mitchell), 1963; papers on fuel cells for World Power Conf., Royal Instn, Nature, two UN Confs, Amer. Inst. of Chem. Eng, Inst. of Fuel, Electrochimica Acta, Royal Soc., 5th World Hydrogen Energy Conf. *Recreations:* hill walking, music, photography, gardening. *Address:* Trees, 34 High Street, Little Shelford, Cambridge CB2 5ES. *T:* Cambridge (0223) 843116. *Club:* Athenæum.
Died 24 May 1992.

BADENOCH, Alec William, MA, MD, ChM, FRCS; *b* 23 June 1903; *s* of late John Alexander Badenoch, chartered accountant, Banff; *m* 1942, Jean McKinnell Brunton, MB, ChB (Edinburgh), *d* of late Alexander Brunton; two *s* (and one *s* decd). *Educ:* Banff Academy; Aberdeen Univ. Pres. Student Representation Council of Scotland, 1926. Served RAFVR, 1937–45, as Temp. Wing Comdr, i/c Surgical Divs, RAF Hosps Rauceby, Wroughton and St Athan; Surgeon: Royal Hosp. of St Bartholomew, 1947–68; St Peter's Hosp. for Stone and other Urological Diseases, 1946–68; Visiting Urologist: Royal Masonic Hosp., 1950–70; King Edward VII's Hosp. for Officers, 1947–77; Visiting Professor: Cairo, 1962; Dallas, Texas, 1967; Guest Lectr, Amer. Urological Assoc., 1968; Hon. Civilian Consultant in Urology to RAF. Hunterian Prof., RCS, 1948; Hon. Fellow, British Assoc. of Urological Surgeons (Pres., 1968–69; St Peter's Medal, 1974); Hon. FRSocMed (Hon. Treasurer, 1971–76; Hon. Mem. and Past Pres. Section of Urology); Hon. Fellow, Hunterian Soc. (Pres. 1949; Vice-Pres. and Orator, 1957); Member: BMA (Vice-Pres. Section of Urology, 1955); Internat. Soc. of Urology (Treas. London Congress, 1964; British Delegate, 1966–74; Hon. Fellow); (Founder Mem.) Cttee of Management, European Soc. of Urology, 1972; Council, RCS, 1963–71 (Patron, 1975); GMC, 1966–71; GDC, 1969–71. Mem., Bd of Governors, St Peter's Hosp. Gp, 1948–73; Chm., Management Cttee, Inst. of Urology, 1968–72. Hon. Mem. Peruvian, American and French Urological Assocs; Corresp. Mem., Mexican Urological Assoc. and Amer. Assoc. of Genito Urinary Surgeons. Chm., Editorial Bd, British Jl of Urology, 1969–72 (Treasurer, 1961–67); Founding Jt Editor, European Jl of Urology, 1974–78. *Publications:* Manual of Urology, 1953, 2nd edn 1974; contrib. to British Surgery, Modern Operative Surgery, and Modern Trends in Urology; articles in scientific jls. *Recreations:* gardening, music, swimming. *Address:* Church Hayes, Lea, Malmesbury, Wilts SN16 9PF. *T:* Malmesbury (0666) 822289. *Club:* Royal Air Force. *Died 16 Feb. 1991.*

BADHAM, Leonard; Vice Chairman, J. Lyons & Company Ltd, 1984–87; Director, Allied-Lyons PLC (formerly Allied Breweries), 1978–87; *b* 10 June 1923; *s* of John Randall Badham and Emily Louise Badham; *m* 1944, Joyce Rose Lowrie; two *d*. *Educ:* Wandsworth Grammar Sch. Commnd E Surrey Regt, 1943; Royal W Kent Regt, 5th Indian Div., 1944–46; SO II Stats, Burma Comd, 1946–47. J. Lyons & Co. Ltd: Management Trainee, 1939; Main Bd, 1965; Chief Comptroller, 1965; Tech. and Commercial Co-ordinator, 1967; Exec. Dir, Finance and Admin, 1970; Asst Gp Man. Dir, 1971; Dep. Gp Man. Dir, 1975; Man Dir, 1977. Gov., S Thames Coll., 1990–. FHCIMA; CIMgt. *Recreations:* bridge, gardening. *Address:* 26 Vicarage Drive, East Sheen, SW14 8RX. *T:* 0181-876 4373. *Died 11 June 1992.*

BAERLEIN, Richard Edgar; Racing Writer: The Observer, since 1963; The Guardian, since 1968; *b* 15 Sept. 1915; *s* of Edgar Baerlein and Dorothy Baerlein (*née* Dixon); *m* 1948, Lillian Laurette de Tankerville Chamberlain. *Educ:* Eton; Sidney Sussex Coll., Cambridge. Sporting Chronicle, 1936–39. Served RAF, Sqdn Ldr, 1940–47 (despatches). Racing writer, Evening Standard, 1947–57; started farm and stud, 1948; Racing Manager to Basil Mavrolem. *Publications:* Nijinsky, 1972; Shergar, 1983; Joe Mercer, 1987. *Recreations:* shooting, golf. *Address:* Shergar, 2nd Avenue, Summerley, Felpham, near Middleton-on-Sea, West Sussex PO22 7LJ. *Clubs:* Clermont; Sunningdale. *Died 10 March 1995.*

BAILEY, Harold, CMG 1960; Under-Secretary, Department of Trade and Industry, 1970–74, retired; *b* 26 Feb. 1914; *yr s* of late John Bailey and Elizabeth Watson, Preston, Lancashire; *m* 1946, Rosemary Margaret, *d* of Harold and Irene Brown, Shotesham St Mary, Norfolk; two *s* one *d*. *Educ:* Preston Grammar Sch.; Christ Church, Oxford. Asst Principal Air Ministry, 1937; Principal, Min. of Aircraft Production, 1942; served Royal Air Force, 1942–45; Private Sec. to Minister of Supply and Aircraft Production, 1945–47; Asst Sec., 1947; Min. of Supply Rep. and Adviser (Defence Supplies) to UK High Comr, Ottawa, 1953–55; Under-Secretary: Ministry of Supply, 1957; BoT, 1958; British Senior Trade Comr in India, and Economic Adviser to the British High Comr, 1958–63. *Address:* Hollies, Hurstbourne Tarrant, Hants SP11 0AX. *T:* Hurstbourne Tarrant (0126476) 482.
Died 28 May 1995.

BAILEY, Wilfrid; Chairman, Southern Gas Region (formerly Southern Gas Board), 1969–75; chartered accountant; *b* 9 March 1910; *s* of late Harry Bailey and Martha Bailey (*née* Pighills); *m* 1934, Vera (*née* Manchester); two *s* one *d*. *Educ:* Keighley Grammar Sch. Borough Treasurer, Bexley BC, 1945–47; Chief Financial Officer, Crawley Development Corp., 1947–49; Gas Council: Chief Accountant, 1949–58; Secretary, 1958–61; Dep. Chm., Southern Gas Bd, 1961–69. FCA 1935. *Recreations:* cricket, motoring, music, photography, gardening. *Address:* Bramble Way, Clease Way, Compton Down, near Winchester SO21 2AL. *T:* Twyford (0962) 713382. *Died 26 April 1993.*

BAINBRIDGE, Maj.-Gen. Henry, CB 1948; CBE 1944; psc; late Corps of Royal Engineers; *b* 1903; *m* Margaret Letitia (*d* 1976); two *s*. 2nd Lieut Royal Engineers, 1923. Served War of 1939–45, 1939–44 (despatches twice, CBE). Dir of Man-power Planning, War Office, 1949–52; DQMG, War Office, 1952–55, retired 1955. *Address:* Brizlee, Hoe Lane, Peaslake, Surrey GU5 9SW.
Died 12 Sept. 1993.

BAKAR, Datuk Jamaluddin A.; *see* Abu Bakar.

BAKER, Alexander Shelley, CB 1977; OBE 1958; DFC 1944; Assistant Under Secretary of State, Home Office, 1973–77, retired; *b* 5 June 1915; *s* of late Rev. William Shelley Baker and Mrs Winifred Baker, Staines and Stratford E15; *m* 1944, Cynthia, 2nd *d* of late Charles Mould, Great Easton, Leics; two *d*. *Educ:* West Ham Secondary School. Served RAF, 1939–65 (despatches, 1944; 2 citations French Croix de Guerre); comd No 4, 16, 37 and 224 Sqdns and RAF North Front, Gibraltar; retd as Group Captain. Principal, Home Office, 1965; Asst Sec., 1969–73. Reader, Church of England. *Recreations:* gardening, bridge. *Address:* High View, Foxearth, near Sudbury, Suffolk CO10 7JB. *T:* Sudbury (0787) 72548. *Club:* Royal Air Force. *Died 22 Dec. 1992.*

BAKER, Sir (Allan) Ivor, Kt 1972; CBE 1944; JP; DL; Chairman, Baker Perkins Holdings Ltd, 1944–75; *b* 2 June 1908; *s* of late Allan Richard Baker; *m* 1935, Josephine, *d* of late A. M. Harley, KC; three *s* one *d*. *Educ:* Bootham Sch., York; King's Coll., Cambridge; Harvard, USA. Baker Perkins: student apprentice, 1931; Director, 1935; Jt Man. Dir., 1942–67. British Engineers' Assoc.: Mem. Council, 1943–68; Pres., 1960–61; Director: Lloyds Bank Ltd, 1973–79; Lloyds Bank Eastern Region, 1953–73 (Chm., 1973–79); Mitchell Construction Holdings Ltd, 1963–85. Member: Economic Planning Council for East Anglia, 1965–69; Peterborough Development Corp., 1968–78. JP Huntingdon and Peterborough, 1954; High Sheriff, 1968–69, DL 1973, Cambridgeshire. *Recreations:* golf, gardening. *Address:* 214 Thorpe Road, Peterborough PE3 6LW. *T:* Peterborough (0733) 262437.
Died 12 Jan. 1994.

BALDRY, Prof. Harold Caparne; Emeritus Professor of Classics, University of Southampton; *b* 4 March 1907; *s* of William and Gertrude Mary Baldry, Nottingham; *m* 1934, Carina Hetley (*née* Pearson) (*d* 1985); one *s* one *d* (and one *d* decd). *Educ:* Nottingham High Sch.; Trinity Hall, Cambridge (Warr Schol.; MA). Editor Cambridge Review, 1931. Educational Staff, Trinity Hall, Cambridge, 1931–34; Asst Lecturer in Classics, University Coll. of Swansea, 1934–35; Univ. of Cape Town: Lecturer in Classics, 1936–48; Prof. of Classics, 1948–54; Univ. of Southampton: Prof. of Classics, 1954–72; Dean of Faculty of Arts, 1959–62; Dep. Vice-Chancellor, 1963–66; Public Orator, 1959–67. Chm., Council of University Classical Depts, 1969–72; Pres., Orbilian Soc., 1970; Vice-Pres., Classical Assoc., 1972–; Mem., Arts Council of GB, 1973–78 (Chm. Regional Cttee, 1975–78); Chm., Southern Arts Assoc., 1972–74. Hon. DLitt Southampton, 1975. *Publications:* The Classics in the Modern World (an Inaugural Lecture), 1949; Greek Literature for the Modern Reader, 1951; Ancient Utopias (an Inaugural Lecture), 1956; The Unity of Mankind in Greek Thought, 1965; Ancient Greek Literature in its Living Context, 1968; The Greek Tragic Theatre, 1971; The Case for the Arts, 1981; articles and reviews in classical journals. *Address:* 19 Uplands Way, Southampton SO2 1QW. *T:* (0703) 555290. *Died 28 Nov. 1991.*

BALFOUR, Hon. Mark Robin; Chairman: Finglands Services Ltd, since 1981; Light Trades House Ltd, since 1973; *b* 16 July 1927; *s* of 2nd Baron Riverdale and Nancy Marguerite (*d* 1928), *d* of Rear-Adm. Mark Rundle, DSO; *m* 1959, Susan Ann Phillips; one *s* two *d. Educ:* Aysgarth Sch., Yorks; Lisgar Collegiate, Ottawa, Canada; Trinity Coll. Sch., Port Hope, Ont; Millfield Sch.; Rotherham Technical Coll. (Intermediate Cert. in Metallurgy). Served RN, 1944–47. Arthur Balfour & Co. Ltd: Dir, 1955; Manager, London Office, Home and Export, 1957; Asst Man. Dir, 1959; negotiated merger with Darwins Group Ltd, 1960; Man. Dir, Balfour Darwins Ltd, 1961, Chm. 1971–75; following formation of Sheffield Rolling Mills Ltd (consortium of BSC, James Neill subsid., Balfour Darwins Ltd subsid.), 1969, Chm. 1970–74; non-exec. Dir, Special Steels Div., BSC, 1971–73; negotiated sale of Sheffield Rolling Mills Ltd to BSC, 1973; Dir, Overseas Ops, Edgar Allen Balfour Ltd (formed by merger of Balfour Darwins Ltd and Edgar Allen Ltd), 1975–79. British Independent Steel Producers' Association: Mem., Exec. Cttee, 1969–75; Mem., Product Group (Special Steels), 1962–75 (Chm., 1970–71); Mem., Steelmakers' Cttee, 1970–75. Pres., National Fedn of Engineers' Tool Manufrs, 1974–76; Member: EDC for Machine Tools, 1976–78; Council, Fedn of British Hand Tool Manufrs, 1972–77; Econs and Management Cttee, Iron and Steel Inst., 1970–75; Iron and Steel Industry Regional Trng Bd, 1964–68; Sheffield and Dist Br. Cttee, Inst. of Dirs, 1969–77; Council, Sheffield Chamber of Commerce, 1959–93 (Pres., 1978); Australian British Trade Assoc. Council, BOTB, 1975–85; ANZ Trade Adv. Cttee, BOTB, 1975–85. Mem. Council, Yorkshire Cancer Res. Campaign, 1991–. Chm., Ashdell Schs Trust, 1985–. Master, Cutlers' Co. of Hallamshire, 1969–70; Mem., Worshipful Co. of Blacksmiths, 1972–; Freeman, City of London, 1972. High Sheriff, S Yorks, 1986–87. Vice-Consul for Finland in Sheffield, 1962–, Consul, 1994. Order of the Lion, Finland, 1975. Silver Jubilee Medal, 1977. *Recreations:* fishing, shooting. *Address:* Fairways, Saltergate, Bamford, near Sheffield S30 2BE. *T:* Hope Valley (01433) 651314. *Club:* The Club (Sheffield). *Died 30 Sept. 1995.*

BALFOUR, Sir (Robert George) Victor F.; *see* FitzGeorge-Balfour.

BALMER, Sir Joseph (Reginald), Kt 1965; JP; retired insurance official; *b* 22 Sept. 1899; *s* of Joseph Balmer; *m* 1927, Dora, *d* of A. Johnson; no *c. Educ:* King Edward's Grammar Sch., Birmingham. North British and Mercantile Insurance Co. Ltd, 1916–60; National Chairman Guild of Insurance Officials, 1943–47. Pres. Birmingham Borough Labour Party, 1946–54; elected to Birmingham City Council, 1945, 1949, 1952; Alderman, 1952–74; Chairman Finance Cttee, 1955–64; Lord Mayor of Birmingham, 1954–55; Hon. Alderman, 1974; City Magistrate, 1956. Hon. Life Mem. Court, Birmingham Univ.; formerly Governor, King Edward VI Schs, Birmingham; Member or ex-member various cttees. Served European War, 1914–18, overseas with RASC and Somerset Light Infantry. *Recreation:* reading. *Address:* c/o 578 Bromford Lane, Ward End, Birmingham B8 2DS. *T:* 021–784 2354. *Died 25 Sept. 1993.*

BAMMEL, Caroline Penrose, PhD; FBA 1994; Reader in Early Church History, since 1992, and Fellow of Girton College, since 1968, University of Cambridge; *b* 6 July 1940; *d* of Prof. Nicholas Geoffrey Lemprière Hammond, CBE, DSO, FBA and Margaret Campbell, *d* of J. W. J. Townley, CBE; *m* 1979, Prof. Ernst Bammel. *Educ:* Clifton High Sch., Bristol; Girton Coll., Cambridge (MA; PhD 1966). Girton College, Cambridge: Res. Fellow, 1966–68; Lectr in Classics, 1968–; Dir of Studies in Theology, 1976–; Asst Lectr, 1975–80, Lectr, 1980–92, in Early Church History, Cambridge Univ. Faculty of Divinity. *Publications:* Der Römerbriefext des Rufin and seine Origenesübersetzung, 1985; Origenis in Epistulam Pauli ad Romanos explanationum libri, Vol. I, 1990; contrib. Jl of Theol Studies, Augustinianum, Zeitschrift für Kirchengeschichte, etc. *Address:* Girton College, Cambridge CB3 0JG. *T:* Cambridge (01223) 338999. *Died 31 Oct. 1995.*

BANGOR, 7th Viscount *cr* 1781; **Edward Henry Harold Ward;** Baron, 1770; free-lance journalist (as Edward Ward); *b* 5 Nov. 1905; *s* of 6th Viscount Bangor, OBE, PC (NI) and Agnes Elizabeth (*d* 1972), 3rd *d* of late Dacre Hamilton, Cornacassa, Monaghan; *S* father, 1950; *m* 1st, 1933, Elizabeth (who obtained a divorce, 1937), *e d* of T. Balfour, Wrockwardine Hall, Wellington, Salop; 2nd, 1937, Mary Kathleen (marr. diss. 1947), *d* of W. Middleton, Shanghai; 3rd, 1947, Leila Mary (marr. diss. 1951; she *d* 1959), *d* of David R. Heaton, Brookfield, Crownhill, S Devon; one *s*; 4th, 1951, Mrs Marjorie Alice Simpson (*d* 1991), *d* of late Peter Banks, St Leonards-on-Sea; one *s* one *d. Educ:* Harrow; RMA, Woolwich. Formerly Reuters correspondent in China and the Far East; BBC War Correspondent in Finland, 1939–40, ME, 1940–41, and Foreign Correspondent all over world, 1946–60. *Publications:* 1940 Despatches from Finland, 1946; Give Me Air, 1946; Chinese Crackers, 1957; The New Eldorado, 1957; Oil is Where They Find It, 1959; Sahara Story, 1962; Number One Boy, 1969; I've lived like a Lord, 1970; with his wife, Marjorie Ward: Europe on Record, 1950; The US and Us 1951; Danger is Our Business, 1955. *Heir: s* Hon. William Maxwell David Ward [*b* 9 Aug. 1948; *m* 1976, Mrs Sarah Bradford]. *Address:* 59 Cadogan Square, SW1X 0HZ. *T:* 071–235 3202. *Clubs:* Savile, Garrick. *Died 8 May 1993.*

BANK-ANTHONY, Sir Mobolaji, KBE 1963 (OBE 1956); company director, Lagos, Nigeria; *b* 11 June 1907; *e s* of Alfred Bank-Anthony and Rabiatu Aleshinloye Williams, Lagos; *m* 1935, Olamide Adeshigbin. *Educ:* Methodist Boys' High Sch., Lagos; CMS Gram. Sch., Lagos; Ijebu-Ode Gram. Sch. Postal Clerk in Nigerian Postal and Telegraphic Dept, 1924; course in Palm Oil cultivation methods, in England, 1931–33, when returned to Nigeria, and gradually built up extensive business, opening stores in many parts of Lagos; Dir of some leading local companies. Fellow of Royal Commonwealth Society; FRSA; FInstD. Stella della Solidarieta (Italy), 1957. *Recreations:* working, reading, newspapers, dancing. *Address:* Executive House, 2a Oil Mill Street, Lagos, Nigeria. *T:* Lagos 24660, 24669; Fountainpen House, 29

Okotie-Eboh Street, Ikoyi, Lagos, Nigeria. *T:* Lagos 21900, 21363. *Clubs:* Royal Automobile; Rotary, Metropolitan, Island, Lagos Race, Lagos Motor, Lagos Amateur Cricket, Yoruba Tennis, Skal, Lodge Academic (Lagos). *Died 26 May 1991.*

BANKS, Sir Maurice (Alfred Lister), Kt 1971; *b* 11 Aug. 1901; *s* of Alfred Banks, FRCS and Elizabeth Maud (*née* Davey); *m* 1933, Ruth Hall (*d* 1991), Philadelphia, USA; one *s* two *d. Educ:* Westminster Sch.; Coll. of Technology, Manchester Univ.; BSc Tech. FRIC, MIChemE. Coal Research Fellowship under DSIR, 1923; joined Anglo Persian Oil Co., 1924. British Petroleum: a Man. Dir, 1960; a Dep. Chm., 1965; retd from BP, 1967. Chairman: Adv. Council on Calibration for Min. of Technology, 1965–66; Adv. Cttee on Hovercraft for Min. of Technology, 1967–68; BoT Departmental Cttee to enquire into Patent Law and Procedure, 1967–70. Chm., Laird Gp Ltd, 1970–75. *Recreations:* golf, gardening. *Address:* Beech Coppice, Kingswood, Surrey. *T:* Mogador (0737) 832270. *Clubs:* Athenæum; Walton Heath Golf.
Died 11 Aug. 1991.

BARBER, Hon. Sir (Edward Hamilton) Esler, Kt 1976; Puisne Judge, Supreme Court of Victoria, Australia, 1965–77; *b* Hamilton, Vic, 26 July 1905; *s* of late Rev. John Andrew Barber and Maggie Rorke; *m* 1954, Constance, *d* of Captain C. W. Palmer; one *s* one *d. Educ:* Hamilton Coll., Victoria; Scots Coll., Sydney; Scotch Coll., Melbourne; Melbourne Univ. Barrister-at-law, 1929; QC (Vic) 1955, (Tas) 1956; Judge, County Court, Vic, 1957–65; Actg Judge, 1964–65. Dep. Chm. Parole Bd, Vic, 1969–77; Mem. Council of Legal Educn, 1968–77. Chairman: Royal Commn into Failure of King's Bridge, 1962–63; Royal Commn into West Gate Bridge Disaster, 1970–71; Bd of Inquiry into causes and origins of bush and grass fires in Vic. during Jan.-Feb. 1977, 1977. *Publications:* articles on matrimonial law, incl. Divorce— the Changing Law, 1968. *Address:* 1 St George's Court, Toorak, Vic 3142, Australia. *T:* 24–5104. *Club:* Australian (Melbourne). *Died 1 Dec. 1991.*

BARBER, Rear-Adm. John L.; *see* Lee-Barber.

BARBER, Prof. Michael, FRS 1985; Professor of Physical Chemistry, since 1985, and Scientific Director, Centre for Mass Spectrometry, since 1991, University of Manchester Institute of Science and Technology; *b* 3 Nov. 1934; *s* of Joseph and Alice Anne Barber; *m* 1958, Joan (*née* Gaskell); one *s* two *d. Educ:* Manchester Grammar Sch.; The Queen's Coll., Oxford (DPhil). Joined AEI Scientific Apparatus Dept, Trafford Park, Manchester, 1961; Hon. Lectr, Chemistry Dept, Univ. of Manchester, 1970–73; Lectr 1973, Reader 1977, Chem. Dept, UMIST. Royal Soc. of Chemistry: Perkin Elmer Award and Medal for analytical science and instrumentation, 1979; Strock Medal and Award for Applied Spectroscopy, 1983; Dist. Scientist Award, Amer. Mass Spectrometry Soc., 1991. *Recreations:* lacrosse; organist and choirmaster of St Michael and All Angels, Wythenshawe. *Address:* Chemistry Department, UMIST, PO Box 88, Sackville Street, Manchester M60 1QD. *T:* 061-200 4585; (home) 29 New Forest Road, Manchester M23 9JT. *T:* 061-962 5881. *Died 8 May 1991.*

BARBER, Col Sir William (Francis), 2nd Bt *cr* 1960, of Greasley, Nottingham; TD; JP; CEng, MIMinE; *b* 20 Nov. 1905; *yr* and *o* surv. *s* of Sir (Thomas) Philip Barber, 1st Bt, DSO, TD, JP, DL, and Beatrice Mary (*d* 1962), *d* of Lieut-Col W. Ingersoll Merritt; *S* father, 1961; *m* 1st, 1936, Diana Constance (marr. diss. 1978; she *d* 1984), *d* of late Lieut-Col Thomas Owen Lloyd, CMG, Minard Castle, Argyll; one *s* one *d*; 2nd, 1978, Jean Marie, *widow* of Dr H. C. Nott, Adelaide, S Australia. *Educ:* Eton Coll. South Nottinghamshire Hussars Yeomanry (commnd,

1924); Royal Horse Artillery; served in Palestine, Egypt, North Africa, NW Europe; Lieut-Col 1947; Hon. Col, South Nottinghamshire Hussars Yeomanry, 1961–66. JP Notts, 1952; High Sheriff, Notts, 1964. *Heir: s* (Thomas) David Barber [*b* 18 Nov. 1937; *m* 1st, 1972, Amanda Mary (*née* Rabone) (marr. diss. 1976), *widow* of Maj. Michael Healing; one *s*; 2nd, 1978, Jeannine Mary Boyle, *d* of Captain T. J. Gurney; one *s* one *d*]. *Address:* Lamb Close House, Eastwood, Notts NG16 3QX. *T:* Langley Mill (01773) 712011. *Died 1 April 1995.*

BARDEEN, Prof. John; Professor of Physics and Electrical Engineering, University of Illinois, 1951–75, then Emeritus; *b* Madison, Wisconsin, 23 May 1908; *s* of Dr Charles R. Bardeen and Althea Bardeen (*née* Harmer); *m* 1938, Jane Maxwell; two *s* one *d. Educ:* Univ. of Wisconsin; Princeton Univ. BS 1928, MS 1929, Univ. of Wisconsin; PhD 1936, Princeton Univ. Geophysicist, Gulf Research and Development Corp., Pittsburgh, Pa, 1930–33; Junior Fellow, Soc. of Fellows, Harvard Univ., 1935–38; Asst Prof. of Physics, Univ. of Minnesota, 1938–41; Physicist, Naval Ordnance Laboratory, Washington, DC, 1941–45; Research Physicist, Bell Telephone Laboratories, Murray Hill, NJ, 1945–51. Foreign Member: Royal Soc., 1973; Indian Nat. Sci. Acad., 1976; Japan Acad., 1977; Acad. of Scis, USSR, 1982; Venezuelan Acad.; Acad. of Scis, Pakistan; Corresponding Member: Acad. of Sci., Hungary; Acad. of Sci., Austria. Hon. doctorates. Nobel Prize for Physics: (with W. H. Brattain and W. Shockley), 1956; (with L. N. Cooper and J. R. Schrieffer), 1972; Founder's Award, Nat. Acad. Engrg, 1984; Lomonosov Prize, Acad. of Scis, USSR, 1988. National Medal of Science, 1965; Presidential Medal of Freedom, 1977. *Publications:* articles on solid state physics, including semi-conductors, metals, superconductivity in Physical Review and other periodicals and books. *Address:* 337 Loomis Laboratory, 1110 W Green Street, Urbana, Ill 61801, USA; 55 Greencroft, Champaign, Illinois 61821, USA. *T:* Champaign 352–6497. *Died 30 Jan. 1991.*

BARDSLEY, Rt Rev. Cuthbert Killick Norman, CBE 1952; DD; *b* 28 March 1907; *yr s* of late Canon J. U. N. Bardsley and Mabel Killick; *m* 1972, Ellen Mitchell. *Educ:* Eton; New Coll., Oxford (DD 1957). Deacon, 1932; priest, 1933; Curate of All Hallows, Barking by the Tower, 1932–34; Rector of Woolwich, 1940–44; Provost of Southwark Cathedral, 1944–47; Suffragan Bishop of Croydon, 1947–56; Bishop of Coventry, 1956–76. Hon. Canon in Canterbury Cathedral, 1948–56; Archbishop of Canterbury's Episcopal Representative with the three Armed Forces, 1948–56; Hon. Chaplain Siemens Bros, 1943–46; Proctor in Convocation, 1945–46. Select Preacher, University of Cambridge, 1958. ChStJ 1976. Hon. DLitt Warwick Univ., 1976. *Publications:* Bishop's Move, 1952; Sundry Times, Sundry Places, 1962; Him We Declare, 1967; I Believe in Mission, 1970; *relevant publication:* Cuthbert Bardsley by Lord Coggan, 1989. *Recreations:* golf, sketching. *Address:* Grey Walls, Berkeley Road, Cirencester, Gloucestershire GL7 1TY. *T:* Cirencester (0285) 653520. *Died 9 Jan. 1991.*

BARFORD, Sir Leonard, Kt 1967; Deputy Chairman, Horserace Totalisator Board, 1974–77 (Member, 1973–77); Chief Inspector of Taxes, Board of Inland Revenue, 1964–73; Commissioner of Inland Revenue, 1970–73; *b* 1 Aug. 1908; *s* of William and Ada Barford, Finsbury Park; *m* 1939, Betty Edna Crichton, Plymouth; two *s. Educ:* Dame Alice Owen's Sch.; St Catharine's Coll., Cambridge Univ. (Exhibitioner in History). Asst Inspector of Taxes, 1930; Administrative Staff Coll., Henley, 1948; Principal Inspector of Taxes, 1953; Senior Principal Inspector of Taxes, 1957; Deputy Chief Inspector, 1960. President, Assoc. of HM Inspectors of

Taxes, 1951–53. *Publication:* (jointly) Essay on Management in Tax Offices, 1950. *Recreations:* badminton, tennis, chess, bridge. *Address:* Harley House, 79 Sutton Road, Seaford, East Sussex BN25 4QH. *T:* Seaford (0323) 893364. *Club:* Civil Service.
Died 3 April 1992.

BARING, Lady Rose (Gwendolen Louisa), DCVO 1972 (CVO 1964); Extra Woman of the Bedchamber to the Queen, since 1973; *b* 23 May 1909; *er d* of 12th Earl of Antrim and Margaret Isabel (*d* 1974), *y d* of late Rt Hon. John Gilbert Talbot; *m* 1933, Francis Anthony Baring (killed in action, 1940); two *s* one *d*. Woman of the Bedchamber to the Queen, 1953–73. *Address:* 43 Pembroke Square, W8. *Died 2 Nov. 1993.*

BARK, Evelyn (Elizabeth Patricia), CMG 1967; OBE 1952; retired as Director International Affairs Department of British Red Cross (1950–66); *b* 26 Dec. 1900; *e d* of late Frederick William Bark. *Educ:* privately. On staff of Swedish Match Co. (at home and abroad) until 1939, when joined British Red Cross. Served War, 1939–44, VAD (Stars: of 1939–45, of France, and of Germany; Defence Medal, and War Medal, 1939–45). Foreign Relations Officer, 1944–48; Commissioner, NW Europe, 1948–49; Foreign Relations and Relief Adviser, 1950 (title later changed to Dir International Affairs). Serving Sister of St John's, 1953; British Red Cross Certificate First Class, 1966. *Publication:* No Time to Kill, 1960. *Recreations:* reading, music, Nordic languages. *Address:* c/o 15 Holly Hill Drive, Banstead, Surrey SM7 2BD.
Died 7 June 1993.

BARKER, George Granville; writer; *b* 26 Feb. 1913; *s* of George Barker and Marion Frances Barker (*née* Taaffe); *m* 1933, Jessica Winifred Theresa Woodward; three *s* three *d*; *m* 1964, Elspeth Langlands. *Educ:* Marlborough Road London County Council Sch., Chelsea. Prof. of English Literature at Imperial Tohoku Univ., Japan, 1939; visited America, 1940; returned to England, 1943; lived in Rome, 1960–65; Arts Fellow, York Univ., 1966–67; Vis. Prof., Florida Internat. Univ., 1974. *Publications:* Thirty Preliminary Poems, 1933; Alanna Autumnal, 1933; Poems, 1935; Janus, 1935; Calamiterror, 1937; Lament and Triumph, 1940; Eros in Dogma, 1944; News of the World, 1950; The Dead Seagull, 1950; The True Confession of George Barker, 1950; A Vision of Beasts and Gods, 1954; Collected Poems, 1930–55, 1957; The True Confession of George Barker, Book II, 1957; Two Plays, 1958; The View from a Blind I, 1962; Dreams of a Summer Night, 1966; The Golden Chains, 1968; Essays, 1970; Runes & Rhymes & Tunes & Chimes, 1970; To Aylsham Fair, 1970; At Thurgarton Church, 1970; Poems of Places and People, 1971; The Alphabetical Zoo, 1972; In Memory of David Archer, 1973; Dialogues etc, 1976; Villa Stellar, 1978; Anno Domini, 1983; Collected Poems, 1987; Seventeen, 1988; *posthumous publication:* Street Ballads, 1992. *Address:* Bintry House, Itteringham, Aylsham, Norfolk NR11 7AT. *T:* Saxthorpe (026387) 240. *Died 27 Oct. 1991.*

BARKER, Sir Harry Heaton, KBE 1978 (CBE 1972; OBE 1964); JP; New Zealand journalist; chairman various organisations; *b* Nelson, NZ, 18 July 1898; *s* of J. H. Barker; *m* 1926, Anita (MBE), *d* of H. Greaves; no *c*. *Educ:* Wellington and Auckland; New Plymouth Boys' High Sch. Served NZEF, 1917–19. Entered journalism, working with NZ Herald and country newspapers, 1916–17, 1919–23; Gisborne Herald: joined, 1923; subeditor, 1926; Leader Writer, Associate Editor, 1930; Editor, 1935–43, resigned. Mayor of Gisborne, 1950; reelected, 1953, 1956, 1959, 1962, 1965, 1968, 1971, 1974. Contested Gisborne seat, 1943, 1946. Member: Cook Hospital Board, 1944–71; King George V Health Camps Federation Board, 1953–69; Exec., Dist Roads Council,

1953–78; East Coast Planning Council, 1972–77. Chairman: Barrington Miller Educnl Trust, 1950–77; Gisborne Airport Cttee, 1958–77; cttee organising nat. celebration, Cook Bicentenary celebration, 1969. Executive Mem., NZ Municipalities Assoc., and Dir, Municipalities Insurance Co., 1959–69. Knighted for services to the City of Gisborne, NZ, and local government. *Publications:* To-Days and Yesterdays, 1978; political articles. *Recreations:* reading, writing, gardening. *Address:* Leighton House, Cheeseman Road, Gisborne, New Zealand. *T:* 8677697. *Club:* Victoria League.
Died 18 May 1994.

BARKER, John Michael Adrian; His Honour Judge Barker; a Circuit Judge, since 1979; *b* 4 Nov. 1932; *s* of Robert Henry Barker and Annie Robson Barker (*née* Charlton); *m* 1971, Gillian Marsha (*née* Greenstone). *Educ:* Marist Coll., Hull Univs of Sheffield and Hull. BSc, LLB. Called to Bar, Middle Temple, 1959. Schoolmaster, Stonyhurst Coll., 1957–59; Lectr in Law, Univ. of Hull, 1960–63. A Recorder of the Crown Court, 1974–79. Mem., Hull CC, 1965–71. *Publications:* articles in Conveyancer and Property Lawyer, Solicitors' Jl, Criminal Law Review and Solicitor. *Recreations:* walking, gardening. *Address:* Combined Court Centre, Lowgate, Hull HU1 2EZ. *Died 15 June 1994.*

BARKER, Susan Vera; *see* Cooper, Susie.

BARKER, Sir William, KCMG 1967 (CMG 1958); OBE 1949; Bowes Professor of Russian, University of Liverpool, 1969–76, retired; *b* 19 July 1909; *s* of Alfred Barker; *m* 1939, Margaret Beirne; one *s* one *d*. *Educ:* Universities of Liverpool and Prague. Employed in Foreign Office, 1943; First Sec., Prague, 1945; Foreign Service Officer, Grade 7, Senior Branch of Foreign Service, 1946; Chargé d'Affaires, Prague, 1947; transferred Moscow, Aug. 1947; granted rank of Counsellor, Dec. 1948; Grade 6, 1950; Counsellor, Oslo, 1951, also Chargé d'Affaires; Consul-Gen., Boston, Mass, Sept. 1954; Counsellor, Washington, 1955; Minister, Moscow, 1960–63; Fellow, Center for Internat. Affairs, Harvard Univ., 1963–64; Asst Under-Sec. of State, FO, 1965–66; Ambassador to Czechoslovakia, 1966–68. *Address:* 19 Moors Way, Woodbridge, Suffolk IP12 4HQ.
Died 8 Jan. 1992.

BARLEY, Prof. Maurice Willmore, MA; Professor of Archaeology, University of Nottingham, 1971–74, then Emeritus; *b* 19 Aug. 1909; *s* of late Levi Baldwin and Alice Barley, Lincoln; *m* 1934, Diana, *e d* of late A. E. Morgan; two *s* one *d*. *Educ:* Lincoln Sch.; Reading Univ. (BA). Asst Lectr, UC Hull, 1935–40; Mins of Information and Labour, 1940–45; Adult Educn Dept, Nottingham, 1946–62; Classics Dept, Nottingham Univ., 1962–74. Sec. 1954–64, Pres. 1964–67, Council for British Archaeology; Vice-Pres., Soc. of Antiquaries, 1965–68; Mem. Royal Commn on Hist. Monuments, 1966–76. FSA 1941. Hon. FRIBA 1987. *Publications:* Parochial Documents of the East Riding, 1939; Lincolnshire and the Fens, 1952, repr. 1972; Documents relating to Newark on Trent, 1956; The English Farmhouse and Cottage, 1961, repr. 1986; The House and Home, 1963, repr. 1971; Guide to British Topographical Collections, 1974; The Plans and Topography of Medieval Towns in England and Wales, 1975; European Towns, their Archaeology and early History, 1977; Houses and History, 1986; contrib. Agrarian History of England vols IV and V, Antiquaries Jl and other learned jls. *Address:* 60 Park Road, Chilwell, Nottingham NG9 4DD. *T:* Nottingham (0602) 257501.
Died 23 June 1991.

BARLOW, Donald Spiers Monteagle, MS; FRCS; Consulting Surgeon: Hospitals for Diseases of the Chest, since 1971 (Consultant Surgeon, 1947–71); Southend

Group of Hospitals, since 1970 (Consultant Surgeon, 1936–70); Luton Group of Hospitals, since 1970 (Consultant Surgeon, 1940–70); Italian Hospital, since 1970 (Hon. Consultant Thoracic Surgeon 1955–70); Penrose-May Surgical Tutor to the Royal College of Surgeons of England, since 1969 (Surgical Tutor, 1962–69); *b* 4 July 1905; *s* of late Leonard Barlow, MIEE, and Katharine Barlow; *m* 1934, Violet Elizabeth (*née* Maciver); one *s* three *d* (and one *d* decd). *Educ:* Whitgift Sch.; University Coll. Hospital and Medical Sch. MRCS, LRCP 1927; MB, BS London 1928; MS London 1930; FRCS 1930. Formerly: RMO, Wimbledon Hosp., 1927; House Phys., UCH, 1928; House Surg., UCH, 1929; Ho. Surg., Norfolk and Norwich Hosp., 1930–31; Resident Asst Surg., West London Hosp., 1931–35; Surg. Registrar London Lock Hosp., 1936; Research work at UCL, 1936–37; Hon. Surg., St John's Hosp., Lewisham, 1937–47; Cons. Thoracic Surg., LCC, 1945–48. Teacher, 1964–67, Lectr, 1967–71, Inst. of Diseases of the Chest, Univ. of London. Chm., S Beds Div., BMA, 1971–72. Coronation Medal, 1953. *Publications:* contribs to: Progress of Clinical Surgery, 1960 (ed Rodney Smith); Operative Surgery, 2nd edn 1969 (ed Rob and Smith); many publications in learned jls mostly concerning diseases of oesophagus, chest and abdomen; also 3 reports (Ceylon Govt White Papers), 1952, 1954, 1967. *Recreations:* golf (Captain, Harpenden Golf Club, 1971–72, Pres., 1976–79), painting. *Address:* Deacons Field, High Elms, Harpenden, Herts AL5 2JU. *T:* Harpenden (05827) 3400. *Died 5 July 1994.*

BARNARD, Sir (Arthur) Thomas, Kt 1958; CB 1954; OBE 1946; Director-General of Inspection, Ministry of Supply, 1956–58, retired; *b* 28 Sept. 1893; *s* of late Arthur Barnard; *m* 1921, Grace (*d* 1986), *d* of William Magerkorth, Belvedere, Kent. *Educ:* Erith Technical Coll. Chartered Civil Engineer. Chief Superintendent, Royal Ordnance Factories, Woolwich, 1951–55; Dep. Dir-Gen., Royal Ordnance Factories, Adelphi, London, 1955–56. *Died 6 July 1995.*

BARNARD, Captain Sir George (Edward), Kt 1968; Deputy Master of Trinity House, 1961–72; *b* 11 Aug. 1907; 2nd *s* of Michael and Alice Louise Barnard; *m* 1940, Barbara Emma Hughes (*d* 1976); one *s*. Apprenticed at sea, 1922; 1st Command, Blue Star Line, 1945. Elder Brother of Trinity House, 1958–. Trustee, Nat. Maritime Museum, 1967–74; Treasurer, Internat. Assoc. of Lighthouse Authorities, 1961–72; Hon. Sec., King George's Fund for Sailors, 1967–75; first Chm., Nautical Inst., 1972–73, Pres., 1973–75, Fellow, 1975; former Mem. Cttee of Management, RNLI. FRSA 1969. *Address:* 10 Breakspear Court, The Crescent, Abbots Langley, Herts WD5 0DP. *T:* Kings Langley (01923) 270706. *Died 14 April 1995.*

BARNARD, Sir Thomas; see Barnard, Sir A. T.

BARNEBY, Lt-Col Henry Habington, TD 1946; retired from HM Forces 1955; Vice Lord-Lieutenant of Hereford and Worcester, 1974–77; *b* 19 June 1909; *er s* of Richard Hicks Barneby, Longworth Hall, Hereford; *m* 1st, 1935, Evelyn Georgina Heywood; 2nd, 1944, Angela Margaret Campbell (*d* 1979); four *s* one *d* (and one *s* decd); 3rd, 1991, Patricia Thornton. *Educ:* Radley Coll.; RMC Sandhurst. QALAS 1939. 2nd Lieut KSLI 1929, retd 1935; Lieut Hereford Regt TA 1936; commanded: Hereford Regt (TA), 1945–46; Hereford LI (TA), 1947–51; Jamaica Bn, 1951–53; regranted commn in KSLI as Major, 1947; retd 1955. Mem., Herefordshire T&AFA, 1955–68; Mem., W Midlands T&AVR, 1968–77. Member: Hereford RDC, 1955–67 (Chm., 1964–67); Dore and Bredwardine RDC, 1966–73; S Herefordshire RDC, 1973–76. DL Herefordshire 1958–83, Vice Lieut, 1973–74, High Sheriff 1972; JP Hereford County PSD, 1957–79 (Chm.,

1977–79). *Address:* Llanerch-y-Coed, Dorstone, Herefordshire HR3 6AG. *T:* Clifford (01497) 831215. *Died 27 April 1995.*

BARNES, Sir Denis (Charles), KCB 1967 (CB 1964); Director: Glynwed Ltd; General Accident, Fire & Life Assurance Corporation, 1976–85; President, Manpower Society, since 1976; *b* 15 Dec. 1914; *s* of Frederick Charles Barnes; *m* 1938, Patricia Abercrombie. *Educ:* Hulme Gram. Sch., Manchester; Merton Coll., Oxford. BA, 1st Cl. Mod. History, 1936; PPE 1937. Chambers Postmaster, Merton Coll., Oxford, 1933–37. Entered Min. of Labour, 1937; Private Sec. to Minister of Labour, 1945–47; Dep. Sec., Min. of Labour, 1963, Permanent Sec. 1966; Permanent Sec., Dept of Employment, 1968–73; Chm., Manpower Services Commn, 1974–76. Member: Council, Manchester Business Sch., 1975; Council, Zoological Soc. of London, 1978–81. FIPM 1974. Commonwealth Fellowship, 1953. *Publication:* Governments and Trade Unions, 1980. *Address:* The Old Inn, 30 The Street, Wittersham, Kent TN30 7ED. *T:* Wittersham (07977) 528. *Club:* Savile. *Died 6 May 1992.*

BARNES, Sir (Ernest) John (Ward), KCMG 1974; MBE (mil.) 1946; HM Diplomatic Service, retired; *b* 22 June 1917; *er s* of Rt Rev. Ernest William Barnes, 3rd Bishop of Birmingham, and Adelaide, *d* of Sir Adolphus Ward, Master of Peterhouse, Cambridge; *m* 1948, Cynthia Margaret Ray (JP E Sussex, CStJ), *d* of Sir Herbert Stewart, CIE; two *s* three *d*. *Educ:* Dragon Sch., Oxford; Winchester; Trinity Coll., Cambridge. Classical Tripos, Pts I and II, Class I; Porson Scholar, 1939. Royal Artillery, 1939–46 (Lt-Col, MBE, US Bronze Star). HM Foreign Service, 1946; served Washington, Beirut, Bonn and Harvard Univ. (Center for International Affairs); Ambassador to Israel, 1969–72; Ambassador to the Netherlands, 1972–77. Director: Alliance Investment Co., 1977–87; Whiteaway Laidlaw Ltd, 1979–88. Chairman: Sussex Rural Community Council, 1982–87; Governors, Hurstpierpoint Coll., 1983–87. Member: Chichester Diocesan Synod, 1978–90; Council, Sussex Univ., 1981–85 (Vice-Chm. 1982–84). *Publication:* Ahead of his Age, 1979. *Address:* Hampton Lodge, Hurstpierpoint, Sussex BN6 9QN; 20 Thurloe Place Mews, SW7 2HL. *Clubs:* Athenæum, Beefsteak, Brooks's, MCC. *Died 11 June 1992.*

BARNES, James Edwin; Under-Secretary, Small Firms and Regional Development Grants, Department of Industry, 1974–75; retired; *b* 23 Nov. 1917; *s* of James Barnes and Kate (*née* Davies); *m* 1943, Gloria Parkinson; two *s* one *d*. *Educ:* King Edward VI Sch., Nuneaton. Joined Civil Service as Executive Officer, War Office, 1936; Higher Executive Officer, Min. of Supply, 1942; Sen. Exec. Officer 1945; Principal, 1946; Asst Sec. 1952; Under-Secretary: Min. of Aviation, 1964–66; BoT, 1966–70; DTI, 1970–74. Coronation Medal, 1953. *Address:* 28 Sandown Road, Deal, Kent CT14 6PG. *T:* Deal (0304) 369308. *Died 12 April 1991.*

BARNES, Sir James George, Kt 1976; MBE (mil.) 1946; JP; Mayor of Dunedin, New Zealand, 1968–77; sharebroker; *b* Dunedin, NZ, 1908; *s* of Richard R. Barnes; *m* 1938, Elsie, *d* of James D. Clark; one *d*. *Educ:* King Edward Technical High Sch. Served War, RNZAF 75 Sqdn, 1940–46 (POW, 1942–45). Mem., Dunedin City Council, 1947–53 and 1959–80 (Dep. Mayor 1951–53 and 1959–68); MP, 1951–57. Exec. Mem.: Otago Peninsula Trust; NZ Fedn for the Blind; Chm., Bd of Ocean Beach Domain. Past Pres., Otago Savings Bank. Chm. or Dir, Sch. Bds and Youth orgs. NZ mile champion, 1932; NZ Cross Country Champion, 1933; Manager NZ Empire Games Team, 1950; Asst Man., NZ Olympic Team, 1956; Past Pres., NZ AAA; Mem. Otago AAA;

Mem. NZ Trotting Conf. (Pres., 1979–80); Sen. Vice Pres., Aust. Trotting Council, 1977–80; Exec. Mem., World Trotting Congress, 1980; Past Pres., Forbury Park Trotting Club. CStJ 1979. *Recreations:* golf, trotting. *Address:* 35 Cliffs Road, Dunedin, New Zealand. *T:* (3) 4558638; PO Box 221, Dunedin.

Died 6 June 1995.

BARNES, Sir John; *see* Barnes, Sir E. J. W.

BARNETT, Air Chief Marshal Sir Denis Hensley Fulton, GCB 1964 (KCB 1957; CB 1956); CBE 1945; DFC 1940; Royal Air Force, retired; Member for Weapons Research and Development, Atomic Energy Authority, 1965–72; *b* 11 Feb. 1906; *y s* of late Sir Louis Edward Barnett, CMG and Mabel Violet, *d* of Hon. James Fulton; *m* 1939, Pamela, OBE, *y d* of late Sir Allan John Grant; one *s* two *d. Educ:* Christ's Coll., NZ; Clare Coll., Cambridge (BA 1929, MA 1935). Perm. Commn, RAF, 1929; Flt Lieut, 1934; Sqdn Ldr 1938; comd 84 Sqdn, Shaibah, 1938; served War of 1939–45: Sqdn Comdr, Stn Comdr and G/C Ops, Bomber Comd, 1939–44; Dep. Dir Bomber Ops, Air Min., 1944; Dep. SASO at HQ Bomber Comd, 1945; Actg Wing Cdr, 1940; Gp Capt., 1941; Air Cdre, 1945; Dir of Ops at Air Min., 1945–46; Air Staff, India, 1946–47; Jt Services Staff Coll., 1948; Comdt Central Bomber Estabt, 1949; Dir of Ops Air Min., 1950–52; idc, 1952; Representative of UK Chiefs of Staff at HQ, UN Command, Tokyo, 1952–54; AOC, No 205 Group, Middle East Air Force, 1954–56; Commandant, RAF Staff Coll., Bracknell, 1956; Commander Allied Air Task Force, Near East, 1956; Air Secretary, Air Ministry, 1957–59; AOC-in-C, RAF Transport Command, 1959–62; Air Officer Commanding-in-Chief, RAF Near East; Commander, British Forces Cyprus, and Administrator of the Sovereign Base Areas, 1962–64; Subst. Air Commodore, 1950; Air Vice-Marshal, 1953; Air Marshal, 1959; Air Chief Marshal, 1962. Comdr, US Legion of Merit, 1954; French Légion d'Honneur (Commandeur) and Croix de Guerre, 1958. *Address:* River House, Rushall, Pewsey, Wilts SN9 6EN. *Died 31 Dec. 1992.*

BARNETT, Sir Oliver (Charles), Kt 1968; CBE 1954 (OBE 1946); QC 1956; *b* 7 Feb. 1907; *er s* of Charles Frederick Robert Barnett, 2nd Lieut Gloucestershire Regt (TA) (killed in action, 1915), and late Cicely Frances Barnett (*née* Cornish); *m* 1945, Joan, *o* surv. *c* of Capt. W. H. Eve, 13th Hussars (killed in action, 1917), *o s* of late Rt Hon. Sir Harry Trelawney Eve, a Judge of the High Court. *Educ:* Eton. Called to Bar, Middle Temple, 1928; Bencher, Middle Temple, 1964; Oxford Circuit; Central Criminal Court Sessions; Dir of Public Prosecutions Office, 1931; Legal Asst, Judge Advocate General's Office, 1934; Second Deputy Judge Advocate, 1937; First Deputy Judge Advocate, 1938; RAF, 1939–47 (OBE); Wing Comdr (RAFVR); Asst Judge Advocate Gen. (RAF), 1942–47; Asst Judge Advocate Gen. (Army and RAF), 1947–54; Deputy Judge Advocate Gen. (Army and RAF), BAOR, British Troops in Austria and 2nd TAF, 1953–54; Vice Judge Advocate Gen., 1955–62; Judge Advocate Gen., 1963–68; Dep. Chm., Somerset QS, 1967–71. *Address:* The Almonry, Stogumber, Taunton, Somerset TA4 3SZ. *T:* Stogumber (01984) 56291. *Clubs:* Brooks's, Pratt's. *Died 3 Feb. 1995.*

BARNSLEY, Thomas Edward, OBE 1975; FCA; Director, H. P. Bulmer Holdings, 1980–87; a Managing Director, Tube Investments Ltd, 1974–82; *b* 1 Sept. 1919; *s* of Alfred E. Barnsley and Ada F. Nightingale; *m* 1947, Margaret Gwyneth Llewellin; one *s* one *d. Educ:* Wednesbury Boys' High Sch. ACMA. Friends' Ambulance Unit, 1940–45. Price Waterhouse Peat & Co., South America, 1948–49; Asst Sec., 1958–62, Group Financial Controller, 1962–65, Tube Investments Ltd; Chm. and Man. Dir, Raleigh Industries Ltd, 1968–74.

Chm., Nat. Industrial Cttee, Nat. Savings Movement, 1975–78. *Recreation:* gardening. *Address:* The Old Rectory, Llanelidan, near Ruthin, Clwyd LL15 2PT.

Died 31 Aug. 1992.

BARR, Ian; Chairman, Scottish Post Office Board (formerly Post Office Scotland), 1984–88; Board Member, National Girobank Scotland, 1984–88; *b* 6 April 1927; *s* of late Peter McAlpine Barr and Isobel Baillie; *m* 1st, 1951, Gertrud Karla (marr. diss. 1988), *d* of late August Otto Odefey, Schleswig-Holstein; two *d*; 2nd, 1988, cousin Margaret Annie McAlpine, *d* of late Andrew McAlpine Barr and Ann Jane Brodie-Scott. *Educ:* Boroughmuir High Sch., Edinburgh. Post Office: Asst Postal Controller, N Western Region, 1955; Inspector of Postal Services, 1957; Asst Controller, Planning, 1962; Principal, 1966; Mem., CS Selection Bd, 1966–71; Post Office: Asst Sec., 1971; Regional Dir, Eastern Region, 1976; Dir, Bldgs, Mechanisation and Transport, 1978; Dir, Estates Exec., 1981–84. Chairman: PO National Arts Cttee, 1976–87; Scottish Cttee, Assoc. for Business Sponsorship of the Arts, 1986–88; CEPT (Bâtiments), 1982–86; Saltire Soc., 1986–87; Member: British Materials Handling Board, 1978–81; Scottish Council, CBI, 1984–88. Director: St Mary's Music School, Edinburgh, 1987–92 (Chm., Management Cttee, 1988–90); Friedman Camerata of St Andrew, 1988–89; Scottish Nat. Orch., 1988–90; Mem., Edinburgh Fest. Council, 1988–89. Mem., Scottish Convention Cttee, 1988, leading to establishment of Scottish Constitutional Convention, 1989– (report, A Claim of Right for Scotland, 1988). Director: Endocrine Res. Trust, Western Gen. Hosp., Edinburgh, 1987–92; Lamp of Lothian Collegiate Trust, Haddington, 1988–92. FInstD 1984. *Recreations:* composing serial music, constructing a metaphysical system, agitating for an independent Scotland. *Address:* Number Ten, Duke Street, Hawick, Roxburghshire TD9 9PY.

Died 3 April 1995.

BARR, Prof. Murray Llewellyn, OC 1968; FRS 1972; Professor of Anatomy, University of Western Ontario, 1949–79, then Emeritus Professor; *b* 20 June 1908; *s* of William Llewellyn Barr and Margaret McLellan; Canadian; *m* 1934, Ruth Vivian King; three *s* one *d. Educ:* Univ. of Western Ontario (BA, MD, MSc). FRSC 1958; FRCP(C) 1964; FACP 1965; FRCOG 1972. Served War of 1939–45 as MO, RCAF (Wing Comdr). Univ. of Western Ontario: Instructor in Anatomy, 1936–45; Associate Prof. of Anatomy, 1945–49 (Chm., Dept of Anatomy, 1951–67). Hon. degrees: LLD Queen's, 1963; LLD Toronto, 1964; Dr med Basel, 1966; LLD Alberta, 1967; LLD Dalhousie, 1968; LLD Saskatchewan, 1973; DSc Western Ontario, 1974. *Publications:* The Human Nervous System: an anatomical viewpoint, 1972, 5th edn (with J. A. Kiernan) 1988; A Century of Medicine at Western, 1977; numerous scientific papers. *Address:* 411–312 Oxford Street W, London, Ontario N6H 4N7, Canada. *T:* (519) 6450084. *Club:* Harvey (London, Ont).

Died 4 May 1995.

BARRATT, Herbert George Harold, OBE 1966; General Secretary, Confederation of Shipbuilding and Engineering Unions, 1957–69; *b* 12 Jan. 1905; *m* 1926; one *s* three *d. Educ:* Vicarage Street Church of England Sch., Nuneaton. Nuneaton Borough Councillor, 1945–47; Chm. Nuneaton Labour Party, 1944–46. Mem. Nat. Cttee, AEU, 1943–48; Delegate to USSR, 1946; Coventry Dist Cttee, AEU, 1943–49; elected Nat. Organiser AEU, 1949–57. Shop Steward Convener, Daimler Motors, 1940–49; Appeals Board Assessor during war years; Nat. Insurance Tribunal Assessor. Formerly Member: Gas Adv. Council; Shipbuilding and Shiprepairing Council; Nat. Adv. Council for the Motor Manufacturing Industry; Motor Industry Joint Labour Council; British Railways

Productivity Council; Econ. Develt Cttee for Mech. Engrg Industry; Econ. Develt Cttee for Electrical Engrg Industry; Econ. Develt Cttee for Motor Manufacturing Industry; Industrial Training Board, Engrg; Industrial Training Board, Shipbuilding; British Productivity team to Swedish Shipyards, 1959; visited German Federal Railways, 1960; Exchange Leader Scheme visitor to USA, 1961; Vice-Chm., Sub-Cttee on Programme and Planning, Metal Trades Cttee, ILO, Geneva, 1965. *Recreation:* gardening. *Address:* 7 Rosebery Close, Sittingbourne, Kent ME10 3DB. *Died July 1993.*

BARRAULT, Jean-Louis; Officer of the Legion of Honour; actor, director, producer; Director, Compagnie du théâtre du Rond-Point (formerly Compagnie Madeleine Renaud-Jean-Louis Barrault), since 1947; *b* Vésinet, France, 8 Sept. 1910; *s* of Jules Barrault and Marcelle Hélène Valette; *m* 1940, Madeleine Renaud. *Educ:* public sch., Paris; Collège Chaptal. Taught at Collège Chaptal, 1931; Atelier Dramatic Sch. and Theatre (schol.), 1931–35; formed experimental theatrical company; served War, 1939–40; with Comédie-Française as producer-director, 1940–46; at instigation of French Govt formed company with Madeleine Renaud, 1947; Dir, Théâtre Marigny, 1947–56; Co-Dir, Théâtre du Palais-Royal, 1958; Director: Théâtre de France, 1959–68; Théâtre des Nations, 1965–67, 1972–74; (also Founder), Théâtre d'Orsay, 1974–81. Appeared: Venice; Edinburgh Festival, 1948, 1957 and 1985; St James's Theatre, London, 1951; Palace Theatre, London, 1956, etc; produced Duel of Angels, Apollo, 1958; World Theatre Season, Aldwych, 1965, 1968; Rabelais, Paris, 1968–69, tours in Japan and USA, 1969, London, 1971; toured Western Europe, S America, Canada and US. Films include: Les Beaux Jours, Hélène, Les Perles de la couronne, La Symphonie fantastique, Les Enfants du Paradis, D'Hommes à hommes, Versailles, Chappaqua, Le Puritain, La route de Varennes. *Publications include:* Une Troupe et ses auteurs, 1950; Reflections on the Theatre (autobiography), 1951; Memories for Tomorrow: the memoirs of Jean-Louis Barrault, 1974; articles in theatrical publications. *Address:* 18 avenue du Président Wilson, 75116 Paris, France.
Died 22 Jan. 1994.

BARRETT, (Arthur) Michael, PhD; FIBiol; Vice-Chancellor, 1985–91, Professor Emeritus, since 1991, University of Buckingham; *b* 1 April 1932; *s* of Arthur Cowley Barrett and late Doris Annie Barrett; *m* 1960, Patricia Lillian Harris (*d* 1989); one *s* one *d*. *Educ:* Cheltenham Grammar Sch.; Sch. of Pharmacy, Univ. of London (BPharm 1st Cl. Hons, PhD). Rotary Foundn Fellow, Western Reserve Univ., Cleveland, Ohio, 1956–57; Asst Lectr in Pharmacology, 1958–59, Lectr, 1959–61, Sch. of Pharmacy, London Univ.; Res. Pharmacologist, Pharmaceuticals Div., ICI Ltd, 1961–70; Head of Pharmacology, Organon Internat. BV, 1970; Prof. and Hd of Dept of Pharmacology, 1970–84, Pro-Vice-Chancellor, 1979–81, Leeds Univ. Chm., Leeds Eastern Health Authority, 1981–84; Vice-Chairman: Kirklees AHA, 1978–79 (Mem., 1974–79); Aylesbury Vale HA, 1990–93; Mem., Gen. Sales List Cttee, Medicines Commn, DHSS, 1971–74; Assessor to Inquiry on LD50 Test, Home Office, 1977–79. Sec. Gen., Internat. Union of Pharmacology, 1981–87; Member: British Pharmacol Soc., 1963– (Meetings Sec., 1977–79); Gen. Sec., 1980–82); Soc. for Endocrinology, 1959–. Mem. Bd Governors, 1985–, Chm., Academic Bd, 1987–89, RAC, Cirencester; Mem. Academic Adv. Cttee, Bellerby's Coll., Hove; Governor: Beachborough Sch., Westbury, 1986–; Dixon's City Technology Coll., Bradford, 1989–; Chm. Trustees, Lorch Foundn, 1986–91; Trustee, Lloyd's of London Tercentenary Foundn, 1988–. FIBiol 1984; FRSA 1985. *Publications:* The Pharmacology of Beta-adrenoceptor blockade, 1975; papers in pharmacol and

endocrinol jls. *Recreations:* models, gardening, music. *Address:* Thene House, Shalstone, Buckingham MK18 5LU. *T:* Brackley (0280) 700551.
Died 21 July 1994.

BARRETT, Denis Everett; a Special Commissioner of Income Tax, 1967–71; *b* 7 Jan. 1911; *o s* of late Walter Everett Barrett, London, and Julia Barrett (*née* MacCarthy), Cork; *m* 1st, 1947, Eilish (*d* 1974), *y d* of late William and Margaret Phelan, Co. Laois; one *s* two *d*; 2nd, 1977, Patricia Madeline (*née* Ruddin), widow of H. A. Cowan, FRCS. *Educ:* Wimbledon Coll.; London Univ. Entered Inland Revenue Dept, 1930; Asst Sec., 1948. *Address:* c/o The Pump House, Bone Mill Lane, Enborne, Newbury, Berks RG15 0EU. *Died 23 Nov. 1991.*

BARRETT, Michael; *see* Barrett, A. M.

BARRON, Douglas Shield, CIE 1945; Chairman, Godfrey Phillips, India, Ltd, retired 1973; *b* 18 March 1904; *s* of Thomas Barron; *m* 1934, Doris Katherine (*d* 1970), *o d* of late Henry Deakin; no *c*. *Educ:* Holgate Grammar Sch.; Corpus Christi Coll., Cambridge. Joined Indian Civil Service, 1926; retired, 1948. *Address:* Sundial Cottage, Cross Lanes, Mockbeggar, Ringwood, Hants BH24 3NQ. *T:* Ringwood (0425) 3885. *Club:* Bombay Yacht.
Died 3 Feb. 1991.

BARRON, Rt Rev. Patrick Harold Falkiner; *b* 13 Nov. 1911; *s* of Albert Harold and Mary Isabel Barron; *m* 1942, Kathleen May Larter; two *s* one *d*. *Educ:* King Edward VII Sch., Johannesburg; Leeds Univ. (BA); College of the Resurrection, Mirfield. Deacon, 1938; priest, 1939; Curate: Holy Redeemer, Clerkenwell, London, 1938–40; Boksburg, S Africa, 1940–41; CF (S African), 1941–46; Rector: Zeerust, S Africa, 1946–50; Potchefstroom, 1950–51; Blyvooruitzicht, 1951–55; St Cyprian's Mission, Johannesburg, 1956–59; Archdeacon of Germiston, 1957–58; Dean of Johannesburg, 1959–64; Bishop Suffragan of Cape Town, 1965–66; Bishop of George, 1966–77. *Recreation:* gardening. *Address:* E37 Edinight, Queen Road, Rondebosch, 7700, South Africa. *T:* 689.1820. *Died 27 Aug. 1991.*

BARROW, Dame (Ruth) Nita, DA 1980; GCMG 1990; FRCN 1980; Governor General of Barbados, since 1990; *b* 15 Nov. 1916. *Educ:* St Michael's Girls' School; Basic Nursing, Barbados (SRN), 1935–41; Midwifery Preparation, Trinidad Registered Midwife, 1941–42; Public Health Diploma, 1943–44, Nursing Educn, 1944–45, Univ. of Toronto; Sister Tutor's Diploma, Edinburgh, 1951–52; BSc Nursing, Columbia Univ., NY, 1962–63. Staff Nurse, Barbados Gen. Hosp., Private Duty Nursing, 1940–41; Nursing Instr, Basic Sch. of Public Health, Jamaica, 1945–51; Sister Tutor, Kingston Sch. of Nursing, Jamaica, 1952–54; Matron, UCH, Jamaica, 1954–56; Principal Nursing Officer, Jamaica, 1956–63; WHO Nursing Advr, Caribbean Area, Region of the Americas, 1964–71; Associate Dir, 1971–75, Dir, 1975–81, Med. Commn, WCC. Ambassador Extraordinary and Plenipotentiary and Permanent Rep. of Barbados to UN, 1986–90. Mem., Editl Bd, Contact, Christian Med. Commn, Geneva. Gamaliel Lectr, Wisconsin, 1983. Hon. LLD: Univ. of W Indies, 1975; Toronto, 1987; Winnipeg, 1988; Spelman Coll., Atlanta; York Univ., Canada, 1990; Smith Coll., USA, 1991; Queen's Univ., Canada, 1991; LLD (*hc*) Adelphi Univ., NY, 1994; Hon. DSc McMaster, 1983; Hon. DHum: Maurice Brown, Ga, 1987; Mount St Vincent, Canada, 1988; Hon. DHumLit, Morris Brown Univ., Atlanta, 1987; Hon. DLitt, Wilfrid Laurier Univ., Canada, 1994; numerous honours and awards from local and national organizations, including: Presidential Medal, Brooklyn Coll., 1988; Christiane Reiman Award, Internat. Council of Nurses, Geneva, 1989; McManus Medal, Columbia

Univ., 1990. Order of the Caribbean Community, 1994. *Publications:* papers on Nursing Educn and Primary Health Care. *Recreations:* travel, reading. *Address:* Government House, Barbados.
Died 19 Dec. 1995.

BARRY, Sir Philip Stuart M.; *see* Milner-Barry.

BARTELL, Lt-Col (Hon.) Kenneth George William, CBE 1977; FCIB; Past President, British Chambers of Commerce in Continental Europe; Past President (twice) and Honorary Vice-President, British Chamber of Commerce, France; *b* 5 Dec. 1914; *s* of William Richard Aust Bartell and Daisy Florence (*née* Kendall); *m* 1955, Lucie Adèle George (*d* 1990). *Educ:* Cooper's Company's Sch. BCom London. Westminster Bank Ltd, London, 1933. Served War, RAOC: France, 1939–40, Egypt and Middle East, 1940–46 (despatches twice); demobilised Hon. Lt-Col. Westminster Bank Ltd, London, 1946–49; Westminster Foreign Bank Ltd: Paris, 1950–51; Lyons, 1952–53; Bordeaux, 1954–55; Manager, State Commercial Bank, Rangoon, Burma, 1955–59; Man., then Chief Man., Westminster Foreign Bank, Paris, 1960–74; Gen. Man., Internat. Westminster Bank Ltd, France, 1974–76, retired. Freeman: Coopers' Co., 1981; City of London, 1981. *Recreations:* swimming, bridge. *Address:* 5 avenue Saint-Honoré-d'Eylau, Paris 75116, France. *T:* (1) 45 53 69 48. *Clubs:* Army and Navy, Royal Automobile; Cercle de l'Union Interalliée (Paris).
Died 18 March 1993.

BARTON, Margaret, LRAM; writer; *b* 1897; *y d* of Thomas Lloyd Barton and Fanny Roberta Isaacs. *Educ:* St Paul's Girls' Sch.; Royal Academy of Music. *Publications:* Tunbridge Wells, 1937; Garrick, 1948; (with Sir Osbert Sitwell): Sober Truth, 1930; Victoriana, 1931; Brighton, 1935. *Address:* 8 Penywern Road, SW5 9ST.
Deceased.

BASTEN, Sir Henry (Bolton), Kt 1966; CMG 1947; MA Oxon and Adelaide; retired, 1982; University of Adelaide, 1953–67, Vice-Chancellor, 1958–67; *b* 2 May 1903; *s* of G. H. Cohen, London. *Educ:* City of London Sch.; Merton Coll., Oxford (BA 1925); Adelaide Univ. Formerly Chairman and General Manager, Singapore & Penang Harbour Boards. Investigated conditions in Australian ports for Commonwealth Government, 1951–52, report published, 1952. Chm., Aust. Univs Commn, 1968–71; Foundn Chm. Council, Australian Inst. of Marine Science, 1972–77. Hon. DLitt Flinders Univ., S Australia, 1967. *Address:* Unit 34, Lindfield Gardens, 2 Ulmarra Place, East Lindfield, NSW 2070, Australia.
Died 8 April 1992.

BATES, Allan Frederick, CMG 1958; BA (Hons); *b* 15 July 1911; *s* of John Frederick Lawes and Ethel Hannah Bates; *m* 1937, Ena Edith, *d* of John Richard Boxall; three *s*. *Educ:* Woolwich Central Sch.; London Univ. Qualified as Certified Accountant, 1938; practised in London, 1938–44; joined Colonial Service (later Overseas Civil Service), 1944; Deputy Comptroller Inland Revenue, Cyprus, 1944–48; Comptroller Inland Revenue, Cyprus, 1948–52; Financial Secretary: Cyprus, 1952–60; Mauritius, 1960–64; Man. Dir, Develt Bank of Mauritius, 1964–70; Financial Advr (IMF) to Govt of Bahamas, 1971–75; Budget Advr (IMF) to Govt of Lesotho, 1975–76. Accounts Adviser, British Exec. Service Overseas, to Govt of Belize, 1982. Fellow Inst. of Taxation 1950; Mem., Inst. of Directors. *Recreations:* painting, carving. *Address:* 5 Redford Avenue, Coulsdon, Surrey. *T:* 081–660 7421. *Club:* Commonwealth Trust.
Died 1 Oct. 1991.

BATES, Prof. Sir David (Robert), Kt 1978; MSc, DSc; FRS 1955; MRIA; Research Professor, Queen's University, Belfast, 1976–82, then Emeritus; *b* Omagh,

Co. Tyrone, N Ireland, 18 Nov. 1916; *s* of late Walter Vivian Bates and Mary Olive Bates; *m* 1956, Barbara Bailey Morris; one *s* one *d*. *Educ:* Royal Belfast Academical Institution; Queen's Univ., Belfast; University Coll., London. Engaged at Admiralty Research Laboratory, 1939–41, and at Mine Design Department, 1941–45; Lecturer in Mathematics, University Coll., London, 1945–50; Consultant at US Naval Ordnance Test Station, Inyokern, Calif, 1950; Reader in Physics, University Coll., London, 1951; Queen's Univ., Belfast: Prof. of Applied Mathematics, 1951–68; Prof. of Theoretical Physics, 1968–74. Smithsonian Regent's Fellow, Center for Astrophysics, Cambridge, Mass, and Vis. Scholar in Atmospheric Scis, Harvard Univ., 1982–83. Chm., Adv. Bd Postgrad. Awards, NI Dept of Educn, 1974–82; Mem., UGC Working Party on Higher Educn in NI, 1983–87. Vice-Pres., RIA, 1976–77; Pres., Section A, British Assoc., 1987. Lectures: Chapman Meml, Univ. of Colorado, 1973; Kistiakowsky, Harvard Univ., 1983; Larmor, QUB, 1990. Hon. Pres., Sanibel Symposium, Florida, 1983. Vice-Pres., Alliance Party of NI, 1971. Mem., Internat. Acad. Astronautics, 1961; Sen. Mem., Internat. Acad. of Quantum Molecular Sci., 1985; Hon. Mem., Eur. Geophys Soc., 1990; Hon. Foreign Mem., Amer. Acad. of Arts and Scis, 1974; Associate Mem., Royal Acad., Belgium, 1979; Foreign Associate, Nat. Acad. of Scis, USA, 1984. Hon. DSc: Ulster, 1972; NUI, 1975; York (Ontario), 1983; QUB, 1984; Hon. ScD Dublin, 1979; Hon. LLD Glasgow, 1979; DUniv: York, 1983; Stirling, 1986; Essex, 1989. Hughes Medal, Royal Soc., 1970; Chree Medal, Inst. Physics, 1973; Gold Medal, Royal Astron. Soc., 1977; Fleming Medal, Amer. Geophys. Union, 1987. Annual eponymous medal estabd by Eur. Geophys Soc., 1992. Editor-in-Chief, Planetary and Space Science, 1962–92; (ed with B. Bederson) Advances in Atomic, Molecular and Optical Physics, 1965–92. *Publications:* papers in astrophysical, geophysical and physical journals. *Recreations:* reading, listening to radio. *Address:* 1 Newforge Grange, Belfast BT9 5QB. *T:* Belfast (0232) 665640.
Died 5 Jan. 1994.

BATES, Maj.-Gen. Sir (Edward) John (Hunter), KBE 1969 (OBE 1952); CB 1965; MC 1944; Director, Thomson Regional Newspapers, 1969–77; *b* 5 Dec. 1911; *s* of Ernest Bates, FRIBA; *m* 1947, Sheila Ann Norman; two *s* two *d*. *Educ:* Wellington Coll.; Corpus Christi Coll., Cambridge. BA 1933; MA 1963. Commissioned, 1932; Pre-war service in UK and Malaya; War Service in Africa, Middle East, Sicily, Italy and Greece; Senior Army Instructor, JSSC, 1954–57; Student, IDC, 1958; CRA, 2 Div., 1959; CCRA 1 (British) Corps, 1960–61; Dir, RA, War Office, 1961–64; Comdt of RMCS, 1964–67; Dir, Royal Defence Acad., 1967–68. Special Comr, Duke of York's Royal Military Sch., 1972–. Col Comdt, RA 1966–76. Mem. Ct of Assts, 1972–, Warden, 1977, Master, 1979, Worshipful Co. of Haberdashers. Chm., RUSI 1976–78. *Recreation:* fishing. *Address:* Chaffenden, Frensham Road, Rolvenden Layne, Cranbrook, Kent. *T:* Cranbrook (0580) 241536. *Clubs:* Army and Navy; Rye Golf.
Died 28 Jan. 1992.

BATES, Sir John (David), Kt 1969; CBE 1962; VRD; Australian Consul-General in New York, 1970–73; *b* 1 March 1904; *s* of H. W. Bates, Plymouth, Devon; *m* 1930, Phyllis Helen Muller; one *s*. *Educ:* Plymouth. Joined sea staff of Orient Line, 1925; transf. to shore staff, in Australia, 1929; RANVR, 1932–57, Comdr; Gen. Manager in Australia of Orient Line, 1954–60; Dep. Chm., P & O Lines of Australia, 1960–67; Chm., Hon. Bd of Australian Nat. Travel Assoc., 1956–67; Chm. Australian Tourist Commn, 1967–69. Federal Pres., Navy League of Australia, 1950–56; Trustee, Art Gallery of NSW,

1962–70; Lay Member, Trade Practices Tribunal, 1968–70. *Recreations:* reading, walking. *Club:* Union (Sydney). *Died 28 March 1992.*

BATES, William Stanley, CMG 1971; HM Diplomatic Service, retired; *b* 7 Sept. 1920; *m* 1970, Suzanne Elston. *Educ:* Christ's Hospital; Corpus Christi Coll., Cambridge. Asst Principal, Colonial Office, 1948; Principal, 1951; Commonwealth Relations Office, 1956; Canberra, 1956–59; Asst Sec., 1962; British Deputy High Commissioner, Northern Nigeria, 1963–65; Imperial Defence Coll., 1966; Head of Communications Dept, FCO, 1967–70; High Comr in Guyana, 1970–75; Ambassador to Korea, 1975–80. *Address:* 3 Houndean Close, Lewes, East Sussex BN7 1EZ.
Died 18 July 1993.

BATESON, Andrew James, QC 1971; *b* 29 June 1925; *m* 1954, Janette Mary Poupart (*d* 1970); one *s* three *d. Educ:* Eton. Called to the Bar, Middle Temple, 1951; Bencher, 1977. *Recreations:* shooting, fishing, gardening. *Address:* Little Foxwarren, Redhill Road, Cobham, Surrey KT11 1EG. *Club:* Flyfishers'. *Died 22 June 1995.*

BATH, 6th Marquess of, *cr* 1789; **Henry Frederick Thynne,** JP; Bt 1641; Viscount Weymouth and Baron Thynne, 1682; Major Royal Wiltshire Yeomanry; *b* 26 Jan. 1905; *o* surv. *s* of 5th Marquess, KG, CB, PC and Violet Caroline (*d* 1928), *d* of Sir Charles Mordaunt, 10th Bt; *S* father, 1946; *m* 1st, 1927, Hon. Daphne (marr. diss. 1953; she *m* 2nd, 1953, Major A. W. Fielding, DSO), *er d* of 4th Baron Vivian, DSO; two *s* one *d* (and one *s* decd); 2nd, 1953, Mrs Virginia Penelope Tennant, *d* of late Alan L. R. Parsons; one *d. Educ:* Harrow; Christ Church, Oxford. MP (U) Frome Division, Som, 1931–35. Served War of 1939–45 (wounded). Chm., Football Pools Panel, 1967–87. Life-long interest in forestry; some of the best private woodland in the country at Longleat. *Heir:* s Viscount Weymouth [*b* 6 May 1932; *m* 1969, Anna Gael Gyarmathy; one *s* one *d*]. *Address:* Job's Mill, Warminster, Wilts BA12 8BB. *T:* Warminster (0985) 212279; Longleat, Warminster, Wilts. *Club:* White's.
Died 30 June 1992.

BATHURST, Sir Frederick Peter Methuen Hervey-, 6th Bt, *cr* 1818; *b* 26 Jan. 1903; *s* of Sir Frederick Edward William Hervey-Bathurst, 5th Bt, DSO and Hon. Moira O'Brien, 2nd *d* of 14th Baron Inchiquin; *S* father 1956; *m* 1st, 1933, Maureen (marr. diss. 1956), *d* of Charles Gordon, Boveridge Park, Salisbury; one *s* one *d*; 2nd, 1958, Mrs Cornelia Shepard Riker, *widow* of Dr John Lawrence Riker, Rumson, NJ, USA. *Educ:* Eton. Served War of 1939–45, Capt. Grenadier Guards. *Recreations:* sailing, riding, ski-ing, flying. *Heir:* s Frederick John Charles Gordon Hervey-Bathurst [*b* 23 April 1934; *m* 1957, Caroline Myrtle, *d* of Lieut-Col Sir William Starkey, 2nd Bt, and late Irene Myrtle Francklin; one *s* two *d*]. *Address:* PO Box 236, Rumson, NJ 07760, USA. *T:* (908) 2914194. *Clubs:* Cavalry and Guards, Royal Ocean Racing. *Died 27 Dec. 1995.*

BATSFORD, Sir Brian (Caldwell Cook), Kt 1974; painter; *b* 18 Dec. 1910; *s* of late Arthur Caldwell Cook, Gerrards Cross, Bucks; assumed mother's maiden name of Batsford by Deed Poll, 1946; *m* 1945, Joan (Wendy), *o d* of late Norman Cunliffe, DSc, Oxford; two *d. Educ:* Repton Sch.; Central Sch. of Arts and Crafts. Dip., Paris Exhibn, 1935. Joined B. T. Batsford Ltd, Booksellers and Publishers, 1928; Chairman, 1952–74; President, 1974–77. As Brian Cook, illustrated topographical books; designed over 100 book jackets, and posters for LNER and British Travel and Holidays Assoc. Lectured in Canada under auspices Canadian National Council of Education, 1935, 1937; lectured in Scandinavia and Baltic States under auspices of British Council, 1940. Hon. Sec. Empire Youth Sunday

Cttee, 1938; Chm. Youth City Cttee of Enquiry, 1939. RAF, 1941–46. Contested Chelmsford Div. of Essex for Nat. Govt, 1945; MP (C) Ealing South, 1958–Feb. 1974; PPS to Minister of Works, 1959–60; Asst Govt Whip, 1962–64; Opposition Deputy Chief Whip, 1964–67; Chairman: Adv. Cttee on Works of Art in House of Commons, 1970; House of Commons Library Cttee, 1970–74. Alderman, GLC, and Parly Rep. of GLC Majority Party, 1967–70; co-opted Mem., GLC Arts and Recreation Cttee, 1970–72. Pres., London Appreciation Soc., 1955. FRSA 1955 (Mem. Council, 1967; Treasurer, 1971–73; Chm., 1973–75; Vice-Pres., 1975); SGA 1933; FSIAD 1971 (MSIA 1936). Mem., Post Office Stamp Adv. Cttee, 1967–80. Pres., Old Reptonian Soc., 1973; Mem., Governing Body, Repton Sch., 1973. Vice-Pres., Questors' Theatre, Ealing, 1978; Pres., Rye Conservation Soc., 1983– (Chm., 1978–83). Hon. RI 1985. *Publication:* The Britain of Brian Cook, 1987. *Recreations:* painting (two paintings included in Arts Council Exhibn, Landscape in Britain 1850–1950, Hayward Gall., 1983; retrospective exhibn, Michael Parkin Gall., 1987), gardening. *Address:* Buckland House, Mill Road, Winchelsea, E Sussex TN36 4HJ. *T:* Rye (0797) 226131. *Club:* Pratt's.
Died 5 March 1991.

BATT, Reginald Joseph Alexander; barrister; a Recorder of the Crown Court, since 1982; *b* 22 July 1920; *o s* of late Benjamin and Alice Harriett Batt; *m* 1951, Mary Margaret (*née* Canning), actress; one *d. Educ:* local authority schs; privately. Called to the Bar, Inner Temple, 1952, Bencher, 1986. *Publications:* articles on law of real property and on landlord and tenant. *Recreations:* walking, tennis, antiques, music. *Address:* 6 King's Bench Walk, Temple, EC4Y 7DR. *T:* 071–583 0410.
Died 13 June 1991.

BATTEN, Mark Wilfrid, RBA 1962; FRBS 1952 (ARBS 1950); sculptor, direct carver in stone; *b* 21 July 1905; *s* of Edward Batten; *m* 1933, Elsie May Owston Thorneloe (*d* 1961); one *d. Educ:* Chelsea Sch. of Art. Commenced to experiment individually with stone carving, 1927; exhibited only drawings and paintings until 1934; combined experiment in sculpture with learning craft of stone carving mainly in granite mason's yards in Cornwall; first exhibited sculpture, 1936; collaborated with Eric Gill, 1939; first exhibited sculpture at Royal Academy, 1939; exhibited Paris Salon, 1949, and thereafter frequently at Royal Acad. and many sculpture exhibitions in Paris, London and provincial cities; many commissions for stone sculptures on public buildings; works in museums and art galleries. President, RBS, 1956–61, Mem. Council, 1953–; Mem. Council, RBA, 1964–. Société des Artistes Français: Gold Medal for Sculpture, 1977 (Silver Medal, 1952); Associate, 1970. Hon. Mem. National Sculpture Soc. of the USA, 1956. FRSA 1936. Syracuse Univ., USA, estab. Mark Batten Manuscripts Collection, 1965, also Wichita State Univ., 1971. War Service in Life Guards, 1940–45. *Publications:* Stone Sculpture by Direct Carving, 1957; Direct Carving in Stone, 1966; articles in art magazines. *Recreations:* country life, travel, contemplation of other men's sculptures. *Address:* 22c Grosvenor Road, W4 4EH. *Club:* Chelsea Arts. *Died 4 Jan. 1993.*

BAVERSTOCK, Donald Leighton; Executive Producer, Television, BBC Manchester, 1975–77; *b* 18 Jan. 1924; *s* of Thomas Philip Baverstock and Sarah Ann; *m* 1957, Gillian Mary (marr. diss. 1994), *d* of late Enid Blyton, (Mrs K. D. Waters); one *s* two *d* (and one *s* decd). *Educ:* Canton High Sch., Cardiff; Christ Church, Oxford (MA). Served with RAF, 1943–46; completed tour of operations Bomber Command, 1944; Instructor, Navigation, 1944–46. History Master, Wellington Coll., 1949; Producer, BBC General Overseas Service, 1950–54; Producer, BBC Television Service, 1954–57; Editor,

Tonight Programme, 1957–61; Asst Controller, Television Programmes, BBC, 1961–63; Chief of Programmes BBC TV (1), 1963–65; Partner, Jay, Baverstock, Milne & Co., 1965–67; Dir of Programmes, Yorkshire TV, 1967–73; Man. Dir, Granada Video Ltd, 1974–75. *Address:* Low Hall, Middleton, Ilkley, Yorks. *T:* Ilkley (01943) 608037.
Died 16 March 1995.

BAXANDALL, David Kighley, CBE 1959; Director of National Galleries of Scotland, 1952–70, retired; *b* 11 Oct. 1905; *m* 1931, Isobel (*d* 1990), *d* of Canon D. J. Thomas; one *s* twin *d. Educ:* King's Coll. Sch., Wimbledon; King's Coll., University of London. Asst Keeper, 1929–39, Keeper of the Department of Art, 1939–41, National Museum of Wales. Served in RAF, 1941–45. Dir of Manchester City Art Galleries, 1945–52. *Publications:* Ben Nicholson, 1962; numerous articles, gallery handbooks, catalogues and broadcast talks. *Address:* 24 Guardian Court, Ferrers Street, Hereford HR1 2LP. *T:* Hereford (0432) 357881. *Died 17 Oct. 1992.*

BAXTER, Jeremy Richard; Assistant Director, Nationalised Industries' Chairmen's Group, 1984–90; *b* 20 Jan. 1929; *s* of late Andrew Paterson Baxter and Ann Winifred Baxter; *m* 1965, Faith Elizabeth Graham; two *s* one *d. Educ:* Sedbergh Sch.; St John's Coll., Cambridge (BA Class. Tripos). Asst Principal, Post Office, 1952; Asst Private Sec. to Postmaster-Gen., 1956; Private Sec. to Asst Postmaster-Gen., 1957; Principal, Post Office, 1958; Principal, Treasury, 1964; Asst Sec., Post Office, 1967; Dir, Postal Personnel, 1971; Dir of Personnel, European Commn, 1973–81; Sec., Post Office, 1982–84. *Recreations:* sailing, gardening. *Address:* Spring Grove Farm, Mursley, Milton Keynes MK17 0SA. *Club:* Travellers'. *Died 4 Jan. 1991.*

BAXTER, Walter; author; *b* 17 May 1915; *s* of G. G. Baxter. *Educ:* St Lawrence, Ramsgate; Trinity Hall, Cambridge. Worked in the City, 1936–39; served War of 1939–45, with KOYLI in Burma; afterwards, in India, ADC to General Slim, and on Staff of a Corps HQ during re-conquest of Burma. After completion of first novel, returned to India to work temporarily on a mission. *Publications:* Look Down in Mercy, 1951; The Image and The Search, 1953. *Address:* Huish House, Oare, Marlborough, Wilts SN8 4JN.
Died 25 July 1994.

BAYNE, John; advocate; Sheriff of Glasgow and Strathkelvin, 1975–79; Sheriff (formerly Sheriff-Substitute) of Lanarkshire at Glasgow, 1959–74. *Address:* Winsford, 7 Milrig Road, Rutherglen G73 2NQ.
Died 29 March 1994.

BAYNE-POWELL, Robert Lane, CB 1981; Senior Registrar of the Family Division, High Court of Justice, 1976–82, retired (Registrar, 1964–76); *b* 10 Oct. 1910; 2nd *s* of William Maurice and Rosamond Alicia Bayne-Powell; *m* 1938, Nancy Geraldine (*d* 1979), *d* of late Lt-Col J. L. Philips, DSO; one *s* two *d. Educ:* Charterhouse; Trinity Coll., Cambridge (BA). Called to Bar, Middle Temple, 1935; Mem., Senate of Inns of Court and the Bar, 1978–81. Served War of 1939–45, Intell. Corps; Major 1944; Allied Commn for Austria, 1945. Mem., Reviewing Cttee on Export of Works of Art, 1975–81; Hon. Keeper of the Miniatures, Fitzwilliam Museum, Cambridge, 1980–. *Publications:* (special editor) Williams and Mortimer on Executors and Probate, 1970; Catalogue of Miniatures in the Fitzwilliam Museum, Cambridge, 1985. *Recreations:* gardening, miniature collecting, wine-tasting. *Address:* The Mount, Borough Green, Sevenoaks, Kent. *T:* Borough Green (0732) 882045. *Club:* Athenæum.
Died 30 Jan. 1994.

BEACH, Surgeon Rear-Adm. William Vincent, CB 1962; OBE 1949; MRCS; LRCP; FRCSE; retired; *b* 22 Nov.

1903; *yr s* of late William Henry Beach; *m* 1931, Daphne Muriel (*d* 1992), *yr d* of late Eustace Ackworth Joseph, ICS; two *d. Educ:* Seaford Coll.; Guy's Hospital, London. Joined RN Medical Service, 1928. Served War of 1939–45 as Surgical specialist in Hospital ships, Atlantic and Pacific Fleets. Surgical Registrar, Royal Victoria Infirmary, Newcastle upon Tyne; Senior Specialist in Surgery, RN Hospitals, Chatham, Haslar, Malta, Portland; Senior Medical Officer, RN Hospital, Malta; Medical Officer i/c RN Hospital, Portland; Sen. Medical Officer, Surgical Division, RN Hospital, Haslar; Medical Officer in charge of Royal Naval Hospital, Chatham, and Command MO on staff of C-in-C the Nore Command, 1960–61; MO i/c RN Hospital, Malta, and on staff of C-in-C, Mediterranean and as Medical Adviser to C-in-C, Allied Forces, Mediterranean, 1961–63. Surg. Rear-Admiral, 1960. QHS 1960. Senior Surgeon i/c Shaw Savill Passenger Liners, 1966–75. Fellow, Assoc. of Surgeons of Great Britain and Ireland, 1947, Senior Fellow, 1963. *Publications:* Urgent Surgery of the Hand, 1940; Inguinal Hernia—a new operation, 1946; The Treatment of Burns, 1950. *Recreations:* shooting, fishing. *Address:* Cherrytree Cottage, Easton, Winchester SO21 1EG. *T:* Itchen Abbas (01962) 779222. *Club:* Naval and Military.
Died 28 Oct. 1995.

BEALE, Sir William (Francis), Kt 1956; OBE 1945; *b* 27 Jan. 1908; *y s* of late George and Elizabeth Beale, Potterspury Lodge, Northants; *m* 1934, Dèva Zaloudek; one *s* one *d. Educ:* Downside Sch.; Pembroke Coll., Cambridge. Joined Green's Stores (Ilford) Ltd, Dir, 1929–63 (Chm., 1950–63). Navy, Army and Air Force Institutes, UK, 1940–41 (Dir, 1949–61; Chm. 1953–61); EFI, GHQ West Africa, 1942–43; EFI, 21st Army Gp, 1944–46. *Recreations:* hunting, shooting; formerly Rugby football (Eastern Counties Cap, 1932). *Address:* The Old Rectory, Woodborough, Pewsey, Wilts SN9 5PH. *Club:* Army and Navy. *Died 15 Jan. 1992.*

BEAM, Jacob Dyneley; US Ambassador to USSR, 1969–73; *b* Princeton, NJ, 24 March 1908; *s* of Jacob Newton Beam and Mary Prince; *m* 1952, Margaret Glassford; one *s. Educ:* Kent Sch., USA; Princeton Univ. (BA 1929); Cambridge Univ., England (1929–30). Vice-Consul, Geneva, 1931–34; Third Sec., Berlin, 1934–40; Second Sec., London, 1941–45; Asst Political Adviser, HQ, US Forces, Germany, 1945–47; Chief of Central European Div., Dept of State, 1947–49; Counsellor and Consul-Gen., US Embassy, Djakarta, 1949–51; Actg US Rep., UN Commn for Indonesia, 1951; Counsellor, Belgrade, 1951–52; Minister-Counsellor, US Embassy, Moscow, 1952–53 (actg head); Dep. Asst Sec. of State, 1953–57; US Ambassador to Poland, 1957–61; Asst Dir, Internat. Relations Bureau, Arms Control and Disarmament Agency, USA, 1962–66; US Ambassador to Czechoslovakia, 1966–68. Chm., US Delegn to Internat. Telecomm. Union Plenipotentiary Conf., Malaga, 1973. Dir, Radio Free Europe, 1974–77. LLB *hc* Princeton, 1970. *Publication:* Multiple Exposure, 1978. *Address:* 3129 'O' Street NW, Washington, DC 20007, USA. *Club:* Metropolitan (Washington, DC).
Died 16 Aug. 1993.

BEARDS, Paul Francis Richmond; *b* 1 Dec. 1916; *s* of late Dr Clifford Beards and Dorothy (*née* Richmond); *m* 1950, Margaret Elizabeth, *y d* of late V. R. Aronson, CBE, KC; one *s* one *d. Educ:* Marlborough; Queen's Coll., Oxford (Open Scholar; 1st cl. hons Mod. Hist.). Entered Admin. Class of Home Civil Service, 1938; Asst Prin., War Office; served in Army, 1940–44; Principal War Office, 1945; Asst Private Sec. to successive Prime Ministers, 1945–48; Prin. Private Sec. to successive Secs of State for War, 1951–54; Asst Sec., 1954; Imp. Def. Coll., 1961; Asst Under-Sec. of State, MoD, 1964–69;

Comr for Administration and Finance, Forestry Commn, 1969; retd, 1970. Coronation Medal, 1953. *Recreations:* fishing, gardening, archæology. *Address:* Thrale Cottage, Budleigh Salterton, Devon EX9 6EA. *T:* Budleigh Salterton (03954) 2084. *Club:* Commonwealth Trust.
Died 6 Nov. 1993.

BEATTIE, (William) John (Hunt Montgomery), MA Cantab; MD, FRCS, FRCOG, FRCGP; retired; Consultant Gynæcologist and Obstetric Surgeon, St Bartholomew's Hospital; Gynæcologist: Leatherhead Hospital; Florence Nightingale Hospital; *b* 25 Oct. 1902. *Educ:* Cambridge Univ.; London Univ. MRCS, LRCP 1927; BCh (Cantab) 1928; FRCS 1929; MB 1930; MD 1933; FRCOG 1942. Examiner: Central Midwives' Board; Univs of Oxford, Cambridge and London (Obst. and Gynæcol.); Conjoint Board (Midwifery and Gynæcol.). *Publications:* (jt) Diseases of Women by Ten Teachers, 1941; articles in medical journals. *Address:* 89 West Street, Reigate, Surrey RH2 9DA. *Died 5 Jan. 1993.*

BEAVAN, family name of **Baron Ardwick.**

BECK, (Rudolph) Rolf, (Baron Rolf Beck); Chairman and Managing Director of Slip and Molyslip Group of Companies since 1939; *b* 25 March 1914; *s* of Baron Dr Otto Beck (famous industrialist and politician in Austrian and Hungarian Empire; also special Envoy and Representative in Switzerland of Emperor Franz Josef of Austria during 1914–18 War) and Baroness Margaret Beck; *m* 1st, 1944, Elizabeth Lesley Brenchley (marr. diss; decd), *d* of Captain Fletcher, RN; one *s*; 2nd, 1979, Countess Mariana von Rosen (marr. diss.), *d* of Count and Countess Mörner, Bjorksund, Sweden; 3rd, 1990, Susan Caroline Cleland (*née* Owtram). *Educ:* Theresanium Mil. Acad.; Univs of Geneva, Lausanne, Vienna. Degrees in Engrg and Chem. Whilst still at univ. took up racing and rally driving seriously in a Skoda car; became well known amateur driver, 1935; came to London as rep. of Skoda works to make Skoda cars in UK with 51 per cent British parts and labour and 49 per cent Czechoslovakian parts; outbreak of war ended this develt, 1938; founded Slip Products Ltd, 1939; discovered Milex (petrol economiser), 1940, and Dieslip (fuel additive of interest to the Admty and Min. of War Transport); apptd Adviser on gas producer research, 1940; acted as export adviser to Rolls Royce and toured USA twice; formed cos, Slip Products and Engrg, Slip Trading and Shipping, also Slip Auto Sales and Engrg, 1948–49; invented for automobiles or oil drilling: Molyslip (lubricant); Copaslip (compound), 1959; founded: Slip Internat. Ltd; Molyslip Trading, 1961; Molyslip Holdings, 1964; Molyslip Chemicals Ltd, 1967; Molytex Internat., 1970; on 1 Nov. 1980 a 50/50 company formed between Molyslip Holdings Ltd and Jet-Lube Lubricants Ltd, Maidenhead, called Molyslip Internat. Sales Ltd; introduced additives: Multiglide and Molyglide, 1972; invented Molyslip 2001 (a metal treatment to be added to oil which considerably reduces engine wear, petrol and oil consumption, water and oil temps), 1984. Fellow of Scientific Exploration Soc.; FZS. *Recreations:* skiing, water skiing, shooting, sailing. *Address:* 62 Bishops Mansions, Bishops Park Road, SW6. *T:* 071–731 3021; Cap Davia, Marine de Davia, Ile Rousse, Corsica. *T:* Ile Rousse 600625. *Clubs:* Royal Automobile, Hurlingham; Royal Scottish Automobile (Glasgow); Royal Harwich Yacht; West Mersey Yacht; Union Interalliée (Paris); Princeton (NY). *Died 25 April 1991.*

BECKETT, John Michael; Chairman and Chief Executive, Woolworth Holdings plc, 1982–86; *b* 22 June 1929; *yr s* of H. N. Beckett, MBE, and C. L. Beckett; *m* 1955, Joan Mary, *o d* of Percy and F. M. Rogerson; five *d*. *Educ:* Wolverhampton Grammar Sch.; Magdalen Coll., Oxford (BA 1953, MA 1957). Nat. Service and Reg. Commn RA, 1947–50; TA, 1950–60. Called to Bar, Gray's Inn, 1954.

Bar, 1954–55; Tootal Ltd, 1955–58; Tarmac Ltd, 1958–75 (Dir, 1963–82, non-exec., 1975–82); Chief Exec., British Sugar Corp. Ltd, 1975–82. Dir, Johnson Matthey, 1985–86. Hon. FIQ; FRSA; CBIM.
Died 15 Nov. 1991.

BECKWITH, John Gordon, FBA 1974; FSA 1968; Keeper, Department of Architecture and Sculpture, Victoria and Albert Museum, 1974–79; *b* 2 Dec. 1918; *s* of late John Frederick Beckwith. *Educ:* Ampleforth Coll., York; Exeter Coll., Oxford (Loscombe Richards Exhibnr; Amelia Jackson Student). MA. Served with The Duke of Wellington's Regt, 1939–45. Victoria and Albert Museum: Asst Keeper, Dept of Textiles, 1948; Asst Keeper, Dept of Architecture and Sculpture, 1955, Dep. Keeper, 1958. Vis. Fellow of Harvard Univ. at Dumbarton Oaks Res. Library and Collection, Washington, DC, 1950–51; Visiting Professor: Harvard Univ. (Fogg Museum of Art), 1964; Univ. of Missouri, Columbia, Mo, 1968–69; Slade Prof. of Fine Art, Oxford Univ., 1978–79. Reynolds-Stephens Meml Lecture, RBS, 1965. Mem., Centre International des Etudes des Textils Anciens, Lyon, 1953–. *Publications:* The Andrews Diptych, 1958; Coptic Textiles, 1959; Caskets from Cordoba, 1960; The Art of Constantinople, 1961; The Veroli Casket, 1962; Coptic Sculpture, 1963; The Basilewsky Situla, 1963; Early Medieval Art, 1964; The Adoration of the Magi in Whalebone, 1966; Early Christian and Byzantine Art, Pelican History of Art, 1970; Ivory Carvings in Early Medieval England, 1972; Catalogue of Exhibition, Ivory Carvings in Early Medieval England 700–1200, 1974; contrib. Art Bulletin, Burlington Magazine, etc. *Recreation:* music. *Address:* Flat 12, 77 Ladbroke Grove, W11 2PF. *T:* 071–727 7277. *Died 20 Feb. 1991.*

BEDBROOK, Sir George (Montario), Kt 1978; OBE 1963; FRCS, FRACS; Director, Prevention of Spinal Injuries Programme, Royal Perth Rehabilitation Hospital, since 1990; *b* 8 Nov. 1921; *s* of Arthur Bedbrook and Ethel (*née* Prince); *m* 1946, Jessie Violet (*née* Page); two *s* three *d*. *Educ:* University High Sch., Melbourne; Medical Sch., Univ. of Melbourne (MB BS (Hons) 1944; J. P. Ryan Schol. in Surgery; MS 1950). FRACS 1950; FRCS 1951. Dip. Physical and Rehabilitation Med. (Sydney) 1970. Resident MO, Royal Melb. Hosp., Vic, 1944–45; Lectr in Anatomy, Univ. of Melb., Vic, 1946–50; Resident MO, Nat. Orthopaedic Hosp., London, 1951; Registrar, Orthopaedic Dept, Croydon Gp Hosps, 1951–53; private practice in Perth, WA; Mem. Orthopaedic Dept, Royal Perth Hosp., 1953; began Paraplegic Service, Royal Perth Hosp., 1954; Head, Dept of Paraplegia, Royal Perth Rehabilitation Hosp., 1954–72, resigned; Royal Perth Hospital and Royal Perth Rehabilitation Hospital: Chm., Dept of Orthopaedic Surgery, 1965–79; Sen. Surgeon, Spinal Unit, 1972–86; Sen. Orthopaedic Consultant, 1972–86, then Consultant Emeritus; Clinical Sub-Dean, Royal Perth Hosp. and Univ. of WA, 1987–89. Pres., Aust. Orthopaedic Assoc., 1977; Vice Chm., Nat. Adv. Council for the Handicapped, 1975–83; Vice-Pres., Australian Council for the Rehabilitation of the Disabled, 1970–80; Pres., Internat. Med. Soc. of Paraplegia, 1981–84; Chm., W Australian Cttee, Internat. Year of Disabled Persons, 1981. Hon. FRCSE 1981; Hon. Fellow, Coll. of Rehabilitation Medicine, 1987; Hon. MD, WA, 1973; Hon. DTech Curtin Univ., 1984. OStJ 1972. Betts Medal, Aust. Orthopaedic Assoc., 1972. *Publications:* Care and Management of Spinal Cord Injuries, 1981; Lifetime Care of the Paraplegic Patient, 1985; numerous (114) papers and contribs to medical and scientific jls, especially relating to spinal injuries with paraplegia. *Recreations:* reading, music, travel, sports for the disabled. *Address:* (home) 29 Ulster Road, Floreat Park, WA 6014,

Australia. *T:* 3873582; (office) 13 Colin Grove, West Perth, WA 6005, Australia. *T:* 3217543.
Died 6 Oct. 1991.

BEDDOES, Air Vice-Marshal John Geoffrey Genior, CB 1981; FRAeS; aviation consultant; *b* 21 May 1925; *s* of Algernon Geoffrey Beddoes and Lucy Isobel (*née* Collier); *m* 1948, Betty Morris Kendrick; three *s. Educ:* Wirral Grammar Sch., Bebington, Cheshire. Pilot training in Rhodesia and Egypt, 1943–45; No 114 Sqdn, Italy and Aden, Bostons and Mosquitos, 1945–46; No 30 Sqdn, Abingdon and Berlin Airlift, Dakotas, 1947–49; Central Flying Sch., 1949; Flying Instr, RAF Coll., Cranwell and Central Flying Sch., 1950–55; Flight Comdr, No 57 Sqdn, Canberras, 1955; Air Ministry, 1956–57; Flying Coll., 1958; Flt Comdr No 57 Sqdn, Victor Mk 1, 1959–61; sc Bracknell, 1962; OC No 139 (Jamaica) Sqdn, Victor Mk 2, 1963–64; Wing Comdr Ops HQ No 3 Gp, 1965–67; Directing Staff Coll. of Air Warfare, 1968–69; OC RAF Laarbruch, 1969–71; Dep. Dir, Operational Requirements, MoD, 1971–73; Asst COS Offensive Operations, HQ 2 ATAF, 1974–75; Director of Operational Requirements, MoD, 1975–78; Dir Gen. Aircraft (2), MoD PE, 1978–80; retired RAF, 1981. Mem., Norfolk CC, 1989– (Chm., Highways Cttee, 1991–). Chm., St Gregory's Trust, Norwich, 1988–. FIMgt. *Recreations:* music, cricket, DIY, golf, gardening. *Address:* White Stables, Stow Bedon, Norfolk NR17 1HP. *T:* Caston 524. *Club:* Royal Air Force.
Died 20 May 1993.

BEDINGFIELD, Christopher Ohl Macredie, TD 1968; QC 1976; a Recorder of the Crown Court, since 1972; *b* 2 June 1935; *s* of late Norman Macredie Bedingfield, Nantygroes, Radnorshire and Mrs Macredie Bedingfield. *Educ:* Rugby; University Coll., Oxford (MA). Called to Bar, Gray's Inn, 1957, Bencher, 1986; Wales and Chester Circuit. Commnd 2 Mon R; NS 24th Regt; Staff Captain TA, 1960–64; Coy Comdr 4 RWF, 1964–69; Lt-Col TAVR, 1973–76, Co. Comdt Denbigh and Flint ACF 1973, Clwyd ACF 1974–76 (resigned on appt as QC). *Recreations:* riding, squash. *Address:* 21 Whitefriars, Chester CH1 1NZ. *T:* Chester (01244) 342020; (residence) Nantygroes, near Knighton, Powys. *T:* Whitton (01547) 560220. *Club:* Reform. *Died 12 Nov. 1995.*

BEEBY, George Harry, CBE 1974; PhD, BSc; CEng, FIChemE, CChem, FRSC; Chairman, Inveresk Research Foundation, 1977–84; *b* 9 Sept. 1902; *s* of George Beeby and Lucy Beeby (*née* Monk); *m* 1929, Helen Elizabeth Edwards (*d* 1992); one *d. Educ:* Loughborough Grammar Sch.; Loughborough Coll. BSc Hons 1922; PhD 1924, London Univ. Various appts in rubber and chemical industries, 1924–84; Chm., Thorium Ltd and Radiochemical Centre (later Amersham Internat.), 1949–57; Divisional Chm., ICI, 1954–57; Chm., British Titan Ltd, 1957–69. Chm., EDC for Chemical Industry, 1964–67; Member: Robens Cttee on Safety and Health at Work, 1970–72; Parly and Sci. Cttee, 1971–83; Windeyer Cttee on lead poisoning, 1972. Chairman: Nat. Sulphuric Acid Assoc., 1963–65; British Standards Instn, 1967–70 (Dep. Pres. 1970–73). Pres., Soc. of Chemical Industry, 1970–72 (Vice-Pres., 1966–69); Vice-Pres., RoSPA, 1969–; Hon. Mem., Chemical Industries Assoc. FRSA 1969. Hon. DTech Loughborough Univ. of Technology, 1969. Soc. of Chemical Industry Medal, 1973. *Publications:* contribs to various jls on industrial safety, industrial economics and business administration. *Address:* The Laurels, Sandy Drive, Cobham, Surrey KT11 2ET. *T:* Oxshott (0372) 842346.
Died 14 June 1994.

BEECH, Patrick Mervyn, CBE 1970; Controller, English Regions, BBC, 1969–72, retired; *b* 31 Oct. 1912; *s* of Howard Worcester Mervyn Beech and Stella Patrick Campbell; *m* 1st, 1935, Sigrid Gunnel Christenson (*d*

1959); two *d*; 2nd, 1960, Merle-Mary Barnes; one *d. Educ:* Stowe; Exeter Coll., Oxford. Joined BBC as Producer, West Region, 1935; News Editor, West Region, 1945; Asst Head of Programmes, West Region, 1954; Controller, Midland Region, 1964–69. *Recreations:* photography, music, theatre. *Address:* Mill Bank, Cradley, near Malvern, Worcs WR13 5NL. *T:* Ridgway Cross (0886) 880234. *Died 10 May 1993.*

BEESTON, Prof. Alfred Felix Landon, MA, DPhil; FBA 1965; Laudian Professor of Arabic, Oxford, 1955–78; Emeritus Fellow, St John's College, Oxford, 1978 (Fellow, 1955–78); *b* 23 Feb. 1911; *o s* of Herbert Arthur Beeston and Edith Mary Landon. *Educ:* Westminster Sch.; Christ Church, Oxford. James Mew Arabic Scholarship, Oxford, 1934; MA (Oxford), 1936; DPhil (Oxford), 1937. Lieut, Intell. Corps, 1940; Capt., 1943. Asst in Dept of Oriental Books, Bodleian Library, Oxford, 1935–40; Sub-Librarian and Keeper of Oriental Books, Bodleian Library, 1946–55. Mem., Governing Body, SOAS, Univ. of London, 1980–84 (Hon. Fellow 1980). Hon. Mem., Hungarian Oriental Soc., 1993. Lidzbarski Medal for Semitic Epigraphy, Deutsche Morgenländische Ges., 1983. *Publications:* Baidāwī's Commentary on Sūrah 12, 1963; Written Arabic, 1968; The Arabic Language Today, 1970; Selections from the Poetry of Baššār, 1977; Samples of Arabic Prose, 1977; The 'Epistle on Singing Girls' of Jāhiz, 1980; Sabaic Grammar, 1984; many articles. *Address:* St John's College, Oxford OX1 3JP.
Died 29 Sept. 1995.

BEEVOR, Miles; retired solicitor and director of companies; *b* 8 March 1900; 2nd *s* of Rowland Beevor; *m* 1st, 1924, Margaret Florence Platt (*d* 1934); one *s* (one *d* decd); 2nd, 1935, Sybil Gilliat (*d* 1991); two *s* one *d. Educ:* Winchester (Scholar); New Coll., Oxford (Scholar). BA 1921. Admitted a Solicitor, 1925. Served European War, 1914–18, in Army (RE Officer Cadet Battalion), 1918; War of 1939–45, RAFVR (Flt-Lieut Admin. and Special Duties Br.), 1941–43. Chief Legal Adviser, LNER, 1943–47; Actg Chief General Manager, LNER, 1947; Chief Sec. and Legal Adviser, British Transport Commission, 1947–51; Managing Dir, Brush Electrical Engineering Co. Ltd (which became The Brush Group Ltd), 1952–56, Deputy Chm. and Joint Managing Dir, 1956–57. *Address:* Badger Farmhouse, Badger, near Wolverhampton WV6 7JS. *T:* Ackelton (07465) 240.
Died 9 Sept. 1994.

BEGG, Sir Neil (Colquhoun), KBE 1986 (OBE 1973); Director of Medical Services, Royal New Zealand Plunket Society, 1956–76, retired; *b* 13 April 1915; *s* of Charles Mackie Begg, CB, CMG, Croix de Guerre, and Lillian Helen Lawrance Begg; *m* 1942, Margaret Milne MacLean; two *s* two *d. Educ:* John McGlashan Coll., Dunedin, NZ; Otago Univ. Med. Sch. (MB ChB 1940); postgrad. paediatrics, London and Edinburgh, 1947–48. DCH, MRCP London, MRCPE. Served 2 NZ Expedn Force, 1942–46, Med. Corps, ME and Italy. Paediatrician, Dunedin Public Hosp., 1949–56. Chm., NZ Historic Places Trust, 1978–86. Hon. FRCPE 1958, Hon. FRCP 1977. *Publications:* (with A. C. Begg) Dusky Bay, 1966; (with A. C. Begg) James Cook and New Zealand, 1969; Child and his Family, 1970, 8th edn 1975; (with A. C. Begg) Port Preservation, 1973; (with A. C. Begg) The World of John Boultbee, 1979; The Intervening Years, 1992; contribs to NZ Med. Jl. *Recreation:* trout fishing. *Address:* 86 Newington Avenue, Dunedin 9001, New Zealand. *T:* (3) 4672089. *Died 25 June 1995.*

BEGG, Admiral of the Fleet Sir Varyl (Cargill), GCB 1965 (KCB 1962; CB 1959); DSO 1952; DSC 1941; Governor and Commander-in-Chief of Gibraltar, 1969–73; *b* 1 Oct. 1908; *s* of Francis Cargill Begg and Muriel Clare Robinson; *m* 1943, Rosemary Cowan, CStJ; two *s. Educ:*

St Andrews Sch., Eastbourne; Malvern Coll. Entered RN, special entry, 1926; Qualified Gunnery Officer, 1933; HMS Glasgow, 1939–40; HMS Warspite, 1940–43; Comdr Dec. 1942; Capt. 1947; commanded HM Gunnery Sch., Chatham, 1948–50; 8th Destroyer Flotilla, 1950–52; HMS Excellent, 1952–54; HMS Triumph, 1955–56; idc 1954; Rear-Adm. 1957; Chief of Staff to C-in-C Portsmouth 1957–58; Flag Officer Commanding Fifth Cruiser Squadron and Flag Officer Second-in-Command, Far East Station, 1958–60; Vice-Adm. 1960; a Lord Commissioner of the Admiralty and Vice-Chief of Naval Staff, 1961–63; Admiral, 1963; C-in-C, British Forces in the Far East, and UK Military Adviser to SEATO, 1963–65; C-in-C, Portsmouth, and Allied C-in-C, Channel, 1965–66; Chief of Naval Staff and First Sea Lord, 1966–68. KStJ 1969. PMN 1966. *Recreations:* fishing, gardening. *Address:* Copyhold Cottage, Chilbolton, Stockbridge, Hants SO20 6BA. *Club:* Army and Navy.
Died 13 July 1995.

BEGIN, Menachem, MJr; Prime Minister, State of Israel, 1977–83; *b* Brest-Litovsk, Poland, 16 Aug. 1913; *s* of Ze'ev-Dov and Hassia Begin; *m* 1939, Aliza Arnold (*d* 1982); one *s* two *d. Educ:* Mizrachi Hebrew Sch.; Polish Gymnasium (High Sch.); Univ. of Warsaw (MJr). Belonged to Hashomer Hatza'ir scout movement as a boy, joining Betar, the Zionist Youth Movement, when 16; head of Organization Dept of Betar for Poland, 1932; also delegated to Czechoslovakia to head movement there; returned to Poland, 1937, and after spell of imprisonment for leading demonstration against British policy in Eretz Israel became head of the movement in Poland, 1939; on outbreak of World War II, arrested by Russian NKVD (People's Commissariat of Internal Affairs) and later confined in concentration camps in Siberia, 1941–42; subseq. released under Stalin-Sikorski agreement; joined Polish Army, 1942, his brigade being posted to Eretz Israel; after demobilization assumed comd of IZL, the National Military Organization, directing from underground headquarters operations against the British; met members of UN Inquiry Cttee and foreign press, secretly, to explain his movement's outlook; after estabt of State of Israel, 1948, he and his colleagues founded the Herut Movement and he headed that party's list of candidates for the Knesset; a member of the Knesset from the first elections; on eve of Six Day War, 1 June 1967, joined Govt of Nat. Unity, serving as Minister without Portfolio, until Aug. 1970; presented his Coalition to the Knesset, June 1977, winning necessary vote of confidence to become Prime Minister; re-elected Prime Minister following nat. elections, June 1981. Nobel Peace Prize (jtly, with Mohamed Anwar El-Sadat), 1978. *Publications:* The Revolt, 1949 (trans. several languages); White Nights (describing his wartime experience in Europe), 1955; numerous articles. *Address:* c/o Herut Movement Headquarters, Beit Jabotinsky, 38 King George Street, Tel Aviv, Israel.   *Died 9 March 1992.*

BEIT, Sir Alfred Lane, 2nd Bt, *cr* 1924, of Tewin Water, Welwyn, Co. Hertford; Trustee of the Beit Trust; Trustee of Beit Fellowships for scientific research; *b* London, 19 Jan. 1903; *o* surv. *s* of 1st Bt and Lilian (*d* 1946), *d* of late T. L. Carter, New Orleans, USA; *S* father, 1930; *m* 1939, Clementine, 2nd *d* of late Major Hon. Clement Mitford, DSO and Lady Helen Nutting. *Educ:* Eton; Christ Church, Oxford. Contested West Islington in LCC election, 1928; South-East St Pancras (C) in general election, 1929; MP (U) St Pancras South-East, 1931–45. Mem., Board of Governors and Guardians, Nat. Gallery of Ireland. FIC 1993. Hon. LLD: Nat. Univ. of Ireland, 1979; TCD, 1993. *Heir:* none. *Address:* Russborough, Blessington, Co. Wicklow, Eire. *Clubs:* Brooks's, Carlton; Kildare Street and University (Dublin); Civil Service (Cape Town).
Died 12 May 1994 (ext).

BELAM, Noël Stephen; Under-Secretary, Department of Industry, 1975–79, retired; *b* 19 Jan. 1920; *s* of Dr Francis Arthur Belam and Hilda Mary Belam; *m* 1948, Anne Coaker; one *s* one *d. Educ:* Cranleigh Sch.; St Edmund Hall, Oxford (MA). Royal Artillery (T/Captain), 1940–46. Board of Trade, 1947; Trade Comr, Karachi, 1955–58; Private Sec. to successive Ministers of State, BoT, 1961–63; Asst Sec., 1963; Principal Trade Comr, Vancouver, 1963–67; Board of Trade: Regional Controller NW Region, 1967–70; Asst Sec., London, 1970–75; Under Sec., 1975. *Recreations:* fishing, Dartmoor ponies. *Address:* Fore Stoke Farm, Holne, Newton Abbot, Devon TQ13 7SS. *T:* Poundsgate (03643) 394.
Died 15 March 1991.

BELL, Douglas Maurice, CBE 1972; Chairman and Chief Executive, Tioxide Group Ltd (formerly British Titan Ltd), 1973–78; Chairman, Tinsley Wire Industries Group, 1981–87 (Director, since 1978); *b* Shanghai, China, 15 April 1914; *s* of Alexander Dunlop Bell; *m* 1947, Elizabeth Mary Edelsten; one *s* two *d. Educ:* Edinburgh Academy; St Andrews Univ. War Dept Chemist, Woolwich Arsenal, 1936; Imperial Chemical Industries: Dyestuffs Div., 1937–42; Regional Sales Manager, 1946–53; Billingham Dir, 1953; Billingham Man. Dir, 1955–57; Heavy Organic Chemicals Managing Dir, 1958–61; Chm. of European Council, Imperial Chemical Industries Ltd, 1960–65; Chief Executive, ICI (Europa) Ltd, 1965–72. Director: British Titan Products Ltd, 1968–78; Tioxide Australia Pty Ltd, 1973–78; Tioxide of Canada Ltd, 1973–78; Tioxide SA, 1973–78; Titanio SA, 1973–78. Hon. Dir, NV Bekaert SA, 1979–. Soc. of Chemical Industry: Vice-Pres., 1975–76; Pres., 1976–78; Mem. Council, Chemical Industry Assoc., 1973–78. Member, Governing Board: British Sch. of Brussels, 1971–; Maison de la Chemie Française, 1972–. FBIM 1974; FRSA 1976; Hon. FIChemE 1977. Hon. LLD St Andrews, 1977. Comendador de Numero de la Orden de Merito Civil (Spain), 1967; Commandeur, Ordre de Léopold II (Belgium), 1973. *Recreations:* sports, gardens. *Address:* Stocks Cottage, Church Street, West Chiltington, Sussex RH20 2JW. *T:* West Chiltington (0798) 812284. *Clubs:* Anglo-Belgian; Cercle Royal Gaulois (Brussels); Royal Waterloo Golf, West Sussex Golf.
Died 25 Feb. 1993.

BELL, Prof. Frank, DSc, PhD; FRSC; FSAScot; FRSE; Professor of Chemistry, Heriot-Watt University (formerly College), Edinburgh, 1950–66 (then Emeritus); *b* 24 Dec. 1904; *o s* of Thomas Bell, Derby; *m* 1930, May Perryman; one *s* one *d. Educ:* Crypt Grammar Sch., Glos; Queen Mary Coll., University of London. Head of Science Dept, Blackburn Tech. Coll. 1935–41; Principal, Lancaster Tech. Coll., 1941–46; Prof. of Chemistry, Belfast Coll. of Tech., 1947–50. *Publications:* original papers mainly in Journal of Chemical Soc. *Recreations:* numismatics, walking, field-club activities (Past Pres., Cotteswold Naturalists' Field Club; Past Pres., Edinburgh Natural History Soc.). *Address:* Hilcot, Finchcroft Lane, Prestbury, Cheltenham, Glos.   *Died 27 Jan. 1992.*

BELL, Sir Gawain (Westray), KCMG 1957; CBE 1955 (MBE mil. 1942); Secretary-General, South Pacific Commission, 1966–70; *b* 21 Jan. 1909; *s* of late William Westray and Emily Helen Bell; *m* 1945, Silvia, *d* of Major Adrian Cornwell-Clyne; three *d. Educ:* Winchester; Hertford Coll., Oxford. Sudan Political Service, 1931; seconded to the Government of Palestine, 1938 (attached Palestine Police, DSP; i/c Beersheba Camel Gendarmerie, 1939–41); Military Service in Middle East, 1941–45; Kaimakam (Col): Arab Legion, 1942–45; District Comr, Sudan Political Service, 1945–49; Dep. Sudan Agent, Cairo, 1949–51; Dep. Civil Sec., Sudan Government, 1953–54; Permanent Under-Sec., Ministry of the Interior,

1954–55; HM Political Agent, Kuwait, 1955–57; Governor, Northern Nigeria, 1957–62; Sec Gen., Council for Middle East Trade, 1963–64; engaged, with Sir Ralph Hone, as Constitutional Adviser to Govt of Fedn of S Arabia, 1965–66. Various missions to Arab world, 1970–. Vice-President: LEPRA, 1984– (Chm. Exec. Cttee, 1972–84); Anglo-Jordanian Soc., 1985–. Mem., Governing Body, SOAS, London Univ., 1971–81; part-time Chm., CS Selection Bds, 1972–77. Mem., Chapter Gen., Order of St John, 1964–66, 1970–89 (KStJ 1958). 2nd Lieut TA, 1929–32; RARO, 1949–59. Order of Independence 3rd Class (Trans Jordan), 1944. *Publications:* Shadows on the Sand, 1984; An Imperial Twilight, 1989; contribs to DNB, and learned jls. *Recreations:* walking, riding, shooting, rifle shooting (Capt. Oxford Univ., 1931; shot for Sudan). *Address:* 6 Hildesley Court, East Ilsley, Berks RG16 0LA. *T:* Newbury (01635) 281554. *Club:* Army and Navy.
Died 26 July 1995.

BELL, George Douglas Hutton, CBE 1965; PhD; FRS 1965; Director, Plant Breeding Institute, Cambridge, 1947–71, retired; a Vice President, Royal Society, 1976–78; *b* 18 Oct. 1905; *er s* of George Henry and Lilian Mary Matilda Bell; *m* 1934, Eileen Gertrude Wright; two *d. Educ:* Bishop Gore's Grammar Sch., Swansea; Univ. Coll. of North Wales, Bangor (BSc 1928); University of Cambridge (PhD 1931). Research Officer, Plant Breeding Inst., 1931; University Demonstrator, Cambridge, 1933, Lectr, 1944; Fellow of Selwyn Coll., Cambridge, 1944–54, Hon. Fellow, 1965. Research Medal, Royal Agricultural Soc. of England, 1956; Royal Society Mullard Medal, 1967. Hon. DSc: Reading Univ., 1968; Univ. of Wales, 1968; Liverpool Univ., 1970; Hon. ScD Cambridge, 1978. Massey-Ferguson National Award, 1973. *Publications:* Cultivated Plants of the Farm, 1948; The Breeding of Barley Varieties in Barley and Malt, 1962; Cereal Breeding in Vistas in Botany, Vol. II, 1963; Phylogeny of Temperate Cereals in Crop Plant Evolution, 1965; (contrib.) Wheat Breeding: the scientific basis, 1987; papers on barley and breeding in Jl of Agricultural Science, etc. *Recreations:* natural history, theatre, music. *Address:* 6 Worts Causeway, Cambridge CB1 4RL. *T:* Cambridge (0223) 247449.
Died 27 June 1993.

BELL, John Geoffrey Y.; *see* Yates-Bell.

BELL, Prof. Robert Edward, CC 1971; FRS 1965; FRSC 1955; Emeritus Professor of Physics, McGill University, Montreal, since 1983; *b* 29 Nov. 1918; *s* of Edward Richardson Bell and Edith E. Rich, British Columbia; *m* 1947, Jeanne Atkinson; one *d. Educ:* Univ. of British Columbia (BA 1939, MA 1941); McGill Univ. (PhD 1948). Wartime Radar development, Nat. Research Council, Ottawa, 1941–45; Sen. Research Officer, Chalk River Nuclear Laboratories, 1946–56; McGill University: seconded to Foster Radiation Lab., 1952–56; Associate Prof. of Physics, 1956–60; Dir, Foster Radiation Lab., 1960–69; Vice-Dean for Physical Scis, 1964–67; Dean, Fac. of Grad. Studies and Research, 1969–70; Rutherford Prof. of Physics, 1960–83; Principal and Vice-Chancellor, 1970–79. Dir, Arts, Sciences and Technol. Centre, Vancouver, 1983–85. Visiting Scientist, Copenhagen Univ. Inst. for Theoretical Physics, under Niels Bohr, 1958–59. President: Royal Society of Canada, 1978–81 (Sec., Section III (Science), 1962–64); Canadian Assoc. of Physicists, 1965–66. Fellow, American Physical Soc. Hon. DSc: Univ. of New Brunswick, 1971; Université Laval, 1973; Université de Montréal, 1976; Univ. of BC, 1978; McMaster Univ., McGill Univ., 1979; Carleton Univ., 1980; Hon. LLD: Univ. of Toronto, 1971; Concordia Univ., 1979; Hon. DCL Bishop's Univ., 1976. *Publications:* contribs to books: Annual Reviews of Nuclear Science, 1954; Beta and Gamma Ray

Spectroscopy, 1955; Alpha, Beta and Gamma Ray Spectroscopy, 1964; papers on nuclear physics and allied topics in scientific jls. *Address:* 822 Tsawwassen Beach, Delta, BC V4M 2J3, Canada. *T:* (604) 943–0667.
Died 1 April 1992.

BELL, Stewart Edward; QC (Scot.) 1982; Sheriff Principal of Grampian, Highland and Islands, 1983–88; *b* 4 Aug. 1919; *yr s* of late Charles Edward Bell, shipowner, and Rosalind Stewart; *m* 1st, 1948, Isla (*d* 1983), 2nd *d* of late James Spencer and Adeline Kelly; three *d*; 2nd, 1985, Mavis Kydd, *d* of late A. St Clair Jameson, WS, and widow of Sheriff R. R. Kydd; two step *d. Educ:* Kelvinside Academy, Glasgow; Trinity Hall, Cambridge; Glasgow Univ. Trinity Hall, 1937–39 and 1946 (MA Cantab), Glasgow Univ., 1946–48 (LLB). Commissioned, Loyal Regt, 1939; served with 2nd Bn in Singapore and Malaya, 1940–42 (wounded, POW in Singapore and Korea, 1942–45). Admitted Advocate, 1948; practised: in Malacca, Malaya as Advocate and Solicitor, 1949–51; at Scottish Bar, 1951–61; Sheriff of Lanarks at Glasgow, later of Glasgow and Strathkelvin, 1961–82. Chm., Scottish Far East POW Assoc., 1988–. *Publication:* (contrib.) The Laws of Scotland: Stair Memorial Encyclopedia, vol. 17, 1989. *Recreation:* Highland bagpipe (Hon. Pipe-major, The Royal Scottish Pipers' Soc., 1975–77). *Address:* 14 Napier Road, Edinburgh EH10 5AY. *T:* 031–229 9822. *Clubs:* New (Edinburgh); Nairn Golf.
Died 27 April 1992.

BELLEW, Hon. Sir George (Rothe), KCB 1961; KCVO 1953 (CVO 1950; MVO 1935); Kt 1950; FSA 1950; Garter Principal King of Arms, 1950–61; *b* 13 Dec. 1899; *s* of late Hon. Richard Bellew and Gwendoline, *d* of William R. J. Fitzherbert Herbert-Huddleston of Clytha; *m* 1935, Ursula Kennard, *e d* of late Anders Eric Knös Cull, Warfield House, Bracknell; one *s. Educ:* Wellington Coll.; Christ Church, Oxford. Served War of 1939–45: Squadron Leader RAFVR, 1940–45 (despatches). Portcullis Pursuivant of Arms, 1922; Somerset Herald, 1926; Registrar of the Coll. of Arms, 1935–46; Knight Principal, Imperial Soc. of Knights Bachelor, 1957–62 (Dep. Knight Principal, 1962–71); Inspector of Regimental Colours, 1957–61; Sec., Order of the Garter, 1961–74. Dir of all civil ceremonies in Westminster Abbey for HM Coronation, 1953. KStJ 1951 (Mem. Chapter Gen., 1951–). *Address:* The Grange, Old Park Lane, Farnham, Surrey GU9 0AH. *T:* Farnham (0252) 715146.
Died 6 Feb. 1993.

BENCE, Cyril Raymond; *b* 26 Nov. 1902; *s* of Harris Bryant Bence; *m* 1st, 1926, Florence Maud Bowler (*d* 1974); one *s* one *d*; 2nd, 1975, Mrs I. N. Hall (*née* Lewis) (decd). *Educ:* Pontywaen Sch.; Newport High Sch., Mon. Apprenticed to Ashworth Son & Co. Ltd of Dock Street, Newport, Mon, Weighing Machine Manufacturers; moved to Birmingham, 1937. Member of National Union of Scalemakers; Mem. of AEU; Pres. Witton Branch AEU. Mem. of Birmingham Trades Council, 1942–45. Contested (Lab) Handsworth Div. of Birmingham, at Gen. Elections of 1945 and 1950, and Bye-election Nov. 1950; MP (Lab) Dunbartonshire East, 1951–70. *Address:* Leda, Sweethay Close, Staplehay, Taunton, Som TA3 7HG.
Died 7 Sept. 1992.

BENJAMIN, Brooke; *see* Benjamin, T. B.

BENJAMIN, Louis; President, 1985–89, Managing Director, 1970–81, and Chief Executive, 1981–85, Stoll Moss Theatres Ltd (The London Palladium, Theatre Royal, Drury Lane, Victoria Palace, Apollo, Her Majesty's, Lyric, Globe, Queen's, Duchess, Garrick, Royalty and Cambridge Theatres); *b* 17 Oct. 1922; *s* of Benjamin and Harriet Benjamin; *m* 1954, Vera Doreen Ketteman; two *d. Educ:* Highbury County Sec. Sch. Served Second World

War: RAC, India, Burma and Singapore. Joined Moss Empires Ltd, 1937; entered theatrical management as Second Asst Manager, London Palladium, 1945; Asst Man., then Box Office Man., Victoria Palace, 1948; Gen. Man., Winter Gardens, Morecambe, 1953; Pye Records: Sales Controller, 1959; Gen. Man., 1962; Man. Dir, 1963; Chm., Pye Records Gp, 1975–80; a Jt Man. Dir, ATV Corp., 1975; Mem., Exec. Bd, Associated Communications Corp., 1982–85; Director: ATV Music Ltd, 1962–85; Bermans & Nathans Ltd, 1973–84; Precision Records & Tapes Ltd, 1982–85; Precision Video Ltd, 1983–86. Entertainment Artistes Benevolent Fund: Vice-Pres., 1971–82; Life Governor, 1982; Presenter of Royal Variety Perf., annually, 1979–85, and of Children's Royal Variety Perf., 1981 and 1982; producer, HM Queen Mother's 90th Birthday Tribute, London Palladium, 1990. Companion, Grand Order of Water Rats. Hon. Council Mem., NSPCC. *Died 20 June 1994.*

BENJAMIN, Prof. (Thomas) Brooke, MEng, MA, PhD; FRS 1966; Sedleian Professor of Natural Philosophy, University of Oxford, since 1979; Fellow, Queen's College, Oxford, since 1979; Adjunct Professor, Pennsylvania State University, since 1987; *b* 15 April 1929; *s* of Thomas Joseph Benjamin and Ethel Mary Benjamin (*née* Brooke); *m* 1st, 1956, Helen Gilda-Marie Rakower Ginsburg (marr. diss. 1974); one *s* two *d;* 2nd, 1978, Natalia Marie-Thérèse Court; one *d. Educ:* Wallasey Grammar Sch.; University of Liverpool; Yale Univ. (USA); University of Cambridge. BEng (Liverpool) 1950; MEng (Yale) 1952; PhD (Cantab) 1955; MA (Oxon) 1979. Fellow of King's Coll., Cambridge, 1955–64; Asst Dir of Research, University of Cambridge, 1958–67; Reader in Hydrodynamics, Univ. of Cambridge, 1967–70; Prof. of Maths, and Dir, Fluid Mechanics Res. Inst., Essex Univ., 1970–78. Visiting Professor: Univ. of Wisconsin, 1980–81; Univ. of Houston, 1985; Univ. of Calif, Berkeley, 1986. Chairman: Mathematics Cttee, SRC, 1975–78; Jt Royal Soc./IMA Mathematical Educn Cttee, 1979–85; Nat. Conf. of Univ. Profs, 1989–91; a Vice-Pres., Royal Soc., 1990–91. For. Mem., French Acad. of Scis, 1992; Hon. Mem., ASME, 1994. Editor, Journal of Fluid Mechanics, 1960–65; Consultant to English Electric Co., 1956–67. FRSA 1992. Hon. DSc: Bath, 1989; Brunel, 1991; Liverpool, 1993. William Hopkins Prize, Cambridge Philosophical Soc., 1969. *Publications:* various papers on theoretical and experimental fluid mechanics. *Recreation:* music. *Address:* Mathematical Institute, 24–29 St Giles', Oxford OX1 3LB. *T:* Oxford (01865) 273525; *Fax:* (01865) 273583; 8 Hernes Road, Oxford OX2 7PU. *T:* Oxford (01865) 54439. *Died 16 Aug. 1995.*

BENN, John Meriton, CB 1969; Pro-Chancellor, Queen's University, Belfast, 1979–86 (Senator, 1973–86); *b* 16 July 1908; *s* of late Ernest and Emily Louise Benn, Burnley; *m* 1933, Valentine Rosemary, *d* of late William Seward, Hanwell; two *d. Educ:* Burnley Gram. Sch.; Christ's Coll., Cambridge (Scholar; Modern Languages Tripos, 1st Cl. Hons French, 2nd Cl. Hons German). Asst Master, Exeter Sch., 1931–34; Lektor, Halle Univ., Germany, 1934; Asst Master, Regent Street Polytechnic Secondary Sch., 1935; Inspector of Schs, Ministry of Education for Northern Ireland, 1935–44; Principal, 1944–51; Asst Sec., 1951–59; Senior Asst Sec., 1959–64; Permanent Sec., 1964–69; Comr for Complaints, NI, 1969–73; Parly Comr for Admin, NI, 1972–73. Chm., NI Schools Exams Council, 1974–81. Chairman Board of Governors: Rupert Stanley Coll. of Further Educn, Belfast, 1986–91; Sullivan Upper Sch., Holywood, 1987–89. Hon. LLD QUB, 1972. *Publication:* Practical French Proses, 1935. *Address:* 7 Tudor Oaks, Holywood, Co. Down BT18 0PA. *T:* Holywood (02317) 2817. *Died 16 Sept. 1992.*

BENN, Captain Sir Patrick (Ion Hamilton), 2nd Bt *cr* 1920, of Rollesby, co. Norfolk; Captain, Reserve of Officers, late Duke of Cornwall's Light Infantry; Major, Norfolk Army Cadet Force, 1960; *b* 26 Feb. 1922; *o s* of late Col Ion Bridges Hamilton Benn, JP (*o s* of 1st Bt), Broad Farm, Rollesby, Gt Yarmouth, and Theresa Dorothy, *d* of late Major F. H. Blacker, Johnstown, Co. Kildare; *S* grandfather, 1961; *m* 1959, Edel Jørgine, *d* of late Col W. S. Løbach, formerly of The Royal Norwegian Army, Andenes, Vesteraalen; one *s* one *d* (both adopted). *Educ:* Rugby. Served War of 1939–45 (despatches): North Africa, Italy, Greece, 1941–45; Capt. 1943; served Korea, 1951–52; retd, 1955. *Recreations:* shooting, fishing. *Heir:* none. *Address:* Rollesby Hall, Great Yarmouth, Norfolk NR29 5DT. *T:* Great Yarmouth (0493) 740313. *Died 10 April 1992 (ext).*

BENNETT, (Frederick Onslow) Alexander (Godwyn), TD; Chairman: Whitbread & Co. Ltd, 1972–77; Whitbread Investment Co. Ltd, 1977–88 (Director, since 1956); *b* 21 Dec. 1913; *s* of Alfred Bennett, banker and Marjorie Muir Bremner; *m* 1942, Rosemary, *d* of Sir Malcolm Perks, 2nd Bt, and Neysa Gilbert (*née* Cheney); one *s* four *d. Educ:* Winchester Coll.; Trinity Coll., Cambridge (BA). Commnd 2nd Bn London Rifle Bde TA, 1938; Lt-Col 1944; GSO1 SHAEF and 21 Army Gp (despatches twice). Joined Whitbread & Co. Ltd, 1935: Man. Dir, 1949; Dep. Chm., 1958; Chief Exec., 1967–75. Pres., Kent CCC, 1983–. Master, Brewers' Company, 1963–64; Chm., Brewers' Soc., 1972–74. US Bronze Star, 1944. *Recreations:* garden and countryside, music. *Address:* Grove House, Selling, Faversham, Kent ME13 9RN. *T:* Canterbury (0227) 752250. *Club:* MCC. *Died 17 March 1993.*

BENNETT, William John, OBE 1946; LLD; retired 1977; Consultant, Iron Ore Company of Canada, Montreal; Chairman, C. D. Howe Institute; Director: Canadian Reynolds Metals Co. Ltd; Eldorado Nuclear Ltd; Peterson, Howell & Heather Canada Inc.; *b* 3 Nov. 1911; *s* of Carl Edward Bennett and Mary Agnes Downey; *m* 1936, Elizabeth Josephine Palleck; three *s* four *d. Educ:* University of Toronto (BA Hons). Private Sec., Minister of Transport, 1935–39; Chief Exec. Asst to Minister of Munitions and Supply, 1939–46; Vice-Pres. and Gen. Man., 1946, Pres. and Man. Dir, 1947–58, Eldorado Mining & Refining Ltd; President: Atomic Energy of Canada Ltd, 1953–58; Canadian British Aluminium Co. Ltd, 1958–60. Hon. LLD, Toronto Univ., 1955; Hon. Dr of Science, St Francis Xavier Univ., Antigonish, NS, 1956; Hon Dr of Laws, University of Ottawa, 1957. *Recreations:* ski-ing, music. *Address:* 1321 Sherbrooke Street West, Apt F41, Montreal, Quebec H3G 1J4, Canada. *Club:* Mount Royal (Montreal). *Died 23 April 1991.*

BENNITT, Mortimer Wilmot; Secretary, Islington Archaeology Society; *b* 28 Aug. 1910; *s* of Rev. F. W. and Honoria Bennitt. *Educ:* Charterhouse; Trinity Coll., Oxford. Entered Office of Works, 1934; Private Sec. to Sir Philip Sassoon, 1937–38. Served War of 1939–45: RAF, 1943–45. Under Sec., 1951; Dep. Dir, Land Commn, 1967–71; retired 1971. Chairman: Little Theatre Guild of Gt Britain, 1959–60; Tavistock Repertory Company, London, 1975–77. Patron of St Mary's, Bletchley. *Publication:* Guide to Canonbury Tower, 1980. *Recreation:* theatre. *Address:* 3/5 Highbury Grove, N5 1HH. *T:* 0171–704 1335. *Clubs:* United Oxford & Cambridge University, Tower Theatre. *Died 13 Nov. 1995.*

BENSON, Baron *cr* 1981 (Life Peer), of Drovers in the County of W Sussex; **Henry Alexander Benson,** GBE 1971 (CBE 1946); Kt 1964; FCA; Partner, Coopers and Lybrand (formerly Cooper Brothers & Co.), Chartered

Accountants, 1934–75; Adviser to the Governor of the Bank of England, 1975–83; *b* 2 Aug. 1909; *s* of Alexander Stanley Benson and Florence Mary (*née* Cooper); *m* 1939, Anne Virginia Macleod; two *s* one *d*. *Educ:* Johannesburg, South Africa. ACA (Hons) 1932; FCA 1939. Commissioned Grenadier Guards, 1940–45; seconded from Army to Min. of Supply to advise on reorganisation of accounts of Royal Ordnance Factories, 1943–44, and in Dec. 1943 apptd Dir Ordnance Factories, to carry out reorganisation; apptd Controller of Building Materials, Min. of Works, 1945; Special appt to advise Minister of Health on housing production, 1945, and subseq. other appts, also Mem. Cttee (Wilson Cttee) to review work done on, and to make recommendations for further research into, processes for transformation of coal into oil, chemicals and gas, 1959–60. Mem., Crawley Development Corp., 1947–50; Mem., Royal Ordnance Factories Board, 1952–56; Dep. Chm. Advisory Cttee (Fleck Cttee) to consider organisation of National Coal Board, 1953–55. Dir Hudson's Bay Co., 1953–62 (Dep. Governor 1955–62); Director: Finance Corporation for Industry Ltd, 1953–79; Industrial and Commercial Finance Corp., 1974–79; Hawker Siddeley Gp, 1975–81; Council, Institute of Chartered Accountants, 1956–75 (Pres., 1966); Mem. Advisory Cttee on Legal Aid, 1956–60; Mem. Tribunal under Prevention of Fraud (Investments) Act 1939, 1957–75; Mem. Special Advisory Cttee to examine structure, finance and working of organisations controlled by British Transport Commission, 1960; apptd by Minister of Commerce, N Ireland, to investigate position of railways, to make recommendations about their future, and to report on effect which recommendations will have on transport system of Ulster Transport Authority, 1961; apptd Chm. of a Cttee to examine possible economies in the shipping and ancillary services engaged in meat, dairy products and fruit trades of New Zealand, 1962; Mem. Cttee apptd by Chancellor of the Exchequer to investigate practical effects of introduction of a turnover tax, 1963. Chm., Royal Commn on Legal Services, 1976–79. Joint Comr to advise on integration of Nat. Assoc. of Brit. Manufrs, FBI, Brit. Employers' Confedn, and on formation of a Nat. Industrial Organisation (CBI), 1963; Joint Inspector, Bd of Trade, to investigate affairs of Rolls Razor Ltd, 1964; Indep. Chm. of British Iron and Steel Fedn Development Co-ordinating Cttee, 1966; Indep. Chm., Internat. Accounting Standards Cttee, 1973–76; Dir, Finance for Industry Ltd, 1974–79; Member: Permanent Jt Hops Cttee, 1967–74; Dockyard Policy Bd, 1970–75; NCB team of inquiry into Bd's purchasing procedures, 1973; CBI Company Affairs Cttee, 1972; City Liaison Cttee, 1974–75; Chm., Exec. Cttee of Accountants' Jt Disciplinary Scheme to review cases involving public concern, 1979–86; Vice-Pres., Union Européene des Experts Comptables économiques et financiers, 1969; Member: Cttee to enquire into admin and organisation of MoD; Cttee on Fraud Trials (Roskill Cttee), 1984–85; Council of Legal Educn, 1989–92. Apptd by Nat. Trust as Chm. of adv. cttee to review management, organisation and responsibilities of Nat. Trust, 1967; apptd by Jt Turf Authorities as Chm. of The Racing Industry Cttee of Inquiry to make detailed study of financial structure and requirements of racing industry, 1967. Treasurer, Open Univ., 1975–79. Trustee, Times Trust, 1967–81. Hon. Bencher, Inner Temple, 1983; Freeman, City of London, 1986. Distinguished Service Award, Univ. of Hartford, 1977; Mem., Accounting Hall of Fame, Ohio State Univ., 1984; Founding Societies' Centenary Award, ICA, 1984. *Publication:* Accounting for Life (autobiog.), 1989. *Recreations:* shooting, golf, sailing. *Address:* 9 Durward House, 31 Kensington Court, W8 5BH. *T:* 0171–937 4850. *Clubs:* Brooks's, Jockey; Royal Yacht Squadron. *Died 5 March 1995.*

BENSON, Sir (William) Jeffrey, Kt 1987; FCIB; Chairman, The 600 Group, 1987–93 (Director, 1983–93; Vice Chairman, 1985–87); *b* 15 July 1922; *s* of Herbert Benson and Lilian (*née* Goodson); *m* 1947, Audrey Winifred Parsons; two *s*. *Educ:* West Leeds High Sch. FCIB (FIB 1976). Served War, RAF, 1941–46. Joined National Provincial Bank Ltd, 1939; Asst Gen. Manager, 1965–68; National Westminster Bank: Reg. Exec. Dir, 1968–73; Gen. Man., Management Services Div., 1973–75; Dir, 1975–87; Dep. Chief Exec., 1975–77; Gp Chief Exec., 1978–82; a Dep. Chm., 1983–87. Chm., Export Guarantees Adv. Council, 1982–87; Pres., Inst. of Bankers, 1983–85. *Recreations:* golf, swimming. *Address:* Auben, Spencer Walk, The Drive, Rickmansworth, Herts WD3 4EE. *T:* Rickmansworth (01923) 778260. *Club:* Phyllis Court (Henley). *Died 13 Nov. 1994.*

BENTALL, (Leonard Edward) Rowan, DL; President, Bentalls PLC, since 1978 (Chairman, 1968–78 and Managing Director, 1963–78); *b* 27 Nov. 1911; *yr s* of late Leonard H. Bentall and Mrs Bentall; *m* 1st, 1937, Adelia Elizabeth (*d* 1986), *yr d* of late David Hawes and Mrs Hawes; three *s* two *d*; 2nd, 1987, Katherine Christina Allan, MCSP, SRP. *Educ:* Aldro Sch.; Eastbourne Coll. Joined family business, 1930. Served War of 1939–45: joined East Surrey Regt, 1940; commissioned, Royal Welch Fusiliers, 1941; served Middle E, N Africa, Sicily, Italy, France, Belgium, Holland, 231 (Malta) Inf. Bde; latterly Hon. Captain, Royal Welch Fusiliers. Bentalls: Dep. Chm., 1950; Merchandise Dir, 1946–63. Pres., Surrey Br., Inst. of Directors, 1979–84. Mem. Nat. Exec. Cttee, Forces Help Soc. and Lord Roberts Workshops, 1984–88. Patron, 8th Army Veterans' Assoc., Portsmouth & Dist. DUniv Kingston, 1993. Freeman of City of London, 1972. FRSA. DL Greater London, 1977, Rep. for Kingston-upon-Thames 1979–84. Cavaliere, Order Al Merito della Repubblica Italiana, 1970. *Publication:* My Store of Memories, 1974. *Recreations:* gardening, ornithology. *Address:* Hill House, Broughton, near Stockbridge, Hants SO20 8DA. *Clubs:* Royal Automobile, Institute of Directors.

Died 24 July 1993.

BENTHALL, Sir (Arthur) Paul, KBE 1950; FLS; Chairman, Bird & Co. (London) Ltd, 1953–73; *b* 25 Jan. 1902; *s* of Rev. Charles Francis Benthall and Annie Theodosia Benthall; *m* 1932, Mary Lucy (*d* 1988), *d* of John A. Pringle, Horam, Sussex; four *s*. *Educ:* Eton; Christ Church, Oxford. Joined Bird & Co. and F. W. Heilgers & Co., Calcutta, 1924; partner (later dir) of both firms, 1934–53; Pres., Bengal Chamber of Commerce, and of Associated Chambers of Commerce of India, 1948 and 1950; Mem. Central Board, Imperial Bank of India, 1948 and 1950–53; Chm. All India Board of Technical Studies in Commerce and Business Administration, 1950–53; Pres. Royal Agri-Horticultural Society of India, 1945–47; Pres., UK Citizens' Assoc. (India), 1952. Chm., Amalgamated Metal Corporation Ltd, 1959–72; Director: Chartered Bank, 1953–72; Royal Insurance Co. and Associated Cos, 1953–72. Trustee: Victoria Meml, Calcutta, 1950–53; Gandhi Meml Fund, India, 1948–63; Vice Chm., Indo-British Historical Soc., Madras, 1985–. Medal, Internationales Burgen Institut, 1978. Certified blind, 1985. *Publication:* The Trees of Calcutta, 1946. *Address:* Benthall Hall, Broseley, Salop. *T:* Telford (0952) 882254. *Club:* Oriental. *Died 7 Jan. 1992.*

BERE, Rennie Montague, CMG 1957; retired; *b* 28 Nov. 1907; *s* of late Rev. M. A. Bere; *m* 1936, Anne Maree Barber; no *c*. *Educ:* Marlborough Coll.; Selwyn Coll., Cambridge (MA). Colonial Administrative Service, Uganda, 1930–55; Asst District Officer, 1930; District Officer, 1942; Commandant, Polish Refugee Settlements, 1943–44; Provincial Commissioner, Uganda, 1951–55;

Dir and Chief Warden, Uganda National Parks, 1955–60. Pres., Cornwall Naturalists' Trust, 1967–70. *Publications:* The Wild Mammals of Uganda, 1961; The African Elephant, 1966; Wild Animals in an African National Park, 1966; The Way to the Mountains of the Moon, 1966; Birds in an African National Park, 1969; Antelopes, 1970; Wildlife in Cornwall, 1971; Crocodile's Eggs for Supper, 1973; The Mammals of East and Central Africa, 1975; (with B. D. Stamp) The Book of Bude and Stratton, 1980; The Nature of Cornwall, 1982; A Cuckoo's Parting Cry, 1990; articles (chiefly of mountaineering and wild life and anthropological interest) in Alpine Jl, Uganda Jl, Oryx, Animals, etc. *Recreations:* mountaineering, game and bird watching, cricket. *Address:* West Cottage, Bude Haven, Bude, Cornwall. *T:* Bude (0288) 2082. *Clubs:* Alpine, Commonwealth Trust; Uganda Kobs (Past Pres.).

Died 23 March 1991.

BÉRÉGOVOY, Pierre Eugène; Prime Minister of France, 1992–93; *b* 23 Dec. 1925; *s* of Adrien Bérégovoy and Irène (*née* Baudelin); *m* 1948, Gilberte Bonnet; one *s* two *d*. *Educ:* Ecole primaire, supérieure, Elbeuf; Institut du travail, Faculté de Droit, Strasbourg. Head of Sub-div., subseq. Asst to Dir, Soc. pour le développement de l'industrie du gaz, 1958–78; Chargé de mission, Gaz de France, 1978–81. Sec. Gen. to Presidency, 1981–82; Minister: of Social Affairs and Nat. Solidarity, 1982; for Economy, Finance and Budget, 1984–86 and 1988–92; Deputy for Nièvre, 1986, re-elected 1988, 1993. Mem., Econ. and Social Council, 1979–81. Founder Mem., Parti Socialiste Autonome, 1958; Member: Secretariat, Parti Socialiste Unifié, 1963–67; Parti Socialiste: Mem., Managing Cttee and Exec. Bd, 1969; Nat. Sec. for Social Affairs, 1973–75; in charge of External Affairs, 1975–81; responsible for party to Liaison Cttee of the Left. Founder, Socialisme moderne, 1967. *Publication:* contrib. Economy and Liberty periodical. *Recreations:* rural antiquities, football, cycling, cross-country running. *Address:* 139 rue de Bercy, 75012 Paris, France. *T:* 40040404.

Died 1 May 1993.

BERKELEY, Baroness (17th in line) *cr* 1421 (called out of abeyance, 1967); **Mary Lalle Foley-Berkeley;** *b* 9 Oct. 1905; *e d* of Col Frank Wigram Foley, CBE, DSO (*d* 1949), Royal Berks Regt, and Eva Mary Fitzhardinge, Baroness Berkeley; assumed by deed poll additional surname of Berkeley, 1951; *S* mother, Baroness Berkeley (16th in line), 1964. *Heir presumptive: nephew* Anthony Fitzhardinge Gueterbock, OBE [*b* 20 Sept. 1939; *m* 1965, Diana Christine, *e d* of Eric William John Townsend; two *s* one *d*]. *Address:* Pickade Cottage, Great Kimble, Aylesbury, Bucks HP17 0XS. *T:* Princes Risborough (08444) 3051. *Died 17 Oct. 1992.*

BERKELEY, (Augustus Fitzhardinge) Maurice, CB 1975; MA; Chief Registrar of the High Court in Bankruptcy, 1966–75; Registrar of the Companies Court, 1957–75 and Clerk of the Restrictive Practices Court, 1965–75; *b* 26 Feb. 1903; *s* of late Dr Augustus Frederic Millard Berkeley and Anna Louisa Berkeley; *m* 1st, 1931, Elaine Emily (*d* 1985), *d* of Adin Simmonds; no *c*; 2nd, 1985, Margaret Mary Thérèse, *d* of Edward Cyril Arthur Crookes. *Educ:* Aldenham Sch.; Pembroke Coll., Cambridge. Called to the Bar, Inner Temple, 1927. Served War of 1939–45: in the Welch Regiment, 1940–45; Temp. Lieut-Col; AAG, AG3d, War Office. Junior Counsel in Chancery Matters to Ministry of Agriculture, Fisheries and Food, the Commissioners of Crown Lands and the Forestry Commissioners, 1956–57. Bar Council, 1955–57. *Recreations:* watching cricket, travel, theatre, reading. *Address:* 22 Boyes Croft, White Street, Great Dunmow, Essex CM6 1BD. *T:* Great Dunmow (0371) 3654. *Clubs:* Garrick, MCC. *Died 2 Sept. 1991.*

BERKELEY, Humphry John; author; Director, Sharon Allen Leukaemia Trust, since 1984; *b* 21 Feb. 1926; *s* of late Reginald Berkeley, author and playwright, former MP (L), and Mrs Hildegarde Tinne. *Educ:* Dragon Sch., Oxford; Malvern; Pembroke Coll., Cambridge (Exhibitioner). BA 1947, MA 1963; Pres., Cambridge Union, 1948; Chm., Cambridge Univ. Conservative Assoc., 1948. Held various appointments at Conservative Political Centre, 1949–56; Dir Gen., UK Council of European Movement, 1956–57; Chairman of Coningsby Club, 1952–55; Hon. Sec., Carlton Club Political Cttee, 1954–59. MP (C) Lancaster, 1959–66; seconded Act of Parlt which abolished death penalty for murder, 1965; introduced Private Members Bill to make homosexual conduct between consenting male adults no longer a crime, which obtained second reading in H of C, 1966; Member, British Parly Delegn to Council of Europe and Council of WEU, 1963–66; personal representative of Colonial Secretary in constitutional talks in Seychelles, 1965; Hon. Sec., Cons. Parly West Africa Cttee, 1959–64; Hon. Sec., UN Parly Gp, 1962–64; joined Labour Party, July 1970; contested (Lab) N Fylde, Oct. 1974; joined SDP, 1981; contested (SDP) Southend East, 1987; rejoined Labour Party, Dec. 1988. Director: Caspair Ltd; Island Developments Ltd. Mem., Prince Philip's Cttee on Overseas Volunteers, 1966–70; Chm., UNA of GB and NI, 1966–70; Vice-Chm, Nat. Coordinating Cttee for 25th Anniversary of UN, 1970; Mem., UK Nat. Commn for Unesco, 1966–71. Patron, Internat. Centre for Child Studies, 1984–. Hon. Treasurer, Howard League for Penal Reform, 1965–71; Mem. Governing Body, Inst. for Study of Internat. Relations, Sussex Univ., 1969–. *Publications:* The Power of the Prime Minister, 1968; Crossing the Floor, 1972; The Life and Death of Rochester Sneath, 1974; The Odyssey of Enoch: a political memoir, 1977; The Myth that will not Die: the formation of the National Government 1931, 1978; (with Jeffrey Archer) Faces of the Eighties, 1987. *Address:* 3 Pages Yard, Church Street, Chiswick, W4 2PA. *Club:* Savile.

Died 15 Nov. 1994.

BERKELEY, Maurice; *see* Berkeley, A. F. M.

BERKHOUWER, Cornelis; Chevalier, Order of the Netherlands Lion, 1966; Commander, Order of Orange–Nassau, 1979; Member, European Parliament, 1963–84, elected Member, 1979–84; *b* Alkmaar, Holland, 19 March 1919; *m* 1966, Michelle Martel; one *s*. *Educ:* Amsterdam Univ. Dr of Law 1946. Barrister, High Court of Amsterdam, 1942. Pres., European Parliament, 1973–75, Vice-Pres., 1975–79. Grand Cross of Merit (Italy), 1974; Grand Cross of Merit (Spain), 1981. *Publications:* Conversion of Void Legal Acts (thesis), 1946; Medical Responsibilities, 1951; Civil Responsibility for Illegal Publicity, 1954. *Recreations:* tennis, ancient literature, swimming, bibliothèque, vinothèque, chess. *Address:* 56 Stationsweg, Heiloo, Netherlands. *Clubs:* National Liberal; de Witte (The Hague); Cercle Gaulois (Brussels); Cercle Interallié (Paris).

Died 5 Oct. 1992.

BERNERS, Baroness (15th in line) *cr* 1455; **Vera Ruby Williams;** *b* 25 Dec. 1901; *d* of late Hon. Rupert Tyrwhitt, Major RA (5th *s* of Emma Harriet, Baroness Berners (12th in line)) and Louise I. F. (*née* Wells); *S* cousin, 1950; *m* 1927, Harold Williams, Colonial Civil Service; two *d*. *Educ:* Ladies' Coll., Eastbourne; St Agnes' Sch., East Grinstead. *Co-heiresses: d* Hon. Mrs Michael Kirkham [*b* (Pamela Vivian Williams) 30 Sept. 1929; *m* 1952; two *s* one *d*]; and *d* Hon. Mrs Kelvin Pollock [*b* (Rosemary Tyrwhitt Williams) 20 July 1931; *m* 1959; two *s*]. *Address:* Ashwellthorpe, Charlton Lane, Cheltenham, Glos GL53 9EE. *T:* Cheltenham (0242) 519595.

Died 20 Feb. 1992.

BERNSTEIN, Baron cr 1969 (Life Peer), of Leigh; **Sidney Lewis Bernstein,** LLD; President, Granada Group PLC, since 1979, Chairman, 1934–79 (Granada Television, Granada Theatres, Granada TV Rental, Granada Motorway Services, Novello & Co.); b 30 Jan. 1899; s of Alexander and Jane Bernstein; m 1st, 1936, Zoë Farmer (marr. diss.; she d 1972); 2nd, 1954, Sandra (d 1991), d of Charles and Charlotte Malone, Toronto; one s two d. A founder, Film Society, 1924. Mem., Mddx CC, 1925–31. Films Adviser, Min. of Inf., 1940–45; Liaison, British Embassy, Washington, 1942; Chief, Film Section, AFHQ N Africa, 1942–43; Chief, Film Section, SHAEF, 1943–45. Lectr on Film and Internat. Affairs, New York Univ. and Yale. Mem., Resources for Learning Cons. Cttee, Nuffield Foundn, 1965–72. Governor, Sevenoaks Sch., 1964–74. Fellow, BFI, 1984. *Address:* 36 Golden Square, W1R 4AH. *Club:* Garrick.   *Died 5 Feb. 1993.*

BESSBOROUGH, 10th Earl of, cr 1739 (Ire.), Earl (UK), cr 1937; **Frederick Edward Neuflize Ponsonby,** DL; Baron Bessborough (Ire.) 1721; Viscount Duncannon 1722; Baron Ponsonby (GB), 1749; Baron Duncannon (UK), 1834; Chairman, Stansted Park Foundation, since 1984; b 29 March 1913; s of 9th Earl of Bessborough, GCMG, PC, and Roberte de Neuflize, GCStJ (d 1979), d of late Baron Jean de Neuflize; S father, 1956; m 1948, Mary, d of Charles A. Munn, USA; one d. *Educ:* Eton; Trinity Coll., Cambridge (MA). Performed many leading parts for Stansted Players, Marlowe Soc., Montreal Rep., Ottawa Little Theatre, 1931–35. Contested W Div. Islington (Nat. Govt), 1935. Joined Sussex Yeomanry (TA), 1936; Sec., League of Nations High Commission for Refugees, 1936–39. Served War of 1939–45, France, Flanders and Dunkirk; ADC to Comdr, Canadian Corps; Experimental Officer (Capt.) Tank Gunnery; GSO2 (liaison) in West and North Africa; Second and subsequently First Sec., British Embassy, Paris, 1944–49. Formerly: with Robert Benson, Lonsdale and Co. Ltd and Overseas Adviser to Pye Gp of Cos (interests incl. communications in ME and establishing first TV stn in Baghdad); Director: High Definition Films; Associated Broadcasting Development Co. Ltd; ATV; Planned Communications; Glyndebourne Arts Trust; Sherek Players, Ltd; English Stage Co. Ltd; Chm., Southdown Radio Ltd; Chm., Inst. for Educnl TV. Chm. of Governors, British Soc. for Internat. Understanding, 1951–71; Chm., International Atlantic Cttee, 1952–55, and 1989–; Chm. and Pres., European Atlantic Group, 1954–61, Co-Pres., 1988, Pres. 1989–; Vice-Pres., British Atlantic Cttee, 1957–. Mem. of UK Parly Delegn to USSR, 1960, and subseq. visits on trade, sci. and technol, incl. setting up London–Moscow TV link and visits to Siberian Res. Insts. Parly Sec. for Science, Oct. 1963; Jt Parly Under-Sec. of State for Educn and Science, 1964; Cons. front bench spokesman on Science, Technology, Power, Foreign and Commonwealth Affairs, 1964–70; Minister of State, Min. of Technology, June-Oct. 1970; led delegns to European space confs in Brussels and Washington, 1970. Dep. Chm., Metrication Board, 1969–70 (Chm., Agricl Cttee); Chm., Cttee of Inquiry into the Res. Assocs, 1972–73; Pres., Parly and Scientific Cttee (Vice-Pres., thrice); Member: European Parliament, 1972–79 (Vice-Pres., 1973–76; Dep. Leader, European Cons. Gp, 1972–77; Chm., Euro–Arab dialogue, 1977–79; Chm., Cttee on Dual Mandate, 1977–79; Mem. Cttees on Budgets, Energy, Research and Technology); House of Lords Select Cttees on European Communities and Science and Technology, 1979–85 (Sub-Cttees on Sci. and Govt, Energy Research, Remote Sensing by Satellite); Adv. Bd, Parly Office of Sci. and Technology, 1988–. Led missions to People's Republic of China, 1977, 1984; lectured throughout world on British science and industry. Member: Amer. Philosophical Soc.; Soc. of Dilettanti. President: SE Assoc.

of Building Socs; Men of the Trees; Chichester Cons. Assoc.; Chichester Festival Theatre Trust; Chichester Operatic Soc.; British Theatre Assoc.; Emsworth Maritime and Historical Trust; Trustee, Shakespeare Globe Trust; Patron of British Art, Tate Gall. Chm. of Governors, Dulwich Coll., 1972–73. DL West Sussex, 1977. OStJ; Chevalier Legion of Honour; MRI; FRSA; FRGS. *Plays and publications:* Nebuchadnezzar (with Muriel Jenkins), 1939 (broadcast by BBC); The Four Men (after H. Belloc), for Fest. of Britain, 1951; Like Stars Appearing, 1953 (perf. Glyndebourne 1954); The Noon is Night, 1954; Darker the Sky, 1955; Triptych, 1957; A Place in the Forest, 1958; Return to the Forest, 1962; (with Clive Aslet) Enchanted Forest, 1984; articles, reviews. *Heir presumptive:* cousin Arthur Mountifort Longfield Ponsonby [b 11 Dec. 1912; m 1st, 1939, Patricia (d 1952), d of Col Fitzhugh Lee Minnigerode, Va, USA; one s one d; 2nd, 1956, Princess Anne Marie Galitzine (marr. diss., 1963), d of late Baron Sir Rudolph Slatin Pasha; 3rd, 1963, Madeleine, d of Maj.-Gen. Laurence Grand, CB, CIE, CBE; two s]. *Address:* 4 Westminster Gardens, SW1P 4JA. *T:* 071–828 5959; Stansted Park, Rowland's Castle, Hants PO9 6DX. *T:* Rowlands Castle (0705) 412223. *Clubs:* Turf, Garrick, Beefsteak, Roxburghe.
            Died 5 Dec. 1993 (UK Earldom ext).

BEST, Alfred Charles, CBE 1962 (OBE 1953); DSc (Wales); Director of Services, Meteorological Office, 1960–66; b 7 March 1904; s of late Charles William Best, Barry, Glam; m 1932, Renée Margaret, d of late John Laughton Parry, Blaina, Mon; two s. *Educ:* Barry Grammar Sch.; University Coll., Cardiff. Professional Asst, Meteorological Office, 1926; appointments: Shoeburyness, 1926; Porton, 1928; Air Min., 1933; Malta, 1936; Larkhill, 1939; Air Min., 1940; Wing Comdr RAFVR, ACSEA, 1945; Air Min., 1945; Research, 1945–54; Meteorological Office Services, 1955–66. *Publications:* Physics in Meteorology, 1957; meteorological papers in jls. *Recreation:* photography. *Address:* 10 Flintgrove, Bracknell, Berks RG12 2JN. *T:* Bracknell (0344) 421772.   *Died 7 June 1993.*

BEST, Edward Wallace, CMG 1971; JP; Deputy Chairman, Melbourne and Metropolitan Board of Works, 1975–79; b 11 Sept. 1917; s of Edward Lewis Best and Mary Best (née Wallace); m 1940, Joan Winifred Ramsay; three d. *Educ:* Trinity Grammar Sch. and Wesley Coll., Melbourne. Served War 6 years with AIF; 3½ years POW (Lieut). Elected to Melbourne City Council, 1960; Lord Mayor of Melbourne, 1969–71; served on numerous cttees: Electric Supply, Finance, Civic Square Bldg, Victoria Market Redevelopment Cttees; Melbourne and Metropolitan Bd of Works Finance and Publicity Cttee; Sidney Myer Music Bowl, 1967– (Chm. 1969); Victorian Olympic Park Cttee of Management, 1967–; Chm., Sports and Recreation Council to Victoria State Govt; Trustee for Olympic Park (Exec. Mem. on Vic. Olympic Cttee which applied for 1956 Melbourne Olympic Games; Mem. Publicity and Pentathlon Cttees at Melbourne Games); Chm., Exhibn Buildings, 1973–75; Melbourne Moomba Festival, 1969– (Pres. 1969–71); Lord Mayor's Holiday Camp, 1969– (Chm. 1969–71); associated 25 years with Lord Mayor's Fund, in an adv. capacity, for appeals; Mem. Cttee: Royal Agricultural Soc. Council, 1970–; Equestrian Fedn of Australia, 1965–75. Visited Edinburgh, Commonwealth Games, 1970 to present Melbourne's application for 1974 Commonwealth Games; Victorian Dem., 1972 Aust. Olympic Appeal, 1971–72, 1974 Commonwealth Games Appeal; Pres., XXth World Congress of Sports Medicine; Chm., Victorian Olympic Council, 1970–75. *Recreations:* racing, hunting, farming; athletics (rep. Australia at 1938 Empire Games; former Victorian champion sprinter). *Address:* Eildon Hills, Maddens Lane, Coldstream, Vic 3770, Australia. *Clubs:* Australian, Bendigo Jockey,

Melbourne Cricket, Moonee Valley Racing (Mem. Cttee, 1975–), Victorian Amateur Turf, Victoria Racing, Royal Automobile Club of Victoria. *Died 1 June 1992.*

BESTOR, Arthur (Eugene); Professor of History, University of Washington, 1962–76, then Emeritus; *b* 20 Sept. 1908; *s* of Arthur Eugene and Jeanette Louise Lemon Bestor; *m* 1st, 1931, Dorothea Nolte (marr. diss.); 2nd, 1939, Anne Carr (*d* 1948); two *s*; 3rd, 1949, Dorothy Alden Koch; one *s*. *Educ:* Yale Univ. PhB 1930; PhD 1938. Yale University: Instructor in English, 1930–31; Instructor in History, 1934–36; Teachers Coll., Columbia University: Associate in History, 1936–37; Asst Prof. of History, 1937–42; Stanford University: Asst Prof. of Humanities, 1942–45; Associate Prof. of History, 1945–46; Lectr in American History, Univ. of Wisconsin, 1947; University of Illinois: Associate Prof. of History, 1947–51; Prof. of History, 1951–62. Harold Vyvyan Harmsworth Prof. of American History, Oxford, 1956–57; Fulbright Vis. Prof., University of Tokyo, 1967. Editor-in-chief, Chautauquan Daily, Chautauqua, NY, 1931–33. Fellow, Newberry Library, Chicago, Ill, 1946; John Simon Guggenheim Memorial Fellow, 1953–54, 1961–62. President: Ill State Historical Soc., 1954–55; Council for Basic Education, 1956–57; Pacific Coast Branch, Amer. Historical Assoc., 1976. MA (Oxon) by decree, 1956; LLD Lincoln Univ. (Pa), 1959; LittD Univ. of Southern Indiana, 1988. John Addison Porter Prize, Yale Univ., 1938; Albert J. Beveridge Award, Amer. Historical Assoc., 1946. *Publications:* Chautauqua Publications, 1934; David Jacks of Monterey, 1945; Education and Reform at New Harmony, 1948; Backwoods Utopias, 1950, 2nd edn 1970; Educational Wastelands, 1953, 2nd edn 1985; The Restoration of Learning, 1955; State Sovereignty and Slavery (in Jl Ill State Historical Soc.), 1961; The American Civil War as a Constitutional Crisis (in Amer. Historical Review), 1964; Separation of Powers in the Realm of Foreign Affairs (in Seton Hall Law Review), 1974; Respective Roles of Senate and President in the Making and Abrogation of Treaties (in Washington Law Review), 1979; jointly: Problems in American History, 1952, 3rd edn 1966; Three Presidents and Their Books, 1955; The Heritage of the Middle West, 1958; Education in the Age of Science, 1959; Interpreting and Teaching American History, 1961; The American Territorial System, 1973; contribs to Amer. Hist. Review, Jl of Hist. of Ideas, Amer. Jl of Internat. Law, William and Mary Quarterly, Encounter, Proc. Amer. Philosophical Soc., American Scholar, Daedalus, Washington Law Review, New England Quarterly, Jl of Southern History, Harvard Educational Review, New Republic, Scientific Monthly, School and Society. *Recreations:* photography, walking. *Address:* Department of History, DP-20, Smith Hall, University of Washington, Seattle, Washington 98195, USA; (home) 4553 55th Avenue NE, Seattle, Washington 98105–3836, USA. *Club:* Elizabethan (New Haven).
Died 13 Dec. 1994.

BESWICK, John Reginald, CBE 1973; FCIArb; FIMgt; *b* 16 Aug. 1919; *s* of Malcolm Holland Beswick and Edythe Beswick (*née* Bednall); *m* 1943, Nadine Caruth Moore Pryde; one *s* two *d*. *Educ:* Manchester Grammar Sch.; Rossall Sch.; Trinity College, Cambridge (MA). Sub-Lt RNVR, 1940–42: anti submarine trawlers, N and S Atlantic; Lt RNVR, 1942–46: submarines, home waters and Far East. Called to Bar, Lincoln's Inn, 1947. Practised at Chancery Bar, 1947–51. Sec., Mullard Ltd, 1951–62; Jt Sec., Philips Electrical Industries Ltd, 1953–62; Dir, Mullard Equipment Ltd, 1955–62; Dir, Soc. of Motor Manufrs & Traders Ltd, 1963–79; Dir-Gen., British Ports Assoc., 1980–83; Dir, Mersey Docks and Harbour Co., 1984–87. Member: CBI Council, 1965–79; Council, Inst. of Advanced Motorists, 1966–76. UK delegate, Bureau Permanent International des Constructeurs d'Automobiles,

1966–79. FCIArb 1978. FRSA 1954; FIMgt (FBIM 1982). Asst, Worshipful Co. of Coachmakers, 1973–79. *Recreations:* golf, garden maintenance, reading. *Address:* White House, Redhill, near Buntingford, Herts SG9 0TG. *T:* Broadfield (076388) 256. *Clubs:* Naval and Military; East Herts Golf. *Died 14 March 1994.*

BETTLEY, F(rancis) Ray, TD 1945; MD; FRCP; Physician for Diseases of the Skin, Middlesex Hospital, London, 1946–74, then Emeritus; Physician, St John's Hospital for Diseases of the Skin, London, 1947–74, then Emeritus; formerly Dean, Institute of Dermatology, British Postgraduate Medical Federation; Lieutenant-Colonel Royal Army Medical Corps, Territorial Army Reserve of Officers; *b* 18 Aug. 1909; *yr s* of late Francis James Bettley; *m* 1951, Jean Rogers, 2nd *d* of late Archibald Barnet McIntyre; one *s* (one *d* decd), and one adopted *d*. *Educ:* Whitgift Sch., Croydon; University Coll., London; University Coll. Hosp. Medically qualified, 1932; MD 1935; FRCP 1948. Gazetted RAMC TA, 1932. Resident house appointments, 1932–33; Radcliffe-Crocker Student (Vienna, Strasbourg), 1936; Hon. Dermatologist to Cardiff Royal Infirmary, 1937; various military hosps in UK and Middle East, 1939–44; Dermatologist and Venereologist, E Africa Comd, 1944–45. Malcolm Morris Lectr, 1959 and 1970; Watson Smith Lectr, RCP, 1960. Emeritus Mem., and former Pres., Brit. Assoc. of Dermatologists; Hon. or Corresp. Mem. of dermatological assocs of Belgium, Denmark, France, Netherlands, India, Israel, Poland, USA, Venezuela. Editor, British Jl of Dermatology, 1949–59. *Publications:* Skin Diseases in General Practice, 1949; medical papers in various medical jls. *Recreation:* painting. *Address:* The Dower House, Headbourne Worthy, Winchester, Hants SO23 7JG. *T:* Winchester (0962) 885423. *Club:* Athenæum.
Died 17 Dec. 1993.

BEVAN, Rt Rev. Kenneth Graham; *b* 27 Sept. 1898; *s* of late Rev. James Alfred Bevan, MA; *m* 1927, Jocelyn Duncan Barber (*d* 1992); three *d*. *Educ:* The Grammar Sch., Great Yarmouth; London Coll. of Divinity. Deacon, 1923; priest, 1924; Curate of Holy Trinity, Tunbridge Wells, 1923–25; Missionary, Diocese of Western China, 1925–36, Diocese of Eastern Szechwan, 1936–40; Bishop of Eastern Szechwan, 1940–50; Vicar of Woolhope, 1951–66; Rural Dean, Hereford (South), 1955–66; Prebendary de Moreton et Whaddon, Hereford Cathedral, 1956–66; Master of Archbishop Holgate's Hosp., Wakefield, 1966–77; Asst Bp, dio. of Wakefield, 1968–77. *Address:* Manormead, Tilford Road, Hindhead, Surrey GU26 6RA. *Died 3 Dec. 1993.*

BEVAN, Michael Guy Molesworth; Lord Lieutenant of Cambridgeshire, since 1985; *b* 23 Aug. 1926; *s* of late Temple Percy Molesworth Bevan and Amy Florence Bevan (*née* Briscoe); *m* 1948, Mary Brocklebank; three *s* one *d*. *Educ:* Eton College. Grenadier Guards, 1944–47. Joined City of London company, 1948; Director, Briscoes Ltd, Walford Maritime Hldgs Ltd, 1953–85; farmer, 1957–. Governor, 1962–91, Chm., 1980–91, Vice Pres., 1991–, Papworth Trust (formerly Papworth Village Settlement). Syndic, Fitzwilliam Mus., 1985–. KStJ 1986. *Recreations:* classical music, cricket, bridge. *Address:* Longstowe Hall, Longstowe, Cambridge CB3 7UH. *T:* Caxton (0954) 719203. *Died 2 March 1992.*

BEVERTON, Prof. Raymond John Heaphy, CBE 1986; FRS 1975; FIBiol 1973; Emeritus Professor of Fisheries Science, University of Wales, since 1990; *b* 29 Aug. 1922; *s* of Edgar John Beverton and Dorothy Sybil Mary Beverton; *m* 1947, Kathleen Edith Marner; three *d*. *Educ:* Forest Sch., Snaresbrook; Downing Coll., Cambridge (MA). Cambridge, 1940–42 and 1946–47. Joined Fisheries Research Lab. (MAFF), 1947; Dep. Dir, Fisheries Res., 1959–65; Sec., NERC, 1965–80; Sen. Res. Fellow, Univ.

of Bristol, engaged on study of change and adaptation in scientific res. careers, 1981–82; Prog. Integrator, Internat. Fedn of Insts for Advanced Study, 1982–84; Hon. Professorial Fellow, UWIST, 1982–84; Prof. of Fisheries Science, 1984–89, Head of Sch. of Pure and Applied Biol., 1988–89, Univ. of Wales Coll. of Cardiff (formerly at UWIST); Chm., Management Cttee, Millport Biol. Lab., 1985–91. Hon. posts during research career: Chm., Comparative Fishing Cttee of ICES, 1957–62; Chm., Res. and Statistics Cttee of Internat. Commn for Northwest Atlantic Fisheries, 1960–63. Member: MAFF Fisheries R&D Bd, 1972–79; NRPB, 1976–80. Head of UK delegn to Intergovernmental Oceanographic Commn, 1981–84; Vis. Lectr in fish population dynamics, Univ. of Southampton, 1982–86. Chm., Nat. Scis Adv. Cttee for UNESCO, 1984–85. President: Fisheries Soc. of British Isles, 1983–88; Challenger Soc. for Marine Sci., 1990–92; Vice-Pres., Freshwater Biological Assoc., 1980–; Mem. Council, Scottish Marine Biol. Assoc., 1984–86; Trustee, World Wildlife Fund UK, 1983–85. Editor, Jl ICES, 1983–91. Hon. DSc Wales, 1989. Award of Excellence, Amer. Fisheries Soc., 1993. *Publications:* (with S. J. Holt) On the Dynamics of Exploited Fish Populations, 1957; (with G. W. D. Findlay) Funding and Policy for Research in the Natural Sciences (in The Future of Research, ed Geoffrey Oldham), 1982; papers on mathematical basis of fish population dynamics, theory and practice of fisheries conservation and various fisheries research topics. *Recreations:* fishing, sailing, golf, music. *Address:* Montana, Old Roman Road, Langstone, Gwent NP6 2JU.
Died 23 July 1995.

BEYNON, Ven. James Royston; Archdeacon of Winchester, 1962–73, then Emeritus; *b* 16 Sept. 1907; *s* of James Samuel and Catherine Beynon; *m* 1933, Mildred Maud Fromings (*d* 1986); four *d. Educ:* St Augustine's Coll., Canterbury. LTh Durham. Deacon, 1931; priest, 1932; Chaplain, Indian Eccl. Estabt, 1933; Senior Chaplain: Peshawar, 1941; Quetta, 1943; Archdeacon of Lahore, 1946–48; Vicar of Twyford, Winchester, 1948–73; Rural Dean of Winchester, 1958–62. Hon. CF, 1945. *Address:* 1511 Geary Avenue, London, Ontario N5X 1G6, Canada. *Died 2 Dec. 1991.*

BEYTAGH, Rev. Canon Gonville Aubie ff.; *see* ffrench-Beytagh.

BICKNELL, Gioconda, (Mrs J. D. Bicknell); *see* De Vito, G.

BIGGS; *see* Ewart-Biggs.

BILLING, Melvin George, CMG 1961; retired as Provincial Commissioner, Provincial Administration, Northern Rhodesia (1951–62); *b* 24 June 1906; *s* of Stuart Morrison Billing and Gertrude Roswell Billing; *m* 1934, Kathleen Jane, *d* of late A. N. Brand; no *c. Educ:* Dulwich Coll.; Worcester Coll., Oxford. Provincial Administration, Northern Rhodesia: Cadet, 1930; District Officer, 1932; Grade II, 1942; Grade I, 1946; Senior, 1950. *Recreations:* bowls, photography. *Address:* Formosa Garden Village, Box 416, Plettenberg Bay, Cape 6600, S Africa. *Club:* Commonwealth Trust. *Died 28 Aug. 1992.*

BINGHAM, His Honour Richard Martin, TD 1949; QC 1958; a Circuit Judge, 1972–88; *b* 26 Oct. 1915; *s* of late John and Dorothy Ann Bingham; *m* 1949, Elinor Stephenson; one *d. Educ:* Harrow; Clare Coll., Cambridge. Called to Bar, Inner Temple, 1940; Bencher, 1964. Joined Northern Circuit, 1946; Recorder of Oldham, 1960–71; Judge of Appeal, IoM, 1965–72. Served with 59th Med. Regt, RA (TA), 1937–46 and 1947–49: Major from 1945; campaigns, Dunkirk and NW Europe (despatches, 1944). Mem. of Liverpool City Council, 1946–49. MP (C) Garston Division of Liverpool, Dec. 1957–March 1966. Member: Home Office Departmental Cttee on Coroners,

1965; Royal Commn on Assizes and Quarter Sessions, 1966. *Publications:* Cases on Negligence, 1961, 3rd edn 1978; Cases and Statutes on Crime, 1980; Crown Court Law and Practice, 1987. *Address:* Hook End, Gayton, Merseyside L60 3SR. *T:* 051–342 5793. *Clubs:* Royal Automobile; Royal Liverpool Golf.
Died 26 July 1992.

BINNS, St John, MBE 1977; JP; Member, West Yorkshire County Council, 1974–86 (Chairman, 1984–85); *b* 25 July 1914; *s* of John William and Lena Binns; *m* 1938, Gwendoline, *e d* of Fred and Minnie Clough; one *s. Educ:* Holbeck Junior Technical School. Amalgamated Union of Engineering Workers: Leeds District Pres., 1948, Sec., 1953; Divisional Organiser, 1970. Councillor, Leeds City Council, 1956 (Chm., Civic Catering, Plans, Licensing, Fire Cttees); Alderman, 1972; W Yorks Metropolitan County Council: Chm., Leeds Area Cttee, 1976; Chm., Personnel Cttee and Chief Whip, 1981–84. JP Leeds, 1959. *Recreation:* gardening. *Address:* 146 West Park Drive (West), Roundhay, Leeds LS8 2DA.
Died 10 Sept. 1993.

BIRCH, Alexander Hope, CMG 1970; OBE 1961; HM Diplomatic Service, retired; *b* 19 Jan. 1913; *s* of Denys Goldney and Lucy Helen Booth Birch; *m* 1st, 1940, Honor Pengelley (marr. diss., 1948); 2nd, 1953, Joan Hastings-Hungerford (*d* 1982); no *c. Educ:* St Catherine's and St Mark's Colls, Alexandria, and privately. Appointed to: HM Embassy, Cairo, 1937; Addis Ababa, 1942; Moscow, 1946; Budapest, 1947; Tel-Aviv, 1949; Second Sec. (Inf.), Baghdad, 1950; First Sec. and Consul, Seoul, 1951, and Djakarta, 1954; First Sec. (Commercial), Khartoum, 1956, and Paris, 1961; Counsellor (Commercial), Paris, 1962, and Baghdad, 1965; Counsellor (Economic and Commercial), Accra, 1967–70; Dep. High Comr, Perth, WA, 1970–73; Administrative Adviser to Premier of Antigua, 1973–75. *Recreations:* international affairs, reading, walking. *Address:* Woodrow, Edgehill Road, Clevedon, Avon BS21 7BZ. *Died 6 March 1995.*

BIRCH, Prof. Arthur John, AC 1987; CMG 1979; DPhil (Oxon); FRS 1958; FAA, FRACI; Professor of Organic Chemistry, Australian National University, 1967–80, then Emeritus; Professorial Fellow, Lincoln College, Oxford, since 1980; *b* 3 Aug. 1915; *s* of Arthur Spencer and Lily Birch; *m* 1948, Jessie Williams; three *s* two *d. Educ:* Sydney Technical High Sch.; Sydney Univ. MA Oxon 1981; MSc: Sydney, 1939; Manchester, 1957. Scholar of the Royal Commission for the Exhibition of 1851, Oxford, 1938–41; Research Fellow, Oxford, 1941–45; ICI Research Fellow, Oxford, 1945–48; Smithson Fellow of the Royal Society, Cambridge, 1949–52; Prof. of Organic Chemistry, University of Sydney, 1952–55; Prof. of Organic Chemistry, Manchester Univ., 1955–67; Dean, Research Sch. of Chemistry, ANU, Canberra, 1967–70, 1973–76; Newton Abraham Prof., Univ. of Oxford, 1980–81. Treas., Australian Acad. Science, 1969–73, Pres., 1982–86; Pres., RACI, 1978. Chairman: Ind. Enquiry into CSIRO, 1976–; Aust. Marine Sciences and Technologies Adv. Cttee, 1978–81. UNDP Consultant, People's Republic of China, 1980, 1982, 1984, 1986; OECD Examiner, Denmark, 1987. Foreign Mem., USSR Acad. of Science, 1976; Foreign Fellow, Indian Nat. Sci. Acad., 1990; Hon. FRCS 1980. Hon. DSc: Sydney, 1977; Manchester, 1982; Monash, 1982. Davy Medal, Royal Soc., 1972; Tetrahedron Prize, Tetrahedron Jl, 1987; ANZAAS Medal, 1990. *Publications:* How Chemistry Works, 1950; 426 original scientific communications, chiefly in Journal of Chemical Soc. and Australian Journal of Chemistry. *Address:* Department of Chemistry, Australian National University, PO Box 4, Canberra, ACT 0200, Australia. *Died 8 Dec. 1995.*

BIRCH, Reginald; Chairman, Communist Party of Britain (Marxist Leninist), 1968; Member, General Council of the TUC, 1975–79; Member, Executive Council, AUEW, 1966–79; *b* 7 June 1914; *s* of Charles and Anne Birch; *m* 1942, Dorothy; three *s. Educ:* St Augustine's Elementary Sch., Kilburn. Apprentice toolmaker, 1929; at trade (toolmaker), until 1960. Divisional Organiser, AEU, 1960–66. Mem., Energy Commn, 1977–79. *Recreations:* swimming, growing herbs. *Address:* 29 Langley Park, NW7 2AA. *T:* 081–959 7058.   *Died 1 June 1994.*

BIRCHALL, Prof. (James) Derek, OBE 1990; FRS 1982; FRSC; FIM; Professor of Inorganic Chemistry, Keele University, since 1992; Non-executive Director, Ceram Research, since 1994; *b* 7 Oct. 1930; *s* of David Birchall and Dora Mary Birchall; *m* 1956, Pauline Mary Jones (*d* 1990); two *s.* ICI, 1956–92: Research Leader, 1965; Research Associate, 1970; Sen. Res. Associate, Mond Div., 1975–92. Visiting Professor: Univ. of Surrey, 1976–88; MIT, 1984–86; Univ. of Durham, 1987–; Univ. of Liverpool, 1991–; Professor Associate: Brunel Univ., 1983–; Sheffield Univ., 1989–; Industrial Fellow, Wolfson Coll., Oxford, 1977–79, Mem., Common Room, 1979–. Mem., Individual Merit Panel, HM Treasury, 1988–89. Lectures: John D. Rose Meml, SCI, 1983; Mellor Meml, Inst. of Ceramics, 1984; Hurter Meml, SCI, Univ. of Liverpool, 1989; Sir Eric Rideal Meml, SCI, 1989; Katritzky, UEA, 1991; Industrial Endowed Lectr, RSC, 1992–93; Orton Meml, American Ceramic Soc., 1993. Hon. ScD UEA, 1994. Ambrose Congreve Energy Award, 1983; RSC Award: for Solids and Materials Processing, 1990; for Materials Science, 1991; Royal Soc. Armourers and Braziers Award, 1993. *Publications:* A Classification of Fire Hazards, 1952, 2nd edn 1961; contribs to various encyclopedias and to learned jls, ie Nature, on inorganic chemistry and materials science. *Recreations:* old books, new cars. *Address:* Braeside, Stable Lane, Mouldsworth, Chester CH3 8AN. *T:* Manley (01928) 740320. *Club:* Athenæum.   *Died 7 Dec. 1995.*

BIRD, Michael Gwynne, CBE 1985; Chairman, Varity Holdings Ltd (formerly Massey-Ferguson Holdings Ltd), since 1980; *b* 16 Aug. 1921; *s* of Edward Gwynne Bird, Chaplain, RN, and Brenda Bird (*née* Rumney); *m* 1944, Frances Yvonne Townley; one *s* two *d. Educ:* Harrow Sch.; St Catharine's Coll., Cambridge. Served War: commnd, Rifle Bde, 1941; demobilised (Major), 1946. Colonial Service (Administration), Malawi, 1948–54; called to the Bar, Inner Temple, 1955; joined Massey-Ferguson, 1955; Director: Legal Services, Massey-Ferguson Ltd, 1977; Varity Corp. (formerly Massey-Ferguson Ltd), 1988– (Chm., European Cos, 1982–90). *Address:* Broad Oak, Clive Road, Esher, Surrey KT10 8PS. *T:* Esher (0372) 466241. *Clubs:* Oriental, MCC.
Died 26 Nov. 1991.

BIRD, Sir Richard Dawnay M.; *see* Martin-Bird.

BIRKINSHAW, Prof. John Howard, DSc; FRSC; Professor of Biochemistry and Head of Department of Biochemistry, London School of Hygiene and Tropical Medicine, University of London, 1956–62, then Emeritus; *b* 8 Oct. 1894; *s* of John Thomas and Madeline Birkinshaw, Garforth, near Leeds; *m* 1929, Elizabeth Goodwin Guthrie, Ardrossan, Ayrshire; one *s* one *d. Educ:* Leeds Modern Sch.; Leeds Univ. War service, 1915, West Yorks Regt and Machine Gun Corps (POW); demobilised, 1919. BSc Hons 1920, MSc 1921, DSc 1929, Leeds. Research Biochemist to Nobel's Explosives Co. (later ICI), 1920–30; Research Asst to Prof. Raistrick, London Sch. of Hygiene and Tropical Medicine, 1931; Senior Lecturer, 1938; Reader, 1945. *Publications:* about 60 scientific papers in Biochemical Journal, Philos. Trans. Royal Society, etc.

Recreation: photography. *Address:* 87 Barrow Point Avenue, Pinner, Mddx HA5 3HE. *T:* 0181–866 4784.
Died 20 Sept. 1995.

BIRKMYRE, Sir Henry, 2nd Bt *cr* 1921, of Dalmunzie, Co. Perth; *b* 24 March 1898; *er s* of Sir Archibald Birkmyre, 1st Bt and Anne, *e d* of Capt. James Black; *S* father, 1935; *m* 1922, Doris Gertrude (*d* 1992), *er d* of late Col Herbert Austen Smith, CIE; one *s* one *d. Educ:* Wellington. War Service in France with RFA, 1917. *Heir: s* Archibald Birkmyre [*b* 12 Feb. 1923; *m* 1953, Gillian Mary, *o d* of Eric Downes, OBE; one *s* two *d*]. *Recreation:* golf. *Address:* Tudor Rest, 2 Calverley Park Gardens, Tunbridge Wells TN1 2DE.
Died 10 March 1992.

BIRLEY, Prof. Eric, MBE 1943; FSA 1931; FBA 1969; Professor of Roman-British History and Archæology, University of Durham, 1956–71, later Professor Emeritus; *b* 12 Jan. 1906; *y s* of J. Harold Birley; *m* 1934, Margaret Isabel, *d* of Rev. James Goodlet; two *s. Educ:* Clifton Coll.; Brasenose Coll., Oxford (Hon. Fellow, 1987). Lecturer, University of Durham, 1931; Reader, 1943. War of 1939–45: Military Intelligence, Lt-Col, GSO1 Military Intelligence Research Section; Chief of German Military Document Section, War Dept. Vice-Master, Hatfield Coll., Durham, 1947–49, Master, 1949–56; first Dean of Faculty of Social Sciences, Univ. of Durham, 1968–70. President: Soc. of Antiquaries of Newcastle upon Tyne, 1957–59; Cumberland and Westmorland Antiquarian and Archaeological Soc., 1957–60; Architectural and Archæological Soc. of Durham and Northumberland, 1959–63; Member: German Archæological Inst.; Ancient Monuments Board for England, 1966–76; Hon. Member, Gesellschaft Pro Vindonissa (Switzerland); Hon. FSAScot, 1980; Chm., Vindolanda Trust, 1970–; Hon. Life Pres., Internat. Congress of Roman Frontier Studies, 1974. Hon. Dr Phil Freiburg i Br, 1970; Hon. DLitt Leicester, 1971; Dr *hc* Heidelberg, 1986. Polonia Restituta, 1944; Legion of Merit, 1947. *Publications:* The Centenary Pilgrimage of Hadrian's Wall, 1949; Roman Britain and the Roman Army, 1953; (ed) The Congress of Roman Frontier Studies 1949, 1952; Research on Hadrian's Wall, 1961; (jt ed) Roman Frontier Studies 1969, 1974; Fifty-one Ballades, 1980; The Roman Army: papers 1929–1986, 1988; numerous papers on Roman Britain and on the Roman army, excavation reports, etc. *Recreation:* archæology. *Address:* Carvoran House, Greenhead, Carlisle CA6 7JB. *T:* Gilsland (016977) 47594.   *Died 20 Oct. 1995.*

BISHOP, Alan; *see* Bishop, T. A. M.

BISHOP, Rt Rev. Clifford Leofric Purdy; *b* 11 June 1908; *s* of Rev. E. J. Bishop; *m* 1949, Ivy Winifred Adams. *Educ:* St John's, Leatherhead; Christ's Coll., Cambridge (MA); Lincoln Theological Coll. Deacon, 1932; priest, 1933; Curacies, 1932–41; Vicar, St George, Camberwell, 1941–49; Rural Dean of Camberwell, 1943–49; Curate-in-charge, All Saints, Newington, 1944–47; Rector of: Blakeney, 1949–53 (Rural Dean of Walsingham, 1951–53); Bishop Wearmouth, 1953–62 (Rural Dean of Wearmouth and Surrogate, 1953–62); Hon. Canon of Durham, 1958–62; Bishop Suffragan of Malmesbury, 1962–73; Canon of Bristol, 1962–73. *Address:* Rectory Cottage, Cley-next-Sea, Holt, Norfolk NR25 7BA. *T:* Cley (0263) 740250.   *Died 1 Sept. 1994.*

BISHOP, Dame (Margaret) Joyce, DBE 1963 (CBE 1953); MA Oxon; Head Mistress of the Godolphin and Latymer School, Hammersmith, W6, 1935–63, retired; *b* 28 July 1896; 2nd *d* of Charles Benjamin and Amy Bishop. *Educ:* Edgbaston High Sch., Birmingham; Lady Margaret Hall, Oxford. English Mistress, Hertfordshire and Essex High Sch., 1918–24; Head Mistress, Holly Lodge High Sch., Smethwick, Staffs, 1924–35. Member Working Party set up by Minister of Education to enquire into Recruitment of Women to Teaching Profession, 1947. President, Association of Head Mistresses, 1950–52. Member: Secondary School Examinations Council, 1950–62; University Grants Cttee, 1961–63; Council for Professions Supplementary to Medicine, 1961–70; TV Research Cttee set up by Home Secretary, 1963–69. Chairman, Joint Cttee of the Four Secondary Associations, 1956–58. FKC 1973. *Recreations:* listening to cassettes and radio, the theatre. *Address:* 22 Malbrook Road, Putney, SW15 6UF. *T:* 081–788 5862.   *Died 7 June 1993.*

BISHOP, (Terence) Alan (Martyn), FBA 1971; *b* 10 Nov. 1907; *s* of Cosby Martyn Bishop. *Educ:* Christ's Hospital; Keble Coll., Oxford. 2nd Mods, 1928; 2nd Hist. 1930; BA 1931, MA 1947; MA Cantab 1947. Asst Master, Glenalmond Coll., 1930–31. Served War of 1939–45: 2nd Lieut, RA, 1940; Capt., 1944. Lectr in Medieval Hist., Balliol Coll., Oxford, 1946–47; Reader in Palaeography and Diplomatic, Dept of History, Cambridge Univ., 1947–73. *Publications:* books and articles on palaeography, etc, incl.: Facsimiles of English Royal Writs to AD 1100 (with P. Chaplais), 1957; Scriptores Regis, 1961; (ed) Umbrae Codicum Occidentalium (Vol. 10), 1966 (Holland); English Caroline Minuscule, 1971.
Died 29 March 1994.

BISHOP, Instr Rear-Adm. Sir William (Alfred), KBE 1955 (OBE 1941); CB 1950; MA; Director of Naval Education Service, 1948–56, retired; *b* 29 May 1899; *s* of late Alfred Bishop, Purley, Surrey; *m* 1929, Stella Margaret Macfarlane, MBE (*d* 1985); no *c*. *Educ:* Whitgift Sch.; Corpus Christi Coll., Cambridge. 2nd Lieut, RE Signals, 1918. Cambridge, 1919. Entered RN as Instructor Lieut, 1922; Instructor Lieut-Comdr, 1928; Instructor Comdr, 1936; Instructor Captain, 1945; Instructor Rear-Adm., 1951. Chief Naval Meteorological Officer, South Atlantic Station, 1939; Asst Director of Naval Meteorological Service, 1944; Dep. Director of Education Dept; 1947; Naval ADC to the King, 1950; retired Sept. 1956. *Address:* Windmill Court, St Minver, Wadebridge, Cornwall PL27 6RD. *T:* Trebetherick (0208) 862890.
Died 22 May 1991.

BLACK, Sir Cyril (Wilson), Kt 1959; JP; DL; *b* 8 April 1902; *s* of Robert Wilson Black, JP, and Annie Louise Black (*née* North); *m* 1930, Dorothy Joyce, *d* of Thomas Birkett, Wigston Hall, Leicester; one *s* two *d*. *Educ:* King's College Sch. Chartered Surveyor; FRICS. Chairman: Temperance Permanent Building Soc., 1939–73; Beaumont Properties Ltd, 1933–80; London Shop Property Trust Ltd, 1951–79; M. F. North Ltd, 1948–81, and other companies. Member Wimbledon Borough Council, 1942–65; Mayor, 1945–46, 1946–47; Alderman, 1942–65; Member, London Borough of Merton Council, 1965–78; Mayor, 1965–66; Member Surrey County Council, 1943–65; County Alderman, 1952–65, and Chm., 1956–59; MP (C) Wimbledon, 1950–70. JP County of London, 1942; DL Surrey, 1957–66; DL Greater London, 1966. Governor of King's College Sch., Wimbledon Coll., Ursuline Convent Sch., Wimbledon, and other schools. Freedom of City of London, 1943; Freedom of Wimbledon, 1957. Hon. Mem., Houses of Parliament Christian Fellowship; Patron: Wimbledon Youth Cttee; Wimbledon Community Assoc.; Member: SW Metrop. Regional Hospital Board, 1959–62; Baptist Union Council (Pres., 1970–71); Free Church Federal Council; Vice-President: Girls' Bde, 1969– (Hon. Treasurer, 1939–69); Boys' Bde, (Hon. Treasurer, 1962–69). Pres., United Nations Association (London Region), 1964–65. *Recreations:* public work, music, reading. *Address:* Rosewall, Calonne Road, Wimbledon, SW19. *T:* 081–946 2588.   *Died 29 Oct. 1991.*

BLACK, Prof. Duncan, PhD; FBA 1989; Professor of Economics, University College of North Wales, Bangor, 1953–68, then Emeritus; *b* 23 May 1908; *s* of Duncan Black and Margaret Brown Muir; *m* 1946, Almut G. A. E. Uffenorde. *Educ:* Dalziel High Sch., Motherwell; Glasgow Univ. (MA, 2nd cl. Hons Maths and Phys; 1st cl. Hons Econs and Pols). Fellow, Econometric Soc. Asst Lectr, Sch. of Econs, Dundee, 1932–34; Asst and Lectr in Econs, UCNW, Bangor, 1934–45; Sen. Lectr, QUB, 1945–46; Sen. Lectr in Econs, Glasgow Univ., 1946–53 (periods in Civil Service). Formerly Dist. Vis. Prof. of Econs, USA univs. Corresp. Fellow, Amer. Acad. of Arts and Scis; Fellow, Lynceorum Academia, Rome. Duncan Black Chair in Econs created at George Mason Univ., Fairfax, Va. *Publications:* The Incidence of Income Taxes, 1939; (with R. A. Newing) Committee Decisions with Complementary Valuation, 1951; The Theory of Committees and Elections, 1958; articles in economic jls. *Recreation:* cricket. *Address:* 22 Marine Parade, Paignton, Devon TQ3 2NU. *T:* Paignton (0803) 556108.
Died 14 Jan. 1991.

BLACK, Eugene R(obert); banker, United States; Chairman: Blackwell Land Co. Inc.; Scandinavian Securities Corp.; Director, Warner Communications; *b* Atlanta, Ga, USA, 1 May 1898; *s* of Eugene R. Black and Gussie Grady; *m* 1st, 1918, Elizabeth Blalock (*d* 1928); one *s* one *d*; 2nd, 1930, Susette Heath; one *s*. *Educ:* Univ. of Georgia. Atlanta Office, Harris, Forbes & Co. (NY Investment Bankers), 1919; Manager, Atlanta Office, Chase-Harris, Forbes Corp., in charge of Atlanta, New Orleans, Houston and Dallas offices, 1933; Chase National Bank of the City of NY: 2nd Vice-Pres., 1933; Vice-Pres., 1937; Senior Vice-Pres., 1949, resigned; US Executive Director, Internat. Bank for Reconstruction and Development, 1947–49, President, 1949–62; Consultant and Dir, Chase Manhattan Bank, 1963–70; Consultant, American Express Co., 1970–78. Special Adviser to President Johnson on SE Asia development, 1965–69. Trustee, Corporate Property Investors, and other financial trusteeships. Medal of Freedom (US), 1969. Numerous hon. doctorates; decorated by many countries. *Publications:* The Diplomacy of Economic Development, 1963 (trans. other languages); Alternative in Southeast Asia, 1969. *Recreations:* golf, fishing, student of William Shakespeare. *Address:* PO Box 753, Southampton, NY 11969–0753, USA. *Clubs:* Athenæum; Lotos, River (New York); International (Washington, DC); National Golf Links of America (Southampton, NY), etc.
Died 20 Feb. 1992.

BLACK, Margaret McLeod; Head Mistress, Bradford Girls' Grammar School, 1955–75; *b* 1 May 1912; *d* of James Black and Elizabeth Malcolm. *Educ:* Kelso High Sch.; Edinburgh Univ. (MA). Classics Mistress, Lancaster Girls' Grammar Sch., 1936–44, and Manchester High Sch. for Girls, 1944–50; Head Mistress, Great Yarmouth Girls' High Sch., 1950–55. President: Leeds Branch of Classical Assoc., 1963–65; Joint Assoc. of Classical Teachers, 1967–69; Yorkshire Divl Union of Soroptimist Clubs, 1968–69. *Recreation:* music. *Club:* Royal Over-Seas League.   *Died 10 May 1993.*

BLACK, Rev. Prof. Matthew, DD, DLitt, DTheol, LLD; FRSE; FBA 1955; Professor of Divinity and Biblical Criticism, and Principal of St Mary's College, University of St Andrews, 1954–78, then Emeritus; Dean of the Faculty of Divinity, 1963–67; *b* 3 Sept. 1908; *s* of late James and Helen Black, Kilmarnock, Ayrshire; *m* 1938, Ethel M., *d* of late Lt-Comdr A. H. Hall, Royal Indian Navy; one *s* one *d*. *Educ:* Kilmarnock Academy; Glasgow Univ. Glasgow: 1st cl. hons MA Classics, 1930; 2nd cl. hons Mental Philosophy, 1931; BD with distinction in Old Testament, 1934; DLitt 1944; Dr Phil Bonn, 1937.

Buchanan Prize, Moral Philosophy, 1929; Caird Scholar, Classics, 1930; Crombie Scholar, Biblical Criticism, 1933 (St Andrews award); Brown Downie Fellow, 1934; Maxwell Forsyth Fellow and Kerr Travelling Scholarship, Trinity Coll., Glasgow, 1934. Asst to Prof. of Hebrew, Glasgow, 1935–37; Warden of Church of Scotland Students' Residence, 1936–37; Asst Lecturer in Semitic Languages and Literatures, University of Manchester, 1937–39; Bruce Lectr, Trinity Coll., Glasgow, 1940; Lectr in Hebrew and Biblical Criticism, Univ. of Aberdeen, 1939–42; Minister of Dunbarney, Church of Scotland, 1942–47; Officiating CF, Bridge of Earn, 1943–47; Lecturer in New Testament Language and Literature, Leeds Univ., 1947–52; Prof. of Biblical Criticism and Biblical Antiquities, University of Edinburgh, 1952–54. Editor, New Testament Studies, 1954–77. Chm., Adv. Cttee of Peshitta Project of Univ. of Leiden, 1968–78. Morse Lectr, 1956 and De Hoyt Lectr, 1963, Union Theological Seminary, NY; Thomas Burns Lectr, Otago, 1967. Pres., Soc. for Old Testament Study, 1968. FRSE 1977. Pres., SNTS, 1970–71; Corresp. Mem., Göttingen Akademie der Wissenschaften, 1957; Mem., Royal Soc. of Scis, Uppsala, 1979; Hon. Member: Amer. Soc. of Biblical Exegesis, 1958; American Bible Soc., 1966. Hon. DTheol Münster, 1960; Hon. LLD St Andrews, 1980; Hon. DD: Glasgow, 1954; Cambridge, 1965; Queen's, Ontario, 1967. British Academy Burkitt Medal for Biblical Studies, 1962. *Publications:* Rituale Melchitarum (Stuttgart), 1938; An Aramaic Approach to the Gospels and Acts, 3rd edn, 1967 (Die Muttersprache Jesu, 1982); A Christian Palestinian Syriac Horologion (Texts and Studies, Contributions to Patristic Literature, New Series, Vol. I), 1954; The Scrolls and Christian Origins, 1961, repr. 1983; General and New Testament Editor, Peake's Commentary on the Bible, revised edn, 1962; Bible Societies' edn of the Greek New Testament (Stuttgart), 1966; (ed jtly) In Memoriam Paul Kahle (Berlin), 1968; (ed and contrib.) The Scrolls and Christianity, 1968; (with A. M. Denis) Apocalypsis Henochi Graece Fragmenta Pseudepigraphorum, 1970; Commentary on Romans, 1973, 2nd edn 1989; (ed with William A. Smalley) On Language, Religion and Culture, in honor Eugene A. Nida, 1974; (organising Editor) The History of the Jewish People in the Age of Jesus Christ: vol. I, ed by G. Vermes and F. Millar, 1973; vol. II, ed jtly with G. Vermes and F. Millar, 1979; vol. III, ed by G. Vermes, F. Millar and M. Goodman, Part 1, 1986, Part 2, 1987; (jtly) The Book of Enoch or I Enoch, 1985; articles in learned journals. *Address:* St Michael's, 40 Buchanan Gardens, St Andrews, Fife KY16 9LX. *Club:* Royal and Ancient.

Died 2 Oct. 1994.

BLACKBURN, (Albert) Raymond; *b* 11 March 1915; *s* of Dr A. E. Blackburn, Bournemouth; *m* 1st, 1939, Barbara Mary (marr. diss. 1954), *d* of Gerald Robison; two *s* one *d*; 2nd, 1956, Marianne Ferguson (marr. diss. 1959); 3rd, 1959, Tessa Hume; two *s* three *d*. *Educ:* Rugby; London Univ. Served War of 1939–45, E Yorks Regt; Capt. 1940; Major, 1944. Admitted solicitor, 1937; with Blackburn, Wyatt & Co., London. MP (Lab) Birmingham, King's Norton, 1945–50; MP (Ind.) Birmingham, Northfield, 1950–51. *Publications:* I am an Alcoholic, 1959; The Erosion of Freedom, 1964. *Died 3 Nov. 1991.*

BLACKBURN, Guy, MBE (mil.) 1944; MChir, FRCS; Consultant Surgeon Emeritus, Guy's Hospital; *b* 20 Nov. 1911; *s* of Dr A. E. Blackburn, Beckenham; *m* 1953, Joan, *d* of Arthur Bowen, Pontycymmer, Wales; one *d* (and one *s* (decd) by a previous marriage). *Educ:* Rugby; Clare Coll., Cambridge (MA). MRCS, LRCP 1935; MB, BChir 1935; FRCS 1937; MChir 1941. House appointments, St Bartholomew's Hospital, 1935–37; Brackenbury Scholar in Surgery, 1935; Demonstrator of Anatomy and Chief Asst in Surgery, 1938–39; Military Service, 1942–46: Lt-

Col i/c Surgical Div., 1945–46; served in N Africa and Italy. Hunterian Prof., RCS, 1946; late Examiner in Surgery, Univs of Cambridge and London; Member Court of Examiners, RCS, 1962–68. Hon. Visiting Surgeon, Johns Hopkins Hospital, Baltimore, USA, 1957; Hon. Consulting Surgeon, British Army at Home, 1967–76. President: Medical Soc. of London, 1964–65; Assoc. of Surgeons of GB and Ireland, 1976–77. Master, Soc. of Apothecaries, 1980–81. *Publications:* (co-ed) A Textbook of Surgery, 1958; (co-ed) Field Surgery Pocket Book, 1981; various publications in medical jls and books. *Address:* 4 Holly Lodge Gardens, N6 6AA. *T:* 081–340 9071. *Died 2 May 1994.*

BLACKBURN, John Graham, PhD; MP (C) Dudley West, since May 1979; *b* 2 Sept. 1933; *s* of Charles Frederick Blackburn and Grace Blackburn; *m* 1958, Marjorie (*née* Thompson); one *s* one *d*. *Educ:* Liverpool Collegiate Sch.; Liverpool Univ.; Berlin Univ. (PhD). Staff/Sgt, Special Investigation Br., Royal Military Police, 1949–53; D/Sgt, Liverpool Police, 1953–65; National Sales Manager with an Internat. Public Engrg Gp, 1965–79; Sales Dir, Solway Engrg Co. Ltd, 1965–. Member, Wolverhampton Council, 1970–80. Member: Home Affairs Select Cttee, 1980–83; Select Cttee for Services, 1987–92; Select Cttee for Heritage, 1992–; Chairman's Panel, 1992–; Jt Chm., All Party Parly Glass Gp, 1994–; Vice Chm., Cons. Parly Cttee for Arts and Heritage, 1986– (Sec., 1980–86). Vice-Pres., Cons. Friends of Israel, 1989– (Chm., 1985–89); Mem., Council of Europe, 1983–85. Member: POUNC, 1972–80; Ecclesiastical Council, 1979–. Freeman: City of London, 1980; City of Tel Aviv, 1981. FInstM 1979; FISE 1975; FInstMSM 1976; FRSA 1984. *Recreation:* keen yachtsman. *Address:* 129 Canterbury Road, Penn, Wolverhampton WV4 4EQ. *T:* Wolverhampton (01902) 36222. *Clubs:* Wolverhampton and Bilston Athletic (Vice-President); Traeth Coch Yacht (Executive Member).

Died 12 Oct. 1994.

BLACKBURN, Raymond; *see* Blackburn, A. R.

BLACKBURN, Ronald Henry Albert; a Planning Appeals Commissioner for Northern Ireland, 1980–89, retired; *b* 9 Feb. 1924; *s* of late Sidney James and Ellen Margaret Selina Blackburn; *m* 1950, Annabell Hunter; two *s*. *Educ:* Royal Belfast Academical Institution; Univ. of London (LLB Hons). Intelligence Service, 1943; Dept of the Foreign Office, 1944–46. Parly Reporting Staff (NI), 1946–52; Second Clerk Asst, Parlt of NI, 1952–62; Clerk Asst, 1962–71; Clerk of the Parliaments, 1971–73; Clerk to NI Assembly, 1973–79; Clerk to NI Constitutional Convention, 1975–76. *Recreations:* golf, gardening. *Address:* Trelawn, Jordanstown Road, Newtownabbey, Co. Antrim, N Ireland BT37 0QD. *T:* Whiteabbey (0232) 862035. *Died 6 Sept. 1993.*

BLACKBURNE, Rt Rev. Hugh Charles; *b* 4 June 1912; *s* of late Very Rev. Harry William Blackburne; *m* 1944, Doris Freda, *widow* of Pilot Officer H. L. N. Davis; two *s* one *d*. *Educ:* Marlborough; Clare Coll., Cambridge (MA); Westcott House, Cambridge. Deacon, 1937; Priest, 1938; Curate of Almondbury, Yorks, 1937–39. Chaplain to the Forces, 1939–47; served with 1st Guards Bde, 11th Armoured Div., HQ Anti-Aircraft Comd, and as Chaplain, RMC, Sandhurst. Rector, Milton, Hants, 1947–53; Vicar, St Mary's, Harrow, 1953–61. Rector of the Hilborough Group, 1961–72; Vicar of Ranworth and Chaplain for the Norfolk Broads, 1972–77; Hon. Canon of Norwich, 1965–77; Chaplain to the Queen, 1962–77. Bishop Suffragan of Thetford, 1977–80. *Recreations:* sailing, bird-watching. *Address:* 4 Goodrick Place, Swaffham, Norfolk PE37 7RP. *Died 15 Oct. 1995.*

BLACKETT, Major Sir Francis Hugh, 11th Bt *cr* 1673, of Newcastle, Co. Northumberland; *b* 16 Oct. 1907; *3rd s* of Sir Hugh Douglas Blackett, 8th Bt and Helen Katherine (*d* 1943), *d* of George Lowther; *S* brother, 1994; *m* 1st, 1950, Elizabeth Eily Barrie (*d* 1982), 2nd *d* of late Howard Dennison; two *s* two *d*; 2nd, 1985, Mrs Joan Chowdry. *Educ:* Eton. Served War, 1939–45, The Royals (Major). *Heir: s* Hugh Francis Blackett [*b* 11 Feb. 1955; *m* 1982, Anna, *yr d* of J. St G. Coldwell; one *s* three *d*]. *Address:* Brewhouse, Halton Castle, Corbridge, Northumberland NE45 5PH.   *Died 9 Feb. 1995.*

BLACKETT, Sir George (William), 10th Bt *cr* 1673, of Newcastle, Northumberland; *b* 26 April 1906; *s* of Sir Hugh Douglas Blackett, 8th Bt, and Helen Katherine (*d* 1943), *d* of late George Lowther; *S* brother, 1968; *m* 1st, 1933, Euphemia Cicely (*d* 1960), *d* of late Major Nicholas Robinson; 2nd, 1964, Daphne Laing, *d* of late Major Guy Laing Bradley, TD, Hexham, Northumberland. Served with Shropshire Yeomanry and CMP, 1939–45. *Recreations:* hunting, forestry, farming. *Heir: b* Major Francis Hugh Blackett [*b* 16 Oct. 1907; *m* 1st, 1950, Elizabeth Eily Barrie (*d* 1982), 2nd *d* of late Howard Dennison; two *s* two *d*; 2nd, 1985, Mrs Joan Chowdry]. *Address:* Colwyn, Corbridge, Northumberland. *T:* Corbridge (043471) 2252. *Club:* English-Speaking Union.   *Died 22 Jan. 1994.*

BLAIR, Rt Rev. James Douglas, CBE 1975; *b* 22 Jan. 1906; *s* of Rev. A. A. Blair; unmarried. *Educ:* Marlborough; Keble Coll., Oxford; Cuddesdon Coll. 2nd class Lit.Hum., 1928. Deacon, Penistone, Yorks, 1929; priest, 1930; Oxford Mission Brotherhood of the Epiphany, Calcutta, 1932–; Asst Bishop of Calcutta, with charge of East Bengal, 1951; Bishop of East Bengal, 1956; title of diocese changed to Dacca, 1960; retired as Bishop of Dacca, 1975. *Recreation:* walking. *Address:* Oxford Mission, Barisha, Calcutta 700008, India.
Died 12 Jan. 1991.

BLAIR-KERR, Sir William Alexander, (Sir Alastair), Kt 1973; President of the Court of Appeal for Bermuda, 1979–89; *b* 1 Dec. 1911; *s* of William Alexander Milne Kerr and Annie Kerr (*née* Blair), Dunblane, Perthshire, Scotland; *m* 1942, Esther Margaret Fowler Wright (*d* 1990); one *s* one *d*. *Educ:* McLaren High Sch., Callander; Edinburgh Univ. (MA, LLB). Solicitor in Scotland, 1939; Advocate (Scots Bar), 1951. Advocate and solicitor, Singapore, 1939–41; Straits Settlements Volunteer Force, 1941–42; escaped from Singapore, 1942; Indian Army: Staff Capt. "A" Bombay Dist HQ, 1942–43; DAAG 107 Line of Communication area HQ, Poona, 1943–44; British Army: GSO2, War Office, 1944–45; SO1 Judicial, BMA Malaya, 1945–46. Colonial Legal Service (HM Overseas Service), Hong Kong: Magistrate, 1946–48; Crown Counsel, 1949; Pres. Tenancy Tribunal, 1950; Crown Counsel, 1951–53; Sen. Crown Counsel, 1953–59; District Judge, 1959–61; Puisne Judge, Supreme Court, 1961–71; Sen. Puisne Judge, Supreme Court, 1971–73; President: Court of Appeal: for the Bahamas, 1978–80; for Belize, 1978–81; for Turks and Caicos Islands, 1978–81; Mem., Ct of Appeal for Gibraltar, 1982–87; sometime Actg Chief Justice of Hong Kong. Pres., various Commns of Inquiry. *Recreations:* golf, walking, music. *Address:* Gairn, Kinbuck, Dunblane, Perthshire FK15 0NQ. *T:* Dunblane (0786) 823377. *Club:* Royal Over-Seas League.
Died 1 Dec. 1992.

BLAKE, Charles Henry, CB 1966; a Commissioner of Customs and Excise, 1968–72; European Adviser, British American Tobacco Co., 1972–76; *b* 29 Nov. 1912; *s* of Henry and Lily Blake, Westbury on Trym, Bristol; *m* 1938, M. Jayne McKinney (*d* 1974), *d* of James and Ellen McKinney, Castle Finn, Co. Donegal; three *d*. *Educ:* Cotham Grammar Sch.; Jesus Coll., Cambridge (Major Scholar). Administrative Class, Home Civil Service, 1936; HM Customs and Excise: Principal, 1941; Asst Sec., 1948;

Comr and Sec., 1957–64; Asst Under-Sec. of State, Air Force Dept, MoD, 1964–68. *Recreation:* gardens. *Address:* 33 Grenville Court, Chorleywood, Herts WD3 5PZ. *Clubs:* United Oxford & Cambridge University; Moor Park.
Died 15 March 1994.

BLAKE, John Clifford, CB 1958; *b* 12 July 1901; *s* of late Alfred Harold and Ada Blake, Prestwich, Lancs; *m* 1928, Mary Lilian Rothwell; one *s* two *d*. *Educ:* Manchester Grammar Sch.; Queen's Coll., Oxford (MA). Admitted solicitor, 1927. Ministry of Health Solicitor's Dept, 1929; Solicitor and Legal Adviser to Ministries of Health and Housing and Local Government, and to Registrar Gen., 1957–65; Mem., Treasurer and Jt Exec. Sec., Anglican-Methodist Unity Commn, 1965–69; Vice-Pres., Methodist Conference, 1968. *Recreation:* music, especially organ and choral. *Address:* 3 Clifton Court, 297 Clifton Drive South, St Anne's on Sea, Lancs FY8 1HN. *T:* St Anne's (0253) 728365.   *Died 13 March 1993.*

BLANCH, Baron *cr* 1983 (Life Peer), of Bishopthorpe in the county of North Yorkshire; **Rt Rev. and Rt Hon. Stuart Yarworth Blanch,** PC 1975; *b* 2 Feb. 1918; *s* of late William Edwin and Elizabeth Blanch; *m* 1943, Brenda Gertrude, *d* of late William Arthur Coyte; one *s* three *d* (and one *d* decd). *Educ:* Alleyns Sch., Dulwich; Oxford Univ. (BA 1st cl. Theo. 1948, MA 1952). Employee of Law Fire Insurance Soc. Ltd, 1936–40; navigator in RAF, 1940–46; St Catherine's Coll., Oxford, 1946–49 (Hon. Fellow, 1975). Deacon, 1949; priest, 1950; Curate of Highfield, Oxford, 1949–52; Vicar of Eynsham, Oxon, 1952–57; Tutor and Vice-Principal of Wycliffe Hall, Oxford, 1957–60 (Chm. 1967–); Oriel Canon of Rochester and Warden of Rochester Theological Coll., 1960–66; Bishop of Liverpool, 1966–75; Archbishop of York, 1975–83. Sub-Prelate, OStJ, 1975–88. Chm., Sandford St Martin Trust, 1988–. Hon. Fellow, St Peter's Coll., Oxford, 1983. Hon. LLD Liverpool, 1975; Hon. DD: Hull, 1977; Wycliffe Coll., Toronto, 1979; Manchester, 1984; DUniv York, 1979. *Publications:* The World Our Orphanage, 1972; For All Mankind, 1976; The Christian Militant, 1978; The Burning Bush, 1978; The Trumpet in the Morning, 1979; The Ten Commandments, 1981; Living by Faith, 1983; Way of Blessedness, 1985; Encounters with Christ, 1988. *Recreations:* sport, meteorology, walking, music. *Address:* Bryn Celyn, The Level, Shenington, near Banbury, Oxfordshire OX15 6NA. *Club:* Commonwealth Trust.   *Died 3 June 1994.*

BLANKENHORN, Herbert, Hon. GCVO 1965; Member and Vice-President, Executive Board, UNESCO, 1970–76; *b* 15 Dec. 1904; *s* of Erich Blankenhorn; *m* 1944, Gisela Krug; two *s* two *d*. *Educ:* Gymnasiums in Strasbourg, Berlin and Karlsruhe; Universities of Munich, London, Heidelberg and Paris. Entered Foreign Service, 1929; served in: Athens, 1932–35; Washington, 1935–39; Helsinki, 1940; Berne, 1940–43; Foreign Office, Berlin (Protocol Section), 1943–45; Dep. Sec.-Gen., Zonal Advisory Council, Hamburg, 1946–48; Sec.-Gen. Christian Democratic Party (British Zone), 1948; Private Sec. to President of Parliamentary Council, Bonn (Dr Adenauer), 1948–49; Political Dir, Foreign Office, 1950–55; German Ambassador: to NATO, 1955–58; to France, 1958–63; to Italy, 1963–65; to UK, 1965–70. *Publication:* (political memoirs) Verständnis und Verständigung, 1980. *Address:* 7847 Badenweiler, Hintere Au 2, Germany.   *Died 10 Aug. 1991.*

BLASCHKO, Hermann Karl Felix, (Hugh), MD; FRS 1962; Emeritus Reader in Biochemical Pharmacology, Oxford University, and Emeritus Fellow, Linacre College, Oxford, since 1967 (Hon. Fellow, 1990); *b* Berlin, 4 Jan. 1900; *o s* of late Prof. Alfred Blaschko, MD and Johanna Litthauer; *m* 1944, Mary Douglas Black, *d* of late John Robert Black, Yelverton, S Devon; no *c*. *Educ:*

Universities of Berlin, Freiburg im Breisgau and Göttingen. MD Freiburg; PhD Cambridge; MA Oxon. Research Asst to late Prof. O. Meyerhof at Berlin-Dahlem and Heidelberg at various periods, 1925–32; University Asst in Physiology, Univ. of Jena, 1928–29; worked at UCL, 1929–30 and 1933–34; Physiological Lab., Cambridge Univ., 1934–44; came to Oxford, 1944. Visiting Professor: Yale Univ., 1967–68; Upstate Medical Center, Syracuse, NY, 1968; RCS, 1968–73; Univ. of Pennsylvania, 1969; Univ. of Bergen, Norway, 1969–70. Hon. Prof., Faculty of Medicine, Heidelberg, 1966. Member of Editorial Board: Pharmacological Reviews, 1957–64; British Journal of Pharmacology and Chemotherapy, 1959–65; Journal of Physiology, 1965–72; Neuropharmacology, 1962–72; Naunyn-Schmiedebergs Arch. Exp. Pharmak., 1966–85; Molecular Pharmacol., 1966–77. Mem. Neuropharmacology Panel, International Brain Research Organisation. Hon. FRSocMed, 1978; Hon. Member: British Pharmacological Soc., 1979; Hungarian Pharm. Soc., 1979; Physiological Soc., 1980; Berliner Medizinische Ges., 1980; Corresp. Mem., German Pharmacol Soc., 1972; Hon. Pres., Internat. Catecholamine Symposium, Göteborg, 1983. Hon. Mem., Sidcot Old Scholars' Assoc., 1958. First Thudichum Lectr and Medallist, London, 1974; Aschoff Lectr, Freiburg, 1974; Wellcome Gold Medal in Pharmacology, 1990. Hon. MD: Berlin (Free Univ.), 1966; Bern, 1984; Freiburg im Breisgau, 1990. *Publications:* numerous papers in scientific publications. *Address:* Department of Pharmacology, Mansfield Road, Oxford OX1 3QT; 24 Park Town, Oxford OX2 6SH.

Died 18 April 1993.

BLAXTER, Sir Kenneth (Lyon), Kt 1977; FRS 1967; FRSE 1965; Director, 1965–82, Hon. Research Associate, since 1982, Rowett Research Institute, Bucksburn, Aberdeen, and Consultant Director, Commonwealth Bureau of Nutrition; *b* 19 June 1919; *s* of Gaspard Culling Blaxter and Charlotte Ellen Blaxter; *m* 1957, Mildred Lillington Hall; two *s* one *d. Educ:* City of Norwich Sch.; University of Reading; University of Illinois. BSc(Agric.), PhD, DSc; NDA (Hons). Scientific Officer, Nat. Inst. for Research in Dairying, 1939–40 and 1941–44. Served RA, 1940–41. Research Officer, Ministry of Agriculture Veterinary Laboratory, 1944–46; Commonwealth Fellow, University of Ill, 1946–47; Head of Dept of Nutrition, Hannah Inst., Ayr, Scotland, 1948–65. Vis. Prof., Univ. of Newcastle, 1982–. Chm., Individual Merit Promotion Panel, HM Treasury. President: British Soc. of Animal Production, 1970–71; Nutrition Soc., 1974; RSE, 1979–82; Inst. of Biology, 1986–88. Foreign Member: Lenin Acad. of Agricl Sciences, 1970; Dutch Soc. of Scis, 1982. Hon. DSc: QUB, 1974; Leeds, 1977; Newcastle, 1984; Hon. LLD Aberdeen, 1981; Hon. DAgric Agricl Univ., Norway, 1975. Hon. MRCVS 1978. Thomas Baxter Prize and Gold Medal, 1960; Gold Medal, RASE, 1964; Wooldridge Gold Medal, British Vet. Assoc., 1973; De Laval Medal, Royal Swedish Acad. Engrg Scis, 1976; Messel Medal, Soc. of Chem. Industry, 1976; Keith Medal and Prize, RSE, 1977; Massey-Ferguson Award, 1977; Wolf Foundn Internat. Prize, 1979. *Publications:* Energy Metabolism of Ruminants, 1962; Energy Metabolism, 1965; People, Food and Resources, 1986; Energy Metabolism in Animals and Man, 1989; scientific papers in Jl Endocrinology, Jl Agricultural Science, British Jl Nutrition, Research in Veterinary Science, etc. *Recreation:* painting. *Address:* Stradbroke Hall, Stradbroke, near Eye, Suffolk IP21 5HH. *Club:* Farmers'.

Died 18 April 1991.

BLENNERHASSETT, His Honour Francis Alfred, (Frank), QC 1965; a Circuit Judge, 1978–89; *b* 7 July 1916; 2nd *s* of John and Annie Elizabeth Blennerhassett; *m* 1948, Betty Muriel Bray; two *d. Educ:* Solihull Sch.

Served War of 1939–45, RA and Royal Warwicks Regt, Britain and East Africa (Captain). Called to Bar, Middle Temple, 1946; Bencher, 1971; Oxford Circuit. Dep. Chm., Staffordshire QS, 1963–71; Recorder of New Windsor, 1965–71; a Recorder of the Crown Court, 1972–78; Hon. Recorder of New Windsor, 1972–76; Hon. Recorder of Windsor and Maidenhead, 1976–89. Legal Assessor to GMC and Dental Council, 1971–78; Chm., Govt Cttee on Drinking and Driving, 1975–76; Member: Parole Bd, 1981–83; Home Office Cttee on Magistrates' Courts Procedure, 1989–92. *Recreation:* golf. *Address:* Manor Cottage, Hampton in Arden, Solihull, Warwickshire BG2 0AE. *T:* Hampton in Arden (0675) 442660. *Club:* Copt Heath Golf. *Died 13 June 1993.*

BLISSETT, Alfreda Rose; *see* Hodgson, A. R.

BLOCK, Maj.-Gen. Adam Johnstone Cheyne, CB 1962; CBE 1959 (OBE 1951); DSO 1945; *b* 13 June 1908; *s* of late Col Arthur Hugh Block, RA; *m* 1945, Pauline Bingham, *d* of late Col Norman Kennedy, CBE, DSO, TD, DL, Doonholm, Ayr; two *d* (and one *d* decd). *Educ:* Blundell's; RMA Woolwich. 2nd Lieut RA 1928; served War of 1939–45 (France, UK, N Africa and Italy); CO 24th Field Regt, RA, 1943–45; GSO1, RA and AMS, GHQ, 1945–47; AQMG and GSO1 Trg AA Comd, 1947–50; Lieut-Col, 1950; Senior Directing Staff (Army). Joint Services Staff College, 1950–53; Col, 1953; CRA 6 Armd Div., 1953; Comdt, School of Artillery, Larkhill, 1956; Maj.-Gen. 1959; GOC Troops, Malta and Libya, 1959–62; retd. PA to Chm., David Brown Corp., 1963–65; Chief Inf. Officer, Church Assembly, then Gen. Synod, 1965–73. Mem. Basingstoke DC, 1973–75. Col Comdt, Royal Regt of Artillery, 1965–73. *Recreations:* all country pursuits. *Address:* St Cross House, Whitchurch, Hants RG28 7AS. *T:* Whitchurch (01256) 892344.

Died 14 Oct. 1994.

BLOMFIELD, Brig. John Reginald, OBE 1957; MC 1944; *b* 10 Jan. 1916; *s* of late Douglas John Blomfield, CIE, and Coralie, *d* of F. H. Tucker, Indian Police; *m* 1939, Patricia Mary McKim; two *d. Educ:* Clifton Coll.; RMA, Woolwich; Peterhouse, Cambridge (MA). Commissioned Royal Engineers, 1936; Lt-Col 1955; Col 1961; Brig. 1965. Retired as Dep. Director, Military Engineering Experimental Establishment, 1969. New Towns Commn Manager, Hemel Hempstead, 1969–78. MBIM 1966. *Recreations:* cruising, ocean racing. *Address:* 9 Armstrong Close, Brockenhurst, Hants. *Clubs:* Royal Ocean Racing; Royal Lymington Yacht. *Died 11 Nov. 1992.*

BLOOM, G(eorge) Cromarty, CBE 1974; General Manager and Chief Executive, The Press Association Ltd, 1961–75; *b* 8 June 1910; *s* of late George Highfield Bloom and Jessie Bloom (*née* Cromarty); *m* 1st, 1940, Patricia Suzanne Ramplin (*d* 1957); two *s*; 2nd, 1961, Sheila Louise Curran; one *s. Educ:* Australia and China, privately; Keble Coll., Oxford. With Reuters Ltd, 1933–60. Dep. Chm., London Broadcasting Co., 1976–81. Vice-Chm., Internat. Press Telecommunications Council, 1971–75; Vice-Pres., Alliance Européenne des Agences de Presse, 1971–75; Chm., CPU Telecommunications Cttee, 1973–77. *Address:* 20 The Pavilions, Sandford Road, Cheltenham GL53 7AJ. *T:* Cheltenham (0242) 239413.

Died 18 Oct. 1992.

BLOOM, Ronald; HM Diplomatic Service, retired; freelance political/commercial consultant; Director: Trefoil Partnership Ltd, since 1982; Eastasia Technology Inc. (Hong Kong), since 1984; Risk & Crisis Analysis Ltd, since 1992; Partner, RFP Associates Ltd Partnership, since 1986; *b* 21 Jan. 1926; *s* of John Bloom and Marjorie Bloom (*née* Barker); *m* 1956, Shirley Evelyn Edge; one *s* two *d. Educ:* inadequately, then Indian Mil. Acad. HM Forces, DLI, E Yorks Regt, 1943–57. Joined HM

Diplomatic Service, 1958; Hong Kong, 1958–61; Singapore, 1961–63; FO, 1963–65; Zomba, 1965–67; FO, 1967–69; Kuala Lumpur, 1969–71; Singapore, 1971–74; Counsellor, FO, 1974–81. UK Representative: The Parvus Co., USA; Internat. Trade & Communications Inc., USA. *Publications:* reviews in Man (Royal Anthropol Inst.); occasional articles on uniforms and model soldiers. *Address:* The Old House, Deep Street, Prestbury, Glos GL52 3AW. *T:* Cheltenham (0242) 244141; Trefoil Partnership Ltd, 3/13 Phillimore Place, W8 7BY. *T:* 071–937 3926. *Clubs:* Brooks's, Special Forces.

Died 8 July 1993.

BLOY, Rt Rev. Francis Eric Irving, DD, STD; *b* Birchington, Isle of Thanet, Kent, 17 Dec. 1904; *s* of Rev. Francis Joseph Field Bloy and Alice Mary (*née* Poynter); *m* 1929, Frances Forbes Cox, Alexandria, Va; no *c*. *Educ:* University of Missouri (BA); Georgetown Univ. of Foreign Service; Virginia Theological Seminary (BD). Rector, All Saints Ch., Reisterstown, Maryland, 1929–33; Assoc. Rector, St James-by-the-Sea, La Jolla, Calif, 1933–35, Rector, 1935–37; Dean, St Paul's Cathedral, Los Angeles, Calif, 1937–48; Bishop of Los Angeles, 1948–73. DD: Ch. Divinity Sch. of the Pacific, Berkeley, Calif, 1942; Occidental Coll., Los Angeles, 1953; Va Theol Sem., 1953; STD: Ch. Divinity Sch. of the Pacific, 1948; Univ. of S Calif, 1955. Pres., Church Federation of Los Angeles, 1946–47; Pres., Univ. Religious Conf., 1956; Hon. Chm. Bd of Trustees, Good Samaritan Hosp.; Mem. Town Hall. *Address:* 3919 Starland Drive, Flintridge, CA 91011, USA. *Club:* California (Los Angeles).

Died 23 May 1993.

BLUNDELL, Sir Michael, KBE 1962 (MBE 1943); *b* 7 April 1907; *s* of Alfred Herbert Blundell and Amelia Woodward Blundell (*née* Richardson); *m* 1946, Geraldine Lötte Robarts (*d* 1983); one *d*. *Educ:* Wellington Coll. Settled in Kenya as farmer, 1925. 2nd Lieut, RE, 1940; Major, 1940; Lieut-Col, 1941; Col, 1944; served Abyssinian campaign and SEAC. Commissioner, European Settlement, 1946–47; MLC, Rift Valley Constituency, Kenya, 1948–63; Leader European Members, 1952–54; Minister on Emergency War Council, Kenya, 1954–55; Minister of Agriculture, Kenya, 1955–59 and April 1961–June 1963; Leader of New Kenya Group, 1959–63. Chairman: Pyrethrum Board of Kenya, 1949–54; Egerton Agricultural Coll., 1962–72; EA Breweries Ltd, 1964–77; Uganda Breweries Ltd, 1965–76; Dir, Barclays Bank of Kenya Ltd, 1968–82. Chm., Kenya Soc. for the Blind, 1977–81. Freeman, Goldsmiths' Co., 1950. Hon. Col, 3rd KAR, 1955–61. Judge, Guernsey cattle, RASE, 1977. *Publications:* So Rough a Wind, 1964; The Wild Flowers of Kenya, 1982; Collins Guide to The Wild Flowers of East Africa, 1987. *Recreations:* gardening, music, 18th century English porcelain. *Address:* Box 30181, Nairobi, Kenya. *T:* Nairobi 512278. *Clubs:* Lansdowne; Muthaiga (Nairobi).

Died 1 Feb. 1993.

BOARDMAN, Harold; *b* 12 June 1907; *m* 1936, Winifred May, *d* of Jesse Thorlby, Derbys; one *d*. *Educ:* Bolton and Derby. Formerly Trade Union Official. For 3 yrs Mem. Derby Town Council. MP (Lab) Leigh, 1945–79; PPS to Ministry of Labour, 1947–51. ILO Confs in Geneva, 1947, 1949, 1950, and San Francisco, 1948; Delegate to Council of Europe, 1960, 1961. Former Exec. Mem., NW Industrial Develt Assoc. *Died 1 Aug. 1994.*

BOARDMAN, Sir Kenneth (Ormrod), Kt 1981; DL; Founder Chairman, Planned Giving Ltd, 1959–93; *b* 18 May 1914; *s* of Edgar Nicholas Boardman and Emily Boardman; *m* 1939, Lucy Stafford; one *s* one *d* (and one *d* decd). *Educ:* St Peter's Sch., Swinton, Lancs. Trooper, Duke of Lancaster's Own Yeomanry, 1932–33; served War 1939–45, Major RA, 1942–46. Chm., K. O. Boardman

Internat. Ltd, 1954–78. Hon. Treasurer, NW Area of Conservative Party, 1977–84; Member: Nat. Union of Cons. and Unionist Assocs, 1975–84 (Patron NW Area, 1984–93; Life Patron, Hazel Grove Cons. Assoc., 1975); NW Industrial Council, 1967–84; several Cons. constituency offices 1984. Pres., Manchester E Euro Constituency, 1984–. Dist Chm., NSPCC 100th Anniv. Appeal, 1984; President: Stockport & Dist NSPCC, 1985–; Stockport Cancer Res. Campaign, 1990–; Appeals Chm., John Charnley Trust, 1985–; Founder Mem., RA Heritage Appeal, 1991–; Patron, Hallé 125th Anniv. Appeal, 1984. Chm., Stockport Parish Church Restoration Fund, 1974–. Liveryman, Farriers Co., 1965–. *Recreations:* gardening, reading and writing, horse racing.

Died 12 July 1995.

BODDINGTON, Lewis, CBE 1956; *b* 13 Nov. 1907; *s* of James and Anne Boddington; *m* 1936, Morfydd, *d* of William Murray; no *c*. *Educ:* Lewis' Sch., Pengam; City of Cardiff Technical Coll.; University Coll. of S Wales and Monmouthshire. Pupil Engineer, Fraser & Chalmers Engineering Works, Erith, 1928–31; Asst to Major H. N. Wylie, 1931–36; Royal Aircraft Establishment, 1936; Head of Catapult Section, 1938; Supt of Design Offices, 1942–45; Head of Naval Aircraft Dept, 1945–51; Asst Dir (R&D) Naval, Min. of Supply, 1951–53; Dir Aircraft R&D (RN), 1953–59; Dir-Gen., Aircraft R&D, 1959–60; Dir and Consultant, Westland Aircraft, 1961–72. Medal of Freedom of USA (Bronze Palm), 1958. *Address:* Flat 6, Penarth House, Stanwell Road, Penarth CF6 2EY.

Died 7 Jan. 1994.

BODEN, Thomas Bennion, OBE 1978; Deputy President, National Farmers' Union of England and Wales, 1979; Chairman, European Economic Community Advisory Committee on Questions of Agricultural Structure Policy, 1985–89; *b* 23 Oct. 1915; *s* of late Harry Bertram Boden and Florence Nellie Mosley; *m* 1939, Dorothy Eileen Ball; one *s* two *d*. *Educ:* Alleynes Grammar Sch., Uttoxeter; Nottingham Univ. BSc course up to final year, when moved into farming on death of father, 1936; became involved in agricultural politics through NFU, 1948; office holder of NFU, 1977. JP Staffs 1957–85. *Publications:* Memories of a Political Farmer, 1995; articles on agricultural taxation, farm structures in EEC, farm finance, young new entrants into farming. *Recreations:* cricket, tennis, swimming, hockey. *Address:* Denstone Hall, Denstone, Uttoxeter, Staffs ST14 5HF. *T:* Rocester (01889) 590243. *Clubs:* Farmers', NFU.

Died 18 May 1995.

BOERMA, Addeke Hendrik; Commander, Order of the Netherlands Lion, 1975; Director-General, Food and Agriculture Organisation of the United Nations, 1968–75; *b* 3 April 1912; *m* 1953, Dinah Johnston; five *d*. *Educ:* Agricultural Univ., Wageningen. Netherlands Farmers' Organisation, 1935–38; Ministry of Agriculture of the Netherlands, 1938–45; Commissioner for Foreign Agricultural Relations, 1946; FAO positions: Regional Representative for Europe, 1948–51; Dir, Economics Div., 1951–58; Head of Programme and Budgetary Service, 1958–62; Asst Dir-Gen., 1960; Exec. Dir, World Food Programme, 1962–67. Hon. degrees from univs in USA, Netherlands, Belgium, Hungary, Canada, Italy and Greece. Wateler Peace Prize, Carnegie Foundn, The Hague, 1976. Commander, Order of Leopold II, Belgium; Officer, Ordre Mérite Agricole, France; Cavaliere di Gran Croce (Italy). *Address:* Prinz Eugenstrasse 44/10, 1040 Vienna, Austria. *Died 8 May 1992.*

BOHM, Prof. David (Joseph), PhD; FRS 1990; Professor of Theoretical Physics, Birkbeck College, University of London, 1961–83, then Emeritus; *b* 20 Dec. 1917; *s* of Samuel and Freda Bohm; *m* 1956, Sarah Woolfson; no *c*. *Educ:* Pennsylvania State Coll. (BS); University of Calif

(PhD). Research Physicist, University of Calif, Radiation Laboratory, 1943–47; Asst Prof., Princeton Univ., 1947–51; Prof., University de São Paulo, Brazil, 1951–55; Prof., Technion, Haifa, Israel, 1955–57; Research Fellow, Bristol Univ., 1957–61. Elliot Cresson Medal, Franklin Inst., 1991. *Publications:* Quantum Theory, 1951; Causality and Chance in Modern Physics, 1957; Special Theory of Relativity, 1965; Fragmentation and Wholeness, 1976; Wholeness and Order: cosmos and consciousness, 1979; Wholeness and the Implicate Order, 1980; (jtly) Science Order and Creativity, 1987; various papers in Physical Review, Nuovo Cimento, Progress of Theoretical Physics, British Jl for Philosophy of Science, etc, inc. papers on Implicate Order and A New Mode of Description in Physics. *Recreations:* walking, conversation, music (listener), art (viewer). *Address:* c/o Physics Department, Birkbeck College, Malet Street, WC1.
Died 27 Oct. 1992.

BOLITHO, Major Simon Edward, MC 1945; JP; DL; Director: Barclays Bank, 1959–86; English China Clays, 1963–86; Vice-Lord-Lieutenant of Cornwall, since 1970; *b* 13 March 1916; *s* of late Lieut-Col Sir Edward Bolitho, KBE, CB, DSO and Agnes Hamilton, *d* of G. Randall Johnson; *m* 1953, Elizabeth Margaret, *d* of late Rear-Adm. G. H. Creswell, CB, DSO, DSC; two *s* two *d*. *Educ:* Royal Naval Coll., Dartmouth; RMC Sandhurst. Grenadier Guards, 1936–49; Lt-Col, DCLI, 1957–60. Hon. Air Cdre, No 2625 (Co. of Cornwall) RAuxAF Regt Sqdn, 1984–. High Sheriff of Cornwall, 1956–57; JP 1959; DL 1964; CC, 1953–67. *Recreations:* shooting, fishing, hunting, sailing, gardening. *Address:* Trengwainton, Penzance, Cornwall. *T:* Penzance (0736) 63106. *Clubs:* Pratt's, MCC; Royal Yacht Squadron.
Died 20 Feb. 1991.

BOLLAND, John; His Honour Judge Bolland; a Circuit Judge since 1974; *b* 30 March 1920; *s* of late Dominic Gerald Bolland and Gladys Bolland; *m* 1947, Audrey Jean Toyne (*née* Pearson) (*d* 1989); one *s*, and one step *s* one step *d*. *Educ:* Malvern Coll.; Trinity Hall, Cambridge (BA). Commnd Royal Warwicks Regt, 1939; 2nd Bn 6th Gurkha Rifles, 1941–46. Called to Bar, Middle Temple, 1948. *Recreations:* cricket, Rugby, golf, theatre. *Address:* 11 Firle Road, North Lancing, Sussex BN15 0NY. *T:* Lancing (0903) 755337.
Died 3 April 1993.

BOLT, Rear-Adm. Arthur Seymour, CB 1958; DSO 1951; DSC 1940 and bar 1941; *b* 26 Nov. 1907; *s* of Charles W. Bolt, Alverstoke, Hants; *m* 1933, Evelyn Mary June, *d* of Robert Ellis, Wakefield, Yorks; four *d*. *Educ:* Nautical Coll., Pangbourne; RN Coll., Dartmouth. Joined RN, 1923; served War of 1939–45: HMS Glorious and Warspite (DSC and Bar), and at Admiralty; Capt. HMS Theseus (Korea), 1949–51; Dir Naval Air Warfare, Admty, 1951–53; Chief of Staff to Flag Officer Air (Home), 1954–56; Dep. Controller of Military Aircraft, Min. of Supply, 1957–60; retd. Capt. 1947; Rear-Adm. 1956. *Recreations:* tennis, squash, sailing. *Address:* 12 Mount Boone Way, Dartmouth, Devon TQ6 6PL. *T:* Dartmouth (0803) 833448. *Clubs:* Royal Naval and Royal Albert Yacht (Portsmouth); Royal Naval Sailing Association; Dartmouth Yacht.
Died 25 March 1994.

BOLT, Robert Oxton, CBE 1972; playwright; *b* 15 Aug. 1924; *s* of Ralph Bolt and Leah Binnion; *m* 1st, 1949, Celia Ann Roberts (marr. diss. 1967); one *s* one *d* (and one *d* decd); 2nd, 1967, Sarah Miles (marr. diss. 1976); one *s*; 3rd, 1980, Ann Zane (marr. diss. 1985); remarried, 1988, Sarah Miles. *Educ:* Manchester Grammar Sch. Left sch., 1941; Sun Life Assurance Office, Manchester, 1942; Manchester Univ., 1943; RAF and Army, 1943–46; Manchester Univ., 1946–49; Exeter Univ., 1949–50; teaching, 1950–58; English teacher, Millfield Sch., 1952–58. Hon. LLD Exeter, 1977. *Plays:* The Critic and

the Heart, Oxford Playhouse, 1957; Flowering Cherry, Haymarket, 1958; A Man for All Seasons, Globe, 1960 (filmed 1967); The Tiger and The Horse, Queen's, 1960; Gentle Jack, Queen's, 1963; The Thwarting of Baron Bolligrew, 1966; Vivat! Vivat Regina!, Piccadilly, 1970; State of Revolution, Nat. Theatre, 1977; *screenplays:* Lawrence of Arabia, 1962; Dr Zhivago, 1965 (Academy Award); Man for all Seasons, 1967 (Academy Award); Ryan's Daughter, 1970; Lady Caroline Lamb, 1972 (also dir.); The Bounty, 1984; The Mission, 1986; TV and radio plays. *Address:* c/o Casarotto Ramsay Ltd, National House, 60–66 Wardour Street, W1V 3HP. *Club:* The Spares (Somerset) (Hon. Life Mem.).
Died 20 Feb. 1995.

BONAR, Sir Herbert (Vernon), Kt 1967; CBE 1946; Chairman, 1949–74, and Managing Director, 1938–73, The Low & Bonar Group Ltd; retired 1974; *b* 26 Feb. 1907; *s* of George Bonar and Julia (*née* Seehusen); *m* 1935, Marjory (*née* East) (*d* 1990); two *s*. *Educ:* Fettes Coll.; Brasenose Coll., Oxford (BA). Joined Low & Bonar Ltd, 1929; Director, 1934. Jute Control, 1939–46 (Jute Controller, 1942–46). Trustee, WWF, UK, 1974–80 (Vice Pres. 1981). Hon. LLD: St Andrews, 1955; Birmingham, 1974; Dundee, 1985. Comdr, Order of the Golden Ark, Netherlands, 1974. *Recreations:* golf, fishing, photography, wild life preservation. *Address:* St Kitts, 24A Albany Road, Broughty Ferry, Dundee, Angus DD5 1NT. *T:* Dundee (0382) 79947. *Clubs:* Blairgowrie Golf; Panmure Golf.
Died 28 April 1993.

BONE, Mary, (Mrs Stephen Bone); *see* Adshead, M.

BONHAM-CARTER, Baron *cr* 1986 (Life Peer), of Yarnbury in the county of Wiltshire; **Mark Raymond Bonham Carter;** Chairman, Governors of The Royal Ballet, since 1985 (Governor, since 1960); *b* 11 Feb. 1922; *e s* of late Sir Maurice Bonham Carter, KCB, KCVO, and Violet, (Baroness Asquith of Yarnbury, DBE), *d* of 1st Earl of Oxford and Asquith, KG, PC; *m* 1955, Leslie, *d* of Condé Nast, NY; three *d*, and one step *d*. *Educ:* Winchester; Balliol Coll., Oxford (Scholar); University of Chicago (Commonwealth Fund Fellowship). Served Grenadier Guards, 1941–45: 8th Army (Africa) and 21st Army Group (NW Europe); captured, 1943; escaped; (despatches). Contested (L) Barnstaple, 1945; MP (L) Torrington Div. of Devonshire, March 1958–1959; Mem., UK Delegn to the Council of Europe, 1958–59; contested (L) Torrington, 1964. Director, Wm Collins & Co. Ltd, 1955–58. First Chm., Race Relations Bd, 1966–70; Chm., Community Relations Commn, 1971–77; Mem. Council, Inst. of Race Relations, 1966–72. Vice-Pres., Consumers' Assoc., 1972– (Mem. Council, 1966–71); Jt Chm., Anglo-Polish Round Table Conf., 1971–91; Chm., Writers and Scholars Educnl Trust, 1977–89. A Dir, Royal Opera House, Covent Garden, 1958–82; Vice Chm. and a Governor, BBC, 1975–81. Chm., Outer Circle Policy Unit, 1976–80. Mem. Court of Governors, LSE, 1970–81. Hon. Fellow: Manchester Metropolitan Univ.; Wolfson Coll., Oxford, 1990. Hon. LLD Dundee, 1978. *Publications:* (ed) The Autobiography of Margot Asquith, 1962; (contrib.) Radical Alternative (essays), 1962; articles, reviews in various jls. *Address:* 13 Clarendon Road, W11 4JB. *T:* 071–229 5200. *Clubs:* Brooks's, MCC.
Died 4 Sept. 1994.

BONHAM CARTER, Richard Erskine; Physician to the Hospital for Sick Children, Great Ormond Street, 1947–75, to University College Hospital, 1948–66; *b* 27 Aug. 1910; *s* of late Capt. A. E. Bonham-Carter and M. E. Bonham-Carter (*née* Malcolm); *m* 1946, Margaret (*née* Stace); three *d*. *Educ:* Clifton Coll.; Peterhouse, Cambridge; St Thomas' Hospital. Resident Asst Physician, Hospital for Sick Children, Great Ormond Street, 1938. Served War of 1939–45 in RAMC; DADMS 1 Airborne Div., 1942–45;

despatches, 1944. *Publications:* contributions to textbooks of pædiatrics and to medical journals. *Recreations:* gardening, fishing. *Address:* Castle Sweyn Cottage, Achnamara, Argyll PA31 8PT.
Died 18 Dec. 1994.

BONSEY, Mary, (Mrs Lionel Bonsey); *see* Norton, M.

BONY, Prof. Jean V., MA; Professor of the History of Art, University of California at Berkeley, 1962–80, then Emeritus; *b* Le Mans, France, 1 Nov. 1908; *s* of Henri Bony and Marie Normand; *m* 1st, 1936, Clotilde Roure (*d* 1942); one *d*; 2nd, 1953, Mary England. *Educ:* Lycée Louis-le-Grand, Paris; Sorbonne. Agrégé d'Histoire Paris; MA Cantab; Hon. FSA; Corres. Fellow, British Academy. Bulteau-Lavisse Research Scholarship, 1935–37; Asst Master, Eton Coll., 1937–39 and 1945–46. Served War of 1939–45; 1st Lieut, French Infantry, 1939–44; POW, Germany, June 1940–Dec. 1943. Research Scholar, Centre Nat. de la Recherche Scientifique, 1944–45; Lecturer in History of Art at the French Inst. in London, 1946–61; Lecturer in History of Art at the University of Lille, France, 1961–62. Focillon Fellow and Vis. Lectr, Yale Univ., 1949; Slade Prof. of Fine Art, University of Cambridge, and Fellow of St John's Coll., Cambridge, 1958–61; Vis. Prof. and Mathews Lectr, Columbia Univ., 1961; Wrightsman Lectr, New York Univ., 1969; Vis. Fellow, Humanities Res. Centre, ANU, 1978; John Simon Guggenheim Meml Fellow, 1981; Kress Prof., Nat. Gall. of Art, Washington, 1982; Vis. Andrew W. Mellon Prof. of Fine Arts, Univ. of Pittsburgh, 1983; Algur H. Meadows Prof. of Art Hist., Southern Methodist Univ., Dallas, 1984–87; Getty Lectr in Art, Univ. of Southern California, LA, 1988. *Publications:* Notre-Dame de Mantes, 1946; French Cathedrals (with M. Hürlimann and P. Meyer), 1951 (revised edn, 1967); (ed) H. Focillon: The Art of the West in the Middle Ages, English edn 1963, new edn 1969; The English Decorated Style, 1979; French Gothic Architecture of the 12th and 13th Centuries, 1983; articles in Bulletin Monumental, Congrès Archéologiques de France, Journal of Warburg and Courtauld Institutes, Journal of British Archæological Assoc., etc. *Address:* Department of History of Art, University of California, Berkeley, California 94720, USA.
Died 7 July 1995.

BOON, George Counsell, FSA; FRHistS; FRNS; Hon. Research Associate, National Museum of Wales, since 1989 (Keeper of Archaeology and Numismatics, 1976–86, Senior Keeper and Curator, 1987–89); *b* 20 Sept. 1927; *s* of Ronald Hudson Boon and Evaline Counsell; *m* 1956, Diana Margaret Martyn; two *s* one *d. Educ:* Bristol Univ. BA Hons (Latin). FRNS 1954; FSA 1955; FRHistS 1978. Archaeological Assistant, Reading Museum and Art Gallery, 1950–56; Asst Keeper, Dept of Archaeology, 1957–76. Member: Ancient Monuments Bd for Wales, 1979–90; Royal Commn on Ancient and Historical Monuments (Wales), 1979–90. Pres., Cambrian Archaeol Assoc., 1986–87. Vice-President: Soc. for Promotion of Roman Studies, 1977–; Soc. of Antiquaries, 1979–83. Corresp. Mem., German Archaeological Inst., 1968. *Publications:* Roman Silchester, 1957, 2nd edn 1974; Isca, the Roman Legionary Fortress at Caerleon, Mon, 1972; Welsh Tokens of the Seventeenth Century, 1973; Cardiganshire Silver and the Aberystwyth Mint in Peace and War, 1981; Welsh Hoards 1979–1981, 1986; contribs to learned journals. *Recreations:* none worth mention. *Address:* 43 Westbourne Road, Penarth, South Glam CF64 3HA. *T:* Penarth (0222) 709588. *Clubs:* unclubbable.
Died 31 Aug. 1994.

BOON, Dr William Robert, FRS 1974; retired; *b* 20 March 1911; *s* of Walter and Ellen Boon; *m* 1938, Marjorie Betty Oury; one *s* two *d. Educ:* St Dunstan's Coll., Catford; King's Coll., London. BSc, PhD; FRSC; FKC 1976.

Research, Chemotherapy and Crop Protection, ICI, 1936–69; Dir, Jealott's Hill Res. Station, 1964–69; Man. Dir, Plant Protection Ltd, 1969–73. Vis. Prof., Reading Univ., 1968. Member: Adv. Bd for the Research Councils, 1972–76; NERC, 1976–79. Hon. DSc Cranfield, 1981. Mullard Medal of Royal Society, 1972; Medal, British Crop Protection Council, 1987. *Publications:* papers in Jl Chem. Soc., Jl Soc. Chem. Ind., etc. *Recreation:* reading. *Address:* The Gables, Sid Road, Sidmouth, Devon EX10 9AQ. *T:* Sidmouth (01395) 514069.
Died 28 Oct. 1994.

BOORMAN, Henry Roy Pratt, CBE 1966 (MBE 1945); President, Kent Messenger Group, since 1982 (Chairman, 1970–82); *b* 21 Sept. 1900; *s* of Barham Pratt Boorman and Elizabeth Rogers; *m* 1st, 1933, Enid Starke; one *s*; 2nd, 1947, Evelyn Clinch; one *d. Educ:* Leys Sch., Cambridge; Queens' Coll., Cambridge (MA). FJI 1936. Entered journalism, 1922; Proprietor and Editor, Kent Messenger, 1928; Chairman, South Eastern Gazette, 1929. Chairman, Kent Newspaper Proprietors' Assoc., 1931, 1932 and 1951; Mem. Council, Newspaper Soc., 1958, President, 1960. War Service: Regional Information Officer, SE Region, Tunbridge Wells, 1939; Dep. Welfare Officer for Kent, 1941; Major 1944; War Correspondent in Europe, 1939–40 and 1944, Berlin, 1949. Association of Men of Kent and Kentish Men: Editor, Journal Kent, 1931–62 (Chm. Council, 1949–51); Association's Sir Edward Hardy Gold Medal, 1964; in 1981, tenor bell in renewed peal in Canterbury Cathedral presented in his name by Kent Messenger staff. Maidstone Town Council: Councillor, 1934–46 and 1961–70; Mayor of Maidstone, 1962, Alderman, 1964. Liveryman, Worshipful Co. of Stationers and Newspaper Makers, 1933 (Mem. Ct of Assts, 1966–72). JP Maidstone Div. of Kent 1962; DL Kent, 1968–82. SBStJ 1946 (Mem. Council, 1960–66). *Publications:* Merry America (Royal Tour of Canada and United States), 1939; Hell's Corner, 1940; Kent—Our Glorious Heritage, 1951; Kentish Pride, 1952; Kent and the Cinque Ports, 1958; Kent Messenger Centenary, 1959; Kent—a Royal County, 1966; Spirit of Kent—Lord Cornwallis, 1968; Kent Our County, 1979. *Recreation:* world travel. *Address:* St Augustine's Priory, Bilsington, Ashford, Kent TN25 7AU. *T:* Aldington (0233) 720252. *Club:* Commonwealth Trust.
Died 18 June 1992.

BOOTH, Rev. Canon David Herbert, (Peter), MBE 1944; Provost, Shoreham College (formerly Shoreham Grammar School), Sussex, since 1977 (Headmaster, 1972–77); Chaplain to the Queen, 1957–77; *b* 26 Jan. 1907; *s* of Robert and Clara Booth; *m* 1942, Diana Mary Chard; two *s* one *d. Educ:* Bedford Sch.; Pembroke Coll., Cambridge; Ely Theological Coll. BA (3rd cl. Hist. Trip. part II), 1931; MA 1936. Deacon, 1932; priest, 1933; Curate, All Saints', Hampton, 1932–34; Chaplain, Tonbridge Sch., 1935–40; Chaplain, RNVR, 1940–45; Rector of Stepney, 1945–53; Vicar of Brighton, 1953–59; Prebendary of Waltham in Chichester Cathedral, 1953–59; Archdeacon of Lewes, 1959–71; Prebendary of Bury in Chichester Cathedral, 1972–76; Canon Emeritus of Chichester, 1976. Select Preacher, University of Cambridge, 1947. Mem. of Archbishop's Commission on South East, 1965. Pres., Nat. Schs Jumping Championship, 1963–. *Recreation:* family life. *Address:* Courtyard Cottage, School Road, Charing, near Ashford, Kent TN27 0HX. *T:* Charing (023371) 3349.
Died 24 March 1993.

BOOTH, John Wells; Director, Alfred Booth & Co. Ltd, 1935–79 (Chairman, 1952–74); *b* 19 May 1903; *s* of late Charles and Grace Wells Booth, Liverpool; *m* 1929, Margaret (*d* 1993), *d* of late Mr and Mrs S. J. Lawry; two *s* (one *d* decd). *Educ:* Royal Naval Colls Osborne and Dartmouth. Royal Navy, 1917–25 (Lieut Comdr); Booth Steamship Co. Ltd, 1926–45 (Chm., 1939–45); Civil

Aviation, 1945–50: Chm., British South American Airways Corporation, 1946–49; Dep. Chm., BOAC, 1949–50; Bd Mem., BOAC, 1950–65. Dir, Phoenix Assurance Co. Ltd, 1945–73. Former Chairman: Liverpool Seamens' Welfare Cttee (Mem. Seamens' Welfare Bd); Liverpool Steamship Owners' Assoc.; former JP for Co. of Cheshire. *Address:* Hilary Lodge, Somerton Road, Hartest, Bury St Edmunds IP29 4NA. *T:* Bury St Edmunds (01284) 830426. *Club:* Flyfishers'.

Died 15 Dec. 1994.

BOOTH, Rev. Canon Peter; *see* Booth, Rev. Canon D. H.

BOREHAM, Sir (Arthur) John, KCB 1980 (CB 1974); Director, Central Statistical Office, and Head of the Government Statistical Service, 1978–85, retired; *b* 30 July 1925; 3rd *s* of late Ven. Frederick Boreham, Archdeacon of Cornwall and Chaplain to the Queen, and Caroline Mildred Boreham; *m* 1948, Heather, *o d* of Harold Edwin Horth, FRIBA, and Muriel Horth; three *s* one *d. Educ:* Marlborough; Trinity Coll., Oxford. Agricultural Economics Research Inst., Oxford, 1950; Min. of Food, 1951; Min. of Agric., 1952; Gen. Register Office, 1955; Central Statistical Office, 1958; Chief Statistician, Gen. Register Office, 1963; Dir of Economics and Statistics, Min. of Technology, 1967–71; Central Statistical Office: Asst Dir, 1971–72; Dep. Dir, 1972–78. Regl Co-ordinator, Caribbean Statistical Trng Prog., 1989–90; Management Consultant, Dept of Statistics, Bahamas, 1992–93. Vis. Fellow, Nuffield Coll., Oxford, 1981–88. President: Inst. of Statisticians, 1984–92; Assoc. of Social Res. Orgns, 1990–. *Recreations:* music, golf. *Address:* Piperscroft, Brittain's Lane, Sevenoaks, Kent TN13 2NG. *T:* Sevenoaks (0732) 454678.

Died 8 June 1994.

BORRADAILE, Maj.-Gen. Hugh Alastair, CB 1959; DSO 1946; Vice Adjutant-General, War Office, 1960–63, retired; *b* 22 June 1907; *s* of late Lt-Col Basil Borradaile, RE, Walnut Cottage, Wylye, Wilts; *m* 1936, Elizabeth Barbara, *d* of late R. Powell-Williams, Woodcroft, Yelverton, Devon; one *s* one *d. Educ:* Wellington Coll.; RMC Sandhurst. Commissioned Devon Regt, 1926; King's African Rifles, 1931–37; Staff Coll., Camberley, 1939; GSO1, GHQ West Africa, 1942–43; CO 5, E Lancs Regt, 1944; CO 7 Somrset LI, 1944–45; GSO1, 30 Corps 1945; Asst Chief of Staff (Exec.), CCG, 1945–46; CO 1 Devon, 1946–48; Dep. Chief Intelligence Div., CCG, 1948–50; National Defence Coll., Canada, 1950–51; Brig. AQ AA Command 1951–53; Comd 24 Inf. Bde, 1953–55; Dept Military Sec. (A), War Office, 1955–57; Gen. Officer Commanding South-West District and 43rd (Wessex) Infantry Div., TA, 1957–60. Col, Devon and Dorset Regt, 1962–67. Master, Worshipful Co. of Drapers, 1971–72 (Liveryman, 1956–). *Recreations:* reading, watching TV. *Address:* Waterstreet Farm, Curry Rivel, Langport, Somerset TA10 0HH. *T:* Langport (0458) 251268. *Club:* Army and Navy. *Died 13 Dec. 1993.*

BOTTOMLEY, Baron *cr* 1984 (Life Peer), of Middlesbrough in the County of Cleveland; **Arthur George Bottomley,** OBE 1941; PC 1951; *b* 7 Feb. 1907; *s* of late George Howard Bottomley and Alice Bottomley; *m* 1936, Bessie Ellen Wiles (Lady Bottomley, DBE); no *c. Educ:* Gamuel Road Council Sch.; Extension Classes at Toynbee Hall. London Organiser of National Union of Public Employees, 1935–45, 1959–62. Walthamstow Borough Council, 1929–49; Mayor of Walthamstow, 1945–46; Chairman of Emergency Cttee and ARP Controller, 1939–41. Dep. Regional Commissioner for S-E England, 1941–45. MP (Lab): Chatham Division of Rochester, 1945–50, Rochester and Chatham 1950–59; Middlesbrough East, 1962–74, Teesside, Middlesbrough, 1974–83. Parliamentary Under-Secretary of State for Dominions, 1946–47; Sec. for Overseas Trade, Board of

Trade, 1947–51; Sec. of State for Commonwealth Affairs, 1964–66; Minister of Overseas Develt, 1966–67. Land Tax Comr, Becontree Div. of Essex; Special Govt Mission to Burma, 1947; Deleg. to UN, New York, 1946, 1947 and 1949; Leader: UK delegation to World Trade and Employment Conference, Havana, 1947; UK Delegn to Commonwealth Conference, Delhi, 1949; Trade Mission to Pakistan, 1950; Special Mission to West Indies, 1951; Member: Consultative Assembly, Council of Europe, 1952, 1953 and 1954; Leader: Parliamentary Labour Party Mission to Burma, 1962, to Malaysia, 1963; UK Delegation to CPA Conferences, Australia, Canada, Malawi, Malaysia, Mauritius; Member, Parliamentary Missions to: India, 1946; Kenya, 1954; Ghana, 1959; Cyprus, 1963; Hong Kong, 1964; China, 1983. Chairman: Commonwealth Relations and Colonies Group, Parly Labour Party, 1963; Select Parly Cttee on Race Relations and Immigration, 1969; Select Cttee on Cyprus, 1975; Special Parly Cttee on Admin and Orgn of House of Commons Services, 1976; House of Commons Commn, 1980–83; Treasurer, Commonwealth Parly Assoc., 1974 (Vice-Chm., UK Branch, 1968 and 1974–77). Chm., Attlee Foundn, 1978–; President: Britain-India Forum, 1981–; Britain-Burma Soc., 1981–. Hon. Fellow, Hunterian Soc., 1985. Hon. Freeman of Chatham, 1959; Freeman: City of London, 1975; Middlesbrough, 1976. Awarded title of Aung San Tagun, Burma, 1981. *Publications:* Why Britain should Join the Common Market, 1959; Two Roads to Colonialism, 1960; The Use and Abuse of Trade Unions, 1961; Commonwealth Comrades and Friends, 1986. *Recreations:* walking and theatre-going. *Address:* 19 Lichfield Road, Woodford Green, Essex IG8 9SU. *Died 3 Nov. 1995.*

BOTVINNIK, Mikhail Moisseyevich; Order of Lenin, 1957; Order of the Badge of Honour, 1936 and 1945; Order of the Red Banner of Labour, 1961; Order of the October Revolution, 1981; Senior Scientist, All-Union (formerly USSR) Research Institute for Electroenergetics, since 1955; *b* Repino, near St Petersburg, 17 Aug. 1911; *s* of Moisey Botvinnik, dental technician and Serafina Botvinnik; *m* 1935, Gayane Ananova; one *d. Educ:* Leningrad Polytechnical Institute (Grad.). Thesis for degree of: Candidate of Technical Sciences, 1937; Doctor of Technical Sciences, 1952; Professor, 1972. Chess master title, 1927; Chess grandmaster title, 1935. Won Soviet chess championship in 1931, 1933, 1939, 1941, 1944, 1945, 1952; World chess title, 1948–57, 1958–60 and 1961–63. Honoured Master of Sport of the USSR, 1945. *Publications:* Flohr-Botvinnik Match, 1934; Alekhin-Euwe Return Match, 1938; Selected Games, 1937, 1945, 1960; Eleventh Soviet Chess Championship, 1939; Tournament Match for the Absolute Champion Title, 1945; Regulation of Excitation and Static Stability of Syndronous Machines, 1950; Botvinnik-Smyslov Match, 1955; Smyslov-Botvinnik Return Match, 1960; Asynchronized Synchronous Machines, 1960; Algorithm Play of Chess, 1968; Controlled AC Machines (with Y. Shakarian), 1969; Computers, Chess and Long-Range Planning, 1971; Botvinnik's Best Games 1947–70, 1972; Three matches of Anatoly Karpov, 1975; On Cybernetic Goal of Game, 1975; A Half Century in Chess, 1979; On Solving of Inexact Search, 1979; Fifteen Games and their History, 1981; Selected Games 1967–70, 1981; Achieving the Aim, 1981; Analytical and Critical Works 1923–41, 1984, 1942–56, 1985, 1957–70, 1986; Chess Method of Solution Search Problems, 1989. *Address:* 3 Frunsenskaja 7 (flat 154), Moscow G-270, Russia. *T:* 2421586.

Died 5 May 1995.

BOURDILLON, Henry Townsend, CMG 1952; Assistant Under-Secretary of State, Department of Education and Science, 1964–73; *b* 19 Aug. 1913; 2nd *s* of late Sir Bernard Henry Bourdillon, GCMG, KBE, and Lady

(Violet Grace) Bourdillon; *m* 1942, Margareta d'Almaine (*née* Tham); one *s* two *d. Educ:* Rugby Sch.; Corpus Christi Coll., Oxford. Asst Principal, Colonial Office, 1937; Acting Principal, Colonial Office, 1940; lent to: Foreign Office, 1942; Cabinet Office, 1943; Ministry of Production, 1944; returned to Colonial Office, 1944; Asst Secretary, 1947–54; Asst Under-Secretary of State, Colonial Office, 1954–59; Deputy UK Commissioner for Singapore, 1959–61; returned to Colonial Office, 1961; Under-Secretary, Ministry of Education, 1962–64. *Recreations:* writing, music. *Address:* 67 The Retreat, Princes Risborough, Bucks HP17 0JQ. *T:* Princes Risborough (08444) 5416. *Died 14 Feb. 1991.*

BOURNE, James Gerald, MA, MD (Cantab); FFARCS, FDSRCS; Consulting Anæsthetist: St Thomas' Hospital, London; Salisbury Hospital Group; *b* 6 March 1906; *y s* of late W. W. Bourne, Garston Manor, Herts and Clara (*née* Hollingsworth); *m* 1957, Jenny Liddell (*d* 1967); one *s; m* 1968, Susan Clarke; two *s. Educ:* Rugby; Corpus Christi Coll., Cambridge; St Thomas' Hospital. 1st class Geographical Tripos Part I, 1925; 1st class Geographical Tripos Part II, 1926; Exhibition and Prizes; MRCS, LRCP 1937; MB, BChir Cantab 1939; DA 1945; FFARCS 1953; MD (Cantab), 1960; FDSRCS 1986. Major RAMC, 1939–45. *Publications:* Nitrous Oxide in Dentistry: Its Danger and Alternatives, 1960; Studies in Anæsthetics, 1967; contributions to medical literature. *Recreations:* fishing, walking, music. *Address:* Melstock, Nunton, Salisbury, Wilts SP5 4HN. *T:* Salisbury (01722) 329734.
Died 5 July 1995.

BOURNE, Prof. Kenneth, FRHistS; FBA 1984; Professor of International History, London School of Economics and Political Science, University of London, since 1976 (Vice-Chairman, Academic Board, 1985–88); *b* 17 March 1930; *s* of Clarence Arthur Bourne and Doris (*née* English); *m* 1955, Eleanor Anne (*née* Wells); one *s* one *d. Educ:* Southend High Sch.; University College of South West; LSE. BA Exeter and London; PhD London. Research Fellow: Inst. of Hist. Research, Univ. of London, 1955–56; Reading Univ., 1956; Asst Lectr, then Lectr, LSE, 1957–69; Reader in Internat. History, Univ. of London, 1969–76; Chm., Bd of Studies in History, London Univ., 1983–84. Fulbright Fellow and Sen. Research Fellow, British Assoc. for American Studies, 1961–62; Vis. Lectr, Univ. of California, Davis, 1966–67; Scaife Distinguished Vis. Lectr, Kenyon Coll., 1971; Kratter Prof., Stanford Univ., 1979; Vis. Prof., Univ. of S Mississippi, 1981; Griffin Lectr, Stanford Univ., 1983; Vis. Prof., Univ. of S Alabama, 1983; Albert Biever Meml Lectr, Loyola Univ., 1983; James Pinckney Harrison Prof., Coll. of William and Mary, 1984–85; Distinguished Vis. Prof. in Humanities, Univ. of Colorado, 1988; J. Richardson Dilworth Fellow, Inst. for Advanced Study, Princeton, 1989; Nuffield Foundn Social Scis Res. Fellow, 1991. Member: Council, List and Index Soc., 1986–; British Nat. Cttee, Internat. Congress of Hist. Scis, 1987–88; Archives and Manuscripts Cttee, Univ. of Southampton, 1988–. Member: Senate, Univ. of London, 1987–91; Council, SSEES, 1987–92. Governor: Wilson's Grammar Sch., Camberwell, 1964–74; Wilson's Sch., Sutton, 1972–84; LSE, 1986–90. *Publications:*Britain and the Balance of Power in North America, 1967 (Albert B. Corey Prize); (with D. C. Watt) Studies in International History, 1967; The Foreign Policy of Victorian England, 1970; The Blackmailing of the Chancellor, 1975; Letters of Viscount Palmerston, 1979; Palmerston: the early years, 1982; (ed, with D. C. Watt) British Documents on Foreign Affairs, 1983–. *Recreation:* book-collecting. *Address:* 15 Oakcroft Road, SE13 7ED. *T:* 081–852 6116.
Died 13 Dec. 1992.

BOURTON, Cyril Leonard, CB 1977; Deputy Secretary (Finance), and Accountant General, Department of Health and Social Security, 1974–76; *b* 28 Dec. 1916; *s* of late Leonard Victor Bourton; *m* 1940, Elizabeth Iris Savage; two *s* one *d. Educ:* St Dunstan's Coll., Catford. Nat. Debt Office, 1933–37; Min. of Health, later DHSS: Dep. Accountant-Gen., 1958; Asst Sec., Exec. Councils Div., 1964; Under-Sec. for Finance and Accountant Gen., 1967. *Recreations:* fishing, photography, genealogy. *Address:* 19 Mytten Close, Cuckfield, Haywards Heath, West Sussex RH17 5LN. *T:* Haywards Heath (01444) 456030.
Died 26 Feb. 1995.

BOVET, Prof. Daniel; Hon. Professor, University of Rome, Italy; *b* Neuchâtel, Switzerland, 23 March 1907; *s* of Pierre Bovet and Amy Babut; Italian citizen; *m* Filomena Nitti; three *s.* Institut Pasteur, Paris, 1929–47 (first as an asst and afterwards Chief of the Laboratory of Therapeutic Chemistry); Chief of the Laboratory of Therapeutic Chemistry, Istituto Superiore di Sanità, Rome, 1947–64; Prof. of Pharmacology, Fac. of Medicine, Univ. of Sassari, Italy, 1964–71; Prof. of Psychobiol., Faculty of Sci., Rome Univ., 1971–77. Mem. of the Accademia Nazionale dei XL, 1949; Mem. of Accademia Naz. dei Lincei, 1958; Foreign Mem., Royal Soc., 1962. Nobel Prize for Physiology or Medicine, 1957. Grande Ufficiale dell' Ordine della Repubblica Italiana, 1959; Comdr, Légion d'Honneur, 1980. *Publications:* (in collaboration with F. Bovet-Nitti) Structure chimique et activité pharmacodynamique du système nerveux végétatif, 1948 (Basle, Switzerland); (in collaboration with F. Bovet-Nitti and G. B. Marini-Bettolo) Curare and Curare-like Agents, 1957 (Amsterdam, Holland); (in collaboration with R. Blum and others) Controlling Drugs, 1974 (San Francisco); Une chimie qui guérit—histoire des sulfamides, 1989 (Paris). *Recreation:* wandering in Amazonia. *Address:* 33 Piazza S Apollinare, 00186 Rome, Italy. *T:* 6865297.
Died 8 April 1992.

BOWDEN, family name of **Baron Aylestone.**

BOWEN, Edward George, CBE 1962; PhD; FRS 1975; FAA; Counsellor (Scientific) at the Australian Embassy in Washington, DC, USA, 1973–76; *b* 14 Jan. 1911; *s* of G. Bowen, Swansea. *Educ:* Univ. of Wales (MSc); London Univ. (PhD). DSc Sydney. FKC 1981. Mem., Radar Develt Team, 1935; Air Ministry Research Station, Bawdsey, 1936–40; British Air Commn, Washington, 1940–42; Radiation Lab., MIT, 1943; Chief, Div. of Radiophysics, CSIRO, 1946–71. Chm., Anglo-Australian Telescope Board, 1967–73. Vice-Pres., Aust. Acad. of Science, 1962–63; Foreign Member: Amer. Acad. of Arts and Scis; US Nat. Acad. of Engrg. Thurlow Award, Amer. Inst. of Navigation, 1950. US Medal for Freedom, 1947. *Address:* c/o 60 The Bulwark, Castlecrag, NSW 2068, Australia. *Club:* Athenæum. *Died 12 Aug. 1991.*

BOWEN, Rear-Adm. Frank; *b* 25 Jan. 1930; *s* of Alfred and Lily Bowen; *m* 1954, Elizabeth Lilian Richards; one *s* two *d. Educ:* Cowley Sch., St Helen's; Royal Naval Engineering Coll. CEng; MIMechE; FIMgt. RNC Dartmouth, 1948; served various ships and RN establishments incl. HMS Eagle and Excellent, 1956–60, and Scylla, 1971–73; served in Washington, 1968–70 and 1976–78; i/c HMS Collingwood, 1981–82; Special Project Dir, MoD, PE; Captain 1974; Rear-Adm., 1982–84. Dir, Dowty-Cap Ltd, 1985–89; Chm., Sea, Air and Land Systems Ltd, 1990–94; Non-exec. Dir, Crew Services Ltd, 1991–95. MInstD. *Recreations:* amateur stage, social golf. *Died 21 May 1995.*

BOWEN, Gordon, CB 1962; CMG 1956; Director, Metrication Board, 1969–74; *b* 17 June 1910; *e s* of late Arthur Thomas Bowen and Dora Drinkwater; *m* 1938, Elsa Catriona (*d* 1987), *y d* of late Rev. Dr Alexander

Grieve, MA, PhD and Euphemia Logan Ross Grieve; one *s* (and one *s* decd). *Educ:* Birkenhead Institute Sch.; University of Liverpool. Asst Lecturer in Geography, University of Glasgow, 1933–36; Commonwealth Fund Fellow, University of Calif, 1936–38; Lecturer in Geography, University of Glasgow, 1938–41; Principal, Board of Trade, 1941–44; Asst Sec., Board of Trade, 1944–53; United Kingdom Senior Trade Commissioner in Canada, 1953–58; Under Secretary: Board of Trade, 1958–66; Min. of Technology, 1966–69. *Address:* 5 Knowehead Gardens, Albert Drive, Pollokshields, Glasgow G41 5RE.　　　　　　　　　*Died 29 June 1991.*

BOWEN, Very Rev. Lawrence; Dean of St Davids Cathedral, 1972–84; *b* 9 Sept. 1914; *s* of William and Elizabeth Ann Bowen; *m* 1941, Hilary Myrtle (*née* Bowen); two *d*. *Educ:* Llanelli Gram. Sch.; Univ. Coll. of Wales, Aberystwyth (BA 1st Cl.); St Michael's Coll., Llandaff (Crossley Exhibnr and Sen. Student). Ordained deacon in St Davids Cathedral, 1938; priest, 1939; Curate of Pembrey, 1938–40; Minor Canon, St Davids Cathedral, 1940–46; Vicar of St Clears with Llanginning, 1946–64; Rector of Tenby, 1964–72; Rector of Rectorial Benefice of Tenby with Gumfreston and Penally, 1970–72; Canon of St Davids Cathedral (Mathry), 1972. Surrogate. *Recreations:* golf, cricket, writing Welsh poetry. *Address:* Saddle Point, Slade Way, Fishguard, Dyfed SA65 9NY.
　　　　　　　　　　　　　　　　　Died 26 Sept. 1994.

BOWEN, Hon. Sir Nigel (Hubert), AC 1988; KBE 1976; Chief Justice (formerly Chief Judge), Federal Court of Australia, 1976–90; *b* Summerland, BC, Canada, 26 May 1911; *s* of late O. P. Bowen, Ludlow, England, and Dorothy Joan Bowen; *m* 1st, 1947, Eileen Cecily (*d* 1983), *d* of F. J. Mullens; three *d*; 2nd, 1984, Ermyn Krippner. *Educ:* King's Sch., Sydney; St Paul's Coll., Sydney Univ. (BA, LLB). Served 2nd AIF, 1942–46 (Captain). Admitted NSW Bar 1936, Victorian Bar 1954; QC (Austr.) 1953; Vice-Pres., Law Council of Australia, 1957–60; Pres., NSW Bar Council, 1959–61. Editor, Australian Law Jl, 1946–58. MHR (L) Australia for Parramatta, NSW, 1964–73, retired; Attorney-General, Australia, 1966–69 and March-Aug. 1971; Minister for Educn and Science, 1969–71; Minister for Foreign Affairs, Aug. 1971–Dec. 1972. Judge of Court of Appeal of NSW, 1973–76; Chief Judge in Equity, 1974–76. Hon. LLD Sydney Univ. *Recreations:* swimming, music. *Club:* Union (Sydney).
　　　　　　　　　　　　　　　　　Died 27 Sept. 1994.

BOWEN, Stanley, CBE 1972; Hon. Sheriff, Lothian and Borders, since 1975; *b* Carnoustie, Angus, 4 Aug. 1910; *s* of late Edward Bowen and Ellen Esther Bowen (*née* Powles), Birmingham; *m* 1943, Mary Shepherd Greig, *d* of late Alexander Greig and Mary Shand Greig (*née* Shepherd), Carnoustie; two *s* one *d*. *Educ:* Barry Sch., Angus; Grove Academy, Dundee; University Coll., Dundee. Enrolled Solicitor, in Scotland, 1932; entered Procurator Fiscal Service, in Scotland, 1933; Procurator Fiscal Depute at Hamilton, Lanarkshire, 1937; Interim Procurator Fiscal at Airdrie, Lanarkshire, 1938; Crown Office, Edinburgh: Legal Asst, 1941; Principal Asst, 1945; Crown Agent for Scotland, 1967–74. Chm., Sec. of State for Scotland's working party on forensic pathology services, 1975; Member: Sec. of State for the Environment's working party on drinking and driving offences, 1975; Sub-Cttee for legislation on transplantation of human tissues, Council of Europe, 1975–76; Police Adv. Bd for Scotland, 1976–83 (sub-cttee on police discipline, 1976, and working party on Cadet entry, 1979); Sec. of State for Scotland's working group on identification evidence in criminal cases, 1977; Council, Scottish Assoc. for Care and Resettlement of Offenders, 1978–83; Council, Corstorphine Trust, 1978–90 (Chm., 1982–90); Hon. Vice-Pres., 1990). *Recreations:* golf, gardening. *Address:*

Achray, 20 Dovecot Road, Corstorphine, Edinburgh EH12 7LE. *T:* 0131–334 4096. *Clubs:* New, Press (Edinburgh); Carnoustie Golf.　　　　　　　　　　*Died 19 Nov. 1995.*

BOWER, Air Marshal Sir Leslie (William Clement), KCB 1962 (CB 1954); DSO 1945; DFC 1944; *b* 11 July 1909; *s* of William Clarke Bower, Co. Cork, Eire; *m* 1947, Phyllis Maud (marr. diss.), *d* of Rev. David Roberts, Cardiff; *m* 1963, Clare (*d* 1971), *d* of H. W. Etkins, OBE, Curlews, Constantine Bay, N Cornwall, and *widow* of Commander Jasper Abbott, RN, Uppaton, Yelverton, S Devon; *m* 1979, Patricia Fearon, *widow* of Wing Comdr D. N. Fearon. *Educ:* The Harvey Grammar Sch., Folkestone; Cranwell; RAF Staff Coll., 1946; USAF War Coll., 1947–50. Royal Air Force 1929; No 11 Sqn, NW Frontier India, 1931–32; CFS Course, 1933; Cambridge Univ. Sqn (Flying Instructor), 1933–34; Instructional Staff, CFS, 1934–36; No 202 Flying Boat Sqn, Malta, 1936–39; Senior Personnel SO, Air HQ Malta, 1939–41; served War of 1939–45 (despatches twice, DFC, DSO), in Europe and Canada; OC 217 (TB) Sqdn, 1941–42; Dir Op. Trg, HQ, RCAF, Ottawa, 1942–43; OC 138 Wing 2nd TAF, 1943–45; AOC 81 (Fighter) Group, 1952–54; Senior Air Staff Officer, HQ Fighter Command, 1954–57; Senior Air Staff Officer, MEAF, 1957–58; Dep. Commander-in-Chief, Middle East Air Force, 1958–59; Air Officer Commanding No 19 Group, RAF Coastal Command, 1959–61; UK Representative in Ankara on Permanent Military Deputies Group of Central Treaty Organisation (Cento), 1962–65; retired. Air Marshal, 1962. *Address:* c/o Lloyds Bank, Cox's & King's Branch, 6 Pall Mall, SW1. *Club:* Royal Air Force.
　　　　　　　　　　　　　　　　　Died 17 Feb. 1991.

BOWER, Stephen Ernest D.; *see* Dykes Bower.

BOWERS, Prof. Fredson Thayer; Linden Kent Professor of Literature, University of Virginia, USA, 1968–75, then Emeritus; *b* 25 April 1905; *s* of Fredson Eugene Bowers and Hattie May Quigley; *m* 1st, 1924, Hyacinth Sutphen; three *s* one *d*; 2nd, 1942, Nancy Hale (*d* 1988). *Educ:* Brown Univ. (PhB); Harvard Univ. (PhD). USNR, Comdr, 1942–46. Instructor in English: Harvard Univ., 1926–36; Princeton Univ., 1936–38; Asst Prof., Univ. of Virginia, 1938–46, Associate Prof., 1946–48, Prof., 1948–75, Alumni Prof., 1959–68 (Dean of the Faculty, 1968–69). Fulbright Fellow for Research in UK, 1953; Guggenheim Fellow, 1959, 1972; Sandars Reader in Bibliography, Cambridge, 1958; Lyell Reader in Bibliography, Oxford, 1959; Vis. Fellow, All Souls Coll., Oxford, 1972, 1974; Fellow Commoner, Churchill Coll., Cambridge, 1975. Mem. Exec. Council, Mod. Lang. Assoc. of Amer., 1964–68 (Pres., S Atlantic MLA, 1969); Pres., Soc. for Textual Scholarship, 1985–87. Corresp. FBA, 1968; Fellow: Amer. Acad. Arts and Scis, 1972; Amer. Antiquarian Soc., 1973. Bicentennial Medal, Brown Univ., 1964; Gold Medal, Bibliographical Soc., 1969; Thomas Jefferson Award, Virginia Univ., 1971; Julian P. Boyd Award, Assoc. for Documentary Editing, 1986. Hon. DLitt: Brown, 1970; Clark, 1970; Hon. MA Oxon, 1972; Hon. LHD Chicago, 1973. Editor, Studies in Bibliography, 1948–. *Publications:* Elizabethan Revenge Tragedy, 1940; Randolph's Fairy Knight (ed), 1942; Principles of Bibliographical Description, 1949; George Sandys: a Bibliographical Catalogue, 1950; Dramatic Works of Thomas Dekker (ed, 4 vols), 1953–61; On Editing Shakespeare and the Elizabethan Dramatists, 1955; Whitman's Manuscripts, 1955; Textual and Literary Criticism, 1959; Works of Nathaniel Hawthorne (text editor, 11 vols), 1962–74; Bibliography and Textual Criticism, 1964; Dramatic Works in the Beaumont and Fletcher Canon (general editor), 1966–; Works of Stephen Crane (ed, 10 vols), 1969–75; Works of Christopher Marlowe (ed, 2 vols), 1973, rev. edn 1981; Tom Jones (text editor), 1975; Works of William James (text editor, 19 vols), 1975–88; Essays in Bibliography, Text and Editing, 1975; (ed) Lectures in Literature by V. Nabokov, 1980; (ed) Lectures in Russian Literature by V. Nabokov, 1981; (ed) Lectures on Don Quixote by V. Nabokov, 1983; Elizabethan Drama (gen. ed.), 1988; Jacobean and Caroline Drama (gen. ed.), 1988; Hamlet as Minister and Scourge, 1989. *Recreation:* music. *Address:* Woodburn, Route 14, Box 7, Charlottesville, Virginia 22901, USA. *T:* (804) 9733629. *Clubs:* Elizabethan (Yale); Tudor and Stuart (Johns Hopkins).   *Died 11 April 1991.*

BOWICK, David Marshall, CBE 1977; Member, British Railways Board, 1976–80; retired; *b* 30 June 1923; *s* of George Bowick, Corstorphine, Edinburgh; *m* Gladys May (*née* Jeffries) (*d* 1988); one *d. Educ:* Boroughmuir Sch., Edinburgh; Heriot-Watt Coll., Edinburgh. Served with Fleet Air Arm, 1942–46. Movements Supt, Kings Cross, 1962; Planning Officer, British Railways Board Headquarters, 1963; Asst Gen. Man., London Midland Region, BR, 1965; Exec. Dir, Personnel, BRB Headquarters, 1969; Gen. Manager, London Midland Region, BR, 1971; Chief Exec. (Railways), BR, 1971–78; Vice-Chm. (Rail), BRB, 1978–80. Pres., Group of Nine EEC Railways, 1978–80. Mem. Council, Manchester Business Sch. Col RE, T&AVR. FREconS; FCIT; CIMgt; FRSA. *Recreations:* sailing, swimming, golf, travel, theatre. *Address:* 23 Arnewood Court, 9 West Cliff Road, Bournemouth BH2 5ET.   *Died 9 March 1995.*

BOWKER, Alfred Johnstone, (John), MC 1944; Regional Chairman of Industrial Tribunals, Southampton, 1978–87; *b* 9 April 1922; *s* of Alfred Bowker and Isabel Florence (*née* Brett); *m* 1947, Ann, *er d* of late John Christopher Fairweather and Gunhild Fairweather; one *s* one *d. Educ:* Winchester Coll.; Christ Church, Oxford (MA). Served War, Coldstream Guards, 1941–47: Italian Campaign; Captain. Solicitor in private practice, Winchester, 1949–57; Resident Magistrate, Northern Rhodesia, 1957–65; solicitor in private practice, Salisbury, Wilts, 1965–71; Chm. of Indust. Tribunals, Newcastle upon Tyne, 1972–75. Winchester City Councillor (C), 1954–57; Hants County Councillor (C), 1989–93. Liveryman, Skinners' Co., 1943. Master, Meon Valley Beagles, 1954–56; Jt Master, Hursley Foxhounds, 1968–69 and 1970–71. *Recreations:* hunting, reading history.
                                                           Died 13 Nov. 1993.

BOWLBY, Sir Anthony Hugh Mostyn, 2nd Bt, *cr* 1923, of Manchester Square, St Marylebone; *b* 13 Jan. 1906; *e s* of Sir Anthony Bowlby, 1st Bt and Maria Bridget (*d* 1957), *d* of Rev. Canon Hon. Hugh W. Mostyn; *S* father, 1929; *m* 1930, Dora Evelyn, *d* of John Charles Allen; two *d. Educ:* Wellington Coll.; New Coll., Oxford. *Heir:* *nephew* Richard Peregrine Longstaff Bowlby [*b* 11 Aug. 1941; *m* 1963, Xenia, *o d* of R. P. A. Garrett; one *s* one *d*]. *Address:* The Old Rectory, Ozleworth, near Wotton-under-Edge, Glos.   *Died 17 Aug. 1993.*

BOWMAN, Sir John Paget, 4th Bt, *cr* 1884, of Holmbury St Mary, Surrey; *b* 12 Feb. 1904; *s* of Rev. Sir Paget Mervyn Bowman, 3rd Bt, and Rachel Katherine (*d* 1936), *d* of late James Hanning, Kilcrone, Co. Cork; *S* father 1955; *m* 1st, 1931, Countess Cajetana Hoyos (*d* 1948), *d* of Count Edgar Hoyos, Schloss Soos, Lower Austria; one *d* (one *s* decd); 2nd, 1948, Frances Edith Marian (*d* 1992), *d* of Sir Beethom Whitehead, KCMG, Efford Park, Lymington; 3rd, 1993, Christian, *d* of Sir Arthur Grant, 10th Bt, CBE, DSO and *widow* of John G. O. Miller. *Educ:* Eton. Formerly 2nd Lieut 98th (Surrey and Sussex Yeomanry) Field Brigade, RA. *Heir:* *cousin* Paul Humphrey Armytage Bowman [*b* 10 Aug. 1921; *m* 1st, 1943, Felicité Anne Araminta MacMichael (marr. diss.); 2nd, 1947, Gabrielle May Currie (marr. diss.); one *d*; 3rd,

1974, Elizabeth Deirdre Churchill]. *Address:* Bishops Green House, Newbury, Berks RG15 8HS.
                                                           Died 16 Aug. 1994.

BOX, Donald Stewart; Member, The Stock Exchange, since 1945; Senior Partner, Lyddon, Stockbrokers, 1978–86 (Partner, 1966–86); *b* 22 Nov. 1917; *s* of late Stanley Carter Box and Elizabeth Mary Stewart Box; *m* 1st, 1940, Margaret Kennington Bates (marr. diss. 1947); 2nd, 1948, Peggy Farr (*née* Gooding) (marr. diss. 1973); 3rd, 1973, Margaret Rose Davies; one *d. Educ:* Llandaff Cathedral Sch.; St John's Sch., Pinner; County Sch., Harrow. RAF ranks, 1939, commissioned, 1941; overseas service Egypt, Palestine, Transjordan, 1941–44; demobbed with rank of Flt-Lieut, 1945. Partner, Henry J. Thomas & Co., stockbrokers, 1945–66. MP (C) Cardiff North, 1959–66. Non-exec. Dir, N. M. Rothschild & Sons (Wales) Ltd, 1988–92. *Recreations:* indifferent tennis, studying race form, doodling and doggerel. *Address:* Laburnum Cottage, Sully Road, Penarth, S Glam CF64 2TQ. *T:* Penarth (0222) 707966; (office) Douglas Buildings, Royal Stuart Lane, Cardiff CF1 6EL. *T:* Cardiff (0222) 494822. *Club:* Cardiff and County (Cardiff).
                                                           Died 12 July 1993.

BOXALL, Bernard, CBE 1963; Deputy Chairman, Lancer Boss Group Ltd, 1974–93; *b* 17 Aug. 1906; *s* of late Arthur Sidney Boxall and Maud Mary Boxall (*née* Mills); *m* 1931, Marjorie Lilian, *d* of late William George Emery and Mrs Emery; one *s* one *d. Educ:* King's Coll. Sch., Wimbledon; Imperial Coll., London Univ. (BSc (Hons); Fellow 1971). FCGI. James Howden & Co. Ltd, 1928–33; J. A. King & Co. Ltd, 1934–42; Production-Engineering Ltd, 1942–59; management consultant, 1959–; Chm., British United Trawlers Ltd, 1969–71; Dir, Lindustries Ltd, and Chm. of its engineering cos, 1960–71. Member: Highland Transport Bd, 1963–66; IRC, 1966–71; Scottish Economic Planning Council, 1967–71; Monopolies Commn, 1969–74. Mem., Company of Coachmakers and Coach Harness Makers (Master, 1977–78). FIMechE, FIProdE. *Recreation:* golf. *T:* Cranleigh (0483) 274340. *Club:* Walton Heath Golf.   *Died 3 Aug. 1994.*

BOYCE, James; MP (Lab) Rotherham, since 1992; *b* Paisley, 6 Sept. 1947; *s* of late James and Helen Boyce; *m* (marr. diss.); two *s*; *m* 1993, Barbara Roxburgh. *Educ:* St Mirrens Acad.; Northern Coll. (Pres., Students' Union); Sheffield Univ. Part-time travel assistant; ex-foundry worker. Dep. Pres., Sheffield Br., Foundry Sect., AEU. Mem. (Lab) Sheffield CC, 1984– (Chm., Operational Services; Dep. Chm., Lab. Gp; Mem., Policy Cttee). *Address:* House of Commons, SW1A 0AA. *Clubs:* Rotherham Central Labour; Rotherham East Dene Workingmen's; Wortley Hall.
                                                           Died 25 Jan. 1994.

BOYD, Sir Francis; *see* Boyd, Sir J. F.

BOYD, Gavin, CBE 1977; Consultant, Boyds, solicitors, since 1978; Director, Scottish Opera Theatre Royal Ltd, since 1973 (Chairman, 1973–88); *b* 4 Aug. 1928; *s* of Gavin and Margaret Boyd; *m* 1954, Kathleen Elizabeth Skinner; one *s. Educ:* Glasgow Acad.; Univ. of Glasgow. MA (Hons); LLB. Partner, Boyds, solicitors, Glasgow, 1955–77. Director: Stenhouse Holdings Ltd, 1970–79 (Chm., 1971–78); Scottish Opera, 1970–88; North Sea Assets plc, 1972–88 (Dep. Chm., 1981–88); Paterson Jenks plc, 1972–81; Scottish Television plc, 1973–92; Ferranti plc, 1975–88; British Carpets plc, 1977–81; Merchant House of Glasgow, 1982–90. Trustee, Scottish Hosps Endowment Res. Trust, 1978–90. Mem. Court, Univ. of Strathclyde, 1973–90 (Convener, Finance Cttee, 1979–83; Chm. Court, 1983–88). Mem., Law Soc. of Scotland. Hon. LLD Strathclyde, 1982. *Recreations:* music

and the performing arts, particularly opera, hill walking. *Address:* Tigh Geal, 6 Milton Hill, Dumbarton G82 2TS.
Died 1 March 1993.

BOYD, Sir (John) Francis, Kt 1976; a Vice-President, Open Spaces Society, since 1982; *b* 11 July 1910; *s* of John Crichton Dick Boyd and Kate Boyd, Ilkley, Yorks; *m* 1946, Margaret, *d* of George Dobson and Agnes Dobson, Scarborough, Yorks; one *s* two *d*. *Educ:* Ilkley Grammar Sch.; Silcoates Sch., near Wakefield, Yorks. Reporter: Leeds Mercury, 1928–34; Manchester Guardian, 1934–37; Parly Correspondent, Manchester Guardian, 1937–39. Aux. Fire Service, London, 1939; Monitoring Unit, BBC, 1940; Army, 1940–45. Political Correspondent, Manchester Guardian and Guardian, 1945–72; Political Editor, 1972–75. Chm., Lobby Journalists, 1949–50. Hon. LLD Leeds, 1973. *Publications:* Richard Austen Butler, 1956; (ed) The Glory of Parliament, by Harry Boardman, 1960; British Politics in Transition, 1964. *Recreations:* reading, walking, gardening. *Address:* 7 Summerlee Avenue, N2 9QP. *T:* 0181-444 8601. *Died 10 Dec. 1995.*

BOYDEN, (Harold) James; *b* 19 Oct. 1910; *s* of late Claude James and Frances Mary Boyden; *m* 1st, 1935, Emily Pemberton (*d* 1988); 2nd, 1990, Mrs Sue Hay. *Educ:* Elementary Sch., Tiffin Boys, Kingston; King's Coll., London. BA (History), 1932; BSc (Econ), London External, 1943. Barrister-at-law, Lincoln's Inn, 1947. Pres., King's Coll. Union Soc., 1931–32. Master: Henry Mellish Grammar Sch., 1933–35; Tiffin Boys Sch., 1935–40; Lectr, Extra-Mural Depts of London, Nottingham and Southampton Univs, 1934–47. RAF, 1940–45: Sqdn-Ldr, 1944–45. Chief Training Officer, Admiralty, 1945–47; Dir Extra-Mural Studies, Durham Univ., 1947–59. Durham City and County Magistrate, 1951; CC for Durham City, 1952–59; Chm. Durham County Education Cttee, 1959 (Vice-Chm. 1957–59); Chm., Exec. Cttee Nat. Inst. for Adult Education, 1958–61; Mem. Newcastle Regional Hospital Board, 1958–64; Fabian Soc. Executive, 1961–65. MP (Lab) Bishop Auckland, 1959–79; Jt Parly Under-Sec. of State, Dept of Education and Science, 1964–65; Parliamentary Sec., Ministry of Public Building and Works, 1965–67; Parly Under-Sec. (Army), MoD, 1967–69; Chm., Select Cttee of Expenditure, 1974–79; Sec., Anglo-French Parly Cttee, 1974–79. Overseas Lecture Tours: for Foreign Office, Germany, 1955 and 1957; for British Council, Ghana, Sierra Leone, 1956; Sierra Leone, 1961; for Admiralty, Malta, 1959. Member: WEA; Fabian Soc.; Nat. Union of General and Municipal Workers; National Trust; Council of Europe, 1970–73; WEU, 1970–73. FKC 1969. *Recreations:* walking, gardening, foreign travel, swimming. *Address:* 18 Salisbury Crescent, Oxford OX2 7TL. *T:* Oxford (0865) 58408. *Clubs:* South Church Workman's, Eldon Lane Workman's (Bishop Auckland); Southerne (Newton Aycliffe).
Died 26 Sept. 1993.

BOYLE, Andrew Philip More; author, journalist, broadcaster; *b* Dundee, 27 May 1919; *er s* of Andrew Boyle and Rose McCann; *m* 1st, 1943, Christina (*d* 1984), *y d* of Jack Galvin; one *s* one *d*; 2nd, 1986, Eleanor Frances Ransome. *Educ:* Blairs, Aberdeen; Paris Univ. Escaped from France as student, June 1940. RAFVR, 1941–43; Military Intelligence, Far East, 1944–45; also Military Corresp., Far East (Major), 1945–46. Joined BBC as scriptwriter/producer, Radio Newsreel, 1947; Asst Editor, 1954; Founding Editor, World At One, 1965, World This Weekend, PM, etc, 1967–75; Head of News and Current Affairs (Radio and TV), BBC Scotland, 1976. Successfully resisted Inland Revenue's attempt to tax literary prizes in 1978 Test Case. Work published, 1979, led to exposure of the Blunt affair. *Publications:* No

Passing Glory, biography of Group Captain Cheshire, VC, 1955; Trenchard, Man of Vision, 1962; Montagu Norman: a biography, 1967; Only the Wind will Listen: Reith of the BBC, 1972; Poor, Dear Brendan: the quest for Brendan Bracken, 1974 (Whitbread Award for Biography, 1974); The Riddle of Erskine Childers, 1976; The Climate of Treason, 1979, rev. edn 1980; The Fourth Man: a study of Robert Parsons, 1986; co-author of four other books; occasional contribs to Observer, Sunday Times, Times, Spectator, Listener, Washington Post, and formerly to Catholic Herald, Tablet, etc. *Recreations:* walking, swimming, conversation, music, watching bad football matches from public terraces, especially at Fulham. *Address:* 39 Lansdowne Road, W11 2LQ. *T:* 071-727 5758. *Died 22 April 1991.*

BOYLE, Marshal of the Royal Air Force Sir Dermot (Alexander), GCB 1957 (CB 1946); KCVO 1953; KBE 1953 (CBE 1945); AFC 1939; Vice-Chairman, British Aircraft Corporation, 1962–71; *b* 2 Oct. 1904; 2nd and *e* surv. *s* of A. F. Boyle, Belmont House, Queen's Co., Ireland; *m* 1931, Una Carey; two *s* one *d* (and one *s* decd). *Educ:* St Columba's Coll., Ireland; RAF (Cadet) Coll., Cranwell. Commissioned RAF, 1924; Air Commodore, 1944; Air Vice-Marshal, 1949; Air Marshal, 1954; Air Chief Marshal, 1956; Marshal of the Royal Air Force, 1958. Air ADC to the King, 1943; Dir-Gen. of Personnel, Air Ministry, 1948–49; Dir-Gen of Manning, Air Ministry, 1949–51; AOC No. 1 Group Bomber Command, 1951–53; AOC-in-C, Fighter Command, 1953–55; Chief of Air Staff, 1956–59. Master, Guild of Air Pilots and Air Navigators, 1965–66. Chairman: Bd of Trustees, RAF Museum, 1965–74; Ct of Governors, Mill Hill Sch., 1969–76; Dep. Chm., RAF Benevolent Fund, 1971–80. J. P. Robertson Meml Trophy, Air Public Relations Assoc., 1973. *Address:* Fair Gallop, Brighton Road, Sway, Hants SO41 6EA. *Club:* Royal Air Force.
Died 5 May 1993.

BOYLE, John Sebastian; Sheriff of South Strathclyde, Dumfries and Galloway at Airdrie, since 1983; *b* 29 March 1933; *s* of Edward Joseph Boyle and Constance Mary Hook; *m* 1st, 1955, Catherine Denise Croall; one *s* two *d*; 2nd, 1978, Isobel Margaret Ryan; one *d* (one *s* decd). *Educ:* St Aloysius College, Glasgow; Glasgow University. BL 1955. Solicitor, Glasgow, 1955–83. Pres., Glasgow Bar Assoc., 1962–63; Member: Council, Law Society of Scotland, 1968–75; Criminal Injuries Compensation Board, 1975–83. Mem., Scottish Arts Council, 1966–72; Dir, Scottish Opera, 1984–; Chm., Westbourne Music, 1988–. Gov., RSAMD, 1989–. *Address:* 5 Great Western Terrace, Glasgow G12 0UP. *T:* 041-357 1459.
Died 2 April 1991.

BOYLE, Kay, (Baroness Joseph von Franckenstein); writer; Professor in English Department, San Francisco State University, 1963–80, then Emeritus; *b* St Paul, Minn, USA, 19 Feb. 1902; *d* of Howard Peterson Boyle and Katherine (*née* Evans); *m* 1st, 1923, Richard Brault (marr. diss.); 2nd, 1931, Laurence Vail (marr. diss.); one *s* four *d* (and one *d* decd); 3rd, Baron Joseph von Franckenstein (*d* 1963). Member: National Institute of Arts and Letters, 1958; Amer. Acad. and Inst. of Arts and Letters, 1978. O. Henry Memorial Prize for best short story of the year, 1936, 1941; Guggenheim Fellowship, 1934, 1961; Center for Advanced Studies Wesleyan Univ. Fellowship, 1963; Radcliffe Inst. for Independent Study, 1964, 1965. Writer-in-residence: Hollins Coll., Virginia, 1970–71; Bowling Green State Univ., Ohio, 1986. Hon. DLitt: Columbia Coll., Chicago, 1971; Southern Illinois, 1982; Bowling Green State Univ., 1986; Hon. DHL Skidmore Coll., 1977. San Francisco Art Commn Award of Honor, 1978; Amer. Book Award, 1983; Lannan Foundn Award, 1989. *Publications: novels:* Plagued by the Nightingale, 1931;

Year Before Last, 1932; Gentlemen, I Address You Privately, 1933; My Next Bride, 1934; Death of a Man, 1936; Monday Night, 1938; His Human Majesty, 1939; The Crazy Hunter, 1940; Primer for Combat, 1942; Avalanche, 1943; A French Man Must Die, 1945; ''1939'', 1947; The Seagull on the Step, 1955; Three Short Novels, 1958; Generation Without Farewell, 1959; The Underground Woman, 1975; *volumes of short stories:* Wedding Day, 1930; The First Lover; The White Horses of Vienna, 1937; The Crazy Hunter; Thirty Stories, 1946; Nothing Ever Breaks Except the Heart, 1966; Fifty Stories, 1980; Life Being the Best, 1988; *essays:* The Smoking Mountain, 1951; Breaking the Silence, 1962; The Long Walk at San Francisco State and other essays, 1970; Words That Must Somehow Be Said, 1985; *memoirs:* The Autobiography of Emanuel Carnevali, 1967; Being Geniuses Together, 1968; *poetry:* A Glad Day, 1930; American Citizen, 1944; Collected Poems, 1962; Testament for my Students and other poems, 1970; This is Not a Letter, 1985; *for children:* The Youngest Camel, 1959; Pinky, the Cat Who Liked to Sleep, 1966; Pinky in Persia, 1968. *Recreations:* ski-ing, mountain climbing. *Address:* c/o Watkins/Loomis Agency Inc., 150 East 35th Street, New York, NY 10016, USA.

Died 27 Dec. 1992.

BOYNE, 10th Viscount *cr* 1717; **Gustavus Michael George Hamilton-Russell,** KCVO 1995; DL; JP; Baron Hamilton, 1715; Baron Brancepeth, 1866; a Lord in Waiting, since 1981; Lord-Lieutenant of Shropshire, since 1994; *b* 10 Dec. 1931; *s* of late Hon. Gustavus Lascelles Hamilton-Russell and *g s* of 9th Viscount; *S* grandfather, 1942; *m* 1956, Rosemary Anne, 2nd *d* of Major Sir Dennis Stucley, 5th Bt; one *s* two *d* (and one *d* decd). *Educ:* Eton; Sandhurst; Royal Agricl Coll., Cirencester. Commissioned Grenadier Guards, 1952. Director: Nat. Westminster Bank, 1976–90 (Chm., W Midlands and Wales Regional Bd, 1976–90); Private Patients Plan Ltd, 1986–; Priplan Investments, 1987–; Chairman: Ludlow Race Club Ltd, 1987–; Harper Adams Agricl Coll., 1990–. Mem., 1963–83, Dep. Chm., 1975–82, Telford Develt Corp. Governor, Wrekin Coll., Telford, 1965–86. KStJ. JP 1961, DL 1965, Salop. *Heir:* s Hon. Gustavus Michael Stucley Hamilton-Russell [*b* 27 May 1965; *m* 1991, Lucy, *d* of George Potter; one *d*]. *Address:* Burwarton House, Bridgnorth, Salop WV16 6QH. *T:* Burwarton (01746) 787203. *Club:* White's.   *Died 14 Dec. 1995.*

BOYS SMITH, Rev. John Sandwith, MA; Master of St John's College, Cambridge, 1959–69 (Fellow, 1927–59 and since 1969; Senior Bursar, 1944–59); Vice-Chancellor, University of Cambridge, 1963–65; Canon Emeritus of Ely Cathedral since 1948; *b* 8 Jan. 1901; *e s* of late Rev. E. P. Boys-Smith, formerly Vicar of Hordle, Hants, and Charlotte Cecilia, *e d* of late T. B. Maunde CB; *m* 1942, Gwendolen Sara, *o d* of late W. J. Wynn; two *s. Educ:* Sherborne Sch.; St John's Coll., Cambridge. Economics Tripos Part I, Class II, division 2, 1921; BA, Theological Tripos, Part I, Sec. B, Class I, 1922; Scholar and Naden Student in Divinity, St John's Coll., 1922; Theological Tripos Part II, Sec. V, Class 1, 1924; Burney Student, 1924; Marburg University, 1924–25. Deacon, 1926; Curate of Sutton Coldfield, Birmingham, 1926–27; priest, 1927; St John's College, Cambridge: Chaplain, 1927–34; Director of Theological Studies, 1927–40, and 1944–52; Assistant Tutor, 1931–34; Tutor, 1934–39; Junior Bursar, 1939–40; University Lecturer in Divinity, Cambridge, 1931–40; Stanton Lecturer in the Philosophy of Religion, Cambridge Univ., 1934–37; Ely Professor of Divinity in the University of Cambridge and Canon of Ely Cathedral, 1940–43. Hon. Fellow: Trinity Coll., Dublin, 1968; Darwin Coll., Cambridge, 1969; New Hall, Cambridge, 1987. Hon. LLD Cambridge, 1970. *Publications:* Religious Thought in the Eighteenth Century

(with J. M. Creed), 1934; Memories of St John's College Cambridge 1919–1969, 1983. *Address:* 1 Dulwich Mead, Half Moon Lane, SE24 9HS. *T:* 071–274 9334; St John's College, Cambridge.   *Died 3 Nov. 1991.*

BRADBROOK, Prof. Muriel Clara, MA; PhD 1933; LittD Cantab 1955; FBA 1990; *b* 27 April 1909; *d* of Samuel Bradbrook, Supt HM Waterguard at Liverpool and Glasgow, and Annie (*née* Harvey); *Educ:* Hutchesons' Sch., Glasgow; Oldershaw Sch., Wallasey; Girton Coll., Cambridge. English Tripos, Class I, 1929; Harness Prize, 1931; Allen Scholar, 1935–36; in residence, Somerville Coll., Oxford, 1935–36. Cambridge University: Univ. Lecturer, 1945–62; Reader, 1962–65; Professor of English, 1965–76; Mistress of Girton College, 1968–76 (Vice-Mistress, 1962–66; Fellow, 1932–35, 1936–68, and 1976–). Board of Trade, Industries and Manufactures Depts 2 and 3, 1941–45; in residence at Folger Library, Washington, and Huntington Library, California, 1958–59; Fellow, Nat. Humanities Center, N Carolina, 1979. Tour of the Far East for Shakespeare's Fourth Centenary, 1964; Trustee, Shakespeare's Birthplace, 1967–82, 1985–. Visiting Professor: Santa Cruz, California, 1966; Kuwait, 1969; Tokyo, 1975; Kenyon Coll., USA, 1977; Rhodes Univ., SA, 1979; Clark Lecturer, Trinity Coll., Cambridge, 1968. Hon. Prof., Graduate Sch. of Renaissance Studies, Warwick Univ., 1987–90. Foreign Mem., Norwegian Acad. of Arts and Scis, 1966; Hon. Mem., Mod. Lang. Assoc. of America, 1974. FRSL 1947. Hon. LittD: Liverpool, 1964; Sussex, 1972; London, 1973; Hon. LLD Smith Coll., USA, 1965; Hon. PhD Gothenburg, 1975; Hon. LHD Kenyon Coll., USA, 1977. Freedom, City of Hiroshima. *Publications:* Elizabethan Stage Conditions, 1932; Themes and Conventions of Elizabethan Tragedy, 1934; The School of Night, 1936; Andrew Marvell (with M. G. Lloyd Thomas), 1940; Joseph Conrad, 1941; Ibsen the Norwegian, 1947; T. S. Eliot, 1950; Shakespeare and Elizabethan Poetry, 1951; The Queen's Garland, 1953; The Growth and Structure of Elizabethan Comedy, 1955; Sir Thomas Malory, 1957; The Rise of the Common Player, 1962; English Dramatic Form, 1965; That Infidel Place, 1969; Shakespeare the Craftsman, 1969; Literature in Action, 1972; Malcolm Lowry: his art and early life, 1974; The Living Monument, 1976; Shakespeare: the poet in his world, 1978; John Webster, Citizen and Dramatist, 1980; Collected Papers, 4 vols, 1982–89; Muriel Bradbrook on Shakespeare, 1984; numerous articles and reviews. *Recreations:* travel, theatre. *Address:* 91 Chesterton Road, Cambridge CB4 3AP. *T:* Cambridge (0223) 352765. *Clubs:* University Women's; Amateur Dramatic (Cambridge).   *Died 11 June 1993.*

BRADBURY, 2nd Baron *cr* 1925, of Winsford, Co. Chester; **John Bradbury;** *b* 7 Jan. 1914; *s* of 1st Baron Bradbury, GCB, and Hilda (*d* 1949), 2nd *d* of W. A. Kirby; *S* father 1950; *m* 1st, 1939, Joan, *o d* of W. D. Knight, Darley, Addlestone, Surrey; one *s* one *d*; 2nd, 1946, Gwerfyl, *d* of late E. Stanton Roberts, Gellifor, Ruthin; one *d. Educ:* Westminster; Brasenose Coll., Oxford. *Heir:* s Hon. John Bradbury [*b* 17 March 1940; *m* 1968, Susan, *d* of late W. Liddiard, East Shefford, Berks; two *s*]. *Address:* 1 Irakli Street, Engomi, Nicosia, Cyprus. *T:* Nicosia 355753.

Died 31 March 1994.

BRADDON, Russell Reading; author; *b* 25 Jan. 1921; *s* of Henry Russell Braddon and Thelma Doris Braddon (*née* Reading). *Educ:* Sydney Church of England Grammar Sch.; Sydney Univ. (BA). Failed Law finals; began writing, by chance, 1949; scripted, narrated and presented television documentaries, 1984–, inc. contrib. to Great Rivers of the World series, BBC, 1985. *Publications:* The Piddingtons, 1950; The Naked Island, 1951; Those in Peril, 1954; Cheshire, VC, 1954; Out of the Storm, 1956;

Nancy Wake, 1956; End of a Hate, 1958; Gabriel Comes to 24, 1958; Proud American Boy, 1960; Joan Sutherland, 1962; The Year of the Angry Rabbit, 1964; Roy Thomson of Fleet Street, 1965; Committal Chamber, 1966; When the Enemy is Tired, 1968; The Inseparables, 1968; Will You Walk a Little Faster, 1969; The Siege, 1969; Prelude and Fugue for Lovers, 1971; The Progress of Private Lilyworth, 1971; End Play, 1972; Suez: splitting of a nation, 1973; The Hundred Days of Darien, 1974; All the Queen's Men, 1977; The Finalists, 1977; The Shepherd's Bush Case, 1978; The Predator, 1980; The Other Hundred Years War, 1983; Thomas Baines, 1986; Images of Australia, 1988; Funnelweb, 1990. *Recreation:* not writing. *Address:* c/o John Farquharson Ltd, 162–168 Regent Street, W1R 5TB.   *Died 20 March 1995.*

BRADEN, Bernard; free-lance performer and dabbler; *b* 16 May 1916; *s* of Rev. Dr Edwin Donald Braden and Mary Evelyn Chastey; *m* 1942, Barbara Kelly; one *s* two *d*. *Educ:* Maple Grove Public Sch., Point Grey Junior High Sch., Magee High Sch., Vancouver, Canada. Radio engineer, announcer, singer, actor in Vancouver, Canada, 1937–43; wrote and performed in plays for Canadian Broadcasting Corporation, 1940–43, in Vancouver and Toronto, 1943–49; moved to England, 1949. London plays include: A Streetcar Named Desire; Biggest Thief in Town; The Man; No News From Father; Anniversary Waltz; The Gimmick; Period of Adjustment; Spoon River Anthology; Apple Cart; BBC radio programmes include: Breakfast with Braden; Bedtime with Braden; Braden Beside Himself; TV includes: inauguration of BBC School's broadcasts; The Brains Trust; Early to Braden; On the Braden Beat; Braden's Week; All Our Yesterdays. Man. Dir, Adanac Productions Ltd; Dir, Prime Performers Ltd. Hon. Chancellor, London School of Economics, 1955. BAFTA Features Personality Award; British Variety Club Light Entertainment Personality; RTS Award for artistry in front of the camera. *Publications:* These English, 1948; The Kindness of Strangers, 1990. *Recreations:* family, tennis, finding time. *Address:* 2 Ovington Square, SW3 1LN.   *Died 2 Feb. 1993.*

BRADFORD HILL, Sir Austin; *see* Hill.

BRADLAW, Prof. Sir Robert (Vivian), Kt 1965; CBE 1950; Hon. Professor of Oral Pathology, Royal College of Surgeons of England, since 1948; Emeritus Professor of Oral Medicine, University of London; Emeritus Consultant, Royal Navy; *b* 14 April 1905; *s* of Philip Archibald Bradlaw, Blackrock, Co. Dublin; unmarried. *Educ:* Cranleigh; Guy's Hosp.; University of London. Hilton Prize, etc, Guy's Hosp. Fellow, Royal Colleges of Surgeons of England (1949), Edinburgh (1949), Glasgow (1967), Ireland (1965), etc; Hon. Fellow, RSM, 1975. Tomes Prize for Research, RCS 1939–41; Howard Mummery Prize for Research, BDA, 1948–53; Colyer Gold Medal, RCS; Hunterian Prof., RCS 1955; Hon. Gold Medal, RCS, 1972. Hon. degrees, Univs of Belfast, Birmingham, Boston, Durham, Leeds, Malta, Melbourne, Meshed, Montreal and Newcastle upon Tyne. Chevalier de la Santé Publique (France), 1950; Knight, Order of St Olaf (Norway); Commander, Order of Homayoun (Iran). *Recreations:* fishing, golf, orchids, oriental ceramics. *Address:* The Manse, Stoke Goldington, Newport Pagnell, Bucks.   *Died 12 Feb. 1992.*

BRADSHAW, Maurice Bernard, OBE 1978; Secretary-General, 1958–79, Governor, 1979–81, a Director, 1981–83, Federation of British Artists; Hon. Member Extraordinary, Royal Society of Portrait Painters, 1983; *b* 7 Feb. 1903; 7th *s* of John Bradshaw; *m* 1927, Gladys (*d* 1983), 2nd *d* of Henry Harvey Frost; one *d*. *Educ:* Christ's Coll., Finchley. Jun. Clerk, Furness Withy & Co., 1918. Dir, Art Exhibns Bureau, 1926–; Asst Sec., British Artists Exhibns, 1927–35; Organising Sec., Floating Art Gall.

aboard Berengaria, 1928; Secretary: Empire Art Loan Exhibn Soc., 1932; Modern Architectural Res. Gp, 1938; Royal Inst. Oil Painters, 1966–74; Royal Inst. Painters in Watercolours, 1969–79; Royal Soc. British Artists, 1958–74; Royal Soc. Marine Artists, 1938–72; Royal Soc. Portrait Painters, 1955–83; Royal Soc. Miniature Painters, Sculptors and Gravers, 1959–72; Royal British Colonial Soc. of Artists (temp. known as Commonwealth Soc. of Artists), 1930–83; Artists of Chelsea, 1949–72; National Soc., 1968–74; New English Art Club, 1955–74; Pastel Soc., 1968–77; Soc. Aviation Artists, 1954–83; Soc. Graphic Artists, 1968–75; Soc. Mural Painters, 1968–; Soc. Portrait Sculptors, 1969–83; Soc. Wildlife Artists, 1963–80; Soc. Women Artists, 1968–79; Senefelder Gp, 1968–83. Commissioned RAFVR, 1941–45. *Recreations:* woodwork, philately. *Address:* Holbrook Park House, Holbrook, near Horsham, W Sussex RH12 4PW.
Died 23 Nov. 1991.

BRAHAM, Harold, CBE 1960; HM Diplomatic Service, retired; *b* Constantinople, 11 Oct. 1907; *er s* of late D. D. Braham, of The Times, and Julie, (Stella), Swift, *d* of H. J. Whiteside; *m* 1941, Cicely Edith Norton Webber (*d* 1990); one *s* one *d*. *Educ:* St Peter's Coll., Adelaide; New College, Oxford. Entered HM Consular Service, China, 1931; retired as HM Consul-Gen., Paris, 1966. *Address:* Caserio Torret 19, 07710 San Luis, Menorca, Spain.
Died 16 Jan. 1995.

BRAMMER, Leonard Griffith, RE 1956 (ARE 1932); painter and etcher; Supervisor of Art and Crafts, Stoke-on-Trent Education Authority, 1952–69; retired; *b* 4 July 1906; *s* of Frederick William Brammer and Minnie Griffith; *m* 1934, Florence May, *d* of William and Mary Barnett, Hanley; one *d*. *Educ:* Burslem Sch. of Art; Royal College of Art (Diploma Associate); awarded Travelling Scholarship, School of Engraving, Royal College of Art, 1930. Represented in Tate Gallery, British Museum, Victoria and Albert Museum, Ashmolean, Oxford, City of Stoke-on-Trent Art Gallery, City of Carlisle Art Gallery, Wedgwood Museum, Barlaston, Keele Univ., Gladstone Pottery Museum, Collection of Contemporary Art Soc., Collections of The British Council, etc; was exhibitor at Royal Academy and all leading English and American exhibitions. *Address:* Sŵn-y-Wylan, Beach Road, Morfa Bychan, Porthmadog, Gwynedd LL49 9YA.
Died 23 May 1994.

BRANCH, Sir William Allan Patrick, Kt 1977; Managing Director and Grenada Representative on the Windward Islands Banana Association (Mirabeau, Capitol, Hope Development and Dougaldston Estates); *b* 17 Feb. 1915; *m* Thelma (*née* Rapier); one *s*. *Educ:* Grenada Boys' Secondary Sch. Dep. Manager, Mt Horne Agricl Estate, 1936; Manager Mt Horne, Boulogne, Colombier, Industry and Grand Bras Agricl Estates, 1941. Chairman, Eastern Dist Agricl Rehabilitation Cttee; Dep. Chm. Bd of Dirs, Grenada Banana Co-op Soc.; Director: Grenada Cocoa Industry; Parochial and Island Anglican Church Council; Managing Cttee: Grenada Boy Scouts Assoc.; St Andrew's Anglican Secondary Sch.; Member, Central Agricl Rehabilitation Cttee. Knighthood awarded for services to agriculture, Grenada, Windward Islands. *Address:* Dougaldston, Gouyave, St John's, Grenada.
Died 27 Jan. 1993.

BRANDON, (Oscar) Henry, CBE 1985; Columnist, New York Times World Syndicate, since 1983; Associate Editor and Chief American correspondent of the Sunday Times, retired 1983; *b* 9 March 1916; *m* 1970, Mabel Hobart Wentworth; one *d*. *Educ:* Univ. of Prague and Lausanne. Joined Sunday Times, 1939; War Correspondent, N Africa and W Europe, 1943–45; Paris Correspondent, 1945–46; Roving Diplomatic Correspondent, 1947–49; Washington Correspondent,

1950–83; Syndicated Columnist for Washington Star, 1979–81. Guest scholar, The Brookings Instn, Washington, DC, 1983–. Hon. LittD Williams Coll., 1979. Foreign corresp. award, Univ. of California, Los Angeles, 1957; award, Lincoln Univ., Jefferson City, Missouri, 1962; Hannen Swaffer award, 1964; Sigma Delta Chi Soc. award, 1983. *Publications:* As We Are, 1961; In The Red, 1966; Conversations with Henry Brandon, 1966; The Anatomy of Error, 1970; The Retreat of American Power, 1973; Special Relationships, 1989; (ed) In Search of a New World Order: the future of US-European relations, 1992. *Recreations:* ski-ing, tennis, swimming, photography. *Died 20 April 1993.*

BRANDON, Prof. Percy Samuel, (Peter); Professor of Electrical Engineering, 1971–84, Head of Electrical Division, 1981–84, University of Cambridge, then Professor Emeritus; *b* 9 Nov. 1916; *s* of P. S. Brandon, OBE; *m* 1942, Joan Edith Marriage, GRSM (London), LRAM; two *s. Educ:* Chigwell Sch.; Jesus Coll., Cambridge (MA). Joined The Marconi Company, 1939; Research Div., 1940–71; Frequency Measurement, 1940–44; Aerial Section, 1944–45; FM Radar, 1945–53; Chief of Guidance Systems, 1953–57; Chief of Mathematics and Systems Analysis Gp, 1957–65; Manager of Theoretical Sciences Laboratory, 1965–68; Asst Dir of Research, 1965–68; Manager of Research Div. of GEC-Marconi Electronics, 1968–71. Part-time lecturing at Mid-Essex Technical Coll., and others, 1945–66. FInstP, FIEE. *Publications:* contribs to Marconi Review, IEE Proc., Agardograph, Electronic Engineering, etc. *Recreations:* colour photography, hi-fi, using computers. *Address:* New Courts, 8 Bridge Lane, Little Shelford, Cambridge CB2 5HE. *T:* Cambridge (0223) 842541.

Died 21 Dec. 1991.

BRANDT, Willy; Chairman, Social Democratic Party (SPD), Federal Republic of Germany, 1964–87, Hon. Chairman since 1987; Member, German Federal Parliament, 1949–57, and since 1969; *b* 18 Dec. 1913; *s* of Martha Frahm; named Herbert Ernst Karl Frahm; *m* 1st, 1941, Carlota Thorkildsen (marr. diss. 1944); one *d*; 2nd, 1948, Rut Hansen (marr. diss.); three *s*; 3rd, 1983, Brigitte Seebacher. *Educ:* Johanneum, Lübeck; University of Oslo. Fled from Lübeck to Norway, 1933. Chief Editor, Berliner Stadtblatt, 1950–51. Mem., Social Democratic Party (SPD), 1931–; Rep. Federal Board of SPD, in Berlin, 1948–49, Deputy Chairman of SPD, 1962–63. President Berlin House of Representatives, 1955–57; Governing Mayor of W Berlin, 1957–66; President German Conference of Mayors, 1958–63; President German Federal Council, 1957–58; Vice-Chancellor and Foreign Minister, 1966–69, Chancellor 1969–74, Federal Republic of Germany; Mem., European Parlt, 1979–83. Pres., Socialist International, 1976–92. Chm., Commn on Develt Issues (which produced Brandt reports, North-South: a programme for survival, 1980, and Common Crisis: North-South: cooperation for world recovery, 1983), 1977–79. Dr (*hc*): Pennsylvania Univ., 1959; Maryland Univ., 1960; Harvard Univ., 1963; Hon. DCL: Oxford Univ., 1969; Leeds, 1982, etc. Nobel Prize for Peace, 1971. Grosskreuz des Verdienstordens der Bundesrepublik Deutschland, 1959. *Publications:* Efter segern, 1944; Forbrytere og andre Tyskere, 1946; (with Richard Löwenthal) Ernst Reuter: Ein Leben für die Freiheit, 1957; Von Bonn nach Berlin, 1957; Mein Weg nach Berlin (recorded by Leo Lania), 1960; Plädoyer für die Zukunft, 1961; The Ordeal of Co-existence, 1963; Begegnungen mit Kennedy, 1964; (with Günter Struve) Draussen, 1966 (UK, as In Exile, 1971); Friedenspolitik in Europa, 1968; Essays, Reflections and Letters 1933–47, 1971; Der Wille zum Frieden, 1971; Über den Tag hinaus, 1974; Begegnungen und Einsichten, 1976 (UK, as People and Politics, 1978); Frauen heute, 1978; Links und frei, 1982; World Armament and World Hunger, 1986; Menschenrechte misshandelt und missbraucht, 1987; Erinnerungen, 1989 (UK, as My Life in Politics, 1992); many publications on topical questions in Sweden and Norway; articles in home and foreign journals. *Address:* (office) Bundeshaus, 5300 Bonn 1, Germany. *T:* 162758. *Died 8 Oct. 1992.*

BRANNAN, Charles Franklin; lawyer; *b* 23 Aug. 1903; *s* of John Brannan and Ella Louise Street; *m* 1932, Eda Seltzer; no *c. Educ:* Regis Coll.; University of Denver Law Sch., Denver, Colorado, USA. Private law practice, Denver, Colorado, 1929–35; Asst Regional Attorney: Resettlement Administration, Denver, 1935–37; Regional Attorney, Office of the Solicitor, US Dept of Agriculture, Denver, 1937–41; Regional Director of Farm Security Administration, US Dept of Agriculture, Denver, 1941–44; Asst Administrator, Farm Security Administration, US Dept of Agriculture, Washington, DC, April-June 1944; Asst Secretary of Agriculture, Washington, DC, 1944–48; Secretary of Agriculture, USA, 1948–Jan. 1953. Pres., Bd of Water Commissioners, Denver, 1976. Hon. Degrees: Doctor of Laws from the University of Denver and Doctor of Science from the Colorado Agricultural and Mechanical Coll. Hon. Phi Beta Kappa. *Address:* (home) 3131 East Alameda, Denver, Colorado 80209, USA; (office) 3773 Cherry Creek North Drive, Denver, Colo 80239. *Club:* Denver Athletic (Denver, Colorado).

Died 2 July 1992.

BRASSEY, Lt-Col Hon. Peter (Esmé); Lord-Lieutenant of Cambridgeshire, 1975–81; *b* 5 Dec. 1907; *yr* surv. *s* of 1st Baron Brassey of Apethorpe and Lady Violet Gordon Lennox, 2nd *d* of 7th Duke of Richmond and Gordon; *m* 1944, Lady Romayne Cecil (OBE 1986), 2nd *d* of 5th Marquess of Exeter, KG, CMG; two *s* one *d. Educ:* Eton; Magdalene Coll., Cambridge. Barrister-at-Law, Inner Temple, 1930; Midland Circuit, 1931. Northamptonshire Yeomanry, Lieut.-Col, 1945; served NW Europe (wounded). Dir, The Essex Water Co. Ltd, 1970–85 (Chm., 1981–85). DL 1961, High Sheriff, 1966, and Vice-Lieutenant, 1966–74, County of Huntingdon and Peterborough. KStJ 1976. *Recreations:* shooting, fishing. *Address:* Pond House, Barnack, Stamford, Lincs PE9 3DN. *T:* Stamford (01780) 740238. *Club:* Carlton.

Died 14 March 1995.

BRATBY, John Randall, RA 1971 (ARA 1959); ARCA; FIAL; RBA; FRSA; painter and writer; Member of London Group; Editor in Chief, Art Quarterly, since 1987; *b* 19 July 1928; *s* of George Alfred Bratby and Lily Beryl Randall; *m* 1953, Jean Esme Oregon Cooke, RA (marr. diss. 1977); three *s* one *d*; *m* 1977, Patti Prime. *Educ:* Tiffin Boys' Sch.; Kingston School of Art; Royal College of Art. Teacher: Carlisle College of Art, 1956; Royal College of Art, 1957–58. Gained prizes and scholarships, 1954–58: Guggenheim Award for Great Britain, 1956 and 1958; won junior section of John Moore's Liverpool Exhibn, 1957. Numerous one-man exhibitions at Beaux Arts Gallery from 1954; Zwemmer Gallery from 1959; Thackeray Gallery; Furneaux Gallery; Nat. Theatre (twice); Phoenix Gall., London and Lavenham; Albemarle Gall.; also in galleries abroad; exhibited: Royal Academy (yearly) from 1955; Nat. Portrait Gall. (retrospective), 1991; pictures in various international exhibitions and festivals (Venice Biennale, 1956); works in public collections: Tate Gallery; Arts Council of Great Britain; British Council; Contemporary Arts Society; National Galleries, Canada, New Zealand, NSW and Victoria; galleries in many cities and towns of Great Britain; Victoria and Albert Museum; Ashmolean Museum; Museum of Modern Art, New York; also in many other public and private art collections, in Great Britain, the Commonwealth and USA. Paintings for film: The Horse's Mouth, 1958; Mistral's Daughter, 1984. Television appearances and sound broadcasts. Hon. DLitt Birmingham, 1992. *Publications: fiction:* Breakdown, 1960; Breakfast and Elevenses, 1961; Break-Pedal Down, 1962 (also TV play); Break 50 Kill, 1963; *non-fiction:* studio publication of colour reproductions of own work, 1961; Stanley Spencer, 1969; *illustrator:* Horse's Mouth, 1965; (contrib.) Oxford Illustrated Old Testament, 1968; The Devils, 1984; Apocryphal Letters, by Edward Lowerby, 1985. *Recreations:* watching TV, cider, buying clothes for my wife. *Address:* Les Ateliers, The Cupola, Belmont Road, Hastings, Sussex TN35 5NR. *T:* Hastings (0424) 434037.   *Died 20 July 1992.*

BRAY, Hon. Dr John Jefferson, AC 1979; Chancellor of the University of Adelaide, 1968–83; *b* 16 Sept. 1912; *s* of Harry Midwinter Bray and Gertrude Eleonore Bray (*née* Stow). *Educ:* St Peter's Coll., Adelaide; Univ. of Adelaide. LLB 1932, LLB Hons 1933, LLD 1937. Admitted to South Australian Bar, 1933; QC 1957. Univ. of Adelaide: Actg Lectr in Jurisprudence, 1941, 1943, 1945, 1951; Actg Lectr in Legal History, 1957–58; Lectr in Roman Law, 1959–66; Chief Justice of Supreme Court of SA, 1967–78. DUniv Adelaide, 1983. Adelaide Fest. Award for Literature (non-fiction), 1990. *Publications:* Poems, 1962; Poems 1961–1971, 1972; Poems 1972–1979, 1979; (ed jtly) No 7 Friendly Street Poetry Reader, 1983; The Bay of Salamis and Other Poems, 1986; Satura: selected poetry and prose, 1988; The Emperor's Doorkeeper, 1988; Seventy Seven (poems), 1990; contribs to: Well and Truly Tried, 1982 (Festschrift for Sir Richard Eggleston); Adelaide Law School Centenary Essays, 1983; Australian Law Jl. *Address:* 39 Hurtle Square, Adelaide, SA 5000, Australia. *Club:* University of Adelaide.   *Died 26 June 1995.*

BRAYNEN, Sir Alvin (Rudolph), Kt 1975; JP; Consultant to Shell, Bahamas, 1969–82; High Commissioner for the Commonwealth of the Bahamas in London, 1973–77; *b* 6 Dec. 1904; *s* of William Rudolph Braynen and Lulu Isabelle Braynen (*née* Griffin); *m* 1969, Ena Estelle (*née* Elden); (one *s* one *d* by a previous marriage). *Educ:* Public Sch., The Current, Eleuthera, Bahamas; Boys' Central Sch., Nassau, Bahamas (teacher trng). Public sch. headmaster, 1923–25; entered commercial world, 1925, as clerk; founded his own petroleum commn firm, 1930, disposing of it in 1965. MP for Cat Island, 1935–42 and constituency for what was later known as St John, 1942–72; Dep. Speaker of House of Assembly, 1949–53, and 1963–66; MEC, 1953–58; Speaker of House of Assembly, 1967–72; during years 1952–58 he was Chairman of several Boards, incl. those responsible for Educn, Public Works, Prisons and Traffic; past Member, Bds of Agriculture, Health, Tourism, Out Island Develt and Educn; Mem., both Constitutional Confs from the Bahamas to London in 1963 and 1968; Chm., Exec. Cttee of Conf. of Commonwealth Caribbean Parliamentary Heads and Clerks; also served as either Chm. or Dep. Chm. of important Nat. Festivities for many years, such as Coronation of the Queen, visit of Princess Margaret, First Constitutional Day, 1964, and supervised arrangements for Conf. of Delegates of Commonwealth Parliamentary Conf. held at Nassau, 1968. Organised Bahamas Chamber of Commerce (first Exec. Sec.); Founder and first Pres., Nassau Mutual Aid Assoc.; first Pres., Kiwanis Club (Montague Branch). JP Bahamas, 1952. *Recreations:* swimming, collector of books on the Bahamas, collector of coins and stamps. *Address:* PO Box N42, Nassau, Bahamas.   *Died 9 Oct. 1992.*

BRAYSHAW, (Alfred) Joseph, CBE 1975 (OBE 1964); JP; DL; Secretary, The Magistrates' Association, 1965–77; *b* Manchester, 20 Dec. 1912; *er s* of late Shipley Neave Brayshaw and Ruth Cotterell (*née* Holmes), JP; *m* 1st, Joan Hawkes (*d* 1940); 2nd, 1943, Marion Spencer, *y d* of

late Spencer Johnson, Bury St Edmunds; three *s. Educ:* Sidcot Sch., Somerset; engineering factories; Dalton Hall, Univ. of Manchester. Brayshaw Furnaces & Tools Ltd, 1934–40; CBCO, 1941–46; Asst Sec., then Gen. Sec., Friends' Relief Service, 1946–48; Gen. Sec., Nat. Marriage Guidance Council, 1949–64 (a Vice-Pres., 1964–); Pres., Guildford and District Marriage Guidance Council, 1983–87. JP Surrey, 1958; DL Surrey, 1983; Chairman: Farnham Bench, 1979–82; Surrey Magistrates' Soc., 1979–83. *Publication:* Public Policy and Family Life, 1980. *Recreation:* gardening. *Address:* Apple Trees, Beech Road, Haslemere, Surrey GU27 2BX. *T:* Haslemere (0428) 642677.   *Died 20 May 1994.*

BREARE, William Robert Ackrill; Chairman and Managing Director: R. Ackrill Ltd, 1955–82; Lawrence & Hall Ltd, 1963–81; *b* 5 July 1916; *s* of late Robert Ackrill Breare and Emily Breare (*née* Waddington); *m* 1942, Sybella Jessie Macduff Roddick, *d* of late John Roddick, Annan; one *s* two *d. Educ:* Old College, Windermere; Charterhouse; Wadham Coll., Oxford (BCL 1938; MA). Sub-Lt RNVSR, 1935–39; Comdr RNVR, 1942–44. Dir, R. Ackrill Ltd, newspaper publishers, 1938. Pres., Yorks Newspaper Soc., 1953 and 1972; Mem. Council, Newspaper Soc., 1967–81; Mem. Press Council, 1972–81. Contested (C) Rother Valley, 1950. *Recreations:* music, sailing. *Address:* Harrison Hill House, Starbeck, Harrogate, N Yorks. *T:* Harrogate (0423) 883302.
                    Died 7 March 1993.

BREEN, Dame Marie (Freda), DBE 1979 (OBE 1958); *b* 3 Nov. 1902; *d* of Frederick and Jeanne Chamberlin; *m* 1928, Robert Tweeddale Breen (*d* 1968); three *d. Educ:* St Michael's C of E Girls' Grammar Sch. Senator for Victoria, 1962–68, retired. Hon. Internat. Sec., Nat. Council of Women of Victoria, 1948–52, Pres., 1954–58, then Hon. Member; Vice-Pres., Australian/Asian Assoc. of Victoria, 1956–74; Chm., UNICEF Victorian Cttee, 1969–73; President: Victorian Family Council, 1958–78; Victorian Assoc. of Citizens' Advice Bureaux, 1970–78; Australian Assoc. of Citizens' Advice Bureaux, 1973–75, 1977–79; Victorian Family Planning Assoc., 1970–71; Patron, FPA of Victoria, 1985–; Executive Mem. and Vice-Pres., Queen Elizabeth Hosp. for Mothers and Babies, 1943–78; Chm., Victorian Consultative Cttee on Social Develt, 1980–82. Mayoress of Brighton, Vic, 1941–42; JP 1948. *Recreations:* music, reading. *Address:* 51 Carpenter Street, Brighton, Victoria 3186, Australia. *T:* 592 2314. *Club:* Lyceum (Melbourne).
                    Died 17 June 1993.

BREMRIDGE, Sir John (Henry), KBE 1983 (OBE 1976); *b* 12 July 1925; *s* of Godfrey Bremridge and Monica (*née* Bennett); *m* 1956, Jacqueline Everard (MBE 1987); two *s* two *d. Educ:* Dragon Sch.; Cheltenham Coll.; St John's Coll., Oxford (MA). Army service: The Rifle Brigade, 1943–47. Joined John Swire & Sons, 1949; retired as Chm., John Swire & Sons (HK) Ltd, Swire Pacific Ltd, and Cathay Pacific Airways Ltd, 1980. Financial Sec., Hong Kong, 1981–86. Director: John Swire and Sons, 1987–89; Orient Express Hotels, 1986–89; Schroders, 1987–89. Hon. DSocSc Chinese Univ., 1980; Hon. DCL Hong Kong Univ., 1982. *Recreation:* bad golf. *Address:* Church House, Bradford-on-Avon, Wilts BA15 1LN. *T:* Bradford-on-Avon (0225) 866136. *Clubs:* Oriental; Hong Kong.   *Died 6 May 1994.*

BRETHERTON, Russell Frederick, CB 1951; Under-Secretary, HM Treasury, 1961–68; *b* 3 Feb. 1906; *s* of F. H. Bretherton, solicitor, Gloucester; *m* 1930, Jocelyn Nina Mathews (*d* 1990); three *s* one *d. Educ:* Clifton College; Wadham College, Oxford. Fellow of Wadham College, 1928–45, Lecturer and Tutor in Economics and Modern History; University Research Lecturer, 1936–39. Temporary Civil Servant, Ministry of Supply and Board of Trade, 1939–45; Under-Secretary, Raw Materials Dept, Board of Trade, 1946–48; Cabinet Office (Economic Section), 1949–51; Under-Secretary: Min. of Materials, 1951–54; Board of Trade, 1954–61; Treasury, 1961–68. *Publications:* (with R. V. Lennard and others) Englishmen at Rest and Play (17th Century Studies), 1932; (with Burchardt and Rutherford) Public Investment and the Trade Cycle, 1941; (contrib.) Moths and Butterflies of Great Britain and Ireland, vol. 9 1979, vol. 10 1983, vol. 7 1988; articles in Social Survey of Oxford, Economic Journal, Econometrica, and in various entomological journals, etc. *Recreations:* walking, mountaineering, entomology. *Address:* Folly Hill, Birtley Green, Bramley, Guildford, Surrey GU5 0LE. *T:* Guildford (0483) 893377. *Died 11 Jan. 1991.*

BRETT, Jeremy, (Peter Jeremy William Huggins); actor; *b* 3 Nov. 1935; *s* of Lt-Col H. W. Huggins, DSO, MC, DL, and late Elizabeth Huggins; *m* 1st, 1958, Anna Massey (marr. diss. 1963); one *s*; 2nd, 1978, Joan Wilson Sullivan (*d* 1985); one *s*. *Educ:* Eton; Central Sch. of Drama. National Theatre, 1967–71: Orlando, in As You Like It; Berowne, in Love's Labour's Lost; Tesman, in Hedda Gabler; Bassanio, in The Merchant of Venice; Che Guevara, in Macrune's Guevara; The Son, in Voyage round my Father, Haymarket, 1972; Otto, in Design for Living, Phoenix, 1973–74; The Way of the World, Stratford, Ont, 1976; Prospero, in The Tempest, Toronto, 1982; narrator, Martha Graham ballet, Song, New York, 1985; Willie, in Aren't We All, Broadway, 1985; title rôle in The Secret of Sherlock Holmes, Wyndham's, 1988. *Films include:* Nicholas, in War and Peace, 1955; Freddie, in My Fair Lady, 1965; *also TV appearances, including:* Max de Winter in Rebecca, 1978; George, Duke of Bristol, in On Approval, 1980; Edward Ashburnham in The Good Soldier, 1981; title rôle in Macbeth, The Last Visitor, 1982; Robert Browning in The Barretts of Wimpole Street, 1982; title rôle in William Pitt the Younger, 1983; title rôle in series (40 films): The Adventures of Sherlock Holmes, 1984, The Return of Sherlock Holmes, 1986, The Casebook of Sherlock Holmes, 1991, The Memoirs of Sherlock Holmes, 1993–94; Mr Nightingale, in Florence Nightingale; Brian Foxworth, in Deceptions, 1986; Sherlock Holmes, in The Sign of Four, 1987. *Recreation:* archery. *Address:* c/o William Morris Agency, 31 Soho Square, W1V 5DG. *Club:* Woodmen of Arden (Meriden). *Died 12 Sept. 1995.*

BREWSTER, George, CVO 1969; MD; practitioner of medicine, retired 1977; Surgeon Apothecary to HM Household at Holyrood Palace, Edinburgh, 1954–70; formerly Medical Officer to French Consulate-General in Scotland; *b* 27 Sept. 1899; *s* of James Brewster; *m* 1930, Maisie Hutchison Taylor (*d* 1976); two *s*. *Educ:* High School, Stirling; Edinburgh Univ. MB, ChB, Edin., 1921; DPH Edin., 1924; MD (with distinction) Edin., 1926. House Surgeon, Edin. Royal Infirmary. Chevalier de la Légion d'Honneur (France), 1957. *Address:* 83 Home Ross House, Mount Grange, Strathearn Road, Edinburgh EH9 2QY. *T:* 031–441 6183. *Died 18 Jan. 1991.*

BRIANT, (Bernard) Christian, CVO 1977 (MVO 1974); MBE 1945; FRICS; Consultant, Messrs Daniel Smith, Chartered Surveyors, 1982–93; Church Commissioner, 1981–89; *b* 11 April 1917; *s* of Bernard Briant and Cecily (*née* Christian); *m* 1942, Margaret Emslie, *d* of A. S. Rawle; one *s* two *d*. *Educ:* Stowe Sch.; Trinity Coll., Oxford (MA). FRICS 1948. Served War, 1939–45: Tunisia, Italy and Austria; Major, Intell. Corps (despatches). Joined Briant & Son, Chartered Surveyors, 1938, Partner 1948; Partner, Daniel Smith, 1970, Sen. Partner, 1976–82. Mem. various cttees, RICS, 1948–70 (Mem. Council, 1962–70); Clerk, Co. of Chartered Surveyors, 1980–85. Director: C of E Bldg Soc., 1953–67;

S of England Building Soc., 1967–80; London and S of England Bldg Soc., 1980–83; Anglia Bldg Soc., 1983–87; Nationwide Anglia Bldg Soc., 1987–88; Mem., Cttee of Management, Lambeth and Southwark Housing Soc., 1971–89 (Vice-Chm., 1983–86). Land Steward, Manor of Kennington of Duchy of Cornwall, 1963–76; Agent, All Souls Coll., Oxford, 1966–79. Governor, Polytechnic of South Bank, 1980–88. *Recreations:* golf, walking, reading. *Address:* 33 The Terrace, Aldeburgh, Suffolk IP15 5HJ. *Clubs:* United Oxford & Cambridge University; Aldeburgh Golf, Rye Golf. *Died 23 July 1993.*

BRICKHILL, Paul Chester Jerome; author; *b* 20 Dec. 1916; 3rd *s* of G. R. Brickhill, Sydney, Aust.; *m* 1950, Margaret Olive Slater (marr. diss. 1964), Sydney; one *s* one *d*. *Educ:* North Sydney High School; Sydney University. Journalist in Sydney, 1935–40; joined RAAF 1940: service in United Kingdom and Middle East as fighter pilot; shot down in Tunisia, 1943; POW Germany; Flight Lieut; Foreign Correspondent in Europe and USA, 1945–47; left journalism to concentrate on books, 1949. *Publications:* Escape to Danger (with Conrad Norton), 1946; The Great Escape, 1951; The Dam Busters, 1951; Escape or Die, 1952; Reach for the Sky, 1954; The Deadline, 1962. *Recreations:* reading, swimming. *Address:* c/o David Higham Associates Ltd, 5–8 Lower John Street, Golden Square, W1R 4HA.
Died 23 April 1991.

BRIDGEMAN, John Wilfred, CBE 1960; BSc London; AKC; Principal, Loughborough Training College, 1950–63, retired; Principal, Loughborough Summer School, 1931–63; *b* 25 Jan. 1895; *s* of late John Edward Bridgeman and Alice Bridgeman, Bournemouth; *m* 1st, 1928, Mary Jane Wallace (*d* 1961); one *s*; 2nd, 1963, Helen Ida Mary Wallace. *Educ:* King's College, University of London; London Day Training College. Industry, 1910–15; taught at technical colleges, Bournemouth, Bath and Weymouth, 1915–20; Asst Master, Lyme Regis Grammar School, 1923; Senior Maths Master, Wolverhampton Secondary Gram. Sch., 1926; Head of Dept for Training of Teachers, Loughborough Coll., 1930. Chm., Assoc. of Teachers in Colls and Depts of Education, 1952; Leader of Staff Panel, Pelham Cttee, 1955–63. Hon. MA Nottingham, 1961; Hon. DLitt Loughborough, 1978. *Recreations:* chess, reading. *Address:* Flat 3, Laleham Court, Woking, Surrey GU21 4AX. *T:* Woking (0483) 721523. *Died 31 Jan. 1992.*

BRIERLEY, Sir Zachry, Kt 1987; CBE 1978 (MBE 1969); Chairman, Z. Brierley Ltd, 1957–90 (Chairman and Managing Director, 1957–73); *b* 16 April 1920; *s* of late Zachry Brierley and of Nellie (*née* Ashworth); *m* 1946, Iris Macara; one *d*. *Educ:* Rydal Sch., Colwyn Bay. Served War: commnd RAF, 1941. Joined family business, Z. Brierley Ltd, 1938: Dir, 1952. Dir, Develt Corp. for Wales, 1974–77. Chairman: Small and Medium Firms Commn, Union des Industries de la Communauté Européenne, Brussels, 1975–77; Wales Adv. Cttee, Design Council, 1977–86 (Mem. Design Council, 1976–86). Member: Welsh Indust. Develt Bd, Welsh Office, 1972–82; Welsh Develt Agency, 1975–86; Bd, Civic Trust for Wales, 1976–; Cttee to Review Functioning of Financial Instns, 1977–80; Council, Machine Tool Trade Assoc., 1977–80; Bd of Governors, Llandrillo Tech. Coll., 1975–82; Bd of Governors, Penrhos Coll., 1980–. Chairman: Conservative Pol Centre (Wales), 1975–79; Conwy Cons. and Unionist Assoc., 1980–82 (also past Chm. and Vice Pres.); Wales Area Cons. Council, 1982–86 (Pres., 1986–); N Wales Business Club, 1984–. Vice Chm., North Wales Medical Centre, 1979–87. Liveryman, Basketmakers' Co., 1978–; Freeman, City of London, 1977. CBIM 1990. *Recreations:* philately, travel, reading, sketching. *Address:* West Point,

Gloddaeth Avenue, Llandudno, Gwynedd, N Wales LL30 2AN. *T:* Llandudno (0492) 76970. *Club:* Carlton.

Died 5 Feb. 1993.

BRIGGS, Sir Geoffrey (Gould), Kt 1974; President, Pensions Appeal Tribunals for England and Wales, 1980–87; Justice of Appeal, Court of Appeal of Gibraltar, 1983–88; *b* 6 May 1914; 2nd *s* of late Reverend C. E. and Mrs Briggs, Amersham, Buckinghamshire; unmarried. *Educ:* Sherborne; Christ Church, Oxford (BA, BCL; MA 1984). Called to Bar, Gray's Inn, 1938. Served War of 1939–45, County of London Yeomanry (Major). Attorney-General, E Region, Nigeria, 1954–58; QC (Nigeria), 1955; Puisne Judge, Sarawak, N Borneo and Brunei, 1958–62; Chief Justice of the Western Pacific, 1962–65; a Puisne Judge, Hong Kong, 1965–73; Chief Justice: Hong Kong, 1973–79; Brunei, 1973–79; Pres., Brunei Court of Appeal, 1979–88. DSNB 1974. FRSA 1984. *Address:* 1 Farley Court, Melbury Road, Kensington, W14 8LJ. *Club:* Wig and Pen. *Died 12 May 1993.*

BRIGINSHAW, Baron *cr* 1974 (Life Peer), of Southwark, Greater London; **Richard William Briginshaw;** General Secretary, National Society of Operative Printers, Graphical and Media Personnel, 1951–75; Member Council, Advisory, Conciliation and Arbitration Service, 1974–76; *b* Lambeth, 15 May 1908; *m* 1931, Catherine Morritt (*d* 1989); three *s*; one *s* by Kathleen Maybin; one *s* one *d* by Joan Wing. *Educ:* Stuart School, London. Later studied economics, trade union and industrial law, and physical anthropology (UCL diploma course). Elected Asst Secretary, London Machine Branch of Union, 1938. Joined Services, 1940; subseq. in Army, saw service overseas in India, Iraq, Persia, Palestine, Egypt, France, etc; left Army, 1946. Returned to printing trade; re-elected to full-time trade union position, 1949. Vice-Pres., 1961–72, Mem. Exec. Council, 1951–72, Printing and Kindred Trades Fedn; Trades Union Congress: Mem. Gen. Council, 1965–75; Member of Finance and General Purposes, Economic, Organisation, and International Cttees. Member: BOTB, 1975–77; British Nat. Oil Corp., 1976–79. Pres. of two London Confs on World Trade Development, 1963. Member: Joint Committee on Manpower, 1965–70; Parly and Scientific Cttee, 1985–; Parly Gp for Energy Studies, 1979–. Patron, Coll. of Osteopaths, 1975–. Member: Bd of Govs, Dulwich Coll., 1967–72; Court, Cranfield Inst. of Technology. Hon. LLD New Brunswick, 1968. *Publications:* (four booklets): Britain's World Rating, 1962; Britain and the World Trade Conference, 1963; Britain's World Rating, 1964; Britain's Oil, the Big Sell Out?, 1979. *Recreations:* swimming, painting, music. *Address:* House of Lords, SW1A 0PW.

Died 27 March 1992.

BRIMELOW, Baron *cr* 1976 (Life Peer), of Tyldesley, Lancs; **Thomas Brimelow,** GCMG 1975 (KCMG 1968; CMG 1959); OBE 1954; Chairman, Occupational Pensions Board, 1978–82; *b* 25 Oct. 1915; *s* of late William Brimelow and Hannah Smith; *m* 1945, Jean E. Cull (*d* 1993); two *d*. *Educ:* New Mills Grammar School; Oriel College, Oxford (Hon. Fellow, 1973). Laming Travelling Fellow of the Queen's College, Oxford, 1937, Hon. Fellow, 1974. Probationer Vice-Consul, Danzig, 1938; served in Consulate, Riga, 1939 and Consulate-Gen., New York, 1940; in charge of Consular Section of Embassy, Moscow, 1942–45; Foreign Office, 1945; Foreign Service Officer, Grade 7, 1946; First Sec. (Commercial), and Consul, Havana, 1948; transf. to Moscow, 1951; Counsellor (Commercial), Ankara, 1954; Head of Northern Department of the Foreign Office, 1956; Counsellor, Washington, 1960–63; Minister, British Embassy, Moscow, 1963–66; Ambassador to Poland, 1966–69; Dep. Under-Sec. of State, FCO, 1969–73; Permanent Under-Sec. of State, FCO, and Head of the

Diplomatic Service, 1973–75. Mem., European Parlt, 1977–78. *Address:* 12 West Hill Court, Millfield Lane, N6 6JJ. *Club:* Athenæum. *Died 2 Aug. 1995.*

BRINK, Prof. Charles Oscar, LittD Cambridge; PhD Berlin; FBA 1964; Kennedy Professor of Latin in the University of Cambridge, 1954–74, then Kennedy Professor Emeritus; Fellow of Gonville and Caius College, Cambridge, since 1955; *b* 13 March 1907; *m* 1942, Daphne Hope Harvey; three *s*. *Educ:* School and University, Berlin; Travelling Scholarship, Oxford. MA Oxford (decree, 1944); MA Cambridge (BIII 6), 1954. Member of editorial staff, Thesaurus Linguæ Latinæ, 1933–38; Member of editorial staff, Oxford Latin Dictionary, 1938–41; Acting Classical Tutor, Magdalen College, Oxford, 1941–45; Member of Faculty of Literæ Humaniores, Oxford, 1941–48; Senior Classics Master, Magdalen College School, Oxford, 1943–48; Senior Lecturer in Humanity, University of St Andrews, 1948–51; Professor of Latin, University of Liverpool, 1951–54. Member Inst. for Advanced Study, Princeton, US, 1960–61, 1966. De Carle Lecturer, University of Otago, NZ, 1965; Vis. Prof., Univ. of Bonn, 1970; Professore Ospite Linceo, Scuola Normale Superiore, Pisa, 1977; James C. Loeb Lectr, Harvard Univ., 1978; Woodward Lectr, Yale Univ., 1989. Hon. Member, Jt Assoc. of Classical Teachers (Pres. 1969–71). Chm., Classics Committee, Schools Council, 1965–69; Trustee, Robinson Coll., Cambridge, 1973–85 (Chm., 1975–85; Hon. Fellow, 1985–). Pres., Internat. Commn, Thesaurus Linguæ Latinæ, 1988– (Vice-Pres., 1979–88). Corresp. Mem., Bayerische Akad. der Wissenschaften, Munich, 1972–. Founding Jt Editor, Cambridge Classical Texts and Commentaries, 1963–87. *Publications:* Imagination and Imitation (Inaug. Lect., Liverpool, 1952), 1953; Latin Studies and the Humanities (Inaug. Lect., Cambridge, 1956), 1957; On reading a Horatian Satire, 1965; Horace on Poetry: vol. I, Prolegomena, 1963; vol. II, The Ars Poetica, 1971; vol III, Epistles Book II, 1982; Studi classici e critica testuale in Inghilterra (Pisa), 1978; English Classical Scholarship: historical reflections on Bentley, Porson, and Housman, 1986; papers on Latin and Greek subjects. *Address:* Gonville and Caius College, Cambridge CB2 1TA. *Died 2 March 1994.*

BRISCO, Sir Donald Gilfrid, 8th Bt *cr* 1782; JP; *b* 15 Sept. 1920; *s* of Sir Hylton (Musgrave Campbell) Brisco, 7th Bt and Kathleen (*d* 1982), *d* of W. Fenwick McAllum, New Zealand; *S* father, 1968; *m* 1945, Irene, *o d* of Henry John Gage, Ermine Park, Brockworth, Gloucestershire; three *d*. Served War of 1939–45 with Royal New Zealand Air Force and Royal Air Force (prisoner of war in Germany and Italy). Retired farmer. JP Hawke's Bay, 1967. *Heir:* cousin Campbell Howard Brisco [*b* 1944; *m* 1969, Kay Janette, *d* of Ewan W. McFadzien; two *s* one *d*]. *Address:* 27a Chambers Street, PO Box 8165, Havelock North, Hawke's Bay, New Zealand. *Died 24 June 1995.*

BRISCOE, Sir (John) James, 5th Bt *cr* 1910, of Bourn Hall, Bourn, Co. Cambridge; FCA; Partner, Newman Sumpter & Co., Chartered Accountants, since 1989; *b* 15 July 1951; *s* of Sir John Leigh Charlton Briscoe, 4th Bt, DFC, MA, FCIT and of Teresa Mary Violet Briscoe (*née* Home), OBE; *S* father, 1993; *m* 1985, Felicity Mary, *e d* of D. M. Watkinson, Norfolk; one *d*. *Educ:* Oratory Sch., Woodcote; University College, London. FCA 1988 (ACA 1978). Manager: Knox Cropper, Chartered Accountants, 1973–79; Peat Marwick Mitchell & Co., London, 1979–82; Chief Accountant, Otis Pressure Control Ltd, 1982–87; Manager, Beavis Walker, Chartered Accountants, London, 1987–89. *Recreations:* shooting, vintage cars, ocean racing. *Heir:* *b* Edward Home Briscoe [*b* 27 March 1955; *m* 1979, Anne Lister (marr. diss. 1989); one *s* one *d*]. *Address:* Hall Barn, Swainsthorpe, Norwich,

Norfolk NR14 8QA. *T:* Swainsthorpe (0508) 471310. *Clubs:* Royal Ocean Racing; Norfolk (Norwich).
Died 3 July 1994.

BRISCOE, Sir John (Leigh Charlton), 4th Bt *cr* 1910, of Bourn Hall, Bourn, Co. Cambridge; DFC 1945; *b* 3 Dec. 1911; *er s* of Sir Charlton Briscoe, 3rd Bt, MD, FRCP, and Grace Maud (*d* 1973), *d* of late Rev. W. S. Stagg; *S* father 1960; *m* 1948, Teresa Mary Violet, OBE 1972, *d* of late Brig.-Gen. Sir Archibald Home, KCVO, CB, CMG, DSO; two *s* one *d. Educ:* Harrow; Magdalen College, Oxford. BA 1933; ACA 1937; MA 1949. Served War of 1939–45 (DFC): RAFVR, 1942–46. Director of Aerodromes, Ministry of Aviation, 1961–66; Dir of Operations, British Airports Authy, 1966–72. *Recreations:* old cars, castles, carpets. *Heir: s* John James Briscoe [*b* 15 July 1951; *m* 1985, Felicity Mary, *e d* of D. M. Watkinson]. *Address:* Little Acres, Grays Park Road, Stoke Poges, Bucks. *T:* Farnham Common (02814) 2394. *Club:* Royal Air Force.
Died 7 Feb. 1993.

BRITTEN, Maj.-Gen. Robert Wallace Tudor, CB 1977; MC; *b* 28 Feb. 1922; *s* of Lt-Col Wallace Ernest Britten, OBE; *m* 1947, Elizabeth Mary, (Jane), *d* of Edward H. Davies, Pentre, Rhondda; one *s* one *d. Educ:* Wellington Coll.; Trinity Coll., Cambridge. CIMgt; CompICE. 2nd Lieut RE, 1941; served War of 1939–45, Madras Sappers and Miners, 19th Indian Div., India and Burma; Comdr 21 Fd Pk Sqn and 5 Fd Sqn RE, 1947–50; on staff WO, 1951–53; British Liaison Officer to US Corps of Engrs, 1953–56; comd 50 Fd Sqn RE, 1956–58; on staff WO, 1958–61; on staff of 1 (BR) Corps BAOR, 1961–64; Lt-Col in comd 1 Trg Regt RE, 1964–65; GSO1 (DS), Jt Services Staff Coll., 1965–67; Comd 30 Engr Bde (V) and Chief Engr Western Comd, 1967; idc 1969; Dir of Equipment Management, MoD (Army), 1970–71; DQMG, 1971–73; GOC West Midland Dist, 1973–76, retired. Brig. 1967; Maj.-Gen. 1971. Col Comdt, RE, 1977–82. Chm., RE Assoc., 1978–83. Hon. Col, Birmingham Univ. OTC, 1978–87. *Recreations:* bridge building, fishing, dowsing (Vice Pres., Brit. Soc. Dowsers). *T:* Haslemere (01428) 642261. *Club:* Army and Navy.
Died 11 July 1995.

BROADBENT, Donald Eric, CBE 1974; MA, ScD; FRS 1968; External Staff, Medical Research Council, 1974–91, retired; *b* 6 May 1926; *s* of Herbert Arthur Broadbent and Hannah Elizabeth (*née* Williams); *m* 1st, 1949, Margaret Elizabeth Wright; one *d* (and one *d* decd); 2nd, 1972, Margaret Hope Pattison Gregory. *Educ:* Winchester College; Pembroke College, Cambridge. RAF Engrg short course, 1st cl., 1944; Moral Science Tripos (Psychology), 1st cl., 1949. Scientific Staff, Applied Psychology Res. Unit, 1949–58 (Dir, 1958–74). Fellow, Pembroke College, Cambridge, 1965–74; Vis. Fellow, All Souls College, Oxford, 1967–68; Fellow, Wolfson Coll., Oxford, 1974–91, then Emeritus Fellow. Mem., SSRC, 1973–75; Chm., ESRC/MRC/SERC Initiative on Cognitive Science, 1987–91; Mem., Adv. Cttee on Safety of Nuclear Installations, 1987–. Pres., Sect. J, BAAS, 1967; Fellow, Acoustical Soc. of Amer.; past or present Council Member: Royal Soc.; British Acoustical Soc.; British Psychol Soc. (Pres., 1965); Ergonomics Res. Soc.; Experimental Psychology Soc.; Fellow, Human Factors Soc.; For. Associate, US Nat. Acad. Sci., 1971; Hon. FFOM 1982; Hon. FRCPsych 1985. Hon. DSc: Southampton, 1974; York, 1979; Loughborough, 1982; City, 1983; Brussels, 1985; Cranfield, Wales, 1991; Leuven, Dundee, 1992; Sussex, 1993. APA Dist. Scientist Award, 1975. *Publications:* Perception and Communication, 1958; Behaviour, 1961; Decision and Stress, 1971; In Defence of Empirical Psychology, 1973; many papers in jls of above societies and of Amer. Psychol Assoc. *Recreations:* reading, camping, photography. *Address:* c/o Department

of Experimental Psychology, South Parks Road, Oxford OX1 3UD.
Died 10 April 1993.

BROADBENT, Sir Ewen, KCB 1984 (CB 1973); CMG 1965; Chairman, International Military Services Ltd, since 1991; *b* 9 Aug. 1924; *s* of late Rev. W. Broadbent and of Mrs Mary Broadbent; *m* 1951, Squadron Officer Barbara David, *d* of F. A. David, Weston-super-Mare; one *s. Educ:* King Edward VI School, Nuneaton; St John's College, Cambridge. Served with Gordon Highlanders, 1943–47 (Captain); Cambridge, 1942–43 and 1947–49; Air Ministry, 1949; Private Sec. to Secretary of State for Air, 1955–59; Asst Secretary, 1959; Dep. Chief Officer, Sovereign Base Areas, Cyprus, 1961, Chief Officer, 1964; Ministry of Defence, 1965–84: Private Sec. to Sec. of State for Defence, 1967–68; Asst Under-Sec. of State, 1969–72; Dep. Under-Sec. of State (Air), 1972–75; Dep. Under-Sec. of State (Civilian Management), 1975–82; Second Perm. Under-Sec. of State, 1982–84. Trustee, RAF Mus., 1985–. Chairman: Look Ahead Housing Assoc., 1988–; Council for Voluntary Welfare Work, 1989–. Vice-Chm. Council, RUSI, 1990–. Trustee, Maxwell Pensioner Trust, 1992–. *Publication:* The Military and Government, from Macmillan to Heseltine, 1988. *Recreation:* golf. *Address:* 18 Park Hill, Ealing, W5 2JN. *T:* 081–997 1978. *Clubs:* Commonwealth Trust, Army and Navy.
Died 27 Feb. 1993.

BROADBENT, Sir George (Walter), 4th Bt *cr* 1893, of Brook Street, co. London and Longwood, co. Yorkshire; AFC 1979; Squadron Leader, Royal Air Force; *b* 23 April 1935; *s* of John Graham Monroe Broadbent (*d* 1967) (*g s* of 1st Bt) and Elizabeth Mary Beatrice Broadbent (*née* Dendy) (*d* 1976); *S* cousin, 1987; *m* 1962, Valerie Anne, *o d* of Cecil Frank Ward; one *s* one *d. Educ:* Stamford School. Joined RAF, 1954. *Recreations:* walking, music. *Heir: s* Andrew George Broadbent, Captain 1 PWO, *b* 26 Jan. 1963. *Address:* 98 Heworth Green, York YO3 7TQ.
Died 20 May 1992.

BROADHURST, Air Chief Marshal Sir Harry, GCB 1960 (KCB 1955; CB 1944); KBE 1945; DSO and Bar, 1941; DFC 1940, and Bar, 1942; AFC 1937; Managing Director, A. V. Roe & Co. Ltd, 1961–66; Director, 1961–76, Deputy Managing Director 1965–76, Hawker Siddeley Aviation Ltd; Director, Hawker Siddeley Group Ltd, 1968–76; *b* 28 Oct. 1905; *s* of Capt. Harry Broadhurst; *m* 1st, 1929, Doris Kathleen French (marr. diss. 1945); one *d*; 2nd, 1946, Jean Elizabeth Townley; one *d.* Joined RAF, 1926; served with: No 11 (B) Sqdn, UK, 1926–28, India, 1928–31; 41 (F) Sqdn, 1932–33; 19 (F) Sqdn, 1933–36; Chief Instr, No 4 FTS, Egypt, 1937; RAF Staff Coll., 1938; served War: OC No 111 (F) Sqdn, 1939–40; Wing Comdr Trng No 11 (F) Gp, Jan.–May 1940; OC No 60 (F) Wing, France, May 1940; OC Fighter Sector, Wittering, June–Dec. 1940, Hornchurch, 1940–42; Dep. SASO No 11 (F) Gp, May–Oct. 1942; SASO and AOC Western Desert, 1942–43; 83 Group Commander Allied Expeditionary Air Force, 1944–45; AO i/c Admin Fighter Command, 1945–46; AOC 61 Group, 1947–48; idc 1949; SASO, BAFO (later 2nd TAF), Germany, 1950–51; ACAS (Ops), 1952–53; C-in-C 2nd Tactical Air Force, Germany, 1954–56; Air Officer Commanding-in-Chief, Bomber Command, Jan. 1956–May 1959; Comdr Allied Air Forces, Central Europe, 1959–61. Vice-Pres., 1973–74, Pres., 1974–75, Dep. Pres., 1975–76, SBAC. Kt Grand Cross of Order of Orange Nassau, 1948; Legion of Merit (US). *Address:* Lock's End House, Birdham, Chichester, W Sussex PO20 7BB. *T:* Birdham (01243) 512717. *Club:* Royal Air Force.
Died 29 Aug. 1995.

BROCK, Arthur Guy C.; *see* Clutton-Brock.

BROCKBANK, (James) Tyrrell; solicitor; Vice Lord-Lieutenant of Durham, since 1990; *b* 14 Dec. 1920; *y s* of late James Lindow Brockbank; *m* 1950, Pamela, *yr d* of late Lt-Col J. Oxley Parker, TD, and Mary Monica (*née* Hills); four *s. Educ:* St Peter's Sch., York; St John's Coll., Cambridge (MA). Served War of 1939–45 with Sherwood Foresters and Inns of Court Regt. Asst Solicitor, Wolverhampton, 1949–51; Asst Clerk, Hertfordshire, 1951–54; Dep. Clerk, Nottinghamshire, 1954–61; Clerk of the Peace, Durham, 1961–71; Clerk of Durham CC, 1961–74; Clerk to the Lieutenancy, 1964–88; DL 1970, High Sheriff, 1989, Durham. Member, Local Govt Boundary Commn for England, 1976–85. *Recreations:* fishing, shooting, golf. *Address:* The Old Post Office, Shincliffe Village, Durham DH1 2NN. *T:* 0191–386 5569. *Clubs:* Travellers'; Durham County (Durham).
Died 24 Dec. 1995.

BROCKLEHURST, Robert James, DM; Emeritus Professor of Physiology, University of Bristol, since 1965; *b* Liverpool, 16 Sept. 1899; *e s* of George and Sarah Huger Brocklehurst, Liverpool; *m* 1st, 1928, Sybille (*d* 1968), *y d* of Captain R. H. L. Risk, CBE, RN; two *s* one *d*; 2nd, 1970, Dora Millicent (*d* 1986), *y d* of late Alexander Watts. *Educ:* Harrow Sch.; University College, Oxford (Scholar; 1st Class Honours in Physiology); St Bartholomew's Hospital. BA 1921; MA, BM, BCh, 1924; DM, 1928; MRCS, LRCP, 1925; Demonstrator of Physiology, St Bartholomew's Hosp. Medical Coll., 1925–26; Radcliffe Travelling Fellow, 1926–28; Lecturer, 1928–29, and Senior Lecturer, 1929–30, in Dept of Physiology and Biochemistry, Univ. Coll., London; Prof. of Physiology, 1930–65, and Dean of Med. Fac., 1934–47, Univ. of Bristol, and Univ. Rep. on GMC, 1935–65 (Jt Treas., 1962–65); Long Fox Meml Lectr, 1952; Mem. Inter-departmental Cttee on Dentistry, 1943; Mem. Dental Bd of UK, 1945–56; Additional Mem., GDC, 1956–65; Pres., Bath, Bristol and Somerset Branch, BMA 1959; Fellow BMA, 1967; Pres. Bristol Medico-Chirurgical Society, 1960; Member Council, 1958–63, and President Sect. I (Physiology), 1950, British Association; Mem., S-W Regional Hosp. Bd, and Bd of Govs of United Bristol Hosps, 1947–66; Chm, Moorhaven Hosp. Management Cttee, 1966–71; a representative of Diocese of Bristol in the Church Assembly, 1945–65; Member, Central Board of Finance, 1957–65; Chm., Bristol Diocesan Bd of Finance, 1951–65. Mem., Council Westonbirt School, 1955–75 (Chm., 1956–68); Member Council, Christ Church College, Canterbury, 1961–73; Churchwarden, St Mary's, Stoke Bishop, 1939–60; a Vice-President Gloucester and Bristol Diocesan Association of Church Bell Ringers. Chm., Glos, Somerset and N Devon Regional Group, YHA, 1934–45. Served in Tank Corps, 1918–19. *Publications:* papers on physiological, biochemical and educational subjects in medical and scientific jls. *Recreation:* gardening. *Address:* Cleeve, Court Road, Newton Ferrers, Plymouth, Devon PL8 1DE. *T:* Plymouth (01752) 872397. *Clubs:* Alpine, Commonwealth Trust, Royal Over-Seas League.
Died 21 Oct. 1995.

BROCKMAN, Hon. Sir Thomas Charles D.; *see* Drake-Brockman.

BRODIE, Maj.-Gen. Thomas, CB 1954; CBE 1949; DSO 1951; late The Cheshire Regiment; *b* 20 Oct. 1903; *s* of Thomas Brodie, Bellingham, Northumberland; *m* 1938, Jane Margaret Chapman-Walker (*d* 1992); three *s* one *d. Educ:* Durham Univ. (BA 1924). Adjutant, The Cheshire Regt, 1935–37; Instructor, RMA Sandhurst, 1938–39; commanded: 2 Manchester Regt, 1942–43; 14th Infantry Brigade in Wingate Expedition, Burma, 1944; 1 Cheshire Regt, 1946–47; Palestine, 1947–48 (CBE and despatches); commanded 29 Inf. Bde, Korea, 1951 (DSO, US Silver Star Medal, US Legion of Merit); GOC 1 Infantry Div.,

MELF, 1952–55; Colonel, The Cheshire Regiment, 1955–61; retired 1957. Economic League, 1957–84. *Address:* Frith Common Farm, Wolverton, Basingstoke, Hants RG26 5RX. *Club:* Army and Navy.
Died 1 Sept. 1993.

BRODRICK, His Honour Norman John Lee, QC 1960; JP; MA; a Circuit Judge (formerly a Judge of the Central Criminal Court), 1967–82; *b* 4 Feb. 1912; 4th *s* of late William John Henry Brodrick, OBE; *m* 1940, Ruth Severn, *d* of late Sir Stanley Unwin, KCMG; three *s* one *d. Educ:* Charterhouse; Merton College, Oxford. Called to Bar, Lincoln's Inn, 1935, Bencher, 1965; Western Circuit, 1935; Temporary Civil Servant (Ministry of Economic Warfare and Admiralty), 1939–45; Recorder: of Penzance, 1957–59; of Bridgwater, 1959–62; of Plymouth, 1962–64; Chairman, Mental Health Review Tribunal, Wessex Region, 1960–63; Deputy Chairman, Middlesex Quarter Sessions, 1961–65; Recorder of Portsmouth, 1964–67; Chm., IoW QS, 1964–67, Dep. Chm. 1967–71. Chm., Deptl Cttee on Death Certification and Coroners, 1965–71. Member: Bar Council, 1950–54, 1962–66; Senate of Four Inns of Court, 1970–71. JP Hants, 1967. *Recreations:* gardening, model railways. *Address:* Slade Lane Cottage, Rogate, near Petersfield, Hants GU31 5BL. *T:* Rogate (0730) 821605.
Died 27 June 1992.

BROGAN, Lt-Gen. Sir Mervyn (Francis), KBE 1972 (CBE 1964; OBE 1944); CB 1970; Chief of the General Staff, Australia, 1971–73, retired; *b* 10 Jan. 1915; *s* of Bernard Brogan, Dubbo, NSW; *m* 1941, Sheila, *d* of David S. Jones, Canberra; two *s. Educ:* RMC Duntroon (Sword of Honour, 1935); Wesley Coll., Univ. of Sydney. Commnd 1935; BEng Sydney, 1938. Served War of 1939–45: New Guinea, 1942–45 (despatches 1943); trng UK and BAOR, 1946–47; Chief Instructor, Sch. of Mil. Engrg, 1947–49; trng UK and USA, 1950–52; jssc 1952; Chief Engr, Southern Comd, 1953–54; Dir of Mil. Trng, 1954–55; BGS: Army HQ, 1956; FARELF, 1956–58; idc 1959; Comdt Australian Staff Coll., 1960–62; GOC Northern Comd, 1962–64; Dir Jt Service Plans, Dept of Defence, 1965–66; QMG, 1966–68; GOC Eastern Comd, 1968–71. Hon. FIEAust; CPEng. JP. *Recreations:* surfing, tennis. *Address:* 71/53 Ocean Avenue, Double Bay, NSW 2028, Australia. *T:* 3639509. *Clubs:* Union, Australian Jockey, Tattersall's, Royal Sydney Golf, City Tattersall's, Australasian Pioneers (Sydney).
Died 8 March 1994.

BROOK, William Edward; British Council Officer, retired; *b* 18 Jan. 1922; *s* of William Stafford Brook and Dorothy Mary (*née* Thompson); *m* 1950, Rene Dorothy Drew; two *s* one *d. Educ:* Highgate Sch.; St Edmund Hall, Oxford (BA Mod. Langs, 1949; MA 1953). Served RAF, 1940–46: Africa, ME and Italy. Apptd to British Council, 1949; Lectr, Salonika, 1949–51; Asst Dir, Northern Provinces, Nigeria, 1951–56; Lecturer: Kuwait, 1956–59; Tripoli, Libya, 1959–62; Regional Director: Moshi, Tanganyika, 1962–67; Frankfurt, W Germany, 1967–72; Rep., Bahrain (with Qatar, UAE and Oman), 1972–76; Dir, Overseas Educnl Appts Dept, 1976; Controller, Appts Div., 1977–79; Representative, Canada, and Counsellor (Cultural), Ottawa, 1979; retd 1982. *Recreations:* music, gardening, bird-watching. *Address:* Clarke's Cottage, Rimpton, near Yeovil, Somerset BA22 8AD. *T:* Marston Magna (0935) 850828.
Died 18 April 1993.

BROOKS, Prof. Cleanth; Gray Professor of Rhetoric, Yale University, USA, 1947–75, then Emeritus Professor; *b* 16 Oct. 1906; *s* of Rev. Cleanth and Bessie Lee Witherspoon Brooks; *m* 1934, Edith Amy Blanchard (*d* 1986); no *c. Educ:* The McTyeire School; Vanderbilt, Tulane and Oxford Universities. Rhodes Scholar, Louisiana and Exeter, 1929; Lecturer, later Prof., Louisiana State Univ.,

1932–47; Prof. of English, later Gray Prof. of Rhetoric, Yale Univ., 1947–75. Visiting Professor: Univ. of Texas; Univ. of Michigan; Univ. of Chicago; Univ. of Southern California; Bread Loaf School of English; Univ. of South Carolina, 1975; Tulane Univ., 1976; Univ. of North Carolina, 1977; Univ. of Tennessee, 1978. Cultural Attaché at the American Embassy, London, 1964–66. Managing Editor and Editor (with Robert Penn Warren), The Southern Review, 1935–42. Fellow, Library of Congress, 1953–63; Guggenheim Fellow, 1953 and 1960; Sen. Fellow, Nat. Endowment for the Humanities, 1975; Mellon Fellow, Nat. Humanities Center, 1980–81. Mem. Council of Scholars, Library of Congress, 1986–88. Member: Amer. Acad. of Arts and Scis; Amer. Acad. of Arts and Letters; Amer. Philos. Soc.; RSL. Lamar Lectr, 1984; Jefferson Lectr, Nat. Endowment for the Humanities, 1985. Hon. DLitt: Upsala Coll., 1963; Kentucky, 1963; Exeter, 1966; Washington and Lee, 1968; Tulane, 1969; Univ. of the South, 1974; Newberry Coll., 1979; Adelphi Univ., 1992; Hon. LHD: St Louis, 1968; Centenary Coll., 1972; Oglethorpe Univ., 1976; St Peter's Coll., 1978; Lehigh Univ., 1980; Millsaps Coll., 1983; Univ. of New Haven, 1984; Univ. of S Carolina, 1984; Indiana State Univ., 1992. *Publications:* Modern Poetry and the Tradition, 1939; (ed) Thomas Percy and Richard Farmer, 1946; The Well Wrought Urn, 1947; (with R. P. Warren) Understanding Poetry, 1938; (with R. P. Warren) Modern Rhetoric, 1950; (with W. K. Wimsatt, Jr) Literary Criticism: A Short History, 1957; The Hidden God, 1963; William Faulkner: The Yoknapatawpha Country, 1963; A Shaping Joy, 1971; (with R. W. B. Lewis and R. P. Warren) American Literature: the Makers and the Making, 1973; (ed) Thomas Percy and William Shenstone, 1977; William Faulkner: Toward Yoknapatawpha and Beyond, 1978; William Faulkner: First Encounters, 1983; The Language of the American South, 1985; On the Prejudices, Predilections, and Firm Beliefs of William Faulkner, 1987; Historical Evidence and the Reading of Seventeenth-Century Poetry, 1991; (Gen. Editor, with David N. Smith and A. F. Falconer) The Percy Letters, 1942–; contrib. articles, reviews to literary magazines, journals. *Address:* 70 Ogden Street, New Haven, Conn 06511, USA. *Club:* Athenæum. *Died 10 May 1994.*

BROOKS, William Donald Wykeham, CBE 1956; MA, DM (Oxon); FRCP; retired; Consulting Physician: St Mary's Hospital; Brompton Hospital; to the Royal Navy; to the King Edward VII Convalescent Home for Officers, Osborne; Chief Medical Officer, Eagle Star Insurance Co.; *b* 3 Aug. 1905; *er s* of A. E. Brooks, MA (Oxon), Maidenhead, Berks; *m* 1934, Phyllis Kathleen, *e d* of late F. A. Juler, CVO; two *s* two *d. Educ:* Reading School; St John's College, Oxford (White Scholar); St Mary's Hospital, London (University Scholar); Strong Memorial Hospital, Rochester, New York. First Class Honours, Final Honour School of Physiology, 1928; Cheadle Gold Medallist, St Mary's Hosp., 1931. Fereday Fellow St John's College, Oxford, 1931–34; Rockefeller Travelling Fellow, 1932–33. Royal College of Physicians: Asst Registrar, 1946–50; Censor, 1961–; Mem. Council, 1959–61; Senior Vice-President and Senior Censor, 1965; Goulstonian Lectr, 1940; Marc Daniels Lectr, 1957. Member Association of Physicians of Great Britain and Ireland. Served War 1940–45 as Surgeon Captain, RNVR. Editor, Quarterly Jl of Medicine, 1946–67. *Publications:* sections on Chest Wounds, Respiratory Diseases and Tuberculosis, in Conybeare's Textbook of Medicine; Respiratory Diseases section in the Official Naval Medical History of the War; numerous articles on general medical topics and on chest diseases in various medical journals. *Recreations:* golf, shooting, gardening, bridge. *Address:*

Two Acres, Fryern Road, Storrington, W Sussex RH20 4NT. *T:* Storrington (0903) 742159.
Died 28 May 1993.

BROOMHALL, Maj.-Gen. William Maurice, CB 1950; DSO 1945; OBE 1932; *b* 16 July 1897; *o s* of late Alfred Edward Broomhall, London, and Florence Mary (*née* Chalk). *Educ:* St Paul's School; Royal Military Academy, Woolwich. Commissioned Royal Engineers, 1915; France and Belgium, 1914–21 (wounded twice); Waziristan, 1921–24 (medal and clasp); NW Frontier of India, 1929–31 (despatches, clasp, OBE); Staff College, Camberley, 1932–33; served North-West Europe, 1939–45 (despatches, DSO); Chief Engineer, Allied Forces, Italy, 1946; Chief Engineer, British Army of the Rhine, 1947–48; Chief Engineer, Middle East Land Forces, 1948–51; retired, 1951. Pres., Colditz Assoc., 1993. *Address:* The Cottage, Park Lane, Beaconsfield, Bucks HP9 2HR. *Club:* Army and Navy. *Died 13 Jan. 1996.*

BROPHY, Brigid (Antonia), (Lady Levey), FRSL; author and playwright; *b* 12 June 1929; *o c* of late John Brophy; *m* 1954, Sir Michael Levey, LVO, FBA; one *d. Educ:* St Paul's Girls' Sch.; St Hugh's Coll., Oxford. Awarded Jubilee Scholarship at St Hugh's Coll., Oxford, 1947 and read classics. Co-organiser, Writers Action Gp campaign for Public Lending Right, 1972–82; Exec. Councillor, Writers' Guild of GB, 1975–78; a Vice-Chm., British Copyright Council, 1976–80. A Vice-Pres., Nat. Anti-Vivisection Soc., 1974–. Awarded Cheltenham Literary Festival First Prize for a first novel, 1954; London Magazine Prize for Prose, 1962. *Publications: fiction:* Hackenfeller's Ape, 1953, new edn 1992; The King of a Rainy Country, 1956, new edn 1990; Flesh, 1962; The Finishing Touch, 1963; The Snow Ball, 1964; In Transit, 1969; The Adventures of God in his Search for the Black Girl, and other fables, 1973; Pussy Owl, 1976; Palace Without Chairs, 1978; *non-fiction:* Black Ship to Hell, 1962; Mozart the Dramatist, 1964, 2nd edn 1988; Don't Never Forget, 1966; (with Michael Levey and Charles Osborne) Fifty Works of English Literature We Could Do Without, 1967; Black and White: a portrait of Aubrey Beardsley, 1968; Prancing Novelist, 1973; Beardsley and his World, 1976; The Prince and the Wild Geese, 1983; A Guide to Public Lending Right, 1983; Baroque 'n' Roll, 1987; Reads, 1989; *plays:* The Burglar, Vaudeville, 1967 (published with preface, 1968); The Waste Disposal Unit, Radio (published 1968); *visual art:* (with Maureen Duffy) Prop Art exhibn, London, 1969. *Address:* Fir Close, 2 Westgate, Louth, Lincolnshire LN11 9YH.
Died 7 Aug. 1995.

BROUGHSHANE, 2nd Baron (UK), *cr* 1945; **Patrick Owen Alexander Davison;** *b* 18 June 1903; *er s* of 1st Baron and Beatrice Mary, *d* of Sir Owen Roberts; *S* father, 1953; *m* 1929, Bettine (*d* 1994), *d* of Sir Arthur Russell, 6th Bt; (one *s* decd). *Educ:* Winchester; Magdalen College, Oxford. Barrister, Inner Temple, 1926. Served War of 1939–45: with Irish Guards, 1939–41; Assistant Secretary (Military), War Cabinet, 1942–45. Has US Legion of Merit. *Heir: b* Hon. (William) Kensington Davison, DSO, DFC, *b* 25 Nov. 1914. *Address:* 28 Fisher Street, Sandwich, Kent CT13 9EJ. *Club:* White's.
Died 22 Sept. 1995.

BROUGHTON, Major Sir Evelyn Delves, 12th Bt *cr* 1660, of Broughton, Staffordshire; *b* 2 Oct. 1915; *s* of Major Sir Henry Delves Broughton, 11th Bt, and Vera Edyth Boscawen (*d* 1968); *S* father, 1942; *m* 1st, 1947, Hon. Elizabeth Florence Marion Cholmondeley (marr. diss. 1953; she *d* 1988), *er d* of 4th Baron Delamere; 2nd, 1955, Helen Mary (marr. diss. 1974), *d* of J. Shore, Wilmslow, Cheshire; three *d* (one *s* decd); 3rd, 1974, Mrs Rona Crammond. *Educ:* Eton; Trinity Coll., Cambridge. Formerly 2nd Lieut Irish Guards and Major RASC. *Heir*

presumptive: kinsman David Delves Broughton [*b* 7 May 1942; *m* 1969, Diane, *d* of R. L. Nicol]. *Address:* 37 Kensington Square, W8 5HP. *T:* 071–937 8883; Doddington, Nantwich, Cheshire. *T:* Nantwich (0270) 841258. *Clubs:* Brooks's, White's; Tarporley Hunt.
Died 5 Jan. 1993.

BROWN, (Albert) Peter (Graeme); Consultant in Press and Public Relations to the Imperial Cancer Research Fund, 1978–83; Press Officer to Royal Commission on National Health Service, 1979; *b* 5 April 1913; *s* of William Edward Graeme Brown, accountant, and Amy Powell Brown; unmarried. *Educ:* Queen Elizabeth's Sch., Darlington. Reporter, Sub-Editor, Dep. Chief Sub-Editor, Westminster Press, 1932–40. Served War of 1939–45: Royal Navy, Officer, Western Approaches; Normandy; Far East; destroyers and assault ships. Information Divs, Ministries of Health, Local Govt and Planning, also Housing and Local Govt, 1946; Chief Press and Inf. Officer, Min. of Housing and Local Govt, 1958; Dir of Information, DHSS, and Advr to Sec. of State for Social Services, 1968–77. *Recreations:* cricket, opera (Mem., Friends of Covent Garden), classical music, art (Mem., Friends of Royal Academy). *Address:* 107 Hamilton Terrace, St John's Wood, NW8. *T:* 071–286 9192. *Club:* MCC. *Died 21 May 1993.*

BROWN, Arthur Godfrey Kilner, MA; Headmaster, Worcester Royal Grammar School, 1950–78; *b* 21 Feb. 1915; *s* of Rev. Arthur E. Brown, CIE, MA, BSc, and Mrs E. G. Brown, MA, formerly of Bankura, India; *m* 1939, Mary Denholm Armstrong (*d* 1993); one *s* three *d. Educ:* Warwick Sch.; Peterhouse, Cambridge. BA Cantab 1938; MA 1950. Assistant Master, Bedford School, 1938–39; King's School, Rochester, 1939–43; Cheltenham College, 1943–50. Elected to Headmasters' Conference, 1950. Founder Mem., Worcester Civic Soc. (Chm., 1960–66); Foundn Trustee, Swan Theatre, Worcester (Chm., 1965–70 and 1977–82); Pres., Worcester Rotary Club, 1975. *Recreations:* athletics (Silver Medal, 400 metres, and Gold Medal, 1,600 metres relay, Olympic Games, 1936; Gold Medal, 400 metres, World Student Games, 1937, and European Championships, 1938); music, gardening, house maintenance, following sport, walking. *Address:* Palmer's Cottage, Coneyhurst, near Billingshurst, West Sussex RH14 9DN. *Clubs:* Achilles; Hawks (Cambridge) (Pres., 1937); Probus (Horsham Weald).
Died 4 Feb. 1995.

BROWN, Sir David, Kt 1968; Chairman, David Brown Holdings Ltd, and Vosper Ltd, until going to live abroad in 1978; *b* 10 May 1904; *s* of Francis Edwin, (Frank), and Caroline Brown; *m* 1st, 1926, Daisie Muriel Firth (marr. diss. 1955); one *s* one *d*; 2nd, 1955, Marjorie Deans (marr. diss. 1980); 3rd, 1980, Paula Benton Stone. *Educ:* Rossall School; private tutor in engineering; Huddersfield Technical Coll. FIMechE. Apprentice, David Brown and Sons (Huddersfield), Ltd, 1921; Dir, 1929; Man. Dir, 1932; founded David Brown Tractors Ltd (first company to manufacture an all-British tractor in England), 1935; Chm., Aston Martin Lagonda Ltd, 1946–72; formed, 1951, The David Brown Corp. Ltd (Chm.), embracing gears, machine tools, castings, etc; Pres., Vosper Ltd, and Chm., Vosper Private Ltd, Singapore, 1978–86; Director: David Brown Corp. of Australia Ltd, 1965–; David Brown Gear Industries Pty Ltd (Australia), 1963–; David Brown Gear Industries (Pty) Ltd (South Africa), 1969–. Past Member: Board of Governors of Huddersfield Royal Infirmary; Council of Huddersfield Chamber of Commerce. Life Governor, RASE. First Englishman to open Canadian Farm and Industrial Equipment Trade Show, Toronto, 1959; inaugurated Chief Flying Sun of Iroquois Tribe of Mohawk Nation, Toronto, 1959. Hon. Dato SPMJ (Johore), 1978. *Address:* L'Estoril, 31 Avenue Princesse

Grace, Monte Carlo, MC 98000, Monaco. *Clubs:* Guards Polo (Life Mem.); International des Anciens Pilotes de Grand Prix (Bergamo); Monte Carlo Country (Roquebrune-Cap-Martin); Monaco Yacht, Monaco Automobile. *Died 3 Sept. 1993.*

BROWN, Sir Edward (Joseph), Kt 1961; MBE 1958; JP; laboratory technician (non-ferrous metals); company director; *b* 15 April 1913; *s* of Edward Brown; *m* 1940, Rosa, *d* of Samuel Feldman; one *s* one *d. Educ:* Greencoat Elementary; Morley College (Day Continuation). Leading Aircraftsman, RAF, 1942–46. Formerly Mem. Assoc. Supervisory Staffs Executives and Technicians (Chm., Enfield Branch, 1953–63); Dist Councillor for Union. Member Tottenham Borough Council, 1956–64. Chm., National Union of Conservative and Unionist Associations, 1959, 1960; Chm. Conservative Party Conference, 1960; former Vice-Chm., Assoc. of Conservative Clubs. Contested Stalybridge and Hyde (C), 1959; MP (C) Bath, 1964–79. JP Middlesex, 1963. *Recreation:* campanology. *Clubs:* Naval and Military; Tottenham Conservative; Harringay-West Green Constitutional. *Died 27 Aug. 1991.*

BROWN, Sir (Ernest) Henry Phelps, Kt 1976; MBE 1945; FBA 1960; Professor of Economics of Labour, University of London, 1947–68, then Emeritus Professor; *b* 10 Feb. 1906; *s* of E. W. Brown, Calne, Wiltshire; *m* 1932, Dorothy Evelyn Mostyn, *d* of Sir Anthony Bowlby, 1st Bt, KCB; two *s* one *d. Educ:* Taunton School; Wadham College, Oxford (Scholar; Hon. Fellow, 1969). Secretary of Oxford Union, 1928; 1st Class Hons Modern History, 1927; Philosophy, Politics and Economics, 1929. Fellow of New College, Oxford, 1930–47 (Hon. Fellow, 1987); Rockefeller Travelling Fellow in USA, 1930–31. Served War of 1939–45, with Royal Artillery; BEF; ADGB; First Army; Eighth Army (MBE). Member: Council on Prices, Productivity and Incomes, 1959; Nat. Economic Development Council, 1962; Royal Commn on Distribn of Income and Wealth, 1974–78. Chairman, Tavistock Inst. of Human Relations, 1966–68. Pres., Royal Economic Soc., 1970–72. Hon. DLitt Heriot-Watt, 1972; Hon. DCL Durham, 1981. *Publications:* The Framework of the Pricing System, 1936; A Course in Applied Economics, 1951; The Balloon (novel), 1953; The Growth of British Industrial Relations, 1959; The Economics of Labor, 1963; A Century of Pay, 1968; The Inequality of Pay, 1977; The Origins of Trade Union Power, 1983; Egalitarianism and the Generation of Inequality, 1988. *Recreations:* walking; represented Oxford *v* Cambridge cross-country running, 1926. *Address:* 16 Bradmore Road, Oxford OX2 6QP. *T:* Oxford (01865) 56320. *Died 15 Dec. 1994.*

BROWN, Hon. Geoffrey E.; *see* Ellman-Brown.

BROWN, George Frederick William, CMG 1974; Member, Melbourne Underground Railway Loop Authority, since 1971; *b* 12 April 1908; *s* of late G. Brown; *m* 1933, Catherine Mills; one *d* (and one *d* decd). *Educ:* Christian Brothers' Coll., Essendon; Phahran Tech. Coll.; Royal Melbourne Inst. Technology. FIEAust, AMIMechE (Aust.), FCIT. Victorian Railways, 1923; Asst Engr 1929; Country Roads Bd, 1934; Plant Engr Newport Workshops, 1939–43; Supt Loco. Maintenance, 1943–53; Chief Mech. Engr, 1953–58; Comr, 1958–61; Dep. Chm., 1961–67; Chm., 1967–73; Mem., Victorian Railway Bd, 1973–77. Mem. Council, Royal Melb. Inst. Technology, 1958–74, Pres. 1970. *Publications:* articles in tech. jls on rail transport. *Recreation:* golf. *Address:* Unit 1, 10 Lucas Street, East Brighton, Victoria 3187, Australia. *Clubs:* Kelvin Victoria, Victoria Golf, MCC (Victoria).
Died 13 Oct. 1991.

BROWN, Sir Henry Phelps; *see* Brown, Sir E. H. P.

BROWN, Prof. H(oward) Mayer; Ferdinand Schevill Distinguished Service Professor of Music, University of Chicago, since 1976 (Professor of Music, since 1974); *b* 13 April 1930; *s* of Alfred R. and Florence Mayer Brown; unmarried. *Educ:* Harvard Univ. AB 1951, AM 1954, PhD 1959. Walter Naumburg Trav. Fellow, Harvard, 1951–53; Instructor in Music, Wellesley Coll., Mass, 1958–60; Univesity of Chicago: Asst Prof., 1960–63; Associate Prof., 1963–66; Prof., 1967–72; Chm., 1970–72; Dir of Collegium Musicum, 1960–83; King Edward Prof. of Music, KCL, 1972–74. Guggenheim Fellow, Florence, 1963–64; Villa I Tatti Fellow, Florence, 1969–70; Andrew D. White Prof.-at-large, Cornell Univ., 1972–76. Pres., Amer. Musicological Soc., 1978–80; Vice-Pres., Internat. Musicological Soc., 1982–87. Fellow, Amer. Acad. of Arts and Scis, 1983–. Hon. DMus Bates Coll., Maine, 1989. Galileo Galilei Prize, Univ. of Pisa, 1987. *Publications:* Music in the French Secular Theater, 1963; Theatrical Chansons, 1963; Instrumental Music Printed Before 1600, 1965; (with Joan Lascelle) Musical Iconography, 1972; Sixteenth-Century Instrumentation, 1972; Music in the Renaissance, 1976; Embellishing Sixteenth-Century Music, 1976; Chansonnier from the Time of Lorenzo the Magnificent, 2 vols, 1983; contrib. Jl Amer. Musicological Soc., Acta Musicologica, Musical Quarterly, etc. *Address:* 5000 East End Avenue, Chicago, Ill 60615, USA. *Club:* Reform.

Died 20 Feb. 1993.

BROWN, Jack, MBE 1985; JP; General Secretary, Amalgamated Textile Workers' Union, 1976–86; *b* 10 Nov. 1929; *s* of Maurice Brown and Edith (*née* Horrocks); *m* 1952, Alice (*née* Brown); one *s. Educ:* Pennington C of E Primary Sch., Leigh, Lancs; Leigh C of E Secondary Sch., Leigh. Commenced employment in cotton industry as operative, Dec. 1943; Royal Artillery, 1949–51; full-time Trade Union Official (Organiser), 1954; District Sec., Nat. Union of Textile and Allied Workers, 1961–72; Asst Gen. Sec., 1972–76. Non-exec. Mem., NW Electricity Bd, 1984–90. JP Greater Manchester, 1967. *Recreations:* reading, Rugby League football. *Address:* 11 Thomas Street, Atherton, Manchester M29 9DP. *T:* Atherton (0942) 870218. *Club:* Soldiers and Sailors (Atherton).

Died 4 Sept. 1991.

BROWN, Rt Rev. Laurence Ambrose, MA; *b* 1 Nov. 1907; 2nd *s* of Frederick James Brown; *m* 1935, Florence Blanche, *d* of late William Gordon Marshall; three *d. Educ:* Luton Grammar School; Queens' College, Cambridge (MA); Cuddesdon Theological College, Oxford. Deacon, 1932; priest, 1933; Asst Curate, St John-the-Divine, Kennington, 1932–35; Curate-in-Charge, St Peter, Luton, Beds, 1935–40; Vicar, Hatfield Hyde, Welwyn Garden City, 1940–46; Sec. Southwark Dio. Reorganisation Cttee, 1946–60; Sec. S London Church Fund and Southwark Dio. Bd of Finance, 1952–60; Canon Residentiary, Southwark, 1950–60; Archdeacon of Lewisham and Vice-Provost of Southwark, 1955–60; Suffragan Bishop of Warrington, 1960–69; Bishop of Birmingham, 1969–77; Priest-in-Charge of Odstock with Nunton and Bodenham, dio. Salisbury, 1977–84. Mem. Church Assembly, later General Synod, and Proctor in Convocation, 1954–77; Chairman: Advisory Council for Church's Ministry, 1966–71; Industrial Christian Fellowship, 1971–77; Mem., Religious Adv. Bd, Scout Assoc., 1953–83. Mem., House of Lords, 1973–77. *Publications:* pamphlets on church building in post-war period. *Address:* 7 St Nicholas Road, Salisbury, Wilts SP1 2SN. *T:* Salisbury (0722) 333138.

Died 7 Feb. 1994.

BROWN, Leslie F.; *see* Farrer-Brown.

BROWN, Maj.-Gen. Michael, FRCP, FRCPE; Director of Army Medicine, 1988–90, retired; *b* 17 Jan. 1931; *s* of Eric Charles Brown and Winifred Ethel Brown (*née* Kemp); *m* 1955, Jill Evelyn; two *s. Educ:* Bedford Sch.; University Coll. Hosp. London (MB BS; BSc Physiol.). DTM&H. House posts, UCH, 1954–55; RAMC, 1956; Consultant Physician, 1966; Jt Prof. of Military Medicine, RCP and RAMC Coll., 1981–85; Consultant Physician, BAOR, 1985–88. QHP, 1988–90. Fellow, UCL, 1991. OStJ 1990. *Recreations:* golf, photography. *Address:* c/o Royal Bank of Scotland, Farnborough, Hants GU14 7NR.

Died 13 June 1993.

BROWN, Peter; *see* Brown, A. P. G.

BROWN, Sir Raymond (Frederick), Kt 1969; OBE; CompIEE; FIERE; Chairman, Muirhead plc, 1972–85 (Chief Executive and Managing Director, 1970–82); Executive Director, STC PLC (formerly Standard Telephones and Cables Ltd), 1985–90; *b* 19 July 1920; *s* of Frederick and Susan Evelyn Brown; *m* 1942, Evelyn Jennings (marr. diss. 1949); (one *d* decd); *m* 1953, Carol Jacquelin Elizabeth, *d* of H. R. Sprinks, Paris; two *s* one *d. Educ:* Morden Terrace LCC School; SE London Technical College; Morley College. Joined Redifon as engineering apprentice, 1934; Sales Man., Communications Div., Plessey Ltd, 1949–50; formerly Chm., Man. Dir and Pres., Racal Electronics Ltd (Joint Founder, 1950), and subsidiary companies; Head of Defence Sales, MoD, 1966–69; Chm., Racecourse Technical Services, 1970–84; Dir, National Westminster Bank, Outer London Region, 1978–84. Consultant Adviser on commercial policy and exports to DHSS, 1969–72; Mem., BOTB Working Gp on Innovation and Exports, 1972–74; Adviser to NEDO, to promote export of equipment purchased by nationalised industries, 1976–. Pres., Electronic Engrg Assoc., 1975; Pres., Egham and Thorpe Royal Agricl and Hortl Assoc., 1977–79. Liveryman: Scriveners' Co.; Scientific Instrument Makers' Co. Governor, SE London Technical Coll., 1980–81. Hon. DSc Bath, 1980. *Recreations:* golf, farming, shooting, polo. *Clubs:* City Livery, Canada, Australia; Ends of the Earth, Pilgrims; Sunningdale Golf; Guards Polo (life mem.); Swinley Forest Golf.

Died 3 Sept. 1991.

BROWN, Thomas Walter Falconer, CBE 1958; consultant in marine engineering; *b* 10 May 1901; *s* of Walter Falconer Brown, MB, ChB, DPH, and Catherine Edith (*née* McGhie); *m* 1947, Lucy Mason (*née* Dickie); one *s* one *d. Educ:* Ayr Academy; Glasgow University; Harvard University. BSc (special dist. in Nat. Philos.), 1921; DSc (Glas.), 1927; SM (Harvard), 1928; ARTC, 1922. Asst General Manager, Alex Stephen & Sons Ltd, Linthouse, 1928–35; Technical Manager, R. & W. Hawthorn Leslie & Co. Ltd, Newcastle upon Tyne, 1935–44; Director of Parsons and Marine Engineering Turbine Research and Development Assoc., Wallsend, 1944–62; Director of Marine Engineering Research (BSRA), Wallsend Research Station, 1962–66. Liveryman, Worshipful Co. of Shipwrights, Freedom City of London, 1946. Eng Lieut, and Eng Lt-Comdr RNVR, Clyde Div., 1924–36. De Laval Gold Medal, Sweden, 1957. *Publications:* various technical papers in: Trans Instn Mech. Engineers, Inst. Marine Engineers, NE Coast Instn of Engineers & Shipbuilders, etc. *Recreations:* model-making, gardening. *Address:* 12 The Dene, Wylam, Northumberland NE41 8JB. *T:* Wylam (01661) 2228.

Died 18 May 1995.

BROWN, W(illiam) Glanville, TD; barrister-at-law; *b* 19 July 1907; *s* of late Cecil George Brown, formerly Town Clerk of Cardiff, and Edith Tyndale Brown; *m* 1st, 1935, Theresa Margaret Mary Harrison (decd); one *s*; 2nd, 1948, Margaret Isabel Dilks, JP (*d* 1988), *o d* of late Thomas Bruce Dilks, Bridgwater. *Educ:* Llandaff Cathedral School; Magdalen College School and Magdalen College, Oxford; in France, Germany and Italy. Called to Bar,

Middle Temple, 1932. Contested (L) Cardiff Central, 1935, St Albans, 1964. Served War of 1939–45, in Army (TA), Aug. 1939–Dec. 1945; attached to Intelligence Corps; served overseas 3½ years in E Africa Command, Middle East and North-West Europe. Junior Prosecutor for UK Internat. Military Tribunal for the Far East, Tokyo, 1946–48; Member: the National Arbitration Tribunal, 1949–51; Industrial Disputes Tribunal, 1959; Deputy-Chairman of various Wages Councils, 1950–64; Joint Legal Editor of English Translation of Common Market Documents for Foreign Office, 1962–63; Lectr in Germany on behalf of HM Embassy, Bonn, 1965–73. Mem., Mental Health Review Tribunal for NE Metropolitan RHB Area, 1960–79. Life Mem., RIIA. Fellow, Inst. of Linguists. *Publication:* translation of Brunschweig's French Colonialism, 1871–1914, Myths and Realities. *Recreations:* walking, reading, watching cricket, travel. *Address:* 36 Chester Road, Northwood, Mddx HA6 1BQ. *Club:* National Liberal. *Died 10 July 1995.*

BROWNE, Coral (Edith), (Mrs Vincent Price); actress; *b* Melbourne, Australia, 23 July 1913; *d* of Leslie Clarence Brown and Victoria Elizabeth (*née* Bennett); *m* 1950, Philip Westrope Pearman (*d* 1964); *m* 1974, Vincent Price. *Educ:* Claremont Ladies' Coll., Melb. Studied painting in Melbourne. First stage appearance, in Loyalties, Comedy Theatre, Melb., 1931; acted in 28 plays in Australia, 1931–34; first London appearance in Lover's Leap, Vaudeville, 1934, and then continued for some years playing in the West End; from 1940, successes included: The Man Who Came to Dinner, 1941; My Sister Eileen, 1943; The Last of Mrs Cheyney, 1944; Lady Frederick, 1946; Canaries Sometimes Sing, 1947; Jonathan, 1948; Castle in the Air, 1949; Othello, 1951; King Lear, 1952; Affairs of State, 1952; Simon and Laura, 1954; Nina, 1955; Macbeth, 1956; Troilus and Cressida, 1956; (Old Vic season) Hamlet, A Midsummer Night's Dream and King Lear, 1957–58; The Pleasure of His Company, 1959; Toys in the Attic, 1960; Bonne Soupe, 1961–62; The Rehearsal, 1963; The Right Honourable Gentleman, 1964–66; Lady Windermere's Fan, 1966; What the Butler Saw, 1969; My Darling Daisy, 1970; Mrs Warren's Profession, 1970; The Sea, 1973; The Waltz of the Toreadors, 1974; Ardèle, 1975; Charley's Aunt, 1976; The Importance of Being Earnest, 1977; Travesties, 1977; also appeared in United States and Moscow. *Films:* Auntie Mame; The Roman Spring of Mrs Stone; Dr Crippen; The Night of the Generals; The Legend of Lylah Clare; The Killing of Sister George, 1969; The Ruling Class, 1972; Theatre of Blood, 1973; The Drowning Pool, 1975; Dreamchild, 1985; *TV series:* Time Express, 1979; *TV films:* Elenor, First Lady of the World, 1982; An Englishman Abroad, 1983. *Recreation:* needlepoint. *Died 29 May 1991.*

BROWNE, (Edward) Michael (Andrew); QC 1970; *b* 29 Nov. 1910; *yr s* of Edward Granville Browne, Fellow of Pembroke Coll., Cambridge, and Alice Caroline Browne (*née* Blackburne Daniell); *m* 1937, Anna Florence Augusta, *d* of James Little Luddington; two *d. Educ:* Eton; Pembroke Coll., Cambridge (Scholar). 1st class History Tripos, 1932; MA. Barrister, Inner Temple, 1934, *ad eundem* Lincoln's Inn; Bencher, Inner Temple, 1964. Practised (mainly in Chancery Div.) until retirement in 1984. FCIArb. Served War of 1939–45: RA (anti aircraft) and GS, War Office (finally GSO3, Capt.). *Address:* 19 Wallgrave Road, SW5 0RF. *T:* 071–373 3055. *Club:* Athenæum. *Died 1 April 1992.*

BROXBOURNE, Baron *cr* 1983 (Life Peer), of Broxbourne in the County of Hertfordshire; **Derek Colclough Walker-Smith; Bt** 1960; TD; PC 1957; QC 1955; Director, William Weston Gallery Ltd, since 1967; *b* 13 April 1910; *y s* of late Sir Jonah Walker-Smith; *m* 1938, Dorothy, *d* of

late L. J. W. Etherton, Rowlands Castle, Hants; one *s* two *d. Educ:* Rossall; Christ Church, Oxford. 1st Class Hons Modern History, 1931. Called to the Bar, Middle Temple, 1934, Bencher 1963. MP (C) Hertford, 1945–55, Herts East, 1955–83; Parly Sec. to the Board of Trade, 1955–Nov. 1956; Economic Secretary to HM Treasury, Nov. 1956–Jan. 1957; Minister of State, Board of Trade, 1957; Minister of Health, 1957–60. Chairman: Cons. Adv. Cttee on Local Govt, 1954–55; 1922 Cttee, 1951–55. Mem., European Parlt, 1973–79 (Chm. of Legal Cttee, 1975–79). Chm., Soc. of Conservative Lawyers, 1969–75; Chm., Nat. House Building Council, 1973–78. ARICS, FCIArb; FIQS. *Publications include:* (jtly) Walker-Smith on the Standard Forms of Building Contracts, 1987; The Protectionist Case in the 1840s; Out of Step (novel). *Heir* (to baronetcy only): *s* John Jonah Walker-Smith [*b* 6 Sept. 1939; *m* 1974, Aileen Marie Smith; one *s* one *d*]. *Address:* 7 Kepplestone, The Meads, Eastbourne; 20 Albany Court, Palmer Street, SW1. *Club:* Garrick.

Died 22 Jan. 1992.

BRUCE, Alexander Robson, CMG 1961; OBE 1948; Assistant Secretary, Board of Trade, 1963–67, retired; *b* 17 April 1907; *s* of Robert Bruce; *m* 1936, Isobel Mary Goldie (*d* 1988); four *d. Educ:* Rutherford Coll., Newcastle upon Tyne; Durham Univ. Asst Trade Comr, 1933–42, Trade Commissioner, 1942–43, Montreal; Commercial Sec., British Embassy, Madrid, 1943–46; Trade Comr, Ottawa, 1946–50; Asst Sec., Bd of Trade, 1950–54; Principal British Trade Commissioner in NSW, 1955–63. *Recreation:* golf. *Address:* 37 North Road, Highgate, N6 4BE. *Club:* Highgate Golf. *Died 26 Nov. 1991.*

BRUCE, Sir Arthur Atkinson, KBE 1943; MC 1917; Director: Wallace Brothers & Co. Ltd, 1947–65; Chartered Bank of India, 1949–70; *b* 26 March 1895; *s* of late John Davidson Bruce, Jarrow-on-Tyne; *m* 1928, Kathleen Frances (*d* 1952), *d* of John Emeris Houldey, ICS (retd), Penn, Bucks; three *d. Educ:* Cambridge. Director Reserve Bank of India, 1935–46. Chairman Burma Chamber of Commerce, 1936, 1942, 1946; Member of Council, London Chamber of Commerce, 1960–65. *Address:* Silverthorne, 5 Grenfell Road, Beaconsfield, Bucks. *Club:* Oriental. *Died 3 Jan. 1992.*

BRUCE LOCKHART, John Macgregor, CB 1966; CMG 1951; OBE 1944; *b* 9 May 1914; *e s* of late John Harold Bruce Lockhart and Mona Brougham; *m* 1939, Margaret Evelyn, *d* of late Rt Rev. C. R. Hone; two *s* one *d. Educ:* Rugby School (Captain XV); St Andrews University (Harkness Scholar). MA (Hons) French and German, 1937. Asst Master, Rugby School, 1937–39; TA Commission, Seaforth Highlanders, 1938; served War of 1939–45, in UK, Middle East, North Africa, Italy (Lt-Col); Asst Military Attaché, British Embassy, Paris, 1945–47; Control Commission Germany, 1948–51; First Secretary, British Embassy, Washington, 1951–53; served Foreign Office, London, until resignation from the Diplomatic Service, 1965; in charge of planning and development, Univ. of Warwick, 1965–67; Head of Central Staff Dept, Courtaulds Ltd, 1967–71. Visitor, HM Prison Onley, 1972–76. Dir, Post Experience Programme, City Univ. Business Sch., 1971–80 (Hon. Fellow, City Univ., 1980); Chm., Business Educn Council, 1974–80; Member: Schools Council, 1975–80; Naval Educn Adv. Cttee, 1973–80. Vis. Scholar, St Andrews Univ., 1981; Vis. Lectr, Rand Afrikaans Univ., 1983. President: Flecknoe Cricket Club, 1966–76; Rugby Football Club, 1972–76. *Publications:* articles and lectures on strategic studies at RCDS, RUSI, Kennedy Inst. of Politics, Harvard and Georgetown Univ., Washington, DC. *Recreations:* music, real tennis, golf, pictures. *Address:* 37 Fair Meadow, Rye, Sussex TN31 7NL. *Clubs:* Reform; Rye Golf. *Died 7 May 1995.*

BRUCE-MITFORD, Rupert Leo Scott, FBA 1976; Research Keeper in the British Museum, 1975–77 (Keeper of British and Mediæval Antiquities, 1954–69, of Mediæval and Later Antiquities, 1969–75); *b* 14 June 1914; 4th *s* of C. E. Bruce-Mitford, Madras, and Beatrice (Allison), *e d* of John Fall, British Columbia; *m* 1st, 1941, Kathleen Dent (marr. diss. 1972); one *s* two *d*; 2nd, 1975, Marilyn Roberta (marr. diss. 1984), *o d* of Robert J. Luscombe, Walton on the Hill, Staffs; 3rd, 1988, Margaret Edna, *o d* of Charles A. Adams, Trowbridge, Wilts. *Educ:* Christ's Hospital; Hertford College, Oxford (Baring Scholar; Hon. Fellow, 1984). DLitt Oxon 1987. FSA 1947 (Sec., 1950–54; Vice-Pres., 1972–76); FSAScot. Temp. Asst Keeper, Ashmolean Museum, 1937; Asst Keeper, Dept of British and Mediæval Antiquities, British Museum, 1938; Royal Signals, 1939–45; Deputy Keeper, British Museum, 1954. Slade Professor of Fine Art, Univ. of Cambridge, 1978–79; Vis. Fellow, All Souls Coll., Oxford, 1978–79; Professorial Fellow, Emmanuel Coll., Cambridge, 1978–79; Faculty Visitor, Dept of English, ANU, Canberra, 1981. Excavations: Seacourt, Berks, 1938–39; Mawgan Porth, Cornwall, 1949–54; Chapter House graves, Lincoln Cathedral, 1955; Sutton Hoo, Suffolk, 1965–68. Pres., Soc. for Mediæval Archæol., 1957–59; Vice-Pres., UISPP World Archaeol Congress, 1986 (resigned, S African non-participation issue). Member: Ancient Monuments Bd, 1954–77; Perm. Council, UISPP, 1957–79; German Archæological Inst.; Italian Inst. of Prehistory and Protohistory; Corresp. Member, Jutland Archæological Society; Hon. Mem., Suffolk Inst. of Archaeology; For. Corresp. Mem., Acad. du Var; For. Trustee, Instituto de Valencia de Don Juan, Madrid, 1954–75. Lectures: Dalrymple, Glasgow, 1961; Thomas Davis Radio, Dublin, 1964; Jarrow, 1967; O'Donnell, Wales, 1971; Garmonsway, York, 1973; Crake, Mount Allison Univ., NB, 1980. Liveryman, Worshipful Co. of Clockmakers. Hon. LittD Dublin 1966. *Publications:* The Society of Antiquaries of London: Notes on its History and Possessions (with others), 1952; (ed and contrib.) Recent Archæological Excavations in Britain, 1956; (with T. J. Brown, A. S. C. Ross and others) Codex Lindisfarnensis (Swiss facsimile edn), 1957–61; (trans. from Danish) The Bog People, by P. V. Glob, 1969; The Sutton Hoo Ship-burial, a handbook, 1972, rev. edn 1979; Aspects of Anglo-Saxon Archaeology, 1974; The Sutton Hoo Ship-burial, Vol. I, 1975, Vol. II, 1978, Vol. III, 1983; (ed) Recent Archaeological Excavations in Europe, 1975; papers and reviews in learned journals; *posthumous publications:* Mawgan Porth: a tenth and eleventh century hamlet on the North Cornish coast, 1994; A Corpus of late-Celtic hanging-bowls, 1994. *Recreations:* reading, chess, watching sport, travel. *Address:* Eton House, Broad Street, Bampton, Oxford OX8 2LX. *Clubs:* Athenæum, Garrick, MCC.   *Died 10 March 1994.*

BRULLER, Jean; *see* Vercors.

BRUNTISFIELD, 1st Baron *cr* 1942, of Boroughmuir; **Victor Alexander George Anthony Warrender,** MC 1918; Bt 1715; late Grenadier Guards; *b* 23 June 1899; *s* of Sir George John Scott Warrender, 7th Bt KCB, KCVO, and Lady (Ethel) Maud Warrender (*d* 1945), *y d* of 8th Earl of Shaftesbury; *S* to father's Baronetcy, 1917; *m* 1920, Dorothy (marr. diss. 1945), *y d* of late Colonel R. H. Rawson, MP, and Lady Beatrice Rawson; three *s*; *m* 1948, Tania, *yr d* of late Dr M. Kolin, St Jacob, Dubrovnik, Jugoslavia; one *s* one *d*. *Educ:* Eton. Served European War, 1917–18 (MC, Russian Order of St Stanislas, Star of Roumania, St Ann of Russia with sword); MP (U) Grantham Division of Kesteven and Rutland, 1923–42; an assistant Whip, 1928–31; Junior Lord of the Treasury, 1931–32; Vice-Chamberlain of HM Household, 1932–35; Comptroller of HM Household, 1935; Parliamentary and Financial Secretary to Admiralty, 1935; Financial

Secretary, War Office, 1935–40; Parliamentary and Financial Secretary, Admiralty, 1940–42; Parliamentary Secretary, Admiralty, 1942–45. *Heir: s* Hon. John Robert Warrender, OBE, MC, TD, DL [*b* 7 Feb. 1921; *m* 1st, 1948, (Anne) Moireen Campbell (*d* 1976), 2nd *d* of Sir Walter Campbell, KCIE; two *s* two *d*; 2nd, 1977, Mrs Shirley Crawley (*d* 1981), *o d* of E. J. L. Ross; 3rd, 1985, Mrs (Kathleen) Joanna Graham, *o d* of David Chancellor]. *Address:* Résidence Le Village, CH-1837 Château-d'Oex, Switzerland. *Club:* Turf.   *Died 14 Jan. 1993.*

BRYANT, Rear-Adm. Benjamin, CB 1956; DSO 1942 (two bars, 1943); DSC 1940; *b* 16 Sept. 1905; *s* of J. F. Bryant, MA, FRGS, ICS (retd); *m* 1st, 1929, Marjorie Dagmar Mynors (*née* Symonds) (*d* 1965); one *s* one *d*; 2nd, 1966, Heather Elizabeth Williams (*née* Hance) (*d* 1989). *Educ:* Oundle; RN Colls Osborne and Dartmouth. Entered submarine branch of RN, 1927; commanded: HM Submarine Sea Lion, 1939–41; HM Submarine Safari, 1941–43; comd 7th and 3rd Submarine Flotillas, 1943–44; comd 4th Submarine Flotilla, British Pacific Fleet, 1945–47; comd HMS Dolphin Submarine School, and 5th Submarine Flotilla, 1947–49; Commodore (submarines), 1948; idc 1950; Commodore, RN Barracks, Devonport, 1951–53; Flag Captain to C-in-C Mediterranean, 1953–54; Rear-Admiral, 1954; Deputy Chief of Naval Personnel (Training and Manning), 1954–57; retired, 1957. Staff Personnel Manager, Rolls Royce Scottish Factories, 1957–68. *Publication:* One Man Band (memoirs), 1958, new edn as Submarine Command, 1975. *Recreations:* fishing, golf, shooting. *Address:* Quarry Cottage, Kithurst Lane, Storrington, West Sussex RH20 4LP.
          Died 23 Nov. 1994.

BUCHAN-HEPBURN, Sir Ninian (Buchan Archibald John), 6th Bt *cr* 1815, of Smeaton-Hepburn; painter; Member, Queen's Body Guard for Scotland, Royal Company of Archers; *b* 8 Oct. 1922; *s* of Sir John Karslake Thomas Buchan-Hepburn, 5th Bt, and Jessie Lawrence, *d* of Francis William Smith, MD; *S* father 1961; *m* 1st, 1958, Bridget (*d* 1976), *er d* of late Sir Louis Greig, KBE, CVO; 2nd, 1991, Mrs Angela Richard. *Educ:* St Aubyn's, Rottingdean, Sussex; Canford School, Wimborne, Dorset. Served Queen's Own Cameron Hldrs, India and Burma, 1939–45 (wounded, 1944). Studied painting, Byam Shaw School of Art. Exhibited at Royal Academy, Royal Scottish Academy, London galleries; work in many public and private collections. *Recreations:* music, gardening, shooting. *Heir: kinsman* John Alastair Trant Kidd Buchan-Hepburn [*b* 27 June 1931; *m* 1957, Georgina Elizabeth Turner; one *s* three *d*]. *Address:* Logan, Port Logan, Wigtownshire DG9 9ND. *T:* Ardwell (077686) 239. *Club:* New (Edinburgh).   *Died 22 Feb. 1992.*

BUCHANAN-SMITH, Rt Hon. Alick (Laidlaw); PC 1981; MP (C) Kincardine and Deeside, since 1983 (North Angus and Mearns, 1964–83); *b* 8 April 1932; 2nd *s* of late Baron Balerno, CBE, TD, and Mary Kathleen, *d* of Captain George Smith of Pittodrie; *m* 1956, Janet, *d* of late Thomas Lawrie, CBE; one *s* three *d*. *Educ:* Edinburgh Academy; Trinity College, Glenalmond; Pembroke College, Cambridge; Edinburgh University. Commissioned Gordon Highlanders, National Service, 1951; subseq. Captain, TA (5th/6th Gordon Highlanders). Contested (C), W Fife, 1959. Parly Under-Sec. of State, Scottish Office, 1970–74; Minister of State: MAFF, 1979–83; Dept of Energy, 1983–87. *Address:* House of Commons, SW1A 0AA.
          Died 29 Aug. 1991.

BUCK, Albert Charles; business consultant; *b* 1 March 1910; *y s* of William and Mary Buck; *m* 1st, 1937, Margaret Court Hartley; one *d*; 2nd, 1951, Joan McIntyre; one *d*; 3rd, 1970, Mrs Aileen Ogilvy. *Educ:* Alderman Newton's Sch., Leicester; Selwyn Coll., Cambridge (MA). Joined J. J. Colman Ltd, as management trainee, 1931;

Export Manager, 1939; Director: Reckitt & Sons Ltd, 1941; Joseph Farrow & Co. Ltd, 1947–69; Thomas Green & Son, 1950–60; Reckitt & Colman (Household) Div.; Industrial Adviser to HM Govt (Dep. Sec.), 1969–73. Member: Incorporated Soc. of British Advertisers (Pres., 1961–63); Internat. Union of Advertiser Societies (Pres. 1963–65); Advertising Standards Authority, 1962–71; Internat. Foundation for Research in Advertising (Pres., 1965–71). Mackintosh Medal for personal and public services to Advertising, 1965. *Publications:* sundry articles to jls and newspapers. *Recreations:* winter sports, shooting, fishing. *Address:* 46 Pearson Park, Hull HU5 2TG. *T:* Hull (0482) 470828.   *Died 20 Feb. 1992.*

BUCKINGHAM, Prof. Richard Arthur; Professor of Computer Education, Birkbeck College, University of London, 1974–78, then Professor Emeritus; *b* 17 July 1911; *s* of George Herbert Buckingham and Alice Mary Watson (*née* King); *m* 1939 Christina O'Brien; one *s* two *d. Educ:* Gresham's Sch., Holt; St John's Coll., Cambridge. Asst Lecturer in Mathematical Physics, Queen's University, Belfast, 1935–38; Senior 1851 Exhibitioner, University College, London and MIT, 1938–40; Admiralty Research Laboratory, Teddington, and Mine Design Dept, Havant, 1940–45; University College London: Lecturer in Mathematics, 1945–50; Lecturer in Physics, 1950–51; Reader in Physics, 1951–57; Dir, Univ. of London Computer Unit, later Inst. of Computer Science, 1957–73, and Prof. of Computing Science, 1963–74. CEng; FBCS; FRSA. *Publications:* Numerical Methods, 1957; (jtly) Information Systems Education, 1987; papers in Proc. Royal Soc., Proc. Phys. Soc., Jl Chem. Physics, Trans Faraday Soc., Computer Journal, etc. *Address:* 21 Plainwood Close, Chichester, West Sussex PO19 4YB.
                    Died 13 Aug. 1994.

BUCKLE, Maj.-Gen. Denys Herbert Vintcent, CB 1955; CBE 1948 (OBE 1945); FCIT; Trustee, South Africa Foundation, since 1969; Director, Prince Vintcent & Co. (Pty) Ltd, Mossel Bay; *b* Cape, South Africa, 16 July 1902; *s* of Major H. S. Buckle, RMLI and ASC and Agnes Buckle (*née* Vintcent), Cape Town; *m* 1928, Frances Margaret Butterworth (*d* 1990); one *d. Educ:* Boxgrove School, Guildford; Charterhouse, Godalming; RMC Sandhurst. 2nd Lieut, E Surrey Regt, 1923; transf. to RASC, 1926; Shanghai Def. Force, 1927–28; Asst Adjt, RASC Trg Centre, 1929–32; Adjt 44th (Home Counties) Divnl RASC, TA, 1932–36; Student Staff Coll., Camberley, 1936–37; Adjt Ceylon ASC, 1938; Bde Maj., Malaya Inf. Bde, 1938–40; GSO 2, Trg Directorate, WO, 1940; AA&QMG, 8th Armd Div., 1940–41; GSO 1, Staff Coll., Camberley, 1941–42; Brig. Admin. Plans, GHQ Home Forces, "Cossac" and SHAEF, 1942–44; Brig. Q Ops, WO, 1944; DDST and Brig. Q, 21 Army Gp and BAOR, 1945–46; DQMG, FARELF, 1946–48; DDST, S Comd, 1948–49; Spec. Appts (Brig.), USA, 1949–50; Dir of Equipment, WO, 1950–51, and special appt, Paris, 1951; Comdt RASC Trg Centre, 1952–53; DST, MELF, 1953–56; Maj.-Gen. i/c Admin, GHQ, MELF, 1956–58; despatches, 1956 (Suez); retd 1958; ADC to King George VI, 1951, to the Queen, 1952–54. FCIT 1971. Bursar, Church of England Training Colleges, Cheltenham, 1958–59. Divisional Manager SE Division, British Waterways, 1961–63; Director of Reorganisation, British Waterways, 1963–65. Dir, UK-S Africa Trade Assoc., 1965–68; Administrative Mem., Southern Africa Cttee, BNEC, 1967–68. Col Comdt RASC, 1959–64; Representative Col Comdt, RASC, 1961; Hon. Col 44th (Home Counties), RASC, 1962–65, Regt, RCT, 1965–67. Legion of Merit (USA), 1944. *Publications:* History of 44th Division, RASC, TA, 1932; The Vintcents of Mossel Bay, 1986. *Recreations:* reading, broadcasting, writing, walking, swimming, travel. *Address:* Flat A, 636 St Martini Gardens, Queen Victoria Street, Cape Town,

8001, South Africa. *T:* 246745. *Clubs:* Army and Navy; Western Province Sports (Cape Town).
                    Died 18 Dec. 1994.

BUCKLE, Rt Rev. Edward Gilbert; Bishop in the Northern Region, Diocese of Auckland, New Zealand, 1981–92; *b* 20 July 1926; *s* of Douglas Gordon Buckle and Claire Ettie Wellman; *m* 1949, Mona Ann Cain; one *s* three *d. Educ:* Hurstville Central Coll.; Moore Theological Coll., Univ. of Sydney (LTh); St Augustine's College, Canterbury, England (DipCC). Served War, RAAF, 1944–45. Rector of Koorawatha, 1950–51; Chaplain, Snowy Mountains Hydro-Electric Authority, 1952–54; Rector, All Saints, Canberra, 1955–62; Canon, St Saviour's Cathedral, Goulburn, 1959; Dir of Adult Education for Gen. Bd of Religious Education, Melbourne, 1962–65; New Zealand: Vicar, St Matthew's-in-the-City, Auckland, 1966–67; Bishop's Executive Officer, 1967–70; Diocesan and Ecumenical Develt Officer, 1970–81; Archdeacon of Auckland, 1970–81. *Publications:* The Disturber: The Episcopacy of Ernest Henry Burgmann, Bishop of Canberra and Goulburn, 1957; A Station of the Cross, 1959; Cost of Living, study material on MRI; Family Affair, 1966; Urban Development, 1968; Interview 69, 1969; The Churches and East Coast Bays, 1970; The Isthmus and Redevelopment, 1973; Inner City Churches, 1973; Otara and the Churches, 1974; The Churches East of the Tamaki, 1974; Paroikia—the house alongside, 1978. *Recreations:* reading, sailing, squash. *Address:* 14 Kiwi Avenue, Maunu, Whangarei, Northland, New Zealand. *T:* (89) 485922. *Club:* Wellesley (Wellington, NZ).
                    Died 27 Nov. 1993.

BUCKLEY, George James, JP; MP (Lab) Hemsworth, since 1987; *b* 6 April 1935; *m*; one *s* one *d. Educ:* Leeds Univ. Former miner. Joined Labour Party, 1966. Mem., Wakefield Dist Council, 1973–87. Member: Yorks Regl TUC, 1972–; NUM, 1965–. *Address:* House of Commons, SW1A 0AA; 128 Barnsley Road, South Kirkby, Pontefract WF9 3AR.   *Died 14 Sept. 1991.*

BUCKLEY, Rear-Adm. Sir Kenneth (Robertson), KBE 1961; *b* 24 May 1904; 2nd *s* of late L. E. Buckley, CSI, TD; *m* 1937, Bettie Helen Radclyffe Dugmore; one *s* two *d. Educ:* RN Colleges, Osborne and Dartmouth. Joined Navy, Jan. 1918; served War of 1939–45 (despatches); ADC to the Queen, 1956–58; Director of Engineering and Electrical Training of the Navy, and Senior Naval Electrical Officer, 1959–62. Comdr 1942; Capt. 1949; Rear-Adm. 1958. *Recreations:* golf, gardening. *Address:* Meadow Cottage, Cherque Lane, Lee-on-Solent, Hants. *T:* Lee-on-Solent (0705) 550646.
                    Died 28 Aug. 1992.

BUCKLEY, Dr Trevor, CB 1993; CEng, FIEE; Assistant Chief Scientific Adviser (Research), Ministry of Defence, 1991–92; *b* 4 Feb. 1938; *s* of Harold Buckley and Selina (*née* Follos); *m* 1960, Mary Pauline Stubbs; one *s* one *d. Educ:* Barmouth Grammar Sch.; UCNW Bangor (BSc Hons Electronic Engrg, PhD). RRE, 1962–76 (Head of ATC Res. Div., 1972–76); Admiralty Underwater Weapons Estabt, 1976–82 (Head of Sonar Data Processing Res. Div., 1976–80, Dep. Dir Underwater Weapons Projects (SM), 1980–82); RCDS, 1983; Dir Gen., Air Weapons and Electronic Systems, 1984–86, Dep. Controller Res., 1986–91, MoD (PE). *Recreations:* photography, musical appreciation, fixing things. *Address:* 46 Moreland Drive, Gerrards Cross, Bucks SL9 8BD. *T:* Gerrards Cross (0753) 885920.
                    Died 24 Jan. 1993.

BUCKMASTER, Rev. Cuthbert Harold Septimus; *b* 15 July 1903; *s* of Charles John and Evelyn Jean Buckmaster; *m* 1942, Katharine Mary Zoë (*d* 1974), 3rd *d* of Rev. Canon T. N. R. Prentice, Stratford-on-Avon; two *d. Educ:*

RN Colls, Osborne and Dartmouth. Deacon, 1926; priest, 1927; Asst Curate St John's, Middlesbrough, 1927–30; Curate of Wigan, 1930–33; Chaplain of Denstone Coll., 1933–35; Warden of St Michael's Coll., Tenbury, Worcs, 1935–46; Rector of: Ashprington, with Cornworthy, 1957–59; Chagford, 1959–71. Chaplain RNVR, 1940; RN 1947. *Address:* 47 Carlyle Street, Byron Bay, NSW 2481, Australia. *Died 20 Dec. 1994.*

BUCKMASTER, Col Maurice James, OBE 1943; independent public relations consultant, 1960–89, retired; *b* 11 Jan. 1902; *s* of Henry James Buckmaster and Eva Matilda (*née* Nason); *m* 1st, 1927, May Dorothy (*née* Steed); one *s* two *d*; 2nd, 1941, Anna Cecilia (*née* Reinstein) (*d* 1988). *Educ:* Eton College. J. Henry Schroder & Co., Merchant Bankers, 1923–29; Asst to Chairman, Ford Motor Co. Ltd, 1929–32; Manager, Ford Motor Co. (France), 1932–36; Head of European Dept, Ford Motor Co. Ltd, 1936–39 and 1945–50; Dir of Public Relations, 1950–60. Served War of 1939–45: 50th Div., G3I, Intelligence, 1939–40 (despatches); Intelligence Officer (Captain), Dakar expedition; Special Operations Executive, Head of French Section, 1941–45. Chevalier de la Légion d'Honneur, 1945, Officier 1978 (France); Croix de Guerre with Palms, Médaille de la Résistance (France), 1945; Legion of Merit (US), 1945. *Publications:* Specially Employed, 1961; They Fought Alone, 1964. *Recreation:* family life. *Died 17 April 1992.*

BUCKTON, Raymond William, FCIT; General Secretary, Associated Society of Locomotive Engineers and Firemen, 1970–87, retired; *b* 20 Oct. 1922; *s* of W. E. and H. Buckton; *m* 1954, Barbara Langfield; two *s*. *Educ:* Appleton Roebuck School. FCIT 1982. Employed in Motive Power Department, British Railways, 1940–60. Elected Irish Officer of ASLEF, 1960 (Dublin); District Organiser, York, Jan. 1963; Assistant General Secretary, July 1963; General Secretary, 1970. Member: Gen. Council, TUC, 1973–86 (Chm., 1983–84); IBA Gen. Adv. Council, 1976–81; Occupational Pensions Bd, 1976–82; Health Services Bd, 1977–80; Health and Safety Commn, 1982–86. Member: Council, Industrial Soc., 1973–; Standing Adv. Cttee, TUC Centenary Inst. of Occupational Health, 1974–; Nat. Adv. Council on Employment of Disabled People, 1975–; Industrial Injuries Adv. Council, 1976–; Dangerous Substances Adv. Cttee, 1976–; Adv. Cttee on Alcoholism, 1977–; Railway Industry Adv. Cttee, 1977–82; TUC Internat. Cttee, 1978–86; EEC Economic and Social Cttee, 1978–82; Exec., ETUC, 1982–; Commonwealth TUC, 1982–. Director: Transport 2000, 1985; Nirex, 1986–92. Mem., Adv. Council for Transport of Radioactive Materials, 1986–89. Councillor, York City Council, 1952–55, Alderman, 1955–57. *Address:* 86 Hillside Gardens, Edgware, Middlesex HA8 8HD. *Died 7 May 1995.*

BUFTON, Air Vice-Marshal Sydney Osborne, CB 1945; DFC 1940; FRAeS; *b* 12 Jan. 1908; 2nd *s* of late J. O. Bufton, JP, Llandrindod Wells, Radnor; *m* 1943, Susan Maureen, *d* of Colonel E. M. Browne, DSO, Chelsea; two *d*. *Educ:* Dean Close School, Cheltenham. Commissioned RAF, 1927; psa 1939; idc 1946; served War of 1939–45, Bomber Command: Nos 10 and 76 Sqdns, RAF Station, Pocklington, 1940–41; Dep. Dir Bomber Ops, 1941–43; Dir of Bomber Ops, Air Min., 1943–45; AOC Egypt, 1945–46; Central Bomber Establishment, RAF Marham, Norfolk, 1947–48; Dep. Chief of Staff (Ops/Plans), Air Forces Western Europe, 1948–51; Dir of Weapons, Air Min., 1951–52; AOA Bomber Command, 1952–53; AOC Brit. Forces, Aden, 1953–55; Senior Air Staff Officer, Bomber Comd, 1955–58; Assistant Chief of Air Staff (Intelligence), 1958–61; retired Oct. 1961. Temp. Gp Capt. 1941; Temp. Air Cdre 1943; Substantive Gp Capt. 1946; Air Cdre 1948; Actg Air Vice-Marshal, 1952; Air

Vice-Marshal, 1953. Invented radio and electronic construction system (Radionic), 1961–62; Man. Dir, Radionic Products Ltd, 1962–70. FRAeS 1970. High Sheriff of Radnorshire, 1967. Comdr Legion of Merit (US); Comdr Order of Orange Nassau (with swords) (Netherlands). *Recreations:* hockey (Welsh International 1931–37; Combined Services, RAF), golf, squash. *Address:* 1 Castle Keep, London Road, Reigate, Surrey RH2 9PU. *T:* Reigate (0737) 243707. *Club:* Royal Air Force. *Died 29 March 1993.*

BUGOTU, Francis, CBE 1979; Cross of Solomon Islands, 1988; Permanent Representative of Solomon Islands to United Nations, since 1990; *b* 27 June 1937; *s* of Tione Kalapalua Bugotu and Rachael Samoa; *m* 1962, Ella Vehe; one *s* one *d*. *Educ:* NZ, Australia, Scotland, England and Solomon Is. Teacher and Inspector of Mission Schs for Ch. of Melanesia (Anglican), 1959–60; Mem., 1st Legislative Council, 1960–62; Lectr, Solomon Is Teachers Coll., 1964–68; Chief Educn Officer and Perm. Sec., Min. of Educn, 1968–75; Perm. Sec. to Chief Minister and Council of Ministers, and titular Head of Civil Service, 1976–78; Sec. for For. Affairs and Roving Ambassador/High Comr of Solomon Is, 1978–82; Sec.-Gen., S Pacific Commn, 1982–86. Chairman: Review Cttee on Educn, 1974–75; Solomon Is Tourist Authority, 1970–73; Solomon Is Scholarship Cttee, 1969–75. Consultant, esp. for S Pacific Commn; Founder Mem. and Chief Adviser, Kakamora Youth Club, 1968–75; Chief Comr of Scouts for Solomon Is, 1970–77. Chm., Solomon Is S Pacific Fest. of Arts Cttee; Dep. Chm., Solomon Is Airlines. Lay Rep., Ch. of Melanesia. *Publications:* (with A. V. Hughes) This Man (play), 1970 (also award winning film); papers on: impact of Western culture on Solomon Is; politics, economics and social aspects in Solomons; recolonising and decolonising; Solomon Is Pidgin. *Recreations:* interested in most ball games (soccer, cricket, basketball, Rugby, tennis, table-tennis, softball, snooker), swimming, music, dancing. *Address:* PO Box 528, Honiara, Solomon Islands. *Died 9 July 1992.*

BULKELEY, Sir Richard Harry David W.; *see* Williams-Bulkeley.

BULL, Megan Patricia, (Lady Bull), OBE 1982; Governor, Holloway Prison, 1973–82; *b* Naaupoort, S Africa, 17 March 1922; *d* of Dr Thomas and Letitia Jones; *m* 1947, Sir Graham MacGregor Bull (*d* 1987); three *s* one *d*. *Educ:* Good Hope Seminary, Cape Town; Univ. of Cape Town. MB, ChB Cape Town 1944, DCH London 1947, MSc QUB 1961, DPM London 1970, MRCP 1974. Lectr in Physiology, Belfast Coll. of Technology, 1954–61; Med. Officer, Student Health Dept, QUB, 1961–66; Prison Med. Officer, Holloway Prison, 1967–73. *Publications:* papers in various medical jls. *Address:* c/o 17 High Road, NI5 5LT. *Died 8 Aug. 1995.*

BULL, Sir Walter (Edward Avenon), KCVO 1977 (CVO 1964); FRICS; Consultant, Walter Bull & Co., chartered surveyors, since 1987; *b* 17 March 1902; *s* of Walter Bull, FRICS, and Florence Bull; *m* 1933, Moira Christian, *d* of William John Irwin and Margaret Irwin, Dungannon, N Ireland; one *s*. *Educ:* Gresham's Sch.; Aldenham. Sen. Partner, Vigers, 1942–74, Consultant, 1974–87. Dir, City of London Building Soc., 1957–74. Mem. Council, Duchy of Lancaster, 1957–74. Pres., RICS, 1956. Dep. Comr, War Damage Commn, 1952–75. Liveryman, Merchant Taylors' Co. Silver Jubilee Medal, 1977. *Publications:* papers to RICS on Landlord and Tenant Acts. *Recreations:* music, golf, bowls. *Address:* The Garden House, 1 Park Crescent, Brighton BN2 3HA. *T:* Brighton (01273) 681196. *Died 9 Jan. 1995.*

BULLARD, Denys Gradwell; Member, Anglian Water Authority and Chairman, Broads Committee, 1974–83; *b*

15 Aug. 1912; *s* of John Henry Bullard; *m* 1970, Diana Patricia Cox; one *s* one *d*. *Educ:* Wisbech Grammar Sch.; Cambridge Univ. Farmer. Broadcaster on agricultural matters both at home and overseas. MP (C) SW Div. of Norfolk, 1951–55; MP (C) King's Lynn, 1959–64. PPS: to Financial Sec., Treasury, 1955; to Min. of Housing and Local Govt, 1959–64. *Recreation:* gardening. *Address:* Elm House, Elm, Wisbech, Cambs PE14 0AB. *T:* Wisbech (01945) 583021.   *Died 2 Nov. 1994.*

BULLARD, Sir Giles (Lionel), KCVO 1985; CMG 1981; HM Diplomatic Service, retired; *b* 24 Aug. 1926; 2nd *s* of Sir Reader Bullard, KCB, KCMG, CIE, and late Miriam (*née* Smith); *m* 1st, 1952, Hilary Chadwick Brooks (*d* 1978); two *s* two *d*, 1982, Linda Rannells Lewis. *Educ:* Blundell's Sch.; Balliol Coll., Oxford. Army service, 1944–48; Oxford Univ., 1948–51 (Capt. OURFC); H. Clarkson & Co. Ltd, 1952–55; HM Foreign (later Diplomatic) Service, 1955; 3rd Sec., Bucharest, 1957; 2nd Sec., Brussels, 1958; 1st Sec., Panama City, 1960; FO, 1964; DSAO, 1965; Head of Chancery, Bangkok, 1967; Counsellor and Head of Chancery, Islamabad, 1969; FCO Fellow, Centre of South Asian Studies, Cambridge, 1973; Inspectorate, FCO, 1974; Consul-Gen., Boston, 1977; Ambassador, Sofia, 1980; High Comr, Bridgetown, 1983–86. *Recreation:* village life. *Address:* Manor House, West Hendred, Wantage, Oxon OX12 8RP. *Club:* Huntercombe Golf.   *Died 11 Nov. 1992.*

BULLEN, Dr William Alexander; Managing Director, 1967–77, Deputy Chairman, 1974, Chairman, 1975–81, Thomas Borthwick & Sons plc; *b* 22 Sept. 1918; *s* of Francis Lisle Bullen and Amelia Morgan; *m* 1st, 1943, Phyllis (marr. diss. 1955), *d* of George Leeson; three *d*; 2nd, 1956, Mary (marr. diss. 1983), *d* of Leigh Crutchley; 3rd, 1983, Rosalind, *d* of Lawrence Gates. *Educ:* Merchant Taylors' Sch., Crosby; London Hosp. Med. Coll. MRCS, LRCP, MRCGP. Royal Tank Regt, UK and Middle East, 1939–45 (Hon. Major). Med. Dir, Boehringer Pfizer, 1957, Sales Man. 1958; Pres., Pfizer Canada, 1962; Gen. Man., Pfizer Consumer Options UK, 1964–66; Chm., Coty (England), 1965; Man. Dir, Scribbans Kemp, 1966. Chm., Whitburgh Investments, 1976–80; Président-Directeur Général, Boucheries Bernard, 1977–81. FBIM 1975. Liveryman, Butchers' Co.; Freeman, City of London. *Publication:* paper on acute heart failure in London Hosp. Gazette. *Recreations:* sailing, viticulture, music. *Club:* Royal Thames Yacht.   *Died 30 Oct. 1992.*

BULMER-THOMAS, Ivor, CBE 1984; FSA 1970; writer; Hon. Director, Friends of Friendless Churches, since 1957; Vice-President, Church Union; *b* 30 Nov. 1905; *s* of late A. E. Thomas, Cwmbran, Newport, Mon and Zipporah (*née* Jones); assumed additional surname Bulmer by deed poll, 1952; *m* 1st, 1932, Dilys (*d* 1938), *d* of late Dr W. Llewelyn Jones, Merthyr Tydfil; one *s*; 2nd, 1940, Margaret Joan, *d* of late E. F. Bulmer, Adam's Hill, Hereford; one *s* two *d*. *Educ:* West Monmouth Sch., Pontypool; Scholar of St John's Coll. (Hon. Fellow, 1985) and Senior Demy of Magdalen Coll., Oxford. 1st Class Math. Mods, 1925; 1st Class Lit. Hum., 1928; Liddon Student, 1928; Ellerton Essayist, 1929; Junior Denyer and Johnson Scholar, 1930; MA 1937. Represented Oxford against Cambridge at Cross-country Running, 1925–27, and Athletics, 1926–28, winning Three Miles in 1927; Welsh International Cross-country Runner, 1926. Gladstone Research Student at St Deiniol's Library, Hawarden, 1929–30; on editorial staff of The Times, 1930–37; chief leader writer to News Chronicle, 1937–39; acting deputy editor, Daily Telegraph, 1953–54. Served War of 1939–45 with Royal Fusiliers, 1939–40 (Fusilier), and Royal Norfolk Regt, 1940–42, 1945 (Captain, 1941). Contested (Lab) Spen Valley div., 1935; MP Keighley, 1942–50 (Lab 1942–48; C 1949–50); contested (C)

Newport, Mon, 1950. Parliamentary Secretary, Ministry of Civil Aviation, 1945–46; Parliamentary Under-Sec. of State for the Colonies, 1946–47. Delegate to Gen. Assembly, UN, 1946; first UK Mem., Trusteeship Council, 1947. Mem. of the House of Laity of the Church Assembly, 1950–70, of General Synod, 1970–85. Lately Chairman: Faith Press; Executive Cttee, Historic Churches Preservation Trust; Chairman: Redundant Churches Fund, 1969–76; Ancient Monuments Soc., 1975–90. Hon. DSc Warwick, 1979; Hon. DLitt Wales, 1992. Stella della Solidarietà Italiana, 1948. *Publications:* Coal in the New Era, 1934; Gladstone of Hawarden, 1936; Top Sawyer, a biography of David Davies of Llandinam, 1938; Greek Mathematics (Loeb Library), 1939–42; Warfare by Words, 1942; The Problem of Italy, 1946; The Socialist Tragedy, 1949;(ed) E. J. Webb, The Names of the Stars, 1952; The Party System in Great Britain, 1953; The Growth of the British Party System, 1965; (ed) St Paul, Teacher and Traveller, 1975; East Shefford Church, 1978; Dilysia: a threnody, 1987; contrib. to Dictionary of Scientific Biography, vol. 37 of Aufstieg und Niedergang der römischen Welt, Classical Review, Classical Qly, Isis. *Address:* 12 Edwardes Square, W8 6HG. *T:* 071–602 6267; Old School House, Farnborough, Wantage, Oxon OX12 8NX. *Clubs:* Athenæum; Vincent's (Oxford).
                              Died 7 Oct. 1993.

BUNFORD, John Farrant, MA; FIA; Hon. FFA; Director, National Provident Institution for Mutual Life Assurance, 1964–85, retired (Manager and Actuary 1946–64); *b* 4 June 1901; *s* of late John Henry Bunford and Ethel Farrant Bunford; *m* 1929, Florence Louise, *d* of late John and Annie Pearson, Mayfield, Cork; two *s* one *d*. *Educ:* Christ's Hosp.; St Catharine's Coll., Cambridge. (MA). Scottish Amicable Life Assurance Soc., 1923–29; Royal Exchange Assurance, 1929–32; National Provident Institution: Dep. Asst Actuary, 1932; Asst Sec., 1933; Asst Manager, 1937. Institute of Actuaries: Fellow, 1930; Hon. Sec., 1944–45; Vice-Pres., 1948–50; Treas., 1952–53; Pres., 1954–56. Hon. Fellow, Faculty of Actuaries, 1956. *Recreation:* gardening. *Address:* 14 Shepherds Way, Liphook, Hants GU30 7HF. *T:* Liphook (0428) 722594.   *Died 5 July 1992.*

BUNTING, Sir (Edward) John, AC 1982; KBE 1977 (CBE 1960); Kt 1964; BA; Australian civil servant (retired); Chairman, Official Establishments Trust, 1983–92; National Co-ordinator, Sir Robert Menzies Memorial Foundation, since 1978; *b* Ballarat, Vic, 13 Aug. 1918; *s* of late G. B. Bunting; *m* 1942, Pauline, (Peggy), *d* of late D. C. MacGruer; three *s*. *Educ:* Trinity Grammar School, Melbourne; Trinity Coll., Univ. of Melbourne (BA Hons; Hon. Fellow 1981). Asst Sec., Prime Minister's Dept, Canberra, 1949–53; Official Sec., Office of the High Commissioner for Australia, London, 1953–55; Deputy Sec., Prime Minister's Dept, Canberra, 1955–58; Secretary: Australian Cabinet, 1959–75; Prime Minister's Dept, 1959–68; Dept of the Cabinet Office, 1968–71; Dept of the Prime Minister and Cabinet, 1971–75; High Comr for Australia in UK, 1975–77. Chm., Roche-Maag Ltd, 1978–83. Mem., Australia Council, 1978–82. *Publication:* R. G. Menzies: a portrait, 1988. *Recreations:* cricket, music, reading. *Address:* 3 Wickham Crescent, Red Hill, ACT 2603, Australia. *Clubs:* Commonwealth (Canberra); Athenæum (Melbourne); Melbourne Cricket.
                              Died 2 May 1995.

BURBURY, Hon. Sir Stanley Charles, KCMG 1981; KCVO 1977; KBE 1958; Governor of Tasmania, 1973–82; *b* 2 Dec. 1909; *s* of Daniel Charles Burbury and Mary Burbury (*née* Cunningham); *m* 1934, Pearl Christine Barren; no *c*. *Educ:* Hutchins Sch., Hobart; Univ. of Tasmania (LLB 1933; Hon. LLD 1970). Admitted to Bar, 1934; QC 1950; Solicitor-Gen. for Tasmania, 1952; Chief

Justice, Supreme Court of Tasmania, 1956–73. Pres., Nat. Heart Foundn of Australia, 1967–73; Nat. Pres., Winston Churchill Memorial Trust, 1980–85. KStJ 1974. Hon. Col, Royal Tasmanian Regt, 1974–82. *Recreations:* music, lawn bowls. *Address:* 3 Mona Street, Kingston, Tasmania 7050, Australia. *Clubs:* Tasmanian, Athenæum, Royal Hobart Bowls (Hobart).   *Died 24 April 1995.*

BURCHMORE, Air Cdre Eric, CBE 1972 (OBE 1963; MBE 1945); JP; Royal Air Force, retired; *b* 18 June 1920; *s* of Percy William Burchmore and Olive Eva Ingledew; *m* 1941, Margaret Ovendale; one *d. Educ:* Robert Atkinson Sch., Thornaby; RAF Halton; Heriot-Watt Coll., Edinburgh. CEng, MRAeS. Royal Air Force: Aircraft Apprentice, 1936–39; Fitter 2, 1939–41; Engr Officer, 1941: served in Fighter Comd; Air Comd SE Asia, 1943–45; Air Min. and various home postings; Far East, 1952–55; London and Staff Coll.; Near East, 1960–62; comd RAF Sealand, 1963–66; Far East, 1967–68; Dir RAF Project (subseq. Dir Harrier Projects), MoD(PE), 1969–75; retired 1975. Dep. Dir of Housing, London Borough of Camden, 1975–80; Manager, Defence Support Services, Technicare Internat., 1981–84. JP Godstone, Surrey, 1979. *Address:* 28 Dorin Court, Landscape Road, Warlingham, Surrey CR3 9JT. *Club:* Royal Air Force.   *Died 11 Oct. 1994.*

BURDEN, 2nd Baron *cr* 1950, of Hazlebarrow, Derby; **Philip William Burden;** *b* 21 June 1916; *s* of 1st Baron Burden, CBE, and Augusta (*d* 1976), *d* of David Sime, Aberdeen; *S* father, 1970; *m* 1951, Audrey Elsworth, *d* of Major W. E. Sykes; three *s* three *d. Educ:* Raines Foundation School. *Heir: s* Hon. Andrew Philip Burden, *b* 20 July 1959.   *Died 25 June 1995.*

BURFORD, Eleanor; *see* Hibbert, E.

BURGER, Warren Earl; Chief Justice of the United States, 1969–86; Chairman, Commission on the Bicentennial of the United States Constitution, 1985–92; *b* St Paul, Minn, 17 Sept. 1907; *s* of Charles Joseph Burger and Katharine Schnittger; *m* 1933, Elvera Stromberg (*d* 1994); one *s* one *d. Educ:* Univ. of Minnesota; St Paul Coll. of Law, later Mitchell Coll. of Law (LLB *magna cum laude,* LLD). Admitted to Bar of Minnesota, 1931; Mem. Faculty, Mitchell Coll. of Law, 1931–46; Partner in Faricy, Burger, Moore & Costello, 1931–53; Asst Attorney-Gen. of US, 1953–56; Judge, US Court of Appeals, Washington, DC, 1956–69. Chm., ABA Proj. Standards for Criminal Justice. Past Lectr, Law Schools in US and Europe. Hon. Master of the Bench of the Middle Temple, 1966 and King's Inn, Dublin, 1986. Pres. Bentham Club, UCL, 1972–73. Chancellor and Regent, Smithsonian Instn, Washington, DC, 1969–86; Chancellor, Coll. of William and Mary, Williamsburg, Va, 1986–93; Hon. Chm., Inst. of Judicial Admin; Trustee: Nat. Gall. of Art, Washington, DC, 1969–86; Nat. Geographic Soc., 1969–; Trustee Emeritus: Mitchell Coll. of Law, St Paul, Minn; Macalester Coll., St Paul, Minn; Mayo Foundn, Rochester, Minn. *Publications:* articles in legal and professional jls. *Address:* c/o Supreme Court, Washington, DC 20543, USA.   *Died 25 June 1995.*

BURGESS, Anthony, CLit 1991; BA; novelist and critic; *b* 25 Feb. 1917; *s* of Joseph Wilson and Elizabeth Burgess; *m* 1942, Llewela Isherwood Jones, BA (*d* 1968); *m* 1968, Liliana Macellari, *d* of Contessa Maria Lucrezia Pasi della Pergola; one *s. Educ:* Xaverian Coll., Manchester; Manchester Univ. Served Army, 1940–46. Lecturer: Birmingham Univ. Extra-Mural Dept, 1946–48; Ministry of Education, 1948–50; English Master, Banbury Grammar Sch., 1950–54; Education Officer, Malaya and Brunei, 1954–59. Vis. Fellow, Princeton Univ., 1970–71; Distinguished Prof., City Coll., NY, 1972–73. Hon. DLitt: Manchester, 1982; Birmingham, 1986; St Andrews, 1991.

Commandeur: de Mérite Culturel, Monaco, 1986; des Arts et des Lettres, France, 1986. TV scripts, Moses the Lawgiver and Jesus of Nazareth (series), 1977; Blooms of Dublin, 1982 (a musical for radio). *Publications:* Time for a Tiger, 1956; The Enemy in the Blanket, 1958; Beds in the East, 1959 (these three, as The Malayan Trilogy, 1972, and as The Long Day Wanes, 1982); The Right to an Answer, 1960; The Doctor is Sick, 1960; The Worm and the Ring, 1961; Devil of a State, 1961; A Clockwork Orange, 1962 (filmed, 1971, adapted for stage, 1990); The Wanting Seed, 1962; Honey for the Bears, 1963; The Novel Today, 1963; Language Made Plain, 1964; Nothing like the Sun, 1964; The Eve of Saint Venus, 1964; A Vision of Battlements, 1965; Here Comes Everybody— an introduction to James Joyce, 1965; Tremor of Intent, 1966; A Shorter Finnegans Wake, 1966; The Novel Now, 1967; Enderby Outside, 1968; Urgent Copy, 1968; Shakespeare, 1970; MF, 1971; Joysprick, 1973; Napoleon Symphony, 1974; The Clockwork Testament, 1974; Moses, 1976; A Long Trip to Teatime, 1976; Beard's Roman Women, 1976; ABBA ABBA, 1977; New York, 1977; L'Homme de Nazareth, 1977 (Man of Nazareth, 1979); Ernest Hemingway and His World, 1978; 1985, 1978; They Wrote in English (Italy), 1979; The Land Where the Ice Cream Grows, 1979; Earthly Powers, 1980; On Going to Bed, 1982; This Man and Music, 1982; The End of the World News, 1982; Enderby's Dark Lady, 1984; Ninety-Nine Novels, 1984; The Kingdom of the Wicked, 1985; Flame into Being, 1985; The Pianoplayers, 1986; Homage to Qwert Yuiop (essays), 1986; Little Wilson and Big God, (autobiog.), 1987; Any Old Iron, 1989; The Devil's Mode, 1989; You've Had Your Time (autobiog.), 1990; Mozart and the Wolf Gang, 1991; A Mouthful of Air, 1992; A Dead Man in Deptford, 1993; *posthumous publication:* Byrne, 1995; *translations of stage plays:* Rostand, Cyrano de Bergerac, 1971; Sophocles, Oedipus the King, 1973; Griboyedov, Chatsky, 1993; *translation of libretto:* Carmen, 1986; as *Joseph Kell:* One Hand Clapping, 1961; Inside Mr Enderby, 1963; as *John Burgess Wilson:* English Literature: A Survey for Students, 1958; contributor to Observer, Spectator, Encounter, Queen, Times Literary Supplement, Hudson Review, Holiday, Playboy, American Scholar, Corriere della Sera, Le Monde, etc. *Recreations:* music composition, piano-playing, cooking, language-learning. *Address:* 44 rue Grimaldi, MC 98000, Monaco; Postfach 77 9642, Lugano, Switzerland.   *Died 22 Nov. 1993.*

BURKE, Sir Joseph (Terence Anthony), KBE 1980 (CBE 1973; OBE 1946); MA; Professor of Fine Arts, University of Melbourne, 1946–78, then Emeritus Professor; Fellow, Trinity College, Melbourne, since 1973; consultant in Art; *b* 14 July 1913; *s* of late R. M. J. Burke; *m* 1940, Agnes, *d* of late Rev. James Middleton, New Brunswick, Canada; one *s. Educ:* Ealing Priory Sch.; King's Coll., Univ. of London; Courtauld Institute of Art; Yale Univ., USA (Henry Fellow, 1936–37). Entered Victoria and Albert Museum, 1938; lent to Home Office and Min. of Home Security, Sept. 1939; Private Sec. to successive Lord Presidents of the Council (Rt Hon. Sir John Anderson, Rt Hon. C. R. Attlee, Rt Hon. Lord Woolton), 1942–45, and to the Prime Minister (Rt Hon. C. R. Attlee), 1945–46. Trustee of Felton Bequest; Fellow, Australian Acad. of the Humanities, Pres., 1971–73. Hon. DLitt Monash, 1977; Hon. DCL Melbourne. *Publications:* Hogarth and Reynolds: a Contrast in English Art Theory, 1943; (ed) William Hogarth's Analysis of Beauty and Autobiographical Notes, 1955; (with Colin Caldwell) Hogarth: The Complete Engravings, 1968; vol. IX, Oxford History of English Art, 1714–1800, 1976; articles in Burlington Magazine, Warburg Journal and elsewhere. *Recreations:* reading, nature study. *Address:* Dormers,

Falls Road, Mount Dandenong, Victoria 3767, Australia. *Clubs:* Athenæum; Melbourne (Melbourne).
Died 25 March 1992.

BURKILL, John Charles, ScD; FRS 1953; Honorary Fellow, Peterhouse, Cambridge; Emeritus Reader in Mathematical Analysis, Cambridge; *b* 1 Feb. 1900; *s* of Hugh Roberson Burkill and Bertha Burkill (*nee* Bourne); *m* 1928, Margareta, (*d* 1984), *d* of Dr Braun; one *s* (two *d* decd). *Educ:* St Paul's; Trinity Coll., Cambridge (Fellow 1922–28). Professor of Pure Mathematics in the University of Liverpool, 1924–29; Fellow of Peterhouse, 1929–67; Master of Peterhouse, 1968–73. Smith's Prize, 1923; Adams Prize, 1949. *Address:* 2 Archway Court, Barton Road, Cambridge CB3 9LW. *Died 6 April 1993.*

BURKITT, Denis Parsons, CMG 1974; MD, FRCSE; FRS 1972; Medical Research Council External Scientific Staff, 1964–76; Hon. Senior Research Fellow, St Thomas's Hospital Medical School, 1976–84; *b* Enniskillen, NI, 28 Feb. 1911; *s* of James Parsons Burkitt and Gwendoline (*nee* Hill); *m* 1943, Olive Mary (*nee* Rogers); three *d. Educ:* Dean Close Sch., Cheltenham; Dublin Univ. BA 1933; MB, BCh, BAO 1935; FRCSE 1938; MD 1946. Surgeon, RAMC, 1941–46. Joined HM Colonial Service: Govt Surgeon, in Uganda, 1946–64, and Lectr in Surgery, Makerere University Coll. Med. Sch.; final appt, Sen. Consultant Surgeon to Min. of Health, Uganda, 1961. First described a form of cancer common in children in Africa, now named Burkitt's Lymphoma. Foundn and Hon. Fellow, E Africa Assoc. of Surgeons; Hon. Fellow, Sudan Assoc. of Surgeons; Hon. FRCSI 1973; Hon. FRCPI 1977; Hon. FRCP&S (Canada), 1992; Foreign Associate Mem., Académie des Sciences, France. Former Pres., Christian Medical Fellowship; a Vice-Pres., CMS. Harrison Prize, ENT Section of RSM, 1966; Stuart Prize, 1966, Gold Medal, 1978, BMA; Arnott Gold Medal, Irish Hosps and Med. Schs Assoc., 1968; Katharine Berkan Judd Award, Sloan-Kettering Inst., New York, 1969; Robert de Villiers Award, Amer. Leukaemia Soc., 1970; Walker Prize for 1966–70, RCS, 1971; Paul Ehrlich-Ludwig Darmstaedter Prize, Paul Ehrlich Foundn, Frankfurt, 1972; Soc. of Apothecaries' Medal, 1972; Albert Lasker Clinical Chemotherapy Award, 1972; Gairdner Foundn Award, 1973; (jtly) Bristol-Myers Award for Cancer Research, 1982; Charles S. Mott Prize, Gen. Motors Cancer Res. Foundn, 1982; Diplôme de Médaille d'Or, Académie de Médecine, France, 1982; Beaumont Bonelli Award for Cancer Research, Beaumont Foundn, Italy, 1983. Le Prix Mondiale Cino del Duca, France, 1987; Buchanan Medal, Royal Soc., 1992; Bower Science Award, Franklin Inst., Philadelphia, 1993. Hon. FTCD. Hon. MD Bristol, 1979; Hon. DSc: E Africa, 1970; Leeds, 1982; Ulster, 1989; Hon. DSc (Med) London, 1984. Co-editor, Fibre-depleted Foods and Disease (dietary film), 1985. *Publications:* co-editor: Treatment of Burkitt's Lymphoma (UICC Monograph 8), 1967; Burkitt's Lymphoma, 1970; Refined Carbohydrate Foods and Disease, 1975; Don't Forget the Fibre in your Diet, 1979; Western Diseases, their emergence and prevention, 1981; over 300 contribs to scientific jls. *Address:* Hartwell Cottage, Bisley, Glos GL6 7AG. *T:* Gloucester (0452) 770245. *Died 23 March 1993.*

BURLEIGH, George Hall; HM Diplomatic Service, retired; Counsellor, Foreign and Commonwealth Office, 1981–91; *b* 24 June 1928; *s* of William Burleigh and Hannah (*nee* Hall); *m* 1957, Barbara Patricia Rigby; two *d. Educ:* Friends Sch., Lisburn; Trinity Coll., Dublin (MA); Trinity Coll., Cambridge. HM Colonial Service (later HMOCS), 1951–62: Asst Dist Comr, Gambaga, Northern Territories, Gold Coast, 1951; Dist Comr, Navrongo, 1952; Govt Agent, Salaga, 1953–54, Tamale, 1955, Zuarungu, 1955–56, Lawra, 1957 and Gambaga, 1958; Sen. (later

Principal) Asst Sec., Min. of Communications and Works, 1959–62; FO, 1962–64; Aden, 1965; FO, 1965–68; First Sec., Dubai, 1968–70 and Bahrain, 1970; FCO, 1971; First Sec., Jakarta, 1972–75 and Stockholm, 1976–81. *Recreations:* books, cricket, travel. *Address:* Buckingham House, 1 Royal Chase, Tunbridge Wells, Kent TN4 8AX. *T:* Tunbridge Wells (0892) 22359. *Clubs:* Travellers', Commonwealth Trust. *Died 28 June 1991.*

BURMAN, Sir Stephen (France), Kt 1973; CBE 1954 (MBE 1943); MA; Chairman, Serck Ltd, Birmingham, 1962–70; Director: Averys, Ltd, 1951–73; Imperial Chemical Industries Ltd, 1953–75; Imperial Metal Industries Ltd, 1962–75; J. Lucas Industries Ltd, 1952–75, and other industrial companies; *b* 27 Dec. 1904; *s* of Henry Burman; *m* 1931, Joan Margaret Rogers (*d* 1992); one *s* (and one *s* decd). *Educ:* Oundle. Pres. Birmingham Chamber of Commerce, 1950–51 (Vice-Pres. 1949); Chm. United Birmingham Hosps., 1948–53, Dep. Chm. 1953–56; Governor Birmingham Children's Hosp., 1944–48; Dep. Chm. Teaching Hosps Assoc., 1949–53. Dir, Midland Bank Ltd, 1959–76; Member, Midlands Electricity Board, 1948–65; Chm. Birmingham and District Advisory Cttee for Industry, 1947–49; Member Midland Regional Board for Industry, 1949–65, Vice-Chm. 1951–65; Member of Council and Governor, Univ. of Birmingham, 1949–76, Pro-Chancellor, 1955–66. General Commissioner for Income Tax, 1950–68. Member Royal Commission on Civil Service, 1953–56. Hon. LLD Birmingham, 1972. *Recreation:* gardening. *Address:* 12 Cherry Hill Road, Barnt Green, Birmingham B45 8LJ. *T:* 021–445 1529. *Died 16 Dec. 1992.*

BURN, Andrew Robert, (Robin), DLitt, FSA 1979; historian; *b* 25 Sept. 1902; *s* of Rev. A. E. Burn and Celia Mary, *d* of Edward Richardson; *m* 1938, Mary, *d* of Wynn Thomas, OBE, Ministry of Agriculture. *Educ:* Uppingham Sch.; Christ Church, Oxford. DLitt Oxon, 1982. Sen. Classical Master, Uppingham Sch., 1927–40; British Council Rep. in Greece, 1940–41; Intelligence Corps, Middle East, 1941–44; 2nd Sec., British Embassy, Athens, 1944–46; Sen. Lectr and sole Mem. Dept of Ancient History, Univ. of Glasgow, 1946; Reader, 1965; resigned, 1969. Vis. Prof. at "A College Year in Athens", Athens, Greece, 1969–72. Pres. Glasgow Archæological Soc., 1966–69. Silver Cross of Order of Phoenix (Greece). *Publications:* Minoans, Philistines and Greeks, 1930; The Romans in Britain, 1932; The World of Hesiod, 1936; This Scepter'd Isle: an Anthology, 1940 (Athens); The Modern Greeks, 1942 (Alexandria); Alexander and the Hellenistic World, 1947; Pericles and Athens, 1948; Agricola and Roman Britain, 1953; The Lyric Age of Greece, 1960; Persia and the Greeks, 1962; The Pelican History of Greece, 1966; The Warring States of Greece (illustrated), 1968; Greece and Rome (History of Civilisation Vol. II), 1970 (Chicago); (with Mary W. Burn) The Living Past of Greece, 1980; contributions to encyclopædias and historical journals. *Recreations:* travel, reading, classical music (radio). *Address:* 23 Ritchie Court, 380 Banbury Road, Oxford OX2 7PW. *T:* Oxford (0865) 510423. *Died 17 June 1991.*

BURN, Robin; *see* Burn, A. R.

BURNET, Pauline Ruth, CBE 1970; JP; President, Cambridgeshire Mental Welfare Association, since 1977 (Chairman, 1964–76); Chairman, Cambridge Society for Mentally Handicapped Children, since 1982; *b* 23 Aug. 1920; *d* of Rev. Edmund Willis and Constance Marjorie Willis (*nee* Bostock); *m* 1940, John Forbes Burnet (*d* 1989), Fellow of Magdalene Coll., Cambridge; one *s* one *d* (and one *s* decd). *Educ:* St Stephen's Coll., Folkestone (later at Broadstairs), Kent. Chm., Cambridgeshire AHA(T), 1973–82; Member: Windsor and Eton Hosp. Management Cttee, 1948–50; Fulbourn and Ida Darwin

HMC, 1951–74 (Chm., 1969–74); E Anglian Regional Hosp. Bd, 1968–74; Bd of Governors of United Cambridge Hosps, 1966–74; Council, Assoc. of Hosp. Management Cttees until 1974 (Chm., 1966–68); Cambs FPC, 1985–87. Mem., Farleigh Hosp. Cttee of Inquiry, 1970. JP City of Cambridge, 1957; Chm., Cambs Magistrates' Courts Cttee, 1978–80. *Recreations:* walking, swimming. *Address:* Grange House, Selwyn Gardens, Cambridge CB3 9AZ. *T:* Cambridge (0223) 350726. *Died 20 Nov. 1991.*

BURNETT, Most Rev. Bill Bendyshe, MA; LTh; *b* 31 May 1917; *s* of Richard Evelyn Burnett and Louisa Dobinson; *m* 1945, Sheila Fulton Trollip; two *s* one *d. Educ:* Bishop's College (Rondebosch); Michaelhouse (Natal); Rhodes University College; St Paul's Theological College, Grahamstown; Queen's College, Birmingham. Schoolmaster, St John's College, Umtata, 1940; Army, 1940–45; deacon, 1946; priest, 1947; Assistant Priest, St Thomas', Durban, 1946–50; Chaplain, Michaelhouse, 1950–54; Vicar of Ladysmith, 1954–57; Bishop of Bloemfontein, 1957–67; Gen. Secretary, S African Council of Churches, 1967–69; Asst Bishop of Johannesburg, 1967–69; Bishop of Grahamstown, 1969–74; Archbishop of Cape Town and Metropolitan of S Africa, 1974–81. ChStJ 1975. Hon. DD Rhodes, 1980. *Publications:* Anglicans in Natal, 1953; (contrib.) Bishop's Move, 1978; (ed) By My Spirit: Renewal in the Worldwide Anglican Church, 1988; The Rock that is higher than I (autobiog.), 1993. *Recreation:* gardening. *Address:* 20 Milner Street, Grahamstown, 6140, South Africa.
Died 23 Aug. 1994.

BURNETT, Rev. Canon (Philip) Stephen; Church of England Board of Education, 1970–80; *b* 8 Jan. 1914; *s* of late Philip Burnett and Mrs Burnett, Salton, York; *m* 1954, Joan Hardy, *e d* of C. F. Hardy, Sheffield; one *s* one *d. Educ:* Scarborough Coll.; Balliol Coll., Oxford; Westcott House, Cambridge. Admitted Solicitor, 1936; Lay Missionary, Dio. Saskatchewan, Canada, 1939–41. Intelligence Corps, 1942–44; Staff Capt., GHQ, New Delhi, 1944–45. Deacon, 1947, priest, 1948; Curate of St Andrew's, Chesterton, Cambridge, and Staff Sec., Student Christian Movement, 1947–49; Asst Gen. Sec., SCM, 1949–52; Vicar of St Mary, Bramall Lane, Sheffield, 1952–61; Rural Dean of Ecclesall, 1959–65; Canon Residentiary of Sheffield Cathedral, and Educn Secretary, Diocese of Sheffield, 1961–70, Canon Emeritus 1970–. Hon. Sec., Fellowship of the Maple Leaf, 1965–. *Address:* 91 Chelverton Road, Putney, SW15 1RW. *T:* 081–789 9934. *Died 13 Dec. 1991.*

BURNHAM, 5th Baron, *cr* 1903, of Hall Barn, Beaconsfield, Bucks; **William Edward Harry Lawson,** JP; DL; Bt 1892; Lieutenant-Colonel, Scots Guards, retired 1968; *b* 22 Oct. 1920; *er s* of 4th Baron Burnham, CB, DSO, MC, TD, and (Marie) Enid, Lady Burnham, CBE (*d* 1979), *d* of Hugh Scott Robson, Buenos Aires; *S* father, 1963; *m* 1942, Anne, *yr d* of late Major Gerald Petherick, The Mill House, St Cross, Winchester; three *d* (one *s* decd). *Educ:* Eton. Royal Bucks Yeomanry, 1939–41; Scots Guards, 1941–68; commanded 1st Bn, 1959–62. Chairman: Sail Training Assoc., 1977–; Masonic Housing Assoc., 1980–. JP Bucks, 1970; DL Bucks, 1977. *Recreations:* sailing, shooting, ski-ing. *Heir: b* Hon. Hugh John Frederick Lawson [*b* 15 Aug. 1931; *m* 1955, Hilary Mary, *d* of Alan Hunter; one *s* two *d*]. *Address:* Hall Barn, Beaconsfield, Bucks HP9 2SG. *T:* Beaconsfield (0494) 673315. *Clubs:* Garrick, Turf; Royal Yacht Squadron.
Died 18 June 1993.

BURNISTON, George Garrett, CMG 1972; OBE 1968; consultant physician in rehabilitation medicine; Senior Consultant in Rehabilitation Medicine, Prince Henry and Prince of Wales Hospitals, Sydney; Life Consultant in Rehabilitation Medicine, St George Hospital, Sydney, and Emeritus Consultant in Rehabilitation Medicine, Sutherland Hospital; *b* Sydney, NSW, 23 Nov. 1914; *s* of George Benjamin Burniston, Melbourne, Vic; unmarried. *Educ:* Sydney High Sch.; Sydney Univ. (MB, BS). Served in RAAF Medical Service, 1940–47 (RAF Orthopaedic Service, UK, 1941–43); Gp Captain, RAAF Med. Reserve (retired). Dep. Co-ordinator of Rehabilitation, Min. of Post-War Reconstruction (Aust.), 1946–48; SMO, Dept of Social Services, 1948–53; Fulbright Fellow, USA and UK, 1953–54; PMO, Dept of Social Services, 1954–62; Chairman and Director, Division of Rehabilitation Medicine, Department of Medicine, Prince Henry, Prince of Wales and Eastern Suburbs Hospitals, Sydney, 1963–79; Sen. Lectr, 1963–77, Associate Prof., 1977–79, Sch. of Community Medicine, Univ. of NSW. Member: WHO Expert Advisory Panel on Medical Rehabilitation, 1958–84; Council, Cumberland Coll. of Health Sciences, Sydney, 1970–85 (Chm., 1980–85); Bd of Trustees, Cumberland Coll. Foundn, 1979–; Nat. Adv. Council for the Handicapped, Aust., 1977–83; Advanced Educn Council, Tertiary Educn Commn, 1979–86. Vice-Pres., Internat. Rehabilitation Med. Assoc., 1978–82; Pres., Aust. Coll. of Rehabilitation Med., 1980–82. Foundation Fellow: Aust. Coll. of Med. Administrators, 1968; Australasian Coll. of Rehabilitation Medicine, 1980. Foundn Diplomate, Physical and Rehabilitation Medicine, 1971; FRSH 1973; FRACP 1976; Hon. Fellow, Cumberland Coll. of Health Sciences, Sydney, 1987. *Recreations:* golf, swimming, painting, reading. *Address:* 701 Tradewinds, Boorima Place, Cronulla, NSW 2230, Australia. *T:* (02) 5238383; Suite 804, 135 Macquarie Street, Sydney, NSW 2000, Australia. *T:* (02) 2471951. *Club:* University (Sydney). *Died 27 June 1992.*

BURNS, James, CBE 1967; GM 1941; Chairman, Southern Gas Board, 1967–69, retired; *b* 27 Feb. 1902; *s* of William Wilson Burns and Isobella MacDonald; *m* 1934, Kathleen Ida Holt (*d* 1976); one *d* (one *s* decd). *Educ:* Inverness Royal Academy; Aberdeen Univ.; Cambridge Univ. BSc 1st cl. Hons 1925, PhD 1928, Aberdeen. Entered Research Dept, Gas Light & Coke Co., 1929; worked as Chem. Engr with Chemical Reactions Ltd, in Germany, 1930–32; Production Engr, Gas Light & Coke Co., 1941, Dep. Chief Engr, 1945; Chief Engr, North Thames Gas Board, 1949, Dep-Chm. 1960–62; Chm, Northern Gas Board, 1962–67. President: Instn Gas Engrs, 1957–58; Inst. Fuel, 1961–62, etc. *Publications:* contrib. Jls Instn Gas Engrs, Inst. Fuel, etc. *Recreations:* golf, shooting, country pursuits. *Address:* 4 Corfu, Chaddesley Glen, Canford Cliffs, Dorset BH13 7PG. *T:* Canford Cliffs (0202) 707370.
Died 27 April 1994.

BURNS, Sir John (Crawford), Kt 1957; Director, James Finlay & Co. Ltd, 1957–74; *b* 29 Aug. 1903; *s* of William Barr Burns and Elizabeth Crawford; *m* 1941, Eleanor Margaret Haughton James; one *s* three *d. Educ:* Glasgow High Sch. Commissioned 2/16th Punjab Regt (Indian Army), 1940–46 (despatches). *Recreations:* golf, fishing. *Address:* Blairalan, Dargai Terrace, Dunblane, Perthshire FK15 0AU. *Club:* Oriental. *Died 25 July 1991.*

BURNS, Thomas Ferrier, OBE 1983; Editor of The Tablet, 1967–82; Chairman of Burns & Oates Ltd, 1948–67; Director, The Tablet Publishing Company, 1935–85; *b* 21 April 1906; *s* of late David Burns and late Clara (*née* Swinburne); *m* 1944, Mabel Marañón; three *s* one *d. Educ:* Stonyhurst. Press Attaché, British Embassy, Madrid, 1940–45. *Publication:* The Use of Memory, 1993. *Recreations:* painting, gardening. *Address:* Flat 7, 36 Buckingham Gate, SW1E 6PB. *T:* 0171–834 1385. *Club:* Garrick. *Died 8 Dec. 1995.*

BURNSIDE, Dame Edith, DBE 1976 (OBE 1957); *d* of G. H. Edwards; *m* W. K. Burnside; one *s* one *d. Educ:* St Michael's C of E Girls' Grammar Sch. President: Prince

Henry's Hosp. Central Council of Auxiliary, 1952 (retired); Royal Melbourne Hosp. Almoner Ambulance, 1952–. Member of a number of cttees and socs for charities, the arts, and internat. friendship. *Address:* Grevisfield RSD, Wildwood Road, Sunbury, Vic 3429, Australia. *Died 10 May 1992.*

BURT-ANDREWS, Air Cdre Charles Beresford Eaton, CB 1962; CBE 1959; Royal Air Force, retired; *b* 21 March 1913; *s* of late Major C. Burt-Andrews, RE; *m* 1st, 1941, Elizabeth Alsina Helen, *d* of late Sir Maurice Linford Gwyer, GCIE, KCB, KCSI; one *s* one *d*; 2nd, 1977, Joan Trésor (*née* Cayzer-Evans). *Educ:* Lindisfarne Coll.; Collège des Frères Chrétiens Sophia. Commnd RAF, 1935; served NWF India, 1937–42; S Waziristan ops, 1937; Burma, 1942; comd Army Co-op. Sqdn RAF, 1943; special ops, 1943–44; Air Attaché, British Embassy, Warsaw, 1945–47; Staff Coll., 1948; Sec. Gen. Allied Air Forces Central Europe, Fontainebleau, 1950–52; directing Staff RAF Staff Coll., 1953–55; Head of Far East Defence Secretariat, Singapore, 1955–58; First Comdt, Pakistan Air Force Staff Coll., 1959–61; UK Nat. Mil. Rep., SHAPE, Paris, 1962–65; Asst Comdt, RAF Staff Coll., Bracknell, 1965–68; retd, 1968. *Recreations:* painting, glass engraving. *Address:* 9 Erimi Close, Erimi Village, Limassol District, Cyprus. *Club:* Royal Air Force.
Died 7 Jan. 1995.

BURTON OF COVENTRY, Baroness, *cr* 1962, (Life Peer) of Coventry; **Elaine Frances Burton;** Chairman, Mail Order Publishers' Authority, and President, Association of Mail Order Publishers, 1970–84; President, Institute of Travel Managers in Industry and Commerce, 1977–86; *b* Scarborough, 2 March 1904; *d* of Leslie and Frances Burton. *Educ:* Leeds Girls' Modern Sch.; City of Leeds Training Coll. Leeds elementary schools and evening institutes, 1924–35; South Wales Council of Social Service and educational settlements, 1935–37; National Fitness Council, 1938–39; John Lewis Partnership, 1940–45; writer, lecturer, broadcaster, public relations consultant, 1945–50. MP (Lab) Coventry South, 1950–59; Member of parliamentary delegation to: Netherlands, 1952; Soviet Union, 1954; Siam, 1956; South America, 1958; deleg. to Council of Europe; first woman Chm., Select Cttee on Estimates (sub-Cttee); Mem., Select Cttee on Practice and Procedure (House of Lords). Chairman: Domestic Coal Consumers' Council, 1962–65; Council on Tribunals, 1967–73; Member: Council Industrial Design, 1963–68; ITA, 1964–69; Sports Council, 1965–71; Air Transport Users Cttee, 1973–79 (Hon. Consultant, 1979–). Founder Mem., Social Democratic Party, 1981. Consultant to: John Waddington Ltd, 1959–61; The Reader's Digest, 1969–70; Courtaulds Ltd, 1960–73; Director: Consultancy Ltd, 1949–73; Imperial Domestic Appliances Ltd, 1963–66. *Publications:* What of the Women, 1941; And Your Verdict?, 1943; articles for press, magazines and political journals. *Recreations:* reading, ballet, opera; World's Sprint Champion, 1920; Yorkshire 1st XI (hockey), 1924–32. *Address:* 18 Vincent Court, Seymour Place, W1H 5WR. *T:* 071–262 0864. *Died 6 Oct. 1991.*

BURTON, Air Marshal Sir Harry, KCB 1971 (CB 1970); CBE 1963 (MBE 1943); DSO 1941; Air Officer Commanding-in-Chief, Air Support Command, 1970–73, retired; *b* 2 May 1919; *s* of Robert Reid Burton, Rutherglen; *m* 1st, 1945, Jean (*d* 1987), *d* of Tom Dobie; one *s* one *d*; 2nd, 1988, Sandra Robertson, *d* of Thomas McGlashan. *Educ:* Glasgow High Sch. Joined RAF, 1937; served War of 1939–45, Europe, India, and Pacific (POW, 1940, escaped 1941; despatches, 1942); CO, RAF Scampton, 1960–62; SASO 3 (Bomber) Group, RAF, 1963–65; Air Executive to Deputy for Nuclear Affairs, SHAPE, 1965–67; AOC 23 Group, RAF, 1967–70. Group Captain 1958; Air Cdre 1963; Air Vice-Marshal 1965; Air Marshal

1971. *Address:* Mayfield, West Drive, Middleton-on-Sea, Sussex PO22 7TS. *Club:* Royal Air Force.
Died 29 Nov. 1993.

BURTON, Rev. John Harold Stanley, MA Oxon; General Secretary, Church Lads' Brigade, 1954–64 and 1973–Jan. 1977; Member, Church of England Youth Council, 1954–64; *b* 6 Feb. 1913; *o s* of John Stanley Burton, Grenadier Guards (killed in action 1916), and Lilian Bostock; *m* 1st, 1943, Susan Lella (*d* 1960), *o d* of Sir John Crisp, 3rd Bt; two *d*; 2nd, 1960, Jacqueline Mary Margaret, *o d* of P. L. Forte, Clifton, Bristol; one *d*. *Educ:* Marlborough; University Coll., Oxford; Westcott House, Cambridge. BA 2nd Class Hons in Theology, Oxford, 1935; MA 1937. Deacon, 1936; priest, 1938; Curate of Christ Church, Woburn Square, WC1, 1936–39; Cranleigh, Surrey, 1939–40; Head of Cambridge Univ. Settlement, Camberwell, 1940–43; Chaplain RAFVR, 1943; Fighter Command, 1943–44; 2nd Tactical Air Force, 1944; Bomber Command, 1945; Ordination Secretary, Air Command, SE Asia, and Chaplain 9 RAF General Hospital, Calcutta, 1945–46; demobilised Aug. 1946; Chaplain of Middlesex Hospital, W1, 1946–50; Chaplain of the Royal Free Hospital, 1950–54; Chairman of Hospital Chaplains Fellowship, 1953–54. *Publications:* (contrib.) A Priest's Work in Hospital, 1955; (contrib.) Trends in Youth Work, 1967. *Recreations:* beagling, fishing, shooting, most games. *Address:* 45 Westbourne Terrace, W2 3UR. *T:* 071–262 5780. *Club:* Royal Air Force.
Died 24 March 1993.

BURTON, Maurice, DSc; Zoology Department, British Museum (Natural History), 1927–58, retired; *b* 28 March 1898; *s* of William Francis and Jane Burton; *m* 1929, Margaret Rosalie Maclean; two *s* one *d*. *Educ:* Holloway County Sch.; London Univ. Biology Master, Latymer Foundation, Hammersmith, 1924–27. Science Editor, Illustrated London News, 1946–64; Nature Correspondent, Daily Telegraph, 1949–90. FZS. Kt of Mark Twain, 1980. *Publications:* The Story of Animal Life, 1949; Animal Courtship, 1953; Living Fossils, 1954; Margins of the Sea, 1954; Animal Legends, 1955; Infancy in Animals, 1956; More Animal Legends, 1959; Phœnix Re-born, 1959; Under the Sea, 1960; Animal Senses, 1961; The Elusive Monster, 1961; Systematic Dictionary of Mammals, 1962; (jtly) Purnell's Encyclopedia of Animal Life, 1968–70; Wild Animals of the British Isles, 1968; The Hedgehog, 1969; Encyclopaedia of Animals, 1972; Introduction to Nature (for children), 1972; Prehistoric Animals, 1974; Deserts, 1974; The Colourful World of Animals, 1974; How Mammals Live, 1975; Just Like an Animal, 1978; A Zoo at Home, 1979; *juveniles:* When Dumb Animals Talk, 1955; British Mammals, 1958; Life in the Deep, 1958; In their Element, 1960; The Life of Birds, 1974; upwards of 100 non-technical books on natural history; numerous publications on sponges in a variety of scientific journals. *Recreation:* gardening. *Address:* Weston House, Albury, Guildford, Surrey GU5 9AE. *T:* Shere (048641) 2369.
Died 9 Sept. 1992.

BURTON-TAYLOR, Sir Alvin, Kt 1972; FCA; FAIM; Director: New South Wales Division, National Heart Foundation of Australia; O'Connell Street Associates Pty Ltd; *b* 17 Aug. 1912; *s* of A. A. W. Taylor, Adelaide, and Ruby Ella Burton, Adelaide; *m* 1949, Joan Lorraine Toole; two *s* one *d* (and one *d* decd). *Educ:* Sydney Church of England Grammar Sch. Cooper Bros Way & Hardie, 1930–37; Asst Gen. Manager, then Gen. Manager, Rheem Aust. Ltd, 1937–57; Man. Dir, Email Ltd (Group), 1957–74. *Recreations:* fishing, bowls, gardening. *Address:* Unit 6 Gainsborough, 50–58 Upper Pitt Street, Kirribilli,

NSW 2061, Australia. *Clubs:* Union, Royal Sydney Yacht Squadron, Elanora Country (all in NSW).
Died 29 May 1991.

BUSBY, Sir Matthew, Kt 1968; CBE 1958; President, Manchester United Football Club, since 1980; *b* 26 May 1909; *s* of Alexander and Helen Busby; *m* 1931, Jean Busby (*d* 1988); one *s* one *d* (and four *s* decd). *Educ:* St Brides, Bothwell. Footballer: Manchester City, 1929–36; Liverpool, 1936–39. Served Army, 1939–45. Manchester United Football Club: Manager, 1945–69; Gen. Manager, 1969–71; Dir, 1971–82. Mem., Football League Management Cttee, 1981–82. Freeman of Manchester, 1967. KCSG. *Publication:* My Story, 1957. *Recreations:* golf, theatre. *Address:* 6 Harboro Road, Sale, Cheshire M33 5AB. *Died 20 Jan. 1994.*

BUSH, Alan Dudley; Composer; Conductor; Pianist; Professor of Composition, Royal Academy of Music, 1925–78; *b* 22 Dec. 1900; *s* of Alfred Walter Bush and Alice Maud (*née* Brinsley); *m* 1931, Nancy Rachel Head (*d* 1991); two *d* (and one *d* decd). *Educ:* Highgate Sch.; Royal Academy of Music; Univ. of Berlin. ARAM 1922; Carnegie Award 1924; FRAM 1938; BMus London, 1940; DMus London, 1968. Arts Council Opera Award, 1951; Händel Prize, City Council of Halle (Saale), 1962; Corresp. Member, Deutsche Akademie der Künste, 1955. FRSA 1966. Hon. DMus Dunelm, 1970. Appeared as piano-recitalist, London, Berlin, etc., 1927–33; played solo part in own Piano Concerto, BBC, 1938, with Sir Adrian Boult conducting. Toured Ceylon, India, Australia as Examiner for Assoc. Board of Royal Schools of Music, London, 1932–33; concert tours as orchestral conductor, introducing British Music and own compositions, to USSR, 1938, 1939, 1963, 1967, 1969, 1973, Czechoslovakia, Yugoslavia, Poland, Bulgaria, 1947, Czechoslovakia and Bulgaria again, 1949, Holland, 1950, Vienna, 1951, Berlin (German Democratic Republic) and Hungary, 1952, and Berlin again, 1958; Première of opera Wat Tyler at the Leipzig Opera House, 1953 (British première, 1974); Première of opera Men of Blackmoor at the German National Theatre, Weimar, 1956; Première of opera The Sugar Reapers at the Leipzig Opera House, 1966; Première of opera Joe Hill (The Man Who Never Died), German State Opera, Berlin, 1970. Musical Adviser, London Labour Choral Union, 1929–40; Chairman Workers' Music Assoc., 1936–41 (President 1941–). Chairman Composers' Guild of Great Britain, 1947–48. *Publications:* In My Eighth Decade and Other Essays, 1980; *operas:* Wat Tyler; Men of Blackmoor; The Sugar Reapers; Joe Hill (The Man Who Never Died); and children's operettas; *choral works:* The Winter Journey, Op. 29; Song of Friendship, Op. 34; The Ballad of Freedom's Soldier, Op. 44 (mixed voices); The Dream of Llewelyn ap Gruffydd, Op. 35 (male voices); The Alps and Andes of the Living World, Op. 66 (mixed chorus); Song for Angela Davis; Africa is my Name, Op. 85; Turkish Workers' Marching Song (chorus and piano), Op. 101; The Earth in Shadow (mixed chorus and orch.), Op. 102; Mandela Speaking, to text by Nelson Mandela (baritone solo, mixed chorus and orch.), Op. 110; Folksong arrangements; *song cycles:* Voices of the Prophets, for tenor and piano, Op. 41; Seafarers' Songs for baritone and piano, Op. 57; The Freight of Harvest, for tenor and piano, Op. 69; Life's Span, for mezzo-soprano and piano, Op. 77; Three Songs for baritone and piano, Op. 86; Woman's Life, for soprano and piano, Op. 87; Two Shakespeare Sonnets, Op. 91; *orchestral works:* Dance Overture, Op. 12; Piano Concerto, Op. 18; Symphony No 1 in C, Op. 21; Overture, Resolution, Op. 25; English Suite for strings, Op. 28; Piers Plowman's Day Suite, Op. 30; Violin Concerto, Op. 32; Symphony No 2, The Nottingham, Op. 33; Concert Suite for 'cello and orchestra, Op. 37; Dorian Passacaglia and Fugue, Op. 52; Symphony No 3, The

Byron Symphony, op. 53; Variations, Nocturne and Finale on an English Sea Song for piano and orchestra, Op. 60; Partita Concertante, Op. 63; Time Remembered for Chamber Orchestra, Op. 67; Scherzo for Wind Orchestra with Percussion, Op. 68; Africa: Symphonic Movement for piano and orchestra, Op. 73; Concert Overture for an Occasion, Op. 74; The Liverpool Overture, Op. 76; Lascaux Symphony, Op. 98; Meditation in Memory of Anna Ambrose, Op. 107; Song Poem and Dance Poem for string orch. and piano, Op. 109; Serenade and Duet for string orch. and piano, Op. 111; *chamber music:* String Quartet, Op. 4; Piano Quartet, Op. 5; Five Pieces for Violin, Viola, Cello, Clarinet and Horn, Op. 6; Dialectic for string quartet, Op. 15; Three Concert Studies for piano trio, Op. 31; Suite for Two Pianos, Op. 65; Serenade for String Quartet, Op. 70; Suite of six for String Quartet, Op. 81; Compass Points, Suite for Pipes, Op. 83; Trio for clarinet, cello and piano, Op. 91; Concertino for two violins and piano, Op. 94; Piano Quintet, Op. 104; Octet for flute, clarinet, horn, string quartet and piano, Op. 105; Canzona for flute, clarinet, violin, cello and piano, Op. 106; *instrumental solos and duos:* Prelude and Fugue for piano, Op. 9; Relinquishment for piano, Op. 11; Concert Piece for 'cello and piano, Op. 17; Meditation on a German song of 1848 for violin and String Orchestra or piano, Op. 22; Lyric Interlude for violin and piano, Op. 26; Le Quatorze Juillet for piano, Op. 38; Trent's Broad Reaches for horn and piano, Op. 36; Three English Song Preludes for organ, Op. 40; Northumbrian Impressions for oboe and piano, Op. 42a; Autumn Poem for horn and piano, Op. 45; Two Ballads of the Sea for piano, Op. 50; Two Melodies for viola with piano accompaniment, Op. 47; Suite for harpsichord or piano, Op. 54; Three African Sketches for flute with piano accompaniment, Op. 55; Two Occasional Pieces for organ, Op. 56; For a Festal Occasion for organ, Op. 58A; Prelude, Air and Dance for violin with accompaniment for string quartet and percussion, Op. 61; Two Dances for Cimbalom, Op. 64; Pianoforte Sonata in A flat, Op. 71; Corentyne Kwe-Kwe for piano, Op. 75; Sonatina for recorders and piano, Op. 82; Twenty-four Preludes for Piano, Op. 84; Sonatina for viola and piano, Op. 88; Rhapsody for cello and piano, Op. 89; Meditation and Scherzo for double-bass and piano, Op. 93; Scots Jigganspiel for piano, Op. 95; Six Short Pieces for piano, Op. 99; Summer Fields and Hedgerows, Two Impressions for clarinet and piano, Op.100; Serenade and Duet for violin and piano, Op. 111; Distant Fields for piano, Op. 112; Piano Sonata in G, Op. 114; Two Pieces for Nancy for piano solo, Op. 115; Prelude and Concert Piece for organ, Op. 116; Suite for organ, Op. 117; Three Five Beat First Year Pieces for piano, Op. 118; Sonata for Piano, Op. 119; Sonata for cello and piano, Op. 120; Two Preludes and Fugues for piano, Op. 121; The Six Modes for piano duet, Op. 122; A Heart's Expression for piano, Op. 123; *textbook:* Strict Counterpoint in Palestrina Style; *essays:* In My Eighth Decade and other essays, 1980. *Recreations:* walking, foreign travel. *Address:* 25 Christchurch Crescent, Radlett, Herts WD7 8AQ. *T:* Radlett (01923) 856422. *Died 31 Oct. 1995.*

BUSHELL, John Christopher Wyndowe, CMG 1971; HM Diplomatic Service, retired; Ambassador to Pakistan, 1976–79; *b* 27 Sept. 1919; *s* of late Colonel C. W. Bushell, RE, and Mrs Bushell, Netherbury, Dorset; *m* 1964, Mrs Theodora Todd, *d* of late Mr and Mrs Senior; one *s*, and one step *s* one step *d. Educ:* Winchester; Clare Coll., Cambridge. Served War of 1939–45, RAF. Entered FO, 1945; served in Moscow, Rome, FO; 1st Sec., 1950; NATO Defence Coll., Paris, 1953–54; Deputy Sec.-Gen., CENTO, 1957–59; Counsellor, 1961; Political Adviser to the Commander-in-Chief, Middle East, 1961–64; UK Delegn to NATO, Brussels, 1964–68; seconded to Cabinet Office, 1968–70; Minister and Deputy Commandant,

British Mil. Govt, Berlin, 1970–74; Ambassador to Vietnam, 1974–75; FCO 1975–76. *Recreations:* varied. *Address:* 19 Bradbourne Street, SW6 3TF. *Club:* Travellers'. *Died 14 Dec. 1995.*

BUTE, 6th Marquess of, *cr* 1796; **John Crichton-Stuart,** KBE 1993; JP; Viscount Ayr, 1622; Bt (NS), 1627; Earl of Dumfries, Lord Crichton of Sanquhar and Cumnock, 1633; Earl of Bute, Viscount Kingarth, Lord Mountstuart, Cumrae, and Inchmarnock, 1703; Baron Mountstuart, 1761; Baron Cardiff, 1776; Earl of Windsor, Viscount Mountjoy, 1796; Hereditary Sheriff of Bute; Hereditary Keeper of Rothesay Castle; Lieutenant (RARO) Scots Guards, 1953; Lord-Lieutenant of Argyll and Bute, since 1990; *b* 27 Feb. 1933; *er s* (twin) of 5th Marquess of Bute and Eileen, Marchioness of Bute (*d* 1993), *yr d* of 8th Earl of Granard; *S* father, 1956; *m* 1st, 1955, (Beatrice) Nicola (Grace) (marr. diss. 1977), *o d* of late Lt-Comdr W. B. C. Weld-Forester, CBE; two *s* one *d* (and one *d* decd); 2nd, 1978, Mrs Jennifer Percy. *Educ:* Ampleforth Coll.; Trinity Coll., Cambridge. FRSE 1992. President: Scottish Standing Cttee for Voluntary Internat. Aid, 1968–75 (Chm., 1964–68); National Trust for Scotland, 1991– (Chm., Council and Exec. Cttee, 1969–84; Vice-Pres., 1984–91); Chairman: Scottish Cttee, National Fund for Res. into Crippling Diseases, 1966–; Historic Bldgs Council for Scotland, 1983–88; Museums Adv. Bd (Scotland), 1984–85; Member: Countryside Commission for Scotland, 1970–78; Design Council, Scottish Cttee, 1972–76; Development Commission, 1973–78; Oil Develt Council for Scotland, 1973–78; Bd, British Council, 1987–92 (Chm., Scottish Adv. Cttee, 1987–92); Council, RSA, 1990–92. Trustee, Nat. Galleries of Scotland, 1980–87; Chm. Trustees, Nat. Museums of Scotland, 1985–. Hon. Sheriff-Substitute, County of Bute, 1976. Fellow, Inst. of Marketing, 1967; Hon. FIStructE 1976; Hon. FRIAS 1985. Pres., Scottish Veterans' Garden City Assoc. (Inc.), 1971–. Buteshire CC, 1956–75; Convener, 1967–70; DL Bute, 1961; Lord Lieutenant, 1967–75; JP Bute 1967. Hon. LLD Glasgow, 1970. *Heir:* s Earl of Dumfries [*b* 26 April 1958; *m* 1984, Carolyn E. R. M., *d* of late Bryson Waddell; one *s* two *d*]. *Address:* Mount Stuart, Rothesay, Isle of Bute PA20 9LR. *T:* Rothesay (0700) 502730. *Clubs:* Turf, White's; New, Puffin's (Edinburgh); Cardiff and County (Cardiff).
Died 21 July 1993.

BUTENANDT, Prof. Adolf Friedrich Johann, Dr phil.; President, Max Planck Society, 1960–72, Hon. President since 1972; Director, Max Planck Institute for Biochemistry, München (formerly Kaiser Wilhelm Institute for Biochemistry, Berlin-Dahlem), 1936–72; Professor of Physiological Chemistry, München, 1956–71, then Emeritus; *b* Bremerhaven-Lehe, 24 March 1903; *s* of Otto Butenandt and Wilhelmine (*née* Thornfohrde); *m* 1931, Erika von Ziegner; two *s* five *d. Educ:* Universities of Marburg and Göttingen. Privatdozent, Univ. of Göttingen, 1931; Prof. Ord. of Organic Chemistry, Technische Hochschule, Danzig, 1933; Honorarprofessor, Univ. Berlin, 1938; Prof. Ord. of Physiological Chemistry, Tübingen, 1945. Foreign Member: Royal Society, 1968; Académie des Sciences, Paris, 1974. Dr med. *hc;* Dr med. vet. *hc;* Dr rer. nat. *hc;* Dr phil. *hc;* Dr sci. *hc;* Dr ing. *eh.* Nobel Prize for Chemistry, 1939. *Publications:* numerous contribs to Hoppe-Seyler, Liebigs Annalen, Berichte der deutschen chemischen Gesellschaft, Zeitschrift für Naturforschung, etc. *Address:* 81245 München, Marsop Strasse 5, Germany. *T:* (089) 885490.
Died 18 Jan. 1995.

BUTLER, Rt Rev. Arthur Hamilton, MBE 1944; DD; MA; *b* 8 March 1912; *s* of George Booker and Anne Maude Butler; *m* 1938, Betty (*d* 1976), *d* of Seton Pringle, FRCSI; (one *s* decd); *m* 1979, Dr Elizabeth Mayne. *Educ:* Friars School, Bangor; Trinity Coll., Dublin. Deacon, 1935; priest, 1936; Curate: Monkstown, Dublin, 1935–37; Christ Church, Crouch End, N8, 1937; Holy Trinity, Brompton, SW3, 1938–39. Army, 1939–45: Chaplain, 2nd DCLI, 1939–43; Senior Chaplain, 1st Div., 1943–45. Incumbent of Monkstown, 1945–58; Bishop of Tuam, Killala and Achonry, 1958–69; Bishop of Connor, 1969–81. *Recreation:* golf. *Address:* 1 Spa Grange, Ballynahinch, Co. Down BT24 8PD. *T:* Ballynahinch (0238) 562966. *Club:* Ulster (Belfast).
Died 6 July 1991.

BUTLER, Joyce Shore; Chairman, Hornsey Housing Trust, 1980–88; *b* 13 Dec. 1910; *née* Wells; *m* Victor Butler; one *s* one *d. Educ:* King Edward's High Sch., Birmingham. Mem., Wood Green Council, 1947–64 (Leader, 1954–55; Deputy Mayor, 1962–63); first Chm., London Borough of Haringey, 1964–65; first Mayoress, 1965–66. MP (Lab & Co-op) Wood Green, 1955–74, Haringey, Wood Green, 1974–79; Vice-Chm., Labour Parly Housing and Local Govt Gp, 1959–64; Member: Estimates Cttee, 1959–60; Chairman's Panel, House of Commons, 1964–79; Jt Chm., Parly Cttee on Pollution, 1970–79; PPS to Minister for Land and Natural Resources, 1965. A Vice-Chm., Parly Labour Party, 1968–70. Exec. Mem., Housing and Town Planning Council; Founder and first Pres., Women's Nat. Cancer Control Campaign; Vice-Chm., Wood Green Age Concern; President: London Passenger Action Concern; Buller Road Over-60 Club, Wood Green. *Address:* 8 Blenheim Close, N21 2HQ. *Club:* University Women's.
Died 2 Jan. 1992.

BUTLER, Col Sir Thomas Pierce, 12th Bt *cr* 1628 (Ire.), of Cloughgrenan, Co. Carlow; CVO 1970; DSO 1944; OBE 1954; Resident Governor and Major, HM Tower of London, 1961–71, Keeper of the Jewel House, 1968–71; *b* 18 Sept. 1910; *o s* of Sir Richard Pierce Butler, 11th Bt, OBE, DL, and Alice Dudley (*d* 1965), *d* of Very Rev. Hon. James Wentworth Leigh, DD; *S* father, 1955; *m* 1937, Rosemary Liège Woodgate Davidson-Houston (marr. diss. 1972; remarried 1973), *d* of late Major J. H. Davidson-Houston, Pembury Hall, Kent; one *s* two *d. Educ:* Harrow; Trinity Coll., Cambridge. BA (Hons) Cantab, 1933. Grenadier Guards, 1933; served War of 1939–45 (wounded, POW, escaped); BEF France; 6th Bn, Egypt, Syria, Tripoli, N Africa; Staff Coll., 1944 (psc); Comd Guards Composite Bn, Norway, 1945–46; Comd 2nd Bn Grenadier Guards, BAOR, 1949–52; AQMG, London District, 1952–55; Col, Lt-Col Comdg the Grenadier Guards, 1955–58; Military Adviser to UK High Comr in New Zealand, 1959–61. Pres., London (Prince of Wales's) District, St John Ambulance Brigade. JP Co. of London 1961–71. CStJ. *Recreations:* fishing, travelling. *Heir:* s Richard Pierce Butler [*b* 22 July 1940; *m* 1965, Diana, *yr d* of Col S. J. Borg; three *s* one *d*]. *Address:* 6 Thurloe Square, SW7 2TA. *T:* 071–584 1225; Ballin Temple, Co. Carlow. *Club:* Cavalry and Guards.
Died 9 April 1994.

BUTTERWORTH, Sir (George) Neville, Kt 1973; DL; Chairman, Tootal Ltd (formerly English Calico Ltd), 1968–74; *b* 27 Dec. 1911; *s* of Richard Butterworth and Hannah (*née* Wright); *m* 1947, Barbara Mary Briggs; two *s. Educ:* Malvern; St John's Coll., Cambridge. Served with Royal Artillery, at home and overseas, 1939–45. Joined English Sewing Cotton Co. Ltd, 1933; Man. Dir, 1966; Dep. Chm., 1967; Chm., 1968, on merger with The Calico Printers' Assoc. Ltd. Dir, National Westminster Bank (North Regional Board), 1969–82; Mem., Royal Commn on Distribution of Income and Wealth, 1974–79. Chm., NW Regional Council of CBI, 1968–70; Former Mem., Grand Council of CBI; Trustee, Civic Trust for the North-West, 1967; Mem., Textile Council, 1970; CompTI 1973. Member: Court of Governors, Manchester Univ.,

1973–79; Council, UMIST, 1973–79. CIMgt (FBIM 1968). High Sheriff 1974, DL 1974, Greater Manchester. *Address:* Oak Farm, Ollerton, Knutsford, Cheshire WA16 8SQ. *T:* Knutsford (01565) 633150.

Died 25 July 1995.

BUTTON, Air Vice-Marshal Arthur Daniel, CB 1976; OBE 1959; CEng; Director of Royal Air Force Education Branch, 1972–76; *b* 26 May 1916; *o s* of late Leonard Daniel Button and of Agnes Ann (*née* Derbyshire); *m* 1944, Eira Guelph Waterhouse, *o d* of late Reginald Waterhouse Jones; (one *s* decd). *Educ:* County High Sch., Ilford; University Coll., Southampton (BSc Hons (Lond.)). Joined RAF Educnl Service, 1938; Gen. Duties Br., RAF, 1941–46 (Queen's Commendation for Valuable Service in the Air, 1946); returned to RAF Educn Br., 1946. Dir, ARELS Examinations Trust, 1976–86. Member Council: RAF Benevolent Fund, 1980–89; RAF Assoc., 1980–89; Lord Kitchener Nat. Meml Fund, 1983–. Hon. Pres., ARELS–FELCO, 1990–. Governor, Duke of Kent School, 1981–86. *Recreations:* music, do-it-myself. *Address:* 7 Parsonage Court, Tring, Herts HP23 5BG. *Club:* Royal Air Force. *Died 27 May 1991.*

BYAM SHAW, (John) James, CBE 1972; *b* 12 Jan. 1903; *o* surv. *s* of John Byam Shaw and Evelyn Pyke-Nott; *m* 1st, 1929, Eveline (marr. diss. 1938), *d* of Capt. Arthur Dodgson, RN; 2nd, 1945, Margaret (*d* 1965), *d* of Arthur Saunders, MRCVS; one *s*; 3rd, 1967, Christina, *d* of Francis Ogilvy and *widow* of William P. Gibson. *Educ:* Westminster; Christ Church, Oxford. Scholar of Westminster and Christ Church; MA 1925; Hon. DLitt Oxford, 1977. Worked independently in principal museums of Europe, 1925–33; Lecturer and Assistant to the Director, Courtauld Institute of Art, Univ. of London, 1933–34; joined P. & D. Colnaghi & Co., 1934, Director, 1937–68. Served in Royal Scots, UK, India and Burma, 1940–46 (wounded); Major, 1944. Lectr, 1964–73, Associate Curator of Pictures, 1973–74, Hon. Student, 1976, Christ Church, Oxford. Member: Council of the Byam Shaw Sch. of Art, 1957–77; Exec. Cttee, Nat. Art Collections Fund, 1968–85; Council, British Museum Soc., 1969–74; Gulbenkian Cttee on conservation of paintings and drawings, 1970–72; Conservation Cttee, Council for Places of Worship, 1970–77; Adv. Cttee, London Diocesan Council for Care of Churches, 1974–76; Cons. Cttee, Burlington Magazine, 1984–; Chm., Adv. Cttee, Master Drawings (NY), 1981 (Chm. Emeritus, 1987). Trustee, Watts Gall., 1957–88. FSA; FRSA. Hon. Fellow: Pierpont Morgan Library, NY; Ateneo Veneto. Grande Ufficiale, Ordine al Merito (Republic of Italy), 1982. Nat. Art Collections Fund Award, 1987. *Publications:* The Drawings of Francesco Guardi, 1951; The Drawings of Domenico Tiepolo, 1962; Catalogue of Paintings by Old Masters at Christ Church, Oxford, 1967; Catalogue of Drawings by Old Masters at Christ Church, Oxford, 1976; Catalogue of exhibition, Disegni Veneti della Collezione Lugt, Venice, 1981; Catalogue of Italian Drawings at the Fondation Custodia (Lugt Collection), Institut Néerlandais, Paris, 1983 (Premio Salimbeni, 1984); (with George Knox) Italian 18th Century Drawings in the Robert Lehman Collection, Metropolitan Museum, New York, 1987; publications in Old Master Drawings (1926–39), Print Collectors' Quarterly, Burlington Magazine, Apollo, Master Drawings (New York), Art Quarterly (Detroit), Arte Veneta, etc. *Address:* 4 Abingdon Villas, Kensington, W8 6BX. *T:* 071–937 6128. *Club:* Athenæum. *Died 18 March 1992.*

C

CADBURY, George Woodall, OC 1990; Chairman Emeritus, Governing Body of International Planned Parenthood Federation, since 1975 (Chairman, 1969–75, Vice-Chairman, and Chairman of the Executive, 1963–69, and Special Representative, since 1960); *b* 19 Jan. 1907; *s* of George Cadbury and Edith Caroline Cadbury (*née* Woodall); *m* 1935, Mary Barbara Pearce; two *d. Educ:* Leighton Park Sch., Reading; King's Coll., Cambridge (personal pupil of J. M. Keynes; MA Economics Tripos); Wharton Sch. of Finance and Commerce, Univ. of Pennsylvania. Man. Dir, British Canners Ltd, 1929–35; Marketing Controller and Man. Dir, Alfred Bird & Sons Ltd, 1935–45; Auxiliary, later Nat., Fire Service, 1939–41; Dep. Dir Material Production, Min. of Aircraft Production and British Air Commn (USA), 1941–45; Chm. Economic Advisory and Planning Bd, and Chief Industrial Executive, Prov. of Saskatchewan, 1945–51; Dir, Technical Assistance Administration, UN, 1951–60 (Dir of Ops, 1951–54; Adviser to Govts of Ceylon, Burma, Indonesia and Barbados, 1954–60; Advr to Govt of Jamaica, 1955–60). New Democratic Party of Canada: Pres., Ont, 1961–66; Fed. Treasurer, 1965–69; Mem., Fed. Exec., 1961–71; Life Mem., 1980. Chm., 1972–74 and 1976–78, Pres., 1978–82, Conservation Council of Ontario. Trustee: Bournville Village Trust, 1928–85; Youth Hostels Trust, 1931–; Sponsor and Council Mem., Minority Rights Group, 1967–; Hon. Director, 1961–: Planned Parenthood Fedn of Canada; Planned Parenthood, Toronto; Planned Parenthood Soc., Hamilton, Ont. Member: TGWU, 1925, Life Mem., 1973; League for Industrial Democracy, NY, 1928, Bd Mem., 1951–. Mem. Meetings Cttee, RIIA, 1931–35; Sec., W Midland Group for Post-War Reconstruction and Planning, 1939–41; Resident, Toynbee Hall, 1929–35, 1941–43. *Publications:* (jointly) When We Build Again, 1940; English County, 1942; Conurbation, 1942; Essays on the Left, 1971; A Population Policy for Canada, 1973. *Recreation:* railway practice and history. *Address:* Suite 308, 345 Church Street, Oakville, Ont L6J 7G4, Canada. *T:* (416) 8459845.

Died 24 Feb. 1995.

CADBURY, Kenneth Hotham, CBE 1974; MC 1944; Assistant Managing Director, 1975–77, Deputy Managing Director, 1978–79, Telecommunications, Post Office; *b* 25 Feb. 1919; *s* of J. Hotham Cadbury, manufacturer, Birmingham; *m* 1st, 1947, Margaret R. King (marr. diss. 1955); one *s* one *d*; 2nd, 1955, Marjorie I. Lilley; three *d. Educ:* Bootham Sch., York; Univ. of Birmingham (BCom 1940); Open Univ. (BA Hons 1986). Served in Royal Artillery in Middle East and Italy, 1939–46 (despatches; MC; Major). Joined Foreign Service, 1946; transferred to GPO, 1947; served in Personnel Dept and Inland Telecommunications Dept; Cabinet Office, 1952–55; PPS to PMG, 1956–57; Dep. Director, 1960, Director, 1962, Wales and Border Counties GPO; Director: Clerical Mechanisation and Buildings, GPO, 1964–65; Inland Telecommunications, GPO, 1965–67; Purchasing and Supply, GPO, 1967–69; Sen. Dir, Planning and Purchasing, PO, 1969–75. Trustee, PO Staff Superannuation Fund, 1969–75. *Recreation:* gardening.

Died 9 June 1991.

CADWALLADER, Sir John, Kt 1967; Chairman and Managing Director of Allied Mills Ltd and subsidiaries, 1949–78; President, Bank of New South Wales, 1959–78, retired; *b* 25 Aug. 1902; *s* of Daniel Cadwallader; *m* 1935, Helen Sheila Moxham; two *s* one *d. Educ:* Sydney Church of England Grammar Sch., NSW. *Recreations:* reading, golf. *Address:* 27 Marian Street, Killara, NSW 2071, Australia. *T:* 4981974. *Clubs:* Commonwealth (Canberra, ACT); Australian, Union, Royal Sydney Golf (all Sydney, NSW); Elanora Country (NSW).

Died 22 Oct. 1991.

CAFFIN, Albert Edward, CIE 1947; OBE 1946; Indian Police (retired); *b* 16 June 1902; *s* of Claud Carter and Lilian Edith Caffin, Southsea; *m* 1929, Hilda Elizabeth Wheeler, Bournemouth; no *c. Educ:* Portsmouth. Joined Indian Police as Asst Supt, Bombay Province, 1922; Asst Inspector General, Poona, 1939; Dep. Comr, Bombay, 1944; Comr of Police, Bombay, 1947. *Recreation:* bowls. *Address:* C22 San Remo Towers, Sea Road, Boscombe, Bournemouth, Dorset BH5 1JT. *Club:* Royal Bombay Yacht.

Died 14 April 1992.

CAHILL, John Conway; Chairman, Trans World Airlines, since 1995; *b* 8 Jan. 1930; *m* 1956, Giovanna Caterina, *d* of late Riccardo Lenardon; three *d*. Joined BTR Industries, 1955; Dep. Overseas Gen. Manager, 1963; Board of Directors, 1968; Dep. Managing Dir, 1976; Vice-Pres., BTR Inc., USA, 1978; Pres. and Chief Exec., BTR Inc., and Chm., BTR Pan American operations, 1979–86; non-exec. Chm., BTR Inc., 1987–92; Chief Exec., BTR plc, 1987–90; Chm., British Aerospace, 1992–94. *Recreations:* reading, gardening, music.

Died 4 Nov. 1995.

CAHN, Sammy; lyric writer; *b* New York, 18 June 1913; *s* of Abraham and Alice Cohen; *m* 1st, 1945, Gloria Delson (marr. diss. 1964); one *s* one *d*; 2nd, 1970, Tita Curtis. *Educ:* NY public schools. Violinist. Early songs (with Saul Chaplin): Rhythm is our Business; Bei Mir Bist Du Schon; songs with Jule Styne include: Let it Snow; I'll Walk Alone; It's Magic; Academy Award songs: Three Coins in the Fountain, 1954; All the Way, 1957; High Hopes, 1959; Call Me Irresponsible, 1963; Emmy Award song: Love and Marriage; numerous songs for Frank Sinatra, for cinema, for US and UK productions. Pres., Songwriters' Hall of Fame; Mem., Bd of Dirs, ASCAP. *Publications:* I Should Care (autobiog.), 1974; The Songwriter's Rhyming Dictionary, 1984. *Address:* c/o ASCAP, 1 Lincoln Plaza, New York, NY 10023, USA.

Died 15 Jan. 1993.

CAINE, Sir Sydney, KCMG 1947 (CMG 1945); Director of the London School of Economics and Political Science, 1957–67; *b* 27 June 1902; *s* of Harry Edward Caine; *m* 1st, 1925, Muriel Anne (*d* 1962), *d* of A. H. Harris, MA; one *s*; 2nd, 1965, Doris Winifred Folkard (*d* 1973); 3rd, 1975, Elizabeth, *d* of late J. Crane Nicholls and *widow* of Sir Eric Bowyer, KCB, KBE. *Educ:* Harrow County Sch.; London Sch. of Economics. BSc (Econ) 1st Class Hons 1922. Asst Inspector of Taxes, 1923–26; entered Colonial Office, 1926; Sec., West Indian Sugar Commn, 1929; Sec., UK Sugar Industry Inquiry Cttee, 1934; Financial Sec., Hong Kong, 1937; Asst Sec., Colonial Office, 1940; Member Anglo-American Caribbean Commission, 1942; Financial Adviser to Sec. of State for the Colonies, 1942; Assistant Under-Secretary of State, Colonial Office, 1944; Deputy Under-Secretary of State, Colonial Office, 1947–48; Third Secretary, HM Treasury, 1948; Head of UK Treasury and Supply Delegn, Washington, 1949–51;

Chief, World Bank Mission to Ceylon, 1951; Vice-Chancellor, Univ. of Malaya, 1952–56. Chairman: British Caribbean Federation Fiscal Commission, 1955; Grassland Utilisation Cttee, 1957–58; Internat. Inst. of Educational Planning, 1963–70; Governor (new bd), Reserve Bank of Rhodesia, 1965–67; Coordinator, Indonesian Sugar Study, 1971–72. Mem., Planning Bd of Independent Univ., 1969–73; Chm., Governing Body, Univ. Coll. at Buckingham (Mem. Bd, Univ. of Buckingham, 1973–83); Mem., ITA, 1960–67 (Dep. Chm., 1964–67). Hon. LLD Univ. of Malaya, 1956; DSc *hc* Univ. of Buckingham, 1980. Grand Officer, Orange Nassau (Netherlands), 1947; Comdr, Order of Dannebrog (Denmark), 1965. *Publications:* The Foundation of the London School of Economics, 1963; British Universities: Purpose and Prospects, 1969; The Price of Stability . . . ?, 1983. *Recreations:* reading, walking. *Address:* Buckland House, Tarn Road, Hindhead, Surrey GU26 6TP. *Club:* Reform.
Died 2 Jan. 1991.

CAIRNS, James George Hamilton Dickson; Chief Architect and Director of Works, Home Office, 1975–80; *b* 17 Sept. 1920; *s* of Percival Cairns and Christina Elliot Cairns; *m* 1944, G. Elizabeth Goodman; one *d. Educ:* Hillhead High Sch., Glasgow; London Polytechnic. ARIBA. Served War, Royal Corps of Signals (Intell.), 1941–46. Architects' Dept, GLC, 1946–75. Divisional Architect, Thamesmead New Town, awarded Sir Patrick Abercrombie Prize by Internat. Union of Architects, 1969. *Recreations:* golf, sailing. *Address:* Elmsleigh, 12 Elmstead Park Road, West Wittering, W Sussex PO20 8NQ. *T:* Birdham (01243) 513316. *Clubs:* Goodwood Golf; West Wittering Sailing.
Died 10 April 1995.

CALDER-MARSHALL, Arthur; author; *b* 19 Aug. 1908; *s* of late Arthur Grotjan Calder-Marshall and Alice Poole; *m* 1934, Violet Nancy Sales; two *d. Educ:* St Paul's Sch.; Hertford Coll., Oxford. *Publications: novels:* Two of a Kind, 1933; About Levy, 1933; At Sea, 1934; Dead Centre, 1935; Pie in the Sky, 1937; The Way to Santiago, 1940; A Man Reprieved, 1949; Occasion of Glory, 1955; The Scarlet Boy, 1961, rev. edn 1962; *short stories:* Crime against Cania, 1934; A Pink Doll, 1935; A Date with a Duchess, 1937; *for children:* The Man from Devil's Island, 1958; Fair to Middling, 1959; Lone Wolf: the story of Jack London, 1961; *travel:* Glory Dead, 1939; The Watershed, 1947; *biography:* No Earthly Command, 1957; Havelock Ellis, 1959; The Enthusiast, 1962; The Innocent Eye, 1963; Lewd, Blasphemous and Obscene, 1972; The Two Duchesses, 1978; *autobiography:* The Magic of My Youth, 1951, repr. 1990; *miscellaneous:* Challenge to Schools: public school education, 1935; The Changing Scene, 1937; The Book Front, ed J. Lindsay, 1947; Wish You Were Here: the art of Donald McGill, 1966; Prepare to Shed Them Now . . .: the biography and ballads of George R. Sims, 1968; The Grand Century of the Lady, 1976; *essays:* Sterne, in The English Novelists, ed D. Verschoyle, 1936; Films, in Mind in Chains, ed C. Day Lewis; *edited:* Tobias Smollett, Selected Writings, 1950; J. London, The Bodley Head Jack London, Vols 1–4, 1963–66; Charles Dickens, David Copperfield, 1967, Nicholas Nickleby, 1968, Oliver Twist, 1970, Bleak House, 1976; The Life of Benvenuto Cellini, 1968; Jack London, The Call of the Wild, and other stories, 1969; Jane Austen, Emma, 1970; Thomas Paine, Common Sense and the Rights of Man, 1970. *Address:* c/o Elaine Greene Ltd, 27 Goldhawk Road, W4 8QQ.
Died 17 April 1992.

CALLAGHAN, Sir Allan (Robert), Kt 1972; CMG 1945; agricultural consultant, retired; *b* 24 Nov. 1903; *s* of late Phillip George Callaghan and Jane Peacock; *m* 1st, 1928, Zillah May Sampson (*d* 1964); two *s* one *d* (and one *s*

decd); 2nd, 1965, Doreen Rhys Draper. *Educ:* Bathurst High Sch., NSW; St Paul's Coll., Univ. of Sydney (BScAgr 1924); St John's Coll., Oxford (Rhodes Scholar, BSc 1926, DPhil 1928). Asst Plant Breeder, NSW, Dept of Agriculture, 1928–32; Principal, Roseworthy Agricultural Coll., South Australia, 1932–49; Asst Dir (Rural Industry) in Commonwealth Dept of War Organisation of Industry, 1943; Chm., Land Development Executive in South Australia, 1945–51; Dir of Agriculture, South Australia, 1949–59; Commercial Counsellor, Australian Embassy, Washington, DC, 1959–65; Chm., Australian Wheat Bd, 1965–71. Farrer Medal (for distinguished service to Australian Agriculture), 1954. FAIAS 1959. *Publications:* (with A. J. Millington) The Wheat Industry in Australia, 1956; numerous articles in scientific and agricultural jls on agricultural and animal husbandry matters. *Recreations:* swimming, riding, gardening. *Address:* 11 Wattle Grove, 1 Wynyard Grove, Wattle Park, SA 5066, Australia. *T:* 3327435.
Died 18 July 1993.

CALLAGHAN, Sir Bede (Bertrand), Kt 1976; CBE 1968; Managing Director, Commonwealth Banking Corporation, 1965–76; Chancellor of the University of Newcastle, New South Wales, 1977–88; *b* 16 March 1912; *s* of S. K. Callaghan and Amy M. Ryan; *m* 1940, Mary T. Brewer; three *d. Educ:* Newcastle High Sch. FAIB; FAIM. Commonwealth Bank, 1927. Mem. Board Executive Directors, IMF and World Bank, 1954–59; Gen. Man., Commonwealth Develt Bank of Australia, 1959–65; Chm., Aust. European Finance Corp. Ltd, 1971–76; Chm., Foreign Investment Review Bd, 1976–. Chm., Lewisham Hospital Adv. Bd, 1975–87. Chairman: Aust. Admin. Staff Coll., 1969–76; Inst. of Industrial Economics, 1976–88; Mem. Council, Univ. of Newcastle, NSW, 1966–88, Dep. Chancellor, 1973–77. Hon. DSc Newcastle, 1973. KCGSS 1992. *Recreation:* lawn bowls. *Address:* 69 Darnley Street, Gordon, NSW 2072, Australia. *T:* (2) 4987583. *Club:* Union (Sydney).
Died 9 Sept. 1993.

CALLAN, Prof. Harold Garnet, FRS 1963; FRSE; MA, DSc; Professor of Natural History, St Salvator's College, St Andrews, 1950–82, then Emeritus (Master, United College of St Salvator's and St Leonard's, 1967–68); *b* 5 March 1917; *s* of Garnet George Callan and Winifred Edith Brazier; *m* 1944, Amarillis Maria Speranza, *d* of Dr R. Dohrn, Stazione Zoologica, Naples, Italy; one *s* two *d. Educ:* King's Coll. Sch., Wimbledon; St John's Coll., Oxford (Exhibitioner). Casberd Scholar, St John's Coll., 1937; Naples Biological Scholar, 1938, 1939; Hon. Fellow, St John's Coll., 1988. Served War of 1939–45: Telecommunications Research Establishment, 1940–45; Hon. Commission, RAFVR. Senior Scientific Officer, ARC, Inst. of Animal Genetics, Edinburgh, 1946–50. Member: Advisory Council on Scientific Policy, 1963–64; SRC, 1972–76; Council, Royal Soc., 1974–76. Trustee, British Museum (Natural History), 1963–66. Vis. Prof., Univ. of Indiana, Bloomington, USA, 1964–65. Hon. Foreign Member: American Acad. of Arts and Scis, 1974; Accademia Nazionale dei Lincei, 1982. Hon. DSc St Andrews, 1984. *Publications:* Lampbrush Chromosomes, 1986; scientific papers, mostly on cytology and cell physiology. *Recreations:* shooting, carpentry. *Address:* 2 St Mary's Street, St Andrews, Fife KY16 8AY. *T:* St Andrews (0334) 72311.
Died 3 Nov. 1993.

CALLINAN, Sir Bernard (James), AC 1986; Kt 1977; CBE 1971; DSO 1945; MC 1943; retired; Consultant, Gutteridge, Haskins & Davey Pty Ltd, 1978–81 (Chairman and Managing Director, 1971–78); *b* 2 Feb. 1913; *s* of Michael Joseph Callinan and Mary Callinan (*née* Prendergast); *m* 1943, Naomi Marian (*née* Cullinan); five *s. Educ:* Univ. of Melbourne (BCE; Dip. Town and

Regional Planning). Hon. FIEAust (Pres., 1971–72; P. N. Russell Meml Medal, 1973); FICE; FTS. Lieut to Lt-Col, AIF, 1940–46. Asst Engr, A. Gordon Gutteridge, 1934; Associate, 1946, Sen. Partner, 1948–71, Gutteridge, Haskins & Davey. Chm., CCI Insurances Ltd, 1984–; Director: West Gate Bridge Authority, 1965–82 (Dep. Chm., 1971–81, Chm., 1981–82); British Petroleum Co. of Aust. Ltd, 1969–85; CSR Ltd, 1978–85. Commissioner: State Electricity Commn, 1963–83; Royal Commn of Inquiry, Aust. PO, 1973–74; Aust. Atomic Energy Commn, 1976–82; Australian Broadcasting Commn, 1977–82; Victorian Post Secondary Educn Commn, 1979–82. Chm., New Parlt House Authority (Canberra), 1979–85. Special Advr, Aust. Overseas Project Corp., 1978–82. Pres., Royal Humane Soc. of Australasia, 1986– (Dir, 1979–). Mem., Pontifical Commn on Justice and Peace, Rome, 1977–82. Councillor: La Trobe Univ., 1964–72; Melbourne Univ., 1976–81. Hon. Col, 4/19 Prince of Wales's Light Horse Regt, 1973–78. Hon. DEng Monash, 1984; Hon. LLD Melbourne, 1987. Kernot Meml Medal, Melbourne Univ., 1982. *Publications:* Independent Company, 1953, 3rd impression 1989; John Monash, 1981; contribs to Jl Instn of Engrs, Aust., Jl Royal Soc. of Vic. *Address:* 111 Sackville Street, Kew, Vic 3101, Australia. *T:* 8171230. *Clubs:* Melbourne, Australian, Naval and Military (Melbourne); Melbourne Cricket (Pres., 1979–85). *Died 20 July 1995.*

CALMAN, Mel; artist, writer; cartoonist for The Times and others; *b* 19 May 1931; *s* of Clement and Anna Calman; *m* 1st, 1957, Pat McNeill (marr. diss.); two *d;* 2nd, Karen Usborne (marr. diss. 1982). *Educ:* Perse School, Cambridge; St Martin's School of Art, London (NDD); Goldsmiths' Coll., London (ATD). Cartoonist for: Daily Express, 1957–63; BBC Tonight Programme, 1963–64; Sunday Telegraph, 1964–65; Observer, 1965–66; Sunday Times, 1969–84; The Times, 1979–; freelance cartoonist for various magazines and newspapers, 1957–; also designer of book-jackets, advertising campaigns, and illustrator of books; started The Workshop-gallery, later The Cartoon Gall., devoted to original cartoons, illustrations etc, 1970; produced animated cartoon, The Arrow; syndicated feature, Men & Women, USA, 1976–82; original radio plays: Sweet Tooth, BBC Radio 3, 1987; Rabbit Man, BBC Radio 3, 1989; Pawnshop Blues, BBC Radio 4, 1993. FRSA; FSIA; AGI. *Publications:* Through The Telephone Directory, 1962; Bed-Sit, 1963; Boxes, 1964; Calman & Women, 1967; The Penguin Calman, 1968; (contrib.) The Evacuees, ed B. S. Johnson, 1968; My God, 1970; Couples, 1972; This Pestered Isle, 1973; (contrib.) All Bull, ed B. S. Johnson, 1973; The New Penguin Calman, 1977; Dictionary of Psychoanalysis, 1979; "But It's My Turn to Leave You", 1980; "How About a Little Quarrel before Bed?", 1981; Help!, 1982; Calman Revisited, 1983; The Big Novel, 1983 (dramatised for radio, 1986); It's Only You That's Incompatible, 1984; "What Else Do You Do?" (autobiog.), 1986; Modern Times, 1988; Calman at the Movies, 1990; Merrie England plc, 1990; Calman at the Royal Opera House, 1990; (ed) Sex?, 1993; *posthumous publication:* Calman's Savoy Sketchbook, 1994. *Recreations:* brooding, worrying. *Address:* 44 Museum Street, WC1A 1LY. *T:* 071–242 5335. *Club:* Garrick.
Died 10 Feb. 1994.

CALOVSKI, Mitko; Yugoslav Ambassador to the Court of St James's and to the Republic of Ireland, 1985–89; *b* 3 April 1930; *m* Ilvana; one *s* one *d. Educ:* Higher School of Journalism and Diplomacy, Univ. of Belgrade. Posts with Federal Agencies, 1952–63; with Federal Board, later with Federal Conf. of Socialist Alliance of Working People of Yugoslavia, 1963–67; Consul-General in Toronto, Canada, 1967–71; Dir of Analysis and Policy Planning, Fed. Secretariat for Foreign Affairs, 1971–74;

Dep. Sec.-Gen. of the Presidency, 1974–77; Ambassador to Canada, 1977–81; Mem., Federal Exec. Council and Federal Sec. for Information, 1982–85. Mem. of Yugoslavian Delegns to UN Gen. Assembly, non-aligned Summit and ministerial confs. *Address:* Flat C, Clifton Gardens, W9 1DT. *T:* 0171–266 3226.
Died 25 Dec. 1994.

CALVERT, Henry Reginald, Dr Phil; Keeper of Department of Astronomy and Geophysics in Science Museum, South Kensington, 1949–67; Keeper Emeritus, 1967–69; *b* 25 Jan. 1904; *e s* of late H. T. Calvert, MBE, DSc, of Min. of Health; *m* 1938, Eileen Mary Frow (*d* 1990); two *d. Educ:* Bridlington Sch., East Yorks; St John's Coll., Oxford (Scholar, MA); Univ. of Göttingen, Germany (Dr Phil). 1st Cl. Hons BSc (External) London, 1925; Goldsmiths' Company's Exhibitioner, 1925. Research Physicist, ICI, 1928–30; Research Physicist, Callender's Cable & Construction Co., 1932–34; entered Science Museum, 1934; Dep. Keeper, 1946. Ballistics research for Min. of Supply, 1940–46. Hon. Treas., British Soc. for History of Science, 1952–63. Fellow Royal Astronomical Soc. *Publications:* Astronomy, Globes, Orreries and other Models, 1967; Scientific Trade Cards, 1971; papers in learned journals. *Recreations:* chess, bridge, croquet, gardening. *Address:* 17 Burnham Drive, Reigate, Surrey RH2 9HD. *T:* Reigate (0737) 246893.
Died 15 Aug. 1992.

CAMERON, Gordon Stewart, RSA 1971 (ARSA 1958); Senior Lecturer, School of Drawing and Painting, Duncan of Jordanstone College of Art, Dundee, 1952–81, retired; *b* Aberdeen, 27 April 1916; *s* of John Roderick Cameron; *m* 1962, Ellen Malcolm, RSA. *Educ:* Robert Gordon's Coll., Aberdeen; Gray's Sch. of Art, Aberdeen. Part-time teaching, Gray's Sch. of Art, 1945–50; engaged on anatomical illustrations for Lockhart's Anatomy of the Human Body, 1945–48; apptd Lectr in Duncan of Jordanstone Coll. of Art, 1952. Work in Public Galleries: Aberdeen, Dundee, Perth, Edinburgh, Glasgow; also in private collections in Scotland, England, Ireland and America. Davidson Gold Medal, 1939; Guthrie Award, 1944; Carnegie Travelling Schol., 1946. *Recreation:* gardening. *Address:* 7 Auburn Terrace, Invergowrie, Dundee DD2 5AB. *T:* Dundee (0382) 562318.
Died 1 April 1994.

CAMERON, Sir James Clark, Kt 1979; CBE 1969; TD 1947; Visitor to Council, British Medical Association (past Chairman of Council, 1976–79); *b* 8 April 1905; *s* of Malcolm Clark Cameron, Rannoch, Perthshire; *m* 1933, Irene (*d* 1986), *d* of Arthur Ferguson, Perth; one *s* two *d. Educ:* Perth Academy; St Andrews Univ. (MB, ChB). FRCGP. Served War of 1939–45, as Captain RAMC attached to 1st Bn, The Rifle Bde (despatches), Calais; POW, 1940. Chm., Gen. Med. Services Cttee, BMA, 1964–74, and Hon. Life Member; Chm., Adv. Cttee for Gen. Practice, Council for Post Grad. Med. Educn (England and Wales), 1971–79; Mem., Adv. Cttee on Med. Trng, Commn of the European Communities, 1976–82. Hon. Mem. Council, Cameron Fund Ltd, 1974. Gold Medal for distinguished merit, BMA, 1974. *Address:* 62 Haven Green Court, Haven Green, Ealing, W5 2UY. *T:* 081–997 8262. *Died 22 Oct. 1991.*

CAMERON, Prof. James Munro; University Professor, St Michael's College, University of Toronto, 1971–78, then Emeritus; *b* 14 Nov. 1910; *o s* of Alan and Jane Helen Cameron; *m* 1933, Vera Shaw (*d* 1985); one *d* (one *s* decd). *Educ:* Central Secondary Sch., Sheffield; Keighley Grammar Sch.; Balliol Coll., Oxford (Scholar). Tutor, Workers' Educational Assoc., 1931–32; Staff Tutor, Univ. Coll., Southampton, 1932–35; Staff Tutor, Vaughan Coll., Leicester (Dept of Adult Education, Univ. Coll., Leicester), 1935–43; University of Leeds: Staff Tutor for Tutorial

Classes, 1943–47; Lectr in Philosophy, 1947–60 (Sen. Lectr from 1952); Acting Head of Dept of Philosophy, 1954–55 and 1959–60; Prof. of Philosophy, 1960–67; Master of Rutherford Coll., and Prof. of Philosophy, Univ. of Kent at Canterbury, 1967–71. Vis. Prof., Univ. of Notre Dame, Indiana, 1957–58, 1965; Terry Lectr, Yale Univ., 1964–65. Newman Fellow, Univ. of Melbourne, 1968; Christian Culture Award, Univ. of Windsor, Ont, 1972. Hon. DLittS St Michael's Coll., Univ. of Toronto, 1990. *Publications:* Scrutiny of Marxism, 1948; (trans. with Marianne Kuschnitzky) Max Picard, The Flight from God, 1951; John Henry Newman, 1956; The Night Battle, 1962; Images of Authority, 1966; (ed) Essay on Development (1845 edn), by J. H. Newman, 1974; On the Idea of a University, 1978; The Music is in the Sadness (poems), 1988; Nuclear Catholics and other Essays, 1990; articles and papers in many periodicals. *Address:* 360 Bloor Street E, Apt 409, Toronto, Ontario M4W 3M3, Canada.
Died 14 Dec. 1995.

CAMPBELL OF ESKAN, Baron *cr* 1966 (Life Peer), of Camis Eskan; **John, (Jock), Middleton Campbell,** Kt 1957; Chairman, Commonwealth Sugar Exporters' Association, 1950–84; *b* 8 Aug. 1912; *e s* of late Colin Algernon Campbell, Colgrain, Dunbartonshire and Underriver House, Sevenoaks, Kent and Mary Charlotte Gladys (*née* Barrington); *m* 1st, 1938, Barbara Noel (marr. diss. 1948), *d* of late Leslie Arden Roffey; two *s* two *d*; 2nd, 1949, Phyllis Jacqueline Gilmour Taylor (*d* 1983), *d* of late Henry Boyd, CBE. *Educ:* Eton; Exeter Coll., Oxford (Hon. Fellow, 1973). Chairman: Booker McConnell Ltd, 1952–66 (Pres., 1967–79); Statesman and Nation Publishing Co. Ltd, 1964–77; Statesman Publishing Co. Ltd, 1964–81; Director: London Weekend TV Ltd, 1967–74 (Dep. Chm., 1969–73); Commonwealth Develt Corp., 1968–81. Mem., Community Relations Commn, 1968–77 (a Dep. Chm., 1968–71); New Towns Assoc., 1975–77; President: W India Cttee, 1957–77; Town and Country Planning Assoc., 1980–89. Trustee, Chequers Trust, 1964–91; Chm., Governing Body, Imperial Coll. of Tropical Agriculture, 1945–55. First Freeman of Milton Keynes, 1982. DUniv Open, 1973. *Recreations:* reading, hitting balls, painting. *Address:* Lawers, Crocker End, Nettlebed, Oxfordshire RG9 5BJ. *T:* Nettlebed (01491) 641202. *Club:* All England Lawn Tennis.
Died 26 Dec. 1994.

CAMPBELL, Archibald, CMG 1966; Assistant Under-Secretary of State, Ministry of Defence, 1969–74, retired; *b* 10 Dec. 1914; *s* of late Archibald Campbell and Jessie Sanders Campbell (*née* Halsall); *m* 1939, Peggie Phyllis Hussey; two *s* one *d. Educ:* Berkhamsted Sch.; Hertford Coll., Oxford. BA Oxford, 1935. Barrister at Law, Middle Temple, 1947. Administrative Service, Gold Coast, 1936–46; Colonial Office, 1946; Colonial Attaché, British Embassy, Washington, 1953–56; Asst Secretary, Colonial Office, 1956–59 and 1962–67; Chief Secretary, Malta, 1959–62; Asst Sec., MoD, 1967–69. Mem., British observer team, Rhodesian Elections, 1980. *Recreations:* cricket (capped for Bucks in Minor County Competition, 1951), walking, gardening. *Address:* Bransbury, Long Park, Chesham Bois, Bucks HP6 5LF. *T:* Amersham (0494) 727727. *Club:* MCC. *Died 2 May 1994.*

CAMPBELL, Sir Clifford (Clarence), ON 1988; GCMG 1962; GCVO 1966; Governor-General of Jamaica, 1962–73; *b* 28 June 1892; *s* of late James Campbell, civil servant, and Blanche, *d* of John Ruddock, agriculturist; *m* 1920, Alice Esthephene (*d* 1976), *d* of late William Jolly, planter; two *s* two *d. Educ:* Petersfield Sch.; Mico Training Coll., Jamaica. Headmaster: Fullersfield Govt Sch., 1916–18; Friendship Elementary Sch., 1918–28; Grange Hill Govt Sch., 1928–44. Member Jamaica House of Representatives (Jamaica Labour Party) for Westmoreland

Western, 1944–49; Chm., House Cttee on Education, 1945–49; first Vice-President, Elected Members Assoc., 1945; re-elected 1949; Speaker of the House of Representatives, 1950; Senator and President of the Senate, 1962. KStJ. *Recreations:* agricultural pursuits, reading. *Address:* 8 Cherry Gardens Avenue, Kingston 8, Jamaica. *Clubs:* (Hon. Member) Caymanas Golf and Country, Ex-Services, Kingston Cricket, Liguanea, Rotary, St Andrew's, Trelawny (all in Jamaica).
Died 28 Sept. 1991.

CAMPBELL, David John G.; *see* Graham-Campbell.

CAMPBELL, Prof. Fergus William, FRS 1978; Professor of Neurosensory Physiology, Physiological Laboratory, University of Cambridge, 1983–91, then Professor Emeritus; Fellow of St John's College, Cambridge, since 1955; *b* 30 Jan. 1924; *s* of William Campbell and Anne Fleming; *m* 1948, Helen Margaret Cunningham; one *s* two *d* (and one *d* decd). *Educ:* Univ. of Glasgow (MA, MD, PhD, DOMS). Casualty and Eye Resident Surg., Western Infirmary, Glasgow, 1946–47; Asst, Inst. of Physiol., Glasgow, 1947–49, Lectr, 1949–52; Res. Graduate, Nuffield Lab. of Ophthalmology, Oxford, 1952–53; Univ. Lectr, 1953–72, Reader in Neurosensory Physiol., 1973–83, Physiol Lab., Cambridge. Hon. FBCO 1962. Hon. DSc: Glasgow, 1986; Aston, 1987. Tillyer Medal, Optical Soc. of America, 1980. *Publications:* papers on neurophysiology and psychophysics of vision in Jl Physiol., and Vision Res. *Recreations:* music, photography. *Address:* 96 Queen Ediths Way, Cambridge CB1 4PP. *T:* Cambridge (0223) 247578.
Died 3 May 1993.

CAMPBELL, Freda Kunzlen, (Mrs Ian McIvor Campbell); *see* Corbet, F. K.

CAMPBELL, Sir Guy (Theophilus Halswell), 5th Bt *cr* 1815; OBE 1954; MC 1941; Colonel, late 60th Rifles, El Kaimakam Bey, Camel Corps, Sudan Defence Force, and Kenya Regiment; *b* 18 Jan. 1910; *s* of Major Sir Guy Colin Campbell, 4th Bt, late 60th Rifles, and Mary Arabella Swinnerton Kemeys-Tynte, *sister* of 8th Lord Wharton; *S* father, 1960; *m* 1956, Lizbeth Webb, Bickenhall Mansions, W1; two *s. Educ:* St Aubyn's, Rottingdean; Eton Coll.; St Andrews Univ. Served in KOYLI, 1931–42; 1st Bn, KOYLI, Gibraltar, 1935–39; War of 1939–45 (wounded); seconded to Camel Corps, Sudan Defence Force, 1939–47; comd 2/7 and 7 Nuba Bns, 1943–47; Shifta Ops, Eritrea, 1946; Acting Brig., 1945, HQ SDF Group (N Africa); Palestine, 1948; Mil. Adviser to Count Folke Bernadotte and Dr Ralph Bunche of United Nations, 1948; attached British Embassy as Civil Affairs Officer, Cairo, 1948; British Mil. Mission to Ethiopia, in Ogaden Province, 1949–51; 2nd i/c 1/60th Rifles, BAOR, 1951; comd Kenya Regt (TF), 1952–56, Mau Mau ops; Head of British Mil. Mission to Libya, 1956–60; retired Aug. 1960. MoD, 1965–72. Col R of O, 60th Rifles. Provided historical research, costume, weapons etc for United Artists film Khartoum, 1964. C-in-C's (MELF) Commendation, 1945; Gold Medal of Emperor Haile Selassie (non-wearable). *Recreations:* painting, writing, watching cricket, Rugby football, golf. *Heir: s* Lachlan Philip Kemeys Campbell, The Royal Green Jackets [*b* 9 Oct. 1958; *m* 1986, Harriet Jane Sarah, *o d* of F. E. J. Girling, Malvern; one *s*]. *Address:* 18 Lansdown Terrace, Malvern Road, Cheltenham, Glos GL50 2JT. *Clubs:* Army and Navy, Special Forces, MCC, I Zingari; Puffins (Edinburgh); Royal and Ancient (St Andrews). *Died 19 July 1993.*

CAMPBELL, Maj.-Gen. Rev. Sir Hamish Manus, KBE 1963 (CBE 1958); CB 1961; Order of Prémontré (White Canons), since 1984; ordained priest, 1988; *b* 6 Jan. 1905; *s* of late Major A. C. J. Campbell, Middlesex Regt and

Army Pay Dept, and Alice, *d* of late Comdr Yelverton O'Keeffe, RN; *m* 1929, Marcelle (*d* 1983), *d* of late Charles Ortlieb, Neuchâtel, Switzerland; one *s. Educ:* Downside School; New Coll., Oxford. Commissioned in Argyll and Sutherland Highlanders, 1927; transferred to Royal Army Pay Corps, 1937; Lieut-Colonel and Staff Paymaster (1st Class), temp. 1945, substantive 1951; Colonel and Chief Paymaster, temp. 1954, substantive 1955; Major-General, 1959; Command Paymaster: Sierra Leone, 1940–42; Burma, 1946–48; Malta, 1953; Deputy Chief, Budget and Finance Division, SHAPE, 1954–56; Commandant, RAPC Training Centre, 1956–59; Paymaster-in-Chief, War Office, 1959–63; retired, 1963. Col Comdt, RAPC, 1963–70. *Address:* Our Lady of England Priory, Storrington, Pulborough, West Sussex RH20 4LN. *T:* Storrington (0903) 742150.
Died 10 May 1993.

CAMPBELL, Ian Macdonald, CVO 1977; BSc; FEng 1980; FICE; Member, Economic and Social Committee, EEC, 1983–90; *b* 13 July 1922; *s* of late John Isdale Campbell; *m* 1946, Hilda Ann Williams; one *s* three *d. Educ:* University Coll., London (Fellow, 1984). BSc(Eng). British Rail: Chief Civil Engr, Scottish Region, 1965–68; Gen. Manager, E Region, 1970–73; Exec. Dir, BR, 1973–76; Bd Mem., 1977–87; Chm., Scottish Bd, 1983–88. Pres., ICE, 1981–82 (Vice-Pres., 1978–81). *Address:* Lochearnside, St Fillans, Perthshire PH6 2NF.
Died 1 April 1994.

CAMPBELL, Leila; Chairman, Inner London Education Authority, 1977–78 (Vice-Chairman, 1967–77); *b* 10 Aug. 1911; *d* of Myer and Rebecca Jaffe; *m* 1940, Andrew Campbell (*d* 1968); one *d. Educ:* Belvedere Sch., Liverpool. Art Teacher's Dip. Dress designer. Elected (Lab), Hampstead Bor. Council, 1961–65; elected new London Bor. of Camden, 1964–78 (later Alderman); elected LCC for Holborn and S St Pancras, 1958–65; elected GLC for Camden, 1964–67; rep. Camden on ILEA, 1970–78. *Recreations:* cooking, theatre, opera, jazz. *Address:* 56 Belsize Park, NW3 4EH. *T:* 071–722 7038. *Died 2 Oct. 1993.*

CAMPBELL of Airds, Brig. Lorne Maclaine, VC 1943; DSO 1940; OBE 1968; TD 1941; Argyll and Sutherland Highlanders (TA); *b* 22 July 1902; *s* of late Col Ian Maxwell Campbell, CBE and Hilda Mary Wade; *m* 1935, Amy Muriel Jordan (*d* 1950), *d* of Alastair Magnus Campbell, Auchendarroch, Argyll; two *s. Educ:* Dulwich Coll.; Merton Coll., Oxford (Postmaster, MA). 8th Bn Argyll and Sutherland Highlanders, 1921–42; War of 1939–45 (despatches four times, DSO and Bar, VC): commanded 7th Bn, 1942–43, and 13th Inf. Brigade, 1943–44; BGS, British Army Staff, Washington, 1944–45. Hon. Col 8th Bn Argyll and Sutherland Highlanders, 1954–67. Past Master of Vintners' Company (Hon. Vintner). Officer US Legion of Merit. *Address:* 95 Trinity Road, Edinburgh EH5 3JX. *T:* 031–552 6851. *Club:* New (Edinburgh). *Died 25 May 1991.*

CAMPBELL ORDE, Alan Colin, CBE 1943; AFC 1919; FRAeS; *b* Lochgilphead, Argyll, NB, 4 Oct. 1898; *s* of Colin Ridley Campbell Orde and Winifred Harriet, *d* of Capt. John C. Stewart; *m* 1951, Mrs Beatrice McClure (*d* 1989), *e d* of late Rev. H. M. Eliott-Drake Briscoe. *Educ:* Sherborne. Served European War, 1916–18: Flight Sub-Lieut, Royal Navy, and Flying Officer, Royal Air Force; active service in Belgium, 1917; one of original commercial Pilots on London-Paris route with Aircraft Transport & Travel Ltd, 1919–20; Instructor and Adviser to Chinese Govt in Peking, 1921–23; Instructor and latterly Chief Test Pilot to Sir W. G. Armstrong-Whitworth Aircraft, Ltd, Coventry, 1924–36; Operational Manager, British Airways, Ltd, 1936–39; subseq. Operations Manager, Imperial Airways Ltd; was Ops Director BOAC,

during first 4 years after its inception in 1939; thereafter responsible for technical development as Development Dir until resignation from BOAC, Dec. 1957. *Recreation:* reading in bed. *Address:* Smugglers Mead, Stepleton, Blandford, Dorset. *T:* Child Okeford (0258) 860268. *Club:* Boodle's. *Died 18 April 1992.*

CAMPOLI, Alfredo; violinist, retired; *b* 20 Oct. 1906; *s* of Prof. Romeo Campoli, Prof. of Violin at Accademia di Santa Cecilia, Rome, and Elvira Campoli, dramatic soprano; *m* 1942, Joy Burbridge. Came to London, 1911; gave regular public recitals as a child; Gold Medal, London Musical Festival, 1919; toured British Isles with Dame Nellie Melba and with Dame Clara Butt, and was engaged for series of International Celebrity Concerts at age of 15. Played all over the world. First broadcast from Savoy Hill, 1930; subsequently made frequent broadcasts and television appearances, and made many gramophone records. *Recreations:* bridge, cine-photography, table tennis, billiards, croquet. *Died 27 March 1991.*

CAMROSE, 2nd Viscount, *cr* 1941, of Hackwood Park; **John Seymour Berry,** TD; Bt 1921; Baron 1929; Director, The Daily Telegraph plc; *b* 12 July 1909; *e s* of 1st Viscount Camrose and Mary Agnes (*d* 1962), *e d* of late Thomas Corns, 2 Bolton Street, W; *S* father, 1954; *m* 1986, Princess Joan Aly Khan, *e d* of 3rd Baron Churston, MVO, OBE. *Educ:* Eton; Christ Church, Oxford. Major, City of London Yeomanry, 1941–45. Served War of 1939–45, North African and Italian Campaigns, 1942–45 (despatches). MP (C) for Hitchin Division, Herts, 1941–45. Dep. Chm., The Daily Telegraph Ltd, 1939–87; Vice-Chm. Amalgamated Press Ltd, 1942–59. Younger Brother, Trinity House. *Heir: b* Baron Hartwell [*b* 18 May 1911; *m* 1936, Lady Pamela Margaret Elizabeth Smith (*d* 1982), *yr d* of 1st Earl of Birkenhead, GCSI, PC, KC; two *s* two *d*]. *Address:* 8a Hobart Place, SW1H 0HH. *T:* 0171–235 9900; Hackwood, Basingstoke, Hampshire RG25 2JY. *T:* Basingstoke (01256) 464630. *Clubs:* Buck's, White's, Beefsteak, MCC; Royal Yacht Squadron (Trustee).
Died 15 Feb. 1995.

CANETTI, Elias; writer; *b* Ruschuk, Bulgaria, 25 July 1905; *e s* of late Jacques Canetti and Mathilde (*née* Arditi); *m* 1st, 1934, Venetia Taubner-Calderón (*d* 1963); 2nd, Hera Buschor; one *d. Educ:* schs in Manchester, Vienna and Zurich; Univ. of Vienna (DSc 1929). Settled in London, 1939. Prizes include: Prix Internat. de Paris, 1949; Austrian Prize for Literature, 1968; Kafka Prize, Austria, 1981; Nobel Prize for Literature, 1981. *Publications: plays:* Hochzeit, 1932; Komödie der Eitelkeit, 1934; Die Befristeten, 1952 (The Numbered, 1956); *novel:* Bie Blendung, 1935 (Auto da Fé, 1946); *non-fiction:* Fritz Wotruba, 1955; Masse und Macht, 1960 (Crowds and Power, 1962); Die Stimmen von Marrakesch, 1967 (The Voices of Marrakesh, 1978); Der andere Prozess, 1969 (Kafka's Other Trial, 1974); Die Provinz des Menschen: Aufzeichnungen 1942–1972, 1973 (The Human Province, 1979); Der Ohrenzeuge: 50 Charaktere, 1974 (Earwitness, 1979); *autobiography:* Die gerettete Zunge, 1977 (The Tongue set Free, 1979); Die Fackel im Ohr, 1980 (The Torch in my Ear, 1989); Das Augenspiel, 1985 (The Play of the Eyes, 1990). *Address:* c/o André Deutsch, 105–106 Great Russell Street, WC1B 3LJ.
Died 14 Aug. 1994.

CANHAM, Bryan Frederick, (Peter), MC 1943; FCIS; Non-Executive Director, Eurofi (formerly Eurofi UK) plc, since 1991 (Chairman, 1981–91); *b* 11 April 1920; *s* of Frederick William Canham and Emma Louisa Martin; *m* 1944, Rita Gwendoline Huggett; one *s. Educ:* Trinity County Sch. FCIS 1968 (ACIS 1950). Served War, 1939–46: N Africa, Italy and NW Europe; Captain 1st Royal Tank Regt. Accounting and financial appts, Shell cos in Kenya, Tanzania and French W Africa, 1947–56;

Controller, S Europe and N Africa, Shell Internat. Petroleum Co., 1956–60; Finance Dir, Shell Philippines and Associated Cos, 1960–63; Finance Dir, Shell Malaysia and Associated Cos, 1963–68; Personnel Adviser, finance and computer staff, Shell Internat. Pet. Co., 1968–73; Div. Hd, Loans, Directorate Gen. XVIII, Commn of European Communities, 1973–76, Dir, Investment and Loans, 1976–80. *Recreations:* reading, chess, pottering. *Address:* The Old Laundry, Penshurst, Kent TN11 8HY. *T:* Penshurst (0892) 870239; The Cottage, Stedham Hall, Stedham, W Sussex. *Club:* Muthaiga Country (Nairobi).
Died 11 Aug. 1993.

CANHAM, Peter; *see* Canham, B. F.

CANNAN, Rt Rev. Edward Alexander Capparis; Assistant Bishop, Diocese of Hereford, since 1986; *b* 25 Dec. 1920; *s* of Alexander and Mabel Capparis; *m* 1941, Eunice Mary Blandford; three *s. Educ:* St Marylebone Grammar School; King's College, London (BD, AKC). Served RAF, 1937–46 (despatches). Deacon 1950, priest 1951, dio. Salisbury; Curate, Blandford Forum, Dorset, 1950–53; Chaplain, RAF, 1953–74: RAF Cosford, 1953–54; Padgate, 1954–57; HQ 2 Gp, Germany, 1957–58; Lecturer, RAF Chaplains' Sch., 1958–60; RAF Gan, Maldive Islands, 1960–61; RAF Halton, 1961–62; Hereford, 1962–64; Khormaksar, Aden, 1964–66; Vice-Principal, RAF Chaplains' School, 1966–69; Asst Chaplain-in-Chief, 1969–74; Far East Air Force, Singapore, 1969–72; HQ Training Comd, 1972–73; Principal, RAF Chaplains' Sch., 1973–74; Hon. Chaplain to the Queen, 1972–74; Chaplain, St Margaret's Sch., Bushey, 1974–79; Bishop of St Helena, 1979–85. *Publications:* A History of the Diocese of St Helena and its Precursors 1502–1984, 1985; The Churches of the South Atlantic Islands 1502–1991, 1992. *Recreations:* gardening, house maintenance, photography. *Address:* Church Cottage, Allensmore, Hereford HR2 9AQ. *T:* Hereford (0432) 277357. *Club:* Royal Air Force.
Died 18 July 1992.

CANSDALE, George Soper, BA, BSc, FLS; *b* 29 Nov. 1909; *y s* of G. W. Cansdale, Paignton, Devon, and Alice Louisa Cansdale; *m* 1940, Margaret Sheila, *o d* of R. M. Williamson, Indian Forest Service; two *s. Educ:* Brentwood Sch.; St Edmund Hall, Oxford. Colonial Forest Service, Gold Coast, 1934–48; Superintendent to Zoological Society of London, Regent's Park, 1948–53. TV presenter, 1948–89. Inventor, SWS Filtration Unit, 1975. IBM Award for Sustainable Development. *Publications:* The Black Poplars, 1938; Animals of West Africa, 1946; Animals and Man, 1952; George Cansdale's Zoo Book, 1953; Belinda the Bushbaby, 1953; Reptiles of West Africa, 1955; West African Snakes, 1961; Behind the Scenes at a Zoo, 1965; Animals of Bible Lands, 1970; articles in The Field, Geographical Magazine, Zoo Life, Nigerian Field, Natural History, etc. *Recreations:* natural history, photography, sailing. *Address:* Dove Cottage, Great Chesterford, Essex CB10 1PL. *T:* Saffron Walden (0799) 30274. *Club:* Commonwealth Trust.
Died 24 Aug. 1993.

CANTLAY, George Thomson, CBE 1973; Partner, Murray & Co., 1979–83, subsequently Consultant; former Director: Parkfield Foundries (Tees-side) Ltd (Chairman, to 1984); A. B. Electronic Products Group PLC; Christie-Tyler Ltd; Welsh National Opera Ltd; *b* 2 Aug. 1907; *s* of G. and A. Cantlay; *m* 1934, Sibyl Gwendoline Alsop Stoker; one *s* one *d. Educ:* Glasgow High Sch. Member of Stock Exchange. Vice-Pres., Welsh Region, Inst. of Directors. KStJ 1985; FRSA. *Recreations:* music (opera), gardening. *Address:* 8 Park Road, Penarth CF6 2BD. *Clubs:* Carlton; Cardiff and County (Cardiff).
Died 5 March 1992.

CANTLEY, Sir Joseph (Donaldson), Kt 1965; OBE 1945; Judge of the High Court of Justice, Queen's Bench Division, 1965–85; *b* 8 Aug. 1910; *er s* of Dr Joseph Cantley, Crumpsall, Manchester, and Georgina Cantley (*née* Kean); *m* 1966, Lady (Hilda Goodwin) Gerrard, *widow* of Sir Denis Gerrard; one step *s. Educ:* Manchester Grammar Sch.; Manchester Univ. Studentship and Certificate of Honour, Council of Legal Education, 1933; Barrister, Middle Temple, 1933 (Bencher 1963; Treasurer 1981); QC 1954. Served throughout War of 1939–45: Royal Artillery and on Staff; commnd 2nd Lieut RA, 1940; N Africa and Italy, 1942–45 (despatches twice); Lieut-Colonel and AAG, 1943–45. Recorder of Oldham, 1959–60; Judge of Salford Hundred Court of Record, 1960–65; Judge of Appeal, Isle of Man, 1962–65; Presiding Judge: Northern Circuit, 1970–74; South Eastern Circuit, 1980. Member, General Council of the Bar, 1957–61. Hon. Col, Manchester and Salford Univs OTC, 1971–77. Hon. LLD Manchester, 1968. *Club:* Travellers'.
Died 6 Jan. 1993.

CAPRA, Frank R., Legion of Merit, 1943; DSM 1945; Hon. OBE (mil.) 1946; writer, director and producer of motion pictures; President of own producing company, Liberty Films Inc.; *b* Palermo, Italy, 18 May 1897; *s* of Salvatore Capra; *m* 1924, Helen Howell (marr. diss.); *m* 1932, Lucille Rayburn Warner (*d* 1984); two *s* one *d* (and one *s* decd). *Educ:* California Institute of Technology. Came to US, 1903. Col, Signal Corps, US Army; released from Army, spring of 1945. Produced and directed following pictures: Submarine, The Strong Man, Flight, Dirigible, Ladies of Leisure, Platinum Blonde, American Madness, Lady for a Day, It Happened One Night, Mr Deeds Goes to Town, Broadway Bill, Lost Horizon, You Can't Take It With You, Mr Smith Goes to Washington, Meet John Doe, Arsenic and Old Lace, It's a Wonderful Life, State of the Union, Here Comes the Groom, A Hole in the Head, Pocketful of Miracles; created: Why We Fight (film series), 1941–46; science series films widely used in schools, incl. Our Mr Sun, Hemo the Magnificent, The Strange Case of Cosmic Rays, The Unchained Goddess, 1956–58. Member of Motion Picture Academy and of Directors' Guild. Hon. Dr Arts Temple Univ., 1971; Hon. Dr Fine Arts Carthage Coll., 1972. Winner of six Academy Awards. *Publication:* Frank Capra: the name above the title (autobiog.), 1971. *Recreations:* hunting, fishing, music. *Address:* PO Box 980, La Quinta, Calif 92253, USA.
Died 3 Sept. 1991.

CARBONELL, William Leycester Rouse, CMG 1956; Commissioner of Police, Federation of Malaya, 1953–58, retired; *b* 14 Aug. 1912; *s* of John Carbonell; *m* 1937, Elsa Agnes, *d* of John William Curdie, Vic, Australia; two *s. Educ:* Shrewsbury Sch.; St Catharine's Coll., Cambridge. Probationary Assistant Commissioner of Police, 1935; (title changed to) Asst Superintendent, 1938; Superintendent, 1949; Asst Commissioner, 1952: Senior Commissioner, 1952; Commissioner, 1953. King's Police Medal, 1950. Perlawan Mangku Negara Malaya, 1958. *Address:* 6 Stratford Court, Avon Road, Farnham, Surrey GU9 8PG.
Died 30 Sept. 1994.

CARDEN, (Graham) Stephen (Paul), CBE 1986; TD 1968; DL; Partner, Cazenove & Co., since 1964; *b* 14 May 1935; *s* of late Paul Carden and Lilias Kathleen Carden. *Educ:* Harrow School. 9th Lancers, 1954–56. Cazenove & Co., 1956–; Dir, Greenfriar Investment Co., 1966–. City of London Yeomanry (Rough Riders) and on amalgamation, Inns of Court & City Yeomanry, 1956–74 (Jt Hon. Col, 1989–); Col, TA, 1976–78; Chm., 1981–88, Vice Pres., 1988–, Greater London TAVRA; Vice-Chairman: Council, TAVRA, 1984–88; ACFA, 1989–; Hon. Col 71st (Yeomanry) Signal Regt, TA, 1989–. Comr, Royal Hosp., Chelsea, 1986–; Vice-Pres., Yeomanry

Benevolent Fund, 1986–. Chm., Fairbridge Soc., 1986–87 (Hon. Treas., 1964–87), Vice Chm. and Hon. Treas., Fairbridge Drake Soc., 1987–; Chm., London House for Overseas Graduates, 1990– (Gov., 1975–). DL Gtr London, 1983. *Recreations:* equestrian (mainly hunting), fishing, sailing, watching cricket. *Address:* 12 Warwick Square, SW1V 2AA. *T:* 071–834 8919. *Clubs:* Cavalry and Guards, White's, City of London, MCC, Royal Yacht Squadron. *Died 10 May 1992.*

CARDEN, Sir Henry (Christopher), 4th Bt *cr* 1887, of Molesley, Surrey; OBE (mil.) 1945; Regular Army Officer (17th/21st Lancers), retired; *b* 16 Oct. 1908; *o s* of Sir Frederick Henry Walter Carden, 3rd Bt, and Winifred Mary, 4th *d* of Philip Wroughton, Woolley Park, Berks; *S* father, 1966; *m* 1st, 1943, Jane St Care Daniell (whom he divorced, 1960); one *s* one *d*; 2nd, 1962, Gwyneth S. Emerson (*née* Acland), *widow* of Flt-Lt Emerson (killed in action, RAF, 1944), Argentina. *Educ:* Eton; RMC Sandhurst. 2/Lieut, 17/21 Lancers, 1928; served Egypt and India, 1930–39; Staff Coll., 1941; comd, 2 Armoured Delivery Regt, in France, 1944–45; CO 17/21 Lancers, in Greece and Palestine, 1947–48; War Office, 1948–51; Military Attaché in Stockholm, 1951–55; retired 1956. Comdr of the Order of the Sword (Sweden), 1954. *Recreations:* most field sports and games. *Heir: s* Christopher Robert Carden [*b* 24 Nov. 1946; *m* 1st, 1972, Sainimere Rokotuibau (marr. diss. 1979), Suva, Fiji; 2nd, 1981, Clarita Eriksen, Manila, Philippines]. *Address:* Moongrove, East Woodhay, near Newbury, Berks. *T:* Highclere (0635) 253661. *Club:* Cavalry and Guards.
Died 4 Feb. 1993.

CARDEN, Stephen; *see* Carden, G. S. P.

CAREW, 6th Baron (UK) *cr* 1838; **William Francis Conolly-Carew,** CBE 1966; Baron Carew (Ire.), 1834; Brevet Major retired, Duke of Cornwall's Light Infantry; *b* 23 April 1905; *e s* of 5th Baron and Catherine (*d* 1947), *o d* of late Thomas Conolly, MP, Castletown, Co. Kildare; *S* father, 1927; *m* 1937, Lady Sylvia Maitland, CStJ (*d* 1991), *o d* of 15th Earl of Lauderdale; two *s* two *d*. *Educ:* Wellington; Sandhurst. Gazetted DCLI 1925; ADC to Governor and Comdr-in-Chief of Bermuda, 1931–36. Chm., British Legion, 1963–66; British Govt Trustee, Irish Sailors' and Soldiers' Land Trust. Pres., Irish Grassland Assoc., 1949. CStJ. *Heir: s* Hon. Patrick Thomas Conolly-Carew, Captain Royal Horse Guards, retd [*b* 6 March 1938; *m* 1962, Celia, *d* of late Col Hon. (Charles) Guy Cubitt, CBE, DSO, TD; one *s* three *d*]. *Address:* The Dower House, Donadea House, Naas, Co. Kildare, Ireland. *T:* Naas (045) 68300.
Died 27 June 1994.

CAREW POLE, Col Sir John (Gawen), 12th Bt *cr* 1628, of Shute House, Devonshire; DSO 1944; TD; JP; Lord-Lieutenant of Cornwall, 1962–77; Member of the Prince of Wales's Council, 1952–68; Member, Jockey Club (incorporating National Hunt Committee), since 1969; *b* 4 March 1902; *e s* of late Lt-Gen. Sir Reginald Pole-Carew, KCB, Antony, Cornwall, and Lady Beatrice Pole-Carew, *er d* of 3rd Marquess of Ormonde; *S* kinsman, 1926; *m* 1st, 1928, Cynthia Mary (OBE 1959) (*d* 1977), *o d* of Walter Burns, North Mymms Park, Hatfield; one *s* two *d*; 2nd, 1979, Joan, *widow* of Lt-Col Anthony Fulford, Dunsford, Devon. *Educ:* Eton; RMC, Sandhurst. Coldstream Guards, 1923–39; ADC to Commander-in-Chief in India, 1924–25; Comptroller to Governor-General, Union of S Africa, 1935–36; Palestine, 1936; commanded 5th Bn Duke of Cornwall's LI (TA), 1939–43; commanded 2nd Bn Devonshire Regt, 1944; Colonel, Second Army, 1944–45; Normandy, France, Belgium, Holland, Germany, 1944–45 (despatches, immediate DSO); raised and commanded post-war TA Bn, 4/5 Bn DCLI, 1946–47; Hon. Col, 4/5 Bn DCLI (TA), 1958–60;

Hon. Col DCLI (TA) 1960–67. Director: Lloyd's Bank, 1956–72 (Chm., Devon and Cornwall Cttee, 1956–72); English China Clays Ltd, 1969–73; Keith Prowse, 1969; Vice-Chm., Westward Television Ltd, 1960–72. Member: Central Transport Consultative Cttee for Great Britain, 1948–54; SW Electricity Consultative Council, 1949–52 (Vice-Chairman, 1951–52); Western Area Board, British Transport Commission, 1955–61. Steward, National Hunt Committee, 1953–56; Member, Garden Society. JP 1939, DL 1947, CA 1954–66, Cornwall; High Sheriff, Cornwall, 1947–48; Vice-Lt, Cornwall, 1950–62; Chairman Cornwall County Council, 1952–63. A Gentleman of HM Bodyguard of the Honourable Corps of Gentlemen-at-Arms, 1950–72, Standard Bearer, 1968–72. Prime Warden Worshipful Company of Fishmongers, 1969–70. KStJ 1972. Hon. LLD Exeter, 1979. *Recreations:* gardening, shooting, travel. *Heir: s* (John) Richard (Walter Reginald) Carew Pole [*b* 2 Dec. 1938; *m* 1st, 1966, Hon. Victoria Marion Ann Lever (marr. diss. 1974), *d* of 3rd Viscount Leverhulme; 2nd, 1974, Mary (MVO 1983), *d* of Lt-Col Ronald Dawnay; two *s*]. *Address:* Horson House, Antony, Torpoint, Cornwall PL11 2PE. *T:* Plymouth (0752) 812406. *Clubs:* Army and Navy, Pratt's, MCC.
Died 26 Jan. 1993.

CAREY-FOSTER, George Arthur, CMG 1952; DFC 1944; AFC 1941; Counsellor, HM Diplomatic (formerly Foreign) Service, 1946–68; *b* 18 Nov. 1907; *s* of George Muir Foster, FRCS, MRCP, and Marie Thérèse Mutin; *m* 1936, Margaret Aloysius Barry Egan; one *d*. *Educ:* Clifton Coll., Bristol. Royal Air Force, 1929–35; Reserve of Air Force Officers, 1935–39; served War of 1939–45: Royal Air Force, 1939–46 (despatches, AFC, DFC); Group Capt. Served at Foreign Office, as Consul General at Hanover, as Counsellor and Chargé d'Affaires at Rio de Janeiro, Warsaw and The Hague, 1946–68; retired, 1968. *Recreations:* wine, gardening. *Address:* 25 Saffrons Court, Compton Place Road, Eastbourne, East Sussex BN21 1DX. *Clubs:* Royal Air Force; Haagsche (The Hague).
Died 14 Jan. 1994.

CARLISLE, 12th Earl of, *cr* 1661; **Charles James Ruthven Howard,** MC 1945; DL; Viscount Howard of Morpeth, Baron Dacre of Gillesland, 1661; Lord Ruthven of Freeland, 1651; *b* 21 Feb. 1923; *o s* of 11th Earl of Carlisle, and Lady Ruthven of Freeland, 11th in line (*d* 1982); *S* father, 1963; *m* 1945, Hon. Ela Beaumont, OStJ, *o d* of 2nd Viscount Allendale, KG, CB, CBE, MC; two *s* two *d*. *Educ:* Eton. Served War of 1939–45 (wounded twice, MC). Lieut late Rifle Brigade. Forestry Comr, 1967–70. DL Cumbria, 1984. FRICS (FLAS 1953). *Heir: s* Viscount Morpeth, *b* 15 Feb. 1949. *Address:* Naworth Castle, Brampton, Cumbria CA8 2HF. *T:* Brampton (016977) 2621.
Died 28 Nov. 1994.

CARNWATH, Sir Andrew Hunter, KCVO 1975; DL; a Managing Director, Baring Brothers & Co. Ltd, 1955–74; Chairman, London Multinational Bank, 1971–74; *b* 26 Oct. 1909; *s* of late Dr Thomas Carnwath, DSO, Dep. CMO, Min. of Health, and Margaret Ethel (*née* McKee); *m* 1st, 1939, Kathleen Marianne Armstrong (*d* 1968); five *s* one *d*; 2nd, 1973, Joan Gertrude Wetherell-Pepper (Joan Alexander, author). *Educ:* Eton (King's Scholar; Hon. Fellow 1981). Served RAF (Coastal Comd Intelligence), 1939–45. Joined Baring Bros & Co. Ltd, 1928; rejoined as Head of New Issues Dept, 1945. Chm., Save and Prosper Group Ltd, 1961–80 (Dir, 1960–80); Director: Equity & Law Life Assurance Soc. Ltd, 1955–83; Scottish Agricultural Industries Ltd, 1969–75; Great Portland Estates Ltd, 1977–89. Member: London Cttee, Hongkong and Shanghai Banking Corp., 1967–74; Council, Inst. of Bankers, 1955– (Dep. Chm., 1969–70, Pres., 1970–72, Vice-Pres., 1972–); Cttee on Consumer Credit; Central Bd of Finance of Church of England (Chm., Investment

Management Cttee), 1960–74; Chm., Chelmsford Diocesan Bd of Finance, 1969–75 (Vice-Chm., 1967–68). Member: Council, King Edward's Hosp. Fund for London, 1962–89 (Treasurer, 1965–74; Governor, 1976–85); Royal Commn for Exhibn of 1851, 1964–85; Council, Friends of Tate Gall., 1962–84 (Treasurer, 1966–82). Trustee: Imp. War Graves Endowment Fund, 1963–74, Chm., 1964–74; Thalidomide Children's Trust, 1980–85; Chairman: Manor Charitable Trustees, 1969–88; Baring Foundn, 1982–85. A Governor, Felsted Sch., 1965–81; Treasurer, Essex Univ., 1973–82 (DU Essex, 1983). Pres., Saffron Walden Conservative Assoc. until 1977. Musicians Company: Mem., Ct of Assts, 1973–; Master, 1981–82. Mem., Essex CC, 1973–77; High Sheriff, 1965, DL Essex, 1972–85. FCIB; FRSA. DU Essex, 1983. *Recreations:* crosswords, struggling with the piano, pictures. *Address:* 37 Riverview Gardens, Barnes, SW13 9QY. *T:* 0181–748 8927. *Club:* Athenæum.

Died 29 Dec. 1995.

CARPENTER, George Frederick, ERD 1954; Assistant Under-Secretary of State, Ministry of Defence, 1971–77; *b* 18 May 1917; *s* of late Frederick and Ada Carpenter; *m* 1949, Alison Elizabeth (*d* 1978), *d* of late Colonel Sidney Smith, DSO, MC, TD and Elizabeth Smith, Longridge, Lancs; two step *d. Educ:* Bec Sch.; Trinity Coll., Cambridge (MA). Commnd Royal Artillery (Supplementary Reserve), July 1939; War Service, 1939–46, France, 1940 and AA Comd; joined War Office, 1946; Asst Sec., 1958; Comd Sec., Northern Comd, 1961–65; Inspector of Establishments (A), MoD, 1965–71. Silver Jubilee Medal, 1977. *Address:* 10 Park Meadow, Hatfield, Herts AL9 5HA. *T:* Hatfield (07072) 65581.

Died 22 April 1992.

CARPENTER, Rt Rev. Harry James, DD; *b* 20 Oct. 1901; *s* of William and Elizabeth Carpenter; *m* 1940, Urith Monica Trevelyan; one *s. Educ:* Churcher's Coll., Petersfield; Queen's Coll., Oxford; Cuddesdon Coll. Deacon, 1927; priest, 1928; Tutor of Keble Coll., Oxford, 1927–29, Fellow, 1930, Warden, 1939–55, Hon. Fellow, 1955; Hon. Fellow, Queen's Coll., Oxford, 1955; Canon Theologian of Leicester Cathedral, 1941–55; Bishop of Oxford, 1955–70. Hon. DD Oxon, 1955; Hon. DLitt Southampton, 1985. *Publications:* (ed) Bicknell, Thirty Nine Articles, 1955; contrib. to: Oxford Dictionary of the Christian Church, ed Cross, 1957; A Theological Word Book of the Bible, ed Richardson, 1963; The Interpretation of the Bible, ed Dugmore, 1944; Jl of Theological Studies. *Address:* St John's Home, St Mary's Road, Oxford OX4 1QE.

Died 24 May 1993.

CARR, Frank George Griffith, CB 1967; CBE 1954; MA, LLB; FSA; FRAS; ARINA; FRIN; Founder and Chairman, World Ship Trust, since 1978; *e s* of Frank Carr, MA, LLD, and Agnes Maud Todd, Cambridge; *m* 1932, Ruth, *d* of Harold Hamilton Burkitt, Ballycastle, Co. Antrim; no *c. Educ:* Perse and Trinity Hall, Cambridge. BA 1926; LLB 1928; MA 1939. Studied at LCC Sch. of Navigation and took Yacht Master's (Deep Sea) BoT Certificate, 1927; Cambridge Univ.: Squire Law Scholar, 1922; Capt. of Boats, Trinity Hall, 1926; Pres., Law Soc., 1924; Vice-Pres., Conservative Assoc., 1925; Pres., Nat. Union of Students, 1925; Ed., The Cambridge Gownsman, 1925. Served War of 1939–45, RNVR, Lt-Comdr. Asst Librarian, House of Lords, 1929–47; Dir, Nat. Maritime Museum, Greenwich, 1947–66. Chm., Cutty Sark Ship Management Cttee, 1952–72; Mem., HMS Victory Advisory Technical Cttee, 1948–76; Vice-President: Soc. for Nautical Research; Foudroyant Trust; Internat. Sailing Craft Assoc.; Mariners International, 1978; Internat. Chm., Ship Trust Cttee, 1978–; President: Thames Shiplovers and Ship Model Soc., 1982–; Thames Barge Sailing Club, 1984–. Governor, HMS Unicorn

Preservation Soc. James Monroe Award, 1974. *Publications:* Sailing Barges, 1931; Vanishing Craft, 1934; A Yachtsman's Log, 1935; The Yachtsman's England, 1936; The Yacht Master's Guide, 1940; (jtly) The Medley of Mast and Sail, 1976; Leslie A. Wilcox, RI, RSMA, 1977; numerous articles in yachting periodicals, etc. *Recreations:* historic ship preservation, nautical research. *Address:* Lime Tree House, 10 Park Gate, Blackheath, SE3 9XB. *T:* 081–852 5181. *Clubs:* Athenæum, Royal Cruising, Cruising Association; Cambridge University Cruising (Cambridge).

Died 9 July 1991.

CARR, James Lloyd; publisher and novelist; *b* 20 May 1912; *s* of Joseph Carr and Elizabeth Carr (*née* Welbourn); *m* 1945, Sally (*d* 1981), *d* of W. H. Sexton, Frating Hall, Essex; one *s. Educ:* Carlton Miniott, North Riding, Village Sch.; Castleford Secondary Sch. Teacher, Hampshire, Birmingham, S Dakota, 1933–39; Intelligence Officer, RAF, 1940–46; Headmaster, Northants, 1951–67; publisher and novelist, 1964–. Hon. Sec., Northants Historic Churches Trust, 1984–. Hon MA Leicester, 1983; Hon. DLitt Huron, S Dakota, 1992. *Publications:* A Day in Summer, 1964; A Season in Sinji, 1967; The Harpole Report, 1972; How Steeple Sinderby Wanderers Won the FA Cup, 1975; A Month in the Country, 1980; The Battle of Pollocks Crossing, 1985; What Hetty Did, 1989; Harpole and Foxberrow, General Publishers, 1992. *Recreation:* stone carving. *Address:* 27 Milldale Road, Kettering, Northants NN15 6QD. *T:* Kettering (0536) 514995.

Died 26 Feb. 1994.

CARR, Philippa; *see* Hibbert, Eleanor.

CARRICK, 9th Earl of, *cr* 1748; **Brian Stuart Theobald Somerset Caher Butler;** Viscount Ikerrin, 1629; Baron Butler (UK), 1912; *b* 17 Aug. 1931; *o s* of 8th Earl of Carrick; *S* father, 1957; *m* 1st, 1951, (Mary) Belinda (marr. diss. 1976), *e d* of Major David Constable-Maxwell, TD, Bosworth Hall, near Rugby; one *s* one *d*; 2nd, 1986, Gillian, *er d* of Leonard Grimes. *Educ:* Downside. Chm., Balfour Maclaine Corp.; Director: Bowater Inc.; Bowater plc; Cargill plc; Cargill Financial Services Corp. Ltd; Chloride Eastern Industries Ltd. *Heir: s* Viscount Ikerrin [*b* 9 Jan. 1953; *m* 1975, Philippa V. J., *yr d* of Wing Comdr L. V. Craxton; three *s* (incl. twin *s*]. *Address:* 10 Netherton Grove, SW10. *T:* 071–352 6328. *Clubs:* White's, Brooks's, Pratt's.

Died 5 Oct. 1992.

CARRUTHERS, George, OBE 1979; FCIT; Member of Board, 1979–82, Deputy Chief Executive, 1981–82, Consultant, 1983–84, National Bus Company; *b* 15 Nov. 1917; *s* of James and Dinah Carruthers; *m* 1941, Gabriel Joan Heath; one *s* one *d. Educ:* Nelson Sch., Wigton, Cumbria; St Edmund Hall, Oxford (BA). FBIM. Served War, Border Regt and Cameronians (Major), 1939–46 (despatches). Various management posts, Bus Industry (all at subsid. cos or Headquarters NBC): Eastern Counties, Norwich, 1946–59; Wilts and Dorset Omnibus Co., 1959–63; Dep. Gen. Manager, Hants and Dorset Omnibus Co., 1963–66; Gen. Manager, United Welsh-Swansea, 1967–69; Vice-Chm., South Wales (NBC), 1969–72; Regional Exec., Western Region, NBC, 1972–73; Gp Exec., 1973–74, Director of Manpower, 1974–79, NBC Headquarters; Mem. for Personnel Services, 1979–81. Pres., Bus and Coach Council, 1983–84. *Publications:* papers for Jl and meetings of CIT (Road Passenger award for a paper, 1978). *Recreation:* the countryside. *Address:* 2 Mallard Close, Lower Street, Harnham, Salisbury, Wilts SP2 8JB. *T:* Salisbury (0722) 323084.

Died 10 Nov. 1992.

CARSON, Air Cdre Robert John, CBE 1974; AFC 1964; Director, Leicestershire Medical Research Foundation, University of Leicester, since 1980; *b* 3 Aug. 1924; *e s* of

Robert George and Margaret Etta Helena Carson; *m* 1945, Jane, *yr d* of James and Jane Bailie; three *d*. *Educ:* Regent House Sch., Newtownards, NI; RAF. MRAeS; MBIM; MIOM. India, Burma, Malaya, 1945–48; Rhodesia, 1949–50; Queens Univ. Air Sqdn, 1951–52; RAF HC Examining Unit, 1952–53; AHQ Iraq, 1953–54; RAF Staff Coll., 1955; Plans, Air Min., 1956–59; 16 Sqdn, Laarbruch, Germany, 1959–62; Wing Comdr Flying, RAF Swinderby, 1962–64; Air Warfare Coll., Manby, 1964; Chief Nuclear Ops, 2 ATAF Germany, 1964–67; JSSC Latimer, 1967; Chief Air Planner, UK Delegn, Live Oak, SHAPE, 1968–71; Station Comdr, RAF Leeming, 1971–73; Overseas Coll. Defence Studies, Canada, 1973–74; Air Adviser, British High Commission, Ottawa, 1974–75; Defence Advr to British High Comr in Canada, 1975–78; Manager, Panavia Office, Ottawa, and Grumman Aerospace Corp., NY, 1978–80. County Chm., SSAFA, Leics, 1982–; Regional Rep., SSAFA, Midland (2), 1986–; Pres., Aircrew Assoc., Leics, 1984–. Queen's Commendation (Air), 1962. *Recreations:* Rugby, tennis, golf, gardening. *Address:* 20 Meadow Drive, Scruton, near Northallerton, North Yorks DL7 0QW. *T:* Northallerton (0609) 748656; c/o Lloyds Bank, 118 High Street, Northallerton, N Yorks DL7 8PW. *Clubs:* Royal Air Force; Royal Ottawa (Ottawa).

Died 18 Nov. 1991.

CARSTAIRS, Charles Young, CB 1968; CMG 1950; *b* 30 Oct. 1910; *s* of late Rev. Dr George Carstairs, DD and Elizabeth Huntly Carstairs (*née* Young); *m* 1939, Frances Mary (*d* 1981), *o d* of late Dr Claude Lionel Coode, Stroud, Glos; one *s* one *d*. *Educ:* George Watson's Boys' Coll., Edinburgh; Edinburgh Univ. Entered Home Civil Service, 1934, Dominions Office; transf. Colonial Office, 1935; Asst Private Sec. to Sec. of State for the Colonies, 1936; Private Sec. to Perm. Under-Sec. of State for the Colonies, 1937; Asst Sec., West India Royal Commn, 1938–39; West Indian, Prodn, Res. and Mediterranean Depts, 1939–47; Administrative Sec., Development and Welfare Organisation, British West Indies, 1947–50; Sec., British Caribbean Standing Closer Assoc. Cttee, 1948–49; Dir of Information Services, Colonial Office, 1951–53; Asst Under-Sec., 1953–62; Deputy Sec., Medical Research Council, 1962–65; Under-Secretary, Ministry of Public Building and Works: Directorate-Gen., R&D, 1965–67; Construction Economics, 1967–70; Special Advr, Expenditure Cttee, House of Commons, 1971–75; Clerk to Select Cttee on Commodity Prices, House of Lords, 1976–77. *Publications:* (contrib.) The New Select Committees, ed Gavin Drewry, 1985; (ed jtly) Parliament and International Relations, 1991. *Recreation:* bad watercolours. *Address:* 4 Church Court, 31 Monks Walk, Reigate, Surrey RH2 0ST. *T:* Reigate (0737) 244896. *Club:* Athenæum. *Died 15 Feb. 1993.*

CARSTAIRS, Dr George Morrison, MD; FRCPE, FRCPsych; Vice-Chancellor, University of York, 1973–78; *b* Mussoorie, India, 18 June 1916; *s* of late Rev. Dr George Carstairs, DD, K-i-H, and Elizabeth Huntly Carstairs; *m* 1950, Vera Hunt; two *s* one *d*. *Educ:* George Watson's Coll., Edinburgh; Edinburgh Univ. Asst Phys., Royal Edinburgh Hosp., 1942; MO, RAF, 1942–46; Commonwealth Fellow, USA, 1948–49; Rockefeller Research Fellow, 1950–51; Henderson Res. Schol., 1951–52; Sen. Registrar, Maudsley Hosp., 1953; Scientific Staff, MRC, 1954–60; Prof. of Psychiatry, Univ. of Edinburgh, 1961–73. Dir, MRC Unit for Research on Epidemiological Aspects of Psychiatry, 1960–71. Vis. Prof. of Psychiatry, Post Grad. Insts, Bangalore, Chandigarh and New Delhi, India, 1979–81; Fellow, Woodrow Wilson Center, Smithsonian Instn, Washington, 1981–82. Reith Lectr, BBC, 1962. Pres., World Federation for Mental Health, 1967–71. *Publications:* The Twice Born, 1957; This Island Now, 1963; (with R.L. Kapur)

The Great Universe of Kota, 1976; Death of a Witch, 1983; chapters and articles in medical publications. *Recreations:* travel, theatre, formerly athletics. *Address:* 23 Lancaster Grove, NW3. *Died 17 April 1991.*

CARSTENS, Prof. Dr Karl; President of the Federal Republic of Germany, 1979–84; *b* 14 Dec. 1914; *s* of Dr Karl Carstens, teacher, and Gertrud (*née* Clausen); *m* 1944, Dr Veronica Carstens (*née* Prior). *Educ:* Univs of Frankfurt, Dijon, München, Königsberg, Hamburg, Yale. Dr Laws Hamburg, 1936; LLM Yale, 1949. Served with Army, 1939–45; lawyer, Bremen, 1945–49; rep. of Bremen in Bonn, 1949–54; rep. of Fed. Republic of Germany to Council of Europe, Strasbourg, 1954–55; teaching at Cologne Univ., 1950–73; Prof. of Constitutional and Internat. Law, 1960–73; FO, Bonn, 1955–60 (State Sec., 1960–66); Dep. Defence Minister, 1966–67; Head of Chancellor's Office, Bonn, 1968–69; Dir Research Inst., German Foreign Policy Assoc., 1969–72; Mem. (CDU) German Bundestag, 1972–79; Leader of the Opposition, 1973–76; Pres. of Bundestag, 1976–79. Hon. Citizen: Berlin, Bonn. Charlemagne Prize, 1984; Bremische Senatsmedaille in Gold, 1985; Robert Schuman Prize, 1985; Stresemann Medaille, 1985; Schleyer Prize, 1987. Sonderstufe Grosskreuz Bundesverdienstkreuz, 1979; Ehrenkreuz Bundeswehr in Gold, 1987. Dr *hc* Univs of Tokyo, Coimbra, St Louis, Dijon and Speyer. *Publications:* Grundgedanken der amerikanischen Verfassung und ihre Verwirklichung, 1954; Das Recht des Europarats, 1956; Politische Führung—Erfahrungen im Dienst der Bundesregierung, 1971; Bundestagsreden und Zeitdokumente, 1977; Reden und Interviews, 5 vols, 1980–84; Anthologie Deutsche Gedichte, 1983; Wanderungen in Deutschland, 1985; Vom Geist der Freiheit, 1989. *Address:* 5300 Bonn 1, Bundeshaus, Germany. *Died 30 May 1992.*

CARTER; *see* Bonham-Carter and Bonham Carter.

CARTER, Angela Olive; author and reviewer; *b* 7 May 1940; *d* of Hugh Stalker; *m* 1st, 1960, Paul Carter (marr. diss. 1972); 2nd, 1991, Mark Pearce; one *s*. *Educ:* Bristol Univ. Fellow in Creative Writing, Sheffield Univ., 1976–78. Judge, Booker McConnell Prize, 1983. Screenplay (jtly), The Company of Wolves, 1984. *Publications: fiction: novels:* Shadow Dance, 1966; The Magic Toyshop (John Llewellyn Rhys Prize), 1967 (screenplay, 1986); Several Perceptions (Somerset Maugham Award), 1968; Heroes and Villains, 1969; Miss Z, the Dark Young Lady, 1970; Love, 1971; The Infernal Desire Machines of Doctor Hoffman, 1972; The Passion of New Eve, 1977; Nights at the Circus (jtly, James Tait Black Meml Prize), 1984; Wise Children, 1991; *short stories:* Fireworks, 1974; The Bloody Chamber and other stories (Cheltenham Fest. of Lit. Award), 1979; Black Venus, 1985; (ed) Wayward Girls and Wicked Women, 1986; (contrib.) The Virago Book of Ghost Stories, 1987; (ed) The Virago Book of Fairy Stories, 1990; Come unto these Yellow Sands: four radio plays, 1984; *for children:* (jtly) Martin Leman's Comic and Curious Cats, 1979; (jtly) Moonshadow, 1982; (jtly) Sleeping Beauty and other favourite fairy tales (Kate Greenaway Medal), 1983; *nonfiction:* The Sadeian Woman: an exercise in cultural history, 1979; Nothing Sacred: selected writings, 1982; contrib. New Society, Guardian, etc; *posthumous publications:* Expletives Deleted: selected writings, 1992; (ed) The Second Virago Book of Fairy Tales, 1992; American Ghosts and Old World Wonders (miscellaneous), 1993. *Address:* c/o Virago Press Ltd, Centro House, 20–23 Mandela Street, Camden Town, NW1 0HQ. *Died 16 Feb. 1992.*

CARTER, Dorothy Ethel Fleming, (Jane); energy adviser; World Bank consultant; Partner, International Energy Efficiency Consultants, since 1983; Vice President, British

Institute of Energy Economics, since 1980; *b* 29 Aug. 1928; *d* of late Charles Edward Starkey and Doris Alma Starkey (*nee* Fleming); *m* 1952, Frank Arthur, (Nick), Carter; two *d*. *Educ:* Dame Allen's Girls' Sch.; Swansea High Sch.; LSE (BSc (Econ) 1951). Joined CS as Exec. Officer, BoT, 1947; Principal, 1966; Min. of Technology, 1969–70; DTI, 1970–73; Asst Sec., Pay Bd, 1973–74; Dept of Energy, 1974–82, Under Sec., 1979–82. Ecole Nat. d'Admin, Paris, 1976. Vis. Prof., Institut d'Economie et de Politique de l'Energie, Grenoble, 1987–88. Pres., Internat. Assoc. of Energy Economists, 1986–. *Recreations:* travelling, reading. *Address:* 27 Gilkes Crescent, Dulwich Village, SE21 7BP. *T:* 0181–693 1889. *Club:* Reform. *Died 14 May 1995.*

CARTER, Frank Ernest Lovell, CBE 1956 (OBE 1949); FSA; Director General of the Overseas Audit Service, 1963–71; *b* 6 Oct. 1909; *s* of Ernest and Florence Carter; *m* 1966, Gerda (*née* Gruen) (*d* 1981). *Educ:* Chigwell Sch.; Hertford Coll., Oxford. Served in Overseas Audit Service in: Nigeria, 1933–42; Sierra Leone, 1943; Palestine, 1944–45; Aden and Somaliland, 1946–49; Tanganyika, 1950–54; Hong Kong, 1955–59; Deputy Director in London, 1960–62. Part-time Adviser: FCO, 1972–76; ODM, 1977–81. FSA 1983. *Address:* Stuart House, 149 London Road, St Albans, Herts AL1 1TA. *T:* St Albans (01727) 830174. *Club:* East India. *Died 29 Jan. 1995.*

CARTER, Maj.-Gen. James Norman, CB 1958; CBE 1955 (OBE 1946); *b* 26 June 1906; *s* of Capt. N. H. Carter, RN; *m* 1929, Barbara Violet Bovill (*d* 1990); two *d*. *Educ:* Charterhouse; RMC Sandhurst. Commissioned The Dorset Regt, 1926; Captain, The Royal Warwickshire Regt, 1936; Lieut-Colonel, 1948; Colonel, 1950; Brigadier, 1954; Maj.-General, 1957; Asst Chief of Staff, Organisation and Training Div., SHAPE, 1955–57; Commander British Army Staff, British Joint Services Mission, Washington, 1958–60; Military Attaché, Washington, Jan.-July 1960; General Secretary, The Officers' Assoc., 1961–63. *Died 29 June 1994.*

CARTER, Jane; *see* Carter, D. E. F.

CARTIER, Rudolph; drama producer, television, since 1953; also producer, television operas, since 1956; *b* Vienna, Austria, 17 April 1904; *s* of Joseph Cartier; *m*; one *d*; *m* 1949, Margaret Pepper; one *d*. *Educ:* Vienna Academy of Music and Dramatic Art (Max Reinhardt's Master-class). Film director and scenario writer in pre-war Berlin; came to Britain, 1935; joined BBC Television. Productions include: Arrow to the Heart, Dybbuk, Portrait of Peter Perowne, 1952; It is Midnight, Doctor Schweitzer, L'Aiglon, The Quatermass Experiment, Wuthering Heights, 1953; Such Men are Dangerous, That Lady, Captain Banner, Nineteen-Eightyfour, 1954; Moment of Truth, The Creature, Vale of Shadows, Quatermass II, The Devil's General, 1955; The White Falcon, The Mayerling Affair, The Public Prosecutor, The Fugitive, The Cold Light, The Saint of Bleecker Street, Dark Victory, Clive of India, The Queen and the Rebels, 1956; Salome, Ordeal by Fire, Counsellor-at-Law, 1957; Captain of Koepenick, The Winslow Boy, A Tale of Two Cities, Midsummer Night's Dream, 1958; Quatermass and the Pit, Philadelphia Story, Mother Courage and her Children, (Verdi's) Othello, 1959; The White Guard, Glorious Morning, Tobias and the Angel (opera), 1960; Rashomon, Adventure Story, Anna Karenina, Cross of Iron, 1961; Doctor Korczuk and the Children, Sword of Vengeance, Carmen, 1962; Anna Christie, Night Express, Stalingrad, 1963; Lady of the Camelias, The Midnight Men, The July Plot, 1964; Wings of the Dove, Ironhand, The Joel Brand Story, 1965; Gordon of Khartoum, Lee Oswald, Assassin, 1966; Firebrand, The Burning Bush, 1967; The Fanatics, Triumph of Death, The Naked Sun, The Rebel, 1968;

Conversation at Night, An Ideal Husband, 1969; Rembrandt, The Bear (opera), The Year of the Crow, 1970; The Proposal, 1971; Lady Windermere's Fan, 1972; The Deep Blue Sea, 1973; Fall of Eagles (episodes Dress Rehearsal, End Game), 1974; Loyalties, 1976; Gaslight, 1977. Prod film, Corridor of Mirrors; directed film, Passionate Summer. Guild of Television Producers and Directors "Oscar" as best drama producer of 1957. *Recreations:* motoring, serious music, going to films or watching television, stamp-collecting. *Address:* 26 Lowther Road, Barnes, SW13 9ND. *Died 7 June 1994.*

CASE, Captain Richard Vere Essex, DSO 1942; DSC 1940; RD; Royal Naval Reserve, retired; Royal Naval Reserve ADC to the Queen, 1958; Chief Marine Superintendent, Coast Lines Ltd and Associated Companies, 1953–69; *b* 13 April 1904; *s* of late Prof. Robert Hope Case and Hilda, *d* of Thomas Trew, Axbridge; *m* 1940, Olive May (*d* 1991), *d* of H. W. Griggs, Preston, near Canterbury, Kent; one *s* one *d*. *Educ:* Thames Nautical Training Coll., HMS Worcester. Joined RNR, 1920; commenced service in Merchant Service, 1920; Master's Certificate of Competency, 1928; Captain RNR, 1953; served War of 1939–45 (DSO, DSC and Bar, RD and Clasp). *Recreation:* bowls. *Address:* 14 Aigburth Hall Road, Liverpool L19 9DQ. *T:* 051–427 1016. *Clubs:* Athenæum (Liverpool); Liverpool Cricket. *Died 30 Oct. 1991.*

CASSELS, Prof. James Macdonald, FRS 1959; Lyon Jones Professor of Physics, University of Liverpool, 1960–82, Emeritus Professor, since 1982; Chairman, Igitur Ltd, 1986–92; *b* 9 Sept. 1924; *s* of Alastair Macdonald Cassels and Ada White Cassels (*née* Scott); *m* 1st, 1947, Jane Helen Thera Lawrence (*d* 1977); one *s* one *d*; 2nd, 1986, Analesia Theresa Bestman (marr. diss. 1989). *Educ:* Rochester House Sch., Edinburgh; St Lawrence Coll., Ramsgate; Trinity College, Cambridge (Coutts Trotter Student, 1948–49). BA, MA, PhD (Cantab). Harwell Fellow and Principal Scientific Officer, Atomic Energy Research Establishment, Harwell, 1949–53; Lecturer, 1953, subseq. Senior Lecturer, University of Liverpool; Prof. of Experimental Physics, University of Liverpool, 1956–59; Extraordinary Fellow, Churchill Coll., Cambridge, 1959–60; Visiting Prof., Cornell Univ., 1959–60. Royal Soc. Adv. Cttee on foundn of CERN, 1953: Member: Design Cttee for CERN synchrocyclotron, 1953–57; CERN Physics Cttee, 1960–63. Mem., Combined Heat and Power Cttee, Dept of Energy, 1974–79; Royal Soc. Mem., working party on energy, Nat. Academies Policy Adv. Gp, 1993–. Mem. Council, Royal Soc., 1968–69. Hon. Mem., Combined Heat and Power Assoc., 1979–. Hon. Fellow, Univ. of Liverpool, 1982–83. Rutherford Medal, Inst. of Physics, 1973. *Publications:* Basic Quantum Mechanics, 1970; contributions to: scientific journals on atomic, nuclear and elementary particle physics; govt reports on district heating and combined heat and power. *Recreations:* fishing, classic cars, talking. *Address:* 8 St Michael at Plea, Norwich NR3 1EP. *T:* Norwich (01603) 660999; Igitur Ltd, 29 Sandy Way, Skelmersdale, Lancs WN8 8LF. *T:* Skelmersdale (01695) 22251. *Died 19 Oct. 1994.*

CASTLE, Mrs G. L.; *see* Sharp, Margery.

CATCHESIDE, David Guthrie, DSc London; FRS 1951; Hon. Research Associate, Waite Agricultural Research Institute, South Australia, 1975–81; *b* 31 May 1907; *s* of late David Guthrie Catcheside and Florence Susanna (*née* Boxwell); *m* 1931, Kathleen Mary Whiteman; one *s* one *d*. *Educ:* Strand Sch.; King's Coll., University of London. Asst to Professor of Botany, Glasgow Univ., 1928–30; Asst Lecturer, 1931–33, and Lecturer in Botany, 1933–36, University of London (King's Coll.); International Fellow of Rockefeller Foundation, 1936–37; Lecturer in Botany, University of Cambridge, 1937–50; Lecturer and Fellow, Trinity Coll., Cambridge, 1944–51; Reader in Plant Cytogenetics, Cambridge Univ., 1950–51; Prof. of Genetics, Adelaide Univ., S. Australia, 1952–55; Prof. of Microbiology, Univ. of Birmingham, 1956–64; Prof. of Genetics, 1964–72, Dir, 1967–72, Vis. Fellow, 1973–75, Res. Sch. of Biol Scis, ANU. Research Associate, Carnegie Instn of Washington, 1958. Visiting Professor, California Inst. of Technology, 1961. Foreign Associate, Nat. Acad. of Sciences of USA, 1974. Foundation FAA 1954; FKC 1959. *Publications:* Botanical Technique in Bolles Lee's Microtomists' Vade-Mecum, 1937–50; Genetics of Micro-organisms, 1951; Genetics of Recombination, 1977; Mosses of South Australia, 1980; papers on genetics and cytology. *Address:* 16 Rodger Avenue, Leabrook, SA 5068, Australia. *Died 1 June 1994.*

CATTANACH, Brig. Helen, CB 1976; RRC 1963; Matron-in-Chief (Army) and Director of Army Nursing Services, Queen Alexandra's Royal Army Nursing Corps, 1973–76; *b* 21 June 1920; *d* of late Francis Cattanach and Marjory Cattanach (*née* Grant). *Educ:* Elgin Academy; trained Woodend Hospital, Aberdeen. Joined QAIMNS (R), 1945; service in India, Java, United Kingdom, Singapore, Hong Kong and Germany, 1945–52; MELF, Gibraltar and UK, 1953–57; Staff Officer, MoD, 1958–61; Inspector of Recruiting, QARANC, 1961–62; Hong Kong, 1963–64; Matron: BMH Munster, 1968; Cambridge Military Hosp., Aldershot, 1969–71; Dir of Studies, QARANC, 1971–72. QHNS, 1973–76. Col Comdt QARANC, 1978–81. Pres., Not Forgotten Assoc., 1991–. Governor, Royal Scottish Corp., 1976–. CStJ 1976 (OStJ 1971). *Died 4 May 1994.*

CATTERMOLE, Lancelot Harry Mosse, ROI 1938; painter and illustrator; *b* 19 July 1898; *s* of Sidney and Josephine Cattermole; *g s* of George Cattermole (1800–1868), painter in water-colours and oils and illustrator of works by Charles Dickens and Sir Walter Scott; *m* 1937, Lydia Alice Winifred Coles, BA; no *c.* *Educ:* Holmsdale House Sch., Worthing, Sussex; The Robert May Grammar Sch., Odiham, Hants. Senior Art Scholarship to Slade Faculty of Fine Art, University of London, and Central School of Arts and Crafts, London, 1923–26. Exhibitor Royal Acad., Royal Inst. of Oil Painters, Royal Soc. of British Artists, Royal Soc. of Portrait Painters, etc, and provincial art galleries; works acquired by National Army Mus., London, and Royal Naval Mus., Portsmouth. Signed work Lance Cattermole. *Recreations:* reading, bridge. *Address:* Horizon, 17 Palmers Way, High Salvington, Worthing, W Sussex BN13 3DP. *T:* Worthing (0903) 260436. *Died 27 June 1992.*

CAUGHEY, Sir Harcourt; *see* Caughey, Sir T. H. C.

CAUGHEY, Sir (Thomas) Harcourt (Clarke), KBE 1972 (OBE 1966); JP; Executive Chairman, Smith & Caughey Ltd, since 1975 (Managing Director, 1962–85); *b* Auckland, 4 July 1911; *s* of James Marsden Caughey and Kathleen Elizabeth Mitchell; *m* 1939, Patricia Mary, *d* of Hon. Sir George Panton Finlay; one *s* two *d.* *Educ:* King's Coll., Auckland; Auckland Univ. Major, Fiji Military Forces (Pacific), 1942–44. Director: New Zealand Insurance Corp., 1981–86 (Dep. Chm., 1981–86); South British Insurance Co., 1963–81; New Zealand Guardian Trust Co., 1963–86. Member: Caughey Preston Trust Bd, 1950–79 (Chm., 1954–79); Eden Park Trustees; Auckland Hosps Bd, 1953–74 (Chm., 1959–74); Hosps Adv. Council, 1960–74; Vice-Pres., NZ Exec. Hosps Bds Assoc., 1960–74; Chairman: NZ MRC, 1966–71; Social Council of NZ, 1971–73; Pres., Auckland Med. Res. Foundn, 1978–84. CStJ. Hon. LLD Auckland, 1986. Mem., All Black Rugby Team, 1932–37. *Recreations:*

gardening, swimming. *Address:* 7 Judges Bay Road, Auckland, NZ. *Club:* Northern (Auckland, NZ).
Died 4 Aug. 1993.

CAULFIELD, Sir Bernard, Kt 1968; Judge of the High Court of Justice, Queen's Bench Division, 1968–89; Presiding Judge, Northern Circuit, 1976–80; *b* 24 April 1914; *y s* of late John Caulfield and Catherine Quinn; *m* 1953, Sheila Mary, *o d* of Dr J. F. J. Herbert; three *s* one *d.* *Educ:* St Francis Xavier's Coll.; University of Liverpool. LLB 1938, LLM 1940, Hon. LLD 1980. Solicitor, 1940. Army Service, 1940–46; Home and MEF; commnd, Dec. 1942, RAOC; released with Hon. rank of Major. Barrister-at-Law, Lincoln's Inn, 1947 (Bencher, 1968); joined Midland Circuit, 1949; QC 1961; Recorder of Coventry, 1963–68; Dep. Chairman QS, County of Lincoln (Parts of Lindsey), 1963–71; Leader, Midland Circuit, 1965–68; Comr of Assize, 1967. Mem., General Council of Bar, 1965–68; Mem. Senate, 1984, Treasurer and Dean of Chapel, Lincoln's Inn, 1987; Mem. Inns of Court Council, 1987. Hon. Mem., Northern Circuit Bar Mess, 1979. *Address:* Ingleby, near Lincoln, LN1 2PQ. *Died 17 Oct. 1994.*

CAWDOR, 6th Earl *cr* 1827; **Hugh John Vaughan Campbell,** FSA; FRICS; Baron Cawdor, 1796; Viscount Emlyn, 1827; *b* 6 Sept. 1932; *s* of 5th Earl Cawdor, TD, FSA, and Wilma Mairi (*d* 1982), *e d* of late Vincent C. Vickers; *S* father, 1970; *m* 1st, 1957, Cathryn (marr. diss. 1979), 2nd *d* of Maj.-Gen. Sir Robert Hinde, KBE, CB, DSO; two *s* three *d*; 2nd, 1979, Countess Angelika Ilona Lazansky von Bukowa. *Educ:* Eton; Magdalen Coll., Oxford; Royal Agricultural Coll., Cirencester. FRSA. High Sheriff of Carmarthenshire, 1964. *Heir:* *s* Viscount Emlyn, *b* 30 June 1962. *Address:* Cawdor Castle, Nairn IV12 5RD. *Clubs:* Pratt's, White's, Beefsteak.
Died 20 June 1993.

CAYLEY, Henry Douglas, OBE 1946; *b* 20 Jan. 1904; *s* of late Cyril Henry Cayley, MD; *m* 1940, Nora Innes Paton, *d* of Nigel F. Paton; one *s* two *d.* *Educ:* Epsom Coll. Joined National Bank of India Ltd, London, 1922; Eastern Staff, 1926; Dep. Exchange Controller, Reserve Bank of India, 1939–48; rejoined National Bank of India, 1948; appointed to London Head Office, 1952; Asst Gen. Manager 1957, Dep. Gen. Manager 1960, Chief Gen. Manager 1964–69, Director 1966–72, National & Grindlays Bank Ltd. *Recreations:* gardening, walking. *Address:* 63 Beluga Street, Mount Eliza, Vic 3930, Australia. *Died 31 March 1991.*

CECIL, Robert, CMG 1959; author; HM Diplomatic Service, retired; Chairman, Institute for Cultural Research, since 1968; *b* 25 March 1913; *s* of late Charles Cecil; *m* 1938, Kathleen, *d* of late Col C. C. Marindin, CBE, DSO; one *s* two *d.* *Educ:* Wellington Coll.; Gonville and Caius Coll., Cambridge. BA Cantab 1935, MA 1961. Entered HM Foreign Service, 1936; served in Foreign Office, 1939–45; First Sec., HM Embassy, Washington, 1945–48; assigned to Foreign Office, 1948; Counsellor and Head of American Dept, 1951; Counsellor, HM Embassy, Copenhagen, 1953–55; HM Consul-Gen., Hanover, 1955–57; Counsellor, HM Embassy, Bonn, 1957–59; Dir-Gen., British Information Services, New York, 1959–61; Head of Cultural Relations Dept, FO, 1962–67. Reader in Contemp. German Hist., 1968–78, Chm., Grad. Sch. of Contemp. European Studies, 1976–78, Reading Univ. *Publications:* Levant and other Poems, 1940; Time and other Poems, 1955; Life in Edwardian England, 1969; The Myth of the Master Race: Alfred Rosenberg and Nazi ideology, 1972; Hitler's Decision to Invade Russia, 1941, 1976; (ed) The King's Son (anthology), 1980; (contrib.) The Missing Dimension, 1984; A Divided Life: a biography of Donald Maclean, 1988; The Masks of Death: changing attitudes in the 19th century, 1991. *Recreations:*

gardening, chess, etc. *Address:* Hambledon, Hants PO7 4RW. *T:* Hambledon (0705) 632669. *Club:* Royal Automobile. *Died 28 Feb. 1994.*

CHADDOCK, Prof. Dennis Hilliar, CBE 1962; Professor of Engineering Design, University of Technology, Loughborough, 1966–73, retired; Professor Emeritus, 1974; Consultant Proprietor, Quorn Engineering, since 1974; *b* 28 July 1908; *s* of Herbert Dennis Chaddock, London; *m* 1937, Stella Edith Dorrington; one *s* one *d* (and one *s* decd). *Educ:* University Coll. Sch. BSc (Eng) Hons, London, 1933; MSc (Eng) London, 1938. Engineering Apprentice, Sa Adolph Saurer, Switzerland, 1927–30; Research Engineer, Morris Commercial Cars Ltd, Birmingham, 1930–32; Asst Road Motor Engineer, LMS Railway Co., Euston, 1932–41; HM Forces, 1941–46: Inspecting Officer, Chief Inspector of Armaments, 1941–43; Dep. Chief Inspecting Officer, 1943–45; Chief Design Officer, Armament Design Estabt, 1945–46; relinquished commission with rank of Lieut-Col, 1946; Superintendent, Carriage Design Branch of Armament Design Estabt, 1947–50; Imperial Defence Coll., 1951; Dep. Chief Engineer, 1952–55; Principal Superintendent, Weapons and Ammunition Div., Armament Research and Development Estabt, 1955–62; Dir of Artillery Research and Development, Ministry of Defence (Army) 1962–66. *Recreation:* model engineering. *Address:* 29 Paddock Close, Quorndon, Leics LE12 8BJ. *T:* Quorn (0509) 412607. *Died 19 Sept. 1992.*

CHADWICK, Rt Rev. William Frank Percival; Bishop of Barking, 1959–75; *b* 1905. *Educ:* Wadham College, Oxford; Harvard Univ., USA (Davison Scholar). Deacon, 1929, priest, 1930, Diocese Liverpool; Curate, St Helens, 1929–34; Vicar: Widnes, 1934–38; Christ Church, Crouch End, N8, 1938–47; Barking, 1947–59. Proctor, Diocese of London, 1946, Diocese of Chelmsford, 1951; Examining Chaplain to Bishop of Chelmsford, 1951; Asst RD, Barking, 1950–53; RD, Barking, 1953; Hon. Canon of Chelmsford, 1954; Pro-Prolocutor, Lower House of Canterbury, 1956; Exchange Preacher, USA, British Council of Churches, 1958; Chm., Church of England's Commn on Roman Catholic Relations, 1968–75; Mem., Dioceses Commn, 1978–80. *Publication:* The Inner Life. *Recreation:* golf. *Address:* Harvard House, Acton, Long Melford, Suffolk CO10 0AU. *T:* Sudbury (0787) 77015. *Club:* Commonwealth Trust. *Died 12 Feb. 1991.*

CHALK, Hon. Sir Gordon (William Wesley), KBE 1971; company director and business consultant; Minister for Transport, Government of Queensland, 1957–65, Deputy Premier and Treasurer, 1965–76; Leader, Liberal Party of Australia (Queensland Division), 1965–76; voluntarily retired, 1976; *b* 16 May 1913; of British parentage; *s* of S. Chalk; *m* 1937, Ellen Clare Grant; one *s* one *d. Educ:* Gatton Senior High Sch., Qld. MLA (L) E Toowoomba, 1947–50, Lockyer, 1950–76. Formerly: Queensland Sales Manager, Toowoomba Foundry Pty Ltd; Registered Taxation Agent. Mem. Senate, Griffith Univ., 1976–84. Hon. LLD Queensland Univ., 1974. *Address:* 277 Indooroopilly Road, Indooroopilly, Qld 4068, Australia. *T:* Brisbane 3711598. *Clubs:* Tattersall's (Brisbane, Qld); Rotary International (Gatton, Qld); Southport Yacht. *Died 26 April 1991.*

CHALLIS, Margaret Joan, MA; Headmistress of Queen Anne's School, Caversham, 1958–77; *b* 14 April 1917; *d* of R. S. Challis and L. Challis (*née* Fairbairn). *Educ:* Girton Coll., Cambridge. BA Hons English Tripos, 1939, MA 1943, Cambridge. English Mistress: Christ's Hospital, Hertford, 1940–44; Dartford Grammar School for Girls, 1944–45; Cheltenham Ladies' Coll., 1945–57 (Housemistress, 1949–57). *Recreations:* local history, music, old churches, gardening. *Address:* 30 Eldorado

Crescent, Cheltenham, Glos GL50 2PY. *T:* Cheltenham (0242) 245605. *Died 14 Sept. 1994.*

CHALMERS, Thomas Wightman, CBE 1957; *b* 29 April 1913; *s* of Thomas Wightman Chalmers and Susan Florence Colman. *Educ:* Bradfield Coll.; King's Coll., London. Organ Scholar, King's Coll., London, 1934–36; BSc (Engineering), 1936. Joined BBC programme staff, 1936; successively announcer, Belfast and London; Overseas Presentation Director; Chief Assistant, Light Programme, 1945, Controller, 1948–50; Director, Nigerian Broadcasting Service, 1950–56, on secondment from BBC; Controller, North Region, BBC, 1956–58; Director of the Tanganyika Broadcasting Corporation, 1958–62; Deputy Regional Representative, UN Technical Assistance Board, East and Central Africa, 1962–64; Special Asst, Overseas and Foreign Relations, BBC, 1964–71; Chief Exec., Radio Services, United Newspapers Ltd, and Dir, Radio Fleet Productions Ltd, 1971–75. *Recreations:* travel, literature, music. *Died 30 Aug. 1995.*

CHAMBERLAIN, Rev. Elsie Dorothea; *see* Chamberlain-Garrington, Rev. E. D.

CHAMBERLAIN, George Digby, CMG 1950; Chief Secretary, Western Pacific High Commission, 1947–52; *b* 13 Feb. 1898; *s* of Digby Chamberlain, late Knockfin, Knaresborough; *m* 1931, Kirsteen Miller Holmes (decd); one *d* (one *s* decd). *Educ:* St Catharine's Coll., Cambridge. War Service, 1917–19, with Rifle Brigade, Lieut RARO. Asst District Commissioner, Gold Coast, 1925; Asst Principal, Colonial Office, 1930–32; Asst Colonial Secretary, Gold Coast, 1932; Asst Chief Secretary, Northern Rhodesia, 1939; Colonial Secretary, Gambia, 1943–47; Acting Governor, Gambia, July-Nov. 1943, and June-Aug. 1944; Acting High Commissioner, Western Pacific, Jan.-April, and Sept. 1951–July 1952; retired 1952. *Recreations:* shooting, fishing. *Address:* 18 Douglas Crescent, Edinburgh EH12 5BA. *Club:* New (Edinburgh). *Died 1994.*

CHAMBERLAIN, Air Vice-Marshal George Philip, CB 1946; OBE 1941; RAF, retired; *b* 18 Aug. 1905; *s* of G. A. R. Chamberlain, MA, FLAS, FRICS, Enville, Staffordshire; *m* 1930, Alfreda Rosamond Kedward; one *s* one *d. Educ:* Denstone Coll.; Royal Air Force Coll., Cranwell. Commissioned RAF, 1925. On loan to Min. of Civil Aviation, 1947–48; Imperial Defence Coll., 1949; AOA 205 Group, MEAF, 1950; AOC Transport Wing, MEAF, 1951–52; Commandant, RAF Staff Coll., Andover, 1953–54; AO i/c A, HQ Fighter Command, 1954–57; Dep. Controller of Electronics, Min. of Supply, 1957–59, Min. of Aviation, 1959–60; Managing Director, Collins Radio Co. of England, 1961–66, non-executive director, 1967–75. *Recreations:* gardening, walking. *Address:* Little Orchard, 12 Adelaide Close, Stanmore, Middlesex HA7 3EL. *T:* 0181–954 0710. *Club:* Royal Air Force. *Died 2 Nov. 1995.*

CHAMBERLAIN, Hon. Sir (Reginald) Roderic (St Clair), Kt 1970; Judge of the Supreme Court of South Australia, 1959–71; *b* 17 June 1901; *s* of late Henry Chamberlain; *m* 1929, Leila Macdonald Haining; one *d. Educ:* St Peter's Coll.; Adelaide Univ. Crown Prosecutor, 1928; KC 1945; Crown Solicitor, 1952–59; Chm., SA Parole Board, 1970–75. Chm., Anti-Cancer Foundn. *Publication:* The Stuart Affair, 1973. *Recreations:* golf, bridge. *Address:* 72 Moseley Street, Glenelg South, SA 5045, Australia. *T:* 95.2036. *Clubs:* Adelaide, Royal Adelaide Golf (Adelaide). *Died 26 Feb. 1991.*

CHAMBERLAIN-GARRINGTON, Rev. Elsie Dorothea, BD (London); Minister, Congregational Centre Church, Nottingham, since 1983; Chairman, Congregational Federation Council, 1978–85 (President, 1973–75);

b 3 March 1910; *m* 1947, Rev. J. L. St C. Garrington (*d* 1978). *Educ:* Channing Sch.; King's Coll., London (BD). Asst Minister Berkeley Street, Liverpool, 1939–41; Minister: Christ Church, Friern Barnet, 1941–46; Vineyard Congregational Church, Richmond, 1947–54; BBC Religious Dept, 1950–67; Associate Minister, The City Temple, 1968–70; Minister: Hutton Free Church, Brentwood, 1971–80; Chulmleigh, 1980–83; North Street, Taunton, 1980–86. 1st woman chaplain, HM Forces, 1946–47. Chm., Congregational Union of England and Wales, 1956–57; Nat. Pres., Free Church Women's Council, 1984–85. *Publications:* (ed) Lift Up Your Hearts, 1959; (ed) Calm Delight: devotional anthology, 1959; (ed) 12 Mini-Commentaries on the Jerusalem Bible, 1970. *Recreation:* music. *Address:* 4 Castle Gate, Nottingham NG1 7AS. *T:* Nottingham (0602) 413801.

Died 10 April 1991.

CHAMPION, John Stuart, CMG 1977; OBE 1963; HM Diplomatic Service, retired; *b* 17 May 1921; *er s* of Rev. Sir Reginald Champion, KCMG, OBE and Margaret, *d* of late Very Rev. W. M. Macgregor, DD, LLD; *m* 1944, Olive Lawrencina, *o d* of late Lawrence Durning Holt, Liverpool; five *s* two *d. Educ:* Shrewsbury Sch.; Balliol Coll., Oxford (Schol., BA). Commnd 11 Hussars PAO, 1941–46. Colonial Service (later HMOCS), Uganda, 1946–63: District Officer; Secretariat, 1949–52; Private Sec. to Governor, 1952; Asst Financial Sec., 1956; Actg Perm. Sec., Min. of Health, 1959; Perm. Sec., Min. of Internal Affairs, 1960; retd 1963; Principal, CRO, 1963; 1st Sec., FCO, 1965; Head of Chancery, Tehran, 1968; Counsellor, Amman, 1971; FCO, 1973; British Resident Comr, Anglo/French Condominium of the New Hebrides, 1975–78. Mem., West Midlands RHA, 1980–81; Chm., Herefordshire HA, 1982–86. Governor, Royal National Coll. for the Blind, 1980–93 (Vice-Chm., 1985–93); Chairman: St John Council for Hereford and Worcester, 1987–93; Council, Friends of Hereford Cathedral, 1988–93. CStJ 1993. *Recreations:* hill walking, golf, music. *Address:* Farmore, Callow, Hereford HR2 8DB. *T:* Hereford (0432) 274875. *Club:* Commonwealth Trust.

Died 18 April 1994.

CHANDLER, Edwin George, CBE 1979; FRIBA, FRTPI; City Architect, City of London, 1961–79; *b* 28 Aug. 1914; *e s* of Edwin and Honor Chandler; *m* 1938, Iris Dorothy, *o d* of Herbert William Grubb; one *d. Educ:* Selhurst Grammar Sch., Croydon. Gained distinction in thesis, ARIBA 1942; FRIBA 1961. Asst Architect, Hants County Council and City of Portsmouth, 1936–39. Served in HMS Vernon, Mine Design Dept, 1940–45. Dep. Architect and Planning Officer, West Ham, 1945–47; City Architect and Planning Officer, City of Oxford, 1947–61. Member: RIBA Council, 1950–52; Univ. Social Survey Cttee, Oxford; City of London Archaeological Trust; Trustee, Silver Jubilee Walkway Trust; Chm., Bd of Alleyn's Estate, Dulwich; Gov., James Allen's Sch., Dulwich. Liveryman, Gardeners' Co. (Master, 1988–89); Mem., Court of Common Council, Corp. of London (Cornhill Ward), 1982–, Deputy, 1986–. *Publications:* Housing for Old Age, 1939; City of Oxford Development Plan, 1950; articles contrib. to press and professional jls. *Recreations:* landscaping, travel, swimming. *Clubs:* Guildhall, Dulwich. *Died 6 Nov. 1991.*

CHANDLER, George, MA, PhD; FLA, FRHistS; FRSA; international adviser and editor in library and information science; *b* England, 2 July 1915; *s* of William and Florence W. Chandler; *m* 1937, Dorothy Lowe; one *s. Educ:* Central Grammar Sch., Birmingham; Leeds Coll. of Commerce; University of London. ALAA 1974. Birmingham Public Libraries, 1931–37; Leeds Public Libraries, 1937–46; WEA Tutor Organiser, 1946–47; Borough Librarian, Dudley, 1947–50; Dep. City Librarian, Liverpool,

1950–52, City Librarian, 1952–74; Dir-Gen., Nat. Library of Australia, 1974–80. Sec. Dudley Arts Club, 1948–50; Pres., Internat. Assoc. of Met. City Libraries, 1968–71; Pres. 1962–71 (Hon. Sec. 1957–62), Soc. of Municipal and County Chief Librarians; Dir, 1962–74 (Hon. Sec. 1955–62), Liverpool and District Scientific, Industrial and Research Library Advisory Council; Hon. Librarian, 1957–74 (Hon. Sec. 1950–57), Historic Soc. of Lancashire and Cheshire; Chm. Exec. Cttee, 1965–70, President, 1971, Library Assoc.; Member: DES Library Adv. Council for England and Wales, 1965–72; British Library Organising Cttee, 1972–73; British Library Bd, 1973–74. Hon. Editor, Internat. Library Review, 1969–. Unesco expert in Tunisia, 1964. *Publications:* Dudley, 1949; William Roscoe, 1953; Liverpool 1207–1957, 1957; Liverpool Shipping, 1960; Liverpool under James I, 1960; How to Find Out, 1963, 5th edn 1982; Four Centuries of Banking: Martins Bank, Vol. I, 1964, Vol. II, 1968; Liverpool under Charles I, 1965; Libraries in the Modern World, 1965; How to Find Out About Literature, 1968; Libraries in the East, 1971; Libraries, Bibliography and Documentation in the USSR, 1972; Victorian and Edwardian Liverpool and the North West, 1972; An Illustrated History of Liverpool, 1972; (ed) International Librarianship, 1972; Merchant Venturers, 1973; Victorian and Edwardian Manchester, 1974; Liverpool and Literature, 1974; Recent Developments in International and National Library and Information Services, 1982; (ed) International Series of Monographs on Library and Information Science; (ed) series, Recent Advances in Library and Information Services, 1981–; contributions to educnl and library press. *Recreations:* writing, research, walking, foreign travel. *Address:* 43 Saxon Close, Stratford-upon-Avon, Warwickshire CV37 7DX.

Died 9 Oct. 1992.

CHANDOS-POLE, Lt-Col John, CVO 1979; OBE 1951; JP; Lord-Lieutenant for Northamptonshire, 1967–84; *b* 20 July 1909; *s* of late Brig.-Gen. Harry Anthony Chandos-Pole, CBE, JP, DL, and Ada Ismay, Heverswood, Brasted, Kent; *m* 1952, Josephine Sylvia (*d* 1990), *d* of late Brig.-Gen. Cyril Randell Crofton, CBE, Limerick House, Milborne Port, near Sherborne; two step *d. Educ:* Eton; Magdalene Coll., Cambridge (MA). 2nd Lieut Coldstream Guards, 1933; Aide-de-camp: to Governor of Bombay, May-Nov. 1937; to Governor of Bengal, Nov. 1937–June 1938, Oct. 1938–Feb. 1939; to Viceroy of India, June–Oct. 1938; served War of 1939–45: France and Belgium (wounded); Palestine, 1948 (wounded, despatches); commanded 1st Bn, Coldstream Guards, 1947–48; Guards Depot, 1948–50; 2nd Bn, Coldstream Guards, 1950–52. Lieut-Col 1949; retired, 1953. A Member of the Hon. Corps of Gentlemen-at-Arms, 1956–79 (Harbinger, 1966–79). JP 1957, DL 1965, Northants. KStJ 1975. *Recreations:* racing, travel. *Address:* Newnham Hall, Daventry, Northants NN11 6HQ. *T:* Daventry (0327) 702711. *Clubs:* Boodle's, Pratt's.

Died 17 Dec. 1993.

CHANDOS-POLE, Major John Walkelyne, JP; DL; *b* 4 Nov. 1913; *o s* of late Col Reginald Walkelyne Chandos-Pole, TD, JP, Radburne Hall; *m* 1947, Ilsa Jill, *er d* of Emil Ernst Barstz, Zürich; one *d* (one *s* decd). *Educ:* Eton; RMC, Sandhurst. Commissioned Grenadier Guards, 1933; ADC to Viceroy of India, 1938–39; retired, 1947. JP 1951, DL 1961, Derbys; High Sheriff of Derbys, 1959. *Recreation:* shooting. *Address:* Radburne Hall, Kirk Langley, Derby DE6 4LZ. *T:* Derby (0332) 824246. *Clubs:* Army and Navy, Lansdowne, MCC; County (Derby). *Died 1 Sept. 1994.*

CHANDRASEKHAR, Subrahmanyan, FRS 1944; Morton D. Hull Distinguished Service Professor of Theoretical Astrophysics, University of Chicago, USA, 1937–85, then

Emeritus; *b* 19 Oct. 1910; US citizen, 1953; *m* 1936, Lalitha Doraiswamy. *Educ:* Presidency Coll., Madras; Trinity Coll., Cambridge (Government of Madras Research Scholar, PhD 1933, ScD 1942). Fellow of Trinity Coll., Cambridge, 1933–37, Hon. Fellow 1981. Managing Editor Astrophysical Journal, 1952–71. Nehru Memorial Lecture, India, 1968. Member: Nat. Acad. of Sciences (Henry Draper Medal, 1971); Amer. Philosophical Soc.; Amer. Acad. of Arts and Sciences (Rumford Medal, 1957). Hon. DSc Oxon 1972. Bruce Gold Medal, Astronomical Soc. of the Pacific, 1952; Gold Medal, Royal Astronomical Soc., 1953; Royal Medal, Royal Society, 1962; Nat. Medal of Science (USA), 1966; Heineman Prize, Amer. Physical Soc., 1974; (jtly) Nobel Prize for Physics, 1983; Copley Medal, Royal Soc., 1984; Dr Tomalla Prize, Eidgenössische Technische Hochschule, Zürich, 1984. *Publications:* An Introduction to the Study of Stellar Structure, 1939; Principles of Stellar Dynamics, 1942; Radiative Transfer, 1950; Hydrodynamic and Hydromagnetic Stability, 1961; Ellipsoidal Figures of Equilibrium, 1969; The Mathematical Theory of Black Holes, 1983; Eddington: the most distinguished astrophysicist of his time, 1983; Truth and Beauty: aesthetics and motivations in science, 1987; Selected Papers, 6 vols, 1989–90; various papers in current scientific periodicals. *Address:* Laboratory for Astrophysics and Space Research, University of Chicago, 933 East 56th Street, Chicago, IL 60637, USA. *T:* (312) 7027860. *Club:* Quadrangle (Chicago). *Died 21 Aug. 1995.*

CHAPLIN, (Sybil) Judith, OBE 1992; MP (C) Newbury, since 1992; *b* 19 Aug. 1939; *d* of Theodore and Sybil Schofield; *m* 1st, 1962, Hon. Robin Walpole (later 10th Baron Walpole) (marr. diss. 1979); two *s* two *d*; 2nd, 1984, Michael Chaplin, CBE, JP, RIBA. *Educ:* Wycombe Abbey; Girton Coll., Cambridge (MA Econs); Univ. of E Anglia (DipEcon). Headmistress, nursery and preparatory sch., 1967–74; Martin & Acock, Accountants, 1977–81; partner in family farm; Conservative Res. Dept, 1983–86; Hd, Policy Unit, Inst. of Dirs, 1986–88; Special Advr to Chancellor of Exchequer, 1988–90 (Rt Hon. Nigel Lawson, 1988–89, Rt Hon. John Major, 1989–90); Head of Prime Minister's Political Office, 1990–92. Norfolk County Councillor, 1974–85 (Chm., Educn Cttee); Member: ACC, 1977–84 (Vice-Chm., Educn Cttee; Mem., Burnham Cttee); Secondary Examn Council, 1983–86; Interim Adv. Body on Teachers' Pay, 1987–88. *Recreations:* walking, riding, opera.
Died 19 Feb. 1993.

CHAPMAN, Sir Stephen, Kt 1966; Judge of the High Court of Justice, Queen's Bench Division, 1966–81; *b* 5 June 1907; 2nd *s* of late Sir Sydney John Chapman, KCB, CBE, and Lady (Mabel Gwendoline) Chapman, JP; *m* 1963, Mrs Pauline Frances Niewiarowski, *d* of late Lt-Col H. Allcard and Mrs A. B. M. Allcard, and *widow* of Dmitri de Lobel Niewiarowski. *Educ:* Westminster; Trinity Coll., Cambridge. King's Scholar and Capt. Westminster; Entrance Scholar and Major Scholar, Trinity Coll., Cambridge; Browne Univ. Gold Medallist, 1927 and 1928; John Stuart of Rannoch Univ. Scholar, 1928; 1st Cl. Classical Tripos, Pt I, 1927, and Pt II, 1929. Entrance Scholar, Inner Temple, 1929; Jardine student, 1931; 1st Cl. and Certificate of Honour, Bar Final, 1931; called to Bar, Inner Temple, 1931. SE Circuit, Herts-Essex Sessions; Asst Legal Adviser, Min. of Pensions, 1939–46; Prosecuting Counsel for Post Office on SE Circuit, 1947–50 (Leader, Circuit, 1962); QC 1955; Comr of Assize, Winchester, Autumn, 1961; Recorder of Rochester, 1959–61, of Cambridge, 1961–63; Judge of the Crown Court and Recorder of Liverpool, 1963–66; Dep. Chm. Herts QS, 1963. Mem. Bar Council, 1956; Hon. Treas. 1958; Vice-Chm. 1959–60. *Publications:* Auctioneers and Brokers, in Atkin's Encyclopædia of

Court Forms, vol. 3, 1938; Insurance (non-marine), in Halsbury's Laws of England, 3rd edn, vol. 22, 1958; Statutes on the Law of Torts, 1962. *Recreation:* gardening. *Address:* 72 Thomas More House, Barbican, EC2Y 8BT. *T:* 071–628 9251. *Club:* United Oxford & Cambridge University. *Died 23 March 1991.*

CHAPPELL, (Edwin) Philip, CBE 1976; Adviser, Association of Investment Trust Companies, 1986–92; Chairman, Thames Customer Service Committee, 1990–92; *b* 12 June 1929; *s* of late Rev. C. R. Chappell; *m* 1962, Julia Clavering House, *d* of late H. W. House, DSO, MC; one *s* three *d. Educ:* Marlborough Coll.; Christ Church, Oxford (MA). Joined Morgan Grenfell, 1954; Dir, Morgan Grenfell & Co. Ltd, 1964–85; a Vice-Chm., Morgan Grenfell Hldgs, 1975–85; Chm., ICL, 1980–81; non-exec. Dir, various cos. Chairman: Nat. Ports Council, 1971–77; EDC for Food and Drink Manufacturing Industry, 1976–80. Member: Council, Institute of Bankers, 1971–85; Business Educn Council, 1974–80; SITPRO Board, 1974–77; (non exec.) British Rail Property Bd, 1986–. Governor of BBC, 1976–81. Treasurer, RSA, 1982–87. *Publication:* Pensions and Privilege, 1988. *Address:* 22 Frognal Lane, NW3 7DT. *T:* 071–435 8627. *Clubs:* Athenæum, Garrick. *Died 7 May 1993.*

CHAPPELL, William; dancer, designer, producer; *b* Wolverhampton, 27 Sept. 1908; *s* of Archibald Chappell and Edith Eva Clara Blair-Staples. *Educ:* Chelsea School of Art. Studied dancing under Marie Rambert. First appearance on stage, 1929; toured Europe with Ida Rubinstein's company, working under Massine and Nijinska; danced in many ballets, London, 1929–34; joined Sadler's Wells Co., 1934, and appeared there every season; Army service, 1940–45; designed scenery and costumes: at Sadler's Wells, 1934–, and Covent Garden, 1947–, including Les Rendezvous, Les Patineurs, Coppelia, Giselle, Handel's Samson, Frederick Ashton's Walk to the Paradise Garden, and Ashton's Rhapsody (costumes); for many revues and London plays; produced: Lyric Revue, 1951, Globe Revue, 1952, High Spirits, Hippodrome, 1953, At the Lyric, 1953, Going to Town, St Martin's, 1954 (also arranging dances for many of these); An Evening with Beatrice Lillie, Globe, 1954 (asst prod.); Time Remembered, New, 1955; Moby Dick, Duke of York's, 1955 (with Orson Welles); The Buccaneer, Lyric, Hammersmith, 1955; The Rivals, Saville; Beaux' Stratagem, Chichester; Violins of St Jacques (also wrote libretto), Sadler's Wells; English Eccentrics; Love and a Bottle; Passion Flower Hotel, Prince of Wales Theatre; Travelling Light; Espresso Bongo; Living for Pleasure, Saville and Garrick Theatres; Where's Charley?; The Chalk Garden, Haymarket, 1971; Offenbach's Robinson Crusoe (1st English perf.), Camden Festival, 1973; Cockie, Vaudeville, 1973; Oh, Kay!, Westminster, 1974; national tour, In Praise of Love, 1974; Fallen Angels, Gate Theatre, Dublin, 1975; Marriage of Figaro (designed and directed), Sadler's Wells, 1977; The Master's Voice, Dublin, 1977; Memoir, Ambassadors, 1978; Gianni Schicci, Sadler's Wells, 1978; Nijinsky (film), 1979; Same Time Next Year, Dublin, 1980; A Little Bit on the Side (revue, with Beryl Reid), 1983; for Dublin Theatre Festival: A Moon for the Misbegotten, 1976; The Rivals, 1976; Speak of the Devil (musical); designs for Giselle, inc. 2 prodns for Anton Dolin, 1980; dir. Arsenic and Old Lace, 1985; design for Merle Park's costume as Fanny Ellsler, Vienna Opera House, 1985; choreographed: Travesties, RSC Aldwych, 1974, NY, 1975; Bloomsbury, Phoenix, 1974; directed, designed costumes and choreographed: Purcell's Fairy Queen, London Opera Centre, 1974; Donizetti's Torquato Tasso, Camden Festival, 1975; Lully's Alceste, London Opera Centre, 1975; restaged original designs for Ashton's Capriole Suite and Valses Nobles et Sentimentales, Sadler's Wells Royal Ballet, 1987; teacher and adviser for: Nureyev season, 1979; Joffrey Ballet, NY, 1979. Appeared in and assisted Orson Welles with film The Trial, 1963. TV shows. *Publications:* Studies in Ballet, 1948; Fonteyn, 1951; (ed and jt author) Edward Burra: a painter remembered by his friends, 1982; (ed) Well, Dearie: the letters of Edward Burra, 1985; illustrator of several books. *Recreations:* reading, cinema, painting. *Address:* 25 Rosenau Road, Battersea, SW11 4QN.

Died 1 Jan. 1994.

CHARLES, Sir Joseph (Quentin), Kt 1984; Managing Director, J. Q. Charles Ltd; *b* 25 Nov. 1908; *s* of Martineau Charles; *m* 1934, Albertha L. Yorke; three *s* two *d. Educ:* St Mary's Coll., St Lucia. Commission agent's clerk, 1927–33; started J. Q. Charles as a small provision wholesale and retail business, 1933, incorporated 1944; business grew to become classified retailer of cars, foods, building materials and hardware, dry goods and wearing apparel; also started several light manufacturing industries; St Lucia Co-operative Bank, 1937 (Founding Director for 43 years; Pres., 1974–79); Past Chm., St Lucia Agricl & Industrial Bank; Chm., St Lucia Banana Growers Assoc., 1963–67; Dir, Copra Manufacturers Ltd. Mem., Castries City Council. *Address:* c/o J. Q. Charles Ltd, PO Box 279, Castries, St Lucia, West Indies. *T:* (home) 20656.

Died 11 Jan. 1993.

CHARLESTON, Robert Jesse, FSA; FSGT; Keeper of the Department of Ceramics, Victoria and Albert Museum, 1963–76; *b* 3 April 1916; *s* of late Sidney James Charleston, Lektor, Stockholms Högskola; *m* 1941, Joan Randle (*d* 1994); one *s* one *d. Educ:* Berkhamsted Sch., Herts; New College, Oxford. Army (Major, RAPC), 1940–46; Asst, Bristol Museum, 1947; Asst Keeper, Victoria and Albert Museum, 1948, Deputy Keeper, 1959. W. E. S. Turner Meml Lectr, Sheffield Univ., 1979. Mem., Reviewing Cttee on Export of Works of Art, 1979–84. President: The Glass Circle, 1957–; Fellows of the Corning Mus. of Glass, 1980–. Award winner, Glass Sellers' Co., 1986. *Publications:* Roman Pottery, 1955; (ed) English Porcelain, 1745–1850, 1965; (ed) World Ceramics, 1968; (with Donald Towner) English Ceramics, 1580–1830, 1977; Islamic Pottery, 1979; Masterpieces of Glass, 1980; The James A. de Rothschild Collection: (with J. G. Ayers) Meissen and Oriental Porcelain, 1971; (with Michael Archer and M. Marcheix) Glass and Enamels, 1977; Maioliche e Porcellane: Inghilterra, Paesi Scandinavi, Russia, 1982; English Glass, 1984; numerous articles and reviews in The Connoisseur, Jl of Glass Studies, Burlington Magazine, etc. *Recreation:* music. *Address:* Whittington Court, Whittington, near Cheltenham, Glos GL54 4HF.

Died 4 Dec. 1994.

CHARLESWORTH, Stanley, OBE 1980; National Secretary, National Council of YMCAs, 1975–80; *b* 20 March 1920; *s* of Ernest and Amy Charlesworth; *m* 1942, Vera Bridge; three *d. Educ:* Ashton under Lyne Grammar Sch.; Manchester Coll. of Commerce. YMCA: Area Sec., Community Services, 1943–52, Dep. Sec., 1952–57; Asst Regional Sec., NW Region, 1957–67, Regional Sec., 1967–75. *Recreations:* sailing, golf, walking, gardening. *Address:* Inchcape, Maes Y Cnwce, Newport, Dyfed SA42 0RS. *Clubs:* Rotary (Fishguard and Goodwick); YMCA (Manchester). *Died 30 May 1992.*

CHARTERIS, Leslie, FRSA; author; *b* Singapore, 12 May 1907; *s* of Dr S. C. Yin; changed surname to Charteris by deed-poll, 1926; US citizen, 1946; *m* 1st, 1931, Pauline Schishkin (divorced, 1937); one *d*; 2nd, 1939, Barbara Meyer (divorced, 1941); 3rd, 1943, Elizabeth Bryant Borst (divorced, 1951); 4th, 1952, Audrey Long. *Educ:* Rossall; Cambridge Univ. Many years of entertaining, but usually unprofitable, travel and adventure; after one or two false starts created character of "The Saint" (trans. into 15 languages besides those of films, radio, television, and the

comic strip). Supervising Editor of the Saint Magazine, 1953–67; Editorial Consultant of the (new) Saint Magazine, 1984–85; columnist, Gourmet Magazine, 1966–68; concurrently worked as special correspondent and Hollywood scenarist. *Publications:* Meet the Tiger, 1928; Enter the Saint, 1931; The Last Hero, 1931; Knight Templar; Featuring the Saint; Alias the Saint; She was a Lady (filmed 1938 as The Saint Strikes Back); The Holy Terror (filmed 1939 as The Saint in London); Getaway; Once More the Saint; The Brighter Buccaneer; The Misfortunes of Mr Teal; Boodle; The Saint Goes On; The Saint in New York (filmed 1938); Saint Overboard, 1936; The Ace of Knaves, 1937; Thieves Picnic, 1937; (trans., with introd.) Juan Belmonte, Killer of Bulls: The Autobiography of a Matador, 1937; Prelude for War, 1938; Follow the Saint, 1938; The Happy Highwayman, 1939; The First Saint Omnibus, 1939; The Saint in Miami, 1941; The Saint Goes West, 1942; The Saint Steps In, 1944; The Saint on Guard, 1945; The Saint Sees it Through, 1946; Call for the Saint, 1948; Saint Errant, 1948; The Second Saint Omnibus, 1952; The Saint on the Spanish Main, 1955; The Saint around the World, 1957; Thanks to the Saint, 1958; Señor Saint, 1959; The Saint to the Rescue, 1961; Trust the Saint, 1962; The Saint in the Sun, 1964; Vendetta for the Saint, 1965 (filmed 1968); The Saint on TV, 1968; The Saint Returns, 1969; The Saint and the Fiction Makers, 1969; The Saint Abroad, 1970; The Saint in Pursuit, 1971; The Saint and the People Importers, 1971; Paleneo, 1972; Saints Alive, 1974; Catch the Saint, 1975; The Saint and the Hapsburg Necklace, 1976; Send for the Saint, 1977; The Saint in Trouble, 1978; The Saint and the Templar Treasure, 1979; Count on the Saint, 1980; The Fantastic Saint, 1982; Salvage for the Saint, 1983; contributor to leading English and American magazines and newspapers. *Recreations:* eating, drinking, horseracing, loafing. *Address:* 3/4 Great Marlborough Street, W1V 2AR. *Clubs:* Mensa; Yacht Club de Cannes. *Died 15 April 1993.*

CHATT, Prof. Joseph, CBE 1978; ScD; FRS 1961; Professor of Chemistry, University of Sussex, 1964–80, then Emeritus; Director, Research Unit of Nitrogen Fixation, Agricultural Research Council, 1963–80 (in Sussex, 1964–80); *b* 6 Nov. 1914; *s* of Joseph and M. Elsie Chatt; *m* 1947, Ethel, *y d* of Hugh Williams; one *s* one *d. Educ:* Nelson Sch., Wigton, Cumberland; Emmanuel Coll., Cambridge (PhD 1940; ScD 1956; Hon. Fellow, 1978). Research Chemist, Woolwich Arsenal, 1941–42; Dep. Chief Chemist, later Chief Chemist, Peter Spence & Sons Ltd, Widnes, 1942–46; ICI Research Fellow, Imperial Coll., London, 1946–47; Head of Inorganic Chemistry Dept, Butterwick, later Akers, Research Laboratories, ICI Ltd, 1947–60; Group Manager, Research Dept, Heavy Organic Chemicals Div., ICI Ltd, 1961–62; Prof. of Inorganic Chem., QMC, Univ. of London, 1964. Visiting Professor: Pennsylvania State Univ., 1960; Yale Univ., 1963; (Royal Society Leverhulme), Univ. of Rajasthan, India, 1966–67; Univ. of S Carolina, 1968. Royal Society of Chemistry (formerly Chemical Society): Mem. Council, 1952–65, 1972–76; Hon. Sec., 1956–62; Vice-Pres., 1962–65, 1972–74; first Pres. Dalton Div., 1972–74; Organometallic Chem. Award, 1970. Pres., Section B, BAAS, 1974–75; Member: Chemical Council, 1958–60; Commn on Nomenclature of Inorganic Chemistry, Internat. Union of Pure and Applied Chemistry, 1959–81 (Hon-Sec., 1959–63; Chm., 1976–81); ARC Adv. Cttee on Plants and Soils, 1964–67; Comité de Direction du Laboratoire de Chimie de Coordination, Toulouse, 1974–77; Council, Royal Soc., 1975–77; national and internat. cttees concerned with chemistry, incl. Parly and Scientific Cttee. Founder, Internat. Confs on Coordination Chemistry, 1950. Pres., Hove Civic Soc., 1993. Lectures: Tilden, 1961–62;

Liversidge, 1971–72; Debye, Cornell, 1975; Nyholm, 1976–77; Arthur D. Little, MIT, 1977; Julius Steiglitz, Chicago, 1978; Columbia, 1978 (and Chandler Medal); Univ. of Western Ontario, 1978; John Stauffer, S California, 1979; Dwyer Meml Lectr and Medallist, Univ. of NSW, 1980; Sunner Meml Lectr, Univ. of Lund, 1982. Gordon Wigan Prize for Res. in Chem., Cambridge, 1939; Amer. Chem. Soc. Award for dist. service to Inorganic Chemistry, 1971; Chugaev Commem. Dipl. and Medal, Kurnakov Inst. of Gen. and Inorganic Chemistry, Soviet Acad. of Sciences, 1976; Davy Medal of Royal Soc., 1979; Wolf Foundn Prize for Chemistry, 1981; G.W. Wheland Award (lecture, medal and prize), Univ. of Chicago, 1983. Hon. DSc: East Anglia, 1974; Sussex, 1982; Hon. Dr Pierre et Marie Curie, Paris, 1981; Filosofie Doctor *hc* Lund, Sweden, 1986. Sócio corresp., Academia das Ciêncas de Lisboa, 1978; Hon. Life Mem., NY Acad. of Sciences, 1978; For. Fellow, Indian Nat. Science Acad., 1980; Hon. Fellow, Indian Chem. Soc., 1983; Hon. Mem., Royal Physiographical Soc., Lund, 1984; Hon. For. Mem., Amer. Acad. of Arts and Scis, 1985. *Publications:* 370 scientific, mainly in Jl Chem. Soc.; also a few on World War I peace medals in Spink Numismatic Circular. *Recreations:* numismatics, art, history, travel. *Address:* 16 Tongdean Road, Hove, East Sussex BN3 6QE. *T:* Brighton (0273) 554377. *Club:* Civil Service.

Died 19 May 1994.

CHEADLE, Sir Eric (Wallers), Kt 1978; CBE 1973; DL; Deputy Managing Director, International Thomson Organisation Ltd, 1959–74; retired 1974 after 50 years service with the same company (Hultons/Allied Newspapers/Kemsleys/The Thomson Organisation); Director, Thomson International Press Consultancy Ltd; *b* 14 May 1908; *s* of Edgar and Nellie Cheadle; *m* 1938, Pamela, *d* of Alfred and Charlotte Hulme; two *s. Educ:* Farnworth Grammar Sch. Editorial Staff, Evening Chronicle and Daily Dispatch, Manchester, 1924–30; Publicity Manager, Allied Newspapers Ltd, 1931–37; Publicity Manager-in-Chief, Allied Newspapers Group, 1938; Organiser, War Fund for the Services, 1939; served War, RAFVR, Sqdn Ldr, 1941–46; Dir and Gen. Manager, Kemsley Newspapers Ltd, 1947–53. Member: Council, Newspaper Publishers Assoc., 1947–74; Council, Newspaper Soc., 1959–78 (Pres., 1970–71; Chm., Editorial Cttee, 1971–78; Mem., Appeal Cttee, 1979–); Council, NEDC for Printing and Publishing Industry; Jt Bd for Nat. Newspaper Industry, 1965–67; Bd, FIEJ/INCA, 1972–76; Caxton Quincentenary Commem. Cttee, 1976; UK Newsprint Users' Cttee (Founder Mem.); Science Mus. Adv. Cttee (Printing); Chm., Jt Cttee, Newspaper and Periodicals Publishers and Distributors, 1979–85; President: Manchester Publicity Assoc., 1972–74 (former Hon. Sec.; Gold Medal, 1973); Printers' Charitable Corp., 1973–74 (Life Vice-Pres., 1975; Chm. of Council, 1975–81; Trustee, 1981–). Member: London Adv. Bd, Nat. and Provincial Building Soc.; Council, Imperial Soc. of Kts Bachelor, 1979–; Appeal Council, Coll. of Arms Quincentenary Appeal, 1982; Special Cttee, Herts Isotope Cancer Scanner Appeal, 1982–84; Children's Assessment Clinic Appeal, 1984–86; St Albans City Hosp. Rehabilitation Unit Appeal, 1986–88; Cttee, St Bride's Appeal for Restoration and Develt, 1987–90; Council, 1981–, Exec. Cttee, 1992– Stroke (formerly Chest, Heart and Stroke) Assoc. (Chm., Appeal Adv. Cttee); Chairman: Nat. Stroke Campaign, 1986–88; St Albans Women Against Cancer Appeal, 1988–89; Trustees and Management Group, St Albans Cathedral Trust; Soc. of St Michaels; Vice Chm., Shrine of St Alban Restoration Appeal, 1990–; Vice-Pres. and Mem. Appeal Cttee, Runcie Appeal for a Macmillan Cancer Care Centre (formerly NW Herts Macmillan Cancer Centre Appeal), 1991–; Trustee, Herts Groundwork Trust, 1986–; Dir,

Herts Building Preservation Trust Ltd, 1981–84; Mem., Ver Valley Soc. Hon. Life Member: Friends of St Albans City Hosp., 1984; Independent Adoption Soc., 1978; Hon. Chm., PS Tattershall Castle (Victoria Embankment) Trust. President: Assoc. of Lancastrians in London, 1959 and 1973–74; Herts Br., ESU, 1989–. Hon. Lay Canon, Cathedral and Abbey Church of St Alban, 1989. DL Hertford, 1985. Editor, Chivalry Newspaper, 1986–. *Publication:* (ed) The Roll of Knights Bachelor, 1981. *Recreations:* watching cricket, talking newspapers. *Address:* The Old Church House, 172 Fishpool Street, St Albans, Herts AL3 4SB. *T:* St Albans (0727) 59639. *Clubs:* Wig and Pen, Press, Variety, MCC; Porters Park Golf (Captain, 1974–75).

Died 25 Jan. 1992.

CHEKE, Dudley John, CMG 1961; MA Cantab; HM Diplomatic Service, retired; *b* 14 June 1912; *s* of late Thomas William Cheke, FRIC; *m* 1944, Yvonne de Méric (*d* 1991), *d* of late Rear-Adm. M. J. C. de Méric, MVO; two *s. Educ:* St Christopher's, Letchworth; Emmanuel Coll., Cambridge. Entered HM Consular Service, 1934; served in Japan, Manchuria, Korea, 1935–41; served 1942–44, in East Africa and Ceylon; Foreign Office, 1945–49 and 1958–61; UK delegation to OEEC, Paris, 1949–50; Commissioner-Gen.'s Office, Singapore, 1950–51; idc 1952; HM Consul-Gen., Frankfurt-am-Main, 1953–55, Osaka-Kobe, 1956–58; Mem. of Foreign Service Corps of Inspectors, 1961–63; Minister, Tokyo, 1963–67; Ambassador to the Ivory Coast, Niger and Upper Volta, 1967–70. Chm., Japan Soc., 1979–82. *Publication:* Joséphine and Emilie (biog.), 1993. *Recreations:* theatre, birdwatching, gardening. *Address:* Honey Farm, Bramley, Basingstoke, Hants RG26 5DE. *Clubs:* United Oxford & Cambridge University; Union Society (Cambridge).

Died 20 Aug. 1993.

CHERKASSKY, Shura; pianist; *b* 7 Oct. 1911; *s* of late Isaac and Lydia Cherkassky; *m* 1946, Genia Ganz (marr. diss. 1948). *Educ:* Curtis Institute of Music, Pa, USA (diploma). Played with the principal orchestras and conductors of the world and in all the major series and festivals in Asia, America, Australia and Europe. Made numerous recordings. *Address:* c/o Lies Askonas, 6 Henrietta Street, WC2E 8LA.

Died 27 Dec. 1995.

CHESHIRE, Baron *cr* 1991 (Life Peer), of Woodhall in the county of Lincolnshire; **Geoffrey Leonard Cheshire**, VC 1944; OM 1981; DSO 1940 and two Bars 1941, 1943; DFC 1941; Royal Air Force, retired; *b* 7 Sept. 1917; *s* of late Geoffrey Chevalier Cheshire, DCL, FBA, and Primrose Barstow; *m* 1st, 1941, Constance Binney (marr. diss.); *m* 2nd, 1959, (Margaret) Susan Ryder (later Baroness Ryder of Warsaw); one *s* one *d. Educ:* Stowe Sch.; Merton Coll., Oxford. 2nd Class Hons Sch. of Jurisprudence, 1939. OU Air Sqdn, 1936; RAFVR, 1937; Perm. Commn RAF, 1939; trained Hullavington; served Bomber Comd, 1940–45: 102 Sqdn, 1940; 35 Sqdn, 1941; CO 76 Sqdn, 1942; RAF Station, Marston Moor, 1943; CO 617 Sqdn (Dambusters), 1943; attached Eastern Air Command, South-East Asia, 1944; British Joint Staff Mission, Washington, 1945; official British observer at dropping of Atomic Bomb on Nagasaki, 1945; retd Dec. 1945. Founder of Cheshire Foundation Homes (270 Homes in 50 countries); Co-founder of Ryder Cheshire Mission for the Relief of Suffering; Founder Chm., Meml Fund for Disaster Relief, 1989–; Pres., SPARKS. Member: Pathfinders Assoc.; Air Crew Assoc. Pres., British Soc. of the Turin Shroud. Hon. LLD: Liverpool, 1973; Manchester Polytechnic, 1979; Nottingham, 1981; Birmingham, 1986; Hon. DCL: Oxon, 1984; Kent, 1986. Variety Club Humanitarian Award (jtly with wife), 1975. *Publications:* Bomber Pilot, 1943; Pilgrimage to the Shroud, 1956; The Face of Victory, 1961; The Hidden World, 1981; The

Light of Many Suns, 1985; Where is God in all this?, 1991; *relevant publications:* Cheshire, VC, by Russell Braddon, 1954; No Passing Glory, by Andrew Boyle, 1955; New Lives for Old, by W. W. Russell, 1963. *Recreation:* tennis. *Address:* 26 Maunsel Street, SW1P 2QN. *T:* 071–828 1822. *Clubs:* Royal Air Force, Queen's (Hon. Life Mem.), All England Lawn Tennis.

Died 31 July 1992.

CHESTER, Prof. Theodore Edward, CBE 1967; DJur; MA (Econ) Manchester; Diploma in Commerce; Director, Management Programme for Clinicians, since 1979; Professor of Social Administration, University of Manchester, 1955–75, then Emeritus Professor (Senior Research Fellow, 1976–78); Member, Council and Finance and General Purposes Committee, Manchester Business School, 1964–86; *b* 28 June 1908; *m* 1940, Mimi; one *s.* Teaching and research in law and administration, 1931–39. Service with HM Forces, 1940–45. Asst Man. in London city firm, 1946–48; Acton Soc. Trust: Senior Research Worker, 1948–52; Dir, 1952–55; Dean, Faculty of Economic and Social Studies, Univ. of Manchester, 1962–63. Research work into problems of large-scale administration in private and public undertakings including the hosp. and educn service in Britain and comparative studies abroad, as well as into the problems of training managers and administrators. Vis. Prof. at many foreign univs and institutions, notably in the United States, Western Europe, Canada, and Australia, 1959–; Kenneth Pray Vis. Prof., Univ. of Pa, 1968; (first) Kellogg Vis. Prof., Washington Univ., St Louis, 1969 and 1970. Mem. Summer Fac., Sloan Inst. of Health Service Admin, Cornell Univ., 1972. Ford Foundn Travelling Fellowships, 1960, 1967. WHO Staff Training Programme, 1963; UN Res. Inst. for Economic and Social Studies, 1968. Member: National Selection Cttee for the Recruitment of Sen. Hospital Administrative Staff, 1956–66; Advisory Cttee on Management Efficiency in the Health Service, 1959–65; Cttee of Inquiry into recruitment, training and promotion of clerical and administrative staffs in the Hospital Service, 1962–63; Programme Cttee of Internat. Hosp. Fedn and Chm. study group into problems of trng in hosp. admin, 1959–65; Trng Council for Social Workers and Health Visitors, 1963–65; Cttee on Technical Coll. Resources, 1964–69; Inter Agency Inst. of Fed. Health Execs, USA, 1980–84; Pres., Corp. of Secs, 1956–66; Adviser: Social Affairs Div., OECD, 1965–66; Turkish State Planning Org. on Health and Welfare Problems, 1964. Broadcasts on social problems in Britain and abroad. Golden Needle of Honour, Austrian Hosp. Dirs Assoc., 1970. The Grand Gold Komturcross for services to the Health Service (Austria), 1980. *Publications:* Training and Promotion in Nationalised Industry (for Acton Soc. Trust), 1951; Patterns of Organisation, 1952; Management under Nationalization, 1953; (with H. A. Clegg) The Future of Nationalization, 1953; Background and Blueprint: A Study of Hospital Organisation under the National Health Service, 1955; The Impact of the Change (co-author), 1956; Groups, Regions and Committees, 1957; (with H. A. Clegg) Wage Policy and the Health Service, 1957; The Central Control of the Service, 1958; Post War Growth of Management in Western Europe, 1961; Graduate Education for Hospital Administration in the United States: Trends, 1969; The British National Health Service, 1970; The Swedish National Health Service, 1970; Organisation for Change: preparation for reorganisation, 1974 (OECD); (contrib.) Management for Clinicians, 1982; (contrib.) Management for Health Service Administrators, 1983; Alternative Systems in Organising and Controlling Health Services: public health systems in a democratic society, 1985; The Prospects for Rationing— an international review, 1986; Restructuring the American Health Services: a synopsis of policies, methods and outcome, 1987; regular contribs to scientific and other jls. *Recreations:* travel, music, swimming, detective stories. *Address:* 189 Grove Lane, Hale, Altrincham, Cheshire. *T:* 061–980 2828. *Died 8 Aug. 1991.*

CHESTERFIELD, Arthur Desborough, CBE 1962; Director: Singer & Friedlander Ltd, 1967–86 (Chairman, 1967–76); Clifford Property Co. Ltd, since 1973 (Chairman); Percy Bilton Ltd, 1977–87 (Chairman, 1983–86; President, since 1986); *b* 21 Aug. 1905; *s* of Arthur William and Ellen Harvey Chesterfield; *m* 1932, Betty (*d* 1980), *d* of John Henry Downey; two *s* three *d.* *Educ:* Hastings Grammar Sch. Entered Westminster Bank Ltd, 1923; Joint Gen. Manager, 1947; Chief Gen. Manager, 1950–65, retired; Director: Nat. Westminster Bank, 1963–69 (Local Dir, Inner London, 1969–74); Woolwich Equitable Bldg Soc., 1966–80 (Vice-Chm., 1976–80); Singer & Friedlander (Holdings) Ltd, 1967–84 (Chm., 1967–76). Member: Export Guarantees Adv. Council, 1952–63; Nat. Savings Cttee, 1954–67; Chm., City of London Savings Cttee, 1962–72. FIB (Mem. Council, 1950–65). *Recreations:* music, gardening. *Died 21 July 1991.*

CHESTERS, Prof. Charles Geddes Coull, OBE 1977; BSc, MSc, PhD; FRSE; FLS, FInstBiol; Professor of Botany, University of Nottingham, 1944–69, then Emeritus Professor; *b* 9 March 1904; *s* of Charles and Margaret Geddes Chesters; *m* 1928, Margarita Mercedes Cathie Maclean; one *s* one *d.* *Educ:* Hyndland Sch.; Univ. of Glasgow. Lecturer in Botany, 1930, Reader in Mycology, 1942, Univ. of Birmingham. *Publications:* scientific papers on mycology and microbiology, mainly in Trans British Myc. Soc., Annals Applied Biol., Jl Gen. Microbiol. *Recreations:* photography, collecting fungi. *Address:* Grandage Cottages, Quenington, near Cirencester, Glos GL7 5DB. *Died 13 Feb. 1993.*

CHESTERS, Dr John Hugh, OBE 1970; FRS 1969; FEng 1978; consultant, since 1971; *b* 16 Oct. 1906; 2nd *s* of Rev. George M. Chesters; *m* 1936, Nell Knight, Minnesota, USA; three *s* one *d.* *Educ:* High Pavement Sch., Nottingham; King Edward VII Sch., Sheffield; Univ. of Sheffield. BSc Hons Physics, 1928; PhD 1931; DSc Tech 1945; Hon. DSc 1975. Metropolitan-Vickers Research Schol., Univ. of Sheffield, 1928–31; Robert Blair Fellowship, Kaiser-Wilhelm Inst. für Silikatforschung, Berlin, 1931–32; Commonwealth Fund Fellowship, Univ. of Illinois, 1932–34; United Steel Cos Ltd: in charge of Refractories Section, 1934–45; Asst Dir of Research, 1945–62; Dep. Dir of Research, United Steel Cos Ltd, 1962–67, Midland Group, British Steel Corporation, 1967–70; Dir, Corporate Labs, BISRA, 1970–71. Chm., Watt Cttee on Energy, 1976–86. President: Brit. Ceramic Soc., 1951–52; Inst. of Ceramics, 1961–63; Iron and Steel Inst., 1968–69; Inst. of Fuel, 1972–73. Foreign Associate, Nat. Acad. of Engineering, USA, 1977. SFInstF, FIM, FICeram; Fellow, Amer. Ceramic Soc. Hon. FInstE 1986. Bessemer Gold Medal, Iron and Steel Inst., 1966; John Wilkinson Gold Medal, Staffs Iron and Steel Inst., 1971; American Inst. Metallurgical Engineers: Robert Hunt Award, 1952; Benjamin Fairless Award, 1973. *Publications:* Steelplant Refractories, 1945, 2nd edn 1957; Iron and Steel, 1948; Refractories: production and properties, 1973; Refractories for Iron- and Steelmaking, 1974; numerous articles in Jl of Iron and Steel Inst., Trans Brit. Cer. Soc., Jl Amer. Cer. Soc., Jl Inst. of Fuel, etc. *Recreations:* foreign travel, fishing. *Address:* 21 Slayleigh Lane, Sheffield S10 3RF. *T:* Sheffield (0114) 230 1257. *Died 14 Dec. 1994.*

CHESWORTH, Donald Piers, OBE 1987; Consultant, Toynbee Hall (Warden, 1977–87); *b* 30 Jan. 1923; *s* of late Frederick Gladstone and Daisy Chesworth. *Educ:*

King Edward VI Sch., Camp Hill, Birmingham; London Sch. of Economics. War of 1939–45: Nat. Fire Service; Royal Air Force. Mem., LCC (Kensington N Div.), 1952–65 (Whip and Mem. Policy Cttee). Labour Adviser: Tanganyika Govt (and Chm., Territorial Minimum Wages Bd), 1961–62; Mauritius Govt (and Chm., Sugar Wages Councils), 1962–65; Mem. Economics Br., ILO, Geneva, 1967; Dir, Notting Hill Social Council, 1968–77; Chairman: (part time) Mauritius Salaries Commn, 1973–77; Mauritius Govt Enquiry into position of families without wage earners, 1981; pt-time Govt Salaries Comr, Mauritius, 1987–88. Co-opted Mem., ILEA Educn Cttee, 1970–77 (Jt Chm., Appts Principals and Sch. Heads Section; Chm., Res. and Statistics Section); Chm., Tower Hamlets ILEA Tertiary Educn Council, and Mem., Tertiary Educn Bd, 1987–; Alderman, Royal Bor. of Kensington and Chelsea, 1971–77. Student and Overseas Sec., Internat. Union of Socialist Youth, 1947–51. Chairman: Nat. Assoc. of Labour Student Orgns, 1947; Assoc. for Neighbourhood Councils, 1972–74; Asha E London Educn Project, 1986–; Adv. Cttee, QMC project to expand further and higher educn taken up by E London youth, 1987–; Spitalfields Heritage Centre, 1987–; Tower Hamlets Befrienders, 1987–; Vice-Chm., Toynbee Housing Assoc., 1977–86; Member: Council, War on Want, 1965–76 (Chm., 1967, 1968, 1970–74); Exec. Bd, Voluntary Cttee on Overseas Aid and Develt, 1969–76; Nat. Cttee, UK Freedom from Hunger Campaigns, 1969–76; S Metropolitan Conciliation Cttee, Race Relations Bd, 1975–77; Member Executive: Tower Hamlets Trng Forum and Workshops, 1986–; Tower Hamlets Educn and Careers Centre, 1986–; Citicare, St Clements EC4, 1987–; Mem. Educn Cttee, Tower Hamlets Assoc. for Racial Equality, 1986–. Mem. Exec., Britain–Tanzania Soc., 1978–. Chm., World Development Political Action Trust, 1971–75; Trustee: UK Bangladesh Fund, 1971–72; Campden Charities, 1971–77; Attlee Meml Foundn, 1977– (Director, 1979–81; Treas., 1984–); Hilden Charitable Fund, 1978–; Aldgate Freedom Foundn, 1980–. Social Affairs Consultant, Kumagai Gumi UK, 1987–. Mem. Bd of Visitors, Hewell Grange Borstal, 1950–52; Chm. Managers, Mayford Home Office Approved Sch., 1952–58. Chairman of Governors: Isaac Newton Sch., N Kensington, 1971–77; Paddington Sch., 1972–76; Mem., Ct of Governors, LSE, 1973–78; Governor: Tower Hamlets Adult Educn Inst., 1978– (Chm., 1987); City and E London Coll., 1978–. Parly Cand. (Lab): Warwick and Leamington, 1945; Bromsgrove, 1950 and 1951. *Publications:* (contrib.) Statutory Wage Fixing in Developing Countries (ILO), 1968; contribs to Internat. Labour Review. *Recreation:* travel. *Address:* 16 Evershed House, Old Castle Street, E1 7NU. *T:* 071–247 4580. *Club:* Reform.

Died 24 May 1991.

CHETWYND-TALBOT, Richard Michael Arthur; *see* Talbot.

CHEVELEY, Stephen William, OBE 1946; farmer; Agricultural Consultant, Cheveley & Co., 1959–72, retired; *b* 29 March 1900; *s* of George Edward Cheveley and Arabella Cheveley; *m* 1926, Joan Hardy (*d* 1977); two *s* one *d*. *Educ:* Leeds Modern Sch.; Leeds Univ. (BSc 1922; MSc). Served War, HAC, 1917–18. Min. of Agric. Scholarship, Farm Costings Res., 1922–23; British Sulphate of Ammonia Fedn, 1924–26; ICI Ltd, 1927–59: Chm., ICI Central Agricultural Control, 1952–59; Man. Dir, Plant Protection Ltd, 1945–51. Mem., Min. of Agric. Technical Develt Cttee, 1941–46; Chm., Foot and Mouth Res. Inst., 1950–58. Governor, Wye Coll., 1963–78, Fellow, 1977; Chm., Appeal Cttee, Centre for European Agric. Studies, 1973–75. Chm., Farmers' Club, 1956. Master, Worshipful Co. of Farmers, 1961. *Publications:* Grass Drying, 1937; Out of a Wilderness, 1939; A Garden Goes to War, 1940; (with O. T. W. Price) Capital in UK

Agriculture, 1956. *Recreations:* farming, fishing, painting. *Address:* Dunorlan Farm, Tunbridge Wells, Kent. *T:* Tunbridge Wells (0892) 26632. *Club:* Farmers'.

Died 7 June 1991.

CHILD, Clifton James, OBE 1949; MA, PhM; FRHistS; Administrative Officer, Cabinet Office Historical Section, 1969–76, retired; *b* Birmingham, 20 June 1912; *s* of late Joseph and Georgina Child; *m* 1938, Hilde Hurwitz; two *s*. *Educ:* Moseley Grammar Sch.; Universities of Birmingham, Berlin and Wisconsin. Univ. of Birmingham: Entrance Schol., 1929; Kenrick Prizeman, 1930; BA 1st class hons, 1932; Francis Corder Clayton Research Schol., 1932–34; MA 1934; Univ. of Wisconsin: Commonwealth Fund Fellow, 1936–38; PhM 1938. Educn Officer, Lancs Community Council, 1939–40; joined Foreign Office, 1941; Head of American Section, Research Dept, 1946–58; African Section, 1958–62; Dep. Librarian and Departmental Record Officer, 1962; Librarian and Keeper of the Papers, 1965–69; Cabinet Office, 1969–76. FRHistS 1965. *Publications:* The German-Americans in Politics, 1939; (with Arnold Toynbee and others) Hitler's Europe, 1954; contribs to learned periodicals in Britain and US. *Recreations:* gardening, foreign travel. *Address:* Westcroft, Westhall Road, Warlingham, Surrey CR6 9HB. *T:* Upper Warlingham (0883) 622540.

Died 7 Feb. 1994.

CHILTON, Air Marshal Sir (Charles) Edward, KBE 1959 (CBE 1945); CB 1951; Royal Air Force (retired); *b* 1906; *o s* of J. C. Chilton; *m* 1st, 1929, Betty Ursula (*d* 1963), 2nd *d* of late Bernard Temple Wrinch; one *s*; 2nd, 1964, Joyce Cornforth. Royal Air Force General Duties Branch; Air Commodore, 1950; Air Vice-Marshal, 1954; Air Marshal, 1959. Dep. Air Officer i/c Administration, Air Command, SE Asia, 1944; AOC Ceylon, 1946; Imperial Defence Coll., 1951; AOC Gibraltar, 1952; Asst Chief of the Air Staff (Policy), 1953–54; SASO, HQ Coastal Command, 1955; AOC Royal Air Force, Malta, Fortress Comdr, Malta, and Dep. Comdr-in-Chief (Air), Allied Forces Mediterranean, 1957–59; AOC-in-C, Coastal Command and Maritime Air Commander Eastern Atlantic Area, and Commander Maritime Air, Channel and Southern North Sea, 1959–62. Consultant and Dir, IBM (Rentals) UK, 1963–78. Specialist navigator (Air Master navigator certificate) and Founder Fellow, Royal Institute of Navigation (Vice-Pres. 1949–51, 1959–61, 1963–65). Pres. RAF Rowing Club, 1956; Vice-Adm. and Hon. Life Mem. RAF Sailing Assoc.; Hon. Vice-Pres. RAF Swimming Assoc. FInstD. Freeman, City of London. Grand Cross of Prince Henry the Navigator (Portugal), 1960; Order of Polonia Restituta (Poland), 1980. *Publications:* numerous contributions to Service and other journals, on maritime-air operations and air navigation, and biographical papers on Rear-Adm. Sir Murray Sueter, Wing Comdr J. C. Porte, Air Chief Marshal Sir Philip Joubert, and Air Chief Marshal Hon. Sir Ralph Cochrane. *Recreations:* sailing, sea fishing, country walking. *Address:* 11 Charles House, Phyllis Court Drive, Henley-on-Thames, Oxon. *Clubs:* Royal Air Force; Phyllis Court (Henley); (Vice-Patron) Royal Gibraltar Yacht.

Died 4 Aug. 1992.

CHISHOLM, Archibald Hugh Tennent, CBE (mil.) 1946; MA; *b* 17 Aug. 1902; 2nd *s* of late Hugh Chisholm and Mrs Chisholm (*née* Harrison), Rush Park, Co. Antrim; *m* 1939, Josephine (*d* 1983), *e d* of J. E. Goudge, OBE, ICS; one *s* one *d* (and one *d* decd). *Educ:* Westminster (Exhibnr and Mure Schol.); Christ Church, Oxford (Schol.). Wall Street Journal of NY, 1925–27; Anglo-Persian/Anglo-Iranian Oil Co., later British Petroleum Co., Iran and Kuwait, 1928–36 and London, 1945–72; Editor of The Financial Times, 1937–40; Army, 1940–45 (despatches twice, CBE). FZS; FInstPet. Chevalier, Légion d'Honneur.

Publication: The First Kuwait Oil Concession Agreement: a Record of the Negotiations, 1911–1934, 1975. *Address:* 107 Hamilton Terrace, NW8 9QY. *T:* 071–289 0713; The Coach House, Charlton House, Tetbury, Glos. *T:* Tetbury (0666) 54339. *Clubs:* Athenæum, Naval and Military, Beefsteak, MCC. *Died 22 Nov. 1992.*

CHISHOLM, Prof. Geoffrey Duncan, CBE 1992; FRSE, FRCSE, FRCPE, FRCS, FRCPSGlas; Professor of Surgery, University of Edinburgh, since 1977; Director, Nuffield Transplant Unit, Edinburgh, since 1977; *b* 30 Sept. 1931; *s* of Sedman Arthur Chisholm and Ellen Marion Chisholm (*née* Friston); *m* 1962, Angela Jane Holden; two *s. Educ:* Scots Coll., Wellington, NZ; Malvern Coll.; St Andrews Univ. (MB ChB 1955, ChM 1965). FRCSE 1959, FRCS 1960, FRCPE 1990, FRCPSGlas 1991; FRSE 1994. BPMF Travelling Fellow, 1961–62; Res. Fellow, Johns Hopkins Hosp., Baltimore, 1961–62; Consultant Urol Surgeon, Hammersmith Hosp., 1967–77; Hon. Consultant Urol Surgeon, Western Gen. Hosp., Edinburgh, 1977–; Chairman: Lister Postgrad. Inst., Edinburgh, 1991–; Med. Adv. Cttee, SE Scotland Cttee for Postgrad. Medical and Dental Educn, 1993–. Hon. Sen. Lecturer: RPMS, 1967–77; Inst. of Urology, Univ. of London, 1972–. Chairman: British Prostate Gp, 1975–80; Conf. Roy. Colls and Faculties (Scotland), 1989–91; Jt Cttee on Higher Surgical Trng, 1991–94; Vice-Pres., British Assoc. of Surgical Oncologists, 1980–81; Chm., European Soc. of Urol Oncology and Endocrinology, 1984–85; President: British Assoc. of Urol Surgeons, 1986–88; RCSE 1988–91 (Mem. Council, 1984–92; Regent, 1992–); Harveian Soc. of Edinburgh, 1991–92; Scottish Urol Soc., 1992–93; FRSocMed (Mem. Council, 1974–76; Pres., Urol Sect., 1995–96); Fellow, Assoc. Surg. GB and Ireland, 1967; Founder Mem., British Transplant Soc., 1972; Corresp. Mem., Amer. Assoc. Genito-urinary Surg., 1980; Hon. Member: Dutch, Australasian, Greek, S African, American, Roumanian and Portuguese Urol Assocs; Assoc. of Surgeons of India, 1991; Acad. Med. Malaysia, 1993; Member: Internat. Soc. of Urology; Internat. Continence Soc. (Mem. Scottish Sub-Cttee, Adv. Cttee on Distinction Awards). Hon. FRACS 1990; Hon. FCSSA 1990; Hon. FACS 1994. Vis. Professorships include Rotterdam, Strasbourg, Aachen, Cairo, San Diego, Dallas, New Haven, RPMS, UCLA. Memorial Lectures: Sir Alexander Haddow, RSocMed (Sect. of Oncology), 1990; Sir Peter Freyer, UC, Galway, 1991; Sir Stanford Cade, RCS, 1991; Keith Yeates, N of England Urological Soc., 1991; Ian Aird, RPMS, 1992; Bodo von Garelts, Huddinge Univ., Sweden, 1994; lectured in UK, USA, Australia, Malaysia and Hong Kong. Trustee: Sir Henry Wade Pilmuir Trust, 1991–; Melville Trust for Care and Cure of Cancer, 1992–. Managing Editor, Urological Research, 1977–81; Editor, British Jl of Urology, 1977–93; Series Editor, Clinical Practice in Urology, 1981– (13 vols). Francisco Diaz Medal, Spanish Assoc. of Urology, 1985; Pybus Medal, N of England Surgical Soc., 1986; St Peter's Medal, British Assoc. of Urol Surgeons, 1989; Silver Medal, Danish Surgical Soc., 1989. *Publications:* Tutorials in Postgraduate Medicine, 1980; (jtly) Scientific Foundations of Urology, 1982, 3rd edn 1990; (jtly) Surgical Management, 1984, 2nd edn 1991; contribs to learned jls. *Recreations:* medical journalism, wine tasting. *Address:* University Department of Surgery/Urology, Western General Hospital, Edinburgh EH4 2XU. *T:* 0131–315 2522; 153 Whitehouse Loan, Edinburgh EH9 2EY. *T:* 0131–447 0292. *Club:* New (Edinburgh). *Died 10 Nov. 1994.*

CHISHOLM, Roderick Æneas, CBE 1946; DSO 1944; DFC and bar; AE; BSc; ARCS; *b* 23 Nov. 1911; *s* of Edward Consitt Chisholm and Edith Maud Mary Cary-Elwes; *m* 1945, (Phillis Mary) Sanchia (SO, WAAF), *d* of late Geoffrey A. Whitworth, CBE; one *s* two *d. Educ:*

Ampleforth Coll.; Imperial Coll. of Science and Technology, London. AAF, 1932–40; Royal Air Force, 1940–46 (Air Cdre). *Publication:* Cover of Darkness, 1953. *Address:* Ladywell House, Alresford, Hants SO24 9DF. *Died 7 Dec. 1994.*

CHOLMELEY, John Adye, FRCS; Surgeon, Royal National Orthopædic Hospital, 1948–70, Hon. Consulting Surgeon, since 1970; Chairman of Joint Examining Board for Orthopædic Nursing, 1959–83; *b* 31 Oct. 1902; *s* of Montague Adye Cholmeley and Mary Bertha Gordon-Cumming; unmarried. *Educ:* St Paul's Sch.; St Bartholomew's Hosp. MRCS, LRCP 1926; MB, BS London 1927; FRCS 1935. Resident appts St Bart's Hosp., 1928–30; Assistant Medical Officer: Lord Mayor Treloar Cripples' Hosp., Alton, 1930–32; Alexandra Orth. Hosp., Swanley, 1933–34; Resident Surg. and Med. Supt, Country Br., Royal Nat. Orth. Hosp., Stanmore, 1940–48 (Asst Res. Surg., 1936–39); former Orthopædic Surg., Clare Hall Hosp., Neasden Hosp. Mem. Internat. Soc. of Orthopædic Surgery and Trauma (Société Internationale de Chirurgie Orthopédique et de Traumatologie, SICOT); FRSocMed (Pres. Orthopædic Sect., 1957–58); Fellow Brit. Orth. Assoc. *Publications:* History of the Royal National Orthopaedic Hospital, 1985; articles on orthopædic subjects, particularly tuberculosis and poliomyelitis in med. jls. *Address:* 14 Warren Fields, Valencia Road, Stanmore, Mddx HA7 4JQ. *T:* 0181–954 6920. *Died 12 Oct. 1995.*

CHORLEY, Francis Kenneth, CBE 1982; FEng, FIEE; Board Member (part-time), Civil Aviation Authority, since 1987; Chairman: 3 NET Ltd, since 1987; Waycom Holdings Ltd, since 1989; *b* 29 July 1926; *s* of late Francis Henry Chorley and Eva Ellen Chorley; *m* 1954, Lorna Stella Brooks; two *s. Educ:* Rutlish Sch., Merton. With Plessey Co., 1951–60; Tech. Dir, Epsylon Industries, 1960–63; Divl Manager, GEC Electronics Ltd, 1963–64; Dir and Gen. Manager, then Man. Dir, GEC-AEI Electronics Ltd, 1964–67; Dir and Gen. Manager, GEC-AEI Telecommunications Ltd, 1967–74; Man. Dir, Plessey Avionics and Communications Div., 1974–78; Man. Dir and Dep. Chm., Plessey Electronic Systems Ltd, 1979–83; Exec. Chm., Plessey Telecommunications & Office Systems Ltd, 1983–86; Bd Mem., 1978–86, Dep. Chief Exec., 1983–86, The Plessey Co. plc; Dir, Pirelli Focom, 1987–. Member: Engineering Council, 1986–; Council, CGLI, 1983–. Pres., IERE, 1987–88; Vice-Pres., TEMA, 1986–87. FInstD; FRSA; CBIM. Prince Philip Medal, CGLI, 1983. *Recreations:* photography, music, sailing. *Address:* 22 Marryat Square, SW6 6UA. *T:* 071–386 7298. *Club:* East India. *Died 19 March 1993.*

CHRISTIE, Charles Henry; Director of Studies, Britannia Royal Naval College, Dartmouth, 1978–86; *b* 1 Sept. 1924; *s* of late Lieut-Comdr C. P. Christie and Mrs C. S. Christie; *m* 1950, Naida Joan Bentley; one *s* three *d. Educ:* Westminster Sch. (King's Scholar); Trinity Coll., Cambridge (Exhibitioner). Served 1943–46, RNVR (despatches, 1945). Trinity Coll., Cambridge, 1946–49; Asst Master, Eton Coll., 1949–57; Under Master and Master of Queen's Scholars, Westminster Sch., 1957–63; Headmaster, Brighton Coll., 1963–71; Warden, St Edward's Sch., Oxford, 1971–78. Vis. Prof., US Naval Acad., Annapolis, 1986–88. Prime Warden, Dyers' Co., 1983–84. *Address:* 8 Paddox Close, Squitchey Lane, Oxford OX2 7LR. *Died 12 April 1992.*

CHRISTIE, John Arthur Kingsley; Under-Secretary, Ministry of Agriculture, Fisheries and Food, 1970–75; *b* 8 Feb. 1915; *s* of Harold Douglas Christie and Enid Marian (*née* Hall); *m* 1971, Enid Margaret (*née* Owen); one *s* two *d. Educ:* Rugby Sch.; Magdalen Coll., Oxford. BA (1st cl. Hon. Mods, 1st cl. Lit. Hum.). Asst Principal, Min. of Agriculture, 1937–41; Sub-Lt, RNVR, 1941–45; Asst

Private Sec. to Lord President of the Council, 1945–47; Min. of Agriculture: Principal, 1947–52; Asst Sec., 1952–70. *Recreation:* music. *Address:* Westfield, 16 Knole Road, Sevenoaks, Kent TN13 3XH. *T:* Sevenoaks (0732) 451423. *Died 17 April 1994.*

CHRISTIE, Hon. Sir Vernon (Howard Colville), Kt 1972; Speaker of the Legislative Assembly, Victoria, 1967–73; MLA (L) for Ivanhoe, Victoria, 1955–73; *b* Manly, NSW, 17 Dec. 1909; *s* of C. Christie, Sydney; *m* 1936, Joyce, *d* of F. H. Hamlin; one *s* one *d*. Chm. Cttees, Legislative Assembly, 1956–61, 1965–68; Director: Australian Elizabethan Theatre Trust, 1969–78; Australian Ballet Foundn, 1969–84; Qld Ballet. Hon. Life Mem., Victoria Br., CPA. AASA; FCIS; AFAIM. *Recreations:* bowls, sailing, music, ballet and the arts, conservation, fly fishing. *Address:* Rothes, 51 Colburn Avenue, Victoria Point, Qld 4165, Australia. *Club:* Queensland (Brisbane).
Died 4 Nov. 1994.

CHRISTISON, Gen. Sir (Alexander Frank) Philip, 4th Bt *cr* 1871, of Moray Place, Edinburgh; GBE 1948 (KBE 1944); CB 1943; DSO 1945; MC (and Bar); DL; *b* 17 Nov. 1893; *s* of Sir Alexander Christison, 2nd Bt, and 2nd wife, Florence (*d* 1949), *d* of F. T. Elworthy; *S* half-brother, 1945; *m* 1st, 1916, Betty (*d* 1974), *d* of late Rt Rev. Anthony Mitchell, Bishop of Aberdeen and Orkney; (one *s* killed in action in Burma, 7 March 1942) two *d* (and one *d* decd); 2nd, 1974, Vida Wallace Smith, MBE (*d* 1992). *Educ:* Edinburgh Academy; Oxford Univ. (BA). Hon. Fellow, University Coll., Oxford, 1973. 2nd Lieut Cameron Highlanders, 1914; Capt. 1915; Bt Major, 1930; Bt Lt-Col 1933; Lt-Col Duke of Wellington's Regt, 1937; Col 1938; comd Quetta Bde, 1938–40; Comdt Staff Coll., Quetta, 1940–41; Brig. Gen. Staff, 1941; Maj.-Gen. 1941; Lt-Gen. 1942; Gen. 1947; comd XXXIII and XV Indian Corps, 1942–45; Temp. Comdr 14th Army, 1945; C-in-C, ALFSEA, 1945; Allied Comdr Netherland East Indies, 1945–46; GOC-in-C Northern Command, 1946; GOC-in-C Scottish Command and Governor of Edinburgh Castle, 1947–49; ADC Gen. to the King, 1947–49; retired pay, 1949. Col, The Duke of Wellington's Regt, 1947–57; Col, 10th Princess Mary's Own Gurkha Rifles, 1947–57; Hon. Col, 414 Coast Regt Royal Artillery, 1950–57. Dir, Cochran and Co. Ltd, 1951–66; Chm., Alban Timber Ltd, 1953–78. Fruit farmer, 1949–. President: Scottish Unionist Party, 1957–58; Army Cadet Force, Scotland; Earl Haig Fund; Vice-President: Burma Star Assoc.; Officers' Assoc.; Scottish Salmon Angling Fedn, 1969; Chm., Lodge Trust for Ornithology, 1969; Chm. and Pres., Clarsach Soc., 1947–. DL Roxburghshire, 1956. FSAScot 1957. Chinese Order of Cloud and Banner with Grand Cordon, 1949. Hon. Fellow, Mark Twain Soc., USA, 1977. *Publications:* Birds of Northern Baluchistan, 1940; Birds of Arakan (with Aubrey Buxton), 1946. *Heir:* none. *Recreations:* ornithology, Celtic languages, field sports. *Address:* St John's Rest Home, Melrose, Roxburghshire TD6 9SQ. *Died 21 Dec. 1993 (ext).*

CHRISTMAS, Arthur Napier, BSc(Eng); CEng, FIEE, FRAeS; Chief Scientific Officer and Director of Materials Quality Assurance, Ministry of Defence, 1971–74, retired; *b* 16 May 1913; *s* of Ernest Napier and Florence Elizabeth Christmas; *m* 1940, Betty Margaret Christmas (*née* Bradbrook); one *s* one *d*. *Educ:* Holloway Sch.; Northampton Technical Coll., London (BSc (Hons)). British Electrical and Allied Industries' Research Assoc., 1934–37; Post Office Research Station, 1937–46; Prin. Scientific Officer, Min. of Supply, 1946–51; Sec., British Washington Guided Missile Cttee, 1951–54; SPSO, Armament Research and Develt Estabt, 1954–59, DCSO, 1959; Dir, Guided Weapons Research and Techniques, Min. of Aviation, 1959–62; Dir for Engrg Develt, European Launcher Develt Org., 1962–67; Prin. Supt,

Royal Armament Research and Develt Estabt, 1967–71. *Recreations:* sailing, mountain walking, music. *Address:* Old Farm Cottage, Itchenor, Sussex. *T:* Birdham (0243) 512224. *Clubs:* Itchenor Sailing, Island Sailing.
Died 1 March 1993.

CHRISTOFAS, Sir Kenneth (Cavendish), KCMG 1983 (CMG 1969); MBE 1944; HM Diplomatic Service, retired; *b* 18 Aug. 1917; *o s* of late Edward Julius Goodwin and Lillian Christofas; step *s* of late Alexander Christofas; *m* 1948, Jessica Laura (*née* Sparshott); two *d*. *Educ:* Merchant Taylors' Sch.; University Coll., London (Fellow, 1976). Served War of 1939–45 (MBE): commissioned in The Queen's Own Royal West Kent Regt, 1939; Adjt 1940; Staff Capt. 1941; DAAG 1942; Staff Coll., Quetta, 1944; AAG 1944; GSO1, War Office, 1946; resigned from Army with Hon. rank of Lieut-Col and joined Sen. Br. of HM Foreign Service, 1948 (HM Diplomatic Service after 1965); served in Foreign Office, 1948–49 and 1951–55; Rio de Janeiro, 1949–51; Rome, 1955–59; Dep. Head of UK Delegn to European Communities, Brussels, 1959–61; seconded to CRO for service as Counsellor in the British High Commn, Lagos, 1961–64 and to Colonial Office as Head of Economic Dept, 1965–66; on sabbatical year at Univ. of London, 1964–65; Counsellor in Commonwealth Office, then in FCO, 1966–69; Minister and Dep. Head of UK Delegn to EEC, 1969–72 (acting Head, March-Oct. 1971); Cabinet Office, on secondment, 1972–73; Director General, Secretariat, Council of Ministers of the European Communities, 1973–82, Hon. Dir Gen. 1982–. Pres., Crabtree Foundn, 1985; Hon. Pres. UK Branch, Assoc. of Former Officials of European Communities, 1986–. Gold Medal, Eur. Parlt, 1982. Order of Polonia Restituta (Poland), 1944. *Recreations:* railways, music. *Address:* 3 The Ridge, Bolsover Road, Eastbourne, Sussex BN20 7JE. *T:* Eastbourne (0323) 722384. *Club:* East India, Devonshire, Sports and Public Schools.
Died 3 Nov. 1992.

CHRISTOFF, Boris; opera singer (bass); *b* Plovdiv, near Sofia, Bulgaria, 18 May 1914; *s* of Kyryl and Rayna Teodorova; *m* Franca, *d* of Raffaello de Rensis. *Educ:* Univ. of Sofia (Doctor of Law). Joined Gussla Choir and Sofia Cathedral Choir as soloist; obtained scholarship, through King Boris III of Bulgaria, to study singing in Rome under Riccardo Stracciari; made concert début at St Cecilia Academy in Rome, 1946 and operatic début, 1946; Covent Garden début, 1950, as Boris Godunov and Philip II; subsequently appeared at all leading European and American opera houses; American début, Metropolitan Opera House, 1950; as Boris Godunov, San Francisco, 1956. Principal rôles include: Boris Godunov, King Philip, Galitzky, Konchak, Don Quixote, Dositheus, Ivan the Terrible, Ivan Susanin, Mephistopheles, Moses, Don Basilio, Pizarro, Simon Boccanegra. Made numerous recordings, including opera and songs, winning many prix du disque; these include particularly the complete lyric works of the five great Russian composers; also concert appearances. Hon. Mem. Théâtre de l'Opéra, Paris; Mem. La Scala, Milan. Holder of foreign decorations. Commendatore della Repubblica Italiana. *Address:* Villa Leccio, Buggiano (PT), Italy.
Died 28 June 1993.

CHURCHILL, Diana (Josephine); actress, stage and screen; *b* Wembley, 21 Aug. 1913; *d* of Joseph H. Churchill, MRCS, LRCP and Ethel Mary Nunn; *m* Barry K. Barnes (*d* 1965); *m* 1976, Mervyn Johns (*d* 1992). *Educ:* St Mary's Sch., Wantage; Guildhall Sch. of Music (scholarship). First professional appearance in Champion North, Royalty, 1931; subsequently in West End and in Repertory; Old Vic Season, 1949–50, New Theatre, as Rosaline in Love's Labour's Lost, Miss Kate Hardcastle in She Stoops to Conquer, Lizaveta Bogdanovna in A

Month in the Country and Elise in The Miser; High Spirits, London Hippodrome, 1953; The Desperate Hours, London Hippodrome, 1955; Hamlet, Stratford-on-Avon Festival, 1956; Lady Fidget in The Country Wife, Royal Court Theatre, 1956; The Rehearsal, Globe Theatre, 1961; The Winter's Tale, Cambridge, 1966; The Farmer's Wife, Chichester, 1967; Heartbreak House, Chichester, later Lyric, 1967. Also appeared in several films. *Address:* c/o Stella Richards Management, 42 Hazlebury Road, SW6 2ND.   *Died 8 Oct. 1994.*

CHURCHILL, John George Spencer; mural, portrait, townscape and landscape painter; sculptor, lecturer and author since 1932; *b* 31 May 1909; *s* of John Strange Spencer Churchill and Lady Gwendoline Bertie; *m* 1st, 1934, Angela Culme Seymour; one *d*; 2nd, 1941, Mary Cookson; 3rd, 1953, Kathlyn Tandy (*d* 1957); 4th, 1958, Lullan Boston (marr. diss. 1972). *Educ:* Harrow School; Pembroke Coll., Oxford; Royal Coll. of Art; Central Sch. of Art; Westminster Sch. of Art; Ruskin Sch. of Art, Oxford; private pupil of Meninsky, Hubbard, Nicholson and Lutyens. Stock Exchange, 1930–32. Served War, Major GSO, RE, 1939–45. Mural and portrait, townscape and landscape paintings in England, France, Spain, Portugal, Italy, Switzerland, Belgium and America, 1932–80. Lectr in America, 1961–69. *Work includes:* incised relief carving on slate and cement cast busts, in Marlborough Pavilion at Chartwell, Westerham, Kent (National Trust), 1949; reportage illustrations and paintings of Spanish Revolution, 1936, and Evacuation of BEF from Dunkirk, 1940 (in Illustrated London News); London from the South Bank, in Simpsons, Piccadilly, 1957; painting of forest destruction for WWF, 1985. Mem., Soc. of Mural Painters. *Publications:* Crowded Canvas, 1960; A Churchill Canvas, 1961 (USA), serialised in Sunday Dispatch and Atlantic Monthly, USA; Varnishing Day, 1986; contrib. illustrations to Country Life, Connoisseur, etc. *Recreations:* music, travel. *Address:* (professional) 40 Elsham Road, W14. *T:* 071–602 4666; (domicile) Appartement Churchill, 83360 Grimaud, France. *T:* 94432131. *Clubs:* Press, Chelsea Arts; Cincinatti (Washington, DC, USA).
Died 23 June 1992.

CHURSTON, 4th Baron *cr* 1858; **Richard Francis Roger Yarde-Buller,** VRD; Bt 1790; Lieutenant-Commander Royal Naval Volunteer Reserve, retired; *b* 12 Feb. 1910; *er s* of 3rd Baron and Jessie (who *m* 2nd, 1928, Theodore William Wessel), *o d* of Alfred Smither; *S* father, 1930; *m* 1st, 1933, Elizabeth Mary (from whom he obtained a divorce, 1943, and who *m* 1943, Lieut-Col P. Laycock; she *d* 1951), 2nd *d* of late W. B. du Pre; one *s* one *d*; 2nd, 1949, Mrs Jack Dunfee (*d* 1979); 3rd, Mrs Olga Alice Muriel Blair. *Educ:* Eton Coll. *Heir:* *s* Hon. John Francis Yarde-Buller [*b* 29 Dec. 1934; *m* 1973, Alexandra, *d* of A. Contomichalos; one *s* two *d*]. *Address:* Pendragon, Fort George, Guernsey, Channel Isles. *Club:* Royal Yacht Squadron.   *Died 9 April 1991.*

CHUTE, Marchette Gaylord; author, retired; *b* 16 Aug. 1909; *d* of William Young Chute and Edith Mary Pickburn; unmarried. *Educ:* Univ. of Minnesota (BA). Doctor of Letters: Western Coll., 1952; Carleton Coll., 1957; Dickinson Coll., 1964. Mem., American Acad. of Arts and Letters. Outstanding Achievement Award, Univ. of Minnesota, 1958; co-winner of Constance Lindsay Skinner Award, 1959. FRSA. *Publications:* Rhymes about Ourselves, 1932; The Search for God, 1941; Rhymes about the Country, 1941; The Innocent Wayfaring, 1943; Geoffrey Chaucer of England, 1946; Rhymes about the City, 1946; The End of the Search, 1947; Shakespeare of London, 1950; An Introduction to Shakespeare, 1951 (English title: Shakespeare and his Stage); Ben Jonson of Westminster, 1953; The Wonderful Winter, 1954; Stories

from Shakespeare, 1956; Around and About, 1957; Two Gentle Men: the Lives of George Herbert and Robert Herrick, 1959; Jesus of Israel, 1961; The Worlds of Shakespeare (with Ernestine Perrie), 1963; The First Liberty: a history of the right to vote in America, 1619–1850, 1969; The Green Tree of Democracy, 1971; PEN American Center: a history of the first fifty years, 1972; Rhymes About Us, 1974; various articles in Saturday Review, Virginia Quarterly Review, etc. *Address:* 66 Glenbrook Road, Morris Plains, NJ 07950, USA. *T:* (201) 5401069. *Clubs:* PEN, Renaissance Society of America (New York).   *Died 6 May 1994.*

CLANCARTY, 8th Earl of, *cr* 1803; **William Francis Brinsley Le Poer Trench;** Baron Kilconnel, 1797; Viscount Dunlo, 1801; Baron Trench (UK), 1815; Viscount Clancarty (UK), 1823; Marquess of Heusden (Kingdom of the Netherlands), 1818; author; *b* 18 Sept. 1911; 5th *s* of 5th Earl of Clancarty and *er s* of 2nd wife, Mary Gwatkin (*d* 1974), *d* of late W. F. Rosslewin Ellis; *S* half-brother, 1975; *m* 1st, 1940, Diana Joan (marr. diss. 1947), *yr d* of Sir William Younger, 2nd Bt; 2nd, 1961, Mrs Wilma Dorothy Millen Belknap (marr. diss. 1969), *d* of S. R. Vermilyea, USA; 3rd, 1974, Mrs Mildred Alleyn Spong (*d* 1975); 4th, 1976, May, *o d* of late E. Radonicich, and *widow* of Commander Frank M. Beasley, RN. *Educ:* Nautical Coll., Pangbourne. Founder Pres., Contact International; Chm., House of Lords UFO Study Gp. *Publications:* (as Brinsley Le Poer Trench): The Sky People, 1960; Men Among Mankind, 1962; Forgotten Heritage, 1964; The Flying Saucer Story, 1966; Operation Earth, 1969; The Eternal Subject, 1973; Secret of the Ages, 1974. *Recreations:* ufology, travel, walking. *Heir:* nephew Nicholas Power Richard Le Poer Trench, *b* 1 May 1952. *Address:* 51 Eaton Place, Belgravia, SW1X 8DE. *Club:* Buck's.   *Died 18 May 1995.*

CLARE, Ernest E. S.; *see* Sabben-Clare.

CLARK, Sir Colin (Douglas), 4th Bt *cr* 1917, of Dunlambert, City of Belfast; MC 1945; *b* 20 July 1918; 2nd *s* of Sir George Ernest Clark, 2nd Bt and Norah Anne (*d* 1966), *d* of W. G. Wilson; *S* brother, 1991; *m* 1946, Margaret Coleman, *d* of Maj.-Gen. Sir Charlton Watson Spinks, KBE, DSO and *widow* of Maj. G. W. Threlfall, MC; one *s* two *d*. *Educ:* Eton; Cambridge Univ. (BA 1939; MA 1944). Served War 1939–45; Major RE; despatches, 1944. Formerly: Man. Dir, G. Heyn & Sons, Belfast; Director: Ulster Steamship Co. Ltd; Northern Irish and Scottish Investment Trust Ltd, and other cos. Mem., Belfast Harbour Comrs, 1961–79. *Heir:* *s* Jonathan George Clark [*b* 9 Oct. 1947; *m* 1971, Susan Joy, *d* of Brig. T. I. G. Gray; one *s* two *d*].
Died 26 April 1995.

CLARK, Douglas Henderson, MD, FRCSEd, FRCSGlas, FRCPEd; Consultant Surgeon, Western Infirmary, Glasgow, since 1950; *b* 20 Jan. 1917; *s* of William and Jean Clark; *m* 1950, Morag Clark (decd); three *s*. *Educ:* Ayr Acad.; Glasgow Univ. (ChM 1950, MD Hons 1956). FRCSEd, FRCSGlas 1947; FRCPEd 1982. Captain RAMC, 1941–47. Miners Welfare Scholar, 1936; Fulbright Scholar, 1952; William Stewart Halsted Fellow, Johns Hopkins Hosp., 1952–53. Vis. Lectr in America, S Africa, Australia and NZ. Pres., RCPGlas 1980–82; Dir, James IV Assoc. of Surgeons, 1979–. Hon. FRCS 1982; Hon. FRCSI 1982. Hon. DSc Glasgow, 1983. *Publications:* papers on gastro-enterology and thyroid disease; chapters in text-books. *Address:* 36 Southbrae Drive, Glasgow G13 1PZ. *T:* 041–959 3556.
Died 10 March 1991.

CLARK, Sir George Anthony, 3rd Bt *cr* 1917, of Dunlambert, City of Belfast; DL; Captain Reserve of Officers, Black Watch, 1939–64; Senator, Northern Ireland

Parliament, 1951–69; *b* 24 Jan. 1914; *e s* of Sir George Ernest Clark, 2nd Bt and Norah Anne (*d* 1966), *d* of W. G. Wilson, Glasgow; *S* father 1950; *m* 1949, Nancy Catherine, 2nd *d* of George W. N. Clark, Carnabane, Upperlands, Co. Derry; one *d*. *Educ:* Canford. Pres., Ulster Unionist Council, 1980. DL Belfast, 1961. *Recreations:* golf, tennis. *Heir: b* Colin Douglas Clark, MC, MA [*b* 20 July 1918; *m* 1946, Margaret Coleman, *d* of late Maj.-Gen. Sir Charlton Watson Spinks, KBE, DSO, and *widow* of Major G. W. Threlfall, MC; one *s* two *d*]. *Address:* Tullygirvan House, Ballygowan, Newtownards, Co. Down, Northern Ireland BT23 6NR. *T:* Ballygowan (0238) 528267. *Clubs:* Naval and Military; Royal Ulster Yacht (Bangor, Co. Down). *Died 20 Feb. 1991.*

CLARK, Sir Grahame; *see* Clark, Sir J. G. D.

CLARK, James McAdam, CVO 1972; MC 1944; HM Diplomatic Service, retired; *b* 13 Sept. 1916; *er s* of late James Heriot Clark of Wester Coltfield, and late Ella Catherine McAdam; *m* 1946, Denise Thérèse (*d* 1994), *d* of late Dr Léon Dufournier, Paris; two *d*. *Educ:* Edinburgh Acad.; Edinburgh Univ. BSc (Hons) Tech. Chemistry, 1938. Asst Lectr, Edinburgh Univ., 1938–39. Served Royal Artillery, 1939–46 (MC), rank of Capt.; Royal Mil. Coll. of Science, 1945–46 (pac). Min. of Fuel and Power, 1947–48; entered Foreign (later Diplomatic) Service, 1948; FO, 1948–50; Head of Chancery, Quito, 1950–53; FO, 1953–56; Head of Chancery, Lisbon, 1956–60; Counsellor, UK Rep. to and Alternate Gov. of Internat. Atomic Energy Agency, Vienna, 1960–64; Head of Scientific Relations Dept, FO, 1964–66; Counsellor on secondment to Min. of Technology, 1966–70; Consul-Gen., Paris, 1970–77. Officer, Order of Christ of Portugal, 1957. *Publications:* a number of poems and articles. *Recreations:* golf, sailing, music, disputation. *Address:* Hill Lodge, Aldeburgh, Suffolk IP15 5DU. *Clubs:* Aldeburgh Yacht, Aldeburgh Golf.
Died 15 Oct. 1995.

CLARK, Sir John (Douglas), 4th Bt *cr* 1886, of Melville Crescent, Edinburgh; *b* 9 Jan. 1923; *s* of Sir Thomas Clark, 3rd Bt and Ellen Mercy (*d* 1987), *d* of late Francis Drake; *S* father, 1977; *m* 1969, Anne, *d* of Angus and Christina Gordon, Aberfawn, Beauly, Inverness-shire. *Educ:* Gordonstoun School; Edinburgh University. Entered firm of T. & T. Clark, Publishers, Edinburgh, 1953; Partner, 1958; retired through ill-health. *Heir: b* Francis Drake Clark [*b* 16 July 1924; *m* 1958, Mary, *d* of late John Alban Andrews, MC, FRCS; one s]. *Address:* 52 Ormidale Terrace, Edinburgh EH12 6EF. *T:* 031–337 5610. *Died 17 Jan. 1991.*

CLARK, Sir (John) Grahame (Douglas), Kt 1992; CBE 1971; MA, PhD, ScD (Cantab); FBA 1951; Master of Peterhouse, 1973–80 (Fellow, 1950–73, Honorary Fellow, 1980); *b* 28 July 1907; *s* of Lt-Col Charles Douglas Clark and Maude Ethel Grahame Clark (*née* Shaw); *m* 1936, Gwladys Maude (*née* White); two *s* one *d*. *Educ:* Marlborough Coll.; Peterhouse, Cambridge. Served War of 1939–45, RAFVR, in Photographic Interpretation, 1941–43, and Air Historical Br., 1943–45. Research Student, 1930–32, and Bye-Fellow, 1933–35, of Peterhouse; Faculty Asst Lectr in Archæology, Cambridge, 1935–46, and Univ. Lectr, 1946–52; Disney Prof. of Archæology, Cambridge, 1952–74; Head of Dept of Archæology and Anthropology, Cambridge, 1956–61 and 1968–71. Lectures: Munro, in Archæology, Edinburgh Univ., 1949; Reckitt, British Acad., 1954; Dalrymple, in Archæology, Glasgow Univ., 1955; G. Grant MacCurdy, Harvard, 1957; Mortimer Wheeler Meml, New Delhi, 1978; William Evans Vis. Prof., Univ. of Otago, NZ, 1964; Commonwealth Vis. Fellow, Australia, 1964; Hitchcock Prof., Univ. of California, Berkeley, 1969; Leverhulme Vis. Prof., Uppsala, 1972. Member: Ancient

Monuments Board, 1954–77; Royal Commn on Historical Monuments, 1957–69; a Trustee, BM, 1975–80; Pres., Prehistoric Soc., 1958–62; Vice-Pres., Soc. of Antiquaries, 1959–62. Hon. Editor, Proceedings Prehistoric Soc., 1935–70. Hon. Corr. Mem., Royal Soc. Northern Antiquaries, Copenhagen, 1946, and of Swiss Prehistoric Soc., 1951; Fellow, German Archæological Inst., 1954; Hon. Member: RIA, 1955; Archæol. Inst. of America, 1977; Foreign Member: Finnish Archæological Soc., 1958; Amer. Acad. of Arts and Sciences (Hon.) 1961; Royal Danish Acad. of Sciences and Letters, 1964; Royal Netherlands Acad. of Sciences, 1964; For. Fellow, Royal Society of Sciences, Uppsala, 1964; For. Associate, Nat. Acad. of Sciences, USA, 1974; Royal Soc. of Humane Letters, Lund, 1976. Hon. DLitt: Sheffield, 1971; National Univ. of Ireland, 1976; Fil dr, Uppsala, 1977. Hodgkins Medal, Smithsonian Institution, 1967; Viking Medal, Wenner-Gren Foundn, 1971; Lucy Wharton Drexel Gold Medal, Museum, Univ. of Pennsylvania, 1974; Gold Medal, Soc. of Antiquaries, 1978; Chanda Medal, Asiatic Soc., Calcutta, 1979; Erasmus Prize, Netherlands Foundn, 1991. Comdr, Order of the Dannebrog (Denmark), 1961. *Publications:* The Mesolithic Settlement of Northern Europe, 1936; Archæology and Society 1939, 3rd edn 1957; Prehistoric England, 1940, 1962; From Savagery to Civilization, 1946; Prehistoric Europe, The Economic Basis, 1952; Excavations at Star Carr, 1954; The Study of Prehistory, 1954; World Prehistory, An Outline, 1961; (with Stuart Piggott) Prehistoric Societies, 1965; The Stone Age Hunters, 1967; World Prehistory, a new outline, 1969; Aspects of Prehistory, 1970; The Earlier Stone Age Settlement of Scandinavia, 1975; World Prehistory in New Perspective, 1977; Sir Mortimer and Indian Archaeology (Wheeler Memorial Lectures, 1978), 1979; Mesolithic Prelude, 1980; The Identity of Man: as seen by an archaeologist, 1982; Symbols of Excellence, 1986; Economic Prehistory, 1989; Prehistoric Archaeology at Cambridge and Beyond, 1989; Space, Time and Man: a prehistorian's view, 1992; numerous papers in archæological journals. *Recreations:* gardening, travel, contemporary art. *Address:* 36 Millington Road, Cambridge CB3 9HP. *Club:* United Oxford & Cambridge University. *Died 12 Sept. 1995.*

CLARK, Leslie Joseph, CBE 1977; BEM 1942; FEng; Chairman, Victor Products (Wallsend) Ltd, 1977–79; Special Adviser on the international gas industry to the Chairman of British Gas, since 1975; Chairman, Northern Gas Region (formerly Northern Gas Board), 1967–75; *b* 21 May 1914; *s* of Joseph George Clark and Elizabeth (*née* Winslow); *m* 1940, Mary M. Peacock; one *s* one *d*. *Educ:* Stationers' Company's Sch.; King's Coll., London. BSc(Eng), 1st Cl. Hons, 1934; MSc 1948. Engineer, Gas Light & Coke Co., later North Thames Gas Board; Chief Engineer, North Thames Gas Board, 1962–65 (pioneered work for development of sea transportation of liquefied natural gas, 1954–63), Dep. Chm., 1965–67. Pres., Instn of Gas Engineers, 1965–66; Pres., IGU, 1973–76 (Vice-Pres., 1970–73). Member: Court, Univ. of Newcastle upon Tyne, 1972–; Council, Univ. of Durham, 1975–78. CEng, FICE, FIMechE, FIGasE, FInstE, MIEE, AMIChemE. Founder Fellow, Fellowship of Engineering, 1976. Elmer Sperry Award, USA, 1979. *Publications:* technical papers to Instns of Gas Engineers and Mech. Engrs, Inst. of Fuel, World Energy Conf., Internat. Gas Union, etc. *Recreations:* model engineering, walking, photography, music. *Address:* Hillway, New Ridley Road, Stocksfield, Northumberland NE43 7QB. *T:* Stocksfield (0661) 842339. *Died 1 Feb. 1992.*

CLARK, Ven. Sidney H.; *see* Harvie-Clark.

CLARK-EDDINGTON, Paul; *see* Eddington.

CLARKE, Arthur Grenfell, CMG 1953; *b* 17 Aug. 1906; *s* of Harry Clarke; *m* 1st, 1934, Rhoda McLean Arnott (*d* 1980); 2nd, 1980, Violet Louise Riley. *Educ:* Mountjoy Sch., Dublin; Dublin Univ. Appointed Cadet Officer, Hong Kong, 1929; entered service of Hong Kong Government, 1929; interned in Stanley Camp during Japanese occupation; Financial Sec., 1952–62; retired, 1962. *Address:* Foxdene, Brighton Road, Foxrock, Dublin 18. *T:* Dublin 2894368. *Died 15 Aug. 1993.*

CLARKE, Sir Ashley; *see* Clarke, Sir H. A.

CLARKE, Elizabeth Bleckly, CVO 1969; JP; MA; Headmistress, Benenden School, Kent, 1954–Dec. 1975; *b* 26 May 1915; *d* of Kenneth Bleckly Clarke, JP, MRCS, LRCP, Cranborne, Dorset, and Dorothy Milborough (*née* Hasluck). *Educ:* Grovely Manor Sch., Boscombe, Hants; St Hilda's Coll., Oxford, 1933–37. BA 1936, BLitt and MA 1940. Asst Mistress: The Grove Sch., Hindhead, 1937–39; Benenden Sch., 1940–47; called to the Bar, Middle Temple, 1949; Vice-Principal, Cheltenham Ladies' Coll., 1950–54. JP County of Kent, 1956. *Recreations:* walking, gardening, local history. *Address:* Minden, 1 Waterloo Place, Cranbrook, Kent TN17 3JH. *T:* Cranbook (0580) 712139. *Club:* English-Speaking Union. *Died 18 Oct. 1993.*

CLARKE, Sir (Henry) Ashley, GCMG 1962 (KCMG 1952; CMG 1946); GCVO 1961; FSA; HM Diplomatic Service, retired; President, Venice in Peril Fund, since 1983 (Vice-Chairman, 1970–83); *b* 26 June 1903; *e s* of H. R. Clarke, MD and Rachel Hill Duncan; *m* 1st, 1937, Virginia (marr. diss. 1960), *d* of Edward Bell, New York; 2nd, 1962, Frances (OBE 1984), *d* of John Molyneux, Stourbridge, Worcs. *Educ:* Repton; Pembroke Coll., Cambridge (Hon. Fellow, 1962). Entered Diplomatic Service, 1925; 3rd Sec., Budapest and Warsaw; 2nd Sec., Constantinople, FO and Gen. Disarmament Conf, Geneva; 1st Sec., Tokyo; Counsellor, FO; Minister, Lisbon and Paris; Deputy Under-Sec., FO; Ambassador to Italy, 1953–62, retd. London Adviser, Banca Commerciale Italiana, 1962–71; Sec.-Gen., Europa Nostra, 1969–70. Governor: BBC, 1962–67; Brit. Inst. of Recorded Sound, 1964–67; Member: Council, British Sch. at Rome, 1962–78; Exec. Cttee, Keats-Shelley Assoc., 1962–71; D'Oyly Carte Trust, 1964–71; Adv. Council, V&A Mus., 1969–73; Nat. Theatre Bd, 1962–66; Governing Body, RAM, 1967–73; Chairman: British-Italian Soc., 1962–67; Italian Art and Archives Rescue Fund, 1966–70; Royal Acad. of Dancing, 1964–69. Mem. Gen. Bd, Assicurazioni Generali of Trieste, 1964–84. Hon. Academician, Accademia Filarmonica Romana, 1962; FSA 1985; Hon. Fellow: Ancient Monuments Soc., 1969– (Vice-Pres., 1982–); Royal Acad. of Music, 1971; Ateneo Veneto, 1973. Freeman, City of Venice, 1985. Hon. Dr of Political Science, Genoa, 1956; Hon. DLitt Venice, 1991. Pietro Torta Prize, 1974 and Bolla Award, 1976 (for conservation in Venice). Knight Grand Cross of the Order of Merit of the Republic of Italy, 1957; Knight Grand Cross, Order of St Gregory the Great, 1976; Knight of St Mark, 1979. *Publication:* Restoring Venice: the Madonna dell'Orto (with P. Rylands), 1977. *Recreation:* music. *Address:* Bushy Cottage, The Green, Hampton Court, Surrey KT8 9BS. *T:* 081–943 2709; Fondamenta Bonlini 1113, Dorsoduro, 30123 Venice, Italy. *T:* (41) 5206530. *Clubs:* Athenæum, Garrick. *Died 20 Jan. 1994.*

CLARKE, Hilton Swift, CBE 1984; President, Atlantic International Bank Ltd, since 1987 (Director, 1969–86; Chairman, 1973–86); *b* 1 April 1909; *yr s* of Frederick Job Clarke; *m* 1st, 1934, Sibyl Muriel (*d* 1975), *d* of late C. J. C. Salter; one *s*; 2nd, 1984, Ann Elizabeth, *d* of late Leonard James Marchant. *Educ:* Highgate School. FCIB. Bank of England, 1927–67; Mem. UK Delegn, OEEC, Paris, 1948–49. Director: Charterhouse Group Ltd,

1967–82 (Chm. Charterhouse Japhet Ltd, 1971–73); United Dominions Trust Ltd, 1967–81; Guthrie Corp., 1967–79; Bank of Scotland Ltd (London Bd), 1967–79; Chairman: Astley & Pearce, 1981–86 (Dir, 1975–86); Exco International plc, 1981–84 (Dir, 1981–86). Freeman, City of London, 1973. Hon. FRCGP 1975. *Recreation:* gardening. *Address:* 4 Coverdale Avenue, Cooden, Bexhill, E Sussex TN39 4TY. *T:* Bexhill (01424) 845030. *Clubs:* Bankers', Sloane; Cooden Beach Golf. *Died 6 Dec. 1995.*

CLARKE, Norman Eley, CB 1985; Deputy Secretary, Department of Health and Social Security, later Department of Social Security, 1982–88; *b* 11 Feb. 1930; *s* of Thomas John Laurence Clarke and May (*née* Eley); *m* 1953, Pamela Muriel Colwill; three *s* one *d*. *Educ:* Hampton Grammar Sch. Grade 5 Officer, Min. of Labour and National Service, 1948–56; Asst Principal, Principal, Asst Sec., Under Sec., 1956–82, with Nat. Assistance Bd, Cabinet Office, Min. of Social Security, DHSS and DSS. Vice-Chm., Civil Service Sports Council, 1991–; Chm.; First Div. Pensioners' Gp, 1991–. *Recreations:* reading, bridge, watching Queens Park Rangers, talking. *Address:* Northwood, Dartnell Avenue, West Byfleet, Surrey KT14 6PJ. *T:* Byfleet (0932) 346043. *Died 10 June 1993.*

CLARKE, Samuel Harrison, CBE 1956; MSc; Hon. MIFireE; *b* 5 Sept. 1903; *s* of Samuel Clarke and Mary Clarke (*née* Clarke); *m* 1st, 1928, Frances Mary Blowers (*d* 1972); one *s* two *d*; 2nd, 1977, Mrs Beryl N. Wood; two step *d*. *Educ:* The Brunts Sch., Mansfield; University Coll., Nottingham (MSc London). Forest Products Res. Laboratory of DSIR, 1927; Fire Research Div., Research and Experiments Dept, Ministry of Home Security, 1940; Dir of Fire Research, DSIR, and Fire Offices Cttee, 1946–58; Dir of Fuel Research Station, DSIR, 1958; Dir, Warren Spring Laboratory, DSIR, 1958–63; Careers Officer, Min. of Technology, 1963–67 (DSIR, 1964–65). Mem. Stevenage Development Corporation, 1962–71; Vice-Pres., Herts Assoc. for Care and Resettlement of Offenders. *Publications:* papers in scientific and technical jls. *Recreations:* exchanging ideas, painting. *Address:* 14 Silam Road, Stevenage, Herts SG1 1JH. *Died 19 July 1994.*

CLARKE, Brig. Terence Hugh, CBE 1943; *b* 17 Feb. 1904; *e s* of late Col Hugh Clarke, AM, Royal Artillery, and Mrs Hugh Clarke, Bunces, Kennel Ride, Ascot; *m* 1928, Eileen Armistead (*d* 1982), Hopelands, Woodville, NZ; two *d*. *Educ:* Temple Grove; Haileybury Coll.; RMA Sandhurst. 2nd Lieut Glos Regt, 1924; served India, 1924–27; China, 1928; India, 1928–31, in IA Ordnance Corps; England, 1931–33, Glos Regt; transferred to RAOC, 1933; Norway, 1940 (despatches); DDOS 1st Army, 1942, as Brig. (despatches, CBE); DDOS 2nd Army, 1944; Normandy to Luneberg, Germany (despatches); comd RAOC Training Centre, 1946; DDOS Southern Command, 1948–50; retired from Army, 1950, to enter industry as a Dir of public and private companies, retired. MP (C) Portsmouth West, 1950–66; contested (C) Portsmouth West, 1966, 1970. *Recreations:* capped six times for the Army at Rugby and boxed heavyweight for Army; sailing, ski-ing, horse racing. *Died 26 May 1992.*

CLARKE, Tom; freelance screenwriter, playwright; *b* 7 Nov. 1918; *s* of Herman C. Clarke and May Dora Carter; *m* 1st, 1945, B. D. Gordon; one *s* three *d*; 2nd, 1953, J. I. Hampton; two *s*; 3rd, 1960, Ann Wiltshire; one *d*. *Educ:* Tonbridge School. Served War, Royal Artillery, 1939–46 (Captain). Called to the Bar, Gray's Inn, 1951. Freelance writer, 1958–. TV plays and films include: Mad Jack, 1971; Stocker's Copper, 1972; Billion Dollar Bubble, 1975; Muck and Brass, 1982; Past Caring, 1986; stage play, Come Again, 1983. Grand Prize, Monte Carlo TV Festival, 1972; UNRRA Silver Dove, 1972; Mention d'Honneur, Prague TV Festival, 1973; Writer's Guild Award, 1973; BAFTA Award, 1973; Mention d'Honneur, Venice Film Festival, 1985; Best Screenplay, Prague TV Fest., 1987. *Recreations:* nursing hypochondria, awaiting fulfilment of optimistic astrological predictions. *Address:* c/o Judy Daish Associates, 83 Eastbourne Mews, W2 6LQ. *T:* 071–262 1101. *Died 15 Jan. 1993.*

CLAVELL, James du Maresq; author, screenwriter, film director and producer; *b* 10 Oct. 1924; *s* of late Comdr R. C. Clavell, OBE, RN and Eileen Ross Clavell; *m* 1953, April, *d* of late Comdr W. S. Stride, DSO, RN; two *d. Educ:* Portsmouth Grammar Sch. Served World War II, Captain, RA; POW Far East, 1941–45. Emigrated to USA, 1953. Screenwriter: The Fly, 1958; Watussi, 1958; The Great Escape, 1960; Satan Bug, 1962; 633 Squadron, 1963; director, Where's Jack?, 1968; writer/producer/director: Five Gates to Hell, 1959; Walk Like a Dragon, 1960; To Sir with Love, 1966; Last Valley, 1969; Children's Story . . . But Not for Children, 1982; exec. producer, Shōgun (TV series), 1980 (Emmy, Peabody, Critics, Golden Globe Awards, 1981); Noble House (TV series), 1986; producer, Shōgun (musical), 1990. Pilot: Multi-engine, Instrument Rating, Helicopter. Hon. DLitt: Maryland, 1980; Bradford, 1986. Goldener Eiger (Austria), 1972. *Publications:* King Rat, 1962; Tai-Pan, 1966; Shōgun, 1976; Noble House, 1980; The Children's Story but not for Children (novella), 1982; (foreword to) Sun Tsu; the Art of War, 1983; Thrump-O-moto (fantasy), 1985; Whirlwind, 1986; Gai-Jin, 1993. *Address:* c/o Foreign Rights, Inc., 60 Arch Street, Greenwich, Connecticut, USA.
Died 6 Sept. 1994.

CLAXTON, Rt Rev. Charles Robert, MA, DD; *b* 16 Nov. 1903; *s* of Herbert Bailey and Frances Ann Claxton; *m* 1930, Agnes Jane Stevenson; two *s* two *d. Educ:* Monkton Combe Sch.; Weymouth Coll.; Queens' Coll., Cambridge. Deacon, 1927; priest, 1928; Curate: St John's, Stratford, E15, 1927–29; St John, Redhill, 1929–33; St Martin-in-the-Fields, 1944–46; Vicar, Holy Trinity, Bristol, 1933–38; Hon. Canon of Bristol Cathedral, 1942–46; Hon. Chaplain to Bishop of Bristol, 1938–46; Hon. Chaplain to Bishop of Rochester, 1943–46; Rector of Halsall, near Ormskirk, Lancs, 1948–59; Suffragan Bishop of Warrington, 1946–60; Bishop of Blackburn, 1960–71; Asst Bishop, dio. of Exeter, 1972–89. Hon. Officiating Chaplain, RN, 1978. *Recreation:* golf. *Address:* St Martins, 18 Prestbury Park, Collar House Drive, Prestbury, Cheshire SK10 4AP. *T:* Prestbury (0625) 829864.
Died 7 March 1992.

CLAXTON, John Francis, CB 1969; Deputy Director of Public Prosecutions 1966–71; *b* 11 Jan. 1911; *s* of late Alfred John Claxton, OBE, and Dorothy Frances O. Claxton (*née* Roberts); *m* 1937, Norma Margaret Rawlinson (*d* 1983); no *c. Educ:* Tonbridge Sch.; Exeter Coll., Oxford (BA). Called to Bar, 1935. Joined Dept of Dir of Public Prosecutions, 1937; Asst Dir, 1956–66. *Recreations:* model making, gardening. *Address:* White Lodge, Bisham Road, Marlow, Bucks SL7 7RP. *T:* Marlow (0628) 898462; (office) Marlow (0628) 898281.
Died 18 Jan. 1991.

CLAY, Trevor Reginald, CBE 1990; MPhil; RN; FRCN; General Secretary to the Royal College of Nursing of the United Kingdom, 1982–89 (Deputy General Secretary, 1979–82); *b* 10 May 1936; *s* of Joseph Reginald George and Florence Emma Clay. *Educ:* Nuneaton and Bethlem Royal and Maudsley Hosps (SRN 1957; RMN 1960). MPhil Brunel Univ. 1976. FRCN 1985. Staff Nurse and Charge Nurse, Guy's Hosp., London, 1960–65; Asst Matron in charge of Psychiatric Unit, Queen Elizabeth II Hosp., Welwyn Garden City, 1965–67; Asst Regional Nursing Officer, NW Metropolitan Regional Hosp. Board, 1967–69; Director of Nursing, Whittington Hosp., London, 1969–70; Chief Nursing Officer, N London Group HMC, 1970–74; Area Nursing Officer, Camden and Islington Area Health Authority, 1974–79. First Vice-Pres., Internat. Council of Nurses, 1989–93 (Mem. Bd, 1985–89); Member: Council, Royal Nat. Pension Fund for Nurses, 1989–; Council, British Lung Foundn, 1989–; Non-exec. Mem., Whittington Hosp. Bd, 1993–. Pres., Breathe Easy, 1991–. Patron, London Lighthouse, 1992–. Hon. DArt Bristol Polytechnic, 1990. *Publications:* Nurses: power and politics, 1987; thesis on The Workings of the Nursing and Midwifery Advisory Committees in the NHS since 1974; various articles on nursing and health care. *Recreations:* breathing, good friends, Mozart and Sondheim. *Address:* c/o The Royal College of Nursing, 20 Cavendish Square, W1M 0AB.
Died 23 April 1994.

CLAYTON, Air Marshal Sir Gareth (Thomas Butler), KCB 1970 (CB 1962); DFC 1940, and Bar, 1944; Air Secretary, Ministry of Defence, 1970–72, retired; *b* 13 Nov. 1914; *s* of Thomas and Katherine Clayton; *m* 1938, Elisabeth Marian Keates (*d* 1990); three *d. Educ:* Rossall Sch. Entered RAF, 1936; served in various Bomber and Fighter Squadrons, 1936–44; RAF Staff Coll., 1944; Air Attaché, Lisbon, 1946–48; various command and staff appts, 1948–58; idc 1959; Air Ministry, 1960–61; Air Officer Commanding No 11 Group, RAF, 1962–63; Chief of Staff, Second Allied Tactical Air Force, Germany, 1963–66; Dir-Gen., RAF Personal Services, 1966–69; Chief of Staff, HQ RAF Strike Command, 1969–70. Life Vice-Pres., RAFA (Chm., 1978–80). *Address:* Polstead, near Colchester CO6 5AD. *Club:* Royal Air Force.
Died 5 Feb. 1992.

CLAYTON, Jack; film director; *b* 1 March 1921; *m* 1st, Christine Norden (marr. diss.); 2nd, Katherine Kath (marr. diss.); 3rd, Haya Harareet. Entered film industry, 1935. Served War of 1939–45, RAF Film Unit. Production Manager, An Ideal Husband, 1947; Associate Producer: Queen of Spades, 1948; Flesh and Blood; Moulin Rouge, 1952; Beat the Devil; The Good Die Young; I am a Camera, 1955; Producer and Director: The Bespoke Overcoat, 1955; The Innocents, 1961; Our Mother's House, 1967; Director: Room at the Top, 1958; The Pumpkin Eater, 1964; The Great Gatsby, 1974; Something Wicked This Way Comes, 1983; The Lonely Passion of Judith Hearne, 1989. *Address:* c/o Batya Films, Heron's Flight, Highfield, Marlow, Bucks SL7 2LE.
Died 25 Feb. 1995.

CLAYTON, Michael Thomas Emilius, CB 1976; OBE 1958; *b* 15 Sept. 1917; *s* of Lt-Col Emilius Clayton, OBE, RA and Irene Dorothy Constance (*née* Strong); *m* 1942, Mary Margery Pate (*d* 1994); one *d. Educ:* Bradfield College, Berks. Attached War Office, 1939 and Ministry of Defence, 1964–76. *Recreations:* philately, country pursuits generally. *Address:* Hillside Cottage, Marshwood, Bridport, Dorset DT6 5QF. *T:* Hawkchurch (01297) 678452. *Died 27 May 1995.*

CLAYTON, Richard Henry Michael, (William Haggard); writer; *b* 11 Aug. 1907; *o s* of late Rev. Henry James Clayton and Mabel Sarah Clayton (*née* Haggard); *m* 1936, Barbara (*d* 1989), *e d* of late Edward Sant, Downton, Wilts; one *s* one *d. Educ:* Lancing; Christ Church, Oxford. Indian Civil Service, 1931–39; Indian Army, 1939–46 (GS01 1943); BoT, 1947–69 (Controller of Enemy Property, 1965–69). *Publications:* Slow Burner, The Telemann Touch, 1958; Venetian Blind, 1959; Closed Circuit, 1960; The Arena, 1961; The Unquiet Sleep, 1962; The High Wire, 1963; The Antagonists, 1964; The Hard Sell, The Powder Barrel, 1965; The Power House, 1966;

The Conspirators, The Haggard Omnibus, 1967; A Cool Day For Killing, 1968; The Doubtful Disciple, Haggard For Your Holiday, 1969; The Hardliners, 1970; The Bitter Harvest, 1971; The Protectors, 1972; The Little Rug Book (non-fiction), 1972; The Old Masters, 1973; The Kinsmen, 1974; The Scorpion's Tail, 1975; Yesterday's Enemy, 1976; The Poison People, 1977; Visa to Limbo, 1978; The Median Line, 1979; The Money Men, 1981; The Mischief Makers, 1982; The Heirloom, 1983; The Need to Know, 1984; The Meritocrats, 1985; The Martello Tower, 1986; The Diplomatist, 1987; The Expatriates, 1989; The Vendettists, 1990. *Address:* 3 Linkside, Frinton-on-Sea, Essex CO13 9EN. *Club:* Travellers'.

Died 27 Oct. 1993.

CLEARY, Rt Rev. Joseph Francis; Auxiliary Bishop of Birmingham, (RC), 1965–87; Titular Bishop of Cresima; *b* 4 Sept. 1912; *s* of William Cleary and Ellen (*née* Rogers). *Educ:* Dublin; Oscott Coll., Sutton Coldfield. Ordained priest, 1939. Asst, St Chad's Cathedral, 1939–41; Archbishop's Sec., 1941–51; Parish Priest, SS Mary and John's, Wolverhampton, 1951–; Diocesan Treasurer, 1963–65; Provost of Diocesan Chapter, 1966–88. Pres., RC Internat. Justice and Peace Commn of England and Wales, 1978–80. *Address:* Presbytery, Snow Hill, Wolverhampton WV2 4AD. *T:* Wolverhampton (0902) 21676.   *Died 25 Feb. 1991.*

CLEARY, Sir Joseph Jackson, Kt 1965; *b* 26 Oct. 1902; *s* of Joseph Cleary, JP; *m* 1945, Ethel McColl. *Educ:* Holy Trinity C of E Sch., Anfield, Liverpool; Skerry's Coll., Liverpool. Alderman 1941, JP 1927, for Liverpool; Lord Mayor of Liverpool, 1949–50. Contested East Toxteth Div., Liverpool, March 1929 and May 1929; West Derby, Oct. 1931; MP (Lab) Wavertree Div. of Liverpool, Feb.-Oct. 1935. Lecture tour to Forces in Middle East, 1945. Freeman, City of Liverpool, 1970. *Recreations:* football (Association), tennis. *Address:* 115 Riverview Heights, Liverpool L19 0LQ. *T:* 051–427 2133.

Died 9 Feb. 1993.

CLEAVER, Leonard Harry, JP; FCA; *b* 27 Oct. 1909; *s* of late Harry Cleaver, OBE, JP; *m* 1938, Mary Richards Matthews; one *s. Educ:* Bilton Grange; Rugby. Chartered Accountant: articled Agar, Bates, Neal & Co., Birmingham; Sec. and Chief Accountant, Chance Bros Ltd, 1935–51; Partner, Heathcote & Coleman, 1951–59. MP (C) Yardley Div. of Birmingham, 1959–64; PPS to Parly Sec. to Min. of Housing and Local Govt, 1963–64; contested Yardley Div. of Birmingham, 1964, 1966. Member: Smethwick Nat. Savings Cttee, 1939–45; Birmingham Probation Cttee, 1955–73; Central Council, Probation and After-Care Cttees for England and Wales, 1966–73. Treasurer: Deritend Unionist Assoc., 1945–48; Yardley Div. Unionist Assoc., 1971–73 (Chm., 1973–74). Governor, Yardley Educnl Foundn, 1966–70. JP Birmingham, 1954; City Councillor, Birmingham, 1966–70. *Recreations:* Rugby football, fishing, philately. *Address:* 6 The Retreat, Leamington Road, Broadway, Worcs WR12 7DZ. *T:* Broadway (0386) 852090.

Died 7 July 1993.

CLEGG, Prof. Hugh Armstrong; Emeritus Professor of Industrial Relations, University of Warwick, since 1983; *b* 22 May 1920; *s* of late Rev. Herbert Hobson Clegg and of Mabel (*née* Duckering); *m* 1941, Mary Matilda (*née* Shaw); two *s* two *d. Educ:* Kingswood Sch., Bath; Magdalen Coll., Oxford. Served War, 1940–45; Official Fellow, Nuffield Coll., Oxford, 1949–66, Emeritus Fellow, 1966–; Prof. of Industrial Relns, Univ. of Warwick, 1967–79, Titular Prof. and Leverhulme Res. Fellow, 1979–83. Chm., Civil Service Arbitration Tribunal, 1968–71; Dir, Industrial Relations Res. Unit, SSRC, 1970–74; Member: Royal Commn on Trade Unions and Employers' Assocs, 1965–68; Cttee of Inquiry into Port

Transport Industry, 1964–65; Ct of Inquiry into Seamen's Dispute, 1966–67; Nat. Board for Prices and Incomes, 1966–67; Ct of Inquiry into Local Authorities' Manual Workers' Pay Dispute, 1970; Council, ACAS, 1974–79; Chm., Standing Commn on Pay Comparability, 1979–80. Hon. DLitt Warwick, 1987. *Publications:* Labour Relations in London Transport, 1950; Industrial Democracy and Nationalisation, 1951; The Future of Nationalisation (with T. E. Chester), 1953; General Union, 1954; Wage Policy in the Health Service (with T. E. Chester), 1957; The Employers' Challenge (with R. Adams), 1957; A New Approach to Industrial Democracy, 1960; Trade Union Officers (with A. J. Killick and R. Adams), 1961; General Union in a Changing Society, 1964; A History of British Trade Unions: Vol. I (with A. Fox and A. F. Thompson), 1964, Vol. II, 1985, vol. III, 1994; The System of Industrial Relations in Great Britain, 1970; How to run an Incomes Policy and Why we made such a Mess of the Last One, 1971; Workplace and Union (with I. Boraston and M. Rimmer), 1975; Trade Unionism under Collective Bargaining, 1976; The Changing System of Industrial Relations in Great Britain, 1979. *Recreations:* walking, beer. *Address:* 7 John Nash Square, Regency Drive, Kenilworth, Warwicks CV8 1JE. *T:* Kenilworth (01926) 50794.   *Died 9 Dec. 1995.*

CLEGG, Ronald Anthony, (Tony), OBE 1995; Chairman, United Leeds Teaching Hospitals NHS Trust, since 1990; *b* 8 April 1937; *s* of Stanley and Cicely Clegg; *m* 1963, Dorothy Eve Glaze; three *d. Educ:* Bickerton House, Southport, Lancs. Joined Mountain Mills Co. Ltd as manager, 1961; Dir, 1963; Dir, Leigh Mills Co. Ltd (a publicly quoted co.), when Mountain Gp merged with it, 1966; Jt Man. Dir, Leigh Mills Co. Ltd, 1972, subseq. Mountleigh Gp, Chm. and Chief Exec., 1983–89. Chm., E & F Securities, 1978–. Member: Develt Bd, Cancer Relief Macmillan Fund, 1991–; Council, Critical Care Trust, 1992–; Special Trustee, Leeds Teaching Hosps, 1992–; Dep. Chm. and Trustee, Prince's Youth Business Trust, 1990–. Mem. Court, Univ. of Leeds, 1992–. Governor: Royal Agricl Coll., 1991–; Nat. Children's Orchestra, 1992–. Chm., Appeal Cttee, Dales Countryside Mus. and Educn Centre, 1990–; Mem. Council, Yorks Agricl Soc., 1984–; Patron: Leeds Br., Riding for the Disabled, 1989–; Marrick Priory Appeal, 1992–. FInstD; CIMgt. Liveryman: Co. of Turners; Co. of Woolmen. *Recreations:* equestrian sport, music, antiques, architecture. *Address:* Low Farm, Stammergate Lane, Linton, Wetherby LS22 4JB. *Clubs:* Carlton, Mark's.

Died 1 June 1995.

CLEGG, Sir Walter, Kt 1980; *b* 18 April 1920; *s* of Edwin Clegg; *m* 1951, Elise Margaret Hargreaves (*d* 1993). *Educ:* Bury Grammar Sch.; Arnold Sch., Blackpool; Manchester Univ. Law Sch. Served in Royal Artillery, 1939–46 (commnd 1940). Articled to Town Clerk, Barrow-in-Furness, 1937; qualified as Solicitor, 1947; subsequently in practice. Lancashire CC, 1955–61. MP (C): N Fylde, 1966–83; Wyre, 1983–87; Opposition Whip, 1967–69; a Lord Comr, HM Treasury, 1970–72; Vice-Chamberlain, HM Household, 1972–73, Comptroller, 1973–74; an Opposition Whip, March-Oct. 1974. Hon. Sec., Cons. Housing and Local Govt Cttee, 1968–69; Mem. Exec., 1922 Cttee, 1975–76, Hon. Treasurer, 1976–87; Chm., Cons. NW Members Group, 1977–87; Mem. Exec., IPU, 1980–85, CPA, 1980–85; Chm., Parly All-Party Solicitors Gp, 1979–87; Vice-Chm., Assoc. of Conservative Clubs, 1969–71, Pres. 1977–78, Vice-Pres. 1982; Pres., Cons. NW Provincial Area, 1982–. Pres., Central and W Lancs Chamber of Commerce, 1981. *Recreation:* reading. *Address:* Beech House, Raikes Road, Little Thornton, near Blackpool, Lancs FY5 5LU. *T:* Cleveleys (0253) 826131. *Club:* Garrick.   *Died 15 April 1994.*

CLEMENTS, Rt Rev. Kenneth John; *b* 21 Dec. 1905; *s* of John Edwin Clements and Ethel Evelyn Clark; *m* 1935, Rosalind Elizabeth Cakebread; one *s* two *d. Educ:* Highgate Sch., London; St Paul's Coll., University of Sydney. BA (Hons) 1933; ThD 1949. Ordained deacon, 1933; priest, 1934; Registrar, Diocese of Riverina, 1933–37; Rector: Narrandera, NSW, 1937–39; Tumbarumba, NSW, 1939–43; Gunning, NSW, 1943–44; Director of Studies, Canberra Grammar Sch., Canberra, ACT, 1945; Registrar, Diocese of Canberra and Goulburn, 1946–56; Archdeacon of Goulburn, 1946–56; Asst Bishop of Canberra and Goulburn, 1949–56; Bishop of Grafton, NSW, 1956–61; Bishop of Canberra and Goulburn, 1961–71; retired, 1971. *Address:* 5 Quorn Close, Buderim, Qld 4556, Australia.   *Died 8 Jan. 1992.*

CLIFFORD-TURNER, Raymond; solicitor; Senior Partner, Clifford-Turner, 1941–81; *b* 7 Feb. 1906; *s* of Harry Clifford-Turner, solicitor; *m* 1st, 1933, Zoë Vachell (*d* 1984); one *s* two *d*; 2nd, 1988, Diana Dumergue Edwards. *Educ:* Rugby Sch.; Trinity Coll., Cambridge. Solicitor, 1930; Partner, Clifford-Turner & Co., 1931. Dir, Transport Holding Co., 1962–73. Wing Commander, RAFVR. *Recreations:* golf, racing. *Address:* Garden Flat, 86 Eaton Place, SW1X 8LN. *T:* 0171–235 2443; Childown, Longcross, near Chertsey, Surrey KT16 0EH. *T:* Ottershaw (01932) 872608. *Clubs:* Portland; Berkshire; Swinley.   *Died 18 April 1995.*

CLODE, Dame (Emma) Frances (Heather), DBE 1974 (CBE 1969; OBE 1955; MBE 1951); Chairman, Women's Royal Voluntary Service, 1971–74; *b* 12 Aug. 1903; *d* of Alexander and Florence Marc; *m* 1927, Capt. (later Col) Charles Mathew Clode, MC (decd), Royal Norfolk Regt, *s* of Sir Walter Baker Clode, KC; one *s. Educ:* privately. Joined WRVS, 1939; served in Cambridge, 1940–45; WRVS Headquarters, 1945; Vice-Chm. 1967. CStJ 1973. *Address:* 19 Rusher's Close, Pershore, Worcs WR10 1HF.   *Died 10 Sept. 1994.*

CLOVER, His Honour (Robert) Gordon, TD 1951; QC 1958; JP; a Circuit Judge (formerly Judge of County Courts), 1965–82; *b* 14 Nov. 1911; *s* of Lt-Col Henry Edward Clover and Catherine Clifford Clover; *m* 1947, Elizabeth Suzanne (*née* McCorquodale); two *s. Educ:* Lancing Coll.; Exeter Coll., Oxford. MA, BCL Oxford. Called to Bar, Lincoln's Inn, 1935. Served in RA, 1939–45 (despatches, 1944). Practised on Northern Circuit, 1935–61; Recorder of Blackpool, 1960–61; Dep. Comr for purposes of Nat. Insurance Acts, 1961–65; Dep. Chm., Bucks QS, 1969–71; Chm., Marlow Magistrates Court, 1972–79. JP Bucks, 1969. *Address:* 10 Westcliff, Sheringham, Norfolk NR26 8JT.

Died 25 July 1993.

CLOWES, Col Sir Henry (Nelson), KCVO 1981 (CVO 1977); DSO 1945; OBE 1953; *b* 21 Oct. 1911; *yr s* of late Major E. W. Clowes, DSO, Bradley Hall, Ashbourne, Derbys; *m* 1941, Diana Katharine, MBE, *er d* of late Major Basil Kerr, DSC; one *s. Educ:* Eton; Sandhurst. Served in Scots Guards, 1931–57: Adjt RMA Sandhurst, 1940–41; psc 1941; Bde Major 4th Inf. Bde, 1942–44; comd 2nd Bn Scots Guards, 1944–46; jssc 1947; comd 1st Bn Scots Guards, 1947–50; War Office (AG4), 1950–52; AAG Scottish Comd, 1952–54; Lt-Col comdg Scots Guards, 1954–57; retired 1957. Mem., HM Body Guard for Scotland, 1961: Clerk of the Cheque and Adjt, 1966; Standard Bearer, 1973–76; Lieut, 1976–81. *Recreations:* shooting, fishing. *Address:* 57 Perrymead Street, SW6 3SN. *T:* 071–736 7901. *Clubs:* Cavalry and Guards, Pratt's, Shikar.   *Died 8 Jan. 1993.*

CLUTTERBUCK, Edmund Harry Michael, OBE 1957; Director, Scottish & Newcastle Breweries Ltd, 1960–80 (Deputy Chairman, 1973–77); *b* 22 July 1920; *s* of late Maj.-Gen. Walter Edmond Clutterbuck, DSO, MC; *m* 1945, Anne Agatha Woodsend; one *s* three *d. Educ:* Winchester Coll.; New Coll., Oxford (MA). HM Forces, 1940–46. Joined William Younger & Co. Ltd, 1947; Dir, Scottish Brewers Ltd, 1955; Scottish & Newcastle Breweries Ltd: Techn. Man. Dir, 1965; Jt Man. Dir, 1970; Director: Scottish American Mortgage Co., 1962; Scottish Eastern Investment Trust, 1965; Scottish Widows' Fund, 1965 (Chm., 1979–81; Dep. Chm., 1981–82). Pres., European Brewery Convention, 1971. Member: Heriot-Watt Univ. Court, 1959; Herring Industry Bd, 1963–81; White Fish Authority, 1973–81; Dep. Chm., Royal Inst. of Internat. Affairs (Scottish Br.), 1969. *Recreations:* music, fishing, shooting, travel, languages. *Address:* 5 Moray Place, Edinburgh EH3 6DS. *Club:* New (Edinburgh).   *Died 20 Feb. 1991.*

CLUTTON-BROCK, (Arthur) Guy; independent social worker, 1965–72, retired; *b* 5 April 1906; *s* of late Henry Alan Clutton-Brock and Rosa Clutton-Brock; *m* 1934, Francys Mary Allen; one *d. Educ:* Rugby Sch.; Magdalene Coll., Cambridge (Hon. Fellow, 1973). Cambridge House, 1927; Rugby House, 1929; Borstal Service, 1933; Principal Probation Officer for the Metropolitan Police Court District, 1936; Head of Oxford House, 1940; Christian Reconstruction in Europe, 1946; Agricultural Labourer, 1947; Agriculturalist at St Faith's Mission, 1949; Field Worker of African Development Trust, 1959–65; deported from Rhodesia by rebel regime, 1971. Treasurer, Cold Comfort Farm Soc., 1966. *Publications:* Dawn in Nyasaland, 1959; Cold Comfort Confronted, 1973. *Address:* 10 Wynne's Parc Cottages, Brookhouse Road, Denbigh, Clwyd LL16 4YB.   *Died 29 Jan. 1995.*

COATES, Sir Ernest (William), Kt 1973; CMG 1970; State Director of Finance and Permanent Head of Victoria Treasury, Australia, 1959–77; *b* 30 Nov. 1916; *s* of Thomas Atlee Coates; *m* 1st, 1943, Phylis E. Morris (*d* 1971); one *s* three *d*; 2nd, 1974, Patricia Ann (*d* 1986), *d* of late C. A. Fisher, Herts. *Educ:* Ballarat High Sch.; Univ. of Melbourne. BCom. Member: Bd of State Savings Bank of Victoria, 1960–77; Nat. Debt Commn, Australia, 1963–78; Australian Universities Commn, 1968–77; Aust. Administrative Appeals Tribunal, 1978–86. Dir, Equity Trustees Executors and Agency Co. Ltd, 1978–89. Chairman: Australian Selection Cttee, Harkness Fellowships, 1975–83; Rhodes Scholarship Selection Cttee (Victoria), 1981 (Mem., 1977–81). Hon. LLD Melbourne, 1979. *Recreations:* golf, music. *Address:* 64 Molesworth Street, Kew, Victoria 3101, Australia. *T:* 8538226. *Club:* Melbourne (Melbourne).

Died 10 Feb. 1994.

COATES, Brig. Sir Frederick (Gregory Lindsay), 2nd Bt *cr* 1921, of Haypark, City of Belfast; *b* 19 May 1916; *o s* of Sir William Frederick Coates, 1st Bt, Belfast, N Ireland, and Elsie Millicent (*d* 1958), *yr d* of Col Frederick William Gregory, Essex Regt; *S* father, 1932; *m* 1940, Joan Nugent, *d* of late Maj.-Gen. Sir Charlton Spinks, KBE, DSO; one *s* two *d. Educ:* Eton; Sandhurst. Commissioned Royal Tank Regt, 1936; served War of 1939–45, North Africa and NW Europe (wounded twice); Min. of Supply, 1947–53; Asst Military Attaché, Stockholm, 1953–56; British Joint Services Mission, Washington, 1956–58; Comdt, RAC School of Tank Technology, 1958–61; Asst Dir of Fighting Vehicles, and Col GS, War Office and MoD, 1961–66; Brig., British Defence Staff, Washington, DC, 1966–69; Mil. Dep. to Head of Defence Sales, 1969–71; retired 1971. *Heir: s* David Charlton Frederick Coates [*b* 16 Feb. 1948; *m* 1973, Christine Helen, *d* of Lewis F. Marshall; two *s*]. *Address:* Launchfield, Briantspuddle, Dorchester, Dorset DT2 7HN. *Clubs:* Royal Ocean Racing; Royal Yacht Squadron; Royal Motor

Yacht; Royal Lymington Yacht; Island Sailing; Royal Armoured Corps Yacht. *Died 23 June 1994.*

COBBOLD, (Michael) David (Nevill), CBE 1983; DL; MA; Consultant, Beachcroft Stanleys (formerly Beachcrofts), Solicitors, since 1983; Senior Partner, Stileman Neate & Topping, 1959–83; *b* 21 Oct. 1919; *s* of late Geoffrey Wyndham Nevill Cobbold and Cicely Helen Cobbold; *m* 1949, Ann Rosemary Trevor; two *s* one *d* (and one *s* decd). *Educ:* Charterhouse; New Coll., Oxford (MA); RMA, Sandhurst. War of 1939–45: commissioned and served with 2nd Bn, The Buffs, 1940–45. Admitted Solicitor, 1949. Westminster City Council: Member, 1949–86; Leader, 1964–65, 1976–83; Alderman, 1962–78; Mayor of Westminster, 1958–59; Lord Mayor and Dep. High Steward of Westminster, 1973–74. London Boroughs Association: Hon. Treas., 1977–84; Chm., Gen. Purposes Cttee, 1978–86; Dep. Chm., 1984–86. Chairman: London Boroughs Grants Cttee, 1985–86; London Area Social Responsibility Cttee, 1988–92; Member: DoE Housing Act Gp, 1970–76; Adv. Cttee on Local Govt Audit, 1979–82; Royal Parks Constabulary Cttee, 1985–89. Pres., Beckenham Conservative Assoc., 1974–91. DL Greater London, 1967. *Recreations:* watching grandchildren and weeds grow: encouraging the former, discouraging the latter. *Address:* Tudor House, Childrey, Wantage OX12 9XQ.
     Died 2 Feb. 1994.

COBBOLD, Patrick Mark; *b* 20 June 1934; *s* of late Captain J. M. Cobbold and Lady Blanche Cobbold, 2nd *d* of 9th Duke of Devonshire. *Educ:* Eton. Served Scots Guards, 1953–57; ADC to the Governor of the Bahamas, 1957–60; Tolly Cobbold Breweries, 1961–89. Chm., Ipswich Town FC, 1976–90. *Recreations:* fishing, shooting, football. *Address:* Glemham Hall, Woodbridge, Suffolk IP13 0BT. *T:* Wickham Market (01728) 746219. *Clubs:* White's, Pratt's. *Died 16 Dec. 1994.*

COBURN, Prof. Kathleen, OC 1974; Professor of English, Victoria College, University of Toronto, 1953–71, then Emeritus; author; *b* 7 Sept. 1905; *d* of Rev. John Coburn and Susannah Coburn. *Educ:* University of Toronto (MA); Oxford University (BLitt). Imperial Order of the Daughters of the Empire Travelling Scholarship, 1930–31. Formerly Lectr, Asst Prof., and Associate Prof. of English, Victoria College, University of Toronto. University Women's Internat. Senior Fellowship, 1948–49; John Simon Guggenheim Memorial Fellowship, 1953–54, renewed, 1957–58; Commonwealth Visiting Fellowship (Univ. of London), 1962–63. FRSC 1958. Hon. Fellow, St Hugh's Coll., Oxford, 1970; Hon. Fellow, Champlain Coll., Trent Univ., Ont, 1972; Corresp. FBA 1973. DHL: Haverford, 1972; Princeton, 1983; Hon. LLD Queen's Univ., Kingston, Ontario, 1964; Hon. DLitt: Trent Univ., 1972; Cambridge, 1975; Toronto, 1978; Hon. DSL Toronto, 1986. Rose Mary Crawshay Prize for English Literature, Brit. Acad., 1958, 1990; Chauveau Medal, RSC. *Publications:* (ed) The Philosophical Lectures of S. T. Coleridge, 1949; Inquiring Spirit, 1951, rev. edn 1979; (ed) The Letters of Sara Hutchinson, 1954; (ed) The Notebooks of S. T. Coleridge, vol. i, 1957, vol. ii, 1961, vol. iii, 1973, vol. iv, 1990; Coleridge: a Collection of Critical Essays, 1967; The Self-Conscious Imagination (Riddell Meml Lectures), 1972; Coleridge, a Bridge Between Science and Poetry: reflections on the bicentenary of his birth, Discourse, Royal Institution, 1972; In Pursuit of Coleridge, 1977; Experience into Thought: perspectives in the Coleridge notebooks, Alexander Lectures, 1979; general editor, The Collected Coleridge, 1968–. *Address:* Victoria College, 73 Queen's Park Crescent, Toronto, Ontario M5S 1K7, Canada. *Died 23 Sept. 1991.*

COCKBURN, Sir Robert, KBE 1960 (OBE 1946); CB 1953; PhD, MSc, MA; FEng 1977; FInstP; Senior Research Fellow, Churchill College, Cambridge, 1970–77; Chairman, National Computing Centre, 1970–77; *b* 31 March 1909; 2nd *s* of late Rev. R. T. Cockburn, Columba Manse, Belford, Northumberland; *m* 1935, Phyllis Hoyland; two *d. Educ:* Southern Secondary Sch. and Municipal Coll., Portsmouth; London Univ. BSc 1928, MSc 1935, PhD 1939, London; MA Cantab, 1973. Taught science at West Ham Municipal Coll., 1930–37; research in communications at RAE Farnborough, 1937–39; in radar at TRE Malvern, Worcs, 1939–45; in atomic energy at AERE Harwell, 1945–48; Scientific Adviser to Air Min., 1948–53; Prin. Dir of Scientific Research (Guided Weapons and Electronics), Ministry of Supply, 1954–55; Deputy Controller of Electronics, Ministry of Supply, 1955–56; Controller of Guided Weapons and Electronics, Ministry of Supply, 1956–59; Chief Scientist of Ministry of Aviation, 1959–64; Dir, RAE Farnborough, 1964–69. Chairman: Television Adv. Cttee for Posts and Telecommunications, 1971–73; BBC Engineering Adv. Cttee, 1973–81. Hon. FRAeS 1970. Congressional Medal for Merit, 1947. *Publications:* scientific papers. *Recreations:* sailing, modelling. *Address:* 1 Firethorn Close, Longmead, Fleet, Hants GU13 9TR. *T:* Fleet (0252) 615518. *Clubs:* Athenæum; Offshore Cruising.
     Died 21 March 1994.

COHEN, His Honour Arthur; *see* Cohen, His Honour N. A. J.

COHEN, Sir Bernard Nathaniel W.; *see* Waley-Cohen.

COHEN, His Honour (Nathaniel) Arthur (Jim), JP; County Court Judge, Circuit No 38, 1955–56, Circuit No 43, 1956–60, Circuit No 56, 1960–70, retired; *b* 19 Jan. 1898; 2nd *s* of late Sir Benjamin Arthur Cohen, KC, and Lady Cohen; *m* 1st, 1927, Judith Luard (marr. diss.); one *s* (and one *s* decd); 2nd, 1936, Joyce Collingridge. *Educ:* Rugby; CCC, Oxford (BA). Served European War, 1916–19, Royal Navy. Called to Bar, Inner Temple, 1923. War of 1939–45: recalled to RN and placed on Emergency List with rank of Commander. Legal Adviser to UNRRA, 1946–49; Dep. Chm., Foreign Compensation Commn, 1950–55. JP Surrey, 1958. *Recreations:* golf, music. *Address:* Bay Tree Cottage, Crockham Hill, Edenbridge, Kent. *Club:* United Oxford & Cambridge University.
     Died 11 June 1995.

COHEN, Ruth Louisa, CBE 1969; MA; Principal, Newnham College, Cambridge, 1954–72; University Lecturer in Economics, Cambridge, 1945–74; *b* 10 Nov. 1906; *d* of late Walter Samuel Cohen and Lucy Margaret Cohen. *Educ:* Hayes Court, Kent; Newnham Coll., Cambridge. Commonwealth Fund Fellow, Stanford and Cornell Univs, USA, 1930–32; Research Officer, Agricultural Economics Research Inst., Oxford, 1933–39; Fellow of Newnham Coll., Cambridge, 1939–54; Min. of Food, 1939–42; Board of Trade, 1942–45. Lay Mem., Gen. Medical Council, 1961–76. City Cllr, Cambridge, 1973–87. *Publications:* History of Milk Prices, 1936; Economics of Agriculture, 1939; articles in Economic Journal, etc. *Address:* 2 Croft Lodge, Cambridge CB3 9LA. *T:* Cambridge (0223) 62699. *Club:* University Women's. *Died 27 July 1991.*

COLAHAN, Air Vice-Marshal William Edward, CB 1978; CBE 1973; DFC 1945; Royal Air Force, retired; Member, Lord Chancellor's Panel of Independent Inquiry Inspectors, since 1983; *b* 7 Aug. 1923; *er s* of Dr W. E. and Dr G. C. J. Colahan; *m* 1949, Kathleen Anne Butler; one *s* two *d. Educ:* Templeton High Sch., S Africa; Univ. of Cape Town. S African Air Force, 1941–46: service in Italy, France (Temp. Captain); Royal Air Force, 1947–83: Flt-Lt 1947; Sqdn Ldr 1952; psa 1957; Wing Comdr 1959; jssc 1962; Gp Captain 1965; Air Cdr 1970; idc 1970; Air Comdr Malta, 1971–73; Air Vice-Marshal 1973; ACAS

(Operations), 1973–75; AOC and Commandant, RAF College Cranwell, 1975–78; Officer Careers Counsellor (RAF), 1978–83. Mem. Council, St Dunstans, 1978–. Vice Chm. (Air), E Midlands TAVRA, 1983–88; Comdr, St John Ambulance, Lincs, 1985–88. OStJ 1986. *Club:* Royal Air Force.   *Died 20 Feb. 1991.*

COLBECK-WELCH, Air Vice-Marshal Edward Lawrence, CB 1961; OBE 1948; DFC 1941; Royal Air Force, retired; *b* 29 Jan. 1914; *s* of Major G. S. M. Colbeck-Welch, MC, Collingham, Yorks; *m* 1938, Doreen (*d* 1988), *d* of T. G. Jenkin, Sliema, Malta; one *s* two *d.* *Educ:* Leeds Grammar Sch. Commnd RAF, 1933; No 22 Sqdn, RAF, 1934–37; CFS Instructor Course, 1937; Flying Instr RAuxAF Sqdns, 1937–39; Staff duties, 1940; OC No 29 Night Fighter Sqdn, 1941–42; Staff Coll., 1942; Staff duties, 1943–44; Staff duties in 2nd TAF and OC No 139 (Bomber) Wing, 1944–45; Dep. Dir Air Defence, Air Min., 1945–47; Staff duties in USA, 1947–50; OC Fighter Stations (2), 1950–53; Personnel Staff duties, Air Min., 1954–55; student, idc 1956; Comdt Central Fighter Estab., 1957–58; SASO, HQ No 13 (F) Group, 1959; SASO, HQ Fighter Comd RAF, 1960–63. *Recreation:* sailing. *Address:* La Côte au Palier, St Martin, Jersey, CI. *Clubs:* Royal Channel Islands Yacht, St Helier Yacht.
                                          Died 16 April 1994.

COLCHESTER, Rev. Halsey Sparrowe, CMG 1968; OBE 1960; MA Oxon; retired; *b* 5 March 1918; *s* of late Ernest Charles Colchester; *m* 1946, Rozanne Felicity Hastings Medhurst, *d* of late Air Chief Marshal Sir Charles Medhurst, KCB, OBE, MC; four *s* one *d.* *Educ:* Uppingham Sch.; Magdalen Coll., Oxford. Served Oxf. and Bucks Lt Inf., 1940–43; 2nd SAS Regt, 1944–46 (despatches); Captain. Joined Diplomatic Service, 1947; FO 1948–50; 2nd Sec., Istanbul, 1950–54; FO 1954–56; Consul, Zürich, 1956–60; 1st Sec., Athens, 1960–64; FO, 1964–68; Counsellor, Paris, 1968–72; retired from Diplomatic Service, 1972; ordinand at Cuddesdon Theological Coll., 1972–73; deacon, 1973; priest, 1974; Curate, Minchinhampton, Glos, 1973–76; Vicar of Bollington, Cheshire, 1976–81; Priest in Charge, Great Tew, Oxfordshire, 1981–87 and 1990–91. *Recreations:* theatre-going, wild flowers. *Address:* Southrop House, Hook Norton, Banbury, Oxford OX15 5PP. *T:* Hook Norton (01608) 737264.   *Died 27 Jan. 1995.*

COLE, Maj.-Gen. Eric Stuart, CB 1960; CBE 1945; retired; Director of Telecommunications, War Office, 1958–61; *b* 10 Feb. 1906; *s* of John William Cole; *m* 1941, Doris Cole (*d* 1986). Served Palestine, 1936–39; War of 1939–45 in Italy, France, Greece (despatches, CBE); Maj.-Gen., 1958. Col Comdt Royal Corps of Signals, 1962–67. Pres., Radio Soc. of GB, 1961. Pres., Army Golf Soc., 1971–73. *Address:* 28 Royal Avenue, Chelsea, SW3. *Clubs:* Army and Navy, MCC, Roehampton.
                                          Died 19 Dec. 1992.

COLE, James S.; *see* Stuart-Cole.

COLE, Prof. Monica Mary; Professor of Geography, 1964–87, and Director of Research in Geobotany, Terrain Analysis and related Resource Use, 1975–87, Royal Holloway and Bedford New College (formerly at Bedford College), University of London, then Professor Emeritus; Leverhulme Emeritus Professorial Research Fellow, since 1988; *b* 5 May 1922; *d* of William Henry Parnall Cole and Dorothy Mary Cole (*née* Thomas). *Educ:* Wimbledon County Grammar Sch.; Bedford Coll., Univ. of London. Research Asst, Min. of Town and Country Planning, Cambridge, 1944–45; Postgrad. study, Univ. of London, 1945–46; Lectr in Geography: Univ. of Capetown, 1947; Univ. of Witwatersrand, 1948–51; Univ. of Keele, 1951–64. Associate Prof., Univ. of Idaho summer sch., 1952; Vis. Lectr, Univs of Queensland, Melbourne, and

Adelaide, 1960. Mem. British delegation International Geographical Congress in: Washington, 1952; Rio de Janeiro, 1956; London, 1964; New Delhi, 1968; Montreal, 1972; Tokyo, 1980; Paris, 1984; Participant, Internat. Savannas Symposia, Venezuela, 1964, S Africa, 1979, Australia, 1984. Research: savannas, vegetation, soils and geomorphology: S Africa, 1948–51; Brazil, 1956, 1965; Central and E Africa, 1959; Australia, 1960, 1962, 1963, 1965, 1966, 1967, 1968, 1971, 1972, 1975, 1976, 1980, 1984; Venezuela, 1964; Southern Africa, 1967, 1968, 1978, 1979, 1980, 1983; plant indicators of mineralization: Australia, Africa, Brazil, UK, Finland, Japan, 1964–73, 1977, 1978, 1980, 1984, 1985; remote sensing for terrain analysis: Australia, UK, 1970–76, 1983–85, China, 1981. Principal Investigator, SPOT IMAGE, 1986–. *Publications:* The Transvaal Lowveld, 1956; South Africa, 1961, 1966; The Savannas: biogeography and geobotany, 1986; (contrib.) Ecology of Areas with Serpentinized Rocks (ed B. A. Roberts and J. Proctor), 1992; contribs to Geograph. Jl, Geography, Trans Inst. Brit. Geographers, S African Geograph. Jl, Trans Instn Mining and Metallurgy, Proc. Royal Soc., Jl Applied Ecology, ESRO, Proc. Symposium Frascati, Jl Biogeography, S Africa Geol Soc., CIMM and COSPAR Conf. Proc., Advances in Space Res., Ecological Studies, Environmental Pollution, and many papers in conf. proc. *Recreations:* painting, photography, tennis, walking, climbing. *Address:* Royal Holloway and Bedford New College, Egham Hill, Egham, Surrey TW20 0EX.   *Died 8 Jan. 1994.*

COLE, Maj.-Gen. William Scott, CB 1949; CBE 1946; *b* 29 March 1902; *s* of late William Scott Cole; *m* 1st, 1948, Kathleen Winifred Coleing (marr. diss. 1970); one *d*; 2nd, 1971, Alice Rose Pitts, *widow* of Dr G. T. Pitts. *Educ:* Victoria Coll., Jersey; RMA Woolwich. Commissioned into the Corps of Royal Engineers, 1921; served War of 1939–45: Temp. Brig., 1943; Substantive Col, 1945; Subs. Brig., 1951; Temp. Maj.-Gen., 1955; Subs. Maj.-Gen., 1956; retd 1958. *Club:* Army and Navy.
                                          Died 26 Dec. 1992.

COLE-HAMILTON, John, CBE 1954; DL; Senior Partner, Brechin Cole-Hamilton, Chartered Accountants, Glasgow; *b* 15 Oct. 1899; *s* of late Col A. R. Cole-Hamilton; *m* 1930, Gladys Cowie (decd); one *s* two *d.* *Educ:* Royal Academy, Irvine. Served European War, 1914–19, with RFC and RAF. Major, Home Guard, 1942. Former Provost of Kilwinning; Mem., Ayrshire CC. DL for County of Ayr, 1951. *Address:* Beltrim House, Kilwinning, Ayrshire.   *Died 10 Nov. 1991.*

COLEMAN, Prof. Donald Cuthbert, LittD; FBA 1972; Professor of Economic History, Cambridge University, 1971–81, then Emeritus; Fellow of Pembroke College, Cambridge; *b* 21 Jan. 1920; *s* of Hugh Augustus Coleman and Marian Stella Agnes Cuthbert; *m* 1954, Jessie Ann Matilda Child (*née* Stevens). *Educ:* Haberdashers' Aske's, Hampstead; London Sch. of Economics, Univ. of London (BSc (Econ), 1st Cl. Hons, 1949; PhD 1951). Worked in London, in insurance, 1937–39; admitted LSE, 1939; served War, in Army, 1940–46: commissioned Royal Warwickshire Regt, 1941; transf. RA, 1942; active service in N Africa, Italy and Greece; returned to LSE, 1946; Leverhulme Research Studentship, 1949–51; Lectr in Industrial History, 1951–58, Reader in Economic History, 1958–69, Prof. of Economic History, 1969–71, LSE; Hon. Fellow, LSE, 1984. Visiting Associate Prof. of Economics, Yale Univ., 1957–58. Lectures: Neale, UCL, 1979; Creighton, Univ. of London, 1989. Governor, Pasold Research Fund, 1977–93, Chm. of Governors, 1986–93. Member advisory committee on history of: BP, 1976–; British Rail, 1979–85; Schroders, 1983–92; brewing industry (Brewers' Soc.), 1989–93. English Editor, Scandinavian Economic History Review, 1952–61; Editor,

Economic History Review, 1967–72. FRHistS. *Publications:* The British Paper Industry, 1495–1860, 1958; Sir John Banks: Baronet and Businessman, 1963; Courtaulds: an economic and social history, vols 1 & 2, 1969, vol. 3, 1980; What Has Happened to Economic History? (Inaug. Lect.), 1972; Industry in Tudor and Stuart England, 1975; The Economy of England 1450–1750, 1977; (ed with A. H. John) Trade, Government and Economy in Pre-Industrial England, 1977; (ed with P. Mathias) Enterprise and History, 1984; History and the Economic Past, 1987; Myth, History and the Industrial Revolution, 1992; numerous articles in: Economic History Review, Economica, Historical Jl, etc. *Recreations:* music, gardening, reading. *Address:* Over Hall, Cavendish, Sudbury, Suffolk CO10 8BP. *T:* Glemsford (01787) 280325.   *Died 3 Sept. 1995.*

COLEMAN, Donald Richard, CBE 1979; JP; DL; MP (Lab) Neath since 1964; *b* 19 Sept. 1925; *s* of late Albert Archer Coleman and of Winifred Marguerite Coleman; *m* 1st, 1949, Phyllis Eileen (*née* Williams) (*d* 1963); one *s*; 2nd, 1966, Margaret Elizabeth Morgan; one *d*. *Educ:* Cadoxton Boys' Sch., Barry; Cardiff Technical Coll. Laboratory Technician, Welsh National Sch. of Medicine, Cardiff, 1940–42; Central Tuberculosis Laboratory, Cardiff, 1942–46; Sen. Technician, Swansea Technical Coll., 1946–50; University Coll., Swansea, 1950–54; Metallurgist, Research Dept, Steel Co. of Wales Ltd, Abbey Works, Port Talbot, 1954 until election to Parliament. PPS to Minister of State for Wales (later Secretary of State for Wales), 1967–70; an Opposition Whip, 1970–74; a Lord Comr, HM Treasury, 1974–79, Vice-Chamberlain of the Household, 1978–79; Opposition Spokesman on Welsh Affairs, 1981–83; Mem., Panel of Chairmen, H of C, 1984–; Delegate to Council of Europe and WEU, 1968–73 and 1983; Chm., Cttee on Parly and Public Relations, Council of Europe, 1986–90. JP City of Swansea, 1962; DL West Glamorgan, 1985. *Address:* Penderyn, 18 Penywern Road, Bryncoch, Neath, West Glamorgan. *T:* Neath (0639) 4599.

Died 14 Jan. 1991.

COLEMAN, Rt Rev. Prof. William Robert, DD; Professor of Humanities, York University, Toronto, 1966–86, then Emeritus; *b* Ulverton, Quebec, 16 Aug. 1917; *s* of Rev. Stanley Harold Coleman and Mary Ann Coleman (*née* Armstrong); *m* 1947, Mary Elizabeth Charmes, *er d* of Thomas Summers and Marion Wilson; one *s* two *d*; *m* 1986, Joan Alison Ives. *Educ:* St Mary's Collegiate Inst.; Brantford Collegiate Inst.; University Coll. and Wycliffe Coll. (BD); Univ. of Toronto (MA); Union Theological Seminary, New York (STM); Univs of Cambridge and Edinburgh. Deacon, 1942; priest, 1943; Curate, Church of the Epiphany, Sudbury, Ont, 1942–43; Priest-in-charge, 1943–45; post-graduate study, 1945–47; Prof. of Religious Philosophy and Ethics, Wycliffe Coll., 1947–50; Dean of Divinity and Harold Prof., Bishop's Coll., Lennoxville, Quebec, 1950–52; Principal, Huron Coll., London, Ont, 1952–61; Bishop of Kootenay, 1961–65. FRSA. DD Wycliffe Coll., 1951; DD (Hon.) Huron Coll., 1961; DD (Hon.) Trinity Coll., Toronto, 1962. *Publications:* contributed to: In Such an Age (ed W. C. Lockhart), 1951; The Church in the Sixties (ed. P. Jefferson), 1962. *Address:* Box 52, Newboro, Ont K0G 1P0, Canada.

Died 21 July 1992.

COLES, Dame Mabel Irene, DBE 1971 (CBE 1965); President: Royal Women's Hospital, Melbourne, 1968–72; Australian Women's Liberal Club, since 1965; Director, Asthma Foundation of Victoria, 1965; *d* of late E. Johnston; *m* 1927, Sir Edgar Coles (*d* 1981); one *s* two *d*. Associated with Royal Women's Hosp. for 30 years; Chairman: Ladies Cttee for (two) $1,000,000 appeals; (two) Door Knock Appeals; Asthma Ladies' Appeal Cttee;

Patroness: Family Planning Assoc. of Vic; Rheumatism and Arthritis Assoc. of Vic; Frankston Musical Soc. Life Mem., Australian Nat. Meml Theatre Ltd. Trustee, Mayfield Centre. *Recreations:* dogs, horses, walking. *Address:* Hendra, Williams Road, Mount Eliza, Vic 3930, Australia. *Clubs:* Alexandra, Peninsula Country (Melbourne).   *Died 17 June 1993.*

COLIN, Rt Rev. Gerald Fitzmaurice, MA; an Assistant Bishop, Diocese of Lincoln, 1979–94; *b* 19 July 1913; *s* of Frederick Constant Colin and Jemima Fitzmaurice; *m* 1941, Iris Susan Stuart Weir; three *s* two *d*. *Educ:* Mountjoy Sch.; Trinity Coll., Dublin. MA (TCD) 1946. Deacon, 1936; Priest, 1937. St George's, Dublin, 1938; Chancellor's Vicar, St Patrick's Cathedral, Dublin, 1938; RAFVR, 1939–47; Vicar of Frodingham, Dio. of Lincoln, 1947–66; Bishop Suffragan of Grimsby, 1966–78. Canon of Lincoln Cathedral, 1960; Rural Dean of Manlake, 1960; Proctor in Convocation, 1960–65, 1966–70. *Recreation:* fishing. *Address:* 11 Upton Close, Norwich NR4 7PD. *T:* Norwich (01603) 51612.   *Died 19 Dec. 1995.*

COLLIER, John Gordon, FRS 1990; FEng 1985; Chairman, Nuclear Electric plc, since 1990; *b* London, 22 Jan. 1935; *s* of John Collier and Edith Georgina (*née* de Ville); *m* 1956, Ellen Alice Mary Mitchell; one *s* one *d*. *Educ:* St Paul's Sch., Hammersmith; University Coll. London (BScEng). FIMechE, FIChemE, FINucE; FInstE. AERE, Harwell: apprenticeship in mech. and chem. engrg, 1951–56; SO, then SSO, Chem. Engrg Div., 1957–62; Sect. Hd, then Br. Hd, Exptl Engrg Br., Adv. Reactor Engrg Div., Atomic Energy of Canada Ltd (on leave of absence from UKAEA), 1962–64; SSO, then PSO, Chem. Engrg Div., AERE, Harwell, 1964–66; Hd, Engrg Div., Atomic Power Constructions Ltd, R&D Lab., Heston, 1966–70; UKAEA, Harwell: Hd of Engrg Scis Gp, later Engrg Scis Br., 1970–75; Hd of Chem. Engrg Div., 1975–77; Mem., Atomic Energy Technical Unit responsible to Dep. Chm., UKAEA, 1977–79; Hd, Atomic Energy Technical Unit, 1979–81; Dir of Technical Studies, UKAEA, Harwell, 1981–82; Dir, Safety and Reliability Directorate, UKAEA, Culcheth, 1982–83; Dir Gen., Generation Develt and Construction Div. of CEGB, Barnwood, Glos, 1983–86; Dep. Chm., 1986, Chm., 1987–90, UKAEA. Chm., Nationalised Industries Chairmen's Gp, 1990–92. Calvin Rice Lectr, ASME/AIChE Nat. Heat Transfer Conf., USA, 1993. Hon. Life Mem., ASME, 1993. Hon. DSc Cranfield, 1988; Hon. DEng Bristol, 1993. *Publications:* Convective Boiling and Condensation, 1972, 2nd edn 1981; (jtly) Introduction to Nuclear Power, 1987. *Recreations:* cricket, music. *Address:* Nuclear Electric plc, Barnett Way, Barnwood, Glos GL4 7RS.   *Died 18 Nov. 1995.*

COLLINS, Maj.-Gen. Joseph Clinton, CB 1953; CBE 1951 (OBE 1946); *b* 8 Jan. 1895; *s* of Edward Collins; British; *m* 1925, Eileen Patricia Williams; two *d*. *Educ:* London Hosp. Served European War, 1914–18: France and Belgium, 1914; Surgeon Probationer, RNVR, 1915–16; Lieut, RAMC, 1917; Egyptian Army, 1923–33; DDMS, BAOR, 1946–49; DMS FARELF, 1949–51; DMS Northern Command, 1951–53; KHS, 1951–54; Dir Medical Services, BAOR, 1953–Dec. 1954, retired. CStJ 1948. 3rd Class Order of Nile.

Died 21 May 1991.

COLLISON, Baron (Life Peer) *cr* 1964, of Cheshunt; **Harold Francis Collison,** CBE 1961; Chairman, Supplementary Benefits Commission, 1969–75; *b* 10 May 1909; *m* 1946, Ivy Kate Hanks. *Educ:* The Hay Currie LCC Sch.; Crypt Sch., Gloucester. Firstly worked in a commercial office in London; farm worker in Glos, 1934–53. National Union of Agricultural Workers (later Nat. Union of Agricultural and Allied Workers): District Organiser in Gloucester and Worcs, 1944; Nat. Officer,

1946; General Secretary, 1953–69. Mem., TUC Gen. Council, 1953–69 (Chm., 1964–65); Chm., Social Insce and Industrial Welfare Cttee of TUC, 1957–69. President: Internat. Fedn of Plantation, Agricultural and Allied Workers, 1960–76; Assoc. of Agriculture, 1976–84; Member: Coun. on Tribunals, 1959–69; Nat. Insce Adv. Cttee, 1959–69; Governing Body of ILO, 1960–69; Pilkington Cttee on Broadcasting, 1960–62; Central Transport Consultative Cttee, 1962–70; Agric. Adv. Council, 1962–80; Adv. Cttee on Agricultural Educn, 1963; Royal Commn on Trades Unions and Employers' Assocs, 1965–68; Home-Grown Cereals Authority, 1965–78; former Member: Industrial Health Adv. Cttee; Economic Develt for Agriculture; Industrial Consultative Cttee, Approach to Europe; Overseas Labour Consultative Cttee; Agric. Productivity Cttee, British Productivity Council; Chairman: Land Settlement Assoc., 1977–79 (Vice-Chm., 1964–77); Agric. Apprenticeship Council, 1968–74; Mem., N Thames Gas Board (part-time), 1961–72. Mem., Governing Body, Brooklands Technical Coll., Weybridge, 1970–85 (Chm., 1977–85). *Recreations:* gardening, chess. *Address:* Honeywood, 163 Old Nazeing Road, Broxbourne, Herts EN10 6QT. *T:* Hoddesdon (01992) 463597. *Died 29 Dec. 1995.*

COLMAN, David Stacy, MA; retired; *b* Broughty Ferry, Angus, 1 May 1906; *yr s* of Dr H. C. Colman; *m* 1934, Sallie Edwards (*d* 1970). *Educ:* Shrewsbury Sch.; Balliol Coll., Oxford (Scholar). 1st Class Hon. Mods, 1926; 1st Class Lit. Hum., 1928. Asst Master at Shrewsbury Sch., 1928–31 and 1935–36; Fellow of Queen's Coll., Oxford and Praelector in Classics and Ancient History, 1931–34; Headmaster, C of E Grammar Sch., Melbourne, 1937–38; Shrewsbury School: Asst Master, 1938–66; Master of Day Boys, 1949–61; Librarian, 1961–66. Member Council: Soc. for Promotion of Roman Studies, 1958–61; Classical Assoc., 1961–64. *Publication:* Sabrinae Corolla: the Classics at Shrewsbury School under Dr Butler and Dr Kennedy, 1950. *Address:* 19 Woodfield Road, Shrewsbury SY3 8HZ. *T:* Shrewsbury (0743) 353749. *Clubs:* National Liberal; Leander (Henley-on-Thames); Salop (Shrewsbury). *Died 18 July 1993.*

COLMAN, (Elijah) Alec, JP; Chairman, E. Alec Colman Group of Companies; *b* Tipton, Staffs, 7 Jan. 1903; *s* of Abraham and Leah Colman; *m* 1956, Eileen Amelia Graham; no *c*. *Educ:* Tipton Green Council Sch., Staffs. Dir of numerous charitable organisations; concerned with rehabilitation of refugees throughout the world; Pres., British Friends of Bar-Ilan Univ., 1981–; Exec. Mem., Jt Palestine Appeal; Vice Pres., British-Israel (formerly Anglo-Israel) Chamber of Commerce, 1981–. Mem. Ct, Patternmakers' Co. JP Inner London, 1962. Hon. PhD Bar-Ilan Univ., 1974. *Recreations:* reading, philosophy. *Clubs:* East India, Devonshire, Sports and Public Schools, City Livery. *Died 25 July 1991.*

COMBS, Sir Willis (Ide), KCVO 1974; CMG 1962; HM Diplomatic Service, retired; *b* Melbourne, 6 May 1916; *s* of Willis Ide Combs, Napier, New Zealand; *m* 1942, Grace Willis; two *d. Educ:* Dannevirke High Sch.; Victoria Coll., NZ; St John's Coll., Cambridge. Served in HM Forces, 1940–46. Apptd Mem. Foreign Service, 1947; transf. to Paris as 2nd Sec. (Commercial), Dec. 1947; 1st Sec., Nov. 1948; transf. to Rio de Janeiro, as 1st Sec., 1951; to Peking as 1st Sec. and Consul, 1953 (Chargé d'Affaires, 1954); Foreign Office, 1956; to Baghdad as Counsellor (Commercial), 1959; Diplomatic Service Inspector, 1963; Counsellor, British Embassy, Rangoon, 1965; Asst Under-Sec. of State, FCO, 1968; Ambassador to Indonesia, 1970–75. *Address:* Sunset, Wadhurst Park, Wadhurst, East Sussex. *Club:* United Oxford & Cambridge University. *Died 13 Jan. 1994.*

COMFORT, Dr Charles Fraser, OC 1972; RCA; artist and author; Emeritus Director, National Gallery of Canada, 1965; *b* Edinburgh, 22 July 1900; *m* 1924, Louise Chase, Winnipeg; two *d. Educ:* Winnipeg Sch. of Art and Art Students' League, New York. Cadet Officer, Univ. of Toronto Contingent of Canadian OTC, 1939; commnd Instr in Infantry Weapons, 1940; Sen. Canadian War Artist (Army), Major, 1942–46 (UK, Italy and NW Europe). Head of Dept of Mural Painting, Ontario Coll. of Art, 1935–38; Associate Prof., Dept of Art and Archaeology, Univ. of Toronto, 1946–60 (Mem. staff, 1938); Dir, Nat. Gall. of Canada, 1959. Gold Medal and cash award, Great Lakes Exhibn, Albright Gall., Buffalo, NY, 1938; travelled widely in Europe; Royal Society Fellowship to continue research into problems of Netherlandish painting, 1955–56; studied under Dr William Heckscher of Kunsthistorisch Inst., Utrecht. *Works include:* landscape painting and portraiture (oils and water colour); mural paintings and stone carvings in many public buildings. Pres., Royal Canadian Academy of Arts, 1957–60; Past Pres., Canadian Soc. of Painters in Water Colour; Past Pres. and Charter Mem., Canadian Group of Painters; Mem., Ontario Soc. of Artists. Dr of Laws *hc:* Mount Allison Univ., 1958; Royal Military Coll., Canada, 1980. Medaglia Benemerito della culturale (Italy), 1963; Univ. of Alberta National Award in painting and related arts, 1963. Centennial Medal, 1967; Queen's Jubilee Medal, 1978. *Publications:* Artist at War, 1956 (Toronto); contrib. to Royal Commission Studies Report on National Development in the Arts, Letters and Sciences, Vol. II, 1951; contrib. various art and literary publications. *Died 5 July 1994.*

COMPTON, Sir Edmund (Gerald), GCB 1971 (KCB 1965; CB 1948); KBE 1955; MA; Hon. FRAM; FRCM; *b* 30 July 1906; *er s* of late Edmund Spencer Compton, MC, Pailton House, Rugby; *m* 1934, Betty Tresyllian, CBE (*d* 1987), 2nd *d* of late Hakewill Tresyllian Williams, JP, DL, Churchill Court, Kidderminster; one *s* four *d. Educ:* Rugby (Scholar); New Coll., Oxford (Scholar; 1st Class Lit. Hum., 1929; Hon. Fellow 1972). Entered Home Civil Service, 1929; Colonial Office, 1930; transf. to HM Treasury, 1931; Private Sec. to Financial Sec. to HM Treasury, 1934–36; seconded to Min. of Aircraft Production as Private Sec. to Minister, 1940; Min. of Supply, 1941; Asst Sec., HM Treasury, 1942, Under-Sec., 1947, Third Sec., 1949–58; Comptroller and Auditor General, Exchequer and Audit Dept, 1958–66; Parly Comr for Administration, 1967–71, and in NI, 1969–71. Chm., English Local Govt Boundary Commn, 1971–78. Chairman: Irish Sailors and Soldiers Land Trust, 1946–86; Milibern Trust, 1968–88; BBC Programmes Complaints Commn, 1972–81; Governing Body, Royal Acad. of Music, 1975–81. *Recreations:* music, water-colour sketching. *Address:* 1/80 Elm Park Gardens, SW10 9PD. *T:* 071–351 3790. *Clubs:* Athenæum, Boodle's. *Died 11 March 1994.*

COMPTON MILLER, Sir John (Francis), Kt 1969; MBE (mil.) 1945; TD; MA Oxon; barrister-at-law; Senior Registrar, The Family Division (formerly Probate, Divorce and Admiralty Division), 1964–72 (Registrar, 1946–64), retired 1972; *b* 11 May 1900; 3rd *s* of Frederic Richard Miller, MD and Effie Anne, *d* of Samson Rickard Stuttaford; *m* 1st, 1925, Alice Irene Mary (*d* 1931), *er d* of John Scales Bakewell; one *s*; 2nd, 1936, Mary, *e d* of Rev. Alexander MacEwen Baird-Smith; one *s* one *d. Educ:* Colet Court; St Paul's Sch.; New Coll., Oxford. Called to Bar, Inner Temple, 1923; went the Western Circuit, practised Criminal, Common Law, Probate and Divorce Courts. Major, Inns of Court Regt, TA, 1936; OC No 21 Reception Unit; Asst Comdt, Army Tech. Sch. (Boys), Chepstow. A Deputy Judge Advocate, United Kingdom and North West Europe, 1969. Examiner,

Council of Legal Education, 1951–64. UK Rep., Council of Europe Sub-Cttee on Registration of Wills, 1970. *Publications:* I Tried My Hand at Verse, 1968; Further Verse, 1970; The Miraculous Cornfield, 1978; The Chinese Saucer, 1980; Poems '81, 1981; Selected Poems, 1982; Miscellany, 1983; And So It Went, 1985; An Ambit Small, 1986. *Recreations:* painting (Dip., City of London Art Exhibn, 1979); versing, heraldic art. *Address:* 2 Crown Office Row, Temple, EC4. *T:* 071–583 1352. *Club:* Garrick (Life Mem.). *Died 5 Oct. 1992.*

CONI, Peter Richard Carstairs, OBE 1987; QC 1980; a Recorder, since 1985; *b* 20 Nov. 1935; *s* of late Eric Charles Coni and Leslie Sybil Carstairs (*née* Pearson). *Educ:* Uppingham; St Catharine's Coll., Cambridge (MA). Called to the Bar, Inner Temple, 1960, Bencher, 1986. Steward, Henley Royal Regatta, 1974 (Chm. Cttee of Management, 1978–93); Pres., London Rowing Club, 1988–; Chm., 1986 World Rowing Championships Cttee (FISA Medal of Honour, 1986); Member: Exec. Cttee, Amateur Rowing Assoc., 1968– (Chm., 1970–77); Exec. Cttee, Central Council of Physical Recreation, 1978–80; Nat. Olympic Cttee, 1990–. Mem., Thames Water Authority, 1978–83. Treas., FISA, 1990–. Mem., Ct of Assts, Needlemakers' Co., 1983–. *Recreations:* rowing, sports administration, good food, modern art. *Address:* 3 Churton Place, SW1V 2LN. *T:* 071–828 2135. *Clubs:* London Rowing; Leander (Henley-on-Thames). *Died 13 July 1993.*

CONN, Prof. John Farquhar Christie, DSc; CEng; FRINA; John Elder Professor of Naval Architecture, University of Glasgow, 1957–73; *b* 5 July 1903; *s* of Alexander Aberdein Conn and Margaret Rhind Wilson; *m* 1935, Doris Maude Yeatman; one *s* one *d*. *Educ:* Robert Gordon's Coll., Aberdeen; Glasgow Univ. Apprenticeship at Alexander Hall and Co. Ltd, Aberdeen, 1920–25; employed in several shipyards; Scientific staff, Ship Div., National Physical Laboratory, 1929–44; Chief Naval Architect, British Shipbuilding Research Association, 1945–57. Hon. Vice-Pres., RINA. *Publications:* various papers in Trans of Royal Instn of Naval Architects and other learned societies. *Recreations:* music, reading. *Address:* 14 Elm Walk, Bearsden, Glasgow G61 3BQ. *T:* 041–942 4640. *Died 27 March 1993.*

CONNALLY, John Bowden; lawyer; *b* 27 Feb. 1917; *s* of John Bowden Connally and Lela (*née* Wright); *m* 1940, Idanell Brill; two *s* one *d*. *Educ:* Univ. of Texas (LLB). Served US Navy, 1941–46. Pres. and Gen. Manager, KVET radio stn, 1946–49; Admin. Asst to Lyndon Johnson, 1949; employed with Powell, Wirtz & Rauhut, 1950–52; Attorney to Richardson & Bass, oil merchants, 1952–61; Sec. US Navy, 1961; Governor of Texas, 1962–68; Secretary of the Treasury, USA, 1971–72. Member: President's Adv. Cttee on Exec. Organisation, 1969–70; President's Foreign Intelligence Adv. Bd, 1972–74 and 1976–77; US Adv. Cttee on reform of Internat. Monetary System, 1973–74; Partner, Vinson Elkins, 1969–71, 1972–85; Director: The Methodist Hospital, 1977–; Ford Motor Co., 1981–87; Coastal Corp., 1988–; Maxxam Inc., 1988–; Kaiser Tech, 1988–; Kaiser Aluminum and Chemical, 1988. *Address:* 5847 San Felipe, Suite 2600, Houston, Texas 77057, USA. *Died 15 June 1993.*

CONNELLY, Thomas John; Director of Services, General and Municipal Workers' Union, 1978–85, retired; *b* 24 Dec. 1925; *s* of William and Jane Connelly; *m* 1952, Naomi Shakow; one *s* one *d*. *Educ:* Priory St Elementary Sch., Colchester; Ruskin Coll.; Lincoln Coll., Oxford. BA 1955. Research Officer: Amalgamated Soc. of Woodworkers, 1955–63; G&MWU, 1963–66; Adviser, Industrial Relations, Prices and Incomes Bd, 1966–68; various posts, finally as Chief Officer, Race Relations Bd,

1968–77; apptd Chief Executive, Commn for Racial Equality, 1977, but withdrew from appt. *Publication:* The Woodworkers 1860–1960, 1960. *Recreations:* reading, music. *Address:* 2 Caroline Court, 25 Lovelace Road, Surbiton, Surrey. *T:* 081–399 9223. *Died 14 Oct. 1991.*

CONNER, Rearden; *see* Connor, Patrick Reardon.

CONNOR, Patrick Reardon, (Rearden Conner), MBE 1967; novelist and short-story writer; *b* 19 Feb. 1907; *s* of John and Bridie Connor; *m* 1942, Malinka Marie Smith; no *c*. *Educ:* Christian Brothers Schs; Presentation Coll., Cork. Worked in Min. of Aircraft Production, during War, in research and development of equipment; carried on in this field, after war, in Min. of Supply, and later in Min. of Aviation and Min. of Technology. Critic of fiction, The Fortnightly, 1935–37, also on Books of the Month; Reader of fiction for Cassell, 1948–56. Work included in: Best Short Stories Anthology (twice); Pick of To-Day's Short Stories; Whit Burnett anthology (USA), Stories of the Forties. *Publications:* Shake Hands with The Devil, 1933 (Literary Guild Selection in USA; filmed, 1958); Rude Earth, 1934; Salute to Aphrodite, 1935 (USA); I am Death, 1936; Time to Kill, 1936 (USA); Men Must Live, 1937; The Sword of Love, 1938; Wife of Colum, 1939; The Devil Among the Tailors, 1947; My Love to the Gallows, 1949; Hunger of the Heart, 1950; The Singing Stone, 1951; The House of Cain, 1952; (under *pseudonym* Peter Malin): To Kill is My Vocation, 1939; River, Sing Me a Song, 1939; Kobo the Brave, 1950. *Recreations:* listening to music, going to the theatre. *Address:* 79 Balsdean Road, Woodingdean, Brighton, Sussex BN2 6PG. *T:* Brighton (0273) 34032. *Died 29 Aug. 1991.*

CONSTABLE, Sir Robert Frederick S.; *see* Strickland-Constable.

CONSTANTINE, Air Chief Marshal Sir Hugh (Alex), KBE 1958 (CBE 1944); CB 1946; DSO 1942; Co-ordinator, Anglo-American Community Relations, Ministry of Defence (Air), 1964–77; *b* 23 May 1908; *s* of Fleet Paymaster Henry Constantine, RN, and Alice Louise Squire; *m* 1937, Helen, *d* of J. W. Bourke, Sydney, Australia; one *d*. *Educ:* Christ's Hosp.; Royal Air Force Coll., Cranwell. Pilot Officer in RAF, 1927; 56 (F) Sqdn, 1928–29; Flying Instructor, RAF Coll., 1930–31; CFS Instructor, 1932–33 and 1937; No 1 Armoured Car Co. (Iraq), 1934–36 (Palestine, despatches); Sqdn Ldr, 1936; 214 Bomber Sqdn, 1937–38; Sqdn Ldr Examining Wing, CFS, 1939; graduated Staff Coll., Andover, 1940; served in Bomber Comd, 1940–45 (Gp Capt. 1941; despatches four times); Wing Comdr (Ops) No 3 Gp, 1940, (Flying) No 11 OTU, 1941; comd RAF Elsham Wolds, 1941–42; SASO No 1 (B) Gp, 1943; Dep. SASO Bomber Comd, 1944; Air Vice-Marshal, Jan. 1945, and commanded No 5 (B) Group Bomber Command; Chief Intelligence Officer, BAFO and Control Commission, Germany, 1946; idc 1947; SASO, 205 Gp (Egypt), 1948–49; Dir of Intelligence, Air Min., 1950–51; AO i/c A, Fighter Comd, 1952–53; AOC No 25 Group, Flying Training Command, 1954–56; Deputy Chief of Staff (Plans and Operations), SHAPE, NATO, 1956–59; Comdt, ATC, 1959–60; AOC-in-C, Flying Trng Comd, 1959–61; Commandant, Imperial Defence Coll., 1962–64; retired 1964. Air Marshal, 1957; Air Chief Marshal, 1961. Patron, Central Flying Sch. Assoc., 1979–84. Governor, Christ's Hospital, 1963– (Almoner, 1969–85). Hon. LLD Warwick, 1978. Order of Polonia Restituta (2nd Class), 1945. *Recreations:* Rugby (English Trial, 1934, Eastern Counties, RAF and Leicester) golf. *Address:* 14 Cadogan Court, Draycott Avenue, SW3 3BX. *T:* 071–581 8821. *Club:* Royal Air Force. *Died 16 April 1992.*

COOK, (Alfred) Melville, MusDoc; FRCO; Hon. FRCCO; Organist and Choirmaster of the Metropolitan United, Toronto, 1967–86; *b* 18 June 1912; *s* of Harry Melville and Vera Louis Cook; *m* 1944, Marion Weir Moncrieff (*d* 1985); no *c. Educ:* King's Sch., Gloucester. MusDoc Durham, 1940. Served War in RA, 1941–46. Chorister, 1923–28, Asst Organist, 1932–37, Gloucester Cathedral; Organist and Choirmaster: All Saints, Cheltenham, 1935–37; Leeds Parish Church, 1937–56; Organist and Master of the Choristers, Hereford Cathedral, 1956–66. Conductor, Three Choirs Festival, Hereford, 1958, 1961, 1964; Conductor, Hereford Choral Soc., 1957–66. Organist and Choirmaster, All Saints', Winnipeg; Conductor of the Winnipeg Philharmonic Choir, Canada, 1966. *Recreation:* walking. *Address:* Flat 6, The Gate House, East Approach Drive, Pittville, Cheltenham GL52 3JE. *Died 22 May 1993.*

COOK, Brian (Caldwell); *see* Batsford, Sir B. C. C.

COOK, John Edward E.; *see* Evan-Cook.

COOK, Prof. John Manuel, FSA; FBA 1974; Professor of Ancient History and Classical Archæology, Bristol University, 1958–76 (formerly Reader); *b* 11 Dec. 1910; *s* of late Rev. Charles R. Cook and Mary M. Arnold; *m* 1st, 1939, Enid May (*d* 1976), *d* of Dr W. A. Robertson; two *s;* 2nd, 1977, Nancy Easton Law, MA, *widow of* Ralph Hamilton Law. *Educ:* Marlborough; King's Coll., Cambridge. Sir William Browne's Medal for Greek Ode, 1933; Members' Latin Essay Prize, 1933; Augustus Austen Leigh Student in King's Coll., 1934. Asst in Humanity and Lectr in Classical Archæology, Edinburgh Univ., 1936–46; Dir of British Sch. of Archæology at Athens, 1946–54; Dean, Faculty of Arts, 1966–68, Pro-Vice-Chancellor, 1972–75, Bristol Univ. C. E. Norton Lectr of the Archaeological Inst. of America, 1961–62; Visiting Prof., Yale Univ., 1965; Gray Memorial Lectr, Cambridge, 1969; Geddes-Harrower Prof., Univ. of Aberdeen, 1977. Served in Royal Scots, Force 133 (despatches), and HQ Land Forces, Greece (Lt-Col). *Publications:* The Greeks in Ionia and the East, 1962; (with W. H. Plommer) The Sanctuary of Hemithea at Kastabos, 1966; The Troad, an archaeological and historical study, 1973; The Persian Empire, 1983; chapters in: Cambridge Ancient History; Cambridge History of Iran. *Address:* 8 Dalrymple Crescent, Edinburgh EH9 2NU.
Died 2 Jan. 1994.

COOK, Melville; *see* Cook, A. M.

COOK, Norman Charles, BA; FSA, FMA; *b* 24 Jan. 1906; *s* of George and Emily Cook; *m* 1934, Dorothy Ida Waters; one *s* one *d. Educ:* Maidstone Grammar Sch. Maidstone Museum, 1924–37; Morven Institute of Archaeological Research, Avebury, 1937–39; Curator, Southampton Museum, 1947–50; Director: Guildhall Museum, 1950–71; Museum of London, 1970–72. Hon. Sec., 1954–59, Pres., 1964–65, Museums Assoc. Vice-Pres., Soc. of Antiquaries, 1967–72. Hon. Curator, Wells Mus., Som, 1972–82. *Recreation:* archæology. *Address:* 6 St Thomas Terrace, Wells, Somerset BA5 2XG.
Died 27 May 1994.

COOK, Norman Edgar, CBE 1980; writer; *b* 4 March 1920; *s* of Edgar James and Kate Cook; *m* 1942, Mildred Warburton; three *s. Educ:* Cowley Grammar Sch., St Helens. TA (Royal Corps of Signals), 1939; served war, UK, Sierra Leone, Gold Coast. Min. of Information, 1943–45; Editor, Northwich Guardian, 1945–47; Liverpool Daily Post, 1947–49; Information Officer, Air Ministry, 1949–53; Liverpool Daily Post and Echo: Night News Editor, 1953–55; Dep. News Editor, 1955–59; London Editor, 1959–72; Exec. News Editor, 1972–77; Editor, 1978–79, retired 1979, then chief book critic, 1980–90, Liverpool Daily Post. *Publications:* numerous

articles and reviews. *Recreations:* walking, reading, playing the piano. *Address:* 7 Trinity Gardens, Southport, Lancashire PR8 1AU. *T:* Southport (01704) 531268. *Club:* Athenæum (Liverpool). *Died 6 May 1995.*

COOK, Peter Edward; writer, entertainer, publisher; *b* 17 Nov. 1937; *s* of Alexander and Margaret Cook; *m* 1st, 1964, Wendy Snowden; two *d;* 2nd, 1973, Judy Huxtable; 3rd, 1989, Lin Chong. *Educ:* Radley Coll.; Pembroke Coll., Cambridge (BA). Founder, The Establishment, 1960; majority shareholder, Private Eye. Co-author and appeared in: *revues:* Pieces of Eight, 1958; One Over the Eight, 1959; Beyond the Fringe, 1959–64 (London and New York); Behind the Fridge, 1971–72 (Australia and London); Good Evening, 1973–75 (US); *television:* Not Only but Also (four series, BBC), 1965–71; Revolver (ITV series), 1978; The Two of Us (CBS series), 1981; Gone to Seed (LWT series), 1992. *Films:* The Wrong Box, 1965; Bedazzled, 1967; A Dandy in Aspic, 1969; Monte Carlo or Bust, 1969; The Bed-Sitting Room, 1970; The Rise and Rise of Michael Rimmer, 1971; The Hound of the Baskervilles, 1978; Secret Policeman's Ball, 1980; Derek and Clive, 1980; Yellowbeard, 1982; Supergirl, 1983; Whoops Apocalypse, 1985; Mr Jolly Lives Next Door, 1986; Princess Bride, 1986; Without a Clue, 1988; Getting It Right, 1988; Great Balls of Fire, 1989; Black Beauty, 1993. *Publications:* Beyond the Fringe, 1962; Dud and Pete: The Dagenham Dialogues, 1971; Good Evening, 1977. *Recreations:* gambling, gossip, golf. *Address:* c/o Private Eye, 6 Carlisle Street, W1V 5RG.
Died 9 Jan. 1995.

COOKE, Cecil; *see* Cooke, R. C.

COOKE, George William, CBE 1975; FRS 1969; Chief Scientific Officer, Agricultural Research Council, 1975–81, retired; *b* 6 Jan. 1916; *s* of late William Harry Cooke and Sarah Jane Cooke (*née* Whittaker); *m* 1944, Elizabeth Hannah Hill; one *s* one *d. Educ:* Loughborough Grammar Sch.; University Coll., Nottingham. BSc Chem. London Univ., 1937; PhD London, 1940. Awarded Min. of Agric. Research Schol., tenable at Rothamsted Experimental Station, 1938; apptd Scientific Officer there, 1941, and Prin. Sci. Officer, 1951; Head of Chemistry Dept, 1956–75; Deputy Dir, 1962–75 (acting Dir, 1972–73). Chm., Agriculture Group of Soc. of Chem. Industry, 1956–58; President: Fertiliser Soc., London, 1961–62; British Soc. of Soil Science, 1976–78. Lectures: Amos Meml, East Malling Res. Station, 1967; Francis New Meml, Fertiliser Soc., 1971; Clive Behrens, Univ. of Leeds, 1972–73; Scott Robertson Meml, QUB, 1973; Macaulay, Macaulay Inst. for Soil Res., 1979; Blackman, Oxford Univ., 1980; Boyd Orr Meml, Nutrition Soc., 1981. Hon. MRIA 1980; Hon. FRAgS 1981; For. Mem., Lenin All-Union Acad. of Agric. Scis, USSR, 1972. Research Medal of Royal Agricultural Soc., 1967; Soc. of Chem. Industry Medal, 1983. *Publications:* Fertilizers and Profitable Farming, 1960; The Control of Soil Fertility, 1967; Fertilizing for Maximum Yield, 1972, 3rd edn 1982 (trans. Japanese, 1986); many papers in scientific jls on soil science, crop nutrition and fertilizers. *Recreation:* boats. *Address:* 33 Topstreet Way, Harpenden, Herts AL5 5TU. *T:* Harpenden (0582) 712899. *Club:* Farmers'.
Died 10 Feb. 1992.

COOKE, Peter Maurice; Regional Administrator, Oxford Regional Health Authority, 1980–85; *b* 23 Feb. 1927; *s* of late Reginald and Grace Cooke; *m* 1956, Daphne Joyce (*née* Annoot); two *s. Educ:* Bristol Grammar Sch.; Corpus Christi Coll., Oxford (MA). 3rd Royal Tank Regt, 1946–48. FHSM. Admin. Assistant, Central Middlesex and Taunton HMCs, 1951–59; Asst Sec., NW Met. Regional Hosp. Bd, 1959–63; Group Secretary, W Suffolk and Ipswich and District HMCs, 1963–73; Area Administrator, Suffolk AHA, 1973–80. *Recreations:* golf,

choral singing. *Address:* Haremire House, Buckland, near Faringdon, Oxon SN7 8QS. *T:* Buckland (0136787) 603.
Died 14 July 1995.

COOKE, (Roland) Cecil, CMG 1959; CBE 1952; Director of Exhibitions, Central Office of Information, 1946–61, retired; *b* 28 June 1899; *s* of Arthur Cooke; *m* 1924, Doris Marjorie Fewings (*d* 1982); *m* 1986, Violet Tebbutt. Architectural Asst, LCC, 1921; Dir of Publicity, Catesbys, Ltd, 1935; Dir of Exhibitions Div., Ministry of Information, 1945. Dir of Exhibitions, Festival of Britain, 1949–51; Dir, Festival Gardens Co., 1951; Dir of Exhibitions, British Government Pavilion, Brussels, 1958; UK representative, International Jury, Brussels Exhibition, 1958; Comr Gen., British Pavilion, Seattle World's Fair, 1962. *Publications:* contrib. to periodicals and press, illustrated stories for children, political and strip cartoons. *Recreation: painting. Address:* 6 Wells Close, Eastbourne, East Sussex BN20 7TX. *T:* Eastbourne (0323) 30258.
Died 28 Feb. 1991.

COOKE, Thomas Fitzpatrick, TD 1946; Lord Lieutenant, City of Londonderry, 1975–86; *b* 10 July 1911; *s* of Thomas Fitzpatrick Cooke and Aileen Frances Cooke; *m* 1946, Ruth, *d* of Rt Hon. Sir Anthony Brutus Babington, QC; one *s* one *d*. *Educ:* Stowe; Trinity Coll., Dublin (Dip. in Commerce). Served War, 1939–46, Captain, RA. Chm., Londonderry Port and Harbour Commissioners, 1967–73. Alderman, Londonderry Corp., 1946–52; High Sheriff, County of Londerry, 1949; DL 1950, High Sheriff, 1971–72, City of Londonderry. *Recreations:* gardening, shooting, fishing. *Address:* The Lodge, 5 Edenreagh Road, Eglinton, Londonderry BT47 3AR. *T:* Eglinton (01504) 810256. *Died 20 Feb. 1994.*

COOKSLEY, Clarence Harrington, CBE 1973; QPM 1969; DL; one of HM Inspectors of Constabulary, 1975–77; *b* 16 Dec. 1915; *e s* of late Clarence Harrington Cooksley and Elsie Cooksley, Nottingham; *m* 1st, 1940, Eunice May White (*d* 1986), Nottingham; two *s*; 2nd, 1988, Barbara May Tovee. *Educ:* Nottingham. Joined Nottinghamshire Constabulary, 1938; served Duke of Wellington's Regt and Dep. Asst Provost Marshal, Special Investigation Branch, Royal Corps of Military Police, 1942–46; Dir of Dept of Law, Police Coll., Bramshill, 1961; Dep. Chief Constable of Hertfordshire, 1961–63; Chief Constable: Northumberland County Constabulary, 1963–69; Northumberland Constabulary, 1969–74; Northumbria Police, 1974–75. DL Northumberland, 1971. OStJ 1966. *Address:* 8 Sandringham Way, Ponteland, Newcastle upon Tyne NE20 9AE.
Died 19 May 1991.

COOKSON, Roland Antony, CBE 1974 (OBE 1946); Chairman, Lead Industries Group Ltd (until 1967 known as Goodlass Wall & Lead Industries Ltd), 1962–73 (Director, 1948–80, a Managing Director, 1952–62); Chairman, Consett Iron Co. Ltd, 1966–67 (Director 1955; Acting Chairman 1964); Director of Lloyds Bank Ltd, 1964–79 (Chairman, Northern Regional Board, 1965–79); *b* 12 Dec. 1908; *s* of late Bryan Cookson; *m* 1st, 1931, Rosamond Gwladys (*d* 1973), *er d* of late Sir John S. Barwick, 2nd Bt; one *d*; 2nd, 1974, Dr Anne Aitchison, *widow* of Sir Stephen Charles de Lancey Aitchison, 3rd Bt. *Educ:* Harrow; Magdalen Coll., Oxford. Vice-Chm., Northern Regional Board for Industry, 1949–65; Mem., Northern Economic Planning Council, 1965–68; Pres., Tyneside Chamber of Commerce, 1955–57; Chm., Northern Regional Council, CBI, 1970–72 (Vice-Chm., 1968–70); Mem., Port of Tyne Authority, 1968–74. Mem., Court and Council, Univ. of Newcastle upon Tyne (Vice-Chm. of Council, 1985–); Chm., Careers Adv. Board, Univs of Newcastle upon Tyne and Durham, 1962–73. Hon. DCL Newcastle, 1974. *Recreations:* music, fishing. *Address:* The Brow, Wylam, Northumberland NE41 8DQ.

T: Wylam (0661) 853888. *Clubs:* Brooks's; Northern Counties (Newcastle upon Tyne).
Died 16 Nov. 1991.

COOLS-LARTIGUE, Sir Louis, Kt 1968; OBE 1955; Governor of Dominica, 1967–78; *b* 18 Jan. 1905; *s* of Theodore Cools-Lartigue and Emily (*née* Giraud); *m* 1932, Eugene (*née* Royer); two *s* four *d*. *Educ:* Convents, St Lucia and Dominica; Dominica Grammar Sch. Clerk, Dominica Civil Service, 1924; Chief Clerk to Administrator and Clerk of Councils, 1932; Colonial Treas., Dominica, 1940, St Vincent, 1945; Asst Administrator, St Lucia, 1949; Chief Sec., Windward Is, 1951, retd 1960 on abolition of office; performed duties of Governor's Dep., Windward Is, over fifty times; Speaker of Legislative Council, Dominica, 1961–67; Speaker of House of Assembly, Dominica, March-Oct. 1967. KStJ 1975. *Recreations:* tennis, swimming. *Address:* 7 Virgin Lane, Roseau, Commonwealth of Dominica, West Indies. *Died 21 Aug. 1993.*

COOPER, Prof. Kenneth Ernest; Emeritus Professor of Bacteriology, Bristol University, 1968; *b* 8 July 1903; *s* of E. Cooper; *m* 1930, Jessie Griffiths; no *c*. *Educ:* Tadcaster Grammar Sch.; Leeds Univ. BSc 1925, PhD 1927, Leeds; LRCP, MRCS 1936; FIBiol. Leeds University: Research Asst in Chemotherapy, 1928–31; Research Asst in Bacteriology, 1931–36; Lectr in Bacteriology, 1936–38; Bristol University: Lectr in Bacteriology, 1938–46; Reader in Bacteriology, 1946–50; Prof. of Bacteriology, 1951–68; Dep. Dean of the Faculty of Science, 1955–58. Hon. Gen. Sec. of Soc. for Gen. Microbiology, 1954–60, Hon. Treas., 1961–68, Hon. Mem., 1969. *Publications:* numerous papers in medical, chemical and bacteriological journals. *Recreations:* golf, chess. *Address:* Flat 22, Oaklands, Elton Road, Clevedon, Avon BS21 7QZ. *T:* Clevedon (0272) 343310. *Died 26 June 1993.*

COOPER, Susie, (Mrs Susan Vera Barker), OBE 1979; RDI 1940; FRSA; Senior Designer for Josiah Wedgwood & Sons Ltd, since 1966; *b* 29 Oct. 1902; *d* of John Cooper and Mary-Ann (*née* Adams); *m* 1938, Cecil Barker (*d* 1972); one *s*. *Educ:* Mollart House, Hanley; Burslem School of Art. Resident designer, Gray's Pottery, 1924; founded Susie Cooper Pottery, 1929; designed and produced tableware for Royal Pavilion, Festival of Britain, on South Bank, 1951. Dr RCA 1987; Hon. DLitt Staffordshire, 1993. *Recreations:* gardening, seed painting, textile design. *Died 28 July 1995.*

COOPER, Dame Whina, ONZ 1991; DBE 1981 (CBE 1974; MBE 1953); JP; New Zealand President, Maori Land Rights, since 1975; *b* 9 Dec. 1895; *d* of Heremia Te Wake, JP (a Chief of Ngati-Manawa hapu of Te Rarawa tribe) and Kare Pouro; *m* 1st, 1916, Richard Gilbert (*d* 1935); one *d* (one *s* decd); 2nd, 1935, William Cooper (*d* 1949); two *s* two *d*. *Educ:* St Joseph's Coll., Greenmeadows, Napier, NZ. Proficiency Cert.; qualified as school teacher. Teacher, Pawarenga Sch., Northland, 1917; postmistress and storekeeper, Panguru, 1940 (Pres., Panguru Federated Farmers, 1940). Active in Maori land develt schemes, 1930; President: (first), Maori Women's Welfare League, 1952; Te Unga Waka Marae Soc., 1960; Maori Progressive Cultural Org., 1966; Pres. and Maori Land Rights Leader who led the Great Maori Land March to Parliament, 1975. Had the honour of being the first woman to cross the threshold of Waitangi House, 1949. Pres., Hokianga Rugby Union, 1947; Mem., Whangarei Gun Club, 1930–38. JP Auckland, 1952. *Publication:* Notable New Zealanders, 1979; *relevant publication:* Whina, by Michael King, 1983. *Recreations:* hockey, netball, table tennis. *Address:* c/o PO Panguru, Hokianga, Northland, New Zealand. *T:* (9) 4095393.
Died 26 March 1994.

COOPER, Prof. Sir William M.; *see* Mansfield Cooper.

COOTE, John Oldham; Captain, Royal Navy; *b* 13 Aug. 1921; *o s* of F. Stanley Coote, OBE, KStJ and Edith F. Coote; *m* 1944, Sylvia Mary (*née* Syson); three *d*. *Educ:* China Inland Mission Sch., Chefoo; Felsted. Royal Navy, as submarine specialist, 1940–60 (despatches 1944). Joined Beaverbrook Newspapers, 1960: Vice-Chm. and Man. Dir, 1968–74; Dep. Chm. and Gp Man. Dir, 1974–75. Mem., Newspaper Publishers Assoc., 1968–75; Chm., Newsvendors Benevolent Inst. Festival Appeal, 1974. Dir Gen., British Film Prodn Assoc., 1976–77. Consultant, Boeing Marine Systems, 1980–87. Mem. Council, King George's Fund for Sailors, 1968–90 (Chm. Appeal Cttee, 1983–88); Trustee: Submarine Meml Museum, 1968–90; Devas Boys' Club, 1967–85; Chm., Petworth House Tennis Court, 1986–. *Publications:* Shell Pilot to the English Channel: Part 1 (South Coast), 1982; Part 2 (N France and Channel Islands), 1985; Shell Guide to Yacht Navigation, 1987; (ed and contrib.) The Faber Book of the Sea, 1989; (ed and contrib.) The Faber Book of Tales of the Sea, 1991; Submariner, 1991; Altering Course, 1992; contrib. defence and yachting pubns. *Recreations:* performing arts, offshore sailing, Real tennis. *Address:* Titty Hill, Iping, Midhurst, W Sussex GU29 0PL. *Clubs:* Garrick, Royal Ocean Racing; Royal Yacht Squadron; Cruising of America.   *Died 11 June 1993.*

COPAS, Most Rev. Virgil, KBE 1982; DD; MSC; Archbishop Emeritus (RC) of Port Moresby and of Kerema; *b* 19 March 1915; *s* of Cornelius Copas and Kathleen (*née* Daly). *Educ:* St Mary's Coll. and Downlands Coll., Toowoomba, Queensland. Sec. to Bp L. Scharmach, Rabaul, New Britain, New Guinea, 1945–51; Religious Superior, Dio. of Darwin, Australia, 1954–60; Bishop of Port Moresby, 1960–66; Archbishop of Port Moresby, 1966–76, resigned in favour of a national archbishop; Archbishop of Kerema, 1976–88. Hon. Mil. Chaplain, Australian Forces, New Guinea, 1945–48; Reserve Naval Chaplain, Darwin, 1954–59. Member: St Vincent de Paul Soc.; Rotary Internat. Initiated into 3 tribal gps of people in Papua New Guinea. *Publications:* articles on peoples, culture and religion of Papua New Guinea. *Address:* 12/64 Esplanade, Surfers Paradise, Qld 4217, Australia.
                    Died 3 Oct. 1993.

COPE, Maclachlan Alan Carl S.; *see* Silverwood-Cope.

COPLESTON, Rev. Frederick Charles, CBE 1993; MA Oxon, DPhil Rome, Gregorian Univ.; FBA 1970; SJ; Principal of Heythrop College, University of London, 1970–74; Emeritus Professor of University of London, 1974; *b* 10 April 1907; *s* of F. S. Copleston, former Chief Judge of Lower Burma, and N. M. Little. *Educ:* Marlborough Coll.; St John's Coll., Oxford (Hon. Fellow, 1975). Entered Catholic Church, 1925; Soc. of Jesus, 1930; ordained 1937. Prof. of History of Philosophy: Heythrop Coll., Oxford, 1939–70, and Univ. of London, 1972–74; Gregorian Univ., Rome, 1952–68; Dean of Faculty of Theology, Univ. of London, 1972–74. Visiting Professor: Univ. of Santa Clara, Calif, 1974–75 and 1977–82; Univ. of Hawaii, 1976; Gifford Lectr, Univ. of Aberdeen, 1979–80. Hon. Dr (Theology), Uppsala, Sweden, 1983; Hon. DLitt St Andrews, 1990. *Publications:* Friedrich Nietzsche, Philosopher of Culture, 1942, new edn 1975; St Thomas and Nietzsche, 1944; Arthur Schopenhauer, Philosopher of Pessimism, 1946; A History of Philosophy: vol. 1, Greece and Rome, 1946, rev. edn 1947; vol. 2, Augustine to Scotus, 1950; vol. 3, Ockham to Suárez, 1953; vol. 4, Descartes to Leibniz, 1958; vol. 5, Hobbes to Hume, 1959; vol. 6, Wolff to Kant, 1960; vol. 7, Fichte to Nietzsche, 1963; vol. 8, Bentham to Russell, 1966; vol. 9, Maine de Biran to Sartre, 1975; Existentialism and Modern Man, 1948; Medieval Philosophy, 1952; Aquinas (Pelican), 1955;

Contemporary Philosophy, 1956, rev. edn 1972; A History of Medieval Philosophy, 1972; Religion and Philosophy, 1974; Philosophers and Philosophies, 1976; On the History of Philosophy, 1979; Philosophies and Cultures, 1980; Religion and the One, 1982; Philosophy in Russia, 1986; Russian Religious Philosophy, 1988; Memoirs, 1993; articles in learned journals. *Address:* 114 Mount Street, W1Y 6AH. *T:* 071-493 7811.   *Died 3 Feb. 1994.*

CORBET, Freda Kunzlen, (Mrs Ian McIvor Campbell), JP; BA; *b* 15 Nov. 1900; *d* of James Mansell; *m* 1925, William Corbet (*d* 1957); *m* 1962, Ian McIvor Campbell (*d* 1976). *Educ:* Wimbledon County Sch.; University Coll., London. Called to the Bar, Inner Temple, 1932. MP (Lab) NW Camberwell, later Peckham Div. of Camberwell, 1945–Feb. 1974. Awarded Freedom of Southwark, 1974. JP Co. London, 1940. *Address:* 39 Gravel Road, Bromley, Kent BR2 8PE.
                    Died 1 Nov. 1993.

CORBETT, Prof. Peter Edgar; Yates Professor of Classical Art and Archaeology in the University of London (University College), 1961–82, then Professor Emeritus; *b* 19 June 1920; 2nd *s* of Ernest Oliver Corbett and Margaret Edgar; *m* 1944, Albertha Yates (*d* 1961); one *s* one *d*; *m* 1962, Margery Martin. *Educ:* Bedford Sch.; St John's Coll., Oxford. Royal Artillery, 1940–41, RAFVR, 1942–45. Thomas Whitcombe Greene Scholar, and Macmillan Student of British School at Athens, 1947–49; Asst Keeper in Dept of Greek and Roman Antiquities, British Museum, 1949–61. Lectr in Classics, Univ. of Calif, Los Angeles, 1956. Pres., Soc. for Promotion of Hellenic Studies, 1980–83. *Publications:* The Sculpture of the Parthenon, 1959; (with A. Birchall) Greek Gods and Heroes, 1974; articles in Jl of Hellenic Studies, Hesperia, Annual of Brit. School at Athens, BM Quarterly, Bulletin of the Inst. of Classical Studies. *Address:* 30 The Terrace, Barnes, SW13 0NR.   *Died 31 Aug. 1992.*

CORDEIRO, His Eminence Cardinal Joseph; RC Archbishop of Karachi, from 1958; *b* Bombay, India, 19 Jan. 1918. *Educ:* St Patrick's High School; D. J. College, Karachi; Papal Seminary, Kandy, Ceylon. Priest, 1946; Asst Chaplain, St Francis Xavier's, Hyderabad, Sind, 1947; Asst Principal, St Patrick's High School, Karachi, 1948; Student at Oxford, 1948; Asst Principal, St Patrick's High Sch., 1950; Principal, Grammar Sch., and Rector, Diocesan Seminary, Quetta, 1952. Cardinal, 1973. *Address:* St Patrick's Cathedral, Karachi 3, Pakistan. *T:* 515870.   *Died 11 Feb. 1994.*

CORK AND ORRERY, 13th Earl of, *cr* 1620; **Patrick Reginald Boyle;** Baron Boyle of Youghall, 1616; Viscount Dungarvan, 1620; Baron Boyle of Broghill, 1621; Viscount Boyle of Kinalmeaky and Baron of Bandon Bridge, 1621; Earl of Orrery, 1660 (all Ire.); Baron Boyle of Marston (GB), 1711; writer, artist and broadcaster; *b* 7 Feb. 1910; *s* of Major Hon. Reginald Courtenay Boyle, MBE, MC (*d* 1946), and Violet (*d* 1974), *d* of late Arthur Flower; *S* uncle, 1967; *m* 1952, Dorothy Kate (*d* 1978), *o d* of late Robert Ramsden, Meltham, Yorks; *m* 1978, Mary Gabrielle Walker, *o d* of late Louis Ginnett, and *widow* of Kenneth Macfarlane Walker. *Educ:* Harrow Sch.; Royal Military College, Sandhurst. Royal Ulster Rifles, 1930–33; Capt. London Irish Rifles, Royal Ulster Rifles (TA), 1935–38; served War of 1939–45 with Royal Ulster Rifles and Parachute Regt. Dep. Speaker and Dep. Chm. of Cttees, House of Lords, 1973–78; Mem., British Delegn to Inter-Parly Conf., Tokyo, 1974, Madrid, 1976. Pres. and Exec. Chm., British Cancer Council, 1973–77; Dir, Cancer Research Campaign; Mem., Council of Management, St Christopher's Hospice, Sydenham (Vice Pres., 1988–). Hereditary Life Governor and Exec. Chm., Christian Faith Soc. (Vice-Pres., 1988). FRSA 1947. *Publications:* (author

and illustrator) Sailing in a Nutshell, 1935; (jointly) Jungle, Jungle, Little Chindit, 1946; contribs to the Hibbert Jl. *Recreations:* oil-painting, gardening. *Heir: b* Hon. John William Boyle, DSC [*b* 12 May 1916; *m* 1943, Mary Leslie, *d* of late Gen. Sir Robert Gordon Finlayson, KCB, CMG, DSO; three *s*]. *Address:* Flint House, Heyshott, Midhurst, W Sussex. *Club:* Cork and County (Cork).
Died 8 Aug. 1995.

CORK, Sir Kenneth (Russell), GBE 1978; FCA; Chairman: Advent Eurofund, since 1982; Advent Capital, since 1985; Advent Management Ltd, since 1988; Richmount Enterprize Zone Managers Ltd, since 1988; Laser Richmount Ltd, since 1990; Vice-Chairman, Ladbroke Group, since 1986; Senior Partner, Cork Gully, Chartered Accountants, 1980–83 (Senior Partner, W. H. Cork, Gully & Co., 1946–80); Lord Mayor of London for 1978–79; *b* 21 Aug. 1913; *s* of William Henry Cork and Maud Alice (*née* Nunn); *m* 1937, Nina Lippold; one *s* one *d. Educ:* Berkhamsted. ACA 1937, FCA 1946 (Founding Socs' Centenary Award, 1981). Enlisted HAC, 1938; called up, 1939; served in North Africa and Italy, 1939–45 (rank Lt-Col). Common Councilman, City of London, 1951–70; Alderman, City of London (Ward of Tower), 1970; Sheriff, City of London, 1975–76; Liveryman, Worshipful Co. of Horners (Mem. Court, 1970, Renter Warden, 1978, Master, 1980); Master, Worshipful Co. of Chartered Accountants in England and Wales, 1984–85 (Sen. Warden, 1983–84); one of HM Lieutenants, City of London, 1979–. Chairman: EEC Bankruptcy Convention Adv. Cttee to Dept of Trade, 1973; Insolvency Law Review Cttee, 1977–82. Chairman: NI Finance Corp., 1974–76; NI Develt Agency, 1976–77 (Hon. Consultant, 1977–). Mem., Cttee to Review the Functioning of Financial Institutions, 1977–. President: Inst. of Credit Management Ltd; City Branch, Inst. of Dirs, 1981–. Director: Aitken Hume International; Brent Walker Hldgs, 1986–89. Vice-Chm., Arts Council of GB, 1986–87 (Mem., 1985–87); Chm., Arts Council Enquiry into Professional Theatre in England, 1986–87; Governor, Royal Shakespeare Theatre, 1967–89 (Chm., 1975–85; Pres., 1986–89); Dir, Shakespeare Theatre Trust (Chm. 1967–75); Treas., Royal Concert, 1970. Chm. of Governors, Berkhamsted Sch. FRSA 1970; FICM; CBIM 1979 (President: S Bucks Br.; City Br., 1986–); FCIS 1979; FInstD. KStJ 1979. Hon. DLitt City Univ., 1978. Hon. GSM. Insol Scroll of Honour, 1989. Commandeur de l'Ordre du Merite (France); Order of Rio Branco, cl. III (Brazil); Grande Oficiàl da Ordem Militare de Cristo (Portugal); Order of Diplomatic Service Merit Gwanghwa Medal (Korea). *Publication:* Cork on Cork (autobiog.), 1988. *Recreations:* sailing, photography, painting. *Address:* Cherry Trees, Grimms Hill, Great Missenden, Bucks HP16 9BG. *T:* Great Missenden (02406) 2628. *Clubs:* Athenæum, Royal Thames Yacht, City Livery, Cornhill (Pres. 1984), Little Ship; Itchenor Sailing, Royal Southern Yacht (Southampton).
Died 13 Oct. 1991.

CORMACK, Sir Magnus (Cameron), KBE 1970; *b* Caithness, Scotland, 12 Feb. 1906; *s* of William Petrie Cormack and Violet McDonald Cameron; *m* 1935, Mary Gordon Macmeiken; one *s* three *d. Educ:* St Peter's Sch., Adelaide, S Aust. Farmer and grazier. Served War, 1940–44; Aust. Imperial Forces, SW Pacific Area, Major. Pres., Liberal Party Organisation, 1947–49; Senator for Victoria, 1951–53 and 1962–78; President of the Senate, 1971–74. *Recreation:* deep sea sailing. *Club:* Australian (Melbourne).
Died 26 Nov. 1994.

CORNISH, William Herbert, CB 1955; Receiver for the Metropolitan Police District, 1961–67; *b* 2 Jan. 1906; *s* of late Rev. Herbert H. Cornish and Susan Emerson; *m* 1938, Eileen May Elizabeth Cooney (*d* 1991); two *d. Educ:* Wesley Coll., Dublin; Trinity Coll., Dublin. Scholar, 1st

Cl. Moderator with Large Gold Medal in Modern History and Political Science. Entered Home Office, 1930; Asst Sec., 1942; Asst Under-Sec. of State, 1952–60. *Recreations:* gardening, music. *Address:* 2 Tormead, Dene Road, Northwood, Mddx HA6 2BX. *T:* Northwood (01923) 821933.
Died 7 Jan. 1995.

CORNWALL, Ian Wolfran, PhD London; Reader in Human Environment, University of London, 1965–74; *b* 28 Nov. 1909; *s* of Lt-Col J. W. Cornwall, CIE, IMS, and Effie E. C. (*née* Sinclair), *d* of Surg.-Gen. D. Sinclair, IMS; *m* 1st, 1937, Anna Margareta (*née* Callear) (*d* 1967); two *s*; 2nd, 1974, Mary L. Reynolds (*née* Miller). *Educ:* private sch.; Wellington Coll., Berks; St John's Coll., Cambridge (BA). Teaching, clerking, pharmaceutical manufacturing, selling, 1931–39; Postal and Telegraph Censorship, Press Censorship, MOI, 1939–45; London Univ. Inst. of Archaeology: Student, 1945–47 (Diploma, 1947); Secretary, 1948–51; University teacher and researcher, 1951–74, retd (PhD London, 1952). Life Mem., Geologists' Assoc. Henry Stopes Memorial Medal, Geologists' Assoc., 1970. *Publications:* Bones for the Archaeologist, 1956, rev. edn 1975; Soils for the Archaeologist, 1958; The Making of Man, 1960 (Carnegie Medal of Library Assoc.); The World of Ancient Man, 1964; Hunter's Half Moon (fiction), 1967; Prehistoric Animals and their Hunters, 1968; Ice Ages, 1970; contribs to specialist jls. *Recreations:* geology, gardening, photography. *Address:* 2 Forest Walk, Elmbridge Village, Cranleigh, Surrey GU6 8TF.
Died 18 Nov. 1994.

CORRIN, John Bowes, OBE 1983; *b* 26 Oct. 1922; *s* of Harold R. Corrin and Mabel F. Corrin; *m* 1948, José M. Sharman; one *s* one *d. Educ:* Berkhamsted. FCA 1945 (Auditing Prize). Partner, Thornton Baker, later Grant Thornton, 1949–87; Dir, Anglia, later Nationwide Anglia Building Soc., 1964–89 (Chm., 1981–85). Pres., Leics and Northants Soc. of Chartered Accountants, 1959; Past Pres., Northampton Conservative Assoc. Mayor, Northampton, 1964–65; Hon. Freeman, Borough of Northampton, 1972. *Recreations:* golf, bridge. *Address:* Tynwald, Sandy Lane, Church Brampton, Northampton NN6 8AX. *T:* Northampton (0604) 845301. *Clubs:* Northampton County; Northamptonshire County Golf.
Died 31 July 1994.

CORY, Sir Clinton James Donald, 4th Bt, *cr* 1919, of Coryton, Whitchurch, Glamorgan; *b* 1 March 1909; 2nd *s* of Sir Donald Cory, 2nd Bt, shipowner of Llandaff, Glam, and Gertrude (*d* 1981), *d* of Henry Thomas Box; *S* brother, 1941; *m* 1935, Mary, *o d* of Dr A. Douglas Hunt, Park Grange, Derby; one *s. Educ:* Brighton Coll.; abroad. *Heir: s* (Clinton Charles) Donald Cory, *b* 13 Sept. 1937. *Address:* 18 Cloisters Road, Letchworth, Herts SG6 3JS. *T:* Letchworth (0462) 677206.
Died 28 Aug. 1991.

COSTAR, Sir Norman (Edgar), KCMG 1963 (CMG 1953); *b* 18 May 1909; *s* of E. T. Costar. *Educ:* Battersea Grammar School; Jesus Coll., Cambridge. Asst Principal, Colonial Office, 1932; Private Sec. to Permanent Under Sec., Dominions Office, 1935; served in UK High Commissioner's Offices, Australia, 1937–39, New Zealand, 1945–47; Principal, 1938; Asst Sec., 1946; Dep. High Commissioner, Ceylon, 1953–57; Asst Under-Sec., Commonwealth Relations Office, 1958–60; Dep. High Commissioner in Australia, 1960–62; High Commissioner: Trinidad and Tobago, 1962–66; Cyprus, 1967–69. Adjudicator, Immigration Appeals, 1970–81. *Club:* United Oxford & Cambridge University.
Died 5 July 1995.

COT, Pierre Donatien Alphonse; Commander Legion of Honour; Croix de Guerre; Hon. MVO; Ingénieur général des ponts et chaussées; *b* 10 Sept. 1911; *s* of late Donatien

Cot, Engr-Gen. and Naval Hydrographer, Membre de l'Institut, and Yvonne (*née* Bunout); *m* 1939, Claude Bouguen; two *s* two *d*. *Educ:* Lycée Louis-le-Grand, Paris; Ecole Polytechnique, Paris. Licencié ès Sciences. Govt Civil Engr, Paris, 1936; Chief Engineer of Port of Le Havre, 1945; Techn. Manager, 1951, Dir-Gen., 1955–67, and Administrator, 1967–75, Paris Airport Authority; Pres., Air France, 1967–74; Pres.-Dir-Gen., Soc. Gén. d'Entreprises, 1974–79, then Président d'Honneur. Pres., Institut géographique national, 1967–75. Médaille de l'Aéronautique; Officier du Mérite Touristique; Médaille de vermeil de la Ville de Paris, 1972. *Address:* 69 rue de l'Assomption, 75016 Paris, France.

Died 22 June 1993.

COTTESLOE, 4th Baron (UK) *cr* 1874; **John Walgrave Halford Fremantle**, GBE 1960; TD; Bt 1821; Baron of Austrian Empire 1816; *b* 2 March 1900; *s* of 3rd Baron Cottesloe, CB and Florence (*d* 1956), *d* of Thomas Tapling; *S* father 1956; *m* 1st, 1926, Lady Elizabeth Harris (marr. diss. 1945; she *d* 1983), *o d* of 5th Earl of Malmesbury; one *s* one *d*; 2nd, 1959, Gloria Jean Irene Dunn, *o d* of W. E. Hill, Barnstaple; one *s* two *d*. *Educ:* Eton; Trinity Coll., Cambridge. BA (Hons) Mechanical Sciences 1921; MA 1924. Served as OC 251 (Bucks) AA Battery RA (TA), 1938–39; GSO 1 attached 2nd Armoured Division, 1940; Senior Military Liaison Officer to Regional Commissioner, NE Region, 1940–41; GSO 1 (Technical) AA Command, 1941–42; Commanding Officer, 20 LAA Regt RA, 1942–44; GSO 1 (Radar) War Office, 1944–45. Mem. LCC, 1945–55. Chm., Thomas Tapling & Co. Ltd; Vice-Chm., PLA, 1956–67. Chairman: Tate Gallery, 1959–60; Arts Council of Gt Britain, 1960–65; South Bank Theatre Bd (from inception), 1962–77 (Cottesloe theatre part of Nat. Theatre complex was opened 1976); Adv. Council and Reviewing Cttee on Export of Works of Art, 1954–72; Heritage in Danger, 1973–; Royal Postgrad. Med. Sch., 1949–58 (Fellow); NW Met. Reg. Hosp. Bd, 1953–60; Hammersmith and St Mark's Hospital, 1968–74; Northwick Park Hosp. Adv. Cttee, 1970–74; a Governor, King Edward's Hosp. Fund for London, 1973–83. Chairman: British Postgraduate Medical Fedn, 1958–72; Nat. Rifle Assoc., 1960–72; Vice-Chm., City Parochial Foundn, 1972–77; Pres., Hospital Saving Assoc., 1973–; Hon. Sec. Amateur Rowing Assoc., 1932–46; a Steward of Henley Royal Regatta; Chm., The Dogs' Home, Battersea, 1970–83. Former DL County of London (later Greater London). *Recreations:* rowed in winning crews in Oxford and Cambridge Boat Race, 1921 and 1922 and in Grand Challenge Cup, Henley, 1922; Captain of English VIII at Bisley on 25 occasions and shot in English VIII on 37 occasions and won Match Rifle Championship six times, with many other first prizes for long-range shooting. *Heir: s* Comdr Hon. John Tapling Fremantle [*b* 22 Jan. 1927; *m* 1958, Elizabeth Ann, *e d* of late Lt-Col H. S. Barker, DSO; one *s* two *d*]. *Address:* Oak House, Well Road, Crondall, near Farnham, Surrey GU10 5PN. *Clubs:* Travellers'; Leander (Pres., 1957–62).

Died 22 April 1994.

COTTON, **Henry Egerton**, JP; Lord-Lieutenant and Custos Rotulorum, Metropolitan County of Merseyside, since 1989; *b* 21 July 1929; *yr s* of late Vere Egerton Cotton, CBE, TD, LLD, and Elfreda Helen Cotton (*née* Moore); *m* 1955, (Elizabeth Margaret) Susan Peard; one *s* one *d*. *Educ:* Durnford and Brockhurst Prep. Schs; Rugby Sch.; Magdalene Coll., Cambridge (MA). National Service, RA, 1947–49; Territorials, 59th Med. Regt RA (Lieut), 1949–55. Owen Owen Ltd, 1952–89; Development Dir, T. J. Hughes & Co., 1986–89. Liverpool Playhouse: Dir, 1967–73; Chm., 1973–82; Pres., 1989–; Dir, Northern Ballet Th., 1977–; Chancellor, Liverpool John Moores Univ., 1992– (Gov., Liverpool Polytechnic, 1988–92); Gov., Blue Coat Sch., Liverpool, 1970–; Vice-Pres. and

Life Gov., Liverpool Coll., 1989–. Trustee: Childwall Open Spaces Trust, 1970–93; Skelton Bounty, 1988–; Nat. Museums and Galls on Merseyside, 1991–; Chairman: Local Radio Council (Radio Merseyside), 1976–79; Drama Panel, Merseyside Arts Assoc., 1980–82. Vice Chm., Liverpool Dio. Bd of Finance, 1968–75; Chm., Liverpool Cathedral Exec. Cttee, 1979–; Dir, Liverpool Cathedral Estates, 1991–. Patron, St Mary's Ch., Grassendale, Liverpool, 1969–. Hon. Col, Merseyside ACF, 1991–. High Sheriff of Merseyside, 1986–87. KStJ 1989. *Recreations:* travel, theatre, canals, gardening. *Address:* Norwood, Grassendale Park, Liverpool L19 0LP. *T:* 051–427 3122.

Died 3 Aug. 1993.

COTTON, **Leonard Thomas**, MCh; FRCS; Surgeon, King's College Hospital, since 1957; Surgeon, Queen Victoria Hospital, East Grinstead, and St Luke's Nursing Home for the Clergy; Dean, King's College Hospital Medical School, 1978–87 (Vice-Dean, 1976–77); *b* 5 Dec. 1922; *s* of Edward Cotton and Elizabeth (*née* Webb); *m* 1946, Frances Joanna Bryan; one *s* two *d*. *Educ:* King's College Sch., Wimbledon; Oriel Coll., Oxford; King's Coll. Hospital. MRCS, LRCP 1946; BM, BCh Oxon 1946; FRCS 1950; MCh Oxon 1957. House Surgeon, King's College Hospital, 1946; Resident Surgical Officer, Royal Waterloo Hospital, 1947; Resident Surgical Officer, Weymouth and District Hospital, 1948; National Service, Surgical Specialist RAMC, 1949–51; Senior Registrar and Registrar, King's College Hospital, 1951–57; Surgical Tutor, King's Coll. Hospital Medical Sch., 1957–65. FRSM; Member: Surgical Research Soc.; Assoc. of Surgeons; Vascular Surgical Soc.; Ct of Examiners, RCS. Hunterian Prof., RCS. FKC 1983. *Publications:* (ed) Hey Groves' Synopsis of Surgery; co-author, short text-book of Surgery; contributions to medical journals. *Recreations:* gardening, reading. *Address:* 3 Dome Hill Park, Sydenham Hill, SE26 6SP. *T:* 081-778 8047; Private Wing, King's College Hospital, Denmark Hill, SE5 8RX. *T:* 071–274 8670.

Died 9 Nov. 1992.

COTTS, **Sir (Robert) Crichton Mitchell**, 3rd Bt, *cr* 1921, of Coldharbour Wood, Rogate, Sussex; *b* 20 Oct. 1903; *yr s* of Sir William Dingwall Mitchell Cotts, 1st Bt, KBE, MP (*d* 1932), and Agnes Nivison (*d* 1966), 2nd *d* of late Robert Sloane; *S* brother, 1964; *m* 1942, Barbara (*d* 1982), *o d* of late Capt. Herbert J. A. Throckmorton, Royal Navy; two *s* two *d* (and one *d* decd). Late Temp. Major, Irish Guards; USSR, White Sea, 1941–42. *Heir: s* Richard Crichton Mitchell Cotts, *b* 26 July 1946. *Address:* 16 High Street, Needham Market, Suffolk IP6 8AP.

Died 17 Jan. 1995.

COULTHARD, **William Henderson**, CBE 1968; MSc, CEng, FIMechE, FRPS; Deputy Director, Royal Armament Research and Development Establishment, 1962–74; *b* 24 Nov. 1913; *s* of William and Louise Coulthard, Flimby, Cumberland; *m* 1942, Peggie Frances Platts Taylor, Chiselhurst; one *d* (one *s* decd). *Educ:* Flimby, Workington Schs; Armstrong Coll., University of Durham. Mather Schol., University of Durham, 1932. Linen Industry Research Assoc., 1934; Instrument Dept, Royal Aircraft Estabt, 1935; Air Ministry HQ, 1939; Sqdn Ldr RAFVR, 1944; Official German Translator, 1945; Air Photography Div., RAE, 1946; Supt, later Dep. Dir, Fighting Vehicles Research and Development Estabt, 1951. *Publications:* Aircraft Instrument Design, 1951; Aircraft Engineer's Handbook, 1953; (trans.) Mathematical Instruments (Capellen), 1948; (trans.) Gyroscopes (Grammel), 1950; articles in technical journals. *Recreations:* art history (Diploma in History of Art, London Univ., 1964), languages. *Address:* Argyll, Francis Close, Ewell, Surrey. *T:* 081–337 4909.

Died 28 Feb. 1993.

COUNSELL, His Honour Paul Hayward, QC 1963; a Circuit Judge, 1973–90; *b* 13 Nov. 1926; twin *s* of Frederick Charles Counsell and Edna Counsell; *m* 1959, Joan Agnes Strachan; one *s* two *d*. *Educ:* Colston Sch., Bristol; Queen's Coll., Oxford (MA). Served RAF, 1944–48. Admitted Solicitor, 1951; called to the Bar, Inner Temple, 1962. Northern Rhodesia: Crown Solicitor, 1955–56; Crown Counsel, 1956–61; Resident Magistrate, 1958; Dir of Public Prosecutions, 1962–63; Solicitor General, 1963–64; Acting Attorney General, 1964; Solicitor-General, Zambia, 1964; MLC, 1963–64; in chambers of Lord Hailsham, Temple, 1965–73; Dep. Circuit Judge, 1971–73. Chm., Industrial Tribunal, 1970–73. *Recreation:* model engineering.
Died 11 March 1993.

COURAGE, Richard Hubert, DL; *b* 23 Jan. 1915; *s* of Raymond Courage and Mildred Frances Courage (formerly Fisher); *m* 1st, 1941, Jean Elizabeth Agnes Watson (*d* 1977), *d* of late Sir Charles Cuningham Watson, KCIE, CSI, ICS; three *s* (and one *s* decd); 2nd, 1978, Phyllida Anne, *widow* of J. D. Derouet. *Educ:* Eton. Served War of 1939–45: Northants Yeomanry, 1939–46; Major (despatches). Director: Courage Ltd, 1948–75 (Chm., 1959–75); Imperial Group Ltd, 1972–75; Norwich Union Insce Group, 1975–80; Chm., London Adv. Bd, Norwich Union Insce Gp, 1975–80 (Dir, 1964–80). Governor, Brentwood Sch., Essex, 1959–90 (Chm., 1976–89). JP Essex, 1955–85; DL Essex, 1977. *Recreations:* yachting, shooting. *Address:* Chainbridge, Mountnessing, near Brentwood, Essex CM15 8SG. *T:* Brentwood (0277) 222206. *Died 5 Sept. 1994.*

COURCEL, Baron de; (Geoffroy Louis Chodron de Courcel), Grand' Croix de la Légion d'Honneur, 1980; Compagnon de la Libération, 1943; Croix de Guerre, 1939–45; Hon. GCVO 1950; MC 1943; Ambassadeur de France, 1965; President, Institute Charles de Gaulle, since 1985; *b* Tours, Indre-et-Loire, 11 Sept. 1912; *s* of Louis Chodron de Courcel, Officer, and Alice Lambert-Champy; *m* 1954, Martine Hallade; two *s*. *Educ:* Stanislas Coll., Paris; University of Paris. DenDr, LèsL, Dip. Ecole des Sciences Politiques. Attaché, Warsaw, 1937; Sec., Athens, 1938–39; Armée du Levant, 1939; joined Free French Forces, June 1940; Chef de Cabinet, Gén. de Gaulle, London, 1940–41; Captain 1st Spahis marocains Regt, Egypt, Libya and Tunisia, 1941–43; Dep.-Dir of Cabinet, Gén de Gaulle, Algiers, 1943–44; Mem. Conseil de l'Ordre de la Libération, 1944; Regional Comr for Liberated Territories, 1944; in charge of Alsace-Lorraine Dept, Min. of Interior, 1944–45; Counsellor, 1945; Ministry of Foreign Affairs: Dep. Dir Central and N European Sections, 1945–47; First Counsellor, Rome, 1947–50; Minister Plen., 1951; Dir Bilateral Trade Agreements Section, 1951; Dir African and ME Section, 1953; Dir Gen., Polit. and Econ. Affairs, Min. of Moroccan and Tunisian Affairs, 1954; Perm. Sec., Nat. Defence, 1955–58; Ambassador, Perm. Rep. to NATO, 1958; Sec.-Gen. Présidence de la République, 1959–62; Ambassador to London, 1962–72; Sec.-Gen., Min. of For. Affairs, 1973–76. Pres., France–GB Assoc., 1978–87. Hon. DCL Oxon, 1970; Hon. LLD Birmingham, 1972. *Publication:* L'influence de la Conférence de Berlin de 1885 sur le droit Colonial International, 1936. *Recreations:* shooting, swimming. *Address:* 7 rue de Médicis, 75006 Paris, France; La Ravinière, Fontaines en Sologne, 41250 Bracieux, France. *Died 9 Dec. 1992.*

COURT, Prof. (Seymour) Donald (Mayneord), CBE 1969; MD; FRCP; Emeritus Professor, University of Newcastle upon Tyne, 1972; *b* 4 Jan. 1912; *s* of David Henry and Ethel Court; *m* 1939, Dr Frances Edith Radcliffe; two *s* one *d*. *Educ:* Adams Grammar Sch., Wem; Birmingham Univ (MB, ChB 1936; MD 1947).

FRCP 1956. Resident hosp. appts Birmingham Gen. Hosps, and Hosp. for Sick Children, London, 1936–38; Paediatric Registrar, Wander Scholar, Westminster Hosp., 1938–39; Physician, EMS, 1939–46; Nuffield Fellow in Child Health, 1946–47; Reader in Child Health, University of Durham, 1947–55; James Spence Prof. of Child Health, Univ. of Newcastle upon Tyne, 1955–72. Chm., Child Health Services Cttee for England and Wales, 1973–76. Pres., British Paediatric Assoc., 1973–76. FRCGP *ad eundem* 1982; Hon. FRSM 1986. James Spence Medal, British Paed. Assoc., 1978; Nils Rosén von Rosenstein Medal, Swedish Paed. Assoc., 1979. *Publications:* (jointly) Growing Up in Newcastle upon Tyne, 1960; (ed) The Medical Care of Children, 1963; (ed jointly) Paediatrics in the Seventies, 1972; (jointly) The School Years in Newcastle upon Tyne, 1974; (ed jtly) Fit for the Future, 1976; contributions to special jls and text books on respiratory infection in childhood. *Recreations:* walking, natural history, poetry. *Address:* 8 Towers Avenue, Jesmond, Newcastle upon Tyne NE2 3QE. *T:* Newcastle upon Tyne (091) 2814884. *Died 9 Sept. 1994.*

COWAN, Sir Robert, Kt 1989; Chairman, Highlands and Islands Enterprise (formerly Highlands and Islands Development Board), Inverness, 1982–92; *b* 27 July 1932; *s* of Dr John McQueen Cowan and May Cowan; *m* 1959, Margaret Morton (*née* Dewar); two *d*. *Educ:* Edinburgh Academy; Edinburgh Univ. (MA). Fisons Ltd, 1958–62; Wolsey Ltd, 1962–64; PA Management Consultants Ltd, 1965–82. Member: Bd, Scottish Develt Agency, 1982–91; BBC Broadcasting Council for Scotland, 1984–89; BBC Gen. Adv. Council, 1989–; Scottish PO Bd, 1990–. Mem. Court, Aberdeen Univ., 1989–; Gov., Napier Coll., Edinburgh, 1989–. Hon. LLD Aberdeen, 1987. *Recreation:* sailing. *Address:* The Old Manse, Farr, Inverness-shire IV1 2XA. *Clubs:* New (Edinburgh); Highland (Inverness); Hong Kong (Hong Kong).
Died 7 Jan. 1993.

COWDRAY, 3rd Viscount, *cr* 1917; **Weetman John Churchill Pearson,** TD; Bt 1894; Baron 1910; Captain, Sussex Yeomanry; Chairman, S. Pearson & Son Ltd, 1954–77; President, Pearson Plc, since 1983; *b* 27 Feb. 1910 (twin); *s* of 2nd Viscount and Agnes Beryl (*d* 1948), *d* of Lord Edward Spencer Churchill; *S* father, 1933; *m* 1st, 1939, Lady Anne Bridgeman (marr. diss. 1950), *d* of 5th Earl of Bradford; one *s* two *d*; 2nd, 1953, Elizabeth Georgiana Mather, 2nd *d* of Sir Anthony Mather-Jackson, 6th Bt; one *s* two *d*. *Educ:* Eton; Christ Church, Oxford. Parliamentary Private Sec. to Under-Sec. of State for Air, 1941–42. *Recreations:* polo, shooting, fishing. *Heir: s* Hon. Michael Orlando Weetman Pearson [*b* 17 June 1944; *m* 1977, Ellen (marr. diss.), *yr d* of late Hermann Erhardt; *m* 1987, Marina, *d* of John H. Cordle, and Mrs H. J. Ross Skinner; one *s* three *d*]. *Address:* Cowdray Park, Midhurst, West Sussex GU29 0AX. *T:* Midhurst (01730) 812461; Dunecht, Skene, Aberdeenshire AB32 7DD. *T:* Dunecht (01330) 860244. *Clubs:* Cavalry and Guards, White's.
Died 19 Jan. 1995.

COWLEY, Rev. Canon Colin Patrick; Rector of Wonston, Winchester, 1955–71; Canon of Winchester, 1950–55, Hon. Canon, 1955, Canon Emeritus, 1971; *b* 3 Aug. 1902; *er s* of Rev. H. G. B. Cowley; *m* 1930, Dorothea Minna Pott (*d* 1980); three *d*. *Educ:* Winchester; Hertford Coll., Oxford. Deacon, 1926; priest, 1927; Curate at St Mary's, Bridport, 1926–28; Curate at St Mary Abbots, Kensington, 1928–35; Rector of Shenfield, Essex, 1935–50. Chaplain to the Forces, 1940–45. *Recreation:* coping with old age. *Address:* Brendon House, Park Road, Winchester, Hants.
Died 26 Feb. 1993.

COWLEY, Lt-Gen. Sir John Guise, GC (AM 1935); KBE 1958 (CBE 1946; OBE 1943); CB 1954; late Royal Engineers; Chairman, Polamco Ltd, since 1976; *b* 20 Aug.

1905; *s* of Rev. Henry Guise Beatson Cowley, Fourgates, Dorchester, Dorset; *m* 1941, Irene Sybil, *d* of Percy Dreuille Millen, Berkhamsted, Herts; one *s* three *d*. *Educ:* Wellington Coll.; RMA Woolwich. 2nd Lieut RE, 1925; Capt. 1936; Major 1940; Lieut-Col 1941; Brig. 1943; Maj.-Gen. 1953; Lieut-Gen. 1957. Served War of 1939–45, Middle East, Italy, and North-West Europe (despatches four times, OBE). Chief of Staff, HQ Eastern Command, 1953–56; VQMG, 1956–57; Controller of Munitions, Ministry of Supply, 1957–60; Master-Gen. of the Ordnance, War Office, 1960–62; retd, 1962. Colonel Commandant: Royal Pioneer Corps, 1961–67; Royal Engineers, 1961–70. Chairman: Bowmaker Ltd, 1962–71; Wilverley Securities Ltd, 1970–73; Keith and Henderson Ltd, 1973–76; Director: British Oxygen Ltd, 1962–76; Alastair Watson Ltd, 1962–70; C. T. Bowring and Co. Ltd, 1969–71. Pres., New Forest Preservation Soc., 1982–. Governor, Wellington Coll., 1960–76 (Vice-Pres. and Chm. of Governors, 1969–76); Pres. OW Soc. 1979–; Chairman of Governors: Eagle House Sch., 1968–76; Bigshotte Sch., 1968–76; Brockenhurst Sixth Form Coll., 1977–84. Knight Comdr Order of Orange Nassau (Netherlands). FRSA. *Recreations:* bridge, croquet. *Address:* Whitemoor, Sandy Down, Boldre, Lymington, Hants SO41 8PN. *T:* Lymington (0590) 23369.
Died 7 Jan. 1993.

COX, His Honour Albert Edward; a Circuit Judge, 1977–89; *b* 26 Sept. 1916; *s* of Frederick Stringer Cox; *m* 2nd, 1962, Alwyne Winifred Cox, JP; one step *s*. Admitted Solicitor, 1938; Principal Partner, Claude Hornby & Cox, 1946–76; a Recorder of the Crown Court, 1972–77. President: London Criminal Courts Solicitors' Assoc., 1967–68; British Acad. of Forensic Science, 1977–78; Mem., Parole Board, 1971–75; Chm., London (Metropolis) Licensing Planning Cttee, 1979–84. *Address:* 38 Carlton Hill, NW8 0JY; Petit Bois, Teilhet, Arriège, France.
Died 10 Aug. 1992.

COX, Sir Anthony (Wakefield), Kt 1983; CBE 1972; FRIBA, AADip; Consultant, Architects' Co-Partnership, since 1980; *b* 18 July 1915; *s* of late William Edward Cox, CBE, and of Elsie Gertrude Wakefield; *m* 1943, Susan Babington Smith, ARIBA, AA Dip.; two *d*. *Educ:* Mill Hill Sch.; Architectural Association Sch. of Architecture, London. RIBA Journal, 1938–39; Jt Editor of Focus, 1938–39; founder partner, Architects' Co-Partnership, 1939; Sir Alexander Gibb & Partners, ordnance factories and hostels, 1940–42; served War: Royal Engineers, Western Europe and India, 1943–46; Hertfordshire CC Schools, 1946–47; reabsorbed in Architects' Co-Partnership, 1947; part-time teaching AA Sch. of Architecture, 1948–54. Member Council: Architectural Assoc., 1956–64 (Pres. 1962–63); RIBA, 1967–72; Member: Bd of Educn, RIBA, 1967–73; Royal Fine Art Commn, 1970–85; Bd, Property Services Agency, 1979–81, Adv. Bd, 1981–84. *Works include:* Departments of: Chemistry at Univ. of Leicester and University Coll., London; Chemistry and Biochemistry at Imperial Coll. of Science and Technology; buildings for: Inst. of Psychiatry, London; Maudsley Hosp., London. *Publications:* (jtly) Design for Health Care, 1981; Hospitals and Health Care Facilities, 1990. *Recreations:* reading, listening, looking, making. *Address:* 5 Bacon's Lane, Highgate, N6 6BL. *T:* 081–340 2543. *Died 5 Jan. 1993.*

COX, Sir (George) Trenchard, Kt 1961; CBE 1954; MA; FRSA (Vice-President 1964–68); FMA; FSA; Director and Secretary, Victoria and Albert Museum, 1956–66; *b* 31 July 1905; *s* of late William Pallett Cox and Marion Beverley; *m* 1935, Mary Désirée (*d* 1973), *d* of late Sir Hugh Anderson, Master of Gonville and Caius Coll., Cambridge. *Educ:* Eton; King's Coll., Cambridge. Worked as volunteer at the National Gallery and Brit. Museum

(Dept of Prints and Drawings), 1929–32; spent a semester at the University of Berlin in the Dept of Arts, 1930; Asst to the Keeper, Wallace Collection, 1932–39; seconded for war-time duties, to Home Office, 1940–44; Dir of Birmingham Museum and Art Gallery, 1944–55. Member: Ancient Monuments Board for England, 1959–69; Standing Commn on Museums and Galleries, 1967–77. People's Warden, St Martin-in-the-Fields, 1968–79. Hon. DLitt Birmingham, 1956. Hon. Fellow, Royal Acad., 1981. Chevalier, Légion d'Honneur, 1967. *Publications:* The National Gallery, a Room-to-Room Guide, 1930; Jehan Foucquet, Native of Tours, 1931; part editor of the Catalogue to the Exhibition of French Art at Burlington House, Jan.-March 1932; The Renaissance in Europe, 1933; A General Guide to the Wallace Collection, 1933; A Short Illustrated History of the Wallace Collection and its Founders, 1936; David Cox, 1947; Peter Bruegel, 1951; Pictures: a Handbook for Curators, 1956. *Recreations:* reading, travelling. *Address:* 33 Queen's Gate Gardens, SW7 5RR. *T:* 0171–584 0231. *Club:* Athenæum.
Died 21 Dec. 1995.

COX, Surg. Rear-Adm. James, OBE 1964; FFARCS; Surgeon Rear Admiral, Support Medical Services, 1983–84, retired; *b* 4 Feb. 1928; *s* of James Wolseley Cox and Gladys May Cox (*née* Watkinson); *m* 1952, Elizabeth Jennings; one *s* one *d*. *Educ:* Durham Sch.; Durham Univ. (MB, BS 1951). FFARCS 1960. HMS Birmingham, 1952–54; Consultant Anaesthetist, RN Hospitals: Plymouth, 1955–59; Chatham, 1959–61; Plymouth, 1962–65; Gibraltar, 1965–69; Plymouth, 1969–71; Principal Medical Officer, HMS Bulwark, 1971–72; Consultant Anaesthetist, RN Hospitals: Plymouth, 1972–75; Haslar, 1975–77; Staff Medical Officer to Major-Gen. Royal Marines Commando Forces, 1977–80; Medical Officer in Charge, RN Hospital Stonehouse, 1980–82; Surgeon Rear-Adm. (Naval Medicine and Trng), 1982–83. QHS, 1982–84. *Recreations:* fishing, gardening. *Address:* c/o National Westminster Bank, 87 Grey Street, Newcastle upon Tyne NE1 6ER.
Died 22 Nov. 1991.

COX, Sir Mencea Ethereal, Kt 1980; Member of the Senate, Barbados; *b* 28 Nov. 1906; *s* of James William Cox and Charlotte Matilda Cox, Plymouth Brethren. *Educ:* elementary and private (languages: English, Latin, French, Spanish). Formerly worked in carpentry, engineering and hired car driving, and as garage owner; also in wholesale and retail business. Elected to Barbados Parliament, 1944; Member of the then Governor's Exec. Council, 1948; following the introduction of ministerial system of Govt in 1954, apptd Minister of Communications, Works and Housing, 1954, then Minister of Trade, Industry, Tourism and Labour, 1956–61; concurrently, 1958–61, Dep. Premier and Leader of House of Assembly. *Recreations:* horse racing, cricket. *Address:* Ambury, Clapham St Michael, Barbados, WI. *T:* 77766.
Died 2 March 1994.

COX, Ronald; Director-General, Greater Glasgow Passenger Transport Executive, 1973–77, retired; *b* St Helens, Lancs, 3 Feb. 1916; *s* of Frederick Nisbet Cox and Annie Cox; *m* 1941, Edna Frances Heaton; one *s* one *d*. *Educ:* Higher Grade Boys' Sch., St Helens, Lancs (Oxford Univ. Cert., 6 credits); Trainee Transport Officer, St Helens Corp. Transport (Endorsed Cert. in Commerce, NC Engrg). Served War, Flt Lt (Tech.), RAF Transport Command, 1940–46. Sen. Traffic Officer, St Helens Corp. Transport, 1946–48; Traffic Supt, Salford City Transport, 1948–53; Dep. Engr and Gen. Manager, Rochdale Corp. Transport, 1953–54, Engr and Gen. Manager, 1954–62; Gen. Manager, Bournemouth Corp. Transport, 1962–64; Transport Manager, Edinburgh Corp. Transport, 1964–73. President: Scottish Road Passenger Transport Assoc.,

1973–74; Incorp. Assoc. of Public Passenger Transport, 1974–75. RSA Dip. (prizewinner transport subjects); MIRTE, MInstT, FCIT. *Recreation:* sailing. *Address:* 6 Stonehanger Court, Devon Road, Salcombe, Devon TQ8 8HJ. *T:* Salcombe (054884) 3456.

Died 15 July 1991.

COX, Sir Trenchard; *see* Cox, Sir G. T.

COZENS, Brig. Dame (Florence) Barbara, DBE 1963; RRC 1958; *b* 24 Dec. 1906; *d* of late Capt. A. Cozens, S Staffs. *Educ:* Seabury Sch., Worthing. Nurse training, The Nightingale Sch., St Thomas' Hosp., London, 1928–32; joined QAIMNS, 1933; served War of 1939–45, England and Continent; Lieut-Col 1954; Col 1958; Brig. 1960; Matron-in-Chief and Dir of Army Nursing Services, 1960–64, retd; Chief Nursing Officer to St John Ambulance Brigade, 1965–72. Col Commandant, QARANC, 1966–69. DStJ 1972.

Died 18 July 1995.

COZENS, Air Cdre Henry Iliffe, CB 1946; AFC 1939; Royal Air Force, retired; *b* 13 March 1904; *s* of Wing George Cozens; *m* 1956, Gillian Mary, *o d* of Wing Comdr O. R. Pigott, Wokingham, Berks; one *s* two *d*. *Educ:* St Dunstan's Coll.; Downing Coll., Cambridge. MA 1934. Commissioned in RAF, 1923; Mem. of British Arctic Air Route Expedition, 1930–31; served War of 1939–45 (AFC, CB); idc 1947. Vice-Pres., British Schs Exploring Soc., 1969–90. *Address:* Horley Manor, Banbury, Oxon OX15 6BJ. *Club:* Royal Air Force.

Died 21 June 1995.

CRAIG, Very Rev. Prof. Robert, CBE 1981; Moderator of the General Assembly of the Church of Scotland, 1986–87; Minister, St Andrew's Scots Memorial Church, Jerusalem, 1980–85; Principal and Vice-Chancellor, 1969–80, Professor of Theology, 1963–80, University of Zimbabwe (formerly University of Rhodesia), then Emeritus; *b* 22 March 1917; *s* of late John Craig, stone-mason, and Anne Peggie, linen-weaver; *m* 1950, Olga Wanda, *d* of late Michael and of Helena Strzelec; one *s* one *d*. *Educ:* Fife CC schs; St Andrews Univ.; Union Theol Seminary, NY. MA (Ordinary) 1938, BD with distinction in Systematic Theology 1941, PhD 1950, St Andrews; STM *magna cum laude* Union Theol Seminary 1948. Pres., Students' Rep. Council, Chm. Union Debating Soc., Berry Schol. in Theology, St Andrews Univ., 1941; Asst Minister, St John's Kirk, Perth, 1941–42, ordained 1942; Chaplain (4th class), Army, 1942–47: infantry bns, NW Europe, 1944–45 (despatches, Normandy, 1944); Palestine, Egypt, 1945–47; HCF 1947; Hugh Black Fellow and Instructor in Systematic Theology, Union Theol Seminary, 1947–48; Dep. Leader, Iona Community, Scotland, 1948–50; Natal Univ.: Prof. of Divinity, 1950–57; College Dean, Adviser of Students and personal rep. of Principal and Vice-Chancellor, 1953–54; Prof. of Religion, Smith Coll., Mass, 1958–63; UC Rhodesia and Nyasaland: Prof. of Theology, 1963; Dean, Faculty of Arts, 1965; Vice-Principal, 1966; Actg Principal, 1967 and 1969. External Examiner: Boston, Cape Town, London, McGill, Natal, Rhodes, S Africa, Surrey, Witwatersrand Univs, various times, 1950–90. Vis. Lectr, Ecumenical Inst., Bossey, Switz., 1955; John Dewey Meml Lectr, Vermont Univ., 1961; Ainslie Meml Lectr, Rhodes Univ., 1965. Jerusalem appointments: Pres., Ecumenical Theol Res. Fraternity, 1983–85 (Mem. 1980–85); Member: Ecumenical Friends Gp, 1980–85; Council, Interfaith Cttee, 1981–85; Bd of Dirs, Internat. YMCA, 1982–85 (Vice-Chm., 1984, Chm., 1984–85); Exec. Cttee, Spafford Community Centre, 1982–85; Chm., Church of Scotland Israel Council, 1981–85; Jt Pres., Soc. of Friends of St Andrew's Church, Jerusalem, 1985–; Moderator, Presbytery of Jerusalem, 1982–84; Mem., Jerusalem Cttee, Jerusalem Foundn, 1989–. Brit. Council Commonwealth Interchange Fellow,

Cambridge Univ., 1966. Hon. Chaplain: Kingdom and Angus Br., Normandy Veterans' Assoc., 1987– (Hon. Life Mem., 1992); Scottish Br., Palestine Police Assoc., 1988– (Hon. Life Mem., 1989). Hon. DD St Andrews, 1967; Hon. LLD: Witwatersrand 1979; Birmingham, 1980; Natal, 1981; Hon. DLitt Zimbabwe, 1981. Hon. Fellow, Zimbabwe Inst. of Engineers, 1976. Golden Jubilee Medal, Witwatersrand Univ., 1977; City of Jerusalem Medal, 1985. *Publications:* The Reasonableness of True Religion, 1954; Social Concern in the Thought of William Temple, 1963; Religion: Its Reality and Its Relevance, 1965; The Church: Unity in Integrity, 1966; Religion and Politics: a Christian view, 1972; On Belonging to a University, 1974; The Task of the Church in Today's World, 1989. *Recreations:* the cinema, theatre, contemporary and recent history, light classical music, listening and talking to people. *Address:* West Port, Falkland, Fife KY7 7BL. *T:* Falkland (01337) 57238. *Clubs:* Kate Kennedy, University Staff, Students' Union (St Andrews); YMCA, Rainbow (Jerusalem). *Died 30 Jan. 1995.*

CRAIG, Thomas Rae, CBE 1969 (OBE 1945); TD; DL; retired; Deputy Governor, The Bank of Scotland, 1972–77; *b* 11 July 1906; *s* of Sir John Craig, CBE, and Jessie Craig (*née* Sommerville); *m* 1931, Christina Gay (*née* Moodie); three *s* one *d*. *Educ:* Glasgow Academy; Lycée Malherbe, Caen, Normandy. Served War of 1939–45: Lt-Col 6th Cameronians; AA&QMG 52nd (Lowland) Div. Dir of Colvilles Ltd, 1935; Man. Dir, 1958; Dep. Chm., 1961; Chm. and Man. Dir, 1965–68. Mem. Bd, BSC, 1967–72. Formerly dir of companies. Mem., Convocation of Strathclyde Univ. DL Dunbartonshire, 1973. Hon. LLD: Strathclyde, 1968; Glasgow, 1970. OStJ. *Recreation:* farming. *Address:* Invergare, Rhu, Dunbartonshire G84 8LL. *T:* Rhu (0436) 820427. *Club:* Royal Scottish Automobile (Glasgow). *Died 28 Feb. 1994.*

CRAIGIE, Dr Hugh Brechin, CBE 1965; Principal Medical Officer, Mental Health Division, Scottish Home and Health Department, retired; *b* 19 May 1908; *s* of late Hugh Craigie; *m* 1st, 1933, Lillia Campbell (*d* 1958), *d* of Dr George Campbell Murray; two *s* (and one *s* decd); 2nd, 1962, Eileen (MBE 1950), *d* of F. S. Lyons. *Educ:* Manchester Grammar Sch.; Manchester Univ. House Physician, Manchester Royal Infirmary, 1931–32; Asst Medical Officer, Monsall Fever Hosp., Manchester, 1932–33; Senior Medical Officer, County Mental Hosp., Lancaster, 1933–46; Dep. Med. Supt, County Mental Hosp., Whittingham, 1946; HM Senior Medical Commissioner, General Board of Control for Scotland, 1947. Served War of 1939–45 (despatches), RAMC (Hon. Lieut-Col). *Publications:* various papers on psychiatry. *Address:* Saviskaill, Westerdunes Park, North Berwick EH39 5HJ. *Died 20 Nov. 1993.*

CRAIGTON, Baron, *cr* 1959 (Life Peer), of Renfield, co. of City of Glasgow; **Jack Nixon Browne,** CBE 1944; PC 1961; *b* 3 Sept. 1904; *s* of Edwin Gilbert Izod; adopted surname Browne, 1920; *m* 1st, 1936, Helen Anne (marr. diss. 1949), *d* of G. J. Inglis; one *s*; 2nd, 1950, Eileen Nolan, *d* of late Henry Whitford Nolan, London. *Educ:* Cheltenham Coll. Served War of 1939–45, RAF (Balloon Command), Actg Group Capt. Contested (C) Govan Div., Glasgow, 1945; MP (C) Govan Div., 1950–55; MP (C) Craigton Div. of Glasgow, 1955–Sept. 1959; Parly Private Sec. to Sec. of State for Scotland, 1952–April 1955; Parly Under-Sec., Scottish Office, April 1955–Oct. 1959; Minister of State, Scottish Office, Nov. 1959–Oct. 1964. Westminster Chamber of Commerce: Mem., General Purposes Cttee, 1948; Mem., Exec. Cttee, 1950; Chm., 1954; Pres., 1966–83. Chm., United Biscuits (Holdings) Ltd, 1967–72. Pres., Commercial Travellers Benevolent Instn, 1976–. Vice-Pres., World Wildlife Fund (British Nat. Appeal), 1979; Chm., Fauna Preservation Soc.,

1981–83 (Vice-Chm., 1970–80); Chairman: Council for Environmental Conservation, 1972–83; All-Party Conservation Group of both Houses of Parliament, 1972–; Fedn of Zoological Gardens, 1975–81; Mem., Jersey Wildlife Preservation Trust Council, 1970– (Internat. Trustee, 1972–). Mem. Council, 1975–81, Environment Cttee, 1975–83, RSA. *Recreation:* gardening. *Address:* Friary House, Friary Island, Wraysbury, near Staines, Middlesex TW19 5JR. *T:* Wraysbury (0784) 482213. *Club:* Buck's.   *Died 28 July 1993.*

CRAM, Alastair Lorimer, MC 1945; Appellate Judge, Supreme Court of Appeal, Malawi, 1964–68, retired; in private practice at Scots Bar, Edinburgh; *b* 25 Aug. 1909; *m* 1951, Isobel Nicholson; no *c. Educ:* Perth Academy; Edinburgh University (LLB). Solicitor, 1933; private practice, 1935–39; admitted Scots Bar, 1946. Served in HM Army, 1939–48: POW, successful escapes; RA, SAS, Intelligence Corps, Counsel War Crimes Group NW Europe, Major, GSO 2. Resident Magistrate, Kenya, 1948; Actg Puisne Judge, 1953–56; Sen. Resident Magistrate, Kenya, 1956; Temp. Puisne Judge, 1958–60; Puisne Judge, High Court of Nyasaland, 1960; acting Chief Justice and (briefly) Governor-General, Malawi, 1965; Legal Dept, Scottish Office, 1971–74. Athlete, climber, and traveller: in Alps, 1930–60, and Himalayas, 1960 and 1963; in African, Asian and South American deserts, 1940–66; in Amazon basin and Peruvian Andes, 1966; in Atlas Mts, 1971; in Great Dividing Range, Australia, N–S traverse, 1981–84. Editor, Kenya Law Reports, 1952–56. *Publications:* contribs law reports, legal and mountaineering jls. *Recreations:* shooting, sound-recordings, photography (still and cine), orchid-collecting, languages. *Address:* 5 Upper Dean Terrace, Edinburgh EH4 1NU. *T:* 031–332 5441. *Clubs:* Alpine; Scottish Mountaineering (Edinburgh).

Died 17 March 1994.

CRAMER, Hon. Sir John (Oscar), Kt 1964; FREI; QRV; MHR (L) for Bennelong, New South Wales, 1949–74; Managing Director, Cramer Brothers, real estate auctioneers; *b* Quirindi, NSW, 18 Feb. 1897; *s* of J. N. Cramer, Quirindi; *m* 1921, Mary, (Dame Mary Cramer, DBE) (*d* 1984), *d* of William M. Earls; one *s* two *d* (and one *s* decd). *Educ:* state public schs; business coll. Mayor of North Sydney, 1940–41; Member: Sydney County Council, 1935–56 (Chm., 1946–49); Statutory Cttee on Public Works, 1949–56 (Chm., 1955–56); Executive Building Industry Congress of New South Wales; Executive of Liberal Party of Australia, NSW Division (a founder of Provisional Exec.). Minister for the Army, 1956–63. Patron: Anzac Meml Club, N Sydney; RSL, N Ryde, NSW. *Recreation:* bowls. *Address:* Unit 2, 5 Morton Street, Wollstonecraft, NSW 2065, Australia. *T:*(2) 9572774. *Club:* Rotary.   *Died 18 May 1994.*

CRANE, Geoffrey David; Head of Freight Directorate, Department of Transport, 1989–90; *b* 13 Oct. 1934; *s* of late Frederick David Crane and Marion Doris Crane; *m* 1962, Gillian Margaret, *d* of late Harry Thomas Austin; one *d. Educ:* City of London Sch. (John Carpenter Schol.); Trinity Hall, Cambridge (Schol., MA). Served RAF, 1956–58, Flying Officer. Assistant Principal, Min. of Works, 1958; Asst Private Sec. to Minister of Works, 1961–62; Principal, 1962; Secretary, Historic Buildings Council for Scotland and Ancient Monuments Bd for Scotland, 1962–66; Private Sec. to Minister of Public Building and Works, 1968–69; Asst Sec., Machinery of Govt Div., CSD, 1970–72; Dep. Dir, Central Unit on Environmental Pollution, DoE, 1972–76; Personnel Management and Trng, 1976–78, Under Sec. and Dir of Res. Ops, 1978–80, Dir, Personnel Management and Trng, 1981–85, Regl Dir, Eastern Region, 1985–89, DoE and Dept of Transport. *Recreations:* music, industrial

archaeology, mathematics. *Address:* 6 The Paddock, Datchet, Berks SL3 9DL. *Clubs:* Royal Air Force, Civil Service.   *Died 27 Oct. 1995.*

CRANSTON, Prof. Maurice (William); Professor of Political Science at the London School of Economics, 1969–85 (seconded as Professor of Political Science, European University Institute, 1978–81), Hon. Fellow, 1991; *b* 8 May 1920; *o c* of William Cranston and Catherine Harris; *m* Helga; *m* 1958, Baroness Maximiliana von and zu Fraunberg; two *s. Educ:* London Univ.; St Catherine's Coll., Oxford (MA, BLitt; Hon. Fellow, 1984). London Civil Defence during war, 1939–45. Lecturer (part-time) in Social Philosophy, London Univ., 1950–59; Reader (previously Lecturer) in Political Science at London Sch. of Economics, 1959–69. Visiting Professor of Government: Harvard Univ., 1965–66; Dartmouth Coll., USA, 1970–71; Univ. of British Columbia, 1973–74; Univ. of California, 1976; Ecole des Hautes Etudes, Paris, 1977; Woodrow Wilson Center, Washington, 1982; Fondation Thiers, Paris, 1983; Univ. of California, 1986–93; Carlyle Lectr, Oxford Univ., 1984. Pres., Institut International de Philosophie Politique, 1976–79; Vice-Pres. de l'Alliance Française en Angleterre, 1964–. Literary Adviser to Methuen Ltd, 1959–69. FRSL. Foreign Hon. Mem., Amer. Acad. of Arts and Sciences, 1970–. Commandeur de l'Ordre des Palmes Académiques (France), 1986. *Publications:* Tomorrow We'll Be Sober, 1946; Philosopher's Hemlock, 1946; Freedom, 1953; Human Rights Today, 1954, rev. edn 1962; John Locke: a biography, 1957 (James Tait Black Memorial Prize); Jean-Paul Sartre, 1962; What Are Human Rights?, 1963 (New York), 2nd rev. edn 1973 (London); (ed) Western Political Philosophers, 1964; A Glossary of Political Terms, 1966; Rousseau's Social Contract, 1967; Political Dialogues, 1968; La Quintessence de Sartre, 1969 (Montreal); Language and Philosophy, 1969 (Toronto); (ed) The New Left, 1970; (ed with R. S. Peters) Hobbes and Rousseau, 1972; The Mask of Politics, 1973; (ed with P. Mair) Idéologie et Politique, 1980; Langage et Politique, 1981; (ed with Lea Boralevi) Culture et Politique, 1982; Jean-Jacques: the early life and work of Jean-Jacques Rousseau 1712–1754, 1983; Rousseau's Discourse on Inequality, 1984; Philosophers and Pamphleteers, 1986; The Noble Savage: Jean-Jacques Rousseau 1754–1762, 1991. *Recreation:* walking. *Address:* 1A Kent Terrace, Regent's Park, NW1 4RP. *T:* 071–262 2698. *Club:* Garrick.

Died 5 Nov. 1993.

CRAWFORD, Hon. Sir George (Hunter), Kt 1972; Judge of the Supreme Court of Tasmania 1958–81; *b* 12 Dec. 1911; *s* of Frederick Charles Crawford and Ruby Priscilla (*née* Simpson); *m* 1st, 1936, Helen Zoë (*d* 1976), *d* of Dr Bruce Arnold Anderson; two *s* one *d*; 2nd, 1979, Nancy Jean Garrott (*née* Findlay). *Educ:* East Launceston State Sch.; Launceston Church Grammar Sch.; Univ. of Tasmania (LLB). Barrister and Solicitor, 1934–58; Mem. Cttee, Northern Law Society, 1946–58 (Vice-Pres. 1957–58). Served (including War): AMF, 1929–40; AIF, 1940–44, Lt-Col. Councillor, Northern Br., Royal Soc. of Tasmania, 1954–72 (Chm., 1957–58 and 1966–68); Mem. Cttee, Tasmanian Historical Res. Assoc., 1960–62 (Chm., 1961–62); Mem. Bd, Launceston Church Grammar Sch., 1946–71 (Chm., 1958–65); Mem. Bd, Cradle Mountain-Lake St Clair Nat. Park; Mem. Adv. Cttee, Cradle Mountain, 1956–71; Pres., N Tasmania Branch, Roy. Commonwealth Soc., 1974–76. Col Comdt, Royal Regt of Australian Artillery, in Tasmania Command, 1972–78. *Recreations:* music, historical research. *Address:* 1/39 David Street, Launceston, Tasmania 7250, Australia. *T:* (03) 312271. *Club:* Launceston (Launceston).

Died 21 Oct. 1993.

CRAWFORD, Maj.-Gen. George Oswald, CB 1956; CBE 1944; Director of Ordnance Services, War Office, 1958–61; *b* 12 Nov. 1902; *s* of late Col Arthur Gosset Crawford, Nailsworth, Glos; *m* Sophie Cecilia (*d* 1974), *d* of J. C. Yorke, JP, Langton, Dwrbach, Pembs; two *s* one *d*; *m* 1974, Ella Brown. *Educ:* Bradfield; RMC. 2nd Lieut Glos Regt, 1922; transf. RAOC 1928; served CMF, 1942–45; Lieut-Col 1942; Brig. 1943; Dep. Dir of Ordnance Services, Western Command, 1947–51; DDOS, Southern Command, 1951–55; ADC to the Queen, 1954–55; Maj.-Gen. 1955; Inspector, Royal Army Ordnance Corps, 1955–57; Commandant Mechanical Transport Organisation, Chilwell, 1957–58; Col Comdt RAOC, 1960–66. *Address:* Gwyers, Dinton, Wilts.
Died 26 Dec. 1994.

CRAWFORD, Prof. Sir Theodore, (Sir Theo), Kt 1973; Professor of Pathology in the University of London, 1948–77, Professor Emeritus, 1977; Director of Pathological Services, St George's Hospital and Medical School, 1946–77; *b* 23 Dec. 1911; *s* of late Theodore Crawford and Sarah Mansfield; *m* 1st, 1938, Margaret Donald Green, MD (*d* 1973); two *s* three *d*; 2nd, 1974, Priscilla Leathley Chater. *Educ:* St Peter's Sch., York; Glasgow Academy; Glasgow Univ. BSc 1932; MB, ChB 1935; Hon. LLD 1979. FRFPSG 1938; MD 1941; Bellahouston Gold Medal (Glasgow Univ.), 1941; MRCP 1960; FRCPath 1963; FRCP 1964; FRCPA 1972. Hall Tutorial and Research Fellow, 1936–38; Asst Physician, Royal Hosp. for Sick Children, Glasgow, 1936–38; Lecturer in Pathology, Glasgow Univ., 1939–46. Served War of 1939–45: Major RAMC, 1941–45. Mem. of the Medical Research Council, 1960–64 (and Mem. Cell Board, 1974–78); Registrar, Coll. of Pathologists, 1963–68; Consultant Adviser in Pathology to Dept of Health and Social Security and Chm. of its Central Pathology Cttee, 1969–78. Royal Society of Medicine: Pres. Section of Pathology, 1961–62; Royal College of Pathologists: Vice-Pres., 1968–69; Pres., 1969–72; Hon. Fellow, 1983; Mem., Pathological Soc. of Great Britain, etc; Chm., Scientific Cttee, British Empire Cancer Campaign, 1969–78 (Hon. Sec., 1955–67; Hon. Sec. of the Campaign, 1967–70); Vice-Pres., Cancer Res. Campaign, 1979–. Member: Council, Epsom Coll., 1949–71; Standing Medical Advisory Cttee, Health Services Council, 1964–69; Cttee on Safety of Medicines, 1969–77 (Vice-Chm., 1976–77); Army Pathology Adv. Cttee, 1970–75; DHSS Cttee on Smoking and Health, 1973–79; Chm., Medical Adv. Gp to The Brewers' Soc., 1982–87 (Mem., 1972–87). *Publications:* (ed) Modern Trends in Pathology, 1967; Pathology of Ischaemic Heart Disease, 1977; scientific papers in Lancet, British Medical Journal, British Journal of Surgery, Archives of Disease in Childhood, British Journal of Opthalmology, Journal of Pathology and Bacteriology, etc. *Recreations:* horticulture, growing trees, walking, music. *Address:* 9 Asher Reeds, Langton Green, Tunbridge Wells, Kent TN3 0AL. *T:* Langton (0892) 863341. *Club:* Sloane.
Died 27 July 1993.

CRAWLEY, Aidan Merivale, MBE; Chairman, London Weekend Television, 1967–71, President 1971–73; *b* 10 April 1908; *s* of late Canon Arthur Stafford Crawley and Anstice Katharine, 2nd *d* of Antony Gibbs; *m* 1945, Virginia Cowles, OBE (*d* 1983); one *d* (two *s* decd). *Educ:* Harrow; Trinity Coll., Oxford. Journalist, 1930–36; Educational Film Producer, 1936–39; AAF, 601 Sqdn, 1936–40; Asst Air Attaché, Ankara, Belgrade (resident Sofia), May 1940–March 1941; joined 73 (F) Sqdn, Egypt; shot down July 1941; prisoner until May 1945. MP (Lab) Buckingham Div. of N Bucks, 1945–51; Parliamentary Private Sec. to successive Secs of State for the Colonies, 1945 and 1946–47; Parliamentary Under-Sec. of State for Air, 1950–51; resigned from the Labour Party, 1957; MP

(C) West Derbyshire, June 1962–Oct. 1967; Editor-in-Chief, Independent Television News Ltd, 1955–56; making television documentaries for BBC, 1956–60; Mem. Monckton Commission on Federation of Rhodesia and Nyasaland, 1960. Pres., MCC, 1973. *Publications:* Escape from Germany, 1956; De Gaulle: a Biography, 1969; The Rise of Western Germany 1945–72, 1973; Dial 200–200, 1980; Leap Before You Look (autobiog.), 1988. *Recreation:* cricket (Co-Founder, Haig Nat. Village Cricket Championship, 1971). *Address:* Oak Cottage, Queen Street, Farthinghoe, Northants NN13 5NY. *T:* Banbury (0295) 710419. *Clubs:* Clermont, MCC, Queen's.
Died 3 Nov. 1993.

CRAWLEY, Charles William; University Lecturer in History, University of Cambridge, 1931–66; Vice-Master of Trinity Hall, Cambridge, 1950–66, Emeritus Fellow, 1966, Hon. Fellow, 1971; *b* 1 April 1899; *s* of Charles Crawley, barrister of Lincoln's Inn, and Augusta, *d* of Rt Rev. Samuel Butcher, Bishop of Meath; *m* 1930, Kathleen Elizabeth (*d* 1982), *d* of Lieut-Col H. G. Leahy, OBE, RA; four *s* one *d*. *Educ:* Winchester (Scholar); Trinity Coll., Cambridge (Scholar). Fellow of Trinity Hall, Cambridge, 1924–66: Asst Tutor, 1927; Acting Senior Tutor, 1940; Senior Tutor, 1946–58. *Publications:* The Question of Greek Independence, 1821–1833, 1930, repr. 1973; (ed) New Cambridge Modern History, Vol. IX, 1965; John Capodistrias: unpublished documents, 1970; Trinity Hall: the history of a Cambridge College, 1350–1975, 1976. *Address:* 93 Castelnau, SW13 9EL.
Died 6 Oct. 1992.

CRAWLEY, Desmond John Chetwode, CMG 1964; CVO 1961; HM Diplomatic Service, retired; *b* 2 June 1917; *s* of late Lieutenant-Colonel C. G. C. Crawley, OBE and Agnes Luke; *m* 1945, Daphne Lesley (*d* 1989), *y d* of late Sir Vere Mockett, MBE, and Ethel Norah Gaddum Tomkinson; two *s* one *d*. *Educ:* King's Sch., Ely; Queen's Coll., Oxford. Entered Indian Civil Service, serving in Madras Presidency, 1939; entered Indian Political Service, serving in Baluchistan, 1946; entered Commonwealth Relations Office, 1947, and served in London, Calcutta, and on loan to the Foreign Office in Washington; Principal Private Secretary to Sec. of State for Commonwealth Relations, 1952–53; British Dep. High Commissioner in Lahore, Pakistan, 1958–61; Imperial Defence Coll., 1962; British High Commissioner in Sierra Leone, 1963–66; Ambassador to Bulgaria, 1966–70; Minister to Holy See, 1970–75. Coronation Medal, 1953. Knight Grand Cross, Order of St Gregory the Great (Holy See), 1973. *Address:* 35 Chartfield Avenue, SW15. *T:* 081–788 9529. *Club:* United Oxford & Cambridge University.
Died 26 April 1993.

CRAWSHAW, Sir (Edward) Daniel (Weston), Kt 1964; QC (Aden) 1949; *b* 10 Sept. 1903; *s* of Godfrey Edward Crawshaw; *m* 1942, Rosemary Treffry; one *s* two *d* (and one *s* decd). *Educ:* St Bees Sch.; Selwyn Coll., Cambridge. Solicitor, Supreme Court of Judicature, England, 1929; Barrister-at-Law, Gray's Inn, 1946; Solicitor, Northern Rhodesia, 1930–32; Colonial Legal Service, Tanganyika, 1933–39; Zanzibar, 1939–47; Attorney-Gen., Aden, 1947–52; Puisne Judge, Tanganyika, 1952–60; Justice of Appeal, Court of Appeal for Eastern Africa, 1960–65. Commissioner, Foreign Compensation Commission, 1965–75. Brilliant Star of Zanzibar, 1947; Coronation Medal, 1953. *Recreation:* reading. *Address:* 1 Fort Road, Guildford, Surrey GU1 3TB. *T:* Guildford (0483) 576883. *Clubs:* Royal Over-Seas League; County (Guildford).
Died 4 April 1991.

CREEGGAN, Rt Rev. Jack Burnett; *b* 10 Nov. 1902; *s* of Alfred Henry Creeggan and Mary Laura (*née* Sheffield); *m* 1931, Dorothy Jarman (*née* Embury); one *s* one *d*. *Educ:* Deseronto (Ont) Public and High Schs; Queen's

Univ. (BA); Bishop's Univ. (LST). Priest, 1928; served in many parishes in Dio. Ontario; Canon, St George's Cathedral, Kingston, Ont, 1952; Archdeacon of: Ontario, 1953; Frontenac, 1962; Kingston, 1969; Bishop of Ontario, 1970–74. Prolocutor, Lower House, Provincial Synod of Ont, 1963. Hon. DCL, Bishop's Univ., Lennoxville, PQ, 1971. *Recreations:* curling, golf. *Address:* Apt 112, 32 Ontario Street, Kingston, Ontario K7L 2Y1, Canada. *T:* (613) 5425319. *Died 18 July 1994.*

CRESPI, (Caesar) James, QC 1984; a Recorder of the Crown Court, since 1973; *b* 1928. *Educ:* Trinity Hall, Cambridge (BA). Called to the Bar, Middle Temple, 1951, South Eastern Circuit. *Address:* 5 Paper Buildings, Temple, EC4Y 7HB. *T:* 071–583 6117. *Club:* Garrick.
Died 3 July 1992.

CRICHTON, Sir Andrew Maitland-Makgill-, Kt 1963; Director, P&OSN Co., 1957–81; Vice-Chairman, Port of London Authority, 1967–76 (Member, 1964–67); *b* 28 Dec. 1910; *s* of late Lt-Col D. M.-M.-Crichton, Queen's Own Cameron Highldrs, and Phyllis (*née* Cuthbert); *m* 1948, Isabel, *d* of Andrew McGill, Sydney, NSW. *Educ:* Wellington Coll. Joined Gray, Dawes & Co., 1929; transf. India to Mackinnon Mackenzie & Co. (Agents of BI Co. and for P & O on Indian Continent and in parts of Far East), 1931. Joined IA, 1940; DDM (Shipping), Col, at GHQ India, 1944. Mackinnon Mackenzie, Calcutta, 1945–48; P&O Co., UK (Gen. Manager, 1951); Chm., Overseas Containers Ltd, 1965–73; former Director: Standard Chartered Group; Inchcape Insurance Hldgs Ltd; London Tin Corp.; Dir, Butler's Warehousing & Distrib. Ltd. Chairman: Nat. Assoc. Port Employers, 1958–65; EDC for GPO, 1965–70; Vice-Chm., British Transport Docks Bd, 1963–68; Member: Baltic Exchange; Nat. Freight Corp., 1969–73; Court of The Chartered Bank; Police Council for GB (Arbitrator), 1969–79; Industrial Arbitration Bd. FRSA; FCIT (a past Vice-Pres.). *Recreations:* golf, music. Freeman, Co. of Watermen and Lightermen. *Address:* 55 Hans Place, Knightsbridge, SW1X 0LA. *T:* 0171–584 1209. *Clubs:* City of London, Caledonian. *Died 29 Oct. 1995.*

CRICK, Alan John Pitts, OBE 1956; *b* 14 May 1913; *er s* of Owen John Pitts Crick and Margaret Crick (*née* Daw), late of Minehead, Somerset; *m* 1941, Norah (*née* Atkins) (*d* 1984); two *d*. *Educ:* Latymer Upper Sch.; King's Coll., London Univ. (MA); Heidelberg Univ. (Dr.phil). Vice-Consul, British Consulate-Gen., Free City of Danzig, 1938–39. Served War, Army, 1939–46: Egypt and Libya, 1941–43, HQ Eighth Army; NW Europe, 1944–46 (despatches); Major, GSO2, Intell., SHAEF; HQ 21 Army Group and HQ BAOR. Min. of Defence Jt Intell. Bureau, 1946–63; jssc, 1948; British Jt Services Mission, Washington, 1953–56; Asst Dir, Jt Intell. Bureau, 1957–63; idc, 1960; Counsellor, British Embassy, Washington, 1963–65; Asst Sec., Cabinet Office, 1965–68; Def. Intell. Staff, MoD, 1968–73; Director of Economic Intelligence, MoD, 1970–73. Adviser to Commercial Union Assurance Co., 1973–78. *Recreations:* travel, antiquarian interests, books. *Address:* 16 Church Square, Rye, East Sussex TN31 7HE. *T:* Rye (01797) 222050. *Club:* Naval and Military. *Died 14 Oct. 1995.*

CRIPPS, Sir John Stafford, Kt 1978; CBE 1968; Chairman, Countryside Commission, 1970–77; *b* 10 May 1912; *s* of late Rt Hon. Sir Stafford Cripps, CH, FC, FRS, QC, and Isobel (Dame Isobel Cripps, GBE); *m* 1st, 1936, Ursula (marr. diss. 1971), *d* of late Arthur C. Davy; three *s* two *d* (and one *s* decd); 2nd, 1971, Ann Elizabeth Farwell. *Educ:* Winchester; Balliol Coll., Oxford. 1st Class Hons Politics, Philosophy and Economics (Modern Greats). Editor, The Countryman, 1947–71. Filkins Parish Councillor, 1946–87; Witney Rural District Councillor, 1946–74; Chairman: Rural District Councils' Association, 1967–70;

Rural Cttee of Nat. Council of Social Service; Member: Oxfordshire Planning Cttee, 1948–69; W Oxfordshire Technical Coll. Governors, 1951–70; South East Economic Planning Council, 1966–73; Nature Conservancy, 1970–73; Exec. Cttee, CPRE, 1963–69; Inland Waterways Amenity Advisory Council, 1968–73; Defence Lands Cttee, 1971–73; Water Space Amenities Commn, 1977–80; Development Commn, 1978–82. President: Oxfordshire Rural Community Council, 1982–; Camping and Caravanning Club of GB and Ireland, 1981–91. Prepared report on Accommodation for Gypsies, 1976. *Address:* Fox House, Filkins, Lechlade, Glos GL7 3JQ. *TA:* Filkins. *T:* Faringdon (0367) 860209. *Club:* Farmers'. *Died 9 Aug. 1993.*

CRITCHLEY, Thomas Alan, JP; Assistant Under-Secretary of State, Home Office, 1972–76; *b* 11 March 1919; *y s* of Thomas Critchley and Annie Louisa Darvell; *m* 1942, Margaret Carol Robinson; one *s* two *d*. *Educ:* Queen Elizabeth's Grammar Sch., Barnet. Entered Civil Service, 1936. Served War, 1940–46 (commnd in RAOC). Asst Principal, Home Office, 1947; Principal, 1948; Cabinet Office, 1954–56; Principal Private Sec. to Rt Hon. R. A. Butler, Home Secretary, 1957–60; Asst Sec., 1958; Sec., Royal Commn on Police, 1960–62; Sec. to Lord Denning's Enquiry into the Profumo Affair, 1963; Sec. of the Gaming Board for Great Britain, 1971–72; Director (and Mem.), Uganda Resettlement Board, 1972–74; held enquiry into UK Immigrants Adv. Service, 1976. Vice-Chm., WRVS, 1977–81; Chm., Mddx Area Probation Cttee, 1983–85. JP Middlesex 1977. *Publications:* The Civil Service Today, 1951; A History of Police in England and Wales, 1967, 2nd edn 1978 (Amer. edn, 1972); The Conquest of Violence, 1970; (with P. D. James) The Maul and the Pear Tree, 1971; contributor to: The Police We Deserve, 1973, and various jls. *Recreations:* reading, gardening, walking. *Address:* 26 Temple Fortune Lane, NW11 7UD. *T:* 081–455 4894. *Clubs:* Reform, Civil Service. *Died 28 June 1991.*

CROCKFORD, Brig. Allen Lepard, CBE 1955 (OBE 1945); DSO 1943; MC 1916; TD 1942; late Hon. Colonel Royal Army Medical Corps, 54 and 56 Division (TA); *b* 11 Sept. 1897; *s* of late J. A. V. Crockford, West Worthing, Sussex; *m* 1924, Doris Ellen Brookes-Smith; one *s* two *d*. *Educ:* Gresham's Sch.; King's Coll., Cambridge; St Thomas' Hosp. BA Cantab, 1920; MA 1926; MB, BCh Cantab, 1922. Glos Regt, BEF (Capt.; wounded), 1915–19. Gen. Practice, 1924–39; RAMC (TA): served with 43rd, Guards Armoured, 46th and 56th Divs, BNAF and CMF (Col), 1939–45; Gen. Practice, 1945–46; Medical Sec., St Thomas' Hosp. Medical Sch., London, SE1, 1946–64. Col (TA), ADMS, 56 Armoured Div., 1947; Brig. (TA); DDMS AA Comd, 1949; KHS 1952; QHS 1952–57. OStJ 1954. *Recreations:* walking, climbing, sailing, wildfowling, gardening, bird-watching, cassette playing. *Address:* Overstone, Elvaston Road, Hexham, Northumberland NE46 2HH.

Died 27 Sept. 1992.

CROFTON, Denis Hayes, OBE 1948 (MBE 1943); retired Home and Indian Civil Servant; Member, Panel of Inspectors, Department of the Environment, 1969–79; President, Tunbridge Wells and District Branch, Civil Service Retirement Fellowship, since 1985 (Chairman, 1972–85); *b* 14 Dec. 1908; *s* of late Richard Hayes Crofton, Colonial Civil Service and Mabel Annie Crofton (*née* Smith); *m* 1933, Alison Carr, *d* of late Andrew McClure and Ethel McClure; three *s* one *d*. *Educ:* Tonbridge Sch.; Corpus Christi Coll., Oxford (Class. Mods, Lit. Hum., MA). Indian Civil Service, 1932; served in Bihar; subdivisional Magistrate, Giridih, 1934, Jamshedpur, 1935; Under-Sec. to Govt of Bihar, Polit. and Appt Depts, 1936; Under-Sec. to Govt of India, Dept of Labour, 1939; Private Sec. to Indian Mem., Eastern Gp Supply Council, 1941; Dist Mag. and Collector, Shahabad, Bihar, 1942; Sec. to Gov. of Bihar, 1944; apptd to Home Civil Service, 1947; Principal, Min. of Fuel and Power, Petroleum Div. 1948; Asst Sec., Petroleum Div. and Chm., OEEC Oil Cttee, Paris, 1950–53; Asst Sec., Monopolies and Restrictive Practices Commn, 1953; Asst Sec., Min. of Fuel and Power, Electricity Div., 1956; Petroleum Div., 1961; Accountant General and Under-Secretary for Finance, 1962–68. *Publications:* The Children of Edmonstown Park: memoirs of an Irish family, 1981; Andrew Hayes leaves the King's County: some footnotes on a diaspora, 1990; Souvenirs of a Competition Wallah: letters and sketches from India 1932–1947, 1994; edited: The Surgery at Aberffrwd: some encounters of a colliery doctor, 1982; A GP's Progress to the Black Country, 1984 (both by Francis Maylett Smith). *Recreations:* reading, gardening. *Address:* 26 Vauxhall Gardens, Tonbridge, Kent TN11 0LZ. *T:* Tonbridge (01732) 353465. *Club:* Commonwealth Trust. *Died 15 Nov. 1995.*

CROKER, Edgar Alfred, (Ted), CBE 1989; Secretary and Chief Executive of the Football Association, 1973–89; *b* 13 Feb. 1924; *s* of late Harry and Winifred Croker; *m* 1952, Kathleen Mullins; one *s* two *d. Educ:* Kingston Technical Coll. Served War: Flt Lieut, RAF, 1942–46; Flt Lieut, RAFVR, 1947–55. Professional footballer: Charlton Athletic, 1947–51; Headington United, 1951–56; Sales Dir, Douglas Equipment, 1956–61; Chairman and Managing Dir, Liner-Croker Ltd, 1961–73; Chairman: Liner Concrete Machinery Co. Ltd, 1971–73; Harrington Kilbride Ltd, Publishers, 1989–; PEL Stadium Seating PLC, 1991–. King's Commendation for brave conduct, 1946. *Publication:* The First Voice You Will Hear Is . . . (autobiog.), 1987. *Recreations:* golf, tennis, bridge. *Address:* South Court, The Park, Cheltenham, Glos GL50 2SD. *T:* Cheltenham (0242) 224907. *Clubs:* Royal Air Force; New (Cheltenham). *Died 25 Dec. 1992.*

CROLL, Hon. David Arnold, PC (Can.) 1990; QC (Ont); BA, LLB; Senator; Chairman, Senate Committees on: Poverty, since 1968; Aging, since 1963; Retirement Age Policies, since 1977; *b* Moscow, 12 March 1900; *s* of Hillel and Minnie Croll; *m* 1925, Sarah Levin (*d* 1987); three *d. Educ:* public schs and Patterson Collegiate Institute, Windsor; Osgoode Hall, Toronto; University of Toronto. Emigrated to Canada with family, 1906, settling at Windsor, Ont; first and only commercial venture was operation of news-stand, which greatly facilitated secondary education; after high school and course, articled to solicitor; graduation from Osgoode Hall Law Sch. followed by practice at Windsor, 1925–30; formerly senior partner with Croll and Croll, Windsor, Ont, and with Croll, Borins and Shiff, later Croll and Godfrey, Toronto, Ont; KC 1934. Mayor of Windsor, Ont, 1930–34 and 1938–41; Mem. for Windsor-Walkerville, Ont Legislature, 1934–44; Minister of Labour, Public Welfare and Municipal Affairs for the Province of Ont; Mem. of House of Commons for Toronto Spadina, 1945–55 when appointed to Senate; was youngest and first Jewish Cabinet Minister and first Jewish Senator in Canada. Served War of 1939–45, with Canadian Army overseas, enlisting as Private in Sept. 1939 and discharged in rank of Col in Sept. 1945. Hon. LLD St Thomas Univ., 1980. *Recreations:* golf and the more strenuous sports. *Address:* 4th Floor, The First City Building, 151 Yonge Street, Toronto, Ont M5C 2W7, Canada. *Club:* Primrose (Toronto).

Died 11 June 1991.

CROMER, 3rd Earl of, *cr* 1901; **George Rowland Stanley Baring,** KG 1977; GCMG 1974 (KCMG 1971); MBE (Mil.) 1945; PC 1966; Baron Cromer, 1892; Viscount Cromer, 1899; Viscount Errington, 1901; Chairman: Royal Trust Co., Jersey, since 1987; Royal Trust Bank, Jersey,

since 1987; Advisor to Baring Brothers & Co. Ltd, since 1974; International Advisor to Marsh & McLennan Cos, NY, 1978–89; *b* 28 July 1918 (HM King George V stood sponsor); *o s* of 2nd Earl of Cromer, GCB, GCIE, GCVO, PC, and Lady Ruby Elliot, 2nd *d* of 4th Earl of Minto, KG, GCSI, GCMG, PC; *S* father, 1953; *m* 1942, Hon. Esmé Harmsworth (CVO 1980), 2nd *d* of 2nd Viscount Rothermere and of Margaret Hunam (*née* Redhead); two *s* (one *d* decd). *Educ:* Eton Coll.; Trinity Coll., Cambridge. Page of Honour: to King George V, 1931–35; to Queen Mary at Coronation, 1937; Private Sec. to Marquess of Willingdon representing HMG on missions to Argentina, Uruguay, Brazil, 1938, and to NZ and Aust., 1940. Served War, 1939–45: Grenadier Guards; Staff Col., Camberley; NW Europe (despatches, MBE); demob. 1945, Lt-Col. Joined Baring Brothers & Co. Ltd, 1938, rejoined 1945; seconded to: J. P. Morgan & Co.; Kidder Peabody & Co.; Morgan Stanley & Co.; Chemical Bank (all of NYC); Man. Dir, Baring Brothers & Co. Ltd, 1948–61; Bank of Internat. Settlements, Basle, 1961–66; Sen. Partner and Man. Dir, Baring Brothers & Co. Ltd, 1967–70. Mem., Inter-Parly Mission to Brazil, 1954; Econ. Minister and Head of Treasury and Supply Delegn, Washington, 1959–61; UK Exec. Dir, IMF, IBRD, and IFC, 1959–61; Head, UK Delegn to Internat. Coffee Conf., Washington, 1960; Governor of Bank of England, 1961–66; UK Governor, IBRD, IFC, and IDA, 1961–66; HM Ambassador, Washington, 1971–74. Author of report for Pres. of BoT, 1967, and for Cttee of Lloyd's, 1968. Chairman: IBM (UK) Ltd, 1967–70 and 1974–79; London Multinational Bank Ltd, 1967–70; Security & Prosper Fund SA, Luxembourg, 1967–70; Hon. Chm., Harris & Partners Ltd, Toronto, 1967–70; Chm., Internat. Adv. Council, Morgan Guaranty Trust Co. of NY, 1977–87; Director, 1949–59: Anglo-Newfoundland Develt Co. Ltd; Royal Ins. Co. Ltd; Liverpool, London & Globe Ins. Co. Ltd; Lewis Investment Trust Ltd; Director: Daily Mail & Gen. Trust Ltd, 1949–61, 1966–70 and 1974–; Union Carbide Corp. of NY, 1967–70; Associated Financial Services, Geneva, 1967–70; Imperial Group Ltd, 1974–80; P&O Steam Navigation Co. Ltd, 1974–80; Shell Trans. & Trading Co. Ltd, 1974–89; Compagnie Financière de Suez, Paris, 1974–82; Robeco Gp of Investment Trusts, Rotterdam, 1977–88; Barfield Trust Co. Ltd, Guernsey, 1979–88; Baring Henderson Gilt Fund, 1979–84; IBM World Trade (Eur./ME/Africa) Corp., NY, 1977–83 (Mem., IBM Eur. Adv. Council, 1967–70 and 1974–88). Chairman: Accepting House Cttee, 1967–70; OECD High Level Cttee on Capital Movements, 1967–70; Churchill Meml Trust, 1979; Member: Inst. Internat. d'Etudes Bancaires, 1967–70; Special Cttee on Trans-national Corps, Internat. Chamber of Commerce, 1967–69; Finance Cttee, UCL, 1954–57; British Inst. in Paris, 1952–57. Eur. Advisor to Govt Res. Corp., Washington, DC, 1974–81. A Governor: Atlantic Inst. for Internat. Affairs; Member: The Pilgrims (Mem. Exec. Cttee); Overseas Bankers Club; Trustee: King George's Jubilee Trust; Brain Res. Trust; Comr, Trilateral Commn. HM Lieut, City of London, 1961–; DL Kent, 1968–79. FIB; Hon. LLD New York Univ., 1966. *Heir: s* Viscount Errington [*b* 3 June 1946; *m* 1971, Plern Isarangkun Na Ayudhya, *e d* of late Dr Charanphat Isarangkun Na Ayudhya]. *Address:* 1 Douro Place, W8 5PH. *T:* 071–376 1290. *Clubs:* White's, Brooks's, Beefsteak; United (Jersey); Brook (NY); Metropolitan (Washington).

Died 16 March 1991.

CROMPTON, Air Cdre Roy Hartley, OBE 1962; Group Director, Emergency Planning, Civil (formerly Home) Defence College, Easingwold, York, 1976–85, retired; *b* 24 April 1921; *er s* of Frank and Ann Crompton, Bedford; *m* 1961, Rita Mabel Leslie; one *d*, and two *s* one *d* from previous marriage. *Educ:* Bedford Sch.; University Coll.,

London (BA Hons). PSO to C-in-C Fighter Comd, 1956–59; OC Flying No 5 FTS, 1959–61; jssc 1962; Chiefs of Staff Secretariat, 1962–64; Stn Comdr No 1 FTS, 1965–67; sowc 1967; Dep. Dir Defence Policy Staff, 1968–70; Gp Dir RAF Staff Coll., 1970; Project Officer, Nat. Defence Coll., 1970–71; AOC and Comdt, Central Flying Sch., RAF, 1972–74. Directing Staff, Home Defence Coll., York, 1974–76. Home Office Consultant, 1987–88. *Recreations:* golf, music, horticulture. *Address:* Sharnford Lodge, Huby, York YO6 1HT. *Club:* Royal Air Force.   *Died 17 Feb. 1992.*

CROOKS, Rev. John Robert Megaw; Dean of Armagh and Keeper of the Library, 1979–89; *b* 9 July 1914; *s* of Rev. Canon Louis Warden Crooks, OBE, MA, and Maria Kathleen Megaw; *m* 1941, Elizabeth Catherine Vance; two *s. Educ:* Campbell College, Belfast; Trinity College Dublin (MA). Deacon, 1938; priest, 1939; Curate Assistant, St Peter's, Dublin, 1938–43; Hon. Vicar Choral, St Patrick's Cathedral, Dublin, 1939–43; Catechist, High School, Dublin, 1939–43; Curate Assistant, Leighlin, 1943–44; Incumbent, Killylea, Dio. Armagh, 1944–56; Vicar Choral, St Patrick's Cathedral, 1956–73; Diocesan Sec., 1963–79; Hon. Clerical Sec., General Synod, 1970–89; Prebendary of Ballymore, 1971, of Mullabrack 1972; Archdeacon of Armagh, 1973–79. *Recreation:* golf. *Address:* 44 Abbey Street, Armagh BT61 7DZ. *T:* Armagh (01861) 522540. *Club:* Kildare Street and University (Dublin).   *Died 17 March 1995.*

CROOKS, Air Vice-Marshal Lewis M.; *see* Mackenzie Crooks.

CROOM-JOHNSON, Henry Powell, CMG 1964; CBE 1954 (OBE 1944); TD 1948; *b* 15 Dec. 1910; *e s* of late Hon. Sir Reginald Croom-Johnson, sometime Judge of High Court, and Lady (Ruby) Croom-Johnson; *m* 1947, Jane, *er d* of late Archibald George Mandry; two *s. Educ:* Stowe Sch.; Trinity Hall, Cambridge. Asst Master, Bedford Sch., 1932–34. Joined staff of British Council, 1935. Served with Queen's Westminsters and King's Royal Rifle Corps, 1939–46 (staff Sicily, Italy, Greece; Lt-Col). Rejoined British Council, 1946: Controller Finance Div., 1951; Controller European Div., 1956; Representative in India, 1957–64; Controller, Overseas Div. B, 1964; Asst Dir-Gen., 1966–72, retired 1973. *Recreations:* climbing, books, music. *Address:* 3a Ravenscourt Square, W6 0TW. *T:* 081–748 3677. *Club:* Savile.
                                                    Died 22 March 1994.

CROSBY, Prof. Theo, RA 1990 (ARA 1982); RIBA, FCSD; Partner, Pentagram Design, since 1972; *b* 3 April 1925; *s* of N. J. Crosby and N. J. A. Goosen; *m* 1st, 1960, Finella Anne Buchanan (marr. diss. 1988); one *d* (one *s* decd); 2nd, 1990, Polly Hope. *Educ:* Univ. of the Witwatersrand (BArch 1947). RIBA 1948; FCSD (FSIAD 1964). Technical Editor, Architectural Design, 1953–62; then engaged in private architectural practice in exhibns, interiors and conservation. Prof. of Architecture and Design, RCA, 1990–93. Mem., Berlin Acad., 1977–. Triennale of Milan Gran Premio, 1964; 2 Architectural Heritage Year Awards, 1973. *Publications:* Architecture: City Sense, 1965; The Necessary Monument, 1970; How to Play the Environment Game, 1973; Let's Build a Monument, 1987; (with Prof. P. Lloyd-Jones) Stonehenge Tomorrow, 1992. *Recreation:* art. *Address:* Tower 3, Whitehall Court, SW1A 2EL. *T:* 071–930 0730 and 071–229 3477; Pentagram Design Ltd, 11 Needham Road, W11 2RP.   *Died 12 Sept. 1994.*

CROSS, Alexander Urquhart, TD 1959; JP; Lord Provost of Perth, 1972–75; *b* 24 Dec. 1906; *m* 1936; one *s* one *d. Educ:* Univ. of Glasgow (MA). Owner of private school, 1931–70 (except war years, 1939–45). JP 1972, DL

1972–75, Hon. Sheriff, 1974–, Perth. CStJ 1981. *Address:* 6 Craigie Road, Perth PH2 0BH. *T:* Perth (0738) 25013.
                                                    Died 21 Dec. 1992.

CROSS, Sir Barry (Albert), Kt 1989; CBE 1981; FRS 1975; Fellow, Corpus Christi College, Cambridge, 1962–67 and since 1974; *b* 17 March 1925; *s* of Hubert Charles and Elsie May Cross; *m* 1949, Audrey Lilian Crow; one *s* two *d. Educ:* Reigate Grammar Sch.; Royal Veterinary Coll., London (MRCVS; BSc (Vet. Sci.)); St John's Coll., Cambridge (BA Hons, MA, PhD). ScD 1964. ICI Research Fellow, Physiological Lab., Cambridge, 1949–51, Gedge Prize 1952; Demonstrator, Zoological Lab., Cambridge, 1951–55, Lectr, 1955–58; Rockefeller Fellow at UCLA, 1957–58; Lectr, Dept of Anatomy, Cambridge, 1958–67; Supervisor in Physiology at St John's Coll., 1955–67; Corpus Christi College, Cambridge: Tutor for Advanced Students, 1964–67; Warden of Leckhampton, 1975–80; Pres., 1987–92; Prof. and Head of Dept of Anatomy, Univ. of Bristol, 1967–74, and Chm., Sch. of Preclinical Studies, 1969–73; Dir, AFRC Inst. of Animal Physiology, Babraham, 1974–86; Dir of Animal Physiology and Genetics Res., AFRC, 1986–89. Consultant: WHO, Geneva, 1964; in agricl biotechnology, OECD, 1989–91. Lectures: Share Jones, RCVS, 1967; Charnock Bradley, Edinburgh Univ., 1968; Glaxo, 1975; Entwhistle, Cambridge, 1976; McFadyean, London Univ., 1976; Wilmott, 1978, Long Fox, 1980, Bristol Univ.; Hunterian, London Hunterian Soc., 1988. Mem. Council, 1985–88, Sec., 1988–92, Zool Soc. of London; Member: Council, Anatomical Soc., 1968–73 (Vice Pres. 1973–74); Council, Assoc. for Study of Animal Behaviour, 1959–62, 1973–75; Cttee, Soc. for Study of Fertility, 1961–65; Cttee, Physiological Soc., 1971–75 (Chm. 1974–75); Internat. Soc. for Neuroendocrinology (Vice-Pres., 1972–75, Pres., 1976–80); Adv. Cttee, Inst. of Zoology, 1982–88; Farm Animals Welfare Adv. Cttee, MAFF, 1975–78; UGC Wkg Party on Veterinary Educn, 1987–89. Chm. Trustees, Strangeways Lab., Cambridge, 1992– (Trustee, 1990–92; Gov., 1987–90). FIBiol 1975; FRVC 1979. Hon. FRASE 1987; Hon. Mem., BVA, 1986. Bledisloe Veterinary Award, RASE, 1982. Chevalier, Order of Dannebrog (Denmark), 1968; Comdr d'honneur de l'Ordre du Bontemps de Médoc et des Graves, 1973. *Publications:* sci. papers on neuroendocrine topics in various biol jls. *Address:* Grosvenor Lodge, 6 Babraham Road, Cambridge CB2 2RA.   *Died 27 April 1994.*

CROSS, Joan, CBE 1951; opera singer; *b* 7 Sept. 1900. *Educ:* St Paul's Girls' Sch. Principal soprano, Old Vic and Sadler's Wells, 1924–44; Dir of Opera, Sadler's Wells, 1941–44; Principal soprano, English Opera Gp; Jt Founder, Opera Sch., 1948, subsequently Principal, National Sch. of Opera (Ltd), Morley Coll., London, resigned. Created rôles in Peter Grimes, The Rape of Lucretia, Albert Herring, Gloriana and The Turn of the Screw. *Address:* Garrett House, Park Road, Aldeburgh, Suffolk.
                                                    Died 12 Dec. 1993.

CROZIER, Eric John, OBE 1991; writer and lecturer; *b* 14 Nov. 1914; *m* Margaret Johns (marr. diss.); two *d*; *m* 1949, Nancy Evans (OBE 1991). Play producer for BBC Television Service, 1936–39. Produced plays and operas for Sadler's Wells Opera, Stratford-on-Avon Meml Theatre, Glyndebourne Opera and other theatres, 1944–46. Closely associated with Benjamin Britten as producer or author of his operas, 1945–51, and was co-founder with him of The English Opera Group, 1947, and The Aldeburgh Festival of Music and the Arts, 1948. *Publications:* Christmas in the Market Place (adapted from French of Henri Ghéon), 1944; The Life and Legends of Saint Nicolas, 1949; Noah Gives Thanks, a play, 1950; (with Benjamin Britten): Albert Herring, a comic opera in three acts, 1947; Saint Nicolas, a cantata, 1948; Let's Make an

Opera, an entertainment for children, 1949; (with E. M. Forster and Benjamin Britten) Billy Budd, an opera in four acts, 1951; many opera translations. *Recreations:* listening to music, walking, writing verse. *Address:* 4 The Timberyard, Great Glemham, Saxmundham, Suffolk IP17 2DL. *T:* Rendham (0728) 663618.

Died 7 Sept. 1994.

CRUICKSHANK, Herbert James, CBE 1969; CEng, FIMechE; FCIOB; retired; *b* 12 July 1912; *s* of late James William Cruickshank and Dorothy Adeline Cruickshank; *m* 1st, 1939, Jean Alexandra Payne (*d* 1978); no *c*; 2nd, 1985, Susan Elizabeth Bullen. *Educ:* Regent Street Polytechnic (Schol.). Bovis Ltd: Staff Trainee, 1931; Plant and Labour Controller, 1937; Gilbert-Ash Ltd: (formed within Bovis Gp), 1945; Director, 1949; Civil Engineering Works in Nyasaland, 1949–55; Managing Dir, UK, 1960–63; Chm. and Man. Dir, 1964; Dir, Bovis Holdings, 1964–72; Group Man. Dir, 1966, Dep. Chm. 1970–72. Member: Metrication Bd, 1969–73; SE Thames RHA, 1972–78; BSI Quality Assurance Council, 1976–81. FRSA. *Recreations:* travel, photography, sketching. *Address:* 45 Bidborough Ridge, Tunbridge Wells, Kent TN4 0UU. *T:* Tunbridge Wells (01892) 527270. *Clubs:* MCC, Lord's Taverners. *Died 5 Aug. 1995.*

CRUICKSHANK, Prof. John; Professor of French, University of Sussex, 1962–89, retired; *b* Belfast, N Ireland, 18 July 1924; *s* of Arthur Cruickshank, parliamentary reporter, and Eva Cruickshank (*née* Shummacher); *m* 1st, 1949, Kathleen Mary Gutteridge; one *s*; 2nd, 1972, Marguerite Doreen Penny. *Educ:* Royal Belfast Academical Institution; Trinity Coll., Dublin. Awarded Mod. Lang. Sizarship, TCD, 1943; 1st class Moderatorship in Mod. Langs (French and German) and 2nd class Moderatorship (Mental and Moral Science), TCD, 1948. Cryptographer in Mil. Intell., 1943–45. Lecteur d'Anglais, Ecole Normale Supérieure, Paris, 1948–49; Asst Lectr in French and German, Univ. of Southampton, 1951; Sen. Lectr in French, Univ. of Southampton, 1961. Mem., UGC, 1970–77. *Publications:* Albert Camus and the Literature of Revolt, 1959; Critical Readings in the Modern French Novel, 1961; The Novelist as Philosopher, 1962; Montherlant, 1964; (ed) French Literature and Its Background: vols 1–6, 1968–70; Aspects of the Modern European Mind, 1969; Benjamin Constant, 1974; Variations on Catastrophe, 1982; Pascal: Pensées, 1983; articles in: French Studies, Modern Language Review, Times Literary Supplement, Times Higher Education Supplement, etc. *Recreations:* bird-watching, watching cricket. *Address:* Woodpeckers, East Hoathly, Sussex BN8 6QL. *T:* Halland (01825) 840364.

Died 11 July 1995.

CRYER, (George) Robert; MP (Lab) Bradford South, since 1987; *b* 3 Dec. 1934; *m* 1963, Ann (*née* Place); one *s* one *d*. *Educ:* Salt High Sch., Shipley; Hull Univ. BSc Econ Hons; Certif. Educn. Secondary sch. teacher, Hull, 1959, Bradford, 1961 and Keighley, 1962; Asst Personnel Officer, 1960; Dewsbury Techn. Coll., 1963; Blackburn Coll. of Technology, 1964–65; Keighley Techn. Coll., 1965–74. MP (Lab) Keighley, Feb. 1974–1983; Parly Under-Sec. of State, DoI, 1976–78; Chm., Jt and Select Cttees on Statutory Instruments, 1979–83, and 1987–. Parliamentary Labour Party: Chair, CND, 1990–; Vice-Chairman: Defence Group, 1980–83; Industry Gp, 1982–83; Employment Gp, 1987–90. Contested (Lab): Darwen Div. of Lancs, 1964; Keighley, 1983. MEP (Lab) Sheffield, 1984–89. Labour Councillor, Keighley Borough Council, 1971–74. Gov., BFI, 1992–. *Publications:* Steam in the Worth Valley, Vol. 1 1969, Vol. 2 1972; Queensbury Lines, 1984. *Recreations:* working on Worth Valley Railway, cinematography, film appreciation, nurturing elderly cars. *Address:* 6 Ashfield Avenue, Shipley, Yorks

BD18 3AL. *T:* Bradford (0734) 584701. *Club:* North Bierley East Labour. *Died 12 April 1994.*

CULHANE, Rosalind, (Lady Padmore), LVO 1938; OBE 1949; Treasury Welfare Adviser, 1943–64; *y d* of late F. W. S. Culhane, MRCS, LRCP, Hastings, Sussex; *m* 1964, Sir Thomas Padmore, GCB. Joined Treasury in 1923 and attached to office of Chancellor of Exchequer; Asst Private Sec. to Rt Hon. Neville Chamberlain, 1934, Rt Hon. Sir John Simon (later 1st Viscount Simon), 1937, Rt Hon. Sir Kingsley Wood, 1940. *Address:* 39 Cholmeley Crescent, N6 5EX. *T:* 0181–340 6587.

Died 4 March 1995.

CULLEN, Gordon; see Cullen, T. G.

CULLEN, James Reynolds; *b* 13 June 1900; *s* of Rev. James Harris Cullen, London Missionary Society; *m* 1931, Inez (*d* 1980), *e d* of M. G. Zarifi, MBE; one *s* two *d*. *Educ:* Weimar Gymnasium; The School, Bishop's Stortford (Rhodes Schol.); Tonbridge Sch.; Balliol Coll., Oxford (Scholar). Hertford Schol., 1919; Craven Schol., 1920; 1st class Hon. Mods, 1920; 2nd class Lit.Hum. 1922; MA 1925. Asst Master, Winchester Coll., 1922–30; archæological expeditions to Asia Minor, 1925, and Mytilene, 1930; Dir of Education, Cyprus, 1930–45; Dir of Education, Uganda, 1945–52; Asst Master, Oundle Sch., 1953–60, Cranbrook and Benenden Schs, 1960–68. *Address:* Bayleaf Rest Home, 16 Whyke Road, Chichester, W Sussex PO19 2MN. *Club:* Commonwealth Trust.

Died 8 April 1995.

CULLEN, (Thomas) Gordon, CBE 1978; RDI 1976; planning consultant, artist and writer; *b* 9 Aug. 1914; *s* of Rev. T. H. Cullen and Mary Anne (*née* Moffatt); *m* 1955, Comtesse Jacqueline de Chabaneix du Chambon; three *d*. *Educ:* Prince Henry's Grammar Sch., Otley, Yorks; Regent Street Polytechnic Sch. of Architecture, London. Fraternal Delegate, Runcorn Trades Council, 1942; Mem. Planning Div., Develt and Welfare, Barbados, 1944–46; Asst Editor, Architectural Rev., 1946–56. Townscape Consultant: with Ford Foundn, New Delhi, 1960, and Calcutta, 1962; Liverpool, Llantrisant, Tenterden, Peterborough and Ware, 1962–76; London Docklands, 1981–82; Glasgow, 1983–84. Dir, Price and Cullen, architects, 1985–91. Exhib. drawings, Paris Salon, Royal Acad.; One-Man Exhibition: Sweden and Holland, 1976; London, 1985. Member: Eton RDC, 1963–73; Wraysbury Parish Council, 1960–89. Hon. FRIBA 1972. Hon. LittD Sheffield, 1975; Hon. LLD Strathclyde, 1988; Hon. Dr ing Munich, 1973. Amer. Inst. of Architects Gold Medal, 1976. *Publications:* Townscape, 1964; planning reports.

Died 11 Aug. 1994.

CULLITON, Hon. Edward Milton, CC 1981; QC (Sask) 1947; retired; Chief Justice of Saskatchewan, 1962–81; *b* Grand Forks, Minnesota, USA, 9 April 1906; *s* of John J. Culliton and Katherine Mary Kelly, Canadians; *m* 1939, Katherine Mary Hector. *Educ:* primary educn in towns in Saskatchewan; Univ. of Saskatchewan. BA 1926, LLB 1928. Practised law in Gravelbourg, Sask, 1930–51. Served War: Canadian Armed Forces (active, overseas, Judges' Advocate Br.), 1941–46. MLA for Gravelbourg, 1935–44, re-elected, 1948; Mem. Opposition until 1951; Provincial Sec., 1938–41; Minister without portfolio, 1941–44. Apptd Judge of Court of Appeal for Sask, 1951; Chm., Sask Revision of Statutes Cttee, 1963–65, and again 1974 until completion 1975–76. Chm., Sask Jubilee Cttee, 1952–55. Univ. of Saskatchewan: Mem. Bd of Governors, 1955–61; Chancellor, 1963–69; Mem. Bd, Can. Nat. Inst. for the Blind, 1955– (Pres. Sask Div., 1962–); Chm., Adv. Bd, Martha House (unmarried mothers), 1955–. Mem., Knights of Columbus, 1930–. Hon. DCL Saskatchewan, 1962. Kt Comdr of St Gregory (Papal), 1963. *Recreations:* golf, curling, interested in football. *Address:* 1303–1830 College Avenue, Regina, Saskatchewan S4P 1C2, Canada. *T:* 569–1758. *Clubs:* Wascana Country, Assiniboia, Royal United Services Institute (all Regina, Sask). *Died 14 March 1991.*

CUMBER, Sir John Alfred, Kt 1985; CMG 1966; MBE 1954; TD; Director-General, Save the Children Fund, 1976–85; *b* 30 Sept. 1920; *s* of A. J. Cumber, FRIBA, AMICE; *m* 1945, Margaret Anne Tripp; two *s*. *Educ:* Richmond County Sch.; LSE. Served War of 1939–46 (Major). HMOCS, Kenya, 1947–63 (Sen. District Comr); Administrator of the Cayman Islands, 1964–68; Comr in Anguilla, 1969; Dep. Election Comr, Southern Rhodesia/Zimbabwe, 1979–80. *Recreations:* art, music. *Address:* 7 Barton Cottages, Throwleigh, Devon EX20 2HS. *Club:* Commonwealth Trust. *Died 18 May 1991.*

CUMMING, (John) Alan, CBE 1983; CA; FCBSI; CIMgt; Director, Woolwich (formerly Woolwich Equitable) Building Society, since 1978; *b* 6 March 1932; *s* of John Cumming; *m* 1958, Isobel Beaumont Sked; three *s*. *Educ:* George Watson's Coll., Edinburgh. CA 1956; FCBSI 1971; CIMgt (FBIM 1976). Woolwich Equitable Building Society, 1958–: Gen. Manager's Asst, 1965; Asst Gen. Man., 1967; Chief Exec., 1969–86; Exec. Vice-Chm., 1986–91. Chairman: Woolwich Homes, 1989–; URC Trust, 1978–; Cavendish Wates 1st Assured, 1988–; Cavendish Wates 3rd Assured, 1989–; Thamesmead Town, 1990–93; Director: Value and Income Trust, 1986–; Woolwich (Europe), 1990–. Chairman: Metrop. Assoc. of Bldg Socs., 1977–78; Bldg Socs Assoc., 1981–83 (Mem. Council, 1970–90); President: Bldg Socs Inst., 1973–74; Europ. Community Mortgage Fedn, 1984–87; Internat. Union of Housing Finance Inst., 1990–92. Chm., Bromley HA, 1991–. *Recreations:* golf, bridge. *Address:* 8 Prince Consort Drive, Chislehurst, Kent BR7 5SB. *T:* 081–467 8382. *Club:* Caledonian. *Died 4 Nov. 1993.*

CUNLIFFE, His Honour Christopher Joseph; a Circuit Judge (formerly County Court Judge), 1966–82; *b* 28 Feb. 1916; *s* of Lt-Col E. N. Cunliffe, OBE, RAMC, Buckingham Crescent, Manchester, and Harriet Cunliffe (*née* Clegg); *m* 1942, Margaret Hamer Barber; two *d*. *Educ:* Rugby Sch.; Trinity Hall, Cambridge (BA 1937). Called to the Bar, Lincoln's Inn, 1938. Legal Cadet, Br. North Borneo Civil Service. 1939–40. Served RAFVR, 1941–46; Intelligence, Judge Advocate General's Branch. Practised on Northern Circuit, 1946; Dep. Coroner, City of Liverpool, 1953; Chairman: National Insurance Tribunal, Bootle, 1956–; Mental Health Review Tribunal for SW Lancs and W Ches, 1961–. *Recreations:* golf, gardening. *Address:* Field House, Compton, W Sussex PO18 9HE. *T:* Compton (01705) 631270.
Died 23 Sept. 1995.

CUNLIFFE, His Honour Thomas Alfred; a Circuit Judge (formerly County Court Judge), 1963–75; *b* 9 March 1905; *s* of Thomas and Elizabeth Cunliffe, Preston; *m* 1938, Constance Isabella Carden; one *s* one *d*. *Educ:* Lancaster Royal Grammar Sch.; Sidney Sussex Coll., Cambridge (Classical Scholar). Inner Temple: Profumo Prize, 1926; Paul Methven Prize, 1926; called to the Bar, 1927; Yarborough Anderson Scholar, 1927. Practised Northern Circuit, 1927–63; Dep. Chm., Lancs County Quarter Sessions, 1961–63; Recorder, Barrow-in-Furness, 1962–63. RAFVR (Squadron Leader), 1940–45. *Recreation:* music. *Address:* 30 Red Dale, Dale Avenue, Heswall, Wirral, Merseyside L60 7TA. *T:* 051–342 3949. *Died 11 April 1993.*

CUNLIFFE-JONES, Rev. Prof. Hubert; Professor of Theology, University of Manchester, 1968–73, then Professor Emeritus; *b* Strathfield, Sydney, NSW, Australia, 30 March 1905; *s* of Rev. Walter and Maud Cunliffe-Jones; *m* 1933, Maude Edith Clifton, BSc, DipEd Sydney

(*d* 1989); two *s* two *d*. *Educ:* Newington Coll., Sydney; Sydney and Oxford Univs; Camden Coll., Sydney; Mansfield Coll., Oxford. Congregational Minister, Warrnambool, Vic, Australia, 1928–29; Travelling Sec., Australian SCM, 1929–30; Congregational Minister, Witney, Oxon, 1933–37; Tutor in Systematic Theology, Yorks United Independent Coll., Bradford, 1937–47; Principal, Yorks United Independent Coll., Bradford, 1947–58; Associate Principal, Northern Congregational Coll., Manchester, 1958–66; Prof., History of Doctrine, Univ. of Manchester, 1966–68 (Lectr, 1958–66). Chm. of the Congregational Union of England and Wales, 1957–58. Hon. DD Edinburgh, 1956. *Publications:* The Holy Spirit, 1943; The Authority of the Biblical Revelation, 1945; Deuteronomy, 1951; Jeremiah, 1960; Technology, Community and Church, 1961; Christian Theology since 1600, 1970; (ed) History of Christian Doctrine, 1979; articles in Theology, Expository Times, etc. *Recreation:* drama. *Address:* 58 Norsey View Drive, Billericay, Essex CM12 0QS. *Died 3 Jan. 1991.*

CUNNINGHAM, David, CB 1983; Solicitor to the Secretary of State for Scotland, 1980–84; *b* 26 Feb. 1924; *s* of Robert Cunningham and Elizabeth (*née* Shields); *m* 1955, Ruth Branwell Crawford; one *s* two *d*. *Educ:* High School of Glasgow; Univ. of Glasgow (MA, LLB). Served War, 1942–47: commnd, Cameronians, 1943; Intelligence Corps (Captain), and Control Commission for Germany, 1945–47. Admitted Solicitor, 1951; entered Office of Solicitor to Secretary of State for Scotland as Legal Asst, 1954; Sen. Legal Asst, 1960; Asst Solicitor, 1966; Cabinet Office Constitution Unit, 1975–77; Dep. Solicitor, 1978–80. *Recreations:* hill walking, reading, theatre, motor-cars. *Address:* The Green Gates, Innerleithen, Peeblesshire, Scotland EH44 6NH. *T:* Innerleithen (01896) 830436. *Died 21 March 1995.*

CUNNINGHAM, Prof. George John, MBE 1945; Professor and Chairman, Department of Academic Pathology, Virginia Commonwealth University, Richmond, 1974–77, then Emeritus Professor; Conservator of Pathological Collection, Royal College of Surgeons; Consultant Pathologist to South East and South West Regional Health Authorities; *b* 7 Sept. 1906; *s* of George S. Cunningham and Blanche A. Harvey; *m* 2nd, 1957, Patricia Champion, Brisbane, Australia. *Educ:* Royal Belfast Academical Institution; Dean Close Sch., Cheltenham; St Bartholomew's Hospital Medical Coll. MRCS, LRCP 1931; MB, BS London, 1933; MD London, 1937; FRCPath 1964. Asst Pathologist, Royal Sussex County Hosp., Brighton, 1934–42. War Service, RAMC, Middle East and Italy (temp. Lt-Col). Senior Lectr in Pathology, St Bartholomew's Hosp., London, 1946–55; Sir William Collins Prof. of Pathology, Univ. of London, at RCS, 1955–68; Prof. of Pathology, Medical Coll. of Virginia, and Chief of Laboratory Service, McGuire Hosp., Richmond, Va, 1968–74. Dorothy Temple Cross Travelling Fellow in America, 1951–52; Vis. Prof., New York State Univ., 1961; Vis. Prof., Cairo Univ., 1963. Past Pres., Assoc. of Clin. Path., Internat. Acad. of Pathology, Quekett Microscopical Club. Freeman, City of London. *Publications:* chapter on Gen. Pathology of Malignant Tumours, in Cancer, Vol. 2, 1957; chapter on Microradiography, in Tools of Biological Research, Vol. 2, 1960; and several articles on pathology, in medical press. *Recreation:* golf. *Clubs:* National Liberal; Royal Blackheath Golf. *Died 24 Feb. 1994.*

CUNYNGHAME, Hon. Pamela Margaret, (Hon. Lady Cunynghame); *see* Stanley, Hon. P. M.

CURRIE, Prof. Sir Alastair (Robert), Kt 1979; Professor of Pathology, Edinburgh University, 1972–86, then Emeritus; Pathologist, Royal Infirmary of Edinburgh; Consultant Pathologist, Lothian Health Board; *b* 8 Oct.

1921; *s* of late John Currie and Maggie Mactaggart; *m* 1949, Jeanne Marion Clarke, MB, ChB; three *s* one *d* (and one *d* decd). *Educ:* Port Ellen Public Sch.; High Sch. and Univ. of Glasgow. BSc; MB, ChB Glasgow; FRCPE; FRCPGlas; FRCP; FRCPath; FRSE. RAMC, 1949–51. Lectr in Pathology, Univ. of Glasgow, 1947–54; Sen. Lectr in Pathology, Univ. of Glasgow, and Cons. Pathologist, Royal Infirmary, Glasgow, 1954–59; Head, Div. of Pathology, Imperial Cancer Research Fund, London, 1959–62; Regius Prof. of Pathology, Univ. of Aberdeen, 1962–72. Chairman: Standing Adv. Cttee on Laboratory Services, 1968–72; Biomedical Res. Cttee, 1975–78; Jt MRC and NRPB Cttee on Radiological Protection, 1974–81; MRC/CRC Cttee for Jtly Supported Insts, 1978–80; CRC/MRC Cttee for Inst. of Cancer Research, 1980–83; Co-ordinating Cttee for Cancer Res., 1980–81; Scottish Cancer Co-ordinating and Adv. Cttee, 1991–; Member: MRC, 1964–68 and 1976–80 (Chm., Cell Biology and Disorders Bd, 1976–78); Scottish NE Regional Hosp. Bd, 1966–71; Council, RCPath, 1968–71; Scottish Health Services Council, 1969–72; Chief Scientist's Cttee, Scottish Home and Health Dept, 1974–78; Court, Edinburgh Univ., 1975–78; Bd of Dirs, Inveresk Research International, 1980–89; Sci. Adv. Council, Alberta Heritage Foundn for Med. Res., 1982–88; Assembly, Gen. Motors Cancer Research Foundn, 1982–86; UK Co-ordinating Cttee for Cancer Res., 1984–88; Cancer Research Campaign: Mem. Council, 1976–91; Mem. Exec. Cttee, 1976–88 (Chm., 1983–88); Mem., 1969–83, Chm., 1978–83, Scientific Cttee; Hon. Treasurer, 1988–91; Vice-Pres., 1991–; Royal Society of Edinburgh: Mem. Council, 1980–83; a Vice-Pres., 1988–90; Pres., 1991–. Chairman: Bd of Govs, Beatson Inst. for Cancer Res., 1984–91; Council, Paterson Inst. for Cancer Res., 1990–92; Dep. Chm., Caledonian Res. Foundn, 1989–. Trustee, Islay Museums, 1987–. Hon. DSc: Birmingham, 1983; Aberdeen, 1985; Hon. LLD Glasgow, 1987; Dr *hc* Edinburgh, 1991. *Publications:* papers in scientific and med. jls. *Address:* 42 Murrayfield Avenue, Edinburgh EH12 6AY. *T:* 031–337 3100; Grianan, Strathlachlan, Strachur, Argyll. *T:* Strachur (036986) 769. *Club:* New (Edinburgh).

Died 12 Jan. 1994.

CURRIE, Rear-Adm. Robert Alexander, CB 1957; DSC 1944, bar 1945; DL; *b* 29 April 1905; 5th *s* of John Currie, Glasgow, and Rachel Thomson, Dundee; *m* 1944, Lady (Edith Margaret) Beevor (*d* 1985), *d* of Frank Agnew, Eccles, Norfolk, and *widow* of Sir Thomas Beevor, 6th Bt; one step *s* (Sir Thomas Beevor, 7th Bt) three step *d*. *Educ:* RN Colleges, Osborne and Dartmouth. Specialised in Gunnery, 1930; served War, 1939–45: HMS Hood; HMS Warspite, 2nd Battle of Narvik; Plans Division, Admiralty; Convoy Escort Comdr; Assault Gp Comdr, Far East; Captain RN, 1945; Captain (D) Fifth Flotilla, 1948–49; idc 1950; Director, Royal Naval Staff Coll., 1951–52; Comdg Officer, HMS Cumberland, 1953; Rear-Adm., 1954; Chief of Staff to Chairman, British Joint Service Mission, Washington, DC, 1954–57; retired, 1957. Member: Cttee of Enquiry into the Fishing Industry, 1958–60; W Suffolk County Council, 1962–74. DL, Suffolk, 1968. King Haakon VII Liberty Cross, Norway, 1945. *Recreation:* painting. *Address:* Saffron Pane, Hall Road, Lavenham, Suffolk CO10 9QU.

Died 7 Feb. 1995.

CURRY, John Anthony, OBE 1976; actor, ice skater; *b* 9 Sept. 1949; *s* of Joseph Henry Curry and Rita Agnes Pritchard. *Educ:* Solihull Sch. British, European, World, and Olympic Figure Skating Champion, 1976. Founder and Director: John Curry Theatre of Skating, 1977; John Curry Sch. of Skating, 1978; Artistic Dir, John Curry Skating Co. Appeared in: A Midsummer Night's Dream, Nottingham and Open Air Theatre, Regent's Park; As You Like It, Open Air Theatre, Regent's Park; A Symphony On Ice, Royal Albert Hall, Metropolitan Opera House, NY, 1984; Cinderella, Liverpool Playhouse, 1986; Hard Times, Lyric Theatre, Belfast and King's Head, 1987. Nat. Advr, Nat. Skating Assoc., 1988–. *Publication:* (with photographs by Keith Money) John Curry, 1978. *Recreations:* theatre, reading. *Address:* c/o London Management, 235 Regent Street, W1.

Died 15 April 1994.

CUTHBERTSON, Sir Harold (Alexander), Kt 1983; Managing Director, Blundstone Pty Ltd, since 1957; Chairman and Director, Essential Oils of Tasmania Pty Ltd, 1985–90; Director, Tasmania University Research Co. Pty Ltd; *b* 16 Nov. 1911; *s* of Thomas Alexander Cuthbertson and Vera Rose Cuthbertson; *m* 1937, Jean Westbrook; two *d*. *Educ:* Hutchins Sch., Hobart. Entered family business, Blundstone Pty Ltd, 1932; after tertiary training, became Dir, 1939. Dir of cos, public and private. Pres., Tas Chamber of Manufrs, 1964–67; Vice Pres., Assoc. of Aust. Chambers of Manufrs, 1966–67; Mem., Commonwealth Immigration Planning Council, 1968–75; Warden, Marine Bd of Hobart, 1963–75. *Recreations:* bowls, fishing. *Address:* 3 David Avenue, Sandy Bay, Tas 7005, Australia. *T:* (02) 251619. *Clubs:* Tasmanian, Athenæum (Pres. 1970), Rotary (Pres., 1959–60) (Hobart).

Died 14 March 1994.

CUTTELL, Rev. Canon Colin, OBE 1977; Vicar of All Hallows, Barking-by-the-Tower, Guild Church of Toc H, 1963–76; *b* 24 Sept. 1908; *s* of late Maurice John Cuttell, Cheltenham, Glos, and Blanche Vickers; unmarried. *Educ:* Bishop's Univ., Lennoxville (BA; STM 1968). Deacon, 1937; priest, 1938; Missioner of Wabamun, Canada, 1937–42; Domestic Chaplain to the Archbishop of Quebec, 1942–43; Chaplain to the Forces, 1943–44; Priest Vicar, Southwark Cathedral, 1945–49; Bishop of Southwark's Chaplain for Industrial Relations, 1948–63; Canon Residentiary and Librarian of Southwark Cathedral, 1954–63, Canon Emeritus, 1976; Sabbatical year, 1960; Acting Provost, Southwark, 1961. Commissary for Bishop of Qu'Appelle, 1951; Founder and Senior Chaplain, S London Industrial Mission, 1950; Acting Chaplain, Lincoln Coll., Oxford. Field Commissioner, Toc H, 1962; Deputy Admin. Padre, Toc H, 1963. Editor of Over the Bridge, 1948. *Publications:* Ministry Without Portfolio, 1962. *Recreations:* swimming, sketching, walking.

Died 15 Aug. 1992.

CZIFFRA, György, (Georges); Chevalier de la Légion d'Honneur, 1973; Comdr, Ordre des Arts et des Lettres, 1975; pianist; *b* Budapest, Hungary, 5 Nov. 1921; *s* of Julius Cziffra and Helen Nagy, naturalized French citizen, 1968; *m* 1942, Soleyka Abdin (Madame Soleyka Cziffra); (one *s* decd). *Educ:* Academy of Music Franz Liszt, Budapest. Gave recitals and took part in concerts at the Festival Hall, London, and throughout the world: USA, Canada, France, Israel, Benelux, Germany, Italy, Switzerland, Hungary, Austria, Japan, S America, also BBC and BBC Television, London. Recorded for HMV: Liszt, Grieg, Tchaikowski, Rackmaninof, Beethoven, Schumann, paraphrases by G. Cziffra, Brahms's Hungarian dances, transciption by Cziffra, etc. Founded, 1968, biennial Concours International de Piano, Versailles, for young pianists; Founder, with son, 1966, Festival of La Chaise Dieu; undertook the creation, in the Chapelle Royale Saint Frambourg, Senlis, of an Auditorium Franz Liszt, 1973; first cultural exchanges between France and Hungary (Foundation Cziffra of Budapest), 1983; Pres., Foundation Cziffra, 1975– (created for young artists). Médaille d'or de l'Académie Française, 1981. *Publication:* Des canons et des fleurs, 1977. *Address:* 1 place Saint Pierre, 60300 Senlis, France. *T:* 44533999.

Died 16 Jan. 1994.

D

d'ABREU, Francis Arthur, ERD 1954; Consultant Surgeon, Westminster Hospital, 1946–69, retired; Surgeon, Hospital of St John and St Elizabeth, 1950–69, then Emeritus; *b* 1 Oct. 1904; *s* of Dr John Francis d'Abreu and Teresa d'Abreu; *m* 1945, Margaret Ann, *d* of Hon. Patrick Bowes-Lyon, 5th *s* of 13th Earl of Strathmore; one *s* one *d* (and one *d* decd). *Educ:* Stonyhurst Coll.; Birmingham Univ. (MB, ChB 1929; ChM 1935). MRCS, LRCP 1929; FRCS, 1932. House Surgeon, Gen. Hosp., Birmingham, 1929; Res. Surgical Officer, Gen. and Queen's Hosps, Birmingham, 1930–34; Surg. Registrar, St Bartholomew's Hosp., London, and Westminster Hosp., 1934–39. Formerly: Examiner to Soc. of Apothecaries; Examiner to Univs of Cambridge and London; Mem., Ct of Examiners, RCS. Mem. Bd of Management, Inst. of Sports Medicine. Lieut RAMC (Supp. Reserve), 1939. Served War of 1939–45: Major, RAMC, 1939, Lt-Col 1942–45. Kt of Magistral Grace, SMO Malta; Kt Comdr, Order of St Gregory (Holy See), 1977. *Publications:* contrib. to various medical jls. *Recreation:* gardening. *Address:* 36 Cumberland Terrace, Regent's Park, NW1 4HP. *Died 16 Nov. 1995.*

DADZIE, Kenneth Kweku Sinaman; High Commissioner for Ghana in London, since 1994; *b* 10 Sept. 1930; *s* of Kwesi Sinaman Dadzie and Sarah Eyaah. *Educ:* Achimoto Coll., Ghana; Queens' Coll., Cambridge (Econs Tripos) (Hon. Fellow, 1991). Various posts in Ghana CS, 1952–56; Ghana Foreign Service, 1957–64; Chargé d'Affaires, Paris, 1957–58; Dep. Perm. Rep., UN, NY, 1960–64; various posts in Foreign Service alternating with posts on secondment to UN Secretariat, 1964–75; Ambassador to Switzerland and concurrently to Austria, and Perm. Rep. to UN in Geneva, 1975–78; UN Dir-Gen. for Develt and Internat. Econ. Co-operation, 1978–82; High Comr, London (with rank of Sec. of State), 1982–86; Sec.-Gen., UNCTAD, 1986–94. Member Council: ODI, 1995–; VSO, 1995–. Order of the Volta (Ghana), 1978. *Publications:* contribs to learned jls and compilations on internat. develt policy and on UN. *Address:* Ghana High Commission, 104 Highgate Hill, N6 5HE. *T:* 0181–342 8686. *Clubs:* United Oxford & Cambridge University, Travellers'. *Died 25 Oct. 1995.*

DAHL, Murdoch Edgcumbe; *b* 11 March 1914; *s* of Oscar Horace and Edith Gladys Dahl; *m* 1940, Joan, *d* of Daniel Charles and Edith Marion Woollaston; three *s*. *Educ:* Royal Grammar Sch., Newcastle upon Tyne; Armstrong Coll. (subseq. King's Coll.), Newcastle upon Tyne; St John's Coll., Durham. BA 1936, MA 1956, Durham. Deacon 1937; priest 1938. Curate of: St Paul, Astley Bridge, 1937–39; Fallowfield, 1939–43; Harpenden, 1943–49; Vicar of Arlesey and Rector of Astwick, 1949–51; Minister, St Oswald's, Croxley Green, 1951–56; Vicar of Great with Little Hormead and Rector of Wyddial, 1956–65; Examining Chaplain to Bishop of St Albans, 1959; Hon. Canon of St Albans, 1963–65; Canon Residentiary, 1965–68; Canon Theologian, 1968–79; Canon Emeritus, 1979. Resigned all ecclesiastical (C of E) titles, Dec. 1982, when he became a Roman Catholic. *Publications:* Resurrection of the Body, 1962; Sin Streamlined, 1966; The Christian Materialist, 1968; Final Loss—Final Gain, 1980; Daughter of Love, 1989. *Address:* 25 Elvaston Road, Hexham, Northumberland NE46 2HA. *T:* Hexham (0434) 606514. *Died 20 June 1991.*

DALAIS, Sir (Adrien) Pierre, Kt 1989; Chairman: Beau Champ Group of Companies (Sugar), Mauritius, since 1984; Floréal Group of Companies (Textile), since 1972; *b* 12 April 1929; *s* of Pierre Adrien Clement Piat Dalais and Simone de la Hogue Rey; *m* 1954, Clotilde Adam; four *s* one *d. Educ:* St Esprit Coll., Mauritius. Certified Secretary at Cape Town, 1952. Developed textile industry in Mauritius, the Floreal Gp employing 11,000 people in wool spinning, dyeing and knitting; succeeded his father as Chm. of Beau Champ Co. Sugar. Chairman: Mauritius Chamber of Agriculture, 1977–87; Mauritius Commercial Bank Ltd, 1986–89; Ireland Blyth Ltd, 1976–80 and 1987–88. *Recreations:* yachting, golf, tennis. *Address:* Forest Lane, Floréal, Mauritius. *T:* 864904. *Clubs:* Mauritius Turf, Grand Baie Yacht, Dodo, Gymkhana (Mauritius). *Died 7 Nov. 1991.*

DALGLISH, Captain James Stephen, CVO 1955; CBE 1963; RN; *b* 1 Oct. 1913; *e s* of late Rear-Adm. Robin Dalglish, CB; *m* 1939, Evelyn Mary, *e d* of late Rev. A. Ll. Meyricke, Vicar of Aislaby, near Whitby; one *s* one *d. Educ:* RN Coll., Dartmouth. Commanded HMS Aisne, 1952–53; HM Yacht Britannia, 1954; HMS Woodbridge Haven and Inshore Flotilla, 1958–59; HMS Excellent, 1959–61; HMS Bulwark, 1961–63; jssc 1950; idc 1957; retired from RN, 1963. Welfare Officer, Metropolitan Police, 1963–73. *Publication:* Life Story of a Fish (autobiog.), 1992. *Recreations:* gardening, painting. *Address:* Park Hall, Aislaby, Whitby, North Yorks YO21 1SW. *T:* Whitby (01947) 810213. *Died 6 Oct. 1995.*

DALTON, Vice-Adm. Sir Norman (Eric), KCB 1959 (CB 1956); OBE 1944; *b* 1 Feb. 1904; *s* of late William John Henry Dalton, Portsmouth; *m* 1927, Teresa Elizabeth (*d* 1982), *d* of late Richard Jenkins, Portsmouth; one *s* one *d. Educ:* RN Colls Osborne and Dartmouth. Joined RN, 1917; Capt. 1946; Rear-Adm. 1954; Vice-Adm. 1957; Deputy Engineer-in-Chief of the Fleet, 1955–57; Engineer-in-Chief of the Fleet, 1957–59; Dir-Gen. of Training, 1959–60; retired 1960. *Address:* New Lodge, Peppard Lane, Henley-on-Thames, Oxon. *T:* Henley (0491) 575552. *Club:* Army and Navy. *Died 27 Jan. 1992.*

DALY, Rt Rev. John Charles Sydney; *b* 13 Jan. 1903; *s* of S. Owen Daly. *Educ:* Gresham's Sch., Holt; King's Coll., Cambridge; Cuddesdon Coll., Oxford. Deacon, 1926; priest, 1927; Curate, St Mary's Church, Tyne Dock, South Shields, 1926–29; Vicar, Airedale with Fryston, Yorks, 1929–35; Bishop of Gambia, 1935–51; Bishop of Accra, 1951–55; Bishop in Korea, 1955–65, of Taejon (Korea), 1965–68; Priest-in-charge of Honington with Idlicote and Whatcote, 1968–70; Vicar of Bishop's Tachbrook, 1970–75. *Died 15 Aug. 1993.*

DALZIEL, Dr Keith, FRS 1975; Reader in Biochemistry, University of Oxford, 1978–83; Fellow of Wolfson College, Oxford, 1970–83, then Emeritus; *b* 24 Aug. 1921; *s* of late Gilbert and Edith Dalziel; *m* 1945, Sallie Farnworth; two *d. Educ:* Grecian Street Central Sch., Salford; Royal Techn. Coll., Salford. 1st cl. hons BSc London 1944; PhD London; MA Oxon. Lab. Technician, Manchester Victoria Meml Jewish Hosp., 1935–44, Biochemist 1944–45; Asst Biochemist, Radcliffe Infirmary, Oxford, 1945–47; Res. Asst, Nuffield

Haematology Res. Fund, Oxford, 1947–58; Rockefeller Trav. Fellowship in Medicine, Nobel Inst., Stockholm, 1955–57; Sorby Res. Fellow of Royal Soc., Sheffield Univ., 1958–63; Univ. Lectr in Biochem., Oxford, 1963–78. Vis. Prof. of Biochemistry, Univ. of Michigan, 1967. Member: Enzyme Chem. and Tech. Cttee, SRC, 1974; Council, Royal Soc., 1979–80; Editorial Bds, European Jl of Biochemistry and Biochimica Biophysica Acta, 1971–74; Adv. Bd, Jl Theor. Biol., 1976–79; an Associate Editor, Royal Soc., 1983–87. *Publications:* sci. papers in Biochem. Jl, European Jl of Biochemistry, etc. *Recreations:* music, golf, walking. *Address:* 25 Hampden Drive, Kidlington, Oxford OX5 2LR. *T:* Kidlington (08675) 2623. *Died 7 Jan. 1994.*

DANIEL, Norman Alexander, CBE 1974 (OBE 1968); PhD; historian of the Middle Ages and intercultural relations; *b* 8 May 1919; *s* of George Frederick Daniel and Winifred Evelyn (*née* Jones); *m* 1st, 1941, Marion Ruth (*d* 1981), *d* of Harold Wadham Pethybridge; one *s*; 2nd, 1988, Morna Mackenzie Wales, *d* of Ronald Neil Mackenzie Murray, MC. *Educ:* Frensham Heights Sch.; Queen's Coll., Oxford (BA); Edinburgh Univ. (PhD). Asst Dir, British Inst., Basra, 1947; British Council Asst Representative: Baghdad, 1948; Beirut, 1952; Edinburgh, 1953; Dir, Brit. Inst., Baghdad, 1957; Dep. Rep., Brit. Council, Scotland, 1960; Brit. Council Rep., Sudan, 1962; Vis. Fellow, University Coll., Cambridge, 1969–70; Dir, Visitors Dept, Brit. Council, London, 1970; Cultural Attaché, Cairo, 1971; British Council Rep. and Cultural Counsellor, British Embassy, Cairo, 1973–79. Planning Advr, 1979–84, Consultant, 1984–, Hassan Khalifa; Gen. Sec., Coptic Archaeological Soc., Cairo, 1979–83. Green Vis Prof., Univ. of British Columbia, 1982. Egyptian Order of Merit, 2nd class, 1977. *Publications:* Islam and the West: the making of an image, 1960, 3rd edn 1966, repr. 1980; Islam, Europe and Empire, 1966; The Arabs and Mediaeval Europe, 1975, enlarged and rev. edn 1979, 3rd edn 1986, trans. Italian (Premio Lao Silesu Terzo Mondo, 1981); The Cultural Barrier, 1975; Heroes and Saracens, 1984; contributions to: Islam: Past Influence and Future Challenge (ed Cachia), 1979; History of the Crusades, vol. 6 (ed Zacour and Hazard), 1990; The Iraqi Revolution of 1958 (ed Furnea and Louis), 1991; D'un orient l'autre, 1991; contrib. to learned jls. *Address:* Le Grammont, rue Nationale, St Gingolph, 74500 Evian, France. *T:* 50767262; 225 Davenport #602, Toronto, Ont M5R 3R2, Canada. *T:* (416) 9242023. *Died 11 Aug. 1992.*

DANIELL, Roy Lorentz, CBE 1957; barrister-at-law; Charity Commissioner, 1953–62; *s* of late Edward Cecil Daniell, Abbotswood, Speen, Bucks; *m* 1936, Sheila Moore-Gwyn, *d* of late Major J. G. Moore-Gwyn, Clayton Court, Liss, Hants. *Educ:* Gresham's Sch., Holt; New Coll., Oxford. Called to the Bar, Inner Temple, 1927. *Address:* Common Side, Russell's Water, Henley on Thames, Oxon RG9 6ER. *T:* Nettlebed (0491) 641696. *Club:* United Oxford & Cambridge University. *Died 22 Feb. 1992.*

DANIELS, Laurence John, CB 1979; OBE 1970; Secretary, Department of Capital Territory, Australia, 1977–81, retired; *b* 11 Aug. 1916; *s* of Leslie Daniels and Margaret (*née* Bradley); *m* 1943, Joyce Carey; two *s* eight *d. Educ:* Rostrevor Coll., South Australia; Sydney Univ. (BEc 1943). AASA 1939. Commonwealth (Australian) Taxation Office, 1934–53; Commonwealth Dept of Health, 1953–72; Director-General, Dept of Social Security, 1973–77. *Address:* 5 Nares Crest, Forrest, ACT 2603, Australia. *T:* (62) 951896. *Died 16 Sept. 1994.*

DANIELS, Robert George Reginald, CBE 1984; JP; DL; Chairman, Dartford Tunnel Joint Committee, 1974–88 (Member, 1968–88, Vice-Chairman, 1970–74); *b* 17 Nov.

1916; *s* of Robert Henry Daniels and Edith Daniels; *m* 1940, Dora Ellen Hancock; one *d. Educ:* private and state. Insurance Representative, Prudential Assurance, 1938–76, retd. Mem., Essex CC, 1965–89 (Alderman, 1969; Vice-Chm., 1977–80, Chm. 1980–83). Member: Theydon Bois Parish Council, 1952– (Chm., 1969–); Epping RDC, 1952–55 and Epping and Ongar RDC, 1955–74 (Vice-Chm., 1958–59 and 1964–65; Chm., 1959–60 and 1965–66); Epping Forest District Council, 1974–79. Chm., Gen. Comrs of Income Tax for Epping Div., 1988– (Comr, 1970–). President: Theydon Bois Br., British Legion, 1985– (Chm., 1973–85); Outward Bound Trust, Essex, 1985–; Mem., Chelmsford Engrg Soc., 1980–. JP Essex (Epping and Ongar Bench), 1969; DL Essex, 1980. *Recreation:* reading. *Address:* 42 Dukes Avenue, Theydon Bois, Epping CM16 7HF. *T:* Theydon Bois (037881) 3123. *Club:* Essex (Chelmsford). *Died 13 Feb. 1993.*

DARBOURNE, John William Charles, CBE 1977; RIBA; Principal, John Darbourne Partnership, Architects, Landscape Architects and Planners; *b* 1 Jan. 1935; *s* of late William Leslie Darbourne and Violet Yorke; *m* 1960, Noreen Fifield (marr. diss. 1989); one *s* three *d. Educ:* Battersea Grammar Sch.; University Coll., London Univ. (BA Hons Arch. 1958); Harvard (MLA). RIBA 1960; AILA. Asst Architect in private practice, 1958–60; Post-grad. study in landscape arch. and planning, Harvard, 1960, completed degree course, 1964; successful entry in Lillington (Westminster) national architect competition whilst in USA; founded own practice, 1961, inviting Geoffrey Darke into partnership; practice moved to Richmond, 1963, and from 1966, grew steadily to undertake several large commns, particularly public housing, offices, corporate headquarters, medical and recreational buildings; latterly practice expanded into Europe (through internat. competitions), building in Stuttgart, Hannover and Bolzano; partnership of Darbourne & Darke dissolved, 1987; formed Darbourne & Partners, subseq. John Darbourne Partnership, 1987, which continued major work in UK and Europe. Architectural and Landscape Consultant to City of Bath. Involved in professional and local cttees, and national confs. Fritz Schumacher Award, 1979. *Recreations:* working late, the piano, golf, ski-ing. *Address:* 6 The Green, Richmond, Surrey TW9 1PL. *T:* 081–940 7182. *Clubs:* Athenæum, Reform. *Died 29 Sept. 1991.*

DARBY, Prof. Sir Clifford; *see* Darby, Prof. Sir H. C.

DARBY, Rt Rev. Harold Richard; Bishop Suffragan of Sherwood, 1975–89; an Assistant Bishop, Diocese of Lincoln, since 1989; *b* 28 Feb. 1919; *s* of late William and Miriam Darby; *m* 1949, Audrey Elizabeth Lesley Green; two *s* three *d. Educ:* Cathedral School, Shanghai; St John's Coll., Durham (BA). Military service, 1939–45; Durham Univ., 1946–50. Deacon 1950; priest 1951; Curate of Leyton, 1950–51; Curate of Harlow, 1951–53; Vicar of Shrub End, Colchester, 1953–59; Vicar of Waltham Abbey, 1959–70; Dean of Battle, 1970–75. Hon. DD Nottingham, 1988. *Recreation:* vintage cars. *Address:* Sherwood, Main Street, Claypole, Lincs NG23 5BJ. *Died 26 Dec. 1993.*

DARBY, Prof. Sir (Henry) Clifford, Kt 1988; CBE 1978 (OBE 1946); LittD 1960; FBA 1967; Professor of Geography in the University of Cambridge, 1966–76, then Emeritus; Honorary Fellow: St Catharine's College, Cambridge, 1960; King's College, Cambridge, 1983; *b* 7 Feb. 1909; *s* of Evan Darby and Janet Darby (*née* Thomas); *m* 1941, Eva Constance Thomson; two *d. Educ:* Neath County Sch.; St Catharine's Coll., Cambridge. 1st Class Geographical Tripos, Parts I, 1926, II, 1928; PhD 1931; MA 1932. Lecturer in Geography, University of Cambridge, 1931–45; Fellow, King's Coll.,

Cambridge, 1932–45, 1966–81; Intelligence Corps, 1940–41 (Capt.); Admiralty, 1941–45; John Rankin Prof. of Geography, University of Liverpool, 1945–49; Prof. of Geography, University Coll. London, 1949–66. Leverhulme Research Fellow, 1946–48; Visiting Prof., Univ. of Chicago, 1952, Harvard Univ., 1959, 1964–65, and Univ. of Washington, 1963. Member: Royal Commission on Historical Monuments (England), 1953–77; National Parks Commn, 1958–63; Water Resources Board, 1964–68. President: Institute of British Geographers, 1961; Section E British Assoc., 1963; English Place-Name Soc., 1985–86; Chm., British National Cttee for Geography, 1973–78. Carl Sauer Lectr, Univ. of Calif, Berkeley, 1985; Ralph Brown Lectr, Univ. of Minnesota, 1987. Mem., Academia Europaea. Hon. Member: Croatian Geog. Soc., 1957; Royal Netherlands Geog. Soc., 1958; RGS, 1976; Inst. of British Geographers, 1977. Victoria Medal, RGS, 1963; Daly Medal, American Geog. Soc., 1963; Honors Award, Assoc. of Amer. Geographers, 1977. Hon. degrees: Chicago, 1967; Liverpool, 1968; Durham, 1970; Hull, 1975; Ulster, 1977; Wales, 1979; London, 1987. *Publications:* An Historical Geography of England before AD 1800 (ed and contrib.), 1936; (with H. Fullard) The University Atlas, 1937, 22nd edn 1983; (with H. Fullard) The Library Atlas, 1937, 15th edn 1981; The Cambridge Region (ed and contrib.), 1938; The Medieval Fenland, 1940; The Draining of the Fens, 1940, 3rd edn 1968; (with H. Fullard) The New Cambridge Modern History Atlas, 1970; (ed and contrib.) A New Historical Geography of England, 1973, 2 vol. edn 1976; The Changing Fenland, 1983; General Editor and Contributor, The Domesday Geography of England, 7 vols, 1952–77; articles in geographical and historical journals. *Address:* 60 Storey's Way, Cambridge CB3 0DX. *T:* Cambridge (0223) 354745.

Died 14 April 1992.

DARLING, Henry Shillington, CBE 1967; Director-General, International Centre for Agricultural Research in Dry Areas, 1977–81, retired; Fellow of Wye College, since 1982; *b* 22 June 1914; *s* of late John Singleton Darling, MD, FRCS, and Marjorie Shillington Darling, BA, Lurgan, N Ireland; *m* 1940, Vera Thompson Chapman, LDS, Belfast; one *s* two *d. Educ:* Watts' Endowed Sch.; Greenmount Agric. Coll., N Ireland; Queen's Univ., Belfast; Imp. Coll. Tropical Agriculture, Trinidad. BSc (1st Hons), 1938, BAgr (1st Hons) 1939, MAgr 1950, Belfast; AICTA 1942; PhD London, 1959. Middle East Anti-Locust Unit, Iran and Arabia, 1942–44; Research Div., Dept of Agriculture: Uganda, 1944–47; Sudan, 1947–49; Faculty of Agriculture, University Coll., Khartoum, 1949–54; Head of Hop Research Dept, Wye Coll., London Univ., 1954–62; Prof. of Agriculture and Dir of Inst. for Agric. Research, Ahmadu Bello Univ., Zaria, Nigeria, 1962–68; Dep. Vice-Chancellor, Ahmadu Bello Univ., 1967–68; Principal, Wye College, Univ. of London, 1968–77. Technical Adviser, Parly Select Cttee for Overseas Develt, 1970–71. Chairman: Agricultural Panel, Intermediate Technology Develt Gp; British Council Agricl Adv. Panel; Member: Senate and Collegiate Council, London Univ. (Chm., Senate European Studies Cttee), and other univ. cttees; Council, Royal Veterinary Coll.; Council, Ahmadu Bello Univ.; Exec. Cttee, and Acad. Policy Cttee, Inter-Univ. Council for Higher Educn Overseas (also Chm., W African Gp and Mem., working parties and gps); Kent Educn Cttee; Exec. Cttee East Malling Res. Station; Council S and E Kent Productivity Assoc. Pres., Agricultural Sect., British Assoc., 1971–72. Technical Adviser: Tear Fund; Methodist Missionary Soc.; Pres., Inter-Collegiate Christian Fellowship, 1971–72. FInstBiol 1968. Hon. DSc: Ahmadu Bello Univ., 1968; Queen's Univ. Belfast, 1984. Order of the Hop, 1959. *Publications:* many papers in jls and reports dealing with applied biology, entomology, agricultural science and rural development in the Third World. *Recreations:* reading, Christian dialogue. *Address:* 1A Jemmett Road, Ashford, Kent TN23 4QA. *T:* Ashford (01233) 632982. *Clubs:* Farmers'; Samaru (Nigeria).

Died 4 Aug. 1995.

DARLING, Sir James Ralph, Kt 1968; CMG 1958; OBE 1953; MA Oxon; Hon. DCL, Hon. LLD; FACE; Headmaster, Geelong Church of England Grammar School, Corio, Victoria, Australia, 1930–61; *b* 18 June 1899; *s* of late Augustine Major Darling and Jane Baird Nimmo; *m* 1935, Margaret Dunlop, *er d* of late John Dewar Campbell; one *s* three *d. Educ:* Repton Sch.; Oriel Coll., Oxford (Hon. Fellow, 1986). 2nd Lieut Royal Field Artillery, 1918–19, France and Germany; Asst Master Merchant Taylors' Sch., Crosby, Liverpool, 1921–24; Asst Master Charterhouse Sch., Godalming, 1924–29; in charge of Public Schs Empire Tour to NZ, 1929; Hon. Sec. Headmasters' Conference of Australia, 1931–45, Chm., 1946–48; Member: Melbourne Univ. Council, 1933–71 (Hon. MA Melbourne); Commonwealth Univs Commission, 1942–51; Commonwealth Immigration Advisory Council, 1952–68; Australian Broadcasting Control Board, 1955–61. President: Australian Coll. of Educn, 1959–63 (Hon. Fellow 1970); Australian Road Safety Council, 1961–70; Chairman: Australian Expert Gp on Road Safety, 1970–71; Australian Frontier Commission, 1962–71 (President, 1971–73); Australian Broadcasting Commission, 1961–67; Commonwealth Immigration Publicity Council, 1962–71; Pres., Elizabethan Trust, 1970–82. Mem. Council, Marcus Oldham Farm Management (formerly Agricl) Coll., 1961–91; Chm. (Victoria), United World Colls, 1972–91. Hon. DCL Oxon, 1948; Hon. LLD Melbourne, 1973; Hon. DLitt Deakin, 1989. *Publications:* The Education of a Civilized Man, 1962; Timbertop (with E. H. Montgomery), 1967; Richly Rewarding, 1978; Reflections for the Age, 1991. *Address:* 3 Myamyn Street, Armadale, Victoria 3143, Australia. *T:* (3) 8226262. *Clubs:* Australian (Sydney); Melbourne (Melbourne).

Died 1 Nov. 1995.

DARWIN, Henry Galton, CMG 1977; MA; barrister; Second Legal Adviser, Foreign and Commonwealth Office, 1984–89; *b* 6 Nov. 1929; *s* of late Sir Charles Darwin, KBE, MC, FRS and Katharine, *d* of F. W. Pember; *m* 1958, Jane Sophia Christie; three *d. Educ:* Marlborough Coll.; Trinity Coll., Cambridge. Called to Bar, Lincoln's Inn, 1953. Asst Legal Adviser, FO, 1954–60 and 1963–67; Legal Adviser, British Embassy, Bonn, 1960–63; Legal Counsellor: UK Mission to UN, 1967–70; FCO, 1970–73; a Dir-Gen., Legal Service, Council Secretariat, European Communities, Brussels, 1973–76; Dep. Legal Adviser, FCO, 1976–84. *Publications:* contribs in Report of a Study Group on the Peaceful Settlement of International Disputes, 1966 and International Regulation of Frontier Disputes, 1970; notes in British Yearbook of International Law and American Jl of International Law. *Address:* 30 Hereford Square, SW7 4NB. *T:* 071–373 1140; 4/5 Gray's Inn Square, WC1R 5AY. *Club:* Athenæum. *Died 17 Sept. 1992.*

DARYNGTON, 2nd Baron, *cr* 1923, of Witley; **Jocelyn Arthur Pike Pease;** *b* 30 May 1908; *s* of 1st Baron Daryngton, PC and Alice (*d* 1948), 2nd *d* of Very Rev. H. Mortimer Luckock, sometime Dean of Lichfield; *S* father 1949. *Educ:* Eton; privately; Trinity Coll., Cambridge (MA). Member Inner Temple, 1932. *Heir:* none. *Address:* Oldfield, Wadesmill, Ware, Herts SG12 0TT.

Died 5 April 1994 (ext).

DAVEY, Jocelyn; *see* Raphael, Chaim.

DAVID, Elizabeth, CBE 1986 (OBE 1976); FRSL 1982; *b* 26 Dec. 1913; 2nd *d* of Rupert Sackville Gwynne, MP, and Hon. Stella Ridley; *m* 1944, Lt-Col Ivor Anthony David (marr. diss. 1960). DUniv Essex, 1979; Hon. DLitt Bristol, 1990. Chevalier du Mérite Agricole (France), 1977. *Publications:* A Book of Mediterranean Food, 1950, rev. edn 1988; French Country Cooking, 1951, rev. edn 1987; Italian Food, 1954, rev. illus. edn 1987; Summer Cooking, 1955, rev. edn 1988; French Provincial Cooking, 1960; English Potted Meats and Fish Pastes, 1968; The Baking of an English Loaf, 1969; English Cooking, Ancient and Modern, vol. I (Spices, Salt and Aromatics in the English Kitchen), 1970, new edn as Spices, Salt and Aromatics in the English Kitchen, 1987; English Bread and Yeast Cookery, 1977; An Omelette and a Glass of Wine, 1984. *Address:* c/o Penguin Books Ltd, 27 Wright's Lane, W8 5TZ. *Died 22 May 1992.*

DAVID, Richard (William), CBE 1967; formerly Publisher to the University, Cambridge University Press; Fellow of Clare Hall, Cambridge; *b* 28 Jan. 1912; *e s* of Rev. F. P. and Mary W. David, Winchester; *m* 1935, Nora Blakesley (later Baroness David); two *s* two *d. Educ:* Winchester Coll. (Scholar); Corpus Christi Coll., Cambridge (Scholar). Joined editorial staff, CUP, 1936. Served RNVR, 1940–46: in Mediterranean and Western Approaches; qualified navigator, 1944; Lt-Comdr, 1945. Transferred to London Office of CUP, 1946; London Manager, 1948–63; Sec. to the Syndics of the Press, 1963–70. Member of Council of Publishers' Assoc., 1953–63; Chairman of Export Research Cttee, 1956–59; President, 1959–61. Pres., Botanical Soc. of British Isles, 1979–81. *Publications:* The Janus of Poets, 1935; Love's Labour's Lost (The Arden Edition of Shakespeare), 1951; Shakespeare in the Theatre, 1978; (ed) Hakluyt's Voyages: a selection, 1981; (jtly) Review of the Cornish Flora, 1981; (ed jtly) John Raven: by his friends, 1981; (jtly) Sedges of the British Isles, 1982; journal articles on the production of Shakespeare plays, and on botanical subjects, especially carex. *Recreations:* music, botanising, fly-fishing. *Address:* 50 Highsett, Cambridge CB2 1NZ. *Club:* Garrick. *Died 25 April 1993.*

DAVIDSON, Brian, CBE 1965; *b* 14 Sept. 1909; *o s* of late Edward Fitzwilliam Davidson and late Esther Davidson (*née* Schofield); *m* 1935, Priscilla Margaret (*d* 1981), *d* of late Arthur Farquhar and Florence Chilver; one *s* one *d* (and one *s* decd). *Educ:* Winchester Coll. (Scholar); New Coll., Oxford (Scholar). Gaisford Prize for Greek Verse; 1st class Honour Mods.; 2nd class LitHum; President, Oxford Union Society; President OU Conservative Assoc.; BA 1932. Cholmeley Student, Lincoln's Inn; Barrister-at-Law, 1933; Law Society Sheffield Prize; Solicitor, 1939; Air Ministry and Ministry of Aircraft Production, 1940. With Bristol Aeroplane Co., 1943–68: Business Manager, 1946; Director, 1950–68; Director, Bristol Siddeley Engines Ltd, 1959–68. Solicitor with Gas Council, later British Gas Corp., 1969–75. Member: Monopolies Commission, 1954–68; Gloucestershire CC (and Chairman Rating Valuation Appeals Cttee), 1953–60; Cttee Wine Society, 1966–83. *Recreations:* fox-hunting, sailing (represented Oxford Univ.), Scottish country dancing, bridge. *Address:* Sands Court, Dodington, Avon BS17 6SE. *T:* Chipping Sodbury (01454) 313077. *Died 1 Dec. 1995.*

DAVIDSON, Howard William, CMG 1961; MBE 1942; *b* 30 July 1911; *s* of late Joseph Christopher Davidson, Johannesburg, and Helen, *d* of James Forbes; *m* 1st, 1941, Anne Elizabeth, *d* of late Captain R. C. Power; one *d*; 2nd, 1956, Dorothy (marr. diss. 1972), *d* of Sir William Polson, KCMG; one step *s. Educ:* King Edward VII Sch., Johannesburg; Witwatersrand Univ.; Oriel Coll., Oxford (1st cl. Greats 1934; MA 1984). Cadet, Colonial Admin.

Service, Sierra Leone, 1935; District Commissioner, 1942; Dep. Fin. Secretary, 1949; Fin. Secretary, Fiji, 1952; Fin. Secretary, N Borneo, 1958; State Financial Secretary and Member Cabinet, Sabah, Malaysia, 1963–64; Financial Adviser, 1964–65; Member of Inter-Governmental Cttee which led to establishment of new Federation of Malaysia; retired, 1965. Inspector (part-time) Min. of Housing and Local Government, 1967–70. Consultant with Peat, Marwick Mitchell & Co, to report on finances of Antigua, 1973. Appointed PDK (with title of Datuk) in first Sabah State Honours List, 1963, latterly SPDK. *Recreations:* cricket, croquet, gardening, learning. *Clubs:* East India; Sussex County Cricket, Sussex County Croquet. *Died 24 June 1995.*

DAVIDSON-HOUSTON, Major Aubrey Claud; portrait painter since 1952; *b* 2 Feb. 1906; *s* of late Lt-Col Wilfred Bennett Davidson-Houston, CMG, and Annie Henrietta Hunt; *m* 1938, Georgina Louie Ethel (*d* 1961), *d* of late Capt. H. S. Dobson; one *d. Educ:* St Edward's Sch., Oxford; RMC, Sandhurst; Slade Sch. of Fine Art. 2nd Lieut, Royal Sussex Regt, 1925; ADC to Governor of Western Australia, 1927–30; Nigeria Regt, RWAFF, 1933–37; POW (Germany), 1940–45; Sch. of Inf., 1946–47; MS Branch, WO, 1948–49; retd, 1949. Slade Sch. of Fine Art, 1949–52 (diploma). *Portraits include:* The Queen, for RWF; The Duke of Edinburgh, for 8th King's Royal Irish Hussars, for Duke of Edinburgh's Royal Regt, for the House of Lords, and for United Oxford & Cambridge University Club; Queen Elizabeth, The Queen Mother, for Black Watch of Canada; The Prince of Wales, for Royal Regt of Wales (twice); Princess Mary, The Princess Royal, for WRAC; Prince Henry, Duke of Gloucester, for Royal Inniskilling Fusiliers, for Scots Guards and for Trinity House; The Duchess of Kent for ACC; also portraits for Lincoln Coll., Keble Coll., and St Cross Coll., Oxford, and for Selwyn Coll., Cambridge; also for a number of other regts and for City Livery cos, schools, etc. Founder Trustee, Jt Educn Trust, 1971–86. *Address:* Hillview, West End Lane, Esher, Surrey KT10 8LA. *T:* Esher (01372) 464769. *Clubs:* Buck's, MCC. *Died 10 June 1995.*

DAVIE, Prof. Donald Alfred, FBA 1987; Andrew W. Mellon Professor of Humanities, Vanderbilt University, 1978–88; *b* 17 July 1922; *s* of George Clarke Davie and Alice (*née* Sugden); *m* 1945, Doreen John; two *s* one *d. Educ:* Barnsley Holgate Gram. Sch.; St Catharine's Coll., Cambridge (BA 1947; PhD 1951; Hon. Fellow, 1973). Served with Royal Navy, 1941–46 (Sub-Lieut RNVR). Lecturer in Dublin Univ., 1950–57; Fellow of Trinity Coll., Dublin, 1954–57 (Hon. Fellow, 1978); Vis. Prof., University of Calif., 1957–58; Lecturer, Cambridge Univ., 1958–64; Fellow of Gonville and Caius Coll., Cambridge, 1959–64; George Elliston Lecturer, University of Cincinnati, 1963; Prof. of Literature, 1964–68, Pro-Vice-Chancellor, 1965–68, University of Essex; Prof. of English, 1968–74, Olive H. Palmer Prof. in Humanities, 1974–78, Stanford Univ. Clark Lectr, Trinity Coll., Cambridge, 1976. Fellow, Amer. Acad. of Arts and Scis, 1973. Hon. DLitt Univ. of Southern California, 1978. *Publications: poetry:* Brides of Reason, 1955; A Winter Talent, 1957; The Forests of Lithuania, 1959; A Sequence for Francis Parkman, 1961; Events and Wisdoms, 1964; Essex Poems, 1969; Six Epistles to Eva Hesse, 1970; Collected Poems, 1972; The Shires, 1975; In the Stopping Train, 1977; Three for Water-Music, 1981; Collected Poems 1971–1983, 1983; To Scorch or Freeze, 1989; Collected Poems, 1990; *criticism and literary history:* Purity of Diction in English Verse, 1952; Articulate Energy, 1957, 2nd edn 1976; The Heyday of Sir Walter Scott, 1961; Ezra Pound: Poet as Sculptor, 1965; Introduction to The Necklace by Charles Tomlinson, 1955; Thomas Hardy and British Poetry, 1972; Pound,

1976; The Poet in the Imaginary Museum: essays of two decades, 1978; A Gathered Church: the literature of the English dissenting interest 1700–1930, 1978; Trying to Explain (essays), 1980; Dissentient Voice, 1982; Czeslaw Milosz and the Insufficiency of Lyric, 1986; Under Briggflatts, 1989; Slavic Excursions, 1990; The Eighteenth-Century Hymn in England, 1994; *anthologies:* The Late Augustans, 1958; (with Angela Livingstone) Modern Judgements: Pasternak, 1969; Augustan Lyric, 1974; The New Oxford Book of Christian Verse, 1981. *Recreations:* verse-translation, literary politics, travel. *Address:* 4 High Street, Silverton, Exeter EX5 4JB. *Club:* Savile.   *Died 18 Sept. 1995.*

DAVIES; *see* Edmund-Davies.

DAVIES OF PENRHYS, Baron *cr* 1974 (Life Peer), of Rhondda; **Gwilym Elfed Davies;** *b* 9 Oct. 1913; *s* of David Davies and Miriam Elizabeth (*née* Williams); *m* 1940, Gwyneth Rees, *d* of Daniel and Agnes Janet Rees; two *s* one *d*. *Educ:* Tylorstown Boys' Sch. Branch Official Tylorstown Lodge, NUM, 1935–59. Member Glamorgan CC, 1954–61; Chairman Local Government Cttee, 1959–61. MP (Lab) Rhondda East, Oct. 1959–Feb. 1974; PPS to Minister of Labour, 1964–68, to Minister of Power, 1968. Part-time Mem., S Wales Electricity Bd, 1974–80; Mem., Nat. Sports Council for Wales, 1978–84. Freeman, Borough of Rhondda, 1975. *Recreations:* Rugby football, cricket. *Address:* Maes-y-Ffrwd, Ferndale Road, Tylorstown, Rhondda, Glam. *T:* Ferndale (0443) 730254.
                                              Died 28 April 1992.

DAVIES, Ven. Carlyle W.; *see* Witton-Davies.

DAVIES, Sir David (Joseph), Kt 1969; Chairman, Wales Tourist Board, 1965–70; *b* 30 Aug. 1896; *s* of David and Catherine Davies; *m* 1924, Eleanor Irene (*née* Bowen) (decd); one *s*. *Educ:* Maesteg Higher Grade and Bridgend County Schools. Served in Welch Regt, 1915–19, Acting Captain. Mem. Court, University Coll., Cardiff, 1959–76; Mem. Court and Council, National Museum of Wales, 1961–73. *Address:* 28 Queen Anne Square, Cardiff CF1 3ED. *T:* Cardiff (0222) 382695. *Club:* Cardiff and County (Cardiff).   *Died 17 Aug. 1991.*

DAVIES, David Ronald, MB, BS, FRCS; Surgeon, University College Hospital, London, 1946–75, retired; *b* Clydach, Swansea, 11 May 1910; 3rd *s* of late Evan Llewelyn and Agnes Jane Davies; *m* 1940, Alice Christine, 2nd *d* of Rev. John Thomson; three *s*. *Educ:* University Coll. and University Coll. Hosp., London. MRCS, LRCP 1934; MB BS London, 1934; FRCS, 1937. House appts at UCH; Asst, Surgical Unit, UCH, 1937–39; Asst Surg. EMS at UCH and Hampstead Gen. Hosp., 1939–41; served RAMC, Surgical Specialist and Officer-in-Charge Surgical Div., 1941–46; Surgeon: Queen Mary's Hospital, Roehampton, 1947–69; Harrow Hosp., 1946–69. Mem., BMA. Fellow: University Coll. London; Assoc. of Surgeons; RSocMed; British Assoc. of Urological Surgeons; Internat. Assoc. of Urologists. *Publications:* The Operations of Surgery (with A. J. Gardham), 1963; various papers on surgical subjects. *Address:* Newland Farm, Withypool, Somerset TA24 7QU. *T:* Exford (0164383) 352. *Club:* Oriental.
                                              Died 8 Sept. 1994.

DAVIES, Elidir (Leslie Wish), FRIBA, FRSA; chartered architect in private practice; *b* 3 Jan. 1907; *yr s* of late Rev. Thomas John Landy Davies and Hetty Boucher (*née* Wish); *m* 1st, 1934, Vera (*née* Goodwin) (*d* 1974); 2nd, 1976, Kathleen Burke-Collis (*d* 1989). *Educ:* privately; Colchester Sch.; Bartlett Sch. of Architecture, University of London (under Prof. Albert Richardson). Min. of Supply, Air Defence, 1939–44; Min. of Town and Country Planning, London and Wales, 1944–47; University Lectr and Cons. to Argentinian and Uruguay Govts on planning

and low cost housing, 1947–49; private practice (Devereux and Davies): rebuilding of Serjeants' Inn, Fleet Street; Royal Vet. Coll., London Univ. (Research and Field Labs); King's Coll. Sch., Wimbledon (Jun. Sch. and Sci. Labs); St James's Hosp., Balham (Out-patients' and other Depts); St Benedict's Hosp. (Hydrotherapy Dept), 1950–61; West Indies: 5-year Hospital prog. for Trinidad (incl. new gen. and maternity hosps, trg schs, specialist depts, and hosp. services); Cons. Arch., Hosps, to Govts of Guiana, Barbados and Grenada, 1957–63; private practice (Elidir L. W. Davies & Partners): architect to: St David's Coll., Lampeter, restoration and new bldgs; London Borough of Camden; Central Library, Shaw Theatre and Arts Centre; Mermaid Theatre; Dynevor Castle, Carmarthen, Wales; new arts centre for drama and films; Chigwell Central Public Library; church work: The Temple, White Eagle Lodge, Hants; rebuilding of Wren's church, St Michael Paternoster Royal; Burrswood Nursing Home of Healing, Groombridge, Kent; Century House, Waterloo; BP Offices, 100 Euston Road; private houses and housing developments in London and the country. Chm., Soc. of Theatre Consultants, 1969–71; Mem. of Exec., Assoc. of British Theatre Technicians, 1965–71. Bronze Medal, RIBA, 1953. *Publications:* lectures and articles; contrib. to pubn relating to hospital architecture. *Recreations:* theatre, travel, sailing, visual arts. *Address:* St David's, Burrswood, Groombridge, Kent TN3 9PY. *T:* Groombridge (0892) 864810. *Clubs:* Garrick, Art Workers' Guild.   *Died 29 Dec. 1993.*

DAVIES, Emlyn Glyndwr, MSc; Chief Scientific Officer, Controller, Forensic Science Service, Home Office, 1974–76; *b* 20 March 1916; *yr s* of late William and Elizabeth Davies; *m* 1940, Edwina, *d* of late Lemuel and Alice Morgan, Blaengarw; two *s*. *Educ:* Bargoed Grammar Sch.; Maesycwmmer Grammar Sch.; University Coll of Wales, Aberystwyth (MSc). Asst Master, Ardwyn Sch., 1939–42; Ministry of Supply, 1942–44; Forensic Science Laboratory, Cardiff, 1944–58; Director, Forensic Science Laboratories: Nottingham, 1958–59; Preston, 1959–63; Forensic Science Adviser, Home Office, 1963–74. Pres., Forensic Science Soc., 1975–77. *Publications:* contribs to scientific jls. *Recreation:* Rugby football. *Address:* 14 Church Hill Close, Llanblethian, Cowbridge, S Glamorgan CF7 7JH. *T:* Cowbridge (0446) 772234.
                                              Died 13 May 1993.

DAVIES, Ernest Albert John; journalist, author; *b* London, 18 May 1902; *s* of late Alderman Albert Emil Davies; *m* 1st, 1926, Natalie Rossin (marr. diss. 1944; she *d* 1955), New York; two *s* one *d*; 2nd, 1944, Peggy Yeo (*d* 1963); (one *d* decd). *Educ:* Wycliffe Coll.; London Univ. (Diploma in Journalism). Editor Clarion, 1929–32; Associate Editor, New Clarion, 1932; Managing Editor, Traffic Engineering and Control, 1960–76; Managing Editor, Antique Finder, 1962–72. Served on Fabian Soc. Exec., 1940; Gov. National Froebel Foundation, 1938–40. With British Broadcasting Corporation, 1940–45, and its North American Service Organiser, 1944–45. Contested (Lab) Peterborough, 1935; MP (Lab) Enfield Division of Middx, 1945–50, East Enfield, 1950–59. Parly Private Sec. to Minister of State, FO, 1946–50; Parliamentary Under-Sec. of State, Foreign Office, 1950–51. Chm. Transport Group Parliamentary Labour Party, 1945–50 and 1951–59; Jt Chm. Parliamentary Roads Study Group, 1957–59; Mem. Select Cttee on Nationalised Industries, 1952–59; Vice-Pres., British Yugoslav Soc., 1980– (Chm., 1957–80); Mem., Exec. Cttee, European-Atlantic Gp, 1958–65 (Vice-Pres., 1966–82). Mem. British Delegation to Gen. Assembly, UN, 1947, 1948–49 and 1950; Dep. Leader British Delegn to UN Conf. on Freedom of Information, 1948; Mem. British Delegn to London Conf. 1950; Leader UK Delegn, Economic Commn for Europe, Geneva, 1950; UK Representative at Foreign Ministers'

Deputies' Four Power Talks, Paris, 1951. Managing Dir, Printerhall Ltd. Vice-Chm., British Parking Assoc., 1969–71, 1976–77 (Pres., 1977–80; Hon. Sec. 1971–76; Mem. Council, 1968–80); Hon. FIHT. Orden de la Liberatión de España, Republican Govt, 1960; Ordenom Jugoslovenske Zvezde sa zlatnim vencem (Yugoslavia), 1976. *Publications:* How Much Compensation, 1935; National Capitalism, 1939; The State and the Railways, 1940; American Labour, 1943; British Transport, 1945; National Enterprise, 1946; Problems of Public Ownership, 1952; (ed) Roads and Their Traffic, 1960; Transport in Greater London, 1962; (ed) Traffic Engineering Practice, 1963, new edn 1968; contrib. Encyclopaedia Britannica. *Address:* 16 Redcliffe Square, SW10 9JZ. *T:* 071–373 3962. *Died 16 Sept. 1991.*

DAVIES, Dame Gwen F.; *see* Ffrangcon-Davies.

DAVIES, Ven. Ivor Gordon; Archdeacon Emeritus; *b* 21 July 1917; *m* 1946, Kristine Wiley, SRN; one *s* two *d*. *Educ:* University of Wales (BA); St Stephen's House, Oxford; London Univ. (BD). Deacon 1941, priest 1942, Llandaff; Curate of St Paul's, Cardiff, 1941–44; CF, 1944–47; Curate of St John the Baptist, Felixstowe, 1947–49; Vicar of St Thomas', Ipswich, 1950–57; Residentiary Canon of Southwark Cathedral and Diocesan Missioner, 1957–72; Dean of Lewisham, 1970–72; Archdeacon of Lewisham, 1972–85. *Address:* 10 Garfield Road, Felixstowe, Suffolk. *T:* Felixstowe (0394) 271546. *Died 27 June 1992.*

DAVIES, Jack Gale Wilmot, OBE 1946; Executive Director of the Bank of England, 1969–76; *b* 10 Sept. 1911; *s* of Langford George Davies, MD, BCh, MRCS, LRCP, and Lily Barnes Davies; *m* 1949, Georgette O'Dell (*née* Vanson); one *s. Educ:* Tonbridge Sch.; St John's Coll., Cambridge. Nat. Institute of Industrial Psychol., 1935–39. Regimental service, The Middlesex Regt, 1940–42; Chief Psychologist, Directorate for Selection of Personnel, War Office, 1942–46. Bureau of Personnel, UN Secretariat, 1946–48; Secretariat, Human Factors Panel, Cttee on Industrial Productivity, 1948–49; Staff Training Section, UN Secretariat, 1950–52; Secretary, Cambridge Univ. Appointments Board, 1952–68; Asst to the Governor, Bank of England, 1968. Director: Portals Holdings Ltd, 1976–83; Portals Water Treatment Ltd, 1983–90. Hon. FBPsS 1990 (FBPsS 1946). Fellow St John's Coll., Cambridge, 1959–68; Dep. Pro-Chancellor, City Univ., 1984–89. Hon. DLitt City, 1976. *Publications:* articles in Occupational Psychology and similar journals. *Recreations:* cricket, golf, music. *Address:* 31 Wingate Way, Cambridge. *Clubs:* Royal Automobile, MCC (Pres., 1985–86). *Died 5 Nov. 1992.*

DAVIES, John Henry Vaughan, CB 1981; Deputy Secretary, Ministry of Agriculture, Fisheries and Food, 1979–81; *b* 15 Sept. 1921; *s* of late Rev. James Henry Davies and Ethel Sarah Davies; *m* 1st, 1950, Dorothy Rosa Mary Levy (marr. diss.); 2nd, 1959, Claire Daphne Bates (marr. diss.); one *d*; 3rd, 1971, Barbara Ann, *o d* of late David L. Davies, Portland, Oregon. *Educ:* Monkton Combe Sch.; Worcester Coll., Oxford (MA). Served Royal Air Force, 1942–46 (FO). Entered Ministry of Agriculture and Fisheries as Asst Principal, 1947; Principal, 1951; Asst Sec., 1964; Under Sec., 1970. Chairman, Joint FAO/WHO Codex Alimentarius Commn, 1968–70. *Publications:* contributor to The Country Seat, 1970; articles on architecture. *Recreations:* reading, architecture. *Address:* 17 Cherrywood Drive, SW15 6DS. *T:* 081–789 1529. *Died 10 April 1994.*

DAVIES, Kenneth Arthur, CMG 1952; OBE 1946; *b* 28 Jan. 1897; *s* of William and Alice Davies; *m* 1932, Edna Myfanwy, *d* of Rev. T. Rowlands; one *s. Educ:* Pontypridd Grammar Sch.; University Coll. of Wales, Aberystwyth;

Trinity Coll., Cambridge. 1st Class Hons Geology BSc 1922, MSc 1925, University Coll., Aberystwyth; PhD Cantab, 1928. Served European War, 1914–18, with RFA in France and Belgium, 1916–19. Research Scholar, 1923–26; Fellow of University of Wales, 1926; Field Geologist, Govt of Uganda, 1929; Senior Geologist, 1936; Director, Geological Survey, 1939, retired 1951. Adviser on Mineral Development to Uganda Govt, 1952–54 and 1965; Commonwealth Geological Liaison Officer, 1954; Dep.-Dir Overseas Geological Surveys, 1957–65. Adviser to United Nations, 1966. Fellow, Geological Society, 1928; FIMM 1950. Murchison Medallist, Geological Society, 1954. *Publications:* various on stratigraphy of Central Wales and graptolites in British geological journals, and on African geology in British and American journals. *Recreation:* gardening. *Address:* The Thatchers, Thrigby Road, Filby, Great Yarmouth, Norfolk NR29 3HJ. *Died 19 July 1991.*

DAVIES, Col Lucy Myfanwy, CBE 1968 (OBE 1962); Deputy Controller Commandant, Women's Royal Army Corps, 1967–77; *b* 8 April 1913; *d* of late Col A. M. O. Anwyl-Passingham, CBE, DL, JP, and Margaret Anwyl-Passingham; *m* 1955, Major D. W. Davies, TD, RAMC (*d* 1959); no *c. Educ:* Francis Holland Graham Street Sch. Driver FANY, 1939; commnd ATS, 1941; served in Egypt, 1945–48; Asst Director, WRAC Middle East (Cyprus), 1957–59; Comdt WRAC Depot, 1961–64; Dep. Director WRAC, 1964–68; retired, 1968. An Underwriting Member of Lloyd's, 1971–. OStJ 1938. *Recreations:* travel, racing, reading. *Address:* 6 Elm Place, SW7 3QH. *T:* 0171–373 5731. *Died 2 Aug. 1995.*

DAVIES, Peter; *see* Davies, R. P. H.

DAVIES, Peter George; Director General, Carroll Historical Institute, 1989–93; *b* 7 April 1927; *s* of George Llewellyn Davies and Alicia (*née* Galloway); *m* 1952, Norma Joyce Brown; one *s* two *d. Educ:* London School of Economics and Political Science. BSc Econ, 1st Class Hons 1948. Editorial Asst, News Chronicle, 1950–53; Deputy City Editor, The Times, 1953–55; HM Treasury, 1955; Asst Sec., Fiscal Policy Group, 1975–78; Press Sec. to Chancellor of the Exchequer and Head of Information, 1978–80; Under Secretary, 1980; seconded to NEDO as Sec. to NEDC and Administrative Dir, 1980–82; Fellow Commoner, Downing College, Cambridge, 1982–83; Dir Gen., Nat. Assoc. of British and Irish Millers, 1984–89. *Recreations:* walking, music, theatre. *Died 3 March 1994.*

DAVIES, Sir Richard Harries, KCVO 1984 (CVO 1982); CBE 1962; BSc; CEng, FIEE; an Extra Equerry to the Duke of Edinburgh, since 1984; *b* 28 June 1916; *s* of Thomas Henry Davies and Minnie Oakley (*née* Morgan); *m* 1st, 1944, Hon. Annie Butcher, (Nan), Macpherson (*d* 1976), *e d* of 1st Baron Macpherson of Drumochter; two *s* two *d*; 2nd, 1979, Mrs Patricia P. Ogier. *Educ:* Porth County Sch.; Cardiff Technical Coll. Scientific Civil Service, 1939–46; British Air Commn, Washington, DC, 1941–45; Vice Pres., Ferranti Electric Inc., New York, 1948–63; Dir, Ferranti Ltd, 1970–76. Duke of Edinburgh's Household: Asst Private Sec., 1977–82; Treasurer, 1982–84. Pres., British Amer. Chamber of Commerce, New York, 1959–62; Vice Pres., Manchester Chamber of Commerce, 1976. Pres., Radio Soc. of GB, 1988. *Recreations:* gardening, amateur radio. *Address:* Haven House, Thorpeness, Suffolk IP16 4NR. *T:* Aldeburgh (01728) 453603. *Club:* Athenæum. *Died 29 Jan. 1995.*

DAVIES, Prof. Robert Ernest, FRS 1966; Benjamin Franklin Professor of Molecular Biology and University Professor, University of Pennsylvania, 1977–90, then

Emeritus, and Chairman, Research Advisory Board, Institute for Environmental Medicine, School of Medicine, 1970–90; *b* 17 Aug. 1919; *s* of William Owen Davies and Stella Davies; *m* 1961, Helen C. (*née* Rogoff); two step *s*. *Educ:* Manchester Grammar Sch.; Univ. of Manchester and Univ. of Sheffield. BSc(Chem.) Manchester, 1941; MSc Manchester, 1942; PhD Sheffield, 1949; DSc Manchester, 1952; MA Oxon, 1956; MA Penn, 1971. Temp. Asst Lectr in Chemistry, Univ. of Sheffield; half-time research (Ministry of Supply, Chemical Defence Research Dept), 1942; full-time research on temp. staff, Medical Research Unit for Research in Cell Metabolism, 1945; apptd to Estab. Staff of MRC, 1947; Hon. Lectr in Biochemistry, Univ. of Sheffield, 1948–54; Vis. Prof., Pharmakologisches Inst., Univ. Heidelberg, March-May 1954; University of Pennsylvania, 1955–: Prof. of Biochemistry, Sch. of Medicine, 1955–62, Grad. Sch. of Medicine, 1962–70; Prof. of Molecular Biology, 1970–77; Chm., Dept of Animal Biology, Sch. of Vet. Medicine, 1962–73; Chairman: Grad. Group Cttee on Molecular Biology, 1962–72; Faculty Senate, 1989–90. Chm., Benjamin Franklin Professors, 1978–; Mem., Bd of Dirs, Assoc. for Women in Science Educnl Foundn, 1978–. Hon. Life Mem., NY Acad. of Scis. *Publications:* very many: in bioastronomy, chemistry, biochemistry, physiology and biology journals concerning secretion, muscle contraction, kidneys, etc. *Recreations:* mountaineering, caving, underwater swimming, white water boating. *Address:* Department of Animal Biology, School of Veterinary Medicine, 3800 Spruce Street, University of Pennsylvania, Philadelphia, Pa 19104–6046, USA. *T:* (215) 8987861; 7053 McCallum Street, Philadelphia, Pa 19119, USA. *Clubs:* Fell and Rock-climbing Club of the English Lake District; Cave Diving Group; Manchester University Mountaineering; Explorers' (New York).   *Died 7 March 1993.*

DAVIES, (Roger) Peter (Havard), OBE 1978; Human Rights consultant; Founder Director, Project Mala (India), 1988–92; *b* 4 Oct. 1919; *s* of Arthur William Davies and Edith Mary Davies (*née* Mealand); *m* 1956, Ferelith Mary Helen Short; two *s* two *d. Educ:* Bromsgrove Sch., Worcs; St Edmund Hall, Oxford (MA). Army service, N Africa, Italy, NW Europe, Captain RA (AOD), 1939–46. Joined British Council, 1949; served Hungary, Israel, Sarawak, Finland, Chile, India (Calcutta); Director: Drama and Music Dept, 1965–69; Information Dept, 1974–75; retired, 1980. Dir, Anti-Slavery Soc., 1980–87. Mem. Exec. Cttee, UNA, 1985–90; Chairman: Human Rights Cttee, UNA, 1985–90; Exec. Council, Internat. Service for Human Rights, Geneva, 1987–; Vice-Chm., Friends of UNESCO, 1990–. *Publications:* (ed) Human Rights, 1988; occasional articles and broadcasts. *Recreations:* family life, music, golf. *Address:* Ley Cottage, Elmore Road, Chipstead, Surrey CR5 3SG. *T:* Downland (07375) 53905. *Clubs:* Commonwealth Trust; Bengal (Calcutta).
                Died 9 Oct. 1993.

DAVIES, Rev. Rupert Eric; Warden, John Wesley's Chapel, Bristol, 1976–82, retired; *b* 29 Nov. 1909; *s* of Walter Pierce and Elizabeth Miriam Davies; *m* 1937, Margaret Price Holt; two *s* two *d. Educ:* St Paul's Sch.; Balliol Coll., Oxford (Class. Schol.; 1st cl. Hons Mods, Classics, 1930; 2nd cl. Lit.Hum., 1932); Wesley House, Cambridge (1st cl. Theology, Pt II, 1934); Univ. of Tübingen, Germany, 1934–35 (Travelling Schol. in Germany). BD Cantab 1946. Chaplain, Kingswood Sch., Bath, 1935–47; Methodist minister, Bristol, 1947–52 and 1973–76; Tutor, Didsbury Coll., Bristol, 1952–67; Principal, Wesley Coll., Bristol, 1967–73. Select Preacher to Univs of Cambridge, 1962, Oxford, 1969. Pres., Methodist Conf., 1970–71; Mem. Exec. Cttee, World Methodist Council, 1956–76; Mem., Anglican-Methodist Unity Commn, 1965–68; World Council of Churches:

Mem., Faith and Order Commn, 1965–74; Deleg. to Fourth Assembly, 1968. Hon DLitt Bristol, 1992. *Publications:* The Problem of Authority in the Continental Reformers, 1946; (ed) Catholicity of Protestantism, 1950; (ed) Approach to Christian Education, 1956; (ed) John Scott Lidgett, 1957; The Church in Bristol, 1960; Methodists and Unity, 1962; Methodism, 1963, 2nd edn 1985; (ed) History of the Methodist Church in Great Britain, vol. I, 1965, vol. II, 1978, vol. III, 1983, vol. IV, 1988; (ed) We Believe in God, 1968; Religious Authority in an Age of Doubt, 1968; A Christian Theology of Education, 1974; What Methodists Believe, 1976, 2nd edn 1988; The Church in Our Times, 1979; (with M. P. Davies) Circles of Community, 1982; (ed) The Testing of the Churches 1932–82, 1982; The Church of England Observed, 1984; (with M. Morgan) Will You Walk a Little Faster?, 1984; Making Sense of the Creeds, 1987; (ed) The Works of John Wesley, vol. 9, 1989; Making Sense of the Commandments, 1990; (with K. Clements and D. Thompson) The Truth in Tradition, 1992; Methodism and Ministry, 1993; contrib. Epworth Review, Proc. of Wesley Hist. Soc., Modern Churchpeople's Magazine, Ad Familiares. *Recreation:* theatre. *Address:* 6 Elmtree Drive, Bishopsworth, Bristol, Avon BS13 8LY. *T:* Bristol (0272) 641087.   *Died 4 July 1994.*

DAVIES, Stuart Duncan, CBE 1968; BSc; FEng 1977; Hon. FRAeS; Past President, Royal Aeronautical Society, 1972–73 (President, 1971–72); *b* 5 Dec. 1906; *s* of William Lewis Davies and Alice Dryden Duncan; *m* 1935, Ethel Rosalie Ann Radcliffe; one *d. Educ:* Westminster City Sch.; London Univ. (BSc Eng). Vickers (Aviation) Ltd, 1925–31; Hawker Aircraft Ltd, 1931–36; A. V. Roe and Co. Ltd, 1938–55, Chief Designer, 1945–55; with Dowty Group Ltd, 1955–58, as Managing Director of Dowty Fuel Systems Ltd; Technical Director: Hawker Siddeley Aviation Ltd, 1958–64; Dowty Rotol Ltd, 1965–72. British Gold Medal for Aeronautics, 1958. *Address:* Sheridans, 4 Arun Way, Aldwick Bay, Bognor Regis, W Sussex PO21 4HF.   *Died 22 Jan. 1995.*

DAVIES, William Rupert R.; *see* Rees-Davies.

DAVIES, Zelma Ince, CB 1989; Under Secretary, Department of Health and Social Services, Northern Ireland, 1984–90, retired; *b* 22 Aug. 1930; *d* of Walter Davies and Ena Davies (*née* Ince). *Educ:* Princess Gardens Sch., Belfast; Queen's Univ., Belfast (BA Hons). Entered NICS, 1955; Principal, Min. of Finance, 1965; Asst Sec., CS Management Div., 1971; Asst and Under Sec., Central Secretariat, 1979–81; Under Sec., Office of the Parly Comr for Admin, 1983–84. *Recreations:* music, reading.
                Died 18 Jan. 1994.

DAVIS, Sir Allan; *see* Davis, Sir W. A.

DAVIS, Prof. Derek Russell, MD, FRCP; Norah Cooke Hurle Professor of Mental Health, University of Bristol, 1962–79 (Dean of Medicine, 1970–72); *b* 20 April 1914; *s* of late Edward David Darelan Davis, FRCS, and Alice Mildred (*née* Russell); *m* 1939, Marit, *d* of Iver M. Iversen, Oslo, Norway; one *s* one *d. Educ:* Stowe Sch., Buckingham; Clare Coll., Cambridge (major entrance and foundn schol.); Middlesex Hosp. Med. Sch. MA, MD; FRCP; FRCPsych; FBPsS. Ho. Phys., Mddx Hosp., 1938, Addenbrooke's Hosp., Cambridge, 1939; Asst Physician, Runwell Hosp., 1939; Mem. Scientific Staff, MRC, 1940; Lectr in Psychopathology, Univ. of Cambridge, 1948; Reader in Clinical Psychology, 1950; Dir, Med. Psychology Research Unit, 1958; Consultant Psychiatrist, United Cambridge Hosps, 1948; Editor, Quarterly Jl of Experimental Psychology, 1949–57. Visiting Professor: Univ. of Virginia, 1958; Univ. of Dundee, 1976; Univ. of Otago, 1977. Fellow, Clare Coll., Cambridge, 1961. Member: Avon AHA (Teaching), 1974–79; Council of

Management, MIND, 1975–; Pres., Fedn of Mental Health Workers, 1972. Adolf Meyer Lectr, Amer. Psychiatric Assoc., 1967. *Publications:* An Introduction to Psychopathology, 1957, 4th edn 1984; Scenes of Madness: a psychiatrist at the theatre, 1991; many articles in scientific and med. jls. *Address:* 9 Clyde Road, Bristol BS6 6RJ. *T:* Bristol (0272) 734744.

Died 3 Feb. 1993.

DAVIS, Sir John (Henry Harris), Kt 1971; CVO 1985; Director, The Rank Foundation, since 1953; President, The Rank Organisation plc, Subsidiary and Associated Cos, 1977–83 (Chief Executive, 1962–74; Chairman, 1962–77); Joint President, Rank Xerox, 1972–83 (Joint Chairman, 1957–72); *b* 10 Nov. 1906; *s* of Sydney Myering Davis and Emily Harris; *m* Kathleen Coryn; one *s* one *d*; *m* Joan Buckingham; one *s*; *m* 1947, Marion Gavid; two *d*; *m* 1954, Dinah Sheridan (marr. diss. 1965); *m* 1976, Mrs Felicity Rutland. *Educ:* City of London Sch. British Thomson-Houston Group, 1932–38; joined Odeon Theatres (predecessor of The Rank Organisation Ltd): Chief Accountant, Jan. 1938; Sec., June 1938; Jt Managing Dir, 1942; Man. Dir, 1948–62 and Dep. Chm., 1951–62, The Rank Organisation Ltd. Director: Southern Television Ltd, 1968–76; Eagle Star Insurance Co. Ltd, 1948–82; Chm., Children's Film Foundation, 1951–80; Chm. and Trustee, The Rank Prize Funds, 1972–. Trustee, Westminster Abbey Trust, 1973–85 (Chm., fund raising cttee, Westminster Abbey Appeal, 1973–85). President: The Advertising Assoc., 1973–76; Cinema and Television Benevolent Fund, 1981–83; East Surrey Cons. Assoc., 1982–87. FCIS 1939. Commandeur de l'Ordre de la Couronne (Belgium), 1974; KStJ. Hon. DTech Loughborough, 1975. *Recreations:* farming, gardening, reading, travel, music. *Address:* 4 Selwood Terrace, SW7. *Club:* Royal Automobile. *Died 27 May 1993.*

DAVIS, Prof. Ralph Henry Carless, FBA 1975; Professor of Medieval History, University of Birmingham, 1970–84, then Professor Emeritus; Emeritus Fellow, Merton College, Oxford, since 1984; *b* 7 Oct. 1918; *s* of late Prof. Henry William Carless Davis and Rosa Jennie Davis; *m* 1949, Eleanor Maud Megaw; two *s. Educ:* Leighton Park Sch.; Balliol Coll., Oxford. Friends' Ambulance Unit, 1939–45. Asst Master, Christ's Hosp., Horsham, 1947–48; Lectr, University Coll., London, 1948–56; Fellow and Tutor, Merton Coll., Oxford, 1956–70. Member: Hebdomodal Council, Oxford Univ., 1967–69; Reviewing Cttee on the Export of Arts, 1983–89. Pres., Historical Assoc., 1979–82. Editor, History, 1968–78. *Publications:* The Mosques of Cairo, 1944; (ed) The Kalendar of Abbot Samson of Bury St Edmunds, 1954; A History of Medieval Europe, 1957; King Stephen, 1967; (ed with H. A. Cronne) Regesta Regum Anglo-Normannorum, vol. iii, 1968, vol. iv, 1969; The Normans and their Myth, 1976; (ed jtly) The Writing of History in the Middle Ages: essays presented to Richard William Southern, 1981; (ed jtly) The Blackwell Dictionary of Historians, 1988; The Medieval Warhorse, 1989; articles in historical and archæological jls. *Recreations:* travel, archæology, architecture. *Address:* 349 Banbury Road, Oxford OX2 7PL. *Died 12 March 1991.*

DAVIS, Sir (William) Allan, GBE 1985; CA; Director, Davis Consultancy Ltd, since 1986; Lord Mayor of London, 1985–86; *b* 19 June 1921; *s* of Wilfred Egwin Davis and Annie Helen Davis; *m* 1944, Audrey Pamela Louch; two *s* one *d. Educ:* Cardinal Vaughan Sch., Kensington. Mem., Inst. of Accountants and Actuaries, Glasgow (later Inst. of Chartered Accountants of Scotland), 1949; FCA; FTII; CIMgt. FRSA. Served War, Pilot RNVR FAA, 1940–44. Joined Barclays Bank, 1939; Dunn Wylie & Co.: apprentice, 1944; Partner, 1952; Sen. Partner, 1972–76; Armitage & Norton, London: Partner, 1976;

Sen. Partner, 1979–86. Director: City of London Heliport Ltd; Crowning Tea Co. Ltd; Dunkelman & Son Ltd; Internatio-Muller UK Ltd and UK subsidiaries. Common Councilman, Ward of Queenhithe, 1971–76; Alderman, Ward of Cripplegate, 1976–91; Sheriff, City of London, 1982–83; HM Lieut, City of London, 1986. Chairman: Port and City of London Health Cttee and Social Services Cttee, 1974–77; Management Cttee, London Homes for the Elderly, 1975–88; Res. into Ageing, 1987–89 (Vice Pres., 1989–); Winged Fellowship, 1987–89 (Vice-Patron, 1989–); Queenhithe Ward Club, 1976–77; Barbican Youth Club, 1979–82; Mem. Court, HAC, 1976–91; Gov., Honourable The Irish Soc., 1986–91. City of London Centre, St John Ambulance Association: Hon. Treas., 1979–82, 1983–84; Vice-Chm., 1984–88; Chm., 1988–92; Mem. Council, Order of St John for London, 1987–89. Liveryman, Worshipful Co. of Painter-Stainers, 1960 (Mem. Court, 1962–; Hon. Treas., 1962–91); Hon. Liveryman: Co. of Chartered Accountants in England and Wales, 1983; Co. of Launderers, 1987; Co. of Constructors, 1990. Chancellor, 1985–86, Mem. Council, 1986–92, City Univ.; Governor: Bridewell Royal Hosp., 1976–91; Cripplegate Foundn, 1976– (Chm., 1981–83); Cardinal Vaughan Meml Sch., 1968–81, 1985–88; Lady Eleanor Holles Sch., 1979–91 (Chm., 1989–91); Trustee, Sir John Soane's Mus., 1979–92. Vice Pres., Lancia Motor Club; Dep. Pres., Publicity Club of London, 1987–. Hon. DSc City, 1985. KCSG 1979; KCHS 1977 (Kt, English Lieutenancy, 1972); KStJ 1986. Knight Commander: Order of Isabel the Catholic, Spain, 1986; Order of Merit, German Federal Republic, 1986; Comdr, Order of Orange-Nassau, Netherlands, 1982; Order of Merit (Class I), State of Qatar, 1985. *Recreations:* reading, travel. *Address:* 168 Defoe House, Barbican, EC2Y 8DN. *T:* 071–638 5354. *Clubs:* Oriental, City Livery. *Died 14 Aug. 1994.*

DAVISON, Prof. Alan Nelson, PhD, DSc; FRCPath; Professor of Neurochemistry, Institute of Neurology, University of London, at the National Hospital, Queen Square, and Consulting Neurochemist, National Hospital, 1971–90; Emeritus Professor, Hunterian Institute, since 1990; *b* 6 June 1925; *s* of Alfred N. Davison and Ada E. W. Davison; *m* 1948, Patricia Joyce Pickering; one *s* two *d. Educ:* Univ. of Nottingham; Univ. of London (BSc Hons, BPharm; PhD 1954; DSc 1962). FRCPath 1979. Staff of MRC Toxicology Unit, 1950–54; MRC Exchange Fellow, Sorbonne, Paris, 1954; Dept of Pathology, 1957–60, Dept of Biochemistry, 1960–65, Guy's Hosp. Med. Sch. (Reader in Biochem., 1962–65); Prof. of Biochem., Charing Cross Hosp. Med. Sch., 1965–71. Sec., Biochemical Soc., 1968. Chief Editor, Jl of Neurochem., 1970–75; Mem. Editorial Boards: Jl of Pharmacy and Pharmacology, 1960–62; Jl of Neurology, Neurosurgery and Psychiatry, 1965–67; Acta Neuropathologica, 1977–; Brain, 1976–81. Dhole-Eddleston Prize (for most deserving publd work of med. res. appertaining to needs of aged people), 1980. *Publications:* (jtly) Applied Neurochemistry, 1968; (jtly) Myelination, 1970; Biochemistry of Neurological Disease, 1976; Biochemical Correlates of Brain Structure and Function, 1977; The Molecular Basis of Neuropathology, 1981; papers on neurochem. of multiple sclerosis and on ageing and senile dementia. *Recreations:* choral singing, painting.

Died 21 Dec. 1993.

DAVISON, Arthur Clifford Percival, CBE 1974; FRAM; FWCMD; Musical Director and Conductor: Royal Orchestral Society, since 1956; Little Symphony of London, since 1964; Virtuosi of England, since 1970; *b* Montreal, Canada, 1918; *s* of late Arthur Mackay Davison and Hazel Edith Smith; *m* 1st, 1950, Barbara June (marr. diss.), *d* of Sir William Hildred, CB, OBE; one *s* two *d*; 2nd, 1978, Elizabeth Blanche. *Educ:* Conservatory of Music, McGill Univ.; Conservatoire de Musique,

Montreal; Royal Associated Board Scholar at Royal Acad. of Music, London; later studies in Europe. LRSM 1947; ARCM 1950; FRAM 1966; FWCMD 1991. A Dir and Dep. Leader, London Philharmonic Orch., 1957–65; Guest Conductor, Royal Danish Ballet and Orch., 1964; Asst Conductor, Bournemouth Symphony Orch., 1965–66. Guest Conductor of Orchestras: London Philharmonic; London Symphony; Philharmonia; Royal Philharmonic; BBC Orchs; Birmingham Symphony; Bournemouth Symphony and Sinfonietta; Ulster; Royal Liverpool Philharmonic; New York City Ballet; CBC Radio and Television Orchs; Royal Danish. Founder of Arthur Davison Concerts for Children, subseq. Arthur Davison Family Concerts, 1966; Dir and Conductor, Nat. Youth Orch. of Wales, 1966–90 (conducted Investiture Week Symphony concert in presence of HRH Prince of Wales, 1969; Guild for Promotion of Welsh Music Award for long and distinguished service, 1976; Music Dir, Corralls Concerts, Bournemouth Symphony, 1966–; conducted official Silver Jubilee concert, Fairfield Halls, 1977, and in presence of the Queen and HRH Duke of Edinburgh, Poole Arts Centre, Dorset, 1979; conducted Royal Over-Seas League 70th Anniversary concert, St James's Palace, in presence of HRH Princess Alexandra, 1980; conducted concert for Charter centenery of Borough of Croydon, in presence of the Queen, Fairfield Halls, 1983. Conductor and Lectr, London Univ., Goldsmiths' Coll., 1971–85; Conductor, 1971–84, Gov., 1975–89, Welsh Coll. of Music and Drama; Orchestral Dir, Symphony Orchestra, Birmingham Sch. of Music, 1981–83. EMI/CFP award for sale of half a million classical records, 1973; Gold Disc for sale of one million classical records, 1977. Tour of Europe recorded for BBC TV. FRSA 1977. Hon. Master of Music, Univ. of Wales, 1974. *Publications:* various articles in musical jls. *Recreations:* reading, theatre-going, fishing, boating on Thames, antiques. *Address:* Glencairn, Shepherd's Hill, Merstham, Surrey RH1 3AD. *T:* Merstham (0737) 644434, 642206. *Clubs:* Savage, Royal Over-Seas League.   *Died 23 Aug. 1992.*

DAVY, Humphrey Augustine A.; *see* Arthington-Davy.

DAWSON, Richard Leonard Goodhugh, MB, FRCS; plastic surgeon, retired; *b* 24 Aug. 1916; *s* of L. G. Dawson and Freda Hollis; *m* 1945, Betty Marie Freeman-Mathews; two *s. Educ:* Bishop's Stortford Coll., Herts; University Coll., London; University College Hospital. MRCS, LRCP 1939; MB London 1940; FRCS 1947; BS London 1948. Royal Army Medical Corps, 1941–46: service in England and Far East (4 years); POW in Japanese hands, 1942–45. Plastic Surgeon: Mt Vernon Centre for Plastic Surgery, Northwood, 1953–82; Royal Free Hosp., London, 1958–76; Royal Nat. Orthopaedic Hosp., Stanmore, 1954–76. Member, British Assoc. Plastic Surgeons (President, 1974). *Publications:* chapters in Operative Surgery, 1957; numerous contributions to Lancet, BMJ, British Journal Plastic Surgery and other journals. *Recreations:* squash, golf, gardening. *Address:* 15 The Willows, Maidenhead Road, Windsor, Berks SL4 5TP. *T:* Windsor (0753) 853554.   *Died 21 June 1992.*

DAWSON, Air Chief Marshal Sir Walter Lloyd, KCB 1954 (CB 1945); CBE 1943; DSO 1948; *b* 6 May 1902; *s* of late W. J. Dawson, Sunderland; *m* 1927, Elizabeth Leslie (*d* 1975), *d* of late D. V. McIntyre, MA, MB, ChB; one *d* (one *s* decd). Enlisted in RAF as boy mechanic, 1919; commissioned from Cranwell, 1922; Station Comdr St Eval, Coastal Command, 1942–43; Dir, Anti-U-Boat Operations, 1943; Dir of Plans, 1944–46; AOC Levant, 1946–48; Commandant, School of Land/Air Warfare, Old Sarum, 1948–50; idc, 1950–51 (RAF Instructor); Asst Chief of the Air Staff (Policy), 1951–53; Deputy Chief of Staff (Plans and Operations), SHAPE, 1953–56; Inspector-General of RAF, 1956–57; Air Member for Supply and

Organisation, 1958–60, retired. Chm., Handley Page, 1966–69 (Vice-Chm., 1964–66). Dir, Southern Electricity Bd, 1961–72. *Address:* Woodlands, Heathfield Avenue, Sunninghill, Berks SL5 0AL. *T:* Ascot (0344) 20030. *Club:* Royal Air Force.   *Died 10 June 1994.*

DEAKIN, Maj.-Gen. Cecil Martin Fothergill, CB 1961; CBE 1956; *b* 20 Dec. 1910; *y s* of William Deakin; *m* 1934, Evelyn (*d* 1984), *e d* of late Sir Arthur Grant, 10th Bt, of Monymusk, Aberdeenshire; one *s* one *d. Educ:* Winchester Coll. Commissioned into Grenadier Guards, 1931; served with Regt, NW Europe, 1944–45 (despatches); commanded: 2nd Bn Grenadier Guards, 1945–46; 1st Bn, 1947–50; 32nd Guards Bde, 1953–55; 29th Infantry Bde, 1955–57 (Suez Expedition, despatches); Brigadier, General Staff, War Office, 1957–59; Director of Military Training, 1959; GOC 56th London Div., TA, 1960; Director Territorial Army, Cadets and Home Guard, 1960–62; Commandant of JSSC, Latimer, 1962–65. Pres., Grenadier Guards Assoc., 1966–81. *Address:* Lettre Cottage, Killearn, Stirlingshire G63 9LE. *Club:* Royal Yacht Squadron.   *Died 8 Sept. 1992.*

DEAN, David Edis; Director, British Architectural Library, Royal Institute of British Architects, 1969–83; *b* 18 June 1922; *y s* of Arthur Edis Dean, CBE, MA, MLitt, and Elsie Georgina Musgrave Wood; *m* 1945, Sylvia Mummery Gray. *Educ:* Bryanston; Wadham Coll., Oxford (MA); Reading Univ. (DipEd). Served War, RAF Photographic Interpretation, 1943–46. Schoolmaster, 1950–54; Cataloguer, then Dep. Librarian, Royal Commonwealth Soc., 1954–60; Dep. Librarian, RIBA, 1960–69. Hon. FRIBA. *Publications:* English Shopfronts, 1970; The Thirties: recalling the English architectural scene, 1983; The Architect as Stand Designer, 1985; articles, reviews. *Recreations:* book collecting, music, birdwatching. *Address:* 181 Morrell Avenue, Oxford OX4 1NG. *T:* Oxford (01865) 247029.

Died 30 Nov. 1994.

DEAN, Eric Walter, CB 1968; CBE 1958; Chairman Member, Surrey and Sussex Rent Assessment Panel, 1968–78; *b* 5 March 1906; *s* of late Thomas W. Dean, London; *m* 1935, Joan Mary, *d* of late L. A. Stanley, Folkestone; one *d. Educ:* Forest Sch.; Exeter Coll., Oxford (MA). Called to Bar, Inner Temple, 1931. Solicitors Dept, Board of Trade, 1935–68: Asst Solicitor, 1947–61; Principal Asst Solicitor, 1961–68, retired. *Recreations:* music, horse-racing. *Address:* 31 Hove Manor, Hove Street, Hove, Sussex BN3 2DG. *T:* Brighton (0273) 721783.   *Died 31 May 1993.*

DEAN, (Frederick) Harold, CB 1976; QC 1979; Chairman, Redundant Churches Uses Committee, Diocese of Oxford, since 1983; *b* 5 Nov. 1908; *o c* of late Frederick Richard Dean and Alice Dean (*née* Baron), Manchester; *m* 1st, 1939, Gwendoline Mary Eayrs Williams (marr. diss., 1966; she *d* 1975), 3rd *d* of late Rev. W. Williams, Kingsley, Staffs; one *s* (one *d* decd); 2nd, 1966, Sybil Marshall Dennis (*d* 1977), *o c* of late Col F. B. M. Chatterton, CMG, CBE; 3rd, 1978, Mary-Rose Lester, *y d* of late Comdr F. L. Merriman, RN. *Educ:* Manchester Grammar Sch.; Manchester Univ. LLB 1930; LLM 1932. Called to Bar, Middle Temple, 1933. Practised on Northern Circuit, 1934–40 and 1945–50. Served in RAFVR, 1940–45 in UK, Iraq, Egypt and E Africa (Sqdn Ldr). AJAG, 1950; DJAG: Far East, 1954–57 and 1962–65; Middle East, 1958–61; Germany, 1967–68; Vice JAG, 1968–72; Judge Advocate General, 1972–79. A Comr, Duke of York's Royal Mil. Sch., 1972–79. Chm., Disciplinary Appeal Cttee, ICA, 1980–87. *Publications:* Bibliography of the History of Military and Martial Law (in composite vol., Guide to the Sources of British Military History, 1971, Supplement, 1987); (jtly) Royal Forces in Halsbury's Laws of England, 1983. *Recreations:* travel, music, reading. *Address:* Gullsway, 32 Callis Court Road, Broadstairs, Kent CT10 3AF. *T:* Broadstairs (01843) 862565. *Club:* Athenæum.   *Died 29 Oct. 1994.*

DEAN, Sir Patrick (Henry), GCMG 1963 (KCMG 1957; CMG 1947); Director, Taylor Woodrow, 1969–86 (Consultant, 1986–93); International Adviser, American Express, 1969–93; *b* 16 March 1909; *o s* of late Professor H. R. Dean and Irene, *d* of Charles Arthur Wilson; *m* 1947, Patricia Wallace, *y d* of late T. Frame Jackson; two *s. Educ:* Rugby Sch.; Gonville and Caius Coll., Cambridge. First Class Hons, Classical Tripos Part I; Law Tripos Parts 1 and 2, 1929–32. Fellow of Clare Coll., Cambridge, 1932–35; called to the Bar, Lincoln's Inn, 1934; Barstow Law Scholar, Inns of Court, 1934; practised at Bar, 1934–39; Asst Legal Adviser, Foreign Office, 1939–45; Head of German Political Dept, FO, 1946–50; Minister at HM Embassy, Rome, 1950–51; Senior Civilian Instructor at Imperial Defence Coll., 1952–53; Asst Under-Secretary of State, Foreign Office, 1953–56; Dep. Under-Secretary of State, Foreign Office, 1956–60; Permanent Representative of the United Kingdom to the United Nations, 1960–64; Ambassador in Washington, 1965–69. Mem., Departmental Cttee to examine operation of Section 2 of Official Secrets Act, 1971. Chm., Cambridge Petroleum Royalties, 1975–82; Dep. Pres., English-Speaking Union, 1984– (Chm., 1973–83). Trustee, The Economist, 1971–90; Mem., Cttee of Award, Harkness Fellowship, 1970–78. Mem., Governing Body, Rugby School, 1939–84 (Chm. 1972–84). Hon. Fellow, Clare Coll. and Gonville and Caius Coll., Cambridge, 1965. Hon. Bencher, Lincoln's Inn, 1965. Hon. LLD Lincoln Wesleyan Univ., 1961, Chattanooga Univ., 1962, Hofstra Univ., 1964, Columbia Univ., 1965, University of South Carolina, 1967, College of William and Mary, 1968. KStJ 1971. *Publications:* various articles and notes in the Law Quarterly Review. *Recreations:* mountains, walking. *Address:* 5 Bentinck Mansions, Bentinck Street, W1M 5RJ. *T:* 0171–935 0881. *Club:* Brooks's.

Died 5 Nov. 1994.

DEANS, Rodger William, CB 1977; Regional Chairman, Social Security Appeal Tribunals and Medical Appeal Tribunals (Scotland), 1984–90, retired; *b* 21 Dec. 1917; *s* of Andrew and Elizabeth Deans, Perth; *m* 1943, Joan Radley; one *s* one *d. Educ:* Perth Academy; Edinburgh Univ. Qual. Solicitor in Scotland, 1939. Served in RA and REME, 1939–46 (Major); Mil. Prosecutor, Palestine, 1945–46; Procurator Fiscal Depute, Edinburgh, 1946–47; entered Office of Solicitor to Sec. of State for Scotland, 1947; Scottish Office: Legal Asst, 1947–50; Sen. Legal Asst, 1951–62; Asst Solicitor, 1962–71; Solicitor to Secretary of State for Scotland and Solicitor in Scotland to HM Treasury, 1971–80. Consultant Editor, Green & Son, Edinburgh, 1981–82; Sen. Chm., Supplementary Benefit Appeal Tribunals (Scotland), 1982–84. *Recreations:* hill walking, travelling, gardening. *Address:* 25 Grange Road, Edinburgh EH9 1UQ. *T:* 0131–667 1893. *Clubs:* Scottish Arts, Edinburgh University Staff (Edinburgh).   *Died 7 June 1995.*

DEAVIN, Stanley Gwynne, CBE 1971 (OBE 1958); FCA; chartered accountant; Chairman, North Eastern Gas Board, 1966–71, retired (Deputy Chairman, 1961–66); *b* 8 Aug. 1905; *s* of Percy John Deavin and Annie (*née* Crayton); *m* 1st, 1934, Louise Faviell (*d* 1982); one *s* one *d*; 2nd, 1982, Hilda Jenkins (*née* Grace). *Educ:* Hymer's Coll., Hull. Firm of Chartered Accountants, 1921–33; Secretary and Accountant, Preston Gas Co., 1933–49; North Western Gas Board: Secretary, 1949–61; Member Board, 1960–61. OStJ. *Recreations:* cricket, Rugby football, theatre. *Address:* 18 Harlow Grange Park, Otley Road, Harrogate, North Yorks HG3 1PX. *T:* Harrogate (0423) 531345.

Died 18 Dec. 1991.

de BRUYNE, Dirk, Hon. CBE 1983; Commander, Order of Orange Nassau, 1982; Knight, Order of Netherlands Lion, 1976; Chairman, 1987–91, Director, 1982–91, Royal Dutch Petroleum Co., The Hague; Chairman, ABN–AMRO Holding NV, Netherlands, 1990–92 (Chairman, ABN, 1983–90); Deputy Chairman, Ocean Transport & Trading, 1983–91; *b* Rotterdam, Netherlands, 1 Sept. 1920; *s* of Dirk E. de Bruyne and Maria van Alphen, Rotterdam; *m* 1945, Geertje Straub; one *s* one *d. Educ:* Erasmus Univ., Rotterdam (Grad. Econ.). Joined Royal Dutch/Shell Gp of Companies, 1945: served in: The Hague, 1945–55; Indonesia, 1955–58; London, 1958–60 (Dep. Gp Treasurer); The Hague, 1960–62 (Finance Manager); Italy, 1962–65 (Exec. Vice-Pres., Shell Italiana); London, 1965–68 (Regional Co-ordinator: Oil, Africa); Germany, 1968–70 (Pres., Deutsche Shell); Dir of Finance, Shell Petroleum Co. Ltd, 1970; Man. Dir, 1971–79, Chm., Cttee of Man. Dirs, 1979–82, Royal Dutch/Shell Gp of Cos; Man. Dir, 1974–77, Pres., 1977–82, Royal Dutch Petroleum Co.; Director: Shell Transport & Trading Co. Ltd, 1971–74; Shell Canada Ltd, 1977–82; Chm., Shell Oil Co., USA, 1977–82. *Recreations:* swimming, reading. *Clubs:* Dutch (London); De Witte (The Hague).   *Died 20 Feb. 1993.*

de CHAIR, Somerset Struben; *b* 22 Aug. 1911; *s* of late Admiral Sir Dudley de Chair, former Governor of NSW, and Enid, *y d* of H. W. Struben; *m* 1st, 1932, Thelma Arbuthnot (marr. diss. 1950); one *s* (and one *s* decd); 2nd, 1950, Carmen Appleton (*née* Bowen) (marr. diss. 1958); two *s*; 3rd, 1958, Mrs Margaret Patricia Manlove (*née* Field-Hart) (marr. diss. 1974); one *d*; 4th, 1974, Juliet, Marchioness of Bristol, *o d* of 8th Earl Fitzwilliam, DSC; one *d. Educ:* King's Sch., Paramatta, New South Wales; Balliol Coll., Oxford. MP (Nat. C) for S West Norfolk, 1935–45; Parliamentary Private Secretary to Rt Hon. Oliver Lyttelton MP, Minister of Production, 1942–44; MP (C) South Paddington, 1950–51. 2nd Lieut Supp. Res. RHG, 1938; served with Household Cavalry in the Middle East, during Iraqi and Syrian campaigns (wounded), IO to 4th Cavalry Bde, 1940–41; Captain GS (I), 1942. Chairman National Appeal Cttee of UN Assoc., and member of National Exec., 1947–50; Chm., Kent Assoc. of Boys' Clubs, 1945–48; Governor, Wye Agricl Coll., 1946–48. *Publications: fiction:* Enter Napoleon, 1934; Red Tie in the Morning, 1936; The Teetotalitarian State, 1947; The Dome of the Rock, 1948; The Story of a Lifetime, 1954; Bring Back the Gods, 1962; Friends, Romans, Concubines, 1973; The Star of the Wind, 1974; Legend of the Yellow River, 1979; *non-fiction:* The Impending Storm, 1930; Divided Europe, 1931; The Golden Carpet, 1943; The Silver Crescent, 1943; A Mind on the March, 1945; edited and translated: The First Crusade, 1945; Napoleon's Memoirs, 1945; Napoleon's Supper at Beaucaire, 1945; Julius Caesar's Commentaries, 1951; Napoleon on Napoleon, 1991; *biography:* (ed) The Sea is Strong (memoirs of Admiral de Chair), 1961; (ed) Getty on Getty, 1989; *autobiography:* Buried Pleasure, 1985; Morning Glory, 1988; Die? I Thought I'd Laugh, 1993; *drama:* Peter Public, 1932; *poetry:* The Millennium, 1949; Collected Verse, 1970; Sounds of Summer, 1992. *Address:* Bourne Park, Bishopsbourne, near Canterbury, Kent CT4 5BJ; St Osyth Priory, St Osyth, Essex CO16 8MZ; The Lake House, 46 Lake Street, Cooperstown, Otsego County, New York, NY 13326, USA. *Club:* Carlton (Hon. Mem.).   *Died 5 Jan. 1995.*

DECIES, 6th Baron *cr* 1812 (Ire.); **Arthur George Marcus Douglas de la Poer Beresford,** DFC (USA); Ex-Flying Officer, Royal Air Force Volunteer Reserve; *b* 24 April 1915; *s* of 5th Baron Decies and Helen Vivien (*d* 1931), *d* of late George Jay Gould; *S* father, 1944; *m* 1st, 1937, Ann Trevor (*d* 1945); 2nd, 1945, Mrs Diana Galsworthy; one *s* two *d. Heir: s* Hon. Marcus Hugh Tristram de la

Poer Beresford [*b* 5 Aug. 1948; *m* 1st, 1970, Sarah Jane (marr. diss. 1974), *o d* of Col Basil Gunnell, New Romney, Kent; 2nd, 1981, Edel Jeannette, *d* of late Vincent Hendron; one *s* one *d*]. *Address:* c/o Coutts & Co., 1 Old Park Lane, W1Y 4BS.   *Died 7 Nov. 1992.*

de COURCEL, Baron; *see* Courcel.

DEED, Basil Lingard, OBE 1946; TD; MA; Chairman, Oxfordshire County Council, 1983–84; *b* 1909; *s* of late S. G. Deed, Maldon; *m* 1937, Elizabeth Mary, *d* of late S. P. Cherrington, Berkhamsted; four *d*. *Educ:* Haileybury Coll.; Peterhouse, Cambridge. 2nd Class Classical Tripos Part I; 1st Class Classical Tripos Part II. Asst Master, Berkhamsted School, 1931–37; Asst Master, Shrewsbury Sch., 1937–47; served War of 1939–45, mostly on General Staff: Lt-Col MEF, 1943; Italy, 1944–45; Headmaster, Stamford Sch., 1947–68. Councillor (Ind.), 1972–85, Vice-Chm., 1981–83, Oxfordshire CC. *Address:* Bendor, Warborough, Oxon OX10 7DY. *T:* Warborough (086732) 8514. *Club:* Blackwater Sailing.
Died 17 March 1991.

DEEGAN, Joseph William, CMG 1956; CVO 1954; QPM; Inspector-General of Colonial Police, 1966–67; *b* 8 Feb. 1899; *s* of John and Sarah Deegan; *m* 1926, Elinor Elsie Goodson; one *s* two *d*. *Educ:* St Paul's and St Gabriel's Schs, Dublin. Army, 1919–25 (seconded to King's African Rifles, 1922–25); Tanganyika Police, 1925–38; Uganda Police, 1938–56 (Commissioner of Police, 1950–56); Dep. Inspector-Gen. of Colonial Police, 1956–61, 1963–65. Colonial Police Medal, 1942; King's Police Medal, 1950. *Address:* Tuffshard, Cuckmere Road, Seaford, East Sussex. *T:* Seaford (0323) 894180.
Died 14 April 1992.

DEER, Sir (Arthur) Frederick, Kt 1979; CMG 1973; Director, The Mutual Life and Citizens' Assurance Co. Ltd, Australia, 1956–83; *b* 15 June 1910; *s* of Andrew and Maude Deer; *m* 1936, Elizabeth Christine (*d* 1990), *d* of G. C. Whitney; one *s* three *d*. *Educ:* Sydney Boys' High Sch.; Univ. of Sydney (BA, LLB, BEc, Hon. DSc Econ). FAII, FAIM. Admitted to Bar of NSW, 1934. The Mutual Life and Citizens' Assurance Co. Ltd: joined Company, 1930; apptd Manager for S Australia, 1943, and Asst to Gen. Manager, 1954; Gen. Man., 1955–74. Chm., Life Offices' Assoc. for Australasia, 1960–61, 1967–68; Pres., Australian Insurance Inst., 1966 (Hon. Life Mem., 1967). Chm., Cargo Movement Co-ordination Cttee, NSW, 1974–82; Member: Cttee Review of Parly Salaries, NSW, 1971; Admin. Review Council, 1976–82; Fellow, Senate of Univ. of Sydney, 1959–83 (Chm. Finance Cttee of the Univ., 1960–83). Dir, James N. Kirby Foundn, 1967–. Nat. Pres., Australia-Britain Soc., 1973–81; Mem., Salvation Army Sydney Adv. Bd, 1970–95 (Chm., 1970–83). *Recreation:* golf. *Address:* 1179 Pacific Highway, Turramurra, NSW 2074, Australia. *T:* (2) 442912. *Clubs:* Union, University, Avondale, Elanora (all in Sydney).   *Died 29 March 1995.*

de GREY, Sir Roger, KCVO 1991; PPRA (RA 1969; ARA 1962); President of the Royal Academy, 1984–93; Principal, City and Guilds of London Art School, since 1973; *b* 18 April 1918; *s* of late Nigel de Grey, CMG, OBE, and Florence Emily Frances (*née* Gore); *m* 1942, Flavia Hatt (*née* Irwin); two *s* one *d*. *Educ:* Eton Coll.; Chelsea Sch. of Art. Served War of 1939–45: Royal West Kent Yeomanry, 1939–42; RAC, 1942–45 (US Bronze Star, 1945). Lecturer, Dept of Fine Art, King's Coll., Newcastle upon Tyne, 1947–51; Master of Painting, King's Coll., 1951–53; Senior Tutor, later Reader in Painting, Royal Coll. of Art, 1953–73. Treasurer, Royal Acad., 1976–84. Trustee, Nat. Portrait Gall., 1984–93. Member: Fabric Adv. Cttee, St Paul's Cathedral, 1991–; Rochester Cathedral Adv. Cttee, 1991–; Lambeth Chapel Adv. Cttee,

1987–. Pictures in the following collections: Tate Gall.; Nat. Portrait Gall.; Govt Art Collections Fund; HM The Queen; Arts Council; Contemporary Arts Society; Chantrey Bequest; Queensland Gallery, Brisbane; Manchester, Carlisle, Bradford and other provincial galleries. One man shows: Royal Acad., Grosvenor Gall., New Art Centre, Leicester Galls, Agnews, Gallery 10. Liveryman: Fishmongers' Co., 1985; Painter–Stainers' Co., 1985. Sen. FRCA 1985 (Hon. ARCA, 1959). Hon. FRIBA 1994; Hon. Fellow, C&G, 1994. Hon. DCL Kent, 1989; Hon. LLD Reading, 1992. Cavaliere Officale, Order of Merit (Italy), 1992. *Address:* City and Guilds of London Art School, 124 Kennington Park Road, SE11 4DJ. *T:* 0171–735 2306; 0171–735 5210.
Died 14 Feb. 1995.

de GUICHE, Lillian; *see* Gish, L.

DELACOMBE, Maj.-Gen. Sir Rohan, KCMG 1964; KCVO 1970; KBE 1961 (CBE 1951; MBE 1939); CB 1957; DSO 1944; Governor of Victoria, Australia, 1963–74; Administrator of the Commonwealth of Australia on four occasions; *b* 25 Oct. 1906; *s* of late Lieut-Col Addis Delacombe, DSO, Shrewton Manor, near Salisbury, and Emma Louise Mary, *o d* of John Smallman Leland, MD, Kirkby Stephen, Westmorland; *m* 1941, Eleanor Joyce (CStJ), *d* of late R. Lionel Foster, JP, Egton Manor, Whitby; one *s* one *d*. *Educ:* Harrow; RMC Sandhurst. 2nd Lieut The Royal Scots, 1926; served Egypt, N China, India and UK, 1926–37; active service Palestine, 1937–39 (despatches, MBE); France, Norway, Normandy, Italy, 1939–45: Lieut-Col comd 8th Bn and 2nd Bn The Royal Scots, 1943–45; GSO1, 2nd Infantry Div., Far East, 1945–47; Colonel GS, HQ BAOR, 1949–50; Brig. Comd 5 Inf. Bde, Germany, 1950–53; Dep. Mil. Sec., War Office, 1953–55; Maj.-Gen. 1956; GOC 52 Lowland Div. and Lowland District, 1955–58; GOC Berlin (Brit. Sector), 1959–62. Mem. Queen's Body Guard for Scotland, Royal Company of Archers, 1957; Col The Royal Scots, 1956–64. Pres., Royal British Legion (Wilts), 1974–85. FRAIA. KStJ 1963. Freeman, City of Melbourne, 1974. Hon. Col 1st Armoured Regt (Australian Army), 1963–74; Hon. Air Cdre RAAF. LLD *hc* Melbourne; LLD *hc* Monash. *Recreations:* normal. *Address:* Shrewton Manor, near Salisbury, Wilts SP3 4DB. *T:* Shrewton (0980) 620253. *Clubs:* Army and Navy; Victoria Racing (Melbourne).
Died 10 Nov. 1991.

de la MARE, Sir Arthur (James), KCMG 1968 (CMG 1957); KCVO 1972; HM Diplomatic Service, retired; *b* 15 Feb. 1914; *s* of late Walter H. de la Mare, Trinity, Jersey, Channel Islands, and Laura Vibert Syvret; *m* 1940, Katherine Elisabeth Sherwood (*d* 1992); three *d*. *Educ:* Victoria Coll., Jersey; Pembroke Coll., Cambridge. Joined HM Foreign Service, 1936; HM Vice-Consul: Tokyo, 1936–38; Seoul, Korea, 1938–39; USA 1942–43; First Sec., Foreign Service, 1945; HM Consul, San Francisco, 1947–50; HM Embassy, Tokyo, 1951–53; Counsellor, HM Foreign Service, 1953–63; Head of Security Dept, Foreign Office, 1953–56; Counsellor, HM Embassy, Washington, 1956–60; Head of Far Eastern Dept, Foreign Office, 1960–63; Ambassador to Afghanistan, 1963–65; Asst Under-Sec. of State, Foreign Office, 1965–67; High Comr in Singapore, 1968–70; Ambassador to Thailand, 1970–73. Chairman: Anglo-Thai Soc., 1976–82; Royal Soc. for Asian Affairs, 1978–84; Jersey Soc. in London, 1980–86; Pres., Jersey Br., Royal Commonwealth Soc., 1990–92. Mem. (cl. 1), Most Exalted Order of the White Elephant (Thailand), 1972. *Recreation:* promotion of and publications in Norman-French language. *Address:* Havre de Grace, Rue des Fontaines, Trinity, Jersey, CI JE3 5AQ. *Clubs:* Commonwealth Trust; Tokyo (Tokyo, Japan).
Died 15 Dec. 1994.

DELAMERE, Sir Monita (Eru), KBE 1990; JP; Officiating Minister, Ringate Church, New Zealand, since 1953; Member, Waitangi Tribunal, since 1986; b 17 June 1921; s of late Paul and Hannah Delamere; m 1943, Mary; four s (one d decd). *Educ:* Maraenui and Omaio Native Schools (school Proficiency). Farm hand, 1937–42; soldier, 1942–45; farmer, 1945–55; dry cleaner, 1956–77. Borough Councillor, Kawerau, 1971–80; Sec., Whakatohea Trust Board, 1980–85; Treasurer: Kawerau Credit Union, 1968–79; Opotiki Credit Union, 1979, 1990–. *Recreations:* Rugby (NZ Maori Team, 1945–49), tennis. *Address:* 151 Ford Street, Opotiki, Bay of Plenty, New Zealand. *T:* 07656630.   *Died 28 April 1991.*

DE LA WARR, Sylvia Countess; Sylvia Margaret Sackville, DBE 1957; d of William Reginald Harrison, Liverpool; m 1st, 1925, David Patrick Maxwell Fyfe (later 1st and last Earl of Kilmuir), GCVO, PC (d 1967); two d (and one d decd); 2nd, 1968, 9th Earl De La Warr, GBE, PC (d 1976). *Address:* Ludshott Manor, Bramshott, Hampshire GU30 7RD.   *Died 10 June 1992.*

DELFONT, Baron cr 1976 (Life Peer), of Stepney; **Bernard Delfont,** Kt 1974; President, First Leisure Corporation (formerly Trusthouse Forte Leisure Ltd), March–Nov. 1988 and since 1992 (Chairman and Chief Executive, 1980–86; Executive Chairman, 1986–88; Chairman, 1988–92); Director, Bernard Delfont Organisation; b Tokmak, Russia, 5 Sept. 1909; named Boris; s of late Isaac and Olga Winogradsky; m 1946, Carole Lynne; one s two d. Entered theatrical management, 1941; presented over 200 shows in London (and NY), including 50 musicals; also presented summer resort shows; converted London Hippodrome into Talk of the Town Restaurant, 1958. Chief Exec., EMI Ltd, May 1979–Dec. 1980. Past Chief Barker (Pres.), Variety Club of GB, (1969); Life Pres., Entertainment Artistes' Benevolent Fund, for which presented annual Royal Variety Performance, 1958–78; Pres., Entertainment Charities Fund, 1983–91; Companion, Grand Order of Water Rats; Member, Saints and Sinners; Pres., Printers Charitable Corp., 1979. *Address:* 7 Soho Street, Soho Square, W1V 5FA. *T:* 071–437 9727.   *Died 28 July 1994.*

DE L'ISLE, 1st Viscount, cr 1956; **William Philip Sidney,** VC 1944; KG 1968; GCMG 1961; GCVO 1963; PC 1951; Baron De L'Isle and Dudley, 1835; Bt 1806; Bt 1818; Chancellor, Order of St Michael and St George, 1968–84; Governor-General of Australia, 1961–65; b 23 May 1909; o s of 5th Baron De L'Isle and Dudley and Winifred (d 1959), e d of Roland Yorke Bevan and Hon. Agneta Kinnaird, 4th d of 10th Baron Kinnaird; S father, 1945; m 1st 1940, Hon. Jacqueline Corinne Yvonne Vereker (d 1962), o d of late Field Marshal Viscount Gort of Hamsterley, VC, GCB, CBE, DSO, MVO, MC; one s four d; 2nd 1966, Margaret Lady Glanusk, d of Maj.-Gen. Thomas Herbert Shoubridge, CB, CMG, DSO, and widow of 3rd Baron Glanusk, DSO. *Educ:* Eton; Magdalene Coll., Cambridge. Commissioned Supplementary Reserve, Grenadier Guards, 1929, and served War of 1939–45 with Regt. MP (C) Chelsea, 1944–45; Parly Sec., Ministry of Pensions, 1945; Sec. of State for Air, Oct. 1951–Dec. 1955. Chairman: Phoenix Assurance Co. Ltd, 1966–78; No 1 Poultry Ltd; Palmerston Property Development PLC, later Etonbrook Properties, 1985–. Pres., Freedom Assoc., 1984– (Chm., 1975–84); Dep. Pres., VC and GC Assoc., 1983–; Chairman of Trustees: Churchill Memorial Trust, 1975–; Tower Armouries Mus., 1984–86; former Trustee: British Museum; Nat. Portrait Gall.; RAF Museum. Hon. Fellow Magdalene Coll., Cambridge, 1955. FCA; Hon. FRIBA. Hon. LLD: Sydney, 1963; Hampden Sydney Coll., Va, 1982. KStJ 1961. *Heir:* s Major Hon. Philip John Algernon Sidney, MBE 1977 [b 21 April 1945; m 1980, Isobel, y d of Sir Edmund Compton, GCB, KBE;

one s one d. Grenadier Guards, 1966–79]. *Address:* Penshurst Place, near Tonbridge, Kent; Glanusk Park, Crickhowell, Brecon.   *Died 5 April 1991.*

DEL MAR, Norman Rene, CBE 1975; freelance conductor; Conductor and Professor of Conducting, Royal College of Music, 1972–90; b 31 July 1919; m 1947, Pauline Mann; two s. *Educ:* Marlborough; Royal College of Music. Asst to Sir Thomas Beecham, Royal Philharmonic Orchestra, 1947; Principal Conductor, English Opera Group, 1949–54; Conductor and Prof. of Conducting, Guildhall Sch. of Music, 1953–60; Conductor: Yorkshire Symphony Orchestra, 1954; BBC Scottish Orchestra, 1960–65; Royal Acad. of Music, 1974–77; Principal Conductor, Acad. of BBC, 1974–77; Artistic Dir and Principal Conductor, Aarhus Symfoniorkester, Denmark, 1985–88, Conductor of Honour, 1989–; Artistic Dir, Norfolk and Norwich Triennial, 1979, 1982. Principal Guest Conductor, Bournemouth Sinfonietta, 1983–85. FRCM; FGSM; Hon. RAM. Hon. DMus: Glasgow, 1974; Bristol, 1978; Edinburgh, 1983; Hon. DLitt Sussex, 1977. Audio Award, 1980; Distinguished Musician of the Year, ISM, 1990. *Publications:* Richard Strauss, 3 vols, 1962–72; Mahler's Sixth Symphony: a study, 1980; Orchestral Variations, 1981; Anatomy of the Orchestra, 1981; Companion to the Orchestra, 1987; Conducting Beethoven, 1992. *Recreations:* writing, chamber music. *Address:* Witchings, Hadley Common, Herts EN5 5QL. *T:* 081–449 4836.
                                        Died 7 Feb. 1994.

de LOTBINIÈRE, Lt-Col Sir Edmond J.; *see* Joly de Lotbinière.

DELVE, Sir Frederick (William), Kt 1962; CBE 1942; Chief Officer, London Fire Brigade, 1948–62, retired; Hon. President, Securicor plc, since 1985 (Director and Vice-Chairman, 1962–82, Vice-President, 1982–85); b 28 Oct. 1902; s of Frederick John Delve, Master Tailor, Brighton; m 1924, Ethel Lillian Morden (d 1980); no c. *Educ:* Brighton. Royal Navy, 1918–23; Fire Service since 1923; Chief Officer, Croydon Fire Brigade, 1934–41; Dep. Inspector-in-Chief of NFS, 1941–43; Chief Regional Fire Officer, No 5 London Region, National Fire Service, 1943–48. Pres., Institution of Fire Engineers, 1941–42. King's Police and Fire Services Medal, 1940. *Address:* 53 Ashley Court, Grand Avenue, Hove, East Sussex BN3 2NL. *T:* Brighton (01273) 774605.
                                        Died 2 Oct. 1995.

DELVES BROUGHTON, Major Sir Evelyn; *see* Broughton.

de MAJO, William Maks, (Willy), MBE (mil.) 1946; FCSD; Principal, W. M. de Majo Associates, since 1989 (Chairman and Managing Director, 1946–89); Consultant: John Millar & Sons (1844) Ltd, 1953–89; Charles Letts & Co., 1967–87; Ti-Well Ltd, 1974–91; b 25 July 1917; s of Maks de Majo and Josefine (née Ganz); m 1941, Veronica Mary Booker (d 1992); three d. *Educ:* Commercial Academy, Vienna. Chartered Designer. In practice as graphic and industrial designer on continent, 1935–39; news typist and broadcaster with BBC Overseas Service, 1940–41; war service as pilot and liaison officer, Royal Yugoslav Air Force, UK, Africa, ME, 1941–45 (Actg Chief Air Sect.); transf. to RAF, SO SHAEF and CCG HQ, 1945–46; re-established practice London, on demobilisation, 1946. Cons. designer to various nat. and internat. cos; guest lectr on design; co-ordinating designer, Fest. of Britain, 1951 (Ulster farm and factory); guest speaker: Internat. Design Conf., Aspen, Colo, 1953; Biennale of Graphic Design, Brno, 1988; designer, Baden-Powell Mus., 1961; designer-in-chief and co-ordinator, internat. exhibits, 1950–75; Member Jury: Canada Olympic Coins Comp., 1976; Crystal Design Awards, 1988; work exhibited on 5 continents. Founder and Pres.,

Internat. Council of Graphic Design Assocs, 1963–66 (Chm. Steering Cttee and Internat. Design Archive); first Vice-Pres., Internat. Inst. for Inf. Design, Vienna. Past Mem., Internat. Relations Bd, SIAD. Hon. FSTD 1991; Hon. Member: Assoc. of Graphic Designers, Netherlands, 1959; Assoc. of Swedish Art Dirs and Designers, 1965; Chambre Belges des Graphistes, 1966; Graphic Design Austria, 1988. SIAD Design Medal, 1969; ZPAP Polish Designers' Assoc. Commemorative Medal, 1983; winner of numerous nat. and internat. design competitions. *Publications:* contrib. Packaging (design of the gift pack), 1959 (Zürich); articles on graphic and industrial design to most leading jls in GB and abroad. *Recreations:* travelling, cooking, fostering good international relations. *Address:* 99 Archel Road, W14 9QL. *T:* 071–385 0394.

Died 17 Oct. 1993.

de MARGERIE, Emmanuel Jacquin, Hon. GCVO 1984; Officier de la Légion d'Honneur; Officier de l'Ordre National du Mérite; Commandeur de l'Ordre des Arts et des Lettres; Ambassadeur de France; Chairman, Christie's Europe, and Christie's France, since 1990; *b* 25 Dec. 1924; *s* of late Roland de Margerie, CVO and Jenny, *d* of Edmond Fabre-Luce; *m* 1953, Hélène Hottinguer; one *s* one *d. Educ:* Lycée Français de Londres; Univ. Aurore, Shanghai; Sorbonne; Institut d'Etudes Politiques, Paris. Ecole Nat. d'Administration, 1949–51; joined Min. of Foreign Affairs, 1951; Sec., French Embassy, London, 1954–59; Moscow, 1959–61; Quai d'Orsay, 1961–67; Minister, Tokyo, 1967–70; Minister, Washington, 1970–72; Dir, European Dept, Quai d'Orsay, 1972–74; Dir Gen. of French Museums, 1975–77; Ambassador: to Madrid, 1978–81; to UK, 1981–84; to Washington, 1984–89. Grand Cross, Order of Isabel la Católica (Spain), 1980, and various other foreign orders. *Address:* Christie's Europe, 6 rue Paul Baudry, 75008 Paris, France.

Died 2 Dec. 1991.

de MAYO, Prof. Paul, FRS 1975; FRSC 1971; Professor of Chemistry, University of Western Ontario, 1959–90, Professor Emeritus, since 1990; *b* 8 Aug. 1924; *s* of Nissim and Anna de Mayo; *m* 1949, Mary Turnbull; one *s* one *d. Educ:* Univ. of London. BSc, MSc, PhD London; DèsS Paris. Asst Lectr, Birkbeck Coll., London, 1954–55; Lectr, Univ. of Glasgow, 1955–57; Lectr, Imperial Coll., London, 1957–59; Dir, Photochemistry Unit, Univ. of Western Ontario, 1969–72. Chemical Institute of Canada: Merck Lecture Award, 1966; Medal, 1982; E. W. R. Steacie Award for Photochemistry, 1985; E. W. R. Steacie Award for Chemistry, 1992. Centennial Medal, Govt of Canada, 1967. *Publications:* Mono- and Sesquiter-penoids, 1959; The Higher Terpenoids, 1959; (ed) Molecular Rearrangements, 1963; (ed) Rearrangements in Ground and Excited States, vols 1–3, 1980; numerous papers in learned jls. *Address:* 436 St George Street, London, Ontario N6A 3B4, Canada. *T:* (office) 6612171, (home) 6799026. *Died 26 July 1994.*

de MILLE, Agnes George, (Mrs W. F. Prude); choreographer and author; *b* New York City, 18 Sept. 1905; *d* of William C. and Anna George de Mille; *m* 1943, Walter F. Prude (*d* 1988); one *s. Educ:* University of Calif (AB *cum laude*). Dance concerts USA, England, Denmark, France, 1929–40; founded and directed Agnes de Mille Dance Theatre, 1953–54; Agnes de Mille Heritage Dance Theater, 1973–74. Choreographed: Black Crook, 1929; Nymph Errant, 1933; Romeo and Juliet 1936; Oklahoma, 1943, 1980; One Touch of Venus, 1943; Bloomer Girl, 1944; Carousel, 1945; Brigadoon, 1947; Gentlemen Prefer Blondes, 1949; Paint Your Wagon, 1951; The Girl in Pink Tights, 1954; Oklahoma (film), 1955; Goldilocks, 1958; Juno, 1959; Kwamina, 1961; One Hundred and Ten in the Shade, 1963; Come Summer, 1968; directed: Allegro, 1947; The Rape of Lucretia, 1948; Out of This World,

1950; Come Summer, 1968; ballets composed: Black Ritual, 1940; Three Virgins and a Devil, 1941; Drums Sound in Hackensack, 1941; Rodeo, 1942; Tally-Ho, 1944; Fall River Legend, 1948; The Harvest According, 1952; The Rib of Eve, 1956; The Bitter Wierd, 1963; The Wind in the Mountains, 1965; The Four Marys, 1965; The Golden Age, 1966; A Rose for Miss Emily, 1970; Texas Fourth, 1976; A Bridegroom called Death, 1979; Inconsequentials, 1982; The Informer, 1988; The Others, 1992, etc. Television shows, for Omnibus, etc. Mem., Nat. Adv. Council of the Arts, 1965–66; Founding Mem., Soc. for Stage Directors and Choreographers (Pres., 1966–67). Hon. degrees: Mills Coll., 1952; Russell Sage College, 1953; Smith Coll., 1954; Northwestern Univ., 1960; Goucher Coll., 1961; University of Calif., 1962; Clark Univ., 1962; Franklin and Marshall Coll., 1966; Western Michigan Univ., 1967; Nasson Coll., 1971; Dartmouth Coll., 1974; Duke Univ., 1975; Univ. of North Carolina, 1980; New York Univ., 1981. New York Critics Award, 1943, 1944, 1945; Antoinette Perry Award, 1962; Handel Medallion, 1976; Kennedy Arts Award, 1981; Emmy Award, 1987; and numerous other awards, 1943–58. *Publications:* Dance to the Piper, 1952; And Promenade Home, 1958; To a Young Dancer, 1962; The Book of the Dance, 1963; Lizzie Borden, Dance of Death, 1968; Dance in America, 1970; Russian Journals, 1970; Speak to me, Dance with me, 1973; Where the Wings Grow, 1978; America Dances, 1981; Reprieve, 1981; Portrait Gallery, 1990; Martha: the life and work of Martha Graham, 1991; articles in Vogue, Atlantic Monthly, Good Housekeeping, New York Times, McCall's, Horizon, Esquire. *Club:* Merriewold Country (NY). *Died 7 Oct. 1993.*

DENBIGH, 11th Earl of, *cr* 1622 **AND DESMOND,** 10th Earl of, *cr* 1622; **William Rudolph Michael Feilding;** Baron Feilding 1620; Viscount Feilding 1620; Viscount Callan 1622; Baron St Liz 1663; *b* 2 Aug. 1943; *s* of 10th Earl of Denbigh and Verena Barbara, (Betty) (*d* 1995), *d* of W. E. Price; *S* father, 1966; *m* 1965, Caroline Judith Vivienne, *o d* of Lt-Col Geoffrey Cooke; one *s* two *d. Educ:* Eton. *Heir: s* Viscount Feilding, *b* 4 Nov. 1970. *Address:* 21 Moore Park Road, SW6 2HU; Newnham Paddox, Monks Kirby, Rugby, Warwickshire CV23 0RX. *T:* Rugby (01788) 832173. *Died 23 March 1995.*

DENHAM, Captain Henry Mangles, CMG 1945; Royal Navy, retired; *b* 9 Sept. 1897; *s* of Henry Mangles Denham and Helen Clara Lowndes; *m* 1924, Estelle Margaret Sibbald Currie; one *s* two *d. Educ:* RN Coll., Dartmouth. Went to sea at beginning of European War, serving at Dardanelles in HMS Agamemnon and destroyer Racoon; occupation of the Rhine in HM Rhine Flotilla; round the world cruise with the Prince of Wales in HMS Renown, 1921; served in Mediterranean for long period largely in HMS Queen Elizabeth and Warspite; at Staff Coll., 1935; Comdr of HMS Penelope, 1936–39; Naval Attaché, Scandinavian Countries, 1940; Naval Attaché, Stockholm, 1940–47; retd list, 1947. *Publications:* The Aegean, 1963, 5th edn 1983; Eastern Mediterranean, 1964; The Adriatic, 1967; The Tyrrhenian Sea, 1969; The Ionian Islands to Rhodes, 1972; Southern Turkey, the Levant and Cyprus, 1973; Ionian Islands to Anatolian Coast, 1982; Inside the Nazi Ring, 1984. *Recreation:* yachting. *Clubs:* Royal Automobile, Royal Cruising; Royal Yacht Squadron (Cowes). *Died 15 July 1993.*

DENNISON, Mervyn William, CBE 1967; MC 1944; DL; *b* 13 July 1914; *er s* of Reverend W. Telford Dennison and Hester Mary (*née* Coulter); *m* 1944, Helen Maud, *d* of Claud George Spiller, Earley, Berks; one *s* one *d. Educ:* Methodist Coll., Belfast; Queen's Univ., Belfast (BA); Middle Temple. Called to the Bar: Northern Ireland, 1945; Middle Temple, 1964. Served War of 1939–45, with Royal Ulster Rifles and Parachute Regt (POW Arnhem,

1944). Crown Counsel, N Rhodesia, 1947; Legal Draftsman, 1952; Senior Crown Counsel and Parliamentary Draftsman, Federal Govt of Rhodesia and Nyasaland, 1953; Federal Solicitor-Gen., 1959; QC (N Rhodesia) 1960; also Chm. Road Service Bd, N Rhodesia, and Mem. Central African Air Authority; High Court Judge, Zambia, 1961–67. Secretary, Fermanagh CC, NI, 1967–73; Chief Comr, Planning Appeals Commn and Water Appeals Commn, 1973–80; Chm., Industrial Tribunals in N Ireland, 1981–84. Mem. Senate, Queen's Univ., Belfast 1979–87. Hon. Col, The Zambia Regt, 1964–66. JP, 1969–73, DL 1972, Co. Fermanagh. KStJ 1978 (CStJ 1964). *Recreation:* fishing. *Address:* Creevyloughgare, Saintfield, Ballynahinch, Co. Down BT24 7NB. *T:* Saintfield (0238) 510397. *Club:* Harare (Zimbabwe). *Died 12 Jan. 1993.*

DENNISON, Stanley Raymond, CBE 1946; Vice-Chancellor, 1972–79, and Honorary Professor, 1974–79, University of Hull, then Emeritus Professor; Vice-Chairman, Committee of Vice-Chancellors and Principals of the United Kingdom, 1977–79; *b* 15 June 1912; *o s* of late Stanley Dennison and Florence Ann Dennison, North Shields; unmarried. *Educ:* University of Durham; Trinity College, Cambridge. Lecturer in Economics, Manchester University, 1935–39; Professor of Economics, University Coll. of Swansea, 1939–45; Lecturer in Economics, Cambridge Univ., 1945–58; Fellow of Gonville and Caius Coll., 1945–58; Prof. of Economics, Queen's Univ. of Belfast, 1958–61; David Dale Prof. of Economics, Univ. of Newcastle upon Tyne, 1962–72, Pro-Vice-Chancellor, 1966–72. Chief Economic Asst, War Cabinet Secretariat, 1940–46. Member: University Grants Cttee, 1964–68; North Eastern Electricity Board, 1965–72; Review Body on Remuneration of Doctors and Dentists, 1962–70; Verdon Smith Cttee on Marketing and Distribution of Fatstock and Carcase Meat, 1964; Scott Cttee on Land Utilisation in Rural Areas, 1942 (Minority Report); Beaver Cttee on Air Pollution, 1954; Waverley Cttee on Med. Services for the Armed Forces, 1955. Chm. Governors, Royal Grammar Sch., Newcastle upon Tyne, 1969–87. Hon. LLD Hull, 1980. *Publications:* The Location of Industry and the Depressed Areas, 1939; (with Sir Dennis Robertson) The Control of Industry, 1960; Choice in Education, 1984; (with John R. Presley) Robertson on Economic Policy, 1992; various articles, etc, on economic questions. *Recreation:* music. *Address:* 22 Percy Gardens, Tynemouth, Tyne and Wear NE30 4HQ. *Died 22 Nov. 1992.*

DENNY, Sir Alistair (Maurice Archibald), 3rd Bt, *cr* 1913, of Dumbarton, co. Dumbarton; *b* 11 Sept. 1922; *er s* of Sir Maurice Edward Denny, 2nd Bt, KBE and Lady (Marjorie) Denny (*d* 1982), Gateside House, Drymen, Stirlingshire; *S* father, 1955; *m* 1949, Elizabeth, *y d* of Sir Guy Lloyd, 1st Bt, DSO; one *s* (and two *s* decd). *Educ:* Marlborough. Started engineering training with William Denny & Bros; served War in Fleet Air Arm, 1944–46; continued engineering training with Alexander Stephen & Sons, Glasgow, and Sulzer Bros, Winterthur, Switzerland; returned to William Denny & Bros, 1948; left, Sept. 1963, when firm went into liquidation. Chm., St Andrews Links Management Cttee, 1980–81. Council Mem., St Leonard's Sch., St Andrews, 1982–89. *Recreations:* golf, gardening, photography. *Heir: s* Charles Alistair Maurice Denny [*b* 7 Oct. 1950; *m* 1981, Belinda, *yr d* of J. P. McDonald, Walkinstown, Dublin; one *s* one *d*]. *Address:* Crombie Cottage, Abercrombie, by St Monans, Fife KY10 2DE. *T:* St Monans (01333) 730631. *Club:* Royal and Ancient Golf (St Andrews). *Died 29 Aug. 1995.*

DENNYS, Cyril George, CB 1949; MC 1918; retired as Under-Secretary; *b* 25 March 1897; *s* of Lieut-Col A. H. Dennys, IA, and Lena Mary Isabel (*née* Harrison); *m*

1920, Sylvia Maitland (*née* Waterlow) (*d* 1980); two *d* (and one *d* decd). *Educ:* Malvern Coll.; Trinity Coll., Oxford. Served European War, 1914–18, as Lieut, RGA, 1917–18. Entered Ministry of Labour as Asst Principal, 1919; Principal Private Sec. to Minister of Labour, 1938; Asst Sec., 1938; Principal Asst Sec., Ministry of Supply, 1942–45; Under-Secretary: Ministry of Labour, 1946; Ministry of National Insurance, 1946; Ministry of Pensions and National Insurance, 1953; retired 1962. *Address:* 38 Belsize Grove, Hampstead, NW3. *T:* 071–722 3964. *Club:* United Oxford & Cambridge University. *Died 4 Sept. 1991.*

DENNYS, Rodney Onslow, CVO 1982 (MVO 1969); OBE (mil.) 1943; FSA, FSG; Arundel Herald of Arms Extraordinary, since 1982 (Somerset Herald of Arms, 1967–82); *b* 16 July 1911; *s* of late Frederick Onslow Brooke Dennys, late Malayan Civil Service, and Claire (*née* de Paula); *m* 1944, Elisabeth Katharine (served FO 1938–41; GHQ MEF, 1941–44, awarded certificate for outstandingly good service by C-in-C MEF; Allied Forces HQ N Africa, Algiers, 1944; FO 1944–45), *d* of late Charles Henry Greene; one *s* two *d*. *Educ:* Canford Sch.; LSE. Apptd to FO, 1937; HM Legation, The Hague, 1937–40; FO, 1940–41. Commissioned in Intell. Corps, 1941; Lt-Col 1944; RARO, 1946. Reapptd, FO, 1947; 1st Sec. British Middle East Office, Egypt, 1948–50; 1st Sec. HM Embassy: Turkey, 1950–53; Paris, 1955–57; resigned, 1957. Asst to Garter King of Arms, 1958–61; Rouge Croix Pursuivant of Arms, 1961–67. Served on Earl Marshal's Staff for State Funeral of Sir Winston Churchill, 1965, and for the Prince of Wales' Investiture, 1969. Dep. Dir, Heralds' Museum, 1978–83, Dir, 1983–91. Advised Queensland Govt on design of first Mace of Qld Leg. Assembly, and in attendance, in Tabard, on Governor of Qld for inauguration of Mace in Qld Parlt, 1978. Mem. Court, Sussex Univ., 1972–77. Council for the Protection of Rural England, 1972–: Mem., Nat. Exec., 1973–78; Chm., 1972–77, Vice-Pres., 1977, Sussex Br. Dir, Arundel Castle Trustees Ltd, 1977–87; Member: Exec. Cttee, Sussex Historic Churches Trust, 1973–83; Council, Harleian Soc. (Chm. 1977–84); Devon Assoc.; Académicien, Académie Internationale d'Héraldique; Mem. Council, Shrievalty Assoc., 1984–93. FRSA. Freeman of City of London; Liveryman and Freeman of Scriveners' Co. (Mem., Ct of Assistants, 1988–). High Sheriff E Sussex, 1983–84. *Publications:* Flags and Emblems of the World; (jt) Royal and Princely Heraldry of Wales, 1969; The Heraldic Imagination, 1975; Heraldry and the Heralds, 1982; articles in jls on heraldry and kindred subjects. *Recreations:* heraldry, ornithology. *Address:* College of Arms, EC4V 4BT. *T:* 071–248 1912. *Clubs:* Garrick; Sussex. *Died 13 Aug. 1993.*

DENSON, John Boyd, CMG 1972; OBE 1965; HM Diplomatic Service, retired; *b* 13 Aug. 1926; *o s* of late George Denson and Alice Denson (*née* Boyd); *m* 1957, Joyce Myra Symondson; no *c. Educ:* Perse Sch.; St John's Coll., Cambridge. Royal Regt of Artillery, 1944; Intelligence Corps, 1946; Cambridge, 1947–51 (English and Oriental Langs Triposes). Joined HM Foreign (later Diplomatic) Service, 1951; served in Hong Kong, Tokyo, Peking, London, Helsinki, Washington, Vientiane; Asst Head of Far Eastern Dept, Foreign Office, 1965–68; Chargé d'Affaires, Peking, 1969–71; Royal Coll. of Defence Studies, 1972; Counsellor and Consul-Gen., Athens, 1973–77; Ambassador to Nepal, 1977–83. Pres., Himalayan Communities Trust, 1986. Gorkha Dakshina Bahu, 1st cl., 1980. *Recreations:* looking at pictures, the theatre, wine. *Address:* Little Hermitage, Scar Hill, Minchinhampton, Stroud, Glos GL6 9AH. *T:* Stroud (0453) 833829. *Club:* Royal Over-Seas League. *Died 24 April 1992.*

DENT, Harold Collett; *b* 14 Nov. 1894; *s* of Rev. F. G. T. and Susan Dent; *m* 1922, Loveday Winifred Martin; one *s* one *d*. *Educ:* public elementary schs; Kingswood Sch., Bath; London Univ. (external student). BA. Asst master in secondary schs, 1911–25 (War Service, 1914–19); Head of Junior Dept, Brighton, Hove and Sussex Grammar Sch., 1925–28; first Headmaster, Gateway School, Leicester, 1928–31; freelance journalist, 1931–35; Asst Ed., Book Dept Odhams Press, 1935–40; Ed., The Times Educational Supplement, 1940–51; Educational Correspondent, The Times, 1952–55; Professor of Education and Dir of the Inst. of Education, University of Sheffield, 1956–60; Senior Research Fellow, Inst. of Education, University of Leeds, 1960–62; Asst Dean, Inst. of Education, University of London, 1962–65; Visiting Prof., University of Dublin, 1966. FRSA; Hon. FCP; Hon. FEIS. *Publications:* A New Order in English Education, 1942; The Education Act 1944, 1944; Education in Transition, 1944; To be a Teacher, 1947; Secondary Education for All, 1949; Secondary Modern Schools, 1958; The Educational System of England and Wales, 1961; Universities in Transition, 1961; British Education, 1962; 1870–1970, Century of Growth in English Education, 1970; The Training of Teachers in England and Wales 1700–1975, 1977; Education in England and Wales, 1977. *Recreation:* reading. *Address:* Barns Croft, Goblin Lane, Cullompton, Devon EX15 1BB. *T:* Cullompton (01884) 32075.
Died 23 Jan. 1995.

DENT, (Robert) Stanley (Gorrell), RWS 1986 (ARWS 1983); RE 1946 (ARE 1935); RWA 1954 (ARWA 1951); ARCA 1933; Principal, Gloucestershire College of Art and Design, 1950–74, retired; *b* 1 July 1909; *o c* of Robert and Phoebe Dent; *m* Doris, *o c* of Clement and Mabel Wenban; two *s*. *Educ:* The Newport Technical Coll.; The Newport, Mon, Sch. of Art and Crafts; Royal College of Art. Runner up in Prix-de-Rome Scholarship, 1935; awarded the British Institution Scholarship in Engraving for the year 1933. Works shown at the Royal Academy, Royal Soc. of Painters in Water-Colours, The Royal Scottish Academy, The Royal West of England Academy and other leading Art Exhibitions in GB and abroad, with paintings and etchings in many permanent and private collections, galleries, universities and schools. Ministry of Education Intermediate Assessor, 1957–60; Panel Mem. (Fine Art), National Council for Diplomas in Art and Design, 1962–65; Chief Examiner A Level Art and Design, 1963–76. *Recreations:* golf, travel, painting, music, spectator sports. *Address:* 5 Timbercombe Mews, Little Herberts Road, Charlton Kings, Cheltenham, Glos GL53 8EL. *T:* Cheltenham (0242) 524742.
Died 29 April 1991.

DE RAMSEY, 3rd Baron *cr* 1887, of Ramsey Abbey, Huntingdon; **Ailwyn Edward Fellowes,** KBE 1974 (for services to agriculture); TD; DL; Captain Royal Artillery; Lord Lieutenant of Huntingdon and Peterborough, 1965–68 (of Huntingdonshire, 1947–65); *b* 16 March 1910; *s* of late Hon. Coulson Churchill Fellowes and Gwendolen Dorothy, *d* of H. W. Jefferson; *S* grandfather, 1925; *m* 1937, Lilah (*d* 1987), *d* of Frank Labouchere, 15 Draycott Avenue, SW; two *s* two *d*. Served War of 1939–45 (prisoner, Far East). Pres. Country Landowners' Assoc., Sept. 1963–1965. DL Hunts and Peterborough, 1973, Cambs 1974. *Heir: s* Hon. John Ailwyn Fellowes [*b* 27 Feb. 1942; *m* 1st, 1973, Phyllida Mary (marr. diss. 1983), *d* of Dr Philip A. Forsyth, Newmarket, Suffolk; one *s*; 2nd, 1984, Alison Mary, *er d* of Archibald Birkmyre, Hebron Cottage, West Ilsley, Berks; one *s* two *d*]. *Address:* Abbots Ripton Hall, Huntingdon, Cambs PE17 2PQ. *T:* Abbots Ripton 234. *Club:* Buck's.
Died 31 March 1993.

DERBY, 18th Earl of *cr* 1485; **Edward John Stanley,** MC 1944; DL; Bt 1627; Baron Stanley 1832; Baron Stanley of Preston, 1886; Major late Grenadier Guards; Constable of Lancaster Castle, since 1972; *b* 21 April 1918; *s* of Lord Stanley, MC, PC (*d* 1938), and Sibyl Louise Beatrix Cadogan (*d* 1969), *e d* of Henry Arthur, late Viscount Chelsea, and Hon. Lady Meux; *g s* of 17th Earl of Derby, KG, GCB, GCVO, PC; *S* grandfather, 1948; *m* 1948, Lady Isabel Milles-Lade (*d* 1990), *yr d* of late Hon. Henry Milles-Lade, and *sister* of 4th Earl Sondes. *Educ:* Eton; Oxford Univ. Left Army with rank of Major, 1946. President: Liverpool Chamber of Commerce, 1948–; NW Area Conservative Assoc., 1969–72. Pro-Chancellor, Lancaster Univ., 1964–71. Lord Lieut and Custos Rotulorum of Lancaster, 1951–68. Alderman, Lancashire CC, 1968–74. Commanded 5th Bn The King's Regt, TA, 1947–51, Hon. Col, 1951–67; Hon. Captain, RNR (Mersey Div., 1955–90); Hon. Colonel: 1st Bn The Liverpool Scottish Regt, TA, 1964–67; Lancastrian Volunteers, 1967–75; 5th/8th (V) Bn The King's Regt, 1975–88; 4th (V) Bn The Queen's Lancashire Regt, 1975–86; Chm., NW of England and IoM TAVR Assoc., 1979–83. President: Rugby Football League, 1948–; Professional Golfers' Assoc., 1964–. DL Lancs 1946. Hon. LLD: Liverpool, 1949; Lancaster, 1972. Hon. Freeman, City of Manchester, 1961. *Heir: nephew* Edward Richard William Stanley, *b* 10 Oct. 1962. *Address:* Knowsley, Prescot, Merseyside L34 4AF. *T:* 0151–489 6147; Stanley House, Newmarket, Suffolk. *T:* Newmarket (01638) 663011. *Clubs:* White's; Jockey (Newmarket).
Died 28 Nov. 1994.

DESAI, Shri Morarji Ranchhodji, BA; Prime Minister of India, 1977–79; *b* Bhadeli, Gujarat, 29 Feb. 1896; *e s* of Shri Ranchhodji and Vajiyaben Desai; *m* 1911, Gajraben Desai; one *s* one *d*. *Educ:* Wilson Coll., Bombay; Univ. of Bombay. Entered Provincial Civil Service of Govt of Bombay, 1918; resigned to join the Civil Disobedience Campaign of Mahatma Gandhi, 1930; convicted for taking part in the Movement during 1930–34; Sec., Gujarat Pradesh Congress Cttee, 1931–37 and 1939–46; Minister for Revenue, Co-operation, Agriculture and Forests, Bombay, 1937–39; convicted, 1940–41, and detained in prison, 1942–45; Minister for Home and Revenue, Bombay, 1946–52; Chief Minister of Bombay, 1952–56; Mem., 2nd, 3rd and 4th Lok Sabha, 1957–70; Minister of Commerce and Industry, Government of India, 1956–58; Treasurer, All India Congress Cttee, 1950–58; Minister of Finance, Government of India, 1958–63; resigned from Govt (under plan to strengthen Congress) Aug. 1963; Chm., Administrative Reforms Commn, Govt of India, 1966; Dep. Prime Minister and Minister of Finance, Government of India, 1967–69; Chm., Parly Gp, Congress Party (Opposition), 1969–77; elected to 5th Lok Sabha, 1971–79; detained in solitary confinement, 1975–77, under State of Emergency; Founder-Chairman, Janata Party, 1977. Hon. Fellow, College of Physicians and Surgeons, Bombay, 1956; Hon. LLD Karnatak Univ., 1957. *Publications:* books include: A View of the Gita; In My View; A Minister and His Responsibilities (Jawaharlal Nehru Meml Lectures); The Story of My Life (2 vols), 1978; Indian Unity: From Dream to Reality (Patel Meml Lectures); book on Nature Cure. *Recreations:* spinning on Charkha; follower of sport and classical Indian dancing. *Address:* Oceana, Marine Drive, Bombay 400020, India.
Died 10 April 1995.

de SAUMAREZ, 6th Baron *cr* 1831; **James Victor Broke Saumarez;** Bt 1801; *b* 28 April 1924; *s* of 5th Baron de Saumarez and Gunhild (*d* 1985), *d* of late Maj.-Gen. V. G. Balck, Stockholm; *S* father, 1969; *m* 1953, Julia, *d* of late D. R. Charlton, Gt Holland-on-Sea, Essex; twin *s* one *d*. *Educ:* Eton Coll.; Millfield; Magdalene Coll., Cambridge (MA). Farmer; Director, Shrubland Health

Clinic Ltd. *Recreations:* swimming, gardening, photography. *Heir: s* Hon. Eric Douglas Saumarez [*b* 13 Aug. 1956; *m* 1982, Christine (marr. diss. 1989), *yr d* of B. N. Halliday]. *Address:* Shrubland Vista, Coddenham, Ipswich, Suffolk. *T:* Ipswich (0473) 830220.
Died 20 Jan. 1991.

DESTY, Prof. Denis Henry, OBE 1983; FRS 1984; FInstPet; Senior Research Associate, Special Projects, British Petroleum Co. Ltd, 1965–82; *b* 21 Oct. 1923; *s* of Ernest James Desty and Alice Q. R. Desty; *m* 1945, Doreen (*née* Scott); one *s* (one *d* decd). *Educ:* Taunton's Sch., Southampton; University Coll., Southampton (BSc Hons Chemistry, London, 1948). FInstPet 1974. Served War, RAF, 1942–46: Signals Officer, UK and India. Research Centre, British Petroleum Co. Ltd: Physical Chemist, 1948; Gp Leader, 1952; Sen. Chemist, 1962; retd 1982. Research consultant: technical and indust. orgns, 1982–; Janus Consultancy, 1982–. Chm., Gas Chromatography Discussion Gp, 1958–68 (Special Parchment Award, 1970). M. S. Tswett Chromatography Medal, USA 1974 and USSR 1978; Award for Combustion Chemistry, RSC, 1980; MacRobert Award, Fellowship of Engrg, 1982; Merit Award, Chicago Chromatography Disc Gp, 1986; Martin Medal, Chromatographic Soc., 1991. Silver Jubilee Medal, 1977. Editor, Proc. Internat. Gas Chromatography Symposia, 1956 and 1958. *Publications:* about 50 papers and 60 patents. *Recreations:* boating, camping. *Address:* 16 Albury Road, Burwood Park, Walton-on-Thames, Surrey KT12 5DT. *T:* Walton-on-Thames (0932) 229687, *Fax:* Walton-on-Thames (0932) 245848.
Died 18 Jan. 1994.

DEVENPORT, Martyn Herbert, MA; Headmaster, Victoria College, Jersey, Channel Islands, since Sept. 1967; *b* 11 Jan. 1931; *s* of Horace Devenport and Marjorie Violet (*née* Fergusson); *m* 1957, Mary Margaret Lord; three *s* one *d*. *Educ:* Maidstone Gram. Sch.; Gonville and Caius Coll., Cambridge. Asst Master at Eton Coll., 1957–67. *Recreations:* photography, squash, sailing. *Address:* Victoria College, Jersey, CI. *T:* 37591.
Died 9 May 1991.

DEVERELL, Sir Colville (Montgomery), GBE 1963 (OBE 1946); KCMG 1957 (CMG 1955); CVO 1953; retired from Government Service, Nov. 1962; Secretary-General, International Planned Parenthood Federation, 1964–69; *b* 21 Feb. 1907; *s* of George Robert Deverell and Maude (*née* Cooke); *m* 1935, Margaret Wynne, *d* of D. A. Wynne Willson; two *s* (and one *s* decd). *Educ:* Portora Sch., Enniskillen, Ulster; Trinity Coll., Dublin (LLB); Trinity Coll., Cambridge. District Officer, Kenya, 1931; Clerk to Exec. and Legislative Councils, 1938–39; Civil Affairs Branch, E Africa Comd, 1941–46, serving Italian Somaliland, British Somaliland, Ethiopia; Mem. Lord de la Warr's Delegation, Ethiopia, 1944; seconded War Office in connection Italian Peace Treaty, 1946. Sec., Development and Reconstruction Authority, Kenya, 1946; acted as Financial Sec. and Chief Native Comr, 1949; Administrative Secretary, Kenya, 1949; Colonial Sec., Jamaica, 1952–55; Governor and Comdr-in-Chief, Windward Islands, 1955–59; Governor and Comdr-in-Chief, Mauritius, 1959–62. Chm. UN(FP) Mission to India, 1965; Mem., UN Mission on Need for World Population Inst., 1970; Chairman: UN Family Planning Evaluation Mission to Ceylon, 1971; UN Family Planning Assoc. Feasability Mission, Al Azhar Univ., Cairo, 1972. Constitutional Adviser: Seychelles, 1966; British Virgin Islands, 1973. LLD *jure dignitatis*, Dublin, 1964. *Recreations:* cricket, tennis, squash, golf, fishing.
Died 18 Dec. 1995.

de VERE WHITE, Terence; *see* White.

DE VITO, Gioconda; violinist; Professor of Corso di Perfezionamento of Violin at Accademia Di Santa Cecilia, Rome, 1946–61; *b* 26 July 1907; *d* of Giacomo and Emilia De Vito (*née* Del Guidice), Martina Franca Puglia, Italy; *m* 1949, (James) David Bicknell (*d* 1988); no *c*. *Educ:* Conservatorio Di Musica Rossini, Pesaro. Began to play violin at age of 8½; final examinations (distinction), Conservatorio Pesaro, 1921; first concert, 1921; teacher, Instituto Musicale Nicolo Piccinni, Bari, 1924–34; first prize, Internat. Competition, Vienna, 1932; Prof. of Violin, Conservatorio Di Santa Cecilia, Rome, 1935–46. World wide musical activities since debut with London Philharmonic Orchestra, 1948 (concert conducted by Victor de Sabata); Royal Philharmonic Soc., 1950; Edinburgh Festival, 1949, 1951, 1953 (took part, 1953, in Festival of the Violin with Yehudi Menuhin and Isaac Stern), and 1960; played at Bath Fest. and Festival Hall with Yehudi Menuhin, 1955; Jury, Tchaikowsky Internat. Violin Competition, Moscow, and recitals Moscow and Leningrad, 1958; Soloist, Adelaide Centenary Fest., and toured Australia, 1960; concerts, Buenos Aires, 1961; last concerts: Gt Brit., Swansea Festival, Oct. 1961; Continent, Basle Philharmonic, Nov. 1961; retired, 1961. Many recordings. Diploma di Medaglia d'Oro del Ministero della Pubblica Istruzione for services to Art, 1957; Academician, Accademia Nazionale di Santa Cecilia, Rome, 1976. Gold Medal, Premium Amadeas, 1991. *Recreation:* bird watching. *Address:* Via Cassia 595, Rome. *T:* 3660937.
Died 14 Oct. 1994.

DEVITT, Lt-Col Sir Thomas Gordon, 2nd Bt, *cr* 1916; Partner of Devitt & Moore, Shipbrokers; *b* 27 Dec. 1902; *e s* of Arthur Devitt (*d* 1921), *e s* of 1st Bt and Florence Emmeline (*d* 1951), *e d* of late William Forbes Gordon, Manar, NSW; *S* grandfather, 1923; *m* 1st, 1930, Joan Mary (who obtained a divorce, 1936), 2nd *d* of late Charles Reginald Freemantle, Hayes Barton, Pyrford, Surrey; 2nd, 1937, Lydia Mary (marr. diss. 1953; she *d* 1995), *o d* of late Edward Milligen Beloe, King's Lynn, Norfolk; two *d*; 3rd, 1953, Janet Lilian, *o d* of late Col H. S. Ellis, CBE, MC; one *s* one *d*. *Educ:* Sherborne; Corpus Christi Coll., Cambridge. 1939–45 War as Lt-Col, Seaforth Highlanders and OC Raiding Support Regt. Royal Order of Phœnix of Greece with swords. Chm. Macers Ltd, 1961–70. Chairman: Board of Governors, The Devitt and Moore Nautical Coll., Pangbourne, 1948–61; Nat. Service for Seafarers, 1948–77. Governor, Sherborne Sch., 1967–75. *Recreations:* shooting, fishing. *Heir: s* James Hugh Thomas Devitt [*b* 18 Sept. 1956; *m* 1985, Susan Carol, *d* of Dr Michael Duffus; two *s* one *d*]. *Address:* 49 Lexden Road, Colchester, Essex CO3 3PY. *T:* Colchester (01206) 577958. *Club:* MCC.
Died 23 Dec. 1995.

DEVLIN, Baron (Life Peer) *cr* 1961, of West Wick; **Patrick Arthur Devlin,** Kt 1948; PC 1960; FBA 1963; High Steward of Cambridge University, 1966–91; *b* 25 Nov. 1905; *e s* of W. J. Devlin; *m* 1932, Madeleine, *yr d* of Sir Bernard Oppenheimer, 1st Bt; four *s* twin *d*. *Educ:* Stonyhurst Coll.; Christ's Coll., Cambridge. President of Cambridge Union, 1926. Called to Bar, Gray's Inn, 1929; KC 1945; Master of the Bench, Gray's Inn, 1947; Treasurer of Gray's Inn, 1963. Prosecuting Counsel to the Mint, 1931–39; Legal Dept, Min. of Supply, 1940–42; Junior Counsel to the Ministries of War Transport, Food and Supply, 1942–45; Attorney-Gen., Duchy of Cornwall, 1947–48; Justice of the High Court, Queen's Bench Div., 1948–60; Pres. of the Restrictive Practices Court, 1956–60; a Lord Justice of Appeal, 1960–61; a Lord of Appeal in Ordinary, 1961–64, retd; Chm. Wiltshire QS, 1955–71. A Judge of the Administrative Tribunal of the ILO, 1964–86; Chm., Commn apptd under constn of ILO to examine complaints concerning observance by Greece of Freedom of Assoc. and similar Conventions, 1969–71. Chairman: Cttee of Inquiry into Dock Labour Scheme, 1955–56;

Nyasaland Inquiry Commn, 1959; Cttee of inquiry into the port transport industry, 1964–65; Jt Bd for the Nat. Newspaper Industry, 1965–69; Commn of Inquiry into Industrial Representation, 1971–72; Cttee on Identification in criminal cases, 1974–76. Chm., Press Council, 1964–69. Chm. of Council, Bedford Coll., University of London, 1953–59. Pres., British Maritime Law Assoc., 1962–76; Chm., Assoc. Average Adjusters, 1966–67. Hon. LLD: Glasgow, 1962; Toronto, 1962; Cambridge, 1966; Leicester, 1966; Sussex 1966; Durham, 1968; Liverpool, 1970; St Louis, 1980; Hon. DCL Oxon, 1965. *Publications:* Trial by Jury (Hamlyn Lectures), 1956; The Criminal Prosecution in England (Sherrill Lectures), 1957; Samples of Lawmaking (Lloyd Roberts and other lectures), 1962; The Enforcement of Morals (Maccabean and other lectures), 1965; The House of Lords and the Naval Prize Bill, 1911 (Rede Lecture), 1968; Too Proud to Fight: Woodrow Wilson's Neutrality, 1974; The Judge (Chorley and other lectures), 1979; Easing the Passing: the trial of Dr John Bodkin Adams, 1985. *Address:* West Wick House, Pewsey, Wilts SN9 5JZ.
Died 9 Aug. 1992.

DE VRIES, Peter; writer; *b* Chicago, 27 Feb. 1910; *s* of Joost De Vries and Henrietta (*née* Eldersveld); *m* 1943, Katinka Loeser; two *s* one *d. Educ:* Calvin College, Michigan (AB); Northwestern University. Editor, community newspaper, Chicago, 1931; freelance writer, 1931–; associate editor Poetry Magazine, 1938, co-editor, 1942; joined editorial staff New Yorker Magazine, 1944. Mem., Amer. Acad. and Inst. of Arts and Letters. *Publications:* No But I saw the Movie, 1952; The Tunnel of Love, 1954; Comfort Me with Apples, 1956; The Mackerel Plaza, 1958; The Tents of Wickedness, 1959; Through the Fields of Clover, 1961; The Blood of the Lamb, 1962; Reuben, Reuben, 1964 (filmed, 1984); Let Me Count the Ways, 1965; The Vale of Laughter, 1967; The Cat's Pajamas and Witch's Milk, 1968 (filmed as Pete and Tillie, 1982); Mrs Wallop, 1970; Into Your Tent I'll Creep, 1971; Without a Stitch in Time, 1972; Forever Panting, 1973; The Glory of the Hummingbird, 1975; I Hear America Swinging, 1976; Madder Music, 1978; Consenting Adults, 1980; Sauce for the Goose, 1981; Slouching Towards Kalamazoo, 1983; The Prick of Noon, 1985; Peckham's Marbles, 1986.
Died 28 Sept. 1993.

DEWHURST, Timothy Littleton, MC 1945; Chief Registrar of the High Court of Justice in Bankruptcy, 1988–93, retired (Registrar, 1981–93); *b* 4 March 1920; *s* of late Robert Cyril Dewhurst and Rhoda Joan Dewhurst; *m* 1949, Pandora Laetitia Oldfield (*d* 1984); four *d. Educ:* Stowe Sch.; Magdalen Coll., Oxford (MA). Called to Bar, Lincoln's Inn, 1950, Bencher, 1988. Served with Rifle Brigade, 1941–46, N Africa and Italy (despatches 1944). Mem. Bar Council, 1977–79; Conveyancing Counsel of the Court, 1980–81. *Died 13 Nov. 1993.*

DEXTRAZE, Gen. Jacques Alfred, CC 1978; CBE 1964 (OBE 1952); CMM 1972; DSO (and Bar) 1945; CD; President, J. A. Dextraze and Associates, since 1984; *b* 15 Aug. 1919; *s* of Alfred and Amanda Dextraze; *m* 1942, Frances Helena Pare; three *s* (and one *s* decd). *Educ:* St Joseph de Berthier; MacDonald Business Coll., Montreal. With Dominion Rubber Co, 1938–40. Served War of 1939–45: Fusiliers, Mt Royal, 1939–45, Lt-Col and Comdg Officer, 1944–45; Comdg Officer, Hastings and Prince Edward Regt, 1945. With Singer Mfg Co., 1945–50; Manager, Forest Ops, 1947–50. Resumed mil. career as Comdg Officer, 2nd Bn Royal 22e Regt, 1950–52; Chief of Staff HQ, UN ops in Congo, 1963–64; Chief of Personnel, Can. Forces HQ, 1970–72; Chief of Defence Staff, 1972–77, retired. Chm., Canadian Nat. Rlys, 1977–82. Hon. ADC to the Governor-Gen., 1958. Hon.

LLD Wilfred Laurier Univ.; Hon. PhD (Business Admin) Sherbrooke Univ. KStJ; KCLJ. Cross of Grand Officer, Order of the Crown (Belgium), 1977. *Address:* 467 Crestview Road, Ottawa, Ontario K1H 5G7, Canada.
Died 24 May 1993.

DICK, Sir John (Alexander), Kt 1987; MC 1944; QC (Scot.) 1963; Sheriff Principal of Glasgow and Strathkelvin, 1980–86; *b* 1 Jan. 1920; *y s* of Rev. David Auchinvole Dick and Blanche Hay Spence; *m* 1951, Rosemary Benzie Sutherland (*d* 1991); no *c. Educ:* Waid Academy, Anstruther; University of Edinburgh. Enlisted in London Scottish, 1940; commissioned Royal Scots, 1942; Italy, 1944; Palestine, 1945–46; released 1946. MA (1st Cl. Hons Economics) 1947, LLB (with distinction) 1949, Univ. of Edinburgh. Called to Scots Bar, 1949; Lecturer in Public Law, Univ. of Edinburgh, 1953–60; Junior Counsel in Scotland to HM Commissioners of Customs and Excise, 1956–63; Comr under Terrorism (N Ireland) Order 1972, 1972–73; Sheriff of the Lothians and Borders at Edinburgh, 1969–78; Sheriff Principal of North Strathclyde, 1978–82. Hon. LLD Glasgow, 1987. *Recreation:* hill-walking. *Address:* 3 St Margaret's Court, North Berwick, East Lothian EH39 4QH. *T:* North Berwick (0620) 5249. *Club:* Royal Scots (Edinburgh).
Died 16 June 1994.

DICK, Rear-Adm. Royer Mylius, CB 1951; CBE 1943; DSC 1918; *b* 14 Oct. 1897; *s* of Louis Henry Mylius Dick and Edith Alice Guy; *m* 1928, Agnes Mary Harben; (one *s* killed on active service one *d* decd); *m* 1955, Vera (*d* 1990), *d* of Sir John Henry, DL, and *widow* of Col Bertram Pott. *Educ:* RN Colls, Osborne and Dartmouth. Midshipman, 1914; at sea, 1914–18 (Falklands, Jutland, North Russia) (DSC); Lieut 1918; Comdr 1933; Capt. 1940; Dep. Chief of Staff, Mediterranean Station, 1940–42 (Matapan); Commodore 1st cl. 1942; British Admty Delegn to Washington, 1942; Chief of Staff to Adm. Sir Andrew Cunningham, Mediterranean Stn, 1942–44 (despatches twice, CBE); HMS Belfast, 1944–46; Dir Tactical and Staff Duties, Admiralty, 1947–48; Chief of Staff to Flag Officer, Western Europe, 1948–50; Rear-Adm. 1949; Naval ADC to the King, 1949; Flag Officer, Training Sqdn, 1951–52; Standing Group Liaison Officer to North Atlantic Council, 1952–55; Vice-Adm. (Acting), 1953; retired list, 1955. Dep. Comr-in-Chief, 1957–62, Comr-in-Chief, 1962–67, SJAB. Dep. Chm., Horticultural Marketing Council, 1960–63; Chairman: Royal United Service Institution, 1965–67; St John Council for London, 1971–75; a Vice-Pres., Royal UK Beneficent Assoc., 1979. KStJ 1961; Bailiff Grand Cross, Order of Hosp. of St John of Jerusalem, 1967. Officer Legion of Merit (US), 1943; Officer Legion of Honour (France), 1943; Croix de Guerre avec palme, 1946. *Address:* The Dower House, Headbourne Worthy, Winchester, Hants SO23 7JG. *T:* Winchester (0962) 882848. *Clubs:* Army and Navy, Royal Automobile. *Died 23 April 1991.*

DICKENS, Geoffrey Kenneth, JP; MP (C) Littleborough and Saddleworth, since 1983 (Huddersfield West, 1979–83); company director, engineering industry; *b* 26 Aug. 1931; *s* of John Wilfred and Laura Avril Dickens; *m* 1956, Norma Evelyn Boothby; two *s. Educ:* Park Lane and Byron Court Primary; East Lane Sch., Wembley; Harrow and Acton Technical Colls. Chairman: Sandridge Parish Council, 1968–69; St Albans Rural District Council, 1970–71 (Leader, 1967–70); Councillor, Hertfordshire CC, 1970–75; Hon. Alderman, City and District of St Albans, 1976. Contested (C): Teesside Middlesbrough, Feb. 1974, and Ealing North, Oct. 1974, general elections. Vice Chm., Assoc. of Conservative Clubs; Vice-Pres., NW Conservative Clubs Council. Royal Humane Soc. Testimonial on Vellum for saving lives, 1972. JP St

Albans, later Barnsley, then Oldham, 1968. *Address:* c/o House of Commons, SW1A 0AA.

Died 17 May 1995.

DICKENS, Monica Enid, (Mrs R. O. Stratton), MBE 1981; writer; Founder of The Samaritans, in the USA, Boston, Mass, 1974; *b* 10 May 1915; *d* of late Henry Charles Dickens, Barrister-at-law, and Fanny Runge; *m* 1951, Comdr Roy Olin Stratton (*d* 1985), US Navy; two *d. Educ:* St Paul's Girls' Sch., Hammersmith. *Publications:* One Pair of Hands, 1939; Mariana, 1940; One Pair of Feet, 1942; The Fancy, 1943; Thursday Afternoons, 1945; The Happy Prisoner, 1946; Joy and Josephine, 1948; Flowers on the Grass, 1949; My Turn to Make the Tea, 1951; No More Meadows, 1953; The Winds of Heaven, 1955; The Angel in the Corner, 1956; Man Overboard, 1958; The Heart of London, 1961; Cobbler's Dream, 1963; Kate and Emma, 1964; The Room Upstairs, 1966; The Landlord's Daughter, 1968; The Listeners, 1970; The House at World's End, 1970; Summer at World's End, 1971; Follyfoot, 1971; World's End in Winter, 1972; Dora at Follyfoot, 1972; Spring Comes to World's End, 1973; Talking of Horses, 1973; Last Year when I was Young, 1974; The Horse of Follyfoot, 1975; Stranger at Follyfoot, 1976; An Open Book, 1978; The Messenger, 1985; The Ballad of Favour, 1985; Miracles of Courage, 1985; The Haunting of Bellamy 4, 1986; Dear Doctor Lily, 1988; Enchantment, 1989; Closed at Dusk, 1990; Scarred, 1991; One of the Family, 1993. *Recreation:* gardening. *Address:* Lavender Cottage, Brightwalton, Berks RG16 0BY. *Died 25 Dec. 1992.*

DICKIE, Rev. Edgar Primrose, MC; MA, BD (Edinburgh); BA Oxon; Emeritus Professor of Divinity, St Mary's College, University of St Andrews, since 1967 (Professor, 1935–67, retired); Extra Chaplain to the Queen in Scotland since 1967 (Chaplain, 1956–67, retired); *b* 12 Aug. 1897; *y* and *o* surv. *s* of William Dickie, editor of Dumfries and Galloway Standard, and Jane Paterson; *m* 1927, Ishbel Graham Holmes (*d* 1985), *d* of Andrew Frier Johnston and Magdalene Ross Holmes, Edinburgh. *Educ:* Dumfries Academy; Edinburgh University; Christ Church, Oxford; New Coll., Edinburgh; Marburg; Tübingen. MA Edinburgh, First Class Hons in Classics; Vans Dunlop Scholar; BA Oxford, First Class in Literae Humaniores; at New Coll., Edinburgh, Hamilton Scholar; Fullarton Scholar in Hebrew; Tutor in Greek, 1925–26; Hons Diploma; Senior Cunningham Fellow, 1926. Asst Minister, New North Church, Edinburgh; ordained, 1927; Minister of St Cuthbert's Church, Lockerbie, 1927–33; Minister of St Anne's Church, Corstorphine, Edinburgh, 1933–35. External Examiner: in Biblical Criticism, Edinburgh Univ., 1931–34 and 1934–35; in New Testament Greek, New Coll., Edinburgh, 1931–34; in History of Doctrine, Univ. of Manchester, 1939–41; in Ethics, Queen's Univ., Belfast, 1941; in Systematic Theology, Univ. of Aberdeen, 1942; in Theology, Univ. of Glasgow, 1948, Belfast, 1953. Kerr Lectr, 1936–39; Murtle Lectr, Univ. of Aberdeen, 1941; Captain St Andrews Univ. OTC, 1941; Convener, Church of Scotland Youth Cttee, 1945–50. Founder-mem., Studiorum Novi Testamenti Societas, 1937. Pres. Scottish Sunday School Union, 1955–57; Vice-Pres. Scottish Universities Athletic Club. Governor, St Leonards Sch. Hon. DD Edinburgh, 1946; Hon. LLD St Andrews, 1969. Hon. Life Mem., Students' Union, St Andrews; Hon. Blue, Athletic Union, St Andrews. Served War of 1914–18 with rank of Captain, 3rd and 1/5th KOSB, Palestine, Flanders, France (wounded, MC); mentioned in despatches; World War II, Gen. Supt of work of Church of Scotland in BEF, 1940, and with BLA, 1944–45 (mentioned in despatches). Companion of Merit and Canon, Order St Lazarus of Jerusalem. *Publications:* Psammyforshort: Rex. Imp.: A Nonsense Story, 1928; The New Divine Order, 1930;

translation of Karl Heim's Die Neue Welt Gottes; The Seven Words from the Cross, 1931; Spirit and Truth, 1935; translation of Heim's Das Wesen des Evangelischen Christentums; God Transcendent; translation of Heim's Glaube und Denken (3rd edn); Revelation and Response, 1938; One Year's Talks to Children, 1940; Scottish Life and Character, 1942; A Second Year's Talks to Children, 1943; The Paper Boat, 1943; The Obedience of a Christian Man, 1944; Normandy to Nijmegen, 1946; The Fellowship of Youth, 1947; Mister Bannock: A Nonsense Story, 1947; I Promise (Girl Guides), 1949; It was New to me (Church of Scotland), 1949; God is Light: Studies in Revelation and Personal Conviction, 1953; Thou art the Christ, 1954; A Safe Stronghold, 1955; introductory essay to McLeod Campbell, The Nature of the Atonement, 1959; The Unchanging Gospel, 1960; The Father Everlasting, 1965; Remembrance, 1966; occasional articles in Punch, The Scots Magazine, and other periodicals. *Recreations:* hill-walking, winter sports. *Address:* Craigmount, The Scores, St Andrews, Fife KY16 9AS.

Died 28 June 1991.

DICKINSON, Rt Rev. John Hubert, MA; Vicar of Chollerton, 1959–71; Hon. Canon in Newcastle Cathedral, 1947–71; *b* 1901; *m* 1937, Frances Victoria (*d* 1991), *d* of late Rev. C. F. Thorp; two *d. Educ:* Jesus Coll., Oxford; Cuddesdon Coll. Deacon, 1925; priest, 1926; Curate of St John, Middlesbrough, 1925–29; SPG Missionary, South Tokyo, 1929–31; Asst Bishop of Melanesia, 1931–37; Vicar of Felkirk-with-Brierley, 1937–42; Vicar of Warkworth, 1942–59. *Died 31 May 1993.*

DICKINSON, Patric (Thomas); poet, playwright and freelance broadcaster; *b* 26 Dec. 1914; *s* of Major A. T. S. Dickinson, 51 Sikhs, FF, IA, and Eileen Constance Kirwan; *m* 1945, Sheila Dunbar Shannon; one *s* one *d. Educ:* St Catharine's Coll., Cambridge (Crabtree Exhibitioner). Asst schoolmaster, 1936–39. Artists' Rifles, 1939–40. BBC, 1942–48 (Feature and Drama Dept); Acting Poetry Editor, 1945–48. Sometime Gresham Prof. in Rhetoric at the City University. Libretti: (for Malcolm Arnold) The Return of Odysseus, 1977; (for Stephen Dodgson) The Miller's Secret, 1973; (for Alan Ridout): Creation, 1973; Good King Wenceslas, 1979. Atlantic Award in Literature, 1948; Cholmondeley Award for Poets, 1973. *Publications: poetry:* The Seven Days of Jericho, 1944; Soldier's Verse (anthology), 1945; Theseus and the Minotaur: play and poems, 1946; Stone in the Midst: play and poems, 1949; (ed) Byron (selected anthology), 1949; A Round of Golf Courses, 1951; The Sailing Race, 1952; The Scale of Things, 1955; (ed with Sheila Shannon) Poems to Remember, 1958; The World I See, 1960; This Cold Universe, 1964; (ed with Sheila Shannon) Poets' Choice: an anthology of English poetry from Spenser to the present day, 1967; (ed) C. Day Lewis Selections from his Poetry, 1967; Selected Poems, 1968; More Than Time, 1970; A Wintering Tree, 1973; The Bearing Beast, 1976; Our Living John, 1979; Poems from Rye, 1980; Winter Hostages, 1980; (ed and introd) Selected Poems of Henry Newbolt, 1981; A Rift in Time, 1982; To Go Hidden, 1984; A Sun Dog, 1988; Two into One (with drawings by John Ward, RA), 1989; Not Hereafter, 1991; *translations:* Aristophanes, Against War, 1957; The Aeneid of Vergil, 1960; Aristophanes, vols I and II, 1970; *play:* A Durable Fire, 1962; *autobiography:* The Good Minute, 1965. *Recreation:* following golf (Cambridge Blue, 1935). *Address:* 38 Church Square, Rye, East Sussex TN31 7HF. *T:* Rye (0797) 222194. *Club:* Savile.

Died 28 Jan. 1994.

DICKSON, Alexander Graeme, (Alec), CBE 1967 (MBE 1945); MA Oxon; Hon. President, Community Service Volunteers, since 1982 (Hon. Director, 1962–82); *b* 23 May 1914; *y s* of late Norman Dickson and Anne Higgins;

m 1951, Mora Hope Robertson, artist, author of numerous travel books and biographies. *Educ:* Rugby; New Coll., Oxford. Private Sec. to Alec Paterson, 1935; editorial staff: Yorkshire Post, 1936–37; Daily Telegraph, 1937–38, Germany; refugee relief, Czechoslovakia, winter 1938–39; served War of 1939–45: Cameron Highlanders; 1st KAR (Abyssinian Campaign); led E Africa Comd mobile educn unit; Displaced Persons Directorate, Berlin, 1946–48; introd Mass Educn, Gold Coast, 1948–49; founded Man O' War Bay Training Centre, Cameroons and Nigeria, 1950–54; Chief Unesco Mission, Iraq, 1955–56; refugee relief, Austro-Hungarian frontier, winter 1956–57; Founder and first Dir, Voluntary Service Overseas, 1958–62; founded Community Service Volunteers, 1962, developing concept of 'A Year Between' for students, linking curriculum to human needs, promoting tutoring in schools, involving disadvantaged and unemployed young people in social service. Shared experience with US Peace Corps, 1961, 1969; India, 1968, 1972; Hong Kong, 1968, 1974, 1980; Israel, 1970, 1980; Nigeria, 1970, 1975, 1976; Malta, 1971; Nepal, 1972; New Zealand, 1972; Papua New Guinea, 1973; Bahamas, 1975; US Nat. Student Volunteer Program, Washington DC and Alaska, 1975; Ontario, 1975, 1981, 1982, 1983; Sri Lanka, Australia, 1976; Japan, 1976, 1980, 1983; Univ. of the South Pacific, 1978; W Germany, Denmark, 1979; Finland, 1980; Sweden, 1982; Malaysia, 1983. Hon. Chm., Nat. Youth Leadership Council (US), 1984–. Consultant to Commonwealth Secretariat, 1974–77; Hon. Consultant: Partnership for Service-Learning (US), 1984–; Inst. for Social Inventions (UK), 1984–; Hon. Advr, Internat. Baccalaureate schs, 1984–. Hon. LLD: Leeds, 1970; Bristol, 1980. Niwano Peace Foundn Award, 1982; Kurt Hahn Centenary Award, 1986. *Publications:* (with Mora Dickson) A Community Service Handbook, 1967; School in the Round, 1969; A Chance to Serve, 1976; Volunteers, 1983; articles on community development and youth service. *Recreations:* identical with work—involving young people in community service, at home or overseas. *Address:* 19 Blenheim Road, W4 1UB. *T:* 0181–994 7437; (office) 0171–278 6601.   *Died 23 Sept. 1994.*

DICKSON, John Abernethy, CB 1970; Director-General and Deputy Chairman, Forestry Commission, 1968–76; *b* 19 Sept. 1915; *yr s* of late John and Williamina Dickson; *m* 1942, Helen Drummond, *o d* of Peter Drummond Jardine; two *d. Educ:* Robert Gordon's Coll., Aberdeen; Aberdeen Univ. MA 1936; BSc (Forestry) 1938. Joined Forestry Commn, 1938; District Officer, 1940; seconded to Min. of Supply, Home Grown Timber Production Dept, 1940–46; Divisional Officer, 1951; Conservator, 1956; Dir (Scotland), 1963; Comr Harvesting and Marketing, 1965. Director: Economic Forestry (Scotland), 1977–84; Forest Thinnings Ltd, 1979–86 (Chm., 1981–86). Chm., Standing Cttee on Commonwealth Forestry, 1968–76; Vice-Pres., Commonwealth Forestry Assoc., 1975–(Chm., 1972–75). Hon. LLD Aberdeen, 1969. FIMgt (FBIM 1975). *Recreation:* gardening. *Address:* 56 Oxgangs Road, Edinburgh EH10 7AY. *T:* 031–445 1067.
Died 25 March 1994.

DICKSON, Dame Violet (Penelope), DBE 1976 (CBE 1964; MBE 1942); *b* Gautby, Lincs, 3 Sept. 1896; *d* of Neville Lucas-Calcraft and Emily Delmar Lindley; *m* 1920, Captain Harold Richard Patrick Dickson, CIE (*d* 1959); one *s* one *d. Educ:* Miss Lunn's High Sch., Woodhall Spa; Les Charmettes, Vevey, Switzerland. Mesopotamia, 1921–22; Quetta, Baluchistan, 1923–24; Bikaner, Rajputana, 1924–28; Bushire, Iran, 1928–29; Kuwait, 1929–. FRZS; Mem. RCAS. *Publications:* Wild Flowers of Kuwait and Bahrain, 1955; Forty Years in Kuwait, 1971. *Recreations:* shooting, riding, tennis, swimming. *Address:* Seef, Kuwait, Arabia. *T:* 2432310.
Died 4 Jan. 1991.

DIETRICH, Maria Magdalena, (Marlene); actress; *b* Berlin, 27 Dec. 1901; *d* of Louis Erich Otto Dietrich and Josephine Felsing; step *d* of Eduard von Losch; naturalised as an American, 1937; *m* 1924, Rudolph Sieber (*d* 1976); one *d. Educ:* Berlin; Weimar; Max Reinhardt Sch. of Theatre. Stage, Berlin and Vienna; first notable film, The Blue Angel, 1930; films in America since 1930, incl. Desire, Destry Rides Again, Foreign Affair, Garden of Allah, Golden Earrings, Rancho Notorious, Scarlet Empress, Shanghai Express, Stage Fright, Witness for the Prosecution, Just a Gigolo; numerous stage appearances in Europe, Great Britain, America and all continents. Special Tony Award, 1967–68. Commandeur, Légion d'Honneur, 1990 (Officier, 1972); US Medal of Freedom. *Publications:* Marlene Dietrich's ABC, 1962; My Life (autobiog.), 1989. *Recreation:* tennis.
Died 6 May 1992.

DILL, Sir (Nicholas) Bayard, Kt 1955; CBE 1951; JP; Senior Partner, Conyers, Dill & Pearman, Barristers-at-Law, since 1948; *b* 28 Dec. 1905; *s* of Thomas Melville and Ruth Rapalje Dill; *m* 1930, Lucy Clare, *d* of Sir Henry Watlington, OBE, Bermuda; two *s. Educ:* Saltus Grammar Sch., Bermuda; Trinity Hall, Cambridge. Law Tripos Cantab, 1926. Called to the Bar, Middle Temple, 1927; Mem. Colonial Parliament (for Devonshire Parish), Bermuda, 1938–68; Mem. HM Exec. Council, 1944–54; Chairman: Board of Trade, 1935–42, also Bd of Educn, 1940, and Board of Works, 1942–48, Bermuda; St David's Island Cttee, 1940–43; Public Works Planning Commn, 1942–49; Board of Civil Aviation, 1944–63; Bermuda Trade Development Bd, 1957–59; Mem., Legislative Council, Bermuda, 1968–73. Served as Capt., Bermuda Volunteer Engrs, 1936–44. Chancellor of Diocese of Bermuda, 1950–84. Life Mem., Internat. Biographical Assoc. JP Hamilton, Bermuda, 1949. *Recreations:* sailing, golf. *Address:* Newbold Place, Devonshire, Bermuda. *T:* 924463. *Clubs:* Anglo-Belgian, Royal Thames Yacht; Royal Bermuda Yacht (Commodore, 1936–38), Mid-Ocean, Royal Hamilton Amateur Dinghy (Bermuda); India House, Canadian, Cruising of America, Metropolitan (NYC).   *Died 10 Sept. 1993.*

DILLISTONE, Rev. Canon Frederick William, DD; Fellow and Chaplain, Oriel College, Oxford, 1964–70; Fellow Emeritus, 1970; Canon Emeritus of Liverpool Cathedral since 1964; *b* 9 May 1903; *s* of late Frederick Dillistone; *m* 1931, Enid Mary, *d* of late Rev. Cecil Francis Ayerst; two *s* one *d. Educ:* Brighton Coll.; BNC, Oxford (Scholar). BA 1924; BD 1933; DD 1951. Deacon, 1927; priest, 1928; Vicar of St Andrew, Oxford, 1934–38; Prof. of Theology, Wycliffe Coll., Toronto, 1938–45; Prof. of Theology, Episcopal Theological Sch., Cambridge, Mass, 1947–52; Canon Residentiary and Chancellor of Liverpool Cathedral, 1952–56; Dean of Liverpool, 1956–63. Hulsean Preacher, Cambridge, 1953; Select Preacher, Oxford, 1953–55; Select Preacher, Cambridge, 1960; Stephenson Lectr, Univ. of Sheffield, 1966; Bampton Lectr, Univ. of Oxford, 1968; Vis. Fellow, Clare Hall, Cambridge, 1970; Zabriskie Lectr, Virginia Theol Seminary, 1971. Asst Editor, Theology Today, 1951–61. Hon. DD: Knox Coll., Toronto, 1946; Episcopal Theological Sch., Cambridge, Mass, 1967; Virginia Theol Seminary, 1979. Chaplain OStJ, 1958. *Publications:* The Significance of the Cross, 1945; The Holy Spirit in the Life of To-day, 1946; Revelation and Evangelism, 1948; The Structure of the Divine Society, 1951; Jesus Christ and His Cross, 1953; Christianity and Symbolism, 1955, repr. 1985; Christianity and Communication, 1956; The Novelist and the Passion Story, 1960; The Christian Faith, 1964; Dramas of Salvation, 1967; The Christian Understanding of Atonement, 1968; Modern Answers to Basic Questions, 1972; Traditional Symbols and the Contemporary World, 1972; Charles Raven: a biography, 1975; C. H. Dodd: a biography, 1977; Into all the World: a biography of Max Warren, 1980; Religious Experience and Christian Faith, 1982; Afire for God: the life of Joe Fison, 1983; The Power of Symbols, 1986; edited: Scripture and Tradition, 1955; Myth and Symbol, 1966; contributor to: The Doctrine of Justification by Faith, 1954; A Companion to the Study of St Augustine, 1955; Steps to Christian Understanding, 1958; The Ecumenical Era in Church and Society, 1959; Metaphor and Symbol, 1961; The Theology of the Christian Mission, 1961; Christianity and the Visual Arts, 1964; Mansions of the Spirit, 1966; Christianity in its Social Context, 1967; Studies in Christian History and Interpretation, 1967; Christ for us Today, 1968; Grounds of Hope, 1968; Man, Fallen and Free, 1969; Sociology, Theology and Conflict, 1969; Christ and Spirit in the New Testament, 1973; Religion and Art as Communication, 1974; Theolinguistics, 1981; God's Truth, 1988; Language and the Worship of the Church, 1990. *Recreation:* gardening. *Address:* 11 Eyot Place, Iffley Fields, Oxford OX4 1SA. *T:* Oxford (0865) 241324.

Died 5 Oct. 1993.

DILLON, Sir John (Vincent), Kt 1980; CMG 1974; Ombudsman for Victoria (Commissioner for Administrative Investigations), 1973–80; *b* 6 Aug. 1908; *s* of Roger Dillon and Ellen (*née* Egan); *m* 1935, Sheila Lorraine D'Arcy; three *s* one *d. Educ:* Christian Brothers Coll., Melbourne. AASA. Mem. Public Service Bd, 1941–54; Stipendiary Magistrate City Court, 1947–61; Chm., Medical Salaries Cttee, 1959–62; Under-Sec., Chief Sec.'s Dept, Vic, 1961–73; Chm., Racecourses Licences Bd, 1961–73. Hon. LLD Melbourne, 1982. *Recreations:* racing, golf, reading. *Address:* 25 Kelvin Grove, Armadale, Vic 3143, Australia. *Clubs:* Athenæum, Victoria Racing, Victoria Amateur Turf, Moonee Valley Racing, Melbourne Cricket, Metropolitan Golf (Melbourne).

Died 20 Nov. 1992.

DINSDALE, Richard Lewis; Chairman, West of England Newspapers Ltd, 1969–72; *b* 23 June 1907; *m* 1930, Irene Laverack (*d* 1984); one *d. Educ:* Hull Technical Coll. Joined Hull Daily Mail as reporter, 1926; Editorial posts: Newcastle Evening World; Chief Sub-editor, Manchester Evening News; Dep. Chief Sub-editor, Daily Express, Manchester; Evening News, London; Daily Mirror, 1940–42; War Service, 1942–46; Copy-taster, Daily Mirror, 1946, successively Chief Sub-editor, Dep. Night Editor, Night Editor; Dep. Editor, 1955; seconded Daily Herald as Editorial Adviser, 1961; Dep. Editor, Daily Herald, 1962; Dep. Editor, The Sun, 1964, Editor, 1965–69. *Recreation:* strolling. *Address:* Southlands Court, 33 Hastings Road, Bexhill-on-Sea, E Sussex TN40 2HJ. *Died 2 Dec. 1995.*

DINWIDDY, Thomas Lutwyche; Master of the Supreme Court (Chancery Division), 1958–73; *b* 27 Aug. 1905; *o c* of late Harry Lutwyche Dinwiddy, Solicitor, and Ethel Maude (*née* McArthur); *m* 1935, Ruth, *d* of late Charles Ernest Rowland Abbott, Barrister-at-Law and Bencher of Lincoln's Inn; three *s. Educ:* Winchester; New Coll., Oxford (BA). Solicitor, Dec. 1930; Partner in Frere Cholmeley & Co., 28 Lincoln's Inn Fields, WC2, 1933–57. Mem. Council of Law Soc., 1953–57. Served RA (TA), 1939–45; Staff Coll., Camberley, 1943; demobilised as Major. *Address:* Allonsfield House, Campsea Ashe, Woodbridge, Suffolk IP13 0PX.

Died 16 Aug. 1992.

DIX, Bernard Hubert; Assistant General Secretary, National Union of Public Employees, 1975–82; *b* 30 March 1925; *s* of Thomas Herbert John Dix and Gertrude Turner; *m* 1979, Eileen Veronica Smith; three *s*; two *s* one *d* by prev. marriage. *Educ:* LCC elem. schs; LSE (TUC Scholar). Engrg industry, 1939–55 (served Army, 1941–47); Deptl Asst, TUC, 1955–63; Res. Officer,

NUPE, 1963–75. Member: Health Services Bd, 1976–80; Hotel and Catering Industry EDC, 1973–79; TUC Local Govt Cttee, 1970–81; TUC Hotel and Catering Industry Cttee, 1973–79; Labour Party NEC, 1981; Bd of Tribune, 1975–82. Mem., Llanddarog Community Council, 1987–94. Governor, Ruskin Coll., 1969–84. Associate Fellow, Warwick Univ., 1982–84. *Publications:* (with Alan W. Fisher) Low Pay and How to End It, 1974; (jtly) The Forward March of Labour Halted?, 1981; (with Stephen Williams) Serving the Public, Building the Union, 1987. *Address:* Pant Tawel, Mynydd Cerrig, Dyfed SA15 5BD. *T:* Pontyberem (01269) 870122. *Club:* Mynydd Cerrig Workingmen's. *Died 20 April 1995.*

DIX, Victor Wilkinson, MA, MB, BChir Cantab; FRCS, MRCP; retired; Professor Emeritus, University of London; *m*; one *s* two *d.* Assistant Surgeon, The London Hospital, 1930–37; Surgeon, The London Hospital, 1937–64. *Address:* 8 Shandon Close, Tunbridge Wells, Kent. *T:* Tunbridge Wells (0892) 30839.

Died 29 June 1992.

DIXON, Guy Holford, JP; barrister-at-law; Honorary Recorder of Newark-on-Trent, since 1972; *b* 20 March 1902; *s* of late Dr Montague Dixon, Melton Mowbray; unmarried. *Educ:* Abbotsholme Sch., Derbs; Repton Sch.; University Coll., Oxford. BA (History) Oxon, 1925. Called to the Bar, Inner Temple, 1929. Recorder of Newark-on-Trent, 1965–71; Deputy Chairman: Leics QS, 1960–71; Northampton County QS, 1966–71; a Recorder, 1972–75; a Dep. Circuit Judge, 1975–77. Lay Canon, Leicester Cathedral, 1962. JP Leics, 1960. *Recreation:* looking at and collecting pictures. *Address:* The Old Rectory, Brampton Ash, Market Harborough, Leics LE16 8PD. *T:* Dingley (085885) 200. *Club:* Reform.

Died 7 June 1993.

DOBSON, Sir Denis (William), KCB 1969 (CB 1959); OBE 1945; QC 1971; Clerk of the Crown in Chancery and Permanent Secretary to the Lord Chancellor, 1968–77; *b* 17 Oct. 1908; *s* of late William Gordon Dobson, Newcastle upon Tyne; *m* 1st, 1934, Thelma (marr. diss. 1947), *d* of Charles Swinburne, Newcastle upon Tyne; one *s* one *d*; 2nd, 1948, Mary Elizabeth, *d* of J. A. Allen, Haywards Heath; two *s* one *d. Educ:* Charterhouse; Trinity Coll., Cambridge (MA, LLB). Solicitor, 1933. Served in RAF, 1940–45 (Desert Air Force, 1942–45). Called to the Bar, Middle Temple, 1951; Bencher, 1968; Dep. Clerk of the Crown in Chancery and Asst Permanent Sec. to Lord Chancellor, 1954–68. Mem., Adv. Council on Public Records, 1977–83. *Address:* 50 Egerton Crescent, SW3 2ED. *T:* 0171–589 7990. *Club:* Athenæum.

Died 15 Dec. 1995.

DOBSON, Sir Richard (Portway), Kt 1976; President, BAT Industries Ltd, 1976–79; *b* 11 Feb. 1914; *s* of Prof. J. F. Dobson and Dina, *e d* of H. H. Portway, JP, Halstead, Essex; *m* 1946, Emily Margaret Carver; one step *d. Educ:* Clifton Coll.; King's Coll., Cambridge. Flt-Lt, RAF, 1941–45 (pilot). Joined British American Tobacco Co. Ltd, 1935: served in China, 1936–40; China, Rhodesia and London, 1946–76; Dir, 1955; Dep. Chm., 1962; Vice-Chm., 1968; Chm., 1970–76. Director: Molins Ltd, 1970–84; Commonwealth Development Finance, 1974–79; Exxon Corporation (USA), 1975–84; Davy Corp. Ltd, 1975–85; Foseco Minsep, 1976–85; Lloyds Bank International, 1976–84; Chm., British Leyland Ltd, 1976–77. Chm., British-North American Res. Assoc., 1976–80. *Publication:* China Cycle, 1946. *Recreations:* fly fishing, golf. *Address:* 16 Marchmont Road, Richmond upon Thames, Surrey TW10 6HQ. *T:* 081–940 1504. *Clubs:* United Oxford & Cambridge University; Richmond Golf. *Died 24 Oct. 1993.*

DODD, Air Vice-Marshal Frank Leslie, CBE 1968; DSO 1944; DFC 1945; AFC 1944 and Bars, 1955 and 1958; AE 1945; LRPS 1987; Administrator, MacRobert Trusts, 1974–85; *b* 5 March 1919; *s* of Frank H. Dodd and Lilian (*née* Willis); *m* 1942, Joyce L. Banyard; one *s* three *d.* *Educ:* King Edward VI Sch., Stafford; Reading University. RAFVR, 1938; CFS course and Flying Instructor, 1940–44; No 544 Sqdn (photo-reconnaissance), 1944–46; CO 45 Sqdn (Beaufighters), 1947–48; CFS Staff and HQ Flying Trng Comd, 1948–52; pfc 1952–53; Chief Instructor CFS, 1953–55; psc 1955; CO 230 OCU Waddington (Vulcans), 1955–59; Gp Captain Trng HQ Bomber Comd, 1959–61; CO RAF Coningsby (Vulcans), 1961–63; idc 1964; AOC and Comdt CFS, 1965–68; MoD (Dir Estabs), 1968–70. Dir Gen., Linesman Project, 1970–74, retired. *Recreations:* golf, music, photography. *Address:* c/o Barclays Bank, 15 Market Square, Stafford ST16 2BE. *Club:* Royal Air Force.
Died 30 April 1993.

DODDS, George Christopher Buchanan, CMG 1977; Assistant Under-Secretary of State, Ministry of Defence, 1964–76; *b* 8 Oct. 1916; *o s* of George Hepple Dodds and Gladys Marion (*née* Ferguson), Newcastle upon Tyne; *m* 1944, Olive Florence Wilmot Ling; no *c.* *Educ:* Rugby; Gonville and Caius Coll., Cambridge (BA). Entered Secretary's Dept, Admiralty, 1939; Royal Marines, 1940–41; Private Sec. to Sec. of the Admiralty, 1941–43; Asst Private Sec. to Prime Minister, June-Aug. 1944; Asst Sec., 1951; idc, 1959. *Recreations:* bird-watching, walking, golf, bridge. *Address:* 5 Bryanston Square, W1H 7FE. *T:* 0171–262 2852. *Club:* Royal Mid-Surrey Golf.
Died 29 June 1995.

DODGE, John Vilas; Senior Editorial Consultant, Encyclopædia Britannica, since 1972; Chairman, Board of Editors, Encyclopædia Britannica Publishers, since 1977; *b* 25 Sept. 1909; *s* of George Dannel Dodge and Mary Helen Porter; *m* 1935, Jean Elizabeth Plate; two *s* two *d.* *Educ:* Northwestern Univ., Evanston, Ill, USA; Univ. of Bordeaux, Bordeaux, France. Free-lance writer, 1931–32; Editor, Northwestern Alumni News and official publications of Northwestern Univ., 1932–35; Exec. Sec., Northwestern Univ. Alumni Assoc., 1937–38; Asst Editor, Encyclopædia Britannica, and Associate Editor, Britannica Book of the Year, 1938–43; US Army, 1943–46 (Intelligence); Associate Editor, Ten Eventful Years and Asst Editor, Encyclopædia Britannica, 1946–50; Editor, Britannica World Language Dictionary, 1954; Managing Editor, Encyclopædia Britannica, 1950–60; Executive Editor, 1960–64; Senior Vice-Pres., Editorial, 1964–65; Senior Editorial Consultant, 1965–70; Vice-Pres., Editorial, 1970–72. Conseiller Editorial, Encyclopædia Universalis (Paris), 1968–; Editorial Advisor: Britannica Internat. Encyclopædia (in Japanese), Tokyo, 1969–; Enciclopedia Mirador (Rio de Janeiro) and Enciclopedia Barsa (Mexico City), 1974–; Chm., Editl Bd, Enciclopedia Hispánica (Mexico City and Madrid-Barcelona), 1989–. *Address:* 3851 Mission Hills Road, Northbrook, Ill 60062, USA. *T:* (708) 272–0254. *Died 23 April 1991.*

DODWELL, Prof. Charles Reginald, MA, PhD, LittD; FBA 1973; FRHistS, FSA; Pilkington Professor of History of Art and Director of Whitworth Gallery, University of Manchester, 1966–89, then Professor Emeritus; *b* 3 Feb. 1922; *s* of William Henry Walter and Blanche Dodwell; *m* 1942, Sheila Juliet Fletcher; one *s* one *d.* *Educ:* Gonville and Caius Coll., Cambridge (MA, PhD, LittD). Served War, Navy, 1941–45. Research Fellow, Caius Coll., 1950–51; Sen. Research Fellow, Warburg Inst., 1950–53; Lambeth Librarian, 1953–58; Fellow, Lectr, Librarian, Trinity Coll., Cambridge, 1958–66. Visiting Scholar, Inst. of Advanced Studies, Princeton, USA, 1965–66. *Publications:* The Canterbury School of Illumination,

1954; Lambeth Palace, 1958; The Great Lambeth Bible, 1959; The St Albans Psalter (section 2), 1960; Theophilus: De Diversis Artibus, 1961; Reichenau Reconsidered, 1965; Painting in Europe 800–1200, 1971; Early English Manuscripts in Facsimile, vol. xviii (section 2), 1972; Anglo-Saxon Art: a new perspective, 1982; The Pictorial Arts of the West 800–1200, 1993; Anglo-Saxon Gestures and the Roman Stage, 1994; articles in Burlington Magazine, Gazette des Beaux Arts, Atti del 18 Congresso Internazionale di studi sull'alto medioevo (Spoleto), Jumièges, Congrès Scientifique du 13 Centenaire, L'Archéologie, etc. *Recreations:* opera, Shakespearean studies. *Address:* The Yews, 37 South Road, Taunton, Somerset TA1 3DU. *T:* Taunton (0823) 323640.
Died 22 April 1994.

DOLLING, Francis Robert; Director: Barclays International (Chairman, 1985–86); Barclays Bank PLC (Deputy Chairman, 1983–85); Chairman, Barclays Merchant Bank Ltd, 1980–85; *b* 21 Jan. 1923; *s* of Frederick George Dolling and Edith Lilian Auriel; *m* 1949, Maisie Alice Noquet; two *d.* *Educ:* Tottenham County School. Served RAF, 1940–47. Joined Barclays Bank DCO, 1947; served in various overseas territories; Managing Director, Barclays National Bank Ltd, South Africa, 1974; Director and Sen. General Manager, Barclays Bank Internat. Ltd, and Director, Barclays Bank Ltd, 1976; Vice-Chm., Barclays Bank, 1980–83.
Died 30 Jan. 1994.

DOMETT, Rear-Adm. Douglas Brian, CB 1989; CBE 1984; Chief of Naval Staff, Royal New Zealand Navy, 1987–89; *b* 12 May 1932; *s* of Samuel and Hazel Marion Domett; *m* 1986, Merrion Ranwell Clark; four *s* one *d* by previous marriage. *Educ:* Putaruru High Sch.; Palmerston North Boys' High Sch.; RNC Dartmouth. Joined RNZN 1950; served in HMNZ Ships Black Prince, Pukaki, Hawea, Rotoiti and Endeavour; specialist training, UK, 1959–62; HMNZS Otago; Ops School, Auckland; RNZAF Comd and Staff Coll., 1967; Dep. Dir, Defence Intelligence, 1968–69; US Armed Forces Staff Coll., 1970; Naval Attaché, Washington, 1970–72; in Comd, HMNZ Ships Waikato, 1972–73, Canterbury, 1974; COS to Commodore, Auckland, 1974–76; Dir, Resources Policy, 1976–79; RCDS 1980; ACDS (Personnel), 1981–83; Dep. Chief of Naval Staff, 1983–87. US Legion of Merit, 1973; Korean Order of Nat. Security Merit Medal, 1988. *Recreations:* all sports, farming, gardening, fishing. *Address:* Station Road, Paparoa RD1, Northland, New Zealand. *T:* (9) 4316851. *Clubs:* Auckland Officers (Auckland); Northland Officers (Whangarei).
Died 6 Dec. 1994.

DONALD, Prof. Kenneth William, OBE 1983; DSC 1940; MA, MD, DSc; FRCP, FRCPE, FRSE; Professor of Medicine, University of Edinburgh, 1959–76, then Emeritus Professor; Senior Physician, Royal Infirmary, Edinburgh; Physician to the Queen in Scotland, 1967–76; *b* 25 Nov. 1911; *s* of Col William Donald, MC, RA and Julia Jane Donald, Sandgate; *m* 1942, Rêthe Pearl, *d* of D. H. Evans, Regents Park. *Educ:* Cambridge Univ.; St Bartholomew's Hosp. Kitchener Scholar and State Scholar, 1930; Senior Scholar, Emmanuel Coll., Cambridge, 1933. Served with Royal Navy, 1939–45: Senior MO, 2nd and 5th Flotilla of Destroyers; Senior MO, Admiralty Experimental Diving Unit. Chief Asst, Med. Prof. Unit and Cattlin Research Fellow, St Bartholomew's Hosp., 1946–48; Rockefeller Travelling Research Fellow, Columbia Univ., 1948–49; Senior Lecturer in Medicine, Inst. Diseases of the Chest, Brompton Hosp., 1949–50; Reader in Medicine, Univ. of Birmingham and Physician, Queen Elizabeth Hosp., Birmingham, 1950–59. Scientific Consultant to the Royal Navy; Physician to the Royal Navy in Scotland. Medical

Consultant to Scottish Dept of Home and Health; Member: Commonwealth Scholarship Commn; Medical Sub-Cttee, UGC; RN Personnel Research Cttee (Chm.) of MRC; Scottish Adv. Cttee on Med. Research; Council and Scientific Adv. Cttee, British Heart Foundn; Scottish Gen. Nursing Council; Chairman: Under-Water Physiology Sub-Cttee of MRC; Adv. Gp to Sec. of State for Scotland on Health Care Aspects of Industrial Developments in North Sea. Governor, Inst. of Occupational Medicine, Edinburgh. *Publications:* Oxygen and the Diver, 1992; contribs to scientific and medical jls concerning normal and abnormal function of the lungs, the heart and the circulation and high pressure physiology in relation to diving and submarines, drowning, resuscitation. *Recreations:* reading, theatre, fishing. *Address:* Nant-y-Celyn, Cloddiau, Welshpool, Powys SY21 9JE. *T:* Welshpool (0938) 552859. *Club:* Athenæum.

Died 17 July 1994.

DONALDSON OF KINGSBRIDGE, Lady; *see* Donaldson, Frances Annesley.

DONALDSON, Air Cdre Edward Mortlock, CB 1960; CBE 1954; DSO 1940; AFC 1941 (and bar 1947); Air Correspondent, The Daily Telegraph, 1961–79; *b* 22 Feb. 1912; *s* of C. E. Donaldson, Malay Civil Service; *m* 1st, 1936, Winifred Constant (marr. diss. 1944); two *d*; 2nd, 1944, Estellee Holland (marr. diss. 1956); one *s*; 3rd, 1957, Anne, Sofie Stapleton (marr. diss. 1982). *Educ:* King's Sch., Rochester; Christ's Hosp., Horsham; McGill Univ., Canada. Joined RAF, 1931; 3 Sqdn, Upavon, Kenley and Sudan until 1936; won RAF air firing trophy, 1933 and 1934; Flight Comdr, 1 Sqdn, 1936–38; led flight aerobatic team, Hendon and Zürich, 1937; Flight-Lieut 1936; Sqdn Leader 1938; Comdr, 151 Squdn, 1938–40, Battle of Britain; Wing Comdr, 1940; Chief Instructor, 5 Flying Training Sch., 1941; went to US to build four air Gunnery Schs, 1941, and teach USAF combat techniques; Group Capt., 1942; Mem. USAF Board and Directing Staff at US Sch. of Applied Tactics, 1944; Comdr RAF Station, Colerne, RAF first jet station, 1944; in comd RAF Station, Milfield, 1946; in comd RAF High Speed Flight, 1946; holder of World's Speed Record, 1946; SASO, No 12 Group, 1946–49; in comd Air Cadet Corps and CCF, 1949–51; in comd RAF Station, Fassberg, Germany, 1951–54; Joint Services Staff Coll., 1954; Dir of Operational Training, Air Ministry, 1954–56; Air Cdre, 1954; Dep. Comdr Air Forces, Arabian Peninsular Command, 1956–58; Commandant, Royal Air Force Flying Coll., Manby, 1958–61; retd. Legion of Merit (US), 1948. *Recreations:* shooting, sailing, golf. *Address:* 3 Fair Oak Court, Tower Close, Alverstoke, Gosport PO12 2TX; Suite Royal 4011, El Palmar, Denia, Alicante, Spain. *Clubs:* Royal Air Force; Island Sailing (Cowes).

Died 2 June 1992.

DONALDSON, Frances Annesley, (Lady Donaldson of Kingsbridge); *b* 13 Jan. 1907; *d* of Frederick Lonsdale and Leslie Lonsdale (*née* Hoggan); *m* 1935, John George Stuart Donaldson (Baron Donaldson of Kingsbridge); one *s* two *d*. *Publications:* Approach to Farming, 1941, 6th edn 1946; Four Years' Harvest, 1945; Milk Without Tears, 1955; Freddy Lonsdale, 1957; Child of the Twenties, 1959; The Marconi Scandal, 1962; Evelyn Waugh: portrait of a country neighbour, 1967; Actor Managers, 1970; Edward VIII, 1974 (Wolfson History Award, 1975); King George VI and Queen Elizabeth, 1977; Edward VIII: the road to abdication, 1978; P. G. Wodehouse, 1982; The British Council: the First Fifty Years, 1984; The Royal Opera House in the Twentieth Century, 1988; (ed) Yours, Plum: the letters of P. G. Wodehouse, 1990; A Twentieth Century Life (autobiog.), 1992. *Address:* 17 Edna Street, SW11 3DP. *T:* 071-223 0259.

Died 27 March 1994.

DONALDSON, Prof. Gordon, CBE 1988; FRSE 1978; FBA 1976; Professor of Scottish History and Palæography, University of Edinburgh, 1963–79, then Professor Emeritus; Historiographer to HM the Queen in Scotland, since 1979; *b* 13 April 1913; *s* of Magnus Donaldson and Rachel Hetherington Swan. *Educ:* Royal High Sch., Edinburgh; Universities of Edinburgh and London. Asst in HM Gen. Register House, Edinburgh, 1938; Lecturer in Scottish History, University of Edinburgh, 1947, Reader, 1955. Birkbeck Lectr, Cambridge, 1958. Member: Royal Commission on the Ancient and Historical Monuments of Scotland, 1964–82; Scottish Records Adv. Council, 1964–87; President: Scottish Ecclesiological Soc., 1963–65; Scottish Church History Soc., 1964–67; Scottish History Soc., 1968–72; Scottish Record Soc., 1981–; Stair Soc., 1987–. Editor, Scottish Historical Review, 1972–77. Hon. DLitt Aberdeen, 1976; DUniv Stirling, 1988. *Publications:* The Making of the Scottish Prayer Book of 1637, 1954; A Source Book of Scottish History, 1952–61; Register of the Privy Seal of Scotland, vols v-viii, 1957–82; Shetland Life under Earl Patrick, 1958; Scotland: Church and Nation through sixteen centuries, 1960, 2nd edn 1972; The Scottish Reformation, 1960, repr. 1972; Scotland—James V to James VII, 1965, repr. 1971; The Scots Overseas, 1966; Northwards by Sea, 1966, 2nd edn 1978; Scottish Kings, 1967, repr. 1977; The First Trial of Mary Queen of Scots, 1969; Memoirs of Sir James Melville of Halhill, 1969; (compiled) Scottish Historical Documents, 1970; Mary Queen of Scots, 1974; Who's Who in Scottish History, 1974; Scotland: The Shaping of a Nation, 1974, 2nd edn 1980; Dictionary of Scottish History, 1977; All the Queen's Men, 1983; Isles of Home, 1983; Sir William Fraser, 1985; Scottish Church History, 1985; Reformed by Bishops, 1988; The Faith of the Scots, 1990; A Northern Commonwealth: Scotland and Norway, 1990; contribs to Scottish Historical Review, English Historical Review, Transactions of Royal Historical Society, etc. *Address:* 6 Pan Ha', Dysart, Fife KY1 2TL. *T:* Kirkcaldy (0592) 52685.

Died 16 March 1993.

DONALDSON, Rear-Adm. Vernon D'Arcy; *b* 1 Feb. 1906; *s* of Adm. Leonard Andrew Boyd Donaldson, CB, CMG, and Mary Mitchell, *d* of Prof. D'Arcy Thompson, Queen's Coll., Galway; *m* 1946, Joan Cranfield Monypenny of Pitmilly, (The Lady Pitmilly) (*d* 1986), *d* of James Egerton Howard Monypenny. *Educ:* RN Colls, Osborne and Dartmouth. Entered Royal Navy, Sept. 1919; Midshipman, 1923; Sub-Lieut 1927; Lieut 1928; specialised in torpedoes and served as Torpedo Officer in HMS Vernon, 8th Destroyer Flotilla, China Stn, and HMS Glorious; Comdr Dec. 1939, and served in Plans Div. Admty, as exec. officer HM Ships Birmingham and Frobisher in Eastern Fleet, and on staff of C-in-C Eastern Fleet; Capt. Dec. 1944. Asst-Dir, Torpedo Anti-Submarine Warfare Div., Naval Staff, 1945–47; Naval Attaché, China, 1948–49; commanded HMS Gambia, 1950–51; Dir Torpedo Anti-Submarine Warfare Div., Naval Staff, 1952–54; ADC to the Queen, 1953–54; Dep. Chief of Supplies and Transport, Admiralty (acting Rear-Adm.), 1955–57; retired, 1957. *Address:* 19 Collingwood Court, Melbourne Road, Royston, Herts SG8 7BY.

Died 30 April 1992.

DONEGAN, Rt Rev. Horace W(illiam) B(aden), Hon. CBE 1957; DD; *b* Matlock, Derbyshire, England, 17 May 1900; *s* of Horace George Donegan and Pembroke Capes Hand. *Educ:* St Stephen's, Annandale, NY; Oxford University, England; Harvard Divinity School; Episcopal Theological Seminary. Rector, Christ Church, Baltimore, 1929–33; Rector, St James' Church, NYC, 1933–47; Suffragan Bishop of New York, 1947–49; Bishop Coadjutor of New York, 1949–50; Bishop of New York, 1950–72. Vice-Pres., Pilgrims, USA; President: St Hilda's and St Hugh's Sch., NY; House of Redeemer, NY; Episcopal Actors Guild, NY; Chaplain, Veterans of Foreign Wars; Episcopal Visitor: Sisters of St Helena; Community of the Holy Spirit; Trustee: St Luke's Hosp., NY; Episcopal Sch., NY; Contemporary Club, NY. Award, Conf. of Christians and Jews; Medal of City of New York; Medal of Merit, St Nicholas Society, NY; Citation, NY Hospital Assoc.; Harlem Arts & Culture Award. Churchill Fellow, Westminster Coll., Fulton, Mo. Hon. degrees: DD: New York Univ., 1940; Univ. of South, 1949; Trinity, 1950; Bard Coll., 1957; King's Univ., Halifax, 1958; Berkley Divinity School, New Haven, Conn, 1969; STD: Hobart Coll., 1948; General Theological Seminary, 1949; Columbia Univ., 1960; DCL Nashotah, 1956. Sub Prelate OStJ, 1956; Grand Cross St Joanikije, 1956; Legion of Honour, France, 1957; Silver Medal of Red Cross of Japan, 1959; Holy Pagania from Armenian Church, 1960; Grand Kt, Order of St Denys of Zante (Greece), 1959. *Publications:* articles in religious publications. *Recreations:* golf, swimming, painting. *Address:* Manhattan House, 200 E 66th Street, New York, NY 10021, USA; 3145 Twin Lakes Lane, Sanibel Island, Florida 33957, USA. *Clubs:* Athenæum, Royal Automobile, American, Kennel (London); Union, Union League, Pilgrims, Century Association, Columbia Faculty, Tuxedo Park (all of New York).

Died 11 Nov. 1991.

DONNISON, (Frank Siegfried) Vernon, CBE 1943; Indian Civil Service (retired); *b* 3 July 1898; *s* of Frank Samuel and Edith Donnison; *m* 1923, Ruth Seruya Singer, MBE, JP (*d* 1968); one *s* one *d*. *Educ:* Marlborough Coll.; Corpus Christi Coll., Oxford. Served with Grenadier Guards, 1917–19; ICS (Burma), 1922; Chief Sec. to Govt of Burma, 1946; military service, Burma, 1944–45 (despatches). Historian, Cabinet Office, Historical Section, 1949–66. *Publications:* Public Administration in Burma, 1953; British Military Administration in the Far East, 1943–46, 1956; Civil Affairs and Military Government, North-West Europe, 1944–46, 1961; Civil Affairs and Military Government, Central Organization and Planning, 1966; Burma, 1970. *Recreation:* music. *Address:* The Old Vicarage, Moulsford, Wallingford, Oxon OX10 9JB.

Died 11 June 1993.

DOOLITTLE, Gen. James H., Hon. KCB 1945; Trustee, Aerospace Corporation, 1963–69 (Chairman of Executive Committee and Vice-Chairman, Board of Trustees, 1965–69); Chairman of Board, Space Technology Laboratories, Inc., 1959–62; Emeritus Director: Mutual of Omaha Insurance Co.; United Benefit Life Insurance Co.; Tele-Trip Co., Inc.; *b* 14 Dec. 1896; *s* of Frank H. Doolittle and Rosa C. Shephard; *m* 1917, Josephine E. Daniels; two *s*. *Educ:* University of California (AB); MIT (MS, ScD). US Army Air Force, 1917–30; Manager, Aviation Dept, Shell Oil Co., 1930–40; USAAF, 1940–45; Dir, Shell Oil Company, 1946–67 (Vice-Pres., 1946–59). *Publications:* various scientific. *Recreations:* shooting, fishing. *Address:* PO Box 566, Pebble Beach, Calif 93953, USA.

Died 27 Sept. 1993.

DORAN, John Frederick, CEng, FInstGasE, MInstM; Chairman, East Midlands Gas Region, 1974–77; *b* 28 July 1916; *s* of Henry Joseph and Clara Doran; *m* 1940, Eileen Brotherton; two *s*. *Educ:* Wandsworth Technical Coll.; Wimbledon Technical Coll. Served War, Fleet Air Arm, 1943–46. Various appts Gas Light & Coke Co. (subseq. North Thames Gas Bd), 1935–53; Dist Manager, Hornsey Dist, North Thames Gas Bd, 1953; Regional Sales Manager, North Western Div., North Thames Gas Bd, 1955–57; Southern Gas Board: Regional Sales and Service Manager, Southampton Region and Dorset and Bournemouth Regions, 1957–65; Marketing Manager, 1965–67; Commercial Manager, 1968–69; Commercial

Dir, 1970–71; Commercial Dir and Bd Mem., 1971–73; Dep. Chm., East Midlands Gas Region, 1973. Founder, John Doran Gas Museum, Leicester. *Publications:* technical papers to Instn Gas Engrs. *Recreations:* golf, gardening. *Address:* 14 Oberfield Road, Brockenhurst, Hants SO42 7QF. *T:* Lymington (01590) 623185.

Died 23 May 1995.

DORMAN, Sir Maurice Henry, GCMG 1961 (KCMG 1957; CMG 1955); GCVO 1961; DL; MA; retired; Governor-General, Malta, 1964–71; *b* 7 Aug. 1912; *s* of late John Ehrenfried and Madeleine Louise Dorman; *m* 1937, Florence Monica Churchward Smith (DStJ 1968); one *s* three *d*. *Educ:* Sedbergh Sch.; Magdalene Coll., Cambridge. Administrative Officer, Tanganyika Territory, 1935; Clerk of Councils, Tanganyika, 1940–45; Asst to the Lt-Governor, Malta, 1945; Principal Asst Sec., Palestine, 1947; seconded to Colonial Office as Asst Sec., Social Services Dept, 1948; Dir of Social Welfare and Community Develt, Gold Coast, 1950; Colonial Sec., Trinidad and Tobago, 1952–56; Actg Governor of Trinidad, 1954, 1955; Governor, Comdr-in-Chief and Vice-Adm., Sierra Leone, 1956–61, after independence, Governor-Gen., 1961–62; Gov. and C-in-C, Malta, 1962–64. Dep. Chm., Pearce Commn on Rhodesia, 1971–72; Chm., British observers of Zimbabwe independence elecns, 1980. Chairman: Swindon HMC, 1972–74; Wilts AHA, 1974–82; Swindon HA, 1982–88. Chm., West of England (formerly Ramsbury) Bldg Soc., 1983–87 (Dir, 1972–87; Vice-Chm., 1981–83). Vice Pres., Badminton Sch., 1966– (Chm. Bd of Govs, 1975–81); Governor, Monkton Combe Sch., 1984–92; a Trustee, Imperial War Museum, 1972–85. Venerable Order of St John of Jerusalem: Almoner, 1972–75; Chief Comdr, St John Ambulance, 1975–80; Lord Prior, 1980–86; Mem., Chapter-Gen., 1972–. DL Wilts, 1978. Hon. DCL Durham, 1962; Hon. LLD Royal Univ. Malta, 1964. GCStJ 1978 (KStJ 1957). Gran Croce Al Merito Melitense (Soc. Ordine Militaire di Malta), 1966. *Recreations:* once sailing and squash, sometimes golf. *Address:* The Old Manor, Overton, Marlborough, Wilts SN8 4ER. *T:* Lockeridge (067286) 600. *Clubs:* Athenæum; Casino Maltese (Valletta). *Died 26 Oct. 1993.*

DORMER, 16th Baron *cr* 1615; **Joseph Spencer Philip Dormer;** Bt 1615; landowner and farmer; *b* 4 Sept. 1914; *s* of 14th Baron Dormer, CBE, and Caroline May (*d* 1951), *y d* of Sir Robert Cavendish Spencer Clifford, 3rd Bt; *S* brother, 1975. *Educ:* Ampleforth; Christ Church, Oxford. Served World War II, Scots Guards. Consultant, Thomas Comely & Sons Ltd. Pres., Warwick and Leamington Conservative Assoc., 1983–. Formerly Mem. Council, West Midlands Area Conservative Assoc. Hon. Vice-Pres., Worcs Br., Grenadier Gds Assoc. Kt of Honour and Devotion, SMO Malta, 1989. *Heir: cousin* Geoffrey Henry Dormer [*b* 13 May 1920; *m* 1st, 1947, Janet (marr. diss. 1957), *yr d* of James F. A. Readman; two *d*; 2nd, 1958, Pamela, *d* of late Wallace Levick Simpson; two *s*]. *Address:* Grove Park, Warwick CV35 8RF. *Club:* Cavalry and Guards. *Died 21 Dec. 1995.*

dos SANTOS, Sir Errol Lionel, Kt 1946; CBE 1939; Consultant, Alstons Ltd; *b* 1 Sept. 1890; *s* of Solomon and Margaret dos Santos; *m* 1st, 1915; one *s* one *d*; 2nd, 1939, Enid Hilda Jenkin, Bath, England; two *d*. *Educ:* St Mary's Coll., Trinidad. Entered Trinidad Civil Service as a junior clerk in the Treasury; Financial Sec., 1941; Colonial Sec., 1947; retired from Colonial Service, 1948. Dir, Alstons Ltd, 1948, Chm. 1953–61. *Address:* Flat 3, 7 Bryanston Square, W1. *Clubs:* MCC; Union, Queen's Park Cricket, Portuguese (Trinidad). *Died 19 Nov. 1992.*

DOUGLAS, Arthur John Alexander, CMG 1965; OBE 1962; Assistant Secretary, Overseas Development Administration, Foreign and Commonwealth Office (formerly Ministry of Overseas Development), 1975–80; *b* 31 May 1920; *s* of Alexander and Eileen Douglas; *m* 1948, Christine Scott Dyke; two *d. Educ:* Dumfries Academy; Edinburgh Univ. Royal Navy, 1940–45. District Officer, Basutoland, 1946; seconded Colonial Office, 1957; Administration Sec., Bechuanaland, 1959; Government Sec. and Chief Sec. 1962–65; Dep. Commissioner for Bechuanaland, 1965–66; ODM, then ODA, 1967–80, retired. *Address:* 13 Pickers Green, Lindfield, West Sussex RH16 2BS. *Club:* Commonwealth Trust. *Died 13 Feb. 1995.*

DOUGLAS, Sir Donald (Macleod), Kt 1972; MBE 1943; ChM St Andrews, MS Minn; FRCSE, FRCS; FRSE 1973; Surgeon to the Queen in Scotland, 1965–76; an Extra Surgeon to the Queen in Scotland, since 1977; Professor of Surgery, University of Dundee (formerly Queen's College), 1951–76, Emeritus Professor, 1977; Surgeon, Ninewells Hospital, Dundee, 1951–76; *b* 28 June 1911; *s* of William Douglas and Christina Broom; *m* 1945, Margaret Diana Whitley; two *s* two *d. Educ:* Madras Coll.; Universities of St Andrews and Minnesota. Commonwealth Fellow in Surgery, Mayo Clinic, University of Minnesota, USA, 1937–39; First Asst in Surgery, British Postgraduate Medical Sch., 1939–40; RAMC, 1941–45; Reader in Experimental Surgery, University of Edinburgh, 1945–51; Asst Surgeon, Edinburgh Municipal Hospitals, 1945; formerly Surgeon, Royal Infirmary, Dundee; Dean of Faculty of Medicine, Univ. of Dundee, 1969–70. Associate Asst Surgeon, Royal Infirmary, Edinburgh. President: RCSE, 1971–73; Assoc. of Surgeons of GB and Ireland, 1964; Surgical Research Soc. of GB, 1966–69; Harveian Soc., 1974. Trustee, Thalidomide Trust, 1973– (Chm., Health and Welfare). Hon. FACS 1972; Hon. FRCS (SA) 1972; Hon. FRCSI 1973. Hon. DSc St Andrews, 1972. *Publications:* Wound Healing, 1965; The Thoughtful Surgeon, 1970; Surgical Departments in Hospitals, 1971. *Address:* The Whitehouse of Nevay, Newtyle, Angus PH12 8SJ. *T:* Newtyle (08285) 315. *Died 28 Jan. 1993.*

DOUGLAS, Ronald Albert Neale, DFC 1944; JP; Agent General for Western Australia in London, 1982–86; *b* 18 Sept. 1922; *s* of Edwyn William Albert Douglas and Kate Maria Douglas; *m* 1st, 1944 (marr. diss. 1966); one *s* one *d*; 2nd, Pamela Joy Carroll; one *s. Educ:* Albany High Sch., WA. Served War, RAAF, 1941–46 (Sqdn Ldr). Joined Shell Co. of Australia, 1938; sales rep., 1946–50; various appts, incl. Aviation Manager and Dist Manager, WA and NSW, 1950–60; appts with Shell Cos, France and USA, 1960–61; Sales Man., WA, 1961–65; Commercial Man., Shell Malaysia, 1965–66; Marketing Man., Shell Singapore, 1966–67; Retail Man., Vic/Tas, 1967–71; Chm.'s Rep. and Commercial Man., Shell Gp of Cos in WA, 1971–82. JP WA, 1982. *Recreations:* cricket, golf, fishing, farming. *Address:* 12 Jarrad Street, Cottesloe, Perth, WA 6011, Australia. *T:* 384 9986. *Clubs:* Weld, West Australian, Royal Aero (Perth); Lake Karrinyup Country (WA). *Died 30 June 1993.*

DOUGLAS-HOME, family name of **Baron Home of the Hirsel.**

DOUGLAS-HOME, Hon. William; *see* Home.

DOUGLAS-MANN, Keith John Sholto, FRICS; Chairman, Jones Lang Wootton International and of the London Partnership, 1981–90; *b* 19 Oct. 1931; *s* of late Captain Leslie Douglas-Mann and of Lallie Douglas-Mann; *m* 1962, Shirley Mary Westhead (*née* McDonald); one *s* one *d. Educ:* Westminster Sch. Commnd, Royal Dragoons, 1955. Joined Jones Lang Wootton, 1961. *Recreations:* farming, shooting, rowing. *Clubs:* Cavalry and Guards; Leander (Henley-on-Thames).

Died 11 Feb. 1992.

DOWDALLS, Edward Joseph; Principal, Coatbridge College (formerly Coatbridge Technical College), 1973–89; *b* 6 March 1926; *s* of late Alexander Dowdalls and Helen Dowdalls; *m* 1953, Sarah Quinn; one *s. Educ:* Our Lady's High Sch., Motherwell; Glasgow Univ. (BSc). Member, Coatbridge Town Council, 1958, Provost, 1967–70. Mem., Scottish Economic Planning Council, 1968–71; Chm., Lanarkshire Area Health Bd, 1977–81 (Mem., 1974–81). Hon. Sheriff, S Strathclyde and Galloway, 1975–. *Recreations:* reading, watching sport. *Address:* 72 Drumpellier Avenue, Coatbridge, Lanarkshire ML5 1JS. *Clubs:* Drumpellier Cricket, Drumpellier Rugby (Coatbridge). *Died 16 June 1994.*

DOWDING, 2nd Baron *cr* 1943, of Bentley Priory, Middlesex; **Derek Hugh Tremenheere Dowding;** Wing Commander, Royal Air Force, retired; *b* 9 Jan. 1919; *s* of (Air Chief Marshal) 1st Baron Dowding, GCB, GCVO, CMG, and Clarice Maud (*d* 1920), *d* of Captain John Williams, IA; *S* father, 1970; *m* 1st, 1940, Joan Myrle (marr. diss. 1946), *d* of Donald James Stuart, Nairn; 2nd, 1947, Alison Margaret (marr. diss. 1960), *d* of Dr James Bannerman, Norwich and *widow* of Major R. M. H. Peebles; two *s*; 3rd, 1961, Odette L. M. S. Hughes, *d* of Louis Joseph Houles. *Educ:* Winchester; RAF College, Cranwell. Served War of 1939–45, UK and Middle East; in comd No 49 (B) Sqdn, 1950; Wing Commander, 1951. Gen. Sec., Sea Cadet Assoc. (formerly Navy League), 1977–. *Heir: s* Hon. Piers Hugh Tremenheere Dowding, *b* 18 Feb. 1948. *Address:* c/o Lloyds Bank, 6 Pall Mall, SW1. *Died 22 Nov. 1992.*

DOWDING, Michael Frederick, CBE 1973; *b* 19 Nov. 1918; *s* of late Guy Francis Dowding and of Frances Constance Dowding (*née* Bragger); *m* 1947, Rosemary, *d* of Somerville Hastings, MS, FRCS; one *s* two *d. Educ:* Westminster; Magdalene Coll., Cambridge. MA Cantab. CEng, FIMechE; FIM. Served War, 1939–45, Major RA (despatches, 1945). Joined Davy & United Engineering Co., 1946: Man. Dir, 1961–64; Chm., Davy Ashmore International, 1964–70; Dir, Davy Ashmore Ltd, 1962–72; formerly Chm., Michael Dowding Associates Ltd, consulting engineers. Mem., Finnish British Technological Cttee, 1969. Vice-Pres., Iron and Steel Inst., 1965; Pres., The Metals Soc., 1978–79. Commander, Knights of Finnish Lion, 1st Class, 1969. *Publications:* various technical papers to Iron and Steel Inst. and foreign metallurgical socs. *Recreations:* painting, shooting, fishing. *Address:* Lowlands, Bath Road, Marlborough, Wilts SN8 1NR. *T:* Marlborough (0672) 513278; Bod Isaf, Aberdaron, Gwynedd. *Clubs:* Brooks's, MCC. *Died 8 Feb. 1991.*

DOWN, Barbara Langdon; *see* Littlewood, Barbara, (Lady Littlewood).

DOWNES, Ralph (William), CBE 1969; retired; Organist, Brompton Oratory, 1936–78, subseq. Organist Emeritus; appointed Curator-Organist, Royal Festival Hall, 1954; *b* 16 Aug. 1904; *s* of James William and Constance Edith Downes; *m* 1929, Agnes Mary (*née* Rix) (*d* 1980); one *s. Educ:* Derby Municipal Secondary Sch. (Scholar); Royal College of Music, London (Schol.); Keble Coll., Oxford. ARCM 1925, FRCM 1969; MA 1931, BMus 1935. Asst Organist, Southwark Cathedral, 1924; Organ Scholar, Keble Coll., 1925–28; Director of Chapel Music and Lecturer, Princeton Univ., USA, 1928–35; Organ Prof., RCM, 1954–75. Organ Curator to LCC, 1949. Consultant to: the Corporation of Croydon, 1960; Cardiff City Council (St David's Hall), 1977; Designer and Supervisor of organs in: Buckfast Abbey, 1952; Royal Festival Hall, 1954; Brompton Oratory, 1954; St John's Cathedral, Valletta, Malta, 1961; St Albans Cathedral, 1963, 1981; Fairfield Halls, 1964; Paisley Abbey, 1968; Gloucester Cathedral, 1971, and others. Recitals and performances in: Aldeburgh, 1948–85; Belgium, France, Germany, Holland, Italy, Switzerland; also radio and TV. Jury mem., organ festivals, Amsterdam, Haarlem, Munich, St Albans, Manchester. External Examiner: Birmingham Sch. of Music; RAM; Univs of Cambridge and Reading. Received into the Catholic Church, 1930. Hon. RAM 1965; Hon. FRCO 1966. KSG 1970. *Publications:* Baroque Tricks (Adventures with the Organ Builders), 1983; miscellaneous articles on the organ, compositions for keyboard and chorus.   *Died 24 Dec. 1993.*

DOWNS, Leslie Hall, CBE 1942; MA Cantab; FIMechE; Chairman, Rose, Downs & Thompson Ltd, Old Foundry, Hull, 1936–71, retired; former Chairman, Rose Downs (Holdings) Ltd, Hull; *b* 6 June 1900; *s* of late Charles Downs, Hull and Bridlington; *m* 1930, Kathleen Mary Lewis; three *d. Educ:* Abbotsholme Sch., Derbys; Christ's Coll., Cambridge (Scholar; BA 1922, MA 1927). European War, Artists' Rifles; served engineering apprenticeship and subsequently employed in various positions with Rose, Downs & Thompson Ltd; former Chm., Barnsley Canister Co. Ltd; former Vice-Chm., Davy-Ashmore Ltd; former Director: Blundell-Permoglaze (Holdings) Ltd; Ashmore Benson Pease & Co. Ltd; Power Gas Corp. Ltd. Past President Hull Chamber of Commerce and Shipping; Custodian Trustee, Hull Trustee Savings Bank; former Treasurer and Member of Council, Hull Univ., retd 1976. Hon. DSc Hull Univ. *Recreations:* fly-fishing, cabinet making, reading. *Address:* Brierley House, Hutton-le-Hole, N Yorks YO6 6UA. *T:* Lastingham (07515) 580.
Died 9 Sept. 1992.

DRAIN, Geoffrey Ayrton, CBE 1981; JP; General Secretary, National and Local Government Officers Association, 1973–83; Visiting Professor, Imperial College of Science and Technology, 1983–88; *b* 26 Nov. 1918; *s* of late Charles Henry Herbert Drain, MBE, and Ann Ayrton; *m* 1950, Dredagh Joan Rafferty (marr. diss. 1959); one *s. Educ:* Preston Grammar Sch.; Bournemouth Sch.; Skipton Grammar Sch.; Queen Mary Coll., Univ. of London (BA, LLB; Fellow, QMC, 1980). Called to Bar, Inner Temple, 1955. Served War, 1940–46. Asst Sec., Inst. of Hosp. Administrators, 1946–52; Exec., Milton Antiseptic Ltd, 1952–58; Dep. Gen.-Sec., NALGO, 1958–73; Mem. Gen. Council, TUC, 1973–83; Pres., Nat. Fedn. of Professional Workers, 1973–75; Staff Side Sec., Health Service Admin and Clerical Staffs, Whitley Council, 1962–72; Comr, Crown Prosecution Service Staff Commn, 1985–87. Director: Bank of England, 1978–86; Co-operative Press Ltd, 1983–84; Collins-Wilde, 1985–88 (Dep. Chm.); Ferguson and Partners, 1986–88 (Dep. Chm.); Home Bridging PLC, 1986–89 (Chm.); Bracken Nominees Ltd, 1986–88 (Chm.); Commercial Bridging PLC (Chm.), 1987–89; Corporate Funding Finance Ltd, 1988–89. Member: NW Metropolitan Regional Hosp. Bd and N London Hosp. Management Cttee, 1967–74; Lord Chancellor's Adv. Cttee on Legal Aid, 1974–76; Layfield Cttee of Inquiry into Local Govt Finance, 1974–76; NEDO Sector Working Party for Paper and Board Ind., 1976–88 (Chm.); Insolvency Law Review Cttee, 1976–82; Council, Industrial Soc., 1974–83; Energy Commn, 1977–79; NEDC, 1977–83; Central Arbitration Cttee, 1977–89; Cttee on Finance for Industry, 1978–83; Engrg Council, 1981–83; Exec. Cttee, Public Services Internat., 1981–85; Employment Appeal Tribunal, 1982–89; Audit Commn, 1983–88; Appeals Panel, FIMBRA (formerly NASDIM), 1985–87. Member: Bd, Volunteer Centre, 1977– (Treas.); British-North American Cttee, 1978–84; Franco British Council, 1978–88; Trilateral Commn, 1979–; Jt Hon. Treasurer, European Movement, 1979–83, Dep. Chm., 1983–90; Trustee: Community Develt Foundn, 1974–; Trident Trust, 1979–. Mem., Exec. Cttee, Age Endeavour, 1988–; Chm., Norman Hart Meml Fund, 1990–. Mem., Goldsmiths' Coll. Delegacy, 1985–88. Hampstead

Borough Councillor, 1956–58; contested (Lab) Chippenham, 1950; JP N Westminster, 1966. Freeman of City of London and Liveryman of Coopers' Company. *Publication:* The Organization and Practice of Local Government, 1966. *Recreations:* cricket, football, walking, studying birds, bridge. *Address:* Flat 3, Centre Heights, Swiss Cottage, NW3 6JG. *T:* 071–722 2081. *Clubs:* Reform, MCC.   *Died 2 April 1993.*

DRAKE, John Edmund Bernard, CBE 1973; DSC 1945; *b* 15 Nov. 1917; *s* of late D. H. C. Drake, CIE; *m* 1942, Pauline Marjory Swift; three *s. Educ:* Blundells Sch.; Exeter Coll., Oxford (BA). Served War, RNVR. Executive, Burmah-Shell, India, 1945–57; Gen. Manager, Shell Co of Ceylon, 1955; Overseas Staff Manager, Burmah Shell, 1957–62; Gen. Manager Personnel, Shell Mex and BP, 1962–69; Special Advr on Personnel Management to CS, 1970–73; Partner, Tyzack & Partners Ltd, 1974–81. *Recreations:* travel, sailing, reading, music. *Address:* Farm House, Coldharbour Lane, Hildenborough, Kent TN11 9JX. *T:* Hildenborough (0732) 832102.
Died 21 April 1991.

DRAKE-BROCKMAN, Hon. Sir Thomas Charles, Kt 1979; DFC 1944; Senator (Country Party) for West Australia, 1958–78; *b* 15 May 1919; *s* of R. J. Drake-Brockman; *m* 1st, 1942, Edith Sykes (marr. diss.); one *s* four *d*; 2nd, 1972, Mary McGinnity. *Educ:* Guildford Grammar School. Farmer, 1938; RAAF 1941. Minister for Air, 1969–72; Minister for Administrative Services and Minister for Aboriginal Affairs, Nov.-Dec. 1975; Dep. Pres. of the Senate, 1965–69, 1976–78. Gen. Pres., Nat. Country Party (WA) Inc., 1978–81; Federal Pres., Nat. Country Party of Aust., 1978–81. Former Wool President and Exec. Mem., WA Farmers' Union; Vice-Pres., Aust. Wool and Meat Producers' Fedn, 1956–57. State Pres., Australia-Britain Soc., 1982–90. *Address:* 80 Basildon Road, Lesmurdie, WA 6076, Australia.
Died 28 Aug. 1992.

DRESCHFIELD, Ralph Leonard Emmanuel, CMG 1957; QC (Uganda) 1950; *b* 18 March 1911; *s* of late Henry Theodore and Jessie Mindelle Dreschfield; unmarried. *Educ:* Merchiston Castle Sch.; Trinity Hall, Cambridge (BA). Called to the Bar, Middle Temple, 1933; entered Colonial Service, 1938, and apptd resident Magistrate, Uganda; served in War of 1939–45, in 4th King's African Rifles; Crown Counsel, Uganda, 1948; Solicitor-Gen., Uganda, 1949; Attorney-Gen., Uganda, 1951–62. Chm. Trustees of Uganda National Parks, 1952–62. Parly Counsel, Law Reform, Bermuda, 1976–79. Sec., Community Council of Essex, 1963–76. Sec., Essex Playing Fields Assoc., 1982–90. *Recreation:* yachting. *Address:* 5 Fairhaven Court, West Mersea, Colchester, Essex. *Clubs:* Royal Ocean Racing, Bar Yacht, Little Ship; West Mersea Yacht.   *Died 31 Dec. 1991.*

DREVER, James; first Principal and Vice-Chancellor, University of Dundee, 1967–78; *b* 29 Jan. 1910; *s* of late Prof. James Drever; *m* 1936, Joan Isabel Mackay Budge; one *s* one *d. Educ:* Royal High Sch., Edinburgh; Universities of Edinburgh (MA Hons Philosophy, 1932) and Cambridge (MA Moral Science Tripos, 1934). LLD Dundee, 1979. FRSE. Asst, Dept of Philosophy, Edinburgh, 1934–38; Lecturer in Philosophy and Psychology, King's Coll., Newcastle, 1938–41; Royal Navy, 1941–45; Prof. of Psychology, Univ. of Edinburgh, 1944–66. Visiting Professor, Princeton Univ., 1954–55. Editor, British Journal of Psychology, 1954–58; President: British Psychological Soc., 1960–61; Internat. Union of Scientific Psychology, 1963–66. Member: Cttee on Higher Education, 1961–63; SSRC, 1965–69; Adv. Council, Civil Service Coll., 1973–; Oil Develt Council for Scotland, 1973–77; Perm. Cttee of Conf. of European Rectors, 1975–78; Chm., Advisory Council on Social Work, in

Scotland, 1970–74. Dir, Grampian Television Ltd, 1973–80. *Publications:* papers and reviews. *Address:* East Ardblair, 494 Perth Road, Dundee DD2 1LR.

Died 5 Nov. 1991.

DREW, Sir Arthur (Charles Walter), KCB 1964 (CB 1958); Chairman, Museum of Empire and Commonwealth, since 1985; *b* 2 Sept. 1912; *er s* of late Arthur Drew, Mexico City, and Louise Schulte-Ummingen; *m* 1943, Rachel, *er d* of late G. W. Lambert, CB; one *s* three *d*. *Educ:* Christ's Hospital; King's Coll., Cambridge. Asst Principal, War Office, 1936; Private Sec. to successive Secs of State for War, 1944–49; IDC, 1949; International Staff, NATO, 1951–53; Dep. Under Sec. of State, Home Office, 1961–63; last Permanent Under Sec. of State, War Office, 1963–64; Permanent Under-Sec. of State (Army), MoD, 1964–68; Perm. Under-Sec. of State (Administration), MoD, and Mem., Admiralty, Army (from 1964) and Air Force Boards, 1968–72. Administrator, J. Paul Getty Jr Charitable Trust, 1986–88. Chairman: Beacon Hostels Housing Assoc., 1974–88; Voluntary Welfare Work Council, 1979–89. Chairman: Museums and Galls Commn (formerly Standing Commn on Museums and Galls), 1978–84 (Mem., 1973–84); Ancient Monuments Bd for England, 1978–84; Pres., Museums Assoc., 1984–86, Hon. FMA 1986; Trustee: British Museum (Natural History), 1972–83; British Museum, 1973–86; Imperial War Museum, 1973–84; Nat. Army Museum, 1975–; RAF Museum, 1976–; Member: Council, Nat. Trust, 1974–84; Historic Houses Assoc., 1981–84; Science Mus. Adv. Council, 1981–84; Council, Zool Soc., 1982–87; Historic Buildings Council, 1982–84; Historic Buildings and Monuments Commn, 1984–86. Chm. of Govs, QMC, Univ. of London, 1982–89; Fellow, QMW, 1990. Master, Drapers' Co., 1977–78. JP 1963, 1973–83, Richmond. Coronation Medal, 1953. *Recreation:* following Baedeker. *Address:* 2 Branstone Road, Kew, Surrey TW9 3LB. *T:* 081–940 1210. *Club:* Reform. *Died 15 Oct. 1993.*

DREW, John Alexander, CB 1957; *b* 19 July 1907; *s* of Charles Edward Drew, Okehampton, Devon, and Ethel Margaret Drew; *m* 1930, Edith Waud Marriott; two *s* (and one *s* decd). *Educ:* Gram. Sch., Okehampton. Entered CS, 1928; Secretaries' Office, HM Customs and Excise, 1935–40; employed on special duties, 1940–45; Asst Sec., Cabinet Office, 1945–48; Bd of Trade, 1948–50; Asst Under-Sec. of State, Ministry of Defence, 1951–67, retired, 1967. US Medal of Freedom with Bronze Palm, 1946. *Address:* 28 Montague Avenue, Sanderstead, Surrey CR2 9NH. *T:* 0181–657 3264. *Died 26 Jan. 1995.*

DREW, Lt-Gen. Sir (William) Robert (Macfarlane), KCB 1965 (CB 1962); CBE 1952 (OBE 1940); FRCP; company director, since 1977; *b* 4 Oct. 1907; *s* of late William Hughes Drew and Ethel Macfarlane; *m* 1934, Dorothy (*d* 1990), *d* of late Alfred E. Dakingsmith, Bowral, NSW; one *s* (one *d* decd). *Educ:* Sydney Gram. Sch.; Sydney Univ. (BSc 1929; MB, BS (Hons) 1930). DTM&H 1938; MRCP 1938; FRCP 1945; FRCPEd 1966; FRACP 1966; Hon. FACP 1966; Hon. FRCS 1970. Joined RAMC, 1931; one of the first House Physicians appointed at Postgrad. Med. Sch., London, 1935; served India, France (Dunkirk), Iraq, MELF; MO, War Cabinet Offices, 1943–46; Consulting Physician to the Army, 1959–60; Commandant, Royal Army Medical Coll., 1960–63; Dir of Medical Services, British Army of the Rhine, 1963–64; Dir-Gen., Army Medical Services, 1965–69; QHP, 1959–69. Dep. Dir, British Postgraduate Med. Fedn, 1970–76 (Mem. Governing Body, 1954–56, 1967–69). Leishman Prize, Royal Army Medical Coll., 1938; Goulstonian Lecturer, RCP, 1946; Mitchener Medallist, RCS, 1955; Lettsomian Lecturer, Medical Soc., London, 1961. Prof. Medicine, Royal Faculty of Med., Baghdad,

1946–52; Lectr Westminster Med. Sch., 1954–59; Pres. Clin. Section, Royal Society of Medicine, 1968–70. Hon. Sec. and later Councillor: Royal Society of Tropical Medicine and Hygiene (Pres., 1971–73); Med. Soc. of London (Pres., 1967–68); Australia and NZ Med. Assoc. (Chm.); Councillor: Royal Society of Medicine; RCP (Vice-Pres., 1970–71); Hunterian Soc.; Mem. Bd of Governors: Hospital for Sick Children, Gt Ormond Street, London; Moorfields Eye Hosp.; Royal Sch. for Daughters of Officers of the Army; Member: Assoc. Physicians Gt Britain and Ireland; Exec. Cttee, Forces Help Soc.; Control Bd, Army Benevolent Fund; Bd, Kennedy Inst. of Rheumatology; Cttee, St John Ophthalmic Hospital of Jerusalem; Cttee of Management, Sir Oswald Stoll Foundn; Mem. Council, Royal Blind Soc., NSW, 1978–; Mem., Aust. Soc. of Genealogists, 1978–. Life Member: Dunkirk Veterans Assoc.; Officers' Pension Soc.; HM Comr, The Royal Hosp., Chelsea, 1965–69 and 1970–76. Orator: York Med. Soc., 1963; Harrogate Med. Soc., 1963; Hunterian, Hunterian Soc., 1966. Extraordinary Mem., Assoc. of Clin. Pathologists; Hon. Member: Sydney Univ. Med. Soc., 1965; Anglo-German Med. Soc., 1970; Founder Mem., Sydney Univ. Med. Graduates' Assoc., 1988–; Foundation Mem., Silver Soc. of Australia, 1988–. Trustee, Commonwealth Philharmonic Orch. Trust, 1974–; Mem. Aust. Ctte, Australian Musical Foundn in London, 1985. Mem. Chapter-Gen., Order of St John, 1977–84; KStJ 1977 (CStJ 1965). FRSA 1965. Comdr Order of El-Rafidain (Iraq), 1951. *Publications:* Roll of Medical Officers in the British Army 1660–1960, 1968; articles in medical journals. *Recreations:* travel, gardening. *Address:* 5B and 5C Wakefield Apartments, 26–28 Etham Avenue, Darling Point, NSW 2027, Australia. *Clubs:* Army and Navy (Hon. Life Mem.); Australian (Hon. Librarian, 1983–), Royal Sydney Golf (Sydney).

Died 27 July 1991.

DREYFUS, Pierre; Grand Officier, Légion d'Honneur; Conseiller à la Président de la République, since 1982; *b* Paris, 18 Nov. 1907; *s* of Emmanuel Dreyfus, banker, and Madeleine (*née* Bernard); *m* 1936, Laure Ullmo; one *d*. *Educ:* Lycée Janson-de-Sailly; Faculty of Law, Univ. of Paris (Dip., Dr of Law). Inspector-Gen. of Industry and Commerce, Chief of Gen. Inspectorate, and Dir of Cabinet to Minister of Industry and Commerce, M Robert Lacoste, 1947–49; Pres., Commn of Energy of the Plan, and Dir of the Cabinet to Minister of Industry and Commerce, M Bourgès-Maunoury, 1954. President: Houillères de Lorraine, 1950–55; Charbonnages de France, 1954; Société des Aciers Fins de l'Est, 1955. President Director-General, Régie Nationale des Usines Renault, 1955–75; Pres., Renault-Finance, 1976–80; Minister of Industry, 1981–82. *Address:* 12 rue Duroc, 75007 Paris, France.

Died 25 Dec. 1994.

DRING, Lt-Col Sir (Arthur) John, KBE 1952; CIE 1943; JP; DL; *b* 4 Nov. 1902; *s* of late Sir William Arthur Dring, KCIE, VD and Jane Reid Greenshields Alston; *m* 1st, 1934, Marjorie Wadham (*d* 1943); two *d*; 2nd, 1946, Alice Deborah, *o d* of late Maj.-Gen. Gerald Cree, CB, CMG, and *widow* of Maj.-Gen. John Stuart Marshall, CB, DSO, OBE. *Educ:* Winchester Coll.; RMC, Sandhurst. Joined Guides Cavalry, 1923; Indian Political Service, 1927; Asst Private Sec. to Viceroy, 1930–32; Deputy Commissioner, Dera Ismail Khan, 1935–36; Sec. to Governor, NWFP, 1937–40; Political Agent, South Waziristan, 1940–42 (despatches); Sec. to NWFP Govt Development Depts; Revenue Commissioner, NWFP; Chief Sec. NWFP, 1947; Prime Minister of Bahawalpur, 1948–52; Adviser to Governor of Gold Coast on Togoland Plebiscite, 1955–56. Adviser to Governor-Gen. of Nigeria and the Governor of the Northern Region for the N and S Cameroons Plebiscite, 1959. JP 1954, DL 1973, Hants. *Recreations:* riding,

gardening. *Address:* Ava Cottage, Purbrook, Hants PO7 5RX. *T:* Waterlooville (0705) 263000.
Died 16 June 1991.

DRINKROW, John; *see under* Hardwick, Michael.

DRUMMOND, William Norman, CB 1987; Under Secretary (formerly Deputy Secretary), Department of Economic Development (formerly Department of Commerce), Northern Ireland, 1979–87; *b* 10 July 1927; *s* of Thomas and Martha Drummond, Lurgan; *m* 1958, Pamela Joyce Burnham; two *d. Educ:* Lurgan Coll.; Queen's Univ. Belfast (BSc (Hons)). Physicist, Iraq Petroleum Co., Kirkuk, Iraq, 1950–54; Reed's Sch., Cobham, 1954–57; Northern Ireland Civil Service, 1957–87: Dep. Sec., Dept of Manpower Services, NI, 1974–79. Chm., Public Service Training Council, 1988–. Mem., Planning Appeals Commn (NI), 1988–. *Recreations:* gardening, reading. *Address:* 8 Magheralave Park East, Lisburn BT28 3BT. *T:* Lisburn (0846) 664104.
Died 10 Aug. 1993.

DRURY, Hon. Charles Mills, OC 1981; CBE 1946 (MBE 1942); DSO 1944; ED 1956; PC 1963; Chairman, National Capital Commission, Canada, 1978; *b* 17 May 1912; *s* of Victor Montague Drury, Montreal, and Pansy Jessie Mills, Ottawa; *m* 1939, Jane Ferrier Counsell (decd); two *s* two *d. Educ:* Bishops Coll. Sch., Lennoxville, Quebec; Royal Military Coll. of Canada, Kingston, Ontario; McGill Univ., Montreal (BCL); University of Paris, France. Practised at law, 1936–39; served War of 1939–45, Canadian Army (final rank Brig.). Chief of UNRRA Mission to Poland, 1945–46; Dept of External Affairs, Canada, 1947–48; Dep. Minister of National Defence, Canada, 1949–55; Pres. and Man. Dir, Provincial Transport Co., 1955–60; Pres., Avis Transport of Canada Ltd, 1960–62; MP (L), Montreal St Antoine-Westmount, 1962–78; Minister, Dept of Defence Production, and Minister of Industry, 1963–68; Pres., Treasury Bd, 1968–74; Minister of Public Works, Canada, and Minister of State for Science and Technol., 1974–76; responsible for Nat. Res. Council of Canada, 1963–76. Chevalier de la Légion d'Honneur (France), 1946; Order of Polonia Restituta (Poland), 1946. *Address:* 71 Somerset Street West, Apt 1002, Ottawa, Ont K2P 2G2, Canada. *Club:* St James (Montreal).
Died 12 Jan. 1991.

DuBRIDGE, Lee A(lvin); President, 1946–69, President Emeritus, 1969, California Institute of Technology, Pasadena; *b* 21 Sept. 1901; *s* of Frederick A. and Elizabeth Browne DuBridge; *m* 1st, 1925, Doris May Koht (*d* 1973); one *s* one *d*; 2nd, 1974, Arrola B. Cole. *Educ:* Cornell Coll., Mt Vernon, Ia (BA); University of Wisconsin (MA, PhD). Instructor in Physics, University of Wisconsin, 1925–26; Nat. Research Council Fellow at Calif Inst. of Tech., 1926–28; Asst Prof. Physics, Washington Univ. (St Louis, Mo), 1928–33; Associate Prof., Washington Univ., 1933–34; Prof. of Physics and Dep. Chm., University of Rochester (NY), 1934–46; Dean of Faculty, University of Rochester, 1938–42; on leave from University of Rochester, 1940–45, as Dir of Radiation Lab. of Nat. Def. Research Cttee, MIT, Cambridge; Science Adviser to President of USA, 1969–70. Hon. ScD: Cornell Coll.; Mt Vernon, Iowa, 1940; Wesleyan Univ., Middletown, Conn, 1946; Polytechnic Inst. of Brooklyn, New York, 1946; University of Brit. Columbia, Can., 1947; Washington Univ., St Louis, Mo, 1948; Occidental Coll., 1952; Maryland, 1955; Columbia, 1957; Indiana, 1957; Wisconsin, 1957; Pennsylvania Mil. Coll., Chester, Pa, 1962; DePauw, Indiana, 1962; Pomona Coll., Claremont, Calif, 1965; Carnegie Inst. of Techn., Pittsburgh, 1965; Hon. LLD: California, 1948; Rochester, 1953; Southern California, 1957; Northwestern, 1958; Loyola, Los Angeles, 1963; Notre Dame, Indiana, 1967; Illinois Inst. Technology, 1968; Hon. LHD: University Judaism, Los Angeles, 1958; Redlands, 1958; Hon. DCL Union Coll., Schenectady, NY, 1961; Hon. DSc: Rockefeller Institute, NY, 1965; Tufts Univ., 1969; Syracuse Univ., 1969; Rensselaer Polytech. Inst., 1970. King's Medal, 1946; Research Corp. Award, 1947; Medal for Merit of US Govt, 1948; Golden Key Award, 1959; Leif Erikson Award, 1959; Arthur Noble Award, 1961; Golden Plate Award, 1973; Vannevar Bush Award, 1982. *Publications:* Photoelectric Phenomena (with A. L. Hughes), 1932; New Theories of Photoelectric Effect (Paris), 1934; Introduction to Space, 1960; articles in various scientific and other journals. *Address:* 1563 Royal Oaks Drive, Duarte, Calif 91110, USA. *Clubs:* Sunset (Los Angeles); Bohemian (San Francisco).
Died 23 Jan. 1994.

Du CANN, Richard Dillon Lott, QC 1975; a Recorder of the Crown Court, 1982–92; *b* 27 Jan. 1929; *yr s* of late C. G. L. Du Cann; *m* 1955, Charlotte Mary Sawtell; two *s* two *d. Educ:* Steyning Grammar Sch.; Clare Coll., Cambridge. Called to Bar, Gray's Inn, 1953; Bencher, 1980; Treasury Counsel, Inner London QS, 1966–70; Treasury Counsel, Central Criminal Court, 1970–75. Chairman: Criminal Bar Assoc., 1977–80; Bar of England and Wales, 1980–81. *Publications:* (with B. Hayhoe) The Young Marrieds, 1954; The Art of the Advocate, 1964. *Address:* 3 Raymond Buildings, Gray's Inn, WC1R 5BH. *T:* 071–831 3833.
Died 4 Aug. 1994.

DUCIE, 6th Earl of, *cr* 1837; **Basil Howard Moreton;** Baron Ducie, 1763; Baron Moreton, 1837; *b* 15 Nov. 1917; *s* of Hon. Algernon Howard Moreton (2nd *s* of 4th Earl) (*d* 1951), and Dorothy Edith Annie, *d* of late Robert Bell; *S* uncle 1952; *m* 1950, Alison May, *d* of L. A. Bates, Pialba, Queensland; three *s* one *d. Heir: s* Lord Moreton [*b* 20 Sept. 1951; *m* 1975, Helen, *er d* of M. L. Duchesne; one *s* one *d*]. *Address:* Tortworth House, Tortworth, Wotton-under-Edge, Glos.
Died 12 Nov. 1991.

DUCKER, Herbert Charles, BSc London; NDA; Field Officer Groundnut Research, under the Federal Ministry of Agriculture, Rhodesia and Nyasaland, retired; *b* 13 May 1900; *s* of Charles Richard and Gertrude Louise Ducker; *m* 1925, Marjorie, *y d* of late Charles Tuckfield, AMICE; two *s* one *d. Educ:* Kingston Grammar Sch., Kingston-on-Thames; South-Eastern Agricultural Coll., Wye; Imperial Coll. of Science, South Kensington. British Cotton Industry Research Assoc. Laboratories; Asst Cotton Specialist, Nyasaland, 1922; Cotton Specialist, Empire Cotton Growing Corporation, Nyasaland, 1925–56; Superintendent-Curator of the National Botanic Gardens, Salisbury, Southern Rhodesia, under the Federal Ministry of Agriculture, of Rhodesia and Nyasaland, 1957. *Publications:* Annual Reports on Cotton Research work 1925–55, carried out in Nyasaland; articles on cotton growing. *Recreation:* fishing. *Address:* Pleasant Ways, MP 13, Mount Pleasant, Harare, Zimbabwe. *Club:* Royal Over-Seas League.
Died 1 July 1993.

DUCKMANTON, Sir Talbot (Sydney), Kt 1980; CBE 1971; General Manager, Australian Broadcasting Commission, 1965–82 (Deputy General Manager, 1964–65); *b* 26 Oct. 1921; *s* of Sydney James Duckmanton; *m* 1947, Florence Simmonds (*d* 1978); one *s* three *d; m* 1979, Janet Strickland (marr. diss. 1981), *d* of R. Cohen; *m* 1984, Carolyn Wright (marr. diss.), *d* of R. Pumfrey). Joined Australian Broadcasting Commission, 1939. War Service: AIF and RAAF. President: Asia-Pacific Broadcasting Union, 1973–77; Commonwealth Broadcasting Assoc., 1975–82. Pres., Sydney Legacy, 1964–65; Mem. Council, Aust. Administrative Staff Coll., 1967–82. Trustee, Visnews, 1965–82; Hon. Life Trustee, Cttee for Economic Develt of Australia. FAIM. *Address:* PO Box A2148, Sydney South, NSW 2000, Australia. *Clubs:* Legacy, Australian, City Tattersall's (Sydney).
Died 12 June 1995.

DUFF, Patrick William; Fellow of Trinity College, Cambridge; *b* 21 Feb. 1901; 3rd *s* of J. D. Duff, Fellow of Trinity College, Cambridge, and Laura, *d* of Sir William Lenox-Conyngham, KCB. *Educ:* Winchester; Trinity Coll., Cambridge; Munich Univ.; Harvard Law Sch. 1st Class, Classical Tripos Parts I and II; Craven and Whewell Scholar; Tancred Scholar of Lincoln's Inn. Called to the Bar, 1933. Fellow of Trinity Coll., Cambridge, 1925; Lecturer, 1927; Tutor, 1938; Senior Tutor, 1945; Dean of Coll., 1950; Vice-Master, 1960; Regius Prof. of Civil Law, Cambridge, 1945–68; Fellow of Winchester Coll., 1948–76; Warden, 1959–62. Pres. Soc. of Public Teachers of Law, 1957–58. Hon. Bencher of Lincoln's Inn, 1959. Cambridge Borough Councillor, 1947–51. *Publications:* The Charitable Foundations of Byzantium (in Cambridge Legal Essays presented to Dr Bond, Prof. Buckland and Prof. Kenny), 1926; The Personality of an Idol (in Cambridge Law Journal), 1927; Delegata Potestas Non Potest Delegari (in Cornell Law Quarterly), 1929; Personality in Roman Private Law, 1938; Roman Law Today (in Tulane Law Review), 1947. *Recreation:* scouting. *Address:* Trinity College, Cambridge.
Died 28 Aug. 1991.

DUFFERIN AND CLANDEBOYE, 10th Baron *cr* 1800 (Ire.); **Francis George Blackwood;** Bt (Ire.) 1763; Bt (UK) 1814; retired chemical engineer; in private practice as a consulting engineer; *b* 20 May 1916; *s* of Captain Maurice Baldwin Raymond Blackwood, DSO, RN (*d* 1941) (3rd *s* of 4th Bt) and Dorothea (*d* 1967), *d* of Hon. G. Bertrand Edwards, Sydney, NSW; *S* to baronetcy of cousin, 1979 and to barony of kinsman, 5th Marquess of Dufferin and Ava, 1988; *m* 1941, Margaret Alice, *d* of Hector Kirkpatrick, Lindfield, NSW; two *s* one *d. Educ:* Knox Grammar School; Sydney Technical Coll. (ASTC). ARACI, FIEAust. Worked in the chemical industry, mainly for Union Carbide, Australia Ltd (formerly Timbrol Ltd) as a design engineer, 1936–78. *Recreations:* community service and domestic. *Heir: s* Hon. John Francis Blackwood, architect [*b* 18 Oct. 1944; *m* 1971, Kay Greenhill; one *s* one *d.*]. *Address:* 408 Bobbin Head Road, North Turramurra, NSW 2074, Australia. *T:* 44 5189. *Club:* Royal Automobile of Australia.
Died 13 Nov. 1991.

DUFTY, (Arthur) Richard, CBE 1971; FSA; Master of the Armouries in HM Tower of London, 1963–76; *b* 23 June 1911; *s* of T. E. Dufty and Beatrice (*née* Holmes); *m* 1st, 1937, Kate Brazley (*née* Ainsworth) (*d* 1991); one *s* two *d*; 2nd, 1991, Jean Wells (*née* Hughes). *Educ:* Rugby; Liverpool School of Architecture. War service in RN. On staff of Royal Commn on Historical Monuments, 1937–73, Sec. and Gen. Editor 1962–73, with responsibility for Nat. Monuments Record, inc. Nat. Buildings Record, 1964–73. Pres., Soc. of Antiquaries, 1978–81; Member: Ancient Monuments Bd for England, 1962–73 and 1977–80; Council for Places of Worship, 1976–81; Council, Nat. Army Museum, 1963–83; Royal Commn on Historical Monuments, 1975–85. Vice-Chm., Cathedrals Advisory Commission, 1981–88. Chairman: Farnham (Buildings Preservation) Trust, 1968–91 (recipient of The Times Conservation Award, 1986); British Cttee, Corpus Vitrearum Medii Aevi, 1970–84 (sponsored by British Acad.); London Dio. Adv. Cttee, 1973–84; Standing Cttee on Conservation of West Front of Wells Cathedral, 1974–85. Trustee: Coll. of Arms Trust, 1978–; Marc Fitch Fund, 1978–. Directed, for Soc. of Antiquaries, repair and rehabilitation of Kelmscott, William Morris's home in Oxfordshire, 1964–67. Hon. Freeman, Armourers and Brasiers' Co., 1974. Hon. Mem., Art Workers' Guild, 1977. ARIBA 1935–74; FSA 1946. DLitt Lambeth, 1988. London Conservation Award, GLC, 1984. *Publications:* Kelmscott Manor: an illustrated guide, 1970; Morris Embroideries: the prototypes, 1985; Exoticism and a Chair

by Philip Webb, 1986; Account of St George's Church, Kelmscott, 1991; ed 5 RCHM Inventories and 5 occasional publications; Introductory Vol. to Morris's Story of Cupid and Psyche, 1974. *Recreations:* viewing sales, taking pleasure in Victoriana and Art Nouveau, music. *Address:* Church Cottage, Kelmscott, Oxon GL7 3HE. *Clubs:* Athenæum, Naval.
Died 5 Oct. 1993.

DUGDALE, Sir John (Robert Stratford), KCVO 1994; Lord-Lieutenant of Shropshire, 1975–94; *b* 10 May 1923; 2nd *s* of Sir William Francis Stratford Dugdale, 1st Bt, and Margaret, 2nd *d* of Sir Robert Gordon Gilmour, 1st Bt; *m* 1956, Kathryn Edith Helen, *d* of Rt Hon. Oliver Stanley, MC, PC; two *s* two *d. Educ:* Eton; Christ Church, Oxford. Chm., Telford Develt Corp., 1971–75. KStJ 1976. *Recreation:* sleeping. *Address:* Tickwood Hall, Much Wenlock, Salop TF13 6NZ. *T:* Telford (01952) 882644. *Clubs:* Brooks's, White's.
Died 13 Dec. 1994.

DUGDALE, Norman, CB 1974; Trustee, The Pushkin Prizes, since 1987; Permanent Secretary, Department (formerly Ministry) of Health and Social Services, Northern Ireland, 1970–84; *b* 6 Feb. 1921; *yr s* of William and Eva Dugdale, Burnley, Lancs; *m* 1949, Mary Whitehead. *Educ:* Burnley Grammar Sch.; Manchester Univ. (BA). Asst Principal, Bd of Trade, 1941; Min. of Commerce, NI, 1948; Asst Sec., Min. of Health and Local Govt, NI, 1955; Sen. Asst Sec., Min. of Health and Local Govt, NI, 1964; Second Sec., Min. of Health and Social Services, 1968. Chm., Bryson House, Belfast, 1985–93. Mem. Bd, British Council, 1986–92 (founder Mem., 1987–, Chm., 1988–92, NI Cttee). Governor, Nat. Inst. for Social Work, London, 1965–84; Mem. Court, NUU, 1971–84. Hon. DLitt NUU, 1983. *Publications:* poems: The Disposition of the Weather, 1967; A Prospect of the West, 1970; Night-Ferry, 1974; Corncrake in October, 1978; Running Repairs, 1983; Limbo, 1991; contribs to various literary periodicals. *Recreations:* procrastinating, next week-end.
Died 27 Oct. 1995.

DUKE, Maj.-Gen. Sir Gerald (William), KBE 1966 (CBE 1945); CB 1962; DSO 1945; DL; *b* 12 Nov. 1910; *e s* of late Lieut-Col A. A. G. Duke, Indian Army; *m* 1946, Mary Elizabeth (*d* 1979), *er d* of late E. M. Burn, Church Stretton; one *s* one *d. Educ:* Dover Coll.; RMA Woolwich; Jesus Coll., Cambridge. Commissioned RE, 1931; served Egypt and Palestine, 1936–39; War of 1939–45, in Western Desert and Italy; BGS Eighth Army, 1944; North West Europe, Brig. Q (Movements), 21st Army Group, 1944; CRE 49th Div., 1945; Chief Engineer, Malaya Comd, 1946; idc 1948; Mil. Attaché, Cairo, 1952–54; Comdt Sch. of Mil. Engineering, 1956–59; DPS, WO, 1959–62; Engineer-in-Chief (Army), 1963.–65; retired. Col Comdt, RE, 1966–75; Commodore Royal Engineer Yacht Club, 1957–60. Chm., SS&AFA, Kent, 1973–85; Pres., Scout Assoc., Kent, 1974–86; Vice-Pres., Hockey Assoc., 1965–. Governor of Dover Coll. FICE. DL Kent, 1970. *Recreations:* sailing, golf. *Address:* Skaith, Newton Stewart, Wigtownshire DG8 0QP. *T:* Newton Stewart (0671) 2774. *Clubs:* Royal Ocean Racing; Rye Golf.
Died 30 April 1992.

DULVERTON, 2nd Baron, *cr* 1929, of Batsford; **Frederick Anthony Hamilton Wills,** CBE 1974; TD; DL; MA Oxon; Bt 1897; *b* 19 Dec. 1915; *s* of 1st Baron Dulverton, OBE, and Victoria May, OBE (*d* 1968), 3rd *d* of Rear-Adm. Sir Edward Chichester, 9th Bt, CB, CMG; *S* father, 1956; *m* 1st, 1939, Judith Betty (marr. diss. 1960; she *d* 1983), *e d* of late Lieut-Col Hon. Ian Leslie Melville, TD; two *s* one *d* (and one *d* decd); 2nd, 1962, Ruth Violet, *o d* of Sir Walter Farquhar, 5th Bt. *Educ:* Eton; Magdalen Coll., Oxford (MA; Waynflete Fellow, 1982). Commissioned Lovat Scouts (TA), 1935; Major, 1943. President: Timber Growers' Orgn Ltd, 1976–78; Bath and West and Southern Counties Agric. Soc., 1973; British

Deer Soc., 1973–87; Three Counties Agric. Soc., 1975; Gloucestershire Trust for Nature Conservation, 1979–; Member, Red Deer Commn, 1972–87; Chairman: Forestry Cttee of GB, 1978–80; Dulverton Trust, 1956–; Trustee, Wildfowl Trust; former Trustee, World Wildlife Fund (UK); Hon. Pres., Timber Growers UK, 1983–. Joint Master: N Cotswold Foxhounds, 1950–56; Heythrop Foxhounds, 1967–70. DL Gloucester, 1979. Commander, Order of Golden Ark (Netherlands), 1985. *Heir: s* Hon. (Gilbert) Michael Hamilton Wills [*b* 2 May 1944; *m* 1980, Rosalind van der Velde-Oliver; one *s* one *d*]. *Address:* Batsford Park, Moreton-in-Marsh, Glos. *T:* Moreton-in-Marsh (0608) 50303; Fassfern, Kinlocheil, Fort William, Inverness-shire. *T:* Kinlocheil (039783) 232. *Clubs:* Boodle's, Pratt's, Army and Navy.

Died 17 Feb. 1992.

DULY, Sidney John, MA; consultant on the carriage of goods by sea; *b* London, 30 Oct. 1891; *s* of Henry Charles and Emily Marion Duly; *m* 1916, Florence Lily Smith (*d* 1980). *Educ:* St Olave's Grammar Sch.; Corpus Christi Coll., Cambridge; Berlin Univ. (Advanced Physics under Rector Prof. Max Planck, 1913–14). War, 1914–18: involved with manufacture of TNT and gun-cotton, and chosen by Stafford Cripps to manage largest contract ever placed for sulphuric acid and oleum, United Alkali Co. Ltd, Widnes, Flint and St Helens; War, 1939–45: Sqdn Ldr; worked on Operation Enigma; with US Strategic Air Force, took surrender of German Air Force Gen. Staff. Head, Dept for Scientific Study of Commercial Products, City of London Coll., 1918–45. Sole Scientific Consultant, Shipowners' Protection and Indemnity Assoc., 1919–68; dealt with over 1,200 cases of cargo damage, covering world's cargo ships (40 cases were decided in court on author's scientific evidence in favour of shipowners); main discovery was that cargoes, in order to be kept rust- and mould-free, and at no extra cost, must not be ventilated when the dew point of the atmosphere is greater than the temperature of the cargo (George V Medal, 1926). Fellow, Inst. of Refrigeration. *Publication:* The Natural Wealth of Britain. *Address:* 34 Sheldon Court, Bath Road, Worthing, West Sussex BN11 3PB. *Club:* Royal Air Force.

Died 25 June 1991.

DUNALLEY, 6th Baron *cr* 1800 (Ire.), of Kilboy, Tipperary; **Henry Desmond Graham Prittie;** Lieutenant-Colonel (retired); late The Rifle Brigade; *b* 14 Oct. 1912; *er s* of 5th Baron Dunalley, DSO, and Beatrix Evelyn (*d* 1967), *e d* of late James N. Graham of Carfin, Lanarkshire; *S* father, 1948; *m* 1947, Philippa, *o d* of late Hon. Philip Cary; two *s* one *d*. *Educ:* Stowe; RMC, Sandhurst. Retd 1953. *Recreation:* fishing. *Heir: s* Hon. Henry Francis Cornelius Prittie [*b* 30 May 1948; *m* 1978, Sally Louise, *er d* of Ronald Vere; one *s* three *d*]. *Address:* Church End House, Swerford, Oxfordshire OX7 4AX. *T:* Hook Norton (0608) 730005. *Clubs:* Kildare Street and University (Dublin); Christchurch (NZ) (Hon. Mem.).

Died 26 June 1992.

DUNBAR of Mochrum, Sir Jean Ivor, 13th Bt *cr* 1694 (NS), of Mochrum, Wigtownshire; *b* 4 April 1918; *s* of Sir Adrian Ivor Dunbar of Mochrum, 12th Bt and Emma Marie (*d* 1925), *d* of Jean Wittevrongel; *S* father, 1977; *m* 1st, 1944, Rose Jeanne (marr. diss. 1979), *d* of Henry William Hertsch; two *s* one *d*; 2nd, 1987, Vivianna Patricia (marr. diss.). Formerly Sergeant, Mountain Engineers, US Army. *Recreation:* horsemanship. *Heir: s* Col James Michael Dunbar, USAF [*b* 17 Jan. 1950; *m* 1st, 1978, Margaret Jacobs (decd); two *s* one *d*; 2nd, 1989, Margaret, *d* of Roger Gordon Talbot; one *d*].

Died 15 Aug. 1993.

DUNCAN, Prof. Archibald Sutherland, DSC 1943; FRCSE, FRCPE, FRCOG; Executive Dean of the Faculty of Medicine and Professor of Medical Education,

Edinburgh University, 1966–76, then Emeritus; *b* 17 July 1914; *y s* of late Rev. H. C. Duncan, K-i-H, DD and Rose Elsie Edwards; *m* 1939, Barbara, *d* of late John Gibson Holliday, JP, Penrith, Cumberland. *Educ:* Merchiston Castle Sch.; Edinburgh Univ. MB, ChB Edinburgh, 1936. Resident hosp. appts in Edinburgh and London, 1936–41. Served RNVR, Surg. Lieut-Comdr (surg. specialist), 1941–45 (DSC). Temp. Cons. in Obs and Gynæ., Inverness, 1946; Lectr in Univ. and part-time Cons. Obstetrician and Gynæcologist, Aberdeen, 1946–50; Sen. Lectr, University of Edinburgh, and Obstetr. and Gynæcol. to Western Gen. Hosp., Edinburgh 1950–53; Prof. of Obstetrics and Gynæcology in the Welsh National Sch. of Medicine, Univ. of Wales, 1953–66; Cons. Obstetrician and Gynæcologist, United Cardiff Hosps, 1953–66; Advisor in Obstetrics and Gynæcology to Welsh Hosp. Board, 1953–66. Member: Clin. Res. Bd of MRC, 1965–69; Council, RCSE, 1968–73; GMC, 1974–78; Lothian Health Bd, 1977–83 (Vice-Chm., 1981–83). Chm., Scottish Council on Disability, 1977–80. Vice-Pres., Inst. of Medical Ethics, 1985–. Hon. Pres., Brit. Med. Students Assoc., 1965–66. Mem. Court, Edinburgh Univ., 1979–83; Hon. Pres. (life), Graduates' Assoc., Edinburgh Univ., 1986. Mem., James IV Assoc. of Surgeons; Hon. Mem., Alpha Omega Alpha Honor Med. Soc. Hon. MD Edinburgh, 1984. Associate Editor, British Jl of Medical Education, 1971–75; Consulting Editor, Jl of Medical Ethics, 1975–81. *Publications:* (ed jtly) Dictionary of Medical Ethics, 1977, 2nd edn 1981; contribs on scientific and allied subjects in various med. jls and books. *Recreations:* mountains, photography. *Address:* 1 Walker Street, Edinburgh EH3 7JY. *T:* 031–225 7657. *Club:* New (Edinburgh).

Died 1 Oct. 1992.

DUNCAN, Michael John Freeman; HM Diplomatic Service, retired; *b* 9 Jan. 1926; *s* of late John Colley Duncan and of Blanche (*née* Freeman); *m* 1964, Sally Ilbert Crosse; one *s* one *d*. *Educ:* Hurstpierpoint (Scholar); Christ Church, Oxford (Scholar; MA); Ecole Nationale des Langues Orientales, Paris (Diplôme des Langues Slaves). Attaché, Moscow, 1949; entered HM Diplomatic Service, 1951; FO, 1951; Germany, 1952; FO, 1954; Moscow, 1959; FO, 1961; UN Disarmament Conf., Geneva, 1964; FO, 1966; Caracas, 1969; FCO, 1973; Counsellor, Moscow, 1982–83; Regional Dir, Res. Dept, FCO, 1983–87. Vis. Fellow, Centre for Caribbean Studies, Warwick Univ., 1987–88. Order of St Cecilia, Estado de Miranda, Venezuela, 1972. *Publications:* Ilf and Petrov, 1964; The Bay Island or The Gentle Art of Cutting the Paper, 1990; *translations:* Trotsky Papers, 1964; Paustovsky, Story of a Life, 1964; Lydia Ginzburg, Within the Whirlwind, 1981; E. B. Pasternak, Boris Pasternak: the tragic years, 1990; various articles. *Recreations:* reading, linguistics, mushrooms, gardening. *Address:* c/o Lloyds Bank, 39 Threadneedle Street, EC2R 8AU.

Died 6 May 1991.

DUNDAS, Sir Hugh (Spencer Lisle), Kt 1987; CBE 1977; DSO 1944 and Bar 1945; DFC 1941; DL; Royal Air Force, retired; Chairman, 1982–87; Managing Director, 1973–82, Deputy Chairman, 1981–82, BET Public Limited Company; *b* 22 July 1920; *s* of late Frederick James Dundas and Sylvia Mary (*née* March-Phillipps); *m* 1950, Hon. Enid Rosamond Lawrence, 2nd *d* of 1st Baron Oaksey and 3rd Baron Trevethin; one *s* two *d*. *Educ:* Stowe. Joined 616 (S Yorks) Sqdn AAF 1939; served in UK Fighter Comd Sqdns, 1939–43; N Africa, Malta, Sicily, Italy, 1943–46; perm. commn 1944; comd 244 Wing, Italy, 1944–46 (Gp Captain; despatches 1945); retd 1947. Comd 601 (Co. London) Sqdn RAuxAF, 1947–50. Beaverbrook Newspapers, 1948–60: various editorial and managerial posts; joined Exec. Staff, Rediffusion Ltd, 1961: Dir, 1966; Dep. Man. Dir, 1968; Man. Dir, 1970–74; Chm., 1978–85; Chm., Thames Television Ltd, 1981–87

(Dir, 1968–87). Mem. Council, and F and GP Cttee, RAF Benevolent Fund, 1976–89; Cancer Relief Macmillan Fund (formerly Nat. Soc. for Cancer Relief): Mem. Council, 1976– (Chm., 1988–91); Trustee, 1983–89; Chm., Bd of Management, 1989–91; Vice-Pres., 1991–. Trustee: Prince's Youth Business Trust (Chm. of Trustees, 1987–90); Home Farm Trust Develt Trust, 1987–90. DL 1969, High Sheriff 1989, Surrey. *Publication:* Flying Start (autobiog.), 1988. *Address:* 55 Iverna Court, W8 6TS. *T:* 0171–937 0773; The Schoolroom, Dockenfield, Farnham, Surrey GU10 4HX. *T:* Farnham (01252) 792331. *Clubs:* White's, Royal Air Force. *Died 10 July 1995.*

DUNKERLEY, George William, MC 1942; Chairman, Oil and Pipelines Agency, 1985–88; Director: STC plc, 1985–89; Scandinavian Bank Group plc, 1986–89; *b* 14 June 1919; *s* of Harold and Eva Dunkerley; *m* 1947, Diana Margaret Lang; two *s. Educ:* Felsted School, Essex. FCA. War Service, 1939–46, with RA (The Northumberland Hussars) in N Africa, Sicily, Northern Europe; Major. With Peat Marwick Mitchell & Co., 1948–85, Dep. Senior Partner (UK), 1982–85. *Recreations:* gardening, forestry, travel. *Address:* 31 The Priory, Priory Road, Abbots Kerswell, Newton Abbot, Devon TQ12 5PP. *Club:* Lansdowne. *Died 29 Aug. 1994.*

DUNKLEY, Captain James Lewis, CBE 1970 (OBE 1946); RD 1943; Marine Manager, P&O Lines, 1971–72 (Marine Superintendent, 1968–71); *b* 13 Sept. 1908; *s* of William E. Dunkley, Thurlaston Grange, Warwickshire; *m* 1937, Phyllis Mary Cale; one *d. Educ:* Lawrence Sheriff Sch., Rugby; Thames Nautical Training Coll., HMS Worcester. Junior Officer, P&O Line, 1928; Captain, 1954; Cdre, 1964. RNR: Sub-Lt, 1931; Comdr, 1951; Captain, 1956. Master, Honourable Co. of Master Mariners, 1970. *Recreations:* gardening, collecting. *Address:* 1 Collindale Gardens, Clacton-on-Sea, Essex CO15 5BH. *T:* Clacton-on-Sea (0255) 813950. *Club:* City Livery. *Died 26 Sept. 1994.*

DUNLEATH, 4th Baron, *cr* 1892; **Charles Edward Henry John Mulholland,** TD; Chairman: Dunleath Estates Ltd; Ulster & General Holdings Ltd; Vice Lord-Lieutenant of County Down, since 1990; *b* 23 June 1933; *s* of 3rd Baron Dunleath, CBE, DSO, and 2nd wife, Henrietta Grace (*d* 1969), *d* of late Most Rev. C. F. D'Arcy, Archbishop of Armagh; *S* father, 1956; *m* 1959, Dorinda Margery, *d* of late Lieut-Gen. A. E. Percival, CB, DSO and Bar, OBE, MC. *Educ:* Eton; Cambridge Univ. Served with 11th Hussars, 1952–53, with N Irish Horse, 1954–69, Lt-Col 1967–69; Captain, Ulster Defence Regt, 1971–73; Lt-Col, North Irish Horse, RARO, 1973–88, Hon. Col 1981–86. Member (Alliance): N Down, NI Assembly, 1973–75; N Down, NI Constitutional Convention, 1975–76; resigned from Alliance Party, 1979, rejoined 1981; Mem. (Alliance) for N Down, and Asst Speaker, NI Assembly, 1982–86. Mem., Ards Borough Council, 1977–81 (Independent 1979–81). Chairman: Carreras Rothmans of NI, 1974–84; NI Independent Television Ltd, 1979–83; Dir, Northern Bank Ltd, 1974–91. Governor of BBC for N Ireland, 1967–73; Mem. Admin. Council, King George's Jubilee Trust, 1974–75; President: Royal Ulster Agric. Soc., 1973–76; Lagan Coll., 1982–86. DL Co. Down, 1964. *Heir:* cousin Major Sir Michael (Henry) Mulholland, 2nd Bt [*b* 15 Oct. 1915; *m* 1st, 1942, Rosemary Ker (marr. diss. 1948); 2nd, 1949, Elizabeth (*d* 1989), *d* of Laurence B. Hyde; one *s*]. *Address:* Ballywalter Park, Newtownards, Co. Down BT22 2PP. *T:* Ballywalter (02477) 58203. *Club:* Cavalry and Guards. *Died 9 Jan. 1993.*

DUNLOP, Sir (Ernest) Edward, AC 1987; Kt 1969; CMG 1965; OBE 1947; consultant surgeon; Consultant, Royal Melbourne Hospital, since 1967; *b* Wangaratta, Australia, 12 July 1907; *s* of James Henry and Alice Emily Maud Dunlop; *m* 1945, Helen Raeburn Ferguson (*d* 1990), *d* of Mephan Ferguson; two *s. Educ:* Benalla High Sch.; Victorian Coll. of Pharmacy, Melbourne; Ormond Coll., Melbourne Univ.; St Bartholomew's, London. Qual. in Pharmacy, Gold Medallist, 1928; MB, BS Melbourne Univ., 1st Cl. Hons and Exhibn 1934; MS Melbourne 1937; FRCS 1938; FRACS 1947; FACS 1964. Ho. Surg. and Registrar, Royal Melbourne Hosp., 1935–36; Royal Children's, Melbourne, 1937; Brit. Post-Grad. Med. Sch., Hammersmith, 1938; Specialist Surgeon, EMS London, St Mary's, Paddington, 1939; served War, 1939–46 (despatches, OBE); RAAMC (Capt. to Col), Europe, Middle East and Far East; Hon. Surg. Royal Melbourne Hosp., 1946, Senior Hon. Surg. 1964–67; Hon. Surg. Victorian Eye and Ear Hosp., 1949, Hon. Life Governor, 1967; Cons. Surg., Peter MacCallum Clinic, Cancer and Repatriation Dept. Colombo Plan Adviser, Thailand and Ceylon 1956, India 1960–64; Team Leader, Australian Surgical Team, South Vietnam, 1969; CMO, British Phosphate Commn, 1974–81. Dir, Microsurgery Foundn, 1976–. Pres., Victorian Anti-Cancer Council, 1980–83 (Vice-Pres., 1966–74, Chm. Executive, 1975–80); Vice-Pres., Internat. Soc. of Surgeons, 1981–83. Membre Titulaire, Internat. Soc. of Surgeons, 1963–; Mem., James IV Assoc. of Surgeons, 1971–; Mem., Internat. Med. Scis Acad., 1981–. Sir Edward Dunlop Res. Foundn, Heidelberg Repatriation Hosp., launched 1985; Dunlop/Boon Pong Medical Exchange Foundn, Australia–Thailand, launched 1986. Cecil Joll Prize and Lectr, RCS 1960; Gordon Taylor Lectr, Malaysia, 1978; Chapman Meml Lecture and Medal, Australian Instn of Engineers, 1978; Sir Wallace Kyle Meml Oration, Perth, 1989; Jennings Group Public Lecture, 1991. Pres. Aust.-Asian Assoc., Victoria, 1995–; Pres. Ex-POW and Relatives Assoc., Victoria, 1946–; Hon. Life Mem., RSL, 1979; Chm., Prime Minister's POW Relief Fund; President: Australian Ex-POW Assoc., 1971–73, 1986–88; Scottish Far East POW Assoc., 1991–; Victorian Foundn on Alcoholism and Drug Dependence; Chm., Adv. Cttee on Drug Educn, Victorian Min. of Health, 1970, 1977; Patron, Australian Foundn on Alcoholism and Drug Dependency; Mem., Standing Cttee on Health Problems of Alcohol, Nat. Health and Medical Res. Council, 1973. Hon. Pres., Melbourne Council for Overseas Students, 1987– (Pres., 1982–85); Member: Council, Ormond Coll.; Cttee, Nurses' Meml Centre, Melbourne; Exec., Vic. Red Cross Soc.; Victorian Cttee, Queen's Jubilee Appeal, 1977; Dir, Queen Elizabeth II Silver Jubilee Trust for Young Australians, 1977–; Vice-President: 3rd Asian Pacific Congress of Gastroenterology, 1968; Melbourne Scots Soc., 1974–77. Vice Pres., Victorian Rugby Union, 1946–; Pres., Victorian Schs RU Assoc., 1986–. Gov., Aust. Adv. Council of Elders, 1983–. Paul Harris Fellow, Rotary, 1988; FIC 1991. Hon. Mem., Assoc. of Surgeons of India, 1974. Hon. Fellow: Pharmaceutical Soc. of Victoria, 1946; AMA, 1973; Coll. of Surgeons of Sri Lanka, 1985; Royal Coll. of Surgs of Thailand, 1988; RCSE, 1991. Hon. DSc Punjab, 1966; LLD (*hc*) Melbourne, 1988. Freedom of City: Wanganui, NZ, 1962; Prahran, 1988. KCSJ 1987. Australian of the Year Award, 1977; Medal for Service, RACS, 1987; World Veterans Fedn Rehabilitation Award, 1988; Dixon Medal, QUB, 1989; Medal of Merit, Internat. Assoc. of Lions Clubs, 1989. Named in 200 Great Australians, Bicentenary, 1988. Kt Grand Cross (1st Cl.), Thailand, 1993. *Publications:* Carcinoma of the Oesophagus; Reflections upon Surgical Treatment, 1960; Appendix of Into the Smother, 1963; The War Diaries of Sir Edward ("Weary") Dunlop, 1986; contribs to med. and surg. jls. *Recreations:* farming, travelling, golf, Rugby Union football (Blue, Aust. Caps 1932–34, British Barbarians 1939); formerly boxing (Blue). *Address:* (home) 605 Toorak Road, Toorak, Victoria 3142, Australia. *T:* 822 4749; (professional) 14 Parliament Place, East Melbourne, Victoria 3002,

Australia. *T:* 650 1214. *Clubs:* Melbourne, Naval and Military, Peninsula Golf, Melbourne Cricket (Melbourne); Barbarian Football. *Died 2 July 1993.*

DUNLOP, (Norman) Gordon (Edward), CBE 1989; Director: Centrewrite Ltd, since 1991; Tracker Network plc, since 1993; *b* 16 April 1928; *s* of Ross Munn Dunlop, CA and May Dunlop; *m* 1952, Jean (*née* Taylor); one *s* one *d*. *Educ:* Trinity Coll., Glenalmond. CA 1951, Scotland. Thomson McLintock & Co., Glasgow, 1945–56; De Havilland and Hawker Siddeley Aviation Companies, 1956–64; Commercial Union Assce Co. Ltd, 1964–77, Chief Exec., 1972–77; Dir, Inchcape Berhad, Singapore, 1979–82; British Airways: Chief Financial Officer, 1982–83; Finance Dir, 1983–89. Mem., Council of Lloyd's, 1990–92. *Recreations:* gardening, fishing, ski-ing, ballet. *Address:* Bridle Cottage, Horseshoe Lane, Ibthorpe, Hants SP11 0BY. *T:* Hurstbourne Tarrant (01264) 736560. *Clubs:* Caledonian, Buck's.
Died 31 Aug. 1995.

DUNMORE, 11th Earl of, *cr* 1686; **Kenneth Randolph Murray;** Viscount Fincastle, Lord Murray of Blair, Moulin and Tillemett, 1686; retired; *b* 6 June 1913; *s* of Arthur Charles Murray (*d* 1964), *g g s* of 4th Earl, and Susan Maud (*d* 1922), *d* of Edward Richards, Tasmania; *S* brother, 1981; *m* 1938, Margaret Joy (*d* 1976), *d* of late P. D. Cousins, Burnie, Tasmania; two *s*. *Educ:* Tasmanian State School. Sgt, 12th/50th Bn, AIF, 1939–45. Former Post-master, Tasmania. Past Master, Tamar Valley Masonic Lodge 42 Tasmanian Constitution, 1957–58. Patron: NSW Combined Scottish Soc.; Exeter RSL Bowls Club. JP Beaconsfield, Tasmania, 1963. *Heir: s* Viscount Fincastle [*b* 17 Sept. 1946; *m* 1970, Joy Anne, *d* of A. Partridge; one *s* one *d*]. *Address:* c/o PO Box 100E, East Devonport, Tas 7310, Australia. *Club:* Exeter RSL (Exeter, Tasmania). *Died 28 Sept. 1995.*

DUNN, Lt-Col Sir (Francis) Vivian, KCVO 1969 (CVO 1954; MVO 1939); OBE 1960; FRAM; Royal Marines, retired; *b* 24 Dec. 1908; *s* of Captain William James, (Paddy), Dunn, MVO, MC, Director of Music, Royal Horse Guards, and Beatrice Maud Dunn; *g s* of Sgt Thomas Dunn, Band Sgt, 1st Bn 33rd (W Riding) Regt of Foot (over a century in succession in military music); *m* 1938, Margery Kathleen Halliday; one *s* two *d*. *Educ:* Peter Symonds Coll.; Winchester; Konservatorium der Musik, Cologne; Royal Acad. of Music. ARAM 1932, FRAM 1953; Hon. GSM. Played with Queen's Hall Prom. Orch., 1927, BBC Symph. Orch., 1930 (founder mem., 1st violin section); Lieut RM and Director of Music, 1931; addtl duties in cypher work, War of 1939–45; with HMS Vanguard for Royal Tour of S Africa, 1947; toured Canada and USA, 1949; Lt-Col and Principal Director of Music, RM, 1953; Royal Tour of Commonwealth countries, 1953; retired 1968. FRSA 1988. Liveryman, 1956, Mem. Court, 1981–, Master, 1988–89, Worshipful Co. of Musicians. Hon. Mem., Amer. Bandmasters' Assoc., 1969; Pres., International Military Music Soc., 1977–. Guest conductor with principal British orchestras and at Univs in Canada and USA; composer and arranger of ceremonial music for RM. EMI Gold Disc Award, 1969; J. P. Sousa Foundn Award of Merit, 1987. *Address:* 16 West Common, Haywards Heath, Sussex RH16 2AH. *T:* Haywards Heath (01444) 412987. *Clubs:* Army and Navy, MCC.
Died 3 April 1995.

DUNN, Col George Willoughby, CBE 1959; DSO 1943 and Bar 1944; MC 1943; TD 1949; DL; Consultant, Thorntons, WS (formerly Clark Oliver, then Thornton Oliver, Solicitors), Arbroath, since 1984 (Partner, 1939–84); former Chairman: The Alliance Trust; The Second Alliance Trust; Member of Queen's Body Guard for Scotland (Royal Company of Archers); *b* 27 March 1914; *s* of Willoughby Middleton Dunn, coal owner,

Lanarkshire; *m* 1944, Louise Wilson, *er d* of Alexander Stephen MacLellan, LLD, ship builder and engr, Glasgow; two *d*. *Educ:* Trinity Coll., Glenalmond; Glasgow Univ. BL 1937; Solicitor, 1937. Served War of 1939–45 with 51st Highland Div., Middle East, N Africa, Sicily and NW Europe; Col late TA The Black Watch. Chm., Royal British Legion Scotland, 1971–74. DL Angus, 1971. *Recreations:* golf, fishing. *Address:* David's Hill, St Vigeans, Arbroath, Angus DD11 4RG. *T:* Arbroath (0241) 72538. *Clubs:* Naval and Military; New (Edinburgh).
Died 1 April 1994.

DUNN, Sir Vivian; *see* Dunn, Sir F. V.

DUNNET, Prof. George Mackenzie, CBE 1994 (OBE 1986); DSc; Regius Professor of Natural History, University of Aberdeen, 1974–92, subseq. Professor Emeritus; *b* 19 April 1928; *s* of John George and Christina I. Dunnet; *m* 1953, Margaret Henderson Thomson, MA; one *s* two *d*. *Educ:* Peterhead Academy; Aberdeen Univ. BSc (1st cl. hons) 1949; PhD 1952; DSc 1984. Research Officer, CSIRO, Australia, 1953–58; University of Aberdeen: Lectr in Ecology, 1958–66; Dir, Culterty Field Stn, 1958–88; Sen. Lectr, 1966–71; Prof. of Zoology, 1971–74; Sen. Research Fellow, DSIR, NZ, 1968–69. Member: Red Deer Commn, 1975–80; NERC, 1975–77; Council, Scottish Marine Biol Assoc., 1979–86; Scottish Adv. Cttee of Nature Conservancy Council, 1979–84; Nature Conservancy Council for Scotland, 1991–92 (Chm., Sci. R&D Bd, 1991–92); Scottish Natural Heritage, 1992–95 (Chm., Res. Bd, 1992–95); Chairman: Shetland Oil Terminal Environment Adv. Gp, 1977–; Adv. Cttees on Protection of Birds, 1979–81; Salmon Adv. Cttee, 1986–; Fish Farming Adv. Cttee, 1990–. Pres., British Ecological Soc., 1980–81. FRSE 1970; FIBiol 1974; FRSA 1981. Hon. FRZSScot 1992. DUniv Stirling, 1994. *Publications:* contrib. Ibis, Jl Animal Ecology, Jl Applied Ecol., Aust. Jl Zool. *Recreations:* walking, photography, croquet. *Address:* Whinhill, Inverebrie, Ellon, Aberdeenshire AB41 8PT. *T:* Schivas (01358) 761215. *Club:* Commonwealth Trust. *Died 11 Sept. 1995.*

DUNNING, John Ernest Patrick, CBE 1973; retired; Director, Rocket Propulsion Establishment, Westcott, 1955–72; *b* 19 Sept. 1912; *s* of late Rev. E. M. Dunning, MA, sometime Rector of Cumberworth and Denby Dale, Yorks; *m* 1939, Mary Meikle Robertson (*d* 1987). *Educ:* Wheelwright Gram. Sch., Dewsbury; Downing Coll., Cambridge (Exhibr, MA). 1st cl. hons Mech. Scis Tripos, 1935. Blackstone Ltd, Stamford, 1935–37; Bristol Aeroplane Co. Ltd (Engines), 1937–38; Armstrong Whitworth Securities Ltd (Kadenacy Dept), 1938–40; RAE, 1940–50; Asst Dir, Min. of Supply, 1950–55; Dir, Engine Research, Min. of Supply, 1955. FRAeS, FIMechE; FRSA. *Publications:* scientific and technical papers, including: RAF Techl Note AERO 1872, SD54, a suggested method of measuring high temperature in high velocity gas streams at low pressure conditions, 1947; Rocket Propulsion, in Chemistry and Industry (jl), 1961. *Address:* 24 Coombe Hill Crescent, Thame, Oxon OX9 2EH. *T:* Thame (084421) 3893. *Club:* North Oxford Golf. *Died 30 May 1992.*

DUNPARK, Hon. Lord; Alastair McPherson Johnston, TD; BA, LLB; FSAScot; a Senator of the College of Justice in Scotland and Lord of Session, 1971–90; *b* 15 Dec. 1915; *s* of late Rev. A. M. Johnston, BD, Stirling; *m* 1939, Katharine Margaret, (Bunty) (*d* 1983), *d* of Charles Mitchell, Chislehurst; three *s*; *m* 1984, Kathleen Macfie, *widow* of John S. Macfie, WS. *Educ:* Merchiston Castle Sch.; Jesus Coll., Cambridge; Edinburgh Univ. RA (TA), 1939–46 (despatches); Staff Coll., Haifa, 1943; Major 1943. Mem. of Faculty of Advocates, 1946; QC (Scot.) 1958. Sheriff of Dumfries and Galloway, 1966–68; Mem., Scottish Law Commn, 1968–71. Chairman: The Cockburn

Assoc. (Edinburgh Civic Trust), 1969–74; Royal Artillery Assoc., E of Scotland District, 1946–60, Scottish Region, 1962–78; Edinburgh Marriage Guidance Council, 1969–72 (Pres., 1973–86); Council, St George's Sch. for Girls, Edinburgh, 1973–89; Edinburgh Legal Dispensary, 1961–; Pres., Scottish Univs' Law Inst., 1978–91. Hon. Fellow, Dept of Law, Edinburgh Univ., 1969. *Publications:* Jt Editor, 3rd edn of Walton's Law of Husband and Wife, 1951; Jt Editor, 7th edn of Gloag and Henderson's Introduction to Law of Scotland, 1968. *Recreation:* reading. *Address:* 17 Heriot Row, Edinburgh EH3 6HP. *T:* 031–556 1896. *Club:* New (Edinburgh).
Died 31 Aug. 1991.

DUPPA-MILLER, John Bryan Peter; *see* Miller.

DUPUCH, Sir (Alfred) Etienne (Jerome), Kt 1965; OBE 1949; Editor, 1919–72, Contributing Editor since 1972, The Tribune, Nassau, Bahamas; *b* Nassau, 16 Feb. 1899; *s* of Leon Edward Hartman Dupuch, Founder of The Tribune, and Elizabeth Harriet Saunders Dupuch; *m* 1928, Marie Plouse, USA; three *s* three *d*. *Educ:* Boys' Central Sch., Nassau; St John's Univ., Collegeville, Minn, USA. Served War, 1914–18, Eastern and Western Fronts, BWI Regt. Rep. for Inagua and Mayaguana, House of Assembly, Bahamas, 1925–42; Eastern District, New Providence, 1949–56; MLC, 1960–64; Mem. Senate, 1964–68. Mem., US Nat. Adv. Bd, Amer. Security Council, 1981. Board Member: ESU, Miami; United World Colls, NY. Hon. Member: East Nassau Rotary Club; Coral Gables Rotary Club; Lions Club, Pennsylvania. Hon. LittD, Hon. LLD. Inter-American Press Association Award: for breaking down racial discrimination in Bahamas, 1956; for successful defence of Freedom of Press, 1969; Citation from Associated Press N American Editors' Assoc. for outstanding coverage of fire on SS Yarmouth Castle, 1965; Paul Harris Award for work in social services (Rotary Club of Lucaya, Freeport); listed in Guinness Book of Records as longest serving editor in history of journalism. RSA medal, and several decorations from governments of three nations. Kt, SMO Malta, 1977; KCSG; OTL; CHM. *Publications:* We Call Him Friend (tribute to Rt Hon. Lord Beaverbrook), 1961; The Tribune Story, 1967; A Salute to Friend and Foe, 1981. *Address:* Camperdown Heights, PO Box N-3207, Nassau, NP, Bahamas; 700 Coral Way, Coral Gables, Florida, USA.
Died 23 Aug. 1991.

DURACK, Dame Mary, (Mrs Horrie Miller), AC 1989; DBE 1978 (OBE 1966); novelist and historian; *b* 20 Feb. 1913; *d* of Michael Patrick Durack and Bessie Ida Muriel (*née* Johnstone); *m* 1938, Captain H. C. Miller (*d* 1980); two *s* two *d* (and two *d* decd). *Educ:* Loreto Convent, Perth. Formerly: lived at Argyle and Ivanhoe Stns, E Kimberley; mem. staff, West Australian Newspapers Ltd. Member: Aust. Soc. of Authors; National Trust; Royal Western Aust. Hist. Soc. Formerly Exec. Mem., Aboriginal Cultural Foundn. Dir, Aust. Stockman's Hall of Fame. Emeritus Fellow, Literature Bd of Australia Council, 1983–86 and 1987–; Foundn Fellow, Curtin Univ. of Technol., 1978. Hon. Life Member: WA Br., Fellowship of Aust. Writers (Pres., 1958–63); Internat. PEN, Australia (Mem., WA Br.). Patron, Friends of Battye Liby of WA, 1989–. Commonwealth Lit. Grant, 1973, 1977 and Australian Research Grants Cttee Grant, 1980 and 1984. Hon. DLitt Univ. of WA, 1978. Alice Award, Soc. of Women Writers (Australia), 1982. *Publications:* (E Kimberley District stories illus. by sister, Elizabeth Durack): All-about, 1935; Chunuma, 1936; Son of Djaro, 1938; The Way of the Whirlwind, 1941, new edn 1979; Piccaninnies, 1943; The Magic Trumpet, 1944; (with Florence Rutter) Child Artists of the Australian Bush, 1952; (novel) Keep Him My Country, 1955; (family documentary) Kings in Grass Castles, 1959; To Ride a

Fine Horse, 1963; The Courteous Savage, 1964 (new edn as Yagan of the Bibbulmun, 1976); Kookanoo and Kangaroo, 1963; An Australian Settler, 1964 (pub. Australia, A Pastoral Emigrant); The Rock and the Sand, 1969; (with Ingrid Drysdale) The End of Dreaming, 1974; To Be Heirs Forever, 1976; Tjakamarra—boy between two worlds, 1977; Sons in the Saddle, 1983; *plays:* The Ship of Dreams, 1968; Swan River Saga, 1972; scripts for ABC drama dept; libretto for opera, Dalgerie (music by James Penberthy), 1966; six dramatised Kookanoo stories on tape and record, 1973. *Address:* 12 Bellevue Avenue, Nedlands, WA 6009, Australia. *T:* (9) 3861117.
Died 16 Dec. 1994.

DURAND, Rev. Sir (Henry Mortimer) Dickon (Marion St George), 4th Bt *cr* 1892, of Ruckley Grange, Salop; Rector, Youghal Union of Parishes, Co. Cork, 1982–92; *b* 19 June 1934; *s* of Lt-Comdr Mortimer Henry Marion Durand, RN (*y s* of 1st Bt) (*d* 1969), and Beatrice Garvan-Sheridan, *d* of Judge Sheridan, Sydney, NSW; *S* uncle, 1971; *m* 1971, Stella Evelyn, *d* of Captain C. C. L'Estrange; two *s* two *d*. *Educ:* Wellington College; Sydney University; Salisbury Theological College. Deacon, 1969; priest, 1970; Curate: All Saints, Fulham, 1969–72; St Leonard's, Heston, 1972–74; Curate-in-Charge, St Benedict's, Ashford, Mddx, 1975–79; Bishop's Curate, Kilbixy Union of Parishes, Co. Westmeath, 1979–82. *Recreations:* heraldry, philately, model railways, printing, militaria, painting, fiction writing, travel. *Heir: s* Edward Alan Christopher David Percy Durand, *b* 21 Feb. 1974. *Address:* Lisnalurg House, Sligo, Ireland.
Died 24 Oct. 1992.

DURAND, Victor Albert Charles, QC 1958; *b* 16 Oct. 1907; *s* of Victor and Blanche Durand; *m* 1935, Betty Joan Kirchner (*d* 1986); one *s* one *d*. *Educ:* Howard High Sch. (Kitchener Scholar). LLB, BSc, AMInstCE. Served War 1939–45 with RE. Called to Bar, Inner Temple, 1939, Bencher, 1985. Dep. Chm., Warwicks QS, 1961.
Died 1 Oct. 1994.

DURRANT, Sir William Henry Estridge, 7th Bt, *cr* 1784, of Scottow, Norfolk; JP (NSW); *b* 1 April 1901; *s* of Sir William Durrant, 6th Bt; *S* father 1953; *m* 1927, Georgina Beryl Gwendoline (*d* 1968), *d* of Alexander Purse, Kircubbin, Co. Down, N Ireland; one *s* one *d*. Served War of 1939–45 (Pacific Area). NSW Registrar, Australian Inst. of Company Dirs, 1959. *Heir: s* William Alexander Estridge Durrant [*b* 26 Nov. 1929; *m* 1953, Dorothy (BA), *d* of Ronal Croker, Quirindi, NSW; one *s* one *d*]. *Address:* 1634 Pacific Highway, Wahroonga, NSW 2076, Australia.
Died 13 July 1994.

DURRELL, Gerald Malcolm, OBE 1983; zoologist and writer since 1946; regular contributor to BBC Sound and TV Services; *b* Jamshedpur, India, 7 Jan. 1925; *s* of Lawrence Samuel Durrell, Civil Engineer, and Louisa Florence Dixie; *m* 1st, 1951, Jacqueline Sonia Rasen (marr. diss. 1979); no *c*; 2nd, 1979, Lee Wilson McGeorge. *Educ:* by private tutors, in Greece. Student Keeper, Whipsnade, 1945–46; 1st Animal Collecting Expedition, British Cameroons, 1947–48; 2nd Cameroon Expedition, 1948–49; collecting trip to British Guiana, 1949–50; began writing, script writing and broadcasting, 1950–53; trip with wife to Argentine and Paraguay, 1953–54; filming in Cyprus, 1955; 3rd Cameroon Expedition with wife, 1957; Trans-Argentine Expedition, 1958–59; expedition in conjunction with BBC Natural History Unit, Sierra Leone, 1965; collecting trip to Mexico, 1968; Aust. Expedn, 1969–70; expedns to Mauritius, 1976 and 1977, Assam, 1978, Mexico, 1979, Madagascar, 1981, 1990. Founder and Hon. Director: Jersey Zoological Park, 1958; Jersey Wildlife Preservation Trust, 1964. Founder Chm., Wildlife Preservation Trust Internat. (formerly SAFE Internat. USA), 1972–. FZS; (Life) FIAL; FRGS; FRSL 1972;

MBOU; MIBiol. Hon. LHD Yale, 1977; Hon. DSc: Durham, 1988; Kent, 1989. *Films for TV:* 1st series, 1956; Two in the Bush, 1962; Catch Me a Colobus, 1966; Animal People-Menagerie Manor, 1967; Garden of the Gods, 1967; The Stationary Ark, 1976; The Ark on the Move, 1981; The Amateur Naturalist (series), 1983; Durrell in Russia (series), 1986; Ourselves and Other Animals (series), 1987; Durrell's Ark, 1987. *Publications:* The Overloaded Ark, 1953; Three Singles to Adventure, 1954; The Bafut Beagles, 1954; The New Noah, 1955; The Drunken Forest, 1956; My Family and Other Animals, 1956 (televised, 1987); Encounters with Animals, 1958; A Zoo in my Luggage, 1960; The Whispering Land, 1961; Island Zoo, 1961; Look at Zoos, 1961; My Favourite Animal Stories, 1962; Menagerie Manor, 1964; Two in the Bush, 1966; Rosy is My Relative, 1968; The Donkey Rustlers, 1968; Birds, Beasts and Relatives, 1969; Fillets of Plaice, 1971; Catch Me a Colobus, 1972; Beasts in My Belfry, 1973; The Talking Parcel, 1974; The Stationary Ark, 1976; Golden Bats and Pink Pigeons, 1977; The Garden of the Gods, 1978; The Picnic & Suchlike Pandemonium, 1979; The Mockery Bird, 1981; The Amateur Naturalist, 1982; Ark on the Move, 1983; How to Shoot an Amateur Naturalist, 1984; (with Lee Durrell) Durrell in Russia, 1986; The Fantastic Flying Journey, 1987; (ed) Best Dog Stories, 1990; The Ark's Anniversary, 1990; Marrying Off Mother and other stories, 1991; The Aye-Aye and I, 1992; contribs to Zoo Life, etc. *Recreations:* reading, filming, drawing, swimming, study of the history and maintenance of zoological gardens. *Address:* Les Augres Manor, Trinity, Jersey, Channel Isles. *T:* Jersey (01534) 864666.

Died 30 Jan. 1995.

du SAUTOY, Peter Francis, CBE 1971 (OBE 1964); *b* 19 Feb. 1912; *s* of late Col E. F. du Sautoy, OBE, TD, DL and Mabel (*née* Howse); *m* 1937, Phyllis Mary, (Mollie), *d* of late Sir Francis Floud, KCB, KCSI, KCMG and Phyllis (*née* Ford); two *s. Educ:* Uppingham (Foundn Schol.); Wadham Coll., Oxford (Sen. Class. Schol.; MA, 1st cl. Lit. Hum). Dept of Printed Books, British Museum, 1935–36; Asst Educn Officer, City of Oxford, 1937–40; RAF, 1940–45; joined Faber & Faber Ltd, 1946; Dir, Dec. 1946; Vice-Chm., 1960–71; Chm., 1971–77, editorial consultant, 1977–; Chm., Faber and Faber (Publishers) Ltd, 1971–77; Mem. Bd, Faber Music Ltd, 1966–87 (Chm., 1971–77; Vice Chm., 1977–81); Trustee, Yale Univ. Press, London, 1984–92 (Mem. Bd, 1977–84). Mem. Council, Publishers Assoc., 1957–63, 1965–77 (Pres., 1967–69); Mem. Exec. Cttee, Internat. Publishers Assoc., 1972–76; Pres., Groupe des Editeurs de Livres de la CEE, 1973–75. Official visits on behalf of Publishers Assoc. and British Council to Australia, USSR, Finland, Hungary, Nigeria, China. Vice-Pres., Aldeburgh Foundn

Ltd, 1987– (Mem. Council, 1976–87; Vice-Chm., 1977–80; Dep. Chm., 1982–87); Pres., Suffolk Book League, 1986–94 (Vice-Pres., 1982–85); Hon. Treasurer, The William Blake Trust, 1959–83; Trustee: The James Joyce Estate, 1970–89; The Alison Uttley Estate. Liveryman, Stationers' Co., 1973; Freeman, City of London, 1973. *Publications:* various articles on publishing. *Address:* 31 Lee Road, Aldeburgh, Suffolk IP15 5EY. *T:* Aldeburgh (01728) 452838. *Club:* Garrick.

Died 17 July 1995.

DYDE, John Horsfall, CBE 1970 (OBE 1957); Chairman, Eastern Gas Board, 1959–69; *b* 4 June 1905; *m* 1930, Ethel May Hewitt; two *s. Educ:* Scarborough High Sch.; University of Leeds (MSc). Engineer and Manager, North Middlesex Gas Co., 1937–42; prior to nationalisation was Engineer and Gen. Manager of Uxbridge, Maidenhead, Wycombe & District Gas Co. and Slough Gas & Coke Co.; also Technical Director of group of undertakings of the South Eastern Gas Corp. Ltd; Dep.-Chm., Eastern Gas Board, 1949. President: Western Junior Gas Assoc., 1935–36; Southern Assoc. of Gas Engineers and Managers, 1949–50; Institution of Gas Engineers, 1951–52; British Road Tar Association. CEng, FIChemE; Hon. FIGasE. *Recreations:* golf, fishing. *Address:* Stable End, Thellusson Lodge, Aldeburgh, Suffolk IP15 5DT. *T:* Aldeburgh (0728) 453148.

Died 28 Jan. 1995.

DYKES BOWER, S(tephen) E(rnest), MA; FRIBA; FSA; Surveyor of the Fabric of Westminster Abbey, 1951–73, then Emeritus; Consulting Architect, Carlisle Cathedral, 1947–75; *b* 18 April 1903; 2nd *s* of Ernest Dykes Bower, MD; unmarried. *Educ:* Cheltenham Coll.; Merton Coll., Oxford (Organ Schol.); Architectural Assoc. Sch. of Architecture. Private practice as architect, 1931–: work chiefly domestic and ecclesiastical. Architect for: new High Altar, Baldachino and American Memorial Chapel, St Paul's Cathedral (with W. Godfrey Allen); enlargement of Bury St Edmunds Cathedral; Cathedral Library and Bishop's Palace, Exeter; completion of Lancing Coll. Chapel; re-building of Gt Yarmouth Parish Church; St Vedast, Foster Lane, EC; and other churches in London and country; work in Canterbury, Winchester, Norwich, Ely, Gloucester, Wells, Oxford, Carlisle, Peterborough and other cathedrals, Oxford and Cambridge colls, public schs, halls of City Livery cos, etc. Lay Canon of St Edmundsbury Cathedral, 1979–84. Pres., Ecclesiological Soc., 1983–. Hon. RCO 1986. DLitt Cantuar, 1993. *Publications:* papers and addresses on architectural subjects. *Address:* Quendon Court, Quendon, near Saffron Walden, Essex CB11 3XJ. *T:* Rickling (0179988) 242. *Clubs:* Athenæum, United Oxford & Cambridge University.

Died 11 Nov. 1994.

E

EADEN, Maurice Bryan, CBE 1983; HM Diplomatic Service, retired; Consul General, Amsterdam, 1980–83; *b* 9 Feb. 1923; *s* of William Eaden and Florence Ada Eaden (*née* Hudson); *m* 1947, Nelly Margaretha Dorgelo (*d* 1992); three *s. Educ:* Bemrose Sch., Derby. Served Army, 1942–47. Foreign Office, 1947; Vice-Consul, Leopoldville, 1955; First Secretary (Commercial): Addis Ababa, 1958; Beirut, 1963; FO, 1967; First Sec. (Commercial), Bombay, 1970; Counsellor (Administration), Brussels, 1972–75; Consul-Gen., Karachi, 1975–79. *Recreations:* walking in Derbyshire, languages. *Address:* New Houses, Cressbrook, Buxton, Derbyshire. *T:* Tideswell (0298) 871404.

Died 6 Sept. 1993.

EAGGER, Brig. Arthur Austin, CBE 1944 (OBE 1940); TD 1945; *b* 14 March 1898; *s* of Edward and Elsie Eagger; *m* 1st, 1935, Kate Mortimer Hare (*d* 1946); three *s;* 2nd, 1948, Barbara Noel Hare. *Educ:* Aberdeen Univ. (MB, ChB 1922). Lieut 6th Bn Gordon Highlanders. Commissioned RAMC (TA), 1928; late DDMS 1 Airborne Corps. Medical Dir, Slough Industrial Health Service, retired 1963, Consultant 1963–79. Bronze Star (USA), 1945. *Publications:* Industrial Resettlement (Proc. RSM), 1952; Health in the Factory (Jl Royal Institute of Public Health and Hygiene), 1953; Venture in Industry, 1965. *Address:* 1 Underwood Close, Dawlish, Devon EX7 9RY. *T:* Dawlish (0626) 864597. *Died 8 Oct. 1993.*

EARDLEY-WILMOT, Sir John (Assheton), 5th Bt *cr* 1821; LVO 1956; DSC 1943; Staff of Monopolies Commission, 1967–82; *b* 2 Jan. 1917; *s* of Commander Frederick Neville Eardley-Wilmot (*d* 1956) (*s* of 3rd Bt) and Dorothy Little (*d* 1959), formerly of Brooksby, Double Bay, Sydney; *S* uncle, 1970; *m* 1939, Diana Elizabeth, *d* of Commander Aubrey Moore, RN, and Mrs O. Bassett; one *s* one *d. Educ:* Stubbington; RNC, Dartmouth. Motor Torpedo Boats, 1939–43; served HMS Apollo, 1944; HMS Fencer, 1945–46; RN Staff Course, 1950; Commander 1950; HMS Opossum, 1951–53; Cabinet Office, 1954–57; Admiralty, 1958–67; retired 1967, as Deputy Director Naval Administrative Planning. MIMgt (MBIM 1978); FRSA 1970. Freeman, City of London (by Redemption). Norwegian War Medal. *Recreation:* fishing. *Heir: s* Michael John Assheton Eardley-Wilmot [*b* 13 Jan. 1941; *m* 1971, Wendy (marr. diss. 1987), *y d* of A. J. Wolstenholme; two *s* one *d; m* 1987, Diana Margaret, *d* of Robert Graham Wallis; one *d*]. *Address:* 41 Margravine Gardens, W6 8RN. *T:* 0181–748 3723.

Died 20 Dec. 1995.

EARLE, Ven. E(dward) E(rnest) Maples; Archdeacon of Tonbridge, 1953–76, Archdeacon Emeritus since 1977; Vicar of Shipbourne, Kent, 1959–86; *b* 22 Dec. 1900; 2nd *s* of Ernest William Earle and Lilian Geraldine Earle (*née* Hudson); *m* 1966, Mrs Jocelyn Mary Offer, *widow* of Canon C. J. Offer. *Educ:* London Coll. of Divinity; St John's Coll., Durham University (LTh, MA). Deacon, 1924; priest, 1925; Vicar of: St John, Bexley, 1936–39; Rainham (Kent), 1939–44; Secretary, Rochester Diocesan Reorganisation Cttee, 1944–52, Great Appeal Cttee, etc, 1944–49; Hon. Canon, Rochester Cathedral, 1949; Rector of Chatham, 1950–52; Proctor in Convocation, 1950–53; Rector of Wrotham 1952–59. *Recreations:* artistic and architectural interests. *Address:* Butcher's Cottage, Stumble Hill, Shipbourne, Tonbridge, Kent TN11 9PE.

Died 15 March 1994.

EASON, His Honour Robert Kinley; HM's First Deemster, Clerk of the Rolls and Deputy Governor of the Isle of Man, 1974–80; *b* 12 April 1908; 2nd *s* of Henry Alexander Eason and Eleanor Jane Eason (*née* Kinley); *m* 1937, Nora Muriel, *d* of Robert Raisbeck Coffey, Douglas, IOM. *Educ:* Douglas High Sch.; King William's Coll., IOM; University Coll. London. LLB (Hons). Called to Bar, Gray's Inn, 1929; Advocate, Manx Bar, 1930; High Bailiff and Chief Magistrate, Isle of Man, 1961–69; HM's Second Deemster, IOM, 1969–74; retired from practice, 1982. Chairman: Criminal Injuries Compensation Tribunal, IOM, 1969–74; IOM Income Tax Appeal Comrs, 1974–80; IOM Unit Trust Tribunal, 1968–74; Tourist (IOM) Appeal Tribunal, 1969–74; Tynwald Arrangements Cttee, 1974–80; Chm. of Trustees: Cunningham House Scout and Guide Headquarters, 1964–90; Ellan Vannin Home, 1971–86; Trustee, Manx Marine Soc., 1974–90. President: Ellynyn Ny Gael, 1974–84; IOM Anti-Cancer Assoc., 1969–85; Wireless Telegraphy Appeal Bd for IOM, 1971–80; Legion Players, 1971–81; SS&AFA, IOM Br., 1973–90; Licensing Appeal Court, 1969–74; King William's College Soc., 1978–80; Past Pres., IOM Soc. for Prevention of Cruelty to Animals. Queen's Silver Jubilee Medal, 1977. *Recreation:* organ music. *Address:* Greenacres, Highfield Drive, Baldrine, Lonan, Isle of Man. *T:* Laxey (0624) 861622. *Clubs:* Ellan Vannin, Manx Automobile (Douglas).

Died 28 Aug. 1991.

EAST, Gerald Reginald Ricketts; Civil Service Commissioner, 1974–78, retired; Chairman, Incorporated Froebel Educational Institute, since 1979; *b* 17 Feb. 1917; *s* of late R. B. East and Dora East (*née* Ricketts); *m* 1944, Anna Elder Smyth; one *s* two *d. Educ:* Peter Symonds' Sch.; St Edmund Hall, Oxford. Goldsmiths' Company's Exhibnr; MA 1945. Royal Artillery, 1939–46; Control Commn for Germany, 1946–47; Asst Principal, War Office, Oct. 1947; Private Sec. to Under-Sec. of State for War, 1949; Directing Staff Imperial Defence Coll., 1952–54; Private Sec. to Sec. of State for War, 1954–55; Asst Sec. (Inspector of Establishments), 1958; Comd Sec., BAOR, 1961–64; Asst Sec. (Establishments), MoD, 1965–70; Asst Under-Sec. of State, MoD, 1970–74. *Address:* Appleden, 4 Dibdale Road, Neasham, Darlington, Co. Durham DL2 1PF. *T:* Darlington (0325) 720577. *Died 1 June 1991.*

EAST, Grahame Richard, CMG 1961; Special Commissioner of Income Tax, 1962–73; *b* 1908; 2nd *s* of William Robert and Eleanor East; *m* 1937, Cynthia Mildred, *d* of Adam Louis Beck, OBE; two *s* two *d. Educ:* Bristol Grammar Sch.; Corpus Christi Coll., Oxford. Asst Master, Royal Belfast Academical Institution, Belfast, 1929; Inland Revenue Dept, Secretaries Office, 1930, Asst Sec., 1941. *Address:* 22 Ormsby, Stanley Road, Sutton, Surrey SM2 6TJ. *T:* 081–643 3047.

Died 21 June 1993.

EASTHAM, Hon. Sir (Thomas) Michael, Kt 1978; **Hon. Mr Justice Eastham;** a Judge of the High Court of Justice, Family Division, since 1978; *b* 26 June 1920; *y s* of late His Honour Sir Tom Eastham, QC, and Margaret

Ernestine, 3rd *d* of A. E. Smith, JP, St Anne's-on-Sea, Lancs; *m* 1942, Mary Pamela, *o d* of late Dr H. C. Billings; two *d* (and one *d* decd). *Educ:* Harrow; Trinity Hall, Cambridge. Served with Queen's Royal Regiment, 1940–46 (Capt.). Called to the Bar, Lincoln's Inn, 1947, Bencher, 1972; QC 1964. Recorder: of Deal, 1968–71; of Cambridge, 1971; Hon. Recorder of Cambridge, 1972; a Recorder of the Crown Court, 1972–78. *Address:* 7a Porchester Terrace, W2 3TH. *T:* 071–723 0770. *Club:* Garrick. *Died 4 March 1993.*

EASTMAN, Ven. Derek Ian Tennent, MC 1945; Archdeacon Emeritus, Diocese of Oxford, since 1985; Canon of St George's Chapel, Windsor, 1977–85; *b* 22 Jan. 1919; *s* of Archibald Tennent Eastman and Gertrude Towler Eastman (*née* Gambling); *m* 1949, Judith Mary, *e d* of Canon Philip David Bevington Miller; three *s* one *d.* *Educ:* Winchester; Christ Church, Oxford; Cuddesdon Theol. Coll. BA 1941; MA 1946. Coldstream Guards, 1940–46: Guards Armoured Div., Temp. Major. Cuddesdon Theol. Coll., 1946–48; deacon 1948; priest 1949; Asst Curate, Brighouse, 1948–51; Priest-in-Charge, St Andrew's, Caversham, 1951–56; Vicar: Headington, Oxford, 1956–64; Banbury, 1964–70; Archdeacon of Buckingham, and Vicar of Chilton and Dorton, 1970–77. Proctor in Convocation for Dio. of Oxford, 1964–70. Mem., General Synod, 1975–77. *Recreations:* English history, gardening. *Address:* 43 Clay Lane, Beaminster, Dorset DT8 3BX. *T:* Beaminster (0308) 862443.
Died 7 Jan. 1991.

EASTON, John Francis; Under-Secretary (Legal), Solicitor's Office, Inland Revenue, 1980–88, retired; Chairman (part-time), VAT Tribunals, since 1988; *b* 20 Aug. 1928; *s* of Rev. Cecil Gordon Easton and Nora Gladys Easton (*née* Hall); *m* 1960, Hon. Caroline Ina Maud, *e d* of 9th Baron Hawke; one *s* one *d.* *Educ:* City of London Sch.; Keble Coll., Oxford (MA). Called to Bar, Middle Temple, 1951. National Service, RASC, 1951–53. Joined Inland Revenue Solicitor's Office, 1955. Member, General Synod of Church of England, 1970–75; Licensed Diocesan Reader, dio. of St Albans, 1969–93; received into RC Church, 1993. *Recreations:* theology, foreign languages, swimming. *Address:* The Old Hall, Barley, Royston, Herts SG8 8JA. *T:* Royston (0763) 848368.
Died 13 May 1994.

EASTWOOD, Sir John (Bealby), Kt 1975; DL; Chairman, Adam Eastwood & Sons Ltd, Builders, since 1946; *b* 9 Jan. 1909; *s* of William Eastwood and Elizabeth Townroe Eastwood (*née* Bealby); *m* 1st, 1929, Constance Mary (*née* Tilley) (*d* 1981); two *d*; 2nd, 1983, Joan Mary (*née* Hayward) (*d* 1986), *widow* of Capt. Arthur McGowan. *Educ:* Queen Elizabeth's Grammar Sch., Mansfield. Civil Engr and Contractor, 1925; founded W. & J. B. Eastwood Ltd, 1945. DL Notts, 1981. OStJ 1972. *Address:* Hexgreave Hall, Farnsfield, Newark, Notts NG22 8LW. *Club:* Farmers'. *Died 6 Aug. 1995.*

EATHER, Maj.-Gen. Kenneth William, CB 1947; CBE 1943; DSO 1941; Executive Director, Water Research Foundation of Australia, 1958–79; *b* 1901; *m* 1st, 1924, Adeline Mabel, *d* of Gustavus Lewis; one *s* one *d* (and one *s* decd); 2nd, 1968, Kathleen, *d* of M. F. Carroll. Served War of 1939–45: AMF, Middle East and SW Pacific (despatches, DSO, CBE). *Club:* Imperial Service (Sydney). *Died 13 May 1993.*

EATON, Air Vice-Marshal Brian Alexander, CB 1969; CBE 1959; DSO 1944, and Bar 1945; DFC; *b* Launceston, Tas, 15 Dec. 1916; *s* of S. A. Eaton; *m* 1952, Josephine Rumbles; one *s* two *d.* *Educ:* Carey Grammar Sch., Melbourne; RAAF Coll., Pt Cook. Served War of 1939–45: CO 3 Sqdn N Africa-Medit., 1943; CO 239 Wing RAF Italy, 1944–45; UK, 1945–46; OC 81 Fighter Wing, Japan,

1948; OC 1948–49; OC 78 Wing Malta, 1952–54; Dir of Ops, RAAF HQ, 1955; OC Williamtown RAAF and Comdt Sch. of Land-Air Warfare, 1957–58; Dir Joint Service Plans, 1959–60; Imp. Defence Coll., 1961; Dir-Gen. of Operational Requirements, 1962; Deputy Chief of Air Staff, 1966–67; AOC HQ 224 Mobile Group (RAF) Far East Air Force, Singapore, 1967–68; Chief of Staff HQFEAF, 1968–69; Air Mem. for Personnel, Dept of Air, Canberra, 1969–73; AOC Operational Comd, RAAF, 1973–74. American Silver Star. *Recreations:* shooting, fishing. *Address:* 125 Mugga Way, Red Hill, ACT 2603, Australia. *Club:* Commonwealth (Canberra).
Died 17 Oct. 1992.

EATON, Peter; owner of the largest antiquarian bookstore in England; *b* 24 Jan. 1914; *m* 1st, Ann Wilkinson; 2nd, Valerie Carruthers; two *s*; 3rd, Margaret Taylor; two *d.* *Educ:* elementary sch.; Municipal Sch. (later Coll.) of Technology, Manchester Univ. (expelled). Born in London at 8 York Gate, Regent's Park; advertised for adoption in Nursing Times, Feb. 1914; brought up in Rochdale, where became apprentice printer; became a tramp; in London, later helped found now defunct Domestic Workers Union; advised on start of Tribune newspaper; mem. of Labour Party for 40 yrs; Conscientious Objector, tried at Royal Courts of Justice, 1939; voluntarily joined London Rescue Squad for duration of War and helped Bomb Disposal Squad; started bookselling in Portobello Road when it was predominantly a fruit and vegetable market, 1945; bought Queen Victoria's books from Kensington Palace (later in Victoria State Library, Australia); bought part or all of libraries of Bernard Shaw, H. G. Wells, Marie Stopes and R. H. Tawney; formed many important collections of books, incl. world's largest collection of books on the atom (later in Texas Univ.). Pres., Private Libraries Assoc., 1989–92. Travelled in many parts of the world, incl. Alaska, India and African jungles; FRGS 1950. *Publications:* Marie Stopes: a bibliographical list of her books, 1977; History of Lilies, 1982; articles in trade jls. *Recreations:* taking the dog for a walk, watching my wife play tennis. *Address:* Lilies, Weedon, Aylesbury, Bucks HP22 4NS. *T:* Aylesbury (0296) 641393. *Club:* Reform.
Died 23 Oct. 1993.

EBBISHAM, 2nd Baron, *cr* 1928, of Cobham, Surrey; **Rowland Roberts Blades,** TD; MA; Bt 1922; *b* 3 Sept. 1912; *o s* of 1st Baron Ebbisham, GBE, and Margaret (MBE 1943, Officer Legion of Honour, OStJ) (*d* 1965), *d* of Arthur Reiner, Sutton, Surrey; *S* father, 1953; *m* 1949, Flavia Mary, *y d* of Charles Meade, Pen y lan, Meifod, Montgomeryshire; three *d.* *Educ:* Winchester; Christ Church, Oxford (MA). Served War of 1939–45: Lieut 98th (Surrey and Sussex Yeo.) Field Regt, RA. Master, Mercers' Co., 1963; Common Councilman, City of London, 1947–83; Chm., City Lands Cttee, and Chief Commoner, Corp. of London, 1967–68; one of HM Lieutenants, City of London, 1966–. President: London Chamber of Commerce, 1958–61; Assoc. of British Chambers of Commerce, 1968–70; British Importers' Confedn, 1978–81; Mem., European Trade Cttee, BOTB, 1973–82; Hon. Treasurer, BPIF, 1971–81; Dir, Williams, Lea Ltd; Chm., Anglo-Dal Ltd. Vice-Pres. The London Record Society. Captain, Surrey II XI (cricket), 1946–54. Hon. DSc City Univ., 1984. Order of Yugoslav Flag with gold wreath, 1976; Comdr, Order of Orange-Nassau, Netherlands, 1982. *Heir:* none. *Address:* St Ann's, Church Street, Mere, Wiltshire BA12 6DS. *T:* Mere (0747) 860376. *Club:* MCC. *Died 12 April 1991 (ext).*

EBURNE, Sir Sidney (Alfred William), Kt 1983; MC 1944; Senior Crown Agent and Chairman of the Crown Agents for Oversea Governments and Administrations, 1978–83; *b* 26 Nov. 1918; *s* of Alfred Edmund Eburne and Ellen Francis Eburne; *m* 1942, Phoebe Freda (*née*

Beeton Dilley); one *s* one *d*. *Educ:* Downhills School. Served War, 1939–46; Captain, RA. Joined Morgan Grenfell & Co. Ltd, 1946; Director: Morgan Grenfell & Co. Ltd, 1968–75; Morgan Grenfell Holdings Ltd, 1971–75; Peachey Property Corp. Ltd, 1983–88. Crown Agents: Dir of Finance, 1975; Man. Dir, 1976. Governor, Peabody Trust, 1984. *Recreations:* golf, travelling. *Address:* Motts Farm, Eridge, East Sussex TN3 9LJ. *Club:* Carlton.   *Died 19 Dec. 1994.*

EDDEN, Alan John, CMG 1957; HM Diplomatic Service, retired; *b* 2 Dec. 1912; *s* of late Thomas Frederick Edden and Nellie Shipway; *m* 1939, Pauline Klay; one *s*. *Educ:* Latymer Sch., Edmonton; Gonville and Caius Coll., Cambridge (Exhibitioner). Served at HM Legation, Bangkok, 1935; Batavia, 1938; Foreign Office, 1939; HM Legation, Bangkok, 1940; HM Legation, Tehran, 1942; Kermanshah, 1944; with SHAEF, May 1945; Actg Consul-Gen. Amsterdam, June 1945; Foreign Office, Oct. 1945; HM Embassy, Warsaw, 1948; Brit. Information Services, New York, 1951; FO, 1953; Counsellor, Foreign Office, 1954–58; Counsellor, HM Embassy, Beirut, 1958–62; HM Consul-Gen., Durban, 1962–66; HM Ambassador to: Cameroon, Central African Republic, Gabon and Chad, 1966–70; Equatorial Guinea, 1969–70; Lebanon, 1970–71. *Recreation:* music. *Address:* c/o Barclays Bank, Lower Edmonton Branch, 3/4 South Mall, N9 0NJ; Eden Gardens, Marriott Road, Durban, South Africa.   *Died 10 Aug. 1991.*

EDDINGTON, Paul Clark-, CBE 1987; actor; *b* 18 June 1927; *s* of Albert Clark Eddington and Frances Mary (*née* Roberts); *m* 1952, Patricia Scott; three *s* one *d*. *Educ:* Holy Child Convent, Cavendish Sq., W1; Friends (Quaker) Sch., Sibford Ferris, Banbury, Oxon; RADA. First appearance on stage with ENSA, 1944; joined Birmingham Repertory Th., 1945; has played with several other rep. theatres during subseq. 30 years; first appearance in West End in The 10th Man, Comedy Th., 1961; first (and only, so far) appearance in New York in A Severed Head, 1964; joined National Theatre to play in revival of Who's Afraid of Virginia Woolf?, 1981; Noises Off, Savoy, 1982; Lovers Dancing, Albery, 1983; Forty Years On, Queen's, 1984; Jumpers, Aldwych, 1985; HMS Pinafore, Victoria State Opera, Australia, 1987 (tour); The Browning Version, and Harlequinade (double-bill), Royalty, 1988, subseq. Australia; London Assurance, Chichester Fest., 1989, transf. Theatre Royal, Haymarket, 1989; The Double Dealer, Ipswich, 1990; Tartuffe, Playhouse, 1991; No Man's Land, Almeida, 1992, transf. Comedy, 1993 (Critics' Circle Best Actor Award, 1993); Home, Wyndhams, 1994. Many TV appearances, including series, The Good Life, Yes Minister, Yes, Prime Minister and The Camomile Lawn. Chm., Internat. Cttee for Artists' Freedom, Equity, 1985–; Member: Council, Equity, 1972–75; Artistic Bd, Internat. Shakespeare Globe Centre, 1993–; Council, Howard League for Penal Reform, 1993–. Governor, Bristol Old Vic Theatre Trust, 1975–84. Hon. Prof. of Drama, Sheffield Univ., 1993–94. Hon. MA Sheffield, 1987. *Publication:* So Far So Good (autobiog.), 1995. *Recreations:* listening to music, reading, washing up, lying down and thinking what ought to be done in the garden. *Address:* c/o ICM Ltd, 388/396 Oxford Street, W1N 9HE. *T:* 0171–629 8080. *Club:* Garrick.   *Died 4 Nov. 1995.*

EDEN, Conrad William, TD; DMus Lambeth 1973; BMus Oxon; Hon. FRCO; Organist, Durham Cathedral, 1936–74, retired; *b* 4 May 1905; *m* 1932, Joyce Phoebe Hindley Cooke; *m* 1943, Barbara L., *d* of late Rev. R. L. Jones, Shepton Mallet; one *s* one *d*. *Educ:* Wells Cath. Sch.; Rugby; RCM; St John's Coll., Oxford. Teacher, Dragon Sch.; Asst Organist, 1928–33, Organist, 1933–36, Wells

Cathedral. *Address:* The Vale, Highmore Road, Sherborne, Dorset DT9 4BT. *T:* Sherborne (01935) 813488.   *Died 16 Oct. 1994.*

EDGEWORTH JOHNSTONE, Robert; *see* Johnstone.

EDMENSON, Sir Walter Alexander, Kt 1958; CBE 1944; shipowner; *b* 1892; 2nd *s* of late Robert Robson Edmenson; *m* 1918, Doris Davidson (*d* 1975); one *d* (one *s* killed in action, 1940). Served European War, 1914–18, RFA (despatches). Min. of War Transport Rep., N Ireland, 1939–45. President: The Ulster Steamship Co. Ltd; G. Heyn & Sons Ltd; Director: Clyde Shipping Co., 1946–64; The Belfast Banking Co. Ltd, 1946–70; The North Continental Shipping Co. Ltd, 1946–70; The Belfast Bank Executor & Trustee Co. Ltd, 1946–70; Commercial Insurance Co. of Ireland Ltd, 1964–72; Member Board: BEA, 1946–63; Gallaher Ltd, 1946–66. Chm., N Ireland Civil Aviation Adv. Council, 1946–61; Member: Bd, Ulster Transport Authority, 1948–64; Council, Chamber of Shipping, 1943–73; Lloyd's Register of Shipping, 1949–74. Belfast Harbour Comr, 1940–61; Irish Lights Comr, 1949–85. DL Belfast, 1951–87. Amer. Medal of Freedom with Palms, 1945. *Address:* 101 Bryansford Road, Newcastle, Co. Down BT33 0LF. *T:* Newcastle (Co. Down) (03967) 22769.   *Died 6 Oct. 1992.*

EDMUND-DAVIES, Baron *cr* 1974 (Life Peer), of Aberpennar, Mid Glamorgan; **Herbert Edmund Edmund-Davies,** Kt 1958; PC 1966; a Lord of Appeal; Life Governor and Fellow, King's College, London University; Hon. Fellow, Exeter College, Oxford; *b* 15 July 1906; 3rd *s* of Morgan John Davies and Elizabeth Maud Edmunds; *m* 1935, Eurwen Williams-James (*d* 1991); three *d*. *Educ:* Mountain Ash Grammar Sch.; King's Coll., London; Exeter Coll., Oxford. LLB (London) and Postgraduate Research Scholar, 1926; LLD London, 1928; BCL (Oxon) and Vinerian Scholar, 1929. Called to the Bar, Gray's Inn, 1929; Bencher, 1948; Treasurer, 1965; Lecturer and Examiner, London School of Economics, 1930–31. Army Officers' Emergency Reserve, 1938; Infantry OCTU; commissioned in Royal Welch Fusiliers, 1940; later seconded to JAG's Dept; Asst Judge Advocate-General, 1944–45 (Lt-Col 1944). QC 1943; Recorder: of Merthyr Tydfil, 1942–44; of Swansea, 1944–53; of Cardiff, 1953–58; Chm., QS for Denbighshire, 1953–64; Judge of High Court of Justice, Queen's Bench Division, 1958–66; a Lord Justice of Appeal, 1966–74; a Lord of Appeal in Ordinary, 1974–81. Foreign Office Observer, Cairo espionage trials, 1957. Chairman: Transport Users' Consultative Cttee for Wales, 1959–61; Lord Chancellor's Cttee on Limitation of Actions, 1961; Tribunal of Inquiry into Aberfan Disaster, 1966; Council of Law Reporting 1967–72; Home Secretary's Criminal Law Revision Cttee, 1969–77; Home Sec.'s Police Inquiry Cttee, 1977–79; Mem., Royal Commn on Penal Reform, 1964–66; conducted Use of Welsh in Courts Inquiry, 1973. President: London Welsh Trust/London Welsh Assoc., 1982–; University College of Swansea, 1965–75; Hon. Standing Counsel, Univ. of Wales, 1947–57; Pro-Chancellor, Univ. of Wales, 1974–85. Hon. Life Member, Canadian Bar Assoc.; CIBA Foundn Trustee; Hamlyn Trustee, 1969–87; Fellow, Royal Soc. of Medicine. Hon. LLD: Wales, 1959; Buckingham, 1989. *Publications:* Law of Distress for Rent and Rates, 1931; miscellaneous legal writings.   *Died 26 Dec. 1992.*

EDWARDS, Derek, FEng 1986; FIM; Director, 1974–91, Industrial Director, 1987–91, RTZ Corp. PLC; *b* 28 March 1931; *s* of L. R. Edwards and M. N. Edwards; *m* 1956, Julia Maureen Wynn; one *s* two *d*. *Educ:* Newport High Sch.; UC Swansea, Univ. of Wales (BSc Metallurgy). RAF, 1952–54. Alcan (UK), 1954–60; Alcan (W Africa), 1960–62; Pillar Ltd, 1962–70; RTZ Pillar, 1970–91 (Chm., 1981–91). Non-executive Director: TI Group, 1984–;

Bridon Ltd, 1985–; Henlys Gp, 1992–; National Express Gp, 1992–. Mem., Glos HA, 1992–. *Recreations:* sport, music, art. *Address:* Kings Lawn, Sandy Lane Road, Charlton Kings, Cheltenham, Glos GL53 9DB. *Clubs:* East India, MCC. *Died 20 July 1993.*

EDWARDS, Donald Isaac, CBE 1965 (OBE 1958); Managing Director, Independent Television News, 1968–71; *b* 27 Sept. 1904; *s* of late Isaac Edwards, Bolton, Lancs; *m* 1930, Enid Bent; two *s. Educ:* Bolton Sch.; Emmanuel Coll., Cambridge (MA). Tillotsons Newspapers, 1926–28; Daily News, 1928–30; Allied Newspapers, 1930–33; Daily Telegraph, 1933–39; BBC: Asst European News Editor, 1940–42; European News Editor, 1942–45; Correspondent in India, 1946; Dir, European News, 1946–48; Head of External Services, News Dept, 1948–58; Editor, News, 1958–60, News and Current Affairs, 1960–67; Gen. Man., Local Radio Development, 1967–68. *Publications:* The Two Worlds of Donald Edwards (autobiography), 1970; contribs to various books on journalism and broadcasting. *Recreations:* gardening, music, chess, walking. *Address:* Spindles, Miles Lane, Cobham, Surrey KT11 2EF. *T:* Cobham (0932) 862257. *Died 14 Sept. 1991.*

EDWARDS, William Philip Neville, CBE 1949; *b* 5 Aug. 1904; *s* of late Neville P. Edwards, Orford, Littlehampton, Sussex; *m* 1st, 1931, Hon. Sheila Cary (*d* 1976), 2nd *d* of 13th Viscount Falkland; one *s* (and one *s* decd); 2nd, 1976, Joan, *widow* of Norman Mullins. *Educ:* Rugby Sch.; Corpus Christi Coll., Cambridge; Princeton Univ., USA (Davison Scholar). Joined Underground Electric group of companies, 1927; shortly afterwards appointed Sec. to 1st Baron Ashfield, Chm. of Board; First Sec. of Standing Jt Cttee of Main Line Railway Companies and of LPTB, 1933; Officer of Board as Personal Asst to Gen. Manager of Railways, 1937; Outdoor Supt of Railways, 1938; Public Relations Officer of Board, 1939; Asst to Chm. of Supply Council of Min. of Supply, 1941–42; Head of Industrial Information Div. of Min. of Production and Alternate Dir of Information of British Supply Council in N America, 1943–45; Dir of Overseas Information Div. of BoT, 1945–46; Head of British Information Services in USA, 1946–49. A Dir, Confedn of British Industry (previously FBI), 1949–66; Man. Dir, British Overseas Fairs Ltd, 1959–66, Chm., 1966–68. UK Associate Dir, Business International SA, 1968–75; Chm., Public Relations (Industrial) Ltd, 1970–75. Chevalier (1st class) of Order of Dannebrog (Denmark), 1955; Commander of Order of Vasa (Sweden), 1962. *Recreations:* golf, gardening. *Address:* Four Winds, Kithurst Lane, Storrington, Sussex RH20 4LP. *Club:* Carlton. *Died 24 Jan. 1995.*

EDWARDS-JONES, Ian, QC 1967; The Banking Ombudsman, 1985–88; *b* 17 April 1923; *o s* of late Col H. V. Edwards-Jones, MC, DL, Swansea, Glam; *m* 1950, Susan Vera Catharine McClintock, *o d* of E. S. McClintock and of Mrs A. MacRossie; three *s. Educ:* Rugby Sch.; Trinity Coll., Cambridge (BA). Capt., RA, N Africa, Italy, Palestine, 1942–47. Called to Bar, Middle Temple, Lincoln's Inn, 1948, Bencher, Lincoln's Inn, 1975. A Social Security (formerly Nat. Insurance) Comr, 1979–85. *Recreations:* fishing, photography, amateur wine growing. *Address:* c/o Ground Floor, 7 Stone Buildings, Lincoln's Inn, WC2A 3SZ. *T:* 0171–405 3886/7. *Clubs:* United Oxford & Cambridge University; Bar Yacht. *Died 3 March 1995.*

EELES, Air Cdre Henry, CB 1956; CBE 1943; retired as Director of Administrative Plans, Air Ministry, 1959; *b* 12 May 1910; *yr s* of Henry Eeles, Newcastle upon Tyne; *m* 1st, 1940, Janet (*d* 1960), *d* of Major J. H. Norton; two *s* one *d*; 2nd, 1963, Pamela Clarice, *d* of Comdr G. A. Matthew, Royal Navy. *Educ:* Harrow. Entered RAF Coll.,

1929; commnd Dec. 1930; Sqdn Ldr 1938; Group Capt. 1949; Air Cdre 1955; Comdt RAF Coll. and AOC RAF Cranwell, 1952–56. *Address:* The Cottage, Sutton Veny, Warminster, Wilts BA12 7AU. *Died 15 July 1992.*

EGGLESTON, Hon. Sir Richard (Moulton), Kt 1971; Consultant, Faculty of Law, Monash University, 1974–83 (Chancellor, 1975–83); *b* Hampton, Vic, Australia, 8 Aug. 1909; *s* of late John Bakewell Eggleston and Elizabeth Bothwell Eggleston (*née* McCutcheon); *m* 1934, Marjorie, *d* of late F. E. Thom; one *s* three *d. Educ:* Wesley Coll., Melbourne; Univ. of Melbourne (LLB). Barrister, 1932–41 and 1945–60. Staff of Defence Dept, 1942–45; Indep. Lectr in Equity, Melbourne Univ., 1940–49; KC 1950. Judge: Supreme Ct of Norfolk Is, 1960–69; Supreme Ct of ACT, 1960–74; Commonwealth Industrial Ct, 1960–74; Pres., Trade Practices Tribunal, 1966–74. Dir, Barclays Australia Ltd, 1974–80. Hon. Treas., Victorian Bar Council, 1953–56 (Chm., 1956–58); Mem., Bd of Aust. Elizabethan Theatre Trust, 1961–67; Fellow, Queen's Coll., Univ. of Melbourne, 1964–; Pro-Chancellor, ANU, 1968–72. Chm., Company Law Adv. Cttee, 1967–73. FASSA 1981; Hon. FIArbA 1977. Hon. LLD: Melbourne, 1973; Monash, 1983. *Publication:* Evidence, Proof and Probability, 1978, 2nd edn 1983. *Recreations:* painting, golf, billiards, music. *Address:* 3 Willow Street, Malvern, Vic 3144, Australia. *Clubs:* Australian (Melbourne); Commonwealth (Canberra). *Died 16 Jan. 1991.*

ELAM, His Honour Henry; a Circuit Judge (formerly Deputy Chairman of the Court of Quarter Sessions, Inner London), 1953–76; barrister-at-law; *b* 29 Nov. 1903; *o s* of Thomas Henry Elam, 33 Sackville Street, W1; *m* 1st, 1930, Eunice (*d* 1975), *yr d* of J. G. Matthews, 41 Redington Road, NW3; one *d*; 2nd, 1975, Doris A. Horsford. *Educ:* Charterhouse; Lincoln Coll., Oxford (MA). Called to Bar, Inner Temple, 1927; Western Circuit; Junior Prosecuting Counsel to the Treasury, Central Criminal Court, 1937; late Dep. Judge Advocate, RAF; Recorder of Poole, 1941–46; 2nd Junior Prosecuting Counsel, 1942–45; 1st Junior, 1945–50; 3rd Senior, Jan.-March 1950; 2nd Senior, 1950–53; Recorder of Exeter, 1946–53; Dep. Chm., West Kent QS, 1947–53. *Recreation:* flyfishing. *Address:* Clymshurst, Burwash Common, East Sussex TN19 7NB. *T:* Burwash (0435) 883335. *Died 13 Aug. 1993.*

ELDRIDGE, Eric William, CB 1965; OBE 1948; Public Trustee, 1963–71; *b* 15 April 1906; *o s* of late William Eldridge; *m* 1936, Doris Margaret Kerr; one *s* one *d. Educ:* Millfields Central Sch.; City of London Coll. Admitted Solicitor (Hons), 1934. Chief Administrative Officer, Public Trustee Office, 1955–60; Asst Public Trustee, 1960–63. Consultant, Lee and Pembertons, solicitors, 1971–88, retd. *Address:* Old Stocks, Gorelands Lane, Chalfont St Giles, Bucks HP8 4HQ. *T:* Chalfont St Giles (02407) 2159. *Died 20 Dec. 1991.*

ELEK, Prof. Stephen Dyonis, MD, DSc; FRCP; Professor of Medical Microbiology in the University of London, 1957–74, then Emeritus; Consultant Bacteriologist, St George's Hospital, SW1, 1948–73; *b* 24 March 1914; *s* of Dezso and Anna Elek; *m* 1947, Sarah Joanna Hall; three *d. Educ:* Lutheran High Sch., Budapest, Hungary; St George's Hosp. Med. Sch., Univ. of London. MB, BS 1940; MD 1943; PhD 1948; DPH 1943; DSc 1958; MRCP 1960; FRCPath 1964. Clinical Pathologist, Maida Vale Hosp. for Nervous Diseases, 1946–47; Laking-Dakin Fellow, 1942–43; Fulbright Fellow, Harvard Medical Sch., 1956. Member: Pathological Soc. of Great Britain; American Society for Microbiology; New York Academy of Sciences; Soc. of Gen. Microbiology, etc. Editor, Jl of Medical Microbiology, 1972–74. Introduced immuno-diffusion as a new analytical tool in serology, 1948.

Publications: Staphylococcus pyogenes and its Relation to Disease, 1959; scientific papers relating to diphtheria, leprosy, vaccination against mental retardation due to CM Virus infection during pregnancy, etc, in Lancet, BMJ, Jl Path. and Bact., Brit. Jl Exper. Path. *Recreations:* sculpting, walking. *Address:* Avenue de Cour 155, 1007 Lausanne, Switzerland. *T:* 265814. *Club:* Athenæum.

Died 21 Jan. 1992.

ELIAS, Dr Taslim Olawale, GCON 1983; CFR 1963; NNMA 1979; QC 1961; Judge, International Court of Justice, since 1976 (Vice-President, 1979–82, President, 1982–85); *b* Lagos, 11 Nov. 1914; *s* of Momolesho Elias Frowoshere; *m* 1959, Ganiat Yetunde Elias; three *s* two *d.* *Educ:* Igbobi Coll., Lagos; University Coll. London (BA, LLM, PhD; Fellow, 1983); Inst. of Advanced Legal Studies, London. Called to the Bar, Inner Temple, 1947 (Hon. Bencher 1982). Simon Res. Fellow, Manchester Univ., 1951–53; Oppenheim Res. Fellow, Oxford, 1954–60; Federal Attorney-Gen. and Minister of Justice, Nigeria, 1960–66; Attorney-Gen., 1966–72; Mem., Fed. Exec. Council, 1967–72; Comr for Justice, 1967–72; Prof. and Dean of Faculty of Law, Univ. of Lagos, 1966–72; Chief Justice of Supreme Court, 1972–75. Vis. Prof., Delhi Univ., 1956. Sen. Gen. Editor, Nigerian Law Jl 1967–73. Member: Internat. Law Commn, UN, 1961–76 (Chm. 1970); Exec., Inst. of Human Rights, Strasbourg, 1969; Exec., Internat. Commn of Jurists, 1975–; Inst. of Internat. Law, 1969–; Council of Management, British Inst. of Internat. and Comparative Law, 1983–; Mem., Delegn to Nigerian Constitutional Conf., London, 1958; Chm., UN Cttee of Constitnl Experts to draft Congo Constitution, 1961–62; Mem., Expert Cttee drafting OAU Charter, 1963. President: World Assoc. of Judges, 1975; Nigerian Soc. of Internat. Law; Chm., African Inst. of Internat. Law. Chm., Governing Council, Nigerian Inst. of Internat. Affairs, 1972–; Governor, SOAS, 1958–61; Mem., Governing Council, Univ. of Nigeria, 1959–66; Hon. Fellow, Nigerian Inst. of Advanced Legal Studies, 1981; Hon. Member: Amer. Soc. of Internat. Law, 1973; Soc. of Public Teachers of Law, 1981. Hon. LLD: Dakar, 1964; Ahmadu Bello, 1972; Ife, 1974; Howard, 1975; Jodhpur, 1976; Hull, 1980; Dalhousie, Halifax, 1983; Nairobi, 1983; Manchester, 1984; Buckingham, 1986; Hon. DSc (Econ.) London, 1983; Hon. DLitt: Ibadan, 1969; Nigeria (Nsukka), 1973; Lagos 1974. World Jurist Award, 1973; Nigerian Nat. Merit Award, 1979. *Publications:* Nigerian Land Law and Custom, 1951; Nigerian Legal System, 1954; Makers of Nigerian Law, 1956; Nature of African Customary Law, 1956, 2nd edn 1962; (jtly) British Legal Papers, 1958; The Impact of English Law upon Nigerian Customary Law, 1960; Government and Politics in Africa, 1961, 2nd edn 1963; Ghana and Sierra Leone: development of their laws and constitutions, 1962; British Colonial Law: a comparative study, 1962; (jtly) International Law in a Changing World, 1963; Nigeria: development of its laws and constitution, 1965; (jtly) Sovereignty within the Law, 1965; (jtly) African Law: adaptation and development, 1965; (jtly) Law, Justice and Equity, 1967; (jtly) Nigerian Prison System, 1968; (jtly) Nigerian Press Law, 1969; Problems concerning the Validity of Treaties, 1971; Nigerian Magistrate and the Offender, 1972; Law and Social Change in Nigeria, 1972; Africa and the Development of International Law, 1972; Law in a Developing Society, 1973; Modern Law of Treaties, 1974; Judicial Process in Commonwealth Africa, 1976; New Horizons in International Law, 1979; Africa before the World Court, 1981; (jtly) International Law: teaching and practice, 1982; The International Court of Justice and Some Contemporary Problems, 1983; (jtly) Essays in International Law in Honour of Judge Manfred Lachs, 1984; (jtly) Encyclopedia of Public International Law,

1984; (jtly) Essays on Third World Perspectives in Jurisprudence; (jtly) Africa and the West: the legacies of Empire, 1986; contribs to legal jls. *Address:* c/o International Court of Justice, Peace Palace, The Hague, Netherlands; (home) 20 Ozumba Mbadiwe Street, Victoria Island, Lagos, Nigeria. *T:* 612389.

Died 14 Aug. 1991.

ELIOT, Ven. Canon Peter Charles, MBE 1945; TD 1945; Archdeacon of Worcester, 1961–75, then Archdeacon Emeritus; Residentiary Canon, Worcester Cathedral, 1965–75, then Canon Emeritus; *b* 30 Oct. 1910; *s* of late Hon. Edward Granville Eliot and late Mrs Eliot; *m* 1934, Lady Alethea Constance Dorothy Sydney Buxton, *d* of 1st and last Earl Buxton, PC, GCMG, and late Countess Buxton; no *c. Educ:* Wellington Coll.; Magdalene Coll., Cambridge. Commissioned in Kent Yeomanry (Lt-Col Comdg, 1949–52), 1933. Admitted Solicitor, 1934; Partner in City firm until 1953. Studied at Westcott House, Cambridge, 1954; made Deacon to serve in Parish of St Martin-in-the-Fields, London, 1954; Priest, 1955; Vicar of Cockermouth, 1957–61; Rural Dean of Cockermouth and Workington, 1960–61; Vicar of Cropthorne with Charlton, 1961–65. *Recreations:* amateur acting, sketching, sight-seeing, gardening. *Address:* The Old House, Kingsland, Leominster, Herefordshire HR6 9QS. *T:* Kingsland (01568) 708285. *Club:* Travellers'.

Died 16 Dec. 1995.

ELKINGTON, (Reginald) Geoffrey, CB 1962; *b* 24 Dec. 1907; *s* of Harold and Millicent Elkington; *m* 1935, Bertha Phyllis (*d* 1990), *d* of William and Bertha Dyason; one adopted *s* one adopted *d. Educ:* Battersea Grammar Sch.; Fitzwilliam Coll., Cambridge. Inland Revenue, 1929–42; Min. of Supply, 1942–57 (Under-Sec., 1954); Dept of Scientific Res., 1957–64; Principal Establishment Officer, Min. of Technology, 1964–67; retired from Civil Service, 1967; Estabt Officer (part-time), Monopolies Commn, 1968–73. Sec., AERE Harwell, 1948–51. *Address:* Maranwood, Highfield Road, West Byfleet, Surrey KT14 6QT. *T:* Byfleet (0932) 343766.

Died 14 June 1993.

ELLIOT OF HARWOOD, Baroness *cr* 1958 (Life Peer), of Rulewater, Co. Roxburgh; **Katharine Elliot,** DBE 1958 (CBE 1946); JP; *b* 15 Jan. 1903; *d* of Sir Charles Tennant, 1st Bt, Innerleithen, Peeblesshire, and Mrs Geoffrey Lubbock; *m* 1934, Rt Hon. Walter Elliot, CH, MC, PC, LLD, FRS, MP (*d* 1958); no *c. Educ:* Abbot's Hill, Hemel Hempstead; Paris. Chairman: Nat. Assoc. of Mixed Clubs and Girls' Clubs, 1939–49; Adv. Cttee on Child Care for Scotland, 1956–65; Women's Nat. Adv. Cttee of Conservative Party, 1954–57; Nat. Union of Conservative and Unionist Assocs, 1956–67; Consumer Council, 1963–68. Chm., Lawrie & Symington Ltd, Lanark, 1958–85. Member: Women's Consultative Cttee, Dept of Employment and Productivity (formerly Min. of Labour), 1941–51, 1958–70; Home Office Adv. Cttee on Treatment of Offenders, 1946–62; King George V Jubilee Trust, 1936–68; NFU; Trustee and Mem. Council, Carnegie UK Trust (Exec. Trustee, 1940–86). Pres., Royal Highland Agricl Soc., 1986. UK Delegate to Gen. Assembly of UN, New York, 1954, 1956 and 1957. Contested (C) Kelvingrove Div. of Glasgow, March 1958. Roxburghshire: CC, 1946–75 (Vice-Convener, 1974); JP 1968. Farmer in Roxburghshire. FRSA 1964. Hon. LLD: Glasgow, 1959; Selly Oak Colls, Birmingham, 1986. Grand Silver Cross, Austrian Order of Merit, 1963. *Publication:* Tennants Stalk, 1973. *Recreations:* foxhunting, golf, music. *Address:* Harwood, Bonchester Bridge, Hawick, Roxburghshire TD9 9TL; 17 Lord North Street, Westminster, SW1P 3LD. *T:* 071–222 3230.

Died 3 Jan. 1994.

ELLIOTT, Bruce John, CBE 1988; TD 1963; District Judge (formerly District Registrar), High Court of Justice and County Courts, since 1961; a Recorder, since 1986; *b* 8 Feb. 1927; *s* of John Thomas Girvan Elliott and Zena Phyllis Elliott; *m* 1st, 1951, Joy Manderson; 2nd, 1955, Joy Redpath; two *s*; 3rd, 1975, Alison Jane Furniss. *Educ:* Charminster Council Sch.; Bournemouth Secondary Sch.; Law Soc. Sch. of Law. Joined Army, 1945; commissioned in India, 1946; served India, Egypt and Palestine to 1948 (Captain, Hampshire Regt). Admitted Solicitor, 1951; Asst Recorder, 1979; former JP; Hon. Sec., Registrars' Assoc., 1969–87. Territorial Army: 14th Bn, Parachute Regt, 1951; qualified parachutist; Major, Royal Hampshire Regt, 1955; 5th Bn, Royal Northumberland Fusiliers, 1961; qualified pilot and glider pilot, 1963; RAF Cadet Reserve Instructor; Company Comdr; subseq. Lt-Col comdg 5th Bn Beds and Herts Regt, 1965; Col Comdt, Beds Army Cadet Force, 1967. Various social work. *Recreations:* the simplest outdoor pursuits. *Address:* Luton County Court, Cresta House, Alma Street, Luton, Beds LU1 2PU. *T:* Luton (0582) 35671.

Died 5 Sept. 1993.

ELLIOTT, Dr Charles Kennedy; Physician to HM the Queen, 1980–86; *b* 14 May 1919; *e s* of late Charles Harper Elliott and Martha Elliott; *m* 1949, Elizabeth Margaret Kyle. *Educ:* Campbell Coll., Belfast; Trinity Coll., Dublin (BA 1941; MA 1970; MB, BCh 1942). MRCGP; MLCOM; MFHom; AFOM RCP. Sir Patrick Dun's Hosp., Dublin, 1943; Captain, RAMC, attached SEAC, 1944; general practitioner, Wisbech, 1949–69; Editor, Rural Medicine, 1969–72; Clinical Asst, Royal London Homoeopathic Hosp., 1973–81; Sub Dean, Faculty of Homoeopathy, 1976–79; Area Surgeon, Cambridgeshire St John Ambulance, 1974–81. Chm., Organizing Cttee, VI Internat. Congress Rural Medicine, Cambridge, 1975; Pres., Internat. Assoc. of Agricl Medicine and Rural Health, 1972–78; Trustee: Rehabilitation Trust of Gt Britain, 1977–; Inst. for Complementary Medicine, 1982–. Hon. DLitt Central Sch. of Religion, 1987. SBStJ 1970; Chevalier de l'Ordre Militaire et Hospitalier de St Lazare de Jerusalem, 1975. *Publications:* (ed jtly) Classical Homoeopathy, 1986, rev. edn 1990; articles in internat. med. pubns and nat. jls. *Recreations:* heraldry, history. *Club:* Royal Society of Medicine. *Died 8 Dec. 1992.*

ELLIOTT, Denholm Mitchell, CBE 1988; actor, stage and films; *b* 31 May 1922; *s* of Myles Layman Farr Elliott and Nina Mitchell; *m* 1954, Virginia McKenna (marr. diss. 1957; she *m* 1957, Bill Travers); *m* 1962, Susan Robinson; one *s* one *d. Educ:* Malvern. *Plays:* The Guinea-Pig, Criterion, 1946; Venus Observed, St James's, 1949; Ring Round the Moon, Martin Beck, New York, 1950; Sleep of Prisoners, St Thomas's, Regent Street, 1950; Third Person, Criterion, 1951; Confidential Clerk, Lyric, 1954; South, Arts, 1955; Who Cares, Fortune, 1956; Camino Real, Phœnix, 1957; Traveller Without Luggage, Arts, 1958; The Ark, Westminster, 1959; Stratford-on-Avon Season, 1960; Write Me a Murder, Belasco Theatre, New York, 1961; The Seagull, The Crucible, Ring Round the Moon, Nat. Repertory Co., New York, 1963–64; Come as You Are, New, 1970; Chez Nous, Globe, 1974; The Return of A. J. Raffles, Aldwych, 1975; Heaven and Hell, Greenwich, 1976; The Father, Open Space, 1979; A Life in the Theatre, Haymarket, 1989; *films:* Sound Barrier, 1949; The Cruel Sea, 1952; They Who Dare, 1953; Pacific Destiny, 1955; Scent of Mystery, 1959; Station Six Sahara, 1962; Nothing But the Best, 1963; King Rat, 1964; The High Bright Sun, 1964; You Must Be Joking, 1965; Alfie, 1966; Here we go round the Mulberry Bush, 1967; The Seagull, 1968; Too Late the Hero, 1969; Madame Sin, 1972; A Doll's House, 1973; The Apprenticeship of Duddy Kravitz, 1974; Russian Roulette, 1976; Sweeney

II, Saint Jack, The Hound of the Baskervilles, Zulu Dawn, A Game for Vultures, Cuba, 1978; Bad Timing, Sunday Lovers, 1980; Trading Places, 1982; The Missionary, The Wicked Lady, 1983; A Private Function, 1984; Defence of the Realm, A Room with a View, 1986; Maurice, September, 1987; Indiana Jones and the Last Crusade, 1988; Toy Soldiers, 1991; *television:* series incl. Bleak House, 1987; Bangkok Hilton, 1990; also plays. Awards, London and New York, incl. BAFTA Best TV Actor, New Standard Best Film Actor, 1981, BAFTA Best Supporting Film Actor, 1984, 1985, 1986. *Recreations:* ski-ing, golf. *Address:* c/o London Management, 235 Regent Street, W1. *Club:* Garrick.

Died 6 Oct. 1992.

ELLIOTT, Harold William, CBE 1967; *b* 24 Nov. 1905; *s* of late W. J. Elliott and Ellen Elliott; *m* 1st, 1929, Mary Molyneux (marr. diss. 1935); one *s* one *d*; 2nd, 1937, Betty (*d* 1976), *d* of late C. J. Thumling; one *s*; 3rd, 1978, Helen Bridget, *y d* of Sir Lionel Faudel-Phillips, 3rd Bt, and *widow* of 5th Earl of Kilmorey. *Educ:* Brighton Coll. Apprenticed to Adolf Saurer, AG Arbon, Switz., 1924; joined Pickfords Ltd, 1926. Mem., Road and Rail Central Conf., 1938; Mem., Transport Adv. Cttee, Food Defence Plans Dept, BoT, 1939; Asst Divisional Food Officer (Transport), London, 1940; Controller of Road Transport, Min. of Supply, 1941; Mem., Salvage Bd; Dir of Transport, Middle East Supply Centre, Cairo, 1943–44, with responsibility, within this Anglo-Amer. orgn which covered some 16 countries of ME, for adequacy of civilian transport for food distribn and other basic needs of wartime economy of area, incl. locust control and Aid to Russia convoys from Persian Gulf; crossed Saudi Arabia via Riyadh, 1943. Mem., Road Haulage Central Wages Bd and Vice-Chm., Meat Transport Organisation Ltd, 1945; Gen. Man., Hay's Wharf Cartage Co. Ltd, Pickfords Ltd and Carter Paterson & Co. Ltd, 1947; Chief Officer (Freight), Road Transport Exec.; Mem., Coastal Shipping Adv. Cttee, 1948; Mem. Bd of Management, Brit. Road Services, and Dir, Atlantic Steam Navigation Co. Ltd, 1959; Man. Dir, Pickfords Ltd, 1963–70, Chm., 1970. Vice-Pres., CIT, 1970–71; Life Mem., Road Haulage Assoc. Trustee, Sutton Housing Trust, 1971–79; Chm., Holmwood Common Management Cttee, 1971–79; Governor, Brighton Coll., 1955 (Chm. Governors, 1974–78; a Vice Patron, 1980). Liveryman, Worshipful Co. of Carmen, 1939–84; Freeman, City of London, 1939. *Address:* Ombla, Moushill Lane, Milford, Godalming, Surrey GU8 5BH. *T:* Godalming (0483) 420723.

Died 19 Sept. 1991.

ELLIOTT, Sir Norman (Randall), Kt 1967; CBE 1957 (OBE 1946); MA; Chairman of the Electricity Council, 1968–72; Chairman, Howden Group, 1973–83; *b* 19 July 1903; *s* of William Randall Elliott and Catherine Dunsmore; *m* 1963, Phyllis Clarke (decd). *Educ:* privately; St Catharine's Coll., Cambridge. Called to the Bar, Middle Temple, 1932 (J. J. Powell Prizeman, A. J. Powell Exhibitioner). London Passenger Transport Board; London and Home Counties Joint Electricity Authority; Yorkshire Electric Power Co.; 21 Army Group: first as CRE, then, as Col, Deputy Dir of Works, 21 Army Group (OBE); Chief Engineer and Manager, Wimbledon Borough Council; Gen. Manager and Chief Engineer, London and Home Counties Joint Electricity Authority and sometime Chm. and Dir, Isle of Thanet Electric Supply Co., and Dir, James Howden & Co. Ltd; Chairman: S-E Electricity Bd, 1948–62; S of Scotland Electricity Bd, 1962–67; Member: Brit. Electricity Authority, 1950 and 1951; Central Electricity Authority, 1956 and 1957; Electricity Council, 1958–62; N of Scotland Hydro-Electric Bd, 1965–69. Director: Newarthill & McAlpine Group, 1972–89; Slumberger Ltd, 1977–84. *Publication:* Electricity Statutes, Orders and Regulations, 1947, rev.

edn 1951. *Recreations:* ball games, the theatre. *Clubs:* Athenæum; Western (Glasgow); Royal Northern Yacht.
Died 23 March 1992.

ELLIS, Joseph Stanley, CMG 1967; OBE 1962; Head of News Department, Commonwealth Office, 1967; retired; *b* 29 Nov. 1907; *s* of Joseph Ellis, Chorley, Lancs; *m* 1933, Gladys Harcombe (*d* 1983); one *s*. *Educ:* Woodhouse Grove, Bradford; University Coll., University of London. Journalist, Manchester Evening News, 1930–40; Publications Div., Min. of Inf., 1941–45; seconded to Dominions Office for service in Australia until 1949; Central Office of Information, 1949–51; Regional Information Officer, Karachi, 1952; Dir, British Information Services: Pakistan, 1953–55; Canberra, Australia, 1955–58; Kuala Lumpur, Malaya, 1958–62; Head, Information Services Dept, Commonwealth Office, 1962–66. *Recreation:* cricket. *Address:* Coxhill Manor, Station Road, Chobham, Surrey GU24 8AJ.
Died 22 Aug. 1993.

ELLIS, Raymond Joseph; *b* 17 Dec. 1923; *s* of Harold and Ellen Ellis; *m* 1946, Cynthia (*née* Lax); four *c*. *Educ:* elementary school; Sheffield Univ.; Ruskin Coll., Oxford. Coal miner, 1938–79. National Union of Mineworkers: Branch Secretary, Highmoor, 1959–79; Pres., Derbyshire Area, 1972–79. Councillor, South Yorkshire CC, 1976–79. MP (Lab) Derbyshire NE, 1979–87. *Address:* Oakdene, 3 The Villas, Mansfield Road, Wales Bar, Kiveton, Sheffield S31 8RL.
Died 20 April 1994.

ELLISON, Rt Rev. and Rt Hon. Gerald Alexander, KCVO 1981; PC 1973; *b* 19 Aug. 1910; *s* of late Preb. John Henry Joshua Ellison, CVO, Chaplain in Ordinary to the King, Rector of St Michael's, Cornhill, and Sara Dorothy Graham Ellison (*née* Crum); *m* 1947, Jane Elizabeth, *d* of late Brig. John Houghton Gibbon, DSO; one *s* two *d*. *Educ:* St George's, Windsor; Westminster Sch.; New Coll., Oxford (Hon. Fellow, 1974); Westcott House, Cambridge. Deacon, 1935; priest, 1936; Curate, Sherborne Abbey, 1935–37; Domestic Chaplain to the Bishop of Winchester, 1937–39; Chaplain RNVR, 1940–43 (despatches); Domestic Chaplain to Archbishop of York, 1943–46; Vicar, St Mark's, Portsea, 1946–50; Hon. Chaplain to Archbishop of York, 1946–50; Canon of Portsmouth, 1950; Examining Chaplain to Bishop of Portsmouth, 1949–50; Bishop Suffragan of Willesden, 1950–55; Bishop of Chester, 1955–73; Bishop of London, 1973–81; Dean of the Chapels Royal, 1973–81; Prelate, Order of the British Empire, 1973–81; Prelate, Imperial Soc. of Knights Bachelor, 1973–85; Episcopal Canon of Jerusalem, 1973–81; Vicar General of Diocese of Bermuda, 1983–84. Select Preacher: Oxford Univ., 1940, 1961, 1972; Cambridge Univ., 1957. Chaplain and Sub-Prelate, Order of St John, 1973–. Hon. Chaplain, RNR. Mem. Wolfenden Cttee on Sport, 1960; Chairman: Bd of Governors, Westfield Coll., Univ. of London, 1953–67; Council of King's Coll., London, 1973–80 (FKC 1968; Vice-Chm. newly constituted Council, 1980–88); Governor, Sherborne Sch., 1982–85. Chm., Archbishop's Commn on Women and Holy Orders, 1963–66; Mem., Archbishop's Commn on Church and State, 1967; President: Actors' Church Union, 1973–81; Pedestrians Assoc. for Road Safety, 1964–75; Nat. Fedn of Housing Assocs, 1981–. Hon. Bencher Middle Temple, 1976. Freeman, Drapers' Co.; Hon. Liveryman: Merchant Taylors' Co.; Glass Sellers' Co. (Chaplain, 1951–73); Painter Stainers' Co.; Mem., Master Mariners' Co. (Chaplain, 1946–73). Chm., Oxford Soc., 1973–85. A Steward of Henley Regatta. *Publications:* The Churchman's Duty, 1957; The Anglican Communion, 1960. *Recreations:* oarsmanship, walking, music, watching television, tapestry, reading. *Address:* Billeys House, 16 Long Street, Cerne Abbas, Dorset. *T:* Cerne

Abbas (0300) 341247. *Clubs:* Army and Navy; Leander (Henley-on-Thames).
Died 18 Oct. 1992.

ELLMAN-BROWN, Hon. Geoffrey, CMG 1959; OBE 1945; FCA 1950 (ACA 1934); *b* 20 Dec. 1910; *s* of John and Violet Ellman-Brown; *m* 1936, Hilda Rosamond Fairbrother; two *s* one *d*. *Educ:* Plumtree Sch., S Rhodesia. Articled to firm of Chartered Accountants in London, 1929–34; final Chartered Accountant exam. and admitted as Mem. Inst. of Chartered Accountants of England and Wales, 1934; Rhodesia Air Force (rising to rank of Group Capt.), 1939–46; resumed practice as Chartered Accountant, 1946–53. Entered S Rhodesia Parliament holding ministerial office (Portfolios of Roads, Irrigation, Local Government and Housing), 1953–58; re-entered Parliament, 1962, Minister of Finance; re-elected, 1962–65, in Opposition Party. Pres. Rhodesia Cricket Union, 1950–52; Mem. S African Cricket Board of Control, 1951–52. Chairman: The Zimbabwe Sugar Assoc.; Industrial Promotion Corp. Central Africa Ltd; Director: RAL Merchant Bank Ltd; Hippo Valley Estates Ltd; Freight Services Ltd. *Recreations:* cricket, golf, shooting, fishing. *Address:* 42 Steppes Road, Chisipite, Harare, Zimbabwe. *T:* (4) 706381. *Clubs:* Harare, Royal Harare Golf (Harare, Zimbabwe); Ruwa Country.
Died 1 July 1994.

ELLWOOD, Air Marshal Sir Aubrey (Beauclerk), KCB 1949 (CB 1944); DSC; DL; *b* 3 July 1897; *s* of late Rev. C. E. Ellwood, Rector of Cottesmore, Rutland, 1888–1926; *m* 1920, Lesley Mary Joan Matthews (*d* 1982); one *s* one *d* (and one *s* decd). *Educ:* Cheam Sch.; Marlborough Coll. Joined Royal Naval Air Service, 1916; permanent commission RAF, 1919; served India, 1919–23 and 1931–36 in RAF; RAF Staff Coll., Air Min., Army Co-operation Comd variously, 1938–42; AOC No 18 Group RAF, 1943–44; Temp. Air Vice-Marshal, 1943; SASO HQ Coastal Comd RAF, 1944–45; Actg Air Marshal, 1947; a Dir-Gen. of Personnel, Air Ministry, 1945–47; Air Marshal, 1949; AOC-in-C, Bomber Command, 1947–50; AOC-in-C, Transport Command, 1950–52; retired, 1952. Governor and Commandant, The Church Lads' Brigade, 1954–70. DL Somerset, 1960. *Recreations:* riding, fishing, music. *Address:* The Old House, North Perrott, Crewkerne, Somerset. *T:* Crewkerne (0460) 73600. *Club:* Naval and Military.
Died 20 Dec. 1992.

ELPHINSTONE, 18th Lord *cr* 1509; **James Alexander Elphinstone;** Baron (UK) 1885; *b* 22 April 1953; *s* of Rev. Hon. Andrew Charles Victor Elphinstone (*d* 1975) (2nd *s* of 16th Lord) and of Jean Frances Woodroffe, CVO (who *m* 3rd, Lt-Col John William Richard Woodroffe (*d* 1990)); *S* uncle, 1975; *m* 1978, Willa, 4th *d* of Major David Chetwode, Upper Slaughter, Cheltenham; three *s* one *d*. *Educ:* Eton Coll.; Royal Agricultural Coll., Cirencester. FRICS 1992 (ARICS 1979). FRSA. *Heir: s* Master of Elphinstone, *b* 15 April 1980. *Address:* Drumkilbo, Meigle, Blairgowrie, Perthshire PH12 8QS. *T:* Meigle (018284) 216. *Club:* Turf.
Died 19 Dec. 1994.

ELPHINSTONE, Sir (Maurice) Douglas (Warburton), 5th Bt *cr* 1816; TD 1946; retired, 1973; *b* 13 April 1909; *s* of Rev. Canon Maurice Curteis Elphinstone (4th *s* of 3rd Bt) (*d* 1969), and Christiana Georgiana (*née* Almond); *S* cousin, 1975; *m* 1943, Helen Barbara, *d* of late George Ramsay Main; one *s* one *d*. *Educ:* Loretto School, Musselburgh; Jesus Coll., Cambridge (MA). FFA; FRSE. Actuary engaged in Life Assurance companies until 1956 (with the exception of the war); Member of Stock Exchange, London, 1957–74. War service with London Scottish and Sierra Leone Regt, RWAFF, mainly in W Africa and India. *Publications:* technical papers mainly in Trans Faculty of Actuaries and Jl Inst. of Actuaries. *Heir:*

s John Howard Main Elphinstone [*b* 25 Feb. 1949; *m* 1990, Diane Barbara Quilliam Callow]. *Address:* 11 Scotby Green Steading, Scotby, Carlisle CA4 8EH. *T:* Scotby (01228) 513141. *Died 5 Dec. 1995.*

ELTON, Charles Sutherland, FRS 1953; Director, Bureau of Animal Population, Department of Zoological Field Studies, 1932–67, and Reader in Animal Ecology, Oxford University, 1936–67; Senior Research Fellow, Corpus Christi College, Oxford, 1936–67, Hon. Fellow since Oct. 1967; *b* 29 March 1900; *s* of late Oliver Elton; *m* 1st, 1928, Rose Montague (marr. diss.); no *c*; 2nd, 1937, Edith Joy, *d* of Rev. Canon F. G. Scovell; one *s* one *d*. *Educ:* Liverpool Coll.; New Coll., Oxford. First Class Hons Zoology, Oxford, 1922. Served as ecologist on: Oxford Univ. Expedition to Spitsbergen, 1921; Merton Coll. Arctic Expedition, 1923; Oxford Univ. Arctic Expedition, 1924; Oxford Univ. Lapland Expedition, 1930; Founding Mem., Oxford Univ. Exploration Club, 1927. Mem. Nature Conservancy, 1949–56 (Mem., Scientific Policy Cttee, 1950–67). Vis. Fellow, Smithsonian Inst., 1968. Hon. Member: NY Zool Soc., 1931; Chicago Acad. of Scis, 1946; Wildlife Soc., 1949; British Ecol Soc., 1960; Ecol Soc. of Amer., 1961 (and as Eminent Ecologist, 1961); Amer. Soc. of Mammalogists, 1973; Inst. of Biology, 1983; Amer. Soc. of Zool., 1985. Foreign Hon. Mem., Amer. Acad. of Arts and Sciences, 1968. Murchison Grant, RGS, 1929; Linnean Soc. Gold Medal, 1967; Darwin Medal, Royal Soc., 1970; John and Alice Tyler Ecology Award, 1976; Edward W. Browning Achievement Award, for Conserving the Environment, 1977. *Publications:* Animal Ecology, 1927; Animal Ecology and Evolution, 1930; The Ecology of Animals, 1933; Exploring the Animal World, 1933; Voles, Mice and Lemmings, 1942; The Ecology of Invasions by Animals and Plants, 1958; The Pattern of Animal Communities, 1966. *Recreations:* natural history, gardening, reading. *Address:* 61 Park Town, Oxford OX2 6SL. *T:* Oxford (0865) 57644. *Died 1 May 1991.*

ELTON, Prof. Sir Geoffrey (Rudolph), Kt 1986; LittD; PhD; FBA 1967; Regius Professor of Modern History, Cambridge, 1983–88; Fellow of Clare College, Cambridge, since 1954; *b* 17 Aug. 1921; *er s* of late Prof. Victor Ehrenberg, PhD, and Eva Dorothea Sommer; changed name to Elton under Army Council Instruction, 1944; *m* 1952, Sheila Lambert; no *c*. *Educ:* Prague; Rydal Sch. London External BA (1st Cl. Hons) 1943; PhD London, 1949; LittD Cantab 1960. Asst Master, Rydal Sch., 1940–43; service in E Surrey Regt and Int. Corps (Sgt), 1944–46; Derby Student, University Coll. London, 1946–48; Asst in History, Glasgow Univ., 1948–49; Univ. Asst Lectr, Cambridge, 1949–53, Lectr, 1953–63, Reader in Tudor Studies, 1963–67, Prof. of English Constitutional History, 1967–83. Visiting Amundson Prof., Univ. of Pittsburgh, Sept.-Dec. 1963; Vis. Hill Prof., Univ. of Minnesota, 1976. Lectures: Ford's, Oxford, 1972; Wiles, Belfast, 1972; Hagey, Waterloo, 1974; Tanner, Utah, 1987. Publications Sec., British Acad., 1981–90. Member: Adv. Council on Public Records, 1977–85; Library and Inf. Services Council, 1986–88. FRHistS 1954 (Pres., 1972–76); Founder and Pres., List & Index Soc., 1965–93; President: Selden Soc., 1983–85; Ecclesiastical Hist. Soc., 1983–84. Fellow, UCL, 1978. Hon. DLitt: Glasgow, 1979; Newcastle, 1981; Bristol, 1981; London, 1985; Göttingen, 1987; Hon. DCL Cambridge, 1992. For. Mem., Amer. Acad. Arts and Scis, 1975; Hon. Mem., American Historical Assoc., 1982. *Publications:* The Tudor Revolution in Government, 1953; England under the Tudors, 1955; (ed) New Cambridge Modern History, vol. 2, 1958, new edn 1975; Star Chamber Stories, 1958; The Tudor Constitution, 1960, 2nd edn 1982; Henry VIII: an essay in revision, 1962; Renaissance and Reformation (Ideas and Institutions in Western Civilization), 1963;

Reformation Europe, 1963; The Practice of History, 1967; The Future of the Past, 1968; The Sources of History: England 1200–1640, 1969; Political History: Principles and Practice, 1970; Modern Historians on British History 1485–1945: a critical bibliography 1945–1969, 1970; Policy and Police: the enforcement of the Reformation in the age of Thomas Cromwell, 1972; Reform and Renewal, 1973; Studies in Tudor and Stuart Politics and Government: papers and reviews, 1946–1972, 2 vols, 1974, vol. 3, 1973–1981, 1983, vol. 4, 1982–1990, 1992; Reform and Reformation: England 1509–1558, 1977; The History of England (inaug. lecture), 1984; (with R. W. Fogel) Which Road to the Past?, 1984; F. W. Maitland, 1985; The Parliament of England 1559–1581, 1986; Return to Essentials, 1991; The English, 1992; contribs to English Hist. Review, Econ. Hist. Rev., History, Hist. Jl, Times Lit. Supplement, Listener, NY Review of Books, etc; recipient of five festschriften. *Recreations:* squash rackets (latterly forbidden), joinery, gardening, beer. *Address:* Clare College, Cambridge CB2 1TL; 30 Millington Road, Cambridge CB3 9HP. *T:* Cambridge (01223) 352109. *Died 4 Dec. 1994.*

ELTON, Air Vice-Marshal John Goodenough, CB 1955; CBE 1945; DFC 1940; AFC 1935; *b* 5 May 1905; *s* of late Rev. George G. Elton, MA Oxon; *m* 1st, 1927, Helen Whitfield (marr. diss.); one *s*; 2nd, 1949, Francesca Cavallero. *Educ:* St John's, Leatherhead. Entered RAF, 1926; service in UK, 1926–31; Singapore, 1932–35 (AFC); Irak, 1939; served War of 1939–45 (despatches twice, DFC, CBE); CO 47 Sqdn, Sudan, 1940; HQ, ME, Cairo, 1941; comd in succession Nos 242, 238 and 248 Wings, N Africa, 1942; CO RAF Turnhouse, Scotland, 1943; CO RAF Silloth, Cumberland, 1944; AOA, HQ Mediterranean Allied Coastal Air Force, 1945–46; idc 1947; Dep. Dir, Air Min., 1948; RAF Mem., UK Delegn, Western Union Military Cttee, 1949–50; Comdt, Sch. of Tech. Training, Halton, 1951; Air Attaché, Paris, 1952; Air Officer i/c Administration, HQ Bomber Comd, 1953–56; Chief of Staff to the Head of British Jt Services Mission, Washington, DC, 1956–59; retired, 1959. *Address:* 64 Lexham Gardens, W8 5JA. *Club:* Royal Air Force. *Died 16 April 1994.*

ELWORTHY, Baron *cr* 1972 (Life Peer), of Timaru in New Zealand, and of Elworthy, Co. of Somerset; **Marshal of the Royal Air Force Samuel Charles Elworthy,** KG 1977; GCB 1962 (KCB 1961; CB 1960); CBE 1946; DSO 1941; LVO 1953; DFC 1941; AFC 1941; *b* 23 March 1911; *e s* of late P. A. Elworthy, Gordon's Valley, Timaru, New Zealand, and Bertha Victoria (*née* Julius); *m* 1936, Audrey (*d* 1986), *o d* of late A. J. Hutchinson, OBE; three *s* one *d*. *Educ:* Marlborough; Trinity Coll., Cambridge (MA). Commissioned in RAFO 1933, transferred to Auxiliary Air Force (600 Sqdn), 1934; called to Bar, Lincoln's Inn, 1935, Hon. Bencher 1970; permanent commission in RAF, 1936; War Service in Bomber Comd; Comdt RAF Staff Coll., Bracknell, 1957–59; Deputy Chief of Air Staff, 1959–60; C-in-C, Unified Command, Middle East, 1960–63; Chief of Air Staff, 1963–67; Chief of the Defence Staff, 1967–71. Acting Air Cdre, 1944; Air Vice-Marshal, 1957; Air Marshal, 1960; Air Chief Marshal, 1962; Marshal of the RAF, 1967. Constable and Governor, Windsor Castle, 1971–78; Lord-Lieutenant of Greater London, 1973–78. Chairman: Royal Commn for the Exhibition of 1851, 1971–78; King Edward VII Hospital for Officers, 1971–78; Royal Over-Seas League, 1971–76. Sometime Governor: Bradfield Coll.; Wellington Coll.; Marlborough Coll. Hon. Freeman, Skinners' Co., 1968–, Master 1973–74. KStJ 1976. Retired to live in NZ, 1978. *Address:* Gordon's Valley, RD2, Timaru, South Canterbury, New Zealand. *Clubs:* Royal Air Force; Leander (Henley-on-Thames); South Canterbury (NZ); Christchurch (NZ). *Died 4 April 1993.*

EMELEUS, Prof. Harry Julius, CBE 1958; FRS 1946; MA, DSc; Professor of Inorganic Chemistry, University of Cambridge, 1945–70, then Professor Emeritus; Fellow of Sidney Sussex College, Cambridge; Fellow of Imperial College, London; *b* 22 June 1903; *s* of Karl Henry Emeleus and Ellen Biggs; *m* 1931, Mary Catherine Horton (*d* 1991); two *s* two *d. Educ:* Hastings Grammar Sch.; Imperial Coll., London. 1851 Exhibition Senior Student, Imperial Coll. and Technische Hochschule, Karlsruhe, 1926–29; Commonwealth Fund Fellow, Princeton Univ., 1929–31; Member of Staff of Imperial Coll., 1931–45. President: Chemical Society, 1958; Royal Institute of Chemistry, 1963–65. Trustee, British Museum, 1963–72. Hon. Fellow, Manchester Institute of Science and Technology. Hon. Member: Austrian, Finnish, Indian, Bangladesh and French Chemical Societies; Finnish Scientific Academy; Gesellschaft Deutscher Chemiker; Royal Academy of Belgium; Akademie der Naturforscher Leopoldina, Halle; Akademie der Wissenschaften, Göttingen; Austrian Acad. of Scis; Acad. of Scis in Catania; Spanish Royal Society for Physics and Chemistry. Hon. Doctor: Ghent; Kiel; Lille; Paris; Technische Hochschule, Aachen; Marquette; Kent. Lavoisier Medal, French Chem. Society; Stock Medal, Gesellschaft Deutscher Chemiker; Davy Medal, Royal Society, 1962. *Publications:* scientific papers in chemical journals. *Recreation:* reading. *Address:* Meadowcroft, 16 Trumpington Road, Cambridge CB2 2AQ. *T:* Cambridge (0223) 321351. *Died 2 Dec. 1993.*

EMMETT, Harold Leslie; Assistant Under-Secretary of State, Ministry of Defence, 1972–79; *b* 20 Sept. 1919; 4th *s* of Alfred and Charlotte Emmett (*née* Frith); *m* 1943, Phyllis Mabel (*née* Tranah); three *s* one *d. Educ:* Gillingham Grammar Sch., Kent. Joined Civil Service (Admiralty), 1938; transf. to War Office, 1948; Principal, 1951; Asst Sec., 1960; Command Sec., HQ BAOR, 1964–67; Imperial Defence College, 1968; seconded to Home Office for service with New Scotland Yard, 1969–70. *Recreation:* golf. *Address:* 9 Oakdale Road, Tunbridge Wells, Kent TN4 8DS. *T:* Tunbridge Wells (0892) 22658. *Died 28 June 1991.*

EMSON, Air Marshal Sir Reginald (Herbert Embleton), KBE 1966 (CBE 1946); CB 1959; AFC 1941; Inspector-General of the Royal Air Force, 1967–69; *b* 11 Jan. 1912; *s* of Francis Reginald Emson, Hitcham, Buckinghamshire; *m* 1934, Doreen Marjory (*d* 1991), *d* of Hugh Duke, Holyport, Maidenhead, Berkshire; two *s* two *d. Educ:* Christ's Hospital; RAF Coll., Cranwell. Joined RAF, 1931; served War of 1939–45 in Aeroplane Armament Establishment Gunnery Research Unit, Exeter; Fighter Command Headquarters and Central Fighter Establishment; Director, Armament Research and Development (Air), Ministry of Supply, 1950–59; Commander RAF Staff and Air Attaché, British Defence Staffs, Washington, 1961–63; Asst Chief of Air Staff (Operational Requirements), 1963–66; Dep. Chief Air Staff, 1966–67. Group Captain, 1943; Air Commodore, 1958; Air Vice-Marshal, 1962; Air Marshal (Acting), 1966. *Address:* Vor Cottage, Holyport, Maidenhead, Berks. *T:* Maidenhead (0628) 21992. *Club:* Royal Air Force. *Died 27 March 1995.*

ENGLAND, Frank Raymond Wilton; *b* 24 Aug. 1911; *s* of Joseph and Florence England; *m* 1st, 1939, Margaretta Helen Wells (marr. diss.); one *d*; 2nd, Doris. *Educ:* Christ's Coll., Finchley. Served War, Pilot, RAF, 1941–45. Apprenticeship with Daimler Co. Ltd, Hendon, 1927–32; Racing Mechanic to: Sir Henry Birkin, Whitney Straight, ERA Ltd, Richard Seaman, B. Bira, 1932–38; Service Engr, Service Dept Supt, Alvis Limited, 1938–40; Service Manager, Jaguar Cars Ltd, 1946–56; Service Dir, 1956–61; Asst Man. Dir, 1961–66; Dep. Man. Dir, 1966–67; Jt

Man. Dir, 1967; Dep. Chm., 1968; Chm. and Chief Executive, 1972; retd as Chm., Jan. 1974. *Recreation:* motor sport. *Address:* Tannachweg 1, 4813 Altmünster, Austria. *T:* (7612) 88316. *Club:* Royal Air Force. *Died 30 May 1995.*

ENNALS, Baron *cr* 1983 (Life Peer), of Norwich in the County of Norfolk; **David Hedley Ennals;** PC 1970; President, National Association for Mental Health (MIND), since 1989 (Campaign Director, 1970–73; Chairman, 1984); Chairman, Gandhi Foundation, since 1984; Vice-Chairman, United Nations Association, since 1991; *b* 19 Aug. 1922; *s* of A. F. Ennals, 8 Victoria Terrace, Walsall, Staffs, and Jessie Ennals; *m* 1st, 1950, Eleanor Maud Caddick (marr. diss. 1977); three *s* one *d*; 2nd 1977, Katherine Gene Tranoy. *Educ:* Queen Mary's Grammar School, Walsall; Loomis Inst., Windsor, Conn, USA. Served with HM Forces, 1941–46: Captain, RAC. Secretary, Council for Education in World Citizenship, 1947–52; Secretary, United Nations Association, 1952–57; Overseas Sec., Labour Party, 1957–64. MP (Lab): Dover, 1964–70; Norwich North, Feb. 1974–1983; PPS to Minister of Overseas Development, 1964; Parly Under-Sec. of State, Army, 1966–67; Parly Under-Sec., Home Office, 1967–68; Minister of State: DHSS, 1968–70; FCO, 1974–76; Sec. of State for Social Services, 1976–79. President: Parly Food and Health Forum, 1985–; Parly Alternative Medicine Gp, 1989–; All Party Parly Gp for Tibet. Chm., John Bellers Ltd, 1972–74; non-exec. Dir, Takare, 1991–. Chairman: Anti-Apartheid Movement, 1960–64; Campaign for Homeless and Rootless, 1972–74; Children's Medical Charity, 1984–; Anglia Telethon Trust, 1988–; Asia Cttee, British Refugee Council; Co-Chm., Global Co-operation for a Better World, 1987; Mem. Council, Counsel and Care for the Elderly, 1990–; Pres., Coll. of Occupational Therapy, 1984–. President: Nat. Soc. of Non Smokers (QUIT); Tibet Soc., 1988–. Trustee, Biopolitics Internat. Orgns. Patron: Altzheimer's Disease Soc., 1990–; Peter Bedford Project, 1990–. Gov., Ditchley Foundn. *Publications:* Strengthening the United Nations, 1957; Middle East Issues, 1958; United Nations Peace Force, 1960; United Nations on Trial, 1962; Out of Mind, 1973. *Address:* 16 Ingram Road, N2 9QA.
Died 17 June 1995.

ENNALS, Kenneth Frederick John, CB 1983; Member, Local Government Commission for England, since 1992; Deputy Secretary, Department of the Environment, 1980–87; *b* 10 Jan. 1932; *s* of Ernest Ennals and Elsie Dorothy Ennals; *m* 1958, Mavis Euphemia; one *s* two *d. Educ:* Alleyn's Sch., Dulwich; LSE. Joined Export Credits Guarantee Dept, 1952; Principal, DEA, 1965–69; Min. of Housing and Local Govt, later DoE, 1969; Asst Sec., 1970, Under Sec., 1976–80, DoE. Mem., Local Govt Boundary Commn for England, 1987–92 (Chm., 1992). *Recreations:* reading, painting. *Address:* Skitreadons, Petworth Road, Haslemere, Surrey GU27 3AU. *T:* Haslemere (01428) 642733. *Clubs:* Commonwealth Trust, Royal Over-Seas League. *Died 7 Dec. 1995.*

ENNALS, Prof. Martin; Ariel F. Sallows Professor of Human Rights, University of Saskatchewan, 1991; *b* 27 July 1927; *s* of A. Ford Ennals and Jessie E. Ennals (*née* Taylor); *m* 1951, Jacqueline B. (*née* Morris); one *s* one *d. Educ:* Queen Mary's Sch., Walsall; London Sch. of Economics. BScEcon (Internat. Relations). UNESCO, 1951–59; Gen. Sec., National Council for Civil Liberties, 1960–66; Information Officer, Nat. Cttee for Commonwealth Immigrants, 1966–68; Sec. Gen., Amnesty International (Nobel Peace Prize, 1977), 1968–80; Head of Police Cttee Support Unit, GLC, 1982–85; Sec.-Gen., International Alert, 1985–91. *Recreations:* escapist television, ski-ing. *Address:* 16 Patterdale, Robert Street, NW1 3QJ; Law Faculty,

University of Saskatchewan, Saskatoon, Saskatchewan, S7N 0W0, Canada.   *Died 5 Oct. 1991.*

ENRIGHT, Derek Anthony; MP (Lab) Hemsworth, since Nov. 1991; *b* 2 Aug. 1935; *s* of Lawrence and Helen Enright; *m* 1963, Jane Maureen (*née* Simmons); two *s* two *d*. *Educ:* St Michael's Coll., Leeds; Wadham Coll., Oxford (BA, DipEd). Head of Classics, John Fisher Sch., Purley, Surrey, 1959–67; Dep. Head of St Wilfrid's, North Featherstone, W Yorks, 1967–79; Mem. (Lab) Leeds, Eur. Parlt, 1979–84; Brit. Labour Group Spokesman on third world affairs and women's rights, 1979–84; EEC deleg. in Guinea Bissau, 1985–87; Special Advr to EEC on The Third World, 1988–91. Contested (Lab) Kent East, European elecn, 1984. Mem., Select Cttee on European Legislation, 1991–. Chm., Lab Movt in Europe, 1994–; Mem., Exec. Cttee, European Movt. Order of Merit (Guinea Bissau), 1987. *Publications:* reports on: fishing agreements in West Africa; EEC relations with non ACP developing countries; Namibia after independence. *Recreations:* reading the Guardian, Staffordshire Bull Terriers, watching Featherstone Rovers Rugby league. *Address:* The Hollies, 112 Carleton Road, Pontefract, W Yorks WF8 3NQ. *T:* Pontefract (01977) 702096.
Died 31 Oct. 1995.

ENSOR WALTERS, Peter Hugh Bennetts; *see* Walters.

ENTWISTLE, Sir (John Nuttall) Maxwell, Kt 1963; Under-writing Member of Lloyd's, 1964–92; *b* 8 Jan. 1910; *s* of Isaac and Hannah Entwistle; *m* 1940, Jean Cunliffe McAlpine, JP (*d* 1993), *d* of late Dr John and Amy Margaret Penman; two *s*. *Educ:* Merchant Taylors' Sch., Great Crosby. Solicitor, 1931; Notary Public, 1976. Liverpool City: Councillor, 1938; Alderman, 1960; Leader of Liverpool City Council, 1961–63, when initiated preparation of devlt plan for City centre. Councillor, Cumbria County, 1979–82. Chairman: Merseyside Development Cttee; Mersey Tunnel Cttee, 1961–63; Abbeyfield Liverpool Soc. Ltd, 1970–75; Council of Management, League of Welldoers, 1972–74. Mem., Liverpool Univ. Court and Council, 1955–64. President: Edge Hill Liverpool Conservative Assoc., 1963–71; Liverpool Clerks Assoc., 1964–78. Merchant Taylors' School: Chm., Appeal Cttee, 1969–74; Pres., Old Boys' Assoc., 1969–70; Governor, 1969–75. *Recreation:* gardening. *Address:* Stone Hall, Sedbergh, Cumbria LA10 5LJ. *T:* Sedbergh (05396) 20700.
Died 10 Feb. 1994.

ERI, Sir (Vincent) Serei, GCMG 1990 (CMG 1982); Governor-General of Papua New Guinea, 1990–91; *b* 12 Sept 1936; *s* of Eri Haiveta and Morasuru Lafe; *m* Margaret Karulaka Pukari; four *s* two *d*. *Educ:* Terapo and Moveave Catholic Schools; teacher training, Sogeri; Port Moresby Teachers' College; Univ. of Papua New Guinea (BA 1971). Teacher, Sogeri Secondary Sch., 1956–67; Dep. Head Teacher, Ihu Primary Sch., 1959–60; Dep. Headmaster, Coronation High Sch., Kerema, 1961–62; training as Schools Inspector, 1962; served Eastern Highlands and Central Provinces, 1963–64; Port Moresby Teachers' Coll., training then Lectr, 1965–66; Supt of Primary Educn, Dept of Educn, 1971–72 (acting Dir, 1972); Head, Dept of Inf. and Extn Services, 1973–74; Consul, then Consul-Gen., Sydney, 1974–76; PNG High Comr in Canberra, 1976–79; Head, Transport and Civil Aviation, PNG, 1979–80; Sec., Dept of Defence, 1980–82; Harrisons & Crosfield (PNG), 1982–90. Served on internat. bodies on educn matters; Chm., PNG Univ. Finance Cttee, 1984–90; Pres., People's Action Party, 1986–90. *Address:* c/o Government House, PO Box 79, Port Moresby, Papua New Guinea.   *Died 25 May 1993.*

ERRINGTON, Richard Percy, CMG 1955; Chartered Accountant (FCA), retired; *b* 17 May 1904; 2nd *s* of Robert George Errington and Edna Mary Errington (*née* Warr); *m* 1935, Ursula, *d* of Henry Joseph Laws Curtis and Grace Barton Curtis (*née* Macgregor); one *d*. *Educ:* Sidcot Sch. Asst Treasurer, Nigeria Government, 1929–37; Colonial Administrative Service: Nigeria, 1937–46; Nyasaland, 1946–48; Financial Sec. to Govt of Aden Colony (also Mem. Bd of Trustees of Port of Aden), 1948–51; Chm., Aden Port Trust, 1951–60. Mem. Governor's Exec. Council, Aden, 1948–58; Unofficial Mem. Aden Colony Legislative Council, 1951–60 (Official Mem., 1948–51). Chairman: Aden Soc. for the Blind, 1951–60; Aden Lab. Advisory Bd, 1951–57. Area Comr, St John Amb. Bde, 1964–71. SBStJ, 1965. *Recreation:* walking. *Address:* Whitecliffs, Wodehouse Road, Old Hunstanton, Norfolk PE36 6JD. *T:* Hunstanton (01485) 532356.
Died 25 Jan. 1995.

ERSKINE OF RERRICK, 2nd Baron *cr* 1964; **Iain Maxwell Erskine;** Bt 1961; professional photographer, management consultant and director of companies; *b* 22 Jan. 1926; *o s* of 1st Baron Erskine of Rerrick, GBE, and of Henrietta, *d* of late William Dunnett, Caithness; *S* father, 1980; *m* 1st, 1955, Marie Elisabeth (marr. diss. 1964), *d* of Major Burton Allen (she *m* 2nd, 1964, 6th Earl of Caledon; no *c*; 2nd, 1974, Maria Josephine (marr. diss. 1989), *d* of late Dr Josef Klupt, Richmond, Surrey; three *d*; 3rd, 1993, Debra, *d* of Gordon Owen Knight. *Educ:* Harrow. Served War of 1939–45; served Regular Army, 1943–65 (2nd Lieut Grenadier Guards, 1944; Temp. Lt-Col, 1961); ADC, RMA, Sandhurst, 1951–52; Comptroller to Governor-Gen. of New Zealand, 1960–62; retd as Major, 1963. PRO to Household Bde, 1963–65; Account Exec., CS Services Ltd PR (involved in setting up Advertising Standards Authority), 1965; Higher Exec. Officer, MoD, 1964–66; Advertising and PR Dir, Saward Baker Ltd, 1966–72; attended Ashridges Management Court, 1967; Man. Dir, Lonrho Ltd, Iran, 1972–73; London Manager, Marples Ridgway Construction Ltd, 1974–85; Chairman: Strabo Ltd (Trading), 1976; Erskine Associates; Caledonian Commodities Ltd (Trading), 1979–82; DK Financial Services (Dai-Ichi Kangyo), 1988–89; Director: Wansdyke Security Ltd, 1974–85; Bath, Portland and Debenham Gp, 1974–85; Ardil Ltd, 1984; Crighton Internat. Ltd, 1984; WSTV Productions Ltd, 1988–91; ISICAD (Computers), 1989–91; CDA Internat. Ltd. Qualified pilot; Mem. Cttee, De Haviland Aircraft Museum (BAe) (Dir, 1967–88); Trustee: RAF Mus. (Bomber Comd); David Tolkien Trust, Stoke Mandeville Hosp.; Transport Trust; Patron: PHAB (Scot.); Orchestra of the World. Chm., Guards' Flying Club, 1959–65. Col, Confederate States Air Force, 1983. Life Mem., Nat. Trust for Scotland; Mem. Cttee and Life Mem., Royal Photographic Soc; Mem., RAF Historical Soc. MInstM, MIPR and FInstD, 1967–75. Chevalier, Legion of Honour. OStJ. *Recreations:* fly-fishing, good food, aviation, photography. *Heir:* none. *Address:* 10 Chesham Place, SW1X 8HN.
Died 7 June 1995 (ext).

ERVINE-ANDREWS, Lt-Col Harold Marcus, VC 1940; East Lancashire Regiment, retired; *b* 29 July 1911; *s* of late C. C. Ervine-Andrews, New Ross, Wexford, Southern Ireland; *m* 1st, 1939, Betty (marr. diss. 1952; she *d* 1975), *er d* of R. I. Torrie; one *s* one *d*; 2nd, 1981, Margaret Gregory. *Educ:* Stonyhurst Coll.; Royal Military Coll., Sandhurst. 2nd Lieut East Lancs Regt, 1932; Captain 1940; Temp. Major, 1940; War Subst. Major, 1942; Temp. Lieut-Col 1942; served with RAF during North-West Frontier of India Operations, 1936–37 (medal and two clasps, despatches) and NW Frontier, 1938–39; served in France with BEF (VC); attached to RAF in UK, 1940; on loan to Australian Military Forces, 1941; attached RAAF, 1942; GSO 1 Air HQ Allied Land Forces in South-West Pacific Area, 1943; commanding No 61 Carrier-Borne

Army Liaison Section, 1944; SALO in 21st Aircraft Carrier Squadron (East Indies), 1945; Lieut-Col Commanding No 18 Infantry Holding Bn, 1946; attached to The Army Mobile Information Unit, 1948; Asst Dir of Public Relations to BAOR, 1951, as a Lieut-Col; retired pay, 1952. *Address:* Treveor Cot, Gorran, St Austell, Cornwall PL26 6LW. *T:* Mevagissey (01726) 842140.
Died 30 March 1995.

ESCRITT, Maj.-Gen. Frederick Knowles, CB 1953; OBE 1943; MRCS; late Royal Army Medical Corps, retired Nov. 1953; *b* 29 Nov. 1893; *s* of Harold Teal Escritt; *m* 1931, Elsa Alfrida, *d* of Director J. A. Larssen, Stockholm; one *d. Educ:* Dulwich Coll.; Guy's Hosp. MRCS, LRCP 1918. Joined RAMC, Aug. 1918 (1914–15 Star, British War and Victory Medals); served War of 1939–45 (Gen. Service Iraq, 1939–45 Star, Burma Star, Defence and War Medals); ADMS Eastern and 14 Armies, 1942–45; DDMS 1 Corps Dist, BAOR, 1945–47; Inspector of Training, AMS, 1950–51; DDMS, Eastern Command, 1951–53. QHS, 1952–53. Order of St John (Officer Brother), 1952.
Died 26 March 1993.

ESSEX, Francis William, CMG 1959; retired from HM Overseas Civil Service; *b* 29 June 1916; *s* of Frank Essex; *m* 1st, 1947, Marjorie Muriel Joyce Lewis (*d* 1987); two *s*; 2nd, 1987, Mary Frances Payton. *Educ:* Royal Grammar Sch., High Wycombe; Reading Univ.; Exeter Coll., Oxford. Joined Colonial Administrative Service, Sierra Leone, 1939; Asst District Commissioner, 1942; District Commissioner, 1948; Principal, HM Treasury, 1951–53; Dep. Financial Sec., Sierra Leone, 1953–56; Financial Sec., British Guiana, 1956–60; Financial Sec. to High Comr for Basutoland, Bechuanaland and Swaziland, 1960–64; Counsellor, British Embassy, South Africa, 1964–65; Sec. for Finance and Development, later Permanent Sec., Min. of Finance, Commerce and Industry, Swaziland, 1965–68; Principal, ODM, 1968–76. Mem., Pearce Commn on Rhodesian opinion, 1971–72. Short term British Technical Co-operation assignments, British Virgin Is, 1977, Tuvalu, 1978 and 1979, Antigua and Barbuda, 1981. *Address:* Cobblestones, Chagford, Devon TQ13 8AW. *Died 10 July 1995.*

EURICH, Richard Ernst, OBE 1984; RA 1953 (ARA 1942); artist (painter); *b* Bradford, 14 March 1903; *s* of late Professor Frederick William Eurich and Margaret Guendolen Carter-Squire; *m* 1934, Mavis Llewellyn Pope; two *d* (one *s* decd). *Educ:* St George's Sch., Harpenden; Bradford Grammar Sch. Studied art at Bradford Sch. of Arts and Crafts, and Slade Sch., London; held One Man Show of drawings at Goupil Gallery in 1929, and several exhibitions of paintings at Redfern Gallery; exhibited at Royal Academy, New English Art Club and London Group; Retrospective Exhibitions: Bradford, 1951; Bradford, Glasgow, London (Fine Art Soc.), Southampton, 1980–81; Imperial War Museum, 1991; works purchased by Contemporary Art Soc. and Chantrey Bequest; painting, Dunkirk Beach 1940, purchased for Canadian Government; Official War Artist, 1941–45; representative works in various public galleries. Hon. DLitt Bradford, 1989. *Recreations:* music, gardening. *Address:* Appletreewick, Dibden Purlieu, Southampton. *T:* Hythe (Hants) (0703) 842291. *Died 6 June 1992.*

EVAN-COOK, John Edward, JP; *b* 25 Oct. 1902; 2nd *s* of late Evan Cook, JP, London; *m* 1928, Winifred Elizabeth (*d* 1985), *d* of Joseph Samuel Pointon; no *c. Educ:* Westminster City Sch. Served War, 1940–46, Major, RAOC; Adviser on Packaging, War Office, 1940–46. Chm., Evan-Cook Group, retd. Vice-Chm. London District Rotary, 1950–52; Pres. Rotary Club of Camberwell, 1948. Chairman: Bd of Visitors, HM Prison, Brixton, 1967–73; Inst. of Packaging (Nat. Chm., 1954, President, 1954–57); Min. of Labour and Nat. Service Local Disablement Cttee,

1959–67. Estates Governor, Dulwich, 1973–90. Chief Scouts' Medal of Merit, 1962; Silver Acorn, 1968. Past Master, Worshipful Company of Paviors; Liveryman: Worshipful Co. of Carmen; Worshipful Co. of Farmers. Sheriff of London, 1958–59; Common Councilman, City of London, 1960–66 and 1972–77. JP City of London, 1950. Order of Homayoun, 3rd Class (Iran); Grand Cross of Merit, Order of Merit (Federal Republic of Germany). *Address:* Deaks Manor, Deaks Lane, Cuckfield, W Sussex RH17 5JA. *T:* Haywards Heath (0444) 452044. *Clubs:* City Livery (Pres., 1964–65), United Wards, Royal Automobile, Bentley Drivers', Institute of Advanced Motorists. *Died 16 Oct. 1991.*

EVANS OF CLAUGHTON, Baron *cr* 1978 (Life Peer), of Claughton in the County of Merseyside; **David Thomas Gruffydd Evans,** JP; DL; President of the Liberal Party, 1977–78; Liberal Party Spokesman in House of Lords on Local Government and Housing; *b* 9 Feb. 1928; *s* of John Cynlais Evans and Nellie Euronwy Evans; *m* 1956, Moira Elizabeth (*née* Rankin); one *s* three *d. Educ:* Birkenhead Prep. Sch.; Birkenhead Sch.; Friars Sch., Bangor; Univ. of Liverpool (LLB 1949). Solicitors' final exam., 1952. Pilot Officer, RAF, 1952–54. Hon. Sec., Lancs, Cheshire and N West Liberal Fedn, 1956–60; Chm., Nat. League of Young Liberals, 1960–61. Councillor: Birkenhead CBC, 1957–74; Wirral BC, 1973–78 (Leader Lib. Gp, 1973–77); Merseyside CC, 1973–81 (Leader Lib. Gp, 1977–81). Introduced Leasehold Reform Bill, 1981. Chairman: Nat. Exec. 1965–68, Assembly Cttee 1971–74, Gen. Election Cttee of the Liberal Party, 1977–79 and 1983; President: Welsh Liberal Party, 1986–87 (Vice-Pres., 1979–86); Birkenhead & Merseyside Soc & Lib Dem, 1988. Dir, Granada TV, 1985–. Mem. Court, Liverpool Univ., 1977–83; Governor, Birkenhead Sch., 1974–78, 1988–; Chairman: Birkenhead Council of Voluntary Service, 1964–73; Abbeyfield Soc. (Birkenhead), 1970–74; Liverpool Luncheon Club, 1980–81; Marcher Sound Radio, 1980–. Pres., Oxton CC, 1988–91. JP Wirral, 1960; DL Merseyside, 1989. *Publications:* booklets: Local Finance for Local Government, 1981; Power and Responsibility to Local Government, 1982. *Recreations:* golf, Welsh Rugby, Liverpool FC. *Address:* Sunridge, 69 Bidston Road, Claughton, Birkenhead, Merseyside L43 6TR. *T:* 051–652 3425. *Clubs:* National Liberal, MCC; Oxton Cricket (Patron, 1991–), Wirral Ladies' Golf (Birkenhead). *Died 22 March 1992.*

EVANS, Rt Rev. Bruce Read; Bishop of Port Elizabeth, since 1975; *b* 10 Nov. 1929; *s* of Roy Leslie and Lilia Evans; *m* 1955, Joan Vanda Erlangsen; two *s* one *d. Educ:* King Edward Sch., Johannesburg; Univ. of the Witwatersrand, Johannesburg; Oak Hill Theological Coll., London. ACIS 1952; DipTh 1958; Diploma of Journalism, 1964. Director of companies, 1952–54. Ordained into C of E, Southwark, 1957; Curate, Holy Trinity, Redhill, Surrey, 1957–59; Senior Curate, St Paul's, Portman Square, W1, and Chaplain to West End Business Houses in London, 1959–61; Curate-in-Charge: St Luke's, Diep River, Cape, 1962; Christ Church, Kenilworth, Cape, 1963–69; Rector of St John's, Wynberg, Cape, 1969–75. Co-Chm., Cape Regional Peace Accord, 1991–; Pres., East Cape Hospice Assoc., 1990–. International speaker. *Publications:* (jointly): I Will Heal their Land, 1974; The Earth is the Lord's, 1975; Facing the New Challenges, 1978; The Church and the Alternative Society, 1979; articles in national, internat. and church papers and magazines. *Recreations:* painting; formerly boxing and hockey. *Address:* Bishop's House, 75 River Road, Walmer, Port Elizabeth, CP, 6070, South Africa. *T:* (41) 514296. *Club:* Port Elizabeth.
Died 25 Aug. 1993.

EVANS, Sir Charles; *see* Evans, Sir R. C.

EVANS, Sir Francis Loring G.; see Gwynne-Evans.

EVANS, Sir Geraint Llewellyn, Kt 1969; CBE 1959; retired opera singer; Principal Baritone, Royal Opera House, Covent Garden, 1948–84; *b* 16 Feb. 1922; *m* 1948, Brenda Evans Davies; two *s*. *Educ:* Guildhall Sch. of Music. Opera singer: Royal Opera House, Covent Garden (1948–84); Glyndebourne Festival Opera; Vienna State Opera; La Scala, Milan; Metropolitan Opera, New York; San Francisco Opera; Lyric Opera, Chicago; Salzburg Festival Opera; Edinburgh Festival Opera; Paris Opera; Teatro Colon, Buenos Aires; Mexico City Opera; Welsh Nat. Opera; Scottish Opera; Berlin Opera; Teatr Wielki, Warsaw. Vice-Pres., Kidney Research Unit for Wales Foundn. Mem., Gorsedd of Bards, Royal Nat. Eisteddfod of Wales; Patron, Churchill Theatre, Bromley; Governor, University Coll. of Wales, Aberystwyth. FGSM 1960; FRNCM 1978; FRCM 1981; FRSA 1984; FTCL 1987; Fellow: University Coll., Cardiff, 1976; Aberystwyth, 1988; UC, Swansea, 1990; Hon. Fellow, Jesus Coll., Oxford, 1979. Freeman, City of London, 1984. Hon. DMus: Wales, 1965; Leicester, 1969; Oxford, 1985; CNAA, 1980; London, 1982. Hon. RAM 1969. Worshipful Company of Musicians Sir Charles Santley Meml Award, 1963; Harriet Cohen Internat. Music Award (Opera Medal), 1967; Fidelio Medal, Internat. Assoc. of Opera Dirs, 1980; San Francisco Opera Medal, 1981; Soc. of Cymmrodorion Medal, 1984. OStJ 1986. *Publication:* (with Noël Goodwin) Sir Geraint Evans: a knight at the opera, 1984. *Recreations:* Rugby, sailing. *Address:* Trelawney, Aberaeron, Dyfed SA46 0BD.

Died 19 Sept. 1992.

EVANS, John Isaac Glyn; Director of Weapons Production (Naval), Ministry of Defence, 1970–79; *b* 1 April 1919; *s* of William Evans; *m* 1943, Hilda Garratt Evans (*née* Lee); two *s* one *d*. *Educ:* Ystalyfera Grammar Sch.; University Coll., Swansea (BSc Physics, BSc Elec. Engineering). Engineer, GEC, 1940–41; served War, Captain REME, 1941–46; Development Engineer, GEC, 1946–50; Works Group Engineer, Admiralty, 1950–53; main grade, 1953–59; senior grade, 1959–64; superintending grade, 1964–67; Dep. Dir, 1967–70. FIEE. *Recreations:* tennis, badminton, cricket. *Address:* 16 Woodland Grove, Claverton Down, Bath, Avon.

Died 27 Dec. 1991.

EVANS, Laurence James, CBE 1977; HM Diplomatic Service, retired; *b* 16 Dec. 1917; *s* of Albert Victor and Margaret Evans; *m* 1940, Clare Mary (*née* Kolb); one *d*. *Educ:* Alsop High Sch., Liverpool; Univ. of Liverpool (BA Hons French); Univ. of Rennes (Diploma). Reader in the Faculté des Lettres, Univ. of Rennes, 1938–39. HM Forces (Intell. Corps), 1939–45. Foreign Office, Asst Principal, 1946–47; Bd of Inland Revenue (HM Inspector of Taxes), 1947–49; rejoined Foreign Service and apptd to Brussels, 1950–51; HM Vice-Consul, Khorramshahr, 1951–52; FO, 1952–54; Second Sec. and Vice-Consul, Ciudad Trujillo, Dominican Republic, 1954–57 (Chargé d'Affaires, 1955 and 1957); FO, 1957–63 (Asst Head of Communications, 1959); HM Consul, New York, 1963–66; Asst Head of Personnel Dept (Ops), DSAO, 1966–69; HM Consul-Gen., Geneva, 1969–73; HM Consul-General at Barcelona and Andorra, 1973–77 (Doyen, Barcelona Consular Corps, 1974–76, Hon. Doyen, 1976–77); Staff Assessor, FCO, 1978–82. *Recreation:* music. *Address:* 7 Worsham Court, Mansell Close, Cooden Sea Road, Bexhill-on-Sea, East Sussex TN39 4XB. *T:* Cooden (04243) 6141. *Club:* Civil Service.

Died 28 July 1991.

EVANS, Raymond John Morda, MA, PhD; Headmaster, Silcoates School, 1960–78; *b* 1 Oct. 1917; 2nd *s* of late Rev. J. Morda Evans, Congregational Minister; *m* 1942, Catherine Mair Gernos Davies (*d* 1988), *er d* of late Rev.

J. Gernos Davies, Congregational Minister; one *s* two *d* (and one *s* decd). *Educ:* Silcoates Sch., near Wakefield; (Casberd Scholar) St John's Coll., Oxford. BA Oxon (Mod. Langs), 1939, MA 1942; MA, PhD London (Russian Lang. and Lit.), 1959. Dauntsey's Sch., 1939–40; Intelligence Corps (Captain), 1940–46; Leeds Grammar School, 1946–52; Head of Dept of Modern Languages, Royal Naval Coll., Greenwich, 1952–60. JP Wakefield, 1964–87. *Publications:* contrib. to Slavonic and Eastern European Review, and to Mariners' Mirror. *Recreation:* swimming. *Address:* 16 Kepstorn Road, West Park, Leeds LS16 5HL.   *Died 25 Jan. 1992.*

EVANS, Prof. Rhydwyn Harding, CBE 1958; MSc, DSc Manchester, PhD Leeds; FICE, FIMechE, FIStructE; Professor of Civil Engineering and Administrative Head of Engineering Departments, University of Leeds, 1946–68, Emeritus Professor, 1968; *b* 9 Oct. 1900; *s* of late David Evans, Tygwyn, Pontardulais, Glam; *m* 1929, Dilys Elizabeth, *o c* of late George Rees, Welsh poet and hymnologist, and Kate Ann Rees, London; one *s*. *Educ:* Llanelly Grammar Sch.; University of Manchester. BSc top 1st class Graduate Prizeman, 1923; MSc 1928; PhD 1932; DSc 1943. Mercantile Marine, 1918–20. Demonstrator, Asst Lecturer, Lecturer, Senior Lecturer and Reader in Civil Engineering, University of Leeds, 1926–46, Dean, Faculty of Tech., 1948–51, Pro-Vice-Chancellor, 1961–65. Lectures: Unwin Meml, ICE, 1960; first George Hondros Meml, WA, 1970. Institution of Structural Engineers: Vice-Pres., 1948–49; Chm., Yorks Br., 1940–41, 1955–56 and 1958–59 (Yorkshire Br. Prize, 1946–47 and 1950–51); Institution of Civil Engineers: Chm. Yorks Assoc., 1942–43 and 1952–53; Mem. Council, 1949–52. Mem., Joint Matriculation Bd, Manchester, 1946–68; Chm., Leeds Univ. Min. of Labour and NS Bd, 1949–60; first Chm., Trng Consultative Cttee, Cement and Concrete Assoc., 1966–73. Consulting Editor in Civil Engineering: McGraw-Hill Book Co. (UK) Ltd, 1975–; Routledge Chapman Hall, 1987. Mem., Soc. of Civil Engrs, France; Hon. Mem., Concrete Soc., 1970; Hon. MIMM. Hon. DèsSc Ghent, 1953; Hon. DTech Bradford, 1971. Rugby Engrg Soc. Student's Prize, 1925; Telford Premiums, 1942–43–44; Medal, Ghent Univ., 1949, 1953; Instn Premium, Institution of Water Engineers, 1953; George Stephenson Gold Medal, 1956; Reinforced Concrete Assoc. Medal, 1961; Institution of Structural Engineers: Research Diploma, 1965; Certif. of Commendation, 1970; Henry Adams Award, 1971. *Publications:* Prestressed Concrete (with E. W. Bennett), 1962; Concrete Plain, Reinforced Prestressed, Shell (with C. B. Wilby), 1963; Reinforced and Prestressed Concrete (with F. K. Kong), 1975, 3rd edn 1987; (jtly) Handbook of Structural Concrete, 1983; papers on: elasticity and plasticity of concrete and other building materials; strain and stress distribution in reinforced concrete beams and arches; pre-stressed concrete; extensibility, cracking and tensile stress-strain of concrete; bond stresses; shear stresses; combined bending and shear stresses; torsional stresses; preflexed pre-stressed concrete beams; lightweight aggregate concrete; vibration and pressure moulding of concrete; in Journals of Institutions of Civil, Struct. and Water Engineers, Concrete Soc., Philosophical Magazine, Engineer, Engineering, Civil Engineering and Public Works. *Recreations:* motoring, travel, gardening. *Address:* 23 Christopher Rise, Pontlliw, Swansea, West Glamorgan SA4 1EN. *T:* Gorseinon (0792) 891961.

Died 22 May 1993.

EVANS, Sir (Robert) Charles, Kt 1969; MA, FRCS; Principal, University College of North Wales, 1958–84; Vice-Chancellor, University of Wales, 1965–67, and 1971–73; *b* 19 Oct. 1918; *o s* of late R. C. Evans and Mrs Charles Evans; *m* 1957, Denise Nea Morin; three *s*. *Educ:* Shrewsbury Sch.; University Coll., Oxford. BM, BCh

Oxon 1943; MA Oxon 1947; FRCS 1949. RAMC, 1943–46 (despatches). Surgical Registrar, United Liverpool Hosps, and Liverpool Regional Hosps, 1947–57. Hunterian Prof., Royal College Surg. Eng., 1953. Dep. Leader, Mt Everest Expedition, 1953; Leader, Kangchenjunga Expedition, 1955; Pres., Alpine Club, 1967–70; Mem. Council, Royal Geog. Society, 1960–61. Hon. DSc Wales, 1956. Cullum Medal, American Geog. Soc., 1954; Livingstone Medal, Scottish Geog. Soc., 1955; Founder's Medal, Royal Geog. Society, 1956. *Publications:* Eye on Everest, 1955; On Climbing, 1956; Kangchenjunga—The Untrodden Peak, 1956; articles in Alpine Journal, Geographical Journal, etc. *Address:* Ardincaple, Capel Curig, N Wales LL24 0EU. *Club:* Alpine. *Died 5 Dec. 1995.*

EVANS, Thomas Henry, CBE 1957; DL; LLM; Clerk of the Peace, Clerk of the County Council, and Clerk to Lieutenancy for Staffordshire, 1942–72; Clerk of Staffordshire Magistrates Courts Committee, 1952–72; Clerk of Staffordshire County and Stoke-on-Trent Police Authority, 1968–72; *b* 1907; *s* of late Henry Evans, Bootle, Lancs. *Educ:* Merchant Taylors' Sch., Crosby, Lancs; University of Liverpool (LLM). Admitted Solicitor, 1930. Asst Solicitor with Surrey County Council, 1930–35; Asst County Solicitor and later Dep. Clerk of Staffs County Council, 1935–42. Member: Cttee on Consolidation of Highway Law, 1958; Interdepartmental Cttee (Streatfeild) on business of Criminal Courts, 1958; Nat. Advisory Coun. on Training of Magistrates, 1964–73. DL Staffs, 1947. *Publication:* contributor to Macmillan's Local Government Law and Administration. *Address:* 108 Holland Road, Hove, East Sussex.

Died 13 Jan. 1992.

EVELYN, (John) Michael, CB 1976; Assistant Director of Public Prosecutions, 1969–76, retired (Under-Secretary, 1972); *b* 2 June 1916; *s* of Edward Ernest Evelyn and Kate Rosa Underwood. *Educ:* Charterhouse; Christ Church, Oxford (MA). Called to Bar, 1939. Army service, 1939–46. Dept of Dir of Public Prosecutions, 1946–76. *Publications:* (under pseudonym Michael Underwood): Murder on Trial, 1954; Murder Made Absolute, 1955; Death on Remand, 1956; False Witness, 1957; Lawful Pursuit, 1958; Arm of the Law, 1959; Cause of Death, 1960; Death by Misadventure, 1960; Adam's Case, 1961; The Case against Phillip Quest, 1962; Girl Found Dead, 1963; The Crime of Colin Wise, 1964; The Unprofessional Spy, 1965; The Anxious Conspirator, 1965; A Crime Apart, 1966; The Man who Died on Friday, 1967; The Man who Killed Too Soon, 1968; The Shadow Game, 1969; The Silent Liars, 1970; Shem's Demise, 1970; A Trout in the Milk, 1971; Reward for a Defector, 1973; A Pinch of Snuff, 1974; The Juror, 1975; Menaces, Menaces, 1976; Murder with Malice, 1977; The Fatal Trip, 1977; Crooked Wood, 1978; Anything but the Truth, 1978; Smooth Justice, 1979; Victim of Circumstance, 1979; A Clear Case of Suicide, 1980; Crime upon Crime, 1980; Double Jeopardy, 1981; Hand of Fate, 1981; Goddess of Death, 1982; A Party to Murder, 1983; Death in Camera, 1984; The Hidden Man, 1985; Death at Deepwood Grange, 1986; The Uninvited Corpse, 1987; The Injudicious Judge, 1987; Dual Enigma, 1988; A Compelling Case, 1989; Rosa's Dilemma, 1990; A Dangerous Business, 1990; The Seeds of Murder, 1991; Guilty Conscience, 1992. *Recreations:* writing, reading, opera, cinema, travel. *Address:* 100 Ashdown, Eaton Road, Hove, Sussex BN3 3AR. *Clubs:* Garrick, Detection. *Died 28 Nov. 1992.*

EVERSLEY, David Edward Charles, PhD; social researcher; *b* 22 Nov. 1921; *s* of Dr Otto Eberstadt and Dela Morel; *m* 1st, 1945, Edith Wembridge (*d* 1978); one *s* three *d*; 2nd, 1986, Barbara Rojo (marr. diss. 1990); 3rd, 1994, Marion Bennathan. *Educ:* Goethe-Gymnasium,

Frankfurt/Main; Leighton Park Sch., Reading; London Sch. of Economics. BSc (Econ) (London), PhD (Birmingham). Asst Lectr, Lectr, then Reader, in Economic (and then Social) Hist., Univ. of Birmingham, 1949–66; Dir, W Midlands Social and Polit. Res. Unit, 1962–65; Reader in Population and Regional Studies, Univ. of Sussex, 1966; Dir, Social Research Unit, Univ. of Sussex, 1967–69, Prof., 1969. Hon. Sec., Midlands New Towns Soc., 1958–62; Chief Planner (Strategy), Greater London Council, 1969–72; Senior Research Fellow: Centre for Environmental Studies, 1972–76; PSI, 1976–81; Vivien Stewart Bursar, Dept of Land Economy, Univ. of Cambridge, 1981–82. Visiting Professor: of Demography, Univ. of California at Berkeley, 1965; Bartlett Sch. of Architecture and Planning, University Coll. London, 1976–79; Dept of Town and Country Planning, QUB, 1984–85; Univ. of Trento, Italy, 1991–92; Vis. Schol., Population Reference Bureau, Washington, 1986. Mem., W Midlands Economic Planning Coun., 1965–66; Corr. Mem., German Acad. for Urban and Regional Planning, 1972–; Pres., Commn sur la Démographie Historique, Internat. Congress of Hist. Sciences, 1965–70. Chm., Regional Studies Assoc., 1972–75, Vice-Chm., 1975–90. Chm., Social Responsibility Council, Society of Friends (Quakers), 1972–75; Pres., British Soc. for Population Studies, 1981–83. Hon. Planning Advr, 1988–90, Hon. Dir, 1991–94, Herts Soc. Hon. MRTPI 1978, Mem. Council, 1979–88. *Publications:* Rents and Social Policy, 1955; Social Theories of Fertility and the Malthusian Debate, 1959, new US edn 1975; (with D. Keate) The Overspill Problem in the West Midlands, 1958; (ed and contrib. with D. V. Glass) Population in History, 1965; (with Lomas and Jackson) Population Growth and Planning Policy, 1965; (with F. Sukdeo) The Dependants of the Coloured Commonwealth Population of England and Wales, 1969; (ed and contrib. with D. Donnison) London: urban patterns, problems and policies, 1973; The Planner in Society, 1973; A Question of Numbers?, 1973; (ed and contrib. with J. Platts) Public Resources and Private Lives, 1976; (ed and contrib. with Alan Evans) The Inner City, Industry and Employment, 1980; (ed and contrib. with W. Koellmann) Population Change and Social Planning, 1982; Changes in the Composition of Households and the Cycle of Family Life, 1984; Religion and Employment in Northern Ireland, 1989; (with R. Vann) Friends in Life and Death, 1992; numerous chapters in collected vols; contribs to Victoria History of the Counties of England; articles in jls of history, demography and planning. *Recreations:* walking, talking, working. *Address:* The Kiln House, Mill Street, Ashwell, Baldock, Herts SG7 5LU. *T:* Ashwell (01462) 742631.

Died 3 July 1995.

EWART, Gavin Buchanan, FRSL; freelance writer (poet), since 1971; *b* 4 Feb. 1916; *s* of George Arthur Ewart and Dorothy Hannah (*née* Turner); *m* 1956, Margaret Adelaide Bennett; one *s* one *d*. *Educ:* Wellington Coll.; Christ's Coll., Cambridge (BA Hons 1937, MA 1942). FRSL 1981. Salesman, Contemporary Lithographs, 1938; served War, Royal Artillery, 1940–46; Production Manager, Editions Poetry, London, 1946; British Council, 1946–52; Advertising copywriter in London advertising agencies, 1952–71. Cholmondeley Award for Poetry, 1971; Michael Braude Award for Light Verse, AAIL, 1991. *Publications:* Poems and Songs, 1939; Londoners, 1964; Pleasures of the Flesh, 1966; The Deceptive Grin of the Gravel Porters, 1968; The Gavin Ewart Show, 1971; Be My Guest!, 1975; No Fool Like An Old Fool, 1976; Or Where a Young Penguin Lies Screaming, 1978; All My Little Ones, 1978; The Collected Ewart 1933–1980, 1980, 2nd edn 1982; The New Ewart, 1982; More Little Ones, 1983; Other People's Clerihews, 1983; The Ewart Quarto, 1984; The Young Pobble's Guide to His Toes, 1985; The Complete

Little Ones of Gavin Ewart, 1986; The Learnèd Hippopotamus, 1987; Late Pickings, 1987; Penultimate Poems, 1989; Caterpillar Stew, 1990; Collected Poems 1980–1990, 1991; Like It Or Not, 1992; 85 Poems, 1993. *Recreations:* reading, listening to music. *Address:* 57 Kenilworth Court, Lower Richmond Road, SW15 1EN. *T:* 0181–788 7071. *Died 23 Oct. 1995.*

EWART, Sir (William) Ivan (Cecil), 6th Bt, *cr* 1887; DSC 1945; JP; *b* 18 July 1919; *s* of late Major William Basil Ewart, *y s* of late Frederick William Ewart, 7th *s* of 1st Bt; *S* kinsman, Sir Talbot Ewart, 5th Bt, 1959; *m* 1948, Pauline Chevallier (*d* 1964), *e d* of late Wing Comdr Raphael Chevallier Preston, OBE, AFC, JP; one *s* two *d. Educ:* Radley. Ulster Div., RNVR, 1938. Served War of 1939–45; Lieut, RNVR; service in Coastal Forces (Motor Torpedo-Boats), 1939–42 (DSC); POW, Germany, 1942–45. Chairman: William Ewart & Son Ltd, Linen Manufacturers, 1968–73 (Dir, 1954–73); William Ewart Investments Ltd, Belfast, 1973–77; Ewart New Northern Ltd, Belfast, 1973–77; E Africa Resident Rep., Royal Commonwealth Soc. for the Blind, 1977–84; Administrator, Ngora Freda Carr Hosp., Uganda (Assoc. of Surgeons of E Africa), 1985–89. Non-exec. Dir, Ewart plc, Belfast, 1986–92. Pres., NI Chamber of Commerce and Industry, 1974. A Northern Ireland Delegate to the Duke of Edinburgh's Study Conf. on the Human Problems of Industrial Communities within the Commonwealth and Empire, Oxford, 1956; Pres., Church of Ireland's Young Men's Soc., 1951–61 and 1975–77; Chm. Flax Spinners Assoc., 1961–66; Pres., Oldpark Unionist Assoc., 1950–68. Belfast Harbour Comr, 1968–77. High Sheriff for County Antrim, 1976. *Heir: s* William Michael Ewart, *b* 10 June 1953. *Address:* Hill House, Hillsborough, Co. Down BT26 6AE. *T:* Hillsborough (01846) 683000; PO Box 30171, Nairobi, Kenya. *T:* 725726. *Clubs:* Naval; Ulster Reform (Belfast); Nairobi.

Died 29 Nov. 1995.

EWART-BIGGS, Baroness *cr* 1981 (Life Peer), of Ellis Green in the County of Essex; **Felicity Jane Ewart-Biggs;** *b* 22 Aug. 1929; *d* of Major Basil Randall; *m* 1960, Christopher Ewart-Biggs, CMG, OBE (HM Diplomatic Service) (*d* 1976); one *s* two *d*; *m* 1992, Kevin O'Sullivan. *Educ:* Downe House School, Cold Ash, Newbury, Berks. Lived in Algiers, Brussels, Paris and Dublin, 1960–76, during husband's service overseas. In 1976, established Christopher Ewart-Biggs Memorial Literary Prize. Labour Party spokesman on: home affairs, 1983–; consumer affairs, 1987–; overseas develt, 1987–; an opposition whip, 1988–. Pres., British Cttee, UNICEF, 1984–. Hon. DLitt, New Univ. of Ulster, 1978. *Publications:* autobiography: Pay, Pack and Follow, 1984; Lady in the Lords, 1988. *Recreations:* travel, discussion. *Address:* 63a Abingdon Villas, W8 6XA. *Died 8 Oct. 1992.*

EWEN, Peter; chartered accountant; *b* 4 June 1903; *s* of Alexander H. and Elizabeth Ewen, Liverpool; *m* 1932, Janet Howat (*née* Allan) (*d* 1982); two *d. Educ:* Merchant Taylors', Crosby. Qualified as Chartered Accountant, 1927; after 4 years in India joined Allan Charlesworth & Co., 1931; Partner, 1938; Senior Partner, 1953; retired, 1969. Dir of companies; Chm., Westinghouse Brake and Signal Co. Ltd, 1962–74. *Address:* Kestor, Moretonhampstead, Devon TQ13 8PP. *T:* Moretonhampstead (0647) 40307. *Club:* Oriental.

Died 10 May 1993.

EWENS, John Qualtrough, CMG 1971; CBE 1959; QC 1983; First Parliamentary Counsel, Commonwealth of Australia, 1948–72; *b* 18 Nov. 1907; *er s* of L. J. Ewens, Adelaide; *m* 1935, Gwendoline, *e d* of W. A. Wilson, Adelaide; two *s. Educ:* St Peter's Coll., Adelaide; Univ. of Adelaide. LLB 1929. Barrister and Solicitor, S Australia, 1929. Legal Asst, Attorney-General's Dept, Commonwealth of Australia, 1933; Sen. Legal Officer, 1939; Asst Parly Draftsman, 1945; Principal Asst Parly Draftsman, 1948; First Parly Counsel (formerly called Parly Draftsman), 1948–72; Actg Solicitor-Gen. and Actg Sec., Commonwealth of Australia Attorney-Gen.'s Dept, numerous occasions, 1953–70. Mem. Council: Canberra UC, 1947–60; Australian Nat. Univ., 1960–75; Mem., Australian Law Reform Commn, 1978–80; Consultant (Legislative Drafting): Norfolk Island Admin, 1979–85; Australian Law Reform Commn, 1980–; Constitutional Commn, 1987–88. *Publications:* articles in legal periodicals. *Recreations:* reading, music. *Address:* 8/167 La Perouse Street, Red Hill, ACT 2603, Australia. *T:* Canberra 295 9283. *Club:* University House (Canberra).

Died 16 Aug. 1992.

EYRE, Ronald; freelance theatre and television director; writer; *b* 13 April 1929; *s* of Christopher Eyre and Mabel Smith. *Educ:* Queen Elizabeth Grammar Sch., Wakefield, Yorks; University Coll., Oxford (MA English Lang. and Lit.). English Master, Queen Elizabeth Grammar Sch., Blackburn, 1952–54; Sen. English Master, Bromsgrove Sch., 1954–56; Producer, BBC Television, 1956–64. *Theatre Director: RSC:* Much Ado About Nothing, 1971; London Assurance, London, 1972 and New York, 1974; The Marquis of Keith, 1974; Saratoga, 1978; Othello, 1979; The Winter's Tale, 1981; *West End:* Enjoy; Three Months Gone, 1970 (also Royal Court); Voyage Round My Father, 1971; Habeas Corpus, 1973; The Secret Policeman's Other Ball, 1981; Hobson's Choice, 1982; Messiah, 1983; A Patriot for Me, 1983 (also Chichester Fest.); When We Are Married, 1986 (SWET Award for Comedy); J. J. Farr, 1987; The Sneeze, 1988; A Walk in the Woods, 1989; *Theatre Royal, Stratford East:* Widower's Houses, 1965; *Hampstead Theatre Club:* Events While Guarding the Bofors Gun, 1966; Bakke's Night of Fame, 1968; *Royal Court:* Veterans, 1972; A Pagan Place, 1972; *National Theatre:* Mrs Warren's Profession, 1970; Saint Joan, 1984; *Stratford, Ontario:* The Government Inspector, 1985; *Shochiku Co., Tokyo:* The Dresser, 1988. *Opera Producer:* Beatrice and Benedict, Buxton, 1980 (also translator); Mussorgsky's Marriage, Nexus Opera, 1981; Falstaff, Los Angeles and Covent Garden, 1982 and Teatro Communale, Florence, 1983, new prodn, Covent Garden, 1984; Jason, Buxton, 1984 (also translator); Curlew River, Nexus Opera and BBC, 1986; Peter Grimes, Opera North, 1989. *Playwright:* theatre: Something's Burning, 1973; television: I'm not Stopping, 1963; A Crack in the Ice, 1964 (theatre, 1966); Bruno, 1965; The Single Passion, 1967; The Glory of Llewellyn Smiley, 1967. Writer and Presenter: The Long Search, BBC, 1977; Seven Ages, BBC, 1987; Midweek, 1988; Frontiers: the Irish border, 1990; Not on Sunday, Channel 4, 1990–91; Faith, Hope and Charity, Channel 4, 1991–92. John Harriott Award for Religious Broadcasting, Channel 4 and The Tablet, 1992. *Publication:* Ronald Eyre on The Long Search, 1979. *Address:* c/o L. Dalzell, Suite 12, 17 Broad Court, Covent Garden, WC2. *T:* 071–379 0875. *Died 8 April 1992.*

F

FAGG, William Buller, CMG 1967; ethnologist, tribal art historian and consultant; Keeper, Ethnography Department (from 1972 the Museum of Mankind), British Museum, 1969–74 (Deputy Keeper, 1955–69); *b* 28 April 1914; *s* of late William Percy Fagg and Lilian Fagg. *Educ:* Dulwich Coll.; Magdalene Coll., Cambridge. Sir Wm Browne's Medal for Latin Epigram; Montagu Butler Prize for Latin Hexameters; BA Classics, 1936, Archaeology and Anthropology, 1937; MA 1939. Asst Keeper Dept of Ethnography, BM, 1938; seconded to Bd of Trade, Industries and Manufactures Dept, 1940–45. Royal Anthropological Institute: Hon. Sec., 1939–56; Mem. Council, 1966–69, 1972–75, 1976–79; Vice-Pres., 1969–72; Patron's Medal, 1966; Hon. Editor, Man: A Monthly Record of Anthropological Science, 1947–65; Hon. Librarian, 1976–. Chm., UK Cttee for First World Festival of Negro Arts, Dakar, 1966; Trustee: UK African Festival Trust, 1973–77; Chm., African Fine Art Gallery Trust, 1974–; Consulting Fellow in African Art, Museum of Primitive Art, NY, 1957–70. Consultant on Tribal Art to Christies, 1974–. Fieldwork: Nigeria and Congo, 1949–50; Nigeria, 1953, 1958–59, 1971, 1974, 1981; Cameroon, 1966; Mali, 1969. Organised and arranged many loan exhibns including: Nigerian Art (Arts Council), London, Manchester, Bristol, 1960, Munich, Basel, 1961; African Art, Berlin Festival, 1964, Musée des Arts Décoratifs, Paris, 1964–65; African Sculpture, Nat. Gall. of Art, Washington, DC, Kansas City Art Gall., and Brooklyn Museum, 1970. FRSA (Silver-Medallist, 1951). Member: Royal African Soc.; RIIA; Internat. African Inst.; Museums Assoc.; African Studies Assoc.; China Soc.; ICA; Assoc. of Art Historians. Leadership Award, Arts Council of African Studies Assoc., USA, 1986. *Publications:* The Webster Plass Collection of African Art, British Museum, 1953; (with E. Elisofon) The Sculpture of Africa, 1958; Afro-Portuguese Ivories, 1959; Nigerian Images, 1963 (awarded P. A. Talbot Prize, 1964, and grand prize for best work on African art at World Festival of Negro Arts, Dakar, 1966); (with Margaret Plass) African Sculpture: An Anthology, 1964; Tribes and Forms in African Art, 1966; African Tribal Sculptures, 2 vols, 1967; Arts of Western Africa, Arts of Central Africa (UNESCO), 1967; African Tribal Images (The Katherine White Reswick Collection of African Art), 1968; African Sculpture (Washington, DC), 1970; Miniature Wood Carvings of Africa, 1970; The Tribal Image: wooden figure sculpture of the world, 1970; African Sculpture from the Tara Collection, 1971; (ed) The Living Arts of Nigeria, 1971; Eskimo Art in the British Museum, 1972; Yoruba Beadwork, 1980; Masques d'Afrique, 1980; African Majesty: from grassland and forest, 1981; Yoruba Sculpture of West Africa, 1982; Africa and the Renaissance, 1988; numerous exhibn catalogues, articles in Man, etc. *Recreations:* photography (esp. of art, incl. ancient churches), listening to music, cycling, travel, geopolitics. *Address:* 6 Galata Road, Barnes, SW13 9NQ. *T:* 081-748 6620. *Club:* Travellers'.

Died 10 July 1992.

FAIRBAIRN, David; Metropolitan Stipendiary Magistrate, 1971–89; Deputy Circuit Judge, 1972–89; *b* 9 Aug. 1924; *s* of late Ernest Hulford Fairbairn and Iva May Fairbairn; *m* 1946, Helen Merriel de la Cour Collingwood, *d* of Harold Lewis Collingwood; two *s* two *d*. *Educ:* Haileybury Coll.; Trinity Hall, Cambridge (MA). Served War of 1939–45, Lieut, RNVR, in Mediterranean. Called to Bar, Middle Temple, 1949; Central Criminal Court Bar Mess; South Eastern Circuit; Herts and Essex QS; Dep. Chm., Surrey QS, 1969–71. Liveryman, Gold and Silver Wyre Drawers' Company, 1957–. *Recreations:* golf, tennis, country life. *Address:* c/o National Westminster Bank, Cranleigh, Surrey GU6 8RH.

Died 8 May 1993.

FAIRBAIRN, Douglas Foakes, CBE 1971; *b* 9 Oct. 1919; *s* of William and Florence Fairbairn; *m* 1947, Gertrude Betty Buswell; two *s*. *Educ:* John Lyon Sch., Harrow; Royal School of Mines, Imperial Coll., London Univ. BSc (Hons), ARSM. Served War, RAF (Sqdn Ldr), 1940–46. Commonwealth Development Corp., 1949–83; Regional Controller: Central Africa, 1959–66; West Africa, 1966–71; Co-ordinator of Operations, 1971–83. Dir, Bank of Rhodesia and Nyasaland, 1961–63; Chm., Central African Airways, 1964–68; Mem., Central African Power Corp., 1961–77; Chm., Springwood Cellulose Co. Ltd, 1983–87; Dir, Town and Commercial Property Services Ltd, 1986–91. *Recreation:* golf. *Address:* 11 Portland Terrace, The Green, Richmond, Surrey TW9 1QQ. *T:* 0181–948 1921. *Club:* Richmond Golf.

Died 30 Nov. 1994.

FAIRBAIRN, Sir Nicholas (Hardwick), Kt 1988; QC (Scot.) 1972; MP (C) Perth and Kinross, since 1983 (Kinross and Perthshire West, Oct. 1974–1983); *b* 24 Dec. 1933; *s* of William Ronald Dodds Fairbairn, DPsych, and Mary Ann More-Gordon, Charleton and Kinnaber; *m* 1st, 1962, Hon. Elizabeth Mary Mackay (marr. diss. 1979), *e d* of 13th Baron Reay; three *d* (and one *s* one *d* decd); 2nd, 1983, Suzanne Mary Wheeler. *Educ:* Loretto; Edinburgh Univ.; MA, LLB. Author, forester, painter, poet, TV and radio broadcaster, journalist, dress-designer, landscape gardener, bon viveur, raconteur and wit. Called to Scots Bar 1957. Cons. Candidate, Central Edinburgh, 1964, 1966. HM Solicitor Gen. for Scotland, 1979–82. Comr of Northern Lighthouses, 1979–82. Mem., Council of World Population Crisis, 1968–70. Founder and Hon. Pres., Soc. for Preservation of Duddingston Village; Member: Edinburgh Festival Council, 1971–; Bd, Edinburgh Brook Adv. Centre (Chm., 1968–75). Chairman: Traverse Theatre, 1964–72; Waverley Broadcasting Co., 1973–74; Historic Buildings Council for Scotland, 1988–; Dir, Ledlanet Nights, 1960–73. Chm., Scottish Soc. for Defence of Literature and the Arts. Pres., Dysart and Dundonald Pipe Band; Life Pres., Edinburgh Brook Adv. Centre, 1975 (Chm., 1968–75). Vice Pres., Scottish Women's Soc. of Artists, 1988–. Trustee, Scottish Museums, 1987–. Private exhibns throughout Britain, 1960–; and in public exhibns. KLJ; KStJ; FSAScot. Hon. Fellow, Internat. Acad. of Trial Lawyers, 1984. Kt Chevalier, Order of Polonia Restituta (Poland), 1988. *Publications:* A Life is Too Short (autobiog.), 1987; contrib., Alistair Maclean Introduces Scotland, 1972. *Recreations:* languishing and sandwiching. *Address:* Fordell Castle, by Dunfermline, Fife KY11 5EY. *Clubs:* Puffin's, Beefsteak, Chatham Dining; New (Edinburgh).

Died 19 Feb. 1995.

FAIRFAX, Sir Vincent Charles, Kt 1971; CMG 1960; company director and pastoralist, Australia; *b* 26 Dec. 1909; *s* of late J. H. F. Fairfax; *m* 1939, Nancy, *d* late Dr C. B. Heald, CBE, FRCP; two *s* two *d*. *Educ:* Geelong

Church of England Grammar Sch., Australia; Brasenose Coll., Oxford Univ. (BA). Staff, John Fairfax & Sons Pty Ltd, 1933; Advertising Manager, 1937–38. Major, Australian Imperial Forces, 1940–46. Director: John Fairfax & Sons Pty Ltd, 1946–53; John Fairfax Ltd (Publishers, Sydney Morning Herald), 1956–87; Chm. Australian Sect., Commonwealth Press Union, 1950–73; Chm., Stanbroke Pastoral Co. Pty Ltd, 1964–82; Director: Bank of NSW, 1953–82; Australian Mutual Provident Soc., 1956–82 (Chm. 1966–82). Chief Comr Scout Assoc., for NSW, 1958–68, for Australia, 1969–73; Pres., Nat. Council, Scout Assoc. of Australia, 1977–86; Dep. Pres., Royal Agric. Society of Commonwealth, 1966–90; Mem. C of E Property Trust, 1950–71; Trustee, Walter and Eliza Hall Trust, 1953–; Mem. Council: Art Gall. Soc. of NSW, 1953–69; Royal Flying Doctor Service, 1954–71; Royal Agric. Society of NSW, 1956 (Pres., 1970–79, Vice-Patron, 1979); Mem., Glebe Administration Bd, 1962–73; Rector's Warden, St Mark's, Darling Point, 1948–71. *Recreations:* tennis, golf, trout fishing. *Address:* Elaine, 550 New South Head Road, Double Bay, Sydney, NSW 2028, Australia. *T:* 3271416. *Clubs:* Leander (Henley-on-Thames); Commonwealth (Canberra); Melbourne (Melbourne); Union, Royal Sydney Golf (Sydney); Queensland (Brisbane). *Died 12 April 1993.*

FAIRLIE, Prof. Alison (Anna Bowie), FBA 1984; Emeritus Professor of French, University of Cambridge, since 1980 (Professor, 1972–80), and Life Fellow, Girton College, since 1980; *b* 23 May 1917; *e d* of Rev. Robert Paul Fairlie, MA, Minister of the Church of Scotland, and Florence A. A. Wilson. *Educ:* Ardrossan Acad.; Dumfries Acad.; Penrhos Coll.; St Hugh's Coll. Oxford; Sorbonne. BA 1st Cl. in Final Hons Sch. of Medieval and Mod. Langs, Oxon; MA, DPhil (Oxon). Doctoral Research: in Paris, 1938–40 (interruptions for voluntary war-work); in Oxford, 1940–42; Temp. Admin. Officer, Foreign Office, 1942–44; Girton College, Cambridge: Lectr in French, 1944–67; Staff Fellow, 1946–80; Dir of Studies in Mod. Langs, 1946–67; Professorial Fellow, 1972–80; Univ. Lectr in French, Cambridge, 1948–67, Reader in French, 1967–72. Vice-Pres., Soc. for French Studies, 1965–66 and 1968–69, Pres., 1966–68; Mem. Council, 1969–, Vice Pres., 1983–, Assoc. Internationale des Etudes françaises; Member: Editorial Bd, French Studies, 1972–80, Adv. Bd 1980–; Adv. Bd, Romance Studies, 1982–. Hon. Fellow, St Hugh's Coll., Oxford, 1972. *Publications:* Leconte de Lisle's Poems on the Barbarian Races, 1947; Baudelaire: Les Fleurs du Mal, 1960 (repr. 1975); Flaubert: Madame Bovary, 1962 (repr. 1976); Imagination and Language, 1981; (ed jtly) Baudelaire, Mallarmé, Valéry—New Essays in honour of Lloyd Austin, 1982; contributions: to Acta of colloquia, on Baudelaire, Constant, Flaubert, Nerval, etc; to presentation vols; to learned jls in France, England, Italy, USA, Australia, etc. *Recreations:* reading, travel. *Address:* 11 Parker Street, Cambridge CB1 1JL. *T:* Cambridge (0223) 358465. *Died 21 Feb. 1993.*

FAIRLIE, Hugh, OBE 1984; MA, MEd; *b* 14 Dec. 1919; *s* of Thomas and Joanna Fairlie; *m* 1947, Jemima Peden; two *s*. *Educ:* Univ. of Edinburgh. MA (Hons Maths and NatPhil); MEd (Dist.). FEIS 1975. Teacher, Maybole Carrick Academy, 1947–49; Asst Director of Education: Morayshire, 1949–52; Fife, 1952–57; Depute Dir of Educn, 1957–64, Dir of Educn, 1964–75, Renfrewshire; Lectr, Jordanhill Coll. of Educn, 1975–82. Chairman: Scottish Council for Research in Education, 1978–84; Renfrew District Arts Guild, 1980–. *Recreations:* golf, gardens. *Address:* 26 Thornly Park Avenue, Paisley, Scotland PA2 7SE. *T:* 041–884 2494. *Clubs:* Royal Over-Seas League; Paisley Burns; Western Gailes Golf. *Died 5 July 1993.*

FALKNER, Sir (Donald) Keith, Kt 1967; Hon. DMus Oxon, 1969; FRCM; Director, Royal College of Music, 1960–74, Vice President, since 1984; professional singer; *b* Sawston, Cambs, 1 March 1900; *y s* of late John Charles Falkner; *m* 1930, Christabel Margaret (*d* 1990), *o d* of Thomas Fletcher Fullard, MA; two *d*. *Educ:* New Coll. Sch.; Perse Sch.; Royal College of Music; Berlin, Vienna, Paris. Sang at all principal festivals in England, and many European cities; toured USA eight times, including concerts with Boston Symphony, New York Philharmonic, Cincinnati, St Louis, and Philadelphia Orchestras; toured: South Africa, 1935, 1939, 1955, 1962, 1974; Canada in 1953; New Zealand in 1956; starred in three Warner Bros musicals, 1937–39. British Council Music Officer for Italy, 1946–50. Prof. of the Dept of Music at Cornell Univ., USA, 1950–60. An Artistic Dir, King's Lynn Fest., 1981–83. FRSA 1979. Hon. RAM; Hon. GSM; Hon. FTCL; Hon. FLCM. Hon. Mem., Assoc. Européene des Conservatoires de Musique, Académies, et Musikhochschulen, 1976. Served European War, 1914–18, in RNAS, 1917–19; War of 1939–45, RAFVR, 1940–45. *Publication:* (ed) Voice, 1983. *Recreations:* cricket, golf, lawn tennis, squash rackets, walking. *Address:* Low Cottages, Ilketshall St Margaret, Bungay, Suffolk NR35 1PL. *T:* Bungay (0986) 892573. *Clubs:* Athenæum, Royal Automobile, MCC; Norfolk (Norwich). *Died 17 May 1994.*

FALLSIDE, Prof. Frank, PhD; CEng, FIWEM; Professor of Information Engineering, since 1983, and Fellow of Trinity Hall, since 1962, University of Cambridge; *b* 2 Jan. 1932; *s* of William Thomas Fallside, Leith and Daisy Helen Janet Kinnear Madden, Edinburgh; *m* 1958, Maureen Helen Couttie, Edinburgh; two *s* one *d*. *Educ:* George Heriot's Sch., Edinburgh; Edinburgh Univ. (BSc). PhD Wales; MA Cantab. MIEE 1968; CEng, FIWES 1983. Engr, English Electric Co., 1957–58; Cambridge University: Sen. Asst in Res., 1958–61; Lectr in Engrg, 1961–72; Reader in Electrical Engrg, 1972–83; Tutor for grad. students, Trinity Hall, 1966–72. Director: Cambridge Water Co., 1969–; Cambridge Microprocessor Courses, 1979–; Eastcam Systems, 1983–. *Publications:* (ed with W. A. Woods) Computer Speech Processing, 1985; various tech. papers in engrg and speech science. *Recreations:* sailing, maritime history. *Address:* 37 Earl Street, Cambridge CB1 1JR. *T:* Cambridge (0223) 353966. *Died 24 March 1993.*

FANE, Harry Frank Brien, CMG 1967; OBE 1957 (MBE 1945); Department of Employment and Productivity, retired 1968; *b* 21 Aug. 1915; *s* of late Harry Lawson Fane and Edith (*née* Stovold); *m* 1947, Stella, *yr d* of late John Hopwood; two *d*. *Educ:* William Ellis Sch.; Birkbeck Coll., London. Joined Ministry of Labour, 1933. HM Forces, 1940–45: Major, Royal Corps of Signals (despatches); served in N Africa, Italy and Austria. British Embassy, Washington: First Sec. (Labour), 1950–56; Counsellor (Labour), 1960–66; Regional Controller, Dept of Employment and Productivity (formerly Min. of Labour), Birmingham, 1966–68. *Address:* 40 Winterbourne Road, Solihull, West Midlands B91 1LU. *Died 16 March 1993.*

FANSHAWE, Maj.-Gen. George Drew, CB 1954; DSO 1944; OBE 1944; *b* 27 Sept. 1901; *s* of Lt-Col Edward Cardwell Fanshawe; *m* 1934, Dorothy Elizabeth Norman-Walker; one *s* one *d*. *Educ:* Tonbridge. 2nd Lieut, RFA, 1922, Lieut 1924; RHA, 1928; Capt. 1935; Adjt Herts Yeomanry, 1935; Brigade-Major, RA, 1939, CO 1942; CRA, 3 Div., 1945; 5th Anti-Aircraft Bde, 1949; BRA Southern Comd, 1950; Comdr 1st Anti-Aircraft Group, 1952–55; retired 1955. Col Comdt, Royal Artillery, 1956–66 (Representative Col Comdt, 1961–62). High Sheriff, Wilts, 1961–62; Alderman, Wilts CC. CStJ. Order

of Merit (US). *Address:* Farley Farm, Farley, Wilts SP5 1AD. *T:* Farley (072272) 202. *Club:* Army and Navy.
Died 20 Feb. 1991.

FARRER-BROWN, Leslie, CBE 1960; consultant; Director: Nuffield Foundation, 1944–64; Alliance Building Society, 1969–83 (Chairman, 1975–81); *b* 2 April 1904; *er s* of late Sydney and Annie Brown; *m* 1928, Doris Evelyn (*d* 1986), *o d* of late Herbert Jamieson; two *s. Educ:* LSE (BSc Econ.; Hon. Fellow 1975); Gray's Inn (Barrister-at-Law, 1932). Asst Registrar, LSE, 1927–28; on Administrative Staff, Univ. of London, 1928–36; Sec., Central Midwives Bd, 1936–44; seconded to Min. of Health, 1941–44. Pres., Surrey and Sussex Rent Assessment Panel, 1965–76. Sec., Interdepartmental Cttee on Med. Schs, 1942–44. Chairman: Malta Med. Services Commn, 1956; Highgate Juvenile Court, 1952–61; Highgate Court, 1961–65; Nat. Council of Social Service, 1960–73; Centre for Educational Television Overseas, 1962–70; Overseas Visual Aid Centre, 1958–70; Voluntary Cttee on Overseas Aid and Develt, 1965–76; Centre for Information on Language Teaching, 1966–72; Cttee for Res. and Develt in Modern Languages, 1964–70; Rhodesia Med. Sch. Cttee, 1956–57; Univ. of London Inst. of Child Health, 1966–76; Inst. of Race Relations, 1968–72. Member: Colonial Adv. Med. Cttee, 1946–61; Colonial Social Science Res. Council, 1954–61; Med. Educn Cttee of UGC, 1945–52; Rating of Charities Cttee, 1958–59; Adv. Council, BBC, 1956–65; Court of Governors, LSE; Chm. Council and Sen. Pro-Chancellor, Univ. of Sussex, 1976–80. Trustee, Nuffield Provincial Hospitals Trust, 1955–67; UK Governor, Commonwealth Foundn, 1966–89. JP: Middx, 1947–65; East Sussex, 1966–81. Hon. FDSRCS. Hon. LLD: Birmingham; Witwatersrand; Sussex; Hon. DSc Keele. *Publication:* (jt) A Short Textbook on Public Health and Social Services. *Recreations:* travel, painting. *Address:* 3 Kennet Court, Woosehill, Wokingham, Berks RG11 9BD. *Clubs:* Athenæum, Commonwealth Trust (Life Vice-Pres., 1969). *Died 20 April 1994.*

FAULKNER, Sir Eric (Odin), Kt 1974; MBE 1945; TD 1945 and Bar 1951; Director, Lloyds Bank Ltd, 1968–84 (Chairman, 1969–77); Advisory Director, Unilever, 1978–84; *b* 21 April 1914; *s* of late Sir Alfred Faulkner, CB, CBE and Florence Edith, *d* of A. A. Nicoll; *m* 1939, Joan Mary (*d* 1991), *d* of Lt-Col F. A. M. Webster; one *s* one *d. Educ:* Bradfield; Corpus Christi Coll., Cambridge (Hon. Fellow, 1975). Joined Glyn, Mills & Co., 1936. Served War of 1939–45, Royal Artillery and Leics Yeomanry; Staff Coll.; Bde Major RA, GSO2; commanded 91 Field Regt RA. Rejoined Glyn, Mills & Co., 1946; Local Dir, 1947–50; Exec. Dir, 1950–68; Dep. Chm., 1959–63; Chm., 1963–68. Chm., Cttee of London Clearing Bankers, 1972–74. Pres., British Bankers' Assoc., 1972–73, 1980–84. Director: Union Discount Co. of London Ltd, 1949–70 (Chm., 1959–70); Hudsons Bay Co., 1950–70 (Dep. Governor, 1952–56); Vickers Ltd, 1957–79. Chairman: Industrial Soc., 1973–76; City Communications Organisation, 1976–79. Warden of Bradfield Coll., 1965–84; Trustee, Winston Churchill Meml Trust, 1973–84. *Recreations:* fishing, walking; formerly cricket, Association football (CUAFC XI 1935). *Address:* Farriers Field, Sevenoaks Road, Ightham, Kent TN15 9AA. *Died 7 Aug. 1994.*

FAULKNER, Dr Hugh Charles, FRCGP; Consultant to Regional Health Authority, Tuscany and to Unità Sanitaria Locale del Chianti; Editorial Board, Salute e Territorio; Hon. Lecturer in Social Medicine, Bedford College, University of London, since 1976; Medical Secretary, Medical Practitioners' Union (ASTMS), and Medical Editor of Medical World, 1971–76; *b* 22 Sept. 1912; *s* of Frank Whitehead Faulkner and Emily Maud Knibb; *m*;

one *s* two *d. Educ:* Oundle Sch.; London Hosp. MRCS, LRCP 1943; FRCGP 1979. Boys' Club manager, 1932–35. Served War, RAMC, 1944–46. Gen. practitioner, 1948–76. Mem. Council of Medical Practitioners' Union, 1948–76. Trustee, Community Health Foundn, 1991–. Mem., Ordine dei Medici (Firenze), 1981. *Publications:* Medicina di Base in due paesi, Gran Bretagna e l'URSS, 1977; Against All Odds, 1992; articles in Medical World, Lancet, etc. *Recreation:* attacking the Establishment. *Address:* La Galera, Passo del Sugame, Greve-in-Chianti, Firenze, Italy. *Died 18 April 1994.*

FAWCETT, Sir James (Edmund Sandford), Kt 1984; DSC 1942; QC 1985; President, European Commission of Human Rights, 1972–81 (Member, 1962–84); *b* 16 April 1913; *s* of Rev. Joseph Fawcett and Edith Fawcett; *m* 1937, Frances Beatrice, 2nd *d* of late Dr E. A. Lowe; one *s* four *d. Educ:* Rugby Sch.; New Coll., Oxford. Called to the Bar, 1938. Fellow of All Souls Coll., Oxford, 1938. Served War of 1939–45, Royal Navy. Asst Legal Adviser to FO, 1945–50 (to UK Delegn to UN and British Embassy, Washington, 1948–50); Gen. Counsel, IMF, 1955–60; Fellow of All Souls Coll., Oxford, 1960–69; Dir of Studies, RIIA, 1969–73; Prof. of Internat. Law, King's Coll., London, 1976–80, Emeritus Professor 1980. Mem., Inst. of Internat. Law, 1973–; Chm., British Inst. of Human Rights, 1977–81. Pres., UK Immigrants Advisory Service, 1985–. *Publications:* British Commonwealth in International Law, 1963; International Law and the Uses of Outer Space, 1968; The Law of Nations (Penguin), 1968; The Application of the European Convention on Human Rights, 1969; International Economic Conflicts, 1977; Law and Power in International Relations, 1981; Outer Space: new perspectives, 1984; numerous articles. *Recreations:* astronomy, piano. *Address:* Murray Court, 80 Banbury Road, Oxford. *Died 24 June 1991.*

FAY, John David, CMG 1985; Director for Publications Policy, Organisation for Economic Co-operation and Development, Paris, 1980–84; *b* 5 July 1919; *s* of late Stanley John Fay and Muriel Etrenne (*née* Nicholson); *m* 1949, Valerie Joyce Stroud; one *s* two *d. Educ:* Stowe Sch.; King's Coll., Cambridge (Minor Scholar; BA 1941, 1st Cl. both parts Historical Tripos; MA 1983). BoT, London, 1941–46 (Asst Private Sec. to Pres., 1944–46); Washington, 1946–48; Internat. Secretariat of OECD (formerly OEEC), Paris, 1949–84: Head of Country Studies Div., 1952; Dir, Econs Br., 1957; Dep. Head of Econs and Statistics Dept, 1968, Head of Dept, 1975. *Publications:* extensive unsigned contribs to OEEC and OECD econ. pubns; editorials for Internat. Herald Tribune. *Recreations:* gardening, gastronomy, helping economists to write English. *Address:* 31 avenue du Cardinal de Retz, 78600 Maisons-Laffitte, France. *T:* 3962 27 28. *Club:* Athenæum. *Died 27 Aug. 1991.*

FEA, William Wallace; Director, Guest, Keen & Nettlefolds Ltd, 1958–72 (Deputy Chairman, 1968–72); *b* Cordova, Argentina, 3 Feb. 1907; *s* of Herbert Reginald Fea and Hilda Florence Fea (*née* Norton); *m* 1935, Norah Anne, *d* of Richard Festing; one *s* (and one *s* decd). *Educ:* Cheltenham Coll. (scholar); Brasenose Coll., Oxford (scholar; BA). ACA 1932; FCA. Member: Council, Inst. of Chartered Accountants, 1953–71; Council, BIM, 1969–73; Management Cttee, AA, 1971–77. *Recreation:* listening to music, particularly opera. *Address:* The Lowe, Worfield, near Bridgnorth, Salop WV15 5NS. *T:* Worfield (07464) 241. *Club:* Lansdowne.
Died 21 June 1993.

FEDRICK, Geoffrey Courtis; HM Diplomatic Service, retired; Counsellor (Management), Brussels, 1989–93; *b* 21 Aug. 1937; *s* of Roy Townsend Fedrick and Vera May Fedrick (*née* Tope); *m* 1st, 1961, Elizabeth Louise Moore; two *s*; 2nd, 1984, Margaret Elizabeth Hearnden (*née*

Pawley); one *s. Educ:* Plymouth College. HM Forces, 1956–58. Govt Actuary's Dept, 1958–60; CRO, 1960; Salisbury, S Rhodesia, 1961–64; Peshawar, Pakistan, 1965–66; 2nd Sec., Washington, 1967–70; FCO, 1971–75; Consul, Toronto, 1975–79; FCO, 1980–83; First Sec., Lagos, 1983–86; FCO, 1986–88. *Recreations:* golf, bridge, choral singing. *Address:* Greystones, Kings Stanley, Glos. *Died 25 July 1994.*

FEENY, Max Howard; barrister; *b* 5 Nov. 1928; *s* of late Howard Raymond John Feeny and Frances Kate Feeny (*née* Muspratt); *m* 1952, June Elizabeth (*née* Camplin) (*d* 1986); three *s* four *d. Educ:* Stonyhurst Coll.; Oratory Sch.; Univ. of Birmingham (LLB). Called to Bar, Inner Temple, 1953. A Recorder of the Crown Court, 1972–78. Senior Lectr, Inst. of Professional Legal Studies, Queen's Univ. of Belfast, 1982–91. Chm. (part-time), Med. Appeals Tribunal, 1987–91. Mem., Council of Legal Educn (NI), 1983–87. *Recreations:* gardening, surf fishing. *Address:* Urlee, Lisselton, near Listowel, Co. Kerry, Eire.
Died 24 March 1995.

FELDBERG, Wilhelm Siegmund, CBE 1963; MA Cantab; MD Berlin; FRS 1947; FRCP 1978; Professor Emeritus; Personal Grant Holder, National Institute for Medical Research, London, 1967–91; *b* 19 Nov. 1900; *s* of Emil Daniel Feldberg; *m* 1925, Katherine (*d* 1976), *d* of late Karl Scheffler; one *d* (one *s* decd); *m* 1977, Kim O'Rourke (*d* 1981). Reader in Physiology, Cambridge Univ., until 1949; Head of Physiology and Pharmacology Division, National Institute for Medical Research, London, 1949–65 (Hon. Head of Division, 1965–66); Head, Lab. of Neuropharmacology, Nat. Inst. for Med. Res., 1966–74. Hon. Lectr, London Univ., 1950–. Lectures: Dunham, Harvard, 1953; Evarts Graham Meml, Washington Univ., St Louis, USA, 1961; Aschoff Meml, Freiburg Univ., 1961; Dixon Meml, RSM, 1964; William Withering, 1966; Nat. Research Council of Canada/Nuffield Foundn, 1970–71; Ferrier, Royal Soc., 1974; Sherrington, 1980. Hon. Member: British Pharmacol Soc.; RSM; Physiol. Soc.; Soc. française d'allergie; Deutsche Physiologische Gesellschaft; Deutsche Pharm. Gesell.; Berliner Medizinische Gesell.; Berliner Phys. Gesell. Hon. MD: Freiburg, 1961; Berlin, and Cologne, 1963; Würzburg; Heidelberg; Liège, 1969; Hon. DSc: Bradford, 1973; London, 1979; Hon. LLD: Glasgow, 1976; Aberdeen, 1977. Grand Cross, Order of Merit of German Federal Republic, 1961. Baly Medal, 1963; Schmiedeberg Plakette, 1969; Stöhr Medal, 1970; Royal Medal, Royal Soc., 1983. *Publications:* Histamin (with E. Schilf); A Pharmacological Approach to the Brain from its Inner and Outer Surface, 1963; articles in med. and scientific jls. *Address:* Lavenham, 74 Marsh Lane, Mill Hill, NW7 4NT. *T:* 081–959 5545. *Died 23 Oct. 1993.*

FELLINI, Federico; film director since 1950; *b* 20 Jan. 1920; *s* of late Urbano Fellini and Ida Barbiani; *m* 1943, Giulietta Masina. *Educ:* Bologna, Italy. Journalist, 1937–39; radio-author, scenario writer, etc, 1939–42. Fellow, BAFTA, 1987; gained many prizes and awards in every part of the world including four "Oscars" (1957, 1958, 1964, 1975) for films La Strada, Le Notti di Cabiria, 8½ and Amarcord. Films include: (as Assistant Director and writer): Quarta Pagina, 1942; Roma Città Aperta, 1944–45; Paisà, 1946; Il Delitto di Giovanni Episcopo, 1947; In Nome della Legge, 1948–49; La Città si Defende, 1951; Il Brigante di Tacca di Lupo, 1953; San Francesco Giullare di Dio, 1954; Fortunella, 1956; (as Director): Luci del Varietà, 1950; Lo Sceicco Bianco, 1952; I Vitelloni, 1953; Agenzia Matrimoniale, 1953; La Strada, 1954; Il Bidone, 1955; Cabiria, 1957; La Dolce Vita, 1960; The Temptation of Dr Antonio, 1962; 8½, 1963 (foreign awards); Giulietta Degli Spiriti, 1965; Never Bet the Devil Your Head, 1968; Director's Blocknotes, 1969;

Satyricon, 1969; The Clowns, 1970; Fellini's Roma, 1972; Amarcord, 1974; Casanova, 1976; Orchestra Rehearsal, 1979; La citta delle donne, 1980; E la nave vá, 1983; Ginger and Fred, 1986; Interview, 1987; The Voice of the Moon, 1990. *Publications:* Amarcord (trans. Nina Rootes), 1974; Quattro film, 1975. *Address:* Via Margutta 110, Rome, Italy. *Died 31 Oct. 1993.*

FENNELL, Prof. John Lister Illingworth, MA, PhD Cantab; FRSL; Professor of Russian, Oxford University, 1967–85; Emeritus Fellow of New College, Oxford, since 1985 (Fellow, 1967); *b* 30 May 1918; *s* of Dr C. H. Fennell and Sylvia Mitchell; *m* 1947, Marina Lopukhin; one *s* one *d. Educ:* Radley Coll.; Trinity Coll., Cambridge. FRSL 1980; FRHistS 1985. Served with Army, 1939–45. Asst Lectr, Dept of Slavonic Studies, Cambridge Univ., 1947–52; Reader in Russian and Head of Dept of Slavonic Languages, Nottingham Univ., 1952–56; Lectr in Russian, Oxford Univ., 1956–67; Fellow and Praelector in Russian, University Coll., Oxford, 1964–67. Vis. Lectr, Harvard Univ., 1963–64; Visiting Professor: Univ. of Calif at Berkeley, 1971, 1977; Virginia Univ., 1974; (Bonsall and Kratter), Stanford Univ., 1982–83; Univ. of Texas at Austin, 1986. Organiser, 3rd Internat. Conf. of Historians of Muscovy, Oxford, 1975. Joint Editor: Oxford Slavonic Papers, 1968–86; Russia Mediaevalis. *Publications:* The Correspondence between Prince A. M. Kurbsky and Ivan IV, 1955; Ivan the Great of Moscow, 1961; The Penguin Russian Course, 1961; Pushkin, 1964; Kurbsky's History of Ivan IV, 1965; The Emergence of Moscow, 1968; (ed jtly) Historical Russian Reader, 1969; (ed) Nineteenth Century Russian Literature, 1973; (with A. Stokes) Early Russian Literature, 1974; (ed jtly) The Cambridge Encyclopaedia of Russia and the Soviet Union, 1982; The Crisis of Medieval Russia, 1983; Cambridge Modern History, Vol. II, Chap. 19; articles in Slavonic and East European Review, Jahrbücher für Geschichte Osteuropas, etc. *Recreation:* music. *Address:* 8 Canterbury Road, Oxford OX2 6LU. *T:* Oxford (0865) 56149.
Died 9 Aug. 1992.

FENTON, Air Cdre Harold Arthur, CBE 1946; DSO 1943; DFC 1942; BA; AFRAeS; *b* Gallegos, Patagonia, Argentine, 9 Feb. 1909; *s* of Dr E. G. Fenton, FRCSI, DPH, Co. Sligo and J. Ormsby, Glen Lodge, Ballina, Co. Mayo; *m* 1935, H. de Carteret; no *c. Educ:* Sandford Park Sch.; Trinity Coll., Dublin (BA 1927). Joined RAF 1928. Served India, 1930–33. Flying Instructor at Air Service Training Ltd, Hamble, until outbreak of war. During war commanded: Fighter Sqdn, Battle of Britain; Fighter Wing, and Fighter Group, Western Desert and Libya; Fighter Sector, London Area. Finished war as Senior Staff Officer, Germany (83 Group) (despatches thrice). Managing Dir, Deccan Airways Ltd, Hyderabad, Deccan, until 1947; Gen. Manager of Airways Training Ltd, 1947–48; Operations Manager, BOAC, 1949–52; Managing Dir, Peter Jones, 1952–58. *Recreation:* gardening. *Address:* Le Vallon, St Brelade, Jersey, Channel Islands. *T:* Jersey (0534) 41172.
Died 11 Dec. 1995.

FERENS, Sir Thomas (Robinson), Kt 1957; CBE 1952; *b* 4 Jan. 1903; *e s* of late J. J. T. Ferens, Hull; *m* 1934, Jessie (*d* 1982), *d* of P. G. Sanderson, Hull and Scarborough; two *d. Educ:* Rydal; Leeds Univ. (BSc Eng). Hon. Treasurer: Hull Seamen's and General Orphanage, 1933–48; Hull Conservative Fedn, 1945–52 (Dep. Chm., 1951–62). Director: Shipham and Co. Ltd, Hull; George Clark and Sons (Hull) Ltd. *Recreation:* fly-fishing. *Address:* Sunderlandwick, Driffield, North Humberside. *T:* Driffield (0377) 42323. *Died 1 June 1992.*

FERGUSON, Dr James Brown Provan; Chief Administrative Medical Officer and Director of Public Health, Lanarkshire, since 1988; *b* 23 Oct. 1935; *s* of Peter

William Ferguson and Sarah Ferguson (*née* Brown); *m* 1960, Sheila Capstick; three *d. Educ:* Univ. of Edinburgh (MB ChB; DipSocMed). FFPHM. Principal SMO, SE Regl Hosp. Bd, 1972–74; Dist MO, N Lothian Dist, 1974–83; SMO, SHHD, 1983–88. W. K. Kellogg Foundn Fellow, 1983; Hon. Sen. Lectr, Univ. of Glasgow, 1988. *Publications:* contribs to BMJ, British Jl of Surgery. *Recreations:* walking, cinema, reading, print collecting. *Address:* Lanarkshire Health Board, 14 Beckford Street, Hamilton ML3 0TA. *T:* Hamilton (0698) 281313.

Died 11 Feb. 1994.

FERGUSON, Sir Neil Edward J.; *see* Johnson-Ferguson.

FERGUSSON, James David, CB 1982; *b* 14 Jan. 1923; *s* of James Thomson Fergusson and Agnes Eva Fergusson; *m* 1946, Jean Barbara Debnam; two *s* one *d. Educ:* Montrose Acad.; St Andrews Univ. (BSc). Temp. Experimental Officer, Admiralty, 1943–47; Patent Office Examining Staff, 1947–69; Asst Comptroller, Patent Office, 1969–83. *Address:* 8 The Warrens, Kirby Cross, Frinton-on-Sea, Essex CO13 0PJ. *T:* Frinton-on-Sea (0255) 678271. *Died 30 Aug. 1991.*

FERMOY, Ruth Lady; Ruth Sylvia Roche, DCVO 1979 (CVO 1966); OBE 1952; JP; Woman of the Bedchamber to Queen Elizabeth the Queen Mother since 1960 (an extra Woman of the Bedchamber, 1956–60); *b* 2 Oct. 1908; *y d* of late William Smith Gill, CB, VD, Dalhebity, Bieldside, Aberdeenshire; *m* 1931, Edmund Maurice Burke Roche, 4th Baron Fermoy (*d* 1955); two *d* (one *s* decd). JP Norfolk, 1944. Freedom of King's Lynn, 1963. Hon. RAM 1968; FRCM 1983. Hon. MusD Univ. of East Anglia, 1975. *Died 6 July 1993.*

FERNS, Prof. Henry Stanley, MA, PhD Cantab; Professor of Political Science, University of Birmingham, 1961–81, then Emeritus Professor; *b* Calgary, Alberta, 16 Dec. 1913; *er s* of Stanley and Janie Ferns; *m* 1940, Helen Maureen, *d* of John and Eleanor Jack; three *s* one *d. Educ:* St John's High Sch., Winnipeg; Univ. of Manitoba; Trinity Coll., Cambridge. Research Scholar, Trinity Coll., Cambridge, 1938; Secretarial staff of Prime Minister of Canada, 1940; Asst Prof. of History and Government, Univ. of Manitoba, 1945; Fellow, Canadian Social Science Research Council, 1949; Lectr in Modern History and Government, Univ. of Birmingham, 1950; successively Sen. Lectr, Head of Dept and Prof. of Political Science; Dean, Faculty of Commerce and Social Sci., 1961–65. Pres., Bd of Dirs, Winnipeg Citizens' Cooperative Publishing Co. Ltd, 1946–48; Member of various Conciliation Boards appointed by Minister of Labour of Govt of Manitoba, 1947–49. Past Pres., British Assoc. of Canadian Studies. Hon. DLitt Buckingham, 1983. *Publications:* (with B. Ostry) The Age of McKenzie King: The Rise of the Leader, 1955 (Toronto and London), 2nd edn 1976; Britain and Argentina in the Nineteenth Century, 1960 (Oxford); Towards an Independent University, 1969; Argentina, 1969; The Argentine Republic 1516–1971, 1973; The Disease of Government, 1978; How Much Freedom for Universities?, 1982; Reading from Left to Right, 1983; (with K. W. Watkins) What Politics is About, 1985; articles in learned jls. *Recreations:* journalism, idling, pottering about. *Address:* 1 Kesteven Close, Sir Harry's Road, Birmingham B15 2UT. *T:* 021–440 1016.

Died 19 Feb. 1992.

FERNYHOUGH, Rt Hon. Ernest, PC 1970; *b* 24 Dec. 1908; British; *m* 1934, Ethel Edwards; one *s* one *d* (and one *s* decd). *Educ:* Wood Lane Council Sch. Full-time official, Union of Shop, Distributive and Allied Workers, 1936–47. MP (Lab) Jarrow, May 1947–1979; PPS to the Prime Minister, 1964–67; Jt Parly Under-Sec. of State, Dept of Employment and Productivity (formerly Min. of Labour), 1967–69. Mem., Council of Europe, 1970–73.

Freeman, Borough of Jarrow, 1972. *Address:* 35 Edwards Road, Lache Park, Chester CH4 8HW.

Died 16 Aug. 1993.

FERRER, José Vicente; actor, director and producer, USA; *b* 8 Jan. 1912; *s* of Rafael Ferrer and Maria Providencia (*née* Cintrón); *m* 1st, 1938, Uta Hagen (marr. diss. 1948); one *d*; 2nd, 1948, Phyllis Hill (marr. diss. 1953); 3rd, 1953, Rosemary Clooney (marr. diss. 1967); three *s* two *d*; 4th, Stella Daphne Magee. *Educ:* Princeton Univ. AB (architecture), 1933. First appearance, The Periwinkle, Long Island show-boat, 1934; Asst Stage Manager Summer Theatre Stock Co., NY, 1935; first appearance NY stage, 1935; A Slight Case of Murder, 1935; Boy Meets Girl, 1935; Spring Dance, Brother Rat, 1936; In Clover, 1937; Dir Princeton Univ. Triangle Club's Fol-de-Rol, 1937; How To Get Tough About It, Missouri Legend, 1938; Mamba's Daughters, Key Largo, 1939; first star rôle, Lord Fancourt Babberley, Charley's Aunt, 1940; producer and dir, The Admiral Had A Wife, 1941; staged and co-starred, Vickie, 1942; Let's Face It, 1943; played Iago to Paul Robeson's Othello, Theatre Guild, 1943, 1944, 1945; producer and dir Strange Fruit, 1945; Play's The Thing, Richard III, Green Goddess, 1946; producer and star, Cyrano, 1946; Design For Living, Goodbye Again, 1947; Gen. dir to NY Theatre Co., City Centre, 1948; Silver Whistle, Theatre Guild, 1948; produced, directed and appeared in Twentieth Century, 1950; produced, directed, Stalag 17; The Fourposter, 1951; producer, dir and appeared in The Shrike, 1952; The Chase, 1952; staged My 3 Angels, 1953; dir and co-author, Oh Captain, 1958; producer, dir, and starred in, Edwin Booth, 1959; dir, The Andersonville Trial, 1960; starred in, The Girl Who Came to Supper, 1963–64; Man of La Mancha, 1966; dir, Cyrano de Bergerac, Chichester, 1975; British stage début as Messerschmann, Ring Round the Moon, Chichester, 1988; Born Again, Chichester, 1990; *films include:* Joan of Arc, 1947; Whirlpool, 1949; Crisis, Cyrano, 1950; Anything Can Happen, 1951; Moulin Rouge, 1952; Miss Sadie Thompson (Rain), Caine Mutiny, 1953; Deep in My Heart, 1955; Cockleshell Heroes, The Great Man, 1957; The High Cost of Loving, I Accuse, The Shrike (Dir, starred), 1958; Return to Peyton Place (Dir), 1962; State Fair (Dir), 1963; Nine Hours to Rama, Lawrence of Arabia, 1963; Cyrano et D'Artagnan, Train 349 From Berlin, The Greatest Story Ever Told, 1964; Ship of Fools, Enter Laughing, 1966; The Fifth Musketeer, 1976; Fedora, 1977; The Amazing Captain Nemo, 1979; The Big Brawl, 1980; A Midsummer Night's Sex Comedy, 1981; To Be Or Not To Be, Dune, 1983. Pres., Players Club, NY, 1983–. Mem., Acad. of Arts and Scis of Puerto Rico, 1974. Hon. degrees. Various awards for acting, etc, 1944–, include: American Academy of Arts and Letters Gold Medal, 1949; Academy Award, 1950 (Best Actor, Cyrano); Theatre Hall of Fame, 1981; Ambassador of the Arts, State of Florida, 1983; Hispanic Heritage Festival Don Quixote Award, Florida, 1984; National Medal of Arts, 1985; Florida Prize, New York Times, 1990. *Recreations:* tennis, golf. *Address:* PO Box 616, Miami, Florida 33133, USA. *Died 26 Jan. 1992.*

FERRIE, Maj.-Gen. Alexander Martin, CBE 1971; Royal Army Medical Corps, retired; *b* 30 Nov. 1923; *s* of late Archibald Ferrie and Elizabeth Ferrie (*née* Martin). *Educ:* Glasgow Academy; Univ. of Glasgow (MB ChB). MFCM 1974. Commissioned RAMC, 1947; Commanding Officer, Queen Alexandra Military Hospital, Millbank, 1973–75; Director of Medical Supply, Min. of Defence, 1975–77; Dep. Dir of Medical Services, UKLF, and Inspector of Trng, TA Medical Services, 1977–81; QHS 1978–83; DMS, UKLF, 1981–82; Comdt, RAMC Trng Gp, and PMO, UKLF, 1982–83. *Recreation:* gardening. *Address:* c/o Barclays Bank, 47 Church Road, Hove, E Sussex BN3 2BQ. *Died 29 June 1995.*

FERRIER, Baron *cr* 1958 (Life Peer), of Culter; **Victor Ferrier Noel-Paton,** ED; DL; *b* Edinburgh, 1900; *s* of late Frederick Waller Ferrier Noel-Paton, Dir-Gen. of Commercial Intelligence to the Govt of India; *m* 1932, Joane Mary (*d* 1984), *d* of late Sir Gilbert Wiles, KCIE, CSI; one *s* three *d. Educ:* Cargilfield and The Edinburgh Academy. Served: RE, 1918–19; Indian Auxiliary Force (Major, ED), 1920–46; and IARO. Commercial and industrial management, Bombay, 1920–51; one time dir and chm. of a number of cos in India and UK; Pres., Bombay Chamber of Commerce. Mem., Legislative Council, Bombay, 1936 and Hon. ADC to Governor of Bombay; Past Chairman: Federation of Electricity Undertakings of India; Indian Roads and Transport Develt Assoc., Bombay. A Dep. Speaker and Chm. of Cttees, House of Lords, 1970–73. Mem. of Queen's Body Guard for Scotland, Royal Company of Archers. DL Lanarks, 1960. *Recreations:* field sports. *Address:* Kilkerran, Maybole, Ayrshire KA19 7SJ. *T:* Crosshill (06554) 515. *Clubs:* Cavalry and Guards, Beefsteak; New (Edinburgh). *Died 4 June 1992.*

FERRY, Alexander, MBE 1977; General Secretary, Confederation of Shipbuilding and Engineering Unions, 1978–93; Member of Board, Harland and Wolff plc, Shipbuilders and Engineers, Belfast, since 1984; *b* 14 Feb. 1931; *s* of Alexander and Susan Ferry; *m* 1958, Mary O'Kane McAlaney; one *s* two *d* (and one *s* decd). *Educ:* St Patrick's High, Senior Secondary, Dunbartonshire. Apprentice engineer, 1947–52; served Royal Air Force, 1952–54; engineer, 1954–64; full-time officer, AUEW, 1964–78. Part-time Mem., Monopolies and Mergers Commn, 1986–; Mem., Employment Appeal Tribunal, 1991–. *Publication:* The Red Paper on Scotland (co-author), 1975. *Recreation:* golf. *Address:* 190 Brampton Road, Bexley Heath, Kent DA2 4SY. *T:* 081–303 5338. *Died 18 July 1994.*

FFRANGCON-DAVIES, Dame Gwen, DBE 1991; actress; *b* 25 Jan. 1891; *d* of David Ffrangcon-Davies, the famous singer, and Annie Frances Rayner. *Educ:* South Hampstead High Sch.; abroad. First London success The Immortal Hour, 1922; created the part of Eve in Shaw's Back to Methuselah; principal successes as Tess, in Tess of the D'Urbervilles, Elizabeth Barrett, in The Barretts of Wimpole Street, Anne of Bohemia, in Richard of Bordeaux, Juliet, in Romeo and Juliet; played Lady Macbeth to Macbeth of John Gielgud, Piccadilly, 1942; appeared, in association with Marda Vanne, in leading parts in various plays in S Africa, 1943–46; returned to England, 1949; played in Adventure Story, St James's, 1949; Stratford Festival, 1950, as Katharine in King Henry VIII; Portia in Julius Cæsar, Regan in King Lear (again Katharine, Old Vic, 1953); Madame Ranevsky in The Cherry Orchard, Lyric, 1954; Aunt Cleofe in Summertime, Apollo, 1955; Rose Padley in The Mulberry Bush, Royal Court, 1956; Agatha in The Family Reunion, Phoenix, 1956; Miss Madrigal in The Chalk Garden, Haymarket, 1957; Mrs Callifer in The Potting Shed, Globe Theatre, 1958; Mary Tyrone in Long Day's Journey into Night, Edinburgh Fest. and Globe, 1958; Queen Isolde in Ondine, Aldwych, 1961; Queen Mother in Becket, Aldwych, 1961; Hester Bellboys in A Penny for a Song, Aldwych, 1962; Mrs Candour in School for Scandal, Majestic, NY, 1963; Beatrice in Season of Goodwill, Queen's, 1964; Amanda in The Glass Menagerie, Haymarket, 1965; Uncle Vanya, Royal Court, 1970. *Films:* The Burning, 1967; Leo the Last, 1969. Numerous radio and TV plays; Omnibus profile: A Juliet Remembered, BBC TV, 1988. *Recreation:* gardening. *Address:* c/o Larry Dalzell, Suite 12, 17 Broad Court, WC2B 5QN. *Died 27 Jan. 1992.*

FFRENCH-BEYTAGH, Rev. Canon Gonville Aubie; Rector of St Vedast-alias-Foster, London, 1974–86;

retired; Hon. Canon of Johannesburg, since 1972 and of Canterbury, since 1973; *b* 26 Jan. 1912; *s* of Leo Michael and Edith ffrench-Beytagh; unmarried. *Educ:* Monkton Combe Sch., Bath; Bristol Grammar Sch.; St Paul's Theol Coll., Grahamstown (LTh). Deacon, 1938; priest, 1939. Tramp and casual labourer, New Zealand, 1929–33; clerk in Johannesburg, 1933–36; Parish Priest and Diocesan Missioner, Johannesburg Dio., 1939–54; Dean of Salisbury, Rhodesia, 1955–65; Dean of Johannesburg, 1965–72; detained, tried, convicted and sentenced to 5 yrs imprisonment under SA Terrorism Act, 1971–72; conviction and sentence quashed by Appellate Div. and returned to England, 1972. *Publications:* Encountering Darkness, 1973; Encountering Light, 1975; Facing Depression, 1978; A Glimpse of Glory, 1986; Tree of Glory, 1988; Out of the Depths: encountering depression, 1990. *Recreations:* drink, companionship, science fiction. *Address:* 56 Tredegar Square, E3 5AE. *T:* 081–980 4051. *Died 11 May 1991.*

FIELD, John, CBE 1967; ARAD; Artistic Director, British Ballet Organisation, since 1984; *b* 22 Oct. 1921; *s* of late William Greenfield; stage-name, John Field; *m* 1958, Anne Heaton. *Educ:* Wheatley Boys' Sch., Doncaster. Sadler's Wells Ballet Co., 1939; RAF, 1942–46; Principal, Sadler's Wells Ballet Co., 1947–56; Resident Dir, Sadler's Wells Theatre Ballet, 1956–57; Asst Dir, 1957–70, Co-Dir, July-Dec. 1970, Royal Ballet Co.; Dir of Ballet, La Scala, Milan, 1971–74; Artistic Dir, 1975–76, Dir, 1976–79, Royal Acad. of Dancing; Artistic Dir, 1979–81, Director, 1982–84, London Festival Ballet. *Address:* c/o Yorkshire Bank, 56 Cheapside, EC2P 2BA. *Died 3 Aug. 1991.*

FIELDHOUSE, Baron *cr* 1990 (Life Peer), of Gosport in the County of Hampshire; **Admiral of the Fleet John David Elliott Fieldhouse,** GCB 1982 (KCB 1980); GBE 1982; Chief of the Defence Staff, 1985–88; retired 1989; *b* 12 Feb. 1928; *s* of Sir Harold Fieldhouse, KBE, CB and Mabel Elaine Elliott; *m* 1953, Margaret Ellen Cull; one *s* two *d. Educ:* RNC Dartmouth. MINucE. Midshipman, E Indies Fleet, 1945–46; entered Submarine Service, 1948; comd HMS Acheron, 1955; CO HMS Dreadnought, 1964–66; Exec. Officer, HMS Hermes, 1967; Captain SM10 (Polaris Sqdn), 1968–70; Captain HMS Diomede, 1971; Comdr, Standing Naval Force Atlantic, 1972–73; Dir, Naval Warfare, 1973–74; Flag Officer, Second Flotilla, 1974–76; Flag Officer, Submarines, and Comdr Submarine Force, E Atlantic Area, 1976–78; Controller of the Navy, 1979–81; C-in-C Fleet, and Allied C-in-C, Channel and Eastern Atlantic, 1981–82; Chief of Naval Staff and First Sea Lord, 1982–85. First and Principal Naval ADC to the Queen, 1982–85. Consultant, Vosper Thornycroft (UK) Ltd, 1990–; non-exec. Dir, DESC Ltd, 1991–. Chm., White Ensign Assoc., 1990–. Liveryman: Shipwrights' Co., 1982–; Glovers' Co., 1983–; Freeman, Clockmakers' Co., 1984. Hon. DSc (Eng) London, 1989. *Recreations:* home, family, friends. *Clubs:* Army and Navy; Royal Yacht Squadron.

Died 17 Feb. 1992.

FIELDHOUSE, Sir Harold, KBE 1949 (OBE 1934); CB 1947; Secretary, National Assistance Board, 1946–59, retired; Member of Letchworth Garden City, Welwyn Garden City and Hatfield Corporations, retired; *b* Leeds, Yorks, 18 Aug. 1892; *e s* of Frank and Mary Ellen Fieldhouse; *m* 1922, Mabel Elaine Elliott, Conisborough, Yorks; two *s. Educ:* Armley Higher Grade Sch., Leeds. Asst Clerk, Leeds Board of Guardians, 1909–30; Public Assistance Officer, City of Leeds, 1930–34; Regional Officer, Asst Sec. and Under-Sec., Assistance Board, 1934–46. Liveryman, Clockmakers' Co., 1959. *Recreations:* golf, bridge, music, reading. *Address:* Holcombe, Woodchester Park, Knotty Green,

Beaconsfield, Bucks HP9 2TN. *T:* Beaconsfield (0494) 677194. *Clubs:* City Livery; Grim's Dyke Golf, West Hill Golf. *Died 20 March 1991.*

FIENNES, Sir Maurice (Alberic Twisleton-Wykeham-), Kt 1965; CEng; FIMechE; engineering and industrial consultant; Chairman and Managing Director of Davy-Ashmore Ltd, 1961–69; Associate Consultant, L. H. Manderstam & Partners Ltd, 1977–80; retired; *b* 1 March 1907; *s* of Alberic Arthur Twisleton-Wykeham-Fiennes and Gertrude Theodosia Colley; *m* 1st, 1932, Sylvia Mabel Joan (marr. diss. 1964), *d* of late Major David Finlay, 7th Dragoon Guards. two *s* three *d*; 2nd, 1967, Erika Hueller von Huellenried, *d* of late Dr Herbert Hueller, Vienna. *Educ:* Repton; Armstrong Coll., Newcastle upon Tyne. Apprenticeship with Ransomes and Rapier Ltd, Ipswich; joined Sir W. G. Armstrong, Whitworth & Co Ltd (Engineers), Newcastle-upon-Tyne, 1930; with The United Steel Companies Ltd, 1937, first as Commercial Asst to Managing Dir, then in charge Gun Forgings and Gun Dept at Steel Peech & Tozer; Gen. Works Dir, Brush Electrical Engineering Co. Ltd, 1942; Managing Dir, Davy and United Engineering Co. Ltd, 1945; Managing Dir, Davy-Ashmore Ltd, 1960. Steel Industry Advr for UN Industrial Develt Orgn to Govt of Peru, 1974–75; Engineering Advisor for World Bank to Venezuelan Investment Fund, 1976–77. Mem. Economic Develt Cttee for Mech. Engrg, 1964–67; Pres. of Iron and Steel Institute, 1962–63; Chairman: Athlone Fellowships Cttee, 1966–71; Overseas Scholarships Bd, CBI, 1970–76; Mem., Reserve Pension Bd, 1974–75. Governor, Yehudi Menuhin School, 1969–84. *Recreations:* music, grandchildren. *Address:* 11 Heath Rise, Kersfield Road, Putney Hill, SW15 3HF. *T:* 081-785 7489. *Died 14 Sept. 1994.*

FIFOOT, (Erik) Richard (Sidney), MC 1945; MA; ALA; Bodley's Librarian, and Professorial Fellow of Exeter College, Oxford, 1979–81; *b* 14 June 1925; *s* of Cecil Herbert Stuart Fifoot and Hjördis (*née* Eriksen); *m* 1949, Jean, *o d* of Lt-Col J. S. Thain; two *d. Educ:* Berkhamsted Sch.; Oxford Univ. (MA); London Univ. (DipLib). HM Coldstream Guards, 1943–46. Leeds University Library: Asst Librarian, 1950–52; Sub-Librarian, 1952–58; Dep. Librarian, Nottingham Univ., 1958–60; Librarian, Univ. of Edinburgh, 1960–79. Chm., Standing Conf. of Nat. and Univ. Libraries, 1979–81; Mem., Exec. Bd, Internat. Fedn of Library Assocs and Instns, 1979–83. Founder and Dir, Three Rivers Books Ltd, 1981–90. *Publications:* A Bibliography of Edith, Osbert and Sacheverell Sitwell, 1963, 2nd edn 1971; articles and reviews in library, architectural and educnl jls, symposia, and encycs. *Address:* Castle View, Bridge Street, Bampton, Oxon OX8 2HA. *Died 24 June 1992.*

FINER, Prof. Samuel Edward, FBA 1982; Gladstone Professor of Government and Public Administration, University of Oxford, 1974–82, then Professor Emeritus; Fellow, All Souls College, Oxford, 1974–82, then Emeritus; *b* 22 Sept. 1915; *y s* of Max and Fanny Finer, 210a Green Lanes, N4; *m* 1st, 1949, Margaret Ann (marr. diss. 1975), 2nd *d* of Sir Andrew McFadyean; two *s* one *d*; 2nd, 1977, Dr Catherine J. Jones, 2nd *d* of T. P. Jones, Prestatyn. *Educ:* Holloway Sch., London; Trinity Coll., Oxford. BA (Oxon) 1st Class Hons Mod. Greats, 1937; 1st Cl. Hons Mod. Hist., 1938; MA (Oxon) 1946; DLitt 1979; Sen. George Webb-Medley Schol., 1938–40. Served War, 1940–46; Capt. Royal Signals, 1945. Lecturer in Politics, Balliol Coll., Oxford, 1946–49, Junior Research Fellow, 1949–50; Prof. of Political Institutions, University of Keele, 1950–66 (Dep. Vice-Chancellor, 1962–64); Prof. of Government, Univ. of Manchester, 1966–74. Visiting Prof. and Faculty Mem., Institute of Social Studies, The Hague, Netherlands, 1957–59; Visiting Professor in Government: Cornell Univ., 1962; Hebrew Univ.,

Jerusalem, 1969; Simon Fraser Univ., BC, 1976; Europ. Univ. Inst., Florence, 1977; Stanford Univ., 1979; Hong Kong Univ., 1980; Vis. Schweitzer Prof., Columbia Univ., 1982. Chm. Political Studies Assoc. of UK, 1965–69. FRHistS. DU Essex, 1982. *Publications:* A Primer of Public Administration, 1950; The Life and Times of Sir Edwin Chadwick, 1952; (with Sir John Maud) Local Government in England and Wales, 1953; Anonymous Empire—a Study of the Lobby in Britain, 1958, 2nd edn 1966; Private Industry and Political Power, 1958; (with D. J. Bartholomew and H. B. Berrington) Backbench Opinion in the House of Commons, 1955–59, 1961; The Man on Horseback: The Rôle of The Military in Politics, 1962, 2nd edn 1976; Great Britain, in Modern Political Systems: Europe, ed Macridis and Ward, 1963, 1968, 1972, 1980; (ed) Siéyès: What is the Third Estate, 1963; Pareto: Sociological Writings, 1966; Comparative Government, 1970; Adversary Government and Electoral Reform, 1975; Five Constitutions, 1979; Britain's Changing Party System, 1980. *Recreation:* oil-painting. *Address:* All Souls College, Oxford OX1 4AL; 48 Lonsdale Road, Oxford. *T:* Oxford (0865) 58060. *Died 9 June 1993.*

FINLAY, Maj.-Gen. Charles Hector, CB 1966; CBE 1958 (OBE 1942); retired; Trustee, Returned Services League of Australia, since 1985 (Hon. National Treasurer, 1969–84); *b* 6 Oct. 1910; 3rd *s* of Frank J. Finlay and Margaret A. Stephenson; *m* 1935, Helen M., *d* of Arthur P. and Edith M. Adams; two *s. Educ:* Sydney; RMC Duntroon, Australia. Graduated RMC, 1931; Light Horse and Cavalry service, 1931–39; ADC to Gov.-Gen., 1932–35; with 14th/20th Hussars, India, 1935–36; served War of 1939–45: Western Desert, Syria, New Guinea, Philippines, Borneo; Comd 2/24 Inf. Bn, 1942–43; Exchange duty, Canada, 1946–49; DMI, 1950–53; Comd Aust. Component, British Commonwealth Forces in Korea, 1953–54; attended Imperial Def. Coll., 1955; Aust. Army Rep., London, 1956–57; Quartermaster Gen. AMF, 1957–62; Commandant Royal Military Coll., Duntroon, Australia, 1962–67. Hon. Col, Australian Intelligence Corps, 1973–77. *Recreation:* cricket. *Address:* 29 The Grange, Deakin, ACT 2600, Australia. *Club:* Commonwealth (Canberra). *Died 22 Nov. 1993.*

FINLAY, (William) Ian (Robertson), CBE 1965; MA; HRSA; Director of the Royal Scottish Museum, 1961–71 (Keeper of the Department of Art and Ethnography, 1955–61); Professor of Antiquities to the Royal Scottish Academy, since 1971; *b* Auckland, New Zealand, 2 Dec. 1906; *s* of William R. Finlay and Annie M. Somerville; *m* 1933, Mary Scott, *d* of late W. Henderson Pringle, barrister-at-law; two *s* one *d. Educ:* Edinburgh Academy; Edinburgh Univ. Joined staff of Royal Scottish Museum, 1932; Deputy Regional Officer for Scotland, Ministry of Information, 1942–44; Vice-Chairman, Scottish Arts Council, 1967; Secretary, Royal Fine Art Commission for Scotland, 1953–61. Guest of State Department in US, 1960. Freeman of City of London; Member of Livery, Worshipful Company of Goldsmiths, London; Mem., Edinburgh Festival Council, 1968–71. FRSA 1971. *Publications:* Scotland, World To-Day Series, 1945; Scottish Art (for British Council), 1945; Art in Scotland, 1948; Scottish Crafts, 1948; The Scottish Tradition in Silver (Saltire booklet), 1948; Scottish Architecture (for schools), 1951; Treasures in Edinburgh, 1951; Scotland, Young Traveller Series, 1953; A History of Scottish Gold and Silver Work, 1956, 2nd edn 1991; Scotland, 1957; The Lothians, 1960; The Highlands, 1963; The Young Robert Louis Stevenson, 1965; The Lowlands, 1967; Celtic Art: an introduction, 1973; The Central Highlands, 1976; Priceless Heritage: the future of museums, 1977; Columba, 1979, new edn 1990; articles, reviews and broadcast talks on art and general subjects. *Address:*

Currie Riggs, Balerno, Midlothian EH14 5AG. *T:*
0131–449 4249.   *Died 10 Dec. 1995.*

FINLEY, Sir Peter (Hamilton), Kt 1981; OBE 1974; DFC
1944; FCA; *b* 6 Dec. 1919; *s* of Cecil Aubert Finley and
Evelyn Finley (*née* Daniels); *m* 1947, Berenice Mitchell
Finley (*née* Armstrong); one *s* one *d. Educ:* The King's
Sch., Parramatta. Served RAAF with RAF Bomber
Command and RAAF SW Pacific Area, 1941–45. With
W. V. Armstrong & Co., Chartered Accountants, 1946–48,
Peat, Marwick, Mitchell & Co. (formerly Smith Johnson
& Co.), 1949–55, P. H. Finley & Co., 1955–72, when
virtually ceased practice. Chairman: Hygienic Lily Ltd,
1970–86; Avery Aust. Ltd, 1972–92; Email Ltd, 1974–93
(Dir, 1966); T. R. Services Pty Ltd, 1975–91; Boral Ltd,
1976–91 (Dir, 1968); Vice Chm., Nat. Australia Bank Ltd,
1986–92 (Dir, 1970); Deputy Chairman: Cadbury
Schweppes Aust. Ltd, 1971–89; AWA Ltd, 1978–86 (Dir,
1974); Dir, Burns Philp & Co. Ltd, 1980–93. Dir, Sir
Robert Menzies Meml Trust, 1978–91. *Recreations:*
cricket, reading, bridge. *Address:* 2F Greenoaks Avenue,
Darling Point, NSW 2027, Australia. *T:* 3286819. *Clubs:*
Australian (Sydney); Melbourne (Melbourne).
                                        Died 27 April 1994.

FINNISTON, Sir (Harold) Montague, (Sir Monty), Kt
1975; BSc, PhD; FRS 1969; FRSE 1978; FEng 1983;
business industrial consultant since 1980; Chairman: H.
M. Finniston Ltd, since 1980; Finance for Housing Ltd
(formerly Building Trust Management Co.), since 1981;
KCA Drilling Group PLC, since 1983; Industrial
Technology Securities Ltd, since 1984; Sherwood BC,
since 1986; Mulholland Ltd, since 1987; Nene Instruments,
since 1987; ABACUS Simulations Ltd, since 1988;
Tricuspid Systems Ltd, since 1989; Director: Cluff
Resources PLC, since 1976; Caledonian Heritable Estates
Ltd, since 1982; British Nutrition Foundation, since 1982;
Combined Capital Ltd, since 1983; Information
Technology Training Accreditation Council, since 1985;
Harold Hartley Engineering Centre Ltd, since 1985; *b* 15
Aug. 1912; *s* of late Robert and Esther Finniston; *m* 1936,
Miriam Singer; one *s* one *d. Educ:* Allan Glen's Sch.,
Glasgow; Glasgow Univ.; Royal College of Science and
Technology, Glasgow. Lecturer in Metallurgy, Royal
College of Science and Technology, 1933–35;
Metallurgist, Stewart & Lloyds, 1935–37; Chief Research
Officer, Scottish Coke Research Cttee, 1937–40;
Metallurgist, RN Scientific Service, 1940–46; seconded to
Ministry of Supply, Chalk River, Canada, 1946–47; Chief
Metallurgist, UKAEA, Harwell, 1948–58; Man. Director,
International Research and Development Co. (Chm.
1968–77), and Technical Director, C. A. Parsons & Co.
Ltd, 1959–67; Director, C. A. Parsons & Co. Ltd; Mem.
Board of Thorn-Parsons Co. Ltd and Northern Economic
Planning Council, 1963–67; Dep. Chm. (Technical), BSC,
1967–71; Dep. Chm. and Chief Executive, 1971–73,
Chm., 1973–76, BSC; Dir, Sears Hldgs Ltd, and Chm.,
Sears Engrg Ltd, 1976–79; Director: GKN PLC, 1976–83;
Bodycote Internat. PLC, 1980–84; Chairman: Anderson
Strathclyde PLC, 1980–83; Drake & Scull Holdings,
1980–83; Butterfield-Harvey, 1981–84; Future
Technology Systems, 1981–85; Metal Sciences (Holdings)
PLC, 1983–85; Taddale Investments PLC, 1983–87; Clyde
Cablevision, 1983–87; Engrg Council Award Co.,
1984–89. Member: Council British Non-Ferrous Metals
Research Assoc., 1965–72 (Vice-Chm. 1969–72; Chm.
Research Board, 1965–70); NRDC, 1963–73; NEDC,
1973–76; Advisory Council, R&D (Fuel and Power), Dept
of Trade and Industry (formerly Ministry of Power),
1965–74; SRC University Science and Technology Board,
1965–67; NPL Steering Cttee, 1966–68; Iron and Steel
Adv. Cttee, 1969–73; Academic Adv. Cttee, Cranfield
Inst. of Technology, 1970–75; BBC Science Consultative
Group, 1971–74; Royal Instn of GB, 1978; Chairman:

Policy Studies Inst. (formerly PEP), 1975–84 (Exec. Cttee
1968–74); Council, Scottish Business Sch., 1976–87; Govt
Cttee of Inquiry into engineering profession, 1977–79;
Building EDC, 1980–87; Prison Reform Trust, 1981–88;
Urban Trust, 1987–; Fellow, Smallpeice Trust, 1985;
President: Ironbridge Gorge Mus. Develt Trust, 1977–81;
Inst. of Metals, 1967–68; Metals Soc., 1974–75 (Hon.
Mem., 1980); Inst. Metallurgists, 1975–76; ASLIB,
1976–78 (Vice-Pres., 1974–76); Inst. of Management
Services, 1977–82; Design and Industries Assoc., 1978–84
(Pres. of Honour, 1984); Indust. Marketing Res. Assoc.,
1982–; Indust. Bldg Bureau, 1983–; Occupnl Pensions
Adv. Service, 1983–; ABCC, 1980–83; BISFA, 1980–87;
IMGTechE, 1984–88; British Exporters Assoc., 1984–89;
Assoc. of Project Managers, 1984–; EIA, 1984–; Surrey
Retirement Assoc., 1985–; Soc. of Environmental Engrs,
1986–; Welding Inst., 1989–; Vice President: Iron and
Steel Inst., 1968–73; Inst. of Marketing, 1979–89; Gen.
Sec., BAAS, 1970–73 (Life Mem.); Mem., Soc. of Chem.
Industry, 1974. A Vice-Pres., Royal Soc., 1971–72.
Freeman, City of London, 1972; Mem., Court of Assts,
Worshipful Co. of Tinplate Workers, 1974–; Liveryman,
Worshipful Co. of Engineers, 1986. Gov., Carmel Coll.,
1973– (Chm., 1980–82). Vis. Fellow, Univ. of Lancaster,
1970–; Pro-Chancellor, Surrey Univ., 1978–85;
Chancellor, Stirling Univ., 1978–88; Mem. Council,
King's Coll. London, 1985–90 (FKC 1988). ARTC; FIM;
FInstP; FIChemE; FBIM; life FRSA 1975; MRI 1978.
Hon. Member: American Iron and Steel Inst., 1974; Japan
Iron and Steel Inst., 1975 (Tawara Gold Medal, 1975);
Indian Inst. of Metals, 1976; Smeatonian Soc. of Civil
Engrs, 1977. Hon. Fellow: UMIST, 1973; Sunderland
Polytech., 1975; Imp. Coll. of Science and Technology,
1979; St Cross Coll., Oxford, 1981. Hon. FSIAD 1984
Hon. FIED 1985. Hon. DSc: Strathclyde, 1968; Aston,
1971; City, 1974; Cranfield, 1976; Bath, 1977; Sussex,
1981; Open, 1982; DUniv: Surrey, 1969; Stirling, 1979;
Hon. DCL Newcastle, 1976; Hon. DEng Liverpool, 1978;
Hon. LLD: Glasgow, 1978; Hull, 1980; Hon. DMet
Sheffield, 1979; Hon. DSc(Eng) QUB, 1985. Hon. CGIA
1987. Bessemer Medal, Metals Soc., 1974; Silver Medal,
Inst. Sheet Metal Engrg, 1975; Eichner Medal, Soc.
Française de Metallurgie, 1976; A. A. Griffiths Silver
Medal, Material Sci. Club, 1976; Glazebrook Medal, Inst.
of Physics, 1976; Leonardo da Vinci Medal, 1986.
Publications: various scientific and engineering papers.
Recreations: reading, writing, spectator interest in sport.
Address: (office) 6 Manchester Square, W1A 1AU. *T:*
071–486 3658; Flat 72, Prince Albert Court, 33 Prince
Albert Road, NW8. *T:* 071–722 8197. *Club:* Athenæum.
                                        Died 2 Feb. 1991.

FIRTH, Maj.-Gen. Charles Edward Anson, CB 1951;
CBE 1945; DSO 1943; *b* 9 Oct. 1902; *s* of late Major E.
W. A. Firth, Indian Army; *m* 1933, Mary Kathleen (*d*
1977), *d* of late Commander W. St J. Fraser, RN; two *s.*
Educ: Wellington Coll., Berks; RMC Sandhurst. 2nd Lieut
The Gloucestershire Regt, 1923; Lieut, 1925; Captain,
1935; Staff Coll., 1936–37; War Office, 1938–40; Major,
1940; Middle East: Temp. Lieut-Colonel; AA&QMG 50
Div., 1941–42; OC 1st Royal Sussex Regt in Middle East,
1942–43; Temp. Brigadier, 7th Indian Infantry Bde, 1943;
Comd 167 Infantry Bde, 1943–44 (Italy); Comd 21 Tank
Bde, 1944 (N Africa); Comd 2 Infantry Bde, 1944 (Italy);
Comdr and Dep. Comdr British Military Mission to
Greece, 1944–45; mentioned in despatches three times,
1941–45; Colonel 1946; War Office, 1946–48; Comd
Area Troops, Berlin (British Sector), 1948–50; Maj.-
General, 1950; Comd East Anglian Dist, 1950; GOC
Salisbury Plain Dist, 1951–53; Director of Personal
Services, War Office, 1953–56. Colonel The
Gloucestershire Regt, 1954–64; first Colonel Comdt,
Military Provost Staff Corps, 1956–61. Chairman: Inter-

Services VC Centenary Cttee, 1954–55; Inter-Services Cttee on Resistance to Interrogation, 1955–56. Governor, Dauntsey's Sch., 1961–77 (Vice-Chairman, 1965–77). Grand Commander Order of the Phoenix (Greek), 1946. *Recreations:* gardening, writing, fishing. *Address:* Garden Cottage, Church Street, Great Bedwyn, Marlborough, Wilts SN8 3PF. *T:* Marlborough (0672) 870270. *Club:* Army and Navy. *Died 13 Oct. 1991.*

FIRTH, Edward Michael Tyndall, CB 1951; *b* 17 Feb. 1903; *s* of Edward H. Firth, Sheffield; *m* 1929, Eileen Marie (*d* 1982), *d* of Edward Newman, Hove; two *s*. *Educ:* King Edward VII Sch., Sheffield; University College, Oxford. Classical Scholar, 1922–26. Inland Revenue, 1926; Ministry of Health, 1945; Under Secretary, 1947–58; Registrar General, 1958–63. *Died 7 Oct. 1991.*

FISCHER, Annie; Hungarian pianist; *b* Budapest, 5 July 1914; *m* Aladár Toth (decd). *Educ:* Franz Liszt Landemusikhochschule, Budapest. Studied under Arnold Székely and Ernst von Dohnanyi. Concert début, Budapest, at age of eight (performed Beethoven's C Major Concerto), 1922; began international career as a concert pianist, Zurich, 1926; toured and played in most European Music centres, 1926–39; concert pianist, Sweden, during War of 1939–45; returned to Hungary after War and made concert tours to all parts of the world. Hon. Prof., Acad. of Music, Budapest, 1965. Awarded 1st prize, Internat. Liszt Competition, Budapest, 1933; Kossuth Prizes 1949, 1955, 1965. Eminent Artist; Red Banner, Order of Labour, 1974. *Address:* c/o Terry Harrison Artists Management, The Orchard, Market Street, Charlbury, Oxon OX7 3PJ. *Died 10 April 1995.*

FISH, Anthony, CBE 1991; PhD; Director, Shell Research Ltd, 1989–90; *b* 18 Feb. 1937; *s* of Leonard and Enid Irene Towrass Fish; *m* 1959, Yvonne Angela Stock. *Educ:* Chesterfield Sch.; Queens' Coll., Cambridge (MA); Imperial College of Science and Technology (PhD). Asst Lectr, Imperial Coll., 1960–63; Lectr, Hatfield Coll., 1963–64; Shell companies in UK, 1964; secondment to Central Policy Rev. Staff, Cabinet Office, 1970–71; Dir, Shell Toxicology Laboratory, 1978–80; Shell Internat. Petroleum Co. Ltd, 1980–85; Man. Dir, Sittingbourne Res. Centre, Shell Res., 1985–89. Corday-Morgan Medallist, RSC, 1964. *Publications:* papers in Proc. Royal Soc., Proc. Royal Institution, Trans Faraday Soc., Jl Chem. Soc., Internat. Symposia on Combustion, Qly Revs Chem. Soc., Jl Catalysis, Angewandte Chemie. *Recreations:* horse racing, ornithology, painting, opera. *Address:* c/o Shell Research Ltd, Shell Centre, SE1 7NA. *T:* 071–934 4954. *Club:* Newbury Race. *Died 21 July 1991.*

FISHER, Anne; see Fisher, P. A.

FISHER, Fredy; see Fisher, M. H.

FISHER, Margery Lilian Edith; free-lance writer; *b* 21 March 1913; *d* of late Sir Henry Samuel Edwin Turner and Edith Rose; *m* 1936, James Maxwell McConnell Fisher (*d* 1970); two *s* three *d* (and one *s* decd). *Educ:* Rangi Ruru Sch., Christchurch, NZ; Amberley House Sch., NZ; Somerville Coll., Oxford (1st Cl. Hons English; MA, BLitt). Taught English at Queen Anne's Sch., Caversham, and Oundle Sch., 1939–45; coach for university scholarships and entrance exams; some broadcasting (BBC) of book reviews, free-lance lectr; Editor and proprietor of Growing Point (private jl reviewing children's books), 1962–92. Eleanor Farjeon Award, 1966; May Arbuthnot Award, USA, 1970. *Publications:* (with James Fisher) Shackleton, a biography, 1957; Intent upon Reading (criticism), 1961, rev. edn 1964; Field Day (novel), 1951; Matters of Fact, 1972; Who's Who in Children's Books, 1975; The Bright Face of Danger (criticism), 1986; monographs on: Classics; Henry Treece; John Masefield. *Recreations:* music,

gardening. *Address:* Ashton Manor, Northampton NN7 2JL. *T:* Roade (0604) 862277.
Died 24 Dec. 1992.

FISHER, Max Henry, (Fredy); Director, S. G. Warburg & Co. Ltd, since 1981; *b* 30 May 1922; *s* of Fritz and Sophia Fischer; *m* 1952, Rosemary Margaret Maxwell; two *s* one *d*. *Educ:* Fichte-Gymnasium, Berlin; Rendcomb Coll.; Lincoln Coll., Oxford. FO Library, working on German War Documents project, 1949–56; Vis. Lectr, Melbourne Univ., 1956; Financial Times, 1957–80, Editor, 1973–80. Director: Commercial Union Assurance Co., 1981–91; Booker (formerly Booker McConnell), 1981–92. Governor, LSE, 1981–91. *Publication:* (ed with N. R. Rich) The Holstein Papers. *Recreations:* reading, listening to music. *Address:* 16 Somerset Square, Addison Road, W14 8EE. *T:* 071–603 9841. *Club:* Royal Automobile.
Died 29 Aug. 1993.

FISHER, Marian, (Mrs Orpheus H. Fisher); see Anderson, Marian.

FISHER, Patricia, (Lady Fisher); Founder and Chairman, Women Caring Trust, 1972–91 (President, 1991); *b* 5 April 1921; *d* of late Lieut-Col Sir Walter Smiles, CIE, DSO, DL, MP for N Down; *m* 1st, 1941, Neville M. Ford (marr. diss., 1956), 2nd *s* of late Dr Lionel Ford, Headmaster of Harrow and Dean of York; two *d*; 2nd, 1956, Sir Nigel Fisher, MC. *Educ:* privately and abroad. MP (UU) North Down (unopposed return), April 1953–55 (as Mrs Patricia Ford). *Recreations:* sailing, travel. *Address:* 45 Exeter House, Putney Heath, SW15 3SX.
Died 23 May 1995.

FISHER, (Phyllis) Anne; Headmistress, Wycombe Abbey School, 1962–74; *b* 8 March 1913; *d* of Rev. L. A. Fisher, Rector of Higham on the Hill, Nuneaton, and Beatrice Fisher (*née* Eustace). *Educ:* Sch. of St Mary and St Anne, Abbots Bromley; Bristol Univ. BA History Hons, 1938. Senior History Mistress: St Helen's, Northwood, 1938–41; St Anne's Coll., Natal, SA, 1941–44; Headmistress, St Winifred's Sch., George, SA, 1944–45; Joint Headmistress, St George's, Ascot, 1946–49; Headmistress, Limuru Girls' Sch., Limuru, Kenya, 1949–57; Headmistress, Arundel Sch., Salisbury, Rhodesia, 1957–61. *Recreations:* study of old churches, the history of painting. *Died 25 April 1994.*

FISHER, Richard Colomb; HM Diplomatic Service, retired; *b* Hankow, 11 Nov. 1923; *s* of Comdr Richard Fisher, RN and late Phillipa (*née* Colomb), Lee-on-Solent; *m* 1946, Edwine Kempers; two *s*. *Educ:* RNC Dartmouth. Joined Navy, 1937; to sea as Midshipman, 1941; War Service in submarines, 1943–45, Far East; flying trng, 1946–47; specialised in navigation/direction, 1948; Comdr 1958; retd from RN and joined Diplomatic Service, 1969; 1st Sec., Bonn, 1970–73; Commercial Counsellor, Warsaw, 1973–76, Rome, 1976–79. *Recreations:* history, languages. *Died 3 April 1992.*

FISKE, Dudley Astley; education consultant; *b* 16 June 1929; *s* of Tom Fiske and late Barbara Fiske; *m* 1958, Patricia Elizabeth, *d* of late Donald MacIver and of Helen MacIver, Weybridge; two *s* one *d*. *Educ:* Berkhamsted Sch.; Merton Coll., Oxford (MA). Asst Master, Barnard Castle Sch., 1953–56; Asst Tutor, Oxford Univ. Dept of Educn, 1956–58; Admin. Asst, East Sussex, 1959–60; Asst Educn Officer, Berkshire, 1961–65; Dep. Educn Officer, Leeds, 1965–68; Chief Educn Officer, Manchester, 1968–82; Educn Officer, AMA, 1983. Pres., Educnl Develt Assoc., 1969–74; Mem., Business Educn Council, 1974–80; President: British Educnl Equipment Assoc., 1973–74; Soc. of Educn Officers, 1978; Commonwealth Educn Fellow in Australia, 1974. *Address:*

Farthings, High Street, Hook Norton, Oxon OX15 5NF. *T:* Hook Norton (0608) 737613.
Died 2 Jan. 1991.

FISTOULARI, Anatole; Principal Conductor of London Philharmonic Orchestra, 1943, then guest conductor; *b* Kiev, Russia, 20 Aug. 1907; *s* of Gregor and Sophie Fistoulari; obtained British nationality, 1948; *m* 1st, 1942, Anna Mahler (marr. diss., 1956); one *d*; 2nd, 1957, Mary Elizabeth, *y d* of late James Lockhart, Edinburgh. *Educ:* Kiev, Berlin, and Paris. Conducted first concert at age of 7 at Opera House in Kiev and later all over Russia; at 13 gave concerts in Germany and Holland; at 24 conducted Grand Opera Russe in Paris at the Châtelet Theatre with Colonne Orchestra and Chaliapin with whom he then toured France and Spain; then conducted the Ballet de Monte-Carlo with Massine in Drury Lane and Covent Garden before the War; toured with same company all over America, France, and Italy; in England in 1941 started opera production of Sorotchinsky Fair by Moussorgsky; March 1942 gave first Symphony Concert with London Symphony Orchestra and later conducted it regularly at Cambridge Theatre; first concert with London Philharmonic Orchestra in Bristol, Jan. 1943; concert engagements in numerous countries, from 1949; Founder, 1946, and Principal Conductor, London Internat. Orch.; Guest Conductor for Sadler's Wells Ballet, Royal Opera House, Covent Garden and NY Metropolitan Opera House, 1955; on tour with London Philharmonic Orchestra, to Moscow, Leningrad, Paris, 1956. Made recordings for several firms. *Recreation:* listening to good concerts. *Address:* Flat 4, 65 Redington Road, NW3 7RP. *Club:* Savage. *Died 21 Aug. 1995.*

FITCH, Marcus Felix Brudenell, (Marc), CBE 1977; *b* 5 Jan. 1908; *s* of Hugh Bernard Fitch and Bertha Violet (*née* James); *m* Evelyn Murray; one *s* one *d*; *m* Ismene Georgalopoulo. *Educ:* Repton; Vienna and Geneva. FSG 1947; FSA 1952. Gold Staff Officer, Coronations of 1937 and 1953. Served Intel. Corps, Belgian Congo, Eritrea and GHQ ME, 1940–46. Chm., Soc. of Genealogists, 1956; founded Marc Fitch Fund, 1956; with Fund founded English Surnames Survey, Leicester Univ., 1965; with Dame Joan Evans estabd Stratigraphical Mus., Knossos, 1966; founded Fitch Archaeological Lab., Athens, 1974; assisted rural re-foundn of St Catherine's British Embassy Sch., Athens, 1974. Master, Tallow Chandlers' Co., 1957. Associate Mem., All Souls Coll., Oxford, 1973. Hon. Fellow, St Cross Coll., Oxford, 1981. Hon. FBA 1978. Hon. DLitt Leicester, 1973; Hon. MA Oxford, 1987. *Publications:* ed 10 vols for British Record Soc., 1959–86. *Clubs:* Athenæum, Garrick, Royal Automobile.
Died 2 April 1994.

FITCH, Admiral Sir Richard (George Alison), KCB 1985; Second Sea Lord, Chief of Naval Personnel and Admiral President, Royal Naval College, Greenwich, 1986–88, retired; *b* 2 June 1929; *s* of Edward William Fitch and Agnes Jamieson Fitch; *m* 1969, Kathleen Marie-Louise Igert; one *s*. *Educ:* Royal Naval College, Dartmouth. Seagoing appointments, 1946–66; HMS Berwick in Command, 1966–67; Staff of Flag Officer, Second in Command, Far East Fleet, 1967–69; Directorate of Naval Plans, MoD, 1969–71; RCDS 1972; HMS Apollo in Command, 1973–74; Naval Asst to First Sea Lord, 1974–76; HMS Hermes in Command, 1976–78; Dir of Naval Warfare, 1978–80; Naval Secretary, 1980–83; Flag Officer, Third Flotilla and Comdr Anti-Submarine Group Two, 1983–85. Liveryman, Coachmakers' and Coach Harness Makers' Co. CIMgt. *Recreations:* gardening, philately, following sport. *Died 15 Feb. 1994.*

FITT, Robert Louis, CMG 1975; FEng 1978; *b* 9 Aug. 1905; *s* of late R. F. Fitt; *m* 1936, Elsie Ockleshaw, *d* of late William Ockleshaw, Liverpool; one *s*. *Educ:*

Launceston and Barnstaple Grammar Schs; City and Guilds Coll., London. BSc; FCGI. Engineer: with Sudan Govt, 1927–31; with Mott Hay & Anderson, on Mersey Tunnel and London Underground Extensions, 1931–39; joined Sir Alexander Gibb & Partners, 1939; Partner, 1946; retired, 1978; responsible for industrial develts, irrigation works, water supplies, thermal and hydro-electric power projects, airports, and economic develt surveys, in countries incl. UK, Iran, Iraq, Sudan, Argentina, Kenya, Tanzania, Swaziland, Rhodesia, Australia and Jamaica. Chm., Assoc. of Consulting Engineers, 1961–62; Vice-Pres., Middle East Assoc., 1972; Pres., Internat. Fedn of Consulting Engrs, 1972–74. FICE (Vice-Pres., 1976–78). Order of Homayoun, Iran, Third Class, 1955. *Recreations:* gardening, golf. *Address:* 27 Longdown Lane North, Ewell, Surrey KT17 3HY. *T:* 081–393 1727.
Died 24 Sept. 1994.

FITZER, Herbert Clyde, CB 1971; OBE 1958; Head of Royal Naval Engineering Service, 1970–71, Director of Engineering (Ships), Navy Department, Ministry of Defence, 1968–71, retired; *b* 3 Nov. 1910; *s* of Herbert John Fitzer; *m* 1938, Queenie Stent; one *d*. *Educ:* Portsmouth Royal Dockyard Sch.; RNC Greenwich; London Univ. 1st cl. hons BSc (Eng) London, 1932; Greenwich Professional Certif. in Electrical Engrg, 1933. CEng, FIEE 1959. Asst Elec. Engr, Admty, 1936; Sheerness Dockyard, 1938; Elec. Engr, Submarine Design, Admty, 1939; Shore Estabs, 1945; Suptg Elec. Engr, Submarine Design, 1950; Asst Dir of Elec. Engrg, Ships Power Systems, 1961; Polaris Project, 1963; Dep. Dir of Elec. Engrg, 1966. Licensed Lay Reader, Dio. Bath and Wells. *Publication:* Christian Flarepath, 1956. *Address:* Longacre House, 16 Sharvells Road, Milford-on-Sea, Lymington, Hants SO41 0PE. *T:* Lymington (0590) 644875. *Died 20 March 1994.*

FitzGEORGE-BALFOUR, Gen. Sir (Robert George) Victor, KCB 1968 (CB 1965); CBE 1945; DSO 1950; MC 1939; DL; Chairman, National Fund for Research into Crippling Diseases, 1975–89; *b* 15 Sept. 1913; *s* of Robert S. Balfour and Iris (*née* FitzGeorge), 47 Wilton Crescent, SW1; *m* 1943, Mary (Diana) (*d* 1994), *er d* of Rear-Adm. Arthur Christian, 3 Sloane Gardens, SW3; one *s* one *d*. *Educ:* Eton; King's Coll., Cambridge (BA). Commissioned 2nd Lieut Coldstream Guards, 1934; Palestine, 1936; Middle East, 1937–43; France and NW Germany, 1944–46; commanded 2nd Bn Coldstream Guards, Malaya, 1948–50; idc 1955; Chief of Staff to Governor of Cyprus, 1956; commanded 1st Guards Brigade, 1957; Chief of Staff, HQ Southern Comd, 1962–63; Dir of Military Operations, Ministry of Defence, 1964–66; Senior Army Instructor, IDC, 1966–68; Vice-Chief of the General Staff, 1968–70; UK Mil. Representative, NATO, 1971–73. ADC (Gen.), 1972–73. Col Comdt, HAC, 1976–84. DL West Sussex, 1977. Knight Commander of the Order of Orange Nassau with swords (Netherlands), 1946. *Address:* The Old Rectory, West Chiltington, West Sussex RH20 2QA. *T:* West Chiltington (01798) 812255. *Club:* Army and Navy.
Died 28 Dec. 1994.

FITZGERALD, Charles Patrick; Professor of Far Eastern History, Australian National University, 1953–67, then Emeritus; Visiting Fellow, Department of International Relations, Australian National University, 1968–69; *b* 5 March 1902; *s* of Dr H. Sauer Fitzgerald and Josephine Fitzpatrick; *m* 1941, Pamela Sara Knollys (*d* 1980); two *d* (and one *d* decd). *Educ:* Clifton. DLitt ANU, 1968. Lived in China, 1923–27, 1930–32, 1936–38, 1946–50. Leverhulme Fellowship for Anthropological Research in South-West China, 1936–39. *Publications:* Son of Heaven, 1932; China, a Cultural History, 1935, rev. edn 1950, repr. 1986; The Tower of Five Glories, 1941; (with George

Yeh) Introducing China, 1948; Revolution in China, 1951 (revised version (Penguin) as The Birth of Communist China, 1965); The Empress Wu, 1955; Flood Tide in China, 1958; Barbarian Beds: the origin of the chair in China, 1965; A Concise History of Eastern Asia, 1965; The Third China, Chinese Communities in SE Asia, 1965; Des Mantchous à Mao Tse-tong, 1968; History of China, 1969; Communism Takes China, 1970; The Southern Expansion of the Chinese People: Southern Fields and Southern Ocean, 1972; Mao Tsetung and China, 1976; Ancient China, 1978; Why China?, 1985. *Address:* 4 St Paul's Street, Randwick, NSW 2031, Australia. *Club:* Savile. *Died 13 April 1992.*

FITZGERALD, William Knight, CBE 1981; JP; DL; Convener, Tayside Regional Council, 1978–86; *b* 19 March 1909; *e s* of John Alexander Fitzgerald and Janet Fitzgerald; *m* 1st, 1938, Elizabeth (*d* 1980), *d* of Alexander Grant; three *s*; 2nd, 1984, Margaret Eleanor Bell. *Educ:* Robertson Grammar Sch., S Africa. Assessor, Dundee Repertory Theatre, 1967–77; Member: Tayside Economic Consultative Group, 1970–77; Dundee Harbour Trust, 1970–73; University Court, Dundee, 1970–86; Dundee Town Council, 1956; City Treasurer, Dundee, 1967–70; Lord Provost of Dundee, and Lord Lieutenant of County of the City of Dundee, 1970–73; Chairman: Tay Road Bridge Joint Board, 1970–73 and 1975–86; Dundee High Sch. Directors, 1970–73; Vice-Chairman: Dundee Coll. of Art and Technology, 1970–75; Scottish Council on Alcoholism, 1972–; E Scotland Water Bd, 1973–75. President: Convention of Scottish Local Authorities, 1979–82; Dundee Bn, Boys' Brigade, 1976–. Dundee: JP 1948; DL 1974. Hon. LLD Dundee, 1981. *Recreations:* gardening, reading. *Address:* Morven, Roxburgh Terrace, Dundee DD2 1NZ. *T:* Dundee (0382) 68475. *Club:* University (Dundee). *Died 25 June 1991.*

FITZMAURICE, Lt-Col Sir Desmond FitzJohn, Kt 1946; CIE 1941; late Royal Engineers; *b* 17 Aug. 1893; *s* of John Day Stokes Fitzmaurice, ICS, Tralee, Co. Kerry; *m* 1926, Nancy (*d* 1975), *d* of Rev. John Sherlock Leake, Grayswood, Surrey; one *s* three *d. Educ:* Bradfield; RMA, Woolwich; Cambridge Univ. Joined RE, 1914; served in France, Belgium and Italy, European War, 1914–18 (despatches); Instructor, RMA Woolwich, 1918–20; Cambridge Univ., 1920–22; Instructor, Sch. of Military Engineering, Chatham, 1923, 1924; half pay list, 1925; Deputy Mint Master, Bombay, 1929–30, Calcutta, 1931–32; Deputy Master, Security Printing, India, 1932; Master, Security Printing and Controller of Stamps, India, 1934; retired. *Address:* Lincombe Lodge, Fox Lane, Boars Hill, Oxford OX1 5DN. *Died 10 Oct. 1991.*

FITZSIMMONS, Rt Hon. William Kennedy, PC (N Ireland) 1965; JP; *b* 31 Jan. 1909; *m* 1935, May Elizabeth Lynd; two *d. Educ:* Skegoniell National Sch.; Belfast Techn. Sch. Mem., Belfast City and Dist Water Comrs, 1948–57 (Chm. 1954–55); Pres., Duncairn Unionist Assoc.; N Ireland Parliament: MP (U) Duncairn Div. of Belfast, 1956–72; Dep. Govt Whip, 1961–63; Parliamentary Secretary: Min. of Commerce, 1961–65; Min. of Home Affairs, 1963–64; Min. of Develt, 1964–65; Min. of Education, 1965–66 and 1968–69; Minister of Development, 1966–68; Minister of Health and Social Services, 1969–72. JP Belfast, 1951. *Address:* 16 Cleaver Court, Cleaver Avenue, Malone Road, Belfast, Northern Ireland BT9 5JA. *Died 21 Feb. 1992.*

FLANDERS, Dennis, RWS 1976 (ARWS 1970); RBA 1970; artist: townscapes and landscapes in pencil and water-colour; *b* 2 July 1915; *s* of late Bernard C. Flanders, ARAM (pianist), and Jessie Marguarite Flanders, ARMS (artist); *m* Peggy Louise Salaman (marr. diss.; she *d* 1990); *m* 1952, Dalma J. Darnley, *o d* of late J. Darnley Taylor and of Mrs Joan Darnley Taylor; one *s* one *d. Educ:*

Merchant Taylors' Sch.; Regent Street Polytechnic; St Martin's Art Sch.; Central Sch. of Arts and Crafts. Princess Louise Gold Medal at age of 7. Mem. of St Paul's Watch, 1940–42; Royal Engineers, 1942–46. Occasional drawings for Daily Telegraph and other journals; series of drawings for Yorkshire Post, 1949; Birmingham Post, 1950–51; "Famous Streets," Sunday Times, 1952–53; Special artist to the Illustrated London News, 1956–64. Water-colours (reproduced as prints) of: RMA Sandhurst; Police Coll., Bramshill; St Edward's Sch., Oxford; Glencorse Barracks, Midlothian; Hampstead; Nottingham, Loughborough, Essex and Leicester Univs; Somerville, Wadham, Jesus, St Cross and Hertford Colls, Oxford; Wolfson Coll., Cambridge; prints of City of London Sch. for Boys, Sherborne Sch.; facsimile prints of schools and colleges (Wellington, King's (Canterbury and Ely), Whitgift, Caterham, Christ's (Brecon), Worcester and Hertford Colls, Oxford). Drawings in private collections and Nat. War Collection (1939–45), Guildhall Library, Bank of England, Nat. Library of Wales, and Museums at Exeter, York, Lincoln, Kensington, St Marylebone, Walthamstow, Wolverhampton, and Bury, Lancs. Exhibitor, Royal Acad. and in provinces; one-man shows: London galleries: Colnaghi's, 1947; J. A. Tooth's, 1951; Coombs & Percival, 1953, 1955; Royal Soc. of British Artists, 1964, 1967; Catto, 1986, 1990; Bedford, 1965, 1966, 1985; Boston (Lincs), 1966; Southport, 1969; Buxton-Lammas, Norfolk, 1972; Worthing, 1972; Cambridge, 1980; York, 1981; Fine Art Soc., London and Edin., 1984; George's Art Bookshop, Bristol, 1985; Bedford, 1986. Member: Art Workers Guild (Master 1975); Soc. for Protection of Ancient Buildings. Freeman: City of London, 1970; Painter Stainers' Co., 1970. Lord Mayor's Art Award, 1966. *Publications: illustrations:* Bolton Abbey, 1947; Chelsea by Richard Edmonds, 1956; Soho for East Anglia by Michael Brander, 1963; A Westminster Childhood by John Raynor, 1973; The Twelve Great Livery Companies of London, 1973; (artist and author) Dennis Flanders' Britannia, 1984. *Recreations:* walking, riding, reading Who's Who. *Address:* 51 Great Ormond Street, WC1N 3HZ. *T:* 071–405 9317; Baker's Cross House, Cranbrook, Kent TN17 3AQ. *T:* Cranbrook (0580) 712018. *Died 13 Aug. 1994.*

FLATLEY, Derek Comedy, MBE 1989; FJI; Public Affairs Correspondent, Southend Evening Echo, since 1970; *b* 16 Oct. 1920; *m* 1959, Valerie Eve Stevens; one *d. Educ:* Grammar sch. Trained West Essex Gazette, 1936. Served War of 1939–45: Household Cavalry, 1945. Army newspaper unit, Southend Standard, 1947; Chief Reporter, 1949. Mem., Press Council, 1968–72; Mem. Council (rep. Essex), Inst. of Journalists, 1957– (Pres. 1966–67); also Chairman: Salaries and Conditions Bd of the Inst., 1958–67; Estabt Cttee, 1963–65; Exec., 1967–70. Fellow, Inst. of Journalists, 1962. *Recreations:* football, cricket, tennis. *Address:* Windyridge House, 22 Earls Hall Avenue, Southend-on-Sea, Essex SS2 6PD. *T:* Southend-on-Sea (0702) 343485. *Died 12 June 1992.*

FLAVELL, Geoffrey, FRCS; FRCP; Hon. Consulting Cardio-Thoracic Surgeon to: The Royal London Hospital; Chelmsford and Harlow Districts Health Authorities; Whipps Cross Hospital; *b* 23 Feb. 1913; *o surv. s* of late W. A. Flavell, JP, Wellington, NZ; *m* 1943, Joan Margaret, *o d* of S. Ewart Adams, Hawkwell, Essex; no *c. Educ:* Waitaki; Otago; University of New Zealand; St Bartholomew's Hospital, London. Qualified in medicine, 1937; house appts, St Bartholomew's Hosp., 1937–39; Resident Surgical Officer, Brompton Hosp., 1940–41; Surgeon Specialist, RAF, 1942, o/c Surgical Divs RAF Gen. Hosps, Carthage and Algiers, 1943; RAF Gen. Hosp., Cairo; Adviser in Surgery RAF Med. and Middle East Command, 1944 (retired rank of Wing Comdr, 1958); Consultant Thoracic Surgeon, British Legion Hosp., and to LCC, 1946; Senior Registrar to London Hosp., 1947; Sen. Surgeon, Dept of Cardiovascular and Thoracic Surgery, London Hosp., 1950–78 (Chm., Surgical Div., 1974–77); Mem., Faculty of Med., Univ. of London, 1953; Consultant Thoracic Surgeon, Royal Masonic Hosp., 1957–78; Sen. Thoracic Surgeon, Broomfield Hosp., 1947–78. Visiting Thoracic Surgeon to: Whipps Cross Hosp.; St Margaret's Hosp., Epping; Harold Wood Hosp.; Harts Hosp.; Oldchurch Hosp., Romford. Consultant, Qatar Govt, 1969. Chm., Adv. Cttee on Cardiothoracic Surgery to NE Thames RHA, 1970–78; Sen. Mem., Soc. of Thoracic Surgeons of GB and Ireland. Touring Lectr for British Council, Middle and Far Eastern Univs, 1961; Ivor Lewis Lectr, N Mddx Hosp., 1978. Liveryman, Hon. Soc. of Apothecaries; Freeman, City of London. *Publications:* Introduction to Chest Surgery, 1957; Basic Surgery (Thoracic section), 1958; The Oesophagus, 1963; many contribs to surgical textbooks and med. jls; various articles on travel, wine and food, in lay periodicals. *Recreations:* history, architecture, literature and art, indulging the senses. *Address:* 9 Camden Crescent, Bath BA1 5HY. *T:* Bath (01225) 444903. *Clubs:* Royal Air Force; Bath and County (Bath).

Died 28 Nov. 1994.

FLEETWOOD, Susan Maureen; actress; Hon. Associate Member, Royal Shakespeare Company, since 1988 (Associate Member, 1980–88); *b* 21 Sept. 1944; *d* of John Joseph Kells Fleetwood and Bridget Maureen (*née* Brereton), St Andrews, Scotland. *Educ:* sixteen schs, incl. Convent of the Nativity, Sittingbourne, Kent; RADA (Bancroft Gold Medal). Rosalind, in As You Like It, and Lady Macbeth, in Macbeth, tour, Arizona, USA, 1964; Founder Mem., Liverpool Everyman, 1965–67: Lady Percy, in Henry IV; Gwendolen, in The Importance of Being Earnest; Alison, in Look Back in Anger; Liz, in Fando and Liz; Margaret, in The Great God Brown; chorus leader, in Murder in the Cathedral; The Woman, in The Four Seasons; Lady Macbeth, in Macbeth; RSC, 1967–68: Regan, in King Lear; Marina/Thaisa, in Pericles; Julia, in The Two Gentlemen of Verona (tour); Beba, in Criminals; Amanda, in The Relapse; RSC, 1972: Portia, in The Merchant of Venice; chorus leader, in Murder in the Cathedral; The Bondwoman, in The Island of the Mighty; RSC, 1975–76: Katharina, in The Taming of the Shrew; Kaleria, in Summerfolk; Princess of France, in Love's Labour's Lost (also US tour); Imogen, in Cymbeline; National Theatre, 1976–78: Pegeen Mike, in Playboy of the Western World; Ophelia, in Hamlet; Jo, in Watch it Come Down; Zenocrate, in Tamburlaine the Great; Nora, in The Plough and the Stars; Clare, in Lavender Blue; Ismene, in The Woman; RSC, 1980–82: Rosalind, in As You Like It; Varya, in The Cherry Orchard; wife, in La Ronde; National Theatre, 1982–83: June Taylor, in Way Upstream; Titania, in A Midsummer Night's Dream; National Theatre, 1988–89: Laura, in The Father; RSC, 1990–91: Beatrice, in Much Ado About Nothing; Madame Arkadina, in The Seagull; Ella, in Curse of the Starving Class; other roles: Nina, in The Seagull, Cambridge Theatre Co., 1970; Ophelia, in Hamlet, Prospect Theatre Co., 1970–71; Clara, in I'm NOT Rappaport, Apollo, 1986; Kitty Twombley, in The Cabinet Minister, Royal Exchange, Manchester, 1988. Films include: Clash of the Titans; Heat and Dust; Young Sherlock Holmes; The Sacrifice; White Mischief; Dream Demons; The Krays; television serials and series include: Eustace and Hilda; The Good Soldier; Strangers and Brothers; Murder of a Moderate Man; Summer's Lease; Inspector Alleyn; The Buddha of Suburbia; Chandler and Co.; TV plays: Watercress Girl; Don't be Silly; Dangerous Corner; Flying in the Branches; Six Characters in Search of an Author; A Landing on the Sun; A Few Short Journeys of the Heart; Persuasion; many radio plays. *Recreations:* listening to music, going to the theatre, travelling, doing everything I can't do when working. *Address:* c/o ICM, Duncan Heath, Oxford House, 76 Oxford Street, W1R 1RB. *T:* 0171–636 6565.

Died 29 Sept. 1995.

FLEMING, Ian, RSA 1956 (ARSA 1947); RSW 1947; RWA 1975; RGI 1986; Head, Gray's School of Art, Aberdeen, 1954–71, retired; *b* 19 Nov. 1906; *s* of John and Catherine Fleming; *m* 1943, Catherine Margaret Weetch; one *s* two *d. Educ:* Hyndland Sch., Glasgow; Glasgow Sch. of Art. Served War, 1941–46 (Normandy, Belgium, Holland, Germany). Lectr, Glasgow Sch. of Art, 1931–48; Warden, Patrick Allan-Fraser Art Coll., Hospitalfield, Arbroath, 1948–54. Chm., Peacock Printmakers Workshop (Aberdeen), 1973–86. Hon. LLD Aberdeen, 1984. *Recreation:* anything Scottish. *Address:* 15 Fonthill Road, Aberdeen AB1 2UN. *T:* Aberdeen (0224) 580680.

Died 24 July 1994.

FLEMING, Rear-Adm. Sir John, KBE 1960; DSC 1944; Director of the Naval Education Service, 1956–60; *b* 2 May 1904; *s* of late James Fleming; *m* 1930, Jean Law (*d* 1986), *d* of late James Stuart Gillitt, South Shields; no *c. Educ:* Jarrow Grammar Sch.; St John's Coll., Cambridge. BA 1925, MA 1957. Entered RN as Instructor Lieut, 1925; Instr Lieut-Comdr, 1931; Instr Comdr, 1939; Instr Capt., 1950; Instr Rear-Adm., 1956. Asst Dir Naval Weather Service, 1945, Dep. Dir, 1947; Fleet Instructor Officer and Fleet Meteorological Officer, Home Fleet, 1950; Command Instructor Officer, The Nore, 1951; Education Dept, Admiralty, 1952. *Recreation:* gardening. *Address:* Mullion Cottage, Tanners Lane, Haslemere, Surrey. *T:* Haslemere (01428) 2412.

Died 3 Nov. 1994.

FLEMINGTON, Roger; Director, 1988–92, Deputy Group Chief Executive, 1990–92, National Westminster Bank; *b* 7 May 1932; *s* of late Walter Harold Flemington and Mary Elizabeth Julia Flemington (*née* Stone); *m* 1st, 1955, Doreen Helen Smyter (*d* 1990); 2nd, 1992, Rosemary Ann Moxon. *Educ:* Nantwich and Acton Grammar School. FCIB. RAF, 1950–52. National Westminster Bank Group, 1948–92: Man. Dir, Diners Club, 1975–77; Sen. Internat. Exec., 1978–79; Chief Internat. Exec., Asia, Australasia and Africa, 1979–81; Asst Gen. Manager, Internat. Banking Div., 1981–84; Dir, Westments, 1984–92; Gen. Manager, Premises Div., 1984–86, Domestic Banking Div., 1986–88; Chief Exec., UK Financial Services, 1989–90. Director: Coutts & Co., 1986–; Lombard North Central, 1989–. Pres., CIB, 1991–92 (Member: Council, 1986–; Gen. Purposes Cttee, 1987–92; Dep. Chm., 1990–91; Vice Pres., 1992–); Member: London & Scottish Bankers Cttee on Private Finance for Housing, 1988–91; Exec. Cttee, BBA, 1989–91 (Chm., Remuneration Sub-Cttee, 1990–92); City Adv. Gp, CBI, 1990–92. Trustee, Indep. Broadcasting Telethon Trust, 1989–92. Freeman, City of London, 1979; Liveryman, Woolmen's Co. FRSA. *Recreations:* music, flyfishing, country pursuits, antiques, travel, reading. *Address:* Larkrise, Rectory Lane, Buckland, Betchworth, Surrey RH3 7BH. *T:* Betchworth (0737) 844522. *Clubs:* Bankers', MCC.

Died 13 Sept. 1994.

FLEMINGTON, Rev. William Frederick, MA Oxon, BD Cantab; Principal of Wesley House, Cambridge, 1955–67; held Greenhalgh Chair of New Testament Language and Literature, Wesley House, Cambridge, 1937–67, retired; *b* 24 May 1901; *er s* of Rev. William Frederick Flemington and Annie Mary Geden Bate; *m* 1930, Ethel Phyllis Goodenough, *er d* of Rev. John Henry Doddrell; one *s* one *d. Educ:* Liverpool Coll.; Jesus Coll., Oxford (Exhibitioner; 2nd Cl. Classical Hon. Mods; 2nd Cl. Lit. Hum.); Jesus Coll., Fitzwilliam Coll. and Wesley House, Cambridge (Carus Greek Testament Prize; 1st Cl. Theological Tripos, Pt II, Sect. 2, New Testament). Entered Wesleyan Methodist Ministry, 1925; Asst Tutor,

Handsworth Coll., Birmingham, 1926–30; Minister in Stourbridge Circuit (Cradley), 1930–33; West Bromwich Circuit, 1933–37; Tutor, Wesley House, 1937–55. Select Preacher, Cambridge Univ., 1944, 1950, 1954. Pres. of Cambridge Theological Soc., 1963–65. *Publications:* The New Testament Doctrine of Baptism, 1948; contributor to Prayer and Worship, 1945; articles and reviews in Expository Times and Jl of Theological Studies. *Recreations:* walking, reading. *Address:* 204 Chesterton Road, Cambridge. *Died 14 May 1991.*

FLETCHER, Hon. Sir Alan (Roy), Kt 1972; Minister for Education and Cultural Activities, Queensland, 1968–74, retired 1975; MLA (Country Party) for Cunningham, Queensland, 1953–74; *b* Pittsworth, 26 Jan. 1907; *s* of Alexander Roy Fletcher, Pittsworth, and Rosina Wilhemina (*née* McIntyre); *m* 1934, Enid Phair, *d* of James Thompson, Ashburton, NZ; two *s* two *d*. *Educ:* Irongate State Sch.; Scots Coll., Warwick, Qld. Pittsworth Shire: Councillor, 1945–57, Chm., 1949–57. Speaker, Legislative Assembly, Qld, 1957–60; Minister for Lands, 1960–68. Dir, Queensland Co-op. Milling Assoc., 1951–65. Member: Presbyterian Schs Council, Warwick, 1951– (Chm., 1958–61); Council, Darling Downs Inst. of Advanced Educn, 1975–. Pres., Old Boys' Assoc., Scots Coll., Warwick, 1948–. *Recreations:* shooting, croquet. *Address:* 3/11 Beresford Street, Pittsworth, Queensland 4356, Australia. *T:* (76) 931091.

Died 7 Oct. 1991.

FLETCHER, Col Archibald Ian, OBE 1967; JP; Lord-Lieutenant for Strathclyde Region (District of Argyll and Bute), since 1993 (Vice Lord-Lieutenant, 1990–93); Consultant and Adviser, Dunans Farming & Forestry, since 1987; *b* 9 April 1924; *s* of Ian Archibald Fletcher and Isabelle Douglas-Dick, *widow* of Ralph Gladwin; *m* 1952, Helen Clare de Salis; one *s* two *d*. *Educ:* Ampleforth Coll. Joined Army, Scots Guards, 1942; Guards Depot, commnd 1943 into 3rd Bn; Tank Troop Comdr, NW Europe, 1944–45; served Palestine, Malaya, 1946–51; E Africa, 1961–63; commanded: 1st Bn, 1963–66; Borneo, 1964–65; Regt, 1967–70; retired to farm in Argyllshire. Dir, Argyll and the Is Enterprise Co. Ltd, 1990–95. Mem., Nat. Council and Scottish Bd, Timber Growers UK, 1985–91. Chm., Colintraive and Glendaruel Community Council, 1977–91. Hon. Pres., NFU of Scotland, 1985–86. Mem., Argyll CC, 1972–75. JP 1971, DL 1974, Argyll. Hon. Sheriff, Rothesay, 1994. Chevalier, Mil. Order of Aviz (Portugal), 1955. *Recreations:* country pursuits. *Address:* Dunans, Glendaruel, Argyll PA22 3AD. *Clubs:* New (Edinburgh); Semengo (Sarawak).

Died 27 April 1995.

FLETCHER, Charles Montague, CBE 1952; MD, FRCP, FFPHM; Physician to Hammersmith Hospital, 1952–76; Professor of Clinical Epidemiology, University of London at Royal Postgraduate Medical School, 1973–76 (Reader, 1952–73), now Professor Emeritus; *b* 5 June 1911; *s* of late Sir Walter Morley Fletcher, FRS and late Mary Frances Fletcher (*née* Cropper); *m* Louisa Mary Sylvia Seely, *d* of 1st Baron Mottistone; one *s* two *d*. *Educ:* Eton Coll.; Trinity Coll., Cambridge (Sen. Schol.; rowed in Univ. Boat, 1933); St Bartholomew's Hospital. MA 1936, MD 1945, Cantab; MRCP 1942; FRCP 1947; FFPHM (FFCM 1974). Michael Foster Research Student, Trinity Coll., 1934–36; Nuffield Res. Student, Oxford, 1940–42. Asst Phys., EMS, 1943–44; Dir, MRC Pneumoconiosis Res. Unit, 1945–52; Sec., MRC Cttee on Bronchitis Res., 1954–76. Royal Coll. of Physicians: Mem. Council, 1959–62; 2nd Vice Pres., 1975; Sec., Cttee on Smoking and Health, 1961–71; Goulstonian Lectr, 1947; Bissett Hawkins Gold Medal, 1969. WHO Consultant: Pulmonary Heart Disease, 1960; Chronic Bronchitis, 1962; Smoking and Health, 1970. Mem., Central Health Services Council

and Standing Med. Adv. Cttee, 1966–76; Vice-Chm., Health Educn Council, 1967; Pres., ASH, 1979– (Chm., 1971–78); Member: Exec. Cttee, Asthma Soc., 1980–89; Council, British Diabetic Assoc., 1983–88 (Chm., Educn Sect., 1983–88); Wkg Party on Prolonging Life and Assisting Death, Inst. of Med. Ethics, 1989–93. Introd. many TV med. programmes incl. Hurt Mind, 1955, Your Life in Their Hands, 1958–65, Television Doctor, 1969–70. Consulting Ed. Jl of Med. Ethics, 1975–81. *Publications:* Communication in Medicine, 1973; Natural History of Chronic Bronchitis and Emphysema, 1976; many papers on: first use of penicillin, 1941; dust disease of lungs, 1946–55; bronchitis and emphysema, 1952–76. *Recreations:* music, gardening. *Address:* 24 West Square, SE11 4SN. *T:* 0171–735 8753; 2 Coastguard Cottages, Newtown, IoW PO30 4PA. *T:* Calbourne (01983) 531321. *Club:* Brooks's. *Died 15 Dec. 1995.*

FLETCHER, Geoffrey Bernard Abbott, MA Cantab; *b* Hampstead, 28 Nov. 1903; *s* of J. Alexander Fletcher and Ursula Constance, *d* of William Richard Rickett; *cousin* of Rt Hon. Sir Joseph Compton-Rickett, MP. *Educ:* Rugby Sch.; King's Coll., Cambridge (Senior Scholar). First Class, Classical Tripos, Part I, 1924; First Class Classical Tripos, Part 2, 1926; Prendergast Student, 1926. Asst Lectr in Classics, University of Leeds, 1927–28; Lectr in Greek, University of Liverpool, 1928–36; Prof. of Classics in the University of Durham, King's Coll., Newcastle upon Tyne, 1937–46, Prof. of Latin, 1946–63; Prof. of Latin, University of Newcastle upon Tyne, 1963–69, then Emeritus Prof. Examiner in Greek, University of Leeds, 1940–42; Examiner in Latin, Queen's Univ., Belfast, 1949–51, University of Wales, 1954–56, Bristol, 1961–63; Dean of Faculty of Arts, University of Durham, 1945–47; Public Orator, University of Durham, 1956–58. *Publications:* an appendix on Housman's Poetry in Housman, 1897–1936, by Grant Richards, 1941; Annotations on Tacitus, 1964; many contributions to classical and other periodicals, British and foreign, and to co-operative works. *Recreations:* music, reading, art galleries. *Address:* Thirlmere Lodge, Elmfield Road, Gosforth, Newcastle upon Tyne NE3 4BB. *T:* 0191–285 2873. *Club:* Athenæum. *Died 8 Feb. 1995.*

FLETCHER, Sir John Henry Lancelot A.; *see* Aubrey-Fletcher.

FLETCHER, (Leopold) Raymond; journalist; *b* 3 Dec. 1921; *s* of Leopold Raymond Fletcher, Ruddington, Notts; *m* 1st, 1947, Johanna Klara Elisabeth (*d* 1973), *d* of Karl Ising, Berlin; 2nd, 1977, Dr Catherine Elliott, *widow* of Jasper Fenn. *Educ:* abroad. Served 1941–48 in Indian and British forces. Former Columnist on The Times and contributor to other journals at home and abroad. MP (Lab) Ilkeston, 1964–83. Vice-Pres., Assembly of Council of Europe, 1974–76; Leader, UK Delegn to Council of Europe and WEU, 1974–76; Leader, Socialist Gp in Council of Europe, 1974–76. Founder and Council Mem., Airship Assoc. *Publications:* The Prussian Officer (play), 1948; Sixty Pounds a Second on Defence, 1963; Wege ins Neve Zukunft, 1963; (contrib.) Confrontation, 1978. *Recreation:* theatre. *Address:* Brooklands, Ilkeston Road, Heanor, Derbyshire DE7 7DT.

Died 16 March 1991.

FODEN-PATTINSON, Peter Lawrence; a Deputy Chairman of Lloyd's, 1976; *b* 14 June 1925; *s* of late Hubert Foden-Pattinson; *m* 1956, Joana Pryor (*née* Henderson); one *s*. *Educ:* Downside. Irish Guards, 1943–47. Lloyd's, 1942–: Underwriting Mem., 1956; Mem., Cttee of Lloyd's, 1973–76; Mem., Cttee of Lloyd's Non-Marine Assoc., 1965, Chm. 1971, Dep. Chm. 1970 and 1972. *Recreations:* boating, music. *Address:* 123 Pier House, Cheyne Walk, SW3 5HM. *T:* 071–351 1313. *Club:* Royal Yacht Squadron. *Died 19 Oct. 1992.*

FOLDES, Andor; international concert pianist since 1933; Head of Piano Master Class, Conservatory, Saarbrücken, 1957–65; *b* Budapest, Hungary, 21 Dec. 1913; *s* of Emil Foldes and Valerie Foldes (*née* Ipolyi); US citizen, 1948; *m* 1940, Lili Rendy (writer); no *c. Educ:* Franz Liszt Academy of Music, Budapest. Started piano playing at 5; first appeared with Budapest Phil. Orch. at 8; studied with Ernest von Dohnanyi, received Master Diploma (Franz Liszt Acad. of Music, Budapest), 1932. Concerts all over Europe, 1933–39; US debut (NBC Orch.), 1940; toured US extensively, 1940–48; concerts, since, all over the world, incl. three recitals in Peking, 1978; Beethoven concerts, Bonn Festival and throughout Europe. Recordings of all Beethoven Sonatas, and works of Mozart and Schubert. Grand Prix du Disque, Paris, for Bartok Complete Works (piano solo), 1957. Order of Merit, First Class, 1956, Grand Cross, 1964 (Germany); Commandeur, Mérite Culturel et Artistique (City of Paris), 1968; Médaille d'Argent de la Ville de Paris, 1971. *Publications:* Two on a Continent (with Lili Foldes), 1947; Keys to the Keyboard, 1950; Cadenzas to Mozart Piano Concertos (W Germany); Is there a Contemporary Style of Beethoven-playing?, 1963; various piano compositions; *relevant publication:* Wolf-Eberhard von Lewinski, Andor Foldes, 1970. *Recreations:* collecting art, reading, writing on musical subjects, swimming, hiking. *Address:* 8704 Herrliberg, Zürich, Switzerland.   *Died 9 Feb. 1992.*

FOLEY, Most Rev. William J.; Archbishop of Perth (Australia), (RC), since 1983; *b* 20 June 1931; *s* of Maurice and Augusta Foley. *Educ:* Christian Brothers' Coll., Perth, WA; St Charles Seminary, Guildford, WA; Brignole-Sale Coll., Genoa, Italy. Diocesan Director of Mission Aid Societies and Catholic Migration and Welfare Assoc., Perth, 1962–69; Diocesan Promoter of Vocations, Perth, 1969–71; Parish Priest, Maddington-Lynwood, 1971–76; Dean/Administrator, St Mary's Cathedral, 1976–81; Bishop of Geraldton, WA, 1981–83. Diocesan Priest Adviser to Christian Life Groups, Perth; State Chaplain, Knights of Southern Cross; Chm., Senate of Priests. Mem., Australian Catholic Bishops' Conf. Central Commn and Cttee for Justice, Develt and Peace. *Recreation:* golf. *Address:* St Mary's Cathedral, Victoria Square, Perth, WA 6000, Australia. *T:* 3259557.   *Died 10 Feb. 1991.*

FOLEY-BERKELEY, family name of **Baroness Berkeley.**

FONTEYN, Dame Margot; *see* Arias, Dame Margot Fonteyn de.

FOOTE, Maj.-Gen. Henry Robert Bowreman, VC 1944; CB 1952; DSO 1942; *b* 5 Dec. 1904; *s* of Lieut-Col H. B. Foote, late RA; *m* 1st, 1944, Anita Flint Howard (*d* 1970); 2nd, 1981, Mrs Audrey May Ashwell. *Educ:* Bedford Sch. Royal Tank Corps; 2nd Lieut, 1925; Lieut, 1927; Capt., 1936; Staff Coll., 1939; GSO3, WO, 1939; GSO2, WO, 1940; GSO2, Staff Coll., 1940–41; GSO1, 10th Armd Div., 1941–42; OC 7th Royal Tank Regt, 1942; Subst. Major, 1942; GSO1, AFHQ, Italy, 1944; 2 i/c, 9th Armd Bde, 1945; Brig. RAC, MELF, 1945–47; Subst. Lieut-Col, 1946; Subst. Col, 1948; OC 2nd Royal Tank Regt, 1947–48; OC Automotive Wing, Fighting Vehicles Proving Establishment, Ministry of Supply, 1948–49; Comd 7th Armd Bde, 1949–50; Maj.-Gen. 1951; Comd 11th Armoured Div., 1950–53; Dir-Gen. of Fighting Vehicles, Min. of Supply, 1953–55; Dir, Royal Armoured Corps, at the War Office, 1955–58; retd. *Address:* Furzefield, West Chiltington Common, Pulborough, West Sussex RH20 2QY. *Club:* Army and Navy.
          Died 22 Nov. 1993.

FORBES of Craigievar, Hon. Sir Ewan, 11th Bt *cr* 1630 (NS), of Craigievar, Aberdeenshire; JP; landowner and farmer; *b* 6 Sept. 1912; 2nd *s* of 18th Lord Sempill and Gwendolen, *d* of Herbert Prodgers, Wilts; *S* to Baronetcy

of brother, 19th Lord Sempill, 1965; *m* 1952, Isabella, *d* of A. Mitchell, Glenrinnes, Banffshire. *Educ:* Dresden; Univ. of Munich; Univ. of Aberdeen. MB, ChB 1944. Senior Casualty Officer, Aberdeen Royal Infirmary, 1944–45; Medical Practitioner, Alford, Aberdeenshire, 1945–55. JP Aberdeenshire, 1969. *Recreations:* shooting, fishing, ski-ing, skating. *Heir: kinsman* John Alexander Cumnock Forbes-Sempill [*b* 29 Aug. 1927; *m* 1st, 1956, Penelope Margaret Ann (marr. diss. 1963), *d* of A. G. Grey-Pennington; 2nd, 1966, Jane Carolyn, *o d* of C. Gordon Evans]. *Address:* Brux, Alford, Aberdeenshire. *T:* Kildrummy (03365) 223.   *Died 12 Sept. 1991.*

FORBES, Muriel Rose, CBE 1963; JP; Alderman, London Borough of Brent, 1972–74; *b* 20 April 1894; *yr d* of John Henry Cheeseright; *m* 1923, Charles Gilbert Forbes (*d* 1957); two *d. Educ:* Gateshead Grammar Sch.; Southlands Teacher Training Coll. Member: Willesden Borough Council, 1936–47; Middlesex CC, 1934–65 (Chm., 1960–61); GLC, 1964–67 (Vice-Chm., 1964–66). Chairman: St Charles's Gp Hosp. Management Cttee, 1968–69; Paddington Gp Hosp. Management Cttee, 1963–68; Mem., Central Middx Hosp. Management Cttee, 1948–63 (Vice-Chm., 1952–63). JP County of Middx, 1946. Hon. DTech Brunel Univ., 1966. *Address:* 9 Rosemary Road, Halesowen, West Midlands B63 1BN.
          Died 18 April 1991.

FORD, Sir Aubrey St C.; *see* St Clair-Ford.

FORD, Elbur; *see* Hibbert, Eleanor.

FORD, Harold Frank; Sheriff at Perth, 1971–80 (Sheriff Substitute at Forfar and Arbroath, 1951–71); *b* 17 May 1915; *s* of Sir Patrick Ford, 1st Bt, and Jessie Hamilton (*d* 1962), *d* of Henry Field, WS; *m* 1948, Lucy Mary, *d* of late Sheriff J. R. Wardlaw Burnet, KC; one *s* three *d. Educ:* Winchester Coll.; University Coll., Oxford (BA); Edinburgh Univ. (LLB). War service with Lothians and Border Yeomanry (Prisoner of War, 1940–45): Hon. Capt. Scottish Bar, 1945; Legal Adviser to UNRRA and IRO in British Zone of Germany, 1947. *Recreations:* golf, gardening. *Address:* Millhill, Meikleour, Perthshire PH2 6EF. *T:* Caputh (073871) 311. *Clubs:* New (Edinburgh); Honourable Company of Edinburgh Golfers, Royal Perth Golfing Society.   *Died 19 June 1994.*

FORD, Joseph Francis, CMG 1960; OBE 1949; HM Diplomatic Service, retired 1970; *b* 11 Oct. 1912; *s* of J. W. Ford, Chesterfield, Derbs; *m* 1938, Mary Margaret (*née* Taylor); two *s. Educ:* Chesterfield Grammar Sch.; Emmanuel Coll., Cambridge (BA). BA (Hons) Modern Chinese, London, 1958. Appointed probationer Vice-Consul to Peking, Nov. 1935; served at Shanghai, Chungking, Washington, Peking, Hanoi, New Orleans and Saigon; Dir, Res. Dept, FCO (formerly Jt Res. Dept, FO/CO), 1967–70; Director: Univs Service Centre, Hong Kong, 1970–72; Great Britain-China Centre, London, 1974–78; Chm., China Soc., 1982–85. *Address:* 10 Raymond Road, Wimbledon, SW19 3RF.
          Died 30 April 1993.

FORD, Raymond Eustace, CBE 1963; MD, MRCP; Principal Medical Officer i/c Regional Medical Service, Ministry of Health, 1946–63, retired; *b* 24 April 1898; *s* of Rev. George Ford; *m* 1924, Elsie (*née* Tipping) (decd); two *s* one *d. Educ:* Sheffield Univ. *Recreations:* crosswords, the garden. *Address:* Philbeach, Hythe, Kent CT21 5UE.   *Died 21 Dec. 1994.*

FORD-ROBERTSON, Francis Calder, OBE 1959; *b* 19 March 1901; 3rd *s* of Dr W. Ford Robertson, MD, and Marion Elam; *m* 1928, Cynthia Mary de Courcy Ireland (*d* 1977); two *s*; *m* 1977, Nora Aline de Courcy Chapman (*née* Ireland). *Educ:* Edinburgh Academy; Edinburgh

Univ. Appointed to Indian Forest Service as probationer, 1923; IFS, 1924–47; Director: Commonwealth Forestry Bureau, Oxford, 1947–64; Dir-Editor, Multilingual Forestry Terminology Project, at Commonwealth Forestry Inst., Oxford and Washington, DC, USA, 1964–70. Hon. Mem., Soc. of American Foresters, 1970. Hon. MA Oxford, 1952. *Publications:* Our Forests, 1934; (ed) The Terminology of Forest Science, Technology, Practice and Products (English lang. version), 1971; also sundry scientific, mainly bibliographical, articles. *Recreations:* choral singing, gardening, local history and archaeology, Oxford guiding. *Address:* 17 Emden House, Barton Lane, Headington, Oxford OX3 9JU. *T:* Oxford (0865) 62431.
Died 7 July 1993.

FORMBY, Myles Landseer, CBE 1962; TD 1946; consulting otolaryngologist, retired: Consultant Emeritus to the Army, since 1971; Surgeon: University College Hospital, 1933–66, then Hon. Consulting Surgeon; Royal Masonic Hospital, 1948–66; *b* 13 March 1901; *s* of Arthur Formby, South Australia; *m* 1st, 1931, Dorothy Hussey Essex (marr. diss. 1952; she *d* 1991); one *s* one *d*; 2nd, 1974, Phyllis Mary Helps (*d* 1986), *d* of late Engr-Comdr G. S. Holgate, RN. *Educ:* St Peter's Coll., Adelaide, South Australia; Univ. of Adelaide; Magdalen Coll., Oxford. Elder Scholarship, Univ. of Adelaide, 1920 and 1921, Everard Scholarship, 1924; MB, BS Adelaide, 1924; Rhodes Scholar for S Australia, 1925; BA Oxford, 1927; BSc Oxford, 1928; FRCS 1930; MA Oxford, 1953. Hon. Asst Surg., Ear, Nose and Throat Hosp., Golden Square, 1931; Hon. Surg., Ear, Nose and Throat, Miller Gen. Hosp., 1932; Hon. Asst Surg., Ear, Nose and Throat Dept, University Coll. Hosp., 1933, Hon. Surg., 1940; Hon. Surg., Ear, Nose and Throat Dept, Royal Masonic Hosp., 1948. RAMC TA, Lieut, 1932; Capt., 1933; Major, 1939; Lieut-Col, 1941; Brig. Consulting Oto-Rhino-Laryngologist to the Army, 1943; served in the Middle East, Italy, North West Europe and India, in War of 1939–45; Hon. Civilian Consultant to War Office, 1946. Mem. Court of Examiners, Royal College of Surgeons, 1947–53, Mem. Council, 1952–57; Royal Society of Medicine: Hon. Dir of Photography, 1958–61; Pres., Section of Laryngology, 1959–60; Hon. Treas., 1962–68; Hon. Fellow, 1970; Hon. Laryngologist to Royal Academy of Music; Pres., British Assoc. of Otolaryngologists. Bronze Star, USA, 1945. *Publications:* Dental Infection in the Aetiology of Maxillary Sinusitis, 1934; Treatment of Otitis Media, 1938; Nasal Allergy, 1943; chapters in Diseases of the Ear, Nose and Throat, 1952; The Maxillary Sinus, 1960; Ultrasonic Destruction of the Labyrinth, 1963. *Recreations:* rowing, lacrosse, golf. *Address:* Thorndene, Kithurst Lane, Storrington, West Sussex RH20 4LP. *T:* Storrington (09066) 2564. *Clubs:* Royal Automobile; Leander (Henley-on-Thames).
Died 20 Jan. 1994.

FORMSTON, Prof. Clifford; Professor of Veterinary Surgery in the University of London, 1943–74, then Emeritus; former Vice-Principal, Royal Veterinary College (1963); *b* 15 Jan. 1907; *s* of Alfred and Annie Formston; *m* 1934, Irene Pembleton (*d* 1973), *d* of Capt. Roland Wood; one *s* one *d*. *Educ:* Chester City Grammar Sch.; Royal Veterinary College, London. MRCVS 1928; FRCVS 1944. Mem. of Royal Veterinary Coll. staff, 1928–74, Fellow, 1974. Member of Council: BVA, 1949–55; RCVS, 1954–62. John Jeyes' Travel Scholarship, 1937; Visiting Professor: Univ. of Cairo, 1960; Univ. of Thessaloniki, 1966; Pahlavi Univ., Iran, 1975; Alfateh Univ., Libya, 1977, 1981; Sir Frederick Hobday Meml Lectr, 1971. Examiner in Veterinary Surgery, Nairobi Univ., 1977. Past President: Royal Counties Veterinary Assoc.; Central Veterinary Soc.; British Equine Veterinary Assoc. Examiner in veterinary surgery to Univs of Bristol, Cambridge, Dublin, Glasgow,

Liverpool, London, Edinburgh and Khartoum; Hon. Res. Fellow, Inst. of Ophthalmology; Hon. Cons. Veterinary Surg. to Childe-Beale Trust. Pres., 1975–86, Patron, 1986–, Vet. Benevolent Fund; Life Vice-Pres., Riding for the Disabled Assoc.; Veterinary Patron, Diamond Riding Centre for the Handicapped; Vice-Pres., Battersea Dogs Home. Hon. Fellow, Farriers' Co., 1984. Blaine Award, 1971; John Henry Steel Meml Medallist, 1973; Simon Award, 1974; Victory Medal, Central Vet. Soc., 1975. *Publications:* contrib. scientific jls on general surgery and ophthalmology. *Recreations:* golf, gardening, reading. *Address:* 4 Marlow Court, Chase Side, Southgate, N14 5HR.
Died 22 Nov. 1993.

FORREST, John Samuel, MA, DSc; FRS 1966; FEng 1976; FInstP; Visiting Professor of Electrical Engineering, University of Strathclyde, 1964–90, then Emeritus; *b* 20 Aug. 1907; *m* 1st, 1940, Ivy May Olding (*d* 1976); one *s*; 2nd, 1985, Joan Mary Downie. *Educ:* Hamilton Acad.; Glasgow Univ. Physicist, Central Electricity Board: Glasgow, 1930; London, 1931; i/c of CEB Research Lab., 1934–40; Founder, 1940, Central Electricity Research Labs, Leatherhead, Dir, 1940–73; Sec., Electricity Supply Research Council, 1949–72. Hunter Memorial Lectr, 1961; Baird Memorial Lectr, 1963, 1975, 1979; Faraday Lectures, 1963–64; Kelvin Lecture, Royal Philosophical Soc. of Glasgow, 1971; Maurice Lubbock Meml Lecture, 1975. Mem. Bd, Inst. of Physics, 1945–49; Chm., London Br. Inst. of Physics, 1954–58; Chm., Supply Sect. of IEE, 1961–62; Chm., British Nat. Cttee, Conférence Internationale des Grands Réseaux Electriques, 1972–76; Pres., Sect. A, Brit. Assoc., 1963; Member Council: IEE; Royal Meteorological Society, 1945–47; Research Associations; Vice-Pres., Royal Soc., 1972–75. Hon. FIEE. Foreign Associate, Nat. Acad. of Engrg of USA, 1979. Hon. DSc: Strathclyde, 1969; Heriot-Watt, 1972. Coopers Hill War Memorial Prize and Medal, 1941; Willans Medal, 1958. *Publications:* papers on electrical power transmission and insulation. *Address:* Arbores, Portsmouth Road, Thames Ditton, Surrey KT7 0EG. *T:* 081–398 4389.
Died 11 Nov. 1992.

FORSTER, Norvela Felicia; Founder Chairman and Managing Director of consultancy company researching into marketing and management problems in Europe and overseas; *b* 1931; *m* 1981, Michael, *s* of Norman and Margaret Jones. *Educ:* South Wilts Grammar School, Salisbury; London Univ. BSc Hons. Pres., Bedford Coll. Union Soc. Mem. (C) Birmingham South, European Parlt, 1979–84; contested (C) Birmingham East, European Parly elecn, 1984. Past Member: Hampstead Borough Council; Council, Bow Group. Mem. Council, Management Consultancies Assoc. *Publication:* Chambers of Commerce: a comparative study of their role in the UK and in other EEC countries, 1983. *Address:* IAL Consultants Ltd, 14 Buckingham Palace Road, SW1W 0QP. *T:* 071–828 5036; 6 Regency House, Regency Street, SW1. *T:* 071–821 5749. *Clubs:* Royal Ocean Racing; Royal Mid-Surrey Golf.
Died 30 April 1993.

FORSYTH, William Douglass, OBE 1955; Australian Ambassador, retired 1969; *b* Casterton, Australia, 5 Jan. 1909; of Australian parents; *m* 1935, Thelma Joyce (*née* Sherry); one *s* two *d*. *Educ:* Ballarat High Sch.; Melbourne Univ. (MA, DipEd); Balliol Coll., Oxford (BLitt). Teacher of History, 1931–35; Rockefeller Fellow, Social Studies, Europe, 1936–37 and 1939; Research Fellow, Melbourne Univ., 1940; Editor Austral-Asiatic Bulletin, Melbourne, 1940; Research Sec., Aust. Inst. International Affairs, 1940–41; Australian Dept of Information, 1941–42; Australian Dept of External Affairs, 1942–69: First Sec., 1946; Counsellor, Aust. Embassy, Washington, 1947–48; Aust. rep. Trusteeship Council, 1948 and 1952–55; Sec.-Gen., South Pacific Commission, 1948–51; Australian

Member UN Population Commission, 1946–47; Mem., Australian Delegns to UN General Assembly, 1946–48 and 1951–58, to San Francisco UN Confs, 1945 and 1955; Minister, Australian Mission to UN, 1951–55; Asst-Sec., Dept of External Affairs, Canberra, 1956–59, 1961–63; Australian Minister to Laos, 1959–60; Australian Ambassador to Viet-Nam, 1959–61; Sec.-Gen., South Pacific Commn, Nouméa, 1963–66; Australian Ambassador to Lebanon, 1967–68. South Pacific Consultant, Dept of Foreign Affairs, 1973–74. Vis. Fellow, ANU, 1975. *Publications:* Governor Arthur's Convict System, 1935, reprinted 1970; The Myth of Open Spaces, 1942; Captain Cook's Australian Landfalls, 1970; articles in Economic Record, etc. *Address:* 88 Banks Street, Yarralumla, Canberra, ACT 2600, Australia.

Died 3 March 1993.

FORTESCUE, 7th Earl *cr* 1789; **Richard Archibald Fortescue,** JP; Baron Fortescue 1746; Viscount Ebrington 1789; *b* 14 April 1922; *s* of 6th Earl Fortescue, MC, TD, and 1st wife, Marjorie, OBE (*d* 1964), *d* of late Col C. W. Trotter, CB, TD; *S* father, 1977; *m* 1st, 1949, Penelope Jane (*d* 1959), *d* of late Robert Evelyn Henderson; one *s* one *d*; 2nd, 1961, Margaret Anne (marr. diss. 1987), *d* of Michael Stratton; two *d*; 3rd, 1989, Carolyn Mary, *d* of Clement Hill. *Educ:* Eton; Christ Church, Oxford. Captain Coldstream Guards (Reserve). JP Oxon, 1964. *Heir: s* Viscount Ebrington [*b* 10 May 1951; *m* 1974, Julia, *er d* of Air Cdre J. A. Sowrey; three *d*]. *Address:* House of Lords, SW1. *Club:* White's.   *Died 7 March 1993.*

FORTEVIOT, 3rd Baron *cr* 1917, of Dupplin, Perthshire; **Henry Evelyn Alexander Dewar,** MBE 1943; DL; Bt 1907; Chairman, John Dewar & Sons Ltd, 1954–76; former Director, Distillers Co. Ltd; *b* 23 Feb. 1906; *s* of 1st Baron Forteviot and 2nd wife, Margaret Elizabeth, *d* of late Henry Holland; *S* half-brother 1947; *m* 1933, Cynthia Monica (*d* 1986), *e d* of late Cecil Starkie, Hethe Place, Cowden, Kent; two *s* two *d*. *Educ:* Eton; St John's Coll., Oxford (BA). Served War of 1939–45, with Black Watch (RHR) (MBE). DL Perth, 1961. *Heir: s* Hon. John James Evelyn Dewar [*b* 5 April 1938; *m* 1963, Lady Elisabeth Waldegrave, 3rd *d* of 12th Earl Waldegrave; one *s* three *d*]. *Address:* Dupplin Castle, Perth, Perthshire. *Club:* Brooks's; Royal (Perth).

Died 25 March 1993.

FOSTER, George Arthur C.; *see* Carey-Foster.

FOSTER, Maj.-Gen. Norman Leslie, CB 1961; DSO 1945; *b* 26 Aug. 1909; *s* of late Col A. L. Foster, Wimbledon; *m* 1937, Joan Constance (*d* 1991), *d* of late Canon T. W. E. Drury; two *s*. *Educ:* Westminster; RMA Woolwich. 2nd Lieut, RA, 1929; served War of 1939–45 in Egypt and Italy; CRA 11th Armoured Division, 1955–56; Deputy Military Sec., War Office, 1958–59; Maj.-Gen., 1959; GOC Royal Nigerian Army, 1959–62; Pres., Regular Commissions Board, 1962–65; retired, 1965. Dir of Security (Army), MoD, 1965–73. Security Advr, CSD, 1974–79. Col Comdt, Royal Regt of Artillery, 1966–74. Pres., Truman and Knightley Educnl Trust Ltd, 1982–87 (Chm., 1976–80). *Address:* Besborough, Heath End, Farnham, Surrey GU9 9AR.   *Died 3 Jan. 1995.*

FOSTER-SUTTON, Sir Stafford William Powell, KBE 1957 (OBE (mil.) 1945); Kt 1951; CMG 1948; QC (Jamaica, 1938, Fedn Malaya, 1948); *b* 24 Dec. 1897; *s* of late G. Foster Sutton and Mrs Foster Sutton; *m* 1919, Linda Dorothy, *d* of late John Humber Allwood, OBE, and Mrs Allwood, Enfield, St Ann, Jamaica; one *d* (one *s* decd). *Educ:* St Mary Magdalen Sch.; private tutor. HM Army, 1914–26; served European War, 1914–18, Infantry, RFC and RAF, active service. Called to the Bar, Gray's Inn, 1926; private practice, 1926–36; Solicitor Gen., Jamaica, 1936; Attorney-Gen., Cyprus, 1940; Col Comdg

Cyprus Volunteer Force and Inspector Cyprus Forces, 1941–44; Dir of Man-Power, Kenya, 1944–45; Chm. Labour Advisory Board, Kenya, and Kenya European Service Advisory Board, 1944–48; Mem. for Law and Order and Attorney-Gen., Kenya, 1944–48; Actg Governor, Aug. and Sept. 1947; Attorney-Gen., Malaya, 1948–50; Officer Administering Govt, Malaya, Sept., Dec. 1950; Chief Justice, Fedn of Malaya, 1950–51; Pres. of the West African Court of Appeal, 1951–55; Chief Justice, Fedn of Nigeria, 1955–58; Actg Governor-Gen., Nigeria, May-June 1957. Pres., Pensions Appeal Tribunals for England and Wales, 1958–73. Chairman: Zanzibar Commn of Inquiry, 1961; Kenya Regional and Electorial Commns, 1962; Referendum Observers, Malta, 1964; Vice Pres., Britain-Nigeria Assoc., 1982–. Mem. Court, Tallow Chandlers' Co. (Master, 1981). *Address:* 7 London Road, Saffron Walden, Essex.   *Died 6 Nov. 1991.*

FOWLER, Prof. Gerald Teasdale; Professor Emeritus, University of East London, since 1992; Partner, Enterprise Education Conferences, since 1992; *b* 1 Jan. 1935; *s* of James A. Fowler, Long Buckby, Northants, and Alfreda (*née* Teasdale); *m* 1968, Julie Marguerite, *d* of Wilfrid Brining Slough; *m* 1982, Lorna, *d* of William Lloyd, Preston. *Educ:* Northampton Grammar Sch.; Lincoln Coll., Oxford; University of Frankfurt-am-Main. Craven Fellowship, Oxford Univ., 1957–59; part-time Lectr, Pembroke Coll., Oxford, 1958–59; Lectr, Hertford and Lincoln Colls, Oxford, 1959–65; Lectr, Univ. of Lancaster, 1965–66; Asst Dir, The Polytechnic, Huddersfield, 1970–72; Prof. of Educnl Studies, Open Univ., 1972–74; Prof. Associate, Dept of Government, Brunel Univ., 1977–80; Dep. Dir, Preston Polytechnic, 1980–81; Rector, NE London Poly., subseq. Poly. of E London, 1982–92. Vis. Prof., Dept of Admin, Strathclyde Univ., 1970–74. Chm., Cttee of Dirs of Polytechnics, 1988–90 (Vice Chm., 1986–88). Oxford City Councillor, 1960–64; Councillor, The Wrekin DC, 1973–76, Leader, 1973–74; Councillor, Shropshire CC, 1979–85. Contested (Lab) Banbury, 1964; MP (Lab) The Wrekin, 1966–70, Feb. 1974–1979; Jt Parly Sec., Min. of Technology, 1967–69; Minister of State: Dept of Educn and Science, Oct. 1969–June 1970, March-Oct. 1974 and Jan.-Sept. 1976; Privy Council Office, 1974–76. President: Assoc. for Teaching of Social Science, 1976–79; Assoc. for Recurrent Educn, 1976–78, 1981–85; Assoc. for Liberal Educn, 1977–79; Comparative Educn in Europe Soc. (British Section), 1980; Vice-Pres., Soc. for Research into Higher Educn, 1983–. Chm., Youthaid, 1977–80; Vice Chm., Nat. Parly Youth Lobby, 1978–79. Trustee, Community Projects Foundn, 1978–80. Vice-Chm., Assoc. of Business Executives, 1982– (Pres., 1979–81; Hon. Fellow 1983). FIMgt (FBIM 1984); FRSA 1985. Hon. Fellow, Nene Coll., 1991. *Address:* 4 Princess Road, NW1 8JJ. *T:* (home) 071–722 2606; (business) 071–483 1349.   *Died 1 May 1993.*

FOWLER, Prof. William Alfred, PhD; Institute Professor Emeritus of Physics, California Institute of Technology, since 1982 (Institute Professor of Physics, 1970–82); *b* Pittsburgh, Pa, 9 Aug. 1911; *s* of late John McLeod Fowler and Jennie Summers (*née* Watson); *m* 1st, 1940, Ardiane Foy Olmsted (*d* 1988), Pasadena, Calif; two *d*; 2nd, 1989, Mary Dutcher, Flushing, NY. *Educ:* Ohio State Univ. (BEngPhys); California Inst. of Technology (PhD Phys). Member: Tau Kappa Epsilon; Tau Beta Pi; Sigma Xi. California Inst. of Technology: Research Fellow in Nuclear Physics, 1936–39; Asst Prof. of Physics, 1939–42; Associate Prof. of Physics, 1942–46; Prof. of Physics, 1946–70. Defense record: research and develt proximity fuses, rocket ordnance, and atomic weapons; Research staff mem.: Sect. T, and Div. 4, Nat. Def. Res. Cttee, 1941; Asst Dir of Research, Sect. L. Div. 3, Nat. Def. Res. Cttee, 1941–45; Techn. Observer, Office of Field Services and New Develts Div., War Dept, in South and Southwestern

Pacific Theatres, 1944; Actg Supervisor, Ord. Div., R&D, Naval Ordnance Test Stn, 1945; Sci. Dir, Project VISTA, Dept Defense, 1951–52. Guggenheim Fellow and Fulbright Lectr, Pembroke Coll. and Cavendish Laboratory, Univ. of Cambridge, Eng., 1954–55; Guggenheim Fellow, St John's Coll., and Dept Applied Math. and Theor. Phys., Univ. of Cambridge, Eng., 1961–62; Walker-Ames Prof. of Physics, Univ. of Washington, 1963; Visitor, The Observatories, Univ. of Cambridge, Summer 1964; Vis. Prof. of Physics, Mass Inst. of Technology, 1966; Vis. Fellow, Inst. of Theoretical Astronomy, Univ. of Cambridge, Summers 1967–72. Numerous lectureships in USA, 1957–; those given abroad include: Lectr, Internat. Sch. of Physics "Enrico Fermi", Varenna, 1965; Lectr, Advanced Sch. on Cosmic Physics, Erice, Italy, 1969, 1982, in addition to past lectures at Cavendish Laboratory, Cambridge; also Lectr at Research Sch. of Physical Sciences, Australian National Univ., Canberra, 1965; Jubilee Lectr, 50th Anniversary, Niels Bohr Inst., Copenhagen, 1970; Scott Lectr, Cavendish Laboratory, Cambridge Univ., 1971; George Darwin Lectr, RAS, 1973; E. A. Milne Lectr, Milne Soc., 1986; 22nd Liège Internat. Astrophysical Symposium, 1978; Vis. Scholar, Phi Beta Kappa, 1980–81. Member: Nat. Science Bd, Nat. Science Foundation, USA, 1968–74; Space Science Bd, Nat. Academy of Sciences, 1970–73 and 1977–80; Space Program Adv. Council, NASA, 1971–74; Bd of Directors, American Friends of Cambridge Univ., 1970–78; Governing Bd, Amer. Inst. of Physics, 1974–80; Cttee Chm., Nuclear Science Adv. Cttee, Nat. Science Foundn/Dept of Energy, USA, 1977–79; Chm., Off. Phys. Sci., Nat. Acad. Sci., 1981–82; Mem. Review Cttee APS Study: Radionuclide Release in Severe Accidents of Nuclear Power Reactors, 1984. Attended numerous conferences, congresses and assemblies. Member: Internat. Astron. Union; Amer. Assoc. for Advancement of Science; Amer. Assoc. of Univ. Professors; Nat. Acad. of Sciences; Mem. corres., Soc. Royale des Sciences de Liège; Fellow: Amer. Physical Soc. (Pres., 1976); Amer. Acad. of Arts and Sciences; British Assoc. for Advancement of Science; Benjamin Franklin Fellow, RSA; ARAS. Hon. Member: Mark Twain Soc.; Soc. Amer. Baseball Res., 1980; Naturvetenskapliga Foreningen, 1984. Hon. Fellow, Pembroke Coll., Cambridge, 1992. Hon. DSc: Chicago, 1976; Ohio State, 1978; Denison, 1982; Arizona State, 1985; Georgetown, 1986; Massachusetts, 1987; Williams Coll., 1988; Dr hc: Liège, 1981; Observatory of Paris, 1981. Various awards and medals for science etc, both at home and abroad, including Medal for Merit, USA, 1948; Vetlesen Prize, 1973; Nat. Medal of Sci., 1974; Eddington Medal, RAS, 1978; Bruce Gold Medal, Astron. Soc. Pacific, 1979; (jtly) Nobel Prize for Physics, 1983; Sullivant Medal, Ohio State Univ., 1985; first William A. Fowler Award for Excellence in Physics, Ohio section, APS, 1986. Officier, Légion d'Honneur (France), 1989. *Publications:* contributor to: Physical Review, Astrophysical Jl, Proc. Nat. Acad. of Sciences, Amer. Jl of Physics, Geophysical Jl, Nature, Royal Astronomical Soc., etc. *Address:* Kellogg Radiation Laboratory 106–38, California Institute of Technology, Pasadena, CA 91125, USA. *Clubs:* Cosmos (Washington, DC); Athenæum (Pasadena, Calif); Cambridge and District Model Engineering Society. *Died 14 March 1995.*

FOX, Prof. Leslie, DSc Oxon; Professor of Numerical Analysis, Oxford University, and Professorial Fellow, Balliol College, 1963–83, then Emeritus Fellow; Director, Oxford University Computing Laboratory, 1957–82; *b* 30 Sept. 1918; *m* 1st, 1943, Paulene Dennis; 2nd, 1973, Mrs Clemency Clements, *er d* of Thomas Fox. *Educ:* Wheelwright Grammar Sch., Dewsbury; Christ Church, Oxford. Admiralty Computing Service, 1943–45; Mathematics Div., Nat. Physical Laboratory, 1945–56;

Associate Prof., Univ. of California, Berkeley, 1956–57; Research Prof., Univ. of Illinois, 1961–62; Vis. Prof., Open Univ., 1970–71. Pres., Math./Phys Section, BAAS, 1975. Hon. Chm., 10th Canadian Conf. on Applied Mechanics, Univ. of Western Ontario, 1985. Hon. FIMA 1989. DUniv Open, 1986. *Publications:* Numerical Solution of Boundary-value Problems in Ordinary Differential Equations, 1957; (ed) Numerical Solution of Ordinary and Partial Differential Equations, 1962; An Introduction to Numerical Linear Algebra, 1964; (ed) Advances in Programming and Non-Numerical Computation, 1966; Chebyshev Polynomials in Numerical Analysis (with I. J. Parker), 1968; Computing Methods for Scientists and Engineers (with D. F. Mayers), 1968; Numerical Solution of Ordinary Differential Equations for Scientists and Engineers (with D. F. Mayers), 1987; numerous papers in learned journals. *Recreations:* sport, music, literature. *Address:* 2 Elsfield Road, Marston, Oxford OX3 0PR. *T:* Oxford (0865) 722668.
Died 1 Aug. 1992.

FOX, William; President, Football League, since 1989; *b* 6 Jan. 1928; *s* of Thomas Fox and Doris Fox (*née* Jones); *m* 1953, Marjorie Hindle; one *s* three *d.* *Educ:* Queen Elizabeth's Grammar Sch., Blackburn. Enlisted 1946, Ballykinlar (Nat. Service), RA; transf. to East Lancs Regt, Corp. 1947, demob. 1948 as small arms instructor. Joined family potato business, 1943; Chm., Wholesale Potato Co., 1968–88, retired. Nat. Fruit and Potato Trades Fedn Rep. on Jt Consultative and Ware Imports Cttees, Potato Marketing Bd; Man. Dir, Fox Commercial Vehicles (Renault main dealers), 1980–88. Bd Mem., Blackburn Rovers FC, 1976– (Vice-Chm., 1979–82; Chm., 1982–); Member: FA (Vice-Pres.); Football League Management Cttee, 1986–. *Recreation:* football only. *Address:* Treetops, Billinge End Road, Blackburn BB2 6PT.
Died 8 Dec. 1991.

FRAME, Sir Alistair (Gilchrist), Kt 1981; MA, BSc; FEng 1978; Chairman: RTZ (formerly Rio Tinto-Zinc) Corporation, 1985–91 (non-executive, 1990–91); Wellcome plc, 1990–93; British Steel, 1992–93 (Director, 1991–93); *b* Dalmuir, Dunbartonshire, 3 April 1929; *s* of Alexander Frame and Mary (*née* Fraser); *m* 1953, Sheila (*née* Mathieson); one *d.* *Educ:* Glasgow and Cambridge Univs (Hon. Fellow, Fitzwilliam Coll., Cambridge, 1985). Director, Reactor and Research Groups, UK Atomic Energy Authority, 1964–68; joined Rio Tinto-Zinc Corp., 1968; appointed to main Board, 1973, Chief Exec. and Dep. Chm., 1978–85. Chm., Davy Corp., 1990–91; Director: Plessey Co., 1978–88; Britoil, 1983–84; Eurotunnel, 1990–. Member: NEB, 1978–79; Engineering Council, 1982–83; Chm., Council of Mining and Metall. Instns, 1983–. Hon. DEng Birmingham, 1989; Hon. DSc: Glasgow, 1990; Buckingham, 1992. *Recreations:* tennis, gardening, walking. *Club:* Royal Automobile.
Died 26 Dec. 1993.

FRANCIS, Sir Richard (Trevor Langford), KCMG 1989; Director-General, British Council, since 1987; *b* 10 March 1934; *s* of Eric Roland Francis and Esther Joy (*née* Todd); *m* 1st, 1958, Beate Ohlhagen (marr. diss.); two *s*; 2nd, 1974, Elizabeth Penelope Anne Fairfax Crone; two *s.* *Educ:* Uppingham Sch.; University Coll., Oxford. BA 1956, MA 1960. Commissioned in RA, 1957. BBC Trainee, 1958–60; BBC Television: Prodn Asst, 1960–62; Producer: afternoon programmes, 1962–63; Panorama, 1963–65; Asst Editor: Panorama, 1965–66; 24 Hours, 1966–67; Projects Editor, Current Affairs, 1967–70; Head, EBU Operations for US Elections and Apollo, 1968–69; Head of Special Projects, Current Affairs, 1970–71; Asst Head, Current Affairs Group, 1971–73; Head, EBU Operations for US Elections, 1972; Controller, BBC NI, 1973–77; Dir, News and Current Affairs, BBC, 1977–82;

Man. Dir, BBC Radio, 1982–86. Visnews: Dir, 1978; Dep. Chm., 1979–82. Member: British Exec., IPI, 1978–82 (Dep. Chm., 1982–86); Press Complaints Commn, 1991–. Hon. Pres., Radio Acad., 1986–. Trustee, Charities Aid Foundn, 1991–. Gov., Westminster Coll., Oxford, 1990–. Hon. Freeman, City of Freetown, Sierra Leone, 1991. CBIM 1984; FRSA 1988; FKC 1991. *Recreations:* offshore sailing, photography, listening to music 6 miles high. *Address:* c/o British Council, 10 Spring Gardens, SW1A 2BN. *Clubs:* Reform, Garrick, Arts; Chichester Yacht. *Died 26 June 1992.*

FRANCKENSTEIN, Baroness Joseph von; *see* Boyle, Kay.

FRANKEL, Dr Paul Herzberg, CBE 1981; FInstPet; Life President, PEL Group, since 1987; *b* 1 Nov. 1903; *s* of Ludwig and Teresa Herzberg-Frankel; *m* 1931, Helen Spitzer; one *s* four *d. Educ:* Vienna Univ. (Dr of Polit. Econ.). FInstPet 1941. Actively engaged in oil industry, mainly in oil refining and marketing, first on Continent and then in UK, mid 1930s-; Dir of Manchester Oil Refinery Ltd and associated cos in UK and on Continent until 1955; founded Petroleum Economics Ltd, the London internat. consulting firm, 1955, Chm., 1955–80, Pres., 1980–87. Chevalier de la Légion d'Honneur, 1976; Grosses Verdienstkreuz des Verdienstordens, Bundesrepublik Deutschland, 1977; Grosses Ehrenzeichen für Verdienste, Republik Osterreich, 1978; Cavaliere Ufficiale dell'Ordine al Merito della Repubblica Italiana, 1988; Goldenes Ehrenzeichen fuer Verdienste um Das Land Wien, 1988. Cadman Medal, Inst. of Petroleum, 1973; Award for outstanding contributions to profession of energy economics and its literature, Internat. Assoc. of Energy Economists, 1985. *Publications:* Essentials of Petroleum, 1946; Oil: the facts of life, 1962; Mattei: oil and power politics, 1966; Paul Frankel: a common carrier of common sense, 1989. *Recreations:* walking, music. *Address:* 30 Dunstall Road, SW20 0HR. *T:* 081–946 5805. *Club:* Reform. *Died 21 Oct. 1992.*

FRANKLIN, Richard Harrington, CBE 1973; Consultant Emeritus to the Royal Navy (Consulting Surgeon, 1961–81); Hon. Visiting Surgeon, Royal Postgraduate Medical School (Surgeon, 1945–71); Emeritus Consultant Surgeon to Kingston and Long Grove Group of Hospitals (Surgeon, Kingston, 1946–71); *b* 3 April 1906; *s* of late P. C. Franklin; *m* 1933, Helen Margaret Kimber (*d* 1987), *d* of Sir Henry Dixon Kimber, 2nd Bt; one *s* (and one *s* decd). *Educ:* Merchant Taylors' Sch.; St Thomas' Hosp., London Univ. MRCS, LRCP 1930; MB, BS 1930; FRCS 1934. First Asst, Brit. Postgrad. Med. Sch., 1936; Surgeon EMS, 1940–45. Hunterian Prof., RCS, 1947; Bradshaw Lectr, 1973; Grey-Turner Lectr, Internat. Soc. Surg., 1973; Hunterian Orator, RCS, 1977. Vis. Prof., Univ. of California, 1972. Mem. Ct of Examrs, RCS, 1956–66; Examr in Surgery, Cambridge Univ., 1958–69. Vice-Pres. 1960, Pres. 1969–70, Sect. of Surgery, RSM; Mem. Council, RCS, 1965–77, Vice-Pres., 1974–76; Mem. Council, Imperial Cancer Research Fund, 1967–82 (Vice-Chm., 1975–79), Life Governor, 1975. Hon. Consulting Surgeon, Star and Garter Home, Richmond, 1957–85, Governor, 1969–85. Hon. Mem., Hellenic Surgical Soc. *Publications:* Surgery of the Oesophagus, 1952; articles in various med. jls and text books. *Recreation:* sailing. *Address:* The Stern Walk, Crespigny Road, Aldeburgh, Suffolk IP15 5EZ. *T:* Aldeburgh (072885) 2600. *Clubs:* Ranelagh Sailing, Aldeburgh Yacht.
Died 15 Sept. 1991.

FRANKS, Baron *cr* 1962 (Life Peer), of Headington ; **Oliver Shewell Franks,** OM 1977; GCMG 1952; KCB 1946; KCVO 1985; CBE 1942; PC 1949; DL; FBA 1960; Provost of Worcester College, Oxford, 1962–76; Chancellor of East Anglia University, 1965–84; Lord

Warden of the Stannaries and Keeper of the Privy Seal of the Duke of Cornwall, 1983–85; *b* 16 Feb. 1905; *s* of late Rev. R. S. Franks and Katharine Shewell; *m* 1931, Barbara Mary Tanner (*d* 1987); two *d. Educ:* Bristol Grammar Sch.; Queen's Coll., Oxford (MA). Fellow and Praelector in Philosophy, Queen's College, Oxford, 1927–37; University Lecturer in Philosophy, Oxford, 1935–37; Visiting Prof., Univ. of Chicago, 1935; Prof. of Moral Philosophy, University of Glasgow, 1937–45; temp. Civil Servant, Ministry of Supply, 1939–46; Permanent Sec. Ministry of Supply, 1945–46; Provost of Queen's Coll., Oxford, 1946–48; British Ambassador at Washington, 1948–52; Director: Lloyds Bank Ltd, 1953–75 (Chm., 1954–62); Schroders, 1969–84; Chm., Friends' Provident & Century Life Office, 1955–62; Cttee of London Clearing Bankers, 1960–62. Mem. of Rhodes Trust 1957–73; Chairman: Bd of Governors, United Oxford Hosps, 1958–64; Wellcome Trust, 1965–82 (Trustee, 1963–65); Commission of Inquiry into Oxford Univ., 1964–66; Cttee on Official Secrets Act, Section 2, 1971–72; Cttee on Ministerial Memoirs, 1976; Political Honours Scrutiny Cttee, 1976–87; Falkland Is Review Cttee, 1982. Mem., National Economic Development Council, 1962–64. Mem. Council, Duchy of Cornwall, 1966–85. Pres., Kennedy Memorial Cttee, 1963; Trustee: Pilgrim Trust, 1947–79; Rockefeller Foundn, 1961–70. Hon. Fellow: Queen's Coll., Oxford, 1948; St Catharine's Coll., Cambridge, 1966; Wolfson Coll., Oxford, 1967; Worcester Coll., Oxford, 1976; Lady Margaret Hall, Oxford, 1978; London Business Sch., 1988; Visiting Fellow, Nuffield Coll., 1959. Hon. DCL Oxford, and other honorary doctorates. DL Oxfordshire, 1978. *Address:* Blackhall Farm, Garford Road, Oxford OX2 6UY. *T:* Oxford (0865) 511286. *Club:* Athenæum. *Died 15 Oct. 1992.*

FRASER, Sir Basil (Malcolm), 2nd Bt, *cr* 1921, of Cromarty; *b* 2 Jan. 1920; *s* of Sir (John) Malcolm Fraser, 1st Bt, GBE, and Irene, *d* of C. E. Brightman of South Kensington; *S* father, 1949. *Educ:* Northaw, Pluckley, Kent; Eton Coll.; Queens' Coll., Cambridge (MA 1950). Served War of 1939–45: RE, 1940–42; Madras Sappers and Miners, 1942–46 (despatches). Mem. AA and RAC. *Recreations:* motoring, music, electronic reproduction of sound. *Heir:* none. *Address:* 175 Beach Street, Deal, Kent CT14 6LE. *Club:* Roadfarers'.
Died 9 April 1992 (ext).

FRASER, Sir Bruce (Donald), KCB 1961 (CB 1956); *b* 18 Nov. 1910; *s* of late Maj.-Gen. Sir Theodore Fraser, KCB and Constance Ruth Fraser (*née* Stevenson); *m* 1939, Audrey (*d* 1982), *d* of late Lieut-Col E. L. Croslegh; (one *s* decd one *d* decd). *Educ:* Bedford Sch.; Trinity Coll., Cambridge (Scholar); First Class in Classical Tripos Part I, 1930 and in English Tripos Part II, 1932; BA 1932, MA 1964. Ed., Granta, 1932. Entered Civil Service as Asst Principal, Scottish Office, 1933; transf. to HM Treasury, 1936; Private Sec. to Financial Sec., 1937, and to Permanent Sec., 1941; Asst Sec., 1945; Under Sec., 1951; Third Sec., 1956–60; Dep. Sec., Ministry of Aviation, Jan.-April 1960; Permanent Sec., Ministry of Health, 1960–64; Joint Permanent Under-Sec. of State, Dept of Education and Science, 1964–65; Permanent Sec., Ministry of Land and Natural Resources, 1965–66; Comptroller and Auditor-General, Exchequer and Audit Dept, 1966–71. Hon. DLitt Wales, 1989. *Publication:* Sir Ernest Gowers' The Complete Plain Words, rev. edn 1973. *Address:* Jonathan, St Dogmael's, Cardigan SA43 3LF. *T:* Cardigan (0239) 612387. *Died 22 Aug. 1993.*

FRASER, Col Hugh Vincent, CMG 1957; OBE 1946; TD 1947; retired 1960; *b* 20 Sept. 1908; *yr s* of William Neilson and Maude Fraser; *m* 1941, Noreen, *d* of Col M. O'C. Tandy; one *s* one *d. Educ:* Sherborne Sch. Commissioned into Royal Tank Regt; served War of

1939–45, India and Burma, with 14th Army. Military Attaché, Cairo, 1954–56; NATO, Washington DC, 1957–60. *Recreations:* hunting (Master Aldershot Command Beagles, 1939), shooting. *Address:* Cheyney Holt, Steeple Morden, Herts SG8 0LX.

Died 7 Feb. 1993.

FRASER, Prof. (Thomas) Russell (Cumming), MD, FRCP; Deputy Director, Medical Research Council, New Zealand, 1975–81, retired; *b* 25 Dec. 1908; *s* of Malcolm Fraser and Caroline (*née* Watson). *Educ:* Otago Univ. Medical School. MB, ChB (distinction) 1932; MRCP 1936; DPM (Eng.) 1937; MD (NZ) 1945; FRCP 1948. Hallett Prize, 1935; NZ University Travel Fellowship, 1935; Rockefeller Travel Fellowship, 1938. Formerly Asst Med. Officer, Maudsley Hosp.; Research Fellow in Medicine, Harvard Univ.; Reader in Medicine, Postgrad. Med. Sch., London; Prof. of Clinical Endocrinology in Univ. of London, RPMS, 1957–74. Member: Assoc. Physicians of Gt Brit.; Med. Research Soc. Hon. DSc NZ, 1975. *Publications:* contribs to medical journals. *Address:* 19B Long Drive, St Heliers, Auckland 5, New Zealand.

Died 26 June 1994.

FRASER-TYTLER, Christian Helen, CBE (mil.) 1941; TD; Senior Controller Auxiliary Territorial Service, retired; *b* 23 Aug. 1897; *d* of John Campbell Shairp, Houstoun; *m* 1919, Col Neil Fraser-Tytler, DSO, Croix de Guerre (*d* 1937); two *d*. *Educ:* home. Foreign Office, 1917–19; War Office, 1939–43 (Dep. Dir of Orgns, ATS, 1941–43); ATS/AA Command, 1943–45 (TD). *Recreation:* fishing. *Address:* Craigmount, The Scores, St Andrews KY16 9AS. *T:* St Andrews (01334) 76826.

Died 30 June 1995.

FREEBODY, Air Vice-Marshal Wilfred Leslie, CB 1951; CBE 1943; AFC; retired; *b* 28 Feb. 1906. RAF Technical Branch; Director of Work Study, at Air Ministry; Squadron Leader, 1937; Acting Air Commodore commanding 226 Group, Air Cdre, 1949; Actg Air Vice-Marshal, 1956; Air Vice-Marshal, 1957. Order of Polonia Restituta 3rd class, Poland. *Club:* Royal Air Force.

Died 8 May 1991.

FREEDMAN, Hon. Samuel; Chief Justice of Manitoba, 1971–83; Counsel to Aikins, MacAulay & Thorvaldson, 1983–88, retired; *b* Russia, 16 April 1908; *s* of Nathan Freedman and Ada (*née* Foxman); came to Canada, 1911; *m* 1934, Claris Brownie Udow; one *s* two *d*. *Educ:* Winnipeg schs; Univ. of Manitoba. BA 1929, LLB 1933. Called to Manitoba Bar, 1933; KC (Canada) 1944; Judge, Court of Queen's Bench, Manitoba, 1952, Court of Appeal 1960. Chancellor, Univ. of Manitoba, 1959–68; Pres., Manitoba Bar Assoc., 1951–52; Mem. Bd of Governors, Hebrew Univ., Jerusalem, 1955; Chm., Rhodes Scholarship Selection Cttee, Manitoba, 1956–66; Pres., Medico-Legal Soc. of Manitoba, 1954–55; Mem. Adv. Bd, Centre of Criminology, Univ. of Toronto; Mem. Bd of Dirs, Confedn Centre of the Arts in Charlottetown; one-man Industrial Inquiry Commn, CNR run-throughs, 1964–65. Numerous hon. degrees. *Publications:* Report of Industrial Inquiry Commission on Canadian National Railways Run-Throughs, 1965; (chapter) Admissions and Confessions, in, Studies in Canadian Criminal Evidence, ed Salhany and Carter, 1972; contrib. Canadian Bar Review. *Recreations:* walking, golf, reading. *Address:* 6B–221 Wellington Crescent, Winnipeg, Manitoba R3M 0A1, Canada. *Club:* Glendale Country (Winnipeg).

Died 6 March 1993.

FREEMAN, (Edgar) James (Albert), MC 1945; Regional Chairman of Industrial Tribunals, Bury St Edmunds, 1984–90; *b* 31 Dec. 1917; *yr s* of Horace Freeman and Beatrice Mary Freeman, Cricklewood; *m* 1948, Shirley Lake Whatmough (*d* 1988), *d* of William Henry

Whatmough, PhD, and Agnes Caroline Whatmough, Streatham; one *s* two *d*. *Educ:* Westminster Sch.; Trinity Coll., Cambridge (BA). Served in DLI, UK, India and Burma, 1940–46. Called to Bar, Lincoln's Inn, 1947; practised Chancery Bar, 1947–72; Vice-Pres., Value Added Tax Tribunals (England and Wales), 1972–90; full-time Chm. of Industrial Tribunals, 1975–90. *Recreations:* sailing, cycling. *Address:* 45 Nightingale Avenue, Cambridge CB1 4SG. *Clubs:* Royal Cruising, Bar Yacht.

Died 29 Feb. 1992.

FREEMAN, Harold Webber; author; *b* 28 March 1899; *s* of Charles Albert Freeman and Emma Mary Ann Mills; *m* Elizabeth Boedecker. *Educ:* City of London Sch.; Christ Church, Oxford (classical scholar). 1st class Hon. Mods, 2nd class Lit. Hum. Main background was work on the land, mostly organic gardening; travelled in Europe (foot and bicycle); casual work as linguist (translation, monitoring, travel trade). Lived mostly in Suffolk, but also, for long periods, in Italy. *Publications:* Joseph and His Brethren, 1928; Down in the Valley, 1930; Fathers of Their People, 1932; Pond Hall's Progress, 1933; Hester and Her Family, 1936; Andrew to the Lions, 1938; Chaffinch's, 1941; Blenheim Orange, 1949; The Poor Scholar's Tale, 1954; Round the Island: Sardinia Re-explored, 1956. *Address:* c/o National Westminster Bank, 2 Tavern Street, Ipswich.

Died 18 Feb. 1994.

FREEMAN, James; see Freeman, E. J. A.

FREEMAN, His Eminence Cardinal Sir James Darcy, KBE 1977; *b* 19 Nov. 1907; *s* of Robert Freeman and Margaret Smith. *Educ:* Christian Brothers' High School, St Mary's Cathedral, Sydney; St Columba's Coll., Springwood, NSW; St Patrick's Coll., Manly, NSW. Priest, 1930; Private Secretary to HE Cardinal Gilroy, Archbishop of Sydney, 1941–46; Auxiliary Bishop to HE Cardinal Gilroy, 1957; Bishop of Armidale, 1968; Archbishop of Sydney, 1971–83. Cardinal, 1973. KHS 1965. Hon. DD 1957. *Address:* PO Box 246, Randwick, NSW 2031, Australia. *T:* 3998564.

Died 16 March 1991.

FRERE, James Arnold, FSA, FRGS; *b* 20 April 1920; *e s* of late John Geoffrey Frere. *Educ:* Eton Coll.; Trinity Coll., Cambridge. Lieut Intelligence Corps, 1944–47; Regular Army R of O, 1949–67. Bluemantle Pursuivant of Arms, 1948–56; Earl Marshal's Office for the Queen's Coronation and i/c robing arrangements in Westminster Abbey, 1952–53; Chester Herald of Arms, 1956–60; an Officer of Supreme Court of Judicature, 1966–70. Member: Surrey Archæological Soc. (Council, 1949–53, 1954–58 and 1959–63); American Soc. of Authors; Council of the Harleian Soc., 1951–66; Hon. Mem. Heraldry Soc. of Southern Africa, 1953–; a Vice-Pres. of Museum of Costume, 1952–60. Press Sec., New Gallery Clinic, 1967–70. Liveryman, Worshipful Co. of Scriveners, 1950 (latterly Sen. Liveryman). Hon. Consul for Poland (in exile), Powys, 1984–90. Mountjoy King of Arms and Judge-at-Arms, Internat. Coll. of Arms of Noblesse, 1982–; Rey de Armas y Cronista de Perpiñan, 1986; Pres., Real Colegio Heraldicó de Aragona, 1987; Head of Ceremonial and Protocol, Royal House of Aragon, 1988; Grand Master of Ceremonies, Supreme Military Order of Temple of Jerusalem. Marqués de la Unión, Spain, 1808; Marchese de la Unión, Aragón, 1986; Marchese Frere, Aragon, 1989. KM 1959; Knight Grand Cross, and Clairvaux King of Arms, SMO of Temple of Jerusalem, 1981; Kt of Justice of Our Lady of Monteza, 1988; Kt, Royal Order of James I of Aragon, 1989; Kt, Order of St George and the Double Crown, 1990; Knight Grand Cross: Mil. Order of the Collar of St Agatha of Paterno', 1987; Order of the Royal Crown of the Balearics, 1987. Commander's Cross, Polonia Restituta, 1983; Polish Gold Cross of Merit, 1983. *Publications:* The British Monarchy at Home, 1963; (with the Duchess of Bedford) Now . . . The Duchesses, 1964. *Recreations:* walking, painting, archæology. *Address:* c/o Society of Antiquaries, Burlington House, Piccadilly, W1V 0HS. *Club:* City Livery.   *Died 26 Nov. 1994.*

FRETWELL, Sir George (Herbert), KBE 1953; CB 1950; Director General of Works, Air Ministry, 1947–59, retired; *b* 21 March 1900; *s* of late Herbert Fretwell, Ripley, Derbyshire; *m* 1930, Constance Mabel, *d* of late George Ratcliffe, Woodford Green, Essex; no *c. Educ:* Heanor Grammar Sch., Derbs. Entered Air Ministry as Asst Civil Engineer, 1928; service in Inland area RAF, Aden, South Arabia and Air Defence Gp; Civil Engineer, 1934; Superintending Engineer, RAF Malaya, 1937; Chief Engineer, Far East Command, 1940; Chief Supt of Design (Works), 1941; Chief Engr ADGB/Fighter Command, 1944; Dep. Dir of Works, Air Min., 1945, Dir, 1946. *Address:* North Lodge, 2 North Street, Sheringham, Norfolk NR26 8LW. *T:* Sheringham (0263) 822336.
                                      Died 16 March 1991.

FREYBERG, 2nd Baron, *cr* 1951, of Wellington, New Zealand, and of Munstead in the Co. of Surrey; **Paul Richard Freyberg,** OBE 1965; MC 1945; *b* 27 May 1923; *s* of 1st Baron Freyberg, VC, GCMG, KCB, KBE, DSO (and 3 bars), and Barbara, GBE (*d* 1973), *d* of Sir Herbert Jekyll, KCMG, and Lady Jekyll, DBE; *S* father, 1963; *m* 1960, Ivry Perronelle Katharine Guild, Aspall Hall, Debenham, Suffolk; one *s* three *d. Educ:* Eton Coll. Joined NZ Army, 1940; served with 2nd NZEF: Greece, 1941; Western Desert, 1941–42; transferred to British Army, 1942; Grenadier Guards; North Africa, 1943; Italy, 1943–45 (MC); Palestine, 1947–48; Cyprus, 1956–58; British Cameroons, 1961; Comd HAC Infantry Battalion, 1965–68; Defence Policy Staff, MoD, 1968–71; Dir Volunteers, Territorials and Cadets, 1971–75; Col, Gen. Staff, 1975–78, retired. Staff Coll., 1952; jssc 1958; sowc 1971. *Publication:* Bernard Freyberg, VC: soldier of two nations, 1991. *Heir: s* Hon. Valerian Bernard Freyberg, *b* 15 Dec. 1970. *Address:* Munstead House, Godalming, Surrey GU8 4AR. *T:* Godalming (0483) 416004. *Clubs:* Boodle's, Royal Automobile.   *Died 26 May 1993.*

FRIEND, Bernard Ernest, CBE 1986; Chairman: Supervisory Board, Ballast Nedam (Holland), since 1989; Brooke Tool Engineering (Holdings), since 1990 (Director, since 1989); *b* 18 May 1924; *s* of Richard Friend and Ada Florence Friend; *m* 1951, Pamela Florence Amor; one *s* two *d. Educ:* Dover Grammar Sch. Chartered Accountant. Flying Officer, RAF, 1943–47. Arthur Young & Co., Chartered Accountants, 1948–55; Comptroller, Esso Petroleum Co. Ltd, 1961–66; Dep. Controller, Esso Europe, 1967–68; Man. Dir, Essoheat, 1968–69; Vice-Pres., Esso Chemicals, Brussels, 1970–73; Chm. and Man. Dir, Esso Chemicals Ltd, 1974–76; Dir, British Aerospace, 1977–89 (Finance Dir, 1977–88). Chm., Graham Rintoul Investment Trust, 1987–. Non-Executive Director: Iron Trades Insurance Gp, 1980–; SD-Scicon, 1988–. *Address:* 27 Archer House, Vicarage Crescent, Battersea, SW11 3LF. *Club:* Royal Air Force.   *Died 23 Dec. 1993.*

FRINK, Dame Elisabeth (Jean), CH 1992; DBE 1982 (CBE 1969); RA 1977 (ARA 1971); sculptor; *b* Thurlow, Suffolk, 14 Nov. 1930; British; *m* 1st, 1955, Michel Jammet (marr. diss. 1963); one *s*; 2nd, 1964, Edward Pool, MC (marr. diss. 1974); 3rd, 1974, Alexander Csáky (*d* 1993). *Educ:* Convent of The Holy Family, Exmouth. Guildford Sch. of Art, 1947–49; Chelsea Sch. of Art, 1949–53. Exhibitions: Beaux Arts Gallery, 1952; *one-man exhibitions:* St George's Gallery, 1955; Waddington Galls, 1959, 1961, 1963, 1967, 1968, 1971, 1972, 1976, 1980, 1981; Royal Academy, 1985; Fischer Fine Art, 1989; also in provinces, and NY, Washington (Nat. Museum of Women in the Arts), Los Angeles,

Johannesburg, Amsterdam, Montreal, Toronto and Sydney; retrospective, Hong Kong, 1989; undertook many commns worldwide, and illus. various books; represented in collections in USA, Australia, Holland, Sweden, Germany and Tate Gallery, London. Member: Bd Trustees, British Museum, 1975–89; Royal Fine Art Commn, 1976–81. Hon. Fellow: St Hilda's Coll., Oxford, 1986; Newnham Coll., Cambridge, 1986. Hon. LittD Cambridge, 1988; Hon. Dr RCA, 1982; DU Essex, 1988; Hon. DLitt Oxford, 1989; Hon. LLD Manchester, 1990; Hon. DLit Bristol, 1991. *Publications:* The Art of Elisabeth Frink, 1972; Elisabeth Frink: catalogue raisonné, 1985; *posthumous publication:* (with E. Lucie-Smith) Frink: a portrait, 1994. *Address:* PO Box 558, Blandford Forum, Dorset DT11 7XT.   *Died 18 April 1993.*

FRIPP, Alfred Thomas, BM; FRCS; *b* 3 July 1899; *s* of late Sir Alfred Fripp, KCVO, and late Lady M. S. Fripp, *d* of late T. B. Haywood; *m* 1931, Kathleen Kimpton, (Jennie) (*d* 1986); one *s* two *d. Educ:* Winchester; Christ Church, Oxford. 2nd Lieut 1st Life Guards, 1917–18. Christ Church, Oxford, 1919–21; Guy's Hospital, 1921; Surg., Royal National Orthopædic Hospital, 1934–64. Mem., Pensions Appeal Tribunal, 1966–74. FRCS 1927. Pres. Orthopædic Section, RSocMed, 1950–51. *Recreations:* gardening, rowing. *Address:* Shalesbrook, Forest Row, Sussex RH18 5LS. *Club:* Leander (Henley-on-Thames).   *Died 31 Dec. 1995.*

FRÖHLICH, Herbert, DPhil; FRS 1951; Professor of Theoretical Physics, University of Liverpool, 1948–73, Professor Emeritus, since 1973; *b* 9 Dec. 1905; *m* 1950, Fanchon Aungst. *Educ:* Munich. Studied Theoretical Physics at University of Munich; DPhil 1930; subsequently Privatdozent at Freiburg Univ. Left Germany in 1933. Research Physicist, Lecturer, and Reader in Theoretical Physics, University of Bristol, 1935–48; Prof. of Solid State Electronics, Univ. of Salford, 1973–76, Vis. Fellow, 1976–81. For. Mem., Max-Planck-Inst., Stuttgart, 1980–. Hon. Dr of Science, Rennes, 1955; Hon. LLD Alberta, 1968; Hon. ScD Dublin, 1969; Dr rer. nat. *hc* Stuttgart, 1980; Hon. DSc Purdue, 1981. Max Planck Medal, 1972. *Publications:* Theory of Dielectrics (monograph), 1949, 2nd edn 1958; various books, scientific papers. *Address:* Department of Physics, Oliver Lodge Laboratory, The University, Oxford Street, PO Box 147, Liverpool L69 3BX.   *Died 23 Jan. 1991.*

FROST, Maj.-Gen. John Dutton, CB 1964; DSO 1943 and Bar, 1945; MC 1942; DL; farmer; *b* 31 Dec. 1912; *s* of late Brig.-Gen. F. D. Frost, CBE, MC and Elsie Dora Bright; *m* 1947, Jean MacGregor Lyle; one *s* one *d. Educ:* Wellington Coll.; RMC Sandhurst. Commissioned The Cameronians, Sept. 1932; Capt., Iraq Levies, 1938–41; Major and Lt-Col, Parachute Regt, 1941–45 (Bruneval raid, 1942; Oudna, 1942; Tunisian campaign, 1942–43; Primosole Bridge, 1943; Italian campaign, 1943; Arnhem Bridge, 1944); Staff Coll., Camberley, 1946; GSO2, HQ Lowland Dist, 1948–49; GSO2, Senior Officers' Sch., 1949–52; AA&QMG, 17 Gurkha Div., 1952–53; GSO1, 17 Gurkha Div., 1953–55; Comd, Netheravon, 1955–57; Comd, 44 Parachute Bde, 1958–61; Comdr 52nd Lowland Div./District, 1961–64; GOC Troops in Malta and Libya, 1964–66; Comdr Malta Land Force, 1965; retired, 1967. DL West Sussex, 1982. Cross of Grand Officer, SMO, Malta, 1966. *Publications:* A Drop Too Many, 1980; Two Para-Falklands, 1983; Nearly There, 1992. *Recreations:* field sports, polo, golf. *Address:* Northend Farm, Milland, Liphook, Hants GU30 7LT. *Club:* Army and Navy.
                                      Died 21 May 1993.

FRY, Donald William, CBE 1970; Director, Atomic Energy Establishment, Winfrith, 1959–73; *b* 30 Nov. 1910; *s* of William Joseph Fry; *m* 1934, Jessie Florence (*née* Wright); three *s. Educ:* Weymouth Gram. Sch.; King's Coll.,

London. Research Physicist, GEC Laboratories, 1932; RAE Farnborough (Radio Dept), 1936; Air Min. Research Establishment (later the Telecommunications Research Establishment, TRE), Swanage, 1940; moved with the Estab. to Malvern, 1942; joined staff of AERE, Malvern, 1946; demonstrated with other mems of group a new Principle for accelerating particles: the travelling wave linear accelerator, 1947; Head of Gen. Physics Div. at AERE Harwell, 1950; Chief Physicist, 1954, Dep. Dir, 1958, AERE Harwell. CEng, FIEE 1946; FIEEE 1960; FInstP 1970. Awarded Duddell Medal of Physical Soc., 1950. Hon. Freeman of Weymouth, 1958. FKC London, 1959. *Publications:* papers in learned journals. *Address:* Coveway Lodge, 25 Bowleaze Coveway, Overcombe, near Weymouth, Dorset DT3 6PL. *T:* Preston (Weymouth) (0305) 833276.   *Died 25 Dec. 1992.*

FRY, John, CBE 1988 (OBE 1975); MD, FRCS, FRCGP; general practitioner, 1947–92, retired; *b* 16 June 1922; *s* of Ansel and Barbara Fry; *m* 1st, 1944, Joan (*d* 1989), *d* of James and Catherine Sabel; one *s* one *d*; 2nd, 1989, Gertrude A. Amiel (*née* Schwer). *Educ:* Whitgift Middle Sch., Croydon; Guy's Hosp., Univ. of London (MD). FRCS 1947, FRCGP 1967. Hon. Consultant in Gen. Practice to the Army, 1968–87; Consultant to WHO, 1965–83; Trustee, Nuffield Provincial Hosps Trust, 1956– (Queen Elizabeth the Queen Mother Fellowship, 1988). Regents Lectr, Univ. of Calif, San Francisco, 1992. Mem., GMC, 1970–92 (Sen. Treasurer, 1975–92); Councillor, RCGP, 1960–92. Guthrie Medal, RAMC, 1987; Foundn Council Award, RCGP, 1993. *Publications:* The Catarrhal Child, 1961; Profiles of Disease, 1966; Medicine in Three Societies, 1969; Common Diseases, 1974, 5th edn 1993; Textbook of Medical Practice, 1976; Scientific Foundations of Family Medicine, 1978; A New Approach to Medicine, 1978; Primary Care, 1980; Family Good Health Guide, 1982; The Health Care Manual, 1983; Common Dilemmas in Family Medicine, 1983; A History of the Royal College of General Practitioners, 1983; NHS Data Book, 1984; Early Diagnosis, 1985; Disease Data Book, 1985; Primary Health Care: 2000, 1986; GP Data Book, 1988; Primary Medical Care, 1988; General Practice: the facts, 1992; Primary Care: in twelve countries, 1993; Medicine in Two Societies: primary care US and UK, 1994. *Recreations:* reading, writing, researching, running. *Address:* 3 Kings Court, Kelsey Park Avenue, Beckenham, Kent BR3 2TT. *T:* 081–650 5414.
Died 28 April 1994.

FRYER, Maj.-Gen. Wilfred George, CB 1956; CBE 1951 (OBE 1941); Chairman, Warminster Press, since 1965; *b* 1 May 1900; *s* of James and Marion Fryer, Kington, Herefordshire; *m* 1931, Jean Eleanore Graham (*d* 1992), *d* of Graham Binny, RSW, Edinburgh; two *s* (and one *s* decd). *Educ:* Christ Coll., Brecon; RMA Woolwich. Commissioned 2nd Lieut RE, 1919, Regular Army; served in India, Royal Bombay Sappers and Miners, 1933–38; Major RE, Instructor, Sch. of Mil. Engineering, Chatham, 1938; served War of 1939–45: Lt-Col RE, ADWE&M, GHQ, Middle East, 1941; SO1 to Chief Engineer, Eighth Army, Western Desert Campaign (OBE), 1941; Col DDWE&M, GHQ, Middle East, 1942; GSO1 to Scientific Adviser to Army Council, 1944; ADWE&M, GHQ and Dep. Chief Engineer, 8 Corps, NW Europe Campaign (despatches), 1944–45; Brig.-Chief Engr, Brit. Army Staff, Washington, DC, 1945; Col E (Equipment), War Office, 1946–48; Brig.-Chief Engr, Singapore Dist, 1948–51; Brig.-Chief Engr, Southern Comd, UK, 1951–53; Maj.-Gen. 1954; Chief Engineer, Middle East Land Forces, 1954–57. "A" Licence air pilot, 1942. MIEE 1952. Nat. Champion, Wayfarer Dinghy, 1960. *Recreations:* ocean racing (Transatlantic Race, 1931), ski-ing (Lauberhorn Cup, 1928), tennis. *Address:* Warminster Press Ltd, Station

Road, Warminster BA12 8BR. *Clubs:* Royal Ocean Racing, Hurlingham; Royal Lymington Yacht.
Died 19 Feb. 1993.

FULBRIGHT, J(ames) William, Hon. KBE 1975; US Senator (Democrat) for Arkansas, 1945–74; *b* Sumner, Mo, 9 April 1905; *s* of Jay Fulbright and Roberta (*née* Waugh); *m* 1st, 1932, Elizabeth Kremer Williams (*d* 1985); two *d*; 2nd, 1990, Harriet Mayor. *Educ:* public schools of Fayetteville, Arkansas; University of Arkansas (AB); (Rhodes Scholar) Pembroke Coll., Oxford Univ. (BA, MA); George Washington Univ. Sch. of Law (LLB). Special Attorney, Dept of Justice, 1934–35; Lectr in Law, George Washington Univ., 1935–36; Mem. Law Sch. Faculty, University of Arkansas, 1936–39, and Pres. of University, 1939–41. Elected to Congress for 3rd Dist of Arkansas, 1942; Mem. Foreign Affairs Cttee; elected to Senate, 1945, and subsequently; Mem. US Delegn to Gen. Assembly, UN, 1954; Chm. Banking and Currency Cttee of Senate, 1955–59, resigning to become Chm. Senate Cttee on Foreign Relations, also Mem. Finance Cttee and Jt Economic Cttee. First McCallum Meml Lectr, Oxford, 1975. Hon. Fellow, Pembroke Coll., Oxford, 1949; Fellow, Amer. Acad. of Arts and Sciences (Boston), 1950; Award by Nat. Inst. of Arts and Letters, 1954. Over fifty hon. degrees, including DCL Oxford, 1953, and LLD Cantab, 1971. *Publications:* Old Myths and New Realities, 1964; Prospects for the West, 1965; The Arrogance of Power, 1967; The Pentagon Propaganda Machine, 1970; The Crippled Giant, 1972; The Price of Empire, 1989. *Address:* Hogan & Hartson, 555 13th Street NW, Washington, DC 20004, USA.   *Died 9 Feb. 1995.*

FULLER, Roy Broadbent, CBE 1970; MA Oxon (by Decree); FRSL; poet and author; solicitor; Professor of Poetry, University of Oxford, 1968–73; *b* 11 Feb. 1912; *e* *s* of late Leopold Charles Fuller, Oldham; *m* 1936, Kathleen Smith; one *s*. *Educ:* Blackpool High Sch. Admitted a solicitor, 1934. Served Royal Navy, 1941–46; Lieut, RNVR, 1944. Asst Solicitor to Woolwich Equitable Building Soc., 1938–58, Solicitor, 1958–69, Director, 1969–87. Vice-Pres., Bldg Socs Assoc., 1969–87 (Chm. Legal Adv. Panel, 1958–69). A Governor of the BBC, 1972–79; Mem., Arts Council, 1976–77 (Chm., Literature Panel, 1976–77); Mem., Library Adv. Council for England, 1977–79. Hon. DLitt Kent, 1986. Queen's Gold Medal for Poetry, 1970; Cholmondeley Award, Soc. of Authors, 1980. *Publications: fiction:* Savage Gold, 1946; With My Little Eye, 1948; The Second Curtain, 1953; Fantasy and Fugue, 1954; Image of a Society, 1956; The Ruined Boys, 1959; The Father's Comedy, 1961; The Perfect Fool, 1963; My Child, My Sister, 1965; Catspaw, 1966; The Carnal Island, 1970; The Other Planet, 1979; Stares, 1990; *non fiction:* Questions and Answers in Building Soc. Law and Practice, 1949; Owls and Artificers: Oxford lectures on poetry, 1971; Professors and Gods: last Oxford lectures on poetry, 1973; (ed with John Lehmann) The Penguin New Writing, 1985; (ed) The Building Societies Act, various dates; *poetry:* Poems, 1939; The Middle of a War, 1942; A Lost Season, 1944; Epitaphs and Occasions, 1949; Counterparts, 1954; Brutus's Orchard, 1957; Collected Poems, 1962; Buff, 1965; New Poems (Duff Cooper Meml Prize), 1968; Off Course, 1969; Seen Grandpa Lately?, 1972; Tiny Tears, 1973; From the Joke Shop, 1975; An Ill-Governed Coast, 1976; Poor Roy, 1977; The Reign of Sparrows, 1980; The Individual and His Times (selected poems), 1982; (with Barbara Giles and Adrian Rumble) Upright Downfall, 1983; New and Collected Poems 1934–84, 1985; Subsequent to Summer, 1985; Consolations, 1987; Available for Dreams (jtly, W. H. Heinemann Award), 1989; The World Through the Window: collected poems for children, 1989; *anthologies:* Byron for Today, 1948; Fellow Mortals: an anthology of animal verse, 1981; *autobiography:* Souvenirs, 1980;

Vamp Till Ready, 1982; Home and Dry, 1984; The Strange and the Good: complete memoirs, 1989; Spanner and Pen: post-war memoirs, 1991. *Address:* 37 Langton Way, Blackheath, SE3. *T:* 081–858 2334. *Club:* Athenæum. *Died 27 Sept. 1991.*

FUNSTON, G(eorge) Keith; *b* Waterloo, Iowa, USA, 12 Oct. 1910; *s* of George Edwin and Genevieve (Keith) Funston; *m* 1939, Elizabeth Kennedy; one *s* two *d. Educ:* Trinity Coll., Hartford, Conn. AB 1932; MBA (*cum laude*), Harvard, 1934. Mem. Research Staff, Harvard Business Sch., 1934–35; Asst to VP Sales, then Asst to Treas., American Radiator & Standard Sanitary, 1935–40; Dir, Purchases & Supplies, Sylvania Electronics, 1940–44; Special Asst to Chm., War Production Bd, 1941–44; Lt-Comdr, US Navy, 1944–46; Pres., Trinity Coll., Hartford, 1944–51; Pres. and Governor, New York Stock Exchange, 1951–67; Chm., Olin Corp., 1967–72; formerly Director: IBM; Metropolitan Life; Republic Steel; AVCO Corp.; Illinois Central Industries; Chemical Bank; Putnam Trust; Hartford Steam Boiler & Insurance Co.; Winn-Dixie Stores; Paul Revere Investors; First Florida Banks. Numerous hon. doctorates. *Recreations:* riding, reading, ski-ing, tennis. *Address:* (home) 911 Strangler Fig Lane, Sanibel, Fla 33957, USA. *Clubs:* Round Hill (Greenwich, Conn); University, The Century Association, The Links (New York). *Died 15 May 1992.*

FÜRER-HAIMENDORF, Prof. Christoph von, DPhil Vienna; Emeritus Professor and Hon. Fellow, School of Oriental and African Studies, University of London, since 1976; *b* 27 July 1909; *s* of Rudolf Fürer von Haimendorf und Wolkersdorf; *m* 1938, Elizabeth Barnardo (*d* 1987); one *s. Educ:* Theresianische Akademie, Vienna. Asst Lecturer, Vienna Univ., 1931–34; Rockefeller Foundation Fellowship, 1935–37; Lecturer, Vienna University, 1938; Anthropological Fieldwork in Hyderabad and Orissa, 1939–43; Special Officer Subansiri, External Affairs Dept, Govt of India, 1944–45; Adviser to HEH the Nizam's Govt and Prof. of Anthropology in the Osmania Univ., 1945–49; Reader in Anthropology with special reference to India, University of London, 1949–51; Prof. of Asian Anthropology, School of Oriental and African Studies, 1951–76 (Dean of Sch., 1969–74, acting Director, 1974–75). Anthropological Research: in India and Nepal, 1953; in Nepal, 1957, 1962, 1966, 1972, 1976, 1981, 1983; in the Philippines, 1968; in India, 1970, 1976–. Munro Lectr, Edinburgh Univ., 1959; Visiting Prof., Colegio de Mexico, 1964, 1966. Pres., Royal Anthropological Inst., 1975–77. Corresponding Member: Austrian Academy of Science, 1964; Anthropological Soc. of Vienna, 1970. Rivers Memorial Medal of Royal Anthropological Institute, 1949; S. C. Roy Gold Medal, Asiatic Soc., Calcutta, 1964; Sir Percy Sykes Memorial Medal, Royal Central Asian Soc., 1965; King Birendra Prize, Royal Nepal Acad., 1976; Annandale Medal, Asiatic Soc. of Bengal, 1979. Austrian Order of Merit for Art and

Science, 1982. *Publications:* The Naked Nagas, 1939; The Chenchus, 1943; The Reddis of the Bison Hills, 1945; The Raj Gonds of Adilabad, 1948; Himalayan Barbary, 1955; The Apa Tanis, 1962; (joint author) Mount Everest, 1963; The Sherpas of Nepal, 1964; (ed and jt author) Caste and Kin in Nepal, India and Ceylon, 1966; Morals and Merit, 1967; The Konyak Nagas, 1969; (ed and jt author) Peoples of the Earth, vol. 12: The Indian Sub-continent, 1973; (ed and jt author) Contributions to the Anthropology of Nepal, 1974; Himalayan Traders, 1975; Return to the Naked Nagas, 1976; The Gonds of Andhra Pradesh, 1979; A Himalayan Tribe, 1980; (ed and jt author) Asian Highland Societies, 1981; Highlanders of Arunachal Pradesh, 1982; Tribes of India, 1982; Himalayan Adventure, 1983; The Sherpas Transformed, 1984; Tribal Populations and Cultures of the Indian Subcontinent, 1985; (jtly) Gonds and their Neighbours, 1987; An Autobiography of an Anthropologist in India, 1989; Exploratory Travels in Nepal, 1989; articles in Journal of Royal Anthropological Inst., Man, Anthropos, Geographical Jl, Man in India. *Recreation:* music. *Died 11 June 1995.*

FURNESS, 2nd Viscount, *cr* 1918; **William Anthony Furness;** Baron Furness 1910; *b* 31 March 1929; *s* of 1st Viscount and Thelma (*d* 1970), *d* of late Harry Hays Morgan, American Consul-Gen. at Buenos Aires; *S* father, 1940. *Educ:* Downside; USA. Served as Guardsman, Welsh Guards (invalided, 1947). Delegate to Inter-Parliamentary Union Conferences, Washington, 1953, Vienna, 1954, Helsinki, 1955, Warsaw, 1959, Brussels, 1961, Belgrade, 1963. Mem. Council, Hansard Soc. for Parliamentary Govt, 1955–67. Founder Chm., Anglo-Mongolian Soc., 1963; Vice-President: Tibet Soc. of the UK; Catholic Stage Guild. Sovereign Military Order of Malta: joined 1954; Sec., Assoc. of Brit. Members, 1956–65, Sec.-Gen. 1965–78; Regent, Brit. Sub-Priory of Blessed Adrian Fortescue, 1980–88; Mem. Sovereign Council, 1960–62; Mem. Board of Auditors, 1979–80; Grand Cross, Order of Merit, 1984, Kt of Justice, 1977 (Solemn Vows, 1982). Grand Officer, Order of Merit, Italy, 1961; KStJ 1971 (CStJ 1964); KCSG 1966. *Heir:* none. *Address:* c/o Midland Bank, 69 Pall Mall, SW1Y 5EY. *Clubs:* Boodle's, Carlton; Travellers' (Paris). *Died 1 May 1995 (ext).*

FURTADO, Robert Audley, CB 1970; Special Commissioner, 1946–77, Presiding Commissioner, 1963–77; *b* 20 August 1912; *yr s* of Montague C. Furtado; *m* 1945, Marcelle Elizabeth (*d* 1992), *d* of W. Randall Whitteridge; one *s* one *d. Educ:* Whitgift Sch.; University Coll., London. LLB London Univ., 1933; called to Bar, Gray's Inn, 1934. Served War of 1939–45, in Army in India and Burma (despatches); demobilised rank of Lieut-Col, 1945. *Recreation:* bricolage. *Address:* Hillfold, Langton Herring, Weymouth, Dorset DT3 4JD. *T:* Abbotsbury (0305) 871502. *Died 6 May 1992.*

G

GABB, (William) Harry, CVO 1974 (MVO 1961); DMus (Lambeth), 1974; Organist, Choirmaster and Composer at HM Chapels Royal, 1953–Easter 1974; Sub-Organist, St Paul's Cathedral, London, 1946–Easter 1974; adjudicator and recitalist; *b* 5 April 1909; *m* 1936, Helen Burnaford Mutton; one *s. Educ:* Scholarship at Royal Coll. of Music for Organ and Composition. ARCO 1928; FRCO 1930; ARCM Solo Organ, 1931. Organist, St Jude's, West Norwood, 1925; Organist and Choirmaster, Christ Church, Gypsy Hill, 1928; Sub-Organist, Exeter Cathedral, also Organist, Church of St Leonard's, Exeter and Heavitree Parish Church, 1929–37; Organist and Master of the Choristers, Llandaff Cathedral, 1937; Lectr, St Michael's Theological Coll., Llandaff; Royal Armoured Corps, War of 1939–45; returned from Army to Llandaff, Jan. 1946. Professor and Examiner of Organ Playing at the Trinity College of Music, London; Special Commissioner for Royal School of Church Music; Member, Council of the Royal College of Organists. Played organ at the Coronation of Elizabeth II and at many Royal Weddings and Baptisms. Hon. FTCL, 1954. *Address:* Kettlewell House, Kettlewell Hill, Chobham Road, Woking, Surrey GU21 4HX. *T:* Woking (01483) 756116. *Died 16 March 1995.*

GADD, John, CBE 1988; Regional Chairman, British Gas North Thames, 1977–88, retired; *b* 9 June 1925; *s* of late George Gadd and of Winifred Gadd (*née* Bowyer), Dunstable, Bedfordshire; *m* 1959, Nancy Jean, *d* of late Pryce Davies, Henley-on-Thames. *Educ:* Cedars Sch., Leighton Buzzard; Cambridgeshire Technical Coll. FIGasE 1967; MIPM 1975; CBIM 1979. Served War, RNVR, 1943–46. Joined Gas Industry, 1941; Southern Gas Bd, 1946–69: various engineering appts; Personnel Manager, 1962; Dep. Chm., 1969; Chm., Eastern Gas, 1973–77. Administrative Staff Coll., Henley-on-Thames, 1961. FRSA 1985. *Recreations:* gardening, walking. *Address:* The Orchard, Rotherfield Road, Henley-on-Thames, Oxon RG9 1NR. *Clubs:* City Livery; Leander, Phyllis Court (Henley-on-Thames).
Died 6 Dec. 1994.

GAGE, 7th Viscount *cr* 1720 (Ire.); **George John St Clere Gage;** Bt 1622; Baron Gage (Ire.) 1720; Baron Gage (GB), 1790; *b* 8 July 1932; *s* of 6th Viscount Gage, KCVO, and Hon. Alexandra Imogen Clare Grenfell (*d* 1969), *yr d* of 1st Baron Desborough, KG, GCVO; *S* father, 1982; *m* 1971, Valerie Ann (marr. diss. 1975), *yr d* of J. E. Dutch. *Educ:* Eton. *Heir: b* Hon. Henry Nicolas Gage [*b* 9 April 1934; *m* 1974, Lady Diana Adrienne Beatty, *d* of 2nd Earl Beatty; two *s*]. *Address:* Firle Place, Firle, Lewes, East Sussex BN8 6LP.
Died 30 Nov. 1993.

GAGE, Sir Berkeley (Everard Foley), KCMG 1955 (CMG 1949); HM Diplomatic Service, retired; *b* 27 Feb. 1904; *s* of late Brig.-Gen. M. F. Gage, DSO and 1st wife, Anne Massie, *d* of William Everard Strong, New York; *m* 1931, Maria von Chapuis (marr. diss. 1954), Liegnitz, Silesia; two *s*; *m* 1954, Mrs Lillian Riggs Miller (*née* Vukmirovic), Dubrovnik. *Educ:* Eton Coll.; Trinity Coll., Cambridge. 3rd Sec. Foreign Office or Diplomatic Service, 1928; appointed to Rome, 1928; transferred to Foreign Office, 1931; 2nd Sec., 1933; Private Sec. to Parly Under-Sec. of State, 1934; served Peking, 1935; FO 1938; China, 1941; FO, 1944; UK Deleg., Dumbarton Oaks Conf., 1944; UK Deleg., San Francisco Conf., April-June 1945; Foreign Service Officer, Grade 5, 1950; Counsellor, British Embassy, The Hague, 1947–50; Chargé d'Affaires, The Hague, in 1947 and 1948; Consul-Gen., Chicago, 1950–54; Ambassador to Thailand, 1954–57; Ambassador to Peru, 1958–63. Chairman: Latin America Cttee, BNEC, 1964–66; Anglo-Peruvian Soc., 1969–71; Member: Council for Volunteers Overseas, 1964–66; Council of Fauna Preservation Soc., 1969–73. Grand Cross, Order of the Sun (Peru), 1964. *Recreation:* swimming. *Address:* 24 Ovington Gardens, SW3 1LE. *T:* 071–589 0361. *Clubs:* Beefsteak (Life Hon. Mem.), Buck's; Tavern (Chicago).
Died 3 March 1994.

GALLAGHER, Patrick Joseph, DFC 1943; Chairman, Company Solutions Ltd, since 1983; *b* 15 April 1921; *s* of Patrick Gallagher and Mary Bernadine Donnellan; *m* 1950, Veronica Frances Bateman (*d* 1981); one *s. Educ:* Prior Park, Bath. Served War, 1941–46: Flt Lieut; Pilot, RAFVR. Principal, HM Treasury, 1948–58: ASC, 1956; Adviser, Raisman Commn, Nigeria, 1957–58; Consultant, Urwick, Orr & Partners Ltd, 1958–60; Dir, Ogilvy, Benson & Mather, 1960–65; Man. Dir, Glendinning Internat. Ltd, 1965–69; Pres., Glendinning Cos Inc., 1970–74; Managing Director: London Broadcasting Co. Ltd, 1975–79; Independent Radio News Ltd, 1975–79; Chm., Radio Sales & Marketing Ltd, 1976–79. *Recreations:* music, travel. *Address:* 29 Gloucester Place, W1H 3PB. *T:* 071–935 2429. *Club:* Royal Air Force.
Died 14 Jan. 1993.

GALPERN, Baron *cr* 1979 (Life Peer), of Shettleston in the District of the City of Glasgow; **Myer Galpern,** Kt 1960; JP; DL; *b* 1 Jan. 1903; *m* 1940, Alice Campbell Stewart; one *s* one *d. Educ:* Glasgow Univ. Lord Provost of Glasgow and Lord Lieut for the County of the City of Glasgow, 1958–60. MP (Lab) Glasgow, Shettleston, 1959–79; Second Dep. Chm. of Ways and Means, 1974–76, First Dep. Chm., 1976–79. Mem. of the Court of Glasgow Univ.; Mem., Advisory Cttee on Education in Scotland. Hon. LLD Glasgow, 1961; Hon. FEIS 1960. DL Co. of City of Glasgow, 1962; JP Glasgow. *Address:* House of Lords, SW1. *Died 23 Sept. 1993.*

GALSWORTHY, Sir John (Edgar), KCVO 1975; CMG 1968; HM Diplomatic Service, retired; *b* 19 June 1919; *s* of Arthur Galsworthy; *m* 1942, Jennifer Ruth Johnstone; one *s* three *d. Educ:* Emanuel Sch.; Corpus Christi Coll., Cambridge. HM Forces 1939–41; Foreign Office, 1941–46; Third Sec., Madrid, 1946; Second Sec., Vienna, 1949; First Sec., Athens, 1951; Foreign Office, 1954; Bangkok, 1958; Counsellor, Brussels (UK Delegation to EEC), 1962; Counsellor (Economic), Bonn, 1964–67; Counsellor and subsequently Minister (European Econ. Affairs), Paris, 1967–71; Ambassador to Mexico, 1972–77. Business consultant, 1978–82. UK Observer to El Salvador elections, March 1982. *Recreation:* fishing. *Address:* Lanzeague, St Just in Roseland, Truro, Cornwall TR2 5JD. *Died 18 May 1992.*

GAMINARA, Albert William, CMG 1963; HM Overseas Civil Service (retired); *b* 1 Dec. 1913; *s* of late Albert Sidney Gaminara and Katherine Helen Copeman; *m* 1947, Monica (*née* Watson); one *s* three *d. Educ:* City of London Sch.; St John's Coll., Cambridge; Oriel Coll., Oxford. MA Cantab 1943. Appointed to Sierra Leone as Administrative

Cadet, 1936; seconded to Colonial Office as Principal, 1947–50; transferred as Administrative Officer to N Rhodesia, 1950; Mem. of Legislative Council, 1963; Admin. Sec. to Govt of Northern Rhodesia, 1961–63; Sec. to the Cabinet, 1964, Adviser, Cabinet Office, 1965, Zambia. *Address:* Stratton House, Over Stratton, South Petherton, Somerset TA13 5LQ. *Club:* Hawks (Cambridge).   *Died 22 Dec. 1993.*

GANDEE, John Stephen, CMG 1967; OBE 1958; HM Diplomatic Service, retired; British High Commissioner in Botswana, 1966–69; *b* 8 Dec. 1909; *s* of John Stephen and Constance Garfield Gandee; *m* 1st, May Degenhardt (*d* 1954); one *s* two *d*; 2nd, Junia Henman (*née* Devine); two *d* (and one step *s* one step *d*). *Educ:* Dorking High Sch. Post Office, Dorking, 1923–30; India Office, 1930–47; Private Sec. to Parly Under-Sec. of State, 1946–47 and 1947–49; Asst Private Sec. to Sec. of State, 1947; First Sec., Ottawa, 1952–54; seconded to Bechuanaland Protectorate, 1958–60 and 1961; seconded to Office of High Comr for Basutoland, Bechuanaland Protectorate and Swaziland, 1960–61; Head of Administration Dept, CRO, 1961–64; Head of Office Services and Supply Dept, Diplomatic Service Administration, 1965–66. *Recreations:* walking, gardening. *Address:* Fulbrook, King's Lane, Coldwaltham, Pulborough, W Sussex RH20 1LE. *T:* Pulborough (0798) 873972.   *Died 4 April 1994.*

GANDHI, Rajiv; Prime Minister of India, 1984–89; Member (Indian National Congress I Party) for Amethi, Uttar Pradesh, Lok Sabha, since 1981; *b* 20 Aug. 1944; *er s* of Feroze and Indira Gandhi; *m* 1968, Sonia Maino; one *s* one *d. Educ:* Shiv Niketan School, New Delhi; Imperial College of Science and Technology, Univ. of London; Trinity College, Cambridge. Pilot with Indian Airlines, 1972–81. Former ministries include: Atomic Energy, Electronics, Ocean Develt, Personnel, Sci. and Technology, and Space; Gen. Sec., 1983–84, Pres., 1984–, Indian Nat. Congress. *Address:* 10 Janpath, New Delhi 110011, India; (office) 24 Akbar Road, New Delhi 110011, India.   *Died 21 May 1991.*

GANILAU, Ratu Sir Penaia Kanatabatu, GCMG 1983 (CMG 1968); KCVO 1982 (CVO 1970); KBE 1974 (OBE 1960); DSO 1956; ED 1974; President of the Republic of Fiji, since 1987; *b* 28 July 1918; Fijian; *m* 1st, 1949, Adi Laisa Delaisomosomo Yavaca (decd); five *s* two *d*; 2nd, 1975, Adi Asilina Davila Liliwaimanu Vunivalu (decd); 3rd, 1985, Veniana Bale Cagilaba. *Educ:* Provincial Sch. Northern; Queen Victoria Meml Sch., Fiji. Devonshire Course for Admin. Officers, Wadham Coll., Oxford Univ., 1947. Served with FIR, 1940; demobilised, retained rank of Captain, 1946. Colonial Admin. Service, 1947; District Officer, 1948–53; Mem. Cttee on Fijian Post Primary Educn in the Colony, 1953. Service with Fiji Mil. Forces, 1953–56; demobilised, retained rank of Temp. Lt-Col, 1956; Hon. Col, 2nd Bn (Territorial), FIR, 1973. Seconded to post of Fijian Econ. Develt Officer and Roko Tui Cakaudrove conjoint, 1956; Tour Manager and Govt Rep., Fiji Rugby football tour of NZ, 1957; Dep. Sec. for Fijian Affairs, 1961; Minister for Fijian Affairs and Local Govt, 1965; Leader of Govt Business and Minister for Home Affairs, Lands and Mineral Resources, 1970; Minister for Communications, Works and Tourism, 1972; Dep. Prime Minister, 1973–83; Minister for: Home Affairs, 1975–83; Fijian Affairs and Rural Develt, 1977–83; Governor-Gen., 1983–87. Member: House of Representatives; Council of Ministers; Official Mem., Legislative Council; Chairman: Fijian Affairs Bd; Fijian Develt Fund Bd; Native Land Trust Bd; Great Council of Chiefs. KStJ 1983. *Recreation:* Rugby football (rep. Fiji against Maori All Black, 1938 and during Rugby tour of NZ, 1939). *Address:* Office of

the President, Suva, Republic of Fiji. *Clubs:* Fiji, Defence (Suva, Fiji).   *Died 15 Dec. 1993.*

GAON, Dr Solomon; Haham (Chief Rabbi) of the Communities affiliated to the World Sephardi Federation in the Diaspora, since 1978; *b* 15 Dec. 1912; *s* of Isaac and Rachael Gaon; *m* 1944, Regina Hassan; one *s* one *d. Educ:* Jesuit Secondary Sch., Travnik, Yugoslavia; Jewish Teachers Seminary, Sarajevo, Yugoslavia; Jews' Coll., London Univ. (BA 1941, PhD 1943; Rabbinic Dip. 1948). Spanish and Portuguese Jews Congregation: Student Minister, 1934–41; Asst Minister, 1941–44; Minister, 1944–46; Sen. Minister, 1946–49; Haham of Spanish and Portuguese Jews Congregation and Associated Sephardi Congregations, 1949–77; Haham, Assoc. of Sephardi Congregations, 1977–80. Pres., Union of Sephardi Communities of England, N America and Canada, 1969–; Vice-Pres., World Sephardi Fedn, 1965–. Prof. of Sephardi Studies, Yeshiva Univ., New York, 1970–, Head of Sephardi Dept, 1977–. Hon. DD Yeshiva Univ., 1974. Alfonso el Sabio (for Cultural Work with and on Spanish Jewry), Spain, 1964. *Publications:* Influence of Alfonso Tostado on Isaac Abravanel, 1944; The Development of Jewish Prayer, 1949; Relations between the Spanish & Portuguese Synagogue in London and its Sister Congregation in New York, 1964; (ed) Book of Prayer of the Spanish & Portuguese Jews' Congregation, London, 1965; Edgar Joshua Nathan, Jr (1891–1965), 1965; Abravanel and the Renaissance, 1974; The Contribution of the English Sephardim to Anglo-Jewry, 1975; Minhath Shelomo, Commentary on Book of Prayer of Spanish & Portuguese Jews, 1990. *Recreations:* walking, tennis, music. *Address:* Barclays Bank, 53 Maida Vale, W9 1SL.   *Died 21 Dec. 1994.*

GARCÍA ROBLES, Alfonso, LLD; Permanent Representative of Mexico to Disarmament Conference, Geneva, since 1977; *b* 20 March 1911; *s* of Quirino and Teresa Robles de García; *m* 1950, Juana Maria de Szyslo; two *s. Educ:* Univ. Nacional Autónoma de México (LLB); Univ. of Paris (LLD 1937); Acad. of International Law, The Hague. Foreign Service, 1939; Sweden, 1939–41; Head, Dept of Internat. Organisations, later Dir-Gen., Political Affairs and Diplomatic Service, 1941–46; Dir, Div. of Political Affairs, UN Secretariat, 1946–57; Head, Dept for Europe, Asia and Africa, Mexican Min. of Foreign Affairs, 1957–61; Ambassador to Brazil, 1961–64; Under-Sec. for Foreign Affairs, 1964–70; Perm. Rep. to UN, 1971–75; Sec. for Foreign Affairs, 1975–76. Pres., Preparatory Commn for Denuclearization of Latin America, 1964–67; Chm., Mexican Delegn to UN Gen. Assembly special session on disarmament, NY, 1978; Mem., Colegio Nacional, México. Nobel Peace Prize (jointly), 1982. *Publications:* Le Panaméricanisme et la Politique de Bon Voisinage, 1938; La Question du Pétrole au Mexique et le Droit International, 1939; La Sorbona Ayer y Hoy, 1943; México en la Postguerra, 1944; La Conferencia de San Francisco y su Obra, 1946; Política Internacional de México, 1946; Ecos del Viejo Mundo, 1946; El Mundo de la Postguerra, 2 vols, 1946; La Conferencia de Ginebra y la Anchura del Mar Territorial, 1959; La Anchura del Mar Territorial, 1966; The Denuclearization of Latin America, 1967; El Tratado de Tlatelolco: génesis, alcance y propósitos de la proscripción de las armas nucléares en la América Latina, 1967; México en las Naciones Unidas, 2 vols, 1970; Mesures de Désarmement dans des Zones Particulières: le traité visant l'interdiction des armes nucléaires en Amérique Latine, 1971; La Proscripción de las Armas Nucleares en América Latina, 1975; Seis Años de la Política Exterior de México 1970–1976, 1976; La Conferencia de Revisión del Tratado sobre la no Proliferación de las Armas Nucleares, 1977; 338 Días de Tlatelolco, 1977; La Asamblea General del Desarme, 1979; El Comité de

Desarme, 1980. *Address:* 13 Avenue de Budé, Geneva, Switzerland. *T:* 345740. *Died 3 Sept. 1991.*

GARDHAM, Air Vice-Marshal Marcus Maxwell, CB 1972; CBE 1965; *b* 5 Nov. 1916; *s* of late Arthur Gardham, High Wycombe; *m* 1954, Rosemary Hilda (*née* Wilkins); one *s. Educ:* Royal Grammar Sch., High Wycombe. Commissioned RAF (Accountant Br.), 1939; RAF Ferry Command, 1941; HQ AEAF, 1944; BJSM, Washington, 1946 (SO Admin); RAPO, 1949; psc 1952; No 16 MU, 1953; 2nd TAF (Org. Staff), 1955; Air Ministry (Personnel Staff), 1957; jssc 1957; Technical Trng Command (Org. Staff), 1959; FEAF (Command Accountant), 1965; Dir of Personal Services, MoD (Air), 1966; Head of RAF Secretarial Br., 1971–72; AOA, RAF Trng Comd, 1969–72. Registrar, Ashridge Management Coll., 1972–82. *Recreations:* gardening, book collecting. *Address:* Four Winds, The Hamlet, Potten End, Berkhamsted, Herts HP4 2RD. *T:* Berkhamsted (0442) 862456. *Club:* Royal Air Force.

Died 5 May 1991.

GARDINI, Dr Raul; industrialist and financier; *b* Ravenna, 7 June 1933; *m* 1957, Idina Ferruzzi; one *s* two *d.* Former Chairman: Ferruzzi Gp; Montedison Gp; Chm., Gardini Srl, 1991–, specialising in fresh and frozen food, agroindustry and services, controlling: in France: Société Centrale d'Investissements; Barry and Vital/Sogéviandes; in Italy: Garma; Isa; Sandiego. Hon. degree in agriculture, Bologna, 1987. Won World Maxi Championship, 1988, World America's Cup Class Championship and Fastnet Race, 1991, Louis Vuitton Cup, 1992; America's Cup Challenger, 1992. *Recreations:* hunting, yachting. *Address:* Via Massimo D'Azeglio 10, 48100 Ravenna, Italy. *T:* (544) 423239, *Fax:* (544) 590301. *Club:* Europa Yacht (Pres.). *Died 23 July 1993.*

GARDNER, James; *see* Gardner, L. J.

GARDNER, Kenneth Burslam; Deputy Keeper of Oriental MSS and Printed Books, The British Library, 1974–86, retired; *b* 5 June 1924; *s* of D. V. Gardner; *m* 1949, Cleone Winifred Adams; two *s* two *d. Educ:* Alleyne's Grammar Sch., Stevenage; University College, London; School of Oriental and African Studies, Univ. of London (BA Hons Japanese). War service, Intelligence Corps (Captain), 1943–47. Assistant Librarian, School of Oriental and African Studies, 1949–54; Assistant Keeper, Department of Oriental Printed Books and MSS, British Museum, 1955–57, Keeper, 1957–70; Principal Keeper of Printed Books, British Museum (later The British Library), 1970–74. Yamagata Banto Prize, Osaka Prefectural Govt, 1995. Order of the Sacred Treasure (3rd class), Japan, 1979. *Publications:* Edo jidai no sashie hangaka-tachi (in Japanese, on book illustration in Japan and related topics), 1977; Descriptive catalogue of Japanese books in the British Library printed before 1700, 1993; contrib. to jls of oriental studies, art and librarianship. *Address:* The Old Stables, 15 Farquhar Street, Bengeo, Hertford SG14 3BN. *T:* Hertford (01992) 583591. *Died 19 April 1995.*

GARDNER, (Leslie) James, CBE 1959; RDI 1947; industrial designer and consultant; *b* 29 Dec. 1907; *s* of Frederic James Gardner; *m* 1935, Mary Williams (decd); two *s. Educ:* Chiswick and Westminster Schools of Art. Jewellery Designer, Cartier Ltd, 1924–31. Served War of 1939–45: Major RE; Chief Deception Officer, Army Camouflage, 1941–46. Designer, Britain Can Make It Exhibition, 1946; Chief Designer, Festival Gardens, Battersea, 1950; British Pavilion, Brussels, 1958; British Pavilion, Expo '67, Montreal; responsible for: Evoluon Museum, Eindhoven, Netherlands; St Helens Glass Museum, Lancs; main display Geological Museum, London, 1972; visual design of QE2 and sternwheeler Riverboat Mississippi Queen; Mus. of Diaspora, Tel Aviv;

Mus. of Natural Sci., Taiwan; Mus. of Tolerance, LA, 1993. Sen. Fellow, RCA, 1987. Minerva Medal, as Designer of the Year, CSD, 1989. *Publications:* Elephants in the Attic, 1983; The Artful Designer, 1993. *Address:* The Studio, 144 Haverstock Hill, Hampstead, NW3 2AY. *Died 25 March 1995.*

GARDNER-MEDWIN, Prof. Robert Joseph, RIBA, FRTPI; architect and town planning consultant; Professor Emeritus, Liverpool University, since 1973; *b* 10 April 1907; *s* of late Dr and Mrs F. M. Gardner-Medwin; *m* 1935, Margaret, *d* of late Mr Justice and Mrs Kilgour, Winnipeg; four *s. Educ:* Rossall Sch., Lancashire; School of Architecture, Liverpool Univ. (BArch, DipCD). Commonwealth Fund Fellowship in City Planning and Landscape Design, Harvard Univ., 1933–35; private practice, and architectural teaching at Architectural Association and Regent Street Polytechnic, 1936–40; served War of 1939–45, with Royal Engineers (Major, RE), 1940–43; Adviser in Town Planning and Housing to Comptroller of Development and Welfare in the British West Indies, 1944–47; Chief Architect and Planning Officer to Department of Health for Scotland, 1947–52; Roscoe Prof. of Architecture, Liverpool Univ., 1952–73. President, Liverpool Architectural Society, 1966; Chm., Merseyside Civic Soc., 1972–76, 1979–86. FRSA. Golden Order of Merit, Poland, 1976. *Publications:* (with H. Myles Wright) Design of Nursery and Elementary Schools, 1938; contributions to Town Planning Review, Architects' Journal, Journals of the RIBA and the RTPI, etc. *Address:* 6 Kirby Mount, West Kirby, Wirral, Merseyside L48 2HU. *Died 29 June 1995.*

GARDNER-THORPE, Col and Alderman Sir Ronald (Laurence), GBE 1980; TD 1948 (3 bars); JP; company director; *b* 13 May 1917; *s* of Joseph Gardner and Hannah Coulthurst Thorpe; *m* 1938, Hazel Mary (*née* Dees); one *s. Educ:* De la Salle Coll. Commnd Hants Heavy Regt, 1938; served War, 1939–45: France, Germany, Italy, British Army Staff Washington; 1945–47: AA&QMG 56 London Div., and XIII Corps; Grade 1 SO XIII Corps; GSO 1 GHQ CMF; comd 5th Bn The Buffs, 1956–60; Col 1960. City of London: Alderman, Ward of Bishopsgate, 1972 (Pres., Bishopsgate Ward Club, 1975); Sheriff, 1978–79; Lord Mayor, 1980–81; HM Lieut, 1980–. Vice-Pres., City of London Red Cross, 1977–. Underwriting Mem. of Lloyd's, 1977–. Contested (L): Eastbourne, 1959; West Derbyshire, June 1962. Member: Lord Lieuts Cttee, 1955–; Council, Magistrates' Assoc., 1972–82; London Court of Arbitration, 1975–85; Public Sch. Governing Body, 1963–; Governor: St John's Coll., Southsea, 1963– (Vice-Chm. Governors, 1976–); St Joseph's, Beulah Hill, 1966–76; Christ's Hosp., 1972–; Trustee: United Westminster Schs, 1974–; The Buffs (Royal East Kent Regt) Museum, 1976–; Morden Coll., 1979–89; Rowland Hill Benevolent Fund, 1979–85; Mental Health Foundn, 1981–; Royal Foundn of Greycoat Hosp., 1981–; Duke of Edinburgh's Award, 1982–; President: 25th Anniv. Appeal Fund, The Duke of Edinburgh's Award, 1980–82; David Isaacs Fund, 1982–86 (Vice-Pres., 1973–82); Central London Br., SSAFA, 1983; League of Friends, Hosp. of St John and St Elizabeth, 1983–; Vice-Pres., Variety Club of GB, 1982–86; Chm. Council, Distressed Gentlefolks' Aid Assoc., 1984–87. Chancellor, City Univ., 1980–81; Adm., Port of London, 1980–81. Member: Kent Territorial Assoc., 1954–62 (Mem., Finance Cttee, 1954); City of London T&AVR Assoc., 1977–86; Hon. Col, Kansas Cavalry, 1981–. Hon. Citizen: Baltimore; Kansas City; Arizona; Norfolk, Va; Cuzco, Peru. JP Inner London, 1964 (Dep. Chm. 1968); JP City of London, 1969 (Dep. Chm. 1970); Hon. Treas., Inner London Magistrates, 1972– (Vice Chm., 1977). Freeman, City of London, 1971; Liveryman and Member of Court: Worshipful Co.

of Painter Stainers, 1972–; Worshipful Co. of Builders Merchants, 1979–; Mem. Court, Hon. Artillery Co., 1972; Hon. Freeman and Liveryman, Leathersellers' Co., 1986. Hon. FRCP 1986. KStJ 1980; Kt of Magistral Grace, SMO, 1982. Kt Comdr, Royal Order of the Dannebrog, 1960; Kt Comdr, Order of Infant Henri, Portugal, 1979; Kt Comdr, Right Hand of the Ghurka, Nepal, 1980; Kt Comdr, Royal Order of King Abdul Aziz, Saudi Arabia, 1981; Kt Grand Cordon of the Swan, USA, 1984; Kt Grand Cross, Holy Order of the Cross of Jerusalem, USA, 1985; Grand Officer of Merit, Il Melito Melitensi, Italy, 1986. Hon. DCL City, 1980; Hon. DH Lewis, Chicago, 1981. *Publications:* The City and the Buffs, 1985; My Lord Mayor, 1988. *Recreations:* interest in Fine Arts and in City of London tradition. *Address:* 8 Cadogan Square, SW1X 0JU. *Clubs:* Belfry, City Livery, United Wards, Bishopsgate Ward. *Died 11 Dec. 1991.*

GARNER, Frederic Francis, CMG 1959; Ambassador to Costa Rica, 1961–67; retired; *b* 9 July 1910; *o s* of Frank Hastings Garner, Santa Cruz, Canary Islands; *m* 1946, Muriel (*née* Merrick). *Educ:* Rugby Sch.; Worcester Coll., Oxford. Joined HM Consular Service in China, 1932; served at Peking, Canton, Shanghai; POW in Japan, 1942–45; Consul, Tangier, 1947–50; First Secretary, Bogota, 1950–54; Consul-General, Shanghai, 1954–56; Head of Consular Department, Foreign Office, 1956–58; Ambassador at Phnom Penh, 1958–61. *Address:* c/o National Westminster Bank, 111 Western Road, Brighton, E Sussex BN1 2AF. *Died 1 April 1993.*

GARNER, Ronald Arthur, CB 1981; FRICS; Chief Valuer, Valuation Office, Inland Revenue, 1979–81; *b* 25 Feb. 1920; *s* of John Henry Garner, Lieut, RN, and Eliza Kate Garner; *m* 1946, Patricia Mary O'Brien. *Educ:* Devonport High Sch., Plymouth. Served with Royal Signals, 1940–46 (despatches, 1945). Joined Valuation Office, Inland Revenue, Plymouth, 1936; Superintending Valuer, 1966; Asst Chief Valuer, 1972; Dep. Chief Valuer, 1974. *Address:* St Ives, Cornwall. *Died 31 Oct. 1944.*

GARNETT-ORME, Ion Hunter Touchet, CBE 1983; Vice-President, St Dunstan's, since 1983 (Member of Council, 1958–83; Chairman, 1975–83); Director, Brown Shipley Holdings Limited, 1960–81 (Chairman, 1963–75), retired; *b* 23 Jan. 1910; *er s* of George Hunter Garnett-Orme and Alice Richmond (*née* Brown); *m* 1946, Katharine Clifton, *d* of Brig.-Gen. Howard Clifton Brown. *Educ:* Eton; Magdalene Coll., Cambridge. Served War, Welsh Guards, 1939–45. Dir, 1951, Chm., 1958–78, United States Debenture Corp. Ltd. Joined: Brown, Shipley & Co., Merchant Bankers, 1945; Bd of London Scottish American Trust Ltd and United States Debenture Corp. Ltd, 1951; Bd of Avon Rubber Co. Ltd, 1956–66; Dir, Ellerman Lines Ltd, 1971–75. *Address:* Cheriton Cottage, Cheriton, near Alresford, Hants SO24 0PR. *Club:* Carlton. *Died 10 Feb. 1991.*

GARNHAM, Prof. Percy Cyril Claude, CMG 1964; FRS 1964; MD; Professor of Medical Protozoology, London University, and Head of Department of Parasitology, London School of Hygiene and Tropical Medicine, 1952–68, then Emeritus Professor (Hon. Fellow, 1976); Senior Research Fellow, Imperial College of Science and Technology, 1968–79 (Hon. Fellow, 1979); Visiting Professor, Department of Biology, University of Strathclyde, 1970–87; *b* 15 Jan. 1901; *s* of late Lieut P. C. Garnham, RN Division, and Edith Masham; *m* 1924, Esther Long Price, Talley, Carms; two *s* four *d. Educ:* privately; St Bartholomew's Hospital. MRCS, LRCP, 1923, MB, BS London, 1923, DPH Eng. 1924, MD London, 1928 (University Gold Medal); Dipl. de Méd. Malariol., University of Paris, 1931; DSc London, 1952; FIBiol 1962; FRCP 1967. Colonial Medical Service, 1925–47; on staff of London School of Hygiene and Tropical Medicine, first as Reader, then as Professor, 1947–68. Heath Clark Lectr, Univ. of London, 1968; Fogarty Internat. Scholar, Nat. Insts of Health, Maryland, 1970, 1972; Manson Orator, 1969; Theobald Smith Orator, 1970; Ross Orator, 1980; Swellengrebel Orator, 1986. Member, Expert Panel of Parasitic Diseases, of WHO; Hon. Pres., European Fedn of Parasitologists; Past President: British Soc. of Parasitologists; Royal Society of Tropical Medicine and Hygiene; Vice-President: World Federation of Parasitologists; International Association against Filariasis; Corresponding Member: Académie Royale des Sciences d'Outre Mer, Belgium; Accad. Lancisiana, Rome; Soc. de Geografia da Lisboa; Hon. Member: Royal Entomol Soc. of London, 1979; Amer. Soc. Tropical Medicine; Société Belge de Médecine Tropicale; Brazilian Soc. Tropical Medicine; Soc. Ital. Medicina Tropicale; Soc. of Protozoologists; Société de Pathologie Exotique (Médaille d'Or, 1971); Acad. Nationale de Médecine, France (Médaille en Vermeil, 1972); Amer. Soc. of Parasitology; Mexican Soc. of Parasitologists; Polish Soc. of Parasitologists; British Soc. of Parasitologists; Groupement des Protistologues de la Langue Française; Foreign Member: Danish Royal Acad. of Sciences and Letters, 1976; Acad. Royale de Médecine, Belgium, 1979. Hon. FRCPE 1966. Freedom, City of London in Farriers Co., 1964. Hon. Dr: Univ. of Bordeaux, 1965; Univ. of Montpellier, 1980; Academician of Pontifical Acad. of Sciences, 1970. KLJ 1979. Darling Medal and Prize, WHO, 1951; Bernhard Nocht Medal, Hamburg, 1957; Gaspar Vianna Medal, Brazil, 1962; Manson Medal, 1965; Emile Brumpt Prize, Paris, 1970; Laveran Medal, 1971; Mary Kingsley Medal, Liverpool, 1973; Rudolf Leuckart Medal, Germany, 1974; Frink Medal, Zool Soc., 1985; Linnean Medal, Linnean Soc., 1986; H. Aragão Medalo, 1991; Le Prince Medal, 1991. *Publications:* Malaria Parasites, 1966; Progress in Parasitology, 1970; Garnham Collection of Malaria Parasites (catalogue), 1986; numerous papers on parasitology in medical journals. *Recreations:* chamber music, European travel. *Address:* Southernwood, Farnham Common, Bucks SL2 3PA. *T:* Farnham Common (012814) 3863. *Club:* Nairobi (Kenya).

Died 25 Dec. 1994.

GARNONS WILLIAMS, Basil Hugh; Headmaster of Berkhamsted School, 1953–72; *b* 1 July 1906; 5th *s* of Rev. A. Garnons Williams, Rector of New Radnor; *m* 1943, Margaret Olive Shearme (*d* 1981); one *s* two *d. Educ:* Winchester Coll. (Scholar); Hertford Coll., Oxford (Scholar). 1st Hon. Classical Moderations 1927; 2nd Lit.Hum. 1929; BA 1929; BLitt 1933; MA 1938. Classical VI Form Master, Sedbergh Sch., 1930–35; Marlborough Coll., 1935–45; Headmaster of Plymouth Coll., 1945–53. *Publications:* A History of Berkhamsted School, 1541–1972, 1980; Berkhamsted School for Girls, a Centenary History (1888–1988), 1988; contributor to History of the World (ed by W. N. Weech), 1944; articles in Classical Quarterly and Greece and Rome. *Address:* Remenham Place, Remenham Hill, near Henley-on-Thames, Berks RG9 3EU. *T:* Henley-on-Thames (0491) 572875. *Died 15 March 1992.*

GARRAN, Sir (Isham) Peter, KCMG 1961 (CMG 1954); HM Diplomatic Service, retired; *b* 15 Jan. 1910; *s* of late Sir Robert Randolph Garran, GCMG, QC and Hilda, 3rd *d* of John Shield Robson, Monkwearmouth, Durham; *m* 1935, Mary Elisabeth (*d* 1991), *d* of late Sir Richard Rawdon Stawell, KBE, MD; two *s* one *d. Educ:* Melbourne Grammar Sch.; Trinity Coll., Melbourne Univ. (BA 1st cl. Hons). Joined Foreign Office, 1934; Foreign posts: Belgrade, 1937–41; Lisbon, 1941–44; Berlin (seconded to CCG as Chief of Political Div.), 1947–50; The Hague, 1950–52; Inspector in HM Foreign Service, 1952–54; Minister (Commercial), Washington, 1955–60;

Ambassador to Mexico, 1960–64; Ambassador to the Netherlands, 1964–70. Director: Lend-Lease Corp., NSW, 1970–78; UK Br., Australian Mutual Provident Soc., 1970–82; Chairman: Securicor Nederland BV, 1976–82; Quality Assurance Council, BSI, 1971–82. *Recreation:* gardening. *Address:* The Coach House, Collingbeams, Donhead St Mary, Shaftesbury, Dorset SP7 9DX. *T:* Donhead (0747) 828108.   *Died 5 July 1991.*

GARRARD, Rev. Lancelot Austin, BD, MA; Professor of Philosophy and Religion, Emerson College, Boston, USA, 1965–71, then Emeritus; *b* 31 May 1904; *s* of late Rev. W. A. Garrard; *m* 1932, Muriel Walsh (*d* 1984); two *s*. *Educ:* Felsted (Scholar); Wadham Coll., Oxford (Exhibitioner); Manchester Coll., Oxford; Marburg (Hibbert Scholar). 2nd Class, Classical Mods; 2nd Class Lit.Hum.; Abbot Scholar; BD, MA (Oxon). Asst Master: Edinburgh Acad., 1927; St Paul's Sch., 1928; Unitarian Minister, Dover, 1932–33; Tutor and Bursar, Manchester Coll., Oxford, 1933–43; Minister, Lewins Mead Meeting, Bristol, 1941–43; Liverpool, Ancient Chapel of Toxteth, 1943–52; Tutor, Unitarian Coll., Manchester, 1945–51; Manchester Coll., Oxford, 1952–56; Principal of Manchester Coll., Oxford, 1956–65, Pres., 1980–86; Editor of The Hibbert Journal, 1951–62. Hon. Chief, Chickasaw Nation. Hon. LLD (Emerson Coll., Boston). *Publications:* Duty and the Will of God, 1935; The Interpreted Bible, 1946; The Gospels To-day, 1953; The Historical Jesus: Schweitzer's Quest and Ours, 1956; Athens or Jerusalem?, 1965; Aide-de-Camp to Sir Stamford Raffles: Lt-Col R. C. Garnham, 1985; Index to The Hibbert Journal, 1987. *Address:* 7 Bancroft Court, Reigate, Surrey RH2 7RW. *T:* Reigate (0737) 249672.
                                                    Died 7 Jan. 1993.

GARRETT, Hon. Sir Raymond (William), Kt 1973; AFC; AEA; JP; President, Legislative Council of Victoria, Australia, 1968–76 (Chairman of Committees, 1964–68); Chairman, Parliamentary Library Committee and Vice-Chairman, House Committee, 1968–76; *b* 19 Oct. 1900; *s* of J. J. P. Garrett, Kew, Australia; *m* 1934, Vera H., *d* of C. E. Lugton; one *s* two *d*. *Educ:* Royal Melbourne Technical Coll.; Univ. of Melbourne. Grad. RAAF Flying Sch., Point Cook, 1926; Citizen Air Force, 1927–37; Commercial Air Pilot, 1927–46. Founded Gliding Club of Vic, and Vic Gliding Assoc., 1928; British Empire Glider Duration Record, 1931. Served War of 1939–45, RAAF; retd as Gp Captain, 1945 (AFC, AEA). Pres., No 2 Squadron RAAF Assoc. Councillor, Shire of Doncaster and Templestone, 1954–60; Pres. and Chief Magistrate, 1955–56. Member Legislative Council: for Southern Province, Vic, 1958–70; for Templestowe Province, 1970–76. Member, Statute Law Revision Cttee, 1963–64; Govt Rep. on Council of Monash Univ., 1967–71. Knighted for services in politics, civic affairs and defence, Victoria. Life Governor, Lady Nell Seeing Eye Dog School. Chairman of Directors: Ilford (Aust.) Pty Ltd, 1965–75; Cine Service Pty Ltd. Pres., Victorian Parly Former Members' Assoc.; Pres., Baden Powell Guild, Victoria. FInstD. Freeman (first), Doncaster and Templestowe, Vic, 1988. *Recreations:* photography, sports cars. *Address:* Elgar Court, 614 Elgar Road, Box Hill North, Vic 3129, Australia. *Clubs:* Royal Automobile; Air Force (Vic.).   *Died 12 Oct. 1994.*

GARRETT, William Edward; DL; Director, Northumberland Waste Management Co., since 1992; *b* 21 March 1920; *s* of John Garrett, coal miner, and Frances (*née* Barwise); *m* 1st, 1946, Beatrice Kelly (*d* 1978); one *s*; 2nd, 1980, Noel Stephanie Ann Johnson. *Educ:* Prudhoe Elementary Sch.; London Sch. of Economics. Commenced work in coal mines, 1934; served engineering apprenticeship, 1936–40; employed by ICI, 1946–64; Union Organiser at ICI, 1946–64; Mem. of AEU. Member:

Prudhoe UDC, 1946–64; Northumberland County Council, 1955–64. Mem. of Labour Party, 1939–; Labour Candidate for Hexham 1953–55, Doncaster 1957–64; MP (Lab) Wallsend, 1964–92. Member: Select Cttee on Agriculture, 1966–69; Expenditure Cttee, 1971–79; Sec., All-Party Group for Chem. Industry. Member: Council of Europe, 1979–92; WEU, 1979–92. Parliamentary Adviser, Machine Tools Trades Assoc., 1970–72. DL Northumberland, 1992. *Recreations:* gardening, walking, reading. *Address:* 84 Broomhill Road, Prudhoe-on-Tyne, Northumberland NE42 5HX. *T:* Prudhoe (0661) 32580. *Club:* Prudhoe Working Men's.
                                                    Died 30 May 1993.

GARRINGTON, Rev. Elsie Dorothea C.; *see* Chamberlain-Garrington.

GARRY, Robert Campbell, OBE 1976; Regius Professor of Physiology, University of Glasgow, 1947–70, retired; *b* April 1900; *s* of Robert Garry and Mary Campbell; *m* 1928, Flora Macdonald, *d* of Archibald and Helen Campbell; one *s*. *Educ:* Glasgow Univ. MB, ChB with Hons, Glasgow Univ., 1922; Brunton Memorial Prize; DSc, Glasgow Univ., 1933; continued studies in Freiburg im Breisgau, Germany; University Coll., London; Medical Sch., Leeds. Asst and then Lectr, Institute of Physiology, Glasgow Univ.; Head of Physiology Dept, Rowett Research Institute, Aberdeen, 1933–35; Lectr on the Physiology of Nutrition, University of Aberdeen, 1933–35; Prof. of Physiology, University Coll., Dundee, The University of St Andrews, 1935–47. Member: MRC, 1955–59; Sci. Adv. Cttee on Med. Res. in Scotland, 1948–52, 1955–59; Physiol. Sub-Cttee of Flying Personnel Res. Cttee, 1951–75 (Chm., 1967–75); Bd of Management, Hill Farming Res. Orgn, 1963–72. Hon. Mem. Physiol. Soc., 1925; Foundn Mem., Nutrition Soc., 1941, Pres., 1950–53, Hon. Mem., 1981. FRSE 1937; FRCPGlas 1948. Hon. LLD Dundee, 1992. *Publications:* Life in Physiology (memoirs), 1992; papers in scientific periodicals, dealing especially with gastrointestinal physiology and nutrition. *Recreations:* gardening, reading. *Address:* Laich Dyke, Dalginross, Comrie, Crieff, Perthshire PH6 2HR. *T:* Comrie (0764) 70474.   *Died 16 April 1993.*

GARSTANG, Walter Lucian, (Tim), BSc, MA; Headmaster of the Roan School, Greenwich, 1959–68, retired 1968; *b* 2 Sept. 1908; *o s* of late Walter Garstang, MA, DSc; *m* 1933, Barbara Mary, *d* of late Dr S. E. Denyer, CMG, MD; one *s* two *d* (and one *s* decd). *Educ:* Oundle Sch.; Oxford (Scholar of Trinity Coll., 1927–31). Research chemist, The Gas Light and Coke Co., 1931–37; asst master, Oundle Sch., 1937–44; asst master, Merchant Taylors' Sch., 1944–46; senior science master, Maidstone Grammar Sch., 1946–48; Headmaster, Owen's Sch., 1949–54; Headmaster, Loughborough Grammar Sch., 1955–58. *Address:* 21 Wells Close, Cheltenham GL51 5BX.   *Died 19 Sept. 1991.*

GARTHWAITE, Sir William, 2nd Bt, *cr* 1919, of Durham; DSC 1941 and Bar, 1942; former Chairman, Sir William Garthwaite (Holdings) Ltd; *b* 3 Jan. 1906; *o s* of Sir William Garthwaite, 1st Bt and Francesca Margherita, *d* of James Parfett; *S* father 1956; *m* 1st, 1931, Hon. Dorothy Duveen (marr. diss. 1937) (*d* 1985), *d* of 1st Baron Duveen; 2nd, 1945, Patricia Leonard (marr. diss. 1952); one *s*; 3rd, 1957, Patricia Merriel, *d* of Sir Philip d'Ambrumenil; three *s* (one *d* decd). *Educ:* Bradfield Coll., Berks; Hertford Coll., Oxford. Lloyd's Underwriter and Insur. Broker at Lloyd's, 1926–. Farmer. Contested (C): Hemsworth Div. of W Riding of Yorks, 1931; Isle of Ely, 1935; E Div. of Wolverhampton, 1945; Pres., Royal Tunbridge Wells Cons. Assoc. Served War of 1939–45 as pilot, Fleet Air Arm (DSC and bar, despatches thrice, Air Crew Europe Star, Atlantic Star, Africa Star, 1939–45 Star, Defence Medal). Coronation Medal, 1953.

Recreations: flying, ski-ing, golf, sailing. *Heir: s* William Mark Charles Garthwaite [*b* 4 Nov. 1946; *m* 1979, Mrs Victoria Lisette Hohler, *e d* of Gen. Sir Harry Tuzo, GCB, OBE, MC; one *s* two *d*]. *Address:* Matfield House, Matfield, Kent TN12 7JT. *T:* Brenchley (089272) 2454. *Clubs:* Portland, Naval, Royal Thames; Jockey (Paris).
Died 15 Dec. 1993.

GARVEY, Sir Ronald Herbert, KCMG 1950 (CMG 1947); KCVO 1953; MBE 1941; *b* 4 July 1903; *s* of Rev. H. R. Garvey, MA, and Alice M. Lofthouse; *m* 1934, Patricia Dorothy Edge, *d* of late Dr V. W. T. McGusty, CMG, OBE; one *s* three *d*. *Educ:* Trent Coll.; Emmanuel Coll., Cambridge. MA 1930. Appointed to Colonial Service, 1926, and attached to Western Pacific High Commission, Suva, Fiji; District Officer British Solomon Islands, 1927–32; Asst Sec. Western Pacific High Commission, 1932–40; acted on various occasions as Res. Comr, Gilbert and Ellice Islands Colony; Asst to Res. Comr New Hebrides Condominium, 1940–41; acted as British Res. Comr, New Hebrides, on various occasions; District Officer, Nyasaland Protectorate, 1942–44; Administrator, St Vincent, Windward Islands, BWI, 1944–48; acted as Governor of Windward Is, 1946, 1948; Governor and C-in-C, British Honduras, 1948–52; Governor and C-in-C, Fiji, Governor, Pitcairn Is, Consul-Gen. for Western Pacific, and Senior Commissioner for UK on South Pacific Commission, 1952–58; Ambassador Plenipotentiary for Tonga, 1958; Lieutenant-Governor of the Isle of Man, 1959–66; Sec., Soil Assoc., 1967–71. Dir, Garvey (London) SA Ltd, 1966. Hon. Mem., E Anglia Tourist Bd. KStJ. *Publications:* autobiography: Gentleman Pauper, 1984; Happy Days in the Isle of Man, 1988. *Recreations:* golf, deep-sea fishing, gardening. *Address:* The Priory, Wrentham, Beccles, Suffolk NR34 7LR.
Died 31 May 1991.

GASS, Prof. Ian Graham, PhD, DSc; FRS 1983; Professor of Earth Sciences and Head of Discipline, Open University, 1969–82, Personal Chair, 1982–92, then Professor Emeritus; *b* 20 March 1926; *s* of John George and Lillian Robinson Gass; *m* 1955, Florence Mary Pearce; one *s* one *d*. *Educ:* Royal Grammar Sch., Newcastle upon Tyne; Almondbury Grammar Sch.; Leeds Univ. (BSc 1952, MSc 1955, PhD 1960, DSc 1972). Armed Forces, 1944–48. Undergrad., 1948–52; Geologist: Sudan Geol Survey, 1952–55; Cyprus Geol Survey, 1955–60; Asst Lectr, Leicester Univ., 1960–61; Lectr, then Sen. Lectr, Leeds Univ., 1961–69. Hon. Vis. Prof., Leeds Univ., 1992–. Mem., NERC, 1985–87. A Vice-Pres., Royal Soc., 1985–86. Led Royal Soc. Expedn to Tristan da Cunha, 1962. Prestwich Medal, 1979, Murchison Medal, 1988, Geol Soc. *Publications:* (ed with T. N. Clifford) African Magmatism and Tectonics, 1970; (ed with P. J. Smith and R. C. L. Wilson) Understanding the Earth, 1971, 2nd edn 1972; articles in scientific jls. *Address:* 12 Greenacres, Bedford MK41 9AJ. *T:* Bedford (0234) 352712.
Died 8 Oct. 1992.

GAUNT SUDDARDS, Henry; *see* Suddards.

GAUVAIN, Timothy John Lund; Executive Director, St John Ambulance, since 1990; *b* 23 June 1942; *s* of Sqdn Ldr John Henry Percival Gauvain and Barbara Lund (*née* Roberts); *m* 1st, 1967, Sandra Gay Duff (marr. diss. 1992); one *s*; 2nd, 1993, Catherine Emma Macher; one *s*. *Educ:* Stowe Sch.; Magdalene Coll., Cambridge (BA Hons 1964; MA 1969). Served RAF, 1964–82: No 111 Sqdn, Wattisham, 1966–69; ADC to AOC 22 Gp, Market Drayton, 1969–71; Flt Comdr, No 5 Sqdn, Binbrook, 1972–74; Canadian Forces Staff Coll., Toronto, 1974–75; Personal Air Sec. to RAF Minister, MoD, 1975–77; OC No 19 Sqdn, Wildenrath, Germany, 1978–80; Air Warfare Course, RAF Coll., Cranwell, 1981; Forward Policy Directorate (RAF), MoD, 1981–82; retired 1982, Wing Comdr. Dir, Nat. Management Office, BDO Binder Hamlyn, 1985–90. Man. Dir, Eskimo Ice Ltd, 1978–90. *Recreations:* flying, playing the organ, travel. *Address:* 73 Whitton Road, Twickenham, Middlesex TW1 1BT. *T:* 0181–891 1077. *Club:* Royal Air Force.
Died 15 Nov. 1994.

GEDDES, William George Nicholson, CBE 1979; FRSE; FEng 1978; FICE, FIStructE; Senior Partner, Babtie Shaw and Morton, Consulting Engineers, 1976–79, retired (Partner, 1950–76); *b* 29 July 1913; *s* of William Brydon Geddes and Ina (*née* Nicholson); *m* 1942, Margaret Gilchrist Wilson; one *s* one *d*. *Educ:* Dunbar High Sch.; Univ. of Edinburgh (BSc, 1st Cl. Hons). Engineer: Sir William Arrol & Co., F. A. Macdonald & Partners, Shell Oil Co., ICI, Babtie Shaw and Morton, 1935–79. President: Instn of Structural Engrs, 1971–72; Instn of Engrs and Shipbuilders in Scotland, 1977–79; Instn of Civil Engrs, 1979–80. Visiting Professor, Univ. of Strathclyde, 1978. Pres., Queen's Park Football Club, 1985–88. Hon. DSc Edinburgh, 1980. *Publications:* numerous papers to engrg instns and learned socs both at home and abroad. *Recreations:* fly-fishing, golf, hill-walking. *Address:* 17 Beechlands Avenue, Netherlee, Glasgow G44 3YT. *T:* 041–637 1526. *Club:* Royal Scottish Automobile (Glasgow).
Died 10 Nov. 1993.

GELLNER, Prof. Ernest André, FBA 1974; William Wyse Professor of Social Anthropology, Cambridge University, 1984–93; Supernumerary Fellow, King's College, Cambridge, 1992–95 (Professorial Fellow, 1984–92); *b* Paris, 9 Dec. 1925; *s* of Rudolf Gellner and Anna (*née* Fantl), Prague; *m* 1954, Susan Ryan; two *s* two *d*. *Educ:* Prague English Grammar Sch.; St Albans County (now Verulam) Sch.; Balliol Coll., Oxford (Open schol.; Univ. John Locke Scholar; MA); PhD (Lond). Pte, Czech. Armoured Brig., BLA, 1944–45. On staff of London School of Economics, 1949–84 (Hon. Fellow 1986), Prof. of Philosophy, 1962–84. Res. Prof., and Dir, Centre for Study of Nationalism, Central European Univ., Prague, 1993– (pt-time, 1991–93); Vis. Lectr, Center for European Studies, Harvard, 1994; Erasmus Vis. Prof., Warsaw Univ., 1995; Visiting Fellow: Harvard, 1952–53; Univ. of California, Berkeley, 1968; Centre de Recherches et d'Études sur les Sociétés Méditerranéens, Aix-en-Provence, 1978–79; Vis. Schol., Inst. of Advanced Studies, Tel Aviv Univ., 1982; Guest of Acad. of Scis of USSR, Moscow, 1988–89. Member: Council, SSRC (later ESRC), 1980–86 (Chm., Internat. Activities Cttee, 1982–84); Council, British Acad., 1981–84; Senate, Acad. of Scis of Czech Republic, 1994–. Pres., RAI, 1991–94; First Pres., Soc. for Moroccan Studies, 1990–. Tanner Lectr, Harvard Univ., 1990; Memorial Lectures: Frazer; Radcliffe-Brown; Marett; Myers; M. Stuchlík; H. Arendt; A. Little; H. Enayat; E. Westermarck; Marie Curie; B. Blackwood; L. Schapiro; Munro; E. H. Carr; A. Sakharov; M. Cummings; A. Harriman; J. Monnet. MAE 1989; Member: Amer. Philosophical Soc., 1992; Academia Scientiarum et Artium Europaea, Salzburg, 1993. Hon. For. Mem., Amer. Acad. of Arts and Scis, 1988. FRSA 1992. Hon. DSc Bristol, 1986; Hon. DLit QUB, 1989. Mem., Editorial or Adv. Boards: British Jl of Sociol.; Amer. Jl of Sociol.; Inquiry; Middle Eastern Studies; Jl of Peasant Studies; Society and Theory; Govt and Opposition; Philosophy of the Social Scis; Cambridge Archæological Jl; Jl of Mediterranean Studies; Third World Review; Nations and Nationalism; Anthropology and Archaeology of Eurasia; Sociological Papers; Modern iyzzazio e Sviluppo; Co-Editor: Europ. Jl of Sociol., 1966–84; Govt and Opposition, 1980–. *Publications:* Words and Things, 1959; Thought and Change, 1964; Saints of the Atlas, 1969; (ed with G. Ionescu) Populism, 1969; (ed with C. Micaud) Arabs and Berbers, 1973; Cause and Meaning in the Social Sciences, 1973, 2nd edn, as The Concept of Kinship and other essays, 1986; Contemporary Thought and Politics, 1974; The Devil in Modern Philosophy, 1974; Legitimation of Belief, 1975; (ed with J. Waterbury) Patrons and Clients, 1977; Spectacles and Predicaments, 1979; (ed) Soviet and Western Anthropology, 1980; Muslim Society, 1981; Nations and Nationalism, 1983; (ed) Islamic Dilemmas: reformers, nationalists and industrialisation, 1985; The Psychoanalytic Movement, 1985; Culture, Identity and Politics, 1987; State and Society in Soviet Thought, 1988; Plough, Sword and Book, 1988; (ed jtly) Malinowski between Two Worlds, 1988; Reason and Culture, 1992; Postmodernism, Reason and Religion, 1992; Conditions of Liberty, 1994; Encounters with Nationalism, 1994; Anthropology and Politics, 1995; numerous contributions to learned jls. *Address:* King's College, Cambridge CB2 1ST. *Club:* Reform. *Died 5 Nov. 1995.*

GENTRY, Maj.-Gen. Sir William George, KBE 1958 (CBE 1950); CB 1954; DSO 1942, and Bar 1945; *b* 20 Feb. 1899; *e s* of late Major F. C. Gentry, MBE and Mrs F. C. Gentry; *m* 1926, Alexandra Nina Caverhill; one *s* one *d. Educ:* Wellington Coll., NZ; RMC of Australia. Commissioned NZ Army, Dec. 1919; attached Indian Army and served in Waziristan, 1921, and Malabar, 1921; served War of 1939–45 with 2nd NZ Div. (Middle East and Italy): GSO 2 and AA&QMG, 1940; GSO 1, 1941–42; Comd 6 NZ Inf. Bde, 1942–43; DCGS, Army HQ, NZ, 1943–44; Comd 9 NZ Inf. Bde (Italy), 1945; Adjutant Gen., NZ Army, 1949–52; Chief of the Gen. Staff, NZ Army, 1952; retired, 1955. Greek Military Cross, 1941; United States Bronze Star, 1945. *Address:* 52 Kings Crescent, Lower Hutt, New Zealand. *T:* 660208. *Clubs:* Wellington, United Services (Wellington, NZ). *Died 13 Oct. 1991.*

GEORGE, Griffith Owen, TD; DL; a Recorder of the Crown Court, 1972–74; *b* 5 Dec. 1902; *s* of late John and Emiah Owen George, Hirwaun, Glam; *m* 1937, Anne Elinor (*d* 1990), *e d* of late Charles and Anne Edwards, Llandaff; one *s. Educ:* Westminster Sch.; Christ Church, Oxford (MA). Beit Prize Essay, 1923. Barrister, Gray's Inn, 1927; Wales and Chester Circuit. Served War of 1939–45, 2nd Lieut RA, 1939; Capt. 1941; Major 1943; on JAG's staff, N Africa, Italy, Middle East, 1943–45. Commissioner in Wales under the National Insurance Acts, 1950–67; Dep. Chm., Glamorgan Quarter Sessions, 1956–66, Chm., 1966–71. JP Glamorgan, 1952–72; DL Glamorgan, 1970. Contested (Nat. C) Llanelly, 1945. *Address:* Glanyrafon, Ponterwyd, Aberystwyth SY23 3JS. *T:* Ponterwyd (0197085) 661. *Died 6 Dec. 1994.*

GERARD, 4th Baron, *cr* 1876; **Robert William Frederick Alwyn Gerard;** Bt 1611; *b* 23 May 1918; *o s* of 3rd Baron Gerard, MC, and Mary Frances Emma, *d* of Sir Martin Le Marchant Hadsley Gosselin, GCVO, KCMG, CB; *S* father, 1953. *Heir: cousin* Anthony Robert Hugo Gerard [*b* 3 Dec. 1949; *m* 1976, Kathleen, *e d* of Dr Bernard Ryan, New York, USA; two *s*]. *Address:* Blakesware, Ware, Herts. *T:* Ware (0920) 3665. *Died 11 July 1992.*

GERARD, (William) Geoffrey, CMG 1963; Founder, Gerard Industries Pty Ltd, S Australia (Managing Director, 1930–76; Chairman, 1950–80); *b* 16 June 1907; *s* of late A. E. Gerard; *m* 1932, Elsie Lesetta, *d* of late A. Lowe; one *s* one *d. Educ:* Adelaide Technical High Sch. President: Electrical Manufrs' Assoc. of SA, 1949–52; Electrical Develt Assoc. of SA, 1952; SA Chamber of Manufactures, 1953–54; Associated Chambers of Manufactures of Aust., 1955; SA Metal Industries Assoc., 1952 and 1957; Aust.-Amer. Assoc. in SA Incorp., 1961–63; Aust. Metal Industries Assoc., 1962–64; Vice-Chm., Standards Assoc. of Aust., 1956–79; Chm., Nat. Employers' Assoc., 1964–66; Member: SA Industries Adv. Cttee, 1952–53; Commonwealth Immigration Planning Council, 1956–74;

Commonwealth Manufg Industries Advisory Coun., 1958–62; Nat. Employers' Policy Cttee, 1964–66; Commonwealth Electrical Industries Adv. Council, 1977–80. Pres., Prince Alfred Coll. Foundn, 1975–80. Pres., Liberal and Country League, SA Div., 1961–64. Rotary Governor's representative in founding Barossa Valley Club, 1956. FAIM. *Recreations:* golf, tennis. *Address:* 9 Robe Terrace, Medindie, SA 5081, Australia. *T:* 44 2560. *Clubs:* Adelaide, Commonwealth (Adelaide); Kooyonga Golf (SA) (Captain, 1953–55, Pres., 1976–78); Rotary (Prospect) (Pres., 1954). *Died 21 Feb. 1994.*

GERE, John Arthur Giles, FBA 1979; FSA; Keeper, Department of Prints and Drawings, British Museum, 1973–81; *b* 7 Oct. 1921; *o s* of Arnold Gere and Carol Giles; *m* 1958, Charlotte Douie; one *s* one *d. Educ:* Winchester; Balliol College, Oxford. Assistant Keeper, British Museum, 1946; Deputy Keeper, 1966. *Publications:* (with Robin Ironside) Pre-Raphaelite Painters, 1948; (with Philip Pouncey) Italian Drawings in the British Museum: vol. iii: Raphael and his Circle, 1962; vol. v: Artists Working in Rome c 1550–c 1640, 1983; Taddeo Zuccaro: his development studied in his drawings, 1969; I disegni dei maestri: il manierismo a Roma, 1971; (ed with John Sparrow) Geoffrey Madan's Notebooks, 1981; (with Nicholas Turner) Drawings by Raphael in English Collections, 1983; various exhibition catalogues; contribs to Burlington Magazine, Master Drawings, etc. *Address:* 21 Lamont Road, SW10 0HR. *T:* 0171–352 5107. *Died 11 Jan. 1995.*

GERNSHEIM, Helmut Erich Robert; photo-historian and author; *b* Munich, 1 March 1913; 3rd *s* of Karl Gernsheim, historian of literature at Munich Univ., and Hermine Gernsheim (*née* Scholz); became British subject, 1946; *m* 1945, Alison Eames (*d* 1969), London; no *c; m* 1971, Irène Guénin, Geneva. *Educ:* St Anne's Coll., Augsburg; State Sch. of Photography, Munich. Settled in England as free-lance photographer, 1937; during War of 1939–45 made photogr. surveys of historic bldgs and monuments for Warburg Inst. (London Univ.); exhibns of these at Churchill Club and Courtauld Inst., 1945 and 1946, Nat. Gall., 1944; one-man show at Royal Photogr. Society 1948; built up Gernsheim photo-historical collection, 1945–, at University of Texas, Austin, 1964–; selections were shown at art museums, Europe and America; retrospective exhibn of own photographs 1935–82, Hamburg, 1983, Hanover and Munich, 1984, Freiburg/Breisgau, 1986. Re-discovered world's first photograph (taken in 1826), 1952 and Lewis Carroll's chief hobby, 1948. Co-ed. Photography Yearbook, 1953–55; British Representative World Exhibition of Photography, Lucerne, 1952, Biennale and Unesco Conference on Photography, Paris, 1955, etc. Photographic adviser to Granada TV on first British action still films, 1958–62. Editorial Adviser, Encyclopædia Britannica and several Museums and Universities. Chm., History of Photo. Seminar, Rencontres Internat. de la Photo.: Arles, 1978; Venice, 1979; Frankfurt, 1981. Distinguished Visiting Professor: Univ. of Texas at Austin, 1979; Arizona State Univ., 1981 (Adjunct Prof., 1985); Regents Prof., Univ. of California, at Riverside, 1984, and at Santa Barbara, 1985, 1989. Dir, Photo-Graphic Editions, London. Trustee: Swiss Foundn for Photography, 1975–81; Alimari Mus., Florence, 1985–. Hon. MSc Brooks Inst., Santa Barbara, Calif., 1984; Hon. Dr Bradford, 1989. Hon. Fellow: Club Daguerre, Frankfurt, 1981; Amer. Photohist. Soc., 1979; Europ. Soc. for History of Photography, 1985. First German cultural prize for photography, 1959; Gold Medal, Accademia Italia delle Belle Arte, Parma, 1980; Hill Medal, German Acad. of Photography, 1983; Daguerre Medal, Soc. L. J. M. Daguerre, 1989; Grand Prize for Photography, San Marino,

1991; Sudek Medal, Czecho-Slovak Govt, 1991; Leitz Silver Medal, 1995. Cross of Merit, Germany, 1970. *Publications include:* New Photo Vision, 1942; Julia Margaret Cameron, 1948, rev. and enlarged edn, 1975; Lewis Carroll—Photographer, 1949, 3rd edn 1969; Beautiful London, 1950; Masterpieces of Victorian Photography, 1951; Those Impossible English, 1952; Churchill, His Life in Photographs, 1955; Creative Photography, 1962, 3rd edn 1991; (with Alison Gernsheim): Roger Fenton, 1954, 2nd edn 1973; The History of Photography, 1955, 3rd edn 1969, enlarged edns, 1983 (Berlin), 1985 (Milan, NY); L. J. M. Daguerre, 1956, 2nd edn 1968; Queen Victoria, a Biography in Word and Picture, 1959; Historic Events, 1960; Edward VII and Queen Alexandra, 1962; Fashion and Reality, 1963, 2nd edn 1981; Concise History of Photography, 1965, 3rd edn, NY, 1987; Alvin Langdon Coburn, photographer, 1966, 2nd edn 1978; The Origins of Photography, 1982; Incunabula of British Photographic Literature, 1984; The Rise of Photography, 1988; contrib. Oxford History of Technology, 19th and 20th century; numerous articles in art and photographic journals in many countries. *Recreations:* travelling, classic music, opera. *Address:* Residenza Tamporiva, Via Tamporiva 28, 6976 Castagnola, Ticino, Switzerland. *T:* Lugano (91) 515904.
Died 20 July 1995.

GERRARD, His Honour Basil Harding; a Circuit Judge (formerly a Judge of County Courts), 1970–82; *b* 10 July 1919; *s* of late Lawrence Allen Gerrard and Mary (*née* Harding); *m* Sheila Mary Patricia (*née* Coggins), widow of Walter Dring, DSO, DFC (killed in action, 1945); one *s* two *d* and one step *d. Educ:* Bryanston Sch.; Caius Coll., Cambridge (BA). Royal Navy, 1940–46. Called to Bar, Gray's Inn, 1947; Recorder of Barrow-in-Furness, 1969–70. Mem., Parole Bd for England and Wales, 1974–76. Chm., Selcare Trust, 1971–78, Vice Pres. 1978–; a Chm., Residential Home Tribunal, 1985–. *Recreation:* gardening. *Address:* Northwood, Toft Road, Knutsford, Cheshire WA16 6EB. *Clubs:* Knutsford Golf; Bowdon Croquet.
Died 29 June 1994.

GIBB, Andrew (McArthur); barrister; *b* 8 Sept. 1927; *s* of late William and of Ruth Gibb; *m* 1956, Olga Mary (*née* Morris); three *d. Educ:* Sedbergh; Queens' Coll., Cambridge (MA). Called to the Bar, Middle Temple, 1952. A Recorder of the Crown Court, 1977–82. Chm., Cttee of Public Inquiry into fire at Wensley Lodge, Hessle, Humberside, 1977. *Recreations:* golf, reading, music. *Address:* 263 Colne Road, Sough, Earby, via Colne, Lancs BB8 6SY. *Clubs:* MCC; Lancashire County Cricket.
Died 6 July 1992.

GIBB, William Eric, MA, DM Oxon; FRCP; Consulting Physician, St Bartholomew's Hospital, since 1976; *b* 30 April 1911; *s* of late James Glenny Gibb, MD, FRCS, and Georgina Henman; *m* 1952, Mary Edith Gertrude Feetham; two *s* (and one *s* decd). *Educ:* Rugby Sch.; Oriel Coll., Oxford; St Bartholomew's Hosp. BA Oxon 1st Cl. Hons Final Sch. of Nat. Science; BM, BCh Oxon 1936; MRCP 1940; DM Oxon 1947; FRCP 1949. George Herbert Hunt Travelling Schol., University of Oxford, 1938. War Service with RAFVR Med. Br., 1941–46; Actg Wing-Comdr i/c a Med. Div. Res. house appts, St Bart's Hosp. and Brompton Chest Hosp.; Cattlin Research Scholar, 1947; Physician: St Bart's Hosp., 1947–76; The Metropolitan Hosp., 1952–76. Mem., Pensions Appeal Tribunal, 1976–85. Examiner in Medicine: University of Oxford, 1952–59; Examg Bd of England; RCP; Soc. of Apothecaries. Fellow, Royal Soc. Med. *Publications:* various articles in medical journals. *Recreation:* gardening. *Address:* 1 Bacon's Lane, Highgate, N6 6BL. *Club:* Osler.
Died 13 July 1992.

GIBBINS, Elizabeth Mary, BA; Headmistress, St Mary's School, Calne, Wilts, 1946–72; *b* 2 May 1911; *d* of late Kenneth Mayoh Gibbins, MB, BS. *Educ:* Sandecotes Sch., Parkstone; Westfield Coll., University of London; Cambridge Univ. Training Coll. for Women (Postgraduate). History Mistress, St Brandons Clergy Daughters' Sch., Bristol, 1935–38; Headmistress, Diocesan Girls' Sch., Hongkong, 1939–45, Acting Headmistress, Oct. 1972–May 1973. Hon. Sec., Hong Kong Diocesan Assoc., 1974–80. *Address:* 8 Moreton Road, Old Bosham, Chichester, West Sussex PO18 8LL. *T:* Bosham (0243) 573038.
Died 18 March 1992.

GIBBS, Air Marshal Sir Gerald Ernest, KBE 1954 (CBE 1945); CIE 1946; MC; *b* 3 Sept. 1896; *s* of Ernest William Cecil and Fanny Wilmina Gibbs; *m* 1938, Margaret Jean Bradshaw; one *s* one *d.* Served European War, 1914–18: transferred from Army to RFC 1916, and RAF 1918 (MC and 2 bars, Légion d'Honneur, Croix de Guerre); ADC to Marshal of the Royal Air Force Sir Hugh Trenchard (later 1st Viscount Trenchard), 1927–28; served in Air Staff Plans, Air Ministry, under Gp Capt. C. F. A. Portal (later 1st Viscount Portal of Hungerford), and then Gp Capt. A. T. Harris (later Marshal of the Royal Air Force Sir Arthur Harris, Bt), 1930–34; served various overseas periods with RAF in Iraq, Palestine, Sudan and Kenya between the two wars; commanded No 47 Sqdn RAF Sudan and RAF Kenya; Senior Air Staff Officer of No 11 Group, Fighter Command, 1940–41 during Battle of Britain; Dir of Overseas Operations, Air Ministry, 1942–43; Senior Air Staff Officer, HQ 3rd Tactical Air Force, South-East Asia, 1943–44; Chief Air Staff Officer to Admiral Mountbatten (later Earl Mountbatten of Burma), Supreme HQ, SEAC, 1945–46; Senior Air Staff Officer, HQ, RAF Transport Command, 1946–48; Head of Service Advisers to UK Delegation and Chm. UK Members of Military Staff Cttee, UN, 1948–51; Chief of Air Staff and Commander-in-Chief, Indian Air Force, 1951–54, retired 1954. *Publication:* Survivor's Story, 1956. *Recreations:* golf, ski-ing, sailing. *Address:* Lone Oak, 170 Coombe Lane West, Kingston-upon-Thames, Surrey. *Clubs:* Royal Air Force; Royal Wimbledon Golf (Wimbledon); Seaford Golf (East Blatchington); Trevose Golf (Cornwall).
Died 10 Oct. 1992.

GIBBS, Sir Martin St John Valentine, KCVO 1991; CB 1958; DSO 1942; TD; JP; Lord-Lieutenant of Gloucestershire, since 1978; *b* 14 Feb. 1917; *er s* of late Major G. M. Gibbs, Parkleaze, Ewen, Cirencester; *m* 1947, Mary Margaret, *er d* of late Col Philip Mitford, and widow of late Captain M. D. H. Wills, MC; two *d. Educ:* Eton. 2nd Lieut, Royal Wilts Yeomanry, 1937; served War of 1939–45 with Royal Wilts Yeo.; Major 1942, Lieut-Col 1951, Brevet-Col 1955, Col 1958; Hon. Colonel: Royal Wilts Yeomanry Sqdn, T&AVR, 1972–82; The Royal Yeomanry, RAC, T&AVR, 1975–82; Col Comdt Yeomanry, RAC, 1975–82. JP 1965, High Sheriff, 1958, Gloucestershire; DL Wilts 1972. *Recreations:* country pursuits. *Address:* Ewen Manor, Ewen, Cirencester, Glos. *T:* Cirencester (0285) 770206. *Clubs:* Cavalry and Guards, MCC.
Died 8 Feb. 1992.

GIBBS, Oswald Moxley, CMG 1976; development and trade consultant, since 1990; High Commissioner for Grenada in London, 1974–78 and 1984–90; Ambassador for Grenada to the European Economic Community, 1985–90; *b* St George's, Grenada, 15 Oct. 1927; *s* of Michael Gibbs and Emelda Mary (*née* Cobb); *m* 1955, Dearest Agatha Mitchell (*d* 1989); two *s* two *d. Educ:* Happy Hill RC Sch.; St George's RC Sen. Boys' Sch.; Grenada Boys' Secondary Sch.; Christy Trades Sch., Chicago (Technical Drafting Dip.); City of London Coll. BScEcon London. Solicitors' Clerk, Grenada, 1948–51; petroleum refining, Royal Dutch Shell Co., Curaçao,

Netherlands Antilles, 1951–55; Civil Servant, Agricl Rehabilitation Dept, Grenada, 1955–57; Transport Worker, London Transport, and Postman, London, 1957–60; Civil Servant, WI Federal Commn, London, 1961–62; Consular Officer, Commn for Eastern Caribbean Govts, London, 1965–75; Welfare Officer, 1965–67; Trade Sec., 1967–72; Dep. Comr, 1972–73; Actg Comr, 1973–75. Rep. Govt of St Kitts-Nevis-Anguilla on London Cttee of Commonwealth Sugar Producing Countries, 1971–75; Consultant, Centre for Industrial Develt, Lomé Convention, Brussels, 1979–80 (signed Lomé III Convention for Grenada, 1984); Deleg., 9th Commonwealth Conf. on Develt and Human Ecology, Univ. of Edinburgh, 1989; Head of Delegn, Commonwealth Heads of Govt Meeting, Kuala Lumpur, 1989; Admin. Dir, N Kensington Family Centre and Unity Assoc., 1980–83; Business Develt Manager, UK Caribbean Chamber of Commerce, 1983–84. Chairman: Civil Service Salaries Revision Commn, Grenada, 1970; Notting Hill Carnival and Arts Cttee, 1981–84. Member: Exec., Commonwealth Human Ecology Council, 1989–; Governing Council, Internat. Fund for Agricl Develt (Rome), 1986–90. Mem., delegns to constitutional, Commonwealth and ACP/EEC meetings and confs. Silver Jubilee Medal, 1977. *Publication:* occasional paper on envmtl concerns of small states. *Recreations:* environment, development economics, DIY, photography, gardening. *Address:* 73A Woodside Green, SE25 5HU.

Died 6 Oct. 1995.

GIBSON, Sir Alexander (Drummond), Kt 1977; CBE 1967; FRSE 1978; Founder, 1962 and Music Director, 1985–87, Scottish Opera Company (Artistic Director, 1962–85), Conductor Laureate, since 1987; *b* 11 Feb. 1926; *s* of late James McClure Gibson and of Wilhelmina Gibson (*née* Williams); *m* 1959, Ann Veronica Waggett; three *s* one *d*. *Educ:* Dalziel; Glasgow Univ.; Royal College of Music; Mozarteum, Salzburg, Austria; Accademia Chigiano, Siena, Italy. Served with Royal Signals, 1944–48. Repetiteur and Asst Conductor, Sadler's Wells Opera, 1951–52; Asst Conductor, BBC Scottish Orchestra, Glasgow, 1952–54; Staff Conductor, Sadler's Wells Opera, 1954–57; Musical Dir, Sadler's Wells Opera, 1957–59; Principal Conductor and Musical Dir, Scottish Nat. Orch., 1959–84 (Hon. Pres., 1985–). Principal Guest Conductor, Houston Symphony Orch., 1981–83. FRSA 1980. Hon. RAM 1969; Hon. FRCM, 1973; Hon. FRSAMD, 1973 (Pres., 1991–); Hon. RSA, 1975. Hon. LLD Aberdeen, 1968; Hon. DMus: Glasgow, 1972; Newcastle, 1990; DUniv: Stirling, 1972; Open, 1978; York, 1991. St Mungo Prize, 1970; ISM Distinguished Musician Award, 1976; Sibelius Medal, 1978. *Recreation:* reading. *Address:* 15 Cleveden Gardens, Glasgow G12 0PU. *T:* 0141–339 6668. *Clubs:* Garrick, Oriental.

Died 14 Jan. 1995.

GIBSON, Sir Christopher (Herbert), 3rd Bt *cr* 1931, of Linconia, Argentina, and of Faccombe, Southampton; Sales Representative, National Homes Ltd, Abbotsford, BC, Canada; *b* 2 Feb. 1921; *s* of Sir Christopher H. Gibson, 2nd Bt, and Lady (Dorothy Edith Orme) Gibson (*née* Bruce); *S* father, 1962; *m* 1941, Lilian Lake Young, *d* of Dr George Byron Young, Colchester; one *s* three *d*. *Educ:* St Cyprian's, Eastbourne; St George's Coll., Argentina. Served, 1941–45 (5 war medals and stars): 28th Canadian Armd Regt (BCR), Lieut. Sugar Cane Plantation Manager, Leach's Argentine Estates, 1946–51; Manager, Encyclopædia Britannica, 1952–55; Design Draughtsman, Babcock & Wilcox, USA, 1956–57; Tea Plantation Manager, Liebig's, 1958–60; Ranch Manager, Liebig's Extract of Meat Co., 1961–64; Building Inspector, Industrias Kaiser, Argentina, 1964–68; Manager and part-owner, Lakanto Poultry Farms, 1969–76. *Recreations:*

shooting, fishing, tennis, cricket. *Heir: s* Rev. Christopher Herbert Gibson, CP, *b* Argentina, 17 July 1948.

Died 26 June 1994.

GIBSON, Sir Donald (Evelyn Edward), Kt 1962; CBE 1951; MA; FRIBA (Distinction Town Planning), FRTPI; Controller General, Ministry of Public Building and Works, 1967–69, then Consultant; *b* 11 Oct. 1908; *s* of late Prof. Arnold Hartley Gibson; *m* 1st, 1936, Winifred Mary (*née* McGowan) (decd); three *s* one *d*; 2nd, 1978, Grace Haines. *Educ:* Manchester Gram. Sch.; Manchester Univ. BA Hons Architecture; MA. Work in USA, 1931; private practice, 1933; professional Civil Service (Building Research), 1935; Dep. County Architect, Isle of Ely, 1937; City Architect and Town Planning Officer, County and City of Coventry, 1939; County Architect, Notts, 1955; Dir-Gen. of Works, War Office, 1958–62; Dir-Gen., R&D, MPBW, 1962–67; Hoffmann Wood Prof. of Architecture, University of Leeds, 1967–68. Mem. Central Housing Advisory Cttee, 1951, 1953 and 1954. President: RIBA, 1964–65; Dist Heating Assoc., 1971–. Hon. FLI 1968. Hon. DCL Durham. *Publications:* various publications dealing with housing, planning and architecture in RIBA and RTPI Journals. *Recreation:* model railways. *Address:* Bryn Castell, Llanddona, Beaumaris, Gwynedd LL58 8TR. *T:* Beaumaris (0248) 810399.

Died 22 Dec. 1991.

GIBSON, Harold Leslie George, OBE 1978 (MBE 1971); General President, National Union of Hosiery and Knitwear Workers, 1975–82; *b* 15 July 1917; *s* of George Robert and Ellen Millicent Gibson; *m* 1941, Edith Lunt (decd); one *s* one *d*. *Educ:* elementary and grammar schools, Liverpool. Officer of National Union of Hosiery and Knitwear Workers, 1949; General Secretary, 1962–75. Member: Monopolies and Mergers Commn, 1978–86; Management Cttee, Gen. Fedn of Trade Unions; TUC Textile Cttee; Exec. Cttee, British Textile Confedn; Knitting, Lace and Net Industry Training Board; Strategy Working Party for the Hosiery Industry. Pres., Internat. Textile, Garment and Leather Workers' Fedn, Brussels. Hon. LLM Leicester, 1982. JP, 1949–77. *Recreations:* photography, golf, music. *Address:* 15 Links Road, Kibworth Beauchamp, Leicester LE8 0LD. *T:* Kibworth (0533) 792149. *Died 11 Jan. 1994.*

GIBSON, Col Leonard Young, CBE (mil.) 1961 (MBE (mil.) 1940); TD 1947; DL; President of Newcastle and District Beagles, since 1983 (Master, 1946–83); *b* 4 Dec. 1911; *s* of late William McLure Gibson and Wilhelmina Mitchell, Gosforth; *m* 1949, Pauline Mary Anthony; one *s* one *d*. *Educ:* Royal Grammar Sch., Newcastle upon Tyne; France and Germany. Service in TA, 1932–61: 72nd (N) Field Regt RA, 1932–39; Staff Coll., Camberley, 1938–39; tsc; Bde Major RA: 50th (N) Div., rearguard Dunkirk, 1939–40 (MBE, despatches); 43rd (W) Div., 1941–42; GSO2, SE Army, 1942; GSO2 (DS), Staff Coll., Camberley, 1942–43 (psc†); GSO1 Ops Eastern Comd, 1943–44; 2nd in Comd 107 Med. Regt S Notts Hussars, RHA TA, France, Belgium, Holland, Germany, 1944–45 (despatches; Croix de Guerre with Gold Star, France, 1944); GSO1 Mil. Govt Germany, 1945; Battery Comd, The Elswick Battery, 1947–51; OC 272 (N) Field Regt RA TA, 1956–58; Dep. Comdr RA 50th Inf. Div. TA, 1959–61; Colonel TA, retd. Mem., Northumberland T&AFA, 1958–68. Pres., Masters of Harriers and Beagles Assoc., 1968–69. DL Northumberland, 1971. *Recreations:* hunting, breeding horses and hounds. *Address:* The Shieling, Humshaugh, Hexham, Northumberland NE46 4AA. *T:* Hexham (0434) 681402.

Died 13 Feb. 1993.

GIBSON, Captain Michael Bradford; Managing Director of Racquet Sports International Ltd, since 1975; *b* 20 March 1929; *s* of Lt-Col B. T. Gibson; *m* 1953, Mary

Helen Elizabeth Legg; two *s. Educ:* Taunton Sch.; RMA Sandhurst; Sidney Sussex Coll., Cambridge (BA). Commnd into RE, 1948, retd 1961. Official Referee to Lawn Tennis Assoc. and All England Lawn Tennis Club, 1961–75. Mem., Inst. of Directors. *Recreations:* hunting, boating. *Address:* Peppercorn Cottage, 8 School Hill, Warnham, Horsham, Sussex RH12 3QN. *T:* Horsham (0403) 65589. *Clubs:* All England Lawn Tennis and Croquet; Cottesmore Golf. *Died 29 Aug. 1993.*

GIBSON, Thomas, FRCSE, FRCSGlas, FRSE; Director, Glasgow and West of Scotland Regional Plastic and Maxillofacial Surgery Service, 1970–80; Consultant Plastic Surgeon to Greater Glasgow Health Board (formerly Western Regional Hospital Board), 1947–80; *b* 24 Nov. 1915; *s* of late Thomas Gibson and Mary Munn; *m* 1944, Patricia Muriel McFeat; two *s* two *d. Educ:* Paisley Grammar Sch.; Glasgow Univ. (MB, ChB 1938). FRCSE 1941, FRFPSG 1955, FRCSGlas 1962; FRSE 1974. House Surg. and Phys., Western Infirmary, Glasgow, 1939–40; Asst Lectr in Surg., Glasgow Univ., and Extra Dispensary Surg., Western Infirm., Glasgow, 1941–42; full-time appt with MRC, Burns Unit, Glasgow Royal Infirm., 1942–44; RAMC, 1944–47: Lieut, rank of Major 1945; OC No 1 Indian Maxillofacial Unit, 1945–47; Emeritus Prof., Bioengrg Unit, Univ. of Strathclyde, 1985– (Vis. Prof., 1966–85). Royal Coll. of Physicians and Surgeons of Glasgow: Hon. Librarian, 1963–73; Visitor, 1975–76; Pres., 1977–78. Hon. FRACS 1977; Hon. FRCS 1988. Hon. DSc Strathclyde, 1972. Editor, British Jl of Plastic Surgery, 1968–79. *Publications:* Modern Trends in Plastic Surgery: vol. 1, 1964; vol. 2, 1966; The Royal College of Physicians and Surgeons of Glasgow, 1983; contrib. med. and surg. jls. *Recreations:* history, horticulture, handicrafts. *Address:* c/o Bryce, 22 Gadloch Avenue, Lenzie, Glasgow G66 5NP. *T:* 041–777 6865. *Died 13 Feb. 1993.*

GILBERT, John Orman, CMG 1958; retired; *b* London, 21 Oct. 1907; *s* of Rev. T. H. Gilbert, late of Chedgrave Manor, Norfolk; *m* 1935, Winifred Mary Harris, Dublin; two *s* two *d. Educ:* Felsted Sch., Essex; Pembroke Coll., Oxford. Joined Sarawak Civil Service, 1928; various posts, from Cadet, to District Officer in 1940. During War of 1939–45 served in Bengal Sappers and Miners stationed in India and attained rank of Major. Came back to Sarawak with BM Administration, 1946; Resident, 4th Div., Sarawak, 1946–53; British Resident, Brunei, 1953–58; retd 1959. Coronation Medal, 1953. *Recreations:* conservation of wild life, animal welfare. *Address:* PO Box 100, Somerset West, Cape, South Africa. *Died 16 Sept. 1995.*

GILBERTSON, Sir Geoffrey, Kt 1981; CBE 1972; *b* 29 May 1918; *s* of A. J. and M. O. Gilbertson; *m* 1940, Dorothy Ness Barkes; two *s* two *d. Educ:* Durham Sch.; Jesus Coll., Cambridge. Served War, 4th/7th Royal Dragoon Guards, 1940–45, Captain. Imperial Chemical Industries, 1946–74: Director, Agricl Div., 1960–67; Plant Protection Ltd, 1964–67; Group General Manager, 1967–74. Dir, Guildway Ltd, 1979–83. Member, Pay Board, 1973–74. Chairman: NEDC (Ship building), 1974–77; Nat. Adv. Cttee, Employment of Disabled People, 1975–81; Fit for Work Award Scheme, 1980–84. FRSA; FIPM. Croix de Guerre (Gold Star), 1944. *Recreation:* fishing. *Address:* Greta Bridge, Barnard Castle, County Durham DL12 9SD. *T:* Teesdale (0833) 27276. *Clubs:* Flyfishers'; Leander (Henley-on-Thames); Hawks (Cambridge). *Died 2 Feb. 1991.*

GILBEY, Sir (Walter) Derek, 3rd Bt, *cr* 1893, of Elsenham Hall, Essex; Lieutenant 2nd Battalion Black Watch; *b* 11 March 1913; *s* of Walter Ewart Gilbey and Dorothy Coysgarne Sim; *S* grandfather, 1945; *m* 1948, Elizabeth Mary, *d* of Col Keith Campbell and Marjorie Syfret; one *s* one *d. Educ:* Eton. Served War of 1939–45 (prisoner). *Heir: s* (Walter) Gavin Gilbey [*b* 14 April 1949; *m* 1st, 1980, Mary Pacetti (marr. diss. 1984), *d* of late William E. E. Pacetti and of Mrs Mary Greer; 2nd, 1984, Mrs Anna Olsson, *d* of Edmund Prosser]. *Address:* Grovelands, Wineham, near Henfield, Sussex BN5 9AW. *T:* Bolney (0444) 881311. *Died 27 Oct. 1991.*

GILCHRIST, Sir Andrew (Graham), KCMG 1964 (CMG 1956); HM Diplomatic Service, retired; formerly Ambassador and administrator; *b* 19 April 1910; *e s* of late James Graham Gilchrist, Kerse, Lesmahagow; *m* 1946, Freda Grace (*d* 1987), *d* of late Alfred Slack; two *s* one *d. Educ:* Edinburgh Acad.; Exeter Coll., Oxford. Diplomatic career, 1933–70, included junior posts in Bangkok, Paris, Marseilles, Rabat, Stuttgart, Singapore, Chicago, also in FO; subseq. Ambassador at Reykjavik, Djakarta and Dublin, retired. Chm., Highlands and Islands Develt Bd, 1970–76. War Service as Major, Force 136 in SE Asia (despatches). *Publications: memoirs:* Bangkok Top Secret, 1970; Cod Wars and How to Lose Them, 1978 (Icelandic edn 1977); *history:* Malaya 1941: the fall of a fighting empire, 1991; *novels:* The Russian Professor, 1984; The Watercress File, 1985; The Ultimate Hostage, 1986; South of Three Pagodas, 1987; Death of an Admiral, 1988; Did Van Gogh Paint His Bed?, 1991. *Address:* Arthur's Crag, Hazelbank, by Lanark ML11 9XL. *T:* Crossford (055586) 263. *Clubs:* Special Forces; New (Edinburgh). *Died 6 March 1993.*

GILCHRIST, (Andrew) Rae, CBE 1961; MD Edinburgh; FRCPE, FRCP; Consulting Physician Royal Infirmary, Edinburgh; *b* 7 July 1899; *o s* of late Rev. Andrew Gilchrist, BA, Edinburgh; *m* 1st, 1931, Emily Faulds (*d* 1967), *yr d* of late W. Work Slater, Edinburgh and Innerleithen, Peeblesshire; one *s* one *d*; 2nd, 1975, Elspeth, widow of Dr Arthur Wightman. *Educ:* Belfast, Edinburgh, New York. MB, ChB Edinburgh, 1921; Lauder-Brunton Prizeman, Milner-Fothergill Medallist, McCunn Medical Res. Scholar, Edinburgh Univ., 1924; MD (gold medal) 1933; FRCPE 1929; FRCP 1944. RFA, 1917–18. Resident hospital appointments at Addenbrooke's Hosp., Cambridge, Princess Elizabeth Hosp. for Children, London, E1, and at Royal Infirmary, Edinburgh, 1922–24; Resident Asst Physician Rockefeller Hosp. for Medical Research, New York, USA, 1926–27; Asst Physician, 1930, Physician, Royal Infirmary, Edinburgh, 1939–64. Gibson Lecturer RCPE, 1944; Lecturer: Canadian Heart Assoc., 1955; Litchfield Lecture, Oxford Univ., 1956; Californian Heart Assoc., 1957; St Cyres Lecturer, National Heart Hosp., London, 1957; Hall Overseas Lecturer, Australia and NZ, 1959; Carey Coombs Memorial Lecture, Bristol Univ., 1960; Gwladys and Olwen Williams Lecture in Medicine, Liverpool Univ., 1961; Orford Lectr, College of Physicians of S Africa, 1962. William Cullen Prize, 1962 (shared). Pres. of the Royal College of Physicians of Edinburgh, 1957–60. Examr in Med. in Univs of Edinburgh, Glasgow, Aberdeen, St Andrews, East Africa (Makerere Coll.), and Baghdad. Member: Assoc. of Physicians of Gt Brit.; Brit. Cardiac Soc. Hon. Mem. Cardiac Soc. of Australia and NZ. Hon. FRACP 1959; Hon. FRFPSG 1961. *Publications:* numerous contributions on disorders of heart and circulation, in British and American medical journals. *Recreation:* fishing. *Address:* 16 Winton Terrace, Edinburgh EH10 7AP. *T:* 0131–445 1119. *Clubs:* Flyfishers'; New (Edinburgh). *Died 1 March 1995.*

GILES; *see* Giles, Carl Ronald.

GILES, Carl Ronald, OBE 1959; Cartoonist, Daily and Sunday Express, since 1943; *b* 29 Sept. 1916; *m* 1942, Sylvia Joan Clarke (*d* 1994). Trained as animated cartoonist; Animator for Alexander Korda, 1935;

Cartoonist, Reynolds News, 1937–43. Cartoons extensively reproduced in US and syndicated throughout world. Produced and animated Documentary Films for Min. of Information, also War Correspondent-cartoonist in France, Belgium, Holland and Germany, War of 1939–45. *Publications:* "Giles" Annual, 1945–; various overseas collections. *Recreations:* sailing, workshops. *Address:* Express Newspapers, Ludgate House, 245 Blackfriars Road, SE1 9UX. *Clubs:* Saints & Sinners, Lord's Taverners; British Racing Drivers'.

Died 27 Aug. 1995.

GILES, Prof. Geoffrey Reginald, FRCS; Professor of Surgery, and Head, University of Leeds Department of Surgery, St James's Hospital, Leeds, since 1973; *b* 17 Dec. 1936; *s* of Reginald Samuel Giles and Phyllis May Giles; *m* 1966, Pamela Billie Hoey; three *s. Educ:* Bablake Sch., Coventry; Manchester Univ. (MB ChB, MD). FRCS 1964. Postgrad. trng, Manchester Royal Inf., 1962–64; Gen. Inf., Leeds, 1964–68; Fellow: Harvard Med. Sch., Boston, 1968–69; Univ. of Colorado, 1969–71; Sen. Lectr, Univ. of Leeds, 1971–73. *Publication:* Essential Surgical Practice (with Cuschieri and Moosa), 1982, 2nd edn 1986. *Recreation:* game fishing. *Address:* 1 North Park Avenue, Roundhay, Leeds LS8 1DN. *T:* Leeds (0532) 661883. *Club:* East India.   *Died 2 April 1992.*

GILL, Cyril James, CB 1965; Senior Lecturer in Education, University of Keele, 1968–71, retired (Gulbenkian Lecturer in Education, 1965–68); *b* 29 March 1904; *s* of William Gill, Carnforth, Lancs; *m* 1939, Phyllis Mary (*d* 1992), *d* of Joseph Windsor, Ramsey, Isle of Man. *Educ:* Ulverston Grammar Sch.; Liverpool Univ. Sch. Master, Ramsey, IOM and Archbishop Tenison's, London, 1926–42; Head Master, Salford Grammar Sch., 1942–45; HM Inspectorate of Schools, 1945–65: Midland Divisional Inspector, 1954–61; Chief Inspector (Teacher Training), 1961–65. *Publications:* articles on counselling and guidance. *Recreations:* gardening, walking, photography, theatre. *Address:* Grosvenor House, Ballure Road, Ramsey, Isle of Man IM8 1NB.

Died 17 Nov. 1994.

GILLAM, Group Captain Denys Edgar, DSO 1940 (and 2 bars); DFC 1940 (and bar); AFC 1938; DL; Director, Homfray & Co. Ltd, 1950–81 (Chairman, 1971–81); retired; *b* 18 Nov. 1915; *s* of Maj. T. H. J. and D. Gillam; *m* 1st, 1945, Nancye Joan Short (*d* 1982); one *s* two *d*; 2nd, 1983, Irene Scott. *Educ:* Bramcote, Scarborough; Wrekin Coll., Salop. Joined RAF, 1935; trained No 1 FTS Netheravon; served 29 Fighter Sqdn, Middle East, 1937–39, Meteorological Flight Aldergrove (AFC); 616 Sqdn (Fighter), 1939–40 (DFC, after Battle of Britain); 312 Sqdn (F), 1940–41; HQ 9 Group till March 1941, rank Sqdn Ldr; commanded 306 Sqdn (Polish), then 615 Sqdn (F) (bar DFC and DSO for shipping attacks in Channel); RAF Staff Coll.; then commanded first Typhoon Wing (despatches); graduated US Command and Gen. Staff Coll.; commanded Tangmere Wing (Typhoons), Jan.-March 1944 (bar to DSO for attacks on V-weapon sites); promoted Group Capt., commanded 20 Sector 2nd TAF, then 146 Wing 2 TAF (Typhoon) till March 1945 (2nd bar DSO); then Group Capt. Ops 84 Group (Main) 2nd TAF. DL for West Riding of Yorks and the City and County of York, 1959. *Recreations:* fishing, shooting, sailing. *Address:* The Glebe, Brawby, Malton, North Yorks YO17 0QA. *T:* Kirbymoorside (0751) 31530. *Club:* Royal Ocean Racing.   *Died 2 July 1991.*

GILLIAT, Lt-Col Sir Martin (John), GCVO 1981 (KCVO 1962; CVO 1954); MBE 1946; DL; Private Secretary to Queen Elizabeth the Queen Mother since 1956; Vice-Lieutenant of Hertfordshire, 1971–86; *b* 8 Feb. 1913; *s* of late Lieut-Col John Babington Gilliat and Muriel Helen Lycette Gilliat; unmarried. *Educ:* Eton; RMC, Sandhurst.

Joined KRRC, 1933. Served War of 1939–45 (despatches, Prisoner of War). Dep. Military Sec. to Viceroy and Governor-Gen. of India, 1947–48; Comptroller to Commissioner-Gen. for UK in South-East Asia, 1948–51; Mil. Sec. to Governor-Gen. of Australia, 1953–55. Hon. Bencher, Middle Temple, 1977. Hon. LLD London, 1977. DL Herts, 1963. *Address:* 66 Eaton Square, SW1; 31A St James's Palace, SW1. *T:* 071–235 0727. *Clubs:* Travellers', Buck's, Brooks's.

Died 27 May 1993.

GILLIATT, Penelope Ann Douglass Conner, FRAM, FRSL; fiction writer for the New Yorker, since 1967; also employed by The Sunday Times and The Observer; freelance fiction writer of books, plays and films; *b* London, 25 March 1932; UK citizen; *d* of late Cyril Conner and Mary Stephanie Douglass; *m* 1st, 1954, Prof. R. W. Gilliatt, MC (marr. diss.; he *d* 1991); 2nd, 1963, John Osborne (marr. diss.), dramatist; one *d. Educ:* Queen's Coll., Harley St, London; Bennington Coll., Vermont. FRSL 1978. Contributor to New Statesman, Spectator, Guardian, Sight and Sound, Encore, Grand Street, Encounter, London Magazine, London Review of Books, etc; film critic, Observer, 1961–65 and 1966–67, theatre critic, 1965–66; film critic, New Yorker, 1967–79 (six months of each yr). Mem., Bd of Adv. Sponsors, Symphony of UN, 1985–. Mem., Labour Party. Property, and Nobody's Business (plays), perf. Amer. Place Theatre, New York, 1980; But When All's Said and Done (play), Actor's Studio, 1981; BBC plays incl. Living on the Box, The Flight Fund, 1978, and In the Unlikely Event of an Emergency, 1979; Beach of Aurora (original libretto, with music by Tom Eastwood), ENO, 1982. Grant for creative achievement in fiction, National Inst. of Arts and Letters, 1972. *Publications: novels:* One by One, 1965; A State of Change, 1967; The Cutting Edge, 1979; Mortal Matters, 1983; A Woman of Singular Occupation, 1988; *short story collections:* What's It Like Out?, 1968 (Come Back If It Doesn't Get Better, NY 1967); Nobody's Business, 1972; Splendid Lives, 1978; Quotations from Other Lives, 1982; They Sleep Without Dreaming, 1985; 22 stories, 1986; Lingo, 1990; selected as contributor to: Penguin Modern Stories, 1970; Best Short Stories of 1987; Best Short Stories of 1988; Best Short Stories of 1989; *non-fiction:* Unholy Fools: film and theatre, 1975; Jean Renoir: essays, conversations, reviews, 1975; Jacques Tati, 1977; Three-Quarter Face: profiles and reflections (with much additional material), 1980; To Wit, 1990; *screenplay:* Sunday Bloody Sunday, 1971 (Oscar nomination for best orig. screenplay; awards for best orig. screenplay, NY Film Critics Circle, Nat. Soc. of Film Critics, USA, and British Soc. of Film Critics), repr. entitled with new essay by author Making Sunday Bloody Sunday, 1986; lengthy essays in Grand Street about Northumberland, Polish films, new British film-makers; profiles: in New Yorker on Jean Renoir, Woody Allen, Jean-Luc Godard, Jacques Tati, Henri Langlois of the French Cinemathèque, Jeanne Moreau, Diane Keaton, Graham Greene, Luis Buñuel, John Cleese, and Jonathan Miller; in Sunday Telegraph Magazine on John Huston; in Observer on Fred Astaire, Fellini, Whoopi Goldberg, Woody Allen, Stanley Kubrick. *Address:* c/o New Yorker Magazine, 20 West 43rd Street, New York, NY 10036, USA; 29 Burnham Court, Moscow Road, W2 4SW.   *Died 9 May 1993.*

GILLIATT, Prof. Roger William, MC; DM; FRCP; Professor of Clinical Neurology, University of London, 1962–87, then Emeritus; Visiting Scientist, National Institutes of Health, Bethesda, USA, since 1988; Hon. Consulting Physician, National Hospital, Queen Square; *b* 30 July 1922; *o s* of late Sir William Gilliatt, KCVO and Anne Louise, *d* of John Kann, Lyne, Surrey; *m* 1st, 1954, Penelope Ann Douglass Conner (marr. diss.); 2nd, 1963, Mary Elizabeth, *er d* of A. J. W. Green; one *s* two *d. Educ:*

Rugby; Magdalen Coll., Oxford (BA 1st Cl. Hons Nat. Sci.; BM, BCh Oxon 1949; MA). MRCP 1951, FRCP 1961; DM 1955. Served in KRRC, 1942–45 (MC, despatches). Mem., Association of British Neurologists (Pres., 1984–85); Corr. Mem., Amer. Neurological Assoc.; Hon. Member: Amer. Acad. of Neurology; Amer. Assoc. of Electromyography and Electrodiagnosis; Société Française de Neurologie; Australian Assoc. of Neurologists; Soc. Suisse de Neurologie; Acad. Royale de Médecine, Belgium. *Publications:* contribs on neurological topics to medical and scientific jls. *Address:* National Institutes of Health, Bethesda, Md 20892, USA; Flat 3, 34 Queen's Gate Gardens, SW7.

Died 19 Aug. 1991.

GILMARTIN, Hugh, OBE 1981; HM Diplomatic Service, retired; *b* 20 Nov. 1923; *s* of late Edward Gilmartin and Catherine Gilmartin (*née* McFadyen); *m* 1962, Olga, *d* of late Nicholas Alexander Plotnikoff; two *s* one *d*. *Educ:* Holy Cross Academy; Edinburgh Univ. Entered HM Diplomatic Service, 1945; Rome, 1945; Vienna, 1945–47; FO, 1947; UN Special Cttee on the Balkans, 1948; Bahrain, 1949–50; FO, 1951–53; Jakarta, 1953–55; Buenos Aires, 1955–57; Second Secretary, Asuncion, 1957–58; Bahrain, 1959–60; Panama, 1961–63; FO, 1963–65; First Sec. and Head of Chancery, Tegucigalpa, 1965–67; Zürich, 1968–73; First Sec., Office of UK Permanent Representative to the European Communities, Brussels, 1973–75; Asst Head of Training Dept, FO, 1975–79; Basle, 1979–80; Consul-Gen., Brisbane, 1980–83; retired 1983; assigned to Falkland Is Dept, FCO, 1984–85. Governor, Rye St Antony Sch., Oxford. Life Mem., Nat. Trust for Scotland. *Recreations:* walking, swimming, gardening. *Address:* 19 Phillimore Road, Emmer Green, Reading, Berks RG4 8UR. *T:* Reading (0734) 476902. *Clubs:* Civil Service; Royal Commonwealth Society (Queensland).

Died 8 June 1992.

GINSBURG, David; company director; economic, marketing and market research consultant; broadcaster; *b* 18 March 1921; *o s* of late N. Ginsburg; *m* 1954, Louise, *er d* of late S. P. Cassy. *Educ:* University Coll. Sch.; Balliol Coll., Oxford. Chm. OU Democratic Socialist Club, 1941; 2nd Cl, Hons Sch. of Politics, Philosophy and Economics, 1941. Commissioned Oxford and Bucks LI, 1942; Capt. Intelligence duties, 1944–45. Senior Research Officer, Govt Social Survey, 1946–52; Sec. of Research Dept of Labour Party and Sec. of Home Policy Sub-Cttee of National Executive Cttee, 1952–59. MP Dewsbury, 1959–83 (Lab, 1959–81, SDP, 1981–83). Chm., Parly and Scientific Cttee, 1968–71 (Life Mem., 1984); Mem., Select Cttee, Parly Comr for Admin, 1982–83. Contested (SDP) Dewsbury, 1983. Chm., Alax Health Care Ltd, 1990–; Consultant: IMS Internat., 1966–; Saatchi and Saatchi, 1991–. FRSM 1986. *Publications:* miscellaneous articles and book reviews in contemporary publications. *Recreations:* walking, swimming, opera. *Address:* 3 Bell Moor, East Heath Road, NW3 1DY. *Club:* Reform.

Died 18 March 1994.

GINSBURY, Norman; playwright; *b* 8 Nov. 1902; *s* of late J. S. and Rachel Cecily Ginsbury; *m* 1945, Dorothy Jennings. *Educ:* Grocers' Co. Sch.; London University (BSc Hons). Plays produced: Viceroy Sarah, Arts Theatre, 1934, Whitehall Theatre, 1935; Walk in the Sun, "Q", and Embassy, 1939; Take Back Your Freedom (written with Winifred Holtby), Neighbourhood, 1940; The Firstcomers, Bradford Civic Playhouse, 1944; The First Gentleman (written, 1935), New and Savoy, 1945; Belasco, New York, 1956; The Gambler (from the story of Dostoievsky), Embassy, 1946; The Happy Man, New, 1948; Portrait by Lawrence (with M. Moiseiwitsch), Theatre Royal, Stratford, 1949; School for Rivals, Bath

Assembly and Old Vic, Bristol, 1949; also following adaptations of plays by Henrik Ibsen: Ghosts, Vaudeville, 1937; Enemy of the People, Old Vic, 1939; Peer Gynt, Old Vic Season at New Theatre, 1944; A Doll's House, Winter Garden, 1946; John Gabriel Borkman, Mermaid, 1961; a new version of Strindberg's Dance of Death at Tyrone Guthrie Theatre, Minneapolis; and at Yvonne Arnaud Theatre, Guildford, 1966; for the Mayflower 350th anniv., The Forefathers, Athenaeum Theatre, Plymouth, 1970; The Wisest Fool, Yvonne Arnaud, 1974. *Publications:* Viceroy Sarah, 1934; Take Back Your Freedom (collab.), 1939; The First Gentleman, 1946; and the following versions of plays by Ibsen: Ghosts, 1938; Enemy of the People, 1939; Peer Gynt, 1945; A Doll's House, 1950; John Gabriel Borkman, 1960; Rosmersholm, 1961; Pillars of Society, 1962. The Old Lags' League (from a story by W. Pett Ridge), in The Best One-Act Plays of 1960–61; version of Dance of Death by Strindberg in Plays of the Year, 1966; The Shoemaker and The Devil (from a story by Tchehov), in The Best Short Plays of 1968 (NY); The Safety Match (from a story by Tchehov), in Best Short Plays of the World Theatre 1968–73 (NY). *Address:* c/o Messrs Goodman Derrick & Co., 9–11 Fulwood Place, Gray's Inn, WC1V 6HQ. *T:* 071–404 0606. *Club:* Dramatists'. *Died 15 Oct. 1991.*

GIRLING, Maj.-Gen. Peter Howard, CB 1972; OBE 1961; CEng, FIMechE, FIEE; Director of Operations, Open University, 1972–80; *b* 18 May 1915; *m* 1942, Stella Muriel (*née* Hope); two *d*. Commissioned, RAOC, 1939; transferred to REME, 1942; served War of 1939–45; India, 1945–47; Staff Coll., Camberley, 1948; Egypt, 1949–52; JSSC, Latimer, 1953; BAOR, 1953–55; Col, 1961; WO, 1961–65; HQ FARELF, 1965–67; Brig., 1965; Comd Berkshire Sub-District, 1967–68; Comdt, REME Training Centre, 1967–69; Maj.-Gen., 1969; Dir of Electrical and Mechanical Engineering (Army), 1969–72; Col Comdt, REME, 1972–77. Freeman of City of London, 1973; Liveryman, Turners' Co., 1973–. Hon. MA Open Univ., 1982. *Club:* Army and Navy. *Died 9 July 1991.*

GISH, Lillian Diana; actress; *b* 14 Oct. 1893; *née* de Guiche. *Educ:* privately. Began acting in theatre at five years of age and at twelve entered motion pictures; Katrina in Crime and Punishment (with John Gielgud), 1948; Ophelia to John Gielgud's Hamlet, The Curious Savage, 1950; Miss Mabel, 1951 (USA); acting mainly on television, 1952; in play, The Trip to Bountiful (for the Theatre Guild), 1953–54; The Chalk Garden, 1957; The Family Reunion, 1958; directed, The Beggar's Opera, 1958; All the Way House, 1960–61 (won Drama Critics and Pulitzer prize as best play); A Passage to India, play (Chicago), 1962–63; Too True to be Good (G. B. Shaw's play) (New York), 1963; Romeo and Juliet (Stratford Festival Theatre), 1965; Anya (musical), 1967; I Never Sang for my Father, 1968; Uncle Vanya, NY, 1973; A Musical Jubilee (musical), NY, 1975. Lillian Gish and the Movies: the art of film, 1900–28 (concert programmes), Moscow, Paris, London and USA, 1969–73; QE2 World tour, 1975; lecturing and performing for The Theatre Guild at Sea on the Rotterdam, 1975; Celebration, Metropolitan Opera 100th Gala Benefit (Spectre de la Rose, with Patrick DuPond), 1984. *Early films include:* Birth of a Nation, 1914; Intolerance, 1916; Souls Triumphant; Hearts of the World, 1918; The Great Love, 1918; Broken Blossoms, 1918; Way Down East, 1920; The Orphans of the Storm, 1922; The White Sister, 1923; Romola, 1924; The Wind, 1928; *later films include:* The Night of the Hunter, 1954; The Cobweb, 1955; Orders to Kill, 1957; The Unforgiven, 1959; Follow Me Boys, 1966; Warning Shot, 1966; The Comedians, 1967; A Wedding, 1978; Hambone and Hillie, 1984; Sweet Liberty, 1986; The Whales of August, 1987. *Television:* frequent appearances include three plays, 1962; plays, 1963;

Arsenic and Old Lace, 1969; Sparrow, CBS, 1978; Love Boat, and Thin Ice, CBS, 1980. Life of Lillian Gish (documentary film by Jeanne Moreau); Hommage à Lillian Gish (ballet by Catherine Berge), France, 1984. Dorothy and Lillian Gish Film Theatre, founded Bowling Green State Univ., Ohio, 1976. Hon. AFD, Rollins Coll., Fla; Hon. HHD, Holyoke Coll.; Hon. Dr of Performing Arts, Bowling Green State Univ., Ohio, 1976. Hon. Oscar, Acad. Motion Picture Arts and Scis, 1971; Life Achievement Award, AFI, 1984; Handel Medallion, NYC, 1973; Medal of Arts and Letters (France), 1983. *Publications:* Lillian Gish: an autobiography, 1968; Lillian Gish, The Movies, Mr Griffith and Me, 1969; Dorothy and Lillian Gish, 1973; An Actor's Life for Me!, 1987. *Recreation:* travel. *Address:* 430 East 57th Street, New York, NY 10022, USA. *Died 27 Feb. 1993.*

GITTINGS, Robert (William Victor), CBE 1970; LittD Cantab, 1970; poet, biographer, playwright; *b* 1 Feb. 1911; *s* of late Surg.-Capt. Fred Claude Bromley Gittings, RN (retd) and Dora Mary Brayshaw; *m* 1st, 1934, Katherine Edith Cambell (marr. diss.); two *s*; 2nd, 1949, Joan Grenville Manton; one *d. Educ:* St Edward's Sch., Oxford; Jesus Coll., Cambridge (Scholar). 1st Cl. Historical Tripos, 1933. Research Student, and Research Fellow, 1933–38, Supervisor in History, 1938–40, Hon. Fellow, 1979, Jesus Coll., Cambridge (Leslie Stephen Lectr, 1980); writer and producer for broadcasting, 1940–63. Professor: Vanderbilt University, Tennessee, 1966; Boston Univ., 1970; Univ. of Washington, 1972, 1974 and 1977 (Danz Lectr); Meiji Univ., Tokyo, 1985. Hon. LittD Leeds, 1981. *Publications: poetry and verse-plays:* The Roman Road, 1932; The Story of Psyche, 1936; Wentworth Place, 1950; The Makers of Violence (Canterbury Festival), 1951; Through a Glass Lightly, 1952; Famous Meeting, 1953; Out of This Wood (sequence of plays), 1955; This Tower My Prison, 1961; Matters of Love and Death, 1968; Conflict at Canterbury, 1970; American Journey, 1972; Collected Poems, 1976; People, Places, Personal, 1985; *biography and criticism:* John Keats: The Living Year, 1954; The Mask of Keats, 1956; Shakespeare's Rival, 1960; (ed) The Living Shakespeare, 1960; (ed with E. Hardy) Some Recollections by Emma Hardy, 1961; (with Jo Manton) The Story of John Keats, 1962; The Keats Inheritance, 1964; (ed) Selected Poems and Letters of John Keats, 1966; John Keats, 1968 (W. H. Smith Literary Award, 1969); John Keats: Selected Letters, 1970; The Odes of Keats, 1970; Young Thomas Hardy, 1975 (Christian Gauss Award, Phi Beta Kappa, 1975); The Older Hardy, 1978 (RSL Heinemann Award, 1979, James Tait Black Meml Prize, 1979); The Nature of Biography, 1978; (with Jo Manton) The Second Mrs Hardy, 1979; (ed with J. Reeves) Selected Poems of Thomas Hardy, 1981; (with Jo Manton) Dorothy Wordsworth, 1985 (Southern Arts Literary Prize, 1987); contrib. to Keats-Shelley Memorial Bulletin, Keats-Shelley Journal, Harvard Library Bulletin, etc; *posthumous publication:* (with Jo Manton) Claire Clairmont and the Shelleys, 1992. *Recreations:* outdoor pursuits except blood-sports. *Address:* The Stables, East Dean, Chichester, West Sussex. *T:* Singleton (024363) 328. *Died 18 Feb. 1992.*

GLANVILLE BROWN, William; *see* Brown.

GLASS, Ven. Edward Brown; Archdeacon of Man, 1964–78, then Emeritus; Rector of Kirk Andreas, Isle of Man, 1964–78; *b* 1 July 1913; *s* of William and Phoebe Harriet Glass; *m* 1940, Frances Katharine Calvert; one *s* two *d. Educ:* King William's Coll., IoM; Durham Univ. (MA). Deacon 1937, priest 1938, dio. Manchester; Curate: St Mary's, Wardleworth, Rochdale, 1937; Gorton Parish Church, Manchester, 1937–42; Vicar: St John's, Hopwood, Heywood, Manchester, 1942–51; St Olave's, Ramsey, IoM, 1951–55; Castletown, IoM, 1955–64. Sec.,

Diocesan Convocation, 1958–64; Proctor for Clergy, Convocation of York, 1959–64; Member, Church Assembly and General Synod, 1959–78; Warden of Diocesan Readers, 1969–78; Chm., Diocesan Advisory Cttee, 1975–78. *Recreations:* gardening, ornithology, touring in Norway. *Address:* c/o Mrs E. Clucas, Carhonnag, Regaby, near Ramsey, Isle of Man IM7 4EJ. *Died 2 June 1995.*

GLASSE, Thomas Henry, CMG 1961; MVO 1955; MBE 1946; retired as Counsellor in HM Diplomatic Service, and Head of Protocol Department, Foreign Office (1957–61); *b* 14 July 1898; *s* of late Thomas and Harriette Glasse; *m* 1st, 1935, Elsie May Dyter (*d* 1965); no *c*; 2nd, 1966, Ethel Alice Needham (*d* 1985); 3rd, 1988, Maria Philomena Cover. *Educ:* Latymer Foundation Upper Sch., Hammersmith. Entered Civil Service as a Boy Clerk, 1914. Army Service, 1/10th Bn Middx Regt, 1917–19. Joined the Foreign Office, 1921. Delegate of United Kingdom to Vienna Conference on Diplomatic Relations, 1961. *Recreations:* books, music, garden, travel. *Address:* 72 Lynch Road, Farnham, Surrey GU9 8BT. *T:* Farnham (0252) 716662. *Club:* Travellers'.

Died 5 Jan. 1994.

GLENTORAN, 2nd Baron, *cr* 1939, of Ballyalloly; **Daniel Stewart Thomas Bingham Dixon,** KBE 1973; PC (Northern Ireland) 1953; Bt 1903; Lord-Lieutenant, City of Belfast, 1975–85 (HM Lieutenant, 1950–76); *b* 19 Jan. 1912; *s* of 1st Baron Glentoran, OBE, PC and Hon. Emily Ina Florence Bingham (*d* 1957), *d* of 5th Baron Clanmorris; *S* father 1950; *m* 1933, Lady Diana Mary Wellesley, (*d* 1984), *d* of 3rd Earl Cowley; two *s* one *d. Educ:* Eton; RMC Sandhurst. Reg. Army, Grenadier Guards; served War of 1939–45 (despatches); retired 1946 (with hon. rank of Lieut-Col); psc. MP (U) Bloomfield Division of Belfast, NI Parliament, Oct. 1950–Feb. 1961; Parliamentary Sec., Ministry of Commerce, NI, 1952–53; Minister of Commerce, 1953–61; Minister in Senate, NI, 1961–72, Speaker of Senate, 1964–72. Hon. Col 6th Battalion Royal Ulster Rifles, 1956–61, retd rank of Hon. Col. *Heir: s* Hon. Thomas Robin Valerian Dixon [*b* 21 April 1935; *m* 1959, Rona, *d* of Capt. G. C. Colville; three *s*; *m* 1990, Margaret Rainey]. *Address:* Drumadarragh House, Doagh, Co. Antrim, Northern Ireland BT39 0TA. *T:* Ballyclare (019603) 40222. *Club:* Ulster (Belfast).

Died 22 July 1995.

GLOVER, Group Capt. John Neville, CMG 1963; *b* 12 July 1913; *s* of John Robert Glover and Sybil Glover (*née* Cureton); *m* 1st, 1940, Margot Burdick; one *s*; 2nd, 1956, June Patricia Bruce Gaskell. *Educ:* Tonbridge Sch. Commissioned 6th Bn Devonshire Regt (TA), 1933; RAF (Gen. Duties Branch), 1934. Served RAF, 1934–46; RAFRO, 1946–59 (retained rank of Group Capt.). Called to Bar, Gray's Inn, 1949. Appointed to Colonial Legal Service, 1951; served: Ghana (Crown Counsel and Senior Crown Counsel), 1951–57; Western Pacific High Commission (Legal Adviser and Attorney-General, British Solomon Islands Protectorate), 1957–63. QC (Western Pacific), 1962. Retired from HM Overseas Civil Service, 1963. Comr to examine Human Rights Laws in the Bahamas, 1964–65. Legal Draftsman in the Bahamas, 1965–66. Law Revision Comr for certain overseas territories, 1967–91. *Recreation:* fishing. *Address:* Clam End, Trebullett, near Launceston, Cornwall PL15 9QQ. *T:* Coad's Green (01566) 782347. *Club:* Royal Air Force.

Died 30 Nov. 1995.

GLYN, Hilary Beaujolais; *b* 12 Jan. 1916; *s* of Maurice Glyn, *g s* of 1st Baron Wolverton, and Hon. Maud Grosvenor, *d* of 2nd Baron Ebury; *m* 1938, Caroline Bull; one *s* two *d. Educ:* Eton; New Coll., Oxford. DipEconPolSc. Served, RASC Supp. Reserve, 1939–46 (A/Major). Joined Gallaher Ltd, 1937; Director, 1962;

Asst Man. Dir, 1975; retd, 1976. *Recreations:* shooting, horse trials. *Address:* Castle Hill Cottage, Boothby Graffoe, Lincoln LN5 0LF. *T:* Lincoln (01522) 810885.
Died 20 June 1995.

GODDARD, Lt-Gen. Eric Norman, CB 1947; CIE 1944; CBE 1942 (OBE 1919); MVO 1936; MC; Indian Army, retired; *b* 6 July 1897; 3rd *s* of late Arthur Goddard, Chartered Accountant, London; *m* 1939, Elizabeth Lynch, *d* of late Major Lynch Hamilton and Frances Prioleau; one *s. Educ:* Dulwich Coll. Commissioned Indian Army, 1915; service in Mesopotamia, Persia and Kurdistan, 1916–19 (despatches twice, OBE, MC); GSO3 AHQ India, 1923–25; 12th Frontier Force Regt, 1928; Staff Coll., Quetta, 1928–29; Bde Major, Nowshera Bde, 1932–34; Chitral relief, 1932 (despatches, bar to MC); Mohmand operations, 1933 (despatches); Bt Major, 1933; GSO2 Eastern Comd, 1934–36; Officer i/c King's Indian Orderly Officers, 1936 (MVO 4th class); Comdt 4th Bn 15 Punjab Regt, 1936; Bt Col 1939 and Col i/c Administration, Burma Army; Brigade Commander, Oct. 1940; Maj.-Gen. i/c Administration Army in Burma, Dec. 1941; served in Burma and on Eastern front, Dec. 1941–Dec. 1944, including Maj.-Gen. i/c Admin 11th Army Group and Allied Land Forces SE Asia, 1943–44 (despatches four times, CIE, CBE); GOC-in-C Southern Comd, India, 1947–48; Subst. Maj.-Gen. 1944; Actg Lieut-Gen. 1947; retired Nov. 1948 with hon. rank of Lieut-Gen. Special appointment CCG, 1949–53; Dir of Civil Defence, North-Western Region (Manchester), 1955–63; Pres., East Lancs Br., British Red Cross, 1964–66. *Address:* Kent House, Camden Park, Tunbridge Wells, Kent TN2 5AD. *T:* Tunbridge Wells (0892) 513755.
Died 11 June 1992.

GODMAN IRVINE, Rt Hon. Sir Bryant; *see* Irvine.

GODWIN, Dame (Beatrice) Anne, DBE 1962 (OBE 1952); a Governor of the BBC, 1962–68; a full-time Member of the Industrial Court, 1963–69; *b* 1897; *d* of William Godwin. Gen. Sec., Clerical and Administrative Workers' Union, 1956–62. Chm. of the TUC, 1961–62. *Address:* 25 Fullbrooks Avenue, Worcester Park, Surrey KT4 7PE.
Died 11 Jan. 1992.

GOHEL, Sir Jayvantsinhji (Kayaji), Kt 1989; CBE 1984; Director, Meghraj Group Ltd, including Meghraj Bank Ltd and other subsidiaries, since 1960; *b* 14 Aug. 1915; *s* of Kayaji Kesarisinhji Gohel and Nandakunver Kavaji Gohel; *m* 1941, Sajjankunver; two *s. Educ:* schs in India and England; Middle Temple. Barrister at Law, 1941. Judge, Mem. of Administrative Council and Diwan, Morvi princely state, W India, 1942–48; Indian Administrative Services, 1948–60: Dist Collector and Magistrate; Settlements Comr under Min. of Rehabilitation; Perm. Sec. to State Govt of Saurashtra in Educn, Rehabilitation and Communications; Political Adviser with Internat. Commn for Supervision and Control in Indo-China. *Recreation:* working for various charities (Indian and particularly British). *Address:* Meghraj Court, 18 Jockey's Fields, WC1R 4BW. *T:* 0171–831 6881. *Club:* Bankers'.
Died 19 May 1995.

GOLDEN, Grace Lydia, ARCA; *b* 2 April 1904; *d* of H. F. Golden. *Educ:* City of London Sch. for Girls. Art training at Chelsea Art Sch. and Royal College of Art; further studies at Regent Street Polytechnic; black and white illustrator, posters, panoramas; watercolour artist and wood-engraver; Exhibitor at Royal Academy, 1936, 1937, 1938 and 1940; Artists' London, Mus. of London, 1993; Retrospective exhibn, South London Art Gall., 1979; watercolour, Summer Evening, Embankment Gardens, and oil-painting, Free Speech, purchased by Chantry Trustees; work also purchased by V&A Mus., Imp. War Mus., Mus. of London, and S London Art Gall.

Publication: Old Bankside, 1951. *Recreation:* theatre. *Address:* 21 Douglas Waite House, 73–75 Priory Road, NW6 3NJ. *T:* 071–624 3204.
Died 3 June 1993.

GOLDING, Sir William (Gerald), Kt 1988; CBE 1966; CLit 1984; FRSL 1955; author; *b* 19 Sept. 1911; *s* of Alec A. and Mildred A. Golding; *m* 1939, Ann, *e d* of late E. W. Brookfield, The Homestead, Bedford Place, Maidstone; one *s* one *d. Educ:* Marlborough Grammar Sch.; Brasenose Coll., Oxford (MA 1961; Hon. Fellow, 1966). Served RN, War of 1939–45. Former actor, writer and producer with small theatre cos; formerly teacher, Bishop Wordsworth's Sch., Salisbury. Hon. DLitt: Sussex, 1970; Kent, 1974; Warwick, 1981; Oxford, 1983; Sorbonne, 1983; Hon. LLD Bristol, 1984. Nobel Prize for Literature, 1983. *Publications:* Poems, 1934; Lord of the Flies, 1954 (filmed 1963); The Inheritors, 1955; Pincher Martin, 1956; Brass Butterfly (play), 1958; Free Fall, 1959; The Spire, 1964; The Hot Gates (essays), 1965; The Pyramid, 1967; The Scorpion God, 1971; Darkness Visible, 1979 (James Tait Black Memorial Prize, 1980); Rites of Passage, 1980 (Booker McConnell Prize); A Moving Target (essays), 1982; The Paper Men, 1984; An Egyptian Journal (travel), 1985; Close Quarters, 1987; Fire Down Below, 1989; To the Ends of the Earth, 1991; *posthumous publication:* The Double Tongue, 1995. *Recreations:* music, Greek, riding. *Address:* c/o Faber & Faber, 3 Queen Square, WC1N 3AU. *Clubs:* Athenæum, Savile.
Died 19 June 1993.

GOLDSMITH, Maj.-Gen. Robert Frederick Kinglake, CB 1955; CBE 1952; retired; *b* 21 June 1907; *s* of late Col Harry Dundas Goldsmith, CBE, DSO; *m* 1935, Brenda (*d* 1983), *d* of Frank Bartlett, late Ceylon Civil Service; one *s. Educ:* Wellington Coll., Berks. Commnd Duke of Cornwall's LI, 1927; served War of 1939–45, in N Africa, Italy, NW Europe; Dep. Chief of Staff, First Allied Airborne Army, 1944–45; comd 131 Inf. Bde (TA), 1950–51; Chief of Staff, British Troops in Egypt, 1951–54, and of HQ Western Command, 1956–59; GOC Yorks District, 1959–62; Col, Duke of Cornwall's LI, 1958–59; Col Somerset and Cornwall LI, 1960–63. Editor, The Army Quarterly, 1966–73. Comdr, Legion of Merit (US), 1945. *Address:* Brendon, Park Road, Winchester, Hants SO23 7BE. *Club:* Army and Navy.
Died 7 April 1995.

GOLDSTONE, David Israel, CBE 1971; JP; DL; Chairman, Sterling McGregor Ltd Group of Companies; *b* Aug. 1908; *s* of Philip and Bessie Goldstone; *m* 1931, Belle Franks; one *s* two *d.* Manchester Chamber of Commerce and Industry: Pres., 1970–72; Emeritus Dir, 1978; Chm., Pension Bd, 1968; Chm., NW Regions Chambers of Commerce Council, 1970–73; Exec. Mem., Association of British Chambers of Commerce Nat. Council, 1970–73; Exec. Mem., British Nat. Council, Internat. Chambers of Commerce; Mem., NW Telecommunications Bd. Vice-Pres., Greater Manchester Youth Assoc.; Founder Trustee and Vice-Pres., Greater Manchester Museum of Science and Industry; Mem. local tribunals, charitable organisations, etc. JP Manchester, 1958; DL Manchester, 1978; High Sheriff of Greater Manchester, 1980–81. Hon. MA Manchester, 1979. *Address:* Dellstar, Elm Road, Didsbury, Manchester M20 0XD. *T:* 061–445 1868.
Died 1 Sept. 1992.

GOLDTHORPE, Brian Lees, FCIB; Director, Midland Bank, 1983–92; *b* 11 June 1933; *s* of Gordon and Winifred Mary Goldthorpe; *m* 1957, Mary (Molly) Commins; one *s* one *d. Educ:* Wath-on-Dearne Grammar Sch. Midland Bank: joined, 1949; various Br., Reg. and Hd Office posts, 1949–77; Gen. Man. (Operations), 1977–80; Gen. Man., N Div., 1980–81; Sen. Gen. Man. and Chief Exec., Forward Trust Gp, 1981–83; Chief Executive: Gp Risk Management, 1983–86; Corporate Banking, 1986–87; UK

Banking Sector, 1987–89; Dep. Chief Exec., 1989–92. *Recreations:* music, golf. *Address:* c/o Midland Bank, Poultry, EC2P 2BX. *T:* 071–260 8000.

Died 13 Nov. 1992.

GOLOMBEK, Harry, OBE 1966; writer on chess; *b* London, 1 March 1911; *s* of Barnet and Emma Golombek; unmarried. *Educ:* Wilson's Gram. Sch.; London Univ. Served in RA, 1940–42, Foreign Office, 1942–45. Editor British Chess Magazine, 1938, 1939, 1940; Joint Editor, British Chess Magazine, 1949–67; Chess correspondent: The Times, 1945; The Observer, 1955–79. British Chess Champion, 1947, 1949, and 1955 (prize-winner 14 times); Jt British Veteran Chess Champion, 1984; 1st prize in 4 International chess tournaments. Recognized as International Master by Federation Internationale des Echecs, 1948; Internat. Grandmaster, World Chess Fedn, 1985. Represented Great Britain in 9 Chess Olympiads and Capt. Brit. team, Helsinki, 1952, Amsterdam, 1954, Munich, 1958, Leipzig, 1960, Varna, 1962. Pres., Zone 1 World Chess Fedn, 1974–78. *Publications:* 50 Great Games of Modern Chess, 1942; Capablanca's 100 Best Games of Chess, 1947; World Chess Championship 1948, 1949; Pocket Guide to Chess Openings, 1949; Hastings Tournament 1948–49, 1949; Southsea Tournament 1949, 1949; Prague 1946, 1950; Budapest 1952, 1952; Reti's Best Games of Chess, 1954; World Chess Championship 1954, 1954; The Game of Chess, 1954; 22nd USSR Chess Championship, 1956; World Chess Championship 1957, 1957; Modern Opening Chess Strategy, 1959; Fischer *v* Spassky 1972, 1973; A History of Chess, 1976; (with W. Hartston) The Best Games of C. H. O'D. Alexander, 1976; Encyclopedia of Chess, 1977, new edn 1981; Beginning Chess, 1981. *Recreations:* music, the Stock Exchange, the theatre. *Died 7 Jan. 1995.*

GOLT, Sidney, CB 1964; consultant; Director, MGK Trade Consultants Ltd; *b* West Hartlepool, 31 March 1910; *s* of late Wolf and Fanny Golt; *m* 1947, Jean, *d* of Ralph Oliver; two *d. Educ:* Portsmouth Grammar Sch.; Christ Church, Oxford. PPE 1931; James Mew Scholar, Oxford, 1934. Statistician, Tin Producers' Assoc., 1936–40; joined Central Price Regulation Cttee, 1941; Asst Sec., Bd of Trade, 1945–60; Sec., Central Price Regulation Cttee, 1945–46; Under-Sec., Bd of Trade, 1960–68 (Adviser on Commercial Policy, 1964–68), Deputy Secretary, 1968–70. UK Mem., Preparatory Cttee for European Free Trade Assoc., Geneva, 1960; Leader, UK Delegns to UN Conf. on Trade and Development, New Delhi, 1968, and to Trade and Development Bd, 1965–68; UK Mem., Commonwealth Gp of Experts on Internat. Economic Policy, 1975–77; Advr on Internat. Trade, Internat. Chamber of Commerce, 1978–90. Chm., Linked Life Assurance Gp, 1972–81. Ed., Tin, and Tin World Statistics, 1936–40. *Publications:* (jtly) Towards an Open World Economy, 1972; The GATT Negotiations: 1973–75: a guide to the issues, 1974; 1973–79: the closing stage, 1978; The New Mercantilism, 1974; The Developing Countries in the GATT System, 1978; (jtly) Western Economies in Transition, 1980; Trade Issues in the Mid 1980's, 1982; The GATT Negotiations 1986–1990, 1988. *Recreations:* travel, looking at pictures, bridge. *Address:* 37 Rowan Road, W6 7DT. *T:* 0171–602 1410. *Club:* Reform. *Died 4 June 1995.*

GOOD, Prof. Ronald D'Oyley, ScD; Head of Department of Botany, University of Hull, 1928–59, Professor Emeritus, 1959; *b* 5 March 1896; 2nd *s* of William Ernest and Mary Gray Good; *m* 1927, Patty Gwynneth Griffith (*d* 1975); one *d. Educ:* Weymouth Coll.; Downing Coll., Cambridge (Senior Scholar). MA, ScD Cantab. Served European War, 1914–18, 4th Bn Dorset Regt, and 2/5th Bn Lincolnshire Regt (France). Staff of Botany Department, British Museum (Nat. Hist.), 1922–28.

Publications: Plants and Human Economics, 1933; The Old Roads of Dorset, 1940, 1966; Weyland, 1945; The Geography of the Flowering Plants, 1947, rev. new edn, 1974; A Geographical Handbook of the Dorset Flora, 1948; Features of Evolution in the Flowering Plants, 1956, new edn USA, 1974; The Lost Villages of Dorset, 1979; The Philosophy of Evolution, 1981; A Concise Flora of Dorset, 1984; contribs to scientific journals. *Address:* Thamesfield Nursing Home, Wargrave Road, Henley-on-Thames, Oxon RG9 2LX. *Died 11 Dec. 1992.*

GOODALE, Cecil Paul; *b* 29 Dec. 1918; *s* of Cecil Charles Wemyss Goodale and Annie Goodale; *m* 1st, 1946, Ethel Margaret (*née* Studer); 2nd, 1984, Margaret Beatrice (*née* Cook). *Educ:* East Sheen County Sch. War Office, 1936; Min. of Supply, 1939; Min. of Health, later DHSS, 1947–78: Sen. Exec. Officer, 1950; Principal, 1953; Principal Regional Officer, 1962; Asst Sec., 1967; Under-Sec., 1976–78. *Recreations:* music, photography. *Address:* 37 Highfield Drive, Kingsbridge, Devon TQ7 1JR. *T:* Kingsbridge (0548) 853511. *Died 22 Sept. 1992.*

GOODALL, Peter, CBE 1983; TD 1950; Executive Chairman and Chief Executive, 1977–86, and Director, 1970–89, Hepworth Ceramic Holdings PLC; *b* 14 July 1920; *s* of Major Tom Goodall, DSO, MC and Alice (*née* Black); *m* 1948, Sonja Jeanne (*née* Burt); one *s* one *d. Educ:* Ashville Coll., Harrogate. Admitted Solicitor, 1948. Served War, Duke of Wellington's Regt and Parachute Regt, 1939–46 (Captain). Practised as Solicitor with family firm, Goodall & Son, and Whitfield Son & Hallam, 1948–67; Dir, Hepworth Iron Co. Ltd, 1967–70; company merged with General Refractories Group Ltd to form Hepworth Ceramic Holdings Ltd, 1970; Man. Dir, 1971–77. Member Council: CBI, 1981–88; British United Industrialists, 1984–89. *Recreations:* shooting, fishing. *Address:* Springfield House, Sicklinghall Road, Wetherby, W Yorks LS22 6AA. *T:* Wetherby (01937) 581297.

Died 30 Nov. 1995.

GOODCHILD, Lt-Col Sidney, LVO 1969; DL; retired; Vice-Lieutenant of Caernarvonshire, 1969–74; *b* 4 Jan. 1903; *s* of late Charles Goodchild; *m* 1934, Elizabeth G. P. Everett (decd); two *s* one *d. Educ:* Friars Sch.; Staff Coll., Quetta. Commnd Royal Welch Fusiliers, 1923; 14th Punjab Regt, Indian Army, 1930; Staff Captain, 4th Inf. Bde, 1937; DA&QMG (Movements), Army HQ India, 1939; AQMG (Movts), Iraq, 1940; comd 7/14 Punjab Regt, 1942; AQMG, Army HQ India, 1945; comd 1st Sikh LI and 5th Bde, 4th Indian Div., 1946; despatches thrice, 1940–44. Chm., NW Wales War Pensioners' Cttee; Pres., Gwynedd Br., SSAFA, 1969–. Alderman, Caernarvonshire CC, 1972–74. DL Caernarvonshire, 1964; DL Gwynedd, 1974. *Address:* Cwm Caeth, Nantmor, Caernarfon, Gwynedd, N Wales LL55 4YH.

Died 4 Aug. 1994.

GOODINGS, Rt Rev. Allen; Assistant Bishop of Ottawa; Bishop of Quebec, 1977–91; *b* Barrow-in-Furness, Lancs, 7 May 1925; *s* of late Thomas Jackson Goodings and Ada Tate; *m* 1959, Joanne Talbot; one *s* one *d. Educ:* Sir George Williams Univ. (BA); McGill Univ. (BD); Diocesan Theological Coll., Montreal (LTh; Hon. DD). Studied engineering and worked for Vickers Armstrongs (Britain) and Canadian Vickers (Montreal); studied in Montreal and ordained into Ministry of Anglican Church of Canada, 1959. Chaplain, Canadian Grenadier Guards, Montreal, 1966–69; Dean of Holy Trinity Cathedral, Quebec, 1969–77. Played Rugby Union (capped for Lancashire, 1947/8, including County Championship). *Recreations:* skiing, tennis, squash, cycling. *Address:* 1-C Castlebrook Lane, Nepean, Ontario KTG 5E4, Canada. *Clubs:* Mess (Royale 22nd Regiment, Quebec); Quebec Garrison (Hon. Mem.). *Died 15 Dec. 1992.*

GOODMAN, Baron, *cr* 1965 (Life Peer), of the City of Westminster; **Arnold Abraham Goodman,** CH 1972; MA, LLM; Master of University College, Oxford, 1976–86 (Hon. Fellow, 1986); Founder and Consultant, Goodman Derrick and Co., Solicitors; *b* 21 Aug. 1913; *s* of Joseph and Bertha Goodman; unmarried. *Educ:* University Coll., London (Fellow 1967); Downing Coll., Cambridge (Hon. Fellow, 1968). Enlisted Gunner, RA, TA, Sept. 1939, retd as Major, Nov. 1945. Chairman: British Lion Films, 1965–72; Charter Film Productions, 1973–84. Dir, The Observer Ltd, 1976–81; Chairman: Observer Editl Trust, 1967–76; Newspaper Publishers Assoc., 1970–76; Jewish Chronicle Trust, 1970–94. Chairman: Housing Corp., 1973–77; Nat. Building Agency, 1973–78; Mem., IRC, 1969–71. Chairman: Cttee of Inquiry into Charity Law, 1974–76; Motability, 1977–94; Council for Charitable Support, 1986–89. Chm., Arts Council of GB, 1965–72; Dep. Chm., British Council, 1976–91 (Mem., 1967–91); President: NBL, 1972–85; Inst. of Jewish Affairs, 1975–90. Chairman: Cttee (on behalf of Arts Council) on London Orchestras, 1964, reported 1965; Australian Music Foundn, 1975–; Mem., S Bank Theatre Bd, 1968–82; President: Theatres Adv. Council, 1972–; Theatre Investment Fund, 1985– (Chm., 1976–85); ENO, 1986– (Chm., 1977–86); Theatres Trust, 1987– (Chm., 1976–87); Union of Liberal & Progressive Synagogues, 1988–; Assoc. for Business Sponsorship of the Arts, 1989– (Chm., 1976–89); Dir, Royal Opera House, Covent Garden, 1972–83; Gov., Royal Shakespeare Theatre, 1972–94. Gov., Coll. of Law, 1975–84. Life Mem., RPO, 1976. Hon. QC 1993. Hon. LLD: London, 1965; Bath, Liverpool, 1976; Hon. DLitt City, 1975; hon. degrees from other univs. *Publication:* Tell Them I'm On My Way (autobiog.), 1993. *Address:* 90 Fetter Lane, EC4A 1EQ. *T:* 0171–404 0606.   *Died 12 May 1995.*

GOODMAN, Rt Rev. Morse Lamb; *b* Rosedale, Ont, 27 May 1917; *s* of Frederick James Goodman and Mary Mathilda Arkwright; *m* 1943, Patricia May Cunningham; three *s* one *d. Educ:* Trinity Coll., Univ. of Toronto. BA Trin., 1940; LTh Trin., 1942. Deacon, 1942, priest, 1943, Diocese of Algoma; Asst Curate, St Paul's, Ft William, 1942–43; Incumbent, Murillo, Algoma, 1943–46; Rector, St Thomas, Ft William, 1946–53; Rector, St James, Winnipeg, 1953–60; Dean of Brandon, 1960–65; Rector, Christ Church, Edmonton, 1965–67; Bishop of Calgary, 1968–83. Conductor of Canadian Broadcasting Corporation Programme, Family Worship, 1954–68. Patron, Nat. Prayer Book Soc. Hon. DD: Trinity, 1961; Emmanuel and St Chad's, 1968. Companion, Order of Coventry Cross of Nails, 1974; GCLJ. Columnist, Country Guide, 1961–. *Publication:* Let's Think It Over (A Christian's Day Book), 1986. *Recreations:* fishing, walking, photography, enology. *Address:* Box 15, Blind Bay, BC V0E 1H0, Canada. *Club:* Ranchman's.
Died 12 Dec. 1993.

GOODWIN, Prof. Albert, MA; Professor of Modern History in the University of Manchester, 1953–69 (Dean of the Faculty of Arts, 1966–68), then Emeritus Professor; *b* 2 Aug. 1906; 3rd *s* of Albert and Edith Ellen Goodwin; *m* 1st, 1935, Mary Ethelwyn (*d* 1981), *e d* of late Capt. W. Millner, Tettenhall, Staffs; two *s* one *d*; 2nd, 1985, Mrs Barbara Mallows (*d* 1990). *Educ:* King Edward VII School, Sheffield; Jesus Coll., Oxford; Sorbonne. Scholar; Gladstone Memorial Prizeman (Oxford), 1926; 1st Cl. Mod. Hist., 1928; Laming Travelling Fellow, The Queen's Coll., Oxford, 1928–29. Asst Lectr in European History, Univ. of Liverpool, 1929–31; Lectr in Mod. Hist. and Economics, 1931, Fellow and Tutor, Jesus Coll., Oxford, 1933; Junior Dean, Librarian and Dean of Degrees, 1931–39; Univ. Lectr in Mod. French Hist., 1938. Staff Officer (Sqdn Ldr) in RAFVR in Air Ministry War Room, 1940–43; Historical Branch, Air Ministry, 1944–45.

Senior Tutor, 1947–48, and Vice-Principal of Jesus Coll., Oxford, 1949–51. Examiner in Final Hon. Sch. of Mod. Hist. (Oxford) 1948–49, Chm., 1950; Senior Univ. Lectr in Revolutionary and Napoleonic Period, 1948–53; Vis. Fellow, All Souls Coll., Oxford, 1969–70. Member: Council of Royal Historical Soc. (Vice-Pres.); Royal Commn on Historical MSS, 1966–81; Governor of John Rylands Library, Manchester. Pres., Sherborne Hist. Soc.; Chm., Sherborne Museum Council, 1981–82. *Publications:* The Abbey of St Edmundsbury, 1931; The Battle of Britain (Air Ministry Pamphlet 156), 1943; The French Revolution, 1953; The European Nobility in the Eighteenth Century (contrib. and ed), 1953; A select list of works on Europe and Europe Overseas, 1715–1815 (co-editor contributor), 1956; The Friends of Liberty: the English democratic movement in the age of the French Revolution, 1979; (ed and contrib.) Vol. VIII New Cambridge Modern History; articles in Eng. Hist. Review, History, Encyclopædia Britannica, etc. *Recreations:* golf, antiques. *Address:* Tyndale Nursing Home, 36 Preston Road, Yeovil, Somerset BA21 3AQ.
Died 22 Sept. 1995.

GOODWIN, Air Vice-Marshal Edwin Spencer, CB 1944; CBE 1941; AFC; *b* 12 Dec. 1894. Served European War, 1914–19: Flt Sub-Lieut RNAS, 1916; War of 1939–45 (CBE, CB); Air Officer i/c Administration, HQ Bomber Command, 1945; retired, 1948. Group Capt. 1939; Air Commodore, 1941; Air Vice-Marshal, 1948.
Died 17 May 1991.

GOODWIN, Prof. Geoffrey Lawrence, BSc (Econ); Montague Burton Professor of International Relations in the University of London (tenable at London School of Economics), 1962–78, then Emeritus; *b* 14 June 1916; *s* of Rev. J. H. Goodwin and Mrs E. M. Goodwin; *m* 1951, Janet Audrey (*née* Sewell) (*d* 1986); one *s* two *d. Educ:* Marlborough Coll.; RMC, Sandhurst; London Sch. of Economics. Regular Army Officer, 1936–43 (The Suffolk Regt; Army Physical Training Staff; Combined Ops; Major, comdg Indep. Company, Gibraltar). Foreign Office, 1945–48; London Sch. of Economics, 1948–81. Principal, St Catharine's, Windsor Great Park, 1971–72. Comr on Internat. Affairs, World Council of Churches, 1968–76. Mem. Council, 1974–77, Sen. Advr, 1983–84, RIIA; Vis. Mem., Inst. for Advanced Study, Princeton 1959; Vis. Prof., Institut Universitaire des Hautes Etudes Internationales, Geneva, 1962; Vis. Fellow, ANU, Canberra, 1978. Hon. Pres., British Internat. Studies Assoc., 1977–80. *Publications:* (ed) The University Teaching of International Relations, 1951; Britain and the United Nations, 1958; (ed) New Dimensions of World Politics, 1975; (ed) A New International Commodity Regime, 1979; (ed) Ethics and Nuclear Deterrence, 1982; articles in International Affairs, International Organization, Political Studies, etc. *Recreations:* painting, sketching, singing. *Address:* Norton Priory, Church Norton, Selsey, Chichester, W Sussex PO20 9DT.
Died 26 April 1995.

GOODY, Most Rev. Launcelot John, KBE 1977; PhD, DD; former Archbishop of Perth (RC); *b* 5 June 1908; *s* of late Ernest John Goody and Agnes Goody. *Educ:* Christian Brothers' College, Perth, WA; Urban University, Rome. PhD 1927, DD 1931. Ordained priest at Rome, 1930; Asst Parish Priest, Perth Cathedral, 1932–35, Kalgoorlie, 1935–37; Parish Priest, Toodyay, 1937; Director of Seminary, Guildford, 1940–47; Domestic Prelate to the Pope, 1947; Parish Priest, Bedford Park, 1947–51; Auxiliary Bishop of Perth, 1951; first RC Bishop of Bunbury, 1954–68; Archbishop of Perth, 1968–83. *Address:* c/o St Mary's Cathedral, Perth, WA 6000, Australia. *T:* 3259177.   *Died 13 May 1992.*

GOOLD-ADAMS, Richard John Moreton, CBE 1974; MA; Vice-President, SS Great Britain Project, since 1982 (Chairman, 1968–82); *b* Brisbane, Australia, 24 Jan. 1916; *s* of Sir Hamilton Goold-Adams, GCMG, CB, Governor of Qld, and Elsie Riordon, Montreal; *m* 1939, Deenagh Blennerhassett. *Educ:* Winchester; New Coll., Oxford. Served 1939–46 in Army, Major, in Middle East and Italy. The Economist, latterly as an Asst Editor, 1947–55. Councillor: Internat. Inst. for Strategic Studies, 1958–76 (a Founder and Vice-Chm., 1958–62; Chm., 1963–73; Hon. Mem., 1985); National Inst. of Industrial Psychology, 1956–70; Royal Inst. of Internat. Affairs, 1957–81; Soc. for Nautical Research, 1970–73, 1975–78; Chm., British Atlantic Cttee, 1959–62, Vice-Pres., 1963–83. Governor: Atlantic Inst. in Paris, 1962–71; Academic Council, Wilton Park, 1963–83. Dep. Chm., Guthrie Estates Agency Ltd, 1962–63, resigned; re-elected to board, 1964; merged into The Guthrie Corp., 1965; Dir, 1965–69. Formerly lecturing, radio and television in USA etc on current affairs. Hon. MA Bristol, 1992. *Publications:* South Africa To-day and Tomorrow, 1936; Middle East Journey, 1947; The Time of Power: a reappraisal of John Foster Dulles, 1962; The Return of the Great Britain, 1976. *Recreation:* photography. *Address:* c/o National Westminster Bank, 116 Fenchurch Street, EC3M 5AN. *Club:* Travellers'.
Died 23 March 1995.

GORDINE, Dora, (Hon. Mrs Richard Hare), FRBS; FRSA; sculptor and painter; *b* 13 April 1906; *d* of late Mark Gordin, St Petersburg, Russia; *m* 1936, Prof. Hon. Richard Hare (*d* 1966), *s* of 4th Earl of Listowel. Studied sculpture, Paris. First exhibited in the Salon des Tuileries, Paris, 1932; one-man exhibitions: Leicester Galleries, London, 1928, 1933, 1938, 1945, 1949; Flechtheim Gallery, Berlin, 1929; commissioned to decorate with bronzes new Town Hall in Singapore, 1930–35; built studio and sculpture gallery in London according to her own designs, 1936; spent a year in America, executing commissions in Hollywood and delivering lectures on art, 1947; also represented by sculpture in American, Asiatic, African and Australian collections; in England 3 works in Tate Gallery; other bronzes in: Senate House, London Univ.; RIBA; Westminster Infant Welfare Centre; Maternity Ward in Holloway Prison; Esso Petroleum Refinery, Milford Haven; Royal Marsden Hospital, Surrey; Herron Museum of Art, Indianapolis; schs, institutions and many private collections. *Publications:* articles in Journal of Royal Asiatic Society. *Address:* Dorich House, Kingston Vale, SW15. *Died 29 Dec. 1991.*

GORDON, (Alexander) Esmé, RSA 1967 (ARSA 1956); FRIBA, FRIAS; *b* 12 Sept. 1910; *s* of Alexander Shand Gordon, WS and Elizabeth Catherine (*née* Logan); *m* 1937, Betsy (*d* 1990), *d* of James and Bessie McCurry, Belfast; two *s* one *d*. *Educ:* Edinburgh Acad.; School of Arch., Edinburgh Coll. of Art; RIBA. Owen Jones Studentship, 1934. War Service with RE in Europe. Sec., RSA, 1973–78; Pres., Edinburgh AA, 1955–57; Mem. Scottish Cttee, Arts Council of Gt Brit., 1959–65. Hon. SSA. *Work in Edinburgh includes:* Third Extension and other work for Heriot-Watt Coll.; Head Office for Scottish Life Assce Co. Ltd; Head Office and Showroom for S of Scotland Elec. Bd; for the High Kirk of St Giles: East End treatment for National Service in Coronation year, War Memorial Chapel, and (in Chapel of Order of Thistle) Memorial to HM King George VI, and other work. Exhibn of watercolours and drawings, Scottish Gall., Edinburgh, 1988. *Publications:* A Short History of St Giles Cathedral, 1954; The Principles of Church Building, Furnishing, Equipment and Decoration, 1963; The Royal Scottish Academy 1826–1976, 1976; The Making of the Royal Scottish Academy, 1988; occasional papers. *Address:* Flat 23, 2 Barnton Avenue West, Edinburgh EH4 6EB. *T:* 031–339 8073. *Died 31 May 1993.*

GORDON, Rt Rev. Eric; *see* Gordon, Rt Rev. G. E.

GORDON, Esmé; *see* Gordon, A. E.

GORDON, Rt Rev. (George) Eric; *b* 29 July 1905; *s* of George Gordon, Dulwich; *m* 1938, Elizabeth St Charaine (*d* 1970), *d* of Lt-Comdr A. J. Parkes, OBE, RN, Squeen, Ballaugh, Isle of Man; one *d*; *m* 1971, Rose Gwynneth Huxley-Jones, FRBS, *d* of Benjamin Holt, Wednesbury, and *widow* of Thomas Bayliss Huxley-Jones, FRBS, Broomfield, Essex. *Educ:* St Olave's Sch., London; St Catharine's Coll., Cambridge (MA); Wycliffe Hall, Oxford. Deacon, Leicester, 1929; Priest, Peterborough for Leicester, 1930; Vice-Principal, Bishop Wilson Coll., Isle of Man, 1931, Principal, and Domestic Chaplain to Bishop of Sodor and Man, 1935; Rector of Kersal, and Examining Chaplain to Bishop of Manchester, 1942; Rector and Rural Dean of Middleton, Manchester, 1945; Proctor in Convocation, 1948; Provost of Chelmsford Cathedral and Rector of Chelmsford, 1951–66; Bishop of Sodor and Man, 1966–74. *Publication:* Eynsham Abbey 1005–1228: a small window into a large room, 1990. *Recreation:* local history. *Address:* Cobden, Queen Street, Eynsham, Witney, Oxon OX8 1HH. *T:* Oxford (0865) 881378.
Died 6 June 1992.

GORDON, Rt Hon. John Bowie, (Peter), QSO 1989; PC (NZ) 1978; retired politician; company director (banking, investment, tyres); *b* 24 July 1921; *s* of Dr W. P. P. Gordon, CBE, and Dr Doris Gordon, OBE; *m* 1943, Dorothy Elizabeth (*née* Morton); two *s* one *d*. *Educ:* Stratford Primary Sch.; St Andrew's Coll., Christchurch; Lincoln Coll., Canterbury. Served War, RNZAF, 1941–45 (Flt Lt, pilot; mentioned in despatches, 1943). Farming cadet, 1936–39; road transp. industry, 1945–47; farming on own account, 1947–89; Nuffield Scholarship, farming, 1954; co. dir, 1950–60; MP Clutha, 1960–78; Minister: Transport, Railways and Aviation, 1966–72; Marine and Fisheries, 1969–71; Labour and State Services, 1975–78; retd from politics on med. grounds, 1978. Past Pres., Returned Services, Federated Farmers, and A. & P. Show Assoc. Mem., Nat. Transition Cttee, Local Govt Reform, 1988– (Dep. Chm., 1988–90). Mem. Council, Otago Univ., 1980–89. USA Leadership Award, 1964. *Publication:* Some Aspects of Farming in Britain, 1955. *Recreations:* golf, gardening, cooking. *Address:* Tapanui, Otago, New Zealand. *T:* Tapanui 20–48–397. *Club:* Tapanui Services. *Died 17 March 1991.*

GORDON, John Gunn Drummond, CBE 1964; Director: Grindlays Bank Ltd, 1969–79; Steel Brothers Holdings Ltd, 1974–79; *b* 27 April 1909; *s* of late Rev. J. Drummond Gordon, MA, BD, BSc, and A. S. Gordon; *m* 1947, Mary Livingstone Paterson; two *s* one *d*. *Educ:* Edinburgh Academy. Served War, King's African Rifles, 1940–45. Career: spent 30 years out of 45, overseas, mainly in Eastern Africa, but also in India, with Grindlays Bank Ltd, finishing up as Group Managing Director; retired 1974. Mem., Bd of Crown Agents, 1974–77. *Address:* Threeways, Boneashe Lane, St Mary's Platt, near Sevenoaks, Kent TN15 8NW. *T:* Sevenoaks (0732) 884749. *Club:* Nairobi (Nairobi).
Died 16 Sept. 1992.

GORDON, Rt Hon. Peter; *see* Gordon, Rt Hon. J. B.

GORDON, Robert Wilson, MC 1944; Deputy Chairman of the Stock Exchange, London, 1965–68; Partner, Pidgeon de Smitt (Stockbrokers), 1978–80; *b* 3 March 1915; *s* of late Malcolm Gordon and Blanche Fayerweather Gordon; *m* 1st, 1946, Joan Alison (*d* 1965), *d* of late Brig. A. G. Kenchington, CBE, MC; one *d*; 2nd, 1967, Mrs Dianna E. V. Ansell (*née* Tyrwhitt-Drake) (*d* 1980). *Educ:* Harrow. Served War of 1939–45 (despatches): Royal Ulster Rifles, and Parachute Regt; Instructor, Staff Coll., 1943–44. Elected to the Council, Stock Exchange, London, 1956.

Chm., Airborne Forces Security Fund, 1974. *Recreation:* golf. *Address:* 41 Cadogan Square, SW1. *T:* 071–235 4496.   *Died 13 Jan. 1993.*

GORDON-SMITH, Ralph; President, since 1973 (Chairman, 1951–73), Smiths Industries Ltd (formerly Smith and Sons (England) Ltd); *b* 22 May 1905; *s* of late Sir Allan Gordon-Smith, KBE, DL and Hilda Beatrice Cave; *m* 1932, Beryl Mavis Cundy; no *c. Educ:* Bradfield Coll. Joined Smiths Industries, 1927; Dir, 1933. Dir of EMI Ltd, 1951–75. FBHI 1961. *Recreations:* shooting, fishing. *Address:* Brook House, Bosham, West Sussex PO18 8LY. *T:* Bosham 573475; 23 Kingston House East, Princes Gate, SW7 1LJ. *T:* 071–584 9428. *Club:* Bosham Sailing.   *Died 29 March 1993.*

GORE, Sir Richard (Ralph St George), 13th Bt *cr* 1621 (Ire.), of Magherabegg, Co. Donegal; *b* 19 Nov. 1954; *s* of Sir (St George) Ralph Gore, 12th Bt, and of Shirley, *d* of Clement Tabor; *S* father, 1973. *Educ:* The King's Sch., Parramatta; Univ. of New England; Queensland Coll. of Art. *Heir: uncle* Nigel Hugh St George Gore [*b* 23 Dec. 1922; *m* 1952, Beth Allison (*d* 1976), *d* of R. W. Hooper; one *d*]. *Address:* 16 Claremont Street, Red Hill, Queensland 4059, Australia.   *Died 30 Oct. 1993.*

GORMLEY, Baron *cr* 1982 (Life Peer), of Ashton-in-Makerfield in Greater Manchester; **Joseph Gormley,** OBE 1969; President, National Union of Mineworkers, 1971–82; *b* 5 July 1917; *s* of John Gormley; *m* 1937, Sarah Ellen Mather; one *s* one *d. Educ:* St Oswald's Roman Catholic Sch., Ashton-in-Makerfield. Entered mining industry at age of 14 and was employed in practically every underground job in mining. Served as Councillor in Ashton-in-Makerfield. Elected to Nat. Exec. Cttee of Nat. Union of Mineworkers, 1957; Gen. Sec. of North Western Area, 1961, when he relinquished his appt as a JP, owing to other commitments. Mem., Nat. Exec. Cttee, Labour Party, 1963–73; former Chm., Internat. and Organisation Cttee, Labour Party; Mem., TUC Gen. Council, 1973–80. Dir, United Racecourses Ltd, 1982–. *Publication:* Battered Cherub (autobiog.), 1982.
                                                  Died 27 May 1993.

GORT, 8th Viscount (Ire.), *cr* 1816; **Colin Leopold Prendergast Vereker,** JP; Baron Kiltarton 1810; company director; *b* 21 June 1916; *s* of Commander Leopold George Prendergast Vereker, RD, RNR (*d* 1937) (*g s* of 4th Viscount) and Helen Marjorie Campbell (*d* 1958); *S* kinsman, 1975; *m* 1946, Bettine Mary Mackenzie, *d* of late Godfrey Greene; two *s* one *d. Educ:* Sevenoaks. Trained at Air Service Training, Hamble, in Aeronautical Engineering, etc, 1937–39; served Fleet Air Arm, 1939–45 (despatches). Member of House of Keys, IOM, 1966–71. JP IOM 1962. *Recreations:* golf, fishing, gardening. *Heir: s* Hon. Foley Robert Standish Prendergast Vereker [*b* 24 Oct. 1951; *m* 1st, 1979, Julie Denise (marr. diss. 1986), *o d* of D. W. Jones, Ballasalla, IoM; 2nd, 1991, Sharon Quayle]. *Address:* Westwood, The Crofts, Castletown, Isle of Man IM9 1LW. *T:* Castletown (0624) 822545.
                                                  Died 6 April 1995.

GOTTMANN, Prof. Jean, FRGS; FBA 1977; Professor of Geography, University of Oxford, 1968–83, then Emeritus; Fellow of Hertford College, Oxford, 1968–83, then Emeritus (Hon. Fellow, 1993); *b* 10 Oct. 1915; *s* of Elie Gottmann and Sonia-Fanny Ettinger Gottmann; *m* 1957, Bernice Adelson. *Educ:* Lycée Montaigne; Lycée St Louis; Sorbonne. Research Asst Human Geography, Sorbonne, 1937–40; Mem., Inst. for Advanced Study, Princeton, NJ, several times, 1942–65; Lectr, then Associate Prof. in Geography, Johns Hopkins Univ., Baltimore, 1943–48; Dir of Studies and Research, UN Secretariat, NY, 1946–47; Chargé de Recherches, CNRS, Paris, 1948–51; Lectr, then Prof., Institut d'Etudes

Politiques, University of Paris, 1948–56; Research Dir, Twentieth Century Fund, NY, 1956–61; Prof. Ecole des Hautes Etudes, Sorbonne, 1960–84. Pres., World Soc. for Ekistics, 1971–73. Governor, Univ. of Haifa, 1972–. Hon. Member: Amer. Geog. Soc., 1961; Royal Netherlands Geog. Soc., 1963; Soc. Géographique de Liège, 1977; Società Geografica Italiana, 1981; Ateneo Veneto, 1986; For. Hon. Mem., Amer. Acad. of Arts and Sciences, 1972. Hon. LLD Wisconsin, 1968; Hon. DSc S Illinois, 1969; Hon. LittD Liverpool, 1986. Charles Daly Medal of Amer. Geograph. Soc., 1964; Prix Bonaparte-Wyse, 1962; Prix Sully-Olivier de Serre, Min. of Agriculture, France, 1964; Palmes Académiques, 1968; Victoria Medal, RGS, 1980; Grand Prix, Société de Géographie, Paris, 1984. Hon. Citizen: Yokohama, 1976; Guadalajara, 1978. Chevalier, Légion d'Honneur, 1974. *Publications:* Relations Commerciales de la France, 1942; L'Amérique, 1949, 3rd edn 1960; A Geography of Europe, 1950, 4th edn 1969; La politique des Etats et leur géographie, 1952; Virginia at Mid-century, 1955; Megalopolis, 1961; Essais sur l'Aménagement de l'Espace habité, 1966; The Significance of Territory, 1973; Centre and Periphery, 1980; The Coming of the Transactional City, 1983; La Citta invincibile, 1984; Orbits, 1984; Megalopolis Revisited, 1987; (with R. A. Harper) Since Megalopolis, 1990; (with C. Muscara) La Città Prossima Ventura, 1991. *Address:* 19 Belsyre Court, Woodstock Road, Oxford OX2 6HU. *T:* Oxford (0865) 57076. *Club:* United Oxford & Cambridge University.   *Died 28 Feb. 1994.*

GOUGH, John, CBE 1972; Director of Administration, and Secretary, Confederation of British Industry, 1965–74; *b* 18 June 1910; *o s* of H. E. and M. Gough; *m* 1939, Joan Renee Cooper; one *s* one *d. Educ:* Repton Sch.; Keble Coll., Oxford. BA 1st cl. hons History. Senior History Tutor, Stowe Sch., 1933; Fedn of British Industries: Personal Asst to Dir, 1934; Asst Sec., 1940; Sec., 1959. *Recreations:* walking, reading, music. *Address:* West Yard, North Bovey, Newton Abbot, Devon TQ13 8RT. *T:* Moretonhampstead (0647) 40395.
                                                  Died 6 May 1992.

GOULD, Cecil Hilton Monk; Keeper and Deputy Director of the National Gallery, 1973–78; *b* 24 May 1918; *s* of late Lieut Commander R. T. Gould and Muriel Hilda Estall. *Educ:* Westminster Sch. Served in Royal Air Force: France, 1940; Middle East, 1941–43; Italy, 1943–44; Normandy, Belgium and Germany, 1944–46. National Gallery: Asst Keeper, 1946; Dep. Keeper, 1962. Vis. Lectr, Melbourne Univ., 1978. FRSA 1968. *Publications:* An Introduction to Italian Renaissance Painting, 1957; Trophy of Conquest, 1965; Leonardo da Vinci, 1975; The Paintings of Correggio, 1976; Bernini in France, 1981; Parmigianino, 1994; various publications for the National Gallery, including 16th-century Italian Schools catalogue; articles in Encyclopædia Britannica, Chambers's Encyclopedia, Dizionario Biografico degli Italiani, and specialist art journals of Europe and USA. *Recreations:* music, travel. *Address:* Jubilee House, Thorncombe, Dorset TA20 4PP. *Club:* Reform.
                                                  Died 7 April 1994.

GOULD, Maj.-Gen. John Charles, CB 1975; Paymaster-in-Chief and Inspector of Army Pay Services, 1972–75, retired; *b* 27 April 1915; *s* of late Alfred George Webb and Hilda Gould; *m* 1941, Mollie Bannister; one *s* one *d. Educ:* Brighton, Hove and Sussex Grammar School. Surrey and Sussex Yeomanry (TA), 1937; Royal Army Pay Corps, 1941; served: N Africa, Sicily, Italy (despatches), Austria, 1941–46; Egypt, Jordan, Eritrea, 1948–51; Singapore, 1957–59; Dep. Paymaster-in-Chief, 1967–72. *Recreations:* golf, bridge. *Address:* Squirrels

Wood, Ringles Cross, near Uckfield, East Sussex TN22 1HB. *T:* Uckfield (0825) 764592. *Club:* Piltdown Golf.
Died 9 Jan. 1993.

GOWANS, Hon. Sir (Urban) Gregory, Kt 1974; Judge of Supreme Court of Victoria, Australia, 1961–76; *b* 9 Sept. 1904; *s* of late James and Hannah Theresa Gowans; *m* 1937, Mona Ann Freeman; one *s* four *d. Educ:* Christian Brothers Coll., Kalgoorlie, WA; Univs of Western Australia and Melbourne. BA (WA) 1924; LLB (Melb.) 1926. Admitted Victorian Bar, 1928; QC 1949; Mem., Overseas Telecommunications Commn (Aust.), 1947–61; Lectr in Industrial Law, Melb. Univ., 1948–56. Constituted Bd of Inquiry into Housing Commn Land Deals, 1977–78. *Publication:* The Victorian Bar: professional conduct practice and etiquette, 1979. *Club:* Melbourne (Melbourne). *Died 1 April 1994.*

GOWER, Most Rev. Godfrey Philip, DD; *b* 5 Dec. 1899; *s* of William and Sarah Ann Gower; *m* 1932, Margaret Ethel Tanton; two *s* one *d. Educ:* Imperial College, University of London; St John's College, Winnipeg, University of Manitoba. Served RAF, 1918–19. Deacon 1930; priest 1931; Rector and Rural Dean of Camrose, Alta, 1932–35; Rector of Christ Church, Edmonton, Alta, 1935–41; Exam. Chaplain to Bishop of Edmonton, 1938–41; Canon of All Saints' Cathedral, 1940–44; Chaplain, RCAF, 1941–44; Rector of St Paul's, Vancouver, 1944–51; Bishop of New Westminster, 1951–71; Archbishop of New Westminster, and Metropolitan of British Columbia, 1968–71. Hon. doctorates in Divinity. *Address:* 312–15366–17th Avenue, Surrey, BC V4A 1T9, Canada.
Died 29 March 1992.

GOWING, Sir Lawrence (Burnett), Kt 1982; CBE 1952; MA Dunelm 1952; RA 1989 (ARA 1978); painter and writer on painting; Hon. Curator, Royal Academy collections and Chairman, Exhibitions Committee, since 1985; Curatorial Chairman, The Phillips Collection, Washington, DC, 1987–89; *b* 21 April 1918; *s* of late Horace Burnett and Louise Gowing; *m* 1952, Julia Frances (*née* Strachey) (marr. diss. 1967), *widow* of Stephen Tomlin; *m* 1967, Jennifer Akam Wallis; three *d. Educ:* Leighton Park Sch., and as a pupil of William Coldstream. Exhibitions: 1942, 1946, 1948, 1955 (Leicester Gall.), 1965 (Marlborough), 1982 (Waddington); retrospective, Serpentine Gall., 1983; Hatton Gall., Newcastle, Ferens Gall., Hull, Plymouth City Art Gall., 1983; works in collections of Contemp. Art Soc., Tate Gallery, National Portrait Gallery, National Gallery of Canada, National Gallery of South Australia, British Council, Arts Council, Ashmolean and Fitzwilliam Museums, and galleries of Brighton, Bristol, Exeter, Manchester, Middlesbrough, Newcastle, Nottingham, Swindon, Wolverhampton, etc. Prof. of Fine Art, Univ. of Durham, and Principal of King Edward VII Sch. of Art, Newcastle upon Tyne, 1948–58; Principal, Chelsea Sch. of Art, 1958–65; Keeper of the British Collection, and Dep. Dir of the Tate Gallery, 1965–67; Prof. of Fine Art, Leeds Univ., 1967–75; Slade Prof. of Fine Art, UCL, 1975–85; Samuel H. Kress Prof., Centre for Advanced Study in the Visual Arts, Nat. Gall. of Art, Washington, 1986–87. Adjunct Prof. of History of Art, Univ. of Pa, 1977–. Mem. Arts Council, 1970–72 and 1977–81; Mem., Art Panel, 1953–58, 1959–65, 1969–72, 1976–81, Dep. Chm., 1970–72, 1977–81; Chm. Art Films Cttee, 1970–72. Trustee: Tate Gallery, 1953–60 and 1961–64; National Portrait Gallery, 1960–88; British Museum, 1976–81; Member of National Council for Diplomas in Art and Design, 1961–65; Chairman: Adv. Cttee on Painting, Gulbenkian Foundation, 1958–64; Exhibn sub-cttee, RA, 1988–. Pres., Turner Soc., 1990–. Foreign Hon. Mem., Amer. Acad. of Arts and Scis, 1989. Hon. DLitt: Heriot-Watt, 1980; Leicester, 1983. Chevalier

de l'Ordre des Arts et des Lettres, 1987. *Television:* Three Painters, BBC2, 1984, second series, 1986, third series, 1988. *Publications:* Renoir, 1947; Vermeer, 1952; Cézanne (catalogue of Edinburgh and London exhibns), 1954; Constable, 1960; Vermeer, 1961; Goya, 1965; Turner: Imagination and Reality, 1966; Matisse: 64 paintings (Museum of Modern Art, New York), 1966, (Hayward Gallery), 1968; Hogarth (Tate Gallery exhibition), 1971; Watercolours by Cézanne (Newcastle and London exhibn), 1973; Matisse, 1979; Lucian Freud, 1982; The Originality of Thomas Jones, 1986; Paintings in the Louvre, 1987; Paul Cézanne: the Basel sketchbooks (Museum of Modern Art, NY), 1988; Cézanne: the early years, 1988 (exhibn in London (RA), Paris (Musée d'Orsay) and Washington DC (Nat. Gall. of Art); (with Sam Hunter) Francis Bacon, 1989; many exhibition catalogues and writings in periodicals. *Address:* 49 Walham Grove, SW6 1QR. *T:* 071–385 5941; Peaklets, Firle, Sussex. *T:* Ripe (032183) 387.
Died 5 Feb. 1991.

GOWLAND, Rev. William; Founder Principal, Luton Industrial College, 1957–85, Emeritus Principal, 1985; President of the Methodist Conference, 1979–80; *b* 3 Oct. 1911; *s* of George and Jane Gowland; *m* 1939, Helen Margaret Qualtrough; three *s* one *d. Educ:* Darlington Technical Coll.; Hartley Victoria Coll. Methodist Minister: Port Erin, IOM, 1935–39; Tilehurst, Reading, 1939–48; Albert Hall, Manchester, 1948–54; Luton, 1954–; founded Luton Industrial Mission and Community Centre, 1954, and Luton Indust. Coll., 1957. Mem., NUAAW. Patron, European Christian Industrial Movement, 1986–. *Publications:* Militant and Triumphant, 1954 (Australia 1957, USA 1959); San Francisco, 1960 (Glide Lecture); Youth in Community, 1967 (King George VI Meml Lecture); Men, Machines and Ministry, 1971 (Beckley Lecture); Under Sealed Orders, 1986 (Rank/Coulson Lecture); Christ and the Cosmos (research report), 1987; contrib. to jls; research papers. *Recreations:* gardening, photography. *Address:* Luton Industrial College, Chapel Street, Luton, Beds LU1 2SE. *T:* Luton (0582) 29374.
Died 23 May 1991.

GOWLLAND, (George) Mark, LVO 1979; HM Diplomatic Service; Head of Chancery, Rome, since 1990; *b* 24 Feb. 1943; *s* of late G. P. and A. M. Gowlland; *m* 1967, Eleanor Julia Le Mesurier; two *s* one *d. Educ:* Tonbridge Sch.; Balliol Coll., Oxford. Entered Foreign Service, 1964; served Warsaw, Accra, Lomé, Kuala Lumpur, Dubai, Algiers; Overseas Inspectorate, FCO, 1986–90. *Address:* c/o Foreign and Commonwealth Office, SW1A 2AH.
Died 28 March 1994.

GRÆME, Maj.-Gen. Ian Rollo, CB 1967; OBE 1955; *b* 23 May 1913; *s* of late Col J. A. Græme, DSO, late RE; *m* 1941, Elizabeth Jean Dyas (*d* 1991); two *d. Educ:* Boxgrove; Stowe; RMA Woolwich. King's Medal and Benson Memorial Prize, RMA, 1933. 2nd Lt RA, 1933; pre-war service at regimental duty UK; War Service in Singapore, Java, India, Burma, Siam; psc 1942; Instructor Staff Coll., Quetta, 1944; CO 1st Burma Field Regt, 1945–46; OC, K Battery, RHA, 1949; jssc 1952; GSO1, HQ Northern Army Group, 1953–54; CO 27 Regt RA, 1955–57; Col GS Staff Coll., Camberley, 1957–59; idc 1960; Dep. Mil. Sec., WO, 1961–63; Dep. Dir Personnel Admin, WO, 1963–64; Dir Army Recruiting, 1964–67; retd 1967. Mem. Royal Yachting Assoc., 1950–; Life Governor, Royal Life Saving Soc., 1956; Life Mem., British Olympic Assoc., 1958; Chm., Army Holiday Cttee for Ski-ing, 1963–67; Council, Army Ski Assoc., 1958–; Member: Council, Nat. Ski Fedn of GB, 1964–67 (Sec., 1967–78; Life Mem. Fedn); Cttee, Sports Aid Foundn, 1976– (Governor, 1982); Trustee, Sports Aid Trust, 1983–; Vice-President: English Ski Council, 1979–82; British Ski

Fedn, 1981–84. Pres., Old Stoic Soc., 1990. Chm., Hampshire Sch. Trust, 1980–. FBIM; MInstD. Gold Medal, Austrian Govt, 1972. *Recreations:* ski-ing, sailing, mountains. *Clubs:* Army and Navy, English-Speaking Union (Life Mem.); Ski Club of Great Britain, Army Ski Association, Alpbach Visitors Ski, Garvock Ski (Pres. 1969–), Kandahar Ski; Royal Artillery Yacht.
Died 14 May 1993.

GRAESSER, Col Sir Alastair Stewart Durward, Kt 1973; DSO 1945; OBE 1963; MC 1944; TD; DL; President: National Union of Conservative and Unionist Associations, 1984–85 (Chairman, 1974–76; Hon. Vice President, 1976); Wales and Monmouth Conservative and Unionist Council, 1972–77; *b* 17 Nov. 1915; *s* of Norman Hugo Graesser and Annette Stewart Durward; *m* 1939, Diana Aline Elms Neale; one *s* three *d. Educ:* Oundle; Gonville and Caius Coll., Cambridge. Director: Municipal Life Assurance Ltd, 1977–88; Municipal General Assurance Ltd, 1977–88; Managing Trustee, Municipal Mutual Insurance Ltd, 1977–88; Trustee, TSB of Wales and Border Counties, 1970–86; Mem., CBI Regional Council for Wales (Past Chm.). Pres., Wales and Monmouth Conservative Clubs Council, 1972–76. Vice-Chm., Wales and Monmouth TA&VR Assoc.; Hon. Col, 3rd Bn Royal Welch Fusiliers (TA), 1972–80. High Sheriff of Flintshire, 1962; DL 1960, JP 1956–78, Vice Lord-Lieut, 1980–83, Clwyd (formerly Flints). CStJ 1980. *Recreation:* shooting. *Address:* Canton House, New Street, Painswick, Glos GL6 6XH. *T:* Painswick (0452) 813122. *Clubs:* Naval and Military; Hawks (Cambridge); Leander (Henley-on-Thames); Grosvenor (Chester).
Died 8 Jan. 1993.

GRAFTON, Col Martin John, CBE 1976 (OBE 1964; MBE 1944); TD 1958, bar 1963; DL; Director-General, National Federation of Building Trades Employers, 1964–79, retired; *b* 28 June 1919; *o s* of Vincent Charles Grafton and Maud (*née* Brazier); *m* 1948, Jean Margaret, *d* of James Drummond-Smith, OBE, MA, and Edith M. Drummond-Smith, MBE, MA; two *d. Educ:* Bromsgrove Sch. Served War, RE, 1940–46: Normandy and NW Europe, 1944–46 (MBE, Rhine Crossing); served TA RE, 1947–66 (TD, and Bar): Lt-Col 1960, Col 1964; comd 101 Field Engr Regt, 1960–64; Dep. Chief Engr, E Anglian Dist, 1964–66. Joined John Lewis Partnership, 1948: Dir of Bldg, 1954–60; a Man. Dir, 1960–63. Member: Council, CBI, 1964–79; EDC for Building, 1964–75; Nat. Consult. Council for Building and Civil Engrg, 1964–79. Hon. FCIOB 1978. DL Greater London, 1967–83; Freeman, City of London, 1978. *Address:* Urchfont House, Urchfont, Devizes, Wiltshire SN10 4RP. *T:* Devizes (0380) 840404.
Died 21 Dec. 1991.

GRAHAM, Prof. Angus Charles, FBA 1981; Professor of Classical Chinese, School of Oriental and African Studies, London University, 1971–84, retired; *b* 8 July 1919; *s* of Charles Harold and Mabelle Graham; *m* 1955, Der Pao (*née* Chang); one *d. Educ:* Ellesmere Coll., Salop; Corpus Christi Coll., Oxford (MA Theol.); SOAS, London (BA, PhD Chinese). Lectr in Chinese, SOAS, 1950–71. *Publications:* Two Chinese Philosophers: Ch'eng Ming-tao and Ch'eng Yi-ch'uan, 1958; The Book of Lieh Tzŭ, 1960; The Problem of Value, 1961; Poems of the Late T'ang, 1965; Later Mohist Logic, Ethics and Science, 1978; Chuang-tzŭ: the Seven Inner Chapters and other writings from the book *Chuang-tzŭ*, 1981; Reason and Spontaneity, 1985; Studies in Chinese Philosophy and Philosophical Literature, 1986; Yin-Yang and the Nature of Correlative Thinking, 1986. *Address:* PO Box 84, Borehamwood, Herts WD6 3AX.
Died 26 March 1991.

GRAHAM, Clifford; Director, Institute of Health, King's College London, since 1990 (on secondment from Department of Health); *b* 3 April 1937; *s* of late James Mackenzie and Monica Graham; *m* 1st, 1960, Audrey Edith Stubbington (marr. diss. 1990); two *s* one *d*; 2nd, Sarah (*née* Fraenkel); one *s* (posthumous). *Educ:* Alsop High Sch., Liverpool; London Univ. (LLB). Called to the Bar, Gray's Inn, 1969. Nat. Service, RAF, Aden, 1955–57. Clerical Officer, Admiralty, 1954–59; Exec. Officer, Customs and Excise, 1959–65; Higher Exec. Officer, Min. of Health, 1965–68; Principal, 1969–74, Asst Sec., 1975–82, Under Sec., 1983–, DHSS, later Dept of Health; on sabbatical, Senior Res. Fellow, LSE, researching and reporting to govt on ways of improving the planning, management and delivery of the health and social services for the benefit of the consumer, 1985–86. *Publications:* Public Administration and Health Services in England, 1983; contrib. to Oxford Textbook of Public Health, 1984, rev. edn 1990; articles in journals and DHSS reports. *Recreations:* cycling, walking, reading, music. *Address:* Highcroft, Milton Clevedon, Shepton Mallet, Somerset BA4 6NS. *T:* (office) 071–333 4194. *Club:* Gray's Inn.
Died 2 July 1994.

GRAHAM, David Alec, CBE 1983; FCA, FCIT; Director General, Greater Manchester Passenger Transport Executive, since 1976; *b* 18 Jan. 1930; *s* of John Leonard Graham and May Susan (*née* Wymark); *m* 1956, Valerie Monica Dartnall. *Educ:* Sutton High Sch. FCA 1953; FCIT 1970; CIPFA. Accountant/Finance Dir, Threlfalls Chesters Ltd, 1959–69; Dir of Finance and Admin, Greater Manchester Passenger Transp. Exec., 1969–76. *Recreations:* sailing, gardening. *Address:* The Spinney, Rowanside, Castleford Park, Prestbury, Cheshire. *T:* Prestbury (0625) 829963.
Died 19 April 1991.

GRAHAM, Rev. Douglas Leslie, MA (Dublin); retired; *b* 4 Oct. 1909; *s* of late Very Rev. G. F. Graham; *m* 1935, (Gladys Winifred) Ann, *y d* of J. W. Brittain, JP, Kilronan, Donnybrook, Co. Dublin; three *s. Educ:* Portora Royal Sch.; Dublin Univ. (BA; MA and Madden Prizeman, 1934); Munich Univ. Ordained deacon, 1937, priest, 1938. Lectr in Classics, Dublin Univ., 1932–34; Asst Master, Eton Coll., 1934–41; served War as Temp. Chaplain, RNVR, 1941–45: HMS Trinidad, 1941; HMS King Alfred, 1942; HMS Daedalus, 1944; HMS Ferret, 1944; Headmaster, Portora Royal School, 1945–53; Headmaster, Dean Close Sch., 1954–68; Asst Master and Chaplain, Williston Acad., Easthampton, Mass, USA, 1968–72. Select Preacher to the Univs of Dublin, 1945, 1961 and 1965, and Oxford, 1956–57. FRSA. *Publications:* Bacchanalia (trans. from Greek Anthology), 1970; occasional articles on classical subjects. *Recreations:* books, birds, boxing. *Address:* Forest Cottage, West Woods, Lockeridge, near Marlborough, Wilts SN8 4EG. *T:* Lockeridge (067286) 432.
Died 1 July 1991.

GRAHAM, George Boughen, QC 1964; *b* 17 July 1920; *s* of Sydney Boughen and Hannah Graham, Keswick, Cumberland; *m* Mavis, *o d* of late Frederick Worthington, Blackpool. *Educ:* Keswick Sch. Royal Signals, 1940–46. Barrister, Lincoln's Inn, 1950, Bencher, 1972. Chancellor, Diocese of Wakefield, 1959–92, Dio. of Sheffield, 1971–92. Member of Lloyd's, 1968. Comdr, Order of Merit (W Germany); Order of Aztec Eagle (Mexico). *Publications:* Covenants, Settlements and Taxation, 1953; Estate Duty Handbook, 1954. *Address:* Brocklehurst, Keswick, Cumbria CA12 4AN. *T:* Keswick (0768) 772042. *Clubs:* Athenæum; Derwent (Keswick).
Died 28 Feb. 1994.

GRAHAM, Sir (John) Patrick, Kt 1969; Judge of the High Court of Justice, Chancery Division, 1969–81; Senior Patent Judge; *b* 26 Nov. 1906; *s* of Alexander Graham and Mary Adeline Cock; *m* 1931, Annie Elizabeth Newport Willson (*d* 1993); four *s. Educ:* Shrewsbury; Caius Coll., Cambridge. Called to Bar, Middle Temple, 1930; read with Sir Lionel Heald, QC, MP; QC 1953; Treasurer, Middle Temple, 1979. Served War of 1939–45: RAF (VR) and with SHAEF; demobilised, 1945, with rank of Group Capt. Dep.-Chm., Salop Quarter Sessions, 1961–69. Mem., Standing Cttee on Structural Safety, 1975–82. *Publication:* Awards to Inventors, 1946. *Recreations:* golf, tennis, sailing. *Address:* Tall Elms, Radlett, Herts WD7 8JB. *T:* Radlett (0923) 856307. *Died 5 Dec. 1993.*

GRAHAM, Martha; dancer, choreographer; director and teacher of dancing at the Martha Graham School of Contemporary Dance in New York; *b* Pittsburgh, Pa, 11 May 1894; *d* of Dr and Mrs George Graham. *Educ:* privately, and with Ruth St Denis and Ted Shawn. First appeared in Xochitl, New York, 1920; first recital by pupils, 1926; danced lead in Stravinsky's La Sacre du Printemps, 1930; founded Dance Repertory Theatre, 1930; choreographer of over 170 solo and ensemble productions inc. three films (A Dancer's World, 1957; Appalachian Spring, 1958; Night Journey, 1960). Foreign tours, 1954, 1955–56, 1958, 1962, 1963, 1967, 1968, 1979; US tours, 1966, 1970, 1978, 1979; performed and lectured in major cities of Europe, Middle East, Iron Curtain countries, and throughout the Orient; gave solo performances with leading orchestras of United States. Three by Martha Graham, TV, 1969. Teacher: Neighbourhood Playhouse; Juilliard Sch. of Music. Her sch. took students from over forty countries. Guggenheim Fellow, 1932, 1939; many doctorates and awards, including the Capezio Award, 1959, Aspen Award in the Humanities, 1965, and Distinguished Service to Arts Award, Nat. Inst. of Arts and Letters, 1970; Medal of Freedom (USA), 1976. Chevalier, Légion d'Honneur, 1984. *Publication:* The Notebooks of Martha Graham, 1973; *relevant publication:* Martha Graham: Portrait of a Lady as an Artist, by LeRoy Leatherman, 1966; *posthumous publication:* Blood Memory (autobiog.), 1992. *Address:* Martha Graham School of Contemporary Dance, 316 East 63rd Street, New York, NY 10021, USA. *Club:* Cosmopolitan (New York). *Died 1 April 1991.*

GRAHAM, Sir Patrick; *see* Graham, Sir J. P.

GRAHAM, Walter Gerald Cloete, CBE 1952; retired 1975; *b* 13 May 1906; *s* of late Lance Graham Cloete Graham, HBM Consular Service in China; *m* 1st, 1937, Nellor Alice Lee Swan (marr. diss. 1948); one *s*; 2nd, 1949, Cynthia Anne, *d* of Sir George Clayton East, 8th Bt and 4th Bt; one *s* one *d. Educ:* Malvern Coll.; The Queen's Coll., Oxford. Laming Travelling Fellow of Queen's, 1927–29; entered Consular Service in China, 1928; served in Peking, Nanking, Shanghai, Mukden Chefoo and Tientsin; Consul: Port Said, 1942–44; Chengtu, 1944–45; Urumchi (Chinese Turkestan), 1945–47; Consul-General, Mukden, 1947–49; Chinese Counsellor, Peking, 1949–50; Counsellor, Foreign Office, 1951–52; Minister to Republic of Korea, 1952–54; Ambassador to Libya, 1955–59; Asia Adviser to Defence Intelligence Staff (formerly Jt Intell. Bureau), Min. of Defence, 1959–67; Res. Adviser, FCO Res. Dept, 1967–75. *Recreations:* golf, watching cricket, gardening. *Address:* Knabb's Farmhouse, Fletching, Uckfield, Sussex TN22 3SX. *T:* Newick (0182572) 2198. *Died 8 March 1995.*

GRAHAM-CAMPBELL, David John, MA Cantab; Liaison Officer to Schools, Aberdeen University, 1972–76; *b* 18 Feb. 1912; *s* of late Sir Rollo Frederick Graham-Campbell and Catharine Ellen, *d* of Sir Walter Sherburne Prideaux; *m* 1940, Joan Sybil (*d* 1992), *d* of late Major H. F. Maclean; three *s. Educ:* Eton Coll.; Trinity Coll., Cambridge (Exhibitioner). Master, Eton Coll., 1935–64 (Housemaster 1950–64); Warden, Trinity Coll., Glenalmond, 1964–72. Served with 2nd Bn KRRC and on the staff, 1939–45 (Lt-Col). *Publications:* Writing English, 1953; Portrait of Argyll and the Southern Hebrides, 1978;

Portrait of Perth, Angus and Fife, 1979; Scotland's Story in her Monuments, 1982. *Address:* 17 Muirton Bank, Perth, Perthshire PH1 5DW. *Died 11 Jan. 1994.*

GRANARD, 9th Earl of, *cr* 1684 (Ire.); **Arthur Patrick Hastings Forbes,** AFC 1941; Bt (NS) 1628; Viscount Granard and Baron Clanehugh (Ire.), 1675; Baron Granard (UK), 1806; Air Commodore, late Royal Air Force Volunteer Reserve; *b* 10 April 1915; *e s* of 8th Earl of Granard, KP, GCVO, PC, and Beatrice, OBE (*d* 1972), *d* of Ogden Mills, Staatsburg, Dutchess County, USA; *S* father, 1948; *m* 1949, Marie-Madeleine Eugènie (*d* 1990), *y d* of Jean Maurel, Millau, Aveyron, formerly wife of late Prince Humbert de Faucigny Lucinge; two *d. Educ:* Eton; Trinity Coll., Cambridge. Served War of 1939–45 (despatches, AFC). Mem. Jockey Club of France. Commandeur Légion d'Honneur; Croix de Guerre with Palm; Officer Legion of Merit, USA; Croix des Vaillants of Poland; Order of George I of Greece. *Heir: nephew* Peter Arthur Edward Hastings Forbes [*b* 15 March 1957; *m* 1980, Noreen Mitchell; three *s* one *d*]. *Address:* 11 rue Louis de Savoie, 1110 Morges, Switzerland. *Clubs:* White's, Pratt's; Kildare Street and University (Dublin); Royal St George's Yacht, Royal Yacht Squadron. *Died 19 Nov. 1992.*

GRANGER, Stewart, (James Lablache Stewart); actor (stage and films); *b* London, 6 May 1913; *s* of late Major James Stewart, RE, and Frederica Lablache; *m* 1st, 1938, Elspeth March (marr. diss. 1948); one *s* one *d*; 2nd, 1950, Jean Simmons (marr. diss. 1960); one *d*; 3rd, 1964, Viviane Lecerf (marr. diss. 1969); one *d. Educ:* Epsom Coll. Began training as doctor but decided to become an actor. Studied at Webber-Douglas School of Dramatic Art; played at Little Theatre, Hull, and with Birmingham Repertory Company; appeared at Malvern Festival, 1936–37; first London appearance as Captain Hamilton in The Sun Never Sets, Drury Lane, 1938; appeared on London stage, 1938–39; joined Old Vic Company, 1939; Dr Fleming in Tony Draws a Horse, Criterion, 1940; George Winthrop in A House in the Square, St Martin's, 1940; toured, 1940; served War of 1939–45, Army, 1940–42 (invalided); toured, 1942; succeeded Owen Nares as Max de Winter in Rebecca, Lyric, 1942; returned to stage as Clive in The Circle, NY, 1989. Began film career in 1938, and appeared in many films, including: The Man in Grey, The Lamp Still Burns, Fanny by Gaslight, Waterloo Road, Love Story, Madonna of the Seven Moons, Cæsar and Cleopatra, Caravan, The Magic Bow, Captain Boycott, Blanche Fury, Saraband for Dead Lovers, Woman Hater, Adam and Evelyne, King Solomon's Mines, Soldiers Three, Light Touch, Wild North, Scaramouche, Young Bess, Salome, Prisoner of Zenda, All the Brothers were Valiant, Beau Brummell, Footsteps in the Fog, Moonfleet, Green Fire, Bhowani Junction, Last Hunt, The Little Hut, Gun Glory, The Whole Truth, Harry Black and the Tiger, North to Alaska, Sodom and Gomorrah, Swordsman of Siena, The Secret Invasion, The Trygon Factor, Last Safari, The Wild Geese. *Publication:* Sparks Fly Upward (autobiog.), 1981. *Address:* c/o Lindsay Granger, Barry Burnett Organisation Ltd, 42 Grafton House, 2–3 Golden Square, W1R 3AP. *T:* 071-437 7048. *Died 16 Aug. 1993.*

GRANIT, Prof. Ragnar Arthur; Commander, Order of Nordstjernan, Sweden, 1964; Professor Emeritus, Karolinska Institutet, Stockholm, since 1967; *b* 30 Oct. 1900; *s* of Arthur W. Granit and Albertina Helena Granit (*née* Malmberg); *m* 1929, Baroness Marguerite (Daisy) Bruun; one *s. Educ:* Swedish Normallyceum; Helsingfors University. MPhil 1923, MD 1927. Prof. of Physiology, Helsingfors, 1937; Prof. of Neurophysiology, Stockholm, 1940; Dir of Dept of Neurophysiology, Medical Nobel

Inst., 1945; retired, 1967. President, Royal Swedish Acad. of Science, 1963–65. Lectures: Silliman, Yale, 1954; Sherrington, London, 1967; Liverpool, 1971; Murlin, Rochester, NY 1973; Hughlings Jackson, McGill, 1975. Visiting Professor: Rockefeller Univ., NY, 1956–66; St Catherine's Coll., Oxford, 1967; Pacific Medical Center, San Francisco, 1969; Fogarty Internat. Foundn, Nat. Inst. of Health, Bethesda, USA, 1971–72, 1975; Düsseldorf Univ., 1976; Max-Planck Inst., Bad Nauheim, 1977. Foreign Member: Amer. Philosophical Soc., 1954; Royal Soc., 1960; Nat. Acad. Sci., Washington, 1968; Accad. Naz. dei Lincei, 1978; Acad of Finland, 1985; Hon. Member: Amer. Acad. of Arts and Sciences; Indian Acad of Sci., 1964. Mem. and Hon. Mem. of several learned societies. Hon. MD: Oslo, 1951; Loyola, 1969; Pisa, 1970; Göttingen, 1987; Hon. DSc: Oxford, 1956; Hong Kong, 1961; Hon. DPhil Helsingfors, 1982; Catedr. Hon., Lima, Santiago, Bogotá, 1958. Retzius Gold Medal, 1957; Donders Medal, 1957; Jahre Prize (Oslo), 1961; III Internat. St Vincent Prize, 1961; Nobel Prize for Medicine (jointly), 1967; Sherrington Medal, 1967; Purkinje Gold Medal, 1969; Tigerstedt Medal, 1985. Cross of Freedom (Finland), 1918. *Publications:* Ung Mans Väg till Minerva, 1941; Sensory Mechanisms of the Retina, (UK) 1947 (US 1963); Receptors and Sensory Perception, (US) 1955; Charles Scott Sherrington: an Appraisal, (UK) 1966; Basis of Motor Control, (UK) 1970; Regulation of the Discharge of Motoneurons, (UK) 1971; The Purposive Brain, (US) 1977; Hur det kom sig (a memoir), 1983. *Recreations:* island life, gardening. *Address:* 14 Eriksbergsgatan, S-114 30 Stockholm, Sweden. *T:* (8) 213728.

Died 12 March 1991.

GRANT, Alec Alan; a Master of the Supreme Court, Queen's Bench Division, since 1982; *b* 27 July 1932; *s* of late Emil Grant, OBE and Elsie Louise (*née* Marks). *Educ:* Highgate Sch.; Merton Coll., Oxford (MA). National Service, RA, 1951–52. Pres., Oxford Union, 1956. Called to the Bar, Middle Temple, 1957; practised at the Bar, 1958–82. Member: Mddx CC, 1961–65; GLC, 1964–67 and 1970–73; Governing Body, SOAS, 1965– (Vice-Chm., 1978–); Court of Governors, Thames Polytechnic, 1972– (Chm., 1982–85). *Recreations:* hill-walking, watching cricket. *Address:* Royal Courts of Justice, Strand, WC2A 2LL. *Clubs:* MCC; Austrian Alpine.

Died 25 Dec. 1991.

GRANT, Andrew Francis Joseph, CB 1971; BSc; CEng, FICE; *b* 25 Feb. 1911; *er s* of Francis Herbert and Clare Grant; *m* 1934, Mary Harrison; two *s* two *d. Educ:* St Joseph's Coll., Beulah Hill; King's Coll., London. Asst Civil Engr with Contractors on London Underground Rlys, 1931; Port of London Authority, 1935; entered Civil Engineer-in-Chief's Dept, Admiralty, and posted to Singapore, 1937; Suptg Civil Engr, Durban, 1942; Civil Engr Adviser, RN Home Air Comd, 1947; Suptg Civil Engr, Malta, 1951; Asst Dir, Navy Works, 1959; Fleet Navy Works Officer, Mediterranean, 1960; Director for Wales, MPBW, 1963; Regional Director, Far East, 1966; Dir, Home Regional Services, DoE, 1968–71. *Recreations:* painting, golf, travel. *Address:* 48 Cecil Road, Norwich, Norfolk NR1 2QN. *T:* Norwich (0603) 622017. *Club:* Civil Service. *Died 8 Aug. 1992.*

GRANT, Douglas Marr Kelso; Sheriff of South Strathclyde, Dumfries and Galloway (formerly of Ayr and Bute), 1966–88; *b* 5 April 1917; *yr s* of late John Marr Grant, JP and Helen (*née* Kelso), Glasgow; *m* 1952, Audrey Stevenson Law, *o d* of late Mr and Mrs William Law, Rhu, Dunbartonshire; two *s* two *d. Educ:* Rugby; Peterhouse, Cambridge. Entered Colonial Admin. Service, Uganda Protectorate, 1939; Army Service, 1940–46: Kenya Regt, KAR; military admins Ethiopia, Madagascar, Tripolitania, Malaya; Civil Affairs Staff Centre, Cairo and

London; called to Bar, Gray's Inn, 1945; transf. to Colonial Legal Service, Fedn of Malaya, 1946; Judicial and Legal Dept, Malaya, 1946–57: Pres., Sessions Ct, 1947–51; acted High Ct Judge, 1951; Fed. Counsel and Dep. Public Prosecutor, Kuala Lumpur, 1951–52; Legal Advisor and Deputy Public Prosecutor: Penang, 1953; Johore, 1953–55; Fed. Counsel and Dep. Public Prosecutor, Kuala Lumpur; retd from Colonial Service, 1957; admitted to Faculty of Advocates and Scottish Bar, 1959; Jun. Counsel to Sec. of State for Scotland; Comr, NI (Emergency Provisions) Act 1973; Mem. Appeals Tribunal. *Address:* Drumellan House, Maybole, Ayrshire KA19 7JG. *T:* Maybole (01655) 882279. *Died 19 April 1995.*

GRANT, Brig. Eneas Henry George, CBE 1951; DSO 1944 and Bar, 1945; MC 1936; Hon. DL; retired; *b* 14 Aug. 1901; *s* of late Col H. G. Grant, CB, late Seaforth Highlanders and Isabel, *d* of Eneas Mackintosh, Balnespick, Inverness-shire; *m* 1926, Lilian Marion (*d* 1978), *d* of late S. O'Neill, Cumberstown House, Co. Westmeath; one *s* (and *er s,* Lieut Seaforth Highlanders, killed in action, Korea, 1951). *Educ:* Wellington Coll., Berks; RMC, Sandhurst. 2nd Lieut Seaforth Highlanders, 1920; Adjt Lovat Scouts, 1928–33; served in Palestine, 1936; War of 1939–45: France, 1940; France and Germany, 1944–45; Lieut-Colonel 1942 (Subs. 1947); Colonel 1944 (Subs. 1948); Brigadier 1944 (Subs. 1952); Bde Commander, 1944–49; Comdr Gold Coast District, 1949–52; Col Comdt Gold Coast Regt, 1949–52; Deputy Commander, Northumbrian District, 1952–55; retired 1955. JP Inverness-shire, 1957–91; DL Inverness-shire, 1958–80. Chairman Inverness-shire TA and Air Force Association, 1961–65. *Recreations:* country pursuits. *Address:* Inverbrough Lodge, Tomatin, Inverness-shire IV13 7XY. *Club:* Highland (Inverness).

Died 5 Feb. 1994.

GRANT, Maj.-Gen. Ferris Nelson, CB 1967; *b* 25 Dec. 1916; *s* of late Lieut-Gen. H. G. Grant and Mrs N. L. B. Grant (*née* Barker); *m* 1st, 1940, Patricia Anne (*née* Jameson) (*d* 1988); one *s* one *d;* 2nd, 1988, Mrs M. L. Bagwell. *Educ:* Cheltenham Coll. BA. Joined Royal Marines, 1935; Capt., HMS Suffolk, 1940–42; US Marine Corps Staff Coll., Major, 1943; Staff of SACSEA, Lt-Col 1943; Army Staff Coll., Camberley, 1946; 45 Commando, 1947; Chief Instructor, Commando Sch., 1949; CO 41 Commando, Korea, 1950; jssc, 1951; Bde Major, Commando Bde, 1952; Instructor, US Marine Corps Staff Coll., 1958; CO Amphibious Trng Unit, 1960; CO Depot RM, 1961; CO Infantry Trng Centre, 1963; Comdr, Plymouth Group, Royal Marines, 1965–68, retired. Member, panel of independent inspectors for public inquiries, 1983–. Governor, Sch. for Visually Handicapped, 1974–82. Past Pres. RN Boxing Assoc. Lay Reader. Officer of Legion of Merit (US). *Recreations:* sailing, gardening, painting. *Clubs:* Army and Navy; Royal Yacht Squadron, Royal Naval Sailing Association. *Died 9 Sept. 1991.*

GRANT, James Pineo; Executive Director, United Nations Children's Fund (UNICEF), 1980–95; *b* 12 May 1922; *s* of John B. and Charlotte Grant; *m* 1st, 1943, Ethel Henck (decd); three *s;* 2nd, 1989, Ellan Young. *Educ:* Univ. of California, Berkeley (BA); Harvard Univ. (JD). US Army, 1943–45; UN Relief and Rehabilitation Admin, 1946–47; Acting Exec. Sec. to Sino-American Jt Cttee on Rural Reconstruction, 1948–50; Law Associate, Covington and Burling, Washington, DC, 1951–54; Regional Legal Counsel in New Delhi for US aid programs for S Asia, 1954–56; Dir, US aid mission to Ceylon, 1956–58; Dep. to Dir of Internat. Co-operation Admin, 1959–62; Dep. Asst Sec. of State for Near East and S Asian Affairs, 1962–64; Dir, AID program in Turkey, with rank of

Minister, 1964–67; Asst Administrator, AID, 1967–69; Pres., Overseas Develt Council, 1969–80. Hon. Prof., Capital Medical Coll. of China, 1983. Hon. LLD: Notre Dame, 1980; Maryville Coll., 1981; Tufts, 1983; Denison, 1983; Hon. DrSci Hacettepe, Ankara, 1980. Rockefeller Public Service Award, 1980; Boyaca Award, Colombia, 1984; Gold Mercury Internat. Award, Internat. Orgn for Co-operation, 1984; Presidential Citation, APHA, 1985; Tolstoy Award, Russian Children's Fund, 1993; UN Human Rights Prize, 1993. Gran Cruz, Orden Daniel A. Carron (Peru), 1991; Order of the Sacred Treasure, First Class, (Japan), 1991; Order of Aguila Azteca (Mexico), 1993; Hilal-i-Pakistan (Pakistan), 1993. *Publications:* The State of the World's Children Report, annually, 1980–; articles in Foreign Affairs, Foreign Policy, Annals. *Address:* 3 United Nations Plaza, New York, NY 10017, USA. *T:* (212) 3267035. *Clubs:* Metropolitan, Cosmos (Washington, DC). *Died 28 Jan. 1995.*

GRANTCHESTER, 2nd Baron *cr* 1953; **Kenneth Bent Suenson-Taylor,** CBE 1985; QC 1971; a Recorder of the Crown Court, 1975–89; Chairman, Dairy Produce Quota Tribunal, 1984–94; *b* 18 Aug. 1921; *s* of 1st Baron Grantchester, OBE, and of Mara Henriette, (Mamie), *d* of late Albert Suenson, Copenhagen; *S* father, 1976; *m* 1947, Betty, *er d* of Sir John Moores, CBE; three *s* three *d*. *Educ:* Westminster School; Christ's College, Cambridge (MA, LLM). Lieut RA, 1941–45. Called to the Bar, Middle Temple, 1946; admitted *ad eundem* by Lincoln's Inn, 1947. Lecturer in Company Law, Council of Legal Education, 1951–72. Chairman: Licensed Dealers' Tribunal, 1976–88; VAT Tribunals, 1988–90 (Pres., 1972–87); Financial Services Tribunal, 1988–91; Pres., Aircraft and Shipbuilding Ind. Arbitration Tribunal, 1980–83. Dep. Chm. of Cttees, H of L, 1988–94. *Heir: e s* (twin) Hon. Christopher John Suenson-Taylor [*b* 8 April 1951; *m* 1972, Jacqueline, *d* of Dr Leo Jaffé; two *s* two *d*]. *Died 12 Aug. 1995.*

GRANTHAM, Adm. Sir Guy, GCB 1956 (KCB 1952; CB 1942); CBE 1946; DSO 1941; retired; Governor and Commander-in-Chief of Malta, 1959–62; *b* 9 Jan. 1900; *s* of late C. F. Grantham, The Hall, Skegness, Lincs; *m* 1934, Beryl Marjorie (*d* 1991), *d* of late T. C. B. Mackintosh-Walker, Geddes, Nairn; two *d.* Served War of 1939–45 (despatches, twice, DSO, CB, CBE); Chief of Staff to C-in-C, Mediterranean, 1946–48; Naval ADC to the King, 1947–48; Flag Officer (Submarines), 1948–50; Flag Officer, Second-in-Command, Mediterranean Fleet, 1950–51; Vice-Chief of Naval Staff, 1951–54; Comdr-in-Chief, Mediterranean Station, and Allied Forces, Mediterranean, 1954–57; Comdr-in-Chief, Portsmouth, Allied Comdr-in-Chief, Channel and Southern North Sea, 1957–59; First and Principal Naval ADC to the Queen, 1958–59; retired list, 1959. Hon. Freeman of Haberdashers' Company. Mem., Commonwealth War Graves Commn, 1962–70 (Vice-Chm. 1963–70). Governor, Corps of Commissionaires, 1964–. *Address:* Tandem House, 6 High Street, Nayland, Suffolk CO6 4JF. *T:* Nayland (0206) 262511. *Died 8 Sept. 1992.*

GRANTLEY, 7th Baron, *cr* 1782; **John Richard Brinsley Norton,** MC 1944; Baron of Markenfield, 1782; a Member of Lloyd's; *b* 30 July 1923; *o s* of 6th Baron and Jean Mary (*d* 1945), *d* of Sir David Alexander Kinloch, CB, MVO, 11th Bt; *S* father 1954; *m* 1955, Lady Deirdre Mary Freda, *e d* of 5th Earl of Listowel, GCMG, PC; two *s*. *Educ:* Eton; New Coll., Oxford. Served War, 1942–45, in Italy as Capt. Grenadier Guards (MC). *Heir: s* Hon. Richard William Brinsley Norton, *b* 30 Jan. 1956. *Address:* 53 Lower Belgrave Street, SW1W 0LP; Markenfield Hall, Ripon, North Yorks HG4 3AD. *Clubs:* White's, Pratt's. *Died 24 June 1995.*

GRAVES, 8th Baron, *cr* 1794 (Ire.); **Peter George Wellesley Graves;** actor; *b* 21 Oct. 1911; *o s* of 7th Baron Graves and Vera Blanche Neville (*d* 1953), *d* of Alfred Neville Shepp; *S* father, 1963; *m* 1960, Vanessa Lee (*d* 1992). *Educ:* Harrow. First appeared on London stage in 1934, and subsequently played many leading parts. Mem. Windsor repertory co., 1941. Appeared in films, 1940–. *Recreation:* lawn tennis. *Heir: kinsman* Evelyn Paget Graves [*b* 17 May 1926; *m* 1957, Marjorie Ann, *d* of late Dr Sidney Ernest Holder; two *s* two *d*]. *Address:* c/o Messrs Coutts & Co., 440 Strand, WC2R 0QS. *Club:* All England Lawn Tennis. *Died 6 June 1994.*

GRAVESON, Prof. Ronald Harry, CBE 1972; QC 1966; barrister-at-law; Professor Emeritus of Private International Law, King's College, University of London, 1978; *b* 2 Oct. 1911; *o s* of Harry Graveson, Sheffield; *m* 1st, 1937, Muriel (*d* 1986), *o d* of John Saunders, Sheffield; one *s* two *d*; 2nd, 1988, Joan, (Jessie), 4th *d* of William Dickinson Franklin, Sheffield. *Educ:* King Edward VII Sch., Sheffield. LLB 1932, LLM 1933, LLD 1955 Sheffield; SJD Harvard 1936; PhD London 1941; LLD London 1951; Gregory Scholar in International Law of Harvard Univ.; Solicitor (Hons), 1934. Army, 1940–46 (Driver, RE; Lieut-Col RASC, G5 Div. SHAEF; CCG). Called to the Bar, Gray's Inn, 1945; Bencher, 1965; Treas., 1983. Reader in English Law, University Coll., Univ. of London, 1946–47; Prof. of Law, KCL, 1947–74, and of Private Internat. Law, 1974–78 (FKC 1962); Dean of the Faculty of Laws, Univ. of London, 1951–54, 1972–74, and KCL, 1951–58, 1959–63, 1966–70. Vis. Prof., Harvard Law Sch., 1958–59. Chm., UK, National Cttee of Comparative Law, 1955–57. Member: Review Body on pay of doctors and dentists, 1971–81; Cttees of Inquiry into Pay of Nurses and Midwives and of Professions supplementary to Medicine, 1974–75; Pres., Harvard Law Sch. Assoc. of the UK, 1959–61, 1977–81. Jt Editor, Internat. and Comparative Law Quarterly, 1955–61; Consultant Editor of the Law Reports and the Weekly Law Reports, 1970–75. Pres. International Association of Legal Science (UNESCO), 1960–62. Mem. Inst. of International Law; Pres., Soc. of Public Teachers of Law, 1972–73. Member: Polish Acad. of Sci., 1977; Council, Luxembourg Soc.; Institut Grand-Ducal, Luxembourg, 1985–; Council, Anglo–Belgian Soc.; Council, British Inst. of Internat. and Comparative Law; Council, Selden Soc.; Internat. Acad. of Comparative Law. Hon. Life Mem., Instn of RCT; Pres., KCL Assoc., 1982–84. LLD (*hc*): Ghent, 1964; Uppsala, 1977; Leuven, 1978; Dr Juris (*hc*) Freiburg, 1969. JP St Alban's City, 1961–66. Liveryman, Clockmakers' Co. Commandeur de l'Ordre de la Couronne de Chêne (Luxembourg), 1964; Comdr, Order of Oranje Nassau (Netherlands), 1970; Order of National Merit (France), 1970; Grand Cross of Order of Merit (German Federal Republic), 1975; Legion of Honour (France), 1977; Comdr, Order of the Crown (Belgium), 1977. *Publications:* English Legal System, 1939; Conflict of Laws, 1948, 7th edn 1974; Cases on the Conflict of Laws, 1949; The Comparative Evolution of Principles of the Conflict of Laws in England and the USA 1960; General Principles of Private International Law, 1964; (jtly) The Conflict of Laws and International Contracts, 1951; Status in the Common Law, 1953, repr. 1983; (jtly) A Century of Family Law, 1957; Law: an Introduction, 1967; (jtly) Unification of the International Law of Sale, 1968; Problems of Private International Law in Non-unified Legal Systems, 1975; Comparative Conflict of Laws, 1976; One Law, 1976; Gen. Editor, Problems in Private International Law, 1977; various articles, notes or reviews since 1936 in English and foreign law reviews; contributor to various collective volumes including essays in honour of British and foreign colleagues, and to Apollo, Connoisseur. *Recreations:* works of art, international friendship. *Address:* 2 Gray's Inn Square, Gray's Inn, WC1R 5AA. *T:* 071–242 8492; 12 Castle Mount Crescent, Bakewell, Derbys DE4 1AT. *T:* Bakewell (062981) 3593. *Clubs:* Athenæum, Commonwealth Trust, Anglo-Belgian.   *Died 5 Jan. 1991.*

GRAY, Sir (Francis) Anthony, KCVO 1981; Secretary and Keeper of the Records of the Duchy of Cornwall, 1972–81; *b* 3 Aug. 1917; *s* of late Major F. C. Gray; *m* 1947, Marcia, *d* of late Major Hugh Wyld; one *s* two *d. Educ:* Marlborough; Magdalen Coll., Oxford. Treas., Christ Church, Oxford, 1952–72, Emeritus Student, 1972. Mem., Agricultural Adv. Council, 1963–68; Mem. Council, Royal Coll. of Art, 1967–73. *Recreations:* planchette, the trampoline. *Address:* Temple House, Upton Scudamore, Warminster, Wilts BA12 0AQ. *Club:* Travellers'.
                                                    Died 2 Aug. 1992.

GRAY, Geoffrey Leicester, CMG 1958; OBE 1953; Secretary for Local Government, North Borneo (later Sabah), 1956–61, retired; *b* 26 Aug. 1905; *s* of late Leonard Swainson Gray, Resident Magistrate of Kingston, Jamaica, and Marion Scotland, Vale Royal, Kingston, Jamaica; *m* 1932, Penelope Milnes (MBE 1962) (*d* 1971), *o c* of late Philip Henry Townsend, OBE and Gwenyth Gwendoline Roberts. *Educ:* Latymer Upper Sch. Cadet, North Borneo Civil Service, under British North Borneo (Chartered) Co., 1925; after qualifying in Malay and Law, served in various admin. posts, 1925–30; studied Chinese in Canton, 1931; attached Secretariat for Chinese Affairs and Educn Dept, Hong Kong, 1931; Dist Officer, Jesselton, Supt, Govt Printing Office, and Editor, British North Borneo Herald and Official Gazette, 1932–35; Dist Officer, Kudat, 1935; Under-Sec., 1935–38; Govt Sec. Class 1b and *ex-officio* MLC, 1938–46; Additional Sessions and High Court Judge, 1938–46; interned by Japanese, 1941–45; Class 1a, 1946; accredited to HQ Brit. Mil. Admin (Brit. Borneo) at Labuan, 1946; assimilated into HM Colonial Admin. Service (later HM Overseas Service) on cession of North Borneo to the Crown, 1946; Actg Dep. Chief Sec., 1946; Protector of Labour and Sec. for Chinese Affairs, 1947; Resident, E Coast, in addition, 1947; Mem. Advisory Council, 1947–50; Comr of Immigration and Labour, 1948–51; Official MLC and MEC, 1950–61; Actg Fin. Sec., 1951–52; Dep. Chief Sec., Staff Class, 1952–56; represented North Borneo at Coronation, 1953; Chm., Bd of Educn and Town and Country Planning Bd, 1956–61; Actg Chief Sec. (intermittently), 1952–60; administered Govt, 1958, 1959; acted as High Comr, Brunei, 1959; retd, 1961. Life Associate, N Borneo and UK Branches, CPA, 1961. Commissary for Bp of Jesselton (later Sabah), 1961. Incorporated Mem. of USPG (formerly SPG), 1964– (Mem. Council, and various Cttees and Gps, 1965–83); Cttee Mem., Borneo Mission Assoc., 1961– (Chm. 1961–76). *Clubs:* Commonwealth Trust, Travellers'.
                                                    Died 11 March 1994.

GRAY, His Eminence Cardinal Gordon Joseph, MA (Hon.) St Andrews; Hon. DD St Andrews, 1967; retired Archbishop of St Andrews and Edinburgh; *b* 10 August 1910; 2nd *s* of Francis William and Angela Gray. *Educ:* Holy Cross Acad., Edinburgh; St John's Seminary, Wonersh. Assistant-Priest, St Andrews, 1935–41; Parish Priest, Hawick, 1941–47; Rector of Blairs College, Aberdeen (Scottish National Junior Seminary), 1947–51; Archbishop of St Andrews and Edinburgh, 1951–85. Cardinal, 1969. Member: Pontifical Congregation for Evangelization of Peoples; Congregation of the Sacraments; Congregation for Clergy. Hon. FEIS, 1970. DUniv. Heriot-Watt, 1981. *Address:* The Hermitage, Whitehouse Loan, Edinburgh EH9 1BB.
                                                    Died 19 July 1993.

GRAY, Maj.-Gen. John; *see* Gray, Maj.-Gen. R. J.

GRAY, John Magnus, CBE 1971 (MBE 1945); ERD 1946; Chairman, Northern Ireland Electricity Service, 1974–80 (Deputy Chairman, 1973–74); *b* 15 Oct. 1915; *o s* of Lewis Campbell Gray, CA and Ingeborg Sanderson Gray (*née* Ross), Glasgow; *m* 1947, Patricia Mary (OBE 1976), *d* of John Norman Eggar and Emma Frances Eggar (*née* Garrett), Epsom and Godalming, and *widow* of Major Aubrey D. P. Hodges; one *d. Educ:* Horris Hill, Newbury; Winchester College. Served RA, 1939–46 (Major). Joined Wm Ewart & Son Ltd, Linen Manufrs, Belfast, 1934; Dir 1950; Man. Dir, 1958–72. Chairman: Irish Linen Guild, 1958–64; Central Council, Irish Linen Industry, 1968–74 (Mem., 1957; Vice-Chm., 1966–68); Linen Industry Standards Cttee of BSI, 1969–74; Belfast Br., RNLI, 1970–76; Member: Council of Belfast T&AFA, 1948–68; Council of Belfast Chamber of Commerce, 1955–59; Gen. Synod of Church of Ireland, 1955–84; Councils of FBI and CBI, 1956–74, 1979–80; NI Legal Aid Cttee, 1958–59; Export Council for Europe, 1964–70; Northern Ireland Adv. Council for BBC, 1968–72; Design Council, 1974–80; Asst Comr for Commn on Constitution, 1969–73. Captain, Royal Co. Down Golf Club, 1963. *Recreations:* golf, gardening. *Address:* Blairlodge, Dundrum, Newcastle, Co. Down BT33 0NF. *T:* Dundrum (039675) 271. *Club:* Army and Navy.
                                                    Died 8 Dec. 1993.

GRAY, Maj.-Gen. (Reginald) John, CB 1973; Chairman, Royal Army Medical Corps Association, 1980–88; *b* 26 Nov. 1916; *s* of late Dr Cyril Gray and Frances Anne Higgins, Higginsbrook, Co. Meath; *m* 1943, Esme, *d* of late G. R. G. Shipp; one *s* one *d. Educ:* Rossall Sch.; Coll. of Medicine, Univ. of Durham. MB, BS. Commissioned into RAMC, 1939; served War of 1939–45 in India; later Burma, NW Europe, Egypt, Malta, BAOR; comd of 9 (Br.) CCS, 1945; Medical Gold Staff Officer, 1953; Asst Dir-Gen., AMS, WO, AMD3, 1954–57; comd of David Bruce Mil. Hosp., Mtarfa, 1957–60; 14 Field Amb., 4 Guards Bde, 1960–63; Brit. Mil. Hosp., Rinteln, 1963–64; The Queen Alexandra Mil. Hosp., Millbank, 1964–67; Asst Dir-Gen., AMS, Min. of Defence AMD1, 1967–69; Dep. Dir-Gen., AMS, 1969–71. QHS 1970–73; DMS, UK Land Forces, 1972–73, retired. Col Comdt, RAMC, 1977–81. Chief MO, British Red Cross Soc., 1974–83; Chm., BMA Armed Forces Cttee, 1981–85. Dir, International Generics Ltd, 1974–83. Mem., Casualty Surgeons Assoc., 1976–; Hon. Mem., St Andrews Ambulance Assoc., 1982; Life Mem., BRCS, 1983; Hon. Mem., Inst. of Civil Defence, 1983. FRSM; FFPHM (FFCM 1972). CStJ 1971 (OStJ 1957). *Recreation:* gardening slowly. *Address:* 11 Hampton Close, Wimbledon, SW20 0RY. *T:* 0181–946 7429.
                                                    Died 28 Oct. 1994.

GRAY, Roger Ibbotson, QC 1967; a Recorder of the Crown Court, since 1972; *b* 16 June 1921; *o s* of Arthur Gray and Mary Gray (*née* Ibbotson); *m* 1st, 1952, Anne Valerie (marr. diss.), 2nd *d* of late Capt. G. G. P. Hewett, CBE, RN; one *s*; 2nd, 1987, Lynne Jacqueline, *er d* of late Eric Towell, FRIAA, RIBA. *Educ:* Wycliffe Coll.; Queen's Coll., Oxford. 1st cl. hons Jurisprudence, Oxon, 1941. Commissioned RA, 1942; served with Ayrshire Yeomanry, 1942–45; Normandy and NW Europe, 1944–45; GSO3 (Mil. Ops), GHQ, India, 1946. Pres. of Oxford Union, 1947. Called to Bar, Gray's Inn, 1947; South-Eastern Circuit. A Legal Assessor: GNC, 1976–83; UKCC, 1983–91. Contested (C) Dagenham, 1955. *Publication:* (with Major I. A. Graham Young) A Short History of the Ayrshire Yeomanry (Earl of Carrick's Own) 151st Field Regiment, RA, 1939–46, 1947. *Recreations:* cricket, reading, talk. *Address:* The Old Cottage, 20 Friday Street, Minchinhampton, Glos GL6 9JL; Queen Elizabeth Building, Temple, EC4. *T:* 071–583 7837. *Clubs:* Carlton, Pratt's, MCC.   *Died 19 Oct. 1992.*

GRAY, Sylvia Mary, CBE 1975 (MBE 1952); *b* 10 July 1909; *d* of Henry Bunting and Mary Elizabeth Gray. *Educ:* Wroxall Abbey. Chm., Bay Tree Hotels Ltd, 1946–83. Mem., Witney RDC, 1943–54 (Vice-Chm. 1950–54); Chairman: Oxon Fedn Women's Insts, 1951–54; Nat. Fedn of Women's Insts, 1969–74 (Mem., Exec. Cttee, 1955; Hon. Treas., 1958). Member: Keep Britain Tidy Group Exec., 1967–78 (Vice-Chm., 1974); Post Office Users' Nat. Council, 1969–78; National Trust, 1971–81 (Chm., S Midlands Regional Cttee, 1975–81); IBA Advertising Standards Adv. Cttee, 1972; Council for European Architectural Heritage, 1972; Nat. Consumer Council, 1975–77; Redundant Churches Cttee, 1976–84. *Recreation:* reading. *Address:* St Winnow, Burford, Oxon. *T:* Burford (099382) 2210. *Club:* Naval and Military.
Died 27 April 1991.

GRAYSON, Sir Rupert (Stanley Harrington), 4th Bt *cr* 1922, of Ravenspoint, Co. Anglesey; writer; *b* 22 July 1897; *s* of Sir Henry Mulleneux Grayson, 1st Bt, KBE and Dora Beatrice (*d* 1946), *d* of Frederick Harrington; *S* nephew, 1987; *m* 1st, 1919, Ruby Victoria, *d* of Walter Henry Banks; 2nd, 1950, Vari Colette, *d* of Major Henry O'Shea, Royal Dublin Fusiliers and IA. *Educ:* schooled at Harrow, but educated between terms travelling Europe with his father. Joined Irish Guards, 1914; served European War (twice wounded). Signed on as ordinary seaman; served for 3 years with Nelson Line, Leyland and Furness Withy. Composed music for films, Hollywood, 1936. Mem. Performing Right Soc. Served War of 1939–45 as Admiralty Courier and King's Foreign Service Messenger. KHS 1923. *Publications: fiction:* Scarlet Livery; Gun Cotton; Death Rides the Forest; Gun Cotton—Adventurer; Escape with Gun Cotton; Gun Cotton in Hollywood; Gun Cotton—Secret Agent; Murder at the Bank; Introducing Mr Robinson; Adventure Nine; Blind Man's Hood; Ace High; Gun Cotton in Mexico; Secret Airman; Outside the Law; Gun Cotton Goes to Russia; *autobiography:* Voyage Not Completed, 1969; Stand Fast The Holy Ghost. *Recreations:* enjoying the company of friends, travelling. *Heir: nephew* Jeremy Brian Vincent Harrington Grayson [*b* 30 Jan. 1933; *m* 1958, Sara, *d* of C.F. Upton; three *s* three *d*]. *Address:* c/o Midland Bank, Hythe, Kent. *Clubs:* Tropico (Denia, Spain); British (Mexico City).
Died 4 April 1991.

GREEN, Alan, CBE 1974; Chairman: Walmsley (Bury) Group, 1970–78; Beloit Walmsley Ltd; Director: Scapa Group Ltd; Wolstenholme Bronze Powders Ltd (Vice-Chairman); Porritts & Spencer (Asia) Ltd, since 1969; Local Director, Barclays Bank, Manchester District, 1969–74; *b* 29 Sept. 1911; *s* of Edward and Emily Green; *m* 1935, Hilda Mary Wolstenholme (*d* 1990); three *d*. *Educ:* Brighton Coll. Schoolmaster, 1931–35; joined Scapa Dryers Ltd, Blackburn, 1935. Army Service, 1940–45. Formerly: Dir of Scapa Dryers Ltd, 1945; Vice-Chm. of Scapa Dryers Ltd, 1956; Dir of Scapa Dryers Inc., 1955; Dir of companies associated with Walmsley (Bury) Group, 1950; Chm. of Walmsley Operating Companies, 1954. Contested (C): Nelson and Colne, 1950 and 1951; MP (C) Preston S, 1955–64, 1970–Feb. 1974; Parly Sec., Min. of Labour, 1961–62; Minister of State, BoT, 1962–63; Financial Sec. to the Treasury, 1963–64; Member: Select Cttee on Nationalised Industries, 1970–74; Speaker's Conf., 1973. Mem., Australia Cttee, BNEC, 1968–72; frequent business visits to Northern and Western Europe, Australasia, Japan, India and North America. *Recreations:* cricket, golf, tennis, gardening, history. *Address:* The Stables, Sabden, near Blackburn, Lancs. *T:* Padiham (0282) 71528. *Clubs:* Reform, Royal Automobile. *Died 2 Feb. 1991.*

GREEN, Rev. Canon Bryan Stuart Westmacott, BD; DD; Canon Emeritus of Birmingham Cathedral since 1970 (Hon. Canon, 1950–70); *b* 14 Jan. 1901; *s* of late Hubert Westmacott Green and Sarah Kathleen Green (*née* Brockwell); *m* 1926, Winifred Annie Bevan; one *s* one *d*. *Educ:* Merchant Taylors' Sch.; London Univ. BD 1922. Deacon, 1924, priest, 1925; Curate, New Malden, 1924–28; Staff of Children's Special Service Mission, 1928–31; Chap., Oxford Pastorate, 1931–34; Vicar of Christ Church, Crouch End, 1934–38; Vicar of Holy Trinity, Brompton, 1938–48; Rector of Birmingham, 1948–70. Conducted evangelistic campaigns: Canada and America, 1936, 1944, and annually, 1947–; Australia and New Zealand, 1951, 1953, 1958, 1974; West Africa, 1953; S Africa, 1953, 1955, 1956, 1957, 1959 and 1960; Ceylon, 1954, 1959. Hon. DD St John's Coll. Winnipeg, 1961; DD Lambeth, 1985. *Publications:* The Practice of Evangelism, 1951; Being and Believing, 1956; Saints Alive, 1959. *Recreation:* golf. *Address:* West Field, Southern Road, Thame, Oxon OX9 2DZ. *T:* Thame (084421) 2026. *Club:* National.
Died 6 March 1993.

GREEN, Major George Hugh, MBE; MC 1945; TD and 3 bars; DL; Vice-Lieutenant of Caithness, 1973–86; retired; *b* 21 Oct. 1911; *s* of George Green, The Breck, John O'Groats; *m* 1936, Isobel Elizabeth Myron (*d* 1987); two *s. Educ:* Wick High Sch.; Edinburgh Univ. (MA). Retired as schoolmaster, 1977. Commnd into Seaforth Highlanders, TA, 1935; served War of 1939–45 with 5th Seaforths in 51st (H) Div., N Africa, Sicily and NW Europe; retd from TA, 1963. DL Caithness 1965. *Recreations:* gardening, bee-keeping. *Address:* Tjaldur, Halkirk, Caithness KW12 6XQ. *T:* Halkirk (0184783) 639. *Club:* Highland Brigade (Inverness).
Died 5 Feb. 1993.

GREENAWAY, Alan Pearce, JP; Vice-President, Daniel Greenaway & Sons Ltd, 1978–82 (Joint Managing Director, 1951–78; Vice-Chairman, 1965–76; Chairman, 1976–78); *b* 25 Nov. 1913; *yr s* of Sir Percy Walter Greenaway, 1st Bt, and Lydie Amy (*d* 1962), *er d* of James Burdick; *m* 1948, Patricia Frances (*d* 1982), *yr d* of Ald. Sir Frederick Wells, 1st Bt; one *s* one *d. Educ:* Canford. Served in King's Liverpool Regt during War of 1939–45, reaching rank of Captain. Liveryman: Worshipful Co. of Merchant Taylors; Worshipful Co. of Stationers and Newspaper Makers (Under-Warden, 1971–72; Upper Warden, 1972–73; Master, 1973–74). Mem. Court of Common Council for Ward of Bishopsgate, 1952–65; Sheriff for the City of London, 1962–63; JP, Co. London, 1964; Alderman, Lime Street Ward, City of London, 1965–72; Chm. and Treasurer, City of London Sheriffs' Soc., 1979–82. Officier, l'Ordre de la Valeur (Cameroon Republic), 1963; Commandeur, l'Ordre de Léopold Class III (Belgium), 1963; Commander, Royal Order of the Phoenix (Greece), 1964. *Recreations:* golf, fishing, swimming, bowls. *Address:* West Byfleet, Surrey. *Clubs:* City Livery (Vice-Pres. 1971–72, Pres., 1972–73), Royal Automobile, United Wards.
Died 9 Jan. 1994.

GREENAWAY, Sir Derek (Burdick), 2nd Bt *cr* 1933, of Coombe, Surrey; CBE 1974; TD; JP; DL; President, Daniel Greenaway & Sons Ltd, 132 Commercial Street, E1, since 1976 (Chairman, 1956–76); *b* 27 May 1910; *er s* of Sir Percy Walter Greenaway, 1st Bt and Lydie Amy (*d* 1962), *er d* of James Burdick; *S* father 1956; *m* 1937, Sheila Beatrice, *d* of late Richard Cyril Lockett, 58 Cadogan Place, SW1; one *s* one *d. Educ:* Marlborough. Served in Field Artillery during War of 1939–45; Hon. Col: 44 (HC) Signal Regt (Cinque Ports) TA, 1966; 36th (Eastern) Signal Regt (V), 1967–74. Joint Master, Old Surrey and Burstow Foxhounds, 1958–66. Chm. Sevenoaks Constituency Cons. & Unionist Assoc., 1960–63; Pres. 1963–66; Vice Pres., 1966–. Asst Area Treasurer,

SE Area Nat. Union of Cons. Assocs, 1966–69, Area Treasurer, 1969–75, Chm. 1975–79. Master, Stationers' and Newspapermakers' Co., 1974–75 (Silver Medal, 1984). JP County of Kent, 1962; High Sheriff, 1971, DL 1973, Kent. FRSA. Life Mem., Assoc. of Men of Kent and Kentish Men. *Recreations:* hunting, shooting. *Heir: s* John Michael Burdick Greenaway, late Lieut, The Life Guards [*b* 9 Aug. 1944; *m* 1982, Susan M., *d* of Henry Birch, Tattenhall, Cheshire; one *s* one *d*]. *Address:* Dunmore, Four Elms, Edenbridge, Kent. *T:* Four Elms (01732) 700275. *Clubs:* Carlton, City of London, MCC.
Died 19 Nov. 1994.

GREENE, Graham, OM 1986; CH 1966; CLit 1984; author; *b* 2 Oct. 1904; *s* of late Charles Henry Greene; *m* 1927, Vivien Dayrell-Browning; one *s* one *d. Educ:* Berkhamsted; Balliol Coll., Oxford (Hon. Fellow, 1963). On staff of The Times, 1926–30; Literary Editor, The Spectator, 1940–41; department of Foreign Office, 1941–44. Director: Eyre & Spottiswoode Ltd, 1944–48; Bodley Head, 1958–68. Mem., Panamanian delegn to Washington for signing of Canal Treaty, 1977. Hon. LittD, Cambridge, 1962; Hon. DLitt: Edinburgh, 1967; Oxford, 1979; Dr *hc* Moscow, 1988. Chevalier de la Légion d'Honneur, 1967. Shakespeare Prize, Hamburg, 1968; John Dos Passos Prize, 1980; Medal, City of Madrid, 1980; Jerusalem Prize, 1981. Hon. Citizen, Anacapri, 1978. Grand Cross, Order of Vasco Nuñez de Balboa (Panama), 1983; Commandeur des Arts et des Lettres, France, 1984; Order of Ruben Dario (Nicaragua), 1987. *Publications:* Babbling April, 1925; The Man Within, 1929; The Name of Action, 1930; Rumour at Nightfall, 1931; Stamboul Train, 1932; It's a Battlefield, 1934; The Old School (Editor), 1934; The Bear Fell Free (limited edn), 1935; England Made Me, 1935; The Basement Room (short stories), 1935; Journey without Maps (account of a journey through Liberia), 1936; A Gun for Sale, 1936; Brighton Rock, 1938; The Lawless Roads, 1939; The Confidential Agent, 1939; The Power and the Glory, 1940 (Hawthornden Prize for 1940); British Dramatists, 1942; The Ministry of Fear, 1943; Nineteen Stories, 1947; The Heart of the Matter, 1948; The Third Man, 1950; The End of the Affair, 1951; The Lost Childhood and other essays, 1951; Essais Catholiques, 1953; Twenty one Stories, 1954; Loser Takes All, 1955; The Quiet American, 1955; Our Man in Havana, 1958; A Burnt-Out Case, 1961; In Search of a Character: Two African Journals, 1961; A Sense of Reality, 1963; The Comedians, 1966; May we borrow your Husband? And other Comedies of the Sexual Life (short stories), 1967; Collected Essays, 1969; Travels with my Aunt, 1969; A Sort of Life (autobiog.), 1971; The Pleasure-Dome: the collected film criticism 1935–40, ed John Russell Taylor, 1972; Collected Stories, 1972; The Honorary Consul, 1973; Lord Rochester's Monkey, 1974; An Impossible Woman: the Memories of Dottoressa Moor of Capri, 1975; The Human Factor, 1978; Dr Fischer of Geneva, 1980; Ways of Escape (autobiog.), 1980; J'Accuse: the dark side of Nice, 1982; Monsignor Quixote, 1982; Getting to Know the General, 1984; The Tenth Man, 1985; The Captain and the Enemy, 1988; Reflections (collection of journalism), 1990; *plays:* The Living Room, 1953; The Potting Shed, 1957; The Complaisant Lover, 1959; Carving a Statue, 1964; The Return of A. J. Raffles, 1975; Yes and No, 1980; For Whom the Bell Chimes, 1980; The Great Jowett, 1981; *for children:* The Little Train, 1947; The Little Fire Engine, 1950; The Little Horse Bus, 1952; The Little Steamroller, 1953; *film plays:* Brighton Rock, 1948; The Fallen Idol, 1948; The Third Man, 1949; Our Man in Havana, 1960; The Comedians, 1967. *Address:* c/o Reinhardt Books Ltd, 27 Wright's Lane, W8 5TZ.
Died 3 April 1991.

GREENE, Ian Rawdon; *b* 3 March 1909; *o s* of Rawdon Greene and Marie Louise, Rahan, Bray, County Wicklow, Ireland; *m* 1937, Eileen Theodora Stack; one *d. Educ:* Cheltenham Coll.; Trinity Coll., Dublin (BA, LLB). Barrister at Law, Kings Inns, Dublin, 1932; Crown Counsel, Tanganyika, 1935; Resident Magistrate, Zanzibar, 1937. Military Service, Kenya, 1940–41. Sen. Resident Magistrate, Zanzibar, 1950; Actg Asst Judge, Zanzibar, on numerous occasions; Actg Chief Justice, Zanzibar, June 1954, and May-Oct. 1955; Judge-in-charge, Somaliland Protectorate, 1955; Chief Justice, Somaliland Protectorate, 1958–60, retired; Stipendiary Magistrate, North Borneo, 1961–64. Registrar to Dean and Chapter, St Patrick's Cathedral, Dublin, 1973–82. Order of Brilliant Star of Zanzibar (4th Cl.), 1953. *Publications:* Jt Ed., Vols VI and VII, Zanzibar Law Reports. *Recreations:* cricket, golf, bridge, chess. *Address:* Pemba, 2 Glenlucan Court, Bray, Co. Wicklow, Ireland. *Clubs:* English (Zanzibar); Hargeisa (Somaliland).
Died 27 May 1992.

GREENE, Dame Judith; *see* Anderson, Dame F. M.

GREENEWALT, Crawford Hallock; *b* Cummington, Mass, 16 Aug. 1902; *s* of Frank Lindsay and Mary Hallock Greenewalt; *m* 1926, Margaretta Lammot du Pont; two *s* one *d. Educ:* William Penn Charter Sch.; Mass Institute of Technology (BS). With E. I. du Pont de Nemours & Co., Inc., 1922–90: Asst Dir Exptl Station, Central Research Dept, 1939; Dir Chem. Div., Industrial and Biochemicals Dept, 1942; Technical Dir, Explosives Department, 1943; Asst Dir, Development Dept, 1945; Asst Gen. Man. Pigments Dept, 1945–46; Vice-Pres., 1946; Vice-Pres. and Vice-Chm. Exec. Cttee, 1947; Pres., 1948–62; Chm. Exec. Cttee, 1948; Mem. Finance Cttee, 1948–88; Chm. Board, 1962–67; Chm. Finance Cttee, 1967–74; Member Board of Directors of various other organisations. Member: Amer. Acad. of Arts and Sciences, National Academy of Sciences, Amer. Philos. Soc. (Pres., 1984–87). Trustee Emeritus: Nat. Geographic Soc.; Carnegie Inst. of Washington. Hon. degrees in Science, Engineering and Laws, and various scientific awards and medals. *Publications:* The Uncommon Man, 1959; Hummingbirds, 1960; Bird Song: acoustics and physiology, 1969. *Recreation:* photography. *Address:* Box 3652, Greenville, Delaware 19807, USA. *Clubs:* Wilmington, Du Pont Country, Greenville Country (USA).
Died 21 Sept. 1993.

GREENFIELD, Hon. Julius MacDonald, CMG 1954; Judge of the High Court of Rhodesia, 1968–74; *b* Boksburg, Transvaal, 13 July 1907; *s* of late Rev. C. E. Greenfield; *m* 1935, Florence Margaret Couper; two *s* one *d. Educ:* Milton Sch., Bulawayo; Universities of Capetown and Oxford. BA, LLB Cape; Rhodes Scholar, 1929; BA, BCL Oxon. Called to the Bar at Gray's Inn, 1933. QC 1949; practised at Bar in S Rhodesia, 1933–50; elected MP for Hillside, S Rhodesia, 1948, and appointed Minister of Internal Affairs and Justice, 1950; participated in London Conferences on Federation in Central Africa; MP Federal Parliament, in Umguza Constituency, 1953–63; Minister of Law, Federation of Rhodesia and Nyasaland, 1954–63; Minister for Home Affairs, 1962–63. *Publications:* Instant Crime, 1975; Instant Statute Case Law, 1977; Testimony of a Rhodesian Federal, 1978. *Address:* Flat 40 Berkeley Square, 173 Main Road, Rondebosch, Cape, 7700, South Africa. *Clubs:* Bulawayo, Harare (Zimbabwe).
Died 9 Jan. 1993.

GREENHAM, Peter George, CBE 1978; RA 1960 (ARA 1951); PPRBA; RP; NEAC; Keeper of the Royal Academy Schools, 1964–85; *b* 9 Sept. 1909; *s* of George Frederick Greenham, MBE, civil servant; *m* 1964, Jane, *d* of late Dr G. B. Dowling, FRCP, and Mary Elizabeth Kelly; one *s* one *d. Educ:* Dulwich Coll.; Magdalen Coll., Oxford

(Hist. Demy, BA); Byam Shaw Sch. of Art. Pres., RBA, to 1982. Paintings in permanent collections: Tate Gall.; Nat. Portrait Gall.; Arts Council; Contemp. Art Soc.; Carlisle Gall.; Plymouth Gall.; Gulbenkian Collection. *Publication:* Velasquez, 1969. *Address:* c/o Royal Academy, Piccadilly, W1V 0DS.

Died 11 July 1992.

GREENSMITH, Edward William, OBE 1972; BScEng; FCGI; Deputy President, Executive Board of the British Standards Institution, 1973–79 (Chairman, 1970–73); *b* 20 April 1909; *m* 1937, Edna Marjorie Miskin (*d* 1971); three *s*; *m* 1972, Margaret Boaden Miles. Engrg Adviser, ICI, 1964–71. Dir (non-executive), Peter Brotherhood Ltd, 1970–78. *Publications:* contribs to Chemistry Ind., 1957, 1959. *Recreations:* walking, gardening. *Address:* Pound Cottage, Graffham, near Petworth, W Sussex GU28 0QA. *T:* Graffham (017986) 374. *Died 1 Feb. 1995.*

GREENWOOD, (James) Russell, LVO 1975; HM Diplomatic Service, retired; Professor of Asian Studies, Matsusaka University, Japan, since 1983; *b* 30 April 1924; *s* of late J. Greenwood and L. Greenwood (*née* Moffat), Padiham; *m* 1957, Mary Veronica (marr. diss.), *d* of late Dr D. W. Griffith and Dr Grace Griffith, Bures; one *s*. *Educ:* Royal Grammar Sch., Clitheroe; Queen's Coll., Oxford. Army Service, 1943–47. BA, MA (Oxon) 1949. Foreign Office, 1949; subseq. service in Bangkok, 1950–52; Tokyo and Osaka, 1952–54; London, 1955–58; Rangoon, 1958–61; Rome, 1961–63; Bangkok, 1964–68; Counsellor (Information), Tokyo, 1968–73; Consul-General, Osaka, 1973–77. PRO, The APV Company and APV International, 1980–82. Order of Sacred Treasure (3rd cl.) (Japan), 1975. *Recreations:* travel, golf, cricket. *Address:* Faculty of Political Science and Economics, Matsusaka University, 1846 Kubo-Cho, Matsusaka, Mie 515, Japan. *Clubs:* United Oxford & Cambridge University, MCC. *Died 5 March 1993.*

GREENWOOD, John Arnold Charles, OBE 1943; Chief General Manager, Sun Alliance & London Insurance Group, 1971–77; *b* 23 Jan. 1914; *o s* of late Augustus George Greenwood and Adele Ellen O'Neill Arnold; *m* 1940, Dorothy Frederica Pestell; two *d*. *Educ:* King's College Sch., Wimbledon. FCII; FRES. Joined Sun Insce Office Ltd, 1932; posted India, 1937–47; served War of 1939–45, TA, 36th Sikh Regt and AA&QMG 4th Indian Div. (Lt-Col, OBE, despatches); subseq. various appts; a Gen. Man., Sun Alliance & London, 1965; Dep. Chief Gen. Man., 1969. Morgan Owen Medal, 1939. *Publications:* papers on insurance, entomology. *Recreations:* entomology, writing, gardening. *Address:* Hambledon House, Rogate, Petersfield, Hants GU31 5EE. *T:* Rogate (0730) 821744. *Died 14 Feb. 1992.*

GREENWOOD, Peter Humphry, DSc; FRS 1985; FIBiol; Deputy Chief Scientific Officer, Ichthyologist, British Museum (Natural History), 1985–89 (Senior Principal Scientific Officer, 1967–85); *b* 21 April 1927; *s* of Percy Ashworth Greenwood and Joyce May Wilton; *m* 1950, Marjorie George; four *d*. *Educ:* St John's Coll., Johannesburg; Krugersdorp High Sch.; Univ. of Witwatersrand. BSc (Hons), DSc. S African Naval Forces, seconded to RN, 1944–46. Colonial Office Fisheries Res. Student, 1950–51; Res. Officer, E African Fisheries Res. Orgn, Jinja, Uganda, 1951–58; British Museum (Natural History): Sen. Res. Fellow, 1958–59; Sen., later Principal, Scientific Officer and Curator of Fishes, 1959–67. Research Associate: Amer. Mus. of Natural Hist., 1965; J. L. B. Smith Inst. of Ichthyology, S Africa, 1977–; H. B. Bigelow Vis. Prof. of Ichthyology, Harvard Univ., 1979; Adjunct Prof., Univ. of Bergen, 1992–; Vis. Res. Fellow, Natural History Mus., 1990–. Mem., British subcttee on productivity of freshwaters, Internat. Biol Prog., 1964–75; Chm., Royal Soc./Internat. Biol Prog. subcttee on res. in

Lake George, 1967–74. Pres., Linnean Soc. of London, 1976–79. Hon. For. Mem., Amer. Soc. of Ichthyologists and Herpetologists, 1972; For. Mem., Swedish Royal Acad. of Science, 1984. DSc (*hc*) Rhodes Univ., South Africa, 1991. Scientific Medal, Zoological Soc. of London, 1963; Medal for Zoology, Linnean Soc., 1982. *Publications:* Fishes of Uganda, 1958, 2nd edn 1966; The Cichlid Fishes of Lake Victoria: the biology and evolution of a species flock, 1974; (ed) J. R. Norman, A History of Fishes, 1963, 2nd rev. edn 1975; (ed with C. Patterson) Fossil Vertebrates, 1967; (ed with C. Patterson and R. Miles) Interrelationships of Fishes, 1973; The Haplochromine Fishes of the East African Lakes, 1981; numerous papers on taxonomy, anatomy, biology and evolution of fishes. *Recreations:* ballet, art, reading, thinking, model building. *Address:* J. L. B. Smith Institute of Ichthyology, Private Bag 1015, Grahamstown, 6140, South Africa. *T:* (461) 27124; Natural History Museum, Cromwell Road, SW7 5BD. *T:* 0171–938 8825.

Died 3 March 1995.

GREENWOOD, Russell; *see* Greenwood, J. R.

GREEVES, Rev. Derrick Amphlet; Methodist Minister, Langwathby, Cumbria, since 1978; *b* 29 June 1913; *s* of Rev. Edward Greeves, Methodist Minister; *m* 1942, Nancy (*née* Morgans); one *s* three *d*. *Educ:* Bolton Sch.; Preston Gram. Sch.; Manchester Univ. 1931–34 (BA); Cambridge Univ. (Wesley Hse), 1934–37 (MA). Entered Methodist Ministry, 1935; Barnet, 1937; Bristol, 1939; RAF Chaplain, 1943; S Norwood, 1947; Bowes Park, 1952; Superintendent Minister: Westminster Central Hall, 1955; Guildford Circuit, 1964; Worcester Circuit, 1969; Salisbury Circuit, 1974. *Publications:* Christ in Me, a study of the Mind of Christ in Paul, 1962; A Word in Your Ear (broadcast talks), 1970; Preaching through St Paul, 1980. *Address:* Red Barn, Langwathby, Penrith, Cumbria CA10 1LW. *T:* Langwathby (0768) 881707.

Died 14 March 1991.

GREGOIRE, His Eminence Cardinal Paul, OC 1979; Archbishop Emeritus of Montreal (Archbishop, 1968–90); *b* Verdun, 24 Oct. 1911. *Educ:* Ecole Supérieure Richard; Séminaire de Ste-Thérèse; Univ. of Montreal. Priest, 1937; became Professor, but continued his studies (PhD, STL, LèsL, MA (Hist.), dip. in pedagogy); subseq. became Director, Séminaire de Ste-Thérèse; Prof. of Philosophy of Educn at l'Ecole Normale Secondaire and at l'Institut Pédagogique; Chaplain of the Students, Univ. of Montreal, 1950–61; consecrated Bishop, 1961, and became auxiliary to Archbishop of Montreal; Vicar-General and Dir of Office for the Clergy; Apostolic Administrator, Archdiocese of Montreal, Dec. 1967–April 1968. Cardinal, 1988. Pres., Episcopal Commn on Ecumenism (French sector), 1965. Presided over several Diocesan Commns (notably Commn for study of the material situation of the Clergy), 1965–68. Member: Canadian delegn to Bishop's Synod, Rome, 1971–; Congregation for the Clergy, 1978–83; Congregation for Catholic Educn, 1983–; Pontifical Commn for pastoral care of Migrations and of Tourism, 1988–; Congregation for the Oriental Churches, 1989–. Dr *hc:* Univ. of Montreal, 1969; St Michael's Coll., Winooski, Vt, 1970. *Address:* Archbishop's House, 1071 Cathedral Street, Montreal, Quebec H3B 2V4, Canada. *Died 30 Oct. 1993.*

GREIG, Prof. James, MSc (London), PhD (Birmingham); William Siemens Professor of Electrical Engineering, University of London, King's College, 1945–70, then Emeritus Professor; *b* 24 April 1903; *s* of James Alexander Greig and Helen Bruce Meldrum, Edinburgh; *m* 1931, Ethel May, *d* of William Archibald, Edinburgh; (one *d* decd). *Educ:* George Watson's Coll. and Heriot-Watt Coll., Edinburgh; University Coll., University of London. Experience in telephone engineering with Bell Telephone

Company, Montreal, 1924–26; Mem. research staff, General Electric Company, London, 1928–33; Asst Lectr, University Coll., London, 1933–36; Lectr, Univ. of Birmingham, 1936–39; Head of Dept of Electrical Engineering, Northampton Polytechnic, 1939–45. Dean of the Faculty of Engineering, Univ. of London, 1958–62, and Mem. Senate, 1958–70; Mem. Court, Univ. of London, 1967–70. FIEE (Chm. Measurement Section, 1949–50; Mem. Council, 1955–58); MRI; Fellow Heriot-Watt Coll., 1951; FRSE 1956; FKC 1963. Mem., British Assoc. for the Advancement of Science. Chm., Crail Preservation Soc., 1959–74. *Publications:* papers (dealing mainly with subject of electrical and magnetic measurements) to: Jl Inst. Electrical Engineers, The Wireless Engineer, and Engineering. *Address:* Inch of Kinnordy, Kirriemuir, Angus. *T:* Kirriemuir (0575) 72350. *Club:* Athenæum.
Died 12 Dec. 1991.

GRETTON, Vice-Adm. Sir Peter (William), KCB 1963 (CB 1960); DSO 1942; OBE 1941; DSC 1936; MA; *b* 27 Aug. 1912; *s* of Major G. F. Gretton; *m* 1943, D. N. G. Du Vivier; three *s* one *d*. *Educ:* Roper's Preparatory Sch.; RNC, Dartmouth. Prize for Five First Class Certificates as Sub.-Lieut; Comdr 1942; Capt. 1948; Rear-Adm. 1958; Vice-Adm. 1961. Served War of 1939–45 (despatches, OBE, DSO and two Bars); Senior Naval Mem. of Directing Staff of Imperial Defence Coll., 1958–60; Flag Officer, Sea Training, 1960–61; a Lord Commissioner of the Admiralty, Dep. Chief of Naval Staff and Fifth Sea Lord, 1962–63, retd. Domestic Bursar, University Coll., Oxford, 1965–71, Senior Research Fellow, 1971–79. Vice-Pres., Royal Humane Soc. (Testimonial of Royal Humane Society, 1940). *Publications:* Convoy Escort Commander, 1964; Maritime Strategy: A Study of British Defence Problems, 1965; Former Naval Person: Churchill and the Navy, 1968; Crisis Convoy, 1974. *Address:* 29 Northmoor Road, Oxford OX2 6UR.   *Died 11 Nov. 1992.*

GRIEVE, Prof. Sir Robert, Kt 1969; MA, FRSE, FRTPI, MICE; Professor Emeritus, University of Glasgow; Hon. Professor, Heriot-Watt University, since 1986; *b* 11 Dec. 1910; *s* of Peter Grieve and Catherine Boyle; *m* 1933, Mary Lavinia Broughton Blackburn; two *s* two *d*. *Educ:* N. Kelvinside Sch., Glasgow; Royal Coll. of Science and Technology (later Univ. of Strathclyde), Glasgow. Trng and qual. as Civil Engr, eventually Planner. Local Govt posts, 1927–44; preparation of Clyde Valley Regional Plan, 1944–46; Civil Service, 1946–54; Chief Planner, Scottish Office, 1960–64. Prof. of Town and Regional Planning, Glasgow Univ., 1964–74; retired from Chair, 1974. Chairman: Highlands and Islands Develt Bd, 1965–70; Highlands and Islands Development Consultative Council, 1978–86; Royal Fine Art Commn for Scotland, 1978–83; President: Scottish Countryside Rangers Assoc.; Saltire Soc., 1991–; Hon. President: Scottish Rights of Way Soc.; New Glasgow Soc.; Inverness Civic Trust; Stewartry Mountaineering Club; Scottish Branch, RTPI (Vice Pres., 1971–73); Friends of Loch Lomond. Former President: Scottish Mountaineering Council; Scottish Mountaineering Club; Former Vice-Pres., Internat. Soc. of Town and Regional Planners. Hon. Vice-Pres., Scottish Youth Hostels Assoc. Gold Medal, RTPI, 1974. Hon. DLitt Heriot-Watt; Hon. LLD Strathclyde, 1984; Dr *hc* Edinburgh, 1985. Hon. FRIAS; Hon. FRSGS 1989. Lord Provost's Award, Glasgow, 1989. *Publications:* part-author and collaborator in several major professional reports and books; many papers and articles in professional and technical jls. *Recreations:* mountains, poetry. *Address:* 5 Rothesay Terrace, Edinburgh EH3 7RY. *Club:* Scottish Arts (Edinburgh).
Died 25 Oct. 1995.

GRIFFIN, Sir John Bowes, Kt 1955; QC 1938; *b* 19 April 1903; *o s* of late Sir Charles Griffin and Aileen Mary, *o c*

of John Fanning, solicitor, Kilkenny; *m* 1st, Eva Orrell (*d* 1977), 2nd *d* of late John Mellifont Walsh, Wexford; two *d*; 2nd, 1984, Margaret Guthrie (*née* Sinclair) (*d* 1991), *widow* of H. F. Lever. *Educ:* Clongowes; Dublin Univ. (MA, LLD, First Cl. Moderatorship, Gold Medallist); Cambridge. Barrister-at-Law, Inner Temple, 1926. Administrative Officer, Uganda, 1927; Asst District Officer, 1929; Registrar, High Court, 1929; Crown Counsel, 1933; Actg Solicitor-Gen. and Attorney-Gen., various periods; Attorney-Gen., Bahamas, 1936 (Acting Governor and Acting Chief Justice, various periods); Solicitor-Gen., Palestine, 1939, Acting Attorney-Gen., various periods; Attorney-Gen., Hong Kong, 1946; Chief Justice of Uganda, 1952–56; retd Dec. 1956. Secretary: East Africa Law Officers Conference, 1933; Commission of Enquiry, Admin of Justice, East Africa, 1933; Chm. Prisons Enquiry, Bahamas, 1936; miscellaneous Bds and Cttees; Chairman: Tel Aviv Municipal Commn of Enquiry, Palestine, 1942; Review Cttees, Detainees (Defence and Emergency Regulations), Palestine, 1940–46. Actg Chief Justice, N Rhodesia, 1957; Chm. Commn of Enquiry Gwenbe Valley Disturbances, N Rhodesia, 1958; Speaker, Legislative Council, Uganda, 1958–62; Speaker, Uganda National Assembly, 1962–63, retd. Chairman: Public Service Commissions, 1963 and Constitutional Council, 1964, N Rhodesia; retd 1965. CStJ 1960. *Publications:* revised edn of Laws (Uganda), 1935; (joint) Hong Kong, 1950. *Address:* 1 Marina Court, Tigne Sea Front, Sliema, Malta. *Clubs:* East India; Union (Malta).
Died 2 Feb. 1992.

GRIFFIN, Rear-Adm. Michael Harold, CB 1973; antiquarian horologist; *b* 28 Jan. 1921; *s* of late Henry William Griffin and Blanche Celia Griffin (*née* Michael); *m* 1947, Barbara Mary Brewer; two *d*. *Educ:* Plymouth Junior Techn. Coll. CEng, FIMechE, FIMarE. MBHI. Commnd, 1941; HMS Kent, 1942; HM Submarines Trusty, Tactician, Tally Ho, Alderney, 1944–50; Admty, 1950–52; HMS Eagle, 1952–54; staff C-in-C Portsmouth, 1954–57; HM Dockyard, Rosyth, 1957–60; Third Submarine Sqdn, 1960–62; Captain, 1962; HM Dockyard, Chatham, 1963–65; HMS St Vincent, 1966–69; Cdre Supt, Singapore, 1969–71; Dir of Dockyard Production and Support, MoD, 1972–77, retired. Naval Adviser to Vosper Shiprepairers Ltd, 1977–81. *Recreations:* horology, motoring, grandchildren. *Address:* 48 Little Green, Alverstoke, Gosport, Hants PO12 2EX. *T:* Gosport (01705) 646481.   *Died 14 July 1995.*

GRIFFITH, Stewart Cathie, CBE 1975; DFC 1944; TD 1954; Secretary, MCC, 1962–74; *b* 16 June 1914; *yr s* of H. L. A. Griffith, Middleton, Sussex; *m* 1939, Barbara Reynolds; one *s* one *d*. *Educ:* Dulwich Coll.; Pembroke Coll., Cambridge (MA). Asst Master, Dulwich Coll., 1937–39. Army, 1939–46: Glider Pilot Regt, Lieut-Col. Sec., Sussex County Cricket Club, 1946–50; Cricket Correspondent, Sunday Times, 1950–52; Asst Sec., MCC, 1952–62; Secretary: Internat. Cricket Conference, 1962–74; Cricket Council, 1969–74; Test and County Cricket Bd, 1969–73; President: Sussex CCC, 1975–77; MCC, 1979–80. *Recreations:* cricket, golf, real tennis, walking. *Address:* 7 Sea Way, Middleton, Sussex PO22 7RZ. *T:* Middleton-on-Sea (0243) 583000. *Clubs:* East India, Devonshire, Sports and Public Schools, MCC, Hawks (Cambridge), etc.   *Died 7 April 1993.*

GRIFFITHS, Edward; *b* 7 March 1929; Welsh; *m* 1954, Ella Constance Griffiths; one *s* one *d*. *Educ:* University Coll. of N Wales, Bangor. Industrial Chemist, 1951. Mem., Flintshire CC, 1964. MP (Lab) Brightside Div. of Sheffield, June 1968–Sept. 1974; contested (Ind Lab) Sheffield Brightside, Oct. 1974. *Recreation:* sport.
Died 18 Oct. 1995.

GRIFFITHS, Sir (Ernest) Roy, Kt 1985; Deputy Chairman, National Health Service Policy Board, since 1989; Adviser to the Government on the National Health Service, since 1986; *b* 8 July 1926; *s* of Ernest and Florence Griffiths; *m* 1952, Winifred Mary Rigby; one *s* two *d. Educ:* Wolstanton Grammar Sch., N Staffs; Keble Coll., Oxford (Open Scholar; MA, BCL; Hon. Fellow 1987); Columbia Business Sch., New York. Solicitor; FCIS 1959; FIGD 1975 (Pres., 1985–87); CIMgt (CBIM 1980); Hon. FCGI (Technology), 1988. Monsanto Cos, 1956–68: Legal Adviser, 1956; Dir, Monsanto Europe, 1964–68; J. Sainsbury plc, 1968–91: Dir, Personnel, 1969; Man. Dir, 1979–88; Dep. Chm., 1975–91. Chm., Management Enquiry, NHS, 1983 (report publd 1983); Mem., Health Services Supervisory Bd, 1983–89; Dep. Chm., NHS Management Bd, 1986–89. Pres., Age Concern England, 1989–. Provost and Chm. of Governors, London Univ. Sch. of Agric., Wye Coll., Kent, 1989–. Lectures: Redcliffe Maude Meml, RIPA, 1987; Archbishop Child's Meml, Cardiff, 1990; Royal Soc. of Health, 1990; Audit Commn, 1991; Lord Seebohm Meml, London, 1991; James Seth Meml, Edinburgh, 1992. Hon. DCL Kent, 1990; Hon. LLD: Keele, 1991; Hull, 1993; Hon. DSc City, 1993. Jephcott Medal, RSM, 1992. Author of *Community Care: agenda for action* (report to Govt), 1988. *Recreations:* cricket, gardening. *Address:* Little Earlylands, Crockham Hill, Edenbridge, Kent TN8 6SN. *T:* Edenbridge (0732) 866362.   *Died 28 March 1994.*

GRIFFITHS, John Edward Seaton, CMG 1959; MBE 1934; retired; *b* 27 Sept. 1908; *s* of A. E. Griffiths, MA, Cape Town; *m* 1937, Helen Parker, *d* of C. C. Wiles, MA, Grahamstown, SA; two *s* one *d. Educ:* South African Coll. Sch.; Cape Town Univ.; Selwyn Coll., Cambridge. Colonial Service (later HM Overseas Civil Service), Tanganyika, 1931–59; Asst Comr, East African Office, 1960–63; Director of Studies, Royal Inst. Public Administration, 1963–67; Administrative Training Officer, Govt of Botswana, 1967–73. *Publications:* articles in *Tanganyika Notes and Records*, *Botswana Notes and Records* and in *Journal of Administration Overseas. Address:* c/o National Westminster Bank, 249 Banbury Road, Summertown, Oxford. *Clubs:* Commonwealth Trust; Mountain Club of South Africa (Cape Town).
    Died 19 Dec. 1991.

GRIFFITHS, Sir Percival Joseph, KBE 1963; Kt 1947; CIE 1943; Indian Civil Service (retired); formerly President, India, Pakistan and Burma Association; director of various companies; *b* 15 Jan. 1899; *s* of late J. T. Griffiths, Ashford, Middx; *m* 1st, Kathleen Mary (*d* 1979), *d* of late T. R. Wilkes, Kettering; two *s* (and one *s* decd); 2nd, 1985, Marie, *widow* of Sir Hubert Shirley Smith. *Educ:* Peterhouse, Cambridge (MA). BSc London. Entered Indian Civil Service, 1922; retired, 1937. Leader, European Group, Indian Central Legislature, 1946; Central Organiser, National War Front, India, and Publicity Adviser to Government of India; Mem. Indian Legislative Assembly, 1937. Hon. Fellow, SOAS, 1971. *Publications:* The British in India, 1947; The British Impact on India, 1952; Modern India, 1957; The Changing Face of Communism, 1961; The Road to Freedom, 1964; History of the Indian Tea Industry, 1967; Empire into Commonwealth, 1969; To Guard My People: the history of the Indian Police, 1971; A Licence to Trade: the History of English Chartered Companies, 1975; A History of the Inchcape Group, 1977; A History of the Joint Steamer Companies, 1979; Vignettes of India, 1986. *Address:* Dormy House, Ridgemount Road, Sunningdale, Berks SL5 9RL. *Club:* Oriental.   *Died 14 July 1992.*

GRIFFITHS, Sir Reginald (Ernest), Kt 1973; CBE 1965; Secretary, Local Authorities' Advisory Board, 1957–73; *b* 4 April 1910; *s* of Arthur Griffiths; *m* 1935, Jessica

Lilian Broad (*d* 1987); two *s. Educ:* St Marylebone Grammar Sch.; London Univ. (external). Asst Clerk, LCC, 1948–52; Dir of Estabs, LCC, 1952–57. Jt Sec., Police Council, 1957–72; Jt Sec., Nat. Jt Industrial Councils (Local Authorities), 1957–72; Mem., Nat. Industrial Relations Court, 1972–74. *Recreations:* gardening, golf. *Address:* 10 Woolbrook Park, Sidmouth, Devon. *T:* Sidmouth (03955) 4884.   *Died 17 July 1991.*

GRIFFITHS, Sir Roy; *see* Griffiths, Sir E. R.

GRIFFITHS, Trevor, BScEng, CEng, FIMechE, FIEE; registered professional engineer, State of California; Engineer Specialist (retired), Bechtel Power Corporation, Norwalk, California; *b* 17 April 1913; *m* 1939, Evelyn Mary Colborn; one *d. Educ:* Bishop Gore Gram. Sch., Swansea; University Coll., London. Metropolitan Vickers Electrical Co. Ltd, 1934; Air Min., 1938; UKAEA, 1955; Min. of Power, 1960; Min. of Technology, 1969 (Chief Inspector of Nuclear Installations, 1964–71); Dep. Chief Inspector of Nuclear Installations, DTI, 1971–73. *Address:* 12705 SE River Road 512E, Portland, Oregon 97222, USA.   *Died 5 July 1993.*

GRILLER, Sidney Aaron, CBE 1951; Leader of Griller String Quartet since 1928; *b* London, 10 Jan. 1911; *s* of Salter Griller and Hannah (*née* Green); *m* 1932, Elizabeth Honor, *y d* of James Linton, JP, Co. Down, N Ireland; one *s* one *d. Educ:* Royal Academy of Music (FRAM 1945). Toured British Isles, Holland, Germany, Switzerland, France, Italy, 1928–38; first concert tour in USA, 1939. Served War, RAF, 1940–45. Lecturer in Music, University of California, 1949; world tours, 1951, 1953. Prof. of Music: Royal Irish Acad. of Music, 1963; Royal Academy of Music, 1964 (Dir of Chamber Music, 1983–86); Associate Sen. Tutor, Menuhin Sch., 1987–. Worshipful Company of Musicians Medal for Chamber Music, 1944. DUniv York, 1981. *Address:* 63 Marloes Road, W8 6LE. *T:* 071–937 7067.   *Died 20 Nov. 1993.*

GRIMOND, Baron *cr* 1983 (Life Peer), of Firth in the County of Orkney; **Joseph Grimond,** TD 1957; PC 1961; Leader of the Parliamentary Liberal Party, 1956–67, and May-July 1976; Trustee, The Manchester Guardian and Evening News Ltd, 1967–83; Chancellor of University of Kent at Canterbury, 1970–90; *b* 29 July 1913; *s* of Joseph Bowman Grimond and Helen Lydia Richardson; *m* 1938, Hon. Laura Miranda, *d* of late Sir Maurice Bonham Carter, KCB, KCVO, and Baroness Asquith of Yarnbury, DBE; two *s* one *d* (and one *s* decd). *Educ:* Eton; Balliol Coll., Oxford (Brackenbury Scholar; 1st Class Hons (Politics, Philosophy, and Economics); Hon. Fellow 1984). Called to the Bar, Middle Temple (Harmsworth Scholar), 1937. Served War of 1939–45, Fife and Forfar Yeomanry and Staff 53 Div. (Major). Contested Orkney and Shetland (L), 1945; MP (L) Orkney and Shetland, 1950–83. Dir of Personnel, European Office, UNRRA, 1945–47; Sec. of the National Trust for Scotland, 1947–49. Rector: Edinburgh Univ., 1960–63; Aberdeen Univ., 1969–72. Chubb Fellow, Yale; Romanes Lectr, 1980. Hon. LLD: Edinburgh, 1960; Aberdeen, 1972; Birmingham, 1974; Buckingham, 1983; Hon. DCL Kent, 1970; DUniv Stirling, 1984. *Publications:* The Liberal Future, 1959; The Liberal Challenge, 1963; (with B. Neve) The Referendum, 1975; The Common Welfare, 1978; Memoirs, 1979; A Personal Manifesto, 1983; The St Andrews of Jo Grimond, 1992; contributor: The Prime Ministers, 1976; My Oxford, 1977; Britain—a view from Westminster, 1986. *Address:* 24 Priory Avenue, W4 1TY.   *Died 24 Oct. 1993.*

GRINDEA, Miron, OBE 1986 (MBE 1977); Editor: ADAM International Review (Anglo-French literary magazine), since 1941; ADAM Poets, since 1960; *b* 31 Jan. 1909; *m* 1936, Carola Rabinovici, concert pianist; one *d. Educ:* Bucharest Univ.; Sorbonne. Literary and music critic,

1928–39; settled in England, Sept. 1939; together with Benjamin Britten, Stephen Spender and Henry Moore founded the International Arts Guild, 1943; war-time work with BBC European Service and Min. of Information; coast to coast lecture tours, USA. Visiting Lecturer: Univs of Paris, Aix-en-Provence, Athens, Karachi, Kyoto, Montreal, Toronto, Rejkiavik, Jerusalem, etc. Hon. DLitt Kent, 1983. Prix de l'Académie Française, 1955; Lundquist Literary Prize, Sweden, 1965. Chevalier de la Légion d'Honneur, 1974; Comdr, Order of Arts and Letters, France, 1985. *Publications:* Malta Calling, 1943; Henry Wood (a symposium), 1944; Jerusalem, a literary chronicle of 3000 years, 1968, 2nd edn, Jerusalem, the Holy City in literature, preface by Graham Greene, 1982; Natalie Clifford Barney, 1963; The London Library (a symposium), 1978; contrib. The Listener, TLS, Figaro, Les Nouvelles Littéraires, New Statesman, The Times, Independent, Guardian, Sunday Times, Observer, Spectator, Books and Bookmen. *Recreations:* Mozart, lazing in the sun. *Address:* 28 Emperor's Gate, SW7 4HS. *T:* 0171–373 7307. *Died 18 Nov. 1995.*

GRINDLE, Captain John Annesley, CBE 1943; JP; Royal Navy, retired; *b* 17 Sept. 1900; *s* of late George Annesley Grindle and Eveleen Grindle; *m* 1925, Joyce Lilian Alton, *d* of J. W. A. Batchelor, Blackheath; two *s. Educ:* Pembroke Lodge, Southbourne; RN Colleges, Osborne and Dartmouth; Pembroke Coll., Cambridge. Midshipman, 1917; Comdr 1934; Captain 1941; commanded HMS Apollo, 1944–55, Glenearn, 1946, Victorious 1949–50; Dep. Chief of Combined Ops (Naval), 1946–48; retired list, 1950. JP Hants, 1952. *Recreation:* gardening. *Address:* Anchor House, Wicor Path, Castle Street, Portchester, Hants PO16 9QT. *T:* Cosham (0705) 376067.
Died 20 Feb. 1991.

GROSSCHMID-ZSÖGÖD, Prof. Géza (Benjamin), LLD; Professor, 1955–89, then Professor Emeritus, and Chairman, 1978–89, Division of Economic Sciences, Duquesne University, Pittsburgh, USA, retired; *b* Budapest, Hungary, 29 Oct. 1918; *o s* of late Prof. Lajos de Grosschmid and Jolán, *o d* of Géza de Szitányi; US citizen, 1950; *m* 1946, Leonora Martha Nissler, 2nd *d* of Otto Nissler and Annemarie Dudt; one *d. Educ:* Piarist Fathers, Budapest; Royal Hungarian Pázmány Péter Univ., Budapest (LLD 1943). With private industry in Hungary, 1943–44; Royal Hungarian Army, 1944–45; UNRRA, 1946–47; Duquesne University: Asst Prof. of Econs, 1948–52; Associate Prof., 1952–55; Dir, Inst. of African Affairs, 1958–70; Dir, African Language and Area Center, 1960–74; Academic Vice Pres., 1970–75. Ford Foundn Fellow, 1958; Fulbright-Hays Fellow, S Africa, 1965; attended Cambridge Colonial Conf., King's Coll., 1961. Director: World Affairs Council of Pittsburgh, 1974–80; Afuture Fund of Philadelphia, 1976–84. Mem., Bd of Visitors, Coll. of Arts and Sciences, Univ. of Pittsburgh, 1970–86; Governor, Battle of Britain Museum Foundn, 1977–84. Consultore pro lingua hungarica, Collegio Araldico, Rome. Lord of the manors of Brassington and of North Tamerton. Kt of Malta, 1955 (Comdr of Merit, 1956; Kt of Obedience, 1974; Grand Cross of Obedience, 1984); Kt, Sacred Mil. Constantinian Order of St George (Naples), 1959 (Grand Cross of Justice, 1988; Pres., Amer. Assoc., 1978); Kt Comdr of St Gregory, 1968. Order of: Valour, Cameroon, 1967; Zaire, 1970; Equatorial Star, Gabon, 1973; Lion, Senegal, 1977. *Publications:* (jtly) Principles of Economics, 1959; (trans. with P. Colombo) The Spiritual Heritage of the Sovereign Military Order of Malta, 1958; (ed with S. B. Vardy and L. S. Domonkos) Louis the Great King of Hungary and Poland, 1986; contrib. Encyc. Britannica; articles in learned jls. *Recreations:* walking, golf, heraldry, polo. *Address:* 3115 Ashlyn Street, Pittsburgh, Pa 15204, USA. *T:* (412) 3317744. *Clubs:* Athenæum, MCC; Royal Forth Yacht

(Edinburgh); Duquesne (Pittsburgh); Metropolitan, Army and Navy (Washington); Jockey (Vienna).
Died 27 Nov. 1992.

GROVES, Sir Charles (Barnard), Kt 1973; CBE 1968 (OBE 1958); FRCM, Hon. RAM, CRNCM; conductor; Associate Conductor, Royal Philharmonic Orchestra, since 1967; Music Director, Leeds Philharmonic Society, since 1988; *b* 10 March 1915; *s* of Frederick Groves and Annie (*née* Whitehead); *m* 1948, Hilary Hermione Barchard; one *s* two *d. Educ:* St Paul's Cathedral Choir Sch.; Sutton Valence Sch.; Royal College of Music. Freelance accompanist and organist; joined BBC, Chorus-Master Music Productions Unit, 1938; Asst Conductor BBC Theatre Orchestra, 1942; Conductor BBC Revue Orchestra, 1943; Conductor BBC Northern Orchestra, 1944–51; Dir of Music, Bournemouth Corporation, and Conductor, Bournemouth Municipal Orchestra, 1951–54; Conductor of Bournemouth Symphony Orchestra, 1954–61; Resident Musical Dir, Welsh National Opera Company, 1961–63; Musical Dir and Resident Conductor, Royal Liverpool Philharmonic Orchestra, 1963–77; Music Dir, ENO, 1978–79; Pres. and Artistic Advr, English Sinfonia, 1984–; Principal Conductor, Guildford Philharmonic Orchestra, 1987–. President: Nat. Youth Orchestra of GB, 1977–; Incorporated Soc. of Musicians, 1982–83; Life Mem., RPO, 1976; Hon. Mem., Royal Philharmonic Soc., 1990. Hon. Fellow: Manchester Poly., 1973; Liverpool Poly., 1987. FRCM 1961; Hon. RAM 1967; Hon. FTCL 1974; Hon. GSM 1974; CRNCM 1983 (Hon. FRNCM 1974). Conductor of the Year Award, 1968, 1978. Freeman, City of London, 1976. Toured Australia, New Zealand, South Africa, N and S America, Japan and Europe. Hon. DMus Liverpool, 1970; DUniv Open, 1978; Hon. DLitt Salford, 1980. *Recreation:* English literature. *Address:* 12 Camden Square, NW1 9UY.
Died 20 June 1992.

GROVES, Ronald, MA, BSc Oxon; FRSC; FKC; Member of Council, Sir Richard Stapley Educational Trust (Secretary, 1969–83); Fellow, King's College Hospital Medical School (Vice Chairman of Council, 1975–83); *b* 19 Aug. 1908; *s* of late John Ackroyd Groves and Annie Groves, Bradford, *m* 1939, Hilary Annot, *yr d* of late George Smith; two *s. Educ:* Bradford Grammar Sch.; Christ Church, Oxford. 1st Class Hons Nat. Sci. (Chemistry), 1931. Asst Master, Bradfield Coll., 1931–32; Worksop Coll., 1932–35; Senior Science Master and Housemaster, King's Sch., Canterbury, 1935–43 (Bursar, 1937–43); Headmaster, Campbell Coll., Belfast, 1943–54; Master, Dulwich Coll., 1954–66. Adviser, Jt Working Party of Governing Bodies' Assoc. and Headmasters' Conf., 1966–73. Chm., Food Standards Cttee, 1959–62. *Address:* 83 Cumnor Hill, Oxford OX2 9HX.
Died 8 Feb. 1991.

GUINNESS, Bryan; *see* Moyne, 2nd Baron.

GUISE, Sir John, GCMG 1975; KBE 1975 (CBE 1972); MP (Ind), Parliament of Papua New Guinea, since 1977; *b* Papua, 29 Aug. 1914; *m*; five *s* four *d.* Served War, Australian New Guinea Administrative Unit.: Royal Papuan Constabulary, 1946; Mem. contingent attending Queen Elizabeth's Coronation, London, 1953; Sgt Major; later transferred to Dept of Native Affairs for local govt and welfare duties, Port Moresby. Mem., 1st Select Cttee Political Develt, 1961–63, which drew up 1st House of Assembly, 1964; Chm., House of Assembly Select Cttee on Political and Constitutional Develt which drew up 1st Ministerial Govt for 2nd House of Assembly, 1968. Mem. for E Papua, Legislative Council, 1961–63; MHA, Milne Bay District, 1964–67; Speaker, Papua New Guinea House of Assembly, 1968–71; Minister for Interior, 1972–74; later Deputy Chief Minister, to 1975, and Minister for Agriculture, 1974–75; unofficial leader of elected

Members, Papua New Guinea House of Assembly, 1964–68. Governor-General, Papua New Guinea, 1975–77. Delegate, S Pacific Conf., Pago Pago, 1962; Mem., Australian delegn to UN, 1962 and 1963; attended UNESCO Conf., Paris, Geneva, London, 1963. Prominent layman in Anglican Church affairs. Hon. LLD. KStJ 1976. *Address:* National Parliament, Port Moresby, Papua New Guinea; Lalaura Village, Cape Rodney, Central Province, Papua New Guinea.					*Died 7 Feb. 1991.*

GUNN, Peter Nicholson; author; *b* 15 Aug. 1914; 2nd *s* of Frank Lindsay Gunn, CBE, and Adèle Margaret (*née* Dunphy); *m* 1953, Diana Maureen James (writer, as Elizabeth Gunn); one *s*. *Educ:* Melbourne; Trinity Coll., Cambridge (MA). Served War 1939–45: Rifle Bde; POW 1942. Sen. Lectr, RMA, Sandhurst, 1949–54. *Publications:* Naples: a Palimpsest, 1961 (German trans. 1964, Italian trans. 1971); Vernon Lee: a Study, 1964; The Companion Guide to Southern Italy, 1969; My Dearest Augusta: a Biography of Augusta Leigh, Byron's half-sister, 1969; A Concise History of Italy, 1971; (ed) Byron's Prose, 1972; Normandy: Landscape with figures, 1975; Burgundy: Landscape with figures, 1976; The Actons, 1978; Napoleon's Little Pest: The Duchess of Abrantès, 1979; (with R. Beny) Churches of Rome, 1981 (trans. German, Italian and Danish, 1982); Yorkshire Dales: Landscape with figures, 1984; (ed) Lord Byron: Selected Letters and Journals, 1984. *Address:* Gruchet-sur-Arques, Arques-la-Bataille, 76880, France. *T:* 35045710.					*Died 4 Oct. 1995.*

GUNNING, John Edward Maitland, CBE 1960 (OBE 1945); barrister-at-law; *b* 22 Sept. 1904; *s* of late John Elgee Gunning, Manor House, Moneymore, Co. Derry, and Edythe, *er d* of T. J. Reeves, London; *m* 1936, Enid Katherine (*d* 1987), *o d* of George Menhinick; two *s*. *Educ:* Harrow; Magdalene Coll., Cambridge. Called to Bar, Gray's Inn, 1933. Practised South Eastern Circuit, Central Criminal Court, North London Sessions, Herts and Essex Sessions. Joined Judge Advocate General's Office, Oct. 1939; War of 1939–45: served BEF, France, 1939–40; N Africa, 1942–43; Italy, 1943–45 (despatches, OBE); Middle East, 1945–50; Deputy Judge Advocate Gen. with rank of Col, CMF, 1945, Middle East, 1946; Deputy Judge Advocate Gen. (Army and RAF): Germany, 1951–53, 1960–63, 1968–70; Far East, 1957–59, 1965–67; Senior Asst Judge Advocate Gen., 1965–70. *Recreations:* bridge, watching cricket, reading. *Clubs:* Travellers', MCC.					*Died 28 Dec. 1992.*

GUNSTON, Sir Richard (Wellesley), 2nd Bt *cr* 1938, of Wickwar, Co. Gloucester; *b* 15 March 1924; *s* of Sir Derrick Wellesley Gunston, 1st Bt, MC, and of Evelyn Bligh, OBE, *d* of late Howard Bligh St George; *S* father, 1985; *m* 1st, 1947, Elizabeth Mary (marr. diss. 1956), *e d* of late Sir Arthur Colegate; one *d*; 2nd, 1959, Mrs Joan Elizabeth Marie Coldicott (marr. diss.), *o d* of Reginald Forde, Johannesburg; one *s*; 3rd, 1976, Veronica Elizabeth (*née* Haynes), *widow* of Captain V. G. Loyd. *Educ:* Harrow; Clare Coll., Cambridge. Served War in RAF (Aircrew), 1942–45. Entered Colonial Admin. Service,

1946; served N Nigeria, 1948–51; Nyasaland, 1951–63; Bechuanaland, 1964–65; Colonial Office, 1966. Asst Sec., Council for Care of Churches and Cathedrals Adv. Cttee, 1967. *Recreations:* hunting, big game shooting, sailing, gliding, painting, photography, architecture, gardening. *Heir: s* John Wellesley Gunston [*b* 25 July 1962; *m* 1990, Rosalind, *y d* of Edward Gordon Eliott]. *Address:* The Arboretum, Tidebrook, Wadhurst, Sussex. *Club:* East India.					*Died 30 June 1991.*

GUTHRIE, Air Vice-Marshal Kenneth MacGregor, CB 1946; CBE 1944; CD 1948; retired; *b* 9 Aug. 1900; *s* of Rev. Donald and Jean Stirton Guthrie; *m* 1926, Catherine Mary Fidler; one *d*. *Educ:* Baltimore, USA; Montreal and Ottawa, Canada. RFC and RAF, 1917–19; Royal Canadian Army Med. Corps, 1919–20; Canadian Air Board and RCAF, 1920–49: Asst Director of Military and Air Force Intelligence, General Staff, Ottawa, 1935–38; CO, RCAF Station, Rockcliffe, 1938–39; Senior Air Staff Officer, Eastern Air Command, 1939–41; CO, RCAF Station, Gander, Newfoundland, 1941; Air Officer i/c Administration, Western Air Command, 1942; Deputy Air Member Air Staff (Plans) AFHQ, Dec. 1942–1944; AOC Northwest Air Command, RCAF, 1944–49; retired, 1949. Legion of Merit (USA), 1946. *Recreations:* hunting, fishing, gardening. *Club:* United Services Institute (Edmonton and Victoria).					*Died 14 March 1993.*

GUTTERIDGE, Joyce Ada Cooke, CBE 1962; retired; *b* 10 July 1906; *d* of late Harold Cooke Gutteridge, QC, and Mary Louisa Gutteridge (*née* Jackson). *Educ:* Roedean Sch.; Somerville Coll., Oxford. Called to the Bar, Middle Temple, Nov. 1938. Served in HM Forces (ATS), War of 1939–45. Foreign Office: Legal Assistant, 1947–50; Asst Legal Adviser, 1950–60; Legal Counsellor, 1960–61; Counsellor (Legal Adviser), UK Mission to the United Nations, 1961–64; Legal Counsellor, FO, 1964–66; re-employed on legal duties, FO, 1966–67. Hon. LLD Western College for Women, Oxford, Ohio, 1963. *Publications:* The United Nations in a Changing World, 1970; articles in British Year Book of International Law and International and Comparative Law Quarterly. *Address:* 1 Croftgate, Fulbrooke Road, Cambridge CB3 9EG. *Club:* University Women's.

Died 24 Oct. 1992.

GWYNNE-EVANS, Sir Francis Loring, 4th Bt *cr* 1913, of Oaklands Park, Awre, Co. Gloucester; *b* 22 Feb. 1914; *s* of Sir Evan Gwynne Gwynne-Evans, 2nd Bt and Ada Jane (*d* 1977), *d* of Walter Scott Andrews, New York; assumed by deed poll 1943 the names of Francis Loring Gwynne Evans-Tipping, reverted by deed poll to his patronymic, 1958; *S* brother, 1985; *m* 1st, 1937, Elisabeth Fforde (marr. diss. 1958), *d* of J. Fforde Tipping; two *s* one *d*; 2nd, 1958, Gloria Marie Reynolds; one *s* three *d* and one adopted *s*. Career as professional singer under name of Francis Loring. *Heir: s* David Gwynne Evans-Tipping, *b* 25 Nov. 1943. *Address:* Chantry, Aveton Gifford, near Kingsbridge, S Devon TQ7 4EH.

Died 29 Dec. 1993.

H

HADDEN-PATON, Major Adrian Gerard Nigel, JP, DL; *b* 3 Dec. 1918; *s* of late Nigel Fairholt Paton, Covehithe, Suffolk; *m* 1951, Mary-Rose, *d* of Col A. H. MacIlwaine, DSO, MC, Troutbeck, S Rhodesia; two *s*, and one step *s* (and one step *s* decd). *Educ:* Rugby; Worcester Coll., Oxford (BA). 2nd Lt, 1st The Royal Dragoons, 1940; Adjutant, 1943–44; served 1940–45: Western Desert, Tunisia, Italy, France, Belgium, Holland, Germany and Denmark; (despatches); Major 1945; Instructor, RMA, Sandhurst, 1947–50; retired 1950. Mem. Estates Cttee, 1956, Properties Cttee, 1970, Finance Cttee, 1973–82, Nat. Trust; Mem. Exec. Cttee, 1959–73, and Finance Cttee, 1961–73 (Chm. 1962–68), Country Landowners Association. Underwriting Mem. of Lloyd's; Chm. Holland & Holland Ltd, 1962–82. Chm. Hertfordshire Agricultural Soc., 1961–69; Past Pres. Hertfordshire & Middlesex Trust for Nature Conservation; Vice-Pres., Royal Forestry Soc., 1980–82. Chm. of Governors, Berkhamsted Sch. and Berkhamsted Sch. for Girls, 1973–78 (Governor, 1950–78). JP 1951, DL 1962, Herts; High Sheriff, 1961. *Recreations:* shooting, forestry. *Address:* Old Rossway, Berkhamsted, Herts HP4 3TZ. *T:* Berkhamsted (0442) 863264. *Died 6 Sept. 1991.*

HADFIELD, Esmé Havelock, FRCS; formerly: Consultant Ear, Nose and Throat Surgeon, High Wycombe, Amersham and Chalfont Hospitals; Associate Surgeon (Hon.), Ear, Nose and Throat Department, Radcliffe Infirmary, Oxford; retired; *b* 1921; *o d* of late Geoffrey Hadfield, MD. *Educ:* Clifton High Sch.; St Hugh's Coll., Oxford; Radcliffe Infirmary Oxford. BA Oxon 1942; BM, BCh Oxon 1945; FRCS 1951; MA Oxon 1952. House Officer appts, Radcliffe Infirmary, Oxford, 1945; Registrar to ENT Dept, Radcliffe Infirmary, Oxford, 1948; Asst, Ohren, Nase, Hals Klinik, Kantonspital, University of Zurich, 1949; First Asst, ENT Dept, Radcliffe Infirmary, Oxford, 1950. Mem. Court of Examrs, RCS, 1978–84; External Examr, RCSI, 1986–. Pres., Sect. of Laryngology, RSocMed, 1983–84. British Empire Cancer Campaign Travelling Fellow in Canada, 1953; Hunterian Prof., RCS, 1969–70. Hon. Mem., Assoc. of Surgeons of Pakistan, 1982. *Publications:* articles on ENT surgery in medical journals. *Recreation:* travel. *Address:* 20 Hamilton Road, Oxford OX2 7PZ. *T:* Oxford (0865) 57187.
Died 8 April 1992.

HADFIELD, Ven. John Collingwood; Archdeacon of Caithness, Rector of St John the Evangelist, Wick, and Priest-in-Charge of St Peter and The Holy Rood, Thurso, Caithness, since 1977; *b* 2 June 1912; *s* of Reginald Hadfield and Annie Best Hadfield (*née* Gribbin); *m* 1939, Margretta Mainwaring Lewis Matthews; three *s* three *d*. *Educ:* Manchester Grammar School; Jesus Coll., Cambridge (Exhibnr, BA 1st cl. Hons, Classical Tripos Pt 2 1934, MA 1938); Wells Theological College. Deacon 1935, priest 1936, Manchester; Curate of S Chad, Ladybarn, Manchester, 1935–44 (in charge from 1940); Vicar of S Mark, Bolton-le-Moors, Lancs 1944–50; Vicar of S Ann, Belfield, Rochdale, Lancs, 1950–62; Surrogate, 1944–62; Proctor in Convocation for Dio. Manchester, 1950–62; Diocese of Argyll and The Isles: Rector of S Paul, Rothesay, Bute, 1962–64; Itinerant Priest, 1964–77; Canon of S John's Cathedral, Oban, 1965–77; Inspector of Schools, 1966–77; Synod Clerk, 1973–77. *Recreation:*

music. *Address:* 4 Sir Archibald Road, Thurso, Caithness KW14 8HN. *T:* Thurso (0847) 62047.
Died 24 Feb. 1993.

HADOW, Sir Gordon, Kt 1956; CMG 1953; OBE 1945; Deputy Governor of the Gold Coast (Ghana), 1954–57; *b* 23 Sept. 1908; *e s* of late Rev. F. B. Hadow and Una Ethelwyn Durrant; *m* 1946, Marie (*d* 1985), *er d* of late Dr L. H. Moiser; two *s*. *Educ:* Marlborough; Trinity Coll., Oxford. Administrative Service, Gold Coast, 1932; Dep. Financial Sec., Tanganyika, 1946; Under-Sec. Gold Coast, 1948; Sec. for the Civil Service, 1949; Sec. to Governor and to Exec. Council, 1950–54. *Address:* Little Manor, Coat, Martock, Somerset TA12 6AS. *Club:* Athenæum.
Died 6 Nov. 1993.

HADOW, Sir (Reginald) Michael, KCMG 1971 (CMG 1962); HM Diplomatic Service, retired; *b* 17 Aug. 1915; *s* of Malcolm McGregor Hadow and Constance Mary Lund; *m* 1943, Maria Anna Stefania Szemplinska; *m* 1955, Dolores Frances Main; *m* 1976, Hon. Mrs Daphne Sieff (*d* 1988). *Educ:* Berkhamsted Sch.; King's Coll., Cambridge. Selected for ICS, 1937; Private Sec. to HM Ambassador, Moscow, 1942; Under-Sec., External Affairs Dept, Delhi, 1946–47; transferred to Foreign Office, 1948; FO, 1948–52 (Private Sec. to Minister of State, 1949–52); Head of Chancery, Mexico City, 1952–54; FO, 1955; Head of Levant Dept and promoted Counsellor, 1958; Counsellor, Brit. Embassy, Paris, 1959–62; Head of News Dept, FO, 1962–65; Ambassador to Israel, 1965–69; Ambassador to Argentina, 1969–72. *Recreation:* self-administration. *Address:* Old Farm, Ashford Hill, near Newbury, Berks RG15 8AX. *Died 22 Dec. 1993.*

HAFERKAMP, Wilhelm; a Vice-President, Commission of the European Communities, 1970–84; *b* Duisburg, 1 July 1923; *m* 1951, Ursula Bartz. *Educ:* Universität zu Köln. German Trade Union Federation: Head of Division for Social Questions, 1950–63, Dep. Chm. 1953, Chm. 1957, N Rhine–Westphalia Area; Mem. Fed. Exec., 1962–67. Socialist Mem., Landtag of North Rhine–Westphalia, 1958–67; Mem., Commn of European Communities, 1967–84, responsible for Energy policy, Euratom Supply Agency and Euratom Safeguards; Vice-Pres., 1970, resp. for internal market and legal harmonisation; 1973, resp. for economic and financial affairs; 1977, resp. for external relations. *Address:* Rodenwaldstrasse 14, 4033 Hösel bei Düsseldorf, Germany.
Died 18 Jan. 1995.

HAGGARD, William; *see* Clayton, Richard Henry Michael.

HÄGGLÖF, Gunnar, GCVO (Hon.), 1954; Swedish Diplomat; *b* 15 Dec. 1904; *s* of Richard Hägglöf and Sigrid Ryding, Stockholm, Sweden; *m* Anna, *d* of Count Folchi-Vici, Rome. *Educ:* Upsala Univ., Sweden. Entered Swedish Diplomatic Service, 1926; Minister without Portfolio, 1939. During War of 1939–45, led various Swedish delegns to Berlin, London, and Washington; Envoy to Belgian and Dutch Govts, 1944; Envoy in Moscow, 1946; permanent delegate to UN, 1947; Ambassador to Court of St James's, 1948–67; Ambassador to France, 1967–71. Delegate to Conf. for Constitution, European Council, 1949; delegate to Suez Confs, 1956; Mem. of Menzies Cttee to Cairo, 1956. Hon. DCL

Birmingham, 1960. *Publications:* Diplomat, 1972; several books and essays in economics, politics and history. *Recreations:* ski-ing, swimming, reading, writing. *Address:* Vigna Orsini, Bracciano, Rome, Italy.

Died Dec. 1995.

HAIMENDORF, Christoph von F.; *see* Fürer-Haimendorf.

HAINSWORTH, Col John Raymond, CMG 1953; CBE 1945; retired; *b* 14 March 1900; *s* of William Henry Hainsworth, Keighley, Yorks; *m* 1925, Dora Marguerite Skiller (*d* 1989), Rochester, Kent; one *s* one *d. Educ:* Taunton Sch.; RMA, Woolwich. Commissioned in Royal Engineers, 1919; posted to India, 1922; served War of 1939–45 (despatches twice, CBE): Burma Campaign, 1942–45; apptd Dir of Works, GHQ, India, March 1945; seconded to Civil Employment in PWD, NWFP, India, 1946; Chief Engineer and Secretary to Government, PWD, NWFP, Pakistan, 1948–52; retired with rank of Col, 1952. *Recreations:* shooting, fishing. *Address:* The Pines, 104 West Hill, Putney, SW15 2UQ. *T:* 081–877 1951.

Died 15 May 1991.

HALAS, John, OBE 1972; FCSD; Chairman, Halas and Batchelor, since 1940; President: British Federation of Film Societies, since 1980; International Animated Film Association, 1975–85, then Hon. President; *b* Budapest, 16 April 1912; named Janos Halasz; *s* of Victor and Bertha Halas; *m* 1940, Joy Batchelor; one *s* one *d. Educ:* Académie des Beaux-Arts, Paris; Mühely, Budapest. Founded: (with Joy Batchelor) Halas and Batchelor Animation Ltd, 1940; (with Lord Snow, Morris Goldsmith, Joy Batchelor and Roger Manvell) Educational Film Centre, 1960; ASIFA (International Animated Film Assoc.), 1960. Produced 2,000 animated films, 1940–93, incl. first feature-length animated film in GB, Animal Farm, 1954; productions incl.: Autobahn, 1979; First Steps, 1981; Dilemma, 1982 (world's first fully digitized film); Players, 1983; A New Vision: the life and work of Botticelli, 1984; Toulouse-Lautrec, 1985; Leonardo da Vinci, 1985; Masters of Animation series, 1986–87; Light of the World, 1989; A Memory of Moholy-Nagy, 1990. Past President, Internat. Council of Graphic Design Assocs. Sen. Fellow, RCA, 1988. Hon. Fellow, BKSTS, 1972. *Publications:* How to Cartoon, 1959; The Technique of Film Animation, 1961; Film and TV Graphics, 1967; Computer Animation, 1974; Visual Scripting, 1977; Film Animation, a Simplified Approach, 1978; Timing for Animation, 1981; Graphics in Motion, 1981; Masters of Animation, 1987; The Contemporary Animator, 1991. *Recreations:* painting, music. *Address:* 6 Holford Road, Hampstead, NW3 1AD. *T:* 0171–435 8674, *Fax:* 0171–431 6835. *Died 20 Jan. 1995.*

HALL, Adam; *see* Trevor, Elleston.

HALL, Edward, RP 1958; Hon. Secretary, Royal Society of Portrait Painters, since 1985; *b* 5 Feb. 1922; *s* of James and Elizabeth Hall; *m* 1946, Daphne Cynthia Grogan; two *s* one *d. Educ:* Wyggeston Sch., Leicester; Leicester Coll. of Art; Wimbledon Sch. of Art; Slade Sch. of Fine Art. War Service, RAF, 1941–46. Painter of portraits, domestic interiors and landscapes; portrait painting, 1952–; exhibited annually at Royal Academy; part-time teaching and lecturing in various London and provincial art schools, including Sir John Cass School of Art, Chelsea School of Art, Medway Coll. of Design. *Recreation:* music. *Address:* 51 St George's Drive, SW1V 4DE. *T:* 071–834 5366. *Club:* Arts. *Died 3 Sept. 1991.*

HALL, Maj.-Gen. Edward Michael, CB 1970; MBE 1943; DL; *b* 16 July 1915; *s* of late Brig. E. G. Hall, CB, CIE and Elinor Brodrick, *d* of Col W. S. Birdwood, late IA; *m* 1948, Nina Diana (*née* McArthur); three *s. Educ:* Sherborne; RMA; Peterhouse, Cambridge. Commissioned RE, 1935; BA (Cantab) 1937. Served 1939–46, with Royal

Bombay Sappers and Miners: Western Desert, India, Burma; CRE, 10th Armd and 3rd Inf. Div., 1957–59; Comd Training Bde, RE, 1962–63; Chief of Staff, Western Command, 1965–66; Military Deputy to Head of Defence Sales, 1966–70. Col Comdt, RE, 1973–76. Comdr and Comr, St John Ambulance, Cornwall, 1971–80. DL Cornwall, 1971; High Sheriff of Cornwall, 1985–86. KStJ 1981. *Recreation:* country pursuits. *Address:* Treworgey Manor, Liskeard, Cornwall. *Died 31 Jan. 1993.*

HALL, Prof. Reginald, CBE 1989; MD; FRCP; Professor of Medicine, University of Wales College of Medicine (formerly Welsh National School of Medicine), 1980–89, Professor Emeritus, 1989; *b* 1 Oct. 1931; *s* of late Reginald P. Hall and Maggie W. Hall; *m* 1960, Dr Molly Hill; two *s* three *d. Educ:* Univ. of Durham (BSc, MB BS, MD). Harkness Fellow of Commonwealth Fund, Clinical and Research Fellow in Medicine, Harvard, 1960–61; Wellcome Sen. Research Fellow in Clinical Science, Univ. of Newcastle upon Tyne, 1964–67; Cons. Physician, Royal Victoria Infirmary, Newcastle upon Tyne, 1967–79; Prof. of Medicine, Univ. of Newcastle upon Tyne, 1970–79. Hon. Member: Assoc. of Amer. Physicians, 1984; British Diabetic Assoc., 1990; European Thyroid Assoc., 1991. Hon. MD Wales. *Publications:* Fundamentals of Clinical Endocrinology, 1969, 4th edn 1989; Atlas of Endocrinology, 1980, 2nd edn 1990; Picture Tests in Endocrinology, 1991. *Recreations:* bryology, cookery, literature. *Address:* 37 Palace Road, Llandaff, Cardiff CF5 2AG. *T:* Cardiff (0222) 567689.

Died 20 July 1994.

HALL, Dr Trevor Henry, JP; MA, PhD; FSA; FRICS; writer, historian, lecturer; *b* 28 May 1910; *o s* of H. Roxby Hall, Wakefield; *m* 1st, 1937, Dorothy (*d* 1973), *d* of late A. H. Keningley, Nostell; one *s* one *d*; 2nd, 1977, Marguerite, *widow* of Dr R. L. McMorris, Selby; one step *s* one step *d. Educ:* Wakefield Sch.; Trinity Coll., Cambridge (Perrott Student; MA); London Coll. of Estate Management (first place in final prof. exams, 1932). FSA 1978. Served War of 1939–45, Army. Sen. Partner, with Richard Gamble Walker, V. Stanley Walker & Son, chartered surveyors, Leeds, Wakefield, Rothwell and Woodlesford, 1945–82; Pres., Huddersfield & Bradford (later Yorkshire) Building Soc., 1972–74; Chm., Legal & General Assce Soc. (North Regional and Scottish Bds), 1978–80. Cecil Oldman Meml Lectr in bibliography and textual criticism, Univ. of Leeds, 1972–73. One of 300 invited Founder Life Mems, Cambridge Soc., 1977; Mem., Oxford Univ. Soc. of Bibliophiles, 1981 (Lectr, 1980, 1983). Chm., Leeds Cttee, Nat. Trust, 1968–70. Pres., Leeds Library (founded 1768), 1969–85. JP City of Leeds, 1959. Received grant of arms, 1974. *Publications:* The Testament of R. W. Hull, 1945; (with E. J. Dingwall and K. M. Goldney) The Haunting of Borley Rectory: A Critical Survey of the Evidence, 1956; A Bibliography of Books on Conjuring in English from 1580 to 1850, 1957; (with E. J. Dingwall) Four Modern Ghosts, 1958; The Spiritualists: The Story of William Crookes and Florence Cook, 1962; The Strange Case of Edmund Gurney, 1964; The Mystery of the Leeds Library, 1965; New Light on Old Ghosts, 1965; (with J. L. Campbell) Strange Things, 1968; Sherlock Holmes: Ten Literary Studies, 1969; Mathematical Recreations, 1633: An Exercise in 17th Century Bibliography, 1970; The Late Mr Sherlock Holmes, 1971; Old Conjuring Books: a bibliographical and historical study, 1972; The Card Magic of Edward G. Brown, 1973; The Early Years of the Huddersfield Building Society, 1974; A New Era, 1974; The Winder Sale of Old Conjuring Books, 1975; (with Percy H. Muir) Some Printers and Publishers of Conjuring Books and Other Ephemera, 1800–1850, 1976; The Leeds Library, 1977; Sherlock Holmes and his Creator, 1978; Search for

Harry Price, 1978; The Strange Story of Ada Goodrich Freer, 1979; Dorothy L. Sayers: Nine Literary Studies, 1980; Twelve Friends, 1981; The Leeds Library: a checklist of publications relating to its history from 1768 to 1977, 1983; Daniel Home: a Victorian Enigma, 1984; The Mediam and the Scientist, 1984; The Last Case of Sherlock Holmes, 1986. *Recreations:* walking, gardening, book collecting, writing. *Address:* The Lodge, Selby, N Yorks YO8 0PW. *T:* Selby (0757) 703372. *Club:* Leeds (Leeds).   *Died 8 March 1991.*

HALL-THOMPSON, Major (Robert) Lloyd, ERD 1953; TD 1956; JP; *b* 9 April 1920; *s* of Lt-Col Rt Hon. S. H. Hall-Thompson, PC (NI), JP, DL, MP; *m* 1948, Alison F. Leitch, MSR (*d* 1992); one *s* one *d. Educ:* Campbell Coll. Prep. Sch.; Campbell Coll. Royal School. Major, Royal Artillery, 1939–46; TA, 1946–56. Joined Unionist Party, 1938; Vice-Pres., Clifton Unionist Assoc. (Chm. 1954–57); MP (U) Clifton, 1969–73; Mem (U), N Belfast, NI Assembly, 1973–75 (Leader of the House, 1973–74); Chief Whip, NI Executive, 1973–74; Mem. (UPNI) for N Belfast, NI Constitutional Convention, 1975–76. Patron of Friends of the Union, 1986–; Chm., Lagan Valley Cons. Party, NI, 1988–. Director of several companies. Formerly Mem. NI Hosps Authority (Past Vice-Chm. Finance and Gen. Purposes Cttee); Past Vice-Chm., Samaritan Hosp. Management Cttee; Life Governor, Samaritan Hosp.; Pres. and Trustee, North Belfast Working Men's Club, 1954–92; Trustee and Hon. Sec., Belfast Newsboys' Club and W. S. Armour Girls' Club; Vice-Pres., Cliftonville Football and Athletic Club; Founder, Trustee and Pres., Duncairn Friendship Assoc.; Life Mem., Not Forgotten Assoc. (Past Hon. Sec. and Hon. Treas.); Life Mem., Royal Ulster Agric. Soc.; Chm., Dep. Gov., Freeman and Steward, Down Royal Corp. of Horse Breeders; Founder and Pres., Irish Draught Horse Soc.; Founder and Hon. Sec., Half-Bred Horse Breeders' Soc.; Mem. Cttee, NI Nurses Housing Assoc. *Recreations:* horse riding, hunting, racing, eventing, show jumping, horse breeding, golf, reading. *Address:* Maymount, Ballylesson, Belfast, Northern Ireland BT8 8JY. *T:* Drumbo (0232) 826327. *Club:* Ulster (Belfast).   *Died 20 May 1992.*

HALLAM HIPWELL, Hermine; *see* Vivenot, Baroness Raoul de.

HALLETT, Cecil Walter; General Secretary, Amalgamated Engineering Union, 1957–64, retired; *b* 10 Dec. 1899; *m* 1923, Edith Nellie Hallett (*née* Smith) (*d* 1990); two *s* two *d. Educ:* New City Road Elementary Sch., London. Messenger, Commercial Cable Co., 1913–15; apprentice fitter and turner, Gas Light and Coke Co., Becton, N Woolwich, 1916–18; HM Forces, 10th London Regt, 1918–19; journeyman fitter and turner, various firms, 1923–48; Asst Gen. Sec. AEU, 1948–57. Former Editor, AEU Monthly Jl and The Way. *Address:* St Martin's Home, 15 York Avenue, Chatham, Kent ME5 9EP.
                                               Died 5 Dec. 1994.

HALLIFAX, Adm. Sir David (John), KCB 1983; KCVO 1992; KBE 1982; Constable and Governor of Windsor Castle, 1988–92; *b* 3 Sept. 1927; *s* of Ronald H. C. Hallifax and Joanne M. Hallifax; *m* 1962, Anne Blakiston Houston; one *s* one *d* (and one *s* decd). *Educ:* Winchester. Joined RN 1945; minesweeping, Gulf of Salonika, 1949–51; CO MTB 5008, 1953; Long TAS Course, 1954; HMS Salerno, Suez, 1956; Staff Coll., Camberley, 1959; CO HMS Agincourt, 1964–65; RCDS 1972; CO HMS Fife, 1973–75; Flag Officer, First Flotilla, 1978–80; Chief of Staff to C-in-C Fleet, 1980–82; Dep. Supreme Allied Comdr, Atlantic, 1982–84; Comdt, RCDS, 1986–87. *Recreations:* sailing, conchology. *Clubs:* Pratt's, Farmers'; Royal Yacht Squadron.   *Died 23 Aug. 1992.*

HALLOWES, Odette Marie Céline, GC 1946; MBE 1945; Légion d'Honneur, 1950; Vice-President, Women's Transport Services (FANY); Member Royal Society of St George; housewife; *b* 28 April 1912; *d* of Gaston Brailly, Croix-de-Guerre, Médaille Militaire; *m* 1931, Roy Sansom (decd); three *d*; *m* 1947, Captain Peter Churchill, DSO (marr. diss.; he *d* 1972); *m* 1956, Geoffrey Macleod Hallowes. *Educ:* The Convent of Ste Thérèse, Amiens (France) and privately. Entered Special Forces and landed in France, 1942; worked as British agent until capture by Gestapo, 1943; sentenced to death June 1943; endured imprisonment and torture until 28 April 1945, when left Ravensbrück Concentration Camp (MBE, GC). Member: Military Medallists League (Vice-Pres.); Cttee, Victoria Cross and George Cross Assoc.; Pres., 282 (East Ham) Air Cadet Sqdn. Founder Vice-Pres., Women of the Year Luncheon. Hon. Mem., St Dunstan's Ex-Prisoners of War Assoc. *Recreations:* reading, travelling, cooking, trying to learn patience. *Address:* Rosedale, Eriswell Road, Burwood Park, Walton-on-Thames, Surrey. *Clubs:* Naval and Military, FANY, Special Forces.
                                              Died 13 March 1995.

HALPIN, Most Rev. Charles A.; Archbishop (RC) of Regina, since 1973; *b* 30 Aug. 1930; *s* of John S. Halpin and Marie Anne Gervais. *Educ:* St Boniface Coll. (BA); St Boniface Seminary (BTh); Gregorian Univ., Rome (JCL). Priest, 1956; Vice-Chancellor of Archdiocese of Winnipeg and Secretary to Archbishop, 1960; Officialis of Archdiocesan Matrimonial Tribunal, 1962; Chaplain to the Holy Father with title of Monsignor, 1969; ordained Bishop, Nov. 1973; installed as Archbishop of Regina, Dec. 1973. *Address:* 445 Broad Street North, Regina, Saskatchewan S4R 2X8, Canada.
                                              Died 16 April 1994.

HAM, Rear-Adm. John Dudley Nelson, CB 1955; Royal Navy, retired; *b* 7 Sept. 1902; *s* of Engr-Rear-Adm. John William Ham and Lily Florence Nelson; *m* 1927, Margery Lyne Sandercock (*d* 1990); no *c. Educ:* Edinburgh House, Lee-on-Solent; RN Colleges, Osborne and Dartmouth. Junior Service, 1920–37; HMS Ramillies, HMS Ceres; staff of RN Engineering College; Destroyers; Commander, 1937; Engineer Officer, Yangtse, China, 1938–40; served War of 1939–45: Chief Engineer, HMS Danae, 1940–41; Asst Dir Combined Operations Material, 1942; Chief Engineer, HMS Indomitable, 1945; Capt., 1946; Fleet Engineer Officer, Home Fleet, 1949; Staff Air Engineer Officer, 1951; Rear-Admiral, 1953; Dir of Aircraft Maintenance and Repair, 1953–55; Flag Officer Reserve Aircraft, 1955–57, retired. *Recreations:* golf, cabinet-making. *Address:* Green Lane Cottage, Lee-on-Solent, Hants PO13 9JW. *T:* Lee-on-Solent (01705) 550660.
                                               Died 20 Nov. 1994.

HAMBLEDEN, Dowager Viscountess; Patricia, GCVO 1990 (DCVO 1953); Lady of the Bedchamber to HM Queen Elizabeth The Queen Mother, since 1937; *b* 12 Nov. 1904; *d* of 15th Earl of Pembroke, MVO and Lady Beatrice Eleanor Paget, CBE; *m* 1928, William Henry, 3rd Viscount Hambleden (*d* 1948); three *s* two *d. Address:* Hill House, Ewelme, Oxford OX10 6HP. *T:* Wallingford (0491) 839242.   *Died 19 March 1994.*

HAMBLY, Dr Edmund Cadbury, FEng, FICE; consulting engineer with own practice, since 1974; *b* 28 Sept. 1942; *s* of late Edmund Henry Hambly and Elizabeth Mary (*née* Cadbury); *m* 1964, Elizabeth Audrey, *d* of late Victor Alexander and Constance Audrey Gorham; one *s* three *d* (incl. twin *s* and *d*). *Educ:* Eton; Trinity Coll., Cambridge (Scholar; BA 1st Cl. Hons with Dist. 1964; MA 1968; PhD 1969). FIStructE 1982; FEng 1984; FICE 1990; FIMechE 1991. Res. in soil mechanics and Fellow, Emmanuel Coll., Cambridge, 1967–69; Assistant Engineer: Ove Arup & Partners, 1969–70; Kier Ltd,

1970–71; Sen. Engr, Gifford & Partners, 1971–74; consulting engineer, 1974–, troubleshooting offshore platforms, bridge design, underpinning an Oxford college etc. Vis. Prof. in Engrg Design, Univ. of Oxford, 1989–92. Pres., ICE, 1994–; Chm., Offshore Engrg Soc., 1989–90. Trustee, Bournville Village Trust, 1979–88. *Publications:* Bridge Deck Behaviour, 1976, 2nd edn 1992; Bridge Foundations and Substructures, 1979; Structural Analysis by Example, 1994; numerous papers incl. 2 discourses to Royal Instn. *Recreations:* engineering, handiwork, drawing, bullnose, Robert Hooke, history, natural history and gardens, discourse. *Address:* Home Farm House, Little Gaddesden, Berkhamsted, Herts HP4 1PN. *T:* Berkhamsted (01442) 843412, *Fax:* (01442) 842741.
Died 28 March 1995.

HAMBRO, Jocelyn Olaf, MC 1944; Chairman: Waverton Property Co. Ltd; J. O. Hambro & Co., since 1986; *b* 7 March 1919; *s* of late Ronald Olaf Hambro and Winifred Martin-Smith; *m* 1st, 1942, Ann Silvia (*d* 1972), *d* of R. H. Muir; three *s*; 2nd, 1976, Margaret Elisabeth (*d* 1983), *d* of late Frederick Bradshaw McConnel and *widow* of 9th Duke of Roxburghe; 3rd, 1988, Margaret Anne, *d* of Michael Stratton and formerly wife of 7th Earl Fortescue. *Educ:* Eton; Trinity Coll., Cambridge. Coldstream Guards, 1939–45. Joined Hambros Bank Ltd, 1945; Man. Dir, 1947–72; Chm., 1965–72; Chm., Hambros Ltd, 1970–83, Pres. 1983–. Formerly Chairman: The Hambro Trust Ltd; Hambros Investment Trust Ltd; HIT Securities Ltd; Chairman: Phœnix Assurance Co. Ltd, 1978–85; Charter Consolidated, 1982–88 (Dir, 1965–88). Member, Jockey Club. *Recreations:* racing, shooting. *Address:* Waverton House, Moreton in Marsh, Glos GL56 9PB. *T:* Blockley (0386) 700700. *Clubs:* Pratt's, White's.
Died 19 June 1994.

HAMILTON, Anthony Norris; *b* 19 July 1913; 3rd *s* of Capt. Claude Hamilton, RD, RNR, and Kathleen Sophia Hamilton (*née* Mack); *m* 1942, Jean Philippa, 3rd *d* of Rev. David Railton, MC; one *s* three *d*. *Educ:* Kelly Coll.; Exeter Coll., Oxford. Served War of 1939–45: commnd 6 Bn Argyll and Sutherland Highlanders, 1940; Gen. Staff, V Corps HQ, 1942, X Corps HQ 1943, VIII Army HQ, 1944; Ops Editor of VIII Army History of Italian Campaign, 1945. Asst Master, Clifton Coll., 1935–40; House Master, 1946–48; Headmaster, Strathallan Sch., 1948–51; Headmaster, Queen Mary's Grammar Sch., Walsall, 1951–55; Headmaster, Hardye's Sch., Dorchester, 1955–74. *Recreation:* painting. *Address:* Brook Farm, Bromyard, Herefordshire. *Died 2 Feb. 1991.*

HAMILTON, John C.; *see* Cole-Hamilton.

HAMILTON, Adm. Sir John (Graham), GBE 1966 (KBE 1963; CBE 1958); CB 1960; *b* 12 July 1910; *s* of late Col E. G. Hamilton, CMG, DSO, MC, and Ethel Marie (*née* Frith); *m* 1938, Dorothy Nina Turner, 2nd *d* of late Col J. E. Turner, CMG, DSO; no *c*. *Educ:* RN Coll., Dartmouth. Joined RN 1924; specialised in Gunnery, 1936; served War of 1939–45: destroyers; on staff of Adm. Cunningham, Mediterranean; Gunnery Officer, HMS Warspite (despatches); Comdr, 1943; Admiralty; SE Asia, 1945; British Commonwealth Occupation Force, Japan, 1946; in command, HMS Alacrity, Far East, 1947–48; Capt., 1949; Dep. Dir, Radio Equipment, 1950–51; in command, 5th Destroyer Squadron, 1952–53; Dir of Naval Ordnance, Admiralty, 1954–56; in command HMS Newfoundland, Far East, 1956–58; despatches, 1957; Rear-Adm., 1958; Naval Sec. to First Lord of the Admiralty, 1958–60; Vice-Adm., 1961; Flag Officer: Flotillas, Home Fleet, 1960–62; Naval Air Command, 1962–64; C-in-C Mediterranean, and C-in-C Allied Forces, Mediterranean, 1964–67; Adm. 1965. Dir-Gen., 1968–72, Nat. Pres., 1972–75, Inst. of Marketing. Patron, Dorset Expeditionary Soc., 1987–. *Recreations:* walking,

climbing, photography. *Address:* Chapel Barn, Abbotsbury, Weymouth, Dorset DT3 4LF. *T:* Abbotsbury (01305) 871507.
Died 27 Oct. 1994.

HAMILTON, Sir Patrick George, 2nd Bt, *cr* 1937, of Ilford, co. Essex; MA; President, Possum Controls Ltd; Trustee: Eleanor Hamilton Trust; Sidbury Trust; Erna Simon Trust; *b* 17 Nov. 1908; *o s* of Sir George Clements Hamilton, 1st Bt, and Eleanor (*d* 1958), *d* of late Henry Simon and *sister* of 1st Baron Simon of Wythenshawe; *S* father, 1947; *m* 1941, Winifred Mary Stone (CBE, MA), *o c* of Hammond Jenkins, Maddings, Hadstock, Cambs. *Educ:* Eton; Trinity Coll., Oxford (MA). First Managing Director and later Chairman of Tyresoles Ltd, 1934–53 (Dir, Propeller Production, MAP, 1943–44); Director: Simon Engineering Ltd and other Simon cos, 1937–78; Renold Ltd, 1952–78; Lloyds Bank Ltd, 1953–79; Chm., Expanded Metal Co. Ltd, 1955–78. Chm., Advisory Cttee on Commercial Information Overseas, 1957–59; Dep. Chm., Export Publicity Council, 1960–63. Chm., Transport Users Consultative Cttee, NW Area, 1957–64; Mem., Central Transport Consultative Cttee, 1963–64. Treas., Fedn of Commonwealth Chambers of Commerce, 1962–64. Mem., ITA, 1964–69. Chm., Central Mddx Gp Hosp. Management Cttee, 1964–70. *Recreations:* gardening, travel. *Heir:* none. *Address:* 21 Madingley Road, Cambridge CB3 0EG.
Died 10 Jan. 1992 (ext).

HAMILTON, Robert William, FBA 1960; *b* 26 Nov. 1905; *s* of William Stirling Hamilton and Kathleen Hamilton (*née* Elsmie); *heir-pres.* to Sir Malcolm Stirling-Hamilton, 14th Bt; *m* 1935, Eileen Hetty Lowick; three *s* two *d*. *Educ:* Winchester Coll.; Magdalen Coll., Oxford. Chief Insp. of Antiquities, Palestine, 1931–38; Dir of Antiquities, Palestine, 1938–48; Sec.-Librarian, British Sch. of Archæology, Iraq, 1948–49; Senior Lecturer in Near Eastern Archæology, Oxford, 1949–56; Keeper of Dept of Antiquities, 1956–72, Keeper, 1962–72, Ashmolean Museum, Oxford. Fellow Magdalen Coll., Oxford, 1959–72. *Publications:* Samaria-Sebaste, 1944; The Church of the Nativity, Bethlehem, 1947; Structural History of the Aqsa Mosque, 1949; Khirbat al Mafjar, 1959; (with others) Oxford Bible Atlas, 1974; Walid and his Friends: an Umayyad tragedy, 1988; Letters from the Middle East by an Occasional Archaeologist, 1992. *Address:* The Haskers, Westleton, Suffolk IP17 3AP.
Died 25 Sept. 1995.

HAMMER, Rev. Canon Raymond Jack, PhD; Librarian, Worcester Diocesan Library, since 1989; *b* 4 July 1920; *s* of Paul and Lily Hammer; *m* 1949, Vera Winifred (*née* Reed); two *d*. *Educ:* St Peter's Coll., Oxford (MA, Dip.Theol.); Univ. of London (BD, MTh, PhD). Asst Curate, St Mark's, St Helens, 1943–46; Sen. Tutor, St John's Coll., Durham, 1946–49; Lectr in Theol., Univ. of Durham, 1946–49; Prof., Central Theol Coll., Tokyo, 1950–64; Prof. in Doctrine, St Paul's Univ., Tokyo, 1958–64; Chaplain at British Embassy, Tokyo, 1954–64; Hon. Canon, St Michael's Cathedral, Kobe, Japan, 1964–; Lectr, Queen's Coll., Birmingham, and Lectr in Theol., Univ. of Birmingham, 1965–77; Dir, Bible Reading Fellowship, 1977–85. Examining Chaplain to: Bishop of Liverpool, 1965–78; Bishop of Birmingham, 1973–78. Archbishops' Consultant on Relations with Other Faiths, 1978–92; Sec. to Archbishops' Consultants, 1983–92. Tutor, Open Univ., 1978–85; Extra-Mural Lectr, Univs of London and Birmingham, 1985–; Vis. Lectr, Warwick Univ., 1988–91. Treasurer, Studiorum Novi Testamenti Societas, 1970–82. *Publications:* Japan's Religious Ferment, 1961 (US 1962), repr. 1985; The Book of Daniel (commentary), 1976; contributed: Theological Word Book of the Bible, 1950; Oxford Dictionary of the Christian Church, 1957, 2nd edn 1975; Concise Dictionary of the

Bible, 1966; Concise Dictionary of the Christian World Mission, 1970; Man and his Gods, 1971; Shorter Books of the Apocrypha, 1972; Perspectives on World Religions, 1978; The World's Religions, 1982; World Religions, 1982; consultant editor: The Times Atlas of The Bible, 1987; The Illustrated Reader's Bible, 1990. *Recreations:* travel, literature. *Address:* 22 Midsummer Meadow, Inkberrow, Worcs WR7 4HD. *T:* Inkberrow (0386) 792883. *Clubs:* Athenæum; Sion College.

Died 14 Jan. 1994.

HANBURY, Lt-Col Sir Hanmer (Cecil), KCVO 1991 (LVO 1953); MC 1943; JP; HM Lord-Lieutenant of Bedfordshire, 1978–91; *b* 5 Jan. 1916; *yr s* of late Sir Cecil Hanbury, MP, FLS, and Mrs Hanbury-Forbes, OBE, Kingston Maurward, Dorchester, Dorset, and La Mortola, Ventimiglia, Italy; *m* 1939, Prunella Kathleen Charlotte, *d* of late Air Cdre T. C. R. Higgins, CB, CMG, JP, DL, Turvey House, Beds; one *s* one *d. Educ:* Eton; RMC, Sandhurst. 2nd Lieut Grenadier Guards, 1936; served 1939–45 with Grenadier Guards, France, Belgium, N Africa, Italy; Capt. 1943; Temp. Major, 1944; Major 1948; Temp. Lt-Col, 1955–57; retired 1958. BRCS, Bedfordshire: Dir, 1959–71; Dep. Pres., 1972–78; Patron, 1978–; Pres., St John's Council for Bedfordshire, 1979–81; Chm., Beds T&AVR Cttee, 1970–78, Pres., 1978–81; Vice-Pres., E Anglia T&AVRA, 1978–80, 1986 (Vice-Chm., 1970–78; Pres., 1980–86). DL 1958, Vice-Lieut, later Vice Lord-Lieut, 1970–78, JP 1959, Beds; High Sheriff, Beds, 1965. KStJ 1980. *Recreations:* shooting, country pursuits. *Address:* Turvey House, Turvey, Beds MK43 8EL. *T:* Turvey (0234) 881227. *Clubs:* White's, Army and Navy, Pratt's. *Died 15 June 1994.*

HANBURY, Harold Greville, QC 1960; DCL; Vinerian Professor Emeritus of English Law, Oxford; Hon. Fellow, Lincoln College, Oxford; Hon. Master of the Bench, Inner Temple; *b* 19 June 1898; *s* of late Lt-Col Basil Hanbury and Hon. Patience Verney; *m* 1927, Anna Margaret (*d* 1980), *d* of late Hannibal Dreyer, Copenhagen, Denmark. *Educ:* Charterhouse; Brasenose Coll., Oxford (Scholar). Vinerian Law Scholar, 1921; Fellow of Lincoln Coll., Oxford 1921–49; Fellow of All Souls Coll., 1949–64, Emeritus Fellow, 1980; Vinerian Prof. of English Law, Oxford, 1949–64. Visiting Prof., Univ. of Ife, 1962–63; Dean of Law Faculty, Univ. of Nigeria, 1964–66. Barrister-at-Law, Inner Temple, 1922; Rhodes Travelling Fellow, 1931–32; Senior Proctor, Oxford Univ., 1933–34 and 1944–45. President: Bentham Club, UCL, 1954–55 (Hon. Mem., 1988); Soc. of Public Teachers of Law, 1958–59. Chairman: Court of Inquiry into Provincial Omnibus Industry, 1954; Board of Inquiry into West Indian Airways, Trinidad, 1958; Tribunal for Industrials, Gibraltar, 1960; Independent Mem. Commns of Inquiry on Retail Distributive Trades, 1946; Minimum Wage Arbitrator in Nigeria, 1955. Hon. Mem., Mark Twain Soc., 1977. *Publications:* Le Système Actuel de l'Equité dans le Système Juridique de l'Angleterre (trans. Robert Kiéfé), 1929; Essays in Equity, 1934, German edn 1977; Modern Equity, 1935 (13th edn *sub nom.* Hanbury and Maudsley, 1989); Traité Pratique des Divorces et des Successions en Droit Anglais (with R. Moureaux), 1939 (2nd edn 1952); English Courts of Law, 1944 (5th edn *sub nom.* Hanbury and Yardley, 1979); Principles of Agency, 1952 (2nd edn, 1960); The Vinerian Chair and Legal Education, 1958; Biafra: a challenge to the conscience of Britain, 1968; Shakespeare as Historian, 1985; articles in legal periodicals. *Recreations:* reading, aelurophily (Vice-Pres. Oxford and District Cat Club); formerly cricket, travelling. *Address:* 14 Dan Pienaar Road, Kloof, Natal, South Africa. *T:* 7644617. *Died 12 March 1993.*

HANBURY, Sir John (Capel), Kt 1974; CBE 1969; formerly Chairman, Allen and Hanburys Ltd, 1954–73

(Director, 1944); *b* 26 May 1908; *e s* of late Frederick Capel Hanbury; *m* 1st, 1935, Joan Terry Fussell (*d* 1989); two *s* one *d* (and one *s* decd); 2nd, 1990, Rosemary Elizabeth, *widow* of Lt Comdr Paul Coquelle, RN. *Educ:* Downside; Trinity Coll., Cambridge. Mem., Pharmacopoeia Commn, 1948–73; Chm., Central Health Services Council, 1970–76; Pres. Assoc. of Brit. Pharmaceutical Industry, 1950–52; Chm., Assoc. of Brit. Chemical Manufacturers, 1961–63; Pres. Franco-British Pharmaceutical Commn, 1955. Mem., Thames Water Authority, 1974–79. FRSC (FRIC 1947); FPS 1955. Fellow, UCL, 1977. *Recreations:* horticulture, archæology. *Address:* Amwellbury House, Ware, Herts SG12 9RD. *T:* Ware (01920) 462108. *Club:* United Oxford & Cambridge University.

Died 1 March 1995.

HANLEY, Gerald Anthony; author; *b* 17 Feb. 1916; *s* of Edward Michael Hanly and Bridget Maria Roche. *Publications:* Monsoon Victory, 1946; The Consul at Sunset, 1951; The Year of the Lion, 1953; Drinkers of Darkness, 1955; Without Love (Book Society Choice), 1957; The Journey Homeward (Book Society Choice), 1961; Gilligan's Last Elephant, 1962; See You in Yasukuni, 1969; Warriors and Strangers, 1971; Noble Descents, 1982. *Recreations:* music, languages. *Address:* c/o Gillon Aitken, Aitken & Stone, 29 Fernshaw Road, SW10 0TG. *Died 7 Sept. 1992.*

HANNIGAN, Rt Rev. James; RC Bishop of Wrexham, from 1987; *b* Co. Donegal, 15 July 1928. Ordained priest, 1954. Bishop of Menevia, 1983–87. Chm., Catholic Educn Council, 1984–. *Address:* Bishop's House, Sontley Road, Wrexham, Clwyd LL13 7EW. *T:* Wrexham (0978) 262726. *Died 6 March 1994.*

HAPPOLD, Prof. Frank Charles, PhD, DSc (Manchester); Professor of Biochemistry, University of Leeds, 1946–67, Emeritus Professor, 1967; *b* Barrow-in-Furness, 23 Sept. 1902; *s* of Henry Happold and Emma Happold (*née* Ley); *m* 1926, A. Margaret M. Smith, MA (*d* 1988), Brighton; one *s* one *d. Educ:* privately; Barrow Gram. Sch.; University of Manchester. PhD (Manchester) 1927; DSc (Manchester) 1934. Leverhulme Fellowship to Harvard Univ. Post Graduate Medical Sch., 1939. University of Leeds: Department of Bacteriology, 1926–36; Dept of Physiology, 1936–46; Dept of Biochemistry, 1946–67; Research Prof., University of Florida, 1958–59. First Chm., Fedn of European Biochem. Socs, 1964. Visiting Prof., University of Ghana, 1967–70; Royal Soc. Vis. Prof., Univ. of Science and Technology, Kumasi, 1972. Co-founder with wife of International Tramping Tours, 1929. Diplôme d'Honneur, Fedn European Biochem. Socs, 1974. Bronze Medal, Ville de Paris, 1964. *Publications:* numerous scientific publications, mainly in Microbiological Chemistry and Enzymology. *Recreations:* gardening, travel. *Address:* 4 Widcombe Terrace, Bath, Avon BA2 6AJ. *Died 4 March 1991.*

HARCUS, Rear-Adm. Ronald Albert, CB 1976; Royal Navy, retired; *b* 25 Oct. 1921; *s* of Henry Alexander Harcus and Edith Maud (*née* Brough); *m* 1946, Jean Heckman; two *s* two *d. Educ:* St Olave's Grammar Sch.; RNC Greenwich. Entered Royal Navy, 1937; Comdr 1956; Captain 1964; Rear-Adm. 1974; served in HM Ships Nigeria, Jamaica, Ocean, Dainty (despatches, Korea, 1953); Fleet Marine Engr Officer Home Fleet, 1965–67; Dep. Dir Fleet Maintenance, 1968–69; Captain, HMS Sultan, 1971–72; attended Royal Coll. of Defence Studies, 1973; Asst Chief of Fleet Support, MoD (Navy), 1974–76. Managing Director: RWO (Marine Equipment) Ltd, 1976–79; R. W. Owen Ltd, 1976–79. Chairman: Management Cttee, British Seamen's Boys Home, 1981–84; NSPCC South Devon, 1981–91. *Recreations:*

fishing, sailing. *Address:* 2 Church Hill Close, Blackawton, Devon TQ9 7BQ. *Died 21 Aug. 1991.*

HARDEN, Donald Benjamin, CBE 1969 (OBE 1956); MA Cantab, MA Oxon, PhD Mich; Hon. FBA; FSA; Director of the London Museum, 1956–70; Acting Director of the Museum of London, 1965–70; *b* Dublin, 8 July 1901; *er s* of late Rt Rev. John Mason Harden, Bishop of Tuam, Killala and Achonry, and Constance Caroline Sparrow; *m* 1st, 1934, Cecil Ursula (*d* 1963), *e d* of late James Adolphus Harriss; one *d*; 2nd, 1965, Dorothy May, *er d* of late Daniel Herbert McDonald. *Educ:* Kilkenny Coll.; Westminster Sch.; Trinity Coll., Cambridge; University of Michigan. Travelled in Italy and Tunisia, 1923–24; Senior Asst, Dept of Humanity, University of Aberdeen, 1924–26; Commonwealth Fund Fellow, University of Michigan, 1926–28; Asst, University of Michigan Archæol. Expedn to Egypt, 1928–29; Asst Keeper, Dept of Antiquities, Ashmolean Museum, Oxford, 1929–45; Keeper, Dept of Antiquities, and Sec., Griffith Institute, 1945–56. Leverhulme Fellowship for research on ancient glass, 1953. Temp. Civil Servant, Ministries of Supply and Production, 1940–45. Vice-Pres. Soc. of Antiquaries of London, 1949–53, 1964–67; President: Council for British Archæology, 1950–54; Oxford Architectural and Historical Soc., 1952–55; Section H, British Assoc., 1955; London and Middlesex Archæol. Soc., 1959–65; Royal Archæol. Inst., 1966–69; Internat. Assoc. for History of Glass, 1968–74; Chm., Directors' Conf. (Nat. Museums), 1968–70; Hon. Sec. Museums Assoc., 1949–54, Chm. Educn Cttee, 1954–59, Pres. 1960; Hon. Editor, Soc. for Medieval Archæology, 1957–73, Pres., 1975–77; Mem. of Council, British School of Archæology in Iraq, 1949–84; Member: Ancient Monuments Board for England, 1959–74; Royal Commission on Historical Monuments (England), 1963–71; Trustee, RAEC Museum, 1966–84. Mem., German Archaeol. Inst. Hon. FBA 1987. Gold Medal, Soc. of Antiquaries, 1977; Hon. Fellow and Rakow Award, Corning Museum of Glass, NY, 1983. *Publications:* Roman Glass from Karanis, 1936; (with E. T. Leeds) The Anglo-Saxon Cemetery at Abingdon, Berks, 1936; (ed) Dark-Age Britain, 1956; The Phoenicians, 1962, rev. edns 1971, 1980; (jtly) Masterpieces of Glass, British Museum, 1968; Catalogue of Greek and Roman Glass in the British Museum, I, 1981; (jtly) Glass of the Caesars (an exhibition of Master Works of Roman Glass shown in Corning, NY, London, Cologne and Rome, 1987–88), 1987; numerous articles on archæology and museums. *Address:* 12 St Andrew's Mansions, Dorset Street, W1H 3FD. *T:* 071–935 5121. *Club:* Athenæum. *Died 13 April 1994.*

HARDING, Prof. Anita Elizabeth, MD; FRCP; Professor of Clinical Neurology, Institute of Neurology, University of London, since 1990 (Reader, 1987–90); *b* 17 Sept. 1952; *d* of George Alfred Harding and Jean Luton Harding; *m* 1977, Peter Kynaston Thomas. *Educ:* King Edward VI High Sch. for Girls, Birmingham; Royal Free Hosp. Sch. of Medicine, London (MB, BS 1975); MD London, 1981. LRCP 1975, MRCP 1977, FRCP 1989; MRCS 1975. House Officer and Registrar posts at Radcliffe Infirmary, Oxford, and at Royal Free, Westminster, Middlesex and National Hospitals, London, 1975–82; Lectr and Sen. Lectr in Neurology, RPMS and Inst. of Neurol., London, 1983–87. *Publications:* The Hereditary Ataxias and Related Disorders, 1984; (ed) The Molecular Biology of Neurological Disease, 1988; (ed) Genetics in Neurology, 1994; papers on neurogenetics. *Recreations:* music (eclectic), dining, ski-ing. *Address:* Institute of Neurology, Queen Square, WC1N 3BG. *T:* 0171–837 3611. *Died 11 Sept. 1995.*

HARDING, Denys Wyatt, MA; Emeritus Professor of Psychology, University of London, since 1968; *b* 13 July 1906; *s* of Clement and Harriet Harding; *m* 1930, Jessie Muriel Ward (*d* 1992); no *c*. *Educ:* Lowestoft Secondary Sch.; Emmanuel Coll., Cambridge. Investigator and Mem. of research staff, National Institute of Industrial Psychology, 1928–33; Asst (later Lecturer) in Social Psychology, London Sch. of Economics, 1933–38; Senior Lecturer in Psychology, University of Liverpool, 1938–45 (leave of absence for national service, 1941–44); part-time Lecturer in Psychology, University of Manchester, 1940–41 and 1944–45; Prof. of Psychology, Univ. of London, at Bedford Coll., 1945–68. Clark Lectr, Trinity Coll., Cambridge, 1971–72. Hon. Gen. Sec., British Psychological Soc., 1944–48. Mem. of editorial board of Scrutiny, a Quarterly Review, 1933–47; Editor, British Journal of Psychology (Gen. Section) 1948–54. *Publications:* The Impulse to Dominate, 1941; Social Psychology and Individual Values, 1953; Experience into Words: Essays on Poetry, 1963; Words into Rhythm, 1976; (ed with Gordon Bottomley) The Complete Works of Isaac Rosenberg, 1937; (trans. with Erik Mesterton) Guest of Reality, by Pär Lagerkvist, 1936; various papers on psychology and literary criticism. *Address:* Ashbocking Old Vicarage, near Ipswich IP6 9LG. *T:* Ipswich (0473) 890347. *Died 17 April 1993.*

HARDING, His Honour Rowe, LLD; DL; a Circuit Judge (formerly County Court Judge), 1953–76; Chairman, Swansea Porcelain Ltd, since 1976; *b* 10 Sept. 1901; *s* of late Albert Harding, Swansea, and Elizabeth Harding; *m* 1933, Elizabeth Adeline, *d* of John Owen George, Hirwaun, S Wales; one *s* one *d* (and one *s* decd). *Educ:* Gowerton County Sch.; Pembroke Coll., Cambridge. Qualified as solicitor, 1924; called to Bar, Inner Temple, 1928. Captain, Wales, Cambridge and Swansea Rugby football, 1924–28. Home Guard, 1940–44. Contested (Nat. L and C): Swansea East, 1945; Gower, 1950 and 1951. Mem., Swansea Town Council, 1945–48. Deputy Chairman, Quarter Sessions: Haverfordwest, 1945 (Chm., 1948–49): Breconshire, 1953 (Chm., 1955–71); Pembrokeshire, 1953 (Chm., 1971); Carmarthenshire, 1956–65; Glamorganshire, 1959–71; Chm., Radnorshire QS, 1953–59. Dep. Chm., Local Tribunal for Conscientious Objectors in Wales, 1956; Pres., Royal Institution of S Wales, 1960–61; Mem., Nat. Adv. Council on the Training of Magistrates, 1964; Chancellor: Diocese of St David's, 1949–85; Diocese of Swansea and Brecon, 1974–82; former Mem., Governing and Rep. Bodies of Church in Wales; Judge of the Provincial Court of Church in Wales, 1966; Member: Council, Lampeter Coll., 1945–80; Court of Governors, UC Swansea, 1956–81 (Council, 1957), Univ. of Wales, 1971–74; Chm., Welsh Regional Cttee, Cheshire Homes, 1961–63; Trustee, Cheshire Foundation, 1962–70. Vice-Pres., Welsh Rugby Union, 1953–56; Chm., Glamorgan County Cricket Club, 1959–76, Pres., 1977–; Pres., Crawshay's Welsh RFC, 1985–. Life Patron, Swansea Cricket and Football Club, 1978. DL Glamorgan, later West Glamorgan, 1970. Hon. LLD Wales, 1971. *Publications:* Rugby Reminiscences and Opinions, 1929; Rugby in Wales, 1970. *Recreations:* walking, gardening, watching Rugby football and cricket. *Address:* The Old Rectory, Ilston, Gower, near Swansea, West Glamorgan. *T:* Penmaen (0792) 243. *Clubs:* Swansea City and County; Hawks (Cambridge). *Died 10 Feb. 1991.*

HARDINGHAM, Sir Robert (Ernest), Kt 1969; CMG 1953; OBE 1947; Chief Executive, Air Registration Board, 1947–68; *b* 16 Dec. 1903; *s* of late Robert Henry Hardingham and Florence Elizabeth Hardingham; *m* 1929, Ivy Everett; one *s* one *d*. *Educ:* Farnborough; de Havilland Technical Coll. RAE Farnborough, 1918–21; de Havilland Aircraft Co., 1921–34; Air Min., 1934–37; Air Registration Board, 1937–68. Pres., Soc. of Licenced Aircraft Engineers and Technologists, 1968–72.

Liveryman, Guild of Air Pilots and Navigators, 1966. CEng; FRAeS 1949 (Empire and Commonwealth Lecturer, 1952). Wakefield Gold Medal, RAeS, 1965; Silver Medal, Royal Aero Club, 1965. Cavaliere Ordino Merito della Repubblica Italiana. *Publications:* many technical papers. *Recreation:* golf. *Address:* Wortheal House, Southam Lane, Cheltenham GL52 3NY. *T:* Cheltenham (0242) 236765. *Club:* Naval and Military.
Died 6 Dec. 1991.

HARDMAN, Sir Fred, Kt 1982; MBE 1972; Board Member, Telford Development Corporation, since 1980; Chairman, Taws Printers Ltd, Telford, since 1983; *b* 26 Sept. 1914; *s* of Fred Hardman (killed in action, 1915, Hooge; KSLI) and Annie (*née* Walsh); *m* 1941, Ennis Lawson; one *s*. *Educ:* Basle, Switzerland. Served Royal Air Force, 1936–46. Conservative Political Agent, 1946–52; Senior Executive, Lectr and Public Relations, Rentokil, 1952–74; Industrial Relations Consultant, 1974–. Vice-Chm., Severn Navigation Restoration Trust Ltd, 1982–. Pres., W Midlands Cons. Trade Unionists, 1980–; Vice Pres., Nat. Union of Cons. Assocs, 1982– (Chm. 1980–81). Chairman: Conservative Trade Unionists, 1977–80; Conservative Party Conference, Blackpool, 1981. Dir, Ironbridge Gorge Mus. Trust, 1989–. Mem., Madeley Parish Council, 1988–. *Address:* The Old Bakehouse, The Wharfage, Ironbridge TF8 7NH. *T:* Ironbridge (095245) 3423. *Clubs:* St Stephen's Constitutional, Royal Over-Seas League.
Died 6 March 1991.

HARDWICK, Michael John Drinkrow; author and dramatist; *b* 10 Sept. 1924; *s* of George Drinkrow Hardwick and Katharine Augusta Townend; *m* 1961, Mollie Greenhalgh (Mollie Hardwick); one *s*. *Educ:* Leeds Grammar Sch. Morley Observer, 1942–43; Indian Army, 1943–47: served in India and Japan; Captain 1944. Dir, NZ Nat. Film Unit, 1948–53; Freedom Newspaper, NZ, 1953–54; Drama Dept, BBC (Radio), 1958–63; freelance, 1963–. FRSA 1966. *Publications:* The Royal Visit to New Zealand, 1954; Emigrant in Motley: letters of Charles Kean and Ellen Tree, 1954; Seeing New Zealand, 1955; Opportunity in New Zealand, 1955; (ed with Baron Birkett) The Verdict of the Court, 1960; Doctors on Trial, 1961; The Plague and Fire of London, 1966; The World's Greatest Air Mysteries, 1970; The Discovery of Japan, 1970; The Osprey Guide to Gilbert and Sullivan, 1972; The Osprey Guide to Jane Austen, 1973; A Literary Atlas and Gazetteer of the British Isles, 1973; The Osprey Guide to Oscar Wilde, 1973; Upstairs Downstairs: Mr Hudson's Diaries, 1973, Mr Bellamy's Story, 1974, On with the Dance, 1975, Endings and Beginnings, 1975; The Osprey Guide to Anthony Trollope, 1974; The Inheritors, 1974; (abridger) The Pallisers, 1974; The Four Musketeers, 1975; A Christmas Carol (play), 1975; The Man Who Would be King, 1976; The Cedar Tree, 1976; The Cedar Tree: Autumn of an Age, 1977, A Bough Breaks, 1978; Regency Royal, 1978; Prisoner of the Devil, 1979; Regency Rake, 1979; Regency Revenge, 1980; Bergerac, 1981; The Chinese Detective, 1981; Regency Revels, 1982; (abridger) The Barchester Chronicles, 1982; The Private Life of Dr Watson, 1983; Sherlock Holmes: my life and crimes, 1984; Last Tenko, 1984; Complete Guide to Sherlock Holmes, 1986; The Revenge of the Hound, 1987; Nightbone, 1989; *as John Drinkrow:* The Vintage Operetta Book, 1972; The Vintage Musical Comedy Book, 1973; *with Mollie Hardwick:* The Jolly Toper, 1961; The Sherlock Holmes Companion, 1962; Sherlock Holmes Investigates, 1963; The Man Who Was Sherlock Holmes, 1964; Four Sherlock Holmes Plays, 1964; The Charles Dickens Companion, 1965; The World's Greatest Sea Mysteries, 1967; Writers' Houses: a literary journey in England, 1968; Alfred Deller: A Singularity of Voice, 1968, rev. edn 1980; Charles Dickens As They Saw Him,

1969; The Game's Afoot (Sherlock Holmes Plays), 1969; Plays from Dickens, 1970; Dickens's England, 1970; The Private Life of Sherlock Holmes (novel), 1970; Four More Sherlock Holmes Plays, 1973; The Bernard Shaw Companion, 1973; The Charles Dickens Encyclopedia, 1973; The Charles Dickens Quiz Book, 1974; The Upstairs Downstairs Omnibus, 1975; The Gaslight Boy, 1976; The Hound of the Baskervilles and Other Sherlock Holmes Plays, 1982; author of numerous plays and scripts for radio and TV; contribs to many publications. *Address:* 2 Church Street, Wye, Kent TN25 5BJ. *T:* Wye (0233) 813051.
Died 4 March 1991.

HARE, Hon. Alan Victor, MC 1942; Deputy Chairman, The Economist, 1985–89; *b* 14 March 1919; 4th *s* of 4th Earl of Listowel and Hon. Freda, *d* of 2nd Baron Derwent; *m* 1945, Jill Pegotty (*née* North); one *s* one *d*. *Educ:* Eton Coll.; New Coll., Oxford (MA). Army, 1939–45. Foreign Office, 1947–61; Industrial and Trade Fairs, 1961–63; Financial Times, 1963–84; Man. Dir, 1971–78, Chm., 1978–84, and Chief Executive, 1975–83, Financial Times Ltd; Director: Pearson Longman Ltd, 1975–83; Economist Newspaper Ltd, 1975–89; Chm., Industrial and Trade Fairs Holdings, 1979–83 (Dir, 1977–83); Dir, English National Opera, 1982–88; Trustee, Reuters plc, 1985–. Pres., Société Civile du Vignoble de Château Latour, 1983–90. Mem., Press Council, 1975–78. Comdr, Order of Merit (FDR), 1985. *Recreations:* walking, opera, swimming. *Address:* Flat 12, 53 Rutland Gate, SW7 1PL. *T:* 0171–581 2184. *Club:* White's.
Died 10 April 1995.

HARE, Dora, (Hon. Mrs Richard Hare); see Gordine, D.

HARE, Sir Thomas, 5th Bt *cr* 1818, of Stow Hall, Norfolk; *b* 27 July 1930; *s* of Sir Ralph Leigh Hare, 4th Bt, and Doreen Pleasance Anna (*d* 1985), *d* of late Sir Richard Bagge, DSO; *S* father, 1976; *m* 1961, Lady Rose Amanda Bligh, *d* of 9th Earl of Darnley; two *d*. *Educ:* Eton; Magdalene College, Cambridge (MA). ARICS. *Heir:* cousin Philip Leigh Hare [*b* 13 Oct. 1922; *m* 1950, Anne Lisle, *d* of Major Geoffrey Nicholson, CBE, MC; one *s* one *d* (twins)]. *Address:* Stow Bardolph, King's Lynn, Norfolk PE34 3HU.
Died 25 Jan. 1993.

HARFORD, Sir James (Dundas), KBE 1956; CMG 1943; *b* Great Yarmouth, 7 Jan. 1899; *s* of late Rev. Dundas Harford, MA; *m* 1st, 1932, Countess Thelma, *d* of Count Albert Metaxa; one *s*; 2nd, 1937, Lilias Madeline, *d* of Major Archibald Campbell; two *d*. *Educ:* Repton; Balliol Coll., Oxford (Hon. Scholar, MA). Served European War, France and Belgium, 1917–19; Asst Master, Eton Coll., 1922–25; Administrative Service, Nigeria, 1926; District administration, Bornu Province, 1926–29; Asst Sec., Nigerian Secretariat, 1930–34 and Clerk to Exec. and Legislative Councils; seconded to Colonial Office, 1934–36; Administrator of Antigua and Federal Sec. of the Leeward Islands, 1936–40; Administrator, St Kitts-Nevis, 1940–47; administered Government of Leeward Islands, on various occasions; seconded to Colonial Office, 1947–48; administered Government of Mauritius, on various occasions; Colonial Sec., Mauritius, 1948–53; Governor and Commander-in-Chief of St Helena, 1954–58. Conference Organiser, Commonwealth Institute, 1959–64. *Address:* Links Cottage, Rother Road, Seaford, East Sussex BN25 4HT.
Died 26 Nov. 1993.

HARGREAVES, Maj.-Gen. William Herbert, CB 1965; OBE 1945; FRCP; *b* 5 Aug. 1908; *s* of Arthur William Hargreaves; *m* 1946, Pamela Mary Westray; one *s* one *d*. *Educ:* Merchant Taylors' Sch.; St Bartholomew's Hospital. FRCP 1950; FRCPE 1965. Served War of 1939–45. Medical Liaison Officer to Surgeon-Gen., US Army, Washington, DC, 1946–48; Prof. of Medicine, Univ. of Baghdad, 1951–59; Physician to late King Faisal II of

Iraq, 1951–58; Hon. Consulting Physician, Iraqi Army, 1953–59; Consulting Physician to the Army, 1960–65; retd 1965. Lectr in Tropical Medicine, Middlesex Hosp. Med. Sch., 1960–65, and London Hosp. Med. Sch., 1963–65; Hon. Consulting Physician, Royal Hosp., Chelsea, 1961–65; Chief Med. Advr, Shell Internat. Petroleum Co. Ltd, 1965–72. Examiner: RCP, 1964–66; Soc. Apothecaries, 1966–73. Mem. of Council, Royal Society of Medicine, 1966–69, Vice-Pres., Library (Scientific Research) Section, 1967–69. Counsellor, Royal Soc. of Tropical Med. and Hygiene, 1961–65; Member: Hosp. Cttee, St John's Ophthalmic Hosp., Jerusalem, 1968–71; Finance Cttee, RCP. OStJ 1965. Iraq Coronation Medal, 1953. *Publications:* The Practice of Tropical Medicine (with R. J. G. Morrison), 1965; chapters in: Textbook of Medicine (Conybeare), 16th edn 1975; Modern Trends in Gastro-Enterology (Avery Jones), 1951; Medicine in the Tropics (Woodruff), 1974; numerous articles in med. jls. *Recreations:* art, music. *Address:* 6/3 Gladswood Gardens, Double Bay, NSW 2028, Australia.
Died 2 April 1994.

HARINGTON, (Edward Henry) Vernon; *b* 13 Sept. 1907; *er s* of late His Honour Edward Harington; *m* 1st, 1937, Mary Elizabeth (marr. diss. 1949), *d* of late Louis Egerton; one *d* (and one *d* decd); 2nd, 1950, Mary Johanna Jean, JP, *d* of late Lt-Col R. G. S. Cox, MC; two *d. Educ:* Eton. Called to Bar, Inner Temple, 1930. Private Sec. to Lord Chancellor and Dep. Serjeant-at-Arms, House of Lords, 1934–40; served with HM Forces, 1940–45 (Major, Coldstream Guards); WO, 1944–45; Austrian Control Commn, Legal Div., 1945; Asst Sec. to Lord Chancellor for Commns of the Peace, 1945; Dep. Judge Advocate, 1946; Asst Judge Advocate Gen., 1954–73. Dep. Chm., Herefordshire QS, 1969–71; a Recorder of the Crown Court, 1972–75. Chm., Hereford, Worcester, Warwicks and W Midlands Regional Agricl Wages Cttee, 1976–82. Councillor, Malvern Hill DC, 1979–87. JP Herefordshire, 1969–71. *Recreations:* shooting, fishing. *Address:* 16 Lower Mill Lane, Ludlow, Shropshire SY8 1BH. *T:* Ludlow (01584) 878103. *Died 26 Dec. 1995.*

HARKNESS, John Leigh, (Jack), OBE 1986; Director, R. Harkness & Co. Ltd, since 1960; *b* 29 June 1918; *s* of Verney Leigh Harkness and Olivia Amy Harkness (*née* Austin); *m* 1947, Betty Catherine Moore; two *s* one *d. Educ:* Whitgift School. Army service, 1940–46: Hertfordshire Regt; Sherwood Foresters; 2nd Punjab Regt; mentioned in despatches, Burma; released with hon. rank of Major. Apprentice nurseryman, Donard Nursery, 1934–37; rose grower, R. Harkness & Co., Hitchin, 1937–77; rose breeder, Harkness New Roses, 1962–. Roses bred include: Escapade, 1967; Elizabeth Harkness, 1969; Alexander, Southampton, 1972; Compassion, 1973; Yesterday, 1974; Margaret Merril, 1977; Anna Ford, Anne Harkness, 1980; Princess Michael of Kent, 1981; Mountbatten, 1982; Paul Shirville, 1983; Amber Queen, 1984; Armada, City of London, 1988; Jacqueline du Pré, Savoy Hotel, 1989. Sec., British Assoc. of Rose Breeders, 1973–85. Gold Medal Rose Nord, 1978; DHM, 1980; Rose Growers Assoc. Medal, 1987; Australian Rose Award, 1988. Editor, Royal National Rose Society, 1978–83. *Publications:* Growing Roses, 1967; Roses, 1978; The World's Favourite Roses, 1979; How to Grow Roses, 1980; The Rose Directory, 1982; The Makers of Heavenly Roses, 1985; Rose Classes, 1989. *Recreations:* writing, bird watching, wine. *Address:* 1 Bank Alley, Southwold, Suffolk IP18 6JD. *T:* Southwold (0502) 722030. *Died 18 June 1994.*

HARLEY, Sir Thomas (Winlack), Kt 1960; MBE 1944; MC 1918; DL; former Consultant with Simpson North Harley & Co., solicitors, Liverpool and with Stanleys & Simpson North, London, admitted 1922; *b* 27 June 1895;

o s of George Harley and Annie Thomson (*née* Macwatty); *m* 1924, Margaret Hilda (*d* 1981), 2nd *d* of late Canon J. U. N. Bardsley; three *s. Educ:* Birkenhead Sch.; Eton. Served: European War, 1914–19, France and Balkans; Major The King's Own Regt (despatches, MC); War of 1939–45, Major RA (TA); comd (HG) AA Battery (MBE). Mem., Liverpool Regional Hosp. Bd, 1947 (Chm., 1959–68). Mem. Board of Governors, United Liverpool Hosps, 1955–69; Pres., Bebington and Ellesmere Port Conservative Assoc., etc. DL Cheshire (formerly County of Chester), 1962. *Recreation:* gardening. *Address:* Hesketh Haven, Thornton Hough, Merseyside L63 1JA. *T:* 051–336 7932. *Clubs:* Royal Over-Seas League; Royal Liverpool Golf. *Died 13 Jan. 1991.*

HARMAN, John Bishop, FRCS, FRCP; Honorary Consulting Physician, since 1972; *b* 10 Aug. 1907; *s* of late Nathaniel Bishop Harman and Katharine (*née* Chamberlain); *m* 1946, Anna Charlotte Malcolm Spicer; four *d. Educ:* Oundle; St John's Coll., Cambridge (Scholar); St Thomas' Hospital (Scholar). Fearnsides Scholar, Cantab, 1932; 1st Cl. Nat. Sci. Tripos Pt I, 2nd Cl. Pt II, Cantab; MA 1933; MD 1937; FRCS 1932; FRCP 1942. Physician: St Thomas' Hospital, 1938–72; Royal Marsden Hospital, 1947–72. Pres., Medical Defence Union, 1976–81; 2nd Vice Pres., RCP, 1981–82. Late Lt-Col RAMC (despatches). *Publications:* contribs to medical literature. *Recreation:* horticulture. *Address:* 108 Harley Street, W1N 1AF. *T:* 0171–935 7822.
Died 13 Nov. 1994.

HARMER, Sir Dudley; *see* Harmer, Sir J. D.

HARMER, Sir Frederic (Evelyn), Kt 1968; CMG 1945; *b* 3 Nov. 1905; *yr s* of Sir Sidney Frederic Harmer, KBE, FRS; *m* 1st, 1931, Barbara Susan (*d* 1972), *er d* of late Major J. A. C. Hamilton, JP, Fyne Court, Bridgwater, Som; one *s* two *d* (and one *d* decd); 2nd, 1973, Daphne Shelton Agar. *Educ:* Eton (KS); King's Coll., Cambridge (Scholar). Wrangler, Maths Tripos Part II, 1926; Class 1, Div. 1, Econs Tripos Part II 1927; BA 1927; MA 1934. Entered Treasury, Sept. 1939; Temp. Asst Sec., 1943–45; served in Washington, March-June 1944 and again in Sept.-Dec. 1945 for Anglo-American economic and financial negotiations; resigned Dec. 1945 and joined New Zealand Shipping Co. (Chm., 1953–65). Dep. Chm., P&OSN Co., 1957–70. Chairman: Cttee of European Shipowners, 1965–68; Internat. Chamber of Shipping, 1968–71; HM Govt Dir, British Petroleum Co. Ltd, 1953–70. Hon. Fellow, LSE, 1970. *Recreations:* sailing, golf. *Address:* Tiggins Field, Kelsale, Saxmundham, Suffolk IP17 2QX. *T:* Saxmundham (01728) 3156.
Died 24 Feb. 1995.

HARMER, Sir (John) Dudley, Kt 1972; OBE 1963; JP; company director; *b* 27 July 1913; *s* of Ernest George William Harmer and Germaine Stuart Harmer (*née* Wells); *m* 1947, Erika Minder-Lanz, Switzerland; two *s. Educ:* Merchant Taylors' Sch.; Wye College. Cert. Agriculture. Mem. 1956, Dep. Chm. 1964–72, Kent Agric. Exec. Cttee; Mem., Kent CC Agric. and Smallholdings Cttee, 1958 (Chm. of Selection of Tenants and Loans Sub-Cttee); Vice-Chm. 1964–66, Chm. 1966–71, SE Area Conservative Provincial Council; Pres., Kent East Euro Cons. Council, 1983–. Service connected with Home Guard, 1952–56: Hon. Major 1956. Trustee, Develt and Endowment Fund of Kent Inc. Soc. for Promoting Experiments in Horticulture, 1979–. JP Kent, 1962. *Recreations:* gardening, travel. *Address:* Stone Hill, Egerton, Ashford, Kent TN27 9DU. *T:* Egerton (023376) 241. *Died 13 March 1991.*

HARMSWORTH, St John Bernard Vyvyan; a Metropolitan Magistrate, 1961–85; *b* 28 Nov. 1912; *e s* of Vyvyan George Harmsworth and Constance Gwendolen

Mary Catt; *m* 1937, Jane Penelope (*d* 1984), *er d* of Basil Tanfield Berridge Boothby; three *d. Educ:* Harrow; New Coll., Oxford. Called to the Bar, Middle Temple, 1937. Served in RNVR, Lieut-Comdr, Oct. 1939–Feb. 1946. *Recreations:* fly fishing, tennis.

Died 13 June 1995.

HARPER, Prof. Denis Rawnsley, CBE 1975; BArch, PhD, MSc Tech; FRIBA, MRTPI, PPIOB; building consultant; Professor of Building at the University of Manchester Institute of Science and Technology, 1957–74, then Emeritus; *b* 27 May 1907; *s* of James William Harper, Harrogate; *m* 1st, 1934, Joan Mary Coggin (*d* 1968); one *s* one *d*; 2nd, 1971, Dora Phylis Oxenham (widow). *Educ:* Harrogate Grammar Sch.; Univ. of Liverpool Sch. of Architecture. Asst architect in hosp. practice in London, 1930–38; RIBA Saxon Snell Prizeman, 1939; Lectr in Sch. of Architecture, University of Cape Town, 1939–49; in private practice (with Prof. Thornton White), in Cape Town, as architect and town planner, 1940–50; Associate Architect in BBC TV Centre, 1950–52; Chief Architect to Corby New Town, Northants, 1952–57. Hanson Fellow, The Master Builder Fedn of South Africa, 1972. Cttee Mem., CNAA. Mem., Summerland Fire Commn, 1973–74. *Publications:* Building: process and product, 1978; various contribs to technical jls. *Recreations:* gardening, boating. *Address:* 2 Glenfield Drive, Great Doddington, Wellingborough, Northants NN9 7TE. *T:* Wellingborough (0933) 223841.

Died 3 Feb. 1993.

HARPLEY, Sydney Charles, RA 1981 (ARA 1974); sculptor since 1956; *b* 19 April 1927; *s* of Sydney Frederick Harpley, electrical engr and cabinet maker, and Rose Isabel Harpley, milliner; *m* 1956, Sally Holliday (marr. diss. 1968), illustrator; two *s* one *d. Educ:* Royal Coll. of Art. ARCA 1956; FRBS 1963. Realist sculptor, portraits and figure; commnd Smuts Memorial, Cape Town, 1963; sculpture in collections of: Nat. Gallery, NZ; Nat. Gallery, Cape Town; Paul Mellon, USA; Anton Rupert, SA; Princess Grace of Monaco; Fleur Cowles Meyer, London; S. & D. Josefowitz, Geneva; Lady Verulam; Lord Jersey; portraits: Edward Heath for Constitutional Club, 1973; Lee Kwan Yew, Singapore, 1983. Visitors' Choice Prize, Royal Acad. Summer Exhibition, 1978, 1979. *Recreations:* chess, music. *Address:* Belline House, Piltown, Co. Kilkenny, Ireland.

Died 9 March 1992.

HARRIS, 6th Baron *cr* 1815, of Seringapatam and Mysore, and of Belmont, Kent; **George Robert John Harris;** Captain RA, retired; *b* 17 April 1920; *s* of 5th Baron Harris, CBE, MC, and Dorothy Mary (*d* 1981), *d* of Rev. W. J. Crookes; *S* father, 1984. *Educ:* Eton; Christ Church, Oxford. *Heir: cousin* Derek Marshall Harris [*b* 23 July 1916; *m* 1938, Laura Cecilia, *e d* of late Major Edmund Thomas William McCausland, Gurkha Rifles; one *s* one *d*]. *Address:* Huntingfield, Eastling, near Faversham, Kent. *Died 17 Sept. 1995.*

HARRIS, Colin Grendon, CMG 1964; HM Diplomatic Service, retired; *b* 25 Oct. 1912; *s* of John Lindsay Harris; *m* 1941, Adelaide Zamoiska (decd); *m* 1947, Monique Jacqueline Marcuse-Baudoux; four *s* two *d. Educ:* Rossall Sch.; Pembroke Coll., Cambridge. Entered Foreign (subseq. Diplomatic) Service, 1935; served San Francisco, Antwerp, Elisabethville, Leopoldville, Lisbon, Montevideo, Rio de Janeiro, Vienna, Tokyo, Oslo; retired 1969. *Address:* 263 Avenue Defré, Brussels, Belgium.

Died 21 July 1992.

HARRIS, Prof. Harry, FRCP; FRS 1966; Harnwell Professor of Human Genetics, University of Pennsylvania, 1976–90, then Emeritus; *b* 30 Sept. 1919; *s* of Sol and Sarah Harris; *m* 1948, Muriel Hargest; one *s. Educ:*

Manchester Gram. Sch.; Trinity Coll., Cambridge (MA, MD). FRCP 1973. Research Asst, Galton Laboratory, Dept of Eugenics, Biometry, and Genetics, UC, London, 1947–50; Leverhulme Scholar, RCP, 1947–48; Lund Research Fellow, Diabetic Assoc., 1949; Lectr, Dept of Biochem., UC, London, 1950–53; Sen. Lectr, 1953–58, Reader in Biochem. Genetics, 1958–60, Dept of Biochem., The London Hosp. Med. Coll.; Prof. of Biochem., University of London, at King's Coll., 1960–65; Galton Prof. of Human Genetics, London Univ. at UCL, 1965–76. Hon. Lectr, 1950–55, Hon. Research Associate, 1955–60, Dept of Eugenics, Biometry, and Genetics, UCL; Hon. Dir, MRC Human Biochem. Genetics Res. Unit, 1962–76; Hon. Consulting Geneticist, UCH, 1966–76. Joint Editor: Annals of Human Genetics, 1965–79; Advances in Human Genetics, 1970–. Nat. Research Coun. of Canada and Nuffield Foundation Vis. Lectr, British Columbia and McGill, 1967; Fogarty Scholar, Nat. Insts of Health, USA, 1972; Rock Carling Fellowship, Nuffield Provincial Hosps Trust, 1974. Lectures: Thomas Young, St George's Hosp. Med. Sch., 1966; De Frees, University of Pennsylvania, 1966; Walter R. Bloor, Univ. Rochester, 1967; Langdon Brown, RCP, 1968; Sir William Jackson Pope, RSA, 1968; Darwin, Inst. Biol., 1969; Leonard Parsons, Birmingham Univ., 1969; Sidney Ringer, UCH Med. Sch., 1970; T. H. Huxley, Birmingham Univ., 1971; George Frederic Still, British Paediatric Assoc., 1971; L. S. Penrose Meml, Genetical Soc., 1973; Bicentennial, Coll. of Physicians of Pa, 1976; Noble Wiley Jones, Univ. of Oregon, 1978; Rhodes, Emory Univ., 1978; Thomas S. Hall, Washington Univ., St Louis, 1979; Harvey, Harvey Soc., NY, 1981; Karl Beyer, Wisconsin, 1983. For. Associate, Nat. Acad. of Scis, USA, 1976. Hon. Dr Univ. René Descartes, Paris, 1976. William Allan Meml Award, Amer. Soc. of Human Genetics, 1968. *Publications:* An Introduction to Human Biochemical Genetics (Eugenics Laboratory Memoir Series), 1953; Human Biochemical Genetics, 1959; The Principles of Human Biochemical Genetics, 1970, 3rd edn 1980; Prenatal Diagnosis and Selective Abortion, 1975; (with D. A. Hopkinson) Handbook of Enzyme Electrophoresis in Human Genetics, 1976. *Address:* Dunwoody Village CH30, 3500 West Chester Pike, Newtown Square, Pa 19073, USA. *T:* (215) 353–7096. *Died 17 July 1994.*

HARRIS, Noël Hedley V.; *see* Vicars-Harris.

HARRIS, Robert Louis Anstruther; actor since 1922; *b* 28 March 1900; *s* of Alfred H. Harris and Suzanne Amelie (*née* Anstie). *Educ:* Sherborne; New Coll., Oxford. Appeared in Shakespearean rôles with the Old Vic-Sadler's Wells Company and at Stratford-on-Avon, and in the West End (Hamlet, Oberon, Prospero, Angelo, Henry IV, King John, Shylock and Dr Faustus); other parts include: St Bernard, in The Marvellous History of St Bernard; Charles Tritton, in The Wind and The Rain; Eugene Marchbanks, in Candida (NY); Orin Mannon, in Mourning Becomes Electra; Thomas More, in A Man for all Seasons (USA); Pope Pius XII in The Deputy (NY); 40 Years On (Canada); J. Robert Oppenheimer, Fortune Theatre; films include: How he lied to her Husband; Decline and Fall; Morta in Roma; Ransom; Love Among the Ruins. Television serials and radio plays incl.: Old Jolyon in The Forsyte Saga; Prof. Gay in C. P. Snow's Strangers and Brothers; Archdeacon Grantly in The Barchester Chronicles; The Mysterious Death of Charles Bravo; Edward and Mrs Simpson; Duke of Burgundy in Henry V. *Recreation:* travel. *Club:* Garrick.

Died 18 May 1995.

HARRIS, Sir Ronald (Montague Joseph), KCVO 1960 (MVO 1943); CB 1956; First Church Estates Commissioner, 1969–82; Chairman, Central Board of Finance of Church of England, 1978–82; *b* 6 May 1913;

o s of late Rev. J. Montague Harris and Edith Annesley Harris (*née* Malcolmson); *m* 1st, 1939, Margaret Julia Wharton (*d* 1955); one *s* three *d*; 2nd, 1957, Marjorie (*d* 1986), *e d* of Sir Harry Verney, 4th Bt, DSO, and Lady Rachel Verney, and *widow* of Julian Tryon; one step *d* (one step *s* decd). *Educ:* Harrow; Trinity Coll., Oxford. India Office and Burma Office, 1936–38; Private Sec. to Sec. of Cabinet, 1939–43; India Office and Burma Office, 1944–47; Imperial Defence Coll., 1948; HM Treasury, 1949–52; Cabinet Office, 1952–55; Second Crown Estate Commissioner, 1955–60; Third Sec., HM Treasury, 1960–64; Sec. to Church Commissioners, 1964–68. Director: Yorks Insurance Co., 1966–69; Yorkshire General Life Assurance Co., 1969–84; General Accident Fire and Life Assurance Corp. Ltd, 1970–84. Chairman: Benenden Sch. Council, 1971–77; Friends of Yehudi Menuhin Sch., 1972–89 (Pres., 1989–), Governor, 1976– (Vice-Chm., 1984–89, Chm., 1989–90); Painshill Park Educn Trust, 1987–. *Publication:* Memory—Soft The Air, 1987. *Address:* Slyfield Farm House, Stoke D'Abernon, Cobham, Surrey KT11 3QE. *Club:* Boodle's.

Died 22 Jan. 1995.

HARRISON, Albert Norman, CB 1966; CVO 1955; OBE 1946; RCNC; Hon. Vice-President, Royal Institution of Naval Architects; *b* 12 July 1901; *s* of William Arthur and Sarah Jane Harrison, Portsmouth, Hants; *m* 1941, Queenie Perpetua Parker (decd), Luton; one *d. Educ:* Portsmouth; Royal Naval Coll., Greenwich. Asst Constructor, Royal Corps of Naval Constructors, 1926, Constructor, 1937; Principal Ship Overseer, Vickers-Armstrong, Barrow-in-Furness, 1936–39; Staff of RA (D), Home Fleet, 1940–41; Naval Constructor-in-Chief, Royal Canadian Navy, 1942–48; Chief Constructor, Admiralty, 1948–51; Asst Dir of Naval Construction, Admiralty, 1951–61; Dir of Naval Construction, Min. of Defence (N) (formerly Admiralty), 1961–66. *Address:* Whiteoaks, 126 Bloomfield Road, Bath, Avon BA2 2AS. *T:* Bath (0225) 429145. *Club:* Bath and County (Bath).

Died 1 Nov. 1992.

HARRISON, George Anthony, DL; solicitor; Clerk to the Lieutenancy of Greater Manchester, since 1986; Chairman and Director, Central Station Properties Ltd, 1976–88; director of various companies; *b* 20 Aug. 1930; *s* of John and Agnes Catherine Harrison; *m* 1957, Jane Parry; two *s* one *d. Educ:* Roundhay Sch., Leeds; Trinity Coll., Cambridge (MA, LLB). Asst Solicitor, Wolverhampton, 1955–58; ICI, 1958–59; Dep. Town Clerk, Wallasey and Bolton, 1962–65; Town Clerk and Clerk of the Peace, Bolton, 1965–69; Dir-Gen., Greater Manchester Transport Exec., 1969–76; Chief Exec., Greater Manchester Council, 1976–86. DL Manchester, 1978. *Recreations:* music, sailing. *Address:* 16 Park View, Sharples, Bolton. *T:* Bolton (0204) 56996. *Died 6 Feb. 1992.*

HARRISON, George Bagshawe, MA Cantab; PhD London; Emeritus Professor of English, University of Michigan, 1964 (Professor, 1949–64); *b* 14 July 1894; *s* of late Walter Harrison, Brighton; *m* 1919, Dorothy Agnes (*d* 1986), *o d* of late Rev. Thomas Barker; one *d* (three *s* decd). *Educ:* Brighton Coll.; Queens' Coll., Cambridge (Classical Exhibitioner; 1st Class English Tripos, 1920). Commnd to 5th Bn The Queen's Royal Regt, and served in India and Mesopotamia, 1914–19; Staff Capt. 42nd Indian Infantry Brigade (despatches); War of 1939–45, RASC and Intelligence Corps, 1940–43. Asst Master, Felsted Sch., 1920–22; Senior Lecturer in English, St Paul's Training Coll., Cheltenham, 1922–24; Asst Lecturer in English Literature, King's Coll., University of London, 1924–27, Lecturer, 1927–29; Frederic Ives Carpenter Visiting Prof. of English, University of Chicago, 1929; Reader in English Literature, University of London, 1929–43; Head of English Dept and Prof. of English,

Queen's Univ., Kingston, Ont, Canada, 1943–49. Lectured at Sorbonne, 1933, in Holland, 1940; Alexander Lecturer, University of Toronto, Canada, 1947. Mem., Internat. Commn on English in the Liturgy. Hon. LittD: Villanova, 1960; Holy Cross, 1961; Marquette, 1963; Hon. LLD Assumption, 1962. KSG 1981. Campion Award for long and eminent service in cause of Christian literature, 1970. *Publications:* Shakespeare: the Man and his Stage (with E. A. G. Lamborn), 1923; Shakespeare's Fellows, 1923; John Bunyan: a Study in Personality, 1928; England in Shakespeare's Day; An Elizabethan Journal, 1591–94, 1928; A Second Elizabethan Journal, 1595–98, 1931; A Last Elizabethan Journal, 1599–1603, 1933; Shakespeare at Work, 1933; The Life and Death of Robert Devereux, Earl of Essex, 1937; The Day before Yesterday (a Journal of 1936), 1938; Elizabethan Plays and Players, 1940; A Jacobean Journal, 1603–1606, 1941; A Second Jacobean Journal, 1607–1610, 1950; Shakespeare's Tragedies, 1951; Profession of English, 1962; The Fires of Arcadia, 1965; (with John McCabe) Proclaiming the Word: a handbook for church speaking, 1976; One Man in His Time: memoirs of G. B. Harrison 1894–1984, 1985, etc; Editor: The Bodley Head Quartos, 1922–26; The New Readers' Shakespeare (with F. H. Pritchard); The Pilgrim's Progress and Mr Badman; The Church Book of Bunyan Meeting, 1928; Breton's Melancholike Humours, 1929; The Trial of the Lancaster Witches, 1612, 1929; The Earl of Northumberland's Advice to his son; (also trans.) The Journal of De Maisse (with R. A. Jones), 1931; A Companion to Shakespeare Studies (with Harley Granville-Barker), 1934; The Letters of Queen Elizabeth, 1935; The Penguin Shakespeares, 1937–59; Shakespeare—the compleat works, 1968; contributor to The Road to Damascus, 1949; etc. *Address:* 36A Manson Street, Palmerston North, New Zealand. *T:* 75895.

Died 1 Nov. 1991.

HARRISON, John Audley, CB 1976; a Director, Ministry of Defence, 1969–76; *b* 13 May 1917; *s* of John Samuel Harrison and Florence Rose (*née* Samways); *m* 1940, Dorothea Pearl (*née* West); two *s* one *d. Educ:* Caterham Sch., Surrey. Prudential Assce Co. Ltd, 1935–39. London Rifle Bde (TA), 1939–40; York and Lancaster Regt (emergency commn), 1940–46. Attached War Office (later MoD), 1946–76, retd May 1976. *Recreations:* golf, bridge. *Address:* 43 Hovedene, 95 Cromwell Road, Hove, Sussex BN3 3EH. *T:* Brighton (0273) 770491. *Club:* Dyke Golf (Brighton). *Died 10 July 1992.*

HARRISON, Kathleen, (Mrs J. H. Back); leading character actress, stage and films; *b* Blackburn, Lancs, 23 Feb. 1892; *d* of Arthur Harrison, MICE, Civil Engineer, and Alice Maud Harrison (*née* Parker); *m* 1916, John Henry Back, Western Telegraph Co. (*d* 1960); one *s* one *d* (and one *s* decd). *Educ:* St Saviour's and St Olave's Grammar Sch,; Clapham High Sch. RADA, 1914–15 (Du Maurier Bronze Medal). *Notable plays include:* The Cage, Savoy, 1927; Aren't Women Wonderful, Royal Court, 1928; Happy Families, Garrick, 1929; Badger's Green, Prince of Wales Theatre, 1930; Jane's Legacy, Duchess, 1930; Lovers' Meeting, Prince of Wales, 1931; Can the Leopard, Theatre Royal, Haymarket, 1931; The Private Room, Westminster, 1934; Night Must Fall, Duchess, 1935; I Killed the Count, Whitehall, 1937; Comedienne, Theatre Royal, Haymarket, 1938; The Corn is Green, Duchess, 1938; Flare Path, Apollo, 1942; The Winslow Boy, Lyric, 1946; A Woman's Place, Vaudeville, 1949; Flowers for the Living, Duchess, 1950; The Silver Box (revival), Lyric, Hammersmith, 1951; Waters of the Moon, Theatre Royal, Haymarket, 1951; All for Mary, Duke of York's, 1954; Nude with Violin, Globe, 1956; How Say You?, Aldwych, 1959; Watch It, Sailor!, Aldwych, 1960; The Chances, Chichester Festival, 1962; Norman, Duchess, 1963; title rôle in Goodnight Mrs Puffin, New Theatre, Bromley; Harvey,

Richmond Theatre, 1971; She Stoops to Conquer, Young Vic, 1972; toured N Africa and Italy with Emlyn William's ENSA Co., 1944; Chichester Festival Theatre Co., 1962; toured in All for Mary and Goodnight Mrs Puffin, 1970. *Films include:* Our Boys, 1915; Hobson's Choice, 1931; Happy Ever After, 1932; The Man from Toronto, 1932; The Ghoul, 1933; Line Engaged, 1935; Broken Blossoms, 1936; Night Must Fall, 1937; Bank Holiday, 1938; Almost a Gentleman, 1938; A Girl Must Live, 1939; They Came By Night, 1940; Tilly of Bloomsbury, 1940; The Girl in the News, 1940; The Ghost Train, 1941; One a Crook, 1941; I Thank You, 1941; Much Too Shy, 1942; In Which We Serve, 1942; Temptation Harbour, 1947; Holiday Camp, 1947; The Huggett series, from 1948; Oliver Twist, 1948; The Winslow Boy, 1948; Waterfront, 1950; Trio, 1950; Scrooge, 1951; The Pickwick Papers, 1952; Turn the Key Softly, 1953; Lilacs in the Spring, 1954; Cast a Dark Shadow, 1955; All for Mary, 1956; Seven Thunders, 1957; Alive and Kicking, 1958. *TV includes:* title role in Mrs Thursday series, 1966; Martin Chuzzlewit and Our Mutual Friend serials. *Address:* c/o T. Plunket Greene, 4 Ovington Gardens, SW3. *T:* 0171–584 0688.

Died 7 Dec. 1995.

HARRISON, Prof. Richard Martin; Research Professor of Roman Archaeology, University of Oxford, since 1991; Fellow, All Souls College, Oxford, since 1985; *b* 16 May 1935; *s* of George Lawrance Harrison and Doris Waring (*née* Ward); *m* 1959, Elizabeth Anne Harkness Browne; one *s* three *d*. *Educ:* Sherborne Sch.; Lincoln Coll., Oxford (BA Greats 1958, MA 1961). Scholar 1959, and Fellow 1960, Brit. Inst. of Archaeol., Ankara; Rivoira Scholar, Brit. Sch. at Rome, 1960; Controller of Antiquities, Provincial Govt of Cyrenaica, 1960–61; Lectr in Class. Archaeol., Bryn Mawr Coll., 1961–62; Glanville Res. Student, Lincoln Coll., Oxford, 1962–64; Newcastle upon Tyne University: Lectr in Roman and Romano-British History and Archaeol., 1964–68; Prof. of Roman Hist. and Archaeol., 1968–72; Prof. of Archaeology, 1972–85; Prof. of Archaeol. of Roman Empire, Univ. of Oxford, 1985–91. Vis. Fellow, Dumbarton Oaks, 1969. Surveys and excavations: Istanbul, 1964–75, Lycia, 1959–63, 1976–85, Phrygia, 1987–. Society of Antiquaries: Fellow, 1965; Vice-Pres., 1984–88; Frend Medal, 1987. Jerome Lectures (Ann Arbor and Rome), 1990. Corresp. Mem., German Archaeol. Inst., 1973. *Publications:* Excavations at Saraçhane in Istanbul, 1986; A Temple for Byzantium, 1989; articles on Roman and Byzantine archaeol. *Recreation:* hill-walking in Northumberland and Turkey. *Address:* All Souls College, Oxford OX1 4AL.

Died 9 Sept. 1992.

HARROD, Maj.-Gen. Lionel Alexander Digby, OBE 1969; Inspector of Recruiting (Army), 1979–90; Secretary, League of Remembrance, since 1990; *b* 7 Sept. 1924; *s* of Frank Henry Harrod, CBE, and Charlotte Beatrice Emmeline (*née* David); *m* 1952, Anne Priscilla Stormont Gibbs; one *s* two *d*. *Educ:* Bromsgrove Sch. Grenadier Guards, 1944–63; Bde Major, 19 Bde, 1956–58; WO staff, 1959–60; CO 1 Welch, 1966–69; Brit. Def. Staff, Washington, 1969–70; Military Attaché, Baghdad, 1971; Staff HQ UKLF, 1972–73; Chief, Brit. Mission to Gp of Soviet Forces, Germany, 1974–76; ACOS (Intelligence), SHAPE, 1976–79, retired. Col, Royal Regt of Wales, 1977–82. Vice Chm., N Dorset Conservative Assoc., 1985–90; Cttee, Military Commentators Circle; Member: Atlantic Council; European Atlantic Gp; Pilgrims. *Recreations:* sport, country life. *Address:* The Grange, Marnhull, Dorset DT10 1PS. *T:* Marnhull (01258) 820256. *Clubs:* Army and Navy, MCC, Pratt's.

Died 18 Jan. 1995.

HART OF SOUTH LANARK, Baroness *cr* 1988 (Life Peer), of Lanark in the county of Larnark; **Judith**

Constance Mary Hart, DBE 1979; PC 1967; *b* 18 Sept. 1924; *d* of late Harry Ridehalgh and Lily Ridehalgh; *m* 1946, Anthony Bernard Hart; two *s*. *Educ:* Clitheroe Royal Grammar Sch.; London School of Economics, London University (BA Hons 1945). Contested (Lab) Bournemouth West, 1951, and South Aberdeen, 1955. MP (Lab): Lanark Div. of Lanarkshire, 1959–83; Clydesdale, 1983–87. Jt Parly Under-Sec. of State for Scotland, 1964–66; Minister of State, Commonwealth Office, 1966–67; Minister of Social Security, 1967–68; Paymaster-General (in the Cabinet), 1968–69; Minister of Overseas Develt, 1969–70, 1974–75; Minister for Overseas Develt, 1977–79; front bench opposition spokesman on overseas aid, 1979–80. Govt Co-Chm., Women's Nat. Commn, 1969–70. Labour Party: Mem., Nat. Executive, 1969–83; Vice-Chm., 1980–81, Chm., 1981–82. Vice Chm., UNA, 1989– (Chm., Econ. and Social Affairs Cttee, 1985–); Vice-President: World Disarmament Campaign, 1987–; World University Service, 1987–. Hon. Fellow, Inst. of Development Studies, Sussex Univ., 1985. *Publication:* Aid and Liberation, 1973. *Recreations:* theatre, gardening, spending time with her family. *Address:* 3 Ennerdale Road, Kew Gardens, Richmond-upon-Thames, Surrey TW9 3PG.

Died 8 Dec. 1991.

HART, Sir Francis Edmund T.; *see* Turton-Hart.

HART, Prof. Herbert Lionel Adolphus; QC 1984; FBA 1962; Principal, Brasenose College, Oxford, 1973–78, Hon. Fellow 1978; Delegate of the Oxford University Press, 1960–74; *b* 18 July 1907; 3rd *s* of Simeon Hart and Rose (*née* Samson); *m* 1941, Jenifer, 3rd *d* of Sir John Fischer Williams, CBE, KC; three *s* one *d*. *Educ:* Cheltenham Coll.; Bradford Grammar Sch.; New Coll., Oxford (Hon. Fellow 1968). Open Classical Scholar, New Coll., Oxford, 1926; First Class Lit.Hum., 1929. Practised at the Chancery Bar, 1932–40. Served War of 1939–45, in War Office, 1940–45. Fellow and Tutor in Philosophy, New Coll., Oxford, 1945; University Lecturer in Philosophy, Oxford, 1948; Prof. of Jurisprudence, Oxford, 1952–68; Fellow, University Coll., Oxford, 1952–68, Res. Fellow 1969–73, Hon. Fellow, 1973; Sen. Res. Fellow, Nuffield Foundn, 1969–73. Visiting Professor: Harvard Univ., 1956–57; Univ. of California, LA, 1961–62. Mem., Monopolies Commn, 1967–73. Pres., Aristotelian Soc., 1959–60; Vice-Pres., British Acad., 1976–77. Hon. Master of the Bench, Middle Temple, 1963. For. Mem., Amer. Acad. of Arts and Sciences, 1966. Hon. Dr of Law: Stockholm, 1960; Hebrew Univ. of Jerusalem, 1985; Hon. LLD: Glasgow, 1966; Chicago, 1966; Cambridge, 1978; Harvard, 1980; Edinburgh, 1980; Georgetown, 1982; Hon. DLitt: Kent, 1969; Hull, 1979; Bradford, 1980; Hon. Dr, Nat. Autonomous Univ. of Mexico, 1979; Hon. PhD Tel Aviv, 1983. Fellow, Accademia delle Scienze, Turin, 1964; Commonwealth Prestige Fellow (Govt of NZ), 1971. *Publications:* (with A. M. Honoré) Causation in the Law, 1959, 2nd edn 1984; The Concept of Law, 1961; Law, Liberty and Morality, 1963; The Morality of the Criminal Law, 1965; Punishment and Responsibility, 1968; (ed with J. H. Burns) Jeremy Bentham: An Introduction to the Principles of Morals and Legislation, 1970; (ed) Jeremy Bentham: Of Laws in General, 1970; (ed jtly) Jeremy Bentham: A Comment on the Commentaries and A Fragment on Government, 1977; Essays on Bentham: jurisprudence and political theory, 1982; Essays in Jurisprudence and Philosophy, 1983; articles in philosophical and legal journals. *Address:* University College, Oxford; 11 Manor Place, Oxford OX1 3UP. *T:* Oxford (0865) 242402.

Died 19 Dec. 1992.

HART, Rt Rev. Mgr William Andrew; *b* Dumbarton, 9 Sept. 1904; *s* of Daniel Hart and Margaret Gallagher.

Educ: St Mungo's Academy, Glasgow; St Mary's Coll., Blairs, Aberdeen; Royal Scots Coll. and Pontifical Univ., Valladolid, Spain. Asst Priest, St Mary's, Hamilton, 1929–33, St John's, Glasgow, 1933–39; Army Chaplain, 1939–45; Asst Priest, St Michael's, Glasgow, 1945–48; Vice-Rector, Royal Scots Coll., Valladolid, 1948–49; Parish Priest, St Nicholas', Glasgow, 1949–51, St Saviour's, Glasgow, 1951–55; Bishop of Dunkeld, 1955–81. *Died 18 Oct. 1992.*

HARTLEY, Arthur Coulton, CIE 1946; OBE 1943; Indian Civil Service (retired); *b* 24 March 1906; *s* of late John Aspinall Hartley and Jennie Hartley; *m* 1943, Mrs Cecilie Leslie; one *s. Educ:* Cowley Grammar Sch.; Manchester Univ.; Balliol Coll., Oxford. Entered Indian Civil Service, 1929; Asst Magistrate, Comilla, Bengal, 1929–30; Subdivisional Magistrate, Sirajganj, Bengal, 1930–32; Asst Settlement Officer, Rangpur, Bengal, 1932–34; Settlement Officer, Rangpur, Bengal, 1934–37; Asst Sec. to Governor of Bengal, 1938–40; District Magistrate, Howrah, Bengal, 1940–43; Controller of Rationing, Calcutta, Bengal, 1943–45; Dir-Gen. of Food, Bengal, India, 1945–47. *Publication:* Report on Survey and Settlement Operations of Rangpur, 1938. *Recreations:* hill walking, painting. *Address:* 12 Grange Road, Lewes, E Sussex BN7 1TR. *Died 24 May 1994.*

HARTLEY, Ven. Peter Harold Trahair; Archdeacon of Suffolk, 1970–75, then Archdeacon Emeritus; *b* 11 July 1909; *m* 1938, Ursula Mary Trahair; two *d. Educ:* Leys School; University of London (BSc 1935); Queen's College, Oxford (MA 1948); Cuddesdon Theological College. Deacon 1953, priest 1954, Diocese of St Edmundsbury; Curate of Dennington and Badingham, 1953–55; Rector of Badingham, 1955, with Bruisyard, 1960, and Cransford, 1974; Priest-in-Charge, Badingham with Bruisyard and Dennington, 1976–85. Rural Dean of Loes, 1967–70. *Publications:* papers in zoological journals. *Recreations:* natural history, naval and military history. *Address:* 26 Double Street, Framlingham, Woodbridge, Suffolk IP13 9BN. *T:* Framlingham (0728) 723604. *Died 3 Feb. 1994.*

HARTMAN, Dame (Gladys) Marea, DBE 1994 (CBE 1978; MBE 1967); President, Amateur Athletic Association of England, since 1991; *b* 22 June 1920. Competed as a runner for Spartan Athletic Club and Surrey County; team manager, British athletics team at Olympic and European Games and English athletics team at Commonwealth Games, 1956–78; Head of Delegn, World Championships, European Championships, English Internat. athletics teams and Commonwealth Games teams, 1978–. Mem., Women's Commn of Internat. Amateur Athletic Fedn, 1958– (Chm., 1968–81); Hon. Treasurer, British Amateur Athletic Bd, 1972–84 (Life Vice-Pres., 1980; Chm., 1989–91); Hon. Sec., Women's AAA, 1960–91 (Hon. Treasurer, 1950–60; Life Vice-Pres., 1970; Vice-Chm., 1981–91); Hon. Treasurer, CCPR, 1984– (Dep. Chm., 1981–83); Hon. Life Mem., IAAF, 1987. FIPM. *Recreations:* music, reading, theatre. *Address:* c/o Amateur Athletic Association of England, Francis House, Francis Street, SW1P 1DE. *T* and *Fax:* 071–828 4731, *Telex:* 8956058. *Died 29 Aug. 1994.*

HARTWELL, Sir Brodrick William Charles Elwin, 5th Bt, *cr* 1805, of Dale Hall, Essex; *b* 7 Aug. 1909; *s* of Sir Brodrick Cecil Denham Arkwright Hartwell, 4th Bt, and Joan Amy (*d* 1962), *o d* of Robert Milne Jeffrey, Esquimault, Vancouver; *S* father, 1948; *m* 1st, 1937, Marie Josephine, *d* of late S. P. Mullins (marr. diss. 1950); one *s;* 2nd, 1951, Mary Maude, MBE, *d* of J. W. Church, Bedford; (one *d* decd). *Educ:* Bedford Sch. Sometime Pilot Officer RAF; served War of 1939–45: Capt. Leics Regt, 1943. *Heir: s* Francis Antony Charles Peter Hartwell [*b* 1 June 1940; *m* 1968, Barbara Phyllis Rae (marr. diss.

1989), *d* of H. Rae Green; one *s*]. *Address:* Little Dale, 50 High Street, Lavendon, Olney, Bucks.
Died 14 Dec. 1993.

HARVEY OF PRESTBURY, Baron *cr* 1971 (Life Peer), of Prestbury in the County Palatine of Chester; **Arthur Vere Harvey,** Kt 1957; CBE 1942; FRAeS; *b* 31 Jan. 1906; *e s* of A. W. Harvey, Kessingland, Suffolk; *m* 1st, 1940, Jacqueline Anne (marr. diss. 1954), *o d* of W. H. Dunnett; two *s;* 2nd, 1955, Mrs Hilary Charmian Williams (marr. diss. 1977; she *d* 1978); 3rd, 1978, Mrs Carol Cassar Torreggiani; three adopted *d. Educ:* Framlingham Coll. Royal Air Force, 1925–30, qualified as flying instructor; Dir of Far East Aviation Co. Ltd and Far East Flying Training Sch. Ltd, Hong-Kong, 1930–35; Adviser to Southern Chinese Air Forces with hon. rank of Maj.-Gen., 1932–35; Sqdn Leader AAF, 1937, and founded 615 County of Surrey Squadron and commanded the Squadron in France, 1939–40 (despatches twice); Group Captain 1942; Air Commodore 1944. Dep. Chm., Handley-Page Ltd, 1951–57; Chm., Ciba-Geigy (UK) Ltd, 1957–74. MP (C) Macclesfield Div. of Cheshire, 1945–71; Chairman Cons. Members' 1922 Cttee, 1966–70. Vice-Pres. British Air Line Pilots' Assoc., 1965. FRAeS. Hon. Freeman: Macclesfield, 1969; Congleton, 1970. Hon. DSc Salford, 1972. Comdr, Order of Oranje Nassau (Netherlands), 1969. *Recreations:* private flying (4th King's Cup Race, 1937), sailing. *Address:* Rocklands, Les Vardes, St Peter Port, Guernsey, CI. *Clubs:* Royal Air Force; Royal Yacht Squadron (Cowes). *Died 5 April 1994.*

HARVIE-CLARK, Ven. Sidney, MA; Archdeacon of Stow, and Vicar of Hackthorn and Rector of Cold Hanworth, 1967–75, then Archdeacon Emeritus; *b* 26 July 1905; *s* of John Harvie Clark and Minnie Young Hunter, Glasgow and Chiswick, London; *m* 1936, Sheilah Marjorie, *d* of late Dr G. C. L. Lunt, Bishop of Salisbury; one *s* one *d* (and one *d* decd). *Educ:* St Paul's Sch., London; Jesus Coll. and Westcott House, Cambridge. Deacon, 1930; priest, 1931; Curate, St Mary's, Gateshead, Co. Durham, 1930–34; St Mary's, Portsea, 1934–36; Rector, Jarrow-on-Tyne, 1936–40; St John's, Edinburgh, 1940–47; Rector of Wishaw, 1947–48; Archdeacon of Birmingham, 1947–67; Vicar of Harborne, 1948–67. *Recreations:* walking, camping. *Address:* Stow House, Skillington, Grantham, Lincs NG33 5HQ. *T:* Grantham (0476) 860447. *Died 13 Feb. 1991.*

HASLEWOOD, Prof. Geoffrey Arthur Dering; Professor of Biochemistry at Guy's Hospital Medical School, University of London, 1949–77, then Emeritus; *b* 9 July 1910; *s* of N. A. F. Haslewood, architect, and Florence (*née* Hughes); *m* 1943, B. W. Leeburn (*d* 1949); two *d; m* 1953, E. S. Blakiston, Geelong, Vic, Australia. *Educ:* St Marylebone Grammar Sch.; University Coll., London. MSc 1932, PhD 1935, DSc 1946. FRSC (FRIC 1946). Research on polycyclic aromatic hydrocarbons, etc, at Royal Cancer Hosp. (Free), 1933–35; Asst in Pathological Chemistry at British Postgraduate Med. Sch., 1935–39; Reader in Biochemistry at Guy's Hosp. Med. Sch., 1939–49. Mem., Zaire River Expedition, 1974–75. Hon. Member: Japanese Biochem. Soc., 1969; Biochem. Soc., 1993. *Publications:* Bile Salts, 1967; The Biological Importance of Bile Salts, 1978; various articles and original memoirs in scientific literature, mainly on steroids in relation to evolution. *Recreation:* conservation, especially of amphibians and reptiles. *Address:* 28 Old Fort Road, Shoreham-by-Sea, Sussex BN43 5RJ. *T:* Brighton (0273) 453622. *Died 15 Oct. 1993.*

HASLIP, Joan; author; *b* 27 Feb. 1912; *yr d* of late George Ernest Haslip, MD, original planner of the Health Service and Anna, *d* of Maurice von Leinkauf, PC, Imperial Austrian Hungarian Government. *Educ:* privately in London and on the continent. Grew up in Florence. Sub-

editor, *London Mercury*, 1929–39, contributed verse, reviews, etc; travelled extensively Europe, USA, Middle East; Editor, European Service, BBC, 1941–45 (Italian Section); lectured for British Council, Italy and Middle East; broadcast and contributed articles to BBC and various publications and newspapers. FRSL 1958. *Publications:* (several translated): Out of Focus (novel), 1931; Grandfather Steps (novel), 1932 (USA 1933); Lady Hester Stanhope, 1934; Parnell, 1936 (USA 1937); Portrait of Pamela, 1940; Lucrezia Borgia, 1953 (USA 1954); The Sultan, Life of Abdul Hamid, 1958, repr. 1973; The Lonely Empress, a life of Elizabeth of Austria, 1965 (trans. into ten languages); Imperial Adventurer, 1971 (Book of Month choice, USA, 1972); Catherine the Great, 1976; The Emperor and the Actress, 1982; Marie Antoinette, 1987 (trans. 10 languages); Madame Du Barry, 1991. *Recreations:* travelling, conversation. *Address:* 8 Via Piana, Bellosguardo, 50124 Florence, Italy.
Died 19 June 1994.

HASLUCK, Rt Hon. Sir Paul (Meernaa Caedwalla), KG 1979; GCMG 1969; GCVO 1970; PC 1966; Governor-General of Australia, 1969–74; *b* 1 April 1905; *s* of E. M. C. Hasluck and Patience (*née* Wooler); *m* 1932, Alexandra Margaret Martin Darker (AD 1978; DStJ 1971); one *s* (and one *s* decd). *Educ:* University of Western Australia (MA). Journalist until 1938; Lectr in History, University of Western Australia, 1939–40; Australian Diplomatic Service, 1941–47: Head of Australian Mission to United Nations, 1946–47; Representative on Security Council, Atomic Energy Commn, General Assembly, etc; Research Reader in History, University of Western Australia, 1948; Official War Historian. Mem. (L) House of Representatives, 1949–69; Minister for Territories in successive Menzies Governments, 1951–63; Minister for Defence, 1963–64; Minister for External Affairs, 1964–69. Fellow, Aust. Acad. of Social Scis. Hon. Fellow, Aust. Acad. of Humanities; Hon. FRAIA; Hon. FRAHS. KStJ 1969. *Publications:* Black Australians, 1942; Workshop of Security, 1946; The Government and the People (Australian Official War History), vol. 1, 1951, vol. 2, 1970; Collected Verse, 1970; An Open Go, 1971; The Office of the Governor-General (Queale Meml Lecture), 1973, rev. edn 1979; The Poet in Australia, 1975; A Time for Building: Australian administration in Papua New Guinea, 1976; Mucking About (autobiog.), 1977; Sir Robert Menzies (Mannix Lecture), 1980; Diplomatic Witness, 1980; Dark Cottage (verse), 1984; Shades of Darkness: Aboriginal affairs 1925–65, 1988; The Ministerial Role in Australian Government, 1989; Crude Impieties (verse), 1991. *Recreation:* book collecting (Australiana). *Address:* 2 Adams Road, Dalkeith, WA 6009, Australia. *Clubs:* Weld (Perth); Claremont Football. *Died 9 Jan. 1993.*

HASSALL, William Owen; Librarian to Earl of Leicester, Holkham, 1937–83; Bodleian Library, Oxford, 1938–80 (Senior Assistant Librarian); *b* 4 Aug. 1912; *s* of Lt-Col Owen Hassall and Bessie Florence Hassall (*née* Cory); *m* 1936, Averil Grafton Beaves; three *s* one *d. Educ:* Twyford Sch., Hants; Wellington Coll., Berks; (Classical scholar) Corpus Christi Coll., Oxford. Hon. Mods, 1st cl. Modern History, 1936; DPhil 1941. Lent by RA to Min. of Economic Warfare, 1942–46. Formerly: External Examnr in History, Univs of Bristol, Durham, Leicester and Oxford Insts of Educn (Trng Colls); Hon. Editorial Sec., British Records Assoc.; Mem. Council, Special Libraries and Information Bureaux. Hon. Sec., Oxfordshire Record Soc.; 1947–76. FSA 1942; FRHistS. *Publications:* A Cartulary of St Mary Clerkenwell, 1949; A Catalogue of the Library of Sir Edward Coke, 1950; The Holkham Bible Picture Book, 1954; Wheatley Records, 956–1956, 1956; They saw it happen: an anthology of eye-witnesses' accounts for events in British history, 55BC-AD1485, 1957; Who's

Who in History, vol. I, British Isles, 55BC-1485, 1960; (with A. G. Hassall) The Douce Apocalypse, 1961; How they Lived: an anthology of original accounts written before 1485, 1962; Index of Names in Oxfordshire Charters, 1966; History Through Surnames, 1967; The Holkham Library Illuminations and Illustrations in the Manuscript Library of the Earl of Leicester (printed for presentation to the Members of the Roxburghe Club), 1970; (with A. G. Hassall) Treasures from the Bodleian, 1975; (ed jtly) Lordship and Landscape in Norfolk 1250–1350: the early records of Holkham, 1993; contrib. to various learned publications; work on Holkham records, 1250–1600. *Recreation:* grandchildren. *Address:* Manor House, Wheatley, Oxford OX33 1XX. *T:* Wheatley (0865) 872333. *Died 19 July 1994.*

HATCH OF LUSBY, Baron *cr* 1978 (Life Peer), of Oldfield in the County of W Yorks; **John Charles Hatch;** author, lecturer, broadcaster; *b* 1 Nov. 1917; *s* of John James Hatch and Mary White; *m* Eva; two *s* by previous marriage. *Educ:* Keighley Boys' Grammar School; Sidney Sussex Coll., Cambridge (BA). Tutor, Nat. Council of Labour Colls, 1942–44; Nat. Organiser, Independent Labour Party, 1944–48; Lectr, Glasgow Univ., 1948–53; Sec., Commonwealth Dept, Labour Party, 1954–61; Dir, Extra-Mural Dept, Univ. of Sierra Leone, 1961–64; Director: African Studies Programme, Houston, Texas, 1964–70; Inst. of Human Relations, Zambia Univ., 1980–82. Commonwealth Correspondent, New Statesman, 1950–70. Hon. Fellow, School of Peace Studies, Univ. of Bradford, 1976. Hon. DLitt, Univ. of St Thomas, Houston, 1981. *Publications:* The Dilemma of South Africa, 1953; New from Africa, 1956; Everyman's Africa, 1959; Africa Today and Tomorrow, 1960; A History of Post-War Africa, 1964; The History of Britain in Africa, 1966; Africa: the Re-Birth of Self-Rule, 1968; Tanzania, 1969; Nigeria, 1971; Africa Emergent, 1974; Two African Statesmen, 1976. *Recreations:* cricket, music. *Address:* House of Lords, Westminster, SW1A 0PW. *T:* 071–219 5353. *Clubs:* Commonwealth Trust, MCC.
Died 11 Oct. 1992.

HATFIELD, Hon. Richard Bennett; PC (Can.) 1982; Member, Canadian Senate, since 1990; Premier of New Brunswick, 1970–87; MLA (Progressive C) Carleton Centre (formerly Carleton), 1961–87; *b* 9 April 1931; single. *Educ:* Rothesay Collegiate Sch.; Hartland High Sch.; Acadia Univ.; Dalhousie Univ. BA Acadia 1952; LLB Dalhousie 1956. Admitted to Bar of NS, 1956. Joined law firm of Patterson, Smith, Matthews & Grant in Truro, NS, 1956; Exec. Asst to Minister of Trade and Commerce, Ottawa, 1957–58; Sales Man., Hatfield Industries Ltd, 1958–66. Leader, PC Party of New Brunswick, 1969. Chm., Beaverbrook Art Gall., 1988–. Hon. Mem., Course XLI, Nat. Defense Coll., 1988. SBStJ 1989. Hon. LLD: Moncton, 1971; New Brunswick, 1972; St Thomas, 1973; Mount Allison, 1975; Hon. Dr Pol. Sci. Université Sainte-Anne, NS, 1983. Hon. Chief, Micmac and Maliseet Tribes, 1970. Canada-Israel Friendship Award, 1973; Aboriginal Order of Canada, 1985. *Address:* 7 Elmcroft Place, Fredericton, New Brunswick E3B 1Y8, Canada. *T:* (506) 4532144. *Died 25 April 1991.*

HAUGHTON, Surg. Rear-Adm. John Marsden, LVO 1964; FFARCS; retired, 1982; *b* 27 Oct. 1924; *s* of Col Samuel George Steele Haughton, CIE, OBE, IMS, and Marjory Winifred Haughton (*née* Porter); *m* 1956, Lucy Elizabeth Lee, Tackley, Oxon; three *s* one *d. Educ:* Winchester Coll.; St Thomas' Hosp., 1942–48 (MRCS, LRCP, DA). Joined Royal Navy, 1949; 45 Commando RM, Malaya, 1950; Anaesthetic Specialist, RN Hosp., Plymouth, 1952; HMS Superb, 1954; RN Hosps, Haslar, 1956, Chatham, 1958; Sen. Anaesthetist, RN Hosp., Malta, 1959; PMO, Royal Yacht Britannia, 1962; Consultant

Anaesthetist, RN Hospital: Haslar, 1964; Malta, 1968; Haslar, 1970; Comd MO and MO in charge RN Hosp., Malta, 1975; MO in charge RN Hosp., Plymouth, 1978; Surg. Rear-Adm. (Naval Hosps), Haslar, 1980–82. QHP, 1978–82. *Recreations:* fishing, gardening, walking.

Died 19 June 1992.

HAVARD-WILLIAMS, Peter; educational and library management consultant; Professor of Library and Information Studies and Head of Department, University of Botswana, since 1988 (Distinguished Personal Professor, since 1995); *b* 11 July 1922; *s* of Graham Havard-Williams and Elizabeth (*née* James); *m* 1st, 1964, Rosine (*d* 1973), *d* of late Paul Cousin, Croix de Guerre; two *d*; 2nd, 1976, Eileen Elizabeth, *d* of Oliver Cumming; one *d*. *Educ:* Bishop Gore Grammar Sch., Swansea; University Coll. of Swansea (Smith's Charity Scholar; MA Wales, 1950); Oxford Univ.; PhD Loughborough Univ., 1986. FRSA, FIMgt, Associate and FLAI, FIInfSc. Sub-Librarian and Hon. Lectr in French, Univ. of Liverpool, 1951–56; Libr. and Keeper of Hocken Collection and Hon. Lectr in French, Univ. of Otago, 1956–60; Fellow, Knox Coll., Dunedin, 1958–60; Dep. Libr., Univ. of Leeds, 1960–61; Libr., QUB, 1961–71 (Dir, Sch. of Lib. and Inf. Studies, 1964–70); Dean and Prof., Liby Sch., Ottawa Univ., 1971–72; Loughborough University: Foundation Prof. and Head of Dept of Library and Information Studies, 1972–87, then Prof. Emeritus; Dean of Educn and Humanities, 1976–79; Warden, Royce Hall, 1978–87; Project Head, Centre for Library and Information Management, 1979–87; Public Orator, 1980–87; Mem. Court, 1978–. Consultant, Council of Europe, 1986–87. Library Association: Vice-Pres., 1970–82; Chm. Council, 1970–71 and 1974–75; Chm. Exec. Cttee, 1976–78; Chm., Cons. Cttee on Nat. Library Co-ordination 1978–80; Chm., Bd of Assessors, 1981; Chm., NI Br., 1963 (when first all-Ireland liby conf. held at Portrush). President: Internat. Colloquium on Univ. Liby Bldgs, Lausanne, 1971; Internat. Seminar on Children's Lit., Loughborough, 1976; Vice-Pres., Internat. Fedn of Liby Assocs, 1970–77. Mem., Botswana Nat. Liby Bd, 1988 (Chm., 1988–94). Member: Adv. Cttee on Public Liby Service, NI, 1965; Liby Adv. Council, 1976–78; Ct of Governors, UWIST, 1979–88. Liby bldg consultant, UK and abroad, 1961–; Cons. and Mem. Brit. Delegn, Unesco Inter-govtl Conf. on Nat. Inf. Systems, Paris, 1974; Consultant to Unesco, EEC, Council of Europe, British Council and foreign govts and instns, 1974–. Ext. Examr, London, Sheffield, Strathclyde, NUI, CNAA, Kenyatta Univ., Moi Univ., Kenya, and Univs of Ibadan, Natal, WI, Zambia; Lectr, European Inst. of Inf. Management, 1983. Hon. Librarian and Consultant, Cathedral of Holy Cross, Gaborone, 1988–. Editor, IFLA Communications and Publications, 1971–78; Editorial Consultant, Internat. Library Review, 1969–89; Consultant Editor: Library Progress Internat., 1981–; Library Waves, 1986–, etc. Hon. FLA 1986. Hon. PhD Confucian Univ., Seoul, 1982. Officier, Ordre des Arts et des Lettres, 1994. *Publications:* (ed) Marsden and the New Zealand Mission, 1961; Planning Information Manpower, 1974; Departmental Profile, 1981; Development of Public Library Services in Sierra Leone, 1984; Literacy Information and Planning (inaug. lecture, Univ. of Botswana), 1993; articles in Encyclopedia Britannica, Jl of Documentation, Libri, Internat. Liby Rev., Unesco Bull. for Libys, Eng. Studies, Essays in Crit., and Monthly Mus. Record, etc. *Recreations:* collecting Bloomsbury first editions, bears (esp. Winnie the Pooh), music, idling. *Address:* 31 Westfield Drive, Loughborough, Leics LE11 3QJ. *Clubs:* Athenæum, Commonwealth Trust; Gaborone. *Died 16 Aug. 1995.*

HAVERS, Baron *cr* 1987 (Life Peer), of St Edmundsbury in the County of Suffolk; **Robert Michael Oldfield**

Havers, Kt 1972; PC 1977; Lord High Chancellor of Great Britain, 1987; *b* 10 March 1923; 2nd *s* of Sir Cecil Havers, QC, and late Enid Snelling; *m* 1949, Carol Elizabeth, *d* of Stuart Lay, London; two *s*. *Educ:* Westminster Sch.; Corpus Christi Coll., Cambridge (Hon. Fellow, 1988). Lieut RNVR, 1941–46. Called to Bar, Inner Temple, 1948; Master of the Bench, 1971; QC 1964; QC (NI) 1973. Recorder: of Dover, 1962–68; of Norwich, 1968–71; a Recorder, 1972; Chm., West Suffolk QS, 1965–71 (Dep. Chairman, 1961–65). Chancellor of Dioceses of St Edmundsbury and Ipswich, 1965–73, of Ely, 1969–73. MP (C) Wimbledon, 1970–87; Solicitor-General, 1972–74; Shadow Attorney-General and Legal Adviser to Shadow Cabinet, 1974–79; Attorney General, 1979–87; Mem. Privileges Cttee, 1978–87. Chairman: RHM Outhwaite, Lloyd's Underwriters, 1988–; Solicitors Law Stationery Soc., 1988–. Chm., Lakenheath Anglo-American Community Relations Cttee, 1966–71. Chm., Playhouse Theatre, 1988–. *Publications:* (jtly) The Poisoned Life of Mrs Maybrick, 1977; (jtly) The Royal Baccarat Scandal, 1977, new edn, 1988; (jtly) Tragedy in Three Voices: the Rattenbury murder, 1980. *Recreations:* writing, photography, reading. *Address:* House of Lords, SW1A 0PW. *Clubs:* Garrick, Pratt's, Beefsteak.

Died 1 April 1992.

HAWARDEN, 8th Viscount (Ire.), *cr* 1793; **Robert Leslie Eustace Maude;** farming his own estate since 1952; *b* 26 March 1926; *s* of 7th Viscount Hawarden and Viscountess Hawarden (*née* Marion Wright) (*d* 1974); *S* father 1958; *m* 1957, Susannah Caroline Hyde Gardner; two *s* one *d*. *Educ:* Winchester; Christ Church, Oxford. Cirencester Agricultural Coll., 1948–50. Served for a short time in the Coldstream Guards and was invalided out, 1945–46. *Recreation:* shooting. *Heir: s* Hon. Robert Connan Wyndham Leslie Maude, *b* 23 May 1961. *Address:* Wingham Court, near Canterbury, Kent CT3 1BB. *T:* Canterbury (0227) 720222. *Died 6 Sept. 1991.*

HAWKE, 10th Baron, *cr* 1776, of Towton; **Julian Stanhope Theodore Hawke;** *b* 19 Oct. 1904; *s* of 8th Baron Hawke and Frances Alice (*d* 1959), *d* of Col J. R. Wilmer, Survey of India; *S* brother, 1985; *m* 1st, 1933, Griselda (marr. diss. 1946; she *d* 1984), *d* of late Capt. Edmund W. Bury; two *d*; 2nd, 1947, Georgette Margaret, *d* of George S. Davidson; one *s* three *d*. *Educ:* Eton; King's College, Cambridge (BA). With Glazebrook Steel & Co. Ltd, 1926–69, Director 1933–69. Served War of 1939–45 with AAF; Wing Comdr, W Africa. A Commissioner of Taxes, Manchester, for about 25 years until 1974 (for some years Head of Manchester Central Section). *Recreations:* golf (½ Blue Cambridge), shooting. *Heir: s* Hon. Edward George Hawke, ARICS, *b* 25 Jan. 1950. *Address:* The Old Mill House, Cuddington, Northwich, Cheshire. *T:* Northwich (0606) 882248. *Club:* Royal Liverpool Golf.

Died 19 Aug. 1992.

HAWKER, Albert Henry, CMG 1964; OBE 1960; *b* 31 Oct. 1911; *s* of late H. J. Hawker, Cheltenham and Mrs G. A. Hawker, Exeter; *m* 1944, Margaret Janet Olivia (*d* 1980), *d* of late T. J. C. Acton, ICS and Mrs M de C. Acton, BEM, Golden Furlong, Brackley, Northants; two *s*. *Educ:* Pate's Sch., Cheltenham. Served War of 1939–45: Bde Major 12th Bde, 1941–43; Staff Coll., Camberley, 1943–44; Lieut-Col, Mil. Asst to CGS in India, 1944–46; RARO; Lieut-Col The Gordon Highlanders, 1946–61. Barclays Bank Ltd, Birmingham and Oxford Local Districts, 1929–39. Joined HM Overseas Civil Service, 1946; served in: Palestine, 1946–48; N Rhodesia, 1948–52; Zanzibar, 1952–64 (Development Sec., Admin. Sec., Perm. Sec. in Min. of Finance, Prime Minister's Office, Vice-President's Office and President's Office); retd, 1964. Director: Thomson Regional Newspapers Ltd, 1965–69; The Times Ltd and The Sunday Times Ltd,

1968–69; The Thomson Organization, 1969–76. Gold Cross, Royal Order of George I of Greece, 1948; Brilliant Star of Zanzibar, 1957. *Recreations:* sailing (Cdre, Zanzibar Sailing Club, 1955 and 1961), gardening, photography. *Address:* Bowling Green Farm, Cottered, near Buntingford, Herts SG9 9PT. *T:* Cottered (076381) 234. *Clubs:* Commonwealth Trust, Royal Yachting Association. *Died 23 Dec. 1991.*

HAWKER, Sir (Frank) Cyril, Kt 1958; Chairman: The Chartered Bank, 1973–74; The Standard Bank Ltd, 1962–74; Standard and Chartered Banking Group, 1969–74; The Bank of West Africa, 1965–73; Union Zairoise de Banques, 1969–74; Director: Head Wrightson & Co. Ltd, 1962–79; Davy Corporation Ltd, 1977–79; Deputy-Chairman, Midland and International Banks, 1964–72; Vice President, National Playing Fields Association, since 1976 (Hon. Treasurer and Chairman, Finance Committee, 1958–76); *b* 21 July 1900; *s* of late Frank Charley and Bertha Mary Hawker; *m* 1931, Marjorie Ann, *d* of late Thomas Henry and Amelia Harriett Pearce; three *d. Educ:* City of London Sch. Entered service Bank of England, 1920; Dep. Chief Cashier, 1944–48; Chief Accountant, 1948–53; Adviser to Governors, 1953–54; Executive Director, 1954–62. Dep. Chm., Agricultural Mortgage Corporation, 1962–73. High Sheriff of County of London, 1963. President: MCC, 1970–71; Minor Counties Cricket Assoc., 1968–; Amateur Football Alliance, 1971–72; Hon. Vice-Pres., Football Assoc., 1970. *Recreation:* cricket. *Address:* Hadlow Lodge, Burgh Hill, Etchingham, E Sussex TN19 7PE. *T:* Hurst Green (058086) 341. *Clubs:* Athenæum, MCC (Hon. Life Mem.). *Died 22 Feb. 1991.*

HAWKES, (Charles Francis) Christopher, FBA 1948; FSA; Professor of European Archaeology in the University of Oxford, and Fellow of Keble College, 1946–72, Professor Emeritus, since 1972; Hon. Fellow of Keble College, since 1972; Secretary, Committee of Research Laboratory for Archæology and History of Art, 1955–72; *b* 5 June 1905; *o s* of late Charles Pascoe Hawkes; *m* 1st, 1933, Jacquetta (from whom he obtained a divorce 1953), *yr d* of late Sir Frederick Gowland Hopkins, OM; one *s*; 2nd, 1959, Sonia Elizabeth, *o d* of late Albert Andrew Chadwick. *Educ:* Winchester Coll. (Scholar); New Coll., Oxford (Scholar). 1st in Classical Hon. Mods 1926, in Final Lit.Hum. 1928; BA 1928; MA 1931. Entered British Museum, Dept of British and Medieval Antiquities, 1928; Asst Keeper 1st Class, 1938; in charge of Prehistoric and Romano-British Antiquities, 1946; retired from British Museum, 1946. Principal in Ministry of Aircraft Production, 1940–45. I/c Inst. of Archæology, Oxford, 1961–67, 1968–72. FSA 1932; Fellow of Royal Archæological Institute (Hon. Sec. 1930–35, and Hon. Editor of Archæological Journal, 1944–50); Pres., Prehistoric Soc., 1950–54; a National Sec. for Great Britain, 1931–48, Mem. of Permanent Council, 1948–71, and Mem. Cttee of Honour, 1971–, International Union of Prehistoric and Protohistoric Sciences; Hon. Sec. of Colchester Excavation Cttee and in joint charge of its excavations, 1930–61; in charge of, or associated with various excavations, 1925–64, on Roman and prehistoric sites, especially for the Hants Field Club, and near Oxford; conducted archæological expedns in N Portugal, 1958–59. Vis. Lectr, Univ. of Manchester, 1947–49; Lectures: Dalrymple, Univ. of Glasgow, 1948; George Grant McCurdy, Harvard Univ., 1953; Davies, Belfast, 1974; Myres Meml, Oxford, 1975; British Acad., and Accad. Naz. Lincei, Rome, 1975; Mortimer Wheeler, 1975; travelled in Europe as Leverhulme Research Fellow, 1955–58, and as Leverhulme Emeritus Fellow, 1972–73; Guest Academician, Budapest, 1971; Guest Prof., Univ. of Munich, 1974; a Visitor, Ashmolean Museum, 1961–67. President: Section H., Brit. Assoc., 1957; Hants Field Club, 1960–63; Member: Council for British Archæology 1944–72 (Pres., 1961–64; Group 9 Convener, 1964–67); Ancient Monuments Board for England, 1954–69. Mem., German Archaeological Inst.; Corresp. Mem., RIA; Swiss Soc. for Prehistory; Patronal Mem., Univ. of Barcelona Inst. of Archaeology and Prehistory. Editor of Inventaria Archæologica for Great Britain, 1954–76. Hon. Dr Rennes, 1971; Hon. DLitt NUI, 1972. Various British Acad. awards, 1963–; Gold Medal, Soc. of Antiquaries, 1981. *Publications:* St Catharine's Hill, Winchester (with J. N. L. Myres and C. G. Stevens), 1931; Archæology in England and Wales, 1914–31 (with T. D. Kendrick), 1932; Winchester College: An Essay in Description and Appreciation, 1933; The Prehistoric Foundations of Europe, 1940, repr. 1974; Prehistoric Britain (with Jacquetta Hawkes), 1943, new edn 1947, rev. edn 1958; Camulodunum: The Excavations at Colchester, 1930–39 (with M. R. Hull), 1947; (contrib. and ed with Sonia Hawkes) Archaeology into History, vol. I, 1973; (contrib. and ed with P. M. Duval) Celtic Art in Ancient Europe, 1976; (ed and co-author with M. R. Hull) Corpus of Ancient Brooches in Britain, vol. I, 1987; articles in encyclopædias, collaborative books, congress proceedings, and many archæological journals; received complimentary vol. by British and foreign colleagues, 1971; *relevant publication:* Hawkeseye: the early life of Christopher Hawkes, by Diana Bonakis Webster, 1991. *Recreations:* archæology, travelling, music. *Address:* Keble College, Oxford; 19 Walton Street, Oxford OX1 2HQ. *Died 29 March 1992.*

HAWKINS, Sir Humphry (Villiers) Cæsar, 7th Bt, *cr* 1778, of Kelston, Somersetshire; MB, ChB; medical practitioner; *b* 10 Aug. 1923; *s* of Sir Villiers Geoffry Caesar Hawkins, 6th Bt and Blanche Hawkins, *d* of A. E. Hampden-Smithers; *S* father 1955; *m* 1952, Anita, *d* of C. H. Funkey, Johannesburg; two *s* three *d. Educ:* Hilton Coll.; University of Witwatersrand. Served War of 1939–45 with 6th SA Armoured Div. *Heir: s* Howard Cæsar Hawkins, *b* 17 Nov. 1956. *Club:* Johannesburg Country. *Died 23 April 1993.*

HAWKSLEY, John Callis, CBE 1946; PhD, MD, FRCP; formerly Physician, University College Hospital and St Peter's, St Paul's and St Philip's Hospitals, London; *b* 30 Nov. 1903; *s* of late Joseph Hawksley, Great Yarmouth; *m* 1933, Margaret (*d* 1985), *er d* of late Engineer Vice-Adm. Sir Reginald Skelton, KCB, CBE, DSO; two *s* two *d. Educ:* Dulwich Coll.; University Coll., London; University Coll. Hospital. Appts on resident staff, University Coll. Hosp., 1926–28; ship's surg., British India Steam Navigation Co., 1929; research appts, Birmingham Children's Hosp., 1930–32; Sebag-Montefiore Research Fellow, Hospital for Sick Children, Gt Ormond Street, 1933–34; Bilton Pollard Travelling Fellowship, University Coll. Hosp., 1935, devoted to work at Bispebjerg Hosp., Copenhagen; Asst Physician, University Coll. Hosp., 1936–39; Physician to University Coll. Hosp., 1940; Fellow of University Coll., London, 1946; Dean of University Coll. Hosp. Med. Sch., 1949–54; retd, 1969. Temp. commission RAMC, 1939; served with rank of Lieut-Col in MEF, 1941–44 (despatches); Consulting Physician, local Brig., with South East Asia Command, 1945. Senior Vice-Pres., RCP, 1966. *Publications:* contributions to various medical journals. *Recreations:* mountaineering, music. *Address:* Pencombe Hall, Pencombe, near Bromyard, Herefordshire HR7 4RL. *Died 14 April 1993.*

HAY, Sir Arthur Thomas Erroll, 10th Bt (NS), *cr* 1663, of Park, Wigtownshire; ISO 1974; ARIBA 1935; retired Civil Servant; *b* 13 April 1909; *o s* of 9th Bt and Lizabel Annie (*d* 1957), *o d* of late Lachlan Mackinnon Macdonald, Skeabost, Isle of Skye; *S* father, 1923; *m* 1st, 1935, Hertha

Louise (who was granted a divorce, 1942), *d* of late Herr Ludwig Stölzle, Nagelberg, Austria, and H. E. Frau Vaugoin, Vienna; one *s*; 2nd, 1942, (Rosemarie Evelyn) Anne, *d* of late Vice-Adm. Aubrey Lambert and Mrs Lambert. *Educ:* Fettes Coll., Edinburgh. Student of architecture, University of Liverpool, 1927–31; Diploma in Architecture, Architectural Assoc., July 1934. Served War of 1939–45: 2nd Lieut RE, 1943; Lieut 1944; service in Normandy, Belgium, Holland and Germany in 21 Army Group. *Heir:* *s* John Erroll Audley Hay, *b* 3 Dec. 1935. *Address:* c/o Lloyds Bank, Castle Street, Farnham, Surrey.   *Died 4 Feb. 1993.*

HAY, Prof. Denys, MA; FBA 1970; FRSE 1977; Emeritus Professor of Medieval History, University of Edinburgh; *b* 29 Aug. 1915; *s* of Rev. W. K. Hay and Janet Waugh; *m* 1937, Sarah Gwyneth, *d* of S. E. Morley; one *s* two *d*. *Educ:* Royal Grammar Sch., Newcastle upon Tyne; Balliol Coll., Oxford. 1st Cl. hons, Modern History, 1937; senior demy, Magdalen Coll., 1937. Temporary Lecturer, Glasgow Univ., 1938; Bryce Studentship, Oxford Univ., 1939; Asst Lecturer, University Coll., Southampton, 1939; RASC, 1940–42; War Historian (Civil Depts), 1942–45; Lecturer, 1945, Professor of Medieval History, 1954–80, Emeritus Professor 1980, Edinburgh Univ. (Vice-Principal, 1971–75). Literary Dir, RHistS, 1955–58 (Hon. Life Vice-Pres., 1981). Lectures: Italian, British Acad., 1959; Wiles, QUB, 1960; Birkbeck, Trinity Coll., Cambridge, 1971–72; David Murray, Glasgow Univ., 1983; Visiting Professor: Cornell Univ., 1963; Univ. of Virginia, 1980; Prof. of History, European Univ. Inst., Badia Fiesolana, 1980–82; Senior Fellow, Newberry Library, Chicago, 1966. Trustee, Nat. Library of Scotland, 1966–88; President: Historical Association, 1967–70; Ecclesiastical Hist. Soc., 1980–81; Mem., Reviewing Cttee on Export of Works of Art, 1976–80. Editor, English Historical Review, 1958–65. Hon. For. Mem., Amer. Acad. of Arts and Scis, 1974. Hon. DLitt Newcastle, 1970; Hon. Dr Tours Univ., 1982. Comdr, Order of Merit, Italy, 1980. *Publications:* Anglica Historia of P. Vergil, 1950; Polydore Vergil, 1952; From Roman Empire to Renaissance Europe, 1953, 2nd edn as The Medieval Centuries, 1964; (ed) R. K. Hannay's Letters of James V, 1954; Europe: the emergence of an idea, 1957, new edn 1968; (ed) New Cambridge Modern History, Vol. I: The Renaissance, 1493–1520, 1957, new edn 1976; Italian Renaissance in its Historical Background, 1961, new edn 1976; Design and Development of Weapons (History of Second World War) (with M. M. Postan and J. D. Scott), 1964; Europe in the 14th and 15th Centuries, 1966, new edn 1989; (ed with W. K. Smith) Aeneas Sylvius Piccolomini, *De Gestis Concilii Basiliensis*, 1967, 2nd edn 1992; (ed) The Age of the Renaissance, 1967; Annalists and Historians, 1977; Italian Church in the 15th Century, 1977; Renaissance Essays, 1987; (with John Law) Italy in the Age of the Renaissance, 1989; articles in historical journals. *Address:* 5/11 Oswald Road, Edinburgh EH9 2HE. *T:* 031–667 2886. *Club:* United Oxford & Cambridge University.   *Died 14 June 1994.*

HAY, Frances Mary, (Mrs Roy Hay); *see* Perry, F. M.

HAYCRAFT, Colin Berry; Chairman, Gerald Duckworth & Co. Ltd, publishers, since 1971; *b* 12 Jan. 1929; *yr s* of Major W. C. S. Haycraft, MC and Bar, 5/8 Punjab Regt (killed 1929), and late Olive Lillian Esmée (*née* King); *m* 1956, Anna Margaret Lindholm; four *s* one *d* (and one *s* one *d* decd). *Educ:* Wellington Coll. (schol.); The Queen's Coll., Oxford (Open Schol. in Classics; 1st Cl. Classical Mods, 1st Cl. Lit.Hum., MA; Hon. Fellow, 1990). Nat. service (army), 1947–49. Personal Asst to Chm., Cecil H. King, Daily Mirror Newspapers Ltd; Dir, Weidenfeld & Nicolson Ltd and Weidenfeld (Publishers) Ltd (original editor and subseq. Man. Dir, World University Library

Ltd); joined Duckworth, 1968. Pres., Classical Assoc., 1993–94. Public Schs Rackets Champion (singles and pairs), 1946; Oxford blue for Squash Rackets (4 years, Captain OU Squash Rackets Club; Eng. internat.), Lawn Tennis (Devon Co. player) and Rackets. *Address:* 22 Gloucester Crescent, NW1 7DS. *T:* 0171–485 7408. *Clubs:* Beefsteak; Vincent's (Oxford); Jesters; Queen's.
                                        Died 24 Sept. 1994.

HAYEK, Friedrich August (von), CH 1984; FBA 1944; Dr Jur, DScPol, Vienna; DSc (Econ.) London; *b* Vienna, 8 May 1899; *s* of late August von Hayek, Prof. of Botany at University of Vienna, and Felizitas von Juraschek; certificate of naturalisation, 1938; *m* 1st, Hella von Fritsch (*d* 1960); one *s* one *d*; 2nd, Helene Bitterlich. *Educ:* University of Vienna. Austrian Civil Service, 1921–26; Dir, Austrian Institute for Economic Research, 1927–31; Lecturer in Economics, University of Vienna, 1929–31; Tooke Prof. of Economic Science and Statistics in University of London, 1931–50; Prof. of Social and Moral Science, University of Chicago, 1950–62; Prof. of Economics, Univ. of Freiburg, 1962–69. Chm., Adam Smith Inst. Hon. Fellow: LSE; Austrian Acad. of Scis; American Economic Assoc.; Hoover Inst. on War, Revolution and Peace; Argentine Acad. of Economic Sci.; Academia Sinica. Dr jur *hc*: Rikkyo Univ., Tokyo, 1964; Univ. of Salzburg, 1974; Dr Lit. Hum. *hc* Univ. of Dallas, 1975; Hon. Dr Soc. Sci., Marroquin Univ., Guatemala, 1977; Hon. Dr: Santa Maria Univ., Valparaiso, 1977; Univ. of Buenos Aires, 1977; Univ. of Giessen, 1982. Nobel Prize in Economic Science (jtly), 1974. Austrian Distinction for Science and Art, 1975; Mem., Orden pour le Mérite für Wissenschaften und Künste, Fed. Rep. of Germany, 1977; Medal of Merit, Baden-Württemberg, 1981; Ring of Honour, City of Vienna, 1983; Gold Medal, City of Paris, 1984; Grosse Goldene Ehrenzeichen mit dem Stern für Verdienste (Austria), 1990. *Publications:* Prices and Production, 1931; Monetary Theory and the Trade Cycle, 1933 (German edition, 1929); Monetary Nationalism and International Stability, 1937; Profits, Interest, and Investment, 1939; The Pure Theory of Capital, 1941; The Road to Serfdom, 1944; Individualism and Economic Order, 1948; John Stuart Mill and Harriet Taylor, 1950; The Counter-revolution of Science, 1952; The Sensory Order, 1952; The Political Ideal of the Rule of Law, 1955; The Constitution of Liberty, 1960; Studies in Philosophy, Politics and Economics, 1967; Freiburger Studien, 1969; Law, Legislation & Liberty, vol. I: Rules and Order, 1973, Vol II: The Mirage of Social Justice, 1976, Vol. III: The Political Order of a Free People, 1979; De-Nationalisation of Money, 1976; New Studies in Philosophy, Politics, Economics and the History of Ideas, 1978; The Fatal Conceit, 1988; edited: Beiträge zur Geldtheorie, 1933; Collectivist Economic Planning, 1935; Capitalism and the Historians, 1954; and the works of H. H. Gossen, 1927; F. Wieser, 1929; C. Menger, 1933–36; and H. Thornton, 1939; articles in Economic Journal, Economica, and other English and foreign journals. *Address:* Urachstrasse 27, D-7800 Freiburg im Breisgau, West Germany. *Club:* Reform.
                                        Died 23 March 1992.

HAYES, Helen, (Mrs Charles MacArthur); actress; *b* Washington, DC, 10 Oct. 1900; *d* of Francis Van Arnum Brown and Catherine Estelle Hayes; *m* 1928, Charles MacArthur (*d* 1956); one *s* (one *d* decd). *Educ:* Sacred Heart Academy, Washington, DC. As actress appeared in USA in stage plays, among others: Pollyanna, Dear Brutus, Clarence, Bab, Coquette, The Good Fairy, To the Ladies, Young Blood, Mary of Scotland, Victoria Regina, Ladies and Gentlemen, Twelfth Night, Harriet, Happy Birthday; The Wisteria Trees, 1950; Mrs McThing, 1952; first appearance in England in The Glass Menagerie, 1948; also radio actress; appeared in films: Farewell to Arms,

The Sin of Madelon Claudet, Arrowsmith, The Son-Daughter, My Son John, Anastasia, Airport (Best Supporting Actress Award, 1971), Candleshoe, etc. Awarded gold statuette by Motion Picture Academy of Arts and Sciences, 1932, as outstanding actress, based on performance in the Sin of Madelon Claudet. Hon. degrees: Smith Coll., Hamilton Coll., Columbia Univ., Princeton Univ., St Mary's Coll. Medal of Freedom, 1986. *Publications:* A Gift of Joy, 1965; On Reflection, 1968; (with Anita Loos) Twice Over Lightly, 1971; (with Marion Glasserow Gladney) Our Best Years, 1984; (with Katherine Hatch) My Life in Three Acts, 1990; *relevant publication:* Front Page Marriage: Helen Hayes and Charles MacArthur, by Jhan Robbins, 1982. *Address:* Nyack, New York, NY 10960, USA. *Clubs:* Cosmopolitan, River, etc.   *Died 17 March 1993.*

HAYES, Prof. William, FRS 1964; FRSE 1968; FAA 1976; Professor and Head of the Department of Genetics, Research School of Biological Sciences, Australian National University, 1974–78, then Emeritus; *b* 18 Jan. 1913; *s* of William Hayes and Miriam (*née* Harris), Co. Dublin, Ireland; *m* 1941, Honora Lee; one *s. Educ:* College of St Columba, Rathfarnham, Co. Dublin; Dublin Univ. BA (1st Cl. Mods Nat. Sci.) Dublin, 1936; MB, BCh Dublin, 1937; FRCPI 1945; ScD Dublin, 1949. Served in India as Major, RAMC, Specialist in Pathology, 1942–46. Lectr in Bacteriology, Trinity Coll., Dublin, 1947–50; Sen. Lectr in Bacteriology, Postgraduate Medical Sch. of London, 1950–57, later Hon. Senior Lectr; Dir, MRC Molecular Genetics Unit, 1957–68, Hon. Dir 1968–73; Prof. of Molecular Genetics, Univ. of Edinburgh, 1968–73; Sherman Fairchild Dist. Scholar, Div. of Biology, California Inst. of Technology, 1979–80; Vis. Fellow, Botany Dept, ANU, 1980–86; retired 1987. Hon. Mem., Société Française de Microbiologie, 1988. Hon. Fellow, RPMS, 1985; Hon. DSc: Leicester, 1966; NUI, 1973; Kent, 1973; Hon. LLD Dublin, 1970. *Publication:* The Genetics of Bacteria and their Viruses, 1964. *Recreations:* painting, reading or doing nothing. *Address:* 634/40 Pennant Hills Road, Normanhurst, NSW 2076, Australia.
Died 7 Jan. 1994.

HAYMAN, Sir Peter (Telford), KCMG 1971 (CMG 1963); CVO 1965; MBE 1945; HM Diplomatic Service, retired; *b* 14 June 1914; *s* of C. H. T. Hayman, The Manor House, Brackley, Northants; *m* 1942, Rosemary Eardley Blomefield; one *s* one *d. Educ:* Stowe; Worcester Coll., Oxford. Asst Principal: Home Office, 1937–39; Min. of Home Security, 1939–41; Asst Priv. Sec. to Home Sec. (Rt Hon. Herbert Morrison, MP), 1941–42; Principal, Home Office, 1942. Served War, 1942–45, Rifle Bde, Major. Principal, Home Office, 1945–49; transf. to Min. of Defence as Personal Asst to Chief Staff Officer to the Minister, 1949–52; Asst Sec., Min. of Defence, 1950; UK Delegation to NATO, 1952–54; transf. to FO, 1954; Counsellor, Belgrade, 1955–58; seconded for temp. duty with Governor of Malta, 1958; Counsellor, Baghdad, 1959–61; Dir-Gen. of British Information Services, New York, 1961–64; Minister and Dep. Comdt, Brit. Milit. Govt in Berlin, 1964–66; Asst Under-Sec., FO, 1966–69; Dep. Under-Secretary of State, FCO, 1969–70; High Comr in Canada, 1970–74. *Publication:* Soult, Napoleon's Maligned Marshal, 1990. *Recreations:* fishing, travel. *Address:* Uxmore House, Checkendon, Oxon RG8 0TY. *T:* Checkendon (0491) 680658. *Club:* MCC.
Died 6 April 1992.

HAYMAN, Rev. Canon William Samuel; Chaplain to the Queen's Household, 1961–73; *b* 3 June 1903; *s* of late Rev. William Henry Hayman, Rector of Leckford, and Louise Charlotte Hayman; *m* 1930, Rosemary Prideaux Metcalfe; one *s* one *d. Educ:* Merchant Taylors' Sch.; St John's Coll., Oxford (MA). Deacon, 1926; priest, 1927;

Curate: St Matthew, Brixton, 1926–32; Wimbledon (in charge of St Mark), 1932–34; Vicar of Finstall, Worcs, 1934–38; Rector of Cheam, 1938–72; Hon. Canon of Southwark, 1952–60, Canon Emeritus, 1972; Rural Dean of Beddington, 1955–60; Archdeacon of Lewisham, 1960–72. Scouts Silver Acorn, 1971. *Recreations:* fly-fishing, photography, music. *Address:* 8 Black Jack Mews, Cirencester, Glos GL7 2AA. *T:* Cirencester (0285) 655024.   *Died 7 Feb. 1993.*

HAYNES, Denys Eyre Lankester; Keeper of Greek and Roman Antiquities, British Museum, 1956–76; *b* 15 Feb. 1913; 2nd *s* of late Rev. Hugh Lankester Haynes and Emmeline Marianne Chaldecott; *m* 1951, Sybille Edith Overhoff. *Educ:* Marlborough; Trinity Coll., Cambridge. Scholar, British School at Rome, 1936; Asst Keeper: Victoria and Albert Museum, 1937; British Museum, 1939–54 (released for war service, 1939–45); Dep. Keeper, British Museum, 1954. Geddes-Harrower Prof. of Greek Art and Archaeology, Univ. of Aberdeen, 1972–73. Chm., Soc. for Libyan Studies, 1974. Corr. Mem., German Archæological Inst., 1953; Ordinary Mem., 1957. Visitor, Ashmolean Museum, 1979–85. Lectures: Burlington, 1976; Brown and Hayley, Univ. of Puget Sound, 1977. *Publications:* Porta Argentariorum, 1939; Ancient Tripolitania, 1946; Antiquities of Tripolitania, 1956; The Parthenon Frieze, 1958; The Portland Vase, 1964; Fifty Masterpieces of Classical Art, 1970; The Arundel Marbles, 1975; Greek Art and the Idea of Freedom, 1981; The Technique of Greek Bronze Statuary, 1992. *Address:* Flat 17, Murray Court, 80 Banbury Road, Oxford OX2 6LQ.
Died 27 Sept. 1994.

HAYNES, Edwin William George, CB 1971; *b* 10 Dec. 1911; *s* of Frederick William George Haynes and Lilian May Haynes (*née* Armstrong); *m* 1942, Dorothy Kathleen Coombs; one *s* one *d. Educ:* Regent Street Polytechnic Secondary Sch.; University of London (BA, LLM). Barrister-at-law, Lincoln's Inn, 1946. Estate Duty Office, Inland Revenue, 1930–39; Air Min., 1939; Min. of Aircraft Production, 1940; Min. of Supply, 1946; Min. of Aviation, 1959; Under-Sec., 1964; Under-Sec., DTI (formerly Min. of Technology), 1968–71; Chief Exec. Officer, later Sec., Covent Garden Market Authority, 1971–81. *Address:* 92 Malmains Way, Beckenham, Kent. *Club:* Civil Service.
Died 8 May 1992.

HAYTER, Sir William Goodenough, KCMG 1953 (CMG 1948); Warden of New College, Oxford, 1958–76, Hon. Fellow, 1976; *b* 1 Aug. 1906; *s* of late Sir William Goodenough Hayter, KBE and Alethea, 2nd *d* of Rev. J. H. Slessor; *m* 1938, Iris Marie, *d* of late Lieut-Col C. H. Grey (formerly Hoare), DSO; one *d. Educ:* Winchester; New Coll., Oxford. Entered HM Diplomatic Service, 1930; served Foreign Office, 1930; Vienna, 1931; Moscow, 1934; Foreign Office, 1937; China, 1938; Washington, 1941; Foreign Office, 1944 (Asst Under-Sec. of State, 1948); HM Minister, Paris, 1949; Ambassador to USSR, 1953–57; Deputy Under-Sec. of State, Foreign Office, 1957–58. Fellow of Winchester Coll., 1958–76. Trustee, British Museum, 1960–70. Hon. DLitt Bristol, 1976; Grosses Goldenes Ehrenzeichen mit dem Stern für Verdienste (Austria), 1967. *Publications:* The Diplomacy of the Great Powers, 1961; The Kremlin and the Embassy, 1966; Russia and the World, 1970; William of Wykeham, Patron of the Arts, 1970; A Double Life (autobiog.), 1974; Spooner, 1977. *Address:* Bassetts House, Stanton St John, Oxford OX9 1EX. *T:* Oxford (01865) 351598.
Died 28 March 1995.

HAYWARD, Sir Richard (Arthur), Kt 1969; CBE 1966; *b* 14 March 1910; *s* of Richard Bolton Hayward; *m* 1936, Ethel Wheatcroft (*d* 1993); one *s* one *d. Educ:* Catford Central Sch. Post Office: Boy Messenger; Counter Clerk; Union of Post Office Workers: Assistant Secretary, 1947;

Deputy General Secretary, 1951. Secretary General, Civil Service National Whitley Council (Staff Side), 1955–66; Chm., Supplementary Benefits Commn, 1966–69; Member, Post Office Board, 1969–71; Chairman: NHS Staff Commn, 1972–75; New Towns Staff Commn, 1976–77; Member: Civil Service Security Appeals Panel, 1967–82; Home Office Adv. Panel on Security (Immigration Act 1972), 1972–81; Parole Board, England and Wales, 1975–79; Solicitors' Disciplinary Tribunal, 1975–82. UK Rep., Meeting of Experts on Conditions of Work and Service of Public Servants, ILO, 1963; overseas visits, inc. Israel, Mauritius, Canada, to advise on Trade Unionism in Public Services. Life Vice-President: Civil Service Sports Council, 1973 (Chm., 1968–73); Assoc. of Kent Cricket Clubs, 1984 (Pres., 1970–84); President: Civil Service Cricket Assoc., 1967–91; Civil Service Assoc. Football, 1974–91 (Patron, 1991); Hon. Life Member: Nat. Assoc. of Young Cricketers, 1975; XL Club, 1990. Governor, Guy's Hosp., 1949–72. Freedom, City of London, 1980. *Publication:* (with A. J. Phelps) A History of Civil Service Cricket. *Recreation:* topography of Southwark, including collecting 17th century tradesmen's tokens. *Address:* Lower Cowley, Parracombe, Barnstaple, N Devon EX31 4PQ. *T:* Parracombe (05983) 373. *Clubs:* MCC, Civil Service.

Died 26 Feb. 1994.

HEADLEY, 7th Baron *cr* 1797 (Ire.); **Charles Rowland Allanson-Winn;** Bt 1660 and 1776; retired; *b* 19 May 1902; 2nd *s* of 5th Baron Headley and Teresa (*d* 1919), *y d* of late W. H. Johnson; *S* brother, 1969; *m* 1927, Hilda May Wells-Thorpe (*d* 1989); three *d* (one *s* decd). *Educ:* Bedford School. *Recreations:* golf, fishing. *Heir:* none. *Address:* Dreys, 7 Silverwood, West Chiltington, Pulborough, W Sussex RH20 2NG. *T:* West Chiltington (0798) 813083. *Died 23 Feb. 1994 (ext).*

HEAL, Anthony Standerwick; Head of the Business, Heal & Son Holdings plc, 1981–84; *b* 23 Feb. 1907; *s* of Sir Ambrose Heal and 2nd wife, Lady (Edith Florence Digby) Heal; *m* 1941, Theodora Caldwell (*née* Griffin) (*d* 1992); two *s*. *Educ:* Leighton Park Sch., Reading. Joined Heal & Son Ltd 1929; Dir 1936; Chm., Heal & Son, later Heal & Son Hldgs, Ltd, 1952–81. Chm. Council, London and S Eastern Furniture Manufrs Assoc., 1947–48; Master, Furniture Makers Guild (latterly Worshipful Co. of Furniture Makers), 1959–60; Mem. Council of Industrial Design, 1959–67; Mem. Council, City and Guilds of London Inst., 1969–81, Chm., Licentiateship Cttee, 1976–79; Pres., Design and Industries Assoc., 1965; Chm. Indep. Stores Assoc., 1970–72. Hon. FCSD (Hon. FSIA 1974); Hon. FCGI 1981. RSA Bi-Centenary Medal, 1964. Order of White Rose of Finland, 1970; Chevalier (First Class) Order of Dannebrog, 1974. *Recreations:* vintage cars, steam engines. *Address:* Baylins Farm, Knotty Green, Beaconsfield, Bucks HP9 2TN. *Clubs:* Vintage Sports Car, National Traction Engine.

Died 25 March 1995.

HEANEY, Brig. Sheila Anne Elizabeth, CB 1973; MBE 1955; TD; Chairman, Women's Royal Voluntary Service, Scotland, 1977–81; *b* 11 June 1917; 2nd *d* of late Francis James Strong Heaney, MA, MD, FRCSI, Liverpool and Anne Summers McBurney. *Educ:* Huyton Coll.; Liverpool University. BA 1938. Joined ATS, 1939, WRAC, 1949; Director, WRAC, and Hon. ADC to the Queen, 1970–73. *Address:* c/o Midland Bank, 32 Rodney Street, Liverpool L1 2TP. *Died 1 Feb. 1991.*

HEARN, Rear-Adm. Frank Wright, CB 1977; Assistant Chief of Personnel and Logistics, Ministry of Defence, 1974–77; *b* 1 Oct. 1919; *s* of John Henry Hearn, Civil Servant, and Elsie Gertrude Hearn; *m* 1st, 1947, Ann Cynthia Keeble (*d* 1964); two *d*; 2nd, 1965, Ann Christina June St Clair Miller. *Educ:* Abbotsholme Sch., Derbyshire.

Joined RN, 1937; HMS Hood, 1937–39; served War of 1939–45 in various HM Ships in Atlantic, Mediterranean and East Indies; Staff of C-in-C, Home Fleet, 1951–53; Sec. to Flag Officer, Submarines, 1954–56; after service in USA became Sec. to Dir of Naval Intell., 1958–60, when joined HMS Tiger as Supply Officer; Fleet Supply Officer, Western Fleet, 1962–64; subseq. service in Plans Div., MoD (Navy) and CSO (Admin) to Flag Officer, Submarines; IDC 1969; commanded HMS Centurion in rank of Cdre, 1970–73; Chm., Review of Officer Structure Cttee, 1973–74. *Recreations:* golf, tennis, gardening, wine-making. *Address:* Hurstbrook Cottage, Hollybank Lane, Emsworth, Hants PO10 7UE. *T:* Emsworth (0243) 372149. *Died 13 Feb. 1993.*

HEARNSHAW, Prof. Leslie Spencer; Professor of Psychology, University of Liverpool, 1947–75, then Emeritus; *b* Southampton, 9 Dec. 1907; *o s* of late Prof. F. J. C. Hearnshaw, Prof. of History, King's Coll., London, and D. M. Spencer; *m* 1937, Gwenneth R. Dickins, Perth, Western Australia; one *s* three *d*. *Educ:* King's Coll. Sch., Wimbledon; Christ Church, Oxford; King's Coll., London. 1st Class Lit.Hum., 1930; 1st Class Psychology Hons (London), 1932. Investigator, Nat. Institute of Industrial Psychology, London, 1933–38; Lecturer in Psychology, Victoria Univ. Coll., Wellington, NZ, 1939–47; Dir, Industrial Psychology Div., DSIR, Wellington, NZ, 1942–47. Mem. of Council, British Psychological Soc., 1949–57 (Chm., Industrial Section, 1953–54); Pres., British Psychological Soc., 1955–56; Pres. Section J (Psychology), Brit. Assoc., 1954; Hon. Dir, Medical Research Council, Research Group into occupational aspects of ageing, 1955–59, 1963–70. Hobhouse Memorial Lecturer, 1966. Vice-Pres., International Assoc. of Applied Psychology, and Editor of its Journal, 1964–74. *Publications:* (with R. Winterbourn) Human Welfare and Industrial Efficiency, 1945; A Short History of British Psychology, 1840–1940, 1964; Cyril Burt, psychologist, 1979; The Shaping of Modern Psychology, 1987; articles on industrial psychology and the psychology of thinking. *Address:* 1 Devonshire Road, West Kirby, Wirral L48 7HR. *T:* 051-625 5823. *Died 10 June 1991.*

HEARST, William Randolph, Jun.; journalist; Editor-in-Chief, The Hearst Newspapers, and Chairman of the Executive Committee, The Hearst Corporation; *b* NYC, 27 Jan. 1908; *s* of William Randolph Hearst and Millicent Veronica (*née* Willson); *m* 1st, 1928, Alma Walker (marr. diss. 1932); 2nd, 1933, Lorelle McCarver (marr. diss. 1948); 3rd, 1948, Austine McDonnell (*d* 1991); two *s*. *Educ:* Collegiate Sch.; St John's Manlius Mil. Acad., Syracuse; Berkeley High Sch., Berkeley, Calif; Hitchcock Mil. Acad., San Rafael, Calif; University of Calif. Began career with New York American, NYC, as a reporter, 1928; publisher, 1936–37; publisher: NY Journal-American, 1937–56; The American Weekly, 1945–56. War Correspondent, 1943–45; Mem. Bd, United Service Orgn, NY. Permanent Charter Mem., For. Correspondents Club of Japan, 1945–. *Address:* (office) 959 Eighth Avenue, New York, NY 10019, USA. *Clubs:* Press; Overseas Press, Madison Square Garden, Knickerbocker (New York City); Waccabuc (N Salem, NY); Pacific Union (San Francisco); Alaska Press; Tokyo Press.

Died 14 May 1993.

HEATON, Ralph Neville, CB 1951; *b* 4 June 1912; *s* of late Ernest Heaton; *m* 1939, Cecily Margaret Alabaster; three *s* one *d*. *Educ:* Westminster; Christ Church, Oxford. Formerly Deputy Secretary various Govt Depts, including Education, Transport, and Economic Affairs. Commonwealth Fund Fellow, 1951–52. *Address:* 38 Manor Park Avenue, Princes Risborough, Bucks HP27 9AS. *Died 18 Aug. 1994.*

HEBBLETHWAITE, Peter; Vatican Affairs Writer for The National Catholic Reporter (USA), since 1979; *b* 30 Sept. 1930; *s* of Charles and Elsie Ann Hebblethwaite; *m* 1974, Margaret I. M. Speaight; two *s* one *d*. *Educ:* Xaverian Coll., Manchester; Campion Hall, Oxford; Heythrop Coll., Oxon. MA (1st Cl.) Oxford; LTh. Joined SJ, 1948; ordained priest, 1963; Editor, The Month, a Jesuit review of Church and world affairs, 1965–73; resigned from priesthood and SJ, 1974; Asst Editor, Frontier, 1974–76; Lectr in French, Wadham Coll., Oxford, 1976–79; thence to Rome as free-lance and Vatican Affairs Writer, for National Catholic Reporter, 1979–. *Publications:* Georges Bernanos, 1965; The Council Fathers and Atheism, 1966; Theology of the Church, 1968; The Runaway Church, 1975; Christian-Marxist Dialogue and Beyond, 1977; The Year of Three Popes, 1978; The New Inquisition?, 1981; The Papal Year, 1981; Introducing John Paul II, the Populist Pope, 1982; John XXIII, Pope of the Council, 1984; Synod Extraordinary, 1986; In the Vatican, 1986; Paul VI, the first modern Pope, 1993; contribs to TLS, Guardian, Tablet etc. *Recreation:* singing songs, Lieder and chansons. *Address:* 45 Marston Street, Oxford OX4 1JU. *T:* Oxford (01865) 723771, *Fax:* (01865) 200178.

Died 18 Dec. 1994.

HEEPS, William, CBE 1990; Chairman, Thomson Regional Newspapers Ltd, 1984–92 (Chief Executive, 1984–90); Director: The Thomson Corp. (formerly International Thomson plc, and International Thomson Organisation plc), 1984–92; Thomson Television, 1984–92; *b* 4 Dec. 1929; *er s* of late William Headrick Heeps and Margaret Munro Heeps; *m* 1st, 1956, Anne Robertson Paton (*d* 1974); two *d*; 2nd, 1983, Jennifer Rosemary Bartlett; one step *d*. *Educ:* Graeme High School, Falkirk. Journalist, Falkirk Mail, Linlithgowshire Jl and Gazette, Daily Record, Evening News and Dispatch, Edinburgh; Editor, Evening Gazette, Middlesbrough, 1966–68; Managing Director: Celtic Newspapers, 1968–71; North Eastern Evening Gazette, Middlesbrough, 1972–75; Evening Post-Echo, Hemel Hempstead, 1976–78; Thomson Magazines, 1978–80; Thomson Data, 1980–82; Editorial Dir, Thomson Regional Newspapers, 1982, Man. Dir and Editor-in-Chief, 1983. Chairman: IP Ltd, 1993; Cavedene Ltd, 1993. Pres., Newspaper Soc., 1988–89 (Mem. Council, 1984–). Trustee, Thomson Foundn, 1986–. Hon. Vice-Pres., Boys' Bde, 1990. Chm., Royal Caledonian Schools, 1986–. Elder, Church of Scotland. CIMgt (CBIM 1988). *Recreations:* travel, bridge. *Address:* The Old Vicarage, Pipers Hill, Great Gaddesden, Herts HP1 3BY. *T:* Hemel Hempstead (01442) 253524. *Club:* Caledonian.

Died 1 Feb. 1995.

HEFFER, Eric Samuel; MP (Lab) Walton Division of Liverpool, since 1964; *b* 12 Jan. 1922; *s* of William George Heffer and Annie Heffer (*née* Nicholls); *m* 1945, Doris Murray. *Educ:* Bengeo Junior Sch. and Longmore Senior Sch., Hertford. Apprenticed carpenter/joiner, 1936, and worked at the trade until 1964. Served RAF, 1942–45. Pres. Liverpool Trades Council and Labour Party, 1959–60, 1964–65, and Vice-Pres., 1960 and 1964. Liverpool City Councillor, 1960–66. Member: Council of Europe, 1965–68; WEU, 1965–68 (served on political, social and financial cttees). Labour front bench spokesman on industrial relations, 1970–72; Minister of State, Dept of Industry, 1974–75; Mem., Shadow Cabinet, 1981–; Labour spokesman on European affairs, 1981–83, on housing and construction, 1983–. Mem., Lab. Party Nat. Exec. Cttee, 1975–86; Vice-Chm., Labour Party, 1982–83, Chm., 1983–84. *Publications:* (jtly) The Agreeable Autocracies, 1961 (USA); (jtly) Election 70, 1970; The Class Struggle in Parliament, 1973; Labour's Future: socialist—or SDP mark 2?, 1986; (jtly) Faith in Politics, 1987; articles in Tribune, Liverpool Daily Post, The Times,

Guardian, Daily Telegraph, New Statesmen, Spectator, New Outlook, Labour Voice, New Left Review, and in foreign jls; *posthumous publications:* Never a Yes Man: the life and politics of an adopted Liverpudlian (autobiog.), 1991; Why I Am a Christian, 1991. *Recreations:* hill-walking, mountaineering. *Address:* House of Commons, SW1.

Died 27 May 1991.

HELE, Sir Ivor (Henry Thomas), Kt 1983; CBE 1969 (OBE 1954); artist; *b* 13 June 1912; *s* of Arthur Hele and Ethel May Hele; *m* 1957, May E. Weatherly. *Educ:* Prince Alfred Coll., Adelaide. Studied art in Paris, Munich and Italy, 1929–32. Enlisted AIF, 1940; War Artist: ME and New Guinea, 1941–46; Korea, 1952. Work represented in: National War Meml, Canberra; King's Hall, Parlt House, Canberra; various national galls. Archibald Prize, 1951, 1953, 1954, 1955 and 1957. *Relevant publications:* The Art of Ivor Hele, by Vernon Branson, 1966; Ivor Hele: the soldier's artist, by Gavin Fry, 1984. *Recreations:* swimming, gardening. *Address:* Box 35, Aldinga, SA 5173, Australia.

Died 12 Dec. 1993.

HELLYER, Arthur George Lee, MBE 1967; FLS; Gardening Correspondent to the Financial Times; Editor of Amateur Gardening, 1946–67; Editor of Gardening Illustrated, 1947–56; *b* 16 Dec. 1902; *s* of Arthur Lee Hellyer and Maggie Parlett; *m* 1933, Grace Charlotte Bolt (*d* 1977); two *s* one *d*. *Educ:* Dulwich Coll. Farming in Jersey, 1918–21; Nursery work in England, 1921–29; Asst Editor of Commercial Horticulture, 1929; Asst Editor of Amateur Gardening, 1929–46. Associate of Honour of Royal Horticultural Society; Victoria Medal of Honour in Horticulture. *Publications:* Your New Garden, 1937; Your Garden Week by Week, 1938; Amateur Gardening Pocket Guide, 1941, 4th rev. edn 1971; The Amateur Gardener, 1948, 4th rev. edn 1972; Encyclopaedia of Plant Portraits, 1953; Encyclopaedia of Garden Work and Terms, 1954; Flowers in Colour, 1955; English Gardens Open to the Public, 1956; Amateur Gardening Popular Encyclopaedia of Flowering Plants, 1957; Garden Plants in Colour, 1958; Garden Pests and Diseases, 1966; Starting with Roses, 1966; Shrubs in Colour, 1966, rev. edn as The Collingridge Book of Ornamental Garden Shrubs, 1981; Find Out About Gardening, 1967; Gardens to Visit in Britain, 1970; Your Lawn, 1970; Carter's Book for Gardeners, 1970; All Colour Gardening Book, 1972; All Colour Book of Indoor and Greenhouse Plants, 1973; Picture Dictionary of Popular Flowering Plants, 1973; Bulbs Indoors, 1976; The Collingridge Encyclopaedia of Gardening, 1976; Shell Guide to Gardens, 1977; Gardens of Genius, 1980; The Dobies Book of Greenhouses, 1981; Gardening Through the Year, 1981; Garden Shrubs, 1982; Climbing and Wall Plants, 1988. *Recreations:* gardening, photography, travelling. *Address:* Orchard Cottage, Rowfant, near Crawley, West Sussex RH10 4NJ. *T:* Copthorne (0342) 714838.

Died 28 Jan. 1993.

HELMSING, Most Rev. Charles Herman; Bishop (RC) of Kansas City-St Joseph, 1962–77, retired; *b* 23 March 1908; *s* of George Helmsing and Louise Helmsing (*née* Boschert). *Educ:* St Michael's Parochial Sch.; St Louis Preparatory Seminary; Kenrick Seminary. Sec. to Archbishop of St Louis, 1946–49; Auxiliary Bishop to Archbishop of St Louis, and Titular Bishop of Axum, 1949; first Bishop, Diocese of Springfield-Cape Girardeau, Mo, 1956–62. Member: Secretariat of Christian Unity, 1963–76; US Bishops Cttee for Ecumenical Affairs, 1964–76; Preparatory Cttee for Dialogue between Anglican Communion and Roman Catholic Church, 1966–67 (Chm., Roman Catholic Members); Chm., Special Cttee for Dialogue with Episcopal Church, US, 1964–76. Hon. Doctorates: Letters: Avila Coll. 1962; Humanities, Rockhurst Coll., 1963; Law: St Benedict's Coll. 1966. Order of Condor, Bolivia, 1966. *Address:*

Cathedral House, 416 West 12th, Kansas City, MO 64105, USA. *Died 20 Dec. 1993.*

HEMINGWAY, Albert, MSc, MB, ChB; Emeritus Professor, University of Leeds (Professor of Physiology, 1936–67); *b* 27 July 1902; *s* of Herbert Hemingway, Leeds; *m* 1930, Margaret Alice Cooper; one *d. Educ:* University of Leeds. Demonstrator in Physiology, King's Coll., London, 1925; Senior Asst in Physiology, University Coll., London, 1926; Lecturer in Experimental Physiology, Welsh National Sch. of Medicine, 1927. Vis. Prof., Makerere University Coll., Uganda, 1968. Examiner in Physiology, Universities of St Andrews, Birmingham, Bristol, Cambridge, Durham, Glasgow, Liverpool, London, Manchester, Wales and RCS. Mem. various cttees of MRC on work and exercise physiology; Mem. Cttee, Physiological Soc. (Editor, Jl Physiology); Pres., Section I, British Assoc., 1959. *Publications:* original papers on the physiology of the circulation, exercise and the kidney in scientific and medical journals. *Recreation:* travel. *Address:* 4 Helmsley Drive, Leeds LS16 5HY. *T:* Leeds (0532) 785720. *Died 27 Jan. 1993.*

HEMS, Dr (Benjamin) Arthur, FRS 1969; FRIC; Managing Director, Glaxo Research, 1965–75; *b* 29 June 1912; *er s* of B. A. Hems and L. D. Hems; *m* 1937, Jean Douglas Herd; one *s* one *d. Educ:* Glasgow High Sch.; Glasgow Univ. (BSc); Edinburgh Univ. (PhD); DSc 1951. Joined Glaxo, 1937. Former Mem., SRC. Member: Chem. Soc.; SCI. Hon. LLD Glasgow, 1970. *Recreations:* golf, avoiding gardening. *Address:* Ickenham, Middlesex. *Died 2 July 1995.*

HENDERSON, Edward Firth, CMG 1972; HM Diplomatic Service, retired; *b* 12 Dec. 1917; *m* 1960, Jocelyn (*née* Nenk), MBE; two *d. Educ:* Clifton Coll.; BNC, Oxford. Served War of 1939–45 in Army (despatches); served in Arab Legion, 1945–47. With Petroleum Concessions Ltd, in Arabian Gulf, 1948–56; Foreign Service, 1956; served in Middle East posts and in Foreign Office; Political Agent, Qatar, 1969–71, and Ambassador there 1971–74. Lectr and Res. Schol., Sch. of Advanced Internat. Studies, Johns Hopkins Univ., 1976, 1977 and 1979; Lectr, Univs of Texas, NY and Princeton, 1979; Hon. Fellow, LSE, 1980–81. Research specialist, Centre for Documentation and Res., Presidential Court, Abu Dhabi, 1976–81; Dir, Council for the Advancement of Arab-British Understanding, 1981–82; Chm., Amer. Educnl Trust, Washington, DC, 1982–83. Returned to Abu Dhabi as res. specialist, 1984. *Publication:* This Strange Eventful History: memoirs of earlier days in the UAE and Oman, 1988 (trans. Arabic and Japanese). *Address:* 2 The Gallery, Northwick Park, Blockley, Moreton-in-Marsh GL56 9RJ; PO Box 2841, Abu Dhabi, United Arab Emirates. *T:* (2) 478386. *Clubs:* Travellers', Special Forces. *Died 13 April 1995.*

HENDERSON, Ian Dalton, ERD 1960 (1st clasp 1966, 2nd clasp 1972); FRCS; Consultant Surgeon, Tunbridge Wells District, 1956–82, then Honorary Consultant Surgeon; *b* 4 Nov. 1918; *s* of Stewart Dalton Henderson and Grace Aird (*née* Masterson); *m* 1951, Rosa Hertz, MB, BS, MRCOG; two *d. Educ:* Fettes Coll., Edinburgh; Guy's Hosp., Univ. of London (MB, BS 1943). LMSSA 1943; FRCS 1949. Served War, RAMC, 1943–46: served India; Major, 1945–46. Lectr in Anatomy and Surg. Registrar, Guy's Hosp., 1947–50; Sen. Surg. Registrar, Royal Postgrad. Med. Sch. of London, 1952–56. Hon. Surgeon to the Queen, 1971–73. Member: Kent AHA, 1973–82; Société Internat. de Chirurgie, 1972–. FRSM 1947–. Served TA and AER, subseq. T&AVR, 1948–79; former Hon. Col and OC 308 Gen. Hosp., T&AVR. Silver Jubilee Medal, 1978. *Recreations:* archaeology, skiing,

golf, photography. *Address:* 5 Thornbury Court, Chepstow Villas, W11 2RE. *T:* 0171–221 3822.
Died 7 Nov. 1995.

HENDERSON, Sir James Thyne, KBE 1959; CMG 1952; HM Diplomatic Service, retired; *b* 18 Jan. 1901; *s* of late Sir Thomas Henderson and Helen Scott Thyne; *m* 1930, Karen Margrethe Hansen (*d* 1993); one *s* four *d. Educ:* Warriston, Moffat; Sedbergh Sch.; Queen's Coll., Oxford. Entered Diplomatic Service, 1925, apptd to FO; transf. to Tehran, 1927; Athens, 1929; Helsinki, 1932, where acted as Chargé d'Affaires in 1932, 1933, 1934 and 1935; Foreign Office, 1935; First Sec., 1936; attached to Representative of Finland at the Coronation of King George VI, 1937; Tokyo, 1938; Santiago, 1941; Foreign Office, 1944; Stockholm, 1946, Chargé d'Affaires there in 1946 and 1947; Counsellor, 1947; Consul-Gen., Houston, 1949; HM Minister to Iceland, 1953–56; HM Ambassador to Bolivia, 1956–60, retired. *Recreation:* gardening. *Died 26 Aug. 1993.*

HENDERSON, John Stuart Wilmot; Under Secretary, Ministry of Defence, and Director General of Ordnance Factories, Finance, Procurement and Administration, retired 1976; *b* 31 March 1919; *s* of Bruce Wilmot Henderson and Sarah (*née* Marchant); *m* 1st, 1941, Elsie Kathleen (*née* Rose) (*d* 1981); one *s* three *d*; 2nd, 1984, Yvonne Crawley (*née* Smith), *widow* of Victor James Crawley. *Educ:* Wade Deacon Grammar Sch., Widnes. Exec. Officer, Royal Ordnance Factories, 1938–39; served War of 1939–45: Royal Fusiliers, 1939–43; Intell. Corps, 1944–47; various appts in Ministries of Supply, Aviation, Technology and Defence, 1947–76. *Recreations:* gardening, enjoying music. *Address:* Tregaron, Llantrissent, near Usk, Gwent NP5 1LG. *T:* Usk (01291) 672297. *Died 5 Nov. 1995.*

HENDERSON, Admiral Sir Nigel Stuart, GBE 1968 (OBE 1944); KCB 1962 (CB 1959); DL; *b* 1 Aug. 1909; *s* of late Lt-Col Selby Herriott Henderson, IMS; *m* 1939, Catherine Mary Maitland, *d* of Lt-Col C. A. S. Maitland of Dundrennan; one *s* two *d. Educ:* Cheltenham Coll. Entered RN, 1927; served War of 1939–45 in HM Ships and as Fleet Gunnery Officer, Mediterranean; Comdr 1942; Capt. 1948; Naval Attaché, Rome, 1949–51; in comd HMS Protector, 1951; in comd RN Air Station, Bramcote, 1952; Imperial Defence Coll., 1954; in command HMS Kenya, 1955; Rear-Admiral, 1957; Vice-Naval Dep. and Naval Dep. to Supreme Allied Comdr, Europe, 1957–Dec. 1959; Vice-Adm. 1960; Dir-Gen. of Training, Admiralty, 1960–62; C-in-C Plymouth, 1962–65; Adm. 1963; Head of British Defence Staffs, Washington, British Mem., Standing Gp, and UK Rep., Mil. Cttee, NATO, 1965–68; Chm., Mil. Cttee, NATO, 1968–71; retired 1971. Rear-Admiral of the United Kingdom, 1973–76; Vice-Admiral of the United Kingdom, and Lieutenant of the Admiralty, 1976–79. Pres., Royal British Legion, Scotland, 1974–80. DL Stewartry of Kirkcudbright, 1973. *Recreations:* sketching, golf, bird-watching. *Address:* Hensol, Mossdale, Castle Douglas, Kirkcudbrightshire DG7 2NE. *T:* Laurieston (06445) 207. *Died 2 Aug. 1993.*

HENDERSON, William Crichton; advocate; Sheriff of Tayside, Central and Fife (formerly Stirling, Dunbarton and Clackmannan) at Stirling, since 1972 (also at Alloa, 1972–81); *b* 10 June 1931; *s* of late William Henderson, headmaster, and Helen Philp Henderson (*née* Crichton); *m* 1962, Norma Sheila Hope Henderson (*née* Grant) (marr. diss. 1985); two *d. Educ:* George Watson's Boys' Coll., Edinburgh; Edinburgh Univ. MA Edinburgh 1952, LLB Edinburgh 1954. Admitted Solicitor, 1954; Diploma in Administrative Law and Practice, Edinburgh, 1955; called to Scottish Bar, 1957; practised as Advocate, 1957–68; Sheriff of Renfrew and Argyll at Paisley, 1968–72. Pres.,

Sheriffs' Assoc., 1985–88 (formerly Sec. and Vice-Pres.). Chm., Supreme Court Legal Aid Cttee, 1967–68. Associate Mem., Commonwealth Magistrates' and Judges' Assoc. *Recreations:* gardening, travel. *Address:* 7 Magdala Crescent, Edinburgh EH12 5BE. *Clubs:* New, University Staff (Edinburgh). *Died 1 April 1992.*

HENNESSY, Sir John Wyndham P.; *see* Pope-Hennessy.

HENNIKER, Brig. Sir Mark Chandos Auberon, 8th Bt, *cr* 1813, of Newton Hall, Essex; CBE 1953 (OBE 1944); DSO 1944; MC 1933; DL; retired, 1958; *b* 23 Jan. 1906; *s* of late F. C. Henniker, ICS, and Ada Russell (*née* Howell); *S* cousin (Lieut-Col Sir Robert Henniker, 7th Bt, MC) 1958; *m* 1945, Kathleen Denys (*née* Anderson); one *s* one *d. Educ:* Marlborough Coll.; Royal Military Academy, Woolwich; King's Coll., Cambridge. Royal Engineers, 1926; served India, 1928–34 (MC); Aldershot, 1937–39; BEF, 1939–40; North Africa, 1943; Sicily, 1943 (wounded); Italy, 1943 (OBE); NW Europe, 1944–45 (immediate award of DSO, Oct. 1944); India, 1946–47; Malaya, 1952–55 (CBE); Port Said, 1956 (despatches). Hon. Col, Parachute Engineer Regt (TA), 1959–68; Hon. Col, REME (TA), 1964–68. DL Gwent (formerly County of Mon), 1963. *Publications:* Memoirs of a Junior Officer, 1951; Red Shadow over Malaya, 1955; Life in the Army Today, 1957; An Image of War, 1987. *Recreations:* appropriate to age and rank. *Heir: s* Adrian Chandos Henniker [*b* 18 Oct. 1946; *m* 1971, Ann, *d* of Stuart Britton; twin *d*]. *Address:* c/o Lloyds Bank, Cox's & King's Branch, 6 Pall Mall, SW1. *Club:* Athenæum.
Died 18 Oct. 1991.

HENNINGS, Richard Owen, CMG 1957; retired as Deputy Chief Secretary, Kenya (1960–63); *b* 8 Sept. 1911; *s* of W. G. Hennings; *m* 1939, Constance Patricia Milton Sexton (*d* 1992); one *d. Educ:* Cheltenham; New Coll., Oxford. Newdigate Prize Poem, 1932. District Officer, Kenya, 1935; Political Officer, Ethiopia, 1941; Secretary for Agriculture, Kenya, 1953; Permanent Secretary, Ministry of Agriculture, Animal Husbandry and Water Resources, Kenya, 1956. Nominated Member of Kenya Legislative Council, 1960, and of East African Central Legislative Assembly, 1960. Hon. Editor, Ski Notes and Queries, 1964–71; Editor, Ski Survey, 1972–73. *Publications:* Arnold in Africa, 1941; African Morning, 1951; articles in The Geographical Magazine, Journal of African Administration, Corona, British Ski Year Book, Ski Notes and Queries. *Recreations:* ski-ing, tennis, gardening, reefing. *Address:* July Farm House, Great Chesterford, Saffron Walden, Essex CB10 1PH. *Clubs:* Ski Club of Great Britain; Nairobi (Nairobi).
Died 22 Nov. 1993.

HENRY, Thomas Cradock, FDS RCS; MRCS, LRCP; retired; Hon. Consultant Oral Surgeon, Hospital for Sick Children, Great Ormond Street; Consultant Maxillo-Facial Surgeon, Royal Surrey County Hospital; Consultant Oral Surgeon, Italian Hospital, London; *b* 30 Dec. 1910; *s* of late Thomas Henry and Rose Emily Bowdler, Moorgate Park, Retford; *m* 1939, Claire Mary, 7th *c* of late R. A. Caraman, The Grange, Elstree; two *s. Educ:* King Edward VI Grammar Sch., Retford; King's Coll., University of London; Middlesex and Royal Dental Hospital; Saunders Scholar; qualified as Doctor, 1935. Formerly: House Physician, House Surgeon and Resident Anæsthetist, St James's Hosp., London; House Surgeon, St Bartholomew's Hosp.; Squadron Leader and Surgical Specialist, RAFVR, 1939–46: Surgical Registrar, Plastic and Jaw Injuries Centre, East Grinstead, 1941–42; Surgeon in charge of Maxillo-Facial and Burns Unit, RAF Hosp., Cosford, 1942–46; Hunterian Prof., RCS, 1944–45. FRSocMed; Founder Fellow and Pres., British Assoc. of Oral Surgeons; Member: British Assoc. of Plastic Surgeons (Mem. Council); BMA. *Publications:* Fracture of the

Facial Bones (chapter in Fractures and Dislocations in General Practice), 1949; Labial Segment Surgery (chapter in Archer's Oral Surgery), 1971; Melanotic Ameloblastoma (in Trans 3rd Internat. Conf. on Oral Surgery); numerous contribs to leading medical and dental journals, including BMJ and Jl of Bone and Joint Surgery. *Recreations:* shooting, fishing. *Address:* Redwing Cottage, Bridge Road, Cranleigh, Surrey GU6 7HH. *T:* Cranleigh (0483) 277730. *Died 15 Jan. 1993.*

HENSON, Ronald Alfred, MD, FRCP; Physician and Neurologist, 1949–81, Chairman, Section of Neurological Sciences, 1968–81, The London Hospital; Physician, National Hospitals for Nervous Diseases, Maida Vale Hospital, 1952–81; *b* 4 Oct. 1915; *s* of late Alfred and Nellie Henson, Chippenham, Wilts; *m* 1941, Frances, *d* of A. Francis and Jessie Sims, Bath; two *d* (and one *d* decd). *Educ:* King Edward VI Sch., Bath; London Hospital Medical Coll.; Univ. of London (Dip. Hist. Music). Major, RAMC, 1940–46. Mem., Archbishops' Commission on Divine Healing, 1953–57. Dir of Studies, Institute of Neurology, University of London, 1955–64, Chm. Academic Bd, 1974–77; Dir, Cancer Res. Campaign Neuropathological Res. Unit, London Hosp. Med. Coll., 1967–71; Chm., London Hosp. Med. Council, 1974–77. Examiner: RCP, 1965–68, 1969–75; Univ. of London, 1971–74; Langdon-Brown Lectr, RCP, 1977; Fest. Lectr, Univ. of Bergen, 1981; vis. lectr at med. schs and neurological socs in N America, Europe, India, Thailand, Australia, NZ, 1959–86. Member: Med. Appeals Tribunal, 1980–87; Attendance Allowance Bd, 1980–86. Hon. Consulting Neurologist, Royal Soc. Musicians, GB, 1966–81; formerly Mem. Board of Governors: The London Hosp.; Nat. Hosps for Nervous Diseases. Chairman: Advance in Medicine, 1976–83; Scientific Adv. Panel, Action Research, 1983 (Mem., 1977; Vice-Chm., 1981); President: Neurological Section, RSM, 1976–77 (Sec., 1956–58; Vice-Pres. 1974); Assoc. of British Neurologists, 1976–77 (Sec., 1964–68). Commonwealth Fellow 1964. Special Trustee, The London Hosp., 1974–82. Member: Assoc. of Physicians of Great Britain and Ireland; British Neuropathological Soc.; Hon. Corresponding Mem. Amer. Neurological Assoc., 1966; Hon. Member: Canadian Neurological Soc., 1971; Belgian Neurological Soc., 1976; Assoc. of British Neurologists, 1983. Chm., London Bach Soc., 1977–85; Arts Council of GB: Mem., 1981–85; Vice-Chm., Regional Adv. Cttee, 1982–86; Chm., Study Gp on Opera Provision Outside London, 1985. Chm., Cheltenham Internat. Music Fest., 1990–93 (Vice-Chm., 1983–90); Chm., Glos Arts Cttee, 1984–89; Member: Exec. Cttee, Southern Arts, 1982–86; Management Cttee, 1983–86, Music Panel, 1986–88, SW Arts (Chm., Music Sub-Panel, 1986–88). Mem. Bd of Governors, King Edward's Sch., Bath, 1983–89. Dep. Editor, Brain, 1974–81. *Publications:* Music and the Brain (ed jtly), 1977; Cancer and the Nervous System (jtly), 1982; various contributions to the neurological literature. *Address:* The Nab, Church Road, Newnham-on-Severn, Glos GL14 1AY. *Club:* Athenæum. *Died 1 Dec. 1994.*

HEPBURN, Audrey; actress; *b* Brussels, 4 May 1929; *d* of Joseph A. Hepburn and Baroness Ella van Heemstra; *m* 1st, 1954, Mel Ferrer (marr. diss. 1968); one *s*; 2nd, 1969, Dr Andrea Dotti; one *s*. Studied ballet in Amsterdam and in Marie Rambert's ballet sch. First stage part in musical production, High Button Shoes; first film appearance in Laughter in Paradise; played leading rôles in Gigi (play), New York, 1951 (tour of America, Oct. 1952–May 1953); Ondine (play by Jean Giraudoux), 1954. Special Ambassador for UNICEF, 1988–. BAFTA Special Award, 1992. Commander, Order of Arts and Letters (France), 1987. *Films:* One Wild Oat; The Young Wives' Tale; The Secret People; Nous Irons à Monte Carlo; The Lavender Hill Mob, 1951; Roman Holiday, 1953 (Acad. Award, best actress, 1954); Sabrina Fair, 1954; War and Peace, 1956; Funny Face, 1957; Love in the Afternoon, 1957; The Nun's Story, 1958; Green Mansions, 1959; The Unforgiven, 1960; Breakfast at Tiffany's, 1961; Paris When it Sizzles, 1962; Charade, 1962; My Fair Lady, 1964; How to Make a Million, 1966; Two for the Road, 1967; Wait Until Dark, 1968; Robin Hood and Maid Marion, 1975; Bloodline, 1979; They All Laughed, 1980; Always, 1990. *Died 20 Jan. 1993.*

HEPBURN, Bryan Audley St John, CMG 1962; Financial Secretary, Sarawak, 1958–63; Member, Sarawak Legislative and Executive Councils, 1955–63; Member, Inter-Governmental Committee which led to establishment of Federation of Malaysia; *b* 24 Feb. 1911; *s* of A. F. St John Hepburn; *m* 1940, Sybil Isabel Myers; two *d. Educ:* Cornwall Coll., Jamaica. Jamaica Civil Service, 1930; Asst Sec., Colonial Service, 1944; Principal Asst Sec., Sarawak, 1947; Development Sec., 1951. Chm., Sarawak Develt Finance Corp., 1958–63; Chm., Sarawak Electricity Supply Co. Ltd, 1955–63; Dir, Malayan Airways Ltd, 1959–63; Dir, Borneo Airways Ltd, 1958–63; Dep. Chm., Malaysian Tariff Adv. Bd, 1963–65. Ministry of Overseas Development, 1966–73. *Recreations:* golf, fishing. *Address:* 27 Dumbrells Court, North End, Ditchling, Sussex. *Clubs:* Royal Over-Seas League; Haywards Heath Golf; Sarawak (Sarawak). *Died 30 May 1991.*

HEPBURN, Sir Ninian Buchan Archibald John B.; *see* Buchan-Hepburn.

HEPPLE, (Robert) Norman, RA 1961 (ARA 1954); RP 1948; NEAC 1950; *b* 18 May 1908; *s* of Robert Watkin Hepple and Ethel Louise Wardale; *m* 1948, Jillian Constance Marigold Pratt; one *s* one *d. Educ:* Goldsmiths' Coll.; Royal Acad. Schools. Figure subject and portrait painter. Pres., Royal Soc. of Portrait Painters, 1979–83. *Address:* 10 Sheen Common Drive, Richmond, Surrey TW10 5BN. *T:* 081–878 4452. *Died 3 Jan. 1994.*

HEREN, Louis Philip, FRSL; journalist and author; *b* 6 Feb. 1919; *s* of William Heren and Beatrice (*née* Keller); *m* 1948, Patricia Cecilia O'Regan (*d* 1975); one *s* three *d. Educ:* St George's Sch., London. FRSL 1974. Army, 1939–46. Foreign Corresp. of The Times, 1947–70: India, 1947–48; Israel and Middle East, 1948–50; Southeast Asian Corresp., 1951–53; Germany, 1955–60; Chief Washington Corresp. and American Editor, 1960–70; Co-Dep. Editor (Foreign), 1970–73; Dep. Editor and Foreign Editor, 1973–78; Dep. Editor, 1978–81; Associate Editor, and Dir, Times Newspapers Hldgs Ltd, 1981. War Correspondent: Kashmir, 1947; Israel-Arab war, 1948; Korean war, 1950. Hannan Swaffer Award for Internat. Reporting, 1967; John F. Kennedy Memorial Award, 1968. *Publications:* New American Commonwealth, 1968; No Hail, No Farewell, 1970; Growing Up Poor in London, 1973; The Story of America, 1976; Growing Up on The Times, 1978; Alas, Alas for England, 1981; The Power of the Press?, 1985; Memories of Times Past, 1988. *Address:* Fleet House, Vale of Health, NW3 1AZ. *T:* 0171–435 0902. *Club:* Garrick.

Died 26 Jan. 1995.

HERIOT, Alexander John, MS, FRCS, FDSRCS; Senior Surgeon, King's College Hospital, 1969–79; Postgraduate Regional Dean, South East Thames Regional Health Authority, 1973–79; *b* 28 May 1914; *s* of Robert Heriot; *m* 1940, Dr Christine Stacey (*d* 1958); two *s*; *m* 1959, Dr Cynthia Heymeson; one *s* one *d.* Major RAMC. *Address:* 47 Upper Tooting Park, SW17 7SN. *T:* 0181–673 3734.

Died 14 March 1995.

HERITAGE, Rev. Canon Thomas Charles; Canon Residentiary of Portsmouth Cathedral, 1964–76, then Canon Emeritus; *b* 3 March 1908; *s* of Thomas and Sarah Ellen Heritage; *m* 1934, Frances Warrington (*d* 1979);

twin *d. Educ:* The King's Sch., Chester; St Edmund Hall, Oxford. BA 1929; MA 1944; Diploma in Education (Oxford), 1930; ATCL 1931. Deacon, 1934; Priest, 1938. Curate of Christ Church, Chesterfield and Asst Master, Chesterfield Grammar Sch., 1934–38; Asst Master, Portsmouth Grammar Sch., 1938–64; Curate of St Mark, Portsmouth, 1938–40, St Christopher, Bournemouth, 1940–44; Chaplain of Portsmouth Cathedral, 1945–64. Hon. Canon, 1958–64. Examining Chaplain to the Bishop of Portsmouth, 1965–74. Warden, Portsmouth Diocesan Readers' Assoc., 1966–76. *Publications:* A New Testament Lectionary for Schools, 1943; The Early Christians in Britain (with B. E. Dodd), 1966. *Recreations:* music, the theatre, reading. *Address:* 117 The Close, Salisbury, Wilts SP1 2EY. *T:* Salisbury (01722) 329104.

Died 28 Sept. 1995.

HERRIES, Sir Michael Alexander Robert Young-, Kt 1975; OBE 1968; MC 1945; Chairman, The Royal Bank of Scotland Group plc (formerly National and Commercial Banking Group Ltd), 1978–91 (Director, 1976–92); Director, The Royal Bank of Scotland plc, 1976–92 (Vice-Chairman, 1974–75; Deputy Chairman, 1975–76; Chairman, 1976–90); Chairman, Scottish Mortgage and Trust PLC, 1984–93 (Director, 1975–93); Lord-Lieutenant, Dumfries and Galloway Region (District of Stewartry), since 1989; *b* 28 Feb. 1923; *s* of Lt-Col William Dobree Young-Herries and Ruth Mary (*née* Thrupp); *m* 1949, Elizabeth Hilary Russell (*née* Smith); two *s* one *d. Educ:* Eton; Trinity Coll., Cambridge (MA). Served KOSB, 1942–47; Temp. Captain, Actg Maj., Europe and ME; Adjt 5th (Dumfries and Galloway) Battalion and 1st Battalion TARO, 1949. Joined Jardine Matheson & Co. Ltd, 1948; served in Hong Kong, Japan and Singapore; Director, 1959; Managing Director, 1962; Chm. and Man. Dir, 1963–70; Chairman: Jardine Japan Investment Trust Ltd, 1972–76; Crossfriars Trust Ltd, 1972–76; Dep. Chm., Williams & Glyn's Bank, 1978–85; Advr, Jardine Matheson, 1988– (Dir, 1959–88); Director: Matheson & Co. Ltd (Chm., 1971–75); Scottish Widows' Fund and Life Assce Soc., 1974–93 (Chm., 1981–84, Dep. Chm., 1979–81 and 1984–85); Banco de Santander SA, 1989–93. Formerly Mem., Exec. Legislative Council, Hong Kong; Chm., Hong Kong Univ. and Polytechnics Grant Cttee, 1965–73. Former Mem. Council, London Chamber of Commerce and Industry, Hon. Mem., 1980–; Chairman: Scottish Trust for the Physically Disabled, 1981–83; Scottish Disability Foundn, 1982–94; Mem. Council, Missions to Seamen. Mem., Royal Company of Archers (Queen's Body Guard for Scotland), 1973–. DL Dumfries and Galloway, 1983. Hon. LLD: Chinese Univ. of Hong Kong, 1973; Univ. of Hong Kong, 1974. Hon. DLitt Heriot-Watt, 1984. *Recreations:* shooting, walking, swimming. *Address:* Spottes, Castle Douglas, Stewartry of Kirkcudbright DG7 3JX. *T:* Haugh of Urr (0155666) 202; Flat 14, Lochmore House, Cundy Street, SW1W 9JX. *T:* 0171–730 1119. *Clubs:* Caledonian, City of London; New (Edinburgh). *Died 6 May 1995.*

HERRIOT, James; *see* Wight, J. A.

HERRON, Prof. Ronald James, ARIBA; FCSD; architect; Partner, Herron Associates, since 1985; Professor and Head of School of Architecture, University of East London, since 1993; *b* 12 Aug. 1930; *s* of James and Louisa Herron; *m* 1952, Patricia Ginn; two *s. Educ:* Brixton Sch. of Building; Regent Street Poly. Architect with GLC, 1954–61; Founder, with Peter Cook, Dennis Crompton, Mike Webb and David Greene, Archigram Gp, 1960; Dep. Architect, Taylor Woodrow Construction, 1961–65; Associate, Halpern & Partners, 1965–67; Consultant Architect to Colin St John Wilson, Cambridge, 1967; in private practice, London, 1968; Dir of Urban Design, William Pereira & Partners, LA, 1969–70; Partner,

Archigram Architects, 1970–75; in private practice, 1975–77; Partner: Pentagram Design, 1977–80; Derek Walker Associates, 1981–82; Principal, Ron Herron Associates, 1982–85; Partner, Herron Associates, 1985; Herron Associates merged with Imagination Ltd to become Herron Associates at Imagination, 1989, Dir, 1989–93; reformed Herron Associates, 1993. Tutor: AA Sch., 1965–93; N London Poly. Sch. of Architecture, 1968; Vis. Prof., USC, LA, 1968–69; Artist-in-Residence: Univ. of Wisconsin, 1972; USC, LA, 1976, 1977, 1979; Southern Calif. Inst. for Architecture, LA, 1982; Visiting Professor: Thames Poly. Sch. of Architecture, 1991–93; Bartlett Sch. of Architecture, UCL, 1992. Ext. Examnr and Mem., RIBA Visiting Bd, 1987. Principal designs and projects include: South Bank Develt (QEH and Hayward Gall.), 1961–63; master plan for new town for Ford Motor Co., Dearborn, Mich, air terminal at LA Internat. Airport for Pan American Airlines, 1969; entertainment facility for Monte Carlo (Archigram winning design, internat. competition), 1970; play centre, Calverton End, Milton Keynes, 1975; develt of central area, Heathrow Airport, 1976; D. O. M. Office Headquarters, Cologne (competition with Peter Cook and Christine Hawley), 1980; Wonderworld theme park, Corby, Northants, 1981; travelling exhibn, design and construction of The Human Story, with Richard Leakey, Commonwealth Inst., 1985; R&D Labs for Imperial Tobacco, urban design project for Hamburg docks, by invitation of Hamburg City Council, 1985; mobile exhibn structure for BT, proposals for remodelling Thorn House, London, 1987; German Headquarters for L'Oréal, Karlsruhe (competition special award), 1988; proposals for a European cultural centre, Belgium, 1989; Far Eastern Internat. airport terminal, British Airports Services, 1990; conf. facility at Waddesdon Manor for Lord Rothschild, 1990; Canada Water underground stn for London Underground Ltd, 1991; projects for Maichi no Kao, Japan, 1992; Exhibitions: Architectural Assoc., London, 1980; Berlin, 1981; Heinz Gall., London, 1989; Kunsthalle, Vienna, 1994; Pompidou Centre, Paris, 1994. Member: Architecture Club; Architectural Assoc. FRSA. (Jtly) Building of the Year Award, Sunday Times/Royal Fine Art Commn, 1990; Eternit Nat. Award for Architecture, 1990; Critics' Choice, BBC Design Awards, 1990. *Publications:* (ed jtly) Archigram, 1973; (with Andrew and Simon Herron) Japan Notebook and Projects in Japan, 1992; contrib. Pentagram Papers, 1977; articles in professional jls incl. Living Arts, Architectural Design. *Recreations:* cricket, soccer, movies. *Address:* Herron Associates, 28–30 Rivington Street, EC2A 3DU; School of Architecture, University of East London, Holbrook Centre, Holbrook Road, E15 3EA.

Died 1 Oct. 1994.

HERSEY, John Richard; writer; *b* 17 June 1914; *s* of Roscoe M. and Grace B. Hersey; *m* 1st, 1940, Frances Ann Cannon (marr. diss. 1958); three *s* one *d*; 2nd, 1958, Barbara Day Kaufman; one *d*. *Educ:* Yale Univ.; Clare Coll., Cambridge. Secretary to Sinclair Lewis, 1937; Editor, Time, 1937–42; War and Foreign Correspondent, Time, Life, New Yorker, 1942–46. Mem. Council, Authors' League of America, 1946–70 (Vice-Pres., 1948–55, Pres., 1975–80). Fellow, Berkeley Coll., Yale Univ., 1950–65; Master, Pierson Coll., Yale Univ., 1965–70, Fellow, 1965–. Writer in Residence, Amer. Acad. in Rome, 1970–71. Lectr, Yale Univ., 1971–75, Vis. Prof., 1975–76, Adjunct Prof., 1976–84, then Emeritus; Lectr, Salzburg Seminars in Amer. Studies, 1975; Vis. Prof., MIT, 1975. Chm., Connecticut Cttee for the Gifted, 1954–57; Member: Amer. Acad. Arts and Letters, 1953 (Sec., 1962–76; Chancellor, 1981–84); Nat. Inst. Arts and Letters, 1950; Amer. Acad. of Arts and Scis, 1978; Council, Authors' Guild, 1946– (Chm., Contract

Cttee, 1963–87); Yale Univ. Council Cttees on the Humanities, 1951–56, and on Yale Coll., 1959–69 (Chm., 1964–69) and 1981–; Vis. Cttee, Harvard Grad. Sch. of Educn, 1960–65; Vis. Cttee, Loeb Drama Center, 1980–85; Nat. Citizens' Commn for the Public Schs, 1954–56; Bd of Trustees, Putney Sch., 1953–56; Trustee: Nat. Citizens' Council for the Public Schs, 1956–58; Nat. Cttee for the Support of the Public Schs, 1962–68. Delegate: to White House Conf. on Educn, 1955; to PEN Congress, Tokyo, 1958. Comr, Nat. Commn on New Technological Uses of Copyrighted Works, 1975–78. Hon. Fellow, Clare Coll., Cambridge, 1967. Hon. MA Yale Univ., 1947; Hon. LLD: Washington and Jefferson Coll., 1946; Univ. of New Haven, 1975; Hon. LHD: New Sch. for Social Research, 1950; Syracuse Univ., 1983; Hon. DHL Dropsie Coll., 1950; Hon. LittD: Wesleyan Univ., 1957; Bridgeport Univ., 1959; Clarkson Coll. of Technology, 1972; Yale Univ., 1984; Monmouth Coll., 1985; William and Mary Coll., 1987; Albertus Magnus Coll., 1988. Pulitzer Prize for Fiction, 1945; Sidney Hillman Foundn Award, 1951; Howland Medal, Yale Univ., 1952. *Publications:* Men on Bataan, 1942; Into the Valley, 1943; A Bell for Adano, 1944; Hiroshima, 1946; The Wall, 1950; The Marmot Drive, 1953; A Single Pebble, 1956; The War Lover, 1959; The Child Buyer, 1960; Here to Stay, 1962; White Lotus, 1965; Too Far to Walk, 1966; Under the Eye of the Storm, 1967; The Algiers Motel Incident, 1968; The Conspiracy, 1972; The Writer's Craft, 1974; My Petition for More Space, 1974; The President, 1975; The Walnut Door, 1977; Aspects of the Presidency, 1980; The Call, 1985; Blues, 1987; Life Sketches, 1989; Fling and Other Stories, 1990; Antonietta, 1991.

Died 24 March 1993.

HERVEY-BATHURST, Sir Frederick Peter Methuen; *see* Bathurst.

HERZIG, Christopher, CBE 1988; Director, External Relations, International Atomic Energy Agency, Vienna, 1981–87; *b* 24 Oct. 1926; *s* of late L. A. Herzig and Elizabeth Herzig (*née* Hallas); *m* 1952, Rachel Katharine Buxton; four *s* one *d*. *Educ:* Christ's Hosp.; Selwyn Coll., Cambridge (MA). Asst Principal, Min. of Fuel and Power, 1951–56; Principal, Min. of Supply, 1956–58; Min. of Aviation, 1959–61; Private Sec. to Lord President of the Council, 1961–64; Private Sec. to Minister of Technology, 1964–66; Asst Sec., Min. of Technology, 1966–70; Dept of Trade and Industry, 1970–71; Under-Sec., DTI, 1972–73; Under Sec., Dept of Energy, 1974–81. UK Governor, IAEA, 1972–78. *Address:* 13a The Causeway, Horsham, West Sussex RH12 1HE. *T:* Horsham (0403) 65239. *Died 1 Sept. 1993.*

HETHERINGTON, (Arthur) Carleton, CBE 1971 (MBE 1945); Secretary of Association of County Councils, 1974–80; *b* 13 Feb. 1916; *s* of late Arthur Stanley and Mary Venters Hetherington, Silloth, Cumberland; *m* 1941, Xenia, *d* of late Nicholas Gubsky, Barnes; three *s*. *Educ:* St Bees Sch. Admitted Solicitor, 1938. Assistant Solicitor: Peterborough, 1938–39; Stafford, 1939. Served Royal Artillery, 1939–46 (Hon. Lt-Col); Temp. Lt-Col 1944–46. Dep. Clerk of the Peace and Dep. Clerk of County Council of Cumberland, 1946–52, of Cheshire, 1952–59; Clerk of the Peace and Clerk of County Council of Cheshire, 1959–64. Sec., County Councils Assoc., 1964–74. Mem., Departmental Cttee on Jury Service, 1963–64; Sec., Local Authorities Management Services and Computer Cttee, 1965–80. *Recreations:* music, golf, family. *Address:* 33 Campden Hill Court, W8 7HS.

Died 15 Oct. 1995.

HETHERINGTON, Rear-Adm. Derick Henry Fellowes, CB 1961; DSC 1941 (2 Bars 1944, 1945); MA (Oxon), 1963; Domestic Bursar and Fellow of Merton College, Oxford, 1963–76, Emeritus Fellow, 1976; *b* 27 June 1911;

s of Commander H. R. Hetherington, RD, Royal Naval Reserve, and Hilda Fellowes; *m* 1942, Josephine Mary, *d* of Captain Sir Leonard Vavasour, 4th Bt, RN; one *s* three *d* (and one *s* decd). *Educ:* St Neot's, Eversley, Hants; RNC Dartmouth. Cadet, HMS Barham, 1928–29; Midshipman-Comdr (HMS Effingham, Leander, Anthony, Wildfire, Kimberley, Windsor, Lookout, Royal Arthur, Cheviot), 1929–50; Captain 1950; Chief of Staff, Canal Zone, Egypt, 1950–52; Senior British Naval Officer, Ceylon, 1953–55; Captain (D) 4th Destroyer Squadron, 1956–57; Director of Naval Training, Admiralty, 1958–59; Flag Officer, Malta, 1959–61; retired 1961. Croix de Guerre (France), 1945. *Address:* Gatehouse Cottage, Pyrton, Oxford OX9 5AN. *T:* Watlington (049161) 2338.
Died 23 Nov. 1992.

HEUSTON, Prof. Robert Francis Vere, DCL Oxon 1970; MRIA 1978; Regius Professor of Laws, Trinity College, Dublin, 1970–83; *b* Dublin, 17 Nov. 1923; *e s* of late Vere Douglas Heuston and late Dorothy Helen Coulter; *m* 1962, Bridget Nancy (*née* Bolland), widow of Neville Ward-Perkins; four step *c*. *Educ:* St Columba's Coll.; Trinity Coll., Dublin; St John's Coll., Cambridge. Barrister, King's Inns, 1947 (Hon. Bencher, 1983), Gray's Inn, 1951 (Hon. Bencher, 1988); Hon. Member, Western Circuit, 1966. Fellow, Pembroke Coll., Oxford, 1947–65 (Hon. Fellow, 1982), Dean, 1951–57, Pro-Proctor, 1953; Professor of Law, Univ. of Southampton, 1965–70. Arthur Goodhart Prof. of Legal Sci., and Fellow, Jesus Coll., Cambridge, 1986–87. Member, Law Reform Cttee (England), 1968–70, (Ireland), 1975–81. Visiting Professor: Univ. of Melbourne, 1956; Univ. of British Columbia, 1960, 1985; ANU, 1977; Gresham Professor in Law, 1964–70. Corresponding FBA, 1988. Hon. QC 1995. Hon. LLD Buckingham. *Publications:* (ed) Salmond and Heuston on Torts, 11th edn 1953, to 20th edn 1992; Essays in Constitutional Law, 2nd edn 1964; Lives of the Lord Chancellors, vol. I, 1885–1940, 1964, vol. II, 1940–70, 1987; various in learned periodicals. *Address:* Kentstown House, Brownstown, Navan, Co. Meath, Ireland. *T:* Drogheda (41) 25195. *Clubs:* Beefsteak, United Oxford & Cambridge University; Royal Irish Yacht.
Died 21 Dec. 1995.

HEWARD, Air Chief Marshal Sir Anthony Wilkinson, KCB 1972 (CB 1968); OBE 1952; DFC and bar; AFC; Air Member for Supply and Organisation, Ministry of Defence, 1973–76; *b* 1 July 1918; *s* of late Col E. J. Heward; *m* 1944, Clare Myfanwy Wainwright, *d* of late Maj.-Gen. C. B. Wainwright, CB; one *s* one *d*. Gp Captain RAF, 1957; IDC 1962; Air Cdre 1963; Dir of Operations (Bomber and Reconnaissance) MoD (RAF), 1963; Air Vice-Marshal 1966; Dep. Comdr, RAF Germany, 1966–69; AOA, HQ RAF Air Support Command, 1969–70; Air Marshal 1970; Chief of Staff, RAF Strike Command, 1970–72; AOC, No 18 (Maritime) Group, 1972–73; Air Chief Marshal, 1974. County Councillor, Wilts, 1981–89. *Address:* Home Close, Donhead St Mary, near Shaftesbury, Dorset SP7 9DL. *Clubs:* Royal Air Force, Flyfishers'.
Died 27 Oct. 1995.

HEWER, Thomas Frederick, MD (Bristol); FRCP, FLS; Professor of Pathology, 1938–68, and Pro-Vice-Chancellor, 1966–68, University of Bristol; Professor Emeritus, 1968; *b* 12 April 1903; *s* of William Frederick Hewer and Kathleen Braddon Standerwick; *m* 1941, Anne Hiatt Baker (OBE 1977; MA); two *s* two *d*. *Educ:* Bristol Gram. Sch.; University of Bristol. Commonwealth Fund Fellow and Asst Pathologist, Johns Hopkins Univ., USA, 1927–29; Bacteriologist Sudan Government, 1930–35; Sen. Lectr in Pathology, University of Liverpool, 1935–38. Botanical explorer, FAO/UN, 1975–80; consultant, WHO, investigating causation of cancer among Turkoman, NE Iran, making botanical exploration of desert E of Caspian

Sea, 1976–77. Mem. Council and Chm. Animal Cttee, Bristol Zoo, 1953–83. Pres., Bristol Br., ESU (Chm., 1942–67). *Publications:* articles in medical and horticultural journals. *Recreations:* gardening, travel. *Address:* Vine House, Henbury, Bristol BS10 7AD. *T:* Bristol (0272) 503573. *Club:* English-Speaking Union.
Died 15 March 1994.

HEWETSON, Gen. Sir Reginald (Hackett), GCB 1966 (KCB 1962; CB 1958); CBE 1945 (OBE 1943); DSO 1944; Adjutant-General, Ministry of Defence (Army), 1964–67; retired; *b* Shortlands, Kent, 4 Aug. 1908; *s* of late J. Hewetson, ICS, and E. M. M. Hackett-Wilkins; *m* 1935, Patricia Mable, *y d* of late F. H. Burkitt, CIE; one *s* one *d*. *Educ:* Repton; RMA, Woolwich. Regular Commission in RA, 1928; service in India (including Active Service, 1930–32), 1929–35; RA depot and home stations, 1935–39; psc 1939; Staff Capt. RA 4 Div., 1938; Adjt 30 Field Regt and Capt., 1939; France, Oct. 1939–Jan. 1940; 2nd war course at Staff Coll., Camberley, Jan.-April 1940; Brigade Major RA 43 (Wessex) Div., May-Sept. 1940; Temp. Major; various GSO2 appts incl. Instructor Senior Officers Sch., 1940–42; GSO1 (Lieut-Col) HQ L of C North Africa, Sept.-Nov. 1942; 78 Div. (in North Africa), 1942–43 (OBE); Lieut-Col Comdg Field Regt in 56 (London) Div. in Italy, 1943–44 (DSO); BGS HQ 10 Corps, 1944–45; BGS, British Troops, Austria, 1945–47; Student, IDC, 1949; Dep. Dir Staff Duties, WO, 1950–52; CRA 2nd Infantry Div., BAOR, 1953–55; GOC 11th Armoured Div., March 1956; GOC, 4th Infantry Div., 1956–58; Commandant, Staff Coll., Camberley, 1958–61; Commander, British Forces, Hong Kong, Dec. 1961–March 1963; GOC-in-C, Far East Land Forces, 1963–64. Col Comdt, RA, 1962–73; Col Comdt, APTC, 1966–70; ADC (Gen.), 1966–67. Chm., Exec. Cttee, Army Benevolent Fund, 1968–76. Governor and Mem. Administrative Bd, Corps of Commissionaires, 1964–84 (Pres., 1980–84); retd. *Recreations:* cricket (Army and Kent 2nd XI, MCC, IZ), hockey (Norfolk and RA), golf. *Address:* North Manor House, Uckfield, East Sussex TN22 1EH. *Club:* MCC.
Died 19 Jan. 1993.

HEWITT, Cecil Rolph, (C. H. Rolph); writer; *b* London, 23 Aug. 1901; *s* of Frederick Thompson Hewitt and Edith Mary Speed; *m* 1st, 1926, Audrey Mary Buttery (marr. diss., 1946; she *d* 1982); one *d*; 2nd, 1947, Jenifer Wayne (*d* 1982), author and scriptwriter; one *s* two *d*. *Educ:* State schools. City of London Police, 1921–46 (Chief Inspector); editorial staff, New Statesman, 1947–70; editor, The Author, 1956–60; Dir, New Statesman, 1965–80. Mem., Parole Bd, 1967–69; Mem. Council, Soc. of Authors. *Publications:* A Licensing Handbook, 1947; Crime and Punishment, 1950; Towards My Neighbour, 1950; On Gambling, 1951; Personal Identity, 1956; (ed) The Human Sum, 1957; Mental Disorder, 1958; Commonsense About Crime and Punishment, 1961; The Trial of Lady Chatterley, 1961; (with Arthur Koestler) Hanged by the Neck, 1961; All Those in Favour? (The ETU Trial), 1962; The Police and The Public, 1962; Law and the Common Man, 1967; Books in the Dock, 1969; Kingsley, 1973; Believe What You Like, 1973; Living Twice (autobiog.), 1974; Mr Prone, 1977; The Queen's Pardon, 1978; London Particulars (autobiog.), 1980; The Police (child's history), 1980; As I Was Saying, 1985; Further Particulars (autobiog.), 1987; contributor to The Encyclopædia Britannica, Chambers's Encyclopædia, Punch, The Week-End Book, The New Law Journal, The Times Literary Supplement, The Author, The Nation (NY), daily and weekly press. *Recreations:* music, reading, the contemplation of work. *Address:* 33 Hitherwood, Cranleigh, Surrey GU6 8BW. *T:* Cranleigh (0483) 272793.
Died 10 March 1994.

HEWITT, Harold; solicitor; consultant since 1973; *b* 1 Jan. 1908; *m* 1949, Jeannette Myers; one *d. Educ:* Bede Collegiate Sch., Sunderland; Armstrong Coll., Univ. of Durham. Solicitor, admitted 1930. Legal Adviser, High Commissioner for Austria, Allied Commission, 1946–49. Member, Law Society; Past Pres., Bexley and Dartford Law Soc. *Recreation:* social welfare work. *Address:* 121 Dorset House, Gloucester Place, NW1 5AQ.
Died 23 April 1994.

HEWITT, Capt. John Graham, DSO 1940; Royal Navy (retired); *b* 15 Oct. 1902; *s* of J. G. L. Hewitt, SM, Marton, NZ; *m* 1924, Esther Graham Stokes; one *s* (and one *s* decd); *m* 1947, Mrs Anne Rooney (*d* 1989), *widow* of Col J. J. Rooney, IMS. *Educ:* RN Colls, Osborne and Dartmouth. Midshipman, 1919; Comdr, 1936; commanded: HMS Winchelsea, 1937; HMS Auckland, 1940–41; HMS Dauntless, 1941–42; Capt. 1942; HMS Royalist, 1944; HMS Frobisher, 1945–46; Second Naval Member of NZ Navy Board, 1947; Director Tactical Sch., Woolwich, 1949–52; retired list, 1952. Norwegian War Cross, 1942. *Recreation:* fishing. *Address:* 16 Royston Court, Kew Gardens, Richmond, Surrey TW9 3EH. *T:* 081–940 7057.
Died 1 Feb. 1991.

HEWITT, Margaret, PhD; Reader in Social Institutions, University of Exeter, since 1970; *b* 25 Oct. 1928; *d* of Robert Henry Hewitt and Jessie Hewitt. *Educ:* Bedford Coll., London; London Sch. of Economics. BA Hons Sociology (1st Cl.) 1950, PhD Sociology 1953. Univ. of London Postgrad. Studentship in Sociology, 1950–52; Asst Lectr in Sociology, University Coll. of the South West, 1952–54; Lectr in Sociology, Univ. of Exeter, 1954–65, Sen. Lectr, 1965–70. Mem. Council, Univ. of Exeter, 1964–70; Governor: Bedford Coll., 1968–82; St Luke's Coll., Exeter, 1969–78. Member: Church Assembly, 1961–70; Gen. Synod of Church of England, 1970–; Standing Cttee of Gen. Synod, 1976–; Crown Appts Commn, 1977–87. Chm., Reid Trust for Educn of Women, 1980–; President: Exeter Br., Nat. Council for Women, 1978–; William Temple Assoc., 1983–89. Nat. Co-ordinator of Women Against the Ordination of Women, 1986–. Rep. of Univ. of London on Council of Roedean Sch., 1974–84; Member, Governing Body: Trinity Theol Coll., Bristol, 1980–85; Salisbury and Wells Theol Coll., 1985–. *Publications:* Wives and Mothers in Victorian Industry, 1958; (with Ivy Pinchbeck) Children in English Society, Vol. I 1969, Vol. II 1973. *Recreation:* doing nothing. *Address:* 14 Velwell Road, Exeter, Devon EX4 4LE. *T:* Exeter (0392) 54150. *Club:* Royal Over-Seas League.
Died 7 June 1991.

HEWITT, Richard Thornton, OBE 1945; retired; Executive Director, Royal Society of Medicine, 1952–82; Vice-President, The Royal Society of Medicine Foundation, Inc., New York, 1969–89; *b* 1917; *yr s* of late Harold and Elsie Muriel Hewitt, Bramhall, Cheshire. *Educ:* King's Sch., Macclesfield; Magdalen Coll., Oxford (Exhibitioner). Served War, Lt-Col, infantry and special forces, 1939–46. Asst Registrary, Cambridge Univ., 1946 (incorporated MA, Magdalene Coll., Cambridge, 1946); Sec., Oxford Univ. Medical Sch., 1947–52. FKC 1985. Hon. Mem., Honourable Soc. of Middle Temple, 1978; Hon. Fellow: Swedish Med. Soc., 1968; RSocMed, 1985; Chelsea Coll., 1985. Liveryman, Worshipful Society of Apothecaries of London, 1954. Freeman of the City of London, 1954. *Recreations:* gentle golf and gardening, listening to music, contemplating the nature of time. *Address:* The White House, Iffley, Oxford OX4 4EG. *T:* Oxford (01865) 779263. *Clubs:* MCC, Royal Automobile; Frewen (Oxford); Royal and Ancient (St Andrews).
Died 1 Oct. 1994.

HEYGATE, Sir George Lloyd, 5th Bt *cr* 1831, of Southend, Essex; *b* 28 Oct. 1936; *s* of Sir John Edward Nourse Heygate, 4th Bt, and 2nd wife, Gwyneth Eliot, 2nd *d* of J. E. H. Lloyd; *S* father, 1976; *m* 1960, Hildegard Mathilde, *d* of August Anton Kleinjohann, Duisburg, Germany. *Heir: b* Richard John Gage Heygate [*b* 30 Jan. 1940; *m* 1st, 1968, Carol Rosemary (marr. diss. 1972), *d* of Comdr Richard Michell; 2nd, 1974, Jong Ja (marr. diss. 1988), *d* of In Suk, Seoul; one *d*; 3rd, 1988, Susan Fiona, *d* of late Robert Buckley; two *s*].
Died 29 Oct. 1991.

HEYWOOD, Francis Melville, MA; Warden of Lord Mayor Treloar College, 1952–69, retired 1969; *b* 1 Oct. 1908; 4th *s* of late Rt Rev. B. O. F. Heywood, DD; *m* 1937, Dorothea Kathleen (*d* 1983), *e d* of late Sir Basil Mayhew, KBE; one *s* two *d* (and one *s* decd). *Educ:* Haileybury Coll. (Scholar); Gonville and Caius Coll. Cambridge (Scholar), 1st Class Hons, Classical Tripos, Part I, 1929; Part II, 1931; Rugby Football blue, 1928. Asst Master, Haileybury Coll., 1931–35; Fellow, Asst Tutor and Praelector, Trinity Hall, Cambridge, 1935–39; Master of Marlborough Coll., 1939–52. *Publication:* A Load of New Rubbish, 1985. *Recreations:* walking, writing. *Address:* 30 The Bayle, Folkestone, Kent CT20 1SQ.
Died 2 Nov. 1995.

HEYWOOD, Sir Oliver Kerr, 5th Bt, *cr* 1838, of Claremont, Lancashire; *b* 30 June 1920; *s* of late Maj.-Gen. C. P. Heywood, CB, CMG, DSO (2nd *s* of 3rd Bt) and Margaret Vere, *d* of late Arthur Herbert Kerr; *S* uncle 1946; *m* 1947, Denise Wymondham, 2nd *d* of late Jocelyn William Godefroi, MVO; three *s. Educ:* Eton; Trinity Coll., Cambridge (BA). Served in Coldstream Guards, 1940–46 (despatches). Profession: artist. *Heir: s* Peter Heywood [*b* 10 Dec. 1947; *m* 1970, Jacqueline Anne, *d* of Sir Robert Hunt, CBE; two *d*]. *Address:* Rose Cottage, Elcombe, Stroud, Glos GL6 7LA.
Died 22 June 1992.

HEYWORTH, Peter Lawrence Frederick; Music Critic of The Observer, 1955–87; *b* 3 June 1921; *er s* of Lawrence Ormerod Heyworth and Ellie Stern. *Educ:* Charterhouse; Balliol Coll., Oxford. HM Forces, 1940–46; Balliol, 1947–50; University of Göttingen, 1950. Music critic of Times Educational Supplement, 1952–56; Record reviewer for New Statesman, 1956–58; Guest of the Ford Foundation in Berlin, 1964–65. Critic of the Year, British Press Awards, 1980, commendation 1979. *Publications:* (ed) Berlioz, Romantic and Classic: selected writings by Ernest Newman, 1972; (ed) Conversations with Klemperer, 1973; Otto Klemperer: his life and times, Vol. 1 1885–1933, 1983. *Address:* 32 Bryanston Square, W1H 7LS. *T:* 071–262 8906; Yew Tree Cottage, Hinton St Mary, Sturminster Newton, Dorset. *T:* Sturminster Newton (0258) 72203.
Died 2 Oct. 1991.

HIBBERT, Eleanor Alice; author; *b* London, 1 Sept. 1906; *née* Burford; *m* George Hibbert (decd). *Educ:* privately. *Publications: as Jean Plaidy:* Together They Ride, 1945; Beyond The Blue Mountains, 1947; Murder Most Royal (and as The King's Pleasure, USA), 1949; The Goldsmith's Wife, 1950; Madame Serpent, 1951; Daughter of Satan, 1952; The Italian Woman, 1952; Sixth Wife, 1953, new edn 1969; Queen Jezebel, 1953; St Thomas's Eve, 1954; The Spanish Bridegroom, 1954; Gay Lord Robert, 1955; The Royal Road to Fotheringay, 1955, new edn 1968; The Wandering Prince, 1956; A Health Unto His Majesty, 1956; Here Lies Our Sovereign Lord, 1956; Flaunting Extravagant Queen, 1956, new edn 1960; Triptych of Poisoners, 1958, new edn 1970; Madonna of the Seven Hills, 1958; Light on Lucrezia, 1958; Louis the Wellbeloved, 1959; The Road to Compiegne, 1959; The Rise of the Spanish Inquisition, 1959; The Growth of the Spanish Inquisition, 1960; Castile For Isabella, 1960; Spain for the Sovereigns, 1960; The End of the Spanish Inquisition, 1961; Daughters of Spain, 1961; Katherine, The Virgin Widow, 1961; Meg Roper, Daughter of Sir

Thomas More (for children), 1961; The Young Elizabeth (for children), 1961; The Shadow of the Pomegranate, 1962; The King's Secret Matter, 1962; The Young Mary, Queen of Scots, 1962; The Captive Queen of Scots, 1963; Mary, Queen of France, 1964; The Murder in the Tower, 1964; The Thistle and the Rose, 1965; The Three Crowns, 1965; Evergreen Gallant, 1965; The Haunted Sisters, 1966; The Queen's Favourites, 1966; The Princess of Celle, 1967; Queen in Waiting, 1967; The Spanish Inquisition, its Rise, Growth and End (3 vols in one), 1967; Caroline The Queen, 1968; Katharine of Aragon (3 vols in one), 1968; The Prince and the Quakeress, 1968; The Third George, 1969; Catherine de Medici (3 vols in one), 1969; Perdita's Prince, 1969; Sweet Lass of Richmond Hill, 1970; The Regent's Daughter, 1971; Goddess of the Green Room, 1971; Victoria in the Wings, 1972; Charles II (3 vols in one), 1972; The Captive of Kensington Palace, 1972; The Queen and Lord M, 1973; The Queen's Husband, 1973; The Widow of Windsor, 1974; The Bastard King, 1974; The Lion of Justice, 1975; The Passionate Enemies, 1976; The Plantagenet Prelude, 1976; The Revolt of the Eaglets, 1977; The Heart of the Lion, 1977; The Prince of Darkness, 1978; The Battle of the Queens, 1978; The Queen from Provence, 1979; Edward Longshanks, 1979; The Follies of the King, 1980; The Vow on the Heron, 1980; Passage to Pontefract, 1981; Star of Lancaster, 1981; Epitaph for Three Women, 1981; Red Rose of Anjou, 1982; The Sun in Splendour, 1982; Uneasy Lies the Head, 1982; Myself My Enemy, 1983; Queen of this Realm, 1984; Victoria Victorious, 1985; The Lady in the Tower, 1986; The Courts of Love, 1987; In the Shadow of the Crown, 1988; The Queen's Secret, 1989; The Reluctant Queen, 1990; The Pleasures of Love, 1991; William's Wife, 1992; *as Eleanor Burford:* Daughter of Anna, 1941; Passionate Witness, 1941; Married Love, 1942; When All The World Was Young, 1943; So The Dreams Depart, 1944; Not In Our Stars, 1945; Dear Chance, 1947; Alexa, 1948; The House At Cupid's Cross, 1949; Believe The Heart, 1950; Love Child, 1950; Saint Or Sinner?, 1951; Dear Delusion, 1952; Bright Tomorrow, 1952; When We Are Married, 1953; Leave Me My Love, 1953; Castles in Spain, 1954; Hearts Afire, 1954; When Other Hearts, 1955; Two Loves In Her Life, 1955; Married in Haste, 1956; Begin To Live, 1956; To Meet A Stranger, 1957; Pride of the Morning, 1958; Blaze of Noon, 1958; Dawn Chorus, 1959; Red Sky At Night, 1959; Night of Stars, 1960; Now That April's Gone, 1961; Who's Calling?, 1962; *as Ellalice Tate:* Defenders of The Faith, 1956 (under name of Jean Plaidy, 1970); Scarlet Cloak, 1957 (2nd edn, under name of Jean Plaidy, 1969); Queen of Diamonds, 1958; Madame Du Barry, 1959; This Was A Man, 1961; *as Elbur Ford:* The Flesh and The Devil, 1950; Poison in Pimlico, 1950; Bed Disturbed, 1952; Such Bitter Business, 1953 (as Evil in the House, USA 1954); *as Kathleen Kellow:* Danse Macabre, 1952; Rooms At Mrs Oliver's, 1953; Lilith, 1954 (2nd edn, under name of Jean Plaidy, 1967); It Began in Vauxhall Gardens, 1955 (2nd edn under name of Jean Plaidy, 1968); Call of the Blood, 1956; Rochester-The Mad Earl, 1957; Milady Charlotte, 1959; The World's A Stage, 1960; *as Victoria Holt:* Mistress of Mellyn, 1961; Kirkland Revels, 1962; The Bride of Pendorric, 1963; The Legend of the Seventh Virgin, 1965; Menfreya, 1966; The King of the Castle, 1967; The Queen's Confession, 1968; The Shivering Sands, 1969; The Secret Woman, 1971; The Shadow of the Lynx, 1972; On the Night of the Seventh Moon, 1973; The Curse of the Kings, 1973; The House of a Thousand Lanterns, 1974; Lord of the Far Island, 1975; The Pride of the Peacock, 1976; My Enemy the Queen, 1978; The Spring of the Tiger, 1979; The Mask of the Enchantress, 1980; The Judas Kiss, 1981; The Demon Lover, 1982; The Time of the Hunter's Moon, 1983; The Landower Legacy, 1984; The Road to Paradise

Island, 1985; Secret for a Nightingale, 1986; The Silk Vendetta, 1987; The India Fan, 1988; The Captive, 1989; Snare of Serpents, 1990; Daughter of Deceit, 1991; Seven for a Secret, 1992; *as Philippa Carr:* The Miracle at St Bruno's, 1972; Lion Triumphant, 1974; The Witch from the Sea, 1975; Saraband for Two Sisters, 1976; Lament for a Lost Lover, 1977; The Love Child, 1978; The Song of the Siren, 1979; The Drop of the Dice, 1980; The Adulteress, 1981; Zipporah's Daughter, 1983; Voices in a Haunted Room, 1984; Return of the Gypsy, 1985; Midsummer's Eve, 1986; The Pool at St Branok, 1987; The Changeling, 1989; The Black Swan, 1990; A Time for Silence, 1991; The Gossamer Cord, 1992. *Address:* c/o Robert Hale Ltd, 45/47 Clerkenwell Green, EC1.

Died 18 Jan. 1993.

HIDAYATULLAH, Mohammed, OBE 1946; Vice-President of India, 1979–84 (Acting President, 1969 and 1982); *b* 17 Dec. 1905; *y s* of Khan Bahadur Hafiz M. Wilayatullah, ISO; *m* 1948, Pushpa Shah, *d* of A. N. Shah, ICS; one *s* (one *d* decd). *Educ:* Govt High Sch., Raipur; Morris Coll., Nagpur (Phillips Schol.; BA; Malak Gold Medal); Trinity Coll., Cambridge (MA; Pres., Indian Majlis, 1928); Lincoln's Inn (Bencher 1968). Nagpur High Court: Advocate, 1930–46; Govt Pleader, 1942–43; Advocate General, CP and Berar, 1943–46; Puisne Judge, 1946–54; Chief Justice, 1954–56; Chief Justice, Madhya Pradesh High Court, 1956–58; Puisne Judge, Supreme Court of India, 1958–68, Chief Justice, 1968–70. Dean, Faculty of Law, Nagpur Univ., 1950–54; Mem., Faculty of Law, Sagar, Vikram and Aligarh Univs; President: Indian Law Inst., 1968–70; Internat. Law Assoc. (Indian Br.), 1968–70; Indian Soc. of Internat. Law, 1968–70; Member: Internat. Inst. of Space Law, Paris; British Inst. of Internat. and Comparative Law, 1982–; Exec. Council, World Assembly of Judges; Advr, Council for World Peace through Law; rep. India at Internat. Confs at Bangkok, Helsinki, Durham, Geneva, Port of Spain, Belgrade, Venice, Canberra, Melbourne, Washington, New York, Tunis, The Hague, Tokyo and Stockholm; Vice Pres., Heritage Fund, Lincoln's Inn, 1986–. Chancellor: Muslim Nat. Univ., New Delhi, 1968–86; Delhi Univ., 1979–85; Punjab Univ., 1979–85; Hyderabad Central Univ., 1986–91. Associate Mem., Royal Acad. of Morocco. Pres., Indian Red Cross Soc., 1982–; Member: World Assoc. for Orphans and Abandoned Children, Geneva; Internat. Council of Former Scouts and Guides (awarded Silver Elephant, 1948); Chief Scout, All India Boy Scouts Assoc. (awarded Bronze Medal for Gallantry, 1969). Patron-in-Chief: Schizophrenic Foundn for Res., India; India Islamic Cultural Centre; Patron, Hungar Project, India. Kt of Mark Twain, 1985. Fellow, Indian Law Inst., 1986. Hon. LLD: Univ. of Philippines, 1970; Ravishankar Univ., 1970; Rajasthan Univ., 1976; Benares Hindu Univ.; Berhampore Univ.; Kashmir Univ., 1983; Punjab Univ.; Nagpur Univ., 1985; Agra Univ., 1987; Hyderabad Central Univ., 1991; Hon. DLitt: Bhopal Univ.; Kakatiya Univ.; Hon. DCL Delhi Univ. Medallion and Plaque of Merit, Philconsa, Manila; Order of Jugoslav Flag with Sash, 1972; Shromani Award, 1986; Grand Cross (1st class) for Arts and Literature, Austrian People, 1989; Lokshree Award, India, 1989; Singhui Award, Benares Hindu Univ., 1991; Royal Insignia, Acad. of Morocco, 1990. *Publications:* Democracy in India and the Judicial Process, 1966; The South-West Africa Case, 1967; Judicial Methods, 1969; A Judge's Miscellany, vol. 1 1972, second series 1979, third series 1983, fourth series, 1985; USA and India, 1977; 5th and 6th Schedules to Constitution of India 1979; My Own Boswell (memoirs), 1980; (ed) Mulla's Mohamedan Law, 16th–19th edns; Taqrir-o Tabir (Urdu), Right to Property and the Indian Constitution, The Indian Constitution (ed, 3 vols); Miscellanea, 1988; numerous monographs and articles.

Recreations: golf, bridge. *Address:* A-10 Rockside, 112 Walkeshwar Road, Bombay 6, India. *T:* 3678344. *Clubs:* Delhi Gymkhana (New Delhi); Willingdon (Bombay).
Died 18 Sept. 1992.

HIGGINS, Hon. Sir Eoin; *see* Higgins, Hon. Sir J. P. B.

HIGGINS, Frank; *see* Higgins, W. F.

HIGGINS, Hon. Sir John Patrick Basil, (Sir Eoin), Kt 1988; **Hon. Mr Justice Higgins;** a Judge of the High Court of Northern Ireland, since 1984; due to take office as a Lord Justice of Appeal, Northern Ireland, 3 Sept. 1993; Deputy Chairman, Boundary Commission for Northern Ireland, since 1989; *b* 14 June 1927; *e s* of late John A. and Mary Philomena Higgins, Magherafelt; *m* 1960, Bridget, *e d* of late Dr Matthew F. O'Neill, Hollingwood, Chesterfield; two *s* three *d. Educ:* St. Columb's Coll., Derry; Queen's Univ., Belfast (LLB). Called to Bar of N Ireland, 1948, Bencher, 1969–; QC (NI) 1967; County Court Judge, 1971–84: Armagh and Fermanagh, 1976–79; S Antrim, 1979–82; Recorder of Belfast, 1982–84. Chairman: Mental Health Review Tribunal for NI, 1963–71; Legal Aid Adv. Cttee (NI), 1975–82; Council of HM County Court Judges, 1978–84; Member: County Court Rules Cttee (NI), 1973–82 (Chm. 1982–84); Statute Law Cttee of NI, 1975–; Lowry Cttee on Registration of Title in NI, 1958–67; Jones Cttee on County Courts and Magistrates' Courts in NI, 1972–73; Gardiner Cttee on measures to deal with terrorism in NI, 1974. Chm., Voluntary Service, Belfast, 1975–85. Member: Community Peace Conf., 1969; Bd of Management, St Joseph's Coll. of Educn, Belfast, 1969–85; Bd of Governors, Dominican Coll., Portstewart, 1974–84. *Address:* The Royal Courts of Justice (Ulster), Belfast, Northern Ireland. *Died 2 Sept. 1993.*

HIGGINS, Reynold Alleyne, LittD; FBA 1972; FSA; *b* Weybridge, 26 Nov. 1916; *er s* of late Charles Alleyne Higgins and Marjorie Edith (*née* Taylor); *m* 1947, Patricia Mary, *d* of J. C. Williams; three *s* two *d. Educ:* Sherborne Sch.; Pembroke Coll., Cambridge (Scholar). First Cl. Classical Tripos pts I and II, 1937, 1938; MA 1960; LittD 1963. Served War: Queen Victoria's Rifles, KRRC, 1939–46 (Captain, POW). Asst Keeper, Dept of Greek and Roman Antiquities, British Museum, 1947, Dep. Keeper, 1965–77, Acting Keeper, 1976. Visiting Fellow, British School of Archaeology at Athens, 1969, Chm., Managing Cttee, 1975–79; Norton Lectr, Archaeol Inst. of America, 1982–83. Corresp. Mem., German Archaeological Inst. *Publications:* Catalogue of Terracottas in British Museum, vols I and II, 1954, 1959; Greek and Roman Jewellery, 1961, 2nd edn 1980; Greek Terracotta Figures, 1963; Jewellery from Classical Lands, 1965; Greek Terracottas, 1967; Minoan and Mycenaean Art, 1967, 2nd edn 1981; The Greek Bronze Age, 1970; The Archaeology of Minoan Crete, 1973; The Aegina Treasure, 1979; Tanagra and the Figurines, 1986; also articles and reviews in British and foreign periodicals. *Recreation:* travel. *Address:* Hillside Cottage, Dunsfold, near Godalming, Surrey GU8 4PB. *T:* Godalming (0483) 200400. *Died 18 April 1993.*

HIGGINS, (Wilfred) Frank, FCIT 1979; *b* 30 Aug. 1927; *s* of Wilfred and Hilda Higgins; *m* 1948, Betty Pulford; one *s* one *d*; *m* 1985, Margaret Roberts. *Educ:* Hanley High Sch., Stoke-on-Trent; St Paul's Coll., Cheltenham. Teacher: Stoke-on-Trent, 1946; Notts, 1948–58; Organising Sec., Youth Gp, 1958–60; Teacher, Nottingham, Derby, 1960–73; Mem. Nat. Bus Co., 1974–79. Contested (Lab) Harborough 1966, Grantham 1970. Mem., Nottingham City Council, 1971–74, 1979–87 (Chm. Transportation Cttee, 1972–74, 1979–81); Lord Mayor of Nottingham, 1986–87; Mem., Notts CC, 1973–77 and 1981–89 (Chm. Environment Cttee,

1973–77; Chm. Resources Cttee, 1981–86; Chm., Police Cttee, 1987–89); Chm., E Midlands Airport Jt Cttee, 1986–87. Chm., Central Transport Consultative Cttee, 1977–80. Chairman: Bridge Housing Assoc., 1987–; Notts Building Preservation Trust, 1988–. *Recreations:* travelling, talking. *Address:* 8 River View, The Embankment, Nottingham NG2 2GF. *T:* Nottingham (0602) 863135. *Died 11 May 1993.*

HIGGS, Rt Rev. Hubert Laurence, MA Cantab; *b* 23 Nov. 1911; *s* of Frank William and Mary Ann Higgs; *m* 1936, Elizabeth Clare (*née* Rogers); one *s* one *d. Educ:* University Coll. Sch.; Christ's Coll., Cambridge; Ridley Hall, Cambridge. Deacon, 1935; priest, 1936; Curate: Holy Trinity, Richmond, 1935; St Luke's, Redcliffe Square, London, 1936–38; St John's, Boscombe (and Jt Sec. Winchester Youth Council), 1938–39; Vicar, Holy Trinity, Aldershot, 1939–45; Editorial Sec., Church Missionary Soc., 1945–52; Vicar, St John's, Woking, 1952–57 (Rural Dean, 1957); Archdeacon of Bradford and Canon Residentiary of Bradford Cathedral, 1957–65; Bishop Suffragan of Hull, 1965–76; RD of Hull, 1972–76; retired 1976. *Recreations:* history, music-listening, gardening. *Address:* The Farmstead, Chediston, Halesworth, Suffolk IP19 0AS. *T:* Halesworth (09867) 2621.
Died 4 Jan. 1992.

HIGGS, Sir (John) Michael (Clifford), Kt 1969; DL; solicitor, retired; *b* 30 May 1912; *s* of late Alderman A. W. Higgs, Cranford House, Stourton, Staffs; *m* 1st, 1936, Diana Louise Jerrams (*d* 1950); two *d*; 2nd, 1952, Rachel Mary Jones, OBE; one *s* one *d. Educ:* St Cuthberts, Malvern; Shrewsbury. LLB (Birmingham), 1932. Admitted solicitor, 1934. Served War of 1939–45 with 73 HAA Regt RA (TA), 1939–42; JAG Staff, 1942–46; demobilised, 1946, with rank of Lieut-Col. Mem. of Staffs County Council, 1946–49; MP (C) Bromsgrove Div. of Worcs, 1950–55; Member: Worcs CC, 1953–73 (Chm. 1959–73; Alderman, 1963); Hereford and Worcester CC, 1973–85 (Chm., 1973–77); West Midlands Economic Planning Council, 1965–79; Chm., W Midlands Planning Authorities' Conf., 1969–73. DL Worcs 1968, Hereford and Worcester, 1974. *Address:* Pixham Cottage, Callow End, Worcester WR2 4TH. *T:* Worcester (01905) 830645. *Died 20 Oct. 1995.*

HIGHSMITH, Patricia; writer since 1942; *b* 19 Jan. 1921; *o c* of Jay Bernard Plangman and Mary Coates (of German and English-Scots descent respectively); name changed to Highsmith on mother's 2nd marriage; unmarried. *Educ:* Barnard Coll., Columbia Univ., New York. For a year after univ. had a mediocre writing job; after that free-lance until publication of first novel; lived in Europe and America alternately from 1951, and latterly in Switzerland. Prix Littéraire (Deauville), 1987. Officier, l'Ordre des Arts et des Lettres (France), 1990. *Publications: novels:* Strangers on a Train, 1950 (filmed 1951); The Blunderer, 1955; The Talented Mr Ripley, 1956; Deep Water, 1957; A Game for the Living, 1958; This Sweet Sickness, 1960 (filmed 1979); The Cry of the Owl, 1962; The Two Faces of January, 1964; The Glass Cell, 1965; A Suspension of Mercy, 1965; Those Who Walk Away, 1967; The Tremor of Forgery, 1969; Ripley Under Ground, 1971; A Dog's Ransom, 1972; Ripley's Game, 1974 (filmed as The American Friend, 1978); Edith's Diary, 1977; The Boy Who Followed Ripley, 1980; People Who Knock on the Door, 1983; Found in the Street, 1986; Carol, 1990 (published as The Price of Salt, 1953, under pseudonym Claire Morgan); Ripley under Water, 1991; *short stories:* The Animal-Lover's Book of Beastly Murder, 1975; Little Tales of Misogyny, 1977; Slowly, Slowly in the Wind, 1979; The Black House, 1981; Mermaids on the Golf Course, 1985; Plotting and Writing Suspense Fiction,

1966, 2nd edn, 1983; Tales of Natural and Unnatural Catastrophes, 1987; *posthumous publication:* Small g: a summer idyll, 1995. *Recreations:* drawing, some painting, carpentering, snail-watching, travelling by train. *Club:* Detection. *Died 4 Feb. 1995.*

HILARY, David Henry Jephson, CB 1991; Receiver for the Metropolitan Police District, 1987–92; *b* 3 May 1932; *s* of late Robert and Nita Hilary; *m* 1957, Phœbe Leonora, *d* of John J. Buchanan and Phoebe (*née* Messel); two *s* two *d. Educ:* Tonbridge Sch.; King's Coll., Cambridge (Sandys Student 1954, Craven Student 1955; MA). Royal Artillery, 1953–54. Home Office, 1956–87; Cabinet Office, 1967–69 and 1981–83; Asst Under Sec. of State, Home Office, 1975–87. *Recreations:* cricket, bridge, family pursuits. *Address:* 17 Victoria Square, SW1W 0RA. *Clubs:* Royal Automobile, MCC.

Died 21 Oct. 1994.

HILDER, Rowland, OBE 1986; RI 1938; painter; *b* Greatneck, Long Island, USA, 28 June 1905; British parents; *m* 1929, Edith Blenkiron (*d* 1992); one *s* one *d. Educ:* Goldsmiths' Coll. Sch. of Art, London. Exhibited, Hayward Gall., 1983. PRI, 1964–74. *Publications:* illustrated editions of: Moby Dick, 1926; Treasure Island, 1929; Precious Bane, 1930; The Bible for To-day, 1940; The Shell Guide to Flowers of the Countryside (with Edith Hilder), 1955; (jointly) Sketching and Painting Indoors, 1957; Starting with Watercolour, 1966, expanded repr. 1988; Painting Landscapes in Watercolour, 1983 (USA, as Expressing Land, Sea and Sky in Watercolour, 1982); *relevant publications:* Rowland Hilder: painter and illustrator, by John Lewis, 1978; Rowland Hilder's England, by Denis Thomas, 1986; Rowland Hilder Country, ed by Denis Thomas, 1987; Rowland Hilder Sketching Country, ed by Denis Thomas, 1991. *Address:* 7 Kidbrooke Grove, Blackheath, SE3 0PG. *T:* 081–858 3072. *Died 21 April 1993.*

HILDITCH, Clifford Arthur; Director of Social Services, Manchester City Council, 1970–74, Manchester District Council, 1974–83, retired; *b* 3 Feb. 1927; *s* of late Arthur Clifford Hilditch and of Lilian Maud Hilditch (*née* Brockman); *m* 1953, Joyce Hilditch (*née* Burgess); one *s. Educ:* Huntingdon Grammar Sch.; London Univ. Dip. in Applied Social Studies. Army Service, 1944–48 (commissioned into Indian Army, 1945). Service as an Administrative Officer, LCC (Welfare Services) until 1961; Manchester City Council: Dep. Chief Welfare Officer, 1962–64; Chief Welfare Officer, 1965–70. Chm., E Cheshire Hospice Council, 1984–; Mem., Industrial Tribunals, 1983–. Hon. Fellow, Manchester Polytechnic, 1976. *Recreations:* various. *Address:* 14 Priory Road, Wilmslow, Cheshire SK9 5PS. *T:* Wilmslow (0625) 522109. *Died 24 Feb. 1991.*

HILDRETH, Maj.-Gen. Sir (Harold) John (Crossley), KBE 1964 (CBE 1952; OBE 1945); *b* 12 June 1908; *s* of late Lt-Col Harold Crossley Hildreth, DSO, OBE, FRCS, and Mrs Hildreth; *m* 1st, 1932, Joan Elise, *d* of Comdr A. F. Hamilton (marr. diss.); two *s* three *d*; *m* 1950, Mary (*d* 1988), *d* of late G. Wroe. *Educ:* Wellington Coll., Berks; RMA, Woolwich. 2nd Lieut, RA, 1928; transferred to RAOC, 1935, as Captain; War Office: Col, 1942–44; Brig., 1944–47; Inspector of Establishments, 1947–50; Controller of Army Statistics, 1950–51; Comdr RAOC, Ammunition Org., 1951–53; Comdr, Bicester, 1953–57; DOS, BAOR, 1957–60; Inspector, RAOC, War Office, 1960–61; Dir of Ordnance Service, War Office, 1961–64; Major 1944; Lieut-Col 1948; Col 1952; Brig. 1958; Maj.-Gen. 1961; retired, Dec. 1964. Man. Dir, Army Kinema Corp., 1965–70, Services Kinema Corp., 1970–75. Chm. Greater London Br., SS&AFA, 1977–81. Col Commandant, RAOC, 1963–70. Legion of Merit (degree of Officer), USA. *Recreations:* shooting, sailing. *Address:*

56 The Cottages, North Street, Emsworth, Hants PO10 7PJ. *T:* Emsworth (0243) 373466. *Club:* Emsworth Sailing. *Died 11 Oct. 1992.*

HILL, Alan John Wills, CBE 1972; FSA; publishing consultant; consultant to the Heinemann Group of Publishers, 1979–84 and since 1986; *b* 12 Aug. 1912; *s* of William Wills Hill and May Frances Hill; *m* 1939, Enid Adela Malin; two *s* one *d. Educ:* Wyggeston Sch., Leicester; Jesus Coll., Cambridge (Schol.). FSA 1993. RAF, 1940–45: Specialist Armament Officer (Sqdn Ldr). Publishing Asst, Wm Heinemann Ltd, 1936–40; Dir, 1955; Man. Dir, 1959–61; Chm. and Man. Dir, Heinemann Educational Books Ltd, 1961–79; Man. Dir, Heinemann Group of Publishers Ltd, 1973–79; Chairman: Heinemann Educnl Books (Nigeria), 1969–83; Heinemann companies in Australia, Canada, Caribbean, E Africa, Hong Kong, Malaysia, NZ, Singapore and USA, 1964–79; World's Work Ltd, 1973–79; Hill MacGibbon Ltd, 1984–85; Man. Dir, Heinemann Computers in Education Ltd, 1981–84; Consultant to William Collins, 1985–86. Chm., Soc. of Bookmen, 1965–68; Chm., Educational Publishers' Council, 1969–71; Vice-Chm., Educn Technol. Project, 1985–88; Member: Council, Publishers' Assoc., 1972–79; Exec. Cttee, National Book League, 1973–79; British Council Books Adv. Panel, 1973–83; CNAA (Business Studies Panel), 1975–82; UNESCO Cttee on Copyright in third world countries; Cttee, Friends of the Lake District, 1979–. Chm. of Trustees, Ceres Trust, 1988–; Trustee, Maryport Heritage Trust, 1990–. Mem., Council, Prehistoric Soc., 1987– (PRO, 1988–). Governor, Nuffield-Chelsea Trust, 1979–; Mem. Council, Chelsea Coll., London Univ., 1978–85 (Vice-Chm., 1981–85); Mem. Council, King's Coll. London, 1985–89 (Hon. Life Fellow, 1985). Pres., Keswick Amateur Athletic Club, 1977–. Closely involved with Commonwealth literature and educn. *Publications:* (with R. W. Finn) And So Was England Born, 1939; History in Action, 1962; In Pursuit of Publishing (autobiog.), 1988; articles in jls. *Recreations:* swimming, mountain-walking, gardening. *Address:* 56 Northway, NW11 6PA. *T:* 081–455 8388; New House, Rosthwaite, Borrowdale, Cumbria. *Clubs:* Athenæum, Garrick, Royal Air Force, PEN.

Died 17 Dec. 1993.

HILL, Sir Austin Bradford, Kt 1961; CBE 1951; PhD (Econ.) 1926, DSc 1929 (London); FRS 1954; Professor of Medical Statistics, London School of Hygiene and Tropical Medicine, University of London, and Hon. Director, Statistical Research Unit of Medical Research Council, 1945–61, then Emeritus Professor; Dean of the London School of Hygiene and Tropical Medicine, 1955–57, Honorary Fellow, 1976; *b* 8 July 1897; 3rd *s* of late Sir Leonard Erskine Hill, FRS, and Janet Alexander; *m* 1923, Florence Maud (*d* 1980), *d* of late Edward Salmon, OBE; two *s* one *d. Educ:* Chigwell Sch.; privately; University Coll., London. Flight Sub-Lieut in Royal Naval Air Service, 1916–18; on staff of Medical Research Council and its Industrial Health Research Board, 1923–33; Reader in Epidemiology and Vital Statistics, London Sch. of Hygiene and Tropical Medicine, 1933–45; seconded during the war to Research and Experiments Dept, Ministry of Home Security, 1940–42, and to Medical Directorate, RAF, 1943–45. Hon. Civil Consultant in Medical Statistics to RAF and Mem. of Flying Personnel Research Cttee, 1943–78; Civil Consultant in Medical Statistics to RN, 1949–77; Mem., Cttee on Safety of Medicines, 1964–75; Pres. Royal Statistical Soc., 1950–52 (Hon. Sec. 1940–50; Gold Medallist, 1953); Pres. Section of Epidemiology, RSM, 1953–55, Section of Occupational Medicine, 1964–65; Member: Council, MRC, 1954–58; Cttee on Review of Medicines, 1975–78; Fellow of University Coll., London; Hon. FRCP; Hon. FFCM; Hon. FFOM; Hon. FIA; Hon FRSM; Hon. FAPHA; Hon.

Fellow: Soc. of Community Medicine; Soc. of Occupational Medicine; Faculty of Medicine, University of Chile; Society for Social Medicine; Internat. Epidemiological Assoc.; Med. Research Club. Cutter Lecturer, Harvard, 1953; Harben Lecturer RIPH&H, 1957; Alfred Watson Memorial Lectr Inst. of Actuaries, 1962; Marc Daniels Lectr RCP, 1963. Hon. DSc Oxford, 1963; Hon. MD Edinburgh, 1968. Galen Medallist, Soc. of Apothecaries, 1959; Harben Gold Medallist, 1961; Jenner Medallist, RSM, 1965; Heberden Medallist, Heberden Soc., 1965; Alton Ochsner Award, 1988. *Publications:* Internal Migration and its Effects upon the Death Rates, 1925; The Inheritance of Resistance to Bacterial Infection in Animal Species, 1934; Principles of Medical Statistics, 1937, 11th edn, as A Short Textbook of Medical Statistics, 1985; Statistical Methods in Clinical and Preventive Medicine, 1962; reports to Industrial Health Research Board on industrial sickness and numerous papers in scientific journals, especially studies of cigarette smoking and cancer of the lung and of the clinical trial of new drugs. *Recreations:* walking in the countryside, gardening. *Address:* Fairview House, Daltongate, Ulverston, Cumbria LA12 7BE. *T:* Ulverston (0229) 54153.
Died 18 April 1991.

HILL, Brian, CBE 1990; DL; Chief Executive and Clerk, Lancashire County Council, 1977–90; *b* 16 Oct. 1930; *s* of late Joseph and of Bessie Hill; *m* 1954, Barbara (*née* Hickson); one *d. Educ:* Wigan Grammar Sch.; Univ. of Manchester (LLB). Solicitor. Asst Solicitor, Manchester Corp., 1953–56; Lancashire County Council: Sen. Solicitor appts, finally Second Dep. Clerk of CC, 1956–74; Dep. Clerk, 1974–76. Clerk of Lancs Lieutenancy, 1977–90; County Electoral Returning Officer, 1977–90. Secretary: Lancs Adv. Cttee, 1977–90; Lord Chancellor's Adv. Cttee on Gen. Comrs of Income Tax, 1977–91; Lancs Probation and After Care Cttee, 1977–90; Co. Sec., Lancashire County Enterprises Ltd (formerly Lancashire Enterprises), 1982–90, Mem., MSC Area Manpower Bd, 1983–86. Member: Council on Tribunals, 1990–; Local Govt Commn for England, 1992–. Chairman: Local Govt Legal Soc., 1970–71; Soc. of County Secs, 1976–77; NW Br., SOLACE, 1985; Assoc. of County Chief Execs, 1989–90. Mem., Lancs Community Council, 1990–92. Vice-Pres., Lancs Youth Clubs Assoc., 1977–; Clerk to Court, 1977–89, Mem. of Council, 1990–, RNCM, Manchester (Hon. RNCM 1979); Member: Court, Univ. of Lancaster, 1977–; Council, Univ. of Central Lancashire (formerly Lancs Poly.), 1990–93. Chm., S Pennine Pack Horse Trails Trust, 1990–93. Dep. Chm., Hallé Concerts Soc., 1990–. Mem., Rossall Sch. Council, 1990–. DL Lancs, 1977. FRSA 1983; CIMgt (CBIM 1987). Hon. Fellow, Univ. of Central Lancashire (formerly Lancs Poly.), 1990. *Recreation:* music. *Address:* The Cottage, Bruna Hill, Garstang, near Preston, Lancs PR3 1QB. *Club:* Royal Over-Seas League. *Died 26 Oct. 1995.*

HILL, George Geoffrey David, CMG 1971; late Assistant Secretary, Department of the Environment (Head of International Transport Division, Ministry of Transport, 1964); *b* 15 Aug. 1911; *o s* of late William George Hill, JP; *m* 1935, Elisabeth Wilhelmina (*née* Leuwer) (*d* 1988); one *d. Educ:* Manchester Grammar Sch.; Gonville and Caius Coll., Cambridge (BA (Hons)). Entered Ministry of Transport as Asst Principal, 1934; Principal, 1941; Asst Sec., 1954; retired 1972. *Recreations:* bridge, languages. *Address:* 125 Ember Lane, Esher, Surrey KT10 8EH. *T:* 0181–398 1851. *Died 11 Dec. 1995.*

HILL, Harry, OBE 1986; FCCA, FCIS, FTII, CIMgt; Director, Beecham Group, 1979–86; Vice-Chairman, Beecham Products, 1984–86; *b* 22 May 1924; *s* of James and Charlotte Hill; *m* 1944, Vera Brydon; two *d.* War Service, 1942–45: flying duties, Fleet Air Arm; Lieut

RNVR. John Marshall & Co., Newcastle upon Tyne, 1945–50: Professional accounting and auditing; articled clerk, subseq. managing clerk and partner; General Motors Ltd, London, 1950–69: sen. financial appts; Group Gen. Comptroller, 1966–69; Parkinson-Cowan Ltd, London, 1969–71: Dir of Finance and Admin; Beecham Products, Brentford, Mddx: Financial Dir, 1972–76; Admin. Dir. 1976–77; Vice-Chm., Food and Drink Div., 1977–80; Chm., Internat. Div., 1977–84; Chm., Proprietaries Div., 1981–86. FCCA 1964 (ACCA 1949); FCIS 1970; FTII 1976; CBIM 1983. Pres., Assoc. of Certified Accountants, 1975–76; Mem., Price Commn, 1977–79; Chm., Apple and Pear Develt Council, 1983–86. *Recreations:* gardening, reading, motoring. *Address:* 77 Howards Thicket, Gerrards Cross, Bucks SL9 7NU. *T:* Gerrards Cross (0753) 883550.
Died 20 June 1993.

HILL, John Frederick Rowland, CMG 1955; *b* 20 April 1905; *s* of Judge William Henry Hill and Mary Agnes, *d* of Rev. F. W. Quilter; *m* 1930, Phyllys Esmé (*née* Fryer); one *s* two *d. Educ:* Pinewood Sch., Farnborough; Marlborough Coll.; Lincoln Coll., Oxford. BA Oxon, Hon. Sch. Jurisprudence, 1927. Cadet, Colonial Civil Service, Tanganyika, 1928; Asst District Officer, 1930; District Officer, 1940; Dep. Provincial Comr, 1947; Provincial Comr, 1948; Sen. Provincial Comr, 1950; Mem. for Communications, Works and Development Planning, Tanganyika Govt, 1951–56; Chm., Tanganyika Broadcasting Corp. and Dir of Broadcasting, 1956–57; Govt Liaison Officer, Freeport, Bahamas, 1957–58; Supervisor of Elections, Zanzibar, 1959–60.
Died 12 April 1991.

HILL, Norman A.; *see* Ashton Hill.

HILL, Sir Richard (George Rowley), 10th Bt *cr* 1779, of Brook Hall, Londonderry; MBE (mil.) 1974; retired; *b* 18 Dec. 1925; *s* of Sir George Alfred Rowley Hill, 9th Bt, and of Rose Ethel Kathleen, MBE, *d* of late William Spratt; *S* father, 1985; *m* 1st, 1954, Angela Mary (*d* 1974), *d* of late Lt-Col Stanley Herbert Gallon, TD, Berwick-upon-Tweed; 2nd, 1975, Zoreen Joy MacPherson (marr. diss. 1986), *d* of late Norman Warburton Tippett, Kirkland, Berwick-upon-Tweed, and *widow* of Lieut Andrew David Wilson Marshall, KOSB; two *d*; 3rd, 1986, Elizabeth Margaret (*née* Tarbitt) (marr. diss. 1988), *widow* of Laurence Sage, RNVR/FAA. *Recreations:* swimming, riding, reading. *Heir:* half-*b* John Alfred Rowley Hill, *b* 1940. *Address:* c/o Barclays Bank, 28 High Street, Great Missenden, Bucks. *Died 9 March 1992.*

HILL, Robert, ScD Cantab 1942; FRS 1946; biochemist; Member of Scientific Staff of Agricultural Research Council, 1943–66; *b* 2 April 1899; *s* of Joseph Alfred Hill and Clara Maud Jackson; *m* 1935, Amy Priscilla, *d* of Edgar Worthington; two *s* one *d* (and one *d* decd). *Educ:* Bedales Sch.; Emmanuel Coll., Cambridge (Scholar). Served European War, 1914–18: RE pioneer Anti-gas Dept, 1917–18. Emmanuel Coll., Cambridge, 1919–22; Senior Studentship (Exhibn of 1851), 1927; Beit Memorial Research Fellow, 1929; Senior Beit Memorial Research Fellow, 1935; Hon. Fellow of Emmanuel Coll., 1963. Royal Medal, Royal Society, 1963; 1st Award for photosynthesis, Soc. of American Plant Physiologists, 1963; Charles E. Kettering Research Award, 1963; Hon. Member: Amer. Soc. of Biological Chemists, 1964; Comité Internat. de Photobiologie, 1968; American Acad. Arts and Sciences, 1971; For. Associate, Nat. Acad. of Sciences, 1975; For. Mem., Accad. Nazionale dei Lincei, 1975. Copley Medal, Royal Soc., 1987. *Publication:* (with C. P. Whittingham) Photosynthesis, 1955. *Recreations:* growing plants and dyeing with traditional plant dyes, water-colour painting. *Address:* Department of

Biochemistry, Cambridge University, Cambridge CB2 1QW; 1 Comberton Road, Barton, Cambridge CB3 7BA. *Died 15 March 1991.*

HILL, William Sephton; Development Director, International Duty Free Confederation, Brussels, since 1989; *b* 24 July 1926; *s* of late William Thomas and Annie May Hill; *m* 1954, Jean, *d* of Philip Wedgwood; one *d. Educ:* Cowley Sch., St. Helens, Merseyside. BA, LLB Cantab. Served RAF, 1944–48, Japanese interpreter. Called to the Bar, Gray's Inn, 1951; practised Northern Circuit, 1951–54. Joined Solicitor's Office, HM Customs and Excise, 1954; Principal Asst Solicitor, 1980–85; Eur. Affairs Advr, BAT, 1985–89. *Recreations:* golf (ex-captain and ex-champion, Civil Service Golfing Society), bridge, listening to and playing piano. *Address:* 31 Hill Rise, Rickmansworth, Herts WD3 2NY. *T:* Rickmansworth (0923) 774756, 897004. *Club:* Moor Park Golf (Herts). *Died 8 Dec. 1993.*

HILLIER, Jack Ronald; freelance writer and expert on Japanese art, since 1950; *b* 29 Aug. 1912; *s* of Charles Hillier and Minnie Hillier (*née* Davies); *m* 1938, Mary Louise Palmer; one *s* one *d. Educ:* Fulham Central School. Sotheby Consultant on oriental pictorial art, 1953–67. Uchiyama Susumu Award, Tokyo, 1982, 1988. Order of the Rising Sun (Japan), 1993. *Publications:* Old Surrey Water Mills, 1951; Japanese Masters of the Colour Print, 1953; Hokusai Paintings, Drawings and Woodcuts, 1955; The Japanese Print: a new approach, 1960, 4th edn 1975; Utamaro: colour prints and paintings, 1961, 2nd edn 1979; Japanese Drawings: from the 17th to the end of the 19th century, 1965, 3rd edn 1975; Hokusai Drawings, 1966; Catalogue of Japanese Paintings and Prints in Collection of Richard P. Gale, 1970; The Harari Collection of Japanese Paintings and Drawings, 1970–73; Suzuki Harunobu, 1970; The Uninhibited Brush: Japanese art in the Shijō style, 1974; Japanese Prints and Drawings from the Vever Collection, 1976; The Art of Hokusai in Book Illustration, 1980; The Art of the Japanese Book, 1987; The Japanese Picture-book: a selection from the Ravicz Collection, 1991; Japanese and Chinese Prints in the Amstutz Collection, 1991. *Recreations:* wood engraving, water colour painting, classical music (esp. lieder), the English countryside. *Address:* 30 Clarence Road, Meadvale, Surrey RH1 6NG. *T:* Redhill (01737) 241123. *Died 5 Jan. 1995.*

HILLYARD, Patrick Cyril Henry, OBE 1956; Head of Sound Light Entertainment BBC, 1952–64, retired Nov. 1964; *b* 5 May 1900; *s* of Rev. Dr H. J. Hillyard and Louie Charlotte Robinson; *m* 1932, Ena Violet (*d* 1985), *d* of late Rev. C. Porter-Brickwell; one *s. Educ:* The High Sch., Dublin. Studied stage production under Donald Calthrop; stage directed and produced plays and musical comedies in England and America, including: A Midsummer Night's Dream, Twelfth Night, The Fake, Jolly Roger, No More Ladies, The Desert Song, Gay Divorce, On Your Toes, Lilac Time; joined BBC Television Service as Dep. Productions Manager, 1937; Asst Dir of Variety, BBC, 1941; Actg Dir of Variety, BBC, 1946; Dir of Television Presentation, BBC, 1947; Head of Television Light Entertainment, BBC, 1948. Kt of Mark Twain, 1980. *Recreations:* going to the theatre, golf, tennis, swimming. *Address:* c/o 5 Ursula Street, SW11 3DW. *Club:* Malta Union. *Died 2 March 1991.*

HILTON, John Robert, CMG 1965; HM Diplomatic Service (appointed to Foreign Service, 1943), retired 1969; *b* 5 Jan. 1908; *s* of Oscar Hilton, MD, and Louisa Holdsworth Hilton; *m* 1933, Margaret Frances Stephens; one *s* three *d. Educ:* Marlborough Coll.; Corpus Christi Coll., Oxford (MA); Bartlett Sch. of Architecture; University Coll., London (Diploma). ARIBA. Dir of Antiquities, Cyprus, 1934–36; Architect to E. S. & A.

Robinson Ltd and private practice, 1936–41. Capt. RE, 1941–43. Foreign Service, 1943; transferred to Istanbul, 1944; 2nd Sec., Athens, 1945; Foreign Office, 1947; 1st Sec., Istanbul, 1956; Foreign Office, 1960. Mem. Council, National Schizophrenia Fellowship, 1977–81, 1983– (Pres., 1985–91). FRSA. *Publications:* Mind and Analysis, memoir on Louis MacNeice (as appendix to his autobiography, The Strings are False), 1965; articles in Architectural Review and other jls. *Recreations:* philosophy, walking. *Address:* Hope Cottage, Nash Hill, Lacock, Wilts SN15 2QL. *T:* Lacock (024973) 0369. *Died 20 April 1994.*

HILTON, Col Sir Peter, KCVO 1993; MC 1942 and Bars 1943 and 1944; JP; Lord-Lieutenant and Custos Rotulorum of Derbyshire, 1978–94; Managing Director and Company Secretary, 1949–86, Consultant, 1986–93, James Smith (Scotland Nurseries) Ltd; *b* 30 June 1919; *er s* of late Maj.-Gen. Richard Hilton, DSO, MC, DFC (and Bar), and Phyllis Martha (*née* Woodin); *m* 1942, Winifred, *d* of late Ernest Smith, Man. Dir Scotland Nurseries, Tansley; one *s* (and one *s* decd). *Educ:* Malvern Coll.; RMA Woolwich; psc. Commnd RA, 1939; BEF, 1939–40, 1st Div. Dunkirk; Western Desert, 1942–43, 7th Armd Div. Alamein (RHA Jacket 1942); Italy, 1943–44, 5th American Army, Adjt 3rd Regt RHA; Normandy, 1944, OC J Bty RHA (wounded Falaise Gap); Greece, 1946–49 (despatches 1948); Instructor Royal Hellenic Staff Coll.; Col RA 1949, retd; RARO; recalled Korean Emergency, 1950; TA Commn, 1951; CO 528 W Notts Regt, RA (TA), 1951–54; ACF Commn, 1962; Comdt Derbyshire ACF, 1962–66, Hon. Col 1972–77. Nat. Pres., Normandy Veterans Assoc.; President: TA&VRA, E Midlands, 1987–94; 8th Army Veterans; Dunkirk 1940 Veterans; SSAFA; FHS; Boys' Brigade; Royal British Legion: Nat. Vice-Pres.; Pres., Derbyshire. Vice-President: Derbys Boys Clubs; British Heart Foundn, Derbys. President: S Derbys Br., ARC; Derbys Rural Community Council; Derbys Cttee, CPRE; Ashover, Ashbourne and Bakewell Show; Longshaw and Dovedale Sheepdog Trials; Victim Support and Neighbourhood Watch; Belper Musical Theatre. Trustee: Derby New Theatre; Univ. of Derby; Patron: Alfreton Ladies Choir; Dalesmen Male Voice Choir; Present Company Opera Gp; Life Mem., Derby Opera Co.; Gov., Derby Show. JP, High Sheriff 1970–71, DL 1972, Derbys; Mem. Wirksworth Div., Derbys CC, 1967–77. KStJ 1979. Commendation Award, NODA, 1993. Greek Order of Minerva, 1949; Ukrainian Gold Cross, 1992. *Recreations:* ex-Service interests, local activities, horticulture. *Address:* Alton Manor, Idridgehay, Belper, Derbys DE56 2SH. *T:* (home) Matlock (01629) 822435.

Died 30 May 1995.

HIMSWORTH, Eric, CMG 1951; *b* 23 Nov. 1905; *s* of H. Himsworth and M. J. Macdonald; *m* 1941, Ethel Emily, *d* of Major Brook Pratt, DSO, Coldstream Guards; two *s. Educ:* Silcoates Sch., near Wakefield; Merton Coll., Oxford. MA, BCL Oxon; LLB, BSc (Econ.), DPA London. Colonial Administrative Service, 1928–55; Financial Sec., Malaya, 1952–55; UN Technical Assistance Administration, Nepal, 1956–64; IMF Financial Consultant, 1965–71; Consultant, Ta Hing Co., Hong Kong, 1972–84. *Recreation:* travelling. *Address:* 33 Ballachurry Avenue, Onchan, Isle of Man. *Club:* Commonwealth Trust. *Died 7 Aug. 1995.*

HIMSWORTH, Sir Harold (Percival), KCB 1952; MD; FRS 1955; FRCP; Secretary, Medical Research Council, 1949–68, retired (Member and Deputy Chairman, 1967–68); *b* 19 May 1905; *s* of late Arnold Himsworth, Huddersfield, Yorks; *m* 1932, Charlotte (*d* 1988), *yr d* of William Gray, Walmer, Kent; two *s. Educ:* King James' Grammar Sch., Almondbury, Yorks; University Coll. and University Coll. Hosp., London. Asst, Medical Unit,

University Coll. Hosp., 1930; Beit Memorial Research Fellow, 1932–35; William Julius Mickle Fellow, University of London, 1935; Fellow of University Coll., London, 1936; Deputy Dir, Medical Unit, University Coll. Hospital, 1936; Goulstonian Lecturer, 1939; Oliver-Sharpey Lectr, 1949, RCP; Prof. of Medicine, Univ. of London and Dir of the Medical Unit, University Coll. Hospital, London, 1939–49; Mem. of Medical Research Council, 1948–49; Sydney Ringer Lecturer, 1949; Lowell Lecturer, Boston, Mass, 1947; Harveian Orator, Royal College of Physicians, 1962. Pres., Sect. of Experimental Medicine, Royal Society of Medicine, 1946–47. Chm., Bd of Management, London Sch. of Hygiene and Tropical Med., 1969–76. Prime Warden, Goldsmiths Co., 1975. Docteur *hc* Toulouse, 1950; Hon. LLD: Glasgow, 1953; London, 1956; Wales, 1959; Hon. DSc: Manchester, 1956; Leeds, 1968; Univ. of WI, 1968; Hon. ScD, Cambridge, 1964. New York Univ. Medallist, 1958; Conway Evans Prize, RCP, 1968. Member: Norwegian Med. Soc., 1954; Royal Soc. of Arts and Sciences, Göteborg, Sweden, 1957; Hon. Member: Med. Soc. of Sweden, 1949; Amer. Assoc. of Physicians, 1950; For. Mem., Amer. Philosoph. Soc., 1972; For. Hon. Member: Amer. Acad. of Arts and Sciences, 1958; Belgian Royal Acad. of Medicine, 1958. Hon. FRCR 1958; Hon. FRCPE 1960; Hon. FRSM 1961; Hon. FRCS 1965; Hon. FRCPath 1969; Hon. Fellow LSHTM, 1979; Hon. FRSTM, 1981. *Publications:* The Development and Organisation of Scientific Knowledge, 1970; Scientific Knowledge and Philosophic Thought, 1986; medical and scientific papers. *Recreation:* fishing. *Address:* 13 Hamilton Terrace, NW8. *T:* 071–286 6996. *Club:* Athenæum.   *Died 1 Nov. 1993.*

HINCHLIFF, Rev. Prof. Peter Bingham, MA, DD Oxon, PhD Rhodes; Canon of Christ Church and Regius Professor of Ecclesiastical History, Oxford University, since 1992; *b* 25 Feb. 1929; *e s* of Rev. Canon Samuel Bingham Hinchliff and Brenda Hinchliff; *m* 1955, Constance, *d* of E. L. Whitehead, Uitenhage, S Africa; three *s* one *d. Educ:* St Andrew's Coll., Grahamstown, S Africa; Rhodes Univ., Grahamstown; Trinity Coll., Oxford. Deacon, 1952; priest, 1953, in Anglican Church in S Africa; Asst in Parish of Uitenhage, 1952–55. Subwarden, St Paul's Theological Coll., Grahamstown, 1955–59; Lectr in Comparative Religion, Rhodes Univ., 1957–59; Prof. of Ecclesiastical History, Rhodes Univ., 1960–69; Canon and Chancellor, Grahamstown Cathedral, 1964–69; Sec., Missionary and Ecumenical Council of the General Synod (formerly the Church Assembly), 1969–72; Fellow and Tutor, 1972–92, Chaplain, 1972–87, Balliol Coll., Oxford. Examng Chaplain to Bishop of Newcastle, 1973, to Bishop of Oxford, 1974–. Public Orator, Rhodes Univ., 1965; Hulsean Lectr, Cambridge Univ., 1975–76; Bampton Lectr, Oxford Univ., 1982. Provincial Hon. Canon, Cape Town Cathedral, 1959–; Hon. Canon, Grahamstown Cathedral, 1969–; Canon Theologian, Coventry Cathedral, 1972–92. Mem., Gen. Synod, 1988–90. Pres., Oxford Soc. of Historical Theol., 1978–79. *Publications:* The South African Liturgy, 1959; The Anglican Church in South Africa, 1963; John William Colenso, 1964; The One-Sided Reciprocity, 1966; A Calendar of Cape Missionary Correspondence, 1967; The Church in South Africa, 1968; The Journal of John Ayliff, 1970; Cyprian of Carthage, 1974; (with D. Young) The Human Potential, 1981; Holiness and Politics, 1982; Benjamin Jowett and the Christian Religion, 1987; God and History, 1992; contributor to: Jl of Ecclesiastical History; Studia Liturgica, etc. *Recreations:* crossword puzzles, odd jobbery. *Address:* Christ Church, Oxford OX1 1DP.
                      Died 17 Oct. 1995.

HIND, Kenneth, ERD 1955; Senior Director, Employment and Industrial Relations, Post Office, 1973–80; *b* 14 March 1920; *er s* of late Harry and Edith Hind; *m* 1942, Dorothy

Walton; one *s. Educ:* Central Sec. Sch., Sheffield; Queens' Coll., Cambridge (Munro Schol.). Army, 1940–48: Major, REME. General Post Office: Asst Principal, 1948; Principal, 1950; Asst Sec., 1960; Dir, Radio and Broadcasting, 1967; Central Services, 1969; Senior Dir, 1971. *Recreations:* cricket, gardening. *Address:* 64 Chorley Drive, Sheffield S10 3RR. *T:* Sheffield (0742) 304901.   *Died 18 Nov. 1993.*

HINDLIP, 5th Baron *cr* 1886; **Henry Richard Allsopp;** Bt 1880; *b* 1 July 1912; 2nd *s* of 3rd Baron Hindlip and Agatha (*d* 1962), 2nd *d* of late John C. Thynne; *S* brother, 1966; *m* 1939, Cecily Valentine Jane, *o d* of late Lt-Col Malcolm Borwick, DSO, Hazelbech Hill, Northampton; two *s* one *d. Educ:* Eton; RMC Sandhurst. 2nd Lieut, Coldstream Guards, 1932; Major, 1941; retired, 1948. Served War of 1939–45: NW Europe, 1944. JP 1957, DL 1956, Wilts. Bronze Star Medal, USA, 1945. *Recreations:* travel, shooting. *Heir: s* Hon. Charles Henry Allsopp [*b* 5 Aug. 1940; *m* 1968, Fiona Victoria Jean Atherley, *d* of late Hon. William Johnston McGowan; one *s* three *d*]. *Address:* Tytherton House, East Tytherton, Chippenham, Wilts. *T:* Kelloways (024974) 207. *Club:* Turf.
                      Died 19 Dec. 1993.

HINGSTON, Lt-Col Walter George, OBE 1964; FRGS; *b* Radcliffe on Trent, Notts, 15 Feb. 1905; *s* of late Charles Hingston, DL and Mildred (*née* Pleydell Bouverie), Cotgrave, Nottingham; *m* 1939, Elizabeth Margaret, *d* of late Brig. Sir Clinton Lewis, OBE, and Lilian Eyre (*née* Wace); two *d. Educ:* Harrow; RMC Sandhurst; Staff Coll. psc. 2nd Lieut, KOYLI, 1925; Nigeria Regt, RWAFF, 1931–36; 1st Punjab Regt, Indian Army, 1936; served War of 1939–45: 4th Indian Div., North Africa, Eritrea (despatches); Dep. Dir Public Relations, GHQ India, 1942; Chief Information Officer to C-in-C, Ceylon, 1943; retired (invalided), 1945. Chief Information Officer, Dept of Scientific and Industrial Research, 1945–63; Editor, Geographical Magazine, 1963–68. Mem., Marlborough and Ramsbury RDC, 1970–74. *Publications:* The Tiger Strikes, 1942; The Tiger Kills (with G. R. Stevens), 1944; Never Give Up, 1948. *Recreation:* fishing. *Address:* The Old Vicarage, Ramsbury, Marlborough, Wilts SN8 2QH. *Club:* Army and Navy.   *Died 18 June 1992.*

HIPWELL, Hermine Hipwell; *see* Vivenot, Baroness R. de.

HIRSHFIELD, Baron *cr* 1967 (Life Peer), of Holborn in Greater London; **Desmond Barel Hirshfield;** chartered accountant, as Lord Hirshfield, Chartered Accountants; Chairman, Horwath & Horwath (UK) Ltd, 1967–86; International President, Horwath & Horwath International, 1984–86 (President, 1977–84); Founder and Director, Foundation on Automation and Human Development, 1962–87; *b* 17 May 1913; *s* of late Leopold Hirshfield and Lily Hirshfield (*née* Blackford); *m* 1st, 1939, Alma King (marr. diss. 1951); 2nd, 1951, Bronia Eisen. *Educ:* City of London Sch. Chartered Accountant, 1939. Founder and Chm., Trades Union Unit Trust Managers Ltd, 1961–83; Chm., MLH Consultants, 1981–83. Mem., Cttee on Consumer Credit, 1968–71; Dep. Chm., Northampton New Town Develt Corp., 1968–76; Member: Central Adv. Water Cttee, 1969–70; Top Salaries Review Body, 1975–84; Admin. Trustee, Chevening Estate, 1970–81; Pres., Brit. Assoc. of Hotel Accountants, 1969–83; Treasurer: UK Cttee of UNICEF, 1969–83 and 1986–88; Nat. Council for the Unmarried Mother and her Child, 1970–71. President: Norwood Charitable Trust, 1960–83; Norwood Foundn, 1977–83. Gov., LSE, 1975–. Capt., British Team, World Maccabi Games, Prague, 1934. *Publications:* pamphlets and reports on: The Accounts of Charitable Institutions; Avoidance and Evasion of Income Tax; Scheme for Pay as You Earn; Investment of Trade Union Funds; Organisations and Methods Reviews;

articles in periodicals and newspapers. *Recreations:* travel, painting, caricaturing. *Address:* House of Lords, SW1.

Died 6 Dec. 1993.

HITCHCOCK, Prof. Edward Robert, ChM; FRCS, FRCSE; Professor of Neurosurgery, University of Birmingham, since 1978; *b* 10 Feb. 1929; *s* of Edwin Robert and Martha Hitchcock; *m* 1953, Jillian Trenowath; three *s* one *d. Educ:* Lichfield Grammar Sch.; Univ. of Birmingham (MB ChB; ChM 1952). FRCS 1959; FRCSE, *ad eundem,* 1971. Leader, Univ. of Birmingham Spitzbergen Expedn, 1951. Lecturer in Anatomy, Univ. of Birmingham, 1953; Captain, RAMC, 1954–56, MO, 2nd Bn Scots Guards; Registrar: Dept of Traumatic Surgery, General Hosp., Birmingham, 1956; Professorial Surgical Unit, University College Hosp., London, 1957–59; Fellow in Clinical Research, MRC, 1960; 1961–65: Ho. Surg./Registrar/Sen. Registrar, Dept of Neurological Surgery, Radcliffe Inf., Oxford, and Dept of Neurosurgery, Manchester Royal Inf.; Research Fellow, Univ. of Oxford; Sen. Lectr and Reader, Dept of Surgical Neurology, Univ. of Edinburgh, 1966–78. Examiner, FRCS, 1971–, RCSE, Surgical Neurology, 1977–90. Pres., Europ Soc. of Functional and Stereotactic Surg., 1986–90 (Mem., Exec. Cttee, 1975–86); Member: Soc. of British Neurol Surgeons, 1966– (Council, 1988–90); Bd, World Soc. Stereo and Functional Neurosurgery, 1981–; Internat. Assoc. for Study of Pain, 1975–. Chm., BSI cttee on neurosurgical implants, 1989–. Hon. Specialist in Neurosurgery, Brazilian Neurosurg. Soc., 1980–; Hon. Member: Soc. de Neurocirurgia de Levante, 1983; Bolivian Neurosurgical Soc.; Corresp. Member: Amer. Assoc. of Neurol Surgeons, 1975; Scandinavian Neurosurg. Soc., 1972; Amer. Physiological Soc., 1988. Ed., Advances in Stereotactic and Functional Neurosurgery, 1969–. *Publications:* Initial Management of Head Injuries (Folia Traumatologica), 1971; Management of the Unconscious Patient, 1971; papers on pain, neuroprosthetics, stereotactic surgery and tumours, in various jls. *Recreations:* history, capology, fishing. *Address:* Cubbold House, Ombersley, near Droitwich, Worcs WR9 0HJ. *T:* Worcester (0905) 620606. *Died 29 Dec. 1993.*

HOBDEN, Dennis Harry; *b* 21 Jan. 1920; *s* of Charles Hobden and Agnes Hobden (*née* Smith); *m* 1st, 1950, Kathleen Mary Hobden (*née* Holman) (marr. diss. 1970); two *s* two *d;* 2nd, 1977, Sheila Hobden (*née* Tugwell). *Educ:* elementary sch. Entered GPO, 1934; retired 1982. Served as Air Crew, RAF, 1941–46 (Flt Lieut). MP (Lab) Kemptown Div. of Brighton, 1964–70. Mem., Brighton Town Council, 1956–91; Mayor of Brighton, 1979–80; Mem., E Sussex CC, 1973–85; Chairman: Brighton Borough Licensing Cttee, 1986–91; Brighton Race Ground Lessees, 1987–91. Founder, 1967, and Vice-Pres., 1992–, Fest. of Brighton. *Recreations:* politics, gardening, music, reading, Spiritualism. *Address:* Sea Hawk, 40 McWilliam Road, Woodingdean, Brighton, East Sussex BN2 6BE.

Died 20 April 1995.

HOBHOUSE, Sir Charles Chisholm, 6th Bt, *cr* 1812, of Broughton-Gifford, Bradford-on-Avon and of Monkton Farleigh, Wiltshire; TD; *b* 7 Dec. 1906; *s* of Sir Reginald A. Hobhouse, 5th Bt and Marjorie Chisholm Spencer (*d* 1967); *S* father, 1947; *m* 1st, 1946, Mary (*d* 1955), *widow* of Walter Horrocks, Salkeld Hall, Penrith; no *c;* 2nd, 1959, Elspeth Jean, *d* of T. G. Spinney, Mazagan, Morocco; one *s. Educ:* Eton. Commissioned North Somerset Yeomanry, 1926; Major 1940; Hon. Col 1966. *Recreations:* hunting, shooting. *Heir: s* Charles John Spinney Hobhouse, *b* 27 Oct. 1962. *Address:* The Manor, Monkton Farleigh, Bradford-on-Avon, Wilts. *T:* Bath (0225) 858558. *Clubs:* Brooks's, City of London. *Died 5 Jan. 1991.*

HOBLEY, John William Dixon, CMG 1976; QC (Hong Kong); *b* 11 June 1929; *s* of John Wilson Hobley and

Ethel Anne Hobley; *m* 1953, Dorothy Cockhill; one *s* one *d. Educ:* University Sch., Southport, Merseyside; Univ. of Liverpool (LLB). Called to the Bar, Gray's Inn, 1950; Northern Circuit, 1950–53; Hong Kong: Crown Counsel, 1953–62; Sen. Crown Counsel, 1962–65; Principal Crown Counsel, 1965–72; Attorney-Gen., Bermuda, 1972; Solicitor-Gen., 1973, Attorney-Gen., 1973–79, Hong Kong. Principal Legal Advr, Wigan BC, 1985–91. *Recreations:* music, bridge. *Died 4 March 1993.*

HOBSON, Sir Harold, Kt 1977; CBE 1971; Special Writer, The Sunday Times, since 1976 (Drama Critic, 1947–76); contributor to: Times Literary Supplement; Drama; London Drama Critic, The Christian Science Monitor, 1935–74; *b* Thorpe Hesley, near Rotherham, 4 Aug. 1904; *o s* of late Jacob and Minnie Hobson; *m* 1st, 1935, Gladys Bessie (Elizabeth) (*d* 1979), *e d* of late James Johns; one *d;* 2nd, 1981, Nancy Penhale. *Educ:* privately; Oriel Coll., Oxford (Hon. Fellow, 1974). Asst Literary Editor, The Sunday Times, 1942–48; TV Critic, The Listener, 1947–51; for many years took part in BBC Radio programme The Critics. Mem., National Theatre Bd, 1976–79. Hon. DLitt Sheffield, 1977. Chevalier of the Legion of Honour, 1959. Knight of Mark Twain, 1976. *Publications:* The First Three Years of the War, 1942; The Devil in Woodford Wells (novel), 1946; Theatre, 1948; Theatre II, 1950; Verdict at Midnight, 1952; The Theatre Now, 1953; The French Theatre of Today, 1953; (ed) The International Theatre Annual, 1956, 1957, 1958, 1959, 1960; Ralph Richardson, 1958; (with P. Knightly and L. Russell) The Pearl of Days: an intimate memoir of The Sunday Times, 1972; The French Theatre since 1830, 1978; Indirect Journey (autobiog.), 1978; Theatre in Britain: a personal view, 1984. *Recreations:* reading the New Yorker, watching cricket, Stock Exchange. *Address:* Westhampnett Private Nursing Home, Westhampnett, Chichester, W Sussex. *Club:* La Casserole (Paris).

Died 12 March 1992.

HOBSON, Lawrence John, CMG 1965; OBE 1960; with Arab-British Chamber of Commerce, since 1977; *b* 4 May 1921; *er s* of late John Sinton Hobson and Marion Adelaide Crawford; *m* 1946, Patricia Fiona Rosemary Beggs (*née* Green); one step *s* (and one *s* decd). *Educ:* Taunton Sch.; St Catharine's Coll., Cambridge. BA 1946, MA 1950. Served War, 1941–42. ADC and Private Sec. to Gov., Aden, 1942; Political Officer, 1944; Asst Chief Sec., 1956; Aden govt Student Liaison Officer, UK, 1960–62; Political Adviser to High Comr, Aden, 1963–66; retired from HMOCS, 1966. With BP Ltd, 1966–77. Mem., Newbury DC, 1973–. *Address:* Saffron House, Stanford Dingley, near Reading, Berks. *T:* Bradfield (0734) 536.

Died 11 Feb. 1993.

HODGE, David, CBE 1980; JP; DL; Lord Provost of Glasgow, and Lord Lieutenant of County of City of Glasgow, 1977–80; *b* 30 Sept. 1909; *s* of David Hodge and Sarah (*née* Crilly); *m* 1950, Mary Forbes Hodge (*née* Taylor); four *d. Educ:* St Mungo's Acad., Glasgow. Served War, RAF, 1940–46: air crew, Coastal Comd. On staff of Scottish Gas Bd, 1934–50; Prudential Assurance Co. Ltd, 1950–74, retd. Chm., Ruchill Ward and Maryhill Constituency for 20 yrs. Elected to Glasgow Corp., 1971; Magistrate, Corp. of Glasgow, 1972–74; Vice-Chm., Transport Cttee. Mem., City of Glasgow Dist Council, 1974: Chm., Licensing Court, Licensing Cttee, and Justices Cttee; Sec. of Admin; Council Rep., Convention of Scottish Local Authorities, 1974–77. Pres., Marist Centenary Club, Glasgow. JP 1975, DL 1980, Glasgow. Hon. LLD Strathclyde, 1980. OStJ 1978. *Recreations:* interested in all sports (former professional footballer; winner of tennis championships; former swimming and badminton coach); theatre, ballet, music. *Address:* 59 Hillend Road, Glasgow G22 6NY. *T:* 041–336 8727.

Clubs: Royal Automobile, Royal Air Forces Association; Art (Glasgow). *Died 7 Dec. 1991.*

HODGE, Sir John Rowland, 2nd Bt *cr* 1921, of Chipstead, Kent; MBE 1940; FRHS; company director; *b* 1 May 1913; *s* of Sir Rowland Hodge, 1st Bt, and Mabel (*d* 1923), *d* of William Edward Thorpe; *S* father, 1950; *m* 1st, 1936, Peggy Ann (marr. diss. 1939), *o d* of Sydney Raymond Kent; 2nd, 1939, Joan (marr. diss. 1961), *o d* of late Sydney Foster Wilson; three *d*; 3rd, 1962, Jeanne Wood Anderson (marr. diss. 1967), *d* of Comdr W. E. Buchanan; 4th, 1967, Vivien Jill, *d* of A. S. Knightley; one *s* one *d. Educ:* Wrekin Coll.; Switzerland. Lt-Comdr, RNVR, 1938; served War of 1939–45, RNVR; formerly Oxford and Bucks Light Infantry. Mem. Inst. of Directors. Dist Grand Master, Dist Grand Lodge of Freemasons, Malta, 1976–86. Freeman, City of Newcastle upon Tyne. *Heir: s* Andrew Rowland Hodge, *b* 3 Dec. 1968. *Address:* 16 Sutherland Drive, Gunton Park, Lowestoft NR32 4LP. *T:* Lowestoft (01502) 68943. *Clubs:* British Racing Drivers, Naval; Valletta Yacht, Royal Yachting Association, Cruising Association.

Died 1 Jan. 1995.

HODGKIN, Prof. Dorothy Mary Crowfoot, OM 1965; FRS 1947; Emeritus Professor, University of Oxford; Hon. Fellow: Somerville College, Oxford; Linacre College, Oxford; Girton College, Cambridge; Newnham College, Cambridge; Fellow, Wolfson College, Oxford, 1977–82; Chancellor, Bristol University, 1970–88; *b* 12 May 1910; *d* of late J. W. Crowfoot, CBE, and Grace Mary, *d* of Sinclair Frankland Hood, Lincoln; *m* 1937, Thomas Lionel Hodgkin (*d* 1982); two *s* one *d. Educ:* Sir John Leman Sch., Beccles; Somerville Coll., Oxford. Fellow, Somerville Coll., 1936–77, Royal Soc. Wolfson Research Prof., 1960–77, Oxford Univ. Pres., BAAS, 1977–78. Fellow: Australian Academy of Science, 1968; Akad. Leopoldina, 1968; Mem., Ehrenzeichens für Kunst and Wissenschaft, Austria, 1983; Hon. Mem., Royal Instn, 1988; Foreign Member: Royal Netherlands Academy of Science and Letters, 1956; Amer. Acad. of Arts and Sciences, Boston, 1958, and other learned bodies. Hon. Foreign Member: US Nat. Acad. of Scis, 1971; USSR Acad. of Scis, 1976; Bavarian Acad., 1980. Hon. DSc Leeds, Manchester and others; Hon. ScD Cambridge; LLD Bristol; DUniv Zagreb and York; Hon. Dr Medicine and Surgery Modena; Hon. DL Dalhousie; Hon. DSc Oxford. First Freedom of Beccles, 1965. Royal Medallist of the Royal Society, 1956; Nobel Prize for Chemistry, 1964; Copley Medal, Royal Soc., 1976; Mikhail Lomonosov Gold Medal, Soviet Acad. of Science, 1982; Dimitrov Prize, Bulgaria, 1984; Lenin Peace Prize, USSR, 1987. *Publications:* various, on the X-ray crystallographic analysis of structure of molecules, including penicillin, vitamin B_{12} and insulin. *Recreations:* archæology, children. *Address:* Crab Mill, Ilmington, Shipston-on-Stour, Warwicks. *T:* Ilmington (060882) 233.

Died 29 July 1994.

HODGSON, Alfreda Rose, (Mrs Paul Blissett); concert singer; *b* 7 June 1940; *d* of Alfred and Rose Hodgson; *m* 1963, Paul Blissett; two *d. Educ:* Northern School of Music; (Graduate; Hon. Fellow 1972); LRAM. Won Kathleen Ferrier Memorial Scholarship, 1964; first professional concert with Royal Liverpool Philharmonic Orchestra, 1964; subseq. sang with all major orchestras in Britain, also throughout Europe, USA, Canada, Mexico, and elsewhere; Covent Garden début, 1983–84 season (Le Rossignol, and L'Enfant et les Sortilèges). Hon. FRNCM 1989. Sir Charles Santley Meml Gift, Worshipful Co. of Musicians, 1985. *Address:* 16 St Mary's Road, Prestwick, Manchester M25 5AP. *T:* 061-773 1541.

Died 17 April 1992.

HODIN, Prof. Josef Paul, LLD; author, art historian, art critic; *b* 17 Aug. 1905; *s* of Eduard D. Hodin and Rosa (*née* Klug); *m* 1945, Doris Pamela Simms; one *s* one *d. Educ:* Kleinseitner Realschule and Neustädter Realgymnasium, Prague; Charles Univ., Prague; London Univ.; Art Academies of Dresden and Berlin. Press Attaché to Norwegian Govt in London, 1944–45; Dir of Studies and Librarian, Inst. of Contemporary Arts, London, 1949–54; Hon. Mem. Editorial Council of The Journal of Aesthetics and Art Criticism, Cleveland, 1955–; Mem. Exec. Cttee British Soc. of Aesthetics; Pres., British Section, AICA; Editor: Prisme des Arts, Paris, 1956–57; Quadrum, Brussels, 1956–66. 1st internat. prize for art criticism, Biennale, Venice, 1954. Hon. PhD Uppsala, 1969; Hon. Prof. Vienna, 1975. DSM 1st cl. Czechoslovakia, 1947; St Olav Medal, Norway, 1958; Comdr, Order of Merit, Italy, 1966; Grand Cross, Order of Merit, Austria, 1968; Order of Merit, 1st cl., Germany, 1969; Silver Cross of Merit, Austria, 1972; Comdr, Order of Merit, Germany, 1986. *Publications:* Monographs on Sven Erixson (Stockholm), 1940; Ernst Josephson (Stockholm), 1942, Edvard Munch (Stockholm), 1948, (Frankfurt a/M), 1951; Isaac Grünewald (Stockholm), 1949; Art and Criticism (Stockholm), 1944; J. A. Comenius and Our Time (Stockholm), 1944; The Dilemma of Being Modern (London), 1956, (New York), 1959; Henry Moore (Amsterdam, Hamburg), 1956, (London, New York), 1958, (Buenos Aires), 1963; Ben Nicholson (London), 1957; Barbara Hepworth (Neuchatel, London, New York), 1961; Lynn Chadwick (Amsterdam, Hamburg, London, New York), 1961; Bekenntnis zu Kokoschka (Mainz), 1963; Edvard Munch (Mainz), 1963; Oskar Kokoschka: A Biography (London, New York), 1966; Walter Kern (Neuchatel, London), 1966; Ruszkowski (London), 1967; Bernard Leach (London), 1967; Oskar Kokoschka: Sein Leben Seine Zeit (Mainz), 1968; Kafka und Goethe (Hamburg), 1968; Giacomo Manzú (Rome), 1969; Die Brühlsche Terrasse, Ein Künstlerroman, 1970; Emilio Greco, Life and Work (London, New York), 1971; Edvard Munch (London, New York, Oslo), 1972; Modern Art and the Modern Mind (London, Cleveland), 1972; Alfred Manessier (London, NY, Paris), 1972; Bernard Stern (London), 1972; Ludwig Meidner (Darmstadt), 1973; Hilde Goldschmidt (Hamburg), 1974; Paul Berger-Bergner, Leben und Werk (Hamburg), 1974; Die Leute von Elverdingen (Hamburg), 1974; Kokoschka und Hellas (Vienna), 1977; John Milne (London), 1977; Else Meidner, 1979; Elisabeth Frink, 1983; Douglas Portway, 1983; Franz Luby (Vienna), 1983; Dieses Mütterchen hat Krallen, Die Geschichte einer Prager Jugend (Hamburg), 1985; Verlorene Existenzen, Erzählungen (Hamburg), 1986; Friedrich Karl Gotsch (Hamburg), 1987; Manzú Pittore (Bergamo, London, Hamburg), 1988; Jan Brazda (London, Stockholm), 1989; contribs on literary and art subjects to internat. periodicals. *Address:* 12 Eton Avenue, NW3 3EH. *T:* 0171-794 3609. *Clubs:* Athenæum, Reform.

Died 6 Dec. 1995.

HODKIN, Rev. Canon Hedley; Residentiary Canon, Manchester Cathedral, 1957–70, Canon Emeritus, since 1970; Sub-Dean, 1966–70; *b* 3 Jan. 1902; *s* of Walter and Elizabeth Hodkin; *m* 1932, Mary M., *d* of Dr J. A. Findlay; one *s* one *d* (and one *d* decd). *Educ:* University of Sheffield; Christ's Coll. and Westcott House, Cambridge. Curate of: Morpeth, 1935–38; St George's, Newcastle, 1938–40; Vicar of: St Luke's, Newcastle, 1940–47; Holy Trinity, Millhouses, Sheffield, 1947–57. Examining Chaplain: to Bishop of Newcastle, 1939–47; to Bishop of Sheffield, 1951–57; to Bishop of Manchester, 1957. Hon. Canon of Sheffield, 1955–57. Select Preacher, Cambridge, 1968. *Recreation:* music. *Address:* Dulverton Hall, St

Martin's Square, Scarborough YO11 2DQ. T: Scarborough (01723) 360364.
Died 18 Dec. 1995.

HODKINSON, William, CBE 1974 (OBE 1952); Part-time Member, British Gas Corporation, 1973–74; b 11 Aug. 1909; s of late William Hodkinson and Ann Greenwood; m 1934, Ann, d of John Buxton; one s. Educ: St Anne's, Stretford; Salford Technical Coll. Stretford Gas Co.: Technical Asst, 1930–32; Asst Works Manager, 1932–35; UK Gas Corp. Ltd: Chief Technical Officer, 1935–39; Gen. Man., 1939–46; Tech. Dir and Gen. Man., 1946–49; North Western Gas Board (later North Western Gas Region): Chief Technical and Planning Officer, 1949–56; Dep. Chm., 1956–64; Chm., 1964–74. Pres., IGasE, 1963–64. OStJ 1968. Recreation: golf. Address: 19 Harewood Avenue, Sale, Cheshire. T: 061–962 4653.
Died 10 May 1991.

HOGAN, Air Vice-Marshal Henry Algernon Vickers, CB 1955; DFC 1940; retired; b 25 Oct. 1909; s of late Lt-Col Edward M. A. Hogan, IA; m 1939, Margaret Venetia, d of late Vice-Adm. W. Tomkinson, CB, MVO; one s one d. Educ: Malvern Coll.; RAF Coll., Cranwell. Commissioned 1930; served in Fighter Sqdns and Fleet Air Arm; Instructor CFS, 1936–37; Mem. RAF Long Distance Flight (Vickers Wellesleys) to Australia, 1938; commanded No 501 Sqdn throughout Battle of Britain; USA, 1941–43 (Arnold Scheme and RAF Delegation Washington); Asst Comdt, Empire CFS, 1944; commanded No 19 Flying Training Sch., RAF Coll., Cranwell, 1945; Staff Coll., 1946; Air Ministry, 1947–48; Sen. Personnel SO, MEAF, 1949–50; commanded RAF, Wattisham 1951; Air Cdre 1953; Sector Comdr, Northern Sector, 1952–53; AOC No 81 Group, 1954; Air Vice-Marshal, 1956; AOC No 83 Group, 2nd ATAF, Germany, 1955–58; SASO, Flying Training Command, 1958–62. Led RAF Mission to Ghana, 1960, and Joint Services Mission to Ghana, 1961. Regional Dir, Civil Defence (Midland), 1964–68. USA Legion of Merit (Officer), 1945. Recreation: country pursuits. Address: Sugar Hill, Bickley, near Tenbury Wells, Worcs WR15 8LU. T: Newnham Bridge (058479) 432. Club: Royal Air Force.
Died 28 June 1993.

HOGG, Sir Arthur (Ramsay), 7th Bt cr 1846; MBE (mil.) 1945; retired; b 24 Oct. 1896; s of Ernest Charles Hogg (d 1907), g s of 1st Bt, and Lucy (d 1924), d of late William Felton Peel; S cousin, Sir Kenneth Weir Hogg, 6th Bt, OBE, 1985; m 1924, Mary Aileen Hester Lee (d 1980), d of late P. H. Lee Evans; three s one d. Educ: Sherborne; Christ Church, Oxford (BA 1921; MA 1929). Served European War, 1914–18 (twice wounded), Captain Royal West Kent Regt; War of 1939–45 (MBE), Major, General List. Heir: s Michael David Hogg [b 19 Aug. 1925; m 1956, Elizabeth Anne Thérèse, d of Lt-Col Sir Terence Falkiner, 8th Bt; three s]. Address: c/o 19 Woodlands Road, SW13 0JZ.
Died 31 Oct. 1995.

HOLDEN, Maj.-Gen. John Reid, CB 1965; CBE 1960 (OBE 1953); DSO 1941; b 8 Jan. 1913; s of late John Holden, MA, Edinburgh; m 1939, Rosemarie Florence (d 1980), d of late William Henry de Vere Pennefather, Carlow; one d. Educ: Hamilton Academy; Glasgow Univ.; RMC, Sandhurst. 2nd Lieut Royal Tank Corps, 1937; Adjutant, 7th Royal Tank Regt, 1940–41 (despatches, DSO); Bde Major, 32nd Army Tank Bde, 1942; POW, 1942–45; GSO1, GHQ, FARELF, Singapore, 1951–52 (OBE); CO 3rd Royal Tank Regt, BAOR, 1954–57; AAG, War Office, 1958; Comdr, 7th Armoured Bde Group, BAOR, 1958–61 (CBE); Royal Naval War Coll., 1961; Chief of Mission, British Comdrs-in-Chief Mission to the Soviet Forces in Germany, 1961–63; GOC 43 (Wessex) Div. Dist, 1963–65; Dir, RAC, 1965–68, retired 1968. Col Comdt, RTR, 1965–68. Hon. Col, The Queen's Own Lowland Yeomanry, RAC, T&AVR, 1972–75.

Recreations: books, birds. Address: c/o Royal Bank of Scotland, Kirkland House, Whitehall, SW1A 2EB.
Died 18 April 1995.

HOLDSWORTH, His Honour Albert Edward; QC 1969; a Circuit Judge, 1972–82; b 1909; e s of Albert Edward and Catherine Sarah Holdsworth; m 1st, 1941, Barbara Frances (d 1968), e d of Ernest Henry and Beatrice Maud Reeves; one s; 2nd, 1970, Brianne Evelyn Frances, d of Arthur James and Evelyn Lock; two s. Educ: Sir George Monoux Sch., Walthamstow; Gonville and Caius Coll., Cambridge (Exhibitioner). Pres., Cambridge Union, 1932; Economics and Politics tripos; MA. Called to the Bar, Middle Temple, 1936. Formerly journalist, Financial News, 1932–33; Special Correspondent, World Economic Conf., 1933; Yorkshire Post, 1933–46, Polit. Correspondent, later London Editor. Broadcasts for BBC on current affairs topics, 1935–56. Conservative Candidate Ipswich, 1951; moved resolution in favour of UK entry into European Common Market, Conservative Conf., Llandudno, 1962. Dep.-Chm., SW Metropolitan Mental Health Tribunal, 1962–65. Publication: Forward Together, 1983. Address: 2 Middle Temple Lane, Temple, EC4Y 9AA. T: 071–353 7926; Sutton Gate, Sutton, Pulborough, West Sussex RH20 1PN. T: Sutton (West Sussex) (07987) 230. Club: Reform.
Died 9 Jan. 1993.

HOLFORD, Rear-Adm. Frank Douglas, CB 1969; DSC 1944; Director General of Naval Manpower, Ministry of Defence, 1967–69, retired 1970; b 28 June 1916; y s of late Capt. C. F. Holford, DSO, OBE, and Ursula Isobel Holford (née Corbett); m 1942, Sybil Priscilla, d of late Comdr Sir Robert and Lady Micklem; two s. Educ: RN Coll., Dartmouth. Cadet, 1929; Midshipman, HMS Hood, 1933; Sub-Lieut, HMS Wolverine, 1937; Lieutenant: HMS Kent, 1938; HMS Anson, 1941; HMS Sheffield, 1943; Lieut-Comdr: HMS Excellent, 1945; HMS Triumph, 1948; Commander: Admty, Naval Ordnance Dept, 1951; British Joint Services Mission, USA, 1953; HMS Excellent, 1955; Captain: Admty, Dir Guided Weapons, 1957; Naval and Mil. Attaché, Buenos Aires, 1960; Staff C-in-C Portsmouth, 1962; Cdre i/c Hong Kong, 1965; Rear-Adm. 1967. jssc 1947. Address: Little Down Cottage, Shedfield, Hants SO3 2HY. T: Wickham (0329) 832295.
Died 10 Jan. 1991.

HOLGATE, Surg. Rear-Adm. William, CB 1962; OBE 1951; Chief Dental Officer, Ministry of Health, 1961–71, and Ministry of Education and Science, 1963–71; b 6 July 1906; s of Anthony and Jane Holgate; m 1933, Inga Ommanney Davis; one s one d. Educ: Scarborough Coll.; Guy's Hospital. LDS, RCS 1927; FDS RCS 1963. Royal Navy, 1928–61; Director of Dental Services, 1960. Address: 16 Upper Hyde Lane, Shanklin, Isle of Wight PO37 7PR. Club: Savage.
Died 16 June 1993.

HOLLEY, Prof. Robert William, PhD; Resident Fellow, The Salk Institute, since 1968; b 28 Jan. 1922; s of Charles and Viola Holley, Urbana, Ill, USA; m 1945, Ann Dworkin; one s. Educ: Univ. of Illinois (AB); Cornell Univ. (PhD); Washington State Coll. Research Biochemist, Cornell Univ. Med. Coll., 1944–46; Instructor, State Coll. of Washington, 1947–48; Assistant Prof. and Associate Prof. of Organic Chemistry, NY State Agricultural Experimental Station, Cornell Univ., 1948–57; Research Chemist, US Plant, Soil and Nutrition Lab., US Dept of Agric., 1957–64; Prof. of Biochem. and Molecular Biol., Biol. Div., Cornell Univ., 1964–69. Various awards for research, 1965–. Hon. DSc Illinois, 1970. Nobel Prize in Physiology or Medicine, 1968. Publications: many contribs to Jl Amer. Chem. Soc., Science, Jl Biol. Chem., Arch. Biochem., Nature, Proc. Nat. Acad. Sci., etc. Recreations: sculpture; family enjoyed walks along ocean and trips to mountains. Address: The Salk Institute, PO

Box 85800, San Diego, California 92186–5800, USA. *T:* 453–4100 (ext. 341).   *Died 11 Feb. 1993.*

HOLLINGSWORTH, Dorothy Frances, OBE 1958; *b* 10 May 1916; *d* of Arthur Hollingsworth and Dorothy Hollingsworth (*née* Coldwell). *Educ:* Newcastle upon Tyne Church High Sch.; Univ. of Durham (BSc 1937); Royal Infirmary, Edinburgh, Sch. of Dietetics (Dip. in Dietetics). FRSC (FRIC 1956); State Registered Dietitian (SRD), 1963; FIBiol 1968. Hosp. Dietitian, Royal Northern Hosp., London, N7, 1939–41; Govt Service, 1941–70: mainly at Min. of Food until its merger with Min. of Agric. and Fisheries, 1955, to form Min. of Agric., Fisheries and Food; Principal Scientific Officer and Head of a Scientific Br., 1949–70; Dir-Gen., British Nutrition Foundn, 1970–77. Chairman: British Dietetic Assoc., 1947–49; Internat. Cttee of Dietetic Assocs; 3rd Internat. Congress Dietetics, 1961; Nutrition Panel, Food Gp, Soc. Chem. Ind., 1966–69 (Mem. Food Gp Cttee, 1969–72); Member: Nat. Food Survey Cttee, 1951–85; Dietetics Bd, Council for Professions Supp. to Med., 1962–74; Cttee on Med. Aspects of Food Policy, 1970–79; Physiological Systems and Disorders Bd, MRC, 1974–77; Envmtl Medicine Res. Policy Cttee, MRC, 1975–76; Council, Inst. Food Sci. and Technol., 1970–89; Council, Nutrition Soc., 1974–77; (Dep. Chm.) Adv. Cttee on Protein, ODA, FCO, 1970–73; Jt ARC/MRC Cttee on Food and Nutrition Res., 1970–74; Royal Soc. British Nat. Cttee for Nutritional Scis, 1970–89; IBA Med. Adv. Panel, 1970–; Univ. of Reading Delegacy for Nat. Inst. for Res. in Dairying, 1973–85. Sec. Gen., Internat. Union of Nutritional Scis, 1978–85. Fellow, 1968, Vice-Pres., 1978–80, Inst. of Biology; Fellow, 1965, Vice-Pres., 1976–80, Hon. Fellow, 1985, Inst. of Food Science and Technology; Fellow, British Dietetic Assoc., 1979. *Publications:* (ed and prod 2nd rev. edn) The Englishman's Food, by J. C. Drummond and Anne Wilbraham, 1958; (ed with H. M. Sinclair 12th rev. edn) Food and the Principles of Nutrition, by Sir Robert Hutchison and A. Moncrieff, 1969; (ed with Margaret Russell) Nutritional Problems in a Changing World, 1973; (ed with E. Morse) People and Food Tomorrow, 1976; many papers in scientific jls. *Recreations:* talking with intelligent and humorous friends; appreciation of music, theatre and countryside; gardening. *Address:* 2 The Close, Petts Wood, Orpington, Kent BR5 1JA. *T:* Orpington (0689) 823168. *Clubs:* University Women's, Arts Theatre.
                    Died 16 Feb. 1994.

HOLLOWAY, David Richard; Literary Editor of The Daily Telegraph, 1968–88 (Deputy Literary Editor, 1960–68); *b* 3 June 1924; *s* of W. E. Holloway and Margaret Boyd (*née* Schleselman); *m* 1952, Sylvia Eileen, (Sally), Gray; two *s* one *d. Educ:* Westminster; Birkbeck Coll., London; Magdalen Coll., Oxford. Served War, RAF, 1942–46 (navigator). Reporter: Middlesex County Times, 1940–41; Daily Sketch, 1941–42; Daily Mirror, 1949; News Chronicle: Reporter and Leader Writer, 1950–53; Asst Lit. Editor and novel reviewer, 1953–58; Book Page Editor, 1958–60. Chairman: Soc. of Bookmen, 1968–71; Booker Prize Judges, 1970; Registrar, Royal Literary Fund, 1982–93. *Publications:* John Galsworthy, 1968; Lewis and Clark and the Crossing of America, 1971; Derby Day, 1975; Playing the Empire, 1979; (ed) Telegraph Year, 1–3, 1977–79; (with Michael Geare) Nothing So Became Them . . ., 1986; (ed) The Fifties: a unique record of the decade, 1991; (ed) The Sixties: a chronicle of the decade, 1992; The Thirties: a chronicle of a decade, 1993; contrib. Folio Magazine and book trade jls. *Recreation:* listening. *Address:* 95 Lonsdale Road, SW13 9DA. *T:* 0181–748 3711. *Club:* Reform.
                    Died 31 Aug. 1995.

HOLMAN, Norman Frederick; *b* 22 Feb. 1914; *s* of late Walter John and Violet Holman, Taunton; *m* 1940, Louisa Young; one *s* two *d. Educ:* Huish's, Taunton. Entered Post Office as Exec. Officer, 1932; Higher Exec. Officer, 1942. Served in Royal Corps of Signals, 1942–46. Sen. Exec. Officer, 1950; Asst Accountant-Gen., 1953; Dep. Dir, 1956; Dir of Postal Finance, 1967; Dir of Central Finance and Accounts, 1971–74. *Recreations:* bowls, bridge, The Observer crossword. *Address:* Crosswinds, 32 Richmond Road, Exmouth, Devon EX8 2NA. *T:* Exmouth (0395) 275298.   *Died 26 Dec. 1991.*

HOLMES, Prof. Brian, PhD, FCP; Professor of Education, College of Preceptors, since 1981 (Dean, 1980–89); Editor, Education Today, since 1980; *b* 25 April 1920; *s* of Albert and Gertrude Maud Holmes; *m* 1st, 1945, Mary I. Refoy; two *s*; 2nd, 1971, Margaret Hon-Yin Wong; one *d. Educ:* Salt High School, Shipley; University College London (BSc Phys 1941). PhD Univ. of London Inst. of Educn 1962. RAFVR Radar Officer, 1941–45; schoolmaster, St Clement Dane's and King's College School, Wimbledon, 1946–51; Lectr in Educn, Univ. of Durham, 1951–53; Univ. of London Institute of Education: Asst Editor, 1953; Lectr, 1959; Senior Lectr, 1963; Reader, 1964; Professor of Comparative Educn, 1975–85, then Emeritus; Head of Dept of Comparative Educn, 1977–85; Pro-Director, 1983–85; Dean, Faculty of Educn, Univ. of London, 1982–85. Vis. Prof., univs in USA, incl. Univ. of Chicago, 1958–59; Res. Consultant, Univ. of Kyushu, Japan, 1960; Consultant: Unesco; Internat. Bureau of Educn; OECD; foreign govts; professional visits to USSR, 1960–87; Vis. Examr, univs in UK, Australia, India and Singapore. Fellow, Japan Soc. for Promotion of Science, 1987. Pres., Inst. of Educn Soc., 1985–88. *Publications:* Problems in Education, 1965; (ed) Educational Policy and the Mission Schools, 1967; (ed) Diversity and Unity in Education, 1980; International Guide to Educational Systems, 1979; Comparative Education: some considerations of method, 1981; (ed) Equality and Freedom in Education, 1985; (with Martin McLean) Curricula in Comparative Perspective, 1988; (ed jtly) Theories and Methods in Comparative Education, 1988; contribs to Internat. Review of Educn, Comparative Educn Review, Compare, Prospects, foreign periodicals. *Recreation:* antique British clocks. *Address:* 110 Sumatra Road, NW6 1PG. *Club:* Commonwealth Trust.
                    Died 11 July 1993.

HOLMES, Prof. Geoffrey Shorter, DLitt; FBA 1983; FRHistS; Professor of History, University of Lancaster, 1973–83, then Emeritus; *b* 17 July 1928; *s* of Horace and Daisy Lavinia Holmes; *m* 1955, Ella Jean Waddell Scott; one *s* one *d. Educ:* Woodhouse Grammar Sch., Sheffield; Pembroke Coll., Oxford (BA 1948; MA, BLitt 1952; DLitt 1978). FRHistS 1968. Served Army, RASC, 1948–50 (Mil. Adviser's Staff, New Delhi, 1949–50). Personnel Dept, Hadfield's Ltd, Sheffield, 1951–52; Asst Lectr, Lectr and Sen. Lectr, Univ. of Glasgow, 1952–69; Reader in History, Univ. of Lancaster, 1969–72. Vis. Fellow, All Souls Coll., Oxford, 1977–78. Raleigh Lectr, British Acad., 1979; James Ford Special Lectr, Oxford, 1981. Vice-Pres., RHistS, 1985–89 (Mem. Council, 1980–84). *Publications:* British Politics in the Age of Anne, 1967, rev. edn 1987; (with W. A. Speck) The Divided Society, 1967; (ed and jtly) Britain after the Glorious Revolution, 1969; The Trial of Doctor Sacheverell, 1973; The Electorate and the National Will in the First Age of Party, 1976; Augustan England: Professions, State and Society 1680–1730, 1982; (ed with Clyve Jones) The London Diaries of William Nicolson, Bishop of Carlisle, 1702–1718, 1985; Politics, Religion and Society in England 1679–1742, 1986; (contrib.) Stuart England, ed Blair Worden, 1986; The Making of a Great Power: late Stuart and early Georgian Britain 1660–1722, 1993; (with

D. Szechi) The Age of Oligarchy: pre-industrial Britain 1722–1783, 1993; articles and reviews in learned jls. *Recreations:* music, gardening, cricket. *Address:* Tatham Lodge, Burton-in-Lonsdale, Carnforth, Lancs LA6 3LF. *T:* Bentham (05242) 61730. *Died 25 Nov. 1993.*

HOLMES, Brig. Kenneth Soar, CB 1963; CBE 1954; Managing Director, Posts, Postal Headquarters, 1971–72 (Senior Director, 1970–71); *b* 1912; *s* of W. J. Holmes, Ellesmere, Chaddesden Park Road, Derby; *m* 1936, Anne, *d* of C. A. Chapman, Leicester; one *s*. *Educ:* Bemrose Sch., Derby, and at Derby Technical Coll. Entered Post Office as Asst Traffic Superintendent (Telephones), 1930; Asst Surveyor, 1936; served War of 1939–45 as Officer Commanding 43rd Division Postal Unit, then with 21st Army Group and 2nd Army Headquarters, and as Asst Director of Army Postal Services, British Army of the Rhine; Principal, 1947; Asst Secretary, 1950; Director of: Army Postal Services, War Office, 1950–59; Mechanisation and Buildings, GPO, 1956–60; Postal Services, GPO, 1960–65; London Postal Region, 1965–70. Chairman Executive Cttee of Universal Postal Union, 1960–64. *Publication:* Operation Overlord: a postal history, 1984. *Address:* 1 Wanderdown Road, Ovingdean, Brighton BN2 7BT. *T:* Brighton (01273) 307847.
Died 16 Dec. 1994.

HOLMPATRICK, 3rd Baron *cr* 1897; **James Hans Hamilton;** *b* 29 Nov. 1928; *s* of 2nd Baron HolmPatrick and Lady Edina Ainsworth (*d* 1964), 4th *d* of 4th Marquess Conyngham; *S* father, 1942; *m* 1954, Anne Loys Roche, *o d* of Commander J. E. P. Brass, RN (retired); three *s*. *Heir:* *s* Hon. Hans James David Hamilton, [*b* 15 March 1955; *m* 1984, Mrs G. duFeu, *e d* of K. J. Harding]. *Address:* c/o House of Lords, SW1. *Died 16 Feb. 1991.*

HOLT, Arthur Frederick; Chairman, Holt Hosiery Co. Ltd, Bolton, 1971–73; *b* 8 Aug. 1914; *m* 1939, Kathleen Mary, MBE, *d* of A. C. Openshaw, Turton, nr Bolton; one *s* one *d*. *Educ:* Mill Hill Sch.; Manchester Univ. Army Territorial Officer (5th Loyals), 1939–45; taken prisoner, Singapore, 1942–45; despatches twice, 1946. MP (L) Bolton West, 1951–64; Liberal Chief Whip, 1962–63. Pres., Liberal Party, 1974–75. *Recreation:* golf. *Address:* Trees, High Wray, Ambleside, Cumbria LA22 0JQ. *T:* Ambleside (015394) 32258. *Died 23 Aug. 1995.*

HOLT, Jack; *see* Holt, John Lapworth.

HOLT, (James) Richard; MP (C) Langbaurgh, since 1983; personnel consultant, since 1981; *b* 2 Aug. 1931; *m* 1959, Mary June Leathers; one *s* one *d*. *Educ:* Wembley County Grammar Sch. FIPM. Served RN, 1949–54; actor, 1954–57; Personnel trainee, Gen. Motors, 1957–63; various personnel appointments with: Smiths Industries, 1963–65; Rolls Royce, 1965–66; William Hill Orgn, 1966–72; E. Gomme Ltd, 1972–78; Bowater Furniture, 1978–81. Member: Brent BC, 1964–74; High Wycombe BC, 1976–83; Bucks CC, 1981–83. Mem., Thames Water Authy, 1981–83. Contested (C) Brent South, Feb. 1974. FBIM. *Address:* Whitecroft, Newton-under-Roseberry, near Great Ayton, Cleveland; 51 High Street, Marske on Sea, Redcar, Cleveland. *Died 21 Sept. 1991.*

HOLT, Sir John Anthony L.; *see* Langford-Holt.

HOLT, Rear-Adm. John Bayley, CB 1969; DL; *b* 1 June 1912; *s* of Arthur Ogden Holt and Gertrude (*née* Bayley); *m* 1940, Olga Esme Creake; three *d*. *Educ:* William Hulme Grammar Sch., Manchester; Manchester Univ. BScTech (hons) 1933. FIEE. Electrical engineer with various cos and electric power undertakings, 1933–41; joined RN; engaged on degaussing and minesweeping research and development, later on radar and electrical engineering, for Fleet Air Arm, 1941–48; served in HMS Cumberland on Gunnery Trials, Naval Air Stations, HQ and Staff

appointments; comd HMS Ariel, 1961–63; subsequently Director of Naval Officer Appointments (Engineer Officers), and Dir-Gen. Aircraft (Naval), 1967–70, Ministry of Defence. Former Naval ADC to HM The Queen. Commander 1948; Captain 1958; Rear-Admiral 1967. Vice Pres., Surrey Br., SSAFA. DL Surrey, 1981. *Recreations:* sailing, gardening, sacred music. *Address:* Rowley Cottage, Thursley, Godalming, Surrey GU8 6QW. *T:* Elstead (01252) 702140. *Died 28 April 1995.*

HOLT, John Lapworth, (Jack Holt), OBE 1979; Founder and Director of Jack Holt Ltd and Holt group of companies, designers and suppliers of small boats and their fittings (Managing Director, 1946–76); *b* 18 April 1912; *s* of Herbert Holt and Annie (*née* Dawson); *m* 1936, Iris Eileen Thornton; one *s* one *d*. *Educ:* St Peter's Sch., London; Shoreditch Techn. Inst. (Schol.). Joiner, boat builder and designer, 1929–46; formed Jack Holt Ltd, 1946; designed: first British post-war sailing dinghy class, Merlin; first British factory-made do-it-yourself boat building kit to construct Internat. Cadet; for Yachting World magazine; International Enterprise, National Solo and Hornet, Heron, Rambler, Diamond, Lazy E, GP14, Vagabond, International Mirror Dinghy, Mirror 16, and Pacer; Pandamaran, for World Wildlife Fund. Techn. Adviser to Royal Yachting Assoc. dinghy cttee, 1950–. Jt winner (with Beecher Moore) of 12ft Nat. Championship, 1946 and Merlin Championships, 1946, 1947 and 1949; Merlin Silver Tiller series winner, 1954–56; won Solo Dutch Nat. Championships, 1962. Yachtsman's Award for service to yachting, RYA, 1977. *Recreation:* small boat sailing. *Address:* 17 Elmstead Park Road, West Wittering, West Sussex PO20 8NQ. *T:* Birdham (01243) 3559. *Clubs:* Ranelagh Sailing, Wraysbury Lake Sailing, Chichester Yacht, Aldenham Sailing. *Died 14 Nov. 1995.*

HOLT, Richard; *see* Holt, J. R.

HOLT, Victoria; *see* Hibbert, Eleanor.

HOME OF THE HIRSEL, Baron *cr* 1974 (Life Peer), of Coldstream; **Alexander Frederick Douglas-Home,** KT 1962; PC 1951; DL; Chancellor, Order of the Thistle, 1973–92; First Chancellor of Heriot-Watt University, 1966–77; *b* 2 July 1903; *e s* of 13th Earl of Home (*d* 1951), KT, and Lilian (*d* 1966), *d* of 4th Earl of Durham; *S* father, 1951, but disclaimed his peerages for life, 23 Oct. 1963; *m* 1936, Elizabeth Hester (*d* 1990), 2nd *d* of late Very Rev. C. A. Alington, DD; one *s* three *d*. *Educ:* Eton; Christ Church, Oxford. MP (U) South Lanark, 1931–45; MP (C) Lanark Div. of Lanarkshire, 1950–51; Parliamentary Private Sec. to the Prime Minister, 1937–40; Joint Parliamentary Under-Sec., Foreign Office, May–July 1945; Minister of State, Scottish Office, 1951–April 1955; Sec. of State for Commonwealth Relations, 1955–60; Dep. Leader of the House of Lords, 1956–57; Leader of the House of Lords, and Lord Pres. of the Council, 1959–60; Sec. of State for Foreign Affairs, 1960–63; MP (U) Kinross and W Perthshire, Nov. 1963–Sept. 1974; Prime Minister and First Lord of the Treasury, Oct. 1963–64; Leader of the Opposition, Oct. 1964–July 1965; Sec. of State for Foreign and Commonwealth Affairs, 1970–74. Hon. Pres., NATO Council, 1973. Captain, Royal Co. of Archers, Queen's Body Guard for Scotland, 1973. Mem., National Farmers' Union, 1964. DL Lanarkshire, 1960. Hon. DCL Oxon., 1960; Hon. Student of Christ Church, Oxford, 1962; Hon. LLD: Harvard, 1961; Edinburgh, 1962; Aberdeen, 1966; Liverpool, 1967; St Andrews, 1968; Hon. DSc Heriot-Watt, 1966. Hon. Master of the Bench, Inner Temple, 1963; Grand Master, Primrose League, 1966–84; Pres. of MCC, 1966–67. Freedom of Selkirk, 1963; Freedom of Edinburgh, 1969; Freedom of

Coldstream, 1972. Hon. Freeman: Skinners' Co., 1968; Grocers' Co., 1977. *Publications:* The Way the Wind Blows (autobiog.), 1976; Border Reflections, 1979; Letters to a Grandson, 1983. *Heir:* (to disclaimed Earldom) *s* Hon. David Alexander Cospatrick Douglas-Home, *b* 20 Nov. 1943. *Address:* House of Lords, SW1A 0PW; The Hirsel, Coldstream, Berwickshire TD12 4LP. *T:* Coldstream (01890) 882345; Castlemains, Douglas, Lanarkshire. *T:* Douglas, (Lanarks) (01555) 851241.
Died 9 Oct. 1995.

HOME, Capt. Archibald John Fitzwilliam M.; *see* Milne Home.

HOME, Sir David George, 13th Bt, *cr* 1671 (NS), of Blackadder, Co. Berwick; late Temporary Major Argyll and Sutherland Highlanders; *b* 21 Jan. 1904; *o s* of Sir John Home, 12th Bt and Hon. Gwendolina H. R. Mostyn (*d* 1960), *sister* of 7th Baron Vaux of Harrowden; *S* father, 1938; *m* 1933, Sheila, *d* of late Mervyn Campbell Stephen; one *s* one *d* (and one *s* one *d* decd). *Educ:* Harrow; Jesus Coll., Cambridge (BA 1925). Member Royal Company of Archers (HM Body Guard for Scotland). FSAScot. *Heir: g s* William Dundas Home, *b* 19 Feb. 1968. *Address:* Winterfield, North Berwick, East Lothian. *Clubs:* Brooks's; New (Edinburgh); Royal and Ancient (St Andrews). *Died 17 Jan. 1992.*

HOME, Hon. William Douglas-; dramatic author; *b* Edinburgh, 3 June 1912; *s* of 13th Earl of Home, KT, and Lilian, *d* of 4th Earl of Durham; *m* 1951, Rachel Brand (later Baroness Dacre); one *s* three *d. Educ:* Eton; New Coll., Oxford (BA). Studied at Royal Academy of Dramatic Art, and appeared on the West End stage. Formerly Captain RAC. Contested: (Progressive Ind) Cathcart Division of Glasgow, April 1942, Windsor Division of Berks, June 1942, and Clay Cross Division of Derbyshire (Atlantic Charter), April 1944; (L) South Edinburgh, 1957. Author of the following plays: Great Possessions, 1937; Passing By, 1940; Now Barabbas, The Chiltern Hundreds, 1947; Ambassador Extraordinary, 1948; Master of Arts, The Thistle and the Rose, 1949; Caro William, 1952; The Bad Samaritan, 1953; The Manor of Northstead, 1954; The Reluctant Debutante, 1955; The Iron Duchess, 1957; Aunt Edwina, 1959; Up a Gum Tree, 1960; The Bad Soldier Smith, 1961; The Cigarette Girl, 1962; The Drawing Room Tragedy, 1963; The Reluctant Peer, Two Accounts Rendered, 1964; Betzi, 1965; A Friend Indeed, 1966; The Secretary Bird, The Queen's Highland Servant, The Grouse Moor Image, The Bishop and the Actress, 1968; The Jockey Club Stakes, Uncle Dick's Surprise, 1970; The Douglas Cause, 1971; Lloyd George Knew My Father, 1972; At the End of the Day, 1973; The Bank Manager, The Dame of Sark, The Lord's Lieutenant, 1974; In The Red, The Kingfisher, Rolls Hyphen Royce, The Perch, The Consulting Room, 1977; The Editor Regrets, 1978; You're All Right: How am I?, 1981; Four Hearts Doubled, Her Mother Came Too, 1982; The Golf Umbrella, 1983; David and Jonathan, 1984; After the Ball is Over, 1985; Portraits, 1987; A Christmas Truce, 1989. *Publications:* Half Term Report, an autobiography, 1954; Mr Home Pronounced Hume: an autobiography, 1979; Sins of Commission, 1985; Old Men Remember, 1991. *Recreations:* golf, politics. *Address:* Derry House, Kilmeston, near Alresford, Hants. *T:* Bramdean (096279) 256. *Club:* Travellers'. *Died 28 Sept. 1992.*

HONE, Maj.-Gen. Sir (Herbert) Ralph, KCMG 1951; KBE 1946 (CBE Mil. 1943); MC; TD; QC (Gibraltar) 1934, QC (Uganda) 1938; barrister-at-law; *b* 3 May 1896; *s* of late Herbert Hone and Miriam Grace (*née* Dracott); *m* 1st, 1918, Elizabeth Daisy (marr. diss. 1944), *d* of James Matthews; one *s* one *d*; 2nd, 1945, Sybil Mary, *widow* of Wing Commander G. Simond; one *s. Educ:* Varndean Grammar Sch., Brighton; London Univ. LLB (Hons).

Called to the Bar, Middle Temple, 1924. Inns of Court OTC; gazetted London Irish Rifles, 1915; Lieut, 1916; Captain, 1918; served with BEF, France, 1916 and 1917–18 (wounded, MC); Staff Captain, Ministry of Munitions, 1918–20; Major R of O (TA). Asst Treas., Uganda, 1920; barrister, practised and went South Eastern Circuit, 1924–25; Registrar, High Court, Zanzibar, 1925; Resident Magistrate, Zanzibar, 1928; Crown Counsel, Tanganyika Territory, 1930; acted Asst Legal Adviser to the Colonial and Dominions Offices, Jan.-Aug. 1933; Attorney-General, Gibraltar, 1933–36; Commissioner for the Revision of the laws of Gibraltar, 1934; Chm., Gibraltar Govt Commn on Slum Clearance and Rent Restriction, 1936; Acting Chief Justice, Gibraltar, on several occasions; Attorney-General, Uganda, 1937–43; Chairman, Uganda Government Cttee on Museum Policy, 1938; Commandant, Uganda Defence Force, 1940; Chief Legal Adviser, Political Branch, GHQ, Middle East, 1941; Chief Political Officer, GHQ, Middle East, 1942–43; General Staff, War Office, 1943–45; Chief Civil Affairs Officer, Malaya, 1945–46; Maj.-Gen., 1942–46 (despatches twice, CBE (mil.)); Secretary-General to Governor-General of Malaya, 1946–48; Dep. Commissioner-General in SE Asia, 1948–49; Governor and C-in-C, North Borneo, 1949–54; Head of Legal Division, CRO, 1954–61; resumed practice at the Bar, 1961. Vice-Pres., Royal Commonwealth Society; Constitutional Adviser, Kenya Govt, Dec. 1961-Jan. 1962; Constitutional Adviser to Mr Butler's Advisers on Central Africa, July-Oct. 1962; Constitutional Adviser to South Arabian Government, Oct. 1965-Jan. 1966, and to Bermuda Government, July-Nov. 1966; Appeal Comr under Civil Aviation Licensing Act, 1961–71; Standing Counsel, Grand Bahama Port Authority, 1962–75. Retd TA with Hon. rank Maj.-Gen., 1956. GCStJ 1973; Mem. Chapter Gen. Order of St John, 1954–. Jubilee Medal, 1935; Coronation Medal, 1937, 1953. *Publications:* Index to Gibraltar Laws, 1933; revised edn of Laws of Gibraltar, 1935; revised edn of Laws of the Bahamas, 1965; Handbook on Native Courts, etc. *Recreations:* tennis, badminton, philately. *Address:* 1 Paper Buildings, Temple, EC4. *T:* 071–583 7355; 56 Kenilworth Court, Lower Richmond Road, SW15. *T:* 081–788 3367. *Clubs:* Athenæum, Commonwealth Trust.
Died 28 Nov. 1992.

HOOPER, Ven. Charles German, MA; Archdeacon of Ipswich, 1963–76, then Archdeacon Emeritus; *b* 16 April 1911; 2nd *s* of A. C. Hooper, solicitor; *m* 1936, Lilian Mary, *d* of late Sir Harold Brakspear, KCVO; one *s* one *d. Educ:* Lincoln Coll., Oxford (2nd cl. English; MA). Deacon, 1934; priest, 1935; Curacies: Corsham, Wilts, 1934–36; Claremont, CP, South Africa, 1936–39; Rector, Castle Combe, Wilts, 1940; Chaplain, RAFVR, 1942–46 (despatches); Rector, Sandy, Beds, 1946–53; Vicar and Rural Dean, Bishop's Stortford, Herts, 1953–63; Rector of Bildeston, Suffolk, 1963–67; Rector of St Lawrence's and St Stephen's, Ipswich, 1967–74. Chaplain to Cutlers' Co., Sheffield, 1964–65, to Drapers' Co., 1972–73. *Recreations:* painting in water colours, sailing. *Address:* East Green Cottage, Kelsale, Saxmundham, Suffolk IP17 2PJ. *T:* Saxmundham (01728) 602702.
Died 22 March 1995.

HOOPER, Sir Leonard (James), KCMG 1967 (CMG 1962); CBE 1951; a Deputy Secretary, Cabinet Office, 1973–78, retired; *b* 23 July 1914; *s* of James Edmond and Grace Hooper; *m* 1st, 1951, Ena Mary Osborn (marr. diss. 1978); 2nd, 1978, Mary Kathleen Horwood. *Educ:* Alleyn's, Dulwich; Worcester Coll., Oxford. idc. Joined Air Ministry, 1938, transferred Foreign Office, 1942; Imperial Defence Coll., 1953; Dir, Govt Communications HQ, 1965–73. *Recreation:* sport. *Address:* 9 Vittoria

Walk, Cheltenham, Glos GL50 1TL. *T:* Cheltenham (0242) 511007. *Club:* New (Cheltenham).
Died 19 Feb. 1994.

HOPE, Maj.-Gen. Adrian Price Webley, CB 1961; CBE 1952; *b* 21 Jan. 1911; *s* of late Adm. H. W. W. Hope, CB, CVO, DSO, and Katherine, *y d* of Rev. Francis Kewley; *m* 1958, Mary Elizabeth (*d* 1990), *e d* of Graham Partridge, Cotham Lodge, Newport, Pembrokeshire; no *c. Educ:* Winchester Coll.; RMC, Sandhurst. 2/Lt KOSB, 1931; Adjt, 1/KOSB, 1937-38; Staff Capt. A, Palestine, Egypt, 1938-40; DA&QMG (Plans) Egypt, 1940-41; Instructor, Staff Coll., 1941; AQMG, Egypt, Sicily, Italy, 1941-44; Col Asst Quartermaster, Plans, India, 1945; Brig., Quartermaster, SE Asia, 1946; Comdt Sch. of Military Admin, 1947-48; Instructor, JSSC, 1948-50; DQMG, GHQ, MELF, 1951-53; Student, IDC, 1954; Brig. Quartermaster (Ops), War Office, 1955-57; BGS, HQ, BAOR, 1958-59; MGA, GHQ, FARELF, 1959-61; Dir of Equipment Policy, War Office, 1961-64; Dep. Master-Gen. of the Ordnance, Ministry of Defence, 1964-66; retd 1966. *Address:* Monks Place, Charlton Horethorne, Sherborne, Dorset. *Club:* Army and Navy.
Died 12 Dec. 1992.

HOPE, Sir Robert Holms-Kerr, 3rd Bt *cr* 1932, of Kinnettles, Co. Angus; *b* 12 April 1900; *s* of Sir Harry Hope, 1st Bt and Margaret Binnie Holms-Kerr; *S* brother, 1979; *m* 1928, Eleanor (*d* 1967), *d* of late Very Rev. Marshall Lang, DD, Whittingehame, East Lothian. *Heir:* none. *Address:* Old Bridge House, Broxmouth, Dunbar, East Lothian.
Died 8 April 1993 (ext).

HOPKINS, Douglas Edward, DMus (London); FRAM, FRCO, FGSM; Conductor, Stock Exchange Male Voice Choir, since 1956; *b* 23 Dec. 1902; *s* of Edward and Alice Hopkins; unmarried. *Educ:* St Paul's Cathedral Choir Sch.; Dulwich Coll.; Guildhall Sch. of Music (Ernest Palmer and Corporation Scholarships); Royal Academy of Music. Organist, Christ Church, Greyfriars, EC, 1921; Sub-Organist, St Paul's Cathedral, 1927; Prof., Royal Acad. of Music, 1937-78; Examr, Royal Schs of Music, 1937-81; Master of the Music, Peterborough Cathedral, 1946-52; Organist, Canterbury Cathedral, 1953-55; Musical Dir, St Felix Sch., Southwold, 1956-65; Organist, St Marylebone Parish Church, 1965-71; Organist, Royal Meml Chapel, RMA Sandhurst, 1971-76. Founder, Holiday Course for Organists (Dir, 1962-74). From 1957 made many overseas tours, inc. NZ, Africa, Malaysia, W Indies, Singapore and Hong Kong. Conductor of Handel Soc., 1928-33, and, subseq., of various other musical societies. Liveryman, Worshipful Co. of Musicians. *Address:* 244 Mytchett Road, Mytchett, Camberley, Surrey GU16 6AF. *Died 2 Dec. 1992.*

HOPKINS, Prof. Harold Horace, FRS 1973; Emeritus Professor, University of Reading, since 1984 (Professor of Applied Optics, 1967-84 and Head of Department of Physics, 1977-80); *b* 6 Dec. 1918; *s* of William Ernest and Teresa Ellen Hopkins; *m* 1950, Christine Dove Ridsdale; three *s* one *d. Educ:* Gateway Sch., Leicester; Univs of Leicester and London. BSc, PhD, DSc, FInstP. Physicist, Taylor, Taylor & Hobson, 1939-42; Royal Engrs, 1942; Physicist: MAP, 1942-45; W. Watson & Sons, 1945-47; Research Fellow, then Reader in Optics, Imperial Coll., 1947-67. Hon. Papers Sec. and Mem. Council, Physical Soc., 1947-59; President: Internat. Commn for Optics, 1969-72; Maths and Phys Sect., British Assoc., 1977. Thomas Young Orator, Inst. of Physics, 1960; Lister Oration, RCS, 1991. Fellow: Optical Soc. of Amer., 1972; Soc. for Photo-Instrumentation Engrs, 1975; Hon. Member: Amer. Assoc. of Gynæcologic Laparoscopy, 1977; Brit. Assoc. of Urological Surgeons, 1977; Brit. Soc. for Gastroenterology, 1980; Hon. FRCS, 1979; Hon. FRCP, 1983; Hon. FRSM, 1989; Hon. Fellow:

Optical Soc. of India, 1981; Soc. for Engrg Optics, Republic of China, 1987. Hon. DrèsSc Besançon, 1960; Hon. DSc: Bristol, 1980; Liverpool, 1982; Reading, 1986; Hon. Dr Med. Munich, 1980. Ives Medal, Optical Soc. of Amer., 1978; St Peter's Medal, Brit. Assoc. of Urological Surgeons, 1979; First Distinguished Service Award, Amer. Soc. for Gastrointestinal Endoscopy, 1980; Gold Medal, Internat. Soc. for Optical Engineering, 1982; Pro-Meritate Medal, Internat. Soc. of Urologic Endoscopy, 1984; Rumford Medal, Royal Soc., 1984; Distinguished Scientific Achievement Award, Amer. Urological Assoc., 1987; Founder's Medal, Eur. Urol Assoc., 1988; Lister Medal, RCS, 1990. Inventions incl. zoom lenses, fibre optics and medical endoscopes. *Publications:* Wave Theory of Aberrations, 1951; (with J. G. Gow) Handbook of Urological Endoscopy, 1978; papers in Proc. Royal Soc., Proc. Phys. Soc., Optica Acta, Jl Optical Soc. Amer., Jl of Modern Optics, Applied Optics. *Recreations:* keyboard music, sailing, languages, woodwork. *Address:* 26 Cintra Avenue, Reading, Berks RG2 7AU. *T:* Reading (01734) 871913. *Died 22 Oct. 1994.*

HOPKINS, Sir James Sidney Rawdon S.; see Scott-Hopkins.

HOPKINSON, Albert Cyril, CBE 1970; FRIBA; consultant architect; *b* 2 Aug. 1911; *s* of Albert Hopkinson and Isaline Pollard (*née* Cox); *m* 1943, Lesley Evelyn Hill; one *s* one *d. Educ:* Univs of Sheffield and London. BA 1933; MA 1934. FRIBA 1949 (ARIBA 1934); Dipl. Town Planning and Civic Architecture, London, 1938. Min. of Public Building and Works, 1937-64; Dir of Works and Chief Architect, Home Office, 1964-75. *Recreations:* reading, walking. *Club:* Wig and Pen.
Died 22 May 1994.

HOPKINSON, Prof. Ralph Galbraith; Haden-Pilkington Professor of Environmental Design and Engineering, University College London, 1965-76, then Emeritus; *b* 13 Aug. 1913; *s* of late Ralph Galbraith Hopkinson and Beatrice Frances (*née* Wright); *m* 1938, Dora Beryl (*née* Churchill) (*d* 1993); two *s* (and one *s* decd). *Educ:* Erith Grammar Sch.; Faraday House. BSc (Eng), PhD; CEng, FIEE; FRPS. Research Engr, GEC, 1934-47, lighting and radar; Principal Scientific Officer, DSIR Building Research Stn, 1947-64 (Special Merit appointment, 1960); Dean, Faculty of Environmental Studies, UCL, 1972-74. Work on: human response to buildings, leading to concept of environmental design by engr-physicists and architects in collab.; schools with Min. of Educn Develt Gp and on hosps with Nuffield Foundn, 1949-65; lighting design of Tate Gallery extension and Stock Exchange Market Hall (Design Award of Distinction, Illum. Engrg Soc. of USA, 1974); visual and noise intrusion (urban motorways) for DoE, 1970; consultant, DoE Road Construction Unit. Pres., Illuminating Engrg Soc., 1965-66 (Gold Medallist, 1972; Hon. Mem., 1976); Mem., Royal Soc. Study Gp on Human Biology in the Urban Environment, 1972-74. Trustee, British Institution Fund, 1972-77. Hon. FRIBA 1969; Hon. FCIBSE 1977. *Publications:* Architectural Physics: Lighting, 1963; Hospital Lighting, 1964; Daylighting, 1966; (with J. D. Kay) The Lighting of Buildings, 1969; Lighting and Seeing, 1969; The Ergonomics of Lighting, 1970; Visual Intrusion (RTPI), 1972; papers in Nature, Jl Optical Soc. of America, Jl Psychol., Illum. Engrg, etc. *Recreations:* music, human sciences, walking. *Address:* Bartlett School of Architecture and Planning, University College London, Wates House, 22 Gordon Street, WC1H 0QB.
Died 11 June 1994.

HOPPE, Iver; Kt of Danish Dannebrog; Chairman and Chief Executive, Navalicon Ltd A/S, Denmark, 1975-84; *b* Denmark, 25 July 1920; *s* of Arthur Hans Knudsen Hoppe and Gerda (*née* Raun Byberg); *m* 1943, Ingeborg

Lassen; one *d. Educ:* Aarhus Katedralskole; Copenhagen Univ. (Law Faculty), 1944. Acting Lecturer, Copenhagen Univ., 1946; Advocate to High Court and Court of Appeal, 1948; Jurisprudential Lecturer, Copenhagen Univ., 1952–58; study sojourn in Switzerland, 1949. A. P. Møller Concern, Copenhagen, 1955–71: Asst Dir, 1960; Man. Dir of Odense Steel Shipyard, Ltd, Odense and Lindø, 1964–71; Chm. A/S Svendborg Skibsvaerft, 1968–71; Mem. Bd of Dansk Boreselskab A/S and other cos until 1971; Man. Dir and Chief Exec., Harland and Wolff Ltd, Belfast, 1971–74. Member: Bd of Den Danske Landmandsbank A/S, 1970–72; Council of Danish National Bank, 1967–71; Bd of Danish Ship Credit Fund, 1965–71; Assoc. of Danish Shipyards, 1964–71; Assoc. of Employers within the Iron and Metal Industry in Denmark, 1967–71; Assoc. of Danish Industries, 1965–72; West of England Steam Ship Owners Protection and Indemnity Assoc., Ltd, 1960–66; Danish Acad. of Technical Sciences; Shipbuilders and Repairers Nat. Assoc. Exec. Council and Management Bd, 1971–74; British Iron and Steel Consumers' Council, 1971–74; Gen. Cttee, Lloyd's Register of Shipping; British Cttee, Det Norske Veritas; Amer. Bureau of Shipping, and other Danish and foreign instns. Kt of Icelandic Falcon. *Recreations:* reading, swimming, mountain walking, farming. *Address:* Malmmosegaard, Dyreborgvej 7, DK-5600 Faaborg, Denmark.　　　　　　*Died 11 April 1991.*

HOPTHROW, Brig. Harry Ewart, CBE 1946 (OBE 1940); Hon. Life Member, Solent Protection Society (Member Council, 1975–85); *b* 13 Nov. 1896; *s* of Frederick Hopthrow; *m* 1925, Audrey Kassel (*d* 1975), *d* of J. Lewer; one *s* one *d. Educ:* Queen Elizabeth's Grammar Sch., Gainsborough; City Sch., Lincoln; Loughborough Coll. Served European War, 1915–18, RE, France and Flanders. Civil and Mechanical Engineer, ICI Ltd, 1925–39; commanded 107 Co. RE, 1931–35, Major; Asst Dir of Works, GHQ, BEF, 1939–40, Lt-Col; served France and Flanders, 1939–40 and 1944; Dep. Chief Engineer: Home Forces, 1940–41, and Western Comd, 1941; Dep. Controller Mil. Works Services, War Office, 1941–43; Dir of Fortifications and Works, WO, 1943–45; Asst Sec., ICI Ltd, 1945–58; Hon. Secretary and a Vice-Pres., Royal Institution, 1960–68. AMIMechE 1924, FIMechE 1933. Mem. Central Advisory Water Cttee (Min. of Housing and Local Govt), 1951–69; Mem. Cttee of Inquiry into Inland Waterways (Bowes Cttee), 1956–58; Vice-Chm. IoW River and Water Authority, 1964–73; UK Rep. to Council of European Industrial Fedns; Vice-Pres., Round Tables on Pollution, 1965–73. Life Mem., Isle of Wight Soc. Officer of American Legion of Merit, 1946. *Recreations:* intellectual conversation with intelligent ladies, historical research. *Address:* Surrey House, Cowes, Isle of Wight. *T:* Isle of Wight (0983) 292430. *Clubs:* Army and Navy; Royal Engineer Yacht; Royal London Yacht, Island Sailing (Cowes).

　　　　　　　　　　　　　　　　Died 16 Dec. 1992.

HORDERN, Sir Michael (Murray), Kt 1983; CBE 1972; actor; *b* 3 Oct. 1911; *s* of Capt. Edward Joseph Calverly Hordern, CIE, RIN, and Margaret Emily (*née* Murray); *m* 1943, Grace Eveline Mortimer (*d* 1986); one *d. Educ:* Brighton Coll. Formerly in business with The Educational Supply Assoc., playing meanwhile as an amateur at St Pancras People's Theatre; first professional appearance as Lodovico in Othello, People's Palace, 1937; two seasons of repertory at Little Theatre, Bristol, 1937–39; War service in Navy, 1940–46, demobilised as Lieut-Comdr, RNVR; parts include: Mr Toad in Toad of Toad Hall, at Stratford, 1948 and 1949; Ivanov in Ivanov, Arts Theatre, 1950; Stratford Season, 1952: Jacques, Menenius, Caliban; Old Vic Season, 1953–54: Polonius, King John, Malvolio, Prospero; "BB" in The Doctor's Dilemma, Saville, 1956; Old Vic Season, 1958–59: Cassius, Macbeth; Ulysses

(Troilus and Cressida), Edinburgh Fest., 1962; Herbert Georg Beutler in The Physicists, Aldwych, 1963; Southman in Saint's Day, St Martin's, 1965; Relatively Speaking, Duke of York's, 1967; A Delicate Balance, Aldwych, 1969; King Lear, Nottingham Playhouse, 1969; Flint, Criterion, 1970; National Theatre: 1972: Jumpers (also 1976), Gaunt, in Richard II; 1973: The Cherry Orchard; The Ordeal of Gilbert Pinfold, Manchester, 1977, Round House, 1979; RSC Stratford, 1978: Prospero in The Tempest, Armado in Love's Labour's Lost; The Rivals, NT, 1983; You Never Can Tell, Haymarket, 1987; Bookends, Apollo, 1990; Trelawney of the Wells, Comedy, 1992; also many leading parts in films, radio and television. Hon. Fellow, QMC, 1987; Hon. DLitt: Exeter, 1985; Warwick, 1987. *Publication:* A World Elsewhere (autobiog.), 1993. *Recreation:* fishing. *Clubs:* Garrick, Flyfishers'.　　　　　　　　　　*Died 2 May 1995.*

HORLICK, Sir John (James Macdonald), 5th Bt *cr* 1914, of Cowley Manor, Gloucester; Partner, Tournaig Farming Company, since 1973; *b* 9 April 1922; *s* of Lt-Col Sir James Horlick, 4th Bt, OBE, MC, and Flora Macdonald (*d* 1955), *d* of late Col Cunliffe Martin, CB; *S* father, 1972; *m* 1948, June, *d* of late Douglas Cory-Wright, CBE; one *s* two *d. Educ:* Eton; Babson Institute of Business Admin, Wellesley Hills, Mass, USA. Served War as Captain, Coldstream Guards. Dep. Chairman, Horlicks Ltd, retired 1971. CStJ 1977. *Recreations:* military history, model soldier collecting. *Heir: s* James Cunliffe William Horlick [*b* 19 Nov. 1956; *m* 1985, Fiona Rosalie, *e d* of Andrew McLaren, Alcester; three *s*]. *Address:* Tournaig, Poolewe, Achnasheen, Ross-shire IV22 2LH. *T:* Poolewe (0144586) 250; Howberry Lane Cottage, Nuffield, near Nettlebed, Oxon RG9 5SU. *T:* Nettlebed (01491) 641454. *Club:* Beefsteak.　　　　　　　　　*Died 20 Feb. 1995.*

HORN, Alan Bowes, CVO 1971; HM Diplomatic Service, retired; *b* 6 June 1917; *s* of Thomas Horn; *m* 1946, Peggy Boocock; one *s* one *d. Educ:* London Sch. of Economics. Served in Army, 1940–46. Joined Foreign Service, 1946; Vice-Consul, Marseilles, 1948–49; 2nd Sec., HM Embassy, Tel Aviv, 1949; promoted 1st Sec. and later appointed: London, 1951–53; New York, 1953–56; Helsinki, 1957–60; FO, 1960–63; Ambassador to the Malagasy Republic, 1963–67; Counsellor, Warsaw, 1967–70; Consul-General, Istanbul, 1970–73. *Address:* Oak Trees, Shere Road, Ewhurst, Cranleigh, Surrey GU6 7PQ.　　　　　　　　　　　　*Died 5 June 1992.*

HORNBY STEER, William Reed; *see* Steer.

HORSMAN, Dame Dorothea (Jean), DBE 1986; JP; *b* 17 April 1918; *d* of Samuel Morrell and Jean (*née* Morris); *m* 1943, Ernest Alan Horsman; one *s* two *d. Educ:* Univ. of New Zealand (MA History); Trained Teacher's Cert., 1941; Univ. of Otago (MA Russian 1970). Mem., Govt Working Party on Liquor Laws, 1985–86. President: NZ Fedn of University Women, 1973–76; Arthritis and Rheumatism Foundn of NZ, 1980–83; Mem., Bd of Management, 1976, Vice-Pres. 1980, Pres., 1982–86, Nat. Council of Women of NZ. Mem., Winston Churchill Meml Trust Bd, 1983–89. JP 1979. Silver Jubilee Medal, 1977. *Publications:* What Price Equality? (with J. J. Herd) (for Nat. Council of Women, NZ), 1974; Women at Home (with J. J. Herd) (for NZ Fedn of Univ. Women), 1976; (contrib. and ed) Women in Council—a History (NCW), 1982. *Recreations:* reading, listening to music. *Address:* 10 Balmoral Street, Opoho, Dunedin, New Zealand. *T:* (3) 4737119.　　　　　　　　　　　*Died 7 Jan. 1994.*

HORT, Sir James Fenton, 8th Bt *cr* 1767, of Castle Strange, Middlesex; *b* 6 Sept. 1926; *s* of Sir Fenton George Hort, 7th Bt, and Gwendolene (*d* 1982), *d* of late Sir Walter Alcock, MVO; *S* father 1960; *m* 1951, Joan, *d* of late Edwin Peat, Swallownest, Sheffield; two *s* two *d. Educ:*

Marlborough; Trinity Coll., Cambridge. MA, MB, BChir, Cambridge, 1950. *Recreation:* fishing. *Heir: s* Andrew Edwin Fenton Hort [*b* 15 Nov. 1954; *m* 1986, Mary, *d* of Jack Whibley; one *s* one *d*]. *Address:* Poundgate Lodge, Uckfield Road, Crowborough, Sussex TN6 3TA.
Died 19 July 1995.

HOSFORD, John Percival, MS, FRCS; retired; Surgeon, Lecturer on Surgery, St Bartholomew's Hospital, 1936–60; Surgeon, King Edward VII Hospital for Officers and Florence Nightingale Hospital; Consulting Surgeon to Hospitals at Watford, Leatherhead, Hitchin, St Albans and to the Foundling Hospital and Reedham Orphanage; *b* 24 July 1900; 2nd *s* of Dr B. Hosford, Highgate; *m* 1932, Millicent Sacheverell Violet Sybil Claud, *d* of late Brig.-Gen. C. Vaughan Edwards, CMG, DSO; one *s* one *d*. *Educ:* Highgate Sch.; St Bartholomew's Hosp. MB, BS (London) 1922; FRCS 1925; MS (London); University Gold Medal, 1925. Formerly Registrar St Bartholomew's Hosp. and Royal National Orthopædic Hosp. Hunterian Prof., Royal College of Surgeons, 1932. Retired, Oct. 1960. Formerly: Mem. of Court of Examiners of Royal College of Surgeons; Examiner in Surgery at Universities of Oxford, London, Sheffield, Belfast. Fellow Assoc. of Surgeons (on Council) and Royal Society Med. *Publications:* numerous articles in medical and surgical journals and encyclopædias. *Recreation:* gardening. *Address:* 16 Pelham Road, Clavering, Saffron Walden, Essex CB11 4PQ. *Died 10 Feb. 1991.*

HOSIE, James Findlay, CBE 1972 (OBE 1955; MBE 1946); a Director, Science Research Council, 1965–74; *b* 22 Aug. 1913; *s* of James Hosie; *m* 1951, Barbara Mary Mansell. *Educ:* Glasgow Univ. (MA Hons); St John's Coll., Cambridge (BA). Indian Civil Service, 1938–47; Principal, 1947–56, Asst Sec., 1956–58, Min. of Defence, London; Asst Sec. QMG to the Forces, War Office, 1958–61; Office of Minister for Science, later Dept of Educn and Science, 1961–65. *Recreations:* bird-watching, gardening. *Address:* Flat 3, Eastbury Court, Compton, near Guildford, Surrey GU3 1EE. *T:* Guildford (0483) 810331. *Died 31 Oct. 1993.*

HOSKING, Eric (John), OBE 1977; photographer, ornithologist; *b* 2 Oct. 1909; 3rd *s* of late Albert Hosking and Margaret Helen, *d* of William Steggall; *m* 1939, Dorothy, *d* of late Harry Sleigh; two *s* one *d*. *Educ:* Stationers' Company's Sch., London N8. Hon. Fellow, Royal Photographic Society; a Vice-Pres., Royal Society for the Protection of Birds; Hon. Vice-Pres., London Natural History Soc.; a Vice-Pres., British Naturalists' Assoc.; Pres., Nature Photographic Society; Scientific Fellow of Zoological Society; Fellow, British Inst. of Professional Photographers. Exhibited at Royal Photographic Society, 1932– (Council, 1950–56; Fellowship and Associateship Admissions Cttee, 1939–48, 1951–56, 1960–65 and 1967–); Member: BOU, 1935–; Brit. Trust for Ornithology, 1938–; Cornell Laboratory of Ornithology, America, 1961–. Dir of Photography to Coto Doñana Expedn, Spain, 1956 and 1957; Leader of Cazoria Valley Expedition, Spain, 1959; Dir of Photography, British Ornithologists' Expedition to Bulgaria, 1960, to Hungary, 1961; other expeditions: Mountfort-Jordan, 1963; British-Jordan, 1965; Pakistan, 1966; World Wildlife Fund, Pakistan, 1967; Lindblad Galapagos Islands, 1970; Kenya and Rhodesia, 1972; Tanzania and Kenya, 1974 and 1977; Seychelles, 1978; India and Nepal, 1979; Falklands and Antarctic, 1979; circumnavigation of Antarctic, and New Zealand and Australia, 1981; Spitzbergen and Arctic, 1982; Greenland and Canadian Arctic, 1984; Alaska, 1984; Sri Lanka and Israel, 1985; Madagascar, Comoros, Aldabra and Seychelles, 1986; Israel and Kalahari Desert, 1987; Singapore and NZ, 1989. Photographic Editor: of New Naturalist, 1942; of British

Birds, 1960–76. RGS Cherry Kearton Award, 1968; RSPB Gold Medal, 1974; Zoological Soc. Silver Medal, 1975. *Publications:* Intimate Sketches from Bird Life, 1940; The Art of Bird Photography, 1944; Birds of the Day, 1944; Birds of the Night, 1945; More Birds of the Day, 1946; The Swallow, 1946; Masterpieces of Bird Photography, 1947; Birds in Action, 1949; Birds Fighting, 1955; Bird Photography as a Hobby, 1961; Nesting Birds, Eggs and Fledglings, 1967; (with Frank Lane) An Eye for a Bird (autobiog.), 1970; Wildlife Photography, 1973; (with Herbert Axell) Birds of Britain, 1978; Eric Hosking's Birds, 1979; (with J. Flegg) Eric Hosking's Owls, 1982; Antarctic Wildlife, 1982; (with W. G. Hale) Eric Hosking's Waders, 1983; (with R. M. Lockley) Eric Hosking's Seabirds, 1983; Just a Lark, 1984; (with Janet Kear) Eric Hosking's Wildfowl, 1985; (with Peter France) The Encyclopaedia of Bible Animals, 1985; (with J. Flegg and David Hosking) Which Bird, 1986; (with J. Flegg and David Hosking) Eric Hosking's Birds of Prey, 1987; (with J. Flegg and David Hosking) Poles Apart, 1990; illustrator of many books on natural history, by photographs. *Address:* 20 Crouch Hall Road, N8 8HX. *T:* 081–340 7703 *Died 22 Feb. 1991.*

HOSKINS, Prof. William George, CBE 1971; FBA 1969; MA, PhD; *b* Exeter, 22 May 1908; *e s* of late William George Hoskins and Alice Beatrice Dymond; *m* 1933, Frances Jackson; one *d* (one *s* decd). *Educ:* Hele's Sch., Exeter; University Coll., Exeter. Lectr in Economics, University Coll., Leicester, 1931–41, 1946–48; Central Price Regulation Cttee, 1941–45; Reader in English Local History, University Coll. (subseq. Univ.) of Leicester, 1948–51; Reader in Econ. Hist., University of Oxford, 1951–65; Hatton Prof. of English History, University of Leicester, 1965–68, retired in despair, 1968; Emeritus Professor, 1968. BBC TV Series, Landscapes of England, 1976, 1977, 1978. Member: Royal Commission on Common Land, 1955–58; Adv. Cttee on Bldgs of Special Architectural and Historical Interest (Min. of Housing and Local Govt), 1955–64; Vice-Pres. Leicestershire Archæol and Hist. Soc., 1952; President: Dartmoor Preserv. Assoc., 1962–76; Devonshire Assoc., 1978–79; British Agricultural History Soc., 1972–74. Leverhulme Res. Fellow, 1961–63; Leverhulme Emeritus Fellowship, 1970–71. Murchison Award, RGS, 1976. Hon. FRIBA, 1973. Hon. DLitt: Exon, 1974; CNAA, 1976; DUniv Open, 1981. *Publications:* Industry, Trade and People in Exeter, 1935; Heritage of Leicestershire, 1946; Midland England, 1949; Essays in Leicestershire History, 1950; Chilterns to Black Country, 1951; East Midlands and the Peak, 1951; Devonshire Studies, (with H. P. R. Finberg), 1952; Devon (New Survey of England), 1954; The Making of the English Landscape, 1955; The Midland Peasant, 1957; The Leicestershire Landscape, 1957; Exeter in the Seventeenth Century, 1957; Local History in England, 1959; Devon and its People, 1959; Two Thousand Years in Exeter, 1960; The Westward Expansion of Wessex, 1960; Shell Guide to Rutland, 1963; The Common Lands of England and Wales (with L. Dudley Stamp), 1963; Provincial England, 1963; Old Devon, 1966; Fieldwork in Local History, 1967; Shell Guide to Leicestershire, 1970; History from the Farm, 1970; English Landscapes, 1973; The Age of Plunder, 1976; One Man's England, 1978. *Recreations:* remembering, quietly reading.
Died 11 Jan. 1992.

HOTHFIELD, 5th Baron *cr* 1881; **George William Anthony Tufton**, TD 1949 (and Bar); DL; Bt 1851; *b* 28 Oct. 1904; *s* of Hon. Charles Henry Tufton, CMG (*d* 1923) (3rd *s* of 1st Baron) and Stella Josephine Faudel, OBE (*d* 1958), *d* of Sir George Faudel Faudel-Phillips, 1st Bt, GCIE; *S* cousin, 1986; *m* 1936, Evelyn Margarette (*d* 1989), *e d* of late Eustace Charles Mordaunt; two *s* one *d*. *Educ:* Eton; Hertford College, Oxford. Insurance Broker

and Underwriting Member of Lloyd's. DL Herts, 1962. *Heir: s* Hon. Anthony Charles Sackville Tufton [*b* 21 Oct. 1939; *m* 1975, Lucinda Marjorie, *d* of Captain Timothy John Gurney; one *s* one *d*]. *Address:* 11A High Street, Barkway, Royston, Herts SG8 8EA. *T:* Barkway (076384) 266. *Club:* Leander (Henley-on-Thames).
Died 5 Feb. 1991.

HOTSON, Leslie, LittD (Cambridge); FRSL; Shakespearean scholar and writer; *b* Delhi, Ont, Canada, 16 Aug. 1897; *s* of John H. and Lillie S. Hotson; *m* 1919, Mary May, *d* of Frederick W. Peabody. *Educ:* Harvard Univ. Sheldon Travelling Fellow, Harvard, 1923–24; Sterling Research Fellow, Yale, 1926–27; Associate Prof. of English, New York Univ., 1927–29; Guggenheim Memorial Fellow, 1929–31; Prof. of English, Haverford Coll., Pa, 1931–41; served War of 1939–45, 1st Lieut and Capt. Signal Corps, US Army, 1943–46; Fulbright Exchange Scholar, Bedford Coll., London, 1949–50; Research Associate, Yale, 1953; Fellow, King's Coll., Cambridge, 1954–60. *Publications:* The Death of Christopher Marlowe, 1925; The Commonwealth and Restoration Stage, 1928; Shelley's Lost Letters to Harriet, 1930; Shakespeare versus Shallow, 1931; I, William Shakespeare, 1937; Shakespeare's Sonnets Dated, 1949; Shakespeare's Motley, 1952; Queen Elizabeth's Entertainment at Mitcham, 1953; The First Night of Twelfth Night, 1954; Shakespeare's Wooden O, 1959; Mr W. H., 1964; Shakespeare by Hilliard, 1977. *Recreation:* boating. *Address:* 130 White Hollow Road, Northford, Conn 06472, USA. *Died 16 Nov. 1992.*

HOUGHTON, Rev. Alfred Thomas, MA, LTh; General Secretary, Bible Churchmen's Missionary Society, 1945–66, Vice-President, 1968; Hon. Canon, Diocese of Morogoro, Central Tanganyika, 1965; *b* Stafford, 11 April 1896; *s* of Rev. Thomas Houghton (Editor of the Gospel Magazine and Vicar of Whitington, Stoke Ferry, Norfolk) and Elizabeth Ann Houghton; *m* 1924, Coralie Mary, *d* of H. W. Green, and *g d* of Maj.-Gen. Green, Indian Army; two *s* four *d. Educ:* Clarence Sch. (subseq. Canford Sch.); Durham Univ. (University Coll.); London Coll. of Divinity. BA Durham, 1923; MA Durham, 1929. Commissioned 2/5th PA Som LI, Burma, 1917; Staff Officer to Inspector of Infantry, South, AHQ India, 1918; Staff Capt., QMG's Br, AHQ India, 1919; demobilised, 1919. Deacon, 1921; priest, 1922; Missionary Sch. of Medicine, 1923–24; Supt of BCMS Mission in Burma, 1924–40; Asst Bishop-Designate of Rangoon, 1940–44 (cancelled owing to Japanese occupation of Burma); Travelling Sec., Inter-Varsity Fellowship of Evangelical Unions, 1941–44, and Asst Sec., Graduates' Fellowship, 1944–45. Pres. Missionary Sch. of Medicine, 1948–77; Trustee Keswick Convention Council, 1948, and Chm., 1951–69; Chairman: Conference of British Missionary Socs, 1960; Church of England Evangelical Council, 1960–66; Pres. Mt Hermon Missionary Training Coll., 1960–71; Vice-President: Evangelical Alliance; Lord's Day Observance Soc. *Publications:* Tailum Jan, 1930; Dense Jungle Green, 1937; Preparing to be a Missionary, 1956. *Address:* 14 Alston Court, St Albans Road, Barnet, Herts EN5 4LJ. *T:* 081–449 1741.
Died 20 Feb. 1993.

HOUSDEN, Rt Rev. James Alan George, BA; *b* Birmingham, England, 16 Sept. 1904; *s* of William James and Jane Housden; *m* 1935, Elfreda Moira Hennessey; two *s* one *d. Educ:* Essendon High School; University of Queensland; St Francis College. BA 1st class, Mental and Moral Philosophy, 1928; ThL 1st Class, 1929. Deacon, 1928; priest, 1929; Curate, St Paul's Ipswich, Qld, 1928–30; Chaplain, Mitchell River Mission, 1930–32; Curate, All Souls' Cathedral, Thursday Island, 1932–33; Rector of Darwin, NT, 1933–37; Vicar of Coolangatta,

Qld, 1936–40; Rector and Rural Dean, Warwick, 1940–46; Vicar of Christ Church, S Yarra, Melbourne, 1946–47; Bishop of Rockhampton, 1947–58; Bishop of Newcastle, NSW, 1958–72. *Recreation:* bowls. *Address:* 38 Maltman Street, Caloundra, Qld 4551, Australia. *Club:* Australian (Sydney, NSW). *Died 22 April 1994.*

HOUSE, Donald Victor; Lay Member, Restrictive Practices Court, 1962–70, retired; *b* 31 Jan. 1900; *s* of Dr S. H. House, Liverpool; *m* 1925, Cicely May Cox-Moore (*d* 1980); one *s* two *d. Educ:* Liverpool Coll. Lieut, Royal Garrison Artillery, 1918. Mem. (Fellow) Inst. of Chartered Accountants in England and Wales, 1922– (Mem. Council, 1942–62; Pres. 1954–55). Senior Partner, Harmood Banner & Co., 1946–62. Mem. Board of Governors, Guy's Hosp., 1955–74, and Chm. of Finance Cttee, 1957–74; Director: National Film Finance Corporation, 1954–70; Finance Cttee, Friends of the Poor and Gentlefolks Help, 1946–70; Mem., London Rent Assessment Panel, 1967–75. Dir of several public and other companies (to 1962); Chm., House Cttee enquiring into Northern Ireland shipping facilities. Hon. Sec., Herts Golf Union, 1964–75, Pres., 1976–78; Mem. Council, English Golf Union. Special Constabulary Long Service Medal, 1943. *Recreations:* golf, amateur dramatics. *Address:* Theobald House, 75 Theobald Street, Borehamwood, Herts WD6 4SL. *Clubs:* Commonwealth Trust; Sandy Lodge Golf (Hon. Mem.), Porters Park Golf (Hon. Mem.).
Died 2 Jan. 1992.

HOUSTON, Aubrey Claud D.; *see* Davidson-Houston.

HOUSTON, Prof. William John Ballantyne, PhD, FDSRCS, FDSRCSE; Professor of Orthodontics, London University, since 1974; Head of Orthodontic and Children's Department, United Medical and Dental Schools (Guy's), since 1984; *b* 6 June 1938; *s* of George and Mary Houston; *m* 1962, Turid Herdis Böe; one *s* one *d. Educ:* Edinburgh Univ. (BDS); London Univ. (PhD). FDSRCSE 1964. Lectr, Edinburgh Univ., 1962–64; Lectr, London Univ., at Royal Dental Hosp. Sch. of Dental Surg., 1964–66, Sen. Lectr 1966–74, Dean of Sch., 1978–85. Ed., European Jl of Orthodontics, 1985–. *Publications:* Orthodontic Diagnosis, 1976; Orthodontic Notes, 1976; A Textbook of Orthodontics, 1986; papers in Brit. Jl of Orthodontics and Eur. Jl of Orthodontics. *Recreations:* sailing, skiing, music. *Address:* 4 Oaken Coppice, Ashtead, Surrey KT21 1DL. *Died 17 Aug. 1991.*

HOWARD, Francis Alex, (Frankie Howerd), OBE 1977; *b* 6 March 1922. *Educ:* Shooters Hill Sch., Woolwich, London. *Revues:* Out of this World, 1950; Pardon my French, 1953; Way Out in Piccadilly, 1966; *one-man show:* Quite Frankly Frankie Howerd, 1990; *plays:* Charlie's Aunt, 1955; Hotel Paradiso, 1957; A Midsummer Night's Dream (playing Bottom), 1958; Alice in Wonderland, 1960; A Funny Thing Happened on the Way to the Forum, 1963 (Critics' Award for Best Musical Actor, 1964) and 1986; The Wind in the Sassafras Trees, Broadway, 1968; Simple Simon in Jack and the Beanstalk, Palladium, 1973; numerous pantomimes, 1947–83; *opera:* Frosch in Die Fledermaus, Coliseum, 1982; *films:* The Ladykillers, 1956; Runaway Bus, 1956; Touch of the Sun, 1956; Jumping for Joy, 1956; Further up the Creek, 1958; Carry On, Doctor, 1968; Carry on Up the Jungle, 1970; Up Pompeii, 1971; Up the Chastity Belt, 1972; Up the Front, 1972; The House in Nightmare Park, 1973; Sergeant Pepper's Lonely Hearts Club Band, 1978; *TV series:* Fine Goings On, 1959; Up Pompeii, 1970–71; Up the Convicts (Australia), 1975; The Frankie Howerd Show (Canada), 1976; Frankie Howerd Strikes Again, 1981; The Blunders, 1986; in Gilbert and Sullivan series: HMS Pinafore, 1982; Trial by Jury, 1982; Frankie Howerd on Campus, 1990; All Change, 1990 and 1991; Frankie's On…, 1992; *special:* Further Up Pompeii, 1991. Roving reporter for

TV-am, 1983–. Royal Variety Performances, 1950, 1954, 1961, 1966, 1968, 1969, 1978, 1982 Variety Club of GB Award (Show Business Personality of the Year), 1966, 1971; Radio and TV Industries Award (Show Business Personality of the Year), 1971. *Publications:* On the Way I Lost It (autobiog.), 1976; Trumps, 1982. *Recreations:* swimming, music, reading. *Address:* c/o Tessa Le Bars Management, 18 Queen Anne Street, W1M 9LB. *T:* 071–636 3191. *Died 19 April 1992.*

HOWARD, Leonard Henry, RD 1941; retired; *b* 5 Aug. 1904; *m* 1st, 1938, Betty Scourse; one *s* one *d*; 2nd, 1960, Barbara Davies-Colley. *Educ:* Stubbington House Sch.; Nautical Coll., Pangbourne. Sea career in Royal Navy and P&O-Orient Lines (Merchant Navy), 1922–64; commanded several RN units, War of 1939–45; Comdr, troop ship Empire Fowey, and passenger ships Strathmore, Himalaya and Arcadia, P&O Co.; Commodore, P&O-Orient Lines, 1963–64 (subseq. P&O Steam Navigation Co.), retired. *Recreations:* golf, gardening. *Club:* Cowdray Park Golf. *Died 24 July 1993.*

HOWARD, Rev. Canon Ronald Claude; Headmaster, Hurstpierpoint College, 1945–64; *b* 15 Feb. 1902; 2nd *s* of Henry H. and Florence Howard, The Durrant, Sevenoaks. *Educ:* Sidney Sussex Coll., Cambridge; Westcott House, Cambridge. Ordained deacon, 1926; priest, 1927; Curate of Eastbourne, 1926–28; Chaplain, Bradfield Coll., 1928–30; Asst Master, Tonbridge Sch., 1930–37; Asst Master, Marlborough Coll., 1937, Chaplain there, 1938–43; Chaplain and Asst Master, Radley Coll., 1943–45. Canon of Chichester, 1957; Communar of Chichester Cathedral, 1964–67; Canon Emeritus, 1967. *Recreations:* painting, collecting water-colours. *Address:* 52 Wilbury Road, Hove, East Sussex BN3 3PA. *Died 15 June 1995.*

HOWARD, Sir Walter Stewart, Kt 1963; MBE 1944; DL; *b* 25 Nov. 1888; *y s* of late Henry Blunt Howard; *m* 1917, Alison Mary Wall (*d* 1985), *e d* of late Herbert F. Waring, Farningham Hill, Kent. *Educ:* Wellington; Trinity Coll., Cambridge. Vice-Chm., Warwicks CC, 1955 (Chm., 1956–60); Chm. Whiteley Village Trust, 1952–62; Governor: King Edward VI Sch., Birmingham; Warwick Sch.; Pres., Association of Education Cttees, 1962–63. Trustee of Shakespeare's Birthplace. JP 1931, CC 1939, CA 1948, DL 1952, Warwicks. *Recreation:* foreign travel. *Address:* Guy's Nursing Home, 26 Warwick New Road, Leamington Spa CV32 5JJ. *Club:* United Oxford & Cambridge University. *Died 24 Sept. 1992.*

HOWARD-VYSE, Lt-Gen. Sir Edward (Dacre), KBE 1962 (CBE 1955); CB 1958; MC 1941; DL; *b* 27 Nov. 1905; *s* of late Lieut-Col Cecil Howard-Vyse, JP, Langton Hall, Malton, Yorks; *m* 1940, Mary Bridget, *er d* of late Col Hon. Claude Henry Comaraich Willoughby, CVO; two *s* one *d*. *Educ:* Wellington Coll., Berks; RMA. 2nd Lieut, Royal Artillery, 1925; served War of 1939–45: British Expeditionary Force, France, 1939–40; Lieut-Col, 1941; Mediterranean Expeditionary Force, 1941–44; in command 1st Royal Horse Artillery, Central Mediterranean Force, 1944–45; Brigadier, 1949; CRA 7th Armoured Division, BAOR, 1951–53; Commandant, Sch. of Artillery, 1953; Maj.-Gen., Artillery, Northern Army Group, 1956–59; Dir, Royal Artillery, War Office, 1959–61; GOC-in-C, Western Command, 1961–64; Lieut-Gen., 1961; retired, 1964. Colonel Commandant: RA 1962–70; RHA 1968–70. Vice-Pres., Army Cadet Force Assoc., 1974–, Chm., 1964–74; Vice-Pres., Nat. Artillery Assoc., 1965–. DL E Riding of Yorks and Kingston upon Hull, 1964, Vice-Lieut, 1968–74; DL N Yorkshire, 1974–. Mem., British Olympic Equestrian Team, 1936 (Bronze medal). *Recreations:* country pursuits. *Address:* Langton House, Malton, North Yorks YO17 9QW. *Club:* Army and Navy. *Died 26 Dec. 1992.*

HOWARTH, David Armine, FRSL 1982; author; *b* 18 July 1912; *s* of Dr O. J. R. Howarth and Mrs E. K. Howarth; *m* 1st, 1944, Nanette Russell Smith (marr. diss. 1981); one *s* three *d*; 2nd, 1981, Joanna White; one step *s* one step *d*. *Educ:* Tonbridge Sch.; Trinity Coll., Cambridge. BBC Talks Asst etc, 1934–39. War Correspondent, 1939–40; RNVR, 1940–45. Knight 1st class, Order of St Olav (Norway), 1955; Cross of Freedom (Norway), 1945. *Publications:* The Shetland Bus, 1951; We Die Alone (also under title Escape Alone), 1955; The Sledge Patrol, 1957; Dawn of D-Day, 1959; The Shadow of the Dam, 1961; (ed) My Land and My People, by HH The Dalai Lama, 1962; The Desert King, A Biography of Ibn Saud, 1964; The Golden Isthmus, 1966; A Near Run Thing: the Day of Waterloo, 1968; Trafalgar: The Nelson Touch, 1969; Sovereign of the Seas, 1974; The Greek Adventure, 1976; 1066, The Year of the Conquest, 1977; The Voyage of the Armada: the Spanish story, 1981; Tahiti, 1983; Pursued by a Bear (autobiog.), 1986; (with S. Howarth) The Story of P&O, 1987; (with S. Howarth) Nelson, The Immortal Memory, 1988; *fiction:* Group Flashing Two, 1952; One Night in Styria, 1953; *for children:* Heroes of Nowadays, 1957; Great Escapes, 1969. *Address:* Wildlings Wood, Blackboys, Sussex. *T:* Hadlow Down (082585) 233. *Died 2 July 1991.*

HOWE, George Edward; HM Diplomatic Service, retired; Counsellor, Foreign and Commonwealth Office, 1977–82; *b* 18 June 1925; *s* of late George Cuthbert Howe and Florence May (*née* Baston); *m* 1949, Florence Elizabeth Corrish; one *s*. *Educ:* Highbury Grammar Sch.; Westminster Coll. Served British Army, 1943; Indian Army, 2nd Bn The Burma Rifles, 1945–48 (Major). HMOCS, Malaya, 1949; joined Foreign Service, later Diplomatic Service, 1957; served Pnomn Penh, Hong Kong, Singapore, Paris, Milan and FCO. *Recreations:* fishing, shooting, military history. *Clubs:* Army and Navy, Travellers'. *Died 14 Oct. 1995.*

HOWELL, Rt Rev. Kenneth Walter, MA; *b* 4 Feb. 1909; *s* of Frederick John and Florence Sarah Howell; *m* 1st, 1937, Beryl Mary Hope (*d* 1972), *d* of late Capt. Alfred and Mrs Hope, Bedford; two *s* one *d*; 2nd, 1978, Mrs Siri Colvin. *Educ:* St Olave's; St Peter's Hall, Oxford; Wycliffe Hall, Oxford. Deacon, 1933; priest, 1934; Curate of St Mary Magdalene, Peckham, 1933–37; Chaplain of Paraguayan Chaco Mission, 1937–38; Chaplain Quepe Mission, Chile, 1938–40; Superintendent of South American Missionary Society's Mission to Araucanian Indians in S Chile, 1940–47; Vicar of Wandsworth, 1948–63, Rural Dean, 1957–63; Chaplain, Royal Hosp. and Home for Incurables, Putney, 1957–63; Hon. Canon of Southwark, 1962–63; Bishop in Chile, Bolivia and Peru, 1963–71; Minister of St John's, Downshire Hill, Hampstead, 1972–79; an Asst Bishop, Diocese of London, 1976–79. *Address:* The Hope, Brooklands Avenue, Cambridge CB2 2BQ. *Died 15 Sept. 1995.*

HOWELL, Paul Philip, CMG 1964; OBE 1955; *b* 13 Feb. 1917; *s* of Brig.-Gen. Philip Howell, CMG (killed in action, 1916) and Mrs Rosalind Upcher Howell (*née* Buxton); *m* 1949, Bridgit Mary Radclyffe Luard; two *s* two *d*. *Educ:* Westminster Sch.; Trinity Coll., Cambridge (Sen. Schol.; MA, PhD); Christ Church, Oxford (MA, DPhil). Sudan Polit. Service, 1938; commnd in Sudan Defence Force, ADC to Gov.-Gen., 1940; Overseas Enemy Territory Administration, Eritrea, 1941; District Comr, Central Nuer, 1942; District Comr, Baggara, Western Kordofan, 1946; Chm., Jonglei Investigation, 1948; Chm. (Dep. Gov.), Southern Development Investigation, 1953; Asst Chief Sec., Uganda Protectorate, 1955; Min. of Natural Resources, 1955; Perm. Sec., Min. of Corporations and Regional Communications, 1957; Perm. Sec., Min. of Commerce and Industry, 1959; Chm., E African Nile

Waters Co-ordinating Cttee, 1956–61; seconded to FO and Min. of Overseas Development; Head of Middle East Develt Div., Beirut, 1961–69. University of Cambridge: Dir of Develt Studies Courses, 1969–82; Chm., Faculty of Archaeology and Anthropology, 1977–82; Fellow of Wolfson Coll., 1969–83, Emeritus Fellow, 1983. Member: Bd of Governors, Inst. of Development Studies, 1971–85; Council, Overseas Development Inst., 1972–; Bd of Governors, Bell Educnl Trust, 1987–91. Gold Medallion, La Belgique Reconnaissante, 1962. *Publications:* Nuer Law, 1954; (ed) The Equatorial Nile Project and its Effects in the Anglo-Egyptian Sudan, 1954; (ed) Natural Resources and Development Potential in the Southern Sudan, 1955; (ed) The Jonglei Canal: Impact and Opportunity, 1988; contribs to jls on social anthropology and development. *Recreations:* fishing, country pursuits. *Address:* Burfield Hall, Wymondham, Norfolk NR18 9SJ. *T:* Wymondham (0953) 603389. *Club:* Norfolk (Norwich).   *Died 5 April 1994.*

HOWERD, Frankie; *see* Howard, F. A.

HOWIE, Sir James (William), Kt 1969; MD (Aberdeen); FRCP, FRCPGlas, FRCPEd, FRCPath; Director of the Public Health Laboratory Service, 1963–73; *b* 31 Dec. 1907; *s* of late James Milne Howie and Jessie Mowat Robertson; *m* 1935, Isabella Winifred Mitchell, BSc; two *s* one *d. Educ:* Robert Gordon's Coll., Aberdeen; University of Aberdeen. University lectureships in Aberdeen and Glasgow, 1932–40; Pathologist, RAMC, 1941–45 (served Nigeria and War Office); Head of Dept of Pathology and Bacteriology, Rowett Research Institute, Aberdeen, 1946–51; Prof. of Bacteriology, University of Glasgow, 1951–63. Mem. Agricultural Research Council, 1957–63. Convener, Medical Research Council Working Party on Sterilisers, 1957–64; Pres., Royal College of Pathologists, 1966–69 (Vice-Pres., 1962–66); President: BMA, 1969–70; Assoc. of Clinical Pathologists, 1972–73; Inst. of Sterile Services Management, 1983–88. QHP, 1965–68. Hon. ARCVS 1977; Honorary Member: Pathological Soc. of GB and Ireland, 1977; ACP, 1977. Hon. FRCPath, 1983; Hon. LLD Aberdeen, 1969. Gold Medal, BMA, 1984. *Publications:* Portraits from Memory, 1988; various publications in medical and scientific periodicals, particularly on bacteriology and nutrition. *Recreations:* golf, music. *Address:* 34 Redford Avenue, Edinburgh EH13 0BU. *T:* 0131–441 3910.   *Died 17 March 1995.*

HOWLAND, Hon. William Goldwin Carrington, OC 1991; Chief Justice of Ontario, 1977–90; *b* 7 March 1915; *s* of Goldwin William Howland and Margaret Christian Carrington; *m* 1966, Margaret Patricia Greene (*d* 1992). *Educ:* Upper Canada Coll.; Univ. of Toronto (BA 1936, LLB 1939); Osgoode Hall Law Sch. Barrister-at-law. Practised law, McMillan Binch, 1936–75; Justice of Appeal, Court of Appeal, Supreme Court of Ontario, 1975–77. Law Society of Upper Canada: Bencher, 1960, 1965; Life Bencher, 1969; (Head) Treasurer, 1968–70. President: Fedn of Law Socs of Canada, 1973–74; UN Assoc. in Canada, 1959–60. Chm., Adv. Council, Order of Ontario, 1986–90. Hon. Lectr, Osgoode Hall Law Sch., 1951–67. Hon. LLD: Queen's Univ., Kingston, Ont, 1972; Univ. of Toronto, 1981; York Univ., 1984; Law Soc. of Upper Canada, 1985; Hon. DLittS Wycliffe Coll., 1985. CStJ 1984. Human Relations Award, Canadian CCJ, 1990. Order of Ontario, 1991. *Publications:* special Lectures, Law Soc. of Upper Canada, 1951, 1960. *Recreation:* travel. *Address:* 2 Bayview Wood, Toronto, Ontario M4N 1R7, Canada. *T:* 4834696. *Clubs:* Toronto, Toronto Hunt, National (Toronto).   *Died 13 May 1994.*

HOWSON, Rear-Adm. John, CB 1963; DSC 1944; *b* 30 Aug. 1908; *s* of late George Howson and Mary Howson, Glasgow; *m* 1937, Evangeline Collins; one *s* one *d. Educ:*

Kelvinside Academy, Glasgow; Royal Naval College, Dartmouth, 1922–25. Lieut, 1930; specialised in gunnery, 1934; Gunnery Officer, HMS Furious, 1936–38; served War of 1939–45 (despatches, DSC); HMS Newcastle, 1939–41; HMS Nelson, 1943–44; Comdr 1945; Fleet Gunnery Officer, British Pacific Fleet, 1947–48; Staff of C-in-C, Far East Stn, 1948–49; Exec. Officer, HMS Superb, 1949–50; Capt. 1951; served on Ordnance Bd, 1950–52; Comdg Officer, HMS Tamar, 1952–54; at SHAPE, 1955–57; UK Nat. Mil. Rep., RN, 1955–58; Chief of Staff to C-in-C, Plymouth, 1958–61; Rear-Adm. 1961; Comdr, Allied Naval Forces, Northern Europe, 1961–62; Naval Dep. to C-in-C Allied Forces, Northern Europe, 1963–64. Regional Officer, N Midlands, British Productivity Council, 1964–71. FRSA. *Club:* Victory Services.   *Died 24 Jan. 1992.*

HOYLE, Ven. Frederick James; Archdeacon of Bolton, 1982–85, Archdeacon Emeritus, since 1985; *b* 14 Dec. 1918; *s* of Henry and Annie Hoyle; *m* 1939, Lillian Greenlees; two *d. Educ:* S John's College, Univ. of Durham (BA 1947, DipTh 1949, MA 1957). Served War of 1939–45: Imphal, 1944 (despatches). Deacon, 1949; priest, 1950; Asst Curate, S Paul, Withington, 1949; Curate in charge, S Martin, Wythenshawe, 1952; Vicar 1960; Vice-Chm. and Exec. Officer, Diocesan Pastoral Cttee (full-time), 1965–85; Hon. Canon of Manchester, 1967; Vicar of Rochdale, and Rural Dean, 1971; Rector of Rochdale Team Ministry, 1978–82; Team Vicar, East Farnworth and Kearsley, 1982–85. *Recreations:* rowing, sailing, boat building. *Address:* 37 Toll Bar Crescent, Scotforth, Lancaster LA1 4NR. *T:* Lancaster (0524) 37883.   *Died 11 Feb. 1994.*

HSIUNG, Shih I; author; Founder, 1963, President, 1963–81, Tsing Hua College, Hong Kong; Hon. Secretary of China Society, London, since 1936 (Secretary 1934–36); Member of Universities China Committee, London, since 1935; *b* Nanchang, China, 14 Oct. 1902; *s* of Hsiung, Yuen-Yui and Chou, Ti-Ping; *m* 1923, Tsai, Dymia, (author of Flowering Exile, 1952) (*d* 1987); three *s* three *d. Educ:* Teachers' Coll., National Univ., Peking. Associate Manager of Chen Kwang Theatre, Peking, 1920–23; Managing Director of Pantheon Theatre, Shanghai, 1927–29; Special Editor of Commercial Press, Shanghai; Prof. at Agriculture Coll., Nanchang; Prof. at Min-Kuo Univ., Peking, till 1932. Chinese Delegate to International PEN Congress: at Edinburgh, 1934; at Barcelona, 1935; at Prague, 1938; at London, 1941; at Zürich, 1947; Chinese Delegate to First Congress of International Theatre Institute at Prague, 1948; lectured on Modern Chinese and Classical Chinese Drama, University of Cambridge, 1950–53; Visiting Prof., University of Hawaii, Honolulu. Dean, College of Arts, Nanyang Univ., 1954–55; Man.-Dir, Pacific Films Co. Ltd, Hong Kong, 1955–; Dir, Konin Co. Ltd, Hong Kong, 1956–62; Dir, Success Co. Ltd, Hong Kong, 1956–62; Chm., Bd of Dirs Standard Publishers, Ltd (subseq. Cathay Press), Hong Kong, 1961–63. *Publications:* various Chinese books including translations of Bernard Shaw, James Barrie, Thomas Hardy, Benjamin Franklin, etc; English publications: The Money-God, 1934; Lady Precious Stream, 1934; The Western Chamber, 1935; Mencius Was A Bad Boy, 1936; The Professor From Peking, 1939; The Bridge of Heaven, 1941; The Life of Chiang Kai-Shek, 1943; The Gate of Peace, 1945; Changing China: History of China from 1840 to 1911, 1946; The Story of Lady Precious Stream, 1949; Chinese Proverbs, 1952; Lady on the Roof, 1959; Memoirs, vols I and II, 1978. *Recreation:* theatre-going. *Address:* 4000 Tunlaw Road NW, Washington, DC 20007, USA.   *Died 15 Sept. 1991.*

HUBBACK, David Francis, CB 1970; Chairman, Simon Population Trust, since 1983; Clerk of the Financial Committees of the House of Commons, 1979–81 (Special Advisor to the Expenditure Committee, 1976–79); *b* 2 March 1916; *s* of late Francis William and Eva Hubback; *m* 1939, Elais Judith, *d* of late Sir John Fischer Williams; one *s* two *d. Educ:* Westminster Sch.; King's Coll., Cambridge. Mines Dept, Bd of Trade, 1939. War of 1939–45: Army, 1940–44; Capt., Royal Signals; Western Desert, Sicily, Normandy; Cabinet Office, 1944. UK Delegn to OEEC, 1948; Treasury, 1950; Principal Private Sec. to Chancellor of the Exchequer, 1960–62; Under-Sec., Treasury, 1962–68; Board of Trade, 1969, DTI, 1970–71; Dep. Sec., DTI, later Dept of Trade, 1971–76. Mem., London Library Cttee, 1971–78. *Publications:* Population Trends in Great Britain: their policy implications, 1983; No Ordinary Press Baron: a life of Walter Layton, 1985; Time and the Valley: the past, present and future of the Upper Ogwen Valley, 1987. *Recreations:* mountain walking, reading. *Address:* 4 Provost Road, NW3 4ST. *T:* 071–586 4341. *Club:* Reform. *Died 17 March 1991.*

HUCKLE, Sir (Henry) George, Kt 1977; OBE 1969; Chairman: Agricultural Training Board, 1970–80; Home-Grown Cereals Authority, 1977–83; *b* 9 Jan. 1914; *s* of George Henry and Lucy Huckle; *m* 1st, 1935, L. Steel (*d* 1947); one *s*; 2nd, 1949, Mrs Millicent Mary Hunter; one *d*, and one step *d. Educ:* Latymer Sch.; Oxford Univ. (by courtesy of BRCS via Stalag Luft III, Germany). Accountant trng, 1929–33; sales management, 1933–39; RAF bomber pilot, 1940–41; POW, Germany, 1941–45; Shell Group, 1945–70: Man. Dir, Shellstar Ltd, 1965–70, retd. *Address:* One Coopers Court, Kings Road, Sherborne, Dorset DT9 4HU. *T:* Sherborne (01935) 816386. *Club:* Farmers'. *Died 29 May 1995.*

HUDLESTON, Air Chief Marshal Sir Edmund Cuthbert, GCB 1963 (KCB 1958; CB 1945); CBE 1943; Air Aide-de-camp to the Queen, 1962–67, retired 1967; *b* 30 Dec. 1908; *s* of late Ven. Cuthbert Hudleston; *m* 1st, 1936, Nancye Davis (*d* 1980); one *s* one *d*; 2nd, 1981, Mrs Brenda Withrington, *d* of A. Whalley, Darwen. *Educ:* Guildford Sch., W Australia; Royal Air Force Coll., Cranwell. Entered Royal Air Force 1927; served in UK until 1933; India, NWFP, 1933–37 (despatches); RAF Staff Coll., 1938; lent to Turkish Govt 1939–40; served Middle East and N Africa, Sicily, Italy, 1941–43 (despatches thrice); AOC No 84 Group, 2 TAF, Western Front, 1944; Imperial Defence Coll., 1946; Head of UK's military delegation to the Western Union Military Staff Cttee, 1948–50; AOC No 1 Group, Bomber Command, 1950–51; Deputy Chief of Staff, Supreme Headquarters, Allied Command, Europe, 1951–53; AOC No 3 Group, Bomber Command, 1953–56; RAF Instructor, Imperial Defence Coll., 1956–57; Vice-Chief of the Air Staff, 1957–62; Air Officer Commanding-in-Chief, Transport Command, 1962–63; Comdr Allied Air Forces, Central Europe, 1964–67, and C-in-C Allied Forces Central Europe, 1964–65. Dir, Pilkington Bros (Optical Div.), 1971–79. Comdr Legion of Merit (USA), 1944; Knight Commander Order of Orange-Nassau (Netherlands), 1945; Commander Order of Couronne, Croix de Guerre (Belgium), 1945; Officer, Legion of Honour, 1956, Croix de Guerre (France), 1957. *Address:* 156 Marine Court, St Leonards-on-Sea, East Sussex TN38 0DZ. *Club:* Royal Air Force. *Died 14 Dec. 1994.*

HUDSON, Barry; *see* Hudson, W. M. F.

HUDSON, Maurice William Petre; Hon. Consulting Anæsthetist: National Dental Hospital (University College Hospital); Westminster Hospital; St Mary's Hospital; Emeritus Consultant Anæsthetist, Princess Beatrice Hospital; Part-time Consultant Anæsthetist, Queen Mary's Hospital, Roehampton; *b* 8 Nov. 1901; *s* of late Henry Hudson, ARCA, and Anna Martha Rosa (*née* Petre); *m* 1922, Fredrica Helen de Pont; one *s* one *d* (and two *s* decd). *Educ:* Sherborne Sch.; St Thomas' Hosp. MB, BS London, 1925; MRCS, LRCP 1924; DA England, 1936; FFARCS 1948. Formerly: Resident House Surg., Resident Anæsthetist, and Clin. Asst, Nose and Throat Dept, St Thomas' Hosp. Fellow Assoc. Anæsthetists of Gt Brit.; Mem. Royal Soc. Med. *Publications:* contribs to med. jls. *Recreation:* swimming. *Address:* 10 Devonshire Mews South, W1N 1LA. *T:* 071–935 9665.

Died 28 Sept. 1992.

HUDSON, William Meredith Fisher, (Barry), QC 1967; barrister-at-law; *b* 17 Nov. 1916; *o s* of late Lt-Comdr William Henry Fisher Hudson, RN (killed in action, Jutland, 1916); *m* 1st, 1938, Elizabeth Sophie (marr. diss., 1948), *d* of late Reginald Pritchard, Bloemfontein, SA; one *s* one *d*; 2nd, 1949, Pamela Helen, *d* of late William Cecil Edwards, Indian Police; two *d. Educ:* Imperial Service Coll.; Trinity Hall, Cambridge. BA 1938; Harmsworth Law Scholar, 1939; MA 1940. Called to the Bar, Middle Temple, 1943, Bencher, 1972; South Eastern Circuit, 1945; Mem. of Central Criminal Court Bar Mess. Commissioned Royal Artillery (TA), 1939; served War of 1939–45, Eritrea and Sudan. Chm., Blackfriars Settlement, 1970–. *Recreations:* trains, travel, theatre; formerly athletics (Cambridge Blue, Cross Country half Blue; rep. England and Wales, European Student Games, 1938). *Address:* 5 King's Bench Walk, Temple, EC4Y 7DN. *T:* 0171–797 7600; (home) 47 The Street, Hullavington, Chippenham, Wilts SN14 6DP. *T:* Hullavington (01666) 837736. *Clubs:* Achilles; Hawks (Cambridge).

Died 8 May 1995.

HUGGINS, Kenneth Herbert, CMG 1960; *b* 4 Dec. 1908; *s* of Herbert John Huggins; *m* 1934, Gladys E. Walker; one *s* one *d. Educ:* Hitchin Grammar Sch.; Tollington Sch.; University Coll., London. BSc London, 1930; PhD Glasgow, 1940. Asst and Lecturer in Geography, Glasgow Univ., 1930–41; Ministry of Supply, 1941; Staff of Combined Raw Materials Board, Washington, 1942–46; Board of Trade, 1947; Staff of Administrative Staff Coll., Henley, 1954–55; Commercial Counsellor, British Embassy, Washington, 1957–60; UK Trade Commissioner, subsequently Consul-General, Johannesburg, 1960–62. Dir, British Industrial Develt Office, NY, 1962–68. Founder Mem., IBG, 1933 (Hon. Mem., 1982). *Publications:* atlases and articles in geographical journals. *Recreation:* computing. *Address:* 3 Skeyne Mews, Pulborough, W Sussex RH20 2BB. *T:* Pulborough (0798) 872365. *Died 16 Jan. 1993.*

HUGGINS, Peter Jeremy William; *see* Brett, Jeremy.

HUGHES, Andrew Anderson, MA; Chairman, Building and Estates Committee, Heriot-Watt University, since 1981; *b* Pittenweem, Fife, 27 Dec. 1915; *s* of Alexander and Euphemia Hughes; *m* 1st, 1944, Dorothy Murdoch (marr. diss. 1946); 2nd, 1946, Margaret Dorothy Aikman; no *c. Educ:* Waid Academy; St Andrews Univ.; Marburg Univ.; Emmanuel Coll., Cambridge. Colonial Administrative Service, 1939; Private Sec. to Governor, Gold Coast, 1940–42; Colonial Office, 1946; Dept of Health for Scotland, 1947; Asst Sec., 1956; Under-Sec., 1964; Under-Sec., Scottish Development Dept, 1966–69; Man. Dir, Crudens Ltd, 1969–71; Chm., Grampian Construction Ltd, 1971; Director: Grampian Hldgs, 1973–84; Highland Craftpoint Ltd, 1979–85; Cairngorm Chairlift Co., 1981–83; Gilmour and Dean Holdings, 1980–87. Dep. Chm., Scottish Tourist Bd, 1971–81 (Mem., 1969–81); Member: Scottish Council, CBI, 1976–82; Central Arbitration Cttee, 1977–85; Chm., Scottish Crafts Consultative Cttee, 1979–85; Mem., Crafts Council, 1981–85. Mem. Ct, Heriot-Watt Univ., 1981–.

DUniv Heriot-Watt, 1988. *Recreations:* golf, fishing. *Address:* 9 Palmerston Road, Edinburgh EH9 1TL. *T:* 031–667 2353. *Club:* New (Edinburgh).

Died 8 March 1992.

HUGHES, Desmond; *see* Hughes, F. D.

HUGHES, Rev. Edward Marshall, MTh, PhD (London); Vicar of St Mary's, Dover, 1971–84; Chaplain to the Queen, 1973–83; *b* London, 11 Nov. 1913; *o s* of late Edward William Hughes, Newhouse, Mersham, Ashford, Kent, and Mabel Frances (*née* Faggetter); descendant of Edward Hughes, *b* 1719, of Little Swanton, Mersham; unmarried. *Educ:* City of London Sch.; King's Coll., London; Cuddesdon Coll., Oxford. Deacon, 1936, priest, 1937, Canterbury; Curate, St Martin's, Canterbury, 1936–41; Chaplain RAFVR, 1941 (invalided Oct. 1941); Curate Bearsted, Kent, 1941–46; Vicar of Woodnesborough, Kent, 1946–52; Chap. St Bartholomew's Hosp., Sandwich, 1947–52; Offg Chap. RAF Station, Sandwich, 1948–52; Warden of St Peter's Theological Coll., Jamaica, 1952–61; Canon Missioner of Jamaica, 1955–61; Examining Chap. to the Bp of Jamaica, 1953–61; Hon. Chap. Jamaica, RAFA, 1954–61; Mem. Board of Governors Nuttall Memorial Hospital, Kingston, 1956–61, and St Jago High Sch., Spanish Town, 1957–61; Visiting Lecturer, McGill Univ., Canada, 1957; Hon. Lecturer, Union Theological Seminary, Jamaica, 1957–58; Visiting Lecturer, Séminaire de Théologie, Haiti, 1959; Acting Rector, St Matthew's Church, Kingston, and Chap. Kingston Public Hospital, 1959–60; JP (St Andrew, Jamaica), 1959–63; Commissary to Bishop of Jamaica, 1968–90. Fellow (Librarian, 1962–65), St Augustine's Coll., Canterbury (Central Coll. of the Anglican Communion), 1961–65; Hon. helper, RAF Benevolent Fund, for Kent, 1961–65, for London (Croydon), 1965–71, for Kent, 1971–; Divinity Master, VI Forms, The King's Sch., Canterbury, 1962–63; Officiating Chap., Canterbury Garrison, 1963–64; Vicar of St Augustine's, S Croydon, 1965–71. Proctor in Convocation, Dio. Canterbury, 1966–75. Examining Chaplain to Archbishop of Canterbury, 1967–76; Rural Dean of Dover, 1974–80; Hon. Chaplain: East and South Goodwin Lightships, 1979–85; Assoc. of Men of Kent and Kentish Men (of which his father was founder-member, 1897), 1979–. *Publications:* various papers on theological education overseas. *Recreations:* gardening, exercising the dogs, computering. *Address:* Woodlands, Sandwich Road, Woodnesborough, Sandwich, Kent CT13 0LZ. *T:* Sandwich (0304) 617098.   *Died 21 April 1992.*

HUGHES, Air Vice-Marshal (Frederick) Desmond, CB 1972; CBE 1961; DSO 1945; DFC and 2 bars, 1941–43; AFC 1954; DL; *b* Belfast, 6 June 1919; *s* of late Fred C. Hughes, company dir, Donaghadee, Co. Down, and Hilda (*née* Hunter), Ballymore, Co. Donegal; *m* 1941, Pamela, *d* of late Julius Harrison, composer and conductor; two *s* (and one *s* decd). *Educ:* Campbell Coll., Belfast; Pembroke Coll., Cambridge (MA). Joined RAF from Cambridge Univ. Air Sqdn, 1939; Battle of Britain, No 264 Sqdn, 1940; night fighting ops in Britain and Mediterranean theatre, 1941–43; comd No 604 Sqdn in Britain and France, 1944–45; granted perm. commn, 1946; served in Fighter Comd, 1946–53; Directing Staff, RAF Staff Coll., 1954–56; Personal Staff Officer to Chief of Air Staff, 1956–58; comd RAF Stn Geilenkirchen, 1959–61; Dir of Air Staff Plans, Min. of Def., 1962–64; ADC to the Queen, 1963; Air Officer i/c Administration, HQ Flying Training Command, RAF, 1966–68; AOC, No 18 Group, RAF Coastal Command, and Air Officer, Scotland and N Ireland, 1968–70; Comdt, RAF Coll., Cranwell, 1970–72; SASO Near East Air Force, 1972–74, retired. Hon. Air Cdre, No 2503 RAuxAF Regt Sqdn, 1982–. Dir, Trident Trust, 1976–78. DL Lincoln, 1983. *Recreations:* fishing,

shooting, music. *Address:* c/o Midland Bank, Sleaford, Lincs. *Club:* Royal Air Force.

Died 11 Jan. 1992.

HUGHES, Herbert Delauney, MA; Principal of Ruskin College, Oxford, 1950–79; *b* 7 Sept. 1914; *s* of late Arthur Percy Hughes, BSc, and late Maggie Ellen Hughes; *m* 1937, Beryl Parker (*d* 1995). *Educ:* Cheadle Hulme Sch.; Balliol Coll., Oxford (State and County Major Scholar). BA (Hons) in Modern History, 1936. Served War of 1939–45, with 6 Field Regt Royal Artillery. Asst Sec., New Fabian Research Bureau, 1937–39; Organising Sec., Fabian Soc., 1939–46; Mem. Exec. Fabian Soc., 1946– (Vice-Chm. 1950–52, 1958–59, Chm. 1959–60, Vice-Pres., 1971–88, Pres., 1988–93); MP (Lab) Wolverhampton (West), 1945–50; Parliamentary Private Sec. to Minister of Education, 1945–47; to Financial Sec. to War Office, 1948–50; Mem. Lambeth Borough Council, 1937–42. Governor of Educational Foundation for Visual Aids, 1948–56. Member: Civil Service Arbitration Tribunal, 1955–81; Commonwealth Scholarship Commn, 1968–74; Cttee on Adult Educn, 1969–73. Workers' Educational Association: Vice-Pres., 1958–67; Dep. Pres., 1968–71; Pres., 1971–81; Hon. Treasurer, 1981–91; Hon. Mem., 1992–. Chm. Management Cttee, Adult Literacy Resource Agency, 1975–78; Mem., Adv. Council on Adult and Continuing Educn, 1978–83; Vice-Pres., Nat. Inst. of Adult and Continuing Educn, 1986–90. Chm., Webb Meml Trust, 1987–92. Hon. Fellow Sheffield Polytechnic, 1979. *Publications:* (part author) Democratic Sweden, 1937, Anderson's Prisoners, 1940, Six Studies in Czechoslovakia, 1947. Advance in Education, 1947; Towards a Classless Society, 1947; A Socialist Education Policy, 1955; The Settlement of Disputes in The Public Service, 1968; (jt author) Planning for Education in 1980, 1970; (part author) Education Beyond School, 1980. *Recreations:* drinking, reading, foreign travel. *Address:* Crossways, Mill Street, Islip, Oxford OX5 2SZ. *T:* Kidlington (01865) 376935.   *Died 15 Nov. 1995.*

HUGHES, Rt Rev. John George; Area Bishop of Kensington, since 1987; *b* 30 Jan. 1935; *s* of late Joseph Ernest Hughes and of Florence Amy (*née* Fisher); *m* 1963, Maureen Harrison; two *s. Educ:* Queens' Coll., Cambridge (BA 1956, MA 1961); Cuddesdon Theological Coll., Leeds Univ. (PhD 1980). Deacon 1960, priest 1961; Curate, St Martin's, Brighouse, 1960–63; Priest-in-charge, St James's, Brighouse, 1961–65; Vicar of St John's, Clifton, 1963–70; dio. of Wakefield Schs Exec. Sec., 1967–70, actg Dir of Educn, 1970; Selection Secretary, ACCM, 1970–73, Senior Selection Sec., 1973–76; Warden, St Michael's Coll., Llandaff, 1976–87; Lectr in Church Hist., Univ. of Wales, 1976–87; Dean of Faculty of Theology, University Coll., Cardiff, 1984–87; Hon. Canon, Llandaff Cathedral, 1980–87. Member, Governing Body 1977–87, and Doctrinal Commn 1980–87, Church in Wales. *Recreations:* music, cricket, walking, gardening, international cuisine. *Address:* 19 Campden Hill Square, W8 7JY.   *Died 19 Aug. 1994.*

HUGHES, (William) Mark, MA, PhD; *b* 18 Dec. 1932; *s* of late Edward Hughes, sometime Prof. of History at Durham, and Sarah (*née* Hughes), Shincliffe, Durham; *m* 1958, Jennifer Mary, *d* of Dr G. H. Boobyer; one *s* two *d. Educ:* Durham Sch.; Balliol Coll., Oxford (BA Oxon 1956; MA); PhD Newcastle 1963. Sir James Knott Research Fellow, Newcastle-upon-Tyne, 1958–60; Staff Tutor, Manchester Univ. Extra-Mural Dept, 1960–64; Lectr, Durham Univ., 1964–70. MP (Lab): Durham, 1970–83; City of Durham, 1983–87. PPS to Chief Sec. of Treasury, 1974–75; opposition spokesman on agriculture, 1980–86; Member: Select Cttee on Expenditure (Trade and Industry Sub-Cttee), 1970–74; Select Cttee on Parly Comr, 1970–75; Delegn to Consultative Assembly of

Council of Europe and WEU, 1974–75; European Parlt, 1975–79 (Vice-Chm., Agric. Cttee and Chm., Fisheries Sub-Cttee, 1977–79). Member: Exec. Cttee, British Council, 1974–85 (Vice-Chm., 1978–85); Gen. Adv. Council, BBC, 1976–84; Adv. Council on Public Records, 1984–87. An Hon. Associate, BVA, 1976–87. Fellow, Industry and Parliament Trust. *Recreations:* gardening, fishing, birdwatching. *Died 19 March 1993.*

HUIJSMAN, Nicolaas Basil Jacques, CMG 1973; *b* 6 March 1915; *s* of Nikolaas Kornelis Huijsman, Amsterdam and Hendrika Huijsman (*née* Vorkink). *Educ:* Selborne Coll., E London, S Africa; Univ. of Witwatersrand (BCom); Gonville and Caius Coll., Cambridge (Econ. Tripos). Commnd Royal Scots Fusiliers, 1940; HQ 17 Inf. Bde, 1940; GSO3, WO, 1941–42; psc 1942; GSO2, HQ of Chief of Staff to Supreme Comdr (Des) and SHAEF, 1943–45 (despatches 1944); Controller of Press and Publications, Control Commn for Germany, 1945–48; Colonial Office, 1948–62; Principal Private Sec. to Sec. of State for Commonwealth Relations and Colonies, 1962–64; Asst Sec., Min. of Overseas Develt, 1964–70, and 1974–75, Overseas Develt Admin/FCO, 1970–74. Bronze Star, US, 1945. *Recreations:* Byzantine history, music, opera, painting. *Address:* 13 Regent Square, Penzance TR18 4BG. *Club:* Reform.
Died 9 March 1995.

HULME, Dr Henry Rainsford; Chief of Nuclear Research, Atomic Weapons Research Establishment, 1959–73, retired; *b* 9 Aug. 1908; *s* of James Rainsford Hulme and Alice Jane Smith; *m* 1937, Hilda Marion Reavley; one *s* one *d*; *m* 1955, Margery Alice Ducker (decd), *d* of late Sir James A. Cooper, KBE, and of Lady Cooper. *Educ:* Manchester Grammar Sch.; Gonville and Caius Coll., Cambridge; University of Leipzig. BA (Math. Tripos) 1929; Smiths' Prizeman, 1931; PhD (Cambridge) 1932; ScD (Cambridge) 1948. Fellow of Gonville and Caius Coll., Cambridge, 1933–38; Chief Asst Royal Observatory, Greenwich, 1938–45; on loan to Admiralty during War; Scientific Adviser, Air Ministry, 1946–48; Rector, Canterbury Univ. Coll., Christchurch, NZ, 1948–54; Scientist, AWRE, 1954–59. *Publications:* on mathematical physics and astronomy in learned jls. *Recreations:* various. *Address:* Cathay, West End, Sherborne St John, near Basingstoke, Hants RG24 9LE. *T:* Basingstoke (0256) 850422.
Died 8 Jan. 1991.

HULME, Maj.-Gen. Jerrie Anthony, CB 1990; Director General of Ordnance Services, 1988–90; *b* 10 Aug. 1935; *s* of Stanley and Laurel Hulme; *m* 1st, 1959, Margaret Mary, (Maureen) (*née* Turton) (marr. diss. 1974); two *s* two *d*; 2nd, 1974, Janet Kathleen (*née* Mills). *Educ:* King Henry VIII Sch., Coventry. FInstPS. jssc, psc. National Service, RAOC, 1953–56; regtl appts, Kenya, Persian Gulf, Aden, 1956–66; Staff Coll., Camberley, 1966; Staff appts, 1967–70; jssc Latimer, 1970; Directing Staff, Staff Coll., 1971–74; Comdr RAOC HQ 4 Div., 1974–76; Staff appt, 1976–78; Col, Staff Coll., 1978–81; Staff appt, 1981–82; Dep. Dir Gen. of Ordnance Services, 1982–85; Dir of Logistic Ops (Army), MoD, 1985–88. Freeman, City of London, 1987. *Recreations:* music, carpentry, country pursuits. *Address:* c/o Lloyds Bank, 21–23 The Square, Kenilworth, Warwickshire CV8 1EE. *Club:* Army and Navy. *Died 20 Sept. 1995.*

HULTON, Sir Geoffrey (Alan), 4th Bt, *cr* 1905, of Hulton Park, Co. of Lancaster; JP; DL; *b* 21 Jan. 1920; *s* of Sir Roger Braddyll Hulton, 3rd Bt and Hon. Marjorie Evelyn Louise (*d* 1970), *o c* of 6th Viscount Mountmorres; *S* father 1956; *m* 1945, Mary Patricia Reynolds. *Educ:* Marlborough. Entered Royal Marines, Sept. 1938; Lieut, 1940; sunk in HMS Repulse, Dec. 1941; prisoner-of-war, Far East, Feb. 1942–Aug. 1945; Captain, 1948; retired

(ill-health), 1949. Owner of Hulton Park estate. Life Pres., Bolton West Conservative Association; Life Patron, Bolton and District Agricultural Discussion Soc.; Life Vice-Pres., Royal Lancs Agricultural Soc. (Pres., 1974–80). Chief Scout's Comr, 1964–85; President: Greater Manchester North Scout County; Bolton Scout Trust; Vice-President: Greater Manchester West Scout County; CLA (Lancashire); Lancashire County Cricket Club; Bolton Cricket League; St Ann's Hospice Ltd; Hon. Life Vice-Pres., Westhoughton Cricket Club. JP Lancs 1955; DL Lancs, later Greater Manchester, 1974. KCSG 1966. *Recreations:* country pursuits. *Heir:* none. *Address:* The Cottage, Hulton Park, Over Hulton, Bolton BL5 1BE. *T:* Bolton (0204) 651324. *Clubs:* Victory, MCC.
Died 20 Nov. 1993 (ext).

HULTON, John, MA; *b* 28 Dec. 1915; *e s* of late Rev. Samuel Hulton, Knaresborough; *m* 1940, Helen Christian McFarlan; two *d. Educ:* Kingswood Sch., Bath; Hertford Coll., Oxford. DipLA; graduate of Landscape Inst. Leeds City Art Gallery and Temple Newsam House (Hon. Asst), 1937–38. Served War, RA, 1939–46. Keeper at Brighton Art Gall., Museum and Royal Pavilion, 1946–48; British Council Fine Arts Dept, 1948, Dir, 1970–75; resigned to study landscape design; subseq. in private practice. Organised many art exhibns abroad. *Recreations:* looking at painting and sculpture; landscape, gardens. *Address:* 70 Gloucester Crescent, NW1 7EG. *T:* 071–485 6906. *Club:* Athenæum. *Died 4 Aug. 1992.*

HUME, Thomas Andrew, CBE 1977; FSA, FMA; Director, Museum of London, 1972–77; *b* 21 June 1917; *o s* of late Thomas Hume, Burnfoot, Oxton, and Lillias Dodds; *m* 1942, Joyce Margaret Macdonald; two *s* one *d. Educ:* Heaton Grammar Sch.; King's Coll., Univ. of Durham (BA Hons Hist.). Gladstone Prizeman, Joseph Cowen Prizeman. Curator: Kirkstall Abbey House Museum, Leeds, 1949–52; Buckinghamshire County Museum, Aylesbury, 1952–60; Dir, City of Liverpool Museums, 1960–72. Member: Museums and Galleries Commn (formerly Standing Commn on Museums and Galleries), 1977–86; Adv. Cttee, London Transport Museum, 1983–90. Past Pres., NW Fedn of Museums; Past Vice-Pres., Internat. Assoc. of Transport Museums; Past Chm., ICOM British Nat. Cttee; Museum Consultant, Unesco; Dir Mus. Exchange Programme, ICOM, Unesco, 1978–79. Hon. Mem., ICOM, 1983. *Publications:* contribs Thoresby Soc., Records of Bucks; excavation reports and historical articles. *Recreations:* travel, gardening.
Died 16 June 1992.

HUMPHREY, (Frank) Basil, CB 1975; Parliamentary Counsel, 1967–80; *b* 21 Sept. 1918; *s* of late John Hartley Humphrey and Alice Maud Humphrey (*née* Broadbent); *m* 1947, Ol'ga Černá, *y d* of late Frántišek Černý, Trenčín, Czechoslovakia; two *s. Educ:* Brentwood Sch.; St Catharine's Coll., Cambridge (Schol.). 2nd cl. hons Pt I Mod. Langs Tripos, 1st cl. hons Pt II Law Tripos. Served RA, 1939–45: Adjt 23rd Mountain Regt and DAAG 4 Corps, India and Burma. Called to Bar, Middle Temple, 1946 (Harmsworth Schol.). Seconded as First Parly Counsel, Fedn of Nigeria, 1961–64; draftsman of the Constitution of the Federal Republic of Nigeria, 1963; seconded as Counsel-in-charge at Law Commn, 1971–72. *Recreations:* gardening, mountain walking, music. *Address:* 1a The Avenue, Chichester, W Sussex PO19 4PZ. *T:* Chichester (0243) 778783; Traverse des Rouvières, 83600 Bagnols-en-Forêt, France. *T:* 94406583. *Died 20 March 1994.*

HUMPHREY, William Gerald, MA Oxon and Cantab, DPhil Oxon; Assistant Secretary, University of Cambridge Appointments Board, 1962–72; Group Personnel Officer, Fisons Ltd, 1958–62; *b* 2 Aug. 1904; *e s* of late Rev. William Humphrey and Helen Lusher; *m* 1936, Margaret (*d* 1989), *er d* of late William E. Swift, Cornwall, Conn, USA; one *s. Educ:* King Edward VII Sch., Sheffield; Queen's Coll., Oxford (Hastings Scholar, Taberdar, University Sen. Research Student). 1st Class Final Honour Sch. of Natural Science, 1926; DPhil, 1928. Commonwealth Fund Fellow, Harvard Univ., 1929–31; Senior Science Master, Uppingham Sch., 1932–34; Headmaster of The Leys School, Cambridge, 1934–58. Mem. Ministry of Agriculture Cttee on demand for Agricultural Graduates. *Publications:* The Christian and Education, 1940; papers in Journal of the Chemical Soc. *Recreation:* painting. *Address:* Hope Nursing Care Home, Brooklands Avenue, Cambridge CB2 2BQ.

Died 4 July 1995.

HUMPHREYS, (David) Colin, CMG 1977; Deputy Under Secretary of State (Air), Ministry of Defence, 1979–85; *b* 23 April 1925; *s* of late Charles Roland Lloyd Humphreys and Bethia Joan (*née* Bowie); *m* 1952, Jill Allison (*née* Cranmer); two *s* one *d. Educ:* Eton Coll. (King's Scholar); King's Coll., Cambridge (MA). Served Army, 1943–46. Air Min., 1949; Private Sec. to Sec. of State for Air, 1959–60; Counsellor, UK Delegn to NATO, 1960–63; Air Force Dept, 1963–69; IDC, 1970; Dir, Defence Policy Staff, 1971–72; Asst Sec. Gen. (Defence Planning and Policy), NATO, 1972–76; Asst Under Sec. of State (Naval Staff), MoD, 1977–79. Dir of Develt, RIIA, 1985–86. *Address:* Rivendell, North Drive, Virginia Water, Surrey GU25 4NQ. *T:* Wentworth (0344) 842130. *Clubs:* Royal Air Force; Wentworth. *Died 15 Sept. 1992.*

HUMPHREYS, Maj.-Gen. George Charles, CB 1952; CBE 1948 (OBE 1945); *b* 5 Oct. 1899; *s* of late George Humphreys, formerly of Croft House, Croft-on-Tees, Co. Durham, and Caroline Huddart; *m* 1931, Doris Isabelle, *d* of late A. B. Baines, Shanghai; no *c. Educ:* Giggleswick Sch., Yorks; RMC Sandhurst. 2nd Lieut Royal Northumberland Fusiliers, 1918; Lieut 1920; Capt. 1930; Bt-Major, Major 1938; Lieut-Col 1946; Col 1947; Brig. 1951; Maj.-Gen, 1952. Served with 2nd Bn Royal Northumberland Fusiliers, Iraq, India and China, 1919–31, Adjt 1925–28 (Iraq medal and clasp, 1920); Bde Major, E Lancs and Border TA Bde, 1935–37; GSO2 Public Relations, War Office, 1938–39; War of 1939–45, in UK and Italy: GSO1 War Office (Asst Dir, Public Relations), 1939–40; successively (Jan. 1941–May 1946), AA&QMG 55th Inf. Div., 1st and 3rd Armd Gps, 79th Armd Div., Col (Q) ops War Office, Col AQ (BUCO) 21 Army Gp, Col AQ, 1944–46; Allied Commn for Austria, took Advance Party into Vienna, 19 July 1945; Dep. Chief Mil. Div. (Brig.), 1946; Brig. i/c Admin Burma Comd, 1946–48; BGS, HQ Scottish Comd, 1948–51; Maj.-Gen. Adminstration, GHQ Middle East Land Forces, 1951–54; Chairman: PAO and PPO Cttees, Middle East, 1951–54; Military Adviser to Contractors for Canal Base (War Office, July 1954–31 May 1955); retired from Army, June 1955, and appointed General Manager, Suez Contractors Management Co. Ltd; appointed Chief Executive to Governing Body of Suez Contractors (Services) Ltd, Jan. 1956 until Liquidation of Suez enterprise, July 1957; Chief Organizer, Dollar Exports Council Conference, 1958. *Recreations:* reading, travel, shooting. *Address:* Lauriston Cottage, Old Green Lane, Camberley, Surrey. *T:* Camberley (0726) 21078. *Died 8 April 1991.*

HUMPHREYS, John Henry; Chairman, Industrial Tribunals (Ashford, Kent), since 1976; Legal Officer, Law Commission, since 1973; *b* 28 Feb. 1917; British; *m* 1939, Helen Mary Markbreiter; one *s* one *d. Educ:* Cranleigh School. Solicitor. Served with Co. of London Yeomanry, and Northampton Yeomanry, 1939–47; Treasury Solicitor Dept, 1947–73. *Recreations:* sailing, golf, gardening. *Address:* Gate House Cottage, Sandown Road, Sandwich,

Kent CT13 9NT. *T:* Sandwich (0304) 612961. *Club:* Prince's (Sandwich). *Died 17 Sept. 1992.*

HUMPHREYS, Kenneth William, BLitt, MA, PhD; FLA; Librarian, European University Institute, Florence, 1975–81; *b* 4 Dec. 1916; *s* of Joseph Maxmillian Humphreys and Bessie Benfield; *m* 1939, Margaret, *d* of Reginald F. Hill and Dorothy Lucas; two *s. Educ:* Southfield Sch., Oxford; St Catherine's Coll., Oxford. Library Asst, All Souls Coll., Oxford, 1933–36; Asst, Bodleian Library, 1936–50; Dep. Librarian, Brotherton Library, University of Leeds, 1950–52; Librarian, Univ. of Birmingham, 1952–75. Prof. of Library Studies, Haifa Univ., 1982. Hon. Lecturer in Palaeography: University of Leeds, 1950–52; University of Birmingham, 1952–75. Panizzi Lectr, Panizzi Trust, 1987. Hon. Sec., Standing Conf. of Nat. and University Libraries, 1954–69, Vice-Chm., 1969–71; Chm. 1971–73; Mem. Library Adv. Council for England, 1966–71; Mem. Council, Library Assoc., 1964–75, Chm. Council 1973; Chm. Exec. Cttee, West Midlands Regional Library Bureau, 1963–75; Chairman: Jt Standing Conf. and Cttee on Library Cooperation, 1965–75; Nat. Cttee on Regional Library Cooperation, 1970–75; Mem. Comité International de Paléographie, and Colloque International de Paléographie, 1955–; President: Nat. and University Libraries Section, Internat. Fedn of Library Assocs, 1968–69, Pres., University Libraries Sub-Section, 1967–73; Ligue des Bibliothèques Européennes de Recherche, 1974–80; Round Table on Library History, 1978–82. Mem. Cttee, British Acad. Corpus of British Medieval Library Catalogues, 1983– (Sec., 1983–90). Editor, Studies in the History of Libraries and Librarianship; Jt Editor, Series of Reproductions of Medieval and Renaissance Texts. Hon. LittD Dublin (Trinity Coll.), 1967. Hon. FLA 1980; Socio d'onore, Italian Library Assoc., 1982. *Publications:* The Book Provisions of the Medieval Friars, 1964; The Medieval Library of the Carmelites at Florence, 1964; The Library of the Franciscans of the Convent of St Antony, Padua at the Beginning of the fifteenth century, 1966; The Library of the Franciscans of Siena in the Fifteenth Century, 1977; A National Library in Theory and in Practice, 1988; The Friars (Corpus of British Medieval Library Catalogues), 1990; articles in library periodicals. *Recreation:* collection of manuscripts. *Address:* 94 Metchley Lane, Harborne, Birmingham B17 0HS. *T:* 0121–427 2785. *Clubs:* Athenæum; Kildare Street and University (Dublin). *Died 4 Nov. 1994.*

HUNT, Rt Rev. Desmond Charles; a Suffragan Bishop of Toronto, 1981–86; *b* 14 Sept. 1918; *s* of George P. and Kathleen Hunt; *m* 1944, Naomi F. Naylor; two *s* two *d. Educ:* Univ. of Toronto (BA). Deacon, 1942; priest, 1943; Rector: Trinity Church, Quebec City, 1943; St John's, Johnstown, USA, 1949; St James, Kingston, Ont, 1953; Church of the Messiah, Toronto, 1969. Hon. DD Wycliffe Coll., Toronto, 1980. *Publications:* Benefits of His Passion, 1988; More than we can ask or imagine, 1992. *Address:* Bishopslodge, Box 1150, Lakefield, Ontario K0L 2H0, Canada. *T:* (705) 6527372.

Died 25 July 1993.

HUNT, Gilbert Adams, CBE 1967; Director, Equity & General (formerly Emray) PLC, 1982–90; *b* Wolverhampton, 29 Dec. 1914; *s* of late Harold William Hunt, MBE, St Helen's, IoW; *m* 1938, Sarah (marr. diss. 1946), *d* of Capt. Wadman-Taylor; *m* 1946, Olive Doreen, *d* of Maurice Martin O'Brien; *m* 1975, Diane Rosemary, *d* of Eric O. Cook; one *d. Educ:* Old Hall, Wellington; Malvern Coll., Worcester. Director, High Duty Alloys, Slough, 1950–54; Dir and Gen. Man., High Duty Alloys (Dir, HDA, Canada, Northern Steel Scaffold & Engrg Co., all subsids Hawker Siddeley Gp), 1954–60; Man. Dir, Massey-Ferguson (UK) Ltd; Jt Man. Dir, Massey-

Ferguson-Perkins; Dir, Massey-Ferguson Holdings Ltd; Chm. and Man. Dir, Massey-Ferguson (Eire) Ltd; Chm., Massey-Ferguson (Farm Services Ltd), 1960–67; Managing Dir, 1967–73, Chief Exec. Officer, 1967–76, Chm., 1973–79, Rootes Motors Ltd, later Chrysler UK Ltd (Pres., April-June 1979). Chairman: Thurgar Bardex, 1977–85 (Dep. Chm., 1985–89; non-exec. Dir, 1985–90); Hedin Ltd, 1978–85; Dir, Technology Transfer Associates, 1980–88. Chm., Cttee for Industrial Technologies, DTI, 1972–78. President: Agricultural Engrs Association Ltd, 1965; The Society of Motor Manufacturers and Traders Ltd, 1972–74. Freeman, City of London, 1968. CEng, CIMechE, FIProdE, MIBF. Hon. DSc Cranfield, 1973. *Recreations:* golfing, sailing. *Address:* The Dutch House, Sheepstreet Lane, Etchingham, E Sussex TN19 7AZ.
Died 17 Aug. 1995.

HUNT, Hugh (Sydney), CBE 1977; MA; Professor of Drama, University of Manchester, 1961–73, then Emeritus; *b* 25 Sept. 1911; *s* of Captain C. E. Hunt, MC, and late Ethel Helen (née Crookshank); *m* 1940, Janet Mary (née Gordon); one *s* one *d. Educ:* Marlborough Coll.; Magdalen Coll., Oxford. BA Oxon 1934, MA Oxon 1961; Hon. MA Manchester 1965. Pres. of OUDS, 1933–34; Producer: Maddermarket Theatre, Norwich, 1934; Croydon Repertory and Westminster Theatres, 1934–35; Producer, Abbey Theatre, Dublin, 1935–38; produced The White Steed, Cort Theatre, NY. Entered HM Forces, 1939; served War of 1939–45, with Scots Guards, King's Royal Rifle Corps, and Intelligence Service; demobilised, 1945. Director of Bristol Old Vic Company, 1945–49; Director Old Vic Company, London, 1949–53; Adjudicator Canadian Drama Festival Finals, 1954; Executive Officer, Elizabethan Theatre Trust, Australia, 1955–60; Artistic Dir, Abbey Theatre, Dublin, 1969–71. Mem., Welsh Arts Council, 1979–85 (Chm., Drama Cttee, 1982–85). *Produced:* The Cherry Orchard, 1948, Love's Labour's Lost, 1949, Hamlet, 1950, New Theatre; Old Vic Seasons, 1951–53: Twelfth Night, Merry Wives of Windsor, Romeo and Juliet, Merchant of Venice, Julius Caesar; The Living Room, New York, 1954; in Australia, Medea, 1955, Twelfth Night, 1956, Hamlet, 1957, Julius Caesar, 1959; The Shaughraun, World Theatre Season, Dublin, 1968; Abbey Theatre productions include: The Well of the Saints, 1969; The Hostage, 1970; The Morning after Optimism, 1971; Arrah-na-Pogue, 1972; The Silver Tassie, 1972; The Three Sisters, 1973; The Vicar of Wakefield, 1974; Red Roses for Me, 1980; Sydney Opera House: Peer Gynt, 1975; The Plough and the Stars, 1977. *Publications:* Old Vic Prefaces, 1954; The Director in the Theatre, 1954; The Making of Australian Theatre, 1960; The Live Theatre, 1962; The Revels History of Drama in the English Language, vol. VII, sections 1 and 2, 1978; The Abbey, Ireland's National Theatre, 1979; Sean O'Casey, 1980; author or co-author of several Irish plays including The Invincibles and In The Train. *Address:* Cae Terfyn, Criccieth, Gwynedd LL52 0SA.
Died 22 April 1993.

HUNT, James Simon Wallis; BBC television broadcaster, since 1980; *b* 29 Aug. 1947; *s* of Wallis Glyn Gunthorpe Hunt and Susan Noel Wentworth Hunt (née Davis); *m* 1st, 1974, Susan Miller (marr. diss.); 2nd, 1983, Sarah Marian Lomax (marr. diss.); two *s. Educ:* Wellington College. Racing driver with Hesketh and McLaren teams, 1973–79; world motor racing champion, 1976. *Address:* Argon House, Argon Mews, Fulham Broadway SW6 1BJ. *T:* 071–381 6366.
Died 15 June 1993.

HUNT, Rt Rev. (William) Warren, MA; Hon. Assistant Bishop to the Dioceses of Chichester and Portsmouth, since 1978; *b* 22 Jan. 1909; *s* of Harry Hunt, Carlisle; *m* 1939, Mollie, *d* of Edwin Green, Heswall, Cheshire; four *d. Educ:* Carlisle Grammar School; Keble College, Oxford;

Cuddesdon Theological College, Oxford. Deacon 1932; priest 1933; Curate: Kendal Parish Church, 1932–35; St Martin-in-the-Fields, London, 1935–40; Chaplain to the Forces, 1940–44; Vicar, St Nicholas, Radford, Coventry, 1944–48; Vicar, Holy Trinity, Leamington Spa, 1948–57, and Rural Dean of Leamington; Vicar and Rural Dean of Croydon, 1957–65; Bishop Suffragan of Repton, 1965–Jan. 1977. Hon. Canon Canterbury Cathedral, 1957. *Recreations:* golf, vicarage lawn croquet (own rules); travel, reading. *Address:* 15 Lynch Down, Funtington, Chichester, West Sussex PO18 9LR. *T:* Bosham (01243) 575536.
Died 29 Sept. 1994.

HUNTER OF NEWINGTON, Baron *cr* 1978 (Life Peer), of Newington in the District of the City of Edinburgh; **Robert Brockie Hunter,** Kt 1977; MBE (mil.) 1945; DL; FRCP; Vice-Chancellor and Principal, University of Birmingham, 1968–81; *b* 14 July 1915; *s* of Robert Marshall Hunter and Margaret Thorburn Brockie; *m* 1940, Kathleen Margaret Douglas; three *s* one *d. Educ:* George Watson's Coll. MB, ChB Edinburgh, 1938; FRCPE 1950; FRCP 1962; FACP 1963; FRSE 1964; FInstBiol 1968; FFPHM (FFCM 1975). Personal Physician, Field-Marshal Montgomery, NW Europe, 1944–45. Asst Dir, Edinburgh Post-Graduate Bd for Medicine, 1947; Lectr in Therapeutics, University of Edinburgh, 1947; Commonwealth (Harkness) Fellow in Medicine, 1948; Lectr in Clinical Medicine, University of St Andrews, 1948, Dean of the Faculty of Medicine, 1958–62; Prof. of Materia Medica, Pharmacology and Therapeutics, University of St Andrews, 1948–67, and in University of Dundee, 1967–68; late Consultant Physician to Dundee General Hosps and Dir, Post-graduate Medical Education. Hon. Lectr in Physiology, Boston Univ. Sch. of Medicine, USA, 1950. Member: Clinical Res. Bd, MRC, 1960–65; GMC, 1962–68; Ministry of Health Cttee on Safety of Drugs, 1963–68 (Chm., Clinical Trials Sub-Cttee); UGC, 1964–68 (Chm., Medical Sub-Cttee, 1966–68); West Midlands RHA, 1974–78; Nuffield Cttee of Inquiry into Dental Educn, 1977–80; DHSS Working Party on Medical Administrators in Health Service, 1970–72 (Chm.); DHSS Independent Scientific Cttee on Smoking and Health, 1973–80; Med. Adv. Cttee of Cttee of Vice-Chancellors and Principals, 1976–81; Management Cttee, King Edward's Hospital Fund, 1980–84; House of Lords Select Cttee on Science and Technology, 1983–87, on European Communities, 1988–92. Chm., Review Cttee of Medical and Public Health Res. Progs, EEC, 1984–85. Senior Commonwealth Travelling Fellowship, 1960; Vis. Professor of Medicine: Post-Graduate School, University of Adelaide, 1965; McGill Univ., 1968. Malthe Foundn Lectr, Oslo, 1958; Christie Gordon Lectr, Birmingham, 1978; Raymond Priestley Lectr, Birmingham Univ., Goodman Lectr, Royal Soc., 1981; Wade Lectr, Keele Univ., 1982. Editor, Quarterly Journal of Medicine, 1957–67. Fellow (ex-President) Royal Medical Society. Major, Royal Army Medical Corps. Gained Purdue Frederick Medical Achievement Award, 1958. Hon. FCP. DL West Midlands, 1975. Hon. LLD: Dundee, 1969; Birmingham, 1974; Liverpool, 1984; Hon. DSc Aston, 1981. *Publications:* Clinical Science; contribs to BMJ, Lancet, Edinburgh Med. Jl, Quarterly Jl of Medicine. *Recreation:* fishing. *Address:* 3 Oakdene Drive, Barnt Green, Birmingham B45 8LQ. *Club:* Oriental.
Died 24 March 1994.

HUNTER, Adam; miner; *b* 11 Nov. 1908; *m*; one *s* one *d. Educ:* Kelty Public Elem. Sch. Joined Labour Party, 1933; Member: Exec. Cttee, NUM (Scot. Area); Lochgelly Dist Council, 1948–52; Sec., Fife Co-op. Assoc. and Dist Council, 1947–64. MP (Lab) Dunfermline Burghs, 1964–74, Dunfermline, 1974–79. Mem. Fife CC, 1961–64. Voluntary Tutor, Nat. Council of Labour Colls.

Recreation: reading. *Address:* 22 Station Road, Kelty, Fife, Scotland. *Died 9 April 1991.*

HUNTER, Dr Alan, CBE 1975; Director, Royal Greenwich Observatory, 1973–75; *b* 9 Sept. 1912; *s* of late George Hunter and Mary Edwards; *m* 1937, W. Joan Portnell (*d* 1985); four *s. Educ:* Imperial Coll. of Science and Technology. PhD, DIC; FRAS. Research Asst, Applied Mech. Dept, RNC, 1940–46; Royal Observatory, Greenwich: Asst, 1937–61; Chief Asst, 1961–67; Dep. Dir, 1967–73. Editor, The Observatory, 1943–49. Treas., Royal Astronomical Soc., 1967–76 (Sec. 1949–56, Vice-Pres. 1957, 1965, 1976); Pres., British Astronomical Assoc., 1957–59; Chm., Large Telescope Users' Panel, 1974–75 (sec. 1969–73). Liveryman, Worshipful Co. of Clockmakers, 1975. *Recreation:* gardening. *Address:* Thatched Cottage, Frettenham Road, Frettenham, Norwich NR12 7LZ. *T:* Norwich (01603) 890179.

Died 11 Dec. 1995.

HUNTER, Prof. Archibald Macbride, MA, BD, PhD Glasgow; Hon. DD Glasgow; DPhil Oxon; Professor of New Testament Exegesis (formerly Biblical Criticism) in Aberdeen University, 1945–71; Master of Christ's College, Aberdeen, 1957–71; *b* 16 Jan. 1906; *s* of late Rev. Archibald Hunter, Kilwinning, and Crissie Swan MacNeish; *m* 1934, Margaret Wylie Swanson; one *s* one *d. Educ:* Hutchesons' Grammar Sch., Glasgow; Universities of Glasgow, Marburg and Oxford. Minister in Comrie, Perthshire, 1934–37; Prof. of New Testament, in Mansfield Coll., Oxford, 1937–42; Minister in Kinnoull, Perth, 1942–45. Hastie Lecturer, Glasgow Univ., 1938; Lee Lecturer, 1950; Sprunt Lecturer (Richmond, Va), 1954. *Publications:* Paul and His Predecessors, 1940; The Unity of the New Testament, 1943; Introducing the New Testament, 1945; The Gospel according to St Mark, 1949; The Work and Words of Jesus, 1950; Interpreting the New Testament, 1951; Design for Life, 1953; Interpreting Paul's Gospel, 1954; The Epistle to the Romans, 1955; Introducing New Testament Theology, 1957; The Layman's Bible Commentary, Vol. 22, 1959; Interpreting The Parables, 1960; Teaching and Preaching the New Testament, 1963; The Gospel according to John, 1965; The Gospel according to St Paul, 1966; According to John, 1968; Bible and Gospel, 1969; Exploring the New Testament, 1971; The Parables Then and Now, 1971; Taking the Christian View, 1974; On P. T. Forsyth, 1974; The New Testament Today, 1974; Gospel and Apostle, 1975; Jesus Lord and Saviour, 1976; The Gospel Then and Now, 1978; Christ and the Kingdom, 1980; The Fifth Evangelist, 1980; Preaching the New Testament, 1981; The Parables for Today, 1983; Introducing the Christian Faith, 1984; articles and reviews in theological journals. *Recreation:* fishing. *Address:* 55 Schaw Drive, Heatherdene, Bearsden, Glasgow G61 3AT.

Died 14 Sept. 1991.

HUNTER, Dr Colin Graeme, DSC 1939; physician, National Health Service, 1973–82; *b* 31 Jan. 1913; *s* of Robert Hunter and Evelyn Harrison; *m* 1944, Betty Louise Riley; one *s* one *d. Educ:* Scots Coll., Univ. of Otago, New Zealand. MD 1958, DSc 1970. Christchurch Hosp. NZ, 1937–38; Royal Naval Medical Service, 1938–55; Univ. of Toronto, Canada, 1955–58; Shell Research Ltd, 1958–73. Fellow: RCP; Royal Coll. of Pathologists, etc. Freeman of City of London. *Publications:* scientific papers in many jls devoted to chemical and radiation toxicology. *Recreations:* sailing, squash. *Address:* 52 Fort Picklecombe, Maker, Torpoint, Cornwall PL10 1JB. *T:* Plymouth (0752) 823419. *Club:* Royal Naval Sailing Association. *Died 14 Dec. 1991.*

HUNTER, Hon. David Stronach, CBE 1991; **Hon. Mr Justice Hunter;** Justice of Appeal, Supreme Court of Hong Kong, since 1987; *b* 5 Oct. 1926; *s* of late Robert John Hunter and Jayne Evelyn Hunter; *m* 1959, Janet Muriel Faulkner; one *s* two *d. Educ:* Harrow Sch.; Hertford Coll., Oxford (Baring Scholar; MA Jurisprudence). Called to the Bar, Middle Temple, 1951, Bencher, 1979; QC 1971; a Recorder of the Crown Court, 1975–81; Judge of Supreme Court of Hong Kong, 1982–87. *Recreations:* golf, gardening, painting. *Address:* Supreme Court, Hong Kong; 48 Manderly Garden, 48 Deep Water Bay Road, Hong Kong. *Clubs:* MCC; Hong Kong.

Died 2 Oct. 1991.

HUNTER, Guy, CMG 1973; author and consultant; Overseas Development Institute, 1967–83, retired; *b* 7 Nov. 1911; *s* of Lt-Col C. F. Hunter, DSO, and Mrs A. W. Hunter (*née* Cobbett); *m* 1941, Agnes Louisa Merrylees. *Educ:* Winchester Coll.; Trinity Coll., Cambridge. 1st cl. hons Classics, MA. Called to Bar, Middle Temple, 1935. Civil Defence, Regional Officer, Edinburgh and Principal Officer, Glasgow and W Scotland, 1939–43; Dir (Admin), Middle East Supply Centre, GHQ, Cairo, 1943–45; Dir, PEP, 1945–46; Warden, Urchfont Manor, Wilts, and Grantley Hall, Yorks, Adult Colleges, 1946–55; Dir of Studies, 1st Duke of Edinburgh's Conf., 1955–56; from 1957, research and consultancy for developing countries overseas, mainly E, W and Central Africa, India, Pakistan, SE Asia, Fiji; launching and 1st Dir, East African Staff Coll., 1966; Inst. of Race Relations, 1959–66. Visiting Prof., Univ. of Reading, 1969–75. Member: Economic and Social Cttee, EEC, 1975–78; Council for Internat. Develt (ODM), 1977; Bd of Governors, Inst. of Develt Studies, Sussex Univ. *Publications:* Studies in Management, 1961; The New Societies of Tropical Africa, 1962; Education for a Developing Region, 1963; (ed) Industrialization and Race Relations, 1965; South East Asia: Race, Culture and Nation, 1966; The Best of Both Worlds, 1967; Modernising Peasant Societies, 1969; The Administration of Agricultural Development, 1970; (ed jtly) Serving the Small Farmer, 1974; (ed jtly) Policy and Practice in Rural Development, 1976. *Recreations:* gardening, nature, travel. *Address:* The Miller's Cottage, Hartest, Bury St Edmunds, Suffolk. *T:* Bury St Edmunds (0284) 830334. *Club:* Travellers'.

Died 5 Jan. 1992.

HUNTING, (Charles) Patrick (Maule), CBE 1975; TD 1952; FCA; Chairman of Hunting Group, 1962–74; *b* 16 Dec. 1910; *s* of late Sir Percy Hunting and Dorothy Edith, *e d* of Daniel Maule Birkett; *m* 1941, Diana, *d* of late Brig. A. B. P. Pereira, DSO, Tavistock, Devon; two *s* two *d. Educ:* Rugby Sch.; Trinity Coll., Cambridge. BA (Hons) Mod. and Mediaeval Langs; MA 1975; ACA 1936, FCA 1960. Served Royal Sussex Regt, 1939–45: France and Belgium, 1940; 8th Army, Western Desert, 1942; also in Palestine and Persia; Staff Coll., Camberley (psc), 1945. Entered Hunting Group 1936, Dir, 1946, Vice-Chm., 1961; Director: Hunting Associated Industries Ltd (Chm., 1965–74); Hunting Gibson Ltd (Chm., 1970–74); Hunting Gp Ltd (Chm., 1962–74). Mem. Council, Chamber of Shipping of UK, 1960 (Chm. Tramp Tanker Section, 1962); Master, Ironmongers' Company, 1978 (Mem. Court, 1970–). *Recreations:* golf, fishing, formerly cricket. *Clubs:* Naval and Military, MCC; Hawks (Cambridge); Royal Ashdown Forest (Golf).

Died 21 March 1993.

HUNTINGDON, Margaret Countess of; see Lane, M.

HUNTINGFIELD, 6th Baron *cr* 1796 (Ire.); **Gerard Charles Arcedeckne Vanneck;** Bt 1751; international civil servant with United Nations Secretariat, 1946–75; *b* 29 May 1915; *er s* of 5th Baron Huntingfield, KCMG, and Margaret Eleanor (*d* 1943) *o d* of late Judge Ernest Crosby, Grasmere, Rhinebeck, NY; *S* father, 1969; *m* 1941, Janetta Lois, *er d* of Capt. R. H. Errington, RN, Tostock Old Hall, Bury St Edmunds, Suffolk; one *s* two *d* (and one *d* decd).

Educ: Stowe; Trinity College, Cambridge. *Heir: s* Hon. Joshua Charles Vanneck [*b* 10 Aug. 1954; *m* 1982, Arabella, *d* of A. H. J. Fraser, MC, Moniack Castle; four *s* one *d*]. *Address:* 53 Barron's Way, Comberton, Cambridge CB3 7EQ. *Died 1 May 1994.*

HURLL, Alfred William, CVO 1970; CBE 1955; Member of Council, The Scout Association, since 1948 (Chief Executive Commissioner, 1948–70); *b* 10 Sept. 1905; *s* of Charles Alfred Hurll; *m* 1933, Elsie Margaret, *d* of Frederick Sullivan; one *s* one *d*. *Educ:* Grammar Sch., Acton. Joined staff, The Scout Assoc. HQ, 1921; Sec., Home Dept, 1935; Asst Gen. Sec., 1938; Gen. Sec., 1941. *Publication:* (co-author) BP's Scouts, 1961. *Recreations:* cricket, theatre. *Address:* 106 Montrose Avenue, Twickenham TW2 6HD. *T:* 081–894 1957.
Died 1 Jan. 1991.

HUTCHISON, A(lan) Michael Clark; *b* 26 Feb. 1914; *y s* of late Sir George A. Clark Hutchison, KC, MP, Eriska, Argyll, and Margaret, *d* of John Blair, WS, Edinburgh; *m* 1937, Anne (*d* 1989), *yr d* of Rev. A. R. Taylor, DD, Aberdeen; one *s* one *d*. *Educ:* Eton; Trinity Coll., Cambridge. Called to Bar, Gray's Inn, 1937. War of 1939–45 (despatches); served AIF, Middle East and Pacific theatres, psc (Major). Mem. Australian Mil. Mission, Washington, USA, 1945–46. Entered Colonial Admin. Service, 1946, and served as Asst Dist Comr in Palestine till 1948; thereafter as Political Officer and Asst Sec. in Protectorate and Colony of Aden; resigned, 1955. Contested (C) Motherwell Div. of Lanarks, 1955; MP (C) Edinburgh South, May 1957–1979; Parliamentary Private Secretary: to Parliamentary and Financial Sec. to the Admiralty, and to the Civil Lord, 1959; to the Lord Advocate, 1959–60; to Sec. of State for Scotland, 1960–62. Scottish Conservative Members' Committee: Vice-Chm., 1965–66, 1967–68; Chm., 1970–71. Introduced as Private Mem.'s Bills: Solicitors (Scotland) Act; Wills Act; Intestate Succession (Scotland) Act; Confirmation to Small Estates (Scotland) Act. *Recreations:* reading, Disraeliana. *Address:* 12 Stokes View, Pangbourne Hill, Pangbourne, Berks RG8 7RP. *T:* Pangbourne (0734) 845106. *Club:* New (Edinburgh). *Died 21 March 1993.*

HUTCHISON, (William) Bruce, OC 1967; Editor Emeritus, formerly Editorial Director, Vancouver Sun; *b* 5 June 1901; *s* of John and Constance Hutchison; *m* 1925, Dorothy Kidd McDiarmid; one *s* one *d*. *Educ:* public and high schs, Victoria, BC. Political writer: Victoria Times, 1918; Vancouver Province, 1925; Vancouver Sun, 1938; associate editor, Winnipeg Free Press, 1944; editor, Victoria Times, 1950–63. Hon. LLD University of British Columbia, 1951. *Publications:* The Unknown Country, 1943; The Hollow Men (novel), 1944; The Fraser, 1950; The Incredible Canadian, 1952; The Struggle for the Border, 1955; Canada: Tomorrow's Giant, 1957; Mr Prime Minister, 1964; Western Windows, 1967; The Far Side of the Street, 1976; Uncle Percy's Wonderful Town (stories), 1981; The Unfinished Country, 1985; A Life in the Country, 1988; The Cub Reporter Learns a Thing or Two, 1991. *Recreations:* fishing, gardening. *Address:* 810 Rogers Avenue, Victoria, BC, Canada. *T:* 479–2269. *Club:* Union (Victoria). *Died 14 Sept. 1992.*

HUTSON, Sir Francis (Challenor), Kt 1963; CBE 1960; Senior Partner, D. M. Simpson & Co., Consulting Engineers, Barbados, 1943–70, retired; *b* 13 Sept. 1895; *s* of Francis and Alice Sarah Hutson; *m* 1st, 1925, Muriel Allen Simpkin (*d* 1945); two *s* one *d*; 2nd, 1947, Edith Doris Howell. *Educ:* Harrison Coll., Barbados; Derby Technical Coll., Derby. Resident Engineer, Booker Bros, McConnell & Co. Ltd, British Guiana, 1920–30; Consulting Engineer, Barbados, 1930–35; D. M. Simpson & Co., 1935–70. MLC, 1947–62, MEC, 1958–61, Barbados; PC (Barbados), 1961–70. FIMechE.

Recreation: bridge. *Address:* Fleetwood, Erdiston Hill, St Michael, Barbados. *T:* 429 3905. *Clubs:* Bridgetown, Royal Barbados Yacht, Savannah (all in Barbados).
Died 4 Oct. 1992.

HUTSON, Maj.-Gen. Henry Porter Wolseley, CB 1945; DSO 1917; OBE 1919; MC 1915; *b* 22 March 1893; *s* of late Henry Wolseley Hutson, Wimbledon, SW19; *m* 1922, Rowena (*d* 1989), *d* of Surg.-Gen. Percy Hugh Benson, IA; two *s* one *d*. *Educ:* King's Coll. Sch.; RMA. 2nd Lieut RE, 1913; Capt. 1917; Major, 1929; Lieut-Col 1937; Col 1939; Temp. Brig. 1940; Maj.-Gen. 1944. Served European War, 1914–18, France, Belgium, Egypt and Mesopotamia (wounded, despatches thrice, DSO, OBE, MC); employed with Egyptian Army, 1920–24; under Colonial Office (Road Engineer Nigeria), 1926–28; Chief Instructor, Field Works and Bridging, Sch. of Military Engineering, 1934–36; served War of 1939–45 (despatches, CB); retired pay, 1947; Chief Engr, Forestry Commn, 1947–58. *Publications:* The Birds about Delhi, 1954; (ed) The Ornithologist's Guide, 1956; Majority Rule—Why?, 1973; Rhodesia: ending an era, 1978. *Address:* David Gresham House, 226 Pollards Oak Road, Hurst Green, Oxted, Surrey RH8 0JP.
Died 23 Dec. 1991.

HUTTON, Maj.-Gen. Walter Morland, CB 1964; CBE 1960; DSO 1943; MC 1936 and bar, 1942; MA (by decree, 1967); FIL (Arabic); Fellow, 1967–72 and Home Bursar, 1966–72, Jesus College, Oxford; *b* 5 May 1912; *s* of Walter Charles Stritch Hutton and Amy Mary Newton; *m* 1945, Peronelle Marie Stella Luxmoore-Ball; two *s* one *d*. *Educ:* Parkstone Sch.; Allhallows Sch.; RMC Sandhurst. Commissioned into Royal Tank Corps, 1932; served in Palestine, 1936 (MC); 1st Class Army Interpreter in Arabic, 1937; War of 1939–45: Western Desert, Alamein and N Africa (comdg 5 RTR); Italy (comdg 40 RTR); Comdt, Sandhurst, 1944–45; Instructor, Staff Coll., Camberley, 1949–51; BGS, Arab Legion, 1953–56; Imperial Defence Coll., 1957; Deputy Comd (Land), British Forces Arabian Peninsula (Aden), 1957–59; Dir of Administrative Plans, War Office, 1959–60, Dir-Gen. of Fighting Vehicles, 1961–64; Chief Army Instructor, Imperial Defence Coll., 1964–66. Mem., Bd of Governors, United Oxford Hosps, 1969–72.
Died 5 March 1994.

HUXLEY, Anthony Julian; author, free-lance writer, editor and photographer; *b* 2 Dec. 1920; *s* of Sir Julian Huxley, FRS and Marie Juliette Baillot; *m* 1st, 1943, Priscilla Ann Taylor; three *d*; 2nd, 1974, Alyson Ellen Vivian, *d* of late Beavan Archibald; one *d*. *Educ:* Dauntsey's Sch.; Trinity Coll., Cambridge (MA). Operational Research in RAF and Min. of Aircraft Production, 1941–47; Economic Research in BOAC, 1947–48; with Amateur Gardening, 1949–71 (Editor, 1967–71); Ed.-in-chief (formerly Gen. Ed.), RHS Dictionary of Gardening, 1988–92. Vice Pres., RHS, 1991– (Mem., Council, 1979–91); Hon. FRHS 1992. Veitch Meml Medal, RHS, 1979; VMH 1980. *Publications:* (trans.) Exotic Plants of the World, 1955; (gen. editor) Standard Encyclopedia of the World's Mountains, 1962; (gen. editor) Standard Encyclopedia of Oceans and Islands, 1962; Garden Terms Simplified, 1962, 1971; Flowers in Greece: an outline of the Flora, 1964; (with O. Polunin) Flowers of the Mediterranean, 1965; (gen. ed.) Standard Encyclopedia of Rivers and Lakes, 1965; Mountain Flowers, 1967; (ed) Garden Perennials and Water Plants, 1971; (ed) Garden Annuals and Bulbs, 1971; House Plants, Cacti and Succulents, 1972; (ed) Deciduous Garden Trees and Shrubs, 1973; (ed) Evergreen Garden Trees and Shrubs, 1973; Plant and Planet, 1978, 2nd edn 1987; (ed) The Financial Times Book of Garden Design, 1975; (with W. Taylor) Flowers of Greece and the Aegean, 1977, 2nd edn 1989; (ed) The

Encyclopedia of the Plant Kingdom, 1977; (with Alyson Huxley) Huxley's House of Plants, 1978; An Illustrated History of Gardening, 1978; (gen. editor) Success with House Plants, 1979; Penguin Encyclopedia of Gardening, 1981; (with P. and J. Davies) Wild Orchids of Britain and Europe, 1983; (ed) The Macmillan World Guide to House Plants, 1983; Green Inheritance, 1984; The Painted Garden, 1988; (ed) The New Royal Horticultural Society Dictionary of Gardening, 4 vols, 1992. *Recreations:* photography, travel for botany and archaeology, gardening. *Address:* 50 Villiers Avenue, Surbiton, Surrey KT5 8BD. *T:* 081–390 7983. *Died 26 Dec. 1992.*

HUXSTEP, Emily Mary, CBE 1964; BA London: Headmistress of Chislehurst and Sidcup Girls' Grammar School, Kent, 1944–66; *b* 15 Sept. 1906; *d* of George T. and Nellie M. Huxstep (*née* Wood). *Educ:* Chatham Girls' Grammar Sch.; Queen Mary Coll. Headmistress, Hanson Girls' Grammar Sch., Bradford, Yorks, 1938–44. Hon. DCL Kent, 1974. *Address:* The Loose Valley Nursing Home, Linton Road, Loose, Maidstone, Kent ME15 0AG. *Died 2 Oct. 1995.*

HYATT KING, Alexander; *see* King.

HYDE WHITE, Wilfrid; *b* 12 May 1903; *s* of William Edward White, Canon of Gloucester and Ethel Adelaide (*née* Drought); *m* 1927, Blanche Hope Aitken (decd); one *s*; *m* 1957, Ethel Korenman (stage name Ethel Drew); one *s* one *d. Educ:* Marlborough. First appeared in London in Beggar on Horseback, Queen's Theatre, 1925; successful appearances include: Rise Above It, Comedy; It Depends What You Mean, Westminster; Britannus in Cæsar and Cleopatra, St James's, London, and Ziegfield, New York; Affairs of State, Cambridge; Hippo Dancing, Lyric; The Reluctant Debutante, Cambridge, and Henry Miller's Theatre, New York (nominated for Tony award, 1956); Not in the Book, Criterion; Miss Pell is Missing, Criterion; The Doctor's Dilemma, Haymarket; Lady Windermere's Fan, Phoenix; Meeting at Night, Duke of York's; The Jockey Club Stakes, Duke of York's, and Cort Theatre, NYC (nominated for Tony award for best actor, 1973); The Pleasure of his Company, Phoenix; Rolls Hyphen Royce, Shaftesbury. *Films include:* The 3rd Man, The Browning Version, Golden Salamander, The Million Pound Note, Libel, Two Way Stretch, North West Frontier, Let's Make Love, His and Hers, On the Double, Ada, The Castaways, Crooks Anonymous, On the Fiddle, Aliki, My Fair Lady, 10 Little Indians, The Liquidator, In God We Trust. *Address:* c/o Chatto and Linnit Ltd, Prince of Wales Theatre, Coventry Street, W1V 7FE. *Clubs:* Green Room, Buck's.   *Died 6 May 1991.*

I

IBIAM, (Francis) Akanu, GCON 1963; LLD, DLit; medical missionary; Eze Ogo Isiala I: Unwana, and the Osuji of Uburu; Chairman, Imo State Council of Traditional Rulers; Chancellor, Imo State University; *b* Unwana, Afikpo Division, Nigeria, 29 Nov. 1906; *s* of late Ibiam Aka Ibiam and late Alu Owora; *m* 1939, Eudora Olayinka Sasegbon (*d* 1974); one *s* two *d. Educ:* Hope Waddell Training Instn Calabar; King's Coll., Lagos; University of St Andrews, Scotland. FMCP (GP) Nigeria. Medical Missionary with the Church of Scotland Mission, Calabar, Nigeria, 1936; started and built up new Hosp. in Abiriba, Bende Div., under Calabar Mission, 1936–45; Medical Supt, CSM Hosp., Itu, 1945–48; CSM Hosp., Uburu, 1952–57. MLC, Nigeria, 1947–52; MEC, 1949–52; retd from Politics, 1953; Principal, Hope Waddell Training Instn, Calabar, 1957–60; (on leave) Governor, Eastern Nigeria, 1960–66; Adviser to Military Governor of Eastern Provinces, 1966. Founder (1937) and former Pres., Student Christian Movement of Nigeria, now Hon. President; Trustee: Presbyterian Church of Nigeria, 1945–; Queen Elizabeth Hosp., Umuahia-Ibeku, 1953–; Scout Movement of Eastern Nigeria, 1957–; Mem. Bd of Governors: Hope Waddell Trng Instn, Calabar, 1945–60; Queen Elizabeth Hosp., 1950–60; Mem. Provl Council of University Coll., Ibadan, 1948–54; Mem. Privy Council, Eastern Nigeria, 1954–60; Pres., Christian Council of Nigeria, 1955–58; Mem. Calabar Mission Council, 1940–60 (now integrated with Church); Mem. Admin. Cttee of Internat. Missionary Council, 1957–61; Chm. Provisional Cttee of All Africa Churches Conf., 1958–62; Chairman: Council of University of Ibadan, Nigeria, 1958–60; Governing Council of Univ. of Nigeria, Nsukka, 1966; a Pres. of World Council of Churches, 1961; a Pres. of All Africa Church Conf., 1963; Pres., World Council of Christian Educn and Sunday Sch. Assoc.; Chm. Council, United Bible Socs, 1966–72, Vice-Pres. 1972–; Founder and Pres., Bible Soc. of Nigeria, 1963–74, Patron 1974; Founder and former Pres., All Africa Council of Churches; Founder, Nigerian SPCC; President: Soc. for Promotion of Ibo Lang. and Culture; Cancer Soc. of Nigeria. Patron, Akanu Ibiam Nat. Ambulance; Grand Patron, World Women Christian Temperance Union. Presbyterian Church of Nigeria: Mem. Educ. Authority, 1940–; Mem. Missionaries' Cttee, Med. Bd, and Standing Cttee of Synod; Advanced Training Fund Management Cttee of Synod; Elder, 1940–. Appointed OBE 1949, KBE 1951, KCMG 1962, and renounced these honours 1967 in protest at British Govt policy on Biafra. Upper Room Citation, 1966. Hon. LLD Ibadan; Hon. DSc Ife, 1966. Kt of Mark Twain. Humanitarian of Rosicrucian Order. Golden Cross with crown, Order of Orthodox Knights of Holy Sepulchre, Jerusalem, 1965; Golden Star Medal (1st degree), Order of Russian Orthodox Church, 1965. *Recreation:* reading. *Address:* Ganymede, Unwana, Afikpo Local Government Area, PO Box 240, Imo State, Nigeria.

Died 1 July 1995.

IEVERS, Rear-Adm. John Augustine, CB 1962; OBE 1944; *b* 2 Dec. 1912; *s* of Eyre Francis Ievers, Tonbridge, Kent; *m* 1937, Peggy G. Marshall (*d* 1992); one *s* two *d. Educ:* RN Coll., Dartmouth. CO Naval Test Squadron, Boscombe Down, 1945–47; RN Staff Coll., 1948–49; HMS Ocean, 1949; HMS Glory, 1949–50; HMS Burghead Bay, 1951–52; CO, RN Air Station, Lossiemouth,

1952–54; Dep. Dir Naval Air Warfare Div., 1954–57; Captain Air, Mediterranean, 1957–60; Deputy Controller Aircraft, Min. of Aviation, 1960–63; retd, 1964. *Recreation:* golf. *Address:* 3 Hollywood Court, Hollywood Lane, Lymington, Hants SO41 9HD. *T:* Lymington (01590) 677268. *Died 7 Aug. 1995.*

IHAKA, Ven. Sir Kingi (Matutaera), Kt 1989; MBE 1969; JP; Archdeacon of Auckland, New Zealand, 1976–82; *b* 18 Oct. 1921; *s* of Eru Timoko Ihaka and Te Paea Ihaka; *m* Manutuke Sadlier (*d* 1972); two *s* (and one *s* decd). *Educ:* St Stephen's Sch., Bombay; St John's Theol. Coll., Auckland (LTh; Fellow). Curate, St Matthew's, Masterton, 1949–50; Pastor, Wanganui, 1951–57; Maori Missioner, Wellington, 1958–66, Auckland, 1967–75; Director, Maori work, Auckland Dio., 1976–82; Chaplain, Maori Community, Sydney, Aust., 1983–86; retired from parish work, 1987, but remained active in Church and State organisations. JP 1970. *Recreations:* reading, gardening. *Address:* 9 Piccadilly Place, Kohimarama, Auckland 5, New Zealand. *T:* (9) 5213442. *Died 1 Jan. 1993.*

ILLINGWORTH, Sir Charles (Frederick William), Kt 1961; CBE 1946; Regius Professor of Surgery, University of Glasgow, 1939, Emeritus, 1964; Hon. Surgeon to the Queen, in Scotland, 1961–65, Extra Surgeon since 1965; *b* 8 May 1899; *s* of John and Edith Illingworth; *m* 1928, Eleanor Mary Bennett (*d* 1971); four *s. Educ:* Heath Grammar Sch., Halifax; Univ. of Edinburgh. Graduated Medicine, 1922. 2nd Lieut, RFC, 1917. FRCSE 1925; FRCSGlas, 1963. Hon. FACS, 1954; Hon. FRCS, 1958; Hon. FRCSI, 1964; Hon. FRCSCan, 1965; Hon. FCSSA, 1965. DSc (Hon.): University of Sheffield, 1962; University of Belfast, 1963; Hon. LLD (Glasgow, Leeds), 1965. *Publications:* (jtly) Text Book of Surgical Pathology, 1932; Short Text Book of Surgery, 1938; Text Book of Surgical Treatment, 1942; Monograph on Peptic Ulcer, 1953; The Story of William Hunter, 1967; The Sanguine Mystery, 1970; University Statesman: Sir Hector Hetherington, 1971; various contributions to surgical literature, mainly on digestive disorders. *Address:* 57 Winton Drive, Glasgow G12 0QB. *T:* 041–339 3759.

Died 23 Feb. 1991.

IMESON, Kenneth Robert, MA; Headmaster, Nottingham High School, 1954–70; *b* 8 July 1908; *s* of R. W. Imeson; *m* 1st, 1934, Peggy (*d* 1967), *d* of late A. H. Mann, Dulwich; two *d*; 2nd, Peggy (*d* 1979), *d* of late Harold Pow, and *widow* of Duncan MacArthur; 3rd, 1982, Barbara Thorpe, *d* of late Alfred Charles Reynolds. *Educ:* St Olave's; Sidney Sussex Coll., Cambridge (Schol.). Mathematical Tripos, Part 1 1928; Part II 1930. Asst Master, Llandovery Coll., 1930–33; Sen. Mathematical Master, Watford Grammar Sch., 1933–44; Headmaster, Sir Joseph Williamson's Mathematical Sch., 1944–53. Member: Council, SCM in Schools, 1948–58; Oxford and Cambridge Examinations Board, 1957–61, 1962–70; Council, Christian Education Movement, 1965–69; Council, Arts Educational Schools, 1971–88; London Diocesan Bd of Educn, 1971–76; Council of Friends of Rochester Cathedral, 1947–53; Board of Visitors, Nottingham Prison, 1956–57; Teaching Cttee, Mathematical Association, 1950–58; Trustee, Nottingham Mechanics Institution, 1955–70; Mem., Court of Nottingham Univ., 1955–64, 1968–70; Lectr, Univ. of

Third Age, in Cambridge, 1983–86. Member: Cttee, Notts CCC, 1969–72; Central Council of Physical Recreation, 1971–. Governor: Lady Margaret Sch., Parson's Green; Purcell Sch. of Music, 1975–78. *Publications:* The Magic of Number, 1989; articles in Journal of Education. *Recreations:* cricket and other games, music. *Address:* 39 Gretton Court, Girton, Cambridge CB3 0QN. *T:* Cambridge (0223) 277903. *Clubs:* Royal Air Force, MCC, Yellowhammers Cricket, Forty; Cambridge Society.
Died 13 April 1994.

IMMS, George, CB 1964; Commissioner and Director of Establishments and Organisation, HM Customs and Excise, 1965–71; *b* 10 April 1911; *o s* of late George Imms; *m* 1938, Joan Sylvia Lance; two *s. Educ:* Grange High Sch., Bradford; Emmanuel Coll., Cambridge (Scholar). Joined HM Customs and Excise, 1933; Asst Sec., 1946; Commissioner, 1957–65. Mem. Civil Service Appeals Bd, 1971–79. *Address:* 26 Lynceley Grange, Epping, Essex CM16 6RA. *Died 5 July 1995.*

INCH, Sir John Ritchie, Kt 1972; CVO 1969; CBE 1958; QPM 1961; Chief Constable, Edinburgh City Police, 1955–76; *b* 14 May 1911; *s* of James Inch, Lesmahagow, Lanarkshire; *m* 1941, Anne Ferguson Shaw; one *s* two *d. Educ:* Hamilton Academy; Glasgow Univ. (MA, LLB). Joined Lanarkshire Constabulary, 1931; apptd Chief Constable, Dunfermline City Police, 1943, and of combined Fife Constabulary, 1949. OStJ 1964. Comdr, Royal Order of St Olav (Norway), 1962; Comdr, Order of Al-Kawkal Al Urdini (Jordan), 1966; Cavaliere Ufficiale, Order of Merit (Italy), 1969; Comdr, Order of Orange-Nassau (Netherlands), 1971; Order of the Oak Crown Class III (Luxembourg), 1972. *Recreations:* shooting, fishing, golf. *Address:* 2 Orchard Brae, Edinburgh EH4 1HY. *Club:* Royal Scots (Edinburgh).
Died 22 Nov. 1993.

INCHCAPE, 3rd Earl of, *cr* 1929; **Kenneth James William Mackay;** Viscount Glenapp, 1929; Viscount Inchcape, 1924; Baron Inchcape, 1911; Chairman and Chief Executive, Inchcape PLC, 1958–82, then Life President; Chairman: P & O Steam Navigation Co., 1973–83 (Chief Executive, 1978–81; Director, 1957–83); Inchcape Family Investment Ltd, since 1985; Glenapp Estate Company, Edinburgh, since 1979; President, Commonwealth Society for the Deaf; *b* 27 Dec. 1917; *e s* of 2nd Earl and 1st wife, Joan (*d* 1933), *d* of Rt Hon. John Francis Moriarty, PC, KC, Lord Justice of Appeal in Ireland; *S* father 1939; *m* 1st, 1941, Mrs Aline Thorn Hannay (marr. diss. 1954), *d* of Sir Richard Pease, 2nd Bt, and *widow* of Flying Officer P. C. Hannay, AAF; two *s* one *d*; 2nd, 1965, Caroline Cholmeley, *e d* of Cholmeley Dering Harrison, Emo Court, Co. Leix, Eire, and Mrs Corisande Harrison; two *s* and one adopted *s. Educ:* Eton; Trinity Coll., Cambridge (MA). Served War of 1939–45: 12th Royal Lancers BEF France; Major 27th Lancers MEF and Italy. Director: Burmah Oil Co., 1960–75; BP Co., 1965–83. Chm., Council for Middle East Trade, 1963–65; Pres., Gen. Council of British Shipping, 1976–77. Pres., Royal Soc. for India, Pakistan and Ceylon, 1970–76. Prime Warden: Shipwrights' Co., 1967; Fishmongers' Co., 1977–78. One of HM Comrs of Lieutenancy for the City of London, 1980–. Freeman, City of London. *Recreations:* all field sports. *Heir: s* Viscount Glenapp [*b* 23 Jan. 1943; *m* 1966, Georgina, *d* of S. C. Nisbet and late Mrs G. R. Sutton; one *s* two *d*]. *Address:* Starvall Farm, Farmington, Northleach, Cheltenham GL54 3NF; Carlock House, Ballantrae, Girvan, Ayrshire KA26 0NY. *Clubs:* White's, Oriental.
Died 17 March 1994.

INGHAM, John Henry, CMG 1956; MBE 1947; retired; *b* 1910; *m. Educ:* Plumtree School, S Rhodesia; Rhodes University College, S Africa; Brasenose College, Oxford. Administrative Officer, Nyasaland, 1936; Secretary for Agricultural and Natural Resources, Kenya, 1947; Administrative Secretary, 1952; Senior Secretary, East African Royal Commission, 1953–55; Secretary for African Affairs, Nyasaland, 1956–60; MEC, Nyasaland, 1961. Minister of Urban Development, Malawi, 1961. Representative of Beit Trust and Dulverton Trust in Central Africa, 1962–81. Hon. MA Rhodesia, 1979. *Address:* 25 Canterbury Road, Avondale, Harare, Zimbabwe. *Died 4 April 1992.*

INGHAM, Stanley Ainsworth; Deputy Director (Under Secretary), Department for National Savings, 1979–82; *b* 21 Feb. 1920; *s* of David Ingham and Ann (*née* Walshaw); *m* 1944, Ethel Clara (*née* Jordan); one *s. Educ:* King's School, Pontefract, Yorkshire. Clerical Officer, Post Office Savings Bank, 1937; served Royal Artillery, 1940–46; Post Office Savings Bank: Executive Officer, 1946; Higher Executive Officer, 1956; Sen. Executive Officer, 1960; Principal, 1964; Asst Sec., Dept for National Savings, 1972. *Recreations:* Church affairs, gardening. *Address:* 2 Manor Crescent, Surbiton, Surrey KT5 8LQ. *T:* 081–399 1078. *Died 3 April 1991.*

INGLEFIELD, Sir Gilbert (Samuel), GBE 1968; Kt 1965; TD; MA; ARIBA, AADip. *b* 13 March 1909; 2nd *s* of late Adm. Sir Frederick Samuel Inglefield, KCB and Cecil, *d* of J. G. Crompton; *m* 1933, Laura Barbara Frances, *e d* of late Captain Gilbert Thompson, Connaught Rangers; two *s* one *d. Educ:* Eton; Trinity Coll., Cambridge. Architect. Served War of 1939–45 with Sherwood Foresters, France, Far East. British Council Asst Rep. in Egypt, 1946–49 and in London, 1949–56. Alderman, City of London (Aldersgate Ward), 1959–79; Sheriff, 1963–64; Chm., Barbican Cttee, 1963–66; Lord Mayor of London, 1967–68; one of HM Lieutenants for City of London; Church Commissioner for England, 1962–78; Governor: Thomas Coram Foundation; Royal Shakespeare Theatre; Fedn of British Artists, 1972–; Trustee, London Symphony Orchestra; Chm., City Arts Trust, 1968–76; Member: Royal Fine Art Commission, 1968–75; Redundant Churches Fund, 1972–76. Dep. Kt Principal, Imp. Soc. of Knights Bachelor, 1972–86; Hon. Master, Haberdashers' Co., 1972; Master, Musicians' Co., 1974; Assistant, Painter Stainers' Co. Chancellor of the Order of St John of Jerusalem, 1969–78; GCStJ. FRSA; Hon. RBA; Hon. GSM; Hon. FLCM. Hon. DSc City Univ., 1967. Comdr Order of the Falcon (Iceland), 1963; Order of the Two Niles, Class III (Sudan), 1964. *Recreations:* music, travel. *Address:* 6 Rutland House, Marloes Road, W8 5LE. *T:* 071–937 3458. *Clubs:* Athenæum, City Livery.
Died 14 Oct. 1991.

INGLIS, Brian (St John), PhD; FRSL; journalist; *b* 31 July 1916; *s* of late Sir Claude Inglis, CIE, FRS, and Vera St John Blood; *m* 1958, Ruth Langdon; one *s* one *d. Educ:* Shrewsbury Sch.; Magdalen Coll., Oxford. BA 1939. Served in RAF (Coastal Command), 1940–46; Flight Comdr 202 Squadron, 1944–45; Squadron Ldr, 1944–46 (despatches). Irish Times Columnist, 1946–48; Parliamentary Corr., 1950–53. Trinity Coll., Dublin: PhD 1950; Asst to Prof. of Modern History, 1949–53; Lectr in Economics, 1951–53; Spectator: Asst Editor, 1954–59; Editor, 1959–62; Dir, 1962–63. TV Commentator: What the Papers Say, 1956–; All Our Yesterdays, 1962–73. Trustee, Koestler (formerly KIB) Foundn, 1983–. *Publications:* The Freedom of the Press in Ireland, 1954; The Story of Ireland 1956; Revolution in Medicine, 1958; West Briton, 1962; Fringe Medicine, 1964; Private Conscience: Public Morality, 1964; Drugs, Doctors and Disease, 1965; A History of Medicine, 1965; Abdication, 1966; Poverty and the Industrial Revolution, 1971; Roger Casement, 1973; The Forbidden Game: the social history of drugs, 1975; The Opium War, 1976; Natural and Supernatural, 1977; The Book of the Back, 1978; Natural

Medicine, 1979; The Diseases of Civilisation, 1981; (with Ruth West) The Alternative Health Guide, 1983; Science and Parascience, 1984; The Paranormal: an encyclopedia of Psychic Phenomena, 1985; The Hidden Power, 1986; The Power of Dreams, 1987; The Unknown Guest, 1987; Trance, 1989; Downstart (autobiog.), 1990; Coincidence, 1990. *Address:* Garden Flat, 23 Lambolle Road, NW3 4HS. *T:* 071–794 0297.   *Died 11 Feb. 1993.*

INGLIS, Robert Alexander; Sheriff of North Strathclyde (formerly Renfrew and Argyll) at Paisley, 1972–84; *b* 29 June 1918; *m* 1950, Shelagh Constance St Clair Boyd (marriage dissolved, 1956); one *s* one *d*. *Educ:* Malsis Hall, Daniel Stewart's Coll.; Rugby Sch.; Christ Church, Oxford (MA); Glasgow Univ. (LLB). Army, 1940–46; Glasgow Univ., 1946–48; called to Bar, 1948. Interim Sheriff-Sub., Dundee, 1955; perm. appt, 1956; Sheriff of Inverness, Moray, Nairn and Ross and Cromarty, 1968–72. *Recreations:* golf, fishing, bridge. *Address:* 1 Cayzer Court, Ralston, Paisley, Renfrewshire PA1 3DH. *T:* 0141–883 6498.   *Died 6 Dec. 1995.*

INGRAM, Reginald Pepys W.; *see* Winnington-Ingram.

INNES, Fergus Munro, CIE 1946; CBE 1951; Indian Civil Service, retired; *b* 12 May 1903; *s* of late Sir Charles Alexander Innes, KCSI, CIE and Agatha Rosalie, *d* of Col Kenlis Stevenson, IA; *m* 1st, Evangeline (marr. diss.), *d* of A. H. Chaworth-Musters; two *d*; 2nd, Vera, *d* of T. Mahoney; one *s* one *d*. *Educ:* Charterhouse; Brasenose Coll., Oxford. Joined Indian Civil Service, 1926; various posts in Punjab up to 1937; Joint Sec., Commerce Dept, Govt of India, 1944; Mem., Central Board of Revenue, 1947; retired, 1947; Adviser in Pakistan to Central Commercial Cttee, 1947–53; Sec., The West Africa Cttee, 1956–61; Chm., India Gen. Navigation and Railway Co. Ltd, 1973–78. Company director. *Address:* The Hippins, Hook Heath Road, Woking, Surrey GU22 0DP. *T:* Woking (0483) 714626. *Club:* Oriental.

Died 5 May 1994.

INNES, Michael; *see* Stewart, J. I. M.

INNES, Robert Mann, JP; Lord Provost of Glasgow, since 1992; *b* 6 March 1926; *s* of Robert and Mary Innes; *m* 1959, Teresa Clements; two *s*. *Educ:* Glasgow Univ. (BSc 1950). Royal Navy, 1944–47; teaching, 1947–50; teaching, 1951–64; Lectr, Further Educn, 1964–86. Councillor (Lab), Keppochhill Ward, 1974–. JP Glasgow, 1974. *Recreations:* golf, jogging, swimming, reading. *Address:* 528 Sandyhills Road, Glasgow G32 9UA. *T:* 041–778 4027; City Chambers, Glasgow.

Died 6 May 1994.

INSCH, James Ferguson, CBE 1974; CA; Director, Guest Keen & Nettlefolds plc, 1964–82, Deputy Chairman, 1980–82; Chairman, Birmid-Qualcast Ltd, 1977–84 (Deputy Chairman, 1975–77); *b* 10 Sept. 1911; *s* of John Insch and Edina (*née* Hogg); *m* 1937, Jean Baikie Cunningham; one *s* two *d*. *Educ:* Leith Academy. Chartered Accountant (Scot.). Director, number of GKN companies, 1945–66; Guest Keen & Nettlefolds Ltd: Group Man. Dir, 1967; Gp Dep. Chm. and Man. Dir, 1968–74; Jt Dep. Chm., 1979. Pres., Nat. Assoc. of Drop Forgers and Stampers, 1962–63 and 1963–64. *Recreations:* golf, fishing. *Address:* 1 Denehurst Close, Barnt Green, Birmingham B43 8HR. *T:* 0121–445 2517.

Died 14 Dec. 1994.

INSKIP, (John) Hampden; QC 1966; **His Honour Judge Inskip;** a Circuit Judge, since 1982; *b* 1 Feb. 1924; *s* of Sir John Hampden Inskip, KBE, and Hon. Janet, *d* of 1st Baron Maclay, PC; *m* 1947, Ann Howell Davies; one *s* one *d*. *Educ:* Clifton Coll.; King's Coll., Cambridge. BA 1948. Called to the Bar, Inner Temple, 1949; Master of the Bench, 1975. Mem. of Western Circuit; Dep. Chm.,

Hants QS, 1967–71; Recorder of Bournemouth, later of the Crown Court, 1970–82. Mem., Criminal Law Revision Cttee, 1973–82; Pres., Transport Tribunal, 1982–91. *Publication:* Foundation Handbook of Care, 1981. *Address:* Clerks, Bramshott, Liphook, Hants.

Died 1 Oct. 1991.

IONESCO, Eugène; Chevalier de la Légion d'Honneur, 1970; Officier des Arts et des Lettres, 1961; homme de lettres; Membre de l'Académie française, since 1970; *b* 13 Nov. 1912; *s* of Eugène Ionescu and Thérèse Icard; *m* 1936, Rodica Burileano; one *d*. *Educ:* Bucharest and Paris. French citizen living in Paris. Ballet: The Triumph of Death, Copenhagen, 1972. *Publications:* (most of which appear in English and American editions) Théâtre I: La Cantatrice chauve, La Leçon, Jacques ou La Soumission, Les Chaises, Victimes du devoir, Amédée ou Comment s'en débarrasser, Paris, 1956; Théâtre II: L'Impromptu de l'Alma, Tueur sans gages, Le Nouveau Locataire, L'Avenir est dans les œufs, Le Maître, La Jeune Fille à marier, Paris, 1958; Rhinocéros (play) in Collection Manteau d'Arlequin, Paris, 1959; Le Piéton de l'air, 1962; Chemises de Nuit, 1962; Le Roi se meurt, 1962; Notes et Contre-Notes, 1962; Journal en Miettes, 1967; Présent passé passé présent, 1968; Découvertes (essays), 1969; Jeux de Massacre (play), 1970; Macbett (play), 1972; Ce formidable bordel (play), 1974; The Hermit (novel), 1975; The Man with the Suitcase, 1975; (with Claude Bonnefoy) Entre la vie et le rêve, 1977; Antidotes (essays), 1977; L'homme en question (essays), 1979; Variations sur un même thème, 1979; Voyages chez les Morts ou Thème et Variations (play), 1980; Noir et Blanc, 1980; Journeys Among The Dead (play), 1986; contrib. to: Avant-Garde (The experimental theatre in France) by L. C. Pronko, 1962; Modern French Theatre, from J. Giraudoux to Beckett, by Jean Guicharnaud, 1962; author essays and tales; *relevant publications:* The Theatre of the Absurd, by Martin Esslin, 1961; Ionesco, by Richard N. Coe, 1961; Eugène Ionesco, by Ronald Hayman, 1972. *Address:* c/o Editions Gallimard, 5 rue Sébastien Bottin, 75007 Paris, France.   *Died 28 March 1994.*

IRESON, Rev. Canon Gordon Worley; *b* 16 April 1906; *s* of Francis Robert and Julia Letitia Ireson; *m* 1939, Dorothy Elizabeth Walker; two *s* one *d*. *Educ:* Edinburgh Theological Coll.; Hatfield Coll., Durham. Deacon, 1933; priest, 1934; Asst Curate of Sheringham, 1933–36; Senior Chaplain of St Mary's Cathedral, Edinburgh, with charge of Holy Trinity, Dean Bridge, 1936–37; Priest-Lecturer to National Soc., 1937–39; Diocesan Missioner of Exeter Diocese, 1939–46; Hon. Chaplain to Bishop of Exeter, 1941–46; Canon Residentiary of Newcastle Cathedral, 1946–58; Canon-Missioner of St Albans, 1958–73; Warden, Community of the Holy Name, 1974–82. Examining Chaplain to Bishop of Newcastle, 1949–59. *Publications:* Church Worship and the Non-Churchgoer, 1945; Think Again, 1949; How Shall They Hear?, 1957; Strange Victory, 1970; Handbook of Parish Preaching, 1982. *Recreation:* making and mending in the workshop. *Address:* St Barnabas College, Blackberry Lane, Lingfield, Surrey RH7 6NJ.   *Died 22 March 1994.*

IRISH, Sir Ronald (Arthur), Kt 1970; OBE 1963; Partner, Irish Young & Outhwaite, Chartered Accountants, retired; Chairman, Rothmans of Pall Mall (Australia) Ltd, 1955–81, retired; *b* 26 March 1913; *s* of late Arthur Edward Irish; *m* 1960, Noella Jean Austin Fraser; three *s*. *Educ:* Fort Street High School. Chm., Manufacturing Industries Adv. Council, 1966–72. Pres., Inst. of Chartered Accountants in Australia, 1956–58; Pres., Tenth Internat. Congress of Accountants, 1972; Life Member: Australian Soc. of Accountants, 1972; Inst. of Chartered Accountants in Australia, 1974. Hon. Fellow, Univ. of Sydney, 1986. *Publications:* Practical Auditing, 1935; Auditing, 1947,

new edn 1972. *Recreations:* walking, swimming. *Address:* 3/110 Elizabeth Bay Road, Elizabeth Bay, NSW 2011, Australia. *Clubs:* Australian, Union (Sydney).
Died 12 July 1993.

IRONSIDE, Christopher, OBE 1971; FRBS; artist and designer; *b* 11 July 1913; *s* of Dr R. W. Ironside and Mrs P. L. Williamson (2nd *m; née* Cunliffe); *m* 1st, 1939, Janey (*née* Acheson) (marr. diss. 1961); one *d*; 2nd, 1961, Jean (*née* Marsden); one *s* two *d. Educ:* Central Sch. of Arts and Crafts. Served War of 1939–45, Dep. Sen. Design Off., Directorate of Camouflage, Min. of Home Security. In charge of Educn Sect., Coun. of Industrial Design, 1946–48; part-time Teacher, Royal College of Art, 1953–63. Paintings in public and private collections. *One-man shows:* Redfern Gall., 1941; Arthur Jeffries Gall., 1960. *Design work includes:* Royal Coat of Arms, Whitehall and decorations in Pall Mall, Coronation, 1953; coinages for Tanzania, Brunei, Qatar, Dubai and Singapore (reverses, 1985); reverses for Decimal Coinage, UK and Jamaican; many medals, coins and awards; theatrical work (with brother, late R. C. Ironside); various clocks, coats of arms and tapestries; firegrate for Goldsmiths' Co.; brass and marble meml to 16th Duke of Norfolk, Arundel; meml to Earl and Countess Mountbatten of Burma, Westminster Abbey. FSIA 1970; FRBS 1977. *Recreation:* trying to keep abreast of modern scientific development. *Address:* 22 Abingdon Villas, W8 6BX. *T:* 071–937 9418; Church Farm House, Smannell, near Andover, Hants SP11 6JW. *T:* Andover (0264) 23909.   *Died 13 July 1992.*

IRVINE, Rt Hon. Sir Bryant Godman, Kt 1986; PC 1982; barrister-at-law; farmer; *b* Toronto, 25 July 1909; *s* of late W. Henry Irvine and Ada Mary Bryant Irvine, formerly of St Agnes, Cornwall; *m* 1945, Valborg Cecilie (*d* 1990), *d* of late P. F. Carslund; two *d. Educ:* Upper Canada Coll.; St Paul's Sch.; Magdalen Coll., Oxford (MA). Sec. Oxford Union Soc., 1931. Called to Bar, Inner Temple, 1932. Chm. Agricultural Land Tribunal, SE Province, 1954–56. Mem. Executive Cttee, East Sussex NFU, 1947–84; Branch Chm., 1956–58. Chm. Young Conservative Union, 1946–47; Prospective Candidate, Bewdley Div. of Worcs, 1947–49; contested Wood Green and Lower Tottenham, 1951. MP (C) Rye Div., E Sussex, 1955–83; PPS to Minister of Education and to Parly Sec., Ministry of Education, 1957–59, to the Financial Sec. to the Treasury, 1959–60. Mem., Speaker's Panel of Chairmen, House of Commons, 1965–76; a Dep. Chm. of Ways and Means, and a Deputy Speaker, 1976–82; Jt Sec., Exec. Cttee, 1922 Cttee, 1965–68, Hon. Treasurer, 1974–76; Vice-Chm., Cons. Agric. Cttee, and spoke on Agriculture from Opposition Front Bench, 1964–70; Mem., House of Commons Select Cttee on Agriculture, 1967–69; Commonwealth Parliamentary Association: Hon. Treasurer, 1970–73; Mem., General Council, 1970–73; Mem., Exec. Cttee, UK Branch, 1964–76; Jt Sec. or Vice-Chm., Cons. Commonwealth Affairs Cttee, 1957–66; Jt Sec., Foreign and Commonwealth Affairs Cttee, 1967–73 (Vice-Chm., 1973–76); Chairman: Cons. Horticulture Sub-Cttee, 1960–62; All Party Tourist and Resort Cttee, 1964–66. President: British Resorts Assoc., 1962–80; Southern Counties Agricl Trading Soc., 1983–86. Served War of 1939–45, Lt-Comdr RNVR, afloat and on staff of C-in-C Western Approaches and Commander US Naval Forces in Europe. Comp. InstCE, 1936–74. *Recreations:* ski-ing, travel by sea. *Address:* Great Ote Hall, Burgess Hill, West Sussex RH15 0SR. *T:* Burgess Hill (0444) 232179; 91 Millbank Court, 24 John Islip Street, SW1. *T:* 071–834 9221; 2 Dr Johnson's Buildings, Temple, EC4. *Clubs:* Carlton, Pratt's, Naval.   *Died 3 May 1992.*

IRVING, Sir Charles (Graham), Kt 1990; DL; consultant on public affairs; County and District Councillor; *b* 4 May 1924. *Educ:* Glengarth Sch., Cheltenham; Lucton Sch.,

Hereford. Mem. Cheltenham Borough Council, 1947–74 (Alderman 1959–May 1967, and Sept. 1967–74); Mem., Cheltenham DC, 1974–; Mem. Gloucestershire CC, 1948– (Chm., Social Services Cttee, 1974–); Mayor of Cheltenham, 1958–60 and 1971–72; Dep. Mayor, 1959–63; Alderman of Gloucestershire County, 1965–74; contested (C): Bilston, Staffs, 1970; Kingswood, Glos, Feb. 1974; MP (C) Cheltenham, Oct. 1974–1992. Former Member Cons. Parly Cttees: Aviation; Social Services; Mem., Select Cttee on Administration; Chairman: Select Cttee on Catering, 1979–92; All Party Mental Health Cttee, 1979–92; All Party Cttee CHAR. Pres., Cheltenham Young Conservatives. Dir, Cheltenham Art and Literary Festival Co. (responsible for the only contemp. Festival of Music in England); Founder Mem., Univ. Cttee for Gloucestershire; Pres., Cheltenham and Dist Hotels' Assoc. Member: Bridgehead Housing Assoc. Ltd; Nat. Council for the Care and Resettlement of Offenders (Nat. Dep. Chm., 1974); (Chm.) NACRO Regional Council for South West; Nat. Council of St Leonard's Housing Assoc. Ltd; (Chm.) SW Midlands Housing Assoc. Ltd; (Chm.) Cheltenham and Dist Housing Assoc. Ltd, 1972; SW Regional Hosp. Bd, 1971–72; Glos AHA, 1974–; (Chm.) Cheltenham Dist Local Govt Re-Organisation Cttee, 1972; Founder and Chm., Nat. Victims Assoc., 1973; Chm., Stonham Housing Assoc., 1976–. Chairman: Irving Hotels Ltd, 1949–67; Irving Engineering Co., 1949–67; Western Travel, 1986–91; New Bridge, 1990–. Mem. NUJ; MIPR 1964. Hon. MA Cheltenham and Gloucester Coll. of Higher Educn, 1992. Freedom, Borough of Cheltenham, 1977. DL Gloucestershire, 1992. *Publications:* pamphlets (as Chm. SW Region of NACRO and SW Midlands Housing Assoc. Ltd, 1970–73) include: Prisoner and Industry; After-care in the Community; Penal Budgeting; What about the Victim; Dosser's Dream—Planner's Nightmare; pioneered Frontsheet (1st prison newspaper); reported in national papers, Quest, Social Services, Glos Life, etc. *Recreations:* antiques, social work. *Address:* The Grange, Malvern Road, Cheltenham, Glos GL50 2JH. *T:* Cheltenham (01242) 523083. *Club:* St Stephen's Constitutional.   *Died 30 March 1995.*

IRVING, Prof. Harry Munroe Napier Hetherington; Professor of Inorganic and Structural Chemistry, University of Leeds, 1961–71, Professor Emeritus, since 1972; Professor of Analytical Science, University of Cape Town, 1979–85 (of Theoretical Chemistry, 1978); retired; *b* 19 Nov. 1905; *s* of John and Clara Irving; *m* 1st, 1934, Monica Mary Wildsmith (*d* 1972); no *c*; 2nd, 1975, Dr Anne Mawby. *Educ:* St Bees Sch., Cumberland; The Queen's Coll., Oxford. BA 1927; First Class in Final Honour Sch. (Chemistry), 1928; MA, DPhil 1930; DSc 1958 (all Oxon); LRAM 1930. Univ. Demonstrator in Chemistry, Oxford, 1934–61; Lectr in Organic Chemistry, The Queen's Coll., 1930–34; Fellow and Tutor, St Edmund Hall, 1938–51, Vice-Principal, 1951–61, Emeritus-Fellow, 1961–. Member: Chem. Soc., 1935– (Council, 1954; Perkin Elmer Award, 1974); Soc. Chem. Ind., 1935– (Gold Medal, 1980); Soc. for Analytical Chemists, 1950– (Council, 1952–57, 1965–67; Vice-Pres. 1955–57; Gold Medal, 1971); Fellow Royal Inst. of Chemistry, 1948– (Council, 1950–52, 1962–65; Vice-Pres. 1965–67); Mem., S African Chem. Inst., 1979. Has lectured extensively in America, Africa and Europe; broadcasts on scientific subjects. FRSSAf. Hon. DTech Brunel Univ., 1970. *Publications:* (trans.) Schwarzenbach and Flaschka's Complexometric Titrations; Short History of Analytical Chemistry, 1974; Dithizone, 1977; A History of the Halogens, 1993; numerous papers in various learned jls. *Recreations:* music, foreign travel, ice-skating. *Address:* 1 North Grange Mount, Leeds LS6 2BY.
Died 20 June 1993.

IRVING, James Tutin, MA Oxon and Cantab, MD, PhD Cantab; Professor of Physiology in the School of Dental Medicine at Harvard University and the Forsyth Dental Center, 1961–68, Professor Emeritus, 1968, Visiting Lecturer in Oral Biology, 1973–77; Emeritus Professor, National Institute on Aging, Baltimore, 1978–81; *b* Christchurch, New Zealand, 3 May 1902; *s* of Dr William Irving, NZ; *m* 1937, Janet, *d* of Hon. Nicholas O'Connor, New York. *Educ:* Christ's Coll., New Zealand; Caius Coll., Cambridge; Trinity Coll., Oxford; Guy's Hospital. Double First Class Hons, Nat. Sci. Tripos, Cambridge, 1923–24; Scholar and Prizeman, Caius Coll., 1923. Benn. W. Levy and Frank Smart Student, 1924–26; Beit Memorial Fellow, 1926–28; Lecturer in Physiology, Bristol Univ., 1931, and Leeds Univ., 1934; Head of Physiology Dept, Rowett Research Inst., and part-time lecturer, Aberdeen Univ., 1936; Prof. of Physiology, Cape Town Univ., 1939–53, Fellow 1948; Professor of Experimental Odontology, and Dir of the Joint CSIR and Univ. of Witwatersrand Dental Research Unit, 1953–59; Prof. of Anatomy, Harvard Sch. of Dental Med., 1959–61; Visiting Professor: Univ. of Illinois Dental Sch. 1947 and 1956; Univ. of Pennsylvania, 1951; Univ. of California, 1956. Chm., Gordon Conference on Bone and Teeth, 1969. Late Hon. Physiologist to Groote Schuur Hosp. Editor, Archives of Oral Biology, 1962–87. AM (Hon.) Harvard. Fellow Odont. Soc. S Africa. Hon. Life Mem. of New York Academy of Sciences. Mem. of Soc. of Sigma Xi. Hon. Mem. of Soc. of Omicron Kappa Upsilon. S African Medal for war services (non-military), 1948. Isaac Schour Meml Award for Res. in Anatomical Scis, 1972. *Publications:* Calcium Metabolism, 1957; Calcium and Phosphorus Metabolism, 1973; many papers in physiological and medical journals, chiefly on nutrition, and bone and tooth formation; also publications on nautical history. *Recreations:* music, gardening, nautical research. *Address:* (home) 5 Peele House Square, Manchester, Mass 01944, USA; (office) 140 The Fenway, Boston, Mass 02115, USA. *Club:* Inanda (Johannesburg).

Died 13 April 1992.

IRVING, Robert Augustine, DFC and Bar, 1943; Musical Director, New York City Ballet, New York, 1958–89; *b* 28 Aug. 1913; *s* of late R. L. G. Irving; unmarried. *Educ:* Winchester; New Coll., Oxford; Royal College of Music. Répétiteur, Royal Opera House, 1936; Music master, Winchester Coll., 1936–40. RA, 1940–41; RAF (Coastal Command), 1941–45. Associate Conductor, BBC Scottish Orchestra, 1945–48; Conductor, Royal Opera House (The Royal Ballet), 1949–58. Many recordings for HMV and Decca, with Philharmonia and Royal Philharmonic Orchestras, also public concerts with these orchestras, London Philharmonic Orchestra and leading Amer. symphony orchestras. Wrote music for film, Floodtide, 1948; for New York production of As You Like It, 1949. Capezio Award, 1975; Dance Magazine Award, 1984. *Recreations:* racing, bridge, mountaineering. *Address:* c/o New York City Ballet, New York State Theatre, Columbus Avenue and 62nd Street, New York, NY 10023, USA. *Club:* Brooks's.   *Died 13 Sept. 1991.*

IVEAGH, 3rd Earl of, *cr* 1919; **Arthur Francis Benjamin Guinness;** Bt 1885; Baron Iveagh 1891; Viscount Iveagh 1905; Viscount Elveden 1919; Member, Seanad Eireann, 1973–77; Chairman, 1962–86, and President, 1986–92, Guinness PLC; *b* 20 May 1937; *o s* of Viscount Elveden (killed in action, 1945) and Lady Elizabeth Hare (*d* 1990), *yr d* of 4th Earl of Listowel; *S* grandfather, 1967; *m* 1963, Miranda Daphne Jane (marr. diss. 1984), *d* of Major Michael Smiley, Castle Fraser, Aberdeenshire; two *s* two *d*. *Educ:* Eton; Trinity Coll., Cambridge; Univ. of Grenoble. *Heir: s* Viscount Elveden, *b* 10 Aug. 1969. *Address:* St James's Gate, Dublin 8. *Clubs:* White's; Royal Yacht Squadron (Cowes); Kildare Street and University (Dublin).   *Died 18 June 1992.*

IVES, Arthur Glendinning Loveless, CVO 1954 (MVO 1945); Secretary, King Edward's Hospital Fund for London, 1938–60, retired; *b* 19 Aug. 1904; *s* of late Rev. E. J. Ives, Wesleyan Minister; *m* 1929, Doris Marion (*d* 1987), *d* of Thomas Coke Boden; three *s* one *d. Educ:* Kingswood Sch.; Queen's Coll., Oxford (classical scholar; MA). George Webb Medley Junior Scholarship for Economics, Oxford Univ., 1926. London Chamber of Commerce, 1928–29; joined staff of King Edward's Hosp. Fund for London, 1929. Seriously injured in railway accident at Lewisham, Dec. 1957. A Governor of Kingswood Sch., 1954–72. *Publications:* British Hospitals (Britain in Pictures), 1948; Kingswood School in Wesley's Day and Since, 1970; contrib. to The Times, Lancet, etc, on hospital administration and allied topics. *Address:* The Cedars, Bordyke, Tonbridge, Kent. *Club:* Athenæum.

Died 1 Oct. 1991.

J

JACKMAN, Air Marshal Sir Douglas, KBE 1959 (CBE 1943); CB 1946; Air Officer Commanding-in-Chief, Royal Air Force Maintenance Command, 1958–61, retired; *b* 26 Oct. 1902; twin *s* of late A. J. Jackman; *m* 1931, Marjorie Leonore, *d* of late A. Hyland, Kingsdown, Kent. *Educ:* HMS Worcester. Officer Royal Mail Line until 1926; joined RAF, 1926; served in Iraq, 1928–30, in No 55 Squadron; in UK with Wessex Bombing Area and at Cranwell until 1934; to Middle East Command in 1934 and served at Aboukir until 1938, when posted to HQ Middle East until 1943; with Mediterranean Air Command and Mediterranean Allied Air Forces HQ until 1944; HQ Balkan Air Force, 1944–45 (despatches five times, CB, CBE, Comdr Order George 1st of Greece with Swords, AFC [Greek]); Dir of Movements Air Ministry, 1946–47; idc 1948; Dir of Organization (forecasting and planning), Air Ministry, 1949–52; AOC No 40 Group, 1952–55; Dir-Gen. of Equipment, Air Ministry, 1955–58; Co-ordinator, Anglo-American Relations, Air Ministry, 1961–64. *Publication:* technical, on planning, 1942. *Recreations:* golf (Member: RAF Golfing Soc.; Seniors Golfing Soc., Natal), woodworking. *Address:* 226 Ninth Avenue, Greyville, Durban 4001, Republic of South Africa. *Club:* Royal Over-Seas League. *Died 15 June 1991.*

JACKS, Hector Beaumont, MA; Headmaster of Bedales School, 1946–62; *b* 25 June 1903; *s* of late Dr L. P. Jacks; *m* 1st, Mary (*d* 1959), *d* of Rev. G. N. Nuttall Smith; one *s* one *d*; 2nd, Nancy, *d* of F. E. Strudwick. *Educ:* Magdalen Coll. Sch., Oxford; Wadham Coll., Oxford. Asst master, Wellington Coll., Berks, 1925–32; Headmaster of Willaston Sch., Nantwich, 1932–37. *Recreation:* gardening. *Address:* Applegarth, Spotted Cow Lane, Buxted, Sussex. *T:* Buxted (0825) 732296.
Died 9 Jan. 1994.

JACKSON, Adrian Alexander W.; *see* Ward-Jackson.

JACKSON, Prof. Daphne Frances, OBE 1987; FIEE; FInstP; Professor and Head of Department of Physics, University of Surrey, since 1971; *b* 23 Sept. 1936; *d* of Albert Henry Jackson and Frances Ethel Elliott. *Educ:* Peterborough County Grammar Sch.; Imperial Coll. of Sci. and Tech., Univ. of London (BSc Phys 1958; ARCS 1958; DSc 1970); Battersea Coll. of Sci. and Technol. (PhD 1962). FInstP 1976; MIEEE 1982; FIEE 1984. Lectr in Physics, Battersea Coll. of Technol., 1962–66; Surrey University: Reader in Nuclear Physics, 1966–71; Dean, Faculty of Science, 1984–88. Res. Asst Prof., Univ. of Washington, 1963–64; Visiting Professor: Univ. of Maryland, 1970; Univ. de Louvain, 1972; Univ. of Lund, 1980–82. Member: Nuclear Phys Bd, SERC, 1973–76 (Mem., Phys Cttee, Sci. Bd, 1974–76, 1985–88); Metrology and Standards Req. Bd, DTI, 1973–75; NRPB, 1980–85; W Surrey and NE Hants DHA, 1981– (Vice-Chm., 1983–84); Regional Sci. Cttee, 1976–85, Regional Res. Cttee, 1983–87, SW Thames RHA; Ind./Educn Adv. Cttee, DTI, 1983–88; Coordinating Gp for Develt of Training for Women, MSC, 1983–89; Phys. Scis Sub-Cttee, UGC, 1985–89; Sci. Consultative Gp, BBC, 1987–; Adv. Council on R&D for Fuel and Power, Dept of Energy, 1988–; Bd, Meteorol Office Agency, 1990–; Sch. Exams and Assessment Council, 1989–. Director: Surrey Univ. Press, 1984– (Chm., 1984–87); Surrey Medical Imaging Systems Ltd, 1986–. Hon. Sec., Women's Engineering Soc., 1988– (Pres., 1983–85; Vice-Pres., 1981–83); Vice-Pres., Inst. of Physics, 1974–78. FRSA 1984. Liveryman, Co. of Engineers, 1986–. DUniv Open, 1987; Hon. DSc Exeter, 1988. *Publications:* Nuclear Reactions, 1970; (with R. C. Barrett) Nuclear Sizes and Structure, 1977; (with K. Kouris and N. M. Spyrou) Imaging with Ionising Radiations, 1982; (ed) Imaging with Non Ionising Radiations, 1983; Atoms and Quanta, 1989; papers and articles on nuclear physics, med. physics, educn, sci. policy in learned jls. *Recreations:* writing, encouraging women in science and engineering. *Address:* 5 St Omer Road, Guildford, Surrey GU1 2DA. *T:* Guildford (0483) 573996. *Club:* National Liberal.
Died 8 Feb. 1991.

JACKSON, Eric Stead, CB 1954; Under-Secretary, Department of Trade and Industry, 1970–71; *b* 22 Aug. 1909; *yr s* of Stead Jackson, Shipley Glen, Yorks; *m* 1938, Yvonne Renée (*d* 1982), *o d* of Devereaux Doria De Brétigny, Victoria, BC; one *s* one *d*. *Educ:* Bradford Grammar Sch.; Corpus Christi Coll., Oxford (Scholar). 1st Class Hons Math. Mods, Math. Finals and Nat. Sci. Finals, Jun. Math. schol., 1930; MA. Asst Principal, Air Ministry, 1932; Sec., British Air Mission to Australia and NZ, 1939; Private Sec. to Minister of Aircraft Production, 1942, and to Resident Minister in Washington, 1943; Sec., British Supply Council in N America, 1944; Dir-Gen. Aircraft Branch, Control Commission, Berlin, 1945; Dep. Pres. Economic Sub-Commission, 1947; British Head of Bizonal Delegation to OEEC, Paris, 1948; Under Sec., Ministry of Supply, 1950–56; Dir-Gen., Atomic Weapons, Ministry of Supply, 1956–59; Under-Secretary: Min. of Aviation, 1959–67; Min. of Technology, 1967–70. *Address:* 10 Ditchley Road, Charlbury, Oxfordshire. *T:* Charlbury (0608) 810682. *Died 20 June 1991.*

JACKSON, Frederick Hume, CMG 1978; OBE 1966; HM Diplomatic Service, retired; Consul-General, Düsseldorf, 1975–78; *b* 8 Sept. 1918; *o s* of late Maj.-Gen. G. H. N. Jackson, CB, CMG, DSO, Rathmore, Winchcombe, Glos and Eileen, *d* of J. Hume Dudgeon, Merville, Booterstown, Co. Dublin; *m* 1950, Anne Gibson; two *s* one *d* (and one *s* decd). *Educ:* Winchester; Clare Coll., Cambridge (MA). Military service, 1939–46: GSO3 (Intelligence), HQ 1 Corps District; Colonial Service (Tanganyika), 1946–57; FO, 1957–60; Head of Chancery, Saigon, 1960–62; 1st Sec., Washington, 1962–67; Counsellor and Dep. Head, UK Delegn to European Communities, Brussels, 1967–69; UK Resident Representative, Internat. Atomic Energy Agency, 1969–75; UK Perm. Representative to UNIDO, 1971–75. Chm., Sevenoaks Cons. Assoc., 1982–85, Vice-Pres., 1985–. *Recreations:* fishing, shooting. *Address:* Orchard Lodge, Leigh, Tonbridge, Kent TN11 8QJ. *T:* Hildenborough (01732) 833495; c/o Barclays Bank, St Nicholas Street, Scarborough, North Yorks YO11 2HS. *Club:* Flyfishers'. *Died 13 Oct. 1994.*

JACKSON, Sir Gordon; *see* Jackson, Sir R. G.

JACKSON, Prof. Kenneth Hurlstone, CBE 1985; FBA 1957; FSAScot 1951; FRSE 1977; Professor of Celtic Languages, Literatures, History and Antiquities, Edinburgh University, 1950–79; *b* 1 Nov. 1909; *s* of Alan Stuart Jackson and Lucy Hurlstone; *m* 1936, Janet Dall Galloway, Hillside, Kinross-shire; one *s* one *d*. *Educ:* Whitgift Sch., Croydon; St John's Coll., Cambridge

(Exhibitioner and Scholar; Hon. Fellow, 1979). First Cl. Hons with Distinction, Classical Tripos, 1930 and 1931 (Senior Classic, 1931); BA 1931; First Cl. Hons with Distinction, Archaeology and Anthropology Tripos, 1932; Sir William Brown medals for Greek and Latin verse, 1930 (two), 1931; MA 1935; LittD 1954. Allen Research Studentship, 1932–34; research in Celtic at University Colls of North Wales and Dublin; Fellowship at St John's Coll., and Faculty Lectr in Celtic, Cambridge Univ., 1934–39; Lectureship, 1939, Associate Professorship, 1940–49, Professorship, 1949–50, Celtic Languages and Literatures, Harvard Univ. (Hon. AM 1940). Editor of the Journal of Celtic Studies, 1949–57. Corresp. Fellow of Mediæval Acad. of America, 1951; President: Scottish Anthropological and Folklore Soc., 1952–60; English Place-Name Soc., 1979–84 (Vice Pres., 1973–79; Hon. Pres., 1980–85); Internat. Congress of Celtic Studies, 1975–84; Vice-Pres. of Soc. of Antiquaries of Scotland, 1960–63; Mem., Comité Internat. des Sciences Onomastiques, 1955–69, Hon. Mem., 1981; Mem. Council for Name Studies in Great Britain and Ireland, 1961–85; one of HM Commissioners for Ancient Monuments (Scotland), 1963–85. War service in the British Imperial Censorship, Bermuda (Uncommon Languages), 1942–44; in the US censorship, 1944. Hon. DLitt Celt. Ireland, 1958; Hon. DLitt Wales, 1963; Hon. DUniv Haute-Bretagne, 1971. Hon. Mem. Mod. Language Assoc. of America, 1958; Hon. Mem. Royal Irish Academy, 1965; Associate Mem., Royal Belgian Acad. for Scis, Letters and Fine Arts, 1975. Derek Allen Prize, British Acad., 1979. *Publications:* Early Welsh Gnomic Poems, 1935; Studies in Early Celtic Nature Poetry, 1935; Cath Maighe Léna, 1938; Scéalta ón mBlascaod, 1939; A Celtic Miscellany, 1951, rev. 1971; Language and History in Early Britain, 1953; (contrib.) Study of Manx Phonology, 1955; The International Popular Tale and Early Welsh Tradition, 1961; The Oldest Irish Tradition, 1964; A Historical Phonology of Breton, 1967; The Gododdin, 1969; The Gaelic Notes in the Book of Deer, 1972; articles on Celtic languages, literature, history, folklore and archaeology in Zeitschrift für Celtische Philologie, Etudes Celtiques, Bulletin of the Bd of Celtic Studies, Antiquity, Journal of Roman Studies, Folklore, Journal of Celtic Studies, Scottish Gaelic Studies, Speculum, Modern Philology, etc. *Recreation:* walking. *Address:* 34 Cluny Drive, Edinburgh EH10 6DX. *Club:* Edinburgh University Staff. *Died 20 Feb. 1991.*

JACKSON, Laura (Riding); *b* New York City, 16 Jan. 1901; American mother (Sarah) and naturalised (Austrian-born) father (Nathaniel S. Reichenthal); changed surname to Riding, 1927; *m* 1920, Louis Gottschalk (marr. diss. 1925); *m* 1941, Schuyler Brinckerhoff Jackson (*d* 1968) (American writer; poetry-editor of Time, 1938–43). *Educ:* American public schools; Cornell University. First published poems in American poetry magazines; member of group of Southern poets, The Fugitives; went to England in 1926, remaining abroad until 1939; engaging in writing and allied activities, seeking a single terminology of truth to supersede our confused terminological diversity (*eg*, as Editor of Epilogue, a critical miscellany); was co-operator of Seizin Press, first author of A Survey of Modernist Poetry (Robert Graves, collaborator), 1927; devoted herself to helping other poets with their work; subsequently renounced poetry as humanly inadequate and concentrated on direct linguistic handling of truth-problem, studying ways to intensify people's consciousness of word-meanings; working long with husband on a book in which the principles of language and the principles of definition were to be brought into relation, entitled Rational Meaning: A New Foundation for the Definition of Words (unpublished). Mark Rothko Appreciation Award, 1971; Guggenheim Fellowship award, 1973; Nat. Endowment for the Arts Fellowship Award (for writing of her memoirs, then in progress), 1979; Bollinger Prize, 1989–90. *Publications include:* (as Laura Riding, until 1941, thereafter as Laura (Riding) Jackson) individual books of poems (10), from 1926; Contemporaries and Snobs, 1928; Anarchism Is Not Enough, 1928; Experts are Puzzled, 1930; Progress of Stories, 1935, new edn with additional stories, and new prefatory and supplementary material, 1982; A Trojan Ending, 1937, new edn 1984 (Spanish trans., 1986); The World and Ourselves, 1938; Collected Poems, 1938, new edn with new preface and extensive appendix 1980; Lives of Wives, 1939, new edn 1988; The Telling (a personal evangel-complete magazine publication, Chelsea, USA), 1967, enl. edn in book form, UK 1972, USA 1973; Selected Poems: in five sets, 1970, USA 1973; Writings of 50 Years—Author's Miscellany, entire biannual issue, Chelsea (USA), autumn 1976; Description of Life, 1980; Some Communications of Broad Reference, 1983; contribs to magazines. *Address:* Box 35, Wabasso, Florida 32970, USA.
Died 2 Sept. 1991.

JACKSON, Hon. Sir Lawrence (Walter), KCMG 1970; Kt 1964; BA, LLB; Judge, 1949–77, and Chief Justice, 1969–77, Supreme Court of Western Australia; Chancellor, University of Western Australia, 1968–81; *b* Dulwich, South Australia, 27 Sept. 1913; *s* of L. S. Jackson; *m* 1937, Mary, *d* of T. H. Donaldson; one *s* two *d. Educ:* Fort Street High Sch., Sydney; University of Sydney. *Recreations:* swimming, golf. *Address:* 57 Lisle Street, Mount Claremont, WA 6010, Australia. *Club:* Weld (Perth, WA). *Died 5 June 1993.*

JACKSON, Air Vice-Marshal Sir Ralph (Coburn), KBE 1973; CB 1963; Honorary Civil Consultant in Medicine to Royal Air Force; Honorary Consultant (Medicine) to RAF Benevolent Fund; Medical Adviser and Director, French Hospital (La Providence), Rochester; *b* 22 June 1914; *s* of Ralph Coburn Jackson and Phillis Jackson (*née* Dodds); *m* 1939, Joan Lucy Crowley; two *s* two *d. Educ:* Oakmount Sch., Arnside; Guy's Hosp., London. MRCS 1937; FRCPE 1960 (MRCPE 1950); FRCP 1972 (MRCP 1968, LRCP 1937). Qualified in Medicine Guy's Hosp., 1937; House Officer appts, Guy's Hosp., 1937–38; commnd in RAF as MO, Nov. 1938; served in France, 1939–40; Russia, 1941; W Africa, 1942–43 (despatches); Sen. MO, 46 Gp for Brit. Casualty Air Evac., 1944–45 (despatches); Med. Specialist, RAF Hosps Wroughton, Aden and Halton, 1946–52; Consultant in Med., Princess Mary's RAF Hosp. Halton, 1952–63, RAF Hosp., Wegberg, Germany, 1964–66; Consultant Advr in Medicine, 1966–74; Sen. Consultant to RAF, 1971–75; QHP 1969–75. Advr in Medicine to CAA, 1966–75; Consultant Medical Referee: Confedn Life Insce Co., 1973–87; Victory Re-insurance Co., 1975–87. Chm., Defence Med. Services, Postgrad. Council, 1973–75. MacArthur Lectr, Univ. Edinburgh, 1959. Fellow, Assurance Med. Soc.; FRSM; Fellow, Huguenot Soc., 1985; Fellow, RSPB, 1981; Member: Wild Fowl Trust, 1982; Soc. of Genealogists; RAF Histl Soc. Liveryman, Worshipful Soc. of Apothecaries; Freeman, City of London. Lady Cade Medal, RCS, 1960. *Publications:* papers on acute renal failure, the artificial kidney and routine electrocardiography in various medical books and journals, 1959–74. *Recreations:* birdwatching, genealogy. *Address:* Cherry Trees, 15 Ball Road, Pewsey, Wiltshire SN9 5BL. *T:* Marlborough (0672) 62042. *Club:* Royal Air Force. *Died 1 Nov. 1991.*

JACKSON, Comdr Sir Robert (Gillman Allen), AC 1986; KCVO 1962; Kt 1956; CMG 1944; OBE (mil.) 1941; international administrator, retired; Chairman Emeritus: Global Broadcasting Foundation, Washington, DC, since 1987; Society for Multi-Purpose Projects, Cambridge,

Mass, since 1987; Consultant to Volta River Authority, Ghana, since 1962 (Member of Board 1965–76); Senior Consultant to McKinsey & Company since 1970; Counsellor to Interim Mekong Committee, since 1978; *b* 8 Nov. 1911; *s* of Archibald Jackson; *m* 1st, 1937, Margaret (marr. annulled), *o d* of Ronald Dick, Hobart; 2nd, 1950, Barbara Ward (Baroness Jackson of Lodsworth, DBE) (*d* 1981); one *s*. RAN, 1929–37; transf. to Malta and RN, 1937; Chief Staff Officer to Gov. and C-in-C, Malta GC, 1940; planned Malta Comd Defence Scheme; re-armament of the Fortress; develt Co-ordinated Supply Scheme, 1940 (OBE); transf. by Cabinet decision from Navy and Army as Principal Asst to UK Cabinet Minister of State in ME and Dir-Gen., ME Supply Centre (Anglo-American para-mil. orgn for co-ordn civilian and mil. supply ops), 1942–45; develt Aid to Russia Supply route; estab. long-term anti-locust campaign, 1942 (CMG); assisted Bengal famine op., 1943; AFHQ for special duties in Greece, 1944–45; transf. to HM Treasury, 1945; Sen. Dep. Dir-Gen. of UNRRA, 1945–47, and, in 1945, i/c of UNRRA's ops in Europe (inc. 8,500,000 displaced persons); supervised transfer of UNRRA's residual functions to UN, UNESCO, WHO, FAO, and assisted in establishment of IRO (subseq. UNHCR), and International Children's Emergency Fund, 1947 (UNICEF); services recognised by various governments in Europe and Asia; Asst Sec.-Gen. for Co-ordination in the UN, 1948; HM Treasury, for duties with Lord Pres. of Council, 1949; Perm. Sec., Min. of Nat. Development, Australia, 1950–52 (Snowy Mountains Scheme); Adviser to Govt of India on Development Plans, 1952, 1957 and 1962–63, and to Govt of Pakistan, 1952; Chm. of Preparatory Commission for Volta River multi-purpose project, Gold Coast, 1953–56; Chm., Development Commission, Ghana, 1956–61 (Kt); Organisation of Royal Tours in Ghana, 1959 and 1961(KCVO); Advr to Min. of Defence, India, 1962; Mem. Adv. Bd, Mekong Project, SE Asia, 1962–76; Adviser to President of Liberia, 1962–79; Special Consultant in about 50 countries, including to Administrator, UNDP, 1963–72, Special Adviser, 1978–80; Chm., UN gp reporting on Zambia's security, 1963; Comr i/c, Survey of UN Develt System, 1968–71; Under Sec.-Gen. i/c UN Relief Ops in Bangladesh, 1972–74; Under Sec.-Gen. i/c UN assistance to Zambia, 1973–78, to Indo-China, 1975–78, to Cape Verde Is, 1975–78, to São Tomé and Príncipe, 1977–78, to Kampuchea and Thailand, 1979–84; Under Sec. Gen. and Sen. Adviser to Sec. Gen., UN, 1984–87. Lectures: Chisholm Meml, WHO, 1986; Brunel Meml, MIT, 1987; Lord Boyd Orr Meml, Aberdeen, 1987. Member: Cttee, Fédération Mondiale des Villes Jumelées Cités Unies, 1972; IUCN Commn on Environmental Policy, 1972; Overseas Service Bureau, Australia, 1976–; ABC (Assistance to Blind Children in Bangladesh), 1980–; Dag Hammarskjöld Foundn, Stockholm, 1981–. Trustee, Inter-Action (UK), 1986–; Patron, PACE-UK Internat. Affairs, 1983–. Mem. Internat. Jury, Prize of Institut de la Vie, 1972–. Freeman, City of Prague, 1946. Hon. DL Syracuse. *Publications:* An International Development Authority, 1955; Report of the Volta River Preparatory Commission, 1956; A Study of the United Nations Development System, 1969; Report on Sen. Volunteers in UN System, 1978; Report on reinforcement of UN Indust. Develt Orgn, 1979; various articles on development, multi-purpose projects and disaster operations. *Recreations:* reading, deepsea fishing, cricket, welfare of tigers. *Address:* c/o Hon. Robert Jackson, 64 Clarendon Drive, SW15 1AH; United Nations, New York City, NY 10017, USA; Palais des Nations, Geneva, Switzerland. *Clubs:* Victoria (Jersey); Melbourne (Victoria).

Died 12 Jan. 1991.

JACKSON, Sir (Ronald) Gordon, AK 1983 (AC 1976); Chairman, Australian Industry Development Corporation, 1983–90; Member of Board, Reserve Bank of Australia, 1975–90; Chancellor, Australian National University, 1987–90; *b* 5 May 1924; *s* of late R. V. Jackson; *m* 1948, Margaret Pratley; one *s* one *d. Educ:* Brisbane Grammar Sch.; Queensland Univ. (BCom). FASA; FAIM. Served AIF, 1942–46. Joined CSR Ltd, 1941; Gen. Man., 1972–82; Dir, 1972–85; Dep. Chm., 1983–85. Chairman: Hampton Australia Ltd, 1984–86; Interscan Internat. Ltd, 1984–87; Austek Microsystems Ltd, 1984–87; Director: Rothmans Holdings Ltd, 1983–; Rockwell Internat. Pty Ltd, 1985–88; Mem., Pacific Adv. Council, United Technologies Corp., 1984–. Foundn Chm., Bd of Management, Aust. Graduate Sch. of Management, 1976–81; Pres., Order of Australia Assoc., 1983–86 (Foundn Chm., 1980–83); Vice-Pres., Australia/Japan Business Co-operation Cttee, 1977–; Hon. Life Mem., German–Australian Chamber of Industry and Commerce, 1986 (Foundn Pres., 1977–80; Chm. 1980–85); Member: Police Bd of NSW, 1983– (Chm., 1988–); Salvation Army Adv. Bd, 1983– (Chm., Red Shield Appeal, 1981–85; Pres. 1986–). Hon. DSc NSW, 1983. James N. Kirby Meml Award, Instn of Prodn Engrs, 1976; John Storey Medal, Aust. Inst. of Management, 1978; Prime Minister of Japan's Trade Award, 1987. Comdr, Order of Merit (FRG), 1980; Grand Cordon (first class), Order of the Sacred Treasure of Japan, 1987. *Recreations:* sailing, fishing. *Address:* 14 Nithdale Street, Pymble, NSW 2073, Australia. *Clubs:* Union, Australian (Sydney); Queensland (Brisbane); Royal Sydney Yacht.

Died 8 June 1991.

JACKSON-STOPS, Gervase Frank Ashworth, OBE 1987; FSA 1985; Architectural Adviser, National Trust, since 1975; *b* 26 April 1947; 2nd *s* of late Anthony Ashworth Jackson-Stops and Jean Jackson-Stops, JP, DL, ARIBA. *Educ:* Harrow; Christ Church, Oxford (BA 1968; MA 1971). Museums Assoc. Studentship, V&A, 1969–71; Res. Asst, Nat. Trust, 1972–75; regular contributor to Country Life, 1973–. Trustee, Attingham Summer Sch., 1983–90; Curator, Treasure Houses of Britain exhibn, Nat. Gallery of Art, Washington, 1985–86 (Presidential Award for Design, 1986); Curator, Robert Adam and Kedleston exhibn, RIBA, 1987, Amer. Museums, 1988–89; Co-Curator, Courts and Colonies exhibn, NY and Pittsburgh, 1988–89; Curator: An English Arcadia exhibn, Amer. Museums, 1991–92, London, York and Bristol, 1992–93; People and Places (NT centenary exhibn of watercolours), 1995. Member: Historic Buildings Adv. Cttee, English Heritage, 1986–88; Reviewing Cttee on Export of Works of Art, 1988–. Pres., Friends of Northampton Museum and Art Gall., 1986–. Editor: Nat. Trust Year Book, 1975–78; Nat. Trust Studies, 1979–82. *Publications:* The English Country House: a grand tour, 1985; The Country House Garden, 1987; The Country House in Perspective, 1990; Nash's Views of the Royal Pavilion, Brighton, 1991; An English Arcadia: designs for gardens and garden buildings, 1992; (ed) 100 Treasures of the National Trust, 1995. *Recreation:* building arbours and grottoes. *Address:* The Menagerie, Horton, Northampton NN7 2BX. *T:* Northampton (01604) 870486. *Club:* Travellers'.

Died 2 July 1995.

JACOB, Ven. Bernard Victor; Archdeacon of Reigate (title changed from Kingston-upon-Thames, 1986), 1977–88, then Archdeacon Emeritus; *b* 20 Nov. 1921; *m* 1946, Dorothy Joan Carey; one *s* two *d. Educ:* Liverpool Institute; St Peter's College (MA) and Wycliffe Hall, Oxford. Deacon, 1950; priest, 1951; Curate, Middleton, Lancs, 1950–54; Vicar, Ulverston, Lancs, 1954–59; Vicar, Bilston, Staffs, 1959–64; Warden of Scargill House, Yorks, 1964–68; Rector of Mortlake, 1968–77.

Recreations: travel, reading, enjoying life. *Address:* 4 The Peacheries, Chichester, West Sussex PO19 2NP.
Died 7 Dec. 1992.

JACOB, Lt-Gen. Sir (Edward) Ian (Claud), GBE 1960 (KBE 1946; CBE 1942); CB 1944; DL; late Royal Engineers, Colonel, retired and Hon. Lieutenant-General; Chairman, Matthews Holdings Ltd, 1970–76; *b* 27 Sept. 1899; *s* of late Field Marshal Sir Claud Jacob, GCB, GCSI, KCMG and Clara Pauline, *d* of Rev. J. L. Wyatt; *m* 1924, Cecil Bisset Treherne (*d* 1991); two *s. Educ:* Wellington Coll.; RMA, Woolwich; King's Coll., Cambridge (BA). 2nd Lieut, Royal Engineers, 1918; Capt. 1929; Bt Major, 1935; Major, 1938; Bt Lt-Col, 1939; Col, 1943. Waziristan, 1922–23; Staff Coll., 1931–32; GSO3 War Office, 1934–36; Bde-Maj., Canal Bde, Egypt, 1936–38; Military Asst Sec., Cttee of Imperial Defence, 1938; Military Asst Sec. to the War Cabinet, 1939–46; retired pay, 1946. Controller of European Services, BBC, 1946; Dir of Overseas Services, BBC, 1947 (on leave of absence during 1952); Chief Staff Officer to Minister of Defence and Deputy Sec. (Mil.) of the Cabinet during 1952; Dir-Gen. of the BBC, 1952–60; Director: Fisons, 1960–70; EMI, 1960–73; Chm., Covent Garden Market Authority, 1961–66; a Trustee, Imperial War Museum, 1966–73. CC, E Suffolk, 1960–70, Alderman, 1970–74; CC Suffolk, 1974–77. JP Suffolk, 1961–69; DL Suffolk, 1964–84. US Legion of Merit (Comdr). *Address:* The Red House, Woodbridge, Suffolk IP12 4AD. *T:* Woodbridge (0394) 2001. *Club:* Army and Navy.
Died 24 April 1993.

JACQUES, Baron *cr* 1968 (Life Peer), of Portsea Island; **John Henry Jacques;** Chairman of the Co-operative Union Ltd, 1964–70; *b* 11 Jan. 1905; *s* of Thomas Dobson Jacques and Annie Bircham; *m* 1st, 1929, Constance White (*d* 1987); two *s* one *d*; 2nd, 1989, Violet Jacques. *Educ:* Victoria Univ., Manchester; (BA(Com)); Co-operative Coll. Sec-Man., Moorsley Co-operative Society Ltd, 1925–29; Tutor, Co-operative Coll., 1929–42; Accountant, Plymouth Co-operative Soc. Ltd, 1942–45; Chief Executive, Portsea Island Co-operative Soc. Ltd, Portsmouth, 1945–65; Pres., Co-operative Congress, 1961. Pres., Retail Trades Education Council, 1971–75. A Lord in Waiting (Govt Whip), 1974–77 and 1979; a Dep. Chm. of Cttees, 1977–85. JP Portsmouth, 1951–75. *Publications:* Book-Keeping I, II and III, 1940; Management Accounting, 1966; Manual on Co-operative Management, 1969. *Recreations:* walking, snooker, gardening, West-Highland terriers. *Address:* 23 Hartford House, Blount Road, Pembroke Park, Portsmouth PO1 2TN. *T:* Portsmouth (01705) 738111. *Club:* Co-operative (Portsmouth).
Died 20 Dec. 1995.

JACQUES, Robin; artist; illustrator of books; *b* 27 March 1920; *m* 1st, 1943, Patricia Bamford (decd); one *s*; 2nd, 1958, Azetta van der Merwe (decd); 3rd, Alexandra Mann (marr. diss.). *Educ:* Royal Masonic Schools, Bushey, Herts. Art Editor, Strand Mag., 1948–51; Principal Art Editor, COI Mags, 1951–53; *drawings for:* Hans Andersen Stories, 1953; James Joyce's Dubliners, 1954; James Joyce's Portrait of the Artist as a Young Man, 1955; Kipling's Kim, 1958; Thackeray's Vanity Fair, 1963; The Sea, Ships and Sailors, 1966; Collected Poems of W. B. Yeats, 1970; Henry James' The Europeans, 1982; Trollope's Dr Wortley's School, 1988; James' Portrait of a Lady, 1994; many illustrated books for children; graphic work for magazines and newspapers, including The Times, Observer, Strand Mag., Lilliput, Punch, Radio Times, Listener. *Publication:* Illustrators at Work, 1960. *Recreations:* music, reading. *Address:* 5 Abbots Place, NW6 4NP. *T:* 0171–624 7040.
Died 18 March 1995.

JAKEWAY, Sir (Francis) Derek, KCMG 1963 (CMG 1956); OBE 1948; *b* 6 June 1915; *s* of Francis Edward and Adeline Jakeway; *m* 1941, Phyllis Lindsay Watson, CStJ; three *s. Educ:* Hele's Sch., Exeter; Exeter Coll., Oxford (BA Hons Mod. Hist.). Colonial Administrative Service, Nigeria, 1937–54, seconded to Seychelles, 1946–49, to Colonial Office, 1949–51; Chief Sec., British Guiana, 1954–59; Chief Sec., Sarawak, 1959–63; Governor and C-in-C, Fiji, 1964–68. Chm., Devon AHA, 1974–82. KStJ 1964. *Address:* 78 Douglas Avenue, Exmouth, Devon EX8 2HG. *T:* Exmouth (0395) 271342.
Died 6 Nov. 1993.

JAMES OF RUSHOLME, Baron *cr* 1959 (Life Peer), of Fallowfield; **Eric John Francis James,** Kt 1956; Chairman, Royal Fine Art Commission, 1976–79 (Member, 1973–79); *b* 13 April 1909; *yr s* of Francis W. and Lilian James; *m* 1939, Cordelia, *d* of late Maj.-Gen. F. Wintour, CB, CBE; one *s. Educ:* Taunton's School, Southampton; Queen's Coll., Oxford (Exhibitioner and Hon. Scholar, 1927; Hon. Fellow, 1959). Goldsmiths' Exhibitioner, 1929; BA, BSc 1931; MA, DPhil 1933. Asst Master at Winchester Coll., 1933–45; High Master of Manchester Grammar Sch., 1945–62; Vice-Chancellor, Univ. of York, 1962–73. Mem. of University Grants Cttee, 1949–59; Chm. of Headmasters' Conference, 1953–54; Mem. Central Advisory Council on Education, 1957–61; Member: Standing Commission on Museums and Galleries, 1958–61; Press Council, 1963–67; SSRC, 1965–68; Chairman: Personal Social Services Council, 1973–76; Cttee to Inquire into the Training of Teachers, 1970–71. Hon. FRIBA 1979. Hon. LLD: McGill, 1957; York (Toronto), 1970; Hon. DLitt New Brunswick, 1974; DUniv York, 1974. Fellow, Winchester Coll., 1963–69. *Publications:* (in part) Elements of Physical Chemistry, 1938; (in part) Science and Education, 1942; An Essay on the Content of Education, 1949; Education and Leadership, 1951; articles in scientific and educational journals. *Address:* Penhill Cottage, West Witton, Leyburn, N Yorks.
Died 16 May 1992.

JAMES, Edmund Purcell S.; *see* Skone James.

JAMES, (Ernest) Gethin, FRICS; Director, Estate Surveying Services, Property Services Agency, 1977–84, retired; *b* 20 March 1925; *s* of Ernest Bertram James and Gwladys James; *m* 1st, 1949, Phyllis Jane (marr. diss.), *d* of Frederick Lloyd Rice and Kathleen Mary Rice; 2nd, 1981, Mrs Margaret Hollis. *Educ:* Christ Coll., Brecon; Coll. of Estate Management. FRICS 1954. Defence Land Agent: Colchester, 1968–69; Aldershot, 1969–72; Dep. Chief Land Agent, MoD, 1972–74, Chief Land Agent and Valuer, 1974–75; Asst Dir (Estates), PSA, London Reg., 1975–77. *Recreations:* living each day, golf. *Address:* Heath Cottage, Church Lane, Ewshot, Farnham, Surrey GU10 5BJ. *T:* Aldershot (01252) 850548. *Club:* Army Golf (Aldershot).
Died 7 Sept. 1995.

JAMES, Noel David Glaves, OBE 1964; MC 1945; TD 1946; *b* 16 Sept. 1911. *o s* of late Rev. D. T. R. James and Gertrude James; *m* 1949, Laura Cecilia (*d* 1970), *yr d* of late Sir Richard Winn Livingstone; two *s* (and one *s* decd). *Educ:* Haileybury Coll.; Royal Agricultural Coll., Cirencester (Gold Medal and Estate Management Prize). In general practice as a land agent, 1933–39. Served War, 1939–46 (MC, despatches); 68 Field Regt RA (TA), France, Middle East, Italy. Bursar, 1946–51, Fellow, 1950–51, Corpus Christi Coll., Oxford (MA (Oxon) 1946). Land Agent for Oxford Univ., 1951–61; Estates Bursar and Agent for Brasenose Coll., 1959–61; Fellow, Brasenose Coll., Oxford, 1951–61; Agent for Clinton Devon Estates, 1961–76. President: Land Agents Soc., 1957–58; Royal Forestry Soc. of England and Wales and N Ireland, 1962–64; Member: Central Forestry Examination Bd of UK, 1951–75; Regional Advisory

Cttee, Eastern Conservancy, Forestry Commn, 1951–61; Regional Advisory Cttee, SW Conservancy, Forestry Commission, 1962–75; Departmental Cttee on Hedgerow and Farm Timber, 1953; UK Forestry Cttee, 1954–59; Governor Wye Coll., Kent, 1955–61; Governor Westonbirt Sch., 1959–68. FLAS; FRICS (Diploma in Forestry and Watney Gold Medal). Gold Medal for Distinguished Service to Forestry, 1967; Royal Agricultural Coll. Bledisloe Medal for services to agriculture and forestry, 1970. *Publications:* Artillery Observation Posts, 1941; Working Plans for Estate Woodlands, 1948; Notes on Estate Forestry, 1949; An Experiment in Forestry, 1951; The Forester's Companion, 1955, 4th edn 1989; The Trees of Bicton, 1969; The Arboriculturalist's Companion, 1972, 2nd edn 1990; A Book of Trees (anthology), 1973; Before the Echoes Die Away, 1980; A History of English Forestry, 1981; A Forestry Centenary, 1982; Gunners at Larkhill, 1983; Plain Soldiering, 1987; An Historical Dictionary of Forestry and Woodland Terms, 1991. *Recreations:* forestry, shooting. *Address:* Blakemore House, Kersbrook, Budleigh Salterton, Devon EX9 7AB. *T:* Budleigh Salterton (0395) 443886. *Club:* Army and Navy.   *Died 5 March 1993.*

JAMES, Prof. Peter Maunde Coram, VRD 1964; John Humphreys Professor of Dental Health, 1966–87, and Postgraduate Advisor in Dentistry, 1983–86, University of Birmingham (Director, Dental School, 1978–82); *b* 2 April 1922; *s* of Vincent Coram James, MRCS, LRCP, and Mildred Ivy (*née* Gooch); *m* 1945, Denise Mary Bond, LDS; four *s. Educ:* Westminster Sch.; Royal Dental Hosp., Univ. of London (MDS); Univ. of St Andrews (DPD). LDSRCS. House Surgeon, then Sen. House Surg., Royal Dental Hosp., 1945; Surg. Lieut (D) RNVR, 1945–48; Registrar, Res. Asst and Hon. Lectr, Inst. of Dental Surgery (Eastman Dental Hosp.), 1949–55; Gibbs Travelling Scholar, 1952; Royal Dental Hosp. Sch. of Dental Surgery, Univ. of London: Sen. Lectr, 1955–65; Asst Dean, 1958–66; Dir, Dept of Children's Dentistry, 1962–66; Hon. Cons. Dental Surg., 1961–87; Reader in Preventive Dentistry, Univ. of London, 1965; Head, Dept of Dental Health, Univ. of Birmingham, 1966–87. Consultant, Internat. Dental Fedn Commn on Dental Res., 1976–87; Cons. Advisor in Community Dentistry to DHSS, 1977–83; Reg. Advisor (W Midlands), Faculty of Dental Surgery, RCS, 1976–83. President: Brit. Paedodontic Soc., 1962; Central Counties Br., BDA, 1981–82; Founding Pres., Brit. Assoc. for Study of Community Dentistry, 1973. Chm., Specialist Adv. Cttee in Community Dental Health, 1981–86; Vice-Chm., BDA Central Cttee for Univ. Teachers and Res. Workers, 1984–87; Member: Dental Working Party, Cttee on Child Health Services, 1974–77; Standing Panel of Experts in Dentistry, Univ. of London, 1976–; Birmingham AHA (Teaching), 1979–82; Birmingham Central DHA, 1982–85; Jt Cttee for Higher Training in Dentistry, 1981–86. Ext. Assessor, Univ. of Malaya, 1977–87; ext. examr in dental subjects, univs and colls, 1955–. Editor, Community Dental Health, 1983–. *Publications:* contrib. to dental and scientific jls. *Recreations:* music, photography, camping. *Address:* The Pump House, Bishopton Spa, Stratford-upon-Avon, Warwicks CV37 9QY. *T:* Stratford-upon-Avon (0789) 204330. *Club:* Royal Society of Medicine.
          Died 30 Sept. 1993.

JAMISON, Dr Robin Ralph, FRS 1969; FEng 1976; FRAeS; CChem, MRSC; Chief Technical Executive (Research), Rolls Royce (1971) Ltd (formerly Rolls Royce Ltd), Bristol Engine Division, 1971–75, retired; *b* 12 July 1912; *s* of Reginald Jamison, MD, FRCS, and Eanswyth Heyworth; *m* 1937, Hilda Watney Wilson, Cape Town; two *s* two *d. Educ:* South African Coll.; Univ. of Cape Town. BSc, PhD. S African Govt research grant, 1936–37; research and development of aero engines, Rolls Royce

Ltd, 1937–50; Head of Ramjet Dept, Bristol Siddeley Engines Ltd, 1950–62 (Asst Chief Engr, 1956); advanced propulsion res., 1962–65; Chief Engr, Res., 1965–71. Vis. Prof., Bath Univ. of Technology, 1969–73. Herbert Ackroyd-Stuart Prize, RAeS, 1958; Thulin Bronze Medal, Swedish Aero. Soc., 1960; Silver Medal of RAeS, 1965. *Publications:* papers in aeronautical and scientific jls. *Recreations:* sailing, gardening, music. *Address:* 2 The Crescent, Henleaze, Bristol BS9 4RN. *T:* Bristol (0272) 620328.   *Died 18 March 1991.*

JANION, Rear-Adm. Sir Hugh (Penderel), KCVO 1981; Flag Officer, Royal Yachts, 1975–81; *b* 28 Sept. 1923; *s* of late Engr Captain Ralph Penderel Janion, RN, and Mrs Winifred Derwent Janion; *m* 1956, Elizabeth Monica Ferard; one *s* one *d. Educ:* Malvern Link Sch., Worcs; RNC Dartmouth. Served War of 1939–45, Russian convoys, invasions of Sicily and Italy; Korean War, 1950–52, Inchon landing; specialised in navigation; Comdr, 1958, i/c HMS Jewel, and Exec. Officer HMS Ark Royal; Captain, 1966, i/c HMS Aurora and HMS Bristol; Rear-Adm. 1975. Extra Equerry to the Queen, 1975–. Younger Brother, Trinity House, 1976–. *Recreations:* sailing, golf. *Address:* King's Hayes, Batcombe, Shepton Mallet, Somerset BA4 6HF. *T:* Upton Noble (0749) 850300. *Clubs:* Royal Thames Yacht; Royal Yacht Squadron (Cowes); Royal Naval and Royal Albert Yacht (Portsmouth); Imperial Poona Yacht.
          Died 12 Aug. 1994.

JANNER, Lady; Elsie Sybil Janner, CBE 1968; JP; *b* Newcastle upon Tyne, 1 Nov. 1905; *d* of Joseph and Henrietta Cohen; *m* 1927, Barnett Janner (later Baron Janner) (*d* 1982); one *s* one *d. Educ:* Central Newcastle High Sch.; South Hampstead High Sch.; Switzerland. Founder and first Hon. Club Leader, Brady Girls' Club, Whitechapel, 1925 (subseq. Pres., Brady Clubs and Settlement); Jt Pres., Brady/Maccabi Youth and Community Centre, Edgware, 1980–. War of 1939–45: Captain, Mechanised Transp. Corps (Def. Medal). Chm., Bridgehead Housing Assoc., to acquire property for residential purposes for homeless ex-offenders, 1967–75; Stonham Housing Assoc. (amalgamation of S Western Housing Assoc., St Leonards Housing Assoc., and Bridgehead): Chm. Adv. Bd, 1975–83; Pres., 1984–; Chm., Stonham Meml Trust; Mem., Finance and Develt Cttees. Magistrates Assoc.: Vice-Pres.; Hon. Treasurer, 1971–76; formerly Dep. Chm., Road Traffic Cttee, and Mem., Exec. Cttee; Vice Pres., Inner London Br. (former Chm.); former Mem., Jt Standing Cttee, Magistrates Assoc. and Justices' Clerks Soc. JP, Inner London, 1936; contested (Lab), Mile End, LCC, 1947; a Visiting Magistrate to Holloway Women's Prison, 1950–62; Chm., Thames Bench of Magistrates, 1975; Mem., Juvenile Courts Panel, 1944–70 (Chm. 1960–70); Former Member: Inner London and NE London Licensing Planning Cttees; Inner London Licensing Compensation Cttee; Inner London Mem., Cttee of Magistrates. Vice-Pres., Assoc. for Jewish Youth; Hon. Vice-Pres., Fedn of Women Zionists of GB and Ire.; Chm., United Jewish Educnl and Cultural Org. (internat. body to re-construct Jewish educn in countries of Europe which had been occupied by Germans), 1947–50; Member: Central Council of Jewish Religious Educn, 1945–65; Bd of Deputies, British Jews Educn and Youth Cttee (Chm., 1943–66); Dep. Chm., Mitchell City of London Charity and Educnl Foundn, 1984–90 (Trustee, 1950–); Trustee, Barnett Janner Charitable Trust, from foundn, 1983–; Member: Nat. Road Safety Adv. Council, 1965–68; Exec., Inst. Advanced Motorists, 1974–88 (Vice-Chm., 1980–84, Fellow). Freeman, City of London, 1975. *Publication:* Barnett Janner—A Personal Portrait, 1984. *Recreation:*

grandchildren. *Address:* 45 Morpeth Mansions, Morpeth Terrace, SW1P 1ET. *T:* 071–828 8700.

Died 17 July 1994.

JANVRIN, Vice-Adm. Sir (Hugh) Richard (Benest), KCB 1969 (CB 1965); DSC 1940; *b* 9 May 1915; *s* of late Rev. Canon C. W. Janvrin, Fairford, Glos; *m* 1938, Nancy Fielding; two *s*. *Educ:* RNC, Dartmouth. Naval Cadet, 1929; Midshipman, 1933; Sub-Lt, 1936; Lt, 1937; qualified Fleet Air Arm Observer, 1938; served War of 1939–45 (took part in Taranto attack, 1940); In Command: HMS Broadsword, 1951–53; HMS Grenville, 1957–58; RNAS Brawdy, 1958; HMS Victorious, 1959–60; Imperial Defence Coll., 1961; Dir, Tactics and Weapons Policy, Admiralty, 1962–63; Flag Officer, Aircraft Carriers, 1964–66; Dep. Chief of Naval Staff, MoD, 1966–68; Flag Officer, Naval Air Comd, 1968–70; retired 1971. Lieut-Comdr, 1945; Comdr, 1948; Capt., 1954; Rear-Adm., 1964; Vice-Adm. 1967. *Recreation:* gardening. *Address:* Allen's Close, Chalford Hill, near Stroud, Glos GL6 8QJ. *T:* Brimscombe (0453) 882336.

Died 15 Jan. 1993.

JARMAN, (Michael) Derek; painter and film maker; *b* 31 Jan. 1942; *s* of late Lance Jarman and Elizabeth Evelyn Puttock. *Educ:* King's College, Univ. of London; Slade School. Sen. FRCA 1993. Designed: Jazz Calendar, Royal Ballet, 1968; Don Giovanni, ENO, 1968; The Devils, 1971, and Savage Messiah, 1972, for Ken Russell; Rake's Progress, Maggio Musicale, Florence, 1973; *films:* Sebastiane, 1975; Jubilee, 1977; The Tempest, 1979; Imagining October, 1984; The Angelic Conversation, 1985; Caravaggio, 1986; The Last of England, 1987; (jtly) Aria, 1987; War Requiem, 1989; The Garden, 1991; Edward II, 1991; Wittgenstein, 1993; Blue, 1993; Glitterbug, 1994. Directed L'ispirazione, Florence, 1988. Painting exhibns include Edward Totah Gallery, Lisson Gallery, Internat Contemp. Art Fair, Inst. Contemp. Arts, Richard Salmon Gall., Karsten Schubert. *Publications:* Dancing Ledge, 1984; The Last of England, 1987; War Requiem, 1989; Modern Nature (autobiog.), 1991; At Your Own Risk, 1992; Chroma, 1994. *Address:* c/o British Film Institute, 29 Rathbone Place, WC2.

Died 19 Feb. 1994.

JARRETT, Sir Clifford (George), KBE 1956 (CBE 1945); CB 1949; Chairman: Tobacco Research Council, 1971–78; Dover Harbour Board, 1971–80; *b* 1909; *s* of George Henry Jarrett; *m* 1st, 1933, Hilda Alice Goodchild (*d* 1975); one *s* two *d*; 2nd, 1978, Mary, *d* of C. S. Beacock. *Educ:* Dover County Sch.; Sidney Sussex Coll., Cambridge. BA 1931. Entered Civil Service, 1932; Asst Principal, Home Office, 1932–34, Admiralty, 1934–38; Private Sec. to Parly Sec., 1936–38; Principal Private Sec. to First Lord, 1940–44; Principal Establishments Officer, 1946–50; a Dep. Sec., Admiralty, 1950–61; Permanent Sec., Admiralty, 1961–64; Permanent Under-Sec., Min. of Pensions and Nat. Insurance, later Min. of Social Security, then Dept of Health and Social Security, 1964–70. A Trustee, Nat. Maritime Museum, 1969–81. *Address:* The Coach House, Derry Hill, Menston, Ilkley, W Yorks LS29 6NG. *Club:* United Oxford & Cambridge University.

Died 9 July 1995.

JARVIS, Hugh John, FIA; Group Chief Actuary, Prudential Corporation, 1989–91; *b* 4 July 1930; *s* of John James and Muriel Jarvis; *m* 1959, Margita; two *s* one *d*. *Educ:* Southend High School. Mercantile & General Reinsurance Co., various positions, finally Dep. General Manager, 1947–88. *Recreation:* organising and umpiring hockey. *Address:* 15 Daines Way, Thorpe Bay, Essex SS1 3PF. *T:* Southend-on-Sea (0702) 587065.

Died 12 Oct. 1993.

JEFFCOATE, Sir (Thomas) Norman (Arthur), Kt 1970; Professor of Obstetrics and Gynæcology, University of Liverpool, 1945–72, then Emeritus; Hon. Consultant Obstetrical and Gynæcological Surgeon, Liverpool Area Health Authority (Teaching); *b* 25 March 1907; *s* of Arthur Jeffcoate and Mary Ann Oakey; *m* 1937, Josephine Lindsay (*d* 1981); four *s*. *Educ:* King Edward VI Sch., Nuneaton; University of Liverpool. MB, ChB (Liverpool) 1st class Hons 1929; MD (Liverpool) 1932; FRCSE 1932; MRCOG 1932; FRCOG 1939 (Vice-Pres., 1967–69; Pres. 1969–72). Hon. Asst Surgeon: Liverpool Maternity Hosp., 1932–45; Women's Hosp., Liverpool, 1935–45. Lectures: Blair-Bell Memorial, Royal College of Obst. and Gynaec., 1938; Sir Arcot Mudalier, Univ. of Madras, 1955; Margaret Orford, S African Coll. of Physicians, Surgeons and Gynaecologists, 1969; J. Y. Simpson, RCSE, 1976. Joseph Price Orator, Amer. Assoc. of Obstetricians and Gynaecologists, 1966. Sims Black Travelling Commonwealth Prof., 1958; Visiting Professor: New York State Univ., 1955; University of Qld, 1964; Univ. of Melbourne, 1964; Univ. of Texas, 1965; Hon. Visiting Obstetrician and Gynæcologist, Royal Prince Alfred Hospital, Sydney, Australia, 1955–. Chairman, Med. Advisory Council of Liverpool Regional Hosp. Bd, 1962–69; President: N of England Obst. and Gynaec. Soc., 1960; Sect. of Obst. and Gynaec., RSM, 1965–66; Liverpool Med. Inst., 1966–67; Vice-Pres. Family Planning Assoc., 1962–79; Member: Gen. Med. Council, 1951–61; Clinical Research Bd, MRC, 1961–65; Clinical Trials Sub-Cttee of Safety of Drugs Cttee, 1963–69; Bd of Science and Educn, BMA, 1968–69; Standing Maternity and Midwifery Adv. Cttee, Dept of Health and Social Security (formerly Min. of Health), 1963–72 (Chm., 1970–72); Standing Med. Adv. Cttee and Central Health Services Council, Dept of Health and Social Security, 1969–72; Jt Sub-Cttee on Prevention of Haemolytic Disease of the Newborn, 1968–72 (Chm., 1969–72). Hon. FCOG(SA), 1972; Hon. FACOG, 1972; Hon. FRCSCan, 1973; Hon. Member: Amer. Gynec. Club; Amer. Gynec. Soc.; Amer. Assoc. Obst. and Gynec.; Central Assoc. Obst. and Gynec.; Assoc. Surg., Ceylon; Obst. and Gynaec. Socs of: Canada, Finland, Honolulu, Malta, Montreal, Panama, S Africa, Uruguay, Venezuela. Hon. LLD, TCD, 1971. Eardley Holland Gold Medal, RCOG, 1975; Simpson Gold Medal, RCSE, 1976. *Publications:* Principles of Gynæcology, 1957, 4th edn, 1975, 5th edn (rev. V. R. Tindall) as Jeffcoate's Principles of Gynaecology, 1986; communications to medical journals. *Address:* 6 Riversdale Road, Liverpool L19 3QW. *T:* 051–427 1448.

Died 13 Oct. 1992.

JELF, Maj.-Gen. Richard William, CBE 1948 (OBE 1944); *b* 16 June 1904; *s* of late Sir Ernest Jelf, King's Remembrancer and Master of the Supreme Court, and Rose Frances, 2nd *d* of R. W. C. Reeves; *m* 1928, Nowell, *d* of Major Sampson-Way, RM, Manor House, Henbury; three *s* one *d*. *Educ:* Cheltenham Coll.; RMA Woolwich. Commissioned Royal Artillery, 1924; served North-West Frontier, India (Loe Agra), 1934; Staff Coll., Quetta, 1936; served War, NW Europe, 1939–45; Dep. Dir Staff Duties, War Office, 1946; Imperial Defence Coll., 1948; CRA 2nd Division, 1949; Dep. Chief, Organization and Training Div., SHAPE, 1951; Comdr 99 AA Bde (TA), 1953; Chief of Staff, Eastern Command, 1956; Maj.-Gen., 1957; Commandant, Police Coll., Bramshill, 1957–63; Dir of Civil Defence, Southern Region, 1963–68. ADC to the Queen, 1954. Hon. Sec., Lyme Regis RNLI, 1972–84. *Address:* 10 Hill's Place, Guildford Road, Horsham, W Sussex RH12 1XT. *T:* Horsham (0403) 217071.

Died 22 Jan. 1994.

JENKINS, Dennis Frederick M.; *see* Martin-Jenkins.

JENKINS, Garth John, CB 1987; QC 1989; Deputy Secretary and Legal Adviser and Solicitor to Ministry of Agriculture, Fisheries and Food, Forestry Commission, and Intervention Board for Agricultural Produce, 1983–93; *b* 7 Dec. 1933; *s* of John Ernest Jenkins and Amy Elizabeth Jenkins; *m* 1965, Patricia Margaret Lindsay; one *d. Educ:* Birmingham Royal Inst. for the Blind; Royal National College for the Blind; Birmingham Univ. (LLB). Called to Bar, Gray's Inn, 1963. Birmingham Corporation, 1954; South Shields Corporation, 1964; The Land Commission, 1967; MAFF, 1971–93; Under Sec., 1981. *Recreations:* literature, theatre, music, chess; food, drink and conversation.   *Died 11 March 1995.*

JENKINS, Peter George James; Associate Editor and Political Columnist, The Independent, since 1987; *b* 11 May 1934; *s* of Kenneth E. Jenkins and Joan E. Jenkins (*née* Croger); *m* 1st, 1960, Charlotte Strachey (decd; one *d*; 2nd, 1970, Polly Toynbee; one *s* two *d. Educ:* Culford Sch.; Trinity Hall, Cambridge (BA Hist., MA). Journalist, Financial Times, 1958–60; The Guardian: Journalist, 1960; Labour Correspondent, 1963–67; Washington Correspondent, 1972–74; Political Commentator and Policy Editor, 1974–85; Political columnist, The Sunday Times, 1985–87. Theatre Critic, The Spectator, 1978–81. First stage play, Illuminations, performed at Lyric, Hammersmith, 1980; TV series, Struggle, 1983. Vis. Fellow, Nuffield Coll., Oxford, 1980–87. Awards include Granada TV Journalist of the Year, 1978. *Publications:* The Battle of Downing Street, 1970; Mrs Thatcher's Revolution, 1987. *Address:* 1 Crescent Grove, SW4 7AF. *T:* 071–622 6492. *Club:* Garrick.
                    Died 27 May 1992.

JENKINS, Lt-Col Stephen Reginald Martin, MC 1944; farmer; Vice Lord-Lieutenant for Gloucestershire, since 1989; *b* 4 Feb. 1915; *o c* of late Capt. William Reginald Haldane Jenkins and Isabel Mary (*née* Osborne); *m* 1943, Elizabeth, *d* of Rev. A. W. Napier; two *s* two *d. Educ:* Eton; RMA Sandhurst; RAC, Cirencester. Commnd 4th/7th Royal Dragoon Guards, 1935; psc; Lt-Col 1954; retd 1956; Lt-Col RARO. Mem., later Alderman, Glos CC, 1964–74. DL 1969, High Sheriff 1975–76, Glos. *Address:* Hampnett Manor, Northleach, Cheltenham, Glos GL54 3NW.   *Died 26 Dec. 1991.*

JENKS, Sir Richard Atherley, 2nd Bt, *cr* 1932, of Cheape in the City of London; *b* 26 July 1906; *er s* of Sir Maurice Jenks, 1st Bt, and Martha Louise Christabel, *d* of late George Calley Smith; *S* father 1946; *m* 1932, Marjorie Suzanne Arlette, *d* of late Sir Arthur du Cros, 1st Bt; two *s. Educ:* Charterhouse. Chartered Accountant, retired. *Heir: s* Maurice Arthur Brian Jenks [*b* 28 Oct. 1933; *m* 1962, Susan, *e d* of Leslie Allen, Surrey; one *d*]. *Address:* 42 Sussex Square, W2 2SP. *T:* 071–262 8356.
                    Died 9 Nov. 1993.

JENNINGS, Sir Albert (Victor), Kt 1969; Founder and Chairman, Jennings Industries Ltd (formerly A. V. Jennings (Australia) Ltd), 1932–72; *b* 12 Oct. 1896; *s* of John Thomas Jennings; *m* 1922, Ethel Sarah, *d* of George Herbert Johnson; two *s. Educ:* Eastern Road Sch., Melbourne. Served First World War, AIF. Council Mem., Master Builders Assoc., 1943–71; Vice Pres. Housing, Master Builders Fedn of Aust., 1970–71; Member: Commonwealth Building Research and Advisory Cttee, 1948–72; Manufacturing Industries Adv. Council to Australian Govt, 1962–72; Decentralisation and Develt Adv. Cttee to Victorian State Govt, 1965–68; Commonwealth of Aust. Metric Conversion Bd, 1970–72; Trustee, Cttee for Economic Develt of Australia. Fellow: Aust. Inst. of Building (Federal Pres., 1964–65 and 1965–66); UK Inst. of Building, 1971. Aust. Inst. of Building Medal 1970; Urban Land Inst. Total Community Develt Award, 1973; Sir Charles McGrath Award for

Services to Marketing, 1976. *Recreations:* swimming, golf. *Address:* Ranelagh House, Rosserdale Crescent, Mount Eliza, Victoria 3930, Australia. *T:* 7871350. *Clubs:* Commonwealth (Canberra); Melbourne, Savage (Melbourne).   *Died 3 March 1993.*

JENNINGS, Arnold Harry, CBE 1977; MA; Headmaster, Ecclesfield School, Sheffield, 1959–79 (formerly, 1959–67, Ecclesfield Grammar School); *b* 24 May 1915; *s* of Harry Jennings and Alice Mary (*née* Northrop); *m* 1939, Elizabeth Redman; one *d* (one *s* decd). *Educ:* Bradford Grammar Sch.; Corpus Christi Coll., Oxford (Classical Schol.; MA). Tutor, Knutsford Ordination Test Sch., Hawarden, 1939–40; served War, Captain RA, England, N Ireland, France, Belgium, Holland and Germany, 1940–46; Sen. Classical Master, Chesterfield Grammar Sch., 1946–53; Headmaster, Tapton House Sch., Chesterfield, 1953–58; part-time extra-mural Lectr, Sheffield Univ., 1946–54. Mem., NUT Executive, 1958–59 and 1960–72 (Chm., Secondary Adv. Cttee, 1968–72); Secondary Heads Association: Hon Sec., 1978–79; Membership Sec., 1979–81; Hon. Mem., 1981–; President: Head Masters' Assoc., 1977; Jt Assoc. of Classical Teachers, 1975–77; Mem., Secondary Schs Examinations Council, 1961–64; Schools Council: Mem., 1964–84; Dep. Chm. and Acting Chm., 1982–84; Chm., Steering Cttee 'C', 1975–78; Chm., Second Examinations Cttee, 1968–76; Jt Chm., Jt Examinations Sub-Cttee, 1971–76; Chm., Exams Cttee, 1978–83; Chm., Classics Cttee; Convenor, A-level Classics Scrutiny Panel: Secondary Examinations Council, 1984–88; Sch. Exams and Assessment Council, 1988–89. Mem. Court, Sheffield Univ., 1959–78. Sheffield City Councillor, 1949–58 (Mem., Sheffield Educn Cttee, 1988–91); contested (Lab) Heeley, Sheffield, 1950 and 1951. Governor: Richmond Further Educn Coll., Sheffield, 1986–88; High Storrs Sch., Sheffield, 1988–94; Stradbrooke Tertiary Coll., Sheffield, 1989–90. Chm., Sheffield Tertiary Forum, 1990–92; Mem., Sheffield Gypsies and Travellers Support Gp, 1990–92. *Publications:* (ed) Management and Headship in the Secondary School, 1977; (ed) Discipline in Primary and Secondary Schools Today, 1979; articles on educn *passim. Recreations:* work, wine, opera, photography, travel. *Address:* 74 Clarkegrove Road, Sheffield S10 2NJ. *T:* Sheffield (0114) 266 2520.   *Died 7 Nov. 1994.*

JENNINGS, Percival Henry, CBE 1953; *b* 8 Dec. 1903; *s* of late Rev. Canon H. R. Jennings; *m* 1934, Margaret Katharine Musgrave, *d* of late Brig.-Gen. H. S. Rogers, CMG, DSO; three *d. Educ:* Christ's Hospital. Asst Auditor, N Rhodesia, 1927; Asst Auditor, Mauritius, 1931; Auditor, British Honduras, 1934; Dep. Dir of Audit, Gold Coast, 1938; Dep. Dir of Audit, Nigeria, 1945; Dir of Audit, Hong Kong, 1948; Dep. Dir-Gen. of the Overseas Audit Service, 1955; Dir-Gen. of the Overseas Audit Service, 1960–63, retd. *Recreation:* golf. *Address:* Littlewood, Lelant, St Ives, Cornwall TR26 3JU. *T:* Hayle (01736) 753407. *Clubs:* Commonwealth Trust, Royal Over-Seas League.   *Died 1 Nov. 1995.*

JENNINGS, Sir Raymond (Winter), Kt 1968; QC 1945; Master, Court of Protection, 1956–70; *b* 12 Dec. 1897; *o s* of late Sir Arthur Oldham Jennings and Mabel Winter; *m* 1930, Sheila (*d* 1972), *d* of Selwyn S. Grant, OBE; one *s* one *d. Educ:* Rugby; RMC, Sandhurst; Oriel Coll., Oxford (MA, BCL). Served 1916–19 in Royal Fusiliers. Called to the Bar, Inner Temple, 1922; Bencher of Lincoln's Inn, 1951. *Address:* 14C Upper Drive, Hove, East Sussex BN3 6GN. *T:* Brighton (01273) 773361.
                    Died 6 March 1995.

JENOUR, Sir (Arthur) Maynard (Chesterfield), Kt 1959; TD 1950; JP; Director: Aberthaw & Bristol Channel Portland Cement Co. Ltd, 1929–83 (Chairman and Joint Managing Director, 1946–83); T. Beynon & Co. Ltd,

1938–83 (Chairman and Joint Managing Director, 1946–83); Ruthin Quarries (Bridgend) Ltd, 1947–83 (Chairman, 1947–83); Associated Portland Cement Manufacturers Ltd, 1963–75; Blue Jacket Motel (Pty) Ltd, Australia, 1964; *b* 7 Jan. 1905; *s* of Brig.-Gen. A. S. Jenour, CB, CMG, DSO, Crossways, Chepstow and Emily Anna (*née* Beynon); *m* 1948, Margaret Sophie, *d* of H. Stuart Osborne, Sydney, NSW, and *widow* of W. O. Ellis Fielding-Jones; three step *d*. *Educ:* Eton. Entered business, 1924. Served War of 1939–45, in England and Middle East, Royal Artillery, Major. Pres., Cardiff Chamber of Commerce, 1953–54; Chm. Wales & Mon. Industrial Estates Ltd, 1954–60; Mem. Board, Development Corporation for Wales, 1958–81. JP Mon 1946; DL Mon, 1960; High Sheriff of Mon, 1951–52; Vice-Lieut of Mon, 1965–74, Vice Lord-Lieut of Gwent, 1974–79. KStJ 1969. *Recreations:* walking, gardening, shooting. *Address:* Stonycroft, 13 Ridgeway, Newport, Gwent NP9 5AF. *T:* Newport (0633) 263802. *Clubs:* Cardiff and County (Cardiff); Union (Sydney, NSW).

Died 1 Sept. 1992.

JERNE, Prof. Niels Kaj, MD; FRS 1980; *b* London, 23 Dec. 1911; *s* of Hans Jessen Jerne and Else Marie (*née* Lindberg); *m* 1st, Ilse Sonja Wahl (decd); two *s*; 2nd, 1964, Ursula Alexandra (*née* Kohl). *Educ:* Univ. of Leiden, Holland; Univ. of Copenhagen, Denmark (MD). Res. worker, Danish State Serum Inst., 1943–56; Res. Fellow, Calif Inst. of Technol., Pasadena, 1954–55; CMO for Immunology, WHO, Geneva, 1956–62; Prof. of Biophysics, Univ. of Geneva, 1960–62; Chm., Dept of Microbiology, Univ. of Pittsburgh, 1962–66; Prof. of Experimental Therapy, Johann Wolfgang Goethe Univ., Frankfurt, 1966–69; Director: Paul-Ehrlich-Institut, Frankfurt, 1966–69; Basel Inst. for Immunology, 1969–80. Prof., Pasteur Inst., Paris, 1981–82. Member: Amer. Acad. of Arts and Sciences, 1967; Royal Danish Acad. of Sciences, 1968; National Acad. of Sciences, USA, 1975; Amer. Philosophical Soc., 1979; Acad. des Scis de l'Institut de France, 1981; Yugoslav Acad. of Scis and Arts, 1986. DSc *hc:* Chicago, 1972; Columbia, 1978; Copenhagen, 1979; PhD *hc:* Basel, 1981; Weizmann Inst., Israel, 1985; MD *hc* Rotterdam, 1983. Nobel Prize for Physiology or Medicine (jtly), 1984. *Publications:* scientific papers on immunology in learned jls. *Address:* Château de Bellevue, Castillon-du-Gard 30210, France. *T:* 66370075. *Died 7 Oct. 1994.*

JERRAM, Maj.-Gen. Richard Martyn, CB 1984; MBE 1960; DL; retired 1984; *b* Bangalore, India, 14 Aug. 1928; *e s* of late Brig. R. M. Jerram, DSO, MC, and Monica (*née* Gillies); *m* 1987, Susan (*née* Roberts), *widow* of John Naylor. *Educ:* Stubbington House; Marlborough Coll.; RMA, Sandhurst. Commissioned into Royal Tank Regt, 1948; served in 2, 3 or 4 RTRs, or in Staff appts in Hong Kong, Malaya (twice) (MBE), Libya, N Ireland, USA, Germany (four times), MoD (three times); Instr, Staff Coll., Camberley, 1964–67; CO 3 RTR, 1969–71; DRAC, 1981–84. Col Comdt, RTR, 1982–88. Comr, Cornwall SJAB, 1987–93. DL Cornwall, 1993. CStJ 1992. *Recreations:* travel, countryside, literature, chess. *Address:* Trehane, Trevanson, Wadebridge, Cornwall PL27 7HP. *T:* Wadebridge (0208) 812523. *Club:* Army and Navy.

Died 1 Sept. 1993.

JOEL, Harry Joel, (Jim); owner, since 1940, and breeder, 1940–86, Childwick Bury Stud; *b* 4 Sept. 1894; *o s* of Jack Barnato Joel, JP. *Educ:* Malvern Coll. Served European War 1914–18 with 15th Hussars. Formerly: Chm., Johannesburg Consolidated Investment Co. Ltd; Director: De Beers Consolidated Mines Ltd; Johnson Matthey & Co., and other cos. Won first British classic, 1000 guineas, 1944; Leading Flat Owner and Leading Flat Breeder, 1967; Leading Nat. Hunt Owner, 1979–80,

1986–87. *Recreation:* racing. *Address:* The Stud House, Childwick Bury, St Albans, Herts. *Clubs:* Buck's; Jockey (Newmarket). *Died 23 March 1992.*

JOHN, Arthur Walwyn, CBE 1967 (OBE 1945); FCA; company director; Underwriting Member of Lloyd's, since 1977; *b* 1 Dec. 1912; *s* of Oliver Walwyn and Elsie Maud John; *m* 1st, 1949, Elizabeth Rosabelle (*d* 1979), *yr d* of Ernest David and Elsie Winifred Williams; one *s* two *d*; 2nd, 1986, Bonita Lynne, *e c* of Sebastian and Adela Maritano. *Educ:* Marlborough Coll. Mem. Institute of Chartered Accountants, 1934 (Mem. Council, 1965–81). Joined Army, 1939; served War of 1939–45: commissioned, 1940; War Office, 1941; DAQMG First Army, 1942, and HQ Allied Armies in Italy; AQMG Allied Forces HQ, 1944 (despatches, 1943, 1945). Asst to Commercial Manager (Collieries), Powell Duffryn Associated Collieries Ltd, 1936; Chief Accountant, John Lewis & Co. Ltd, 1945; Dep. Dir-Gen. of Finance, National Coal Board, 1946; Dir-Gen. of Finance, 1955; Member, NCB, 1961–68; Chm., NCB Coal Products Div., 1962–68. Director: Unigate Ltd, 1969–75; Property Holding and Investment Trust Ltd, 1976–87 (Chm., 1977–87); Stenhouse Holdings Ltd, 1976–84 (Chm., 1982–84); Reed Stenhouse Companies Ltd, Canada, 1977–84; J. H. Sankey & Son Ltd, 1965–86; Schroder Property Fund, 1971–88; Teamdale Distribution Ltd, 1982– (Chm., 1982–); Chartered Accountants Trustees Ltd, 1982–87; Wincanton Contracts Finance Ltd, 1983–85; Dir and Chm., Chase Property Holdings plc, 1986–87. Mem., Price Commn, 1976–77. Mem. and Court, Worshipful Co. of Chartered Accts in England and Wales, 1977– (Master, 1981–82). *Address:* Limber, Top Park, Gerrards Cross, Bucks SL9 7PW. *T:* Gerrards Cross (0753) 884811. *Club:* Army and Navy.

Died 4 Nov. 1991.

JOHN, David Dilwyn, CBE 1961; TD; DSc; Director, National Museum of Wales, Cardiff, 1948–68; *b* 20 Nov. 1901; *e s* of Thomas John, St Bride's Major, Glam; *m* 1929, Marjorie, *d* of J. W. Page, HMI, Wellington, Salop; one *s* one *d*. *Educ:* Bridgend County Sch.; University Coll. of Wales, Aberystwyth. Zoologist on scientific staff, Discovery Investigations, engaged in oceanographical research in Antarctic waters, 1925–35; awarded Polar Medal. Appointed Asst Keeper in charge of Echinoderms at British Museum (Natural History), 1935; Deputy Keeper, 1948. Pres., Museums Assoc., 1964–65. Joined Territorial Army, 1936; promoted Major, RA, 1942. Pres., Cardiff Naturalists' Soc., 1952–53; Hon. Sec., Challenger Soc., 1946–48. Hon. LLD Univ. of Wales, 1969; Hon. Fellow, UC Cardiff, 1982. *Publications:* papers, chiefly on Echinoderms, in scientific journals. *Address:* 1 Gilfach Hill, Lampeter Velfrey, near Narberth, Dyfed SA67 8UL. *T:* Llanteg (0183483) 789. *Died 2 Oct. 1995.*

JOHN, Michael M.; *see* Morley-John.

JOHN-MACKIE, Baron *cr* 1981 (Life Peer), of Nazeing in the County of Essex; **John John-Mackie;** Chairman, Forestry Commission, 1976–79; *b* 24 Nov. 1909; *s* of late Maitland Mackie, OBE, farmer, and Mary Ann Mackie (*née* Yull); *m* 1934, Jeannie Inglis Milne; three *s* two *d*. *Educ:* Aberdeen Gram. Sch.; North of Scotland Coll. of Agriculture. Chm., Glentworth Scottish Farms Ltd, 1947–68; Managing director of family farming company at Harold's Park Farm, Nazeing, Waltham Abbey, Essex, 1953–, of Vicarage and Plumridge Farms, Hadley Wood, Enfield, 1968–79. MP (Lab) Enfield East, 1959–Feb. 1974; Jt Parly Sec., Min. of Agriculture, 1964–70; opposition frontbench spokesman on agriculture, food, forestry and fisheries, H of L, 1983–88. Mem., Aberdeen and Kincardine Agricl Exec. Cttee, 1939–47; Governor, North of Scotland Coll. of Agriculture, 1942–64, Vice Chm. 1956–64; Chm., Aberdeen and Kincardine Health

Exec. Cttee, 1948–51; Governor, Nat. Inst. of Agricl Engrg, 1949–61; Member: Secretary of State for Scotland's Adv. Council, 1944–54; Plant Cttee on Poultry Diseases, 1963–64. *Publication:* (for Fabian Soc.) Land Nationalisation. *Recreation:* tree planting. *Address:* Harold's Park, Nazeing, Waltham Abbey, Essex EN9 2SF. *T:* Nazeing (099289) 2202. *Club:* Farmers'.
Died 25 May 1994.

JOHNS, Alan Wesley, CMG 1990; OBE 1973; Executive Director, Royal Commonwealth Society for the Blind, 1984–94 (Deputy Director, 1978–83); *b* 27 March 1931; *s* of Harold Wesley and Catherine Louisa Johns; *m* 1954, Joan Margaret (*née* Wheeler); one *s* one *d. Educ:* Farnborough Grammar Sch., Hants. BScEcon, London; CertEd, Southampton Univ. Teaching in secondary schools, Wilts LEA, 1953–61; Educn Officer, Govt of St Helena, 1961–68; Director of Education: Govt of Seychelles, 1968–74; Govt of Gibraltar, 1974–78. Official Mem., Exec. and Adv. Councils, Govt of St Helena, 1963–68. Sec. Gen., Internat. Agency for the Prevention of Blindness, 1994– (Pres., 1990–94); Trustee, Motor Neurone Disease Assoc., 1994–. FRSA 1992. SQA (Pakistan), 1992. *Recreations:* travel in developing countries, house maintenance, sailing. *Address:* Sitwell, Courtmead Road, Cuckfield, West Sussex RH17 5LR. *T:* Haywards Heath (01444) 413355. *Club:* Rotary (Haywards Heath). *Died 17 Oct. 1995.*

JOHNSON, (Denis) Gordon, CBE 1969; Chairman, Geo. Bassett Holdings Ltd, 1955–78 (Managing Director, 1955–71); Chairman: W. R. Wilkinson & Co. Ltd, Pontefract, 1961–78; Drakes Sweets Marketing Ltd, 1961–78; B. V. de Faam, Holland, 1964–78; Barratt & Co. Ltd, London, 1968–78; *b* 8 Oct. 1911; *s* of late Percy Johnson; *m* 1986, Joan Wilde (*née* Barringham). *Educ:* Harrow; Hertford Coll., Oxford (MA). President: Cocoa, Chocolate and Confectionery Alliance, 1964–66 (Hon. Treas., 1972–77); Confectioners' Benevolent Fund, 1967–68; Member: Yorks Electricity Bd, 1965–75; Food Manufacturing Economic Develt Cttee, 1967–70; Council of CBI, 1968–78; Council, Sheffield Univ., 1972–81; Chm., S Yorks Industrialists' Council, 1976–78. Chm., Hallam Conservative Assoc., 1966–69, and 1973–76; Hon. Treas., City of Sheffield Conservative Fedn, 1969–73; Chm., City of Sheffield Cons. Assocs, 1976–78. Pres., Sheffield and Hallamshire Lawn Tennis Club. Vis. Fellow, Yorks and Humberside Regional Management Centre. CIMgt; MInstD. *Publications:* address to British Assoc. (Economics Section), 1964; contributor to: Business Growth (ed Edwards and Townsend), 1966; Pricing Strategy (ed Taylor and Wills), 1969. *Recreations:* walking, travel, philosophy. *Address:* Ivy Cottage, Trolver Croft, Feock, Truro, Cornwall TR3 6RT. *T:* Truro (01872) 865669. *Died 24 Oct. 1995.*

JOHNSON, Eric Alfred George, CBE 1953; retired chartered engineer; specialist in flood control, sea defences and land drainage engineering; *b* 3 Sept. 1911; *s* of Ernest George Johnson and Amelia Rhoda Johnson; *m* 1936, Barbara Mary Robin; one *s. Educ:* Taunton's Sch., Southampton; UC Southampton. Grad. Engrg, 1931; served for periods with Great Ouse and Trent Catchment Boards, 1933–37; joined Min. of Agriculture, 1937; Chief Engr, 1949–72; associated with most major flood alleviation schemes carried out 1931–81, incl. Thames Barrier; Consultant, Sir Murdoch MacDonald & Partners, 1972–82; Vice-Pres., Internat. Commn of Irrigation and Drainage, 1958–61; former chm. of several internat. and nat. cttees. *Publications:* papers in ICE and other professional jls. *Recreation:* visiting the countryside and sea coast to see some of the areas with which he was associated through floods and protection schemes.

Address: 94 Park Avenue, Orpington, Kent BR6 9EF. *T:* Orpington (0689) 823802. *Died 25 March 1994.*

JOHNSON, Gordon; *see* Johnson, D. G.

JOHNSON, Ven. Hayman; Archdeacon of Sheffield, 1963–78, Archdeacon Emeritus 1978; a Canon Residentiary of Sheffield Cathedral, 1975–78; Chaplain to HM The Queen, 1969–82; *b* 29 June 1912; *s* of late W. G. Johnson, Exeter; *m* 1943, Margaret Louise Price; one *d. Educ:* Exeter Sch.; New Coll., Oxon. Chaplain, RAFVR, 1941–46; Chaplain and Vicar Temporal, Hornchurch, 1953–61; Examining Chaplain to Bishop of Sheffield, 1962–78. *Address:* Flat 1, Parklands, 56 Kibbles Lane, Southborough, Tunbridge Wells, Kent TN4 0LQ.
Died 1 April 1993.

JOHNSON, Henry Leslie, FTI; farmer; *b* 4 March 1904; *s* of Henry and Annie Letitia Johnson, formerly of Macclesfield, Cheshire and Coventry; *m* 1939, Mabel Caroline Hawkins, Woking, Surrey; one *s* two *d. Educ:* Rugby. Joined Courtaulds Ltd, 1922; Dir, 1933–68; Managing Dir, 1935–47. Vice-Chm., Warwicks CC, 1974–75. Pres., Textile Institute, 1942 and 1943. Liveryman, Worshipful Co. of Farmers; Freeman, City of London, 1959. *Address:* Offchurch Bury, near Leamington Spa, Warwicks CV33 9AR. *TA* and *T:* Leamington Spa (0926) 424293. *Died 29 July 1991.*

JOHNSON, Henry Powell C.; *see* Croom-Johnson.

JOHNSON, James, BA, DPA; *b* 16 Sept. 1908; *s* of James and Mary Elizabeth Johnson; *m* 1937, Gladys Evelyn Green; one *d. Educ:* Duke's Sch., Alnwick; Leeds Univ. BA 1st Cl. Hons Geography, 1931; Diploma in Education, 1932; Diploma in Public Administration (London), 1944. FRGS. Schoolmaster: Queen Elizabeth Grammar Sch., Atherstone, 1931; Scarborough High Sch., 1934; Bablake Sch., Coventry, 1944; Lecturer, Coventry Tech. Coll., 1948–50. MP (Lab): Rugby Div. of Warwicks, 1950–59; Kingston upon Hull West, 1964–83. Trade Union Advr, Kenya Local Govt Workers, 1959–60; Student Adviser, Republic of Liberia, 1960–64. Treasurer, Commonwealth Parly Assoc., 1979–82; Chm., Anglo-Somali Soc., 1980. Dir, Hull City Football Club, 1982. Freeman, City of Kingston-upon-Hull, 1982. Played soccer for British Univs and Corinthians. Grand Comdr, Order of Star of Africa (Liberia), 1967; Commander's Cross 2nd Class (Austria), 1985; Comdr, Order of Somali Star (Somalia), 1988. *Recreation:* watching soccer and snooker. *Address:* 70 Home Park Road, Wimbledon Park, SW19 7HN. *T:* 0181–946 6221. *Clubs:* Royal Over-Seas League; Humber St Andrews Engineering Social and Recreation.
Died 31 Jan. 1995.

JOHNSON, Michael Howard; a Social Security Commissioner, since 1986; a Child Support Commissioner, since 1993; a Recorder of the Crown Court, since 1980; *b* 9 May 1930; *s* of Howard Sydney Johnson and Nora Winifred Johnson; *m* 1st, 1954, Elisabeth Loewenthal (marr. diss.); two *d*; 2nd, 1962, Margaret Hazel, *d* of late Ernest Seymour Thomas and Marjorie Lillian Thomas. *Educ:* Charterhouse; Chelsea School of Art. Partner, Johnson & Hecht, Designers and Typographers, 1954–64. Called to the Bar, Gray's Inn, 1964. Asst Parliamentary Boundary Commissioner, 1976–84. Chm., Hertfordshire FPC, 1985–86. Jt Hon. Treas., Barristers' Benevolent Assoc., 1991–. *Recreations:* painting, printmaking, music, gardening. *Address:* Office of the Social Security Commissioners, 83–86 Farringdon Street, EC4A 4BL. *T:* 071–353 5145.
Died 27 Jan. 1994.

JOHNSON, Dr Ralph Hudson, FRCPG; FRACP; FRSE; Director of Postgraduate Medical Education and Training, Oxford University, since 1987; Professorial Fellow,

Wadham College, Oxford; Hon. Consultant Physician and Neurologist, Oxford Regional Health Authority and Oxfordshire Health Authority, since 1987; *b* 3 Dec. 1933; *s* of Sydney R. E. Johnson and Phyllis Johnson (*née* Hudson); *m* 1970, Gillian Sydney (*née* Keith); one *s* one *d*. *Educ:* Rugby; St Catharine's Coll., Cambridge (MA, MB, MChir, MD, Lord Kitchener Schol., Drapers' Co. Schol.; University Coll. Hosp. Med. Sch.; Worcester Coll., Oxford (MA, DPhil; DM Oxon 1966; DSc Glasgow 1976. Hosp. appts, 1958-61; Fellow, Nat. Fund for Res. into Crippling Diseases, 1961-63; Oxford Univ.: Schorstein Med. Res. Fellow, 1963-65; MRC Sci. Staff and Asst to Regius Prof., 1964-67; Dean, St Peter's Coll., 1965-68; Lectr in Neurology, 1967-68; Sen. Lectr in Neurology, Glasgow Univ., and Warden, Queen Margaret Hall, 1968-77; Hon. Consultant Neurologist, Inst. of Neurological Scis, Glasgow; Prof. of Medicine, Wellington Sch. of Medicine, Univ. of Otago, NZ, 1977-87 (Dean, 1977-86); Consultant Neurologist, Wellington Hosp. Bd, 1977-87. Wyndham Deedes Schol., Anglo-Israel Assoc., 1963; Arris and Gale Lectr, RCS, 1965; E. G. Fearnsides Schol., Cambridge, 1966-67; T. K. Stubbins Sen. Res. Fellow, RCP, 1968; Visiting Professor: McGill Univ. Montreal Neurological Inst., 1974; Baghdad, 1974, 1976; Mosul, 1979; All India Vis. Fellow, NZ, 1979. Member: Oxfordshire HA, 1989-91; GMC, 1989-; numerous Boards and Cttees, UK and NZ. Appeal Dir, Wadham Coll., Oxford, 1989-92; Trustee, Disability Information Trust, 1991-. Expeditions to Ecuador, 1960, Atlas Mountains, 1961, Jordan, 1967; Mem., exploration and expedition organisations, Oxford, 1966-68. *Publications:* (with J. M. K. Spalding) Disorders of the Automatic Nervous System, 1974; (with Gillian S. Johnson) Living with Disability, 1978; (with D. G. Lambie and J. M. K. Spalding) Neurocardiology, 1984; numerous contribs to sci. jls on clinical neurology, physiology and patient care. *Recreations:* book collecting, sailing. *Address:* Wadham College, Oxford OX1 3PN. *T:* Oxford (0865) 221517. *Died 1 July 1993.*

JOHNSON, Rex; Director of Social Services, Lancashire County Council, 1978-86; *b* 19 Aug. 1921; *s* of Samuel and Ellen Johnson; *m* 1946, Mary Elizabeth Whitney (*d* 1988); two *d*. *Educ:* Accrington Grammar Sch.; St Paul's Trng Coll., Cheltenham (qual. teacher); Leeds Univ. (MA). Served War, RAF, 1942-46; radar mechanic, educn instr; served Ireland, India, Singapore (Burma Star). Asst Master, Darwen, 1946-49; Dep. Supt, Boys' Remand Home, Lincoln, 1949-52; Head of Springfield Reception Centre, Bradford, 1953-64; Home Office Inspector, Children's Dept, 1964-65; Educnl Psychologist, Bradford, 1965-67; Univ. Lectr, Leeds, 1967-69; Social Work Service Officer, DHSS (formerly Home Office Inspector), 1969-72; Dep. Dir of Social Services, Lancs, 1972-78. Mem., Personal Social Services Council, 1977-80. *Publications:* (ed) ABC of Behaviour Problems, 1962 (2nd edn 1969); (ed) ABC of Social Problems and Therapy, 1963; (ed) ABC of Social Services, 1964; articles in Soc. Work Today, Residential Soc. Work, Community Care, Hosp. and Soc. Services Jl, and Jl RSH. *Address:* Teazledown Cottage, Chain House Lane, Whitestake, Preston, Lancs PR4 4LB. *T:* Preston (01772) 35930. *Died 1 March 1995.*

JOHNSON, Robert White, CBE 1962; Director, Cammell Laird & Co. Ltd, 1946-70; Chairman: Cammell Laird & Co. (Shipbuilders and Engineers) Ltd, 1957-68; Cammell Laird (Shiprepairers) Ltd, 1963-68; retired; *b* 16 May 1912; *s* of Sir Robert (Stewart) Johnson, OBE and Lillian Edna White; *m* 1950, Jill Margaret Preston; two *s* one *d*. *Educ:* Rossall Sch. Robt Bradford & Co. Ltd (Insurance Brokers), 1931-35. Served War of 1939-45, Provost Marshal's Dept, RAF, becoming Wing Comdr. Director: Patent Shaft & Axletree Co. Ltd, Wednesbury, Staffs, 1946-51; Metropolitan-Cammell Carriage and Wagon Co.

Ltd, Birmingham, 1946-64; North Western Line (Mersey) Ltd, 1964-70; Bradley Shipping Ltd, 1964-70; formerly Director: Scottish Aviation Ltd; Coast Lines Ltd; English Steel Corp. Ltd; Chm. of North West Tugs Ltd, Liverpool, 1951-66; Mem. Mersey Docks and Harbour Board, 1948-70; Pt-time Mem. Merseyside and North Wales Electricity Board, 1956-66; Chm., Merseyside Chamber of Commerce and Industry, 1972-74. Underwriting Mem., Lloyd's, 1936-. Pres., Shipbuilding Employers' Federation, 1958-59. *Recreations:* fishing, shooting, golf. *Address:* The Oaks, Well Lane, Heswall, Wirral, Merseyside L60 8NE. *T:* 0151-342 3304.
Died 10 June 1995.

JOHNSON, His Honour William; QC; County Court Judge for County Tyrone, 1947-78; *b* 1 April 1903; *s* of late William Johnson, CBE, and Ellen Johnson. *Educ:* Newry Intermediate Sch.; Portora Royal Sch., Enniskillen; Trinity Coll., Dublin (BA; Sen. Moderator Legal and Polit. Sci.; LLB 1st cl.); King's Inns, Dublin (Certif. of Honour at Final Examinations for Call to Bar). Called to Irish Bar and Bar of N Ireland, 1924; Hon. Bencher, Inn of Court of N Ireland. Served War of 1939-45, France, Germany, Holland, Belgium (despatches); ADJAG, Actg Lt-Col. Lectr in Law, QUB, 1933-36; Chm. Court of Referees 1928-30, Dep. Umpire 1930-35, Umpire 1935-47, NI Unemployment Insce and Pensions Acts; KC (Northern Ireland) 1946; Sen. Crown Prosecutor, Co. Antrim, 1947. Chairman: Cttee on Law of Intestate Succession in NI, 1951; Cttee on Law of Family Provision in NI, 1953; Cttee on Examns for Secondary Intermediate Schs in NI, 1958; Vice-Chm., Jt Cttee on Civil and Criminal Jurisdictions in NI, 1971; Chm., Council of HM's County Ct Judges in NI, 1975-78. Held various positions as Leader and Comr in Scout Assoc., 1923-70; Mem., NI Youth Cttee, 1939; Mem. Council, Scout Assoc., 1958; Chief Comr for NI, Boy Scouts Assocs, 1955-65; Vice-Pres., NI Scout Council. *Publications:* contrib. NI Legal Qly. *Address:* Bar Library, Royal Courts of Justice, Belfast BT1 3JX. *Died 27 July 1993.*

JOHNSON, William Harold Barrett; Commissioner of Inland Revenue, 1965-76; *b* 16 May 1916; *s* of late William Harold Johnson and Mary Ellen (*née* Barrett); *m* 1940, Susan Gwendolen, *d* of Rev. H. H. Symonds; one *s* one *d*. *Educ:* Charterhouse; Magdalene Coll., Cambridge. Served in Royal Artillery, 1939-45. Entered Inland Revenue Dept, 1945. Vice-Pres., Cruising Assoc., 1974-77. *Recreation:* pottering. *Address:* 45 Granville Park, SE13 7DY; Barrow Cottage, Ravenglass, Cumbria CA18 1ST. *Died 29 May 1992.*

JOHNSON-FERGUSON, Sir Neil (Edward), 3rd Bt, *cr* 1906, of Springkell, Dumfries, of Kenyon, Newchurch-in-Culceth, Lancaster, and of Wiston, Lanark; TD; Lieutenant-Colonel Royal Corps of Signals; Vice-Lieutenant, Dumfriesshire, 1965-80; *b* 2 May 1905; *s* of Sir Edward Alexander James Johnson-Ferguson, 2nd Bt, and Hon. Elsie Dorothea McLaren (*d* 1973), *d* of 1st Baron Aberconway; *S* father, 1953; *m* 1931, Sheila Marion (*d* 1985), *er d* of late Col H. S. Jervis, MC; four *s*. *Educ:* Winchester; Trinity Coll., Cambridge (BA). Capt. Lanarks Yeomanry, TA, 1928; Major 1937; Major, Royal Signals, 1939; Lt-Col 1945. JP 1954, DL 1957, Dumfriesshire. American Legion of Merit. *Heir:* *s* Ian Edward Johnson-Ferguson [*b* 1 Feb. 1932; *m* 1964, Rosemary Teresa, *d* of C. J. Whitehead, Copthall Place, Clatford, Hants; three *s*]. *Address:* Springkell, Eaglesfield, Dumfriesshire.
Died 18 June 1992.

JOHNSON-MARSHALL, Percy Edwin Alan, CMG 1975; RIBA; FRTPI; Professor of Urban Design and Regional Planning, University of Edinburgh, 1964-85; Director, Patrick Geddes Centre for Planning Studies, University of Edinburgh, since 1985; in practice as planning consultant since 1960; *b* 20 Jan. 1915; *s* of Felix William Norman Johnson-Marshall and Kate Jane Little; *m* 2nd, 1944, April Bridger; three *s* four *d. Educ:* Liverpool Univ. Sch. of Architecture. Dip. in Arch.(Dist); (RIBA) RTPI; (RIBA) DisTP; MA (Edin). Served War: with Royal Engrs (India and Burma), 1942–46. Planning Architect, Coventry, 1938–41; Asst Regional Planner, Min. of Town and Country Planning, 1946–49; Gp Planning Officer, in charge of reconstr. areas gp, LCC, 1949–59 (projects incl.: Lansbury and Stepney/Poplar South Bank, (jtly with City Corp.) Barbican Area, Tower Hill area, etc); Sen. Lectr, Dept of Architecture, Univ. of Edinburgh, 1959, Head, Dept of Urban Design and Regional Planning, 1967–84. Director: Architectural Research Unit, 1961–64; Planning Research Unit, 1962. Consultant on Human Settlements for UN Stockholm Conf. on Environment, 1972. Partner of Architectural and Planning Consultancy, Percy Johnson-Marshall & Partners (projects incl. Edin. Univ. Plan, Kilmarnock and Bathgate Town Centres, Porto Regional Plan, etc). *Publications:* Rebuilding Cities, 1966; contribs to technical jls. *Address:* Bella Vista, Duddingston Village, Edinburgh EH15 3PZ. *T:* 031–661 2019.

Died 14 July 1993.

JOHNSTON, Alastair McPherson; *see* Dunpark, Hon. Lord.

JOHNSTON, Sir Alexander, GCB 1962 (CB 1946); KBE 1953; Chairman, Board of Inland Revenue, 1958–68; *b* 27 Aug. 1905; *s* of Alexander Simpson Johnston and Joan Macdiarmid; *m* 1947, Betty Joan Harris (*see* Lady Johnston); one *s* one *d. Educ:* George Heriot's Sch.; University of Edinburgh. Entered Home Office, 1928; Principal Asst Sec., Office of the Minister of Reconstruction, 1943–45; Under-Sec., Office of Lord Pres. of the Council, 1946–48; Dep. Sec. of the Cabinet, 1948–51; Third Sec., HM Treasury, 1951–58. Deputy Chairman: Monopolies and Mergers Commn, 1969–76; Panel on Take-overs and Mergers, 1970–83; Council for the Securities Industry, 1978–83. Chairman: Univs Academic Salaries Cttee, 1970–87; Jt Negotiating Cttee, Univs Superannuation Scheme, 1975–90. Hon. DSc(Econ) London, 1977; Hon. LLD Leicester, 1986. *Publications:* The Inland Revenue, 1965; The City Take-over Code, 1980; Presbyterians Awake, 1988. *Address:* 18 Mallord Street, SW3 6DU. *T:* 071–352 6840. *Club:* Reform.

Died 7 Sept. 1994.

JOHNSTON, Betty Joan, (Lady Johnston), CBE 1989; JP; President, Girls' Public Day School Trust, since 1992 (Chairman, 1975–91); Standing Counsel to General Synod of Church of England, 1983–88; *b* 18 May 1916; *d* of Edward and Catherine Anne Harris; *m* 1947, Sir Alexander Johnston, *qv;* one *s* one *d. Educ:* Cheltenham Ladies' Coll.; St Hugh's Coll., Oxford (1st cl. Hons Jurisprudence; MA; BCL). Called to Bar, Gray's Inn, 1940 (1st cl., Bar Final exams; Arden and Lord Justice Holker Sen. schols). Asst Parly Counsel, 1942–52; Dep. Parly Counsel, Law Commn, 1975–83. Chm., Francis Holland (Church of England) Schs Trust, 1978–92. Chairman: GBGSA, 1979–89; ISJC, 1983–86 (Chm., Assisted Places Cttee, 1981–91); Mem., Council, Queen's Coll., London, 1963–91. JP Inner London, 1966. *Address:* 18 Mallord Street, SW3 6DU. *T:* 0171–352 6840. *Club:* University Women's.

Died 28 Nov. 1994.

JOHNSTON, Brian (Alexander), CBE 1991 (OBE 1983); MC 1945; freelance broadcaster and commentator; *b* 24 June 1912; *s* of Lt-Col C. E. Johnston, DSO, MC and Pleasance, *y d* of Col W. J. Alt, CB; *m* 1948, Pauline, *d* of late Col William Tozer, CBE, TD; three *s* two *d. Educ:* Eton; New Coll., Oxford (BA). Family coffee business, 1934–39. Served War of 1939–45: in Grenadier Guards; in 2nd Bn throughout, taking part in Normandy Campaign, advance into Brussels, Nijmegen Bridge and Crossing of Rhine into Germany. Joined BBC, 1945, retired 1972; specialised in cricket commentary for TV and radio (BBC Cricket Corresp., 1963–72), interviews, ceremonial commentary (*eg* Funeral of King George VI, 1952; Coronation of Queen Elizabeth II, 1953; Weddings of Princess Margaret, 1960, Princess Anne, 1973, Prince of Wales, 1981; Queen's Silver Jubilee, 1977); Let's Go Somewhere feature in In Town Tonight, 1948–52; Down Your Way, 1972–87; Twenty Questions, 1975–76, etc. Radio Sports Personality Award, Soc. of Authors/Pye Radio, 1981; Radio Personality of the Year Award, Sony, 1983; Radio Sports Commentator of the Year, Daily Mail, 1988. *Publications:* Let's Go Somewhere, 1952; Armchair Cricket, 1957; Stumped for a Tale, 1965; The Wit of Cricket, 1968; All About Cricket, 1972; It's Been a Lot of Fun, 1974; It's a Funny Game . . ., 1978; Rain Stops Play, 1979; Chatterboxes, 1983; Now Here's a Funny Thing, 1984; Guide to Cricket, 1986; It's Been a Piece of Cake, 1989; Down Your Way, 1990; The Tale of Billy Bouncer, 1990; Views from the Boundary, 1990; 45 Summers, 1991; Someone Who Was, 1992; More Views from the Boundary, 1993. *Recreations:* cricket, theatre, reading newspapers. *Address:* 43 Boundary Road, NW8 0JE. *T:* 071–286 2991. *Clubs:* Boodle's, MCC.

Died 5 Jan. 1994.

JOHNSTON, Sir Edward (Alexander), KBE 1989; CB 1975; Government Actuary, 1973–89; Director, Noble Lowndes Actuarial Services Ltd, since 1989; *b* 19 March 1929; 2nd *s* of Edward Hamilton Johnston, DLitt, and Iris Olivia Helena May; *m* 1st, 1956, Veronica Mary Bernays (marr. diss.); two *s* two *d*; 2nd, Christine Elizabeth Nash (*née* Shepherd). *Educ:* Groton Sch., USA; Marlborough Coll.; New Coll., Oxford (BA 1952). FIA 1957; FPMI 1976. Equity & Law Life Assce Soc., 1952–58; Govt Actuary's Dept, 1958–89. Mem. Council: Inst. of Actuaries, 1973–88; Pensions Management Inst., 1983–88 (Pres., 1985–87). *Address:* (office) Norfolk House, Wellesley Road, Croydon CR9 3EB. *Club:* Reform.

Died 11 Nov. 1991.

JOHNSTON, Michael Errington; Under-Secretary, Ministry of Agriculture, Fisheries and Food, 1970–76; *b* 22 Jan. 1916; *s* of late Lt-Col C. E. L. Johnston, RA, and Beatrix Johnston; *m* 1st, 1938, Ida Brown (*d* 1988); two *d*; 2nd, 1992, Clare Cave. *Educ:* Wellington; Peterhouse, Cambridge (Scholar). BA, 1st cl. Hist. Tripos, 1937; MA 1947. Served War of 1939–45, Rifle Bde (Capt., despatches). Asst Principal, Board of Education, 1938; Principal, 1946; Asst Sec., HM Treasury, 1952, Under-Sec., 1962–68; Under-Sec., Civil Service Dept, 1968–70. *Recreations:* painting, birdwatching. *Address:* Flat 7, 151 Mortlake High Street, SW14 8SW. *T:* 081–876 5265.

Died 16 April 1992.

JOHNSTON, Robert William Fairfield, CMG 1960; CBE 1954; MC 1917; TD 1936 (and three Bars, 1947); Assistant Secretary, Ministry of Defence, 1946–62; retired from the Civil Service, 1962; *b* 1 May 1895; *e s* of late Capt. Robert Johnston, Army Pay Dept and Royal Scots; *m* 1922, Agnes Scott (*d* 1980), *o c* of late Peter Justice, Edinburgh; one *s*. Entered Civil Service, Dec. 1910: served in War Office, Bd of Trade, Min. of Labour, Home Office, Office of Minister without Portfolio, Min. of Defence, and seconded to FO, as Counsellor in UK Delegation in Paris to NATO and OEEC, 1953–61. Territorial Army, 1910–47; served European War, 1914–18, The Royal Scots (1st, 9th and 16th Battalions) in France, Flanders, Macedonia and Egypt; commissioned 1917; War of 1939–45, Lieut-Col, Comdg 8th Bn Gordon Highlanders, 1940–42, and 100th (Gordons) Anti-Tank Regt, RA, 1942–44, in 51st (Highland) and 2nd (British) Inf. Divs respectively; retired

as Lieut-Col TA, Sept. 1947. *Address:* 8 Broad Avenue, Queen's Park, Bournemouth, Dorset.
Died 18 Oct. 1991.

JOHNSTONE, David Kirkpatrick; Director of Programmes, Scottish Television plc, 1977–86; *b* 4 July 1926; *s* of John and Isabel Johnstone; *m* 1950, Kay. *Educ:* Ayr Academy; Scottish Radio College. Reporter, Ayrshire Post; Radio Officer, Blue Funnel Line; Reporter, Glasgow Herald; Night News Editor, Scottish Daily Mail; Scottish Feature Writer, News Chronicle; Scottish TV, 1958–: News Editor; Producer/Director; Head of News and Current Affairs; Asst Controller of Programmes; Controller of Programmes. Chm., Regional Programme Controllers Gp, ITV Contractors Assoc., 1984–85. Member, BAFTA, 1978. Elder, Church of Scotland; Clerk to Congregational Bd, Broom Parish Church, 1989–. Pres., Eastwood Probus Club, 1989–90. *Recreations:* golf, travel, television. *Club:* Eastwood Golf (Glasgow).
Died 8 Feb. 1993.

JOHNSTONE, Sir Frederic (Allan George), 10th Bt *cr* 1700, of Westerhall, Dumfriesshire; *b* 23 Feb. 1906; *o s* of Sir George Johnstone, 9th Bt and Ernestine (*d* 1955), *d* of Col A. R. C. Porcelli-Cust; *S* father, 1952; *m* 1st, 1933, Gladys Hands (marr. diss. 1941); 2nd, 1946, Doris, *d* of late W. L. Shortridge; two *s. Educ:* Imperial Service Coll. *Heir: s* (George) Richard (Douglas) Johnstone [*b* 21 Aug. 1948; *m* 1976, Gwyneth Susan Bailey; one *s* one *d*].
Died 19 July 1994.

JOHNSTONE, R(obert) Edgeworth, BScTech (Manchester); MSc, DSc (London); FIChemE; FIMechE; FRSC; Lady Trent Professor of Chemical Engineering, University of Nottingham, 1960–67; *b* 4 Feb. 1900; *e s* of Lieut-Col Sir Walter Edgeworth-Johnstone, KBE, CB and Helen Gunning Walker Waters; *m* 1931, Jessie Marjorie (*d* 1981), *d* of late R. M. T. Greig; one *s* one *d* (and one *s* decd). *Educ:* Wellington; RMA Woolwich; Manchester Coll. of Technology; University Coll., London. Fellow Salters' Inst. of Industrial Chem., 1926–27. Held various posts at home and abroad with Magadi Soda Co., Trinidad Leaseholds, Petrocarbon, Min. of Supply and UK Atomic Energy Authority. Vice-Pres., IChemE, 1951. Liveryman, Worshipful Co. of Salters, 1956. Council Medal, IChemE, 1969, Hon. Fellow, 1981. *Publications:* Continuing Education in Engineering, 1969; (with Prof. M. W. Thring) Pilot Plants, Models and Scale-up Methods in Chemical Engineering, 1957; papers in scientific and engineering jls, especially on distillation, process development and engineering education; *as Robert Johnstone:* The Lost World, 1978; (ed) Samuel Butler on the Resurrection, 1980; The Johnstone Flute, 1993. *Recreations:* music, philosophy. *Address:* 3 rue Basse, 72300 Parcé-sur-Sarthe, France. *Club:* Athenæum. *Died 3 Dec. 1994.*

JOICEY, 4th Baron, *cr* 1906, of Chester-le-Street, Co. Durham; **Michael Edward Joicey,** DL; Bt 1893; *b* 28 Feb. 1925; *s* of 3rd Baron Joicey and Joan (*d* 1967), *y d* of 4th Earl of Durham; *S* father, 1966; *m* 1952, Elisabeth Marion, *y d* of late Lieut-Col Hon. Ian Leslie Melville; two *s* one *d. Educ:* Eton; Christ Church, Oxford. DL Northumberland, 1985. *Heir: s* Hon. James Michael Joicey [*b* 28 June 1953; *m* 1984, Harriet, *yr d* of Rev. William Thompson, Oxnam Manse, Jedburgh; two *s* one *d*]. *Address:* Etal Manor, Berwick-upon-Tweed, Northumberland TD15 2PU. *T:* Crookham (0890) 820205. *Clubs:* Lansdowne, Kennel; Northern Counties (Newcastle upon Tyne). *Died 14 June 1993.*

JOLL, Prof. James Bysse, MA; FBA 1977; Stevenson Professor of International History, University of London, 1967–81, then Professor Emeritus; *b* 21 June 1918; *e s* of Lieut-Col H. H. Joll and Alice Muriel Edwards. *Educ:* Winchester; University of Bordeaux; New Coll., Oxford.

War Service, Devonshire Regt and Special Ops Exec., 1939–45. Fellow and Tutor in Politics, New Coll., Oxford, 1946–50; Fellow, 1951–67, Emeritus Fellow, 1967, Hon. Fellow, 1991, and Sub-Warden, 1951–67, St Antony's Coll., Oxford. Vis. Mem., Inst. for Advanced Study, Princeton, 1954 and 1971; Visiting Professor of History: Stanford Univ., Calif, 1958; Sydney Univ., 1979; Univ. of Iowa, 1980; Vis. Lectr in History, Harvard University, 1962; Benjamin Meaker Vis. Prof., Bristol Univ., 1985. Hon. Prof. of History, Warwick Univ., 1981–87. Hon. Fellow, LSE, 1985. Hon. DLitt Warwick, 1988. *Publications:* The Second International, 1955, rev. edn 1974; Intellectuals in Politics, 1960; The Anarchists, 1964, rev. edn 1979; Europe since 1870, 1973, 4th edn 1990; Gramsci, 1977; The Origins of the First World War, 1984, 2nd edn 1992. *Recreation:* music. *Address:* 24 Ashchurch Park Villas, W12 9SP. *T:* 081–749 5221.
Died 12 July 1994.

JOLLY, Anthony Charles; His Honour Judge Jolly; a Circuit Judge since 1980; *b* 25 May 1932; *s* of Leonard and Emily Jolly; *m* 1962, Rosemary Christine Kernan; two *s* one *d. Educ:* Royal Naval Coll., Dartmouth; Balliol Coll., Oxford (Exhibnr history; MA). Called to Bar, Inner Temple, 1954; a Recorder, 1975–80; Hon. Recorder of Preston, 1989. *Recreations:* sailing, chess. *Address:* (home) Naze House, Freckleton, Lancs PR4 1UN. *T:* Freckleton (0772) 632285. *Died 26 Sept. 1992.*

JOLY de LOTBINIÈRE, Lt-Col Sir Edmond, Kt 1964; Chairman, Eastern Provincial Area Conservative Association, 1961–65, President, 1969–72; Chairman, Bury St Edmunds Division Conservative Association, 1953–72, President, 1972–79; *b* 17 March 1903; *er s* of late Brig.-Gen. H. G. Joly de Lotbinière, DSO and Mildred Louisa, *d* of C. S. Grenfell; *m* 1st, 1928, Hon. Elizabeth Alice Cecilia Jolliffe (marr. diss. 1937), *d* of 3rd Baron Hylton; two *s*; 2nd, 1937, Helen Ruth Mildred Ferrar (*d* 1953); 3rd, 1954, Evelyn Adelaide (*née* Dawnay) (*d* 1985), widow of Lt-Col J. A. Innes, DSO. *Educ:* Eton Coll.; Royal Military Academy, Woolwich. 2nd Lieut Royal Engineers, 1923; served in India; RARO, 1928; re-employed, 1939; served War of 1939–45: in Aden, Abyssinian Campaign and East Africa (despatches); Major 1941; Lieut-Col 1943; retired 1945. Chm. and Managing Dir of several private companies connected with the building trade. *Recreation:* bridge. *Address:* Horringer Manor, Bury St Edmunds, Suffolk. *T:* Horringer (0284) 735208. *Club:* Naval and Military.
Died 13 Feb. 1994.

JONES, (Albert) Arthur; *b* 23 Oct. 1915; *s* of late Frederick Henry Jones and Emma (*née* Shreeves); *m* 1939, Peggy Joyce (*née* Wingate); one *s* one *d. Educ:* Bedford Modern Sch. (Harpur Schol.). Territorial, Beds Yeomanry, RA, 1938; Middle East with First Armd Div., 1941; captured at Alamein, 1942; escaped as POW from Italy, 600 miles walk to Allied Territory. Mem. Bedford RDC, 1946–49; Mem. Bedford Borough Council, 1949–74, Alderman, 1957–74; Mayor of Bedford, 1957–58, 1958–59; Member: Beds CC, 1956–67; Central Housing Advisory Cttee, 1959–62; Internat. Union of Local Authorities; Exec. Cttee, Nat. Union of Cons. and Unionist Assocs, 1963–73; Chm., Local Govt Nat. Adv. Cttee, Cons. Central Office, 1963–73; UK Rep., Consultative Assembly, Council of Europe and Assembly of WEU, 1971–73. Contested (C) Wellingborough, 1955; MP (C) Northants S, Nov. 1962–1974, Daventry, 1974–79; Mem., Speaker's Panel of Chairmen, 1974–79. Member: Select Cttee on Immigration and Race Relations, 1969–70; Select Cttee on Expenditure, 1974–79; Chm., Environment Sub-Cttee, 1974–79; Vice-Chm., Cons. Back-Bench Cttee for the Environment, 1974–79. Dir of private companies. Hon. Treas., Town and Country Planning Assoc., 1975–81;

Founder Mem., UK Housing Assoc., 1972–81; Member: New Towns Commn, 1980–88 (Dep. Chm., 1981–88); Anglian Water Authority, 1980–82. Vice-Pres., IWA, 1970–. Governor: Harpur Charity, 1953–89 (Chm., Estates Cttee, 1960–84; Chm., Finance Cttee, 1984–89); Centre for Policy Studies, 1980–83; St Andrew's Hosp., Northampton, 1979– (Dep. Chm., 1984–91). FSVA. *Publications:* Future of Housing Policy, 1960; War on Waste, 1965; Local Governors at Work, 1968; For the Record: Bedford 1945–74: Land Use and Financial Planning, 1981; Britain's Heritage, 1985. *Address:* Moor Farm, Pavenham, Bedford. *Died 6 Dec. 1991.*

JONES, Maj.-Gen. Basil Douglas, CB 1960; CBE 1950; *b* 14 May 1903; *s* of Rev. B. Jones; *m* 1932, Katherine Holberton (*d* 1986), *d* of Col H. W. Man, CBE, DSO; one *s* two *d. Educ:* Plymouth Coll.; RMC, Sandhurst. 2nd Lieut, Welch Regt, 1924; transferred to RAOC, 1935; Major 1939; served with Australian Military Forces in Australia and New Guinea, 1941–44; Temp. Brig. 1947; Brig. 1955; Maj.-Gen. 1958; Inspector, RAOC, 1958–60, retired. ADC to the Queen, 1956–58. Col Commandant, RAOC, 1963–67. *Recreation:* golf. *Address:* Churchfield, Sutton Courtenay, Abingdon, Oxon OX14 4AG. *T:* Abingdon (0235) 848261. *Died 15 Oct. 1992.*

JONES, David Elwyn L.; *see* Lloyd Jones.

JONES, Captain Desmond V.; *see* Vincent-Jones.

JONES, Edgar Stafford, CBE 1960 (MBE 1953); *b* 11 June 1909; *s* of late Theophilus Jones; *m* 1938, Margaret Aldis, *d* of late Henry Charles Askew; one *s* one *d. Educ:* Liverpool Institute High Sch. Mem. of Local Government Service, 1925–34; joined Assistance Board, 1934; seconded to Air Min., as Hon. Flt-Lt RAFVR, 1943; Hon. Sqdn-Ldr, 1945; transferred to Foreign Office, 1946; transferred to Washington, 1949; Dep. Finance Officer, Foreign Office, 1953; Head of Finance Dept, Foreign Office, 1957 and Diplomatic Service Administration Office, 1965; retired 1968. *Address:* 30 Wingfield Road, Kingston upon Thames, Surrey KT2 5LR. *T:* 081–546 9812. *Clubs:* London Welsh Rugby Football, Rugby; Glamorgan County Cricket. *Died 26 July 1992.*

JONES, Rt Hon. Sir Edward (Warburton), Kt 1973; PC 1979; PC (NI) 1965; Lord Justice of Appeal, Supreme Court of Judicature, Northern Ireland, 1973–84 (Judge of the High Court of Justice in Northern Ireland, 1968–73); *b* 3 July 1912; *s* of late Hume Riversdale Jones and Elizabeth Anne (*née* Phibbs); *m* 1st, 1941, Margaret Anne Crosland Smellie (*d* 1953); three *s*; 2nd, 1953, Ruth Buchan Smellie (*d* 1990); one *s. Educ:* Portora Royal School, Enniskillen, N Ireland; Trinity Coll., Dublin. BA (TCD), with First Class Moderatorship, Legal Science, and LLB (TCD) 1935. Called to Bar of Northern Ireland, 1936; QC (N Ireland), 1948; Bencher, Inn of Court of NI, 1961; called to Bar, Middle Temple, 1964; Hon. Bencher, Middle Temple, 1982. Junior Crown Counsel: County Down, 1939; Belfast, 1945–55. Enlisted, 1939; commissioned Royal Irish Fusiliers, 1940; Staff Coll., Camberley, 1943; AAG, Allied Land Forces, South-East Asia, 1945; released with Hon. rank Lt-Col, 1946. MP (U) Londonderry City, Parliament of Northern Ireland, 1951–68; Attorney-Gen. for Northern Ireland, 1964–68. Chancellor: Dio. Derry and Raphoe, 1945–64; Dio. Connor, 1959–64 and 1978–81; Dio. Clogher, 1973; Lay Mem. Court of Gen. Synod, Church of Ireland. Vice-Pres., College Historical Soc., TCD, 1983–. *Publication:* Jones L. J.: his life and times—an autobiography, 1987. *Recreation:* golf. *Address:* Craig-y-Mor, Trearddur Bay, Anglesey. *T:* Trearddur Bay (0407) 860406. *Clubs:* Army and Navy; Ulster Reform (Belfast); Royal Portrush Golf (Captain, 1956–57). *Died 18 March 1993.*

JONES, Eifion, CMG 1964; OBE 1953; Permanent Secretary, Ministry of Works, Northern Nigeria, 1959–66; Member, Northern Nigerian Development Corporation, 1959–66; retired; *b* Llanelly, Carmarthenshire, 10 June 1912; *s* of I. J. Jones and R. A. Jones (*née* Bassett); *m* 1944, Kathleen, *d* of Donald and E. J. MacCalman, Argyllshire. *Educ:* Llanelli Grammar Sch.; University Coll., Swansea. BSc (Wales). CEng; FICE 1957; FIWEM (FIWE 1957). Executive Engineer, Nigeria, 1942; Colonial Service 2nd Course, Camb. Univ., 1949–50 (Mem. Christ's Coll.); Senior Executive Engineer, 1951; Chief Engineer, 1954; Dep. Dir of Public Works, Nigeria, 1958. Member: Lagos Exec. Develt Bd, 1954–57; Governing Cttee, King's Coll., Lagos, 1956–59; Cttee for Develt of Tourism and Game Reserves in N Nigeria, 1965. Mem., West African Council, ICE, 1960–65. JP N Nigeria, 1963–66. *Recreations:* golf, gardening, reading. *Address:* c/o Barclays Bank, Llanelli, Dyfed SA15 3UE. *Died 6 March 1995.*

JONES, Emrys; *see* Jones, J. E.

JONES, Major Francis, CVO 1969; TD (3 clasps); DL; MA; FSA; Wales Herald Extraordinary since 1963; County Archivist, Carmarthenshire, 1958–74; *b* Trevine, Pembrokeshire, 5 July 1908; *s* of James Jones, Grinston, Pembs, and Martha Jones; *m* Ethel M. S. A. (*d* 1985), *d* of late J. J. Charles, Trewilym, Pembs; two *s* two *d. Educ:* Fishguard County Sch., Pembs. Temp. Archivist of Pembs, 1934–36; Archivist, Nat. Library of Wales, 1936–39. Lt 4th Bn Welch Regt (TA), 1931–39; trans. Pembroke Yeomanry (RA, TA), 1939, Battery Captain; served War of 1939–45: RA (Field), N Africa (despatches), Middle East, Italy; Battery Comdr, and 2nd-in-comd of regt; GSO2 War Office; Mil. Narrator, Hist. Section, Cabinet Office, 1945–58 (compiled Official narrative of Sicilian and Italian Campaigns); Battery Comdr, The Surrey Yeomanry, QMR (RA, TA), 1949–56. Mil. Liaison Officer, Coronation, 1953; served on the Earl Marshal's staff, State Funeral of Sir Winston Churchill, 1965; Mem., Prince of Wales Investiture Cttee, 1967–69. Local Sec. and Mem., Cambrian Assoc.; President: Cambrian Archaeol Assoc., 1985–86; Pembrokeshire Historical Soc., 1988–89; Vice-Pres., Council, Hon. Soc. of Cymmrodorion; Member: Gorsedd, Royal National Eisteddfod of Wales; Court and Council, Nat. Library of Wales, 1967–77; Council, Nat. Museum of Wales; Historical Soc. of the Church in Wales; Carmarthenshire Local History Soc.; Pembrokeshire Records Soc. (Vice-Pres.); Croeso '69 Nat. Cttee; Academie Internationale d'Heraldique; Heraldry Soc. Trustee, Elvet Lewis Memorial (Gangell), 1967–81. Vice-Pres., Dyfed Local Councils, 1974–81. DL Dyfed, 1965. Broadcaster (TV and radio). Hon. MA Univ. of Wales. CStJ. *Publications:* The Holy Wells of Wales, 1954; The History of Llangunnor, 1965; God Bless the Prince of Wales, 1969; The Princes and Principality of Wales, 1969; (jtly) Royal and Princely Heraldry in Wales, 1969; Historic Carmarthenshire Homes and their Families, 1987; numerous articles on historical, genealogical and heraldic matters to learned jls. *Recreations:* genealogical research and heraldry, fly-fishing, study of ancient ruins. *Address:* Hendre, Springfield Road, Carmarthen. *T:* Carmarthen (0267) 237099. *Died 14 Dec. 1993.*

JONES, Air Marshal Sir George, KBE 1953 (CBE 1942); CB 1943; DFC; Royal Australian Air Force; *b* 22 Nov. 1896; *s* of Henry Jones; *m* 1st, 1919, Muriel Agnes Cronan (*d* 1969), *d* of F. Stone; (two *s* decd); 2nd, 1970, Mrs Gwendoline Claire Bauer (*d* 1980). Served Gallipoli and European War, 1914–18 (despatches, DFC); joined RAAF, 1921; Dir Personnel Services, RAAF, 1936–40; Dir of Training, 1940–42; Chief of Air Staff, 1942–52.

Publication: From Private to Air Marshal (autobiog.), 1988. *Club:* Naval and Military (Melbourne).

Died 24 Aug. 1992.

JONES, Sir Glyn (Smallwood), GCMG 1964 (KCMG 1960; CMG 1957); MBE 1944; *b* 9 Jan. 1908; *s* of late G. I. Jones, Chester; *m* 1942, Nancy Madoc, *d* of J. H. Featherstone, CP, South Africa; one *d* (one *s* decd). *Educ:* King's Sch., Chester; St Catherine's Coll., Oxford Univ. (MA; Hon. Fellow, 1977). HM Colonial Service (later HM Overseas Civil Service) N Rhodesia: Cadet, 1931; District Officer, 1933; Commissioner for Native Development, 1950; Acting Development Sec., 1956; Prov. Comr, 1956; Resident Comr, Barotseland, 1957; Sec. for Native Affairs, 1958; Minister of Native Affairs and Chief Comr, 1959; Chief Sec., Nyasaland, 1960–61; Governor, 1961–64; Governor-Gen. and C-in-C of Malawi, 1964–66. Advr on Govt Admin to Prime Minister of Lesotho, 1969–71; Dep. Chm., Lord Pearce Commn on Rhodesian Opinion, 1971–72; British Govt Observer, Zimbabwe Elections, 1980. Founding Chm., Friends of Malawi Assoc, 1968–83; Chairman: Malawi Church Trust, 1970–; Friends of Jairos Jiri Assoc. (Zimbabwe), 1982–; Zimbabwe Trust (London), 1982–; Malaŵi Against Polio Trust, 1984–. Grand Cordon, Order of the Trinity (Ethiopia), 1965; Order of the Epiphany (Central Africa), 1966. KStJ. *Recreations:* shooting, fishing, golf. *Clubs:* Athenæum, Commonwealth Trust, MCC.

Died 10 June 1992.

JONES, (Gwilym) Wyn, CBE 1977; Member, Gwynedd Health Authority, 1982–90, Associate Member, since 1990; *b* 12 July 1926; *s* of late Rev. John Jones, MA, BD, and Elizabeth (*née* Roberts); *m* 1951, Ruth (*née* Thomas); one *s* one *d*. *Educ:* Llanrwst Grammar Sch.; UCNW, Bangor (BA Hons); London Univ. Served RN, 1944–47. Cadet, Colonial Admin. Service, Gilbert and Ellice Islands, 1950; DO, DC and Secretariat in Tarawa, Line Islands, Phoenix Islands and Ocean Island, 1950–61; Solomon Islands, 1961; Asst Sec., 1961–67; Sen. Asst Sec., 1967–74; Dep. Chief Sec., 1974; Sec. to Chief Minister and Council of Ministers, 1974–77; Governor, Montserrat, 1977–80. Administrator, Cwmni Theatr Cymru (Welsh Nat. Theatre), 1982–85. Mem. Court, UCNW Bangor, 1980–86. *Recreation:* walking alone. *Address:* Y Frondeg, Warren Drive, Deganwy, Gwynedd LL31 9ST. *T:* Deganwy (0492) 583377. *Died 23 Oct. 1993.*

JONES, Rev. Prof. Hubert C.; *see* Cunliffe-Jones.

JONES, Rev. Hugh; *see* Jones, Rev. R. W. H.

JONES, Ian E.; *see* Edwards-Jones.

JONES, Sir James (Duncan), KCB 1972 (CB 1964); *b* 28 Oct. 1914; *m* 1943, Jenefer Mary Wade; one *s*. *Educ:* Glasgow High Sch.; Glasgow Univ.; University Coll., Oxford. Admiralty, 1941; Ministry of Town and Country Planning: joined 1946; Prin. Priv. Sec., 1947–50; Under-Sec., Min. of Housing and Local Govt, 1958–63; Sec., Local Govt Commn for England, 1958–61; Dep. Sec., Min. of Housing and Local Govt, 1963–66; Dep. Sec., Min. of Transport, 1966–70; Sec., Local Govt and Develt, DoE, 1970–72; Permanent Sec., DoE, 1972–75. Hon. FRIBA; Hon. FRTPI. *Address:* The Courtyard, Ewelme, Wallingford, Oxon OX10 6HP. *T:* Wallingford (01491) 839270. *Club:* Oxford Union. *Died 6 Sept. 1995.*

JONES, (John) Emrys, CBE 1979; Regional Organiser and Secretary, Labour Party, Wales, 1965–79, retired; *b* 12 March 1914; *s* of William Jones and Elizabeth Susan Jones; *m* 1935, Stella Davies; one *d*. *Educ:* Secondary Sch., Mountain Ash, S Wales. Shop assistant, 1928–29; railwayman, 1929–33; Rootes motor factory, 1933–36; railwayman, 1936–49. Regional Organiser, Labour Party: S West, 1949–60; W Midlands, 1960–65. *Recreations:*

reading, writing. *Address:* 11 Conham Hill, Hanham, Bristol BS15 3AW. *T:* Bristol (0272) 615134.

Died 24 Dec. 1991.

JONES, Sir (John) Kenneth (Trevor), Kt 1965; CBE 1956; QC 1976; Legal Adviser to the Home Office, 1956–77; *b* 11 July 1910; *s* of John Jones and Agnes Morgan; *m* 1940, Menna, *d* of Cyril O. Jones; two *s*. *Educ:* King Henry VIII Grammar Sch., Abergavenny; University Coll. of Wales, Aberystwyth; St John's Coll., Cambridge. Called to the Bar, Lincoln's Inn, 1937. Served Royal Artillery, 1939–45. Entered the Home Office as a Legal Asst, 1945. Mem. of the Standing Cttee on Criminal Law Revision, 1959–80. *Address:* 7 Chilton Court, Walton-on-Thames, Surrey KT12 1NG. *T:* Walton-on-Thames (01932) 226890. *Club:* Athenæum. *Died 25 Oct. 1995.*

JONES, Brig. John Murray R.; *see* Rymer-Jones.

JONES, Rev. Preb. John Stephen Langton; Residentiary Canon and Precentor of Wells Cathedral, 1947–67, Prebendary, since 1967; *b* 21 May 1889; *m* 1921, Jeanne Charlotte Dujardin; three *s* one *d*. *Educ:* Dover College; Jesus College, Cambridge. Deacon, 1914; priest, 1915; Asst Curate of Halifax Parish Church, 1914; Asst Curate, Hambleden, Berks, 1919; Vicar of Yiewsley, Middx, 1921; Rector of W Lydford, Taunton, 1939–47. Proctor in Convocation for Bath and Wells, 1946–50. *Address:* 16 Wimborne Road, Bournemouth BH2 6NT.

Died 26 Sept. 1992.

JONES, Sir Kenneth; *see* Jones, Sir J. K. T.

JONES, Air Marshal Sir Laurence (Alfred), KCB 1987 (CB 1984); AFC 1971; Lieutenant-Governor of the Isle of Man, 1990–95; *b* 18 Jan. 1933; *s* of Benjamin Howel and Irene Dorothy Jones; *m* 1956, Brenda Ann; two *d*. *Educ:* Trinity Sch., Croydon; RAF College, Cranwell. Entry to RAF Coll., 1951, graduated 1953; served as Jun. Officer Pilot with 208 Sqdn in Middle East, 1954–57; Fighter Weapons Sch., 74 Sqdn, until 1961; commanded: No 8 Sqdn, Aden, 1961–63; No 19 Sqdn, RAF Germany, 1967–70; Station Comdr, RAF Wittering, 1975–76; RCDS 1977; Director of Operations (Air Support), MoD, 1978–81; SASO, Strike Command, 1982–84; ACAS(Ops), MoD, 1984; ACDS(Progs), 1985–86; ACAS, 1986–87; Air Member for Personnel, 1987–89, retd. *Recreation:* golf. *Club:* Royal Air Force.

Died 23 Sept. 1995.

JONES, Leslie, JP; MA; Secretary for Welsh Education, Welsh Office and Department of Education and Science, 1970–77; *b* Tumble, Carms, 27 April 1917; *y s* of late William Jones, ME and Joanna (*née* Peregrine); *m* 1948, Glenys, *d* of late D. R. Davies, Swansea; one *s* one *d*. *Educ:* Gwendraeth Valley Grammar Sch.; Univ. of Wales. Served with RN, 1940–46 (Lieut RNVR). UC Swansea, 1937–40 and 1946–47 (1st cl. hons Econs); Lectr in Econs, Univ. of Liverpool, 1947–51; Lectr and Sen. Lectr in Econs, UC Cardiff, 1952–60; Dir, Dept of Extra-Mural Studies, UC Cardiff, 1965–69. Hon. Lectr, Dept of Educn, UC Cardiff, 1977–85. Member: Ancient Monuments Bd for Wales, 1970–77; Court, UWIST, 1978–85; Council, St David's University Coll., 1978–85; Court, Nat. Library of Wales, 1978–; Court, Nat. Mus. of Wales, 1978–85; Council, Dr Barnardo's, 1978–88. Hon. Fellow, UC Cardiff, 1971. JP Cardiff 1966. *Publications:* The British Shipbuilding Industry, 1958; articles on maritime, coal, iron and steel industries; industrial economics generally. *Recreations:* walking, gardening. *Address:* 43 Cyncoed Road, Cardiff CF2 6AB. *Club:* Naval.

Died 18 July 1994.

JONES, Hon. Mrs Miller; *see* Askwith, Hon. B. E.

JONES, Noel Andrew Stephen; HM Diplomatic Service; Ambassador to Kazakhstan, since 1993; *b* 22 Dec. 1940;

s of Ernest Walter Jones and Merlyn Edith (*née* Jones); *m* 1963, Jean Rosemary Cheval; one *s* one *d*. *Educ:* St Joseph's Coll., London. With Jenkins Wood, Chartered Accountants, 1958–61; joined HM Diplomatic Service, 1962; served Zagreb, Hamburg, Bangkok, Taiwan, 1963–72; FCO, 1972–74; Sarajevo (lang. studies), 1975; Third Sec. (Commercial), Belgrade, 1975–79; Second Sec. (Econ. then Pol), Bonn, 1979–83; Russian lang. studies, Sussex Univ., 1984–85; Hd of Chancery and Dep. Hd of Mission, Ulan Baatar, 1985–87; Hd of Post, Seattle, 1987–90; Press Attaché and Hd of Press and Public Affairs, Moscow, 1991–93. *Recreations:* field sports, gardening, travelling, sailing. *Address:* c/o Foreign and Commonwealth Office, King Charles Street, SW1A 2AH. *Died 21 Nov. 1995.*

JONES, Norman William, CBE 1984; TD 1962; FCIB; Director, 1976–91 and Vice Chairman, 1989–91, Lloyds Bank plc; *b* 5 Nov. 1923; *s* of late James William Jones and Mabel Jones; *m* 1950, Evelyn June Hall; two *s*. *Educ:* Gravesend Grammar Sch. FIB 1972. Served War, Army, 1942–47: commnd Beds and Herts Regt, 1943; with Airborne Forces, 1944–47; TA, 1947–64. Entered Lloyds Bank, 1940; Gen. Man., 1973; Asst Chief Gen. Man., 1975; Dep. Group Chief Exec., 1976; Gp Chief Exec., 1978–83; a Dep. Chm., 1984–89. Chairman: Lloyds Merchant Bank (Govt Bonds) Ltd, 1986–87; Lloyds Bank (Stockbrokers) Ltd, 1986–91; Director: Lloyds Bank California, 1974–83; National Bank of New Zealand, 1978–91; Lloyds Bank International, 1984–85; Lloyds Bank NZA Ltd, 1985–90; Lloyds Merchant Bank Hldgs, 1985–91; Lloyds Abbey Life Group, 1988–91. Chm., Aust. and NZ Trade Adv. Cttee, 1985–88. FRSA. *Recreations:* sailing, photography, DIY. *Address:* Rowans, 21 College Avenue, Grays, Essex RM17 5UN. *T:* Grays Thurrock (0375) 373101. *Club:* Overseas Bankers.
Died 7 June 1993.

JONES, Norvela, (Mrs Michael Jones); *see* Forster, N.

JONES, Reginald Ernest, MBE 1942; Chief Scientific Officer, Ministry of Technology, 1965–69, retired; *b* 16 Jan. 1904; *m* 1933, Edith Ernestine Kressig; one *s* one *d*. *Educ:* Marylebone Gram. Sch.; Imperial Coll. of Science and Technology. MSc, DIC, FIEE. International Standard Electric Corp., 1926–33; GPO, 1933–65 (Asst Engr-in-Chief, 1957). Bronze Star (US), 1943. *Recreations:* music, gardening, walking. *Address:* 22 Links Road, Epsom, Surrey KT17 3PS. *T:* Epsom (0372) 723625.
Died 17 Sept. 1993.

JONES, Air Vice-Marshal Richard Ian, CB 1960; AFC 1948; psa; pfc; *b* 21 April 1916; *m* 1940, Margaret Elizabeth Wright. *Educ:* Berkhamsted Sch.; Cranwell. Group Captain, 1955; Air Commodore, 1960; Air Vice-Marshal, 1965. Senior Air Staff Officer, Royal Air Force, Germany (Second Tactical Air Force), Command Headquarters, 1959–62; Dir of Flying Training, 1963–64; AOC No 25 Group, RAF Flying Training Command, 1964–67; SASO, Fighter Command, 1967–68; AOC No 11 (Fighter) Gp, Strike Command, 1969–70; retired 1970. *Recreations:* golf, ski-ing. *Clubs:* Royal Air Force; Victoria (Jersey). *Died 4 June 1993.*

JONES, Maj.-Gen. Richard K.; *see* Keith-Jones.

JONES, Richard S.; *see* Stanton-Jones.

JONES, Rev. (Robert William) Hugh; Moderator of the West Midland Province of the United Reformed Church (formerly of the Congregational Church in England and Wales), 1970–78, retired; *b* 6 May 1911; *s* of Evan Hugh Jones and Sarah Elizabeth Salmon; *m* 1st, 1939, Gaynor Eluned Evans (*d* 1974); one *s* one *d*; 2nd, 1979, Mary Charlotte Pulsford, *widow* of H. E. Pulsford, FIEE. *Educ:* Chester Grammar Sch.; Univs of Wales and Manchester;

Lancashire Independent College. BA Wales, History and Philosophy. Ordained, 1939; Congregational Church: Welholme, Grimsby, 1939–45; Muswell Hill, London, 1945–49; Warwick Road, Coventry, 1949–61; Petts Wood, Orpington, 1961–69; President, Congregational Church in England and Wales, 1969–70; Minister, URC, Foleshill Road, Coventry, 1978–81. Broadcaster, radio and TV; Mem., BBC/ITA Central Religious Adv. Cttee, 1971–75. Guest preacher, USA. *Recreations:* painting, photography. *Address:* 24 Ashdene Gardens, Whitemoor Road, Kenilworth, Warwicks CV8 2TR. *T:* Kenilworth (0926) 851112. *Died 28 Nov. 1993.*

JONES, Sydney T.; *see* Tapper-Jones.

JONES, Wyn; *see* Jones, G. W.

JONES-PARRY, Sir Ernest, Kt 1978; *b* 16 July 1908; *o s* of late John Parry and Charlotte Jones, Rhuddlan; *m* 1938, Mary Powell; two *s*. *Educ:* St Asaph; University of Wales; University of London. MA (Wales) 1932; PhD (London) 1934; FRHistS. Lecturer in History, University Coll. of Wales, 1935–40; Ministry of Food, 1941; Treasury, 1946–47; Asst Sec., Ministry of Food, 1948–57; Under Sec., 1957; Dir of Establishments, Ministry of Agriculture, Fisheries and Food, 1957–61. Exec. Director: Internat. Sugar Council, 1965–68; Internat. Sugar Orgn, 1969–78. *Publications:* The Spanish Marriages, 1841–46, 1936; The Correspondence of Lord Aberdeen and Princess Lieven, 1832–1854 (2 vols), 1938–39; articles and reviews in History and English Historical Review. *Recreations:* reading, watching cricket. *Address:* Flat 3, 34 Sussex Square, Brighton, Sussex BN2 5AD. *T:* Brighton (0273) 688894. *Club:* Athenæum. *Died 6 Aug. 1992.*

JORDAN, Henry; Under-Secretary, Department of Education and Science, 1973–76; *b* 1919; *s* of late Henry Jordan and Mary Ann Jordan (*née* Shields); *m* 1946, Huguette Yvonne Rayée; one *s*. *Educ:* St Patrick's High Sch., Dumbarton. Served War, RA, 1939–46. Home Civil Service, Post Office, 1936; Foreign Office, 1947; Central Land Board and War Damage Commn, 1949; Min. (later Dept) of Educn, 1957. *Address:* 22 Bainfield Road, Cardross, Strathclyde. *Died 4 Oct. 1994.*

JORDAN, Air Marshal Sir Richard Bowen, KCB 1956 (CB 1947); DFC 1941; psa; Royal Air Force, retired; *b* 7 Feb. 1902; *s* of late A. O. Jordan, Besford Ct, Worcestershire; *m* 1932, F. M. M. Haines (*d* 1985); one *d*. *Educ:* Marlborough Coll.; RAF Coll., Cranwell. Joined RAF, 1921. Late AOC the RAF in India and Pakistan; Air Officer Commanding RAF Gibraltar, 1948–49; Commandant of the Royal Observer Corps, 1949–51; ADC to the King, 1949–51; Air Officer Commanding No 25 Group, 1951–53; Dir-Gen. of Organisation, Air Ministry, 1953–55; Air Officer Commanding-in-Chief, Maintenance Command, 1956–58, retd. *Address:* 4 Stonegate Court, Stonegate, Wadhurst, E Sussex TN5 7EQ. *Died 24 April 1994.*

JOSEPH, Baron *cr* 1987 (Life Peer), of Portsoken in the City of London; **Keith Sinjohn Joseph,** CH 1986; PC 1962; Bt 1943; *b* 17 Jan. 1918; *o c* of Sir Samuel George Joseph, 1st Bt, and Edna Cicely (*d* 1981), *yr d* of late P. A. S. Phillips, Portland Place, W1; *S* father, 1944; *m* 1st, 1951, Hellen Louise (marr. diss. 1985), *yr d* of Sigmar Guggenheimer, NY; one *s* three *d*; 2nd, 1990, Mrs Yolanda Sheriff. *Educ:* Harrow; Magdalen Coll., Oxford. War of 1939–45, served 1939–46; Captain RA; Italian campaign (wounded, despatches). Fellow All Souls Coll., Oxford, 1946–60, 1972–; barrister, Middle Temple, 1946. Contested (C) Baron's Court, General Election, 1955. MP (C) Leeds NE, Feb. 1956–1987. PPS to Parly Under-Sec. of State, CRO, 1957–59; Parly Sec., Min. of Housing and Local Govt, 1959–61; Minister of State at Board of Trade, 1961–62; Minister of Housing and Local Govt and

Minister for Welsh Affairs, 1962–64; Secretary of State: for Social Services, DHSS, 1970–74; for Industry, 1979–81; for Educn and Science, 1981–86. Co-Founder and first Chm., Foundation for Management Education, 1959; Founder and first Chm., Mulberry Housing Trust, 1965–69; Founder, and Chm. Management Cttee, Centre for Policy Studies Ltd, 1974–79 (Dir, 1991–). Chm., Bovis Ltd, 1958–59; Dep. Chm., Bovis Holdings Ltd, 1964–70 (Dir, 1951–59); Director: Gilbert-Ash Ltd, 1949–59; Drayton Premier Investment Trust Ltd, 1975–79; Part-time Consultant: Bovis Ltd, 1986–89 (Dir, 1989–); Cable & Wireless PLC, 1986–91; Trusthouse Forte PLC, 1986–89; Metrolands Developments Ltd, 1992 (Dir, 1991–92). FIOB. Common Councilman of City of London for Ward of Portsoken, 1946, Alderman, 1946–49; Liveryman, Vintners' Company. *Publications:* Reversing the Trend: a critical appraisal of Conservative economic and social policies, 1975; (with J. Sumption) Equality, 1979. *Heir* (to baronetcy): *s* Hon. James Samuel Joseph, *b* 27 Jan. 1955. *Address:* House of Lords, SW1A 0PW. *Club:* Athenæum.   *Died 10 Dec. 1994.*

JOSEPH, Sir (Herbert) Leslie, Kt 1952; DL; Vice-Chairman, Trust Houses Forte Ltd, 1970–80; *b* 4 Jan. 1908; *s* of David Ernest and Florence Joseph; *m* 1st, 1934, Emily Irene (*d* 1987), *d* of Dr Patrick Julian Murphy, Cwmbach, Aberdare; two *d*; 2nd, 1989, Christine Jones. *Educ:* The King's Sch. Canterbury. Commissioned RE, 1940–46. Former Pres., Assoc. of Amusement Parks and Piers of Great Britain (formerly Assoc. Amusement Parks Proprietors of GB); Chairman: National Amusements Council, 1950–51; Amusement Caterers' Assoc., 1953, 1954; Housing Production Board for Wales, 1952–53. Member: Council, Swansea Univ.; Art Cttee, Nat. Museum of Wales. High Sheriff, 1975–76, DL, Mid Glamorgan. Governor, King's Sch., Canterbury, 1968–. *Recreations:* horticulture, ceramics. *Address:* Coedargraig, Newton, Porthcawl, Mid Glamorganshire CF36 5SS. *T:* Porthcawl (065671) 2610.   *Died 7 Jan. 1992.*

JOSLING, John Francis; writer on legal subjects; Principal Assistant Solicitor of Inland Revenue, 1965–71; *b* 26 May 1910; *s* of John Richard Josling, Hackney, London, and Florence Alice (*née* Robinson); *m* 1935, Bertha Frearson (*d* 1991); two *s* two *d*. *Educ:* Leyton Co. High Sch. Entered a private Solicitor's office, 1927; articled, 1937; admitted as Solicitor, 1940. Served War of 1939–45 (war stars and medals): RA, 1940–45; JAG's Br., 1945–46. Entered office of Solicitor of Inland Revenue, 1946; Sen. Legal Asst, 1948; Asst Solicitor, 1952. Mem., Law Society. Coronation Medal, 1953. *Publications:* Oyez Practice Notes on Adoption of Children, 1947, (with A. Levy) 11th edn 1992; Execution of a Judgment, 1948, 5th edn 1974; (with C. Caplin) Apportionments for Executors and Trustees, 1948, 3rd edn 1963; Change of Name, 1948, 14th edn 1989; Naturalisation, 1949, 3rd edn 1965; Summary Judgment in the High Court, 1950, 4th edn 1974; Periods of Limitation, 1951, 7th edn 1989; (with L. Alexander) The Law of Clubs, 1964, 6th edn 1987; A History of the Souvenir Normand, 1987; (ed) Caplin's Powers of Attorney, 1954, 4th edn 1971; (ed) Wilkinson's Affiliation Law and Practice, 1971, 4th edn 1977; (ed) Summary Matrimonial and Guardianship Orders, 3rd edn 1973; contribs to: Simon's Income Tax (2nd edn); Halsbury's Laws of England vol. 20 (3rd edn); Pollard's Social Welfare Law, 1977; many contribs to Solicitors' Jl and some other legal jls. *Recreations:* music and musical history, Victorian novels, Georgian children and Elizabethan grand-children. *Address:* Proton, Farley Way, Fairlight, E Sussex TN35 4AS. *T:* Hastings (0424) 812501.   *Died 7 Jan. 1993.*

JOSSET, Lawrence Leon Louis; RE 1951 (ARE 1936); ARCA 1935; free-lance artist; *b* 2 Aug. 1910; *s* of Leon

Antoine Hyppolite and Annie Mary Josset; *m* 1960, Beatrice, *d* of William Alford Taylor. *Educ:* Bromley County Sch. for Boys; Bromley and Beckenham Schs of Art; Royal College of Art (diploma). Engraver's Draughtsman at Waterlow and Son Ltd, Clifton Street, 1930–32; Art Master at Red Hill Sch., East Sutton, near Maidstone, Kent, 1935–36. Mem. of Art Workers' Guild. *Publications:* mezzotints in colours: Flowers, after Fantin-Latour, 1937; The Trimmed Cock, after Ben Marshall, 1939; Brighton Beach and Spring, after Constable, 1947; Carting Timber and Milking Time, after Shayer, 1948; The Pursuit, and Love Letters, after Fragonard, 1949; Spring and Autumn, after Boucher, 1951; A Family, after Zoffany, 1953; Master James Sayer, 1954; HM The Queen after Annigoni, commissioned by the Times, 1956, and plates privately commissioned after de Lazlo, James Gunn and Oswald Birley. *Recreations:* outdoor sketching, cycling, etc. *Address:* The Cottage, Pilgrims Way, Detling, near Maidstone, Kent ME14 3JY.

Died 7 May 1995.

JOY, Michael Gerard Laurie, CMG 1965; MC 1945; HM Diplomatic Service, retired; *b* 27 Oct. 1916; *s* of late Frank Douglas Howarth Joy, Bentley, Hants; *m* 1951, Ann Félise Jacomb; one *s* three *d*. *Educ:* Winchester; New Coll., Oxford. Served RA, 1940–46 (MC, wounded). Foreign Office, 1947; Private Sec. to Permanent Under Sec. of State, 1948–50; Saigon, 1950–53; Washington, 1953–55; IDC, 1956; Foreign Office, 1957–59; Counsellor, 1959; Addis Ababa, 1959–62; Stockholm, 1962–64; seconded to Cabinet Office, 1964–66; Foreign Office, 1966–68. *Recreation:* shooting. *Address:* Marelands, Bentley, Hants GU10 5JB. *T:* Bentley (0420) 23288.

Died 13 March 1993.

JOYCE, Eileen Alannah, CMG 1981; concert pianist; *b* Zeehan, Tasmania, 21 Nov. 1912; *d* of Joseph and Alice Joyce, Western Australia; *m* 1st, 1937, Douglas Leigh Barrett (*d* 1942); one *s*; 2nd, Christopher Mann. *Educ:* Loreto Convent, Perth, Western Australia; Leipzig Conservatoire. Studied in Germany under Teichmuller, and later, Schnabel. Concert début in London at Promenade Concerts under Sir Henry Wood; numerous concert tours, radio performances and gramophone recordings; during War of 1939–45, played in association with London Philharmonic Orchestra, especially in blitzed towns and cities throughout Great Britain; concerts with: all principal orchestras of the UK; Berlin Philharmonic Orchestra in Berlin; Conservatoire and National Orchestras, France; Concertgebouw Orchestra, Holland; La Scala Orchestra, Italy; Philadelphia Orchestra, Carnegie Hall, New York; concert tours in: Australia, 1948; SA, 1950; Scandinavia and Holland, 1951; S Amer., Scandinavia and Finland, 1952; Jugoslavia, 1955; NZ, 1958; USSR, 1961; India, 1962; also performed harpsichord in several concerts Royal Albert Hall and Royal Festival Hall. Adjudicated at music competitions, including Sydney Pianoforte Comp. Contributed to sound tracks of films including: The Seventh Veil, Brief Encounter, Man of Two Worlds, Quartet, Trent's Last Case; appeared in films: Battle for Music, Girl in a Million, Wherever She Goes (biographical). Hon. DMus: Cantab, 1971; Univ. of Western Australia, 1979; Melbourne, 1982.

Died 25 March 1991.

JOYNT, Evelyn Gertrude, MBE 1967; Major (retired), Woman's Royal Army Corps; Director, World Bureau of World Association of Girl Guides and Girl Scouts, 1971–79; *b* 5 Sept. 1919; 2nd *d* of late Rev. George Joynt, Dublin. *Educ:* Collegiate Sch., Enniskillen; Banbridge Academy. Joined ATS, 1942; transf. to WRAC, 1952; jsc, WRAC Staff Coll., 1954; served Middle East and Far East; OC Drivers and Clerks Training Wing, WRAC; DAQMG, Eastern Comd; retired 1967; Nat. Gen. Sec.,

YWCA of GB, 1968–71. *Address:* Bowden House, West Street, Alresford, Hants SO24 9AU.

Died 6 Nov. 1991.

JUDGE, Edward Thomas, MA Cantab; FIM; Director: ETJ Consultancy Services; Cleveland Scientific Institution; *b* 20 Nov. 1908; *o s* of late Thomas Oliver and Florence Judge (*née* Gravestock); *m* 1934, Alice Gertrude Matthews; one *s* (and one *s* decd). *Educ:* Worcester Royal Grammar Sch.; St John's Coll., Cambridge. Joined Dorman Long, 1930, and held various appts, becoming Chief Technical Engr, 1937; Special Dir, 1944; Chief Engr, 1945; Dir, 1947; Asst Man. Dir, Dorman Long (Steel) Ltd, 1959; Jt Man. Dir, 1960; Chm. and Gen. Man. Dir, Dorman Long & Co. Ltd, 1961–67; Dir, Dorman Long Vaderbijl (SA), 1959–79. Chairman: Reyrolle Parsons Ltd, 1969–74 (Dep. Chm., 1968); A. Reyrolle & Co. Ltd, 1969–73; C. A. Parsons & Co. Ltd, 1969–73; Director: BPB Industries, 1967–79; Pilkington Bros, 1968–79; Fibreglass, 1968–79. Mem. Exec. and Develt Cttees of Brit. Iron and Steel Fedn; Rep. of Minister of Transport on Tees Conservancy Commn., 1951–66; part-time Mem. N Eastern Electricity Bd, 1952–62; Vice-Pres., Iron and Steel Inst., 1958; President: British Iron and Steel Federation, 1965, 1966, 1967; British Electrical Allied Manufacturers' Assoc. Ltd, 1970–71 (Dep. Pres., 1969–70). Bessemer Gold Medal, Iron and Steel Inst., 1967. *Publications:* technical papers. *Recreation:* fishing. *Address:* 4 Delamores Acre, Willaston, Cheshire L64 1UB.

Died 8 Jan. 1992.

JUSTHAM, David Gwyn; Chairman, Central Independent Television plc, 1986–91 (Director, 1981–91); *b* 23 Dec. 1923; *s* of John Farquhar Richard and Margaret Anne Justham; *m* 1950, Isobel Thelma, *d* of G. Gordon Thomson, MC; one *s* one *d. Educ:* Bristol Grammar School. Served RAF, Bomber Pilot (Flt Lieut), 1941–46. Admitted Solicitor, 1949; joined ICI, 1955; Asst Secretary, ICI Dyestuffs Div., 1955–59; Secretary: ICI European Council, 1960–61; ICI Nobel Div., 1961–65; Imperial Metal Industries Ltd (subseq. IMI plc), 1965–73 (Dir, 1968–85); various appts with IMI, 1965–81, incl. Chm., C. A. Norgren Co., Littleton, Colo, USA, 1974–81. Chairman: W Midlands Bd of Central Independent Television plc, 1981–85; Midland Regional Bd of National Girobank, 1982–85; Nat. Exhibition Centre Ltd, 1982–89 (Dir, 1979–89); Dir, H. Samuel plc, 1981–84; Pres., Birmingham Chamber of Industry and Commerce, 1974–75 (Mem. Council, 1969–); Chm., Birmingham Hippodrome Theatre Trust, 1979–89; Member, Council: Welsh National Opera, 1979–84; Univ. of Aston, 1982–86 (Mem. Convocation, 1974–); Univ. of Birmingham, 1983– (Mem., 1976–, Hon. Life Mem., 1986, Ct of Governors; Dep. Pro-Chancellor, 1987–89); City of Birmingham Symphony Orch., 1984–89; Mem., W Midlands Economic Planning Council, 1970–74. General Comr of Income Tax, 1972–77. Pres., Birmingham Press Club, 1985–86. High Sheriff of Co. of W Midlands, 1981–82. *Recreations:* opera, theatre. *Address:* 9 Birch Hollow, Edgbaston, Birmingham B15 2QE. *T:* 021–454 0688.

Died 25 Sept. 1991.

K

KABERRY OF ADEL, Baron *cr* 1983 (Life Peer), of Adel in the City of Leeds; **Donald Kaberry,** TD 1946; Bt 1960; DL; *b* 18 Aug. 1907; *s* of Abraham Kaberry; *m* 1940, Lily Margaret Scott; three *s. Educ:* Leeds Grammar Sch. Solicitor (Mem. of Council of The Law Society, 1950–55). Served War of 1939–45, in RA (despatches twice); Battery Comdr, Dunkirk evacuation; Col., Sen. Legal Officer, Hamburg Mil. Govt. Mem. Leeds City Council for 20 years; Hon. Alderman. MP (C) North-West Div. of Leeds, 1950–83; Asst Government Whip, 1951–April 1955; Parliamentary Sec., Board of Trade, April-Oct. 1955; Vice-Chm., Conservative Party, Oct. 1955–1961; Mem., Select Cttee on Nationalised Industries, 1961–79 (Chm. Sub-Cttee C, 1974–79); Chm., Select Cttee on Industry and Trade, 1979–83; Mem., Speaker's Panel of Chairmen, 1974–83. Pres., Yorks Area Council of Conservative Party, 1966–(Chm. 1952–56; Dep. Pres. 1956–65); Patron, Assoc. of Conservative Clubs, 1988– (Chm., 1961–88). Chairman: Yorkshire Chemicals Ltd, 1964–77; W. H. Baxter Ltd. Chm., Bd of Governors, United Leeds Hosps, 1961–74; Leeds Teaching Hosps Special Trustee, 1974–86; Life Pres., Headingly Branch, Royal British Legion. Nat. Pres., Dunkirk Veterans Assoc., 1988– (Hon. Legal Advr; Pres., Leeds Branch (founder Branch), 1973–); Treasurer, Leeds Poppy Day Appeal Fund, 1947–73. Pres., Incorporated Leeds Law Soc., 1952. DL York and West Yorks, 1974. *Heir* (to baronetcy only): *s* Hon. Christopher Donald Kaberry [*b* 14 March 1943; *m* 1967, Gaenor Elizabeth Vowe, *yr d* of C. V. Peake; two *s* one *d*]. *Address:* 1 Otley Road, Harrogate, N Yorks HG2 0DJ. *T:* Harrogate (0423) 503243. *Clubs:* Carlton, St Stephen's Constitutional. *Died 13 March 1991.*

KADOORIE, Baron *cr* 1981 (Life Peer), of Kowloon in Hong Kong and of the City of Westminster; **Lawrence Kadoorie,** Kt 1974; CBE 1970; JP; Joint Proprietor and Director, Sir Elly Kadoorie & Sons; Chairman: Sir Elly Kadoorie Successors Ltd; St George's Building Ltd; *b* Hong Kong, 2 June 1899; *s* of Sir Elly Kadoorie, KBE, and Laura Kadoorie (*née* Mocatta); *m* 1938, Muriel, *d* of David Gubbay, Hong Kong; one *s* one *d. Educ:* Cathedral Sch., Shanghai; Ascham St Vincents, Eastbourne; Clifton Coll., Bristol; Lincoln's Inn. With his brother, Horace, founded New Territories Benevolent Soc. Hon. Life Chm., China Light & Power Co.; former Chairman: Schroders Asia Ltd, Hong Kong Carpet Manufacturers Ltd, Nanyang Cotton Mill Ltd and others. Mem. Council and Court, Univ. of Hong Kong. Fellow, Mem., Patron, Governor, Chm., etc, of numerous other assocs, cttees, etc. JP Hong Kong, 1936; MEC 1954, MLC 1950, 1951, 1954, Hong Kong. Hon. LLD Univ. of Hong Kong, 1961. FInstD (London). KStJ (A) (UK) 1972. Solomon Schechter Award (USA), 1959; Ramon Magsaysay Award (Philippines), 1962. Comdr, Légion d'Honneur (France), 1982 (Officier, 1975; Chevalier, 1939); Officier, Ordre de Léopold (Belgium), 1966; Comdr, Ordre de la Couronne (Belgium), 1983. *Recreations:* sports cars (Life Mem. Hong Kong AA), photography, Chinese works of art. *Address:* St George's Building, 24th floor, 2 Ice House Street, Hong Kong. *T:* 249221. *Clubs:* Royal Automobile; Hong Kong, Hong Kong Country, Royal Hong Kong Jockey, Jewish Recreation, American (Hong Kong); Travellers' Century (USA). *Died 25 Aug. 1993.*

KADOORIE, Sir Horace, Kt 1989; CBE 1976 (OBE); Director, Sir Elly Kadoorie & Sons Ltd; *b* London, 28 Sept. 1902; *s* of Sir Elly Kadoorie, KBE and Laura (*née* Mocatta). *Educ:* Cathedral Sch., Shanghai; Ascham St Vincents, Eastbourne. Hon. Life President: Hongkong and Shanghai Hotels; Peak Tramways Co.; Hon. Chm., Manila Peninsula Hotel Inc.; Director: Hong Kong Carpet (Hldgs); Hutchison Whampoa; Philippine Carpet Manufacturing Corp.; Rotair; St George's Building Ltd; Tai Ping Internat. (HK). Mem. Cttee, Hong Kong Agricl Show, 1956–61, 1969, 1972; Associate Mem., Hong Kong Council of Social Service; Founder Member: Conservancy Assoc.; Kadoorie Agricl Aid Loan Fund; Life Member: FPA of Hong Kong; Hong Kong Anti-Cancer Soc.; Hong Kong AA; Botanical Soc. of S Africa, Kirstenbosch; Johannesburg Garden Soc.; RSPCA (Hong Kong); St John Amb. Assoc. Hon. Pres., HKNT Fish Culture Assoc. Trustee, Ohel Leah Synagogue, Hong Kong. Patron, Alumni Assoc., Ellis Kadoorie Coll., Hong Kong. Hon. DSocScis Hong Kong, 1981. Chevalier, Legion of Honour (France); Officier, Order of Leopold (Belgium). *Publication:* The Art of Ivory Sculpture in Cathay, 1988. *Address:* St George's Building, 24th Floor, 2 Ice House Street, Hong Kong. *T:* 249221. *Clubs:* American, Hong Kong, Jewish Recreation, Royal Hong Kong Jockey (Hong Kong). *Died 22 April 1995.*

KAGAN, Baron *cr* 1976 (Life Peer), of Elland, W Yorks; **Joseph Kagan;** *b* 6 June 1915; *s* of late Benjamin and Miriam Kagan; *m* 1943, Margaret Stromas; two *s* one *d. Educ:* High School, Kaunas, Lithuania; Leeds University. BCom hons (Textiles). Founder of 'Gannex'-Kagan Textiles Limited, 1951, thereafter Chairman and Managing Director. *Recreation:* chess. *Address:* Delamere, 15 Fixby Road, Huddersfield, W Yorks HD2 2JL. *Died 18 Jan. 1995.*

KAPLAN, Prof. Joseph; Professor of Physics, University of California at Los Angeles, 1940–70, then Professor Emeritus; *b* 8 Sept. 1902; *s* of Henry and Rosa Kaplan, Tapolcza, Hungary; *m* 1st, 1933, Katherine Elizabeth Feraud (*d* 1977); no *c*; 2nd, 1978, Frances Irsak Baum (*née* Irsak). *Educ:* Johns Hopkins University, Baltimore, Md (PhD 1927). National Research Fellow, Princeton Univ., 1927–28; University of Calif at Los Angeles: Asst Prof. of Physics, 1928–35; Associate Prof., 1935–40; Prof., 1940–. Chief, Operations Analysis Section, Second Air Force, 1943–45 (Exceptional Civilian Service Medal, US Air Corps, 1947). Chm., US Nat. Cttee for Internat. Geophysical Year, 1953–64. Fellow: Inst. of Aeronautical Sciences, 1957; Amer. Meteorological Soc., 1970 (Pres., 1963–67). Mem. Nat. Acad. of Sciences, 1957; Hon. Mem., Amer. Meteorological Soc., 1967; Vice-Pres., International Union of Geodesy and Geophysics, 1960–63, Pres., 1963; Hon. Governor, Hebrew Univ. of Jerusalem, 1968. Hon. DSc: Notre Dame, 1957; Carleton Coll., 1957; Hon. LHD: Yeshiva Univ. and Hebrew Union Coll., 1958; Univ. of Judaism, 1959. Exceptional Civilian Service Medal (USAF), 1960; Hodgkins Prize and Medal, 1965; Exceptional Civilian Service Medal, 1969; John A. Fleming Medal, Amer. Geophysical Union, 1970; Commemorative Medal, 50th Anniversary, Amer. Meteorological Soc., 1970; Special Award, UCLA Alumni Assoc., 1970. *Publications:* Across the Space Frontier, 1950; Physics and Medicine of the Upper Atmosphere,

1952; (co-author) Great Men of Physics, 1969; publications in Physical Review, Nature, Proc. Nat. Acad. of Sciences, Jl Chemical Physics. *Recreations:* golf, ice-skating, walking. *Address:* 1565 Kelton Avenue, Los Angeles, Calif 90024, USA. *T:* (213) 477–8166. *Club:* Cosmos (Washington, DC). *Died 3 Oct. 1991.*

KAPPEL, Frederick Russell; retired as Chairman of Board: American Telephone & Telegraph Company; International Paper Company; Chairman, Board of Governors, US Postal Service; *b* Albert Lea, Minnesota, 14 Jan. 1902; *s* of Fred A. Kappel and Gertrude M. Towle Kappel; *m* 1st, 1927, Ruth Carolyn Ihm (*d* 1974); two *d*; 2nd, 1978, Alice McW. Harris. *Educ:* University of Minnesota (BSE). Northwestern Bell Telephone Company: various positions in Minnesota, 1924–33; Plant Engineer, Nebraska, S Dakota, 1934; Plant Operations Supervisor (Exec.), Gen. Staff, Omaha, Nebraska, 1937, Asst Vice-Pres. Operations, 1939, Vice-Pres. Operations and Dir, 1942; Amer. Telephone & Telegraph Co., NY: Asst Vice-Pres. (Ops and Engrg), Vice-Pres. (Long Lines), Vice Pres. (Ops and Engrg), 1949; Pres. Western Electric Co., 1954–56; Chm. and Chief Exec. Officer, Amer. Telephone & Telegraph Co., 1956–67, Chm. Exec. Cttee, 1967–69; Chm. Bd, International Paper Co., 1969–71, Chm. Exec. Cttee 1971–74. Director: Amer. Telephone & Telegraph Co., 1956–70; Chase Manhattan Bank, 1956–72; Metropolitan Life Insurance Co., 1958–75; General Foods Corporation, 1961–73; Standard Oil Co. (NJ), 1966–70; Whirlpool Corp., 1967–72; Chase Manhattan Corp., 1969–72; Boys' Club of America; Acad. of Polit. Sciences, 1963–71; Member: Business Council (Chm., 1963–64); Advisory Board of Salvation Army, 1957–73; US Chamber of Commerce; various societies. Trustee: Presbyterian Hospital, 1949–74; Grand Central Art Galleries, Inc., 1957–70; Aerospace Corp., 1967–74; Tax Foundation, 1960–72. Trustee, University of Minnesota Foundation. Numerous hon. doctorates and awards, including: Cross of Comdr of Postal Award, France, 1962; Presidential Medal of Freedom, 1964. *Publications:* Vitality in a Business Enterprise, 1960; Business Purpose and Performance, 1964. *Recreation:* golf. *Address:* Apt 1101, 435 S Gulfstream Avenue, Sarasota, FL 34236, USA. *Clubs:* Triangle, University, Economic (New York); International (Washington); Bird Key Yacht, Sarabay Country (Sarasota, Fla). *Died 10 Nov. 1994.*

KARANJA, Hon. Dr Josphat Njuguna; Vice-President of Kenya, 1988–89; Minister of Home Affairs and National Heritage, 1988–89; *b* 5 Feb. 1931; *s* of Josphat Njuguna; *m* 1966, Beatrice Nyindombi, Fort Portal, Uganda; one *s* two *d*. *Educ:* Alliance High Sch., Kikuyu, Kenya; Makerere Coll., Kampala, Uganda; University of Delhi, India; Atlanta Univ. (MA); Princeton Univ., New Jersey, USA (PhD). Lecturer in African Studies, Farleigh Dickinson Univ., New Jersey, 1961–62; Lecturer in African and Modern European History, University College, Nairobi, Kenya, 1962–63; High Comr for Kenya in London, 1963–70; Vice-Chancellor, Univ. of Nairobi, 1970–79. MP for Mathare, Nairobi, 1986. *Recreations:* golf, tennis. *Address:* c/o General Accident Insurance Co. (Kenya) Ltd, Icea Building, Kenyatta Avenue, PO Box 42166, Nairobi, Kenya. *Died 28 Feb. 1994.*

KATZ, Milton; Director, International Legal Studies, and Henry L. Stimson Professor of Law, Harvard University, 1954–78, then Emeritus; Distinguished Professor of Law, Suffolk University Law School, Boston, Mass, since 1978; *b* 29 Nov. 1907; *s* of Morris Katz and Clara Schiffman; *m* 1933, Vivian Greenberg; three *s*. *Educ:* Harvard Univ. AB 1927; JD 1931. Anthropological Expedition across Central Africa for Peabody Museum, Harvard, 1927–28; Mem. of Bar, 1932–; various official posts, US Government, 1932–39; Prof. of Law, Harvard Univ., 1940–50; served

War of 1939–45, with War Production Board and as US Executive Officer, Combined Production and Resources Board, 1941–43, thereafter Lt-Comdr, USNR, until end of war; Dep. US Special Representative in Europe with rank of Ambassador, 1949–50; Chief US Delegation, Economic Commission for Europe, and US Mem., Defense Financial and Economic Cttee under North Atlantic Treaty, 1950–51; Ambassador of the United States and US Special Representative in Europe for ECA, 1950–51; Associate Dir, Ford Foundation, 1951–54, and Consultant, 1954–66. Dir, Internat. Program in Taxation, 1961–63. Consultant, US Office of Technology Assessment, 1972–82; Chm., Energy Adv. Cttee, 1974–82. Mem. Council, Amer. Acad. of Arts and Sciences, 1982– (Pres., 1979–82); Trustee: Carnegie Endowment for Internat. Peace (Chm. Bd, 1970–78); World Peace Foundation (Exec. Cttee); Citizens Research Foundation (Pres., 1969–78); Brandeis Univ.; Case Western Reserve Univ., 1967–80; International Legal Center (Chm. Bd, 1971–78); Director, Internat. Friendship League; Member: Corp., Boston Museum of Science; Cttee on Foreign Affairs Personnel, 1961–63; Case Inst. of Technology/Western Reserve Univ. Study Commn, 1966–67; Panel on Technology Assessment, Nat. Acad. of Sciences, 1968–69; Cttee on Life Sciences and Social Policy, Nat. Research Council, 1968–75 (Chm.); Vis. Cttee for Humanities, MIT, 1970–73; Adv. Bd, Energy Laboratory, MIT, 1974–85; Cttee on Technology, Internat. Trade and Econ. Issues, Nat. Acad. of Engrg, 1976–; Adv. Bd, Consortium on Competitiveness and Co-operation, Univ. of California, 1986–; Co-Chm., ABA-AAAS Cttee on Science and Law, 1978–82. Sherman Fairchild Dist. Schol., Calif Inst. of Technol., 1974. John Danz Lectr, Univ. of Washington, 1974, Phi Beta Kappa Nat. Vis. Scholar, 1977–78. Hon LLD Brandeis, 1972. Legion of Merit (US Army), 1945; Commendation Ribbon (US Navy), 1945. Order of Merit, Fed. Rep. of Germany, 1968. *Publications:* Cases and Materials on Administrative Law, 1947; (co-author and ed) Government under Law and the Individual, 1957; (with Kingman Brewster, Jr) The Law of International Transactions and Relations, 1960; The Things That are Caesar's, 1966; The Relevance of International Adjudication, 1968; The Modern Foundation: its dual nature, public and private, 1968; (contrib.) Man's Impact on the Global Environment, 1970; (ed) Federal Regulation of Campaign Finance, 1972; (jtly) Assessing Biomedical Technologies, 1975; (jtly) Technology, Trade and the US Economy, 1978; (jtly) Strengthening Conventional Deterrence in Europe, 1983; (contrib.) The Positive Sum Strategy, 1986; articles in legal, business and other jls. *Address:* (business) Harvard Law School, Cambridge, MA 02138, USA; (home) 6 Berkeley Street, Cambridge, MA 02138, USA. *Died 9 Aug. 1995.*

KAULBACK, Ronald John Henry, OBE 1946; *b* 23 July 1909; *er s* of late Lieutenant-Colonel Henry Albert Kaulback, OBE, and Alice Mary, *d* of late Rev. A. J. Townend, CF; *m* 1st, 1940, Audrey Elizabeth (marr. diss. 1984; she *d* 1994), 3rd *d* of late Major H. R. M. Howard-Sneyd, OBE; two *s* two *d*; 2nd, 1984, Joyce Nora, widow of Capt. H. S. Woolley, MC. *Educ:* Rugby; Pembroke Coll., Cambridge. In 1933 journeyed through Assam and Eastern Tibet with Capt. Francis Kingdon-Ward; returned to Tibet, 1935, accompanied by John Hanbury-Tracy, spending eighteen months there in an attempt to discover source of Salween River; 1938 spent eighteen months in Upper Burma hunting and collecting zoological specimens for the British Museum (Natural History); Murchison Grant of Royal Geog. Society, 1937. Served War of 1939–45, Intelligence Corps; Lt-Col, 1943. Ran hotel, then restaurant, at Ardnagashel, Bantry Bay. *Publications:*

Tibetan Trek, 1934; Salween, 1938. *Address:* Altbough, Hoarwithy, Hereford HR2 6QE. *T:* Carey (01432) 840676. *Died 2 Oct. 1995.*

KAY, Air Vice-Marshal Cyril Eyton, CB 1958; CBE 1947; DFC 1940; Chief of Air Staff, with the rank of Air Vice-Marshal, Royal New Zealand Air Force, 1956–58, retired; *b* 25 June 1902; *s* of David Kay and Mary, *d* of Edward Drury Butts; *m* 1932, Florence, *d* of Frank Armfield; two *d. Educ:* Auckland, NZ. Joined RAF, 1926, 5 years Short Service Commn; joined RNZAF, 1935, Permanent Commn; as Flying Officer: flew London-Sydney in Desoutter Light aeroplane, 1930 (with Flying Off. H. L. Piper as Co-pilot; first New Zealanders to accomplish this flight); also, as Flying Off. flew a De Havilland-Dragon Rapide (with Sqdn Ldr J. Hewett) in London-Melbourne Centenary Air Race, 1934; then continued over Tasman Sea to New Zealand (first direct flight England-New Zealand); Comdg Officer No 75 (NZ) Sqdn "Wellington" Bombers stationed Feltwell, Norfolk, England, 1940; IDC, 1946; Air Board Mem. for Supply, RNZAF, 1947; AOC, RNZAF, London HQ, 1950; Air Board Mem. for Personnel, 1953. *Recreation:* The Restless Sky, 1964. *Recreation:* golf. *Address:* c/o Lloyds Bank, 7 Pall Mall, SW1. *Clubs:* Royal Air Force; Officers' (Wellington, NZ). *Died 29 April 1993.*

KAY, Ernest, FRGS; Founder and Director-General, International Biographical Centre, Cambridge, since 1967 (Director-General, New York, 1976–85); *b* 21 June 1915; *s* of Harold and Florence Kay; *m* 1941, Marjorie Peover (*d* 1987); two *s* one *d. Educ:* Spring Bank Central Sch., Darwen, Lancs. Reporter, Darwen News, 1931–34; Ashton-under-Lyne Reporter, 1934–38; Industrial Corresp., Manchester Guardian and Evening News, 1938–41; The Star, London, 1941–47; London Editor, Wolverhampton Express and Star, 1947–52, Managing Editor, 1952–54; Managing Editor, London Evening News, 1954–57; Editor and Publisher, John O'London's, 1957–61; Managing Editor, Time and Tide, 1961–67; Editor: Dictionary of International Biography, 1967–; Dictionary of Caribbean Biography, 1970–; Dictionary of African Biography, 1970–; Dictionary of Scandinavian Biography, 1972–; International Who's Who in Poetry, 1970–; World Who's Who of Women, 1973–; International Who's Who in Music, 1975–; International Authors and Writers Who's Who, 1976–; Women in Education, 1977–; Who's Who in Education, 1978–; International Youth in Achievement, 1981–. Chairman: Kay Sons and Daughter Ltd, 1967–77; Dartmouth Chronicle Group Ltd, 1968–77; Cambridge and Newmarket Radio Ltd, 1981–; Pres., Melrose Press Ltd, 1970–77. Chm., Cambridge Symphony Orchestra Trust, 1979–83. Mem., Acad. of Creative Endeavors, Moscow, 1993. FRSA 1967; FRGS 1975. Hon. DLitt Karachi, 1967; Hon. PhD Hong Kong, 1976. Emperor Haile Selassie Gold Medal, 1971. Key to City of: Las Vegas, 1972; New York, 1975; Miami, 1978; New Orleans (and Hon. Citizen), 1978; Beverly Hills, 1981; LA, 1981. Staff Col and ADC to Governor of Louisiana, 1979; Hon. Senator, State of La, 1986. Gold Medal, Ordre Supreme Imperial Orthodox Constantinian de Saint-Georges (Greece), 1977. *Publications:* Great Men of Yorkshire, 1956, 2nd edn 1960; Isles of Flowers: the story of the Isles of Scilly, 1956, 3rd edn 1977; Pragmatic Premier: an intimate portrait of Harold Wilson, 1967; The Wit of Harold Wilson, 1967. *Recreations:* reading, writing, music, watching cricket, travel. *Address:* Westhurst, 418 Milton Road, Cambridge CB4 1ST. *T:* Cambridge (01223) 424893. *Clubs:* Surrey CC; Lancashire CC; National Arts (New York City). *Died 25 Nov. 1994.*

KAY, John Menzies, MA, PhD; CEng, FIMechE, FIChemE; engineering consultant; Director, GSK Steel Developments Ltd, 1976–83; *b* 4 Sept. 1920; *s* of John

Aiton Kay and Isabel Kay (*née* Menzies). *Educ:* Sherborne Sch.; Trinity Hall Cambridge. University Demonstrator in Chemical Engineering, Cambridge University, 1948; Chief Technical Engineer, Division of Atomic Energy Production, Risley, 1952; Prof. of Nuclear Power, Imperial Coll. of Science and Technology, University of London, 1956; Dir of Engineering Development, Tube Investments Ltd, 1961; Chief Engineer, Richard Thomas & Baldwins Ltd, 1965; Dir-in-charge, Planning Div., BSC, 1968–70; Dir of Engrng, Strip Mills Div., BSC, 1970–76. Mem., Nuclear Safety Adv. Cttee, 1960–76; Chm., Radioactive Waste Study Gp, 1974–81; Mem., Adv. Cttee on Safety of Nuclear Installations, 1980–83. *Publications:* Introduction to Fluid Mechanics and Heat Transfer, 1957, 3rd edn 1974; Fluid Mechanics and Transfer Processes, 1985; contribs to Proc. of Institution of Mechanical Engineers. *Recreations:* hill-walking, tree planting, music. *Address:* Church Farm, St Briavels, near Lydney, Glos GL15 6QE. *Clubs:* Alpine, United Oxford & Cambridge University. *Died 11 Nov. 1995.*

KAYE, Sir David Alexander Gordon, 4th Bt *cr* 1923, of Huddersfield; *b* 26 July 1919; *s* of Sir Henry Gordon Kaye, 2nd Bt and (second wife *d* of Walter H. Scales, Verwood, Bradford; *S* brother, 1983; *m* 1st, 1942, Elizabeth (marr. diss. 1950), *o d* of Captain Malcolm Hurtley; 2nd, 1955, Adelle, *d* of Denis Thomas, Brisbane, Queensland; two *s* four *d. Educ:* Stowe; Trinity Coll., Cambridge (BA). MRCS Eng., LRCP London 1943. *Heir: s* Paul Henry Gordon Kaye [*b* 19 Feb. 1958; *m* 1984, Sally Ann Louise]. *Died 23 June 1994.*

KEARTON, Baron *cr* 1970 (Life Peer), of Whitchurch, Bucks; **Christopher Frank Kearton,** Kt 1966; OBE 1945; FRS 1961; Chancellor, University of Bath, since 1980; *b* 17 Feb. 1911; *s* of Christopher John Kearton and Lilian Hancock; *m* 1936, Agnes Kathleen Brander; two *s* two *d. Educ:* Hanley High Sch.; St John's Coll., Oxford. Joined ICI, Billingham Division, 1933. Worked in Atomic Energy Project, UK and USA, 1940–45. Joined Courtaulds Ltd, i/c of Chemical Engineering, 1946; Dir 1952; Dep. Chm., 1961–64; Chm., 1964–75; Chm. and Chief Exec., British Nat. Oil Corp., 1976–79. Part-time Member: UKAEA, 1955–81; CEGB, 1974–80. Dir, Hill Samuel Gp, 1970–81; Chm., British Printing Corp., 1981. Visitor, DSIR, 1955–61, 1963–68. Chairman: Industrial Reorganisation Corp., 1966–68; Electricity Supply Res. Council, 1960–77 (Mem., 1954–77); Tropical Products Inst. Cttee, 1958–79; East European Trade Council, 1975–77. Member: Windscale Accident Cttee, 1957; Special Advisory Group, British Transport Commn, 1960; Adv. Council on Technology, 1964–70; Council, RIIA, 1964–75; NEDC, 1965–71; Adv. Cttee, Industrial Expansion Bill, 1968–70 (Chm.); Central Adv. Council for Science and Technology, 1974–75; Cttee of Enquiry into Structure of Electricity Supply Industry, 1974–75; Offshore Energy Technology Bd, 1976–79; Energy Commn, 1977–79. Member Council: Royal Soc., 1970; British Heart Foundn, 1977–; Gov., Ditchley Foundn, 1971–91. Mem., Select Cttees, H of L, 1982–92. President: Soc. of Chemical Industry, 1972–74 (Chm., Heavy Organic Chemical Section, 1961–62); RoSPA, 1973–80; BAAS, 1978–79; Aslib, 1980–82; Market Research Soc., 1983–87. Mem. Syndicate, Govt of Univ. of Cambridge, 1988–89. FIC 1976; Hon. Fellow: St John's Coll., Oxford, 1965; Manchester Coll. of Sci. and Techn., 1966; Soc. of Dyers and Colourists, 1974. CompTI, 1965; Hon. FIChemE 1968; Hon. LLD: Leeds, 1966; Strathclyde, 1981; Bristol, 1988; Hon. DSc: Bath, 1966; Aston in Birmingham, 1970; Reading, 1970; Keele, 1973; Ulster, 1975; Hon. DCL Oxon, 1978; DUniv Heriot-Watt, 1979. FRSA 1970; CBIM 1980. Grande Ufficiale, Order of Merit (Italy), 1977. *Address:* The Old House, Church

Headland Lane, Whitchurch, near Aylesbury, Bucks HP22 4JX. *T:* Aylesbury (0296) 641232. *Club:* Athenæum.

Died 2 July 1992.

KEATING, Donald Norman, QC 1972; FCIArb; a Recorder, 1972–87 and since 1993; *b* 24 June 1924; *s* of late Thomas Archer Keating and Anne Keating; *m* 1st, 1945, Betty Katharine (*d* 1975); two *s* one *d*; 2nd, 1978, Kay Rosamond Blundell, *widow* of Edmund Deighton; one *s* (one step *d* decd). *Educ:* Roan Sch.; King's Coll., London. BA (History), 1948. RAFVR, 1943–46 (Flt Lt). Called to Bar, Lincoln's Inn, 1950; Bencher, 1979. Head of chambers, 1976–92. Mem., DTI study team on Professional Liability, 1988–89. *Publications:* Building Contracts, edns 1955, 1963, 1969, 1978 and supps 1982, 1984, consultant to 5th edn 1991; Guide to RIBA Forms, 1959; various articles in legal and other jls. *Recreations:* theatre, music, travel, walking. *Address:* 10 Essex Street, WC2R 3AA. *T:* 0171–240 6981. *Club:* Garrick.

Died 1 Aug. 1995.

KEDOURIE, Prof. Elie, CBE 1991; FBA 1975; Professor of Politics in the University of London, 1965–90, Professor Emeritus, since 1990; Founder, and Editor since 1964, Middle Eastern Studies; *b* 25 Jan. 1926; *er s* of A. Kedourie and L. Dangour, Baghdad; *m* 1950, Sylvia, *d* of Gourgi Haim, Baghdad; two *s* one *d*. *Educ:* Collège A-D Sasson and Shamash Sch., Baghdad; London Sch. of Economics; St Antony's Coll., Oxford (Sen. Scholar). BSc(Econ). Taught at the London Sch. of Economics, 1953–90. Visiting Lecturer: Univ. of California, Los Angeles, 1959; Univ. of Paris, 1959; Visiting Professor: Princeton Univ., 1960–61; Monash Univ., Melb., 1967 and 1989; Harvard Univ., 1968–69; Tel Aviv Univ., 1969; Brandeis Univ., 1985–86; Inst. Raymond Aron, Paris, 1990; Columbia Univ., 1991; Scholar-in-Residence, Brandeis Univ., 1982; Vis. Res. Fellow, All Souls Coll., Oxford, 1989–90; Koret Fellow, Washington Inst. for Near East Policy, 1990–91; Fellow, Woodrow Wilson Center, Washington, 1991–92. Mem., Cttee of Enquiry into Validation of Acad. Degrees in Public Sector Higher Educn, 1984–85. Hist. Advr, Roads to Conflict, BBC TV, 1978. Fellow: Netherlands Inst. for Advanced Study, 1980–81; Sackler Inst. of Advanced Studies, Tel-Aviv Univ., 1983. Dr *hc* Tel-Aviv Univ., 1991. Mem. Editorial Bd, Cambridge Studies in History and Theory of Politics, 1968–82. *Publications:* England and the Middle East, 1956, new edn 1987; Nationalism, 1960 (trans. German, 1968), new edn with afterword, 1985; Afghani and 'Abduh, 1966; The Chatham House Version, 1970, new edn 1984; Nationalism in Asia and Africa, 1971; Arabic Political Memoirs, 1974; In the Anglo-Arab Labyrinth, 1976; (ed) The Middle Eastern Economy, 1977; (ed) The Jewish World, 1979; (ed jtly) Modern Egypt, 1980; Islam in the Modern World, 1980; (ed jtly) Towards a Modern Iran, 1980; (ed jtly) Palestine and Israel in the Nineteenth and Twentieth Centuries, 1982; (ed jtly) Zionism and Arabism in Palestine and Israel, 1982; The Crossman Confessions, 1984; Diamonds into Glass: the Government and the universities, 1988; (ed jtly) Studies in the Economic History of the Middle East, 1989; Perestroika in the Universities, 1989; Politics in the Middle East, 1992; Democracy and Arab Political Culture, 1992; (ed) Spain and the Jews, 1992; *relevant publication:* National and International Politics in the Middle East: essays in honour of Elie Kedourie, ed Edward Ingram, 1986. *Address:* c/o London School of Economics, Houghton Street, Aldwych, WC2A 2AE. *T:* 071–405 7686.

Died 29 June 1992.

KEEBLE, Thomas Whitfield; HM Diplomatic Service, retired 1976; Senior Clerk (Acting), Committee Office, House of Commons, 1976–83; *b* 10 Feb. 1918; *er s* of C. F. A. Keeble, MBE, and Elizabeth Sowerbutts; *m* 1945,

Ursula Scott Morris; two *s*. *Educ:* Sir John Deane's Grammar Sch., Cheshire; St John's Coll., Cambridge (MA); King's Coll., London (PhD). Served, 1940–45, in India, Persia, Iraq and Burma in RA (seconded to Indian Artillery), Captain. Asst Principal, Commonwealth Relations Office, 1948; Private Sec. to Parliamentary Under Sec. of State; Principal, 1949; First Sec., UK High Commn in Pakistan, 1950–53, in Lahore, Peshawar and Karachi; seconded to Foreign Service and posted to UK Mission to the United Nations in New York, 1955–59; Counsellor, 1958; Head of Defence and Western Dept, CRO, 1959–60; British Dep. High Comr in Ghana, 1960–63; Head of Econ. Gen. Dept, CRO, 1963–66; Minister (Commercial), British Embassy, Buenos Aires, 1966–67; Hon. Research Associate, Inst. of Latin American Studies, Univ. of London, 1967–68; Minister, British Embassy, Madrid, 1969–71; Head of UN (Econ. and Social) Dept, FCO, 1971–72, of UN Dept, 1972–74; Sen. Directing Staff (Civil), Nat. Defence Coll., Latimer, 1974–76. *Publications:* British Overseas Territories and South America, 1806–1914, 1970; articles in Hispanic reviews. *Recreations:* Hispanic history and arts, bird watching. *Address:* 49 Station Road, Oakington, Cambridge CB4 5AH. *T:* Cambridge (01223) 234922. *Club:* United Oxford & Cambridge University.

Died 20 Dec. 1994.

KEEGAN, Denis Michael; barrister; General Manager, Mercantile Credit Co. Ltd, 1975–83, retired; *b* 26 Jan. 1924; *o s* of Denis Francis Keegan and Mrs Duncan Campbell; *m* 1st, 1951, Pamela Barbara (marr. diss.), *yr d* of late Percy Bryan, Purley, Surrey; one *s*; 2nd, 1961, Marie Patricia (marr. diss.), *yr d* of late Harold Jennings; one *s*; 3rd, 1972, Ann Irene, *d* of Norman Morris. *Educ:* Oundle Sch.; Queen's University, Kingston, Ontario, Canada (BA). Served RN Fleet Air Arm, 1944–46 (petty officer pilot). Called to Bar, Gray's Inn, 1950. Mem. Nottingham City Council, 1953–55, resigned. MP (C) Nottingham Sth, 1955–Sept. 1959. Dir, HP Information PLC (Chm. 1984). Formerly Dir, Radio and Television Retailers' Assoc. *Recreations:* reading, talking, music. *Address:* 5 Paper Buildings, Temple, EC4Y 7HB. *T:* 071–353 8494.

Died 9 Oct. 1993.

KEENLEYSIDE, Hugh Llewellyn, CC 1969; consultant; *b* 7 July 1898; *s* of Ellis William Keenleyside and Margaret Louise Irvine; *m* 1924, Katherine Hall Pillsbury, BA, BSc (*d* 1977); one *s* three *d*. *Educ:* Langara School and Public Schools, Vancouver, BC; University of British Columbia (BA); Clark University (MA, PhD). Held several hon. degrees in Law, Science. Instructor and Special Lecturer in History, Brown University, Syracuse Univ., and University of British Columbia, 1923–27; Third Sec., Dept of External Affairs, 1928; Second Sec., 1929; First Sec. and First Chargé d'Affaires, Canadian Legation, Tokyo, 1929; Dept of External Affairs and Prime Minister's Office, 1936; Chm, Board of Review to Investigate charges of illegal entry on the Pacific Coast, 1938; Sec., Cttee in charge of Royal Visit to Canada, 1938–39; Counsellor, 1940; Asst Under-Sec. of State for External Affairs, 1941–44; Mem. and Sec., Canadian Section, Canada-United States Permanent Jt Bd on Defence, 1940–44, Acting Chm., 1944–45; Member: North-West Territories Council, 1941–45; Canada-United States Joint Economic Cttees, 1941–44; Special Cttee on Orientals in BC; Canadian Shipping Board, 1939–41; War Scientific and Technical Development Cttee, 1940–45; Canadian Ambassador to Mexico, 1944–47; Deputy Minister of Resources and Development and Comr of Northwest Territories, 1947–50; Head of UN Mission of Technical Assistance to Bolivia, 1950; Dir-Gen., UN Technical Assistance Administration, 1950–58; Under-Sec. Gen. for Public Administration, UN, 1959. Chairman: BC Power Commn, 1959–62; BC Hydro and Power Authy, 1962–69.

Vice-Pres. National Council of the YMCAs of Canada, 1941–45; Vice-Chm., Canadian Youth Commission, 1943–45; Head of Canadian Delegn to UN Scientific Conf. on Conservation and Utilization of Resources, 1949. Life Mem., Asiatic Soc. of Japan; one of founders and mem. of first Board of Governors of Arctic Institute of North America; Vice-Chm., Board of Governors, Carleton Coll., 1943–50; Pres. Assoc. of Canadian Clubs, 1948–50; Mem. Bd of Trustees, Clark Univ., 1953–56; Mem. Senate, University of British Columbia, 1963–69. Hon. Life Mem., Canadian Association for Adult Education; Mem. Board of Governors, Canadian Welfare Council, 1955–69; Member: Canadian National Cttee of World Power Conference; Adv. Bd (BC), Canada Permanent Cos; Hon. Bd of Dirs, Resources for the Future; Dir, Toronto-Dominion Bank, 1960–70. Assoc. Comr General, UN Conf. on Human Settlements, 1975–76 (Hon. Chm. Canadian Nat. Cttee, 1974–77). Chancellor, Notre Dame Univ., Nelson, BC, 1969–76. Dir and Fellow, Royal Canadian Geographic Soc. Haldane Medal, Royal Inst. of Public Administration, 1954; first recipient, Vanier Medal, Inst. of Public Administration of Canada, 1962. *Publications:* Canada and the United States, 1929, revised edn 1952; History of Japanese Education (with A. F. Thomas), 1937; International Aid: a summary, 1966; Memoirs: Vol. 1, Hammer the Golden Day, 1981; Vol. 2, On the Bridge of Time, 1982; various magazine articles. *Recreations:* reading, outdoor sports, cooking, poker. *Address:* 3470 Mayfair Drive, Victoria, BC V8P 1P8, Canada. *T:* 592–9331. *Died 27 Sept. 1992.*

KEIGHLY-PEACH, Captain Charles Lindsey, DSO 1940; OBE 1941; Royal Navy, retired; *b* 6 April 1902; *s* of late Admiral C. W. Keighly-Peach, DSO and Kathleen, *d* of Fleet Paymaster J. R. Dennis; *m* 1st, V. B. Cumbers (marr. diss.); one *s* one *d*; 2nd, Beatrice Mary Harrison (*d* 1974). *Educ:* RN Colleges, Osborne and Dartmouth. Midshipman, 1919; Sub-Lieut 1922; Lieut 1924; 3 Squadron, RAF, 1926; HMS Eagle (402 Sqdn), 1927; H/M S/M M2, 1929; HMS Centaur, 1930; Lieut-Comdr 1932; HMS Glorious (802 Sqdn), 1932; RN Staff Coll., Greenwich, 1934; SO (Ops) to Rear-Adm. Destroyers, 1935; HMS London, 1937; Commander, 1938; RN Air Station Lee-on-Solent, 1939; HMS Eagle, 1940–41; Naval Assistant (Air) to 2nd Sea Lord, 1941–44; Capt. 1943; RN Air Station, Yeovilton, 1944–45; Comdg HMS Sultan, Singapore, 1945–47; in command HMS Troubridge and 3rd Destroyer Flot. Med., 1947–49; Dir Captain, Senior Officer's War Course, RN, 1949–51; Asst Chief Naval Staff (Air) on loan to Royal Canadian Navy, 1951–53. *Recreations:* golf, gardening. *Died 4 Feb. 1995.*

KEITH, David; *see* Steegmuller, Francis.

KEITH-JONES, Maj.-Gen. Richard, CB 1968; MBE 1947; MC 1944; Manager, Management Development, Mardon Packaging International Ltd, 1969–75; *b* 6 Dec. 1913; *o s* of late Brig. Frederick Theodore Jones, CIE, MVO, VD and 1st wife, May Saunders; *m* 1938, Margaret Ridley Harrison; three *d. Educ:* Clifton Coll.; Royal Military Academy Woolwich. Commissioned into Royal Artillery, 1934; served in UK, 1934–42; 1st Airborne Div., 1943–44; War Office, 1944–47; Palestine and Egypt, 1st Regt RHA, 1947–49; Instructor Staff Coll., Camberley, 1949–52; Military Asst to F-M Montgomery, 1953–55; CO 4th Regt, RHA, 1955–57; Senior Army Instructor, JSSC, 1957–59; Dep. Comdr 17 Gurkha Div., Malaya, 1959–61; Student, Imperial Defence Coll., 1962–63; Military Adviser, High Comr, Canada, 1963–64; GOC 50 (Northumbrian) Div. (TA), 1964–66; Comdt, Jt Warfare Establishment, 1966–68; retd 1969. Col Comdt RA, 1970–78; Hon. Col, 266 (Glos Vol. Artillery) Batt., RA, T&AVR, 1975–83. *Recreations:* fishing, shooting, golf.

Address: The White House, Brockley, Backwell, Bristol BS19 3AU. *Clubs:* MCC; Bath and County (Bath). *Died 26 May 1992.*

KELL, Joseph; *see* Burgess, Anthony.

KELLETT, Sir Brian (Smith), Kt 1979; Chairman: Port of London Authority, 1985–92; Unigate PLC, since 1991 (Director, since 1974); Director, Lombard North Central PLC, since 1985; *b* 8 May 1922; *s* of late Harold Lamb Kellett and Amy Elizabeth Kellett (*née* Smith); *m* 1947, Janet Lesly Street; three *d. Educ:* Manchester Grammar Sch.; Trinity Coll., Cambridge (MA). Wrangler and Sen. Scholar, 1942. Exper. Officer, Admty, 1942–46; Asst Principal, Min. of Transport, 1946–48; Sir Robert Watson-Watt & Partners, 1948–49; Pilkington Bros Ltd, 1949–55; joined Tube Investments Ltd, later TI Group plc, 1955, Dir 1965, a Man. Dir, 1968–82, Dep. Chm. and Chief Exec., 1974, Chm., 1976–84; Chm., British Aluminium Co. Ltd, 1972–79. Dir, Nat. Westminster Bank, 1981–92. Chm., British Ports Fedn, 1990–92; Dir, IMRO, 1987–90. Member: Royal Commn on Standards of Conduct in Public Life, 1974–76; PO Review Cttee, 1976–77; Council, Industrial Soc., 1981–84. A Vice-Pres., Engineering Employers' Fedn, 1976–84. Governor: London Business Sch., 1976–84; Imperial Coll., 1979–91. *Address:* The Old Malt House, Deddington, Banbury, Oxon OX15 0TG. *T:* Deddington (0869) 38257. *Club:* United Oxford & Cambridge University.
Died 30 Jan. 1994.

KELLIHER, Sir Henry (Joseph), Kt 1963; Founder, 1929, Life President, 1982, Dominion Breweries Ltd (Chairman to 1980, Managing Director to 1982); *b* 2 March 1896; *s* of Michael Joseph Kelliher; *m* 1917, Evelyn J., *d* of R. S. Sproule; one *s* four *d. Educ:* Clyde Sch. Dir, Bank of New Zealand, 1936–42. Founded League of Health of NZ Youth, 1934 (objective, Free milk scheme for NZ children, in which it succeeded); purchased Puketutu Island, 1938; established Puketutu Ayrshire Stud, 1940, Aberdeen Angus Stud, 1942, Suffolk Stud, 1946; Thoroughbred and Standard Bred Studs, 1969. Founded: Kelliher Art Trust, 1961; Kelliher Charitable Trust, 1963. KStJ 1960. *Publications:* New Zealand at the Cross Roads, 1936; Why your £ buys Less and Less, 1954. *Recreations:* gardening, riding. *Address:* Puketutu Island, Manukau Harbour, Auckland, New Zealand. *T:* 09–2756871.
Died 29 Sept. 1991.

KELLOCK, His Honour Thomas Oslaf; QC 1965; a Circuit Judge, 1976–91; Deputy Senior Judge (non-resident), Sovereign Base Areas, Cyprus, since 1983; *b* 4 July 1923; *s* of late Thomas Herbert Kellock, MA, MD, MCh Cambridge, FRCS LRCP and Margaret, *y d* of Alexander Brooke; *m* 1967, Jane Ursula Kellock, JP. *Educ:* Rugby; Clare Coll., Cambridge. Sub-Lieut (Special Branch), RNVR, 1944–46. Called to the Bar, Inner Temple, 1949, Bencher, 1973. Admitted: Gold Coast (Ghana) Roll of Legal Practitioners, 1955; N Rhodesia (Zambia) Bar, 1956; Nigeria Bar, 1957; Ceylon (Sri Lanka) Roll of Advocates, 1960; Sierra Leone Bar, 1960; Malayan Bar, 1967; Fiji Bar, 1975. Also appeared in courts of Kenya, Malawi, Pakistan, Jammu and Kashmir, Sarawak. Dir, Legal Div., Commonwealth Secretariat, 1969–72; a Recorder of the Crown Court, 1974–76. Constitutional Advr to HH Sultan of Brunei, 1975–76. Mem., Criminal Injuries Compensation Bd, 1991–. Chm., Anti-Apartheid Movement, 1963–65. Contested (L) Torquay, 1959, S Kensington, 1966 and March 1968, Harwich, Oct. 1974. Gov., Nottingham Polytechnic, 1989–91. *Recreation:* travelling. *Address:* 9 King's Bench Walk, Temple, EC4Y 7DU. *T:* 071–353 6997. *Club:* Reform. *Died 12 Jan. 1993.*

KELLOW, Kathleen; *see* Hibbert, Eleanor.

KELSEY, Julian George, CB 1982; Deputy Secretary (Fisheries and Food), Ministry of Agriculture, Fisheries and Food, 1980–82; *b* 28 Aug. 1922; *s* of William and Charlotte Kelsey, Dulwich; *m* 1944, Joan (*née* Singerton) (*d* 1993); one *d*. *Educ:* Brockenhurst. Lord Chancellor's Dept, 1939; War Service, 1941–46: Lancs Fusiliers and RAC; SOE and Force 136; Comdg No 11 Searcher Party Team, Burma; Exec. Officer, Central Land Board, 1948; Asst Principal, MAFF, 1951; Under Sec., 1969; Dir of Establishments, 1971–76; Fisheries Sec., 1976–80. *Address:* Shaston House, St James, Shaftesbury, Dorset SP7 8HL. *T:* Shaftesbury (01747) 851147.

Died 25 March 1995.

KEMP, (Athole) Stephen (Horsford), LVO 1983; OBE 1958 (MBE 1950); Secretary General, Royal Commonwealth Society, 1967–83; *b* 21 Oct. 1917; *o s* of late Sir Joseph Horsford Kemp, CBE, KC, LLD, and Mary Stuart; *m* 1940, Alison, *yr d* of late Geoffrey Bostock, FCA; two *s* one *d*. *Educ:* Westminster Sch.; Christ Church, Oxford (MA). War service, RA, 1939–46; POW Far East (Thailand-Burma Railway). Malayan CS, 1940–64 (Sec. to Govt, 1955–57; Dep. Perm. Sec., PM's Dept, 1957–61). Sec., Royal Commonwealth Soc. Library Trust, 1984–90; Chief Examiner, Royal Commonwealth Soc. Essay Comp., 1986–. Member: Exec. Cttee, Oxford Fieldpaths Soc., 1983– (Chm., 1991–94); Rights of Way Cttee, CPRE (Oxon), 1983–. Clerk to Parish Council, Langford, Oxon, 1987–. Hon. Life Mem., Royal Commonwealth Society. JMN 1958. *Recreations:* gardening, public rights of way, wine. *Address:* Lockey House, Langford, Lechlade, Glos GL7 3LF. *T:* Faringdon (01367) 860239.

Died 23 March 1995.

KEMP, Lt-Comdr Peter Kemp, OBE 1963; FSA, FRHistS; Royal Navy, retired; Head of Naval Historical Branch and Naval Librarian, Ministry of Defence, 1950–68; Editor of Journal of Royal United Service Institution, 1957–68; *b* 11 Feb. 1904; *e s* of Henry and Isabel Kemp; *m* 1st, 1930, Joyce, *d* of Fleming Kemp; 2nd, 1949, Eleanore (*d* 1987), *d* of Frederick Rothwell; two *d* (and one *s* decd). *Educ:* Royal Naval Colleges, Osborne and Dartmouth. Served in submarines till 1928 (invalided); Naval Intelligence Division, 1939–45. Asst Editor, Sporting and Dramatic, 1933–36; Member: Editorial Staff, The Times, 1936–39 and 1945–50; Council of Navy Records Society; Editorial Adv. Board of Military Affairs (US). *Publications:* Prize Money, 1946; Nine Vanguards, 1951; HM Submarines, 1952; Fleet Air Arm, 1954; Boys' Book of the Navy, 1954; HM Destroyers, 1956; Famous Ships of the World, 1956; Victory at Sea, 1958; Famous Harbours of the World, 1958; (with Prof. C. Lloyd) Brethren of the Coast, 1960; History of the Royal Navy, 1969; The British Sailor: a social history of the lower deck, 1970; Escape of the Scharnhorst and Gneisenau, 1975; A History of Ships, 1978; Merchant Ships, 1982; Seamanship, 1983; (with Richard Ormond) The Great Age of Sail, 1986; The Campaign of the Spanish Armada, 1988; regimental histories of: Staffordshire Yeomanry; Royal Norfolk Regiment; Middlesex Regiment; King's Shropshire Light Infantry; Royal Welch Fusiliers; books on sailing; children's novels; *edited:* Hundred Years of Sea Stories; Letters of Admiral Boscawen (Naval Records Soc.); Fisher's First Sea Lord Papers (Naval Records Soc.), Vol. I, 1960, Vol. II, 1964; Oxford Companion to Ships and the Sea, 1976; Encyclopædia of Ships and Seafaring, 1980; (jtly) Pocket Oxford Guide to Sailing Terms, 1987. *Recreations:* sailing, golf. *Address:* 53 Market Hill, Maldon, Essex. *T:* Maldon (0621) 852609. *Clubs:* West Mersea Yacht, Maldon Golf.

Died 15 March 1992.

KEMP, Stephen; *see* Kemp, A. S. H.

KEMPFF, Wilhelm Walter Friedrich; pianist and composer; *b* Jüterbog, Berlin, 25 Nov. 1895; *m* 1926, Baroness Helen Hiller von Gärtringen; seven *c*. *Educ:* Viktoria Gymnasium, Potsdam; Berlin University and Conservatoire (studied under H. Barth and Robert Kahn). Professor and Director of Stuttgart Staatliche Hochschule für Musik, 1924–29; concert tours throughout the world, 1918–; London début, 1951; NY début, 1964. Made numerous recordings. Mem. of Prussian Academy of Arts. Mendelssohn Prize, 1917; Swedish Artibus et Litteris Medal; French Arts et Lettres Medal, 1975; German Maximiliansorden, 1984, etc. Hon. RAM, 1980; Hon. Mem., Bayerische Akad. der schönen Künste, 1980. *Compositions include:* two symphonies; four operas; piano and violin concertos; chamber, vocal and choral works. *Publications:* Unter dem Zimbelstern, Das Werden eines Musikers (autobiog.), 1951; Was ich hörte, was ich sah: Reisebilder eines Pianisten, 1981. *Address:* Wallgraben 14, D-8193 Ammerland-Münsing 2, Germany; c/o Ibbs & Tillett, 18b Pindock Mews, W9 2PY.

Died 23 May 1991.

KENDALL, (William) Denis, PhD; FRSA; FIMechE; Chartered Engineer; *b* Halifax, Yorks, 27 May 1903; *yr s* of J. W. Kendall, Marton, Blackpool; *m* 1952, Margaret Hilda Irene Burden. *Educ:* Trinity Sch.; Halifax Technical Coll. Cadet in Royal Fleet Auxiliary. Asst to Chief Inspector, Budd Manufacturing Corp., Philadelphia, Pa, 1923; Dir of Manufacturing, Citroen Motor Car Co., Paris, 1929–38; Managing Director, British Manufacture and Research Co., Grantham, England (manufacturers of aircraft cannon and shells), 1938–45, and Consultant to Pentagon, Washington, on high velocity small arms. MP (Ind.) Grantham Division of Kesteven and Rutland, 1942–50; Mem., War Cabinet Gun Bd, 1941–45 (decorated for bravery); Executive Vice-Pres., Brunswick Ordnance Corp., New Brunswick, NJ, 1952–55 (also Dir and Vice-Pres. Ops, Mack Truck Corp.); President and Director: American MARC, Inc., 1955–61 (manufacturers of diesel engines, developed and produced the world's first Diesel outboard engine, and also electric generators, etc), Inglewood, Calif; Dynapower Systems Corp. (manufacturers of electro-medical equipment), Santa Monica, Calif, 1961–73; Pres., Kendall Medical International, Los Angeles, Calif, 1973–82. Mem. President's Council, American Management Assoc. Mem. Worshipful Co. of Clockmakers; Freeman City of London, 1943; Governor of King's Sch., Grantham, 1942–52. Mason (30° Shriner-Al Malaika Temple, LA). Religious Society of Friends (Quakers). Chevalier de l'Ordre du Ouissam Alouite Cherifien (Morocco). *Address:* 1319 North Doheny Drive, Los Angeles, CA 90069, USA. *T:* (213) 5508963. *Clubs:* Riviera Country, United British Services (Los Angeles, Calif).

Died 29 July 1995.

KENDRICK, John Bebbington Bernard; Chief Inspector of Audit, Ministry of Housing and Local Government, 1958–65, retired; *b* 12 March 1905; 3rd *s* of late John Baker Kendrick and Lenora Teague, Leominster, Herefordshire; *m* 1932, Amelia Ruth, 4th *d* of late James Kendall, Grange-over-Sands; two *s*. *Educ:* Leominster Grammar Sch.; King's Sch., Chester; Queen's Coll., Oxford (MA). Called to Bar, Middle Temple. Asst District Auditor, 1926; Deputy District Auditor, 1946; District Auditor, 1953; Deputy Chief Inspector of Audit, 1958. *Recreation:* fell walking. *Address:* Green Acres, Old Hall Road, Troutbeck Bridge, Windermere, Cumbria LA23 1HF. *T:* Windermere (019662) 3705.

Died 24 Nov. 1995.

KENNABY, Very Rev. Noel Martin; Dean of St Albans and Rector of the Abbey Church, 1964–73, Dean Emeritus, 1973; *b* 22 Dec. 1905; *s* of Martin and Margaret Agnes

Kennaby; *m* 1st, 1933, Margaret Honess Elliman; 2nd, 1937, Mary Elizabeth Berry (*d* 1991). *Educ:* Queens' Coll., Cambridge; Westcott House, Cambridge. BA 1928; MA 1932. Deacon 1929, priest 1930, Diocese of Guildford; Curate of Epsom, 1929–32; in charge of Christ Church, Scarborough, 1932–36; Vicar of St Andrew's, Handsworth, 1936–42; Tynemouth, 1942–47; Surrogate from 1942; Rural Dean of Tynemouth, 1943–47; Provost and Vicar of Newcastle upon Tyne, 1947–61; Rural Dean of Newcastle upon Tyne, 1947–61; Senior Chaplain to the Archbishop of Canterbury, 1962–64; Hon. Canon, Newcastle Cathedral, 1962–64. Commissary, Jamaica, 1950–67. *Publication:* To Start You Praying, 1951. *Address:* Delapré House, St Andrew's Road, Bridport, Dorset DT6 3BZ. *Died 22 Jan. 1994.*

KENNEDY, Sir Albert (Henry), Kt 1965; QPM; Hon. President, Securicor (Ulster) Ltd; *b* 11 May 1906; *s* of Joseph and Elizabeth Kennedy; *m* 1st, 1931, Elizabeth Freeborn (decd); two *d*; 2nd, 1942, Muriel Lucile Hamilton (decd); one *d*, and one step *s* one step *d*; 3rd, Edythe. Joined Royal Ulster Constabulary, 1924; District Inspector, 1936; County Inspector, 1951; Deputy Commissioner, Belfast, 1954; Deputy Inspector General, 1957; Inspector General, 1961–69. KPM 1947. *Club:* Royal Belfast Golf (Ulster). *Died 11 Oct. 1991.*

KENNEDY, Prof. John (Stodart), FRS 1965; Research Associate, Department of Zoology, University of Oxford, since 1983; Deputy Chief Scientific Officer, Agricultural Research Council, 1967–77, and Professor of Animal Behaviour in the University of London, Imperial College at Silwood Park, Ascot, 1968–77, then Professor Emeritus; *b* 19 May 1912; *s* of James John Stodart Kennedy, MICE, and Edith Roberts Kennedy (*née* Lammers); *m* 1st, 1936, Dorothy Violet Bartholomew (marr. diss. 1946); one *s*; 2nd, 1950, Claude Jacqueline Bloch (*widow, née* Raphäel); one *s* one *d*, and one step *s. Educ:* Westminster Sch.; University Coll., London. BSc (London) 1933; MSc (London) 1936; PhD (Birmingham) 1938; DSc (London) 1956. Locust Investigator for Imperial Inst. of Entomology, University of Birmingham, 1934–36, Anglo-Egyptian Sudan, 1936–37; London Sch. of Hygiene and Trop. Med., 1937–38; Rockefeller Malaria Res. Lab., Tirana, Albania, 1938–39; Wellcome Entomolog. Field Labs, Esher, Surrey, 1939–42; Res. Officer, Middle East Anti-Locust Unit, 1942–44; Chem. Defence Exptl Station, Porton, Wilts, 1944–45; ARC Unit of Insect Physiology, Cambridge, 1946–67. Sen. Res. Fellow, Imperial Coll., 1977–83. Pres. Royal Entomological Society, 1967–69 (Hon. Fellow, 1974; Wigglesworth Medal, 1985). Fellow: University (later Wolfson) Coll., Cambridge, 1966; University Coll., London, 1967; Imperial Coll., London, 1982. Gold Medal, Linnean Soc., 1984. *Publications:* The New Anthropomorphism, 1992; numerous research papers, review articles and essays on the biology of locusts, mosquitos, moths and greenfly, and insect behaviour generally. *Address:* 17 Winchester Road, Oxford OX2 6NA. *T:* Oxford (0865) 54484. *Died 4 Feb. 1993.*

KENNEY, (William) John; United States lawyer; Partner, Squire, Sanders & Dempsey, since 1973; *b* Oklahoma, 16 June 1904; *s* of Franklin R. Kenney and Nelle Kenney (*née* Torrence); *m* 1931, Elinor Craig (*d* 1991); two *s* two *d. Educ:* Lawrenceville Sch., New Jersey; Stanford Univ (AB); Harvard Law Sch. (LLB). Practised law in San Francisco, 1929–36; Head of oil and gas unit, Securities and Exchange Commission, 1936–38; practised law in Los Angeles, 1938–41; Special Asst to Under-Sec. of the Navy, 1941–46; Asst Sec. of the Navy, 1946–47; Under-Sec. of the Navy, 1947–49; Minister in charge of Economic Cooperation Administration Mission to the UK,

1949–50; Deputy Dir for Mutual Security, resigned 1952. Chairman: Democratic Central Cttee of DC, 1960–64; DC Chapter, American Red Cross, 1968–71. Director: Riggs National Bank, 1959–81; Merchants Fund Inc., 1954–; Porter International, 1953–; Trustee, George C. Marshall Foundn, Lexington, Va, 1963–. *Address:* 2700 Calvert Street, NW, Washington, DC 20008; (office) 1201 Pennsylvania Avenue, NW, Washington, DC 20004, USA. *Clubs:* California (Los Angeles); Alibi, Metropolitan, Chevy Chase (Washington). *Died 16 Jan. 1992.*

KENNON, Vice-Adm. Sir James (Edward Campbell), KCB 1983; CBE 1974 (OBE 1962); Chief of Fleet Support, 1981–83; *b* 26 Nov. 1925; *s* of late Robert Kennon, MC, FRCS, and Ethel Kennon, OBE; *m* 1950, Anne (*d* 1990), *e d* of Captain Sir Stuart Paton, KCVO, CBE, RN retd; two *s* one *d. Educ:* Stowe School. Special entry to RN, 1943; Military Assistant to CDS, 1959–62; Supply Officer, HMS Kent, 1963–65; Secretary: to VCNS, 1965–67; to C-in-C Fleet, 1968–70; Admiralty Interview Bd, 1970; Sec. to First Sea Lord, 1971–74; NATO Defence Coll., 1974; Captain, HMS Pembroke, 1974–76; Dir, Naval Administrative Planning, 1976–78; Asst Chief of Naval Staff (Policy), 1978–79; Chief Naval Supply Officer, 1979–81, and Port Adm., Rosyth, 1980–81. Pres., RN Benevolent Trust, 1984–. Governor, Stowe Sch., 1983– (Chm., 1986–). *Recreations:* walking, languages, photography. *Address:* c/o National Westminster Bank, 26 Haymarket, SW1. *Club:* Army and Navy. *Died 22 Jan. 1991.*

KENT, Geoffrey Charles; Director, since 1988, and Chairman, since 1989, Mansfield Brewery plc (Deputy Chairman, 1988–89); Director, 1975–86, Chairman and Chief Executive, 1981–86, Imperial Group plc; *b* 2 Feb. 1922; *s* of late Percival Whitehead and Madge Kent; *m* 1955, Brenda Georgine Conisbee. *Educ:* Blackpool Grammar Sch. CBIM 1976; FCIM (FInstM 1977). Served RAF, 1939–46; Flt Lieut Coastal Comd. Advertising and marketing appts with Colman, Prentis & Varley, Mentor, and Johnson & Johnson, 1947–58; John Player & Son: Advertising Manager, 1958; Marketing Dir, 1964; Asst Man. Dir, 1969; Chm. and Man. Dir, 1975; Chm. and Chief Exec., Courage Ltd, 1978–81; Dep. Chm. and Dir, Corah plc, 1986–89. Director: Lloyds Bank plc, 1981–92; Lloyds Bank International, 1983–85; Lloyds Merchant Bank Holdings Ltd, 1985–88; John Howitt Group Ltd, 1986–; Brewers' Soc., 1978–86, 1989–. Mem., Lloyd's of London, 1985–. *Recreations:* foreign travel, watching television. *Address:* Hill House, Gonalston, Nottingham NG14 7JA. *Died 23 Sept. 1992.*

KENYON, 5th Baron, *cr* 1788; **Lloyd Tyrell-Kenyon,** CBE 1972; FSA; DL; Bt 1784; Baron of Gredington, 1788; Captain late Royal Artillery, TA; *b* 13 Sept. 1917; *o s* of 4th Baron and Gwladys Julia (*d* 1965), *d* of late Col H. R. Lloyd Howard, CB; *S* father, 1927; *m* 1946, Leila Mary, *d* of Comdr John Wyndham Cookson, RN, Strand Hill, Winchelsea, and Mary, *d* of Sir Alan Colquhoun, 6th Bt, KCB, JP, DL, and *widow* of Lt Hugh William Jardine Ethelston Peel, Welsh Guards; two *s* one *d* (and one *s* decd). *Educ:* Eton; Magdalene Coll., Cambridge. BA (Cambridge), 1950. 2nd Lt Shropshire Yeo. 1937; Lt RA, TA, retired (ill-health) 1943 with hon. rank of Captain. Dir, Lloyds Bank Plc, 1962–88 (Chm. North West Bd); President: University Coll. of N Wales, Bangor, 1947–82; Nat. Museum of Wales, 1952–57. Trustee, Nat. Portrait Gall., 1953–88, Chm., 1966–88; Chairman: Wrexham Powys and Mawddach Hosp. Management Cttee, 1960–74; Clwyd AHA, 1974–78; Friends of the Nat. Libraries, 1962–85; Flint Agricultural Exec. Cttee, 1964–73. Member: Standing Commn on Museums and Galleries, 1953–60; Welsh Regional Hosp. Bd, 1958–63; Council for Professions Supplementary to Medicine,

1961–65; Royal Commn on Historical MSS, 1966–92; Ancient Monuments Bd for Wales, 1979–87; Bd of Governors, Welbeck Coll. Chief Comr for Wales, Boy Scouts' Assoc., 1948–65. DL Co. Flint, 1948; County Councillor, Flint, 1946–55 (Chm., 1954–55). Hon. LLD Wales, 1958. *Heir: s* Hon. Lloyd Tyrell-Kenyon, [*b* 13 July 1947; *m* 1971, Sally Carolyn, *e d* of J. F. P. Matthews; two *s*]. *Address:* Cumbers House, Gredington, Whitchurch, Salop SY13 3DH. *TA:* Hanmer 330; *T:* Hanmer (094874) 330. *Clubs:* Brooks's, Cavalry and Guards, Beefsteak.

Died 16 May 1993.

KERR, Sir Alastair B.; *see* Blair-Kerr, Sir W. A.

KERR, Andrew Stevenson, CBE 1976; arbitrator in industrial relations disputes, retired 1993; *b* 28 Aug. 1918; *s* of John S. Kerr and Helen L. Kerr; *m* 1946, Helen Reid Bryden; two *s* two *d*. *Educ:* Spiers' Sch., Beith, Ayrshire; Glasgow Univ. MA (Hons). Served Army, 1940–46. Entered Min. of Labour, 1947; general employment work in the Ministry, in Scotland, 1947–63; Industrial Relns Officer for Scotland, Min. of Labour, 1964–66; Dep. Chief Conciliation Officer, Min. of Labour, 1966–68; Chief Conciliation Officer, Dept of Employment, 1968–71; Controller (Scotland), Dept of Employment, 1972–74; Chief Conciliation Officer, ACAS, 1974–80. *Recreations:* golf, history. *Address:* The Rowans, 1 Maplewood Close, Gonerby Hill Foot, Grantham, Lincs NG31 8GY. *T:* Grantham (01476) 73370. *Died 17 Nov. 1994.*

KERR, Francis Robert Newsam, OBE 1962; MC 1940; JP; farmer, 1949–85, retired; Vice Lord-Lieutenant of Berwickshire, 1970–90; *b* 12 Sept. 1916; *s* of late Henry Francis Hobart Kerr and Gertrude Mary Kerr (*née* Anthony); *m* 1941, Anne Frederica Kitson; two *s* one *d*. *Educ:* Ampleforth College. Regular Officer, The Royal Scots, 1937–49; TA 1952–63; retired as Lt-Col. Member: Berwickshire County Council, 1964–75; SE Scotland Regional Hosp. Bd, 1971–74; Borders Area Health Bd, 1973–81 (Vice-Chm.); Borders Reg. Council, 1974–78; Post Office Users Nat. Council, 1972–73; Whitley Council, 1970–81; Council, Multiple Sclerosis Soc., 1971–93. Sheriff of Berwick upon Tweed, 1974; JP Berwickshire, 1975. *Recreations:* country pursuits. *Address:* The Coach House, Howden, Jedburgh, Roxburghshire TD8 6QP. *T:* Jedburgh (01835) 64193. *Died 19 Oct. 1995.*

KERR, Rt Hon. Sir John (Robert), AK 1976 (AC 1975); GCMG 1976 (KCMG 1974; CMG 1966); GCVO 1977; PC 1977; Governor-General of Australia, 1974–77; *b* 24 Sept. 1914; *s* of late H. Kerr, Sydney; *m* 1st, 1938, Alison (*d* 1974), *d* of F. Worstead, Sydney; one *s* two *d*; 2nd, 1975, Mrs Anne Robson, *d* of J. Taggart. *Educ:* Fort Street Boys' High Sch.; Sydney Univ. LLB First Cl. Hons; Sydney Univ. Medal. Admitted NSW Bar, 1938. Served War of 1939–45: 2nd AIF, 1942–46; Col, 1945–46. First Prin., Australian Sch. of Pacific Admin, 1946–48; Organising Sec., S Pacific Commn, 1946–47, Acting Sec.-Gen., 1948; returned to Bar, 1948; QC (NSW) 1953; Mem. NSW Bar Coun., 1960–64; Vice-Pres., 1962–63, Pres., 1964, NSW Bar Assoc.; Vice-Pres., 1962–64, Pres., 1964–66, Law Coun. of Australia; Judge of Commonwealth Industrial Court and Judge of Supreme Court of ACT, 1966–72; Judge of Courts of Marine Inquiry, 1967–72; Judge of Supreme Court of Northern Territory, 1970–72; Chief Justice, Supreme Court, NSW, 1972–74; Lieutenant Governor, NSW, 1973–74. Chairman: Commonwealth Cttee on Review of Admin. Decisions, 1968–72; Commonwealth Cttee on Review of Pay for Armed Services, 1970; Deputy President: Trades Practices Tribunal, 1966–72; Copyright Tribunal, 1969–72; President: 3rd Commonwealth and Empire Law Conf., Sydney, 1965; Industrial Relations Soc., 1960–63; Industrial Relations Soc. of Aust. (in formation) (*pro tem*), 1964–66; NSW Marriage Guidance Coun., 1961–62; Law

Assoc. for Asia and W Pacific, 1966–70; Member: Bd of Coun. on New Guinea Affairs, 1964–71; Med. Bd of NSW, 1963–66; Hon. Life Mem., Law Soc. of England and Wales, 1965; Hon. Mem., Amer. Bar Assoc., 1967–. World Lawyer Award, World Peace Through Law Conf., Philippines, 1977. KStJ 1974. *Publications:* Matters for Judgment, 1979, new edn with additional preface, 1988; Uniformity in the Law: trends and techniques (Robert Garran Meml Lectr), 1965; Law in Papua and New Guinea (Roy Milne Meml Lectr), 1968; The Ethics of Public Office (Robert Garran Meml Lectr), 1974; various papers and articles on judicial administration, industrial relations, New Guinea affairs, organisation of legal profession, etc. *Address:* Suite 2, 11th Floor, Norwich House, 6–10 O'Connell Street, Sydney, NSW 2000, Australia. *Club:* Union (Sydney). *Died 24 March 1991.*

KERR, Robert Reid, TD; MA, LLB; Sheriff of Tayside, Central and Fife (formerly Stirling, Dumbarton and Clackmannan) at Falkirk, 1969–83; *b* 7 May 1914; *s* of James Reid Kerr, sugar refiner, and Olive Rodger; *m* 1942, Mona Kerr; three *d*. *Educ:* Cargilfield; Trinity Coll., Glenalmond; Oxford Univ. (MA); Glasgow Univ. Sheriff-Substitute: of Inverness, Moray, Nairn and Ross and Cromarty at Fort William, 1952–61; of Aberdeen, Kincardine and Banff at Banff, 1961–69. OStJ. *Address:* Bagatelle, 14 Rennie Street, Falkirk FK1 5QW.

Died 19 Nov. 1995.

KERSH, Cyril; author and journalist; *b* 24 Feb. 1925; *s* of Hyman and Leah Kersh; *m* 1956, Suzanne Fajner. *Educ:* Westcliff High Sch., Essex. Served War, RN, 1943–47. Worked variously for newsagent, baker, woollen merchant and toy manufr, 1939–43; Reporter, then News and Features Editor, The People, 1943–54; Features Editor, Illustrated, 1954–59; Features staff, London Evening Standard, 1959–60; Editor, Men Only, 1960–63; Daily Express (one day), 1963; Features Editor, then Sen. Features Exec., Sunday Mirror, 1963–76; Editor, Reveille, 1976–79 (Fleet Street's 1st photocomposition editor); Asst Editor (Features), 1979–84, Man. Editor, 1984–86, Sunday Mirror. *Publications:* The Aggravations of Minnie Ashe, 1970; The Diabolical Liberties of Uncle Max, 1973; The Soho Summer of Mr Green, 1974; The Shepherd's Bush Connection, 1975; Minnie Ashe at War, 1979; A Few Gross Words, 1990. *Recreations:* talking, walking, reading, writing. *Address:* 14 Ossington Street, W2 4LZ. *T:* 071–229 6582. *Club:* Our Society.

Died 13 May 1993.

KERSHAW, His Honour Henry Aidan; a Circuit Judge, 1976–92; *b* 11 May 1927; *s* of late Rev. H. Kershaw, Bolton; *m* 1960, Daphne Patricia, *widow* of Dr. C. R. Cowan; four *s*. *Educ:* St John's, Leatherhead; Brasenose Coll., Oxford (BA). Served RN, 1946–48. Called to Bar, Inner Temple, 1953. Councillor, Bolton CBC, 1954–57. Asst Recorder of Oldham, 1970–71; a Recorder of the Crown Court, 1972–76. Dep. Chm., Agricultural Land Tribunal, 1972–76. Chm., Lancs Schs Golf Assoc., 1981–84; Vice-Pres., English Schs Golf Assoc., 1984–. *Recreations:* golf, ski-ing, oil-painting. *Address:* Broadhaven, St Andrew's Road, Lostock, Bolton, Lancs BL6 4AB. *Clubs:* Royal and Ancient Golf (St Andrews); Bolton Golf; West Hill Golf. *Died 29 Oct. 1995.*

KETTLEWELL, Richard Wildman, CMG 1955; Colonial Service, retired 1962; *b* 12 Feb. 1910; *s* of late George Wildman Kettlewell and Mildred Frances Atkinson; *m* 1935, Margaret Jessie Palmer (*d* 1990); one *s* one *d*. *Educ:* Clifton Coll.; Reading and Cambridge Univs. BSc 1931; Dip. Agric. Cantab 1932; AICTA 1933. Entered Colonial Agricultural Service, 1934; appointed to Nyasaland; served War of 1939–45 (despatches) with 2nd Bn King's African Rifles, 1939–43; rank of Major; recalled to agricultural duties in Nyasaland, 1943; Dir of Agriculture, 1951–59; Sec. for Natural Resources, 1959–61; Minister for Lands and Surveys, 1961–62. Consultant to Hunting Technical Services, 1963–79. *Address:* Orchard Close, Over Norton, Chipping Norton, Oxon OX7 5PH. *T:* Chipping Norton (01608) 642407. *Died 17 Nov. 1994.*

KEVILLE, Sir (William) Errington, Kt 1962; CBE 1947; *b* 3 Jan. 1901; *s* of William Edwin Keville; *m* 1928, Ailsa Sherwood (*d* 1991), *d* of late Captain John McMillan; three *s* two *d. Educ:* Merchant Taylors'. Pres., Chamber of Shipping, 1961 (Vice-Pres. 1960; Mem. of Council, 1940); Chairman: Gen. Coun. of British Shipping, 1961; International Chamber of Shipping, 1963–68; Cttee of European Shipowners, 1963–65; Member: Executive Council of Shipping Federation Ltd, 1936–68; Board of PLA, 1943–59; National Maritime Board, 1945–68; Mem. of Cttee of Lloyd's Register of Shipping, 1957–68; Director: Shaw Savill & Albion Co. Ltd, 1941–68 (former Dep. Chm.); National Bank of New Zealand Ltd, 1946–75; Economic Insurance Co. Ltd, 1949–68 (Chm., 1962–68); National Mortgage & Agency Co. of NZ Ltd, 1950–68; British Maritime Trust Ltd, 1959–72 (Chm. 1962–68); Furness Withy & Co. Ltd, 1950–68 (Chm., 1962–68); Chm., Air Holdings Ltd, 1968–69. *Recreations:* walking, history. *Address:* c/o Bunts End, Leigh, Surrey RH2 8NS. *Died 31 Jan. 1992.*

KEY, Maj.-Gen. (Clement) Denis, MBE 1945; late Royal Army Ordnance Corps; *b* 6 June 1915; *s* of late William Clement Key, Harborne, Birmingham; *m* 1941, Molly, *d* of late F. Monk, Kettering, Northants; two *s. Educ:* Seaford Coll. Commnd in RAOC, 1940; served in: England, 1940–44; France, Belgium, Burma, Singapore, 1944–48; Staff Coll., Camberley, 1945; England, 1948–51; USA, 1951–54; England, 1954–59; jssc 1954; Belgium, 1959–61; War Office, 1961–64; Dep. Dir of Ordnance Services, War Office, 1964–67; Dep. Dir of Ordnance Services, Southern Comd, 1967; Comdr, UK Base Organisation, RAOC, 1968–70; retd, 1970. Hon. Col, RAOC (T&AVR), 1968–71; Col Comdt, RAOC, 1972–75. Bursar, 1971–76, Clerk to Govrs, 1976–85, Tudor Hall Sch., Banbury. *Recreations:* rowing, gardening, bee-keeping. *Address:* 104 Maidenhead Road, Stratford-upon-Avon, Warwicks CV37 6XY. *T:* Stratford-upon-Avon (01789) 204345. *Died 29 Sept. 1994.*

KEYS, Prof. Ivor Christopher Banfield, CBE 1976; MA, DMus Oxon; FRCO; FRCM; Hon. RAM; Professor of Music, University of Birmingham, 1968–86, then Emeritus; *b* 8 March 1919; *er s* of Christopher Richard Keys, Littlehampton, Sussex; *m* 1944, Margaret Anne Layzell (*d* 1990); two *s* two *d. Educ:* Christ's Hospital, Horsham; Christ Church, Oxford. FRCO 1934; FRCM 1982. Served with Royal Pioneer Corps, 1940–46. Music scholar and asst organist, Christ Church Cathedral, Oxford, 1938–40 and 1946–47; Lecturer in Music, 1947, Reader, 1950, Sir Hamilton Harty Professor of Music, 1951–54, Queen's University of Belfast; Prof. of Music, Nottingham Univ., 1954–68. Vis. Prof., Huddersfield Poly., 1986–89. Pres., RCO, 1968–70. Chairman: Nat. Fedn of Music Socs, 1985–88; BBC Central Music Adv. Cttee, 1985–88. Hon. RAM 1962. Hon. DMus QUB, 1972. *Publications:* The Texture of Music: Purcell to Brahms, 1961; Brahms Chamber Music, 1974; Mozart, 1980; Johannes Brahms, 1989; *compositions:* Sonata for Violoncello and Pianoforte; Completion of Schubert's unfinished song Gretchens Bitte; Concerto for Clarinet and Strings; Prayer for Pentecostal Fire (choir and organ); The Road to the Stable (3 Christmas songs with piano); Magnificat and Nunc Dimittis (choir and organ); editions of music; reviews of music, in Music and Letters, and of books, in

Musical Times and Organists' Review. *Recreation:* bridge. *Address:* 6 Eastern Road, Birmingham B29 7JP. *Died 7 July 1995.*

KHOUINI, Hamadi; Order of Independence, Tunisia; Order of the Republic, Tunisia; Hon. CBE 1980; Ambassador and Permanent Representative of Tunisia to the United Nations, New York, since 1992; *b* 21 May 1943; *m* 1969, Rafika Hamdi; one *s* one *d. Educ:* The Sorbonne, Paris (LèsL). Sec. Gen., Town Hall, Tunis, 1969–72; Head of Department: Min. of Foreign Affairs, 1972–73; Min. of the Interior, 1973–74; Dir of Youth, Min. of Youth and Sport, 1974–78 (Merit of Youth; Merit of Sport); Dir, Population Demographic Office, 1979–80; Governor of Sousse, 1980–83; Gov. of Tunis, 1983–87, and 1989–90; Ambassador to UK, 1987–88; Minister of State, Min. of For. Affairs, 1990–91. Order of Civil Merit (Spain), 1983; National Order of Merit (France), 1984; Senegalese decoration. *Recreation:* sport (football in particular). *Died 1994.*

KIDU, Hon. Sir Buri (William), Kt 1980; Judge of Appeal Courts of Fiji and Vanuatu, since 1993; *b* 8 Aug. 1945; *s* of Kidu Gaudi and Dobi Vagi; *m* 1969, Carol Anne Kidu; three *s* two *d. Educ:* Univ. of Queensland, Australia (LLB). Barrister-at-Law of Supreme Courts of Queensland and Papua New Guinea. Legal Officer, Dept of Law, 1971; Crown Prosecutor, 1972; Deputy Crown Solicitor, 1973–74; Crown Solicitor, 1974–77; Secretary for Justice, 1977–79; Secretary of Prime Minister's Dept, 1979–80; Chief Justice of Papua New Guinea, 1980–93. Vis. Prof. of Law, Univ. of Papua New Guinea, 1994. Chancellor: Anglican Church of Papua New Guinea, 1976–; Univ. of Papua New Guinea, 1981–90. Hon. LLD Univ. of Papua New Guinea, 1991. *Recreations:* reading, swimming. *Address:* PO Box 5223, Boroko, Port Moresby, Papua New Guinea. *T:* 250259. *Died 30 Jan. 1994.*

KIKI, Hon. Sir (Albert) Maori, KBE 1975; Chairman of the Constitutional Commission, Papua New Guinea, since 1976; *b* 21 Sept. 1931; *s* of Erevu Kiki and Eau Ulamare; *m* 1957, Elizabeth Hariai Miro; two *s* three *d. Educ:* London Missionary Soc. Sch.; Sogeri Central Sch., Papua New Guinea; Fiji Sch. of Med. (Pathology); Papua New Guinea Admin. Coll. Medical Orderly, Kerema, Gulf Province, 1948; Teacher Trng, Sogeri, CP, 1950; Central Med. Sch., Fiji, 1951; Dept of Public Health, Port Moresby, 1954. Formed first trade union in Papua New Guinea and Pres., Council of Trade Unions; Welfare Officer, CP, Land Claims work amongst Koiari people, 1964; studied at Admin. Coll., 1964–65; Foundn Mem. and first Gen. Sec. of Pangu Pati (PNG's 1st Political League); Mem., Port Moresby CC, 1971. MP for Port Moresby, 1972; Minister for Lands, Papua New Guinea, 1972; Deputy Prime Minister and Minister for Defence, Foreign Affairs and Trade, 1975–77. Chairman of Directors: Nat. Shipping Corp.; New Guinea Motors Pty Ltd; Credit Corp. (PNG) Ltd; Kwila Insurance Corp. Ltd; Ovameveo Develts Pty Ltd (Property Developers); Maruka Pty Ltd; On Pty Ltd; Mae Pty Ltd; Maho Investments Ltd; Consultants Pty Ltd. Hon. Dr Laws Kyung Hee Univ., South Korea, 1976. *Publications:* Ten Thousand Years in a Lifetime (autobiog.), 1970; (with Ulli Beier) HoHao: art and culture of the Orokolo people, 1972. *Recreations:* care of farm; formerly Rugby (patron and founder of PNG Rugby Union). *Address:* PO Box 1739, Boroko, Papua New Guinea; (private) Granville Farm, 8 Mile, Port Moresby, PNG. *Died 13 March 1993.*

KILFEDDER, Sir James (Alexander), Kt 1992; MP North Down since 1970 (UU 1970–80, UPUP since 1980) (resigned seat Dec. 1985 in protest against Anglo-Irish Agreement; re-elected Jan. 1986); Leader, Ulster Popular Unionist Party, since 1980; barrister-at-law; *b* 16 July 1928; *yr s* of late Robert and Elizabeth Kilfedder;

unmarried. *Educ:* Model Sch. and Portora Royal Sch., Enniskillen, NI; Trinity Coll., Dublin (BA); King's Inn, Dublin. Called to the Bar, Gray's Inn, 1958. MP (UU) Belfast West, 1964–66. Chm., Select Cttee on NI Affairs, 1994–. Mem. (Official Unionist), N Down, NI Assembly, 1973–75; Mem. (UUUC) N Down, NI Constitutional Convention, 1975–76; Mem. (UPUP) N Down and Speaker, NI Assembly, 1982–86. Mem., Exec. Cttee GB Br., IPU, 1990–. *Recreation:* walking in the country. *Address:* 96 Seacliff Road, Bangor, Co. Down B20 5EZ. *T:* Bangor (01247) 451690; House of Commons, SW1A 0AA. *T:* 0171–219 3563.   *Died 20 March 1995.*

KILMARTIN, Terence Kevin, CBE 1987; Literary Editor, The Observer, 1952–86; *b* 10 Jan. 1922; *s* of Ambrose Joseph Kilmartin and Eve (*née* Hyland); *m* 1952, Joanna (*née* Pearce); one *s* one *d*. *Educ:* Xaverian Coll., Mayfield, Sussex. Private tutor, France, 1938–39; Special Operations Executive, 1940–45; Asst Editor, World Review, 1946–47; freelance journalist, Middle East, 1947–48; Asst Editor, Observer Foreign News Service, 1949–50; Asst Literary Editor, 1950–52. *Publications:* A Guide to Proust, 1983; (ed and trans.) Marcel Proust: Selected Letters 1904–1909, 1989; translations of: Henry de Montherlant: The Bachelors, 1960; The Dream, 1962; Chaos and Night, 1964; The Girls, 1968; The Boys, 1974; André Malraux: Anti-Memoirs, 1968; Lazarus, 1977; Charles de Gaulle: Memoirs of Hope, 1971; Marcel Proust: Remembrance of Things Past (rev. trans.), 1981; Albertine Gone, 1989. *Address:* 44 North Side, Clapham Common, SW4. *T:* 071–622 2697; Mas du Prévot, 13810 Eygalières, France. *T:* 90 959375.   *Died 17 Aug. 1991.*

KILMUIR, Countess of; *see* De La Warr, Countess.

KIMBER, Derek Barton, OBE 1945; FEng 1976; Chairman: London & Overseas Freighters Ltd, 1984–95; London & Overseas Freighters (UK) Ltd, since 1992; Short Sea Europe Plc, since 1989; *b* 2 May 1917; *s* of George Kimber and Marion Kimber (*née* Barton); *m* 1943, Gwendoline Margaret Maude Brotherton (*d* 1995); two *d*. *Educ:* Bedford Sch.; Imperial Coll., London Univ; Royal Naval Coll., Greenwich. MSc(Eng), FCGI, DIC; FRINA, FIMechE, FIMarE, FNECInst, FRSA. Royal Corps of Naval Constructors, 1939–49; Consultant, Urwick, Orr & Partners Ltd, 1950–54; Fairfield Shipbuilding & Engineering Co. Ltd: Manager, 1954; Dir, 1961; Dep. Man. Dir, 1963–65; Dir, Harland & Wolff Ltd, 1966–69; Dir Gen., Chemical Industries Assoc., 1970–73; Chairman: Austin & Pickersgill, 1973–83; Bartram & Sons, 1973–83; Sunderland Shipbuilders, 1980–83; Govan Shipbuilders, 1980–83; Smith's Dock, 1980–83; Director: A. & P. Appledore International Ltd, 1974–77; British Ship Research Assoc. (Trustees) Ltd, 1973–81; R. S. Dalgliesh Ltd, 1978–80; Equity Capital for Industry Ltd, 1977–86; Eggar Forrester (Hldgs), 1983–93; Wilks Shipping Co. Ltd, 1986–93; AMARC (TES) Ltd, subseq. Community Industry Ltd, then Rathbone CI, 1986–; Community Industry Ltd, 1990–. Dir, Glasgow Chamber of Commerce, 1962–65. Chm., C. & G. Jt Adv. Cttee for Shipbuilding, 1968–70; Pres., Clyde Shipbuilders Assoc., 1964–65; Lloyds Register of Shipping: Member: Scottish Cttee, 1964–65; Gen. Cttee, 1973–90; Technical Cttee, 1976–80; Exec. Bd, 1978–84; Member: Shipbuilding Industry Trng Bd, 1964–69; Research Council, British Ship Res. Assoc., 1973–81; Brit. Tech. Cttee, Amer. Bureau of Shipping, 1976– (Chm., 1989–94); Standing Cttee, Assoc. of W European Shipbuilders, 1976–89 (Chm., 1983–84); Cttee of EEC Shipbuilders' Assoc., 1985–89; Underwriting Mem., Lloyd's, 1985–; Chm., Management Bd, Shipbuilders & Repairers Nat. Assoc., 1974–76, Vice-Pres., 1976–77; Mem., Jt Industry Cons. Cttee, (SRNA/CSEU), 1966–76. Member: EDC for Chem. Industry, 1970–72; Process Plant Working Party (NEDO),

1970–72; CBI Central Council, 1970–72, 1975–84; CBI Northern Reg. Council, 1973–80 (Chm. 1975–77); Steering Cttee, Internat. Maritime Industries Forum, 1981–. Member: Council, RINA, 1961– (Chm., 1973–75, Pres. RINA 1977–81); Council, Welding Inst., 1959–74, 1976–82; Bd, CEI, 1977–81, Exec. Cttee, 1978–80; C. & G. Senior Awards Cttee, 1970–81; Council, NE Coast Inst. of Engrs and Shipbuilders, 1974–92 (Pres., 1982–84); Vice-Pres., British Maritime League, 1985–87; Life Gov., Marine Soc., 1987. Mem., City of London Br., Royal Soc. of St George, 1985–. Liveryman: Worshipful Co. of Shipwrights, 1967 (Asst to Court 1974–, Prime Warden, 1986–87); Worshipful Co. of Engineers, 1984–. Mem., Smeatonian Soc., 1984–; Pres., Old Centralians, 1985–86. Mem., Propeller Club of US. Mem. Court, City Univ., 1984–; Governor, Imperial Coll., London Univ., 1967–87. Hon. FRINA 1981. RINA Gold Medallist, 1977. *Publications:* papers on shipbuilding subjects in learned soc. trans. *Recreations:* DIY, golf, rough gardening. *Address:* Broughton, Monk's Road, Virginia Water, Surrey GU25 4RR. *T:* Wentworth (01344) 844274. *Clubs:* Brooks's, Caledonian, City Livery, Aldgate Ward, United Wards, Anchorites, MCC; Den Norske; Yacht of Greece.
            Died 21 Dec. 1995.

KINAHAN, Charles Henry Grierson, CBE 1972; JP; DL; retired 1977; Director, Bass Ireland Ltd, Belfast, and subsidiary companies, 1956–77; *b* 10 July 1915; *e s* of Henry Kinahan, Belfast, and Ula, *d* of late Rt Rev. C. T. P. Grierson, Bishop of Down and Connor and Dromore; *m* 1946, Kathleen Blanche McClintock, MB, BS, *e d* of Rev. E. L. L. McClintock; three *s*. *Educ:* Stowe School. Singapore Volunteer Corps, 1939–45; POW Singapore, 1942–45. Commerce, London, 1933–38 and Malaya, 1938–56. Dir, Dunlop Malayan Estates Ltd, 1952–56; Man. Dir, Lyle and Kinahan Ltd, Belfast, 1956–63. Mem. (Alliance) Antrim S, NI Constitutional Convention, 1975–76; contested (Alliance) Antrim S, gen. election 1979. Belfast Harbour Comr, 1966–80; Chm., 1969–73, Pres., 1975–84, NI Marriage Guidance Council; Mem. Senate, QUB, 1968–93; Chairman: NI Historic Buildings Council, 1973–88; Ulster '71 Exhibn, 1971; NI Mountain Rescue: Working Party, 1976–77; Coordinating Cttee, 1978–85; Trustee, Nat. Heritage Memorial Fund, 1980–91. JP 1961, High Sheriff 1971, DL 1977, Co. Antrim; Mem., Antrim District Council (Alliance Party), 1977–81. LLD *hc* QUB, 1993. *Recreations:* mountain trekking, farming, classical music. *Address:* 53 Broadacres, Templepatrick, Co. Antrim BT39 0AY. *T:* Templepatrick (01849) 432379. *Club:* Royal Over-Seas League.

            Died 11 Aug. 1995.

KINDERSLEY, Lt-Col Claude Richard Henry, DSO 1944; MC 1943; DL; Vice Lord-Lieutenant, Isle of Wight, 1980–86; *b* 11 Dec. 1911; *s* of late Lt-Col Archibald Ogilvie Lyttelton Kindersley, CMG, and Edith Mary Kindersley (*née* Craven); *m* 1938, Vivien Mary, *d* of late Charles John Wharton Darwin, Elston Hall, Notts; three *d*. *Educ:* Wellington Coll.; Trinity Coll., Cambridge. MA. Commissioned HLI, 1933; served with 2nd Bn HLI, NW Frontier, Palestine and Middle East, 1936–43, and with 1st Bn HLI, France and Germany, 1944–45; commanded 1st Bn HLI, 1945; comd Infantry Boys' Batt., 1953–54; retd 1955. DL: Hants, 1962–74; Isle of Wight, 1974; High Sheriff, Isle of Wight, 1974–75. President: Country Landowners' Assoc. (IoW Branch), 1978–87; Isle of Wight Scout Assoc., 1966–86. *Recreation:* yachting. *Address:* Hamstead Grange, Yarmouth, Isle of Wight PO41 0YE. *T:* Yarmouth (0983) 760230. *Clubs:* Royal Yacht Squadron; Royal Solent (Yarmouth).
            Died 31 March 1993.

KINDERSLEY, David Guy, MBE 1979; stone-carver and designer of alphabets (self-employed); in partnership with

Lida Lopes Cardozo, since 1981; *b* 11 June 1915; *s* of Guy Molesworth Kindersley and Kathleen Elton; *m* 1st, 1938, Christine Sharpe (marr. diss.); two *s* one *d*; 2nd, 1957, Barbara Pym Eyre Petrie (marr. diss.); 3rd, 1986, Lida Lopes Cardozo; three *s*. *Educ:* St Cyprian's, Eastbourne (prep. sch.); Marlborough Coll., Wilts. Apprenticed to Eric Gill, ARA, 1933–36. Taught at Cambridge Coll. of Arts and Technology, 1946–57; one-time adviser to MoT on street-name alphabets; adviser to Shell Film Unit on design of titles, 1949–58; consultant to Letraset Internat., 1964–88; Dir, Cambridge Super Vision Ltd, 1983–. Sen. Research Fellow, William Andrews Clark Memorial Library, Univ. of California, Los Angeles, 1967; Sen. Fellow, RCA, 1987. Hon. Pres., Wynkyn de Worde Soc. (Chm. 1976). FRSA 1992. *Publications:* Optical Letter Spacing and its Mechanical Application, 1966 (rev. and repub. by Wynkyn de Worde Soc., 1976); Mr Eric Gill, 1967, 3rd edn (Eric Gill—Further Thoughts by an Apprentice), 1990; Graphic Variations, 1979; (with L. L. Cardozo) Letters Slate Cut, 1981, 2nd edn 1991; contribs to Printing Technology, Penrose Annual, Visible Language; limited editions: Variations on the Theme of 26 Letters, edn 50, 1969; Graphic Sayings, edn 130, 1973; *relevant publication:* David Kindersley: his work and workshop, by Montague Shaw, 1989. *Recreation:* archaeology. *Address:* 152 Victoria Road, Cambridge CB4 3DZ. *T:* Cambridge (01223) 62170. *Clubs:* Arts, Double Crown; (Hon. Mem.) Rounce and Coffin (Los Angeles). *Died 2 Feb. 1995.*

KING, Alexander Hyatt, (Alec); musical scholar; a Deputy Keeper, Department of Printed Books, British Museum, 1959–76, retired; *b* 18 July 1911; *s* of Thomas Hyatt King and Mabel Jessie (*née* Brayne); *m* 1943, Evelyn Mary Davies; two *s*. *Educ:* Dulwich Coll.; King's Coll., Cambridge (schol.; MA). Entered Dept of Printed Books, British Museum, 1934; Supt of Music Room, 1944–73; Music Librarian, Ref. Div., British Library, 1973–76. Hon. Sec., British Union Catalogue of Early Music, 1948–57; Mem. Council, Royal Musical Assoc., 1949–, Editor, Proc. of the Assoc., 1952–57, Pres., 1974–78; Pres., Internat. Assoc. of Music Libraries, 1955–59 (Hon. Mem., 1968), Pres., UK Br., 1953–68; Vice-Chm. Jt Cttee, Internat. Musicological Soc. and Internat. Assoc. of Music Libys, for Internat. Inventory of Musical Sources, 1961–76; Chm., Exec. Cttee, Brit. Inst. of Recorded Sound, 1951–62. Sandars Reader in Bibliography, Univ. of Cambridge, 1962. Vice-Chm., Exec. Cttee, Grove's Dictionary of Music, 1970–74; Trustee, Hinrichsen Foundn, 1976–82; Hon. Librarian, Royal Philharmonic Soc., 1969–82. Mem., Zentralinst. für Mozartforschung, 1953. DUniv York, 1978; Hon. DMus St Andrews, 1981. Silver Medal, Mozarteum, Salzburg, 1991. *Publications:* Chamber Music, 1948; (jtly) catalogue: Music in the Hirsch Library, 1951; catalogue: Exhibition of Handel's Messiah, 1951; Mozart in Retrospect, 1955, 3rd edn 1976; Mozart in the British Museum, 1956, repr. 1975; exhibn catalogue: Henry Purcell—G. F. Handel, 1959; Some British Collectors of Music, 1963; 400 Years of Music Printing, 1964, 2nd edn 1968; Handel and his Autographs, 1967; Mozart Chamber Music, 1968, rev. edn 1986; Mozart String and Wind Concertos, 1978, rev. edn 1986; Printed Music in the British Museum: an account of the collections, the catalogues, and their formation, up to 1920, 1979; A Wealth of Music in the various collections of the British Library (Reference Division) and the British Museum, 1983; A Mozart Legacy: aspects of the British Library collections, 1984; Musical Pursuits: selected essays, 1987; *edited:* (jtly) Mozart's Duet Sonata in C K19d, 1953; illustr. edn of Alfred Einstein's Short History of Music, 1953; P. K. Hoffmann's Cadenzas and elaborated slow movements to 6 Mozart piano concertos, 1959; (jtly) 2nd edn of Emily Anderson's Letters of Mozart and his

Family, 1966; Concert Goer's Companion series, 1970–; Auction catalogues of Music, 1973–; *contribs to:* Year's Work in Music, 1947–51; Schubert, a symposium, 1947; Music, Libraries and Instruments, 1961; Deutsch Festschrift, 1963; Essays in honour of Victor Scholderer, 1970; Grasberger Festschrift, 1975; Essays in honour of Sir Jack Westrup, 1976; The New Grove, 1980; Rosenthal Festschrift, 1984; The Library of the British Museum, 1991; various articles; *relevant publication* (ed by Oliver Neighbour) Music and Bibliography: Essays in honour of Alec Hyatt King, 1980. *Recreations:* watching cricket, opera, exploring Suffolk. *Address:* 37 Pier Avenue, Southwold, Suffolk IP18 6BU. *T:* Southwold (01502) 724274. *Club:* MCC. *Died 10 March 1995.*

KING, Alison Elsie, OBE 1978; Co-ordinator Properties, Women's Royal Voluntary Service, 1974–78; Director, WRVS Office Premises Ltd, 1969–78; Member, WRVS Housing Association Management Committee, 1973–83; *b* 20 Aug. 1913. *Educ:* King's House Sch., London; Germany. Flight-Capt., Operations, Air Transport Auxiliary, 1940–45. Dir, Women's Junior Air Corps, 1952–58; Gen. Sec., NFWI, 1959–69. Chm., British Women Pilots' Assoc., 1956–64. *Publications:* Golden Wings, 1956 (repr. 1975); articles in Aeroplane Monthly. *Recreations:* writing, painting in oils. *Address:* 87 Kenilworth Court, SW15 1HA. *Club:* University Women's. *Died 6 April 1992.*

KING, Douglas James Edward, FRICS; FCIArb; Senior Partner, 1963–87, Consultant, since 1987, King & Co., Chartered Surveyors; Director: Bradford & Bingley Building Society, 1982–90; Frogmore Estates plc (formerly Fairview Estates), 1982–90; *b* 12 April 1919; *s* of Herbert James King, OBE, FRICS and Gertrude Carney; *m* 1941, Betty Alice Martin; two *s* one *d*. *Educ:* Hillcrest Prep. Sch., Frinton-on-Sea; Taunton Sch. FRICS 1952. Served War, TA, 1939–46, Captain RA. Chm., Hearts of Oak & Enfield Bldg Soc., 1975–82. A Vice Pres., London Chamber of Commerce and Industry, 1980– (Chm., 1978–80); Chm., London Court of Internat. Arbitration, 1981–82, and of Jt Cttee of Management, 1987–88; Gen. Comr of Income Tax, City of London, 1978–. Master, Wheelwrights' Co., 1985–86. Governor, Queenswood Sch., 1980–. *Recreation:* lives and writings of Johnson, Boswell and Pepys. *Address:* Monkswood Cottage, 73a Camlet Way, Hadley Wood, Herts EN4 0NL. *T:* 081–449 0263. *Clubs:* Carlton, City Livery.

Died 9 March 1992.

KING, Evelyn Mansfield, MA; *b* 30 May 1907; *s* of Harry Percy King and Winifred Elizabeth Paulet; *m* 1935, Hermione Edith (*d* 1989), *d* of late Arthur Felton Crutchley, DSO; one *s* two *d*. *Educ:* Cheltenham Coll.; King's Coll., Cambridge; Inner Temple. Cambridge Univ. Correspondent to the Sunday Times, 1928–30; Asst Master Bedford Sch., 1930; Headmaster and Warden, Clayesmore Sch., 1935–50. Gloucestershire Regt 1940; Acting Lt-Col 1941. MP (Lab) Penryn and Falmouth Div. of Cornwall, 1945–50; Parly Sec., Min. of Town and Country Planning, 1947–50; resigned from Labour Party, 1951, and joined Conservative Party; contested (C) Southampton (Itchen), 1959; MP (C) Dorset S, 1964–79. Member of Parly delegations: Bermuda and Washington, 1946; Tokyo, 1947; Cairo and ME, 1967; Jordan and Persian Gulf, 1968; Kenya and Seychelles, 1969; Malta, 1970 (leader); Malawi, 1971 (leader); Mem. Select Cttee on Overseas Aid, 1971; Chm. Food Cttee, 1971–73. *Publications:* (with J. C. Trewin) Printer to the House (biography of Luke Hansard), 1952; Closest Correspondence, 1989. *Recreations:* boats, riding. *Address:* Embley Manor, near Romsey, Hants SO51 6DL. *T:* Romsey (0794) 512342; 11 Barton Street, SW1P 3NE. *T:* 071–222 4525. *Club:* Carlton. *Died 14 April 1994.*

KING, Prof. Jeffrey William Hitchen, MSc, CEng, FICE, FIStructE; Professor of Civil Engineering, Queen Mary College, University of London, 1953–72, then Emeritus Professor; *b* 28 Sept. 1906; *s* of George and Edith King, Wigan; *m* 1930, Phyllis Morfydd Harris (*d* 1977), *d* of Rev. W. Harris; one *s* one *d. Educ:* Ashton-in-Makerfield Grammar Sch.; Manchester Univ. Engineer and Agent to Cementation Co. Ltd, British Isles, Spain and Egypt, 1927–36; Research Engineer, Michelin Tyre Co. 1936–37; Lecturer in Civil Engineering, University Coll., Nottingham, 1937–47; Reader in Civil Engineering, Queen Mary Coll., London, 1947–53. Governor, Queen Mary Coll., 1962–65; formerly Mem., Academic Board and Vice-Chm., Civil Engineering Cttee of Regional Advisory Council for Higher Technological Education; formerly Mem., Research Cttee, formerly Chm., Concrete Specification Cttee and Cttee on Accelerated Testing of Concrete, Instn of Civil Engineers; formerly Mem. BSI Cttees, CEB/4/4, CEB/21. *Publications:* papers in Journals of Instn of Civil Engineers, Instn of Structural Engineers, and Inst. of Mine Surveyors, and in various technical periodicals. *Recreations:* many and varied. *Address:* The Nook, Crayke Road, Easingwold, York YO6 3PN. *T:* Easingwold (01347) 821151. *Died 14 Feb. 1995.*

KING, John George Maydon, (Jock), CMG 1959; OBE 1953 (MBE 1945); retired from Colonial Agricultural Service; *b* 26 Jan. 1908; 2nd *s* of late Harold Edwin and Elizabeth Lindsay King, Durban, Natal, SA; *m* 1st, 1938, Françoise Charlotte de Rham (*d* 1966), Lausanne; two *s*; 2nd, 1970, Violet (*d* 1990), *widow* of Colin MacPherson, late of Tanganyika Administration Service. *Educ:* University Coll. Sch. (Preparatory); Oundle Sch.; London Univ. (Wye Coll.); Cambridge Univ. (Colonial Office Schol., Cambridge Univ. and Imperial Coll. of Tropical Agric.). Appointed to Colonial Agricultural Service as Agricultural Officer, Tanganyika, 1932–46; seconded to Cambridge Univ. as Lecturer in Tropical Agric. to Colonial Services Courses, 1946–48; Dir of Livestock and Agricultural Services, Basutoland, 1948–54; Dir of Agriculture, Uganda, 1954–60, Swaziland, 1960–63; Regional Manager, Lower Indus Project, Hyderabad-Sind, 1964–66. *Recreations:* walking, photography. *Address:* Brockley House, Nailsworth, near Stroud, Glos GL6 0AR. *T:* Nailsworth (045383) 2407. *Club:* Farmers'.
Died 10 Aug. 1992.

KING, Sir Sydney (Percy), Kt 1975; OBE 1965; JP; District Organiser, National Union of Agricultural and Allied Workers, 1946–80; Chairman, Trent Regional Health Authority, 1973–82; *b* 20 Sept. 1916; *s* of James Edwin King and Florence Emily King; *m* 1944, Millicent Angela Prendergast; two *d. Educ:* Brockley Central School. Member: N Midland Regional Board for Industry (Vice-Chm. 1949); Sheffield Regional Hosp. Bd, 1963–73 (Chm, 1969–73); E Midland Economic Planning Council, 1965; E Midlands Gas Board, 1970; MAFF E Midland Regional Panel, 1972 (Chm., 1977). Pro-Chancellor, Univ. of Leicester, 1987–. JP 1956, Alderman 1967, Kesteven. Hon. LLD: Leicester, 1980; Nottingham, 1981. *Recreations:* reading, music, talking. *Address:* 49 Robertson Drive, Sleaford, Lincs NG34 7AL. *T:* Sleaford (0529) 302056. *Died 24 Oct. 1991.*

KING-MARTIN, Brig. John Douglas, CBE 1966; DSO 1957; MC 1953; Deputy Commander, HQ Eastern District, 1968–70, retired; *b* 9 March 1915; *s* of late Lewis King-Martin, Indian Forest Service; *m* 1940, Jeannie Jemima Sheffield Hollins, *d* of late S. T. Hollins, CIE, Indian Police; one *s* one *d. Educ:* Allhallows Sch.; RMC Sandhurst. Commnd 1935; 3rd Royal Bn 12 Frontier Force Regt, IA, 1936; Waziristan Ops, 1936–37; Eritrea, Western Desert, 1940–42 (despatches); Staff Coll., Quetta, 1944; Bde Major, 1944–46, India, Java; GSO 2, Indian

Inf. Div., Malaya, 1946–47; transf. to RA, 1948; Battery Comdr, 1948–50; DAQMG 2 Inf. Div., 1951–52; Korea, 1952–53; CO, 50 Medium Regt, RA, 1956–57; Suez, Cyprus, 1956–57; Coll. Comdr, RMA Sandhurst, 1958–60; Dep. Comdr and CRA, 17 Gurkha Div., 1961–62; Comdr, 17 Gurkha Div., 1962–64; Comdr, Rhine Area, 1964–67. Lieut-Col 1956; Brig. 1961. ADC to the Queen, 1968–70. *Recreations:* golf, painting, photography. *Address:* White House Farm, Polstead, Suffolk CO6 5DL. *T:* Boxford (0787) 210327. *Club:* East India, Devonshire, Sports and Public Schools.
Died 11 April 1993.

KINGHAM, His Honour James Frederick; DL; freelance lecturer and broadcaster; Teacher on Law, Selwyn College, Cambridge, since 1990; *b* 9 Aug. 1925; *s* of late Charles William and Eileen Eda Kingham; *m* 1958, Vivienne Valerie Tyrrell Brown; two *s* two *d. Educ:* Blaenau Ffestiniog Grammar Sch.; Wycliffe Coll.; Queens' Coll., Cambridge (MA); Graz Univ., Austria. Served with RN, 1943–47. Called to Bar, Gray's Inn, 1951; Mem. Gen. Council of Bar, 1954–58; Mem. Bar Council Sub-Cttee on Sentencing and Penology. Dep. Recorder, Nottingham City QS, 1966–72; a Recorder, 1972–73; a Circuit Judge, 1973–90; Liaison Judge, Beds, 1981–90. Member: Bd, Criminal Injuries Compensation Bd, 1990–; Parole Bd, 1992–. Consultant Editor, Family Court Reports, 1991–. Dep. County Comr, Herts Scouts, 1971–80, formerly Asst County Comr for Venture Scouts; Venture Scout Leader: Harpenden, 1975–86; Kimpton and Wheathampstead, 1986–. Mem. Ct, Cranfield Univ., 1992–. DL Hertford, 1989. *Recreations:* mountain activities, squash, ski-ing, youth work, history, gardening, watching football. *Address:* Stone House, High Street, Kimpton, Hitchin, Herts SG4 8RJ. *T:* Kimpton (01438) 832308. *Clubs:* Union, University Centre (Cambridge); Western (Glasgow). *Died 8 Feb. 1995.*

KINLOCH, Sir John, 4th Bt, *cr* 1873, of Kinloch, co. Perth; *b* 1 Nov. 1907; *e s* of Sir George Kinloch, 3rd Bt, OBE, and Ethel May (*d* 1959), *y d* of late Major J. Hawkins; *S* father, 1948; *m* 1934, Doris Ellaline, *e d* of C. J. Head, London; one *s* two *d. Educ:* Charterhouse; Magdalene Coll., Cambridge. Served with British Ministry of War Transport as their repr. at Abadan, Persia, and also in London. Employed by Butterfield & Swire in China and Hong Kong, 1931–63, and by John Swire & Sons Ltd, London, 1964–73. *Heir:* *s* David Oliphant Kinloch, CA [*b* 15 Jan. 1942; *m* 1st, 1968, Susan Minette (marr. diss. 1979), *y d* of Maj.-Gen. R. E. Urquhart, CB, DSO; three *d*; 2nd, 1983, Sabine, *o d* of Philippe de Loes, Geneva; one *s*]. *Address:* Aldie Cottage, Kinross, Kinross-shire KY13 7QH. *T:* Fossoway (05774) 305.
Died 28 May 1992.

KIPARSKY, Prof. Valentin Julius Alexander, MA, PhD; Finnish writer and Professor, Helsinki, retired 1974; Member of the Finnish Academy, 1977; *b* St Petersburg, 4 July 1904; *s* of Professor René Kiparsky and Hedwig (*née* Sturtzel); *m* 1940, Aina Dagmar, MagPhil, *d* of Rev. Matti Jaatinen and Olga (*née* Jungmann); one *s. Educ:* St Annen-Schule, St Petersburg; St Alexis Sch., Perkjärvi, Finland; Finnish Commercial Sch., Viipuri, Finland; Helsinki Univ.; Prague Univ.; and research work in different countries. Helsinki University: Junior Lectr, 1933, Sen. Lectr, 1938, actg Prof., 1946, Prof., 1947 and again, 1963. Visiting Prof., Indiana Univ., Bloomington, USA, 1952, Minnesota Univ., USA, 1961–62; Prof. of Russian Language and Literature, University of Birmingham, 1952–55, when he returned to Finland; Prof. of Slavonic Philology, Freie Univ., Berlin, 1958–63. Co-Editor: Slavistische Veröffentlichungen (W Berlin), 1958–; Scando-Slavica (Copenhagen), 1963–. Lt Finnish Army, 1939–40, 1941–42; Translator and Interpreter to

Finnish Govt, 1942–44; Director: Finnish Govtl Inst. for studies of USSR, 1948–50; Osteuropa-Institut, W Berlin, 1958–63. Pres., Societas Scientiarum Fennica; Corresp. Member: Akad. der Wissenschaften und der Literatur, Mainz; Internat. Cttee of Slavists. Dr *hc*: Poznań, 1973; Stockholm, 1975. Comdr of the Finnish Lion, 1954; Order Zasługi, Poland, 1974. *Publications:* Die gemein-slavischen Lehnwörter aus dem Germanischen, 1934; Fremdes im Baltendeutsch, 1936; Die Kurenfrage, 1939; Suomi Venäjän Kirjallisuudessa, 1943 and 1945; Venäjän Runotar, 1946; Norden i den Ryska Skönlitteraturen, 1947; Wortakzent der russischen Schriftsprache, 1962; Russische historische Grammatik I, 1963; English and American Characters in Russian Fiction, 1964; Russische historische Grammatik II, 1967, III, 1974; numerous articles in various languages in learned jls. *Recreation:* cycling. *Address:* Maurinkatu 8–12 C 37, Helsinki, Finland. *Died 18 May 1983.*

KIRK, John Henry, CBE 1957; Emeritus Professor of Marketing (with special reference to horticulture), University of London; *b* 11 April 1907; *s* of William Kirk, solicitor; *m* 1946, Wilfrida Margaret Booth; two *s. Educ:* Durban High Sch., S Africa; Universities of S Africa, Cambridge, North Carolina and Chicago. Ministry of Agriculture (from 1934, as economist and administrator); Under-Sec., 1959–65; Prof. of Marketing, Wye Coll., 1965–72. *Publications:* Economic Aspects of Native Segregation, 1929; Agriculture and the Trade Cycle, 1933; United Kingdom Agricultural Policy 1870–1970, 1982; contributions to journals of sociology, economics and agricultural economics. *Recreation:* gardening. *Address:* Yallands Farmhouse, Staplegrove, Taunton, Som TA2 6PZ. *T:* Taunton (01823) 278979.

Died 2 Dec. 1995.

KIRSOP, (Arthur) Michael (Benjamin); Chairman, Forth Thyme Ltd, since 1994; *b* 28 Jan. 1931; *s* of Arthur Kirsop and Sarah (*née* Cauthery); *m* 1957, Patricia (*née* Cooper); two *s. Educ:* St Paul's Sch., Brazil; Glasgow Academy; Univ. of Oxford (BA). Joined English Sewing Cotton Co. Ltd, 1955; Area Sales Man., 1957; Export Sales Man., 1961; Man. Dir, Thread Div., 1964; Dir, English Sewing Cotton Co. Ltd, 1967 (later English Calico Ltd, then Tootal Ltd); Jt Man. Dir, 1973–76; Chief Exec., 1974–76; Chm., Tootal Ltd, 1975–76; Chm. and Man. Dir, Ollerenshaw Threads Ltd, 1981–86. Hon. Consul for the Netherlands, 1971–80. CIMgt (FBIM 1973). *Recreations:* gardening, sport. *Address:* Devonshire House, 237 Ashley Road, Hale, Cheshire WA15 9NE. *T:* 0161–941 5173. *Clubs:* MCC; Lancs CC. *Died 6 July 1995.*

KISCH, Alastair Royalton; conductor of symphony concerts; Artistic Director, Cork Street Art Gallery; *b* London, 20 Jan. 1919; *s* of late E. Royalton Kisch, MC and Pamela Kisch; *m* 1940, Aline, *d* of late Bruce Hylton Stewart and M. F., (Molly), Thornely; one *s* two *d. Educ:* Wellington Coll., Berks; Clare Coll., Cambridge. War service, Captain, KRRC (60th Rifles), 1940–46. Conducted Royal Festival Hall concerts with London Philharmonic Orchestra, London Symphony Orchestra, Philharmonia Orchestra, Royal Philharmonic Orchestra, etc; Guest conductor to Hallé Orchestra, Birmingham Symphony Orchestra, etc; also conducted concerts in Europe with Paris Conservatoire Orchestra, Palestine Symphony Orchestra, Florence Philharmonic Orchestra, Athens State Symphony Orchestra, Pasdeloup Orchestra of Paris, Royal Opera House Orchestra of Rome, San Carlo Symphony Orchestra of Naples, Vienna Symphony Orchestra, etc; broadcast on BBC with London Symphony Orchestra, Royal Philharmonic Orchestra, and Philharmonia Orchestra. Gramophone recordings for Decca. Specialist in English and French paintings of 20th century. *Recreations:* good food and wine. *Address:* 2 Edwardes Square, Kensington, W8 6HE. *T:* 0171–602 6655. *Clubs:* Athenæum, Hurlingham.

Died 21 March 1995.

KISCH, John Marcus, CMG 1965; *b* 27 May 1916; *s* of late Sir Cecil Kisch, KCIE, CB, and Myra Kisch; *m* 1951, Gillian Poyser; four *d. Educ:* Rugby Sch.; King's Coll., Cambridge. Served Royal Corps of Signals, 1939–45. Assistant Principal: Board of Inland Revenue, 1938; Colonial Office, 1939; seconded E Africa High Commission, 1951; Kenya Govt, 1952; Asst Sec., Colonial Office, 1956; seconded CRO, 1964; transferred Min. of Defence, 1965; MoD (Navy Dept), 1965–68; Asst Sec., ODM, later ODA, 1968–72; Planning Inspector, DoE, 1972–79. *Address:* Westwood, Dunsfold, Surrey GU8 4LN. *T:* Dunsfold (0483) 200252; 21 Pembroke Square, W8 6PB. *T:* 071–937 8590. *Died 22 June 1992.*

KISCH, Royalton; *see* Kisch, A. R.

KITCHEN, Frederick Bruford, CBE 1975; *b* Melbourne, 15 July 1912; *o s* of F. W. Kitchen, Malvern, Vic, Australia; *m* 1936, Una Bernice Sloss; two *s* one *d. Educ:* Melbourne Grammar Sch.; Melbourne Univ. (BSc). Joined family firm (in Melb.), J. Kitchen and Sons Pty Ltd, which had become a Unilever soap co., 1934; Sales Dir, Lever Bros Ltd, Canada, 1946; came to England, 1949, as Chm., Crosfields (CWG) Ltd; Chm., Lever Bros Ltd, 1957; Marketing Dir, Lever Bros & Associates Ltd, 1960; Chm., Van den Berghs & Jurgens Ltd, 1962–74. Mem., Price Commn, 1973–75. Past Pres.: Incorp. Soc. of British Advertisers; Internat. Fedn of Margarine Assocs; Margarine and Shortening Manufacturers' Assoc. Associate, Royal Australian Chemical Inst. *Recreations:* gardening, dendrology. *Address:* Southdown, Yal Yal Road, Merricks, Victoria 3916, Australia. *T:* (59) 898411. *Club:* Australian (Melbourne).

Died 23 June 1995.

KITTO, Rt Hon. Sir Frank (Walters), AC 1983; KBE 1955; PC 1963; Chancellor, University of New England, 1970–81; Chairman, Australian Press Council, 1976–82; *b* 30 July 1903; *s* of late James W. Kitto, OBE, Austinmer, New South Wales; *m* 1928, Eleanor (*d* 1982), *d* of late Rev. W. H. Howard; four *d. Educ:* North Sydney High Sch.; Sydney Univ. BA 1924; Wigram Allen Scholar, G. and M. Harris Scholar and Pitt Cobbett Prizes in Faculty of Law, and LLB first class hons, 1927. Called to Bar of NSW, 1927. KC (NSW), 1942. Challis Lecturer in Bankruptcy and Probate, Sydney Univ., 1930–33; Justice of the High Court of Australia, 1950–70. Mem. Council, University of New England, 1967–81, Deputy Chancellor, 1968–70. Hon. DLitt New England, 1982; Hon. LLD Sydney, 1982. *Address:* 18/243 Donnelly Street, Armidale, NSW 2350, Australia. *T:* Armidale (67) 721189.

Died 15 Feb. 1994.

KLEINWORT, Sir Kenneth (Drake), 3rd Bt *cr* 1909, of Bolnore, Cuckfield, Sussex; Director, Kleinwort Benson Group (formerly Kleinwort, Benson, Lonsdale plc), since 1976; *b* 28 May 1935; *s* of Ernest Greverus Kleinwort (*d* 1977) (4th *s* of 1st Bt) and Joan Nightingale Kleinwort, MBE, JP, DL (*d* 1991), *d* of late Prof. Arthur William Crossley, CMG, CBE, FRS; *S* uncle, 1983; *m* 1st, 1959, Lady Davina Pepys (*d* 1973), *d* of 7th Earl of Cottenham; one *s* one *d*; 2nd, 1973, Madeleine Hamilton, *e d* of Ralph Taylor; two *s* one *d. Educ:* Eton College; Grenoble Univ. Joined Kleinwort Sons & Co. Ltd, 1955; Director: Kleinwort Benson Belgium SA (formerly Kleinwort Benson (Europe)), 1970–; Banque Kleinwort Benson SA, Geneva, 1971–; Kleinwort Benson Ltd, 1971–76; Vice Chm., Trebol International Corp., USA (Exec. Dir, 1978–); Pres., Interalia SA, Chile, 1980–. Council Mem., WWF International, Switzerland, 1978–; Vice-Pres., Wildfowl and Wetlands Trust, UK, 1992– (Hon. Treas., 1982–92;

Mem. Council, 1982–92). *Recreations:* travel, photography, skiing, tennis. *Heir:* s Richard Drake Kleinwort, [*b* 4 Nov. 1960; *m* 1989, Lucinda, *d* of William Shand Kydd]. *Address:* La Massellaz, 1126 Vaux-sur-Morges, Switzerland.   *Died 8 July 1994.*

KLIEN, Walter; musician (concert pianist); soloist with leading conductors and orchestras; *b* 27 Nov. 1928; *m* 1981, Chizuko Kojima. *Educ:* Frankfurt-am-Main; Vienna. Concert tours and concerts with leading orchs and conductors in Europe, USA, South America, Japan and Australia; concerts at international music festivals: Salzburg, Vienna, Berlin, Israel, Edinburgh, Prades, Bonn, Athens, NY, Prague, Lucerne. Many recordings, which include complete solo-works by Mozart and Brahms, also the complete Schubert Sonatas. Gold Medal of Honour, Vienna, 1989. *Address:* c/o Kaye Artists Management Ltd, 250 King's Road, SW3 5UE.
                                                    Died 10 Feb. 1991.

KNEIPP, Hon. Sir (Joseph Patrick) George, Kt 1982; a Judge of the Supreme Court of Queensland, 1969–92; *b* 13 Nov. 1922; *s* of A. G. Kneipp and K. B. McHugh; *m* 1948, Ada Joan Crawford Cattermole; two *s* one *d. Educ:* Downlands Coll., Toowoomba; Univ. of Queensland (LLB). Called to the Queensland Bar, 1950; in practice as Barrister-at-Law, 1950–69. Chancellor, James Cook Univ. of N Qld, 1974–93. *Recreations:* reading, gardening. *Address:* 20 Kenilworth Avenue, Hyde Park, Townsville, Qld 4812, Australia. *T:* 794652. *Clubs:* North Queensland, James Cook University, Townsville Turf (Townsville).
                                                    Died 15 Feb. 1993.

KNIGHT, Geoffrey Cureton, MB, BS London; FRCS; FRCPsych; Consulting Neurological Surgeon in London, since 1935; Hon. Consultant Neurosurgeon: West End Hospital for Neurology and Neurosurgery; South-East Metropolitan Regional Neurosurgical Centre; Royal Postgraduate Medical School of London; formerly Teacher of Surgery, University of London; *b* 4 Oct. 1906; *s* of Cureton Overbeck Knight; *m* 1933, Betty, *d* of Francis Cooper Havell, London; two *s. Educ:* Brighton Coll.; St Bartholomew's Hosp. Medical Sch. Brackenbury Surgical Schol. St Bart's Hosp., 1930. Ho. Surg. and Chief Asst, Surgical Professorial Unit at St Bart's Hosp.; Demonstrator in Physiology, St Bart's Hosp. Medical Sch.; Leverhulme Research Scholar, Royal College of Surgeons, 1933–35; Mackenzie Mackinnon Research Scholar, 1936–38; Bernard Baron Research Scholar, 1938; Hunterian Prof., 1935–36 and 1963. FRSocMed; Fellow Soc. Brit. Neurological Surgeons; Fellow Med. Soc. London; Vice-Pres., Internat. Soc. for Psychosurgery. Neurological Surg., Armed Forces of Czecho-Slovakia, 1941; Hon. Fellow, Czecho-Slovak Med. Soc., Prague, 1946; Officer, Order of the White Lion of Czecho-Slovakia, 1946. *Publications:* contrib. med. jls on aetiology and surgical treatment of diseases of the spine and nervous system and the surgical treatment of mental illness. *Recreations:* gardening, swimming. *Address:* 7 Aubrey Road, Campden Hill, W8 7JJ. *T:* 071–727 7719 (Sec., 071–935 7549). *Club:* Hurlingham.   *Died 2 April 1994.*

KNIPE, Sir Leslie Francis, Kt 1980; MBE; farmer; *b* Pontypool, 1913. *Educ:* West Monmouth School, Pontypool. Served War of 1939–45, Burma; RASC, attained rank of Major. President: Conservative Party in Wales (Chairman, 1972–77); Monmouth Conservative and Unionist Assoc. *Address:* Brook Acre, Llanvihangel, Crucorney, Abergavenny, Gwent NP7 8DH.
                                                    Died 20 June 1992.

KNOX, Jean Marcia; *see* Swaythling, Dowager Lady.

KOPAL, Prof. Zdeněk; Professor of Astronomy, University of Manchester, 1951–81, then Emeritus; *b* Litomyšl, 4 April 1914; 2nd *s* of Prof. Joseph Kopal, Charles

University, Prague, and Ludmila (*née* Lelek); *m* 1938, Alena, *o d* of late Judge B. Muldner; three *d. Educ:* Charles University, Prague; University of Cambridge, England; Harvard Univ., USA. Agassiz Research Fellow, Harvard Observatory, 1938–40; Research Associate in Astronomy, Harvard Univ., 1940–46; Lecturer in Astronomy, Harvard Univ., 1948; Associate Prof., Mass Institute of Technology, 1947–51. Pres., Fondation Internationale du Pic-du-Midi; Mem. Internat. Acad. of Astronautical Sciences, New York Acad. of Sciences; Chm., Cttee for Lunar and Planetary Exploration, Brit. Nat. Cttee for Space Research; Mem. Lunar-Planetary Cttee, US Nat. Space Bd. Editor-in-Chief, Astrophysics and Space Science, 1968; Founding Editor: Icarus (internat. jl of solar system); The Moon (internat. jl of lunar studies), 1969. Pahlavi Lectr, Iran, 1977. For. Mem., Greek Nat. Acad. of Athens, 1976; Hon. Mem., Astronomical Soc. of India, 1987. Hon. DSc: Krakow, 1974; Charles Univ., Prague, 1991. Gold Medal, Czechoslovak Acad. of Sciences, 1969; Copernicus Medal, Krakow Univ., 1974. Hon. Citizen of: Delphi, 1978; Litomyšl, 1991. *Publications:* An Introduction to the Study of Eclipsing Variables, 1946 (US); The Computation of Elements of Eclipsing Binary Systems, 1950 (US); Tables of Supersonic Flow of Air Around Cones, 3 vols, 1947–49 (US); Numerical Analysis, 1955; Astronomical Optics, 1956 (Amsterdam); Close Binary Systems, 1959; Figures of Equilibrium of Celestial Bodies, 1960; The Moon, 1960; Physics and Astronomy of the Moon, 1962, 2nd edn 1971; Photographic Atlas of the Moon, 1965; An Introduction to the Study of the Moon, 1966; The Measure of the Moon, 1967; (ed) Advances in Astronomy and Astrophysics, 1968; Telescopes in Space, 1968; Exploration of the Moon by Spacecraft, 1968; Widening Horizons, 1970; A New Photographic Atlas of the Moon, 1971; Man and His Universe, 1972; The Solar System, 1973; Mapping of the Moon, 1974; The Moon in the Post-Apollo Stage, 1974; Dynamics of Close Binary Systems, 1978; The Realm of Terrestrial Planets, 1978; Language of the Stars, 1979; Of Stars and Men: reminiscences of an astronomer, 1986; The Roche Problem, 1989; Mathematical Theory of Stellar Eclipses, 1990; over 400 original papers on astronomy, aerodynamics, and applied mathematics in publications of Harvard Observatory, Astrophysical Journal, Astronomical Journal, Astronomische Nachrichten, Monthly Notices of Royal Astronomical Society, Proc. Amer. Phil. Soc., Proc. Nat. Acad. Sci. (US), Zeitschrift für Astrophysik, etc. *Recreation:* mountaineering. *Address:* Greenfield, Parkway, Wilmslow, Cheshire SK9 1LS. *T:* Wilmslow (0625) 522470. *Club:* Explorers' (NY).
                                                    Died 23 June 1993.

KOSINSKI, Jerzy Nikodem; author; *b* Lodz, Poland, 14 June 1933; naturalised US citizen, 1965; *s* of Mieczyslaw and Elzbieta (Liniecka) Kosinski; *m* 1962, Mary Hayward Weir (marr. diss. 1966; she *d* 1968); *m* 1987, Katherina von Fraunhofer. *Educ:* Univ. of Lodz (MA (Polit. Sci.) 1953; MA (Hist.) 1955). Asst Prof., Inst. Sociology and Cultural Hist., Polish Acad. of Scis, Warsaw, 1955–57; Ford Foundn Fellow, Univ. of Columbia, 1958–60; postgrad. student, 1958–65 (PhD); Guggenheim Lit. Fellow, 1967; Fellow, Center for Advanced Studies, Wesleyan Univ., 1968–69; Sen. Fellow, Council of Humanities. Vis. Lectr in English, Princeton, 1969–70; Vis Prof. in English Prose, Sch. of Drama, Yale, also resident Fellow, Davenport Coll., 1970–73; Fellow, Timothy Dwight Coll., Yale, 1986–. Hon. Chm., Bd, Polish–Jewish Heritage Foundn of America, 1987–; President: Jewish Presence Foundn, 1988–; Polish–American Resources Corp., 1988–. Member: PEN (Pres., 1973–75); Bd, Nat. Writers Club; Bd, Internat. League for Human Rights; Amer. Civil Liberties Union

(Chm., Artists and Writers Cttee; Mem., Nat. Adv. Council); Authors Guild. Film début as Zinoviev in Reds, 1982. Hon. PhD (Hebrew Letters) Spertus Coll., 1982. Literature Award, Amer. Acad. Arts and Letters, 1970; Brith Sholom Humanitarian Freedom Award, 1974; First Amendment Award, Amer. Civil Liberties Union, 1980; Polonia Media Perspectives Award, 1980; Spertus Coll. Internat. Award, 1982. Hon. DHL Potsdam Coll., SUNY, 1989. *Publications:* The Future is Ours, Comrade (under pen-name, Joseph Novak), 1960; No Third Path (under pen-name, Joseph Novak), 1962; *novels:* The Painted Bird, 1965 (Best Foreign Book Award, Paris, 1966); Steps, 1968 (Nat. Book Award, 1969); Being There, 1971 (filmed, 1978; Best Screenplay Awards, Writers Guild of Amer., 1979, and BAFTA, 1980); The Devil Tree, 1973, rev. and enlarged edn 1981; Cockpit, 1975; Blind Date, 1977; Passion Play, 1979 (screenplay, 1987); Pinball, 1982; The Hermit of 69th Street, 1988. *Address:* Hemisphere House (18-k), 60 W 57th Street, New York, NY 10019, USA. *Club:* Century Association (NY).

Died 3 May 1991.

KRAMRISCH, Stella, PhD; Professor of Indian Art, Institute of Fine Arts, New York University, since 1964; Curator Emeritus, Indian Art, Philadelphia Museum of Art, since 1954; *d* of Jacques Kramrisch, scientist, and Berta Kramrisch; *m* 1929, Laszlo Neményi (*d* 1950). *Educ:* Vienna University. Prof. of Indian Art, Univ. of Calcutta, 1923–50; Prof. in the Art of South Asia, Univ. of Pennsylvania, 1950–69; Lectr on Indian Art, Courtauld Inst. of Art, Univ. of London, 1937–41. Public lectures in USA, Canada, India, Nepal, W Germany, including: Aditi Exhibn Seminar, Fest. of India, London, 1982; Fest. of India, Washington, DC, 1985. Mem., Adv. Bd, South Asian Regional Art Studies. Editor: Jl Indian Soc. of Oriental Art, 1932–50; Indian Section, Artibus Asiae, 1959–92. Hon. DLit Visva Bharati Univ., 1974; Hon. LLD Pennsylvania, 1981; Hon. DHL: Smith Coll., 1982; Chicago, 1984; Hon. DLit Columbia, NY, 1985. Cross of Honour for Science and Art, Austria, 1979; Padma Bhushan Award, India, 1982; National Women's Caucus for Art Conf. Award, 1983; Prabala Gorkhadakshina Bahu Award, Nepal, 1984; Charles Lang Freer Medal, Washington, DC, 1985. *Publications:* Principles of Indian Art, 1924; Vishnudharmottara, 1924; History of Indian Art, 1929; Indian Sculpture, 1932; Asian Miniature Painting, 1932; A Survey of Painting in the Deccan, 1937; Indian Terracottas, 1939; Kantha, 1939; The Hindu Temple, 1946, repr. 1976; Arts and Crafts of Travancore, 1948; Dravida and Kerala, 1953; Art of India, 1954; Indian Sculpture in the Philadelphia Museum of Art, 1960; The Triple Structure of Creation, 1962; The Art of Nepal, 1964; Unknown India: Ritual Art in Tribe and Village, 1968; The Presence of Siva, 1981; Manifestations of Shiva, 1981; The Antelope, 1982; (contrib.) Discourses on Siva, ed Michael Meister, 1985; Painted Delight (exhibn catalogue), 1986; various articles; *relevant publication:* Exploring India's Sacred Art: selected writings of Stella Kramrisch, by Barbara Stoler Miller, 1983. *Address:* Philadelphia Museum of Art, PO Box 7646, Philadelphia, Pa 19101, USA.

Died 31 Aug. 1993.

KRESTIN, David, MD (London), BS; MRCP; retired; formerly: Consulting Physician, London Jewish Hospital; Medical Specialist, Ministries of Pensions and of National Insurance; Lecturer in Medicine, North-East London Post-Graduate Medical College; *b* London; *s* of Dr S. Krestin; *m* Ruth Fisher (decd); one *s. Educ:* University of London; London Hosp. Medical Coll.; University of Pennsylvania. Anatomy prize, London Hosp.; MRCS, LRCP 1922; MB, BS London 1923, Hons Medicine and Surgery; MD London 1926; MRCP 1926. Clinical Asst, House Surg., House Physician, Medical Registrar and First Asst, London

Hosp.; Rockefeller Medical Fellowship, 1928–29; Fellow in Pathology, Henry Phipps Institute, University of Penn; Yarrow Research Fellow, London Hosp.; formerly Physician with charge of Out-Patients, Dreadnought Hospital; Medical Registrar, Prince of Wales' Hospital. *Publications:* Pulsation in Superficial Veins, Lancet, 1927; The Seborrhœic facies in Post-Encephalitic Parkinsonism, Qly Jl Med., 1927; Congenital Dextrocardia and Auric. Fibrillation, BMJ, 1927; Latent Pulmonary Tuberculosis, Qly Jl Med., 1929; Glandular Fever, Clinical Jl, 1931 and other medical papers. *Recreation:* fishing. *Address:* 14 Spaniards End, NW3 7JG. *T:* 081–455 1500.

Died 21 Aug. 1991.

KUHN, Heinrich Gerhard, DPhil, MA; FRS 1954; Reader in Physics, Oxford University, 1955–71, then Emeritus; Fellow of Balliol College 1950–71, then Emeritus; *b* 10 March 1904; *s* of Wilhelm Felix and Martha Kuhn; *m* 1931, Marie Bertha Nohl; two *s. Educ:* High Sch., Lueben (Silesia); Universities of Greifswald and Göttingen. Lecturer in Physics, Göttingen Univ., 1931; Research at Clarendon Laboratory, Oxford, 1933–71; Lecturer, University Coll., Oxford, 1938; work for atomic energy project, 1941–45; University Demonstrator, Oxford, 1945–55. Prof. *aD* Göttingen Univ., 1957. Dr *hc* Aix-Marseille, 1958. Holweck Prize, 1967. *Publications:* Atomspektren, 1934 (Akad. Verl. Ges., Leipzig); Atomic Spectra, 1962, 2nd edn 1970; articles on molecular and atomic spectra and on interferometry. *Address:* 25 Victoria Road, Oxford OX2 7QF. *T:* Oxford (0865) 515308.

Died 26 Aug. 1994.

KUSCH, Prof. Polykarp; Regental Professor Emeritus, Department of Physics, University of Texas at Dallas, since 1982; *b* Germany, 26 Jan. 1911; *s* of John Matthias Kusch and Henrietta van der Haas; *m* 1st, 1935, Edith Starr McRoberts (*d* 1959); three *d*; 2nd, 1960, Betty Jane Pezzoni; two *d. Educ:* Case Inst. of Technology, Cleveland (BS); Univ. of Illinois, Urbana (MS, PhD). Asst, Univ. of Illinois, 1931–36; Research Asst, Univ. of Minnesota, 1936–37; Instr in Physics, Columbia Univ., 1937–41; Engr, Westinghouse Electric Corp., 1941–42; Mem. Tech. Staff, Div. of Govt Aided Research, Columbia Univ., 1942–44; Mem. Tech. Staff, Bell Telephone Laboratories, 1944–46; Columbia University: Associate Prof. of Physics, 1946–49; Prof. of Physics, 1949–72; Exec. Officer, Dept of Physics, 1949–52, Chm. 1960–63; Exec. Dir, Columbia Radiation Laboratory, 1952–60; Vice-Pres. and Dean of Faculties, 1969–70; Exec. Vice-Pres. and Provost, 1970–71; University of Texas at Dallas: Prof. of Physics, 1972–74; Eugene McDermott Prof., 1974–80; U. T. System Chair, 1980–82. Member: Nat. Acad. of Sciences, US; American Philosophical Soc.; Amer. Acad. of Arts and Scis. Phi Beta Kappa. Hon. DSc: Case Inst. of Tech., 1956; Ohio State Univ., 1959; Colby Coll., 1961; Univ. of Illinois, 1961; Gustavus Adolphus Coll., 1963; Yeshiva Univ., 1976; Incarnate Word Coll., 1980; Columbia Univ., 1983. (Jointly) Nobel Prize in Physics, 1955. *Publications:* technical articles in Physical Review and other jls. *Address:* University of Texas at Dallas, Department of Physics, PO Box 830688, Richardson, Texas 75083–0688, USA; 7241 Paldao, Dallas, Texas 75240, USA. *T:* (214) 6611247.

Died 20 March 1993.

KUTSCHER, Hans, Dr iur; President, Court of Justice of the European Communities, 1976–80 (Judge of Court, 1970–80), retired 1980; *b* Hamburg, 14 Dec. 1911; *m* 1946, Irmgard Schroeder; two step *d. Educ:* Univ. of Graz, Austria; Univ. of Freiburg-im-Breisgau, Berlin; Königsberg Preussen (Dr. iur). Started career as civil servant; Ministry of: Commerce and Industry, Berlin, 1939; Transport, Baden Württemberg, 1946–51; Foreign Affairs, Bonn, 1951; Sec., Legal Cttee and Conf. Cttee of Bundesrat, 1951–55; Judge, Federal Constitutional Court,

1955–70. Hon. Prof., Univ. of Heidelberg, 1965. Hon. Bencher: Middle Temple, 1976; King's Inns, Dublin, 1977. Hon. Dr. iur Würzburg, 1989. Awarded Grand Cross Verdienstorden of Federal Republic of Germany, 1980. *Publications:* Die Enteignung, 1938; Bonner Vertrag mit Zusatzvereinbarungen, 1952; various contribs to professional jls. *Recreations:* literature, history. *Address:* Viertelstrasse 10, W-7506 Bad Herrenalb 5, Germany.

Died 24 Aug. 1993.

KWAKYE, Dr Emmanuel Bamfo; Project Coordinator, UNESCO, Nairobi, Kenya, since 1985 (Consultant Project Coordinator, 1982–85); *b* 19 March 1933; *s* of Rev. W. H. Kwakye and F. E. A. Kwakye; *m* 1964, Gloria E. (*née* Mensah); two *d. Educ:* a Presbyterian sch., Ghana; Achimota Secondary Sch., Ghana; Technical Univ., Stuttgart, West Germany (DipIng, DrIng). Development Engr, Siemens & Halske, Munich, W Germany, 1960–62; Univ. of Science and Technology, Kumasi: Lectr, 1963; Sen. Lectr, 1964; Associate Prof., 1966; Head of Dept, 1970; Dean of Faculty, 1971; Pro Vice-Chancellor, 1971; Vice-Chancellor, 1974–82. Visiting Prof., Bradley Univ., Peoria, USA, 1981. *Publications:* design and research reports on digital equipment. *Recreations:* reading, indoor games, opera and operetta. *Address:* UNESCO-ROSTA, PO Box 30592, Nairobi, Kenya.

Died 15 Jan. 1993.

L

LACHS, Manfred; Judge, International Court of Justice, since 1967 (President, 1973–76); *b* 21 April 1914; *s* of Ignacy and Zofia Lachs; *m* Halina Kirst. *Educ:* Univ. of Cracow, Poland (LLM 1936, Dr jur 1937); Univ. of Nancy, France (Dr); Univ. of Moscow (DSc Law); Univs of Vienna, London and Cambridge. Legal Adviser, Polish Ministry Internat. Affairs, 1947–66 (Ambassador, 1960–66). Prof., Acad. Polit. Sci., Warsaw, 1949–52; Prof. Internat. Law, Univ. of Warsaw, 1952; Dir, Inst. Legal Scis, Polish Academy of Sciences, 1961–67. Röling Prof., Groningen Univ., 1990. Chm., Legal Cttee, UN Gen. Assemblies, 1949, 1951, 1955; Rep. of Poland, UN Disarmament Cttee, 1962–63; Pres. of Tribunal, Guinea/Guinea-Bissau case, 1983–85. Rapporteur: Gen. Colloquy Internat. Assoc. Juridical Sciences, UNESCO, Rome, 1948; Internat. Law Commn, UN, 1962; Chm., Legal Cttee UN Peaceful Uses of Outer Space, 1962–66; Hon. Sen. Fellow, UNITAR. Pres., Internat. Inst. of Space Law, Paris. Member: Inst. of Internat. Law; Ind. Commn on Internat. Humanitarian Issues, 1983–; Curatorium, Hague Acad. of Internat. Law (Vice-Pres.); Acad. of Bologna; Polish Acad. of Sciences. Hon. Mem., Amer. Soc. Internat. Law; Corresp. Mem., Institut de France; Foreign Mem., Dutch Soc. of Scis, 1982. LLD (Hon.), Univs of: Budapest 1967; Algiers 1969; Delhi 1969; Nice 1972; Halifax, 1973; Bruxelles, 1973; Bucarest, 1974; New York, 1974; Southampton, 1975; Howard (Washington), 1975; Sofia, 1975; Vancouver, 1976; London, 1976; Helsinki, 1980; Vienna, 1984; Cracow, 1986; NY State, 1986; Bridgeport, 1987; Silesia, 1988. Gold medal for outstanding contribs to develt of rule of law for outer space, 1966; World Jurist Award for enormous contrib. to improvement of justice, Washington, 1975; Netherland's Wateler Peace Prize, 1976; Copernicus Medal, 1984; Britannica Award Laureate, 1987; First Prize, Polish Acad. of Scis, 1988; also other awards. *Publications:* War Crimes, 1945; The Geneva Agreements on Indochina, 1954; Multilateral Treaties, 1958; The Law of Outer Space, 1964; Polish-German Frontier, 1964; The Law of Outer Space—an experience in law making, 1972; Teachings and Teaching of International Law, 1977; The Teacher in International Law, 1982 (Cert. of Merit, Amer. Soc. of Internat. Law), 2nd rev. edn 1986; Le Monde de la pensée en droit international—théories et pratique, 1988; numerous essays and articles in eleven languages. *Address:* International Court of Justice, Peace Palace, The Hague 2517 KJ, Holland. *T:* 392–44–41.
Died 14 Jan. 1993.

LAGESEN, Air Marshal Sir Philip (Jacobus), KCB 1979 (CB 1974); DFC 1945; AFC 1959; FIMgt; *b* 25 Aug. 1923; *s* of late Philip J. Lagesen, Johannesburg, South Africa; *m* 1944, Dulcie, *d* of late H. McPherson, Amanzimtoti, Natal, S Africa; one *s* one *d. Educ:* Jeppe, Johannesburg. Served War, 1939–45, South African Air Force; joined RAF, 1951; Flying Instructor, Rhodesia Air Trng Gp, 1952–53; Kenya, 1953–55; No 50 Squadron, 1955–57; Staff, RAF Flying Coll., Manby, 1957–59; PSO, C-in-C Middle East, 1959–61; Comdr, No 12 (B) Sqdn, 1961–64; Wing Comdr Ops, No 1 (B) Group 1964–66; CO, RAF Tengah, Singapore, 1966–69; Sen. PSO, Strike Comd, 1969–70; Dir Ops (S), RAF, MoD, 1970–72; SASO, HQ Strike Comd, 1972–73; Dep. Comdr, RAF Germany, 1973–75; AOC 1 Group, 1975–78; AOC 18

Group, 1978–80. *Recreations:* golf, motoring. *Address:* 10 Mayfair Mews, Heyfield Road, Kloof, Natal 3610, Republic of South Africa. *Clubs:* Royal Air Force; Kloof Country.
Died 9 Oct. 1994.

LAING, Austen, CBE 1973; Director General, British Fishing Federation Ltd, 1962–80; Chairman, Home-Grown Cereals Authority, 1983–89; *b* 27 April 1923; *s* of William and Sarah Ann Laing; *m* 1945, Kathleen Pearson; one *s* one *d. Educ:* Bede Grammar Sch., Sunderland; Newcastle Univ. BA (Social Studies) and BA (Econs). Lectr, Univ. of Durham, 1950–56; Administrator, Distant Water Vessels Develt Scheme, 1956–61. Mem. Cttee of Inquiry into Veterinary Profession, 1971–75. *Address:* Freshfields, 12 Hall Park, Swanland, North Ferriby, North Humberside HU14 3NL.
Died 29 May 1992.

LAIRD, Edgar Ord, (Michael), CMG 1969; MBE 1958; HM Diplomatic Service, retired; *b* 16 Nov. 1915; *s* of late Edgar Balfour Laird; *m* 1940, Heather Lonsdale Forrest; four *d. Educ:* Rossall; Emmanuel Coll., Cambridge. Surveyor, Uganda Protectorate, 1939. Served Army, 1939–46 (Major). Appointed to Malayan Civil Service, 1947; Federation of Malaya: Sec. to Government, 1953–55; Sec. for External Defence, 1956; Sec., Constitutional Commission, 1956–57; Dep. Sec., Prime Minister's Dept, 1957; appointed to Commonwealth Relations Office, 1958; First Sec. (Finance), Office of British High Comr, Ottawa, Canada, 1960–63; High Comr in Brunei, 1963–65; Dep. High Comr, Kaduna, 1965–69; RNC Greenwich, 1969–70; Head of Hong Kong and Indian Ocean Dept, FCO, 1970–72; British Govt Rep., West Indies Associated States, 1972–75. *Recreations:* playing the piano, reading. *Address:* St Jude's Cottage, 87 Fore Street, Topsham, Exeter EX3 0HQ. *Club:* Commonwealth Trust.
Died 8 April 1992.

LAIRD, John Robert, (Robin), TD 1946; FRICS; chartered surveyor; Member, Lands Tribunal, England and Wales, 1956–76; retired; *b* Marlow, Bucks, 3 Sept. 1909; *o s* of late John Laird, JP, and Mary (*née* Wakelin); *m* 1st, 1940, Barbara Joyce Muir (marr. diss. 1965); one *s* one *d*; 2nd, 1966, Betty Caroline McGregor (widow). *Educ:* Sir William Borlase's Sch., Marlow; Coll. of Estate Management, London. Partner, private practice, Lawrence, Son & Laird, Chartered Surveyors, Marlow, 1938–56. Served War: 2nd Lieut RA (TA), 1939; Staff Captain 35 AA Bde, RA, 1941; Acting Lt-Col Eastern Comd, 1945. *Recreations:* hockey (Scottish International, 12 caps, Captain 1935), rowing, sailing, walking. *Address:* 8 Marine Square, Kemp Town, Brighton, E Sussex BN2 1DL. *T:* Brighton (0273) 602065.
Died 12 July 1991.

LAIRD, Michael; see Laird, E. O.

LAIRD, Robin; see Laird, J. R.

LAJTHA, Prof. Laszlo George, CBE 1983; MD, DPhil, FRCPE, FRCPath; Director of Paterson Laboratories, Christie Hospital and Holt Radium Institute, 1962–83; Professor of Experimental Oncology, University of Manchester, 1970–83, then Emeritus Professor; *b* 25 May 1920; *s* of Laszlo John Lajtha and Rose Stephanie Hollos; *m* 1954, Gillian Macpherson Henderson; two *s. Educ:* Presbyterian High School, Budapest; Medical School, Univ. of Budapest (MD 1944); Exeter Coll., Univ. of

Oxford (DPhil 1950). FRCPath 1973; FRCPE 1980. Asst Prof., Dept of Physiology, Univ. of Budapest, 1944–47; Research Associate, Dept of Haematology, Radcliffe Infirmary, Oxford, 1947–50; Head, Radiobiology Laboratory, Churchill Hosp., Oxford, 1950–62; subseq. Research Fellow, Pharmacology, Yale Univ., New Haven, Conn, USA. Editor, British Jl of Cancer, 1972–82. President: British Soc. of Cell Biology, 1977–80; European Orgn for Res. on Treatment of Cancer, 1979–82. Hon. Citizen, Texas, USA; Hon. Member: Amer. Cancer Soc.; German, Italian and Hungarian Socs of Haematology; Hungarian Acad. of Sciences, 1983. Dr hc Szeged Univ., Hungary, 1981. *Publications:* Isotopes in Haematology, 1961; over 250 articles in scientific (medical) jls. *Recreations:* alpine gardening, medieval history, bonsai. *Address:* Brook Cottage, Little Bridge Road, Bloxham, Oxon OX15 4PU. *T:* Banbury (01295) 720311. *Club:* Athenæum.   *Died 14 March 1995.*

LAKEMAN, Enid, OBE 1980; Editorial Consultant and a Vice-President, Electoral Reform Society, since 1979 (Director, 1960–79); *b* 28 Nov. 1903; *d* of Horace B. Lakeman and Evereld Simpson. *Educ:* Tunbridge Wells County Sch.; Bedford Coll., Univ. of London. Posts in chemical industry, 1926–41; WAAF, 1941–45; Electoral Reform Soc., 1945–. Parly candidate (L): St Albans, 1945; Brixton, 1950; Aldershot, 1955 and 1959. *Publications:* When Labour Fails, 1946; (with James D. Lambert) Voting in Democracies, 1955 (2nd edn 1959; 3rd and 4th edns, 1970 and 1974, as sole author, as How Democracies Vote); Nine Democracies, 1973, 4th edn 1991, as, Twelve Democracies; Power to Elect, 1982; pamphlets; articles in polit. jls. *Recreations:* travel, gardening. *Address:* 37 Culverden Avenue, Tunbridge Wells, Kent TN4 9RE. *T:* Tunbridge Wells (01892) 521674. *Club:* National Liberal.   *Died 7 Jan. 1995.*

LALOUETTE, Marie Joseph Gerard; retired; *b* 24 Jan. 1912; 3rd *s* of late Henri Lalouette and Mrs H. Lalouette; *m* 1942, Jeanne Marrier d'Unienville; four *s* two *d. Educ:* Royal Coll., Mauritius; Exeter Coll., Oxford; London School of Economics; Middle Temple. District Magistrate, Mauritius, 1944; Electoral Commissioner, 1956; Addit. Subst. Procureur-General, 1956; Master, and Registrar, Supreme Court, 1958; Assistant Attorney-General, 1959; Solicitor-General, 1960; Puisne Judge, 1961; Senior Puisne Judge, Supreme Court, Mauritius, 1967–70; Attorney, Republic of S Africa, 1973–83; Justice of Appeal, Seychelles, 1977–82. *Publications:* Digest of Decisions of Supreme Court of Mauritius, 1926–43; The Mauritius Digest to 1950; A First Supplement to the Mauritius Digest, 1951–55; A Second Supplement to the Mauritius Digest, 1956–60; The Seychelles Digest, 1982; contrib. Internat. Encyclopedia of Comparative Law. *Recreations:* music, gardening. *Address:* 419 Windermere Centre, Windermere Road, Durban, Republic of South Africa. *T:* (31) 237598.   *Died 1 Aug. 1992.*

LAMB, Prof. John, CBE 1986; FEng; James Watt Professor of Electrical Engineering, since 1961, and Vice-Principal, 1977–80, University of Glasgow; *b* 26 Sept. 1922; *m* 1947, Margaret May Livesey; two *s* one *d. Educ:* Accrington Grammar Sch.; Manchester Univ. BSc (1st class Hons) Manchester Univ. 1943; Fairbairn Prizeman in Engineering; MSc 1944, PhD 1946, DSc 1957, Manchester. Ministry of Supply Extra-Mural Res., 1943–46. Assistant Lecturer, 1946–47, Lecturer, 1947–56, Reader, 1956–61, in Electrical Engineering at Imperial Coll. (London Univ.); Assistant Director, Department of Electrical Engineering, Imperial Coll., 1958–61. Gledden Fellow, Univ. of WA, Perth, 1983. Pres., British Soc. of Rheology, 1970–72. Chm., Scottish Industry Univ. Liaison Cttee in Engrg, 1969–71; Member: Nat. Electronics Council, 1963–78; CNAA, 1964–70; Council, RSE,

1980–83, 1986–; British Nat. Cttee for Radio Sci., 1983–87. Scientific Advr, Scottish Office Industry Dept, 1987–. FInstP 1960; Fellow, Acoustical Society of America, 1960; FRSE 1968 (Vice-Pres., 1989–); FIEE 1983; FEng 1984; Hon. Fellow, Inst. of Acoustics, 1980. *Publications:* contributed: (The Theory and Practice of Ultrasonic Propagation) to Principles and Practice of Nondestructive Testing (ed J. H. Lamble), 1962; (Dispersion and Absorption of Sound by Molecular Processes) to Proc. International School of Physics "Enrico Fermi" Course XXVII (ed D. Sette), 1963; (Thermal Relaxation in Liquids) to Physical Acoustics, Vol. II (ed W. P. Mason), 1965; (Theory of Rheology) to Interdisciplinary Approach to Liquid Lubricant Technology (ed P. M. Ku), 1973; (Viscoelastic and Ultrasonic Relaxation Studies) to Molecular Motions in Liquids (ed J. Lascombe), 1974; (Motions in Low Molecular Weight Fluids and Glass forming Liquids) to Molecular Basis of Transitions and Relaxations (ed D. J. Meier), 1978; Shear Waves of Variable Frequency for Studying the Viscoelastic Relaxation Processes in Liquids and Polymer Melts (ed A. Kawski and A. Sliwinsky), 1979; (Development of Integrated Optical Circuits) to Integrated Optics (ed S. Martellucci and R. N. Chester), 1983; (ed jtly) Proceedings of the Fourth European Conference on Integrated Optics, 1987; numerous pubns in Proc. Royal Society, Trans Faraday Society, Proc. Instn Electrical Engineers, Proc. Physical Society, Journal Acoustical Society of America, Quarterly Reviews of Chem. Society, Nature, Phys. Review, Journal of Polymer Science. *Recreations:* walking, wine-making, music. *Address:* 5 Cleveden Crescent, Glasgow G12 0PD. *T:* 041–339 2101.
                                    Died 18 Dec. 1991.

LAMB, Hon. Kenneth Henry Lowry, CBE 1985; Secretary to the Church Commissioners, 1980–85; *b* 23 Dec. 1923; *y s* of 1st Baron Rochester, CMG and Rosa Dorothea, *y d* of W. J. Hurst, JP, Co. Down; *m* 1952, Elizabeth Anne Saul; one *s* two *d. Educ:* Harrow; Trinity Coll., Oxford (MA). President of the Union, Oxford, 1944. Instructor-Lieut, Royal Navy, 1944–46. Lecturer, then Senior Lecturer in History and English, Royal Naval Coll., Greenwich, 1946–53; Commonwealth Fund Fellow in United States, 1953–55; joined BBC in 1955 as a Talks Producer (Radio); became a Television Talks Producer, 1957, and then Chief Assistant, Current Affairs, TV Talks, 1959–63; Head of Religious Broadcasting, BBC, 1963–66; Secretary to the BBC, 1967–68; Dir, Public Affairs, BBC, 1969–77; Special Adviser (Broadcasting Research), BBC, 1977–80. Chm., Charities Effectiveness Review Trust, 1987–92. *Recreations:* cricket, walking, golf. *Address:* 25 South Terrace, Thurloe Square, SW7 2TB. *T:* 0171–584 7904. *Clubs:* MCC, National Liberal; Royal Fowey Yacht.   *Died 21 June 1995.*

LAMB, Sir Lionel (Henry), KCMG 1953 (CMG 1948); OBE 1944; HM Diplomatic Service, retired; *b* 9 July 1900; *s* of late Sir Harry Lamb, GBE, KCMG and Sabina, *d* of Commendatore Felice Maissa; *m* 1927, Jean Fawcett (*née* MacDonald); one *s. Educ:* Winchester; Queen's Coll., Oxford. Appointed HM Consular Service in China, Dec. 1921; Consul (Gr. II), 1935; served Shanghai, 1935–37, Peking, 1937–40; Consul (Gr. I), 1938; Superintending Consul and Assistant Chinese Secretary, Shanghai, 1940; transferred to St Paul-Minneapolis, 1943; Chinese Counsellor, HM Embassy, Chungking, 1945; HM Minister, Nanking, 1947–49; Chargé d'Affaires, Peking, China, 1951–53; Ambassador to Switzerland, 1953–58, retired. *Address:* Roxford Barn, Hertingfordbury, Herts SG14 2LF.   *Died 27 July 1992.*

LAMB, Captain William John, CVO 1947; OBE 1944; Royal Navy, retired; *b* 26 Dec. 1906; *s* of late Sir Richard Amphlett Lamb, KCSI, CIE, ICS, and Kathleen Maud

Barry; *m* 1948, Bridget, *widow* of Lieut-Commander G. S. Salt, RN; two *d*. *Educ:* St Anthony's, Eastbourne; RNC Osborne and Dartmouth. Commander, 1941; Staff of C-in-C Mediterranean Fleet, 1940–42; Staff of C-in-C, Eastern Fleet, 1942–44; Executive Officer, HMS Vanguard, 1945–47; Deputy Director of Naval Ordnance, 1948–50; Comd HMS Widemouth Bay and Captain (D) 4th Training Flotilla, Rosyth, 1951–52; Commanding Admiralty Signal and Radar Establishment, 1952–54; Commanding HMS Cumberland, 1955–56. Hon. Life Member: BIM, 1974; RNSA, 1985. *Recreation:* sailing. *Clubs:* Naval and Military, Royal Cruising.
Died 2 May 1993.

LAMBERT, Sir Edward (Thomas), KBE 1958 (CBE 1953); CVO 1957; retired from HM Diplomatic Service, 1960; *b* 19 June 1901; *s* of late Brig.-Gen. Thomas Stanton Lambert, CB, CMG and Geraldine Rachel Lambert; *m* 1936, Rhona Patricia Gilmore, *d* of late H. St G. Gilmore and Mrs J. H. Molyneux; one *s* one *d*. *Educ:* Charterhouse; Trinity Coll., Cambridge. Member of HM Diplomatic (formerly Foreign) Service. Entered Far Eastern Consular Service, 1926; served at Bangkok, Batavia, Medan, Curaçao, and The Hague; Consul-General, Geneva, 1949–53, Paris, 1953–59. Commandeur, Légion d'Honneur, 1957. *Recreations:* reading, travel. *Address:* Crag House, Crabbe Street, Aldeburgh, Suffolk IP15 5AB. *T:* Aldeburgh (0728) 452296. *Died 2 May 1994.*

LAMBERT, Hon. Margaret (Barbara), CMG 1965; PhD; British Editor-in-Chief, German Foreign Office Documents, 1951–83; *b* 7 Nov. 1906; *yr d* of 1st Viscount Lambert, PC and Barbara, *d* of G. Stavers, Morpeth; *Educ:* Lady Margaret Hall, Oxford. London School of Economics. BA 1930, PhD 1936. Served during War of 1939–45 in European Service of BBC. Assistant Editor British Documents on Foreign Policy, 1946–50; Lecturer in Modern History, University College of the South-West, 1950–51; Lecturer in Modern European History, St Andrews University, 1956–60. *Publications:* The Saar, 1934; When Victoria began to Reign, 1937; (with Enid Marx) English Popular and Traditional Art, 1946, and English Popular Art, 1952. *Address:* 39 Thornhill Road, Barnsbury Square, N1 1JS. *T:* 0171–607 2286.
Died 22 Jan. 1995.

LAMBERT, Olaf Francis, CBE 1984; DL; Chairman, British Road Federation, 1987–92 (Member, Executive Committee, since 1977); Vice President, The Automobile Association, since 1987; *b* 13 Jan. 1925; *s* of late Walter Lambert and Edith (*née* Gladstone); *m* 1950, Lucy, *d* of late John Adshead, Macclesfield, and Helen Seymour (*née* Ridgway); two *s* two *d*. *Educ:* Caterham Sch.; RMA, Sandhurst (war time). Commnd Royal Tank Regt, 1944; retd with rank of Major, 1959. Joined Automobile Assoc., 1959; Man. Dir, 1973–77; Dir-Gen., 1977–87. Director: Drive Publications Ltd, 1974–87; AA Insurance Services Ltd, 1974–87; AA Travel Services Ltd, 1977–87; AA Pensions Trustees Ltd, 1977–87; AA Executive Pensions Trustees Ltd, 1977–87; Mercantile Credit Co. Ltd, 1980–85; AA Re-insurance Ltd, 1982–87; AA Underwriting Services Ltd, 1982–87; Automobile Association Ltd, 1982–87; Fanum Ltd, 1982–87; AA Pension Investment Trustees Ltd, 1984–87; AA Developments Ltd, 1984–87; AA Financial Services Ltd, 1985–87. Member: Cttee of Management, AA Friendly Soc., 1982– (Chm., 1986–); AA Exec. Cttee, 1982–87; Adv. Bd, DVLA, 1965–89; Council, Inst. of Advanced Motorists, 1968–89; Management Cttee, Alliance Internationale de Tourisme, 1976–87 (Pres., 1983–86); Hampshire Cttee, Army Benevolent Fund, 1980–; Winchester Cathedral Trust Council, 1984–; BHS Develt Council, 1987–90. FIMI 1984 (MIMI 1977); CBIM 1980; FRSA 1984. Freeman, City of London, 1978; Liveryman,

Worshipful Co. of Coachmakers and Coach Harness Makers, 1978. DL Hants, 1989. Hon. Col, RMP (TA), 1984–92. Col, Commonwealth of Kentucky, 1979. *Recreations:* hunting, skiing, walking, travel, music. *Club:* Army and Navy. *Died 3 April 1993.*

LAMBOLL, Alan Seymour, JP; Underwriting Member of Lloyd's; *b* 12 Oct. 1923; *s* of late Frederick Seymour and Charlotte Emily Lamboll. *Educ:* Ascham St Vincents, Eastbourne (preparatory sch.); Marlborough Coll. BBC Engineering Staff, 1941–43. Served War: Royal Signals, East Africa Command (Captain), 1943–47. Dir, family firm of wine merchants, City of London, Slack & Lamboll, Ltd, 1947–54. Lloyd's Insurance Broker, Alexr Howden, Stewart Smith (Home), 1954–57; Director: Anglo-Portuguese Agencies Ltd (Insurance and Reinsurance Agents), 1957–62; Aga Dictating Machine Co. Ltd, 1962–70; Roger Grayson Ltd, Wine Merchants, 1971–74; London Investment Trust Ltd; Ellinger Heath Western (Underwriting Agencies) Ltd, 1974–82; Consultant to Rank Orgn, 1970–72. Mem., Iken Parish Council, 1987–90. JP Inner London, 1965; Chm., S Westminster PSD, 1978–80; Dep. Chm., City of London Commn, 1979–82, Supplemental List, 1982. Mem. Council: City and Guilds of London Inst., 1965–79; Toynbee Hall, 1958–81 (Hon. Sec., 1968–79); Drama Centre London Ltd, 1974–82 (Chm. Council, 1975–82). Dir, City Arts Trust Ltd, 1962–77; Member: Royal Theatrical Fund (formerly Royal Gen. Theatrical Fund Assoc.), 1963– (Vice-Chm., 1967–91; Vice-Pres., 1991–); LSO Adv. Council, 1972–74; Cttee, Industrial Sponsors, 1974–84; Grand Master's Cttee, 1974–83; Chm. of Govs, GSMD, 1957–58; Governor: Mermaid Theatre Trust, 1966–77; Christ's Hospital (Donation Governor, 1971–). Secretary: Ross McWhirter Foundation, 1980–82; Dicey Trust, 1980–82. Hon. Assistant: Worshipful Co. of Distillers, 1991– (Master, 1972–73, Tercentenary Year); Worshipful Co. of Parish Clerks (Master, 1975–76); Freedom of City of London, 1947; Common Council, Ward of Langbourn, 1949–70; Alderman, Ward of Castle Baynard, 1970–78; Sheriff, City of London, 1976–77 (Silver Jubilee Year). St John Council for London, 1971–82; CStJ 1973. FRSA 1970. *Recreations:* writing, swimming, Anubis (Tibetan spaniel). *Address:* Quinta Essência, Azinheiro, Estói, 8000 Faro, Algarve, Portugal. *T:* (89) 97049. *Clubs:* Athenæum, Garrick, Pratt's. *Died 25 Jan. 1994.*

LANCASTER, Joan Cadogan; *see* Lancaster Lewis, J. C.

LANCASTER, Vice-Adm. Sir John (Strike), KBE 1961; CB 1958; retired 1962; *b* 26 June 1903; *s* of George Henry Lancaster; *m* 1927, Edith Laurie Jacobs (*d* 1980); two *d*. *Educ:* King Edward VI Sch., Southampton. Joined RN, 1921; Commander, 1940; Captain, 1951; Rear-Admiral, 1956; Vice-Admiral, 1959. Served War of 1939–45: HMS Gloucester; RN Barracks, Portsmouth; Persian Gulf; HMS Ocean; Rear-Admiral Personnel, Home Air Command, Lee-on-the-Solent, 1956; Director-General of Manpower, 1959–62; Chief Naval Supply and Secretariat Officer, 1959–62. *Recreation:* gardening. *Address:* Moorings, 59 Western Way, Alverstoke, Hants PO12 2NF.
Died 7 Jan. 1992.

LANCASTER LEWIS, Joan Cadogan, CBE 1978; Director, India Office Library and Records, 1972–78; *b* 2 Aug. 1918; *yr d* of Cyril Cadogan Lancaster and Mary Ann Lancaster; *m* 1983, Rev. Kenneth Lionel Lewis, MA. *Educ:* Charles Edward Brooke Sch., London; Westfield Coll., Univ. of London. BA 1940, MA 1943; ALA 1943; FRHistS 1956; FSA 1960. Served War, ATS, 1943–46. Asst Librarian, University Coll., Leicester, and Asst Archivist, the Museum, Leicester, 1940–43; Archivist, City of Coventry, 1946–48; Asst Librarian, Inst. of Historical Research, Univ. of London, 1948–60; Asst Keeper, India Office Records, 1960–67; Dep. Librarian and Dep. Keeper, India Office Library and Records, 1968–72. Reviews Editor, Archives (Jl of British Records Assoc.), 1951–57, Editor, Archives, 1957–63. *Publications:* Guide to St Mary's Hall, Coventry, 1949, rev. edn 1981; Bibliography of historical works issued in the United Kingdom 1946–56 (Inst. of Historical Research), 1957; Guide to lists and catalogues of the India Office Records, 1966; Godiva of Coventry, 1967; India Office Records: Report for the years 1947–67 (FCO), 1970; contribs on Coventry to: Victoria County History, 1969; Historic Towns, vol. 2, 1974; Medieval Coventry— a city divided?, 1981; articles and reviews in Bulletin of Inst. of Historical Research, Archives, Asian Affairs, etc. *Recreations:* music, photography. *Address:* 9 Nostle Road, Northleach, Cheltenham, Glos GL54 3PF. *T:* Cotswold (0451) 60118. *Died 31 Dec. 1992.*

LANCE, Rev. Preb. John Du Boulay, MC 1945; MA; Prebendary of Henstridge in Wells Cathedral, since 1974; Assistant Curate, St Cuthbert, Wells, since 1981; *b* 14 March 1907; *s* of late Rev. Arthur Porcher Lance and Harriet Agatha Lance, Buckland St Mary, Somerset; *m* 1936, Lena Winifred Clifford; one *s. Educ:* Marlborough; Jesus Coll., Cambridge; Cuddesdon Theological Coll. Deacon, 1930; priest, 1932; Assistant Curate, St Peter, Wolverhampton, 1930–34; Missioner, Trinity Coll., Oxford Mission, Stratford, 1934–36; Vicar of Bishops Lydeard, 1936–47; Vicar of St Andrew's, Taunton, 1947–57; Preb. of Wells, 1951–63; Rector of Bathwick, Bath, 1957–63; Archdeacon of Wells and Canon of Wells Cathedral, 1963–73; Diocesan Dir of Ordinands, Wells, 1974–76. Chaplain to the Forces, 1941–46 (despatches). Proctor in Convocation, 1959–64; Diocesan Adviser in Christian Stewardship, 1961–67; Warden, Abbey Retreat House, Glastonbury, 1965–82. *Address:* Danby Rigg, 1B Welsford Avenue, Wells BA5 2HX. *T:* Wells (0749) 75372. *Club:* Hawks (Cambridge).

Died 4 Sept. 1991.

LAND, Edwin Herbert; US physicist and inventor; Founder, President, scientist, The Rowland Institute for Science, since 1981; Founder Chairman of Board and Consulting Director of Basic Research, Polaroid Corporation, retired 1982 (President, 1937–75; Chief Executive Officer and Director of Research, 1937–80); Fellow and Visiting Institute Professor, Massachusetts Institute of Technology, since 1956; *b* Bridgeport, Connecticut, 7 May 1909; *s* of Harry M. and Matha G. Land; *m* 1929, Helen Maislen; two *d. Educ:* Norwich Acad.; Harvard. War of 1941–45, in charge of research into development of weapons and materials, and cons. on missiles to US Navy. Invented polarizer for light in form of extensive synthetic sheet; also camera which produces complete photograph immediately after exposure, 1947. Member: President's Science Adv. Cttee, 1957–59 (Consultant-at-large, 1960–73); President's Foreign Intelligence Adv. Bd, 1961–77; Nat. Commn on Technology, Automation, and Economic Progress, 1964–66; Carnegie Commn on Educational TV, 1966–67; President's Cttee, Nat. Medal of Science, 1969–72. Harvard University: Mem. Vis. Cttee, Dept of Physics, 1949–66, 1968; William James Lectr on Psychol., 1966–67; Morris Loeb Lectr on Physics, 1974. Trustee, Ford Foundn, 1967–75. Fellow: Photographic Soc. of America, 1950–; Amer. Acad. of Arts and Sciences, 1943– (Pres., 1951–53); Royal Photographic Society, 1958–; Nat. Acad. of Sciences, 1953–, etc; Foreign Mem., Royal Soc., 1986. Hon. MRI, 1975; Hon. Mem., Soc. of Photographic Science and Technology, Japan, 1975; Hon. Fellow: Royal Microscopical Society, and many other American and foreign learned bodies. ScD (Hon.) Harvard Univ., 1957, and many other hon. doctorates in science and law. Awards include: Hood Medal and Progress Medal, RPS; Cresson Medal and Potts Medal, Franklin

Inst.; Scott Medal, Philadelphia City Trusts; Rumford Medal, Amer. Acad. of Arts and Scis, 1945; Holley Medal, ASME, 1948; Duddell Medal, British Physical Soc., 1949; Nat. Medal of Science, 1967. Presidential Medal of Freedom, 1963. *Publications:* contributions to Journal Opt. Soc. America, Amer. Scientist, Proceedings of Nat. Acad. of Science. *Recreations:* music, horseback riding. *Address:* 163 Brattle Street, Cambridge, Mass 02138, USA; (office) 100 Cambridge Parkway, Cambridge, Mass 02142. *T:* 617 497–4600. *Clubs:* Harvard (NY and Boston); Century Association (New York); St Botolph, Harvard Faculty (Boston); Cosmos (Washington, DC).

Died 1 March 1991.

LANE, Frank Laurence, CBE 1961; Chairman, Elder Dempster Lines Ltd, 1963–72; *b* 5 May 1912; *s* of late Herbert Allardyce Lane, CIE, and Hilda Gladys Duckle Lane (*née* Wraith); *m* 1938, Gwendolin Elizabeth Peterkin; one *s* (one *d* decd). *Educ:* Wellington Coll., Berks; New Coll., Oxford. Mansfield & Co. Ltd, Singapore and Penang, 1934–42; BOAC, UK and USA, 1942–45; Mansfield & Co. Ltd, Singapore, 1945–61; Elder Dempster Lines Ltd, Liverpool, 1962–72. *Recreations:* golf, fishing. *Address:* Amberwood, Bisterne Close, Burley, Ringwood, Hampshire BH24 4AU. *T:* Burley (0425) 403249.

Died 21 March 1993.

LANE, John, CB 1981; Deputy Director, Central Statistical Office, 1978–81; *b* 23 Oct. 1924; *s* of R. J. I. and M. E. L. Lane; *m* 1954, Ruth Ann Crocker; one *s. Educ:* John Lyon Sch., Harrow; HMS Conway; Univ. of London (BSc(Econ)). Merchant Navy, 1943–47. Joined Ministry of Transport, 1950; Statistician, 1954; Asst Sec. to Council on Prices, Productivity and Incomes, 1959–61; Principal, MoT, 1962; Asst Sec., 1966; Under-Sec., DoE, 1972; Regional Dir, SE Region and Chm., SE Economic Planning Bd, 1973–76; Under Sec., Dept of Transport, 1976–78. *Address:* Fern Hill, 67 Mount Ephraim, Tunbridge Wells, Kent TN4 8BG. *T:* Tunbridge Wells (0892) 527293.

Died 26 Oct. 1992.

LANE, Margaret, (Margaret Countess of Huntingdon); novelist, biographer, journalist; *b* 23 June 1907; *o d* of late H. G. Lane; *m* 1st, 1934, Bryan (marr. diss. 1939), *e s* of Edgar Wallace; 2nd, 1944, 15th Earl of Huntingdon (*d* 1990); two *d. Educ:* St Stephen's, Folkestone; St Hugh's Coll., Oxford (MA). Reporter, Daily Express, 1928–31; special correspondent: in New York and for International News Service, USA, 1931–32; for Daily Mail, 1932–38. President: Women's Press Club, 1958–60; Dickens Fellowship, 1959–61, 1970; Johnson Soc., 1971; Brontë Soc., 1975–79; Jane Austen Soc., 1985–88. *Publications:* Faith, Hope, No Charity (awarded Prix Femina-Vie Heureuse), 1935; At Last the Island, 1937; Edgar Wallace: The Biography of a Phenomenon, 1938; Walk Into My Parlour, 1941; Where Helen Lies, 1944; The Tale of Beatrix Potter, 1946, rev. edn, 1985; The Brontë Story, 1953; A Crown of Convolvulus, 1954; A Calabash of Diamonds, 1961; Life With Ionides, 1963; A Night at Sea, 1964; A Smell of Burning, 1965; Purely for Pleasure, 1966; The Day of the Feast, 1968; Frances Wright and the Great Experiment, 1971; Samuel Johnson and his World, 1975; Flora Thompson, 1976; The Magic Years of Beatrix Potter, 1978; (ed) Flora Thompson's A Country Calendar and other writings, 1979; The Drug-Like Brontë Dream, 1980; Operation Hedgehog, 1981; series natural history for children: The Fox, The Spider, The Stickleback, The Squirrel, The Frog, The Beaver, 1982. *Address:* Blackbridge House, Beaulieu, Hants.

Died 14 Feb. 1994.

LANE, Prof. Ronald Epey, CBE 1957; MD; FRCP; Emeritus Nuffield Professor of Occupational Health, University of Manchester (Professor, 1945–65); *b* 2 July 1897; *s* of E. E. Lane; *m* 1st, 1924, Winifred E. Tickner (*d*

1981); one *s* (one *d* decd); 2nd, 1982, Ida (*d* 1991), *widow* of Arnold Bailey. *Educ:* Simon Langton Sch., Canterbury; Guy's Hospital. MRCP 1925, FRCP 1938; MSc Manchester, 1946; MD London, 1947. Served European War, RFC, 1915–19. Guy's Hospital, 1919–24, qualified, 1923; General Medical practice, 1925–27; Medical Officer, Chloride Elec. Storage Co. Ltd, 1928; Physician, Salford Royal Hospital, 1935. Milroy Lecturer (Royal College of Physicians), 1947, McKenzie Lecturer, 1950. Mem. of various Govt advisory cttees. *Publications:* original papers on lead poisoning, medical education, occupational health and universities, in Lancet, BMJ, Brit. Jl of Industrial Med., Jl of Industrial Hygiene and Toxicology, etc. *Recreations:* golf, fishing. *Address:* 3 Daylesford Road, Cheadle, Cheshire SK8 1LE. *T:* 0161–428 5738. *Club:* Athenæum.
Died 14 March 1995.

LANG, Prof. David Marshall, MA, PhD, DLit, LittD; Professor of Caucasian Studies in the University of London, 1964–84, then Emeritus; Warden of Connaught Hall, University of London, 1955–84; Special Assistant (Georgian), Department of Oriental Collections (formerly Oriental Manuscripts and Printed Books), British Library, 1950–84; *b* 6 May 1924; *s* of Dr David Marshall Lang, Medical Practitioner, Bath, and Mrs May Rena Lang; *m* 1956, Janet, *d* of late George Sugden, Leeds; one *s* two *d* (and one *s* decd). *Educ:* Monkton Combe Sch.; St John's Coll., Cambridge. Actg Vice-Consul, Tabriz, 1944–46; 3rd Sec., British Embassy, Tehran, 1946; Research Fellow, St John's Coll., Cambridge, 1946–52; Lectr in Georgian, School of Oriental and African Studies, University of London, 1949–58; Senior Fellow, Russian Inst., Columbia Univ., 1952–53; Reader in Caucasian Studies, University of London, 1958–64; Vis. Prof. of Caucasian Languages, University of California, Los Angeles, 1964–65. Hon. Sec., Royal Asiatic Society, 1962–64; Vice-Pres., Holborn Soc., 1973–87; Pres., Georgian Cultural Circle, 1974–. Hon. Dr Philological Sciences, Tbilisi State Univ.; Prix Brémond, 1971. *Publications:* Studies in the Numismatic History of Georgia in Transcaucasia, 1955; Lives and Legends of the Georgian Saints, 1956; The Wisdom of Balahvar, 1957; The Last Years of the Georgian Monarchy, 1957; The First Russian Radical: Alexander Radishchev, 1959; A Modern History of Georgia, 1962; Catalogue of the Georgian Books in the British Museum, 1962; The Georgians, 1966; The Balavariani, 1966; Armenia, Cradle of Civilization, 1970, 3rd edn 1980; (with C. Burney) The Peoples of the Hills, 1971; (ed) Guide to Eastern Literatures, 1971; The Bulgarians, 1976; (with C. Walker) The Armenians (Minority Rights Gp report), 1976; The Armenians: a people in exile, 1981; articles in Bulletin of School of Oriental and African Studies, Encyclopædia Britannica, etc. *Recreations:* music, foreign travel. *Address:* (office) School of Oriental and African Studies, University of London, Thornhaugh Street, Russell Square, WC1H 0XG. *T:* 071–637 2388; (home) The Willows, Stocking Pelham, near Buntingford, Herts SG9 0JX. *T:* Brent Pelham (027978) 409. *Club:* Leander.
Died 30 March 1991.

LANG, John Russell, CBE 1963; Deputy Chairman, The Weir Group Ltd, 1968–73; *b* 8 Jan. 1902; *s* of Charles Russell Lang, CBE and Jessie, *d* of John Crow; *m* 1st, 1934, Jenny (*d* 1970), *d* of Sir John Train, MP, Cathkin, Lanarkshire; four *d* (one *s* decd); 2nd, 1973, Gay Mackie (*d* 1979); 3rd, 1981, Kay, *widow* of Norman Macfie. *Educ:* Loretto Sch., Musselburgh; France and USA. Dir, G. & J. Weir Ltd, 1930–67; Chairman, Weir Housing Corp., 1946–66. President, Scottish Engineering Employers' Association, 1963–64. Mem., Toothill Cttee and EDC for Mech. Eng. Lt-Col 277 Field Regt, RA (TA), 1937. *Recreations:* hunting, shooting, golf. *Address:* Cranford Court, The Ferns, Tetbury, Glos GL8 8JE. *T:* Tetbury

(0666) 53227. *Clubs:* Royal Scottish Automobile (Glasgow); Prestwick Golf; Troon Golf.
Died 2 June 1993.

LANGDON, (Augustus) John; chartered surveyor and land agent; *b* 20 April 1913; *e s* of late Rev. Cecil Langdon, MA and Elizabeth Mercer Langdon, MBE; *m*; two *d*; *m* 1949, Doris Edna Clinkard; one *s*. *Educ:* Berkhamsted Sch.; St John's Coll., Cambridge (Nat. Science Tripos; MA). FRICS (Chartered Land Agent); FRSA. Asst to J. Carter Jonas & Sons, Oxford, 1936–37, Partner 1945–48; Suptg Lands Officer, Admty, 1937–45; Regional Land Comr, Min. of Agriculture, 1948–65; Dep. Dir, Agric. Land Service, Min. of Agriculture, 1965–71; Chief Surveyor, Agricultural Develt and Advisory Service, MAFF, 1971–74; with the National Trust in London, 1974–76. Chm., Statutory Cttee on Agricultural Valuation. Royal Institution of Chartered Surveyors: Mem., Gen. Council; Mem., Land Agency and Agricultural Divisional Council, 1971–75. *Publications:* contrib. Rural Estate Management (ed R. C. Walmsley), Fream's Elements of Agriculture, professional and agric. jls. *Recreations:* gardening, walking, collecting. *Address:* Thorn Bank, Long Street, Sherborne, Dorset DT9 3BS. *T:* Sherborne (0935) 812910. *Club:* United Oxford & Cambridge University.
Died 3 Dec. 1992.

LANGDON, Michael, CBE 1973; Principal Bass Soloist, Royal Opera House, Covent Garden, since 1951; *b* 12 Nov. 1920, named Frank Birtles; *s* of Henry Birtles, Wednesfield Road, Wolverhampton; *m* 1947, Vera Duffield, Norwich; two *d*. *Educ:* Bushbury Hill Sch., Wolverhampton. First Principal Contract, Royal Opera House, Covent Garden, 1951; first Gala Performance, before Queen Elizabeth II (Gloriana), 1953; Grand Inquisitor in Visconti Production of Don Carlos, 1958; debut as Baron Ochs (Rosenkavalier), 1960; first International Engagement (Hamburg), 1961; first Glyndebourne Festival, 1961; appeared in international performances in Paris, Berlin, Aix-en-Provence, San Francisco and Los Angeles, 1962; Lausanne, Geneva, Vienna and Budapest, 1963; Zürich, New York, 1964; Geneva, Marseilles, 1965; Seattle, Buenos Aires; Houston, 1975; Gala Performances, 1967, 1969. Dir, 1978–86, Consultant, 1986–87, Nat. Opera Studio. *Publication:* (with Richard Fawkes) Notes from a Low Singer, 1982. *Recreations:* swimming, walking, Association football (latterly only as spectator). *Address:* 34 Warnham Court, Grand Avenue, Hove, East Sussex.
Died 12 March 1991.

LANGDON-DOWN, Barbara; *see* Littlewood, Barbara, (Lady Littlewood).

LANGFORD-HOLT, Sir John (Anthony), Kt 1962; Lieutenant-Commander Royal Navy (retired); *b* 30 June 1916; *s* of late Ernest Langford-Holt; *m* 1944, Elisabeth Charlotte Marie (marr. diss. 1950), *d* of late Ernst Neustadtl, Vienna; *m* 1953, Flora Evelyn Innes (marr. diss. 1969), *d* of late Ian St Clair Stuart; one *s* one *d*; *m* 1971, Betty Ann (marr. diss. 1981), *d* of H. Maxworthy; *m* 1984, Irene, *d* of late David Alexander Kerr. *Educ:* Shrewsbury Sch. Joined RN and Air Branch (FAA), 1939. MP (C) Shrewsbury, 1945–83. Sec. of Conservative Parly Labour Cttee, 1945–50; Member: CPA, 1945–83; IPU, 1945–83, and other Internat. Bodies; Parliamentary and Scientific Cttee, 1945–83; Estimates Cttee, 1964–68; Expenditure Cttee, 1977–79; Chm., Select Cttee on Defence, 1979–81. Chancellor, Primrose League, 1989–92. Chm., Anglo-Austrian Soc., 1960–63, 1971–82. Freeman and Liveryman of City of London. Grand Decoration of Honour, in Silver with Star (Austria), 1980. *Address:* 704 Nelson House, Dolphin Square, SW1V 3PA. *T:* 071–798 8186; New Milton (0425) 621606. *Club:* White's.
Died 23 July 1993.

LANGSTONE, Rt Rev. John Arthur William; *b* 30 Aug. 1913; *s* of Arthur James Langstone and Coullina Cook; *m* 1944, Alice Patricia Whitby; two *s*. *Educ:* Univ. of Toronto (BA); Trinity Coll., Toronto (LTh); Yale Univ. (Master of Divinity). Asst Curate, St John Baptist, Toronto, 1938; Chaplain, Canadian Army, 1943; Exec. Officer, Dio. Toronto, 1947; Rector: Trinity Church, Port Credit, Toronto, 1950; St George's, Edmonton, 1958; St Faith's, Edmonton, 1969; Canon of All Saints' Cathedral, Edmonton, 1963; Archdeacon of Edmonton, 1965; Exec. Archdeacon, 1971; Bishop of Edmonton, 1976–79. Hon. DD Trinity Coll., Toronto, 1977. *Address:* 5112 109 Avenue, Edmonton, Alberta T6A 1S1, Canada. *T:* 4654111. *Died 26 Feb. 1994.*

LAPSLEY, Air Marshal Sir John (Hugh), KBE 1969 (OBE 1944); CB 1966; DFC 1940; AFC 1950; *b* 24 Sept. 1916; *s* of late Edward John Lapsley, Bank of Bengal, Dacca, and Norah Gladis Lapsley; *m* 1st, 1942, Jean Margaret MacIvor (*d* 1979); one *s* one *d*; 2nd, 1980, Millicent Rees (*née* Beadnell), *widow* of T. A Rees. *Educ:* Wolverhampton Sch.; Royal Air Force Coll., Cranwell. Served in Fighter Squadrons in UK, Egypt and Europe, 1938–45; psc 1946; Air Ministry Directorate of Policy, 1946–48; Commander No 74 Fighter Squadron and Air Fighting Development Squadron, 1949–52; HQ Fighter Command Staff, 1952–54; 2nd TAF Germany, 1954–58; Ministry of Defence Joint Planning Staff, 1958–60; Deputy Chief of Staff Air, 2nd Allied TAF, 1960–62; IDC, 1963; Secretary to Chiefs of Staff Cttee and Director of Defence Operations Staff, Ministry of Defence, 1964–66; No 19 Group, RAF Coastal Comd, 1967–68; AOC-in-C, RAF Coastal Comd, 1968–69; Head of British Defence Staff and Defence Attaché, Washington, 1970–73. Mem. Council, Officers' Pension Soc., 1976–87. Dir-Gen., Save the Children Fund, 1974–75. Dir, Falkland Is R&D Assoc. Ltd, 1978–83; Councillor, Suffolk Coastal District Council, 1979–87, Chm. 1983. Fellow RSPB. *Recreations:* golf, fishing, ornithology. *Address:* Milcroft, 149 Saxmundham Road, Aldeburgh, Suffolk IP15 5PB. *T:* Aldeburgh (01728) 453957. *Clubs:* Royal Air Force; Aldeburgh Golf; Suffolk Fly Fishers.
Died 21 Nov. 1995.

LARGE, Maj.-Gen. Stanley Eyre, MBE 1945; retired; *b* 11 Aug. 1917; *s* of late Brig. David Torquil Macleod Large and Constance Lucy Houston; *m* 1941, Janet Mary (*née* Brooks); three *s*. *Educ:* Edinburgh; Cheltenham Coll.; Caius Coll., Cambridge (MA, MD); St Thomas' Hosp. FRCP, FRCPE. Commnd in RAMC, 1942; war service in Tunisia, Italy, Austria, Greece, with field ambs and as Regimental Med. Officer; psc 1948; spec. medicine; served in hosps at home and overseas as med. specialist, later consultant in medicine, with particular interest in diseases of chest, 1950–65; various sen. admin. appts in Cyprus and BAOR, 1965–75; DMS, UKLF, 1975–78. QHP 1974–78. Dir of Med. Servs, King Edward VIII Hosp., Midhurst, 1978–83. *Publications:* King Edward VII Hospital, Midhurst 1901–1986, 1986; contrib. med. literature. *Recreations:* travel, ski-ing, golf, photography; formerly running (half blue, Cambridge v Oxford, mile, 1937). *Address:* Drumcrannog, Colvend, Dalbeattie, Kirkcudbrightshire DG5 4QD.
Died 12 May 1991.

LARSEN, Cyril Anthony; Senior Clerk, House of Commons, 1980–86, retired; *b* 29 Dec. 1919; *s* of late Niels Arthur Larsen and Ella Bessie Larsen (*née* Vaughan); *m* 1956, Patricia Sneade; two *s* three *d*. *Educ:* St Francis Xavier's College, Liverpool. Board of Trade, 1936–38; Min. of Labour, 1938–40; Royal Navy, Lieut, 1940–46; entered administrative class, Dept of Employment, 1947; seconded to HM Treasury, 1950–53; Asst Sec., 1963; seconded to Prices and Incomes Board, 1966–69; Under

Sec., 1971–79. *Address:* 51 Park Hill Road, Wallington, Surrey SM6 0RJ. *T:* 081–647 9380.
Died 10 March 1993.

LARTIGUE, Sir Louis C.; *see* Cools-Lartigue.

LASCELLES, Mary Madge, FBA 1962; Hon. Fellow, Somerville College, 1967; *b* 7 Feb. 1900; *d* of William Horace and Madeline Lascelles. *Educ:* Sherborne School for Girls; Lady Margaret Hall, Oxford. Research Studentship, Westfield Coll., 1923; Assistant Lecturer, Royal Holloway Coll., 1926; Somerville College: Tutor in English Language and Literature, 1931; Fellow, 1932–67; Vice-Principal, 1947–60; University Lecturer in English Literature, 1960–66; Reader, 1966–67. *Publications:* Jane Austen and her Art, 1939; Shakespeare's Measure for Measure, 1953; (ed) The Works of Samuel Johnson, Yale vol. ix, A Journey to the Western Islands of Scotland, 1971; The Adversaries and Other Poems, 1971; Notions and Facts, 1973; The Story-Teller Retrieves the Past, 1980; Further Poems, 1982; Selected Poems, 1990; contributions to learned journals, etc. *Address:* Valley House, Cley, Holt, Norfolk NR25 7TR. *T:* Cley (01263) 740413. *Club:* University Women's. *Died 10 Dec. 1995.*

LAST, Prof. Raymond Jack, FRCS, FRACS; Professor of Applied Anatomy, and Warden, Royal College of Surgeons, 1949–70; *b* 26 May 1903; English; *m* 1st, 1926, Vera Estella Judell (marr. diss.); two *s*; 2nd, 1939, Margret Stewart Milne (decd). *Educ:* Adelaide High Sch., Australia. MB, BS (Adelaide), 1924. Medical practice S Australia, 1927–38; arrived London, 1939; Surgeon, EMS, Northern Hospital, N21, 1939–40; OC Abyssinian Medical Unit, Hon. Surgeon to Emperor Haile Selassie I, also OC Haile Selassie Hospital, Surgeon to British Legation, Addis Ababa, 1941–44; returned to London, Lieut-Colonel, RAMC, 1945; ADMS, British Borneo, 1945–46. Anatomical Curator and Bland Sutton Scholar, RCS, 1946; FRCS 1947; Adviser to Central Government of Pakistan on organization and conduct of primary FRCS instruction, Colombo Plan, 1961. Vis. Prof. of Anatomy: UCLA, 1970–87; Mt Sinai Sch. of Medicine, NY, 1971–72. *Publications:* Anatomy, Regional and Applied, 7th edn 1984; Wolff's Anatomy of Eye and Orbit, 6th edn, 1968; Aids to Anatomy, 12th edn, 1962; contrib. to Journals of Surgery; various articles. *Address:* c/o 49 Westall Street, Unley Park, SA 5061, Australia.
Died 1 Jan. 1993.

LATHAM, Robert Clifford, CBE 1973; FBA 1982; Hon. Fellow of Magdalene College, Cambridge, since 1984 (Research Fellow, 1970–72; Fellow, 1972–84; Pepys Librarian, 1972–82); *b* 11 March 1912; *s* of Edwin Latham and Alice Latham, Audley, Staffs; *m* 1st, 1939, Eileen Frances Redding Ramsay (*d* 1969); one *s* one *d*; 2nd, 1973, Rosalind Frances Birley (*d* 1990). *Educ:* Wolstanton County Grammar Sch., Staffs; Queens' Coll., Cambridge (scholar). Hist. Tripos Pt I 1932, Pt II 1933; MA 1938. Asst Lectr in History, King's Coll., London, 1935, Lectr, 1939; University Reader in History, Royal Holloway Coll., London, 1947–72. Visiting Associate Prof., Univ. of Southern California, Los Angeles, 1955; Prof. of History, Univ. of Toronto, 1968–69. Hon. Fellow, RHBNC, 1989. Wheatley Medal, LA, 1983; Marc Fitch prize, Univ. of Leeds, 1984. *Publications:* (ed) Bristol Charters, 1509–1899 (Bristol Rec. Soc., vol. xii), 1947; (ed) The Diary of Samuel Pepys, vols i-ix (with Prof. W. Matthews), 1970–76, vols x and xi, 1983; (ed) The Illustrated Pepys, 1978; gen. editor, Catalogue of the Pepys Library at Magdalene College, Cambridge, 1978–94; (ed) The Shorter Pepys, 1985; (ed with Linnet Latham) A Pepys Anthology, 1987; articles and reviews in learned and other jls. *Recreations:* music, gossip.

Address: Magdalene College, Cambridge CB3 0AG. *T:* Cambridge (01223) 350357. *Died 4 Jan. 1995.*

LATNER, Prof. Albert Louis; Professor of Clinical Biochemistry, University of Newcastle upon Tyne, 1963–78, then Emeritus Professor, and Director of Cancer Research Unit, 1967–78; Consultant Clinical Biochemist, Royal Victoria Infirmary, Newcastle upon Tyne, 1948–78, Hon. Consultant, since 1978; *b* 5 Dec. 1912; *s* of Harry Latner and Miriam Gordon; *m* 1936, Gertrude Franklin (*d* 1986). *Educ:* Imperial College of Science and University College, London; University of Liverpool. ARCS 1931; MSc (London) 1933; DIC, 1934; MB, ChB (Liverpool) 1939; MD (Liverpool) 1948; FRIC 1953; MRCP 1956; DSc (Liverpool) 1958; FRCPath 1963; FRCP 1964. Lectr in Physiology, Univ. of Liverpool, 1933–36 and 1939–41; Pathologist in RAMC, 1941–46; Sen. Registrar, Postgrad. Medical Sch., 1946–47; Lectr in Chem. Pathol., King's Coll., Univ. of Durham, 1947–55; Reader in Medical Biochemistry, Univ. of Durham, 1955–61; Prof. of Clin. Chem., Univ. of Durham, 1961–63. Vis. Lectr, Amer. Assoc. Clinical Chemists, 1972. Hon. Member: Assoc. of Clinical Biochemists, 1984 (Chm., 1958–61; Pres., 1961–63); British Electrophoresis Soc., 1986; Titular Member, Section of Clinical Chemistry, International Union of Pure and Applied Chemistry, 1967–73; Hon. Fellow, American Nat. Acad. of Clinical Biochemistry, 1977. Member, Editorial Board: Clinica Chimica Acta, 1960–68; Electrophoresis, 1980–88; Med. Sci. Res., 1981–; Co-Editor, Advances in Clinical Chemistry, 1971–84. Wellcome Prize, Royal Soc., 1976. *Publications:* Isoenzymes in Biology and Medicine, 1968 (co-author); Cantarow and Trumper Clinical Biochemistry, 7th edn, 1975; chapter on Metabolic Aspects of Liver Disease in Metabolic Disturbances in Clinical Medicine (ed G. A. Smart), 1958; chapters on Chemical Pathology and Clinical Biochemistry in British Encyclopædia of Medical Practice: Medical Progress (ed Lord Cohen of Birkenhead), 1961, 1962, 1964, 1966 and 1968; chapter on Isoenzymes in Recent Advances in Clinical Pathology, Series IV, 1964; section on Isoenzymes in Advances in Clinical Chemistry (ed C. P. Stewart), 1966; (ed with O. Bodansky and contrib. section on Isoelectric Focusing) Advances in Clinical Chemistry, 1975; contribs to medical and scientific journals dealing with cancer, liver disease, pernicious anæmia, the serum proteins in disease and isoenzymes. *Recreations:* art, photography, gardening. *Address:* Ravenstones, Rectory Road, Gosforth, Newcastle upon Tyne NE3 1XP. *T:* 091–285 8020. *Club:* Athenæum. *Died 10 Dec. 1992.*

LAUCKE, Hon. Sir Condor (Louis), KCMG 1979; Lieutenant-Governor, State of South Australia, 1982–92; *b* 9 Nov. 1914; *s* of Friedrich Laucke and Marie (*née* Jungfer); *m* 1942, Rose Hambour; one *s* one *d*. *Educ:* Immanuel Coll., Adelaide; South Australian School of Mines. Elected to S Australian House of Assembly, 1956, 1959, 1962; Government Whip, 1962–65; Member, Australian Senate for S Australia, 1967–81; Pres. Senate, Parlt of Commonwealth of Australia, 1976–81. Member, Liberal Party Executive, 1972–74. Joint President: CPA, 1976–81 (also Chm., Exec. Cttee, 1976–81); IPU. *Address:* Bunawunda, Greenock, SA 5360, Australia. *T:* (8) 5628143. *Died 30 July 1993.*

LAW-SMITH, Sir (Richard) Robert, Kt 1980; CBE 1965; AFC 1943; Chairman, National Australia Bank Ltd, 1979–86; grazier; *b* Adelaide, 9 July 1914; *s* of W. Law-Smith; *m* 1941, Joan, *d* of Harold Gordon Darling; two *d*. *Educ:* St Edward's Sch., Oxford; Adelaide Univ. Served War, RAAF, 1940–46 (AFC), Sqdn Ldr. Director: Nat. Bank of Australasia, later Nat. Commercial Banking Corp. of Australia, then Nat. Australia Bank, 1959–86 (Vice-Chm., 1968); Australian Mutual Provident Soc., 1960–84

(Chm. Victoria Br., 1977–84); Broken Hill Pty Co. Ltd, 1961–84; Commonwealth Aircraft Corp., 1965–84; Blue Circle Southern Cement Ltd, 1974–84. Mem., Australian National Airlines Commn, 1962–84 (Vice-Chm., 1975–79; Chm., 1979–84). Councillor, Royal Flying Doctor Service (Victorian Div.), 1956–85. *Address:* Field House, Mount Macedon, Vic 3441, Australia. *Clubs:* Australian, Melbourne (Melbourne). *Died 4 Oct. 1992.*

LAWRENCE, Arnold Walter, MA; FSA; Professor of Archæology, University College of Ghana, and Director, National Museum of Ghana, 1951–57; Secretary and Conservator, Monuments and Relics Commission of Ghana, 1952–57; Laurence Professor of Classical Archæology, Cambridge University, 1944–51, and Fellow of Jesus College; *b* 2 May 1900; *s* of T. R. Lawrence; *m* 1925, Barbara Thompson (*d* 1986); (one *d* decd). *Educ:* City of Oxford Sch.; New Coll., Oxford. Student, British Schs of Athens and Rome; Ur excavations, 1923; Craven Fellow, 1924–26; Reader in Classical Archæology, Cambridge Univ., 1930; lectured in Latin America, 1948; Leverhulme Research Fellow, 1951. Corr. Mem., German Archæological Institute. Literary executor of T. E. Lawrence, 1935. Military Intelligence, Middle East, 1940; Scientific Officer, Coastal Command, RAF, 1942; Ministry of Economic Warfare, 1943. Hon. FBA 1982. *Publications:* Later Greek Sculpture and its Influence, 1927; Classical Sculpture, 1929; Herodotus (Rawlinson's translation revised and annotated), 1935; (ed) T. E. Lawrence by his Friends, 1937; Greek Architecture (Pelican History of Art), 1957, rev. edns 1967 and 1974, rev. by R. A. Tomlinson, 1984; (ed) Letters to T. E. Lawrence, 1962; Trade Castles and Forts of West Africa, 1963, abr. as Fortified Trade Posts: the English in West Africa, 1968; Greek and Roman Sculpture, 1972; The Castle of Baghras, in The Armenian Kingdom of Cilicia (ed T. S. R. Boase), 1978; Greek Aims in Fortification, 1980. *Recreation:* going to and fro in the earth and walking up and down in it. *Address:* c/o Barclays Bank, High Street, Pateley Bridge, Harrogate HG3 5LA. *Died 31 March 1991.*

LAWRENCE, Geoffrey Charles, CMG 1963; OBE 1958; *b* 11 Nov. 1915; *s* of Ernest William Lawrence; *m* 1945, Joyce Acland Madge (MBE 1959), *d* of M. H. A. Madge, MC. *Educ:* Stationers' Company's Sch.; Brasenose Coll., Oxford. Served War, 1939–46, Middlesex Yeo. and Brit. Mil. Administration of Occupied Territories (Major). HM Overseas Civil Service (Colonial Administrative Service): Administrative Officer, Somaliland Protectorate, 1946; Asst Chief Sec., 1955; Financial Sec., 1956; Financial Sec., Zanzibar and Mem. of East African Currency Board, 1960–63; Colonial Office, 1964–66; ODM, later ODA, FCO, 1966–73; ODM, 1973–76. *Address:* c/o Barclays Bank, 6 High Street, Haslemere, Surrey GU27 2LY. *Died 5 June 1994.*

LAWRENCE, Air Vice-Marshal Thomas Albert, CB 1945; CD; Royal Canadian Air Force, retired; *b* 1895; *s* of K. J. Lawrence; *m* 1921, Claudine Audrey Jamieson; two *s*. Served War of 1914–18, France; Flight Cadet, RFC, later 24 Fighter Sqdn, RAF; Pilot-Navigator, Canadian Air Bd; one of original gp of officers commnd into perm. RCAF, 1924; comdr, Hudson Strait Expedn, 1927; Liaison Officer, RCAF, Air Ministry, London, 1932–35; served War of 1939–45: Dir, Plans and Ops, Air Force HQ, 1939; CO Trenton, Ont, 1940; AOC, 2 Training Comd, BCATP, 1942–44; AOC, NW Air Comd, Canada, 1944–47, retd. Comdr, Legion of Merit (USA), 1945. Mem., Canada's Aviation Hall of Fame, 1980. *Address:* 10 William Morgan Drive, Toronto, Ont M4H 1E5, Canada. *Died 19 Feb. 1992.*

LAWTON, Ven. John Arthur; Rector of Winwick, 1969–87; Archdeacon of Warrington, 1970–81, Archdeacon Emeritus since 1986; *b* 19 Jan. 1913; *s* of Arthur and Jennie Lawton; unmarried. *Educ:* Rugby; Fitzwilliam House, Cambridge (MA); Cuddesdon Theological College, Oxford. Deacon, 1937; priest, 1938; Curate, St Dunstan, Edgehill, Liverpool, 1937–40; Vicar of St Anne, Wigan, 1940–56; Vicar of St Luke, Southport, 1956–60; Vicar of Kirkby, Liverpool, 1960–69; Canon Diocesan of Liverpool, 1963–87. *Address:* 32 Ringwood Close, Gorse Covert, Warrington WA3 6TQ. *T:* Warrington (01925) 818561.   *Died 29 April 1995.*

LAWTON, Louis David; QC 1973; barrister-at-law; a Recorder of the Crown Court, since 1972; *b* 15 Oct. 1936; *m* 1959, Helen Margaret (*née* Gair); one *s* two *d. Educ:* Repton Sch.; Sidney Sussex Coll., Cambridge (MA). Called to Bar, Lincoln's Inn, 1959; Bencher, Lincoln's Inn, 1981. Mem. Criminal Injuries Compensation Bd, 1981–83. *Address:* 199 Strand, WC2R 1DR. *Club:* United Oxford & Cambridge University.
                                      Died 25 Oct. 1993.

LAWTON, Philip Charles Fenner, CBE 1967; DFC 1941; Group Director and Chairman, BEA, 1972–73; Member: British Airways Board, 1972–73; Board, BOAC, 1972–73; *b* Highgate, London, 18 Sept. 1912; *o s* of late Charles Studdert Lawton and Mabel Harriette Lawton; *m* 1941, Emma Letitia Gertrude, *y d* of late Lieut-Colonel Sir Henry Kenyon Stephenson, 1st Bt, DSO, and Frances, Hassop Hall, Bakewell, Derbyshire; one *s* one *d. Educ:* Westminster Sch. Solicitor, 1934–39. Joined AAF, 1935; served War of 1939–45 (despatches twice, Group Captain): Pilot with 604 Aux. Sqdn (night fighters), 1939–41; Staff Officer HQ, Fighter Command, 1942; Station Commander, RAF Predannock; RAF Portreath; RAF Cranfield and Special Duties for Inspector-General, RAF, 1943–45. Joined BEA, 1946; Commercial and Sales Dir, 1947–71; Mem. Corporation, 1964; Exec. Bd Member, 1971; Chm., BEA Airtours, 1969–72. LLB Hons Degree, 1933; FCIT (MInstT 1955). *Address:* Fenner House, Glebe Way, Wisborough Green, West Sussex RH14 0EA. *T:* Wisborough Green (0403) 700606; 17 Pembroke Walk, W8 6PQ. *T:* 071–937 3091. *Club:* Royal Air Force.
                                       Died 8 Dec. 1993.

LAZARUS, Sir Peter (Esmond), KCB 1985 (CB 1975); FCIT; Director, Manchester Ship Canal Co., 1986–93; Member, Civil Aviation Authority, 1986–92; *b* 2 April 1926; *er s* of late Kenneth M. Lazarus and Mary R. Lazarus (*née* Halsted); *m* 1950, Elizabeth Anne Marjorie Atwell, *e d* of late Leslie H. Atwell, OBE; three *s. Educ:* Westminster Sch.; Wadham Coll., Oxford (Open Exhibition). Served RA, 1945–48. Entered Ministry of Transport, 1949: Secretary, London and Home Counties Traffic Advisory Cttee, 1953–57; Private Secretary to Minister, 1961–62; Asst Sec., 1962; Under-Sec., 1968–70; Under-Sec., Treasury, 1970–72; Deputy Secretary: DoE, 1973–76; Dept of Transport, 1976–82; Perm. Sec., Dept of Transport, 1982–85. Chairman: Assoc. of First Div. Civil Servants, 1969–71; Cttee for Monitoring Agreements on Tobacco Advertising and Sponsorship, 1986–91. Pres., Liberal Jewish Synagogue, St John's Wood, 1994– (Chm. Council, 1972–75, 1987–92); Chm., Jews' Temporary Shelter, 1993–; Comdt, Jewish Lads' and Girls' Brigade, 1987–95. FRSA 1981. *Recreations:* music, reading. *Address:* 28 Woodside Avenue, N6 4SS. *T:* 0181–883 3186. *Club:* Athenæum.   *Died 19 Oct. 1995.*

LAZARUS, Robert Stephen; QC 1958; Social Security (formerly National Insurance) Commissioner, 1966–81; *b* 29 Oct. 1909; *s* of late Solomon and Mabel Lazarus; *m* 1938, Amelia (*née* Isaacs); two *d. Educ:* Marlborough Coll.; Caius Coll., Cambridge. Called to the Bar, at Lincoln's Inn, 1933; Bencher, 1964. Member: Bar Council,

1960–64; Legal Aid Cttee, 1961–66. Served with RASC, 1940–46. *Recreations:* music, gardening. *Address:* 50 Southgrove House, Southgrove, Highgate, N6 6LR.
                                       Died 3 June 1991.

LEAN, Sir David, Kt 1984; CBE 1953; film director; *b* 25 March 1908; *s* of late Francis William le Blount Lean and Helena Annie Tangye; *m* Kay Walsh (marr. diss. 1949); one *s*; *m* 1949, Ann Todd (marr. diss. 1957); *m* 1960, Mrs Leila Matkar (marr. diss. 1978); *m* 1981, Sandra Hotz (marr. diss. 1985); *m* 1990, Sandra Cooke. *Educ:* Leighton Park Sch., Reading. Entered film industry as number board boy, 1928; edited and did commentary for Gaumont Sound News and British Movietone News; then edited Escape Me Never, Pygmalion, 49th Parallel, etc; co-directed, with Noel Coward, In Which We Serve, 1942; *directed:* This Happy Breed, 1943; Blithe Spirit, 1944; Brief Encounter, 1945; Great Expectations, 1946; Oliver Twist, 1947; The Passionate Friends, 1948; Madeleine, 1949; The Sound Barrier (British Film Acad. Award), 1952; Hobson's Choice, 1953; Summer Madness (Amer. title, Summertime), 1955; The Bridge on the River Kwai (US Acad. Award for Best Picture), 1957; Lawrence of Arabia, 1962 (US Acad. Award, 1963; Italian silver ribbon, 1964); Doctor Zhivago, 1965; Ryan's Daughter, 1970; A Passage to India, 1984. Fellow: BAFTA, 1974; BFI, 1983. Hon. DLitt Leeds, 1986. Officier de l'Ordre des Arts et des Lettres, France, 1968.   *Died 16 April 1991.*

LEATHERLAND, Baron, *cr* 1964 (Life Peer), of Dunton; **Charles Edward Leatherland,** OBE 1951; Treasurer and Member of Council, University of Essex, from foundation until 1973; *b* 18 April 1898; *e s* of John Edward Leatherland, Churchover, Warwicks; *m* 1922, Mary Elizabeth (*d* 1987), *d* of Joseph Henry Morgan, Shareshill, Staffs; one *s* one *d. Educ:* Harborne, Birmingham; University Extension Courses. Asst Editor, Daily Herald, until retirement, 1963. Served European War, 1914–19 (despatches, MSM): enlisted, 1914, aged 16; served in France, Belgium, Germany; Company Sgt Major, Royal Warwicks Regt; Essex TA Assoc., 1946–68, and E Anglian TA Assoc., 1968. Chm., Essex County Council, 1960–61 (Vice-Chm. 1952–55 and 1958–60); CA Essex, 1946–68; JP Essex, 1944–70; DL Essex, 1963; Dep. Chm., Epping Magistrates Bench. Mem. Bd of Basildon Development Corporation, 1967–71. Additional Mem., Monopolies Commn, to consider newspaper mergers, 1969. Chm., E Counties Regional Council of the Labour Party, 1950–66. DUniv Essex, 1973. *Publications:* (part author) The Book of the Labour Party, 1925; Labour Party pamphlets; contribs on local govt affairs in Municipal Jl and general press; 4 Prince of Wales Gold Medals 1923 and 1924 for essays on: Measures that may be taken by other countries to promote an improvement in the economic condition of Czecho-Slovakia, 1923; The possibilities of the cinema in the development of commercial education, 1923; Difficulties attending the economic position of Czecho-Slovakia after the Peace Treaty, and the methods adopted to remove them, 1924; Home and foreign trade: their relative importance and interdependence, 1924. *Recreations:* walking; formerly fox hunting. *Address:* 19 Starling Close, Buckhurst Hill, Essex. *T:* 081–504 3164.   *Died 17 Dec. 1992.*

LEBLANC, Rt Rev. Camille André; Chaplain at Caraquet Hospital; *b* Barachois, NB, 25 Aug. 1898. *Educ:* Collège Sainte-Anne, Church Point, NS; Grand Séminaire, Halifax, NS. Priest, 1924; subseq. Curé at Shemogue and the Cathedral of Nôtre Dame de l'Assomption, Moncton; Bishop of Bathurst, 1942–69. *Address:* c/o Hôpital de l'Enfant-Jésus, Caraquet, NB E0B 1K0, Canada.
                                       Died 19 Aug. 1993.

LECKIE, John, CB 1955; *b* 2 Sept. 1911; *o s* of late Alexander M. Leckie; *m* 1937, Elizabeth Mary Murray

Brown; two s. *Educ:* Hamilton Academy; Glasgow Univ. (MA, BSc). Entered Administrative Class, Home Civil Service, by competitive examination, 1934; Customs and Excise Dept, 1934; transferred to Board of Trade, 1940; Head of Board of Trade Delegation, Washington, USA, 1943–45; Adviser on Commercial Policy, 1950; Under-Sec., 1950–60, Second Sec., 1960–64, BoT; Deputy Secretary: Min. of Technology, 1964–70; DTI, 1970–72, retd 1972. *Address:* 1 The Wedges, West Chiltington Lane, Itchingfield, Horsham, Sussex RH13 7TA.
Died 27 May 1992.

LeCOMBER, Prof. Peter George, FRS 1992; FRSE; CEng, FIEE; CPhys, FInstP; Harris Professor of Physics, University of Dundee, since 1991; *b* 19 Feb. 1941; *s* of George Henry LeComber and Florence LeComber (*née* Peck); *m* 1962, Joy Smith; one *s* one *d. Educ:* Univ. of Leicester (BSc, PhD); University of Dundee (DSc). Res. Fellow, Purdue and Leicester Univs, 1965–68; University of Dundee: Lectr, Sen. Lectr and Reader, 1968–85; Personal Chair in Solid State Physics and Electronics, 1986–91. Maxwell Premium, IEE, 1983; Duddell Medal, Inst. Phys, 1984; Rank Prize for Opto-Electronics, 1988. *Publications:* numerous scientific papers, mainly on amorphous materials. *Recreations:* music, fishing, photography. *Address:* The University, Dundee DD1 4HN. *T:* Dundee (0382) 307569.
Died 9 Sept. 1992.

LEDGER, Sir Joseph Francis, (Sir Frank), Kt 1963; retired company director (engineering etc); *b* 29 Oct. 1899; *s* of Edson and Annie Frances Ledger; *m* 1923, Gladys Muriel Lyons (*d* 1981); one *s* two *d. Educ:* Perth Boys' Sch., Perth, WA. President: J. E. Ledger Cos; Mitchell Cotts Gp; Dir, Mitchell Cotts Australia; Governing Dir, Ledger Investments; Past Chm. of Dirs, S Australian Insurance Co.; Director: Chamber of Manufrs Insurance Co.; ARC Engineering Co.; Winget Moxey (WA) Pty Ltd; Lake View and Star Ltd; Member, Past Chairman: WA Branch of Inst. of Directors (London); WA Govt Industrial Develt Adv. Cttee; Pres., Royal Commonwealth Society (WA Branch); Past President: WA Chamber of Manufacturers; WA Employers Federation; Ironmasters Assoc. (WA); Metal Industries Assoc. (WA); Inst. of Foundrymen (WA); Past Vice-Pres., Associated Chamber of Manufacturers (Canberra). Pres., WA Trotting Assoc.; Vice-Pres., Australian Trotting Council. *Recreations:* golfing, sailing. *Address:* 2 The Esplanade, Peppermint Grove, WA 6011, Australia. *Clubs:* Weld, Perth, Royal Freshwater Bay Yacht, Cottesloe Golf, West Australian Turf, West Australian Cricket Association (all in Perth, WA).
Died 8 April 1993.

LEDINGHAM, Prof. John Marshall, MD, FRCP; Consultant Physician, The London Hospital, 1954–81, then Consulting Physician; Professor of Medicine, University of London, at London Hospital Medical College, 1971–81, then Emeritus; *b* 13 Feb. 1916; *s* of late Prof. Sir John C. G. Ledingham, CMG, FRS, The Lister Institute, London, and Lady (Barbara) Ledingham; *m* 1950, Josephine, *d* of late Matthew and Jane Metcalf, Temple Sowerby, Westmorland; two *s. Educ:* Whitgift Sch.; University College, London; The London Hospital. BSc (London) First Class Hons in Physics, 1936; MRCS, LRCP 1942; MD (London), Gold Medal, 1951; FRCP 1957. Service in RAMC as Graded Clinical and Experimental Pathologist, in UK, France, Middle and Far East, 1942–47. Lectr in Medicine, London Hosp. Med. Sch., 1948–53; Univ. Reader in Medicine, 1953–64; Prof. of Experimental Medicine, London Hosp. Med. Coll., London Univ., 1964–71. Vis. Prof., Maiduguri Univ., Nigeria, 1982. Mem., Professional and Linguistic Assessment Bd, GMC, 1984–90. Past Pres., Section of Exptl Med. and Therapeutics, RSM; Bertram Louis

Abrahams Lectr, RCP, 1970; Censor, RCP, 1975. Editor, Dep. Chm. and Chm. Editl Bd, Clinical Science, 1965–70. *Publications:* numerous scientific, mainly in field of hypertension and renal disease, 1938–. *Address:* 11 Montpelier Walk, SW7 1JL. *T:* 071–584 7976.
Died 8 Sept. 1993.

LEE, Arthur James, CBE 1979; DSC (and Bar); Controller of Fisheries Research and Development, Ministry of Agriculture, Fisheries and Food, 1977–80; *b* 17 May 1920; *s* of Arthur Henry and Clara Lee; *m* 1953, Judith Graham; three *d. Educ:* City Boys' Sch., Leicester; St Catharine's Coll., Cambridge (MA). Served War of 1939–45 (DSC and Bar). Apptd: Scientific Officer at Fisheries Laboratory, Lowestoft, 1947; Dep. Dir of Fishery Research, 1965, Dir, 1974–77. *Publications:* (ed) Atlas of the Seas around the British Isles, 1981; contribs to various marine science jls. *Recreation:* gardening. *Address:* 191 Normanston Drive, Oulton Broad, Lowestoft, Suffolk NR32 2PY. *T:* Lowestoft (0502) 574707.
Died 28 Dec. 1993.

LEE, Sir Desmond; see Lee, Sir H. D. P.

LEE, (George) Russell, CMG 1970; Acting Assistant Director, Ministry of Defence, 1967–78, retired; *b* 11 Nov. 1912; *s* of Ernest Harry Lee and Alice Mary Lee (*née* Russell); *m* 1947, Annabella Evelyn (*née* Dargie); one *s* one *d. Educ:* Birkenhead Sch., Cheshire. WO and MoD, 1940–78. *Address:* 13 Abberbury Road, Iffley, Oxford OX4 4ET.
Died 26 Oct. 1995.

LEE, Gilbert Henry Clifton; Chairman, BOAC Associated Cos Ltd, 1964–75; *b* 19 April 1911; *s* of Walter Lee and Sybil Townsend; *m* 1938, Kathleen Cooper; two *d. Educ:* Worksop College. FCIT. Joined Imperial Airways, 1931; served overseas India, E Africa, Pakistan; Gen. Man., West African Airways Corp., 1949–52; BOAC: Traffic Manager, 1953; Gen. Sales Man., 1955; Commercial Dir, 1959; Mem. Bd, BOAC, 1961–73. Chm., European Hotel Corporation NV, 1975–76. *Recreation:* golf. *Address:* Dana, Callow Hill, Virginia Water, Surrey GU25 4LD. *T:* Wentworth (09904) 2195. *Clubs:* Oriental; Wentworth (Virginia Water).
Died 5 Jan. 1991.

LEE, Sir (Henry) Desmond (Pritchard), Kt 1961; MA; President, Hughes Hall, Cambridge, 1973–78; Hon. Fellow 1978; *b* 30 Aug. 1908; *s* of Rev. Canon Henry Burgass Lee; *m* 1935, Elizabeth, *d* of late Colonel A. Crookenden, CBE, DSO; one *s* two *d. Educ:* Repton Sch. (George Denman Scholar); Corpus Christi Coll., Cambridge (Entrance Scholar). 1st Class Part 1 Classical Tripos, 1928; Foundation Scholar of the College; 1st Class Part 2 Classical Tripos, 1930; Charles Oldham Scholar. Fellow of Corpus Christi Coll., 1933, 1948–68, Life Fellow, 1978, Tutor, 1935–48; University Lecturer in Classics, 1937–48; Headmaster of Clifton Coll., 1948–54; Headmaster of Winchester Coll., 1954–68. Fellow, University Coll., later Wolfson Coll., Cambridge, 1968–73, Hon. Fellow, 1974. Regional Comr's Office, Cambridge, 1941–44; Mem. Council of the Senate, 1944–48. Mem. Anderson Cttee on Grants to Students, 1958–59; Chm., Headmasters' Conference, 1959–60, 1967. Hon. DLitt Nottingham, 1963. *Publications:* Zeno of Elea: a Text and Notes, 1935; Aristotle, Meteorologica, 1952; Plato, Republic, 1955, rev. edn 1974; Plato, Timæus and Critias, 1971; Entry and Performance at Oxford and Cambridge, 1966–71, 1972; (ed) Wittgenstein's Lectures 1930–32, 1980. *Address:* 8 Barton Close, Cambridge CB3 9LQ.
Died 8 Dec. 1993.

LEE, Russell; see Lee, G. R.

LEE-BARBER, Rear-Adm. John, CB 1959; DSO 1940 and Bar 1941; Admiral Superintendent, HM Dockyard, Malta, 1957–59, retired; *b* 16 April 1905; *s* of Richard Lee-Barber, Herringfleet, near Great Yarmouth; *m* 1939,

Suzanne (*d* 1976), *d* of Colonel Le Gallais, ADC, MC, La Moye, Jersey, CI; two *d*. *Educ:* Royal Naval Colleges, Osborne and Dartmouth. Service in destroyers and in Yangtze gunboat until 1937; CO Witch, 1937–38; CO Griffin, 1939–40–41; Commander, 1941; CO Opportune, 1942–44; 2nd in Command, HMS King Alfred, 1945; CO, HMS St James, 1946–47; Captain, 1947; Senior Officer Reserve Fleet, Harwich, 1948–49; Naval Attaché, Chile, 1950–52; CO Agincourt and Captain D4, 1952–54; Commodore, Inshore Flotilla, 1954–56; Rear-Admiral, 1957. Polish Cross of Valour, 1940. *Recreation:* sailing. *Address:* Ferry House, The Quay, Wivenhoe, Essex. *T:* Wivenhoe (01206) 822592. *Died 14 Nov. 1995.*

LEECH, Air Vice-Marshal David Bruce, CBE 1978 (OBE 1976); Commandant General, Royal Air Force Regiment and Director General of Security (RAF), 1985–87; retired, 1988; *b* 8 Jan. 1934; *s* of Mrs S. A. Leech; *m* 1958, Shirley Anne (*née* Flitcroft); two *d*. *Educ:* Bolton School, Lancs. Joined RAF 1954, and served with Nos 11 and 20 Sqns, 1956–58; Pilot attack instr, APC Sylt, 1958–61; Mem., RAF 2 TAF Air Gunnery Team, Cazaux, 1958; qualified flying instr, RAF Coll., Cranwell, CFS and Church Fenton, 1961–66; Chief Instr, Canadian Tactical Air Ops Sch., Rivers, Manitoba, 1966–69; RAF Staff Coll., 1969–70; HQ 38 Gp, Ops Staff, 1970–72; OC Ops Wing, RAF Wittering, 1973–75; Stn Comdr, RAF Wildenrath, RAF Gutersloh and Comdr RAF Germany Harrier Force, 1975–77; Dir, Dept of Warfare, RAF Coll., 1977–79; Inspector of Flight Safety, 1979–81; RCDS 1982; Comdr, Allied Sector Ops Centre No 1, Brockzetel, 1983–85. *Recreations:* golf, country pursuits. *Address:* The Annexe, Wellingore, Lincs LN5 0HY. *Club:* Royal Air Force.
Died 14 Aug. 1994.

LEEDALE, Harry Heath, CBE 1972; Controller of Surtax and Inspector of Foreign Dividends, 1968–74; *b* 23 June 1914; *s* of John Leedale and Amy Alice Leedale (*née* Heath), New Malden; *m* 1st, 1940, Audrey Beryl (*née* Platt) (*d* 1970); one *d*; 2nd, 1971, Sheila Tyas Stephen. *Educ:* Henry Thornton Sch., Clapham, London. Served War, RAF, 1941–46. Entered Inland Revenue, 1933; Controller, Assessments Div., 1961; Asst Clerk to Special Commissioners of Income Tax, 1963; Controller, Superannuation Funds Office, 1964. *Recreations:* gardening, foreign travel. *Address:* Lavender Cottage, Rotherfield, Sussex TN6 3QP. *T:* Rotherfield (089285) 2424. *Died 10 Sept. 1991.*

LEES, Prof. Anthony David, FRS 1968; Senior Research Fellow, Imperial College at Silwood Park, since 1982; *b* 27 Feb. 1917; *s* of Alan Henry Lees, MA and Mary Hughes Bomford; *m* 1943, Annzella Pauline Wilson; one *d*. *Educ:* Clifton Coll., Bristol; Trinity Hall, Cambridge (Schol.). BA 1939; PhD (Cantab) 1943; ScD 1966. Mem., ARC Unit of Insect Physiology at Zoology Dept, Cambridge, 1945–67; Lalor Fellow, 1956; Vis. Prof., Adelaide Univ., 1966; Hon. Lectr, London Univ., 1968; DCSO and Prof. of Insect Physiology, ARC at Silwood Park Field Station, Ascot, 1969–82, then Prof. Emeritus. Pres., Royal Entomological Soc., 1973–75, Hon. Fellow 1984. Leverhulme Res. Fellow, 1988–89. *Publications:* scientific papers. *Recreations:* gardening, fossicking. *Address:* Wells Lane Corner, London Road, Ascot, Berks SL5 7DY. *Died 3 Oct. 1992.*

LEES, Air Marshal Sir Ronald Beresford, KCB 1961 (CB 1946); CBE 1943; DFC; Commander-in-Chief, Royal Air Force, Germany, 1963–65, retired; *b* 27 April 1910; *s* of John Thomas and Elizabeth Jane Lees; *m* 1931, Rhoda Lillie Pank; one *s* one *d*. *Educ:* St Peter's Coll., Adelaide, Australia. Joined Royal Australian Air Force, 1930; transferred Royal Air Force, 1931; ADC to the Queen, 1952–53 (to King George VI, 1949–52); AOC No 83 Gp, 2nd TAF in Germany, 1952–55; Asst Chief of Air Staff

(Operations), 1955–58; SASO, Fighter Command, 1958–60; Dep. Chief of the Air Staff, 1960–63; Air Marshal, 1961. *Address:* 1B Penarth Avenue, Beaumont, SA 5066, Australia. *Died 18 May 1991.*

LEESE, John Arthur; Editor-in-Chief, Evening Standard, 1986–91; *b* 4 Jan. 1930; *s* of late Cyril Leese and May Leese; *m* 1959, Maureen Jarvis; one *s* one *d*. *Educ:* Bishop Vesey's School, Warwicks. Editor, Coventry Evening Telegraph, 1964–70; Dep. Editor, Evening News, 1970–76, Editor, 1980; Editor-in-Chief and Publisher, Soho News, NY, 1981–82; Editl Dir, Harmsworth Publishing, 1975–82; Editor, You Magazine and Editor-in-Chief and Man. Dir, Associated Magazines, 1983–86; Editor, Evening News, 1987; Dir, Associated Newspaper Hldgs, 1989–. *Died 23 Sept. 1991.*

LeFANU, Dame Elizabeth; *see* Maconchy, Dame E.

LE GALLIENNE, Eva; theatrical producer, director and actress; *b* London, England, 11 Jan. 1899; *d* of Richard Le Gallienne and Julie Norregaard. *Educ:* Collège Sévigné, Paris, France. Début Prince of Wales Theatre, London, in The Laughter of Fools, 1915; New York Début in The Melody of Youth, 1916; appeared in NY and on tour, in Mr Lazarus, season of 1916–17; with Ethel Barrymore in The Off Chance, 1917–18; Not So Long Ago, 1920–21; Liliom, 1921–22; The Swan, 1923; Hannele in The Assumption of Hannele, by Hauptmann, 1923; Jeanne d'Arc, by Mercedes de Acosta, 1925; The Call of Life, by Schnitzler, 1925; The Master Builder, by Henrik Ibsen, 1925–26; Founder and Director Civic Repertory Theatre, NY, 1926; played in Saturday Night, The Three Sisters, Cradle Song, 2x2–5, The First Stone, Improvisations in June, The Would-Be Gentleman, L'Invitation au Voyage, The Cherry Orchard, Peter Pan, On the High Road, The Lady from Alfaqueque, Katerina, The Open Door, A Sunny Morning, The Master Builder, John Gabriel Borkman, La Locandiera, Twelfth Night, Inheritors, The Good Hope, Hedda Gabler, The Sea Gull, Mlle Bourrat, The Living Corpse, Women Have Their Way, Romeo and Juliet, The Green Cockatoo, Siegfried, Allison's House, Camille, Liliom (revival), Dear Jane, Alice in Wonderland; L'Aiglon, 1934; Rosmersholm, 1935; Uncle Harry, 1942; Cherry Orchard, 1944; Thérèse, 1945; Elizabeth I in Schiller's Mary Stuart, Phœnix Theatre, NYC, 1958, toured in same, 1959–60; Elizabeth the Queen, 1961–62; The Sea Gull, 1963; Ring Round the Moon, 1963; The Mad Woman of Chaillot, 1964; The Trojan Women, 1964; Exit the King, 1967; All's Well That Ends Well, Amer. Shakespeare Theatre, 1970; Mrs Woodfin in The Dream Watcher, 1975; Fanny Cavendish in The Royal Family, NYC, 1976, tour, 1977; To Grandmother's House We Go, NYC, 1981; White Queen in Alice in Wonderland, NYC, 1983 (also dir); Man. Dir of Amer. Repertory Theatre, which did six classic revivals in repertory, NY, 1946 and 1947; Dir The Cherry Orchard, Lyceum Theatre, NY, 1967–68. Resurrection (film), 1980. Hon. MA Tufts Coll., 1927, and several honorary doctorates, 1930–. Member Actors' Equity Assoc. and Managers' Protective Assoc. Gold Medal, Soc. Arts and Sciences, 1926; Amer. Acad. of Arts and Letters Medal for good speech, 1945; Drama League Award, 1976; Handel Medallion, City of NY, 1976; Amer. Nat. Theatre and Acad. Award, 1977; National Medal of Arts Award, 1986. Cross of St Olav (Norway), 1961. *Publications:* At 33 (autobiography), 1934; Flossie and Bossy, (NY) 1949, (London) 1950; With A Quiet Heart, 1953; A Preface to Hedda Gabler, 1953; The Master Builder, a new translation with a Prefatory Study, 1955; trans. Six Plays by Henrik Ibsen, 1957 (NYC); trans. The Wild Duck and Other Plays by Henrik Ibsen, 1961 (NYC); The Mystic in the Theatre: Eleonora Duse, 1966 (NYC and London); trans. The Spider and Other Stories by Carl Evald, 1980; articles for

New York Times, Theatre Arts Monthly, etc. *Recreations:* gardening, painting. *Address:* N Hillside Road, Weston, Conn 06883, USA. *Died 3 June 1991.*

LÉGER, His Eminence Cardinal Paul-Émile; *b* Valleyfield, Quebec, Canada, 26 April 1904; *s* of Ernest Léger and Alda Beauvais. *Educ:* Ste-Thérèse Seminary; Grand Seminary, Montreal. Seminary of Philosophy, Paris, 1930–31; Seminary of Theology, Paris, 1931–32; Asst Master of Novices, Paris, 1932–33; Superior Seminary of Fukuoka, Japan, 1933–39; Prof., Seminary of Philosophy, Montreal, 1939–40; Vicar-Gen., Diocese of Valleyfield, 1940–47; Rector, Canadian Coll., Rome, 1947–50; consecrated bishop in Rome and apptd to See of Montreal, 1950; elevated to Sacred Coll. of Cardinals and given titular Church of St Mary of the Angels, 1953; Archbishop of Montreal, 1950–67; resigned to work as a missionary in Africa; Parish Priest, St Madeleine Sophie Barat parish, Montreal, 1974–75. Hon. Pres., Jules and Paul-Émile Léger Foundn and its subsidiaries, that help the poorest of world. Variety Club award, 1976. Several hon. doctorates both from Canada and abroad. Foreign decorations. *Address:* CP1500–Succursale A, Montréal, PQ H3C 2Z9, Canada. *Died 13 Nov. 1991.*

LEGGETT, Douglas Malcolm Aufrère, MA, PhD, DSc; FRAeS; FIMA; Vice-Chancellor, University of Surrey, 1966–75; *b* 27 May 1912; *s* of George Malcolm Kent Leggett and Winifred Mabel Horsfall; *m* 1943, Enid Vida Southall; one *s* one *d*. *Educ:* Rugby Sch.; Edinburgh Univ.; Trinity Coll., Cambridge. Wrangler, 1934; Fellow of Trinity Coll., Cambridge, 1937; Queen Mary Coll., London, 1937–39; Royal Aircraft Establishment, 1939–45; Royal Aeronautical Society, 1945–50; King's Coll., London, 1950–60; Principal, Battersea Coll. of Technology, 1960–66. Vice-Pres., Scientific and Med-Network, 1992. FKC 1974; DUniv Surrey, 1975. *Publications:* (with C. M. Waterlow) The War Games that Superpowers Play, 1983; (with M. G. Payne) A Forgotten Truth, 1986; The Sacred Quest, 1987; Facing the Future, 1990; contrib. to scientific and technical jls. *Address:* Southlands, Fairoak Lane, Oxshott, Surrey KT22 0TW. *T:* Oxshott (0372) 843061. *Died 21 Aug. 1994.*

LE GRICE, Very Rev. F(rederick) Edwin, MA; Dean Emeritus of Ripon Cathedral, since 1984 (Dean, 1968–84); *b* 14 Dec. 1911; *s* of Frederick and Edith Le Grice; *m* 1940, Joyce Margaret Hildreth; one *s* two *d*. *Educ:* Paston Sch., North Walsham; Queens' Coll., Cambridge; Westcott House, Cambridge. BA (2nd class hons Mathematics, 2nd class hons Theology) 1934; MA 1946. Deacon, 1935; priest, 1936; Asst Curate: St Aidan's, Leeds, 1935–38; Paignton, 1938–46; Vicar of Totteridge, N20, 1946–58; Canon Residentiary and Sub-Dean of St Albans Cathedral, 1958–68; Examining Chaplain to the Bishop of St Albans, 1958–68. A Church Comr, 1973–82; Mem., Church Commn on Crown Appts, 1977–82. *Publications:* Sharp Reflections (poetry), 1989; Five Instant Glorias and a Creed, 1991; Love Unknown (cantata), 1992. *Address:* The West Cottage, Markenfield Hall, Ripon, N Yorks HG4 3AD. *Died 25 June 1992.*

LEICESTER, 6th Earl of, *cr* 1837; **Anthony Louis Lovel Coke;** Viscount Coke 1837; farmer, since 1976; *b* 11 Sept. 1909; *s* of Hon. Arthur George Coke (killed in action, 1915) (2nd *s* of 3rd Earl) and (Phyllis) Hermione (who *m* 2nd, Maj.-Gen. Sir Richard Howard-Vyse), *d* of late Francis Saxham Elwes Drury; *S* cousin, 1976; *m* 1st, 1934, Moyra Joan (marr. diss. 1947) (*d* 1987), *d* of late Douglas Crossley; two *s* one *d*; 2nd, 1947, Vera Haigh (*d* 1984), Harare, Zimbabwe; 3rd, 1985, Elizabeth Hope Johnstone, Addo, Eastern Province, South Africa, *d* of late Clifford Arthur Johnstone. *Educ:* Gresham's School, Holt. Served War of 1939–45 in RAF. Career spent ranching. *Recreations:* general. *Heir:* *s* Viscount Coke [*b* 6 May

1936; *m* 1st, 1962, Valeria Phyllis (marr. diss. 1985), *e d* of late L. A. Potter; two *s* one *d*; 2nd, 1986, Mrs Sarah de Chair]. *Address:* Hillhead, PO Box 544, Plettenberg Bay, 6600, South Africa. *T:* (04457) 32255.
Died 19 June 1994.

LEIGH, Sir John, 2nd Bt, *cr* 1918, of Altrincham, Cheshire; *b* 24 March 1909; *s* of Sir John Leigh, 1st Bt, and Norah Marjorie, CBE (*d* 1954); *S* father 1959; *m* 1959, Ariane, *d* of late Joseph William Allen, Beverly Hills, California, and *widow* of Harold Wallace Ross, NYC. *Educ:* Eton; Balliol Coll., Oxford. *Heir:* *nephew* Richard Henry Leigh [*b* 11 Nov. 1936; *m* 1st, 1962, Barbro Anna Elizabeth (marr. diss. 1977), *e d* of late Stig Carl Sebastian Tham, Sweden; 2nd, 1977, Chérie Rosalind, *e d* of D. D. Dale and *widow* of Alan Reece, RMS]. *Clubs:* Brooks's; Travellers' (Paris). *Died 13 Dec. 1992.*

LEIGH, Sir Neville (Egerton), KCVO 1980 (CVO 1967); Clerk of the Privy Council, 1974–84; *b* 4 June 1922; *s* of late Cecil Egerton Leigh; *m* 1944, Denise Margaret Yvonne, *d* of late Cyril Denzil Branch, MC; two *s* one *d*. *Educ:* Charterhouse. RAFVR, 1942–47 (Flt-Lt). Called to Bar, Inner Temple, 1948. Legal Asst, Treasury Solicitors Dept, 1949–51; Senior Clerk, Privy Council Office, 1951–65; Deputy Clerk of Privy Council, 1965–74. Member: Investigation Cttee, ICA, 1985–90; Press Council, 1986–88; Chm., Central London Valuation and Community Charge Tribunal, 1990–94 (Mem., Central London Valuation Panel, 1986–90). Pres., British Orthoptic Soc., 1984–91. Consultant, Royal Coll. of Nursing of UK, 1985–88. Trustee: R&D Trust for the Young Disabled, Royal Hosp. and Home, Putney, 1986–90; Coll. of Arms Trust, 1987–; Gov., Suttons Hosp., Charterhouse, 1986–. Hon. FCIOB 1982. *Address:* 11 The Crescent, Barnes, SW13 0NN. *T:* 081–876 4271. *Club:* Army and Navy. *Died 1 Aug. 1994.*

LEIGHTON, Ronald; MP (Lab) Newham North-East, since 1979; *b* 24 Jan. 1930; *s* of Charles Leighton and Edith (*née* Sleet); *m* 1951, Erika Wehking; two *s*. *Educ:* Monteagle and Bifrons Sch., Barking. Newspaper printer. Secretary, Labour Cttee for Safeguards on Common Market, 1967–70; Director, All-Party Common Market Safeguards Campaign, 1970–73; Editor, Resistance News, 1973–74; Secretary, Get Britain Out Campaign, 1974–75; National Organiser, National Referendum Campaign, which campaigned for 'No' vote in Referendum, 1975; Chairman: Labour Common Market Safeguards Cttee, 1975–; Select Cttee on Employment, 1984–92. An Opposition Whip on Employment, 1981–84. Sponsored member, Sogat '82. *Publications:* The Labour Case Against Entry to the Common Market; What Labour Should Do About the Common Market; also pamphlets (1963–). *Recreations:* reading, footpath walking. *Address:* c/o House of Commons, SW1A 0AA.
Died 28 Feb. 1994.

LEINSDORF, Erich; orchestral and operatic conductor; *b* Vienna, 4 Feb. 1912; *s* of Ludwig Julius Leinsdorf and Charlotte (*née* Loebl); US citizen, 1942; *m* 1st, 1939, Anne Frohnknecht (marr. diss. 1968); three *s* two *d*; 2nd, 1968, Vera Graf. *Educ:* University of Vienna; State Academy of Music, Vienna (dipl.). Assistant Conductor: Salzburg Festival, 1934–37; Metropolitan Opera, NY, 1937–39; Chief Conductor, German operas, 1939–43; Conductor, Rochester Philharmonic, 1947–56; Director, NYC Opera, 1956; Music Cons. Director, Metropolitan Opera, 1957–62; Music Director, Boston Symphony Orchestra, 1962–69. Director: Berkshire Music Center, Berkshire Music Festival, 1963–69; American Arts Alliance, 1979–; Mem., Nat. Endowment for the Arts, 1980–. Guest appearances with virtually every major orchestra in the USA and Europe, incl. Philadelphia, Los Angeles, St Louis, New Orleans, Chicago, Minneapolis,

Cleveland, New York, Concertgebouw Amsterdam, Israel Philharmonic, London Symphony, New Philharmonia, BBC, San Francisco Opera, Bayreuth, Holland and Prague Festivals. Recorded many symphonies and operas. Former Member Executive Cttee, John F. Kennedy Center for Performing Arts. Fellow, American Academy of Arts and Sciences. Hon. degrees. *Publications:* Cadenza (autobiog.), 1976; The Composer's Advocate, 1981; transcriptions of Brahms Chorale Preludes; contribs to Atlantic Monthly, Saturday Review, New York Times, High Fidelity. *Address:* Hadlaubstrasse 104, CH-8006 Zürich, Switzerland. *Died 11 Sept. 1993.*

LEMIEUX, Most Rev. (Marie-) Joseph; *b* Quebec City, 10 May 1902; *s* of Joseph E. Lemieux and Eva (*née* Berlinguet). *Educ:* College of St Anne de la Pocatière; Dominican House of Studies, Ottawa; College of Angelico, Rome; Blackfriars, Oxford. Missionary to Japan, 1930; Parish Priest, Miyamaecho, Hakodate, Japan, 1931–36; first Bishop of Sendai, 1936; resigned, 1941; Administrator of Diocese of Gravelbourg, Sask, 1942; Bishop of Gravelbourg, 1944–53; Archbishop of Ottawa, 1953–66; Apostolic Nuncio to Haiti, 1966–69; Apostolic Pro-Nuncio in India, 1969–71; Delegate of St Peter's Basilica in Vatican, 1971–73. *Address:* 143 St Patrick, Ottawa, Ontario K1N 5J9, Canada. *Died 7 March 1994.*

LEMMON, Cyril Whitefield, FRIBA, FAIA; architect, Honolulu, Hawaii (private practice), 1946–69, retired; Chairman of the Board, Architects Hawaii Ltd; *b* Kent, 27 Oct. 1901; *s* of T. E. Lemmon and Catherine Whitefield; *m* 1st, 1921, Ethel Belinda Peters (marr. diss. 1936), artist; no *c*; 2nd, 1938, Rebecca Robson Ramsay; two *d. Educ:* University of Pennsylvania, Philadelphia, Pa. Fifth-year Studio Instructor and Lecturer in the School of Architecture, University of Liverpool, 1933–36; Consulting Architect to Government of India for Rebuilding of Quetta, 1936; Consulting Architect to MES for all military buildings in India, 1938. Lieut-Colonel, Royal Indian Engineers, 1941; Director of Civil Camouflage in India, 1943; GSO 1, GHQ, India and 11th Army Group, 1943–44. President, Hawaii Chapter, AIA, 1950; AIA Honour Award, Hawaii State Capitol. Exhibited paintings in Salon des Tuileries, Paris, 1933; travel in United States, Mexico, Europe, N Africa and Asia. Public Lectures on architecture and painting. 32° Mason; Potentate, Aloha Temple, AONMS, 1970. *Publications:* contributions to professional journals on architecture. *Recreations:* golf, swimming. *Address:* 1434 Punahou Street, #1016 Honolulu, Hawaii 96822, USA. *Clubs:* Pacific (Honolulu); Waialae Country.
Died 5 June 1993.

LENDRUM, Prof. Alan Chalmers, MA, MD, BSc; ARPS; FRCPath; Professor of Pathology, University of Dundee, 1967–72, Professor Emeritus, 1972, Honorary Research Fellow, 1972; *b* 3 Nov. 1906; *yr s* of late Rev. Dr Robert Alexander Lendrum and Anna, *e d* of late James Guthrie, Pitforthie, Angus; *m* 1st, 1934, Elizabeth Bertram (*d* 1983), *e d* of late Donald Currie, BA, LLB; two *s* one *d*; 2nd, 1984, Dr Ann Brougham Sandison. *Educ:* High Sch., Glasgow; Ardrossan Acad.; University of Glasgow. Asst to Sir Robert Muir, MD, FRS, 1933; Lecturer in Pathology, University of Glasgow; Prof. of Pathology, Univ. of St Andrews, 1947–67. Visiting Prof. of Pathology, Yale, 1960. Kettle Meml Lecture, RCPath, 1973. Hon. For. Mem. Argentine Soc. of Normal and Pathological Anatomy; Hon. Member: Pathol Soc. of GB and Ireland; Nederlandse Patholoog Anatomen Vereniging; Dialectic Soc., Glasgow Univ.; Forfarshire Medical Assoc.; Hon. Fellow, and ex-Pres., Inst. Med. Lab. Sci. Dean of Guildry of Brechin, 1971–73. Capt. RAMC (TA), retd. Sims Woodhead Medal, 1971. Chm. of Governors, Duncan of Jordanstone Coll. of Art, Dundee, 1975–77. *Publications:*

(co-author) Recent Advances in Clinical Pathology, 1948; Trends in Clinical Pathology, 1969; publications in medical journals. *Address:* Hobstones, Gawthrop, Dent, Sedbergh, Cumbria LA10 5TA. *T:* Dent (05396) 25238.
Died 2 Jan..1994.

LENIHAN, Brian Joseph; Teachta Dala (TD) for Dublin West, Parliament of Ireland, since 1981 (TD for Roscommon/Leitrim, 1961–73), for Dublin (West County), 1977–81); *b* 17 Nov. 1930; *s* of Patrick Lenihan (TD Longford-Westmeath, 1965–70); *m* 1958, Ann Devine; four *s* one *d. Educ:* St Mary's Coll. (Marist Brothers), Athlone; University Coll., Dublin. Member: Roscommon CC, 1955–61; Seanad Eireann (FF), 1957–61 and (as Leader in Seanad, Fianna Fáil), 1973–77; Parly Sec. to Minister for Lands, 1961–64; Minister for: Justice, 1964–68; Educn, 1968–69; Transport and Power, 1969–73; Foreign Affairs, 1973; Fisheries and Forestry, 1977–79; Foreign Affairs, 1979–81; Agriculture, 1982; Foreign Affairs, 1987–89; Defence, 1989–90; Tánaiste (Dep. Prime Minister), 1987–90; Chm., All Party Foreign Affairs Cttee, 1993–. Mem., European Parlt, 1973–77. Dep. Leader, Fianna Fáil Party, 1983–. Contested (FF), Presidency of Ireland, 1990. *Publication:* For the Record, 1991. *Address:* Leinster House, Dublin 2, Eire.
Died 1 Nov. 1995.

LENNON, (John) Dennis, CBE 1968; MC 1942; Senior Partner, Dennis Lennon & Partners, since 1950; *b* 23 June 1918; British; *m* 1947, Else Bull-Andersen; three *s. Educ:* Merchant Taylors' Sch.; University Coll., London. Served Royal Engineers, 1939–45 (despatches): 1st, 7th, 6th Armd Divs; captured in France 1940, later escaped; 7th Armd Div., N Africa; 6th Armd Div., Italy. Dir, Rayon Industry Design Centre, 1948–50; private practice, 1950–. Main Work: Jaeger shops; London Steak Houses; co-ordinator of interior, RMS Queen Elizabeth II; Chalcot Housing Estate, Hampstead; approved plans for Criterion site, Piccadilly Circus; Central Dining Room, Harrow Sch.; Arts Club; Refurbishment of Ritz Hotel, London. Work for stage: set for Capriccio, Glyndebourne; 9 state galas, Royal Opera House. FRIBA, FSIA, FRSA. *Recreations:* arts, design. *Address:* Hamper Mill, Watford, Herts. *T:* Watford (0923) 34445. *Clubs:* Savile, Royal Thames Yacht. *Died 16 April 1991.*

LENTON, (Aylmer) Ingram, PhD; Chairman, Compass Group plc, 1987–94; Deputy Chairman, Board of Crown Agents for Oversea Governments and Administrations, since 1990 (Member, since 1987); *b* 19 May 1927; *s* of Albert Lenton and Olive Lenton; *m* 1951, Ursula Kathleen King; one *s* two *d. Educ:* Leeds Grammar Sch.; Magdalen Coll., Oxford (MA); Leeds Univ. (PhD). Richard Haworth & Co. Ltd, 1951; British Nylon Spinners Ltd, 1956; Managing Director, S African Nylon Spinners Ltd, 1964; Director, ICI Fibres Ltd, 1966; Director, John Heathcoat & Co. Ltd, 1967, Man. Dir, 1971; Bowater Corporation Ltd: Dir, 1979; Man. Dir, 1981–84; Chm. and Man. Dir, Bowater Industries plc (formerly Bowater Corp.), 1984–87; Chairman: Bowater UK Paper Co., 1976; Bowater UK Ltd, 1979; Inveresk Ltd, 1991–94; Watts Blake Bearne & Co., 1991–94 (Dir, 1987–94; Dep. Chm., 1988–91); Director: Atkins Holdings, 1987– (Chm., 1989–); Scapa Gp, 1988–. CIMgt. Hon. Fellow, British Orthopaedic Assoc., 1990. Court Asst, Stationers' and Newspaper Makers' Co. *Recreations:* golf, fell walking, fishing. *Address:* Robin Hill, Hockett Lane, Cookham Dean, Berks SL6 9UF. *Died 11 June 1994.*

LEONARD-WILLIAMS, Air Vice-Marshal Harold Guy, CB 1966; CBE 1946; DL; retired; *b* 10 Sept. 1911; *s* of late Rev. B. G. Leonard-Williams; *m* 1937, Catherine Estelle, *d* of late G. A. M. Levett; one *d. Educ:* Lancing Coll.; RAF Coll., Cranwell. 58 Sqdn, 1932–33; 208 Sqdn, Middle East, 1933–36; No 17 Signals Course, 1936–37;

Instructor, RAF Coll., 1937–38; Advanced Air Striking Force, France, 1939–40 (despatches, 1940); Air Min. (Signals), 1940–43; Chm., Brit. Jt Communications Bd, 1943–46; RAF Staff Coll., 1947; Dep. CSO, RAF Middle East, 1947–50; Jt Services Staff Coll., 1950–51; CO Radio Engrg Unit, 1951–53; Dep. Dir Signals, Air Min., 1953–56; Sen. Techn. Staff Off., 90 Signals Gp, 1956–57; Dir of Signals, Air Min., 1957–59; Comdt No 1 Radio Sch., 1959–61; Comd Electronics Off., Fighter Comd, 1961–63; AOA, HQ Far East Air Force, and AOC, HQ Gp, 1963–65; Dir-Gen. of Manning (RAF), Air Force Dept, 1966–68. Warden, St Michael's Cheshire Home, Axbridge, 1968–72. Mem., Somerset CC, 1973–85 (Chm. 1978–83). Chm., Exmoor Nat. Park, 1978–85. DL Somerset 1975. Officer, Legion of Merit (US), 1945. *Recreations:* gardening, do-it-yourself. *Address:* Openbarrow, Barrows Park, Cheddar, Somerset BS27 3AZ. *T:* Cheddar (01934) 742474. *Club:* Royal Air Force.
Died 21 Nov. 1994.

LE POER TRENCH, Brinsley; *see* Clancarty, 8th Earl of.

LERNER, Max; author; Syndicated newspaper column appeared New York Post, Los Angeles Times Syndicate and elsewhere; Professor of American Civilization and World Politics, Brandeis University, USA, 1949–73, then Emeritus; Professor of Human Behavior, Graduate School of Human Behavior, US International University, San Diego, since 1974; *b* 20 Dec. 1902; *s* of Benjamin Lerner and Bessie Podel; *m* 1st, 1928, Anita Marburg (marr. diss. 1940); two *d* (and one *d* decd); 2nd, 1941, Edna Albers; three *s. Educ:* Yale Univ. (BA); Washington Univ., St Louis (MA); Robert Brookings Graduate Sch. of Economics and Government (PhD). Asst editor, Encyclopædia of Social Sciences, 1927, then managing editor; Mem., Social Science Faculty, Sarah Lawrence Coll., 1932–36; Lectr, Dept of Govt, Harvard, 1935–36; Prof. of Political Science, Williams Coll., 1938–43; Ford Foundation Prof. of Amer. Civilization, Sch. of Internat. Studies, University of Delhi, 1959–60; Ford Foundn res. project on European unity, 1963–64. Welch Prof. of Amer. Studies, Univ. of Notre Dame, 1982–84. Editor of the Nation, 1936–38; Editorial Director PM, 1943–48; Columnist for the New York Star, 1948–49. *Publications:* It is Later Than You Think, 1938, rev. edn, 1943, new edn with afterword, 1989; Ideas are Weapons, 1939, new edn with afterword, 1990; (ed) Machiavelli, Prince and Discourses, 1940; Ideas for the Ice Age, 1941; The Mind and Faith of Justice Holmes, 1943, new edn with afterword, 1989; (ed) Aristotle's Politics, 1943; Public Journal, 1945; The Third Battle for France, 1945; The World of the Great Powers, 1947; The Portable Veblen, 1948; Actions and Passions, 1949; America as a Civilization, 1957, rev. edn, 1987; The Unfinished Country, 1959; (ed) Essential Works of John Stuart Mill, 1961; Education and a Radical Humanism, 1962; The Age of Overkill, 1962; Tocqueville and American Civilization, 1966; (ed) Tocqueville, Democracy in America, 1966; Values in Education, 1976; Ted and the Kennedy Legend, 1980; Wrestling with the Angel, 1990, rev. edn 1991. *Address:* 25 East End Avenue, New York, NY 10028, USA; (office) New York Post, 210 South Street, New York, NY 10002, USA.
Died 5 June 1992.

LESLIE, Prof. David Clement; Director, Turbulence Unit, Queen Mary College, London, 1975–90; Professor Emeritus, London University, since 1984; *b* Melbourne, 18 Dec. 1924; *o s* of Clement and Doris Leslie; *m* 1952, Dorothea Ann Wenborn; three *s* two *d. Educ:* Westminster; Leighton Park; Wadham Coll., Oxford (MA, DPhil). Royal Navy, 1944–47. Postgrad. research in physics, 1948–50; Sir W. G. Armstrong Whitworth Aircraft, Coventry, 1951–54; Guided Weapons Div., RAE Farnborough, 1954–58; UKAEA Harwell and Winfrith, 1958–68; Prof.

of Nuclear Engrg, QMC, 1968–84 (Hd of Dept, 1968–80; Dean, Faculty of Engrg, 1980–83). Member: Scientific and Technical Cttee, EEC, 1973–86 (Chm. 1980–84); Electricity Supply Res. Council, 1981–89 (Dep. Chm. 1984–89); Machines and Power Cttee, SERC, 1985–87. Safety Adviser to the Local Authorities for the Sizewell Inquiry, 1981–87. *Publications:* Developments in the Theory of Turbulence, 1973; papers in Proc. Royal Soc., Jl of Fluid Mechanics, Nature, Nuclear Science and Engrg, etc. *Address:* Berwyns, Clarendon Road, Prestwood, Great Missenden, Bucks HP16 0PL. *T:* Great Missenden (0494) 863415.
Died 27 Aug. 1993.

LESLIE, His Honour Gilbert Frank; retired Circuit Judge (formerly Judge of County Courts); *b* 25 Aug. 1909; *e s* of late F. L. J. Leslie, JP and M. A. Leslie (*née* Gilbert), Harrogate; *m* 1947, Mary Braithwaite, MD, JP, *e d* of late Col W. H. Braithwaite, MC, TD, DL and Mrs E. M. Braithwaite, Harrogate; three *d. Educ:* St Christopher Sch., Letchworth; King's Coll., Cambridge (MA). Called to the Bar, Inner Temple, 1932; joined North-Eastern Circuit. Served War of 1939–45; Private Sherwood Foresters, 1939; commissioned West Yorkshire Regt, 1940; on Judge-Advocate-General's staff from Nov. 1940; finally ADJAG, HQ BAOR; released Nov. 1945 (Lt-Col). Asst Recorder, Newcastle upon Tyne City Quarter Sessions, 1954–60; Sheffield City Quarter Sessions, 1956–60; Recorder of Pontefract, 1958–60; Recorder of Rotherham, 1960; Dep. Chm., West Riding Quarter Sessions, 1960–63; Judge of County Court Circuit 14, 1960, Circuit 46, 1960–63, Circuit 42 (Bloomsbury and Marylebone), 1963–80 (Circuit Judge, 1972); Dep. Chm., Inner London Area Sessions, 1965–71. Dep. Chm., Agricultural Lands Tribunal (Yorkshire Area), 1958–60. Jt Pres., Council of HM Circuit Judges, 1978. Manager, 1974–77, 1980–83, Vice-Pres., 1975–77, 1980–83, Royal Institution. Mem. Board of Faculty of Law and Court of Governors, Sheffield Univ., 1958–61; Governor, 1964–87, Chm. of Governors, 1974–84, Parsons Mead Sch. for Girls. Liveryman, Worshipful Co. of Gardeners, 1963– (Mem. Court, 1978–, Master, 1987–88, Sen. Past Master, 1993). FRSA. *Recreations:* gardening, history. *Address:* Ottways, 26 Ottways Lane, Ashtead, Surrey KT21 2NZ. *T:* Ashtead (01372) 274191. *Club:* Reform.
Died 24 March 1995.

LESLIE, Hon. John Wayland; *b* 16 Dec. 1909; 2nd *s* of 19th Earl of Rothes and Noëlle Lucy Martha, *d* of T. Dyer Edwardes; *m* 1932, Coral Angela, *d* of late G. H. Pinckard, JP, Combe Court, Chiddingfold, Surrey, and 9 Chesterfield Street, Mayfair; one *s* one *d. Educ:* Stowe Sch.; Corpus Christi Coll., Cambridge. Formerly Flt-Lieut, RAFVR; invalided 1943. Mem. of Royal Company of Archers (Queen's Body Guard for Scotland). Mem. Clothworkers' Co. *Recreations:* fishing, shooting. *Address:* Guildford House, Castle Hill, Farnham, Surrey GU9 7JG. *T:* Farnham (0252) 716975. *Club:* Boodle's.
Died 17 June 1991.

LESSER, Sidney Lewis; Vice-President, Royal Automobile Club, since 1979 (Executive Chairman, 1978–79); *b* 23 March 1912; *s* of Joseph and Rachel Lesser; *m* 1938, Nina Lowenthal; two *d.* Solicitor of Supreme Court of Judicature; Comr for Oaths. In sole practice, 1935–82. Mem., Propeller Club of USA. *Recreations:* golf, travel, reading. *Address:* 37 Fairfax Place, Hampstead, NW6 4EJ. *T:* 071–328 2607. *Clubs:* Royal Automobile; Coombe Hill Golf.
Died 19 Oct. 1993.

LESSORE, Helen, OBE 1958; RA 1986; painter; *b* 31 Oct. 1907; *d* of Alfred Brook and Edith Berliner; *m* 1934, Frederick Lessore (*d* 1951); two *s. Educ:* Slade School of Fine Art. Began working at Beaux Arts Gallery, 1931 (founder, Frederick Lessore); director of gallery, 1952–65; full-time artist, 1965–. Exhibitions: with Marlborough

Fine Art, Helen Lessore and the Beaux Arts Gallery, 1968; 12 Duke Street, 1981; retrospective, Fine Art Soc., 1987. *Publication:* A Partial Testament, 1986. *Address:* c/o Royal Academy, Burlington House, Piccadilly, W1V 0DS. *Died 6 May 1994.*

LETSON, Maj.-Gen. Harry Farnham Germaine, CB 1946; CBE 1944; MC; ED; CD; *b* Vancouver, BC, 26 Sept. 1896; *e s* of late J. M. K. Letson, Vancouver, BC; *m* 1928, Sally Lang Nichol; no *c. Educ:* McGill Univ.; University of British Columbia; University of London. BSc (UBC) 1919; PhD (Eng) London, 1923. Active Service Canadian Army, 1916–19; Associate Professor Mechanical and Electrical Engineering, University of BC, 1923–36; on Active Service Canadian Army, 1939–46: Adjt-General Canadian Army, 1942–44; Commander of Canadian Army Staff in Washington, 1944–46; Secretary to Governor-General of Canada, 1946–52; Adviser on Militia, Canadian Army, 1954–58, retired. Hon. Colonel British Columbia Regt, 1963. LLD University of BC, 1945. *Recreation:* fishing. *Address:* 474 Lansdowne Road, Ottawa K1M 0X9, Canada. *Clubs:* Rideau (Ottawa); Vancouver (Vancouver, BC). *Died 11 April 1992.*

LEUCHARS, Sir William (Douglas), KBE 1984 (MBE (mil.) 1959); ED (2 bars); Dominion President, New Zealand Returned Services Association Inc., 1974–88; *b* 8 Aug. 1920; *s* of late James and Isabella Leuchars; *m* 1947, Mary Isbister Walter; three *s* one *d. Educ:* Scots College, NZ. New Zealand Army: Territorial Force, 1939–41; NZEF (to Captain), 1941–46; NZ Scottish Regt, Territorial Force (to Lt-Col), 1946–71; Returned Services Association: Pres., Tawa Branch, Wellington RSA, 1949–60, Life Mem., 1981; Mem. Council, Wellington RSA, 1950–57, 1967–71, Life Mem., 1981 (Mem. numerous Cttees, 1955–); Mem., Dominion Exec. Cttee, 1965–68, Dominion Vice-Pres., 1968–74; NZRSA Rep. on numerous bodies and overseas confs; Gold Star and Cert. of Merit, 1966, Gold Badge and Life Mem., 1985, NZRSA. Chm., Scots Coll. Bd of Governors, 1974–91 (Mem., 1968–); Founder Trustee, Nat. Paraplegic Trust, 1973–90; President: Wellington Regional Employers' Assoc., 1975–77, 1983–84 (Mem., 1973–); NZ Employers' Fedn, 1984–86 (Mem. Exec., 1975–87; Vice-Pres., 1975–77, 1984); Director: Tolley & Son Ltd, 1957–66 (Chm., 1963–66); Tolley Holdings Ltd, 1963–85; Tolley Industries Ltd, 1966–82; ASEA Tolley Electric Co. (subseq. ASEA Electric Co. Ltd), 1985–88; Norwich Winterthur Insurance NZ Ltd, 1977–91. *Recreation:* bowling (Patron, Tawa Services Bowling). *Address:* 45 Lohia Street, Khandallah, Wellington 4, New Zealand. *T:* 792.391. *Clubs:* various service clubs, NZ. *Died 3 Sept. 1991.*

LEUCKERT, Jean Elizabeth, (Mrs Harry Leuckert); *see* Muir, J. E.

LEVER OF MANCHESTER, Baron *cr* 1979 (Life Peer), of Cheetham in the City of Manchester; **Norman Harold Lever,** PC 1969; *b* Manchester, 15 Jan. 1914; *s* of late Bernard and Bertha Lever; *m* 1st, 1939, Ethel Sebrinski (marr. diss.); 2nd, 1945, Billie Featherman (*née* Wolfe) (*d* 1948); one *d;* 3rd, 1962, Diane, *d* of Saleh Bashi; three *d. Educ:* Manchester Grammar Sch.; Manchester Univ. Called to Bar, Middle Temple, 1935. MP (Lab) Manchester Exchange, 1945–50, Manchester, Cheetham, 1950–74, Manchester Central, 1974–79. Promoted Defamation Act, 1952, as a Private Member's Bill. Joint Parliamentary Under-Secretary, Dept of Economic Affairs, 1967; Financial Sec. to Treasury, Sept. 1967–69; Paymaster General, 1969–70; Mem., Shadow Cabinet, 1970–74; Chancellor of the Duchy of Lancaster, 1974–79. Chm., Public Accounts Cttee, 1970–73. Chairman: SDS Bank Ltd (formerly London Interstate Bank) (Sparekassen SDS),

1984–90; Stormgard, 1985–87; Pres., Authority Investments PLC, 1986–91 (Chm., 1984–86); Mem., Internat. Adv. Bd, Creditanstalt-Bankverein, 1982–90; Director: The Guardian and Manchester Evening News, 1979–90; INVESCO MIM (formerly Britannia Arrow Hldgs), 1983–92. Treasurer, Socialist International, 1971–73. Governor: LSE, 1971–; ESU, 1973–86; Trustee, Royal Opera House, 1974–82; Mem. Ct, Manchester Univ., 1975–87. Hon. Fellow, and Chm. Trustees, Royal Acad., 1981–87. Hon. doctorates in Law, Science, Literature and Technology. Grand Cross, Order of Merit, Germany, 1979. *Publication:* (jtly) Debt and Danger, 1985. *Address:* House of Lords, SW1A 0PW. *Died 6 Aug. 1995.*

LEVEY, Brigid, (Lady Levey); *see* Brophy, B. A.

LEVIS, Maj.-Gen. Derek George, CB 1972; OBE 1951; DL; retired; *b* 24 Dec. 1911; *er s* of late Dr George Levis, Lincoln; *m* 1st, 1938, Doris Constance Tall (*d* 1984); one *d;* 2nd, 1984, Charlotte Anne Nichols, *y d* of late Charles Pratt, Lincoln. *Educ:* Stowe Sch.; Trinity Coll., Cambridge; St Thomas' Hospital, London. BA Cantab 1933; MRCS, LRCP 1936; MB, BChir (Cantab), 1937; DPH 1949. Commnd into RAMC, 1936; house appts, St Thomas' Hospital, 1936–37; served in: China, 1937–39; War of 1939–45 (1939–45 Star, Pacific Star, France and Germany Star, Defence and War Medal): Malaya and Java, 1939–42; Ceylon, 1942–43; NW Europe, 1944–45; qualified as specialist in Army Health, Royal Army Med. Coll., 1949; Asst Director Army Health, HQ British Troops Egypt, 1949–51; Deputy Asst Dir Army Health, HQ British Commonwealth Forces, Korea, 1952–53 (Korean Co. Medal and UN Medal); Asst Dir Army Health: Malaya Comd, 1953–55 (Gen. Service Medal, Clasp Malaya, despatches); War Office, 1956–58; Deputy Director, Army Health, HQ, BAOR, 1958–62; Comdt Army School of Health, 1962–66; Director of Army Health, Australian Military Forces, Melbourne, 1966–68; Dep. Director Army Health, HQ Army Strategic Comd, 1968; Director of Army Health, MoD (Army), 1968–70; Dep. Dir, Medical Services, Southern Comd, 1970–71. QHP 1969–71. Col Comdt, RAMC, 1973–76. Co. Comr, St John Ambulance Brigade, Lincs, 1972–85. Mem., Faculty of Community Physicians, RCP, 1971. DL Lincs, 1976. KStJ 1983. *Publications:* contribs to Journal RAMC and Proc. Royal Society Med. *Recreations:* fishing, reading. *Address:* 27 The Green, Welbourn, Lincoln LN5 0NJ. *T:* Loveden (0400) 72673. *Died 24 May 1993.*

LEWES, John Hext, OBE 1944; Lieutenant of Dyfed, 1974–78 (Lord Lieutenant of Cardiganshire, 1956–74); *b* 16 June 1903; *s* of late Colonel John Lewes, RA, and Mrs Lewes (*née* Hext); *m* 1929, Nesta Cecil, *d* of late Captain H. Fitzroy Talbot, DSO, RN; one *s* two *d. Educ:* RN Colleges Osborne and Dartmouth. Sub-Lieut, 1923, Lieut, 1925; specialised in Torpedoes, 1928; Commander, 1939; commanded: HMS Shikari, Intrepid, 1941–42 (despatches); Ameer, 1944–45 (despatches); retired 1947, with war service rank of Captain, RN. Latterly farming. FRAgSs 1972. KStJ 1964. *Address:* Llanllyr, near Lampeter, Dyfed. *T:* Aeron (0570) 470323. *Died 14 March 1992.*

LEWIS, Sir Allen (Montgomery), GCSL 1986; GCMG 1979; GCVO 1985; Kt 1968; Governor-General of St Lucia, 1982–87 (first Governor-General, 1979–80; Governor, 1974–79); *b* 26 Oct. 1909; *s* of George Ferdinand Montgomery Lewis and Ida Louisa (*née* Barton); *m* 1936, Edna Leofrida Theobalds; three *s* two *d. Educ:* St Mary's Coll., St Lucia. LLB Hons (external) London, 1941. Admitted to practice at Bar of Royal Court, St Lucia (later Supreme Court of Windward and Leeward Islands), 1931; called to English Bar, Middle Temple,

1946; in private practice, Windward Islands, 1931–59; Acting Magistrate, St Lucia, 1940–41; Acting Puisne Judge, Windward and Leeward Islands, 1955–56; QC 1956; Judge: of Federal Supreme Court, 1959–62; of British Caribbean Court of Appeal, 1962; of Court of Appeal, Jamaica, 1962–67; Acting President, Court of Appeal, 1966; Acting Chief Justice of Jamaica, 1966; Chief Justice, West Indies Associated States Supreme Court, 1967–72; Chm., Nat. Devslt Corp., St Lucia, 1972–74. MLC, St Lucia, 1943–51; Member, Castries Town Council, 1942–56 (Chairman six times); President W Indies Senate, 1958–59. Served on numerous Government and other public cttees; Comr for reform and revision of laws of St Lucia, 1954–58; rep. St Lucia, Windward Islands, and W Indies at various Conferences. Director, St Lucia Branch, British Red Cross Society, 1955–59; President: Grenada Boy Scouts' Assoc., 1967–72; St John Council for St Lucia, 1975–80. Served as President and/or Cttee Member, cricket, football and athletic associations, St Lucia, 1936–59. Chancellor, Univ. of WI, 1975–89; Hon. LLD Univ. of WI, 1974. Chief Scout, St Lucia, 1976–80, 1984–87. Coronation Medal, 1953; Silver Jubilee Medal, 1977. KStJ 1975; KSG 1991. Order of Andres Bello, 1st cl. (Venezuela), 1986. *Publication:* revised edition of Laws of St Lucia, 1957. *Recreation:* gardening. *Address:* Beaver Lodge, The Morne, PO Box 1076, Castries, St Lucia. *T:* 27285. *Club:* St Lucia Yacht. *Died 18 Feb. 1993.*

LEWIS, Adm. Sir Andrew (Mackenzie), KCB 1971 (CB 1967); Lord-Lieutenant and Custos Rotulorum of Essex, 1978–92; Commander-in-Chief, Naval Home Command, 1972–74; Flag Aide-de-camp to the Queen, 1972–74; *b* 24 Jan. 1918; *s* of late Rev. Cyril Lewis; *m* 1st, 1943, Rachel Elizabeth Leatham (*d* 1983); two *s*; 2nd, 1989, Primrose Robinson (*née* Sadler-Phillips). *Educ:* Haileybury. Director of Plans, Admiralty, 1961–63; in command of HMS Kent, 1964–65; Director-General, Weapons (Naval), 1965–68; Flag Officer, Flotillas, Western Fleet, 1968–69; Second Sea Lord and Chief of Naval Personnel, 1970–71. DL Essex, 1975. DU Essex, 1990. KStJ 1978. *Address:* Coleman's Farm, Finchingfield, Braintree, Essex CM7 4PE. *Club:* Brooks's. *Died 8 Nov. 1993.*

LEWIS, Sir Arthur; *see* Lewis, Sir W. A.

LEWIS, David Malcolm, MA, PhD; FBA 1973; Professor of Ancient History, University of Oxford, since 1985; Student of Christ Church, Oxford, since 1956; *b* London, 7 June 1928; *s* of William and Milly Lewis; *m* 1958, Barbara, *d* of Prof. Samson Wright, MD, FRCP; four *d*. *Educ:* City of London Sch.; Corpus Christi Coll., Oxford (MA); Princeton Univ. (PhD). National Service with RAEC, 1949–51. Mem., Inst. for Advanced Study, Princeton, 1951–52, 1964–65. Student, British Sch. at Athens, 1952–54; Junior Research Fellow, Corpus Christi Coll., Oxford, 1954–55; Tutor in Ancient History, Christ Church, Oxford, 1955–85; Univ. Lectr in Greek Epigraphy, Oxford, 1956–85. Corr. Mem., German Archaeol Inst., 1985. *Publications:* (ed with John Gould) Sir Arthur Pickard-Cambridge, The Dramatic Festivals of Athens, 2nd edn 1968; (with Russell Meiggs) Greek Historical Inscriptions, 1969; Sparta and Persia, 1977; Inscriptiones Graecae I, 1981–94; (ed) Cambridge Ancient History, vol IV, 1988, vol. V, 1992, vol. VI, 1994; The Jews of Europe, 1992; articles in learned jls. *Recreations:* opera, gardening. *Address:* Christ Church, Oxford OX1 1DP. *T:* Oxford (0865) 276212.

Died 12 July 1994.

LEWIS, David Thomas, CB 1963; Hon. Professorial Fellow, Department of Chemistry, University College of Wales, Aberystwyth, 1970–78; *b* 27 March 1909; *s* of Emmanuel Lewis and Mary (*née* Thomas), Breconshire,

Wales; *m* 1st, 1934, Evelyn (*née* Smetham); one *d*; 2nd, 1959, Mary (*née* Sadler). *Educ:* Brynmawr County Sch.; University Coll. of Wales, Aberystwyth. BSc (Wales), 1st Class Hons in Chemistry, 1930; PhD (Wales), 1933; DSc (Wales), 1958. Senior Chemistry Master, Quakers' Yard Secondary Sch., 1934–38; Asst Lecturer, University Coll., Cardiff, 1938–40; various scientific posts (finishing as Principal Scientific Officer, Ministry of Supply), Armaments Research Establishment, 1941–47; Senior Superintendent of Chemistry Div., Atomic Weapons Research Establishment, Aldermaston, 1947–60; Govt Chemist, 1960–70. FRIC 1940; FRSH 1964. Dawes Memorial Lectr, 1965. Scientific Governor, British Nutrition Foundn, 1967; Member: British National Cttee for Chemistry (Royal Society), 1961–70; British Pharmacopœia Commission, 1963–73. *Publications:* Ultimate Particles of Matter, 1959; Mountain Harvest (poems), 1964; analytical research investigations in learned jls; scientific articles in encyclopædias, scientific reviews, etc. *Recreations:* writing, fishing, shooting. *Address:* Green Trees, 24 Highdown Hill Road, Emmer Green, Reading, Berks RG4 8QP. *T:* Reading (0734) 471653. *Died 1 July 1992.*

LEWIS, Gwynedd Margaret; a Recorder of the Crown Court, 1974–81; barrister-at-law; *b* 9 April 1911; *d* of late Samuel David Lewis and Margaret Emma Lewis. *Educ:* King Edward's High Sch., Birmingham; King's Coll., Univ. of London. BA. Called to Bar, Gray's Inn, 1939; Mem., Midland and Oxford Circuit; Dep. Stipendiary Magistrate for City of Birmingham, 1962–74. Legal Mem., Mental Health Review Tribunal for the W Midlands Region, 1972–83. *Recreations:* archaeology, bird-watching. *Address:* Berringtons, Burley Gate, Hereford HR1 3QS. *Died 1 Sept. 1993.*

LEWIS, Prof. Hywel David, MA, BLitt; Professor of History and Philosophy of Religion, in the University of London, 1955–77; *b* 21 May 1910; *s* of Rev. David John and Rebecca Lewis, Waenfawr, Cærnarvon; *m* 1943, Megan Elias Jones, MA (*d* 1962), *d* of J. Elias Jones, Bangor; *m* 1965, K. A. Megan Pritchard, *d* of T. O. Pritchard, Pentrefoelas. *Educ:* University Coll., Bangor; Jesus Coll., Oxford (Hon. Fellow, 1986). Lecturer in Philosophy, University Coll., Bangor, 1936; Senior Lecturer, 1947; Prof. of Philosophy, 1947–55; Fellow of King's Coll., London, 1963; Dean of the Faculty of Theology in the University of London, 1964–68; Dean of the Faculty of Arts, King's Coll., 1966–68, and Faculty of Theology, 1970–72. President: Mind Association, 1948–49; Aristotelian Soc., 1962–63; Chm. Council, Royal Inst. of Philosophy, 1965–88; Soc. for the Study of Theology, 1964–66; President: Oxford Soc. for Historical Theology, 1970–71; London Soc. for Study of Religion, 1970–72; Inst. of Religion and Theology, 1972–75; International Soc. for Metaphysics, 1974–80. Editor, Muirhead Library of Philosophy, 1947–78; Editor, Religious Studies, 1964–79; Leverhulme Fellow, 1954–55; Visiting Professor: Brynmawr Coll., Pa, USA, 1958–59; Yale, 1964–65; University of Miami, 1968; Boston Univ., 1969; Kyoto Univ., 1976; Santiniketan Univ., 1977; Surrey Univ., 1977–83; Emory Univ., 1977–81; Jadavpur Univ., 1979; Vis. Professorial Fellow, UCW Aberystwyth, 1979–84; Lectures: Robert McCahan, Presbyterian Coll., Belfast, 1960; Wilde, in Natural and Comparative Religion, Oxford, 1960–63; Edward Cadbury, Birmingham, 1962–63; Centre for the Study of World Religions, Harvard, 1963; Ker, McMaster Divinity Coll., Ont, 1964; Owen Evans, University Coll., Aberystwyth, 1964–65; Firth Meml, Nottingham, 1966; Gifford, Edinburgh, 1966–68; L. T. Hobhouse Meml, London, 1966–68; Elton, George Washington Univ., 1969; Otis Meml, Wheaton Coll., 1969; Drew, London, 1973–74; Laidlaw, Toronto, 1979. Commemoration Preacher,

University of Southampton, 1958; Commemoration Lectr, Cheshunt Coll., Cambridge, 1960, and Westminster Coll., 1964. Warden, Guild of Graduates, University of Wales, 1974–77; Mem., Advisory Council for Education (Wales), 1964–67. Mem., Gorsedd of Bards. Hon. Vice-Pres., FISP, 1984. Hon. DD St Andrews, 1964; Hon. DLit Emory Univ., USA, 1978. *Publications:* Morals and the New Theology, 1947; Morals and Revelation, 1951; (ed) Contemporary British Philosophy, Vol. III, 1956, Vol. IV, 1976; Our Experience of God, 1959; Freedom and History, 1962; (ed) Clarity is not Enough, 1962; Teach yourself the Philosophy of Religion, 1965; World Religions (with R. L. Slater), 1966; Dreaming and Experience, 1968; The Elusive Mind, 1969; The Self and Immortality, 1973; (ed) Philosophy East and West, 1975; (ed with G. R. Damodaran) The Dynamics of Education, 1975; Persons and Life after Death, 1978; Jesus in the Faith of Christians, 1980; The Elusive Self, 1982; Freedom and Alienation, 1985; *in Welsh:* Gweriniaeth, 1940; Y Wladwriaeth a'i Hawdurdod (with Dr J. A. Thomas), 1943; Ebyrth, 1943; Diogelu Diwylliant, 1945; Crist a Heddwch, 1947; Dilyn Crist, 1951; Gwybod am Dduw, 1952; Hen a Newydd, 1972; Pwy yw Iesu Grist?, 1979; Gofidiau Patsi, 1988; *festschrift:* ed S. Sutherland and T. A. Roberts, Religion, Reason and the Self, 1990; contributions to Mind, Proc. of Aristotelian Society, Philosophy, Ethics, Hibbert Jl, Philosophical Quarterly, Analysis, Efrydiau Athronyddol, Llenor, Traethodydd, etc. *Address:* 1 Normandy Park, Normandy, near Guildford, Surrey GU3 2AL. *T:* Aldershot (0252) 26673. *Died 6 April 1992.*

LEWIS, (Isaiah) Leonard; QC 1969; retired 1982; *b* 11 May 1909; *e s* of Barnet Lewis; *m* 1939, Rita Jeanette Stone; two *s* one *d*. *Educ:* Grocers' Company Sch.; St John's Coll., Cambridge (Major Schol.). Wrangler, Wright's Prizeman, MA Cantab; BSc 1st class Hons London. Called to the Bar, Middle Temple, 1932 and started to practise. Served War of 1939–45, RAF. *Address:* East Park House, Newchapel, near Lingfield, Surrey RH7 6HS. *T:* Lingfield (0342) 832114.
Died 2 Feb. 1994.

LEWIS, Joan; *see* Lancaster Lewis, J. C.

LEWIS, Maj.-Gen. Kenneth Frank Mackay, CB 1951; DSO 1944; MC 1918; retired; *b* 29 Jan. 1897; *s* of Frank Essex Lewis and Anne Florence Mackay; *m* 1930, Pamela Frank Menzies Pyne, *d* of Lt-Col C. E. Menzies Pyne; two *s*. *Educ:* privately. Commissioned 2nd Lieut Royal Highlanders and RFA, 1916; served with 9th Scottish Div., France and Belgium, 1916–18; ADC to GOC Lowland Div., 1921; ADC to GOC Upper Silesia Force, 1922; Iraq Levies, 1923–25; Adjutant, Portsmouth and IOW, 1926–29; Royal West African Frontier Force, Nigeria Regt, 1929–30; Colchester, 1930–33; India, School of Artillery, Quetta 22 Mountain Battery, 1933–37; Military Coll. of Science, UK, 1938; School of Artillery, Larkhill, 1939–41; CO 7th Survey Regt, 1942; CO 185 Field Regt, 1943; CRA 43 and 49 Divisions, 1944 and 1945 (despatches 1946); CCRA Palestine, 1947 and 1948 (despatches 1949); BRA Western Command, UK, 1948; GOC 4th Anti-Aircraft Group, 1949–50; Dir of Royal Artillery, War Office, Dec. 1950–1954; retired, 1954; Col Comdt RA, 1957. OStJ 1955. Order of Leopold, Croix de Guerre (Belgium). *Recreations:* sailing, shooting, books, music. *Address:* 18 Beverley Road, Colchester CO3 3NG. *T:* Colchester (0206) 76507. *Club:* Army and Navy.
Died 3 Jan. 1993.

LEWIS, Leonard; *see* Lewis, I. L.

LEWIS, Michael Samuel, PhD; FGS; educational consultant; *b* 18 Oct. 1937; *s* of Nicholas Samuel Japolsky and Annie Catherine (*née* Lewis; adopted Lewis as surname; *m* 1962, Susan Mary Knowles; one *s* one *d*.

Educ: St Paul's Sch., London; Balliol Coll., Oxford (BA Geology); King's Coll., London (PhD). National Service, RN rating, 1956–58. Management trng, United Steel Cos Ltd, Sheffield, 1961–62; Res. Studentship, KCL, res. into carbonate sediments of The Seychelles, 1962–65; Asst Lectr in Geol., Univ. of Glasgow, 1965–68; Gen. Service Officer, Brit. Council, 1968–75; Asst Rep., Calcutta, 1969–73; Science Officer, Benelux, 1973–75; Asst Sec., S Bank Poly., 1975–78; Asst Registrar, CNAA, 1978–80; Registrar, Oxford Poly., 1980–83; Sec., Cttee of Dirs of Polytechnics, 1983–91; Sec. and a Dir, Polys Central Admissions System, 1984–89. *Publications:* sci. papers on carbonate sedimentology and higher educn. *Recreations:* music, geology, shaping gardens. *Address:* 5 Carr Lane, Sandal, Wakefield WF2 6HJ. *T:* Wakefield (01924) 255183.
Died 6 Aug. 1994.

LEWIS, Captain Roger Curzon, DSO 1939; OBE 1944; Royal Navy, retired; *b* 19 July 1909; *s* of late F. W. and K. M. Lewis; *m* 1944, Marguerite Christiane (*d* 1971), *e d* of late Captain A. D. M. Cherry, RN, retd; two *s*. *Educ:* Royal Naval Coll., Dartmouth. HMS Lowestoft, Africa Station, 1927–29; HMS Vivien and HMS Valentine, 6th Flotilla Home Fleet, 1930–32; Qualifying Lt T 1933; HMS Enterprise, East Indies Station, 1935–37; Staff of HMS Vernon, 1938–39; HMS Florentino, 1939–40; HMS Rodney, 1940–42; Staff of Comdr-in-Chief Mediterranean, 1942–45; HMS Lioness, Sen. Officer, 11th Minesweeping Flotilla, 1945–46; Admiralty, Bath, 1946–48; HMS Seahawk, 1948–49; Superintendent of Torpedo Experimental Establishment, Greenock, 1950–53; CSO to FO, ME, 1953–55; Capt. of the Dockyard and Queen's Harbourmaster, Chatham, 1955–58; retired, 1959. *Address:* Officers' Association, Country House, Huntly, Bishopsteignton, Teignmouth, Devon TQ14 9SJ.
Died 8 Aug. 1994.

LEWIS, Sir (William) Arthur, Kt 1963; PhD; BCom (London); MA (Manchester); James S. McDonnell Distinguished University Professor of Economics and International Affairs, Princeton University, 1982–83, Emeritus since 1983; *b* 23 Jan. 1915; 4th *s* of George F. and Ida Lewis, Castries, St Lucia; *m* 1947, Gladys Jacobs; two *d*. *Educ:* St Mary's Coll., St Lucia; London Sch. of Economics. Lecturer at London Sch. of Economics, 1938–47; Reader in Colonial Economics, University of London, 1947; Stanley Jevons Prof. of Political Economy, University of Manchester, 1948–58; Principal, University Coll. of the West Indies, 1959–62; Vice-Chancellor, University of the West Indies, 1962–63; Princeton University: Prof. of Public and International Affairs, 1963–68; James Madison Prof. of Political Economy, 1968–82. Pres., Caribbean Development Bank, 1970–73. Assigned by United Nations as Economic Adviser to the Prime Minister of Ghana, 1957–58; Dep. Man. Dir, UN Special Fund, 1959–60. Temp. Principal, Board of Trade, 1943, Colonial Office, 1944; Consultant to Caribbean Commn, 1949; Mem. UN Group of Experts on Underdeveloped Countries, 1951; Part-time Mem. Board of Colonial Development Corporation, 1951–53; Mem. Departmental Cttee on National Fuel Policy, 1951–52; Consultant: to UN Economic Commission for Asia and the Far East, 1952; to Gold Coast Govt, 1953; to Govt of Western Nigeria, 1955. Mem. Council, Royal Economic Soc., 1949–58; Pres. Manchester Statistical Soc., 1955–56. Chancellor, Univ. of Guyana, 1966–73. Hon. LHD: Columbia, Boston Coll., Wooster Coll., DePaul, Brandeis; Hon. LLD: Toronto, Wales, Williams, Bristol, Dakar, Leicester, Rutgers, Brussels, Open, Atlanta, Hartford, Bard, Harvard, Howard; Hon. LittD: West Indies, Lagos, Northwestern; Hon. DSc, Manchester; Hon. DSc (Econ) London; Hon. DSocSc Yale. Corresp. Fellow, British Acad., 1974; Hon. Fellow, LSE; For. Fellow Amer. Acad. of Arts and Sciences; Mem., Amer. Phil. Soc.; Hon.

Fellow Weizmann Inst.; Distinguished Fellow, Amer. Economic Assoc., 1970 (Pres. 1983). (Jtly) Nobel Prize for Economics, 1979. *Publications:* Economic Survey, 1918–1939, 1949; Overhead Costs, 1949; The Principles of Economic Planning, 1949; The Theory of Economic Growth, 1955; Politics in West Africa, 1965; Development Planning, 1966; Reflections on the Economic Growth of Nigeria, 1968; Some Aspects of Economic Development, 1969; Tropical Development 1880–1913, 1971; The Evolution of the International Economic Order, 1977; Growth and Fluctuations 1870–1913, 1978; Racial Conflict and Economic Development, 1985; articles in technical, economic and law jls. *Address:* Woodrow Wilson School, Princeton University, Princeton, NJ 08540, USA. *Died 15 June 1991.*

LEWISON, Peter George Hornby, CBE 1977; Chairman, National Dock Labour Board, 1969–77; Member, National Ports Council, 1972–77; *b* 5 July 1911; *s* of late George and Maud Elizabeth Lewison; *m* 1937, Lyndsay Sutton Rothwell; one *s* one *d. Educ:* Dulwich; Magdalen Coll., Oxford. Dunlop Rubber Co., Coventry, 1935–41; Min. of Supply (seconded), 1941–44; RNVR (Special Br.), 1944–46; Min. of Labour, 1946–47; Personnel Manager, British-American Tobacco Co. Ltd, 1947–68, retd. *Recreations:* music, cricket, maintaining a sense of curiosity. *Address:* Court Hill House, East Dean, Chichester, Sussex PO18 0JG. *T:* Singleton (024363) 200. *Club:* MCC. *Died 30 Sept. 1992.*

LE WITT, Jan; painter, poet and designer; *b* 3 April 1907; *s* of Aaron Le Witt and Deborah (*née* Koblenz); British subject, 1947; *m* 1939, Alina Prusicka; one *s. Educ:* autodidact. Began artistic career as self-taught designer in Warsaw, 1927; first one-man exhibn of his graphic work, Soc. of Fine Arts, Warsaw, 1930; co-author and illustrator of children's books, publ. several European langs; settled in England, 1937; Member of Le Witt-Him partnership, 1933–54; in 1955 when at top of his profession, he gave up graphic design to devote himself entirely to painting. During War of 1939–45 executed (in partnership) a series of murals for war factory canteens, posters for Min. of Inf., Home Office, GPO, etc; originator of a range of Britain's World War II anti-invasion defences in 1940 that prevented the Nazis from gaining a foothold on British soil. Co-designer of murals for Festival of Britain, 1951, and Festival Clock, Battersea Park. One-man exhibn, Zwemmer Gall., London, 1947; subseq. Hanover Gall. London, 1951; in Rome, 1952; Zwemmer Gall., 1953; New York, 1954; Milan, 1957; Paris, 1960; Grosvenor Gall., London, 1961; Paris, 1963; Musée d'Antibes (retrospective), 1965; Salon d'Automne, Paris, 1963; Salon de Mai, Paris, 1964; Warsaw (retrosp.), 1967; Venice (retrosp.) (organised by City of Venice), 1970; Paris, 1972; exhibn of Haiku paintings, Fitzwilliam Mus., Cambridge, 1989. *Works at:* Musée National d'Art Moderne, Paris; Nat. Museum, Jerusalem; Nat. Museum, Warsaw; Musée d'Antibes; Museum and Art Gall., Halifax; City Art Gall., Middlesbrough; British Council; Contemp. Art Soc., London; and in private collections; represented in collective exhibns in Tate Gall., London, and many foreign galleries. Other artistic activities: décors and costumes for Sadler's Wells Ballet; glass sculptures Venice (Murano); tapestry designs, Aubusson. Gold Medal, Vienna, 1948; Gold Medal Triennale, Milan, 1954; Member: Alliance Graphique Internationale, 1948–60; Exec. Council, Société Européenne de Culture, Venice, 1961–; Nominated Member Italian Acad. (with Gold Medal), 1980; Fellow, Internat. PEN, 1978. *Publications:* Vegetabull, 1956 (London and New York); A Necklace for Andromeda, 1976; contribs to Poetry Review, Temenos, Adam, Comprendre, Malahat Review, etc; *relevant Publication:* Sir Herbert Read, Jean Cassou, Pierre Emmanuel and John Smith (jointly), Jan Le Witt,

London 1971, Paris 1972, NY 1973. *Recreations:* music, swimming against the current. *Address:* 10 Highfield Avenue, Cambridge CB4 2AL. *T:* Cambridge (0223) 311614. *Club:* PEN. *Died 21 Jan. 1991.*

LEWTHWAITE, Sir William Anthony, 3rd Bt, *cr* 1927, of Broadgate, Thwaites, Co. Cumberland; solicitor, 1937–75; *b* 26 Feb. 1912; *e s* of Sir William Lewthwaite, 2nd Bt, JP, and Beryl Mary Stopford (*d* 1970), *o c* of late Major Stopford Cosby Hickman, JP, DL, Fenloe, Co. Clare; *S* father, 1933; *m* 1936, Lois Mairi, *o c* of late Capt. Robertson Kerr Clark (brother of 1st Baron Inverchapel) and Lady Beatrice Minnie Ponsonby, *d* of 9th Earl of Drogheda (she *m* 2nd, 1st Baron Rankeillour, and *d* 1966); one *d* (and one *d* decd). *Educ:* Rugby; Trinity Coll., Cambridge, BA. Lt, Grenadier Guards, 1943–46. Mem. Council, CLA, 1949–64. Mem. Cttee, Westminster Law Society, 1964–73. *Heir: b* Brig. Rainald Gilfrid Lewthwaite, CVO, OBE, MC [*b* 21 July 1913; *m* 1936, Margaret Elizabeth Edmonds, MBE (*d* 1990); one *s* one *d* (and one *s* one *d* decd)]. *Address:* 114 Cranmer Court, SW3 3HE. *T:* 071–584 2088. *Died 25 Dec. 1993.*

LEWY, Casimir, FBA 1980; Fellow of Trinity College, Cambridge, since 1959; Reader in Philosophy, University of Cambridge, 1972–82, then Emeritus; *b* 26 Feb. 1919; *o c* of Ludwik Lewy and Izabela Lewy (*née* Rybier); *m* 1945, Eleanor Ford; three *s. Educ:* Mikolaj Rej Sch., Warsaw; Fitzwilliam House and Trinity Coll., Cambridge (BA 1939, MA 1943, PhD 1943). Stanton Student, Trinity Coll., Cambridge, 1939–41; Burney Student, Univ. of Cambridge, 1940–42; Sen. Rouse Ball Student, Trinity Coll., Cambridge, 1942–45; Lectr in Philosophy, Univ. of Liverpool, 1945–52; Univ. Lectr in Philosophy, Cambridge, 1952–72, Sidgwick Lectr, 1955–72. Visiting Professor of Philosophy: Univ. of Texas at Austin, 1967; Yale Univ., 1969. *Publications:* Meaning and Modality, 1976; *editor:* G. E. Moore, Commonplace Book 1919–1953, 1962; G. E. Moore, Lectures on Philosophy, 1966; C. D. Broad, Leibniz, 1975; C. D. Broad, Kant, 1978; C. D. Broad, Ethics, 1985; articles in philosophical jls; *relevant publication:* Exercises in Analysis: essays by students of Casimir Lewy, ed Ian Hacking, 1985. *Recreations:* reading, walking. *Address:* Trinity College, Cambridge CB2 1TQ. *T:* Cambridge (0223) 338400. *Died 8 Feb. 1991.*

LEY, Arthur Harris, FRIBA, AADip, FIStructE, MRAeS; former Partner, Ley Colbeck & Partners, Architects; *b* 24 Dec. 1903; *s* of late Algernon Sydney Richard Ley, FRIBA, and Esther Eliza Harris; *m* 1935, Ena Constance Riches (*d* 1988); one *d. Educ:* Westminster City Sch.; AA Coll. of Architecture. Architect for: Principal London Office Barclays Bank DCO; Head Office Nat. Mutual Life Assce Soc.; Palmerston Hse, EC2; Baltic Hse, EC3; Bishops House, Bishopsgate; Broad Street House; Hqrs Marine Soc.; Hqrs SBAC; Hqrs RAeS; Hqrs Instn Struct. Engrs; York Hall, Windsor Gt Park; Aircraft Research Assoc. Estab., Bedford. Factories and Office Blocks for: Vickers Ltd, at Barrow, etc; British Aircraft Corporation at Weybridge and Hurn; Wallpaper Manufrs Ltd; Sir Isaac Pitman & Sons; Decca Radar Ltd; Ever Ready Co.; Charter Consolidated, Ashford, Kent; also numerous office blocks in the City of London, Leeds, Inverness and Vancouver. Banks for: Hambro; Nat. Provincial; Barclays; Bank of Scandinavia; Head London office, Hongkong and Shanghai Bank. Central area develt, Watford and Ashford, Kent. Hospitals: Watford and Harrow. Schools: London, Hertfordshire, Barrow in Furness and Surrey. Mem. Council: Architects Registr. Coun. of UK, 1958–60; Instn Struct. Engrs, 1951–54; London Chamber of Commerce, 1955–79; Associated Owners of City Properties (Pres.), 1971–77). Consultant, Bishopsgate Foundn; Mem. Court, City Univ., to 1988; Liveryman: Worshipful Co. of Paviors

(Master, 1962), and of Upholders (Master, 1966); Hon. Liveryman, Co. of Constructors; Freeman, City of London; Sheriff 1964–65, and Mem. Court of Common Council, City of London, 1964–80; Churchwarden of St Mary-le-Bow, 1960–83. FRSA. Grand Officer of the Order of Merit (Chile). *Publications:* contributions to journals and technical press. *Address:* 14 Fox Close, off Queens Road, Weybridge, Surrey KT13 0AX. *T:* Weybridge (0932) 842701. *Clubs:* City Livery (Pres., 1968–69), Guildhall, United Wards (Pres., 1961), Bishopsgate Ward (Pres., 1966). *Died 28 Sept. 1993.*

LEY, Sir Francis (Douglas), 4th Bt *cr* 1905, of Epperstone, Nottingham; MBE 1961; TD; JP; DL; *b* 5 April 1907; *yr s* of Major Sir Gordon Ley, 2nd Bt, and 1st wife, Rhoda, *d* of Herbert Prodgers, JP, Wilts; *S* brother, 1980; *m* 1931, Violet Geraldine Johnson (*d* 1991); one *s* one *d. Educ:* Eton; Magdalene Coll., Cambridge (MA). JP 1939, DL 1957, Derbyshire. High Sheriff of Derbyshire, 1956. *Heir: s* Ian Francis Ley [*b* 12 June 1934; *m* 1957, Caroline Margaret, *d* of Major George Henry Errington, MC; one *s* one *d*]. *Address:* Pond House, Shirley, Derby DE6 3AS. *T:* Ashbourne (01335) 60327.

Died 10 May 1995.

LEYSER, Prof. Karl Joseph, TD 1963; FBA 1983; Chichele Professor of Medieval History, Oxford University, 1984–88; Fellow, All Souls College, Oxford, 1984–88; *b* 24 Oct. 1920; *s* of late Otto and Emmy Leyser; *m* 1962, Henrietta Louise Valerie Bateman; two *s* two *d. Educ:* Hindenburg Gymnasium, Düsseldorf; St Paul's School; Magdalen College, Oxford. Gibbs Scholar in History, 1946, Bryce Research Student, 1948. FRHistS 1960, FSA 1980. War service: Pioneer Corps, 1940–43 (Cpl); The Black Watch (RHR), 1943; commissioned 1944; service with 7th Bn, 51 Div., NW Europe, 1944–45 (despatches 1945) (Captain); Territorial, 1949–63, 6/7 The Black Watch and HQ 153 Bde (Major 1961). Official Fellow and Tutor in History, Magdalen Coll., Oxford, 1948–84, Senior Dean of Arts, 1951–55, Vice-Pres., 1971–72; University Lectr, 1950–65, and 1975–84 (CUF); Special Lectr, Medieval European Hist., 1965–75; Chm., Faculty of Modern Hist., 1980–82, Vice-Chm. Bd, 1985–88. Distinguished Vis. Prof. of Medieval Studies, Univ. of California, Berkeley, 1987; Vis. Prof., Harvard, 1989. Lectures: Dark Age, Univ. of Kent, 1981; Raleigh, British Acad., 1983; Collège de France, 1984; Denys Hay Seminar in Medieval and Renaissance Hist., Univ. of Edinburgh, 1986; Medieval Acad. of America, 1987 (Corresp. Fellow, 1988); Reichenau, 1988, 1990; Centre d'Etudes Supérieures de Civilisation Médiévale, 1989; Theodor-Schieder-Gedächtnisvorlesung, 1991. Governor: Magdalen Coll. Sch., Oxford, 1971–84; St Paul's Schs, 1974–. Mem. Council: Max-Planck-Inst. für Geschichte, Göttingen, 1978–91; RHistS, 1985–89; German Historical Inst., London, 1985–; Corresp. Mem., Zentral-Direktion, Monumenta Germaniae Historica, 1979–; Mem. Kuratorium, Historisches Kolleg, Munich, 1985–; Corresp. Mem., Akademie der Wissenschaften, Göttingen, 1991. *Publications:* Rule and Conflict in an Early Medieval Society: Ottonian Saxony, 1979 (trans. German 1984); Medieval Germany and its Neighbours 900–1250, 1982; Communications and Power, the European Experience 900–1200, 1992; articles in learned jls. *Address:* Manor House, Islip, Oxford. *T:* Kidlington (08675) 3177. *Club:* Athenæum. *Died 27 May 1992.*

LI, Choh-Ming, Hon. KBE 1973 (Hon. CBE 1967); Founding Vice-Chancellor, The Chinese University of Hong Kong, 1964–78; Professor Emeritus, University of California (Berkeley), since 1974; *b* 17 Feb. 1912; *s* of Kanchi Li and Mewching Tsu; *m* 1938, Sylvia Chi-wan Lu; two *s* one *d. Educ:* Univ. of California at Berkeley (MA, PhD). Prof. of Economics, Nankai and Southwest Associated and Central Univs in China, 1937–43; Mem., China's special mission to USA, Canada and UK, 1943–45; Dep. Dir-Gen., Chinese Nat. Relief and Rehabilitation Admin (CNRRA), 1945–47; China's chief deleg. to UN Relief and Rehabilitation Confs and to UN Econ. Commn for Asia and Far East, 1947–49; Chm., Board of Trustees for Rehabilitation Affairs, Nat. Govt of China, 1949–50; Expert on UN Population Commn and Statistical Commn, 1952–57; Lectr, Associate Prof., and Prof. of Business Admin, and sometime Dir of Center for Chinese Studies, Univ. of California (Berkeley), 1951–63. Mem., Soc. of Berkeley Fellows, Univ. of Calif, 1981–. Hon. Dr of Laws: Hong Kong, 1967; Michigan, 1967; Marquette, 1969; Western Ontario, 1970; Chinese Univ. of Hong Kong, 1978; Hon. Dr Social Science, Pittsburgh, 1969. Hon. Mem., Internat. Mark Twain Soc. Elise and Walter A. Haas Internat. Award, 1974, Clark Kerr Award, 1979, Univ. of Calif; Soong Foundn Hall of Fame Award, 1980. *Publications:* Economic Development of Communist China, 1959; Statistical System of Communist China, 1962; (ed) Industrial Development in Communist China, 1964; (ed) Asian Workshop on Higher Education, 1969; The First Six Years, 1963–69, 1971; The Emerging University, 1970–74, 1975; New Era Begins 1975–78, 1979; C. M. Li's Chinese Dictionary, 1980 (Hong Kong edn 1980, Shanghai edn 1981). *Recreations:* tennis, calligraphy. *Address:* 81 Northampton Avenue, Berkeley, Calif 94707, USA. *Clubs:* American, Country (Hong Kong); Century (New York); International Platform (Cleveland Heights, Ohio). *Died 21 April 1991.*

LIDBURY, Sir John (Towersey), Kt 1971; FRAeS; Vice-Chairman, Hawker Siddeley Group PLC, 1974–83 (Director, 1960; Deputy Managing Director, 1970–81; Consultant, 1983–85); *b* 25 Nov. 1912; *m* 1939, Audrey Joyce (*née* Wigzell); one *s* two *d. Educ:* Owen's Sch. Joined Hawker Aircraft Ltd, 1940; Dir, 1951, Gen. Manager, 1953, Man. Dir, 1959, Chm., 1961; Jt Man. Dir, Hawker Siddeley Aviation Ltd, 1959, Dir and Chief Exec., 1961, Dep. Chm. and Man. Dir, 1963–77; Chairman: Hawker Siddeley Dynamics Ltd, 1971–77 (Dep. Chm., 1970); High Duty Alloys Ltd, 1978–79 (Dep. Chm., 1971); Carlton Industries PLC, 1981–82 (Dir, 1978–82); Director: Hawker Siddeley International Ltd, 1963–82; Smiths Industries PLC, 1978–85; Invergordon Distillers (Hldgs) PLC, 1978–82. Dir, Hawker Siddeley Pensions Trustees Ltd, 1968–82 (Chm., 1975–82). Pres., 1969–70, Mem. Council, 1959–77, Soc. of British Aerospace Companies Ltd. Trustee, Science Museum, 1984–85. CBIM. JP Kingston-upon-Thames, 1952–62.

Died 7 Sept. 1994.

LIDDELL, (John) Robert; author; *b* 13 Oct. 1908; *e s* of late Major J. S. Liddell, CMG, DSO, and Anna Gertrude Morgan. *Educ:* Haileybury Coll.; Corpus Christi Coll., Oxford (MA, BLitt). Lecturer in Universities of Cairo and Alexandria, 1942–51, and assistant professor of English, Cairo Univ., 1951; Head of English Dept, Athens Univ., 1963–68. FRSL. Hon. DLitt Athens, 1987. *Publications: fiction:* The Almond Tree, 1938; The Last Enchantments, 1948; Unreal City, 1952; The Rivers of Babylon, 1959; An Object for a Walk, 1966; The Deep End, 1968; Stepsons, 1969; The Aunts, 1987, and other novels; *non-fiction:* A Treatise on the Novel, 1947; Aegean Greece, 1954; The Novels of I. Compton-Burnett, 1955; Byzantium and Istanbul, 1956; The Morea, 1958; The Novels of Jane Austen, 1963; Mainland Greece, 1965; Cavafy: a critical biography, 1974; The Novels of George Eliot, 1977; Elizabeth and Ivy, 1986; A Mind at Ease: Barbara Pym and her novels, 1989; Twin Spirits: Emily and Anne Brontë, 1990; *translation:* Ferdinand Fabre, The Abbé Tigrane, 1988. *Died 23 July 1992.*

LIDDIARD, Richard England, CBE 1978; non-executive Director, Lion Mark Holdings Ltd (Chairman, 1983–87); Chairman, Bart's Research Development Trust, since 1988; *b* 21 Sept. 1917; *s* of late E. S. Liddiard, MBE, and M. A. Brooke; *m* 1943, Constance Lily, *d* of late Sir William J. Rook; one *s* three *d*. *Educ:* Oundle; Worcester Coll., Oxford (MA). Lt-Col, Royal Signals, 1939–46. Chairman: C. Czarnikow Ltd, 1958–74; Czarnikow Group Ltd, 1974–83; Sugar Assoc. of London, 1960–78; British Fedn of Commodity Assocs, 1962–70, Vice-Chm., 1970–77; London Commodity Exchange, 1972–76; Mem., Cttee on Invisible Exports, 1966–70. Mem. Ct of Assts, Worshipful Co. of Haberdashers, 1958, Master 1978. FRSA. MC (Poland), 1941; Silver Jubilee Medal, 1977. *Recreation:* walking. *Address:* Oxford Lodge, 52 Parkside, Wimbledon, SW19 5NE. *T:* 081–946 3434.
Died 10 Jan. 1993.

LIGGINS, Sir Edmund (Naylor), Kt 1976; TD 1947; solicitor; *b* 21 July 1909; *s* of Arthur William and Hannah Louisa Liggins; *m* 1952, Celia Jean Lawrence (CBE 1991), *d* of William Henry and Millicent Lawrence; three *s* one *d*. *Educ:* King Henry VIII Sch., Coventry; Rydal Sch. Joined TA, 1936; commissioned 45th Bn (Royal Warwicks Regt), RE; served War: comd 399 Battery, RA, subseq. 498 LAA Battery, RA, 1942–45; subseq. commanded 853 Indep. Battery, RA, 1948–51. Consultant, Blythe Liggins, Solicitors, Coventry, Leamington Spa, Balsall Common, Kenilworth, Nuneaton and Warwick. Elected Mem. Council, Law Society, 1963, Vice-Pres., 1974–75, Pres., 1975–76 (Chm., Non-Contentious Business Cttee of Council, 1968–71; Chm., Educn and Trng Cttee, 1973–74); Chm., West Midland Legal Aid Area Cttee, 1963–64; Pres., Warwickshire Law Soc., 1969–70. Mem. Court, Univ. of Warwick, 1964–; Hon. LLD Warwick, 1988. Hon. Mem., Amer. Bar Assoc. *Recreations:* cricket, Rugby football, squash rackets, amateur theatre. *Address:* Hareway Cottage, Hareway Lane, Barford, Warwickshire CV35 8DB. *T:* Barford (0926) 624246. *Clubs:* Army and Navy, MCC, Forty; Coventry and North Warwickshire Cricket, Drapers' (Coventry). *Died 15 Dec. 1991.*

LIGHTBOWN, Sir David Lincoln, Kt 1995; MP (C) Staffordshire South East, since 1983; *b* 30 Nov. 1932; *m* 1960, Margaret Ann. Former Engrg Dir, a public limited co. in West Midlands. Member: Lichfield Dist Council, 1975–86 (Leader of Council, 1977–83); Staffs CC, 1977–85 (formerly Chm., Educn and Finance Cttees). An Assistant Govt Whip, 1986–87; a Lord Comr of HM Treasury (Govt Whip), 1987–90; Vice-Chamberlain, HM Household, 1990; Comptroller of HM Household, 1990–95. *Address:* House of Commons, SW1A 0AA. *T:* 0171–219 6241/4212. *Died 12 Dec. 1995.*

LIGHTON, Sir Christopher Robert, 8th Bt, *cr* 1791 (Ire.), of Merville, Dublin; MBE 1945; *b* 30 June 1897; *o s* of 7th Bt and Helen (*d* 1927), *d* of late James Houldsworth, Coltness, Lanarkshire; *S* father, 1929; *m* 1st, 1926, Rachel Gwendoline (marr. diss. 1953; she *d* 1991), *yr d* of late Rear-Admiral W. S. Goodridge, CIE; two *d*; 2nd, 1953, Horatia Edith (*d* 1981), *d* of A. T. Powlett, Godminster Manor, Bruton, Somerset; one *s*; 3rd, 1985, Eve, *o d* of late Rear-Adm. A. L. P. Mark-Wardlaw, and *widow* of Major Stopford Ram. *Educ:* Eton Coll.; RMC. Late The King's Royal Rifle Corps; rejoined the Army in Aug. 1939 and served War of 1939–45. *Heir: s* Thomas Hamilton Lighton [*b* 4 Nov. 1954; *m* 1990, Belinda, *d* of John Fergusson; twin *s* one *d*]. *Address:* Fairview, Dirleton, East Lothian EH39 5HG. *Died 1 Aug. 1993.*

LINCOLN, Sir Anthony (Handley), KCMG 1965 (CMG 1958); CVO 1957; HM Diplomatic Service, retired; Ambassador to Venezuela, 1964–69; *b* 2 Jan. 1911; *s* of late J. B. Lincoln, OBE; *m* 1948, Lisette Marion Summers;

no *c*. *Educ:* Mill Hill Sch.; Magdalene Coll., Cambridge (BA). Prince Consort and Gladstone Prizes, 1934. Appointed Asst Principal, Home Civil Service, 1934; subsequently transferred to Foreign Service; served in Foreign Office; on UK Delegation to Paris Peace Conf., 1946, and in Buenos Aires; Counsellor, and Head of a Dept of Foreign Office, 1950; Dep. Sec.-Gen., Council of Europe, Strasbourg, France, 1952–55; Counsellor, British Embassy, Copenhagen, 1955–58; British Ambassador to Laos, 1958–60; HM Minister to Bulgaria, 1960–63. Officer Order of Orange Nassau (Netherlands), 1950; Comdr Order of Dannebrog (Denmark), 1957. *Publication:* Some Political and Social Ideas of English Dissent, 1937. *Recreations:* country pursuits. *Clubs:* Brooks's, Reform.
Died 15 Nov. 1993.

LINCOLN, Hon. Sir Anthony (Leslie Julian), Kt 1979; **Hon. Mr Justice Lincoln;** a Judge of the High Court of Justice, Family Division, since 1979; a Judge of the Restrictive Practices Court, since 1980, President, since 1982; writer and broadcaster; *b* 7 April 1920; *s* of Samuel and Ruby Lincoln. *Educ:* Highgate; Queen's Coll., Oxford (Schol., MA). Served Somerset Light Inf. and RA, 1941–45. Called to the Bar, Lincoln's Inn, 1949; Bencher, 1976; QC 1968; Mem. Senate of Inns of Court and the Bar, 1976–80; Chm., Law Reform Cttee of Senate, 1979–81. A Recorder of the Crown Court, 1974–79. Chm., Justice Cttee on Freedom of Information, 1978; Pres., British Br., Internat. Law Assoc., 1981–. Vice-Prin., Working Men's Coll., 1965–60; Chm., Working Men's Coll. Corp., 1969–79; Chm. and Trustee, Harrison Homes for the Elderly, 1963–80 (Patron, 1980–). *Publications:* Wicked, Wicked Libels, 1972; (ed) Lord Eldon's Anecdote Book, 1960; regular contribs to Observer, Spectator and other jls. *Recreations:* fishing, swimming, walking. *Address:* Royal Courts of Justice, Strand, WC2A 2LL; Salisbury, Wilts. *Clubs:* Beefsteak, Lansdowne.
Died 12 Aug. 1991.

LINDARS, Rev. Prof. Frederick Chevallier, (Barnabas Lindars, SSF), DD; Rylands Professor of Biblical Criticism and Exegesis, University of Manchester, 1978–90 (Dean, Faculty of Theology, 1982–84), then Professor Emeritus; *b* 11 June 1923; *s* of Walter St John Lindars and Rose Lindars. *Educ:* Altrincham Grammar Sch.; St John's Coll., Cambridge (Rogerson Scholar, 1941; BA 1945 (1st Cl. Oriental Langs Tripos, Pt I, 1943; 1st Cl. Theol Tripos, Pt I, 1946, 2nd Cl. Pt II, 1947); MA 1948, BD 1961, DD 1973). Served War, 1943–45. Westcott House, Cambridge, 1946–48; deacon 1948, priest 1949; Curate of St Luke's, Pallion, Sunderland, 1948–52; joined Soc. of St Francis (Anglican religious order), taking the name of Barnabas, 1952; Asst Lectr in Divinity, Cambridge Univ., 1961–66, Lectr, 1966–78; Fellow and Dean, Jesus Coll., Cambridge, 1976–78. Proctor for Northern Univs in Convocation of York and Gen. Synod of C of E, 1980–July 1990. Lectures: T. W. Manson Meml, Manchester Univ., 1974; Ethel M. Wood, London Univ., 1983; Peake Meml, Methodist Conf., 1986. Canon Theologian (hon.), Leicester Cathedral, 1977–. Member: Studiorum Novi Testamenti Societas; Soc. for Old Testament Study (Pres., 1986). *Publications:* New Testament Apologetic, 1961, 2nd edn 1973; (ed and contrib.) Church without Walls, 1968; (ed with P. R. Ackroyd, and contrib.) Words and Meanings, 1968; Behind the Fourth Gospel, 1971 (also French edn 1974; Italian edn 1978); The Gospel of John, 1972, 2nd edn 1977; (ed with S. S. Smalley, and contrib.) Christ and Spirit in the New Testament, 1973; Jesus Son of Man, 1983; (with J. Rogerson and C. Rowland) The Study and Use of the Bible, 1988; (ed and contrib.) Law and Religion: essays on the place of the law in Israel and Early Christianity, 1988; John, 1990; The Theology of the Letter to the Hebrews, 1991; articles in Jl Theol Studies, New

Testament Studies, Vetus Testamentum, and Theol. *Recreations:* walking, music. *Address:* The Friary, Hilfield, Dorchester, Dorset DT2 7BE. *T:* Cerne Abbas (0300) 341345.   *Died 21 Oct. 1991.*

LINDLEY, Sir Arnold (Lewis George), Kt 1964; DSc; FCGI; FEng 1976; FIMechE, FIEE; Chairman, GEC, 1961–64, retired; *b* 13 Nov. 1902; *s* of George Dilnot Lindley; *m* 1st, 1927, Winifred May Cowling (*d* 1962); one *s* one *d*; 2nd, 1963, Mrs Phyllis Rand. *Educ:* Woolwich Polytechnic. Chief Engineer, British Gen. Electric Co., South Africa, 1933; Director: East Rand Engineering Co., 1943; British Gen. Electric Co., S Africa, 1945; Gen. Manager Erith Works, GEC, 1949; GEC England, 1953; Vice-Chm. 1959, Managing Dir, 1961–62, GEC. Chairman: BEAMA, 1963–64; Internat. Electrical Assoc., 1962–64; Engineering Industry Trng Bd, 1964–74; Dep. Chm., Motherwell Bridge (Holdings) Ltd, 1965–84. President, Instn of Mechanical Engineers, 1968–69; Chm., Council of Engineering Instns, 1972–73 (Vice-Chm., 1971–72); Member: Council, City Univ., 1969–78; Design Council, 1971. Appointed by Govt to advise on QE2 propulsion turbines, 1969; Associate Consultant, Thames Barrier, 1970. *Recreations:* sailing, golf. *Address:* Heathcote House, 18 Nab Lane, Shipley, W Yorks BD18 4HJ.   *Died 14 May 1995.*

LINDSAY OF BIRKER, 2nd Baron, *cr* 1945, of Low Ground, Co. Cumberland; **Michael Francis Morris Lindsay;** Professor Emeritus in School of International Service, The American University, Washington, DC; *b* 24 Feb. 1909; *e s* of 1st Baron Lindsay of Birker, CBE, LLD, and Erica Violet (*née* Storr) (*d* 1962); *S* father 1952; *m* 1941, Li Hsiao-li, *d* of Col Li Wen-chi of Lishih, Shansi; one *s* two *d*. *Educ:* Gresham's Sch., Holt; Balliol Coll., Oxford. Adult education and economic research work in S Wales, 1935–37; Tutor in Economics, Yenching Univ., Peking, 1938–41; Press Attaché, British Embassy, Chungking, 1940; served War of 1939–45, with Chinese 18th Group Army, 1942–45; Vis. Lectr at Harvard Univ., 1946–47; Lectr in Econs, University Coll., Hull, 1948–51; Sen. Fellow of the Dept of Internat. Relations, ANU, Canberra, 1951–59 (Reader in Internat. Relations, 1959); Prof. of Far Eastern Studies, Amer. Univ., Washington, 1959–74, Chm. of E Asia Programme, 1959–71. Visiting Professor: Yale Univ., 1958; Ball State Univ., Indiana, 1971–72. *Publications:* Educational Problems in Communist China, 1950; The New China, three views, 1950; China and the Cold War, 1955; Is Peaceful Coexistence Possible?, 1960; The Unknown War: North China 1937–45, 1975; Kung-ch'an-chu-i Ts' o-wu ts'ai Na-li, 1976; articles in learned journals. *Heir:* s Hon. James Francis Lindsay [*b* 29 Jan. 1945; *m* 1966, Mary Rose, *d* of W. G. Thomas]. *Address:* 6812 Delaware Street, Chevy Chase, Md 20815, USA. *T:* (301) 6564245.   *Died 13 Feb. 1994.*

LINDSAY, Kenneth Martin; *b* 16 Sept. 1897; *s* of George Michael Lindsay and Anne Theresa Parmiter; unmarried. *Educ:* St Olave's; Worcester Coll., Oxford. Served European War, HAC, 1916–18. Pres., Oxford Union, 1922–23; Leader, First Debating Visit to Amer. Univs. Barnett Research Fellow, Toynbee Hall, 1923–26; Councillor and Guardian, Stepney, 1923–26; Dir of Voluntary Migration Societies, Dominions Office, 1929–31; First Gen. Sec. Political and Economic Planning, 1931–35; MP Kilmarnock Burghs, 1933–45 (Nat. Lab 1933–43, Ind. Nat. 1943–45); MP (Ind.) Combined English Universities, 1945–50; Civil Lord of the Admiralty, 1935–37; Parliamentary Sec., Board of Education, 1937–40; Founder of Youth Service, and of CEMA (later Arts Council); Mem. Council, National Book League; a Vice-President: Educational Interchange Council (Ex-Chm.), 1968–73; Anglo-Israel Assoc. (Dir, 1962–73); Vis.

Prof. at many Amer. Univs. Vice-Pres., Feathers Clubs Assoc. Contested Oxford, Harrow and Worcester. *Publications:* Social Progress and Educational Waste; English Education, 1947; Eldorado-An Agricultural Settlement: Towards a European Parliament, 1958; European Assemblies. *Recreations:* Association Football, Oxford University, 1921–22, and Corinthians; cricket, Authentics. *Address:* Stonepound House, Hassocks, West Sussex BN6 8JG. *T:* Hassocks (07918) 4423. *Club:* Athenæum.   *Died 4 March 1991.*

LING, Maj.-Gen. Fergus Alan Humphrey, CB 1968; CBE 1964; DSO 1944; Defence Services Consultant, Institute for the Study of Conflict, since 1970; *b* 5 Aug. 1914; 3rd *s* of John Richardson and Mabel Ling; *m* 1940, Sheelah Phyllis Sarel (*d* 1990); two *s* three *d*. *Educ:* Stowe Sch.; Royal Military Coll., Sandhurst. Comd 2nd/5th Queen's, 1944; GSO 1 (Ops), GHQ, Middle East, 1945–46; British Liaison Officer, US Infantry Centre, 1948–50; Comd Regt Depot, Queen's Royal Regt, 1951; Directing Staff, Staff Coll., Camberley, 1951–53; Comd 5th Queen's, 1954–57; Asst Military Secretary, War Office, 1957–58; Comd 148 North Midland Brigade (TA), 1958–61; DAG, HQ, BAOR, 1961–65; GOC: 54 (East Anglian) Division/District, 1965–67; East Anglian District, 1967–68; Eastern District, 1968–69. Col, The Queen's Regt, 1973–77 (Dep. Col, 1969–73). Chairman: Surrey T&AVR Cttee, 1973–80; SE T&AVR Assoc., 1978–79. DL Surrey, 1970, Vice Lord-Lieutenant 1975–82. *Recreations:* cricket (Wiltshire and Sandhurst), memories, home affairs, fifteen grandchildren. *Address:* Mystole Coach House, near Canterbury CT4 7DB. *T:* Canterbury (01227) 738496.

            Died 7 May 1995.

LINTOTT, Sir Henry (John Bevis), KCMG 1957 (CMG 1948); *b* 23 Sept. 1908; *s* of late Henry John Lintott, RSA, and Edith Lunn; *m* 1st, 1934, Phyllis Hamerton (marr. diss. 1948); 2nd, 1949, Margaret Orpen; one *s* one *d*. *Educ:* Edinburgh Acad.; Edinburgh Univ.; King's Coll., Cambridge. Entered Customs and Excise Dept, 1932; Board of Trade, 1935–48; Dep. Secretary-General, OEEC, 1948–56. Dep. Under-Secretary of State, Commonwealth Relations Office, 1956–63; British High Commissioner in Canada, 1963–68. *Address:* 47 Grantchester Street, Cambridge CB3 9HZ.   *Died 5 Jan. 1995.*

LIPSCOMB, Air Vice-Marshal Frederick Elvy, CB 1958; CBE 1953; *b* 2 Sept. 1902; *s* of late Arthur Bossley Lipscomb, St Albans; *m* 1931, Dorothy May (*d* 1964), *d* of Frederick Foskett, Berkhamsted, Herts; no *c*. *Educ:* Aldenham Sch.; Middlesex Hospital. MRCS, LRCP 1927; DTM&H, 1933; DPH (London), 1934. Commnd RAF, 1927; psa 1946; served Aden, Malta, Palestine; War of 1939–45, Mediterranean and West Africa (despatches thrice); Director of Hygiene and Research, Air Ministry, 1950; Principal Medical Officer, Far East Air Force, 1951–54; Dep. Director General RAF Medical Services, 1954–55; Principal Medical Officer, Home Command, 1955–57. KHP 1952; QHP 1952–57. CStJ 1952. *Publications:* Tropical Diseases section, Conybeare's Textbook of Medicine, 6th to 9th edns; contributions to British Medical Journal, RAF Quarterly, etc. *Address:* Kilfillan House, Graemsdyke Road, Berkhamsted, Herts HP4 3LZ. *T:* Berkhamsted (0442) 862387.

            Died 19 March 1992.

LIPSON, Prof. Henry Solomon, CBE 1976; FRS 1957; Professor of Physics, University of Manchester Institute of Science and Technology, 1954–77, then Emeritus; *b* 11 March 1910; *s* of Israel Lipson and Sarah (*née* Friedland); *m* 1937, Jane Rosenthal; one *s* one *d* (and one *d* decd). *Educ:* Hawarden Grammar Sch.; Liverpool Univ. BSc 1930, MSc 1931, DSc 1939 (Liverpool); MA Cambridge, 1942; MSc Tech., Manchester, 1958; Oliver Lodge Scholar, Liverpool, 1933; Senior DSIR Grant, Manchester,

1936. Junior Scientific Officer, National Physical Lab., 1937; Asst in Crystallography, Cambridge, 1938; Head of Physics Dept, Manchester College of Technology, 1945; Dean, Faculty of Technology, Manchester Univ., 1975. President Manchester Literary and Philosophical Society, 1960–62, 1977–79. Visiting Professor of Physics: University of Calcutta, 1963–64; Technion, Haifa, 1969. *Publications:* The Interpretation of X-Ray Diffraction Photographs (with Drs Henry and Wooster), 1951; Determination of Crystal Structures (with Dr Cochran), 1953; Fourier Transforms and X-Ray Diffraction (with Prof. Taylor), 1958; Optical Transforms: Their Preparation and Application to X-ray Diffraction Problems (with Prof. Taylor), 1964; Optical Physics (with Prof. S. G. Lipson), 1968; The Great Experiments in Physics, 1968; Interpretation of X-ray Powder Diffraction Patterns (with Dr Steeple), 1970; Crystals and X-rays (with R. M. Lee), 1970; (ed) Optical Transforms, 1972; papers in Royal Society Proceedings, Acta Crystallographica, etc. *Recreations:* cryptic crosswords, D-I-Y, voluntary hospital work, grandchildren. *Address:* 22 Cranmer Road, Manchester M20 0AW. *T:* 061–445 4517.

Died 26 April 1991.

LISSMANN, Hans Werner, FRS 1954; Reader, Department of Zoology, Cambridge, 1966–77, then Emeritus, and Director, Sub-Department of Animal Behaviour, 1969–77; Fellow of Trinity College, Cambridge, since 1955; *b* 30 April 1909; *s* of Robert and Ebba Lissmann; *m* 1949, Corinne Foster-Barham; one *s. Educ:* Kargala and Hamburg. Dr rer.nat., Hamburg, 1932; MA, Cantab, 1947. Asst Director of Research, Dept of Zoology, Cambridge, 1947–55; Lecturer, 1955–66. *Address:* 9 Bulstrode Gardens, Cambridge CB3 0EN. *T:* Cambridge (01223) 356126. *Died 21 April 1995.*

LITCHFIELD, Captain John Shirley Sandys, OBE 1943; RN; *b* 27 Aug. 1903; *e s* of late Rear-Admiral F. S. Litchfield-Speer, CMG, DSO, and Cecilia Sandys; *m* 1939, Margaret, *d* of late Sir Bertram Portal, KCB, DSO, and Hon. Lady Margaret Louisa Portal; one *s* two *d. Educ:* St Aubyns, Rottingdean; RN Colleges Osborne and Dartmouth. Midshipman and Lieut in HMS Renown during Royal Cruise to India and Japan, 1921–22 and to Australia and NZ, 1927; Yangtse river gunboat, 1929–31; RN Staff Coll., 1935; comd naval armoured trains and cars, Palestine, 1936 (despatches); Staff Officer (Ops) to C-in-C Mediterranean, 1936–38; comd HMS Walker, 1939, HMS Norfolk 1943, HMS Tyne, 1946–47 and HMS Vanguard, 1951–53; Naval SO, Supreme War Council, 1939, Joint Planning Staff, 1940; SO (Ops) Western Approaches, 1941; Russian Convoys and N Africa landings, 1941–43; planning staff, Normandy ops, 1944; Combined Chiefs of Staff, Washington, 1945; National War College of US, 1947–48; Dep. Director Naval Intelligence, 1949–50; idc 1951; Director of Ops, Admiralty, 1953–54; retired 1955. CC Kent, 1955–58. MP (C) Chelsea, 1959–66. Liveryman, Vintners' Company. *Address:* Snowfield, Bearsted, Kent ME14 4DH. *Clubs:* Royal Navy Club of 1765 and 1785; Bearsted Cricket. *Died 31 May 1993.*

LITTLE, Prof. Kenneth Lindsay; Professor of African Urban Studies, Edinburgh University, 1971–78, then Emeritus; *b* 19 Sept. 1908; *e s* of late H. Muir Little, Liverpool; *m* 1st, 1939, Birte Hoeck (marr. diss.); one *s* one *d*; 2nd, 1957, Iris May Cadogan (marr. diss. 1979). *Educ:* Liverpool Coll.; Selwyn Coll., Cambridge; Trinity Coll., Cambridge (William Wyse Student). MA Cantab 1944; PhD London 1945. Lectr in Anthropology, LSE, 1946; Reader in Social Anthropology, 1950–65, Professor, 1965–71, Edinburgh Univ.; first Convenor of Centre for Centre of African Studies, Edinburgh Univ., 1962. Frazer Lectr, Cambridge Univ., 1965. Leverhulme Res. Fellow,

1974–76. Vis. Prof., 1949–74, at Univs of New York, California, Washington, North Western, Fisk, Ghana and Khartoum. Chm., Adv. Cttee on Race Relations Research (Home Office), 1968–70. Pres., Sociology Section, British Assoc., 1968. Gen. Editor, CUP series Urbanization in Developing Countries, 1973–80. Hon. DCL Univ. of Sierra Leone, 1982. *Publications:* Negroes in Britain, 1948 (rev. edn, 1972); Behind the Colour Bar, 1950; The Mende of Sierra Leone, 1951 (rev. edn, 1967); Race and Society, 1952; West African Urbanization, 1967; African Women in Towns, 1973; Urbanization as a Social Process, 1974; The Sociology of Urban Women's Image in African Literature, 1980. *Recreations:* Mozart piano concertos, West African drumming and dancing. *Club:* Edinburgh University Staff. *Died 28 Feb. 1991.*

LITTLEWOOD, Barbara, (Lady Littlewood); Consultant with Barlows, Solicitors, of Guildford; *b* 7 Feb. 1909; *d* of Dr Percival Langdon-Down, Teddington; *m* 1934, Sir Sydney Littlewood (*d* 1967); one *s. Educ:* Summerleigh Sch., Teddington; King's Coll., London, (BSc). Admitted solicitor, 1936. Pres. West Surrey Law Soc., 1952–53; Mem. Home Office Departmental Committees on: the Summary Trial of Minor Offences, 1954–55; Matrimonial Proceedings in Magistrates' Courts, 1958–59; Financial Limits prescribed for Maintenance Orders made in Magistrates' Courts, 1966–68. Pres., Nat. Fedn of Business and Professional Women's Clubs of Gt Brit. and N Ire., 1958–60; Pres. Internat. Fedn of Business and Professional Women, 1965–68; Lay Member, Press Council, 1968–74. JP Middx, 1950–. *Recreation:* occasional golf. *Address:* 26 St Margarets, London Road, Guildford, Surrey GU1 1TT. *T:* Guildford (01483) 504348.

Died 17 Oct. 1995.

LIVINGSTON, James Barrett, CBE 1972; DSC 1942; formerly Consultant, Rockware Group Ltd (Director, retired 1970), Director, Rockware Glass Ltd, 1947–72 (Joint Managing Director, 1951–60; Managing Director, 1960–69; Vice-Chairman, 1967–69); *b* 13 Sept. 1906; *yr s* of late Capt. David Liddle Livingston and Ruth Livingston, Bombay and Aberdour; *m* 1933, Joyce Eileen (*d* 1987), fourth *d* of late Arthur and Lilian Birkett, Clements Inn and Southwold; one *s. Educ:* HMS Worcester. Served War of 1939–45, RN: Staff Officer (Ops) 10th Cruiser Sqdn, Norwegian Campaign, North Russian and Malta Convoys (despatches 1943); Ops Div. Admiralty, 1943–45 (Comdr). Joined Rockware Group of Cos, 1945; Exec. Director, British Hartford-Fairmont Ltd, 1947–50. Director: Portland Glass Co. Ltd, 1956–69; Jackson Bros (Knottingley) Ltd, 1968–69 (Chm.); Burwell, Reed & Kinghorn Ltd, 1962–71; Blewis & Shaw (Plastics) Ltd, 1960–70; Automotated Inspection Machinery Ltd, 1962–69; Garston Bottle Co. Ltd, 1966–69 (Chm.); Forsters Glass Co. Ltd, 1967–69; also other Glass and Associated Companies. Member: Bd of Govs, Charing Cross Hospital, 1956–73 (Chm., Medical School Council, 1967–73); Council, Glass Manufacturers' Fedn, 1967 (Pres. 1970–71); Nat. Cttee, Assoc. of Glass Container Manufacturers, 1959–69 (Vice-Pres.); Nat. Jt Industrial Council, 1959–69; Court of Ironmongers' Co., 1946 (Master, 1960–61); Adv. Cttee to Faculty of Materials Technology, Sheffield University, 1969–71; Council, CBI, 1970–71; Furniture Develt Council, 1972; Council, Royal College of Art, 1970–71. *Recreations:* golf, racket re-strings, gardening. *Address:* (home) Ferroners, Beaconsfield, Bucks HP9 1PB. *T:* Beaconsfield (0494) 673853. *Died 12 Feb. 1991.*

LIVINGSTONE, James, CMG 1968; OBE 1951; British Council Service, retired; *b* 4 April 1912; *e s* of late Angus Cook Livingstone, sometime Provost of Bo'ness, Scotland, and Mrs Jean Fraser Aitken Wilson Livingstone; *m* 1945, Dr Mair Eleri Morgan Thomas, MB ChB, BSc, DPH,

FRCPath, *e d* of late John Thomas, DSc, Harlech and Mrs O. M. Thomas, Llanddewi Brefi and Wilmslow; one *d* (one *s* decd). *Educ:* Bo'ness Acad.; Edinburgh Univ.; Moray House Trng Coll., Edinburgh. Adult Educn and School Posts, Scotland and Egypt, 1936–42; British Coun. Service, Egypt and Iran, 1942–45; Middle East Dept, 1945–46; Asst Rep., Palestine, 1946–48; Dep. Dir, 1949, Dir, 1956, Personnel Dept; Controller: Establishments Div., 1962; Overseas A Div. (Middle East and Africa), 1969–72. Mem. Council, British Inst. of Persian Studies, 1977–88 (Hon. Treasurer, 1977–82). *Recreations:* photography, exploring the West Highlands and Islands. *Address:* 21 Park Avenue, NW11 7SL. *T:* 081–455 7600; Tan yr Allt, Llangeitho, Dyfed. *Clubs:* Commonwealth Trust, Travellers'. *Died 4 Oct. 1991.*

LLEWELLYN, Sir David (Treharne), Kt 1960; Captain, late Welsh Guards; journalist; *b* Aberdare, 17 Jan. 1916; 3rd *s* of Sir David Richard Llewellyn, 1st Bt, LLD, JP, and Magdalene Anne (*d* 1966), *yr d* of late Rev. Henry Harries, DD, Porthcawl; *m* Joan Anne Williams, OBE, 2nd *d* of R. H. Williams, Bonvilston House, Bonvilston, near Cardiff; two *s* one *d*. *Educ:* Eton; Trinity Coll., Cambridge. BA 1938; MA 1979. Served War of 1939–45: enlisted Royal Fusiliers, serving in ranks; commissioned Welsh Guards; North-West Europe, 1944–45. Contested (C) Aberavon Div. of Glamorgan, 1945. MP (C) Cardiff, North, 1950–Sept. 1959; Parliamentary Under-Sec. of State, Home Office, 1951–52 (resigned, ill-health). *Publications:* Nye: The Beloved Patrician, 1961; The Adventures of Arthur Artfully, 1974; Book of Racing Quotations, 1988. *Address:* Yattendon, Newbury, Berks. *Died 9 Aug. 1992.*

LLEWELLYN, Rev. John Francis Morgan, LVO 1982; MA; Chaplain at the Chapel Royal of St Peter ad Vincula within HM Tower of London, 1974–89; *b* 4 June 1921; *s* of late Canon D. L. J. Llewellyn; *m* 1955, Audrey Eileen (*née* Binks). *Educ:* King's College Sch., Wimbledon; Pembroke Coll., Cambridge (MA); Ely Theological Coll. Served War, 1941–45, in Royal Welch Fusiliers and in India (Captain). Deacon, 1949; priest, 1950; Curate of Eltham, 1949–52; Chaplain and Asst Master, King's College Sch., Wimbledon, 1952–58; Headmaster, Cathedral Choir Sch., and Minor Canon of St Paul's Cathedral, 1958–74; Sacrist and Warden of College of Minor Canons, 1968–74; Dep. Priest-in-Ordinary to the Queen, 1968–70, 1974–91; Priest-in-Ordinary, 1970–74; Asst Master, Dulwich Coll. Prep. Sch., 1974–86. ChStJ (Sub-Chaplain, 1970–74, Officiating Chaplain, 1974–95); Chaplain: City Solicitors' Co., 1975–91; Builders' Merchants' Co., 1986–91. Freeman, City of London, 1981. *Publications:* (contrib.) The Tower of London: Its Buildings and Institutions, 1978; The Chapel Royal in the Tower, 1987. *Recreations:* golf, fishing. *Address:* The Gate House, Ouseley Lodge, Ouseley Road, Old Windsor, Berks SL4 2SQ. *T:* Windsor (01753) 855681. *Club:* Hawks (Cambridge). *Died 28 June 1995.*

LLEWELLYN, Lt-Col Sir Michael (Rowland Godfrey), 2nd Bt *cr* 1959, of Baglan, Co. Glamorgan; JP; Lord-Lieutenant of West Glamorgan, since 1987 (Vice Lord-Lieutenant, 1985–87); *b* 15 June 1921; *s* of Sir (Robert) Godfrey Llewellyn, 1st Bt, CB, CBE, MC, TD, JP, DL, and Frances Doris (*d* 1969), *d* of Rowland S. Kennard; *S* father, 1986; *m* 1st, 1946, Bronwen Mary (marr. diss. 1951), *d* of Sir (Owen) Watkin Williams-Wynn, 8th Bt; 2nd, 1956, Janet Prudence Edmondes; three *d*. *Educ:* Harrow. Commissioned Grenadier Guards, 1941; served Italian campaign, 1943–44; retired from Army, 1949; Comd 1st Bn Glamorgan Army Cadet Force, 1951–59. Director of companies, 1949–; Gen. Comr of Income Tax, 1965–. Pres., Gower Cons. Assoc., 1967–85; Chm., W Wales Gp of Cons Assocs, 1975–78; Chm., 1978–83,

Pres., 1983–85, Mid and W Wales Cons. European Assoc. Chm., 1967–79, Vice-Pres., 1979–87, Pres., 1987–, St John Council for W Glamorgan. President: W Glamorgan SSAFA, 1987–; W Glamorgan County Scout Council, 1987–; Swansea Br., Royal British Legion, 1987–; TA&VRA for Wales, 1990–; W Glamorgan Magistrates' Assoc., 1988–. KStJ 1991. High Sheriff of W Glamorgan, 1980–81, DL 1982; JP Swansea, 1984. *Recreations:* shooting, gardening. *Heir:* none. *Address:* Glebe House, Penmaen, Swansea, West Glamorgan SA3 2HH. *T:* Penmaen (0792) 371232. *Clubs:* Cardiff and County (Cardiff); Bristol Channel Yacht. *Died 8 Sept. 1994 (ext).*

LLOYD OF HAMPSTEAD, Baron *cr* 1965 (Life Peer), of Hampstead in the London Bor. of Camden; **Dennis Lloyd,** QC 1975; Quain Professor of Jurisprudence in the University of London (University College), 1956–82, then Emeritus; Hon. Research Fellow, University College London, since 1982; *b* 22 Oct. 1915; 2nd *s* of Isaac and Betty Lloyd; *m* 1940, Ruth Emma Cecilia Tulla; two *d*. *Educ:* University Coll. Sch.; University Coll., London; Gonville and Caius Coll., Cambridge. LLB (London) 1935; BA 1937, MA 1941, LLD 1956 (Cantab). Called to the Bar, Inner Temple, 1936; Yorke Prize, 1938; in practice in London, 1937–39 and 1946–82. Served War of 1939–45 in RA and RAOC, Liaison Officer (DADOS) with Free French Forces in Syria and Lebanon, 1944–45. Reader in English Law, University Coll., London, 1947–56; Fellow of University Coll., London; Dean of Faculty of Laws, University of London, 1962–64; Head of Dept of Law, University Coll., 1969–82. Hon. Fellow, Ritsumeikan Univ., Kyoto, Japan, 1978. Member: Law Reform Cttee, 1961–82; Consolidation Bills Cttee, 1965–77; European Communities Cttee, 1973–79, 1984–90, 1991–; Joint Cttee on Theatre Censorship; Joint Cttee on Broadcasting, 1976–81; Select Cttee on Bill of Rights; Interim Action Cttee on Film Industry, 1976–85; Conseil de la Fédération Britannique de l'Alliance Française, 1970–78; Council, BAFTA, 1985–86; British Screen Adv. Council, 1985–; Council, Anglo-Jewish Assoc., 1989–; Chairman: Nat. Film Sch. Cttee; Planning for Nat. Film Sch.; Governors, Nat. Film School, 1970–88 (Hon. Pres., 1988–); British Film Inst., 1973–76 (Governor, 1968–76); Brighton and Hove Arts Trust, 1989–. Pres., Bentham Club (University Coll. London), 1983; Chm. Council, University Coll. Sch., 1971–79. Hon. LLD Ritsumeikan Univ., Kyoto, Japan, 1986. *Publications:* Unincorporated Associations, 1938; Rent Control, 1949, 2nd edition, 1955; Public Policy: A Comparative Study in English and French Law, 1953; United Kingdom: Development of its Laws and Constitution, 1955; Business Lettings, 1956; Introduction to Jurisprudence, 1959, 5th edn 1985; The Idea of Law, 1964, 10 rev. imps, 1968–91, Japanese trans., 1969, Spanish trans., 1987; Law (Concept Series), 1968; contrib. to periodicals. *Recreations:* painting, listening to music, modern Greek. *Address:* House of Lords, SW1A 0PW. *Clubs:* Athenæum, Royal Automobile, PEN (Hon. Life Mem.). *Died 31 Dec. 1992.*

LLOYD OF KILGERRAN, Baron *cr* 1973 (Life Peer), of Llanwenog, Cardigan; **Rhys Gerran Lloyd,** CBE 1953; QC 1961; JP; barrister-at-law; *b* 12 Aug. 1907; *s* of late J. G. Lloyd, Kilgerran, Pembrokeshire; *m* 1940, Phyllis, *d* of late Ronald Shepherd, JP, Hants; two *d*. *Educ:* Sloane Sch.; Selwyn Coll., Cambridge (science scholar). MA Cantab; BSc London. Called to the Bar, Gray's Inn, 1939, *ad eundem* Middle Temple, 1954. Wartime service in scientific research departments, 1939–46. Sec. (part time), Royal Commn on Awards to Inventors, 1946–51. Contested (L) Anglesey, General Election, 1959. In practice at Patent Bar, 1939–68. Director: Strayfield International Ltd; Morgan Marine Ltd; Bracondale Properties Ltd. Chairman: Education Trust; Brantwood

(John Ruskin) Trust. Mem., Sainsbury Cttee on NHS, 1965–67. Vice-Chairman: Victoria League, 1975; House of Lords Select Cttee on Science and Technology, 1980–85; European Communities Cttee, 1975–81; Parly Cttee on Information Technology, 1979–; Dep. Chm., Parly Cttee on Energy, 1980–; Hon. Treas., House of Lords Defence Gp, 1982–; Vice Pres., Parly and Scientific Cttee, 1984–89. Pres., Welsh Liberal Party, 1971–74; Pres., UK Liberal Party, 1973–74, Jt Treas., 1977–83; Liberal Whip, and delegate, Council of Europe and WEU, 1973–75. Vice-Chm., CPA, 1985. President: Inst. of Patentees and Inventors, 1975–; Mobile Radio Users Assoc., 1986–; Industrial Copyright Reform Assoc., 1986–; Chm., Foundn of Science and Technology, 1983 (Pres., 1990–). Hon. Fellow, Selwyn Coll., Cambridge, 1967–. JP Surrey, 1954. *Publications:* Kerly on Trade Marks, 8th edn, 1960; Halsbury's Trade Marks and Designs, 3rd edn, 1962. *Address:* 15 Haymeads Drive, Esher, Surrey. *Clubs:* Reform, Commonwealth Trust, City Livery, National Liberal. *Died 30 Jan. 1991.*

LLOYD, Prof. Antony Charles, FBA 1993; Professor of Philosophy, Liverpool University, 1957–83, then Emeritus; *b* 15 July 1916; *s* of Charles Mostyn Lloyd and Theodosia Harrison-Rowson. *Educ:* Shrewsbury Sch.; Balliol Coll., Oxford. Asst to Prof. of Logic and Metaphysics, Edinburgh Univ., 1938–39 and 1945; served in Army, 1940–45; Lecturer in Philosophy, St Andrews Univ., 1946–57. Visiting Professor: Kansas Univ., 1967; Berkeley, Calif, 1982. *Publications:* Form and Universal in Aristotle, 1981; Anatomy of Neoplatonism, 1990; chapters in Cambridge History of Later Ancient Philosophy, 1967. *Address:* 11 Palmeira Court, 25–28 Palmeira Square, Hove, E Sussex BN3 2JP.
Died 17 Dec. 1994.

LLOYD, Glyn, CBE 1979; retired; Executive Member, Union of Construction, Allied Trades and Technicians, 1953–84; *b* 20 June 1919; *s* of William and Elizabeth Lloyd; *m* 1949, Olwen Howel; one *s. Educ:* Melyn Elementary School; Cwrt Sart Central School. Member: Joint Council, Nat. Joint Council, CBI, 1958 (Vice-Chm., 1970; Chm., Conciliation Panel, 1968); Gen. Council, TUC, 1973–83; Health and Safety Commn, 1974–84; Governing Body, ILO, 1977–84. *Recreations:* reading, sport. *Address:* 25 Furzeland Drive, Bryncoch, Neath, West Glam. *T:* Neath (0639) 642084. *Club:* Brynhyfryd Bowling (Neath). *Died 21 Jan. 1991.*

LLOYD, Maj.-Gen. Richard Eyre, CB 1959; CBE 1957 (OBE 1944); DSO 1945; late Royal Engineers, retired Sept. 1962; Arms Control and Disarmament Research Unit, Foreign and Commonwealth Office, 1966–73; *b* 7 Dec. 1906; *s* of late Lieut-Colonel W. E. Eyre Lloyd; *m* 1939, Gillian, *d* of late Rear-Adm. J. F. C. Patterson, OBE; one *s* two *d. Educ:* Eton; Pembroke Coll. (Cambridge). 2nd Lieut in Royal Engineers, 1927. Served War of 1939–45 on Staff, also with RE in North West Europe; Lieut-Colonel 1942; Colonel, 1951; Brigadier, 1955; Maj.-Gen., 1957. Chief of Staff, Middle East Land Forces, 1957–59; Director of Military Intelligence, 1959–62. Colonel Comdt, Intelligence Corps, 1964–69. *Recreation:* sailing. *Address:* Snooks Farm House, Walhampton, Lymington, Hants SO41 5SF. *T:* Lymington (0590) 673569. *Died 10 April 1991.*

LLOYD JONES, David Elwyn, MC 1946; Under-Secretary, Department of Education and Science, 1969–80; *b* 20 Oct. 1920; *s* of late Daniel and Blodwen Lloyd Jones; *m* 1955, Mrs Elizabeth W. Gallie, *d* of late Prof. Robert Peers, CBE, MC and Mrs F. D. G. Peers, and *widow of* Ian Gallie; no *c* (one step *s*). *Educ:* Ardwyn Grammar Sch., Aberystwyth; University College of Wales, Aberystwyth (BA Hons). War Service, 1941–46, Indian Army: with 1st Bn, The Assam Regt, in Burma Campaign

(Major, MC). Entered Ministry of Education, 1947; Principal Private Sec. to Chancellor of the Duchy of Lancaster, 1960–61; Asst Sec., Min. (later Dept) of Educn and Science, 1961–69. Mem., councils of Royal Acad. of Dancing, 1980–, Froebel Inst., 1980–, and RCM, 1981–. Hon. Sec., Assam Regt Assoc., 1948–. FRCM 1988. *Address:* 5 Playfair Mansions, Queen's Club Gardens, W14 9TR. *T:* 071–385 0586. *Clubs:* Commonwealth Trust, MCC, Roehampton. *Died 8 July 1991.*

LO, Kenneth Hsiao Chien; author, Chinese food critic and consultant; *b* 12 Sept. 1913; *s* of Lo Tsung Hsien and Wei Ying; *m* 1954, Anne Phillipe Brown; two *s* two *d. Educ:* Yenching Univ., Peking (BA); Cambridge Univ. (MA). Student-Consul for China, Liverpool, 1942–46; Vice-Consul for China, Manchester, 1946–49. Man. Director, Cathay Arts Ltd (Chinese Fine Art Publishers), 1951–66; Founder Director: Memories of China restaurant, 1980; Ken Lo's Kitchen, Chinese cookery sch., 1980. Chm., Chinese Gourmet Club, London, 1975–. *Publications include:* Chinese Food, 1972; Peking Cooking, 1973; Chinese Vegetarian Cooking, 1974; Encyclopedia of Chinese Cookery, 1975; Quick and Easy Chinese Cooking, 1973; Cheap Chow, 1977; Love of Chinese Cooking, 1977; Chinese Provincial Cooking, 1979; Chinese Eating and Cooking for Health, 1979; Wok Cookbook, 1981; Chinese Regional Cooking, 1981; The Feast of My Life (autobiog.), 1993; Classic Chinese Cooking, 1993. *Recreation:* tennis (Davis cup for China, 1946; Veteran Doubles Champion of Britain, 1976, 1979, 1981, 1982, 1984; Single for UK in Britannia Cup and Crawford Cup (World Super-Veteran Championships), 1981, 1983, 1984, 1985, 1986). *Address:* 60 Sussex Street, SW1 4RG. *Clubs:* Hurlingham, Queen's. *Died 11 Aug. 1995.*

LOBB, Howard Leslie Vicars, CBE 1952; FRIBA, AIStructE, FRSA; architect; *b* 9 March 1909; *e s* of late Hedley Vicars Lobb and Mary Blanche (*née* Luscombe); *m* 1949, Charmian Isobel (*née* Reilly); three *s. Educ:* privately; Regent Street Polytechnic School of Architecture. Senior Partner, Howard Lobb Partnership, 1950–74. During War of 1939–45, Architect to various ministries: subseq. built numerous schools for County Authorities; HQ of City and Guilds of London Inst., W1; British Pavilion, Brussels International Exhibition, 1958; Cons. Architect for Hunterston Nuclear Power Station, Ayrshire; Dungeness Nuclear Power Station; Newcastle Racecourse; Newmarket Rowley Mile, for Jockey Club; Car park, Savile Row, for City of Westminster; HQ for British Council, SW1; Calgary Exhbn and Stampede, Upper Alberta, Canada. Chairman Architectural Council, Festival of Britain, and later Controller (Constr.) South Bank Exhibition. Member RIBA Council and Executive, 1953–56; Life Vice-Pres. (formerly Chm.), London Group of Building Centres; Chm., Architects' Registr. Council, UK, 1957–60; Vice-Pres., Architects' Benevolent Society, 1980– (Hon. Sec., 1953–80). Freeman of City of London; Master, Worshipful Co. of Masons, 1974–75. Chm., Solent Protection Soc. *Publications:* contrib. various arch. journals, reviews, etc. *Recreations:* sailing, gardening, colour photography, model railways. *Address:* Shallows Cottage, Pilley Hill, Pilley, near Lymington, Hants SO41 5QF. *T:* Lymington (0590) 677595. *Clubs:* Royal Corinthian Yacht (Vice-Cdre, 1960–63); Tamesis (Teddington) (Cdre, 1954–57); Royal Lymington Yacht.
Died 18 Nov. 1992.

LOCH, 4th Baron *cr* 1895, of Drylaw; **Spencer Douglas Loch,** MC 1945; *b* 12 Aug. 1920; *s* of Maj.-Gen. 2nd Baron Loch, CB, CMG, DSO, MVO, and Lady Margaret Compton (*d* 1970), *o d* of 5th Marquess of Northampton, KG; *S brother,* 1982; *m* 1st, 1948, Hon. Rachel (*d* 1976), *yr d* of Gp Captain H. L. Cooper, AFC, and Baroness Lucas of Crudwell (9th in line) and Dingwall; one *d* (two *s* decd); 2nd, 1979, Davina Julia Boughey, *d* of late Fitzherbert Wright and of Hon. Mrs (Doreen Julia) Wright (*d* of 8th Viscount Powerscourt), and *widow* of Sir Richard Boughey, 10th Bt. *Educ:* Wellington College; Trinity College, Cambridge. Served as Major, Grenadier Guards, 1940–46. Called to the Bar, Lincoln's Inn, 1948. *Heir:* none. *Address:* Bratton House, Westbury, Wilts; Lochluichart, Ross-shire. *Clubs:* Cavalry and Guards, Beefsteak. *Died 24 June 1991 (ext).*

LOCKHART, John Macgregor B.; *see* Bruce Lockhart.

LOCKWOOD, Sir Joseph (Flawith), Kt 1960; Chairman, Royal Ballet, 1971–85; *b* 14 Nov. 1904; *s* of Joseph Agnew and Mabel Lockwood. Manager of flour mills in Chile, 1924–28; Technical Manager of Etablissements, Henry Simon Ltd, in Paris and Brussels, 1928–33, Director, 1933; Dir Henry Simon Ltd, Buenos Aires, Chm. Henry Simon (Australia) Ltd, Dir Henry Simon (Engineering Works) Ltd, etc, 1945, Chm. and Managing Dir, Henry Simon Ltd, 1950; Dir, NRDC, 1951–67; Chm., IRC, 1969–71 (Mem., 1966–71); Chm., EMI Ltd and subsidiaries, 1954–74 (Dir, 1954–79); Director: Smiths Industries Ltd, 1959–79; Hawker Siddeley Group, 1963–77; British Domestic Appliances Ltd, 1966–71 (Chm., 1966–70); The Beecham Group, 1966–75; Laird Group Ltd, 1970–84. Member: Engineering Advisory Council, Board of Trade, 1959; Export Council for Europe, 1961–63; Export Credits Guarantee Adv. Council, 1963–67; Council, Imperial Soc. of Knights Bach. Director: Sandown Park Ltd, 1969–83; Epsom Grandstand Assoc. Ltd, 1969–83; United Racecourses Ltd, 1969–83. Hon. Treasurer British Empire Cancer Campaign, 1962–67; Chairman: Royal Ballet Sch. Endowment Fund and Governors, Royal Ballet Sch., 1960–78; Young Vic Theatre Company, 1974–75; South Bank Theatre Bd, 1977–84 (Mem., 1968–85); Vice-Pres., Central Sch. of Speech and Drama (Chm., Governors, 1965–68); Mem., Arts Council, 1967–70. CompIEE. *Publications:* Provender Milling—the Manufacture of Feeding Stuffs for Livestock, 1939; Flour Milling (trans. into various languages), 1945. *Address:* c/o National Westminster Bank, Southwell, Notts. *Died 6 March 1991.*

LODGE, Thomas Cecil S.; *see* Skeffington-Lodge.

LOEHNIS, Sir Clive, KCMG 1962 (CMG 1950); Commander Royal Navy (retired); *b* 24 Aug. 1902; *s* of H. W. Loehnis, Barrister-at-Law, Inner Temple; *m* 1929, Rosemary Beryl, *d* of late Major Hon. R. N. Dudley Ryder, 8th Hussars; one *s* one *d*. *Educ:* Royal Naval Colls, Osborne, Dartmouth and Greenwich. Midshipman, 1920; Lt, 1924; qualified in signal duties, 1928; Lt-Comdr, 1932; retired, 1935; re-employed in Signal Div. Admiralty, 1938; Comdr on retd List, 1942; Naval Intelligence Div., 1942; demobilised and entered Foreign Office, 1945; Dep. Dir, Government Communications Headquarters, 1952–60; Dir, Government Communications HQ, 1960–64. Dep. Chm., Civil Service Selection Bd, 1967–70. AMIEE 1935. *Address:* 12 Eaton Place, SW1X 8AD. *T:* 071–235 6803. *Club:* MCC. *Died 23 May 1992.*

LOGAN, James, OBE 1988; CChem; Director, Scotland The What? Revue Company, since 1970; *b* 28 Oct. 1927; *s* of John and Jean Logan; *m* 1959, Anne Brand, singer; one *s* one *d*. *Educ:* Robert Gordon's Inst., Aberdeen. MRIC. Member, Sen. Scientific Staff, Macaulay Inst. for Soil Research, 1949–81. Chm., Voluntary Service Aberdeen, 1989–91. Member: Arts Council of Great Britain, 1984–88; Scottish Arts Council, 1983–88 (Vice-Chm., 1984–88); Founder/Chm., Friends of Aberdeen Art Gallery and Museums, 1975–77. Queen's Jubilee Medal, 1977. *Recreation:* theatre. *Address:* 53 Fountainhall Road, Aberdeen AB2 4EU. *T:* Aberdeen (0224) 646914. *Died 28 Nov. 1993.*

LONGCROFT, James George Stoddart, FCA; FInstPet; Managing Director, Tournesol Ltd, Bermuda, since 1984; Senior Partner, Longcrofts, Chartered Accountants, since 1969; *b* 25 Oct. 1929; *s* of Reginald Stoddart Longcroft and Annie Mary Longcroft (*née* Thompson); *m* 1963, Valerie Sylvia (*née* Ward); three *s* one *d*; *m* 1993, Anita (*née* Self); two *s*. *Educ:* Wellington Coll., Crowthorne, Berks. FBIM. Partner, Longcrofts, Chartered Accountants, 1955; Director 1964, Managing Director 1969, Chairman, 1980–88, Tricentrol plc. Master, Worshipful Company of Founders, 1978; Mem., Honourable Artillery Co., 1957–. FRSA 1985. *Recreations:* skiing, tennis. *Address:* c/o Longcroft House, Victoria Avenue, Bishopsgate, EC2M 4NS. *Club:* City of London. *Died 13 Jan. 1994.*

LONGLAND, Cedric James, LVO 1949; Surgeon, Glasgow Royal Infirmary, 1954–77; *b* 30 Sept. 1914; *s* of Frank Longland; *m* 1945, Helen Mary Cripps; three *d*. *Educ:* Monkton Combe Sch. MB, BS (Hons in Medicine) London, 1937; FRCS 1939; MS London, 1949. House Surgeon and Demonstrator of Pathology, St Bartholomew's Hosp.; served 1 Airborne Division; Lieut RAMC 1942, Temp. Major, RAMC, 1943; SMO Bermuda Command, 1945; First Assistant, Surgical Professorial Unit, St Bartholomew's Hospital, 1947; Assistant Surgical Professorial Unit, University College Hospital, 1951. Bronze Cross (Holland), 1945. *Publications:* articles in Lancet and British Journal of Surgery. *Address:* Malmesbury Lodge, Grittleton, near Chippenham, Wiltshire SN14 6AW. *T:* Castle Combe (0249) 782624. *Died 14 Jan. 1991.*

LONGLAND, Sir John Laurence, (Sir Jack), Kt 1970; Director of Education, Derbyshire, 1949–70; *b* 26 June 1905; *e s* of late Rev. E. H. Longland and Emily, *e d* of Sir James Crockett; *m* 1934, Margaret Lowrey (*d* 1992), *y d* of late Arthur Harrison, Elvet Garth, Durham; one *s* two *d* (and one *s* decd). *Educ:* King's Sch., Worcester; Jesus Coll., Cambridge (Rustat Exhibitioner and Scholar). 2nd Class, 1st Part Classical Tripos, 1925; 1st Class, 1st Division, Historical Tripos, Part II, 1926; 1st Class with special distinction, English Tripos, 1927. Charles Kingsley Bye-Fellow at Magdalene Coll., Cambridge, 1927–29; Austausch-student, Königsberg Univ., 1929–30; Lectr in English at Durham Univ., 1930–36; Dir Community Service Council for Durham County, 1937–40; Regional Officer of Nat. Council of Social Service, 1939–40; Dep. Educn Officer, Herts, 1940–42; County Educn Officer, Dorset CC, 1942–49. Member: Colonial Office Social Welfare Adv. Cttee, 1942–48; Develt Commn, 1948–78; Adv. Cttee for Educn in RAF, 1950–57; Adv. Cttee for Educn in Germany, 1950–57; Central Adv. Council for Educn in England and Wales, 1948–51; Nat. Adv. Council on the Training and Supply of Teachers, 1951–; Children's Adv. Cttee of the ITA, 1956–60; Wolfenden Cttee on Sport, 1958–60; Outward Bound Trust Council, 1962–73; Central Council of Physical Recreation Council and Exec., 1961–72; Electricity Supply Industry Training Bd, 1965–66; Royal Commn on Local Govt, 1966–69; The Sports Council, 1966–74 (Vice-Chm. 1971–74); Countryside Commn, 1969–74; Commn on Mining and the Environment, 1971–72; Water Space Amenity Commn, 1973–76; President: Assoc. of Educn Officers, 1960–61; British Mountaineering Council, 1962–65 (Hon. Mem., 1983); Chairman: Mountain Leadership Training Bd, 1964–80; Council for Environmental Educn, 1968–75. Chm., My Word, BBC Radio, 1956–76. Athletic Blue; Pres., Cambridge Univ. Mountaineering Club, 1926–27; Member: Mount Everest Expedn, 1933; British East Greenland Expedn, 1935; Pres., Climbers' Club, 1945–48 and Hon. Mem., 1964; Pres., Alpine Club, 1973–76 (Vice-Pres., 1960–61). *Publications:* literary and mountaineering articles in various books and journals. *Recreations:*

walking, books. *Address:* Bridgeway, Bakewell, Derbyshire DE4 1DS. *T:* Bakewell (0629) 812252. *Clubs:* Savile, Alpine, Achilles. *Died 29 Nov. 1993.*

LONGLEY, Sir Norman, Kt 1966; CBE 1954; DL; retired as Chairman, James Longley (Holdings) Ltd, Building and Civil Engineering Contractors, Crawley, Sussex; *b* 14 Oct. 1900; *s* of Charles John Longley and Anna Gibson Marchant; *m* 1925, Dorothy Lilian Baker; two *s* one *d. Educ:* Clifton. West Sussex County Council, 1945–61, Alderman 1957–61. President: National Federation of Building Trades Employers, 1950; International Federation of Building and Public Works Contractors, 1955–57. Hon. Fellow, Institute of Builders. DL West Sussex, 1975. Hon. DSc: Heriot-Watt, 1968; Sussex, 1986. Coronation Medal, 1953. *Recreation:* horticulture. *Address:* The Beeches, Crawley, Sussex RH10 6AR. *T:* Crawley (0293) 520253. *Died 24 Jan. 1994.*

LOOSLEY, Stanley George Henry, MC 1944; MA Cantab; JP Glos; Headmaster of Wycliffe College, 1947–67; *b* 18 July 1910; *s* of Harold D. and Edith M. Loosley; *m* 1938, Margaret Luker; two *s* one *d. Educ:* Wycliffe Coll.; St John's Coll., Cambridge. Asst Master, Wycliffe Coll., 1934–39; War of 1939–45, RA, Sept. 1939–Oct. 1945; Major OC 220 Field Battery, 1941 (despatches, MC); NW Europe Campaign, 1944; sc; Bde Major RA 43 Div., 1945; Senior Asst Master, Wycliffe Coll., 1945–47. A Vice-Pres., Gloucestershire Magistrates Assoc., 1981–. *Publication:* Wycliffe College—The First Hundred Years, 1982. *Recreations:* travel, unskilled gardening, walking, looking, listening. *Address:* Brillings, Chalford Hill, Stroud, Glos GL6 8QJ. *T:* Brimscombe (0453) 883505. *Club:* Royal Over-Seas League.

Died 23 July 1991.

LORD, His Honour John Herent; a Circuit Judge, 1978–93; *b* 5 Nov. 1928; *s* of late Sir Frank Lord, KBE, JP, DL, and Lady Lord (*née* Rosalie Jeanette Herent), Brussels; *m* 1959, June Ann, *d* of late George Caladine and of Ada Caladine, Rochdale; three *s. Educ:* Manchester Grammar Sch.; Merton Coll., Oxford (BA (Jurisprudence), MA). Half Blue, Oxford Univ. lacrosse XII, 1948 and 1949; represented Middlesex, 1950. Called to Bar, Inner Temple, 1951; The Junior of Northern Circuit, 1952; Asst Recorder of Burnley, 1971; a Recorder of the Crown Court, 1972–78. Trustee, Frank Lord Postgraduate Med. Centre. *Recreations:* photography, shooting. *Address:* Three Lanes, Greenfield, Oldham, Lancs OL3 7PB. *T:* Saddleworth (01457) 872198. *Clubs:* St James's (Manchester); Leander. *Died 20 Dec. 1994.*

LORIMER, Hew Martin, OBE 1986; RSA 1957 (ARSA 1946); sculptor; Representative in Fife of National Trust for Scotland; *b* 22 May 1907; 2nd *s* of late Sir Robert Stodart Lorimer, KBE, Hon. LLD, ARA, RSA, architect, and Violet Alicia (*née* Wyld); *m* 1936, Mary McLeod Wylie (*d* 1970), 2nd *d* of H. M. Wylie, Edinburgh; two *s* one *d. Educ:* Loretto; Edinburgh Coll. of Art, Andrew Grant Scholarship, 1933 and Fellowship, 1934–35. National Library of Scotland, Edinburgh, sculptor of the 7 allegorical figures, 1952–55; Our Lady of the Isles, South Uist, 1955–57; St Francis, Dundee, 1957–59. Hon. LLD Dundee, 1983. KSG 1993. *Recreations:* music, travel, home. *Address:* Craigmount Nursing Home, The Scores, St Andrews, Fife KY16 9AS. *Died 1 Sept. 1993.*

LORING, Francis; *see* Gwynne-Evans, Sir F. L.

LOUGHLIN, Charles William; trade union official; retired 1974; *b* 16 Feb. 1914; *s* of late Charles Loughlin, Grimsby; *m* 1945, May, *d* of David Arthur Dunderdale, Leeds; one *s* (one *d* decd). *Educ:* St Mary's Sch., Grimsby; National Council of Labour Colls; Leeds Polytechnic (BA History and Politics, 1989). Area Organiser, Union of Shop, Distributive and Allied Workers, 1945–74. MP (Lab)

Gloucestershire West, 1959–Sept. 1974; Parly Sec., Min. of Health, 1965–67; Jt Parly Sec., Min. of Social Security, then Dept of Health and Social Security, 1967–68; Parly Sec., Min. of Public Building and Works, 1968–70. *Address:* Flat 25, Richmond House, Street Lane, Leeds LS8 1BW. *T:* Leeds (0532) 665327.

Died 23 Sept. 1993.

LOUIS, John Jeffry, Jr; Director: Air Wisconsin, Inc., since 1984; Baxter Travenol Laboratories, since 1984; Gannett Company, Inc., since 1984; Johnson's Wax, since 1961; *b* 10 June 1925; *s* of John Jeffry Louis and Henrietta Louis (*née* Johnson); *m* 1953, Josephine Peters; one *s* two *d. Educ:* Deerfield Academy, Mass; Northwestern Univ., 1943 and 1946; Williams Coll., Mass (BA 1947); Dartmouth Coll., New Hampshire (MBA 1949). Served with AUS, 1943–45. Account Executive, Needham, Louis & Brorby, Inc., Chicago, 1952–58; Director, International Marketing, Johnson's Wax, Wis, 1958–61; Chairman Board: KTAR Broadcasting Co., Ariz, 1961–68; Combined Communications Corp., Chicago, 1968–80; US Ambassador to UK, 1981–83. Trustee: Northwestern Univ., 1967–81, 1984–; Deerfield Acad., 1963–81; Foxcroft Sch., 1975–79; Williams Coll., 1979–81. Trustee, Evanston Hosp., 1959–81, 1984– (Chm., 1962–68). Hon. Master of The Bench, Middle Temple, 1981. *Recreations:* golf, tennis, skiing, shooting. *Address:* Suite 510, One Northfield Plaza, Northfield, IL 60093, USA. *Clubs:* Old Elm (Illinois); Pine Valley Golf (New Jersey); Augusta National Golf (Georgia); Gulfstream Golf (Florida).

Died 15 Feb. 1995.

LOUSADA, Sir Anthony (Baruh), Kt 1975; solicitor; Partner in Stephenson Harwood, 1935–73, Consultant, 1973–81; *b* 4 Nov. 1907; *s* of Julian George Lousada and Maude Reignier Conder; *m* 1st, 1937, Jocelyn (marr. diss. 1960), *d* of late Sir Alan Herbert, CH; one *s* three *d*; 2nd, 1961, Patricia, *d* of late C. J. McBride, USA; one *s* one *d. Educ:* Westminster; New Coll., Oxford. Admitted Solicitor, 1933. Min. of Economic Warfare, 1939–44; Min. of Production and War Cabinet Office, 1944–45. Member: Council, Royal College of Art, 1952–79 (Hon. Fellow, 1957; Sen. Fellow, 1967; Vice-Chm., 1960–72; Treasurer, 1967–72; Chm., 1972–79; Hon. Dr 1977); Cttee, Contemp. Art Soc., 1955–71 (Vice-Chm., 1961–71); Fine Arts Cttee, British Council (visited Japan on behalf of Council, 1970, to set up exhibn of sculpture by Barbara Hepworth); GPO Adv. Cttee on Stamp Design, 1968–80; Chairman: Adv. Cttee, Govt Art Collection, 1976–83; British Art Market Standing Cttee, 1984–90. Mem. Council, Friends of Tate Gallery, 1958– (Hon. Treasurer, 1960–65; Chm., 1971–77); Trustee, Tate Gallery, 1962–69 (Vice-Chm., 1965–69; Chm., 1967–69). One-man exhibns of drawings, Covt Gdn Gall., 1977, 1981. Officer, Order of Belgian Crown, 1945. *Recreations:* painting, music, travel. *Address:* The Tides, Chiswick Mall, W4 2PS. *T:* 081–994 2257. *Clubs:* Garrick; London Corinthian Sailing. *Died 24 June 1994.*

LOUTIT, John Freeman, CBE 1957; FRS 1963; MA, DM, FRCP; External Scientific Staff Medical Research Council, 1969–75, Visitor at Radiobiology Unit, 1975–88; *b* 19 Feb. 1910; *s* of John Freeman Loutit, Perth, WA; *m* 1941, Thelma Salusbury; one *s* two *d. Educ:* C of E Grammar Sch., Guildford, W Australia; Univs of W Australia, Melbourne, Oxford, London. Rhodes Scholar (W Australia), 1930; BA Oxon 1933; BM, BCh Oxon 1935; MA Oxon 1938; DM Oxon 1946; FRCP 1955. Various appointments, London Hosp., 1935–39; Director, South London Blood Supply Depot, 1940–47; Dir, Radiobiological Research Unit, AERE Harwell, 1947–69. Hon. VMD (Dr Vet. Med.) Stockholm, 1965; Hon. DSc St Andrews, 1988. Officer, Order of Orange-Nassau (Netherlands), 1951. *Publications:* Irradiation of Mice and

Men, 1962; Tissue Grafting and Radiation (jointly), 1966; articles in scientific journals. *Recreations:* cooking, gardening. *Address:* 22 Milton Lane, Steventon, Oxon OX13 6SA. *T:* Abingdon (0235) 831279.

Died 11 June 1992.

LOVAT, 17th Lord (S) *cr* 1458–1464 (*de facto* 15th Lord, 17th but for the Attainder); **Simon Christopher Joseph Fraser,** DSO 1942; MC; TD; JP; DL; Baron (UK) 1837; 24th Chief of Clan Fraser of Lovat; *b* 9 July 1911; *s* of 16th Lord Lovat and Hon. Laura Lister (*d* 1965), 2nd *d* of 4th Baron Ribblesdale; *S* father, 1933; *m* 1938, Rosamond, *o d* of Sir Delves Broughton, 11th Bt; two *s* two *d* (and two *s* decd). *Educ:* Ampleforth; Magdalen Coll., Oxford, BA. Lt, Scots Guards, 1932–37, retd; served War of 1939–45: Capt. Lovat Scouts, 1939; Lt-Col 1942; Brig. Commandos, 1943 (wounded, MC, DSO, Order of Suvarov, Légion d'Honneur, Croix de Guerre avec palme, Norway Liberation Cross). Under-Sec. of State for Foreign Affairs, 1945. DL 1942, JP 1944, Inverness. Awarded LLD (Hon.) by Canadian universities. Order of St John of Jerusalem; Knight of Malta; Papal Order of St Gregory with Collar. *Publication:* March Past, 1978. *Heir: g s* Master of Lovat, *b* 13 Feb. 1977. *Address:* Balblair, Beauly, Inverness-shire IV4 7AZ. *Club:* Cavalry and Guards. *Died 16 March 1995.*

LOVAT, Master of; Hon. Simon Augustine Fraser; *b* 28 Aug. 1939; *s* of 17th Baron Lovat and Rosamond, *o d* of Sir Delves Broughton, 11th Bt; *m* 1972, Virginia, *d* of David Grose; two *s* one *d. Educ:* Ampleforth Coll. Lieut Scots Guards, 1960. *Address:* Beaufort Castle, Beauly, Inverness-shire. *Died 26 March 1994.*

LOVE, Charles Marshall; Director and Chief Executive, Clydesdale Bank, since 1992; *b* 27 Oct. 1945; *s* of John and Catherine Love; *m* 1968, June Alexandra Dyball; one *s* one *d. Educ:* Musselburgh Grammar Sch. FCIBS, FCIB; CIMgt. TSB North West, 1976–83; Regl Gen. Manager, Gen. Manager Financial Services, Exec. Dir, Man. Dir, Property and Mortgage Services, TSB England & Wales, 1983–89; Man. Dir, Banking Services, TSB Bank, 1989–90; Regl Dir, Northern Reg., TSB Bank, 1990–91; Chm., TSB Asset Finance, 1989–92; Br. Banking Dir, TSB Bank, 1991–92; Chief Exec., TSB Bank Scotland, 1990–92; Chm., Cttee of Scottish Clearing Bankers, 1992– (Dep. Chm., 1991–92); Mem., CBI Scottish Council, 1990–92. FRSA. *Recreations:* reading, music, theatre. *Address:* Clydesdale Bank, 30 St Vincent Place, Glasgow G1 2HL. *T:* 041-248 7070. *Clubs:* Royal Automobile; Western (Glasgow). *Died 28 Dec. 1993.*

LOVE, Sir (Makere Rangiatea) Ralph, Kt 1987; QSO 1975; JP; Department of Maori Affairs (welfare, Maori Land Court and other administration divisions), New Zealand, 1925–65, retired; *b* 16 Sept. 1907; *s* of Wi Hapi Love, OBE and Ripeka Love, OBE; *m* 1933, Flora Heberley; one *s* one *d. Educ:* Petone District High Sch. Public Service cadet in Native Trust Office, 1925; Accounts; Administrator for Maori lands, Native Dept, 1932; Secretarial Corps of Parlt, 1946. Councillor, Wellington CC, 1962–65; Mayor of Bor. of Petone, 1965–68; Member: Wellington Reg. Authority; Envmt and Planning Services Cttee, Wellington Regl Council. Jt Patron, Wellington 1990 Trust. JP 1946. PM, William Ferguson Massey Lodge no 282. Sir Ralph belonged to the Maori Te Atiawa tribe on his father's side and to the Taranaki tribe on his mother's side. *Recreations:* participant in cricket, rugby, swimming; later an administrator in all these sports (Executive and Council, NZ Rugby Union). *Address:* 17 Rakeiora Grove, Korokoro, Petone, New Zealand. *T:* (4) 691924. *Clubs:* Petone Workingmen's (Life Member), and others.

Died 30 July 1994.

LOVERIDGE, Sir John (Henry), Kt 1975; CBE 1964 (MBE 1945); Bailiff of Guernsey, 1973–82; barrister-at-law; Judge of Appeal for Jersey, 1974–82; *b* 2 Aug. 1912; *e s* of late Henry Thomas and Vera Lilian Loveridge; *m* 1946, Madeleine Melanie, *o d* of late Eugene Joseph C. M. Tanguy; one *s* one *d. Educ:* Elizabeth Coll., Guernsey; Univ. of Caen. Called to Bar, Middle Temple, 1950. Advocate of Royal Court of Guernsey, 1951; HM Solicitor-General, Guernsey, 1954–60; HM Attorney-General, Guernsey, 1960–69; Deputy Bailiff of Guernsey, 1969–73. RAFVR, 1954–59. KStJ 1980. *Recreations:* reading, swimming, sport. *Address:* Kinmount, Sausmarez Road, St Martin's, Guernsey. *T:* Guernsey (0481) 38038. *Club:* Royal Guernsey Golf. *Died 7 Nov. 1994.*

LOWE, Air Vice-Marshal Sir Edgar (Noel), KBE 1962 (CBE 1945); CB 1947; Director General of Supply Co-ordination, Ministry of Defence, 1966–70, retired (Inspector General of Codification and Standardisation, 1964); *b* 22 Dec. 1905; *s* of late Albert Henry Lowe, Church Stretton, Shropshire; *m* 1948, Mary McIlwraith, *o d* of George M. Lockhart, Stair House, Stair, Ayrshire; one *s* one *d.* Served India, 1934–38; psa 1939; served in France 1939–40 (despatches); Air Commodore, Director of Organisation (Forecasting and Planning), Air Ministry, 1945–47; idc 1949; ADC to the King, 1949–52, to the Queen, 1952–57; Directing Staff, RAF Staff Coll., Bracknell, 1950–51; Director of Organisation, Air Ministry, 1951–53; Deputy Asst Chief of Staff (Logistics), SHAPE, 1953–56; Senior Air Staff Officer, HQ No 41 Group, RAF, 1956–58; AOC No 40 Group, RAF, 1958–61; Director-General of Equipment, Air Ministry, 1961–64. *Address:* Wyndford, 97 Harestone Hill, Caterham, Surrey CR3 6DL. *Club:* Royal Air Force.

Died 23 Jan. 1992.

LU, Dr Gwei-Djen; Associate Director, East Asian History of Science Library, Needham Research Institute, Cambridge, since 1976; Fellow of Robinson College, Cambridge, 1979–80, Emeritus Fellow, since 1980; *b* 1 Sept. 1904; *d* of Mou-T'ing Lu and Hsiu-Ying Lu; *m* 1989, Dr Joseph Needham, CH, FRS, FBA. *Educ:* Ming-Tê Sch., Nanking; Ginling Coll., Nanking (BA). PhD Cambridge. Trained as clin. pathologist, Peking Union Med. Coll.; Lectr in Physiology and Biochemistry, St John's Univ., Shanghai; Res. Fellow, Lester Inst. of Med. Research, Shanghai (nutritional biochemistry); research, Cambridge Biochemical Lab., 1937–39, followed by research at Univ. of Calif, Berkeley, Birmingham City Hosp., Alabama, and at Coll. of Physicians and Surgeons, Columbia Univ., NY; staff mem., Sino-British Science Co-operation Office, HM Embassy, Chungking, later Nanking; Prof. of Nutritional Science, Ginling Coll., Nanking, 1947; staff mem., Secretariat, UNESCO, Paris (i/c Nat. Sci. Div., Field Science Co-operation Offices); working with Dr Joseph Needham on Science and Civilisation in China proj., Cambridge, 1957–. Hon. Prof. of History of Science, Academia Sinica, Beijing, China. 1990. Medal for Literature, Ministry of Educn, China. *Publications:* Epicure in China, 1942; (with Dr J. Needham and others) Clerks and Craftsmen in China and the West, 1970; (with Dr J. Needham and others) Science and Civilisation in China, 1971–: Vol. 4, pt 3; Vol. 5, pts 2, 3, 4, 5 and 7; Vol. 6, pts 1, 3 and 4; (with Dr J. Needham) Celestial Lancets: a history and rationale of Acupuncture and Moxa, 1980; Trans-Pacific Echoes and Resonances; Listening Once Again, 1985; The Hall of Heavenly Records: Korean astronomical instruments and clocks 1380–1780, 1986; papers in biochem. and historical jls. *Recreation:* reading, esp. history, economics, politics and sociology. *Address:* 2A Sylvester Road, Cambridge CB3 9AF. *T:* Cambridge (0223) 352183; 8 Sylvester Road, Cambridge CB3 9AF. *T:* Cambridge (0223) 311545.

Died 28 Nov. 1991.

LUARD, (David) Evan (Trant); Fellow of St Antony's College, Oxford, since 1957; writer on international affairs; *b* 31 Oct. 1926; *s* of late Colonel T. B. Luard, DSO, RM. *Educ:* Felsted; King's Coll., Cambridge (Maj. Schol.). Factory worker, 1949–50; HM Foreign Service, 1950–56; served in Hong Kong, Peking, London; resigned, 1956. Oxford City Councillor, 1958–61. Delegate, UN General Assembly, 1967–68. MP (Lab) Oxford, 1966–70 and Oct. 1974–1979; Parly Under-Sec. of State, FCO, 1969–70, 1976–79; contested (SDP) Oxford W and Abingdon, 1983. Apptd by UN Sec.-Gen. to Cttee on Restructuring of UN Economic and Social Activities, 1975; worked for Oxfam, 1980–83. President: Oxford Consumers Gp; Oxford Animal Sanctuary; Oxfordshire Nat. Deaf Children's Soc. *Publications:* (part author) The Economic Development of Communist China, 1959, 2nd edn 1961; Britain and China, 1962; Nationality and Wealth, 1964; (ed) The Cold War, 1965; (ed) First Steps to Disarmament, 1966; (ed) The Evolution of International Organisations, 1967; Conflict and Peace in the Modern International System, 1968, rev. edn 1988; (ed) The International Regulation of Frontier Disputes, 1970; (ed) The International Regulation of Civil Wars, 1972; The Control of the Sea-bed, 1974; Types of International Society, 1976; International Agencies, the Emerging Framework of Interdependence, 1977; The United Nations, 1978; Socialism without the State, 1979; A History of the United Nations, vol I, 1982, vol II, 1989; The Management of the World Economy, 1983; Economic Relationships Among States, 1984; War in International Society, 1986; The Blunted Sword: the erosion of military power in modern world politics, 1988; International Society, 1990; articles in Foreign Affairs, Foreign Policy, International Affairs, World Politics, World Today, The Annals. *Recreations:* music, gardening. *Address:* 35 Observatory Street, Oxford OX2 6EN. *T:* Oxford (0865) 513302.
Died 8 Feb. 1991.

LUCAS OF CRUDWELL, Baroness (10th in line) *cr* 1663, **AND DINGWALL,** Lady (13th in line) *cr* 1609; **Anne Rosemary Palmer;** *b* 28 April 1919; *er d* of Group Captain Howard Lister Cooper, AFC, and Baroness Lucas of Crudwell (9th in line) and Dingwall; *S* mother, 1958; a *co-heir* to Barony of Butler; *m* 1950, Major the Hon. Robert Jocelyn Palmer, MC, DL, late Coldstream Guards, 3rd *s* of 3rd Earl of Selborne, CH, PC; two *s* one *d. Heir:* *s* Hon. Ralph Matthew Palmer [*b* 7 June 1951; *m* 1978, Clarissa Marie, *d* of George Vivian Lockett, TD; one *s* one *d*]. *Address:* The Old House, Wonston, Winchester, Hampshire.   *Died 31 Dec. 1991.*

LUCAS, Ven. John Michael; Archdeacon of Totnes, 1976–81, then Archdeacon Emeritus; *b* 13 June 1921; *s* of Rev. Stainforth John Chadwick Lucas and Dorothy Wybray Mary Lucas; *m* 1952, Catharina Madeleine Bartlett; three *s* (one *d* decd). *Educ:* Kelly Coll., Tavistock; Lichfield Theological Coll. Deacon 1944, priest 1945, dio. Exeter; Asst Curate: Parish of Wolborough, 1944; Parish of Ashburton, 1950; Rector of Weare Giffard with Landcross and Vicar of Monkleigh, 1952; Vicar of Northam, 1962; Vicar of Chudleigh Knighton, 1976–83. *Recreations:* family recreations, garden. *Address:* Wybray House, Shobrooke, Crediton, Devon.
Died 20 Jan. 1992.

LUCEY, Rear-Adm. Martin Noel, CB 1973; DSC 1944; RN retired; *b* 21 Jan. 1920; *s* of A. N. Lucey; *m* 1947, Barbara Mary Key; two *s* one *d. Educ:* Gresham's Sch., Holt. Entered RN, 1938; served War of 1939–45: qualif. in navigation, 1944; "N" 10th Destroyer Sqdn, 1944; Comdr, 1953; Mem. NATO Defence Coll., 1954; Captain, 1961; Captain "F7" HMS Puma, 1964; Cdre, Sen. Naval Officer, West Indies, 1968; Rear-Adm., 1970; Adm. President, RNC Greenwich, 1970–72; Flag Officer,

Scotland and NI, 1972–74. Dir Gen., Nat. Assoc. of British and Irish Millers, 1975–84. *Recreation:* painting. *Address:* Oldways, Houghton, Arundel, West Sussex BN18 9LW.
Died 8 July 1992.

LUFF, Richard William Peter, FRICS; FRSA; Member Board, Commission for New Towns, since 1987; Deputy Chairman, London Regional Transport Property Board, since 1988 (Member, since 1987); Director, Housing Standards Co. Ltd, since 1988; *b* 11 June 1927; *s* of Victor and Clare Luff; *m* 1st, 1950, Betty Chamberlain (*d* 1989); no *c*; 2nd, 1990, Daphne Olivia Louise Andrews (*née* Brough). *Educ:* Hurstpierpoint Coll., Sussex; Coll. of Estate Management. Service in RA, India and UK, 1945–48. Estates and Valuation Dept, MCC, 1949–65; Asst Valuer, GLC, 1968–75; City Surveyor, Corp. of London, 1975–84; Dir of Property, British Telecom, 1984–87. Royal Institution of Chartered Surveyors: Mem., Gen. Practice Divl Council, 1973–83; Chm., Valuation and Rating Cttee, 1974–79; Mem., Gen. Council, 1975–86; Dep. Chm., Public Affairs Cttee, 1975–79; Pres., 1982–83; Pres., Assoc. of Local Authority Valuers and Estate Surveyors, 1978–79; Hon. Vice-Pres., 1983–89, Hon. Mem., 1989–, Cambridge Univ. Land Soc. Dir, London Wall Litigation Claims Ltd, 1988–. Mem., Furniture History Soc. Master, Chartered Surveyors' Co., 1985. Hon. FISM 1983. *Publications:* Furniture in England— the age of the joiner (with S. W. Wolsey), 1968; articles and papers on compensation and allied property matters; nearly 50 articles on furniture history in Antique Collector, Country Life, and Connoisseur, 1961–73. *Recreations:* collecting antiquarian objects, writing and lecturing on English furniture. *Address:* Blossoms, Broomfield Park, Sunningdale, Ascot, Berks SL5 0JT. *T:* Ascot (0344) 23806. *Club:* MCC.   *Died 28 Sept. 1993.*

LUKE, Peter (Ambrose Cyprian), MC 1944; writer and dramatist, freelance since 1967; *b* 12 Aug. 1919, *e s* of late Sir Harry Luke, KCMG, DLitt Oxon and Joyce Fremlin; *m* 1st, Carola Peyton-Jones (decd); 2nd, Lettice Crawshaw (marr. diss.); one *d* (one *s* decd); 3rd, June Tobin; two *s* three *d. Educ:* Eton; Byam Shaw Sch. of Art; Atelier André Lhote, Paris. Served War, 1939–46 with Rifle Bde in ME, Italy and NW Europe. Sub-Editor, Reuters News Desk, 1946–47; wine trade, 1947–57; Story Editor, ABC TV, 1958–62; Editor, The Bookman (ABC TV), 1962–63; Editor, Tempo (ABC TV Arts Programme), 1963–64; Drama Producer, BBC TV, 1963–67. Dir, Edwards-Mac Liammoir Dublin Gate Theatre Co., 1977–80; Dir, Rings for a Spanish Lady, Gaiety Theatre, Dublin, 1978. Author TV plays: Small Fish are Sweet, 1958; Pigs Ear with Flowers, 1960; Roll on Bloomin' Death, 1961; (with William Sansom) A Man on Her Back, 1965; Devil a Monk Wou'd Be, 1966; Honour, Profit and Pleasure, 1985; produced: Hamlet at Elsinore, BBC TV, 1963; Silent Song, BBC TV (Prix Italia, 1967); wrote and directed films: Anach Cuan (about Sean O Riada), BBC TV, 1967; Black Sound—Deep Song (about Federico Garcia Lorca), BBC TV, 1968; wrote stage plays: Hadrian the Seventh, prod. Birmingham Rep. 1967, Mermaid 1968, Theatre Royal, Haymarket and Broadway, 1969 (Antoinette Perry Award nomination, 1968–69), (dir.) Abbey Theatre, Dublin, 1970; Bloomsbury, Phoenix, 1974; Proxopera (adaptation), Dublin Gate Theatre, 1979; Married Love, Thorndyke, Leatherhead, 1985, Wyndham's, 1988; (trans.) Yerma, by Federico García Lorca, NT, 1987; wrote BBC Radio plays: Nymphs and Satyrs Come Away, 1984; The Last of Baron Corvo, 1989 (Sony Radio Award, 1990); It's a Long Way from Talavera, and The Long Road to Waterloo, 1991; A Popish Plot, 1994. OStJ 1940. *Publications:* The Play of Hadrian VII, 1968; Sisyphus and Reilly, an autobiography, 1972; (ed) Enter Certain Players, Edwards-Mac Liammoir 1928–1978, 1978; Paquito and the Wolf (children), 1981;

Telling Tales: selected short stories, 1981; The Other Side of the Hill, a novel of the Peninsular War, 1984; The Mad Pomegranate & the Praying Mantis, Adventure in Andalusia, 1985; translations from the Spanish: Yerma, by Federico García Lorca; Rings for a Spanish Lady (Anillos para Una Dama) by Antonio Gala; short stories in: Envoy, Cornhill, Pick of Today's Short Stories, Winter's Tales, Era, New Irish Writing, The Pen, etc. *Recreations:* gastronomy, tauromachy, grafting citrus trees. *Address:* c/o Lemon Unna & Durbridge Ltd, 24 Pottery Lane, Holland Park, W11 4LZ.
Died 23 Jan. 1995.

LUNT, Rev. Canon Ronald Geoffrey, MC 1943; MA, BD; Rector of Martley, 1974–78; Chief Master, King Edward's School, Birmingham, 1952–74; *b* 25 June 1913; *s* of late Rt Rev. G. C. L. Lunt, DD, Bishop of Salisbury, and Lilias Marjorie Sherbrooke; *m* 1945, Veslemoy Sopp Foss, Oslo, Norway; one *s* two *d. Educ:* Eton (King's Scholar); The Queen's Coll., Oxford (Scholar, 1st class Lit. Hum.); Westcott House, Cambridge. BD (Oxon), 1967. Assistant Master, St George's Sch., Harpenden, 1935; Haberdashers' Sch., Hampstead, 1936–37; deacon, 1938; priest, 1939; Master in Orders at Radley Coll., Abingdon, 1938–40; CF 1940–45: Middle East, 1941–44 (MC); CF 3rd class, SCF 1 Airborne Division, 1945; Headmaster, Liverpool Coll., 1945–52. Won Cromer Greek Prize, 1937; Page Scholar to USA, 1959; Select Preacher: University of Cambridge, 1948, 1960; Oxford, 1951–53, 1983. Chm., Birmingham Council of Churches, 1957–60; Hon. Canon, Birmingham Cathedral, 1969. Mem., Birmingham Educn Cttee, 1952–74. Life Governor, Queen's Coll., Birmingham, 1957; Trustee, 1954, Chm., 1971–74, E. W. Vincent Trust; Governor, 1952, Sen. Vice-Pres., 1971–72, Pres., 1973, Birmingham and Midland Inst. Pres., Incorporated Assoc. of Head Masters, 1962. Mem., Press Council, 1964–69. *Publications:* edition of Marlowe's Dr Faustus, 1937, Edward II, 1938; contrib. to Arts v Science, 1967; articles in Theology, Expository Times, and other journals. *Address:* The Station House, Ledbury, Herefordshire HR8 1AR. *T:* Ledbury (0531) 633174.
Died 19 May 1994.

LURGAN, 5th Baron *cr* 1839, of Lurgan, Co. Armagh; **John Desmond Cavendish Brownlow,** OBE 1950; Lieutenant-Colonel, Grenadier Guards, retired; *b* 29 June 1911; *s* of Captain Hon. Francis Cecil Brownlow (*d* 1932) (3rd *s* of 2nd Baron) and Angela (*d* 1973), *d* of Samuel Radcliffe Platt; *S* cousin, 1984. *Educ:* Eton. *Address:* Pennington House, Lymington, Hants.
Died 17 Sept. 1991 (ext).

LURIA, Prof. Salvador Edward; Sedgwick Professor of Biology, Massachusetts Institute of Technology, 1964–70, Institute Professor since 1970; *b* 13 Aug. 1912; *s* of David Luria and Ester Sacerdote; *m* 1945, Zella Hurwitz; one *s. Educ:* Turin Univ. (MD 1935). Res. Fellow, Inst. of Radium, Paris, 1938–40; Res. Asst, Columbia Univ. Medical School, NY, 1940–42; Guggenheim Fellow, Vanderbilt and Princeton Univs, 1942–43; Instructor in Bacteriology, Indiana Univ., 1943–45, Asst Prof., 1944–47, Associate Prof. 1947–50; Prof. of Bacteriology, Illinois Univ., 1950–59; Prof. and Chm. of Dept of Microbiology, MIT, 1959–64. Fellow of Salk Inst. for Biol Studies, 1965–. Associate Editor, Jl Bacteriology, 1950–55; Editor, Virology, 1955–; Biological Abstracts, 1958–62; Member: Editorial Bd, Exptl Cell Res. Jl, 1948–; Advisory Bd, Jl Molecular Biology, 1958–64; Hon. Editorial Advisory Bd, Jl Photochemistry and Photobiology, 1961–. Lecturer: Univ. of Colorado, 1950; Jesup, Notre Dame, 1950; Nieuwand, Notre Dame 1959; Dyer, Nat. Insts of Health, 1963. Member: Amer. Phil Soc.; Amer. Soc. for Microbiology (Pres. 1967–68); Nat. Acad. of Scis; Amer. Acad. of Arts and Scis; AAAS; Soc.

Genetic Microbiology; Genetics Soc. of America; Amer Assoc. Univ. Profs; Sigma Xi. Prizes: Lepetit, 1935; Lenghi, 1965; Louisa Gross Horowitz of Columbia University; Nobel Prize for Physiology or Medicine (jtly), 1969. Hon. ScD: Chicago, 1967; Rutgers, 1970; Indiana, 1970. *Publications:* General Virology, 1953, rev. edn 1967; Life: the unfinished experiment, 1974. *Recreation:* sculpting. *Address:* Department of Biology, Massachusetts Institute of Technology, Cambridge, Mass 02139, USA.
Died 6 Feb. 1991.

LUSTY, Sir Robert (Frith), Kt 1969; *b* 7 June 1909; *o s* of late Frith Lusty; *m* 1st, 1939, Joan Christie (*d* 1962), *y d* of late Archibald Brownlie, Glasgow; 2nd, 1963, Eileen (*née* Barff), *widow* of Dr Denis Carroll. *Educ:* Society of Friends' Co-educational Sch., Sidcot. Joined editorial staff The Kent Messenger, 1927; abandoned journalism for publishing and entered production and editorial departments Messrs Hutchinson and Company, 1928; appointed manager associated company, Messrs Selwyn & Blount, 1933; left in 1935 to join Michael Joseph Ltd, on its formation, resigned as Deputy Chairman, 1956, to become Man. Dir, Hutchinson Publishing Gp, until retirement in 1973; a Governor of the BBC, 1960–68 (Vice-Chairman, 1966–68); Member Council of Publishers' Assoc., 1955–61; Chairman: National Book League, 1949–51 and of its 1951 Festival Cttee; Soc. of Bookmen, 1962–65; Publication Panel, King Edward's Hosp. Fund for London, 1975–83. Liveryman Stationers' Co., 1945; Freeman of City of London. A Governor and Councillor, Bedford Coll., 1965–71. FRSA 1969. *Publication:* Bound to be Read (autobiog.), 1975. *Address:* Broad Close, Blockley, Moreton-in-Marsh, Glos GL5 6DY. *T:* Blockley (0386) 700335. *Club:* Garrick.
Died 23 July 1991.

LUTOSŁAWSKI, Witold; composer and conductor; *b* Warsaw, 25 Jan. 1913; *s* of Józef and Maria Lutosławski; *m* 1946, Maria Danuta Dygat. *Educ:* Warsaw Conservatoire. Dep. Chief of Music Dept, Polish Radio, 1945–46; teacher of composition: Berkshire Music Center, USA, 1962; Dartington, 1963, 1964; Aarhus, 1968; composer-in-residence: Hopkins Center, USA, 1966; Aldeburgh Fest., 1983. Vice-Pres., Polish Composers' Union, 1973–79. Member: Swedish Royal Acad. of Music; Free Acad. of Arts, Hamburg; Acad. of Arts, Berlin; German Acad. of Arts, E Berlin; Bavarian Acad. of Fine Arts; Amer. Acad. of Arts and Letters; Nat. Inst. of Arts and Letters, NY; Acad. of Fine Arts, France; Acad. Européenne des Scis et des Lettres; Acad. Royale des Sciences, des Lettres et des Beaux Arts de Belgique; Associate Mem., Acad. Naz. di Santa Cecilia. Hon. Member: Polish Composers' Union; Polish Soc. of Contemp. Music; ISCM; Konzerthausges., Vienna; Assoc. of Professional Composers; Serbian Acad. of Sci.; Internat. Music Council; Soc. of Norwegian Composers. FRCM; FRNCM; Hon. RAM 1976; Hon. GSM 1978. Hon. Dr: Cleveland Inst. of Music; Northwestern; Evanston, Chicago; Warsaw; Lancaster; Glasgow; Torún; Durham; Cracow; Cambridge; Duquesnes Univ., Pittsburgh; QUB; Warsaw Acad. of Music; New England Conservatoire of Music, Boston; Univ. des Scis Humaines de Strasbourg. Many prizes include: City of Warsaw Music Prize, 1948; state prizes; Sonning Music Prize, Copenhagen, 1967; Ravel Prize, 1971; Sibelius Prize, 1972; Ernst von Siemens Music Prize, 1983; Solidarność (Solidarity) Prize, 1984 (Poland); Univ. of Louisville Grawemeyer Award for music composition, 1985; (jtly) Gold Medal, Royal Philharmonic Soc., 1985; Queen Sofia of Spain, 1985; High Fidelity Internat. Record Critics' Award for Symphony No 3, 1986; Grammy Award, USA, 1986; Pittsburgh Symphony Orch. Signature Award. Order of Builders of People's Poland, 1977; Comdr des Arts et des Lettres (France). *Compositions* include: *orchestral:*

Symphonic Variations, 1938; 1st Symphony, 1947; Concerto for Orchestra, 1954; Musique Funèbre, 1958; Jeux vénitiens, 1961; 2nd Symphony, 1967; Livre pour orchestre, 1968; Cello concerto, 1970; Les espaces du sommeil for baritone and orch., 1975; Mi-parti, 1976; Novelette, 1979; 3rd Symphony, 1983; Chain 2 for violin and orchestra, 1985; Chain 3 for orchestra, 1986; Concerto for Piano and Orchestra, 1988; Interlude for orch., 1990; 4th Symphony, 1993; *chamber:* Overture, 1949; Three Poems of Henri Michaux for choir and orch., 1963; String Quartet, 1964; Paroles tissées for tenor and chamber orch., 1965; Preludes and Fugues for 13 solo strings, 1972; Double Concerto, 1980; Chain 1, 1983; Partita for violin and piano, 1984 (version for violin and orch., 1988); Tarantella for baritone and piano, 1990; Chantefleurs et chantefables, 1991; vocal and choral works, compositions for piano, and children's music; scores and incidental music for theatre, films and radio. Many recordings, conducting own compositions. *Address:* Ul. Śmiała 39, 01–523 Warsaw, Poland. *Died 7 Feb. 1994.*

LUXTON, William John, CBE 1962; Director, London Chamber of Commerce and Industry, 1964–74 (Secretary, 1958–74); *b* 18 March 1909; *s* of late John Luxton and Emma Luxton (*née* Webber); *m* 1942, Megan, *d* of late John M. Harries and Mary Ann Harries (*née* Lewis); one *s* one *d. Educ:* Shebbear Coll., N Devon; London Univ. Wallace Brothers & Co. Ltd (merchant bankers), 1926–38. Called to the Bar, Lincoln's Inn, 1938; Chancery Bar, 1938–40. Served with Royal Armoured Corps, 1940–45. Legal Parliamentary Secretary, Association of British Chambers of Commerce, 1947–53 (Vice-Pres., 1974); Secretary Birmingham Chamber of Commerce, 1953–58; Dir, Fedn of Commonwealth Chambers of Commerce, 1958–74. *Address:* 19 Brookfields, Crickhowell, Powys NP8 1DJ. *T:* Crickhowell (0873) 811493.
Died 28 Feb. 1992.

LUYT, Sir Richard (Edmonds), GCMG 1966 (KCMG 1964; CMG 1960); KCVO 1966; DCM 1942; Vice-Chancellor and Principal, University of Cape Town, 1968–80; *b* 8 Nov. 1915; *m* 1st, 1948, Jean Mary Wilder (*d* 1951); one *d;* 2nd, 1956, Eileen Betty Reid; two *s. Educ:* Diocesan Coll., Rondebosch, Cape, SA; Univ. of Cape Town (BA); Trinity Coll., Oxford (MA). Rhodes Scholar from S Africa, 1937. Entered Colonial Service and posted to N Rhodesia, 1940; War Service, 1940–45: with Mission 101, in Ethiopia, 1941; remained in Ethiopia with British Military Mission, for remainder of War; returned to N Rhodesia, Colonial Service, 1945; transferred to Kenya, 1953; Labour Commissioner, Kenya, 1954–57; Permanent Secretary to various Ministries of the Kenya Government, 1957–60; Secretary to the Cabinet, 1960–61; Chief Secretary, Northern Rhodesia, 1962–64; Governor and C-in-C, British Guiana, 1964–66, until Guyana Independence; Governor-General of Guyana, May–Oct. 1966. Vice-Pres., South African Inst. of Race Relations, 1983–85; Nat. Pres., Friends of the Nat. Union of South African Students, 1980–88; Governor, Africa Inst. of South Africa, 1968–; Pres. (formerly Patron), Civil Rights League, 1968–. Hon. LLD: Natal, 1972; Witwatersrand, 1980; Hon. DAdmin Univ. of South Africa, 1980; Hon. DLitt Cape Town, 1982. *Recreations:* gardening, sport, particularly Rugby (Oxford Blue, 1938) and cricket (Oxford Captain 1940) (also played for Kenya at cricket). *Address:* Allandale, 64 Alma Road, Rosebank, Cape, 7700, South Africa. *T:* 6866765. *Clubs:* Commonwealth Trust; Nairobi (Kenya); City and Civil Service (Cape Town). *Died 12 Feb. 1994.*

LWOFF, Prof. André Michel; Grand-Croix de la Légion d'Honneur, 1982 (Grand Officier; Commandeur, 1966; Officier, 1960; Chevalier, 1947); Médaille de la Résistance, 1946; Directeur de l'Institut de Recherches Scientifiques sur le Cancer, 1968–72; Professor of Microbiology, Faculté des Sciences, Paris, 1959–68, and Head of Department of Microbial Physiology, Pasteur Institute, 1938–68; *b* Ainay-le-Château, Allier, France, 8 May 1902; *s* of Salomon Lwoff and Marie Simenuvitch; *m* 1925, Marguerite Bourdaleix (decd). *Educ:* (Fac. des Sciences et de Méd.) Univ. of Paris. MD (Paris) 1927; DSc (Paris) 1932. With the Pasteur Institute, 1921–72. Fellow: Rockefeller Foundn, 1933 and 1935; Salk Inst., 1967; Vis. Professor: MIT, 1960; Harvard Univ., Albert Einstein Med. Sch., New York, 1964. Lectures: Dunham, Harvard, 1947; Marjory Stephenson, Soc. for Gen. Microbiol.; Harvey, 1954; Leuwenhoek, Royal Soc., 1966; Dyer, 1969; Penn, University of Pennsylvania, 1969; MacCormick, Univ. of Chicago, 1969. Hon. Member: Soc. for Gen. Microbiol.; Amer. Soc. of Microbiol.; Amer. Botanical Soc.; Amer. Soc. of Biochem.; Corresp. Mem., Acad. of Med. Sciences of USSR; Foreign Member: Royal Soc., 1958; Hungarian Acad. of Science; Indian Acad. of Science; For. Associate, Nat. Acad. of Scis, USA; For. Associate Mem., Amer. Acad. of Arts and Scis. President: Internat. Assoc. of Societies of Microbiology, 1962; Mouvement Français pour le Planning Familial, 1970–74. Exhibitions of paintings: Galerie Alex Maguy, 1960; Galerie Aleph, 1978, 1985. Hon. doctorates in science and law at British and other foreign univs. Awarded several prizes and medals from 1928 onwards, both French and foreign, for his work; Nobel Prize for Medicine (jointly), 1965; Leuwenhoek Medal, Royal Netherlands Acad. of Science; Keilin Medal, Biochemical Soc. *Publications:* (with L. Justin-Besançon) Vitamine antipellagreuse et avitaminoses nocotiniques, 1942; L'Evolution physiologique, Collection de microbiologie, Hermann éd., 1944; Problems of Morphogenesis in Ciliates, The Kinetosomes in Development, Reproduction and Evolution, 1950; Biological Order, 1960; Jeux et combats, 1981. *Recreation:* painting. *Address:* 69 avenue de Suffren, 75007 Paris, France. *T:* 47832782.
Died 30 Sept. 1994.

LYNN, Wilfred; Director, National Westminster Bank Ltd (Outer London Board), 1969–73; *b* 19 May 1905; *s* of late Wilfred Crosland Lynn and Alice Lynn; *m* 1936, Valerie, *e d* of late B. M. A. Critchley; one *s* one *d* (twins). *Educ:* Hull Grammar School. Entered National Provincial Bank Ltd, 1921; Asst General Manager, 1952; Joint General Manager, 1953; Chief General Manager, 1961; Director, 1965–69; Dir, North Central Finance Ltd, 1962–70. FCIB. *Recreation:* golf. *Address:* c/o National Westminster Bank, 15 Bishopsgate, EC2. *Died 13 Oct. 1994.*

LYON, Alexander Ward; Chairman, UK Immigrants Advisory Service, 1978–84; *b* 15 Oct. 1931; *s* of Alexander Pirie and Doris Lyon; *m* 1st, 1951, Hilda Arandall (marr. diss.); two *s* one *d;* 2nd, 1981, Clare Short, sometime MP for Birmingham, Ladywood. Called to the Bar, Inner Temple, 1954. Contested (Lab) York, 1964, 1983. MP (Lab) York, 1966–83; addtl PPS to the Treasury Ministers, 1969; PPS to Paymaster General, 1969; Opposition Spokesman: on African Affairs, 1970; on Home Affairs, 1971; Min. of State, Home Office, 1974–76. Member: Younger Cttee on Intrusions into Privacy; Select Cttee on Home Affairs, 1979; Chm., PLP Home Affairs Gp, 1979. *Address:* 23 Larkhall Rise, SW4 6JB. *T:* 071–720 1525.
Died 30 Sept. 1993.

LYON, Stanley Douglas; Deputy Chairman, Imperial Chemical Industries Ltd, 1972–77 (Director, 1968–77); *b* 22 June 1917; *s* of late Ernest Hutcheon Lyon and Helen Wilson Lyon; *m* 1941, May Alexandra Jack; three *s. Educ:* George Heriot's Sch., Edinburgh; Edinburgh Univ. (BSc Hons Engrg). MICE, CBIM. Major, Royal Engrs, 1939–46. ICI Ltd: Engr, Dyestuffs Div., 1946; Engrg Dir, Wilton Works, 1957; Prodn Dir, Agricl Div., 1962; Dep.

Chm. 1964, Chm. 1966, Agric. Div. *Recreations:* golf, tennis, gardening, sculpture. *Address:* Ghyll Close, West Lane, Danby, Whitby, N Yorks YO21 2LY.
Died 18 Dec. 1991.

LYONS, Hamilton; Sheriff of Renfrew and Argyll, and Ayr and Bute, later North Strathclyde, 1968–84, retired; *b* 3 Aug. 1918; *s* of Richard Lyons and Annie Cathro Thomson; *m* 1943, Jean Cathro Blair; two *s. Educ:* Gourock High Sch.; Greenock High Sch.; Glasgow Univ. (BL 1940). Practised as Solicitor, Greenock, until 1966; Sheriff Substitute of Inverness, Moray, Nairn and Ross and Cromarty at Stornoway and Lochmaddy, 1966–68. Temp. Sheriff, 1984–88. Member: Coun. of Law Soc. of Scotland, 1950–66 (Vice-Pres., 1962–63); Law Reform Cttee for Scotland, 1954–64; Cttee of Inquiry on Children and Young Persons, 1961–64; Cttee of Inquiry on Sheriff Courts, 1963–67; Sheriff Court Rules Coun., 1952–66; Scottish Probation Adv. and Trng Coun., 1959–69. *Address:* 14 Cloch Road, Gourock, Inverclyde PA19 1AB. *T:* Gourock (0475) 32566. *Died 7 Jan. 1992.*

LYONS, His Honour Sir Rudolph, Kt 1976; QC 1953; a Circuit Judge, 1972–82; Honorary Recorder of Manchester, 1977–82; *b* 5 Jan. 1912; *er s* of late G. Lyons, Leeds; *m* 1936, Jeannette, *yr d* of late Philip Dante; one *s* two *d. Educ:* Leeds Grammar Sch.; Leeds Univ. (LLB). Called to Bar, Gray's Inn, 1934; Mem., Gen. Council of the Bar, 1958–70; Master of the Bench, Gray's Inn, 1961–. Recorder of: Sunderland, 1955–56; Newcastle upon Tyne, 1956–61; Sheffield, 1961–65; Leeds, 1965–70; Recorder and Judge of the Crown Ct of Liverpool, 1970–71; Hon. Recorder of Liverpool, 1972–77. Comr, Central Criminal Court, 1962–70; Comr of Assize, 1969; Leader of N Eastern Circuit, 1961–70; Solicitor-Gen., 1961–65, Attorney-Gen., 1965–70, County Palatine of Durham. Jt Pres., Council, HM Circuit Judges, 1974. Hon. Member: Northern Circuit, 1979; N Eastern Circuit, 1983. Mem. Court, Univ. of Manchester, 1980–. Hon. LLD Leeds, 1982. *Recreations:* gardening, paintings, classical music. *Address:* 8 Brookside, Alwoodley, Leeds LS17 8TD. *T:* Leeds (0532) 683274. *Clubs:* Racquet (Liverpool); St James's (Manchester). *Died 25 Jan. 1991.*

LYONS, Terence Patrick; a consultant, since 1983; Director, Industrial Training Services Ltd, since 1980; *b* 2 Sept. 1919; *s* of Maurice Peter Lyons and Maude Mary Elizabeth Lyons (*née* O'Farrell); *m* 1945, Winifred Mary Normile; two *d. Educ:* Wimbledon Coll.; King's College, London; London Sch. of Economics. Companion IPM, FCIB. Indian Armd Corps, 1940–46. Unilever Ltd, 1948–54; Philips Electrical Industries Ltd, 1954–60; Ilford Ltd, 1960–66; Dir of Personnel, Staveley Industries Ltd, 1966–69; Exec. Dir (Personnel), 1969–81, Dir, 1981–82, Williams & Glyn's Bank Ltd. Associate Dir, Hurst Associates (Europe), 1989–. Sen. Vis. Fellow, City Univ. Business Sch., 1983–86. Pres., Inst. of Personnel Management, 1971–73; Mem. Council, Inst. Bankers, 1975–81; Chairman: Manpower Services Adv. Panel, CBI, 1975–82; Educn and Trng Cttee, CBI, 1976–77 (Vice-Chm., 1977–82); Council, Fedn of London Clearing Bank Employers, 1976–78 (Mem., 1971–81); IPM Career Counselling and Outplacement Forum, 1990–. Member: Monopolies and Mergers Commn, 1975–81; MSC, 1981–82; EEC Vocational Trng Cttee, 1981–84. Member Council: Open Univ., 1980–90 (Chm., Council's Staff Cttee, 1980–90); CBI Educn Foundn, 1976–86. DUniv

Open, 1990. *Publications:* The Personnel Function in a Changing Environment, 1971, 2nd edn 1985; contrib. newspapers and personnel management and banking jls. *Recreations:* sailing, golf, music. *Address:* Winter Ride, 2 Rosefield, Kippington Road, Sevenoaks, Kent TN13 2LJ. *Clubs:* Army and Navy; Wildernesse Golf; Royal Eastbourne Golf; Chipstead Sailing.
Died 20 Jan. 1992.

LYTTLE, John Gordon; Secretary for Public Affairs to the Archbishop of Canterbury, since 1987; *b* 15 Jan. 1933; *s* of W. J. and Hilda Lyttle. *Educ:* Oldershaw Grammar Sch., Wallasey; Sheffield Univ. (BJur). Res. Dept, Labour Party, 1963–66; Chief Officer, Race Relations Bd, 1966–73; Political Advr to Rt Hon. Shirley Williams, 1974–79; Chief Press Officer, SDP, then Head of Rt Hon. Roy Jenkins' office, 1981–83; Mem., Police Complaints Authy, 1985–87. *Recreations:* reading, music, talk. *Address:* Lambeth Palace, SE1 7JU. *T:* 071–928 8282.
Died 27 April 1991.

LYTTLETON, Prof. Raymond Arthur, MA, PhD; FRS 1955; Emeritus Professor of Theoretical Astronomy, University of Cambridge (Professor of Theoretical Astronomy, 1969–78); Fellow of St John's College, Cambridge, since 1949; Member, Institute of Astronomy (formerly Institute of Theoretical Astronomy), University of Cambridge, since 1967; *b* 7 May 1911; *o s* of William John Lyttleton and Agnes (*d* of Patrick Joseph Kelly), Warley Woods, near Birmingham, formerly of Ireland; *m* Meave Marguerite, *o d* of F. Hobden, Parkstone, formerly of Shanghai; no *c. Educ:* King Edward's Grammar Sch., Five Ways; King Edward's Sch., Birmingham; Clare Coll., Cambridge. Wrangler; Tyson Medal for Astronomy. Procter Visiting Fellowship, Princeton Univ., USA. Exptl Officer, Min. of Supply, 1940–42; Technical Asst to Scientific Adviser to the Army Council, War Office, 1943–45. Lectr in Mathematics, 1937–59, Stokes Lectr, 1954–59, Reader in Theoretical Astronomy, 1959–69, Univ. of Cambridge. Jacob Siskind Vis. Prof., Brandeis Univ., USA, 1965–66; Vis. Prof., Brown Univ., USA, 1967–68; Halley Lectr, Oxford Univ., 1970; Milne Lectr, Oxford, 1978. Mem. of Council, Royal Society, 1959–61; Geophysical Sec. of Royal Astronomical Soc., 1949–60 and Mem. of Council, 1950–61, 1969–72, Fellow, 1934–; Pres., Milne Soc., 1977–88. Hon. Mem., Mark Twain Soc., 1977. Hopkins Prize (for 1951) of Cambridge Philosophical Soc.; Gold Medallist of Royal Astronomical Soc., 1959; Royal Medallist of Royal Society, 1965. *Publications:* The Comets and their Origin, 1953; The Stability of Rotating Liquid Masses, 1953; The Modern Universe, 1956; Rival Theories of Cosmology, 1960; Man's View of the Universe, 1961; Mysteries of the Solar System, 1968; A Matter of Gravity (play; produced by BBC, 1968); Cambridge Encyclopædia of Astronomy (co-ed and contrib.), 1977; The Earth and Its Mountains, 1982; The Gold Effect, 1990; papers on astrophysics, cosmogony, cosmology, physics, dynamics, and geophysics in Proc. Royal Soc., Monthly Notices of Royal Astron. Soc., Proc. Camb. Phil Soc., etc. *Recreations:* motoring, music; wondering about it all. *Address:* 48 St Alban's Road, Cambridge CB4 2HG. *T:* Cambridge (01223) 354910; St John's College, Cambridge CB2 1TP. *T:* Cambridge (01223) 338600; Institute of Astronomy, Madingley Road, Cambridge CB3 0HA. *T:* Cambridge (01223) 337548, ext. 7519. *Died 16 May 1995.*

M

McADAM CLARK, James; *see* Clark.

McALPINE, Sir Robin, Kt 1969; CBE 1957; Chairman: Sir Robert McAlpine & Sons Ltd, 1967–77; Newarthill plc, 1972–77 (Director, 1972); (*b* 18 March 1906; *s* of late Sir (Thomas) Malcolm McAlpine, KBE, and Lady (Maud) McAlpine; *m* 1st, 1939, Nora Constance (*d* 1966), *d* of F. H. Perse; 2nd, 1970, Mrs Philippa Nicolson (*d* 1987), *d* of Sir Gervais Tennyson D'Eyncourt, 2nd Bt. *Educ:* Charterhouse. Pres., Federation of Civil Engineering Contractors, 1966–71. *Recreation:* owner and breeder of racehorses. *Address:* Aylesfield, Alton, Hants. *Club:* Jockey. *Died 19 Feb. 1993.*

MacARTHUR, Helen, (Mrs Charles MacArthur); *see* Hayes, Helen.

MacBETH, George Mann; writer; *b* Scotland, 1932; *s* of George MacBeth and Amelia Morton Mary Mann; *m* 1955, Prof. Elizabeth Browell Robson, PhD (marr. diss. 1975); *m* 1982, Lisa St Aubin de Téran (marr. diss. 1989); one *s*; *m* 1989, Penelope Ronchetti-Carpenter; one *d*. *Educ:* New Coll., Oxford (read Classics and Philosophy). BBC, 1955–76: Producer, Overseas Talks Dept, 1957; Producer, Talks Dept, 1958; Editor: Poet's Voice, 1958–65; New Comment, 1959–64; Poetry Now, 1965–76. Cholmondeley Award (jtly), 1977. *Publications: poems:* A Form of Words, 1954; The Broken Places, 1963 (Sir Geoffrey Faber Meml Award (jtly), 1964); A Doomsday Book, 1965; The Colour of Blood, 1967; The Night of Stones, 1968; A War Quartet, 1969; The Burning Cone, 1970; Collected Poems 1958–1970, 1971; The Orlando Poems, 1971; Shrapnel, 1973; A Poet's Year, 1973; In The Hours Waiting For The Blood To Come, 1975; Buying a Heart, 1978; Poems of Love and Death, 1980; Poems from Oby, 1982; The Long Darkness, 1983; The Cleaver Garden, 1986; Anatomy of a Divorce, 1988; Collected Poems 1958–82, 1989; Trespassing, 1991; *prose poems:* My Scotland, 1973; *prose:* The Transformation, 1975; The Samurai, 1975; The Survivor, 1977; The Seven Witches, 1978; The Born Losers, 1981; A Kind of Treason, 1982; Anna's Book, 1983; The Lion of Pescara, 1984; Dizzy's Woman, 1986; Another Love Story, 1991; *anthologies:* The Penguin Book of Sick Verse, 1963; (with J. Clemo and E. Lucie-Smith) Penguin Modern Poets VI, 1964; The Penguin Book of Animal Verse, 1965; (with notes) Poetry, 1900–1965, 1967; The Penguin Book of Victorian Verse, 1968; The Falling Splendour, 1970; The Book of Cats, 1976; Poetry, 1900–1975, 1980; Poetry for Today, 1984; *children's books:* Noah's Journey, 1966; Jonah and the Lord, 1969; The Rectory Mice, 1982; The Story of Daniel, 1986; *autobiography:* A Child of the War, 1987 (Angel Literary Award, 1987); *posthumous publication:* The Patient, 1993. *Recreation:* Japanese swords. *Address:* Moyne Park, Tuam, County Galway, Eire. *Died 16 Feb. 1992.*

MacCABE, Brian Farmer, MC and Bar, 1942; Honorary President, Foote, Cone & Belding Ltd (London) (Chairman, 1948–78, President, 1978–80); Director and Senior Vice-President, Foote, Cone & Belding Communications Inc. (New York), 1953–80; *b* 9 Jan. 1914; *s* of late James MacCabe and Katherine MacCabe (*née* Harwood); *m* 1940, Eileen Elizabeth Noel Hunter (*d* 1984); one *s*. *Educ:* Christ's Coll., Finchley. Served War, Major RTR (wounded 3 times, Sqdn Comd, Alamein),

1940–45. Executive, C. R. Casson Ltd, 1934–40; World-wide Advertising Manager, BOAC, 1945–47; Chm., FCB International Inc. (NY), 1967–74. Mem. Council: Inst. of Practitioners in Advertising, 1951–80 (Pres., 1963–65); Advertising Assoc., 1952–69; Internat. Marketing Programme, 1965–80. Mem., Reith Commn on Advertising, 1962–66; Dir, American Chamber of Commerce, 1971–80; Member: Promotion Cttee, BNEC, 1965–68; Marketing Cttee, Ashridge Management Coll., 1965–78; Advertising Standards Authority, 1969–72; Appeals Cttee, Olympic and Commonwealth Games, 1952–80; Management Cttee, British Sports Assoc. for the Disabled, 1962–65; Nat. Council, Brit. Polio Fellowship, 1959–65. Royal Humane Soc. Medal for saving life from drowning, 1934. *Recreations:* finalist: (800 metres) Olympic Games, Berlin, 1936; (880 yards) British Commonwealth Games, Sydney, 1938; golf, fishing. *Address:* Somerford, Penn Road, Beaconsfield, Bucks HP9 2LN. *T:* Beaconsfield (0494) 673365. *Clubs:* Boodle's; Wasps Rugby Football; London Athletic (Vice-Pres.), Bucks Amateur Athletic (Vice-Pres.); Beaconsfield Golf, Denham Golf. *Died 31 Oct. 1992.*

McCALL, Robin Home, CBE 1976 (OBE 1969); retired 1976; *b* 21 March 1912; *s* of late Charles and Dorothy McCall; *m* 1937, Joan Elizabeth Kingdon (*d* 1989); two *s* one *d*. *Educ:* St Edward's Sch., Oxford. Solicitors Final (Hons), 1935. Served War, RAFVR Night Fighter Controller (Sqdn Ldr); D Day landing Normandy, in command of 15083 GCI, 1944. Asst Solicitor: Bexhill Corp., 1935–39; Hastings Corp., 1939–46; Bristol Corp., 1946–47; Dep. Town Clerk, Hastings, 1947–48; Town Clerk and Clerk of the Peace, Winchester, 1948–72; Sec., Assoc. of Municipal Corporations, later Assoc. of Metropolitan Authorities, 1973–76. Hon. Sec., Non-County Boroughs Cttee for England and Wales, 1958–69; Member: Reading Cttee (Highway Law Consolidation); Morris Cttee (Jury Service); Kennett Preservation Gp (Historic Towns Conservation); Exec. Cttee, European Architectural Heritage Year, 1972–; UK delegn to ECLA (Council of Europe); North Hampshire Hosp. Cttee, 1969–72. Governor, St Swithin's Sch., Winchester, 1978–87; Mem., Winchester Excavations Cttee, 1962–. Hon. Freeman, City of Winchester, 1973. *Publications:* contrib. Local Government, Halsbury's Laws, 4th edn, 1980; various articles and reviews on local govt. *Recreations:* gardening, mountains. *Address:* Bernina, St Giles Hill, Winchester SO23 8JW. *T:* Winchester (0962) 854101. *Club:* Alpine. *Died 27 Oct. 1991.*

McCALLUM, Archibald Duncan Dugald, TD 1950; MA; Headmaster, Strathallan School, 1970–75; *b* 26 Nov. 1914; *s* of late Dr A. D. McCallum and Mrs A. D. McCallum; *m* 1950, Rosemary Constance, *d* of William C. Thorne, OBE, Edinburgh, and *widow* of Sqdn Ldr John Rhind, RAF; two *s*, and one step *s*. *Educ:* Fettes Coll., Edinburgh; St John's Coll., Cambridge (Classical Sizar). Served War of 1939–45 (despatches): Home Forces, India, and Burma. Asst Master and Housemaster, Fettes Coll., 1937–39, 1945–51; Second Master, Strathallan Sch., 1951–56; Headmaster: Christ Coll., Brecon, 1956–62; Epsom Coll., 1962–70. FRSA 1969–75. *Recreations:* golf, reading. *Address:* 1 Church Row Cottages, Burnham Market, King's Lynn, Norfolk PE31 8DH. *T:* Fakenham (0328) 738518. *Died 21 April 1993.*

McCALLUM, John, (Ian), BSc, FEng, FRINA, FICE; Eur Ing; consultant naval architect; Chief Ship Surveyor, Lloyd's Register of Shipping, 1970–81; *b* 13 Oct. 1920; *s* of Hugh McCallum and Agnes Falconer McCallum (*née* Walker); *m* 1948, Christine Peggy Sowden (*d* 1989); two *s. Educ:* Allan Glen's Sch., Glasgow; Glasgow Univ. (BSc (First Cl. Hons Naval Architecture) 1943). Apprenticed John Brown & Co., Clydebank, 1938–43; Jun. Lectr, Naval Architecture, Glasgow Univ., 1943–44; Ship Surveyor, Lloyd's Register of Shipping, Newcastle upon Tyne, 1944, Glasgow, 1949, London, 1953; Naval Architect, John Brown & Co., 1961 (Chief Ship Designer, QE2); Technical Dir, John Brown Shipbuilders, 1967, Upper Clyde Shipbuilders, 1969. FRINA (Mem. Council, 1970–; Chm., 1971–73; Vice-Pres., 1975–); FEng 1977; FICE 1978; Eur Ing 1992. FIES 1993 (MIES 1962; past Mem. Council); Member: SNAME, 1970–81, Fellow, 1981–; Smeatonian Soc. of Civil Engrs, 1979–; CEI Cttee on Internat. Affairs, 1980–83; Lloyd's Register Technical Cttee, 1981–. Liveryman, Worshipful Co. of Shipwrights, 1975 (Mem. Educn Cttee, 1975–90). *Publications:* various technical papers to Royal Soc., RINA, NE Coast IES, Assoc. Tech. Maritime et Aéronautique (1978 Medal), and other Europ. learned socs. *Recreations:* golf, piano, pastel art. *Address:* Dala, Garvock Drive, Kippington, Sevenoaks, Kent TN13 2LT. *T and Fax:* Sevenoaks (01732) 455462. *Clubs:* Caledonian, Caledonian Westminster Business. *Died 12 Feb. 1995.*

McCANCE, Robert Alexander, CBE 1953; FRS 1948; Professor of Experimental Medicine, Medical Research Council and University of Cambridge, 1945–66, then Emeritus; Director, MRC Infantile Malnutrition Research Unit, Mulago Hospital, Kampala, 1966–68; Fellow of Sidney Sussex College; *b* near Belfast, Northern Ireland, 9 Dec. 1898; *s* of Mary L. Bristow and J. S. F. McCance, linen merchant, Belfast; *m* 1922, Mary L. MacGregor (*d* 1965); one *s* one *d. Educ:* St Bees Sch., Cumberland; Sidney Sussex Coll., Cambridge. BA 1922, MD 1929, Cambridge; FRCP 1935. RN Air Service and RAF, 1917–18. Biochemical Research, Cambridge, 1922–25; qualified in medicine King's Coll. Hosp., London, 1927; Asst Physician i/c biochemical research, King's Coll. Hosp., London; Reader in Medicine, Cambridge Univ., 1938. Goulstonian Lectr, RCP, 1936; Humphrey Rolleston Lectr, RCP, 1953; Groningen Univ. Lectr, 1958; Leonard Parsons Lectr, Birmingham Univ., 1959; Lumleian Lectr, RCP, 1962. War of 1939–45, worked on medical problems of national importance; visited Spain and Portugal on behalf of British Council, 1943, South Africa, 1965; i/c Medical Research Council Unit, Germany, 1946–49. Hon. FRCOG; Hon. Member: Assoc. of American Physicians; American Pediatric Soc.; Swiss Nutrition Soc.; Brit. Pædiatric Assoc.; Nutrition Soc. Gold Medal, West London Medico-Chirurgical Soc., 1949; Conway Evans Prize, RCP and Royal Society, 1960; James Spence Medal, Brit. Pæd. Assoc., 1961. Hon. DSc Belfast, 1964. *Publications:* Medical Problems in Mineral Metabolism (Goulstonian Lectures), 1936; (with E. M. Widdowson) The Chemical Composition of Foods, 1940; An Experimental Study of Rationing; (jointly) Breads White and Brown, 1956; numerous papers on the physiology of the newborn animal. *Recreations:* mountaineering, cycling, gardening. *Address:* 17 Shelford Lodge, 144 Cambridge Road, Great Shelford, Cambridge CB2 5JU. *Died 5 March 1993.*

McCANN, His Eminence Cardinal Owen, DD, PhD, BCom; Archbishop Emeritus of Cape Town; Cardinal since 1965 (Titular Church, St Praxedes); *b* 26 June 1907; *s* of Edward McCann and Susan Mary Plint. *Educ:* St Joseph's Coll., Rondebosch, CP; Univ. of Cape Town; Collegium Urbanianum de Propaganda Fide, Rome. Priest, 1935. Editor, The Southern Cross, 1940–48 and 1986–;

Administrator, St Mary's Cathedral, Cape Town, 1948–50; Archbishop of Cape Town, 1950–84. Hon. DLitt Univ. of Cape Town, 1968; Hon. Dr Hum. Lett. Coll. of St Joseph, Portland, Maine, USA, 1984. Freeman of City of Cape Town, 1984. *Address:* Oak Lodge, Fair Seat Lane, Wynberg, CP, South Africa; Chancery Office, Cathedral Place, 12 Bouquet Street, Cape Town. *Club:* City and Civil Service (Cape Town).
Died 26 March 1994.

MACCLESFIELD, 8th Earl of *cr* 1721; **George Roger Alexander Thomas Parker;** Baron Parker, 1716; Viscount Parker, 1721; DL; *b* 6 May 1914; *e s* of 7th Earl of Macclesfield and Lilian Joanna Vere (*d* 1974), *d* of Major Charles Boyle; *S* father, 1975; *m* 1938, Hon. Valerie Mansfield, *o d* of 4th Baron Sandhurst, OBE; two *s.* DL Oxfordshire, 1965. *Heir: s* Viscount Parker [*b* 31 May 1943; *m* 1967, Tatiana Cleone, *d* of Major Craig Wheaton-Smith; three *d* (incl. twins); *m* 1986, Mrs Sandra Hope Mead]. *Address:* Shirburn, Watlington, Oxon.
Died 7 Dec. 1992.

McCLUSKIE, Samuel Joseph; Executive Officer, Rail, Maritime and Transport Union, 1990–91; General Secretary, National Union of Seamen, 1986–90 (Assistant General Secretary, 1976–86); *b* 11 Aug. 1932; *s* of James and Agnes McCluskie; *m* 1961, Alice (*née* Potter); one *d* (one *s* decd). *Educ:* St Mary Primary School, Leith; Holy Cross Academy, Edinburgh. Merchant Navy, 1955; Union Delegate, 1963; Mem., Labour Party Nat. Exec. Cttee, 1974–91, Treasurer, 1984–92; Chairman, Labour Party, 1983. *Recreations:* coursing, greyhounds, watching Glasgow Celtic. *Address:* 23/7 Ferryfield, Edinburgh EH5 2PR. *T:* 0131–467 1334. *Died 15 Sept. 1995.*

McCONE, John Alex; US business executive, retired; Chairman, Hendy International Co., 1969–75; *b* 4 Jan. 1902; *s* of Alexander J. McCone and Margaret McCone (*née* Enright); *m* 1938, Rosemary Cooper (*d* 1961); no *c*; *m* 1962, Mrs Theiline McGee Pigott (widow) (*d* 1990). *Educ:* Univ. of California, Coll. of Engineering. Began as construction engineer, Llewellyn Iron Works; supt Consolidated Steel Corp., 1929; Exec. Vice-Pres. and Dir, 1933–37; Pres. of Bechtel-McCone Corp., Los Angeles, 1937–45; Pres. and Dir, California Shipbuilding Corp., 1941–46; Joshua Hendy Corp., Joshua Hendy Iron Works, 1945–69 (Chm., Joshua Hendy Corp., 1961–69). Mem. President's Air Policy Commn, 1947–48; Dep. to Sec. of Defense, March-Nov. 1948; Under Sec. of US Air Force, 1950–51. Chm., US Atomic Energy Commn, 1957–61; Dir, Central Intelligence Agency, 1961–65. Hon. degrees from univs and colls in the US. US Presidential Medal of Freedom, 1987. *Recreation:* golf. *Address:* (home) 1543 Riata Road, PO Box 1499, Pebble Beach, Calif 93953, USA. *T:* (408) 625 3266; Norcliffe, The Highlands, Seattle, Washington; PO Box 19, Rock Sound, Eleuthera, Bahamas. *Clubs:* California, Los Angeles Country (Los Angeles); Pacific Union, Bohemian (San Francisco); Metropolitan (Washington, DC); The Links (NYC); Cypress Point (Pebble Beach, Calif); Seattle Golf, Ranier (Seattle). *Died 14 Feb. 1991.*

McCONNELL, Albert Joseph, MA, ScD; Hon. Fellow of Oriel College, Oxford; Provost of Trinity College, Dublin, 1952–74; Member of Council of State, Ireland, 1973–91; *b* 19 Nov. 1903; *s* of Joseph McConnell; *m* 1st, 1934, Hilda (*d* 1966), *d* of late Francis McGuire; 2nd, 1983, Jean (*d* 1985), *d* of late Robert Shekleton. *Educ:* Ballymena Acad.; Trinity Coll., Dublin (Scholar, First Math. Moderator and Univ. Student); Univ. of Rome. Dr of Univ. of Rome, 1928; ScD (Dublin), 1929; MRIA, 1929. Lectr in Maths, Trinity Coll., Dublin, 1927–30; Fellow of Trinity Coll., Dublin, 1930–52; Prof. of Natural Philosophy, Univ. of Dublin, 1930–57; Special Univ. Lectr, Univ. of London, 1949. Vis. Professor: Univ. of

Alexandria, 1946–47; Univ. of Kuwait, 1970. Chm., Governing Bd, Sch of Theoretical Physics, 1970– (Mem., 1940–); Mem. Council, Dublin Inst. for Advanced Studies, 1970–. Hon. DSc: Belfast; Ulster; Hon. ScD Columbia; Hon. LLD NUI. *Publications:* Applications of the Absolute Differential Calculus, 1931; (ed) The Mathematical Papers of Sir William Rowan Hamilton, vol. II, 1940; Applications of Tensor Analysis, 1957; papers on relativity, geometry and dynamics in various mathematical jls. *Address:* Seafield Lodge, Seafield Road, Killiney, Dublin. *Clubs:* Athenæum; Dublin University (Dublin). *Died 24 Aug. 1993.*

MacCONOCHIE, John Angus, MBE 1943; FCIT; Chairman: Furness Withy & Co. Ltd, 1968–72 (Director, 1964–73); Shaw Savill & Albion Co. Ltd, 1968–73 (Director, 1957–73); *b* 12 April 1908; *m* 1938, Peggy, *d* of late Robert Gunson Martindale, MA, Worthing, Sussex; one *s* one *d*. *Educ:* Royal Caledonian Schools, Bushey, Herts. Joined Shaw Savill Line, 1927. Seconded to Min. of War Transport, 1942; served on Staff of Resident Minister for W Africa, Accra; Min. of War Transport Rep. in Gold Coast (MBE); London, 1944; Min. HQ with 21 Army Group; subseq. Paris, Marseilles, Naples. Returned to Shaw Savill Line, 1945: New Zealand, 1949; subseq. Manager for Australia; Gen. Manager for New Zealand, 1953; returned to Britain, 1958; Dir, 1957. Chm., Royal Mail Lines, 1968–73; Director: Economic Insurance, 1967 (Chm. 1969–73); British Maritime Trust, 1966–73; Pacific Steam Navigation Co. Ltd, 1967–73; Pacific Maritime Services, 1967–73; Houlder Bros & Co. Ltd, 1967–73; Whitehall Insurance Co. Ltd, 1967–73; Manchester Liners Ltd, 1968–73; National Bank of New Zealand, 1970 (NZ Bd, 1973–78). Member: Council, Chamber of Shipping; Council of Management, Ocean Travel Development (past Chm.); Cttee, NZ Society (PP); British Ship Adoption Soc. (past Chm.); Pres., UK Chamber of Shipping, 1972–73 (Pres.-designate 1971). Patron, Auckland Maritime Soc. *Address:* 36 Barlow Place, Chatswood, Auckland 10, New Zealand. *Club:* Northern (Auckland). *Died 14 May 1992.*

McCORMACK, Arthur Gerard; Director, Population and Development Office, Rome, 1973–86; Consultant to United Nations Fund for Population Activities, since 1975; *b* 16 Aug. 1911; *s* of Francis McCormack and Elizabeth Ranard. *Educ:* St Francis Xavier Coll., Liverpool; Durham Univ. (MA Hons History and Econs). Ordained, 1936. Mill Hill Missionary, Africa, 1940–48 (invalided home, 1948); after lengthy illness and convalescence, hosp. chaplain and subseq. teacher-chaplain in secondary modern sch., Widnes; Adviser to Superior Gen., Mill Hill Missionaries, 1963; attended II Vatican Council as expert on population and develt of developing countries, 1963–65; part Founder, Vatican Commn, Justice and Peace (mem. staff for 7 yrs). Special Adviser to Sec. Gen., World Population Conf., Bucharest, 1974. *Publications:* People, Space, Food, 1960; (ed) Christian Responsibility and World Poverty, 1963; World Poverty and the Christian, 1963; Poverty and Population, 1964; The Population Problem, 1970; The Population Explosion and Christian Concern, 1973; Multinational Investment: Boon or Burden for the Developing Countries, 1980; contrib. The Tablet, Population & Develt Rev., Populi, etc. *Recreations:* reading, driving scooter. *Died 11 Dec. 1992.*

McCUNN, Peter Alexander, CBE 1980; Deputy Chairman, Cable and Wireless plc, 1978–82 (Group Managing Director, 1978–81); *b* 11 Nov. 1922; *m* 1943, Margaret Prescott; two *s* (and one *s* decd). *Educ:* Mexborough Grammar Sch.; Edinburgh University. Commnd W Yorks Regt, 1942; served in Normandy, Malta, Italy; left Army, Nov. 1946 (Captain). Joined Cable & Wireless, 1947; Director: Cable & Wireless/Western Union International

Inc. of Puerto Rico, 1968–70; Cable & Wireless, 1969–82 (Exec. Dep. Chm., 1977); Nigerian External Telecommunications Ltd, 1969–72; Sierra Leone External Telecommunications Ltd, 1969–72; Trinidad and Tobago External Telecommunications Ltd, 1972–77; Jamaica International Telecommunications Ltd, 1972–77; Cable and Wireless (Hong Kong) Ltd, 1981–84; Mercury Communications Ltd, 1981–84. *Recreations:* music, gardening, swimming, reading, crosswords. *Address:* Wychelms, 14 Lime Walk, Pinkneys Green, Maidenhead, Berks SL6 6QB. *T:* Maidenhead (0628) 24308. *Clubs:* Exiles (Twickenham); Phyllis Court (Henley). *Died 9 March 1992.*

McDERMID, Rev. Canon Richard Thomas Wright; Vicar of Christ Church, Harrogate, 1970–94; Chaplain to the Queen, since 1986; *b* 10 July 1929; *s* of Lloyd Roberts McDermid and Annie McDermid; *m* 1956, Joyce Margaret (*née* Pretty); one *s* four *d*. *Educ:* St Peter's Sch., York; Univ. of Durham, 1950–55 (MA, DipTh). Served Intelligence Corps, 1947–49. Deacon 1955, priest 1956; Curate of Seacroft, Leeds, 1955–61; Vicar of St Mary's, Hawksworth Wood, Leeds, 1961–70. Hon. Canon of Ripon Cath., 1983–94, then Canon Emeritus. *Publication:* Beverley Minster Fasti, 1991. *Recreations:* local history, brass rubbing, gardening. *Address:* Greystones Mews, Wycar, Bedale, N Yorks DL8 1EP. *T:* Bedale (0677) 426564. *Died 19 July 1994.*

McDONALD, Alexander Gordon, (Alex); Chief Scientific Officer, Department of Health and Social Security, 1975–82; *b* 29 Jan. 1921; *m* 1st, 1942, P. Thomas; 2nd, 1950, J. James; two *d*. *Educ:* Tiffin Sch., Kingston upon Thames; Royal Coll. of Science (BSc, ARCS). Served RNVR, Lieut (A), Fleet Air Arm, 1939–46. Home Office, 1949; Chief of Staffs, MoD, 1956; Police Research and Develt Br., 1963; DHSS, 1970. Sometime Lectr at: Inst. of Criminology, Inst. of Advanced Legal Study, London Hosp. Sch. of Forensic Pathology, London Sch. of Hygiene and Trop. Med., and Univ. of Warwick Sch. of Business Studies. Member, Bd of Studies in Community Med., London. Hon. Prof. in Industrial and Business Studies, and Dir, Res. Centre on Mathematical Modelling of Clinical Trials, Univ. of Warwick. *Publications:* contrib. learned jls on OR and Systems Analysis. *Recreations:* basset hounds, blood hounds, needlework, reading. *Address:* 40 Wolsey Road, East Molesey, Surrey KT8 9EN. *Club:* Kennel. *Died 13 Feb. 1992.*

MACDONALD, Alistair; *b* 23 July 1912; 2nd *s* of late Reginald James Macdonald and Dorothy Bolden; *m* 1941, Myra Jones; one *s* six *d*. *Educ:* King's Sch., Bruton. Called to the Bar, Inner Temple, 1935. Worked with mentally handicapped children, Sunfield Childrens' Homes, Clent, 1936–40; served in RAF, 1940–45: Air Staff (Intelligence), 1943–45 (despatches). Practice at the Bar and journalism, 1946–48; Legal Assistant, Law Officers Dept, 1948; Legal Sec. to Law Officers of the Crown, 1950–58; Secretary, The Council on Tribunals, 1958–70; Mem., Lord Chancellor's Dept. Consultant to: Royal Inst. of Public Admin, 1970–72; Emerson Coll., Forest Row, Sussex, 1973–. *Publication:* (with R. E. Wraith and P. G. Hutchesson) Administrative Tribunals, 1973. *Address:* South Harbour, Priory Road, Forest Row, E Sussex RH18 5HR. *Died 1 May 1991.*

McDONALD, Alistair Ian, CBE 1978; Director: Schroder Global Trust plc (formerly Trans Oceanic Trust), 1981–89; TR Trustees Corporation PLC, 1982–89; *b* 12 Sept. 1921; *s* of late Angus McDonald and Blanche Elizabeth McDonald; *m* 1947, Olwen (*née* Evans); one *d*. *Educ:* Greenwich Sch. Served War, RAF, 1940–46. Church Comrs, 1947–81: Dep. Investments Sec., 1966–68; Investments Sec., 1968–81. Director: Datastream Ltd, 1981–82; Trust Union Ltd, 1981–82; TR Industrial and

Gen. Trust PLC, 1982–89; Chm., Cirkit Hldgs PLC, 1983–87. Royal Coll. of Nursing: Investment Adviser, 1967–90; Vice Pres., 1975–. Chm., Lampada Housing Assoc., 1975–92. *Recreations:* grandsons, gardening, reading. *Club:* Caledonian.   *Died 15 Jan. 1995.*

MacDONALD, Gen. Sir Arthur (Leslie), KBE 1978 (OBE 1953); CB 1969; *b* 30 Jan. 1919; *s* of late Arthur Leslie MacDonald, Yaamba, Queensland; *m* 1940, Joan Bevington, *d* of late Sidney Brady, Brisbane, Queensland; one *d. Educ:* The Southport School, Southport, Queensland; Royal Military College, Duntroon, ACT. Regtl and Staff appts, Aust., ME and New Guinea, 1940–44; Instructor, Staff Coll., Camberley, 1944–45; CO 3rd Bn, The Royal Australian Regt, Korea, 1953–54; Dir of Mil. Ops, AHQ, 1955–56; Senior Aust. Planner, SEATO, Bangkok, 1957–58; Commandant, Jungle Training Centre, Canungra, 1959–60; Dir of Staff Duties, AHQ, 1960–61; Imperial Defence Coll., 1962; Dep. Commander, 1st Div., 1963–64; Commander, Papua New Guinea Comd, 1965–66; Dep. Chief of the General Staff, 1966–67; Commander Australian Force, Viet Nam, 1968–69; Adjutant-Gen., 1969–70; GOC Northern Comd, 1970–73; Chief of Operations, 1973; Vice Chief of Gen. Staff, 1973–75; CGS, 1975–77; Chief of Defence Force Staff, 1977–79, retired. Col Comdt, Royal Aust. Regt, 1981–85. Director: Carricks Ltd and associated cos, 1980–86; Gas Corp. of Qld, 1983–91. *Address: c/o* Mrs M. Beaumont, 25 Bon Accord Avenue, Bondi Junction, NSW 2022, Australia. *Club:* Queensland (Brisbane).   *Died 28 Jan. 1995.*

MACDONALD, Rev. Donald Farquhar Macleod, CBE 1979; Principal Clerk of General Assembly of the Church of Scotland, 1972–85; *b* 1 May 1915; *s* of John Murchison Macdonald and Margaret Macleod; *m* 1948, Anne Jane Vance Sinclair; one *s* two *d. Educ:* North Kelvinside Secondary Sch.; Glasgow Univ. (MA, LLB). Ordained to Glasford Parish, 1948; Clerk to Presbytery of Hamilton, 1952–72; Dep. Clerk of General Assembly, 1955–71. Hon. Fellow and Hon. DLit, Central Sch. of Religion, Worcester, 1985. *Publications:* (ed) Practice and Procedure in the Church of Scotland, 6th edn, 1977; (ed and comp.) Fasti Ecclesiae Scoticanae, vol. X, 1981. *Recreations:* chess, swimming, gardening. *Address:* 29 Auchingramont Road, Hamilton, Lanarkshire ML3 6JP. *T:* Hamilton (01698) 423667; 3 Chapmans Place, Elie, Fife KY9 1BT. *Club:* Royal Scots (Edinburgh).   *Died 26 April 1995.*

MACDONALD, Sir Herbert (George deLorme), KBE 1967 (OBE 1948); JP (Jamaica); retired government officer (Jamaica); company director; sportsman; President Organising Committee, IX Central American and Caribbean Games, 1962, and 8th British Empire and Commonwealth Games, 1966 (compiled and edited history); Chairman, National Sports Ltd (a Government body owning and operating National Stadium and Sports Centre), 1960–67, subsequently President (specially created post); Director: Prospect Beach Ltd; Macdonald Ltd; *b* Kingston, 23 May 1902; *s* of late Ronald Macdonald, JP, planter, and Louise (*née* Alexander). *Educ:* Wolmer's Boys' Sch., Jamaica; Northeast High Sch., Philadelphia, USA. Clerical and planting activities, 1919–43. Published Sportsman Magazine (with Sir Arthur Thelwell). Accompanied Jamaica's team to World Olympics, London, 1948, and (as Manager) to Helsinki, 1952, Melbourne, 1956; Chef de Mission, WI Olympic Team to Rome, 1960; Deleg., Tokyo, 1964. Chief Liaison Officer, BWI Central Lab. Org. (USA), 1943–55; Pres., Jamaica Olympic Assoc., 1940–44 and 1956–58; Pres., WI Olympic Assoc. (from inception), 1958–61 (when Polit. Fedn was broken up). Past Pres. etc, various Jamaican sporting assocs and boards; Mem. Exec. Cttee Pan

American Sports Organisation which controlled Pan American Games; Exec. Sec., Jamaica Tercentenary Celebrations Cttee, 1955. Mem. Bd of Trustees, Wolmer's Sch. Diploma of Merit, 1966 Internat. Olympic Cttee, 1968. Anglican. *Recreations:* all sports (represented Jamaica in football and tennis *v* foreign teams, 1925–32), stamp collecting (athletic stamps). *Address:* 1 Liguanea Row, Kingston 6, Jamaica. *T:* 927–8213. *Clubs:* (Life Mem., past Hon. Sec.) Kingston Cricket (Kingston, Jamaica); Constant Spring Golf.   *Died 26 Oct. 1991.*

McDONALD, Thomas Muirhead; JP; Lord Provost and Lord Lieutenant of Dundee, since 1992; telephone engineer, British Telecom, since 1978; *b* 12 March 1952; *m* 1987, Jill Hannan. *Educ:* St John's High Sch., Dundee. TV engineer, 1966–78; joined PO Telecommunications, 1978. Joined Labour Party, 1969. City of Dundee District Council: Mem., 1974–; Depute Leader of Admin, 1984–86; Leader 1986–88. Member: COSLA, 1984–88; Dundee Rep. Theatre Bd, 1985–86. JP City of Dundee, 1984. *Recreations:* reading, fishing, current affairs. *Address:* City of Dundee District Council, City Chambers, Dundee DD1 3BY. *T:* Dundee (01382) 23141; 1 Viewpark Cottage, Gardners Lane, Dundee DD1 5RE.   *Died 20 June 1995.*

MACDONALD-SMITH, Sydney, CMG 1956; retired; *b* 9 July 1908; *s* of late John Alfred Macdonald-Smith, MB, ChB, FRCSE; *m* 1st, 1935, Joyce (*d* 1966), *d* of Austen Whetham, Bridport, Dorset; one *s* one *d*; 2nd, 1968, Winifred Mary Atkinson, JP, *widow* of Captain T. K. W. Atkinson, RN. *Educ:* Nottingham High Sch.; New Coll., Oxford. Entered Colonial Administrative Service, Nigeria, 1931; Controller of Imports, 1945; Director of Supplies, 1947; Under-Sec., Gold Coast, 1949; Permanent Sec. Ministry of Communications and Works, 1950; Chief Regional Officer, Northern Territories, 1954–57; retired Nov. 1957. *Recreation:* gardening. *Address:* Woodman's, Westbourne, Emsworth, Hants PO10 8RS. *T:* Emsworth (0243) 372943.   *Died 18 Sept. 1994.*

MacDOUGALL, Brig. David Mercer, CMG 1946; MA; *b* 8 Dec. 1904; *m* 1st, 1929, Catherine Crowther; one *d*; 2nd, 1951, Inez Weir, *o d* of late James Hislop Thompson; two *d. Educ:* St Andrews Univ. Cadet Hong Kong Administrative Service, 1928; seconded to Colonial Office as asst principal, Feb. 1937–March 1939; seconded Hong Kong Dept of Information and Sec. Far Eastern Bureau of British Ministry of Information, Oct. 1939; Colonial Office, 1942; British Embassy, Washington, DC, 1943; Dir British Political Warfare Mission, San Francisco, Dec. 1943; Colonial Office, 1944; Brig. Chief Civil Affairs Officer, Hong Kong, 1945; Colonial Sec., Hong Kong, 1946–49; retired, 1949. Order of the Brilliant Star (China), 1946. *Address:* Mercers, Finchingfield, Essex CM7 4JS.   *Died 13 May 1991.*

MacDOUGALL, Laura Margaret, (Lady MacDougall); Hon. Fellow of Somerville College, Oxford, since 1975; *b* 27 Aug. 1910; *d* of George E. Linfoot and Laura Edith Clayton; *m* 1932, Robert L. Hall (later Lord Roberthall, who *d* 1988) (marr. diss. 1968); two *d*; *m* 1977, Sir Donald MacDougall, CBE, FBA. *Educ:* Sheffield Girls' High Sch. and High Storrs Grammar Sch.; Somerville Coll., Oxford. Hon. Scholar, 1st Cl. Hons Philosophy, Politics and Economics; Jun. George Webb Medley Scholar. US Govt Office of Price Admin, 1941–44; UNNRA Planning Div., Washington, DC, Sydney and London, 1944–45; Lectr, Lincoln Coll., Oxford, 1946–47; Lectr, 1947–49, and Fellow and Tutor, 1949–75, Somerville Coll., Oxford; University Lectr in Economics, 1949–75. Consultant, NEDO, 1962–87; Economic Consultant, Distillers' Co. plc, 1978–84. Member: Treasury Purchase Tax Cttee, 1954; Interdeptl Cttee on Economic and Social Research,

1957–58; Gaitskell Indep. Co-operative Commn, 1958; Min. of Agric. Cttee on the Remuneration of Milk Distributors in the UK, 1962; Reith Indep. Commn on Advertising, 1964; Covent Garden Market Authority Adv. Cttee, 1972; Distributive Trades Industrial Trng Bd's Research Cttee, 1972; EDC for Distributive Trades, 1963–87; Monopolies and Mergers Commn, 1973–76; Past Member: Retail Furnishing and Allied Trades Wages Council; Retail Newsagency, Confectioner and Tobacconist Wages Council. Visiting Professor: MIT, USA, 1961–62; in Distributive Studies, Univ. of Stirling, 1984–87 (Hon. Prof., 1987–). Hon. LLD Nottingham, 1979. *Publications:* (US Senate Cttee Print) Effect of War on British Retail Trade, 1943; Distributive Trading: an economic analysis, 1954; Distribution in Great Britain and North America (with Knapp and Winsten), 1961; contribs to: The British Economy, 1945–50, 1952; The British Economy in the 1950s, 1962; (Bolton Cttee, Research Report No 8) The Small Unit in Retail Trade, 1972; numerous contribs to various economic and statistical jls. *Address:* Flat K, 19 Warwick Square, SW1V 2AB. *T:* 0171–821 1998. *Died 8 March 1995.*

McDOWELL, Prof. (Martin Rastall) Coulter, JP; FRAS, FInstP; Professor of Applied Mathematics, 1969–86, then Emeritus, and Head of Department of Mathematics, 1982–86, Royal Holloway and Bedford New College (formerly at Royal Holloway College), University of London; *b* 30 Jan. 1932; *s* of late Richard Whiteside Coulter McDowell and Evelyn Jean McDowell; *m* 1956, Brenda Gordon Blair, *d* of late Robert Cooke Blair and of Mildred Martley Blair; two *s. Educ:* Methodist College, Belfast; Queen's University, Belfast (BSc 1953, PhD 1957); Columbia University, NY (MA 1954). Gassiot Research Fellow, QUB, 1956–57; Lectr in Mathematics, Royal Holloway Coll., 1957–64; apptd Teacher, Univ. of London, 1960; Vis. Scholar, Georgia Inst. of Tech., Atlanta, 1959–60; Reader in Appl. Maths, Univ. of Durham, 1964–69; Senior Research Associate, Goddard Space Flight Center, 1967–68; Dean of Science, 1972–75 and 1982–85, RHC, Univ. of London; Member: Council, RHC, 1973–76, 1984–85; Senate, Univ. of London, 1983–85. JP Surrey, 1981. *Publications:* (ed) Atomic Collision Processes, 1964; (ed with E. W. McDaniel) Case Studies in Atomic Collision Physics, Vol. 1 1969, Vol. 2 1972, Vol. 3 1974, Vol. 4 1975; (with J. P. Coleman) Theory of Ion-Atom Collisions, 1970; (with H. J. W. Kleinpoppen) Electron and Photon Interactions with Matter, 1976; (with A. Ferendici) Atomic Processes in Thermonuclear Plasmas, 1980; (with J. W. Humberston) Positrons in Gases, 1984; (with Prof. B. H. Bransden) Charge Exchange and the Theory of Ion-Atom Collisions, 1992; papers in learned jls. *Recreations:* Roman archaeology, drinking wine. *Died 13 June 1993.*

McELROY, Roy Granville, CMG 1972; LLD, PhD; Pro-Chancellor of the University of Auckland, 1968–74; *b* 2 April 1907; *s* of H. T. G. McElroy and Frances C. Hampton; *m* 1st, Joan H. (decd), *d* of R. O. H. Biss; two *d*; 2nd, 1992, Betty Joan Boyd Macgregor, *d* of John Boyd Macgregor. *Educ:* Auckland Univ.; Clare Coll., Cambridge. LLM NZ 1929; PhD Cantab 1934; LLD NZ 1936. Barrister. Lectr in Law, Auckland Univ., 1936–37. Mem., Auckland City Council, 1938–53; Dep. Mayor of Auckland, 1953, Mayor, 1965–68; Chm., Auckland Metro Planning Cttee, 1953; Mem., Auckland Regional Planning Authority, 1954–66; Chairman: Auckland Old People's Welfare Cttee, 1950–65; NZ Welfare of Aged Persons Distribution Cttee, 1962–75; Sunset Home Inc., 1972–82; Member: Bd of Trustees, NZ Retirement Life Care, 1972–82; Council, Dr Barnardo's in NZ; Auckland Medico-Legal Soc. Consular Agent of France in Auckland, 1948–72; Dean, Auckland Consular Corps, 1965 and 1971. Chm., NZ Section Internat. Commn of Jurists,

1965–72. Chm. Legal Research Foundn, Auckland Univ., 1968–72; Mem., Auckland Univ. Council, 1939–54 and 1960–78; Chm., Auckland Br., NZ Inst. of Internat. Affairs, 1970. FRSA 1971. Hon. DLitt Auckland Univ., 1976. Chevalier de l'Ordre National de la Légion d'Honneur, 1954. *Publications:* Law Reform Act 1936 NZ, 1937; Impossibility of Performance of Contracts, 1942; articles in Modern Law Review, NZ Law Jl, NZ Financial Times. *Recreation:* reading. *Address:* 122 St John's Road, Meadowbank, Auckland, New Zealand. *Club:* Northern (Auckland). *Died 16 May 1994.*

McEVOY, Air Chief Marshal Sir Theodore Newman, KCB 1956 (CB 1951); CBE 1945 (OBE 1941); *b* 21 Nov. 1904; *s* of late Rev. C. McEvoy, MA, Watford; *m* 1935, Marian, *d* of late W. A. E. Coxon, Cairo; one *s* one *d. Educ:* Haberdashers' School; RAF Coll., Cranwell. Served with Fighter Squadrons and in Iraq, 1925–36; psa 1937; Air Ministry, 1938–41; commanded Northolt, 1941; Group Captain Operations, HQ Fighter Command, 1942–43; SASO No 11 Group, 1943; SASO No 84 Group, 1944 (despatches); Air Ministry (DST), 1945–47; idc 1948; AOC No 61 Group, 1949–50; Assistant Chief of Air Staff (Training), 1950–53; RAF Instructor, Imperial Defence Coll., 1954–56; Chief of Staff, Allied Air Forces, Central Europe, 1956–59; Air Secretary, Air Ministry, 1959–62; Air ADC to the Queen, 1959–62; retired, 1962. Vice-President, British Gliding Assoc. Commander Order of Polonia Restituta (Poland), 1942. *Recreations:* gardening, glass engraving. *Address:* Hurstwood, West Drive, Aldwick Bay Estate, Bognor Regis PO21 4LZ. *Club:* Royal Air Force. *Died 28 Sept. 1991.*

McEWAN YOUNGER, Sir William; *see* Younger.

M'EWEN, Ewen, CBE 1975; MScEng; FRSE; consulting engineer, since 1980; *b* 13 Jan. 1916; *e s* of Clement M'Ewen and Doris Margaret Pierce-Hope; *m* 1938, Barbara Dorrien, *d* of W. F. Medhurst; two *s* one *d. Educ:* Merchiston; University Coll., London. BSc (Eng) 1st class Hons, 1935; MSc (Eng) 1948; Head Memorial Medallist and Prizeman, 1935. CEng; FIMechE; FASME. Graduate Apprentice David Brown & Sons (Huddersfield) Ltd, 1935–37, Research Engineer, 1937–40, Asst Works Manager, 1940–42; served War of 1939–45, 1942–46: Lt-Col 1943; Lt-Col (Hon. Col) REME (TA retd); Asst Dir, Dept of Tank Design, 1943–46; Asst Chief Engineer, Fighting Vehicles Design Dept, 1946–47; Prof. of Agricultural Engineering, King's Coll., Univ. of Durham, Newcastle upon Tyne, 1947–54, and Reader in Applied Mechanics, 1952–54; Dir Armament R&D Establishment, Fort Halstead, 1955–58; Dir of Engineering, Massey Ferguson Ltd, 1958–63; Dep. Man. Dir, 1963, Man. Dir, 1965–67, Hobourn Group Ltd; Vice-Chm. (Engrg), Joseph Lucas Ltd, 1967–80. Visiting Professor: Imperial Coll., London, 1971–78; UCL, 1978–. Member: Council, Instn of Mech. Engs, 1961–81 (Vice-Pres., 1970–76; Pres., 1976–77); Design Council, 1971–77; Armed Forces Pay Review Body, 1971–83; Chm., Metrology and Standards Requirements Bd, 1973–77. Commanded REME 50 (N) Infantry Div. (TA), 1949–52. Hon. Col Durham Univ. OTC, 1955–60. Chm., Lanchester Polytechnic, Coventry, 1970–73. Fellow, UCL, 1965; FRSE 1973. Hon. DSc: Heriot-Watt, 1976; Newcastle, 1977. Liveryman, Glaziers' Company; Hammerman, Glasgow. *Publications:* papers and articles in Technical Press. *Recreation:* sailing. *Address:* 45 Pearce Avenue, Poole, Dorset BH14 8EG. *T:* Parkstone (0202) 742067. *Clubs:* Army and Navy, Royal Thames Yacht; Parkstone Yacht, Royal Motor Yacht. *Died 10 July 1993.*

McEWEN, Rev. Prof. James Stevenson, DD; Professor of Church History, University of Aberdeen, 1958–77; Master of Christ's College, Aberdeen, 1971–77; *b* 18 Feb. 1910; *s* of Rev. Thomas McEwen and Marjorie Bissett; *m* 1945,

Martha M. Hunter, Auchendrane, Alexandria; two *s*. *Educ:* George Watson's Coll., Edinburgh Univ. Ordained Church of Scotland, 1940; held parishes at Rathen, Hawick and Invergowrie; Lecturer in Church History at University of Edinburgh, 1953. *Publication:* The Faith of John Knox, 1961. *Address:* 8 Westfield Terrace, Aberdeen AB2 4RU. *T:* Aberdeen (0224) 645413.   *Died 4 May 1993.*

McFADZEAN OF KELVINSIDE, Baron *cr* 1980 (Life Peer), of Kelvinside in the District of the City of Glasgow; **Francis Scott McFadzean,** Kt 1975; Director, Shell Transport and Trading Company Ltd, 1964–86, then non-executive Director; Director: Shell Petroleum Company Ltd, 1964–86; Beecham Group Ltd, 1974–86; Coats Patons Ltd, 1979–86; *b* 26 Nov. 1915; *m* 1st, 1938, Isabel McKenzie Beattie (*d* 1987); one *d*; 2nd, 1988, Sonja Khung. *Educ:* Glasgow Univ. (MA); London Sch. of Economics (Hon. Fellow, 1974). BoT, 1938; Treasury, 1939; War Service, 1940–45; Malayan Govt, 1945; Colonial Develt Corp., 1949; Shell Petroleum Co. Ltd, 1952; Man. Dir, Royal Dutch/Shell Group of Companies, 1964–76; Man. Dir, 1971, Chm., 1972–76, "Shell" Transport and Trading Co. Ltd; Chairman: Shell International Marine Ltd, 1966–76; Shell Canada Ltd, 1970–76; Shell Petroleum Co. Ltd, 1972–76; British Airways, 1976–79 (Dir, 1975); Rolls Royce Ltd, 1980–83; Dir, Shell Oil Co., 1972–76. Chairman: Trade Policy Research Centre, 1971–82; Steering Bd, Strathclyde Div., Scottish Business Sch., 1970–76; Vis. Prof. of Economics, Strathclyde Univ., 1967–76. FRSE 1989. Hon. LLD Strathclyde, 1970. Comdr, Order of Oranje Nassau. *Publications:* Galbraith and the Planners, 1968; Energy in the Seventies, 1971; The Operation of a Multi-National Enterprise, 1971; (jtly) Towards an Open World Economy, 1972; The Economics of John Kenneth Galbraith: a study in fantasy, 1977; (jtly) Global Strategy for Growth: a report on North-South issues, 1981. *Address:* House of Lords, SW1A 0PW.   *Died 23 May 1992.*

MacFARLANE, Donald, CBE 1963; HM Diplomatic Service, retired; *b* 26 Oct. 1910; *s* of late Donald MacFarlane, CIE and Aylmer, *d* of H. H. Lake, MICE, superintending engr, India; *m* 1933, Jean Carmen, *d* of late Charles Young, Pitt Manor, Winchester; (one *s* decd). *Educ:* Stowe; Queens' Coll., Cambridge. Lamson Paragon Supply Co. Ltd, 1932–39. Served in RA and Intelligence Corps, 1939–46 (despatches): North Africa, Sicily, Italy and France; Colonel, head of Anglo-Greek Information Services, Athens, 1945–46. First Secretary, Foreign Service, 1946; British Embassy, China, 1946–49; Foreign Office, 1949–52; British Embassy, Rio de Janeiro, 1952–55; Counsellor (Commercial), Washington, 1955–58; Lisbon, 1958–60; HM Consul-General, Frankfurt-am-Main, 1960–64, Naples, 1964–67; Head of Nationality and Treaty Dept, FCO, 1967–70. *Recreation:* fishing. *Address:* 27 Lennox Gardens, SW1X 0DE. *Clubs:* Flyfishers', Caledonian.   *Died 28 March 1991.*

MACFARLANE, Sir James (Wright), Kt 1973; JP; DL; PhD; FRSE; CEng, FIEE, FIMechE; Managing Director, Cathcart Investment Co. Ltd, since 1964; *b* 2 Oct. 1908; *s* of late James C. Macfarlane, OBE, MIEE, WhSch; *m* 1937, Claire Ross. *Educ:* Allan Glen's Sch.; Royal Technical Coll. (DRTC); Glasgow Univ. (PhD); London Univ. WhSch and WhSen.Sch. FIFireE. War of 1939–45: Home Guard (Major); Intell.; Lt-Col (TA) Comdg Renfrewshire Bn, Army Cadet Force. Apprentice, 1926, subseq. Engineer and Director, Macfarlane Engrg Co. Ltd; Chm., Macfarlane Engrg Co. Ltd, Cathcart, 1967–69. Past Pres., Assoc. of County Councils in Scotland; Past Mem. various instns; Member: Royal Commn on the Police, 1960–62; Departmental Cttee on the Fire Service, 1968–70. JP 1940; entered local govt, 1944; DL 1962, Renfrewshire; Convener, County of Renfrew, 1967–73.

Chm. of Governors, Paisley Coll. of Technology. *Publications:* numerous papers in IEE and IMechE Jls. *Recreations:* motor cycles and cars (vintage), sailing. *Address:* 2 Sandringham Court, Newton Mearns, Glasgow G77 5DT. *T:* 041–639 1842. *Clubs:* RNVR (Scotland); Royal Gourock Yacht (Gourock).
                    Died 17 April 1992.

McGHIE, Hamish; *see* McGhie, J. I.

McGHIE, James Ironside, (Hamish), CMG 1973; HM Diplomatic Service, retired; *b* 12 Oct. 1915; *s* of William I. McGhie and Annie E. Ratcliffe; *m* 1946, Ellen-Johanne Gran, *d* of Maj. T. Gran, MC, Norway, and Ingeborg Gran (*née* Meinich); two *s* one *d*. *Educ:* King Henry VIII Sch., Coventry. Journalist, 1933–39. Army, 1940–46, attached Royal Norwegian Army, 1943–46. Entered Foreign Service, 1946; served: Stockholm, Helsinki, FO, Tokyo, FO, Singapore; Dir, British Information Services, Saigon; Head of Chancery, Bucharest; Consul-General, Seattle; Counsellor, Commercial, Stockholm; Minister (Commercial and Econ.), Tokyo; retired, 1975. Special Advr on Japanese market to BOTB, 1975–77; Co-Chm., Japan Task Force, 1976–77. Order of the Rising Sun (Japan) 3rd class, 1975. *Recreations:* Scandinavian studies and translations. *Address:* Poplars, South Street, Faversham, Kent ME13 9NS. *T:* Canterbury (0227) 751424.   *Died 14 Feb. 1992.*

McGILLIGAN, Denis Brian; Assistant Solicitor, Ministry of Agriculture, Fisheries and Food, 1973–83; *b* 26 June 1921; *s* of Michael McGilligan, SC, and Mary Georgina McGilligan (*née* Musgrave); *m* 1952, Hazel Patricia Pakenham Keady; one *s* two *d*. *Educ:* St Gerard's, Bray, Co. Wicklow; Trinity Coll., Dublin (BA). Practised at Irish Bar, 1945–52; Crown Counsel, Sarawak, and Dep. Legal Adviser, Brunei, 1952–58; Senior Magistrate, Sarawak, 1958–59; Acting Puisne Judge, Combined Judiciary, 1959–60; Senior Magistrate, Sarawak, 1960–63; Puisne Judge, Combined Judiciary of Sarawak, North Borneo and Brunei, March, 1963; Judge of the High Court in Borneo, Malaysia, 1963–66; called to the Bar, Gray's Inn, 1966; Legal Sec., Cabinet Office Cttee drafting Eur. Communities Bill, 1970–72; Legal Advr, Agricl Wages Bd, 1979–83. *Recreations:* conversation, religious study, reading, writing. *Address:* 7 Steward's Rise, Arundel, West Sussex BN18 9ER.   *Died 8 July 1995.*

MacGINNIS, Francis Robert, CMG 1979; HM Diplomatic Service, retired; Minister and Deputy Commandant, British Military Government, Berlin, 1977–83; *b* 6 March 1924; *s* of late Dr Patrick MacGinnis, Murray House, Chesterfield; *m* 1955, Carolyn, *d* of late Col D. W. McEnery, USA; three *s* two *d*. *Educ:* Stonyhurst; Merton Coll., Oxford (MA). Served with Rifle Bde, 1942–47 (Temp. Captain). Joined HM Foreign (subseq. Diplomatic) Service, 1949; served in London, Washington, Paris and Warsaw; Dir-Gen., British Information Services, New York, 1968–72; Counsellor, Bonn, 1972–76; RCDS, 1976. *Address:* Boîte Postale 47, Fayence 83440, Var, France. *T:* 94761705. *Club:* Travellers'.
                    Died 28 July 1993.

McGRATH, Dr Patrick Gerard, CB 1981; CBE 1971; Senior Consultant Psychiatrist and Physician Superintendent, Broadmoor Hospital, 1956–81, then Physician Superintendent Emeritus; *b* 10 June 1916; *s* of late Patrick McGrath and Mary (*née* Murray), Glasgow; *m* 1949, Helen Patricia O'Brien; three *s* one *d*. *Educ:* St Aloysius Coll., Glasgow; Glasgow and Edinburgh Univs. MB, ChB Glasgow 1939; DipPsych Edinburgh 1955; FRCPsych (Vice-Pres., 1978–80), Hon. FRCPsych 1981; FRSocMed. RAMC, 1939–46 (Hon. Lt-Col); various trng posts in psychiatry, Glasgow, London and Colchester, 1946–51; psychiatrist, Ayrshire, 1951–56. Member: Parole

Board, 1982–85; Adv. Council, Inst. of Criminology, Univ. of Cambridge, 1982–86. *Publications:* chapter in: Psychopathic Disorder, 1966; Mentally Abnormal Offender, 1968; contrib. Jl of RSH, Jl of Forensic Psychiatry, Cropwood publications, etc. *Recreation:* golf (purely social). *Address:* 18 Heathermount Drive, Crowthorne, Berks RG11 6HN. *T:* Crowthorne (01344) 774552. *Club:* East Berks Golf.

Died 18 Oct. 1994.

McGUIRE, Robert Ely, CMG 1948; OBE 1943; Indian Civil Service (retired); *b* 22 Aug. 1901; *s* of late Major E. C. McGuire, 2nd Bn York and Lancaster Regt; *m* 1930, Barbara, *d* of late Sir Benjamin Heald, ICS, Judge of the High Court of Judicature, Rangoon; one *s* one *d. Educ:* High Sch., Dublin; Trinity Coll., Dublin. MA (Hons). Entered ICS, 1926; Warden, Burma Oilfields, 1932 and 1940–42; Dep. Commissioner, 1932–42; Secretary to Government of Burma (temp. in India), 1942–45; Dep. Director of Civil Affairs, with rank of Brigadier, British Military Administration in Burma, 1945; Divisional Comr, Burma, 1946–47; Secretary to Governor of Burma, 1947 to 4 Jan. 1948 (date of Independence of Burma). Secretary Cement Makers Federation, 1949–64. *Address:* Pelham House, Cuckfield, West Sussex RH17 5EU. *T:* Haywards Heath (0444) 453692. *Club:* East India.

Died 24 June 1991.

McHUGH, Dr Mary Patricia; Coroner for Southern District of London, 1965–85; *b* 5 June 1915; *d* of J. C. McHugh, MB, BS, BAO, Royal Univ., Dublin, and Madeleine Jeffroy Leblan, Brittany, France; *m* 1943, E. G. Murphy, FRCS (marr. diss., 1952); one *s* two *d. Educ:* Nymphenburg, Munich, Bavaria; Notre Dame, Clapham; Birmingham Univ. MB, ChB 1942; PhD Fac. of Laws, London, 1976. Called to the Bar, Inner Temple, 1959. Birmingham House Physician and Anæsthetist, St Chad's Hospital, Birmingham, 1942–43; General Practice, London, 1944–65. Past Chm., Whole Time Coroners' Assoc.; Mem., British Academy of Forensic Sciences, 1963; Founder Mem., RCGP; Associate, Inst. of Linguists, 1981; Associate to Res. and Adv. Cttee, Cantab Gp of Toxicology and Biosciences, Cambridge, 1983–. Medico Legal Columnist, Pulse, 1981–. *Publication:* Treasure Trove and the Law (Med. Sci. Law vol. 16 no 2), 1976. *Recreations:* cooking, languages. *Address:* 8 Hitherwood Drive, College Road, Dulwich, SE19 1XB. *T:* 081–670 8400. *Died 6 Aug. 1992.*

McILWAIN, Prof. Henry, DSc, PhD; Professor of Biochemistry in the University of London at Institute of Psychiatry, British Postgraduate Medical Federation, 1954–80, then Emeritus; Hon. Senior Research Fellow, Department of Pharmacology, University of Birmingham, since 1987; *b* Newcastle upon Tyne, 20 Dec. 1912; *e s* of John McIlwain, Glasgow, and Louisa (*née* Widdowson), Old Whittington; *m* 1st, 1941, Valerie (*d* 1977), *d* of K. Durston, Bude, Cornwall; two *d*; 2nd, 1979, Marjorie Allan Crennell, *d* of E. A. Crennell, Newcastle upon Tyne. *Educ:* King's Coll., Newcastle upon Tyne (University of Durham); The Queen's Coll., Oxford. Leverhulme Research Fellow and later Mem. of Scientific Staff, Medical Research Council, in Council's Dept of Bacterial Chemistry (Middlesex Hosp., London) and Unit for Research in Cell Metabolism (Univ. of Sheffield), 1937–47; Lectr in Biochemistry, Univ. of Sheffield, 1944–47; Senior Lectr (later Reader) in Biochemistry, Inst. of Psychiatry (British Postgraduate Medical Fedn), Univ. of London, 1948–54. Vis. Prof., St Thomas's Hospital Med. Sch., 1980–87. Hon. Biochemist, Bethlem Royal Hosp. and Maudsley Hosp., 1948–80. Mem. Editorial Bd, Biochemical Jl, 1947–50; Historian, Internat. Soc. for Neurochemistry, 1984–. Research Associate, Univ. of Chicago, 1951; Visiting Lectr, Univ. of Otago,

New Zealand, 1954; Lectr and Medallist, Univ. of Helsinki, 1973; Thudichum Lectr and Medallist, Biochemical Soc., 1975. Dr *hc* Univ. d'Aix-Marseille, 1974. *Publications:* Biochemistry and the Central Nervous System, 1955, 5th edn (with H. S. Bachelard), 1985; Chemotherapy and the Central Nervous System, 1957; (with R. Rodnight) Practical Neurochemistry, 1962; Chemical Exploration of the Brain, 1963; (ed) Practical Neurochemistry, 1975; 250 papers in the Biochemical Journal and other scientific and medical publications. *Address:* 68 Cartway, Bridgnorth, Shropshire WV16 4BG. *T:* Bridgnorth (0746) 761353.

Died 14 Sept. 1992.

McILWRAITH, Arthur Renwick; Sheriff of South Strathclyde, Dumfries and Galloway (formerly Lanark) at Airdrie, 1972–85, retired; Hon. Sheriff at Airdrie, since 1992; *b* 8 April 1914; *s* of Nicholas Renwick McIlwraith and Adaline Gowans McIlwraith; *m* 1950, Thelma Preston or Sargent; one *s* one *d. Educ:* High Sch. of Glasgow; Univ. of Glasgow (MA, LLB). Grad. 1938. Served War: Highland Light Infantry, 1939–45. Solicitor, 1945–72. *Recreation:* fishing. *Address:* 29 Kelvin Court, Anniesland, Glasgow G12 0AB.

Died 11 March 1994.

MacINTOSH, Prof. Frank Campbell, FRS 1954; FRSC 1956; J. M. Drake Professor of Physiology, McGill University, Montreal, Canada, 1949–78, Emeritus Professor since 1980; *b* 24 Dec. 1909; *s* of Rev. C. C. MacIntosh, DD, and Beenie MacIntosh (*née* Matheson); *m* 1938, Mary M. MacKay; two *s* three *d. Educ:* Dalhousie Univ., Halifax, NS (MA); McGill Univ. (PhD). Member of research staff, Medical Research Council of Great Britain, 1938. Hon. LLD: Alberta, 1964; Queen's, 1965; Dalhousie, 1976; St Francis Xavier, 1985; Hon. MD Ottawa, 1974; Hon. DSc McGill, 1980. *Publications:* papers in physiological journals. *Address:* Department of Physiology, McGill University, 3655 Drummond Street, Montreal H3G 1Y6, Canada; 145 Wolseley Avenue, Montreal West, H4X 1V8, Canada. *T:* 481–7939.

Died 11 Sept. 1992.

MACINTYRE, Angus Donald, DPhil; Official Fellow and Tutor in Modern History, since 1963, Senior Fellow, since 1989, Magdalen College, Oxford; Principal Designate, Hertford College, Oxford; *b* 4 May 1935; *e s* of Major Francis Peter Macintyre, OBE, and Evelyn, *d* of Nicholas Synnott, JP, Furness, Naas, Co. Kildare, Eire; *m* 1958, Joanna Musgrave Harvey, *d* of Sir Richard Musgrave Harvey, 2nd Bt; two *s* one *d. Educ:* Wellington; Hertford Coll., Oxford (Baring Scholar); St Antony's Coll., Oxford (MA, DPhil). Coldstream Guards, 1953–55, 1956 (Lieut). Magdalen College, Oxford: Sen. Tutor, 1966–68; Vice-Pres., 1981–82; Actg Pres., Jan–July 1987. Mem., Press Complaints Commn, 1993–. Governor: Magdalen Coll. Sch., Brackley, 1965–77; Wolverhampton Grammar Sch., 1987–93; Magdalen Coll. Sch., Oxford, 1987–92 (Chm., 1987–90). Chm., Thomas Wall Trust, London, 1971–. Gen. Editor, Oxford Historical Monographs, 1971–79; Editor, English Historical Review, 1978–86. FRHistS 1972. *Publications:* The Liberator: Daniel O'Connell and the Irish Parliamentary Party 1830–47, 1965; (ed with Kenneth Garlick) The Diary of Joseph Farington 1793–1821, vols I-II, 1978, vols III-VI, 1979; (contrib.) Thank You Wodehouse by J. H. C. Morris, 1981; (contrib.) Daniel O'Connell: portrait of a Radical, ed Nowlan and O'Connell, 1984; (ed) General Index, English Historical Review, vols LXXI–C, 1956–85, 1986; (jtly) Magdalen College and the Crown, 1988; (contrib.) Pour Jean Malaurie, 1990. *Recreations:* cricket, bibliophily. *Address:* Magdalen College, Oxford OX1 4AU. *T:* Oxford (0865) 276000. *Club:* MCC. *Died 21 Dec. 1994.*

MACK, Prof. Alan Osborne, MDS; FDSRCS; Professor of Dental Prosthetics, Institute of Dental Surgery, University of London, 1967–80, then Emeritus; Consultant Dental Surgeon, Eastman Dental Hospital; Civilian Consultant in Dental Prosthetics to the Royal Air Force since 1976; *b* 24 July 1918; *s* of Arthur Joseph Mack, Glos, and Florence Emily Mack (*née* Norris); *m* 1943, Marjorie Elizabeth (*née* Westacott); two *s* one *d. Educ:* Westbourne Park Sch.; London Univ. LDS RCS 1942; MDS Durham, 1958; FDS RCS 1971. House Surgeon, Royal Dental Hosp., Sch. of Dental Surgery, University of London, 1942–43; served in RAF Dental Branch, 1943–47; Demonstrator, Prosthetics Dept, Royal Dental Hosp., 1948; successively Asst Dir, Prosthetics Dept, and Senior Lecturer, London Univ., Royal Dental Hosp., 1949–56; Prof. of Dental Prosthetics, Univ. of Newcastle upon Tyne (formerly King's Coll., Univ. of Durham), 1956–67; Examiner in Dental Prosthetics, Royal Coll. of Surgeons of England, 1956; Examiner, University of Manchester, 1959, Leeds, 1961, Glasgow, 1961, Liverpool, 1965, London, 1965, Edinburgh, 1968, Lagos, 1970, Singapore, Khartoum, 1977, Benghazi, 1978; Examination Visitor, GDC; Advisor, Univ. of Malaya. Mem. Board of Faculty, Royal College of Surgeons, 1959. Pres. British Soc. for Study of Prosthetic Dentistry, 1963. Hon. Consultant, Stoke Mandeville Hosp., 1976; part-time Consultant, John Radcliffe Hosp., 1980–88. Visiting Professor: Univ. of Singapore, 1981; Univ. of Sci. and Technol., Irbid, Jordan, 1987. Hon. Mem., Amer. Acad. of Implant Dentures, 1966. *Publications:* Full Dentures, 1971; articles in British dental jls. *Recreations:* gardening, pottery, bowls. *Address:* Home Farm, London Road, Aston Clinton, Bucks HP22 5HG.   *Died 18 Jan. 1994.*

MACKAY, Maj.-Gen. Eric MacLachlan, CBE 1971 (MBE 1944); *b* 26 Dec. 1921; *s* of Ian MacLachlan Mackay and Violet Aimée Scott-Smith; *m* 1954, Ruth Thérèse Roth (*d* 1985); one *s*; *m* 1994, Margaret Hadcock (*née* Shepherd). *Educ:* Fettes Coll., Edinburgh. Served War: enlisted Royal Scots Fusiliers, 1940; commissioned Oct. 1941, Royal Engineers; 2/Lieut-Major, 1st Parachute Sqdn, RE, 1941–45, N Africa, Sicily, Italy, Arnhem, PoW (escaped) Norway. OC, Field Company, 20 Indian Div., French Indo-China, 1945–46; 2 i/c 23 Indian Div. Engrs, Java, 1946; OC, 35 Indian Field Company, Malaya, 1947; Supplementary Engrg Course, SME, 1948; GSO 2 Intell., Jt Intell. Bureau, 1949–50; Staff Coll., 1951; GSO 2, Org. and Equipment, HQ, ALFCE, 1952–53; Sen. Instructor Tactics, SME, 1954–55; OC, 33 Field Sqdn, RE, Cyprus, Suez, 1956–58; GSO 2, Wpns, MoD, 1958–60; JSSC, 1960; 2 i/c 2 Div. Engrs, 1961–62; Chief Engr, Malaysian Army, Borneo/Malaya, 1963–65; GSO 1, Co-ord., Master-Gen. of the Ordnance, 1966–67; Col, GS, RSME, 1968–69; Chief Engr (Brig.): Army Strategic Command, 1970–71; UK Land Forces, 1972; Maj.-Gen. 1973; Chief Engr, BAOR, 1973–76, retired. Managing Director: Cementation Sico Oman Ltd, 1977; Galadari Cementation Pte Ltd, Dubai, 1978–83; Forum Develt Pte Ltd, Singapore, 1983–85; Regional Dir Iraq, Engineering Services Internat., 1981–82; Chm., Amorshield Security Products, 1986–90. CEng 1976; MICE 1976. DSC (USA), 1944; Pingat Peringatan Malaysia (PPM), 1965. *Recreations:* motoring, skiing, photography. *Address:* Marston Court, Marston Magna, Yeovil, Somerset BA22 8BZ.
          Died 16 Nov. 1995.

McKAY, Sir James (Wilson), Kt 1971; JP; DL; former Lord Provost of Edinburgh; Lord Lieutenant of the County of the City of Edinburgh, 1969–72; *b* 12 March 1912; *s* of John McKay; *m* 1942, Janette Urquhart; three *d. Educ:* Dunfermline High Sch.; Portobello Secondary Sch., Edinburgh. Insurance Broker; Man. Dir, John McKay (Insurance) Ltd, Edinburgh; Dir, George S. Murdoch & Partners Ltd, Aberdeen. Served with RN, 1941–46 (Lieut, RNVR). Hon. DLitt Heriot-Watt, 1972. JP Edinburgh, 1972; DL County and City of Edinburgh, 1972. Order of

Cross of St Mark (Greek Orthodox Church), 1970; Knight, Order of Orange-Nassau (Netherlands), 1972. *Recreations:* walking, gardening, reading. *Address:* T'Windward, 11 Cammo Gardens, Edinburgh EH4 8EJ. *T:* 031–339 6755. *Clubs:* New (Edinburgh); Caledonian (Hon. Mem.) (San Francisco).
          Died 25 May 1992.

McKAY, Rev. Roy; Hon. Canon, Chichester Cathedral, since 1957; *b* 4 Nov. 1900; *s* of William McKay and Sarah Evelyn (*née* Littlewood); *m* 1927, Mary Oldham Fraser; one *d* (one *s* decd). *Educ:* Marlborough Coll.; Magdalen Coll., Oxford. Deacon, 1926; priest, 1927; Curate, S Paul's, Kingston Hill, 1926; Curate-in-charge and Vicar of St Mark's Londonderry, Smethwick, 1928; Vicar of Mountfield, Sussex, 1932; Chaplain of Christ's Chapel of Alleyn's College of God's Gift, Dulwich, 1937; Vicar of Goring-by-Sea, Sussex, 1943; Chaplain of Canford Sch., 1948; Head of Religious Broadcasting, 1955–63; Preacher to Lincoln's Inn, 1958–59; Rector of St James, Garlickhythe, EC4, 1965–70. *Publications:* Tell John (with Bishop G. F. Allen), 1932; The Pillar of Fire, 1933; Take Care of the Sense, 1964; John Leonard Wilson: Confessor for the Faith, 1973. *Address:* 12 Torkington Gardens, West Street, Stamford, Lincs PE9 2EW.
          Died 5 Nov. 1993.

MACKAY LEWIS, Maj.-Gen. Kenneth Frank; *see* Lewis.

McKENZIE, Sir Alexander, KBE 1962; Dominion President, New Zealand National Party, 1951–62; *b* Invercargill, New Zealand, 26 Oct. 1896; *s* of Alex McKenzie; *m* 1935, Constance Mary Howard; two *s* two *d. Educ:* Isla Bank Primary Sch.; Southland Technical Coll.; Southland Boys' High Sch. Chm., Ponsonby Electorate, NZ Nat. Party, 1938–41; Chm., Auckland Div., NZ Nat. Party, 1941–51. Overseas Rep. for NZ Forest Products Ltd, 1925–29; engaged in Stock and Share Broking, 1929–; Mem. Auckland Stock Exchange; Dir of companies covering finance, merchandising, manufacturing, etc. Mem. Anglican Church. *Recreations:* trout fishing, surfing, bowling, gardening. *Address:* 1/46 King Edward Parade, Devonport, Auckland, New Zealand. *Club:* Auckland (Auckland, NZ).
          Died 20 Aug. 1992.

MACKENZIE, Sir (Alexander George Anthony) Allan, 4th Bt *cr* 1890, of Glen-Muick, Aberdeenshire; CD 1957; retired; *b* 4 Jan. 1913; *s* of late Capt. Allan Keith Mackenzie (3rd *s* of 2nd Bt) and Hon. Louvima (who *m* 2nd, 1922, Richard Henry Spencer Checkley), *o d* of 1st Viscount Knollys; *S* uncle, 1944; *m* 1937, Marjorie McGuire, Vancouver, BC; three *d* (and one *d* decd). *Educ:* Stowe School. Page of Honour to King George V; Member Royal Canadian Mounted Police, 1932–37; served War of 1939–45, with Seaforth Highlanders of Canada (Captain), in Italy and in NW Europe; subsequently Black Watch (RHR) of Canada (Regular Army). Canada Centennial Medal, 1967. *Heir: cousin* James William Guy Mackenzie [*b* 6 Oct. 1946; *m* 1972, Paulene Patricia Simpson (marr. diss. 1980); two *d*].   *Died 5 Jan. 1993.*

MACKENZIE, David James Masterton, CMG 1957; OBE 1947 (MBE 1944); FRCP; Colonial Medical Service, retired; Hon. Research Associate, Department of Medical Microbiology, Medical School, University of Cape Town, 1970–84; Visiting Scientist, Malaria Eradication Program, Communicable Disease Center, Atlanta, Georgia, 1965–69; *b* 23 July 1905; *s* of John Henderson Mackenzie and Agnes Masterton; *m* 1934, Patricia Eleanor Margaret Bailey (decd); two *d. Educ:* Rutherford College School; Edinburgh Univ. MB, ChB Edinburgh, 1929; DPH (Edinburgh), 1948; MRCPE 1956, FRCPE 1959. Edinburgh Royal Infirmary, 1930–31. Joined Colonial

Medical Service, 1934; DDMS, 1944–46, DMS, 1946–49, Bechuanaland Protectorate; DMS Nyasaland, 1949–55; DMS Northern Nigeria, 1955–57; Dir of Med. and Health Services, Hong Kong, 1958–64. *Recreations:* golf, fishing. *Address:* 8 Avondrust Avenue, Bergvliet, 7945, S Africa. *T:* (72) 4541. *Clubs:* Royal Hong Kong Golf; Zomba Gymkhana (Malaŵi).   *Died 10 March 1994.*

MacKENZIE, Rt Hon. (James) Gregor, PC 1977; *b* 15 Nov. 1927; *o s* of late James and Mary MacKenzie; *m* 1958, Joan Swan Provan; one *s* one *d. Educ:* Queen's Park Sch.; Glasgow Univ. (School of Social Studies). Joined Labour Party, 1944. Contested (Lab): East Aberdeenshire, 1950; Kinross and West Perthshire, 1959. Chm., Scottish Labour League of Youth, 1948; Mem. and Magistrate, Glasgow Corporation, 1952–55, 1956–64. MP (Lab): Rutherglen, May 1964–1983; Glasgow, Rutherglen, 1983–87; PPS to Rt Hon. James Callaghan, MP, 1965–70; Opposition spokesman on Posts and Telecommunications, 1970–74; Parly Under-Sec. of State for Industry, 1974–75, Minister of State for Industry, 1975–76; Minister of State, Scottish Office, 1976–79. JP Glasgow, 1962. *Address:* 30/1 Haggswood Avenue, Pollokshields, Glasgow G41 4RH. *T:* 041–427 0485.   *Died 4 May 1992.*

MACKENZIE, Brig. John Alexander, CBE 1955; DSO 1944 and Bar, 1944; MC 1940 and Bar, 1940; retired; *b* 9 March 1915; *s* of late Louis Robert Wilson Mackenzie; *m* 1952, Beryl Cathreen Culver; one *s. Educ:* Nautical Coll., Pangbourne; RMC, Sandhurst. 2nd Bn Gloucestershire Regt, 1935–43; Bn Comd, 2nd Bn Lancs Fusiliers, Tunisia, Sicily and Italy Campaigns, 1943–44 (despatches, 1944); Bde Comd: 11 Inf. Bde, Italy, 1944; 10 Inf. Bde, Greece, 1945–46; psc 1947; GSO1 HQ British Troops, Berlin, 1948–49; AAG (Organisation), HQ, BAOR, 1950; jssc 1951; GSO1 HQ Western Comd, 1951–54; Comd: Britcom Sub-area N, S Korea, 1955; Inf. Trng Team, HQ Jordan Arab Army, 1956; Jt Concealment Centre, 1957–58; Small Arms Sch., Hythe, 1958–59; idc 1960; Comd: 1 Bde, Nigeria, 1961–63; 3 Bde, Congo, 1962; Actg GOC, Royal Nigerian Army, 1963; BGS Army Trng, MoD, 1964–67; ADC to the Queen, 1967–70; Comdt and Inspector of Intelligence, 1967–70; retired 1970. *Recreation:* gardening. *Address:* Slaybrook Hall, Sandling Road, Saltwood, Hythe, Kent CT21 4HG.

Died 3 Dec. 1995.

MACKENZIE, Kenneth Edward, CMG 1970; HM Diplomatic Service, retired; *b* 28 April 1910; *s* of late A. E. Mackenzie, Dundee, and K. M. Mackenzie (*née* Foley); *m* 1935, Phyllis Edith Fawkes; one *s. Educ:* schools in India, Australia and in the UK; University Coll., London. Engineering industry, 1926–29; University Coll., London, 1929–32 (BSc (Hons) in civil and mechanical engineering); Inst. of Civil Engineers, 1932–34; Dept of Overseas Trade, 1934–36; HM Embassy, Brussels, 1936–40; interned in Germany, 1940–41; HM Embassy, Tehran, 1942–45; Trade Commissioner: in India, 1945–48; in Malaya, 1949–54; Asst Sec., Bd of Trade, 1954–66; Counsellor (Commercial), HM Embassy, Stockholm, and Chargé d'Affaires *ad interim*, 1966–70; Counsellor (Investment), 1973; Counsellor (Investment), HM Embassy, Copenhagen, 1974–75. *Address:* 11 St James Close, Pangbourne, Berks RG8 7AP. *T:* Pangbourne (01734) 842228.   *Died 24 April 1995.*

MACKENZIE, Kenneth Roderick, CB 1965; Clerk of Public Bills, House of Commons, 1959–73; *b* 19 April 1908; *s* of late Walter Mackenzie; *m* 1935, Mary Howard, *e d* of late Lt-Col C. H. Coode, RM; three *s* one *d. Educ:* Dulwich Coll.; New Coll., Oxford (scholar). 1st class Classical Moderations; 2nd class Literæ Humaniores. Asst Clerk, House of Commons, 1930; Clerk of Standing Cttees, 1953. Mem., Cttee on Preparation of Legislation, 1973–74. Officer's Cross, Order of Polonia Restituta

(Poland), 1964. *Publications:* The English Parliament, 1950; Parliament, 1959; editions of Sir Bryan Fell's Guide to the Palace of Westminster, 1944–72; verse translations of: Słowacki's In Switzerland, 1953; Mickiewicz's Pan Tadeusz, 1964; Virgil's Georgics, 1969; Dante's Divine Comedy, 1979. *Recreation:* gardening. *Address:* Woodnorton, Mayfield, East Sussex TN20 6EJ. *T:* Mayfield (0435) 872317.   *Died 4 Jan. 1991.*

MACKENZIE, Maxwell Weir, OC 1972; CMG 1946; Director: Canadian Imperial Bank of Commerce, 1955–77, then Emeritus; Canron Ltd, 1961–77; International Multifoods Corp., 1964–77; Royal Trust, 1960–67; Imperial Life, 1962–75; *b* 30 June 1907; *s* of late Hugh Blair Mackenzie, Gen. Man., Bank of Montreal, Montreal, and Maude Marion Weir; *m* 1931, Jean Roger Fairbairn; two *s* two *d. Educ:* Lakefield Preparatory Sch., Lakefield, Ont; Trinity Coll. School, Port Hope, Ont; McGill Univ., Montreal (BCom 1928). Joined McDonald, Currie & Co., Chartered Accountants of Montreal, 1928; Mem. Soc. of Chartered Accountants of the Province of Quebec, 1929; Jun. Partner, McDonald, Currie & Co., Montreal, 1935; on loan to Foreign Exchange Control Board, Ottawa, 1939–42; to Wartime Prices and Trade Board, Ottawa, 1942–44 (Dep. Chm. 1943–44); Mem., Royal Commission on Taxation of Annuities and Family Corporation, 1944; Dep. Minister of Trade and Commerce, 1945–51; Dep. Minister of Defence Production, Canada, 1951–52; Pres., Canadian Chemical & Cellulose Company, Ltd, 1954–59 (Exec. Vice-Pres., 1952–54). Mem., Economic Council of Canada, 1963–71. Dir, C. D. Howe Res. Inst., 1973–80. Chairman: Royal Commission on Security, 1966; Federal Inquiry into Beef Marketing, 1975. Hon. LLD McGill, 1973. *Recreation:* ski-ing. *Address:* 1245 Scollard Drive, Peterborough, Ontario K9H 7K8, Canada. *Club:* Rideau (Ottawa).   *Died 26 March 1991.*

MACKENZIE CROOKS, Air Vice-Marshal Lewis, CBE 1963 (OBE 1950); Consultant Adviser in Orthopaedic Surgery, Royal Air Force, 1966–70, retired; locum consultant in orthopaedic surgery, Cornwall, since 1970; *b* 20 Jan. 1909; *s* of David Mackenzie Crooks and Mary (*née* McKechnie); *m* 1936, Mildred, *d* of A. J. Gwyther; two *s* one *d. Educ:* Epworth Coll.; Liverpool Univ. MB, ChB 1931; FRCS 1937; ChM (Liverpool) 1945. House Surgeon: Northern Hosp., Liverpool, 1931–32; Shropshire Orthop. Hosp., Oswestry, 1932–33; Sen. House Surgeon: Selly Oak Hosp., Birmingham, 1933–34; All Saints Hosp., London, 1934–35; commnd RAF, 1935; surgical hosp. appts in RAF, 1936–52; overseas service: Palestine, 1937–39; Iraq, 1939–42 (despatches 1941); Egypt, 1950–51. Clinical Tutor, Edinburgh Royal Infirmary, 1947; Cons. in Orthop. Surgery, 1952; Sen. Cons. in Orthop. Surgery, 1955. QHS, 1966–70. *Publication:* article on chondromalaca patellae in Jl of Bone and Joint Surgery. *Recreations:* golf, gardening. *Address:* Trelawney, Harlyn Bay, Padstow, Cornwall PL28 8SF. *T:* Padstow (0841) 520631. *Clubs:* Royal Air Force; Trevose Golf, Country (Constantine Bay, Cornwall).

Died 12 March 1992.

McKIE, Rt Rev. John David; Assistant Bishop, Diocese of Coventry, 1960–80; Vicar of Great and Little Packington, 1966–80; *b* 14 May 1909; *s* of Rev. W. McKie, Melbourne, Vic; *m* 1952, Mary Lesley, *d* of late Brig. S. T. W. Goodwin, DSO and Mrs Goodwin, Melbourne, Vic; four *d. Educ:* Melbourne Church of England Grammar Sch.; Trinity Coll., Melbourne Univ.; New Coll., Oxford. BA (Trinity Coll., Melbourne Univ.), 1931; MA (New Coll., Oxford), 1945. Deacon, 1932; priest, 1934; Asst Chap. Melbourne Church of England Grammar Sch., 1932–33; Chap. and lecturer, Trinity Coll., Melbourne, 1936–39; served War of 1939–45 (despatches): AIF, 1939–44; ACG; Vicar, Christ Church, South Yarra, 1944–46;

Coadjutor, Bishop of Melbourne (with title of Bishop of Geelong) and Archdeacon of Melbourne, 1946–60. Chaplain and Sub-Prelate, Order of St John of Jerusalem, 1949. *Address:* 13 Morven Street, Mornington, Victoria 3931, Australia. *Died 30 March 1994.*

MacKINNON, Prof. Donald MacKenzie, MA; FRSE 1984; FBA 1978; Norris-Hulse Professor of Divinity, Cambridge University, 1960–78; Fellow of Corpus Christi College, Cambridge, since 1960; *b* Oban, 27 Aug. 1913; *o s* of late D. M. MacKinnon, Procurator Fiscal, and Grace Isabella Rhind; *m* 1939, Lois, *e d* of late Rev. Oliver Dryer; no *c.* *Educ:* Cargilfield Sch., Edinburgh; Winchester Coll. (scholar); New Coll., Oxford (scholar). Asst in Moral Philosophy (to late Prof. A. E. Taylor) at Edinburgh, 1936–37; Fellow and Tutor in Philosophy at Keble Coll., Oxford, 1937–47; Dir of Course for special courses in Philosophy for RN and RAF cadets at Oxford, 1942–45; Lectr in Philosophy at Balliol Coll., 1945–47; Wilde Lectr in Natural and Comparative Religion at Oxford, 1945–47; Regius Prof. of Moral Philosophy at Aberdeen, 1947–60. Lectures: Scott Holland, 1952; Hobhouse, 1953; Stanton, in the Philosophy of Religion, Cambridge, 1956–59; Gifford, Edinburgh, 1965–66; Prideaux, Exeter, 1966; Coffin, London, 1968; Riddell, Newcastle-upon-Tyne, 1970; D. Owen Evans, Aberystwyth, 1973; Drummond, Stirling, 1977; Martin Wight Meml, LSE, 1979; Boutwood, CCC Cambridge, 1981. President: Aristotelian Soc., 1976–77; Soc. for Study of Theol., 1981–82. Hon. Res. Fellow, Dept of Philosophy, Aberdeen Univ., 1992. Hon. DD: Aberdeen, 1961; Edinburgh, 1988; DUniv Stirling, 1989. Mem., Scottish Episcopal Church. Supporter, CND. *Publications:* (ed) Christian Faith and Communist Faith, 1953; The Notion of a Philosophy of History, 1954; A Study in Ethical Theory, 1957; (with Prof. G. W. H. Lampe) The Resurrection, 1966; Borderlands of Theology and other papers, 1968; The Stripping of the Altars, 1969; The Problem of Metaphysics, 1974; Explorations in Theology, 1979; Creon and Antigone, 1981; Themes in Theology: the threefold cord, 1987; articles, reviews, etc in periodicals and symposia in UK, France, Italy and Germany. *Recreations:* walking, cats, the cinema. *Address:* Dunbar Cottage, 10 Dunbar Street, Old Aberdeen AB2 1UE.
Died 2 March 1994.

MACKINTOSH, Prof. Allan Roy, FRS 1991; Professor of Physics, University of Copenhagen, since 1970; *b* 22 Jan. 1936; *s* of Malcolm Roy Mackintosh and Alice Mackintosh (*née* Williams); *m* 1958, Jette Stannow; one *s* two *d. Educ:* Nottingham High Sch.; Peterhouse, Cambridge (scholar; BA, PhD). Associate Prof., Iowa State Univ., 1960–66; Res. Prof., Technical Univ. of Denmark, 1966–70; Dir, Risø Nat. Lab., Denmark, 1971–76; Dir, Nordic Inst. for Theoretical Physics, 1986–89. Alfred P. Sloan Res. Fellow, 1964–66; Lectures: D. K. C. MacDonald, Canada, 1975; F. H. Spedding, USA, 1983; Vis. Miller Prof., Univ. of California, Berkeley, 1989. Pres., European Phys. Soc., 1980–82. Member: Royal Danish Acad. of Scis and Letters, 1977; Norwegian Acad. of Sci. and Letters, 1993. Fil. Dr *hc* Uppsala, 1980. F. H. Spedding Award for Rare Earth Res., 1986. Kt of the Dannebrog (Denmark), 1975. *Publications:* Rare Earth Magnetism: structures and excitations (with Jens Jensen), 1991; articles on physics in learned jls. *Recreations:* sedate squash, listening to music, reading, walking. *Address:* Henrik Thomsenvej 4, 3460 Birkerød, Denmark. *T:* (45) 42815038; Physics Laboratory, H. C. Ørsted Institute, Universitetsparken 5, 2100 Copenhagen, Denmark. *T:* (45) 35320450.
Died 20 Dec. 1995.

MACKINTOSH, Duncan Robert, CBE 1969 (OBE 1948); *b* 4 Oct. 1902; *s* of Duncan H. Mackintosh; *m* 1937, Mary Isa Grant; one *s* three *d. Educ:* RN Colleges Osborne and

Dartmouth; University Coll., London. Served with Royal Dutch Shell Group of Oil Cos, in China, Middle East and London, 1923–58. Mem. British Council. Chm. Exec. Cttee, Voluntary Service Overseas, 1962–70. *Publications:* (with Alan Ayling): A Collection of Chinese Lyrics, 1965; A Further Collection of Chinese Lyrics, 1969; A Folding Screen, 1974. *Recreations:* bird-watching, gardening. *Address:* Apple Tree Cottage, Oaksey, Malmesbury, Wilts SN16 9TG. *T:* Crudwell (06667) 431. *Club:* Athenæum.
Died 14 Sept. 1991.

MACKINTOSH OF MACKINTOSH, Lt-Comdr Lachlan Ronald Duncan, OBE 1972; JP; 30th Chief of Clan Mackintosh; Lord-Lieutenant of Lochaber, Inverness, Badenoch and Strathspey, since 1985 (Vice-Lieutenant, 1971–85); Chairman, Highland Exhibitions Ltd, 1964–84; *b* 27 June 1928; *o s* of Vice-Adm. Lachlan Donald Mackintosh of Mackintosh, CB, DSO, DSC (*d* 1957); *m* 1962, Mabel Cecilia Helen (Celia), *yr d* of Captain Hon. John Bernard Bruce, RN; one *s* two *d* (and one *d* decd). *Educ:* Elstree; RNC Dartmouth. Flag Lieut to First Sea Lord, 1951; spec. communications, 1954; served in HM Yacht Britannia, 1957; retd 1963. Vice-Pres., Scottish Conservative and Unionist Assoc., 1969–71. DL 1965, CC 1970–75, Inverness-shire; Regional Cllr, Highland Region, 1974–; JP Inverness, 1982. *Heir: s* John Lachlan Mackintosh, younger of Mackintosh, *b* 2 Oct. 1969. *Address:* Moy Hall, Tomatin, Inverness IV13 7YQ. *T:* Tomatin (01808) 511211. *Club:* Naval and Military.
Died 26 Dec. 1995.

McKISSOCK, Sir Wylie, Kt 1971; OBE 1946; MS (London); FRCS; Consulting Neurological Surgeon in London, 1936–71, retired; formerly Neurological Surgeon: National Hospital for Nervous Diseases, Queen Square; Metropolitan Ear, Nose and Throat Hospital; Hospital for Sick Children, Great Ormond Street; St Andrew's Hospital, Northampton; *b* 27 Oct. 1906; *s* of late Alexander Cathie McKissock; *m* 1934, Rachel (*d* 1992), *d* of Leonard Marcus Jones, Beckenham, Kent; one *s* two *d. Educ:* King's Coll. and St George's Hospital, University of London. Junior University Schol., St George's Hospital, 1928; Laking Memorial Prize, 1932–33 and 1933–34; Rockefeller Schol. in Neuro-Surgery, 1937–38; formerly: Casualty Officer, House Surgeon, House Physician, House Surgeon to Ear, Nose, Throat and Eye Depts, Assistant Curator of Museum, Surgical Registrar, Surgical Chief Asst, St George's Hosp.; Surgical Registrar, Maida Vale Hosp. for Nervous Diseases, Hosp. for Sick Children, Great Ormond St, and Victoria Hospital for Children, Tite St; Visiting Neurological Surgeon, Graylingwell Hospital, Chichester, St James's Hospital, Portsmouth, Belmont Hospital, Sutton, and Park Prewett Hospital, Basingstoke; Associate Neurological Surgeon, Royal Marsden Hospital; Director of Institute of Neurology, Queen Square; Surgeon in Charge, Department of Neuro-Surgery, Atkinson Morley Hospital branch of St George's Hospital; Hon. Civil Consultant in Neuro-Surgery to RAF; Hon. Neurological Surgeon, Welsh Regional Hospital Board; Teacher of Surgery, St George's Hospital Medical School (University of London); Member, Panel of Consultants, Royal Navy, British European Airways, British Overseas Airways Corporation. FRSM; Fellow, Society of British Neurological Surgeons (President, 1966); FRCR (Hon.) 1962; Corresponding Member, American Association of Neurological Surgeons, 1968. Hon. DSc, Newcastle upon Tyne, 1966. *Publications:* contributions to medical journals. *Recreations:* wine, food, gardening, ornithology, antagonism to bureaucracy, the enjoyment of retirement. *Address:* Glebelands, 22 Withdean Road, Brighton, Sussex BN1 5BL. *T:* Brighton (0273) 501876.
Died 3 May 1994.

MACKLEN, Victor Harry Burton, CB 1975; consultant to Ministry of Defence, since 1980; *b* 13 July 1919; *s* of H. Macklen and A. C. Macklen, Brighton, Sussex; *m* 1950, Ursula Irene Fellows; one *d. Educ:* Varndean Sch., Brighton; King's Coll., London. Air Defence Experimental Establishment, 1941; Operational Research Group, 1942; served Army, 1943–49; WO Scientific Staff, 1949–51; Head, Operational Research Section, BAOR, 1951–54; MoD Scientific Staff, 1954–60; Head, Technical Secretariat Reactor Group, UKAEA, 1960–64; Dep. Director, Technical Operations Reactor Group, UKAEA, 1966–67; Asst Chief Scientific Adviser (Studies and Nuclear), MoD, 1967–69; Dep. Chief Scientific Adviser (Projects and Nuclear), MoD, 1969–79; Personal Advr to Chm., British Telecom, 1980–87. Chm., Hartlip Parish Council, 1983–91. FRSA 1975. *Club:* Army and Navy.
Died 25 Nov. 1993.

McLACHLAN, Air Vice-Marshal Ian Dougald, CB 1966; CBE 1954; DFC 1940; *b* Melbourne, 23 July 1911; *s* of Dugald McLachlan, author and teacher, and Bertha Frances (*née* Gilliam); *m* 1946, Margaret Helen Chrystal (marr. diss. 1968); one *d. Educ:* Melbourne High Sch.; Royal Military Coll., Duntroon. Imperial Defence Coll., 1954; Dir, Flying Trng, Air Min., London 1955–56; Dep. Chief of Air Staff, Australia, 1959–61; Australian Defence Adviser, Washington, 1962–63; Air Mem. for Supply and Equipment, Australian Air Bd, 1964–68. Consultant, Northrop Corp., 1968–87; Chairman: Mainline Corp., 1970–74; Pokolbin Winemakers, 1971–73; Information Electronics, 1984–87; Director: Capitol Motors, 1969–75; Reef Oil, 1969–75. *Recreations:* tennis, squash, golf. *Address:* 2 Eastbourne Road, Darling Point, NSW 2027, Australia. *T:* (2) 3261860. *Clubs:* Australian (Sydney); Naval and Military (Melbourne); Melbourne Cricket, Royal Sydney Golf, Royal Canberra Golf.
Died 14 July 1991.

MacLEAN, Captain Donald Murdo, DSC 1944; RD 1940; Royal Naval Reserve; retired from Cunard Line, 1962; Commodore Captain Cunard Fleet and commanding RMS Queen Elizabeth, 1960–62; *b* 9 June 1899; *s* of William MacLean and Isobel (*née* Graham); *m* 1929, Bernice Isobel Wellington (decd); one *s* (one *d* decd). *Educ:* The Nicholson Sch., Lewis Island. Apprenticed to Cunard Line, 1917–21; served, as Officer, 1921–39; served War of 1939–45 (despatches): RNR, 1939–46; Trng Comdr RNC, Greenwich, 1941–43; Sen. Officer, 7th Escort Gp, Murmansk and Atlantic and Mediterranean Convoys; Staff Officer C-in-C Mediterranean, 1944–45; returned to Cunard Line, 1946. ADC to Lord High Comr for Scotland, 1946. *Publications:* Queens' Company, 1965; Cachalots and Messmates, 1973. *Recreations:* sailing, fishing, travel. *Address:* 14 Garden Mews, Newtown Road, Warsash, Southampton. *T:* Locks Heath (04895) 3951. *Club:* Master Mariners (Southampton).
Died 4 April 1991.

MacLEAN, Dr John Alexander, CBE 1968; Chairman, Northern Regional Hospital Board (Scotland), 1971–74; *b* 12 Oct. 1903; *s* of Donald MacLean, Achiltibuie, Ross-shire; *m* 1935, Hilda M. L. Munro, BSc, Aberdeen; one *s* one *d. Educ:* Dingwall Academy; Aberdeen Univ. MA, LLB, PhD; FEIS. Aberdeen Educn Authority: Teacher, 1926–39; Asst Dir of Educn, 1939–43; Dir of Educn, Inverness-shire Educn Authority, 1943–68, retd. Member: Exec. Cttee, National Trust for Scotland, 1967–82; Scottish Council, Royal Over-Seas League, 1969–81; Scottish Arts Council, 1964–68; Sec. of State's Council for Care of Children; Council on School Broadcasting. *Publication:* Sources for History of the Highlands in the Seventeenth Century, 1939. *Recreation:* sport. *Address:* 12 Eriskay Road, Inverness IV2 3LX. *T:* Inverness (0463) 231566. *Club:* Royal Over-Seas House (Edinburgh).
Died 11 Aug. 1992.

McLELLAN, His Honour Eric Burns; a Circuit Judge (formerly County Court Judge), 1970–86; *b* 9 April 1918; *s* of late Stanley Morgan McLellan, Christchurch, Newport, Mon; *m* 1949, Elsa Sarah, *d* of late Gustave Mustaki, Alexandria; one *s* one *d. Educ:* Newport High Sch.; New Coll., Oxford. BA 1939; MA 1967. Served RAF, 1940–46, N Africa, Italy, Egypt, 205 Group; Flt-Lt. Called to Bar, Inner Temple, 1947. Dep. Chm., IoW QS, 1967–72. Official Principal, Archdeaconry of Hackney, 1967–72; Dep. Chm., Workmen's Compensation Supplementation Bd and Pneumoconiosis, Byssinosis and Miscellaneous Diseases Benefit Bd, 1969–70; Mem., Dept of Health and Social Security Adv. Group on Use of Fetuses and Fetal Material for Research, 1970. Governor, Portsmouth Grammar Sch., 1980–87. *Publications:* (contrib.) The History of the Royal Air Force; contribs to medico-legal jls. *Recreations:* heraldry, genealogy. *Address:* Spinning Field, Hambledon, near Portsmouth, Hants PO7 6RU. *Clubs:* United Oxford & Cambridge University, Royal Air Force; Leander (Henley-on-Thames).
Died 16 Jan. 1992.

MacLELLAN, Sir (George) Robin (Perronet), Kt 1980; CBE 1969; JP; Chairman: Scottish Industrial and Trade Exhibitions Ltd, since 1981 (Director, 1975–79); Bield Housing Trust, Edinburgh, 1982–90; Scottish Tourist Board, 1974–80; *b* 14 Nov. 1915; *e s* of George Aikman MacLellan, Glasgow, and Irene Dorothy Perronet Miller, Liverpool; *m* 1941, Margaret (*d* 1990), *er d* of Dr Berkeley Robertson, Glasgow; one *s*; *m* 1991, Jennifer, *widow* of Roderick George Scott MacLellan. *Educ:* Ardvreck Sch., Crieff; Clifton Coll.; Ecole de Commerce, Lausanne. Chm., George MacLellan Hldgs Ltd, 1965–76; Dep. Chm., British Airports Authority, 1965–75; Pres., Glasgow Chamber of Commerce, 1970–71; Mem., Scottish Industrial Develt Bd, 1972–74. Director: Scottish National Trust plc, 1970–85; Govan Shipbuilders Ltd, 1972–74; Nationwide Building Society, 1971–84; British Tourist Authority, 1974–80; Melville Retirement Homes Ltd, Edinburgh, 1983–89. Chairman: Crossroads (Scotland) Care Attendant Scheme, 1984–87; Strathclyde Cttee, Tenovus-Scotland, 1986–. Mem. Council, Scottish Business Sch., 1972–75; Mem. Court, Strathclyde Univ., 1972–76. Member: West Central Scotland Plan Steering Cttee, 1970–75; Scottish Econ. Council, 1968–75; BNEC's Cttee for Exports to Canada, 1964–69; Council, Nat. Trust for Scotland, 1974–86 (Dep. Chm., 1980–85); Counsellor Emeritus, 1986–); Gen. Adv. Council, IBA, 1976–79; BR Adv. Bd (Scottish), 1977–81. Pres., Soc. of Friends of Glasgow Cathedral, 1978–87. A Vice-Pres., Assoc. British Chambers of Commerce, 1975–80; Pres., Inst. of Marketing (Strathclyde Branch), 1980–85; Senior Industrialist, Design Advisory Service, Design Council (funded consultancy scheme), 1983–87. Dir and Chm. of Governors, Ardvreck Sch. Ltd, 1970–83; Governor, Clifton Coll.; Pres., Old Cliftonian Soc., 1983–85. Trustee, Mental Health Foundn, 1982–86. Fellow of the Council, Scottish Council (Develt and Industry), 1987. Hon. FRCPSGlas, 1979; Hon. FRIAS, 1989. JP Dunbartonshire, 1973. OStJ 1972. *Publications:* articles on travel and tourism. *Recreations:* looking back gratefully, looking forward hopefully; family motto: "Think On". *Address:* 11 Beechwood Court, Bearsden, Glasgow G61 2RY. *T:* 041–942 3876. *Club:* Western (Glasgow).
Died 12 June 1991.

MacLEOD OF FUINARY, Baron, *cr* 1967 (Life Peer), of Fuinary in Morven; **Very Rev. George Fielden MacLeod,** MC; Bt 1924; BA Oxford; DD (Glasgow); Moderator of the General Assembly of the Church of Scotland, May 1957–May 1958; Founder of the Iona Community (Leader, 1938–67); one of Her Majesty's Chaplains in Scotland; *b* 17 June 1895; 2nd *s* of Sir John MacLeod, 1st Bt and Edith, *d* of Joshua Fielden; *S* nephew, 1944; *m* 1948,

Lorna Helen Janet (*d* 1984), *er d* of late Rev. Donald Macleod, Balvonie of Inshes, Inverness; two *s* one *d*. *Educ:* Winchester; Oriel Coll., Oxford (Hon. Fellow 1969); Edinburgh Univ. Served European War, 1914–18; Captain Argyll and Sutherland Highlanders (MC and Croix de Guerre). Post Graduate Fellow, Union Theological Coll., New York, 1921; Missioner, British Columbia Lumber Camps, 1922; Collegiate Minister, St Cuthbert's Parish Church, Edinburgh, 1926–30; Minister of Govan Parish Church, Glasgow, 1930–38. Warrack Lecturer on Preaching at Edinburgh and St Andrews Universities, 1936; Select Preacher, Cambridge Univ., 1943 and 1963; Cunningham Lecturer on Evangelism, 1954; first holder of Fosdick Professorship (Rockefeller Foundation), Union Theological Seminary, New York, 1954–55; Danforth Lecturer, USA Universities, 1960 and ,1964. Rector of Glasgow Univ., 1968–71. Pres. and Chm. of Council of International Fellowship of Reconciliation, 1963. Templeton Prize for Progress in Religion (jtly), 1989. DLitt Muskingum Univ., USA; Dr of Laws, Iona Coll., New Rochelle, USA. *Publications:* Govan Calling: a book of Broadcast Sermons and Addresses, 1934; Speaking the Truth in Love: a book on Preaching, 1936; We Shall Rebuild (the principles of the Iona Community), 1944; Only One Way Left, 1956; contributor to Way to God Series for the BBC. *Heir* (to Baronetcy only): *s* Hon. (John) Maxwell (Norman) MacLeod, *b* 23 Feb. 1952. *Address:* 23 Learmonth Terrace, Edinburgh EH4 1PG. *T:* 031–332 3262. *Died 27 June 1991.*

MacLEOD, Angus, CBE 1967; Hon. Sheriff of Lothians and Peebles, since 1972; Procurator Fiscal of Edinburgh and Midlothian, 1955–71; *b* 2 April 1906; *s* of late Alexander MacLeod, Glendale, Skye; *m* 1936, Jane Winifred (*d* 1977), *d* of late Sir Robert Bryce Walker, CBE, LLD; three *s*. *Educ:* Hutchesons Grammar Sch.; Glasgow Univ. (MA, LLB). Solicitor, 1929; general practice, 1929–34; Depute Procurator Fiscal, Glasgow and Edinburgh, 1934–42; Procurator Fiscal of Dumfriesshire, 1942–52, of Aberdeenshire, 1952–55; Temp. Sheriff, Scotland, 1973–77. Part-time Chm., VAT Appeal Tribunals, 1973–77. *Recreations:* reading, walking, interested in sport. *Address:* 7 Oxford Terrace, Edinburgh EH4 1PX. *T:* 031–332 5466. *Died 18 Jan. 1991.*

MacLEOD, Air Vice-Marshal Donald Francis Graham, CB 1977; FDSRCSE; Director of Royal Air Force Dental Services, 1973–77, retired; *b* Stornoway, Isle of Lewis, Scotland, 26 Aug. 1917; *s* of Alexander MacLeod; both parents from Isle of Lewis; *m* 1941, Marjorie Eileen (*née* Gracie); one *s* one *d*. *Educ:* Nicolson Inst., Stornoway, Isle of Lewis; St Andrews Univ.; Royal Coll. of Surgeons, Edinburgh. LDS St Andrews, 1940; FDSRCSE 1955. Qualif. in Dental Surgery, 1940; two years in private practice. Joined Royal Air Force Dental Branch, 1942; served in various parts of the world, mainly in hospitals doing oral surgery. QHDS, 1972. Royal Humane Society Resuscitation Certificate for life saving from the sea in the Western Isles, 1937. *Recreations:* golf, gardening; Captain of Soccer, St Andrews Univ., 1938 (full blue), Captain of Badminton, 1939 (half blue). *Address:* 20 Witchford Road, Ely, Cambs CB6 3DP. *T:* Ely (0353) 663164. *Club:* Royal Worlington Golf. *Died 12 June 1993.*

MacLEOD, Sir (Hugh) Roderick, Kt 1989; Chairman, Lloyd's Register of Shipping, since 1983; *b* 20 Sept. 1929; *s* of Neil MacLeod and Ruth MacLeod (*née* Hill); *m* 1958, Josephine Seager Berry (marr. diss. 1985); two *s* one *d*. *Educ:* Bryanston Sch.; St John's Coll., Cambridge. Served 2nd Regt, RHA, 1948–50. Joined The Ben Line Steamers Limited, 1953, Jt Man. Dir, 1964–82; Partner, Wm Thomson & Co., 1959, Director, 1964; Chairman, Associated Container Transportation Ltd, 1975–78. Member: Leith Docks Commn, 1960–65; Forth Ports

Authority, 1967–70; National Ports Council, 1977–80; pt-time Mem. Bd, BR, 1980–86; Chm., Scottish Bd, BR, 1980–82. *Recreations:* outdoor pursuits, music. *Address:* 14 Dawson Place, W2. *Died 22 Jan. 1993.*

McMASTER, Stanley Raymond; *b* 23 Sept. 1926; *o s* of F. R. McMaster, Marlborough Park, Belfast, N Ireland; *m* 1959, Verda Ruth Tynan, SRN, Comber, Co Down, Northern Ireland; two *s* two *d* (and one *d* decd). *Educ:* Campbell Coll., Belfast; Trinity Coll., Dublin (MA, BComm). Called to the Bar, Lincoln's Inn, 1953. Lectr in Company Law, Polytechnic, Regent Street, 1954–59. Parliamentary and Legal Sec., to Finance and Taxation Cttee, Association of British Chambers of Commerce, 1958–59. MP (UU) Belfast E, March 1959–Feb. 1974; contested (UU) Belfast S, Oct. 1974. *Publications:* various articles in legal and commercial journals. *Recreations:* golf, rowing, shooting. *Address:* 31 Embercourt Road, Thames Ditton, Surrey; 10 Marlborough Park North, Belfast. *Clubs:* Knock Golf, etc.
Died 20 Oct. 1992.

McMICHAEL, Sir John, Kt 1965; MD, FRCP, FRCPE; FRS 1957; Director, British Post-graduate Medical Federation, 1966–71; Emeritus Professor of Medicine, University of London; *b* 25 July 1904; *s* of James McMichael and Margaret Sproat; *m* 1942, Sybil E. Blake (*d* 1965); four *s*; *m* 1965, Sheila M. Howarth. *Educ:* Kirkcudbright Acad.; Edinburgh Univ. Ettles Scholar, 1927; Beit Memorial Fellow, 1930–34. MD (Gold Medal) Edinburgh 1933; MD Melbourne 1965; FRCPE 1940 (Hon. FRCPE 1981); FRCP 1946. Johnston and Lawrence Fellow, Royal Society, 1937–39; Univ. teaching appointments in Aberdeen, Edinburgh and London; Dir, Dept of Medicine, Post-grad. Med. Sch. of London, 1946–66. Mem. Medical Research Council, 1949–53. A Vice-Pres., Royal Soc., 1968–70. Pres., World Congress of Cardiology, 1970. Morgan Prof., Nashville, Tenn, 1964. Fellow, Royal Postgrad. Med. Sch., 1972. Hon. Member: American Medical Association, 1947; Medical Soc., Copenhagen, 1953; Norwegian Medical Soc., 1954; Assoc. Amer. Physicians, 1959. For. Mem. Finnish Acad. of Science and Letters, 1963; Hon. For. Mem., Acad. Roy. de Méd. Belgique, 1971; For. Associate, Nat. Acad. Sci., Washington, 1974. Thayer Lectr, Johns Hopkins Hosp., 1948; Oliver Sharpey Lectr, 1952, Croonian Lectr, 1961, Harveian Orator, 1975, RCP; Watson Smith Lectr, RCPEd, 1958. Cullen Prize, RCPEd, 1953. Jacobs Award, Dallas, 1958; Moxon Medal, RCP, 1960; Gairdner Award, Toronto, 1960; Wihuri Internat. Prize, Finland, 1968; Krug Award of Excellence, 1980. Trustee, Wellcome Trust, 1960–77. Hon. FACP; Hon. LLD Edin.; Hon. DSc: Newcastle; Sheffield; Birmingham; Ohio; McGill; Wales; Hon. ScD Dublin. *Publications:* Pharmacology of the Failing Human Heart, 1951; numerous papers on: Splenic Anaemia, 1931–35; Cardiac Output in Health and Disease, 1938–47; Lung Capacity in Man, 1938–39; Liver Circulation and Liver Disease, 1932–43. *Recreation:* gardening. *Address:* 2 North Square, NW11 7AA. *T:* 081–455 8731. *Died 3 March 1993.*

McMILLAN, Col Donald, CB 1959; OBE 1945; Chairman, Cable & Wireless Ltd, and associated companies, 1967–72; *b* 22 Dec. 1906; *s* of Neil Munro McMillan and Isabella Jamieson; *m* 1946, Kathleen Ivy Bingham; one *s*. *Educ:* Sloane Sch., Chelsea; Battersea Polytechnic. Post Office Engineering Dept, 1925–54; Director External Telecommunications, Post Office External Telecommunications Executive, 1954–67. BSc Eng (London); FIEE. *Publications:* contribs to Institution Engineers Journal, Post Office Institution Engineers Journal. *Recreations:* golf, gardening. *Address:* 46 Gatehill

Road, Northwood, Mddx HA6 3QP. *T:* Northwood (01923) 822682. *Club:* Grim's Dyke Golf.

Died 5 Oct. 1995.

McMILLAN, Prof. Duncan; John Orr Professor of French Language and Romance Linguistics, University of Edinburgh, 1955–80, then Emeritus; *b* London, 30 April 1914; *o s* of late Duncan McMillan and Martha (*née* Hastings); *m* 1945, Geneviève, *er d* of late M and Mme Robert Busse, Paris; one *s. Educ:* Holbeach Rd LCC; St Dunstan's Coll.; University Coll., London (Troughton Schol., Rothschild Prizeman, Univ. Postgrad. Student); Sorbonne, Paris (Clothworkers Schol., British Inst. in Paris). BA, PhD (London); Diplôme de l'Ecole des Hautes Etudes, Paris. Army, 1940–46. Lecteur d'anglais, Univ. of Paris, 1938–40; Lectr in French and Romance Philology, Univ. of Aberdeen, 1946–50, Univ. of Edinburgh, 1950–55. Founder Mem., Société Rencesvals, 1955, Pres., British Sect., 1956–59; Member Council: Société des anciens textes français, 1963; Société de Linguistique romane, 1977–83. Chevalier de la Légion d'Honneur, 1958; Médaille d'Honneur, Univ. of Liège, 1962. *Publications:* La Chanson de Guillaume (Société des anciens textes français), 2 vols, 1949–50; (in collaboration with Madame G. McMillan) An Anthology of the Contemporary French Novel, 1950; Le Charroi de Nîmes, 1972, 2nd edn 1978. *Address:* 11 rue des Prés Hauts, 92290 Châtenay Malabry, France. *T:* (1) 46603713. *Club:* Scottish Arts (Edinburgh). *Died 1 June 1993.*

McMILLAN, Prof. Edwin Mattison; Professor of Physics, University of California, 1946–73, then Professor Emeritus; *b* Redondo Beach, Calif, 18 Sept. 1907; *s* of Edwin Harbaugh McMillan and Anna Marie (*née* Mattison); *m* 1941, Elsie Walford Blumer; two *s* one *d. Educ:* Calif Institute of Technology (MS); Princeton Univ. (PhD). Univ. of California: National Research Fellow, 1932–34; Research Associate, 1934–35; Instructor, 1935–36; Asst Prof., 1936–41; Associate Prof., 1941–46. Leave of absence for war research, 1940–45. Mem. of staff of Radiation Laboratory, Univ. of Calif., 1934–: Assoc. Dir, 1954–58; Dir, 1958–71; Dir, Lawrence Berkeley Laboratory, 1971–73. Mem. General Advisory Cttee to Atomic Energy Commission, 1954–58. Member: Commission on High Energy Physics of International Union for Pure and Applied Physics, 1960–66; Scientific Policy Cttee of Stanford Linear Accelerator Center, 1962–66; Physics Adv. Cttee, Nat. Accelerator Lab., 1967–69; Trustee, Univs Research Assoc., 1969–84; Chm., Cl. I, Nat. Acad. of Sciences, 1968–71. Fellow Amer. Physical Soc. Member: Nat. Acad. of Sciences (USA); American Philosophical Soc.; Fellow, Amer. Acad. of Arts and Sciences. Research Corp. 1950 Scientific Award, 1951; (jtly) Nobel Prize in Chemistry, 1951; (jtly) Atoms for Peace Award, 1963; Alumni Dist. Service Award, Calif. Inst. of Tech., 1966; Centennial Citation, Univ. of California, Berkeley, 1968. Hon. DSc, Rensselaer Polytechnic Institute; Hon. DSc, Gustavus Adolphus Coll. *Address:* 1401 Vista Road, El Cerrito, Calif 94530, USA. *Died 7 Sept. 1991.*

MacMILLAN, Sir Kenneth, Kt 1983; Principal Choreographer to the Royal Ballet, Covent Garden, since 1977; Artistic Associate, American Ballet Theatre, since 1984; *b* 11 Dec. 1929; *m* 1974, Deborah Williams; one *d. Educ:* Great Yarmouth Gram. Sch. Started as Dancer, Royal Ballet; became Choreographer, 1953; Dir of Ballet, Deutsche Oper, Berlin, 1966–69; Resident Choreographer, and Dir, Royal Ballet, 1970–77. First professional ballet, Danses Concertantes (Stravinsky-Georgiades). Principal ballets: The Burrow; Solitaire; Agon; The Invitation; Romeo and Juliet; Diversions; La Création du Monde; Images of Love; The Song of the Earth; Concerto; Anastasia; Cain and Abel; Olympiad; Triad; Ballade; The

Poltroon; Manon; Pavanne; Elite Syncopations; The Four Seasons; Rituals; Requiem; Mayerling; My Brother, My Sisters; La Fin du Jour; Gloria; Isadora; Valley of Shadows; Different Drummer; The Wild Boy; Requiem (Andrew Lloyd Webber); The Prince of the Pagodas; Winter Dreams; The Judas Tree. Devised ballets for: Ballet Rambert, American Ballet, Royal Ballet Sch., theatre, television, cinema, musical shows. Directed: Ionesco's plays, The Chairs and The Lesson, New Inn, Ealing, 1982; The Dance of Death, Royal Exchange, Manchester, 1983; The Kingdom of Earth, Hampstead Theatre Club, 1984. Dr *hc:* Edinburgh, 1976; RCA, 1992. Evening Standard Ballet Award, 1979; Ballet Award, SWET Managers, 1980 and 1983. *Recreation:* cinema. *Address:* c/o Royal Opera House, Covent Garden, WC2E 9DD. *Died 29 Oct. 1992.*

MACMILLAN, Wallace, CMG 1956; retired; *b* 16 Oct. 1913; *s* of late David Hutchen Macmillan and Jean Wallace, Newburgh, Fife; *m* 1947, Betty Bryce, *d* of late G. R. Watson and Margaret Bryce; three *s. Educ:* Bell-Baxter Sch.; University of St Andrews; Kiel Univ.; Corpus Christi Coll., Oxford. Administrative Officer, Tanganyika, 1937; District Officer, 1947; Administrator of Grenada, BWI, 1951–57; acted as Governor, Windward Is, periods 1955; Federal Establishment Sec. (subsequently Permanent Sec., Min. of Estabts and Service Matters), Federation of Nigeria, 1957–61. Dir, Management Selection Ltd, 1961–78. *Recreations:* bridge, chess, golf. *Address:* Flat 1, 6 Spylaw Road, Edinburgh EH10 5BL. *Died 14 Nov. 1992.*

McMURTRIE, Group Captain Richard Angus, DSO 1940; DFC 1940; Royal Air Force, retired; *b* 14 Feb. 1909; *s* of Radburn Angus and Ethel Maud McMurtrie; *m* 1st, 1931, Gwenyth Mary (*d* 1958), 3rd *d* of Rev. (Lt-Col) H. J. Philpott; no *c;* 2nd, 1963, Laura, 4th *d* of William H. Gerhardi. *Educ:* Royal Grammar Sch., Newcastle on Tyne. First commissioned in Territorial Army (72nd Brigade, RA), 1927; transferred to Royal Air Force, 1929, as Pilot Officer; served in No 2 (AC) Squadron, 1931–32, and Fleet Air Arm (442 Flight, and 822 Squadron in HMS Furious), 1932–33; Cranwell, 1934–35; Flt Lieut, 1935; Calshot and No 201 (Flying Boat) Squadron, 1935–38; Squadron Leader, 1938, and commanded Recruits Sub-Depot, RAF, Linton-on-Ouse; served War of 1939–45 (despatches thrice, DFC, DSO): No 269 GR Squadron, 1939–41; Wing Commander, 1940; HQ No 18 Group RAF, 1941; Group Captain, commanding RAF Station, Sumburgh (Shetlands), 1942–43; HQ Coastal Command, 1943; RAF Staff Coll., Air Ministry, Whitehall, and HQ Transport Command, 1944; commanded RAF Station, Stoney Cross, Hants, 1945; and formed and commanded No 61 Group (Reserve Command), 1946; Joint Services Mission, Washington, DC, 1946–49; commanded RAF Station, Cardington, 1949–52; HQ No 1 Group, RAF, 1952–54; Royal Naval College, Greenwich, 1954; HQ, Supreme Allied Commander, Atlantic (NATO), Norfolk, Virginia, USA, 1954–56; HQ, Coastal Command, RAF, Northwood, Mddx, 1957–59. Latterly farming. *Recreations:* sailing, photography. *Address:* Rose in Vale Farm, Constantine, Falmouth, Cornwall TR11 5PU. *T:* Falmouth (0326) 40338. *Clubs:* Royal Air Force Yacht (Hon. Life Mem.), Royal Cornwall Yacht.

Died 3 Jan. 1994.

MACNAB, Brig. Sir Geoffrey (Alex Colin), KCMG 1962 (CMG 1955); CB 1951; retired; *b* 23 Dec. 1899; *s* of Brig.-General Colin Macnab, CMG and Beatrice Marian, *d* of Rev. W. B. Bliss, Wicken, Essex; *m* 1930, Norah (*d* 1981), *d* of Captain H. A. Cramer-Roberts, Folkestone. *Educ:* Wellington Coll.; RMC Sandhurst. 1st Commission, Royal Sussex Regt, 1919; Instr, Small Arms Sch., Hythe, 1925–28; Captain, Argyll and Sutherland Highlanders,

1931; Staff Coll., Camberley, 1930–31; GSO 3, WO, 1933–35; BM 10 Infantry Bde, 1935–38; Military Attaché, Prague and Bucharest, 1938–40; served War of 1939–45, campaigns Western Desert, Greece, Crete; Brigadier, 1944; Military Mission, Hungary, 1945; DMI, Middle East, 1945–47; Military Attaché, Rome, 1947–49; Military Attaché, Paris, 1949–54; retired 1954 (also service in Ireland, Germany, Far East, India, Middle East). Secretary, Government Hospitality Fund, 1957–68. *Address:* Stanford House, Stanford, Ashford, Kent TN25 6DF. *T:* Sellindge (0130381) 2118. *Clubs:* Army and Navy, MCC.   *Died 17 Jan. 1995.*

McNAIR, Thomas Jaffrey, CBE 1988; MD; FRCSE, FRCS, FRCPE, FRCPGlas; Surgeon to the Queen in Scotland, 1977–87; Consultant Surgeon, Royal Infirmary of Edinburgh, 1961–87; *b* 1 March 1927; *s* of David McMillan McNair and Helen (*née* Rae); *m* 1951, Dr Sybil Monteith Dick Wood; one *s* one *d*. *Educ:* George Watson's Coll.; Univ. of Edinburgh (MB, ChB, MD). FRCSE 1955: FRCS 1956; FRCPE 1989; FRCPGlas 1989. Served as Flt Lt, RAF, 1950–52. Ho. Surg., Registrar, Clinical Tutor, Royal Infirmary of Edin., 1949–60; MO, Marlu, Gold Coast, 1950; Lectr in Clin. Surgery, Univ. of Edin., 1960; Instr in Surgery, Univ. of Illinois, USA, 1960; Consultant Surgeon: Eastern Gen. Hosp., 1961–64; Chalmers Hosp., 1964–81. Hon. Sen. Lectr in Clin. Surg., Univ. of Edin., 1976–87. Pres., 1985–88, Examr, 1964–88, RCSEd. Hon. FRACS 1988. *Publications:* Emergency Surgery, 8th and 9th edns, 1967 and 1972; various, on surgical subjects. *Recreations:* golf, sailing. *Address:* Easter Carrick, Chapel Green, Earlsferry, Leven, Fife KY9 1AD. *Clubs:* New (Edinburgh); Golf House (Elie).

Died 27 April 1994.

McNAIR-WILSON, Sir (Robert) Michael (Conal), Kt 1988; *b* 12 Oct. 1930; *y s* of late Dr Robert McNair-Wilson and of Mrs Doris McNair-Wilson; *m* 1974, Mrs Deidre Granville; one *d*. *Educ:* Eton College. During national service, 1948–50, was commissioned in Royal Irish Fusiliers. Farmed in Hampshire, 1950–53; journalist on various provincial newspapers, and did freelance work for BBC in Northern Ireland, 1953–55; joined Sidney-Barton Ltd, internat. public relations consultants, 1955, Dir, 1961–79; consultant to various public affairs cos, 1979–92. Contested (C) Lincoln, 1964; MP (C): Walthamstow E, 1969–74; Newbury, 1974–92. PPS to Minister of Agriculture, 1979–83. Mem. Council, Bow Group, 1965–66; Jt Secretary: UN Parly Gp, 1969–70; Cons. Greater London Members Gp, 1970–72; Cons. Constitution Cttee, 1986; Sec., 1969–70, Vice-Chm., 1970–72, Chm., 1972–74, Cons. Aviation Cttee; Member Select Cttee on: Nationalised Industries, 1973–79; Members Interests, 1986–92; Educn, Science and the Arts, 1986–92; Dep. Chm., Air Safety Gp, 1979–92. Led first IPU Parly Delegn to Estonia since 1939, 1991. Member: Council, Air League, 1972–76; Watching Cttee, Friends of Ulster, 1985–. Mem. Ct, Reading Univ., 1979–91. Non-exec. Dir, W Berks Priority Care Services Trust, 1993–; Pres., Nat. Fedn of Kidney Patients Assocs, 1989–; Mem., Unrelated Live Transplant Regulatory Authy, 1989–; Trustee: Transplant Patients Trust, 1989–; Oxford Kidney Unit Trust Fund, 1989–; Donnington Hosp. Trust, 1992–. First MP on kidney dialysis, and first MP with a kidney transplant. Gov., Shaw House Sch., Newbury. *Publications:* Blackshirt, a biography of Mussolini (jointly), 1959; No Tame or Minor Role (Bow Group pamphlet on the Common Market) (jointly), 1963. *Recreations:* gardening, sailing, ski-ing, riding. *Address:* Nine Elms Farmhouse, Bucklebury, Reading RG7 6NS. *T:* Reading (0734) 713357. *Club:* Carlton.

Died 28 March 1993.

McNEIL, John Struthers, CBE 1967; Chief Road Engineer, Scottish Development Department, 1963–69; *b* 4 March 1907; *s* of R. H. McNeil, Troon; *m* 1931, Dorothea Yuille; two *s*. *Educ:* Ayr Academy; Glasgow Univ. BSc Hons, Civil Engineering, 1929; FICE 1955. Contracting and local government experience, 1929–35; joined Ministry of Transport as Asst Engineer, 1935; Divisional Road Engineer, NW Div. of England, 1952–55; Asst Chief Engineer, 1955–57; Dep. Chief Engineer, 1957–63. Telford Gold Medal, ICE. *Publications:* contribs to technical journals. *Recreations:* fishing, gardening. *Address:* 306–250 Douglas Street, Victoria, BC V8V 2P4, Canada.   *Died 29 Aug. 1993.*

MACONCHY, Dame Elizabeth, (Dame Elizabeth LeFanu), DBE 1987 (CBE 1977); FRCM; Hon. RAM; composer of serious music; *b* 19 March 1907; of Irish parentage; *d* of Gerald E. C. Maconchy, lawyer, and Violet M. Poë; *m* 1930, William Richard LeFanu (author of Betsy Sheridan's Journal, 1960, repr. 1986, Bibliography of Nehemiah Grew, 1990, etc); two *d*. *Educ:* privately; Royal College of Music, London. Held Blumenthal Scholarship and won Sullivan Prize, Foli and other exhibitions, at RCM; pupil of Vaughan-Williams; travelled with Octavia Scholarship, 1929–30. First public performance: Piano Concerto with Prague Philharmonic Orchestra, 1930; Sir Henry Wood introduced The Land (suite for orchestra), Promenade Concerts, 1930; works performed at 3 Festivals of International Society for Contemporary Music (Prague, 1935; Paris, 1937; Copenhagen, 1947); largest output in Chamber Music; String Quartets played as a series in BBC Third Programme, 1955, 1975. Chairman: Composers Guild of Great Britain, 1960; Soc. for Promotion of New Music, 1972–75 (Pres., 1977–). Hon. Fellow, St Hilda's Coll., Oxford, 1978. *Compositions:* The Land; Nocturne; Overture, Proud Thames (LCC Coronation Prize, 1953); Dialogue for piano and orchestra; Serenata Concertante for violin and orchestra, 1963; Symphony for double string orchestra; Concertino for: bassoon and string orchestra; Piano and chamber orchestra; Concerto for oboe, bassoon and string orchestra; Variazioni Concertanti for oboe, clarinet, bassoon, horn and strings, 1965; Variations for String Orchestra; twelve String Quartets (No 5, Edwin Evans Prize; No 9, Radcliffe Award, 1969); Oboe Quintet (Daily Telegraph Prize); Violin Sonata; Cello Divertimento; Duo for 2 Violins; Duo for Violin and Cello; Variations for solo cello; Reflections, for oboe, clarinet, viola and harp (Gedok International Prize, 1961); Clarinet Quintet; Carol Cantata, A Christmas Morning; Samson and the Gates of Gaza for chorus and orchestra, 1964; 3 settings of Gerard Manley Hopkins for soprano and chamber orchestra; Sonatina for harpsichord and Notebook for harpsichord, 1965; Three Donne settings, 1965; Nocturnal for unaccompanied chorus, 1965; Music for brass and woodwind, 1966; An Essex Overture, 1966; 6 Miniatures for solo violin, 1966; Duo for piano duet, 1967; Extravaganza, The Birds, after Aristophanes, 1968; And Death shall have no Dominion for chorus and brass, 3 Choirs Festival, 1969; The Jesse Tree, masque for Dorchester Abbey, 1970; Music for double-bass and piano, 1971; Ariadne (C. Day Lewis), for soprano and orch., King's Lynn Festival, 1971; Faustus, scena for tenor and piano, 1971; Prayer Before Birth, for women's voices, 1971; 3 Bagatelles for oboe and harpsichord, 1972; oboe quartet, 1972; songs for voice and harp, 1974; The King of the Golden River, opera for children, 1975; Epyllion, for solo cello and strings, Cheltenham Festival, 1975; Sinfonietta, for Essex Youth Orch., 1976; Pied Beauty, and Heaven Haven (G. M. Hopkins), for choir and brass, Southern Cathedrals Fest., 1976; Morning, Noon and Night, for harp, Aldeburgh Fest., 1977; Sun, Moon and Stars (Traherne), song cycle for soprano and piano, 1977; Heloise and Abelard, for 3 soloists, chorus and orch.,

1977–78; The Leaden Echo & the Golden Echo (Hopkins), for choir and 3 instruments, 1978; Contemplation, for cello and piano, 1978; Colloquy, for flute and piano, 1979; Romanza, for solo viola and 11 instruments, 1979; Creatures, for mixed voices, 1979; Fantasia, for clarinet and piano, 1980; Little Symphony, for Norfolk Youth Orch., 1980; 4 Miniatures for chorus, 1981; Trittico for 2 oboes, bassoon and harpsichord, 1981; Piccola Musica for string trio, 1981; My Dark Heart, for soprano and 6 instruments, for RCM cent., 1982; Wind Quintet, 1982; L'Horloge (Baudelaire), for soprano, clarinet and piano, 1982; Music for Strings, Proms, 1983; 5 Sketches for Solo Viola, 1983; O Time Turn Back, chorus with cello, 1983; Narration for solo cello, 1984; Still Falls the Rain for double choir, 1984; Excursion for solo bassoon, 1985; Life Story for string orchestra, 1985; Two songs by Auden in memory of W. B. Yeats, and It's No Go (MacNeice), 1985; Three One-Act Operas (The Sofa, The Three Strangers, The Departure); songs, piano pieces, etc. *Address:* Shottesbrook, Boreham, Chelmsford, Essex CM3 3EJ. *T:* Chelmsford (01245) 467286.

Died 11 Nov. 1994.

McPETRIE, Sir James (Carnegie), KCMG 1966 (CMG 1961); OBE 1953; HM Diplomatic Service, retired; Honorary Fellow, Department of Public Law, Dundee University, since 1976; *b* 29 June 1911; *er s* of late James Duncan McPetrie and Elizabeth Mary Carnegie; *m* 1941, Elizabeth, *e d* of late John Howie; one *d. Educ:* Madras Coll., St Andrews; Univ. of St Andrews; Jesus Coll., Oxford (Scholar). MA (St Andrews) 1933; BA Oxon 1937, MA 1972; Harmsworth Schol., Middle Temple, 1937; Barrister, Middle Temple, 1938. Served War of 1939–45, Royal Artillery and staff of JAG (India); commissioned, 1940; Major, 1944. Legal Asst, Commonwealth Relations Office and Colonial Office, 1946, Sen. Legal Asst, 1947, Asst Legal Adviser, 1952; Legal Adviser, Colonial Office, 1960, Commonwealth Office, 1966, FCO, 1968–71. Temporary mem. Legal Staff, DoE, 1972–75. Chm., UNESCO Appeals Bd, 1973–79. Mem. Court, Univ. of St Andrews, 1982–86. *Address:* 52 Main Street, Strathkinness, St Andrews, Fife KY16 9SA. *T:* Strathkinness (033485) 235.

Died 26 Aug. 1991.

MACPHERSON, Ian, CA; Chairman and Chief Executive, Watson & Philip plc, 1989–93; *b* 25 March 1936; *s* of William and Isobel Macpherson; *m* 1960, Margaret Petrie; one *s* one *d. Educ:* Morrison's Acad., Crieff, Perthshire. CA 1961. Partner, The Alliance Trust, 1961–67; W. Greenwell & Co., 1967–73; Director: London & European Gp, 1973–75; Provincial Cities Trust, 1973–75; Vice Pres., Manufacturers Hanover Trust, 1976–79; British Linen Bank: Dir, 1979–82; Dep. Chief Exec., 1982–88. Chairman: Low & Bonar plc, 1990– (Dir, 1987–90); VG Distributors Ltd, 1992–; Caledonian Newspaper Publishing Ltd, 1992–; George Outram & Co. Ltd, 1992–; Securities Trust of Scotland plc, 1993– (Dir, 1991–93); Dir, Spar Food Distributors Ltd, 1991–. Bd Mem., Internat. Stock Exchange of UK and Republic of Ireland, 1991–. FInstD 1985 (Mem. Council, 1991–). Mem. Court, Univ. of Dundee, 1991–. *Recreations:* gardening, golf, watching Rugby, reading, music. *Address:* Dinmont, 64 Buchanan Gardens, St Andrews, Fife KY16 9LX. *T:* St Andrews (0334) 72827. *Club:* New (Edinburgh).

Died 30 Jan. 1994.

MACPHERSON, Sir Keith (Duncan), Kt 1981; company director; Consultant, The Herald and Weekly Times Ltd, Melbourne, since 1986; *b* 12 June 1920; *m* 1946, Ena Forester McNair; three *s* two *d. Educ:* Scotch Coll., Melbourne. Joined The Herald and Weekly Times Ltd, 1938; Sec., 1959–64; Asst Gen. Man., 1965–67; Gen. Man., 1968–70; Dir, 1974–86; Chief Exec., 1975–85;

Chm., 1977–86; non-exec. Chm., 1985–86. Chairman: Australian Newsprint Mills Holdings Ltd, 1978–86 (Vice-Chm., 1976–78); West Australian Newspapers Ltd, 1981–86 (Dir, 1970; Man. Dir, 1970–75); South Pacific Post Pty Ltd (New Guinea Newspapers), 1965–70; Queensland Press Ltd, 1983–86 (Dep. Chm., 1981–83; Dir, 1978–86). Director: Tasman Pulp & Paper Co. Ltd, 1977–78; Davies Bros Ltd, 1975–86; New Nation Publishing Ltd, Singapore, 1974–81. Pres., Australian Newspapers Council, 1968–70; Chairman: Newspaper Proprietors' Assoc. of Melbourne, 1968–70; Media Council of Aust., 1969–70. *Recreations:* swimming, gardening. *Address:* Gleneagles, 24 Balwyn Road, Canterbury, Vic 3126, Australia. *T:* 8368571. *Clubs:* Melbourne, Athenæum, Melbourne Cricket, Victoria Automobile of Victoria, Victoria Racing, Victoria Amateur Turf, Moonee Valley Racing (Melbourne); American National (Sydney). *Died 3 Nov. 1993.*

MacPHERSON, Stewart Myles; radio commentator; journalist; variety artist; Special Events Coordinator, Assiniboia Downs Racetrack, Winnipeg; *b* Winnipeg, Canada, 29 Oct. 1908; *m* 1937, Emily Comfort; one *s* one *d. Educ:* Canada. Started broadcasting, 1937, on ice hockey; War correspondent; commentator on national events and world championships; Question Master, Twenty Questions and Ignorance is Bliss; Compère, Royal Command Variety Performance, 1948; Dir of Programs, C-Jay Television, Winnipeg, 1960. *Publication:* The Mike and I, 1948; *relevant publication:* Highlights with Stewart MacPherson, by John Robertson, 1980. *Recreations:* golf, bridge, poker. *Address:* 709–3200 Portage Avenue, Winnipeg, Manitoba, Canada. *T:* (204) 8890210.

Died 16 April 1995.

MACQUEEN, Angus, CMG 1977; Director, The British Bank of the Middle East, 1970–79 (Chairman, 1975–78); Member, London Advisory Committee, The Hongkong and Shanghai Banking Corporation, 1975–78; Chairman, Incotes Ltd, 1975–85; *b* 7 April 1910; *s* of Donald Macqueen and Catherine Thomson; *m* 1st, 1940, Erica A. L. Sutherland (marr. diss.); one *d*; 2nd, 1950, Elizabeth Mary Barber (*d* 1995); one *s* one *d. Educ:* Campbeltown Grammar Sch. Joined Union Bank of Scotland, 1927; Imperial Bank of Persia (later The British Bank of the Middle East), 1930; overseas service in Iraq, Iran, Kuwait, Aden, Lebanon, Morocco; Gen. Manager, 1965–70. Director: The British Bank of the Middle East (Morocco), 1961–70; The Bank of Iran and the Middle East, 1965–74; Bank of North Africa, 1965–70. Member: London Chamber of Commerce (Middle East Section), 1962–66; Council, Anglo-Arab Assoc., 1968–75. AIB (Scot.). Hon. Texas Citizen, 1975. National Cedar Medal, Lebanon, 1960. *Recreations:* walking, foreign travel. *Address:* 18 Montagu Square, W1H 1RD. *T:* 0171–935 9015. *Club:* Oriental. *Died 15 July 1995.*

MACRORY, Sir Patrick (Arthur), Kt 1972; Director, Rothman Carreras Ltd, 1971–82; barrister-at-law; *b* 21 March 1911; *s* of late Lt-Col F. S. N. Macrory, DSO, DL, and Rosie, *d* of Gen. Brabazon Pottinger; *m* 1939, Elizabeth, *d* of late Rev. J. F. O. Lewis; three *s* (one *d* decd). *Educ:* Cheltenham Coll.; Trinity Coll., Oxford (MA). Called to the Bar, Middle Temple, 1937. Served War, 1939–45, Army. Unilever Ltd: joined 1947; Secretary, 1956; Director, 1968–71, retd. Dir, Bank of Ireland Gp, 1971–79; Chm., Merchant Ivory Productions, 1976–92. Mem., Northern Ireland Development Council, 1956–64; Gen. Treasurer, British Assoc. for Advancement of Science, 1960–65; Chm., Review Body on Local Govt in N Ireland, 1970; Pres., Confedn of Ulster Socs, 1980–84 (Chm., 1974–79); Member: Commn of Inquiry into Industrial Representation, 1971–72; Cttee on the Preparation of Legislation, 1973. Mem. Council,

Cheltenham Coll. (Dep. Pres., 1980–83). *Publications:* Borderline, 1937; Signal Catastrophe—the retreat from Kabul 1842, 1966, repr. as Kabul Catastrophe: the retreat of 1842, 1986; (ed) Lady Sale's Journal, 1969; The Siege of Derry, 1980; Days that are Gone, 1983; (with George Pottinger) The Ten Rupee Jezail, 1993. *Recreations:* golf, military history. *Address:* Amberdene, Walton-on-the-Hill, Tadworth, Surrey KT20 7UB. *T:* Tadworth (0737) 813086. *Clubs:* Athenæum; Walton Heath Golf; Castlerock Golf (Co. Londonderry).

Died 3 May 1993.

McWHIRTER, Prof. Robert, CBE 1963; FRCSEd, FRCPEd, FRCR; FRSE; Professor of Medical Radiology, Edinburgh University, 1946–70; Director of Radiotherapy, Royal Infirmary, Edinburgh, 1935–70; President, Medical and Dental Defence Union of Scotland, 1959–90, then Hon. Fellow; *b* 8 Nov. 1904; *s* of Robert McWhirter and Janet Ramsay Gairdner; *m* 1937, Dr Susan Muir MacMurray; one *s. Educ:* Girvan Academy; Glasgow and Cambridge Universities. MB, ChB (High Commendn), Glasgow, 1927; FRCSEd 1932; DMRE Cambridge, 1933; FRCR (FFR 1939); FRCPEd 1965. FRSE 1944. Formerly: Student, Mayo Clinic; British Empire Cancer Campaign Research Student, Holt Radium Institute, Manchester; Chief Assistant, X-Ray Dept, St Bartholomew's Hospital, London. Member, British Institute of Radiology; Pres., Sect. of Radiology, RSM, 1956; Royal College of Radiologists: Pres., 1966–69; Twining Memorial Medal, 1943; Skinner Memorial Lecturer, 1956; Warden, 1961–66; Knox Memorial Lecturer, 1963; Caldwell Memorial Lecturer, American Roentgen Ray Society, 1963; Past Pres., Internat. Radio Therapists Visiting Club; Hon. Member, American Radium Society; Membre Corresp. Etranger, Société Française d'Electro-Radiologie Médicale, 1967; Membro d'onore, Società Italiana della Radiologia Medica e Medicine Nucleare, 1968; Hon. Member: Sociedade Brasileira de Patologia Mamária, 1969; Nippon Societas Radiologica, 1970; Groupe Européen des Radiotherapeutes, 1971; Hon. Fellow: Australasian College of Radiologists, 1954; American College of Radiology, 1965; Faculty of Radiologists, RCSI, 1967. Gold Medal, Nat. Soc. for Cancer Relief, 1985. *Publications:* contribs to medical journals. *Recreation:* golf. *Address:* 2 Orchard Brae, Edinburgh EH4 1NY. *T:* 0131–332 5800. *Club:* University (Edinburgh). *Died 24 Oct. 1994.*

McWILLIAM, (Frederick) Edward, CBE 1966; RA 1989; sculptor; *b* 30 April 1909; *yr s* of Dr William Nicholson McWilliam, Banbridge, County Down, Ireland; *m* 1932, Elizabeth Marion Crowther (*d* 1988); two *d. Educ:* Campbell Coll., Belfast; Slade School of Fine Art; Paris. Served War of 1939–45, RAF, UK and Far East. Member of Staff, Slade Sch. of Fine Art, London Univ., 1947–66. Mem. Art Panel, Arts Council, 1960–68. First one-man exhibn., sculpture, London Gall., 1939; subsequently Hanover Gallery, 1949, 1952, 1956; Waddington Galleries, 1961, 1963, 1966, 1968, 1971, 1973, 1976, 1979, 1984; Dawson Gallery, Dublin; Felix Landau Gallery, Los Angeles; exhibn to mark eightieth birthday, New Art Centre, 1989; Mayor Gall., 1990, 1992; retrospective exhibns: Belfast, Dublin, Londonderry, 1981; Warwick Arts Trust, 1982; Tate Gall., 1989; exhibited in International Open-Air Exhibitions, London, Antwerp, Arnheim, Paris; work included in British Council touring exhibitions, USA, Canada, Germany, South America. Fellow, UCL, 1972. Hon. DLit Belfast, 1964. *Relevant Publication:* McWilliam, Sculptor, by Roland Penrose, 1964. *Address:* 8A Holland Villas Road, W14 8BP. *Died 13 May 1992.*

MADDOCKS, William Henry, MBE 1975; General Secretary, National Union of Dyers, Bleachers and Textile

Workers, 1979–82; *b* 18 Feb. 1921; *m* 1944, Mary Holdsworth; one *d. Educ:* Eastwood Elem. Sch.; Holycroft Council Sch., Keighley. W of England full-time Organiser for National Union of Dyers, Bleachers and Textile Workers, 1963. Mem., TUC Gen. Council, 1978–82. JP Gloucestershire, 1968. *Address:* 50 Waterside, Silsden, Keighley, W Yorks BD20 0LQ. *T:* Steeton (0535) 652893. *Clubs:* Yeadon Trades Hall (Yeadon, W Yorks); Keighley Cricket. *Died 23 Aug. 1992.*

MAGNIAC, Rear-Adm. Vernon St Clair Lane, CB 1961; *b* 21 Dec. 1908; *s* of late Major Francis Arthur Magniac and Mrs Beatrice Caroline Magniac (*née* Davison); *m* 1947, Eileen Eleanor (*née* Witney); one *s* one *d* (and one *d* decd). *Educ:* Clifton Coll. Cadet, RN, 1926; served in HM Ships Courageous, Effingham, Resolution and Diamond, 1931–37; RN Engineering Coll., 1937–39; HMS Renown, 1940–43; Combined Ops, India, 1943–45; HM Ships Fisgard, Gambia, and Nigeria, 1945–50; HM Dockyards Chatham, Malta and Devonport, 1950–62. *Recreations:* golf, fishing. *Address:* Marlborough, Down Park, Yelverton, Devon PL20 6BN.

Died 28 Nov. 1994.

MAGNUS, Samuel Woolf; Justice of Appeal, Court of Appeal for Zambia, 1971; Commissioner, Foreign Compensation Commission, 1977–83; *b* 30 Sept. 1910; *s* of late Samuel Woolf Magnus; *m* 1938, Anna Gertrude, *o d* of Adolph Shane, Cardiff; one *d. Educ:* University Coll., London. BA Hons, 1931. Called to Bar, Gray's Inn, 1937. Served War of 1939–45, Army. Practised in London, 1937–59; partner in legal firm, Northern Rhodesia, 1959–63; subseq. legal consultant. QC 1964, MLC 1962, MP Jan.-Oct. 1964, Northern Rhodesia; MP, Zambia, 1964–68; Puisne Judge, High Court for Zambia, 1968. Treas., Assoc. of Liberal Lawyers, Mem. Council, London Liberal Party and Pres., N Hendon Liberal Assoc., until 1959. Contested (L) Central Hackney, 1945. Chm., Law, Parly and Gen. Purposes Cttee, Bd of Deputies of British Jews, 1979–83. FCIArb 1987. *Publications:* (with M. Estrin) Companies Act 1947, 1947; (with M. Estrin) Companies: Law and Practice, 1948, 5th edn 1978, and Supplement, 1981; (with A. M. Lyons) Advertisement Control, 1949; Magnus on Leasehold Property (Temporary Provisions) Act 1951, 1951; Magnus on Landlord and Tenant Act 1954, 1954; Magnus on Housing Repairs and Rents Act 1954, 1954; Magnus on the Rent Act 1957, 1957; (with F. E. Price) Knight's Annotated Housing Acts, 1958; (with Tovell) Magnus on Housing Finance, 1960; (with M. Estrin) Companies Act 1967, 1967; Magnus on the Rent Act 1968, 1969; Magnus on Business Tenancies, 1970; Magnus on the Rent Act 1977, 1978; Butterworth's Company Forms Manual, 1987; contributor: Law Jl; Halsbury's Laws of England; Encycl. of Forms and Precedents; Atkin's Court Forms and Precedents. *Recreations:* writing, photography, enthusiastic spectator at all games, preferably on TV. *Address:* 33 Apsley House, Finchley Road, St John's Wood, NW8. *T:* 071–586 1679. *Clubs:* MCC, Middlesex CC. *Died 28 Feb. 1992.*

MAGOR, Major (Edward) Walter (Moyle), CMG 1960; OBE 1956 (MBE 1947); DL; *b* 1 June 1911; *e s* of late Edward John Penberthy Magor, JP, Lamellen, St Tudy, Cornwall, and Gilian Sarah Magor, JP; *m* 1939, Daphne Davis (*d* 1972), *d* of late Hector Robert Lushington Graham, Summerhill, Thomastown, Co. Kilkenny; two *d. Educ:* Marlborough; Magdalen Coll., Oxford; Magdalene Coll., Cambridge. MA. Indian Army, 1934–47; RARO, 10th Hussars, 1949–61; Indian Political Service, 1937–39 and 1943–47; Colonial Administrative Service, 1947–61; Asst Chief Secretary, Kenya, 1953; Permanent Secretary, Ministry of Defence, 1954; Acting Minister for Defence, 1956; Secretary to the Cabinet, 1958; Home Civil Service, DTI, formerly BoT, 1961–71; Asst Secretary, 1964; retired

1971. Chm., St John Council for Cornwall, 1973–78. Editor, RHS Rhododendron and Camellia Yearbook, 1974–82; Chm., RHS Rhododendron and Camellia Gp, 1976–80. President: Cornwall Garden Soc., 1981–84; Royal Cornwall Agricl Assoc., 1983. DL Cornwall, 1974; High Sheriff of Cornwall, 1981. CStJ 1978 (OStJ 1975). Médaille de la Belgique Reconnaissante, 1961; Veitch Meml Medal, RHS, 1986. Lord of the Manor of Kellygreen. *Recreation:* gardening (Mem., Garden Soc.). *Address:* Lamellen, St Tudy, Cornwall PL30 3NR. *T:* Bodmin (01208) 850207. *Died 1 May 1995.*

MAHON, Rt Rev. Gerald Thomas; Auxiliary Bishop of Westminster (Bishop in West London) (RC) and Titular Bishop of Eanach Duin since 1970; *b* 4 May 1922; *s* of George Elborne Mahon and Mary Elizabeth (*née* Dooley). *Educ:* Cardinal Vaughan Sch., Kensington; Christ's Coll., Cambridge. Priest, 1946. Teaching, St Peter's Coll., Freshfield, 1950–55; missionary work in Dio. of Kisumu, Kenya, 1955–63; Superior General of St Joseph's Missionary Society of Mill Hill, 1963–70. *Address:* 34 Whitehall Gardens, Acton, W3 9RD.

Died 29 Jan. 1992.

MAIR, Prof. Alexander, OBE 1995; FRSE 1980; Professor of Community and Occupational Medicine (formerly of Public Health and Social Medicine), University of Dundee, 1954–82, then Emeritus; *b* 9 Sept. 1912; *m* 1945, Nancy Waddington; two *s* one *d. Educ:* Aberdeen Univ. MB, ChB, 1942, DPH, 1948, MD (Hons), 1952 (Aberdeen); DIH (London) 1955; FRCPE 1966; FFCM 1976; FFOM 1979. RAMC, 1942–46. Lecturer, Univ. of Aberdeen, 1948–52; Senior Lecturer, Univ. of St Andrews, at Dundee, 1952–54. Formerly Founder and Dir, Scottish Occupational Health Laboratory Service, Ltd; Member: Steering Cttee, East of Scotland Occupational Health Service; Nat. Adv. Cttee for Employment of Disabled; Asbestos Adv. Cttee, 1976; Adv. Cttee, Health and Safety Exec., 1976–82; Industrial Injuries Adv. Council, 1977–82; formerly Chm., Scottish Cttee for Welfare of Disabled and Sub-Cttee on Rehabilitation; Consultant, Occupational Health, to RN in Scotland. First Chm., British Soc. for Agriculture Labour Science. Occasional consultant to WHO, Geneva. Hon. FIOH 1989. *Publications:* Student Health Services in Great Britain and Northern Ireland, 1966; (jointly) Custom and Practice in Medical Care, 1968; Hospital and Community II, 1969; Sir James Mackenzie, MD, 1973 (Abercrombie Award); contrib.: Cerebral Palsy in Childhood and Adolescence, 1961; Further Studies in Hospital and Community, 1962; numerous publications on researches into occupational diseases, especially silicosis, byssinosis, etc. *Address:* Tree Tops, Castle Roy, Broughty Ferry, Dundee DD5 2LQ. *T:* Dundee (01382) 778727. *Club:* Caledonian.

Died 6 Aug. 1995.

MAIS, Baron, *cr* 1967 (Life Peer), of Walbrook, in the City of London; **Alan Raymond Mais,** GBE 1973 (OBE (mil.) 1944); TD 1944; ERD 1958; JP; DL; FEng 1977; Colonel; Director, Royal Bank of Scotland, 1969–81; Chairman, Peachey Property Corporation, 1977–81; *b* July 1911; *s* of late Capt. E. Mais, RNR, Mornington Court, Kensington, and Violet Geraldine, *d* of Walter Thomas, MICE; *m* 1936, Lorna Aline, *d* of late Stanley Aspinall Boardman, Addiscombe, Surrey; two *s* one *d. Educ:* Banister Court, Hants; Coll. of Estate Management, London Univ. Commissioned RARO, Royal West Kent Regt, 1929; transf. RE, 1931; Major 1939, Lt-Col 1941, Col 1944; served War of 1939–45; France, BEF, 1939–40 (despatches); Special Forces, MEF, Iraq and Persia, 1941–43 (despatches); Normandy and NW Europe, 1944–46 (OBE, despatches), wounded; CRE 56 Armd Div., TA, 1947–50; CO 101 Field Engr Regt, 1947–50, Hon. Col, 1950–63; Comd Eng Gp, AER, 1951–54;

DDES, AER, 1954–58. Worked for Richard Costain and other cos on civil engrg works at home and abroad, 1931–38; private practice, A. R. Mais & Partners, Structural Engineers & Surveyors, 1938–39 and 1946–48. Dir Trollope & Colls Ltd, Bldg and Civil Engrg contractors and subsid. cos, 1948–68, Chm. and Man. Dir 1963–68; Chairman: City of London Insurance Co. Ltd, 1970–77; Hay-MSL Consultants, 1969–81; Director: Nat. Commercial Bank of Scotland, 1966–69; Slag Reduction Co. Ltd, 1962–85. Member: EDC Cttee for Constructional Industry, 1964–68; Marshall Aid Commemoration Commn, 1964–74. Treasurer: Royal Masonic Hosp., 1973–86; Fellowship of Engrg, 1977–81. City University: Mem., Court and Council, 1965–; Chancellor, 1972–73; Pro-Chancellor, 1979–84. Governor, The Hon. Irish Soc., 1978–80. Lieut, City of London, 1963–81; Alderman, Ward of Walbrook, 1963–81; Sheriff, 1969–70; Lord Mayor of London, 1972–73. JP London (City Bench), 1963–83; DL: Co. London (later Greater London), 1951–76; Kent, 1976–. Master: Cutlers' Co., 1968–69; Paviors' Co., 1975–76; Marketors' Co., 1983–84. FICE 1953 (Hon. FICE 1975); FIStructE, MSocCE (France), FIArb, FRICS. GCStJ 1987 (KStJ 1973). Hon. DSc: City, 1972; Ulster, 1981. Order of Patriotic War (1st class), USSR, 1942; Order of Aztec Eagle, Mexico, 1973; Order of Merit, Mexico, 1973. *Publications:* Yerbury Foundation Lecture, RIBA, 1960; Bossom Foundation Lecture, 1971. *Recreations:* family, Territorial Army. *Address:* The Penthouse, 12a Copperfields, 48 The Avenue, Beckenham, Kent BR3 2ER. *T:* 081–650 3929. *Clubs:* City Livery, Army and Navy, London Welsh.

Died 28 Nov. 1993.

MAITLAND, Sir Richard John, 9th Bt, *cr* 1818, of Clifton, Midlothian; farmer; *b* 24 Nov. 1952; *s* of Sir Alexander Keith Maitland, 8th Bt, and of Lavender Mary Jex, *y d* of late Francis William Jex Jackson, Kirkbuddo, Forfar; *S* father, 1963; *m* 1981, Carine, *er d* of J. St G. Coldwell, Somerton, Oxford; one *s* one *d. Educ:* Rugby; Exeter Univ. (BA Hons 1975); Edinburgh Sch. of Agriculture. Mem., Queen's Body Guard for Scotland, Royal Co. of Archers, 1987–. *Heir:* *s* Charles Alexander Maitland, *b* 3 June 1986. *Address:* Burnside, Forfar, Angus DD8 2RX.

Died 14 Jan. 1994.

MAITLAND-MAKGILL-CRICHTON, Sir Andrew; *see* Crichton.

MALCOLM, Sir David (Peter Michael), 11th Bt *cr* 1665; *b* 7 July 1919; *s* of Sir Michael Albert James Malcolm, 10th Bt, and Hon. Geraldine Margot (*d* 1965), *d* of 10th Baron Digby; *S* father, 1976; *m* 1959, Hermione, *d* of Sir David Home, 13th Bt; one *d. Educ:* Eton; Magdalene Coll., Cambridge (BA). Served with Scots Guards, 1939–46 (Major). Mem., Inst. of Chartered Accountants of Scotland, 1949. Member: Stock Exchange, 1956–80; Stock Exchange Council, 1971–80. Mem., Queen's Body Guard for Scotland, Royal Co. of Archers, 1952–. *Recreations:* shooting, golf. *Heir: cousin* James William Thomas Alexander Malcolm [*b* 15 May 1930; *m* 1955, Gillian Heather, *d* of Elton Humpherus; two *s* two *d*]. *Address:* Whiteholm, Gullane, East Lothian EH31 2BD. *Club:* New (Edinburgh). *Died 30 Nov. 1995.*

MALCOLMSON, Kenneth Forbes, MA, BMus (Oxon), FRCO; Precentor and Director of Music, Eton College, 1956–71; *b* 29 April 1911; *m* 1972, Mrs B. Dunhill. Organ Scholar, Exeter Coll., Oxford, 1931–35; Commissioner, Royal School of Church Music, 1935–36; Temporary Organist, St Alban's Cathedral, 1936–37; Organist, Halifax Parish Church, 1937–38; Organist and Master of the Music, Newcastle Cathedral, 1938–55. *Recreations:* gardening, swimming, walking. *Address:* Parade House, The Parade, Monmouth, Gwent NP5 3PA. *T:* Monmouth (01600) 716391. *Died 19 Aug. 1995.*

MALIN, Peter; *see* Connor, Reardon.

MALLE, Louis; Film Director; *b* 30 Oct. 1932; *s* of Pierre Malle and Françoise Béghin; *m* 1st, Anne-Marie Deschodt (marr. diss.); one *s*; 2nd, 1980, Candice Bergen; one *d*. *Educ:* Paris Univ.; Institut d'Etudes Politiques. Television, 1953; Asst to Comdt Cousteau on the Calypso, 1953–55. Films: Co-prod. Le Monde du Silence, 1955 (Palme d'Or, Cannes); Collab. techn of Robert Bresson for Un Condamné a mort s'est echappé, 1956; Author and Producer of: Ascenseur pour l'échafaud, 1957 (Prix Louis-Delluc, 1958); Les Amants, 1958 (Prix spécial du Jury du Festival de Venise, 1958); Zazie dans le métro, 1960; Vie privée, 1962; Le Feu Follet (again, Prix spécial, Venise, 1963); Viva Maria, 1965 (Grand Prix du Cinéma français); Le Voleur, 1966; Histoires extraordinaires (sketch), 1968; Calcutta, 1969 (prix de la Fraternité); Phantom India, 1969; Le Souffle au Coeur, 1971 (nominated Best Screenplay, US Acad. Awards, 1972); Humain, trop humain, 1972; Place de la République, 1973; Lacombe Lucien, 1974; Black Moon, 1975; Pretty Baby, 1977; films directed: Atlantic City, 1979 (Jt winner, Golden Lion, Venice Film Fest., 1980; Best Director, BAFTA awards, 1982; nominated Best Film and Best Director, US Acad. Awards, 1982); My Dinner With André, 1981; Crackers, 1984; Alamo Bay, 1985; (also cameraman) God's Country (for Public TV), 1985; And the Pursuit of Happiness, 1986; (also writer) Au Revoir Les Enfants, 1987 (Golden Lion, Venice Film Fest.; Best Film Director, BAFTA Award, 1988); Milou in May, 1990; Damage, 1993; Vanya on 42nd Street, 1994. *Publication:* Malle on Malle, 1993. *Address:* c/o NEF, 15 rue du Louvre, 75001 Paris, France.   *Died 23 Nov. 1995.*

MALLINSON, Dennis Hainsworth; Director, National Engineering Laboratory, East Kilbride, Department of Industry, 1974–80; *b* 22 Aug. 1921; *s* of David and Anne Mallinson; *m* 1945, Rowena Mary Brooke; one *s* two *d*. *Educ:* Leeds Univ. (BSc). RAE, 1942, early jet engines; Power Jets (R&D) Ltd, later Nat. Gas Turbine Estabt, 1944–63; Min. of Aviation and successors: Asst Dir, 1963; Dir, 1964; Dir-Gen., Engines, Procurement Exec., MoD, 1972–74. Vis. Prof., Strathclyde Univ., 1976–82. Mem. Council, Instn Engrs and Shipbuilders in Scotland, 1977–80. *Address:* 19 Rossett Holt Close, Harrogate HG2 9AD.   *Died 8 June 1993.*

MALLINSON, Sir William (John), 4th Bt *cr* 1935, of Walthamstow; *b* 8 Oct. 1942; *s* of Sir William Paul Mallinson, 3rd Bt, FRCP, FRCPsych and Eila Mary (*d* 1985), *d* of Roland Graeme Guy; *S* father, 1989; *m* 1968, Rosalind Angela (marr. diss. 1978), *o d* of Rollo Hoare; one *s* one *d*. *Educ:* Charterhouse. *Recreations:* sailing, tennis, ski-ing. *Heir:* *s* William James Mallinson, *b* 22 April 1970. *Address:* 1 Hollywood Mews, Chelsea, SW10 9HU. *T:* 0171–352 3821; The Watch House, The Point, Bembridge, Isle of Wight PO35 5NQ. *T:* Isle of Wight (01983) 872019. *Club:* Bembridge Sailing.
                                                   Died 17 Nov. 1995.

MANBY, Mervyn Colet, CMG 1964; QPM 1961; retired; *b* 20 Feb. 1915; *s* of late Harold B. and Mary Manby (*née* Mills), late of Petistree, Suffolk; *m* 1949, Peggy Aronson, Eastern Cape, South Africa; one *s* one *d*. *Educ:* Bedford Sch., Bedford; Pembroke Coll., Oxford (MA). Colonial Police Service, 1937; Malaya, 1938–47; Basutoland, 1947–54; Kenya, 1954–64 (Dep. Inspector General, Kenya Police, 1961–64); retired, 1964. United Nations Technical Assistance Adviser to Government of Iran, 1965–70; UN Div. of Narcotic Drugs, 1971–75; special consultant, UN Fund for Drug Abuse Control, 1975. Mem. Council, Inst. for Study of Drug Dependence, 1975–78. *Address:* Old Well Cottage, Barham, Canterbury, Kent CT4 6PB. *T:* Canterbury (0227) 381369.   *Died 1 July 1994.*

MANHOOD, Harold Alfred; writer; *b* 6 May 1904; *m* 1937. *Educ:* elementary schooling. *Publications:* Gay Agony (novel), 1930; short stories: Nightseed, 1928; Apples by Night, 1932; Crack of Whips, 1934; Fierce and Gentle, 1935; Sunday Bugles, 1939; Lunatic Broth, 1944; Selected Stories, 1947; A Long View of Nothing, 1953. *Address:* Holmbush, near Henfield, W Sussex BN5 9NJ.
                                                   Died 5 Jan. 1991.

MANKIEWICZ, Joseph Leo; American writer and film director; *b* 11 Feb. 1909; *s* of Frank Mankiewicz and Johanna (*née* Blumenau; *m* 1934, Elizabeth Young (marr. diss. 1937); one *s*; *m* 1939, Rosa Stradner (*d* 1958); two *s*; *m* 1962, Rosemary Matthews; one *d*. *Educ:* Columbia Univ. (AB 1928). Wrote, directed and produced for the screen, 1929–. President, Screen Directors' Guild of America, 1950. *Films include:* Manhattan Melodrama, Fury, Three Comrades, Philadelphia Story, Woman of the Year, Keys of the Kingdom, The Ghost and Mrs Muir, A Letter to Three Wives (Academy Awards for Best Screenplay and Best Direction), No Way Out, All About Eve (Academy Awards for Best Screenplay and Best Direction), People Will Talk, Five Fingers, Julius Caesar, The Barefoot Contessa, Guys and Dolls, The Quiet American, Suddenly Last Summer, The Honey Pot, There Was a Crooked Man, Sleuth. Directed La Bohème for Metropolitan Opera, 1952. Formed own company, Figaro Inc., 1953, dissolved 1961. Fellow, Yale Univ., 1979–. Work in progress on The Performing Woman (when and how women came to perform the roles of women on the stages of the Western theatre). Received Screen Directors' Guild Award, 1949 and 1950; Screen Writers' Guild Award for best American comedy, 1949 and 1950; Laurel Award, Writers Guild of America, 1963; D. W. Griffith Award, for lifetime achievement, Directors Guild of America, 1986; Leone D'Oro Award, for lifetime achievement, Venice Film Fest., 1987; Akira Kurosawa Award, for lifetime achievement, San Francisco Internat. Film Festival, 1989. Erasmus Award, City of Rotterdam, 1984; Alexander Hamilton Medal, Columbia Coll., NYC, 1986. Order of Merit (Italy), 1965; Hon. Citizen of Avignon (France), 1980; Chevalier de la Légion d'Honneur (France), 1988. *Address:* 419 Guard Hill Road, Bedford, NY 10506, USA.   *Died 7 Feb. 1993.*

MANN, Frederick Alexander, (Francis), CBE 1980; LLD, DrJur; FBA 1974; Solicitor of the Supreme Court, since 1946; Partner, Herbert Smith & Co., 1957–83, then Consultant; Hon. Professor of Law in the University of Bonn, since 1960; *b* 11 Aug. 1907; *s* of Richard Mann and Ida (*née* Ehrlich) (*d* 1980); *m* 1933, Eleonore (*née* Ehrlich) (*d* 1980); one *s* two *d*. *Educ:* Univs of Geneva, Munich, Berlin (DrJur) and London (LLD). Asst, Faculty of Law, Univ. of Berlin, 1929–33; German lawyer, 1933; Internat. Law Consultant, London, 1933–46; Solicitor, 1946; Mem., Legal Div., Allied Control Council (British Element), Berlin, 1946. Member: Lord Chancellor's Standing Cttee for Reform of Private Internat. Law, 1952–64; numerous Working Parties of Law Commn; Council, British Inst. of Internat. and Comparative Law; Rapporteur, Monetary Law Cttee, Internat. Law Assoc., 1952–73. Special Consultant, Cttee on Foreign Money Liabilities, Council of Europe, 1964–67; Chm., Cttee on Place of Payment, Council of Europe, 1968–71. Counsel for Belgium in Barcelona Traction Case, The Hague, 1969–70; Counsel for Federal Republic of Germany in Young Loan Case, Koblenz and Bonn, 1979–80. Mem., Editorial Cttee, British Year Book of International Law. Mem., Institut de Droit International. Lectures at Acad. of Internat. Law at The Hague, 1959, 1964, 1971 and 1984, and at numerous Univs in England, Austria, Belgium, Germany, Hong Kong, Japan, Switzerland and USA; Blackstone Lectr, Oxford, 1978; Hon. Prof. of Legal Ethics, Univ. of Birmingham, 1985–87. Hon. Member: Amer. Soc. of

Internat. Law, 1980; Soc. of Public Teachers of Law, 1987; Associate Mem., Internat. Acad. of Comparative Law, 1987. Hon. Bencher, Gray's Inn, 1991; Hon. QC 1991. Hon. DrJur: Kiel, 1978; Zürich, 1983; Hon. DCL Oxford, 1989. Alexander von Humboldt Prize, Alexander von Humboldt Foundn, Bonn, 1984. Grand Cross of Merit, Federal Republic of Germany, 1977, with Star, 1982. *Publications:* The Legal Aspect of Money, 1938, 5th edn 1992 (trans. German, 1960, Spanish, 1986); Studies in International Law, 1973; Foreign Affairs in English Courts, 1986; Further Studies in International Law, 1990; numerous articles on international law, the conflict of laws, and monetary law in English and foreign legal pubns and periodicals. *Recreations:* music, walking. *Address:* Flat 4, 56 Manchester Street, W1M 5PA. *T:* 071–487 4735. *Club:* Athenæum. *Died 16 Sept. 1991.*

MANN, Keith John Sholto D.; *see* Douglas-Mann.

MANN, Thaddeus Robert Rudolph, CBE 1962; FRS 1951; biochemist; Professor of the Physiology of Reproduction, University of Cambridge, 1967–76, then Emeritus (Reader in Physiology of Animal Reproduction, 1953–67); Hon. Fellow of Trinity Hall, Cambridge, since 1979 (Fellow, 1961–79); Member of the Staff of Agricultural Research Council, 1944–76; *b* 4 Dec. 1908; *s* of late William Mann and Emilia (*née* Quest); *m* 1934, Dr Cecilia Lutwak-Mann. *Educ:* Trin. Hall, Cambridge. MD Lwòw 1935, PhD Cantab 1937, ScD Cantab 1950; Rockefeller Research Fellow, 1935–37; Beit Meml Research Fellow, 1937–44. Dir, ARC Unit of Reproductive Physiology and Biochemistry, Cambridge, 1954–76. Senior Lalor Fellow at Woods Hole Oceanographic Instn, 1960; Vis. Prof. in Biology at Florida State Univ., 1962; Vis. Prof. in Biological Structure and Zoology, Univ. of Washington, 1968; Vis. Scientist, Reproduction Res. Br., Nat. Insts of Health, USA, 1978–82. Gregory Pincus Meml Lectr, 1969; Albert Tyler Meml Lectr, 1970. For. Member: Royal Belgian Acad. of Medicine, 1970; Polish Acad. of Science, 1980. Hon. doctorate: of Veterinary Medicine, Ghent, 1970, Hanover, 1977; of Natural Scis, Cracow, 1973. Awarded Amory Prize of Amer. Academy of Arts and Sciences, 1955. Cavaliere Ufficiale, Order of Merit (Italy), 1966. *Publications:* The Biochemistry of Semen, 1954; The Biochemistry of Semen and of the Male Reproductive Tract, 1964; (with C. Lutwak-Mann) Male Reproductive Function and Semen—Themes and Trends in Physiology, Biochemistry and Investigative Andrology, 1981; Spermatophores—Development, Structure, Biochemical Attributes and Role in the Transfer of Spermatozoa, 1984; papers on carbohydrate metabolism of muscle, yeast and moulds, on metaloprotein enzymes, and on biochemistry of reproduction. *Address:* 1 Courtney Way, Cambridge CB4 2EE. *Died 27 Nov. 1993.*

MANNING, Frederick Allan, CVO 1954; ISO 1971; JP; retired, 1970; Commissioner for Transport, Queensland, 1967–70 (Deputy Commissioner, 1960–67); *b* Gladstone, Qld, Australia, 27 Aug. 1904; British parentage; *m* 1934, Phyllis Maud Fullerton; no *c. Educ:* Central Boys' State Sch. and Boys' Gram. Sch., Rockhampton, Qld. Entered Qld State Public Service as Clerk in Petty Sessions Office, Rockhampton, 1920; Clerk of Petty Sessions and Mining Registrar, 1923; Stipendiary Magistrate and Mining Warden, 1934; Petty Sessions Office, Brisbane, 1926; Relieving Clerk of Petty Sessions and Mining Registrar, 1931 (all parts of State); seconded to Commonwealth Govt for service in Qld Directorate of Rationing Commission, 1942; Asst Dep. Dir of Rationing, 1943. Dep. Dir, 1944, for Qld; returned to Qld Public Service, 1947; Sec., Dept of Transport, 1947–60. JP Qld, 1925. Coronation Medal, 1953; State Dir, Royal Visit to Queensland, 1954 (CVO). Exec. Vice-Chm, Qld Road Safety Coun., and Qld Rep. Aust. Road Safety Coun., 1962. Mem., Greyhound Racing

Control Bd of Queensland, 1971–77. *Recreation:* bowls. *Address:* 126 Indooroopilly Road, Taringa, Brisbane, Qld 4068, Australia. *T:* 370–1936. *Club:* Tattersalls (Brisbane). *Died 1 Aug. 1991.*

MANSEL, Rev. Canon James Seymour Denis, KCVO 1979 (LVO 1972); Extra Chaplain to the Queen, since 1979; Priest Vicar, Westminster Abbey, 1983–88, then Emeritus; *b* 18 June 1907; *e s* of Edward Mansel, FRIBA, Leamington, and Muriel Louisa (*née* Denis Browne); *m* 1942, Ann Monica (*d* 1974), *e d* of Amyas Waterhouse, MD, Boars Hill, Oxford, and Ruth (*née* Gamlen); one *d. Educ:* Brighton Coll.; Exeter Coll., Oxford (MA); Westcott House. Deacon, 1941; priest, 1942. Asst Master, Dulwich Coll., 1934–39; Asst Master, Chaplain and House Master, Winchester Coll., 1939–65; Sub-Dean of HM Chapels Royal, Deputy Clerk of the Closet, Sub-Almoner and Domestic Chaplain to the Queen, 1965–79; Canon and Prebendary of Chichester Cathedral, 1971–81, Canon Emeritus, 1981; Asst Priest, St Margaret's, Westminster, 1980–88. Mem., Winchester City Coun., 1950–56. JP: City of Winchester, 1964; Inner London Commn, 1972. FSA. ChStJ. *Address:* 15 Sandringham Court, Maida Vale, W9 1UA. *Club:* Athenæum. *Died 22 Sept. 1995.*

MANSERGH, Prof. (Philip) Nicholas (Seton), OBE 1945; DPhil 1936; DLitt Oxon 1960; LittD Cantab 1970; FBA 1973; Master of St John's College, Cambridge, 1969–79, Fellow 1955–69 and since 1979; Editor-in-chief, India Office Records on the Transfer of Power, 1967–82 (12 volumes); *b* 27 June 1910; *yr s* of late Philip St George Mansergh and Mrs E. M. Mansergh, Grenane House, Tipperary; *m* 1939, Diana Mary, *d* of late G. H. Keeton, Headmaster's Lodge, Reading; three *s* two *d. Educ:* Abbey Sch., Tipperary; College of St Columba, Dublin; Pembroke Coll., Oxford. Sec. OU Politics Research Cttee and Tutor in Politics, 1937–40; Empire Div., Ministry of Information, 1941–46, Dir, 1944–46; Asst Sec., Dominions Office, 1946–47; Abe Bailey Research Prof. of British Commonwealth Relations, RIIA, 1947–53; Smuts Prof. of History of British Commonwealth, Univ. of Cambridge, 1953–April 1970, then Emeritus Professor. Chm. Faculty Board of History, 1960–62, Bd of Graduate Studies, 1970–73, Cambridge Univ. Visiting Professor: Nat. Univ. of Australia, 1951; Univ. of Toronto, 1953; Duke Univ., NC, 1957 and 1965 (W. K. Boyd Prof. of History); Indian Sch. of International Studies, New Delhi, 1958 and 1966; Jawaharlal Nehru Univ., 1980; Reid Lecturer, Acadia Univ., 1960; Smuts Meml Lectr, Cambridge Univ., 1976. Member: Editorial Board, Annual Register, 1947–73; Gen. Advisory Council, BBC, 1956–62; Adv. Council on Public Records, 1966–76; Councillor, RIIA, 1953–57. Hon. Fellow: Pembroke College, Oxford, 1954; Trinity College, Dublin, 1971. *Publications:* The Irish Free State: Its Government and Politics, 1934; The Government of Northern Ireland, 1936; Ireland in the Age of Reform and Revolution, 1940; Advisory Bodies (Jt Editor), 1941; Britain and Ireland, 1942, 2nd edn 1946; The Commonwealth and the Nations, 1948; The Coming of the First World War, 1949; Survey of British Commonwealth Affairs (2 vols), 1931–39, 1952 and 1939–52, 1958; Documents and Speeches on Commonwealth Affairs, 1931–62 (3 vols), 1953–63; The Multi-Racial Commonwealth, 1955; (jointly) Commonwealth Perspectives, 1958; South Africa, 1906–1961, 1962; The Irish Question, 1840–1921, 1965, 3rd edn 1975; The Commonwealth Experience, 1969, 2nd edn 1982; Prelude to Partition, 1978. *Recreation:* lawn mowing. *Address:* The Lodge, Little Shelford, Cambridge CB2 5EW. *Clubs:* Commonwealth Trust; Kildare Street and University (Dublin). *Died 16 Jan. 1991.*

MANSFIELD COOPER, Prof. Sir William, Kt 1963; LLM; Professor of Industrial Law, University of

Manchester, 1949–70, then Professor Emeritus; Vice-Chancellor of the University, 1956–70; *b* Newton Heath, Manchester, 20 Feb. 1903; *s* of William and Georgina C. Cooper; *m* 1936, Edna Mabel, *o c* of Herbert and Elizabeth Baker; one *s*. *Educ:* elementary sch.; Ruskin Coll., Oxford, 1931–33; Manchester Univ., 1933–36 (LLB, Dauntesey Jun. Law Schol., Dauntesey Special Prizeman in International Law). Grad. Res. Schol., 1936–37; Lecturer WEA (LLM 1938). Called to the Bar, Gray's Inn, 1940. University of Manchester: Asst Lecturer, 1938; Lecturer, 1942; Asst to Vice-Chancellor, 1944; Registrar and Senior Lecturer in Law, 1945; Professor of Industrial and Commercial Law, 1949, continuing as Joint Registrar until 1952; Acting Vice-Chancellor, Nov. 1953–May 1954 and July 1954–Oct. 1954. Chairman John Rylands Library, 1956–70; Chairman Cttee of Vice-Chancellors and Principals, 1961–64; President, Council of Europe Cttee on Higher Education and Research, 1966–67; Vice-President, Standing Conference of European Rectors and Vice-Chancellors, 1964–69. Dep. Chm., Cttee of Inquiry into London Univ., 1970–72. Hon. Mem., Manchester Royal Coll. Music, 1971. Hon. LLD: Manitoba, 1964; Liverpool, 1970; Manchester, 1970; Hon. DLitt Keele, 1967; Hon. DSc Kharkov, 1970; Hon. DHL Rochester, 1970. Hon. Fellow, Manchester Inst. Science and Technology, 1972. *Publications:* Outlines of Industrial Law, 1947, 6th edn by John C. Wood, 1972; papers and reviews in learned journals. *Recreation:* reading. *Address:* Flat 32, The Chestnuts, West Street, Godmanchester, Huntingdon PE18 8HH. *Club:* Athenæum.

Died 14 Nov. 1992.

MANZÙ, Giacomo; sculptor and painter; stage designer; *b* 22 Dec. 1908; *s* of Angelo and Maria Manzoni; *m* 1934, Antonia Oreni (marr. diss. 1952); (three *s* decd); *m* 1958, Inge Schabel; one *s* one *d*. *Educ:* Milan. Professor of Sculpture, Brera Accad., Milan, 1941–54; International Summer Acad., Salzburg, 1954–60. Grazioli Prize, Milan, 1934; Prize of Esposizione Universale, Paris, 1937; Sculpture Prize, Venice Biennale, 1948; Society of Portrait Sculptors' International Award (Jean Masson Davidson Medal), 1965; Internat. Feltrinelli Prize, Nat. Acad. of Arts, Rome, 1984. Works include: Cathedral main door, Salzburg, 1958; re-designing of bronze doors of St Peter's, Rome, 1963 (commission won in open international competition); façade of Palace of Italy, NY, 1965; The Door of Peace and War, St Laurenz Church, Rotterdam, 1968. Exhibitions of Sculptures, Paintings and Drawings: La Cometa, Rome, 1937; Buenos Aires, 1949; Hanover Gall., London, 1953, 1965; NY, 1957; Haus der Kunst, Munich, 1959; Tate Gall., 1960; NY, Tokyo, Moscow, Leningrad, and Kiev, 1966; Bordeaux, 1969; Prague and Tokyo, 1973; Salzburg and Budapest, 1974; Rome, 1975; Moscow and Münster, 1976; (retrospective exhibn) Hamilton, Ont, 1980, and in 8 other Canadian cities, 1981; Tokyo, 1982, 1983; travelling exhibn to 8 Japanese Museums, 1983; Oslo and tour of Norway, 1986; Florence, 1986. Established permanent collection of his most important works at Ardea, near Rome, 1969, donated to the Republic of Italy, 1981; Sala Manzù established at Accademia Carrara, Bergamo, 1982; Bronze figure set up, Chamber of Commerce, Augsburg, 1983; Sala Manzù, Hermitage Mus., Leningrad, 1986. Hon. RA; Hon. RSA; Hon. Member: American Academy of Arts and Letters; National Academies of Argentina, Belgium and Rome; Accademia di Belle Arti Sovietica; Acad. Européenne des Sciences, des Arts et des Lettres, Paris; Akad. der Kunst, Berlin; Acad. des Beaux Arts, Paris; For. Hon. Mem., Amer. Acad. of Arts and Sci., 1978. Hon. Dr RCA 1971. Premio Internazionale Lenin per la pace, 1966. Medaglia d'Oro Benemeriti, Scuola Cultura, Arte (Italy), 1981. *Publication:* La Porta di S Pietro, 1965; *relevant publications include:* J. Rewald, Giacomo Manzù, 1966;

B. Heynold von Graefe, The Doors of Rotterdam, 1969. *Address:* 00040 Ardea, Rome, Italy.

Died 17 Jan. 1991.

MAR, 13th Earl of, *cr* 1565, and KELLIE, 15th Earl of, *cr* 1619; **John Francis Hervey Erskine;** Baron Erskine, 1429; Viscount Fentoun, 1606; Baron Dirleton, 1603; Premier Viscount of Scotland; Hereditary Keeper of Stirling Castle; Representative Peer for Scotland, 1959–63; Major Scots Guards, retired 1954; Major, Argyll and Sutherland Highlanders (TA), retired 1959; Lord Lieutenant of Clackmannan, since 1966; *b* 15 Feb. 1921; *e s* of late Lord Erskine, (John Francis Ashley Erskine), GCSI, GCIE; *S* grandfather, 1955; *m* 1948, Pansy Constance (OBE 1984; Pres., UK Cttee for UNICEF, 1979–84; Chm., Youth at Risk Adv. Gp; Chm. and Vice-Chm., Scottish Standing Conf., Voluntary Youth Orgns, 1967–81; Elder of Church of Scotland; JP 1971; CStJ 1983), *y d* of late General Sir Andrew Thorne, KCB; three *s* one *d*. *Educ:* Eton; Trinity Coll., Cambridge. 2nd Lieut, Scots Guards, 1941; served in Egypt, N Africa, Italy and Germany with 2nd Bn Scots Guards and HQ 201 Guards' Brigade, 1942–45 (wounded, despatches); Staff Coll., Camberley, 1950; DAAG, HQ, 3rd Infantry Div., 1951–52. DL Clackmannanshire, 1954, Vice-Lieutenant, 1957; JP 1962; County Councillor for Clackmannanshire, 1955–75 (Vice-Convener, 1961–64); Chairman: Forth Conservancy Board, 1957–68; Clackmannanshire T&AFA, 1961–68. An Elder of the Church of Scotland. Member of the Queen's Body Guard for Scotland (Royal Company of Archers). KStJ 1966. *Heir: s* Lord Erskine [*b* 10 March 1949; *m* 1974, Mrs Mary Mooney, *yr d* of Dougal McD. Kirk]. *Address:* Claremont House, Alloa, Clackmannanshire FK10 2JF. *T:* Alloa (0259) 212020. *Club:* New (Edinburgh). *Died 22 Dec. 1993.*

MARCH, Sir Derek (Maxwell), KBE 1988 (CBE 1982; OBE 1973); HM Diplomatic Service, retired; High Commissioner in Kampala, 1986–90; *b* 9 Dec. 1930; *s* of Frank March and Vera (*née* Ward); *m* 1955, Sally Annetta Riggs; one *s* two *d*. *Educ:* Devonport High Sch.; Birkbeck Coll., London. National Service, RAF, 1949–51. Joined HM Diplomatic Service, 1949; FO, 1951; Bonn, 1955; Vice Consul, Hanover, 1957; Asst Trade Comr, Salisbury, 1959; Consul, Dakar, 1962; First Secretary: FO, 1964; Rawalpindi, 1968; Peking, 1971; FCO, 1974; Counsellor, seconded to Dept of Trade, 1975; Senior British Trade Comr, Hong Kong, 1977–82; Counsellor, seconded to DTI, 1982–86. *Recreations:* golf, cricket, Rugby Union. *Address:* Soke House, The Soke, Alresford, Hants SO24 9DB. *T:* Alresford (0962) 732588. *Clubs:* MCC, East India, Devonshire, Sports and Public Schools; Hong Kong (Hong Kong); Alresford Golf.

Died 15 Feb. 1992.

MARCHAMLEY, 3rd Baron, *cr* 1908, of Hawkstone; **John William Tattersall Whiteley;** late Lieutenant, Royal Armoured Corps; *b* 24 April 1922; *s* of 2nd Baron and Margaret Clara (*d* 1974), *d* of Thomas Scott Johnstone, Glenmark, Waipara, New Zealand; *S* father, 1949; *m* 1967, Sonia Kathleen Pedrick; one *s*. Served War of 1939–45, Captain, 19th King George V Own Lancers. *Heir: s* Hon. William Francis Whiteley, *b* 27 July 1968. *Address:* Whetcombe, North Huish, South Brent, Devon TQ10 9NG. *Died 26 May 1994.*

MARDON, Lt-Col (John) Kenric La Touche, DSO 1945; TD 1943; JP; DL; MA; Vice Lord-Lieutenant, Avon, 1974–80; Chairman, Mardon, Son & Hall, Ltd, Bristol, 1962–69; Director, Bristol & West Building Society, 1969–82; *b* 29 June 1905; *e s* of late Evelyn John Mardon, Halsway Manor, Crowcombe and Maud Mary (*née* Rothwell); *m* 1933, Dulcie Joan (decd), 3rd *d* of late Maj.-Gen. K. M. Body, CB, CMG, OBE; two *s* one *d*. *Educ:* Clifton; Christ's Coll., Cambridge. Commissioned in

Royal Devon Yeomanry, 1925; Major, 1938; Lieut-Colonel, RA, 1942; served War of 1939–45, in NW Europe, 1944–45 (despatches). JP Somerset, 1948; High Sheriff of Somerset, 1956–57; DL 1962. Master, Society of Merchant Venturers, Bristol, 1959–60; Governor, Clifton Coll., 1957. Pres., Bristol YMCA, 1969–79. *Recreations:* shooting, lawn tennis, squash rackets (rep. Cambridge v Oxford, 1925). *Address:* Cranhill Nursing Home, Weston Road, Bath BA1 2YA. *T:* Bath (0225) 422321. *Club:* Bath and County (Bath).
Died 5 April 1993.

MARJORIBANKS, (Edyth) Leslia, JP; MA; Headmistress, The Henrietta Barnett School, London, 1973–89; *b* 17 Feb. 1927; *d* of late Stewart Dudley Marjoribanks and Nancye (*née* Lee). *Educ:* Cheltenham Ladies' Coll.; Girton Coll., Cambridge (BA Hons Hist. 1951, MA 1955); Hughes Hall, Cambridge (Certif. Educn 1952). Talbot Heath, Bournemouth: Asst History Mistress, 1952–57; Head of History Dept, 1957–68; Headmistress, Holly Lodge High Sch., Liverpool, 1969–73. Mem. Governing Council, Examinations Cttee and Curriculum Sub-Cttee of North-West Sec. Schs Exam. Board, 1969–73. JP City of Liverpool, 1971–73, Inner London, 1976. *Recreations:* gardening, cookery. *Address:* 29 Park Farm Close, N2 0PU. *T:* 081–883 6609. *Died 22 March 1993.*

MARKALL, Most Rev. Francis, SJ; *b* 24 Sept. 1905; *e s* of late Walter James Markall and Alice Mary Gray, London. *Educ:* St Ignatius' College, London. Entered Society of Jesus, 1924; continued classical and philosophical studies, 1926–31; Assistant Master, Stonyhurst College, 1931–34; theological studies, 1934–38; Missionary in Rhodesia, 1939–56; Titular Archbishop of Cotieo and Coadjutor with right of succession to Archbishop of Salisbury, April 1956; Archbishop of Salisbury and Metropolitan of Province of Rhodesia, Nov. 1956; retired, 1976. *Address:* Nazareth House, PO Box HG295, PO Highlands, Harare, Zimbabwe. *T:* (4) 45144. *Died 8 Aug. 1992.*

MARKUS, Rika, (Rixi), MBE 1975 (for services to Bridge); Bridge journalist and author; *b* 27 June 1910; *d* of Michael and Louise Scharfstein; *m* 1929, Salomon Markus (marr. diss. 1947); (one *d* decd). *Educ:* Vienna and Dresden. Turned to bridge after a severe illness; arrived in London, March 1938 (3 days after Hitler occupied Austria; parents lived already in London). Bridge correspondent of: The Guardian and Weekly Guardian, 1955– (organizer of Eastern Bridge Guardian Tournament); Harpers & Queen (organizer of Championship for Women); New York Observer, 1989–; formerly of the Evening Standard; wrote for Express Syndication Gp; commentator and contributor to Daily Bulletin on major European and world championships. Organised annual bridge match between House of Lords and House of Commons (Challenge Cup donated by The Guardian); matches held with parliamentarians and players in other countries, *eg* France, Holland, Dubai, USA, Sweden and Morocco; player in Master Bridge, Channel Four TV series, 1983. Acclaimed as best woman player in the world; European Bridge Champion, 1935 and 1936; World Champion, 1937; 1st Woman Grand Master, 1974; Charles Goren Award for the player of the year, 1976; 5 World titles (incl. 4 gold Olympic medals), 1937, 1962, 1964 and 1974; 3 silver Olympic medals, 1970, 1976; 10 Eur. Championships; first European Grand Master, 1987; many national and internat. titles. *Publications:* Bid Boldly, Play Safe, 1965; Common-Sense Bridge, 1972; Aces and Places, 1972; Bridge around the World, 1977; Improve Your Bridge, 1977; Play Better Bridge with Rixi Markus, 1978; Table Tales by Rixi Markus, 1979; Bridge with Rixi, 1983; More Deadly than the Male, 1984; Best Bridge Hands, 1985; The Rixi Markus Book of Bridge, 1985; A

Vulnerable Game (memoirs), 1988; Better Bridge for Club Players, 1989. *Recreations:* music, cooking, watching all sports, theatre. *Address:* 22 Lowndes Lodge, Cadogan Place, SW1X 9RZ. *T:* 071–235 7377. *Club:* TGR's Bridge. *Died 4 April 1992.*

MARSH, Rt Rev. Henry Hooper, MA, DD; *b* 6 Oct. 1898; *s* of Rev. Canon Charles H. Marsh, DD; *m* Margaret D. Heakes; one *s* one *d. Educ:* University College, Toronto, BA 1921; Wycliffe College, Toronto, 1924, MA 1925; DD 1962. Deacon, 1924; priest, 1925; Curate of St Anne, Toronto, 1924–25; Curate of St Paul, Toronto, 1925–30; Priest-in-charge of St Timothy's Mission, City and Diocese of Toronto, 1930–36; Rector, Church of St Timothy, 1936–62; Canon of Toronto, 1956–62; Bishop of Yukon, 1962–67. Canadian Centennial Medal, 1967. *Recreation:* bird watching. *Died 27 Jan. 1995.*

MARSH, (Henry) John, CBE 1967; international management consultant, writer and lecturer; director of companies; *b* 17 Aug. 1913; *s* of late Jasper W. P. Marsh and Gladys M. Carruthers; *m* 1950, Mary Costerton; two *s* two *d. Educ:* Chefoo Sch., China; Queen Elizabeth's Grammar Sch., Wimborne. Commerce, China, 1930–32; Shanghai Volunteer Force, 1930–32; engineering apprenticeship and apprentice supervisor, Austin Motor Co., 1932–39. Served War of 1939–45, Royal Army Service Corps TA, 48th and 56th Divisions; Singapore Fortress; BEF France, 1940; Malaya, 1941–42 (despatches twice); Prisoner of War, 1942–45; released with rank of Major, 1946. Personnel Officer, BOAC, 1946–47; Dir of Personnel Advisory Services, Institute of Personnel Management, 1947–49; Dir, Industrial (Welfare) Soc., 1950–61; British Institute of Management: Dir, later Dir-Gen., 1961–73; Asst Chm. and Counsellor, 1973–75. Mem., Nat. Coal Board, 1968–74. Hon. Administrator, Duke of Edinburgh's Study Conference, 1954–56; Chairman: Brit. Nat. Conference on Social Work, 1957–60; VSO, 1957–60; Member: Youth Service Cttee, 1958–59; BBC General Advisory Council, 1959–64; Advisory Cttee on Employment of Prisoners, 1960–63; Council for Technical Educn and Training for Overseas Countries, 1961–74; UK Advisory Council on Education for Management, 1962–66; Russell Cttee on Adult Educn, 1969–72; Court, Univ. of Cranfield, 1962–69; Court, Univ. of Surrey, 1969–79; Food Manufacturing EDC, 1967–69; Adv. Council, Civil Service College, 1970–77; UK Mem., Commonwealth Team of Industrial Specialists, 1976–78. Governor, King's Coll. Hosp., 1971–74. British Information Service Lectures: Ardeshir Dalal Meml, India, 1953; Clarke Hall, Lincoln's Inn, 1957; E. W. Hancock, IProdE, 1960; MacLaren Meml, Birmingham, 1962; Tullis Russell, Glasgow, 1967; Allerdale-Wyld, Galashiels, 1972; RSA, 1973; Geden Foster, RSA, 1977; Chester, Sheffield Cathedral, 1978; Stantonbury, Milton Keynes, 1981; lecture tours: India and Pakistan, 1959 and 1963; Nigeria, 1964; Malaysia, 1965; Australia, 1967; Latin America, 1971, 1973; Malaysia, NZ, 1974. FIAM 1969; Hon. Fellow, Canadian Inst. of Management, 1973; CBIM (FBIM 1967); FIMC 1980. Hon. CIPM 1985. Hon. DSc Bradford, 1968. Verulam Medal, 1976. *Publications:* Introduction to Human Relations at Work, 1952; People at Work, 1957; Partners in Work Relations, 1960; Work and Leisure Digest, 1961; Pursuit of God, 1968; Ethics in Business, 1970; Organisations of the Future, 1980; Late Glimpses (verse), 1984; Management of Change, 1989. *Recreations:* writing, music, counselling, idling. *Address:* 13 Frank Dixon Way, Dulwich, SE21 7ET. *Died 19 Aug. 1992.*

MARSH, Rev. Prof. John, CBE 1964; MA (Edinburgh et Oxon), DPhil (Oxon); DD (Hon.) Edinburgh and Nottingham; Moderator, Free Church Federal Council, 1970–71; Principal, Mansfield College, Oxford, 1953–70;

b 5 Nov. 1904; *s* of George Maurice and Florence Elizabeth Ann Marsh, East Grinstead, Sussex; *m* 1934, Gladys Walker, *y d* of George Benson and Mary Walker, Cockermouth, Cumberland; two *s* one *d*. *Educ:* The Skinners Company Sch., Tunbridge Wells; Yorkshire United Coll., Bradford; Edinburgh Univ.; Mansfield Coll. and St Catherine's Soc., Oxford; Marburg Univ. Lecturer, Westhill Training Coll., 1932; Minister, Congregational Church, Otley, Yorks, 1934; Tutor and Chaplain, Mansfield Coll., Oxford, 1938; Prof. of Christian Theology, The University, Nottingham, 1949–53. Gray Lectr, Duke Univ., NC; Reinecke Lectr, Protestant Episc. Seminary, Alexandria, Va, 1958. Delegate: First Assembly, World Council of Churches, Amsterdam, 1948; Second Assembly, Evanston, Ill, 1954; Third Assembly, New Delhi, 1961; Fourth Assembly, Uppsala, 1968. Sec. World Conference on Faith and Order's Commn on "Intercommunion"; Chm., Section 2 of British Council of Churches Commn on Broadcasting, 1949; Mem., Working Cttee, Faith and Order Dept, World Council of Churches, 1953; Sec., European Commission on Christ and the Church, World Council of Churches, 1955; Mem. Central Religious Advisory Cttee to BBC, 1955–60; Mem. Sub-Cttee, Central Religious Adv. Cttee, acting as Religious Advisory Panel to ITA, 1955–65; Chm. British Council of Churches Commn of Faith and Order, 1960–62; Mem. Central Cttee, World Council of Churches, 1961–68; Chm. Division of Studies, World Council of Churches, 1961–68; Select Preacher, University of Oxford, 1962; Chm. Congregational Union of England and Wales, 1962–63; Chairman: Inter-Church Relationships Cttee, Congregational Church in England and Wales, 1964–67; Board of Faculty of Theology, Oxford Univ., 1966–68; Exec. Cttee, Congregational Church in England and Wales, 1966–72; Joint Chm. Joint Cttee for Conversations between Congregationalists and Presbyterians, 1965–72; Lay Vice-Chm., Derwent Deanery Synod, 1979–82. Vice-Pres., Philosophical Soc. of England, 1986–. Chm., Buttermere Parish Council, 1973–80. Governor, Westminster Coll., Oxford, 1967–70. *Publications:* The Living God, 1942; Congregationalism Today, 1943; (jtly) A Book of Congregational Worship, 1948; (contrib.) Biblical Authority Today, 1951; (contrib.) Ways of Worship, 1951; (ed jtly) Intercommunion, 1952; The Fulness of Time, 1952; The Significance of Evanston, 1954; trans. Stauffer, Theology of the New Testament, 1955; A Year with the Bible, 1957; (contrib.) Essays in Christology for Karl Barth, 1957; Amos and Micah, 1959; trans. Bultmann, The History of the Synoptic Tradition, 1963; Pelican Commentary on St John's Gospel, 1968; Jesus in his Lifetime, 1981. *Recreations:* water colour painting, wood turning. *Address:* 5 Diamond Court, 153 Banbury Road, Oxford OX2 7AA. *T:* Oxford (0865) 57479.   *Died 26 Jan. 1994.*

MARSH, John; *see* Marsh, H. J.

MARSHALL, Arthur C.; *see* Calder-Marshall.

MARSHALL, Arthur Hedley, CBE 1956; MA, BSc (Econ), PhD; City Treasurer, Coventry, 1944–64, retired; Senior Research Fellow in Public Administration, Birmingham University, 1964–74; Visiting Lecturer, City University, 1977–83; *b* 6 July 1904; *s* of Rev. Arthur Marshall; *m* 1933, Margaret L. Longhurst (*d* 1987); one *s*. *Educ:* Wolverhampton Grammar Sch.; London Sch. of Economics. Incorporated Accountant (Hons), 1934; Fellow Institute Municipal Treasurers and Accountants and Collins gold medal, 1930 (Pres. 1953–54); DPA (London) 1932. Chm. Royal Institute of Public Administration, 1952–53; Adviser in Local Govt to Sudan Govt, 1948–49, and to Govt of British Guiana, 1955. Chm., Cttee on Highway Maintenance, 1967–70; Member: Colonial Office Local Government Advisory Panel, 1950;

Central Housing Adv. Cttee, 1957–65; Cttee for Training Public Administration in Overseas Countries, 1961–62; Arts Council Drama Panel, 1965–76; Arts Council, 1973–76; Uganda Commission, 1961; Kenya Commission, 1962; Royal Commission on Local Government in England, 1966–69. Hon. LLD Nottingham, 1972. *Publications:* Local Authorities: Internal Financial Control, 1936; Consolidated Loans Funds of Local Authorities (with J. M. Drummond), 1936; Financial Administration in Local Government, 1960; Financial Management in Local Government, 1974; Local Authorities and the Arts, 1974; Report on Local Government in the Sudan, 1949, and on British Guiana, 1955; various contribs to learned jls on local government, accountancy, and administration of the arts. *Recreation:* music.   *Died 15 Jan. 1994.*

MARSHALL, Prof. Herbert Percival James; film, theatre and TV producer, director, scriptwriter, author and translator; *b* London, 20 Jan. 1906; *s* of Percival Charles Marshall and Anne Marshall (*née* Organ); *m* 1935, Fredda Brilliant, sculptor. *Educ:* Elementary Sch., Ilford; evening classes, LCC; Higher Inst. of Cinematography, Moscow, USSR. Began as Asst Film Editor, Empire Marketing Bd Film Unit, 1929–30; Asst Dir various Moscow theatres; Drama Dir, Moscow Radio (English), 1933–35; Founder, Dir, Unity Theatre; prod documentary films, Spanish Civil War; Principal, Unity Theatre Trng Sch.; Lectr, LCC Evening Insts, 1935–39; Founder and Artistic Dir, Neighbourhood Theatre, S Kensington; Script-writer (with Fredda Brilliant) and Associate Producer (Ealing Studios), 1939–40; apptd Dir, Old Vic (theatre bombed); toured England; Dir for Sadler's Wells Opera Co.; Lectr, RADA, 1940–41; i/c of production, Russian, Czech, Polish and Yugoslav films for Europe (8 langs); broadcasts, BBC, in Russian, 1942–45; Lectr on film art, Amer. Univ., Biarritz, 1945–46; Indep. Film Producer: prod for J. Arthur Rank, Min. of Educn, NCB, etc; prod, scripted and dir. (with Fredda Brilliant), Tinker (Edinburgh Festival Award), 1946–50; dir. Man and Superman, Arena Theatre (Fest. of Brit.), 1951; prod official Mahatma Gandhi Biog. Documentary, etc, India, 1951–55; Exec. Producer, TV closed circuit and films for Advision Ltd, London, 1955–56; Film Producer for Govt of India; Principal, Natya Acad. of Dramatic Art, Bombay; Producer, Natya Nat. Theatre Company, 1957–60; Dir, Centre for Soviet and E European Studies, Southern Illinois Univ., apptd Prof., Academic Affairs, 1970, Prof. Emeritus 1979. Theatre Architecture Consultant to various projects: Indian Nat. Theatres, 1955–59; Centre 42, London, 1962; Morrison Civic Arts Centre, Lambeth, 1965; Samuel Beckett Theatre, Oxford Univ., 1968–. Lecturer: RCA and NY Univ., 1965; Univ. of Illinois, and Oxford Univ., 1968; Himachal Pradesh Univ., Hong Kong Univ., La Trobe Univ., Monash Univ., Univ. of Melbourne, 1972. Many well-known actors and actresses have been produced or directed by him. FRSA 1967. Mather Schol. of the Year, Case Western Reserve, Ohio, 1972. *Publications:* (ed) International Library of Cinema and Theatre (20 vols), 1946–56; Mayakovsky and His Poetry, 1964 (London); Hamlet Through the Ages (jointly), 1953 (London); Ira Aldridge, The Negro Tragedian (with Mildred Stock), 1953 (London, New York); Poetry of Voznesensky (London and New York) and Yevtushenko (London and New York), 1965; Stanislavsky Method of Direction (London and New York), 1969; Anthology of Soviet Poetry, 1970; (ed) Pictorial History of the Russian Theatre, 1978; (ed and introd) Battleship Potemkin, 1979; Masters of the Soviet Cinema: crippled creative biographies, 1983; (trans.) Memoirs of Sergei Eisenstein, vol. 1, Immoral Memories, 1983; (trans.) S. M. Eisenstein, Nonindifferent Nature, 1987; *scores:* English Text and Lyrics, Ivan the Terrible (Oratorio by S. Prokoviev and S.

M. Eisenstein), 1962 (Moscow); English Texts: 13th and 14th Symphonies, and Execution of Stepan Razin, by D. Shostakovich; Mayakovsky Oratorio Pathetique, by G. Sviridov, 1974, etc. *Recreations:* reading, TV. *Address:* 1204 Chautauqua Street, Carbondale, Ill 62901, USA; Southern Illinois University, Carbondale, Ill 62901, USA. *Died 28 May 1991.*

MARSHALL, Percy Edwin Alan J.; *see* Johnson-Marshall.

MARSHALL, Maj.-Gen. Roger Sydenham, CB 1974; TD 1948; Director of Army Legal Services, Ministry of Defence, 1971–73, retired; *b* 15 July 1913; 2nd *s* of Robert Sydenham Cole Marshall and Enid Edith Langton Cole; *m* 1940, Beryl Marie, *d* of William Vaughan Rayner; one *d.* Solicitor, Supreme Court, 1938. Commnd N Staffs Regt, TA, 1933; mobilised TA, 1939; comd 365 Batt. 65th Searchlight Regt, RA, 1942–44; transf. Army Legal Services, 1948; DAD, Army Legal Services: HQ MELF, 1948–49; HQ E Africa, 1949–52; GHQ MELF, 1952–53; WO, 1953–55; Assistant Director, Army Legal Services: WO, 1955–56; HQ BAOR, 1956–58; WO, 1960–61; HQ E Africa Comd, 1961–62; Dep. Dir, Army Legal Services, GHQ FARELF, 1962–63; Col Legal Staff, WO, 1964–69; Brig. Legal Staff, 1969–71; Maj.-Gen. 1971. *Recreations:* golf, reading history. *Address:* Aynho Park, Aynho, near Banbury, Oxon. *Died 22 April 1994.*

MARSHALL, Thurgood; Associate Justice of US Supreme Court, 1967–91, retired; *b* 2 July 1908; *s* of William C. and Norma A. Marshall; *m* 1st, 1929, Vivian Burey (*d* 1955); 2nd, 1955, Cecilia A. Suyat; two *s. Educ:* Lincoln Univ. (AB 1930); Howard Univ. Law Sch. Admitted Maryland Bar, 1933. Special Counsel, NAACP, 1938–50 (Asst, 1936–38); Dir, NAACP Legal Defense and Educ. Fund, 1940–61. Judge, 2nd Circuit Court of Appeals, 1961–65; Solicitor-Gen. of USA, 1965–67. Hon. doctorates at many US univs. Spingarn Medal, 1946.
Died 24 Jan. 1993.

MARSHALL, William; Assistant Under-Secretary of State, Ministry of Defence (Navy), 1968–72, retired; *b* 30 Sept. 1912; *e s* of late Allan and Julia Marshall, Whitecraigs, Renfrewshire; *m* 1st, 1940, Jessie Gardner Miller (*d* 1962); one *s;* 2nd, 1963, Doreen Margaret Read. *Educ:* Allan Glen's Sch., Glasgow; Glasgow Univ. MA Glasgow 1932, LLB (*cum laude*) Glasgow 1935. War of 1939–45: Temp. Asst Principal, Air Ministry, 1940; Service with Royal Navy (Ord. Seaman), and Admin. Staff, Admty, 1941. Private Sec. to Permanent Sec. of Admty (Sir J. G. Lang), 1947–48; Principal Private Sec. to successive First Lords of Admty (Lord Hall, Lord Packenham and Rt Hon. J. P. L. Thomas, later Lord Cilcennin), 1951–54; Asst Sec. in Admty, 1954; on loan to HM Treasury, 1958–61; returned to Admiralty, 1961. Chm., cttee to review submarine escape trng, 1974. *Recreations:* golf, travel, gardening. *Address:* 37 West Drive, Cheam, Surrey SM2 7NB. *T:* 0181–642 3399. *Died 30 Dec. 1995.*

MARTIN, Sir Andrew; *see* Martin, Sir R. A. St G.

MARTIN, Brig. John Douglas K.; *see* King-Martin.

MARTIN, Sir John (Miller), KCMG 1952; CB 1945; CVO 1943; British High Commissioner in Malta, 1965–67; *b* 15 Oct. 1904; *s* of late Rev. John Martin; *m* 1943, Rosalind Julia, 3rd *d* of late Sir David Ross, KBE; one *s. Educ:* The Edinburgh Acad.; Corpus Christi Coll., Oxford (Scholar, MA; Hon. Fellow, 1980). Entered Civil Service (Dominions Office), 1927; seconded to Malayan Civil Service, 1931–34; Sec. of Palestine Royal Commission, 1936; Private Sec. to the Prime Minister (Rt Hon. Winston Churchill), 1940–45 (Principal Private Sec. from 1941); Asst Under-Sec. of State, 1945–56, Dep. Under-Sec. of State, 1956–65, Colonial Office. KStJ 1966. *Publications:*

(contrib.) Action This Day—Working with Churchill, 1968; Downing Street, The War Years, 1991. *Address:* The Barn House, Watlington, Oxford OX9 5AA. *T:* Watlington (049161) 2487. *Died 31 March 1991.*

MARTIN, Hon. Paul Joseph James, CC 1976; PC (Canada) 1945; QC (Canada); High Commissioner for Canada in the United Kingdom, 1974–79; *b* Ottawa, 23 June 1903; *s* of Philip Ernest Martin and Lumina Marie Chouinard; *m* 1937, Alice Eleanor Adams; one *s* one *d. Educ:* Pembroke Separate Schs; St Alexandre Coll.; St Michael's Coll.; University of Toronto (MA); Osgoode Hall Law Sch., Toronto; Harvard Univ. (LLM); Trinity Coll., Cambridge; Geneva Sch. of Internat. Studies. Wilder Fellow, 1928; Alfred Zimmern Schol., 1930; Barrister-at-Law; Partner, Martin, Laird & Cowan, Windsor, Ont, 1934–63; QC 1937. Lectr, Assumption Coll., 1931–34. Can. Govt Deleg., 19th Ass. League of Nations, Geneva, 1938; Parly Asst to Minister of Labour, 1943; Deleg. to ILO Confs, Philadelphia, 1944, London, 1945; apptd Sec. of State, 1945; Deleg. to 1st, 4th, 7th, 9th, 10th General Assembly, UN (Chm. Can. Del., 9th, 18th, 19th, 20th, 21st); Deleg. 1st, 3rd, 5th sessions, Economic and Social Council, 1946–47; Minister of National Health and Welfare, Dec. 1946–June 1957; Sec. of State for External Affairs, 1963–68; Pres., N Atlantic Council, 1965–66; Govt Leader in Senate, Canada, 1968–74. First elected to Canadian House of Commons, Gen. Elec., 1935; Rep. Essex East until 1968; apptd to senate, 1968. Chancellor, Wilfrid Laurier Univ., 1972–78. Several hon. doctorates. Hon. Life Mem., Canadian Legion. Christian Culture Award, 1956. Freedom, City of London, 1977. Hon. LLD Cambridge, 1980. *Publications:* A Very Public Life (autobiog.), vol. I 1983, vol. II 1986; London Diaries 1975–1979, 1988. *Address:* 2021 Ontario Street, Windsor, Ontario N8Y 1N3, Canada. *Clubs:* Rideau (Ottawa); Beach Grove Golf and Country (Windsor, Ont).
Died 14 Sept. 1992.

MARTIN, Col Sir (Robert) Andrew (St George), KCVO 1988; OBE 1959 (MBE 1949); JP; Lord-Lieutenant and Custos Rotulorum of Leicestershire, 1965–89; *b* 23 April 1914; *o s* of late Major W. F. Martin, Leics Yeo., and Violet Anne Philippa (*née* Wynter); *m* 1950, Margaret Grace (JP Leics 1967), *e d* of late J. V. Buchanan, MB, ChB and Waiata Buchanan (*née* Godsal); one *s. Educ:* Eton Coll.; RMC Sandhurst. Commissioned Oxf. and Bucks Lt Inf., 1934; ADC to Gov.-Gen. of S Africa, 1938–40; war service 4 Oxf. and Bucks, 1940–42; 2/7 Royal Warwicks Regt, 1942–44; 5 DCLI, 1944–45 in NW Europe (despatches); Staff Coll., Camberley, 1945; DAMS, HQ ALFSEA, 1946; Mil. Asst to C of S, GHQ, SEALF, 1946–49 (MBE); Chief Instr, School of Mil. Admin, 1949–50; 1 Som. LI, 1950–52; AMS, HQ BAOR, 1952–54; 1 Oxf. and Bucks, 1954–55; Military Sec. to Gov.-Gen. of Australia, 1955–57; Comd 1 Oxf. and Bucks Lt Inf. and 1 Green Jackets, 1957–59; Bde Col Green Jackets Bde, 1959–62; Comd Recruiting and Liaison Staff, HQ Western Command, 1962–65. Pres., E Midlands TA&VRA, 1968–86. Pres., Sports Aid Foundn (E Midlands), 1987–. Hon. LLD Leicester, 1984; Hon. DTech Loughborough, 1988. JP Leics, 1965. KStJ 1966 (Pres., Council, Leics, 1966–89). Order of Orange Nassau (Netherlands), 1950. *Recreations:* hunting, shooting, gardening. *Address:* The Brand, Woodhouse Eaves, Loughborough, Leics LE12 8SS. *T:* Woodhouse Eaves (0509) 890269. *Clubs:* Army and Navy, MCC.
Died 13 Dec. 1993.

MARTIN, Rupert Claude, JP; MA; *b* 2 July 1905; *s* of late Col C. B. Martin, CMG and Mary, *d* of J. L. Thomas; *m* 1931, Ellen (*d* 1966), *d* of Henry Wood, Guernsey, CI; one *s* two *d. Educ:* Shrewsbury Sch.; Queen's Coll., Oxford (Classical Scholar), 2nd Class in Greats, 1927.

Asst Master at St Paul's Sch., 1927–37, House Master, 1930–37; Headmaster of King's Sch., Bruton, Som., 1937–46, Governor, 1949–87; representative of British Council in Switzerland, 1946–48; Headmaster, St Dunstan's, Burnham on Sea, 1948–66. Vice-Chm., Incorporated Assoc. of Preparatory Schs, 1957. *Publications:* (Lands and Peoples Series) Switzerland; Italy; Spain; Morocco; Looking at Italy; Looking at Spain. *Recreations:* mountaineering, travel. *Address:* Quantocks, Allandale Road, Burnham on Sea, Som TA8 2HG. *Clubs:* MCC, I Zingari, Free Foresters, Alpine; Vincent's, Authentics (Oxford).　　　　*Died 17 Aug. 1991.*

MARTIN, Sir Sidney (Launcelot), Kt 1979; FRSC; Pro Vice-Chancellor, University of the West Indies, and Principal, Cave Hill Campus, 1964–83, retired; *b* 27 Sept. 1918; *s* of Sidney A. Martin and late Miriam A. Martin (*née* McIntosh); *m* 1944, Olga Brett (*née* Dolphin); three *s. Educ:* Wolmers Boys' Sch., Jamaica (Jamaica schol. 1937); Royal College of Science, Imperial Coll. London, 1938–42 (BScChem, ARCS, DIC; Fellow, 1981); MSc London. FRIC 1949 (ARIC 1940). Materials Research Laboratory, Phillips Electrical Ltd, Surrey, 1942; Head, Phys. Chem. Div., 1946–49; University College of the West Indies, later University of the West Indies: Lectr, 1949–52, Sen. Lectr, 1952–63, in Phys. Chem.; Warden, Taylor Hall, 1954–64; Acting Registrar, on secondment, 1961–63; Registrar, 1963–66; Principal, Cave Hill, and Pro Vice-Chancellor on secondment, 1964–66, substantively, 1966–83; Hon. LLD Univ. of West Indies, 1984. Chairman: Sci. Res. Council of Jamaica, 1961–64; Barbados Nat. Council for Sci. and Technology, 1977–84; Member: Bd of Management, Coll. of Arts, Sci. and Technology, Jamaica, 1958–64; Educnl Adv. Cttee, Jamaica, 1960–64; Public Services Commn of Barbados, 1964–69; Bd of Management, Codrington Coll., Barbados, 1969–84. Member: Faraday Soc., London, 1943–68; Chemical Soc., London, 1942–; RSA, 1972–. Queen's Silver Jubilee Medal, 1977. *Publications:* articles in various chemical and physical jls. *Recreations:* bridge, reading. *Address:* c/o University of the West Indies, Cave Hill Campus, PO Box 64, Barbados. *T:* 425–1310; 2 Balmoral Apartments, Balmoral Gap, Hastings, Christchurch, GPO 28, Barbados. *T:* 429–5288.
　　　　Died 3 Aug. 1991.

MARTIN, Thomas Ballantyne; *b* 13 Nov. 1901; *s* of late Angus Martin, FRCSE, Forest Hall, and Robina, *d* of Thomas Pringle, Middleton Hall, Wooler, Northumberland; *m* 1953, Jean Elisabeth, *e d* of Lt-Col O. D. Bennett and Audrey, *d* of Sir Hamilton Grant, 12th Bt; two *d. Educ:* Cambridge Univ. (MA). MP (C) Blaydon Div. of Co. Durham, 1931–35; Political Correspondent of Daily Telegraph, 1936–40; RAFVR; Squadron Leader, Middle East Intelligence Centre, 1940–43; Adviser on Public Relations to UK High Comr in Australia, 1943–45; Sec. of United Europe Movement, 1947–48; Sec. to British all-party delegn to Congress of Europe at The Hague; Mem., London Stock Exchange, 1949–74, retired. *Address:* Noad's House, Tilshead, Salisbury, Wilts SP3 4RY. *T:* Shrewton (01980) 620258. *Club:* Pratt's.
　　　　Died 28 Jan. 1995.

MARTIN-BIRD, Col Sir Richard Dawnay, Kt 1975; CBE 1971 (OBE (mil.) 1953); TD 1950; DL; President, Yates Brothers Wine Lodges PLC, Manchester; *b* 19 July 1910; *s* of late Richard Martin Bird and Mildred, 2nd *d* of late Peter Peel Yates; *m* 1935, Katharine Blanche, *d* of Sir Arthur Selborne Jelf, CMG; three *d* (two *s* decd). *Educ:* Charterhouse. Served with 8th (Ardwick) Bn, The Manchester Regt (TA), 1936–53; war service 1939–45; Lt-Col comdg, 1947–53; Hon. Col, 1953–67; Hon. Col, The Manchester Regt (Ardwick and Ashton) Territorials, 1967–71; Dep. Comdr, 127 Inf. Bde (TA), 1953–57 and

1959–63; Regtl Councillor, The King's Regt, 1967–; ADC (TA) to the Queen, 1961–65; Chairman: E Lancs T&AFA, 1963–68; TA&VRA for Lancs, Cheshire and IoM, later TA&VRA for NW England and IoM, 1968–75; Vice-Chm., Council, TA&AVR Assocs, 1973–75; Mem., TAVR Adv. Cttee, 1973–75. Pres., Wine and Spirit Assoc. of GB, 1978–79. DL Lancs 1964–74, Cheshire 1974; High Sheriff Greater Manchester, 1976–82. *Address:* Stockinwood, Chelford, Cheshire SK11 9BE. *T:* Chelford (0625) 861523. *Clubs:* Army and Navy; St James's (Manchester); Winckley (Preston).
　　　　Died 3 Dec. 1992.

MARTIN-JENKINS, Dennis Frederick, TD 1945; Chairman, Ellerman Lines Ltd, 1967–81 (Managing Director, 1967–76); formerly chairman or director of many other companies; retired; *b* 7 Jan. 1911; 2nd *s* of late Frederick Martin-Jenkins, CA and Martha Magdalene Martin-Jenkins (*née* Almeida); *m* 1937, Rosemary Clare Walker, MRCS, LRCP; three *s. Educ:* St Bede's Sch., Eastbourne; Marlborough College. FCIT. Served RA, 1939–45 (Lt-Col). Insce, 1930–35; joined Montgomerie & Workman Ltd, 1935; transf. City Line Ltd, 1938; transf. Hall Line Ltd, 1947 (Dir 1949); Dir, Ellerman Lines Ltd and associated cos, 1950. Chamber of Shipping of UK: Mem. 1956 (Hon. Mem., 1975); Vice-Pres. 1964; Pres. 1965; Chm., Deep Sea Liner Section, 1969–76; Chairman: Gen. Council of British Shipping for UK, 1963; Internat. Chamber of Shipping, 1971–77; Past Chm., London Gen. Shipowners' Soc.; formerly Member: Mersey Docks and Harbour Bd; Bd of PLA; Nat. Dock Labour Bd; Exec. Cttee, Nat. Assoc. of Port Employers; Mem., British Transport Docks Bd, 1968–81. Chm. and Trustee, Moorgate Trust Fund; Trustee, New Moorgate Trust Fund. *Recreations:* golf, gardening. *Address:* Maytree House, Woodcote, Guildford Road, Cranleigh, Surrey GU6 8NZ. *T:* Cranleigh (0483) 276278. *Clubs:* United Oxford & Cambridge University; Woking Golf, Thurlestone Golf.
　　　　Died 4 Dec. 1991.

MARTINEZ ZUVIRIA, Gen. Gustavo; historian; Argentine Ambassador to the Court of St James's, 1970–74; *b* 28 Dec. 1915; *s* of Dr Gustavo Martinez Zuviria and Matilde de Iriondo de Martinez Zuviria; *m* 1940, Maria Eugenia Ferrer Deheza; five *s* four *d* (and one *s* decd). *Educ:* Col. El Salvador, Buenos Aires; Mount St Mary's Coll. (nr Sheffield); San Martin Mil. Academy. Promoted to 2nd Lt, 1938; Capt. 1951. He participated in attempt to overthrow the Peron regime; imprisoned, but when Peron was overthrown, he continued career in Army; among other posts he served in: Cavalry Regt No 12, 1940; Granaderos a Caballo, 1944; Cavalry Regt No 7, 1945; Instr of cadets, Military Sch., 1944; Mil. Attaché to Peru, 1955; Chief of 3rd Regt of Cavalry, 1957; Asst Dir and Dir of Mil. Sch., 1958; Chief of Staff, Argentine Cav. Corps, 1961; Dir, in Superior War Staff Coll., 1962; Dir, Sch. of Cav. and Cav. Inspector, 1963; Comdr, 2nd Cav. Div., 1964; 2nd Comdr, 3rd Army Corps, 1965; Comdr, 1st Army Corps, 1966; Comdr, Southern Joint Forces, 1969; retd from Army and was designated Sec. of State in Intelligence (Secretario de Informaciones de Estado), 1970. Presidente dela Comisión de Caballería, 1974–76. Member: Genealogical Studies Centre, 1962; Nat. Sanmartinian Historical Academy, 1966; Nat. Acad. of History, 1978. Lectured in Paris and Brussels, Feb. 1978, on bicentenary of birth of Gen. San Martín. Several foreign orders. *Publications:* numerous (related to professional and historical subjects); notably Los tiempos de Mariano Necochea, 1961 (2nd edn, 1969) (1st award mil. lit. and award Fundación Eguiguren); Retreta del Desierto, 1956 (14 edns); José Pidsudski; San Martin y O'Brien, 1963; Historia de Angel Pacheco, 1969. *Recreations:* riding, shooting. *Address:* Avenida del Libertador 15249, 1640 Acassuso, Buenos Aires, Argentina. *Clubs:* Naval and

Military, Travellers', Hurlingham, Turf (all in London); Cowdray Park Polo (Sussex); Circulo Militar, Jockey (Buenos Aires); Club Social de Paraná (Entre Rios).
Died 27 April 1991.

MARTY, Cardinal François, Officier de la Légion d'honneur; *b* Pachins, Aveyron, 18 May 1904; *s* of François Marty, cultivateur, and Zoé (*née* Gineste). *Educ:* Collège de Graves et Villefranche-de-Rouergue; Séminaire de Rodez; Institut Catholique de Toulouse (Dr en Th.). Priest, 1930. Vicaire: Villefranche-de-Rouergue, 1932; Rodez, 1933; Parish Priest: Bournazel, 1940; Rieupeyroux, 1943; Archpriest, Millau, 1949; Vicar-General, Rodez, 1951; Bishop of Saint Flour, 1952; Coadjutor Archbishop, 1959, and Archbishop of Reims, 1960; Archbishop of Paris, 1968–81. Cardinal, 1969. Pres., Comité Episcopal of Mission de France, 1965; Mem. Bureau, then Vice-Pres., Perm. Council of French Episcopate, 1966, and Pres., French Episcopal Conf., 1969–75, responsable des Catholiques orientaux. Member, Rome Commission for: Revision of Canon Law; Congregations; Divine Worship; Clergy; Eastern Church. *Publications:* Dieu est tenace, 1973; Evangile au présent, 1974; Prophètes de la joie, 1978; l'Evêque dans la ville, 1979; Cardinal Marty: chronique vécue de l'église de France, 1980. *Address:* Monteils, 12200 Villefranche-de-Rouergue, France. *Died 16 Feb. 1994.*

MARWICK, Sir Brian (Allan), KBE 1963 (CBE 1954; OBE 1946); CMG 1958; *b* 18 June 1908; *s* of James Walter Marwick and Elizabeth Jane Flett; *m* 1934, Riva Lee (*d* 1988), *d* of Major H. C. Cooper; two *d. Educ:* University of Cape Town; CCC, Cambridge. Administrative Officer: Swaziland, 1925–36; Nigeria, 1937–40; Swaziland, 1941–46; First Asst Sec.: Swaziland, 1947–48; Basutoland, 1949–52; Dep. Resident Comr and Govt Sec., Basutoland, 1952–55; Administrative Sec. to High Comr for Basutoland, the Bechuanaland Protectorate and Swaziland, 1956; Resident Comr, Swaziland, 1957–63; HM Comr, Swaziland, 1963–64; Permanent Secretary: Min. of Works and Town Planning Dept, Nassau, Bahamas, 1965–68; Min. of Educn, Bahamas, 1968–71. *Publication:* The Swazi, 1940. *Recreation:* golf. *Died 1 April 1992.*

MARWICK, Ewan; Secretary and Chief Executive, Glasgow Chamber of Commerce, since 1983; *b* 23 April 1952; *s* of Kenneth and Valerie Marwick, Edinburgh; *m* 1980, Helen Mary Ma, PhD; four *s* one *d. Educ:* Daniel Stewart's Coll.; Edinburgh Univ. (MA Jt Hons Econs and Econ. Hist. 1974). Post-grad. res. and consultancy work on econ. implications of devolution, 1978; Asst Sec., RICS, 1979–80; Dep. Sec., Glasgow Chamber of Commerce, 1980–83. Sec., Assoc. of Scottish Chambers of Commerce, 1982–. Chm., Certification and Internat. Trade Formalities Cttee, 1991–. Non-Exec. Dir, Edinburgh Financial and General Holdings Ltd; Econ. Advr, Rostov Oblast, 1992–. Hon. Sec., Saints and Sinners Club of Scotland. Contested (C) Paisley North, Nov. 1990. *Publications:* occasional articles on current affairs. *Address:* Chamber of Commerce, 30 George Square, Glasgow G2 1EQ. *T:* 041-204 2121. *Club:* Glasgow Nomads. *Died 12 May 1993.*

MASCALL, Rev. Canon Eric Lionel, DD Oxon, DD Cantab, BSc London; FBA 1974; DGS; an Hon. Canon of Truro Cathedral, with duties of Canon Theologian, 1973–84, then Canon Emeritus; Professor of Historical Theology, London University, at King's College, 1962–73, then Professor Emeritus; Dean, Faculty of Theology, London University, 1968–72; *b* 12 Dec. 1905; *s* of John R. S. Mascall and S. Lilian Mascall (*née* Grundy); unmarried. *Educ:* Latymer Upper Sch., Hammersmith; Pembroke Coll., Cambridge (Scholar); Theological Coll., Ely. BSc (London) 1926; BA (Wrangler) 1927, MA 1931,

BD 1943, DD 1958 Cantab; DD Oxon, 1948. Sen. Maths Master, Bablake Sch., Coventry, 1928–31; ordained deacon, 1932, priest, 1933; Mem., Oratory of the Good Shepherd, 1938–; Asst Curate, St Andrew's, Stockwell Green, 1932–35; St Matthew's, Westminster, 1935–37; Sub-warden, Scholae Cancellarii, Lincoln, 1937–45; Lecturer in Theology, Christ Ch., Oxford, 1945–46; Student and Tutor of Christ Ch., Oxford, 1946–62, Emeritus Student, 1962–; University Lectr in Philosophy of Religion, 1947–62; Chaplain at Oxford to Bishop of Derby, 1947–48; Commissary to Archbishop of Cape Town, 1964–73; Examining Chaplain to: Bishop of Willesden, 1970–73; Bishop of Truro, 1973–81; Bishop of London, 1981–. Visiting Professor: Gregorian Univ., Rome, 1976; Pontifical Coll. Josephinum, Columbus, Ohio, 1977; Lectures: Bampton, Oxford, 1956; Bampton, Columbia, 1958; Boyle, 1965–66; Charles A. Hart Memorial, Cath. Univ. of America, Washington, DC, 1968; Gifford, Univ. of Edinburgh, 1970–71. FKC, 1968–. Hon. DD St Andrews, 1967. *Publications:* Death or Dogma, 1937; A Guide to Mount Carmel, 1939; Man, his Origin and Destiny, 1940; The God-Man, 1940; He Who Is, 1943, rev. edn 1966; Christ, the Christian and the Church, 1946; Existence and Analogy, 1949; Corpus Christi, 1953, rev. edn 1965; Christian Theology and Natural Science, 1956; Via Media, 1956; Words and Images, 1957; The Recovery of Unity, 1958; The Importance of Being Human, 1958; Pi in the High, 1959; Grace and Glory, 1961; Theology and History (Inaugural Lecture), 1962; Theology and Images, 1963; Up and Down in Adria, 1963; The Secularisation of Christianity, 1965; The Christian Universe, 1966; Theology and The Future, 1968; (jt author) Growing into Union, 1970; The Openness of Being, 1971; Nature and Supernature, 1976; Theology and the Gospel of Christ, 1977, rev. edn 1984; Whatever Happened to the Human Mind, 1980; Jesus: who he is and how we know him, 1985; Compliments of the Season, 1985; The Triune God, 1986; Saraband (memoirs), 1993; Editor: The Church of God, 1934; The Mother of God, 1949; The Angels of Light and the Powers of Darkness, 1954; The Blessed Virgin Mary, 1963; contribs to: Man, Woman and Priesthood, 1978; When Will Ye Be Wise?, 1983. *Address:* St Mary's House, Kingsmead, Belgrave Road, Seaford, East Sussex BN25 2ET. *Died 14 Feb. 1993.*

MASON, Sydney, CBE 1994; FSVA; Chairman, The Hammerson Property Investment and Development Corporation plc, 1958–93, Life President, 1993 (Director, 1949–93; Joint Managing Director, 1958–88); *b* 30 Sept. 1920; *s* of Jacob Mason and Annie (*née* Foreman); *m* 1945, Rosalind Victor. FSVA 1962. Manager, Land Securities plc, 1943–49. Mem., 1974, Hon. Life Mem., 1985, Gen. Council, British Property Fedn. Chm. Exec., Lewis W. Hammerson Meml Home for the Elderly, 1959–80; Member: Exec., Norwood Orphanage, 1958–76 (Chm., 1968–76); Special Projects Cttee, Church Urban Fund. Master, Co. of Masons, July 1994–. Hon. Companion, NEAC, 1991. *Recreation:* painting in oils and acrylics. *Address:* Deep River Cottage, Ferry Lane, Wargrave, Berks RG10 8ET. *T:* Wargrave (01734) 402095. *Clubs:* Naval, City Livery, Royal Thames Yacht.
Died 24 Jan. 1995.

MASON, Walter W.; *see* Wynne Mason.

MASSEREENE, 13th Viscount, *cr* 1660, **AND FERRARD,** 6th Viscount, *cr* 1797; **John Clotworthy Talbot Foster Whyte-Melville Skeffington,** Baron of Loughneagh (Ire.), 1660; Baron Oriel (Ire.), 1790; Baron Oriel (UK), 1821; DL; *b* 23 Oct. 1914; *s* of 12th Viscount (*d* 1956) and Jean Barbara (*d* 1937), *e d* of Sir John Stirling Ainsworth, MP, JP, 1st Bt, Ardanaiseig, Argyllshire; *S* father 1956; *m* 1939, Annabelle Kathleen, *er d* of late Mr and Mrs Henry

D. Lewis, Combwell Priory, Hawkhurst, Kent; one *s* one *d*. *Educ:* Eton. Lieut, Black Watch SR, 1933–36, re-employed, 1939–40 (invalided); retired; served in Small Vessels Pool, Royal Navy, 1944. Mem. IPU Delegation to Spain, 1960; Whip, Conservative Peers Cttee (IUP), House of Lords, 1958–65, Jt Dep. Chm., 1965–70; introduced in House of Lords: Deer Act, 1963; Riding Establishments Act, 1964; Export of Animals for Research Bill, 1968; Riding Establishments Act, 1970; Valerie Mary Hill and Alan Monk (Marriage Enabling) Act, 1984; Industrial Training Act, 1986; Protection of Animals (Penalties) Bill, 1987; Southern Water Authority Bill, 1988; moved debates on Overseas Information Services and other matters. Pres., Monday Club, 1981–; Member: CPA delegn to Malaŵi, 1976; Select Cttee on Anglian Water Authority Bill, 1976; Nat. Cttee, 900th Anniversary of Doomesday, 1987. Posts in Cons. Constituency organisations incl. Pres., Brighton, Kemp Town Div., Vice-Pres. and former Treasurer, Ashford Div. Chm. and dir of companies; Chm., Sunset and Vine plc, 1989–. Driver of leading British car, Le Mans Grand Prix, 1937. One of original pioneers in commercial develt of Cape Canaveral, Florida; promoted first scheduled air service Glasgow-Oban-Isle of Mull, 1968; presented operetta Countess Maritza at Palace Theatre, London. Comr, Hunterston Ore Terminal Hearing, Glasgow, 1973. Pres., of Charitable and other organisations incl.: Ponies of Britain, 1970–86; Kent Hotels and Restaurants Assoc., 1975–85. Pres., Canterbury Br., RNLI. Former Mem., Senechal Council, Canterbury Cathedral. Chief, Scottish Clans Assoc. of London, 1974–76. Chm. Kent Branch Victoria League, 1962–87. Treas., Kent Assoc. of Boys' Clubs, 1963–86. Master, Ashford Valley Foxhounds, 1953–54; Vice-Pres., Animal Welfare Year, 1976–77. Commodore, House of Lords Yacht Club, 1972–85. Freeman, City of London, and Mem. Worshipful Company of Shipwrights. Gold Staff Officer, Coronation, 1953. FZS. DL Co. Antrim, 1957. Cross of Comdr, Order of Merit, SMO Malta, 1978. *Publications:* The Lords, 1973; contributed articles to newspapers, chiefly sporting and natural history. *Recreations:* all field sports, farming, forestry, racing. *Heir:* s Hon. John David Clotworthy Whyte-Melville Foster Skeffington [*b* 3 June 1940; *m* 1970, Ann Denise, *er d* of late Norman Rowlandson; two *s* one *d*]. *Address:* Knock, Isle of Mull, Argyll PA71 6HT. *T:* Aros (06803) 356; (Seat) Chilham Castle, Kent. *T:* Canterbury (0227) 730319. *Clubs:* Carlton, Turf, Pratt's; Royal Yacht Squadron.   *Died 27 Dec. 1992.*

MASSEY, William Edmund Devereux, CBE 1961; OStJ; retired from HM Diplomatic Service; *b* 1901; *m* 1942, Ingrid Glad-Block, Oslo; one *d*. Entered Foreign Office, 1922; served in diplomatic and consular posts in Poland, France, Japan, Brazil, Roumania, Sweden, Luxembourg (Chargé d'Affaires), Germany; Ambassador and Consul-General to Nicaragua, 1959–61. Hon. Consul for Nicaragua in London, 1969–79. Freeman of City of London. Chm., UK Permanent Cttee on Geographical Names for Official Use, 1965–81; UK Deleg., 2nd UN Conf. on Geographical Names, 1972. FRGS. OStJ 1945. Grand Ducal Commemorative Medal, Luxembourg, 1953.   *Died 26 April 1991.*

MATHER, Leonard Charles, CBE 1978; Chairman, United Dominions Trust, 1974–81; Director, Midland Bank, 1968–84; a life Vice-President, Institute of Bankers, 1970; *b* 10 Oct. 1909; *s* of Richard and Elizabeth Mather; *m* 1937, Muriel Armor Morris. *Educ:* Oldershaw Sch., Wallasey. BCom (London). Entered Midland Bank, Dale Street, Liverpool, 1926; transf. to London, 1937; served in Gen. Managers' Dept at Head Office, 1937–45; Man., Bolton, 1945–48; Prin., Legal Dept, 1948–50; Asst Gen. Man., 1950–56; Gen. Man., Midland Bank Executor & Trustee Co. Ltd, 1956–58; Jt Gen. Man., Midland Bank

Ltd, 1958–63; Asst Chief Gen. Man., 1964–66; Dep. Chief Gen. Man., 1966–68; Chief Gen. Man., 1968–72; Vice-Chm., 1972–74; Director: Midland Bank Trust Co. Ltd, 1968–74; Midland & International Banks Ltd, 1969–74; Montagu Trust, 1969–74; Chm., European Banks' International Co. SA, 1972–74 (Dir, 1970); Dep. Chm., Euro-Pacific Finance Corp. Ltd, 1970–74. FCIS; FIB (Dep. Chm., 1967–69; Pres., 1969–70); Hon. FIB 1974. Hon. DLitt Loughborough, 1978. *Publications:* The Lending Banker, 1955; Banker and Customer Relationship and the Accounts of Personal Customers, 1956; The Accounts of Limited Company Customers, 1958; Securities Acceptable to the Lending Banker, 1960. *Recreations:* golf, bridge. *Address:* Rochester House, Parkfield, Seal, Sevenoaks, Kent. *T:* Sevenoaks (0732) 61007.   *Died 8 May 1991.*

MATHESON of Matheson, Sir Torquhil (Alexander), 6th Bt *cr* 1882, of Lochalsh, Co. Ross; Chief of Clan Matheson; DL; FSAScot; one of HM Body Guard of the Honourable Corps of Gentlemen at Arms, since 1977, Clerk of the Cheque and Adjutant, since 1990; *b* 15 Aug. 1925; *s* of General Sir Torquhil George Matheson, 5th Bt, KCB, CMG; *S* father, 1963, *S* kinsman as Chief of Clan Matheson, 1975; *m* 1954, Serena Mary Francesca, *o d* of late Lt-Col Sir Michael Peto, 2nd Bt, Barnstaple; two *d*. *Educ:* Eton. FSAScot 1989. Served War of 1939–45: joined Coldstream Guards, July 1943; commnd, March 1944; 5th Bn Coldstream Guards, NW Europe, Dec. 1944–May 1945 (wounded); served with 3rd Bn Coldstream Guards: Palestine, 1945–48 (despatches); Tripoli and Egypt, 1950–53; seconded King's African Rifles, 1961–64. Captain, 1952; Major, 1959; retd 1964. 4th Bn, Wilts Regt, TA, 1965–67; Royal Wilts Territorials (T&AVR III), 1967–69. DL Somerset, 1987. *Heir:* (to Baronetcy and Chiefship): *b* Major Fergus John Matheson, late Coldstream Guards [*b* 22 Feb. 1927; *m* 1952, Hon. Jean Elizabeth Mary Willoughby, *yr d* of 11th Baron Middleton, KG, MC, TD; one *s* two *d*]. *Address:* Standerwick Court, Frome, Som BA11 2PP. *Clubs:* Army and Navy; Leander (Henley-on-Thames).
        Died 9 April 1993.

MATHEWS, Rev. (Arthur) Kenneth, OBE 1942; DSC 1944; Vicar of Thursley, 1968–76; Rural Dean of Godalming, 1969–74; *b* 11 May 1906; *s* of late Reverend Canon A. A. and Mrs Mathews; *m* 1st, 1936, Elisabeth (*d* 1981), *d* of late E. M. Butler and Mrs Butler; no *c*; 2nd, 1987, Diana, *d* of late Maj.-Gen. A. A. Goschen, CB, DSO. *Educ:* Monkton Combe Sch.; Balliol Coll., Oxford (Exhibitioner); Cuddesdon Theol Coll. Deacon 1932, priest 1933, at Wakefield; Asst Curate of Penistone; Padre of the Tanker Fleet of the Anglo-Saxon Petroleum Co. Ltd; licensed to officiate, Diocese of Wakefield, 1935–38; Vicar of Forest Row, 1938–44; Temp. Chaplain, RNVR, 1939–44 (Chaplain HMS Norfolk, 1940–44); on staff of Christian Frontier Council, 1944–46; Vicar of Rogate and Sequestrator of Terwick, 1946–54; Rural Dean of Midhurst, 1950–54; Hon. Chaplain to Bishop of Portsmouth, 1950–55; Commissary to: Bishop of Singapore, 1949–64; Bishop of Wellington, 1962–72; Student of Central Coll. of Anglican Communion at St Augustine's Coll., Canterbury, 1954–55; Dean and Rector of St Albans, 1955–63; Rector of St Peter's, Peebles, 1963–68. Hon. Chaplain to Bishop of Norwich, 1969–71. Member: Council, Marlborough Coll., 1953–74; Governing Body, Monkton Combe Sch., 1959–77. *Recreations:* walking, gardening. *Address:* The Tallat, Westwell, near Burford, Oxon OX8 4JT.
        Died 18 Dec. 1992.

MATHIAS, Lionel Armine, CMG 1953; apple grower, 1962–84, retired; *b* 23 Jan. 1907; *s* of Hugh Henry Mathias and Amy Duncan Mathias (*née* Mathias); *m* 1935, Rebecca

Gordon Rogers (*d* 1984); two *d* (and one *d* decd). *Educ:* Christ's Coll., New Zealand; St Paul's Sch.; Keble Coll., Oxford. Appointed Asst District Commissioner, Uganda, 1929; Labour Commissioner, 1949–53; Member: Uganda Exec. Council, 1948, Legislative Council, 1949–53; Kampala Municipal Council, 1952–53; Uganda Students Adviser, 1953–62; Chm., Uganda Britain Soc., 1964–65. *Address:* Little Copt Farm, Shoreham, Sevenoaks, Kent. *T:* Otford (09592) 2040. *Died 12 Aug. 1991.*

MATHIAS, Sir Richard Hughes, 2nd Bt, *cr* 1917, of Vaendre Hall, St Mellons, Co. Monmouth; Member, London Stock Exchange, 1948–84, retired; *b* 6 April 1905; *s* of Sir Richard Mathias, 1st Bt, and Annie, *y d* of Evan Hughes, Cardiff; *S* father 1942; *m* 1st, 1937, Gladys Cecilia Turton (marr. diss., 1960), *o d* of late Edwin Hart, New Hextalls, Bletchingley, Surrey; two *d*; 2nd, 1960, Mrs Elizabeth Baird Murray (*d* 1972), *er d* of late Dr and Mrs Miles of Hendrescythan, Creigiau, Glamorgan; 3rd, 1973, Mrs Hilary Vines (*d* 1975), Malaga, Spain. *Educ:* Eton; Balliol Coll., Oxford. RAF, 1940–46 (Staff appt Air Ministry, 1942–46). Mem. Council, Royal Nat. Mission to Deep Sea Fishermen, 1953–54. Fellow, Corp. of St Mary and St Nicolas (Woodard Schs), 1965–80; Mem. Council, Hurstpierpoint Coll., 1965–80 (Chm., 1967–74). *Heir:* none. *Address:* 8 Oakwood Court, Abbotsbury Road, W14 8JU. *T:* 071–602 2635. *Club:* Reform (Chm., 1964–67). *Died 4 Jan. 1991 (ext).*

MATHIAS, Prof. William (James), CBE 1985; DMus; FRAM; composer, conductor, pianist; Professor and Head of the Department of Music, University College of North Wales, Bangor, 1970–88; *b* 1 Nov. 1934; *s* of James Hughes Mathias and Marian (*née* Evans); *m* 1959, Margaret Yvonne Collins; one *d*. *Educ:* University Coll. of Wales, Aberystwyth (Robert Bryan Schol.; Fellow, 1990); Royal Academy of Music (Lyell-Taylor Schol.). DMus Wales, 1966; FRAM 1965 (LRAM 1958). Lectr in Music, UC of N Wales, Bangor, 1959–68; Sen. Lectr in Music, Univ. of Edinburgh, 1968–69. Member: Welsh Arts Council, 1974–81 (Chm., Music Cttee, 1982–88); Music Adv. Cttee, British Council, 1974–83; ISCM (British Section), 1976–80; BBC Central Music Adv. Cttee, 1979–86; Welsh Adv. Cttee, British Council, 1979–90; Council, Composers' Guild of GB, 1982–; Bd of Governors, Nat. Museum of Wales, 1973–78; Artistic Dir, N Wales Music Festival, 1972–; Vice-President: British Arts Fests Assoc., 1988– (Vice-Chm., 1983–88); RCO, 1985; Pres., ISM, 1989–90. Governor, NYO of GB, 1985–92. Hon. FWCMD, 1992. Hon. DMus Westminster Choir Coll., Princeton, 1987. Arnold Bax Society Prize, 1968; John Edwards Meml Award, 1982. *Publications include:* Piano Concerto No 2, 1964; Piano Concerto No 3, 1970; Harpsichord Concerto, 1971; Harp Concerto, 1973; Clarinet Concerto, 1976; Horn Concerto, 1984; Organ Concerto, 1984; Oboe Concerto, 1990; Violin Concerto, 1992; Flute Concerto, 1992; *orchestral compositions:* Divertimento for string orch., 1961; Serenade for small orch., 1963; Prelude, Aria and Finale, 1966; Symphony No 1, 1969; Festival Overture, 1973; Celtic Dances, 1974; Vistas, 1977; Laudi, 1978; Vivat Regina (for brass band), 1978; Helios, 1978; Requiescat, 1979; Dance Variations, 1979; Investiture Anniversary Fanfare, 1979; Reflections on a theme by Tomkins, 1981; Symphony No 2: Summer Music (commnd by Royal Liverpool Philharmonic Soc.), 1983; Ceremonial Fanfare (for 2 trumpets), 1983; Anniversary Dances (for centenary of Univ. Coll. Bangor), 1985; Carnival of Wales, 1987; Threnos, for string orch., 1990; Symphony No 3, 1991; In Arcadia, 1992; *chamber compositions:* Sonata for violin and piano, 1963; Piano Sonata, 1965; Divertimento for flute, oboe and piano, 1966; String Quartet, 1970; Capriccio for flute and piano, 1971; Wind Quintet, 1976; Concertino, 1977; Zodiac Trio, 1977; Clarinet Sonatina,

1978; String Quartet No 2, 1981; Piano Sonata No 2, 1984; Violin Sonata No 2, 1984; Piano Trio, 1986; Flute Sonatina, 1986; String Quartet No 3, 1986; Soundings for Brass Quintet, 1988; Little Suite for piano, 1989; Santa Fe Suite for harp, 1989; Summer Dances, for Brass Quintet, 1990; *choral and vocal compositions:* Wassail Carol, 1965; Three Medieval Lyrics, 1966; St Teilo, 1970; Ave Rex, 1970; Sir Christemas, 1970; Culhwch and Olwen, 1971; A Babe is born, 1971; A Vision of Time and Eternity (for contralto and piano), 1974; Ceremony after a fire raid, 1975; This Worlde's Joie, 1975; Carmen Paschale, 1976; Elegy for a Prince (for baritone and orch.), 1976; The Fields of Praise (for tenor and piano), 1977; A Royal Garland, 1978; Nativity Carol, 1978; A May Magnificat, 1980; Shakespeare Songs, 1980; Songs of William Blake (for mezzo-soprano and orch.), 1980; Rex Gloriae (four Latin motets), 1981; Te Deum, for soli, chorus and orchestra (commnd for centenary of the Chapel at Haddo House), 1981; Lux Aeterna, for soli, chorus and orchestra (commnd for Three Choirs Fest.), 1982; Salvator Mundi: a carol sequence, 1983; Angelus, 1984; Four Welsh Folk Songs, 1984; The Echoing Green, 1985; O Aula Nobilis (for opening of Orangery at Westonbirt Sch. by the Prince and Princess of Wales), 1985; Veni Sancte Spiritus (Hereford Three Choirs Fest.), 1985; Gogoneddawg Arglwydd (for Nat. Youth Choir of Wales), 1985; Riddles, 1987; Jonah (a musical morality), 1988; Sweet was the Song, 1988; Learsongs, 1989; World's Fire (poems of Gerard Manley Hopkins) for soprano and baritone soli, SATB chorus and orchestra, 1989; Bell Carol, 1989; Yr Arglwydd yw fy Mugail (male voices and piano), 1989; *organ compositions:* Variations on a Hymn Tune, 1963; Partita, 1963; Postlude, 1964; Processional, 1965; Chorale, 1967; Toccata giocosa, 1968; Jubilate, 1975; Fantasy, 1978; Canzonetta, 1978; Antiphonies, 1982; Organ Concerto, 1984; Berceuse, 1985; Recessional, 1986; A Mathias Organ Album, 1986; Fanfare for organ, 1987; Fenestra, 1989; Carillon, 1989; *anthems and church music:* O Sing unto the Lord, 1965; Make a joyful noise, 1965; Festival Te Deum, 1965; Communion Service in C, 1968; Psalm 150, 1969; Lift up your heads, 1970; O Salutaris Hostia, 1972; Gloria, 1972; Magnificat and Nunc Dimittis, 1973; Alleluya Psallat, 1974; Missa Brevis, 1974; Communion Service (Series III), 1976; Arise, shine, 1978; Let the people praise thee, O God (anthem composed for the wedding of the Prince and Princess of Wales), 1981; Praise ye the Lord, 1982; All Wisdom is from the Lord, 1982; Except the Lord build the House, 1983; A Grace, 1983; Jubilate Deo, 1983; O how amiable, 1983; Tantum ergo, 1984; Let us now praise famous men, 1984; Alleluia! Christ is risen, 1984; Missa Aedis Christi—in memoriam William Walton, 1984; Salve Regina, 1986; O clap your hands, 1986; Let all the world in every corner sing, 1987; Rejoice in the Lord, 1987; I will lift up mine eyes unto the hills, 1987; Cantate Domino, 1987; Thus saith God the Lord—An Orkney anthem, 1987; O Lord our Lord, 1987; As truly as God is our Father, 1987; The Heavens Declare, 1988; I Will Celebrate, 1989; Praise is due to you, O God, 1989; The Doctrine of Wisdom, 1989; Lord, Thou hast been our dwelling place, 1990; In the Time appointed, 1990; Hodie Christus natus est, 1990; In Excelsis Gloria, 1992; Magnificat and Nunc Dimittis (St David's Service), 1992; Come, Holy Ghost, 1992; *opera:* The Servants (libretto by Iris Murdoch), 1980. *Address:* Y Graigwen, Cadnant Road, Menai Bridge, Anglesey, Gwynedd LL59 5NG. *T:* Menai Bridge (0248) 712392. *Club:* Athenæum. *Died 29 July 1992.*

MATILAL, Prof. Bimal Krishna, Padma Bhushan (India), 1990; PhD; Spalding Professor of Eastern Religions and Ethics, University of Oxford, since 1976; Fellow, All Souls College, since 1976; *b* 1 June 1935; *s* of Hare Krishna Matilal and Parimal Matilal; *m* 1958, Karabi

Chatterjee; one *s* one *d. Educ:* Univ. of Calcutta (BA Hons 1954, MA 1956); Harvard Univ. (AM 1963, PhD 1965). Lectr, Sanskrit Coll., Calcutta Univ., 1957–65; Asst Prof., Univ. of Toronto, 1965–67, Associate Prof., 1967–71; Associate Prof., Univ. of Pennsylvania, 1969–70; Vis. Sen. Fellow, SOAS, Univ. of London, 1971–72; Prof., Univ. of Toronto, 1971–77. Visiting Professor: Univ. of California, Berkeley, 1979; Victoria Univ. of Wellington, NZ, 1980; Chicago Univ., 1983; Vis. Fellow, Harvard Univ., 1982 and 1988; Fellow, Japan Soc. for Promotion of Scis, 1984; Sacklar Vis. Fellow, Tel-Aviv Univ., 1985. Mem., Wolfson Coll., Oxford, 1984–. Founder-Editor, Jl of Indian Philosophy, 1971–. *Publications:* The Navya-nyāya Doctrine of Negation, 1968; Epistemology, Logic and Grammar in Indian Philosophical Analysis, 1971; The Logical Illumination of Indian Mysticism, 1977; The Central Philosophy of Jainism, 1981; Logical and Ethical Issues in Indian Religions, 1982; (ed) Analytical Philosophy in Comparative Perspective, 1985; Logic, Language and Reality, 1985; Perception, 1986; Confrontation of Culture, 1988; (ed) Moral Dilemmas in the Mahabharata, 1989; The Word and the World, 1990; contrib. Nyāya-Vaiśesika Literature, Indian and Comparative Philosophy. *Recreation:* gardening. *Address:* Oriental Institute, University of Oxford, Oxford.
Died 8 June 1991.

MATTHEWS, Baron *cr* 1980 (Life Peer), of Southgate in the London Borough of Enfield; **Victor Collin Matthews;** Trafalgar House plc: Deputy Chairman, 1973–85; Group Managing Director, 1968–77; Group Chief Executive, 1977–83; *b* 5 Dec. 1919; *s* of A. and J. Matthews; *m* 1942, Joyce Geraldine (*née* Pilbeam) (*d* 1995); one *s. Educ:* Highbury. Served RNVR, 1939–45. Chairman: Trafalgar House Develt Hldgs, 1970–83; Cunard Steam-Ship Co., 1971–83; Ritz Hotel (London), 1976–83; Trafalgar House Construction Hldgs, 1977–83; Express Newspapers plc, 1977–85 (Chief Exec., 1977–82); Cunard Cruise Ships, 1978–83; Cunard Line, 1978–83; Evening Standard Co. Ltd, 1980–85; Fleet Publishing Internat. Hldgs Ltd, 1978–82; Fleet Hldgs, 1982–85; (non-exec.) Ellerman Hldgs, 1983–86; Director: Associated Container Transportation (Australia) Ltd, 1972–83; Cunard Crusader World Travel Ltd, 1974–85; Racecourse Holdings Trust Ltd, 1977–85; Associated Communications Corp. plc, 1977–82; Goldquill Ltd, 1979–83; Darchart Ltd, 1980–83; Garmaine Ltd, 1980–83. FRSA; CMgt. *Recreations:* racehorse breeder/owner, cricket, golf. *Address:* Waverley Farm, Mont Arthur, St Brelades, Jersey, Channel Islands. *Clubs:* MCC, Royal Automobile; Royal & Ancient Golf.
Died 5 Dec. 1995.

MATTHEWS, Horatio Keith, CMG 1963; MBE 1946; JP; HM Diplomatic Service, 1948–74; *b* 4 April 1917; *s* of late Horatio Matthews, MD and Ruth Matthews (*née* McCurry); *m* 1940, Jean Andrée Batten; two *d. Educ:* Epsom Coll.; Gonville and Caius Coll., Cambridge. Entered Indian Civil Service, 1940, and served in Madras Presidency until 1947; appointed to Foreign Service, 1948; Lisbon, 1949; Bucharest, 1951; Foreign Office, 1953; Imperial Defence Coll., 1955; Political Office with Middle East Forces, Cyprus, 1956; Counsellor, UK High Commission, Canberra, 1959; Political Adviser to GOC Berlin, 1961; Corps of Inspectors, Diplomatic Service, 1964; Minister, Moscow, 1966–67; High Commissioner in Ghana, 1968–70; UN Under-Sec.-Gen. for Admin and Management, 1971–72; Asst Under-Sec. of State, MoD (on secondment), 1973–74. Mem., Bd of Visitors, HM Prison, Albany, 1976–82. JP IoW 1975. *Address:* Elm House, Bembridge, IoW PO35 5UA. *T:* Isle of Wight (01983) 872327.
Died 31 Dec. 1994.

MATTHEWS, Maj.-Gen. Michael, CB 1984; DL; Engineer in Chief (Army), 1983–85; Secretary, Council of TAVR

Associations, since 1986; *b* 22 April 1930; *s* of late W. Matthews and of M. H. Matthews; *m* 1955, Elspeth Rosemary, *d* of late Lt-Col Sir John Maclure, 3rd Bt, OBE, and Lady Maclure; two *s* two *d. Educ:* King's Coll., Taunton, Somerset. CompICE, 1984; FBIM. rcds, psc. Commissioned, Royal Engineers, 1951; served overseas, Egypt, Cyprus, Jordan, Kenya, Aden and BAOR; DAA&QMG HQ 24 Inf. Bde, Kenya, 1962–65; OC, Indep. Para Sqn RE, UK and Aden, 1965–67; GSO1 (DS) Staff College, Camberley, 1968–70; CO 35 Engr Regt, BAOR, 1970–72; Col GS Ops, Exercise Planning Staff and Trg, HQ BAOR, 1972–74; CCRE, HQ1 (BR) Corps, BAOR, 1974–76; RCDS 1977; DQMG HQ BAOR, 1978–80; Dir of Personal Services (Army), 1980–83. Col Comdt, RE, 1985–; Hon. Colonel: Southampton Univ. OTC, 1985–; 131 Indep. Commando Sqn RE (V), 1985–92. DL Hants, 1991. *Recreations:* Rugby, cricket, hockey, hang gliding. *Address:* c/o Lloyds Bank, Chagford, Newton Abbot, Devon. *Clubs:* Army and Navy, MCC; British Sportsman's.
Died 7 Jan. 1993.

MATTHEWS, Prof. Richard Ellis Ford, ONZ 1988; ScD; FRS 1974; FRSNZ; FNZIC; Professor of Microbiology, Department of Cell Biology, University of Auckland, New Zealand, 1962–86, then Emeritus; *b* Hamilton, NZ, 20 Nov. 1921; *s* of Gerald Wilfrid Matthews and Ruby Miriam (*née* Crawford); *m* 1950, Lois Ann Bayley; three *s* one *d. Educ:* Mt Albert Grammar Sch.; Auckland University Coll.; Univ. of Cambridge. MSc (NZ), PhD, ScD (Cantab). Postdoctoral Research Fellow, Univ. of Wisconsin, 1949. Plant Diseases Div., DSIR, Auckland, NZ: Mycologist, 1950–53; Sen. Mycologist, 1954–55; (on leave from DSIR as a visiting worker at ARC Virus Research Unit, Molteno Inst., Cambridge, 1952–56); Sen. Principal Scientific Officer, DSIR, 1956–61; Head of Dept of Cell Biology, Univ. of Auckland, 1962–77, 1983–85. Pres., Internat. Cttee for Taxonomy of Viruses, 1975–81. *Publications:* Plant Virus Serology, 1957; Plant Virology, 1970, 3rd edn 1991; Fundamentals of Plant Virology, 1992; over 130 original papers in scientific jls. *Recreations:* gardening, sea fishing, bee keeping. *Address:* 1019 Beach Road, Torbay, Auckland 1310, New Zealand. *T:* Auckland (9) 4737709; (summer residence) RD4 Hikurangi. *T:* (9) 4037403.
Died 19 Feb. 1995.

MATTHEWS, Ronald Sydney, CB 1978; Deputy Secretary, Department of Health and Social Security, 1976–81; *b* 26 July 1922; *s* of George and Louisa Matthews; *m* 1945, Eleanor Bronwen Shaw (*d* 1989); one *s* one *d. Educ:* Kingsbury County School. RAF, 1940–46. Clerical Officer, Min. of Health, 1939; Principal 1959; Private Sec. to Minister of Health, 1967–68; Private Sec. to Sec. of State for Social Services, 1968–69; Asst Sec. 1968; Under-Sec., DHSS, 1973–76. *Recreations:* walking, gardening, reading. *Address:* 4 Saxon Rise, Winterborne Stickland, Blandford Forum, Dorset DT11 0PQ.
Died 25 May 1995.

MATTHEWS, Thomas Stanley; journalist; *b* 16 Jan. 1901; *s* of late Rt Rev. Paul Matthews, sometime Bishop of New Jersey, and Elsie Procter; *m* 1st, 1925, Juliana Stevens Cuyler (*d* 1949); four *s*; 2nd, 1954, Martha Gellhorn (marr. diss.); 3rd, 1964, Pamela, *widow* of Lt-Col V. Peniakoff. *Educ:* Park Hill, Lyndhurst, Hants; Shattuck Sch. (Minn); St Paul's Sch. (Concord, NH); Princeton Univ.; New Coll., Oxford (MA; Hon. Fellow, 1986). Doctor of Humane Letters, Kenyon Coll., Ohio; Doctor of Letters, Rollins Coll., Florida. Editorial staff: The New Republic, 1925–29; Time, 1929; Exec. Editor, Time, 1942, Managing Editor, 1943–50, Editor, 1950–53. *Publications:* To the Gallows I Must Go, 1931; The Moon's No Fool, 1934; The Sugar Pill, 1957; Name and Address (autobiog.), 1960; O My America!, 1962; The Worst Unsaid (verse), 1962; Why So Gloomy? (verse), 1966; Great Tom: notes towards the

Definition of T. S. Eliot, 1974; Jacks or Better, 1977 (Under the Influence, UK, 1979); Journal to the End of the Day, 1979; Cut Out the Poetry, 1982; Joking Apart, 1983; Tell Me About It, 1985; Angels Unawares, 1985; No Problem—OK?, 1987; Mind Your Head!, 1988. *Address:* Cavendish Hall, Cavendish, Suffolk. *T:* Clare (0787) 296. *Clubs:* Athenæum, Buck's; Princeton (New York); Nassau (Princeton, NJ). *Died 4 Jan. 1991.*

MATTHEWS, Rt Rev. Timothy John; BA, DCL; LST, STh; Chaplain Emeritus, Bishop's College School; *b* 8 July 1907; *s* of John Colmworth Matthews and Ethel May Burns; *m* 1933, Mary Eileen, *d* of Dr T. E. Montgomery; four *s* one *d. Educ:* Bishop's Univ., Lennoxville. Deacon 1932, priest 1933, Edmonton; Vicar of Viking, 1933–37; Incumbent of Edson, 1937–40; Rector of Coaticook, 1940–44; Lake St John, 1944–52; Rector and Archdeacon of Gaspé, 1952–57; Rector of Lennoxville, 1957–71; Archdeacon of St Francis, 1957–71; Bishop of Quebec, 1971–77. Hon. Visitor, Bishops Univ. *Address:* 23 High Street, Lennoxville, PQ J1M 1E6, Canada. *Clubs:* St George's (Sherbrooke); Hole-in-One, Lennoxville Golf, Milby Golf; Lennoxville Curling.

Died 12 Sept. 1991.

MAUDE OF STRATFORD-UPON-AVON, Baron *cr* 1983 (Life Peer), of Stratford-upon-Avon in the county of Warwickshire; **Angus Edmund Upton Maude,** Kt 1981; TD; PC 1979; author and journalist; *b* 8 Sept. 1912; *o c* of late Col Alan Hamer Maude, CMG, DSO, TD, and Dorothy Maude (*née* Upton); *m* 1946, Barbara Elizabeth Earnshaw, *o d* of late John Earnshaw Sutcliffe, Bushey; one *s* two *d* (and one *s* decd). *Educ:* Rugby Sch. (Scholar); Oriel Coll., Oxford (MA). Financial journalist, 1933–39: The Times, 1933–34; Daily Mail, 1935–39. Commissioned in RASC (TA), May 1939; served in RASC, 1939–45, at home and in North Africa (POW, Jan. 1942–May 1945); Major 56th (London) Armd Divl Column RASC (TA), 1947–51. Dep. Dir of PEP, 1948–50; Dir, Cons. Political Centre, 1951–55; Editor, Sydney Morning Herald, 1958–61. MP (C) Ealing (South), 1950–57, (Ind. C), 1957–58, (C) Stratford-upon-Avon, Aug. 1963–1983; a Dep. Chm., Cons. Party, 1975–79 (Chm. Res. Dept, 1975–79); Paymaster Gen., 1979–81. Contested S Dorset, by-election, Nov. 1962. *Publications:* (with Roy Lewis) The English Middle Classes, 1949; Professional People, 1952; (with Enoch Powell) Biography of a Nation, 1955; Good Learning, 1964; South Asia, 1966; The Common Problem, 1969. *Address:* Old Farm, South Newington, near Banbury, Oxon. *Club:* Carlton.

Died 9 Nov. 1993.

MAVOR, Air Marshal Sir Leslie (Deane), KCB 1970 (CB 1964); AFC 1942; DL; FRAeS; *b* 18 Jan. 1916; *s* of William David Mavor, Edinburgh; *m* 1947, June Lilian Blackburn; four *s. Educ:* Aberdeen Grammar Sch. Commissioned RAF 1937; Dir of Air Staff Briefing, Air Ministry, 1961–64; AOC, No 38 Group, 1964–66; Asst CAS (Policy), 1966–69; AOC-in-C, RAF Training Comd, 1969–72; retd Jan. 1973. Principal, Home Office Home Defence Coll., 1973–80; Co-ordinator of Voluntary Effort in Civil Defence, 1981–84. DL N Yorks, 1976. *Recreations:* golf, fishing, shooting, gliding. *Address:* Barlaston House, Alne, York YO6 2HR. *Clubs:* Royal Air Force; Yorkshire. *Died 2 Oct. 1991.*

MAXWELL, Hon. Lord; Peter Maxwell; a Senator of the College of Justice in Scotland, 1973–88; *b* 21 May 1919; *s* of late Comdr and Mrs Herries Maxwell, Munches, Dalbeattie, Kirkcudbrightshire; *m* 1941, Alison Susan Readman; one *s* two *d* (and one *s* decd). *Educ:* Wellington Coll.; Balliol Coll., Oxford; Edinburgh Univ. Served Argyll and Sutherland Highlanders, and late RA, 1939–46. Called to Scottish Bar, 1951; QC (Scotland) 1961; Sheriff-Principal of Dumfries and Galloway, 1970–73. Mem.,

Royal Commn on Legal Services in Scotland, 1976–80; Chm., Scottish Law Commn, 1981–88. *Address:* 19 Oswald Road, Edinburgh EH9 2HE. *T:* 031–667 7444.

Died 2 Jan. 1994.

MAXWELL, Col (Arthur) Terence, TD; *b* 19 Jan. 1905; *s* of late Brig.-Gen. Sir Arthur Maxwell, KCB, CMG, DSO, and Eva Jones; *m* 1935, Beatrice Diane, *d* of late Rt Hon. Sir J. Austen Chamberlain, KG, PC, MP, and Ivy Muriel Dundas, GBE; two *s* one *d. Educ:* Rugby; Trinity Coll., Oxford, MA. Travelled in Africa as James Whitehead travelling student, 1926–27, and in South America; Barrister-at-Law, 1929. Served 7th City of London Regt Post Office Rifles, 1923–35; Captain TA Reserve of Officers, 1935. Capt. KRRC 1940; Staff Coll., 1941; Leader Ministry of Economic Warfare Mission to the Middle East with rank of Counsellor, 1941–42; Col General Staff, AFHQ, 1943–44; Deputy Chief, Military Government Section; attached SHAEF etc. British Rep., Investments Cttee, ILO, 1937–77. A Managing Dir, Glyn, Mills & Co., bankers, until 1945; Chm., Powers-Samas Accounting Machines Ltd, 1952–70; Dep. Chm., International Computers and Tabulators Ltd, 1959–67, Chm., 1967–68; Chm., International Computers (Holdings) Ltd, 1968, Dep. Chm. 1969; Chm. Computer Leasings Ltd, 1963–69; Director: Vickers Ltd, 1934–75; Aust. and NZ Banking Group Ltd, and its predecessors, 1935–76; Steel Co. of Wales, 1948–67; English Steel Corp. Ltd, 1954–67. Vice-Chm. Cttee on Rural Bus Services (1959), Ministry of Transport; Vice-Pres. and Treas. City and Guilds of London Institute, 1959–67; Mem. Delegacy of City and Guilds Coll., Imperial Coll., University of London, 1959–64. *Recreation:* forestry. *Address:* Roveries Hall, Bishop's Castle, Shropshire. *T:* Bishop's Castle (0588) 638402; Flat 7, 52 Onslow Square, SW7. *T:* 071–589 0321. *Club:* Carlton.

Died 27 June 1991.

MAXWELL, (Ian) Robert, MC 1945; Chairman, Mirror Group Newspapers Ltd (publisher of Daily Mirror, Daily Record, Sunday Mail, Sunday Mirror, The People, Sporting Life, Sporting Life Weekender, since 1984); Publisher and Editor in Chief, The European, since 1990; Founder and Publisher, Pergamon Press, Oxford, New York and Paris, 1949–91; Publisher: Magyar Hirlap; Moscow News (English edition), since 1988; Chairman and Chief Executive: Maxwell Communication Corporation plc (formerly The British Printing & Communication Corporation plc), since 1981; Macmillan Inc., since 1988; Chairman: Mirror Colour Print Ltd (formerly British Newspaper Printing Corporation plc), since 1983; British Cable Services Ltd (Rediffusion Cablevision), since 1984; Pergamon Media Trust plc since 1986; Maxwell Pergamon Publishing Corporation plc (formerly Pergamon BPCC Publishing Corporation plc), since 1986; MTV Europe, since 1987; Maxwell Communication Corporation Inc., NY, since 1987; Macmillan Foundation, since 1988; Pergamon AGB plc (formerly Hollis plc), since 1988 (Director, since 1982); Maxwell Macmillan Pergamon International Publishing; Berlitz International Inc., since 1988; Scitex Corporation Ltd, Israel, since 1988; Thomas Cook Travel Inc., since 1989; Official Airline Guides Inc., since 1989; President, State of Israel Bonds (UK), since 1988; *b* 10 June 1923; named Jan Ludvik Hoch; *s* of Michael and Ann Hoch; *m* 1945, Elisabeth (*née* Meynard); three *s* four *d* (and one *s* one *d* decd). *Educ:* self-educated. Served War of 1939–45 (MC). In German Sect. of Foreign Office (Head of Press Sect., Berlin), 1945–47. Chm., Robert Maxwell & Co. Ltd, 1948–86; Director: SelecTV, 1982–; Central Television plc, 1983–; The Solicitors' Law Stationery Soc. plc, 1985–; Mirrorvision, 1985–; Clyde Cablevision Ltd, 1985–; Philip Hill Investment Trust, 1986–; Reuters Holdings plc, 1986–; TF1, 1987–; Maxwell Media, Paris,

1987–; Maxwell Business Communications Gp Ltd, 1989–; Maxwell Consumer Publishing & Communications Ltd, 1989–. Chm., Commonwealth Games (Scotland 1986) Ltd, 1986. Mem. Council, Newspaper Publishers' Assoc., 1984–. MP (Lab) Buckingham, 1964–70. Chm., Labour Nat. Fund Raising Foundn, 1960–69; Chm., Labour Working Party on Science, Govt and Industry, 1963–64; Mem., Council of Europe (Vice-Chm., Cttee on Science and Technology), 1968. Contested (Lab) Buckingham, Feb. and Oct. 1974. Treasurer, The Round House Trust Ltd (formerly Centre 42), 1965–83; Chairman: GB-Sasakawa Foundn, 1985–; Nat. AIDS Trust fundraising gp, 1987–; Trustee, Internat. Centre for Child Studies. Chairman: Oxford Utd FC plc, 1982–87; Derby County FC, 1987–. Kennedy Fellow, Harvard Univ., 1971. Hon. Mem., Acad. of Astronautics, 1974; Member: Club of Rome, 1979– (Exec. Dir, British Gp); Senate, Leeds Univ., 1986–; Bd of Trustees, Polytech. Univ. of NY, 1987–. FIC 1988. Co-produced films: Mozart's Don Giovanni, Salzburg Festival, 1954; Bolshoi Ballet, 1957; Swan Lake, 1968; Producer, DODO the Kid from Outer Space (children's TV series), 1968. Hon. DSc Moscow State Univ., 1983; Hon. Dr of Science, Polytech. Univ. of NY, 1985; Hon. LLD Aberdeen 1988; Dr *hc*: Adama Mickiewicza Univ., 1989; Univ. du Québec à Trois-Rivières, 1989; Hon. Dr of Laws, Temple Univ., Pa, 1989; Hon. Dr, Bar-Ilan, Israel, 1989; Hon. DLitt Plymouth, 1989. Prism Award, NY Univ. Centre for Graphic Arts Management and Technology, 1989; World of Difference Award, Anti-Defamation League, NY, 1989. Royal Swedish Order of Polar Star (Officer 1st class), 1983; Bulgarian People's Republic Order Stara Planina (1st class), 1983; Comdr, Order of Merit with Star, Polish People's Republic, 1986; Order of the White Rose (1st class) (Finland), 1988; Officier de l'Ordre des Arts et des Lettres (France), 1989. Gen. Editor, Leaders of the World series, 1980–. *Publications*: The Economics of Nuclear Power, 1965; Public Sector Purchasing, 1968; (jt author) Man Alive, 1968. *Recreations*: chess, football. *Address*: Holborn Circus, EC1A 1DQ. *T*: 071–353 0246; Headington Hill Hall, Oxford OX3 0BB. *T*: Oxford (0865) 64881; 866 Third Avenue, New York, NY 10022, USA. *T*: 212–702 2000. *Died 5 Nov. 1991.*

MAXWELL, Patrick; solicitor; *b* 12 March 1909; *e s* of late Alderman Patrick Maxwell, Solicitor, Londonderry; *m* 1st, 1935 (wife *d* 1962); two *d*; 2nd, 1969. *Educ*: Convent of Mercy, Artillery Street, Londonderry; Christian Brothers Sch., Brow-of-the-Hill, Londonderry; St Columb's Coll., Londonderry. Solicitor, 1932; entered Londonderry Corporation as Councillor, 1934; resigned as protest against re-distribution scheme, 1937; Leader of Anti-Partition Party in Londonderry Corporation from 1938; did not seek re-election, 1946; first Chairman of Irish Union Association, 1936; Chairman of Derry Catholic Registration Association, 1934–52. MP (N) Foyle Division of Londonderry City, Northern Ireland Parliament, 1937–53. Resident Magistrate, 1968–80. President: Law Society of Northern Ireland, 1967–68 (Vice-Pres., 1966–67); Londonderry Rotary Club, 1958–59; Chm. Rotary in Ireland, 1963–64; Mem., Council, International Bar Association, 1968. *Died 15 Dec. 1991.*

MAXWELL, Peter; *see* Maxwell, Hon. Lord.

MAXWELL, Robert; *see* Maxwell, I. R.

MAXWELL, Sir Robert (Hugh), KBE 1961 (OBE 1942); *b* 2 Jan. 1906; *s* of William Robert and Nancy Dockett Maxwell; *m* 1935, Mary Courtney Jewell; two *s*. Comdr of Order of George I of Greece, 1961; Order of Merit of Syria. *Address*: Court Hay, Charlton Adam, Som TA11 7AS. *Died 19 Feb. 1994.*

MAXWELL, Col Terence; *see* Maxwell, Col A. T.

MAY, Harry Blight, MD, FRCP; retired; Director of Clinical Laboratories, The London Hospital, 1946–74; Consultant Pathologist to Royal Navy, 1950–74; *b* 12 Nov. 1908; *s* of John and Isobel May, Plymouth, Devon; *m* 1949, Dorothy Quartermaine; no *c*. *Educ*: Devonport; St John's Coll., Cambridge (Scholar). 1st cl. Natural Science Tripos, 1929. Postgraduate study Harvard Medical Sch., 1936. Dean, Faculty of Medicine, Univ. of London, 1960–64; Dean of Med. and Dental Sch., The London Hosp. Med. Coll., 1953–68; Mem. Senate, Univ. of London; Mem. Governing Body, Royal Veterinary Coll.; Examiner, Royal College of Physicians of London and Univ. of Oxford. *Publications*: Clinical Pathology (6th edn), 1951; papers on antibacterial agents and other medical subjects. *Address*: 3 Littlemead, Littleworth Road, Esher, Surrey KT10 9PE. *T*: Esher (0372) 62394.
Died 21 June 1991.

MAY, John; Councillor, Tyne and Wear County Council, 1974–86 (Vice-Chairman, 1978–79, Chairman, 1979–80); *b* 24 May 1912; *s* of William and Sara May; *m* 1939, Mary Peacock (*d* 1980); two *s*. *Educ*: Holystone Council Sch., Newcastle upon Tyne. Councillor: Seaton Valley UDC, 1949–74 (Chm., 1963–64 and 1972–73); Northumberland CC, 1970–74; Vice-Chm., 1977–80, Chm., 1980–86, Transport Cttee, Tyne and Wear County Council. *Address*: 12 Cheviot View, Cheviot View Sheltered Home, West Street, West Allotments, North Tyneside. *Died 5 Feb. 1992.*

MAY, Peter Barker Howard, CBE 1981; Lloyd's Insurance Broker since 1953; Underwriting Member of Lloyd's, 1962; Consultant, Willis Corroon Ltd, since 1990; *b* 31 Dec. 1929; *m* 1959, Virginia, *er d* of A. H. H. Gilligan; four *d*. *Educ*: Charterhouse; Pembroke Coll., Cambridge (MA). Cambridge cricket and football XIs v Oxford, 1950, 1951 and 1952; Surrey County Cricket Cap, 1950; played cricket for England v S Africa 1951, v India 1952, v Australia 1953, v W Indies 1953, v Pakistan, Australia and New Zealand 1954; captained England 41 times, incl. v S Africa, 1955, v Australia 1956, v S Africa 1956–57, v W Indies, 1957, v New Zealand 1958, v Australia, 1958–59, v India, 1959, v West Indies, 1959–60, v Australia, 1961. Chm., England Cricket Selection Cttee, 1982–88. *Publications*: Peter May's Book of Cricket, 1956; A Game Enjoyed, 1985. *Recreations*: golf, eventing. *Address*: Hatch House, Liphook, Hants GU30 7EL. *Clubs*: MCC (Pres., 1980–81), Surrey County Cricket.
Died 27 Dec. 1994.

MAYALL, Sir (Alexander) Lees, KCVO 1972 (CVO 1965); CMG 1964; HM Diplomatic Service, retired; Ambassador to Venezuela, 1972–75; *b* 14 Sept. 1915; *s* of late Alexander Mayall, Bealings End, Woodbridge, Suffolk, and Isobel, *d* of F. J. R. Hendy; *m* 1st, 1940, Renée Eileen Burn (marr. diss., 1947); one *d*; 2nd, 1947, Hon. Mary Hermione Ormsby Gore, *e d* of 4th Baron Harlech, KG, GCMG, PC; one *s* two *d*. *Educ*: Eton; Trinity Coll., Oxford (MA). Entered HM Diplomatic Service, 1939; served with armed forces, 1940; transferred to HM Legation, Berne, 1940–44; First Secretary, HM Embassy, Cairo, 1947–49, Paris, 1952–54; Counsellor, HM Embassy: Tokyo, 1958–61; Lisbon, 1961–64; Addis Ababa, 1964–65; Vice-Marshal of the Diplomatic Corps and Head of Protocol and Conference Dept, FCO, 1965–72. Pres., Bath Preservation Trust, 1986–. *Publication*: Fireflies in Amber, 1989. *Recreations*: travelling, reading. *Address*: Sturford Mead, Warminster, Wilts BA12 7QT. *T*: Westbury (0373) 832219. *Club*: Travellers'. *Died 27 Dec. 1992.*

MAYER BROWN, Prof. Howard; *see* Brown.

MAYO, Dame Eileen (Rosemary), DBE 1994; artist, author, printmaker and painter; *b* Norwich, 11 Sept. 1906;

m 1936, Richard Gainsborough (marr. diss. 1952). *Educ:* Clifton High School; Slade School of Art. Exhibited Royal Academy, London Group, United Society of Artists, Festival of Britain, etc; works acquired by British Council, British Museum, Victoria and Albert Museum, Contemporary Art Society, and public galleries in UK, USA, Australia and NZ. Designer of Australian mammals series of postage stamps, 1959–62, and Barrier Reef series, 1966; four Cook Bicentenary stamps, NZ, 1969, and other NZ stamps, 1970–78, and three for Christmas 1985. *Publications:* The Story of Living Things; Shells and How they Live; Animals on the Farm, etc. *Recreations:* printmaking, gardening. *Died 4 Jan. 1994.*

MEADE, Sir Geoffrey; *see* Meade, Sir R. G. A.

MEADE, James Edward, CB 1947; FBA 1951; MA Oxon, MA Cantab; Hon. Dr, Universities of Basel, Bath, East Anglia, Essex, Glasgow, Hull, Oxford and Athens; Hon. Fellow: London School of Economics; Oriel College, Oxford; Hertford College, Oxford; Christ's College, Cambridge; Trinity College, Cambridge; *b* 23 June 1907; *s* of Charles Hippisley Meade and Kathleen Cotton-Stapleton; *m* 1933, Elizabeth Margaret, *d* of Alexander Cowan Wilson; one *s* three *d. Educ:* Malvern Coll.; Oriel Coll., Oxford; Trinity Coll., Cambridge. 1st Class Hon. Mods 1928; 1st Class Philosophy, Politics, and Economics, 1930. Fellow and Lecturer in Economics, 1930–37, and Bursar, 1934–37, Hertford Coll., Oxford; Mem. Economic Section of League of Nations, Geneva, 1938–40. Economic Asst (1940–45), and Dir (1946–47), Economic Section Cabinet Offices. Prof. of Commerce, with special reference to International Trade, London Sch. of Economics, 1947–57; Prof. of Political Economy, Cambridge, 1957–68; Nuffield Res. Fellow, 1969–74, and Fellow, Christ's Coll., Cambridge, 1957–74. Member: Coun. of Royal Economic Society, 1945–62 (Pres., 1964–66, Vice-Pres., 1966–); Council of Eugenics Soc., 1962–68 (Treasurer 1963–67). Visiting Prof., Australian National Univ., 1956. Pres. Section F, British Assoc. for the Advancement of Science, 1957; Chm. Economic Survey Mission, Mauritius, 1960. Trustee of Urwick, Orr and Partners Ltd, 1958–76. Governor: Nat. Inst. of Economic and Social Research, 1947–; LSE, 1960–74; Malvern Coll., 1972–. Chm., Cttee of Inst. for Fiscal Studies, 1975–77 (producing report on The Structure and Reform of Direct Taxation, 1978). Hon. Mem., Amer. Economic Assoc., 1962; For. Hon. Member: Soc. Royale d'Econ. Politique de Belgique, 1958; Amer. Acad. of Arts and Sciences, 1966; For. Associate, Nat. Acad. of Sciences, USA, 1981. (Jtly) Nobel Prize for Economics, 1977. *Publications:* Public Works in their International Aspect, 1933; The Rate of Interest in a Progressive State, 1933; Economic Analysis and Policy, 1936; Consumers' Credits and Unemployment, 1937; League of Nations' World Economic Surveys for 1937–38 and 1938–39; The Economic Basis of a Durable Peace, 1940; (with Richard Stone) National Income and Expenditure, 1944; Planning and the Price Mechanism, 1948; The Theory of International Economic Policy, Vol. I, 1951, Vol. II, 1955; A Geometry of International Trade, 1952; Problems of Economic Union, 1953; The Theory of Customs Unions, 1955; The Control of Inflation, 1958; A Neo-Classical Theory of Economic Growth, 1960; Three Case Studies in European Economic Union, 1962 (Joint Author); Efficiency, Equality, and the Ownership of Property, 1964; Principles of Political Economy, Vol. 1, The Stationary Economy, 1965, Vol. 2, The Growing Economy, 1968, Vol. 3, The Controlled Economy, 1972, Vol. 4, The Just Economy, 1976; The Theory of Indicative Planning, 1970; The Theory of Externalities, 1973; The Intelligent Radical's Guide to Economic Policy, 1975; Stagflation, vol. 1, Wage Fixing, 1982, vol. 2, (jtly) Demand Management, 1983; Alternative Systems of Business

Organisation and of Workers' Remuneration, 1986; Collected Papers, vols 1, 2, 3, 1988, vol. 4, 1989; (jtly) Macroeconomic Policy: inflation, wealth and the exchange rate, 1989; Agathotopia: the economics of partnership, 1989; Liberty, Equality and Efficiency, 1993; Full Employment Regained?, 1995. *Address:* 40 High Street, Little Shelford, Cambridge CB2 5ES. *T:* Cambridge (01223) 842491. *Died 22 Dec. 1995.*

MEADE, Sir (Richard) Geoffrey (Austin), KBE 1963; CMG 1953; CVO 1961; HM Diplomatic Service, retired; *b* 8 March 1902; *s* of late Austin Meade, MA; *m* 1929, Elizabeth Ord, MA Oxon, 2nd *d* of late G. J. Scott, JP; three *d* (one *s* decd). *Educ:* Ecole Alsacienne, Paris; Balliol Coll., Oxford. BA 1925. Entered Consular Service, 1925; served at Tangier, 1927, Salonica, 1929, Aleppo, 1930, Athens, 1931, Salonica, 1933, Tangier, 1935, Valencia, 1939, Crete, 1940, FO, 1941, Dakar, 1943, Tetuan, 1943, Casablanca, 1945, Istanbul, 1947; idc, 1950; Marseilles, 1951; Tangier, 1956; Düsseldorf, 1957; Milan, 1958–62; retired, 1962. *Address:* Baker's Close, 104 Lower Radley, Abingdon, Oxon OX14 3BA. *T:* Abingdon (0235) 521327. *Died 2 Oct. 1992.*

MEADOWS, Swithin Pinder, MD, BSc, FRCP; Consulting Physician: Westminster Hospital; National Hospital, Queen Square; Moorfields Eye Hospital; *b* 18 April 1902; *er s* of late Thomas and Sophia Florence Meadows; *m* 1934, Doris Steward Noble; two *s* two *d. Educ:* Wigan Grammar Sch.; University of Liverpool; St Thomas' Hosp. Kanthack Medal in Pathology; Owen T. Williams Prize. House Physician and House Surgeon, Liverpool Royal Infirmary; House Physician, Royal Liverpool Children's Hospital; Medical Registrar and Tutor, St Thomas' Hosp.; RMO National Hosp., Queen Square; Medical First Asst, London Hosp.; Examiner in Neurology and Medicine, University of London; Hosp. Visitor, King Edward's Hosp. Fund for London; Mem., Assoc. of British Neurologists; Hon. Mem., Aust. Assoc. of Neurologists; Hunterian Prof., Royal College of Surgeons, 1952; Pres., Section of Neurology, Royal Society of Medicine, 1965–66; Visiting Prof., University of California, San Francisco, 1954; Doyne Meml Lectr, Oxford Ophthalmological Congress, 1969. Neurologist, British European Airways. Vice-Pres., Newspaper Press Fund. *Publications:* contributions to medical literature. *Recreations:* walking, music, country life. *Address:* 45 Lanchester Road, Highgate N6 4SX.

Died 1 May 1993.

MEANEY, Sir Patrick (Michael), Kt 1981; Chairman: The Rank Organisation Plc, since 1983 (Director since 1979); A. Kershaw and Sons PLC, since 1983; Mecca Leisure Group PLC, since 1990; Deputy Chairman: Midland Bank, since 1984 (Director, since 1979); Horserace Betting Levy Board, since 1985; *b* 6 May 1925; *m* Mary June Kearney; one *s. Educ:* Wimbledon College; Northern Polytechnic. HM Forces, 1941–47. Joined Thomas Tilling Ltd, 1951; Dir 1961, Man. Dir and Chief Exec. 1973–83. Director: Cable and Wireless PLC, 1978–84; ICI PLC, 1981–; Metropolitan and Country Racecourse Mgt Hldgs Ltd, 1985–; Racecourse Technical Services Ltd, 1985–; MEPC PLC, 1986–; Tarmac PLC, 1990–; Member, Internat. Adv. Board: WEF Foundn, 1979–; CRH PLC (formerly Cement Roadstone), 1985–. Member Council: British North American Cttee and Res. Assoc., 1979–90; CBI, 1979–92; London Chamber of Commerce and Industry, 1977–82; RSA, 1987–; BESO, 1987–; Stock Exchange Listed Cos Adv. Cttee, 1987–; President's Cttee, Advertising Assoc., 1987–; Pres., Chartered Inst. of Marketing (formerly Inst. of Marketing), 1981–91; Chm., Govt Review Cttee on Harland & Wolff, 1980; Mem., Conference Bd, 1982–87. CBIM 1976; FCIM (FInstM 1981; Pres., 1981–91); FRSA 1976. *Recreations:* sport, music, education. *Address:*

Harefield House, Sandridge, Herts AL4 9EG. *T:* (office) 071–706 1111. *Clubs:* Harlequins, British Sportsman's.
Died 16 July 1992.

MEDD, His Honour Patrick William, OBE 1962; QC 1973; a Circuit Judge, 1981–92; *b* 26 May 1919; *s* of E. N. Medd; *m* 1st, 1945, Jeananne Spence Powell (marr. diss.); three *d*; 2nd, 1971, Elizabeth Spinks D'Albuquerque. *Educ:* Uppingham Sch.; Selwyn Coll., Cambridge. Served in Army, 1940–46, S Staffs Regt and E African Artillery, Major. Called to Bar, Middle Temple, 1947, Bencher 1969; Mem. Gen. Council of the Bar, 1965–67. Dep. Chm., Shropshire QS, 1967–71; Jun. Counsel to Comrs of Inland Revenue, 1968–73; Recorder of Abingdon, 1964–71 (Hon. Recorder, 1972–); a Recorder of the Crown Court, 1972–81. Chm., Bd of Referees, and Finance Act 1960 Tribunal, 1978–91; UK rep., panel of arbitrators, Internat. Centre for Settlement of Investment Disputes, 1979–87; Co-Pres., Nat. Reference Tribunal for Coalmining Ind., 1985–; Special Comr of Income Tax, 1986–92 (Presiding Special Comr, 1990–92); Pres., VAT Tribunals, 1988–92. *Publications:* (jtly) The Rule of Law, 1955; (jtly) Murder, 1956; (jtly) A Giant's Strength, 1958; Romilly, 1968. *Recreation:* gardening. *Address:* Little Place, Clifton Hampden, near Abingdon, Oxon OX14 3EQ. *Died 15 Oct. 1995.*

MEDLEY, (Charles) Robert (Owen), CBE 1982; RA 1986; painter and theatrical designer; Chairman, Faculty of Painting, British School at Rome, 1966–77; *b* 19 Dec. 1905; *s* of late C. D. Medley, and A. G. Owen. *Educ:* Gresham's Sch., Holt. Studied art in London and Paris; Art Dir of the Group Theatre and designed the settings and costumes for plays by T. S. Eliot, W. H. Auden, Christopher Isherwood, Louis Macneice, and Verdi's Othello, Sadler's Wells Theatre, Coppelia, Sadler's Wells Theatre Ballet; exhibited in London and New York World's Fair; pictures bought by: Tate Gallery; V&A (collection of drawings); Walker Art Gallery, Liverpool; City Art Gallery, Birmingham, and other provincial galleries; National Gallery of Canada, Ontario; Contemporary Art Society; Arts Council for Festival of Britain, 1951; retrospective exhibitions: Whitechapel Art Gallery, 1963; Mus. of Modern Art, Oxford, then touring, 1984; Coram Gall., London, 1994. Official War Artist, 1940. Diocletian in Sebastiane (film), 1976. *Publications:* (illustr.) Milton's Samson Agonistes, 1981; Drawn from the Life, a memoir (autobiog.), 1983. *Address:* Charterhouse, Charterhouse Square, EC1M 6AN.
Died 20 Oct. 1994.

MEDWIN, Robert Joseph G.; *see* Gardner-Medwin.

MEINERTZHAGEN, Daniel; Chairman: Royal Insurance plc, 1974–85; Alexanders Discount plc, 1981–84; *b* 2 March 1915; *e s* of Louis Ernest Meinertzhagen, Theberton House, Leiston, Suffolk and Gwynedd, *d* of Sir William Llewellyn, PPRA; *m* 1940, Marguerite, *d* of A. E. Leonard; two *s. Educ:* Eton; New Coll., Oxford. Served War of 1939–45, RAFVR (Wing Comdr). Joined Lazard Brothers, 1936; Man. Dir 1954; Dep. Chm. 1971; Chm., 1973–80. Former Chm., Mercantile Credit Co. Ltd, Raeburn Investment Trust Ltd, and Whitehall Trust; former Director: S. Pearson & Son Ltd; Pearson Longman Ltd; W. T. Henley's Telegraph Works Co. Ltd; Rootes Motors Ltd; Trollope & Colls Ltd; Costain Group Ltd; Brixton Estate plc; Tozer Kemsley & Millbourn (Hldgs) plc. *Address:* 82 Old Church Street, Chelsea, SW3 6EP. *T:* 071–352 5150. *Club:* White's.
Died 22 March 1991.

MELDRUM, Andrew, CBE 1962 (OBE 1956); KPM 1952; Chief Inspector of Constabulary for Scotland, 1966–69, retired; *b* 22 April 1909; *s* of late Andrew Meldrum, Burntisland, Fife; *m* 1st, 1937, Janet H. (*d* 1987), *d* of late

Robert Crooks, Grangemouth; one *s* one *d*; 2nd, 1990, Diana Cicely Meldrum, *d* of late Ernest Cecil Meldrum, Mayfield, Sussex. *Educ:* Burntisland, Fife. Joined Stirlingshire Police, 1927; Deputy Chief Constable, Inverness Burgh, 1943, Chief Constable, 1946; Chief Constable, County of Angus, 1949; Chief Constable of Fife, 1955; Inspector of Constabulary for Scotland, 1965–66. *Recreation:* golf. *Clubs:* Royal Burgess Golfing Society of Edinburgh; Royal Guernsey Golf; Royal Channel Islands Yacht (Guernsey).
Died 10 Jan. 1995.

MELLANBY, Kenneth, CBE 1954 (OBE 1945); ScD Cantab; ecological consultant and editor; Hon. Research Fellow, University of Exeter, since 1992; *b* 26 March 1908; *s* of late Emeritus Professor A. L. Mellanby and Annie W. Maunder; *m* 1933, Helen Neilson Dow, MD (marr. diss.); one *d; m* 1948, Jean Copeland, JP, MA; one *s. Educ:* Barnard Castle Sch.; King's Coll., Cambridge (Exhibitioner). Research Worker, London Sch. of Hygiene and Trop. Med., 1930–36 and 1953–55; Wandsworth Fellow, 1933; Sorby Research Fellow of Royal Society of London, 1936; Hon. Lecturer, University of Sheffield; CO (Sqdn Ldr RAFVR) Sheffield Univ. Air Sqdn; Dir Sorby Research Institute, 1941; Major, RAMC (Specialist in Biological Research), overseas service in N Africa, SE Asia, etc; Dep. Dir, Scrub Typhus Research Laboratory, SEAC; Reader in Medical Entomology, University of London, 1945–47; first Principal, University Coll., Ibadan, Nigeria, 1947–53; Head of Dept of Entomology, Rothamsted Experimental Station, Harpenden, Herts, 1955–61; first Dir, Monks Wood Experimental Station, Huntingdon, 1961–74. Vice-Pres. and Mem. Council, Royal Entomological Soc. of London, 1953–56; Pres. Assoc. for Study of Animal Behaviour, 1957–60; Member: Inter-University Council for Higher Education Overseas, 1960–75; ARC Research Cttee on Toxic Chemicals; Council, and Chm., Tropical Group, Brit. Ecological Soc.; Nat. Exec., Cambs Br., CPRE (also Pres.); Council for Science and Technology Insts, 1976–77 (Chm.); Council for Environmental Science and Engrg, 1976– (Chm., 1981–); Pres., Sect. D (Zoology), 1972, and Sect. X (General), 1973, British Assoc.; Vice-Pres. of the Institute of Biology, 1967, Pres., 1972–73; Vice-Pres., Parly and Scientific Cttee; first Hon. Life Mem., Assoc. for Protection of Rural Australia; Pres., British Isles Bee Breeders' Assoc., 1978–. Hon. Professorial Fellow, University Coll. of S Wales; Hon. Prof. of Biology, Univ. of Leicester. Essex Hall Lectr, 1971. Fellow, NERC. Chm., Editorial Bd, Environmental Pollution; Mem. Editorial Bd, New Naturalist series. Hon. Life Prof., Central London Polytechnic, 1980; DUniv Essex, 1980; Hon. DSc: Ibadan, 1963; Bradford, 1970; Leicester, 1972; Sheffield, 1983. First Charter Award, Inst. of Biology, 1981. *Publications:* Scabies, 1943, new edn 1973; Human Guinea Pigs, 1945, new edn 1975; The Birth of Nigeria's University, 1958, new edn 1975; Pesticides and Pollution, 1967; The Mole, 1971; The Biology of Pollution, 1972; Can Britain Feed Itself?, 1975; Talpa, the story of a mole, 1976; Farming and Wildlife, 1981; (ed) Air Pollution, Acid Rain and the Environment, 1988; Waste and Pollution, 1991; The DDT Story, 1992; many scientific papers on insect physiology, ecology, medical and agricultural entomology; ed, Monographs on Biological Subjects; British Editor of Entomologia Experimentalis et Applicata. *Recreation:* austere living. *Address:* 13 Wonford Road, Exeter EX2 4LH. *T:* Exeter (0392) 78715.
Died 23 Dec. 1993.

MENZIES, Dame Pattie (Maie), GBE 1954; *b* 2 March 1899; *d* of late Senator J. W. Leckie; *m* 1920, Robert Gordon Menzies (Rt Hon. Sir Robert Menzies, KT, AK, CH, QC, FRS; Prime Minister of the Commonwealth of Australia, 1939–41 and 1949–66) (*d* 1978); one *d* (two *s*

decd). *Educ:* Fintona Girls' Sch., Melbourne; Presbyterian Ladies' Coll., Melbourne. Awarded GBE for public and charitable work, particularly in support of women throughout Australia. *Address:* Unit 14, St Andrew's Village, Groom Street, Hughes, ACT 2605, Australia. *Club:* Alexandra (Melbourne).

Died 30 Aug. 1995.

MERRETT, Charles Edwin, CBE 1979; Area Organiser, Union of Shop, Distributive and Allied Workers, 1948–83, retired; *b* 26 Jan. 1923; *s* of Charles and Eva Merrett; *m* 1950, Mildred Merrett; two *s*. *Educ:* Palfrey Senior Boys' Sch., Walsall. Bristol City Council: Councillor, 1957–91, Leader, 1974–78; Lord Mayor of Bristol, 1978–79, Dep. Lord Mayor, 1979–80. Member: Policy Cttee, Assoc. of District Councils, 1974–78; Jt Consultative Cttee on Local Govt Finance, 1975–78; Chm., Adv. Council, BBC Radio Bristol, 1979–83. *Recreations:* watching sport, music, theatre. *Address:* 13 Gainsborough Square, Lockleaze, Bristol BS7 9XA. *T:* Bristol (0272) 515195.

Died 6 Feb. 1994.

MESSERVY, Sir (Roney) Godfrey (Collumbell), Kt 1986; Chairman, Strathclyde Institute Ltd, 1990–94; Director, ASDA (formerly ASDA—MFI) Group PLC, 1986–93 (Chairman, 1991); *b* 17 Nov. 1924; *s* of late Roney Forshaw Messervy and Bertha Crosby (*née* Collumbell); *m* 1952, Susan Patricia Gertrude, *d* of late Reginald Arthur Nunn, DSO, DSC, RNVR, and Adeline Frances Nunn; one *s* two *d*. *Educ:* Oundle; Cambridge Univ. Served War, RE, 1943–47: Parachute Sqdn (Captain). CAV (Mem. of Lucas Group): joined as trainee, 1949; Dir of Equipment Sales, 1963; Dir and Gen. Man., 1966 (also dir of various Lucas subsids at home and abroad); Dir, 1972, Man. Dir, 1974–79, Joseph Lucas (Industries) Ltd; Chm. and Chief Exec., Lucas Industries plc, 1980–87; Chm., Costain Group, 1987–90 (Dir, 1978–90). Member: Council, Birmingham Chamber of Industry and Commerce, 1979–95 (Pres., 1982–83); Council, SMMT, 1980– (Vice-Pres., 1984–87; Pres., 1987–88; Dep. Pres., 1988–90); Engrg Industries Council, 1980–87; Nat. Defence Industries Council, 1980–87; Council, CBI, 1982–88; BOTB, 1984–88; Vice-Pres., EEF, 1982–87. Freeman, Worshipful Co. of Ironmongers, 1977, Liveryman, 1979. Hon. DSc: Aston in Birmingham, 1982; City, 1986. *Recreations:* farming, field sports, photography. *Address:* Heath Farm, Ullenhall, Solihull, W Midlands B95 5PR.

Died 22 July 1995.

MESSIAEN, Olivier; Grand Croix de la Légion d'Honneur; Grand Croix de l'Ordre national du Mérite; Commandeur des Arts et des Lettres; Member, Institut de France; composer and organist; *b* Avignon, 10 Dec. 1908; *s* of Pierre Messiaen and Cécile Sauvage; *m* 1st, Claire Delbos (*d* 1959); one *s*; 2nd, 1961, Yvonne Loriod (pianist). *Educ:* Lycée de Grenoble; Conservatoire Nat. supérieur de musique, Paris (7 1st prizes). Organist, Trinité, Paris, 1930–; co-founder Jeune-France Movement, 1936. Professor: Ecole Normale and Schola Cantorum, 1936–39; of Harmony, Paris Conservatoire, 1941–47; of Analysis, Aesthetics and Rhythm, 1947–; of Composition, 1966–. Mem. Council, Order of Arts and Letters, 1975–. Member: Royal Academy; Acads of Brussels, Madrid, Stockholm. Hon. FRCO 1988. Erasmus Prize, 1971; Sibelius Prize, 1971; Von Siemens Prize, 1975; Léonie Sonning Prize, 1977; Bach-Hamburg Prize, 1979; Liebermann Prize, 1983; Wolf Foundn (Israel) Prize, 1983; Académie Berlin Prize, 1984; Inamori of Kyoto Prize, 1985; Paul VI Prize, 1989. *Works for organ include:* Le Banquet Céleste, 1928; Le Diptyque, 1929; L'Ascension, 1933; La Nativité du Seigneur, 1935; Les Corps Glorieux, 1939; Messe de la Pentecôte, 1949; Livre d'Orgue, 1951; Méditations sur le Mystère de la Sainte Trinité, 1969; Le Livre du Saint Sacrement, 1984; *other works include:* Préludes, 1929;

Poèmes pour Mi, 1936; Chants de Terre et de Ciel, 1938; Quatuor pour la Fin du Temps, 1941; Visions de l'Amen, 1943; Vingt Regards sur l'Enfant Jésus, 1944; Trois Petites Liturgies de la Présence Divine, 1944; Harawi, 1945; Turangalila–Symphonie, 1946–48; Cinq Rechants, 1949; Etudes de Rythme, 1949; Réveil des Oiseaux, 1953; Oiseaux exotiques, 1955; Catalogue d'Oiseaux, 1956–58; Chronochromie, 1959; Sept Haïkaï, 1963; Couleurs de la Cité Céleste, 1964; Et Exspecto Resurrectionem Mortuorum, 1965; La Transfiguration de Notre Seigneur, Jésus-Christ, 1969; La Fauvette des Jardins (for piano), 1970; Des Canyons aux Etoiles, 1970–74; Saint François d'Assise (opera), 1975–83; Petites Esquisses d'oiseaux (for piano), 1985–; Un vitrail et des oiseaux (piano and small orch.), 1986; La Ville d'En-Haut (piano and orch.), 1987–; Eclairs sur l'Au-delà (large orch.), 1988–90; Un Sourire (orch.)., 1989–. *Died 28 April 1992.*

MESSITER, Air Cdre Herbert Lindsell, CB 1954; *b* 28 Sept. 1902; 2nd *s* of late Col Charles Bayard Messiter, DSO, OBE, Barwick Park, Yeovil, Som, and Alice Lindsell; *m* 1933, Lucy Brenda Short (decd); one *d*. *Educ:* Bedford Sch. Served War of 1939–45 (despatches 4 times): Egypt, N Africa, Belgium, Germany; Command Engineer Officer, Far East Air Force, 1950–52; Senior Technical Staff Officer, Bomber Command, RAF, 1952–56; Senior Technical Staff Officer, Middle East Air Force, 1956–59, retired. *Address:* Apartado 46, San Pedro de Alcantara, Málaga, Spain. *Club:* Royal Air Force.

Died 15 April 1994.

METHUEN, 6th Baron *cr* 1838; **Anthony John Methuen,** ARICS; *b* 26 Oct. 1925; *s* of 5th Baron Methuen and Grace (*d* 1972), *d* of Sir Richard Holt, 1st Bt; *S* father, 1975. *Educ:* Winchester; Royal Agricultural Coll., Cirencester. Served Scots Guards and Royal Signals, 1943–47. Lands Officer, Air Ministry, 1951–62. QALAS 1954. *Recreation:* shooting. *Heir: b* Hon. Robert Alexander Holt Methuen [*b* 22 July 1931; *m* 1958, Mary Catharine Jane, *d* of Ven. C. G. Hooper; two *d*.] *Address:* Corsham Court, Corsham, Wilts. *Club:* Lansdowne.

Died 24 Aug. 1994.

MEYER, Rollo John Oliver, (Jack), OBE 1967; Founder, Millfield School, 1935, and first Headmaster, 1935–70; *b* 15 March 1905; *s* of Canon Rollo Meyer and Arabella Ward; *m* 1931, Joyce Symons; one *d* (and one *d* decd). *Educ:* Haileybury Coll.; Pembroke Coll., Cambridge. MA 1926. Cottonbroker, Gill & Co., Bombay, 1926–29; Private Tutor, Limbdi and Porbandar, 1929–30; Headmaster, Dhrangadhra Palace Sch., 1930–35; Founder, and first Headmaster of Edgarley Hall Preparatory Sch., Glastonbury, 1945–71; Headmaster, 1973–77, and Pres., 1977–80, Campion Sch., Athens; Founder, 1979, and first Headmaster, St Lawrence Coll., Athens, resigned 1986; Co-founder and first Rector, Byron Coll., Athens, 1986–87, retired. *Recreations:* remedial teaching, chess. *Address:* 12 Milton Lane, Wells, Somerset BA5 2QS. *T:* Wells (0749) 72080. *Club:* MCC. *Died 9 March 1991.*

MICHAELS, Michael Israel, CB 1960; *b* 22 Dec. 1908; *m* 1932, Rosina, *e d* of late Joseph Sturges; one *s* one *d*. *Educ:* City of London College; London Sch. of Economics (Social Science Research Scholar, 1931). Asst Sec., New Survey London Life and Labour, 1932–34; Deputy Director, Programmes and Statistics, Ministry of Supply, 1940–45; Asst Sec., Ministry of Health, 1946–54; Under-Sec., Atomic Energy Office, 1955–59; Office of the Minister for Science (Atomic Energy Division), 1959–64; Under-Sec., Min. of Technology, 1964–71, retired. British Mem., Bd of Governors, Internat. Atomic Energy Agency, 1957–71. *Recreations:* music, gardening, history. *Address:* Tower House, Kelsale, Saxmundham, Suffolk. *T:* Saxmundham (0728) 603142.

Died 21 Nov. 1992.

MICHALOWSKI, Jerzy; Polish diplomat; *b* 26 May 1909; *s* of Andrzej and Maria Michalowski; *m* 1947, Mira Krystyna; two *s*. *Educ:* University of Warsaw. Asst, Polish Inst. of Social Affairs, 1933–36; Dir of Polish Workers Housing Organisation, 1936–39; Chief of Housing Dept of Warsaw City Council, 1945; Counsellor of Polish Embassy in London, 1945–46; Deputy Deleg. of Poland to UN, March-Nov. 1946; Ambassador of Republic of Poland to the Court of St James's 1946–53; Head of a department, Ministry of Foreign Affairs, Warsaw, 1953–54; Under Sec. of State for Educ., 1954–55; Deleg. of Poland to the Internat. Commn in Vietnam, 1955–56; Permanent Representative of Poland to UN, 1956–60; Dir-Gen., in Ministry of Foreign Affairs, Warsaw, 1960–67; Ambassador to USA, 1967–71. Pres., Econ. and Social Council, UN, 1962. *Publications:* Unemployment of Polish Peasants, 1934; Housing Problems in Poland (publ. by League of Nations), 1935; The Big Game for the White House, 1972. *Recreations:* tennis, winter sports. *Address:* Al. I Armii WP 16/20, Warsaw, Poland.

Died 30 March 1993.

MICHENER, Rt Hon. (Daniel) Roland, CC 1967; CMM 1972; CD 1976; Royal Victorian Chain, 1973; PC (Canada) 1962; QC (Canada); Governor-General and Commander-in-Chief of Canada, 1967–Jan. 1974; Barrister associated as Counsel with Lang, Michener, Lash, Johnston (formerly Lang, Michener, Cranston, Farquharson & Wright), Toronto, since 1974; Chairman of Council, Duke of Edinburgh's Fifth Commonwealth Study Conference, Canada 1980; Hon. Chairman of Board: National Trust Co., Toronto; Teck Corporation Ltd; *b* Lacombe, Alta, 19 April 1900; *s* of late Senator Edward Michener and Mary Edith (*née* Roland), Lincoln Co., Ontario; *m* 1927, Norah Evangeline (decd), *d* of Robert Willis, Manitoba; two *d* (and one *d* decd). *Educ:* Universities of Alberta and Oxford. BA (Alta) 1920; Rhodes Scholar for Alta, 1919; BA 1922, BCL 1923, MA 1929, Oxon. Served with RAF, 1918. Called to Bar, Middle Temple, 1923; Barrister, Ontario, 1924; KC 1943. Practising lawyer with Lang, Michener & Cranston, Toronto, 1924–57. Mem. Ontario Legislature for St David, Toronto, 1945–48, and Provincial Sec. for Ontario, 1946–48; elected to Canadian House of Commons, 1953; re-elected 1957 and 1958; elected Speaker, 1957 and May 1958; Canadian High Commissioner to India and Ambassador to Nepal, 1964–67. Chancellor, Queen's Univ., 1974–80. Gen. Sec. for Canada, Rhodes Scholarships, 1936–64. Mem. Bd of Governors, Toronto Stock Exchange, 1974–76. Formerly: Governor, Toronto Western Hosp.; Hon. Counsel, Chm. of Exec. Cttee (Pres., 1974–79), Canadian Inst. of Internat. Affairs; Hon. Counsel, Red Cross Ont Div.; Chm. of Exec., Canadian Assoc. for Adult Educn; Officer and Dir of various Canadian mining and financial companies. Chancellor and Principal Companion, Order of Canada, 1967–74; Chancellor and Comdr, Order of Military Merit, 1972–74. KJStJ (Prior for Canada), 1967. Hon. Fellow: Hertford Coll., Oxford, 1961; Acad. of Medicine, Toronto, 1967; Trinity Coll., Toronto, 1968; Frontier Coll., Toronto, 1972; Royal Canadian Mil. Inst., 1975; Heraldry Soc. of Canada, 1976; Hon. FRCP(C) 1968; Hon. FRAIC, 1968; Hon. FRSC, 1975. Hon. Mem., Canadian Medical Assoc., 1968; Hon. Bencher, Law Soc. of Upper Canada, 1968. Hon. LLD: Ottawa, 1948; Queen's, 1958; Laval, 1960; Alberta, 1967; St Mary's, Halifax, 1968; Toronto, 1968; RMC Canada, 1969; Mount Allison, Sackville, NB, 1969; Brock, 1969; Manitoba, 1970; McGill, 1970; York, Toronto, 1970; British Columbia, 1971; Jewish Theol Seminary of America, 1972; New Brunswick, 1972; Law Soc. of Upper Canada, 1974; Dalhousie, 1974; Hon. DCL: Bishop's, 1968; Windsor, 1969; Oxford Univ., 1970. *Address:* PO Box 10, First Canadian Place, Toronto,

Ontario M5X 1A2, Canada; (home) 24 Thornwood Road, Toronto, Ontario M4W 2S1. *Died 6 Aug. 1991.*

MICKLETHWAIT, Sir Robert (Gore), Kt 1964; QC 1956; Chief National Insurance Commissioner, 1966–75 (Deputy Commissioner, 1959; National Insurance Commissioner and Industrial Injuries Commissioner, 1961); *b* 7 Nov. 1902; 2nd *s* of late St J. G. Micklethwait, KC and Annie Elizabeth Micklethwait (*née* Aldrich-Blake); *m* 1936, Philippa J., 2nd *d* of late Sir Ronald Bosanquet, QC; three *s* one *d*. *Educ:* Clifton Coll.; Trinity Coll., Oxford (2nd Class Lit.Hum., MA). Called to Bar, Middle Temple, 1925, Bencher, 1951; Autumn Reader, 1964; Dep. Treasurer, 1970, Treasurer, 1971. Royal Observer Corps, 1938–40; Civil Asst, WO, 1940–45. Oxford Circuit; Gen. Coun. of the Bar, 1939–40 and 1952–56; Supreme Court Rule Cttee, 1952–56; Recorder of Worcester, 1946–59; Deputy Chm., Court of Quarter Sessions for County of Stafford, 1956–59. Hon. LLD Newcastle upon Tyne, 1975. Hon. Knight, Hon. Soc. of Knights of the Round Table, 1972. *Publication:* The National Insurance Commissioners (Hamlyn Lectures), 1976. *Address:* 71 Harvest Road, Englefield Green, Surrey TW20 0QR. *T:* Egham (0784) 432521.

Died 8 Sept. 1992.

MIDDLETON, Kenneth William Bruce; formerly Sheriff of Lothian and Borders at Edinburgh and Haddington; *b* Strathpeffer, Ross-shire, 1 Oct. 1905; 2nd *s* of W. R. T. Middleton; *m* 1st, 1938, Ruth Beverly (marr. diss. 1972; she *m* 1972, 4th Baron Kinross), *d* of W. H. Mill, SSC; one *s* one *d*; 2nd, 1984, Simona Vere, *d* of T. C. Pakenham, *widow* of N. Iliff. *Educ:* Rossall Sch.; Merton Coll., Oxford; Edinburgh Univ. BA Oxford, LLB Edinburgh. Called to Scottish Bar, 1931; Vans Dunlop Scholar in International Law and Constitutional Law and History, Edinburgh Univ.; Richard Brown Research Scholar in Law, Edinburgh Univ.; served War of 1939–45 with Royal Scots and Seaforth Highlanders; attached to Military Dept, Judge Advocate-Gen.'s Office, 1941–45; Sheriff-Substitute, subseq. Sheriff: Perth and Angus at Forfar, 1946–50; Lothians and Peebles, later Lothian and Borders, at Edinburgh and Haddington, 1950–86. *Publication:* Britain and Russia, 1947. *Address:* Cobblers Cottage, Ledwell, Chipping Norton, Oxon OX7 7AN.

Died 19 Feb. 1995.

MIDDLETON, Sir Stephen Hugh, 9th Bt, *cr* 1662, of Belsay Castle, Northumberland; *b* 20 June 1909; 2nd *s* of Lieut Hugh Jeffery Middleton, RN (3rd *s* of Sir Arthur Middleton, 7th Bt), and Mary Katharine (OBE 1920), *er d* of Rear-Adm. Samuel Long; *S* uncle, 1942; *m* 1962, Mary (*d* 1972), *d* of late Richard Robinson. *Educ:* Eton; Magdalene Coll., Cambridge. *Heir:* *b* Lawrence Monck Middleton [*b* 23 Oct. 1912; *m* 1984, Primrose Westcombe]. *Address:* Belsay Castle, Northumberland.

Died 4 Jan. 1993.

MIKARDO, Ian; *b* 9 July 1908; *m* 1932, Mary Rosette; two *d*. *Educ:* Portsmouth. MP (Lab): Reading, 1945–50, South Div. of Reading, 1950–55, again Reading, 1955–Sept. 1959; Poplar, 1964–74; Tower Hamlets, Bethnal Green and Bow, 1974–83; Bow and Poplar, 1983–87. Member: Nat. Exec. Cttee of Labour Party, 1950–59, and 1960–78 (Chm. 1970–71); Internat Cttee of Labour Party (Chm. 1973–78); Chm., Parly Labour Party, March-Nov. 1974; Chm., Select Cttee on Nationalized Industries, 1966–70. Pres., ASTMS, 1968–73; Vice-Pres., Socialist International, 1978–83 (Hon. Pres. 1983–). *Publications:* Centralised Control of Industry, 1944; Frontiers in the Air, 1946; (with others) Keep Left, 1947; The Second Five Years, 1948; The Problems of Nationalisation, 1948; (jtly) Keeping Left, 1950; The Labour Case, 1950; It's a Mug's Game, 1951; Socialism or Slump, 1959; Back-Bencher (autobiog.), 1988. *Address:* 20 Larchwood, The Crescent, Cheadle, Cheshire SK8 1PU. *T:* 061–428 0433.

Died 6 May 1993.

MILCHSACK, Lisalotte, (Lilo), Hon. DCMG 1972 (Hon. CMG 1968); Hon. CBE 1958; Initiator, 1949, and Hon. Chairman, since 1982, Deutsch-Englische Gesellschaft e V (Hon. Secretary, 1949–77; Chairman, 1977–82); *b* Frankfurt/Main, 1905; *d* of Prof. Dr Paul Duden and Johanna Bertha (*née* Nebe); *m* Hans Milchsack (*d* 1984); two *d. Educ:* Univs of Frankfurt, Geneva and Amsterdam. Awarded Grosses Bundesverdienstkreuz, 1959, with Stern, 1985. *Recreations:* gardening, reading. *Address:* An der Kalvey 11, D-4000 Düsseldorf 31–Wittlaer, Germany. *T:* Düsseldorf 40 13 87. *Died 7 Aug. 1992.*

MILES, Baron *cr* 1979 (Life Peer), of Blackfriars in the City of London; **Bernard James Miles,** Kt 1969; CBE 1953; actor; Founder, with his wife, of the Mermaid Theatre, Puddle Dock, EC4, 1959 (first opened in North London, 1950); *b* 27 Sept. 1907; *s* of Edwin James Miles and Barbara Fletcher; *m* 1931, Josephine Wilson (*d* 1990); one *s* one *d* (and one *d* decd). *Educ:* Uxbridge County Sch.; Pembroke Coll., Oxford (Hon. Fellow, 1969). Hon. DLitt, City Univ., 1974. First stage appearance as Second Messenger in Richard III, New Theatre, 1930; appeared in St Joan, His Majesty's, 1931; spent 5 years in repertory as designer, stage-manager, character-actor, etc; frequent appearances on West End Stage from 1938; entered films, 1937, and wrote for, directed, and acted in them; first went on Music-hall stage, London Palladium, etc, 1950. Mermaid Theatre seasons: Royal Exchange, 1953; Macbeth, Dido and Aeneas, As You Like It, Eastward Ho!; formed Mermaid Theatre Trust which built City of London's first theatre for 300 years, the Mermaid, Puddle Dock, EC4; opened May 1959, with musical play Lock Up Your Daughters. *Publications:* The British Theatre, 1947; God's Brainwave, 1972; Favourite Tales from Shakespeare, 1976; (ed with J. C. Trewin) Curtain Calls, 1981. *Address:* House of Lords, SW1A 0PW.

Died 14 June 1991.

MILES, Dame Margaret, DBE 1970; BA; Headmistress, Mayfield School, Putney, 1952–73; *b* 11 July 1911; 2nd *d* of Rev. E. G. Miles and Annie Miles (*née* Jones). *Educ:* Ipswich High Sch., GPDST; Bedford Coll., Univ. of London (Hon. Fellow, 1983). History teacher: Westcliff High Sch., 1935–39; Badminton Sch., 1939–44; Lectr, Dept of Educn, University of Bristol, 1944–46; Headmistress, Pate's Grammar Sch., Cheltenham, 1946–52. Member: Schools Broadcasting Council, 1958–68; Educ. Adv. Council, ITA, 1962–67; Nat. Adv. Council on Trng and Supply of Teachers, 1962–65; BBC Gen. Adv. Council, 1964–73; Campaign for Comprehensive Educn, 1966 (Chm., 1972; Pres., 1979); RSA Council, 1972–77; British Assoc., 1974–79; Council, Chelsea Coll., Univ. of London, 1965–82; former Mem., Council, Bedford Coll., Univ. of London (Vice-Chm.); Chairman: Adv. Cttee on Develt Educn, ODM, 1977–79; Central Bureau for Educl Visits and Exchanges, 1978–82; Vice-Chm., Educ. Adv. Cttee, UK Nat. Commn for Unesco, 1985. Chm., Meirionnydd Br., Council for Protection of Rural Wales, 1982–91; Pres., British Assoc. for Counselling, 1980–86. Hon. Fellow, Chelsea Coll., London, 1985. Hon. DCL, Univ. of Kent at Canterbury, 1973. *Publications:* And Gladly Teach, 1965; Comprehensive Schooling, Problems and Perspectives, 1968. *Recreations:* opera, films, reading, gardening, golf, walking, travel when possible. *Address:* Tanycraig, Pennal, Machynlleth SY20 9LB. *Clubs:* University Women's; Aberdovey Golf. *Died 26 April 1994.*

MILFORD, 2nd Baron *cr* 1939; **Wogan Philipps;** Bt 1919; farmer and painter; *b* 25 Feb. 1902; *e s* of 1st Baron Milford and Ethel Georgina, *o d* of Rev. Benjamin Speke;

S father, 1962; *m* 1st, 1928, Rosamond Nina Lehmann, CBE (marr. diss. 1944; she *d* 1990); one *s* (one *d* decd); 2nd, 1944, Cristina, Countess of Huntingdon (*d* 1953); 3rd, 1954, Tamara Rust. *Educ:* Eton; Magdalen Coll., Oxford. Member of International Brigade, Spanish Civil War. Former Member of Henley on Thames RDC; Communist Councillor, Cirencester RDC, 1946–49; took active part in building up Nat. Union of Agric. Workers in Gloucestershire and served on its county cttee. Prospective Parly cand. (Lab), Henley on Thames, 1938–39; contested (Com) Cirencester and Tewkesbury, 1950. Held one-man exhibitions of paintings in London, Milan and Cheltenham and shown in many mixed exhibns. *Heir:* *s* Hon. Hugo John Laurence Philipps [*b* 27 Aug. 1929; *m* 1st, 1951, Margaret Heathcote (marr. diss., 1958); one *d*; 2nd, 1959, Mary (marr. diss. 1984), *e d* of 1st Baron Sherfield; three *s* one *d*; 3rd, 1989, Mrs Felicity Leach (*née* Ballantyne)]. *Address:* Flat 2, 8 Lyndhurst Road, Hampstead, NW3 5PX. *Died 30 Nov. 1993.*

MILLAIS, Sir Ralph (Regnault), 5th Bt *cr* 1885, of Palace Gate, Kensington and Saint Ouen, Jersey; *b* 4 March 1905; *s* of Sir Geoffroy William Millais, 4th Bt, and Madeleine Campbell (*d* 1963), *d* of C. H. Grace; *S* father, 1941; *m* 1st, 1939, Felicity Caroline Mary Ward Robinson (marr. diss. 1947), *d* of late Brig.-Gen. W. W. Warner, CMG; one *s* one *d*; 2nd, 1947, Irene Jessie (marr. diss. 1971; she *d* 1985), *er d* of E. A. Stone, FSI; 3rd, 1975, Babette Sefton-Smith, *yr d* of Maj.-Gen. H. F. Salt, CB, CMG, DSO. *Educ:* Marlborough; Trinity Coll., Cambridge. Business career. Joined RAFVR at outbreak of war, 1939, Wing Comdr. *Recreations:* fishing, travel, the restoration of famous vintage and historic cars. *Heir:* *s* Geoffroy Richard Everett Millais, *b* 27 Dec. 1941. *Address:* Gate Cottage, Winchelsea, East Sussex.

Died 14 May 1992.

MILLER of Glenlee, Sir (Frederick William) Macdonald, 7th Bt *cr* 1788, of Glenlee, Kirkcudbrightshire; *b* 21 March 1920; *e s* of Sir Alastair George Lionel Joseph Miller of Glenlee, 6th Bt and 1st wife, Kathleen Daisy, *yr d* of Major Stephen Goodwin Howard, CBE; *S* father, 1964; *m* 1947, Marion Jane Audrey Pettit; one *s* one *d. Educ:* Tonbridge. Conservative Agent for: Whitehaven, 1947–50; Wembley North, 1950–52; North Norfolk, 1952–65; Lowestoft, 1965–82; political consultant, 1982–85. Suffolk County Council: Councillor, 1977–89; Vice-Chm., 1986–88; Chm., 1988–89; Chm. Education Cttee, 1985–88. Chm., Eastern Sea Fisheries Jt Cttee, 1981–83. Mem., Suffolk FPC, 1981–90. *Recreation:* gardening. *Heir:* *s* Stephen William Macdonald Miller of Glenlee, FRCS [*b* 20 June 1953; *m* 1st, 1978, Mary Owen (*d* 1989); one *s* one *d*; 2nd, 1990, Caroline Clark (*née* Chasemore)]. *Address:* Ivy Grange Farm, Westhall, Halesworth, Suffolk IP19 8RN. *T:* Ilketshall (098681) 265. *Died 19 June 1991.*

MILLER, Mrs Horrie; *see* Durack, Dame M.

MILLER, Lt-Comdr John Bryan Peter Duppa-, GC and King's Commendation 1941; *b* 22 May 1903; *er s* of Brian Stothert Miller, JP, Posbury, Devon, and Mary (*née* Sadler); *m* 1st, 1926, Barbara (marr. diss. 1944) (decd), *d* of 1st Baron Buckmaster (later 1st Viscount Buckmaster), GCVO, PC, KC; three *s*; 2nd, 1944, Clare (decd), *d* of Francis Egerton Harding, JP, Old Springs, Market Drayton; 3rd, 1977, Greta, *d* of B. K. G. Landby, Royal Vasa Order, Gothenburg, Sweden. *Educ:* Rugby Sch.; Hertford Coll., Oxford. Dep. County Educn Officer, Hants, 1930–35; Asst Sec., Northants Educn Cttee, 1936–39; Torpedo and Mining Dept, Admty, 1940–45; a Dep. Dir-Gen., Trade and Econs Div., Control Commn for Germany, 1945; Inspector-Gen., Min. of Educn, Addis Ababa, 1945–47; Educn Dept, Kenya, 1947–57; Chm. of European Civil Servants' Assoc., and formation Chm. Staff Side, Central

Whitley Coun. for Civil Service; Sec. to Kenya Coffee Marketing Bd, 1960–61; Sec. to Tanganyika Coffee Bd, 1961–62; Asst Sec. and Marketing Officer, Min. of Lands and Settlement, Kenya, 1963–65. *Publication:* Saints and Parachutes, 1951. *Recreations:* yachting, economics. *Address:* Box 222, Somerset West, 7130, South Africa.
Died 15 Dec. 1994.

MILLER, Sir John Francis C.; *see* Compton Miller.

MILLER of Glenlee, Sir Macdonald; *see* Miller of Glenlee, Sir F. W. M.

MILLER, Richard King; QC (Scot) 1988; *b* 19 Aug. 1949; *s* of late James Cyril King Miller, WS and of Ella Elizabeth Walker or Miller; *m* 1975, Lesley Joan Rist or Miller; two *s. Educ:* Edinburgh Acad.; Magdalene Coll., Cambridge (BA Hons); Edinburgh Univ. (LLB Hons). Called to the Scottish Bar, 1975. Temp. Sheriff of all Sheriffdoms of Scotland, 1988–. *Recreations:* shooting, fishing, tennis, reading and collecting good literature, good wine. *Address:* Leahurst, 16 Gillespie Road, Colinton, Edinburgh EH13 0LL. *T:* 031–441 3737.   *Died 12 July 1992.*

MILLER, Comdr Ronald S.; *see* Scott-Miller.

MILLER, Comdr William Ronald, OBE 1984; Royal Navy (retired); *b* 6 Dec. 1918; *y s* of Col Joseph Miller, DSO and Florence Eva Drabble; *m* 1942, Betty Claelia Otto, Richmond, Natal; one *d. Educ:* Cranleigh Sch., Surrey. Entered RN, 1936; Sec. to Flag Officer (Submarines), 1955–57; Exec. Asst to Dep. Supreme Allied Comdr Atlantic (as Actg Capt.), 1958–60; Sec. to C-in-C Home Fleet (as Actg Capt.), 1960–62; Sec. to C-in-C Portsmouth (as Actg Capt.), 1963–65; retd from RN at own request, 1966. Called to Bar, Lincoln's Inn, 1958. Clerk, Worshipful Co. of Haberdashers, 1966–83 (Liveryman, 1969, Assistant *hc,* 1980). *Recreations:* wine, travel, reading, writing. *Address:* 1 Great George Street, Godalming, Surrey GU7 1EE. *T:* Godalming (0483) 422965.   *Died 26 May 1991.*

MILLER JONES, Hon. Betty Ellen, (Hon. Mrs Keith Miller Jones); *see* Askwith, Hon. B. E.

MILLIGAN, Stephen David Wyatt; MP (C) Eastleigh, since 1992; *b* 12 May 1948; *s* of David Knowles Milligan and Ruth (*née* Seymer). *Educ:* Bradfield Coll.; Magdalen Coll., Oxford. Joined staff, The Economist, 1970: industrial relns corresp., 1972–75; Brussels corresp., 1975–79; Editor, Foreign Report, 1980–81; European Editor, 1982–83; Britain Editor, 1983; Presenter, The World Tonight, Radio 4, 1980–83; The Sunday Times: Foreign Editor, 1984–87; Washington corresp., 1987–88; Europe corresp., BBC TV, 1988–90. *Publication:* The New Barons: British trade unions in the 1970s, 1976. *Recreations:* golf, running, rowing, ski-ing, bird-watching, opera. *Address:* House of Commons, SW1A 0AA. *T:* 071–219 3590. *Clubs:* Royal Mid-Surrey Golf (Richmond); Furnivall Sculling.
Died 7 Feb. 1994.

MILLS, Maj.-Gen. Alan Oswald Gawler; Director-General of Artillery, Ministry of Defence (Army), 1967–69, retired; *b* 11 March 1914; *o s* of John Gawler Mills; *m* 1941, Beata Elizabeth de Courcy Morgan Richards; one *s* (one *d* decd). *Educ:* Marlborough Coll.; RMA, Woolwich. Commissioned RA, 1934; Hong Kong, 1938–45; British Jt Services Mission, USA, 1951–53; Techn SO Grade I, Min. of Supply, 1955–57; Mil. Dir of Studies, RMCS, 1957–61; Sen. Mil. Officer, Royal Armament Research and Develt Estabt, 1961–62; BGS, WO, 1962–65; Dir, Guided Weapons Trials, Min. of Aviation, 1966. *Recreations:* sailing, ski-ing. *Address:* 9 Redburn Street, Chelsea, SW3 4DA. *T:* 071–351 4272. *Club:* Seaview Yacht.   *Died 22 Oct. 1992.*

MILLS, Major Anthony David; *b* 14 Dec. 1918; *y s* of late Maj.-Gen. Sir Arthur Mills, CB, DSO and 1st wife, Winifred Alice, *d* of Col R. H. Carew, DSO; *m* 1948, Anne (*née* Livingstone); two *d. Educ:* Wellington Coll.; RMC, Sandhurst. Commnd Indian Army, 1939, 9th Gurkha Rifles; served War of 1939–45, NW Frontier and Burma, regimental duty and various staff appts; seconded Indian Para. Regt, 1944; retd from Army 1948. Apptd Asst Sec., All England Lawn Tennis Club and Wimbledon Championships, 1948, Sec. Treasurer, and Sec.-Gen., 1963–79. *Recreations:* golf, dog walking, consulting Who's Who. *Address:* c/o All England Lawn Tennis Club, Church Road, Wimbledon, SW19 5AE. *Clubs:* Naval and Military, Queen's (Hon.); All England Lawn Tennis; Royal Wimbledon Golf.   *Died 29 Sept. 1993.*

MILLS, Maj.-Gen. Graham; *see* Mills, Maj.-Gen. W. G. S.

MILLS, (Laurence) John, CBE 1978; FEng 1978; Chairman, Osprey Belt Company Ltd, since 1986; Member, 1974–82, a Deputy Chairman, 1982–84, National Coal Board; *b* 1 Oct. 1920; *s* of late Archibald John and Annie Ellen Mills; *m* 1944, Barbara May (*née* Warner); two *s. Educ:* Portsmouth Grammar Sch.; Birmingham Univ. BSc (Hons); Hon. FIMinE, CIMEMME; CIMgt. Mining Student, Houghton Main Colliery Co. Ltd, 1939; Corps of Royal Engrs, 1942–46, Major 1946; various mining appts, Nat. Coal Bd, 1947–67; Chief Mining Engr, HQ NCB, 1968; Area Dir, N Yorks Area, 1970; Area Dir, Doncaster Area, 1973. Chairman: British Mining Consultants Ltd, 1983–85; Specialist Trng and Technical Services Ltd, 1989–91; Director: Coal Develts (Queensland) Ltd, 1980–84; Capricorn Coal Management Pty Ltd, 1981–84; Coal Develts (German Creek) Pty Ltd, 1980–84; German Creek Pty Ltd, 1981–84; Burnett and Hallamshire Holdings plc, 1986–88. Member: Mining Qualifications Bd, 1975–83; Safety in Mines Res. Adv. Bd, 1975–83; Adv. Council on Res. Develt for Fuel and Power, 1981–83. Pres., IMinE, 1975. Silver Medal, Midland Counties Instn of Engrs, 1959 and 1962; Douglas Hay Medal, IMinE, 1977; Clerk Maxwell Medal, Assoc. of Mining, Electrical and Mech. Engrs (later IMEMME), 1979; Robens Coal Science Lecture Gold Medal, 1981; Institution Medal, IMinE, 1982. *Publications:* techn. papers in Trans IMinE. *Recreation:* coastal and inland waterway cruising. *Address:* Unit 4, Bowers Parade, Harpenden, Herts AL5 2SH.   *Died 27 Jan. 1994.*

MILLS, Air Marshal Sir Nigel (Holroyd), KBE 1991; QHP 1988; FRCGP; FRCP; Surgeon General, 1990–91, and Director General Medical Services (Royal Air Force), 1987–91; *b* 12 Nov. 1932; *s* of Air Chief Marshal Sir George (Holroyd) Mills, GCB, DFC, and Mary Austen Mills (*née* Smith); *m* 1956, Pamela (*née* Jones); three *d. Educ:* Berkhamsted Sch.; Middlesex Hosp. Med. Sch. (MB, BS). FFOM; DipAvMed; FRCGP 1991; FRCP 1991. OC RAF Inst. of Occupational and Community Medicine, 1979–82; OC RAF Med. Rehabilitation Unit, Headley Court, 1982–83; Dep. PMO, HQ RAF Strike Comd, 1983–84; PMO, RAF Germany, 1984–86; RCDS 1987; Dep. Surg. Gen. (Res. and Training, later Health Services), 1987–90. FRSM 1988. CStJ 1987. *Recreations:* sailing/windsurfing, computing. *Address:* c/o Lloyds Bank, Cox's and King's Branch, PO Box 1190, 7 Pall Mall, SW1Y 5NA. *Club:* Royal Air Force.
Died 18 Oct. 1991.

MILLS, Sir Peter (McLay), Kt 1982; *b* 22 Sept. 1921; *m* 1948, Joan Weatherley; one *s* one *d. Educ:* Epsom; Wye Coll. MP (C): Torrington, 1964–74; Devon W, 1974–83; Torridge and W Devon, 1983–87. Parly Sec., MAFF, 1972; Parly Under-Sec. of State, NI Office, 1972–74. Member: European Legislation Cttee, EEC, 1974–79; Select Cttee on Foreign Affairs, 1980–82; Dep. Chm., CPA, 1982–85; Chairman: Cons. Agriculture Cttee,

1979–87; Houses of Parlt Christian Fellowship, 1970–87; Minister of Agric. Panel for SW England, 1988–. Dir, Torridge Trng Ltd, 1987–; Chm., Devon Cable Vision Ltd, 1984–; Regl Chm., Portman Bldg Soc. (formerly Regency and W of England Bldg Soc.), 1988–. *Recreations:* work, staying at home for a short time. *Address:* Priestcombe, Crediton, Devon EX17 5BT.
Died 16 Aug. 1993.

MILLS, Wilbur Daigh; lawyer and politician, USA; tax consultant, Shea & Gould (Mirabelli & Gould), 1977–91; *b* Kensett, Ark, 24 May 1909; *s* of Ardra Pickens Mills and Abbie Lois Daigh; *m* 1934, Clarine Billingsley; two *d. Educ:* Hendrix Coll.; Harvard Law Sch. Admitted to State Bar of Arkansas, 1933; in private legal practice, Searcy; County and Probate Judge, White County, 1934–38; Cashier, Bank of Kensett, 1934–35. Mem., US House of Representatives, 1939–76 (Chm., Ways and Means Cttee, 1958–76). Democrat. *Address:* PO Box 402, Kensett, Arkansas 72082, USA.
Died 2 May 1992.

MILLS, Maj.-Gen. (William) Graham (Stead), CBE 1963; *b* 23 June 1917; *s* of William Stead Mills and Margaret Kennedy Mills; *m* 8 July 1941, Joyce Evelyn (*née* Ransom) (*d* 1981); three *s. Educ:* Merchiston Castle Sch., Edinburgh. Regtl duty, Royal Berks Regt, in India, 1938–43; Staff Coll., India, 1944; GSO2 and GSO1, Ops HQ 14th Army, Burma, 1944–45; despatches, 1945; WO and Washington, USA, 1946–50; Regtl duty with Parachute Regt, comdg 17th Bn, The Parachute Regt, 1958–60; GSO1, 2 Div. BAOR, 1956–58; Regtl Col The Parachute Regt, 1960–62; Comdg TA Brigade, Winchester, 1963–64; Brig. GS, HQ Middle East Comd, Aden, 1965–66; Imperial Defence Coll., Student, 1967; GOC West Midland District, 1968–70. Head of Home, Le Court Cheshire Home, 1972–77; Mem. Management Cttee, Park House Sandringham (Cheshire Foundn Country House Hotel for Disabled People), 1983–88. *Recreations:* normal. *Address:* Inglenook, Field Dalling, Holt, Norfolk. *T:* Binham (0328) 830388.
Died 29 July 1992.

MILLWARD, William, CB 1969; CBE 1954; with Government Communications Headquarters, 1946–74, retired (Superintending Director, 1958–69); *b* 27 Jan. 1909; *s* of William John and Alice Millward; *m* 1937, Nora Florella Harper; one *s* one *d. Educ:* Solihull Sch.; St Catherine's Society, Oxford. Asst Master, Dulwich Coll., 1930–41; RAF, 1941–46. *Recreations:* music, reading, walking. *Address:* 37 Pegasus Court, St Stephen's Road, Cheltenham GL51 5AB. *T:* Cheltenham (0242) 525732.
Died 23 Feb. 1994.

MILNE, Alexander Taylor; Fellow of University College London; Secretary and Librarian, Institute of Historical Research, University of London, 1946–71; *b* 22 Jan. 1906; *s* of late Alexander Milne and Shanny (*née* Taylor); *m* 1960, Joyce Frederica Taylor, Dulwich. *Educ:* Christ's Coll., Finchley; University Coll., London. BA History Hons 1927; Diploma in Education, 1928; MA (London), 1930; FRHistS, 1938. Asst Officer and Librarian, Royal Historical Society, 1935–40; Hon. Librarian, 1965–70. Fellow, Huntington Library, Calif, 1975. Served War of 1939–45: Buffs and Maritime Artillery, 1940–42; Army Bureau of Current Affairs, 1942–44; Research Dept, FO, 1944–46. Vice-Pres., 1956–70, Pres., 1970–73, Historical Assoc. Director, History Today, 1962–79. *Publications:* History of Broadwindsor, Dorset, 1935; Catalogue of the Manuscripts of Jeremy Bentham in the Library of University College, London, 1937, 2nd edn 1961; Writings on British History, 1934–45: a Bibliography (8 vols), 1937–60; Centenary Guide to Publications of Royal Historical Society, 1968; (part-author) Historical Study in the West, 1968; (ed) Librarianship and Literature, essays

in honour of Jack Pafford, 1970; (ed) Correspondence of Jeremy Bentham, vols IV and V, 1788–1797, 1981; contribs to Cambridge History of the British Empire, Encyclopædia Britannica and learned journals. *Recreation:* golf. *Address:* 9 Frank Dixon Close, Dulwich, SE21 7BD. *T:* 081–693 6942. *Clubs:* Athenæum, Dulwich (1772).
Died 9 May 1994.

MILNE, Andrew McNicoll, MA; National Lottery Operations Director, Arts Council of England, since 1994; *b* 9 March 1937; *s* of late John McNicoll Milne and Daviona K. Coutts; *m* 1963, Nicola Charlotte (marr. diss. 1989), 2nd *d* of Ian B. Anderson and Sylvia Spencer; two *d. Educ:* Bishop Wordsworth's Sch., Salisbury; Worcester Coll., Oxford (MA 1961). Oundle: apptd, 1961; Head of History Dept, 1966–70; Housemaster, 1968–75; Second Master, 1975–79; Headmaster, The King's Sch., Worcester, 1979–83; Editor, Conference and Common Room (HMC magazine), 1983–86; Eastern Arts Assoc., 1984–92 (Dir); Exec. Dir, Arts Council of Bophuthatswana, 1992–94. FRSA. *Publications:* Metternich, 1975; contrib. to Practical Approaches to the New History. *Recreations:* music (classical and jazz), reading, writing.
Died 14 May 1995.

MILNE, Prof. Malcolm Davenport, MD, FRCP; FRS 1978; Professor of Medicine, University of London, at Westminster Medical School, 1961–80, then Emeritus; *b* 22 May 1915; *s* of Alexander Milne and Clara Lilian Milne (*née* Gee); *m* 1941 Mary Milne (*née* Thorpe); one *s* one *d. Educ:* Stockport Sch.; Univ. of Manchester (BSc, MD, ChB). Served War, RAMC, 1940–46 (despatches 1942). Ho. Phys., Manchester Royal Inf., 1939–40; Sen. Registrar in Med., Manchester, 1946–49; Lectr in Medicine: Manchester, 1949–52; Postgrad. Med. Sch., London, 1952–61. *Publications:* numerous articles relating to renal and metabolic diseases in appropriate scientific jls. *Recreations:* horticulture, haute cuisine, mathematics. *Address:* 19 Fieldway, Berkhamsted, Herts HP4 2NX. *T:* Berkhamsted (0442) 864704. *Club:* Athenæum.
Died 3 April 1991.

MILNE HOME, Captain Archibald John Fitzwilliam, DL; RN, retired; Member of Queen's Body Guard for Scotland (Royal Company of Archers) since 1963; *b* 4 May 1909; *e s* of late Sir John Milne Home and Mary, *d* of Col Hon. Fitzwilliam Elliot; *m* 1936, Evelyn Elizabeth, *d* of late Comdr A. T. Darley, RN; three *s* one *d. Educ:* RNC Dartmouth. Joined RN, 1923: Comdr 1946; Captain 1952; retd 1962; ADC to the Queen, 1961–62. Chm., Whitbread (Scotland), 1968–73. Chm., SE Region, Scottish Woodland Owners Assoc., 1966–78. DL Selkirkshire, 1970. Cross of Merit, SMO Malta, 1963. *Recreations:* shooting, fishing. *Address:* Flat 1 Hays Park, Shaftesbury, Dorset SP7 9JR. *Died 27 July 1993.*

MILNER, Sir (George Edward) Mordaunt, 9th Bt *cr* 1716; *b* 7 Feb. 1911; *er s* of Brig.-Gen. George Francis Milner, CMG, DSO (*g s* of Sir William Mordaunt Sturt Milner, 4th Bt); *S* cousin, Sir William Frederick Victor Mordaunt Milner, 8th Bt, 1960; *m* 1st, 1935, Barbara Audrey (*d* 1951), *d* of Henry Noel Belsham, Hunstanton, Norfolk; two *s* one *d*; 2nd, 1953, Katherine Moodie Bisset, *d* of D. H. Hoey, Dunfermline. *Educ:* Oundle. Served War of 1939–45, Royal Artillery. Stipendiary Steward, Jockey Club of South Africa, 1954–59; Steward, Cape Turf Club, 1959–75; Steward, Jockey Club of SA, 1977–80. Mem. Council, Thoroughbred Breeders Assoc., 1975–82. *Publications:* Thoroughbred Breeding: notes and comments, 1987; Sons of the Desert, 1987; The Godolphin Arabian, 1989; *novels:* Inspired Information, 1959; Vaulting Ambition, 1962; The Last Furlong, 1965. *Heir:* *s* Timothy William Lycett Milner, *b* 11 Oct. 1936. *Address:*

Natte Valleij, Klapmuts, Cape, S Africa. *T:* 02211–5171. *Clubs:* Rand (Johannesburg); Jockey Club of SA.
Died 18 Dec. 1995.

MILNER-BARRY, Sir (Philip) Stuart, KCVO 1975; CB 1962; OBE 1946; Ceremonial Officer, Civil Service Department (formerly Treasury), 1966–77; *b* 20 Sept. 1906; *s* of late Prof. E. L. Milner-Barry; *m* 1947, Thelma Tennant Wells; one *s* two *d. Educ:* Cheltenham Coll.; Trinity Coll., Cambridge (Major Schol.). 1st Class Hons, Classical Tripos (Pt I), Moral Science Tripos (Pt II). With L. Powell Sons & Co., Stockbrokers, 1929–38; Chess Correspondent, The Times, 1938–45; temporary civil servant, a Dept of the Foreign Office, 1940–45; Principal, HM Treasury, 1945; Asst Sec., 1947; Dir of Organisation and Methods, Treasury, 1954–58; Dir of Establishments and Organisation, Min. of Health, 1958–60; Under-Sec., Treasury, 1954–66. *Recreations:* chess (British Boy Champion, 1923; British Championship Second, 1953; mem. British Internat. teams, 1937–61; Pres. British Chess Fedn, 1970–73), walking. *Address:* 12 Camden Row, SE3 0QA. *T:* 0181–852 5808. *Club:* Brooks's.
Died 25 March 1995.

MILSTEIN, Nathan; violinist; *b* Odessa, Russia, 31 Dec. 1904; *s* of Miron and Maria Milstein; *m* 1945, Thérèse Weldon; one *d. Educ:* with Prof. Stoliarsky, in Odessa; with Leopold Auer, at Royal Conservatory, St Petersburg; studied with Eugène Isaye, Le Zoot, Belgium. Many tours in Russia, 1920–26; left Russia, 1926; annual tours throughout Europe, also in North, Central and South America, from 1920, except for war years. Hon. Mem., Acad. of St Cecilia, Rome, 1963. Commandeur, Légion d'Honneur, 1983 (Officier, 1967); Ehrenkreuz, Austria, 1963. *Address:* c/o Shaw Concerts Inc., 1995 Broadway, New York, NY 10023, USA; 17 Chester Square, SW1W 9HS.
Died 21 Dec. 1992.

MIN; *see* Minhinnick, Sir G. E. G.

MINHINNICK, Sir Gordon (Edward George), ('Min'), KBE 1976 (OBE 1950); Cartoonist, New Zealand Herald, 1930–76, retired; *b* 13 June 1902; *s* of Captain P. C. Minhinnick, RN, and Anne Sealy; *m* 1928, Vernor Helmore; one *s* (one *d* decd). *Educ:* Kelly Coll., Tavistock, Devon. Came to NZ, 1921; studied architecture for 4 years; Cartoonist: NZ Free Lance, 1926; Sun, Christchurch, and Sun, Auckland, 1927. *Address:* Apartment 219, Northbridge, Akoranga Drive, Northcote, Auckland, New Zealand.
Died 19 Feb. 1992.

MISKIN, His Honour Sir James (William), Kt 1983; QC 1967; Recorder of London, 1975–90; *b* 11 March 1925; *s* of late Geoffrey Miskin and Joyce Miskin; *m* 1st, 1951, Mollie Joan Milne; two *s* two *d*; 2nd, 1980, Sheila Joan Collett, widow. *Educ:* Haileybury; Brasenose Coll., Oxford (MA). Sub-Lt, RNVR, 1943–46. Oxford, 1946–49 (Sen. Heath Harrison Exhibnr). Called to Bar, Inner Temple, 1951; Bencher; Mem. of Bar Council, 1964–67, 1970–73. Dep. Chm., Herts QS, 1968–71; a Recorder of the Crown Court, 1972–75; Leader of SE Circuit, 1974–75. City of London Magistrate, 1976. Chm., Bd of Discipline, LSE, 1972–75. Appeals Steward, British Boxing Bd of Control, 1972–75; Chm., Inner London Probation After Care Cttee, 1979–88. One of HM Lieutenants, City of London, 1976–. Liveryman, Worshipful Co. of Curriers; Hon. Liveryman, Worshipful Co. of Cutlers. *Recreation:* golf. *Clubs:* Vincent's (Oxford); All England Lawn Tennis.
Died 21 Nov. 1993.

MITCHAM, Heather; a Metropolitan Stipendiary Magistrate, since 1986; *b* 19 Dec. 1941; *d* of Louis George Pike and Dorothy Evelyn (*née* Milverton); *m* 1964, Anthony John Mitcham; one *s* one *d. Educ:* The King's Sch., Ottery St Mary. Called to the Bar, Gray's Inn, 1964.

Examiner, Estate Duty Office, 1960–67; Dep. Chief Clerk, Inner London Magistrates' Court Service, 1967–78; Chief Clerk, Inner London Juvenile Courts, 1978–85; Senior Chief Clerk: Thames Magistrates' Court, 1985; S Western Magistrates' Court, 1986. *Recreations:* riding, horses, gardening. *Address:* c/o Camberwell Green Magistrates' Court, D'Eynsford Road, SE5 7UP.
Died 17 Aug. 1993.

MITCHELL, Prof. George Archibald Grant, OBE 1945; TD 1950; Professor of Anatomy and Director of Anatomical Laboratories, Manchester University, 1946–74, then Professor Emeritus; late Dean of Medical School and Pro-Vice-Chancellor; *b* 11 Nov. 1906; *s* of George and Agnes Mitchell; *m* 1933, Mary Cumming; one *s* two *d. Educ:* Fordyce Academy; Aberdeen Central Sch.; Aberdeen Univ. MB, ChB (1st Cl. Hons), 1929; ChM 1933; MSc (Manchester); DSc (Aberdeen) 1950; FRCS 1968. Lecturer in Anatomy, 1930–33, in Surgery, 1933–34, Aberdeen Univ.; Surgical Specialist, Co. Caithness, 1934–37; Sen. Lecturer in Anatomy, Aberdeen Univ., 1937–39. Chm., Internat. Anatomical Nomenclature Commn, 1970–75. Pres., 3rd European Anatomical Congress; Pres., S Lancs and E Cheshire BMA Br. Council, 1972–73; Mem. Ct of Examnrs, RCS, 1950–68; Mem. Bd of Governors, United Manchester Hosps, 1955–74; Past President: Anatomical Soc. of GB and Ireland; Manchester Med. Soc. Served War, 1939–45: Surgical Specialist, Officer i/c No 1 Orthopædic Centre, MEF; Officer i/c Surgical Divs, Adviser in Penicillin and Chemotherapy, 21 Army Gp. Hon. Alumnus, Univ. of Louvain, 1944; Hon. Member: Société Med. Chir. du Centre; Assoc. des Anatomistes; Amer. Assoc. Anat.; British Assoc. Clin. Anat. Chevalier First Class Order of the Dannebrog (Denmark). *Publications:* The Anatomy of the Autonomic Nervous System, 1952; Basic Anatomy (with E. L. Patterson), 1954; Cardiovascular Innervation, 1956; ed Symposium, Penicillin Therapy and Control in 21 Army Group, 1945; sections in: Penicillin (by Sir A. Fleming), 1946; Medical Disorders of the Locomotor System (by E. Fletcher), 1947; British Surgical Practice (by Sir Rock Carling and Sir J. Patterson Ross), 1951; Peripheral Vascular Disorders (by Martin, Lynn, Dible and Aird), 1956; Essentials of Neuroanatomy, 1966; Encyclopaedia Britannica, 15th edn; Editor, Nomina Anatomica, 1956–70; numerous articles in Jl Anatomy, British Jl Surg., Jl Bone and Joint Surg., Brit. Jl Radiol., BMJ, Lancet, Acta Anat., Nature, Brit. Jl Urol., Edinburgh Medical Jl, Jl Hist. Med., Aberdeen Univ. Rev., Ann. Méd. Chir. du Centre, etc. *Recreations:* music, studying archaeology.
Died 14 April 1993.

MITCHELL, Harold Charles, CIE 1947; Indian Police (retired); *b* 7 March 1896; *s* of late Daniel Charles Mitchell and Helen Mitchell; *m* 1923, Edna Evadne Bion (*d* 1982); one *d. Educ:* Fairfield. RNVR, Bristol, 1912–19 (Pay Lt). Joined Indian Police, 1920; served as Dist Supt of Police, Bareilly, Benares, Cawnpore, Meerut and other UP districts; Central Intelligence Officer, UP and Ajmer, Home Dept Govt of India; Special Branch, CID, UP; Dep. Inspector-Gen. of Police, CID, UP; Personal Asst to Inspector-Gen. of Police, UP; Dep. Inspector-Gen. of Police, UP HQ and Railways. Pres., Indian Police (UK) Assoc., 1979–. *Recreations:* formerly golf, fishing. *Address:* 41 Clarefield Court, North End Lane, Sunningdale, Ascot, Berks SL5 0EA. *T:* Ascot (0344) 23962. *Club:* Naval.
Died 11 May 1991.

MITCHELL, Prof. John Richard Anthony, (Tony), FRCP; Foundation Professor of Medicine, Nottingham Medical School, 1967–90, then Emeritus; Consultant Physician, Nottingham Hospitals, since 1968; *b* 20 Oct. 1928; *s* of Richard and Elizabeth Mitchell; *m* 1954, Muriel Joyce Gibbon; two *s* two *d. Educ:* Manchester Univ. (BSc,

MB ChB, MD); St Catherine's Coll., Oxford (MA, DPhil). Junior clinical posts, Manchester, 1953–54; Medical Specialist, RAMC, 1955–57; Registrar and Lectr, and Asst to Regius Prof., Oxford, 1957–61; MRC Research Fellow, Oxford, 1961–63; First Asst, Oxford, 1963–68; Fellow, Linacre Coll., Oxford, 1964–68. Adviser in general medicine to DHSS, 1968–81. President: Assoc. of Physicians of GB and Ireland, 1982–83; Nottingham Medico-Chirurgical Soc., 1989–90. Chm., Atherosclerosis Discussion Gp, 1986–89. Moxon Medal, RCP, 1990. *Publications:* Arterial Disease, 1965; numerous papers on aspects of vascular disease. *Recreations:* music, getting on to water (sea and canal), local history, natural history, arguing. *Address:* Department of Public Health, Medicine and Epidemiology, University Hospital, Nottingham NG7 2UH. *T:* Nottingham (0602) 421421.

Died 22 March 1991.

MITCHELL, Dr Peter Dennis, FRS 1974; Chairman and Hon. Director, Glynn Research Foundation, since 1987; *b* 29 Sept. 1920; *s* of Christopher Gibbs Mitchell, Mitcham, Surrey; *m* 1st, Eileen Rollo (marr. diss.); one *s* one *d*; 2nd, 1958, Helen, *d* of Lt-Col Raymond P. T. ffrench, late Indian Army; two *s. Educ:* Queen's Coll., Taunton; Jesus Coll., Cambridge (BA 1943; PhD 1950; Hon. Fellow, 1980). Dept of Biochem., Univ. of Cambridge, 1943–55, Demonstrator 1950–55; Dir of Chem. Biol. Unit, Dept of Zoology, Univ. of Edinburgh, 1955–63, Sen. Lectr 1961–62, Reader 1962–63; Founder and Dir of Res., Glynn Res. Labs, later Glynn Res. Inst., 1964–86. Vis. Prof., KCL, 1987–89. Sir Hans Krebs Lect. and Medal, Fed. European Biochem. Socs, 1978; Fritz Lipmann Lectr, Gesellschaft für Biol. Chem., 1978; Humphry Davy Meml Lectr, RIC and Chilterns and Mddx Sect. of Chem. Soc., at Royal Instn of London, 1980; James Rennie Bequest Lectr, Univ. of Edinburgh, 1980; Croonian Lecture, Royal Soc., 1987. For. Associate, Nat. Acad. of Scis, USA, 1977; Associé Etranger de l'Acad. des Sciences, France, 1989; Foreign Mem., Acad. of Creators, USSR, 1989; Hon. Member: Soc. for Gen. Microbiology, 1984; Japanese Biochem. Soc., 1984; Biochemical Soc. of the USSR, 1991; Hon. Fellow, UMIST, 1990. Hon. Dr rer. nat. Tech. Univ., Berlin, 1976; Hon. DSc: Exeter, 1977; Chicago, 1978; Liverpool, 1979; Bristol, 1980; Edinburgh, 1980; Hull, 1980; Aberdeen, 1990; Hon. ScD: East Anglia, 1981; Cambridge, 1985; DUniv York, 1982. CIBA Medal and Prize, Biochem. Soc., for outstanding research, 1973; (jtly) Warren Trienniel Prize, Trustees of Mass Gen. Hosp., Boston, 1974; Louis and Bert Freedman Foundn Award, NY Acad. of Scis, 1974; Wilhelm Feldberg Foundn Prize, 1976; Lewis S. Rosenstiel Award, Brandeis Univ., 1977; Nobel Prize for Chemistry, 1978; Copley Medal, Royal Society, 1981; Medal of Honour, Athens Municipal Council, 1982. *Publications:* Chemiosmotic Coupling in Oxidative and Photosynthetic Phosphorylation, 1966; Chemiosmotic Coupling and Energy Transduction, 1968; papers in scientific jls. *Recreations:* enjoyment of family life, home-building and creation of wealth and amenity, restoration of buildings of architectural and historical interest, music, thinking, understanding, inventing, making, sailing. *Address:* Glynn House, Bodmin, Cornwall PL30 4AU. *T:* Cardinham (020882) 540. *Club:* Athenæum.

Died 10 April 1992.

MITCHELL, Maj.-Gen. Robert Imrie, OBE 1958 (MBE 1945); retired; *b* 25 Jan. 1916; *s* of James I. Mitchell; *m* 1947, Marion Lyell. *Educ:* Glasgow Academy; Glasgow Univ. BSc 1936, MB, ChB 1939. FFCM. 2/Lt 1937, Lieut 1938 (TA Gen. List); Lieut, RAMC, 1939; served war 1939–45 (despatches 1945); Captain 1940; Major 1947; Lt-Col 1958; Col 1962; Brig. 1968; DDMS, I (British) Corps, BAOR, 1968–69; Maj.-Gen. 1969; DDMS, Army Strategic Command, 1969–71; DMS, BAOR, 1971–73.

QHP 1970–73. Hon. Colonel, Glasgow and Strathclyde Univs. OTC TA, 1977–82. OStJ 1966. *Recreations:* fishing, golf. *Clubs:* Naval and Military; Royal Scottish Automobile (Glasgow). *Died 25 June 1993.*

MITCHELL, Tony; *see* Mitchell, J. R. A.

MITCHELL COTTS, Sir Crichton; *see* Cotts.

MITCHENSON, Francis Joseph Blackett, (Joe); Joint Founder and Director, The Raymond Mander and Joe Mitchenson Theatre Collection, since 1939 (Theatre Collection Trust, since 1977); *b* 4 Oct. 1911; *s* of Francis William Mitchenson and Sarah Roddam. *Educ:* privately; Fay Compton Studio of Dramatic Art. First appeared on stage professionally in Libel, Playhouse, London, 1934; acted in repertory, on tour and in London, until 1948; with Raymond Mander, founded Theatre Collection, 1939; War Service with Royal Horse Artillery, invalided out, 1943; returned to stage, and collab. with Raymond Mander on many BBC progs. Collection subject of an Aquarius programme, 1971; many theatrical exhbns, incl. 50 Years of British Stage Design, for British Council, USSR, 1979. Archivist to: Sadler's Wells; Old Vic. Mem., Soc. of West End Theatre Awards Panel, 1976–78. Several TV appearances, 1987–88. Luncheon party given by theatrical profession to celebrate his work and that of his partner, Raymond Mander, over past 50 years, 1991. *Publications:* with Raymond Mander: Hamlet Through the Ages, 1952 (2nd rev. edn 1955); Theatrical Companion to Shaw, 1954; Theatrical Companion to Maugham, 1955; The Artist and the Theatre, 1955; Theatrical Companion to Coward, 1957; A Picture History of British Theatre, 1957; (with J. C. Trewin) The Gay Twenties, 1958; (with Philip Hope-Wallace) A Picture History of Opera, 1959; (with J. C. Trewin) The Turbulent Thirties, 1960; The Theatres of London, 1961, illus. by Timothy Birdsall (2nd rev. edn, paperback, 1963; 3rd rev. edn 1975); A Picture History of Gilbert and Sullivan, 1962; British Music Hall: A Story in Pictures, 1965 (rev. and enlarged edn 1974); Lost Theatres of London, 1968 (2nd edn, rev. and enlarged, 1976); Musical Comedy: A Story in Pictures, 1969; Revue: A Story in Pictures, 1971; Pantomime: A Story in Pictures, 1973; The Wagner Companion, 1977; Victorian and Edwardian Entertainment from Old Photographs, 1978; Introd. to Plays, by Noël Coward (4 vols), 1979; Guide to the W. Somerset Maugham Theatrical Paintings, 1980; contribs and revs in Encyc. Britannica, Theatre Notebook, and Books and Bookmen. *Recreations:* collecting anything and everything theatrical, sun bathing. *Address:* The Mansion, Beckenham Place, Kent BR3 2BP. *T:* 081–650 9322; (office) 081–658 7725.

Died 7 Oct. 1992.

MITFORD, Rupert Leo Scott B.; *see* Bruce-Mitford.

MOIR, (George) Guthrie, MA; retired; *b* 30 Oct. 1917; *s* of James William and May Flora Moir; *m* 1951, Sheila Maureen Ryan, SRN; one *s* two *d. Educ:* Berkhamsted; Peterhouse, Cambridge. Officer, 5th Suffolk Regt, 1940–46, POW Singapore, 1942. Chief Officer (with Countess (Edwina) Mountbatten of Burma), St John Ambulance Bde Cadets, 1947–50; Dir, European Youth Campaign, 1950–52; Chm., later Pres., World Assembly of Youth, 1952–56; Education Adviser, Hollerith Tab. Machine Co., 1957; adopted Bradenham Manor (Disraeli's) as a training centre; Asst Controller and Exec. Producer, Rediffusion TV, 1958–68; Controller of Educn and Religious Programmes, Thames TV, 1968–76. Serious damage under train in Sept. 1974. Member: Gen. Synod (formerly House of Laity, Church Assembly), 1956–75; Bd of Church Army, 1973–; Mem. Council, Reading Univ. Mem. Cttee Athenæum, 1974–. Contested (L) Aylesbury Div., 1950. CC Bucks, 1949–75; President: Old Berkhamstedians Assoc., 1974; Ivinghoe Beacon

Villages, 1973; started Green Park in adjoining delicious Rothschild country (Chm., Youth Centre). Vice Pres., St John, Bucks. Papal Bene Merenti Medal 1970, for services to religious and educational broadcasting. FRSA 1980. OStJ. Many TV series, including This Week; Dialogue with Doubt; Royalist and Roundhead; Best Sellers; Treasures of the British Museum; (with Nat. Trust) A Place in the Country; A Place in History; A Place in Europe. *Publications:* (ed) Why I Believe, 1964; (ed) Life's Work, 1965; (ed) Teaching and Television: ETV Explained, 1967; The Suffolk Regiment, 1969; Into Television, 1969; (ed) Beyond Hatred, 1969; contribs to Times, Times Ed. Supplement, Church Times, Contemporary Review, Frontier, etc. *Recreations:* golf, poetry, churches, mountains. *Address:* The Old Rectory, Aston Clinton, Aylesbury, Bucks HP22 5JR. *T:* Aylesbury (0296) 630393. *Club:* Nikaean.

Died 29 Nov. 1993.

MOLSON, Baron, *cr* 1961 (Life Peer), of High Peak, co. Derby; **(Arthur) Hugh (Elsdale) Molson,** PC 1956; President, Council for Protection of Rural England, 1971–80 (Chairman, 1968–71); *b* 29 June 1903; *o surv. s* of late Major J. E. Molson, MP, Gainsborough, and Mary, *d* of late A. E. Leeson, MD; *m* 1949, Nancy (decd), *d* of late W. H. Astington, Bramhall, Cheshire. *Educ:* Royal Naval Colleges, Osborne and Dartmouth; Lancing; New Coll., Oxford. Pres. of Oxford Union, 1925; 1st Class Hons Jurisprudence. Served 36 Searchlight Regt, 1939–41; Staff Captain 11 AA, Div., 1941–42. Barrister-at-Law, Inner Temple, 1931. Political Sec., Associated Chambers of Commerce of India, 1926–29; contested Aberdare Div. of Merthyr Tydfil, 1929; MP (U) Doncaster, 1931–35; MP (U) The High Peak Div. of Derbyshire, 1939–61. Parly Sec., Min. of Works, 1951–53; Joint Parly Sec., Min. of Transport and Civil Aviation, Nov. 1953–Jan. 1957; Minister of Works, 1957–Oct. 1959. Mem., Monckton Commission on Rhodesia and Nyasaland, 1960; Chm., Commn of Privy Counsellors on the dispute between Buganda and Bunyoro, 1962. Pres., TCPA, 1963–70. *Publications:* articles in various reviews on political and other subjects. *Address:* 20 Marsham Court, Marsham Street, SW1P 4JY. *T:* 071–828 2008. *Clubs:* Athenæum, Carlton. *Died 13 Oct. 1991.*

MOLYNEUX, Wilfrid, FCA; *b* 26 July 1910; *s* of Charles Molyneux and Mary (*née* Vose); *m* 1937, Kathleen Eleanor Young; one *s* one *d. Educ:* Douai Sch. With Cooper Brothers & Co., 1934–67; Finance Mem., BSC, 1967–71. *Address:* 105 Park Road, Brentwood, Essex CM14 4TT. *Died 7 Feb. 1994.*

MONAGHAN, Rt Rev. James; Titular Bishop of Cell Ausaille, Archdiocese of St Andrews and Edinburgh, 1970–92; Parish Priest of Holy Cross, Edinburgh, 1959–92; *b* Bathgate, 11 July 1914; *s* of Edward and Elizabeth Monaghan. *Educ:* St Aloysius' Coll., Glasgow; Blairs Coll., Aberdeen; Scots Coll., Valladolid; St Kieran's Coll., Kilkenny, Ireland. Priest, 1940; Secretary, 1953; Vicar-Gen. for Archdio. St Andrews and Edinburgh, 1958, Bp Auxiliary, 1970–89. *Address:* 252 Ferry Road, Edinburgh EH5 3AN. *T:* 031–552 3957.

Died 3 June 1994.

MONGER, George William; Head of Industry, Agriculture and Employment Group, HM Treasury, since 1990; *b* 1 April 1937; *s* of George Thomas Monger and Agnes Mary (*née* Bates). *Educ:* Holloway Sch.; Jesus Coll., Cambridge (PhD 1962). Entered Home Civil Service (Admin. Class), 1961: Min. of Power, Min. of Technol., DTI, and Dept of Energy; Principal, 1965; Asst Sec., 1972; Under-Secretary: Electricity Div., 1976, Coal Div., 1979, Dept of Energy; Social Services Gp, 1981, Fiscal Policy Gp, 1983, HM Treasury; Cabinet Office, 1987. Alexander Prize, RHistS, 1962. *Publication:* The End of Isolation: British Foreign

Policy, 1900–1907, 1963. *Address:* c/o HM Treasury, Whitehall, SW1. *Club:* United Oxford & Cambridge University. *Died 1 Sept. 1992.*

MONROE, John George; Social Security (formerly National Insurance) Commissioner, 1973–88; *b* 27 July 1913; *s* of late Canon Horace G. Monroe, Vicar of Wimbledon and Sub-dean of Southwark and Frances Alice Monroe (*née* Stokes); *m* 1943, Jane Reynolds; one *s* two *d. Educ:* Marlborough Coll.; Oriel Coll., Oxford. Called to Bar, Middle Temple, 1937; Master of the Bench, 1967. *Publications:* (ed, with Judge McDonnell) Kerr on Fraud and Mistake, 7th edn 1952; The Law of Stamp Duties, 1954, 5th edn (with R. S. Nock) 1976. *Address:* Highmead, Birchwood Grove Road, Burgess Hill, West Sussex RH15 0DL. *T:* Burgess Hill (0444) 223350.

Died 10 July 1991.

MONSELL, 2nd Viscount *cr* 1935, of Evesham, Co. of Worcester; **Henry Bolton Graham Eyres Monsell;** *b* 21 Nov. 1905; *s* of 1st Viscount Monsell, GBE, PC, and Caroline Mary Sybil, CBE (*d* 1959), *d* of late H. W. Eyres, Dumbleton Hall, Evesham; *S* father, 1969. *Educ:* Eton. Served N Africa and Italy, 1942–45 (despatches); Lt-Col Intelligence Corps. US Medal of Freedom with bronze palm, 1946. *Recreation:* music. *Heir:* none. *Address:* The Mill House, Dumbleton, Evesham, Worcs WR11 6TR. *Club:* Travellers'. *Died 28 Nov. 1993 (ext).*

MONSON, Sir (William Bonnar) Leslie, KCMG 1965 (CMG 1950); CB 1964; HM Diplomatic Service, retired; *b* 28 May 1912; *o s* of late J. W. Monson and Selina L. Monson; *m* 1948, Helen Isobel Browne. *Educ:* Edinburgh Acad.; Hertford Coll., Oxford. Entered Civil Service (Dominions Office) 1935; transferred to Colonial Office, 1939; Asst Sec., 1944; seconded as Chief Sec. to West African Council, 1947–51; Asst Under-Sec. of State, Colonial Office, 1951–64; British High Commissioner in the Republic of Zambia, 1964–66; Dep. Under-Sec. of State, Commonwealth Office, later FCO, 1967–72. Dir, Overseas Relations Branch, St John Ambulance, 1975–81. KStJ 1975. *Address:* Golf House, Goffers Road, Blackheath, SE3 0UA. *Club:* United Oxford & Cambridge University. *Died 3 July 1993.*

MONTAGU, (Alexander) Victor (Edward Paulet); *b* 22 May 1906; *s* of 9th Earl of Sandwich and 1st wife, Alberta, *d* of William Sturges, New York; *S* father, 1962, as 10th Earl of Sandwich, but disclaimed his peerages for life, 24 July 1964; *m* 1st, 1934, Rosemary (marr. diss. 1958), *d* of late Major Ralph Harding Peto; two *s* four *d*; 2nd, 1962, Anne, MBE (marr. annulled, 1965; she *d* 1981), *y d* of 9th Duke of Devonshire, KG, PC. *Educ:* Eton; Trinity Coll., Cambridge. MA (Nat. Sciences). Lt 5th (Hunts) Bn The Northamptonshire Regt, TA, 1926; served France, 1940, and afterwards on Gen. Staff, Home Forces. Private Sec. to Rt Hon. Stanley Baldwin, MP, 1932–34; Treasurer, Junior Imperial League, 1934–35; Chm., Tory Reform Cttee, 1943–44. MP (C) South Dorset Div. (C 1941, Ind. C 1957, C 1958–62); contested (C) Accrington Div. Lancs, Gen. Elec., 1964. *Publications:* Essays in Tory Reform, 1944; The Conservative Dilemma, 1970; articles in Quarterly Review, 1946–47. *Heir:* (to disclaimed peerages): *s* John Edward Hollister Montagu [*b* 11 April 1943; *m* 1968, Caroline, *o d* of Canon P. E. C. Hayman, Beaminster, Dorset; two *s* one *d*]. *Address:* Mapperton, Beaminster, Dorset DT8 3NR.

Died 25 Feb. 1995.

MONTAGU-POLLOCK, Sir William Horace, KCMG 1957 (CMG 1946); Ambassador to Denmark, 1960–62; *b* 12 July 1903; *s* of Sir Montagu Frederick Montagu-Pollock, 3rd Bt and Margaret Angela, *d* of W. A. Bell, Bletchingley; *m* 1st, 1933, Frances Elizabeth Prudence (marr. diss. 1945), *d* of late Sir John Fischer Williams,

CBE, KC; one *s* one *d*; 2nd, 1948, Barbara, *d* of late P. H. Jowett, CBE, FRCA, RWS; one *s*. *Educ:* Marlborough Coll.; Trinity Coll., Cambridge. Served in Diplomatic Service at Rome, Belgrade, Prague, Vienna, Stockholm, Brussels, and at Foreign Office; British Ambassador, Damascus, 1952–53 (Minister, 1950–52); British Ambassador: to Peru, 1953–58; to Switzerland, 1958–60; retired from HM Foreign Service, 1962. Governor, European Cultural Foundation; Chm., British Inst. of Recorded Sound, 1970–73; Vice-Pres., Soc. for Promotion of New Music. *Recreation:* washing up. *Address:* Flat 181, Coleherne Court, SW5 0DU. *T:* 071–373 3685.

Died 26 Sept. 1993.

MONTAGUE, Francis Arnold, CMG 1956; retired; *b* 14 June 1904; *s* of late Charles Edward Montague, OBE, author and journalist, and Madeleine Montague (*née* Scott), Manchester; *m* 1939, Fanny Susanne, *d* of late E. S. Scorer and Mrs C. D. Scorer; one *d*. *Educ:* Cargilfield Sch., Edinburgh; Rugby Sch.; Balliol Coll., Oxford. Tanganyika: served in Game Preservation Dept, 1925–28; Cadet, Colonial Administrative Service, 1928; Dist Officer, 1938; Private Sec. to Governor, 1938–40; Asst Chief Sec., 1948; Administrative Sec., Sierra Leone, 1950–58; retired from Colonial Service, Jan. 1958. Deputy-Chairman: Public Service Commn, Uganda, 1958–63; Public Service Commn, Aden, 1963. Mem., Oxon CC, 1964–73, Witney (Oxon) RDC, 1966–74; W Oxon Dist Council, 1973–76. *Recreation:* gardening. *Address:* Dolphin House, Westhall Hill, Fulbrook OX8 4BJ. *T:* Burford (099382) 2147. *Club:* Lansdowne.

Died 16 June 1991.

MONTEITH, Charles Montgomery; Fellow of All Souls College, Oxford, 1948–88, then Emeritus; *b* 9 Feb. 1921; *s* of late James Monteith and Marian Monteith (*née* Montgomery). *Educ:* Royal Belfast Academical Instn; Magdalen Coll., Oxford (Demy 1939, Sen. Demy 1948, MA 1948, BCL 1949). Sub-Warden, All Souls Coll., Oxford, 1967–69. Served War, Royal Inniskilling Fusiliers, India and Burma (Major), 1940–45. Called to the Bar, Gray's Inn, 1949; joined Faber & Faber, 1953, Dir, 1954, Vice-Chm., 1974–76, Chm., 1977–80, Senior Editorial Consultant, 1981–. Dir, Poetry Book Soc., 1966–81; Member: Literature Panel, Arts Council of GB, 1974–78; Library Adv. Council for England, 1979–81. Hon. DLitt: Ulster, 1980; Kent, 1982. *Address:* c/o Faber & Faber Ltd, 3 Queen Square, WC1N 3AU. *T:* 071–465 0045. *Club:* Garrick. *Died 9 May 1995.*

MONTEITH, Lt-Col (Robert Charles) Michael, OBE 1981; MC 1943; TD 1945; JP; Vice Lord-Lieutenant of Lanarkshire since 1964; land-owner and farmer since 1950; *b* 25 May 1914; *s* of late Major J. B. L. Monteith, CBE, and Dorothy, *d* of Sir Charles Nicholson, 1st Bt; *m* 1950, Mira Elizabeth, *e d* of late John Fanshawe, Sidmount, Moffat; one *s*. *Educ:* Ampleforth Coll., York. CA (Edinburgh), 1939. Served with Lanarkshire Yeomanry, 1939–45: Paiforce, 1942–43; MEF, 1943–44; BLA, 1944–45. Contested (U) Hamilton Division of Lanarkshire, 1950 and 1951. Member: Mental Welfare Commn for Scotland, 1962–84; E Kilbride Develt Corp., 1972–76. DL 1955, JP 1955, CC 1949–64, 1967–74, Lanarkshire; Chm., Lanark DC, later Clydesdale DC, 1974–84. Mem. Queen's Body Guard for Scotland, Royal Company of Archers. Mem. SMO of Knights of Malta; OStJ 1973. *Recreations:* shooting, curling. *Address:* Cranley, Cleghorn, Lanark ML11 7SN. *T:* Carstairs (0555) 870330. *Club:* New (Edinburgh). *Died 19 Dec. 1993.*

MONTGOMERY, Prof. George Lightbody, CBE 1960; TD 1942; MD, PhD; FRCPE, FRCPGlas, FRCPath, FRCSE; FRSE; Professor of Pathology, University of Edinburgh, 1954–71, then Emeritus; *b* 3 Nov. 1905; *o s* of late John Montgomery and Jeanie Lightbody; *m* 1933,

Margaret Sutherland, 3rd *d* of late A. Henry Forbes, Oban; one *s* one *d*. *Educ:* Hillhead High Sch., Glasgow; Glasgow Univ. MB, ChB, 1928; Commendation and RAMC Memorial Prize; PhD (St Andrews), 1937; MD Hons and Bellahouston Gold Medal (Glasgow), 1946. House Physician, House Surgeon, Glasgow Royal Infirmary, 1928–29; Lecturer in Clinical Pathology, Univ. of St Andrews, 1931–37; Lecturer in Pathology of Disease in Infancy and Childhood, Univ. of Glasgow, 1937–48; Asst Pathologist, Glasgow Royal Infirmary, 1929–31; Asst Pathologist, Dundee Royal Infirmary, 1931–37; Pathologist, Royal Hospital for Sick Children, Glasgow, 1937–48; Professor of Pathology (St Mungo-Notman Chair), Univ. of Glasgow, 1948–54. Chm. Scottish Health Services Council, 1954–59. Hon. Member: Pathological Soc. Gt Britain and Ireland; BMA. Col (Hon.) Army Medical Service. *Publications:* Textbook of Pathology, 1965; General Pathology for Students of Dentistry, 3rd edn 1965; numerous contribs to medical and scientific journals. *Recreation:* music. *Address:* 2 Cumin Place, Edinburgh EH9 2JX. *T:* 031–667 6792.

Died 5 Feb. 1993.

MONTROSE, 7th Duke of, *cr* 1707; **James Angus Graham;** Lord Graham 1445; Earl of Montrose, 1505; Bt (NS) 1625; Marquis of Montrose, 1644; Duke of Montrose, Marquis of Graham and Buchanan, Earl of Kincardine, Viscount Dundaff, Baron Aberuthven, Mugdock, and Fintrie, 1707; Earl and Baron Graham (Eng.), 1722; Hereditary Sheriff of Dunbartonshire; *b* 2 May 1907; *e s* of 6th Duke of Montrose, KT, CB, CVO, VD, and Lady Mary Douglas-Hamilton, OBE (*d* 1957), *d* of 12th Duke of Hamilton; *S* father, 1954; *m* 1st, 1930, Isobel Veronica (marr. diss. 1950; she *d* 1990), *yr d* of late Lt-Col T. B. Sellar, CMG, DSO; one *s* one *d*; 2nd, 1952, Susan Mary Jocelyn, *d* of late Dr J. M. Semple, and *widow* of Michael Raleigh Gibbs; two *s* two *d*. *Educ:* Eton; Christ Church, Oxford. Lt-Comdr RNVR. MP for Hartley-Gatooma in Federal Assembly of Federation of Rhodesia and Nyasaland, 1958–62; Minister of Agriculture, Lands, and Natural Resources, S Rhodesia, 1962–63; Minister of Agric., Rhodesia, 1964–65; (apptd in Rhodesia) Minister of External Affairs and Defence, 1966–68. *Heir: s* Marquis of Graham [*b* 6 April 1935; *m* 1970, Catherine Elizabeth MacDonell, *d* of Capt. N. A. T. Young; two *s* one *d*]. *Address:* Nether Tillyrie, Milnathort, Kinross KY13 7RW; (seat) Auchmar, Drymen, Glasgow.

Died 10 Feb. 1992.

MOODY, John Percivale, OBE 1961; producer and director for stage; Counsellor to the Board, Welsh National Opera Co.; *b* 6 April 1906; *s* of Percivale Sadleir Moody; *m* 1937, Helen Pomfret Burra; (one *s* decd). *Educ:* Bromsgrove; Royal Academy Schools. In publishing in the City, 1924–26; painting, Academe Schs, 1927–28, various London Exhibitions; taught at Wimbledon Art Sch., 1928–29; studied opera Webber Douglas Sch. Derby Day under Sir Nigel Playfair, Lyric, Hammersmith, 1931; West End plays include: The Brontës, Royalty, 1932; Hervey House, His Majesty's, 1935; After October, Criterion, 1936; played in Old Vic seasons 1934, 1937; Ascent of F6, Dog Beneath the Skin, Group Theatre, 1935; Auxiliary Fire Service, Clerkenwell, 1940 (wounded and discharged); Dir Old Vic Sch., 1940–42; Producer Old Vic Co., Liverpool, 1942–44; Birmingham Repertory Theatre, 1944–45; Carl Rosa Opera Co., 1945; Sadler's Wells Opera Co., 1945–49; Drama Dir, Arts Council of Great Britain, 1949–54; Dir, Bristol Old Vic Co., 1954–59; Dir of Productions, 1960, and Jt Artistic Dir, 1970, Welsh Nat. Opera. First productions in England of Verdi's Simone Boccanegra, 1948, Nabucco, 1952, and The Battle of Legnano, 1960; Rimsky's May Night, 1960; also for Welsh Nat. Opera: Rossini's William Tell, 1961; Macbeth, 1963; Moses, 1965; Carmen, 1967; Boris Godunov, 1968;

Simone Boccanegra, 1970; Rigoletto, 1972; The Pearl Fishers, 1973; What the Old Man Does is Always Right, Fishguard Festival, 1977. With wife, new translations of Carmen, Simone Boccanegra, Macbeth, La Traviata, The Pearl Fishers, Prince Igor, May Night, Battle of Legnano, William Tell, Moses and Fidelio. *Publications:* (with Helen Moody) translations of: The Pearl Fishers, 1979; Carmen, 1982; Moses, 1986; Songs of Massenet (2 vols) 1988. *Recreations:* swimming, gardening, painting. *Address:* 2 Richmond Park Road, Bristol BS8 3AT. *T:* Bristol (0272) 734436.   *Died 15 April 1993.*

MOON, Sir Peter (James Scott), KCVO 1979; CMG 1979; HM Diplomatic Service, retired; *b* 1 April 1928; *m* 1955, Lucile Worms; three *d.* Home Office, 1952–54; CRO, 1954–56; Second Sec., Cape Town/Pretoria, 1956–58; Principal, CRO, 1958–60; First Sec., Colombo, 1960–63; Private Sec. to Sec. of State for Commonwealth Relations, 1963–65; First Sec., UK Mission to UN, New York, 1965–69; Counsellor, FCO, 1969–70; Private Sec. to Prime Minister, 1970–72; NATO Defence Coll., 1972; seconded to NATO Internat. Staff, Brussels, 1972–75; Counsellor, Cairo, 1975–78; Ambassador to Madagascar (non-resident), 1978–79; High Comr in Tanzania, 1978–82; High Comr in Singapore, 1982–85; Ambassador to Kuwait, 1985–87. *Address:* c/o Bank of Scotland, 332 Oxford Street, W1A 3BW.   *Died 10 July 1991.*

MOON, Philip Burton, FRS 1947; Poynting Professor of Physics in the University of Birmingham, 1950–74, then Emeritus; Dean of the Faculty of Science and Engineering, 1969–72; *b* 17 May 1907; *o s* of late F. D. Moon; *m* 1st, 1937, Winifred F. Barber (*d* 1971); one *s* one *d;* 2nd, 1974, Lorna M. Aldridge. *Educ:* Leyton County High Sch.; Sidney Sussex Coll., Cambridge. Hon. DSc Aston, 1970. Hughes Medal, Royal Soc., 1991. *Publications:* Artificial Radioactivity, 1949; papers (1929–91) on physics and molecular-beam chemistry. *Address:* 4 Severn Court, Corbett Avenue, Droitwich, Worcs WR9 7DL. *T:* Droitwich (01905) 778677.   *Died 9 Oct. 1994.*

MOORE, Bobby; *see* Moore, R. F.

MOORE, Sir Edward Stanton, 2nd Bt *cr* 1923, of Colchester, Co. of Essex; OBE 1970; *b* 28 Dec. 1910; *s* of Major E. C. H. Moore (killed, Vimy Ridge, 1917) and Kathleen Margaret (*d* 1970), *d* of H. S. Oliver, Sudbury, Suffolk; *S* grandfather, 1923; *m* 1946, Margaret, *er d* of T. J. Scott-Cotterell. *Educ:* Mill Hill Sch.; Cambridge. RAF, 1940–46; Wing Comdr Special Duties. Managing Director, Spain and Western Mediterranean, BEA, 1965–72. Pres., British Chamber of Commerce in Spain, 1969–71; Dir, European British Chambers of Commerce, 1970–72. FCIT 1960. *Heir:* none. *Address:* Church House, Sidlesham, Sussex PO20 7RE. *T:* Sidlesham (024356) 369. *Clubs:* Special Forces; Chichester Yacht.

                  Died 3 Nov. 1992 (ext).

MOORE, George Herbert, MSc; FRPharmS; FRSC; *b* 1 June 1903; *s* of late R. Herbert Moore and Mabel Moore, Bath; *m* 1931, Dora, *d* of Frederick and Emily Blackmore, Bath; one *d. Educ:* King Edward's Sch., Bath; Bath Coll. of Chemistry and Pharmacy. FRPharmS (FPS 1928), FRSC (FRIC 1943); MSc Bristol 1953. Merchant Venturers' Technical Coll., Bristol: Lectr in Pharmaceutical Chemistry, 1929–38; Head of Science Dept, 1938–50; Vice-Principal, Bristol Coll. of Technology, 1950–54; Principal, Bristol Coll. of Science and Technology, 1954–66; Vice-Chancellor, Bath Univ., 1966–69. Vice-Pres. Royal Inst. of Chemistry, 1955–57. Hon. LLD Bath, 1968. *Publication:* University of Bath: the formative years 1949–69, 1982. *Recreations:* music, photography. *Address:* Hilcot, Horsecombe Vale, Combe Down, Bath BA2 5QR. *T:* Bath (0225) 837417.

                  Died 6 March 1993.

MOORE, Robert Frederick, (Bobby), OBE 1967; formerly professional footballer; sports commentator, Capital Gold, since 1990; *b* 12 April 1941; *m* 1st, 1962, Christina Elizabeth Dean (marr. diss. 1986); one *s* one *d;* 2nd, 1991, Susan Pareane-Moore. Captained: England Youth, at 17 years old (18 caps); England Under 23 (8 caps); made 108 appearances for England (record number for England until 1989, and a world record until 1978), 90 as Captain (equalling Billy Wright's record). League debut for West Ham against Manchester United, Sept. 1958; England debut against Peru, 1962; played in World Cup, in Chile, 1962; captained England for first time, against Czechoslovakia, 1963. Footballer of the Year, 1963–64; Holder of: FA Cup Winners' medal, 1964; European Cup Winners' medal, 1965; named Player of Players in World Cup (England the Winner), 1966; transferred to Fulham Football Club, 1974–77; played 1,000 matches at senior level. Manager, Oxford City Football Club, 1979–81; Coach: Eastern Ath. FC, Hong Kong, 1982–83; Carolina Lightnin, N Carolina, 1983; Manager and Dir, Southend United FC, 1983–86. Sports Editor, Sunday Sport, 1986–90. *Publication:* Bobby Moore (autobiog.), 1976.

                  Died 24 Feb. 1993.

MOORE, Roy, CBE 1962; *b* 10 Jan. 1908; *s* of Harry Moore and Ellen Harriet Post; *m* 1st, 1934, Muriel Edith (*d* 1959), *d* of late C. E. E. Shill; two *s;* 2nd, 1963, Lydia Elizabeth Newell Park (*d* 1990), *widow* of David Park, Berkeley, Calif. *Educ:* Judd Sch., Tonbridge; King's Coll., London. 2nd Cl. Hons English, 1928; AKC 1928; MA 1931; Carter Prize for English Verse. Chief English Master, Mercers' Sch., London, 1931–40; Head Master: Lawrence Sheriff Sch., Rugby, 1945–51; Mill Hill Sch., 1951–67. Served War of 1939–45, Squadron Leader RAF Bomber Command, 1941–45. Fellow King's Coll., London, 1956. *Club:* Athenæum.   *Died 1 Jan. 1992.*

MOORES, Sir John, Kt 1980; CBE 1972; Founder of the Littlewoods Organisation, 1924, Chairman, 1924–77 and 1980–82, Life President, 1982; *b* Eccles, Lancs, 25 Jan. 1896; *s* of John William Moores and Louisa (*née* Fethney); *m* 1923, Ruby Knowles; two *s* two *d. Educ:* Higher Elementary Sch. Founded: Littlewoods Pools, 1924; Littlewoods Mail Order Stores, 1932; Littlewoods Stores, 1936. Hon. Freeman, City of Liverpool, 1970; Hon. LLB Liverpool, 1973; first winner of Liverpool Gold Medal for Achievement, 1978. *Recreations:* painting, languages, sport, travel. *Address:* c/o The Littlewoods Organisation PLC, JM Centre, Old Hall Street, Liverpool L70 1AB. *T:* 051–235 2222.   *Died 25 Sept. 1993.*

MOORMAN, Mary Caroline; *b* 19 Feb. 1905; *d* of George Macaulay Trevelyan, OM, CBE, FRS, FBA, and Janet Penrose Ward, CH; *m* 1930, Rt Rev. J. R. H. Moorman (*d* 1989). *Educ:* Berkhamsted Sch. for Girls; Somerville Coll., Oxford. BA 1926; MA 1950. Chm., Trustees of Dove Cottage, 1974–77. Hon. Lectr, Sch. of English, Leeds Univ., 1970, and Dept of English, Durham Univ., 1980. Hon. LittD: Leeds, 1967; Durham, 1968. *Publications:* William III and the Defence of Holland, 1672–73, 1930; William Wordsworth, A Biography: vol. 1, The Early Years, 1957, vol. 2, The Later Years, 1965 (James Tait Black Meml Prize, 1965); (ed) Letters of William and Dorothy Wordsworth, vol. II, The Middle Years: Part 1, 1806–1811, 2nd edn (rev. and ed), 1969; vol. III, The Middle Years: Part 2, 1812–1820, 2nd edn (rev. and ed with A. G. Hill), 1970; (ed) The Journals of Dorothy Wordsworth, 1971; George Macaulay Trevelyan, a Memoir, 1980. *Recreations:* reading, bird-watching.

                  Died 21 Jan. 1994.

MOOTHAM, Sir Orby Howell, Kt 1962; *b* 17 Feb. 1901; *s* of Delmé George Mootham, ARIBA; *m* 1st, 1931, Maria Augusta Elisabeth Niemöller (*d* 1973); one *s* one *d;* 2nd, 1977, Beatrix Douglas Ward (*d* 1990), *widow* of Basil

Ward, FRIBA. *Educ:* Leinster House Sch., Putney; London Univ. MSc (Econ). Called to Bar, Inner Temple, 1926 (Yarborough-Anderson Schol., 1924; Hon. Bencher, 1958). An Advocate of Rangoon High Court, 1927–40; DJAG, Army in Burma, 1940–41, thereafter service in Dept of JAG in India and as Chief Judicial Officer, Brit. Mil. Admin, Burma (despatches); Actg Judge, Rangoon High Court, 1945–46; Judge, Allahabad High Court, 1946–55; Chief Justice, 1955–61; Legal Adviser's Dept, CRO, 1961–63; Deputy-Chairman of QS: Essex, 1964–71; Kent, 1965–71; Surrey, 1970–71; a Recorder of the Crown Court, 1972. Chm., Allahabad Univ. Enquiry Cttee, 1953–54; Chm., Med. Appeals Tribunal, 1963–73; Mem. Governing Body, Froebel Educational Inst., 1965–79. *Publications:* Burmese Buddhist Law, 1939; The East India Company's Sadar Courts 1801–34, 1983; articles in Brit. Year Book of Internat. Law and other legal jls. *Address:* 25 Claremont Road, Teddington, Middlesex TW11 8DH. *T:* 0181–977 1665. *Club:* Athenæum.
Died 19 July 1995.

MORGAN; *see* Vaughan-Morgan, family name of Baron Reigate.

MORGAN, Rev. Chandos Clifford Hastings Mansel, CB 1973; MA; Rector, St Margaret Lothbury, City of London, 1983–89; retired; *b* 12 Aug. 1920; *s* of Llewelyn Morgan, Anglesey; *m* 1946, Dorothy Mary (*née* Oliver); one *s*. *Educ:* Stowe; Jesus Coll., Cambridge (MA); Ridley Hall, Cambridge. Curate of Holy Trinity, Tunbridge Wells, 1944–51; staff of Children's Special Service Mission, 1947–51; Chaplain, RN, 1951; served in HM Ships: Pembroke, 1951; Vengeance and Ceylon, 1952; Drake, 1954; Theseus, 1956; Ocean, 1957; Caledonia, 1958; Adamant, 1960; Jufair, 1961; Heron, 1963; Ark Royal, 1965; Collingwood, 1967; Royal Arthur, 1969; Chaplain of the Fleet and Archdeacon of the Royal Navy, 1972–75; QHC 1972–75; Chaplain, Dean Close Sch., Cheltenham, 1976–83. *Recreations:* riding, shooting, sailing, gardening, etc. *Address:* Westwood Farmhouse, West Lydford, Somerton, Somerset TA11 7DL. *T:* Wheathill (096324) 301. *Died 1 Jan. 1993.*

MORGAN, Cyril Dion, OBE 1970; TD 1945; FCIS; Secretary, Institution of Structural Engineers, 1961–82; *b* 30 Aug. 1917; *y s* of late Robert Dymant Morgan and Nell (*née* Barrett); *m* 1948, Anthea Grace Brown; two *d*. *Educ:* Sloane Sch., Chelsea; City of London Coll. Served War, North Africa, Italy, 1939–46. Secretary: Inst. of Road Transport Engineers, 1948–53; British Road Fedn, 1953–61. Hon. Fellow, IStructE, 1983. FRSA. *Publications:* articles/reports in Proc. Instn of Structural Engrs. *Recreation:* thinking about gardening. *Address:* 12 Bartholomew Way, Westminster Park, Chester CH4 7RJ. *T:* Chester (0244) 675260. *Died 19 April 1994.*

MORGAN, Rev. David Lewis, (Dewi); Rector, St Bride's Church, Fleet Street, EC4, 1962–84; a Prebendary of St Paul's Cathedral, 1976–84, then Prebendary Emeritus; *b* 5 Feb. 1916; *s* of David and Anne Morgan; *m* 1942, Doris, *d* of Samuel and Ann Povey; two *d*. *Educ:* Lewis Sch., Pengam; University Coll. Cardiff (BA); St Michael's Coll., Llandaff. Deacon, 1939; priest, 1940; Curate: St Andrew's, Cardiff, 1939–43; Aberdare, 1943–46; Aberavon, 1946–50; Soc. for the Propagation of the Gospel: Press Officer, 1950–52; Editorial and Press Sec., 1952–62. Editor, St Martin's Review, 1953–55; Associate Editor: Church Illustrated, 1955–67; Anglican World, 1960–67; Priest-in-charge, St Dunstan-in-the-West, 1978–80. Hon. FIPR 1984. Publicity Club of London Cup for services to advertising, 1984. Freeman of City of London, 1963. *Publications:* Expanding Frontiers, 1957; The Bishops Come to Lambeth, 1957; Lambeth Speaks, 1958; The Undying Fire, 1959; (ed) They Became Anglicans, 1959; 1662 And All That, 1961; But God

Comes First, 1962; Agenda for Anglicans, 1963; Seeds of Peace, 1965; Arising From the Psalms, 1965; (ed) They Became Christians, 1966; God and Sons, 1967; The Church in Transition, 1970; The Phoenix of Fleet Street, 1973; Where Belonging Begins, 1988. *Recreation:* sleeping. *Address:* 217 Rosendale Road, West Dulwich, SE21 8LW. *T:* 081–670 1308. *Died 8 Jan. 1993.*

MORGAN, Col Frank Stanley, CBE 1940; ERD 1954; JP; DL; *b* 10 Jan. 1893; *s* of F. A. Morgan, Commissioner Imperial Chinese Customs; *m* 1918, Gladys Joan (*d* 1953), *d* of Lt-Col H. M. Warde, CBE, DL Kent; no *c*; *m* 1956, Minnie Helen Pine, MBE, TD, DL, Lt-Col WRAC, The Manor House, Great Barrow, Cheshire. *Educ:* Marlborough; Christ Church, Oxford. Served European War, 1914–18; public work in Wales; Territorial and Reserve Service, 1919–39; Air Formation Signals, France, North Africa, Italy, Middle East, 1939–45. Hon. Col 50 and 81 AF Signal Regts, 1952–60. DL, Glamorgan, 1946; JP 1951. *Address:* Herbert's Lodge, Bishopston, Swansea. *T:* Bishopston (044128) 4222.
Died 16 March 1992.

MORGAN, Geraint; *see* Morgan, W. G. O.

MORGAN, Gwenda, RE 1961; wood engraver; *b* 1 Feb. 1908; *d* of late William David Morgan, JP, and Mary Morgan. *Educ:* Brighton and Hove High Sch. Studied Art at Goldsmiths' Coll. Sch. of Art, and at Grosvenor Sch. of Modern Art under Iain Macnab. Women's Land Army, 1939–46. Work represented in: British Museum; Victoria and Albert Museum; Brighton Art Gallery; Herefordshire Museum; Ashmolean Museum, Oxford; Bodleian Library, Oxford; Whitworth Art Gall., Manchester; Fitzwilliam Mus., Cambridge; Hunterian Art Gall., Glasgow; Art Gall., Greater Victoria, BC; Art Gall., Ontario; Glenbow Mus., Alberta; Winnipeg Art Gall., Manitoba. *Publications:* Pictures and Rhymes, 1936; (illustrator) Gray's Elegy, 1946; (illustrator) Grimm's Other Tales, 1956; The Wood Engravings of Gwenda Morgan, 1985. *Address:* Ridge House, Petworth, West Sussex GU28 0ES. *Died 9 Jan. 1991.*

MORGAN, His Honour Peter Trevor Hopkin; QC 1972; a Circuit Judge, 1972–87; Liaison Judge to Gwent Magistrates, and Justice of the Peace, 1973–87; a Judge of the Provincial Court of the Church in Wales, 1976–87; *b* 5 Feb. 1919; *o s* of Cyril Richard Morgan and Muriel Arceta (*née* Hole); *m* 1942, Josephine Mouncey, *d* of Ben Travers, CBE, AFC; one *s* three *d*. *Educ:* Mill Hill Sch.; Magdalen Coll., Oxford (BA). Called to Bar, Middle Temple, 1949; Wales and Chester Circuit; Lectr in Law, Univ. of Wales (Cardiff and Swansea), 1950–55. Liveryman, Fishmongers' Company. *Recreations:* inland waterways, viniculture, wine making. *Address:* 26 Westmead Lane, Chippenham, Wilts SN15 3HZ.
Died 30 Dec. 1995.

MORGAN, (William) Geraint (Oliver), QC 1971; a Recorder of the Crown Court, since 1972; *b* Nov. 1920; *m* 1957, J. S. M. Maxwell; two *s* two *d*. *Educ:* University Coll. of Wales, Aberystwyth; Trinity Hall, Cambridge (Squire Law Schol.); London Univ. BA, LLB. Served War of 1939–45 with Royal Marines; demobilised with Rank of Major, 1946. Called to the Bar, Gray's Inn, 1947 (Holt Scholar); Northern Circuit. Formerly FCIArb. MP (C) Denbigh, Oct. 1959–1983; Chm., Welsh Parly Party, 1967; resigned from Cons. Party, 1983. Member: Lord Chancellor's Cttee (Payne Cttee) on Recovery of Judgment Debts, 1965–69; Investiture Cttee of HRH The Prince of Wales, 1968–69. Mem., Gorsedd of Bards of Royal Nat. Eisteddfod of Wales, 1969–. *Address:* 13 Owen Road, Prescot, Merseyside L35 0PJ. *Died 2 July 1995.*

MORINI, Erica; concert violinist; *b* Vienna, 5 Jan. 1904; *m* 1938, Felice Siracusano; no *c*. *Educ:* at age of 4 years under father, Prof. Oscar Morini, and then under Prof. Ottocar Sevcik, masterclass of Viennese Conservatory, at age of 8. Début under Arthur Nikisch, at age of 9, in Leipzig Gewandhaus (Beethoven Festival); from there on Concert-tours to: Australia, Asia, Africa, Europe; to USA, 1920. Hon. Mem., Sigma Alpha Beta. Hon. MusD: Smith Coll., Mass, 1955; New England Conservatory of Music, Mass, 1963. Gold Medal, City of NY, 1976. *Recreations:* mountain climbing, chamber music. *Address:* 1200 Fifth Avenue, New York, NY 10029, USA.

Died 1 Nov. 1995.

MORLEY, John; actor and playwright; Pantomime Writer for Triumph Productions Ltd, 1973–87; *b* 24 Dec. 1924; *s* of Austin Morley and Patricia (*née* Bray). *Educ:* Uppingham; St John's Coll., Cambridge; RADA. Served War: commnd Coldstream Guards, 1943. Wrote Coldstream Guards pantomime, Dick Whittington and his kit, 1944; performed in and wrote two revues and pantomime, St John's Coll., Cambridge, 1947–48; perf. in and co-author of Cambridge Footlights Revue, 1948; performed in: Private View, Fortune, 1948; Birmingham Rep., 1949; Bob's Your Uncle, Theatre Royal, Stratford, and Music at Midnight, Her Majesty's, 1950; Victorian Music Hall, Players, 1951; Fancy Free, Prince of Wales, 1951–53; Northampton Rep., 1953; Call Me Madam tour, 1953–54; After the Ball, Globe, 1954; Jubilee Girl, Victoria Palace, 1956; The Crystal Heart, Saville, and Love à la Carte, Richmond, 1958; Marigold, Savoy, 1959; Follow that Girl, Vaudeville, 1960; performer and writer, Café de Paris, 1955–60; pantomime writer for Howerd and Wyndham, 1964–73; author of: songs for The Art of Living, Criterion, 1960–61; (jtly) Puss in Boots, London Palladium, 1963; (jtly) Houdini, Man of Magic, Piccadilly, 1966; (jtly) The Littlest Clown, Fortune House, 1972; Aladdin, BBC Radio, 1980; Big Night Out (Thames Television variety series), 1963–66 (incl. The Beatles Night Out, Blackpool Night Out, Boxing Night Out); BBC Television pantomimes: Babes in the Wood, 1972; The Basil Brush Pantomime, 1980; Aladdin and the Forty Thieves, 1983; BBC Children's Television series: Crazy Bus, 1972; Captain Bonny the pirate, 1973–74; Children's Television Revue, 1975; Basil Brush, 1979–81; wrote 153 pantomimes. *Publications:* (jtly) The Magic of Houdini, 1978; (jtly) The Performing Arts, 1980; Pinocchio (children's musical), 1983; The Wind in the Willows (children's musical), 1984; (jtly) The Encyclopedia of Pantomime, 1993; pantomimes: Aladdin; Jack and the Beanstalk; Sinbad the Sailor; Goldilocks and the Three Bears; Robinson Crusoe; Dick Whittington; Cinderella; Mother Goose; Babes in the Wood; The Sleeping Beauty. *Recreations:* architecture, furniture, travel, New York, Wagnerian opera, history of pantomime, British folklore, the Industrial Revolution. *Address:* 4 Stafford Terrace, W8 4SN. *T:* 071–937 5575.   *Died 16 July 1994.*

MORLEY, Robert Adolf Wilton, CBE 1957; actor-dramatist; *b* Semley, Wilts, 26 May 1908; *s* of Major Robert Morley and Gertrude Emily Fass; *m* 1940, Joan North Buckmaster, *d* of Dame Gladys Cooper, DBE; two *s* one *d*. *Educ:* Wellington Coll. Originally intended for diplomatic career; studied for stage at RADA. First appearance in Treasure Island, Strand Theatre, 1929; appeared in provinces; established repertory (with Peter Bull) at Perranporth, Cornwall; parts include: Oscar Wilde in play of that name, Gate, 1936, and Fulton (first New York appearance), 1938; Alexandre Dumas in The Great Romancer, Strand, 1937; Higgins in Pygmalion, Old Vic, 1937; Sheridan Whiteside in The Man Who Came to Dinner, Savoy, 1941; Prince Regent in The First Gentleman, New, 1945, and Savoy; Arnold Holt in Edward My Son, His Majesty's and Lyric, 1947, Martin Beck Theatre, New York, 1948; toured Australia, 1949–50; The Little Hut, Lyric, 1950; Hippo Dancing, Lyric, 1954; A

Likely Tale, Globe, 1956; Fanny, Drury Lane, 1957; Hook, Line and Sinker, Piccadilly, 1958; A Majority of One, Phœnix, 1960; A Time to Laugh, Piccadilly, 1962; Halfway Up The Tree, Queen's, 1968; How the Other Half Loves, Lyric, 1970; A Ghost on Tiptoe, Savoy, 1974; Banana Ridge, Savoy, 1976. Directed: The Tunnel of Love, Her Majesty's Theatre, 1957; Once More, with Feeling, New Theatre, 1959. Entered films, 1937; *films:* Marie Antoinette; Major Barbara; Young Mr Pitt; Outcast of the Islands; The African Queen; Curtain Up; Mr Gilbert and Mr Sullivan; The Final Test; Beat the Devil; The Rainbow Jacket; Beau Brummell; The Good Die Young; Quentin Durward; Loser Takes All; Law and Disorder; The Journey; The Doctor's Dilemma; Libel; The Battle of the Sexes; Oscar Wilde; Go to Blazes; The Young Ones; The Boys; The Road to Hong Kong; Nine Hours to Rama; The Old Dark House; Murder at the Gallop; Take her, She's Mine; Hot Enough for June; Sold in Egypt; Topkapi; Of Human Bondage; Those Magnificent Men in Their Flying Machines; Ghengis Khan; ABC Murders; The Loved One; Life at the Top; A Study in Terror; Way Way Out; Finders Keepers; Hotel Paradiso; Le Tendre Voyou; Hot Millions; Sinful Davey; Song of Norway; Oliver Cromwell; When Eight Bells Toll; Doctor in Trouble; Theatre of Blood; Too Many Cooks; The Human Factor; Little Dorrit; The Wind. Hon. DLitt Reading, 1980. *Publications:* Short Story, 1935; Goodness How Sad, 1937; Staff Dance, 1944; (with Noel Langley) Edward My Son, 1948; (with Ronald Gow) The Full Treatment, 1953; Hippo Dancing, 1953; (with Dundas Hamilton) Six Months Grace, 1957; (with Sewell Stokes) Responsible Gentleman (autobiography), 1966; A Musing Morley, 1974; Morley Marvels, 1976; (ed) Robert Morley's Book of Bricks, 1978; (ed) Robert Morley's Book of Worries, 1979; Morley Matters, 1980; The Best of Morley, 1981; The Second Book of Bricks, 1981; The Pleasures of Age, 1988. *Recreations:* conversation, horse racing. *Address:* Fairmans, Wargrave, Berks.   *Died 3 June 1992.*

MORLEY, Very Rev. William Fenton, CBE 1980; Dean Emeritus of Salisbury, since 1977; *b* 5 May 1912; *s* of Arthur Fenton and Margaret Morley; *m* 1937, Marjorie Rosa, *d* of Joseph Temple Robinson, Frinton; one *s* one *d*. *Educ:* St David's, Lampeter; Oriel Coll., Oxford; Wycliffe Hall, Oxford; University of London. Ordained deacon, 1935; priest, 1936; Curate of: Ely, Cardiff, 1935–38; Porthcawl, S Wales, 1938–43; Officiating Chaplain to the Forces, 1941–43; Vicar of Penrhiwceiber, 1943–46; Rector of Haseley, Oxon, 1946–50; Director of Music and Lecturer in Hebrew at Cuddesdon Coll., Oxon, 1946–50; Examiner in Hebrew and New Testament Greek, 1947–59 and External Lecturer in Biblical and Religious Studies, 1950–61, Univ. of London; Chaplain and Lecturer of St Gabriel's Training Coll., 1956–61; Education Sec. to Overseas Council of Church Assembly, 1950–56; Warburton Lectr, Lincoln's Inn, 1963–65; Chairman: Church of England Deployment and Payment Commission, 1965–68; Church of England Pensions Bd, 1974–80; Bath and Wells Diocesan Education Council, 1978–82. Public Preacher to Diocese of Rochester, 1950–56; Canon Residentiary and Precentor of Southwark Cathedral, 1956–61; Vicar of Leeds, Rural Dean of Leeds and Hon. Canon of Ripon, 1961–71; Dean of Salisbury, 1971–77. Editor, East and West Review, 1953–64. Chaplain to HM's Household, 1965–71; Church Comr, 1968–77. *Publications:* One Church, One Faith, One Lord, 1953; The Church to Which You Belong, 1955; The Call of God, 1959; Preaching through the Christian Year: Year 4, 1974, Year 6, 1977. *Recreations:* music, writing. *Address:* 21 Capel Court, The Burgage, Prestbury, Cheltenham GL52 3EL. *T:* Cheltenham (01242) 579463.

Died 9 July 1995.

MORLEY-JOHN, Michael, CBE 1979; RD 1970; Judge of the Supreme Court of Hong Kong, 1973–78; *b* 22 May 1923; *s* of late Clifford Morley-John and Norah (*née* Thompson); *m* 1951, Sheila Christine Majendie; one *s* one *d. Educ:* Wycliffe Coll.; Univ. of Bristol (LLB). Called to the Bar, Gray's Inn, 1950. Hong Kong: Crown Counsel, 1951; Dir of Public Prosecutions, 1961; Acting Solicitor Gen., 1966–67; Dist Judge, 1967; Judicial Comr, State of Brunei, 1974. Acting Comdr, RNR, 1973. *Recreations:* tennis, stamp collecting, sailing. *Address:* The Coach House, Woodland Way, Milford-on-Sea, Hants SO41 0NB. *T:* Lymington (0590) 644824. *Clubs:* Milford and South Hants (Milford-on-Sea); Royal Ocean Racing; Bar Yacht; Hong Kong, Hong Kong Kennel (former Pres.) (Hong Kong). *Died 2 April 1993.*

MORLING, Col Leonard Francis, DSO 1940; OBE 1946; TD 1942; architect; *b* 2 Nov. 1904; British; 2nd *s* of late Ernest Charles Morling and Frances Ruth Baldwin; unmarried. *Educ:* Brighton, Hove and Sussex Grammar Sch. Architect, 1927–36; Mem. of firm, C. Morling Ltd, Builders and Contractors, Seaford, 1936–39; social work, in London, 1948–50, Malaya, 1950–55; Personnel and Welfare Work, London, 1956–59, Australia, 1960–63, London, 1964. Commnd, Territorial Army, 1924; Capt. 1930; Major, 1934; Lt-Col, 1943; Col 1946; served France and Flanders (despatches, DSO); Persia, Iraq and India. *Publication:* Sussex Sappers, 1972. *Address:* c/o Lloyds Bank, Seaford, East Sussex BN25 1LJ.
Died 17 May 1994.

MORLING, Norton Arthur; Member, Civil Aviation Authority, 1972–75; *b* 13 Feb. 1909; *o s* of Norton and Edith Morling, Hunsdon, Herts; *m* 1942, Rachel Paterson, *d* of James and Elizabeth Chapman, Johannesburg, SA; one *s* one *d. Educ:* Hertford Grammar Sch.; Cambridge Univ. (MA); Birmingham Univ. (MCom). War Service, N Africa and Italy, 1942–45 (despatches); Lt-Col 1944; ADS&T, AFHQ, 1944–45. Joined Turner & Newall Ltd as Management Trainee, 1931; Dir, and in some cases Chm., of various subsid. and associated companies, UK and overseas, 1946–64, including Turner Brothers Asbestos Co. Ltd and Ferodo Ltd; Gp Dir, 1957–67; Financial Dir, 1964–67; seconded as Industrial Advr to Nat. Economic Develt Office, 1967–70; Mem., Air Transport Licensing Bd, 1971–72. *Recreation:* gardening. *Address:* Little Brook House, Over Wallop, Stockbridge, Hants SO20 8HT. *T:* Andover (0264) 781296.
Died 6 Feb. 1994.

MORRELL, Col (Herbert) William (James), OBE 1954; MC 1944; TD; JP; DL; *b* 1 Aug. 1915; *er s* of James Herbert Morrell, MA, Headington Hill, Oxford; *m* 1947, Pamela Vivien Eleanor, *d* of Richard Stubbs, Willaston, Cheshire; one *s* two *d. Educ:* Eton; Magdalen Coll., Oxford (MA). 2nd Lt RA, 1936; served War of 1939–45 (France, Madagascar, Burma); retired 1948. DL 1961, JP 1959, High Sheriff 1960, Oxon. *Recreations:* hunting, sailing. *Address:* Caphill, Sandford St Martin, Oxon OX7 7AL. *T:* Great Tew (01608) 683291.
Died 20 Nov. 1995.

MORRIS, Prof. (William) Ian (Clinch), TD; FRCSE, FRCOG; Professor of Obstetrics and Gynaecology, University of Manchester, 1949–72, Professor Emeritus since 1972; *b* 10 May 1907; *s* of Dr J. M. Morris, Neath; *m* 1938, Mary Farquharson (*d* 1976); one *d. Educ:* Royal High Sch., Edinburgh; Edinburgh Univ. (MB ChB). FRCSE 1934; FRCOG 1949. Obstetrician to Ayr County Council, 1937–46; Sen. Lectr in Obstetrics and Gynaecology, Univ. of Edinburgh, 1946–49. RAMC (TA) 1935; war service, 1939–43. *Publications:* (jointly) A Combined Text-book of Obstetrics and Gynaecology, 1950; contribs to Jl of Obstetrics and Gynaecology of British Commonwealth, Lancet, Edinburgh Med. Jl, etc.

Address: Edenfield House, Springfield, by Cupar, Fife KY15 5RT. *T:* Cupar (01334) 657517.
Died 20 Nov. 1995.

MORRISON, Rt Hon. Sir Peter (Hugh), Kt 1990; PC 1988; *b* 2 June 1944; 3rd *s* of 1st Baron Margadale, TD and late Hon. Margaret Esther Lucie Smith, 2nd *d* of 2nd Viscount Hambleden. *Educ:* Eton; Keble Coll., Oxford (Hons Law; Hon. Fellow, 1989). Personal Asst to Rt Hon. Peter Walker, MP, 1966–67; investment manager, 1968–70; independent business, 1970–74. MP (C) City of Chester, Feb. 1974–1992. An Opposition Whip, 1976–79; a Lord Comr of HM Treasury, and Govt Pairing Whip, 1979–81; Parly Under-Sec. of State, 1981–83, Minister of State, 1983–85, Dept of Employment; Minister of State, DTI, 1985–86, Dept of Energy, 1987–90; PPS to the Prime Minister, 1990. Sec., NW Cons. Members' Gp, 1974–76; Jt Sec., Cons. Smaller Businesses Cttee, 1974–76. Dep. Chm., Cons. Party, 1986–89. Chairman: Cons. Collegiate Forum, 1987–89; One Nation Forum, 1987–89. Pres., Assoc. of Cons. Clubs, 1986–87; Vice-Pres., Nat. YCs, 1990–. FRSA. *Clubs:* White's, Pratt's.
Died 13 July 1995.

MORRISON-SCOTT, Sir Terence (Charles Stuart), Kt 1965; DSC 1944; DL; DSc; Director, British Museum (Natural History), 1960–68 (Director, Science Museum, 1956–60); *b* Paris, 24 Oct. 1908; *o s* of late R. C. S. Morrison-Scott, DSO, and Douairière Jhr. R. Quarles van Ufford; *m* 1935, Rita, 4th *d* of late E. J. Layton. *Educ:* Eton; Christ Church (MA of the House, 1947), Oxford; Royal College of Science (1st Class Hons Zoology, BSc, ARCS 1935, MSc 1939). FLS 1937; DSc London, 1952. Asst Master, Eton, 1935; Scientific Staff, Brit. Museum (Natural Hist.) in charge of Mammal Room, 1936–39, 1945–55 and part of 1956. Served War of 1939–45, with Royal Navy (DSC); Lt-Comdr RNVR. Treas., Zoological Soc. of London, 1950–76; Treas., XVth Internat. Congress of Zoology, 1958. Trustee, Imp. War Museum, 1956–60; Dir, Arundel Castle Trustees Ltd, 1976–86. Governor, Imperial Coll. of Science and Technology, 1956–76 (Fellow, 1963); Mem., Standing Commn on Museums and Galleries, 1973–76; National Trust: Mem., Properties Cttee, 1968–83; Chm., Nature Cons. Panel, 1970–81; Chm., Architectural Panel, 1973–82. Goodwood Flying Sch. (solo), 1975. DL West Sussex, 1982. *Publications:* Palaearctic and Indian Mammals (with J. R. Ellerman), 1951; Southern African Mammals (with J. R. Ellerman and R. W. Hayman), 1953; papers in scientific jls on taxonomy of mammals. *Address:* Upperfold House, Fernhurst, Haslemere, Surrey GU27 3JH. *Clubs:* Athenæum, Brooks's; Vincent's (Oxford); Leander.
Died 25 Nov. 1991.

MORTIMER, Air Vice-Marshal Roger, CBE 1972; Officer Commanding RAF Institute of Pathology and Tropical Medicine and Consultant Adviser in Pathology and Tropical Medicine, 1969–76; Dean of Air Force Medicine, 1975–76; *b* 2 Nov. 1914; *s* of Henry Roger Mortimer, tea planter, Dooars, India and Lily Rose (*née* Collier); *m* 1942, Agnes Emily Balfour (*d* 1985); two *d. Educ:* Uppingham; St Mary's Hosp. Med. School. MB, BS London, FRCPath, DCP, DTM&H. Joined RAF, 1942; Sqdn Med. Officer to Nos 23 and 85 Sqdns, 1942–44; Service Narrator and Editor to Official RAF Medical History of the War, 1944–47; specialised in Pathology and Tropical Medicine from 1947. Founder Mem. RCPath; Assoc. Editor and Council Mem., British Div. of Internat. Academy of Pathology, 1967–73; Editor, International Pathology, 1970–73; Mem. Council, Royal Soc. Trop. Med. and Hygiene, 1970–73. QHS 1973–76. *Publications:* papers on approved laboratory methods, practical disinfection, blood transfusion and infusion. *Recreations:* cars, anything mechanical, do-it-yourself, laboratory

design. *Address:* 13 Welclose Street, St Albans, Herts AL3 4QD. *T:* St Albans (0727) 864247.
Died 27 May 1992.

MORTLOCK, Herbert Norman; Civil Service, retired; *b* 1926. Ministry of Defence: Superintendent, Royal Armament Research & Development Estabt, 1964–71; Asst Director, Procurement Executive, 1971–73; Dep. Dir., Chemical Defence Estabt, 1973–78; Dep. Dir, 1978–79, Dir, 1979–84, Materials Quality Assurance Directorate; Dir, Quality Assurance (Technical Support), 1984. *Died 5 June 1995.*

MORTON OF SHUNA, Baron *cr* 1985 (Life Peer), of Stockbridge in the District of the City of Edinburgh; **Hugh Drennan Baird Morton;** a Senator of the College of Justice in Scotland, since 1988; *b* 10 April 1930; *s* of late Rev. T. R. Morton, DD, and J. M. M. Morton (*née* Baird); *m* 1956, Muriel Miller; three *s*. *Educ:* Glasgow Academy; Glasgow Univ. (BL). Admitted Faculty of Advocates, 1965; QC (Scot) 1974. *Address:* 25 Royal Circus, Edinburgh EH3 6TL. *T:* 0131–225 5139.
Died 26 April 1995.

MORTON, Alastair; *see* Morton, S. A.

MORTON, Sir Brian, Kt 1973; FRICS; Chairman, Harland & Wolff, 1975–80; *b* 24 Jan. 1912; *s* of Alfred Oscar Morton and Margaret Osborne Hennessy; *m* 1937, Hilda Evelyn Elsie Hillis; one *s* (and one *s* decd). *Educ:* Campbell Coll., Belfast. Estate Agency, Brian Morton & Co., Belfast, 1936; retired, 1964. Elected Councillor (U) Cromac Ward, Belfast Corp., 1967; apptd Mem. Craigavon Development Commn, 1968; Chm., Londonderry Develt Commn, 1969–73. Hon. DSc Ulster, 1987. *Recreations:* golf, sailing, landscape painting, fishing. *Address:* 8 Demesne Gate, Saintfield, Co. Down, N Ireland BT24 7BE. *Clubs:* Royal Automobile; Ulster Reform (Belfast); Royal County Down Golf (Newcastle).
Died 27 July 1991.

MORTON, His Honour (Stephen) Alastair, TD 1949; JP; a Circuit Judge (formerly Deputy Chairman, Greater London Quarter Sessions), 1971–87; *b* 28 July 1913; *o s* of late Philip Morton, Dorchester; *m* 1939, Lily Yarrow Eveline, *o d* of J. S. P. Griffith-Jones, Drews, Beaconsfield, Bucks; one *s* one *d*. *Educ:* private sch.; Trinity Hall, Cambridge. Commnd Dorset Heavy Bde, RA, TA, 1932; served War of 1939–45, Royal Artillery. Called to the Bar, Middle Temple, 1938; Western Circuit, 1938; Master of the Bench, 1964. Counsel to the Crown at County of London Sessions, 1954–59; Central Criminal Court: First Junior Treasury Counsel, 1959–64; Senior Treasury Counsel, 1964–71; Recorder of Devizes, 1957–71; Dep.-Chm. Quarter Sessions: Dorset, 1957–71; Norfolk, 1969–71. JP Dorset, 1957. *Recreation:* painting. *Address:* 1 Church Row, Moore Park Road, SW6 2JW. *T:* 071–736 8109; Cringles, Burnham Overy Staithe, near King's Lynn, Norfolk PE31 8JD. *T:* Fakenham (0328) 738339. *Clubs:* White's, Pratt's. *Died 9 May 1992.*

MORTON, Sir William (David), Kt 1990; CBE 1984; farmer; *b* 13 June 1926; *m* 1952, Catherine Mary Macbeth; three *s*. *Educ:* Northampton Town and County Grammar Sch. Farming in Northants and Bucks. County Chairman: Nat. Fedn of Young Farmers' Clubs, 1953–57; Northants NFU, 1970. Northamptonshire County Council: Member, 1964–; Dep. Leader, 1970–73; Chief Whip, 1973–81; Dep. Leader, 1981–84, Leader, 1984–, Cons. Gp; Chairman: Highways Cttee, 1969–73; Planning and Transportation Cttee, 1977–81. Conservative Party: Chairman: Daventry Constituency, 1975–79 (Dep. Chm., 1969–75); Northants Euro-Constituency, 1978–82; E Midlands Area, 1980–85 (Mem. Exec., 1975–; Treas., 1979–80); Nat. Agricl and Countryside Cttee, 1984–89; Mem., Exec. Cttee, Nat. Union, 1979–. High Sheriff,

Northants, 1984–85. *Address:* Flore Fields House, Flore, Northants NN7 4JX. *T:* Weedon (0327) 40226.
Died 11 Dec. 1993.

MOSES, Dr Kenneth, CBE 1988; FEng 1985; Member, since 1986 and a Joint Deputy Chairman, since 1992, British Coal Corporation; *b* 29 Nov. 1931; *s* of Thomas and Mary Moses; *m* 1949, Mary Price; one *s* two *d*. *Educ:* Cowley Boys Grammar Sch., St Helens; Wigan Mining Coll. (Dip. in Mining; 1st Cl. Cert., Mines and Quarries Act); Nottingham Univ. (MPhil 1988; PhD 1990). Mineworker, 1954; Management Trainee, 1960; Undermanager, 1962; Dep. Manager, 1964; Colliery Manager, 1967; Mem. Directing Staff, NCB Staff Coll., 1971; National Coal Board: Chief Mining Engr, N Yorks, 1974; Dir of Planning, 1978; Dir, N Derbys, 1981. Mem., NRDC, 1990–92. CBIM. Hon. FIMinE, 1990. Laurence Holland Medal, IMinE, 1961; Douglas Hay Medal, IMinE, 1982. *Publications:* contribs to learned journals. *Recreations:* gardening, walking, swimming, reading. *Address:* Oaktrees, 6 Heath Avenue, Mansfield NG18 3EU. *T:* Mansfield (0623) 653843; Flat 22, 36 Buckingham Gate, Westminster, SW1E 6PB.
Died 2 Oct. 1992.

MOSS, David Francis; JP; Assistant Chief Executive, Dockyards, Ministry of Defence, Bath, 1981–82, retired; *b* 11 July 1927; *s* of Frank William and Dorothy May Moss; *m* 1950, Beryl Eloïse (*née* Horsley); one *s* one *d*. *Educ:* Manchester Grammar Sch.; Manchester Univ. (BSc Hons MechEng); RNC Greenwich (Naval Architecture Cert.). Devonport Dockyard, 1952; Director General Ships, Bath, 1956; HM Dockyards: Gibraltar, 1961; Devonport, 1964; Singapore, 1967; Rosyth, 1969; Chatham, 1973; Rosyth, 1975; Portsmouth, 1979. JP Bath 1983. *Recreations:* hill walking, handiwork; material and philosophical aspects of early Mediterranean sea power. *Address:* 16 Beaufort West, Grosvenor, Bath BA1 6QB.
Died 15 Feb. 1992.

MOSS, Edward Herbert St George; Under-Secretary, University Grants Committee, 1971–78; *b* 18 May 1918; *s* of late Sir George Moss, KBE, HM Consular Service in China, and Lady (Gladys Lucy) Moss; *m* 1948, Shirley Evelyn Baskett; two *s* one *d*. *Educ:* Marlborough; Pembroke Coll., Cambridge. PhD Surrey, 1984. Army Service in UK and Middle East, 1940–45; entered HM Foreign (subseq. Diplomatic) Service, 1945; served in Japan, FO, Belgrade (Head of Chancery 1951–55), St Louis, Detroit, FO; transf. to Home Civil Service (MoD), 1960; Asst Sec. 1961; Dept of Educn and Science, 1969. *Publications:* (with Rev. Robert Llewelyn) Fire from a Flint: daily readings with William Law, 1986; Seeing Man Whole: a new model for psychology, 1989; Growing into Freedom: a way to make sense of ourselves, 1993; The Grammar of Consciousness: an exploration of tacit knowing, 1995. *Recreations:* writing, gardening. *Address:* Prospect, 29 Guildown Avenue, Guildford, Surrey GU2 5HA. *T:* Guildford (01483) 66984.
Died 1 April 1995.

MOTE, Harold Trevor, JP, DL; company director, company consultant and engineer, retired; *b* 28 Oct. 1919; *s* of late Harold Roland Mote; *m* 1944, Amplias Pamela, *d* of late Harold Johnson, Oswestry; three *s* one *d*. *Educ:* Upper Latymer Sch.; St Paul's Sch.; Regent Street Polytechnic; Army Staff Coll. RE, TA, 1935–39; Royal Signals, 1940–46 (Lt-Col); TA, 1948–54. Councillor, Harrow, 1953–67, Alderman 1967; 1st Mayor, London Bor. of Harrow, 1965–66; Opposition Leader, Harrow Council, 1971–73, Leader, 1973–77, resigned 1978. Greater London Council: Mem. for Harrow E, 1965–86; Member, Leader's Cttee, 1977–78, 1979–81 (formerly with special responsibility for Law and Order); Dep. Leader, Planning and Communications Policy Cttee,

1977–78, 1980–81; Chm., 1978–79; Chm., London Transport Cttee, 1979–81; Opposition Spokesman on Transport, 1981–82; Technical Services, 1985–86; Member: Staff Cttee, 1981–82; Planning Cttee, 1981–86; Shadow Leaders Cttee, 1981–82 and 1985–86; formerly: Chm., Scrutiny Cttee; Vice-Chm., Public Services Cttee; Member: Policy and Resources Cttee; West and North Area Planning Bds; Opposition Leader, Fire Bde Cttee; Chm., W Area Planning and Transportation Sub-Cttee; Member: Finance and Estabt Cttee; Public Services and Safety Cttee. Mem., Thames Water Authority, 1973–83 (Chm., Personnel Sub-Cttee, 1973–83; Nat. Rep. on Personnel Matters, 1973–83). JP Mddx 1965; DL Greater London 1967; Rep. DL Harrow 1969. *Address:* 3 Manor Park Drive, Harrow, Middlesex HA2 6HT. *T:* 0181–863 1760. *Died 10 Jan. 1995.*

MOTT-RADCLYFFE, Sir Charles (Edward), Kt 1957; DL; Captain Rifle Brigade, Reserve of Officers; *b* 25 Dec. 1911; *o s* of Lt-Col C. E. Radclyffe, DSO, Rifle Brigade (killed in action 1915), Little Park, Wickham, Hants, and Theresa Caroline, *o d* of John Stanley Mott, JP, Barningham Hall, Norfolk; added surname of Mott by deed poll, 1927; *m* 1940, Diana (*d* 1955), *d* of late Lt-Col W. Gibbs, CVO, 7th Hussars; three *d*; *m* 1956, Stella, *d* of late Lionel Harrisson, Caynham Cottage, Ludlow, Salop. *Educ:* Eton; Balliol Coll., Oxford. Hon. Attaché Diplomatic Service, Athens and Rome, 1936–38; Mem. Military Mission to Greece, 1940–41; served as Liaison Officer in Syria, 1941, and with Rifle Brigade in Middle East and Italy, 1943–44; MP (C) Windsor, 1942–70; Parliamentary Private Sec. to Sec. of State for India (Rt Hon. L. S. Amery), Dec. 1944–May 1945; Junior Lord of the Treasury, May-July 1945; Conservative Whip, Aug. 1945–Feb. 1946; Chm. Conservative Parly Foreign Affairs Cttee, 1951–59. Mem., Plowden Commn on Overseas Representational Services, 1963–64. A Governor of Gresham's Sch., Holt, 1957–87; Mem., Historic Buildings Council for England, 1962–70; President: Country Landowners Assoc. (Norfolk Branch), 1972–87; Norfolk CCC, 1972–74 (Chm., 1976–89); Royal Norfolk Show, 1979. High Sheriff, 1974, DL 1977, of Norfolk. Comdr. Order of Phoenix (Greece). *Publication:* Foreign Body in the Eye (a memoir of the Foreign Service), 1975. *Recreations:* cricket (Captain, Lords and Commons Cricket, 1952–70), shooting. *Address:* Barningham Hall, Matlaske, Norfolk. *T:* Matlaske 250; Flat 1, 38 Cadogan Square, SW1. *T:* 071–584 5834. *Clubs:* Turf, Buck's, Pratt's, MCC. *Died 25 Nov. 1992.*

MOULTON, Maj.-Gen. James Louis, CB 1956; DSO 1944; OBE 1950; retired; *b* 3 June 1906; *s* of Capt. J. D. Moulton, RN; *m* 1937, Barbara Aline (*née* Coode); one *s* one *d. Educ:* Sutton Valence Sch. Joined Royal Marines, 1924; Pilot, Fleet Air Arm, 1930; Staff Coll., Camberley, 1938; served War of 1939–45: GSO3 GHQ, BEF, Dunkirk, 1940; GSO1, Force 121 (Madagascar), 1942; Commanding Officer, 48 Commando, NW Europe, 1944–45 (DSO); Comd 4th Commando Bde, NW Europe, 1945 (despatches); CO Commando Sch., 1947–49; Comd 3rd Commando Bde, Middle East, 1952–54; Maj.-Gen. Royal Marines, Portsmouth, 1954–57; Chief of Amphibious Warfare, 1957–61. Rep. Col Comdt RM, 1971–72. Mem. Council, RUSI, 1964–71 (Vice-Chm., 1965–67; Chm., 1967–69). Naval Editor, 1964–69, Editor, 1969–73, Brassey's Annual. *Publications:* Haste to the Battle, 1963; Defence in a Changing World, 1964; The Norwegian Campaign of 1940, 1966; British Maritime Strategy in the 1970s, 1969; The Royal Marines, 1972, 2nd rev. and enl. edn 1981; Battle for Antwerp, 1978. *Address:* Fairmile, Woodham Road, Woking, Surrey GU21 4DN. *T:* Woking (0483) 715174. *Died 22 Nov. 1993.*

MOUNT, Sir James (William Spencer), Kt 1979; CBE 1965; BEM 1946; VMH; *b* 8 Nov. 1908; *s* of Spencer William Mount and Kathleen Mount (*née* Ashenden) *m* 1931, Margaret Geikie (*d* 1973); three *d* (one *s* decd); *m* 1975, Jane Mount. *Educ:* Tonbridge School. Chairman and Director, S. W. Mount & Sons Ltd, 1944–. Chairman: Horticultural Advisory Cttee, MAFF, 1963–69; National Fruit Trials Advisory Cttee, MAFF, 1973–78; Governing Body, E Malling Res. Station, 1960–80. VMH 1982. *Recreations:* fishing, gardening. *Address:* Woolton Farm, Bekesbourne, Canterbury, Kent CT4 5EA. *T:* Canterbury (0227) 830202. *Club:* Farmers'. *Died 26 July 1994.*

MOUNT, Sir William (Malcolm), 2nd Bt, *cr* 1921, of Wasing Place, Reading, Berks; Lieutenant-Colonel Reconnaissance Corps; *b* 28 Dec. 1904; *s* of Sir William Mount, 1st Bt, CBE, and Hilda Lucy Adelaide, OBE (*d* 1950), *y d* of late Malcolm Low, Clatto, Fife; *S* father, 1930; *m* 1929, Elizabeth Nance, *o d* of Owen John Llewellyn, Badminton Vicarage, Glos; three *d. Educ:* Eton; New Coll., Oxford. Berkshire: DL 1946; High Sheriff, 1947–48; Vice-Lieutenant, 1960–76. *Recreation:* fishing. *Heir: nephew* (William Robert) Ferdinand Mount [*b* 2 July 1939; *m* 1968, Julia Margaret, *d* of Archibald Julian and Hon. Mrs Lucas; two *s* one *d* (and one *s* decd)]. *Address:* Wasing Place, Aldermaston, Berks RG7 4NG. *Died 22 June 1993.*

MOUNTFORD, Arnold Robert, CBE 1984; MA; Director, City Museum and Art Gallery, Stoke-on-Trent, 1962–87, retired; *b* 14 Dec. 1922; *s* of Ernest Gerald and Dorothy Gwendoline Mountford; *m* 1943, Joan (*née* Gray); one *s. Educ:* Hanley High School; Univ. of Keele (MA History). Royal Artillery, seconded to Special Liaison Unit and Special Communications Unit, 1942–47; demobilized 1947 (Captain). Joined staff of City Museum and Art Gallery, Stoke-on-Trent, specializing in archaeology and ceramics, 1949. Editor, Jl of Ceramic History, 1968–83. *Publications:* The Illustrated Guide to Staffordshire Saltglazed Stoneware, 1971; various ceramic journals. *Recreations:* touring inland waterways, gardening. *Died 6 Aug. 1991.*

MOURANT, Arthur Ernest, DM, FRCP; FRS 1966; formerly Director, Serological Population Genetics Laboratory; Conseiller Scientifique Etranger, Institut d'Hématologie, Immunologie et Génétique Humaine, Toulouse, since 1974; *b* 11 April 1904; *er s* of Ernest Charles Mourant and Emily Gertrude (*née* Bray); *m* 1978, Mrs Jean E. C. Shimell. *Educ:* Victoria Coll., Jersey; Exeter Coll., Oxford; St Bartholomew's Hosp. Medical Coll. London. 1st cl. hons Chem., 1926; Sen. King Charles I Schol., Exeter Coll., Oxford, 1926; Burdett-Coutts Schol., Oxford Univ., 1926; BA 1925, DPhil (Geol.) 1931, MA 1931, BM, BCh 1943, DM 1948, Oxford; FRCP 1960; FRCPath 1963. Demonstrator in Geology, Univ. of Leeds, 1928–29; Geol Survey of Gt Brit., 1929–31; teaching posts, 1931–34; Dir, Jersey Pathological Lab., 1935–38; Med. Student, 1939–43; House med. appts, 1943–44; Med. Off., Nat. Blood Transfusion Service, 1944–45; Med. Off., Galton Lab. Serum Unit, Cambridge, 1945–46; Dir, Blood Gp Reference Lab., Min. of Health and MRC, 1946–65 (Internat. Blood Gp Reference Lab., WHO, 1952–65); Hon. Adviser, Nuffield Blood Gp Centre, 1952–65; Hon. Sen. Lectr in Haematology, St Bartholomew's Hospital Medical Coll., 1965–77. Visiting Professor: Columbia Univ., 1953; Collège de France, 1978–79. Marett Meml Lectr, Exeter Coll., Oxford, 1978. Pres., Section H (Anthropology), Brit. Assoc., 1956; Vice-Pres., Mineralogical Soc., 1971–73; Mem. Hon., Société Jersiaise (Vice-Pres., 1977–80, 1984–87); Corresp. Mem., Académie des Sciences, Inscriptions et Belles-Lettres, Toulouse; Honorary Member: Internat. Soc. of Blood

Transfusion; British Soc. for Haematology; Peruvian Pathological Soc.; Soc. for Study of Human Biol. (Vice-Pres., 1960–63); Human Biology Council, 1987. Mem. or Past Mem. Editl Bd of eight British, foreign and internat. scientific jls. His bronze bust by John Doubleday, 1990, Jersey Mus. Hon. Citizen, Toulouse, 1985. Oliver Meml Award, 1953; Huxley Memorial Medal, Royal Anthropological Institute, 1961; Landsteiner Meml Award, Amer. Assoc. of Blood Banks, 1973; Osler Meml Medal, Univ. of Oxford, 1980; R. H. Worth Prize, Geolog. Soc., 1982. *Publications:* The Distribution of the Human Blood Groups, 1954, (jtly) 2nd edn, 1976; (jtly) The ABO Blood Groups: Comprehensive Tables and Maps of World Distribution, 1958; (ed jtly) Man and Cattle, 1963; (jtly) Blood Groups and Diseases, 1978; (jtly) The Genetics of the Jews, 1978; Blood Relations, 1983; numerous papers in scientific jls on blood groups and other biol subjects, geology and archæology. *Recreations:* photography, geology, archæology, travel, reading in sciences other than own, alpine gardening. *Address:* The Dower House, Maison de Haut, Longueville, St Saviour, Jersey JE2 7SP, Channel Islands. *T:* Jersey (0534) 52280.

Died 29 Aug. 1994.

MOWER, Brian Leonard, CBE 1992; Head of News Department, Foreign and Commonwealth Office, 1990–92; *b* 24 Aug. 1934; *s* of Samuel William and Nellie Elizabeth Rachel Mower; *m* 1960, Margaret Ann Wildman; one *s* one *d*. *Educ:* Hemel Hempstead Grammar Sch. Royal Air Force, 1954–56. Executive, Service Advertising Co., 1956–66; entered Civil Service, Sen. Information Officer, HM Treasury, 1966; Principal Information Officer, Central Statistical Office, 1969; Dep. Head of Information, HM Treasury, 1978; Head of Information, Dept of Employment, 1980; Dep. Press Sec. to Prime Minister, 1982; Dir of Information, Home Office, 1982. *Recreations:* bridge, reading. *Address:* 34 Wrensfield, Hemel Hempstead, Herts HP1 1RP. *T:* Hemel Hempstead (0442) 252277. *Club:* Reform. *Died 7 May 1993.*

MOYA, (John) Hidalgo, CBE 1966; RIBA 1956; architect; *b* Los Gatos, Calif, 5 May 1920; *s* of Hidalgo Moya; *m* 1st, 1947, Janiffer Innes Mary Hall (marr. diss. 1985); one *s* two *d*; 2nd, 1988, Jean Conder (*née* MacArthur). *Educ:* Oundle Sch.; Royal West of England Coll. of Art; AA Sch. of Architecture; AA Dip., 1943. Partner, Powell and Moya, 1946, Powell Moya and Partners, 1976–. Major works include: Churchill Gardens Flats, Westminster, 1948–62; houses at Chichester, 1950; Toys Hill, 1954; Mayfield Sch., Putney, 1955; Plumstead Manor Sch., Woolwich, 1970; Chichester Festival Theatre, 1962; Public Swimming Baths, Putney, 1967; British Nat. Pavilion, Expo 1970, Osaka; Dining Rooms, Bath Acad. of Art, 1970, Eton Coll., 1974; Psychiatric Hosp. extensions at Fairmile, 1957 and Borocourt, 1965; Brasenose Coll., 1961 and Corpus Christi Coll., 1969, Oxford extensions; Christ Church Coll., Oxford Picture Gall. and undergraduate rooms, 1967; St John's Coll., 1967 and Queens' Coll., 1978, Cambridge, new buildings; Wolfson Coll., Oxford, 1974; General Hosps at Swindon, Slough, High Wycombe, Wythenshawe, Woolwich and Maidstone; new headquarters for London & Manchester Assurance Co., near Exeter, 1978; extensions for Schools for Advanced Urban Studies and of Extra Mural Studies, Univ. of Bristol, 1980; Nat. West. Bank, Shaftesbury Ave, London, 1982; labs etc and Queen's Building, RHBNC, Egham, 1986; Queen Elizabeth II Conf. Centre, Westminster, 1986. Pimlico Housing Scheme, Winning Design in Open Competition, 1946; Skylon, Festival of Britain Winning Design, 1950 (Award, 1951); Mohlg Good Design in Housing Award, 1954; RIBA Bronze Medal, 1958, 1961 (Bucks, Berks, Oxon); Civic Trust Awards (Class I and II), 1961; Architectural Design Project Award, 1965; RIBA Architectural Award (London

and SE Regions), 1967; Royal Gold Medal for Architecture, RIBA, 1974. *Address:* Point Hill South, Rye, E Sussex TN31 7NP. *Died 3 Aug. 1994.*

MOYNE, 2nd Baron, *cr* 1932, of Bury St Edmunds; **Bryan Walter Guinness**, MA; FRSL; poet and novelist; Vice-Chairman of Arthur Guinness, Son and Co., 1949–79, retired (Director, 1934–79); Trustee: Iveagh (Housing) Trust, Dublin; Guinness (Housing) Trust, London; barrister-at-law; *b* 27 Oct. 1905; *e s* of 1st Baron Moyne (3rd *s* of 1st Earl of Iveagh) and Lady Evelyn Erskine (*d* 1939), 3rd *d* of 14th Earl of Buchan; *S* father 1944; *m* 1st, 1929, Diana Freeman-Mitford (marr. diss. 1934); two *s*; 2nd, 1936, Elisabeth Nelson; three *s* five *d* (and one *s* decd). *Educ:* Eton; Christ Church, Oxford. Called to Bar, Inner Temple, 1930. Capt., Royal Sussex Regiment, 1943. A Governor National Gallery of Ireland, 1955; Mem., Irish Acad. of Letters, 1968. Hon. FTCD 1979. Hon. LLD: TCD, 1958; NUI, 1961. *Publications:* (as Bryan Guinness): 23 Poems, 1931; Singing out of Tune, 1933; Landscape with Figures, 1934; Under the Eyelid, 1935; Johnny and Jemima, 1936; A Week by the Sea, 1936; Lady Crushwell's Companion, 1938; The Children in the Desert, 1947; Reflexions, 1947; The Animals' Breakfast, 1950; Story of a Nutcracker, 1953; Collected Poems, 1956; A Fugue of Cinderellas, 1956; Catriona and the Grasshopper, 1957; Priscilla and the Prawn, 1960; Leo and Rosabelle, 1961; The Giant's Eye, 1964; The Rose in the Tree, 1964; The Girl with the Flower, 1966; The Engagement, 1969; The Clock, 1973; Dairy Not Kept, 1975; Hellenic Flirtation, 1978; Potpourri from the Thirties, 1982; Personal Patchwork, 1986; Faithful Rosa, 1991; *plays:* The Fragrant Concubine, 1938; A Riverside Charade, 1954. *Recreation:* travelling. *Heir:* *s* Hon. Jonathan Bryan Guinness [*b* 16 March 1930; *m* 1st, 1951, Ingrid Wyndham (marr. diss. 1962); two *s* one *d*; 2nd, 1964, Suzanne Phillips (*née* Lisney); one *s* one *d*]. *Address:* Biddesden House, Andover, Hants SP11 9DN. *T:* Andover (0264) 790237; Knockmaroon, Castleknock, Co. Dublin. *Clubs:* Athenæum, Carlton; Kildare Street and University (Dublin). *Died 6 July 1992.*

MOYNIHAN, 3rd Baron, *cr* 1929, of Leeds, Co. York; **Antony Patrick Andrew Cairnes Berkeley Moynihan**; Bt 1922; *b* 2 Feb. 1936; *s* of 2nd Baron Moynihan, OBE, TD, and Ierne Helen Candy (*d* 1991); *S* father, 1965; *m* 1st, 1955, Ann Herbert (marr. diss., 1958); 2nd, 1958, Shirin Roshan Berry (marr. diss., 1967); one *d*; 3rd, 1968, Luthgarda Maria Fernandez (marr. diss. 1979); three *d*; 4th, Editha; 5th, Jinna (*née* Sabiaga); one *s*. *Educ:* Stowe. Late 2nd Lt Coldstream Guards. *Recreation:* dog breeding. *Heir:* *s* Hon. Daniel Antony Patrick Berkeley Moynihan, *b* 12 Jan. 1991. *Died 24 Nov. 1991.*

MOYNIHAN, Sir Noël (Henry), Kt 1979; MA, MB, BCh; FRCGP; Chairman, Save the Children Fund, 1977–82 (Member Council, 1972–86, Vice-Chairman, 1972–77); *b* 24 Dec. 1916; *o s* of Dr Edward B. Moynihan and Ellen (*née* Shea), Cork, Ireland; *m* 1941, Margaret Mary Lovelace, JP (*d* 1989), *d* of William John Lovelace, barrister-at-law, and Mary Lovelace, JP, Claygate, Surrey; two *s* two *d*. *Educ:* Ratcliffe; Downing Coll., Cambridge (BA English Tripos 1940, MA 1946; Pres., Downing Coll. Assoc., 1985–86; Associate Fellow, 1986–) (represented Cambridge in athletics (mile) and cross country, v Oxford, 1939, 1940). Medically qual., St Thomas' Hosp., 1954; Newsholme Public Health Prize, 1954; Sutton Sams Prize (Obstet. and Gynaecol.), 1954; MB 1956, BChir 1955 London; MRCS, LRCP 1954, MRCGP 1965, FRCGP 1981. Cambridge Univ. Air Sqdn, 1938–39; served War, RAF, Sqdn Ldr, 1940–46 (despatches twice). Upjohn Travelling Fellow, RCGP, 1967; Leverhulme Travelling Res. Fellow, 1974. Co-Founder, Med. Council on Alcoholism, 1963 (Mem. Council, 1963–79; Hon. Vice-

Pres., 1972–); Mem. Bd, S London Faculty, RCGP, 1958–73; Chm., Public Relations and Fund Raising Cttee, African Med. and Res. Foundn, 1959–64; President: Harveian Soc. of London, 1967 (Mem. Council, 1963–68, 1978–79; Hon. Life Mem., 1988); Chelsea Clinical Soc., 1978 (Mem. Council, 1969–78; Hon. Life Mem., 1987); Hon. Sec., Council, 1981–82, Vice-Pres., 1982–85, Med. Soc. of London. Mem. Exec. Cttee, St Francis Leper Guild, 1964–85 (Vice-Pres., 1981). Mem. Bd, Royal Med. Benevolent Fund, 1973–77. Editor, St Thomas' Hosp. Gazette, 1952–54. Mem., Inner Temple, 1948; Yeoman, Worshipful Soc. of Apothecaries, 1956, Liveryman, 1959; Cttee of Liverymen, 1984–88; Freeman, City of London, 1959. CStJ 1971; Kt SMO Malta 1958 (Officer of Merit, 1964; Comdr of Merit, 1979); KSG 1966. *Publications:* The Light in the West, 1978; Rock Art of the Sahara, 1979; contribs to med. jls, 1953–89. *Recreations:* Save The Children Fund, rock art of the Sahara. *Address:* Herstmonceux Place, Church Road, Flowers Green, near Hailsham, East Sussex BN27 1RL. *T:* Herstmonceux (01323) 832017. *Clubs:* Carlton, MCC; Hawks (Cambridge); Achilles. *Died 5 Oct. 1994.*

MTEKATEKA, Rt Rev. Josiah; *b* 1903; *s* of Village Headman; *m* 1st, 1925, Maude Mwere Nambote (*d* 1940); one *s* four *d*; 2nd, 1944, Alice Monica Chitanda; six *s* two *d* (and five *c* decd). *Educ:* Likoma Island School; S Michael's Teachers' Training Coll., Likoma; St Andrew's Theological Coll., Likoma. Deacon, 1939; priest, 1943; Asst Priest, Nkhotakota, Nyasaland Dio., 1943–45; Chiulu, Tanganyika, 1945–50; Priest, Mlangali, Tanganyika, Nyasaland Dio., 1950–52; Mlangali, SW Tanganyika Dio., 1952–60; rep. SW Tanganyika Dio. at Centenary Celebrations in England, Univs Mission to Central Africa, 1957; Canon of SW Tanganyika Dio., 1959; Priest-in-charge, Manda, 1960–64, Njombe, 1964–65, SW Tanganyika Dio.; Archdeacon of Njombe, 1962–65; Suffragan Bishop, Nkhotakota, Dio. Malawi, 1965–71; Bishop of Lake Malaŵi, 1971–77. *Address:* Madimba 1, PO Box 5, Likoma Island, Malaŵi.

Died 17 June 1995.

MUIR, Jean Elizabeth, (Mrs Harry Leuckert), CBE 1984; RDI 1972; FCSD; Designer-Director and Co-Owner, Jean Muir Ltd, since 1967; *d* of Cyril Muir and Phyllis Coy; *m* 1955, Harry Leuckert. *Educ:* Dame Harper Sch., Bedford. Selling/sketching, Liberty & Co., 1950; Designer, Jaeger Ltd, 1956, then Jane & Jane; with Harry Leuckert as co-director, formed own company, 1966. Member: Art & Design Cttee, TEC, 1978–83; BTEC Bd for Design and Art, 1983–; Design Council, 1983–; Adv. Council, V&A Museum, 1979–83; Trustee, V&A Museum, 1984–. Awards: Dress of the Year, British Fashion Writers' Gp, 1964; Ambassador Award for Achievement, 1965; Harpers Bazaar Trophy, 1965; Maison Blanche Rex Internat. Fashion Award, New Orleans, 1967, 1968 and 1974 (also Hon. Citizen of New Orleans); Churchman's Award as Fashion Designer of the Year, 1970; Neiman Marcus Award, Dallas, Texas, 1973; British Fashion Industry Award for Services to the Industry, 1984; Hommage de la Mode, Féd. Française du Prêt-à-porter Feminin, 1985; Chartered Soc. of Designers' Medal, 1987; Textile Inst. Medal for Design, 1987; Australian Govt Bicentennial Award, 1988. FRSA 1973; FCSD (FSIAD 1978). Hon. Fellow, Duncan of Jordanstone Coll. of Art, Dundee. Hon. Dr RCA, 1981; Hon. DLit Newcastle, 1985; Hon. DLitt: Ulster, 1987; Heriot-Watt, 1992. *Address:* 59/61 Farringdon Road, EC1M 3HD. *T:* 0171–831 0691.

Died 28 May 1995.

MUIR, Sir John (Harling), 3rd Bt, *cr* 1892, of Deanston, Perthshire; TD; Director, James Finlay & Co. Ltd, 1946–81 (Chairman, 1961–75); Member, Queen's Body Guard for Scotland (The Royal Company of Archers); *b* 7 Nov.

1910; *s* of James Finlay Muir (*d* 1948), Braco Castle, Perthshire, and Charlotte Escudier, *d* of J. Harling Turner, CBE; *S* uncle 1951; *m* 1936, Elizabeth Mary, *e d* of late Frederick James Dundas, Dale Cottage, Cawthorne, near Barnsley; five *s* two *d*. *Educ:* Stowe. With James Finlay & Co. Ltd, in India, 1932–40. Served War of 1939–45: joined 3rd Carabiniers, Sept. 1940, Lieut; transferred 25th Dragoons, 1941, Capt.; Major, 1942; transferred RAC Depot, Poona, i/c Sqdn, 1942; transferred to Staff, HQ 109 L of C Area, Bangalore; held various Staff appointments terminating as AA&QMG with actg rank of Lt-Col; demobilised, 1946, with rank of Major. *Recreations:* shooting, fishing, gardening. *Heir: s* Richard James Kay Muir [*b* 25 May 1939; *m* 1965, Susan Elizabeth (marr. diss.), *d* of G. A. Gardner, Leamington Spa; two *d*; *m* 1975, Lady Linda Mary Cole, *d* of 6th Earl of Enniskillen, MBE; two *d*]. *Address:* Bankhead, Blair Drummond, by Stirling, Perthshire FK9 4UX. *T:* Doune (0786) 841207. *Club:* Oriental.

Died 31 May 1994.

MUIRSHIEL, 1st Viscount, *cr* 1964, of Kilmacolm, Co. of Renfrew; **John Scott Maclay,** KT 1973; CH 1962; CMG 1944; PC 1952; DL; Lord-Lieutenant of Renfrewshire, 1967–80; shipowner; *b* 26 Oct. 1905; *s* of 1st Baron Maclay, PC and Martha, *d* of William Strang; *m* 1930, Betty L'Estrange (*d* 1974), *d* of Major Delaval Astley, Wroxham, Norfolk. *Educ:* Winchester; Trinity Coll., Cambridge. MP (NL and C) for Montrose Burghs, 1940–50, for Renfrewshire West, 1950–64. Capt., 57th Searchlight Regt RA, TA, seconded to Min. of War Transport, 1940; Mem., Brit. Merchant Shipping Mission, Washington, 1941, Head of Mission, 1944; Parliamentary Sec., Min. of Production, May-July 1945; Minister of Transport and Civil Aviation, Nov. 1951–May 1952; Minister of State for Colonial Affairs, Oct. 1956–Jan. 1957; Sec. of State for Scotland, Jan. 1957–July 1962. Pres., Assembly of WEU, 1955–56. Pres., National Liberal Council, 1957–67; Chm., Joint Exchequer Board for Northern Ireland, 1965–73. Former Director: Maclay & Macintyre; Nat. Provincial Bank; P&O Steamship Co.; Dir, Clydesdale Bank, 1970–82. Chm., Scottish Civic Trust, 1967–89; Trustee, Nat. Galls of Scotland, 1966–76. DL Renfrewshire, 1981. Hon. LLD: Edinburgh, 1963; Strathclyde, 1966; Glasgow, 1970. *Heir:* none. *Address:* House of Lords, SW1A 0PW; Knapps Wood, Kilmacolm, Renfrewshire PA13 4NQ. *T:* Kilmacolm 2770. *Clubs:* Turf; Western (Glasgow).

Died 17 Aug. 1992 (ext).

MULDOON, Rt Hon. Sir Robert (David), GCMG 1984; CH 1977; PC 1976; Prime Minister, and Minister of Finance, New Zealand, 1975–84; Leader of the National Party, 1974–84; *b* 25 Sept. 1921; *s* of James Henry and Mamie R. Muldoon; *m* 1951, Thea Dale Flyger; one *s* two *d*. *Educ:* Mt Albert Grammar School. FCANZ, CMA, FCIS, FCMA. Chartered Accountant. Pres., NZ Inst. of Cost Accountants, 1956. MP (Nat. Party) Tamaki, 1960–92; Parly Under-Sec. to Minister of Finance, 1963–66; Minister of Tourism, 1967; Minister of Finance, 1967–72; Dep. Prime Minister, Feb.-Nov. 1972; Dep. Leader, National Party and Dep. Leader of the Opposition, 1972–74; Leader of the Opposition, 1974–75 and 1984; Shadow Minister of Foreign Affairs, 1986–92. Chm., Bd of Governors, IMF and World Bank, 1979–80; Chm., Ministerial Council, OECD, 1982. Chm., Global Econ. Action Inst., 1988–91. Pres., NZ Football Assoc., 1986–88. *Publications:* The Rise and Fall of a Young Turk, 1974; Muldoon, 1977; My Way, 1981; The New Zealand Economy: a personal view, 1985; No 38, 1986. *Recreation:* horticulture. *Address:* 7 Homewood Place, Birkenhead, Auckland 10, New Zealand. *Died 5 Aug. 1992.*

MULLEY, Baron *cr* 1984 (Life Peer), of Manor Park in the City of Sheffield; **Frederick William Mulley;** PC 1964; barrister-at-law and economist; *b* 3 July 1918; *er s* of late William and M. A. Mulley, Leamington Spa; son of general labourer; *m* 1948, Joan D., *d* of Alexander and Betty Phillips; two *d. Educ:* Bath Place Church of England Sch.; Warwick Sch. (Schol.); Christ Church, Oxford (Adult Scholar, 1945). 1st Class Hons Philosophy, Politics and Economics, 1947; Research Studentship, Nuffield Coll., Oxford, 1947; Fellowship (Economics), St Catharine's Coll., Cambridge, 1948–50. Called to Bar, Inner Temple, 1954. Clerk, National Health Insurance Cttee, Warwicks, 1936. Served War of 1939–45, Worcs Regt; Lance-Sgt 1940 (prisoner of war in Germany, 1940–45, meanwhile obtaining BSc (Econ.) and becoming Chartered Sec.). Contested (Lab) Sutton Coldfield Division of Warwicks, 1945. MP (Lab) Sheffield, Park, 1950–83; PPS to Minister of Works, 1951; Deputy Defence Sec. and Minister for the Army, 1964–65; Minister of Aviation, Dec. 1965–Jan. 1967; Jt Minister of State, FCO (formerly FO), 1967–69; Minister for Disarmament, 1967–69; Minister of Transport, 1969–70; Minister for Transport, DoE, 1974–75; Sec. of State for Educn and Science, 1975–76; Sec. of State for Defence, 1976–79. Parly deleg. to Germany, 1951, to Kenya, 1957; deleg. to Council of Europe and WEU, 1958–61 and 1979–83; WEU Assembly: Vice-Pres., 1960 (also Vice-Pres., Econ. Cttee); Pres., 1980–83. Mem., Labour Party NEC, 1957–58, 1960–64, 1965–80; Chm., Labour Party, 1974–75. Dep. Chm., Sheffield Develt Corp., 1988–91. Director: Radio Hallam, Sheffield, 1980–90; Brassey's Defence Publications, 1983–. Chm., London Conf. for Overseas Students, 1984–87. *Publications:* The Politics of Western Defence, 1962; articles on economic, defence and socialist subjects. *Address:* House of Lords, SW1A 0PW.

Died 15 March 1995.

MULLIGAN, Most Rev. Patrick; *b* 9 June 1912; *s* of James and Mary Martin. *Educ:* St Macartan's, Monaghan; Maynooth. Prof., St Macartan's, 1938; Bishop's Sec., 1943; Headmaster, Clones, 1948; Headmaster, St Michael's, Enniskillen, 1957; Parish Priest of Machaire Rois and Vicar General and Archdeacon, 1966; Bishop of Clogher, 1970–79. *Publications:* contribs to IER, JLAS, Seanchas Clochair. *Address:* Sacred Hearts' Home, Clones, Co. Monaghan, Ireland.

Died 21 Jan. 1991.

MUMFORD, Rt Rev. Peter; Bishop of Truro, 1981–89; *b* 14 Oct. 1922; *s* of late Peter Walter Mumford, miller, and of Kathleen Eva Mumford (*née* Walshe); *m* 1950, Lilian Jane, *d* of Captain George Henry Glover; two *s* one *d. Educ:* Sherborne School, Dorset; University Coll., Oxford; Cuddesdon Theological Coll. BA 1950, MA 1954 (Hons Theology). War Service, 1942–47, Captain, RA. Deacon, 1951; priest, 1952; Assistant Curate: St Mark, Salisbury, 1951–55; St Alban's Abbey, 1955–57; Vicar: Leagrave, Luton, 1957–63; St Andrew, Bedford, 1963–69; Rector of Crawley, Sussex, 1969–73; Canon and Prebendary of Ferring in Chichester Cathedral, 1972–73; Archdeacon of St Albans, 1973–74; Bishop Suffragan of Hertford, 1974–81. Vice Chm., Central Bd of Finance, 1984–89; Chm., Consultative Cttee, Foundation for Christian Communication, 1981–90. Pres., Royal Cornwall Agricl Assoc., 1985–86. *Address:* Greystones, Zeals, Wilts BA12 6LZ. *T:* Bourton (0747) 840392. *Club:* United Oxford & Cambridge University.   *Died 22 Feb. 1992.*

MUNRO, John Bennet Lorimer, CB 1959; CMG 1953; *b* 20 May 1905; *s* of late Rev. J. L. Munro; *m* 1st, 1929, Gladys Maie Forbes Simmons (*d* 1965); three *s*; 2nd, 1965, Margaret Deacy Ozanne, *d* of John Deacy, Blackfort House, Foxford, County Mayo. *Educ:* Edinburgh

Academy; Edinburgh University; Corpus Christi Coll., Oxford (MA). ICS: entered, 1928; Under-Sec. Public Dept, Fort St George, 1934; HM Treasury, 1939; Min. of Supply, 1943; idc, 1949; Div. of Atomic Energy Production, 1950; Chief Administrative Officer, UK High Commission for Germany, 1951; Under-Sec.: Min. of Supply, 1953; Bd of Trade, 1955–62; Export Credits Guarantee Dept, 1962–65; Consultant, Export Council for Europe, 1966–67. *Address:* 77 Shirley Drive, Hove, Sussex BN3 6UE. *T:* Brighton (0273) 556705.

Died 24 Oct. 1993.

MUNRO OF FOULIS, Captain Patrick, TD 1958; DL 1949; 30th Chief of Clan Munro; landowner and farmer; Vice-Lieutenant of Ross and Cromarty, 1968–77; *b* 30 Aug. 1912; *e s* of late Col C. H. O. Gascoigne, DSO, Seaforth Highlanders, and Eva Marion, *e d* of Sir Hector Munro, 11th Bt; assumed arms and designation of Munro of Foulis on death of his grandfather, 1935; *m* 1947, Eleanor Mary, *d* of Capt. Hon. William French, French Park, Co. Roscommon, Eire; three *s* one *d. Educ:* Imperial Service Coll., Windsor; RMC Sandhurst. 2nd Lt Seaforth Highlanders, 1933; Capt. 1939; served War of 1939–45, France (POW). Mem. Ross and Cromarty T&AFA, 1938. Hon. Sheriff of Ross and Cromarty, 1973. *Address:* Foulis Castle, Evanton, Ross-shire IV16 9UX. *T:* Evanton (01349) 212. *Club:* MCC.   *Died 24 Feb. 1995.*

MUNRO, Sir Robert (Lindsay), Kt 1977; CBE 1962; President of the Senate, Fiji, 1970–82; *b* NZ, 2 April 1907; *s* of Colin Robert Munro and Marie Caroline Munro; *m* 1937, Lucie Ragnhilde Mee; two *s* one *d. Educ:* Auckland Grammar Sch.; Auckland University Coll. (LLB). Barrister and Solicitor, 1929. Served War, 1940–46: 1st Lieut, FMF. Founder Chairman, Fiji: Town Planning Bd, 1946–53; Broadcasting Commn, 1953–61. Member: Educn Bd and Educn Adv. Council, 1943–70; Legislative Council, 1945–46; Nat. Health Adv. Cttee, 1976–80. President: Law Soc., 1960–62 and 1967–69; Family Planning Assoc. of Fiji, 1963–87. Internat. Planned Parenthood Federation: formerly Mem., Governing Body; Regional Vice-Pres., 1973–82. Govt Representative: Bangkok reg. pre-consultation World Population Conf., ECAFE, 1974; World Pop. Conf., Bucharest, 1974; E Asian and Pacific Copyright Seminar, Sydney, 1976. Order of St Olav, Norway, 1966. Rifle shooting Blue; Captain, NZ Hockey Team, 1932. *Recreations:* literature, garden, music. *Address:* Foulis, 6 Milne Road, Suva, Fiji. *T:* 314156. *Club:* Fiji (Suva).   *Died 12 July 1995.*

MUNRO, William, QC (Scot.) 1959; *b* 19 April 1900; *s* of William Munro, JP, Kilmarnock, and Janet Thomson Munro; *m* 1950, Christine Frances, *d* of W. B. Robertson, MC, DL, Colton, Dunfermline; three *d. Educ:* Glasgow High Sch.; Glasgow Univ. (MA, LLB). Called to Scottish Bar, 1925; called to Bar of Straits Settlements, 1927; Johore, 1927. Practised in Singapore and Malaya, 1927–57; Partner, Allen & Gledhill, Singapore. 1933–57 (Prisoner of war, Feb. 1942–Aug. 1945); resumed practice Scottish Bar, 1958. *Recreation:* reading. *Address:* 9 The Hawthorns, Muirfield Park, Gullane EH31 2DZ. *T:* Gullane (0620) 842398. *Clubs:* New (Edinburgh); Hon. Company of Edinburgh Golfers.

Died 17 Oct. 1992.

MURDOCH, Robert, (Robin), TD 1946; MD; FRCSGlas, FRCOG; Consultant Obstetrician and Gynaecologist, Royal Maternity and Royal Samaritan Hospitals, Glasgow, 1946–76; *b* 31 July 1911; *s* of late James Bowman Young Murdoch and Christina Buntin Murdoch (*née* Wood); *m* 1941, Nora Beryl (*née* Woolley); two *s* (and one *s* decd). *Educ:* Hillhead High Sch., Glasgow; Glasgow Univ. MB ChB 1934, MD 1955; MRCOG 1940; FRCSGlas 1959; FRCOG 1961. Pres., Glasgow Univ. Union, 1933. Served War, 1939–45; Major RAMC. Examiner in Obstetrics and

Gynaecology, Univs of Glasgow and Cambridge. Royal College of Gynaecologists: Examiner; Mem. Council, 1954–60, 1968–74; Jun. Vice-Pres., 1974–75; Sen. Vice-Pres., 1975–77. Pres., Scottish AAA, 1956; Mem., British Amateur Athletic Bd, 1956. *Publications:* contribs to medical jls. *Recreations:* angling, golf, gardening, athletics (rep. Scotland (British Empire Games, 1934), and GB (1931, 1933, 1934, 1935, 1938) in 220 yds). *Address:* Carrick Arden, Torwoodhill Road, Rhu, Helensburgh G84 8LE. *T:* Helensburgh (0436) 820481. *Clubs:* Oriental; Royal Scottish Automobile (Glasgow).

Died 13 Sept. 1994.

MURPHY, Most Rev. John Aloysius, DD; Archbishop Emeritus of Cardiff, (RC) (Archbishop, 1961–83); *b* Birkenhead, 21 Dec. 1905; *s* of John and Elizabeth Murphy. *Educ:* The English Coll., Lisbon. Ordained 1931; consecrated as Bishop of Appia and Coadjutor Bishop of Shrewsbury, 1948; Bishop of Shrewsbury, 1949–61. ChStJ 1974. *Address:* Ty Mair, St Joseph's Nursing Home, Malpas, Newport, Gwent NP9 6ZE.

Died 18 Nov. 1995.

MURPHY, Richard Holmes; Chairman, Industrial Tribunals, 1972–84; *b* 9 July 1915; *o s* of Harold Lawson Murphy, KC, and Elsie, 4th *d* of Rt Hon. Lord Justice Holmes; *m* 1967, Irene Sybil, *e d* of Reginald and Elizabeth Swift. *Educ:* Charterhouse; Emmanuel Coll., Cambridge (MA, LLB). Called to Bar, Inner Temple, 1939. Enlisted Inns of Court Regt, 1939; commissioned 3rd County of London Yeomanry, 1940; served Middle East and Italy, 1941–45; Judge Advocate-Gen.'s Dept, WO, 1945–46; released, rank of Major. Resident Magistrate, Tanganyika, 1948; Chief Registrar, Gold Coast Supreme Ct and Registrar of W African Ct of Appeal, 1951; Sen. Magistrate, Gold Coast, 1955; Puisne Judge, Ghana, 1957–60; Judge of High Court, Tanganyika, 1960–64; Senior Lectr in Law, Polytechnic of Central London (formerly Holborn Coll.), 1965–72. *Address:* 3 Abingdon Court, Abingdon Villas, W8 6BS. *T:* 071–937 4540.

Died 9 March 1994.

MURRAY OF NEWHAVEN, Baron *cr* 1964 (Life Peer), of Newhaven, Co. of City of Edinburgh; **Keith Anderson Hope Murray,** KCB 1963; Kt 1955; Chancellor, Southampton University, 1964–74; Visitor, Loughborough University of Technology, 1968–78; *b* 28 July 1903; 2nd surv. *s* of late Rt Hon. Lord Murray, CMG, PC, LLD and Annie Florence, *d* of David Nicolson. *Educ:* Edinburgh Academy; Edinburgh Univ. (BSc). Ministry of Agriculture, 1925–26; Commonwealth Fund Fellowship, 1926–29, at Cornell Univ., New York (PhD); Oriel Coll. and Agricultural Economics Research Institute, 1929–32, University of Oxford (BLitt and MA); Research Officer, 1932–39; Fellow and Bursar, Lincoln Coll., 1937–53, and Rector, 1944–53; Chm., Univ. Grants Cttee, 1953–63. Oxford City Council, 1938–40; Min. of Food, 1939–40; RAFVR 1941–42; Dir of Food and Agriculture, Middle East Supply Centre, GHQ, MEF, 1942–45; Oxfordshire Education Cttee, 1946–49; JP, City of Oxford, 1950–53; Chm., Vice-Chancellor's Commission of Enquiry on Halls of Residence, 1947; Mem. of Commission of Enquiry into Disturbances in the Gold Coast, 1948; Development Commissioner, 1948–53; Chairman: Advisory Cttee on Colonial Colleges of Arts, Science and Technology, 1949–53; RAF Education Advisory Cttee, 1947–53; National Council of Social Service, 1947–53. Member: Advisory Cttees on Agricultural Colls, 1954–60; Harkness Fellowship Cttee of Award, 1957–63; Cttee on Provincial Agricultural Economics Service, 1949–57; Cttee on Australian Univs, 1957; World Univ. Service, 1957–62; Dartmouth Review Cttee, 1958; Pres. Agric. Economics Soc., 1959–60; Pres. Agricultural History Soc., 1959–62; Chairman: Colonial Univ. Grants Cttee, 1964–66; London

Conf. on Overseas Students, 1963–67; Academic Adv. Cttee for Stirling Univ., 1967–75. Vice-Pres., Wellington Coll., 1966–69; Governor, The Charterhouse, 1957–69. Mem. Bd, Wellcome Trustees, 1965–73; Dir, Leverhulme Trust Fund, 1964–72; Hon. Pres., Nat. Union of Students, 1967–70. Chairman: Cttee of Enquiry into Governance of London Univ., 1970–72; Royal Commn for Exhibition of 1851, 1962–71. Director: Bristol Aeroplane Co., 1963–67; Metal Box Co., 1964–68. Hon. Fellow: Downing Coll., Cambridge; Oriel Coll., Oxford; Lincoln Coll., Oxford; Birkbeck Coll., London. Hon. LLD: Western Australia and Bristol, 1963; Cambridge, Hull, Edinburgh, Southampton, Liverpool and Leicester, 1964; Calif, 1966; London and Strathclyde, 1973; Hon. DCL Oxford, 1964; Hon. DLitt Keele, 1966; Hon. DUniv Stirling, 1968; DU Essex, 1971; Hon. FDSRCS, 1964; Hon. FUMIST, 1965. *Address:* 224 Ashley Gardens, SW1P 1PA. *T:* 071–828 4113. *Club:* United Oxford & Cambridge University.

Died 10 Oct. 1993.

MURRAY, Brian; Under Secretary, Minerals and Metals Division, 1983–87, Research and Technology Policy Division, 1987–90, Department of Trade and Industry; *b* 7 Feb. 1931; *s* of Sidney Franklin Murray and Marjorie Manton Murray; *m* 1958, Pamela Anne Woodward (marr. diss. 1982); one *s* two *d*. *Educ:* Queen Mary College, London. BSc Chem. Central Research Labs, Bowater Corp., 1957–64; Dept of Scientific and Industrial Research, 1964–66; Min. of Technology, 1967–70; Cabinet Office, 1971–74. Chm., Northumbria Cttee, The Prince's Trust, 1991–. *Recreations:* food, travel. *Address:* 43 Lindisfarne Close, Newcastle upon Tyne NE2 2HT. *Club:* Royal Automobile.

Died 24 Oct. 1993.

MURRAY, Rear-Adm. Sir Brian (Stewart), AO 1978; KCMG 1982; Governor of Victoria, 1982–85; *b* 26 Dec. 1921; *s* of Alan Stewart Murray and Lily Astria (*née* Fenton); *m* 1st, 1954, Elizabeth Malcolmson (*d* 1962); one *s* two *d*; 2nd, 1973, Janette, *d* of Mr and Mrs J. J. Paris. *Educ:* Hampton High Sch., Vic; Royal Naval Coll., Dartmouth. Joined RAN, 1939; served War, 1939–45: cruisers and destroyers in Pacific, Indian and Atlantic Oceans, North Sea and China Sea; served Korean War, 1952–53: Sen. Air Direction Officer, HMAS Sydney (despatches); CO HMAS Condamine, 1954–55; Staff course, RNC Greenwich, 1958–59; CO HMAS: Queenborough, 1961–62; Parramatta, 1963; Dir of Plans, Navy Office, 1964–65; IDC, London, 1966; CO HMAS Supply, 1967; Aust. Services Attaché, Tokyo, 1968–70; served Vietnam War, 1970: CO HMAS Sydney (troop transport); Hon. ADC to the Queen, 1971–72; Dir, Jt Ops and Plans, Dept of Defence, 1971, Dir of Jt Policy, 1972–73; Naval Officer i/c, Vic, 1974–75; Dep. Chief of Naval Staff, 1975–78; retd RAN, 1978. Owner and winemaker of Doonkuna Estate vineyard and winery at Murrumbateman, on southern tablelands of NSW, 1978–. *Recreation:* breeding thoroughbred horses. *Address:* Doonkuna Estate, Murrumbateman, NSW 2582, Australia.

Died 4 June 1991.

MURRAY, Cecil James Boyd, MS; FRCS; Emeritus Consultant Surgeon, Middlesex Hospital, since 1975 (Surgeon, 1946–75); Surgeon, Royal Masonic Hospital, London, 1958–75; *b* 8 Jan. 1910; *s* of Richard Murray, MIEE; *m* 1940, Bona (*d* 1974), *o d* of Rev. William Askwith, MA, Ripon; two *s*. *Educ:* Warriston Sch., Moffat; King's Sch., Canterbury; Middlesex Hospital Medical Sch. MB, BS, 1935; MS 1936; MRCS, LRCP, 1933, FRCS 1936. Formerly: Surgeon, King Edward Memorial Hospital, Ealing; Lecturer in Operative Surgery, Middlesex Hospital Medical Sch. Served War of 1939–45 (despatches), temp. Lt-Col RAMC. Mem., Court of Examiners, Royal College of Surgeons of England; Fellow, Assoc. of Surgeons of Great Britain; FRSocMed.

Publications: papers in medical journals. *Recreation:* fly-fishing. *Address:* Conifera, Comrie, Perthshire PH6 2LT. *T:* Comrie (0764) 70395. *Clubs:* Flyfishers', MCC.

Died 4 April 1991.

MURRAY, James Patrick, CMG 1958; *b* 10 Oct. 1906; *s* of Brig.-Gen. E. R. B. Murray; *m* 1934, Margaret Ruth Buchanan; three *s. Educ:* St Edward's Sch., Oxford; Christ Church, Oxford. Cadet, Northern Rhodesia, 1929; District Officer, Northern Rhodesia, 1931; Provincial Commissioner, Northern Rhodesia, 1950; Senior Provincial Commissioner, Northern Rhodesia, 1955; Commissioner for Northern Rhodesia in London, 1961–64 (Country became Independent, as Zambia, 1964). *Address:* Trewen, Shaftesbury Road, Woking, Surrey. *T:* Woking (0483) 761988. *Club:* Commonwealth Trust.

Died 8 Jan. 1993.

MURRAY, John (Arnaud Robin Grey), CBE 1975 (MBE 1945); FSA; FRSL; Senior Director of Publishing House of John Murray since 1968; *b* 22 Sept. 1909; *o s* of late Thomas Robinson Grey and Dorothy Evelyn Murray; adopted surname Murray, 1930; *m* 1939, Diana Mary, 3rd *d* of late Col Bernard Ramsden James and Hon. Angela Kay-Shuttleworth; two *s* two *d. Educ:* Eton; Magdalen Coll., Oxford (BA Hist). Joined publishing firm of John Murray, 1930; Asst Editor, Cornhill Magazine, 1931; Asst Editor, Quarterly Review, 1933. Served with Royal Artillery and Army-Air Support, War Office, 1940–45. Relaunched Cornhill Magazine with Peter Quennell, 1945. Member: Council, Publishers' Assoc., to 1976; Council, RGS, to 1978; Pres., English Assoc., 1976. *Publications:* (editor, with Peter Quennell) Byron: A Self-Portrait, 1950; (editor, with Leslie A. Marchand) Complete Letters and Journals of Lord Byron, 12 vols, 1973–81. *Recreations:* Byron, archives, forestry, music. *Address:* (office) 50 Albemarle Street, W1X 4BD. *T:* 071–493 4361; (home) Cannon Lodge, 12 Cannon Place, NW3 1EJ. *T:* 071–435 6537. *Clubs:* Pratt's, Beefsteak, Brooks's; Roxburghe.

Died 22 July 1993.

MURRAY, Peter (John), PhD (London), FSA; Professor of the History of Art at Birkbeck College, University of London, 1967–80, then Emeritus; *b* 23 April 1920; *er s* of John Knowles Murray and Dorothy Catton; *m* 1947, Linda Bramley. *Educ:* King Edward VI Sch., Birmingham; Robert Gordon's Coll., Aberdeen; Gray's Sch. of Art, Aberdeen; Slade Sch. and Courtauld Inst., Univ. of London. Sen. Research Fellow, Warburg Inst., 1961. Trustee, British Architectural Library, 1979–83. Pres., Soc. of Architectural Historians of GB, 1969–72; Chm., Walpole Soc., 1978–81. Rhind Lecturer, Edinburgh, 1967; Vis. Prof., Univ. of Victoria, BC, 1981. *Publications:* Watteau, 1948; Index of Attributions . . . before Vasari, 1959; Dictionary of Art and Artists (with Linda Murray), 1959 (6th edn 1989); History of English Architecture (with P. Kidson), 1962, (with P. Kidson and P. Thomson), 1965; The Art of the Renaissance (with L. Murray), 1963; The Architecture of the Italian Renaissance, 1963, 3rd edn 1986; Renaissance Architecture, 1971; The Dulwich Picture Gallery, a Catalogue, 1980; (ed) J. Burckhardt, The Architecture of the Italian Renaissance, 1985; contribs to New Cambridge Mod. Hist., Encycl. Britannica, etc; translations; articles in Warburg and Courtauld Jl, Burlington Mag., Apollo, foreign jls. *Address:* The Old Rectory, Farnborough, Banbury OX17 1DZ.

Died 20 April 1992.

MURRAY, Dr Ronald Ormiston, MBE (mil.) 1945; MD; FRCPE, DMR, FRCR; Consulting Radiologist: Royal National Orthopaedic Hospital, since 1977 (Consultant Radiologist, 1956–77); Lord Mayor Treloar's Orthopaedic Hospital, Alton, and Heatherwood Hospital, Ascot, since 1977 (Consultant Radiologist, 1951–77); *b* 14 Nov. 1912; *y s* of late John Murray and Elizabeth Ormiston Murray

(*née* MacGibbon); *m* 1st, 1940, Catherine Joan Suzette Gauvain, FFCM (*d* 1980), *d* of late Sir Henry Gauvain, MD, FRCS, and Laura Louise Butler; one *s* two *d*; 2nd, 1981, Jane (*née* Tierney), widow of Dr J. G. Mathewson. *Educ:* Glasgow Acad.; Loretto Sch.; St John's Coll., Cambridge (MA); St Thomas's Hosp. Med. Sch. Casualty Officer and Ho. Surg., St Thomas' Hosp., 1938–39; RAMC (TA), 1939–45, MO 2nd Bn The London Scottish, Hon. Lt-Col. Associate Prof., Radiology, Amer. Univ. Hosp., Beirut, 1954–56; Sen. Lectr in Orthopaedic Radiology, Inst. of Orthopaedics, London Univ., 1963–77. Robert Jones Lectr, RCS, 1973; Baker Travelling Prof. in Radiology, Australasia, 1974; Caldwell Lectr, Amer. Roentgen Ray Soc., 1975, also Corresp. Mem. of the Soc., 1973–; Skinner Lectr, RCR, 1979; other eponymous lectures. Associate Editor, Brit. Jl of Radiology, 1959–71. Founder Vice-Pres., Internat. Skeletal Soc., 1973, Pres., 1977–78. Fellow: Brit. Orthopaedic Assoc.; RSocMed (Pres., Sect. of Radiol., 1978–79); Hon. Fellow: Amer. Coll. of Radiology, 1969; Royal Australasian Coll. of Radiol., 1979; Fac. Radiol., RCSI, 1981; Hon. Member: Mexican and Peruvian Radiol. Socs, 1968; Radiol. Soc. of N Amer., 1975; GETROA, France, 1976. *Publications:* chapters in: Modern Trends in Diagnostic Radiology, 1970; D. Sutton's Textbook of Radiology, 1969, 4th edn 1987; (jtly) Radiology of Skeletal Disorders: exercises in diagnosis, 1971, 3rd edn 1990; (jtly) Orthopaedic Diagnosis, 1984; papers in med. jls, mainly concerning radiological aspects of orthopaedics. *Recreations:* golf; formerly: Rugby football (Cambridge XV 1933–34, Scotland XV 1935), swimming (Cambridge Univ. Team 1933–34, British Univs Team, Turin, 1933). *Address:* Little Court, The Bury, Odiham, Hants RG25 1NB. *T:* Odiham (01256) 702982. *Clubs:* United Oxford & Cambridge University; Hawks (Cambridge); Berkshire Golf, Rye Golf.

Died 5 March 1995.

MURRIE, Sir William (Stuart), GCB 1964 (CB 1946); KBE 1952; Permanent Under-Secretary of State for Scotland, 1959–64, retired; *b* Dundee, 19 Dec. 1903; *s* of Thomas Murrie and Catherine Burgh; *m* 1932, Eleanore Boswell (*d* 1966). *Educ:* S America; Harris Acad., Dundee; Edinburgh Univ.; Balliol Coll., Oxford. Entered Scottish Office, 1927; transferred to Dept of Health for Scotland, 1935; Under-Sec., Offices of War Cabinet, 1944; Deputy Sec. (Civil), Cabinet Office, 1947; Deputy Under-Sec. of State, Home Office, 1948–52; Sec. to the Scottish Education Dept, 1952–57; Sec., Scottish Home Dept, 1957–59. Chm., Board of Trustees for Nat. Galls of Scotland, 1972–75; Member: Council on Tribunals, 1965–77; Adv. Cttee on Rhodesian Travel Restrictions, 1968–79 (Chm., 1979). General Council Assessor, Edinburgh Univ. Court, 1967–75. Hon. LLD, Dundee Univ., 1968. *Address:* St Raphael's, 6 South Oswald Road, Edinburgh EH9 2HE. *T:* 031–667 2612.

Died 6 June 1994.

MUSHIN, Prof. William W(oolf), CBE 1971; MA Oxon, 1946; MB, BS (Hons) London, 1933; FRCS 1966; FFARCS 1948; Professor and Director of Anaesthetics, Welsh National School of Medicine, University of Wales, 1947–75, then Emeritus; *b* London, Sept. 1910; *y s* of Moses Mushin and Jesse (*née* Kalmenson); *m* 1939, Betty Hannah Goldberg; one *s* three *d. Educ:* Davenant Sch.; London Hosp. Med. Sch. (Buxton Prize in Anatomy, Anderson Prize in Clinical Medicine). Various resident hosp. posts; formerly: Anaesthetist, Royal Dental Hosp.; first Asst, Nuffield Dept of Anaesthetists, Univ. of Oxford. Lectures: Clover, RCS, 1955; Kellogg, George Washington Univ., 1950; Guedel, Univ. of Calif, 1957; John Snow, 1964; Baxter Travenol, Internat. Anaesth. Research Soc., 1970; Macgregor, Univ. of Birmingham, 1972; Rovenstine, Amer. Soc. of Anesthesiol., 1973; Crawford Long, Emory Univ., USA, 1981. Visiting

Professor or Consultant to univs, academic and other bodies in USA, Argentine, Uruguay, Brazil, Denmark, NZ, Australia, India, Germany, Ghana, Kenya, S Africa, and Holland. Examiner: Univ. of Oxford for MD and PhD; FFARCS, 1953–73; FFARCSI, 1962–67. Welsh Regional Hospital Board: Cons. Adviser in Anaesthetics, 1948–74; Mem., 1961–74. Member: Central Health Services Council, 1962–72; Safety of Drugs Cttee, Dept of Health and Social Security, 1964–76; Medicines Commn, 1976–83; Assoc. of Anaesthetists, 1936– (Mem. Council, 1946–59 and 1961–73; Vice-Pres., 1953–56); Anaesthetists Group Cttee, BMA, 1950–69; Bd of Governors, United Cardiff Hosps, 1956–65; Court, Univ. of Wales, 1957–58; Commonwealth Scholarships Commn, 1969–78. Welsh National School of Medicine: Mem. Senate, 1947–75; Mem. Council, 1957–58; Vice-Provost, 1958–60; Royal College of Surgeons: Mem. Bd, Faculty of Anaesthetists, 1954–71; Mem. Council, 1961–64; Dean, Faculty of Anaesthetists, 1961–64. Mem. Bd of Management and Consulting Editor, British Jl of Anaesthesia, 1947–75. Hon. Mem., various societies of anaesthetists. Hon. FFARACS 1959; Hon. FFA(SA) 1962; Hon. FFARCSI 1962; Hon. FRSM 1987. Hon. DSc Wales, 1982. John Snow Silver Medal, 1974; Henry Hill Hickman Medal, RSocMed, 1978. *Publications:* Anaesthesia for the Poor Risk, 1948; (with Sir R. Macintosh) Local Analgesia: Brachial Plexus, 1954, 4th edn 1967; Physics for the Anaesthetist, 1946, 4th edn 1987; Automatic Ventilation of Lungs, 1959, 3rd edn 1980; (ed) Thoracic Anaesthesia, 1963; numerous papers on anaesthesia and allied subjects in British and foreign jls. *Address:* 30 Bettws-y-Coed Road, Cardiff CF2 6PL. *T:* Cardiff (0222) 751002.
Died 22 Jan. 1993.

MUSKER, Sir John, Kt 1952; banker; racehorse breeder; Chairman: Cater, Brightwen & Co. Ltd, Bankers, 1938–60; Cater, Ryder & Co., Ltd, Bankers, 1960–71 (Director, 1960–79); *b* 25 Jan. 1906; *o s* of late Capt. Harold Musker,

JP, Snarehill Hall, Thetford, Norfolk; *m* 1st, 1932, Elizabeth (decd), *d* of Captain Loeffler, 51 Grosvenor Square, W1; one *d* (and one *d* decd); 2nd, 1955, Mrs Rosemary Pugh (*d* 1980), *d* of late Maj.-Gen. Merton Beckwith-Smith; 3rd 1982, Hon. Audrey Elizabeth Paget (*d* 1990), *d* of 1st and last Baron Queenborough, GBE. *Educ:* privately; St John's Coll., Cambridge (BA). Mem. LCC for City of London, 1944–49. Lt, RNVR, 1940. Hon. Treas., London Municipal Soc., 1936–46. *Address:* Shadwell Park, Thetford, Norfolk. *T:* Thetford (0842) 753257. *Club:* White's. *Died 20 May 1992.*

MUSSON, Maj.-Gen. Alfred Henry, CB 1958; CBE 1956; pac; late Royal Artillery; President, Ordnance Board, 1957–58, retired (Vice-President, 1955–57); *b* 14 Aug. 1900; *s* of Dr A. W. Musson, Clitheroe, Lancs; *m* 1932, Joan Wright Taylor (*d* 1980); three *s. Educ:* Tonbridge Sch.; RMA Woolwich. Served War of 1939–45. *Address:* Lyndon, 19 The Ridgeway, Tonbridge, Kent TN10 4NH. *T:* Tonbridge (01732) 364978. *Died 6 Aug. 1995.*

MUSSON, Samuel Dixon, CB 1963; MBE 1943; Chief Registrar of Friendly Societies and Industrial Assurance Commissioner, 1963–72; *b* 1 April 1908; *e s* of late R. Dixon Musson, Yockleton, Salop; *m* 1949, Joan I. S., 2nd *d* of late Col D. Davies-Evans, DSO, Penylan, Carmarthenshire. *Educ:* Shrewsbury Sch.; Trinity Hall, Cambridge. Called to Bar, Inner Temple, 1930; practised as Barrister, 1930–46; commnd, Pilot Officer, RAFVR, 1941; served Egypt, N Africa, Italy, 1942–45 (despatches); Ministry of Health: Senior Legal Asst, 1946; Asst Solicitor, 1952; Principal Asst Solicitor, 1957. Vice-Pres., Building Socs Assoc., 1972–87; Mem., Trustee Savings Bank Inspection Cttee, 1972–77. *Recreations:* golf, country pursuits. *Address:* The Beehive, 8 Fairview Road, Headley Down, Bordon, Hants GU35 8JP. *T:* Headley Down (0428) 713183. *Club:* Savile. *Died 31 July 1992.*

N

NAIRNE, Lady (12th in line, of the Lordship *cr* 1681); **Katherine Evelyn Constance Bigham;** *b* 22 June 1912; *d* of 6th Marquess of Lansdowne and Elizabeth (she *m* 2nd, Lord Colum Crichton-Stuart, who *d* 1957; she *d* 1964); *S* to brother's Lordship of Nairne, 1944; *m* 1933, Hon. Edward Bigham (later 3rd Viscount Mersey, who *d* 1979); three *s. Heir: s* 4th Viscount Mersey [*b* 8 July 1934; *m* 1961, Joanna Murray; one *s*]. *Address:* Bignor Park, Pulborough, W Sussex RH20 1HG. *T:* Sutton (Sussex) (017987) 214. *Died 20 Oct. 1995.*

NALDER, Hon. Sir Crawford David, Kt 1974; farmer; active in voluntary and charitable organisations; *b* Katanning, WA, 14 Feb. 1910; *s* of H. A. Nalder, Wagin; *m* 1st, 1934, Olive May (*d* 1973), *d* of S. Irvin; one *s* two *d*; 2nd, 1974, Brenda Wade (*d* 1987). *Educ:* State Sch., Wagin; Wesley Coll., Perth, WA. Sheep, wheat and pig farmer, 1934–; Country rep. for Perth butchers. Entered parliament, 1947; MLA (CP) for Katanning, Parliament of Western Australia, 1950–73 (for Wagin, 1947–50); Dep. Leader, Country Party, 1956; Minister: for War Service Land Settlement, 1959–66; for Agriculture, 1959–71; for Electricity, 1962–71; Leader, Parly Country Party, 1962–73. Chm., Girls College Council. Knighted for services to the state and in local govt. *Recreations:* tennis, gardening. *Address:* 4–7 Dale Place, Booragoon, WA 6154, Australia. *Died 8 Dec. 1994.*

NANCE, His Honour Francis James, LLM; a Circuit Judge (formerly a Judge of County Courts and Commissioner, Liverpool and Manchester Crown Courts), 1966–90; *b* 5 Sept. 1915; *s* of late Herbert James Nance, S Africa, and Margaret Ann Nance, New Brighton; *m* 1st, 1943, Margaret Gertrude Roe (*d* 1978); two *s*; 2nd, 1988, Theodora Wilhelmina Maria McGinty (*née* Marchand) (*d* 1995). *Educ:* St Francis Xavier's College, Liverpool; University of Liverpool (LLM 1938). Called to the Bar, Gray's Inn, 1936. Served War of 1939–45, Royal Corps of Signals (Captain): Normandy invasion, NW Europe (despatches). Practised on Northern Circuit, 1936–66; Deputy Chairman, Lancashire QS, 1963–71; Pres., HM Council of Circuit Judges, 1984. *Recreation:* chess. *Address:* 41 Bower House, Upton, Merseyside L49 4RP. *Club:* Athenæum (Liverpool). *Died 4 June 1995.*

NAPIER, Barbara Langmuir, OBE 1975; Senior Tutor to Women Students in the University of Glasgow, 1964–74; Member, the Industrial Arbitration Board (formerly Industrial Court), 1963–76; *b* 21 Feb. 1914; *y c* of late James Langmuir Napier, consultant engineer, and Siblie Agnes Mowat. *Educ:* Hillhead High Sch., Glasgow; Univ. of Glasgow (MA); Glasgow and West of Scotland Coll. of Domestic Science. Org. Sec. Redlands Hosp., Glasgow, 1937–41; Univ. of Glasgow: Warden, Queen Margaret Hall, 1941–44; Gen. Advr to Women Students, 1942–64; Appts Officer (Women), 1942–65. Founder Mem. Assoc. of Principals, Wardens and Advisers to Univ. Women Students, 1942, Hon. Mem., 1977– (Pres. 1965–68); Local Rep. and later Mem. Coun., Women's Migration and Overseas Appts Soc., 1946–64. Winifred Cullis Lecture Fellowship (midwest USA) of Brit. Amer. Associates, 1950. Founder Dir, West of Scotland Sch. Co. Ltd, 1976–77. Member, Tribunal under National Insurance Acts, 1954–60; President, Standing Conference of Women's Organisations (Glasgow), 1955–57; Member: Scottish Committee, ITA, 1957–64; Executive Cttee, Nat. Advisory Centre on Careers for Women (formerly Women's Employment Fedn), 1963–68, 1972–77; Indep. Member: Flax and Hemp Wages Council (GB), 1962–70 (Dep. Chm. 1964–70); Hat, Cap and Millinery Wages Council (GB), 1963–70; Laundry Wages Council (GB), 1968–70. Governor: Westbourne Sch., Glasgow, 1951–77 (Chm., 1969–77; Hon. Governor, 1981); Notre Dame Coll. of Educn, Glasgow, 1959–64. Admitted as Burgess and Guild Sister (*qua* Hammerman) of Glasgow, and Mem., Grand Antiquity Soc. of Glasgow, 1956. JP Glasgow 1955–75, Stirling 1975–80. *Publications:* (with S. Nisbet) Promise and Progress, 1970; contrib. The College Courant, etc. *Recreations:* reading, travel, gardening, painting, being with cats. *Address:* 67 Brisbane Street, Largs, Ayrshire KA30 8QP. *T:* Largs (01475) 675495. *Club:* College (Glasgow).

Died 7 Nov. 1991.

NAPIER, Sir Robin (Surtees), 5th Bt *cr* 1867, of Merrion Square, Dublin; Consultant, Rothschild Bank, AG (Zurich), since 1994 (UK Representative, 1983–94); *b* 5 March 1932; *s* of Sir Joseph William Lennox Napier, 4th Bt, OBE and of Isabelle Muriel, *yr d* of late Major Siward Surtees; assumed forenames of Robin Surtees in lieu of Robert Aubone Siward; *S* father, 1986; *m* 1971, Jennifer Beryl, *d* of late H. Warwick Daw; one *s. Educ:* Eton College. 2nd Lt Coldstream Guards, 1951–52. Pearl Assurance Co., 1953–56; Charterhouse Japhet, 1956–83. Gen. Comr of Income Tax (Basingstoke), 1993–. *Recreations:* fishing, shooting, gardening. *Heir: s* Charles Joseph Napier, *b* 15 April 1973. *Address:* Upper Chilland House, Martyr Worthy, Winchester, Hants SO21 1EB. *T:* Itchen Abbas (0962779) 307. *Clubs:* City of London, Flyfishers', MCC, British Sportsman's; Union (Sydney, NSW). *Died 2 July 1994.*

NAPLEY, Sir David, Kt 1977; solicitor; Consultant, Kingsley Napley (formerly Senior Partner); President of the Law Society, 1976–77 (Vice-President, 1975–76); *b* 25 July 1915; *s* of late Joseph and Raie Napley; *m* 1940, Leah Rose, *d* of Thomas Reginald Saturley; two *d. Educ:* Burlington College. Solicitor, 1937. Served with Queen's Royal (W Surrey) Regt, 1940; commnd 1942; Indian Army, 1942; Captain 1942; invalided 1945. Contested (C): Rowley Regis and Tipton, 1951; Gloucester, 1955. Pres., London (Criminal Courts) Solicitors Assoc., 1960–63; Chm. Exec. Council, British Academy of Forensic Sciences, 1960–74 (Pres. 1967; Director, 1974–); Mem. Council, Law Soc., 1962–86; Mem. Judicial Exchange with USA, 1963–64; Chm., Law Soc.'s Standing Cttee on Criminal Law, 1963–76; Mem. Editorial Bd, Criminal Law Review, 1967–; Chairman: Contentious Business, Law Soc., 1972–75; Legal Aid Cttee, 1969–72; Exam. Bd, Incorp. Soc. of Valuers and Auctioneers, 1981–84; Mem., Home Office Law Revision Cttee, 1971–. President: City of Westminster Law Soc., 1967–68; Law Services Assoc., 1987–90. Mem. Council and Trustee, Imperial Soc. of Kts Bachelor, 1981–, Chm., 1988–. Chairman: Mario & Franco Restaurants Ltd, 1968–77; Burton-Race Restaurants plc, 1986–; Dir, Covent Garden Fest. Ltd, 1989–. Trustee, W Ham Boys' Club, 1979–, Pres., 1981–; Pres., Burnham Ratepayers Assoc., 1987–91. *Publications:* Law on the Remuneration of Auctioneers and Estate Agents, 1947; (ed) Bateman's Law of Auctions,

1954; The Law of Auctioneers and Estate Agents Commission, 1957; Crime and Criminal Procedure, 1963; Guide to Law and Practice under the Criminal Justice Act, 1967; The Technique of Persuasion, 1970, 4th edn 1991; Not without Prejudice, 1982; The Camden Town Murder, 1987; Murder at the Villa Madeira, 1988; Rasputin in Hollywood, 1990; a section, Halsbury's Laws of England; contrib. legal and forensic scientific jls, press, legal discussions on radio and TV. *Recreations:* painting, reading, writing, music, eating. *Address:* Knights Quarter, 14 St John's Lane, EC1M 4AJ. *T:* 071–814 1200. *Club:* Garrick. *Died 24 Sept. 1994.*

NASH, Thomas Arthur Manly, CMG 1959; OBE 1944; Dr (Science); retired; *b* 18 June 1905; *s* of late Col L. T. M. Nash, CMG, RAMC and Editha Gertrude, *y d* of Rev. Charles Sloggett; *m* 1930, Marjorie Wenda Wayte; (one *s* decd). *Educ:* Wellington Coll.; Royal Coll. of Science. Doctorate of Science, 1933. Entomologist, Dept Tsetse Research and Reclamation, Tanganyika Territory, 1927; Entomologist, Sleeping Sickness Service, Med. Dept, Nigeria, 1933; in charge Anchau Rural Development Scheme, 1937–44; seconded as Chief Entomologist, W African Institute for Trypanosomiasis Research, 1948, Deputy Director, 1953, Director, 1954–59; Dir, Tsetse Research Lab., Univ. of Bristol, Veterinary Field Station, Langford, 1962–71. *Publications:* Tsetse Flies in British West Africa, 1948; Africa's Bane, The Tsetse Fly, 1969; A Zoo without Bars, 1984; numerous scientific publications on tsetse and trypanosomiasis. *Recreation:* fishing. *Address:* Spring Head Farm, Upper Langford, near Bristol BS18 7DN. *T:* Churchill (0934) 852321.
Died 14 Jan. 1993.

NEALE, Sir Alan (Derrett), KCB 1972 (CB 1968); MBE 1945; Deputy Chairman, Association of Futures Brokers and Dealers Ltd, 1987–91, retired; *b* 24 Oct. 1918; *o s* of late W. A. Neale; *m* 1956, Joan, *o d* of late Harry Frost, Wisbech; one *s. Educ:* Highgate School; St John's College, Oxford. War Service, Intelligence Corps, 1940–45. Board of Trade, 1946–68; Second Sec., 1967; Dep. Sec., Treasury, 1968–71, Second Permanent Sec., 1971–72; Perm. Sec., MAFF, 1973–78. A Dep. Chm., Monopolies and Mergers Commn, 1982–86 (Mem., 1981–86). Commonwealth Fund Fellowship, USA, 1952–53; Fellow of Center for Internat. Affairs, Harvard Univ., 1960–61. *Publications:* The Anti-Trust Laws of the USA, 1960; The Flow of Resources from Rich to Poor, 1961; (jtly) International Business and National Jurisdiction, 1988. *Recreations:* music, bridge. *Address:* 95 Swains Lane, N6 6PJ. *T:* 0181–340 5236. *Club:* Reform.
Died 21 March 1995.

NEAVE, Sir Arundell Thomas Clifton, 6th Bt, *cr* 1795, of Dagnam Park, Essex; JP; late Major Welsh Guards; *b* 31 May 1916; *e s* of Col Sir Thomas Lewis Hughes Neave, 5th Bt, and Dorina (*d* 1955) (author of 26 years on the Bosphorus, Remembering Kut, 1937, Romance of the Bosphorus, 1950), *d* of late George H. Clifton; *S* father, 1940; *m* 1946, Richenda Alice Ione, *o c* of Sir Robert J. Paul, 5th Bt; two *s* two *d. Educ:* Eton. Served in 1939–45 War, Welsh Guards (Major); Dunkirk, 1940, retired 1947. JP for Anglesey, 1950. *Heir: s* Paul Arundell Neave [*b* 13 December 1948; *m* 1976, Coralie Jane Louise, *e d* of Sir Robert Kinahan, ERD; two *s*]. *Address:* Greatham Moor, Liss, Hants. *Clubs:* Carlton, Pratt's.
Died 5 Aug. 1992.

NEEDHAM, Gwei-Djen Lu-; *see* Lu, G. D.

NEEDHAM, (Noël) Joseph (Terence Montgomery), CH 1992; MA, PhD, ScD (Cantab); FRS 1941; FBA 1971; Emeritus Director, Needham Research Institute (East Asian History of Science Library), Cambridge (Director, 1976–90); Master of Gonville and Caius College,

Cambridge, 1966–76; Hon. Counsellor, UNESCO; *b* 9 Dec. 1900; *s* of late Joseph Needham, MD, Harley Street and Clapham Park, and Alicia A. Needham; *m* 1st, 1924, Dorothy Mary, ScD, FRS (*d* 1987), *d* of John Moyle, Babbacombe, Devon; 2nd, 1989, Gwei-Djen Lu, PhD (*d* 1991). *Educ:* Oundle School. Fellow Gonville and Caius Coll., 1924–66, 1976– (Librarian, 1959–60, Pres., 1959–66); Univ. Demonstrator in Biochem., 1928–33; Sir William Dunn Reader in Biochemistry, 1933–66, then Emeritus. Vis. Prof. of Biochem. at Stanford Univ., California, USA, 1929; Hitchcock Prof., Univ. of California, 1950; Visiting Professor: Univ. of Lyon, 1951; Univ. of Kyoto, 1971; Collège de France, Paris, 1973; Univ. of British Columbia, Vancouver, 1975; Hon. Professor: Inst. of History of Science, Acad. Sinica, Peking, 1980–; Chinese Acad. of Soc. Sci., 1983–. Lectures: Terry and Carmalt, Yale Univ.; Goldwin-Smith, Cornell Univ.; Mead-Swing, Oberlin College, Ohio, USA, 1935; Oliver Sharpey, RCP, 1935–36; Herbert Spencer, Oxford, 1936–37; for Polskie Towarzystwo Biologicznej in the Universities of Warsaw, Lwów, Kraków and Wilno, 1937; Comte Memorial, London, 1940; Conway Memorial, London, 1947; Boyle, Oxford, 1948; Noguchi, Johns Hopkins Univ., 1950; Hobhouse, London Univ., 1950; Dickinson, Newcomen Soc., 1956; Colombo, Singapore, Peking and Jaipur Universities, 1958; Wilkins, Royal Society, 1958; Wilde, Manchester, 1959; Earl Grey, Newcastle upon Tyne, 1960–61; Henry Myers, Royal Anthropological Institute, 1964; Harveian, London, 1970; Rapkine, Paris, 1971; Bernal, London, 1971; Ballard Matthews, Bangor, 1971; Fremantle, Oxford, 1971; Irvine, St Andrews, 1973; Dressler, Leeds, 1973; Carr-Saunders, London, Gerald Walters, Bath, First John Caius, Padua, 1974; Bowra, Oxford, 1975; Danz, Seattle, 1977; Harris, Northwestern, 1978; First Wickramasinghe, Colombo, 1978; Ch'ien Mu and Huang Chan, Hong Kong, 1979; Creighton, London, 1979; Radhakrishnan, Oxford, 1980; Priestley, London, 1982; First E Asian Hist. of Sci. Foundn, Hongkong, 1983; First Julian Huxley Meml, 1987. Head of the British Scientific Mission in China and Scientific Counsellor, British Embassy, Chungking, and Adviser to the Chinese National Resources Commission, Chinese Army Medical Administration and Chinese Air Force Research Bureau, 1942–46; Director of the Dept of Natural Sciences, UNESCO, 1946–48. Mem., Internat. Commn for Investigation of Bacteriological Warfare in China and Korea, 1952; Chm. Ceylon Government University Policy Commission, 1958. Pres., Internat. Union of Hist. of Science, 1972–75. Foreign Member: Nat. Acad. of Science, USA; Amer. Acad. Arts and Sciences; Amer. Hist. Assoc.; National Academy of China (Academia Sinica); Royal Danish Acad.; Mem. Internat. Academies of Hist. of Science and of Med.; Hon. Member Yale Chapter of Sigma Xi. Hon. Fellow, UMIST. Hon. FRCP 1984. Hon. DSc, Brussels, Norwich, Chinese Univ. of Hong Kong; Hon. LLD Toronto and Salford; Hon. LittD Cambridge, Hongkong, Newcastle upon Tyne, Hull, Chicago, Wilmington, N Carolina and Peradeniya, Ceylon; DUniv Surrey; Hon. PhD Uppsala. Sir William Jones Medallist, Asiatic Society of Bengal, 1963; George Sarton Medallist, Soc. for History of Science, 1968; Leonardo da Vinci Medallist, Soc. for History of Technology, 1968; Dexter Award for History of Chemistry, 1979; Science Award (1st cl.), Nat. Sci. Commn of China, 1984; Fukuoka Municipality Medal for Asian Culture, 1990; UNESCO Einstein Gold Medal, 1994. Order of the Brilliant Star, 3rd grade with sash (China), 1985; Friendship Ambassador, 1990 (title conferred by Chinese People's Cttee for friendship with other countries). *Publications:* Science, Religion and Reality (ed), 1925; Man a Machine, 1927; The Sceptical Biologist, 1929; Chemical Embryology (3 vols), 1931; The Great Amphibium, 1932; A History of Embryology, 1934; Order and Life, 1935;

Christianity and the Social Revolution (ed), 1935; Adventures before Birth (trans.), 1936; Perspectives in Biochemistry (Hopkins Presentation Volume; ed), 1937; Background to Modern Science (ed), 1938; Biochemistry and Morphogenesis, 1942; The Teacher of Nations, addresses and essays in commemoration of John Amos Comenius (ed), 1942; Time, the Refreshing River, 1943; History is on Our Side, 1945; Chinese Science, 1946; Science Outpost, 1948; Hopkins and Biochemistry (ed), 1949; Science and Civilisation in China (7 vols, 25 parts; jtly), 1954–: vol. I, Introductory Orientations, 1954; vol. II, History of Scientific Thought, 1956; vol III, Mathematics and the Sciences of the Heavens and the Earth, 1959; vol. IV, Physics and Physical Technology, part 1, Physics, 1962, part 2, Mechanical Engineering, 1965, part 3, Civil Engineering and Nautics, 1971; vol. V, Chemistry and Chemical Technology, part 1, Paper and Printing, 1985, part 2, Spagyrical Discovery and Invention, 1974, part 3, History of Alchemy, 1976, part 4, Apparatus, Theory and Comparative Macrobiotics, 1980, part 5, Physiological Alchemy, 1983, part 6, Projectiles and Sieges, 1994, part 7, The Gunpowder Epic, 1988; vol. VI, part 1, Botany, 1985, part 2, Agriculture, 1984; The Development of Iron and Steel Technology in China, 1958; Heavenly Clockwork, 1960, rev. edn 1986; Within the Four Seas, 1970; The Grand Titration, 1970; Clerks and Craftsmen in China and the West (jtly), 1970; The Chemistry of Life (ed), 1970; Moulds of Understanding, 1976; Celestial Lancets, a history and rationale of Acupuncture and Moxa (jtly), 1980; The Hall of Heavenly Records: Korean astronomical instruments and clocks 1380–1780 (jtly), 1986; Trans-Pacific Echoes and Resonances, Listening Once Again (jtly), 1986; Chart to illustrate the History of Physiology and Biochemistry, 1926; original papers in scientific, philosophical and sinological journals. *Address:* 2A Sylvester Road, Cambridge CB3 9AF. *T:* Cambridge (01223) 352183; Needham Research Institute (East Asian History of Science Library), 8 Sylvester Road, Cambridge CB3 9AF. *T:* Cambridge (01223) 311545.

Died 24 March 1995.

NELIGAN, Desmond West Edmund, OBE 1961; National Insurance Commissioner, 1961–76, retired; *b* 20 June 1906; *s* of late Rt Rev. M. R. Neligan, DD (one time Bishop of Auckland, NZ), and Mary, *d* of Edmund Macrory, QC; *m* 1st, 1936, Penelope Ann (marr. diss. 1946), *d* of Henry Mason; two *s*; 2nd, 1947, Margaret Elizabeth, *d* of late Captain Snook, RN; one step *d. Educ:* Bradfield Coll.; Jesus Coll., Cambridge. BA Cantab, 1929; Barrister, Middle Temple, 1940. Practising Barrister until 1961. Appointed Umpire under National Service Acts, Nov. 1955; Dep. Comr for National Insurance, 1955–61. Served War of 1939–45, in 2 NZ Division, in Greece, Crete and Western Desert. *Publications:* (ed) 6th, 7th and 8th Editions Dumsday's Parish Councils Handbook; (with Sir A. Safford, QC) Town and Country Planning Act, 1944, and *ibid*, 1947; Social Security Case Law: digest of Commissioners' decisions, 1979; Lawful Lyrics and Cautionary Tales for Lawyers, 1984. *Recreations:* formerly: hockey, cricket, tennis, hunting. *Address:* The Cottage, 61 West Street, Storrington, Pulborough, West Sussex RH20 4DZ. *T:* Storrington (09066) 4514.

Died 20 March 1993.

NELSON OF STAFFORD, 2nd Baron, *cr* 1960; **Henry George Nelson,** MA; FEng 1976; FICE, FRAeS; Bt 1955; *b* Manchester, 2 Jan. 1917; *s* of 1st Baron Nelson of Stafford and Florence Mabel, *o d* of late Henry Howe, JP; *S* father, 1962; *m* 1940, Pamela Roy Bird, *yr d* of late Ernest Roy Bird, formerly MP for Skipton, Yorks; two *s* two *d. Educ:* Oundle; King's Coll., Cambridge. Exhibnr 1935; Mechanical Sciences Tripos, 1937. Practical experience in England, France and Switzerland, 1937–39;

joined the English Electric Co. Ltd, 1939; Supt, Preston Works, 1939–40; Asst Works Man., Preston, 1940–41; Dep. Works Man., Preston, 1941–42; Man. Dir, D. Napier & Son Ltd, 1942–49; Exec. Dir, The Marconi Co. Ltd, 1946–58; Dep. Man. Dir, 1949–56, Man. Dir, 1956–62, Chm. and Chief Exec., 1962–68, The English Electric Co. Ltd; Chm., 1968–83, Dir, 1968–87, GEC. Dep. Chm., British Aircraft Corp., 1960–77; Chm., Royal Worcester Ltd, 1978–84; Director: Internat. Nickel Co. of Canada, 1966–74 and 1975–88; ICL, 1968–74; Nat. Bank of Australasia Ltd (London Bd of Advice), 1950–81; Bank of England, 1961–87; Enserch Corp., 1984–89; Humphreys & Glasgow International, 1991–93. Outside Lectr, Univ. of Cambridge (Mech. Sciences Tripos course on Industrial Management), 1947–49. Chancellor of Aston Univ., 1966–79. Chm., Stafford Enterprise Ltd, 1987–93; Member: Govt Adv. Council on Scientific Policy, 1955–58; Adv. Council on Middle East Trade, 1958–63 (Industrial Leader and Vice-Chm., 1959–63); Civil Service Commn (Part time Mem. Final Selection and Interview Bds), 1956–61; Engrg Adv. Council, 1958–61; Council, Inst. Electrical Engineers, 1959–76 (Vice-Pres. 1957–62 and 1965–70, Pres., 1970–71); Middle East Assoc. (Vice-Pres., 1962–); Gen. Bd of NPL, 1959–66; Council, SBAC, 1943–64 (Pres. 1961–62); Council, Foundn on Automation and Employment Ltd, 1963–68; Council, BEAMA, 1964–78 (Pres., 1966); Adv. Council, Min. of Technology, 1964–70; Engineering Industries Council, 1975–84; H of L Select Cttee on Sci. and Technology, 1984–91; Mem., 1954–87, Chm., 1971–74, British Nat. Cttee, World Power Conf.; Mem., Nat. Def. Industries Council, 1969–77 (Chm., 1971–77); President: Locomotive and Allied Manufacturers Assoc., 1964–66; British Electrical Power Convention, 1965–67; ORGALIME, 1968–70; Sino-British Trade Council, 1973–83. Liveryman: Worshipful Co. of Coachmakers and Coach Harness Makers of London, 1944; Worshipful Co. of Goldsmiths, 1961 (Prime Warden, 1983–84). Lord High Steward of Borough of Stafford, 1966–71. Hon. FIMechE, Hon. FIEE; Hon. DSc: Aston, 1966; Keele, 1967; Cranfield, 1972; Hon. LLD Strathclyde, 1971; Fellow, Imp. Coll. of Science and Technology, 1969. Benjamin Franklin Medal, RSA, 1959. *Recreations:* shooting, fishing. *Heir: s* Hon. Henry Roy George Nelson [*b* 26 Oct. 1943; *m* 1968, Dorothy, *yr d* of Leslie Caley, Tibthorpe Manor, Driffield, Yorks; one *s* one *d*]. *Address:* 244 Cranmer Court, Whiteheads Grove, SW3 3HD. *T:* 0171–581 2551. *Club:* Carlton.

Died 19 Jan. 1995.

NELSON, Campbell Louis; Hon. President, Ultramar plc; *b* 14 Dec. 1910; *s* of George Francis Nelson and Kate Nelson (*née* Wilson); *m* 1939, Pauline Frances Blundell (*d* 1978); one *s* one *d. Educ:* Seaford Coll.; King's Coll., London Univ. FCA. Served War, KRRC (Motor Bns), 1941–44. Partner of Limebeer & Co., Chartered Accountants, 1933–41; Sen. Partner, Limebeer & Co., 1951–74. Dir, 1947–87, Exec. Dir, 1947–60, Man. Dir, 1960–80, and Chm., 1971–80, Ultramar plc; Exec. Dir, 1948–85, Chm., 1957–85, British-Borneo Petroleum Syndicate Ltd; Dir, 1970–81, Chm., 1976–81, Gellatly Hankey & Co. Ltd; Chm., Scottish Offshore Investors Ltd, 1975–85; Dir, Harrisons (Clyde) Ltd, 1981–88. Councillor: Maritime Trust, 1979–; Indonesian Assoc., 1980–; Patron, St James and St Vedast Schools, 1980–. *Recreations:* golf, bridge. *Address:* 2 Chelsea House, 26 Lowndes Street, SW1X 9JD. *T:* 071–235 8260; Queenshill, Sunningdale, Berks. *T:* Ascot (0990) 20088. *Clubs:* City of London; Royal and Ancient Golf (St Andrews), Sunningdale Golf. *Died 11 Jan. 1991.*

NELSON, Maj.-Gen. Sir (Eustace) John (Blois), KCVO 1966 (MVO 1953); CB 1965; DSO 1944; OBE 1948; MC 1943; *b* 15 June 1912; *s* of late Roland Hugh Nelson and Hylda Letitia Blois; *m* 1936, Lady Jane FitzRoy (granted rank and precedence of *d* of a duke, 1931), *er d* of (William Henry Alfred FitzRoy) Viscount Ipswich; two *d. Educ:* Eton; Trinity College, Cambridge. BA (Hons) History, MA 1983. Commissioned Grenadier Guards, Sept. 1933; served 1939–45 with 3rd and 5th Bns, Belgium, N Africa, Italy (wounded three times, despatches); comd 3rd Bn Grenadier Guards, 1944–45, Italy; comd 1st Guards Parachute Bn, 1946–48, Palestine; comd 1st Bn Gren. Gds, 1950–52, Tripoli, N Africa; Planning Staff Standing Group, Washington, DC, 1954–56; Imperial Defence College, 1958; comd 4th Guards Bde, 1959–61, Germany; GOC London District, and Maj.-Gen. comdg Household Brigade 1962–65; GOC Berlin (British Sector), 1966–68. Chm., Christian Youth Challenge Trust; Vice-Pres., Nat. Playing Fields Assoc. (Gen. Sec. 1969–72); Pres., Trident Trust, 1986–92. Contested (C) Whitechapel, 1945. Silver Star (USA), 1944. *Recreations:* the countryside, sailing. *Address:* Tigh Bhaan, Appin, Argyll PA38 4BL. *T:* Appin (063173) 252. *Died 23 Dec. 1993.*

NELSON, Sir William Vernon Hope, 3rd Bt, *cr* 1912, of Acton Park, Acton, Denbigh; OBE 1952; Major (retired), late 8th Hussars; *b* 25 May 1914; *s* of late William Hope Nelson (2nd *s* of 1st Bt) and Dora Violet Venables, *d* of Col Arthur Venables Kyrke, Taunton; *S* uncle, Sir James Hope Nelson, 2nd Bt, 1960; *m* 1945, Elizabeth Ann Bevil, *er d* of 14th Viscount Falkland; three *s* three *d. Educ:* Beaumont; Royal Military College, Sandhurst. Commissioned 2nd Lt, 8th Hussars, 1934; served in Palestine, 1936–39 (despatches, medal with clasp); served War of 1939–45; served Korea, 1950–51 (OBE). *Heir: s* Jamie Charles Vernon Hope Nelson [*b* 23 Oct. 1949; *m* 1983, Marilyn Hodges; one *s*]. *Address:* c/o C. Hoare & Co., Bankers, 37 Fleet Street, EC4.

Died 27 May 1991.

NESS, Air Marshal Sir Charles Ernest, KCB 1980 (CB 1978); CBE 1967 (OBE 1959); Military Adviser: International Computers Ltd, since 1983; DESC, since 1991; *b* 4 April 1924; *s* of late Charles W. Ness and Jessica Ness; *m* 1951, Audrey, *d* of late Roy and Phyllis Parker; one *s. Educ:* George Heriot's Sch.; Edinburgh Univ. CIMgt, MIPM. Joined RAF, 1943; flying and staff appts in Bomber Comd and with USAF, 1944–62; Commander, British Skybolt Trials Force, Florida, 1962–63; Station Commander, Royal Air Force, Steamer Point, Aden, 1965–67; Air Comdr, Gibraltar, 1971–73; Director of Organisation and Administrative Plans (RAF), MoD, 1974–75; Comdr, Southern Maritime Air Region, 1975–76; Dir Gen., Personnel Management (RAF), 1976–80; Air Mem. for Personnel, 1980–83. Chairman: Air League, 1987–90 (Vice Pres., 1991); Educn Cttee, RAF Benevolent Fund, 1987–. Chm., Bd of Govs, Duke of Kent Sch., 1987–. *Address:* Lloyds Bank plc, Cox's & Kings Branch, 7 Pall Mall, SW1Y 5NA. *Club:* Royal Air Force. *Died 13 Sept. 1994.*

NEVE, David Lewis; President, Immigration Appeal Tribunal, 1978–91; *b* 7 Oct. 1920; *s* of Eric Read Neve, QC, and Nellie Victorine Neve (*née* Uridge); *m* 1948, Betsy Davida Bannerman; (one *s* decd). *Educ:* Repton; Emmanuel Coll., Cambridge (BA). Served War, Royal Artillery, 1940–46. Called to Bar, Middle Temple, 1947; Resident Magistrate, Uganda, 1952–59; Sen. Resident Magistrate, Uganda, 1959–62; Acting Judge, Uganda, 1962. Immigration Appeals Adjudicator, 1970; Vice-Pres., Immigration Appeals Tribunal, 1976. *Recreations:* sailing, music, reading. *Address:* Deans, Lewes Road, Ditchling, Hassocks, East Sussex. *Died 26 Nov. 1992.*

NEVILLE, Sir Richard (Lionel John Baines), 3rd Bt *cr* 1927, of Sloley, Co. Norfolk; *b* 15 July 1921; *s* of Sir Reginald James Neville Neville, 1st Bt (*d* 1950), and 2nd wife, Violet Sophia Mary (*d* 1972), *d* of Lt-Col Cuthbert

Johnson Baines, Gloucester Regt, The Lawn, Shirehampton, Glos, and *widow* of Captain Richard Jocelyn Hunter, Rifle Bde; *S* half-brother, 1982; unmarried. *Educ:* Eton; Trinity Coll., Cambridge (BA 1941, MA 1948). Served War of 1939–45: joined Army, 1941; Captain, Oxford and Bucks Light Infantry; seconded Royal West African Frontier Force (1st Gold Coast Regt), Burma Campaign, 1944–45. Journalist and Director of English Broadcasts of Radio-Télévision Française (RTF), Indochina, 1953–55; Dir of Foreign Broadcasts, RTF (English, Spanish and Portuguese), French Equatorial Africa (Congo), 1956–57, Algeria, 1957–60. Master, Worshipful Co. of Bowyers, 1972–74. *Recreations:* history, genealogy, heraldry, supporting lost causes. *Heir:* none. *Address:* Sloley Hall, Norwich NR12 8HA. *T:* Swanton Abbott (069269) 236.

Died 2 Aug. 1994 (ext).

NEWBOLD, Sir Charles Demorée, KBE 1970; Kt 1966; CMG 1957; QC (Jamaica) 1947; President, Court of Appeal for East Africa, 1966–70; *b* 11 June 1909; *s* of late Charles Etches and Laura May Newbold; *m* 1936, Ruth, *d* of Arthur L. Vaughan; two *d. Educ:* The Lodge Sch., Barbados; Keble Coll., Oxford (BA). Called to Bar, Gray's Inn, 1931. Private practice at the Bar, Trinidad, 1931–35; joined Colonial Legal Service, 1936, as Principal Officer, Supreme Court Registry, Trinidad; Magistrate, Trinidad, 1937; Legal Draftsman, Jamaica, 1941; Solicitor-General Jamaica, 1943; Member of Commission of Enquiry into Land Taxation, Jamaica, 1942–43; represented Jamaica at Quarantine Conf. in Trinidad, 1943; at US Bases Conf. in Trinidad, 1944; at Washington, USA, for labour contracts, 1945; Actg Attorney-Gen., 1946; Legal Secretary, East Africa High Commn, 1948–61. Mem. of East Africa Central Legislative Assembly, 1948–61 (Chm. of Committee of Supply, 1948–61); Commissioner for Revision of High Commn Laws, 1951; Vice-Chm. Governing Council of Royal Technical Coll., 1954–59; Justice of Appeal, Court of Appeal for Eastern Africa, 1961–65, Vice-Pres., 1965–66. Star of Africa (Liberia). *Publications:* Joint Editor of Trinidad Law Reports, 1928–33; Editor of East African Tax Cases Reports, 1948–61. *Recreations:* cricket, tennis, croquet, reading. *Address:* 7 St Mary's Garden, Chichester, W Sussex PO19 1NY. *Died 17 Oct. 1993.*

NEWEY, His Honour John Henry Richard, QC 1970; London Official Referee, 1980–93; Senior Official Referee, 1990–93; Commissary General of the City and Diocese of Canterbury, 1971–93; *b* 20 Oct. 1923; *s* of late Lt-Col T. H. Newey, ED and of Mrs I. K. M. Newey (*née* Webb); *m* 1953, Mollie Patricia (*née* Chalk), JP; three *s* two *d. Educ:* Dudley Grammar Sch.; Ellesmere Coll.; Queens' Coll., Cambridge (MA, LLM (1st class); Foundn Scholar). Served Central India Horse, Indian Army, 1942–47 in India, Middle East, Italy and Greece, Captain (US Bronze Star, 1944). Called to Bar, Middle Temple, 1948, Bencher 1977. Prosecuting Counsel to Post Office, South Eastern Circuit, 1963–64; Standing Counsel to Post Office at Common Law, 1964–70; Personal Injuries Junior to Treasury, 1968–70; Dep. Chm., Kent County QS, 1970–71; a Recorder of the Crown Court, 1972–80. Initiated orders for exchanges of statements of witnesses of fact and for meetings of expert witnesses, subseq. adopted throughout High Court and county courts, 1981. Legal Assessor, GMC and GDC, 1973–80; an Advr to the Home Sec. under Prevention of Terrorism Act, 1978–80; Parly Boundary Comr for England, 1980–88. Chm., Cheshire Structure Plan Exam., 1977; Inspector: Calder Valley Motorway Inquiry, 1978; Gatwick Air Port Inquiry, 1980. Legal Mem., Rhodesian Travel Facilities Cttee, 1978–80. Lectr, (part-time), Coll. of Estate Mgt, Univ. of London, 1951–59. Contested (C and L) Cannock Div. of Staffs, 1955. Alternate Chm., Burnham and other

Teachers' Remuneration Cttees, 1969–80. Chairman: Sevenoaks Preservation Soc., 1962–65; Sevenoaks Conservation Council, 1991–; Sevenoaks Div. Conservative Assoc., 1965–68. FCIArb 1989 (ACIArb 1988; Patron, SE Br., 1992–); Vice-Pres., British Acad. of Experts, 1991–. *Publications:* Official Referees Courts—practice and procedure, 1988; (jtly) Construction Disputes, 1989. *Recreations:* history, excursions. *Address:* St David's, 68 The Drive, Sevenoaks, Kent TN13 3AF. *T:* Sevenoaks (0732) 454597. *Died 19 May 1994.*

NEWLEY, Edward Frank, CBE 1960; consultant; *b* 9 June 1913; *s* of Frederick Percy Newley; *m* 1946, Sybil Madge Alvis; two *s* one *d. Educ:* King's Coll., London. 1st class hons BSc; MSc. GPO Engrg Dept, Radio Research Br, 1937–44; GPO Factories Dept, 1944–49; Royal Naval Scientific Service, 1949–55; joined UKAEA, 1955; Dep. Dir, AWRE, 1959; Dir, Atomic Weapons Establishment, Aldermaston, 1965–76. Mem., Nat. Savings Cttee, 1976–78. *Publications:* sundry scientific and technical papers. *Address:* Rosapenna, Leigh Woods, Bristol BS8 3PX. *Died 9 Jan. 1994.*

NEWMAN, Graham Reginald, FICS; Chairman, Tatham Bromage & Co. Ltd and group of companies, since 1953; *b* 26 July 1924; *s* of late A. H. G. Newman and Ethel (*née* Wadey); *m* 1952, Joycelyn Helen Sandison, MB, ChB, DPH. *Educ:* Canford Sch.; Hertford Coll., Oxford. War service, Royal Signals, India and Far East, 1941–46, retd Captain. Elected to Baltic Exchange, 1947; Dir, 1967; Chm., 1977–79; Chm., Baltic Exchange Clerks' Pension Fund, 1966–68. Pres., Baltic Charitable Soc., 1982–84. Mem. Cttee of Management, RNLI and sub-cttees, 1977–. Prime Warden, Shipwrights' Co., 1988–89. *Recreation:* sailing. *Address:* Irwin House, 2nd Floor, 118 Southwark Street, SE1 0SW. *Died 2 June 1992.*

NEWMAN, Philip Harker, CBE 1976; DSO 1940; MC; FRCS; FCSSA; formerly Consulting Orthopædic Surgeon, Middlesex Hospital, Royal National Orthopædic Hospital, King Edward VII's Hospital for Officers, W1, retired; *b* 22 June 1911; *s* of John Harker Newman, Mannofield, Ingatestone, Essex; *m* 1943, Elizabeth Anne, *er d* of Rev. G. H. Basset, Turners, Belchamp St Paul, Suffolk; two *s* one *d. Educ:* Cranleigh; Middlesex Hospital Medical School (Senior Broderip Scholar and 2nd Year Exhibitioner). MRCS, LRCP, 1934; FRCS, 1938. Late Lt-Col RAMC; served War of 1939–45 (DSO, MC). Hunterian Prof., RCS, 1954. FRSM (formerly Pres., Section of Orthopaedics); Fellow Brit. Orthopædic Assoc. (Pres., 1975–76); Chm., British Editorial Soc. of Bone and Joint Surgery, 1973–75; Chm., Medical Br., St John, 1976–82; Member British Medical Association. Corresp. Member: Amer. Orthopaedic Assoc.; S African Orthopaedic Assoc. *Publications:* The Prisoner of War Mentality, 1944; Early Treatment of Wounds of the Knee Joint, 1945; The Etiology of Spondylolisthesis, 1962; The Spine, the Wood and the Trees, 1968; Spinal Fusion, Operative Surgery, 1969; Safer than a Known Way, 1983; Orthopaedic Surgery, in British Encyclopædia of Medical Practice, 1956; (contrib.) Total Hip Replacement, 1971; (contrib.) The Scientific Basis of Medicine, Annual Review, 1973. *Recreations:* sailing, golf. *Address:* 72A Saxmundham Road, Aldeburgh, Suffolk IP15 5PD. *T:* Aldeburgh (01728) 453373. *Died 31 Dec. 1994.*

NEWNHAM, Captain Ian Frederick Montague, CBE 1955; Royal Navy, retired; *b* 20 Feb. 1911; *s* of late John Montague Newnham, OBE, JP, DL, and Hilda Newnham; *m* 1947, Marjorie Warden; no *c. Educ:* RN College, Dartmouth. Served War of 1939–45 (despatches); Captain, 1952; lent to Indian Navy as Chief of Material, 1952–55; Chief of Staff to Admiral, British Joint Service Mission, and Naval Attaché, Washington, 1959–61; retd 1961. Gen. Manager, Precision Engineering Div., Short Brothers and

Harland, Belfast, 1961–68. *Recreation:* fishing. *Address:* The Lodge, Mill Lane, Stedham, Midhurst, West Sussex GU29 0PS. *T:* Midhurst (0730) 813663.
Died 2 June 1993.

NEWSOM, George Harold, QC 1956; Chancellor: Diocese of St Albans, since 1958; Diocese of London, since 1971; Diocese of Bath and Wells, since 1971; *b* 29 Dec. 1909; *e s* of late Rev. G. E. Newsom, Master of Selwyn Coll., Cambridge, and Alethea Mary, *d* of Charles Awdry; *m* 1939, Margaret Amy, *d* of L. A. Allen, OBE; two *s* one *d. Educ:* Marlborough; Merton College, Oxford. 2nd Class Lit.Hum. 1931; 1st Class Jurisprudence, 1932; Harmsworth Senior Scholar; Cholmeley Student, 1933. Called to Bar, Lincoln's Inn, 1934; Bencher, 1962; Treasurer, 1980; practised at Chancery Bar, 1934–79. Min. of Economic Warfare, 1939–40; Trading with the Enemy Dept, Treasury and Bd of Trade, 1940–45; Junior Counsel to Charity Comrs, 1947–56; Conveyancing Counsel to PO, 1947–56; Dep. Chm., Wilts QS, 1964–71; a Recorder of the Crown Court, 1972–74. Member Gen. Council of the Bar, 1952–56. Vis. Prof. in Law, Auckland Univ., NZ, 1971. Contested (L) Dorset W, 1945. *Publications:* Restrictive Covenants affecting freehold land (with C. H. S. Preston), 1940, 7th edn 1982; Limitation of Actions (with C. H. S. Preston), 1939, 2nd edn 1943, 3rd edn (with L. Abel-Smith), 1953; The Discharge and Modification of Restrictive Covenants, 1957; (with J. G. Sherratt) Water Pollution, 1972; The Faculty Jurisdiction of the Church of England, 1988. *Recreations:* wine, walking. *Address:* The Old Vicarage, Bishop's Cannings, Devizes, Wilts SN10 2LA. *T:* Devizes (0380) 860660. *Club:* Athenæum.
Died 14 Feb. 1992.

NEWTON, 4th Baron, *cr* 1892, of Newton-in-Makerfield, Co. Lancaster; JP; **Peter Richard Legh;** *b* 6 April 1915; *er s* of 3rd Baron Newton, TD, JP, DL, and Hon. Helen Meysey-Thompson (*d* 1958); *S* father 1960; *m* 1948, Priscilla, *yr d* of late Capt. John Egerton-Warburton and *widow* of William Matthew Palmer, Viscount Wolmer (*s* of 3rd Earl of Selborne, CH, DC); two *s. Educ:* Eton; Christ Church, Oxford (MA). 2nd Lt, Grenadier Guards (SR), 1937; Captain, 1941; Major, 1945. Chairman East Hampshire Young Conservatives, 1949–50. MP (C) Petersfield Division of Hants, Oct. 1951–June 1960; PPS to Fin. Sec. to Treasury, 1952–53; Asst Govt Whip, 1953–55; a Lord Comr of Treasury, 1955–57; Vice-Chamberlain of the Household, 1957–59; Treasurer of the Household, 1959–60; Capt. Yeomen of the Guard and Govt Asst Chief Whip, 1960–62; (Joint) Parly Sec., Min. of Health, 1962–64; Min. of State for Education and Science, April-Oct. 1964. JP 1951; CC Hampshire, 1949–52 and 1954–55. *Recreations:* photography, clock repairing, making gadgets. *Heir: s* Hon. Richard Thomas Legh [*b* 11 Jan. 1950; *m* 1978, Rosemary Whitfoot Clarke, *yr d* of Herbert Clarke, Eastbourne; one *s* one *d*]. *Address:* Vernon Hill House, Bishop's Waltham, Hampshire. *T:* Bishop's Waltham (04893) 2301. *Clubs:* Carlton, St Stephen's Constitutional, Pratt's; Hampshire (Winchester). *Died 16 June 1992.*

NEWTON, Douglas Anthony, CB 1976; Senior Registrar, Principal Registry, Family Division of High Court, 1972–75, retired; *b* 21 Dec. 1915; *s* of John and Janet May Newton; *m* 1946, Barbara Sutherland; one *s* one *d. Educ:* Westminster Sch. Joined Civil Service, 1934. Served War, British and Indian Armies, 1940–46. Apptd Registrar, 1959; Sen. Registrar, 1972. *Recreations:* beer, boats, building. *Died 20 May 1993.*

NIALL, Sir Horace Lionel Richard, Kt 1974; CBE 1957 (MBE 1943); Civil Servant, retired; *b* 14 Oct. 1904; *s* of late Alfred George Niall and Jane Phyllis Niall; *m* 1st, 1930, Alison, *d* of D. Weir, NSW; 2nd, 1965, Una Lesley (*née* de Salis); one *d. Educ:* Mudgee High Sch., NSW; Sydney Univ., NSW. Served War of 1939–45: with AIF, four yrs in New Guinea, rank Major, No NGX 373, all campaigns in New Guinea. NSW Public Service (Water Conservation Commn), 1923–27; Public Service of Papua, New Guinea, 1927–64: joined as a Cadet and retd as Dist Comr; rep. PNG at South Pacific Commn, 1954, and UN Trusteeship Council, 1957; Mem. for Morobe in first House of Assembly and Speaker First House, 1964. *Recreations:* golf, surfing. *Address:* 9 Commodore, 50 Palm Beach Road, Palm Beach, NSW 2108, Australia. *T:* 9195462. *Clubs:* Palm Beach Golf, RSL Palm Beach (NSW). *Died 30 April 1994.*

NICHOLS, Sir Edward (Henry), Kt 1972; TD; Town Clerk of City of London, 1954–74; *b* 27 Sept. 1911; *o s* of Henry James and Agnes Annie Nichols, Notts; *m* 1941, Gwendoline Hetty, *d* of late Robert Elgar, Leeds; one *s. Educ:* Queen Elizabeth's Gram. Sch., Mansfield; Selwyn Coll., Cambridge (BA, LLB). Articled Town Clerk, Mansfield, 1933; Asst Solicitor, Derby, 1936–40; Dep. Town Clerk, Derby, 1940–48, Leicester, 1948–49; Town Clerk and Clerk of the Peace, Derby, 1949–53. Served War of 1939–45, Hon. Lt-Col RA. Hon. DLitt City Univ., 1974. Chevalier, Order of N Star of Sweden; other foreign orders. *Address:* 4 Victoria Place, Esher Park Avenue, Esher, Surrey KT10 9PX. *T:* Esher (0372) 465102. *Club:* City Livery. *Died 19 Sept. 1992.*

NICHOLSON, Sir Godfrey, 1st Bt, *cr* 1958, of Winterbourne, Berkshire; distiller; *b* 9 Dec. 1901; *s* of late Richard Francis Nicholson, Woodcott, Hants, and Helen Violet Portal; *m* 1936, Lady Katharine Constance Lindsay (*d* 1972), 5th *d* of 27th Earl of Crawford; four *d. Educ:* Winchester; Christ Church, Oxford. Royal Fusiliers, 1939–42. MP (Nat. C) Morpeth, 1931–35; MP (C) Farnham Division of Surrey, 1937–66; retired. Chairman, Estimates Cttee, 1961–64. Pres., British Assoc. of Parascending Clubs, 1973–81. Chm., St Birinus Hosp. Gp (Psychiatric), 1966–74. Chm., Friends of Friendliess Churches, 1962–88. FSA. *Heir:* none. *Address:* Bussock Hill House, Newbury, Berks RG16 9BL. *T:* Chieveley (0635) 248260. *Clubs:* Athenæum, Pratt's.
Died 14 July 1991 (ext).

NICHOLSON, Sir John (Norris), 2nd Bt, *cr* 1912, of Harrington Gardens, Royal Borough of Kensington; KBE 1971; CIE 1946; JP; Lord-Lieutenant, 1980–86, and Keeper of the Rolls, 1974–86, of the Isle of Wight; *b* 19 Feb. 1911; *o c* of late Captain George Crosfield Norris Nicholson, RFC, and Hon. Evelyn Izme Murray, *y d* of 10th Baron and 1st Viscount Elibank (she *m* 2nd, 1st Baron Mottistone, PC); *S* grandfather, 1918; *m* 1938, Vittoria Vivien (*d* 1991), *y d* of late Percy Trewhella, Villa Sant' Andrea, Taormina; two *s* two *d. Educ:* Winchester Coll.; Trinity Coll., Cambridge. Captain 4th Cheshires (TA), 1939–41. BEF Flanders, 1940 (despatches); Min. of War Transport, India and SE Asia, 1942–46. Chairman: Ocean Steam Ship Co. Ltd, 1957–71; Liverpool Port Employers Assoc., 1957–61; Martins Bank Ltd, 1962–64 (Dep. Chm., 1959–62); Management Cttee, HMS Conway, 1958–65; British Liner Cttee, 1963–67; Cttee, European Nat. Shipowners' Assoc., 1965–69; IoW Develt Bd, 1986–88; Mem., Shipping Advisory Panel, 1962–64; Pres., Chamber of Shipping of the UK, 1970–71; Mem., Economic and Social Cttee, EEC, 1973–74. Director: Barclays Bank Ltd, 1969–81; Royal Insurance Co. Ltd, 1955–81. Pres., E Wessex TA&VRA, 1982–84. Governor, IoW Technical Coll., 1974–89. Vice Lord-Lieutenant, IoW, 1974–79. Silver Jubilee Medal, 1977. *Heir: s* Charles Christian Nicholson [*b* 15 Dec. 1941; *m* 1975, Martie, *d* of Stuart Don and *widow* of Niall Anstruther-Gough-Calthorpe]. *Address:* Mottistone Manor, Isle of Wight. *T:*

Isle of Wight (0983) 740322. *Clubs:* Army and Navy; Royal Yacht Squadron (Commodore, 1980–86).
Died 30 Aug. 1993.

NICKERSON, Albert Lindsay; retired as Chairman and Chief Executive Officer, Mobil Oil Corporation; *b* 17 Jan. 1911; *s* of Albert Lindsay Nickerson and Christine (*née* Atkinson); *m* 1936, Elizabeth Perkins; one *s* three *d. Educ:* Noble and Greenough Sch., Mass; Harvard. Joined Socony-Vacuum Oil Co. Inc. as Service Stn Attendant, 1933; Dist Man., 1940; Div. Manager, 1941; Asst General Manager, Eastern Marketing Div., 1944; Director, 1946; name of company changed to Socony Mobil Oil Co. Inc., 1955; President, 1955–61; Chairman Exec. Cttee and Chief Exec. Officer, 1958–69; Chm. Bd, 1961–69; name of company changed to Mobil Oil Corporation, 1966. Chairman, Vacuum Oil Co. Ltd, London (later Mobil Oil Co. Ltd), 1946. Director, Placement Bureau War Manpower Commission, Washington, 1943. Chm., Federal Reserve Bank of NY, and Federal Reserve Agent, 1969–71; Mem., The Business Council (Chm. 1967–69). Director: American Management Assoc., NY, 1948–51, 1953–56, 1958–61; Federal Reserve Board of NY, 1964–67; Metrop. Life Insurance Co., 1965–81; Mobil Oil Corp., 1946–75; Raytheon Co., 1970–90; State Street Investment Corp.; State Street Growth Fund Inc.; Harvard Management Co., 1974–84; Transportation Assoc. of America, 1969; State Street Exchange Fund; Trustee: International House, NY City, 1952–62; Cttee for Economic Development, NY, 1961–65; Brigham and Women's Hosp., Boston, 1969–89; Rockefeller Univ., 1964–84; (Emeritus) Boston Symphony Orch.; American Museum of Natural History, 1958–62, 1964–69; Mem. Emeritus, Corp. of Woods Hole Oceanographic Instn, Mass; former Director and Treas., American Petroleum Institute; former Member: Council on Foreign Relations; National Petroleum Council; Harvard Corp., 1965; Fellow, Harvard Univ., 1965–75; Overseer Harvard Univ., 1959–65. Hon. LLD: Hofstra Univ., 1964; Harvard Univ., 1976. Comdr, Order of Vasa (Sweden), 1963; Grand Cross of the Republic (Italy), 1968. *Recreations:* golfing, fishing, sailing, camping. *Address:* 3 Lexington Road, Lincoln Center, Mass 01773, USA. *T:* (617) 2599664. *Clubs:* Thames Rowing; Harvard Varsity, Cambridge Boat (Cambridge, Mass); Country (Brookline, Mass); Harvard (NY City); Harvard (Boston); 25 Year Club of Petroleum Industry. *Died 7 Aug. 1994.*

NICOL, Abioseh; *see* Nicol, D. S. H. W.

NICOL, Davidson Sylvester Hector Willoughby, CMG 1964; MA, MD, PhD (Cantab); FRCPath; Associate Lecturer, Centre of International Studies, University of Cambridge, since 1985; *b* 14 Sept. 1924; of African parentage; *m* 1950, Marjorie Esme Johnston, MB, ChB; three *s* two *d. Educ:* schools in Nigeria and Sierra Leone; Cambridge and London Univs. Science Master, Prince of Wales Sch., Sierra Leone, 1941–43. Cambridge: Foundation Schol., Prizeman, 1943–47, Fellow and Supervisor in Nat. Sciences and Med., 1957–59, Christ's Coll. (Hon. Fellow, 1972); BA 1946; 1st Cl. Hons (Nat. Sciences), 1947; Beit Meml Fellow for Medical Research, 1954; Benn Levy Univ. Studentship, Cambridge, 1956; Univ. Schol., House Physician (Medical Unit and Clinical Pathology), Receiving Room Officer, and Research Asst (Physiology), London Hosp., 1947–52; Univ. Lectr, Medical School, Ibadan, Nigeria, 1952–54; Sen. Pathologist, Sierra Leone, 1958–60; Principal, Fourah Bay Coll., Sierra Leone, 1960–68, and first Vice-Chancellor, Univ. of Sierra Leone, 1966–68; Perm. Rep. and Ambassador for Sierra Leone to UN, 1969–71 (Security Council, 1970–71, Pres. Sept. 1970; Chm., Cttee of 24 (Decolonisation); Mem., Economic and Social Council, 1969–70); High Comr for Sierra Leone in London, and

Ambassador to Norway, Sweden and Denmark, 1971–72; Under-Sec.-Gen. of UN, and Exec. Dir, UNITAR, 1972–82; Sen. Fellow, UNITAR, 1983. Hon. Consultant Pathologist, Sierra Leone Govt. Chairman: Sierra Leone Nat. Library Bd, 1959–65; Univ. of E Africa Visiting Cttee, 1962; W African Exams Council, 1964–69; Member: Governing Body, Kumasi Univ., Ghana; Public Service Commn, Sierra Leone, 1960–68; W African Council for Medical Research, 1959–62; Exec. Council, Assoc. of Univs of British Commonwealth, 1960 and 1966; Commn for proposed Univ. of Ghana, 1960. Director: Central Bank of Sierra Leone; Consolidated African Selection Trust Ltd (London); Davesme Corp. President: W African Science Assoc., 1964–66; Sierra Leone Red Cross Soc., 1962–66; World Fedn of UNAs, 1983–87 (Hon. Pres., 1987–); Vice-Pres., Royal African Soc., 1986. Consultant, Ford Foundn, NY. Member, Internat. Board: African-Amer. Inst., NY; Fund for Peace, NY. Chm., UN Mission to Angola, July 1976; Conference Delegate to: WHO Assembly, 1960; UNESCO Higher Educn Conf., Tananarive, 1963; Commonwealth Prime Ministers' Conf., London, 1965 and 1969, Singapore 1971. Visiting Lecturer, Univs of Toronto, California (Berkeley), Mayo Clinic, 1958; Aggrey-Fraser-Guggisberg Meml Lectr, Univ. of Ghana, 1963; Danforth Fellowship Lectr in African Affairs, Assoc. of Amer. Colls, USA, 1968–71; Guest Scholar: Woodrow Wilson Internat. Center, Washington, 1983; Hoover Instn, Stanford Univ., 1984; Distinguished Vis. Prof. in Internat. Studies, Calif State Univ., 1987–88; Vis. Fellow, Johns Hopkins Sch. of Advanced Internat. Studies, Washington, 1983; Vis. Prof., Univ. of S Carolina, 1990, 1991, 1992, 1993. Hon. Fellow, Ghana Acad. of Scis. Hon. LLD: Leeds; Barat, Ill; Univ. of West Indies (St Augustine), 1981; Tuskegee, Ala, 1981; Hon. DSc: Newcastle upon Tyne; Kalamazoo, Mich; Laurentian, Ont; Sierra Leone; Hon. DLitt Davis and Elkins Coll., W Va. Margaret Wrong Prize and Medal for Literature in Africa, 1952; World Peace Gold Medal, Indian Fedn of UN Assocs, New Delhi, 1986; Medal of Highest Honour, Kyung Hee Univ., S Korea, 1992. Indep. Medal, Sierra Leone, 1961; Grand Commander: Order of Rokel, Sierra Leone, 1974; Star of Africa, Liberia, 1974. *Publications:* Malnutrition in African Mothers and Children (contrib.), 1954; HRH the Duke of Edinburgh's Study Conference, Vol. 2 (contrib.), 1958; The Mechanism of Action of Insulin, 1960; The Structure of Human Insulin, 1960; Africa, A Subjective View, 1964; Africanus Horton and Black Nationalism (1867), 1969; New and Modern Rôles for Commonwealth and Empire, 1976; The United Nations and Decision Making: the role of women, 1978; Nigeria and the Future of Africa, 1980; (ed) Paths to Peace, 1981; (ed) Essays on the UN Security Council and its Presidency, 1981; (ed) Regionalism and the New International Economic Order, 1981; The United Nations Security Council: towards greater effectiveness, 1981; Creative Women in Changing Societies, 1982; (as Abioseh Nicol): The Truly Married Woman, 1965; Two African Tales, 1965; (contrib.) Modern African Poetry, ed K. Senanu, 1982; contribs to Présence Africaine (Paris), Cambridge Rev. of Internat. Affairs, Peace Forum, Jl Trop. Med., Biochem. Jl, Nature, Jl of Royal African Soc., Times, Guardian, New Statesman, Encounter, West Africa, etc. *Recreation:* creative writing (under *nom-de-plume* Abioseh Nicol). *Address:* Christ's College, Cambridge CB2 3BU. *Clubs:* Athenæum, United Oxford & Cambridge University, Commonwealth Trust; Senior Dinner (Freetown). *Died 20 Sept. 1994.*

NICOLL, Prof. Ronald Ewart, MSc, FRTPI, FRICS; Professor of Urban and Regional Planning, University of Strathclyde, 1966–80; Partner, 1980–85, Consultant, since 1985, PIEDA; *b* 8 May 1921; *s* of William Ewart Nicoll and Edith May Choat; *m* 1943, Isabel Christina McNab;

one *s* one *d. Educ:* Southend Municipal Coll.; Hammersmith Sch. of Architecture and Building; Royal College of Science and Technology, Glasgow. Served War, Royal Navy, 1939–46. Planning Asst, 1949–53: Southend CB; Derbyshire CC; Northamptonshire CC; Dep. Dir of Planning, Glasgow City, 1953–64; Chief Planning Officer, Scottish Development Dept, 1964–66. Consultant to UN and WHO. Member: Scottish Social Advisory Council, 1970; Scottish Council on Crime, 1971; Scottish Council (Develt and Industry), 1971; Glasgow Chamber of Commerce, 1971; Royal Commn on Environmental Pollution, 1973–79. RICS Gold Medal, 1975. FRSA. *Publications:* Oceanspan, 1970; Energy and the Environment, 1975; contribs to: The Future of Development Plans, 1965 (HMSO); How Do You Want to Live?, 1972 (HMSO); A Future for Scotland, 1973. *Recreations:* travel, photography, hill walking. *Address:* 78 Victoria Park Drive North, Glasgow G14 9PJ. *T:* 041–959 7854. *Clubs:* Commonwealth Trust; Western (Glasgow). *Died 21 Dec. 1991.*

NICOLSON, Malise Allen, MC 1945; Chairman: Bangor-on-Dee Races Ltd, 1984–94 (Director, since 1972); *b* 31 Oct. 1921; *e s* of late Sir Kenneth Nicolson, MC; *m* 1946, Vivien Bridget, *y d* of late Arthur Hilton Ridley, CBE; one *s* two *d. Educ:* Eton. Served War, Probyn's Horse, 1940–45 (MC; Burma); served 1st Royal Dragoons, 1946–47. Gladstone, Lyall Ltd, Calcutta, 1948–55; joined Booker McConnell, 1956; Dir, 1968–83; Chairman: Booker Line, 1968–83 (Dir, 1957–83); Coe Metcalf Shipping, 1977–83; McConnell Salmon Ltd, 1980–90 (Dir, 1973–90); Govt 'A' Dir, Mersey Docks and Harbour Co., 1974–80. Chairman: Liverpool Steam Ship Owners, 1971–72; Employers Assoc., Port of Liverpool, 1972–74; Vice-Chm., British Shipping Fedn, 1968–71; Pres., Gen. Council of British Shipping, 1982–83; Mem., Nat. Dock Labour Bd, 1986–90. Dir, The Racecourse Assoc. Ltd, 1984–90. *Recreation:* country sports. *Address:* Frog Hall, Tilston, Malpas, Cheshire SY14 7HB. *T:* Tilston (01829) 250320. *Club:* Army and Navy.

Died 22 Dec. 1995.

NIELD, Sir William (Alan), GCMG 1972; KCB 1968 (CB 1966); Deputy Chairman, Rolls Royce (1971) Ltd, 1973–76; *b* 21 Sept. 1913; *s* of William Herbert Nield, Stockport, Cheshire, and Ada Nield; *m* 1937, Gwyneth Marion Davies (*d* 1994); two *s* two *d. Educ:* Stockport Gram. Sch.; St Edmund Hall, Oxford (Hon. Fellow, 1990). Served Royal Air Force and Royal Canadian Air Force, 1939–46 (despatches, 1944); demobilised as Wing Comdr, 1946. Research and Policy Dept of Labour Party, 1937–39; K-H News Letter Service, 1939; Min. of Food, 1946–47; HM Treasury, 1947–49; Min. of Food and Min. of Agric., Fisheries and Food, 1949–64 (Under-Sec., 1959–64); Dept of Economic Affairs: Under-Sec., 1964–65; Dep. Under-Sec. of State, 1965–66; a Dep. Sec., Cabinet Office, 1966–68; Permanent Under-Sec. of State, DEA, 1968–69; Permanent Secretary: Cabinet Office, 1969–72; NI Office, 1972–73. Pres., St Edmund Hall Assoc., 1981–83. *Address:* South Nevay, Stubbs Wood, Chesham Bois, Bucks HP6 6EY. *T:* Amersham (0494) 433869. *Club:* Farmers'. *Died 13 Sept. 1994.*

NISSEN, Karl Iversen, MD, FRCS; Surgeon, Royal National Orthopædic Hospital, W1, 1946–71, retired; Orthopædic Surgeon: Harrow Hospital 1946–71; Peace Memorial Hospital, Watford, 1948–71; *b* 4 April 1906; *s* of Christian and Caroline Nissen; *m* 1935, Margaret Mary Honor Schofield (*d* 1981); one *s* one *d. Educ:* Otago Boys' High Sch., Dunedin, NZ; Univ. of Otago, NZ. BSc (NZ) 1927; MB, ChB (NZ) 1932; MD (NZ) 1934; FRCS 1936. Served as Orthopædic Specialist, RNVR, 1943–45. Corresp. mem. Belgian, French, Swiss, German, Scandinavian, Norwegian, Finnish, Danish Socs of

Orthopædics. Wrote articles and gave talks on the genetics and cure of primary osteoarthrosis of the hip. *Recreation:* human origins. *Address:* Prospect House, The Avenue, Sherborne, Dorset DT9 3AJ. *T:* Sherborne (01935) 813539. *Club:* Naval. *Died 30 Dec. 1995.*

NIVEN, Sir (Cecil) Rex, Kt 1960; CMG 1953; MC 1918; *b* 20 Nov. 1898; *o s* of late Rev. Dr G. C. and Jeanne Niven, Torquay, Devon; *m* 1st, 1925, Dorothy Marshall (*d* 1977), *e d* of late D. M. Mason, formerly MP (Coventry and E Edinburgh); one *d* (and one *d* decd); 2nd, 1980, Mrs Pamela Beerbohm, *d* of late G. C. Leach, ICS, Sibton Park, Lyminge, Kent and Mrs Leach, and *widow* of Dr O. H. B. Beerbohm. *Educ:* Blundell's Sch., Tiverton; Balliol Coll., Oxford (MA Hons). Served RFA, 1917–19, France and Italy. Colonial Service Nigeria, 1921–54; served Secretariats, and Provinces; PRO, Nigeria, 1943–45; Senior Resident, 1947; twice admin. Northern Govt; Mem. N House of Assembly, 1947–59 (Pres. 1952–58; Speaker, 1958–59); Mem., N Executive Council, 1951–54; Comr for Special Duties in N Nigeria, 1959–62. Dep. Sec., Southwark Dio. Bd of Finance, 1962–68. Life Mem., BRCS; Member: Council, RSA, 1963–69; Council, N Euboea Foundation; Council, Imp. Soc. of Knights Bachelor, 1969–; Gen. Synod of C of E, 1975–80; St Charles's (formerly Paddington) Group Hosp. Management Cttee, 1963–72. Chm., NE Kent Oxford Soc., 1986–89, Pres., 1989–; Patron, Deal Soc., 1985–. FRGS. *Publications:* A Short History of Nigeria, 1937, 12th edn 1971; Nigeria's Story, 1939; Nigeria: the Outline of a Colony, 1946; How Nigeria is Governed, 1950; West Africa, 1958; Short History of the Yoruba Peoples, 1958; You and Your Government, 1958; Nine Great Africans, 1964; Nigeria (in Benn's Nations of the Modern World), 1967; The War of Nigerian Unity, 1970; A Nigerian Kaleidoscope, 1982; (collab.) My Life, by Sardauna of Sokoto, 1962. *Recreations:* walking, architecture, philately. *Address:* 12 Archery Square, Walmer, Kent CT14 7HP. *T:* Deal (0304) 361863. *Club:* Royal Over-Seas League. *Died 22 Feb. 1993.*

NIXON, Richard Milhous; President of the United States of America, 1969–74, resigned Aug. 1974; *b* 9 Jan. 1913; *s* of Francis A. and Hannah Milhous Nixon; *m* 1940, Patricia Ryan (*d* 1993); two *d. Educ:* Whittier Coll., Whittier, California (AB); Duke University Law Sch., Durham, North Carolina (LLB). Lawyer, Whittier, California, 1937–42; Office of Price Administration, 1942; Active duty, US Navy, 1942–46. Member 80th, 81st Congresses, 1947–50; US Senator from California, 1950–53. Vice-President of the USA, 1953–61; Republican candidate for the Presidency of the USA, 1960. Lawyer, Los Angeles, 1961–63; NY, 1963–68. Republican Candidate for Governor of California, 1962. Member: Board of Trustees, Whittier Coll., 1939–68; Society of Friends; Order of Coif. *Publications:* Six Crises, 1962; Memoirs, 1978; The Real War, 1980; Leaders, 1982; Real Peace: a strategy for the West, 1983; No More Vietnams, 1986; 1999: Victory Without War, 1988; In the Arena: a memoir of victory, defeat and renewal, 1990; Seize the moment: America's challenge in a one superpower world, 1992. *Address:* 577 Chestnut Ridge Road, Woodcliff Lake, NJ 07675, USA.
Died 22 April 1994.

NOAKES, His Honour Sidney Henry; a Circuit Judge (formerly County Court Judge), 1968–77; *b* 6 Jan. 1905; *s* of Thomas Frederick Noakes (Civil Servant) and Ada Noakes. *Educ:* Merchant Taylors' Sch.; St John's Coll., Oxford (MA). Called to Bar, Lincoln's Inn, 1928; SE Circuit; Bencher, 1963; Deputy Chairman: Surrey QS, 1963; Herts QS, 1964; Recorder of Margate, 1965–68. War Service, Lt-Col, Intelligence Corps, England and NW Europe. *Publication:* Fire Insurance, 1947. *Recreations:*

regretfully latterly only walking and gardening. *Address:* 14 Meadway Crescent, Hove, E Sussex BN3 7NL. *T:* Brighton (0273) 736143. *Died 16 Feb. 1993.*

NOBLE, Major Sir Marc (Brunel), 5th Bt, *cr* 1902, of Ardmore and Ardadan Noble, Cardross, Co. Dunbarton; CBE 1991; *b* 8 Jan. 1927; *er s* of Sir Humphrey Brunel Noble, 4th Bt, MBE, MC, and Celia (*d* 1982), *d* of late Captain Stewart Weigall, RN; *S* father, 1968; *m* 1956, Jennifer Lorna, (Jane), *yr d* of late John Mein-Austin, Flint Hill, West Haddon, Northants; two *s* one *d* (and one *d* decd). *Educ:* Eton. Commissioned into King's Dragoon Guards as 2nd Lieut, 1947; on amalgamation, transferred Royal Dragoons, 1958. Training Major and Adjutant, Kent and County of London Yeomanry (Sharpshooters), 1963–64; retired 1966. Scout Association: Commonwealth Comr, 1972–; Chm., Cttee of Council, 1979–80; County Pres., Kent, 1986–. Gov., Sibton Park Sch., Lyminge, 1986–. High Sheriff, Kent, 1985. *Heir: s* David Brunel Noble [*b* 25 Dec. 1961; *m* 1987, Virginia Ann, *yr d* of late Roderick Wetherall; one *s*]. *Address:* Deerleap House, Knockholt, Sevenoaks, Kent TN14 7NP. *T:* Knockholt (0959) 33222. *Club:* Cavalry and Guards.
Died 2 Jan. 1991.

NOEL, Rear-Adm. Gambier John Byng, CB 1969; retired; *b* 16 July 1914; *s* of late G. B. E. Noel; *m* 1936, Joan Stevens; four *d. Educ:* Royal Naval Coll., Dartmouth. Joined Royal Navy, 1928; served in War of 1939–45, HMS Aurora and HMS Norfolk (despatches twice); Captain 1959; Imperial Defence Coll., 1962; Staff of Commander Far East Fleet, 1964–67; Rear-Admiral 1967; Chief Staff Officer (Technical) to C-in-C, Western Fleet, 1967–69. *Recreation:* gardening. *Address:* Woodpeckers, Church Lane, Haslemere, Surrey GU27 2BJ. *T:* Haslemere (01428) 643824. *Died 9 Nov. 1995.*

NOEL-PATON, family name of **Baron Ferrier.**

NOLAN, Sir Sidney (Robert), OM 1983; AC 1988; Kt 1981; CBE 1963; RA 1991 (ARA 1987); artist; *b* Melbourne, 22 April 1917; *s* of late Sidney Henry Nolan; *m* 1939, Elizabeth Patterson (marr. diss. 1942); one *d*; *m* 1948, Cynthia Hansen (*d* 1974); *m* 1977, Mary Elizabeth à Beckett Perceval. *Educ:* State and technical schools, Melbourne; National Art Gallery Sch., Victoria. Italian Government Scholar, 1956; Commonwealth Fund Fellow, to USA, 1958; Fellow: ANU, 1965 (Hon. LLD, 1968); York Univ., 1971; Bavarian Academy, 1971. Exhibited: Paris, 1948, 1961; New Delhi, 1953; Pittsburgh International, 1953, 1954, 1955, 1964, 1967, 1970; Venice Biennale, 1954; Rome, 1954; Pacific Loan Exhibition, 1956; Brussels International Exhibition, 1958; Documenta II, Kassel, 1959; Retrospective, Art Gallery of New South Wales, Sydney, 1967; Retrospective, Darmstadt, 1971; Ashmolean Museum, Oxford, 1971; Retrospective, Royal Dublin Soc., 1973; Perth Festival, 1982; Retrospective, Nat. Gall. of Vic, 1987; Tate Gallery, Marlborough New London Gallery, Marlborough Gallery, New York. Ballet designs for: Icare, Sydney, 1941; Orphée (Cocteau), Sydney, 1948; The Guide, Oxford, 1961; Rite of Spring, Covent Garden, 1962, 1987; The Display, Adelaide Festival, 1964; opera designs for: Samson et Delilah, Covent Garden, 1981; Il Trovatore, Sydney Op. House, 1983; Die Entführung aus dem Serail, Covent Garden, 1987; mural for Victorian Cultural Centre Concert Hall, 1982. Works in Tate Gallery, Museum of Modern Art, New York, Australian national galleries, Contemporary Art Society and Arts Council of Great Britain, etc. Film, Nolan at 60, BBC and ABC, 1977. Hon. DLit London, 1971; Hon. DLitt: Sydney, 1977; Perth, 1988. *Publication:* Paradise Garden (poems, drawings and paintings), 1972; *Illustrated:* Near the Ocean, by Robert Lowell, 1966; The Voyage, by Baudelaire, trans. Lowell, 1968; Children's Crusade, by Benjamin Britten, 1973; *Relevant* *publications:* Kenneth Clark, Colin MacInnes, Bryan Robertson: Nolan, 1961; Robert Melville: Ned Kelly, 1964; Elwyn Lynn: Sydney Nolan: Myth and Imagery, 1967; Melville and Lynn: The Darkening Ecliptic: Ern Malley Poems, Sidney Nolan Paintings, 1974; Cynthia Nolan: Open Negative, 1967; Sight of China, 1969; Paradise, and yet, 1971. *Address:* c/o Marlborough Fine Art Ltd, 6 Albemarle Street, W1. *Clubs:* Athenæum, Garrick. *Died 27 Nov. 1992.*

NORFOLK, Lavinia Duchess of; Lavinia Mary Fitzalan-Howard, LG 1990; CBE 1971; Lord-Lieutenant of West Sussex, 1975–90; *b* 22 March 1916; *d* of 3rd Baron Belper and of Eva, Countess of Rosebery, DBE (*d* 1987); *m* 1937, 16th Duke of Norfolk, KG, PC, GCVO, GBE, TD (*d* 1975); four *d*. *Educ:* Abbotshill, Hemel Hempstead, Herts. President: Nat. Canine Defence League, 1969–; Pony Riding for the Disabled Trust, Chigwell, 1964–; BHS, 1980–82. Vice-President: ASBAH, 1970–; Spastic Soc., 1969–; NSPCC, 1967–. Patron, Riding for the Disabled, 1986– (Pres., 1970–86). Vice Pres., King Edward VII Hosp., Midhurst, 1975–. Steward, Goodwood, 1976–78. BRCS Certificate of Honour and Badge, Class 1, 1969. Silver Jubilee Medal, 1977. *Address:* Arundel Park, Sussex. *T:* Arundel (01903) 882041.
Died 10 Dec. 1995.

NORMAN, Lady; Priscilla Cecilia Maria Norman, CBE 1963; JP; *b* 20 March 1899; *o d* of late Major Robert Reyntiens and Lady Alice Bertie, *d* of 7th Earl of Abingdon; *m* 1st, 1921, Alexander Koch de Gooreynd, OBE (marr. diss. 1929); two *s*; 2nd, 1933, 1st and last Baron Norman, DSO, PC (*d* 1950). Member: London County Council, 1925–33; Chelsea Borough Council, 1928–31; Bethlem Royal and the Maudsley Hospital Board, 1951–75; South-East Metropolitan Regional Board, 1951–74; Hon. Pres., World Fedn for Mental Health, 1972. Vice-Chm., Women's Voluntary Services for Civil Defence, 1938–41; Vice-Pres., Royal College of Nursing. JP London, 1944. *Publication:* In the Way of Understanding, 1983. *Address:* 67 Holland Park, W11 3SJ. *Died 5 April 1991.*

NORMAN, Vice-Adm. Sir (Horace) Geoffrey, KCVO 1963; CB 1949; CBE 1943; *b* 25 May 1896; *s* of W. H. Norman; *m* 1924, Noreen Frances, *o d* of late Brig.-General S. Geoghegan; one *s* one *d*. *Educ:* Trent Coll.; RN Coll., Keyham. HMS Queen Elizabeth and destroyers, 1914–18; Long Gunnery Course, 1921; passed RN Staff Coll., 1929; Commander, 1932; Captain, 1938; idc 1939; Rear-Admiral, 1947; Chief of Staff to C-in-C, Mediterranean Station, 1948–50; Admiralty, 1950; Vice-Admiral (retired), 1951. Sec., Nat. Playing Fields Assoc., 1953–63. *Recreations:* fishing, outdoor sports. *Address:* Chantry Cottage, Wickham, Hants PO17 6JA. *T:* Wickham (0329) 832248. *Died 16 April 1992.*

NORMAN, Mark Richard, CBE 1977 (OBE 1945); Managing Director of Lazard Brothers & Co. Ltd, 1960–75; Chairman, Gallaher Ltd, 1963–75; Director of other public companies, 1947–75; Deputy Chairman, National Trust, 1977–80 (Chairman, Finance Committee, 1969–80); *b* 3 April 1910; *s* of late Ronald C. Norman; *m* 1933, Helen, *d* of late Thomas Pinckney Bryan, Richmond, Virginia; two *s* three *d*. *Educ:* Eton; Magdalen Coll., Oxford. With Gallaher Ltd, 1930–32; Lazard Brothers & Co. Ltd, 1932–39. Served War of 1939–45: Hertfordshire Yeomanry; wounded Greece, 1941; an Asst Military Secretary, War Cabinet Offices, 1942–45 (Lieut-Colonel). Partner Edward de Stein & Co., 1946–60. *Address:* Garden House, Moor Place, Much Hadham, Herts SG10 6AA. *T:* Much Hadham (0127984) 2703. *Club:* Brooks's.
Died 6 Dec. 1994.

NORMAN, Sir Richard (Oswald Chandler), KBE 1987; DSc; FRS 1977; CChem, FRSC; Rector, Exeter College, University of Oxford, since 1987; Chief Scientific Adviser, Department of Energy, 1988–93; *b* 27 April 1932; *s* of Oswald George Norman and Violet Maud Chandler; *m* 1982, Jennifer Margaret Tope. *Educ:* St Paul's Sch.; Balliol Coll., Oxford (MA, DSc; Hon. Fellow, 1989). CChem; FRIC 1963. Jun. Res. Fellow, Merton Coll., Oxford, 1956–58, Fellow and Tutor, 1958–65; Univ. Lectr in Chemistry, Oxford, 1958–65; Prof. of Chemistry, Univ. of York, 1965–87; seconded as Chief Scientific Advr, MoD, 1983–88. Mem., SERC, 1983–88. President: RIC, 1978–80; RSC, 1984–86; Dir, Salters' Inst. of Indust. Chemistry, 1975–. Tilden Lectr, Chemical Soc., 1976. Hon. Fellow, Merton Coll., Oxford, 1988. Meldola Medal, RIC, 1961; Corday-Morgan Medal, Chemical Soc., 1967. Encomienda, Orden del Mérito Civil (Spain), 1990. *Publications:* Principles of Organic Synthesis, 1968; (with D. J. Waddington) Modern Organic Chemistry, 1972; papers in Jl Chem. Soc. *Recreations:* cricket, music, gardening. *Address:* The Rector's Lodgings, Exeter College, Oxford OX1 3DP. *T:* Oxford (0865) 279644. *Club:* United Oxford & Cambridge University.
Died 6 June 1993.

NORMANBY, 4th Marquis of, *cr* 1838; **Oswald Constantine John Phipps,** KG 1985; CBE 1974 (MBE (mil.) 1943); Baron Mulgrave (Ire.), 1767; Baron Mulgrave (GB) 1794; Earl of Mulgrave and Viscount Normanby, 1812; Lord-Lieutenant of North Yorkshire, 1974–87 (of North Riding of Yorkshire, 1965–74); *b* 29 July 1912; *o s* of Rev. the 3rd Marquess and Gertrude Stansfeld, OBE, DGStJ (*d* 1948), *d* of Johnston J. Foster, Moor Park, Ludlow; *S* father, 1932; *m* 1951, Hon. Grania Maeve Rosaura Guinness, *d* of 1st Baron Moyne; two *s* five *d*. *Educ:* Eton; Christ Church, Oxford. Served War of 1939–45, The Green Howards (wounded, prisoner, repatriated). PPS to Sec. of State for Dominion Affairs, 1944–45, to Lord President of the Council, 1945; a Lord-in-Waiting to the King, 1945. High Steward of York Minster, 1980–88. Mem., Council of St John for N Yorks (formerly NR of Yorks), 1948–87 (Chm., 1948–77; Pres., 1977–87); Chairman: KCH, 1948–74; Nat. Art-Collections Fund, 1981–86; Pres., Nat. Library for the Blind, 1977–88 (Chm., 1946–77); Vice-President: St Dunstans, 1980– (Mem. Council, 1944–80); RNLI, 1984– (Mem. Cttee of Management, 1972–84). Mem., N Riding CC, 1937–46. Hon. Col Comdt, The Green Howards, 1970–82; Dep. Hon. Col, 2nd Bn Yorks Volunteers, 1971–72; President: TA&VRA for N of England, 1971–74 (Vice-Pres., 1968–71); TA&VRA N Yorks and Humberside, 1980–83. KStJ. Fellow, KCH Med. Sch., 1982. Hon. DCL: Durham Univ, 1963; York Univ., 1985. *Heir: s* Earl of Mulgrave [*b* 24 Feb. 1954; *m* 1990, Mrs Nicola St Aubyn, *d* of Milton Shulman and Drusilla Beyfus; one *d*]. *Address:* Lythe Hall, near Whitby, N Yorks YO21 3RL; Argyll House, 211 King's Road, SW3. *T:* 071–352 5154. *Club:* Yorkshire (York).
Died 30 Jan. 1994.

NORRIS, Herbert Walter; Regional Director, South East Region, National Westminster Bank Ltd, 1969–73; Deputy Chief General Manager, 1962–65, Director, 1965–68, Westminster Bank Ltd; *b* 9 Dec. 1904; *s* of Walter Norris, Farnworth, Widnes, Lancs; *m* 1935, Laura Phyllis Tardif (*d* 1986), *d* of A. Tardif, St Martin's, Guernsey; no *c*. *Educ:* Liverpool Collegiate School. Joined Westminster Bank, Liverpool Office, 1921; Joint General Manager, Westminster Bank Ltd, 1949. FCIB; Mem. Council, Inst. of Bankers, 1952–65, Dep. Chairman, 1959–61. Master of Coopers' Company, 1973–74. *Recreations:* reading, music. *Address:* c/o Ashurst Park Nursing Home, Fordcombe, Tunbridge Wells, Kent TN3 0RD.
Died 17 Dec. 1991.

NORTH, Howard; see Trevor, E.

NORTHESK, 13th Earl of, *cr* 1647; **Robert Andrew Carnegie;** Lord Rosehill and Inglismaldie, 1639; landowner, farmer; *b* 24 June 1926; *yr s* of 12th Earl of Northesk and Dorothy Mary (*d* 1967), *er d* of late Col Sir William Robert Campion, KCMG, DSO; *S* father, 1975; *m* 1st, 1949, Jean Margaret (*d* 1989), *yr d* of Captain (John) Duncan George MacRae, Ballimore, Otter Ferry, Argyll; one *s* two *d* (and one *s* decd); 2nd, 1989, Brownie (*née* Grimason), *widow* of Carl Heimann. *Educ:* Pangbourne RNR Coll.; Tabor Naval Acad., USA. Served with Royal Navy, 1942–45. Member: Council, Fédération Internationale des Assocs d'éleveurs de la race bovine Charolaise; Council, Game Research Assoc., 1955–57; Council, British Charolais Cattle Soc., 1972–74. Chairman of Board: Chandler, Hargreaves (IOM) Ltd, 1980–92; Lowndes Lambert (IOM) Ltd, 1992–; Director: NEL Britannia International Assurance Ltd, 1984–89; Royal Skandia Life Assurance Ltd, 1989–; Member: Bd of Dirs, IOM Bank, 1980–; IOM Br., CPA; Bd of Governors, Buchan Sch., IOM, 1980–86. President: Save the Children Fund, Douglas, IoM, 1977–; Friends of the Physically Disabled, IOM, 1985–. Trustee, Pain Relief Foundn, 1985–. Midhurst RDC, 1968–75 (Chm., 1972–74). *Publication:* Diary of an Island Glen, 1988. *Heir:* s Lord Rosehill [*b* 3 Nov. 1954; *m* 1979, Jacqueline Reid, *d* of Mrs Elizabeth Reid, Sarasota, Florida, USA; one *s* three *d*]. *Address:* Springwaters, Ballamodha, Isle of Man.

Died 26 Jan. 1994.

NORTHROP, Filmer S(tuart) C(uckow), PhD, LittD, LLD; Sterling Professor of Philosophy and Law Emeritus, the Law School and the School of Graduate Studies, Yale University, USA, since 1962; *b* 27 Nov. 1893; *s* of Marshall Ellsworth Northrop and Ruth Cuckow; *m* 1st, 1919, Christine Johnston (decd); two *s*; 2nd, 1969, Marjorie Carey (decd). *Educ:* Beloit Coll. (BA 1915, LittD 1946); Yale (MA 1919); Harvard (MA 1922, PhD 1924); Imperial Coll. of Science and Technology, London; Trinity Coll., Cambridge. Instr at Yale, 1923–26; Asst Prof., Yale, 1926–29; Associate Prof., Yale, 1929–32, Prof., 1932–47; Master of Silliman Coll., 1940–47; Sterling Prof. of Philosophy and Law, Yale, 1947–62. Visiting Professor: summer session, Univ. of Iowa, 1926; Univ. of Michigan, 1932; Univ. of Virginia, 1931–32; Visiting Prof. and Mem. of East-West Conf. on Philosophy at Univ. of Hawaii, 1939; Prof. Extraordinario, La Universidad Nacional Autonoma de Mexico, 1949; Fellow: American Acad. of Arts and Sciences, 1951; American Acad. of Political and Social Science, 1957; Pres., American Philosophical Assoc. (Eastern Div.), 1952. Hon. Founder: Macy Foundn Conferences, 1944–53; Amer. Soc. of Cybernetics, 1964; Mem., SEATO Round Table, Bangkok, 1958. Hon. LLD: Univ. of Hawaii, 1949; Rollins Coll., 1955; Hon. LittD: Beloit Coll., 1946; Pratt Inst., 1961. Order of the Aztec Eagle (Mexico), 1946. *Publications:* Science and First Principles, 1931; The Meeting of East and West, 1946; The Logic of the Sciences and the Humanities, 1947; (ed) Ideological Differences and World Order, 1949; The Taming of the Nations, A Study of the Cultural Bases of International Policy, 1952 (Wilkie Memorial Building Award, 1953); European Union and United States Foreign Policy, 1954; The Complexity of Legal and Ethical Experience, 1959; Philosophical Anthropology and Practical Politics, 1960; Man, Nature and God, 1962; Co-Editor, Cross-cultural Understanding: Epistemology in Anthropology, 1964; Chapter 5 in Contemporary American Philosophy, second series, 1970; (with J. Sinões da Fonseca) Interpersonal Relations in Neuropsychological and Legal Science, 1975; Prolegomena to a Philosophia Naturales, 1985. *Recreations:* travel, baseball. *Address:* 8 Hampton Road, Exeter, NH 03833, USA. *Clubs:* Century (New York);

Beaumont, Berzilius, Elizabethan, Graduates, Mory's (New Haven); American Academy of Arts and Sciences (Philosophy Section) (Boston).

Died 21 July 1992.

NORTHUMBERLAND, 11th Duke of, *cr* 1766; **Henry Alan Walter Richard Percy;** Bt 1660; Baron Percy 1722; Earl of Northumberland, Baron Warkworth 1749; Earl Percy 1766; Earl of Beverly 1790; Lord Lovaine, Baron of Alnwick 1784; *b* 1 July 1953; *s* of 10th Duke of Northumberland, KG, GCVO, TD, PC, FRS and of Lady Elizabeth Diana Montagu-Douglas-Scott, *er d* of 8th Duke of Buccleuch and Queensberry, KT, GCVO, PC; *S* father, 1988. *Educ:* Eton; Christ Church, Oxford. President: Alnwick & Dist Cttee for the Disabled; Alnwick Working Men's Club & Inst.; Northumbria Club; Northumbrian Anglers' Fedn; Natural History Soc. of Northumbria; Northumberland Assoc. of Boys Clubs; Northumberland County Victims' Support Scheme; N of England CRC; Craster Br., RNLI; Surrey Farming & Wildlife Adv. Gp; Royal Northumberland Yacht Club; Tyne Mariners' Benevolent Instn; Vice President: Ancient Monuments Soc.; Internat. Sheep Dog Soc.; Patron: Assoc. of Northumberland Local History Socs; Berwick-upon-Tweed Preservation Trust; Internat. Centre for Child Studies; NE Br., Mental Health Foundn; Northumberland Buildings Preservation Trust; Hounslow and Feltham Victim Support Scheme; Hounslow and Twickenham Br., Arthritis Care; Northern Counties Sch. for the Deaf; Royal Northumberland Fusiliers Aid Soc. and Regimental Assoc.; Theatre W4; Tyneside Cinema. MFH 1989; FRSA 1989. *Recreations:* tennis, shooting, movies (film producer and actor). *Heir: b* Lord Ralph George Algernon Percy [*b* 16 Nov. 1956; *m* 1979, Jane, *d* of John W. M. M. Richard; two *s* two *d*]. *Address:* Alnwick Castle, Northumberland NE66 1NQ; Syon House, Brentford, Mddx TW8 8JF.

Died 31 Oct. 1995.

NORTON, 7th Baron, *cr* 1878; **John Arden Adderley,** OBE 1964; *b* 24 Nov. 1915; *s* of 6th Baron Norton and Elizabeth (*d* 1952), *d* of W. J. Birkbeck; *S* father, 1961; *m* 1946, Betty Margaret, *o d* of late James McKee Hannah; two *s. Educ:* Radley; Magdalen Coll., Oxford (BA). Oxford University Greenland Expedition, 1938. Assistant Master, Oundle School, 1938–39. Served War, 1940–45 (despatches); RE (N Africa, Europe); Major, 1944. Asst Secretary, Country Landowners Assoc., 1947–59. *Recreations:* mountaineering, shooting, heraldry, genealogy. *Heir: s* Hon. James Nigel Arden Adderley [*b* 2 June 1947; *m* 1971, Jacqueline Julie Willett, *e d* of Guy W. Willett, Woking, Surrey; one *s* one *d*]. *Address:* Fillongley Hall, Coventry, West Midlands. *T:* Fillongley (0676) 40303. *Died 24 Sept. 1993.*

NORTON, Mary; children's writer; *b* 10 Dec. 1903; *d* of Reginald Spencer Pearson and Minnie Savile Hughes; *m* 1st, 1926, Robert Charles Norton; two *s* two *d*; 2nd, 1970, Lionel Bonsey (*d* 1989). *Educ:* St Margaret's Convent, East Grinstead. Old Vic Co. under Lilian Baylis, 1925–26; domiciled family home in Portugal, 1926–39; war job and acting for BBC, 1940; war job, British Purchasing Commn, New York, 1941; returned to London, 1942, caring for own children and acting for H. M. Tennant. *Publications:* Bonfires and Broomsticks, 1947; The Borrowers, 1952 (Library Assoc. Carnegie Medal, 1952; Hans Christian Anderson Honours Award); The Borrowers Afield, 1955; The Borrowers Afloat, 1959; The Borrowers Aloft, 1961; Poor Stainless, 1971; Are All the Giants Dead?, 1975; The Borrowers Avenged, 1982. *Recreations:* (formerly) swimming, training for show-jumping. *Address:* 102 West Street, Hartland, N Devon EX39 6BQ. *Clubs:* Lansdowne, Sloane. *Died 29 Aug. 1992.*

NOSSITER, Bernard Daniel; journalist; *b* 10 April 1926; *s* of Murry and Rose (Weingarten) Nossiter; *m* 1950,

Jacqueline Robinson; four *s*. *Educ*: Dartmouth Coll., Hanover, NH (BA); Harvard Univ., Cambridge, Mass (MA Econ). Washington Post: Nat. Econs Corresp., 1955–62; European Econs Corresp., 1964–67; S Asia Corresp., 1967–68; Nat. Bureau Reporter, 1968–71; London Corresp., 1971–79; UN Bureau Chief, NY Times, 1979–83. Nieman Fellow, Harvard, 1962–63. *Publications:* The Mythmakers, 1964; Soft State, 1970; Britain: a future that works, 1978; The Global Struggle for More, 1987; Fat Years and Lean: the economy since Roosevelt, 1990; contribs to Amer. Econ. Rev., Harvard Business Rev., Annals Amer. Acad. Pol. Sci. *Address:* 300 East 75 Street, New York, NY 10021, USA. *T:* 879 1491. *Club:* Reform. *Died 24 June 1992.*

NOVE, Prof. Alexander, (Alec), FRSE 1982; FBA 1978; Professor of Economics, University of Glasgow, 1963–82, then Emeritus; Hon. Senior Research Fellow, Glasgow University, since 1982; *b* Leningrad, 24 Nov. 1915; *s* of Jacob Novakovsky; *m* 1951, Irene MacPherson; three *s*. *Educ:* King Alfred Sch., London; London Sch. of Economics (Hon. Fellow, 1982). BSc (Econ) 1936. Army, 1939–46. Civil Service (mainly BoT), 1947–58; Reader in Russian Social and Economic Studies, Univ. of London, 1958–63. Hon. Dragr. Giessen, 1977; Hon. DrEcon Stockholm Sch. of Econ., 1994. *Publications:* The Soviet Economy, 1961; (with J. A. Newth) The Soviet Middle East, 1965; Was Stalin Really Necessary?, 1965; Economic History of the USSR, 1969, 3rd edn 1993; (ed with D. M. Nuti) Socialist Economics, 1972; Efficiency Criteria for Nationalised Industries, 1973; Stalinism and After, 1976; The Soviet Economic System, 1977, 3rd edn 1986; Political Economy and Soviet Socialism, 1979; The Economics of Feasible Socialism, 1983; Socialism, Economics and Development, 1986; Glasnost in Action, 1989; Economics of Feasible Socialism Revisited, 1991; Studies in Economics and Russia, 1991; (ed) The Stalin Phenomenon, 1993. *Recreations:* walking in Scottish hills, travel, music, theatre, exotic dishes. *Address:* 55 Hamilton Drive, Glasgow G12 8DP. *T:* 041–339 1053. *Club:* Commonwealth Trust. *Died 15 May 1994.*

NUGENT OF GUILDFORD, Baron, *cr* 1966 (Life Peer), of Dunsfold, co. Surrey; **George Richard Hodges Nugent,** PC 1962; Bt 1960; *b* 6 June 1907; *s* of late Colonel George H. Nugent, OBE, RA, and Violet Stella, *d* of Capt. Henry Theophilus Sheppard; *m* 1937, Ruth, *d* of late Hugh G. Stafford, Tilford, Surrey. *Educ:* Imperial Service Coll., Windsor; RMA, Woolwich. Commissioned RA, 1926–29. MP (C) Guildford Division of Surrey, 1950–66. Parliamentary Secretary: Ministry of Agriculture, Fisheries and Food, 1951–57; Min. of Transport, 1957–Oct. 1959; Chm., Select Cttee for Nationalised Industries, 1961–64; a Dep. Speaker, House of Lords. JP Surrey; CC and sometime Alderman, Surrey, 1944–51. Member: Exec. Council, NFU, 1945–51; Agricl Improvement Council, 1947–51; Vice-Chairman: Nat. Fedn of Young Farmers, 1948–51; Wye Agricl Coll., 1946–51; Harper Adams Agricl Coll., 1947–51; Chairman: Thames Conservancy Board, 1960–74; Nat. Water Council, 1973–78; Agricultural Market Development Cttee, 1962–68; Animal Virus Research Institute, 1964–77; Standing Conf. on London and SE Regional Planning, 1962–81; Defence Lands Cttee, 1971–73; President, Assoc. of River Authorities, 1965–74; Chm. Management Bd, Mount Alvernia Hosp., Guildford, 1987–92; Mem., Guildford Diocesan Synod, 1970–93. Pres., Surrey Conservative and Unionist Club, 1992–. Pres., RoSPA, 1980–82. FRSA

1962. Hon. FIWEM (Hon. FIPHE; Hon. FIWES). DUniv Surrey, 1968. Hon. Freeman, Borough of Guildford, 1985. *Address:* Blacknest Cottage, Dunsfold, Godalming, Surrey GU8 4PE. *Club:* Royal Automobile (Vice-Pres., 1974). *Died 16 March 1994 (Btcy ext).*

NUREYEV, Rudolf Hametovich; ballet dancer and choreographer; Directeur Artistique de la Danse, Théâtre National de l'Opéra, Paris, 1983–89; *b* Razdolnaia, 17 March 1938, of a farming family; Austrian citizen, 1982. Joined Kirov Ballet School at age 17; appeared with the Company in 1959; when on tour, in Paris, sought political asylum, June 1961; joined Le Grand Ballet du Marquis de Cuevas Company and made frequent appearances abroad; London debut at Royal Academy of Dancing Gala Matinée, organised by Dame Margot Fonteyn, Dec. 1961; debut at Covent Garden in Giselle with Margot Fonteyn, Feb. 1962; Choreographic productions include: La Bayadère, Raymonda, Swan Lake, Tancredi, Sleeping Beauty, Nutcracker, Don Quixote, Romeo and Juliet, Manfred, The Tempest, Washington Square, Cinderella; guest artist in England and America in wide variety of rôles; danced in many countries of the world. Gold Star, Paris, 1963. *Films:* Romeo and Juliet, 1965; Swan Lake, 1966; I am a Dancer, 1972; Don Quixote, 1972; Valentino, 1977; Exposed, 1983. Légion d'Honneur (France), 1988; Commander, Order of Arts and Letters (France), 1992. *Publication:* Nureyev, 1962. *Recreations:* listening to and playing music. *Address:* c/o S. A. Gorlinsky Ltd, 34 Dover Street, W1X 4NJ. *Died 6 Jan. 1993.*

NURSAW, William George; investment consultant since 1961; financial writer and company director; *b* 5 Sept. 1903; *s* of George Edward Nursaw and Amy Elizabeth (*née* Davis); *m* 1931, Lilian May (*née* Howell); one *s* two *d*. *Educ:* Rushmore Road LCC Primary Sch.; Holloway Grammar Sch. (Schol.). Insurance, 1920–61: Trustee Man., Atlas Assce Co.; subseq. Dir Throgmorton Management (Man. Dir, 1962–71) and Hogg Robinson Gardner Mountain Pensions Management (Chm., 1963–71). Hon. Financial Adviser, RAF Escapers Soc., 1964–83, and National Birthday Trust, 1946–90 (and Hon. Treas.); Co-founder and Hon. Financial Advr, 1945–, Jt Pres., 1987–, Covenanters Educational Trust and Perry Foundn. Freeman, City of London; Past Warden, Loriners' Co.; Deacon, Chingford Congregational Church, 1944–62; Youth Leader, 1942–67; Sec. and Treas., 1934–58, Chm., 1959–79, Chingford and Waltham Forest Playing Fields Assoc. (completed 51 yrs as an hon. officer for the dist); Exec., Essex County Playing Fields Assoc., then Greater London Playing Fields, 1948–85. Civil Defence (Post Warden), 1938–65. FSS; ACII; FCIS (Mem. Council, 1962–70, Chm., London, 1968–69); FCIArb (Mem. Council, 1968–74); Associate Mem., Soc. of Investment Analysts. Mem., Royal Soc. of St George. *Publications:* Investment in Trust: problems and policies, 1961; Art and Practice of Investment, 1962, 4th edn 1974; Purposeful Investment, 1965; Principles of Pension Fund Investment, 1966, 2nd edn 1976; Investment for All, 1972; articles for national press on investment and insurance, incl. over 200 articles for The Guardian, Observer, etc. *Recreations:* rose-growing, cricket (Pres. and Captain, Chingford Park CC), writing, portrait painting, playing-fields movement, 1934–85 (Duke of Edinburgh award). *Address:* 603 Mountjoy House, Barbican, EC2Y 8BP. *T:* 071–628 7638; 6 Carlton Road East, Westgate, Kent. *T:* Thanet (0843) 32105. *Clubs:* City Livery, Aldersgate Ward, MCC, Pen International. *Died 2 Aug. 1994.*

O

O'BEIRNE, Cornelius Banahan, CBE 1964; QC (Gibraltar) 1967; consultant on international and comparative law; *b* 9 September 1915; *e s* of late Captain C. B. O'Beirne, OBE; *m* 1949, Ivanka (*d* 1991), *d* of Miloc Tupanjanin, Belgrade; one *s* one *d*. *Educ:* Stonyhurst Coll. Solicitor, 1940; called to the Bar, Lincoln's Inn, 1952. Served War, 1940–46: Major RA, Europe, ME. Polit. Adviser's Office, Brit. Emb., Athens, 1945–46; Colonial Office, 1947–48; Crown Counsel: Nigeria, 1949–53; High Commn Territories, SA, 1953–59; Solicitor-Gen., 1959; Attorney-General, High Commission Territories, South Africa, 1961–64; Counsellor (Legal), British Embassy, SA, 1964–65; Senior Legal Asst, Lord Chancellor's Office, 1966–71 (seconded as Attorney-Gen., Gibraltar, 1966–70); Council on Tribunals, 1971–78; Asst Dir, British Inst. of Internat. and Comparative Law, 1978–82, Dir of its Commonwealth Legal Adv. Service, 1982–86. QC: Basutoland, Bechuanaland and Swaziland, 1962. Member: RIIA; Justice; Plowden Soc.; Commonwealth Parly Assoc. *Publications:* Laws of Gibraltar, rev. edn 1968; Survey of Extradition and Fugitive Offenders Legislation in the Commonweath, 1982, 3rd edn 1989; contribs to jls. *Recreations:* reading, photography. *Address:* Nanhoran Cottage, 23 Claremont Lane, Esher, Surrey KT10 9DP. *T:* Esher (0372) 462268. *Died 21 Aug. 1992.*

O'BRIEN OF LOTHBURY, Baron *cr* 1973 (Life Peer), of the City of London; **Leslie Kenneth O'Brien,** GBE 1967; PC 1970; President, British Bankers' Association, 1973–80; *b* 8 Feb. 1908; *e s* of late Charles John Grimes O'Brien; *m* 1st, 1932, Isabelle Gertrude Pickett (*d* 1987); one *s*; 2nd, 1989, Marjorie Violet Taylor. *Educ:* Wandsworth School. Entered Bank of England, 1927; Deputy Chief Cashier, 1951; Chief Cashier, 1955; Executive Director, 1962–64; Deputy Governor, 1964–66; Governor, 1966–73; Director: Commonwealth Develt Finance Co. Ltd, 1962–64; The Prudential Assurance Co. Ltd, 1973–80; The Prudential Corp. Ltd, 1979–83; The Rank Organisation, 1974–78; Bank for International Settlements, 1966–73, 1974–83 (Vice-Chm., 1979–83); Saudi Internat. Bank, 1975–84; Vice-Chm., Banque Belge, 1981–88; Mem., Adv. Bd, Unilever Ltd, 1973–78; Consultant to J. P. Morgan & Co., 1973–79; Chm., Internat. Council of Morgan Guaranty Trust Co., NY, 1974–78; Mem. Internat. Adv. Council, Morgan Grenfell & Co. Ltd, 1974–87. Chm., Cttee of Inquiry into export of animals for slaughter, 1973. Member: Finance and Appeal Cttee, RCS, 1973–85; Council, RCM, 1973–90; Bd of National Theatre, 1973–78; Council, Marie Curie Meml Foundn, 1963–78; Investment Adv. Cttee, Mercers' Co., 1973–92; City of London Savings Cttee, 1966–78. A Trustee of Glyndebourne Arts Trust, 1974–78; Hon. Treasurer and Mem. Exec. Cttee, Royal Opera House Develt Appeal, 1977–87. Pres., United Banks' Lawn Tennis Assoc., 1958–81; Vice-Pres., Squash Rackets Assoc., 1972–78. One of HM Lieutenants for City of London, 1966–73; Freeman, City of London in Co. of Mercers; Hon. Liveryman, Leathersellers Co. Hon. DSc City Univ., 1969; Hon. LLD Univ. of Wales, 1973. FRCM 1979. Hon. FCIB. Cavaliere di Gran Croce al Merito della Repubblica Italiana, 1975; Grand Officier, Ordre de la Couronne (Belgium), 1976. *Address:* 3 Peter Avenue, Oxted, Surrey RH8 9LG. *T:* Oxted (01883) 712535. *Clubs:* Boodle's, Grillions, All England Lawn Tennis.
Died 24 Nov. 1995.

OCHOA, Dr Severo; Hon. Director, Centro de Biología Molecular, Universidad Autónoma, Madrid, since 1985; *b* Luarca, Spain, 24 Sept. 1905; *s* of Severo Ochoa and Carmen (*née* Albornoz); US citizen, 1956; *m* 1931, Carmen G. Cobian. *Educ:* Malaga Coll.; University of Madrid. AB, Malaga, 1921; MD, Madrid, 1929. Lecturer in Physiology, University of Madrid Medical School, 1931–35; Head of Physiology Div., Institute for Medical Research, 1935–36; Guest Research Asst, Kaiser Wilhelm Inst., Heidelberg, 1936–37; Marine Biological Lab., Plymouth, July-Dec. 1937; Demonstrator and Nuffield Research Assistant in Biochemistry, University of Oxford Medical School, 1938–41; Instructor and Research Associate in Pharmacology, Washington Univ. School of Medicine, St Louis, 1941–42; New York University School of Medicine: Research Associate in Medicine, 1942–45; Asst Professor of Biochemistry, 1945–46; Professor of Pharmacology, and Chairman of Dept of Pharmacology, 1946–54; Prof. of Biochemistry, and Chm. of Dept of Biochemistry, 1954–74; Distinguished Mem., Roche Inst. of Molecular Biology, New Jersey, 1974–85. Carlos Jimenez Diaz lectr, Madrid Univ., 1969. Pres., Internat. Union of Biochemistry, 1961–67. Member: US National Academy of Sciences; American Academy of Arts and Sciences; American Philosophical Society; Deutsche Akademie der Naturforscher (Leopoldina), etc. Nobel Prize (joint) in Physiology or Medicine, 1959. Hon. degrees from universities and colleges in Argentina, Brazil, Chile, England, Italy, Peru, Philippines, Scotland, Spain and USA. Foreign Member: Royal Society, 1965; USSR Academy of Science, 1966; Polish Acad. of Science; Acad. of Science, DDR, 1977; Acad. of Med. Scis, Argentina, 1977; Chilean Acad. of Scis, 1977; Indian Nat. Sci. Acad., 1977. Hon. Mem., Royal Acad. Med., Sevilla, 1971. Gold Medal, Madrid Univ., 1969; Quevedo Gold Medal, Madrid, 1969; Albert Gallatin Medal, NY Univ., 1970. Order of Rising Sun, 2nd class, 1967. *Publications:* papers on biochemistry and molecular biology. *Recreations:* colour photography, swimming. *Address:* Miguel Angel 1 Bis, 28010 Madrid, Spain. *T:* (1) 4100709; Universidad Autónoma, Campus de Cantoblanco, 28049 Madrid, Spain. *T:* (1) 7349300.

Died 1 Nov. 1993.

O'CONNOR, Rt Rev. Kevin, JCL; Titular Bishop of Glastonbury and an Auxiliary Bishop of Liverpool, (RC), since 1979; *b* 20 May 1929. *Educ:* St Francis Xavier, Liverpool; Junior and Senior Seminaries, Upholland; Gregorian Univ., Rome. Priest, 1954; Member, Archdiocesan Marriage Tribunal; Parish Priest, St Anne's and Chancellor of Archdiocese of Liverpool, 1977. *Address:* 12 Richmond Close, Eccleston, St Helens WA10 5JE. *Died 4 May 1993.*

O'FAOLÁIN, Seán, (John Francis Whelan); writer; *b* Cork, 22 Feb. 1900; *s* of Denis Whelan and Bridget Murphy; *m* 1928, Eileen Gould (*d* 1989); one *s* one *d*. *Educ:* National Univ. of Ireland (MA); Harvard (AM); but mainly by good conversation. Commonwealth Fellow, 1925–28; John Harvard Fellow, 1928–29; Lectr in English, Boston Coll., 1929; Lectr in English, St Mary's Coll.,

Strawberry Hill, Middx, 1929–33. Founder, 1940 and Editor, 1940–46, The Bell. Dir, Arts Council of Ireland, 1957–59. *Publications:* Midsummer Night Madness, 1932; A Nest of Simple Folk, 1933; Constance Markievicz: a biography, 1934; Bird Alone, 1936; A Purse of Coppers, 1937; King of the Beggars: a biography, 1938; She Had to Do Something (play), 1938; An Irish Journey, 1940; Come Back to Erin, 1940; The Great O'Neill: a biography, 1942; Teresa, 1946; The Short Story, 1948; Summer in Italy, 1949; Newman's Way, 1952; South to Sicily, 1953; The Vanishing Hero, 1956; The Stories of Sean O'Faolain, 1958; I Remember! I Remember!, 1962; Vive Moi!, 1965; The Heat of the Sun, 1966; The Talking Trees, 1970; Foreign Affairs and Other Stories, 1976; Selected Stories of Sean O'Faolain, 1978; And Again?, 1979; The Collected Stories, vol. I, 1980, vol. II, 1981, vol. III, 1982. *Address:* 17 Rosmeen Park, Dunlaoire, Dublin.

Died 21 April 1991.

OFFLER, Prof. Hilary Seton, MA; FBA 1974; Professor of Medieval History in the University of Durham, 1956–78, then Professor Emeritus; *b* 3 Feb. 1913; *s* of Horace Offler and late Jenny Whebby; *m* 1951, Betty Elfreda, *d* of late Archibald Jackson, Sawbridgeworth; two *s. Educ:* Hereford High School; Emmanuel College, Cambridge. 1st Cl. Historical Tripos Pt I, 1932, Part II, 1933, Theological Tripos Pt II, 1934; Lightfoot Schol., Cambridge, 1934; Research Fellow, Emmanuel Coll., 1936–40. Served with RA in N Africa, Sicily and NW Europe, 1940–46. Lecturer, Univ. of Bristol, 1946; Reader in Medieval History, Univ. of Durham, 1947. Pres., Surtees Society, 1980–87 (Sec., 1950–66). *Publications:* edited: Ockham, Opera politica, vol. i (jtly) 1940, *ed. altera* 1974; vol. ii (jtly) 1963; vol. iii 1956; (with E. Bonjour and G. R. Potter) A Short History of Switzerland, 1952; Medieval Historians of Durham, 1958; Durham Episcopal Charters 1071–1152, 1968; articles in English and foreign hist. jls. *Address:* 28 Old Elvet, Durham DH1 3HN. *T:* Durham (091) 3846219.

Died 24 Jan. 1991.

OGILVY, Sir David (John Wilfrid), 13th Bt, *cr* 1626 (NS), of Inverquharity, Forfarshire; DL; farmer and landowner; *b* 3 February 1914; *e s* of Gilbert Francis Molyneux Ogilvy (*d* 1953) (4th *s* of 10th Bt) and Marjory Katharine, *d* of late M. B. Clive, Whitfield, Herefordshire; *S* uncle, Sir Herbert Kinnaird Ogilvy, 12th Bt, 1956; *m* 1966, Penelope Mary Ursula, *d* of Arthur Lafone Frank Hills, White Court, Kent; one *s. Educ:* Eton; Trinity College, Oxford. Served in the RNVR in War of 1939–45. JP 1957, DL 1971, East Lothian. *Heir: s* Francis Gilbert Arthur Ogilvy, *b* 22 April 1969. *Address:* Winton Cottage, Pencaitland, East Lothian EH34 5AT. *T:* Pencaitland (0875) 340222. *Died 16 June 1992.*

OGLE-SKAN, Peter Henry, CVO 1972; TD 1948; Director, Scottish Services, Department of the Environment, 1970–75; *b* 4 July 1915; 2nd *s* of Dr H. W. Ogle-Skan, Hendon; *m* 1941, Pamela Moira Heslop; one *s* one *d. Educ:* Merchant Taylors' Sch., London. Clerk with Arbuthnot-Latham & Co. Ltd, London, 1933–39. Commnd into Royal Engineers (TA), 1936; War Service, 1939–46: England, 1939–42; India, 1942–45. Min. of Works: Temp. Principal, 1946; Principal, 1948; Asst Sec., 1955; Under-Sec., Scottish HQ, MPBW, 1966–70. *Recreations:* golf, walking, photography. *Address:* 44 Ravelston Garden, Edinburgh EH4 3LF. *T:* 031–337 6834.

Died 1 March 1992.

O'GORMAN, Rev. Brian Stapleton; President of the Methodist Conference, 1969–70; *b* 4 March 1910; *s* of William Thomas and Annie Maria O'Gorman; *m* 1939, Margaret, *d* of William and Margaret Huggon, Carlisle; two *d. Educ:* Bowdon College, Cheshire; Handsworth Theological College, Birmingham. Porlock, 1931–32;

Handsworth College, 1932–35; Manchester Mission, 1935–40; Islington Mission, London, 1940–43; Longton Mission, Stoke on Trent, 1943–50; Sheffield Mission, 1950–57; Chm., Wolverhampton and Shrewsbury Dist of Methodist Church, 1957–75. *Address:* 9 Trysull Gardens, Wolverhampton WV3 7LD. *T:* Wolverhampton (0902) 762167. *Died 20 Jan. 1991.*

O'HALLORAN, Sir Charles (Ernest), Kt 1982; Chairman, Irvine Development Corporation, 1983–85; *b* 26 May 1924; *s* of Charles and Lily O'Halloran; *m* 1943, Annie Rowan; one *s* two *d. Educ:* Conway St Central Sch., Birkenhead. Telegraphist, RN, 1942–46. Elected Ayr Town Council, 1953; Provost of Ayr, 1964–67; Mem., Strathclyde Regional Council, 1974–82 (Convener, 1978–82). Freeman of Ayr Burgh, 1975. Parly Cand. (Lab) Ayr Burghs, 1966. Dir, Radio Clyde, 1980–85; Mem., BRB(Scot.), 1981–85. *Recreations:* politics, golf, soccer spectating. *Address:* 40 Savoy Park, Ayr. *T:* Ayr (0292) 266234. *Clubs:* Royal Scottish Automobile (Glasgow); Ex-Servicemen's (Ayr).

Died 9 Feb. 1993.

OLIVER, Sir (Frederick) Ernest, Kt 1962; CBE 1955; TD 1942; DL; Chairman, George Oliver (Footwear) Ltd, 1950–73; *b* 31 Oct. 1900; *s* of late Colonel Sir Frederick Oliver and Lady (Mary Louise) Oliver, CBE; *m* 1928, Mary Margaret (*d* 1978), *d* of late H. Simpson; two *d* (one *s* decd). *Educ:* Rugby School. Member Leicester City Council, 1933–73, Lord Mayor, 1950. Officer, Territorial Army, 1922–48; served UK and Burma, 1939–45. President: Multiple Shoe Retailers' Assoc., 1964–65; Leicester YMCA, 1955–76; Leicester Conservative Assoc., 1952–66. Leicester: DL 1950; Hon. Freeman, 1971. *Address:* c/o 20 New Walk, Leicester LE1 6TX. *Club:* Leicestershire (Leicester).

Died 7 Sept. 1994.

OLIVER, Stephen Michael Harding; freelance composer, since 1974; *b* 10 March 1950; *s* of Osborne George Oliver and Charlotte Hester Oliver. *Educ:* St Paul's Cathedral Choir Sch.; Ardingly Coll.; Worcester Coll., Oxford (MA, BMus). Forty operas incl. The Duchess of Malfi, 1971; Tom Jones, 1976; Euridice, 1981; Beauty and the Beast, 1984; Mario and the Magician, 1988; Timon of Athens, 1990; L'Oca del Cairo, 1991; numerous scores for theatre, film and TV, incl. The Lord of the Rings, BBC Radio, 1980; Nicholas Nickleby, RSC, 1980; Peter Pan, RSC, 1982; other works incl. a symphony, several chamber pieces called Ricercare; musical (with Tim Rice) Blondel, 1983. *Recreations:* friends, books. *Address:* 44 Queen's Gate, SW7 5HR. *T:* 071–584 7912.

Died 29 April 1992.

OLUFOSOYE, Most Rev. Timothy Omotayo, OON 1964; *b* 31 March 1918; *s* of Chief D. K. Olufosoye and Felecia O. Olufosoye; *m* 1947, Joan; one *s* three *d. Educ:* St Andrew's Coll., Oyo, Nigeria; Vancouver School of Theology, Univ. of BC (STh). Headmaster, 1942–44; deacon 1946, priest 1947; appointments in Ondo, Lagos, and overseas in St Helens, Lancs, Sheffield Cathedral, Yorks, and Christ Church Cathedral, Vancouver, BC; Canon, 1955; Provost, St Stephen's Cathedral, Ondo, 1959; Vicar-Gen., 1963; Bishop of Gambia and Rio Pongas, 1965–70; Bishop of Ibadan, 1971–88; Archbishop of Nigeria, 1979–88. Member: World Council of Churches; Gen. and Exec. Cttee, All Africa Conf. of Churches. Hon. DD, St Paul's Univ., Tokyo, 1958. Knight Comdr, Humane Order of African Redemption, Republic of Liberia. *Publications:* Egbobi fun Ibanuje, 1967; Glossary of Ecclesiastical Terms, 1988; My Memoirs; editor of the Beacon, Ibadan Ecclesia Anglicana, The Rubric. *Recreation:* poultry farming. *Address:* 12 Awosika

Avenue, Bodija Estate, PO Box 1666, Ibadan, Oyo State, Nigeria. *Club:* Ibadan Dining.
Died 29 Oct. 1992.

O'NEILL, Alan Albert; Clerk to the Drapers' Company, 1973–80, Member, Court of Assistants, since 1981; *b* 11 Jan. 1916; *o s* of late Albert George O'Neill; *m* 1939, Betty Dolbey (*d* 1986); one *s. Educ:* Sir George Monoux Grammar Sch., Walthamstow. Joined staff Drapers' Co., 1933, Dep. Clerk 1967. Clerk to Governors, Bancroft's School, 1951–73, Governor, 1980–; Governor, Queen Mary Coll., 1973–80. Served War of 1939–45, Royal Navy: Telegraphist, RNVR (Wireless), 1939; DEMS Gunnery Officer, SS Aquitania and SS Nieuw Amsterdam; Lt-Comdr, RNVR, 1943; DEMS Staff Officer, Aberdeen and NE Coast Scotland, 1945. *Recreation:* gardening. *Address:* Wickenden, 36 Main Road, Sundridge, Sevenoaks, Kent TN14 6EP. *T:* Westerham (0959) 63530.
Died 25 Oct. 1991.

O'NEILL, Thomas P(hilip), Jr; Speaker, House of Representatives, USA, 1977–86; *b* Cambridge, Mass, 9 Dec. 1912; *s* of Thomas P. O'Neill and Rose Anne (*née* Tolan); *m* 1941, Mildred Anne Miller; three *s* two *d. Educ:* St John's High Sch.; Boston Coll., Mass. Grad. 1936. In business, insurance, in Cambridge, Mass. Mem., State Legislature, Mass, 1936–52: Minority Leader, 1947 and 1948; Speaker of the House, 1948–52. Member, Camb. Sch. Cttee, 1946, 1949. Member of Congresses: 83rd-87th, 11th Dist, Mass; 88th-99th, 8th Dist, Mass. Democrat: Majority Whip, 1971–73, Majority Leader, 1973–77. *Address:* 1310 19th Street NW, Washington, DC 20036–1602, USA.
Died 6 Jan. 1994.

OPPENHEIMER, Sir Philip (Jack), Kt 1970; Chairman, The Diamond Trading Co. (Pty) Ltd, since 1975; *b* 29 Oct. 1911; *s* of Otto and Beatrice Oppenheimer; *m* 1935, Pamela Fenn Stirling; one *s* one *d. Educ:* Harrow; Jesus Coll., Cambridge. Dir, De Beers Consolidated Mines Ltd. Bronze Cross of Holland, 1943; Commandeur, Ordre de Léopold, 1977. *Recreations:* golf, horse-racing and breeding. *Address:* (office) 17 Charterhouse Street, EC1N 6RA. *Clubs:* Jockey, Portland, White's.
Died 8 Oct. 1995.

ORAM, Samuel, MD (London); FRCP; Consultant Cardiologist and Emeritus Lecturer; former Senior Physician, and Director, Cardiac Department, King's College Hospital; former Censor, Royal College of Physicians; Medical Adviser, Rio Tinto Zinc Corporation Ltd; *b* 11 July 1913; *s* of Samuel Henry Nathan Oram, London; *m* 1940, Ivy (*d* 1991), *d* of Raffaele Amato; two *d. Educ:* King's College, London; King's College Hospital, London. Senior Scholar, KCH, London; Sambrooke Medical Registrar, KCH. Served War of 1939–45, as Lt-Col, RAMC. Examiner: in Pharmacology and Materia Medica, The Conjoint Bd; in Medicine: RCP; Univs of Cambridge and London; The Worshipful Soc. of Apothecaries. Member: Assoc. of Physicians; Br. Cardiac Society; American Heart Assoc.; Corresp. Member Australasian Cardiac Soc. Gold Medal, RCP. *Publications:* Clinical Heart Disease (textbook), 1971, 2nd edn 1981; various cardiological and medical articles in Qly Jl Med., British Heart Jl, BMJ, Brit. Encyclopaedia of Medical Practice, The Practitioner, etc. *Recreation:* golf (execrable). *Address:* 73 Harley Street, W1. *T:* 071–935 9942.
Died 8 Nov. 1991.

ORCHARD, Peter Francis, CBE 1982; Chairman, De La Rue plc, since 1987 (Director, since 1963; Chief Executive, 1977–87); *b* 25 March 1927; *s* of Edward Henslowe Orchard and Agnes Marjory Willett; *m* 1955, Helen Sheridan; two *s* two *d. Educ:* Downside Sch., Bath; Magdalene Coll., Cambridge (MA). CBIM. Service, KRRC, 1944–48. Joined Thomas De La Rue & Co. Ltd,

1950; Managing Director: Thomas De La Rue (Brazil), 1959–61; Thomas De La Rue International, 1962–70. Dir, Delta plc, 1981–. Mem., Court of Assistants, Drapers' Co., 1974–, Master 1982. Hon. Col 71st (Yeomanry) Signal Regt, TA, 1984–88. *Recreations:* gardening, swimming, building, cricket. *Address:* Willow Cottage, Little Hallingbury, Bishop's Stortford, Herts CM22 7PX. *T:* Bishop's Stortford (0279) 654101. *Clubs:* Travellers', MCC.
Died 28 Jan. 1993.

ORDE, Alan Colin C.; *see* Campbell Orde.

ORME, Ion Hunter Touchet G.; *see* Garnett-Orme.

ORMROD, Rt Hon. Sir Roger (Fray Greenwood), Kt 1961; PC 1974; a Lord Justice of Appeal, 1974–82; *b* 20 Oct. 1911; *s* of late Oliver Fray Ormrod and Edith Muriel (*née* Pim); *m* 1938, Anne, *d* of Charles Lush; no *c. Educ:* Shrewsbury Sch.; The Queen's Coll., Oxford (Hon. Fellow, 1966). BA Oxon (Jurisprudence) 1935. BM, BCh Oxon, 1941; FRCP 1969. Called to Bar, Inner Temple, 1936. House Physician, Radcliffe Infirmary, Oxford, 1941–42. Served in RAMC, 1942–45, with rank of Major; DADMS 8 Corps. Lecturer in Forensic Medicine, Oxford Medical Sch., 1950–59; QC 1958; Judge of High Court of Justice, Family Div. (formerly Probate, Divorce and Admiralty Div.), 1961–74. Hon. Prof. of Legal Ethics, Univ. of Birmingham, 1973–74. Chairman: Lord Chancellor's Cttee on Legal Education, 1968; Notting Hill Housing Trust, 1968–88. Pres., British Acad. of Forensic Science, 1970–71; Chm., Cttee of Management, Institute of Psychiatry, 1973–84. Visitor, Royal Postgrad. Med. Sch., 1975–90; Chm., British Postgrad. Med. Fedn, 1980–86. Hon. Fellow: RPMS, 1990; Manchester Polytechnic, 1972; Hon. FRCPsych 1975; Hon. FRCPath 1983. Hon. LLD Leicester, 1978. *Publications:* (ed with E. H. Pearce) Dunstan's Law of Hire-Purchase, 1938; (with Harris Walker) National Health Service Act 1946, 1949; (with Jacqueline Burgoyne and Martin Richards) Divorce Matters, 1987. *Address:* 4 Aubrey Road, W8 7JJ. *T:* 071–727 7876. *Club:* Garrick.
Died 6 Jan. 1992.

ORR, Rt Hon. Sir Alan (Stewart), Kt 1965; OBE 1944; PC 1971; a Lord Justice of Appeal, 1971–80; *b* 21 Feb. 1911; *s* of late William Orr and Doris Kemsley, Great Wakering, Essex; *m* 1933, Mariana Frances Lilian (*d* 1986), *d* of late Captain J. C. Lang, KOSB; four *s. Educ:* Fettes; Edinburgh Univ. (1st Class Hons Classics); Balliol Coll., Oxford (1st Class Hons Jurisprudence). Barrister Middle Temple, 1936 (Cert. Hon.); Master of the Bench, 1965; Barstow Law Scholar; Harmsworth Scholar. RAF, 1940–45 (despatches, OBE), Wing Comdr. Lectr in Laws (pt-time), UCL, 1948–50. Member of General Council of the Bar, 1953–57; Junior Counsel (Common Law) to Commissioners of Inland Revenue, 1957–63; QC 1963; Recorder of: New Windsor, 1958–65; Oxford, Jan.-Aug. 1965; Dep. Chairman, Oxford Quarter Sessions, 1964–71; Judge of High Court of Justice, Probate, Divorce and Admiralty Division, 1965–71; Presiding Judge, North-Eastern Circuit, 1970–71. Mem., Chancellor's Law Reform Cttee, 1966–80 (Chm., 1973–80). Chm., Court of Governors, Mill Hill Sch., 1976–79. *Recreation:* golf. *Address:* The Steps, Ratley, Banbury, Oxon OX15 6DT. *T:* Edge Hill (029587) 704. *Club:* United Oxford & Cambridge University.
Died 3 April 1991.

ORR, Sir John Henry, Kt 1979; OBE 1972; QPM 1977; Chief Constable, Lothian and Borders Police, 1975–83; *b* 13 June 1918; *m* 1942, Isobel Margaret Campbell; one *s* one *d. Educ:* George Heriot's Sch., Edinburgh. Edinburgh City Police, 1937; served in RAF 1943–45 (Flying Officer; Defence and War Medals); Chief Constable of Dundee, 1960; of Lothians and Peebles, 1968. Hon. Sec., Assoc. of Chief Police Officers (Scotland), 1974–83. FIMgt (FBIM

1978). Coronation Medal, 1953; Police Long Service and Good Conduct Medal, 1959; Jubilee Medal, 1977; OStJ, 1975. Comdr, Polar Star, class III, Sweden, 1975; Legion of Honour, France, 1976. *Recreations:* Rugby (capped for Scotland; Past Pres., Scottish Rugby Union), golf. *Address:* 24 Foulis Crescent, Juniper Green, Edinburgh EH14 5BN. *Died 26 Sept. 1995.*

OSBORNE, Maj.-Gen. Rev. Coles Alexander, CIE 1945; Indian Army, retired; *b* 29 July 1896; *s* of late W. E. Osborne, formerly of Dover, Kent; *m* 1930, Joyce (*d* 1994), *o d* of late R. H. Meares, Forbes and Sydney, NSW, Australia; two *d. Educ:* Dover County Sch. European War, 1914–18: served with HAC, Royal West Kent Regt, and RFC (wounded); transferred to 15th Sikhs, 1918; served in Afghan War, 1919 and in NW Frontier Operations, 1920–22; Tactics Instructor at Royal Military Coll., Duntroon, Australia, 1928–30; Bt Major 1933; General Staff (Operations), War Office, 1934–38; Bt Lieut-Col 1936; served in: Palestine, 1938; NW Frontier Ops, 1939; Middle East, 1940; Comd 1 Bombay Grenadiers, 1940; Deputy Director Military Training, India, 1940; Colonel, 1940; Commandant, Staff Coll., Quetta, 1941–42; Brigadier, 1941; Director Military Operations, GHQ, India and Burma, 1942–43; Temp. Maj.-Gen. 1942; Comd Kohat District, 1943–45; retired 1946. Student at Moore Theological Coll., Sydney, 1947; ordained, 1947; Hon. Asst Minister St Andrew's Cathedral, Sydney, Australia, 1947–53; Hon. Asst Minister, St Mark's Church, Darling Point, 1953–66; Personal Chaplain to Anglican Archbishop of Sydney, 1959–66. Director, Television Corp., 1956–75. Fellow of St Paul's Coll., Sydney Univ., 1953–69. Chairman, Freedom from Hunger Campaign, NSW, 1970–72. *Address:* 11 Charles Street, Warner's Bay, NSW 2282, Australia. *Club:* Australian (Sydney). *Died 11 June 1994.*

OSBORNE, John (James); dramatist and actor; Director of Woodfall Films; *b* 12 Dec. 1929; *s* of Thomas Godfrey Osborne and Nellie Beatrice Grove; *m* 1st, 1951, Pamela Elizabeth Lane (marr. diss. 1957); 2nd, 1957, Mary Ure (marr. diss. 1963; she *d* 1975); 3rd, 1963, Penelope Gilliatt (marr. diss. 1968; she *d* 1993); one *d*; 4th, 1968, Jill Bennett (marr. diss. 1977; she *d* 1990); 5th, 1978, Helen Dawson. *Educ:* Belmont Coll., Devon. First stage appearance at Lyceum, Sheffield, in No Room at the Inn, 1948; toured and in seasons at Ilfracombe, Bridgwater, Camberwell, Kidderminster, Derby, etc; English Stage Company season at Royal Court: appeared in Death of Satan, Cards of Identity, Good Woman of Setzuan, The Making of Moo, A Cuckoo in the Nest; directed Meals on Wheels, 1965; appeared in: The Parachute (BBC TV), 1967; First Night of Pygmalion (TV), 1969; First Love (film, as Maidanov), 1970; Get Carter (film), 1971; Lady Charlotte (TV), 1977; Tomorrow Never Comes (film), 1978. First play produced, 1949, at Theatre Royal, Huddersfield; other plays include, Personal Enemy, Opera House, Harrogate, 1955. *Plays filmed:* Look Back in Anger, 1958; The Entertainer, 1959, 1975; Inadmissible Evidence, 1965; Luther, 1971. *Film:* Tom Jones, 1964 (Oscar for best screenplay). Hon. Dr RCA, 1970. *Publications: plays:* Look Back in Anger, 1957 (produced 1956); The Entertainer, 1957 (also produced); Epitaph for George Dillon (with A. Creighton), 1958 (produced 1957); The World of Paul Slickey (comedy of manners with music), 1959 (produced 1959); Luther, 1960 (produced 1961, New York, 1964); A Subject of Scandal and Concern (TV), 1960; Plays for England, 1963; Inadmissible Evidence, 1964 (produced 1965); A Patriot for Me, 1964 (produced 1965, 1983); A Bond Honoured (trans. of Lope de Vega, La Fianza Satisfecha), 1966 (produced 1966); The Hotel in Amsterdam, 1967 (produced 1968); Time Present, 1967 (produced 1968); Hedda Gabler (adaptation), 1970 (produced 1972); The

Right Prospectus, and Very Like a Whale (TV), 1971; West of Suez, 1971 (produced 1971); The Gift of Friendship (TV), 1971; A Sense of Detachment, 1972 (produced 1972); A Place Calling Itself Rome, 1972; The Picture of Dorian Gray (adaptation), 1973; Jill and Jack (TV), 1974; The End of Me Old Cigar, 1975; Watch it come down, 1975; You're Not Watching Me, Mummy, and Try a Little Tenderness (TV), 1978; God Rot Tunbridge Wells! (TV), 1985; The Father (adapted and trans.), 1989; Déjàvu, 1991; *prose:* A Better Class of Person: an autobiography 1929–56, 1981; Almost a Gentleman: an autobiography vol. II 1955–1966, 1991; Damn You, England: collected prose, 1994; contrib. to various newspapers, journals. *Address:* The Hurst, Clunton, Craven Arms, Shropshire SY7 0JA. *Club:* Garrick. *Died 24 Dec. 1994.*

OSWALD, Maj.-Gen. Marshall St John, CB 1965; CBE 1961; DSO 1945; MC 1943; retired as Director of Management and Support Intelligence, Ministry of Defence, 1966; *b* 13 Sept. 1911; *s* of William Whitehead Oswald and Katharine Ray Oswald; *m* 1st, 1938, Mary Georgina Baker (*d* 1970); one *s* two *d*; 2nd, 1974, Mrs Barbara Rickards. *Educ:* Rugby Sch.; RMA, Woolwich. Commissioned RA, 1931; served in RHA and Field Artillery, UK and India, 1931–39; served War of 1939–45 (despatches, MC, DSO): Battery Comdr 4 RHA and Staff Officer in Egypt and Western Desert, 1939–42; GSO1, Tactical HQ, 8th Army, 1942–43; 2nd in Comd Field Regt, Italy, 1943–44; CO South Notts Hussars, Western Europe, 1944–45; Col on staff of HQ 21 Army Group, 1945; Mil. Govt Comdr (Col) of Cologne Area, 1946–47; Staff Officer, War Office (Lt-Col), 1948–49; Instructor (Col) Staff Coll., Camberley 1950–52; CO 19 Field Regt, Germany/Korea, 1953–55; GHQ, MELF (Col), 1955–56 (despatches 1957); IDC 1958; CCRA and Chief of Staff (Brig.) 1st Corps in Germany, 1959–62; DMI, War Office, 1962–64, Min. of Defence (Army), 1964–65. *Recreations:* fishing, shooting, ski-ing. *Address:* Eastfield House, Longparish, near Andover, Hants SP11 6NN. *T:* Longparish (026472) 228. *Club:* Army and Navy. *Died 7 Oct. 1991.*

OVENS, Maj.-Gen. Patrick John, OBE 1968; MC 1951; Commandant, Joint Warfare Establishment, 1976–79; retired; *b* 4 Nov. 1922; *s* of late Edward Alec Ovens and Mary Linsell Ovens, Cirencester; *m* 1952, Margaret Mary White; one *s* two *d. Educ:* King's Sch., Bruton. Commnd into Royal Marines, 1941; HMS Illustrious, 1942–43; 46 Commando, 1945; HQ 3rd Commando Bde, 1946–48; 41 Indep. Commando, Korea, 1950–52; HQ Portsmouth Gp, 1952–55; psa 1955–56; Staff of CGRM, 1959–61; Amphibious Warfare Sqdn, 1961–62; 41 Commando, 1963–65, CO 1965–67; C-in-C Fleet Staff, 1968–69; Comdr 3 Commando Bde, 1970–72; RCDS 1973; COS to Comdt Gen., RM, MoD, 1974–76. *Recreations:* sailing, music, gardening. *Died 29 Jan. 1994.*

OVERTON, Sir Hugh (Thomas Arnold), KCMG 1983 (CMG 1975); HM Diplomatic Service, retired; Member of Council, Barnardo's, since 1985 (Executive Finance Committee, since 1988); *b* 2 April 1923; *e s* of late Sir Arnold Overton, KCB, KCMG, MC and Bronwen Cecilie, *d* of Sir Hugh Vincent; *m* 1948, Claire-Marie Binet; one *s* two *d. Educ:* Dragon Sch., Oxford; Winchester; Clare Coll., Cambridge. Royal Signals, 1942–45. HM Diplomatic Service, 1947–83; served: Budapest; UN Delegn to UN, New York; Cairo; Beirut; Disarmament Delegn, Geneva; Warsaw; Bonn; Canadian Nat. Defence Coll.; Head of N America Dept, FCO, 1971–74; Consul-Gen., Düsseldorf, 1974–75; Minister (Econ.), Bonn, 1975–80; Consul-Gen., New York, and Dir-Gen., British Trade Develt in USA, 1980–83. Trustee: Bell Educnl Trust, 1986–; Taverner Concerts Trust, 1987–. Mem.,

RIIA. *Recreations:* reading, handwork, sailing, fishing. *Club:* Royal Automobile. *Died 11 Dec. 1991.*

OWEN, Alun (Davies); writer since 1957; *b* 24 Nov. 1925; *s* of Sidney Owen and Ruth (*née* Davies); *m* 1942, (Theodora) Mary O'Keeffe; two *s. Educ:* Cardigan County School, Wales; Oulton High School, Liverpool. Worked as stage manager, director and actor, in theatre, TV and films, 1942–59. Awards: Screenwriters and Producers Script of the Year, 1960; Screenwriters Guild, 1961; Daily Mirror, 1961; Golden Star, 1967. *Acted in: stage:* Birmingham Rep., 1943–44; Humoresque, 1948; Snow White and the Seven Dwarfs, 1951; Old Vic season, 1953: Tamburlaine the Great; As You Like It; King Lear; Twelfth Night; The Merchant of Venice; Macbeth; The Wandering Jew; The Taming of the Shrew, 1957; Royal Court Season, 1957; Man with a Guitar, The Waiting of Lester Abbs, The Samson Riddle, 1972; The Ladies, 1977; *films:* Every Day Except Christmas, 1957; I'm All Right Jack, 1959; The Servant, 1963; *television:* Glas y Dorlan, BBC Wales. *Author of productions: stage:* The Rough and Ready Lot, 1959 (radio 1958), publ. 1960; Progress to the Park, 1959 (radio 1958), publ. 1962; The Rose Affair, 1966 (TV 1961), publ. 1962; A Little Winter Love, 1963, publ. 1964; Maggie May, 1964; The Game, 1965; The Goose, 1967; Shelter, 1971 (TV 1967), publ. 1968; There'll Be Some Changes Made, 1969; Norma, 1969 (extended version, Nat. Theatre, 1983); We Who Are About To (later title Mixed Doubles), 1969, publ. 1970; The Male of the Species, 1974 (TV 1969), publ. 1972; Lucia, 1982; *screen:* The Criminal, 1960; A Hard Day's Night, 1964 (Oscar nomination); Caribbean Idyll, 1970; *radio:* Two Sons, 1957; It Looks Like Rain, 1959; Earwig (series), 1984; *television:* No Trams to Lime Street, 1959; After the Funeral, 1960; Lena, Oh My Lena, 1960, publ. as Three TV Plays, 1961; The Ruffians, 1960; The Ways of Love, 1961; Dare to be a Daniel, 1962, publ. in Eight Plays, Book 1, 1965; The Hard Knock, You Can't Wind 'em All, 1962; The Strain, Let's Imagine Series, The Stag, A Local Boy, 1963; The Other Fella, The Making of Jericho, 1966; The Wake, 1967, publ. in A Collection of Modern Short Plays, 1972; George's Room, 1967, publ. 1968; The Winner, The Loser, The Fantasist, Stella, Thief, 1967; Charlie, Gareth, Tennyson, Ah There You Are, Alexander, Minding the Shop, Time for the Funny Walk, 1968; Doreen, 1969, publ. in The Best Short Plays, 1971; The Ladies, Joan, Spare Time, Park People, You'll Be the Death of Me, Male of the Species, 1969; Hilda, And a Willow Tree, Just the Job, Female of the Species, Joy, 1970; Ruth, Funny, Pal, Giants and Ogres, The Piano Player, 1971; The Web, 1972; Ronnie Barker Show (3 scripts), Buttons, Flight, 1973; Lucky, Norma, 1974; Left, 1975; Forget Me Not (6 plays), 1976; The Look, 1978; Passing Through, publ. 1979; The Runner, 1980; Sealink, 1980; Lancaster Gate End, 1982; Cafe Society, 1982; Kish-Kisch, 1982; Colleagues, 1982; Soft Impeachment, 1983; Tiger (musical drama), 1984; (adap.) Lovers of the Lake, 1984 (Banff award, 1985); Widowers, 1985; Unexplained Laughter, 1989; (adap.) Come home Charlie, and face them, 1990. *Recreations:* languages, history. *Address:* c/o Felix de Wolfe, Manfield House, 376–378 The Strand, WC2R 0LB. *Club:* Chelsea Arts.
Died 6 Dec. 1994.

OWEN, John Simpson, OBE 1956; conservationist; *b* 31 Dec. 1912; *s* of late Ven. Walter Edwin Owen and Lucy Olive (*née* Walton); *m* 1946, May Patricia, *d* of late Francis Gilbert Burns and May (*née* Malone); three *d. Educ:* Christ's Hospital; Brasenose Coll., Oxford. Sudan Political Service, 1936–55; Director of National Parks, Tanzania, 1960–70, Asst to Director, 1971; Consultant on National Parks in Eastern and Central Africa, 1972–74; Woodrow Wilson Internat. Centre for Scholars, Washington, DC, 1973; Council of the Fauna Preservation

Soc., 1975–80. Founder Mem., Royal Tunbridge Wells Dept of Civic Virtue, 1985. Hon. DSc (Oxon) 1971; World Wildlife Fund Gold Medal, 1971; Special Freedom of Information Award, 1987. *Publications:* papers and articles on National Parks and African zoology. *Recreations:* implacably opposing the Channel Tunnel, walking, reading. *Address:* 5 Calverley Park Crescent, Tunbridge Wells TN1 2NB. *T:* Tunbridge Wells (01892) 29485. *Died 23 Feb. 1995.*

OWEN, Joslyn Grey, CBE 1979; Chief Education Officer, Devon, 1972–89; Visiting Professor, Polytechnic of the South-West, since 1989; *b* 23 Aug. 1928; *s* of W. R. Owen, (Bodwyn), and Nell Evans Owen; *m* 1961, Mary Patricia Brooks; three *s. Educ:* Cardiff High Sch.; Worcester Coll., Oxford (MA). Asst Master, Chigwell Sch., and King's Sch., Canterbury, 1952–58; Asst Educn Officer, Croydon, 1959–62, and Somerset, 1962–66; Jt Sec., Schs Council, 1966–68; Dep. Chief Educn Officer, Devon, 1968–72; Dep. Chief Exec., Devon CC, 1975–89. Adviser, ACC and Council of Local Educn Authorities, 1977–89. Pres., BAAS Educn Section, 1978–79; Chairman: Further Educn Unit, 1982–87; IBA Educnl Adv. Council, 1982–86; County Educn Officers' Soc., 1980–81; Member: Assessment of Perf. Unit Consultative Cttee, 1974–80; NFER Management Cttee, 1973–86; Council of Educnl Technol., 1972–82; Gulbenkian Working Party, Arts in the Curriculum, 1978–81; Macfarlane Working Party, 16–19 Educn, 1979–80; Educnl Research Board of SSRC, 1976–82; Nat. Adv. Bd for Local Auth. Higher Educn, 1982–88; Nat. Joint Council, Further Education, 1980–84; Cttee for Academic Policy, CNAA, 1981–84; Exec., Soc. of Educn Officers, 1987–89; Council of Management, United World Coll. of the Atlantic, 1988–; Bd of Dirs, Exeter and Devon Centre for the Arts, 1989–. Mem. Council, Univ. of Exeter, 1976–. Governor: The Open Sch., 1989–; Dartington Coll. of Arts, 1990–. FRSA 1977; Hon. FCP 1979; Hon. Fellow Plymouth Polytechnic, 1981. OStJ 1985. *Publications:* The Management of Curriculum Development, 1973; many chapters in edited works, papers and contribs to jls. *Address:* 4 The Quadrant, Exeter EX2 4LE. *Club:* Reform. *Died 19 Jan. 1992.*

OWEN, Rowland Hubert, CMG 1948; Deputy Controller, HM Stationery Office, 1959–64, retired; *b* 3 June 1903; *s* of William R. and Jessie M. Owen, Armagh, NI; *m* 1st, 1930, Kathleen Margaret Evaline Scott (*d* 1965); no *c*; 2nd, 1966, Shelagh Myrle Nicholson. *Educ:* Royal Sch., Armagh; Trinity Coll., Dublin (BA, LLB). Entered Dept of Overseas Trade, 1926; Private Secretary to Comptroller-General, 1930; Secretary Gorell Cttee on Art and Industry, 1931; idc, 1934; Commercial Secretary, Residency, Cairo, 1935; Ministry of Economic Warfare, 1939; Rep. of Ministry in Middle East, 1942; Director of Combined (Anglo-American) Economic Warfare Agencies, AFHQ Mediterranean, 1943; transferred to Board of Trade and appointed Senior UK Trade Commissioner in India, Burma and Ceylon, 1944; Economic Adviser to UK High Commissioner in India, 1946; Adviser to UK Delegation at International Trade Conf., Geneva, 1947; Comptroller-General, Export Credits Guarantee Dept, 1953–58; Member Managing Cttee, Union d'Assureurs des Crédits Internationaux, 1954–58. Staff, NPFA, 1964–68. Chm., Haslemere Br., British Heart Foundn Appeal. Vice-President, Tilford Bach Society, 1962–69; Organist: St Mary's, Bramshott, 1964–70; St John the Evangelist, Farncombe, 1970–75; St Luke's, Grayshott, 1975–87; Holy Trinity, Bramley, 1987–94; Pres., Surrey Organists' Assoc., 1976, Secretary, 1977–83. US Medal of Freedom. *Publications:* Economic Surveys of India, 1949 and 1952; Insurance Aspects of Children's Playground Management, 1966; Children's Recreation: Statutes and Constitutions,

1967; miscellaneous church music miniatures. *Recreations:* music, theatre, gardening. *Address:* Oak Tree Cottage, Holdfast Lane, Haslemere, Surrey GU27 2EU.
Died 25 Jan. 1995.

OWENS, Frank Arthur Robert, CBE 1971; Editor, Birmingham Evening Mail, 1956–74; Director, Birmingham Post & Mail Ltd, 1964–75; *b* 31 Dec. 1912; *s* of Arthur Oakes Owens; *m* 1st, 1936, Ruby Lilian Long; two *s*; 2nd, Olwen Evans, BSc; one *s* one *d. Educ:* Hereford Cathedral School. Served with RAF, 1940–46 (despatches). Member: Defence, Press and Broadcasting Cttee, 1964–75; Deptl Cttee on Official Secrets Act 1911, 1970–71; West Midlands Econ. Planning Council, 1975–77; Press Council, 1976–79. Pres., Guild of British Newspaper Editors, 1974–75. Hon. Mem., Mark Twain Soc. Hon. Mem., Barnt Green Fishing and Sailing Club. *Address:* 52 Albany Park Court, 3 Westwood Road, Southampton SO17 1LA.   *Died 26 June 1995.*

P

PADMORE, Rosalind, (Lady Padmore); *see* Culhane, R.

PAFFARD, Rear-Adm. Ronald Wilson, CB 1960; CBE 1943; *b* Ludlow, 14 Feb. 1904; 4th *s* of Murray Paffard and Fanny (*née* Wilson); *m* 1933, Nancy Brenda Malim; one *s* one *d. Educ:* Maidstone Grammar Sch. Paymaster Cadetship in RN, 1922; Paymaster Commander, 1940; Captain (S), 1951; Rear-Admiral, 1957. Secretary to Adm. of the Fleet Lord Tovey in all his Flag appointments, including those throughout the War of 1939–45; Supply Officer of HMS Vengeance, 1946–48; Portsmouth Division, Reserve Fleet, 1948–50; HMS Eagle, 1950–51; Asst Director-General, Supply and Secretarial Branch, 1952–54; Commanding Officer, HMS Ceres, 1954–56; Chief Staff Officer (Administration) on staff of Commander-in-Chief, Portsmouth, 1957–60, retired. *Recreations:* painting, golf. *Address:* 2 Little Green Orchard, Alverstoke, Hants PO12 2EY.

Died 11 Sept. 1994.

PAGE, Sir Alexander Warren, (Sir Alex), Kt 1977; MBE 1943; Chairman, PFC International Portfolio Fund Ltd, since 1985; *b* 1 July 1914; *s* of Sydney E. Page and Phyllis (*née* Spencer); *m* 1st, 1940, Anne Lewis Hickman (marr. diss.); two *s* one *d*; 2nd, 1981, Mrs Andrea Mary Wharton; two step *d. Educ:* Tonbridge; Clare Coll., Cambridge (MA). Served REME, with Guards Armoured Div., 1940–45, Lt-Col REME. Joined The Metal Box Co. Ltd, 1936; joined board as Sales Dir, 1957; Man. Dir 1966; Dep. Chm. 1969; Chief Exec., 1970–77; Chm., 1970–79. Director: J. Lyons & Co. Ltd, Feb.-Oct. 1978; C. Shippam Ltd, 1979–85; Chairman: Electrolux, 1978–82; G. T. Pension Services Ltd, 1981–85; Paine & Co. Ltd, 1981–87. Mem., IBA (formerly ITA), 1970–76; Mem., Food Science and Technology Bd, 1973–. Pres., BFMIRA, 1980. FIMechE; CBIM. Governor, Colfe's Grammar Sch., Lewisham, 1977–. *Recreations:* golf, tennis. *Address:* Beldhamland Farm, Skiff Lane, Wisborough Green, W Sussex RH14 0AJ. *T:* Wisborough Green (0403) 752567; 41 Rosaville Road, SW6. *Club:* Army and Navy.

Died 7 May 1993.

PAGE, Bertram Samuel, (Tony); University Librarian and Keeper of the Brotherton Collection, University of Leeds, 1947–69, Emeritus Librarian, since 1969; *b* 1 Sept. 1904; *s* of Samuel and Catherine Page; *m* 1933, Olga Ethel, *d* of E. W. Mason. *Educ:* King Charles I School, Kidderminster; University of Birmingham. BA 1924, MA 1926. Asst Librarian (later Sub-Librarian), Univ. of Birmingham, 1931–36; Librarian, King's College, Newcastle upon Tyne, 1936–47. Pres. Library Assoc., 1960 (Hon. Fellow, 1961); Chairman: Standing Conf. of Nat. and Univ. Libraries, 1961–63; Exec. Cttee, Nat. Central Library, 1962–72 (Trustee, 1963–75); Librarianship Bd, Council for Nat. Academic Awards, 1966–71. Mem. Court of Univ. of Birmingham, 1954–69. Hon. DUniv York, 1968. *Publications:* contrib. to Stephen MacKenna's trans. of Plotinus, vol. 5, 1930 (revised whole trans. for 2nd, 3rd, 4th edns, 1958, 1962, 1969); A Manual of University and College Library Practice (jt ed.), 1940; articles and reviews in classical and library jls. *Address:* 24 St Anne's Road, Headington, Oxford OX3 8NL. *T:* Oxford (0865) 65981.

Died 13 Oct. 1993.

PAGE, Brig. (Edwin) Kenneth, CBE 1951 (OBE 1946); DSO 1945; MC 1918; *b* 23 Jan. 1898; *s* of G. E. Page,

Baldock, Herts; *m* 1921, Kate Mildred (*d* 1975), *d* of G. H. Arthur, Yorkshire, Barbados, BWI; two *s*; *m* 1987, Joan, *d* of W. H. Goodall and widow of Bryan Rose. *Educ:* Haileybury College; RMA, Woolwich. 2nd Lt, RFA, 1916; BEF, France, 1916–18; Adjt TA, 1924–27; Staff College, Camberley, 1928–29; Staff Captain, India, 1931–35; GSO2, War Office, 1936–39; Lt-Col, 1939; served War of 1939–45: BEF, France, 1940; Col, 1945; Brig., 1946; Dep. Director, WO, 1946–48; Commander, Caribbean Area, 1948–51; employed War Office, 1951; retired pay, 1952. CC 1961–74, CA 1968–74, Dorset. *Address:* Durrant End, Durrant, Sturminster Newton, Dorset DT10 1DQ. *T:* Sturminster Newton (01258) 473146. *Club:* Army and Navy.

Died 26 Jan. 1995.

PAGE, Tony; *see* Page, B. S.

PAGET, Sir John (Starr), 3rd Bt *cr* 1886, of Cranmore Hall, Co. Somerset; CEng, FIMechE; Director, Somerset Fruit Machinery Ltd, since 1986; Proprietor, Sir John Paget Woodworker; Senior Partner, Haygrass Cider Orchards; *b* 24 Nov. 1914; *s* of Sir Richard Paget, 2nd Bt and 1st wife, Lady Muriel Paget, CBE (*d* 1938), *o d* of 12th Earl of Winchilsea; *S* father 1955; *m* 1944, Nancy Mary Parish, JP, *d* of late Lieutenant-Colonel Francis Parish, DSO, MC; two *s* five *d. Educ:* Oundle; Château D'Oex; Trinity College, Cambridge (MA). Joined English Electric Co. Ltd, 1936; Asst Works Supt, English Electric, Preston, 1941; joined D. Napier & Son Ltd, 1943; Assistant Manager, D. Napier & Son Ltd, Liverpool, 1945; Manager, D. Napier & Son Ltd, London Group, 1946; Dir and Gen. Man. D. Napier & Son Ltd, 1959–61; Works Director, Napier Aero Engines, 1961–62. Director: Thermal Syndicate Ltd, Wallsend, 1939–84 (Chm., 1973–80; Chm. Emeritus, 1980–84); Glacier Metal Group, 1963–65; Hilger & Watts, 1965–68; Rank Precision Industries Ltd, 1968–70. Hon. DTech Brunel, 1976. Silver Medal, Instn of Production Engineers, 1950. *Recreations:* music, cooking. *Heir: s* Richard Herbert Paget [*b* 17 February 1957; *m* 1985, Richenda, *d* of Rev. J. T. C. B. Collins; three *d*]. *Address:* Haygrass House, Taunton, Somerset TA3 7BS. *T:* Taunton (0823) 331779. *Club:* Athenæum.

Died 7 Feb. 1992.

PAINE, George, CB 1974; DFC 1944; *b* 14 April 1918; 3rd *s* of late Jack Paine and Helen Margaret (*née* Hadow), East Sutton; *m* 1969, Hilary (*née* Garrod), widow of Dr A. C. Frazer. *Educ:* Bradfield Coll.; Peterhouse, Cambridge. External Ballistics Dept, Ordnance Bd, 1941; RAF, 1942–46; Min. of Agriculture, 1948; Inland Revenue, 1949; Central Statistical Office, 1954; Board of Trade, 1957; Dir of Statistics and Intelligence, Bd of Inland Revenue, 1957–72; Dir, OPCS and Registrar Gen. for Eng. and Wales, 1972–78. Hon. Treasurer, Royal Statistical Soc., 1974–78. *Recreations:* fruit growing, beekeeping. *Address:* Springfield House, Broad Town, near Swindon, Wilts SN4 7RU. *T:* Swindon (0793) 731377.

Died 2 March 1992.

PAINE, Thomas Otten; Chairman, Thomas Paine Associates, Los Angeles, since 1982; *b* 9 Nov. 1921; *s* of George Thomas Paine, Cdre, USN retd and Ada Louise Otten; *m* 1946, Barbara Helen Taunton Pearse; two *s* two *d. Educ:* Maury High, Norfolk, Va; Brown Univ.; Stanford Univ. Served War of 1939–45 (US Navy Commendation

Ribbon 1944; Submarine Combat Award with two stars, 1943–45). Research Associate: Stanford Univ., 1947–49; General Electric Res. Lab., Schenectady, 1949–50; Manager, TEMPO, GE Center for Advanced Studies, Santa Barbara, 1963–67; Dep. Administrator, US Nat. Aeronautics and Space Admin, Washington, 1968, Administrator 1968–70; Group Executive, GEC, Power Generation Group, 1970–73, Sen. Vice-Pres., GEC, 1974–76; Pres. and Chief Operating Officer, Northrop Corp., 1976–82. Member, Board of Directors: Eastern Air Lines, 1981–86; Quotron Systems, Inc., 1982–; RCA, 1982–86; NBC, 1982–86; Director: Arthur D. Little Inc., 1982–85; NIKE Inc., 1982–; Orbital Sciences Corp., 1987–. Chairman: Pacific Forum, 1980–86; US National Commn on Space, 1985–86. MInstMet; Member: Newcomen Soc.; Nat. Acad. of Engineering; Acad. of Sciences, NY; Sigma Xi; Trustee: Occidental Coll.; Brown Univ.; Asian Inst. Tech. Hon. Dr of Science: Brown, 1969; Clarkson Coll. of Tech., 1969; Nebraska Wesleyan, 1970; New Brunswick, 1970; Oklahoma City, 1970; Hon. Dr Engrg: Worcester Polytechnic Inst., 1970; Cheng Kung Univ., 1978. Harvey Mudd Coll. Outstanding Contribution to Industrial Science Award, AAS, 1956; NASA DSM, 1970; Washington Award, Western Soc. of Engrs, 1972; John Fritz Medal, United Engrg Soc., 1976; Faraday Medal, IEE, 1976; NASA Distinguished Public Service Award, 1987; Konstantin Tsiolkovsky Award, USSR, 1987; John F. Kennedy Astronautics Award, Amer. Astronautical Soc., 1987; Assoc. of Space Explorers Award, 1988. Grand Ufficiale della Ordine Al Merito della Repubblica Italiana, 1972. *Publications:* various technical papers and patents. *Recreations:* sailing, beachcombing, skin diving, photography, book collecting, oil painting. *Address:* (office) Thomas Paine Associates, Suite 178, 2401 Colorado Avenue, Santa Monica, Calif 90404, USA; (home) 1275 Las Alturas, Santa Barbara, Calif 93103, USA. *Clubs:* Sky, Lotos, Explorers (New York); Army and Navy, Space, Cosmos (Washington); California, Regency (Los Angeles).

Died 4 May 1992.

PALING, William Thomas; *b* Marehay, Derbys, 28 Oct. 1892; *s* of George Thomas Paling, Sutton-in-Ashfield, Notts; *m* 1919, Gladys Nellie, MBE (decd), *d* of William Frith, James Street, Nuncar Gate, Nottinghamshire; one *s* one *d. Educ:* Central Labour Coll., London (schol.). Former miner and colliery checkweighman. Mem., WR Yorks CC, 1928–45. Contested (Lab) Burton-on-Trent, 1929, 1931. MP (Lab) Dewsbury, 1945–59, retired.

Died 10 April 1992.

PALMER, Arthur Montague Frank, CEng, FIEE, FInstE; *b* 4 Aug. 1912; *s* of late Frank Palmer, Northam, Devon; *m* 1939, Dr Marion Ethel Frances Woollaston, medical consultant; two *d. Educ:* Ashford Gram. Sch.; Brunel Technical College (later Brunel Univ.). Chartered Engineer and Chartered Fuel Technologist. Studied electrical supply engineering, 1932–35, in London; Member technical staff of London Power Co., 1936–45; former Staff Mem., Electrical Power Engineers Assoc. Member Brentford and Chiswick Town Council, 1937–45. MP (Lab) for Wimbledon, 1945–50; MP (Lab and Co-op): Cleveland Div. of Yorks, Oct. 1952–Sept. 1959; Bristol Central, 1964–74; Bristol NE, 1974–83; Frontbench Opposition Spokesman on fuel and power, 1957–59; Chairman: Parly and Scientific Cttee, 1965–68; House of Commons Select Cttee on Science and Technology, 1966–70, 1974–79; Co-operative Parly Gp, 1970–73; Vice-Chm., Select Cttee on Energy, 1979–83. Defence Medal, 1946; Coronation Medal, 1953. *Publications:* The Future of Electricity Supply, 1943; Modern Norway, 1950; Law and the Power Engineer, 1959; Nuclear Power: the reason why, 1984; Energy Policy in the Community, 1985; articles on political, industrial, and economic subjects.

Recreations: walking, motoring, gardening, reading novels, history, politics. *Address:* Manton Thatch, Manton, Marlborough, Wilts SN8 4HR. *T:* Marlborough (0672) 513313. *Club:* Athenæum. *Died 14 Aug. 1994.*

PALMER, Leslie Robert, CBE 1964; Director-General, Defence Accounts, Ministry of Defence, 1969–72; *b* 21 Aug. 1910; *s* of Robert Palmer; *m* 1937, Mary Crick; two *s* one *d. Educ:* Battersea Grammar School; London University. Entered Admiralty Service, 1929; Assistant Dir of Victualling, 1941; Dep. Dir of Victualling, 1954; Dir of Victualling, Admiralty, 1959–61; Principal Dir of Accounts, Admiralty, 1961–64; Principal Dir of Accounts (Navy) MoD, 1964–68. Hon. Treasurer and Chm., Finance and Admin Dept, United Reformed Church, 1973–79; Hon. Treasurer, BCC, 1980–82. *Recreation:* music. *Address:* 3 Trossachs Drive, Bath BA2 6RP. *T:* Bath (0225) 461981. *Died 11 Dec. 1992.*

PALMER, Maj.-Gen. Philip Francis, CB 1957; OBE 1945; Major-General late Royal Army Medical Corps; *b* 8 Aug. 1903. MB, BCh, BAO, Dublin, 1926; DPH 1936. Served North West Frontier of India, 1930–31 (medal and clasp); Adjutant Territorial Army, 1932–36; War of 1939–45 (OBE); Director of Medical Services, Middle East Land Forces, Dec. 1955; QHS, 1956–60, retired. Col Comdt, RAMC, 1963–67. *Address:* c/o Royal Bank of Scotland, Whitehall, SW1. *Died 7 Feb. 1992.*

PALMER, William John, CBE 1973; Judge of Her Majesty's Chief Court for the Persian Gulf, 1967–72; Member, Court of Appeal for Anguilla, 1973–81; *b* 25 April 1909; *o s* of late William Palmer and Mary Louisa Palmer (*née* Dibb), Suffolk House, Cheltenham; *m* 1st, 1935, Zenaida Nicolaevna (*d* 1944), *d* of late Nicolai Maropoulo, Yalta, Russia; 2nd, 1949, Vanda Ianthe Millicent, *d* of late William Matthew Cowton, Kelvin Grove, Queensland; one *s* two *d. Educ:* Pate's Grammar School, Cheltenham; Christ's College, Cambridge (Lady Margaret Scholar). Barrister, Gray's Inn. Joined Indian Civil Service, 1932; Deputy Commissioner, Jalpaiguri, 1943, Chief Presidency Magistrate, Calcutta, 1945; retired from ICS, 1949; joined Colonial Legal Service as Magistrate, Nigeria, 1950; Chief Registrar, High Court, Eastern Region, 1956; Judge, 1958; Acting Chief Justice of Eastern Nigeria, Oct.-Dec. 1963 and Aug.-Nov. 1965; Judge of HM's Court for Bahrain and Assistant Judge of the Chief Court for the Persian Gulf, 1965–67. A part-time Chm. of Industrial Tribunals, 1975–78. *Recreations:* travel, history. *Address:* Guys Farm, Icomb, Glos GL54 1JD. *T:* Cotswold (0451) 30219. *Clubs:* East India, Commonwealth Trust. *Died 30 March 1993.*

PANT, Apasaheb Balasaheb; Padma Shri 1954; retired 1975; *b* 11 Sept. 1912; *s* of Balasaheb Pandit Pant Pratinidhi, Raja of Aundh, and Mainabai Pant Pratinidhi; *m* 1942, Nalini Pant, MB, BS, FRCS; one *s* two *d. Educ:* Univ. of Bombay (BA); Univ. of Oxford (MA). Barrister-at-Law, Lincoln's Inn. Educn Minister, Aundh State; Prime Minister, 1944–48 (when State was merged into Bombay State). Member, AICC, 1948; as alternate Deleg., of India, at UN, 1951 and 1952; Comr for Govt of India in Brit. E Africa, 1948–54; apptd Consul-Gen. for Belgian Congo and Ruanda-Urundi, Nov. 1950, and Comr for Central Africa and Nyasaland, Dec. 1950; Officer on Special Duty, Min. of Ext. Affairs, 1954–55; Polit. Officer in Sikkim and Bhutan with control over Indian Missions in Tibet, 1955–61; Ambassador of India: to Indonesia, Oct. 1961–June 1964; to Norway, 1964–66; to UAR, 1966–69; High Comr in London, 1969–72; Ambassador to Italy, 1972–75. Dr of Laws *hc* Univ. of Syracuse, NY, 1988. *Publications:* Tensions and Tolerance, 1965; Aggression and Violence: Gandhian experiments to fight them, 1968; Yoga, 1968 (Arabic, Italian, German, Danish, Norwegian and Marathi edns); Surya Namaskar, 1969,

2nd edn 1987 (Marathi, Italian, German, Danish, Norwegian, Swahili edns; 3rd edn, as A Yogic Exercise, 1988); Mahatma Gandhi; A Moment in Time, 1973; Mandala, An Awakening, 1976; Progress, Power, Peace and India, 1978; Survival of the Individual, 1981; Un-Diplomatic Incidents, 1985; Story of the Pants: an extended family and fellow pilgrims, 1985; Energy: Intelligence: Love, 1986; An Unusual Raja and the Mahatma, 1987; A Tale of Two Houses, 1990. *Recreations:* photography, yoga, tennis, ski-ing, gliding. *Address:* Natesh, 211 Road No 2, Sindh Society, Aundh, Poona 411 007, India. *T:* 345115.								*Died 5 Oct. 1992.*

PANUFNIK, Sir Andrzej, Kt 1991; composer and conductor; *b* 24 Sept. 1914; 2nd *s* of Tomasz Panufnik and Mathilda Thonnes Panufnik; naturalized British subject, 1961; *m* 1st, 1951, Marie Elizabeth O'Mahoney (marr. diss. 1958); (one *d* decd); 2nd, 1963, Camilla Ruth Jessel, FRPS, *yr d* of late Commander R. F. Jessel, DSO, OBE, DSC, RN; one *s* one *d. Educ:* Warsaw State Conservatoire; Vienna State Acad. for Music (under Professor Felix von Weingartner). Diploma with distinction, Warsaw Conservatoire, 1936. Conductor of the Cracow Philharmonic, 1945–46; Director and Conductor of the Warsaw Philharmonic Orchestra, 1946–47; conducting leading European orchestras such as L'Orchestre National, Paris, Berliner Philharmonisches Orchester, L'Orchestre de la Suisse Romande, Geneva, and all principal British orchestras, 1947–; left Poland and settled in England, 1954; Vice-Chairman of International Music Council of UNESCO, Paris, 1950–53; Musical Director and Conductor, City of Birmingham Symphony Orchestra, 1957–59. Hon. Member of International Mark Twain Society (USA), 1954; Knight of Mark Twain, 1966; Hon. RAM 1984. DPhil *hc* Polish Univ. in Exile, London, 1985. The Sibelius Centenary Medal, 1965; Prix de composition musical Prince Pierre de Monaco, 1983. Polish decorations: Standard of Labor 1st class (1949), twice State Laureate (1951, 1952). *Ballets:* Elegy, NY, 1967; Cain and Abel, Berlin, 1968; Miss Julie, Stuttgart, 1970; Homage to Chopin (SWRB), 1980; Adieu (Royal Ballet), 1980; Polonia (SWRB), 1980; Dances of the Golden Hall (Martha Graham), NY, 1982; Sinfonia Mistica (NY City Ballet), 1987. *Compositions:* Piano Trio, 1934; Five Polish Peasant Songs, 1940; Tragic Overture, 1942; Twelve Miniature Studies for piano, 1947; Nocturne for orchestra, 1947; Lullaby for 29 stringed instruments and 2 harps, 1947; Sinfonia Rustica, 1948; Hommage à Chopin—Five vocalises for soprano and piano, 1949; Old Polish Suite for strings, 1950; Concerto in modo antico, 1951; Heroic Overture, 1952; Rhapsody for orchestra, 1956; Sinfonia Elegiaca, 1957; Polonia—Suite for Orchestra, 1959; Piano Concerto, 1961; Autumn Music, 1962; Landscape, 1962; Two Lyric Pieces, 1963; Sinfonia Sacra, 1963 (first prize, Prix de Composition Musicale, Prince Rainier III de Monaco, 1963); Song to the Virgin Mary, 1964; Katyn Epitaph, 1966; Jagiellonian Triptych, 1966; Reflections for piano, 1967; The Universal Prayer, 1969; Thames Pageant, 1969; Violin Concerto, 1971; Triangles, 1972; Winter Solstice, 1972; Sinfonia Concertante, 1973; Sinfonia di Sfere, 1974; String Quartet No 1, 1976, No 2, 1980, No 3, 1990; Dreamscape, 1976; Sinfonia Mistica, 1977; Metasinfonia, 1978; Concerto Festivo, 1979; Concertino, 1980; Sinfonia Votiva, 1981; A Procession for Peace, 1982; Arbor Cosmica, 1984; Pentasonata, 1985; Bassoon Concerto, 1985; Symphony No 9, 1986; String Sextet, 1987; Symphony No 10, 1988; Harmony, 1989; String Quartet No 3, 1990. *Publication:* Composing Myself (autobiog.), 1987. *Address:* Riverside House, Twickenham, Middlesex TW1 3DJ. *T:* 081–892 1470. *Club:* Garrick.						*Died 27 Oct. 1991.*

PAO, Sir Yue-Kong, Kt 1978; CBE 1976; JP; LLD; Chairman of Supervisory Board, World-Wide Shipping

Group, since 1974; Group Deputy Chairman, Standard Chartered Bank, 1986–88; *b* Chekiang, China, 10 Nov. 1918; *s* of late Sui-Loong Pao and Chung Sau-Gin Pao; *m* 1940, Sue-Ing Haung; four *d. Educ:* Shanghai, China. Banking career in China until went to Hong Kong, 1949; engaged in import and export trade; shipowner, 1955–. Dep. Chm., Hongkong & Shanghai Banking Corp., 1980–84; Adviser, Indust. Bank of Japan. Member: Adv. Council, Nippon Kaiji Kyokai of Japan; (Life), Court of Univ. of Hong Kong; Rockefeller Univ. Council, New York; Hon. Mem., INTERTANKO. Hon. Vice-Pres., Maritime Trust. Overseas Hon. Trustee, Westminster Abbey Trust. Trustee, Hong Kong Arts Centre. Hon. LLD: Univ. of Hong Kong, 1975; Chinese Univ. of Hong Kong, 1977. JP Hong Kong, 1971. Commander: National Order of Cruzeiro do Sul, Brazil, 1977; Order of the Crown, Belgium, 1982; Order of Vasquo Nunez de Balboa, Panama, 1982. *Recreations:* swimming, golf. *Address:* World-Wide Shipping Agency Ltd, Wheelock House, 6/F, 20 Pedder Street, Hong Kong. *T:* 5–8423888. *Clubs:* Royal Automobile; Woking Golf (Surrey); Royal and Ancient Golf (St Andrews, Fife); Sunningdale Golf (Berks).							*Died 23 Sept. 1991.*

PAPE, (Jonathan) Hector (Carruthers), OBE 1980; advocate; Chief General Manager, National Dock Labour Board, 1975–82 (General Manager and Secretary, 1970–75); *b* 8 March 1918; *er s* of Jonathan Pape, MA and Florence Muriel Myrtle; *m* 1st, 1944, Mary Sullins (*née* Jeffries) (*d* 1985); one *s*; 2nd, 1987, Yvonne (*née* Bartlett). *Educ:* Merchant Taylors' Sch., Crosby. Mercantile Marine, 1934–46; Master Mariner (FG), 1944 (Liverpool Qualif.). Manager, Master Stevedoring Co., Liverpool, 1947–51; National Dock Labour Board: Dep. Port Manager, London, 1952–57; Asst Gen. Manager, Bd HQ, 1957–69; Dep. Gen. Manager and Secretary, Bd HQ, 1969. Mem., Honourable Co. of Master Mariners, 1965. Freeman, City of London. *Address:* 65 Albany Court, Robertson Terrace, Hastings, East Sussex TN34 1JH.

Died 19 March 1993.

PARE, Rev. Philip Norris; *b* 13 May 1910; *s* of Frederick William and Florence May Pare; *m* 1943, Nancy Eileen, *d* of late Canon C. Patteson; two *s* two *d. Educ:* Nottingham High Sch.; King's Coll., Cambridge; Cuddesdon Theological Coll. Deacon, 1934; priest, 1935; Curate, All Saints, W Dulwich, 1934–37; Chaplain and Vice-Principal, Bishops Coll., Cheshunt, 1937–39; Curate, St Mary the Less, Cambridge, 1939–40; Chaplain RNVR, 1940–46; Vicar of Cheshunt, Herts, 1946–57; Rural Dean of Ware, 1949–56; Examining Chaplain to Bishop of St Albans, 1952–56; Missioner Canon Stipendiary, Diocese of Wakefield, 1957–62; Diocesan Adviser for Christian Stewardship, 1959–68; Provost, and Vicar of Cathedral Church of All Saints, Wakefield, 1962–71; Vicar of Cholsey, dio. Oxford, 1973–82. A Church Commissioner, 1968–71; Member Board of Ecclesiastical Insurance Office, 1966–83; Provost of Woodard Schools (Northern Div.), 1977–82; Trustee, Ely Stained Glass Museum, 1980–87. *Publications:* Eric Milner-White, A Memoir (with Donald Harris), 1965; Re-Thinking Our Worship, 1967; God Made the Devil?: a ministry of healing, 1985; articles in Theology, The Reader, etc. *Recreations:* modern stained glass and architecture, railways, motor cars, church music. *Address:* 73 Oakland Drive, Ledbury, Herefordshire HR8 2EX. *T:* Ledbury (0531) 3619.

Died 20 April 1992.

PARES, Peter; *b* 6 Sept. 1908; 2nd *s* of late Sir Bernard Pares, KBE, DCL, and Margaret Pares (*née* Dixon); unmarried. *Educ:* Lancing Coll.; Jesus Coll., Cambridge (Scholar). Entered Consular Service, 1930; served in Philadelphia, 1930; Havana, 1932; Consul, Liberec and Bratislava, Czechoslovakia, 1936–39; Budapest, 1939;

Cluj, Rumania, 1940; New York, 1941; Washington, as First Secretary, 1944; Control Commission for Germany, 1946; Foreign Office, 1949; Casablanca, 1952; Strasbourg, 1956; Deputy Consul-General, Frankfurt, 1957; Consul-General, Asmara, Eritrea, 1957–59; Head of Education and Cultural Relations Dept, CRO, 1960–63. *Address:* 3 Ashburnham Gardens, Eastbourne, East Sussex BN21 2NA.   *Died 20 April 1992.*

PARGETER, Edith Mary, OBE 1994; BEM 1944; *b* 28 Sept. 1913; 3rd *c* of Edmund Valentine Pargeter and Edith Hordley; unmarried. *Educ:* Dawley C of E Elementary Sch.; County High School for Girls, Coalbrookdale. Worked as a chemist's assistant, and at twenty succeeded in finding a publisher for first-and unsuccessful-book. WRNS Aug. 1940, teleprinter operator (BEM 1944); dispersed from the Service, Aug. 1945. FIIAL 1962. MA Birmingham, 1994. Gold Medal and Ribbon, Czechoslovak Society for International Relations, 1968. *Publications:* Hortensius, Friend of Nero, Iron Bound, 1936; The City Lies Foursquare, 1939; Ordinary People, 1941; She Goes to War, 1942; The Eighth Champion of Christendom, 1945; Reluctant Odyssey, 1946; Warfare Accomplished, 1947; By Firelight, 1948; The Fair Young Phoenix, 1948; The Coast of Bohemia, 1949; Lost Children, 1950; Fallen Into the Pit, 1951; Holiday with Violence, 1952; This Rough Magic, 1953; Most Loving Mere Folly, 1953; The Soldier at the Door, 1954; A Means of Grace, 1956; Tales of the Little Quarter (trans. from the Czech of Jan Neruda), 1957; Don Juan (trans. from the Czech of Josef Toman), 1958; Assize of the Dying, 1958; The Heaven Tree, 1960; The Green Branch 1962; The Scarlet Seed, 1963; The Terezín Requiem (trans. from the Czech of Josef Bor), 1963; The Lily Hand and other stories, 1965; Close Watch on the Trains (trans from the Czech of Bohumil Hrabal), 1968; Report on my Husband (trans. from the Czech of Josefa Slánská), 1969; A Bloody Field by Shrewsbury, 1972; Sunrise in the West, 1974; The Dragon at Noonday, 1975; The Hounds of Sunset, 1976; Afterglow and Nightfall, 1977; The Marriage of Meggotta, 1979; *as Ellis Peters:* many crime and mystery novels including: Monk's-hood, 1980 (Silver Dagger, Crime Writers Assoc.); Saint Peter's Fair, 1981; The Leper of Saint Giles, 1981; The Virgin in the Ice, 1982; The Sanctuary Sparrow, 1982; The Devil's Novice, 1983; Dead Man's Ransom, 1984; The Pilgrim of Hate, 1984; An Excellent Mystery, 1985; The Raven in the Foregate, 1986; The Rose Rent, 1986; The Hermit of Eyton Forest, 1987; The Confession of Brother Haluin, 1988; The Heretic's Apprentice, 1989; The Potter's Field, 1989; The Summer of the Danes, 1991; The Holy Thief, 1992; Brother Cadfael's Penance, 1994; (with Roy Morgan), non-fiction: Shropshire, 1992; Strongholds and Sanctuaries, 1993. *Recreations:* collecting gramophone records, particularly of voice; reading anything and everything; theatre. *Address:* Troya, 3 Lee Dingle, Madeley, Telford, Salop TF7 5TW. *T:* Telford (01952) 585178.   *Died 15 Oct. 1995.*

PARHAM, Adm. Sir Frederick Robertson, GBE 1959 (CBE 1949); KCB 1955 (CB 1951); DSO 1944; *b* 9 Jan. 1901; *s* of late Frederick James Parham, Bath, and Jessie Esther Brooks Parham (*née* Robertson), Cheltenham; *m* 1st, 1926, Kathleen Dobrée (*d* 1973), *d* of Eugene Edward Carey, Guernsey; one *s*; 2nd, 1978, Mrs Joan Saunders (*née* Charig). *Educ:* RN Colleges, Osborne and Dartmouth. Joined HMS Malaya as Midshipman, 1917; specialised in gunnery, 1925; Commander, 1934; commanded HMS Shikari, 1937, HMS Gurkha, 1938–40; Captain, 1939; commanded HMS Belfast, 1942–44 (despatches), HMS Vanguard, 1947–49; Dep. Chief, Naval Personnel, 1949–51; Rear-Admiral, 1949; Vice-Admiral, 1952; Flag Officer (Flotillas) and 2nd in command, Mediterranean, 1951–52; a Lord Commissioner of the Admiralty, Fourth

Sea Lord and Chief of Supplies and Transport, 1954–55; Commander-in-Chief, The Nore, 1955–58; retired list, 1959. Member British Waterways Board, Jan. 1963–1967, Vice-Chairman (part-time) Aug. 1963–1967. Naval ADC to the King, 1949. Grand Cross of Military Order of Avis (Portugal), 1955; Order of Al Rafidain (Class II, Mil., conferred by the King of Iraq), 1956; Ordine al merito della Repubblica, Grande Ufficiale (Italy), 1958.
                                                    Died 20 March 1991.

PARK, George Maclean; *b* 27 Sept. 1914; *s* of James McKenzie Park and Mary Gorman Park; *m* 1941, Joyce, *d* of Robert Holt Stead and Gertrude Stead; one *d*. *Educ:* Onslow Drive Sch., Glasgow; Coventry Techn. College. Sen. AEU Shop Steward, Chrysler UK Ltd, Ryton, 1968–73. Coventry City Councillor, 1961–74; Coventry District Councillor, 1973–74; Leader of Council Labour Gp, 1967–74; Leader, Coventry City and District Councils, 1972–74; Chm. Policy Adv. Cttee, 1972–74; Mem., W Mids Metropolitan CC, 1973–77; Chm. Coventry and District Disablement Adv. Cttee, 1960–74. MP (Lab) Coventry North East, Feb. 1974–1987. PPS to Dr J. Gilbert, Minister for Transport, 1975–76; PPS to E. Varley, Sec. of State for Industry, 1976–79. Chm., W Midland Regional Council of the Labour Party, 1983–84. Chairman: Coventry Mental Health Assoc. (MIND), 1987–88; Coventry CHC, 1990– (Mem., 1987–; Vice-Chm., 1989–90). Chm. Belgrade Theatre Trust, 1972–74. JP Coventry, 1961–84. AEU Award of Merit, 1967. *Recreations:* reading, walking. *Address:* 170 Binley Road, Coventry CV3 1HG. *T:* Coventry (0203) 458589.
                                                    Died 8 May 1994.

PARK, Trevor; Lecturer in Industrial Relations, 1972–83 and Senior Fellow, 1983–86, Department of Adult Education and Extramural Studies, University of Leeds; *b* 12 Dec. 1927; *s* of late Stephen Clifford Park and Annie Park (*née* Jackson); *m* 1953, Barbara Black; no *c*. *Educ:* Bury Grammar Sch.; Manchester Univ. (MA). History Master, Bacup and Rawtenstall Grammar Sch., 1949–56; WEA Tutor and Organiser (NW District), 1956–60; Lecturer, Extramural Dept, Univ. of Sheffield (politics and internat. relations), 1960–64; WEA Tutor and Organiser, Manchester, 1970–72. Parliamentary Labour Candidate: Altrincham and Sale, General Election, 1955; Darwen, General Election, 1959; MP (Lab) South East Derbyshire, 1964–70. Member: Select Cttees on Nationalised Industries, 1966–68, and on Education and Science, 1968–70; Yorkshire and Humberside Economic Planning Council, 1977–79. Mem. (Lab) Leeds CC, 1979–86 (Chairman: Mun. Services Cttee, 1980–83; Planning and Develt Cttee, 1983–86). Chm. ATAE, 1972–75. *Recreation:* walking.   *Died 6 April 1995.*

PARKER, Sir Karl (Theodore), Kt 1960; CBE 1954; MA, PhD; FBA 1950; Hon. Antiquary to the Royal Academy, 1963; Hon. Fellow, Oriel College, Oxford; Trustee, National Gallery, 1962–69; Keeper of the Ashmolean Museum, Oxford, 1945–62 (retired); Keeper of the Department of Fine Art, Ashmolean Museum, and of the Hope Collection of Engraved Portraits, 1934–62; *b* 1895; *s* of late R. W. Parker, FRCS, and Marie Luling; *m* Audrey (*d* 1976), *d* of late Henry Ashworth James, Hurstmonceux Place; two *d. Educ:* Bedford; Paris; Zürich. Studied art at most continental centres and at the British Museum; edited Old Master Drawings, a Quarterly Magazine for Students and Collectors, since its inception, 1926; late Asst Keeper, Dept of Prints and Drawings, British Museum. Hon. DLitt Oxon, 1972. *Publications:* North Italian Drawings of the Quattrocento; Drawings of the Early German Schools; Alsatian Drawings of the XV and XVI Centuries; Drawings of Antoine Watteau; Catalogue of Drawings in the Ashmolean Museum, Vol. I, 1938, Vol. II, 1956; Catalogue of Holbein's Drawings at Windsor Castle, 1945; The

Drawings of Antonio Canaletto at Windsor Castle, 1948; Antoine Watteau: Catalogue Complet de son œuvre Dessiné, Vol. I (with J. Mathey), 1957, Vol. II, 1958; and articles, mostly on Old Master drawings, in various English and continental periodicals. *Address:* 4 Saffrons Court, Compton Place Road, Eastbourne, E Sussex BN21 1DX. *Died 22 July 1992.*

PARKER, Kenneth Alfred Lamport, CB 1959; Receiver for the Metropolitan Police District, 1967–74; *b* 1 April 1912; *e s* of A. E. A. and Ada Mary Parker; *m* 1938, Freda Silcock (OBE 1975); one *s* one *d. Educ:* Tottenham Grammar Sch.; St John's College, Cambridge (Scholar; MA 1937). Home Office, 1934; London Civil Defence Region, 1938–45; (Assistant Secretary, 1942, Deputy Chief Administrative Officer, 1943); Assistant Under-Secretary of State, Home Office, 1955–67 (Head of Police Dept, 1961–66). Imperial Defence College, 1947. Mem., Chairman's Panel, CS Selection Bd, 1974–82. *Publications:* articles on police matters. *Recreations:* garden, cellar, library. *Address:* 18 Lichfield Road, Kew, Surrey TW9 3JR. *T:* 0181–940 4595. *Club:* United Oxford & Cambridge University. *Died 11 Sept. 1995.*

PARKER, Dame Marjorie Alice Collett, DBE 1977; welfare worker, Tasmania; Deputy-Chairman, Australian National Council of Women, 1960–64 (Life Member, 1974); *b* Ballarat; *d* of W. Shoppee, Ballarat, Vic; *m* 1926, Max Parker; one *s. Educ:* Ballarat State Sch. Announcer and Dir Women's Interests, Radio Launceston, 1941–69; Public Relations Adviser for Girl Guide Assoc., 1954–68; Pres. and Org., Red Cross Meals on Wheels, Launceston, Tas, 1961–71; State Exec. and Public Relations Officer, Good Neighbour Council, Tas, 1964–70; N Regional Pres., Aust. Red Cross Soc., Tas. Div., 1965–68; Pres., Victoria League, Launceston, 1966–69; Exec. Mem., Soc. for Care of Crippled Children (Life Mem. 1973). Past Pres., N Tas. Branch, Royal Commonwealth Soc. Vice-Pres., United Nations Assoc., Launceston, 1964–68. Freeman, City of Launceston, 1985. *Recreation:* gardening. *Address:* Aldersgate Nursing Home, 16 Hobart Road, King's Meadows, Launceston, Tasmania 7250, Australia. *Clubs:* Soroptomist (Pres. 1951), Royal Commonwealth Soc. (Launceston, Tas). *Died 18 March 1991.*

PARKER, Rev. Reginald Boden; *b* Wallasey, Cheshire, 4 June 1901; *s* of Joseph William and Ada Parker. *Educ:* Wallasey Grammar School; St Catherine's College, Oxford University; Ripon Hall, Oxford. BSc (London), 1923; MA (Oxon), 1938. Assistant Master, Ashton Gram. Sch., Lancs, 1925–30; Asst Master, Newton Gram. Sch., Lancs, 1930–32; deacon, 1935; priest, 1936; Curate, Childwall, Liverpool, 1935–37; Curate, St Margaret's, Westminster, 1937–39; Asst Master and Chaplain, Oundle School, 1940–48; Headmaster, Igbobi College, Lagos, 1948–58; Bishop's Chaplain in Liverpool University, 1958–61; Residentiary Canon, Liverpool Cathedral, 1958–61; Precentor, Liverpool Cathedral, 1959–61; Asst Master, Wellington Coll., 1961–64; Rector of Bentham, dio. of Bradford, 1964–72. Hon. Lecturer in Hellenistic Greek, Liverpool University, 1959; Select Preacher, Oxford University, 1960. Member of Headmasters' Conference, 1950. *Publications:* (with J. P. Hodges): The Master and the Disciple, 1938; The King and the Kingdom, 1939; The Holy Spirit and The Kingdom, 1941. *Address:* St Gabriel's Nursing Home, Warrenside, Burbo Bank Road, Blundellsands, Liverpool L23 7TX. *T:* 051–924 8619. *Died 9 Oct. 1993.*

PARKES, Sir Basil (Arthur), Kt 1971; OBE 1966; *b* 20 Feb. 1907; *s* of late Sir Fred Parkes, Boston, Lincs, and Blackpool, Lancs, and Gertrude Mary Parkes (*née* Bailey); *m* 1933, May Lewis McNeill (*d* 1988); two *s* one *d*; *m* 1991, Mrs Jane Ward (*née* Jones). *Educ:* Boston Grammar Sch., Lincs. Joined family trawler owning Co., 1924 (Dir, 1928; Man. Dir, 1946). Pres., North British Maritime Gp Ltd (formerly United Towing Ltd), 1960–. Hon. Brother, Hull Trinity House. Mem., Worshipful Co. of Fishmongers; Mem., Worshipful Co. of Poulters. Officier de l'ordre du Mérite National Français, 1973; Ordre de la Couronne, Belgium, 1979. *Publication:* Trawlings of a Lifetime, 1991. *Recreations:* golf, shooting. *Address:* Hatherleigh, 23 Riverbank Road, Ramsey, Isle of Man. *T:* Ramsey (0624) 815449. *Clubs:* City Livery, St Stephen's Constitutional, Royal Over-Seas League. *Died 5 July 1993.*

PARKES, Norman James, CBE 1976 (OBE 1960); Clerk of the Australian House of Representatives, 1971–76, retired; *b* 29 July 1912; *s* of Ernest William Parkes; *m* 1937, Maida Cleave, *d* of James Nicholas Silk; two *s. Educ:* Victorian State Schools. AASA. Parliamentary officer, 1934: with Reporting Staff, 1934–37; with House of Representatives, 1937–76. *Recreation:* bowls. *Address:* 1/3 Nuyts Street, Red Hill, Canberra, ACT 2603, Australia. *T:* (6) 2957320. *Clubs:* Canberra Bowling, National Press (Canberra). *Died 29 Jan. 1991.*

PARKHURST, Raymond Thurston, BSc(Agr), MSc, PhD; Director of South Central Poultry Research Laboratory, State University, Mississippi, 1960–68, retired; *b* Everett, Massachusetts, USA, 24 April 1898; *o s* of Fred Lincoln and Celeste Elizabeth Parkhurst; *m* 1922, Norma F. Langroise; one *s* one *d*; *m* 1985, Christine Jennings. *Educ:* Fitchburg High School, Mass; Universities of Massachusetts, Idaho and Edinburgh. Extension Poultryman, Iowa State College, 1919–21; Professor of Poultry Husbandry, Experiment Station Poultry Husbandman, and Head, Dept of Poultry Husbandry, University of Idaho, 1921–27; Director, Brit. Nat. Institute of Poultry Husbandry, 1927–32; Head, Department of Agricultural Research, National Oil Products Co., 1932–38; Head, Dept of Poultry Husbandry, University of Massachusetts, Amherst, 1938–44; Director, Nutrition and Research, Flory Milling Co., Bangor, Pa, 1944–49; Director of Nutrition and Research, Lindsey-Robinson and Company, Roanoke, Va, USA, 1949–60. Life Mem., Amer. Feed Industry Assoc. Nutrition Council; Member: Amer. Poultry Science Assoc.; Amer. Assoc. of Retired Persons; Nat. Assoc. of Retired Persons, etc; First President of British Poultry Education Association. *Publications:* Vitamin E in relation to Poultry; The Comparative Value of various Protein Feeds for Laying Hens; Factors Affecting Egg Size; Mixed Protein Foods for Layers; Ricketts and Perosis in Growing Chickens; Rexing the Rabbit; Corn Distillers By-Products in Poultry Rations; Calcium and Manganese in Poultry Nutrition; Crabmeal and Fishmeal in Poultry Nutrition; Commercial Broiler Raising; Gumboro Disease, etc. *Recreations:* roses, bridge, stamps, coins. *Address:* 119 Kirk Side, Starkville, Miss 39759, USA. *Club:* Kiwanis International. *Died 23 Aug. 1993.*

PARKINSON, Cyril Northcote, MA, PhD, FRHistS; author, historian and journalist; Professor Emeritus and Hon. President, Troy State University, Alabama, since 1970; *b* 30 July 1909; *yr s* of late W. Edward Parkinson, ARCA and Rose Emily Mary Curnow; *m* 1st, 1943, Ethelwyn Edith Graves (marr. diss. 1949); one *s* one *d*; 2nd, 1952, Elizabeth Ann Fry (*d* 1983); two *s* one *d*; 3rd, 1985, Iris Hilda, (Ingrid), Waters. *Educ:* St Peter's School, York; Emmanuel College, Cambridge; King's College, London. Fellow of Emmanuel Coll., Cambridge, 1935; Sen. History Master, Blundell's Sch., Tiverton, 1938; Master, RNC, Dartmouth, 1939; commissioned as Captain, Queen's Royal Regt, 1940; Instructor in 166 OCTU; attached RAF, 1942–43; Major, 1943; trans. as GSO2 to War Office (General Staff), 1944; demobilised, 1945;

Lectr in History, Univ. of Liverpool, 1946; Raffles Professor of History, University of Malaya, Singapore, 1950–58. Visiting Professor: Univ. of Harvard, 1958; Univs of Illinois and California, 1959–60. Mem. French Académie de Marine and US Naval Inst.; Mem. Archives Commission of Govt of India. Hon. LLD Maryland, 1974; Hon. DLitt Troy State, 1976. *Plays:* Helier Bonamy, Guernsey, 1967; The Royalist, Guernsey, 1969. *Publications:* many books including: Edward Pellew Viscount Exmouth, 1934; Trade in the Eastern Seas, 1937; (ed) The Trade Winds, 1948; The Rise of the Port of Liverpool, 1952; War in the Eastern Seas, 1954; Britain in the Far East, 1955; Parkinson's Law, the Pursuit of Progress, 1958; The Evolution of Political Thought, 1958; British Intervention in Malaya, 1867–1877, 1960; The Law and the Profits, 1960; In-laws and Outlaws, 1962; East and West, 1963; Ponies Plot, 1965; A Law unto Themselves, 1966; Left Luggage, 1967; Mrs Parkinson's Law, 1968; The Law of Delay, 1970; The Life and Times of Horatio Hornblower, 1970; Big Business, 1974; Gunpowder, Treason and Plot, 1977; Britannia Rules, 1977; The Rise of Big Business, 1977; (with Nigel Rowe) Communicate, 1977; Jeeves: a Gentleman's Personal Gentleman, 1979; (with H. Le Compte) The Law of Longer Life, 1980; *novels:* Devil to Pay, 1973; The Fireship, 1975; Touch and Go, 1977; Dead Reckoning, 1978; So Near So Far, 1981; The Guernseyman, 1982; The Fur-Lined Mousetrap, 1983; Manhunt: wartime adventure on the Isle of Man, 1990; contribs to Encyclopædia Britannica, Economist, Guardian, New York Times, Fortune, Saturday Evening Post, Punch and Foreign Policy. *Recreations:* painting, travel, music. *Address:* Delancey, 36 Harkness Drive, Canterbury, Kent CT2 7RW. *Club:* Army and Navy.

Died 9 March 1993.

PARKINSON, Dr David Hardress; science writer and consultant; Director General, Establishments Resources and Programmes, A, Ministry of Defence, 1973–77; *b* Liverpool, 9 March 1918; *s* of E. R. H. Parkinson; *m* 1st, 1944, Muriel Gwendoline Patricia (*d* 1971), *d* of Captain P. W. Newenham; two *s*; 2nd, 1974, Daphne Margaret Scott-Gall (marr. diss. 1978). *Educ:* Gravesend County Grammar Sch.; Wadham Coll., Oxford (MA, DPhil). CPhys, FInstP. Royal Artillery, 1939–45 (Major); Oxford Univ., 1937–39 and 1945–49. Civil Service: TRE, Malvern, 1949; Supt Low Temp. and Magnetics Div., RRE, Malvern, 1956–63; Head Physics Gp, RRE, 1963–68; Head Physics and Electronics Dept, RRE and Dep. Dir, 1968–72. Hon. Prof. Physics, Birmingham Univ., 1966–73. Chm. Midland Br., Inst. Physics, 1968–70; Vice-Pres. (Exhibns), Inst. Physics, 1973–78; Chm. Adv. Cttee on Physics and Society, European Physical Soc., 1982–88. *Publications:* (with B. Mulhall) Generation High Magnetic Fields, 1967; many scientific papers and articles. *Recreations:* antiques, silversmithing. *Address:* South Bank, 47 Abbey Road, Great Malvern, Worcs WR14 3HH. *T:* Malvern (0684) 575423. *Club:* Commonwealth Trust. *Died 15 Nov. 1993.*

PARKINSON, Desmond Frederick, CMG 1975; HM Diplomatic Service, retired; *b* 26 Oct. 1920; *m* 1st, 1947, Ann Deborah Durnford (marr. diss. 1957); two *s* one *d*; 2nd, 1963, June Rose Bodington (marr. diss. 1969); 3rd, Heather Marguerite Scott (*d* 1977); one *d*; 4th, 1977, Patricia Jean Campbell Taylor. HM Forces, 1939–49; served FO, 1949–51; Rangoon, 1951–53; Jakarta, 1954–55; FO, 1955–57; Rabat, 1957–60; Lagos, 1960–61; FO, 1961–63; Singapore, 1963–65; Delhi, 1965–67; FCO, 1967–78. *Address:* Woodrow, Silchester, near Reading RG7 2ND. *T:* Reading (01734) 700257. *Club:* Huntercombe Golf. *Died 22 Aug. 1995.*

PARNIS, Alexander Edward Libor, CBE 1973; *b* 25 Aug. 1911; *s* of Alexander T. J. Parnis and Hetty Parnis (*née* Dams). *Educ:* Malvern Coll.; London Univ. BSc(Econ); MA (Cantab). Entered HM Consular Service, 1933: Acting British Vice-Consul, Paris, 1933–34; transferred to HM Treasury, 1937; Finance Officer, Friends' Ambulance Unit, 1941–45; returned to HM Treasury, 1945; Sec., Gowers Cttee on Houses of Outstanding Historic or Architectural Interest, 1950; Sec., Waverley Cttee on Export of Works of Art, etc, 1952; Treasurer, Univ. of Cambridge, 1953–62; Fellow, King's Coll., Cambridge, 1959–62; Asst Sec., Univ. Grants Cttee, 1962–72. Sec., Church's Main Cttee, 1973–81. *Recreations:* music, travel, cycling, walking. *Address:* 4 Jordan Close, Kenilworth, Warwicks CV8 2AE. *T:* Kenilworth (01926) 58354. *Club:* Reform. *Died 11 Oct. 1994.*

PARRETT, John; Managing Director and Clerk of the Course, Aintree Racecourse, since 1989; Clerk of the Course, Chester Racecourse, since 1993; *b* 18 Sept. 1947; *s* of Peter John and Gladys Mary Parrett; *m* 1968, Deborah Phyllis Gibb; one *s* one *d. Educ:* Clarks Coll., Southampton. Fellow, Chartered Inst. of Certified Accountants, 1972; Associate, CIMA, 1970. Various management positions and directorships held in engrg and marine industries from 1968 until entered racing, 1983. Exec. Dir, Nottingham Racecourse, 1991–; Dir, Racecourse Communications Ltd, 1992–. *Recreations:* fox hunting, racing, reading, gardening. *Address:* Barrs Farm, Soberton, Southampton SO3 1PN. *T:* Droxford (0489) 878548; Winterbourne Cottage, Aintree Racecourse, Aintree, Liverpool L9 5AS.

Died 8 Dec. 1992.

PARRY, Sir Ernest J.; see Jones-Parry.

PARRY, Sir (Frank) Hugh (Nigel), Kt 1963; CBE 1954; *b* 26 Aug. 1911; *s* of Charles Frank Parry and Lilian Maud Parry (*née* Powell); *m* 1945, Ann Maureen Forshaw; two *d. Educ:* Cheltenham Coll.; Balliol Coll., Oxford. Entered Colonial Administrative Service, 1939; Chief Secretary, Central African Council, Salisbury, S Rhodesia, 1951–53; Secretary, Office of Prime Minister and External Affairs, Federal Government of Rhodesia and Nyasaland, 1953–63; Ministry of Overseas Development, 1965; Acting Head, Middle East Develt Div., 1969–71, retd 1971. *Recreations:* sailing, motoring. *Address:* c/o Grindlays Bank, 13 St James's Square, SW1.

Died 19 April 1992.

PARSONS, Geoffrey Penwill, AO 1990; OBE 1977; concert accompanist; *b* 15 June 1929; *s* of Francis Hedley Parsons and Edith Vera Buckland. *Educ:* Canterbury High Sch., Sydney; State Conservatorium of Music (with Winifred Burston), Sydney. Winner ABC Concerto Competition, 1947; first tour of Australia, 1948; arrived England, 1950; made 30th tour of Australia, 1993; accompanied many of world's greatest singers and instrumentalists, incl. Elisabeth Schwarzkopf, Victoria de los Angeles, Janet Baker, Jessye Norman, Hans Hotter, Olaf Bär, Thomas Hampson, in 40 countries of world on all six continents. Master Classes: South Bank Summer Festival, 1977 and 1978; Sweden, 1984, 1985, 1987, 1989, 1993; Austria, 1985; USA, 1987, 1988; Denmark, 1990; France, 1993; Geoffrey Parsons and Friends, internat. song recital series, Barbican Concert Hall opening season 1982, 1983. FRCM 1987. Hon. RAM, 1975; Hon. GSM, 1983. Instrumentalist of the Year, Royal Philharmonic Soc., 1991. *Address:* 176 Iverson Road, NW6 2HL. *T:* 0171–624 0957.

Died 26 Jan. 1995.

PARSONS-SMITH, (Basil) Gerald, OBE (mil.) 1945; MA, MD, FRCP; Hon. Consulting Neurologist, Charing Cross Hospital; Hon. Consulting Physician, St Mary's Hospital Group; Teacher in Medicine, London University; *b* 19

Nov. 1911; *s* of late Dr Basil Parsons-Smith, FRCP, and Marguerite, *d* of Sir David Burnett, 1st Bt; *m* 1939, Aurea Mary, *d* of late William Stewart Johnston, Sunningdale; two *s* one *d. Educ:* Harrow; Trinity Coll., Cambridge; St George's Hospital (Entrance Exhib., 1933; Brackenbury Prize in Medicine, 1936). MD Cantab 1949 (*Prox. acc.* Raymond Horton Smith Prize). MRCP 1939, FRCP 1955. House Surgeon, House Physician, Med. Registrar, St George's Hosp.; Physician: Western Ophthalmic Hospital (St Mary's), 1938–60; Electro Encephalograph Dept, Middlesex Hospital Medical Sch., 1950–55; Dept of Neurology, West London and Charing Cross Hosps, 1950–77; Graylingwell Hosp., Chichester, 1950; West End Hosp. for Neurology, 1951–72; Neurologist, Florence Nightingale Hosp., 1955. Served War of 1939–45, as Blood Transfusion Officer, Chelsea EMS, then as medical specialist i/c medical divisions in RAF Hospitals in ME; Sqdn Leader RAFVR (despatches, OBE). Examiner, RCP. FRSocMed. Member: Med. Appeals Trib., 1966–83; Vaccine Damage Tribunal, 1979–83; Association of British Neurologists; Ophthalmic Society of UK. Liveryman, Society of Apothecaries. Appeared in Hospital 1922, BBC TV, 1972. *Publications:* EEG of Brain Tumours, 1949; Sir Gordon Holmes, in, Historical Aspects of the Neurosciences, 1982; 60 contribs to medical, neurological and ophthalmic jls mostly on the immediate treatment of acute stroke of the brain (1979) and eye (1952). *Recreation:* managing wife's equitation centre. *Address:* Roughets House, Bletchingley, Surrey RH1 4QX. *T:* Caterham (01883) 343929. *Clubs:* Royal Society of Medicine; Pitt (Cambridge).

Died 21 April 1995.

PARTRIDGE, Rt Rev. Arthur; *see* Partridge, Rt Rev. W. A.

PARTRIDGE, Prof. (Stanley) Miles, FRS 1970; Professor of Biochemistry, University of Bristol, since 1976; *b* Whangarei, NZ, 2 Aug. 1913; *s* of Ernest Joseph Partridge and Eve Partridge (later Eve McCarthy) (*d* 1977); *m* 1940, Ruth Dowling (*d* 1992); four *d. Educ:* Harrow County Sch.; Battersea Coll. of Technology. PhD Chemistry 1937; MA 1946, ScD 1964, Cantab. Beit Memorial Fellow, Lister Inst. of Preventive Medicine, 1940; Techn. Adviser, Govt of India, 1944; returned to Low Temperature Stn, Cambridge, 1946; Principal Scientific Officer 1952; Dep. Chief Scientific Officer, ARC, 1964; Head of Dept of Biochem. and Physiol., ARC Meat Research Inst., 1968–78. Member: Biochemical Soc. Cttee, 1957–61; Nuffield Foundn Rheumatism Cttee, 1965–77. Fourth Tanner Lectr and Award, Inst. of Food Technologists, Chicago, 1964. Hon. DSc Reading, 1984. Laurea ad Honorem in Medicine and Surgery, Univ. of Padua, 1986. *Publications:* scientific papers, mainly in Biochemical Jl. *Recreation:* gardening. *Address:* c/o Millhouse Farm, Rectory Road, Bacton, Stowmarket, Suffolk IP14 4LE.

Died 26 April 1992.

PARTRIDGE, Rt Rev. (William) Arthur; Assistant Bishop of Hereford, 1963–75; Prebendary Emeritus, Hereford Cathedral, since 1977; *b* 12 Feb. 1912; *s* of Alfred and Sarah Partridge; *m* 1945, Annie Eliza Joan Strangwood (*d* 1984); one *s. Educ:* Alcester Grammar Sch.; Birmingham Univ.; Scholæ Cancellarii, Lincoln. Deacon, 1935; priest, 1936; Curate of Lye, Worcs, 1935; SPG Studentship at Birmingham Univ. Education Dept, 1938–39; Educational Missionary, Dio. Madras, 1939–43; Chaplain, RAFVR, 1943–46; Lecturer Meston Training Coll., Madras, 1947–51; Metropolitan's Commissary and Vicar-General in Nandyal, 1951; Asst Bishop of Calcutta (Bishop in Nandyal), 1953–63; Vicar of Ludford, 1963–69. *Publication:* The Way in India, 1962. *Recreation:* the organ. *Address:* Flat 3, Capel Court, The Burgage, Prestbury, Cheltenham, Glos GL52 3EL. *T:* Cheltenham (0242) 576505. *Died 18 Dec. 1992.*

PASQUILL, Frank, DSc; FRS 1977; retired from Meteorological Office, 1974; *b* 8 Sept. 1914; *s* of late Joseph Pasquill and Elizabeth Pasquill (*née* Rudd), both of Atherton, Lancs; *m* 1937, Margaret Alice Turnbull, West Rainton, Co. Durham; two *d. Educ:* Henry Smith Sch., Hartlepool; Durham Univ. BSc (1st Cl. Hons Physics) 1935, MSc, 1949, DSc 1950. Meteorological Office, 1937–74, with posts at Chem. Defence Res. Estabt, Porton, 1937–46 (incl. overseas service in Australia); Sch. of Agric., Cambridge Univ., 1946–49; Atomic Energy Res. Estabt, Harwell, 1949–54; Chem. Defence Res. Estabt, Porton, 1954–61; Meteorological Office HQ Bracknell, 1961–74 (finally Dep. Chief Scientific Officer, and Head of Boundary Layer Research Br.). Visiting Prof., Pennsylvania State Univ., Autumn, 1974, N Carolina State Univ., Spring, 1975; Visiting Scientist, Penn State Univ., 1975, Winter, 1976, Winter, 1977, Savannah River Lab., S Carolina, Winter, 1976. Royal Meteorological Society: Editor, 1961–64; Pres., 1970–72; Hon. Mem., 1978; Chm., Aero Res. Council's Gust Res. Cttee, 1963–68; Chm., CEGB's Adv. Panel on Environmental Res., 1962–80. Symons Medal, RMetS, 1983. *Publications:* Atmospheric Diffusion, 1962, 3rd edn (with F. B. Smith) 1983; papers on atmospheric turbulence and diffusion in various jls. *Address:* Beeston Farm, Marhamchurch, Bude, Cornwall EX23 0ET. *Died 15 Oct 1994.*

PATERSON, (James Edmund) Neil, MA; author; *b* 31 Dec. 1915; *s* of late James Donaldson Paterson, MA, BL; *m* 1939, Rosabelle, MA, 3rd *d* of late David MacKenzie, MC, MA; two *s* one *d. Educ:* Banff Academy; Edinburgh Univ. Served in minesweepers, War of 1939–45, Lieut RNVR, 1940–46. Dir, Grampian Television, 1960–86; Films of Scotland: Mem., 1954–76; Dir, 1976–78; Consultant, 1978–80. Member: Scottish Arts Council, 1967–76 (Vice-Chm., 1974–76; Chm., Literature Cttee, 1968–76); Arts Council of Great Britain, 1974–76; Governor: Nat. Film Sch., 1970–80; Pitlochry Festival Theatre, 1966–76; British Film Institute, 1958–60. Atlantic Award in Literature, 1946; Award of American Academy of Motion Picture Arts and Sciences, 1960. *Publications:* The China Run, 1948; Behold Thy Daughter, 1950; And Delilah, 1951; Man on the Tight Rope, 1953; The Kidnappers, 1957; film stories and screen plays. *Recreations:* golf, fishing. *Address:* St Ronans, Crieff, Perthshire PH7 4AF. *T:* Crieff (01764) 652615.

Died 19 April 1995.

PATERSON, John Allan; Agent-General in London and Deputy Minister Abroad for Province of New Brunswick, 1968–75; *b* Montreal, 20 May 1909; *s* of William A. and M. Ethel Paterson; *m* 1st, 1935, Elizabeth Stewart Messenger; four *s*; 2nd, 1976, Joan Sheila Dewell (*née* Huess). *Educ:* Westmount, Quebec; Mount Allison Univ. (BSc 1932); Queen's Univ. RCAF, 1941–45 (Sqdn Ldr). Prudential Insurance Co. of America, 1934–46; New Brunswick Dept of Industry, 1946–68 (Deputy Minister, 1956); Provincial Co-ordinator of Civil Defence, 1950–55; Bd of Comrs, Oromocto, 1956–63; Chm., Provincial Govts of Canada Trade and Industry Council, 1956–57, 1961–62, 1964–65 and 1966–67. Mem. Bd of Regents, Mount Allison Univ., 1959–63; Pres. Oromocto Develt Corp., 1963–68. *Publication:* (co-author) The New Brunswick Economy, Past Present and Future, 1955. *Recreations:* golf, motoring, fishing. *Address:* The Coach House, Back Lane, Great Malvern, Worcs.

Died 18 Jan. 1991.

PATERSON, Neil; *see* Paterson, J. E. N.

PATERSON, Robert Lancelot, OBE 1980; MC 1945; ERD 1957; part-time Adjudicator, Home Office Immigration Appeals, 1970–83; Director, Merseyside Chamber of Commerce and Industry, 1967–81; *b* 16 May 1918; *e s* of Lancelot Wilson and Sarah Annie Paterson; *m* 1940,

Charlotte Orpha, *d* of James and Elizabeth Nicholas; three *s. Educ:* Monmouth Sch.; University Coll. of Wales, Aberystwyth (BA); London School of Economics. Commissioned into Border Regt, SR, Dec. 1937; served War of 1939–45, 4th Bn, Border Regt, France, ME, Syria, Tobruk, Burma and India (Chindits, 1943–44); Asst Chief Instr 164 (Inf.), OCTU, 1946. Entered Colonial Admin. Service, Tanganyika, 1947; Dist Officer, 1947–60; Principal Asst Sec., Min. of Home Affairs, 1960–62; prematurely retired on attainment of Independence by Tanganyika. Dep. Sec., Liverpool Chamber of Commerce, 1963–67; Member, Nat. Council, Assoc. of Brit. Chambers of Commerce, 1969–81; Pres., Brit. Chambers of Commerce Executives, 1977–79; Governor, Liverpool Coll. of Commerce, 1967–71; Mem., Liverpool Univ. Appts Bd, 1968–72; *Recreations:* archaeology, gardening. *Address:* 4 Belle Vue Road, Henley-on-Thames, Oxon RG9 1JG. *Died 8 Feb. 1995.*

PATON; *see* Noel-Paton.

PATON, Major Adrian Gerard Nigel H.; *see* Hadden-Paton.

PATON, Rev. Canon David Macdonald; Chaplain to the Queen, 1972–83; Rector of St Mary de Crypt and St John the Baptist, Gloucester, 1970–81; Vicar of Christ Church, Gloucester, 1979–81; Hon. Canon of Canterbury Cathedral, 1966–80 (later Canon Emeritus); *b* 9 Sept. 1913; *e s* of late Rev. William Paton, DD and Grace Mackenzie Paton (*née* Macdonald); *m* 1946, Alison Georgina Stewart; three *s. Educ:* Repton; Brasenose Coll., Oxford. BA 1936, MA 1939. SCM Sec., Birmingham, 1936–39; deacon 1939, priest 1941; missionary in China, 1940–44 and 1947–50; Chaplain and Librarian, Westcott House, Cambridge, 1945–46; Vicar of Yardley Wood, Birmingham, 1952–56; Editor, SCM Press, 1956–59; Sec., Council for Ecumenical Co-operation of Church Assembly, 1959–63; Sec., Missionary and Ecumenical Council of Church Assembly, 1964–69. Chairman: Churches' China Study Project, 1972–79; Gloucester Civic Trust, 1972–77. Hon. Fellow, Selly Oak Colls, 1981. *Publications:* Christian Missions and the Judgment of God, 1953; (with John T. Martin) Paragraphs for Sundays and Holy Days, 1957; (ed) Essays in Anglican Self-Criticism, 1958; (ed) The Ministry of the Spirit, 1960; Anglicans and Unity, 1962; (ed) Reform of the Ministry, 1968; (ed) Breaking Barriers (Report of WCC 5th Assembly, Nairobi, 1975), 1976; (ed with C.H. Long) The Compulsion of the Spirit, 1983; (ed) The 1483 Gloucester Charter in History, 1983; R.O.: The Life and Times of Bishop Ronald Hall of Hong Kong, 1985. *Died 18 July 1992.*

PATON, Prof. Sir William (Drummond Macdonald), Kt 1979; CBE 1968; MA, DM; FRS 1956; FRCP 1969; JP; Professor of Pharmacology in the University of Oxford, and Fellow of Balliol College, 1959–84, then Emeritus Professor and Emeritus Fellow; Honorary Director, Wellcome Institute for History of Medicine, 1983–87; *b* 5 May 1917; 3rd *s* of late Rev. William Paton, DD, and Grace Mackenzie Paton; *m* 1942, Phoebe Margaret, *d* of Thomas Rooke and Elizabeth Frances (*née* Pearce); no *c. Educ:* Winchester House Sch., Brackley; Repton Sch.; New Coll., Oxford (Scholar; Hon. Fellow, 1980); University College Hospital Medical Sch. BA (Oxon) Natural Sciences, Physiology, 1st class hons, 1938; Scholarships: Theodore Williams (Physiology), 1938; Christopher Welch, 1939; Jesse Theresa Rowden, 1939; Goldsmid Exhibition, UCH Medical Sch., 1939; Fellowes Gold Medal in Clinical Med., 1941; BM, BCh Oxon, 1942; MA 1948; DM 1953. Demonstrator in Physiology, Oxford, 1938–39; House physician, UCH Med. Unit, 1942; Pathologist King Edward VII Sanatorium, 1943–44; Member scientific staff, National Institute for Medical Research, 1944–52; Reader in Pharmacology, University College and UCH Med. Sch., 1952–54; Professor of Pharmacology, RCS, 1954–59. Delegate, Clarendon Press, 1967–72; Rhodes Trustee, 1968–87 (Chm., 1978–82). Chm., Cttee for Suppression of Doping, 1970–71; Member: Pharmacological Soc. (Chm. Edtl Bd, 1969–74; Hon. Mem., 1981); Physiological Soc. (Hon. Sec. 1951–57; Hon. Mem., 1985); British Toxicological Soc., 1980– (Chm., 1982–83; Hon. Mem., 1987); MRC, 1963–67; Council, Royal Society, 1967–69; British Nat. Cttee for History of Science, 1972–87 (Chm., 1980–85); Council, Inst. Study of Drug Dependence, 1969–75; Central Adv. Council for Science and Technology, 1970; DHSS Independent Cttee on Smoking, 1978–83; Adv. Cttee on Animal Experiments, 1980–85; Advr, HO Breath-alcohol Survey, 1984–85. Pres., Inst. of Animal Technicians, 1969–75, Vice-Pres., 1976–; Chm., Research Defence Soc., 1972–78 (Paget Lectr, 1978, Boyd Medal, 1987). Wellcome Trustee, 1978–87. Consultant, RN (Diving), 1978–82. Hon. Member: Soc. Française d'Allergie; Australian Acad. Forensic Sci.; Corresp. Mem., German Pharmacological Soc.; Hon. Lectr, St Mary's Hosp. Med. Sch., 1950; Visiting Lecturer: Swedish Univs, 1953; Brussels, 1956. Robert Campbell Oration, 1957; Lectures: Clover, 1958; Bertram Louis Abrahams, RCP, 1962; Ivison Macadam, RCSE, 1973; Osler, RCP, 1978; Cass, Dundee, 1981; Scheuler, Tulane, 1981; Hope Winch, Sunderland, 1982. Editor, UCH Magazine, 1941; Jt organizer and jt editor, international cannabis symposia, 1972, 1976, 1979, 1985; Editor with R. V. Jones, Notes and Records of Royal Soc., 1971–89. FRSA 1973; Hon. FFARCS 1975; Hon. FRSM 1982. JP St Albans, 1956. Hon. DSc: London, 1985; Edinburgh, 1987; DUniv Surrey, 1986. Bengue Meml Prize, 1952; Cameron Prize, 1956; Gairdner Foundn Award, 1959; Gold Medal, Soc. of Apothecaries, 1976; Baly Medal, RCP, 1983; Osler Meml Medal, Univ. of Oxford, 1986; Wellcome Gold Medal, British Pharmacol Soc., 1991. *Publications:* Pharmacological Principles and Practice (with J. P. Payne), 1968; Man and Mouse: animals in medical research, 1984, 2nd edn 1993 (Italian edn 1987); papers on diving, caisson disease, histamine, synaptic transmission, drug action, cannabis and drug dependence in physiological and pharmacological journals. *Recreations:* music, old books. *Address:* 13 Staverton Road, Oxford OX2 6XH. *Died 17 Oct. 1993.*

PATTERSON, Rt Rev. Cecil John, CMG 1958; CBE 1954; CFR 1965; DD (Lambeth), 1963; DD (University of Nigeria, Nsukka), 1963; *b* 9 Jan. 1908; *s* of James Bruce Patterson. *Educ:* St Paul's School; St Catharine's Coll., Cambridge; Bishop's Coll., Cheshunt. Deacon, 1931; priest, 1932; London Curacy, 1931–34; Missionary in S Nigeria, 1934–41; Asst Bishop on the Niger, 1942–45; Bishop on the Niger, 1945–69; Archbishop of West Africa, 1961–69; Representative for the Archbishops of Canterbury and York for Community Relations, 1970–72; Hon. Asst Bishop, Diocese of London, 1970–76. Hon. Fellow, St Catharine's Coll., Cambridge, 1963. *Address:* 6 High Park Road, Kew, Surrey TW9 4BH. *T:* 081-876 1697. *Died 11 April 1992.*

PATTINSON, Peter Lawrence F.; *see* Foden-Pattinson.

PATTON, Thomas William Saunderson, OBE 1985; Member, Belfast City Council, since 1973; Lord Mayor of Belfast, 1982–83; *b* 27 July 1914; *s* of Florence and Robert Patton; *m* 1940, Alice Glover; three *s* three *d* (and one *d* decd). *Educ:* Templemore Avenue School, Belfast. Harland and Wolff Ltd, 1932–61; Ulster Folk and Transport Museum, 1962–82. High Sheriff, Belfast, 1992–93. *Recreations:* gardening, football. *Address:* 89 Park Avenue, Belfast BT4 1JJ. *T:* Belfast (0232) 658645. *Died 20 Oct. 1993.*

PAUL, Dr David Manuel; HM Coroner: City of London, since 1966; Northern District of London, since 1968; *b* 8 June 1927; *s* of Kenneth and Rachael Paul; *m* 1948, Gladys Audrey Garton, MCSP; two *d*. *Educ:* Selhurst Grammar Sch. for Boys, Croydon; St Bartholomew's Hosp. Med. Coll.; The London Hosp. Med. Coll. MRCS, LRCP 1953; DRCOG 1962; DA 1962; DMJ (Clin.) 1965. Served Manchester Regt, 1946–49 (Lieut). House Surgeon, Beckenham Hosp., 1954; Obstetric House Surgeon, Luton and Dunstable Hosp., 1955; gen. practice, Drs Duncan & Partners, Croydon, 1955–67; Clin. Asst Anaesthetist, Croydon Gp of Hosps, 1956–68; GP Obstetrician, Purley Hosp., 1958–68; Divl Surgeon, Z Div., Met. Police, 1956–68. Hon. Lectr, Court Practice and Clin. Forensic Medicine, Guy's Hosp. Med. Sch., 1966–91; Hon. Consultant, Clin. Forensic Medicine, Surrey Constab., 1967–93; Hon. Sen. Lectr, Clin. Forensic Medicine, Charing Cross and Westminster Hosp. Med. Sch., 1990–. Chm., Med. Section, 1973–76, Chm., Exec. Council, 1979–83, and 1989–, and Pres., 1987–88, British Acad. of Forensic Sciences. *Publications:* contrib. medico-legal jls and text books on forensic medicine. *Recreations:* travel, equitation, fishing, photography. *Address:* The Coroner's Court, Milton Court, Moor Lane, EC2Y 9BL. *T:* 071–606 3030; The Coroner's Court, Myddelton Road, Hornsey, N8 7PY. *T:* 081–348 4411; Shirley Oaks Hospital, Poppy Lane, Shirley Oaks Village, Croydon CR9 8AB. *T:* 081–655 2255. *Died 17 June 1993.*

PAUL, Prof. Wolfgang, Grosses Verdienstkreuz mit Stern, 1981; Emeritus Professor of Physics, University of Bonn, since 1981; *b* 10 Aug. 1913; *s* of Theodor Paul and Elisabeth (*née* Ruppel); *m* 1st, 1940, Liselotte Hirsche (*d* 1977); two *s* two *d*; 2nd, 1979, Dr Doris Walch. *Educ:* Tech. Hochschule, München (DrIng); Tech. Hochschule, Berlin. Asst, Univ. of Göttingen, 1942–44, Dozent, 1944–52; Prof. of Exptl Physics, Univ. of Bonn, 1952–81; Director: Kern Forschungs Anlage, Tülich, 1960–62; Nuclear Physics Div., CERN, Geneva, 1964–67; DESY, Hamburg, 1970–73. Hon. Degrees: Uppsala, 1978; Aachen, 1981; Poznan, 1990. (Jtly) Nobel Prize for Physics, 1990. *Publications:* numerous in physics jls. *Address:* Stationsweg 13, 53 Bonn, Germany.
Died 7 Dec. 1993.

PAULING, Linus (Carl); Research Professor, Linus Pauling Institute of Science and Medicine, since 1974; *b* 28 Feb. 1901; *s* of Herman William Pauling and Lucy Isabelle Darling; *m* 1923, Ava Helen Miller (*d* 1981); three *s* one *d*. *Educ:* Oregon State Coll.; California Institute of Technology. BS Oregon State Coll., 1922; PhD California Inst. of Technology, 1925. Asst in Chemistry and in Mechanics and Materials, Oregon State Coll., 1919–22; Graduate Asst, California Inst. Technology, 1922–23; Teaching Fellow, 1923–25; Research Associate, 1925–26; Nat. Res. Fellow in Chemistry, 1925–26; Fellow of John Simon Guggenheim Meml Foundn, 1926–27 (Univs of Munich, Zürich, Copenhagen); Asst Prof., California Inst. of Technology, 1927–29; Associate Prof., 1929–31; Prof. of Chemistry, 1931–63; Dir of Gates and Crellin Labs of Chemistry, and Chm., Div. of Chemistry and Chemical Engrg, 1936–58; Prof. of Chemistry, Stanford Univ., 1969–74. George Fisher Baker Lectr in Chemistry, Cornell Univ., Sept. 1937–Feb. 1938; George Eastman Prof., Oxford Univ., Jan.-June 1948, etc. Hon. DSc: Oregon State Coll., 1933; Univ. of Chicago, 1941; Princeton Univ., 1946; Yale, 1947; Cambridge, 1947; London, 1947; Oxford, 1948; Brooklyn Polytechnic Inst., 1955; Humboldt Univ. (Berlin), 1959; Melbourne, 1964; York (Toronto), 1966; LLD Reed Coll., 1959; LHD Tampa, 1949; Dr *hc:* Paris, 1948; Toulouse, 1949; Liège, 1955; Montpellier, 1958; Warsaw, 1969; Lyon, 1970; UJD, NB, 1950; DFA, Chouinard Art Inst., 1958. Amer. Chem. Soc. Award in Pure Chemistry, 1931; William H.

Nichols Medal, 1941; J. Willard Gibbs Medal, 1946; Theodore William Richards Medal, 1947; Davy Medal of Royal Society, 1947; Presidential Medal for Merit, 1948; Gilbert Newton Lewis Medal, 1951; Thomas Addis Medal, 1955; Amedeo Avogadro Medal, 1956; Pierre Fermat Medal; Paul Sabatier Medal, 1957; International Grotius Medal, 1957; Linus Pauling Medal, 1966; Internat. Lenin Peace Prize, 1971; 1st Martin Luther King Jr Medical Award, 1972; Nat. Medal of Science, 1975; Lomonosov Gold Medal, Soviet Acad. of Scis, 1978; Vannevar Bush Medal, Nat. Sci. Bd, 1989. Nobel Prize for Chemistry, 1954; Nobel Peace Prize for 1962, 1963. Member: Nat. Acad. of Sciences; Amer. Phil. Soc.; Amer. Acad. of Arts and Sciences, etc; Hon. Fellow: Chemical Society (London), Royal Institution, etc; For. Member: Royal Society; Akademia Nauk, USSR, etc; Associé étranger, Acad. des Sciences, 1966. War of 1939–45, Official Investigator for projects of National Defense Research Cttee on Medical Research, and Office of Scientific Research and Development. Grand Officer, Order of Merit, Italian Republic. *Publications:* The Structure of Line Spectra (with S. Goudsmit), 1930; Introduction to Quantum Mechanics (with E. B. Wilson, Jr), 1935; The Nature of the Chemical Bond, 1939 (3rd edn, 1960); General Chemistry, 1947 (2nd edn, 1953); College Chemistry, 1950 (3rd edn, 1964); No More War!, 1958 (revised edn, 1962); The Architecture of Molecules (with Roger Hayward), 1964; The Chemical Bond, 1967; Vitamin C and the Common Cold, 1971; (with Peter Pauling) Chemistry, 1975; Vitamin C, the Common Cold and the Flu, 1976; (with Ewan Cameron) Cancer and Vitamin C, 1979; How to Live Longer and Feel Better, 1986; also numerous scientific articles in the fields of chemistry, physics, and biology including the structure of crystals, quantum mechanics, nature of the chemical bond, structure of gas molecules, structure of antibodies and nature of serological reactions, etc. *Address:* Linus Pauling Institute of Science and Medicine, 440 Page Mill Road, Palo Alto, California 94306, USA.
Died 19 Aug. 1994.

PAYNE, Maj.-Gen. George Lefevre, CB 1966; CBE 1963; Director of Ordnance Services, Ministry of Defence, 1964–68; retired, 1968; *b* 23 June 1911; *s* of Dr E. L. Payne, MRCS, LRCP, Brunswick House, Kew, Surrey; *m* 1st, 1938, Betty Maud (*d* 1982), *d* of Surgeon Captain H. A. Kellond-Knight, RN, Eastbourne, Sussex; two *s* (and one *s* decd); 2nd, 1990, Antoinette Georgina, *d* of Roger Cookson, and widow of D. Mitchell. *Educ:* The King's Sch., Canterbury; Royal Mil. Coll., Sandhurst. Royal Leicestershire Regiment: England, Northern Ireland, 1931–33; India, 1933–37; Royal Army Ordnance Corps: England, 1938–39; France, 1939–40; England, 1941; Deputy Director Ordnance Services: HQ, BAOR, 1952–54; War Office, 1955–57; Commandant, Central Ordnance Depot, Chilwell, 1957–59; Deputy Director Ordnance Services, War Office, 1959–63; Commander, Stores Organization, RAOC, 1963–64; Col Comdt, RAOC, 1968–72. *Recreations:* racing, cricket. *Address:* 10 Highlands Heath, Bristol Gardens, SW15 3TG. *T:* 081–785 3196. *Club:* Commonwealth Trust.
Died 10 Sept. 1992.

PEACH, Captain Charles Lindsay K.; *see* Keighly-Peach.

PEACOCK, Sir Geoffrey (Arden), Kt 1981; CVO 1977; MA; Remembrancer, City of London, 1968–81; *b* 7 Feb. 1920; *s* of Warren Turner Peacock and Elsie (*née* Naylor); *m* 1949, Mary Gillian Drew, *d* of Dr Harold Drew Lander, Rock, Cornwall; two *d*. *Educ:* Wellington Coll.; Jesus Coll., Cambridge. Served in War, 1939–46: RA and Royal Lincs Regt; Lt-Col 1945; Pres. of War Crimes Court, Singapore. Called to the Bar, Inner Temple. Legal Asst,

Treasury Solicitor's Dept, 1949; Prin., HM Treasury, 1954; Sen. Legal Asst, Treasury Solicitor's Dept, 1958. Hon. Steward, Westminster Abbey, 1981–. Master: Pewterers' Co., 1985, 1986, 1988; Co. of Watermen and Lightermen, 1986. Chm., Brighton and Storrington Beagles, 1970–73. Various foreign decorations. *Recreations:* beagling, sailing, rowing. *Address:* Haymarsh, Duncton, Petworth, West Sussex GU28 0JY. *T:* Petworth (0798) 42793. *Clubs:* Cruising Association, London Rowing, City Livery; Leander.

Died 27 March 1991.

PEACOCK, Prof. Joseph Henry, MD, FRCS; Professor of Surgical Science, University of Bristol, 1969–84, then Emeritus; *b* 22 Oct. 1918; *s* of Harry James Peacock and Florence Peacock; *m* 1950, Gillian Frances Pinckney; one *s* one *d*. *Educ:* Bristol Grammar Sch.; Univ. of Birmingham (MB, ChB 1941, ChM 1957, MD 1963). MRCS, LRCP 1941, FRCS 1949. House appts, 1942; served RAMC, 1942–47: surgical and orthopaedic specialist, England and Far East; Hon. Major; Demonstr in Anat., Univ. of Birmingham, 1947; Surg. Registrar, 1948–51, and Sen. Surg. Registrar, 1952–53, United Bristol Hosp.; Rockefeller Fellow, Ann Arbor, 1951; Lectr in Surgery, 1953, and Reader in Surg., 1965, Univ. of Bristol; Consultant Surgeon: United Bristol Hosp., 1955; SW Reg. Hosp. Bd, 1960. Member: GMC, 1975–85 (Chm., Sub-cttee F, 1980–85); SW RHA, 1975–84 (Chm., Res. Cttee, 1981–84); Vascular Surgical Soc. of GB (also Pres.); Founder Member: Surgical Res. Soc.; European Soc. of Surg. Res.; Fellow, Assoc. of Surgeons of GB. Royal Coll. of Surgeons: Jacksonian Prize, 1954 and 1967; Hunterian Prof., 1956; Arris and Gale Lectr, 1960; Examr, LDS, 1958–63, and primary FRCS, 1965–71; Mem., Ct of Examrs, 1976–82 (Chm., 1982). Examr in Surg., Univs of Bristol, Birmingham, London, Wales, Ghana, Sudan and Liverpool. *Publications:* Raynaud's Disease: British surgical practice, 1960; scientific pubns on vascular surgery and liver transplantation. *Recreations:* short wave radio, gardening. *Address:* The Old Manor, Ubley, near Bristol BS18 6PJ. *T:* Blagdon (0761) 462733. *Club:* Army and Navy. *Died 6 May 1992.*

PEACOCK, Ronald, MA, LittD (Leeds), MA (Manchester), DrPhil (Marburg); Professor of German, Bedford College, University of London, 1962–75, then Emeritus Professor; Fellow of Bedford College, 1980; *b* 22 Nov. 1907; *s* of Arthur Lorenzo and Elizabeth Peacock; *m* 1933, Ilse Gertrud Eva, *d* of Geheimer Oberregierungsrat Paul Freiwald; no *c*. *Educ:* Leeds Modern Sch.; Universities of Leeds, Berlin, Innsbruck, Marburg. Assistant Lecturer in German, University of Leeds, 1931–38; Lecturer, 1938–39; Professor, 1939–45; Henry Simon Professor of German Language and Literature, University of Manchester, 1945–62; Dean of the Faculty of Arts, 1954–56; Pro-Vice-Chancellor, 1958–62. Visiting Professor of German Literature, Cornell Univ. (USA), 1949; Visiting Professor of German Literature and Comparative Literature, University of Heidelberg, 1960–61; Professor of Modern German Literature, University of Freiburg, 1965, 1967–68. Pres., MHRA, 1983. Hon. LittD Manchester, 1977. *Publications:* The Great War in German Lyrical Poetry, 1934; Das Leitmotiv bei Thomas Mann, 1934; Hölderlin, 1938; The Poet in the Theatre, 1946 (reprinted with additional essays, 1960), 1986; The Art of Drama, 1957; Goethe's Major Plays, 1959; Criticism and Personal Taste, 1972; various articles on literature contributed to reviews and periodicals. *Recreations:* music, theatre, travel. *Address:* Greenshade, Woodhill Avenue, Gerrards Cross, Bucks SL9 8DR. *T:* Gerrards Cross (0753) 884886.

Died 1 June 1993.

PEACOCKE, Rt Rev. Cuthbert Irvine, TD; MA; *b* 26 April 1903; *er s* of late Rt Rev. Joseph Irvine Peacocke, DD and Ada Victoria Stanley, *d* of Lindsey Bucknall Barker; ; *m* 1931, Helen Louise Gaussen (*d* 1988); one *s* one *d*. *Educ:* St Columba's Coll., Dublin; Trinity Coll., Dublin. Deacon, 1926; priest, 1927; Curate, Seapatrick Parish, 1926–30; Head of Southern Mission, 1930–33; Rector, Derriaghy, 1933–35; Rector, St Mark's, Dundela, 1935–56; CF, 1939–45; Archdeacon of Down, 1950–56; Dean of St Anne's Cathedral, Belfast, 1956–69; Bishop of Derry and Raphoe, 1970–75. *Publication:* The Young Parson, 1936. *Recreations:* games, garden, reading. *Address:* 32 Lisburn Road, Hillsborough, Co. Down BT26 6HW. *Died 6 April 1994.*

PEARCE, John Dalziel Wyndham, MA, MD; FRCP, FRCPEd, FRCPsych, DPM, FBPsS; Consulting Psychiatrist: St Mary's Hospital; Queen Elizabeth Hospital for Children; *b* 21 Feb. 1904; *s* of John Alfred Wyndham Pearce and Mary Logan Dalziel; *m* 1929, Grace Fowler (marr. diss., 1964), no *c*; *m* 1964, Ellinor Elizabeth Nancy Draper. *Educ:* George Watson's Coll.; Edinburgh Univ. Formerly: Physician-in-charge, Depts of Psychiatry, St Mary's Hosp. and Queen Elizabeth Hosp. for Children; Cons. Psychiatrist, Royal Masonic Hosp.; Hon. physician, Tavistock Clinic and West End Hospital for Nervous Diseases; Medical co-director Portman Clinic, Institute for Study and Treatment of Delinquency; medico-psychologist, LCC remand homes; Mem. Academic Boards, Inst. of Child Health, and St Mary's Hosp. Med. Sch. (Univ. of London); Examiner in Medicine: RCP; Univ. of London; Royal Coll. of Psychiatrists; Chm., Adv. Cttee on delinquent and maladjusted children, Internat. Union for Child Welfare; Mem., Army Psychiatry Adv. Cttee; Lt-Col, RAMC; adviser in psychiatry, Allied Force HQ, CMF (despatches). Member: Council, National Assoc. for Mental Health; Home Sec's Adv. Council on Treatment of Offenders. *Publications:* Juvenile Delinquency, 1952; technical papers in scientific journals. *Address:* 2/28 Barnton Avenue West, Edinburgh EH4 6EB. *T:* 031–317 7116. *Clubs:* Caledonian; New (Edinburgh). *Died 25 Jan. 1994.*

PEARD, Rear-Adm. Sir Kenyon (Harry Terrell), KBE 1958 (CBE 1951); retired; *b* 1902; *s* of Henry T. Peard; *m* 1935, Mercy Leila Bone; one *s* one *d*. *Educ:* RN Colleges, Osborne and Dartmouth. Went to sea, 1919; Torpedo Specialist, 1929; transferred to Electrical Branch, 1946, Director, Naval Electrical Dept, Admiralty, 1955–58; retired 1958. *Address:* Finstead, Shorefield Crescent, Milford-on-Sea, Hants SO41 0PD.

Died 14 April 1994.

PEARMAN, Sir James (Eugene), Kt 1973; CBE 1960; Senior Partner, Conyers, Dill & Pearman; *b* 24 Nov. 1904; *o s* of Eugene Charles Pearman and Kate Trott; *m* 1st, 1929, Prudence Tucker Appleby (*d* 1976); two *s*; 2nd, 1977, Mrs Antoinette Trott, *d* of Dr and Mrs James Aiguier, Philadelphia, Pa. *Educ:* Saltus Grammar Sch., Bermuda; Bromsgrove Sch., Worcs; Merton Coll., Oxford. Called to the Bar, Middle Temple, 1927; law partnership with N. B. Dill, 1927–29; law partnership with Sir Reginald Conyers and N. B. Dill, 1929, latterly Conyers, Dill & Pearman. Member Colonial Parlt, Bermuda, 1943–72; MEC, 1955–63 and 1968–72; MLC, 1972. Hon. Consul for Bolivia. *Recreations:* deep-sea fishing, bridge. *Address:* Palmetto Cove, 15 Lone Palm Drive, Pembroke HM05, Bermuda. *T:* 21125. *Clubs:* Carlton; Anglers' (New York); Rod and Reel (Miami); Royal Bermuda Yacht. *Died 13 April 1994.*

PEARSON, Sir Denning; *see* Pearson, Sir J. D.

PEARSON, Sir Francis Fenwick, 1st Bt, *cr* 1964, of Gressingham, Co. Palatine of Lancaster; MBE 1945; JP;

DL; Chairman, Central Lancashire New Town Development Corporation, 1971–86; *b* 13 June 1911; *s* of Frank Pearson, solicitor, Kirby Lonsdale, and Susan Mary Pearson; *m* 1938, Katharine Mary Fraser, *d* of the Rev. D. Denholm Fraser, Sproughton, Roxburgh; one *s* one *d*. *Educ:* Uppingham; Trinity Hall, Cambridge. 1st Gurkha Rifles, 1932; ADC to Viceroy of India, 1934–36; Indian Political Service, 1936; Under-Secretary, Political Dept, 1942–45; Chief Minister, Manipur State, 1945–47; retired, 1947. MP (C) Clitheroe, Oct. 1959–1970; Assistant Whip (unpaid), 1960–62; a Lord Commissioner of the Treasury, 1962–63; PPS to Prime Minister, Nov. 1963–Oct. 1964. JP Lancs, 1952; DL Co. Palatine of Lancaster, 1971. *Recreation:* fishing. *Heir:* s Francis Nicholas Fraser Pearson [*b* 28 Aug. 1943; *m* 1978, Henrietta, *d* of Comdr Henry Pasley-Tyler]. *Address:* Beech Cottage, Borwick, Carnforth. *T:* Carnforth (0524) 4191. *Club:* Carlton.

Died 17 Feb. 1991.

PEARSON, Air Cdre Herbert Macdonald, CBE 1944; Royal Air Force, retired; *b* Buenos Aires, Argentina, 17 Nov. 1908; *s* of John Charles Pearson; *m* 1st, 1939, Jane Leslie (*d* 1978); one *s* two *d*; 2nd, 1982, Elizabeth Griffiths, JP, *widow* of E. P. Griffiths, MRCS, LRCP. *Educ:* Cheltenham Coll.; Cranwell. Left Cranwell, 1928; Malta, 1929–31; Central Flying Sch., 1932; Instructor, Cranwell, 1933–34; attached to Peruvian Government, 1935–36; Asst Air Attaché in Spain, 1936–38; comd No 54 Sqdn, 1938–39; War of 1939–45, in Fighter Command; then France, Belgium and Germany (despatches 1942, 1943, 1946); Air Attaché, Lima, Peru, 1946; Deputy Director Air Foreign Liaison, Air Ministry, 1949; Commanding Royal Air Force, Kai Tak, Hong Kong, 1951–53; Assistant Chief of Staff Intelligence, Headquarters of Allied Air Forces, Central Europe, 1953–55; Air Commodore, 1953; retired, 1955. *Publication:* Pilot-Diplomat and Garage Rat, 1989. *Address:* Mapleridge Barn, Horton, Chipping Sodbury, Bristol BS17 6QH. *Club:* Naval and Military.

Died 21 Nov. 1992.

PEARSON, Sir (James) Denning, Kt 1963; JP; FEng 1976; Chairman and Chief Executive, Rolls-Royce Ltd, 1969–70; Chairman, Gamma Associates, 1972–80; *b* 8 Aug. 1908; *s* of James Pearson and Elizabeth Henderson; *m* 1932, Eluned Henry (*d* 1992); two *d*. *Educ:* Canton Secondary Sch., Cardiff; Cardiff Technical Coll. Senior Whitworth Scholarship; BSc Eng. Joined Rolls-Royce Ltd, 1932; Technical Production Engineer, Glasgow Factory, 1941; Chief Quality and Service Engineer (resident in Canada for one year), 1941–45; Gen. Man. Sales and Service, 1946–49; Director, 1949; Director and Gen. Man., Aero Engine Division, 1950; Managing Director (Aero Engine Div.), 1954–65; Chief Exec. and Dep. Chm., 1957–68. President, SBAC, 1963; Mem., NEDC, 1964–67. FRAeS, 1957–64, Hon. FRAeS, 1964; Hon. FIMechE; DrIngEh Brunswick Univ., 1962–86. Member: Council, Manchester Business Sch.; Governing Body, London Graduate Sch. of Business Studies, 1968–70; Governing Body, Admin. Staff Coll., Henley, 1968–73; Council, Voluntary Service Overseas. Fellow, Imperial Coll. of Science and Technology, 1968–; Hon. Fellow, Manchester Univ. Inst. of Science and Technology, 1969; Hon. DSc: Nottingham, 1966; Wales, 1968; Cranfield Inst. of Technology, 1970; Hon. DTech: Loughborough, 1968; CNAA, 1969. Gold Medal, Royal Aero Club, 1969; Benjamin Franklin Medal, RSA, 1970. FRSA 1970. *Recreations:* reading, golf, tennis, sailing. *Address:* Green Acres, Holbrook, Derbyshire DE5 0TF. *T:* Derby (0332) 881137. *Died 1 Aug. 1992.*

PEARSON, Norman Charles, OBE 1944; TD 1944; Member, Air Transport Licensing Board, 1971–72; Lay Member, Restrictive Practices Court, 1968–86; *b* 12 Aug. 1909; *s* of late Max Pearson and Kate Pearson; *m* 1951,

Olive May, *d* of late Kenneth Harper and Ruth Harper, Granston Manor, Co. Leix; one *s* one *d*. *Educ:* Harrow Sch. (Scholar); Gonville and Caius Coll., Cambridge (Sayer Scholar). Commnd Royal Signals (TA), 1932; Middx Yeomanry; served War of 1939–45, N Africa (despatches, OBE), Italy, Greece; Lt-Col, comd 6th Armd Div. Signals, 1942; 10 Corps Signals, 1944; Mil. Comd Athens Signals; 4th Div. Signals, 1945; subseq. re-formed 56 Div. Signals Regt (TA). Boots Pure Drug Co. Ltd, 1931–37; Borax (Holdings) Ltd, 1937–69, Director, 1951–69; Director: UK Provident Instn, 1965–80; Cincinnati Milacron Ltd, 1968–83 (Dep. Chm., 1972–83). *Recreation:* gardening. *Address:* Brook House, Norton, Malmesbury, Wilts SN16 0JP. *Club:* Carlton.

Died 9 Sept. 1992.

PECK, Sir John (Howard), KCMG 1971 (CMG 1956); HM Diplomatic Service, retired; *b* Kuala Lumpur, 16 Feb. 1913; *o s* of late Howard and Dorothea Peck; *m* 1st, 1939, Mariska Caroline (*d* 1979), *e d* of Josef Somló; two *s*; 2nd, 1987, Catherine, *y d* of Edward McLaren. *Educ:* Wellington College; CCC, Oxford. Assistant Private Secretary: to First Lord of Admiralty, 1937–39; to Minister for Coordination of Defence, 1939–40; to the Prime Minister, 1940–46; transferred to Foreign Service, 1946; served in United Nations Dept, 1946–47; in The Hague, 1947–50; Counsellor and Head of Information Research Dept, 1951–54; Counsellor (Defence Liaison) and Head of Political Division, British Middle East Office, 1954–56; Director-General of British Information Services, New York, 1956–59; UK Permanent Representative to the Council of Europe, and Consul-General, Strasbourg, 1959–62; Ambassador to Senegal, 1962–66, and Mauritania, 1962–65; Asst Under-Sec. of State, FO, then FCO, 1966–70; Ambassador to the Republic of Ireland, 1970–73. *Publications:* Dublin from Downing Street (memoirs), 1978; various essays and light verse. *Recreations:* photography, gardening. *Address:* Stratford, Saval Park Road, Dalkey, Co. Dublin. *T:* Dublin 2852000. *Club:* Stephen's Green (Dublin).

Died 13 Jan. 1995.

PEDDER, Vice-Adm. Sir Arthur (Reid), KBE 1959; CB 1956; Commander, Allied Naval Forces, Northern Europe, 1957–59, retired; *b* 6 July 1904; *s* of late Sir John Pedder, KBE, CB and Frances Evelyn, *e d* of W. Arthur Sharpe, Highgate; *m* 1934, Dulcie, *d* of O. L. Bickford; two *s*. *Educ:* Osborne and Dartmouth. Served in various ships, 1921–56: qualified as Naval Observer, 1930; promoted Commander and appointed Admiralty, 1937–40; Executive Officer, HMS Mauritius, 1940–42; Admiralty Asst, Dir of Plans (Air), 1942–45; Capt. 1944; comd HM Ships Khedive and Phoebe, 1945–47; idc 1948; Admiralty (Dep. Dir of Plans), 1949–50; Fourth Naval Member of Australian Commonwealth Naval Board, 1950–52; Rear-Adm. 1953; Asst Chief of Naval Staff (Warfare), Admiralty, 1953–54; Flag Officer, Aircraft Carriers, December 1954–May 1956; Vice-Adm. 1956. *Recreation:* everything outdoors. *Died 22 June 1995.*

PEDLER, Sir Frederick (Johnson), Kt 1969; *b* 10 July 1908; *s* of Charles Henry Pedler and Lucy Marian (*née* Johnson); *m* 1935, Esther Ruth Carling; two *s* one *d*. *Educ:* Watford Grammar School; Caius College, Cambridge (MA). Colonial Office, 1930; seconded to Tanganyika, 1934; Secretary to Commission on Higher Educn in E Africa and Sudan, 1937; Sec. to Lord Privy Seal, 1938; Sec. to Lord Hailey in Africa, 1939, Congo, 1940; Chief Brit. Econ. Representative, Dakar, 1942; Finance Dept, Colonial Office, 1944. Joined United Africa Co., 1947, Director, 1951, Deputy Chairman, 1965–68. Director: Unilever Ltd and NV, 1956–68; William Baird Ltd, 1969–75. Chm., Council for Technical Educn and Training for Overseas Countries, 1962–73. Chm., E Africa and

Mauritius Assoc., 1966–68; Mem., Inter-University Council, 1967–73. Treas., SOAS, Univ. of London, 1969–81, Hon. Fellow, 1976. *Publications:* West Africa, 1951 (2nd edn 1959); Economic Geography of W Africa, 1955; The Lion and the Unicorn in Africa, 1974; Main Currents of West African History 1940–78, 1979; A Pedler Family History, 1984; A Wider Pedler Family History, 1989. *Recreations:* languages, history. *Address:* 36 Russell Road, Moor Park, Northwood, Mddx HA6 2LR. *Died 6 April 1991.*

PEEL, Prof. Edwin Arthur, DLit; Professor of Education, University of Birmingham, 1950–78, and Chairman of School of Education, 1965–70; *b* 11 March 1911; *s* of late Arthur Peel and Mary Ann Miller; *m* 1939, Nora Kathleen Yeadon (*d* 1988); two *s* two *d. Educ:* Prince Henry's Grammar School, Otley, Yorks; Leeds University; London University. MA London, 1938; PhD London 1945; DLit London, 1961. Teaching in various London Schools, 1933–38; LCC School of Building, 1938–41; Ministry of Supply, 1941–45; Part-time Lecturer London Univ. Institute of Education, 1945; Lecturer in Education, King's College, Newcastle, 1946; Reader in Psychology, Durham University, 1946–48; Professor of Educational Psychology, University of Durham, 1948–50. President British Psychological Society 1961–62. *Publications:* The Psychological Basis of Education, 1956; The Pupil's Thinking, 1960; The Nature of Adolescent Judgment, 1971; various in leading British and foreign journals of psychology; Editor and contrib., Educational Review. *Recreation:* painting. *Address:* Callerton Hall Rest Home, High Callerton, Northumberland NE20 9TT. *T:* Ponteland (0661) 72832. *Died 10 June 1992.*

PEEL, Jack Armitage, CBE 1972; DL; European affairs consultant; *b* 8 Jan. 1921; *s* of Martha and George Henry Peel; *m* 1950, Dorothy Mabel Dobson; one *s* one *d. Educ:* elem. and modern sch.; Ruskin Coll., Oxford (Schol., Social Sci.), 1948–49. Railwayman, 1936–47. National Union of Dyers, Bleachers and Textile Workers: full-time Officer, 1950; Asst Gen.-Sec., 1957–66, Gen. Sec., 1966–73; Mem. Gen. Council of TUC, 1966–72; Dir, Industrial Relations, in the Social Affairs Directorate, EEC, 1973–79, Chief Adviser, 1979–81. Part-time Director: British Wool Marketing Board, 1968–73; NCB, 1969–73. Served on several courts of inquiry, incl. Rochdale Cttee of Inquiry into Merchant Navy; Special Adviser to Sec. of State for Transport on long term industrial relns strategy, May 1983-Jan. 1984. Senior Vis. Fellow in Industrial Relns, Bradford Univ., 1984–. Hon. MA Bradford, 1979. DL West Yorks, 1971; JP Bradford, 1960–72. *Publications:* The Real Power Game, 1979; What Makes Man Work?, 1989; Europe—the wider perspective, 1990; What Price Europe?, 1991. *Recreations:* cricket, painting, guitar music, swimming. *Address:* Timberleigh, 39 Old Newbridge Hill, Bath, Avon BA1 3LU. *T:* Bath (0225) 423959. *Died 10 May 1993.*

PEGLER, James Basil Holmes, TD; BA; FIA, FSS, FIS, FIMA; Professor of Actuarial Science, City University, 1976–79, Visiting Professor, 1979–86; *b* 6 Aug. 1912; *s* of late Harold Holmes Pegler and Dorothy Cecil (*née* Francis); *m* 1937, Enid Margaret Dell; one *s* three *d. Educ:* Charterhouse; Open Univ. Joined Clerical, Medical and Gen. Life Assce Soc., 1931; Gen. Man. and Actuary, 1950–69; Man. Dir, 1970–75; non-exec. Dir, 1975–83. War service, Queen's Royal Regt and RA, 1939–45 (Major). Inst. of Actuaries: Fellow, 1939; Hon. Sec., 1955–57; Pres., 1968–70. Chm., Life Offices' Assoc., 1959–61; Chm., Life Gp of Comité Européen des Assurances, 1964–70. *Publications:* contribs to Jl Inst. Actuaries. *Recreations:* mathematics, languages, lawn tennis, tap dancing. *Address:* Dormers, 28 Deepdene

Wood, Dorking, Surrey RH5 4BQ. *T:* Dorking (0306) 885955. *Club:* Army and Navy.

Died 22 Sept. 1992.

PEIERLS, Sir Rudolf (Ernst), Kt 1968; CBE 1946; FRS 1945; MA Cantab, DSc Manchester, DPhil Leipzig; Wykeham Professor of Physics, Oxford University, and Fellow, New College, Oxford, 1963–74, then Emeritus Fellow (Hon. Fellow 1980); Professor of Physics (part-time), University of Washington, Seattle, 1974–77; *b* Berlin, 5 June 1907; *s* of H. Peierls and Elisabeth (*née* Weigert); *m* 1931, Eugenia (*d* 1986), *d* of late N. Kannegiesser; one *s* three *d. Educ:* Humboldt School, Oberschöneweide, Berlin; Universities of Berlin, Munich, Leipzig. Assistant, Federal Institute of Technology, Zürich, 1929–32; Rockefeller Fellow, 1932–33; Honorary Research Fellow, Manchester University, 1933–35; Assistant-in-Research, Royal Society Mond Laboratory, 1935–37; Professor of Mathematical Physics (formerly Applied Mathematics), University of Birmingham, 1937–63; worked on Atomic Energy Project in Birmingham, 1940–43, in USA, 1943–45. Royal Society: Royal Medal, 1959; Copley Medal, 1986; Lorentz Medal of Royal Netherlands Academy of Sciences, 1962; Max Planck Medal, Assoc. of German Physical Societies, 1963; Guthrie Medal, IPPS, 1968; first British recipient of Enrico Fermi Award, US Dept of Energy, 1980. Hon. FInstP 1973 (Paul Dirac Medal, 1991). Hon. DSc: Liverpool, 1960; Birmingham, 1967; Edinburgh, 1969; Sussex, 1978; Chicago, 1981; Coimbra, 1988. Foreign Hon. Mem., American Academy of Arts and Sciences, 1962; Hon. Associate, College of Advanced Technology, Birmingham, 1963; Foreign Associate: Nat. Acad. of Sciences, USA, 1970; French Acad. of Sciences, 1984; Hon. Mem., French Phys. Soc., 1979; Foreign Member: Royal Danish Acad., 1980; USSR (later Russian) Acad. of Sciences, 1988; Mem., Leopoldina Acad., E Germany, 1981; Corresponding Member: Yugoslav (later Croatian) Acad. of Arts and Sciences, 1983; Lisbon Academy of Sciences, 1988. *Publications:* Quantum Theory of Solids, 1955; The Laws of Nature, 1955; Surprises in Theoretical Physics, 1979; Bird of Passage, 1985; More Surprises in Theoretical Physics, 1991; papers on quantum theory. *Address:* Oakenholt, Farmoor OX2 9NT; Nuclear Physics Laboratory, Keble Road, Oxford.

Died 19 Sept. 1995.

PELLY, Major Sir John (Alwyne), 6th Bt *cr* 1840, of Upton, Essex; JP, DL; landowner and farmer; *b* 11 Sept. 1918; *s* of Sir (Harold) Alwyne Pelly, 5th Bt, MC, and Caroline (*d* 1976), *d* of late Richard Heywood Heywood-Jones; *S* father, 1981; *m* 1st, 1945, (Ava) Barbara (Ann) (marr. diss. 1950), *o d* of Brig. Keith Frederick William Dunn, CBE; 2nd, 1950, Elsie May, (Hazel) (*d* 1987), *d* of late L. Thomas Dechow, Rhodesia; one *d* (and two *d* decd); 3rd, 1990, 1st wife Barbara (Mrs Cazenove). *Educ:* Canford; RMC Sandhurst; Royal Agricultural Coll. Commissioned Coldstream Guards, 1938; served War of 1939–45; Malaya, 1948–50; retired (Major), 1950. Rhodesia, 1950–61; Royal Agric. Coll., 1962–63 (Certificate of Merit). Mem., Lands Tribunal, 1981–90. JP 1966, High Sheriff 1970–71, DL 1972, Hants. Lord of the Manors of East Ham, West Ham and Burnells with Plaistow. *Recreation:* shooting. *Heir:* nephew Richard John Pelly [*b* 10 April 1951; *m* 1983, Clare Gemma, *d* of late H. W. Dove; three *s*]. *Address:* The Manor House, Preshaw Park, Upham, Hants SO3 1HP. *T:* Bramdean (0962) 771757. *Club:* Royal Over-Seas League.

Died 1 June 1993.

PEMBROKE, Mary Countess of; Mary Dorothea Herbert, CVO 1947; DL; Extra Lady-in-Waiting to Princess Marina, Duchess of Kent, 1950–68 (Lady-in-Waiting, 1934–50); *b* 1903; *o d* of 1st Marquess of

Linlithgow and Hon. Hersey de Moleyns, 3rd *d* of 4th Lord Ventry; *m* 1936, Lord Herbert (later 16th Earl of Pembroke and Montgomery, who *d* 1969); one *s* one *d*. DL Wilts, 1980. *Address:* The Old Rectory, Wilton, near Salisbury, Wilts SP2 0HT. *T:* Salisbury (01772) 743157.
Died 16 Jan. 1995.

PENMAN, John, FRCP; Consulting Neurologist to The Royal Marsden Hospital; *b* 10 Feb. 1913; *er s* of late William Penman, FIA; *m* 1st, 1938, Joan, *d* of late Claude Johnson (marr. diss. 1975); one *s* two *d*; 2nd, 1975, Elisabeth Quin. *Educ:* Tonbridge Sch.; University College, Oxford (Senior Classical Scholar); Queen Mary Coll., E1; The London Hospital. MB, BS (London) 1944; MRCP 1948, FRCP 1969. Neurologist to The Royal Marsden Hospital, 1954–77. Member of Association of British Neurologists. *Publications:* The Epodes of Horace: a new English version, 1980; A Late Harvest: poems, 1987; section on trigeminal injection, in Operative Surgery, 1957; chapters in Handbook of Clinical Neurology, 1968; contributions to medical journals, mainly on tic douloureux and brain tumours. *Recreations:* poetry, etymology, Japanese flower arrangement. *Address:* Forest View, Upper Chute, Andover, Hants SP11 9EL. *Club:* Royal Automobile.
Died 5 Jan. 1994.

PENN, Lt-Col Sir Eric (Charles William Mackenzie), GCVO 1981 (KCVO 1972; CVO 1965); OBE 1960; MC 1944; Extra Equerry to the Queen since 1963; *b* posthumously 9 Feb. 1916; *o s* of Capt. Eric F. Penn (killed in action 1915), Grenadier Guards, and late Gladys Ebden; *m* 1947, Prudence Stewart-Wilson, *d* of late Aubyn Wilson and Muriel Stewart-Stevens, Balnakeilly, Pitlochry, Perthshire; two *s* one *d*. *Educ:* Eton; Magdalene Coll., Cambridge. Grenadier Guards, 1938–60: France and Belgium, 1939–40; Italy and Austria, 1943–45; Germany, 1945–46; Libya and Egypt, 1950–52; Germany, 1953–55. Assistant Comptroller, Lord Chamberlain's Office, 1960–64, Comptroller, 1964–81. *Address:* Carnbee House, by Anstruther, Fyfe, KY10 2RN. *T:* Arncroach (03338) 350. *Clubs:* White's, Pratt's.
Died 10 May 1993.

PENNEY, Baron, *cr* 1967, (Life Peer) of East Hendred in the Royal Co. of Berks; **William George Penney,** OM 1969; KBE 1952 (OBE 1946); MA; PhD; DSc; FRS 1946; Rector of the Imperial College of Science and Technology, 1967–73; *b* 24 June 1909; *s* of W. A. Penney, Sheerness, Kent and Blanche Evelyn, *d* of Henry Alfred Johnson; *m* 1st, 1935, Adele Minnie Elms (*d* 1944); two *s*; 2nd, 1945, Eleanor Joan Quennell. *Educ:* Tech. School, Sheerness; Royal College of Science, London Univ. (BSc, PhD); Commonwealth Fund Fellowship. University of Wisconsin (MA), 1931–33; Senior Student of 1851 Exhibition, Trinity Coll., Cambridge, 1933–36; PhD (Cambridge), DSc (London), 1935. Stokes Student of Pembroke Coll., 1936; Assistant Professor of Mathematics at Imperial College of Science, London, 1936–45; on loan for scientific work to Ministry of Home Security and Admiralty, 1940–44; Principal Scientific Officer, DSIR, at Los Alamos Laboratory, New Mexico, 1944–45; Chief Superintendent, Armament Research, Ministry of Supply, 1946–52; Director Atomic Weapons Research Establishment, Aldermaston, 1953–59; Member for Weapons R&D, UKAEA, 1954–59; Member for Research, UKAEA, 1959–61; Dep. Chm., 1961–64; Chm., 1964–67. Director: Tube Investments, 1968–79; Standard Telephones and Cables, 1971–83. Treasurer, Royal Society, 1956–60 (Vice-President, 1957–60); Fellow, Imperial Coll.; Fellow, Winchester Coll., 1959; Supernumerary Fellow, St Catherine's Coll., Oxford, 1960; Hon. Fellow: Manchester College of Science and Technology, 1962; Trinity Coll., Cambridge, 1969; Pembroke Coll., Cambridge, 1970; Hon FRSE, 1970; For.

Associate, National Academy of Sciences, USA, 1962. Hon. DSc: Durham, 1957; Oxford, 1959; Bath University of Technology, 1966; Hon. LLD Melbourne, 1956. Rumford Medal, Royal Society, 1966; Glazebrook Medal and Prize, 1969; Kelvin Gold Medal, 1971. *Publications:* articles in scientific journals on theory of molecular structure. *Recreations:* golf, cricket. *Address:* Cat Street, East Hendred, Wantage, Oxford OX12 8JT. *Club:* Athenæum.
Died 3 March 1991.

PENNISON, Clifford Francis, CBE 1977; *b* 28 June 1913; *s* of Henry and Alice Pennison; *m* 1940, Joan Margaret Hopkins; three *d*. *Educ:* Taunton Sch.; Bristol Univ. (BA, 1st Cl. Hons, Hist.). Barrister-at-Law, Inner Temple, 1951. Appointed senior management trainee, Unilever Ltd, 1938. Field Security Officer, Army, 1940–46 (Captain). Principal, Home Civil Service, 1946; Assistant Secretary, and Director of Organisation and Methods, Ministry of Food, 1949; Ministry of Agriculture: Director of Statistics Div., 1953; Director of Public Relations Div., 1958; Director of External Relations Div., 1961; FAO: Permanent UK representative, 1963–66; Director, Economic Analysis Div., 1966–67; Asst Dir-Gen., Admin and Finance, 1967–74; Consultant, EEC/FAO relations, 1974–76; retired 1976. Diplôme, Lettres Modernes, and Diplôme, Langue allemande, Univ. of Nice, 1977–81; Final examination (French), Inst. of Linguists, 1984. *Recreations:* reading, foreign languages. *Address:* 9 Arden Drive, Wylde Green, Sutton Coldfield B73 5ND. *T:* 0121–384 2289.
Died 29 Dec. 1995.

PENNOCK, Baron *cr* 1982 (Life Peer), of Norton in the County of Cleveland; **Raymond William Pennock;** Kt 1978; Senior Adviser, Morgan Grenfell Group plc, since 1990 (Director, 1984–90); *b* 16 June 1920; *s* of Frederick Henry Pennock and Harriet Ann Pennock (*née* Mathison); *m* 1943, Lorna Pearse; one *s* two *d*. *Educ:* Coatham Sch.; Merton Coll., Oxford (Hon. Fellow, 1979). 2nd cl. hons History, MA; Dipl. Educn. Royal Artillery (Captain), 1941–46 (despatches 1945). Joined ICI Ltd, 1947; Personnel Management and Commercial Duties, 1947–61; Commercial Dir, Billingham Div., 1961–64; Dep. Chm., Billingham Div., 1964–68; Chm., Agric. (formerly Billingham) Div. 1968–72; Director, ICI Ltd, 1972, Dep. Chm., 1975–80; Chm., BICC plc, 1980–84; Dep. Chm., Plessey Co., 1985–89 (Dir, 1979–89); Director: Standard Chartered plc, 1982–91 (Dep. Chm., 1989–91); Willis Corroon (formerly Willis Faber) plc, 1985–90; Eurotunnel plc, 1986–91. President: CIA, 1978–79; CBI, 1980–82 (Chm., Economic Situation Cttee, 1977–80); UNICE, 1984–86. Mem., NEDC, 1979–82. Mem. Nat. Council, Oxford Soc. *Recreations:* tennis, music, ballet. *Address:* 23 Great Winchester Street, EC2P 2AX. *Clubs:* Boodle's; Vincent's (Oxford); Queen's, Royal Tennis Court, All England Lawn Tennis & Croquet.
Died 23 Feb. 1993.

PENRICE, Geoffrey, CB 1978; consultant, since 1981, including International Monetary Fund Adviser, Ministry of Finance, Thailand, 1984–86; *b* Wakefield, 28 Feb. 1923; *s* of Harry and Jessie Penrice; *m* 1947, Janet Gillies Allardice; three *s*. *Educ:* Thornes House Grammar Sch.; London Sch. of Economics. Control Commn for Germany, 1947; Asst Lectr in Statistics, LSE, 1952; Statistician, Inland Revenue, 1956; Statistician and Chief Statistician, Central Statistical Office, 1964; Chief Statistician, Min. of Housing and Local Govt, 1968; Under-Sec., BoT, Min. of Technology, DTI, 1968–73; Principal Dir of Stats, DoE, later DoE and Dept of Transport, 1973–78; Dir of Stats, and Dep. Sec., DoE, 1978–81. Statistical Adviser to Cttee on Working of Monetary System, 1957–59; OECD Consultant, Turkey, 1981–83. *Publications:* articles on wages, earnings, financial statistics and housing statistics.

Address: 10 Dartmouth Park Avenue, NW5 1JN. *T:* 071–267 2175. *Club:* Reform.
Died 24 March 1994.

PEPLOE, Denis (Frederic Neil), RSA 1966 (ARSA 1956); former Teacher of drawing and painting at Edinburgh College of Art; *b* 25 March 1914; *s* of late Samuel John Peploe, RSA, and Margaret Peploe (*née* Mackay); *m* 1957, Elizabeth Marion (*née* Barr); one *s* one *d. Educ:* Edinburgh Academy. Studied at Edinburgh College of Art and Académie André Lhote, 1931–37. Served War of 1939–45: Royal Artillery and Intelligence Corps. Lectr, Edinburgh College of Art, 1954–79, retd, Governor 1982–85. *Recreations:* hill-walking, mycology. *Address:* 18 Mayfield Gardens, Edinburgh EH9 2BZ. *T:* 031–667 6164. *Died 22 May 1993.*

PEPYS, Lady (Mary) Rachel, DCVO 1968 (CVO 1954); Lady-in-Waiting to Princess Marina, Duchess of Kent, 1943–68; *b* 27 June 1905; *e d* of 15th Duke of Norfolk, KG, GCVO, PC (*d* 1917) and 2nd wife, 12th Baroness Herries (*d* 1945); *m* 1st, 1939, as Lady Rachel Fitzalan Howard, Lieutenant-Colonel Colin Keppel Davidson, CIE, OBE, RA (killed in action, 1943), *s* of Col Leslie Davidson, CB, RHA, and Lady Theodora, *d* of 7th Earl of Albemarle; one *s* one *d;* 2nd, 1961, Brigadier Anthony Hilton Pepys, DSO (*d* 1967). *Address:* Highfield House, Crossbush, Arundel, W Sussex. *T:* Arundel (0903) 883158. *Died 17 Aug. 1992.*

PERCIVAL, Allen Dain, CBE 1975; Deputy Chairman, Stainer & Bell Publishers, since 1989 (Chairman, 1978–89); *b* 23 April 1925; *s* of Charles and Gertrude Percival, Bradford; *m* 1st, 1952, Rachel Hay (*d* 1987); 2nd, 1990, Margaret Pickett. *Educ:* Bradford Grammar Sch.; Magdalene Coll., Cambridge. MusB Cantab 1948. Served War of 1939–45, RNVR. Music Officer of British Council in France, 1948–50; Music Master, Haileybury and Imp. Service Coll., 1950–51; Dir of Music, Homerton Coll., Cambridge, 1951–62; Conductor, CUMS, 1954–58; Dir of Music Studies, GSM, 1962–65, Principal, GSMD, 1965–78; Gresham Prof. of Music, City Univ., 1980–85; Dir, Hong Kong Academy for Performing Arts, 1987–89. Also professional continuo playing, broadcasting and conducting. Dep. Chm., Musicians' Benevolent Fund, 1985–. Sen. Warden, Musicians' Co., 1992–93. FRCM; FGSM; FLCM 1986; Hon. RAM 1966; Hon. FTCL 1967; Fellow: Hong Kong Conservatory of Music, 1980; Curwen Inst., 1981. Hon. DMus City, 1978. *Publications:* The Orchestra, 1956; The Teach Yourself History of Music, 1961; Music at the Court of Elizabeth I, 1975; Galliard Book of Carols, 1980; English Love Songs, 1980; contribs to musical and educnl jls. *Recreations:* travel, gardening. *Address:* Water Gate, Water Lane, Charlton Horethorne, near Sherborne, Dorset DT9 4NX. *T:* Corton Denham (096322) 219. *Died 19 Sept. 1992.*

PERCIVAL, Sir Anthony (Edward), Kt 1966; CB 1954; Secretary, Export Credits Guarantee Department, 1962–71; *b* 23 Sept. 1910; *s* of Leonard Percival; *m* 1st, 1935, Doris Cuff (*d* 1988); one *d;* 2nd, 1990, Audrey Smith. *Educ:* Manchester Gram. Sch.; Cambridge. Entered Board of Trade, 1933; Assistant Secretary, 1942; Commercial Counsellor, Washington, on secondment, 1946–49; Under-Secretary, Board of Trade, 1949–58. Director: Simon Engineering, 1972–80; Trade Indemnity Co., 1973–81. Pres., Berne Union of Export Credit Insurance Organisations, 1966–68. *Address:* 16 Beckenham Road, Beckenham, Kent BR3 4LS.
Died 24 May 1994.

PEREIRA, Helio Gelli, DrMed; FRS 1973; FIBiol 1975; Consultant, Department of Virology, Fundação Oswaldo Cruz, Rio de Janeiro, 1979–88; *b* 23 Sept. 1918; *s* of Raul Pereira and Maria G. Pereira; *m* 1946, Marguerite

McDonald Scott, MD (*d* 1987); one *s* one *d* (and one *d* decd). *Educ:* Faculdade Fluminense de Medicina, also Instituto Oswaldo Cruz, Rio de Janeiro, Brazil. British Council Scholarship, Dept of Bacteriology, Manchester Univ. and Div. of Bacteriology and Virus Research, Nat. Inst. for Med. Research, London, 1945–47; Rickettsia Laboratory, Instituto Oswaldo Cruz, 1948–51; Asst to Prof. of Microbiology, Faculdade Fluminense de Medicina, 1943–45 and 1948–51; Nat. Inst. for Med. Research, Mill Hill, London: Mem. Scientific Staff, 1951–73; Head of Div. of Virology, 1964–73; Dir, World Influenza Centre, 1961–70; Hd of Dept of Epidemiology and of World Reference Centre for Foot-and-Mouth Disease, Animal Virus Res. Inst., 1973–79. Carlos Findlay Prize, Unesco, 1987. *Publication:* (with C. H. Andrewes) Viruses of Vertebrates, 3rd edn 1972, 4th edn (with C. H. Andrewes and P. Wildy) 1978. *Recreations:* swimming, music. *Address:* 3 Ducks Walk, Twickenham, Mddx TW1 2DD. *T:* 0181–892 4511. *Died 16 Aug. 1994.*

PERKINS, Surg.-Vice-Adm. Sir Derek Duncombe S.; *see* Steele-Perkins.

PERKINS, Francis Layton, CBE 1977; DSC 1940; Chairman: British Insurance Brokers' Association, 1976–80; Insurance Brokers' Registration Council, 1977–84; solicitor since 1937; *b* 7 Feb. 1912; *s* of Montague Thornton and Madge Perkins; *m* 1st, 1941, Josephine Brice Miller (marr. diss. 1971); one *s* two *d;* 2nd, 1971, Jill Patricia Greenish. *Educ:* Charterhouse. Served War of 1939–45, Comdr RNVR, in command of minesweepers. Partner in Clifford Turner & Co., 1946, Consultant, Clifford Chance, 1983; Dir, Hogg Robinson & Capel-Cure Ltd, 1962; Chairman: Hogg Robinson and Gardner Mountain Ltd, 1967–74; Hogg Robinson Group Ltd (formerly Staplegreen Insurance Holdings Ltd), 1971–77; Dir, Transport Holding Co., 1971–73. Dep. Pres., 1971, Pres., 1972–77, Corp. of Insurance Brokers; Chairman: UK Insurance Brokers European Cttee, 1973–80; Common Mkt Cttee, Bureau International des Producteurs d'Assurances et de Réassurances, 1977–79; Dep. Chm., Cttee of Management, Inst. of Laryngology and Otology, 1976–78 (Mem., 1974–78); Mem. Council: Industrial Soc., 1976– (Treasurer, 1976–85); Common Law Inst. of Intellectual Property, 1983–. Governor and Chm. of Cttee, Tonbridge Sch.; Governor: Sutton's Hospital in Charterhouse, 1974–; Royal National Throat, Nose and Ear Hospital, 1974–80; Chairman: Fund Raising Cttee, St Bartholomew's Hosp., 1980; City of London and Thames Estuary Panel, Duke of Edinburgh's 1974 Commonwealth Conf.; Trustee, Barts Res. Develt Trust. Master of Skinners' Company, 1966. *Recreations:* tennis, golf, fishing. *Address:* Flat 4, 34 Sloane Court West, SW3 4TB. *T:* 071–730 9775. *Clubs:* Boodle's, MCC, All England Lawn Tennis; Royal St George's Golf; Hon. Co. of Edinburgh Golfers. *Died 5 Feb. 1994.*

PERKS, His Honour (John) Clifford, MC 1944; TD; a Circuit Judge (formerly County Court Judge), 1970–85, retired; *b* 20 March 1915; *s* of John Hyde Haslewood Perks and Frances Mary Perks; *m* 1940, Ruth Dyke Perks (*née* Appleby); two *s* (and one *s* two *d* decd). *Educ:* Blundell's; Balliol Coll., Oxford. Called to Bar, Inner Temple, 1938; joined Western Circuit; Chancellor, diocese of Bristol, 1950–71; Dep. Chm., Devon QS, 1965–71. *Recreation:* castles. *Address:* 32 Melbury Close, Chislehurst, Kent BR7 5ET. *Died 7 April 1994.*

PEROWNE, Rear-Adm. Benjamin Cubitt, CB 1978; Member, Defence Advisory Group, ML Holdings, since 1988; Chairman, Faversham Oyster Fishery Co., since 1991; *b* 18 Feb. 1921; *s* of late Bernard Cubitt Perowne and of Gertrude Dorothy Perowne; *m* 1946, Phyllis Marjorie, *d* of late Cdre R. D. Peel, RNR, Southampton; two *s* one *d. Educ:* Culford Sch. Joined RN, 1939; Sec. to

Adm. Sir Deric Holland-Martin, GCB, DSO, DSC, 1955–64; Acting Captain, 1957–64, Captain 1966; Staff, Chief of Personnel and Logistics, 1967–70 (Cdre, 1969–70); comd, HMS Cochrane, 1971–73; Dir of Defence Policy, 1973–75 (Cdre); Dir, Management and Support Intelligence, 1976–78, also Chief Naval Supply and Secretariat Officer, 1977–78. Gen. Sec., then Dir, RUKBA, 1978–88. *Recreations:* shooting, gardening. *Address:* c/o Barclays Bank, Haslemere, Surrey. *Club:* Army and Navy. *Died 24 Oct. 1992.*

PEROWNE, Dame Freya; *see* Stark, Dame Freya.

PERRETT, His Honour John, JP; a Circuit Judge (formerly a Judge of County Courts), 1969–81; *b* 22 Oct. 1906; *er s* of late Joseph and Alice Perrett, Birmingham; *m* 1933, Elizabeth Mary, *y d* of late William Seymour, Nenagh, Co. Tipperary; two *s* two *d. Educ:* St Anne's RC and Stratford Road Schools, Birmingham; King's Coll., Strand, WC2. Entered office of Philip Baker & Co., Solicitors, Birmingham, 1922; joined late Alfred W. Fryzer, Solicitor, Arundel St, WC2, 1925; joined Herbert Baron & Co., Solicitors, Queen Victoria St, EC4, 1934; called to Bar, Gray's Inn, 1946; practised in London and on Midland Circuit; Dep. Chm., Warwicks QS, 1970–71. Served War of 1939–45.³RAPC, 1939–45; RASC, 1945. JP Warwicks, 1970. *Address:* 5B Vicar's Close, Lichfield, Staffs WS13 7LE. *T:* Lichfield (0543) 252320.

Died 2 May 1992.

PERRY, Frances Mary, (Mrs Roy Hay), MBE 1962; VMH 1971; horticulturist; *b* 19 Feb. 1907; *d* of Richard and Isabella Everett; *m* 1st, 1930, Gerald Amos Perry (*d* 1964); one *s* (and one *s* decd); 2nd, 1977, Robert Edwin Hay, MBE, VMH (*d* 1989). *Educ:* Enfield County Sch.; Swanley Horticultural Coll. (later Wye Coll.). Diploma in Horticulture. Organiser for Agricl and Horticultural Educn, Mddx CC, 1943; Principal, Norwood Hall Inst. and Coll. of Horticulture, 1953–67. Veitch Meml Medal in Gold, RHS, 1964; Sara Francis Chapman Medal, Garden Club of America, 1973. *Publications:* Water Gardening, 1938; The Herbaceous Border, 1949; The Garden Pool, 1954; The Woman Gardener, 1955; (as Charles Hewitt) Flower Arrangement, 1955; Guide to Border Plants, 1957; Making Things Grow, 1960; Shrubs and Trees for the Smaller Garden, 1961; Penguin Water Gardens, 1962; Colour in the Garden, 1964; Book of Flowering Bulbs, Corms and Tubers, 1966; Flowers of the World, 1972; Gardening in Colour, 1972; Plants & Flowers, 1974; Good Gardeners Guide, 1976; Beautiful Leaved Plants, 1979; Water Garden, 1981; (with Roy Hay) Tropical and Subtropical Plants, 1982; Scent in the Garden, 1989. *Recreations:* flower stamps, photography. *Address:* Lussacombe, Lustleigh, Devon TQ13 9SQ. *Died 11 Oct. 1993.*

PERRY, Frederick John; professional tennis coach, TV and BBC Radio commentator, since 1946; *b* Stockport, 18 May 1909; US citizen; *s* of Samuel Frederick Perry, sometime MP for Kettering, and Hannah Perry; *m* 1935, Helen Vinson (marr. diss. 1938); *m* 1941, Sandra Breaux (marr. diss.); *m* 1945, Lorraine Walsh (marr. diss.); *m* 1952, Barbara Riese; one *d. Educ:* elementary school. Started to play tennis at age of 14; World Table Tennis Champion, 1929; first played at Wimbledon Lawn Tennis championships, 1929; Wimbledon Champion, 1934, 1935, 1936; also won Mixed Doubles, with Dorothy Round, Wimbledon, 1935, 1936; Australian Champion, 1934; French Champion, 1935; American Champion, 1933, 1934, 1936; first player to win all four major titles; Mem., British Davis Cup team , 1931–36; winner: Australian Doubles, 1934, and French Doubles, 1935, with Pat Hughes; French Mixed Doubles, with Betty Nuthall; American Mixed Doubles, with Sarah Palfrey, 1932; became professional, 1936. Co-Founder, with Theodore Wegner, Fred Perry Sportswear, 1950. *Publications:* My Story, 1934; Perry on Tennis, 1934; Perry Wins, 1935; Fred Perry: an autobiography, 1984. *Address:* c/o All England Lawn Tennis Club, Church Road, Wimbledon, SW19 5AE. *Died 2 Feb. 1995.*

PERRY, Peter George, CB 1983; Under Secretary, Department of Health and Social Security, 1975–84; *b* 15 Dec. 1923; *s* of late Joseph and Elsie Perry; *m* 1957, Marjorie Margaret Stevens; no *c. Educ:* Dartford Grammar Sch.; London Univ. (LLB). Normandy with Northants Yeomanry, 1944. Joined Min. of Health, 1947; Private Sec. to Minister of State, 1968–70; Asst Sec., 1971. Chm., Investigation Cttee, 1988–91, Chm., Policy Adv. Cttee, 1991–93, Solicitors' Complaints Bureau; Member: Industrial Tribunals, 1984–93; Parole Bd, 1988–91. JP City of London, 1974–87; Freeman, City of London, 1975. *Recreations:* sailing, squash, opera. *Address:* 50 Great Brownings, College Road, Dulwich, SE21 7HP. *T:* 081–670 3387. *Club:* Little Ship (Commodore, 1984–87; Vice-Pres., 1988–). *Died 19 April 1994.*

PERRY, Prof. Roger, FEng 1994; FRSC; Professor of Environmental Control and Waste Management (formerly of Public Health and Water Technology), Imperial College of Science, Technology and Medicine, since 1981; Director, Centre for Environmental Control and Waste Management (formerly for Toxic Waste Management), since 1990; *b* 21 June 1940; *s* of Charles William and Gladys Perry; *m* (marr. diss.); one *s* one *d. Educ:* King Edward's Grammar Sch., Birmingham; Univ. of Birmingham (BSc, PhD); DSc London 1992. FRSH, FIWEM, FICE. Held number of industrial appts in chem. industry until 1964; Depts of Chemistry and Chem. Engineering, Univ. of Birmingham, 1964–70; Mem., academic staff, Imperial Coll., 1970–. Cons. to number of major chemical and engrg based industries and govt depts, UK and overseas, also to UNEP and WHO, resulting in involvement in major environmental projects in some 30 countries. Mem., Univ. of London Senate and Academic Council, 1984–. *Publications:* Handbook of Air Pollution Analysis (ed jtly with R. Young), 1977, 2nd edn (ed jtly with R. M. Harrison), 1986; approx. 200 papers in various scientific jls. *Recreations:* travel, gardening, cooking, building. *Address:* Imperial College of Science, Technology and Medicine, Centre for Environmental Control and Waste Management, South Kensington, SW7 2BU. *T:* 0171–589 5111. *Club:* Athenæum. *Died 1 Oct. 1995.*

PESTELL; *see* Wells-Pestell.

PETCH, Prof. Norman James, FRS 1974; FEng 1979; Professor of Metallurgy, University of Strathclyde, 1973–82, then Emeritus Professor; *b* 13 Feb. 1917; 3rd *s* of George and Jane Petch, Bearsden, Dunbartonshire; *m* 1st, 1942, Marion Blight (marr. diss. 1947); 2nd, 1949, Eileen Allen (*d* 1975); two *d*; 3rd, 1976, Marjorie Jackson. *Educ:* Queen Mary Coll., London; Sheffield Univ. Research at Cavendish Lab., Cambridge, 1939–42; Royal Aircraft Establishment, 1942–46; Cavendish Laboratory, 1946–48; British Iron and Steel Research Assoc., Sheffield, 1948–49; Reader in Metallurgy, Leeds Univ., 1949–56; First Professor of Metallurgy, Leeds Univ., 1956–59; Cochrane Prof. of Metallurgy, 1959–73, a Pro-Vice-Chancellor, 1968–71, Univ. of Newcastle upon Tyne. Former Member: Basic Properties of Metals Cttee, Interservice Metallurgical Res. Council; Ship Steels Cttee, Admiralty; Physics Cttee, Aeronautical Res. Council; Carbon Steel Cttee, BSC; Plasticity Div. Cttee, Nat. Engrg Lab.; former UK Editor: Acta Metallurgica; Internat. Jl of Fracture. Royal Society: Mem. Council, 1979–81; Chm., Scientific Relief Cttee, 1983–88. Rosenhain Medal, Inst. of Metals, 1963; Gold Medal, Amer. Soc. of Metals, 1990.

Address: Findon Cottage, Culbokie, Conon Bridge, Ross-shire IV7 8JJ. *T:* Culbokie (034987) 259.
Died 9 Dec. 1992.

PETERS, Ellis; *see* Pargeter, E.

PHELPS BROWN, Sir Ernest Henry; *see* Brown.

PHILBIN, Most Rev. William J., DD; *b* 26 Jan. 1907; *s* of late James Philbin and Brigid (*née* O Hora). *Educ:* St Nathy's Coll., Ballaghaderreen; St Patrick's, Maynooth. Priest, 1931; DD Maynooth, 1933. Curate, Eastbourne, 1933; Secondary teacher, Ballaghaderreen, 1934; Prof. of Dogmatic Theology, Maynooth, 1936; Bishop of Clonfert, 1953; Bishop of Down and Connor, 1962–82. *Publications:* Does Conscience Decide?, 1969; To You Simonides, 1973; The Bright Invisible, 1984; Mise Padraig, 3 edns; pamphlets on socio-moral questions; contributor to The Irish Theological Quarterly, Studies, The Irish Ecclesiastical Record. *Address:* 81 Highfield Road, Rathgar, Dublin 6, Ireland.
Died 22 Aug. 1991.

PHILIPPS, Lady Marion (Violet), FRAgS; JP; farmer, since 1946; *b* 1 Feb. 1908; *d* of 12th Earl of Stair, KT, DSO and Violet Evelyn, *o d* of Col Harford; *m* 1930, Hon. (Richard) Hanning Philipps, MBE, 2nd *s* of 1st Baron Milford; one *s* one *d. Educ:* privately. FRAgS 1973. War Service: original Mem., WVS HQ Staff, i/c Canteen and Catering Information Services, 1938–41; Min. of Agriculture, 1942–45. Mem., Narberth Rural Dist Council, 1970–73. Chm., Picton Land & Investment Pty Ltd, WA. Trustee, Picton Castle Trust (Graham Sutherland Gallery), 1976–. Founder Mem., British Polled Hereford Soc., 1950– (also first Pres.); Member: Welsh Council, Historic Houses Assoc., 1975; Gardens Cttee, National Council of Historic Houses Assoc., 1975. Pres., Royal Welsh Agricultural Soc., 1978–. JP Dyfed (formerly Pembrokeshire), 1965. CStJ; Order of Mercy, 1926. *Recreation:* gardening. *Address:* Picton Castle, The Rhos, Haverfordwest, Dyfed SA62 4AS. *T:* Rhos (01437) 751201. *Died 18 June 1995.*

PHILIPSON, Sir Robert James, (Sir Robin), Kt 1976; RA 1980 (ARA 1973); RSA 1962 (ARSA 1952); RSW 1954; Head of the School of Drawing and Painting, The College of Art, Edinburgh, 1960–82; President, Royal Scottish Academy, 1973–83 (Secretary, 1969–73); *b* 17 Dec. 1916; *s* of James Philipson; *m* 1949, Brenda Mark (*d* 1960); *m* 1962, Thora Clyne (marr. diss. 1975); *m* 1976, Diana Mary Pollock; one *s*, and one adopted *s* one adopted *d. Educ:* Whitehaven Secondary School; Dumfries Academy; Edinburgh College of Art, 1936–40. Served War of 1939–45: King's Own Scottish Borderers, 1942–46, in India and Burma; attached to RIASC. Member of teaching staff, Edinburgh College of Art, 1947. Exhibited with Browse & Darby Ltd, London, Scottish Gallery and Fine Art Soc., Edinburgh. Mem., Royal Fine Art Commn for Scotland, 1965–80. Hon. RA 1973; Hon. Mem., RHA 1979; Hon. Mem., RCA 1980. Commandeur de l'Ordre National du Mérite de la République Française, 1976. FRSA 1965; FRSE 1977. DUniv: Stirling, 1976; Heriot-Watt, 1985; Hon. LLD Aberdeen 1977. *Address:* 23 Crawfurd Road, Edinburgh EH16 5PQ. *T:* 031–667 2373. *Club:* Scottish Arts (Edinburgh).
Died 26 May 1992.

PHILLIMORE, 4th Baron *cr* 1918, of Shiplake, Oxfordshire; **Claud Stephen Phillimore;** Bt 1881; architect; *b* 15 Jan. 1911; *s* of 2nd Baron Phillimore and Dorothy Barbara, *d* of Lt-Col A. B. Haig, CMG, CVO; *S* nephew, 1990; *m* 1944, Anne Elizabeth, *e d* of late Maj. Arthur Algernon Dorrien-Smith, DSO; one *s* one *d. Educ:* Winchester Coll.; Trinity Coll., Cambridge. RIBA. Major, City of London Yeomanry, 1939–45. 1939–45 Star; Defence Medal; Africa Star, 8th Army. *Recreation:* travel.

Heir: s Hon. Francis Stephen Phillimore [*b* 25 Nov. 1944; *m* 1971, Nathalie Pequin; two *s* one *d*]. *Address:* 39 Ashley Gardens, SW1P 1QE.*Club:* Brooks's.
Died 29 March 1994.

PHILLIPS, Baroness *cr* 1964 (Life Peer), of Fulham, Co. London; **Norah Phillips,** JP; President (and former General Secretary), National Association of Women's Clubs; President: Institute of Shops, Health and Safety Acts Administration; Association for Research into Restricted Growth; Keep Fit Association; International Professional Security Association; Vice-President: National Chamber of Trade; Fair Play for Children; *b* 12 Aug. 1910; *d* of William and Catherine Lusher; *m* 1930, Morgan Phillips (*d* 1963); one *s* one *d. Educ:* Marist Convent; Hampton Training College. A Baroness in Waiting (Govt Whip), 1965–70. Lord-Lieutenant of Greater London, 1978–85. *Address:* House of Lords, SW1A 0PW. *T:* (office) 081–741 4815.
Died 14 Aug. 1992.

PHILLIPS, Arthur, OBE 1957; MA, PhD; JP; Barrister at Law (Middle Temple); Professor Emeritus, University of Southampton; *b* 29 May 1907; *e s* of Albert William Phillips and Agnes Phillips (*née* Edwards); *m* 1934, Kathleen Hudson; two *s* two *d. Educ:* Highgate School; Trinity College, Oxford. In chambers in Temple, 1929; joined Colonial Service, 1931, and served in Kenya: Dist Officer, 1931; Actg Resident Magistrate, 1933–35; Crown Counsel, 1936; Actg Solicitor-Gen., 1940 and 1946; Judicial Adviser, 1945; Mem. of Kenya Leg. Council, 1940; served in Kenya Regt, Somaliland and Abyssinia, 1940–42; Chm. War Claims Commn, British Somaliland, 1942; retd from Colonial Service on medical grounds and practised at Bar, England, 1947–49; Reader in Law, LSE, Univ. of London, 1949–56; Prof. of English Law, Univ. of Southampton, 1956–67; Dean of Faculty of Law, 1956–62; Deputy Vice-Chancellor, 1961–63. Dep. Chm., Hants QS, 1960–71; a Recorder of the Crown Court, 1972–79. Director of Survey of African Marriage and Family Life, 1948–52. Chairman Milk and Dairies Tribunal, South-Eastern Region, 1961–79; Pres., Southern Rent Assessment Panel, 1965–72. JP Hants; Chairman Winchester County Magistrates' Court, 1956–61. Chancellor, dio. of Winchester, 1964–84; Member, Church Assembly, 1965–70; Lay Reader, Diocese of Winchester, 1960–86; Counsellor to the Dean and Chapter of Winchester, 1963–86. *Publications:* Report on Native Tribunals (Kenya), 1945; (ed and part-author) Survey of African Marriage and Family Life, 1953; (jt) Marriage Laws in Africa, 1971; principal contribr on Ecclesiastical Law, Halsbury's Laws of England, 1975. *Address:* 10 Old Parsonage Court, Otterbourne, Winchester, Hants SO21 2EP. *T:* Twyford (0962) 714945. *Club:* Commonwealth Trust.
Died 16 May 1991.

PHILLIPS, Prof. Charles Garrett, DM; FRCP; FRS 1963; Dr Lee's Professor of Anatomy, University of Oxford, 1975–83, then Emeritus; Fellow of Hertford College, Oxford, 1975–83, then Emeritus; *b* 13 October 1916; *s* of Dr George Ramsey Phillips and Flora (*née* Green); *m* 1942, Cynthia Mary, *d* of L. R. Broster, OBE, DM, FRCS; two *d. Educ:* Bradfield; Magdalen College, Oxford; St Bartholomew's Hospital. Captain, RAMC, 1943–46. Reader in Neurophysiology, 1962–66, Prof., 1966–75, Oxford Univ.; Fellow, Trinity Coll., 1946–75, Emeritus Fellow, 1975. Mem., MRC, 1980–84. Hon. Sec., Physiological Society, 1960–66; President: Sect. of Neurology, RSocMed, 1978–79; Assoc. of British Neurologists, 1980–81. Mem., Norwegian Acad. of Sci. and Letters, 1980; Hon. Member: Canadian Neurol Soc.; Belgian Soc. of Electromyography and Clin. Neurophysiology. Editor, Brain, 1975–81. Hon. DSc Monash, 1971. Lectures: Ferrier, 1968; Hughlings Jackson (and Medal), 1973; Victor Horsley Meml, 1981; Sherrington, Univ. of Liverpool, 1982. Feldberg Prize, 1970. *Publications:* papers on neurophysiology in Jl of Physiology, etc. *Address:* 10 Hawkswell Gardens, Oxford OX2 7EX. *Club:* United Oxford & Cambridge University. *Died 9 Sept. 1994.*

PHILLIPS, Surgeon Rear-Adm. Rex Philip, CB 1972; OBE 1963; Medical Officer-in-Charge, Royal Naval Hospital, Plymouth, 1969–72, retired; *b* 17 May 1913; 2nd *s* of William John Phillips, late Consultant Anaesthetist at Royal Victoria Infirmary, Newcastle upon Tyne, and Nora Graham Phillips; *m* 1939, Gill Foley; two *s. Educ:* Epsom Coll.; Coll. of Med., Newcastle upon Tyne, Univ. of Durham (now Univ. of Newcastle upon Tyne). Qual. MB, BS 1937; Ho. Surg., Ingham Infirmary, S Shields, 1938. Joined RN, 1939; served War of 1939–45: HMS Rochester, 1939–41; Royal Marines, 1941–43; HMS Simba, 1943–45. HMS Excellent, 1945–47; qual. Dip. in Ophthalmology (London), 1948; HMS Implacable, Fleet MO, 1949–51; Specialist in Ophthalmology: HMS Ganges, 1951–53; Central Air Med. Bd, 1953–55; RN Hosp., Malta (Senior), 1955–57; Admty Adv. in Ophth. to Med. Dir-Gen., 1957–65; Surg. Captain 1963; SMO, RN Hosp., Malta, 1965–68; Staff MO to Flag Officer Submarines, 1968–69. QHS 1969–72. CStJ 1970. *Recreations:* golf, bridge. *Address:* Langstone House, 25 Langstone High Street, Havant, Hants PO9 1RY. *T:* Havant (01705) 484668. *Died 22 Dec. 1995.*

PHILLIPS, Sydney William Charles, CB 1955; Second Civil Service Commissioner, 1968–70; *b* 1 Dec. 1908; *s* of late Frederick Charles and Elizabeth Phillips; *m* 1932, Phyllis, *d* of late James Spence; two *s. Educ:* Bridport Grammar Sch.; University College, London. Administrative Asst, University College, Hull, 1932–37; Asst Registrar, Liverpool Univ., 1937–45; seconded to Min. of Works, 1941–43; Min. of Town and Country Planning, 1943–51 (Principal Private Sec. to Minister, 1943–44); Asst Sec., 1944; Under-Sec., Min. of Housing and Local Govt, 1952–68, Dir of Establishments, 1963–68. Fellow, UCL, 1969. *Recreations:* walking, gardening. *Address:* Flat 2, 24 Box Ridge Avenue, Purley, Surrey CR8 3AQ. *T:* 081–660 8617. *Club:* Commonwealth Trust. *Died 5 May 1991.*

PHILPOT, Oliver Lawrence Spurling, MC 1944; DFC 1941; Managing Director, Remploy Ltd, 1974–78; *b* Vancouver, BC, Canada, 6 March 1913; *s* of Lawrence Benjamin Philpot, London, and Catherine Barbara (*née* Spurling), Bedford; *m* 1st, 1938, Margaret Nathalie Owen (marr. diss. 1951); one *s* two *d*; 2nd, 1954, Rosl Widhalm, BA Hons History, PhD (Lond.), Vienna; one *s* one *d. Educ:* Queen Mary Sch., N Vancouver; Aymestrey Court, Worcester; Radley Coll.; Worcester Coll., Oxford (BA Hons PPE; MA). RAFVR: Pilot, 42 Torpedo/Bomber Sqdn, RAF Coastal Comd, 1940; shot down off Norway, 1941; 5 prison camps, Germany and Poland; escaped to Sweden and Scotland, as 3rd man in Wooden Horse, from Stalag Luft III at Sagan, Silesia, 1943; Sen. Scientific Officer, Air Min., 1944 (wrote 33 RAF Stations Manpower Survey, 1944). Management Trainee, Unilever Ltd, 1934; Asst (commercial) Sec., Unilever Home Margarine Exec., 1936; Exec., Maypole Dairy Ltd, 1946; Chm., Trufood Ltd, 1948; Office Manager, Unilever House, EC4, 1950; Gen. Manager (admin.), T. Walls & Sons Ltd, 1951; Coast-to-Coast Lecture Tour in N America on own book, Stolen Journey, with Peat Agency, Canadian Clubs and USAAF, 1952; Dir, Arthur Woollacott & Rappings Ltd, 1953; Chm. and Man. Dir, Spirella Co. of Great Britain Ltd, 1956; Man. Dir, Venesta (later Aluminium) Foils Ltd, 1959; Exec., Union International Ltd, 1962 (also Dep. Chm. and Chief Exec., Fropax Eskimo Frood Ltd, 1965–67), i/c Lonsdale & Thompson Ltd, John Layton

Ltd, Merseyside Food Products Ltd, Union Distribution Co. Ltd, Weddel Pharmaceuticals Ltd, John Gardner (Printers) Ltd, and Union Internat. Res. Centre. Chairman, Royal Air Forces Escaping Soc., and RAFES Charitable Fund, 2 terms, 1963–69. Overseas Administrator, Help the Aged, 1979–82; Manager, St Bride Foundn Inst., 1982–89; Mem., Nat. Adv. Council on Employment of Disabled People, 1978; Chm., London NW Area Cttee for Employment of Disabled People, 1981–86. Mem., Gen. Adv. Council, IBA, 1982–85. Supported European Community; fought local environmental battles. *Publication:* Stolen Journey, 1950 (5th edn 1951, repr. 1970; Swedish, Norwegian and Amer. edns, 1951–52; paperback 1954, repr. 4 times, 1962–66). *Recreations:* political activity incl. canvassing, sculling Boat Race course and return (No 452 in Head of the River Race for Scullers, 1986), talking, idling, listening to sermons, reading Financial Times and obituaries in Lancet. *Address:* 30 Abingdon Villas, Kensington, W8 6BX. *T:* 071–937 6013. *Clubs:* London Rowing, Ends of the Earth, Society of Authors, United Oxford & Cambridge University, Goldfish, Guild of St Bride, RAF Escaping Society, RAF ex-POW Association, Aircrew Association; Worcester College Society (London and Oxford). *Died 29 April 1993.*

PHILPS, Dr Frank Richard, MBE (mil.) 1946; retired; Consultant in Exfoliative Cytology, University College Hospital, WC1, 1960–73; Director, Joint Royal Free and University College Hospitals, Department of Cytology, 1972–73; *b* 9 March 1914; *s* of Francis John Philps and Matilda Ann Philps (*née* Healey); *m* 1941, Emma L. F. M. Schmidt; two *s* one *d. Educ:* Christ's Hospital, Horsham, Sussex. MRCS, LRCP, 1939; MB, BS, 1939; DPH 1947; MD London, 1952; FRCPath, 1966; Fellow, International Academy of Cytology, 1967. RAF Medical Service, 1940–46; Japanese POW, 1942–45. Junior Hospital Appointments, UCH, 1950–54; Consultant Pathologist, Eastbourne, 1954–64; Research Asst, UCH, 1955–60. Hon. Cons. in Cytology, Royal Free Hosp., 1972–73. Producer, with wife, Wild Life Series of Educational Nature Films and films on pottery making, for Educational Foundation for Visual Aids; made BBC films, The Magic of a Dartmoor Stream, 1977, The Magic of a Dartmoor Wood, 1979. Exhibitor in the annual exhibition of the Royal Inst. of Painters in Watercolours, 1980–84. BBC Nature Film Prize, 1963; Council for Nature Film Prize, 1966. *Publications:* A Short Manual of Respiratory Cytology, 1964; Watching Wild Life, 1968, 3rd edn 1984; papers on Cytology to several medical journals, 1954–67. *Recreations:* living in the country; watching wild animals and filming them, painting. *Address:* Woodlands, Sydenham Wood, Lewdown, Okehampton EX20 4PP. *T:* Chillaton (01822) 860347. *Died 16 Oct. 1995.*

PICACHY, His Eminence Cardinal Lawrence Trevor, SJ; former Archibishop of Calcutta; *b* 7 Aug. 1916; Indian. *Educ:* St Joseph's College, Darjeeling and various Indian Seminaries. 1952–60: Headmaster of St Xavier's School, Principal of St Xavier's College, Rector of St Xavier's, Calcutta; Parish Priest of Basanti, large village of West Bengal, 1960–62; (first) Bishop of Jamshedpur, 1962–69, Apostolic Administrator of Jamshedpur, 1969–70; Archibishop of Calcutta, 1969. Cardinal, 1976. Pres., Catholic Bishops' Conf. of India, 1976–81 (Vice-Pres., 1972–75). *Address:* c/o Archbishop's House, 32 Park Street, Calcutta 700016, India.

Died 29 Nov. 1992.

PICKARD, Sir Cyril (Stanley), KCMG 1966 (CMG 1964); HM Diplomatic Service, retired; British High Commissioner in Nigeria, 1971–74; *b* 18 Sept. 1917; *s* of G. W. Pickard and Edith Pickard (*née* Humphrey), Sydenham; *m* 1st, 1941, Helen Elizabeth Strawson (*d*

1982); three *s* one *d* (and one *s* decd); 2nd, 1983, Mary Rosser (*née* Cozens-Hardy). *Educ:* Alleyn's Sch., Dulwich; New Coll., Oxford. 1st Class Hons Modern History, 1939. Asst Principal, Home Office, 1939; War of 1939–45: Royal Artillery, 1940–41, Captain; appointment in Office of Minister of State, Cairo, 1941–44, Principal, 1943; with UNRRA in Middle East and Germany, 1944–45; transf. to Commonwealth Relations Office, 1948; Office of UK High Comr in India, New Delhi, 1950; Local Asst Sec., Office of UK High Comr, Canberra, 1952–55; Commonwealth Relations Office, Head of South Asian Dept, 1955–58; Deputy High Commissioner for the UK in New Zealand, 1958–61; Asst Under Sec. of State, CRO, 1962–66 (Acting High Commissioner in Cyprus, 1964); British High Comr, Pakistan, 1966–71. Vice President: Commonwealth Trust; Parkinson's Disease Soc.; Pakistan Soc.; Tibet Soc. *Recreation:* gardening. *Address:* 3 Orwell Road, Norwich NR2 2ND.
Died 26 Dec. 1992.

PICKAVANCE, Thomas Gerald, CBE 1965; MA, PhD; FRS 1976; Fellow, St Cross College, Oxford, 1967–84, then Emeritus; *b* 19 October 1915; *s* of William and Ethel Pickavance, Lancashire; *m* 1943, Alice Isobel (*née* Boulton); two *s* one *d. Educ:* Cowley School, St Helens; Univ. of Liverpool. BSc (Hons Phys) 1937; PhD 1940. Research Physicist, Tube Alloys Project, 1941–46; Lecturer in Physics, University of Liverpool, 1943–46; Atomic Energy Research Establishment, Harwell: Head of Cyclotron Group, 1946–54; Head of Accelerator Group, 1954–57; Deputy Head of General Physics Division, 1955–57; Dir, Rutherford High Energy Lab., SRC, 1957–69; Dir of Nuclear Physics, SRC, 1969–72. Chm., European Cttee for Future Accelerators, 1970–71. Hon. DSc, City Univ., 1969. *Publications:* papers and articles in learned journals on nuclear physics and particle accelerators. *Recreations:* motoring, travel, photography. *Address:* 3 Kingston Close, Abingdon, Oxon OX14 1ES. *T:* Abingdon (0235) 523934.   *Died 12 Nov. 1991.*

PICKERING, Herbert Kitchener; Chief of Protocol, Government of Alberta, 1983–85; *b* 9 Feb. 1915; *s* of Herbert Pickering, Hull, and Ethel Bowman, Carlisle; *m* 1963, Florence Marion Carr; two *s* two *d. Educ:* Montreal; Bishop's Univ. (Business Admin); Cornell Univ. (Hotel Admin); Michigan State Univ. (Hotel and Business Admin). Canadian National Railways: Gen. Passenger Traffic Dept, Montreal, 1930; various cities in Canada and US; served War of 1939–45, RCAF; returned to CNR; assisted in creation and management of Maple Leaf Tour Dept, 1953–59; created Sales Dept for Canadian National Hotels in Western Canada and then for System, 1960–67; Man., Bessborough Hotel, Saskatoon, 1968; Gen. Man., Jasper Park Lodge, until 1973; Agent-Gen. for Alberta in London, 1973–80; opened Govt Office, Hong Kong, and served as Agent General, 1980–82; Senior Dir, International Operations, Edmonton, 1982–83. Charter Mem., Lion's International; Life Mem., Royal Canadian Legion, 1974 (Mem., 1946); Liveryman, Plaisterers' Co., 1980–; Freeman, City of London, 1978; Hon. Mem., Wheelwrights' Co., 1979. *Recreations:* golf, ski-ing, swimming, philately. *Address:* 3074 McMillan Road, Abbotsford, BC V2S 6A8, Canada. *Clubs:* East India and Sports, MCC; Kelowna Canadian, International Skal (Vancouver, BC).   *Died 22 April 1992.*

PICKERING, His Honour John Robertson; a Circuit Judge, 1972–84; *b* 8 Jan. 1925; *s* of late J. W. H. Pickering and Sarah Lilian Pickering (*née* Dixon); *m* 1951, Hilde (marr. diss. 1989) *widow* of E. M. Wright; one *s*, and two step *s. Educ:* Winchester; Magdalene Coll., Cambridge. Degree in Classics (wartime) and Law, MA. Served War, Lieut RNVR, Russia, Europe and Far East, 1942–47. Called to Bar, Inner Temple, 1949. Subseq. with Nat. Coal

Bd and Dyson Bell & Co (Parliamentary Agents). Mem. Parliamentary Bar. Dep. Chm. of Pneumoconiosis, Byssinosis and Miscellaneous Diseases Benefit Bd, and Workmen's Compensation (Supplementation) Bd, 1970; apptd Dep. Chm. NE London Quarter Sessions, 1971. *Publication:* Mines and Quarries Act 1954, 1957.
Died 25 April 1995.

PICKTHORN, Sir Charles (William Richards), 2nd Bt *cr* 1959, of Orford, Suffolk; *b* 3 March 1927; *s* of Rt Hon. Sir Kenneth William Murray Pickthorn, 1st Bt, and Nancy Catherine Lewis (*d* 1982), *d* of late Lewis Matthew Richards; *S* father, 1975; *m* 1951, Helen Antonia, *o d* of late Sir James Mann, KCVO; one *s* two *d. Educ:* King's Coll. Sch., Cambridge; Eton; Corpus Christi Coll., Cambridge (Major Schol., BA). Served RNVR, 1945–48. Called to the Bar, Middle Temple, 1952. Dir, J. Henry Schroder Wagg & Co. Ltd, 1971–79. Occasional journalism. Contested (C) Hemsworth Div., W Riding of Yorks, 1966. Treas., Salisbury Gp, 1978–. Chm., R. S. Surtees Soc., 1980–. *Recreations:* smoking tobacco, sailing, reading. *Heir: s* James Francis Mann Pickthorn, *b* 18 Feb. 1955. *Address:* Manor House, Nunney, near Frome, Somerset BA11 4NJ. *T:* Frome (01373) 836574; 3 Hobury Street, SW10 0JD. *T:* 0171–352 2795.
Died 20 June 1995.

PIERCE, Rt Rev. Reginald James, Hon. DD (Winnipeg), 1947; retired; *b* 1909; *s* of James Reginald Pierce and Clara (*née* Whitehand), Plymouth; *m* 1932, Ivy Bell, *d* of Edward and Lucy Jackson, Saskatoon, Canada; one *d. Educ:* University of Saskatchewan (BA 1931); Emmanuel Coll., Saskatoon (LTh 1932); Univ. of London (BD 1942). Deacon, 1932; priest, 1934; Curate of Colinton, 1932–33; Priest-in-charge, 1933–34; Rector and Rural Dean of Grande Prairie, 1934–38; Rector of South Saanich, 1938–41; Rector of St Barnabas, Calgary, 1941–43; Canon of St John's Cathedral, Winnipeg, and Warden of St John's Coll., 1943–50; Priest-in-charge of St Barnabas, Winnipeg, 1946–50; Bishop of Athabasca, 1950–74; Acting Rector: All Saints, Victoria, BC, 1975–76; St David's, Victoria, BC, 1976–78. Examining Chaplain: to Bishop of Athabasca, 1935–38; to Archbishop of Rupertsland, 1943–50. *Address:* 1735 Green Oaks Terrace, Victoria, BC V8S 2A9, Canada.
Died 11 Jan. 1992.

PIKE, Rt Rev. St John Surridge, DD *jure dig* 1958; Assistant Bishop, Diocese of Guildford, 1963–83; *b* 27 Dec. 1909; *s* of late Rev. Canon William Pike, Thurles, Co. Tipperary; *m* 1958, Clare, *d* of late William Henry Jones; one *s* one *d* (and one *s* decd). *Educ:* The Abbey, Tipperary; Bishop Foy School, Waterford; Trinity Coll., Dublin (MA). Deacon, 1932; priest, 1934; Curate of Taney, 1932–37; Head of Southern Church Mission, Ballymacarrett, Belfast, 1937–47; SPG Missionary, Diocese of Gambia, 1947–52; Rector of St George's, Belfast, 1952–58; Commissary for Gambia in N Ireland, 1954–58; Bishop of Gambia and the Rio Pongas, 1958–63; Vicar of St Mary the Virgin, Ewshot, 1963–71; Vicar of Holy Trinity, Botleys and Lyne, and Christ Church, Longcross, 1971–83. Hon. Canon, Guildford, 1963–83. *Address:* Wisteria Cottage, Old Rectory Lane, Twyford, near Winchester, Hampshire SO21 1NS. *T:* Twyford (0962) 712253.   *Died 13 Nov. 1992.*

PIKE, Lt-Gen. Sir William (Gregory Huddleston), KCB 1961 (CB 1956); CBE 1952; DSO 1943; Chief Commander, St John Ambulance, 1969–75; *b* 24 June 1905; *s* of late Captain Sydney Royston Pike, RA, and Sarah Elizabeth Pike (*née* Huddleston); *m* 1939, Josephine Margaret, *er d* of late Maj.-Gen. R. H. D. Tompson, CB, CMG, DSO, and Mrs B. D. Tompson; one *s* two *d. Educ:* Bedford School; Marlborough Coll.; RMA Woolwich. Lieutenant RA, 20th and 24th Field Brigades, RA and

"A" Field Brigade, Indian Artillery, 1925–36; Staff College, Camberley, 1937–38; Command and Staff Appointments in UK, France and Belgium, North Africa, USA and Far East, 1939–50; CRA, 1st Commonwealth Div., Korea, 1951–52; idc 1953; Director of Staff Duties, War Office, 1954–57; Chief of Staff, Far East Land Forces, Oct. 1957–1960; Vice-Chief of the Imperial General Staff, 1960–63; Col Comdt RA, 1962–70. Lieutenant of HM Tower of London, 1963–66; Commissioner-in-Chief, St John Ambulance Brigade, 1967–73. Jt Hon. Pres., Anglo-Korean Society, 1963–69. Hon. Col 277 (Argyll and Sutherland Highlanders) Regt RA (TA), 1960–67; Hon. Col Lowland Regt RA (T), 1967–70. Member Honourable Artillery Company; Chm., Lord Mayor Treloar Trust, 1976–82; Corps of Commissionaires, 1964–81 (Mem. Administrative Bd). Officer, US Legion of Merit, 1953. GCStJ 1976. *Recreations:* field sports, gardening. *Address:* Ganwells Cottage, Bentley, Hants.

Died 10 March 1993.

PILCHER, Sir (Charlie) Dennis, Kt 1974; CBE 1968; FRICS; Chairman, Commission for the New Towns, 1971–78; Consultant, late Senior Partner (Partner 1930), Graves, Son & Pilcher (Chartered Surveyors); Director, Save and Prosper Group Ltd, 1970–80; *b* 2 July 1906; *s* of Charlie Edwin Pilcher, Fareham, Hants; *m* 1929, Mary Allison Aumonier (*d* 1991), *d* of William Aumonier, London; two *d. Educ:* Claysemore Sch. Served War: Major, RA (despatches, Normandy), 1940–45. Hemel Hempstead Development Corp., 1949–56; Bracknell Development Corp., 1956–71 (Chm. 1968–71); Dir, Sun Life Assurance Soc. Ltd, 1968–77. Pres., RICS, 1963–64; Mem., Milner Holland Cttee on London Housing, 1963–64; Vice-Pres., London Rent Assessment Panel, 1966–70; Adviser to Business Rents Directorate of DoE, 1973–77. Mem. Council, Glyndebourne Fest. Opera, 1969–. *Recreations:* opera, golf, fishing. *Address:* Brambles, Batts Lane, Mare Hill, Pulborough, West Sussex RH20 2ED. *T:* Pulborough (07982) 2126. *Club:* West Sussex Golf. *Died 5 Jan. 1994.*

PILCHER, Robin Sturtevant, MS, FRCS, FRCP; Emeritus Professor of Surgery, University of London; Professor of Surgery and Director of the Surgical Unit, University College Hospital, London, 1938–67; *b* 22 June 1902; *s* of Thorold and Helena Pilcher; *m* 1929, Mabel Pearks; one *s* one *d. Educ:* St Paul's Sch.; University Coll., London. Fellow University Coll., London. *Publications:* various surgical papers. *Address:* Swanbourne, 21 Church End, Haddenham, Bucks HP17 8AE. *T:* Haddenham (0844) 291048. *Died 10 July 1994.*

PILDITCH, James George Christopher, CBE 1983; Founder, AIDCOM International plc (Chairman, 1980–83); *b* 7 Aug. 1929; *s* of Frederick Henry Pilditch and Marie-Thérèse (*née* Priest); *m* 1st, 1952, Molly (marr. diss.); one *d*; 2nd, 1970, Anne Elisabeth W:son Johnson. *Educ:* Slough Grammar Sch.; Reading Univ. (Fine Arts); INSEAD. Nat. Service, commnd RA, 1950; Royal Canadian Artillery Reserve, 1953–56. Journalism in Canada including Maclean-Hunter Publishing Co., 1952–56; work in design offices, Orr Associates (Toronto), THM Partners (London), Jim Nash Assocs (New York), 1956–59; started Package Design Associates (later Allied International Designers), in London, 1959. Chairman: Design Bd, Business and Technician Educn Council, 1983–86; Furniture EDC, NEDO, 1985–88; Design Working Party, NEDO, 1985–86; Financial Times/London Business Sch. Design Management Award, 1987–; Member: Council, Marketing Gp of GB, 1979–84; Adv. Panel, Design Management Unit, London Business School, 1982–; Design Council, 1984–89; Design Management Gp, CSD (formerly SIAD), 1984–86; Council, RSA, 1984–89; Council, Heritage of London

Trust, 1985–; Chm.'s design panel, BAA, 1987–92; Council, RCA, 1990–; UK Cttee, European Cultural Foundn, 1992–. Final Judge, Prince of Wales' Award for Innovation, 1990–. Trustee, Parnham Trust, 1988. FRSA; Hon FCSD (Hon. FSIAD 1985 (ASIAD 1968)); First Hon. Fellow, Design Management Inst., USA, 1985. Medal of Conf. for Higher Educn in Art and Design, for distinguished services to higher educn, 1988. *Publications:* The Silent Salesman, 1961, 2nd edn 1973; (with Douglas Scott) The Business of Product Design, 1965; Communication By Design, 1970; Talk About Design, 1976; Hold Fast the Heritage, 1982; Winning Ways, 1987, 2nd edn 1989; I'll Be Over in the Morning, 1990. *Recreations:* real tennis, watching West Indies cricket, travel, writing, sketching. *Address:* 62 Cadogan Square, SW1X 0EA. *T:* 0171–584 9279; Brookhampton House, North Cadbury, Som BA22 7DA. *T:* North Cadbury (01963) 40225. *Clubs:* Travellers', MCC, Queen's; Falkland Palace Royal Tennis; Barbados Cricket Assoc.

Died 23 Aug. 1995.

PILKINGTON, Sir Lionel Alexander Bethune, (Sir Alastair), Kt 1970; FRS 1969; President, Pilkington plc (formerly Pilkington Brothers), St Helens, since 1985; Director, British Petroleum, since 1976; *b* 7 Jan. 1920; *yr s* of late Col L. G. Pilkington and Mrs L. G. Pilkington, Newbury, Berks; *m* 1945, Patricia Nicholls (*née* Elliott) (*d* 1977); one *s* one *d*; *m* 1978, Kathleen, *widow* of Eldridge Haynes. *Educ:* Sherborne School; Trinity Coll., Cambridge (Hon. Fellow, 1991). War service, 1939–46. Joined Pilkington Brothers Ltd, Glass Manufacturers, St Helens, 1947; Production Manager and Asst Works Manager, Doncaster, 1949–51; Head Office, 1952; Sub-Director, 1953; Director, 1955–85; Dep. Chm., 1971–73; Chm., 1973–80. Dir, Bank of England, 1974–84. Member: Central Adv. Council for Science and Technology, 1970–; SRC, 1972–; British Railways Bd, 1973–76; Court of Governors, Administrative Staff Coll., 1973–; Chairman: Council for Business in the Community, 1982–85; CNAA, 1984–87; Pres., BAAS, 1983–; Vice-Pres., Foundn of Science and Technology, 1986–. Chm., Cambridge Foundn, 1990–. Pro-Chancellor, Lancaster Univ., 1980–90; Chancellor, Liverpool Univ., 1994–. Hon. FUMIST, 1969; Hon. Fellow: Imperial Coll., 1974; LSE, 1980; Sheffield Poly., 1987; Lancashire Poly., 1987. FIMgt (FBIM 1971). Hon. DTech: Loughborough, 1968; CNAA, 1976; Hon. DEng Liverpool, 1971; Hon. LLD Bristol, 1979; Hon. DSc (Eng) London, 1979. Toledo Glass and Ceramic Award, 1963; Mullard Medal, Royal Soc., 1968; John Scott Medal, 1969; Wilhelm Exner Medal, 1970; Phoenix Award, 1981. *Recreations:* gardening, sailing, music. *Address:* 74 Eaton Place, SW1X 8AU; Goldrill Cottage, Patterdale, near Penrith, Cumbria CA11 0NW. *T:* Glenridding (017684) 82263. *Club:* Athenæum. *Died 5 May 1995.*

PILLAI, Sir (Narayana) Raghavan, KCIE 1946 (CIE 1939); CBE 1937; Padma Vibhushan, 1960; *b* 24 July 1898; *s* of M. C. Narayana Pillai, Trivandrum, S India; *m* 1928, Edith Minnie Arthurs (*d* 1976); two *s. Educ:* Madras Univ.; Trinity Hall, Cambridge (schol.). BA (Madras) 1st Cl. English, 1918; Natural Sciences Tripos Pt 1 (Cambridge), 1st Cl., 1921; Law Tripos Pt 2, 1st Cl., 1922. ICS 1921; various appointments under the Government of Central Provinces and the Government of India; Secretary General, Ministry of External Affairs, New Delhi, 1952–60. Hon. DLitt Kerala University, 1953. Hon. Fellow, Trinity Hall, Cambridge, 1970. *Recreation:* walking. *Address:* 26 Hans Place, SW1X 0JY. *Clubs:* Oriental; Gymkhana (New Delhi).

Died 31 March 1992.

PINAY, Antoine; Médiateur, French Republic, 1973–74; leather manufacturer; *b* Department of the Rhône, 30 Dec.

1891; *s* of Claude Pinay and Marie (*née* Besson); *m* 1917, Marguerite Fouletier (decd); two *d* (one *s* decd). *Educ:* Marist Fathers' Sch., St-Chamond. Joined a tannery business there; became Mayor, 1929–77; later became gen. councillor, Dept of the Loire (Pres. 1949–79); was returned to Chamber of Deputies, 1936, Ind. Radical party; Senator, 1938; elected to 2nd Constituent Assembly, 1946; then to 1st Nat. Assembly; re-elected to Nat. Assembly as an associate of Ind. Republican group; Sec. of State for Economic Affairs, Sept. 1948–Oct. 1949; in several successive ministries, July 1950–Feb. 1952, he was Minister of Public Works, Transportation, and Tourism; Prime Minister of France, March-Dec. 1952; Minister of Foreign Affairs, 1955–56; Minister of Finance and Economic Affairs, 1958–60. Served European War, 1914–18, in artillery as non-commnd officer (Croix de Guerre, Médaille Militaire). *Address:* 17 avenue de Tourville, 75007 Paris, France.

Died 13 Dec. 1994.

PINEAU, Christian Paul Francis, Grand Officier, Légion d'Honneur; Compagnon de la Libération; Croix de Guerre; Médaille de la Résistance (Rosette); Hon. GCMG; French statesman and writer; *b* Chaumont (Haute-Marne), 14 Oct. 1904; *s* of Col Paul Pineau and Suzanne (*née* Boland); *m* 1st, Nadine Desaunais de Guermarquer (marr. diss.); four *s*; 2nd, Arlette Bonamour du Tartre; one *d* (one *s* decd); 3rd, 1962, Mlle Blanche Bloys; one *d.* Minister of Food and Supplies, June-Nov. 1945; General Rapporteur to Budget Commission 1945–46; Chm. Nat. Assembly Finance Commn, 1946–47; Minister of Public Works, Transport, and Tourism (Schuman Cabinet), 1947–48, also (Marie Cabinet) July-Aug. 1948, also (Queuille Cabinet), Sept. 1948, also (Bidault Cabinet), Oct. 1949; Minister of Finance and Economic Affairs (Schuman Cabinet), Aug. 1946; Chm. Nat. Defence Credits Control Commn, 1951–55; designated Premier, Feb. 1955; Minister for Foreign Affairs, Feb. 1956–June 1957. Numerous foreign decorations. *Publications: books for children:* Contes de je ne sais quand; Plume et le saumon; L'Ourse aux pattons verts; Cornerousse le Mystérieux; Histoires de la forêt de Bercé; La Planète aux enfants perdus; La Marelle et le ballon; La Bête à bêtises; Le grand Pan; *other publications:* The SNCF and French Transport; Mon cher député; La simple verite, 1940–45; L'escalier des ombres; Khrouchtchev; 1956: Suez, 1976; economic and financial articles; contrib. to various papers. *Address:* 55 rue Vaneau, 75007 Paris, France.

Died 5 April 1995.

PINNINGTON, Geoffrey Charles; Editor, Sunday People, 1972–82; *b* 21 March 1919; *s* of Charles and Beatrice Pinnington; *m* 1941, Beryl, *d* of Edward and Lilian Clark; two *d. Educ:* Harrow County Sch.; Rock Ferry High Sch., Birkenhead; King's Coll., Univ. of London. Served War as Air Navigator, RAF Bomber and Middle East Commands, 1940–45 (Sqdn Ldr, 1943). On staff of (successively): Middlesex Independent; Kensington Post (Editor); Daily Herald: Dep. News Editor, 1955; Northern Editor, 1957; Dep. Editor, 1958; Daily Mirror: Night Editor, 1961, Assistant Editor, 1964, Dep. Editor, 1968; Dir, Mirror Group Newspapers, 1976–82. Mem., Press Council, 1982–86 (Jt Vice-Chm., 1983–86). *Recreations:* his family, travel, reading, music, theatre and the arts, amateur cine-photography. *Address:* 23 Lauderdale Drive, Richmond, Surrey TW10 7BS.

Died 24 Dec. 1995.

PIPER, Bright Harold, (Peter), CBE 1979; FCIB; Director, 1970–84, Chief Executive, 1973–78, Lloyds Bank Group; *b* 22 Sept. 1918; 2nd *s* of Robert Harold Piper; *m* 1st, 1945, Marjorie Joyce, 2nd *d* of Captain George Arthur; one *s* one *d*; 2nd, 1979, Leonie Mary Lane, *d* of Major C. V. Lane. *Educ:* Maidstone Grammar School. Served with

RN, 1939–46. Entered Lloyds Bank, 1935: Asst Gen. Man., 1963; Jt Gen. Man., 1965; Asst Chief Gen. Man., 1968; Dep. Chief Gen. Man., 1970; Chief Gen. Man., 1973. Director: Lewis' Bank, 1969–75; Lloyds and Scottish, 1970–75; Chm., Lloyds First Western (US), 1973–78. FCIB 1967. Freeman, City of London; Liveryman, Spectacle Makers' Company. *Recreation:* sailing. *Address:* Greenways, Hawkshill Close, Esher, Surrey KT10 8JY. *Clubs:* Overseas Bankers, Australia.

Died 16 June 1993.

PIPER, John Egerton Christmas, CH 1972; painter and writer; Member of the Oxford Diocesan Advisory Committee, since 1950; *b* 13 Dec. 1903; *s* of late C. A. Piper, Solicitor; *m* 1st, 1929, Eileen Holding (marr. diss. 1933); 2nd, 1935, (Mary) Myfanwy Evans; one *s* two *d* (and one *s* decd). *Educ:* Epsom Coll.; Royal College of Art. Paintings, drawings, exhibited in London since 1925; pictures bought by Tate Gallery, Contemporary Art Society, Victoria and Albert Museum, etc; series of watercolours of Windsor Castle commissioned by the Queen, 1941–42; windows for nave of Eton College Chapel commissioned 1958; windows and interior design, Nuffield College Chapel, Oxford, completed, 1961; window, Coventry Cathedral, completed, 1962; windows for King George VI Memorial Chapel, Windsor, 1969; windows for Robinson Coll., Cambridge, 1981; designed Tapestry for High Altar, Chichester Cathedral, 1966, and for Civic Hall, Newcastle upon Tyne; designer for opera and ballet. Mem., Royal Fine Art Commn, 1959–78; a Trustee: Tate Gallery, 1946–53, 1954–61, 1968–74; National Gallery, 1967–74, 1975–78; Arts Council art panel, 1952–57. Hon. Fellow, Robinson Coll., Cambridge, 1980. Hon. ARIBA, 1957, Hon. FRIBA 1971; Hon. ARCA 1959; Hon. DLitt: Leicester, 1960; Oxford, 1966; Sussex, 1974; Reading, 1977; Wales (Cardiff), 1981. *Publications:* Wind in the Trees (poems), 1921; 'Shell Guide' to Oxfordshire, 1938; Brighton Aquatints, 1939; British Romantic Painters, 1942; Buildings and Prospects, 1949; (ed with John Betjeman) Buckinghamshire Architectural Guide, 1948; Berkshire Architectural Guide, 1949; (illus.) The Castles on the Ground by J. M. Richards, 1973; (jtly) Lincolnshire Churches, 1976; (illus.) John Betjeman's Church Poems, 1981; (with Richard Ingrams) Piper's Places: John Piper in England and Wales, 1983; *relevant publications:* John Piper: Paintings, Drawings and Theatre Designs, 1932–54 (arr. S. John Woods), 1955; John Piper, by Anthony West, 1979. *Address:* Fawley Bottom Farmhouse, near Henley-on-Thames, Oxon. *Club:* Athenæum.

Died 28 June 1992.

PIPER, Peter; *see* Piper, B. H.

PIPKIN, (Charles Harry) Broughton, CBE 1973; Chairman: BICC Ltd, 1977–80; Electrak International Ltd, 1982–84 (Director, 1982–85); *b* 29 Nov. 1913; *er s* of late Charles Pipkin and Charlotte Phyllis (*née* Viney), Lewisham; *m* 1941, Viola, *yr d* of Albert and Florence Byatt, Market Harborough; one *s* one *d. Educ:* Christ's Coll., Blackheath; Faraday House. CEng, FIEE; FIMgt. Various appts with BICC, 1936–73; Dep. Chm. and Chief Exec., 1973–77. War service, 1940–46: Major REME, 14th Army (despatches). President: British Non-ferrous Metals Fedn, 1965–66; Electric Cable Makers' Fedn, 1967–68; BEAMA, 1975–76. *Recreations:* travel, reading, racing. *Address:* Pegler's Barn, Bledington, Oxon OX7 6XQ. *T:* Kingham (01608) 658304. *Club:* City Livery.

Died 31 Jan. 1995.

PIRATIN, Philip; *b* 15 May 1907; *s* of Abraham Piratin, tradesman, E London; *m* 1st, 1929, Beatrice Silver (marr. diss.); one *s*; 2nd, 1944, Cecilia Gresser (decd), *d* of late P. Fund, Shoreditch; one *d*, and one step *s* one step *d. Educ:* Davenant Foundation Sch., London, E1. Became political worker for Communist Party, subseq. London

Organiser, 1939; Member (Com), Stepney Borough Council, 1937–49; MP (Com) Mile End Division of Stepney, 1945–50; Circulation Manager, Daily Worker, 1954–56; then in business. *Publication:* Our Flag stays Red (autobiog.), 1948. *Died 10 Dec. 1995.*

PIRIE, Henry Ward; crossword compiler, journalist and broadcaster; Sheriff (formerly Sheriff-Substitute) of Lanarkshire at Glasgow, 1955–74; *b* 13 Feb. 1922; *o* surv. *s* of late William Pirie, Merchant, Leith; *m* 1948, Jean Marion (*d* 1992), *y d* of late Frank Jardine, sometime President of RCS of Edinburgh; four *s. Educ:* Watson's Coll., Edinburgh; Edinburgh Univ. MA 1944; LLB 1947. Served with Royal Scots; commnd Indian Army, 1944; Lieut, Bombay Grenadiers, 1944–46. Called to Scottish Bar, 1947. Sheriff-Substitute of Lanarkshire at Airdrie, 1954–55. OStJ 1967. *Recreations:* curling, golf, bridge. *Address:* 16 Poplar Drive, Lenzie, Kirkintilloch, Dunbartonshire G66 4DN. *T:* 0141–776 2494.
Died 29 Nov. 1995.

PIRIE, Psyche; Consultant Design and Decoration Editor, Woman's Journal (IPC Magazines), 1979–84, retired; *b* 6 Feb. 1918; *d* of late George Quarmby; *m* 1940, James Mansergh Pirie; one *d. Educ:* Kensington High Sch.; Chelsea Sch. of Art. Air Ministry, 1940–44. Teaching, Ealing Sch. of Art and Willesden Sch. of Art, 1944–46; indep. interior designer, 1946–56; Furnishing Editor, Homes and Gardens, 1956–68, Editor, 1968–78. *Recreations:* conversation, cinema, theatre, junk shops; or doing absolutely nothing. *Address:* 2 Chiswick Square, W4 2QG. *T:* 0181–995 7184. *Died 2 June 1995.*

PITCHFORD, John Hereward, CBE 1971; FEng 1980; President, Ricardo Consulting Engineers Ltd, since 1976 (Chairman, 1962–76); *b* 30 Aug. 1904; *s* of John Pitchford and Elizabeth Anne Wilson; *m* 1930, Teresa Agnes Mary, (Betty) Pensotti (*d* 1991); one *s* two *d. Educ:* Brighton Coll.; Christ's Coll., Cambridge (MA). FIMechE (Pres. 1962). Ricardo & Co. Engineers (1927) Ltd: Test Shop Asst, 1926; Asst Research Engr, 1929; Personal Asst to Man. Dir, 1935; Gen. Man., 1939; Dir and Gen. Man., 1941; Man. and Jt Techn. Dir, 1947; Chm. and Man. Dir, 1962; Chm. and Jt Man. Dir, 1965; Chm., 1967. Pres., Fédération Internationale des Sociétés d'Ingénieurs des Techniques de l'Automobile, 1961–63; Chm., Navy Dept Fuels and Lubricants Adv. Cttee, 1964–71. Hon. Mem., Associazione Tecnica Automobile, 1958. *Publications:* papers on all aspects of internal combustion engine. *Recreations:* music, sailing. *Address:* Byeways, Ditchling, East Sussex. *T:* Hassocks (017918) 2177. *Club:* Royal Automobile. *Died 24 Feb. 1995.*

PITCHFORD, John W.; *see* Watkins-Pitchford.

PITMAN, Edwin James George, MA, DSc; FAA; Emeritus Professor of Mathematics, University of Tasmania (Professor, 1926; retired, Dec. 1962); *b* Melbourne, 29 Oct. 1897; *of* English parents; *s* of late Edwin Edward Major Pitman and Ann Ungley Pitman; *m* 1932, Edith Elinor Josephine, *y d* of late William Nevin Tatlow Hurst; two *s* two *d. Educ:* South Melbourne Coll.; Ormond Coll., University of Melbourne. BA with First Class Honours, Dixson scholarship and Wyselaskie scholarship in Mathematics. Enlisted Australian Imperial Forces, 1918; returned from abroad, 1919. Acting-Professor of Mathematics at Canterbury Coll., University of New Zealand, 1922–23; Tutor in Mathematics and Physics at Trinity Coll. and Ormond Coll., University of Melbourne, 1924–25. Visiting Prof. of Mathematical Statistics at Columbia Univ., NY, Univ. of N Carolina, and Princeton Univ., 1948–49; Visiting Prof. of Statistics: Stanford Univ., Stanford, California, 1957; Johns Hopkins Univ., Baltimore, 1963–64; Chicago, 1968–69; Vis. Sen. Res. Fellow, Univ. of Dundee, 1973. Fellow, Inst. Math.

Statistics, 1948; FAA 1954; Vice-Pres., 1960; Mem. International Statistical Institute, 1956; Pres., Australian Mathematical Soc., 1958–59; Hon. Fellow, Royal Statistical Soc., 1965; Hon. Life Member: Statistical Soc. of Australia, 1966 (first Pitman Medal, 1978, for contribs to theory of statistics and probability); Australian Mathematical Soc., 1968. Hon. DSc Tasmania, 1977. *Publication:* Some Basic Theory for Statistical Inference, 1979 (trans. Russian 1986). *Address:* Bishop Davies Court, 27 Redwood Road, Kingston, Tas 7050, Australia. *Died 21 July 1993.*

PITT OF HAMPSTEAD, Baron *cr* 1975 (Life Peer), of Hampstead, in Greater London and in Grenada; **David Thomas Pitt,** TC 1976; JP; DL; MB, ChB Edinburgh, DCH London; general practitioner, London, since 1947; *b* St David's, Grenada, WI, 3 Oct. 1913; *s* of Cyril S. L. Pitt; *m* 1943, Dorothy Elaine Alleyne; one *s* two *d. Educ:* St David's RC Sch., Grenada, WI; Grenada Boys' Secondary Sch.; Edinburgh Univ. First Junior Pres., Student Rep. Council, Edinburgh Univ., 1936–37. Dist Med. Officer, St Vincent, WI, 1938–39; Ho. Phys., San Fernando Hosp., Trinidad, 1939–41; GP, San Fernando, 1941–47. Mem. of San Fernando BC, 1941–47; Dep. Mayor, San Fernando, 1946–47; Pres., West Indian Nat. Party (Trinidad), 1943–47. Mem. LCC, 1961–64, GLC 1964–77, for Hackney (Dep. Chm., 1969–70; Chm. 1974–75). Mem. Nat. Cttee for Commonwealth Immigrants, 1965–67; Chm., Campaign Against Racial Discrimination, 1965; Dep. Chm., Community Relations Commn, 1968–77, Chm. 1977; Mem., Standing Adv. Council on Race Relations, 1977–79. Mem. (part time), PO Bd, 1975–77. Vice-Pres., Shelter, 1990– (Chm., 1979–90). Pres., BMA, 1985–86. JP London, 1966. Contested (Lab): Hampstead, 1959; Clapham (Wandsworth), 1970. Hon. DSc Univ. of West Indies, 1975; Hon. DLitt Bradford, 1977; Hon. LLD: Bristol, 1977; Hull, 1983; Shaw Univ., N Carolina, 1985. DL Greater London, 1988. *Recreations:* reading, watching television, watching cricket, listening to music, theatre. *Address:* 6 Heath Drive, NW3 7SY. *Clubs:* Commonwealth Trust, MCC. *Died 18 Dec. 1994.*

PITTAM, Robert Raymond, MBE 1991; Assistant Under-Secretary of State, Home Office, 1972–79; *b* 14 June 1919; *e s* of Rev. R. G. Pittam and Elsie Emma Pittam (*née* Sale); *m* 1946, Gwendoline Lilian Brown; one *s* one *d. Educ:* Bootle Grammar Sch.; Pembroke Coll., Cambridge. MA; 1st Cl. Law Tripos. War of 1939–45: temp. Civil Servant, and service in RAOC, 1940–46. Home Office, 1946–66: Private Sec. to Home Secretary, 1955–57; Asst Sec., 1957; HM Treasury, 1966–68; CSD, 1968–72. Founder Chm., Home Office Retired Staff Assoc., 1982–. *Address:* 14 Devonshire Way, Shirley, Croydon, Surrey. *Club:* Civil Service.
Died 21 Oct. 1991.

PITTER, Ruth, CBE 1979; CLit 1974; poetess; *b* Ilford, Essex, 7 Nov. 1897; *d* of George Pitter, Elementary Schoolmaster. *Educ:* Elementary Sch.; Coborn Sch., Bow. E. Heinemann Foundation Award, 1954; Queen's Medal for Poetry, 1955. *Publications:* First Poems, 1920; First and Second Poems, 1927; Persephone in Hades (privately printed), 1931; A Mad Lady's Garland, 1934; A Trophy of Arms, 1936 (Hawthornden Prize, 1937); The Spirit Watches, 1939; The Rude Potato, 1941; The Bridge, 1945; Pitter on Cats, 1946; Urania, 1951; The Ermine, 1953; Still By Choice, 1966; Poems 1926–66, 1968; End of Drought, 1975; Collected Poems, 1990. *Recreation:* gardening. *Address:* 71 Chilton Road, Long Crendon, near Aylesbury, Bucks. *T:* Long Crendon (0844) 208 373.
Died 29 Feb. 1992.

PITTS-TUCKER, Robert St John, CBE 1975; *b* 24 June 1909; *e s* of Walter Greame Pitts-Tucker, Solicitor, and Frances Elsie Wallace; *m* 1942, Joan Margery (*d* 1991), *d*

of Frank Furnivall, Civil Engineer, India, and Louisa Cameron Lees; three *s* one *d. Educ:* Haileybury (Schol.); Clare Coll., Cambridge (Schol.). 1st cl. Class. Tripos, Pts I and II, 1930 and 1931. Asst Master, Shrewsbury Sch., 1931–44; Headmaster, Pocklington Sch., 1945–66; Dep. Sec. to HMC and HMA, 1966–69, Sec., 1970–74. Member: ER Yorks Educn Cttee, 1946–66; Herts Educn Cttee, 1974–85; Vice-Chm., Yorks Rural Community Council, 1949–65; Mem., Secondary Schools Examination Council, 1954–57. Mem., House of Laity, Church Assembly, 1956–70; St Albans diocese: Reader; Vice-Pres. of Synod, 1976–79. Governor: Mill Hill Sch.; Haileybury. Mem., GBA Exec. Cttee, 1975–80. *Recreations:* country walks, listening to music, gardening. *Clubs:* Commonwealth Trust, East India, Devonshire, Sports and Public Schools.
Died 5 Aug. 1993.

PIXLEY, Sir Neville (Drake), Kt 1976; MBE (mil.) 1944; VRD 1941; company director; *b* 21 Sept. 1905; *s* of Arthur and Florence Pixley; *m* 1938, Lorna, *d* of Llewellyn Stephens; three *d. Educ:* C of E Grammar Sch., Brisbane. FCIT. Served RANR, 1920–63; War Service, Comd Corvettes, 1939–46 (Comdr 1945). Macdonald, Hamilton & Co. (P&O agents), 1922–59, Managing Partner, 1949–59; Chm., P&O Lines of Australia, 1960–70; Director: Burns Philp & Co. Ltd, 1962–80; Mauri Brothers & Thomson Ltd, 1970–77; NSW Boards of Advice: Nat. Bank of Australasia Ltd, 1970–77; Elder Smith Goldsborough Mort Ltd, 1970–76. Chm. Australian Cttee, Lloyd's Register of Shipping, 1967–80. ADC to King George VI and to the Queen, 1951–54. Order of St John in Australia: KStJ 1963; GCStJ 1984; Bailiff Grand Cross; apptd Receiver-Gen., 1963, Vice-Chancellor, 1978, retired. Pres., Royal Humane Soc. of NSW. *Recreation:* tennis. *Address:* 23 Carlotta Road, Double Bay, Sydney, NSW 2028, Australia. *T:* (2) 3275354. *Clubs:* Union, Australian (Sydney); Queensland (Qld).
Died 12 Aug. 1993.

PIZEY, Admiral Sir (Charles Thomas) Mark, GBE 1957 (KBE 1953); CB 1942; DSO 1942, and bar 1943; DL; Royal Navy, retired; *b* 1899; *s* of late Rev. C. E. Pizey, Mark and Huntspill, Somerset; *m* Phyllis (*d* 1993), *d* of Alfred D'Angibau; two *d.* Served European War, 1914–18, Midshipman, Revenge, 1916–18; Lieut, 1920; HMS Danae Special Service Squadron World Cruise, 1921–22; Flag Lieut to Vice-Admiral Sir Howard Kelly, 2nd in command Mediterranean Fleet, 1929–30; Destroyer Commands Mediterranean and Home Fleets, 1930–39; War of 1939–45: Captain, 1939; commanded HMS Ausonia, Atlantic Patrol and Convoys, 1939–40; Captain (D) 21st Destoyer Flotilla in HMS Campbell, Nore Command, Channel and North Sea Operations, 1940–42 (CB, DSO, despatches twice); commanded HMS Tyne and Chief Staff Officer to Rear-Admiral Destroyers, Home Fleet, Russian convoys, 1942–43 (bar to DSO); Director of Operations (Home) Admiralty Naval Staff, 1944–45; Chief of Staff to C-in-C Home Fleet, 1946; Imperial Defence Coll., 1947 (idc); Rear-Admiral, 1948; Chief of UK Services Liaison Staff, Australia, 1948–49; Flag Officer Commanding First Cruiser Squadron, 1950–51; Vice-Admiral, 1951; Chief of Naval Staff and Commander-in-Chief, Indian Navy, 1951–55; Admiral, 1954; Commander-in-Chief, Plymouth, 1955–58, retired. DL County of Somerset, 1962. *Address:* 1 St Ann's Drive, Burnham on Sea, Somerset TA8 2HR. *Died 17 May 1993.*

PLACE, Rear-Adm. (Basil Charles) Godfrey, VC 1944; CB 1970; CVO 1991; DSC 1943; Lay Observer, Royal Courts of Justice, 1975–78; *b* 19 July 1921; *s* of late Major C. G. M. Place, DSO, MC, and Anna Margaret Place, *d* of W. A. Stuart-William, PWD, India; *m* 1943, Althea Annington, *d* of late Harry Tickler, Grimsby; one *s* two *d. Educ:* The Grange, Folkestone; RNC, Dartmouth.

Midshipman, 1939; 10th and 12th submarine flotillas, 1941–43; Lieut, 1942; Comdr, 1952; HMS Glory (801 Sqn), 1952–53; Comdg HMS Tumult, 1955–56; Exec. Officer, HMS Theseus, 1956–57; HMS Corunna, 1957–58; Captain, 1958; Chief SO to Flag Officer Aircraft Carriers, 1958–60; Deputy Director of Air Warfare, 1960–62; HMS Rothesay and Captain (D), 25th Escort Squadron, 1962–63; HMS Ganges, 1963–65; HMS Albion, 1966–67; Adm. Comdg Reserves, and Dir-Gen., Naval Recruiting, 1968–70. Chm., VC and GC Assoc., 1971–94. Polish Cross of Valour, 1941. *Address:* The Old Bakery, Corton Denham, Sherborne, Dorset DT9 4LR.
Died 27 Dec. 1994.

PLAIDY, Jean; *see* Hibbert, Eleanor.

PLAISTER, Sir Sydney, Kt 1980; CBE 1972; FRICS; chartered quantity surveyor, since 1930; *b* 15 Jan. 1909; *s* of Herbert Plaister; *m* 1937, Coralie Fraser Steele; one *s* one *d. Educ:* Acton and Chiswick Polytechnic; College of Estate Management. Partner, L. C. Wakeman & Partners, 1942, Consultant, 1977. Chairman, Solihull Conservative Assoc., 1951–53 and 1957; West Midlands Conservative Council: Hon. Treasurer, 1967–73; Chairman, 1973–76; President, 1980–83; Pres., Midlands Central Conservative Euro-constituency Council, 1985– (Chm., 1978–85); Mem. Exec. Cttee, Nat. Union of Conservative Associations, 1967–82. Freeman, City of London, 1981; Liveryman, Worshipful Co. of Glaziers, 1982. *Recreations:* gardening, music, travel. *Address:* Turnpike Close, Old Warwick Road, Lapworth, Warwickshire B94 6AP. *T:* Lapworth (05643) 2792.
Died 25 March 1991.

PLATT, Rev. William James; General Secretary, British and Foreign Bible Society, 1948–60; Consultant, 1960–61; retired, 1961; *b* 2 May 1893; *s* of James and Mary Platt; *m* 1921, Hilda Waterhouse (*d* 1975); one *d. Educ:* Rivington Grammar School; Didsbury Theological College, Manchester. Methodist Missionary in West Africa, 1916–30; Chairman and General Superintendent, Methodist District of French West Africa, 1925–30; joined Bible Society Staff as Secretary for Equatorial Africa, 1930; travelled extensively as General Secretary of Bible Society. Chairman of Council, United Bible Societies, 1954–57. Hon. DD, Knox College, Toronto, Canada, 1954. Officer of the Order of Orange Nassau (Netherlands), 1954; Commander, National Order of the Ivory Coast Republic, 1985 (Officer, 1964). *Publications:* An African Prophet; From Fetish to Faith; Whose World?; Three Women in Central Asia; articles in religious and missionary publications. *Address:* Winton House, 51 Dedworth Road, Windsor, Berks SL4 5AZ. *T:* Windsor (0753) 840616. *Club:* Commonwealth Trust.
Died 5 July 1993.

PLAXTON, Ven. Cecil Andrew; Archdeacon of Wiltshire, 1951–74, then Archdeacon Emeritus of the Diocese of Salisbury; *b* 1902; *s* of Rev. J. W. Plaxton, Wells and Langport, Somerset; *m* 1929, Eleanor Joan Elisabeth Sowerby (*d* 1989); one *s* (one *d* decd). *Educ:* Magdalen College School, Oxford; St Edmund Hall, Oxford; Cuddesdon Theological College. BA 1924, MA 1928, Oxford. Deacon, 1926; priest, 1927; Curate of Chard, 1926–28; Curate of St Martin, Salisbury, 1928–32; Vicar of Southbroom, Devizes, 1932–37; Vicar of Holy Trinity, Weymouth, 1937–51; Rural Dean of Weymouth, 1941–51; Rector of Pewsey, 1951–65; Canon of Salisbury and Prebend of Netheravon, 1949. Officiating Chaplain to the Forces, 1932–51. *Publication:* The Treasure of Salisbury: Life and Death of St Edmund of Abingdon, 1971, repr. 1980. *Recreations:* archæology, travelling, music. *Address:* 12 Castle Court, St John's Street, Devizes, Wilts SN10 1DQ. *T:* Devizes (0380) 723391.
Died 2 Feb. 1993.

PLAYER, Denis Sydney, CBE 1967; Hon. President, Newall Engineering Group, 1973 (Chairman 1962–73; Deputy Chairman, 1955); Chairman, Newall Machine Tool Co. Ltd, 1964–73; *b* 13 Nov. 1913; *s* of Sydney Player and Minnie Emma Rowe; *m* 1940, Phyllis Ethel Holmes Brown (*d* 1975); three *d. Educ:* England; Worcester Acad., Mass. Apprenticed to Newall Engrg Co. Ltd, 1930; spent a year with Federal Produce Corp., RI, before rejoining Newall Engrg on Sales side; Man. Dir, Optical Measuring Tools, 1940; formed Sales Div. for whole of Newall Engrg Gp, 1945. Joined Royal Artillery, 1939; invalided out, 1940. CEng, FIProdE, FRSA. High Sheriff of Rutland, 1970–71. *Recreations:* yachting, fishing, shooting. *Address:* c/o National Westminster Bank, 8 Bennetts Hill, Birmingham B2 5RT. *Clubs:* Royal Automobile, Royal Ocean Racing; Island Sailing (Cowes). *Died 30 April 1994.*

PLEASENCE, Donald, OBE 1994; actor; *b* 5 Oct. 1919; *s* of late Thomas Stanley and of Alice Pleasence; *m* 1st, 1940, Miriam Raymond (marr. diss. 1958); two *d*; 2nd, 1959, Josephine Crombie (marr. diss. 1970); two *d*; 3rd, 1970, Meira Shore (marr. diss.); one *d*; 4th, 1989, Linda Woollam. *Educ:* The Grammar School, Ecclesfield, Yorkshire. Made first stage appearance at the Playhouse Theatre, Jersey, CI, May 1939; first London appearance, Twelfth Night, Arts Theatre, 1942. Served with RAF, 1942–46 (Flt Lieut); shot down and taken prisoner, 1944. Returned to stage in The Brothers Karamazov, Lyric, Hammersmith, 1946; Huis Clos, Arts Theatre; Birmingham Repertory Theatre, 1948–50; Bristol Old Vic, 1951; Right Side Up, and Saint's Day, Arts Theatre, 1951; Ziegfeld Theatre, New York (with Laurence Olivier's Co.), 1951; played in own play, Ebb Tide, Edinburgh Festival and Royal Court Theatre, 1952; Stratford-on-Avon season, 1953; Wise Child, NY, 1972; *London appearances:* Hobson's Choice, 1952; Antony and Cleopatra, 1953; The Rules of the Game, 1955; The Lark, 1956; Misalliance, 1957; Restless Heart, 1960; The Caretaker, 1960, New York, 1961; Poor Bitos, also New York; The Man in the Glass Booth, St Martin's, 1967 (London Variety Award for Stage Actor of the Year, 1968), New York, 1968–69; Tea Party, The Basement, 1970; Reflections, Theatre Royal, Haymarket, 1980; The Caretaker, Arts, 1990. Many television appearances, incl. The Barchester Chronicles, 1982, The Falklands Factor, 1983, Scoop, 1987. Named Actor of the Year, 1958. *Films include:* The Beachcomber, Heart of a Child, Manuela, The Great Escape, Doctor Crippen, The Caretaker, The Greatest Story Ever Told, The Hallelujah Trail, Fantastic Voyage, Cul-de-Sac, The Night of the Generals, Eye of the Devil, Will Penny, The Mad Woman of Chaillot, Sleep is Lovely, Arthur! Arthur?, THX 1138, Outback, Soldier Blue, The Pied Piper, The Jerusalem File, Kidnapped, Innocent Bystanders, Death Line, Henry VIII, Wedding in White, The Rainbow Boys, Malachi's Cove, Mutations, Tales From Beyond the Grave, The Black Windmill, Escape to Witch Mountain, I Don't Want to be Born, Journey Into Fear, Hearts of the West, Trial by Combat, The Last Tycoon, The Passover Plot, The Eagle has Landed, Golden Rod, The Devil's Men, Tomorrow Never Comes, Telefon, Sgt Pepper's Lonely Hearts Club Band, Halloween, Power Play, Dracula, Halloween II, The Monster Club, Escape from New York, Race for the Yankee Zephyr, Frankenstein's Great Aunt Tilly, A Rare Breed, Warrior of the Lost World, Creepers, The Ambassador, The Corsican Brothers, Master of the Game, Arch of Triumph, Phenomenon, Honour Thy Father, Nothing Underneath, The Rainbow Four, Into the Darkness, Nosferatu II, Ground Zero, Catacomb, Animale Metropolitani, Gila and Rick, The Return of Djiango, Fuja del'Inferno, Prince of Darkness, Imbalances, Hanna's War, Ground Zero, Commander Search and Destroy,

Halloween IV, Paganini Horror, River of Blood, Murder on Safari, Buried Alive, Fall of the House of Usher, American Rickshaw, Casablanca Express, Halloween V, Women in Arms, Miliardi, Shadows and Fog, Dien Bien Phu, Hour of the Pig, The Big Freeze. *Recreation:* talking too much. *Address:* 219 The Plaza, 535 Kings Road, SW10 0SZ. *Died 2 Feb. 1995.*

PLEVEN, René Jean; Compagnon de la Libération, 1943; Commandeur du Mérite Maritime, 1945; French Statesman; Député des Côtes-du-Nord, 1945–73; Président du Conseil Général des Côtes-du-Nord, 1949; Président du Conseil Régional de Bretagne, 1974; *b* 15 April 1901; *s* of Colonel Jules Pleven and Valérie Andrée Synave; *m* 1924, Anne Bompard (*d* 1966); two *d. Educ:* Faculté de Droit de Paris (LLD); Ecole Libre des Sciences Politiques. Company Director. Deputy chief of French Air Mission to USA, 1939. French National Committee and Comité Français de Libération Nationale (Finances, Colonies, Foreign Affairs), 1941–44; Minister: of Colonies (Provisional Government), 1944; of Finances, 1944–46; of Defence, Nov. 1949 and 1952–54; Président du Conseil, July 1950, Aug. 1951–Jan. 1952; Vice-Président du Conseil, Feb. 1951; Ministre des Affaires Etrangères, 1958; Délégué à l'Assemblée parlementaire européenne, and Chm., Liberal Gp of this Assembly, 1956–69; Ministre de la Justice, et Garde des Sceaux, 1969–73. Grand Officer Order of Leopold (Belgium), 1945; Grand Cross: Le Million d'éléphants (Laos), 1949; Etoile Polaire (Sweden), 1950; Orange-Nassau (Netherlands), 1950; Dannebrog (Denmark), 1950; Ouissam Alaouite (Morocco), 1950; Vietnam, 1951; Order of Merit of the Republic of Italy, 1972; National Order of Ivory Coast, 1972; Order of Central African Republic, 1972; Hon GBE, 1972. *Publications:* Les Ouvriers de l'agriculture anglaise depuis la guerre, 1925; Avenir de la Bretagne, 1962. *Address:* 12 rue Chateaubriand, 22100 Dinan (Côtes d'Armor), France. *Died 13 Jan. 1993.*

PLOWMAN, Sir (John) Anthony, Kt 1961; Judge of the High Court of Justice (Chancery Division), 1961–76, Vice-Chancellor, 1974–76; *b* 27 Dec. 1905; *e s* of late John Tharp Plowman (solicitor); *m* 1933, Vernon (*d* 1988), 3rd *d* of late A. O. Graham, Versailles; three *d. Educ:* Highgate School; Gonville and Caius Coll., Cambridge. Solicitors Final (John Mackrell Prize), 1927; LLB London, 1927; LLB Cantab (1st Cl.), 1929; LLM Cantab 1956. Called to Bar, Lincoln's Inn, 1931 (Tancred and Cholmeley studentships; Buchanan Prize); QC 1954; Bencher of Lincoln's Inn, 1961; Member of General Council of the Bar, 1956–60. Served War, 1940–45, Squadron-Leader, RAF. *Address:* Treetop, Lane End, High Wycombe, Bucks HP14 3HX. *Died 30 Aug. 1993.*

POANANGA, Maj.-Gen. Brian Matauru, CB 1980; CBE 1977 (OBE 1967; MBE 1962); Chief of General Staff, New Zealand Army, 1978–81, retired; *b* 2 Dec. 1924; *s* of Henare and Atareta Poananga; *m* 1949, Doreen Mary Porter (formerly QAIMNS/R); two *s* one *d. Educ:* Royal Military College, Duntroon, Australia. Graduated RMC, 1946; served BCOF, Japan, 1947–48; Commonwealth Div., Korea, 1952–53 (mentioned in despatches, 1952); Staff Coll., Camberley, 1957; 28 Commonwealth Inf. Bde, Malaya, 1959–61; Jt Services Staff Coll., Latimer, 1964; CO 1RNZIR, Malaysia, 1965–67 (mentioned in despatches, Sarawak, 1966); Dir of Army Training, 1968–69; Dir of Services Intelligence, 1969–70; Comdr Army Training Gp, 1970–72; RCDS, 1973; Comdr 1st (NZ) Inf. Bde Gp, 1974; NZ High Commissioner to Papua New Guinea, 1974–76; Deputy Chief of General Staff, 1977–78. *Recreations:* golf, fishing. *Address:* PO Box 397, Taupo, New Zealand. *T:* (74) 48296. *Club:* Taupo (NZ). *Died 5 Sept. 1995.*

POETT, Gen. Sir (Joseph Howard) Nigel, KCB 1959 (CB 1952); DSO and Bar, 1945; idc; psc; *b* 20 Aug. 1907; *s* of late Maj.-Gen. J. H. Poett, CB, CMG, CBE and Julia Baldwin, *d* of Edward Thompson Caswell, USA; *m* 1937, Julia, *d* of E. J. Herrick, Hawkes Bay, NZ; two *s* one *d*. *Educ:* Downside; RMC Sandhurst. 2nd Lieut, DLI, 1927; Operations, NW Frontier, 1930–31; Adjt 2nd Bn DLI, 1934–37; GSO2, 2nd Div., 1940; GSO1, War Office, 1941–42; Comd 11th Bn DLI, 1942–43; Comdr, 5th Parachute Bde, 1943–46; served North-West Europe, 1944–45; Far East, 1945–46; Director of Plans, War Office, 1946–48; idc 1948; Dep.-Commander, British Military Mission, Greece, 1949; Maj.-General, 1951; Chief of Staff, FARELF, 1950–52; GOC 3rd Infantry Division, Middle East Land Forces, 1952–54; Dir of Military Operations, War Office, 1954–56; Commandant, Staff Coll., Camberley, 1957–58; Lt-Gen., 1958; General Officer Commanding-in-Chief, Southern Command, 1958–61; Commander-in-Chief, Far East Land Forces, 1961–63; General, 1962. Colonel, The Durham Light Infantry, 1956–65. Dir, British Productivity Council, 1966–71. Silver Star, USA. *Posthumous publication:* Pure Poett (autobiog.), 1991. *Address:* Swaynes Mead, Great Durnford, Salisbury, Wilts. *Club:* Army and Navy.
Died 29 Oct. 1991.

POLE; *see* Chandos-Pole.

POLE, Col Sir John Gawen C.; *see* Carew Pole.

POLLOCK, David Linton; *b* 7 July 1906; *yr s* of late Rev. C. A. E. Pollock, formerly President of Corpus Christi College, Cambridge, and Mrs G. I. Pollock; *m* 1st, 1933, Lilian Diana Turner; one *s*; 2nd, 1950, Margaret Duncan Curtis-Bennett (*née* Mackintosh). *Educ:* Marlborough Coll.; Trinity Coll., Cambridge. Partner in the firm of Freshfields, 1938–51; served with HM Treasury, 1939–40; War of 1939–45, Commander RNVR (despatches). Member of British Government Economic Mission to Argentina, 1946. Former Director: S. Pearson & Son Ltd; National Westminster Bank Ltd; Vickers Ltd; Legal and General Assurance Soc. Ltd; Industrial and Commercial Finance Corp. Ltd. President, Société Civile du Vignoble de Château Latour. Member of Council: Royal Yachting Assoc., 1950–65; Marlborough College, 1950–71. *Recreation:* sailing. *Address:* The Old Rectory, Wiggonholt, near Pulborough, West Sussex RH20 2EL. *T:* Pulborough (07982) 2531. *Clubs:* Royal Thames Yacht; Itchenor Sailing (Sussex). *Died 17 Sept. 1991.*

POLLOCK, Sir George, Kt 1959; QC 1951; *b* 15 March 1901; *s* of William Mackford Pollock; *m* 1st, 1922, Doris Evelyn Main (*d* 1977); one *s* one *d*; 2nd, 1977, Mollie (*née* Pedder) (*d* 1988), widow of J. A. Van Santen. Served Merchant Navy, 1914–18 War; served Army (Special Forces), 1940–44, Egypt, N Africa, Sicily and Italy (Colonel, Gen. Staff); Chief Judicial Officer, Allied Control Commn, Italy, 1944. Entered journalism as trainee reporter on Leamington Spa Courier; sub-editor Daily Chronicle, 1922–28; called to Bar, Gray's Inn, 1928; Bencher, 1948; Recorder of Sudbury, 1946–51; retired from Bar, 1954; Dir, British Employers' Confedn, 1954–65; Member: Nat. Jt Adv. Council (to advise Minister of Labour), Jt Consultative Cttee (to advise BEC and TUC), Nat. Production Adv. Council on Industry (to advise Pres., BOT), 1955–61; British Productivity Council, 1955–61. Assisted in planning and orgn of newly constituted CBI; Senior Consultant to CBI on Internat. Labour Affairs, 1965–69. Member: Governing Body, ILO, 1963–69; EFTA Consultative Cttee, 1966–69; Royal Commn on Trade Unions and Employers' Organisations. Mem. Council, Sussex Univ., 1974–77. *Publication:* Life of Mr Justice McCardie, 1934. *Address:* Cranhill Nursing Home, Weston Road, Bath, Avon BA1 2YA.
Died 28 April 1991.

POLLOCK, John Denton; General Secretary, Educational Institute of Scotland, 1975–88; a Forestry Commissioner, 1978–91; *b* 21 April 1926; *s* of John Pollock and Elizabeth (*née* Crawford); *m* 1961, Joyce Margaret Sharpe; one *s* one *d*. *Educ:* Ayr Academy; Royal Technical Coll., Glasgow; Glasgow Univ.; Jordanhill Coll. of Education. BSc (Pure Science). FEIS 1971. RE, 1945–48 (commnd). Teacher, Mauchline Secondary Sch., 1951–59; Head Teacher, Kilmaurs Secondary Sch., 1959–65; Rector, Mainholm Acad., 1965–74. Chm., Scottish Labour Party, 1959 and 1971. Vice-Chm., Scottish TUC, 1980–81, Chm., 1981–82 (Mem., Gen. Council, 1975–87). Member: (Annan) Cttee on Future of Broadcasting, 1974–77; Gen. Adv. Council, BBC, 1981–84; Broadcasting Council for Scotland, 1985–89; Manpower Services Cttee Scotland, 1977–88; Employment Appeal Tribunal, 1991–; Council for Tertiary Educn in Scotland, 1979–83; Exec. Bd, European Trade Union Cttee for Educn, 1980–90 (Vice-Pres., 1986–87 and 1989–90); Chm., European Cttee, World Conf. of Orgns of Teaching Profession, 1980–90; Mem. World Exec., World Conf. of Orgns of Teaching Profession, 1986–90. Chm., Network Scotland, 1992– (Dir, 1991–92). Russell Award, for services to internat. educn, Stockholm, 1993. *Address:* 52 Douglas Road, Longniddry, East Lothian, Scotland EH32 0LJ. *T:* Longniddry (01875) 52082. *Died 22 Oct. 1995.*

POLLOCK, Sir William Horace M.; *see* Montagu-Pollock.

POOLE, 1st Baron, *cr* 1958, of Aldgate in the City of London; **Oliver Brian Sanderson Poole,** CBE 1945; TD; PC 1963; Member of Lloyd's; lately Director, S. Pearson & Son Ltd; *b* 11 Aug. 1911; *s* of late Donald Louis Poole, Mem. of Lloyd's and Therese Lilian Frodsham; *m* 1st, 1933, Betty Margaret Gilkison (marr. diss., 1951; she *d* 1988); one *s* three *d*; 2nd, 1952, Mrs Daphne Heber Percy (marr. diss., 1965); 3rd, 1966, Barbara Ann Taylor. *Educ:* Eton; Christ Church, Oxford. Life Guards, 1932–33; joined Warwickshire Yeomanry, 1934; service in 1939–45 in Iraq, Syria, North Africa, Sicily and NW Europe (despatches thrice, MBE, OBE, CBE, US Legion of Merit, Order of Orange Nassau). MP (C) Oswestry Division of Salop, 1945–50. Conservative Party Organisation: Jt Hon. Treas., 1952–55; Chairman, 1955–57; Dep.-Chm., 1957–59; Jt Chm., May-Oct. 1963; Vice-Chm., Oct. 1963–Oct. 1964. Governor of Old Vic, 1948–63; a Trustee, Nat. Gallery, 1973–81. Hon. DSc City Univ., 1970. *Heir:* *s* Hon. David Charles Poole [*b* 6 Jan. 1945; *m* 1st, 1967, Fiona, *d* of John Donald, London SW6; one *s*; 2nd, 1975, Philippa, *d* of Mark Reeve]. *Address:* 24 Campden Hill Gate, Duchess of Bedford Walk, W8. *Clubs:* MCC, Buck's; Royal Yacht Squadron (Cowes).
Died 28 Jan. 1993.

POPE, Andrew Lancelot, (Lance), CMG 1972; CVO 1965; OBE 1959; HM Diplomatic Service, retired; *b* 27 July 1912; *s* of Andrew Noble Pope, OBE; *m* 1st, 1938 (marr. diss.); 2nd, 1948, Ilse Migliarina (*d* 1988); one step *d*. *Educ:* Harrow School. Served War of 1939–45 (despatches): Lieut, Royal Fusiliers, 1939; POW 1940–45. Served in Mil. Govt and Allied High Commn in Germany, 1945–56; entered Foreign (subseq. Diplomatic) Service, 1959; Counsellor, Bonn, 1962–72. Director: Conf. Bd, NY, 1972–80; Gerling Global General and Reinsurance Co. Ltd. Liveryman, Worshipful Co. of Grocers. Order of Merit (Germany), 1965; Order of Merit (Bavaria), 1970; Order of Merit (Lower Saxony), 1972. *Recreations:* shooting, gardening. *Address:* Goldhill Grove, Lower Bourne, Farnham, Surrey. *T:* Farnham (0252) 721662.
Died 2 March 1993.

POPE-HENNESSY, Sir John (Wyndham), Kt 1971; CBE 1959 (MBE 1944); FBA 1955; FSA; FRSL; art historian; *b* 13 Dec. 1913; *er s* of late Major-General L. H. R. Pope-

Hennessy, CB, DSO, and Dame Una Pope-Hennessy, DBE. *Educ:* Downside School; Balliol Coll., Oxford (Hon. Fellow). Served Air Ministry, 1939–45. Joined staff of Victoria and Albert Museum, 1938; Keeper, Dept of Architecture and Sculpture, 1954–66; Dir and Sec., 1967–73; Dir, British Museum, 1974–76; Consultative Chm., Dept of European Paintings, Metropolitan Mus., NY, 1977–86; Prof. of Fine Arts, NY Univ., 1977–92. Slade Professor of Fine Art, Univ. of Oxford, 1956–57; Clark Professor of Art, Williams College, Mass, USA, 1961–62; Slade Professor of Fine Art, and Fellow of Peterhouse, University of Cambridge, 1964–65. Member: Arts Council, 1968–76; Ancient Monuments Bd for England, 1969–72; Dir, Royal Opera House, 1971–76. Fellow, Amer. Acad. of Arts and Scis, 1978; Hon. Fellow, Pierpont Morgan Library, 1975; Life Fellow, Metropolitan Mus., NY, 1983. Corresponding Member: Accademia Senese degli Intronati; Bayerische Akademie der Wissenschaften; Hon. Academician, Accademia del Disegno, Florence; For. Mem., Amer. Philosophical Soc., 1974. Serena Medal of British Academy for Italian Studies, 1961; New York University Medal, 1965; Torch of Learning Award, Hebrew Univ., Jerusalem, 1977; Art Dealers Assoc. Award, 1984; Jerusalem Prize of Arts and Letters, 1984; Premio Galileo Galilei, 1986. Hon. LLD: Aberdeen, 1972; Univ. Cattolica, Milan, 1994; Hon. Dr RCA, 1973. Mangia d'Oro, 1982; Premio della Cultura della Presidenza del Consiglio, 1992. Hon. Citizen: Siena, 1982; Florence, 1994; Grande Ufficiale, Order of Merit of the Republic, Italy, 1988. *Publications:* Giovanni di Paolo, 1937; Sassetta, 1939; Sienese Quattrocento Painting, 1947; A Sienese Codex of the Divine Comedy, 1947; The Drawings of Domenichino at Windsor Castle, 1948; A Lecture on Nicholas Hilliard, 1949; Donatello's Ascension, 1949; The Virgin with the Laughing Child, 1949; edition of the Autobiography of Benvenuto Cellini, 1949; Paolo Uccello, 1950, rev. edn, 1972; Italian Gothic Sculpture in the Victoria and Albert Museum, 1952; Fra Angelico, 1952, rev. edn, 1974; Italian Gothic Sculpture, 1955, rev. edn 1985; Italian Renaissance Sculpture, 1958, rev. edn 1985; Italian High Renaissance and Baroque Sculpture, 1963, rev. edn 1985; Catalogue of Italian Sculpture in the Victoria and Albert Museum, 1964; Renaissance Bronzes in the Kress Collection, 1965; The Portrait in the Renaissance (A. W. Mellon Lectures in the Fine Arts, 1963), 1967; Essays on Italian Sculpture, 1968; Catalogue of Sculpture in the Frick Collection, 1970; Raphael (Wrightsman Lectures), 1970; (with others) Westminster Abbey, 1972; Luca della Robbia, 1980 (Mitchell Prize, 1981); The Study and Criticism of Italian Sculpture, 1980; Cellini, 1985; La Scultura Italiana del Rinascimento, 1986; The Robert Lehman Collection-1, Italian Paintings, 1987; Learning to Look (autobiog.), 1991; The Piero Della Francesca Trail, 1991; Paradiso: the Illuminations to Dante's Divine Comedy by Giovanni di Paolo, 1993; Donatello Sculptor, 1993; On Artists and Art Historians: selected reviews, 1994; contribs to NY Rev. of Books, TLS, etc. *Recreation:* music. *Address:* 28 via de' Bardi, Florence 50125, Italy.

Died 31 Oct. 1994.

POPPER, Prof. Sir Karl (Raimund), CH 1982; Kt 1965; PhD (Vienna), MA (New Zealand), DLit (London); FRS 1976; FBA 1958; Professor of Logic and Scientific Method in the University of London (London School of Economics and Political Science), 1949–69; Emeritus Professor, 1969; Guest Professor in the Theory of Science, University of Vienna, since 1986; Senior Research Fellow, Hoover Institution, Stanford University, since 1986; *b* Vienna, 28 July 1902; *s* of Dr Simon Siegmund Carl Popper, Barrister, Vienna, and Jenny Popper (*née* Schiff); *m* 1930, Josefine Anna Henninger (*d* 1985); no *c*. *Educ:* University of Vienna. Senior Lecturer in Philosophy, Canterbury University College, Christchurch (Univ. of NZ), 1937–45; Reader in Logic and Scientific Method, LSE, Univ. of London, 1945–49. Fellow, Center for Advanced Study in the Behavioral Sciences, Stanford, Calif, 1956–57; Visiting Professor: Harvard (Wm James Lectures in Philosophy), 1950; Univ. of California, Berkeley, 1962; Minnesota Center for Phil. of Science, 1962; Indiana Univ., 1963; Inst. for Advanced Studies, Vienna, 1964; Denver Univ., 1966; Vis. Fellow, The Salk Institute for Biological Studies, 1966–67; Kenan Univ. Prof., Emory Univ., 1969; Jacob Ziskind Vis. Prof. in Philosophy and the History of Thought, Brandeis Univ., 1969; William Evans Vis. Prof., Otago, 1973; Vis. Erskine Fellow, Canterbury, NZ, 1973; Lectures: Yale, Princeton, Chicago, Emory Univs, 1950, 1956; Eleanor Rathbone, Bristol, 1956; Annual Philos. to British Acad., 1960; Herbert Spencer, Oxford, 1961 and 1973; Shearman Meml, UCL, 1961; Farnum, Princeton, 1963; Arthur H. Compton Meml, Washington, 1965; Romanes, Oxford, 1972; Broadhead Meml, Canterbury NZ, 1973; First Darwin, Darwin Coll., Cambridge, 1977; Tanner, Ann Arbor, 1978; Frank Nelson Doubleday, Smithsonian Inst., 1979; first Morrell Meml, York, 1981; first Medawar, Royal Soc., 1986. Member: Editorial Bd: Foundations of Physics; British Jl Phil. of Science; Studi Internat. di Filosofia; Jl of Political Theory; Biologie et Logique; Board of Consulting Editors: Theory and Decision; Idea; Advisory Board: Medical Hypotheses; The Monist; Co-Editor: Ratio; Studies in the Foundations Methodology and Philosophy of Science; Methodology and Science; Rechtstheorie; Schriftenreihe Erfahrung und Denken; Library of Exact Philosophy; Ed. Correspond., Dialectica. Chairman, Phil. of Science Group, 1951–53; President: The Aristotelian Soc., 1958–59; British Society for the Phil. of Science, 1959–61; Mem. Council, Assoc. for Symb. Logic, 1951–55. Mem., Académie Internat. de Philosophie des Sciences, 1949; Hon. Mem., RSNZ, 1965; For. Hon. Mem., Amer. Acad. of Arts and Sciences, 1966; Correspondant de l'Institut de France, 1974–80; Associate Mem., Académie Royale de Belgique, 1976; Membre d'Honneur, Académie Internationale d'Histoire des Sciences, 1977; Hon. Mem., Deutsche Akademie für Sprache und Dichtung, 1979; Membre de l'Académie Européenne des Sciences, des Arts et des Lettres (Delegn of GB), 1980; Membre de l'Institut de France, 1980; Socio Straniero dell'Accademia Nazionale dei Lincei, 1981; Ehrenmitglied, Oesterreichische Akademie der Wissenschaften, 1982; Foreign Associate, Nat. Acad. of Scis, Washington, 1986; Mem., Konrad Lorenz Inst., Altenberg, Austria, 1990; Emeritus Mem., Academia Europaea, 1991; Hon. Mem., Academia Scientiarum et Artium Europaea, Salzburg, 1991; Hon. Mem., Harvard Chapter of Phi Beta Kappa, 1964; Hon. Fellow, LSE, 1972; Hon. Mem., Allgemeine Gesellschaft für Philosophie in Deutschland, 1979; Hon. Fellow, Darwin Coll., Cambridge, 1980; Hon. Research Fellow, Dept of History and Philosophy of Science, KCL, 1982; Hon. Mem., Gesellschaft der Ärzte, Vienna, 1986. Hon. Prof. of Econs, Vienna, 1986. Hon. LLD: Chicago, 1962; Denver, 1966; Hon. LittD: Warwick, 1971; Canterbury, NZ, 1973; Cantab, 1980; Hon. DLitt: Salford, 1976; City Univ., 1976; Guelph, Ontario, 1978; Oxon 1982; Hon. Dr rer.nat, Vienna, 1978; Dr phil (*hc*): Mannheim, 1978; Salzburg, 1979; Eichstätt, 1991; Univ. Complutense de Madrid, 1991; Athens, 1993; Hon. Dr rer.pol, Frankfurt, 1979; Hon. DSc: Gustavus Adolphus Coll., 1981; London, 1986; Dr med. sc. (*hc*) Prague, 1994. Prize of the City of Vienna for 'Geisteswissenschaften' (mental and moral sciences), 1965; Sonning Prize for merit in work that has furthered European civilization, Univ. of Copenhagen, 1973; Lippincott Award, Amer. Pol. Sci. Assoc., 1976; Dr Karl Renner Prize, Vienna, 1978; Gold Medal for Disting. Service to Sci., Amer. Mus. of Nat. Hist., NY, 1979; Dr

Leopold Lucas Prize, Univ. of Tübingen, 1981; Alexis de Tocqueville Prize, Fondation Tocqueville, 1984; International Prize of Catalonia (1st recipient), 1989; Goethe Medal, Goethe Inst., 1992; Kyoto Prize, Inamori Foundn, 1992; Otto Hahn Peace Medal, 1993. Grand Decoration of Honour in Gold (Austria), 1976; Ehrenzeichen für Wissenschaft und Kunst (Austria), 1980; Order of Merit, 1980, Grand Cross with Star, Order of Merit, 1983 (German Fed. Rep.); Ring of Honour, City of Vienna, 1983. *Publications:* (trans. into 26 languages): Logik der Forschung, 1934, rev. 2nd edn 1966, rev. 8th edn 1984; The Open Society and Its Enemies, 1945, rev. 5th edn 1966, 14th impr. 1984; The Poverty of Historicism, 1957, 11th impr. 1984; The Logic of Scientific Discovery, 1959, 12th impr. 1985; On the Sources of Knowledge and of Ignorance, 1961; Conjectures and Refutations, 1963, 9th impr. 1984; Of Clouds and Clocks, 1966; Objective Knowledge, 1972, 7th impr. 1983; Unended Quest: An Intellectual Autobiography, 1976, 7th impr. 1985; (with Sir John Eccles) The Self and Its Brain, 1977, rev. pbk edn (UK), 1984, 3rd impr. rev. edn 1985; Die beiden Grundprobleme der Erkenntnistheorie, 1979, 2nd edn 1991; Postscript to The Logic of Scientific Discovery (ed W. W. Bartley), 3 vols, 1982–83 (vol. 1, Realism and the Aim of Science; vol. 2, The Open Universe; vol. 3, Quantum Theory and the Schism in Physics, 1982); (with F. Kreuzer) Offene Gesellschaft—Offenes Universum, 1982, 3rd edn 1983; A Pocket Popper (ed David Miller), 1983; Auf der Suche nach einer besseren Welt, 1984, 3rd edn 1988; (with Konrad Lorenz) Die Zukunft ist Offen, 1984, 2nd edn 1985; (ed David Miller) Popper Selections, 1985; A World of Propensities, 1990; contribs to: The Philosophy of Karl Popper, Library of Living Philosophers (ed P. A. Schilpp), 1974; learned jls; anthologies. *Recreation:* music. *Address:* c/o London School of Economics, Houghton Street, Aldwych, WC2A 2AE.
Died 17 Sept. 1994.

PORCHER, Michael Somerville, CMG 1962; OBE 1960; Secretary (Operations Division), Royal National Life-Boat Institution, 1964–83, retired; *b* 9 March 1921; *s* of late Geoffrey Lionel Porcher and Marjorie Fownes Porcher (*née* Somerville); *m* 1955, Mary Lorraine Porcher (*née* Tweedy); two *s. Educ:* Cheltenham College; St Edmund Hall, Oxford. Military Service, 1941–42. Joined Colonial Admin. Service: Sierra Leone: Cadet, 1942; Asst Dist Comr, 1945; Dist Comr, 1951; British Guiana: Dep. Colonial Sec., 1952; Governor's Sec. and Clerk Exec. Council, 1953; Dep. Chief Sec., 1956; British Honduras: Colonial Secretary, 1960; Chief Secretary, 1961; retired, 1964. *Recreation:* fishing. *Address:* Bladon, Worth Matravers, near Swanage, Dorset BH19 3LQ.
Died 15 April 1994.

PORRITT, Baron *cr* 1973 (Life Peer), of Wanganui, NZ, and of Hampstead; **Arthur Espie Porritt**, GCMG 1967 (KCMG 1950); GCVO 1970 (KCVO 1957); CBE 1945 (OBE 1943); Bt 1963; President: African Medical and Research Foundation, since 1991 (Chairman, 1973–81; Vice-President, 1981–89); Arthritis and Rheumatism Council, 1979–88 (Chairman, 1973–79); *b* 10 Aug. 1900; *e s* of late E. E. Porritt, VD, MD, FRCS, Wanganui, New Zealand, and Ivy Elizabeth, *d* of Alexander John Mackenzie, Lanarks; *m* 1st, 1926, Mary Frances Wynne, *d* of William Bond; 2nd, 1946, Kathleen Mary, 2nd *d* of late A. S. Peck and Mrs Windley, Spalding, Lincs; two *s* one *d. Educ:* Wanganui Collegiate School, NZ; Otago University, NZ; Magdalen College, Oxford (Rhodes Scholar); St Mary's Hospital, London. MA Oxon.; MCh Oxon; FRCS. Surgeon: St Mary's Hosp.; Hosp. of St John and St Elizabeth; King Edward VII Hosp. for Officers; Royal Masonic Hosp.; Consulting Surgeon: Princess Louise Kensington Hosp. for Children; Paddington Hosps; Royal Chelsea Hosp.; Civil Consulting Surgeon to the Army, 1954–67, Emeritus, 1971; Brigadier, RAMC, 21 Army Group; Surgeon-in-Ordinary to the Duke of York, 1936; Surgeon to HM Household, 1937–46; a Surgeon to King George VI, 1946–52; Sergeant-Surgeon to the Queen, 1952–67; Governor-General of New Zealand, 1967–72. Dir, Sterling Winthrop, 1973–. Chairman: Medical Advisory Cttee, Ministry of Overseas Develt; Medical Services Review Cttee, 1958; Red Cross Comr for NZ in UK; Chapter-Gen., Order of St John; Hunterian Soc., 1934–39 (Past Pres.); President: RCS, 1960–63; BMA, 1960–61 (Gold Medallist, 1964); RSM, 1966–67; Assoc. of Surgeons of Gt Britain and Ireland; Patron, Med. Council on Alcoholism; Pres., Med. Commn on Accident Prevention, 1973–89; Master, Soc. of Apothecaries, 1964–66; Vice-Pres., Royal Commonwealth Soc. Pres., OUAC, 1925–26; holder of 100 yards and 220 yards hurdles records at Oxford and 100 yards Oxford v Cambridge (9 9/10 seconds); represented Oxford in Athletics, 1923–26; Finalist, Olympic 100 metres (Bronze Medallist), Paris, 1924; Captain NZ Olympic Team, Paris, 1924, Amsterdam, 1928, Manager Berlin, 1936; Mem., Internat. Olympic Cttee, British Olympic Council; Vice-Pres., British Empire and Commonwealth Games Federation. Olympic Order (1st cl.), 1985. Fellow: Amer. Surgical Assoc.; Amer. Soc. of Clinical Surgery; French Acad. of Surgery; Hon. FRACS; Hon. FRCSEd; Hon. FACS; Hon. FRCSGlas; Hon. FRCS(C); Hon. FCSSA; Hon. FRCSI; Hon. FRCP; Hon. FRACP; Hon FRCOG; Hon. FRACR; Hon. Fellow, Magdalen College, Oxford, 1961. Hon. LLD: St Andrews; Birmingham; New Zealand; Otago; Hon. MD Bristol; Hon. DSc Oxon. Legion of Merit (USA); KStJ. *Publications:* Athletics (with D. G. A. Lowe), 1929; Essentials of Modern Surgery (with R. M. Handfield-Jones), 1938, 6th edn 1956; various surgical articles in medical jls. *Recreations:* riding, golf, swimming; formerly athletics and Rugby football. *Heir* (to baronetcy only): *s* Hon. Jonathon Espie Porritt [*b* 6 July 1950; *m* 1986, Sarah, *d* of Malcolm Staniforth, Malvern; two *d*]. *Address:* 57 Hamilton Terrace, NW8 9RG. *Club:* Buck's.
Died 1 Jan. 1994.

PORTER, Rt Rev. David Brownfield; *b* 10 May 1906; *s* of Sydney Lawrence Porter and Edith Alice Porter; *m* 1936, Violet Margaret Eliot (*d* 1956); one *s*; *m* 1961, Mrs Pamela Cecil (*née* Lightfoot) (*d* 1974), *widow* of Neil McNeill. *Educ:* Hertford Coll., Oxford. Deacon, 1929; priest, 1930; Curate of St Augustine's, Leeds, 1929; Tutor of Wycliffe Hall, Oxford, 1931; Chaplain, 1933; Chaplain of Wadham Coll., Oxford, 1934; Vicar of All Saints', Highfield, Oxford, 1935; Vicar of Darlington, 1943; Rector of St John's, Princes Street, Edinburgh, 1947–61; Dean of Edinburgh, 1954–61; Bishop Suffragan of Aston, 1962–72. Select Preacher, Oxford Univ., 1964. *Recreations:* fishing, painting. *Address:* Silver Leys, Brockhampton, near Cheltenham GL54 5TH. *T:* Cheltenham (0242) 820431.
Died 14 May 1993.

PORTER, Eric (Richard); actor; *b* London, 8 April 1928; *s* of Richard John Porter and Phoebe Elizabeth (*née* Spall). *Educ:* LCC and Wimbledon Technical College. First professional appearance with Shakespeare Memorial Theatre Company, Arts, Cambridge, 1945; first appearance on London stage as Dunois' Page in Saint Joan with the travelling repertory company, King's, Hammersmith, 1946; Birmingham Repertory Theatre, 1948–50; under contract to H. M. Tennant, Ltd, 1951–53. *Plays include:* The Silver Box, Lyric, Hammersmith, 1951; The Three Sisters, Aldwych, 1951; Thor, With Angels, Lyric, Hammersmith, 1951; title role in Noah, Whitehall, 1951; The Same Sky, Lyric, Hammersmith, 1952; Under the Sycamore Tree, Aldwych, 1952; season at Lyric, Hammersmith (directed by John Gielgud), Richard II, The Way of the World, Venice Preserved, 1953; with Bristol Old Vic Company, 1954, and again 1955–56: parts included title roles in King Lear, Uncle Vanya, Volpone; with Old Vic Company, 1954–55: parts included Jacques in As You Like It, title role in Henry IV, Bolingbroke in Richard II, Christopher Sly in The Taming of the Shrew; Romanoff and Juliet, Piccadilly, 1956; A Man of Distinction, Edinburgh Festival and Princes, 1957; Time and Again, British tour with the Lunts, 1957, and New York in The Visit, 1958; The Coast of Coromandel, English tour, 1959; Rosmersholm, Royal Court, 1959, Comedy, 1960 (Evening Standard Drama Award as Best Actor of 1959); under contract to Royal Shakespeare Company, 1960–65: Malvolio in Twelfth Night, Stratford, 1960, Aldwych, 1961; Duke in The Two Gentlemen of Verona, Stratford, 1960; Leontes in The Winter's Tale, Stratford, 1960; Ulysses in Troilus and Cressida, Stratford, 1960; Ferdinand in The Duchess of Malfi, Stratford, 1960, Aldwych, 1961; Lord Chamberlain in Ondine, Aldwych, 1961; Buckingham in Richard III, Stratford, 1961; title role in Becket, Aldwych, 1961, Globe, 1962; title role in Macbeth, Stratford, 1962; Iachimo in Cymbeline, Stratford, 1962; Pope Pius XII in The Representative, Aldwych, 1963; Stratford Season, 1964: Bolingbroke in Richard II; Henry IV in Henry IV Parts I and II; Chorus in Henry V; Richmond in Richard III; Stratford Season, 1965: Barabas in The Jew of Malta; Shylock in The Merchant of Venice; Chorus in Henry V, Aldwych, 1965; Ossip in The Government Inspector, Aldwych, 1966; Stratford Season, 1968: Lear in King Lear; Faustus in Dr Faustus (US tour, 1969); Paul Thomsen in My Little Boy-My Big Girl (also directed), Fortune, 1969; The Protagonist, Brighton, 1971; Peter Pan, Coliseum, 1971; Malvolio, inaugural season, St George's Elizabethan Theatre, 1976; Big Daddy in Cat on a Hot Tin Roof, National, 1988 (Evening Standard Drama Award, Best Actor); title rôle in King Lear, Old Vic, 1989; Malvolio in Twelfth Night, Playhouse, 1991; Prof. Serebriakov in Uncle Vanya, Nat. Theatre, 1992. *Films:* The Fall of the Roman Empire, 1964; The Pumpkin Eater, 1964; The Heroes of Telemark, 1965; Kaleidoscope, 1966; The Lost Continent, 1968; Hands of the Ripper, Nicholas and Alexandra, Antony and Cleopatra, 1971; Hitler: the last ten days, 1973; The Day of the Jackal, 1973; The Belstone Fox, 1973; Callan, 1974; Hennessy, 1975; The Thirty-Nine Steps, 1978; Little Lord Fauntleroy, 1980; *television parts include:* Soames Forsyte in The Forsyte Saga, BBC (Best Actor Award, Guild of TV Producers and Directors, 1967); Karenin, in Anna Karenina, BBC, 1977; Alanbrooke in Churchill and the Generals, BBC, 1979; Polonius in Hamlet, BBC, 1980; Dep. Governor Danforth in The Crucible, BBC, 1981; Neville Chamberlain in Winston Churchill: The Wilderness Years, 1981; Count Bronowsky in The Jewel in the Crown, 1983; Moriarty in Sherlock Holmes, 1984; Fagin in Oliver Twist, 1985. *Recreations:* walking, model railways. *Address:* c/o Jonathan Altaras Associates, 2 Goodwins Court, WC2N 4LL. *Died 15 May 1995.*

PORTER, Hon. Sir Murray (Victor), Kt 1970; Agent-General for Victoria in London, 1970–76; *b* 20 Dec. 1909; *s* of late V. Porter, Pt Pirie, SA; *m* 1932, Edith Alice Johnston, *d* of late C. A. Johnston; two *d*. *Educ:* Brighton (Victoria) Grammar Sch., Australia. Served War, 2nd AIF, 1941–45. MLA (Liberal) Sandringham, Victoria, 1955–70; Govt Whip, 1955–56; Asst Minister, 1956–58; Minister for: Forests, 1958–59; Local Govt, 1959–64; Public Works, 1964–70. *Recreations:* golf, swimming. *Address:* Flat 7, The Point, 405 Beach Road, Beaumaris, Victoria 3193, Australia. *Clubs:* Royal Automobile of Victoria (Melbourne); Melbourne Cricket, Royal Melbourne Golf. *Died 16 Jan. 1993.*

POSTGATE, Richmond Seymour, MA; FCP; formerly consultant, education and broadcasting; *b* 31 Dec. 1908; *s* of Prof. J. P. Postgate, FBA and Edith Postgate; *m* 1949,

Audrey Winifred Jones; one *s* two *d*. *Educ:* St George's Sch., Harpenden, Herts; Clare Coll., Cambridge. Editorial staff, Manchester Guardian newspaper; teaching in public and elementary schools; County LEA administration; RAFVR; Head of School Broadcasting, etc, BBC; Director-General, Nigerian Broadcasting Corporation, 1959–61; Controller, Educnl Broadcasting, BBC, 1965–72. FCP 1973. *Recreation:* walking. *Address:* 3 Stanford Road, Faringdon, Oxon. *T:* Faringdon (0367) 240172. *Died 10 Dec. 1991.*

POTTER, Dennis (Christopher George); playwright, author and journalist (freelance since 1964); *b* 17 May 1935; *e s* of Walter and Margaret Potter; *m* 1959, Margaret Morgan (*d* 1994); one *s* two *d*. *Educ:* Bell's Grammar Sch., Coleford, Glos; St Clement Danes Grammar Sch.; New Coll., Oxford (Hon. Fellow, 1987). Editor, Isis, 1958; BA (Hons) in PPE Oxon, 1959. BBC TV (current affairs), 1959–61; Daily Herald, feature writer, then TV critic, 1961–64; contested (Lab) East Herts, 1964; Leader writer, The Sun, Sept.-Oct. 1964, then resigned; TV Critic, Sunday Times, 1976–78. First television play, 1965. NFT retrospective, 1980. *Television plays:* Vote Vote Vote for Nigel Barton (also at Bristol Old Vic, 1968; SFTA Award, 1966); Stand Up Nigel Barton; Where the Buffalo Roam; A Beast with Two Backs; Son of Man; Traitor; Paper Roses; Casanova; Follow the Yellow Brick Road; Only Make Believe; Joe's Ark; Schmoedipus; (adapted from novel by Angus Wilson) Late Call, 1975; Brimstone and Treacle, 1976 (transmitted, 1987); Double Dare, 1976; Where Adam Stood, 1976; Pennies from Heaven (sextet), 1978 (BAFTA award, 1978); Blue Remembered Hills, 1979 (BAFTA award, 1980); Blade on the Feather, Rain on the Roof, Cream in my Coffee, 1980 (Prix Italia, 1982); Tender is the Night (sextet, from Scott Fitzgerald), 1985; The Singing Detective (sextet), 1986; Visitors, 1987; Christabel (quartet, from The Past Is Myself, by Christabel Bielenberg), 1988; Blackeyes (quartet), 1989; Lipstick on Your Collar (sextet), 1993; *screenplays:* Pennies from Heaven, 1981; Brimstone and Treacle, 1982; Gorky Park, 1983; Dreamchild, 1985; Track 29, 1988; Blackeyes, 1990; (also directed) Secret Friends, 1992; White Clouds, 1994; *stage play:* Sufficient Carbohydrate, 1983. *Publications:* The Glittering Coffin, 1960; The Changing Forest, 1962; *plays:* The Nigel Barton Plays, 1968; Son of Man, 1970; Brimstone and Treacle, 1979; Sufficient Carbohydrate, 1983; Waiting for the Boat (3 plays), 1984; *novels:* Hide and Seek, 1973; Pennies from Heaven, 1982; Ticket to Ride, 1986; Blackeyes, 1987. *Recreations:* nothing unusual, ie the usual personal pleasures, sought with immoderate fervour. *Address:* Morecambe Lodge, Duxmere, Ross-on-Wye, Herefordshire HR9 5BB. *Died 7 June 1994.*

POTTER, Sir Ian; *see* Potter, Sir W. I.

POTTER, Sir (Joseph) Raymond (Lynden), Kt 1978; Chairman, Halifax Building Society, 1974–83; *b* 21 April 1916; *s* of Rev. Henry Lynden and Mabel Boulton Potter; *m* 1939, Daphne Marguerite, *d* of Sir Crawford Douglas-Jones, CMG; three *s* one *d*. *Educ:* Haileybury Coll.; Clare Coll., Cambridge (MA). War Service, 1939–46, Queen's Own Royal W Kent Regt, England and Middle East; GSO2 Staff Duties, GHQ, MEF; AQMG War Office. Sec., Royal Inst. of Internat. Affairs, 1947–51; joined Halifax Building Soc., 1951; Gen. Man. 1956; Chief Gen. Man., 1960–74; Dir, 1968–83. Mem., Board, Warrington and Runcorn (formerly Warrington) New Town Develt Corp., 1969–86. Vice Pres., Building Socs Assoc., 1981– (Mem. Council, 1965–81; Chm., 1975–77). Freeman, City of London, 1981. Life Governor, Haileybury Coll. *Recreation:* music. *Address:* Oakwood, Chilbolton,

Stockbridge, Hampshire SO20 6BE. *T:* Chilbolton (0264) 860523. *Club:* Hawks (Cambridge).

Died 17 Nov. 1993.

POTTER, Sir (William) Ian, Kt 1962; FAA; stockbroker, Melbourne, Australia; *b* 25 Aug. 1902; *s* of James William Potter and Maria Louisa (*née* McWhinnie); *m* 1975, Primrose Catherine Dunlop, AO, JP, DLJ; two *d* of former *m. Educ:* University of Sydney (BEc). Served RANVR, 1939–44. Economist to Federal Treasury, 1935–36; Commonwealth Rep., Rural Debt Adjustment Cttee, 1936; founded Ian Potter & Co., 1937; Principal Partner, 1937–67. Mem., Internat. Adv. Bd, Chemical Bank, USA, 1967–77. Member: Cttee, Stock Exchange of Melbourne, 1945–62; Melbourne University Council, 1947–71; Commonwealth Immigration Planning Council, 1956–62; Victorian Arts Centre Building Cttee, 1960–78. President, Australian Elizabethan Theatre Trust, 1964–66 and 1983– (Chairman 1968–83); Vice-Pres., Howard Florey Inst., Melbourne. Hon. Life Member: Aust. Ballet; Aust. Opera; Nat. Gall. of Vic. Hon. LLD Melbourne. Kt 1st Cl., Order of the Star of the North (Sweden). *Publications:* contrib. articles on financial and economic subjects to learned journals and press. *Recreations:* yachting, tennis, golfing. *Address:* 99 Spring Street, Melbourne, Victoria 3000, Australia. *Clubs:* Melbourne, Australian, Royal Automobile of Victoria, Royal Melbourne Golf (Melbourne); Australian (Sydney); The Links (NY).

Died 24 Oct. 1994.

POTTS, Archie; Under-Secretary, and Director of Scientific and Technical Intelligence, Ministry of Defence, 1964–74; *b* 28 Dec. 1914; *s* of late Mr and Mrs A. Potts, Newcastle upon Tyne; *m* 1951, Winifred Joan Bishop, MBE, *d* of late Mr and Mrs Reginald Bishop; two *s. Educ:* University of Durham. BSc (Hons) Physics, 1935. Research in Spectroscopy, King's Coll., University of Durham, 1936–39; War of 1939–45: Operational Research in Radar and Allied Fields, Fighter Command, and N Africa and Italy; Hon. Sqdn Leader, RAFVR, 1943–45; Chief Research Officer, Fighter Command, 1946–51; Defence Research Staff, Min. of Defence, 1951–53; Scientific Adviser, Allied Air Forces Central Europe, 1954–56; Asst Scientific Adviser, Air Ministry, 1957; Dep. Director for Atomic Energy, Jt Intell. Bureau, 1957–63. FInstP 1945. *Recreation:* listening to music. *Address:* 3 The Keir, West Side, SW19 4UG. *T:* 081–946 7077. *Club:* Royal Air Force. *Died 24 May 1991.*

POTTS, Thomas Edmund, ERD 1957; company director, retired; *b* 23 March 1908; *s* of late T. E. Potts, Leeds; *m* 1932, Phyllis Margaret, *d* of late J. S. Gebbie, Douglas, Isle of Man; one *s. Educ:* Leeds Modern School. Joined The British Oxygen Co. Ltd, 1928. Commissioned RE, SRO, 1938; served War of 1939–45, Madras Sappers and Miners in India, Eritrea, Western Desert, Tunisia, with 4th and 5th Indian Divs (despatches, 1942 and 1943; Major); CRE 31st Indian Armoured Div., 9th Army (Lt-Col); released from active service and transferred to RARO (resigned Commission, RE, 1950). Rejoined British Oxygen Co. Ltd, London, 1945; Managing Director, African Oxygen Ltd, Johannesburg, 1947; Director, British Oxygen Co. Ltd, 1955; Group Managing Director, British Oxygen Co. Ltd, 1958–63; UK Atomic Energy Authority: Consultant, 1968–78, a Dir, 1971–78, Radiochemical Centre; Dir, Amersham Corp., Chicago, 1968–78. Pres. South African Instn of Welding, 1951; Vice-Pres., Inst. of Welding, 1963–64. CBIM 1979. *Recreations:* golf, gardening. *Address:* Cleeve, Brayfield Road, Bray-on-Thames, Berks SL6 2BW. *T:* Maidenhead (0628) 26887. *Clubs:* Rand (Johannesburg); Temple Golf.

Died 10 Sept. 1993.

POUNDER, Rafton John; Secretary, Northern Ireland Bankers' Association, since 1977; *b* 13 May 1933; *s* of late Cuthbert C. Pounder, Gefion, Ballynahatty, Shaw's Bridge, Belfast; *m* 1959, Valerie Isobel, *d* of late Robert Stewart, MBE, Cherryvalley, Belfast; one *s* one *d. Educ:* Charterhouse; Christ's College, Cambridge. Qualified as a Chartered Accountant, 1959. Chm. Cambridge Univ. Cons. and Unionist Assoc., 1954; Ulster rep. on Young Cons. and Unionist Nat. Adv. Cttee, 1960–63; Hon. Mem., Ulster Young Unionist Council, 1963; Member: UK delegn (C) to Assembly of Council of Europe, and to Assembly of WEU, 1965–68; UK Delegn to European Parlt, Strasbourg, 1973–74; Exec. Cttee, Nat. Union of Cons. and Unionist Assocs, 1967–72; Exec. Cttee, Ulster Unionist Council, 1967–73. MP (UU) Belfast S, Oct. 1963–Feb. 1974; Mem., House of Commons Select Cttee on Public Accounts, 1970–73; Vice-Chm., Cons. Parly Party's Technology Cttee, 1970; PPS to Minister for Industry, 1970–71. Mem. CPA Delegn to: Jamaica and Cayman Is, Nov. 1966; Malawi, Sept. 1968. Hon. Secretary: Ulster Unionist Parly Party at Westminster, 1964–67; Cons. Parly Party's Power Cttee, 1969–70. Pres., Ulster Soc. for Prevention of Cruelty to Animals, 1968–74. Dir, Progressive Building Soc., 1968–77. Lay Member, General Synod of the Church of Ireland, 1966–78. *Recreations:* golf, reading, music, sailing. *Address:* Gunpoint, Coastguard Lane, Orlock, Groomsport, Co. Down BT19 2LR.

Died 16 April 1991.

POWELL, Arthur Barrington, CMG 1967; *b* 24 April 1918; *er s* of late Thomas and Dorothy Powell, Maesteg, Glam; *m* 1945, Jane, *d* of late Gen. Sir George Weir, KCB, CMG, DSO; four *s* one *d. Educ:* Cowbridge; Jesus Coll., Oxford. Indian Civil Service, 1939–47; served in Province of Bihar. Asst Principal, Min. of Fuel and Power, 1947; Principal Private Sec. to Minister, 1949–51; Asst Sec., 1955; Petroleum Div., 1957–68; Petroleum Attaché, HM Embassy, Washington, 1962–64; Gas Div., 1968–72; Reg. Finance Div., DoI, 1972–76; Exec. Dir, Welsh Develt Agency, 1976–83. *Address:* Mulberry House, Pwllmeyric, Chepstow, Gwent NP6 6LA. *Clubs:* United Oxford & Cambridge University; Royal Porthcawl Golf; St Pierre Golf & Country (Chepstow). *Died 4 Nov. 1995.*

POWELL, David; *b* 1914; *s* of Edward Churton Powell and Margaret (*née* Nesfield); *m* 1941, Joan Boileau (*née* Henderson); one *s* four *d. Educ:* Charterhouse. Served War, 1939–46: Lt, Kent Yeomanry RA; Captain and Major on Staff. Qualified as Chartered Accountant, 1939, admitted, 1943; in practice, 1946–47; joined Booker McConnell Ltd, 1947; Finance Dir, 1952; Dep. Chm. 1957; Man. Dir, 1966; Chm. and Chief Exec., 1967, retired 1971. *Recreations:* walking, English water-colours, fishing, reading. *Address:* The Cottage, 20 Coldharbour Lane, Hildenborough, Kent TN11 9JT. *T:* Hildenborough (01732) 833103. *Died 28 June 1995.*

POWELL, (Elizabeth) Dilys, CBE 1974; FRSL; *b* 20 July 1901; *yr d* of late Thomas and Mary Powell; *m* 1st, 1926, Humfry Payne (*d* 1936), later Director of the British School of Archæology at Athens; 2nd, 1943, Leonard Russell (*d* 1974); no *c. Educ:* Bournemouth High School; Somerville College, Oxford (Hon. Fellow, 1991). Sunday Times: Editorial Staff, 1928–31 and 1936–41; Film Critic, 1939–79; Films on TV notes, 1976–; Film Critic, Punch, 1979–92. Lived and travelled extensively in Greece, 1931–36. Member: Bd of Governors of British Film Institute, 1948–52 (Fellow, BFI, 1986); Independent Television Authority, 1954–57; Cinematograph Films Council, 1965–69; President, Classical Association, 1966–67. Hon. Mem., ACTT. Award of Honour, BAFTA, 1984. *Publications:* Descent from Parnassus, 1934; Remember Greece, 1941; The Traveller's Journey is Done, 1943; Coco, 1952; An Affair of the Heart, 1957; The Villa Ariadne, 1973; The Golden Screen (collected reviews),

1989; The Dilys Powell Film Reader (collected reviews), 1991. *Address:* 14 Albion Street, Hyde Park, W2 2AS. *T:* 0171–723 9807. *Died 3 June 1995.*

POWELL, Harry Allan Rose, (Tim), MBE 1944; TD 1973; Chairman, Massey-Ferguson Holdings Ltd, 1970–80 (Managing Director, 1962–78); Director, Holland and Holland Holdings Ltd, 1960–89 (Chairman, 1982–87); *b* 15 Feb. 1912; *er s* of late William Allan Powell and Marjorie (*née* Mitchell); *m* 1936, Elizabeth North Hickley (*d* 1990); two *d. Educ:* Winchester; Pembroke Coll., Cambridge (MA). Joined Corn Products Ltd, 1934. Commissioned Hertfordshire Yeomanry, 1938; Staff Coll., 1942; War Office 1942; Joint Planning Staff, 1943; seconded to War Cabinet Secretariat, 1943–44; Head of Secretariat, Supreme Allied Commander, South East Asia, 1944–45 (Col). Mitchells & Butlers Ltd, 1946–49; Gallaher Ltd, 1949–52; joined Harry Ferguson Ltd, 1952. British Inst. of Management: Fellow, 1963; Vice-Chm., 1970–77. Governor, St Thomas' Hosp., 1971–74. *Recreations:* fishing, lapidary, arguing. *Address:* Ready Token, near Cirencester, Glos GL7 5SX. *T:* Cirencester (0285) 740219. *Clubs:* Buck's, MCC.
Died 19 Nov. 1993.

POWELL, Herbert Marcus, BSc, MA; FRS 1953; Professor of Chemical Crystallography, Oxford University, 1964–74, then Emeritus; *b* 7 Aug. 1906; *s* of William Herbert and Henrietta Powell; *m* 1973, Primrose Jean Dunn. *Educ:* St John's College, Oxford (MA 1931). Reader in Chemical Crystallography in the University of Oxford, 1944–64; Fellow of Hertford College, Oxford, 1963–74, Emeritus Fellow, 1974. *Address:* 46 Davenant Road, Oxford. *Died 10 March 1991.*

POWELL, Robert Lane B.; *see* Bayne-Powell.

POWELL, Tim; *see* Powell, H. A. R.

POWER, Eugene Barnum, Hon. KBE 1977; microphotographer, retired 1970; business executive; *b* Traverse City, Mich, 4 June 1905; *s* of Glenn Warren Power and Annette (*née* Barnum); *m* 1929, Sadye L. Harwick (*d* 1991); one *s. Educ:* Univ. of Mich (AB 1927, MBA 1930). With Edwards Bros, Inc., Ann Arbor, Mich, 1930–38; engaged in expts with methods and uses of microfilm technique for reprodn of materials for res., 1935; Founder: Univ. Microfilms (merged with Xerox Corp. 1962), 1938; Univ. Microfilms, Ltd London, 1952; Dir, Xerox Corp., 1962–68. Organized: 1st large microfilming proj. for libraries, copying all books printed in England before 1640; Microfilms, Inc., as distbn agency, using microfilm as reprodn medium for scientific and technical materials, 1942–62; Projected Books, Inc. (non-profit corp.), for distbn of reading and entertainment materials in photog. form to physically incapacitated, 1944–70; Eskimo Art, Inc. (non-profit corp.). During War 1939–45, dir. large-scale copying of important Brit. MSS in public and private archives, also enemy documents. Pres. and Chm., Power Foundn, 1968–; Mem. Bd of Dirs, Domino's Pizza Inc., Ann Arbor, 1978–92. Special Rep. Co-ordinator of Inf. and of Library of Congress, London 1942, Office of Strategic Services, 1943–45. President: Internat. Micrographic Congress, 1964–65; Nat. Microfilm Assoc., 1946–54. Chm., Mich Co-ordinating Council for State Higher Educn; Regent, Univ. of Michigan, 1956–66. Chm., Ann Arbor Summer Festival Inc., 1978–88 (Trustee, 1978–). Member: Council of Nat. Endowment for the Humanities, 1968–74; Amer. Philos. Soc., 1975. Fellow, Nat. Microfilm Assoc., 1963 (Award of Merit, 1956); Fellow of Merit, Internat. Micrographic Congress, 1978; Paul Harris Fellow, Rotary Internat., 1979. Hon. Fellow: Magdalene Coll., Cambridge, 1967; Northwestern Mich Coll., 1967. Hon. LHD: St John's Univ., 1966; Univ. of Michigan, 1971. First Alumni Achievement Award, Univ.

of Michigan Business Sch., 1990. *Publications:* numerous articles on techniques and uses of microfilm. *Recreations:* swimming, sailing, fishing, hunting, music. *Address:* (home) 989 Forest Road, Barton Hills, Ann Arbor, Mich 48105, USA. *T:* (313) 6622886; (office) 2929 Plymouth Road #300, Ann Arbor, Mich 48105, USA. *T:* (313) 7698424. *Club:* Rotary (Ann Arbor). *Died 6 Dec. 1993.*

POWIS, 7th Earl of, *cr* 1804; **George William Herbert;** Baron Clive (Ire.) 1762; Baron Clive (GB) 1794; Viscount Clive, Baron Herbert of Chirbury, Baron Powis 1804; *b* 4 June 1925; *s* of Rt Rev. Percy Mark Herbert, KCVO (*d* 1968), former Bishop of Norwich, and Hon. Elaine Letitia Algitha (*d* 1984), *d* of 5th Baron Bolton; *S* cousin, 1988; *m* 1949, Hon. Katharine Odeyne de Grey, *d* of 8th Baron Walsingham, DSO, OBE; four *s* two adopted *d. Educ:* Eton; Trinity Coll., Cambridge (MA). FRICS. Served War with Rifle Brigade, 1943–46. Resident Land Agent, 1949–70. *Recreations:* agriculture, genealogy, local history. *Heir:* *s* Viscount Clive [*b* 19 May 1952; *m* 1977, Marijke Sophia, *d* of Maarten Nanne Guther, Canada; one *s* two *d*]. *Address:* Marrington Hall, Chirbury, Montgomery, Powys SY15 6DR. *T:* Chirbury (093872) 256. *Died 13 Aug. 1993.*

POWLES, Sir Guy (Richardson), ONZ 1990; KBE 1961; CMG 1954; ED 1944; first Ombudsman of New Zealand, 1962–75, Chief Ombudsman, 1975–77; *b* 5 April 1905; *s* of late Colonel C. G. Powles, CMG, DSO, New Zealand Staff Corps, and Jessie Mary, *d* of C. T. Richardson, Wellington, NZ; *m* 1931, Eileen, *d* of A. J. Nicholls; two *s. Educ:* Wellington Coll., NZ; Victoria Univ. (LLB). Barrister, Supreme Court, New Zealand, 1929. Served War of 1939–45 with NZ Military Forces, to rank of Colonel; Counsellor, NZ Legation, Washington, DC, USA, 1946–48; High Comr, Western Samoa, 1949–60, for NZ in India, 1960–62, Ceylon, 1960–62, and Ambassador of NZ to Nepal, 1960–62. President, NZ Inst. of Internat. Affairs, 1967–71. NZ Comr, Commn of the Churches on Internat. Affairs, World Council of Churches, 1971–80; Comr, Internat. Commn of Jurists, Geneva, 1975. Race Relations Conciliator, 1971–73. Patron: Amnesty International (NZ); NZ-India Soc.; Environmental Defence Soc. Hon. LLD Victoria Univ. of Wellington, 1969. *Publications:* articles and speeches on international affairs, administrative law and race relations. *Address:* 34 Wesley Road, Wellington, NZ.
Died 24 Oct. 1994.

POWLETT, Rear-Adm. Philip Frederick, CB 1961; DSO 1941 (and Bar 1942); DSC 1941; DL; retired; *b* 13 Nov. 1906; *s* of late Vice-Admiral F. A. Powlett, CBE and Nora, *d* of Ernest Chaplin, Leicester; *m* 1st, 1935, Frances Elizabeth Sykes (*née* Elwell) (*d* 1987); two *s* one *d*; 2nd, 1988, Désirée Kathleen Leyden. *Educ:* Osborne and Dartmouth. War of 1939–45 (DSC, DSO and Bar; Polish Cross of Valour, 1942); in command of destroyers and corvettes, Shearwater, Blankney, Cassandra; Deputy Director of Naval Air Organisation and Training, 1950; Senior Officer, Reserve Fleet, Clyde, 1952–53; Captain (F), 6th Frigate Squadron, 1954–55; Director (RN), Joint Anti-Submarine School, and Senior Naval Officer, Northern Ireland, 1956–58; Flag Officer and Admiral Superintendent, Gibraltar, 1959–62; retired, 1962. DL Norfolk, 1974. *Address:* The Mill House, Lyng, Norwich, Norfolk NR9 5QZ. *T:* Norwich (0603) 872334.
Died 15 Jan. 1991.

PRAIN, Sir Ronald (Lindsay), Kt 1956; OBE 1946; Chief Executive, 1943–68, Chairman, 1950–72, RST international group of companies; Director, Pan-Holding SA, and other companies; *b* Iquiqui, Chile, 3 Sept. 1907; *s* of Arthur Lindsay Prain and Amy Prain (*née* Watson); *m* 1938, Esther Pansy (*d* 1987), *d* of late Norman

Brownrigg, Haslemere; two s. Educ: Cheltenham Coll. Controller (Ministry of Supply): Diamond Die and Tool Control, 1940–45; Quartz Crystal Control, 1943–45. First Chairman: Agricultural Research Council of Rhodesia & Nyasaland, 1959–63; Merchant Bank of Central Africa Ltd, 1956–66; Merchant Bank (Zambia) Ltd, 1966–72; Director: Metal Market & Exchange Co. Ltd, 1943–65; San Francisco Mines of Mexico Ltd, 1944–68; Selection Trust Ltd, 1944–78; Internat. Nickel Co. of Canada Ltd, 1951–72; Wankie Colliery Co. Ltd, 1953–63; Minerals Separation Ltd, 1962–78; Foseco Minsep Ltd, 1969–80; Barclays Bank International, 1971–77. Chairman, Council of Commonwealth Mining and Metallurgical Institutions, 1961–74; President, British Overseas Mining Assoc., 1952; President, Inst. of Metals, 1960–61; Hon. Pres., Copper Develt Assoc.; Hon. Member: Inst. of Metals; Amer. Inst. of Min. and Metall. Engrs. Trustee, Inst. for Archaeo-Metallurgical Studies. Pres. Council, Cheltenham College, 1972–80. ANKH Award, Copper Club, New York, 1964; Gold Medal, 1968, and Hon. Fellow, Instn of Mining and Metallurgy; Platinum Medal, Inst. of Metals, 1969. Publications: Selected Papers (4 Vols); Copper: the anatomy of an industry, 1975 (Japanese trans. 1976; Spanish trans. 1980); Reflections on an Era, 1981. Recreations: formerly cricket, real tennis, travel. Address: Waverley, St George's Hill, Weybridge, Surrey KT13 0QJ. T: Weybridge (0932) 842776. Clubs: White's, MCC. Died 10 May 1991.

PRATT, Very Rev. Francis; see Pratt, Very Rev. J. F. I.

PRATT, His Honour Hugh MacDonald; a Circuit Judge (formerly County Court Judge) 1947–72; b 15 Sept. 1900; o c of late Sir John William Pratt and Elizabeth, d of Hugh Niven, Gosforth; m 1928, Ingeborg (d 1993), e d of late Consul Johannes Sundför, MBE, Haugesund, Norway; one s. Educ: Hillhead High Sch., Glasgow; Aske's Haberdashers' Sch., London; Balliol Coll., Oxford. Called to Bar, Inner Temple, 1924; practised London and Western Circuit; Member General Council of the Bar; Dep. President War Damage (Valuation Appeals) Panel, 1946. Chairman, Devon Quarter Sessions, 1958–64. President, Hardwicke Society; contested Drake Div. of Plymouth, 1929. Hon. LLD Exeter, 1972. Publications: English trans. of Professor Axel Möller's International Law (Vol. I, 1931, Vol. II, 1935); trans. of various articles in Norwegian, Danish and Swedish on commercial and international law. Recreations: reading, gardening. Address: New Pond Farm, New Pond Road, Compton, Surrey GU3 1HY. T: Godalming (0483) 416049.
Died 28 July 1993.

PRATT, Very Rev. (John) Francis (Isaac), MA; Provost of Southwell, 1970–78, Emeritus, since 1978; b 30 June 1913; s of late Rev. J. W. J. Pratt, Churchill, Somerset; m 1939, Norah Elizabeth (d 1981), y d of late F. W. Corfield, Sandford, Somerset; two d. Educ: Keble Coll., Oxford; Wells Theological Coll. Deacon, 1936; priest, 1937. CF, 1st KSLI, 1941–46 (despatches, 1943); SCF, Cyprus, 1946. Vicar of: Rastrick, 1946–49; Wendover, 1949–59; Reading S Mary's (with All Saints, S Saviour's, S Mark's and S Matthew's), 1959–61; Vicar of Chilton with Dorton, 1961–70; Archdeacon of Buckingham, 1961–70; Priest-in-charge, Edingley with Halam, 1975–78. RD of Wendover, 1955–59; Chaplain to High Sheriff of Bucks, 1956, 1962; Examining Chaplain to Bishop of Southwell, 1971–78. Address: Manormead, Tilford Road, Hindhead, Surrey GU26 6RA. Died 3 March 1992.

PRATT, Prof. Peter Lynn, PhD; FInstP; CEng, FIM; Professor of Crystal Physics, Imperial College, London University, 1963–92, then Emeritus; Senior Research Fellow, Imperial College; consultant materials scientist; b 10 March 1927; s of late William Lynn Pratt and Margery Florence Pratt; m 1951, Lydia Elizabeth Anne, y d of late

G. A. Lyon Hatton, Edgbaston; two s. Educ: Cheltenham Coll.; Birmingham Univ. (BSc 1948); Pembroke Coll., Cambridge (PhD 1952). FInstP 1967; FIM 1980; FACerS 1987. Res. Fellow, AERE, 1951–53; Lectr, Univ. of Birmingham, 1953–58; Reader in Physical Metallurgy, Imperial Coll., 1959–63; Dean, Royal Sch. of Mines, and Mem. Governing Body, Imperial Coll., 1977–80; Dir of Continuing Educn, Imperial Coll., 1981–86. Vis. Scientist, N Amer. Aviation Centre, 1963; Vis. Prof., Univ. of Stanford, 1964; Eshbach Soc. Disting. Vis. Schol., Technol Inst. of Northwestern Univ., 1989; Vis. Prof., Univ. of British Columbia, 1991. Consultant at various times to: AERE; DoE; DTI; MoD; Tower of London; Commonwealth Trans-Antarctic Expedn; Commonwealth Develt Corp.; Mary Rose Trust; indust. firms and publishing houses; UK and US lawyers. Dir, London Centre for Marine Technol., 1981–92. Chm., Adv. Cttee on Trng and Qualification of Patent Agents, 1972–73; Member: Continuing Educn and Trng Cttee, Engrg Council, 1986–90; Visitors' Panel, BRE, 1988–; Tech. Adv. Cttee, Marine Technol. Directorate Ltd, 1989–93. Pres., RSM Assoc., 1984–85; Mem. Council and Exec. Cttee, Inst. of Metals, 1987–91. Sir George Beilby Gold Medal and Prize, Institute of Metals, 1964; A. A. Griffith Medal and Prize, Inst. of Metals, 1990. Publications: (ed) Fracture, 1969; technical appendix to Longbow (by Robert Hardy), 1976, contributed to new chapter on Mary Rose bows, 3rd edn 1992; articles on materials science and engrg in learned jls. Recreations: toxophily (esp. the English longbow), sailing, music, motor racing. Address: 20 Westfield Road, Beaconsfield, Bucks HP9 1EF. T: Beaconsfield (01494) 673392.
Died 2 March 1995.

PREMADASA, Hon. Ranasinghe; President of Sri Lanka, since 1989; Minister of Defence, Finance, Local Government, Housing and Construction, Highways, and the Emergency Civil Administration; b 23 June 1924; s of Richard and J. A. Ensinahamine Ranasinghe; m 1964, Hema Wickrematunga; one s one d. Educ: Lorenz Coll., Colombo; St Joseph's Coll., Colombo. Member, Colombo Municipal Council, 1950; Dep. Mayor of Colombo, 1955. Joined United Nat. Party and contested Ruvanwella, 1956; MHR (Colombo Central), 1960, 1965–88; Chief Whip, Govt Parly Gp, 1965; Parly Sec. to Minister of Information and Broadcasting, also to Minister of Local Govt, 1965; Minister of Local Govt, 1968–70; Chief Whip, Opp. Parly Gp, 1970–77; Leader, Nat. State Assembly, 1977–88; Prime Minister, 1978–88; Dep. Leader, United Nat. Party, 1976. Delegate to: Buddha Sangayana, Burma, 1955; China, Soviet Union, 1959; Commonwealth Parly Conf., Canberra, 1970; Commonwealth Heads of Govt meetings, Lusaka, 1979, Aust., 1981; 35th Session, UN Gen. Assembly, 1980; 4th Session, 1980–11th Session, 1988, UN Commn (formerly Conf.) on Human Settlements; 40th Anniv. Session of UN, NY, 1985; Internat. Shelter Seminar, MIT, 1986; 8th Summit of Hds of State of Non-Aligned Nations, Harare, 1986. Publications: numerous books in Sinhalese language. Address: President's House, Colombo, Republic of Sri Lanka.
Died 1 May 1993.

PRENDERGAST, Sir John (Vincent), KBE 1977 (CBE 1960); CMG 1968; GM 1955; CPM 1955; QPM 1963; retired; Deputy Commissioner and Director of Operations, Independent Commission Against Corruption, Hong Kong, 1973–77; b 11 Feb. 1912; y s of late John and Margaret Prendergast; m 1943, Enid Sonia, yr d of Percy and Julia Speed; one s one d. Educ: in Ireland; London Univ. (External). Local Government, London, 1930–39; War Service, 1939–46 (Major); Asst District Comr, Palestine Administration, 1946–47; Colonial Police Service, Palestine and Gold Coast, 1947–52; seconded Army, Canal Zone, on special duties, 1952–53; Colonial

Police Service, Kenya, 1953–58 (Director of Intelligence and Security, 1955–58); Chief of Intelligence, Cyprus, 1958–60; Director, Special Branch, Hong Kong (retired as Dep. Comr of Police), 1960–66; Director of Intelligence, Aden, 1966–67. Dir, G. Heywood Hill Ltd, 1983–91. *Recreations:* racing, collecting first editions. *Address:* 20 Westbourne Terrace, W2 3UP. *T:* 071–262 9514. *Clubs:* East India; Hong Kong, Royal Hong Kong Jockey (Hong Kong). *Died 17 Sept. 1993.*

PRESLAND, John David; Executive Vice-Chairman, Port of London Authority, 1978–82; *b* 3 July 1930; *s* of Leslie and Winifred Presland; *m* 1969, Margaret Brewin. *Educ:* St Albans Sch.; London Sch. of Economics. BScEcon. FCA, IPFA, MBCS. Knox Cropper & Co., Chartered Accountants, 1950–58; Pfizer Ltd (various financial posts), 1958–64; Berk Ltd: Chief Accountant, 1964–67; Financial Controller, 1967–68; Dir and Financial Controller, 1968–71; Port of London Authority: Financial Controller, 1971–73; Asst Dir-Gen. (Finance), 1973–76; Exec. Dir (Finance), 1976–78. Freeman of City of London; Freeman of Company of Watermen and Lightermen of River Thames. *Recreations:* history, natural history, music. *Address:* c/o Pilots' National Pension Fund, New Premier House, 150 Southampton Row, WC1B 5AL. *Club:* Oriental. *Died 15 Oct. 1993.*

PRESTON, F(rederick) Leslie, FRIBA; AADip; formerly Senior Partner in firm of Easton Robertson Preston and Partners, Architects; *b* 27 Nov. 1903; *m* 1927, Rita Lillian (*d* 1982), *d* of late T. H. J. Washbourne; one *d*. *Educ:* Dulwich Coll.; Architectural Association Sch., London. Henry Jarvis Student, 1924; joined firm of Easton & Robertson, 1925, and engaged on: in London: Royal Horticultural Society's New Hall; Royal Bank of Canada; Metropolitan Water Board's Laboratories; in Cambridge: reconstruction of Old Library; Zoological laboratories; School of Anatomy; Gonville and Caius new buildings; in New York: British Pavilion, World's Fair, 1939. Hon. Citizen of City of New York, 1939. Served War of 1939–45, RAF, Wing Comdr, Airfield Construction Branch (despatches). *Principal works:* laboratories for Brewing Industry Research Foundation; laboratories for Coal Research Establishment, NCB, Cheltenham; Bank of England, Bristol; offices for Lloyds Bank, Plymouth; Birmingham; plans for development of Reading University: Faculty of Letters, Library, Windsor Hall, Depts of Physics and Sedimentology, Dept of Mathematics, Applied Physical Science Building, Palmer Building, Whiteknights House, Students Union, Animal Biology and Plant Sciences Buildings, additions to St Patrick's Hall and to Depts of Horticulture and Dairying; buildings for Dulwich Coll.; office building for Salters' Co., London; laboratories and aquarium for Marine Biological Association, Plymouth; offices for Friends' Provident & Century Life Office, Dorking; research laboratories for Messrs Arthur Guinness Son & Co. (Park Royal) Ltd; University of Keele, Library; Midland Hotel, Manchester, alterations; University of Kent at Canterbury, Chemistry Laboratories, Biology Laboratories, Physics 11; Bank of England Printing Works Extension, Debden; Eagle Star Insurance Head Office, City; plans for Aquarium, Rangoon Zoological Gardens. Member of RIBA Practice Cttee, 1951–55; Member Council of Architects' Registration Council of the UK, 1954–60); Pres., Surveyors' Club, 1962. Governor of Westminster Technical College, 1957–67. Hon. DLitt, Reading, 1964. *Recreations:* seeing friends and places of interest, reading. *Address:* Wintershaw, Westcott, Surrey RH4 3NU. *T:* Dorking (0306) 885472. *Club:* Athenæum.
Died 2 Aug. 1994.

PRESTON, Sir Kenneth (Huson), Kt 1959; *b* 19 May 1901; *e s* of late Sir Walter Preston, Tetbury, Glos and

Ella Margaret, *e d* of Huson Morris; *m* 1st, 1922, Beryl Wilmot (decd), *d* of Sir William Wilkinson; one *s* one *d*; 2nd, 1984, Mrs V. E. Dumont (*d* 1992). *Educ:* Rugby; Trinity Coll., Oxford. Dir, J. Stone & Co, 1925; Chm. Platt Bros, 1946; Chm. Stone-Platt Industries, 1958–67; Dir, Midland Bank Ltd, 1945–76. Mem. S Area Bd, BR. Mem. British Olympic Yachting team, 1936 and 1952, Captain 1960. *Recreations:* yachting, hunting. *Address:* Court Lodge, Avening, Tetbury, Glos GL8 8NX. *T:* Nailsworth (0145383) 4402. *Clubs:* Royal Thames Yacht (Vice-Cdre, 1953–56); Royal Yacht Squadron (Vice-Cdre, 1965–71). *Died 6 June 1995.*

PRESTON, Leslie; *see* Preston, F. L.

PRESTT, Ian, CBE 1986; President, Royal Society for the Protection of Birds, since 1991 (Director, subseq. Director General, 1975–91); *b* 26 June 1929; *s* of Arthur Prestt and Jessie Prestt (*née* Miller); *m* 1956, Jennifer Ann Wagstaffe; two *d* (one *s* decd). *Educ:* Bootham School, York; Sch. of Architecture, Liverpool; Univ. of Liverpool (BSc, MSc). FIBiol. 2nd Lt, RA, 1947–49. Joined staff of Nature Conservancy, 1956; Asst Regional Officer (SW England), 1956–59; Asst to Dir-Gen. and Ornithological Officer (GB, HQ), 1959–61; Dep. Regional Officer (N England), 1961–63; PSO, Monks Wood Experimental Station, 1963–70; Dep. Dir, Central Unit on Environmental Pollution, Cabinet Office and DoE, 1970–74; Dep. Dir, Nature Conservancy Council, 1974–75. Member: Council and Exec. Cttee, Wildfowl Trust, 1976–90; Adv. Cttee on Birds, Nature Conservancy Council, 1981–92; Vice Pres., Birdlife Internat. (formerly ICBP), 1990– (Mem., 1979–90, Chm., 1982–90, Exec. Cttee); Pres., Cambridge Branch, CPRE, 1990– (Chm., Huntingdon Div., 1975–90); Chm., Sensory Trust, 1993–; Trustee, Herpetological Conservation Trust, 1992–. *Publications:* scientific papers in ecol and ornithol jls. *Recreations:* sketching, architecture, reading. *Address:* Eastfield House, Tuddenham Road, Barton Mills, Suffolk IP28 6AG. *T:* Mildenhall (01638) 715139. *Club:* Athenæum.
Died 24 Jan. 1995.

PRICE, Coral Edith, (Mrs Vincent Price); *see* Browne, C. E.

PRICE, John Lister Willis, CVO 1965; HM Diplomatic Service, retired; *b* 25 July 1915; *s* of Canon John Willis Price, Croughton, Brackley, Northants, and Maude Katherine, *d* of Rev. E. C. Lister; *m* 1940, Frances Holland (marr. diss.); one *s* one *d*. *Educ:* Bradfield; New College, Oxford. Military Service, 1940–46 (despatches). Joined Foreign Office News Dept, 1946; apptd First Secretary, Paris, 1950; transf. to FO, 1952; to Sofia, 1956; FO, 1959; Counsellor, Head of British Information Services, Bonn, 1962–66; IDC 1967; seconded as Dir of Information, NATO, 1967–72; retired 1972. Dir, Merseyside Develt Office in London, 1972–79. *Recreations:* mountains, hill walking. *Club:* Ski Club of Great Britain (Invitation Life Mem.). *Died 1 March 1995.*

PRICE, (John) Maurice; QC 1976; *b* 4 May 1922; 2nd *s* of Edward Samuel Price and Hilda M. Price, JP; *m* 1945, Mary, *d* of Dr Horace Gibson, DSO and bar, Perth, WA; two *s*. *Educ:* Grove Park Sch., Wrexham; Trinity Coll., Cambridge (MA). Served in Royal Navy, 1941–46 (Submarines, 1943–46), Lieut RNVR. Called to Bar, Gray's Inn, 1949 (Holt Scholar, Holker Sen. Scholar; Bencher 1981), and to Lincoln's Inn (*ad eundem*), 1980; called to Singapore Bar, 1977. Member: Senate of Inns of Court and the Bar, 1975–78; Supreme Court Rules Cttee, 1975–79. FCIArb 1991. *Recreations:* fishing, opera. *Address:* Halls Green Farmhouse, Weald, Sevenoaks, Kent TN14 6NQ; (chambers) 5 Stone Buildings, Lincoln's Inn, WC2A 3XT. *T:* 0171–242 6201. *Club:* Flyfishers'.
Died 15 April 1995.

PRICE, Brig. Rollo Edward Crwys, CBE 1967; DSO 1961; *b* 6 April 1916; *s* of Eardley Edward Carnac Price, CIE and Frances Louisa, *d* of Robert Eastmond Cruwys; *m* 1945, Diana Budden; three *d*. *Educ*: Canford; RMC Sandhurst. Commissioned 2nd Lt in S Wales Borderers, 1936; War Service, Middle East and Italy, 1939–45; Lt-Col and seconded for service with Queen's Own Nigeria Regt, 1959–61; Col 1962; Comdr 160 Inf. Bde, 1964–67; Brig. 1966; Comdr, British Troops, Malta, 1968–69, retired. *Publication:* After Desert Storm, 1992. *Address:* Elsford, Netherton, near Yeovil, Somerset BA22 9QH. *T:* Yetminster (01935) 872377.   *Died 24 Feb. 1995.*

PRICE, Prof. William Charles, FRS 1959; Wheatstone Professor of Physics, University of London, at King's College, 1955–76, then Emeritus; *b* 1 April 1909; *s* of Richard Price and Florence Margaret (*née* Charles); *m* 1939, Nest Myra Davies; one *s* one *d*. *Educ*: Swansea Grammar Sch.; University of Wales, Swansea (Hon. Fellow, 1985); Johns Hopkins University, Baltimore; Trinity Coll., Cambridge. BSc (Wales) 1930; Commonwealth Fellow, 1932; PhD (Johns Hopkins), 1934; Senior 1851 Exhibitioner, Cambridge, 1935; PhD (Cantab) 1937; ScD (Cantab) 1949. University Demonstrator, Cambridge, 1937–43; Prize Fellow, Trinity Coll., 1938; Senior Spectroscopist, ICI (Billingham Div.), 1943–48; Research Associate, University of Chicago, 1946–47; Reader in Physics, University of London (King's Coll.), 1948. FKC 1970. FRIC 1944; FIP 1950. Co-editor, British Bulletin of Spectroscopy, 1950. Hon. DSc Wales, 1970. Meldola Medal of Inst. of Chem., 1938. *Publications:* research and review articles on physics and chemistry in scientific journals. *Address:* 38 Cross Way, Orpington, Kent BR5 1PE. *T:* Orpington (0689) 828815.
                Died 10 March 1993.

PRICHARD, Sir Montague (Illtyd), Kt 1972; CBE 1965; MC 1944; Chairman: Belgrave Holdings PLC, since 1985; Scientific Applied Research plc, since 1985; Perspective International Group Ltd, since 1989; Director, Polysius Ltd, since 1975; *b* 26 Sept. 1915; *s* of late George Montague Prichard; *m* 1942, Kathleen Georgana Hamill; two *s* one *d*. *Educ*: Felsted Sch., Essex. Served War of 1939–45 (despatches thrice, MC): Royal Engineers: Somaliland, India, Burma, Malaya and Far East; Lt-Col as CRE 20 Indian Division. R. A. Lister & Co. Ltd, 1933–53 (excluding war service), Dir, 1950–53; Perkins Engineering Group Ltd, 1953, Man. Dir, 1958, Chm., 1959–75; Dir, Massey-Ferguson Ltd (Canada), 1961–75; retired from exec. capacities, 1975; Dir, Tozer, Kemsley & Millbourn (Holdings) plc, 1976–85 (Chm., 1982–85). Member: British Productivity Council; BNEC, 1965–72; Founder Chairman: Nat. Marketing Council, 1963; British Industry Roads Campaign. Vice-Pres., SMMT, 1966–70; Pres., Motor Industry Res. Assoc., 1972–74. FInstMSM. *Address:* Willowdale House, Apethorpe, Peterborough PE8 5DP. *T:* Kingscliffe (078087) 211. *Club:* East India, Devonshire, Sports and Public Schools.
                Died 12 June 1991.

PRICKMAN, Air Cdre Thomas Bain, CB 1953; CBE 1945; *b* 1902; *m* 1st, Ethel Serica (*d* 1949), *d* of John Cubbon, Douglas, IOM; 2nd, 1952, Dorothy, *d* of John Charles Clarke, and *widow* of Gp Capt. F. C. Read. *Educ*: Blundell's Sch. Joined RAF, 1923; served War of 1939–45, with Fighter Command; RAF Liaison staff in Australia, 1946–48; AOA, Home Command, 1950–54; retired, 1954. *Address:* Tilsmore Cottage, Cross-in-Hand, Heathfield, Sussex TN21 0LS.   *Died 1 Feb. 1992.*

PRIDAY, Christopher Bruton; QC 1986; *b* 7 Aug. 1926; *s* of Arthur Kenneth Priday and Rosemary Priday; *m* 1953, Jill Holroyd Sergeant, *o d* of John Holroyd Sergeant and Kathleen Sergeant; two *s*. *Educ*: Radley College; University College, Oxford (MA). Called to the Bar,

Gray's Inn, 1951, Bencher, 1991; Hon. *ad eundem* Mem., Middle Temple, 1985. Associate, RICS 1987. Hon. Mem., CAAV, 1988. *Publications:* jt editor, publications on law of landlord and tenant. *Recreations:* opera, golf at St Enodoc. *Address:* 61 Chiddingstone Street, SW6 4QT. *T:* 071–736 4681. *Club:* St Enodoc Golf.
                Died 26 March 1992.

PRIDEAUX, Sir John (Francis), Kt 1974; OBE 1945; DL; *b* 30 Dec. 1911; 2nd *s* of Walter Treverbian Prideaux and Marion Fenn (*née* Arbuthnot); *m* 1934, Joan, *er d* of Captain Gordon Hargreaves Brown, MC (killed in action, 1914) (*e s* of Sir Alexander Hargreaves Brown, 1st Bt) and Editha Ivy Pigott (Lady Pigott-Brown); two *s* one *d*. *Educ*: St Aubyns, Rottingdean; Eton. Middlesex Yeomanry, 1933; served War of 1939–45, Colonel Q, 2nd Army, 1944. Joined Arbuthnot Latham & Co. Ltd, Merchant Bankers, 1930, Dir, 1936–69, Chm., 1964–69. Mem., London Adv. Bd, Bank of NSW, 1948–74; Director: Westminster Bank Ltd, later National Westminster Bank Ltd, 1955–81 (Chm., 1971–77); Westminster Foreign Bank Ltd, later Internat. Westminster Bank Ltd, 1955–81 (Chm., 1969–77). Chm., Cttee of London Clearing Bankers, 1974–76; Vice-Pres., British Bankers' Assoc., 1972–77. Pres., Inst. of Bankers, 1974–76. Mem., Wilson Cttee to review functioning of financial instns in the City, 1977–80. Dep. Chm., Commonwealth Develt Corp., 1960–70; Chm., Victoria League for Commonwealth Friendship, 1977–81. Mem., Lambeth, Southwark and Lewisham AHA(T), 1974–82 (Commissioner, Aug. 1979–March 1980); Treasurer and Chm., Bd of Governors, St Thomas' Hosp., 1964–74; Chm., Special Trustees, St Thomas' Hosp., 1974–88. Hon. Fellow UMDS, 1992. Prime Warden, Goldsmiths' Company, 1972. DL Surrey 1976. Legion of Merit, USA, 1945. *Address:* Elderslie, Ockley, Surrey. *T:* Dorking (0306) 711263. *Clubs:* Brooks's, Overseas Bankers (Pres. 1976–77).
                Died 7 Jan. 1993.

PRIDEAUX, Walter Arbuthnot, CBE 1973; MC 1945; TD 1948; *b* 4 Jan. 1910; *e s* of Walter Treverbian Prideaux and Marion Fenn (*née* Arbuthnot); *m* 1937, Anne, *d* of Francis Stewart Cokayne; two *s* two *d*. *Educ*: Eton; Trinity Coll., Cambridge. Solicitor, 1934. Assistant Clerk of the Goldsmiths' Company, 1939–53, Clerk 1953–75. Chm., City Parochial Foundn, 1972–80. Kent Yeomanry, 1936–48. *Recreation:* rowed for Cambridge, 1930, 1931.
                Died 5 Nov. 1995.

PRIESTLAND, Gerald Francis; Religious Affairs Correspondent, BBC, 1977–82; *b* 26 Feb. 1927; *s* of late Frank Priestland and Nelly Priestland (*née* Renny); *m* 1949, Helen Sylvia (*née* Rhodes); two *s* two *d*. *Educ*: Charterhouse; New Coll., Oxford (BA). Subeditor, BBC News, 1949–54; BBC Correspondent: New Delhi, 1954–58; Washington, 1958–61; Beirut, 1961–65; Washington, 1965–70; news presenter on radio and TV, 1970–76. Pulpit column, Sunday Times, 1988–. Hon. Fellow, Manchester Polytechnic, 1978. MUniv Open, 1985. Hon. DD: St Andrews, 1988; Hull, 1988. Sandford St Martin Prize for religious broadcasting, 1982. *Television:* Priestland Right and Wrong (series), 1983. *Publications:* America the Changing Nation, 1968; Frying Tonight (the Saga of Fish and Chips), 1971; The Future of Violence, 1976; Yours Faithfully, Vol. 1, 1979, Vol. 2, 1981; Dilemmas of Journalism, 1979; (with Sylvia Priestland) West of Hayle River, 1980; Priestland's Progress, 1981; Reasonable Uncertainty (Swarthmore Lect.), 1982; Who Needs the Church? (William Barclay Lects), 1983; Gerald Priestland at Large, 1983; Priestland Right and Wrong, 1983; The Case Against God, 1984; For All the Saints (Backhouse Lect.), 1985; Something Understood (autobiog.), 1986; The Unquiet Suitcase, 1988; Praying for Peace, 1991. *Recreation:* being in

Cornwall. *Address:* 4 Temple Fortune Lane, NW11 7UD. *T:* 081–455 3297; The Old Sunday School, Carfury, Cornwall. *T:* Penzance (0736) 69191.

Died 20 June 1991.

PRINCE, (Celestino) Anthony; solicitor; Taxing Master of the Supreme Court, since 1983; *b* 20 Aug. 1921; *s* of Charles Prince and Amelia (*née* Daubenspeck); *m* 1950, Margaret (*née* Walker) (rep., 200 metres, GB in Olympic Games, 1948 and England in British Empire Games, 1950); one *s* one *d. Educ:* Finchley Grammar Sch. Served War, RN, 1939–45: Western Mediterranean in HMS Antelope; Atlantic, Indian Ocean and Pacific in HMS Arbiter; commnd Sub-Lt, 1944. Articled to Kenneth George Rigden of Beaumont Son & Rigden, Fleet Street, 1939; admitted solicitor, 1947; founded firm of C. Anthony Prince & Co., Ealing, 1952; retd as Sen. Partner, 1981. Mem., No 1 (London), later No 14, Legal Aid Area Cttee, 1966–71. Founder Chm., Ealing Family Housing Assoc., 1963. Hon. Sec., Bucks CCC, 1954–69 (played in Minor Counties Comp., 1946–49); Captain, W Mddx Golf Club, 1970–71. Member: RYA; RNLI. *Recreations:* cricket, golf, sailing (Mem., Australian Sardinia Cup team, 1978; Fastnet Race, 1981). *Address:* Royal Courts of Justice, Strand, WC2A 2LL. *Clubs:* MCC; Buckinghamshire CC; Beaconsfield Cricket; West Middlesex Golf.

Died 25 Oct. 1993.

PRING, David Andrew Michael, CB 1980; MC 1943; Clerk of Committees, House of Commons, 1976–87; *b* 6 Dec. 1922; *s* of late Captain John Arthur Pring and Gladys Pring; *m* 1962, Susan Brakspear, Henley-on-Thames; one *s* one *d. Educ:* King's Sch., Rochester; Magdalene Coll., Cambridge (MA). Served Royal Engineers, N Africa, Sicily, Italy, Austria, 1941–46; attached staff Governor-General, Canada, 1946. A Clerk of the House of Commons, 1948–87. *Publications:* include: (as Douglas Perring) The Apostles of Violence, 1957; What's Wrong With Parliament, 1964; (with Kenneth Bradshaw) Parliament and Congress, 1972; two books for children. *Address:* Bushy Platt, Stanford Dingley, Berks RG7 6DY. *T:* Woolhampton (0734) 712585. *Club:* Athenæum.

Died 15 Aug. 1991.

PRINGLE, Dr Derek Hair, CBE 1980; BSc, PhD, DSc; FRSE; CPhys; FInstP; Director, Dunedin Enterprise Investment Trust plc (formerly Melville Street Investments), since 1983; Member, Board of Trustees, National Museums of Scotland, since 1985; *b* 8 Jan. 1926; *s* of Robert Pringle and Lillias Dalgleish Hair; *m* 1949, Anne Collier Caw; three *s* one *d. Educ:* George Heriot's Sch., Edinburgh; Edinburgh Univ. (BSc 1948, PhD 1954). FInstP 1957; FRSE 1970. Res. Physicist, Ferranti Ltd, Edinburgh, 1948–59; Nuclear Enterprises Ltd: Technical Dir, 1960–76; Man. Dir, 1976–78; Chm., 1978–80; Chairman: SEEL Ltd, 1980–92; Bioscot, 1983–86; Director: Amersham Internat., 1978–87; Creative Capital Nominees Ltd, 1982–90. Chairman: Borders Health Bd, 1989–93; Scottish Health Service Cttee on Non-Surgical Management of Cancer in Scotland, 1990–91. Member: Nat. Radiol Protection Bd, Harwell, 1969–81; Council for Applied Science in Scotland, 1981–86; CNAA, 1982–85. Vice-Pres., RSE, 1985–88 (Mem. Council, 1982–88); Mem., Council, Scottish Museums Adv. Bd, 1984–85. Mem., Court, Heriot-Watt Univ., 1968–77. Pres., Edinburgh Chamber of Commerce and Manufactures, 1979–81; Chm., Assoc. of Scottish Chambers of Commerce, 1985–87; Mem. Council, Assoc. of British Chambers of Commerce, 1986–87; Vice-Chm. (Scotland), Industry Matters, 1987–88. Faraday Lectr, 1978–79. FRSA 1991. Hon. FRCSE 1988. Hon. DSc Heriot Watt Univ., 1981. *Publications:* papers on microwave engrg, gas discharge physics and nuclear science in scientific jls. *Recreations:* golf, gardening. *Address:* Earlyvale,

Eddleston, Peeblesshire EH45 8QX. *T:* Eddleston (01721) 730231. *Clubs:* Royal Over-Seas League, English-Speaking Union. *Died 7 July 1995.*

PRITCHARD, Baron *cr* 1975 (Life Peer), of West Haddon, Northamptonshire; **Derek Wilbraham Pritchard;** Kt 1968; DL; *b* 8 June 1910; *s* of Frank Wheelton Pritchard and Ethel Annie Pritchard (*née* Cheetham); *m* 1941, Denise Arfor Pritchard (*née* Huntbach); two *d. Educ:* Clifton College, Bristol. Took over family business of E. Halliday & Son, Wine Merchants, 1929, Man. Dir, 1930–51, Chm., 1947. Called up in TA and served War of 1939–45; demob. as Col and joined Bd of E. K. Cole, Ltd, 1946. Joined Ind Coope Ltd, as Man. Dir of Grants of St James's Ltd, 1949, Chm., 1960–69; Chm., Victoria Wine Co. Ltd, 1959–64. Director: Ind Coope Ltd, 1951; Ind Coope Tetley Ansell Ltd on merger of those companies, 1961, subseq. renamed Allied Breweries Ltd, 1961–80 (Chm., 1968–70); Allied Breweries Investments Ltd, 1961–80; Licences & General Assurance Ltd, 1952–56, subseq. merged with Guardian Assurance Ltd, 1956–80; Guardian Royal Exchange Assurance Ltd, 1956–80; George Sandeman Sons & Co. Ltd, 1952–80; J. & W. Nicholson (Holdings), 1962–82; Carreras Ltd, 1970–72 (Chm.); Dorchester Hotel Ltd, 1976–80 (Chm.); Rothmans of Pall Mall Canada Ltd, 1972–77; Rothmans of Pall Mall (Australia) Ltd, 1972–77; Rothmans of Pall Mall (Malaysia) Berhad, 1972–77; Rothmans of Pall Mall (Singapore) Ltd, 1972–77; Deltec International, 1975–77; London-American Finance Corp., 1976–78; Midland Bank Ltd, 1968–85; Samuel Montagu Ltd, 1969–86; Adelaide Associates Ltd, 1970–; Rothmans International Ltd, 1972–86 (Chm., 1972–75); Rothmans Group Services SA, 1972–86; Rothmans of Pall Mall (London) Ltd, 1972–86; Rothmans Tobacco Hldgs Ltd, 1972–86; Carreras Group (Jamaica) Ltd, 1972–86; Paterson, Zochonis & Co. Ltd, 1977–89; Philips Electronic & Associated Industries Ltd, 1978–85; Lyford Cay Property Owners Assoc. Ltd, 1980–; Tiedmann-Goodnow Internat. Capital Corp., 1980–89 (Chm., 1980–86); Matterhorn Investment Co. Ltd (Chm., 1980–85); Thoroughbred Holdings Internat. Ltd, 1982– (Chm.); Euro-Canadian Bank Inc., 1984–89; Templeton Foundn Adv. Bd, 1980– (Chm., 1984–85); Templeton, Galbraith & Hansberger Ltd, 1987–; Templeton Investments Management Ltd, 1980–; Best Investments Inc.; Chalk International Airlines, 1984–; Equator Hldgs, 1985–; Equator Bank, 1985–; Dextra Bank & Trust Co., 1986–89 (Chm.). Chairman: Dorchester Hotel Bd of Trustees, 1976–87; Dorchester Pension Fund, 1976–86; Rothmans Internat. Adv. Bd, 1986–89; Mem., Salomon Bros Adv. Bd, USA, 1980–83; Dep Chm., British National Export Council, 1965–66, Chm. 1966–68; Member: Nat. Inds Appts Bd, 1973–82; Top Salaries Review Body, 1975–78; House of Lords EEC Cttee, 1975–79, EEC Sub-Cttee A, 1975–80; Cttee, British Foundn for Age Research, 1975–84; British Overseas Trade Adv. Council, 1976–84; Fund Raising Cttee, RCS, 1976–87; Chancellor of the Duchy of Lancaster's Cttee on Business Sponsorship of the Arts, 1980–87; Amer. European Community Assoc., 1981–88; President: British Export Houses Assoc., 1976–83; Northants Co. Branch, Royal Agricl Benevolent Instn, 1981–87; Patron: Northants British Red Cross Soc., 1982– (Pres., 1975–83); Inst. of Directors, 1966– (Pres., 1968–74); Vice-President: Inst. of Export, 1976– (Pres., 1974–76); Wine and Spirit Assoc. of GB, 1964– (Pres., 1962–64); Northants Youth Club Assoc., 1965–; East of England Agricl Soc., 1974–; Co-Chm., UK-Jamaica Cttee, 1981–87; Trustee: Age Action Trust, 1975–80; St Giles Church, Northampton, 1976–86; Patron: Northampton and County Chamber of Commerce, 1978–; Three Shires Indept Hosp., 1978–; Abbeyfield Soc. for the Aged, 1979– (Pres., 1970–79); Governor: Clifton Coll., Bristol; Nene Coll., Northampton. DL Northants, 1974. *Recreations:*

farming, tennis, golf, hunting. *Address:* West Haddon Hall, Northampton NN6 7AU. *T:* West Haddon (01788) 510210.   *Died 18 Oct. 1995.*

PROBYN, Air Cdre Harold Melsome, CB 1944; CBE 1943; DSO 1917; *b* 8 Dec. 1891; *s* of late William Probyn; *m* 1920, Marjory (*d* 1961), *d* of late Francis Evance Savory. Served European War, 1914–17 (despatches, DSO); commanded: 208 (AC) Squadron, Egypt; No 2 (AC) Squadron, Manston; 25 (Fighter) Squadron at Hawkinge; RAF School of Photography, 1932; No 22 Group, RAF, 1932–34; Senior Personnel Staff Officer, Middle East, Cairo, 1934–35; Senior Engineer Staff Officer, Middle East, Cairo, 1935–37; No 12 (Fighter) Group Royal Air Force, Hucknall, Notts, 1937; served War of 1939–45 (despatches); SASO, No 11 Fighter Group, Uxbridge, 1939–40; commanded RAF Station, Cranwell, 1940–44; retired, 1944. *Recreations:* flying, fishing, golf. *Club:* Naval and Military.
                                     Died 24 March 1992.

PROCTOR, Ian Douglas Ben, RDI 1969; FCSD (FSIAD 1969); FRSA 1972; Chairman, Ian Proctor Metal Masts Ltd, 1959–76 and 1981–86 (Director, 1959–86); freelance industrial designer since 1950; *b* 12 July 1918; *s* of Douglas McIntyre Proctor and Mary Albina Louise Proctor (*née* Tredwen); *m* 1943, Elizabeth Anne Gifford Lywood, *d* of Air Vice-Marshal O. G. Lywood, CB, CBE; three *s* one *d. Educ:* Gresham's Sch., Holt; London University. RAFVR (Flying Officer), 1942–46. Man. Dir, Gosport Yacht Co., 1947–48; Joint Editor Yachtsman Magazine, 1948–50; Daily Telegraph Yachting Correspondent, 1950–64. Yachtsman of the Year, 1965; Council of Industrial Design Award, 1967; Design Council Awards, 1977, 1980. *Publications:* Racing Dinghy Handling, 1948; Racing Dinghy Maintenance, 1949; Sailing: Wind and Current, 1950; Boats for Sailing, 1968; Sailing Strategy, 1977. *Recreation:* sailing. *Address:* Ferry House, Duncannon, Stoke Gabriel, near Totnes, Devon TQ9 6QY. *Club:* Stoke Gabriel Boating Assoc.
                                     Died 23 July 1992.

PROCTOR, Sir Roderick (Consett), Kt 1978; MBE 1946; FCA; company director; *b* 28 July 1914; *s* of Frederick William Proctor and Ethel May (*née* Christmas); *m* 1st, 1943, Kathleen Mary (*née* Murphy; *d* 1978); four *s*; 2nd, 1980, Janice Marlene (*née* Pryor). *Educ:* Hale Sch., Perth, WA; Melbourne C of E Grammar Sch., Vic. FCA 1958. Served War, 1939–45. Commenced career as chartered accountant, 1931, as Jun. Clerk with R. Goyne Miller, Perth; joined Clarke & Son, Chartered Accountants, Brisbane, Qld, 1937; Partner, 1950, Sen. Partner, 1966 (firm merged with Aust. national firm, Hungerfords, 1960); retd as Partner, 1976. *Recreations:* surfing, boating. *Address:* 18 Captains Court, Raby Bay, Qld 4163, Australia. *Clubs:* Queensland, Brisbane, United Service (Brisbane); Brisbane Polo; Southport Yacht, Royal Queensland Yacht.   *Died 30 Aug. 1991.*

PROPPER, Arthur, CMG 1965; MBE 1945; *b* 3 Aug. 1910; 2nd *s* of late I. Propper; *m* 1941, Erica Mayer; one *d. Educ:* Owen's Sch.; Peterhouse, Cambridge (schol.). 1st class, Hist. Tripos, Pt 2. With W. S. Crawford Ltd (Advertising Agents), 1933–38, and the J. Walter Thompson Co. Ltd, 1939; Min. of Economic Warfare, 1940; transf. to Min. of Food, 1946 (subseq. to Min. of Agric., Fisheries and Food); established in Home Civil Service, 1949; Asst Sec., 1952; Mem. UK Delegn at Common Market negotiations, with rank of Under-Sec., 1962–63; seconded to Foreign Office, 1963; Counsellor (Agric.), UK Delegn to the European Communities, Brussels, and HM Embassy, Bonn, 1963–64; Under-Sec., Min. of Agriculture, Fisheries and Food, 1964–70; Common Mkt Advr, Unigate Ltd, 1970–73; Sec., Food Panel, Price Commn, 1973–76. *Recreations:* the theatre,

music, buying books, visiting Scotland. *Address:* 3 Hill House, Stanmore Hill, Stanmore, Mddx HA7 3EW. *T:* 081–954 1242.   *Died 30 July 1992.*

PROUD, Air Cdre Harold John Granville Ellis, CBE 1946; *b* 23 Aug. 1906; *s* of late Ralph Henry Proud, Glasgow; *m* 1937, Jenefer Angela Margaret, *d* of late Lt-Col J. Bruce, OBE, 19th Lancers; two *d.* HAC (Inf.), 1924–26; commissioned RAF, pilot, 1926; Staff Coll., 1936; served in: Mediterranean (FAA), 1928; India, 1937 and 1942–45 (Inspector Gen. Indian Air Force, 1942–43; AOA Air HQ, 1943–45); Dir of Ground Def., Air Min., 1945–47; served in Singapore, 1949; AOC 67 (NI) Gp and Senior Air Force Officer N Ire., 1951–54; Provost Marshal and Chief of Air Force Police, 1954; retired 1956; in business, 1957–71. Latterly domiciled in Switzerland; Mem. Council, British Residents Assoc. of Switzerland, 1973–77, Chm., 1974–75. *Address:* Appt 10, Les Libellules, 1837 Château d'Oex, Switzerland. *T:* (029) 46223. *Club:* Royal Air Force.
                                     Died 19 March 1995.

PROUDFOOT, Bruce Falconer; Publicity Officer, Ulster Savings Committee, 1963–69; Editor, Northern Whig and Belfast Post, 1943–63; *b* 1903; 2nd *s* of G. A. Proudfoot, Edinburgh; *m* 1928, Cecilia, *er d* of V. T. T. Thompson, Newcastle on Tyne; twin *s. Educ:* Edinburgh Education Authority's Primary and Secondary Schools. Served with Edinburgh Evening Dispatch, Galloway Gazette (Newton-Stewart) and Newcastle Daily Chronicle before joining Northern Whig, 1925. *Address:* Westgate, Wardlaw Gardens, St Andrews, Fife KY16 9DW. *T:* St Andrews (0334) 73293.   *Died 13 Oct. 1993.*

PRUDE, Agnes George, (Mrs Walter F. Prude); *see* de Mille, A. G.

PUGH, Surg. Rear-Adm. Patterson David Gordon, OBE 1968; surgeon and author; *b* 19 Dec. 1920; *o s* of late W. T. Gordon Pugh, MD, FRCS, Carshalton, and Elaine V. A. Pugh (*née* Hobson), Fort Beaufort, S Africa; *m* 1st, 1948, Margaret Sheena Fraser; three *s* one *d*; 2nd, 1967, Eleanor Margery Jones; one *s* one *d. Educ:* Lancing Coll.; Jesus Coll., Cambridge; Middlesex Hosp. Med. Sch. MA (Cantab), MB, BChir; FRCS, LRCP. Ho. Surg., North Middlesex Hosp., 1944; RNVR, 1945; served, HMS Glasgow and HMS Jamaica, 1945–47; perm. commn, 1950; served, HMS Narvik, 1952, HMS Warrior, 1956; Consultant in Orthopaedics, RN Hospitals: Malta, 1960; Haslar, 1962; Plymouth, 1968; Sen. MO (Admin.), RN Hosp., Plymouth, 1973; MO i/c, RN Hosp., Malta, 1974–75; Surgeon Rear-Adm. (Naval Hosps), 1975–78; QHS, 1975–78; MO, Home Office Prison Dept, 1978–80. Fellow, British Orthopaedic Assoc.; FRSA; Mem., Soc. of Authors. CStJ 1976. *Publications:* Practical Nursing, 16th edn 1945, to 21st edn 1969; Nelson and his Surgeons, 1968; Staffordshire Portrait Figures and Allied Subjects of the Victorian Era, 1970, enlarged edn 1981; Naval Ceramics, 1971; Heraldic China Mementos of the First World War, 1972; Pugh of Carshalton, 1973. *Recreation:* travel. *Address:* 3 Chilworth Road, Camps Bay, Cape Town, 8001, Republic of South Africa. *T:* (21) 4381122.
                                     Died 15 July 1993.

PURCELL, Ven. William Henry Samuel, MA; Archdeacon of Dorking, 1968–82; *b* 22 Jan. 1912; *m* 1941, Kathleen Clough, Leeds; one *s* (and one *s* decd). *Educ:* King Edward VI School, Norwich; Fitzwilliam House, Cambridge (MA). Deacon, 1937; priest, 1938; Asst Curate, St Michael's, Headingley, Leeds, 1937; Minor Canon of Ripon Cathedral, 1940; Vicar: St Matthew, Holbeck, Leeds, 1943; St Matthew, Chapel Allerton, Leeds, 1947; St Martin's, Epsom, 1963. Rural Dean of Epsom, 1965. Hon. Canon of Ripon Cathedral, 1962; Hon. Canon of Guildford Cathedral, 1968, Canon Emeritus,

1982. *Recreations:* walking, travel. *Address:* 55 Windfield, Epsom Road, Leatherhead, Surrey KT22 8UQ. *T:* Leatherhead (0372) 375708. *Died 4 June 1994.*

PURSEGLOVE, John William, CMG 1973; Tropical Crops Specialist, Overseas Development Administration at East Malling Research Station, Kent, 1967–75; *b* 11 Aug. 1912; *s* of late Robert and Kate Purseglove; *m* 1947, Phyllis Agnes Adèle, *d* of late George and Mary Turner, Falkland Is; one *s* (one *d* decd). *Educ:* Lady Manners Sch., Bakewell; Manchester Univ. (BSc Hons Botany); Gonville and Caius Coll, Cambridge; Imperial Coll. of Tropical Agriculture, Trinidad (AICTA). Agricultural and Sen. Agricl Officer, Uganda, 1936–52; Lectr in Tropical Agriculture, Univ. of Cambridge, 1952–54; Dir, Botanic Gardens, Singapore, 1954–57; Prof. of Botany, Imperial Coll. of Tropical Agriculture and Univ. of the West Indies, Trinidad, 1957–67. Pres., Assoc. for Tropical Biology, 1962–65. FLS 1945; FIBiol 1970; Hon. Mem., Trop. Agric. Assoc., 1984. *Publications:* Tobacco in Uganda, 1951; Tropical Crops, Dicotyledons, 2 vols, 1968; Tropical Crops, Monocotyledons, 2 vols, 1972; (with E. G. Brown, C. L. Green and S. R. J. Robbins) Spices, 2 vols, 1981, Japanese edn 1985; papers on land use, ethnobotany, etc, in scientific jls and symposia vols. *Recreations:* gardening, natural history. *Address:* Walnut Trees, Sissinghurst, Cranbrook, Kent TN17 2JL. *T:* Cranbrook (0580) 712836. *Died 27 Nov. 1991.*

PUTT, S(amuel) Gorley, OBE 1966; MA; Fellow, Christ's College, Cambridge, since 1968 (Senior Tutor, 1968–78; Praelector, 1976–80); *b* 9 June 1913; *o c* of late Poole Putt and Ellen Blake Gorley, Brixham. *Educ:* Torquay Grammar School; Christ's College, Cambridge; Yale University. 1st Class English Tripos Pts I and II, MA 1937, Cambridge; Commonwealth Fund Fellow, MA 1936, Yale. BBC Talks Dept, 1936–38; Warden and Sec., Appts Cttee, Queen's Univ. of Belfast, 1939–40; RNVR, 1940–46, Lieut-Comdr; Warden and Tutor to Overseas Students and Director International Summer School, Univ. Coll., Exeter, 1946–49; Warden of Harkness House, 1949–68 and Director, Div. of International Fellowships, The Commonwealth Fund, 1966–68. Chm., 1964–72, Vice-Pres., 1972–78, English Assoc. Visiting Professor: Univ. of Massachusetts, 1968; Univ. of the South, Sewanee, 1976; Univ. of Pisa, 1979; Texas Christian Univ., 1985. Member: English-Speaking Union, London Cttee, 1952–57; UK-US Educational Commn: Travel Grants Cttee, 1955–64; Cttee of Management, Inst. of US Studies, London Univ., 1965–69. Contested (L) Torquay, 1945. FRSL 1952. Cavaliere, Order of Merit of Italy, 1980. *Publications:* Men Dressed As Seamen, 1943; View from Atlantis, 1955; (ed) Cousins and Strangers, 1956; Coastline, 1959; Scholars of the Heart, 1962; (ed) Essays and Studies, 1963; A Reader's Guide to Henry James, 1966; The Golden Age of English Drama, 1981; A Preface to Henry James, 1986; Wings of a Man's Life, 1990; Arthur Mizener, 1991. *Address:* Christ's College, Cambridge CB2 3BU. *T:* Cambridge (01223) 334900. *Club:* Athenæum. *Died 24 April 1995.*

PYKE, Magnus Alfred; OBE 1978; PhD, CChem, FRSC, FInstBiol, FIFST, FRSE; *b* 29 Dec. 1908; *s* of Robert Bond Pyke and Clara Hannah Pyke (*née* Lewis); *m* 1937, Dorothea Mina Vaughan (*d* 1986); one *s* one *d*. *Educ:* St Paul's Sch., London; McGill Univ., Montreal; University Coll. London (Fellow, 1984–). BSc, PhD. Scientific Adviser's Div., Min. of Food, London, 1941–45; Nutritional Adviser, Allied Commn for Austria, Vienna, 1945–46; Principal Scientific Officer (Nutrition), Min. of Food, London, 1946–48; Distillers Co. Ltd: Dep. Manager, Yeast Research Outstation, 1949–55; Manager, Glenochil Research Station, 1955–73; Sec. and Chm. of Council, British Assoc. for the Advancement of Science, 1973–77

(Mem. Council, 1968–77; Pres. Section X, 1965). Member: Soc. for Analytical Chemistry, 1959–61 (Vice-Pres.); Council, Royal Inst. of Chemistry, 1953–56, 1962–65; Council, Royal Soc. of Edinburgh, 1961–64; Council, Soc. of Chemical Industry, 1967–69; (Chm.) Scottish Section, Nutrition Soc., 1954–55; (Vice-Pres.) Assoc. for Liberal Education, 1964–81; (Pres.) Inst. of Food Science and Technology of the UK, 1969–71; Participated in Don't Ask Me, 1974–78, Don't Just Sit There, 1979–80, Yorkshire TV. FInstBiol (Mem. Council, Scottish Sect., 1959–62). Hon. Fellow: Australian IFST, 1973; NZ IFST, 1979. Hon. Senior Mem., Sen. Common Room, Darwin Coll., Univ. of Kent, 1979. DUniv Stirling, 1974; Hon. DSc: Lancaster, 1976; McGill, 1981. Silver Medal, RSA, 1972; Pye Colour TV Award: the most promising newcomer to television, 1975; BBC Multi-Coloured Swap Shop Star Award (Expert of the Year), 1977–78. *Publications:* Manual of Nutrition, 1945; Industrial Nutrition, 1950; Townsman's Food, 1952; Automation, Its Purpose and Future, 1956; Nothing Like Science, 1957; Slaves Unaware, 1959; The Boundaries of Science, 1961; Nutrition, 1962; The Science Myth, 1962; Food Science and Technology, 1964; The Science Century, 1967; Food and Society, 1968; Man and Food, 1970; Synthetic Food, 1970; Technological Eating, 1972; Catering Science and Technology, 1973; Success in Nutrition, 1975; Butter-side Up, 1976; There and Back, 1978; Food for all the Family, 1980; Long Life, 1980; Our Future, 1980; (with P. Moore) Everyman's Scientific Facts and Feats, 1981; Six Lives of Pyke, 1981; Curiouser and Curiouser, 1983; Red Rag to a Bull, 1983; (contrib.) Diet and Health in Modern Britain, ed D. J. Oddy and D. S. Miller, 1985; (contrib.) The World's Food Supply, ed J. Asimov, 1985; Dr Magnus Pyke's 101 Inventions, 1986. *Recreation:* until he was 75 he wrote a page a day and savoured the consequences. *Address:* Elmbank, 38 Carlton Drive, SW15 2BH. *T:* 081–780 9027. *Died 19 Oct. 1992.*

PYLE, Cyril Alfred; Head Master, South East London School, 1970–80; *s* of Alfred John Pyle and Nellie Blanche Pyle; *m* 1940, Jean Alice Cotten; one *s* one *d*. *Educ:* Shooters Hill Grammar Sch.; Goldsmiths' Coll., Univ. of London. Dep. Headmaster, Woolwich Polytechnic Secondary Sch., 1940–66; Headmaster, Bow Sch., 1966–70. Pres., London Teachers' Assoc., 1962; Chm., Council for Educnl Advance, 1964–76; Sec., Conference of London Comprehensive School Heads, 1973–79. *Recreations:* Rotary Club, motoring, gardening. *Address:* Barleyfields, Hartlip, Sittingbourne, Kent ME9 7TH. *T:* Newington (01795) 842719. *Died 11 May 1994.*

PYRAH, Prof. Leslie Norman, CBE 1963; Senior Consultant Surgeon, Department of Urology, Leeds General Infirmary, 1950–64, retired; Hon. Director, Medical Research Council Unit, Leeds General Infirmary, 1956–64; Professor of Urological Surgery, Leeds University, 1956–64, then Emeritus; *b* 11 April 1899; *s* of Arthur Pyrah; *m* 1934, Mary Christopher Batley (*d* 1990); one *s* one *d* (and one *s* decd). *Educ:* University of Leeds; School of Medicine, Leeds. Hon. Asst Surgeon, Leeds Gen. Infirmary, 1934; Hon. Consultant Surgeon, Dewsbury Infirmary, Leeds Public Dispensary, Goole Hosp., and Lecturer in Surgery, Univ. of Leeds, 1934; Hon. Cons. Surgeon, St James' Hosp., Leeds, 1941; Surgeon with charge of Out-patients, Leeds Infirmary, 1944. Weild Lectr, Royal Faculty Physicians and Surgeons, Glasgow, 1955; Ramon Guiteras Lectr, Amer. Urological Assoc., Pittsburgh, USA, 1957; Litchfield Lectr, Univ. of Oxford, 1959; Hunterian Orator, RCS, 1969. Chm., Specialist Adv. Cttee in Urology, Jt Royal Colls of Surgeons of GB and Ireland, 1968–72. Pres., Section of Urology, Royal Soc. Med., 1958; Pres., British Assoc. of Urological Surgeons, 1961, 1962; Pres. Leeds and W Riding Medico-Chirurgical Soc., 1959. Mem. Council (elected), Royal College of

Surgeons of England, 1960–68. Hon. Mem. Soc. Belge de Chirurgie, 1958; Corresponding Member: Amer. Assoc. of Genito-Urinary Surgeons, 1962; Amer. Soc. of Pelvic Surgeons, 1962; Australasian Soc. of Urology, 1963. St Peter's Medal (British Assoc. of Urological Surgeons) for outstanding contributions to urology, 1959; Honorary Medal, RCS, 1975. DSc (*hc*) Leeds, 1965; Hon. FRSM, 1978. *Publications:* British Surgical Progress (contrib.), 1956; Renal Calculus, 1979; numerous contribs to British Journal of Surgery, British Journal of Urology, Proc. Royal Soc. Med., Lancet, BMJ. *Recreations:* tennis, music. *Address:* Fieldhead, 55 Weetwood Lane, Leeds LS16 5NP. *T:* Leeds (0113) 275 2777.

Died 30 April 1995.

Q

QUENNELL, Sir Peter (Courtney), Kt 1992; CBE 1973; writer; *b* March 1905; *s* of late Marjorie and C. H. B. Quennell; *m* 1st (marr. diss. 1935); 2nd, 1935, Marie José Roth (marr. diss. 1937); 3rd, 1938, Joyce Frances Warwick Evans (marr. diss. 1943); one *d*; 4th, 1956, Sonia Geraldine Leon (marr. diss. 1967); 5th, 1967, Joan Marilyn Peak (*née* Kerr); one *s. Educ:* Berkhamsted Grammar Sch.; Balliol Coll., Oxford. Editor, History To-day, 1951–79; edited The Cornhill Magazine, 1944–51. *Publications:* Poems, 1926; Baudelaire and the Symbolists, 1929, 2nd edn 1954; A Superficial Journey through Tokyo and Peking, 1932, 2nd edn 1934; Sympathy, and Other Stories, 1933; Byron, 1934; Byron: the years of fame, 1935, 3rd edn 1967; Victorian Panorama: a survey of life and fashion from contemporary photographs, 1937; Caroline of England, 1939; Byron in Italy, 1941; Four Portraits, 1945, 2nd edn 1965; John Ruskin, 1949; The Singular Preference, 1952; Spring in Sicily, 1952; Hogarth's Progress, 1955; The Sign of the Fish, 1960; Shakespeare: the poet and his background, 1964; Alexander Pope: the education of Genius 1688–1728, 1968; Romantic England, 1970; Casanova in London and other essays, 1971; Samuel Johnson: his friends and enemies, 1972; (with H. Johnson) A History of English Literature, 1973; Byron, 1974; The Marble Foot (autobiog.), 1976; The Wanton Chase (autobiog.), 1980; Customs and Characters, 1982; The Pursuit of Happiness, 1988; *edited:* Aspects of Seventeenth Century Verse, 1933, 2nd edn 1936; The Private Letters of Princess Lieven to Prince Metternich, 1820–1826, 1948; Byron: selected letters and journals, 1949; H. Mayhew, Mayhew's Characters, 1951; Diversions of History, 1954; H. Mayhew, Mayhew's London, 1954; George Borrow, The Bible in Spain, 1959; H. Mayhew, London's Underworld, 1960; G. G. N. Byron, Lord Byron, Byronic Thoughts, 1960; H. de Montherlant, Selected Essays, 1960; W. Hickey, Memoirs, 1960; T. Moore, The Journal of Thomas Moore, 1964; H. Mayhew, Mayhew's Characters, 1967; Marcel Proust, 1871–1922: a centenary volume, 1971; Vladimir Nabokov, his Life, his Work, his World, 1979; Genius in the Drawing Room: the literary salon in the 19th and 20th centuries, 1980; A Lonely Business: a self-portrait of James Pope-Hennessy, 1981. *Address:* 2 Chamberlain Street, Primrose Hill, NW1 8XB. *Club:* White's. *Died 27 Oct. 1993.*

R

RABIN, Yitzhak; Prime Minister and Minister of Defence, Israel, since 1992; *b* Jerusalem, 1 March 1922; *m* 1948, Lea Schlossberg; one *s* one *d. Educ:* Staff Coll., England; Kedoorie Coll., Israel. Palmach Bde, 1941–48, incl. War of Independence; rep. Israel Defence Forces at Rhodes armistice negotiations; Israel Defence Forces: Head, Trng Dept, 1953–56; C-in-C, Northern Comd, 1956–59; Dep. COS and Chief of Ops Br., 1959–63; Maj.-Gen.; COS, 1964–68; Ambassador to USA, 1968–73. Mem., Knesset, 1974–; Chm., Labour Party, 1974–77; Minister of Labour, 1974; Prime Minister, 1974–77; Minister of Defence, 1984–90. Hon. PhD Jerusalem, 1967, and hon. degrees from other colls and univs. (Jtly) Nobel Peace Prize, 1994. *Publication:* Service Notebook: the Rabin memoirs, 1979. *Address:* c/o Prime Minister's Office, Jerusalem, Israel.
Died 4 Nov. 1995.

RABUKAWAQA, Sir Josua Rasilau, KBE 1977 (CBE 1974; MBE 1968); MVO 1970; Ambassador-at-Large for Fiji and Chief of Protocol, Fiji, 1977–80; *b* 2 Dec. 1917; *s* of Dr Aisea Rasilau and Adi Mereoni Dimaicakau, Bau, Fiji; *m* 1944, Mei Tolanivutu; three *s* two *d. Educ:* Suva Methodist Boys' Sch.; Queen Victoria Sch.; Teachers' Trng Coll., Auckland. Diploma in Public and Social Admin, 1958. Teaching in schools throughout Fiji, 1938–52; Co-operatives Inspector, 1952; joined Fiji Mil. Forces, 1953; attached Gloucester Regt at Warminster Sch. of Infantry and Support Weapons Wing, Netheravon; comd Mortar Platoon, Malaya, 1954–55; subseq. Econ. Develt Officer, Fiji, 1957; District Officer, Fiji Admin. Service, 1961; Comr, Central Div., 1968. MLC, Fiji, 1964–66; Delegate, Constitutional Conf., London, 1965; (first) High Comr for Fiji in London, 1970–76. Active worker for Scouts, Red Cross and Methodist Church Choir; formed Phoenix Choir; compiled manual of singing in Fijian language, 1956, and guide for Fijian pronunciation for use by Fiji Broadcasting Commn, 1967; Chm., Fijian Adv. Cttee of Fiji Broadcasting Commn, 1965–70; Chm. Bd of Examrs for High Standard Fijian and Interpreters Exams, 1965–70; Mem., Housing Authority; Mem., Educn Adv. Council. *Recreations:* cricket, Rugby football (toured NZ as player/manager for Fiji, 1967). *Address:* 6 Vunivivi Hill, Nausori, Fiji. *Clubs:* Commonwealth Trust; Defence, Union (Fiji).
Died 30 Sept. 1992.

RACZYNSKI, Count Edward, Hon. GBE 1991; Dr Juris; Hon. President, The Polish Institute and Sikorski Museum, since 1977 (Chairman, 1966–77); Polish President-in-exile, 1979–86; *b* 19 Dec. 1891; *s* of Count Edouard Raczynski and Countess Rose Potocka; *m* 1st, 1925, Joyous (*d* 1930), *d* of Sir Arthur Basil Markham, 1st Bt, and Lucy, CBE, *d* of Captain A. B. Cunningham, late RA; 2nd, 1932, Cecile (*d* 1962), *d* of Edward Jaroszynski and Wanda Countess Sierakowska; three *d*; 3rd, 1991, Aniela Mieczyslawska, *d* of Franeiszek and Halina Wieniawska. *Educ:* Universities of Krakow and Leipzig; London School of Economics and Political Science. Entered Polish Ministry of Foreign Affairs, 1919; served in Copenhagen, London, and Warsaw; Delegate to Disarmament Conference, Geneva, 1932–34; Polish Minister accredited to the League of Nations, 1932–34; Polish Ambassador to the Court of St James's, 1934–45; Acting Polish Minister for Foreign Affairs, 1941–42; Minister of State in charge of Foreign Affairs, Cabinet of Gen. Sikorski, 1942–43; Chief Polish Rep. on Interim Treasury Cttee for Polish Questions, 1945–47; Hon. Chief Polish Adviser, Ministry of Labour and National Service, 1952–Dec. 1956; Chairman: Polish Research Centre, London, 1940–67; Polish Cultural Foundn, 1970–92. Hon. Dr Krakow, 1992. Grand Officier of the Order of Polonia Restituta, Order of White Eagle, Poland, Grand Cross of the Crown of Rumania, Grand Cross, Polish Order of Merit, 1991, Knight Grand Cross, Papal Order of Pius IX, 1992, etc. *Publications:* in Polish: In Allied London: Diary 1939–45, also in English, 1963; Rogalin and its Inhabitants, 1963; Pani Róża, 1969; Book of Verse, 1960; Memoirs of Viridianne Fiszer (translated from French to Polish), 1975; From Narcyz Kulikowski to Winston Churchill, 1976; From Geneva to Yalta: discussion of Count Raczynski with Tadeusz Zenczykowski, 1988; A Time of Great Change: conversations with Krzysztof Muszkowski, 1990. *Recreations:* tennis, golf, skating, ski-ing. *Address:* 8 Lennox Gardens, SW1X 0DG; 5 Krakowskie Przedmieście, Warsaw, Poland.
Died 30 July 1993.

RADCLIFFE, Hugh John Reginald Joseph, MBE 1944; Chairman, Dun and Bradstreet Ltd, 1974–76; *b* 3 March 1911; 2nd *s* of Sir Everard Radcliffe, 5th Bt and Daisy, *d* of Capt. H. Ashton Case, Tewkesbury; *m* 1937, Marie Therese, *d* of late Maj.-Gen. Sir Cecil Pereira, KCB, CMG; five *s* one *d. Educ:* Downside. Dep. Chm., London Stock Exchange, 1967–70. Kt Comdr St Silvester (Papal), 1965; Kt of St Gregory (Papal), 1984. *Address:* The White House, Stoke, Andover, Hants SP11 0LU.
Died 13 Dec. 1993.

RADCLIFFE, Percy, CBE 1985; farmer; Chairman, Isle of Man Government Executive Council (Manx Cabinet), 1981–85; *b* 14 Nov. 1916; *s* of Arthur and Annie Radcliffe; *m* 1942, Barbara Frances Crowe; two *s* one *d. Educ:* Ramsey Grammar Sch., Isle of Man. Member (Ind.) Isle of Man Govt, 1963, re-elected 1966, 1971, 1976; elected by House of Keys to be Mem. Legislative Council, 1980; Chairman: IOM Local Govt Board, 1966–76; Finance Board, 1976–81; elected by Tynwald (Govt of IOM) first Chm. of Manx Cabinet, 1981. Pres., Riding/Driving for Disabled, IOM Gp, 1985–; Member: Isle of Man Agricultural Marketing Soc., 1945–75; British Horse Driving Soc., 1979–. Silver Jubilee Medal, 1977. *Address:* Kellaway, Sulby, Isle of Man. *T:* Sulby (062489) 7257.
Died 4 Dec. 1991.

RADCLYFFE, Sir Charles Edward M.; *see* Mott-Radclyffe.

RADFORD, Sir Ronald (Walter), KCB 1976 (CB 1971); MBE 1947; Hon. Secretary-General, Customs Co-operation Council, since 1983 (Secretary-General, 1978–83); *b* 28 Feb. 1916; *er s* of late George Leonard Radford and Ethel Mary Radford; *m* 1949, Jean Alison Dunlop Strange; one *s* one *d. Educ:* Southend-on-Sea High Sch.; St John's Coll., Cambridge (Schol., Wrangler, MA). Joined ICS, 1939; Dist Magistrate and Collector, Shahabad, Bihar, 1945; on leave, prep. to retirement from ICS, 1947; Admin. Class, Home CS, and posted to HM Customs and Excise, 1947; Asst Sec., 1953; Comr, 1965; Dep. Chm., 1970; Chm., 1973–77. Mem. Management Cttee, RNLI, 1977– (Vice-Chm., 1986–91, Life Vice-Chm., 1991). *Address:* 4 Thomas Close, Brentwood, Essex

CM15 8BS. *T:* Brentwood (01277) 211567. *Clubs:* Reform, Civil Service, City Livery, MCC.

Died 3 Sept. 1995.

RAE, Air Vice-Marshal Ronald Arthur R.; *see* Ramsay Rae.

RAHIMTOOLA, Habib Ibrahim, BA, LLB; FRPS; Diplomatist, Pakistan; *b* 10 March 1912; *s* of late Sir Ibrahim Rahimtoola, GBE, KCSI, CIE, and Lady Kulsum Rahimtoola (*née* Mitha); *m* Zubeida, *d* of Sir Sultan Chinoy; two *s* one *d. Educ:* St Xavier's School and College and Govt Law Coll., Bombay. Pakistan's first High Commissioner in London, 1947–52; Ambassador for Pakistan to France, 1952–53; Governor of Sind Province, 1953–54, of Punjab Province, June-Nov. 1954; Minister for Commerce, Central Govt, Nov. 1954–Aug. 1955; Federal Minister for Commerce and Industries, 1955–56. President: Fedn of Muslim Chambers of Commerce and Industry, New Delhi, 1947–48; Bombay Provincial Muslim Chamber of Commerce, 1944–47; Bombay Provincial Muslim League Parly Board for Local Bodies, 1945–47; Young Men's Muslim Association, 1946–47; Bombay Muslim Students' Union, 1946–47–48. Member: Govt of India Food Delegation to UK and USA, 1946; Govt of India Policy Cttee on Shipping; Govt of Bombay Housing Panel; Civil Aviation Conference, Govt of India, 1947; Cttee on Trade Policy, Govt of India, 1947; Indian Delegation to Internat. Trade and Employment Conference, Geneva, 1947; alternate Leader Indian Delegation Special Cereals Conference, Paris, 1947; Delegate or Leader of Pakistan Delegations: Inter-Allied Reparations Agency, Brussels, 1947–48–49–50–51; FAO, Geneva, 1947; Dollar Talks, London, 1947; Internat. Trade and Employment Conf., Geneva, 1947; Freedom of Information Conf., Geneva, 1948; Safety of Life at Sea (1948), and Sterling Balance (1948, 1949, 1950, 1951) Confs, London; Prime Ministers' Conferences, London, 1948, 1949, 1951; Foreign Ministers' Conference, Ceylon, 1950; ILO, 1950; Commonwealth Finance Ministers' Conf., 1948–52; SE Asia Conf. on Colombo Plan, 1950; Commonwealth Talks on Japanese Peace Treaty, London, 1950; General Agreement on Tariffs and Trade Conf., 1950–52; Supply Ministers' Conf., London, 1951; UNESCO, Paris, 1953; Afro-Asian Conf., Bandung, 1955; Leader Pakistan Trade Delegation to Brit. E Africa, 1956; Leader, Flood Control Conf., New Delhi, 1956. Chairman: Karachi Development Authority, 1958–60; Water Co-ordination Council, 1958–60; Pakistan Govt Shipping Rates Adv. Bd, 1959–71; Pakistan Red Cross, 1970–73. Chm., or Dir, numerous companies. Chairman: Karachi Race Club Ltd, 1958–70 (Pres., 1970–71); Pak-Japan Cultural Assoc., 1959–87. Director, Rotary Club, 1944–46: Chairman Membership Committee, 1945–46, Classification Cttee, 1944–45; Internat. Counsellor, Lions Internat.; District Governor 305W, Lions International, 1964–67. FRSA. Melvin Jones Award, USA; Gold Medal, Pakistan Movt, 1987; several photography awards. Order of Sacred Treasure (1st Cl), Japan. *Recreations:* photography, horse racing, golf, tennis. *Address:* Bandenawaz (Pvt.) Ltd, Standard Insurance House, I. I. Chundrigar Road, PO Box 4792, Karachi 74000, Pakistan. *T:* 2415600/2410779; Kulib, KDA 1, Habib I. Rahimtoola Road, Karachi 8. *T:* 432125. *Clubs:* MCC; Sind, Boat, Gymkhana (Karachi); Willingdon (Bombay).

Died 2 Jan. 1991.

RAILTON, Brig. Dame Mary, DBE 1956 (CBE 1953); *b* 28 May 1906; *d* of late James and Margery Railton. *Educ:* privately. Joined FANY, 1938; commissioned in ATS, 1940; WRAC 1949; Director WRAC, 1954–57; Deputy Controller Commandant, 1961–67. *Address:* 1 Ilsom House, Tetbury, Glos GL8 8RX.

Died 12 Nov. 1992.

RAINE, (Harcourt) Neale, CBE 1986; Chairman, Business and Technician Education Council, 1983–86 (of Technician Education Council, 1976–83); *b* 5 May 1923; *s* of late Harold Raine and Gertrude Maude Healey; *m* 1947, Eileen Daphne, *d* of A. A. Hooper; one *s. Educ:* Dulwich and London. MSc (Eng) London; CEng, FIProdE, MICE, FIMC. Various appts as professional civil engr, 1947–52; Industrial Management Consultant with Production Engrg Ltd, 1953–59; Jt Man. Dir, Mycalex & TIM Ltd, 1959–63; Chief Exec., Car Div., Wilmot Breedon Ltd, 1963; Management Consultancy in assoc. with Production Engrg Ltd, 1964–65; Dep. Man. Dir, 1965, later Chm. and Man. Dir, Brico Engrg Ltd (Associated Engrg Gp); Chm., Coventry Radiator & Presswork Co. Ltd (Associated Engrg Gp), 1968–70; Man. Dir, Alfred Herbert Ltd, 1970–75. Dir, Associated Engineering Ltd and Man.-Dir of Gen. Div., 1968–70; Dir, Stothert & Pitt Ltd, 1978–86. Nat. Chm., IProdE, 1987–89. Pres., Coventry and District Engrg Employers' Assoc., 1975–77. Governor, Lanchester Polytechnic, Coventry and Rugby, 1970–80. *Address:* Penn Lea, The Avenue, Charlton Kings, Cheltenham, Glos GL53 9BJ. *T:* Cheltenham (0242) 526185.

Died 7 July 1994.

RAINSFORD, Surg. Rear-Adm. Seymour Grome, CB 1955; ARC Research Fellow, Bone and Joint Research Unit, London Hospital Medical College, 1975; Hon. Consultant in Coagulation Disorders, Wessex Regional Hospital Board, 1975; *b* 24 April 1900; *s* of Frederick Edward Rainsford, MD, Palmerstown Hse, Co. Dublin; *m* 1st, 1929, Violet Helen (*née* Thomas) (decd); 2nd, 1972, Caroline Mary Herschel, *d* of late Sir Denis Hill, FRCP, FRCPsych; twin *s. Educ:* St Columba's College, Co. Dublin; Trinity College, Dublin. MD 1932; ScD 1939; DPH 1937; FRCPath 1964; FRCP 1977. Joined RN as Surg. Lieut, 1922; Surgeon Rear-Adm. 1952; Deputy Medical Director-General of the Royal Navy, 1952–55. North Persian Forces Memorial Medal, for research on Mediterranean fever, 1933; Gilbert Blane Gold Medal for research on typhoid fever, 1938; Chadwick Gold Medal and Prize for research on typhoid vaccine and on blood transfusion in the Royal Navy, 1939. Chevalier de la Légion d'Honneur, 1948; CStJ 1955. *Publications:* papers on typhoid fever and other tropical diseases, haematology, blood transfusion, blood clotting disorders and physiological problems concerned in diving and submarine escape, in Jl Hygiene, Lancet, BMJ, British Jl of Haematology, Jl Clin. Pathology, Thrombosis et Diathesis and Journal RN Med. Serv. *Recreations:* shooting, golf. *Address:* The Ashes, 25 Colletts Close, Corfe Castle, Wareham, Dorset BH20 5HG. *Club:* Army and Navy.

Died 28 July 1994.

RAMELSON, Baruch, (Bert); Member, Editorial Board, World Marxist Review, published in Prague, and Editor of the English edition, 1977–90, retired; *b* 22 March 1910; named Baruch Rahmilevich Mendelson; *s* of Jacob and Liuba Mendelson; *m* 1st, 1939, Marion Jessop (*d* 1967); 2nd, 1970, Joan Dorothy Smith; one step *s* two step *d. Educ:* Univ. of Alberta. 1st cl. hons LLB. Barrister and solicitor, Edmonton, Alta, 1934–35; Internat. Bde, Mackenzie-Pappinard Bn, Spanish Civil War, 1937–39; Adjt, Canadian Bn of Internat. Bde; Tank Driver, Royal Tank Corps, 1941; captured, Tobruk, 1941; escaped Prison Camp, Italy, 1943; OCTU, Catterick, 1944–45, commnd RA 1945; served in India, 1945–46 (Actg Staff Captain Legal). Communist Party of GB: full-time Sec., Leeds, 1946–53; Sec., Yorks, 1953–65; Mem. Nat. Exec., 1953–78; Mem. Polit. Cttee, 1954–78; National Industrial Organiser, 1965–77; resigned membership following 1991 Congress, when Party became the Party of the Democratic Left. *Publications:* The Case for an Alternative Policy, 1977; Consensus or Socialism, 1987; various pamphlets and booklets; contrib. Communist (Moscow), Marxism

Today, World Marxist Review. *Recreations:* current affairs, political discussions. *Address:* 160A Conisborough Crescent, Catford, SE6 2SF. *T:* 081–698 0738.
Died 13 April 1994.

RAMPTON, Sir Jack (Leslie), KCB 1973 (CB 1969); Director, London Atlantic Investment Trust, 1981–94; *b* 10 July 1920; *s* of late Leonard Wilfrid Rampton and of Sylvia (*née* Davies); *m* 1950, Eileen Joan (*née* Hart); one *s* one *d. Educ:* Tonbridge Sch.; Trinity Coll., Oxford. MA. Treasury, 1941; Asst Priv. Sec. to successive Chancellors of the Exchequer, 1942–43; Priv. Sec. to Financial Sec., 1945–46; Economic and Financial Adv. to Comr-Gen. for SE Asia and to British High Comr, Malaya, 1959–61; Under-Secretary, HM Treasury, 1964–68; Dep. Sec., Min. of Technology (formerly Min. of Power), 1968–70; Dep. Sec., DTI, 1970–72; Second Permanent Sec. and Sec. (Industrial Develt), DTI, 1972–74; Perm. Under-Sec. of State, Dept of Energy, 1974–80. Dep. Chm., Sheerness Steel Co., 1985–87 (Dir, 1982–87); Special Adviser: North Sea Sun Oil Co., 1982–87; Sun Exploration and Development Co. Inc., 1982–87; Magnet Gp, WA, 1981–84; Director: ENO Co., 1982–88; Flextech plc, 1985–. Member: Oxford Energy Policy Club, 1978–; Honeywell UK Adv. Council, 1981–; Energy Industries Club, 1985–. Mem., British Library of Tape Recordings Adv. Council, 1977–88; Council Member: Victoria League, 1981–91 (Dep. Chm. 1985–91); Cook Soc., 1978– (Chm., 1986–87; Dep. Chm., 1988–89); Britain-Australia Soc., 1986– (Hon. Sec., 1986–92; Vice-Chm., 1988–92; Chm., 1992–); Governor: Commonwealth Trust, 1988– (Vice Chm., 1989–91); London House for Overseas Graduates, 1989–92; Advr, Sir Robert Menzies Meml Trust, 1990–. Pres., Tonbridge Civic Soc., 1993–; Chm., Trinity Soc., Oxford, 1992–. CIMgt; CIGasE; FInstPet 1982. Hon. DSc Aston, 1979. *Recreations:* gardening, games, photography, travel; Oxford Squash V (Capt.) 1939–40; Authentic, 1940. *Address:* 17 The Ridgeway, Tonbridge, Kent TN10 4NQ. *T:* Tonbridge (0732) 352117. *Clubs:* Pilgrims, Britain Australia Society, Tuesday; Vincent's (Oxford).   *Died 30 March 1994.*

RAMSAY, Sir Thomas (Meek), Kt 1972; CMG 1965; Chairman, The Kiwi International Company Ltd, Melbourne, 1967–80; *b* Essendon, Victoria, 24 Nov. 1907; *s* of late William Ramsay, Scotland; *m* 1941, Catherine Anne, *d* of John William Richardson, Adelaide, SA; four *s* one *d. Educ:* Malvern Grammar; Scotch Coll.; Melbourne Univ. (BSc). CMF, 1940–41 (Lieut); Asst Controller, Min. of Munitions, 1941–45. Joined The Kiwi Polish Co. Pty Ltd, Melbourne, 1926, Managing Director, 1956–72 (Joint Managing Director, 1945). Chairman: Norwich Union Life Insurance Soc. (Aust. Bd), 1968–79; Collie (Aust.) Ltd Group, 1977–79; Industrial Design Council of Australia, 1969–76; ANZAC Fellowship Selection Cttee, 1971–78; Director: Australian Consolidated Industries Ltd Group, 1965–79; Alex Harvey Industries Group, NZ. President: Associated Chambers of Manufrs of Australia, 1962–63; Victorian Chamber of Manufrs, 1962–64; Mem., Selection Cttee (Industrial), Sir Winston Churchill Fellowships. FRHistS of Queensland, 1964; FRHistS of Victoria, 1965; FAIM; FSAScot; FIMgt; Fellow, Mus. of Victoria (formerly Hon. Sen. Fellow). *Recreations:* gardening, Australian historical research. *Address:* 23 Airlie Street, South Yarra, Victoria 3141, Australia. *T:* (03) 2661751. *Clubs:* Athenæum, Australian, Melbourne (Melbourne).   *Died 27 Jan. 1995.*

RAMSAY RAE, Air Vice-Marshal Ronald Arthur, CB 1960; OBE 1947; *b* 9 Oct. 1910; *s* of late George Ramsay Rae, Lindfield, NSW, and Alice Ramsay Rae (*née* Haselden); *m* 1939, Rosemary Gough Howell, *d* of late Charles Gough Howell, KC, Attorney General, Singapore; one *s* one *d. Educ:* Sydney, New South Wales, Australia.

Served Australian Citizen Force and then as Cadet, RAAF, at Point Cook, 1930–31; transf. to RAF, 1932; flying duties in UK and Middle East with Nos 33 and 142 Sqdns until 1936; Advanced Armament Course; Armament officer in Far East, 1938–42; then Comdr RAF Tengah, Singapore; POW, 1943–45; Gp Captain in comd Central Gunnery Sch., Leconfield, Yorks, 1946; despatches, 1946; RAF Staff Coll., Andover, 1948; Dep. Dir Organisation (Estabt), Middle East; in comd RAF North Luffenham and then RAF Oakington (206 Advanced Flying Sch.); Commandant, Aircraft and Armament Exptl Estabt, Boscombe Down, 1955–57; Dep. Air Sec., Air Min., 1957–59; AOC No 224 Group, RAF, 1959–62, retd. Gen. Sec., NPFA, 1963–71. AFRAeS 1956. *Recreations:* cricket, golf, tennis, winter sports (Cresta Run and ski-ing; Pres., St Moritz Toboganning Club, 1978–84). *Address:* Commonwealth Bank of Australia, 8 Old Jewry, EC2R 8ED; Little Wakestone, Bedham, Fittleworth, W Sussex RH20 1JR. *Club:* Royal Air Force.
Died 19 June 1994.

RAMSDEN, Sarah, (Sally), OBE 1981; Director, North East Broadcasting Co. Ltd (Metro Radio), 1973–81; *b* 10 Jan. 1910; *d* of John Parkin and Hannah Bentley; *m* 1948, Allan Ramsden (decd). *Educ:* Ryhope Grammar Sch.; Neville's Cross Coll., Durham (Teaching Diploma). Teacher, 1930–47; Headmistress, 1947–69; Asst. Group Officer (part time), Nat. Fire Service, 1941–45; Hon. Organiser, Citizens' Advice Bureau, 1971–73; Pres., UK Fedn of Business and Professional Women, 1972–75 (Hon. Mem., NE Div., 1988–); Member: Women's Nat. Commn, 1972–75; Women's Internat. Year Cttee, 1974–75; VAT Tribunals, 1973–84; Royal Commn on Legal Services, 1976–79; Durham Posts and Telecom Adv. Cttee, 1980–. *Recreations:* fly fishing, gardening, reading. *Address:* 1 Westcott Drive, Durham Moor, Durham City DH1 5AG. *T:* Durham (0191) 3842989.
Died 3 Oct. 1995.

RANKING, His Honour Robert Duncan; a Circuit Judge (formerly County Court Judge), 1968–88; Judge of the Mayors and City of London Court, 1980–88; *b* 24 Oct. 1915; *yr s* of Dr R. M. Ranking, Tunbridge Wells, Kent; *m* 1949, Evelyn Mary Tagart (*née* Walker); one *d. Educ:* Cheltenham Coll.; Pembroke Coll., Cambridge (MA). Called to Bar, 1939. Served in Queen's Own Royal W Kent Regt, 1939–46. Dep. Chm. E Sussex QS, 1962–71; Dep. Chm., Agricultural Land Tribunal (S Eastern Area), 1963. *Address:* 4 Arundel Road, Seaford, E Sussex BN25 4PS. *T:* Seaford (0323) 892557.

Died 25 April 1994.

RAPHAEL, Chaim, CBE 1965 (OBE 1951); *b* Middlesbrough, 14 July 1908; *s* of Rev. David Rabinovitch and Rachel Rabinovitch; name Hebraised by deed poll, 1936; *m* 1934, Diana Rose (marr. diss. 1964); one *s* one *d. Educ:* Portsmouth Grammar Sch.; University Coll., Oxford. PPE 1930. James Mew Post-Grad. Schol. in Hebrew, 1931. Kennicott Fellowship, 1933–36, Cowley Lectr in Post-Biblical Hebrew, 1932–39, Oxford Univ.; Liaison Officer for Internment Camps: UK 1940; Canada 1941; Adviser, British Information Services, NY, 1942–45; Dir (Economics), USA, 1945–57; Dep. Head of Information Div., HM Treasury, 1957–59; Head of Information Division: HM Treasury, 1959–68; Civil Service Dept, 1968–69. Research Fellow, Univ. of Sussex, 1969–75. *Publications:* Memoirs of a Special Case, 1962; The Walls of Jerusalem, 1968; A Feast of History, 1972; A Coat of Many Colours, 1979; The Springs of Jewish Life, 1982 (jtly, Wingate Prize, 1983); The Road from Babylon: the story of Sephardi and Oriental Jews, 1985, repr. as The Sephardi Story, 1991; A Jewish Book of Common Prayer, 1986; The Festivals: a history of Jewish celebration, 1990; Minyan: 10 Jewish lives in 20 centuries of history, 1992; *novels:* (under pseudonym Jocelyn Davey): The Undoubted Deed, 1956; The Naked Villany, 1958; A Touch of Stagefright, 1960; A Killing in Hats, 1964; A Treasury Alarm, 1976; Murder in Paradise, 1982; A Dangerous Liaison, 1987. *Recreation:* America. *Address:* 40 St John's Court, Finchley Road, NW3 6LL. *T:* 0171–625 8489. *Club:* Reform.

Died 10 Oct. 1994.

RATHBONE, John Francis Warre, CBE 1966; TD 1950; Secretary of National Trust for Places of Historic Interest or Natural Beauty, 1949–68; President, London Centre of the National Trust, since 1968; *b* 18 July 1909; *e s* of Francis Warre Rathbone and Edith Bertha Hampshire, Allerton Beeches, Liverpool. *Educ:* Marlborough; New College, Oxford. Solicitor, 1934. Served War of 1939–45; AA Comd and staff (Col 1945). Dir Ministry of Justice Control Branch, CCG (British Element), 1946–49. *Recreations:* music, travel. *Died 22 April 1995.*

RATHBONE, Very Rev. Norman Stanley; Dean of Hereford, 1969–82, then Dean Emeritus; *b* 8 Sept. 1914; *er s* of Stanley George and Helen Rathbone; *m* 1952, Christine Olive Gooderson; three *s* two *d. Educ:* Lawrence Sheriff Sch., Rugby; Christ's Coll., Cambridge; Westcott House, Cambridge. BA 1936, MA 1939. Deacon, 1938; priest, 1939; St Mary Magdalen's, Coventry: Curate, 1938; Vicar, 1945; Examining Chaplain to Bp of Coventry, 1944; Canon Theologian, Coventry Cathedral, 1954; Canon Residentiary and Chancellor, Lincoln Cathedral, 1959. *Address:* The Daren, Newton St Margarets, Herefordshire HR2 0QN. *T:* Michaelchurch (01981) 510623. *Died 13 July 1995.*

RATHCAVAN, 2nd Baron *cr* 1953, of The Braid, Co. Antrim; **Phelim Robert Hugh O'Neill;** PC (NI) 1969; Bt 1929; Major, late Royal Artillery; *b* 2 Nov. 1909; *s* of 1st Baron Rathcavan, PC and Sylvia (*d* 1972), *d* of Walter A. Sandeman; *S* father, 1982; *m* 1st, 1934, Clare Désirée (marr. diss. 1944), *d* of late Detmar Blow; one *s* one *d*; 2nd, 1953, Mrs B. D. Edwards-Moss, *d* of late Major Hon. Richard Coke; three *d* (and one *d* decd). *Educ:* Eton. MP (UU) for North Antrim (UK Parliament), 1952–59; MP (U) North Antrim, Parliament of N Ireland, 1959–72; Minister, N Ireland: Education, 1969; Agriculture, 1969–71. *Heir: s* Hon. Hugh Detmar Torrens O'Neill [*b* 14 June 1939; *m* 1983, Sylvie Marie-Thérèse Wichard; one *s*]. *Address:* The Lodge, Killala, Co. Mayo, Ireland. *T:* Ballina 32252. *Died 20 Dec. 1994.*

RATTRAY, Simon; *see* Trevor, E.

RAVEN, Ronald William, OBE (mil.) 1946; TD 1953; FRCS 1931; Consulting Surgeon, Westminster Hospital and Royal Marsden Hospital, since 1969; Surgeon, French Hospital, London, 1936–69; Cons. Surgeon (General Surgeon) Eversfield Chest Hospital 1937–48; Cons. Surgeon, Royal Star and Garter Home for Disabled Sailors, Soldiers and Airmen 1948–69; *b* 28 July 1904; *e s* of late Fredric William Raven and Annie Williams Raven (*née* Mason), Coniston. *Educ:* Ulverston Grammar School; St Bartholomew's Hospital Medical College, Univ. of London. St Bart's Hospital: gained various prizes and Brackenbury surgical schol.; resident surgical appts, 1928–29; Demonstrator in Pathology, 1929–31; Registrar Statistics Nat. Radium Commn, 1931–34; jun. surgical appts, 1931–35; Asst Surg. Gordon Hosp., 1935; Asst Surg. Roy. Cancer Hosp., 1939–46, Surg. 1946–62; Jt Lectr in Surgery, Westminster Med. Sch., Univ. of London, 1951–69; Surgeon, Westminster (Gordon) Hosp., 1947–69; Sen. Surgeon, Royal Marsden Hosp. and Inst. of Cancer Research, Royal Cancer Hosp., 1962–69. Lectr, RIPH&H, 1965–85. Member: DHSS Standing Sub-Cttee on Cancer; DHSS Adv. Cttee on Cancer Registration; Chairman: Jt Nat. Cancer Survey Cttee; Cancer

Rehabilitation and Continuing Care Cttee, UICC, 1982–90. Fellow Assoc. of Surg. of GB; Hon. FRSM 1987 (PP, Section of Proctology, PP, Section of Oncology); Mem. Council, 1968–76, Mem. Court of Patrons, 1976–, RCS; (Founder) Pres., British Assoc. of Surgical Oncology, 1973–77; (Founder) Pres., Assoc. of Head and Neck Oncologists of GB, 1968–71; formerly Member: European Soc. Surgical Oncology: Internat. Soc. of Surgery; President: Marie Curie Meml Foundn, 1990– (Chm. Council, 1961–90; Chm. Exec. Cttee, 1948–61); Epsom Coll., 1990– (Vice-Pres. and Chm., Council, 1954); late Chm., Conjoint Cttee; late Mem. Bd of Governors Royal Marsden Hosp.; formerly Mem. Council of Queen's Institute of District Nursing; Mem. (late Chm.), Cttee of Management Med. Insurance Agency; formerly Mem. Council, Imperial Cancer Res. Fund; Life Pres., Hellenic Soc. of Oncology, 1990; Vice-President: John Grooms Assoc. for the Disabled, 1958–; Malta Meml District Nursing Assoc., 1982–. Surg. EMS, 1939; joined RAMC, 1941, and served in N Africa, Italy and Malta (despatches); o/c Surg. Div. (Lt-Col) and o/c Gen. Hosp. (Col), 1946; Lt-Col RAMC (TA); o/c Surg. Div. Gen. Hosp., 1947–53; Col RAMC (TA); o/c No 57 (Middlesex) General Hospital (TA), 1953–59; Colonel TARO, 1959–62; Hon. Colonel RAMC. OStJ 1946. Hon. Professor National Univ. of Colombia, 1949; Hon. MD Cartagena, 1949; Corresponding Foreign Member: Soc. of Head and Neck Surgeons of USA; Roman Surg. Soc.; Soc. Surg. of Bogotà; Société de Chirurgie de Lyon; Acad. of Athens, 1983; Member: Nat. Acad. Med. of Colombia; NY Acad. of Sciences; Soc. of Surgeons of Colombia; Italian Soc. Thoracic Surg.; Czechoslovak Soc. of J. E. Purkyne; Hon. Mem., Indian Assoc. of Oncology, 1983; Diploma de Socio Honorario, Soc. de Cancerologia de El Salvador, 1983; Diploma de Honor al Merito, Liga Nacional de El Salvador, 1983. Lectures: Arris and Gale, 1933; Erasmus Wilson, 1935, 1946, 1947; Malcolm Morris Meml, 1954; Blair Bell Meml, 1960; Elizabeth Matthai Endowment, Madras Univ., 1965; First W. Emory Burnett Honor, Temple Univ., USA, 1966; Edith A. Ward Meml, 1966; Gerald Townsley Meml, 1974; Bradshaw, RCS, 1975; Ernest Miles Meml, 1980; Honor, Amer. Soc. of Surg. Oncology, 1981; Honor, 1st Congress, Eur. Soc. of Surg. Oncology, Athens, 1982; Honor-Centenary, George N. Papanicolaou, Athens, 1983; First Kitty Cookson Meml, Royal Free Hosp., 1985. Hunterian Prof., RCS, 1948; Vis. Prof. of Surgery: Ein-Shams University, Cairo, 1961; Cancer Inst., Madras, 1965; Maadi Hosp., Cairo, 1974. Surgical missions to: Colombia, 1949; Saudi Arabia, 1961, 1962, 1975, 1976; United Arab Emirates, 1975, 1985. Consulting Editor, Clinical Oncology, 1979–82. FRSA 1987. Mem. Court, 1973–, Master, 1980–81, Worshipful Co. of Barbers; Mem., Livery Consultative Cttee, 1981–86. Freeman, City of London, 1956. Furnished Ronald William Raven Room, Mus. of Royal Crown Derby Porcelain Co., 1987; Ronald Raven Chair in Clinical Oncology, Royal Free Hosp. Sch. of Medicine (London Univ.), established 1990. Hon. Life Mem., Derby Porcelain Internat. Soc., 1988. G. Paparicolaou Gold Medal, 1990. Chevalier de la Légion d'Honneur, 1952. *Publications:* War Wounds and Injuries (jt editor and contrib.), 1940; Treatment of Shock, 1942 (trans. Russian); Surgical Care, 1942, 2nd edn 1952; Cancer in General Practice (jointly), 1952; Surgical Instruments and Appliances (jointly), 1952; chapters on Shock and Malignant Disease in Encyclopædia British Medical Practice, 1952, 1955, 1962–69, and Medical Progress, 1970–71; Handbook on Cancer for Nurses and Health Visitors, 1953; Cancer and Allied Diseases, 1955; chapters in Operative Surgery (Rob and Rodney Smith), 1956–57; (ed and contrib.) Cancer (7 vols), 1957–60; Cancer of the Pharynx, Larynx and Oesophagus and its Surgical Treatment, 1958; (ed) Cancer Progress, 1960 and 1963; (ed jtly) The Prevention of Cancer, 1967; (ed)

Modern Trends in Oncology 1, part 1, Research Progress, part 2, Clinical Progress, 1973; (ed and contrib.) The Dying Patient, 1975 (trans. Japanese and Dutch); (ed and contrib.) Principles of Surgical Oncology, 1977; (ed and contrib.) Foundations of Medicine, 1978; Rehabilitation and Continuing Care in Cancer, 1986; (jtly) Cancer Care—an international survey, 1986; The Gospel of St John, 1987; The Theory and Practice of Oncology: its historical evolution and present principles, 1990; Death Into Life, 1990; Rehabilitation Oncology, 1991; papers on surgical subjects, especially relating to cancer in British and foreign journals. *Recreations:* philately (medallist Internat. Stamp Exhibn, London, 1950), music, ceramics and pictures, travel. *Address:* 29 Harley Street, W1N 1DA. *T:* 071–580 3765; Manor Lodge, Wingrave, Aylesbury, Bucks. *T:* Aylesbury (0296) 681287. *Clubs:* MCC, Pilgrims.

Died 24 Oct. 1991.

RAWNSLEY, Prof. Kenneth, CBE 1984; FRCP, FRCPsych, DPM; Professor and Head of Department of Psychological Medicine, University of Wales College of Medicine (formerly Welsh National School of Medicine), 1964–85, then Emeritus; *b* 1926; *m* 2nd *d* (two *s* one *d* by previous marr.). *Educ:* Burnley Grammar Sch.; Univ. of Manchester Med. Sch. MB ChB Manchester 1948; MRCP 1951; DPM Manchester 1954; FRCP 1967; FRCPsych 1971. Member, Scientific Staff of Medical Research Council, 1954–64; Registrar, Bethlem Royal and Maudsley Hosps; Pres., Royal College of Psychiatrists, 1981–84 (Dean, 1972–77); Vice-Provost, Welsh Nat. Sch. of Medicine, 1979–80; Hon. Consultant Psychiatrist, S Glam AHA(T), 1960–85; Postgrad. Organiser and Clinical Tutor in Psychiatry, S Glam, 1968–85. Chm., Management Cttee, Nat. Counselling Service for Sick Doctors. Hon MD Wales, 1989. *Publications:* contribs to Brit. Jl Psych., Postgrad. Med. Jl, Jl Psychosom. Res., etc. *Address:* 46 Cathedral Road, Cardiff. *T:* Cardiff (0222) 397850. *Club:* Athenæum.

Died 1 April 1992.

RAY, Cyril; *b* 16 March 1908; *e s* of Albert Benson Ray (who changed the family name from Rotenberg, 1913), and Rita Ray; *m* 1953, Elizabeth Mary, JP, *o d* of late Rev. H. C. Brocklehurst; one *s. Educ:* elementary sch., Bury, Lancs; Manchester Grammar Sch. (Foundation schol.); Jesus Coll., Oxford (open schol.). Manchester Guardian and BBC war correspondent: 5th Destroyer Flotilla, 1940 (Hon. Mem. HMS Kelly Reunion); N African landings, 1942; 8th Army, Italy (despatches); US 82nd Airborne Div. (US Army citation, Nijmegen), and 3rd Army, 1944–45. UNESCO missions, Italy, Greece, East, Central and S Africa, 1945–50. Sunday Times, 1949–56 (Moscow Correspondent, 1950–52); Editor, The Compleat Imbiber, 1956–71, 1986–89 (Wine and Food Soc.'s first André Simon Prize, 1964); Asst Editor, The Spectator, 1958–62; Wine Correspondent: The Director, 1958–76; The Observer, 1959–73; Punch, 1978–84; Chief Conslntt, The Good Food Guide, 1968–74; Founder and past President, Circle of Wine Writers. Trustee, Albany, 1967– (Chm. Trustees, 1981–86). Much occasional broadcasting, 1940–62 (The Critics, 1958–62), Southern TV, 1958–59. Hon. Life Mem., NUJ; Mem., Punch Table (old regime). Glenfiddich Wine and Food Writer of the Year, 1979; Special Glenfiddich Award, 1985. Freeman, City of London; Liveryman, Fan-Makers Co. Mem. Labour Party. Commendatore, Italian Order of Merit, 1981 (Cavaliere 1972); Chevalier, French Order of Merit, 1985 (Mérite Agricole, 1974). *Publications:* (ed) Scenes and Characters from Surtees, 1948; From Algiers to Austria: The History of 78 Division, 1952; The Pageant of London, 1958; Merry England, 1960; Regiment of the Line: The Story of the Lancashire Fusiliers, 1963; (ed) The Gourmet's Companion, 1963; (ed) Morton Shand's Book of French Wines, 1964; (ed) Best Murder Stories, 1965; The Wines

of Italy, 1966 (Bologna Trophy, 1967); In a Glass Lightly, 1967; Lafite: The Story of Château Lafite-Rothschild, 1968, rev. edn 1985; Bollinger: the story of a champagne, 1971, rev. edn 1982; Cognac, 1973, rev. edn 1985; Mouton: the story of Mouton-Rothschild, 1974; (with Elizabeth Ray) Wine with Food, 1975; The Wines of France, 1976; The Wines of Germany, 1977; The Complete Book of Spirits and Liqueurs, 1978; The Saint Michael Guide to Wine, 1978; Ruffino: the story of a Chianti, 1979; Lickerish Limericks, with Filthy Pictures by Charles Mozley, 1979; Ray on Wine (Glenfiddich Wine Book of the Year), 1979; The New Book of Italian Wines, 1982; (ed) Vintage Tales, 1984; Robert Mondavi of the Napa Valley, 1984; Bollinger—Tradition of a Champagne Family, 1988. *Recreation:* formerly riding, latterly The Times crossword. *Address:* Albany, Piccadilly, W1V 9RQ. *T:* 071–734 0270. *Clubs:* Athenæum, Brooks's, MCC, Special Forces; Civil Service Riding (Hon. Life Mem.).

Died 24 Sept. 1991.

RAY, Satyajit; Padma Shree, 1957; Padma Bhushan, 1964; Padma Bibhushan, 1976; Indian film producer and film director since 1953; *b* 2 May 1921; *s* of late Sukumar and Suprabha Ray (née Das); *m* 1949, Bijoya (née Das); one *s. Educ:* Ballygunge Govt School; Presidency College, Calcutta. Joined British advertising firm, D. J. Keymer & Co., as visualiser, 1943; Art Director, 1950; in 1952, started first feature film, Pather Panchali, finished in 1955 (Cannes Special Award, 1956, San Francisco, best film, 1957); left advertising for whole-time film-making, 1956. Other films: Aparajito, 1957 (Venice Grand Prix, 1957, San Francisco, best direction); Jalsaghar, 1958; Devi, 1959; Apur Sansar, 1959 (Selznick Award and Sutherland Trophy 1960); Teen Kanya (Two Daughters), 1961; Kanchanjangha, 1962; Mahanagar, 1963; Charulata, 1964; Kapurush-O-Mahapurush (The Coward and The Holy Man), 1965; Nayak (The Hero), 1965; Goopy Gyne and Bagha Byne, 1969; Days and Nights in the Forest, 1970; Pratidwandi (The Adversary), 1970; Company Limited, 1971; Distant Thunder, 1973 (Golden Bear, Berlin Film Festival, 1973); The Golden Fortress, 1974; The Middleman, 1975; The Chess Players, 1977; The Elephant God, 1979; The Kingdom of Diamonds, 1980; Pikoo, Deliverance, 1981; Ghare Baire (The Home and the World), 1984; Ganashatru (Public Enemy), 1989; Shakha-Proshakha (Branches of a Tree), 1990; The Stranger, 1991. Founded first Film Society in Calcutta, 1947. Composed background music for own films. Fellow, BFI, 1983. Hon. DLitt Oxon, 1978. Hon. Academy Award, 1992. Légion d'Honneur, 1989. *Publications:* Our Films, Their Films, 1976; Stories, 1987; The Chess Players and other screenplays, 1989; film articles in Sight and Sound, Sequence; (Editor, 1961–) children's magazine Sandesh, with contributions of stories, poems. *Recreations:* listening to Indian and Western classical music, reading science-fiction. *Address:* Flat 8, 1–1 Bishop Lefroy Road, Calcutta 20, India. *T:* 447–8747.

Died 23 April 1992.

RAYNE, Sir Edward, Kt 1988; CVO 1977; Chairman and Managing Director of H. & M. Rayne Ltd, 1951–87; Executive Chairman, Harvey Nichols, 1979–86; *b* 19 Aug. 1922; *s* of Joseph Edward Rayne and Meta Elizabeth Reddish (American); *m* 1952, Phyllis Cort; two *s. Educ:* Harrow. Pres., 1961–72, Exec. Chm., 1972–86, Rayne-Delman Shoes Inc.; Dir, Debenhams Ltd, 1975–88; Pres., Debenhams Inc., 1976–86; Chairman: Fashion Multiple Div., Debenhams Ltd, 1978–86; Harvey Nichols Ltd, 1978–88; Lotus Ltd, 1978–86. Member: Export Council for Europe, 1962–71; European Trade Cttee, 1972–84; Bd of Governors, Genesco Inc., 1967–73; Franco British Council, 1980–89. Chairman: Incorp. Soc. of London Fashion Designers, 1960; British Fashion Council, 1985–90; Pres., Royal Warrant Holders' Assoc., 1964, Hon. Treas. 1974–91; President: British Footwear

Manufacturers' Fedn, 1965; British Boot and Shoe Instn, 1972–79; Clothing and Footwear Inst., 1979–80. Master, Worshipful Co. of Pattenmakers, 1981. FRSA 1971. Harper's Bazaar Trophy, 1963. Chevalier, l'Ordre Nat. du Mérite, France, 1984. *Recreations:* golf, bridge (Mem., winning British team, European Bridge Championship, 1948, 1949). *Address:* 29 Hartfield Road, Cooden Beach, E Sussex TN39 3EA. *T:* Cooden (04243) 2175. *Clubs:* Portland, White's. *Died 7 Feb. 1992.*

READ, Prof. Alan Ernest Alfred, CBE 1989; MD, FRCP; Chief Medical Officer, London Life Association and Sun Life Assurance Society, since 1992; Professor of Medicine and Director of Medical Professorial Unit, University of Bristol, 1969–92, then Professor Emeritus; *b* 15 Nov. 1926; *s* of Ernest Read and Annie Lydia; *m* 1952, Enid Malein; one *s* two *d*. *Educ:* Wembley County Sch.; St Mary's Hosp. Med. Sch., London. House Phys., St Mary's Hosp., 1950; Med. Registrar, Royal Masonic Hosp., 1951; Mil. Service Med. Specialist, Trieste, 1952–54; Registrar and Sen. Registrar, Central Mddx and Hammersmith Hosps, 1954–60; University of Bristol: Lectr in Medicine and Cons. Phys., 1961; Reader in Medicine, 1966; Dean of Faculty of Medicine, 1983–85; Pro-Vice-Chancellor, 1987–90. Sen. Censor and Sen. Vice-Pres., RCP, 1986–87. Associate Prof. of Medicine, Univ. of Rochester, USA, 1967. *Publications:* Clinical Apprentice (jtly), 1948, 6th edn 1989; (jtly) Basic Gastroenterology, 1965, 3rd edn 1980; (jtly) Modern Medicine, 1975, 3rd edn 1984. *Recreations:* boating, fishing, golf, riding. *Address:* Riverbank, 77 Nore Road, Portishead, Bristol BS20 9JZ. *Died 24 Oct. 1993.*

READ, Prof. Margaret (Helen), CBE 1949; MA (Cantab), PhD (London); *b* 5 Aug. 1889; *d* of Mabyn Read, MD, Worcester, and Isabel Margaret Lawford. *Educ:* Roedean School, Brighton; Newnham College, Cambridge. Social work in India, 1919–24; lecturing on international affairs in Gt Britain and USA, 1924–30; LSE, student of anthropology and occasional lecturer, 1930–34; Research Fellow, Internat. African Inst. and field work in N Rhodesia and Nyasaland, 1934–39; Asst Lecturer, LSE, 1937–40; Prof. and Head of Dept of Educ. in Tropical Areas, Univ. of London Inst. of Educ., 1940–55; Prof. of Educ., Univ. Coll., Ibadan, Nigeria, 1955–56; occasional Consultant to WHO, 1956–62; Consultant to Milbank Memorial Fund, New York, 1964, 1965, 1966, 1967, 1968, 1969. Vis. Prof., Cornell Univ., 1951–52, Northwestern Univ., 1955, Michigan State Univ., 1960, Yale Univ. Medical School, 1965, 1966, 1967, 1968. *Publications:* Indian Peasant Uprooted, 1931; Africans and their Schools, 1953; Education and Social Change in Tropical Areas, 1955; The Ngoni of Nyasaland, 1956; Children of their Fathers, 1959; Culture, Health and Disease, 1966; articles in Africa, Bantu Studies, Journal of Applied Anthropology, Annals of the American Academy, etc. *Recreations:* gardening, music. *Address:* 9 Paradise Walk, Chelsea, SW3. *T:* 071–352 0528. *Died 19 May 1991.*

READWIN, Edgar Seeley, CBE 1971; retired; *b* 7 Nov. 1915; *s* of Ernest Readwin, Master Mariner and Edith Elizabeth Readwin; *m* 1940, Lesley Margaret (*née* Barker); two *s* one *d*. *Educ:* Bracondale Sch., Norwich. FCA. Articled Clerk, Harman & Gowen, Norwich, 1932–37; Asst Auditor, Bengal & North Western Railway, 1938–40; commnd service 14th Punjab Regt, 1941–45, PoW Far East, Singapore, Siam-Burma Railway, 1942–45; Indian Railway Accounts Service, 1945–49; Booker Group of Companies in Guyana: Asst to Accounts Controller, 1950; Finance Dir, 1951–56; Dep. Chm., 1956–62; Chm., 1962–71. Dir, West Indies Sugar Assoc., 1962–71; Finance Dir, Indonesia Sugar Study, 1971–72; Chm., Minvielle & Chastenet Ltd, St Lucia, 1973–76. Hon. Treas., Guyana

Lawn Tennis Assoc., 1951–67, Pres., 1968–70, Hon. Life Vice-Pres., 1971. *Recreations:* lawn tennis, golf, gardening, chess, bridge. *Address:* Puxholt, 2 Halliwick Gardens, Felpham, Bognor Regis, West Sussex PO22 7JE. *Clubs:* Veterans' Lawn Tennis of Great Britain; Bognor Tennis; Littlehampton Golf. *Died 14 June 1992.*

REARDON-SMITH, Sir William; *see* Smith.

REBBECK, Dr Denis, CBE 1952; JP, DL; MA, MSc, PhD, BLitt; FEng 1979; FICE, FIMechE, FRINA, FIMarE, FCIT; *b* 22 Jan. 1914; *er s* of late Sir Frederick Ernest Rebbeck, KBE and Amelia Letitia, *d* of Robert Glover; *m* 1938, Rosamond Annette Kathleen, *e d* of late Henry Jameson, Bangor, Co. Down; four *s*. *Educ:* Campbell Coll., Belfast; Pembroke Coll., Cambridge. BA (Hons) Mech. Sciences Tripos, 1935; MA (Cantab) 1939; MA (Dublin) 1945; BLitt (Dublin) 1946; MSc (Belfast) 1946; PhD (Belfast) 1950. Part-time Post-grad. Research. Harland & Wolff, Ltd: Director, 1946–70; Dep. Man. Director, 1953; Man. Dir, 1962–70; Chm., 1965–66. Chm., 1972–84, Dir, 1950–84, Iron Trades Employers' Insurance Association Ltd and Iron Trades Mutual Insurance Co. Ltd (Vice-Chm., 1969–72); Director: Nat. Shipbuilders Security Ltd, 1952–58; Colvilles Ltd, 1963–67; Brown Brothers & Co. Ltd, 1967–68; Shipbuilding Corporation Ltd, 1963–73; National Commercial Bank of Scotland Ltd, 1965–69; Royal Bank of Scotland Ltd, 1969–84; Belships Co. Ltd, 1970–76 (Chm., 1972–76); John Kelly Ltd, 1968–79 (Dep. Chm., 1968; Chm., 1969–79); Howdens Ltd, 1977–79; Norman Canning Ltd, 1977–79; Nationwide Building Soc., 1980–87; Nationwide Anglia Building Soc., 1987–89; General Underwriting Agencies Ltd, 1984–92 (Chm. 1984–92); Nordic Business Forum for Northern Britain Ltd, 1980–84. Special Consultant, Swan Hunter Group Ltd, 1970–79; Consultant, Ellerman Travel, 1979–84. Belfast Harbour Commissioner, 1962–85. Member Research Council, and Chairman, Design Main Committee, British Ship Research Association, 1965–73; Pres., Shipbuilding Employers' Fedn, 1962–63; Past Chm. Warship Gp, Shipbuilding Conf.; Member: NI Economic Council, 1965–70; Lloyd's Register of Shipping General Cttee, 1962–85 and Technical Cttee, 1964–76; Management Board: Engineering Employers Fedn, 1963–75; Shipbuilders & Repairers Nat. Assoc., 1966–71; Council, RINA, 1964–72; Council for Scientific R&D in NI, 1948–59; Member Inst. of Engineers and Shipbuilders in Scotland; Cambridge Univ. Engineers' Assoc.; Science Masters' Assoc. (Pres. NI Branch, 1954–55); NI Grammar Schools Careers Assoc. (Pres., 1964–65); National Playing Fields Assoc. (NI Exec. Cttee), 1952–77; Chairman: Adv. Cttee on Marine Pilotage, 1977–79; Pilotage Commn, 1979–83; Member: Drummond Technical Investigation Cttee, 1955–56; Lord Coleraine's Committee to enquire into Youth Employment Services in NI, 1957–58; Sir John Lockwood's Cttee on Univ. and Higher Techn. Educn in Northern Ireland, 1963–64; Queen's Univ., Better Equipment Fund Exec. Cttee, 1951–82; Hon. Life Mem., Irish Port Authorities Assoc., 1985; Vice-Pres. of Belfast Savings Council; Past Chm. and Trustee, Belfast Savings Bank; Visitor, Linen Industry Research Assoc., DSIR, 1954–57; President: Belfast Assoc. of Engineers, 1947–48; NI Society of Incorporated Secretaries, 1955–70; Glencraig Curative Schools, NI, 1953–70; World Ship Soc., 1978–81 (Vice Pres., 1956); Past Mem. Council: IMechE; IMarE; Chm. NI Assoc., ICE, 1952–53; FEng 1979. Life Mem. Brit. Assoc. for the Advancement of Science; Member: Smeatonian Soc. of Civil Engrs; Incorp. of Hammermen of Glasgow. Liveryman, Worshipful Company of Shipwrights, 1952– (Prime Warden, 1980–81). Hon. Mem., BUPA, 1984. Vice-Pres., Queen's Univ. Guild, 1951–65; Board Governors Campbell Coll., Belfast, 1952–60 (Vice-Chm. 1957–60); Member of Court,

New Univ. of Ulster. Mem., T&AFA for Belfast, 1947–65; Dep.-Chm. NI Festival of Britain, 1948–51; papers read before British Association, ICE, etc; Akroyd Stuart Award, IMarE, 1943. JP County Borough of Belfast, 1949; DL County of the City of Belfast, 1960. *Recreations:* sailing, worldwide travel. *Address:* The White House, Craigavad, Holywood, County Down, N Ireland BT18 0HE. *T:* Holywood (0232) 422294. *Clubs:* Royal Automobile, City Livery, Den Norske; Cambridge Union; Shippingklubben (Oslo); Royal Norwegian Yacht; Royal North of Ireland Yacht (Cultra, Co. Down).   *Died 10 May 1994.*

REDESDALE, 5th Baron, *cr* 1902; **Clement Napier Bertram Mitford;** Vice President, Corporate Communications Europe, Africa and Middle East, Chase Manhattan Bank, North America; *b* 28 Oct. 1932; *o s of* late Hon. E. R. B. O. Freeman-Mitford (5th *s* of 1st Baron), and Flora, *yr d* of Comdr Gerald Talbot Napier, RN, and *widow* of Henry Lane Eno, USA; *S* uncle, 1963; *m* 1958, Sarah Georgina Cranston Todd; one *s* five *d* (and one *d* decd). *Educ:* Eton. MCAM. Joined Colin Turner (London) Ltd, 1953; joined Erwin Wasey (Advertising), 1955, Associate Director, 1960–64. Pres., Guild of Cleaners and Launderers, 1968–70. Chm., Nat. Council of Royal Soc. of St George, 1970–75, Pres., 1975–79. Governor, Yehudi Menuhin Sch., 1973–. *Heir: s* Hon. Rupert Bertram Mitford, *b* 18 July 1967. *Address:* 2 St Mark's Square, NW1 7TP. *T:* 071–722 1965. *Club:* Lansdowne.   *Died 3 March 1991.*

REDHEAD, Brian; Presenter, Today programme, BBC Radio, since 1975; *b* 28 Dec. 1929; *s* of Leonard Redhead and Janet Fairley; *m* 1954, Jean, (Jenni), Salmon; two *s* one *d* (and one *s* decd). *Educ:* Royal Grammar Sch., Newcastle upon Tyne; Downing Coll., Cambridge. Northern Editor, The Guardian, 1965–69; Editor, Manchester Evening News, 1969–75. BBC Radio, Presenter: A Word in Edgeways; Workforce; The Good Book, 1986; The Pillars of Islam, 1987; The Christian Centuries, 1988; The Wandering Scholar, 1989. Dir, World Wide Pictures, 1980. Former Pres., Council for Nat. Parks; President: Trinity–the Hospice in the Fylde; Cat Action Trust. *Publications:* (with F. Gumley) The Good Book, 1987; (with S. Gooddie) The Summers of Shotton, 1987; A Love of the Lakes, 1988; The National Parks of England and Wales, 1988; (with F. Gumley) The Christian Centuries, 1989. *Address:* 71 Thomas More House, Barbican, EC2Y 8AB. *T:* 071–638 5111. *Club:* Garrick.   *Died 23 Jan. 1994.*

REDSHAW, Prof. Seymour Cunningham, DSc (Wales), PhD (London); FICE, FIStructE, FRAeS; Beale Professor and Head of Civil Engineering Department, University of Birmingham, 1950–69, then Emeritus Professor; Dean of Faculty of Science, 1955–57; Member of Aeronautical Research Council, 1955; *b* 20 March 1906; *s* of Walter James Redshaw and Edith Marion Cunningham; *m* 1935, Mary Elizabeth Jarrold; three *s*. *Educ:* Blundell's School; University of Wales. Technical Assistant, Bristol Aeroplane Co. Ltd, 1927–31; Asst Designer, General Aircraft Ltd, 1931–32; Member of Staff: Imperial College, London, 1933–35; Building Research Station, 1936–40; Boulton Paul Aircraft Ltd, 1940–50: Chief Engineer, 1945; Director, 1949. Mem. Adv. Cttee on Building Research, 1965–67; Mem. Council, Univ. of Aston, 1966–67; Chm., Acad. Adv. Cttee and Mem. Council, Univ. of Bath, 1966; a Governor of Coll. of Aeronautics, 1951–69. Hon. DSc: Bath, 1966; Cranfield, 1976. *Publications:* numerous papers in scientific and engineering journals. *Address:* 22 Newport Street, Brewood, Staffs ST19 9DT. *T:* Brewood (01902) 850274.   *Died 25 Jan. 1995.*

REES, Dr (Florence) Gwendolen, FRS 1971; FIBiol; a Professor of Zoology, University of Wales, at University College of Wales, Aberystwyth, 1971–73, then Emeritus; *b* 3 July 1906; *yr d* of late E. and E. A. Rees; unmarried. *Educ:* Girls' Grammar Sch., Aberdare; UCW Cardiff. BSc 1927; PhD 1930; DSc 1942. FIBiol 1971. UCW, Aberystwyth: Lectr in Zoology, 1930–46; Sen. Lectr, 1946–66; Reader, 1966–71. Vis. Scientist, Univ. of Ghana, 1961. Research grants from Royal Soc., SRC, Shell Grants Cttee, Nat. Research Council, USA. Hon. Member: Amer. Soc. of Parasitologists, 1975; British Soc. for Parasitology, 1976. Linnean Medal for services to zoology, Linnean Soc., 1990. *Publications:* numerous papers on parasitology (helminthology) in scientific jls. *Recreations:* riding, amateur dramatics, the arts. *Address:* Grey Mist, North Road, Aberystwyth, Dyfed SY23 2EE. *T:* Aberystwyth (01970) 612389.   *Died 4 Oct. 1994.*

REES, Haydn; *see* Rees, T. M. H.

REES, Llewellyn; *see* Rees, W. L.

REES, (Thomas Morgan) Haydn, CBE 1975; JP; DL; Chairman, Welsh Water Authority, 1977–82; Member: National Water Council, 1977–82; Water Space Amenity Commission, 1977–82; *b* 22 May 1915; *y s* of late Thomas Rees and Mary Rees, Gorseinon, Swansea; *m* 1941, Marion, *y d* of A. B. Beer, Mumbles, Swansea; one *d*. *Educ:* Swansea Business Coll. Served War, 1939–45. Admitted solicitor, 1946; Sen. Asst Solicitor, Caernarvonshire CC, 1947; Flints County Council, 1948–65: Dep. Clerk, Dep. Clerk of the Peace, Police Authority, Magistrates Courts Cttee, and of Probation Cttee; 1966–74: Chief Exec.; Clerk of Peace (until office abolished, 1971); Clerk, Flints Police Authority (until merger with N Wales Police Authority, 1967); Clerk of Probation, Magistrates Courts, and of Justices Adv. Cttees; Clerk to Lieutenancy; Chief Exec., Clwyd CC, and Clerk, Magistrates Courts Cttee, 1974–77; Clerk to Lieutenancy and of Justices Adv. Cttee, Clwyd, 1974–77. Clerk, N Wales Police Authority, 1967–77; Secretary: Welsh Counties Cttee, 1968–77; (Corresp.) Rep. Body (Ombudsman) Cttee for Wales, 1974–77; Mem., Severn Barrage Cttee, 1978–81. Asst Comr, Royal Commn on Constitution, 1969–73. Chm., New Jobs Team, Shotton Steelworks, 1977–82; part-time Mem. Bd, BSC (Industry) Ltd, 1979–83. Chm., N Wales Arts Assoc., 1981–93. Member: Lord Chancellor's Circuit Cttee for Wales and Chester Circuit, 1972–77; Welsh Council, 1968–79; Welsh Arts Council, 1968–77 (Mem. Regional Cttee 1981–94); Gorsedd, Royal National Eisteddfod for Wales; Prince of Wales Cttee, 1976–79; Welsh Political Archive Adv. Cttee, Nat. Library of Wales, 1989–92; N Wales Music Festival Cttee, 1983–. Clerk, 1974–77, Mem., 1983–, Theatr Clwyd Governors. Chairman: Govt Quality of Life Experiment in Clwyd, 1974–76; Deeside Enterprise Trust Ltd, 1982–89; President: Clwyd Voluntary Services Council, 1980–; Clwyd Pre-Retirement Assoc., 1986–92. DL Flints 1969, Clwyd 1974; JP Mold, 1977 (Dep. Chm., 1978–84; Chm., 1985). *Recreation:* golf. *Address:* Cefn Bryn, Gwernaffield Road, Mold, Clwyd CH7 1RQ. *T:* Mold (01352) 752421.   *Died 27 Oct. 1995.*

REES, (Walter) Llewellyn, MA; actor and theatre administrator; Hon. Life Member: British Actors' Equity Association, 1981 (General Secretary, 1940–46); Theatrical Management Association, 1985; Honorary President of International Theatre Institute since 1951; *b* 18 June 1901; *s* of Walter Francis Rees and Mary Gwendoline Naden; *m* 1961, Madeleine Newbury; one *s* one *d*. *Educ:* King Edward's School, Birmingham; Keble College, Oxford. Private tutor, 1923–26; studied at RADA, 1926–28; actor, 1928–40; Jt Secretary: London Theatre Council, 1940–46; Prov. Theatre Council, 1942–46; Sec. of Fedn of Theatre Unions, 1944–46; Governor of the Old Vic, 1945–47; Drama Director, Arts Council of Great Britain, 1947–49; Administrator of the Old Vic, 1949–51;

Administrator of Arts Theatre, 1951–52; General Administrator, Donald Wolfit's Company, 1952–58; Chairman Executive Committee of International Theatre Institute, 1948–51; Hon. Counsellor to Council of Repertory Theatres, 1951–77. Returned to West End Stage, 1956, as Bishop of Buenos Aires in The Strong are Lonely, Theatre Royal, Haymarket; Olmeda in The Master of Santiago, Lyric Theatre, Hammersmith, 1957; Polonius in Hamlet, Bristol Old Vic, 1958; Dean of College in My Friend Judas, Arts Theatre, 1959; Mr Brandy in Settled out of Court, Strand Theatre, 1960–61; Justice Worthy in Lock Up Your Daughters, Mermaid Theatre and Her Majesty's, 1962–63; Sir Henry James in the Right Honourable Gentleman, Her Majesty's, 1964–65; Father Ambrose in The Servants and the Snow, Greenwich, 1970; Duncan in Macbeth, Greenwich, 1971; Mr Justice Millhouse in Whose Life Is It Anyway?, Savoy, 1978–79. Many film and television appearances. *Recreation:* travel. *Address:* 6 Byfeld Gardens, Barnes, SW13 9HP.
Died 7 Jan. 1994.

REES-DAVIES, William Rupert, QC 1973; barrister-at-law; *b* 19 Nov. 1916; *o s* of late Sir William Rees-Davies, KC, JP, DL (formerly Chief Justice of Hong Kong and Liberal MP for Pembroke) and Lady (Hilda Kathleen) Rees-Davies; *m* 1st, 1959, Jane (marr. diss. 1981), *d* of Mr and Mrs Henry Mander; two *d*; 2nd, 1982, Sharlie Kingsley. *Educ:* Eton; Trinity Coll., Cambridge. Eton Soc., Eton XI, 1934–35; Eton Victor Ludorum; Cambridge Cricket XI, 1938; Honours in History and Law. Called to Bar, Inner Temple, 1939. Commissioned HM Welsh Guards, 1939; served War of 1939–45 (discharged disabled with loss of arm, 1943). Contested (C) South Nottingham in 1950 and 1951. MP (C) Isle of Thanet, March 1953–1974, Thanet W, 1974–83; Cons. Leader, Select Cttee on Health and the Social Services, 1980–83; Chm., Cons. Cttee on Tourism. *Recreations:* racing, collecting pictures and antiques. *Address:* 5 Lord North Street, SW1. *Clubs:* Turf, Guards' Polo, MCC; Hawks, University Pitt (Cambridge).
Died 12 Jan. 1992.

REEVE, Sir (Charles) Trevor, Kt 1973; a Judge of the High Court of Justice, Family Division, 1973–88; *b* 4 July 1915; *o s* of William George Reeve and Elsie (*née* Bowring), Wokingham; *m* 1941, Marjorie (*d* 1990), *d* of Charles Evelyn Browne, Eccles, Lancs. *Educ:* Winchester College; Trinity College, Oxford. Commissioned 10th Royal Hussars (PWO), 1940; served BEF, CMF (Major), 1940–44 (despatches); Staff College, Camberley, 1945. Called to Bar, Inner Temple, 1946, Bencher, 1965; Mem., Bar Council, 1950–54. QC 1965; County Court Judge, 1968; Circuit Judge, 1972. Mem., Appeals Tribunal for E Africa in respect of Commonwealth Immigration Act, 1968. *Recreations:* golf, dancing. *Address:* 95 Abingdon Road, Kensington, W8 6QU. *T:* 071–937 7530. *Clubs:* Garrick; Royal North Devon Golf (Westward Ho!); Sunningdale Golf.
Died 7 Dec. 1993.

REIACH, Alan, OBE 1965; RSA 1986; architect; Senior Partner, Reiach and Hall, 1964–75, retired; *b* 2 March 1910; *s* of Herbert L. Reiach and Marie Barbara Fredenson; *m* 1940, Julie Dittmar; *m* 1949, Patricia Anne Duncan; one *s* one *d*. *Educ:* Edinburgh Acad.; Edinburgh Coll. of Art, 1928–35. Lorimer & Matthew, Edinburgh, 1928–33; Sch. of Architecture, Coll. of Art, 1933–35; Travelling Schol., USA and Europe, 1935–36; worked for Robert Atkinson and Partners, London, 1936–38; Andrew Grant Fellow, Edinburgh, 1938–40; Asst Sec., Scottish Housing Adv. Cttee, Dept of Health, Scottish Office, 1940–44; Planning Asst, Clyde Valley Planning Authy, 1944–46; established own practice, 1949, and joined with Eric Hall and Partners, 1964. *Publication:* Building Scotland (with Robert Hurd), 1940, 2nd edn 1944. *Recreation:* watercolour painting. *Address:* 3 Winton Loan, Edinburgh

EH10 7AN. *T:* 031–445 1006. *Clubs:* New, Scottish Arts (Edinburgh).
Died 24 July 1992.

REID, Archibald Cameron, CMG 1963; CVO 1970; retired 1971; *b* 7 Aug. 1915; *s* of William Reid; *m* 1941, Joan Raymond Charlton; two *s* two *d*. *Educ:* Fettes; Queens' College, Cambridge. Apptd Admin. Officer, Class II, in Colony of Fiji, 1938; Admin. Officer, Class I, 1954; British Agent and Consul, Tonga, 1957–59; Sec. for Fijian Affairs, 1959–65; British Comr and Consul, Tonga, 1965–70; Dep. High Comr, Tonga, 1970–71. Engaged in Pacific history research. *Publication:* Tovata I and II, 1990. *Recreations:* walking, painting. *Address:* 9/10 Minkara Road, Bayview Heights, NSW 2104, Australia. *T:* (2) 9975667.
Died 24 Nov. 1994.

REID, Hon. Sir George Oswald, Kt 1972; QC (Vic) 1971; Attorney-General, Victoria, Australia, 1967–73; barrister and solicitor; *b* Hawthorn, Vic, 22 July 1903; *s* of late George Watson Reid and Lillias Margaret Reid (*née* Easton); *m* 1st, 1930, Beatrix Waring McCay, LLM (*d* 1972), *d* of Lt-Gen. Hon. Sir James McCay; one *d*; 2nd, 1973, Dorothy, *d* of late C. W. F. Ruttledge. *Educ:* Camberwell Grammar Sch. and Scotch Coll., Melbourne; Melbourne Univ. (LLB). Admitted to practice as Barrister and Solicitor, Supreme Ct of Vic, 1926; practised as solicitor in Melbourne, 1929. Served War, RAAF, 1940–46, Wing Comdr. MLA (Liberal) for Box Hill, 1947–52, and 1955–73. Government of Victoria: Minister without Portfolio, 1955–56; Minister: of Labour and Industry and Electrical Undertakings, 1956–65; for Fuel and Power, 1965–67; of Immigration, 1967–70; Chief Secretary, March 9–Apr. 27, 1971. *Recreations:* golf, reading. *Address:* Southern Cross Homes, Broadford Crescent, Macleod, Vic 3085, Australia. *Clubs:* Melbourne, Savage, Melbourne Cricket (Melbourne).
Died 18 Feb. 1993.

REID, Air Vice-Marshal Sir (George) Ranald Macfarlane, KCB 1945 (CB 1941); DSO 1919; MC and bar; Extra Gentleman Usher to the Queen, 1959; Gentleman Usher to the Queen, 1952 (formerly to King George VI, 1952); *b* 25 Oct. 1893; *s* of late George Macfarlane Reid and Gertrude Macquisten, Prestwick; *m* 1934, Leslie Livermore Washburne, *d* of late Hamilton Wright, Washington, DC, USA, and *g d* of Senator William Washburne; one *s* one *d*. *Educ:* Routenburn; Malvern Coll. Regular Officer, 1914–46 in: 4th (SR) Argyll and Sutherland Highlanders; 2nd Black Watch; RFC and RAF; served European War, 1914–18 (wounded, despatches, MC and Bar, DSO); Egypt, 1919–21; Sudan, 1927–29; RAF Staff Coll., 1930; Imperial Defence Coll., 1932; Air Attaché, British Embassy, Washington, 1933–35; AOC Halton, 1936–38; Air Officer Commanding British Forces, Aden, 1938–41; Air Officer Administration Flying Training Command; AOC 54 Group; AOC West Africa, 1944–45; retired from Royal Air Force, 1946. *Address:* c/o R3 Section, Lloyds Bank, 6 Pall Mall, SW1Y 5NH. *Clubs:* Royal Air Force; Weld (Perth, Western Australia).
Died 19 May 1991.

REID, Col Ivo; *see* Reid, Col P. F. I.

REID, Sir John (James Andrew), KCMG 1985; CB 1975; TD 1958; MD, FRCP, FRCPE; Consultant Adviser on International Health, Department of Health (formerly of Health and Social Security), 1986–94; Hon. Consultant in Community Medicine to the Army, 1971–90; Chairman, Review Board for Overseas Qualified Practitioners, 1990–94 (Deputy Chairman, 1986–90); *b* 21 Jan. 1925; *s* of Alexander Scott Reid and Mary Cullen Reid (*née* Andrew); *m* 1st, 1949, Marjorie, MB, ChB (*née* Crumpton) (*d* 1990); one *s* four *d*; 2nd, 1992, Dulcie (*née* Rawle), MB, BS, FFCM, DPH. *Educ:* Bell-Baxter Sch.; Univ. of St Andrews. BSc 1944; MB, ChB 1947; DPH 1952; MD

1961; Hon. DSc 1979; FRCPE 1970; FRCP 1971; FFCM 1972; FRCPGlas 1980. Lt-Col RAMC (TA). Hospital, Army (Nat. Service) and junior Public Health posts, 1947–55; Lectr in Public Health and Social Medicine, Univ. of St Andrews, 1955–59; Dep. County MOH, Northamptonshire, 1959–62; County MOH, Northamptonshire, 1962–67; County MOH, Buckinghamshire, 1967–72; Dep. Chief MO, DHSS, 1972–77; Chief MO, SHHD, 1977–85. Member: GMC (Crown Nominee), 1973–81, 1985; Council for Post-grad. Med. Educn, 1973–77; Scottish Council for Post-grad. Med. Educn, 1977–85; Scottish Health Service Planning Council, 1977–85; Exec. Bd, WHO, 1973–75, 1976–79, 1980–83, 1984–87 (Vice Chm., 1977–78; Chm.), 1978–79; consultant); MRC, 1977–85; EC Adv. Cttee on Med. Training, 1976–85. WHO Fellow, 1962; Mem., Standing Med. Adv. Cttee, DHSS, 1966–72; Chm., Jt Sub-Cttee on Health and Welfare Services for People with Epilepsy (Report, People with Epilepsy, 1969); Chm., Jt Working Party for Health Services in Milton Keynes, 1968–74; Dep. Co-Chm., UK/USSR Cttee on Health Care, 1975–77; Jt Chm., Scottish/Finnish Health Agreement, 1978–85; Mem., Working Party on Medical Administrators (Report, 1972); Public Health Lab. Service Bd, 1974–77; Hospital Management Committees: St Crispins, 1959–69; Northampton, 1962–67; St Johns, 1967–72. Pres., BMA, 1992–93. Vis. Prof. in Health Services Admin, London Sch. of Hygiene and Tropical Medicine, 1973–78 (Governor and Mem., 1977–, Chm., 1989–, Bd of Management); Vis. Lectr and Examr, univs in UK and abroad; Vice-Pres., Liverpool Sch. of Tropical Medicine, 1987–; Governor, United Oxford Hosps, 1962–66. Hon. FRSH 1994. Hon. LLD Dundee, 1985. Léon Bernard Foundn Prize, 1987. *Publications:* papers on public and international health, community medicine, diabetes, epilepsy, etc, in BMJ, Lancet, etc. *Address:* Manor House Cottage, Manor Road, Oving, Aylesbury, Bucks HP22 4HW. *Died 10 July 1994.*

REID, John (Robson), OBE 1992; DL; architect and consultant designer; Partner, John and Sylvia Reid, since 1951; Pageantmaster to the Lord Mayors of London, since 1972; *b* 1 Dec. 1925; *m* 1948, Sylvia Reid (*née* Payne), Dip. Arch., RIBA, FCSD; one *s* twin *d*. *Educ:* Wellingborough Grammar Sch.; Sch. of Architecture, The Polytechnic, WI (Dip. in Architecture with dist.). RIBA, PPCSD, FCIBS. Capt., Green Howards, 1944–47; Mem. HAC, 1980. *Architectural work includes:* hotels, showrooms, museums, houses and pubs: Civic Suite, Wandsworth Town Hall; Savile Room, Merton Coll., Oxford; Great Room, Grosvenor House; Dunhill Res. Lab., Inst. of Dermatology; Westminster Theatre; Lawson House, ICI, Runcorn; Heatherside Shopping Centre; Savoy Grill; Exec. Suite, British Telecoms HQ; Barbican Exhibition Halls, Corporation of City of London; Sherlock Holmes Mus., Meiringen, Switzerland; *industrial design work includes:* furniture, lighting fittings, road and rail transport, carpets, textiles, civic regalia; lighting consultant for Coventry Cathedral; some-time design consultant to Thorn, Rotaflex, Stag, CMC, BR, N General Transport, PO; UNIDO consultant on industrial design in India, Pakistan, Egypt and Turkey, 1977–79; British Council tour, India, 1985. *Exhibitions:* 350th Anniversary Celebration, Jamestown, Virginia, USA, 1957; various exhibns for BR, Cardiff Corp., City of London, etc. Leader, British delegn of design educn in Soviet Union, Anglo-Soviet Cultural Exchange Treaty, 1967. Dean of Art and Design, Middx Polytechnic, 1975–78; some-time mem. of adv. cttees, Central Sch. of Art and Design, Leeds Coll. of Art and Design, Newcastle-upon-Tyne Sch. of Art and Design, and Carleton Univ., Ottawa; Governor, Hornsey Coll. of Art; Trustee, Geffrye Mus., 1990. Lectured in Canada, Czechoslovakia, Eire, Hungary,

Japan, Poland, USA, USSR. PSIAD, 1965–66; Pres., Internat. Council of Socs of Ind. Design, 1969–71; Vice-Pres., Illuminating Engrg Soc., 1969–71. RIBA Mem., Bd of Nat. Inspection Council for Electrical Installation Contracting (Chm., 1972–73). Master, Worshipful Co. of Furniture Makers, 1989–90; Inaugural Master, Worshipful Co. of Chartered Architects, 1988–89. DL Gtr London, 1991. Four CoID Awards; Silver Medals of 12th and 13th Milan Internat. Triennales. *Publications:* International Code of Professional Conduct, 1969; A Guide to Conditions of Contract for Industrial Design, 1971; Industrial Design in India, Pakistan, Egypt and Turkey, 1978; various articles in professional jls. *Recreations:* music, gardening. *Address:* Arnoside House, The Green, Old Southgate, N14 7EG. *T:* 081–882 1083.
Died 14 April 1992.

REID, Col (Percy Fergus) Ivo, OBE 1953; DL; *b* 2 Nov. 1911; *er s* of Col Percy Lester Reid, CBE, JP, DL and K. M. E. Fergusson; *m* 1940, Mary Armida, *d* of Col James Douglas Macindoe, MC; two *s* one *d*. *Educ:* Stowe; Pembroke Coll., Oxford. Joined Irish Guards, 1933; Egypt, 1936–38; served in 2nd World War, Guards Armd Div., Europe (despatches); Staff Coll., 1945; Comdt, Guards Depot, 1950–53; Lt Col 1951; comd Irish Guards and Regt District, 1955–59; Col 1955; retd 1959. Mem., HM Bodyguard of Hon. Corps of Gentlemen at Arms, 1961–81; Harbinger, 1979–81. Northamptonshire: High Sheriff 1967; DL 1969. *Recreations:* hunting, shooting. *Address:* The Glebe House, Marston St Lawrence, Banbury, Oxon OX17 2DA. *T:* Banbury (01295) 710300. *Club:* White's.
Died 9 Dec. 1994.

REID, Air Vice-Marshal Sir Ranald; *see* Reid, Sir G. R. M.

REID, Sir Robert (Basil), Kt 1985; CBE 1980; FCIT; Chairman, British Railways Board, 1983–90; Chairman, West Lambeth Health Authority, 1990–93; *b* 7 Feb. 1921; *s* of Sir Robert Niel Reid, KCSI, KCIE, ICS and Lady (Amy Helen) Reid (*née* Rennie); *m* 1951, Isobel Jean McLachlan (*d* 1976); one *s* one *d*. *Educ:* Malvern Coll.; Brasenose Coll., Oxford (MA; Hon. Fellow, 1985). Commnd Royal Tank Regt, 1941, Captain 1945. Traffic Apprentice, LNER, 1947; Goods Agent, York, 1958; Asst Dist Goods Manager, Glasgow, 1960, Dist Passenger Man., 1961, Divl Commercial Man., 1963; Planning Man., Scottish Region, 1967; Divl Man., Doncaster, 1968; Dep. Gen. Man., Eastern Region, York, 1972; Gen. Manager, Southern Reg., BR, 1974–76; British Railways Board: Exec. Mem. for Marketing, 1977–80; Chief Exec. (Railways), 1980–83; a Vice-Chm., 1983. Director: British Transport Hotels Ltd, 1977–83; Docklands Light Rly, 1991–; Chm., Freightliner Co. Ltd, 1978–80. Chm., Nat. Industries Chairmen's Gp, 1987–88; Pres., European Community Rlys Dirs General, 1988–89. President: CIT, 1982–83; Inst. of Administrative Management, 1989–. Gov., UMDS of Guy's and St Thomas', 1993–. FCIM; CIMgt. CStJ 1985. Freeman, City of London. Master: Information Technologists' Co., 1988–89; Carmen's Co., 1990–91. Hon. DBA Buckingham Internat. Management Centre, 1988; Hon. DEng Bristol, 1990. Hon. Col, 275 Railway Sqn, RCT(V), 1989–91. *Recreations:* fishing, shooting. *Address:* St Thomas' Hospital, Lambeth Palace Road, SE1 7EH. *T:* 071–928 9292. *Club:* Naval and Military. *Died 17 Dec. 1993.*

REIDY, Joseph Patrick Irwin, FRCS; Consulting Plastic Surgeon, retired: Westminster Hospital, 1948–72; Stoke Mandeville Hospital, Bucks, 1942–72 (Director, Plastic Surgery, 1957–72); Oldchurch Hospital, Romford, 1946–72; Consulting Plastic Surgeon (Hon.), St Paul's Hospital, WC, 1959–72; *b* 30 October 1907; 2nd *s* of late Dr Jerome J. Reidy, JP, MD, Co. Limerick and London and Alderman Mrs F. W. Reidy, JP (*née* Dawson), Castle

Dawson, Co. Derry; *m* 1943, Anne (*d* 1970), *e d* of late Mr and Mrs T. Johnson, County Durham; three *d*; *m* 1972, Freda M. Clout (*née* Lowe), Gosfield Hall, Essex. *Educ:* Stonyhurst College, Lancs; St John's Coll., Cambridge; London Hospital. MA (Nat. Sci. Trip.) (Cantab); MD, BCh (Cantab); FRCS 1941. Casualty Officer and Ho. Phys., Poplar Hosp., 1932; Ho. Surg. and Casualty Officer, London Hosp., 1933; Ho. Surg., Leicester Roy. Inf., 1934; General Practitioner, 1934–37; Surgeon H. Div., Metropolitan Police, 1934–37. Hon. Demstr of Anatomy, Med. Sch., Middx Hosp., 1938; Civilian Surg., RAF Hosp., Halton, Bucks, 1939; Resident Surg. Officer: EMS, Albert Dock Hosp., 1939–40; EMS, St Andrew's Hosp., Billericay, 1940–42; Chief Asst, Plastic Surgery, St Thomas' Hosp., 1943–48; Cons. Plastic Surgeon, Essex Co. Hosp., Colchester, 1943–46; Senior Grade Surgeon, Plastic Surg. Unit, Min. of Pensions: Stoke Mandeville Hosp., Bucks, 1942–51; Queen Mary's Hosp., Roehampton, 1942–51. Consulting Plastic Surgeon: Middlesex CC, 1944–48; Nelson Hosp., Kingston, 1948–50; Metropolitan ENT Hosp., 1948–50; West Middlesex Hosp.; Lord Mayor Treloar Hosp., Alton, 1953–56. Hon. Chief MO, Amateur Boxing Association, 1948; Hon. Secretary and Treas. United Hospitals Rugby Football Club, 1957–62. Liveryman Soc. of Apothecaries; Freeman of City of London. FRSocMed; Fellow, Medical Soc.; Fellow Hunterian Soc.; Pres., Chiltern Medical Soc., 1958–60; Pres., Brit. Assoc. of Plastic Surgeons, 1962. Member: BMA; British Assoc. of Surgeons; Brit. Acad. of Forensic Sciences; Colchester Med. Soc. Hunterian Prof., RCS, 1957, 1968; Lecturer, London Univ., 1952; Purkinje Medal, Czechoslovak Acad. of Sciences, 1965. *Publications:* contribs 1944– to: Proc. Roy. Soc. Med., Medical Press, West London Medico-Chirurgical Journal, British Journal of Plastic Surgery, BMJ, Medical History 2nd World War, Monograph Plastic Surgery and Physiotherapy, Annals RCS, etc. *Recreations:* gardening, reading. *Address:* Priory Cottage, Earls Colne, Essex CO6 2PG. *T:* Earls Colne (0787) 222271.

Died 10 Sept. 1991.

REIGATE, Baron *cr* 1970 (Life Peer), of Outwood, Surrey; **John Kenyon Vaughan-Morgan;** PC 1961; Bt 1960; *b* 2 Feb. 1905; *yr s* of late Sir Kenyon Vaughan-Morgan, OBE, DL, MP and Lady (Muriel) Vaughan-Morgan; *m* 1940, Emily, *d* of late Mr and Mrs W. Redmond Cross, New York City; two *d*. *Educ:* Eton; Christ Church, Oxford. Mem. Chelsea Borough Council, 1928; Member of London County Council for Chelsea, 1946–52; Chm. East Fulham Conservative and Unionist Assoc., 1935–38 (Pres. 1945); MP (C) Reigate Div. of Surrey, 1950–70. Parly Sec., Min. of Health, 1957; Minister of State, BoT, 1957–59. Dir, Morgan Crucible Co. Ltd, retired. Chm. Bd of Govs, Westminster Hosp., 1963–74 (Mem., 1960). Pres., Royal Philanthropic Sch., Redhill. Dep. Chm., South Westminster Justices, retired. Mem., Court of Assistants, Merchant Taylors Co. (Master 1970). Hon. Freeman, Borough of Reigate, 1971. Served War of 1939–45; Welsh Guards, 1940; GSO2, War Office; GSO1, HQ 21 Army Group (despatches). *Address:* 36 Eaton Square, SW1W 9DH. *T:* 0171–235 6506. *Clubs:* Brooks's, Beefsteak, Hurlingham. *Died 26 Jan. 1995 (Btcy ext).*

REILLY, Noel Marcus Prowse, (Peter), CMG 1958; *b* 31 Dec. 1902; *s* of late Frederick Reilly and Ellen Prowse; *m* 1st, 1927, Dolores Albra Pratten (marr. diss., 1963); one *s* one *d*; 2nd, 1963, Dorothy Alma Rainsford. *Educ:* University Coll. Sch.; Gonville and Caius College, Cambridge (MA 1928); London Univ. (BSc Econ., 1st Cl. Hons 1946, PhD 1972). Schoolmaster, Boston, Massachusetts, USA, 1924; business in New Zealand, 1926, England, 1928; Secretary, Area Cttee for National Fitness for Oxon, Bucks, and Berks, 1938; Press Censor, Ministry of Information, 1939; Principal, HM Treasury,

1946; Economic Counsellor, Persian Gulf, 1953–59; Financial Counsellor and Dep. Head, UK Treasury Delegation, British Embassy, Washington, 1960–65; Alternate Exec. Dir for the UK, IBRD, and Affiliates, 1962–65. *Publication:* The Key to Prosperity, 1931. *Recreations:* ski-ing, windsurfing, whitewater kayaking. *Address:* North Sandwich, New Hampshire 03259, USA. *T:* 603–284–7730. *Died 22 April 1991.*

REILLY, Peter; *see* Reilly, N. M. P.

REMEZ, Aharon; sculptor; *b* 8 May 1919; *m* 1952, Rita (*née* Levy); one *s* three *d*. *Educ:* Herzliah Grammar Sch., Tel Aviv; New Sch. for Social Res., NY; Business Sch., Harvard Univ.; Woodrow Wilson Sch. of Public and Internat. Affairs, Princeton Univ. Volunteered for service with RAF, and served as fighter pilot in Gt Brit. and in European theatre of war; after end of war with British Occupation forces in Germany. Mem., kibbutz Kfar Blum, 1947–. Dir Planning and of Ops and subseq. Chief of Staff, and C-in-C Israel Air Force (rank Brig.-Gen.), 1948–51; Head of Min. of Defence Purchasing Mission, USA, 1951–53; Aviation Adviser to Minister of Def., 1953–54; Mem. Bd of Dirs, Solel Boneh Ltd, and Exec. Dir, Koor Industries Ltd, 1954–59; MP (Israel Lab Party) for Mapai, 1956–57; Admin. Dir, Weizmann Inst. of Science, Rehovot, 1959–60. Dir, Internat. Co-op. Dept, Min. for Foreign Affairs, Jerusalem, 1960; Adviser on Internat. Co-operation to Min. for Foreign Affairs, also Consultant to OECD, 1964–65; Ambassador of Israel to the Court of St James's, 1965–70. Dir Gen., Israel Ports Authority, 1970–77. Chairman: Nat. Council for Civil Aviation, 1960–65; Bd of Dirs, Airports Authority, 1977–81. *Recreations:* handicrafts, sculpture. *Address:* San Martin Street, Cottage 11, Jerusalem 93341, Israel. *Died 3 April 1994.*

RENAUD, Madeleine, (Mme Jean-Louis Barrault); Officier de la Légion d'Honneur; actress; Joint Founder, Madeleine Renaud-Jean-Louis Barrault Company, 1947, Co-director and player leading parts; *b* Paris, 21 Feb. 1900; *d* of Prof. Jean Renaud; *m* 1st, Charles Gribouval, (Charles Grandval) (marr. diss.); one *s*; 2nd, Pierre Bertin (marr. diss.; he *d* 1984); 3rd, 1940, Jean-Louis Barrault (*d* 1994). *Educ:* Lycée Racine; Conservatoire de Paris (Ier Prix de Comédie). Pensionnaire, Comédie Française, 1921–46. Appeared in classical and modern plays, and in films. Mem., Conseil d'administration, ORTF, 1967–68. Grand Officier de l'ordre national du Mérite; Commandeur des Arts et des Lettres. *Publications:* novels, short stories, plays. *Address:* 18 Avenue du Président Wilson, 75116 Paris, France. *Died 23 Sept. 1994.*

RENDELL, Sir William, Kt 1967; General Manager, Commonwealth Development Corporation, 1953–73, retired; *b* 25 Jan. 1908; *s* of William Reginald Rendell and Hon. Janet Marion Rendell; *m* 1st, 1946, Simone Nicole (*née* Dubois) (marr. diss. 1950); one *s*; 2nd, 1950, Annie Henriette Maria (*née* Thorsen). *Educ:* Winchester; Trinity Coll., Cambridge. FCA. Partner, Whinney Murray & Co., 1947–52. *Recreations:* fishing, gardening. *Address:* Flat 5, Hugo House, 178 Sloane Street, SW1X 9QL. *T:* 0171–235 6340. *Died 20 Jan. 1995.*

RENFREW, Rt Rev. Charles McDonald; Titular Bishop of Abula and Auxiliary to the Archbishop of Glasgow, (RC), since 1977; Vicar General of Archdiocese of Glasgow, since 1974; *b* 21 June 1929; *s* of Alexander Renfrew and Mary (*née* Dougherty). *Educ:* St Aloysius College, Glasgow; Scots College, Rome. PhL, STL (Gregorian). Ordained Rome, 1953; Assistant at Immaculate Conception, Glasgow, 1953–56; Professor and Procurator, Blairs Coll., Aberdeen, 1956–61; First Rector and founder of St Vincent's Coll., Langbank, 1961–74. Sound and television broadcasts for BBC and

STV. Comdr, Order of Merit (Republic of Italy), 1982. *Publications:* St Vincent's Prayer Book, 1971; Rambling Through Life, 1975; Ripples of Life, 1975; Pageant of Holiness, 1975; pamphlets and articles in newspapers and magazines. *Recreation:* music, especially grand and light opera. *Address:* St Joseph's, 38 Mansionhouse Road, Glasgow G41 3DN. *T:* 041–649 2228.
Died 27 Feb. 1992.

RENWICK, Prof. James Harrison, DSc; FRCP, FRCPath; Professor of Human Genetics and Teratology, University of London, 1979–91, then Emeritus; *b* 4 Feb. 1926; *s* of late Raymond Renwick and Edith Helen Renwick; *m* 1st, 1959, Helena Verheyden (marr. diss. 1979); one *s* one *d*; 2nd, 1981, Kathleen Salafia; two *s*. *Educ:* Sedbergh School; Univ. of St Andrews (MB ChB (commendation), 1948); University Coll. London (PhD 1956). DSc London, 1970; FRCP 1972; MFCM 1972; FRCPath 1982. Captain RAMC, Korean War: research on genetical effects of atomic bomb, Hiroshima, 1951–53. Univ. of Glasgow, 1959, Prof. of Human Genetics, 1967–68; London Sch. of Hygiene and Tropical Medicine, 1968, Head of Preventive Teratology Unit, 1977–91. Mem., Med. Res. Club. Hon. Treasurer, Genetical Soc., 1960–65, Hon. Auditor, 1965–72; Hon. Pres., Develtl Pathology Soc., 1989–91. FRSocMed. Freeman, Co. of Stationers and Newspaper Makers. *Publications:* numerous scientific articles on mapping of genes on human chromosomes and on prevention of human congenital malformations. *Recreations:* walking, music. *Address:* Rue des Coteaux 17, Bruxelles 1030, Belgium. *T:* (2) 2187668.
Died 29 Sept. 1994.

RESO, Sidney Joseph; Executive Vice President, since 1986, President, since 1988, Exxon Co. International; *b* 12 Feb. 1935; *s* of late James A. Reso and of J. Agnes Reso; *m* 1955, Patricia M. Armond; two *s* three *d*. *Educ:* Louisiana State Univ. (BS Petroleum Engrg). Joined Humble Oil & Refining Co., Houston, Texas (subseq. Exxon Co., USA), as engineer, 1957; USA and Australia: engrg assignments, 1961–66; managerial assignments, 1967–71; Dir, Esso Australia Ltd, Sydney, 1972; managerial assignments, USA, 1973–74; Vice-Pres., Esso Europe Inc. and Managing Dir, Esso Petroleum Co., 1975–78; Vice-Pres., Exxon Corp., 1978–80; Exxon Co. USA: Vice-Pres., 1980–81; Sen. Vice-Pres., 1981–85; Exec. Vice-Pres., 1985–86. *Recreations:* golf, tennis, photography, reading. *Address:* 200 Park Avenue, Florham Park, NJ 07932–1002, USA. *Club:* River Oaks Country (Houston).
Died May 1992.

REUTER, Prof. Gerd Edzard Harry, MA Cantab; Professor of Mathematics, Imperial College of Science and Technology, London, 1965–83, then Emeritus; *b* 21 Nov. 1921; *s* of Ernst Rudolf Johannes Reuter and Gertrud Charlotte Reuter (*née* Scholz); *m* 1945, Eileen Grace Legard; one *s* three *d*. *Educ:* The Leys School, Cambridge; Trinity College, Cambridge. Mem. of Dept of Mathematics, Univ. of Manchester, 1946–58; Professor of Pure Mathematics, Univ. of Durham, 1959–65. *Publications:* Elementary Differential Equations and Operators, 1958; articles in various mathematical and scientific jls. *Address:* 47 Madingley Road, Cambridge CB3 0EL.
Died 20 April 1992.

REVELSTOKE, 4th Baron *cr* 1885, of Membland, Devon; **Rupert Baring;** *b* 8 Feb. 1911; *o s* of 3rd Baron and Maude (*d* 1922), *d* of late Pierre Lorillard; *S* father, 1934; *m* 1934, Flora (who obtained a divorce 1944; she *d* 1971), 2nd *d* of 1st Baron Hesketh; two *s*. *Educ:* Eton. 2nd Lt Royal Armoured Corps (TA). *Heir: s* Hon. John Baring, *b* 2 Dec. 1934. *Address:* Lambay Island, Rush, Co. Dublin, Ireland.
Died 18 July 1994.

REX, Hon. Sir Robert (Richmond), KBE 1984 (OBE 1973); CMG 1978; Prime Minister of Niue, since 1974; Representative of Alofi South on the Niue Island Council, since 1952; *b* 25 Jan. 1909; *s* of Leslie Lucas Richmond Rex and Monomono Paea; *m* 1941, Tuagatagaloa Patricia Vatolo; two *s* two *d*. *Educ:* Tufukia Technical Sch., Niue. Engrg Apprentice, Rakiraki Sugar-mills, Fiji Islands, 1926; Employee, NZ Steamship Union Co., 1927; farmer, Niue, 1930; Businessman (retailing), R. R. Rex & Sons Ltd, 1952. Clerk and Official Interpreter (Jack-of-all-trades), Niue Govt, 1934; Mem. Exec. Cttee, Niue Island Assembly, 1960; Leader of Govt Business, 1966; known as the longest-serving statesman in the Pacific. Mem., Commonwealth Parly Assoc. *Recreations:* cricket, Rugby, fishing, planting, billiards. *Address:* Alofi South, Niue Island, New Zealand. *T:* 275. *Club:* Niue Sports.
Died 12 Dec. 1992.

REYNOLDS, Eric Vincent, TD 1948; MA; Headmaster of Stowe, 1949–58, retired; *b* 30 April 1904; *o s* of late Arthur John and Lily Reynolds; unmarried. *Educ:* Haileybury College; St John's College, Cambridge. Modern and Mediæval languages Tripos, Parts 1 and 2; MA 1930. Lector in English at University of Leipzig, 1926–27; Assistant Master: Rugby School, 1927–31; Upper Canada College, Toronto, 1931–32; Rugby School, 1932–49 (Housemaster, 1944–49). CO, Rugby School JTC, 1938–44. *Recreations:* ski-ing, mountaineering. *Address:* 48 Lemsford Road, St Albans, Herts AL1 3PR. *T:* St Albans (0727) 53599.
Died 7 Dec. 1992.

REYNOLDS, Frank Arrowsmith, OBE 1974; LLB; HM Diplomatic Service, retired; *b* 30 March 1916; *s* of late Sydney Edward Clyde Reynolds and Bessie (*née* Foster); *m* 1938, Joan Marion Lockyer; one *s* one *d* (and one *d* decd). *Educ:* Addey and Stanhope Sch.; London University. Army, 1941–46 (Lieut, RE). District Officer, Tanganyika, 1950; Commonwealth Relations Office, 1962–63; First Secretary, Bombay, 1964–67; CO, later FCO, 1967–69; Consul-Gen., Seville, 1969–71; Head of Chancery, Maseru, 1971–75. *Publication:* Guide to Super-8 Photography, 1981. *Recreations:* music, sailing, photography. *Address:* 26 Nelson Street, Brightlingsea, Essex CO7 0DZ. *Clubs:* Royal Bombay Yacht; Colne Yacht.
Died 24 Oct. 1994.

RICE, Peter Ronan; Director: Ove Arup Partnership, since 1984; RFR Paris, since 1984; *b* 16 June 1935; *s* of James Patrick Rice and Maureen Kate (*née* Quinn); *m* 1960, Sylvia Watson; one *s* three *d*. *Educ:* Queen's University, Belfast (BSc Eng); DIC 1958. MICE 1973. Ove Arup & Partners, 1956–; Sen. Engr – Analysis, and Resident Engr, Sydney Opera House, 1960–66; Design Associate, 1968–72; Chief Design Engr for Centre Pompidou, Paris, 1972–76; Partner, Atelier Piano & Rice, 1977–78; Dir, Ove Arup & Partners, 1978–84 (Dir, Lightweight Structures Lab., 1978–84). Vis. Schol., Dept of Engrg, Cornell Univ., 1966–67. Projects include: 1978–84: Redevelt of Lloyd's and of St Katherine's, London; Menil Art Collection Mus., Houston; IBM Travelling Exhibn; Schlumberger, Paris; Patscenter, Princeton; Fleetguard, Quimper; Nantes Usine Centre; Stansted Airport steelwork; 1984–: Pavilion of the Future, Expo '92, Seville; Japan Bridge, Paris; KIAC Terminal Bldg, Osaka; Lille TGV Stn Roof; New Groninger Mus.; Marseille Airport Terminal; Charles de Gaulle Aerogare 3, Paris; West Front, Cathédrale Notre Dame de Treille, Lille; Brau & Brunnen Tower, Berlin. Hon. FRIBA 1988; Hon. MRIAI 1990. Médaille d'Argent, Soc. d'Encouragement pour l'Industrie Nat., 1987; Médaille d'Argent de la Recherche et de la Technique, Acad. d'Architecture, 1989; Gold Medal, RIBA, 1992. *Publications:* (with Hugh Dutton) Le Verre Structurel, 1990; contribs on internat. architecture and engrg to books and jls. *Recreations:* horse racing, football, studying wild flowers. *Address:* Ove Arup Partnership, 13 Fitzroy Street, W1P 6BQ. *T:* 071–636 1531.　　　　　　　　　　　　　*Died 25 Oct. 1992.*

RICH, John Rowland, CMG 1978; HM Diplomatic Service, retired; *b* 29 June 1928; *s* of late Rowland William Rich, Winchester, and Phyllis Mary, *e d* of Charles Linstead Chambers, Southgate; *m* 1956, Rosemary Ann, *yr d* of late Bertram Evan Williams, Ferndown, Dorset; two *s* one *d*. *Educ:* Sedbergh; Clare Coll., Cambridge (Foundn Exhibnr 1948). BA 1949, MA 1954. HM Forces, 1949–51; FO, 1951–53; 3rd, later 2nd Sec., Addis Ababa, 1953–56; 2nd, later 1st Sec., Stockholm, 1956–59; FO, 1959–63; 1st Sec. (Economic) and Head of Chancery, Bahrain (Political Residency), 1963–66; FCO, 1966–69; Counsellor and Head of Chancery, Prague, 1969–72; Diplomatic Service Inspector, 1972–74; Commercial Counsellor, Bonn, 1974–78; Consul-Gen., Montreal, 1978–80; Ambassador: to Czechoslovakia, 1980–85; to Switzerland, 1985–88. *Recreations:* walking, wild orchids, steam locomotives. *Address:* 23 Embercourt Road, Thames Ditton, Surrey KT7 0LH. *T:* 0181–398 1205. *Club:* Travellers'.
　　　　　　　　　　　　　　　　　Died 13 May 1995.

RICHARDS, Catherine Margaret; Secretary and Registrar, Institute of Mathematics and its Applications, since 1987; *b* 12 May 1940; *d* of John Phillips Richards and Edna Vivian (*née* Thomas). *Educ:* Newport High Sch. for Girls, Gwent; Bedford Coll., Univ. of London (BSc 1962). CMath, FIMA. Information Officer, British Oxygen Co., 1962–63; Chemistry Mistress, St Joseph's Convent Grammar Sch., Abbeywood, 1963–65; Asst Editor, Soc. for Analytical Chemistry, 1965–70; Dep. Sec., IMA, 1970–87. *Recreation:* reading. *Address:* Institute of Mathematics and its Applications, 16 Nelson Street, Southend-on-Sea, Essex SS1 1EF. *T:* Southend-on-Sea (0702) 354020. *Clubs:* University Women's, Wig and Pen.　　　　　　　　　　　　　*Died 1 April 1993.*

RICHARDS, Hon. Sir Edward (Trenton), Kt 1970; CBE 1967; Premier of Bermuda, 1972–75 (Leader, 1971; Deputy Leader, 1968–71); MP, 1948–76; *b* 4 Oct. 1908; 2nd *s* of late George A. Richards and Millicent Richards, British Guiana; *m* 1940, Madree Elizabeth Williams; one *s* two *d*. *Educ:* Collegiate Sch.; Queen's Coll., Guyana. Called to the Bar, Middle Temple, 1946. Secondary School-teacher, 1930–43. Elected to House of Assembly, Bermuda, 1948; served numerous Select Cttees of Parliament; served on Commns; Member, Exec. Council (later Cabinet), 1963–75; Mem. of Govt responsible for Immigration, Labour and Social Security, 1968–71. Served on many Govt Boards; Chairman: Public Transportation Board; Transport Control Board. Bermuda Representative: CPA Confs, Lagos, 1962, Kuala Lumpur, 1971; Guyana's Independence Celebrations, 1966, Bahamas Independence Celebrations, 1973; Mem., Constitution Conf., 1966; Leader Bermuda Delegn, ILO Confs Geneva, 1969–71. Magistrate, 1958. Chm., Berkeley Educational Soc., 1956–72. Hon. Life Vice-Pres., Bermuda Football Assoc. Hon. LLD, Wilberforce, USA, 1960. *Recreations:* music, reading, walking. *Address:* Wilton, Keith Hall Road, Warwick East, Bermuda. *T:* 2–3645. *Clubs:* Somerset Cricket, Warwick Workman's, Blue Waters Anglers (Bermuda); Royal Hamilton Amateur Dinghy.
　　　　　　　　　　　　　　　　　Died 13 May 1991.

RICHARDS, Prof. Elfyn John, OBE 1958; FEng 1978; FRAeS; FIMechE; Research Professor, Southampton University, and Acoustical Consultant, 1975–84, then Emeritus Professor; *b* Barry, Glamorgan, South Wales, 28 Dec. 1914; *s* of Edward James Richards, Barry, schoolmaster, and of Catherine Richards; *m* 1941, Eluned Gwenddydd Jones (*d* 1978), Aberporth, Cardigan; three *d*; *m* 1979, Rita Alma Irving, Ruthin, Clwyd; *m* 1986, Olive Meakin (*d* 1989); *m* 1990, Miriam Davidson,

Romsey, Hants. *Educ:* Barry County School; Univ. Coll. of Wales, Aberystwyth (BSc); St John's Coll., Cambridge (MA). DSc (Wales), 1959. Research Asst, Bristol Aeroplane Company, 1938–39; Scientific Officer, National Physical Laboratory, Teddington, 1939–45, and Secretary, various Aeronautical Research Council sub-cttees; Chief Aerodynamicist and Asst Chief-Designer, Vickers Armstrong, Ltd, Weybridge, 1945–50; Prof. of Aeronautical Engineering, 1950–64, and Founder Dir, Inst. of Sound and Vibration Research, 1963–67, Univ. of Southampton, also Aeronautical Engineering Consultant; Vice-Chancellor, Loughborough Univ., 1967–75. Res. Prof., Florida Atlantic Univ., 1983. Member: SRC, 1970–74; Noise Adv. Council; Noise Research Council, ARC, 1968–71; Construction Research and Adv. Council, 1968–71; Inland Transport and Develt Council, 1968–71; Gen. Adv. Council of BBC (Chm. Midlands Adv. Council, 1968–71); Cttee of Scientific Advisory Council; Wilson Cttee on Problems of Noise; Planning and Transport Res. Adv. Council, 1971–. Chm., Univs Council for Adult Educn; President: British Acoustical Soc., 1968–70; Soc. of Environmental Engrs, 1971–73. Mem. Leics CC. Hon. FIOA 1978; Hon. Fellow Acoustical Soc. of America, 1980; Hon. FRAeS 1991. Hon. LLD Wales, 1973; Hon. DSc: Southampton, 1973; Heriot-Watt, 1983; Hon. DTech Loughborough, 1975. Taylor Gold Medal, RAeS, 1949; James Watt Medal, ICE, 1963; Silver Medal, RSA, 1971. *Publications:* books and research papers (250) in acoustics, aviation, education. *Address:* 53 The Harrage, Romsey, Hants SO51 8AE.　　　　　　　　　*Died 7 Sept. 1995.*

RICHARDS, Very Rev. Gwynfryn; Dean of Bangor, 1962–71; Archdeacon of Bangor, 1957–62; Rector of Llandudno, 1956–62; *b* 10 Sept. 1902; *er s* of Joshua and Elizabeth Ann Richards, Nantyffyllon, Glam; *m* 1935, Margery Phyllis Evans; one *s* one *d*. *Educ:* Universities of Wales, Oxford and Boston. Scholar, Univ. Coll., Cardiff, 1918–21; BSc (Wales), 1921; Jesus Coll., Oxford, 1921–23; Certificate, School of Geography, Oxford, 1922; BA 1st Cl. Hons School of Natural Science, 1923; MA 1928. In industry (USA), 1923–25. Boston Univ. Sch. of Theology, 1926–28; STB First Cl., 1928. Scholar and Travelling Fellow, 1928–29; Oxford, 1928–29; St Michael's Coll., Llandaff, 1929–30; deacon, 1930; priest, 1931; Curate of: Llanrhos, 1930–34; Aberystwyth, St Michael, 1934–38; Rector of Llanllyfni, 1938–49; Vicar of Conway with Gyffin, 1949–56. Canon of Bangor Cathedral, 1943–62, Treas., 1943–57; Examining Chaplain to Bp of Bangor, 1944–71; Rural Dean of Arllechwedd, 1953–57. Pantyfedwen Lectr, Univ. Coll., Aberystwyth, 1967. *Publications:* Ffurfiau Ordeinio Holl Eglwysi Cymru, 1943; Yr Hen Fam, 1952; Ein Hymraniadau Annedwydd, 1963; Gwir a Diogel Obaith, 1972; Ar Lawer Trywydd, 1973; A Fynn Esgyn, Mynn Ysgol, 1980; contrib. to Journal of the Historical Society of the Church in Wales, Nat. Library of Wales Jl, Trans of Caernarvonshire Hist. Soc. *Recreations:* gardening, photography, local history. *Address:* Llain Werdd, Llandegfan, Menai Bridge, Gwynedd LL59 5LY. *T:* Menai Bridge (0248) 713429.
　　　　　　　　　　　　　　　　　Died 30 Oct. 1992.

RICHARDS, Sir James (Maude), Kt 1972; CBE 1959; FSA 1980; architectural writer, critic and historian; Editor, Architectural Review, 1937–71; Editor, Architects' Journal, 1947–49 (editorial board, 1949–61); Architectural Correspondent, The Times, 1947–71; *b* 13 Aug. 1907; 2nd *s* of late Louis Saurin Richards and Lucy Denes (*née* Clarence); *m* 1st, 1936, Margaret (marr. diss., 1948), *d* of late David Angus; one *d* (one *s* decd); 2nd, 1954, Kathleen Margaret, (Kit), 2nd *d* of late Henry Bryan Godfrey-Faussett-Osborne, Queendown Warren, Sittingbourne, Kent, and widow of late Morland Lewis; (one *s* decd). *Educ:* Gresham's School, Holt; AA School of Architecture.

ARIBA, AADipl 1930. Studied and practised architecture in Canada and USA, 1930–31, London and Dublin, 1931–33; Asst Editor, The Architects' Jl, 1933; The Architectural Review, 1935; Editor, Publications Div., 1942, Director of Publications, Middle East, Cairo, 1943–46, MOI; Gen. Editor, The Architectural Press, 1946. Hoffman Wood Prof. of Architecture, Leeds Univ., 1957–59. Editor, European Heritage, 1973–75. Member: exec. cttee Modern Architectural Research Gp, 1946–54; AA Council, 1948–51, 1958–61, 1973–74; Advisory Council, Inst. of Contemporary Arts, 1947–68; Architecture Council, Festival of Britain, 1949–51; British Cttee, Internat. Union of Architects, 1950–66; Royal Fine Art Commn, 1951–66; Fine Art Cttee, Brit. Council, 1954–78; Council of Industrial Design, 1955–61; Min. of Transport (Worboys) Cttee on traffic signs, 1962–63; World Soc. of Ekistics, 1965–86; Council, Victorian Soc., 1965–; National Trust, 1977–83; Vice-Pres. Nat. Council on Inland Transport, 1963–; Exec. Cttee, Venice in Peril Fund, 1969–; Chm., Arts Council inquiry into provision for the arts in Ireland, 1974–76; British Cttee, Icomos, 1975–88. Broadcaster, television and sound (regular member, BBC Critics panel, 1948–68). FRSA 1970; Hon. AILA, 1955; Hon. FAIA, 1985. Chevalier (First Class), 1960, Comdr, 1985, Order of White Rose of Finland; Gold Medal, Mexican Institute of Architects, 1963; Bicentenary Medal, RSA, 1971. *Publications:* Miniature History of the English House, 1938; (with Eric Ravilious) High Street, 1938; Introduction to Modern Architecture, 1940, new edn 1970 (trans. seven langs); (with John Summerson) The Bombed Buildings of Britain, 1942; Edward Bawden, 1946; The Castles on the Ground, 1946, new enl. edn 1973; The Functional Tradition in Early Industrial Buildings, 1958; (ed) New Building in the Commonwealth, 1961; An Architectural Journey in Japan, 1963; Guide to Finnish Architecture, 1966; A Critic's View, 1970; (ed with Nikolaus Pevsner) The Anti-Rationalists, 1972; Planning and Redevelopment in London's Entertainment Area, 1973 (Arts Council report); The Professions: Architecture, 1974; (ed) Who's Who in Architecture: from 1400 to the present day, 1977; 800 Years of Finnish Architecture, 1978; Memoirs of an Unjust Fella (autobiog.), 1980; The National Trust Book of English Architecture, 1981; Goa, 1982; The National Trust Book of Bridges, 1984. *Recreations:* travel, topography. *Address:* 29 Fawcett Street, SW10 9AY. *T:* 071–352 9874. *Clubs:* Athenæum, Beefsteak.

Died 27 April 1992.

RICHARDS, John Arthur; Under-Secretary, Department of Education and Science, 1973–77; *b* 23 June 1918; *s* of late Alderman A. J. Richards and Mrs Annie Richards, Dulwich; *m* 1946, Sheelagh, *d* of late Patrick McWalter and Katherine McWalter, Balla, Co. Mayo; two *s* one *d*. *Educ:* Brockley Sch.; King's Coll., London. BA, AKC, Dip. in Educn. Hon. Sec., King's Coll. Union Soc., 1939. Served War: Captain RA; Directorate of Personnel Selection, War Office, 1945–46. Temp. Third Sec., Foreign Office, 1946; Staff, Hackney Downs Grammar Sch., 1948; Ministry of Education: Asst Principal and Principal, 1949 (Jt Sec., Secondary Schs Examinations Council, 1956–57); Asst Sec. (also Dept of Educn and Science), 1963–73. *Publications:* occasional verse and contribs to journals. *Recreations:* journalism, writing verse. *Address:* 14 Blacksmiths Hill, Sanderstead, Surrey CR2 9AY. *T:* 0181–657 1275. *Died 11 Oct. 1995.*

RICHARDS, Michael; Director, Samuel Montagu & Co. Ltd, 1960–85; *b* 4 Oct. 1915; *s* of Frank Richards and Jenny Charlotte (*née* Levinsen); *m* 1942, Lucy Helen Quirey; three *d*. *Educ:* Leeds Univ. (LLB). Qualified Solicitor, 1936. Partner, Ashurst, Morris Crisp & Co., Solicitors, City of London, 1936–54; Chm. and Man. Dir, Hart, Son & Co. Ltd, Merchant Bankers, 1954–60. Chm.,

Wood Hall Trust Ltd, 1950–82. *Recreations:* work, farming, collecting works of art. *Address:* Wood Hall, Shenley, Herts WD7 9AY. *T:* Radlett (0923) 856624.

Died 26 June 1994.

RICHARDSON, Cecil Antonio, (Tony); Director, Woodfall Film Productions Ltd, since 1958; *b* 5 June 1928; *s* of Clarence Albert and Elsie Evans Richardson; *m* 1962, Vanessa Redgrave, CBE (marr. diss. 1967); two *d*; one *d* by Grizelda Grimond. *Educ:* Wadham College, Oxford. Associate Artistic Dir, English Stage Co., Royal Court Theatre, 1956–64. *Plays* directed or produced: Look Back in Anger, 1956; The Chairs, 1957; Pericles and Othello (Stratford), 1958; The Entertainer, 1958; A Taste of Honey, NY, 1961; Luther, 1961; Semi-Detached, 1962; Arturo Ui, 1963; Natural Affection, 1963; The Milk Train Doesn't Stop Here Any More, 1963; The Seagull, 1964; St Joan of the Stockyards, 1964; Hamlet, 1968; The Threepenny Opera, Prince of Wales, 1972; I Claudius, Queen's, 1972; Antony and Cleopatra, Bankside Globe, 1973; Lady from the Sea, New York, 1977; As You Like It, Los Angeles, 1979. *Films* directed or produced: Look Back in Anger, 1958; The Entertainer, 1959; Saturday Night and Sunday Morning (prod), 1960; Taste of Honey, 1961; The Loneliness of the Long Distance Runner (prod and dir.), 1962; Tom Jones (dir.), 1962; Girl with Green Eyes (prod), 1964; The Loved One (dir.), 1965; Mademoiselle (dir.), 1965; The Sailor from Gibraltar (dir.), 1965; Red and Blue (dir.) 1966; The Charge of the Light Brigade (dir.), 1968; Laughter in the Dark (dir.), 1969; Hamlet (dir.), 1969; Ned Kelly (dir.), 1969; A Delicate Balance, 1972; Dead Cert, 1974; Joseph Andrews, 1977; A Death in Canaan, 1978; The Border, 1981; The Hotel New Hampshire, 1983. *Films for television:* Penalty Phase, 1986; Shadow on the Sun, 1988; Phantom of the Opera, 1989; Hills Like White Elephants, 1989; Blue Sky, 1990. *Posthumous publication:* Long Distance Runner: a memoir, 1993. *Recreations:* travel, tennis, birds, directing plays and films. *Address:* 1478 North King's Road, Los Angeles, Calif 90069, USA. *Died 14 Nov. 1991.*

RICHARDSON, Gen. Sir Charles (Leslie), GCB 1967 (KCB 1962; CB 1957); CBE 1945; DSO 1943; Member of the Army Board (Quartermaster General to the Forces, then Master-General of the Ordnance), 1965–71; *b* 11 Aug. 1908; *s* of late Lieutenant-Colonel C. W. Richardson, RA, and Mrs Richardson; *m* 1947, Audrey Styles (*née* Jorgensen); one *s* one *d* and one step *d*. *Educ:* Wellington College; Royal Military Acad., Woolwich (King's Medal); Cambridge Univ. Exhibitioner, Clare College, Cambridge, 1930; 1st Cl. Hons Mech Sciences Tripos; BA. Commissioned Royal Engineers, 1928; served France and Belgium, 1939–40; GSO1 Plans HQ, Eighth Army, 1942; BGS Eighth Army, 1943; Deputy Chief of Staff Fifth US Army, 1943; BGS Plans, 21st Army Group, 1944; Brigade Commander, 1953–54; Commandant, Royal Military College of Science, 1955–58; General Officer Commanding Singapore District, 1958–60; Director of Combat Development, War Office, 1960–61; Director-General of Military Training, 1961–63; General Officer Commanding-in-Chief, Northern Command, 1963–65; ADC (General) to the Queen, 1967–70; Chief Royal Engr, 1972–77. Col Comdt, RAOC, 1967–71. Consultant, International Computers Ltd, 1971–76. Treasurer, Kitchener Nat. Meml Fund, 1971–81; Chm., Gordon Boy's Sch., 1977–87. Legion of Merit (US), 1944. *Publications:* Flashback: a soldier's story, 1985; Send for Freddie, 1987; From Churchill's Secret Circle to the BBC: the biography of Gen. Sir Ian Jacob, 1991; contrib. to DNB. *Address:* The Stables, Betchworth, Surrey RH3 7AA. *Club:* Army and Navy. *Died 7 Feb. 1994.*

RICHARDSON, Brig. Charles Walter Philipps, DSO and Bar 1945; *b* 8 Jan. 1905; *s* of W. J. Richardson and E. C.

Philipps; *m* 1st, 1932, Joan Kathleen Constance Lang (from whom he obtained a divorce, 1946); one *s*; 2nd, 1946, Hon. Mrs Averil Diana Going; one *s*. *Educ:* RNC Osborne and Dartmouth; RMC Sandhurst. 2nd Lieut KOSB, 1924; served in Egypt, China and India; Bde Maj. 52nd (Lowland) Div., 1942; Comdr 6th Bn KOSB 15th (Scottish) Div., 1944–46; Colonel 1946; Comdt, Tactical Wing, School of Infantry, Warminster, 1947–48; GSO(1) Singapore District, 1948–49 (despatches, Malaya, 1948); Deputy Comdt Malay Regt, 1949; Dir Amphibious Warfare Trg, 1951; Comdr 158 Inf. Bde (TA), 1952; Brig. 1952; Dep. Comdr Lowland District, 1955–57; retired 1957. Order of Leopold and Belgian Croix de Guerre, 1945; King Haakon Victory Medal (Norway), 1945. *Recreation:* fishing. *Address:* Quintans, Steventon, Hants RG25 3BB. *T:* Dummer (0256) 397473.

Died 11 Feb. 1993.

RICHARDSON, Air Marshal Sir (David) William, KBE 1986; Chief Engineer, Royal Air Force, 1986–88, retired; *b* 10 Feb. 1932; *s* of Herbert Cyril Richardson and Emily Lydia Richardson; *m* 1954, Mary Winifred Parker; two *s* one *d*. *Educ:* Southend Grammar Sch.; Birmingham Univ. (BSc Maths); Cranfield Inst. of Technology (MSc Eng). CEng, FIMechE, FRAeS. Joined RAF from Univ. Air Sqdn, 1953 and completed flying and technical trng; served in Fighter Comd before attending Staff Coll. 1964; Staff: HQ Middle East, 1965–67; HQ RAF Germany, 1969–71; CO, RAF Colerne, 1971–74; RCDS, 1974; AO Engrg and Supply, HQ NEAF, 1975; Dir, Engrg and Supply Policy, 1976–78; AO Engrg and Supply, HQ RAF Germany, 1978–81; AOC Maintenance Gp, RAF Support Comd, 1981–83; AO Engrg, RAF Strike Comd, 1983–86. Dir, Aero and Industrial Technology, 1989–91. Trustee: MONITOR Charity for Motor Neurone Disease sufferers, 1989–; COMPAID Charity to promote the use of computers by the disabled. *Publications:* contrib. RUSI Jl. *Recreation:* formerly sailing (past Cdre, RAF Sailing Assoc.; past Pres., Assoc. of Service Yacht Clubs).

Died 13 March 1993.

RICHARDSON, Graham Edmund; Rector, Dollar Academy, Clackmannanshire, 1962–75; *b* 16 July 1913; *s* of H. W. Richardson, BSc, MIEE, AMIMechE, Studland, Dorset; *m* 1939, Eileen Cynthia, *d* of Lewis Beesly, FRCSE, Brightwalton, Newbury, Berks; one *s* one *d*. *Educ:* Tonbridge School; Strasbourg University; Queen's College, Oxford. Asst Master, Fettes College, Edinburgh, 1935–55; Housemaster, 1946–55; Headmaster, Melville College, Edinburgh, 1955–62. Mem., Scottish Adv. Cttee, IBA, 1968–73. *Recreations:* sailing, fishing, natural history. *Address:* Sunnyholme, Studland, Dorset.

Died 13 March 1992.

RICHARDSON, Ven. John Farquhar, MA; Archdeacon of Derby, 1952–73, then Emeritus; Chaplain to the Queen, 1952–76; First Residentiary Canon of Derby Cathedral, 1954–73; *b* 23 April 1905; 2nd *s* of late William Henry Richardson and Gertrude Richardson (*née* Walker); *m* 1936, Elizabeth Mary, *d* of Henry Roy Dean; one *s* two *d*. *Educ:* Winchester; Trinity Hall, Cambridge; Westcott House, Cambridge. Deacon, 1929; priest, 1930; Curate of Holy Trinity, Cambridge, 1929–32; Chaplain of Repton School, 1932–35; Curate of St Martin-in-the-Fields, 1935–36; Vicar of Christ Church, Hampstead, 1936–41; Rector of Bishopwearmouth, 1941–52; Rural Dean of Wearmouth, 1947–52. Proctor in Convocation, 1950–52; Hon. Canon of Durham, 1951–52. Vice Chm., Trent Coll., 1972–82; Vice Provost, Midlands Div., Woodard Schs, 1971–80. *Recreation:* golf. *Address:* 474 Kedleston Road, Derby DE3 2NE. *T:* Derby (0332) 559135. *Clubs:* Royal Automobile; Jesters; Hawks (Cambridge).

Died 29 April 1991.

RICHARDSON, Josephine; MP (Lab) Barking, since Feb. 1974; *b* 28 Aug. 1923; *d* of J. J. Richardson. *Educ:* Southend-on-Sea High Sch. for Girls. Formerly Mem. and Alderman, Hornsey BC. Contested (Lab): Monmouth, 1951, 1955; Hornchurch, 1959; Harrow E, 1964. Opposition spokesperson on women's rights, 1983–92. Mem., Labour Party NEC, 1979–91; a Vice President, Campaign for Nuclear Disarmament; Chairperson, Tribune Group, 1978–79 (Secretary, 1948–78; formerly Keep Left Group, then Bevan Group); Member: MSF; APEX. *Recreations:* politics, cooking. *Address:* House of Commons, SW1A 0AA. *T:* 071–219 5028.

Died 1 Feb. 1994.

RICHARDSON, Kenneth Albert; QC 1985; **His Honour Judge Richardson;** a Circuit Judge, since 1988; *b* 28 July 1926; *s* of Albert Robert Richardson and Ida Elizabeth Richardson (*née* Williams); *m* 1956, Dr Eileen Mary O'Cleary (*d* 1993), Galway; two *s* one *d* (and one *s* decd). *Educ:* Ruthin Sch.; Merton Coll., Oxford. MA (in English and Jurisprudence). Called to the Bar, Middle Temple, 1952 (Harmsworth Scholar; Bencher, 1975; Treasurer, 1993). Commissioned RWF, 1945 (attached 8th Punjab Regt). Junior Prosecuting Counsel to the Crown, 1967–73; Senior Prosecuting Counsel to the Crown, 1973–81; First Sen. Prosecuting Counsel to the Crown at CCC, 1981–85; a Recorder of the Crown Court, 1980–88. Member: Bar Council, 1972; Senate of the Inns and Bar, 1974–80. Chm., British Suzuki Inst., 1980–84; Pres., Porters Park Golf Club, 1980–82. *Recreations:* ski-ing, golf, sailing, music. *Clubs:* Garrick; Vincent's (Oxford).

Died 6 Dec. 1994.

RICHARDSON, Group Captain Michael Oborne; Royal Air Force, retired; *b* Holmfirth, Yorks, 13 May 1908; *s* of Rev. Canon G. L. Richardson, MA, BD, and Edith Maria (*née* Ellison); *m* 1st, 1935, Nellie Marguerita (*d* 1974), *d* of Walter Ross Somervell, Elizavetgrad, Russia; one *s* one *d*; 2nd, 1979, Gwendolyn Oenone Jane Bevan, *e d* of William Stuart Rashleigh, JP, Menabilly and Stoketon, Cornwall. *Educ:* Lancing Coll.; Keble Coll., Oxford; Guy's Hospital. BA 1929; MRCS, LRCP 1938; DPH 1955; MA Oxon 1963; DPhysMed 1964. Oxford House, Bethnal Green, 1930. Commissioned RAF, 1939; served at Kenley; War Service included HQ Fighter Comd (Unit), S Africa, Western Desert, Malta, Sicily, Italy (despatches); Post-war service in Germany and Aden and comdt various hosps and medical rehabilitation units; Commandant, Royal Star and Garter Home for Disabled Sailors, Soldiers and Airmen, 1967–73. OStJ 1965. *Recreation:* the countryside. *Address:* Tremethek, Penscott Lane, Tregorrick, St Austell, Cornwall PL26 7AH. *T:* St Austell (0726) 63768. *Clubs:* Royal Air Force; Webbe.

Died 6 April 1994.

RICHARDSON, Ronald Frederick, CBE 1973 (MBE 1945); Deputy Chairman, Electricity Council, 1972–76; *b* 1913; *s* of Albert F. Richardson and Elizabeth Jane (*née* Sayer); *m* 1946, Anne Elizabeth McArdle; two *s*. *Educ:* Coopers' Company's School; Northampton Engineering Inst.; Polytechnic Inst.; Administrative Staff College. Served War of 1939–45: Major, Field Park Company RE, 1942–46. Callenders Cables, 1929–36; Central London Electricity, 1936–39, 1946–48; London Electricity Board, 1948–52; British Electricity Authority, 1952–57; South Western Electricity Board, 1957–63; Chm., North Western Electricity Board, 1964–71. Chm., Nat. Inspection Council for Electrical Installation Contracting, 1969–70; Dep. Chm., NW Regional Council, CBI, 1971; Member: North West Economic Planning Council, 1965–70; Adv. Council on Energy Conservation, 1974–76; (part-time): NCB, 1975–77; Electricity Council, 1976; Price Commn, 1977–79. Member: Court of Manchester Univ., 1969–71; Council, 1970–71, Court, 1970–74, Salford Univ.;

Governor, William Temple Coll., 1971–74. *Recreations:* music, the open air. *Died 24 Dec. 1991.*

RICHARDSON, Tony; *see* Richardson, C. A.

RICHARDSON, Air Marshal Sir William; *see* Richardson, Air Marshal Sir D. W.

RICHARDSON, William Eric, CEng, FIEE, FIMgt; Chairman, South Wales Electricity Board, 1968–77; Member, Electricity Council, 1968–77; retired 1977; *b* 21 May 1915; *o s* of William Pryor and Elizabeth Jane Richardson, Hove, Sussex; *m* (she *d* 1975); one *s*; *m* 1976, Barbara Mary Leech. *Educ:* Royal Masonic Sch., Bushey. Engineer with Brighton Corp., 1934–37; Southampton Corp., 1937–39; Norwich Corp., 1939–46; Distribution Engr with Newport (Mon) Corp., 1946–48; Area Engr with S Wales Electricity Bd, 1948–57; Area Manager, 1957–65; Chief Commercial Engr, 1965–67; Dep. Chm., 1967–68. *Recreations:* sailing, golf, gardening. *Address:* 57 Allt-yr-Yn View, Newport, Gwent NP9 5DN. *T:* Newport (Gwent) (01633) 264388.

Died 26 Oct. 1995.

RICHNELL, Donovan Thomas, CBE 1973; Director General, British Library Reference Division, 1974–79; *b* 3 Aug. 1911; *o s* of Thomas Hodgson Richnell and Constance Margaret Richnell (*née* Allen); *m* 1957, Renée Norma Hilton; one *s* one *d*. *Educ:* St Paul's School; Corpus Christi Coll., Cambridge; University Coll., London (Fellow 1975). BA; FLA. Sub-Librarian, Royal Soc. Med., 1946–49; Dep. Librarian, London Univ. Library, 1949–60; Librarian, Univ. of Reading, 1960–67; Dir, and Goldsmiths' Librarian, Univ. of London Library, 1967–74. Library Association: Mem. Council, 1962–71; President 1970; Hon. Fellow 1979; Chm. of Council, Aslib, 1968–70. Member: Library Adv. Council for England, 1966–71, 1974–77; British Library Organising Cttee, 1971–73; Adv. Cttee for Scientific and Technical Information, 1970–74; British Library Bd, 1974–79; Chm., Standing Conf. of Nat. and Univ. Libraries, 1973–75. Hon. DLitt Loughborough, 1977. *Address:* 2 Queen Anne's Gardens, Bedford Park, W4 1TU.

Died 18 Feb. 1994.

RICKETTS, Maj.-Gen. Abdy Henry Gough, CBE 1952; DSO 1945; *b* 8 Dec. 1905; *s* of Lt-Col P. E. Ricketts, DSO, MVO, and L. C. Ricketts (*née* Morant); *m* 1932, Joan Warre, *d* of E. T. Close, Camberley; one *s* one *d*. *Educ:* Winchester. Sandhurst, 1924; Durham LI, 1925; Shanghai Defence Force, 1927; NW Frontier, India (medal and clasp), 1930; Burma "Chindit" campaign, 1944–45; Gen. Service Medal and clasp, Malaya, 1950; comd British Brigade, Korea, 1952; Comdr (temp. Maj.-Gen.), Cyprus District, 1955–56. Col, Durham LI, 1965–68; Dep. Col, The Light Infantry (Durham), 1968–70. DL Somerset, 1968–90. Officer, Legion of Merit (USA), 1953. *Address:* The Old Rectory, Pylle, Shepton Mallet, Som BA4 6TE. *T:* Ditcheat (074986) 248. *Died 16 Jan. 1993.*

RICKS, Sir John (Plowman), Kt 1964; Solicitor to the Post Office, 1953–72; *b* 3 April 1910; *s* of late James Young Ricks; *m* 1st, 1936, May Celia (*d* 1975), *d* of late Robert William Chubb; three *s*; 2nd, 1976, Mrs Doreen Ilsley. *Educ:* Christ's Hosp.; Jesus Coll., Oxford. Admitted Solicitor, 1935; entered Post Office Solicitor's Department, 1935; Assistant Solicitor, Post Office, 1951. *Address:* 8 Sunset View, Barnet, Herts EN5 4LB. *T:* 081–449 6114.

Died 29 Dec. 1991.

RIDDOCH, John Haddow, (Ian), CMG 1963; Under-Secretary, Board of Trade, 1966–69, retired; *b* 4 Feb. 1909; *s* of Joseph Riddoch, Gourock, Renfrewshire; *m* 1st, 1938, Isobel W. Russell (*d* 1972); one *s* two *d*; 2nd, 1975, Margaret C. McKimmie. *Educ:* Greenock Acad.; Glasgow Univ. Entered Inland Revenue Dept (Inspectorate of

Taxes), 1932; Asst Principal in Air Ministry (Dept of Civil Aviation), 1939; Principal, 1942; Asst Sec., Min. of Civil Aviation, 1945; Under-Sec., Min. of Transport and Civil Aviation, 1957, Min. of Aviation, 1959; United Kingdom Representative on the Council of the ICAO, 1957–62 (First Vice-Pres. of Council, 1961–62); Under-Sec., Min. of Aviation, 1962–66. *Recreations:* music, bowls, gardening. *Address:* 10 The Fairway, New Barnet, Herts EN5 1HN. *Died 6 May 1991.*

RIDGWAY, Gen. Matthew Bunker, DSC (with Oak Leaf Cluster); DSM (with 3rd Oak Leaf Cluster); Silver Star (with Oak Leaf Cluster); Legion of Merit; Bronze Star Medal V (with Oak Leaf Cluster); Purple Heart; Hon. KCB 1955 (Hon. CB 1945); Chairman of The Mellon Institute of Industrial Research 1955–60, retired; *b* 3 March 1895; *s* of Thomas Ridgway and Ruth Starbuck Bunker; *m* 1st, 1917; two *d*; 2nd, 1930; one *d*; 3rd, 1947, Mary Anthony; (one *s* decd). *Educ:* United States Military Academy, 1913–17. Inf. School (Company Officers' Course), 1924–25; Mem. Am. Electoral Commn, Nicaragua, 1927–28; Mem. Commn on Bolivian-Paraguayan boundary dispute, 1929; Inf. School (Advanced Course), 1929–30; Liaison Officer to Govt in Philippine Is, Tech. Adviser to Gov.-Gen., 1932–33; Comd and Gen. Staff School, 1933–35; Asst Chief of Staff, 6th Corps Area, 1935–36; Dep. Chief of Staff, Second Army, 1936; Army War College, 1936–37; Assistant Chief of Staff, Fourth Army, 1937–39; accompanied Gen. Marshall on special mission to Brazil, 1939; War Plans Div., War Department Gen. Staff, 1939–42; Asst Div. Comdr, 82nd Inf. Div., 1942; Comdr 1942; Comdg Gen. 82nd Airborne Div., Sicily, Italy, Normandy, 1942–44; Comdr 18th Airborne Corps, Belgium, France, Germany, 1944–45; Comdr Luzon Area Command, 1945; Comdr Medit. Theater, and Dep. Supreme Allied Comdr, Medit., 1945–46; Senior US Army Member Military Staff Cttee, UN, 1946–48; Chm. Inter-Am. Defense Bd, 1946–48; C-in-C Caribbean Command, 1948–49; Dep. Army Chief of Staff for Admin, 1949–50 (and Chm. Inter-Am. Defense Bd, 1950); Comdg Gen. Eighth Army in Korea, 1950–51; Comdr UN Comd in Far East, C-in-C of Far East Comd and Supreme Comdr for Allied Powers in Japan, 1951–52; Supreme Allied Comdr, Europe, 1952–53; Chief of Staff, United States Army, 1953–55, retired. Many American and foreign decorations. *Died 26 July 1993.*

RIDING, Laura; *see* Jackson, L. R.

RIDLEY OF LIDDESDALE, Baron *cr* 1992 (Life Peer), of Willimontswick in the County of Northumberland; **Nicholas Ridley,** PC 1983; *b* 17 Feb. 1929; *yr s* of 3rd Viscount Ridley, CBE, TD and Ursula (OBE 1953) (*d* 1967), 2nd *d* of Sir Edwin Landseer Lutyens, OM, KCIE, architect; *m* 1st, 1950, Hon. Clayre Campbell (marr. diss. 1974), 2nd *d* of 4th Baron Stratheden and Campbell, CBE; three *d*; 2nd, 1979, Judy Kendall. *Educ:* Eton; Balliol College, Oxford. Civil Engineering Contractor, Brims & Co. Ltd, Newcastle upon Tyne, 1950–59, Director, 1954–70; Director: Heenan Group Ltd, 1961–68; Ausonia Finance, 1973–79; Marshall Andrew Ltd, 1975–79. Contested (C) Blyth, Gen. Election, 1955; MP (C) Cirencester and Tewkesbury Div. of Glos, 1959–92. PPS to Minister of Education, 1962–64; Delegate to Council of Europe and WEU, 1962–66; Parly Sec., Min. of Technology, June-Oct. 1970; Parly Under-Sec. of State, DTI, 1970–72; Minister of State, FCO, 1979–81; Financial Sec. to HM Treasury, 1981–83; Secretary of State: for Transport, 1983–86; for the Envmt, 1986–89; for Trade and Industry, 1989–90. Mem., Royal Commn on Historical Manuscripts, 1967–79. *Publication:* My Style of Government: the Thatcher years, 1991. *Recreations:*

painting, architecture, gardening, fishing. *Address:* Kilnholme, Penton, Carlisle CA6 5QZ.

Died 4 March 1993.

RIDLEY, Sir Sidney, Kt 1953; Emeritus Fellow, St John's College, Oxford, 1969 (Fellow, 1962); Indian Civil Service, retired; *b* 26 March 1902; *s* of John William and Elizabeth Janet Ridley; *m* 1929, Dorothy Hoole (*d* 1987); three *d. Educ:* Lancaster Royal Grammar Sch.; Sidney Sussex Coll., Cambridge. MA Cantab, MA Oxon. Joined ICS, 1926; Finance Secretary, Govt of Sind, 1936; Secretary to the Agent-General for India in South Africa, 1936–40; Chief Secretary, Govt of Sind, 1944; Commissioner: Northern Division, Ahmedabad, 1946; Central Div., Poona, 1947; Revenue Commissioner in Sind and Secretary to Government, 1947–54. Representative of W Africa Cttee in Ghana, Sierra Leone and the Gambia, 1957–60; Domestic Bursar, St John's Coll., Oxford, 1960–68. *Recreation:* golf.

Died 9 Oct. 1993.

RIE, Dame Lucie, DBE 1991 (CBE 1981; OBE 1968); studio potter since 1927; *b* 16 March 1902; *d* of Prof. Dr Benjamin and Gisela Gomperz; *m* 1926, Hans Rie (marr. diss. 1940). *Educ:* Vienna Gymnasium (matriculate); Kunstgewerbe Schule. Pottery workshop: Vienna, 1927; London, 1939. Work included in V&A Museum, Fitzwilliam Museum, Cambridge Museum, Boymans-van Beuningen Museum, Stedelijk Museum, Museum of Modern Art, NY, Aust. Nat. Gall., Canberra, and other public collections in England and abroad. Exhibitions include: Arts Council retrospective, 1967; (with Hans Coper) Boymans-van Beuningen Museum, 1967; Expo '70, Osaka, 1970; (with Hans Coper) Museum of Art and Crafts, Hamburg, 1972; Hetjens Museum, Düsseldorf, 1978; retrospective, Sainsbury Centre and V&A Mus, 1981–82; one-woman, Sogetsu-Kai Foundn, Tokyo, 1989; (with Hans Coper and pupils) Sainsbury Centre, 1990, Fitzwilliam Mus., Cambridge, 1991; Crafts Council, 1992; (with Hans Coper) Metropolitan Mus. of Art, NY, 1994–95. Gold medals: Internat. Exhibn, Brussels, 1935; Trienniale, Milan, 1936, 1954; Internat. Exhibn, Munich, 1964. Hon. Doctor, Royal College of Art, 1969; Hon. DLitt Heriot-Watt, 1992. *Relevant publications:* Lucie Rie (ed by John Houston), 1981; Lucie Rie (biography by Tony Birks), 1987, rev. edn 1994.

Died 1 April 1995.

RIMBAULT, Brig. Geoffrey Acworth, CBE 1954; DSO 1945; MC 1936; DL; Director, Army Sport Control Board, 1961–73; *b* 17 April 1908; *s* of late Arthur Henry Rimbault, London; *m* 1933, Joan (*d* 1991), *d* of late Thomas Hallet-Fry, Beckenham, Kent; one *s. Educ:* Dulwich College. 2nd Lieut, The Loyal Regt (N Lancs), 1930; served: India, Waziristan, 1931–36; Palestine, 1937; Staff Coll., Camberley; N Africa, Anzio, Italy and Palestine, 1939–46; Chief Instructor, RMA Sandhurst, 1950–51; Chief of Staff, E Africa, 1952–54; comd 131 Inf. Bde, 1955–57; comd Aldershot Garrison, 1958–61. Colonel, The Loyal Regt, 1959–70. Life Vice-Pres., Surrey CCC (Pres., 1982–83). Liveryman, Mercers' Co., 1961, Master, 1970–71. DL Surrey, 1971. *Recreations:* cricket, tennis, golf, shooting. *Address:* 10 Clarke Place, Elmbridge, Cranleigh, Surrey GU6 8TH. *T:* Cranleigh (0483) 271207. *Clubs:* Army and Navy, MCC.

Died 20 Oct. 1991.

RIMINGTON, Claude, MA, PhD Cantab, DSc London; FRS 1954; Emeritus Professor of Chemical Pathology, University of London; Head of Department of Chemical Pathology, University College Hospital Medical School, 1945–67; *b* 17 Nov. 1902; *s* of George Garthwaite Rimington, Newcastle upon Tyne; *m* 1929, Soffi (decd), *d* of Clemet Andersen, Askerøy, Lyngør, Norway; one *d. Educ:* Emmanuel College, Cambridge. Benn W. Levy

Research Scholar, Univ. of Cambridge, 1926–28; Biochemist, Wool Industries Research Association, Leeds, 1928–30; Empire Marketing Board Senior Research Fellow, then Scientific Research Officer, Division of Veterinary Services, Govt of Union of South Africa, at Onderstepoort Veterinary Research Laboratory, Pretoria, 1931–37; Biochemist, National Institute for Medical Research, Medical Research Council, London, 1937–45. Guest Res. Worker, Inst. for Cancer Res., Norwegian Radium Hosp., Oslo, 1985–. Mem., Norwegian Acad. of Sci. and Letters, 1988. Hon. FRCP Edinburgh, 1967; Hon. Mem. Brit. Assoc. of Dermatology, 1967. Graham Gold Medal, Univ. of London, 1967. Knight (1st Class), Royal Norwegian Order of Merit, 1989. *Publications:* (with A. Goldberg), Diseases of Porphyrin Metabolism, 1962; (with M. R. Moore, K. E. L. McColl and Sir Abraham Goldberg) Disorders of Porphyrin Metabolism, 1987; numerous biochemical and scientific papers. *Recreations:* sailing, languages, Scandinavian literature. *Address:* Fallanveien 30B, Seksjon 62, 0495 Oslo, Norway.

Died 8 Aug. 1993.

RINGWOOD, Prof. Alfred Edward, FAA 1966; FRS 1972; Professor of Geochemistry, Australian National University, since 1967; *b* 19 April 1930; *s* of Alfred Edward Ringwood and Wilhelmena Grace Bruce Ringwood (*née* Robertson); *m* 1960, Gun Ivor Carlsson, Halsingborg, Sweden; one *s* one *d. Educ:* Hawthorn Central Sch., Melbourne; Geelong Grammar Sch.; Melbourne Univ. BSc 1950, MSc 1953, PhD 1956, Melbourne. Research Fellow, Geochemistry, Harvard Univ., 1957–58; Australian National University: Sen. Res. Fellow, 1959; Sen. Fellow, 1960; Personal Prof., 1963; Dir, Res. Sch. of Earth Scis, 1978–84. Lectures: Clark Meml, Royal Soc., NSW, 1969; William Smith, Geol Soc. of London, 1973; Vernadsky, USSR Acad. of Scis, 1975; Centenary, Chem. Soc., London, 1977 (also Medal); Foster Hewitt, Lehigh Univ., Penn, USA, 1978; Matthew Flinders, Australian Acad. of Sci., 1978; Pawsey Meml, Aust. Inst. of Physics, 1980; Sir Maurice Mawby Meml, Mineralogical Soc., Vic, 1981; Hallimond, Mineralogical Soc. of GB, 1983; Bakerian, Royal Soc., 1983; Alix G. Mautner Meml, UCLA, 1990. Commonwealth and Foreign Mem., Geol Soc., London, 1967; Fellow, Amer. Geophysical Union, 1969; Vice-Pres., Australian Acad. of Science, 1971. For. Associate, Nat. Acad. of Scis of Amer., 1975; Hon. Mem., All-Union Mineralogical Soc., USSR, 1976. Hon. DSc Göttingen, 1987. Internat. Co-operation Year Medal, Govt of Canada, 1965; Mineralogical Soc. of America Award, 1967; Britannica Australia Award for Science, 1969; Rosentiel Award, AAAS, 1971; Werner Medal, German Mineralogical Soc., 1972; Bowie Medal, American Geophysical Union, 1974; Day Medal, Geological Soc. of America, 1974; Mueller Medal, Aust. and NZ Assoc. for Advancement of Sci., 1975; Holmes Medal, European Union of Geosciences, 1985; Gold Medal for Research, Royal Soc., Vic, 1985; Wollaston Medal, Geol Soc. Lond., 1988; Ingerson Award, Internat. Assoc. Cosmochem., Geochem., 1988; Goldschmidt Award, Geochem. Soc., 1991; Feltrinelli Internat. Award, Italian Nat. Acad., 1991. *Publications:* Composition and Petrology of the Earth's Mantle, 1975; Safe Disposal of High Level Nuclear Reactor Wastes: a new strategy, 1978; Origin of Earth and Moon, 1979; numerous papers in learned jls dealing with nature of earth's interior, phase transformations under high pressures, origin and evolution of earth, moon, planets and meteorites, and safe immobilization of high level nuclear reactor wastes. *Recreations:* music, travel. *Address:* 3 Vancouver Street, Red Hill, Canberra, ACT 2603, Australia. *T:* Canberra (62) 953635.

Died 12 Nov. 1993.

RIPLEY, Sydney William Leonard; Member, Greater London Council (Kingston-upon-Thames Borough), 1964–86; *b* 17 July 1909; *o s* of late Leonard Ripley; *m* 1st, 1934, Doris Emily (from whom he obtained a divorce, 1966), *d* of late William Gray; one *s* two *d*; 2nd, 1972, Mrs Pida Polkinghorne, *d* of Capt. Peter Russell. *Educ:* King's School, Canterbury; London. Served War of 1939–45, with RAF, Flight-Lieut (despatches). Contested (C) Ipswich, 1950, Watford, 1951; Chairman Malden and Coombe Conservative Assoc., 1938–49, Pres., 1950–; Vice-Pres., Kingston Division, 1955–79, Pres., 1979–. Formerly Chairman Leonard Ripley and Co. Ltd and other printing and outdoor advertising companies, resigned 1973; Dir, Mills and Allen Ltd, 1970–73 (Consultant, 1975–). Member, Malden and Coombe Borough Council, 1938–48, formerly Chm. Finance Cttee; CC 1946, CA 1955, Surrey; Vice-Chm. Surrey CC, 1956–59, Chm., 1959–62; Chm. General Purposes Cttee, 1952–59; Chm., Finance Cttee, 1962–64; Mem., Surrey Jt Standing Cttee, 1959–65; County Council rep. on Metrop. Water Bd, 1956–65; County Councils Assoc., 1958–65; Surrey T&AFA, 1959–65; Governor Westminster Hosp., 1963–65; Jt Dep. Leader, Cons. Opposition, GLC, 1964–66; GLC rep. on Surrey T&AFA, 1965–68; London Tourist Board, 1965–68; Thames Water Authority, 1975–86; Chm., Open Spaces and Recreation Cttee, GLC, 1977–81. Chm., SW Regional Hosp. Bd, 1963–65. Freeman, City of London. JP, 1959–69, DL 1960, Surrey; DL Greater London, 1966–84. *Recreations:* golf, swimming, tennis. *Address:* Apt 145, 3 Whitehall Court, SW1A 2EL. *Clubs:* Brooks's, Carlton.

Died 7 June 1991.

RISHBETH, John, OBE 1985; ScD; FRS 1974; Reader in Plant Pathology, University of Cambridge, 1973–84, then Emeritus; Fellow of Corpus Christi College, Cambridge, since 1964; *b* 10 July 1918; *e s* of late Prof. Oswald Henry Theodore Rishbeth and Kathleen (*née* Haddon), Cambridge; *m* 1946, Barbara Sadler; one *s* one *d*. *Educ:* St Lawrence Coll., Ramsgate; Christ's Coll., Cambridge. MA, PhD, ScD (Cantab). Frank Smart Prize, 1940, and Studentship, 1944, 1946, in Botany. Chemist, Royal Ordnance Factories, 1940–43; Bacteriologist, Scientific Adviser's Div., Min. of Food, 1943–45; Demonstrator in Botany, Univ. of Cambridge, 1947–49; Plant Pathologist, West Indian Banana Research Scheme, 1950–52; Lectr in Botany, Univ. of Cambridge, 1953–73. Visiting Prof. in Forest Pathology, N Carolina State Univ., 1967. Hon. Dr agro Royal Veterinary and Agricl Univ., Copenhagen, 1976. *Publications:* papers on: root diseases, especially of trees, caused by fungi; biological control. *Recreations:* hill walking, tennis. *Address:* Fairfield, Gazeley Lane, Cambridge CB2 2HB. *T:* Cambridge (0223) 841298. *Club:* Hawks (Cambridge). *Died 1 June 1991.*

RISSON, Maj.-Gen. Sir Robert Joseph Henry, Kt 1970; CB 1958; CBE 1945 (OBE 1942); DSO 1942; ED 1948; Chairman Melbourne and Metropolitan Tramways Board, 1949–70; Chairman, National Fitness Council of Victoria, 1961–71; *b* 20 April 1901; *s* of late Robert Risson; *m* 1934, Gwendolyn, *d* of late C. A. Spurgin; no *c*. *Educ:* Gatton High Sch.; Univ. of Queensland. BE (Civil); FICE; FIEAust; FAIM. Served AIF, War of 1939–45: GOC 3 Div. (Australian), 1953–56; Citizen Military Forces Member, Australian Military Board, 1957–58. Chief Commissioner, Boy Scouts, Victoria, 1958–63; Pres., Instn Engineers, Australia, 1962–63. OStJ 1966. *Address:* 39 Somers Street, Burwood, Victoria 3125, Australia. *Clubs:* Australian, Naval and Military (Melbourne); United Service (Brisbane). *Died 18 July 1992.*

RITCHIE, Charles Stewart Almon, CC 1972; FRSL 1982; *b* 23 Sept. 1906; *s* of William Bruce Almon Ritchie, KC and Lilian Constance Harriette Ritchie (*née* Stewart), both of Halifax, Nova Scotia; *m* 1948, Sylvia Catherine Beatrice Smellie; no *c*. *Educ:* University of King's College; Ecole Libre des Sciences Politiques, Paris. BA, MA Oxford 1929; MA Harvard, 1930. Joined Dept of External Affairs, 3rd Sec. Ottawa, 1934; 3rd Sec., Washington, 1936; 2nd Sec., London, 1939; 1st Sec., London, 1943; 1st Sec., Ottawa, 1945; Counsellor, Paris, 1947; Asst Under-Secretary of State for External Affairs, Ottawa, 1950; Deputy Under-Secretary of State for External Affairs, 1952; Ambassador to Federal Republic of Germany, Bonn, and Head of Military Mission, Berlin, 1954; Permanent Rep. to UN, New York 1958; Ambassador of Canada to the United States, 1962; Ambassador and Permanent Representative of Canada to the North Atlantic Council, 1966–67; Canadian High Comr in London, 1967–71; Special Adviser to Privy Council, Canada, 1971–73. Hon. DCL: Univ. of King's College, Halifax, NS; McGill Univ., Montreal. Hon. Fellow, Pembroke College, Oxford. *Publications:* 4 vols of diaries: The Siren Years: undiplomatic diaries 1937–1945, 1974; An Appetite for Life: the education of a young diplomat, 1978; Diplomatic Passport, 1981; Storm Signals, 1983; My Grandfather's House, 1987. *Address:* Apt 10, 216 Metcalfe Street, Ottawa K2P 1R1, Canada. *Clubs:* Brooks's, Beefsteak; Rideau (Ottawa). *Died 8 June 1995.*

RITCHIE, Douglas Malcolm; Chairman (formerly Managing Director), and Chief Executive Officer, British Alcan Aluminium, since 1986; *b* Parry Sound, Ont, 8 Jan. 1941; *s* of Ian David Ritchie and Helen Mary Ritchie (*née* Jamieson); *m* 1965, Cydney Ann Brown; three *s*. *Educ:* McGill University (BSc 1962, MBA 1966). Alcan Group Cos, 1966–73; Vice-Pres. Gen. Manager, 1973–75, Exec. Vice-Pres., 1975–78, Alcan Canada Products; Corp. Vice-Pres., Aluminium Co. Can., 1978–80; Exec. Vice-Pres., 1980–82, Pres., 1982–86, Alcan Smelters & Chems; Dir and Exec. Vice-Pres., Alcan Aluminium, Cleveland, 1985–86. Non-executive Director: Laurentian Gp Corp., Montreal, 1988–; Laurentian Financial Group plc (formerly Laurentian Life), 1989–. *Address:* Chalfont Park, Gerrards Cross, Bucks SL9 0QB. *Died 17 Aug. 1993.*

RITCHIE, Horace David; Professor of Surgery, University of London, 1964–85, then Emeritus; Director of the Surgical Unit at The London Hospital, 1964–85; *b* 24 Sept. 1920; *m* 1953, Jennifer Prentice (marr. diss.); three *s*; *m* 1990, Elizabeth Thompson. *Educ:* Universities of Glasgow, Cambridge and Edinburgh. Dean, London Hosp. Med. Coll. and Dental Sch., 1982–83. *Publications:* contribs to various scientific journals. *Club:* Athenæum. *Died 21 Dec. 1993.*

RITCHIE, Sir James Edward Thomson, 2nd Bt, *cr* 1918 (2nd creation); TD 1943 (2 clasps); FRSA; Chairman M. W. Hardy & Co. Ltd, 1948–78; Director, Wm Ritchie & Son (Textiles) Ltd; Member Court of Assistants, Merchant Taylors' Co. (Master, 1963–64); *b* 16 June 1902; *s* of Sir James William Ritchie, 1st Bt (*er s* of Sir James Thomson Ritchie, 1st Bt of Shanklin, IOW), and 1st wife, Ada Bevan, *d* of late Edward ap Rees Bryant; *S* father, 1937; *m* 1st, 1928, Esme Phyllis (*d* 1939), *o d* of late J. M. Oldham, Ormidale, Ascot; 2nd, 1936, Rosemary, *yr d* of late Col Henry Streatfeild, DSO, TD; two *d*. *Educ:* Rugby; The Queen's Coll., Oxford. Joined Inns of Court Regt, 1936; commissioned, 1938; served 1939–45 (CMF 1944–45), various staff and regimental appts; Lt-Col 1945; re-commissioned, 1949, to command 44 (Home Counties) Div. Provost Co. RCMP (TA); retired 1953. Co-opted Mem. Kent TA&AFA (Mem. General Purposes Cttee), 1953–68. Chm., Chatwood-Milner (formerly Milners Safe Co. Ltd), 1937–70; Director: Caledonian Insurance Co. (London Bd), 1951–67; Guardian Assurance Co. Ltd (Local London Bd, 1967–71). Pres., Royal British Legion,

Ashford (Kent) Br., 1952–75; Patron, Ashford and Dist Caledonian Society. Chm. Finance and General Purposes Cttee and joint Hon. Treas., London School of Hygiene and Tropical Medicine, Univ. of London, 1951–61; co-opted Mem. Bd of Management and Finance and Gen. Purposes Cttee, 1964–67. *Heir:* none.

Died 20 March 1991 (ext).

RITCHIE, (James) Martin; Chairman: British Enkalon Ltd, 1975–83; Haymills Holdings Ltd, 1977–83; Director, Sun Alliance and London Insurance Ltd, 1970–87; *b* 29 May 1917; *s* of late Sir James Ritchie, CBE and Lady (Mary) Ritchie (*née* Gemmell); *m* 1939, Noreen Mary Louise Johnston; three *s. Educ:* Strathallan Sch., Perthshire. Joined Andrew Ritchie & Son Ltd, Glasgow, corrugated fibre container manufrs, 1934; Dir, 1938. TA Officer, 1938; served War of 1939–45: HAA Regt; Capt. 1941; psc 1943; DAA&QMG, MEF, Middle East, 1944–45 (Maj.). Rejoined Andrew Ritchie & Son Ltd, then part of Eburite Organisation; Man. Dir, 1950; Gen. Man., Bowater-Eburite Ltd, on merger with Bowater Organisation, 1956; Bowater Paper Corp. Ltd: Dir, 1959; Man. Dir, 1964; Dep. Chm. and Man. Dir, 1967; Chm. 1969–72. FIMgt (FBIM 1971); FRSA 1971. *Recreations:* golf, fishing. *Address:* Tilehouse, Scotswood Close, Beaconsfield, Bucks HP9 2LJ. *T:* Beaconsfield (0494) 676517. *Club:* Denham Golf. *Died 3 June 1993.*

RIVET, Prof. Albert Lionel Frederick, FBA 1981; Professor of Roman Provincial Studies, University of Keele, 1974–81, then Emeritus; *b* 30 Nov. 1915; *s* of Albert Robert Rivet, MBE and Rose Mary Rivet (*née* Bulow); *m* 1947, Audrey Catherine Webb; one *s* one *d. Educ:* Felsted Sch. (schol.); Oriel Coll., Oxford. BA 1938, MA 1946. FSA 1953; FSAScot 1959. Schoolmaster, 1938–39; ARP, 1939–40; mil. service, mainly in E Africa, 1940–46 (Major, Royal Signals); bookseller, 1946–51; Asst Archaeology Officer, Ordnance Survey, 1951–64; Keele University: Lectr in Classics, 1964–67; Reader in Romano-British Studies, 1967–74. Member: Royal Commn on Historical Monuments (England), 1979–85; Exec. Cttee, British Sch. at Rome, 1974–83. Pres., Soc. for Promotion of Roman Studies, 1977–80. Corresp. Mem., German Archaeol Inst., 1960–. Editor, Proc. of Soc. of Antiquaries of Scotland, 1961–64. *Publications:* Town and Country in Roman Britain, 1958, 2nd edn 1964; (ed) The Iron Age in Northern Britain, 1966; (ed) The Roman Villa in Britain, 1969; (with C. C. Smith) The Place-Names of Roman Britain, 1979; Gallia Narbonensis, 1988; contribs to books, atlases, encyclopaedias and learned journals. *Recreation:* conversation. *Address:* 7 Springpool, Keele, Staffs ST5 5BN.

Died 6 Sept. 1993.

ROBARTS, Eric Kirkby; *b* 20 Jan. 1908; *s* of Charles Martin Robarts and Flora Robarts (*née* Kirkby); *m* 1930, Iris Lucy Swan; five *d. Educ:* Bishops Stortford Coll.; Herts Inst. of Agriculture. Ran family business, C. M. Robarts & Son, until Aug. 1942; joined Express Dairy Co. Ltd, 1942: Dir, 1947–73; Man. Dir, 1960–73; Dep. Chm., 1966; Chm., 1967–73. FRSA; FBIM. *Recreations:* hunting, shooting. *Address:* Frithcote, Watford Road, Northwood, Middx. *T:* Northwood (0923) 822533. *Club:* Farmers'. *Died 30 July 1992.*

ROBERGE, Guy, QC (Can.); Counsel, McCarthy Tétrault, Ottawa (formerly Clarkson Tétrault), Barristers and Solicitors, since 1982; *b* 26 Jan. 1915; *s* of P. A. Roberge and Irène Duchesneau; *m* 1957, Marie Raymond; one *s* one *d. Educ:* Laval Univ., Quebec. Called to Bar of Quebec, 1937; Mem., Quebec Legislative Assembly, 1944–48; Mem., Restrictive Trade Practices Commn of Canada, 1955–57; Chm. and Chief Exec. Officer, Nat. Film Bd of Canada, 1957–66; Agent-General for Govt of PQ in UK, 1966–71; Vice-Pres. (Law), Canadian Transport

Commn, 1971–81. Hon. DCL, Bishop's Univ., 1967; Hon. doctorat d'université, Laval Univ., 1975. *Address:* 555 Wilbrod, Ottawa, Ontario K1N 5R4, Canada. *Club:* Rideau (Ottawa). *Died 21 June 1991.*

ROBERTS, Dr Albert, MSc, PhD; CEng; Head of Department of Mining Engineering, University of Nevada, 1969–75, retired 1975; *b* 25 April 1911; British; *m* 1938, May Taberner; two *s* one *d. Educ:* Wigan Mining and Techn. College. Mining Engr, Wigan Coal Corp., 1931–35, 1938–40; Ashanti Goldfields Corp., 1935–38; Lecturer: Sunderland Techn. Coll., 1940–45; Nottingham Univ., 1945–55; Sheffield Univ., 1955; Dir, Postgraduate Sch. of Mining, Sheffield Univ., 1956–69. Ed., Internat. Jl of Rock Mechanics and Mining Sciences, 1964–68. *Publications:* Geological Structures, 1946; Underground Lighting, 1959; Mine Ventilation, 1959; Mineral Processing, 1965; Geotechnology, 1977; Applied Geotechnology, 1981. *Recreation:* music. *Died 19 March 1992.*

ROBERTS, Ernest Alfred Cecil; *b* 20 April 1912; *s* of Alfred and Florence Roberts; *m* 1st, 1938, Helena Morris (marr. diss.); one *s* one *d;* 2nd, 1953, Joyce Longley; one *d. Educ:* St Chad's Boys' Elementary Sch., Shrewsbury. Engineer, 1925–57; Assistant General Secretary, AUEW, 1957–77. MP (Lab) Hackney North and Stoke Newington, 1979–87. Former Chairman: PLP Health and Social Security Cttee; Lab. Party Parly Assoc. Tom Mann Gold Medal for services to trade unionism, 1943; Special Award for Merit, AEU, 1994. *Publication:* Workers' Control, 1973. *Recreations:* work and politics, reading. *Died 28 Aug. 1994.*

ROBERTS, Air Cdre Sir Geoffrey Newland, Kt 1973; CBE 1946; AFC 1942; Hon. FRAeS; company director, retired; *b* Inglewood, Taranaki, New Zealand, 8 Dec. 1906; *s* of Charles Oxford Roberts, England, and Hilda Marion Newland, New Zealand; *m* 1934, Phyllis Hamilton Bird; one *s* one *d. Educ:* New Plymouth Boys' High Sch., New Plymouth, Taranaki, NZ. In commerce, NZ, 1924–28; RAF, England/India, 1928–34; commerce, UK, 1935–36; commerce, NZ, 1936–39; served War: RNZAF, NZ and Pacific (final rank Air Cdre), 1939–46; Air New Zealand: General Manager, 1946–58; Dir, 1958–65; Chm., 1965–75. Chairman: Lion Breweries Ltd Mimiwhangata Farm Park Trust Board, 1975–86; Kaipara Edible Oils Refinery Ltd, 1978–82; Director: MFL Mutual Fund Ltd, 1971–86; Saudi NZ Capital Corp., 1980–84. Patron: Soc. of Licensed Aircraft Engrs and Technologists, 1964–86; Internat. Fedn of Airworthiness, 1976–84. Hon. FRAeS 1990 (FRAeS 1970). US Legion of Merit, 1944. *Relevant publication:* To Fly a Desk, by Noel Holmes, 1982. *Address:* Puketiro, No 2: RD, Wellsford, North Auckland, New Zealand. *T:* Wellsford 7219. *Clubs:* Northern, Auckland (Auckland, NZ); Probus (Warkworth, NZ). *Died 27 Aug. 1995.*

ROBERTS, John Harvey Polmear; His Honour Judge John Roberts; a Circuit Judge, since 1991; *b* 11 June 1935; *s* of George Edward Polmear Roberts and Mary Harvey Roberts (*née* Sara); *m* 1961, Mary Patricia Gamble; two *s* two *d. Educ:* Blundell's Sch., Tiverton; College of Law. Admitted Solicitor with Hons, 1957; Managing Partner, Winter Taylors, 1984–91. HM Coroner, S Bucks, 1980–91; Regional Chm., Mental Health Review Tribunals, Oxford and East Anglia Regions, 1981–. *Recreations:* golf, football, reading. *Address:* Badgers Hill, Speen, Princes Risborough, Bucks HP27 0SP. *T:* High Wycombe (0494) 488289. *Clubs:* Oriental, Wig and Pen; Phyllis Court (Henley). *Died 6 Sept. 1994.*

ROBERTS, Norman Stafford, MA, DPA; Headmaster, Taunton School, 1970–87; educational consultant; *b* 15 Feb. 1926; *s* of late Walter S. Roberts, LLM and Florence

E. Roberts (*née* Phythian), Calderstones, Liverpool; *m* 1965, Beatrice, *o d* of late George and Winifred Best, Donaghadee, Co. Down; one *s* two *d. Educ:* Quarry Bank High Sch., Liverpool; Hertford Coll., Oxford (Open Exhibnr, History). Served in RA, Egypt and Palestine, 1945–47 (Lieut). 2nd cl. hons PPE 1950; DipEd Oxford 1951; DPA London 1951. Asst Master, Berkhamsted Junior Sch., 1951–55; House Master, Sixth Form Master, Berkhamsted Sch., 1955–59; Walter Hines Page Scholar to USA, 1959, 1980; Senior History Master, Monkton Combe Sch., 1959–65, Housemaster 1962–65 (CO CCF; Hon. Major 1965); Schoolmaster Student, Merton Coll., Oxford, 1964; Headmaster, Sexey's Sch., Bruton, 1965–70. Chm., Bath and Wells Diocese, Church Urban Fund, 1987–90. Pres., Taunton Rotary, 1990–91; Vice Chm., ESU, Taunton. Trustee, SFIA Educnl Trust. Chm. of Govs, St Audries Sch., Som, 1987–91. Governor: Wycliffe Coll., 1988–; King Edward Sch., Witley 1988–. *Recreations:* foreign travel, bridge, hockey, tennis. *Address:* 23 Mount Street, Taunton, Somerset TA1 3QF. *T:* Taunton (0823) 331623. *Club:* Commonwealth Trust.
Died 1 Jan. 1993.

ROBERTS, Rear-Adm. Richard Douglas, CB 1971; CEng; FIMechE; Rear-Admiral Engineering on staff Flag Officer Naval Air Command, 1969–72; *b* 7 Nov. 1916; *s* of Rear-Adm. E. W. Roberts and Mrs R. E. Roberts (*née* Cox); *m* 1943, Mary Norma Wright; one *s* one *d. Educ:* RNC Dartmouth; RNEC Keyham. Frobisher, 1934; RNEC Keyham, 1935–38 (qual. Marine Eng); HM Ships: Kent, 1938–40; Exeter, 1941; Bermuda, 1942; Mauritius, 1943–45; RNEC Manadon, 1945 (qual. Aero Eng); RNAY Donibristle, 1946 (AMIMechE); RNAS Worthy Down, 1947; RNAS Yeovilton, 1948–49; Staff of Rear-Adm. Reserve Aircraft, 1949–50; Comdr, 1950; RN Staff Coll., 1951; RNAY Fleetlands, 1952–53 (Production Man.); HMS Newfoundland, 1954–56 (Engr Officer); Engr-in-Chief's Dept, Bath, 1956–60; Captain 1960; RNAY Belfast, 1961–62 (Supt); idc, 1963 (MIMechE); Dir, Fleet Maintenance, 1964–66; Dir, Naval Officer Appts (E), 1966–68; Naval ADC to the Queen, 1968; Rear-Adm. 1969. FIMgt (FBIM 1982). *Recreations:* sailing (RNSA, 1936), fishing; light railways; Vice Pres., Axe Vale Conservation Soc. *Club:* Army and Navy.
Died 15 Dec. 1995.

ROBERTS, Roy Ernest James, CBE 1986; FEng 1984; FIMechE, FIProdE; AMIBF; Chairman: Simon Engineering plc, since 1987; Dowty Group PLC, 1991–92 (Deputy Chairman, 1986–91); *b* 14 Dec. 1928; *s* of Douglas Henry Roberts and Elsie Florence (*née* Rice); *m* 1950, Winson Madge Smith; two *s. Educ:* Farnham Grammar Sch.; Royal Aircraft Estabt, Farnborough (student apprentice). Management trainee, Guest, Keen and Nettlefolds, 1951–55; Asst to Directors, C. & B. Smith Ltd, 1956–57, Works Director, 1958–66, Dir and Gen. Manager, 1966–70 (C. & B. Smith was acquired by GKN, 1966); Managing Director: GKN Cwmbran Ltd, 1970–72; GKN Engineering Ltd, 1972–74; GKN Gp, 1980–87; Dep. Chm., GKN Gp, 1987–88; Chairman, GKN Engineering Ltd and GKN Building Supplies & Services Ltd, 1974–77; Member, main board of GKN, 1975–88; Group Director, GKN, with special responsibilities for engrg and construction services activities, also for interests in India, Pakistan, S Africa and the Middle East, 1977–79. Mem. (pt-time), UKAEA, 1981–88. Instn of Mechanical Engineers: Pres., 1989–90 (Vice Pres., 1986–89); Chm. Bd, Manufg Industries Div., 1983–86; Mem. Council, 1983–; Instn of Production Engineers: Vice Pres., 1983–89; Mem., Exec. Policy Bd, 1983–89. Chm., Standing Conf. on Schools' Science and Technol., 1988–92; Mem. Exec. Cttee, SMMT, 1983–87; Vice-Pres., Engrg Employers' Fedn, 1988–. Member: Council, Cranfield Inst. of Technol., 1983–89; Engineering

Council, 1986–88. CBIM 1979; FInstD 1980; FRSA 1980. *Recreations:* field sports, music. *Address:* Simon Engineering plc, Buchanan House, 3 St James's Square, SW1Y 4JU. *T:* 071–925 0666. *Club:* Royal Automobile.
Died 9 April 1993.

ROBERTS, Dame Shelagh (Marjorie), DBE 1981; former industrial relations consultant; *b* 13 Oct. 1924; *d* of Glyn and Cecelia Roberts, Ystalyfera. *Educ:* St Wyburn Sch., Birkdale, Lancs. Member: Kensington and Chelsea Borough Council, 1953–71; GLC, 1970–81 (Leader, Planning and Communications Policy Cttee, 1977–79); MEP (C) London SW, Sept. 1979–1989: Vice Chm., Transport Cttee, 1979–84; Chm., Cttee on External Econ. Relations, 1984–87; Dep. Chm., Cons. Gp, 1987–89; contested (C) London SW, European Parly Elecn, 1989. Member: Bd of Basildon Development Corp., 1971–75; Occupational Pensions Bd, 1973–79; Race Relations Bd, 1973–77; Panel of Industrial Tribunals, 1973–79; PLA, 1976–79. Chairman: London Tourist Bd and Convention Bureau, 1989–; Payroll Giving Assoc., 1989–. Chm., National Women's Advisory Cttee of Conservative Party, 1972–75; Pres., Nat. Union of Conservative Party, 1988–89 (Chm., 1976–77). Co-Chm., Jt Cttee Against Racialism, 1978–80. *Publications:* (co-author) Fair Share for the Fair Sex, 1969; More Help for the Cities, 1974. *Recreation:* enjoying the sun and fresh air. *Address:* 47 Shrewsbury House, Cheyne Walk, SW3 5LW. *T:* 071–352 3711. *Clubs:* Hurlingham, St Stephen's Constitutional.
Created Baroness (Life Peer), New Year's Honours List, 1992. *Died 16 Jan. 1992.*

ROBERTS, Wilfrid Hubert Wace, JP; *b* 28 Aug. 1900; *s* of Charles Henry and Lady Cecilia Maude Roberts, *d* of 9th Earl of Carlisle, Boothby, Brampton, Cumberland; *m* 1st, 1923, Margaret Jennings (*d* 1924); one *d*; 2nd, 1928, Anne Constance Jennings (marr. diss. 1957); two *d*; 3rd, Kate Sawyer. *Educ:* Gresham School; Balliol College, Oxford. MP (L) North Cumberland, 1935–50; joined Labour Party, July 1956. *Address:* Boothby Manor House, Brampton, Cumbria.
Died 26 May 1991.

ROBERTSON, Douglas William, CMG 1947; DSO 1918; MC 1918; *b* 30 Nov. 1898; 2nd surv. *s* of late Rev. J. A. Robertson, MA; *m* 1924, Mary Eagland (*d* 1968), *y d* of late W. E. Longbottom, Adelaide; no *c. Educ:* George Watson's College, Edinburgh. 2nd Lt KRRC, 1917; France, 1918 (wounded, MC, DSO, despatches); Administrative Service, Uganda, 1921–50; Resident of Buganda, 1945; Secretary for African Affairs, Uganda, 1947–50, retired, 1950. *Address:* 3a Ravelston Park, Edinburgh EH4 3DX. *Club:* East India, Devonshire, Sports and Public Schools.
Died 19 Sept. 1993.

ROBERTSON, Francis Calder F.; *see* Ford-Robertson.

ROBERTSON, Ian Macbeth, CB 1976; LVO 1956; JP; Secretary of Commissions for Scotland, 1978–83; *b* 1 Feb. 1918; *s* of late Sheriff-Substitute J. A. T. Robertson and Brenda Lewis; *m* 1947, Anne Stewart Marshall. *Educ:* Melville College; Edinburgh University. Served War of 1939–45 in Middle East and Italy; Royal Artillery and London Scottish, Captain. Entered Dept of Health for Scotland, 1946; Private Secretary to Minister of State, Scottish Office, 1951–52 and to Secretary of State for Scotland, 1952–55; Asst Secretary, Dept of Health for Scotland, 1955; Assistant Under-Secretary of State, Scottish Office, 1963–64; Under-Secretary: Scottish Development Department, 1964–65; Scottish Educn Dept, 1966–78. Mem., Williams Cttee on Nat. Museums and Galls in Scotland, 1979–81. Chm. of Governors, Edinburgh Coll. of Art, 1981–88. JP Edinburgh 1978. HRSA 1987. Hon. DLitt Heriot-Watt, 1988. *Address:*

Napier House, 8 Colinton Road, Edinburgh EH10 5DS. *T:* 031–447 4636. *Club:* New (Edinburgh).
Died 31 July 1992.

ROBERTSON, James, CBE 1969; MA; FRCM; *b* 17 June 1912; *s* of Ainslie John Robertson and Phyllis Mary Roughton; *m* 1st, 1949, Rachel June Fraser (*d* 1979); one *s* (and one *s* decd); 2nd, 1980, Oswalda Viktoria Pattrick. *Educ:* Winchester College; Trinity College, Cambridge; Conservatorium, Leipzig; Royal College of Music, London (ARCM 1938). On music staff, Glyndebourne Opera, 1937–39; Conductor, Carl Rosa Opera Co., 1938–39; Conductor, Canadian Broadcasting Corp., 1939–40; Air Ministry, 1940–42; RAFVR (Intelligence), 1942–46; Director and Conductor, Sadler's Wells Opera Company, 1946–54; Conductor of National Orchestra of New Zealand Broadcasting Service, Sept. 1954–Nov. 1957; Conductor, Touring Opera, 1958; Adviser on Opera, Théâtre de la Monnaie, Brussels, 1960–61; Artistic and Musical Director, New Zealand Opera Co., 1962–63; Dir, London Opera Centre, 1964–77, Consultant, 1977–78; Musical Dir, Nat. Opera of NZ, 1979–81. Conductor: Northern Opera Ltd, 1968–85; John Lewis Musical Soc., 1961–86. Hon. FTCL; Hon. GSM; Hon. RAM. *Recreation:* languages. *Address:* Ty Helyg, Llwynmawr, Pontfadog, Llangollen, Clwyd LL20 7BG. *T:* Glynceiriog (069172) 480. *Died 18 May 1991.*

ROBERTSON, Maj.-Gen. John Carnegie; Director of Army Legal Services, Ministry of Defence, 1973–76; *b* 24 Nov. 1917; *s* of late Sir William C. F. Robertson, KCMG and Dora (*née* Whelan); *m* 1961, Teresa Mary Louise, *d* of Cecil T. Porter. *Educ:* Cheltenham Coll.; RMC, Sandhurst. Served War of 1939–45: Officer in Gloucestershire Regt (POW, Germany, 1940). Called to the Bar, Gray's Inn, 1949. Joined Judge Advocate's Dept, 1948; served subseq. in Middle East, BAOR, East Africa and the Far East; Dep. Dir, Army Legal Services, HQ, BAOR, 1971–73. *Address:* Berry House, Nuffield, Henley-on-Thames, Oxon RG9 5SS. *T:* Nettlebed (0491) 641740. *Club:* Huntercombe Golf. *Died 15 July 1994.*

ROBERTSON, Robert Alexander; Lord Provost, City of Aberdeen, 1988–92; *b* 17 June 1922; *m* 1946, Susie Gladys Ivy Edmondson. Freeman, City of London, 1991. JP Aberdeen, 1968. Hon. LLD Aberdeen, 1991. *Address:* 54 Fairview Circle, Danestone, Aberdeen AB22 8ZQ. *T:* Aberdeen (0224) 713882. *Died 24 Aug. 1992.*

ROBERTSON, Ronald Foote, CBE 1980; MD, FRCP, FRCPE, FRCPGlas; Physician to the Queen in Scotland, 1977–85; *b* 27 Dec. 1920; *s* of Thomas Robertson and Mary Foote; *m* 1949, Dorothy Tweedy Wilkinson; two *d* (and one *d* decd). *Educ:* Perth Acad.; Univ. of Edinburgh. MB, ChB (Hons) 1945; MD (High Commendation) 1953; FRCPEd 1952; FRCP 1969; FRCPGlas 1978. Consultant Physician: Leith Hosp., 1959–74; Deaconess Hosp., 1958–83; Royal Infirmary of Edinburgh, 1975–86. Sec., RCPEd, 1958–63; Vice-Pres., 1973–76; Pres., 1976–79. Principal MO, Scottish Life Assce Co., 1968–86. Mem., Assoc. of Phys of Gt Britain and Ireland; Pres., BMA, 1983–84. Served on numerous NHS cttees; Mem. GMC, 1979–89. Hon. Fellow, Coll. of Physicians and Surgeons, Pakistan, 1977; Hon. FACP 1978; Hon. FRCPI 1978; Hon. FRACP 1979; Hon. Mem., Acad. of Medicine, Singapore, 1988. *Publications:* several articles in scientific jls. *Recreations:* gardening, curling, fishing. *Address:* 15 Wester Coates Terrace, Edinburgh EH12 5LR. *T:* 031–337 6377. *Clubs:* New, University Staff (Edinburgh).
Died 11 April 1991.

ROBINSON, Prof. Sir (Edward) Austin (Gossage), Kt 1975; CMG 1947; OBE 1944; FBA 1955; Emeritus Professor of Economics, Cambridge University since 1966 (Professor, 1950–65); Fellow of Sidney Sussex College,

Cambridge, since 1931; Secretary of Royal Economic Society, 1945–70; *b* 20 Nov. 1897; *s* of late Rev. Canon Albert Gossage Robinson and Edith, *d* of Rev. T. W. Sidebotham; *m* 1926, Joan (*d* 1983), *d* of late Major-General Sir Frederick Maurice, KCMG, CB; two *d. Educ:* Marlborough College (Scholar); Christ's College, Cambridge (Scholar). BA 1921; MA 1923. RNAS and RAF (Pilot), 1917–19. Fellow of Corpus Christi Coll., Cambridge, 1923–26; Tutor to HH The Maharaja of Gwalior, 1926–28; University Lecturer, Cambridge, 1929–49; Asst Editor of Economic Journal, 1934–44, Joint Editor, 1944–70; Member of Economic Section, War Cabinet Office, 1939–42; Economic Adviser and Head of Programmes Division, Ministry of Production, 1942–45; Member of British Reparations Mission, Moscow and Berlin, 1945; Economic Adviser to Board of Trade, 1946; returned to Cambridge, Sept. 1946. Mem. of Economic Planning Staff, 1947–48; Treasurer of International Economic Association, 1950–59, President 1959–62; Mem. Council, DSIR, 1954–59; Dir of Economics, Min. of Power, 1967–68. Chairman: Council Nat. Inst. of Economic and Social Research, 1949–62; European Energy Advisory Commn, OEEC, 1957–60; Exec. Cttee, Overseas Develt Inst. *Publications:* The Structure of Competitive Industry, 1931; Monopoly, 1941; Economic Consequences of the Size of Nations, 1960; Economic Development of Africa South of the Sahara, 1964; Problems in Economic Development, 1965; The Economics of Education (with J. E. Vaizey), 1966; Backward Areas in Advanced Countries, 1969; Economic Development in South Asia, 1970; (ed jtly) The Economic Development of Bangladesh within a Socialist Framework, 1974; (ed jtly) Employment Policy in a Developing Country, 1983; contributor to: Modern Industry and the African, 1933; Lord Hailey's African Survey, 1938; articles in Economic Journal, etc. *Address:* Sidney Sussex College, Cambridge CB2 3HU. *T:* Cambridge (0223) 357548. *Club:* Reform. *Died 1 June 1993.*

ROBINSON, Harold George Robert, OBE 1961; FRAeS; CEng, MIEE; consultant on aerospace matters, since 1990; Director-General Research (General), Ministry of Defence (Procurement Executive), and Assistant Chief Scientific Adviser (Research), Ministry of Defence, 1981–84, retired; *b* 2 April 1924; *s* of Harold Arthur Robinson and Winifred Margaret (*née* Ballard); *m* 1955, Sonja (*née* Lapthorn); two *s. Educ:* Portsmouth Northern Grammar Sch.; Imperial Coll., London Univ.; California Inst. of Technology. WhSch 1944; BSc 1948; FCGI 1970. Joined RAE as Scientific Officer, 1948; Head of Satellite Launcher Div., Space Dept, RAE, 1961; Head of Avionics Dept, RAE, 1965–69; Head of Research Planning Div., Min. of Technology, 1969–71; Dir Gen., Aerospace Assessment and Res., DTI, 1971–74; Under-Sec., Space and Air Res., DoI, 1974–76; a Dep. Dir, RAE, 1976–81, Acting Dir, 1981. Sen. Consultant, General Technology Systems Ltd, 1984–90. Pres., Astronautics Commn, FAI, 1969–70 (Paul Tissandier Diploma, 1971); FRAeS 1981 (Bronze Medal, 1961). Pres., Whitworth Soc., 1982–83. *Publications:* various scientific and technical papers, and contribs to books, primarily on rocket and space research. *Recreations:* bowls, photography. *Address:* 39 Crosby Hill Drive, Camberley, Surrey GU15 3TZ. *T:* Camberley (01276) 23771. *Died 4 Jan. 1995.*

ROBOROUGH, 2nd Baron, *cr* 1938, of Maristow; **Massey Henry Edgcumbe Lopes;** Bt 1805; JP; Brevet Major Reserve of Officers Royal Scots Greys; Lord-Lieutenant and Custos Rotulorum of Devon, 1958–78; *b* 4 Oct. 1903; *o s* of 1st Baron and Lady Albertha Louisa Florence Edgcumbe (*d* 1941), *d* of 4th Earl of Mount Edgcumbe; *S* father, 1938; *m* 1936, Helen, *o d* of late Colonel E. A. F. Dawson, Launde Abbey, Leicestershire; two *s* (one *d* decd). *Educ:* Eton Coll.; Christ Church, Oxford (BA).

Served in Royal Scots Greys, 1925–38; served again 1939–45 (twice wounded). ADC to Earl of Clarendon, when Governor of Union of South Africa, 1936–37. CA Devon, 1956–74; DL 1946; Vice-Lieutenant of Devon, 1951; Member of Duchy of Cornwall Council, 1958–68; High Steward of Barnstaple. Chairman: Dartmoor National Park, 1965–74; SW Devon Div. Educn Cttee, 1954–74; Devon Outward Bound, 1960–75; President: SW Reg., YMCA, 1958–67; Devon British Legion, 1958–68; Devon Conservation Forum, 1972–78; President, Devon, 1958–78: Magistrates Cttee; Council of St John; CPRE; Trust for Nature Conservation; Boy Scouts Assoc.; Football Assoc.; Assoc. of Youth Clubs. Governor: Exeter Univ.; Seale-Hayne, Kelly, Plymouth and Exeter Colls. Hon. Col, Devon Army Cadet Force, 1967–78. Hon. LLD Exeter, 1969. KStJ. *Heir: s* Hon. Henry Massey Lopes [*b* 2 Feb. 1940; *m* 1st, 1968, Robyn, *e d* of John Bromwich, Melbourne, Aust.; two *s* two *d*; 2nd, 1986, Sarah Anne Pipon, second *d* of Colin Baker; two *d*]. *Address:* Bickham Barton, Roborough, Plymouth, Devon PL6 7BL. *T:* Yelverton (0822) 852478. *Club:* Cavalry and Guards.
Died 30 June 1992.

ROBSON, Lawrence Fendick; Member, Electricity Council, 1972–76; *b* 23 Jan. 1916; *s* of (William) Bertram Robson and Annie (*née* Fendick); *m* 1945, Lorna Winifred Jagger, Shafton, Yorks; two *s* one *d*. *Educ:* Rotherham Grammar Sch.; Clare Coll., Cambridge (BA). FIEE. North Eastern Electric Supply Co. Ltd, 1937; Royal Corps of Signals, 1939–45; various positions with NE and London Electricity Bds, 1948–65; Commercial Adviser, Electricity Council, 1965–72. *Recreations:* music, open air. *Address:* Millers Hill, Priestman's Lane, Thornton Dale, N Yorks.
Died 8 Oct. 1992.

ROBSON, Nigel John; Chairman, London Committee, Ottoman Bank, since 1987 (Deputy Chairman, 1983–87; Member, since 1959); Member, Board of Banking Supervision, since 1986; London Adviser to Bank of Tokyo Group, since 1984; Vice-Chairman, Automobile Association, since 1990 (Treasurer, 1986–89); *b* 25 Dec. 1926; *s* of late Col the Hon. Harold Burge Robson, TD, JP, DL, Pinewood Hill, Wormley, Surrey, and Iris Robson (*née* Abel Smith); *m* 1957, Anne Gladstone, *yr d* of late Stephen Deiniol and Clair Gladstone; three *s*. *Educ:* Eton. Grenadier Guards, 1945–48. Joined Arbuthnot Latham & Co. Ltd, Merchant Bankers, 1949, a Director, 1953, Chm., 1969–75; Dir, Arbuthnot Latham Holdings Ltd, 1969–81; Dir, Grindlays Bank plc, 1969–83, Dep. Chm., 1975–76, Chm. 1977–83; Director: British Sugar plc, 1982–86; Central Trustee Savings Bank, 1984–86; TSB Gp, 1985–; Royal Trustco Ltd, Toronto, 1985–89; Chairman: Alexander Howden Underwriting, subseq. Alexander Howden & Beck Ltd, 1984–88; Royal Trust Co. of Canada, subseq. Royal Trust Bank, 1984–89; TSB England & Wales, 1986–89. Mem. Council, British Heart Foundn, 1984– (Chm., F & GP Cttee, 1984–89); Hon. Treas., 1985–89); Mem., 250th Anniv. Cttee, Royal London Hosp., 1989–91; Treas., Univ. of Surrey, 1987–. Gov., King Edward's Sch., Witley, 1975–. *Recreations:* tennis, music. *Address:* Pinewood Hill, Wormley, Godalming, Surrey GU8 5UD. *Clubs:* Brooks's, City of London, MCC. *Died 25 Feb. 1993.*

ROBSON, Sir Thomas (Buston), Kt 1954; MBE 1919; FCA; Partner in Price Waterhouse & Co., Chartered Accountants, 1934–66; Chairman, Renold Ltd, 1967–72; *b* Newcastle upon Tyne, 4 Jan. 1896; *s* of late Thomas Robson, Langholm, Dumfriesshire, and Newcastle upon Tyne; *m* 1936, Roberta Cecilia Helen (*d* 1980), *d* of late Rev. Archibald Fleming, DD, St Columba's Church of Scotland, Pont St, SW1; two *d*. *Educ:* Rutherford College, Newcastle upon Tyne; Armstrong Coll., University of Durham. BA Hons, Modern History, 1920; MA 1923.

Served European War, 1914–18, with British Salonika Force in Macedonia; Captain RGA; MBE, despatches 1919. Articled with Sisson & Allden, Chartered Accountants, Newcastle upon Tyne, 1920; W. B. Peat gold medal in final examination of Inst. Chartered Accountants in England and Wales, 1922; joined staff of Price Waterhouse & Co., London, 1923. ACA, 1923, FCA, 1939; Mem. Council of Inst., 1941–66 (Vice-Pres. 1951–52; Pres., 1952–53); rep. Inst. at overseas mtgs of accountants; FCA (Ont). Member: Committee on Amendment of Census of Production Act, Bd of Trade, 1945; Central Valuation Bd for Coal Industry, 1947; Accountancy Advisory Cttee on Companies Act, Bd of Trade, 1948–68 (Chm. 1955–68); Cttee of Inquiry into London Transport Exec., Min. of Transport and Civil Aviation, 1953; Chm. Cttees of Inquiry into Coal Distribution Costs, Min. of Fuel and Power, 1956 and Min. of Commerce, N Ireland, 1956; Mem. Advisory Cttee on Replacement of the "Queen" ships, Min. of Transport and Civil Aviation, 1959; Chm. Economic Development Cttee for Paper and Board Industry under National Economic Development Council, 1964–67. Vice-Pres. Union Européenne des Experts Comptables, Economiques et Financiers, 1963–64; Mem. Transport Tribunal, 1963–69. *Publications:* Garnsey's Holding Companies and their Published Accounts, 3rd edn, 1936; The Construction of Consolidated Accounts, 1936; Consolidated and other Group Accounts, 1946, 4th edn, 1969; numerous papers and addresses on professional subjects. *Recreation:* for many years an active worker in Boy Scout movement (Vice-Pres., Gtr London Central Scout Council). *Address:* 3 Gonville House, Manor Fields, SW15 3NH. *T:* 081–789 0597.
Died 12 April 1991.

ROBSON, Thomas Snowdon, CBE 1986 (OBE 1970; MBE 1964); FEng 1989; FIEE; Director of Engineering, Independent Broadcasting Authority, 1978–86; *b* 6 Aug. 1922; *s* of Thomas Henry Robson and Annie Jessie (*née* Snowdon); *m* 1951, Ruth Bramley; one *s* one *d*. *Educ:* Portsmouth Grammar Sch. BBC, 1941–42; RAF Techn. Br., 1942–46; EMI Research Labs, 1947–57; ITA: Engr in Charge, Black Hill, 1957–58; Sen. Engr, Planning and Construction, 1958–67; Head of Station Design and Construction, 1967–69; Asst Dir of Engrg, 1969–73; IBA, Dep. Dir of Engrg, 1973–77. FRTS 1976; Hon. FBKSTS 1986. Eduard Rhein Prize, Eduard Rhein Foundn, Berlin, 1984. *Recreations:* home computing, walking, gardening, study of history. *Address:* 8 Gloster Drive, Kenilworth, Warwickshire CV8 2TU. *T:* Kenilworth (0926) 56906.
Died 6 Aug. 1992.

ROBSON, Prof. William Wallace, FRSE; Masson Professor of English Literature, University of Edinburgh, 1972–90, then Emeritus; *b* 20 June 1923; *o s* of late W. Robson, LLB, barrister, and Kathleen Ryan; *m* 1962, Anne-Varna Moses, MA; two *s*. *Educ:* Leeds Modern School; New College, Oxford (R. C. Sherriff Scholar; BA 1944, MA 1948). Asst Lectr, King's College London, 1944–46; Lectr, Lincoln College, Oxford, 1946–48, Fellow, 1948–70; Prof. of English, Univ. of Sussex, 1970–72. Visiting Lecturer: Univ. of S California, 1953; Univ. of Adelaide, 1956; Vis. Prof., Univ. of Delaware, 1963–64; Elizabeth Drew Prof., Smith Coll., USA, 1969–70; Vis. Fellow: All Souls Coll., Oxford, 1982; New Coll., Oxford, 1985. FRSE 1988; FRSA 1991. *Publications:* Critical Essays, 1966; The Signs Among Us, 1968; Modern English Literature, 1970, 5th edn 1984; The Definition of Literature, 1982; A Prologue to English Literature, 1986. *Address:* Department of English Literature, The University, Edinburgh EH8 9YL. *T:* 031–667 1011. *Died 31 July 1993.*

ROCHDALE, 1st Viscount *cr* 1960; **John Durival Kemp**, OBE 1945; TD; Baron 1913; *b* 5 June 1906; *s* of 1st Baron Rochdale and Lady Beatrice Egerton, 3rd *d* of 3rd Earl of Ellesmere; *S* father, 1945; *m* 1931, Elinor Dorothea Pease (CBE 1964; JP); one *s* (one *d* decd). *Educ:* Eton; Trin. Coll., Cambridge. Hons degree Nat. Science Tripos. Served War of 1939–45 (despatches); attached USA forces in Pacific with rank of Col, 1944; Temp. Brig., 1945; Hon. Col 251 (Westmorland and Cumberland Yeomanry) Field Regiment, RA, TA, later 851 (Westmorland and Cumberland Yeo.) Field Bty, RA, 1959–67. Joined Kelsall & Kemp Ltd, 1928, Chm., 1952–71; Director: Consett Iron Co. Ltd, 1957–67; Geigy (Hldgs) Ltd, 1959–64; Williams Deacon's Bank Ltd, 1960–70; Nat. and Commercial Banking Gp Ltd, 1971–77; Deputy Chairman: West Riding Worsted & Woollen Mills, 1969–72; Williams & Glyn's Bank Ltd, 1973–77; Chm., Harland & Wolff, 1971–75. Mem., H of L Select Cttee on European Affairs (Chm., sub cttee B), 1981–86. President: National Union of Manufacturers, 1953–56; NW Industrial Develt Assoc., 1974–84; Economic League, 1964–67; Member: Dollar Exports Council, 1953–61; Central Transport Consultative Cttee for GB, 1953–57; Western Hemisphere Exports Council, 1961–64; Chairman: Cotton Board, 1957–62; Docks and Harbours Committee of Inquiry, 1961; National Ports Council, 1963–67; Cttee of Inquiry into Shipping, 1967–70. A Governor of the BBC, 1954–59. Dir, Cumbria Rural Enterprise Agency, 1986–91. Chm., Rosehill Arts Trust, 1970–83. Pres., British Legion, NW Area, 1955–61. Companion, Textile Inst. 1959; MInstT 1964. Upper Bailiff, Weavers' Co., 1949–50, 1956–57. DL Cumberland, 1948–84. Medal, Textile Inst., 1986 *Recreations:* gardening, forestry, music. *Heir: s* Hon. St John Durival Kemp [*b* 15 Jan. 1938; *m* 1st, 1960, Serena Jane Clark-Hall (marr. diss. 1974); two *s* two *d*; 2nd, 1976, Elizabeth Anderton]. *Address:* Lingholm, Keswick, Cumbria CA12 5UA. *T:* Keswick (07687) 72003. *Club:* Lansdowne. *Died 24 May 1993.*

ROCHE, Frederick Lloyd, CBE 1985; Roche Partners, since 1992; *b* 11 March 1931; *s* of John Francis Roche and Margaret Roche; *m* 1955, Sheila Lindsay; one *s* one *d. Educ:* Regent Street Polytechnic. DipArch, ARIBA. Architect (Schools), City of Coventry, 1958–62; Principal Develt Architect, Midlands Housing Consortium, 1962–64; Chief Architect and Planning Officer, Runcorn Develt Corp., 1964–70; Gen. Manager, Milton Keynes Develt Corp., 1970–80; Dep. Chm. and Man. Dir, Conran Roche, 1981–90. Vice-Pres., RIBA, 1983. *Publications:* numerous technical articles. *Address:* Roche Partners, 47 Church Road, Bow Brickhill, Milton Keynes MK17 9LH. *T:* Milton Keynes (0908) 374526.

Died 9 Nov. 1992.

ROCKE, John Roy Mansfield; Vice-Chairman, J. Bibby & Sons, 1975–82, retired; *b* 13 April 1918; *s* of late Frederick Gilbert Rocke and Mary Susan Rocke; *m* 1948, Pauline Diane Berry; no *c. Educ:* Charterhouse; Trinity Coll., Cambridge (BA). War Service, Grenadier Guards, 1940–46 (Maj.). Orme & Eykyn (Stockbrokers), 1946–50; Booker McConnell Ltd, 1950–70, Dir, 1954, Vice-Chm., 1962–70. Mem., BNEC, and Chm., BNEC (Caribbean), 1965–68; Chm., Nat. Econ. Development Cttee for the Food Manufacturing Industry, 1967–71. *Address:* Pendomer Manor, Pendomer, near Yeovil, Somerset BA22 9PH. *Club:* Cavalry and Guards.

Died 19 Aug. 1993.

RODEN, 9th Earl of, *cr* 1771 (Ire.); **Robert William Jocelyn;** Baron Newport, 1743; Viscount Jocelyn, 1755; Bt 1665; Captain Royal Navy; retired; *b* 4 Dec. 1909; *s* of 8th Earl and Elinor Jesse (*d* 1962), 2nd *d* of Joseph Charlton Parr, JP, DL; *S* father, 1956; *m* 1937, Clodagh (*d* 1989), *d* of late Edward Kennedy, Bishopscourt, Co.

Kildare; two *s* (and one *s* decd). Retired 1960. *Heir: s* Viscount Jocelyn [*b* 25 Aug. 1938; *m* 1st, 1970, Sara Cecilia (marr. diss. 1982), *d* of Brig. Andrew Dunlop; one *d*; 2nd, 1986, Ann Margareta Maria, *d* of Dr Gunnar Henning; one *s*]. *Address:* 75 Bryansford Village, Newcastle, Co. Down BT33 0PT. *T:* Newcastle (03967) 23469. *Died 18 Oct. 1993.*

RODERICK, Rev. Charles Edward Morys; Chaplain to the Queen, 1962–80; Rector of Longparish and Hurstbourne Priors, 1971–80; *b* 18 June 1910; *s* of Edward Thomas and Marion Petronella Roderick; *m* 1940, Betty Margaret Arrowsmith; two *s. Educ:* Christ's College, Brecon; Trinity College, Oxford (MA). Schoolmaster, 1932–38; training for ordination, 1938–39; ordained deacon, 1939, priest, 1940; Curate, St Luke's Parish Church of Chelsea, 1939–46; Chaplain to the Forces, 1940–45; Rector of Denham, Bucks, 1946–53; Vicar of St Michael's, Chester Square, London, 1953–71. HCF. *Address:* 135 Little Ann, Abbotts Ann, Andover, Hants SP11 7NW. *Died 13 Jan. 1993.*

RODGERS, Barbara Noel, OBE 1975; Reader in Social Administration, Manchester University, 1965–73, retired; *b* 1912; *d* of F. S. Stancliffe, Wilmslow, Cheshire; *m* 1950, Brian Rodgers (*d* 1987); no *c. Educ:* Wycombe Abbey Sch.; (Exhibitioner) Somerville Coll., Oxford (MA). Social work and travel, 1935–39; Jt appt with Manchester and Salford Council of Social Service and Manchester Univ. (practical work Tutor and special Lectr), 1939–45; Lectr 1945, Sen. Lectr, 1955, Manchester Univ.; Teaching Fellowship in Grad. Sch. of Social Work, Toronto Univ., 1948–49; Sen. Res. Fellow, Centre for Studies in Social Policy, 1973–75. Member: various wages councils and Industrial Tribunal Panel, 1950–85; National Assistance Bd, 1965; Supplementary Benefits Commn, 1966–76. Served on numerous voluntary welfare organisations. *Publications:* (co-author) Till We Build Again, 1948; (with Julia Dixon) Portrait of Social Work, 1960; A Follow Up Study of Manchester Social Administration Students, 1940–60, 1963; Careers of Social Studies Graduates, 1964; (co-author) Comparative Social Administration, 1968; (with June Stevenson) A New Portrait of Social Work, 1973; chapter on Comparative Studies in Social Administration, in Foundations of Social Administration (ed H. Heisler), 1977; The Study of Social Policy: a comparative approach, 1979; numerous articles in learned jls mainly on social security and social services in America, France and Canada. *Recreations:* walking, bird watching, travel. *Address:* 19 High Street, Great Budworth, Cheshire CW9 6HF. *T:* Comberbach (0606) 892068. *Died 18 Feb. 1992.*

RODGERS, Sir John (Charles), 1st Bt, *cr* 1964, of Groombridge, Kent; DL; *b* 5 Oct. 1906; *o s* of Charles and Maud Mary Rodgers; *m* 1930, Betsy (JP, East Sussex), *y d* of Francis W. Aikin-Sneath, JP, and Louisa, *d* of Col W. Langworthy Baker; two *s. Educ:* St Peter's, York; Ecole des Roches, France; Keble College, Oxford (scholar). MA. Sub-Warden, Mary Ward Settlement, 1929; Lectr and Administrative Asst, Univ. of Hull, 1930; FO, 1938–39; Dir, Commercial Relations Div., MOI, 1939–41; Dir, Post-War Export Trade Develt, Dept of Overseas Trade, 1941–42; Head Industrial Inf. Div., Min. of Production, 1942–44; FO, 1944–45; Special Mission to Portugal, December 1945; Foundation Gov. of Administrative Staff Coll.; Exec. Council Member, Foundation for Management Education, 1959; Mem., BBC General Advisory Council, 1946–52; Hon. Secretary Smuts Memorial Committee, 1953; Chm. Cttee on Litter in Royal Parks, 1954; Mem. Exec. Cttee of British Council, 1957–58; Governor, British Film Institute, 1958; Member Tucker Cttee on Proceedings before Examining Justices, 1957; Leader, Parliamentary Panel, and on Exec. and

Coun., Inst. of Dirs, 1955–58; Vice-Chm. Exec. Cttee Political and Economic Planning (PEP), 1962–68; Mem. Exec., London Library, 1963–71. MP (C) Sevenoaks, Kent, 1950–79 (where Winston Churchill was one of his constituents); PPS to Rt Hon. Viscount Eccles (at Ministries of Works, Education and Board of Trade), 1951–57; Parliamentary Sec., Bd of Trade, and Minister for regional development and employment, 1958–60. UK Delegate and Leader of the Conservatives to Parly Assembly, Council of Europe, and Vice-Pres., WEU, 1969–79; Chm., Independent Gp, Council of Europe, 1974–79; Chm., Political Affairs Cttee, 1976–79; Vice-Pres., European League for Econ. Co-operation, 1970–79; Hon. Treasurer, Europe-Atlantic Gp, 1975; Mem., UK Cttee, European Cultural Foundn, 1982–. President: Centre Européen de Documentation et Information, 1963–66; Friends of Free China, 1969–. Dep. Chm., J. Walter Thompson Co. Ltd, 1931–70; Chairman: Cocoa Merchants Ltd, 1959–81; British Market Research Bureau Ltd, 1933–54; New English Library, 1961–70; Radio Luxembourg London, 1979–83 (Hon. Pres., 1983–); Dir of Comweld Ltd and other cos. Mem. Council, Nat. Trust, 1978–83; Vice-Chm., Heritage of London Trust, 1980–. Mem. Court: City Univ., 1969–; Brunel Univ., 1981–84. President: Inst. of Practitioners in Advertising, 1967–69; Soc. for Individual Freedom, 1970–73; Inst. of Statisticians, 1971–77; Master, Worshipful Company of Masons, 1968–69; Freeman of the City of London. DL Kent 1973. CBIM; FSS; FIS; FRSA. Medal of Merit, Council of Europe, 1980. Knight Grand Cross, Order of Civil Merit (Spain), 1965; Grand Cross of Liechtenstein, 1970; Comdr, Order of Dom Infante Henrique (Portugal), 1972; Grand Officier, Order of Leopold II (Belgium), 1978; Order of Brilliant Star (China), 1979; Kt Comdr, 1st cl., Royal Order of North Star, Sweden, 1980; Comdr, 1st cl., Order of Lion of Finland, 1980; Grand Officer, Order of Merit of Grand Duchy of Luxembourg, 1983. *Publications:* Mary Ward Settlement: a history, 1930; The Old Public Schools of England, 1938; The English Woodland, 1941; (jtly) Industry looks at the New Order, 1941; English Rivers, 1948; (jtly) One Nation, 1950; York, 1951; (ed) Thomas Gray, 1953; (jtly) Change is our Ally, 1954; (jtly) Capitalism—Strength and Stress, 1958; One Nation at Work, 1976; and pamphlets. *Recreations:* travel, theatre. *Heir: s* (John Fairlie) Tobias Rodgers, *b* 2 July 1940. *Address:* The Dower House, Groombridge, Kent. *T:* Groombridge (089276) 213. *Clubs:* Brooks's, Pratt's, Beefsteak, Royal Thames Yacht.

Died 29 March 1993.

RODNEY, 9th Baron *cr* 1782; **John Francis Rodney;** Bt 1764; *b* 28 June 1920; *s* of 8th Baron Rodney and Lady Marjorie Lowther (*d* 1968), *d* of 6th Earl of Lonsdale; *S* father, 1973; *m* 1952, Régine, *d* of late Chevalier Pangaert d'Opdorp, Belgium, and Baronne Pangaert d'Opdorp; one *s* one *d. Educ:* Stowe Sch., Buckingham; McGill Univ., Montreal. Served War of 1939–45 with Commandos, Burma, 1943–45 (despatches). Alternate Delegate to Council of Europe and WEU, 1986 (Member: Science and Technology Cttee; Agricl Cttee, Council of Europe); Member: Standing Cttee on Drug Abuse, 1986–; All Party Gp on Pseudo Religious Cults, 1985–. Past Chm. and Council Mem., British Fedn of Printing Machinery and Supplies; Chm., Printing Equipment Educnl Trust, 1986–. *Recreations:* sailing, shooting, gardening, travelling round the world (not all recreation). *Heir: s* Hon. George Brydges Rodney, *b* 3 Jan. 1953. *Address:* 38 Pembroke Road, W8 6NU. *T:* 071–602 4391. *Club:* White's.

Died 13 Oct. 1992.

ROGERS, Hugh Charles Innes, MA, FIMechE; Director, Avon Rubber Co., 1968–79 (Chairman, 1968–78); Vice-Chairman, Bristol and West Building Society, 1972–82; *b* 2 Nov. 1904; *s* of late Hugh Innes Rogers, OBE, MIEE;

m 1930, Iris Monica Seymour; one *s* three *d. Educ:* Marlborough; Clare College, Cambridge. Brecknell Munro & Rogers, 1926–31 (Chairman and Jt Man. Dir, 1931–41); SW Reg. Controller, Min. of Supply, 1941; SW Reg. Controller, Min. of Production and Chm. of Regional Bd, 1942–44; Dep. Controller (Production) in Admiralty, 1944–46; Imperial Tobacco Co. Ltd, Bristol: Chief Engr, 1948; Dir, 1949–67; a Dep. Chm., 1964–67; Dir, British American Tobacco Co., 1964–67. Member Bristol University Council, 1938, Chm., 1968–72. Chairman: SW Regional Housing Bd, 1952–53; SW Regional Council, FBI, 1954. High Sheriff of Avon, 1974. Hon. LLD Bristol, 1971; Hon. DSc Bath, 1971. *Recreations:* sailing, shooting, tennis, farming. *Address:* Beach House, Bitton, near Bristol BS15 6NP. *T:* Bitton (0272) 323127.

Died 20 March 1991.

ROGERS, Murray Rowland Fletcher; Member, Courts of Appeal for the Seychelles, St Helena, The Falkland Islands Colony and Dependencies, and the British Antarctic Territory, 1965–75; *b* 13 Sept. 1899; *s* of Geoffrey Pearson and Adeline Maud Rogers; *m* 1924, Dorothy Lilian Bardsley (*d* 1950); one *s* (one *d* decd). *Educ:* St Edward's School; RMC, Sandhurst (2nd Lieut 8th Hussars, 1918–21); Liverpool Univ. (BA 1924). Schoolmaster until 1929; called to Bar, Gray's Inn, 1929; Northern Circuit until 1937; Magistrate, Nigeria, 1937–42; Chief Magistrate, Palestine, 1942–47; District Judge, Malaya, 1947–49; President Sessions Court, Malaya, 1949–52; Judge of Supreme Court, Sarawak, N Borneo and Brunei, 1952–63, retd. *Publication:* Law Reports of the Seychelles Court of Appeal, vol. 1, 1965–76, 1976. *Address:* Flat 10, 2 Mountview Road, N4. *Clubs:* Athenæum; Artists' (Liverpool).

Died 28 March 1991.

ROGERS, Sir Philip (James), Kt 1961; CBE 1952; Chairman, Tobacco Research Council, 1963–71; *b* 1908; *s* of late James Henry Rogers; *m* 1939, Brenda Mary Sharp, CBE (*d* 1993), *d* of late Ernest Thompson Sharp. *Educ:* Blundell's Sch. Served War (RWAFF and Intell. Corps), 1940–44. MLC, Nigeria, 1947–51; MLC, Kenya, 1957–62; elected Representative, Kenya, East African Legislative Assembly, 1962 and 1963. President: Nigerian Chamber of Commerce, 1948 and 1950 (Vice-Pres. 1947 and 1949); Nairobi Chamber of Commerce, 1957 (Vice-Pres. 1956); AAA of Nigeria, 1951; Dir, Nigerian Elec. Corp., 1951; Governor, Nigeria Coll. of Technology, 1951; Member: Nigerian Exec. Cttee, Rd Transport Bd, 1948–51; Central Council Red Cross Soc. of W Africa, 1950–51; Trades Adv. Cttee, Nigeria, 1950 and 1951; Wages Adv. Bd, Kenya, 1955–61; EA Industrial Council, 1954–63; EA Air Licensing Appeals Trib., 1958–60; EA Air Adv. Council, 1956–60; Kenya Road Authority, 1957–61; Provl Council, Univ. of E Africa, 1961–63; Gov. Council, Roy. Tech. Coll. of E Africa, 1957–58 (Chm. 1958/59/60). Chairman: East African Tobacco Co. Ltd, 1951–63; Rift Valley Cigarette Co. Ltd, 1956–63; EA Rd Fedn, 1954–56; Kenya Cttee on Study and Trg in USA, 1958–63; Bd of Govs, Coll. of Social Studies, 1960–63; Nairobi Special Loans Cttee, 1960–63; African Teachers' Service Bd, 1956–63; Council, Royal College (later University Coll., Nairobi), 1961–63; Trustee, Outward Bound Trust of Kenya, 1959–63; Rep. of Assoc. Chambers of Commerce & Indust. of Eastern Africa; Mem. of Industrial Tribunals, England and Wales, 1966–80. Governor, Plumpton Agric. Coll., 1967–76. Member: E Sussex Educn Cttee, 1969–75; Finance Cttee, UCL, 1972–79; Indep. Schools Careers Orgn, 1972–79; Chairman: Fedn of Sussex Amenity Socs, 1968–80; Age Concern, East Sussex, 1974–80. *Address:* Church Close, Newick, East Sussex BN8 4JZ. *T:* Newick (082572) 2210.

Died 16 April 1994.

ROIJEN, Jan Herman Van; Grand Cross, Order of Orange Nassau; Commander, Order of the Netherlands Lion; Hon. CBE; Netherlands Ambassador to the United Kingdom, 1964–70; Netherlands Ambassador to the Icelandic Republic, 1964–70; Netherlands Permanent Representative to Council of Western European Union, 1964–70; *b* Istanbul, 10 April 1905; *s* of Jan Herman van Roijen (sometime Netherlands Minister to USA), and (American-born) Albertina Winthrop van Roijen; *m* 1934, Anne Snouck Hurgronje; two *s* two *d. Educ:* Univ. of Utrecht. Doctor in Law, 1929. Joined Foreign Service, 1930; Attaché to Neths Legn, Washington, 1930–32; Min. of For. Affairs, 1933–36; Sec. to Neths Legn, Tokyo, 1936–39; Chief of Polit. Div. of Min. of For. Affairs, 1939; jailed during German occupation; escaped to London, 1944; Minister without Portfolio, 1945; Minister of For. Affairs, March-July 1946; Asst Deleg. and Deleg. to UN Conf. and Assemblies, 1945–48; Ambassador to Canada, 1947–50; Leader, Neths Delegn to bring about Netherlands-Indonesian Round Table Conf., Batavia, 1949; Dep. Leader, Neths Delegn at Round Table Conf., The Hague, 1949; Ambassador to the United States, 1950–64; Leader, Neths Delegn in negotiations with Indonesia about W New Guinea, Middleburg (Va) and New York, 1962. Several hon. doctorates in Laws, of Univs and Colls in USA; Gr. Cross, Order of Oak Crown, Luxembourg; Gr. Cross, Order of Falcon, Iceland; Comdr, Order of Holy Treasure, Japan. *Recreations:* reading, theatre, golf. *Address:* Stoephoutflat, Stoeplaan 11, 2243 CW, Wassenaar, Netherlands. *Club:* De Haagsche (The Hague). *Died 16 March 1991.*

ROLPH, Cecil Hewitt; *see* Hewitt, C. R.

ROONEY, Denis Michael Hall, CBE 1977; FEng 1979; FIMechE, FIEE; CIMgt; industrial consultant; *b* 9 Aug. 1919; *s* of late Frederick and Ivy Rooney; *m* 1st, 1942, Ruby Teresa (*née* Lamb) (*d* 1984); three *s* three *d*; 2nd, 1986, Muriel Franklin; one step *d. Educ:* Stonyhurst Coll.; Downing Coll., Cambridge (MA). Served War, Royal Navy, 1941–46 (Lieut Engr). Various appts with BICC Ltd, 1946–69; Balfour Beatty Ltd: Dep. Managing Dir, 1969–72; Man. Dir, 1973–77; Chm., 1975–80; BICC Ltd: Exec. Dir, 1973–80; Exec. Vice-Chm., 1978–80; Chm., BICC Internat., 1978–80; Dep. Chm., Metal Manufactures Ltd, Australia, 1978–80; Chm., Nat. Nuclear Corp., 1980–81; Consultant, Goddard, Kay, Rogers, 1983–85; Chm., Laserfix Ltd, 1984–86. Chm., SE Asia Trade Adv. Gp, BOTB, 1975–79; Member: British Overseas Trade Adv. Council, 1976–80; Overseas Projects Bd, BOTB, 1976–79; BOTB, 1979–80; Council: Export Gp for Construction Industries, 1964–80; Christian Assoc. of Business Execs, 1979–92; Inst. of Business Ethics; W London Cttee for Protection of Children; Batti Wallahs Soc. Liveryman, Worshipful Company of Turners of London. USSR Jubilee Medal, 1988. *Publication:* contrib. (Brazilian Rlwy Electrification) IEE Jl. *Recreation:* golf. *Address:* 36 Edwardes Square, W8 6HH. *T:* 071–603 9971. *Club:* Roehampton. *Died 9 March 1994.*

ROOTES, 2nd Baron *cr* 1959; **William Geoffrey Rootes;** Chairman, Chrysler United Kingdom (formerly Rootes Motors Ltd), 1967–73; *b* 14 June 1917; *s* of 1st Baron Rootes, GBE and 1st wife, Nora (*d* 1964), *d* of Horace Press, Norfolk; *S* father, 1964; *m* 1946, Marian, *d* of late Lt-Col H. R. Hayter, DSO, and *widow* of Wing Comdr J. H. Slater, AFC; one *s* one *d. Educ:* Harrow; Christ Church, Oxford. Served War of 1939–45 in RASC (France, E Africa, Western Desert, Libya, Tunisia and Italy), demobilised, Actg Major, 1946. Rejoined Rootes Group, 1946: Man. Dir, 1962–67; Dep. Chm., 1965–67; Chm. 1967–70. Director: Rank Hovis McDougall, 1973–84; Joseph Lucas Industries Ltd, 1973–85. President: SMMT, 1960–61 (Hon. Officer, 1958–62, Chm. Exec. Cttee,

1972–73); Motor & Cycle Trades Benevolent Fund, 1968–70; Motor Ind. Research Assoc., 1970–71; Inst. of Motor Industry, 1973–75. Member: Nat. Adv. Council, Motor Manufrg Industry, 1964–71; Nat. Economic Development Cttee, Motor Manufacturing Industry, 1968–73; BNEC (Chm., American Cttee, 1969–71); Council, CBI, 1967–74, Europe Cttee, CBI, 1972–76; Council, Inst. of Dirs, 1953–78; Council, Warwick Univ., 1968–74 (Chm., Careers Adv. Bd); Council, Game Conservancy (Chm., 1975–79); Vice-Pres., British Field Sports Soc., 1978–; Mem. Council, WWF UK, 1983–(Trustee, 1983–88; Chm., Educnl Adv. Council, 1984–88). County Pres., St John Ambulance, Berks, 1983–88; KStJ 1988 (CStJ 1983). FRSA; FBIM; FIMI; FIPE. *Recreations:* shooting, fishing. *Heir:* *s* Hon. Nicholas Geoffrey Rootes [*b* 12 July 1951; *m* 1976, Dorothy Anne Burn-Forti, *d* of Cyril Wood]. *Address:* North Standen House, Hungerford, Berks RG17 0QZ. *Clubs:* Buck's, Flyfishers'. *Died 16 Jan. 1992.*

ROPER, Hon. Sir Clinton Marcus, Kt 1985; Chief Justice, High Court of the Cook Islands, since 1988; Acting Judge, High Court of New Zealand, since 1989; *b* Christchurch, 19 June 1921; *s* of Wilfred Marcus Roper; *m* 1947, Joan Elsa Turnbull; one *s* one *d. Educ:* Christchurch West High Sch.; Canterbury Univ.; Victoria Univ. of Wellington. LLB. Served War of 1939–45, Pacific, Italy and Japan (Lieut). Crown Solicitor, Christchurch, 1961–68; Judge: High Court of NZ, 1968–85; Court of Appeal, Fiji, 1985–87; High Court, Cook Islands, 1985–88; Tongan Privy Council Court, 1986–90; Tongan Court of Appeal, 1990–. Chairman: Prisons Parole Bd, 1970–85; Prisons Rev. Cttee, 1987–89; Cttee of Inquiry into Violence, 1985–87. *Address:* 15 Allister Avenue, Christchurch, New Zealand. *Died 6 March 1994.*

ROSE, Sir Alec (Richard), Kt 1968; *b* 13 July 1908; *s* of Ambrose Rose; *m* 1st, 1931, Barbara Kathleen (*née* Baldwin); two *s* two *d*; 2nd, 1960, Dorothy Mabel (*née* Walker). *Educ:* Simon Langton Boys School, Canterbury. Farming in Canada, 1928–30; haulage contractor, 1930–39; served RNVR, 1939–45; market gardener, 1945–57; fruit merchant, 1957–71. Member: Fruiterers' Co.; Worshipful Co. of Basketmakers; Worshipful Co. of Shipwrights. Hon. Life Governor, RNLI, 1975. Freeman, City of London, 1969; Freedom of Portsmouth, 1968. Blue Water Medal, Cruising Club of America, 1969; Seamanship Medal, Royal Cruising Club. *Publication:* My Lively Lady, 1968. *Recreation:* sailing (inc. circumnavigation of world, 1968). *Address:* Woodlands Cottage, Eastleigh Road, Havant, Hants PO9 2NY. *T:* Havant (0705) 477124. *Clubs:* City Livery; Royal Yacht Squadron; Portsmouth County, Royal Naval and Royal Albert Yacht (Portsmouth); Royal Naval Sailing Assoc., Eastney Cruising Assoc., Ocean Cruising (Admiral). *Died 11 Jan. 1991.*

ROSE, Prof. Geoffrey Arthur, CBE 1991; DM; FRCP, FRCGP, FFPHM; Emeritus Professor of Epidemiology, University of London, since 1991; *b* 19 April 1926; *s* of Rev. Arthur Norman Rose and Mary (*née* Wadsworth); *m* 1949, Ceridwen (*née* Coates); two *s* one *d. Educ:* Kingswood Sch.; Queen's Coll., Oxford (MA); St Mary's Hosp. Med. Sch. DM Oxford, 1958; FRCP 1970; FRCGP 1988; FFPHM (FFCM 1974). Professor of Epidemiology: St Mary's Hosp. Med. Sch., 1970–77; London Sch. of Hygiene and Tropical Medicine, 1977–91. Hon. Consultant Physician, St Mary's Hosp., 1964–91. Chairman: WHO Expert Cttees on Heart Disease Prevention, 1982, 1984; Council on Epidemiology and Prevention, Internat. Soc. and Fedn of Cardiology, 1982–86. Hon. Mem., Med. Acad. of Catalonia and Balearic Is, 1981. Hon. DSc Meml Univ. of Newfoundland, 1983; Hon. MD Univ. of Kuopio, Finland, 1991. Purkinje

Medal, Czechoslovak Med. Soc., 1978; Duodecim Medal, Finnish Med. Soc., 1989. *Publications:* (with Prof. H. Blackburn) Cardiovascular Survey Methods, 1968, 2nd edn 1982; (with Prof. D. J. P. Barker) Epidemiology in Medical Practice, 1976, 4th edn 1990; (with Prof. D. J. P. Barker) Epidemiology for the Uninitiated, 1979, 2nd edn 1986; The Strategy of Preventive Medicine, 1992. *Recreations:* lay preaching, rural pursuits. *Address:* Trevalley, Penfold Lane, Holmer Green, High Wycombe, Bucks HP15 6XS. *Died 12 Nov. 1993.*

ROSE, Graham John; gardening correspondent, Sunday Times, since 1978; *b* 28 Jan. 1928; *s* of Herbert Trower Whitfield Rose and Grace Rose (*née* Cain); *m* 1st, 1953, Catherine Marie Louise Degrais; 2nd, 1967, Elizabeth Dorothy Goldbach (*née* Dodd). *Educ:* Dame Allan's School, Newcastle-upon-Tyne; King's College, Durham Univ. (BSc Hons); Gonville and Caius College, Cambridge. Entomologist, ICI (India), Calcutta, 1950–51; Universal Crop Protection, 1951–53; Technical Dir, Micron Sprayers, 1953–57; Consultant: Micron Sprayers, Britten Norman, SDC Pesticides, Opico (UK), 1957–68; agricultural corresp., Sunday Times, 1968–78. *Publications:* Crop Protection, 1955; Landscape with Weeds, 1980; The Low Maintenance Garden, 1983; (with Peter King) Green Words, 1986; Gardener's Almanac, 1986; The Small Garden Planner, 1987; (jtly) Gardening with Style, 1988; The Romantic Garden, 1988; Woodland and Wildflower Gardening, 1988; The Traditional Garden Book, 1989; (with Peter King) The Good Gardens Guide, (annually) 1990–; (with Peter King) The Love of Roses, 1990. *Recreations:* garden designing, building. *Address:* 58 Hugh Street, SW1V 4ER. *T:* 0171–821 9378. *Club:* Pourcairou (France). *Died 3 Dec. 1995.*

ROSE, (Thomas) Stuart, CBE 1974; PPCSD; Design Director, The Post Office, 1968–76; *b* 2 Oct. 1911; *s* of Thomas and Nellie Rose; *m* 1940, Dorothea Winifred, *d* of F. G. Ebsworth, St Petersburg; two *d. Educ:* Choral Scholar, Magdalen College Sch., Oxford; Central Sch. of Arts and Crafts. Designer, Crawfords Advertising, 1934–39; free-lance graphics designer and typographer, 1946–68; Typographer, Cement and Concrete Assoc., 1946–51; Print Consultant, Fedn of British Industries, 1947–68; Art Editor, Design Magazine, 1947–53; Typographic Adviser to Postmaster General, 1962–68; Associate, Design Research Unit, industrial design partnership, 1964–68. Member: Industrial Design Cttee, FBI, 1948–65 (Chm. 1965–68); CoID Stamp Adv. Cttee, 1960–62; Post Office Stamp Adv. Cttee, 1968–76. Mem., Soc. of Industrial Artists and Designers, 1936, Pres. 1965. Governor, Central Sch. of Art and Design, 1965–74 (Vice-Chm., 1971–74). FRSA 1970. Phillips Gold Medal for Stamp Design, 1974. *Publication:* Royal Mail Stamps, 1980. *Recreations:* drawing, music, the country. *Address:* Walpole House, East Street, Coggeshall, Colchester, Essex CO6 1SH. *T:* Coggeshall (0376) 562409. *Club:* Arts (Chairman 1982–85). *Died 10 Sept. 1993.*

ROSENTHAL, Erwin Isak Jacob, LittD, DrPhil, MA; Reader in Oriental Studies, University of Cambridge, 1959–71, then Emeritus Reader; Fellow of Pembroke College, 1962–71, then Emeritus Fellow; *b* 18 Sept. 1904; *y s* of Moses and Amalie Rosenthal; *m* 1933, Elizabeth Charlotte Marx; one *s* one *d. Educ:* Heilbronn; Universities of Heidelberg, Munich, Berlin. Goldsmid Lectr in Hebrew, Lectr in North-Semitic Epigraphy, Head of Dept of Hebrew, University Coll., Univ. of London, 1933–36; Special Lectr, Semitic Langs and Lits, Univ. of Manchester, 1936–44; Lectr, Central Advisory Coun. for Educn, HM Forces, 1940–44; Nat. Service, RASC, 1944–45; attached FO, 1945; German Sect., FO, 1946–48; Tutor, Adult Educn, Univ. Tutorial Class, WEA, London, 1946–48 (part-time); Univ. Lectr in Hebrew, Cambridge,

1948–59. Vis. Professor: Columbia Univ., 1967–68; El Colegio de Mexico, 1968; Leverhulme Emeritus Fellow, 1974, 1975. Pres., British Assoc. for Jewish Studies, 1977. Corresp. Fellow, Amer. Acad. for Jewish Res., 1984; Corresp. Mem., Rhenish-Westphalian Acad. of the Sciences, 1986. *Publications:* Ibn Khalduns Gedanken über den Staat, 1932; Law and Religion, (ed and contrib.) Vol. 3, Judaism and Christianity, 1938; (ed and contrib.) Saadya Studies, 1943; (ed and trans.) Averroes' Commentary on Plato's Republic, 1956, 1966; Political Thought in Medieval Islam, 1958, new edn 1986 (Spanish trans., 1967; Japanese trans., 1970); Griechisches Erbe in der jüdischen Religionsphilosophie des Mittelalters, 1960; Judaism and Islam, 1961; Islam in the Modern National State, 1965; (ed) Judaism section, in Religion in the Middle East, 1969; Studia Semitica (Vol. I: Jewish Themes; Vol. II: Islamic Themes), 1971; articles in learned jls; festschriften. *Recreations:* music, walking, travelling. *Address:* 199 Chesterton Road, Cambridge CB4 1AH; Pembroke College, Cambridge. *T:* Cambridge (0223) 357648. *Died 5 June 1991.*

ROSKILL, Sir Ashton (Wentworth), Kt 1967; QC 1949; MA Oxon; Chairman, Monopolies and Mergers Commission (formerly Monopolies Commission), 1965–75 (Part-time Member, 1960–65); *b* 1 Jan. 1902; *e s* of late John Roskill, KC, and Sybil Mary Wentworth, *d* of late Ashton Dilke, MP; *m* 1st, 1932, Violet Willoughby (*d* 1964), *d* of late Charles W. Waddington, CIE, MVO; one *s* one *d*; 2nd, 1965, Phyllis Sydney (*d* 1990), *y d* of late Sydney Burney, CBE. *Educ:* Winchester; Exeter Coll., Oxford (Schol.; 1st class hons Modern History, 1923; Hon. Fellow, 1989). Barrister-at-Law, Inner Temple, 1925; Certificate of Honour, Council of Legal Education, 1925. Attached War Office, Intelligence Staff, 1940–45. Bencher, Inner Temple, 1958, Treasurer, 1980; Hon. Bencher, Middle Temple, 1980. Chm., Barristers Benevolent Assoc., 1968–79. *Address:* Heath Cottage, Newtown, Newbury, Berks. *T:* Newbury (0635) 40328. *Club:* Reform. *Died 23 June 1991.*

ROSKILL, Oliver Wentworth, CChem, FRSC, CEng, FIChemE, CIMechE, SFInstE, CIMgt, FIMC; Senior Partner, O. W. Roskill Industrial Consultants, 1930–74; Chairman: O. W. Roskill & Co. (Reports) Ltd, 1957–74; Roskill Information Services Ltd, 1971–74; Life President, Exhibition Audience Audits Ltd, 1985; *b* 28 April 1906; *s* of John Roskill, KC, and Sibyl Mary Wentworth, *d* of Ashton Wentworth Dilke, MP. *Educ:* Oundle Sch.; Lincoln Coll., Oxford (scholar). MA, BSc (Oxon) (1st Cl. Hons). Captain, Oxford Univ. Rugby Fives Club, 1927. Imperial Chemical Industries Ltd, 1928–30. Min. of Economic Warfare, Dep. Head, Enemy Countries Intell., 1939–41. Mem. Exec. Cttee of Political and Economic Planning (later Policy Studies Inst.), 1931, Vice-Pres., 1975; Founder Mem. Council, British Inst. of Management, 1947–53 (Chm. Inf. and Research Cttee); Mem. British Nat. Export Council, Caribbean Cttee, 1965–69; Mem. Council, Inst. of Management Consultants, 1963–74 (Pres., 1970–71). Consultant on industrial development projects to Govts of Iran, Pakistan, Malta, Fed. Govt of Rhodesia, Windward Is, and others. *Publications:* founder and part author of 'Who Owns Whom' series of directories; part author of Fifty Years of Political and Economic Planning; author of monographs on economics of metals and minerals (incl. tungsten, titanium, chromium, fluorspar); contributor to many jls of learned societies (incl. Chemical Engr, Inst. Fuel, RIBA, Town Planning Inst.). *Recreations:* mountain walking, playing chamber music, choral singing, real tennis, gardening. *Address:* The Priory, Beech Hill, Reading, Berks RG7 2AY. *T:* Reading (0734) 883146. *Clubs:* Brooks's; Woodmen of Arden; Hampton Court Tennis, Holyport Tennis. *Died 25 May 1994.*

ROSS OF NEWPORT, Baron *cr* 1987 (Life Peer), of Newport in the county of the Isle of Wight; **Stephen Sherlock Ross,** FRICS; *b* 6 July 1926; *s* of Reginald Sherlock Ross and Florence Beryl (*née* Weston); *m* 1949, Brenda Marie Hughes; two *s* two *d*. *Educ:* Bedford Sch. Served War of 1939–45, RN, 1944–48. Articled Nock & Joseland, Kidderminster, 1948–51; Assistant: Heywood & Sons, Stone, Staffs, 1951–53; Sir Francis Pittis & Son, Newport, IoW, 1953–57 (Partner, 1958–73). County Councillor, IoW CC, 1967–74 and 1981–85 (Chm. Policy and Resources Cttee, 1973–74 and 1981–83). MP (L) Isle of Wight, Feb. 1974–1987. Chm., Nat. Housing Forum, 1990–. *Recreations:* cricket; antique porcelain collector. *Address:* Herb Cottage, Skyborry Green, Knighton, Powys LD7 1TW. *T:* Knighton (0547) 528229.

Died 10 May 1993.

ROSS, Sir Alexander, Kt 1971; Chairman: United Dominions Trust Ltd, 1963–74 (Director, 1955; Vice-Chairman, 1962); Australia and New Zealand Banking Group Ltd, 1970–75; Deputy Chairman: Eagle Star Insurance Co. Ltd, 1963–82; Eagle Star Holdings Ltd, retired 1982; *b* 2 Sept. 1907; *s* of William Alexander Ross and Kathleen Ross; *m* 1st, 1933, Nora Bethia Burgess (*d* 1974); two *s* two *d*; 2nd, 1975, Cynthia Alice Barton. *Educ:* Mount Albert Grammar Sch.; Auckland University (Dip. Banking). Joined Nat. Bank of NZ, 1927, and Reserve Bank of NZ on its establishment in 1934; Dep. Gov., 1948–55. Director: Whitbread Investment Trust Ltd, 1972–83; Drayton Far Eastern Trust Ltd (formerly British Aust. Investment Trust Ltd), 1975–82; Power Components Ltd, 1976–82. Rep. NZ on numerous occasions overseas, including Commonwealth Finance Ministers' Conf. in Australia, 1954. Rep. NZ in rowing, at Empire Games, 1930; Manager, NZ team to Commonwealth Games, Vancouver, 1954; NZ rowing selector for Olympic and Commonwealth Games, NZ; Chairman: Commonwealth Games Fedn, 1968–82 (Vice Chm., 1966–68); Cttee for British Exports to NZ, 1965–67; East European Trade Council, 1967–69; British Aust. Soc., 1970–75; Queensland Community Foundn, 1986–92; Vice-Pres., British Export Houses Assoc., 1968–71; Dir, NRDC, 1966–74; Mem., BNEC, 1967–69. Member: New Zealand Soc. (Past Pres.); Council, Dominion Students' Hall Trust; Governor, Royal Caledonian Schs, 1964–69; Trustee, Aust. Musical Soc. Foundn; a past Governor, ESU. Pres., Fellowship of British Motor Industry, 1971–73. Dep. Chm., Central Council, Royal Over-Seas League, 1979–82, Life Vice Pres., 1982. Chm. Ct of Advisers, St Paul's Cathedral, 1981–82. Qld Pres., St John's Ambulance, 1982–92; Life Vice-Pres., Commonwealth Games Fedn. Freeman, City of London. Hon. Mem., NUR. *Recreations:* walking, writing. *Address:* 20 Compass Way, Tweed Heads West, NSW 2485, Australia. *T:* (75) 367430. *Died 10 April 1994.*

ROSS, Alfred William, OBE 1955; MA, MIEE; technical and operational research consultant, 1974–84, retired; Deputy Chief Scientist (Navy), Ministry of Defence, 1972–74; *b* 13 Sept. 1914; *m* 1946, Margaret Elizabeth Wilson; three *d*. *Educ:* King Edward VI School, Stourbridge; Christ's Coll., Cambridge. Joined HM Signal Sch., Portsmouth, 1936; worked on Radar during War at Admiralty Signal and Radar Establishment; Defence Research Policy Staff, Ministry of Defence, 1946–47; Chief Superintendent, Army Operational Research Group, 1951–56; Director, Naval Physical Research, MoD, 1956–68; Chief of Naval Research, MoD, 1968–72. *Publications:* scientific papers on radar, electronics and operational research. *Recreation:* golf. *Address:* 336 Fir Tree Road, Epsom Downs, Surrey KT17 3NW. *T:* Burgh Heath (0737) 356774. *Club:* Walton Heath Golf.

Died 8 Jan. 1991.

ROSS, Rear-Adm. George Campbell, CB 1952; CBE 1945; FRGS; CEng, MIMechE; MRAeS; retired; *b* 9 Aug. 1900; *s* of late Sir Archibald Ross, KBE and Maria, *d* of Col Gousieff; *m* 1st, 1929, Alice Behrens; 2nd, 1950, Lucia Boer (marr. diss. 1969); two *d*; 3rd, 1975, Manolita Harris (*d* 1988). *Educ:* Royal Naval Colleges, Osborne and Dartmouth. Served European War, 1914–18, Grand Fleet (HM Ships Warspite, P59, Vendetta); Engineering Courses at RN College, Greenwich, and RNEC, Keyham, 1919–21; HMS Hawkins, Flagship China Station, 1921–24; Lecturer in Marine Engineering, RNEC, 1924–27; HMS Effingham, Flagship East Indies Station, 1927–29; HM Dockyard, Chatham, 1929–31; HMS Rodney, Atlantic Fleet, 1931–33 (incl. Invergordon Mutiny); Comdr 1933; Asst Naval Attaché, Embassy, Tokyo, 1933–36; Liaison Officer to Japanese Flagship Asigara, Coronation Review, 1937; introduced the Oerlikon 20mm gun to the Royal Navy, 1937 (adopted in 1939 largely owing to Lord Mountbatten and the First Sea Lord, Sir Roger Backhouse); HMS Manchester, E Indies Station, 1937–39; Engineer-in-Chief's Dept, Admiralty, 1939–41; Engineer Officer, HMS Nelson, and Staff Engineer Officer to Flag Officer, Force "H", Malta Convoy, N Africa and Sicily, 1941–Aug. 1943; Capt. 1943; HMS St Angelo, Malta, as Staff Engineer Officer (D), on staff of Captain (D), Force "H", Aug. 1943–Dec. 1943 (first officer to go aboard flagship of Italian Fleet after its surrender); Aircraft Maintenance and Repair Dept, Admiralty, 1943–47; ADC to the King, 1948–49; Chief of Staff to Rear-Admiral Reserve Aircraft, 1948–49; Rear-Adm. (E) 1949; Director of Aircraft Maintenance and Repair, Admiralty, 1949–53; retd, Oct. 1953. Joined Hawker Siddeley group, Nov. 1953, and retd Sept. 1965. Consultant to Grieveson Grant, Stockbrokers, 1965–79, and other cos. Chairman, Combined Services Winter Sports Assoc., 1951–67. Freeman, City of London, 1955. *Recreations:* fishing, travel, painting, writing. *Address:* Meadowbank, 5 Parkgate Road, SW11 4NL. *T:* 071–228 7844. *Club:* Hurlingham. *Died 30 July 1993.*

ROSS, Sir Lewis (Nathan), Kt 1984; CMG 1974; FCA; chartered accountant in public practice, since 1932; company director, New Zealand; *b* 7 March 1911; *e s* of Robert and Raie Ross; *m* 1937, Ella Myrtle Burns, Melbourne, Australia; two *s* one *d*. *Educ:* Auckland Grammar Sch.; Univ. of Auckland. Commenced practice as CA, founding firm (latterly known as Ross, Melville, Bridgman & Co.), 1932; withdrew from partnership in 1965 to practise as consultant. Pres., Associated Chambers of Commerce of NZ, 1955–56; Chm., Govt Cttee: on PAYE taxation, 1964; to review all aspects of Central Govt Taxation in NZ, 1966–67. Chm., Aotea Centre Trust Bd, Auckland, 1984–; Pres., NZ Soc. of Accountants, 1972–73 (Life Mem., 1986). Director: Bank of NZ (Chm.), 1966–87; James Hardie Impey Ltd; Revertex Ind. Ltd. Hon. LLD Auckland, 1983. *Publications:* Taxation—Principles, Purpose and Incidence, 1964 (rev. edn 1973); Finance for Business, 1964; Accounting Problems that arise from Business Combinations, 1973; articles in Accountants' Jl and other business pubns. *Recreations:* bowls, contract bridge. *Address:* (private) 4/198 Remuera Road, Remuera, Auckland, New Zealand. *T:* 524–7449; (business) PO Box 881, Auckland, New Zealand. *T:* 798–665, *Fax:* (09) 393247. *Club:* Northern (Auckland).

Died 26 April 1991.

ROSS, Malcolm Keir; Headmaster of Crown Woods School, London, 1957–71; *b* 8 June 1910; *m* 1937, Isabel Munkley (*d* 1983); two *d*. *Educ:* Grangefield Grammar Sch., Stockton-on-Tees; Keble Coll., Oxford. Schoolmaster: Gordonstoun, 1933–34; Haverfordwest Grammar Sch., 1934–36; Bromley Grammar Sch., 1936–40; war service with RAF, 1940–45; Warden of Village Coll., Sawston, Cambs, 1945–57. Mem., Cttee of Enquiry into conditions

of service life for young servicemen, 1969. Governor, Rachel McMillan Coll. of Education. Book reviewer for The Times Educational Supplement. FRSA. *Recreations:* gardening, reading. *Address:* 45 Winn Road, SE12 9EX.
Died 26 Dec. 1993.

ROSS, Comdr Ronald Douglas, OBE 1984; RN; *b* 30 July 1920; *o s* of Captain James Ross, FRGS, Scottish Horse of Chengtu, Szechwan Province, China; *m* 1952, Elizabeth Mary, *er d* of Canon S. J. S. Groves; one *d. Educ:* Cargilfield; Sedbergh; RN Staff Coll. Joined Accountant Br. of RN and went to sea, 1937; war service in HM Ships Exeter, Devonshire and Tartar. Called to Bar, Middle Temple, 1950; called to the Bar, Supreme Court of Hong Kong, 1963; officiated frequently as Judge Advocate; Admiralty Prize Medal for Naval History, 1957; retired list, 1967. Clerk, Vintners' Co., 1969–84. Mem., Wine Standards Bd, 1973–84. Chevalier du Sacavin d'Anjou, 1974; Citizen and Vintner, 1975. *Publications:* contribs to The Times, Scotsman, New York Times, Investors' Chronicle, Brassey's Naval Annual, etc. *Recreation:* scripophily (collection of old share certificates and defaulted bonds). *Address:* The Limes, Ashley Close, Sevenoaks, Kent TN13 3AP. *T:* Sevenoaks (0732) 455678.
Died 1 April 1994.

ROSTAL, Prof. Max, CBE 1977; Professor at the Guildhall School of Music, London, 1944–58; Professor of the Master-Class, State Academy of Music, Cologne, 1957–82; Professor of the Master-Class, Conservatoire, Berne, Switzerland, 1958–86; *b* 7 Aug. 1905; *m* 1st, Sela Tran (marr. diss.); one *d*; 2nd, 1946, Karoline T. I. (*née* Reichsedle von Hohenblum-Simitsch) (marr. diss.); one *d*; 3rd, 1980, Maria Busato. *Educ:* State Acad., Vienna (Prof. Rosé); State Academy, Berlin (Prof. Flesch). Concert artist from age of 6; gave concerts in all parts of the world; at age of 23 Assistant to Prof. Flesch; Professor at State Academy of Music, Berlin, 1928–33; lived in London, 1934–58; latterly residing in Switzerland. Various recordings for HMV, Decca, Argo, Concert Hall Soc., Deutsche Grammophon and Symposium Records Companies. FGSM 1945. Hon. RAM 1981. Silver Medal, State Acad. of Music, Cologne, 1965; Music Award, City of Berne, Switzerland, 1972; Ehrendiplom 1st Class für Kunst und Wissenschaft, Austrian Government, 1987. Bundesverdienstkreuz 1st Class, 1968, Grand Cross of Merit, 1981, German Federal Govt; Commendatore della Repubblica Italiana, 1984. *Publications:* Thoughts on the interpretation of Beethoven's Violin Sonatas, 1981; many compositions, transcriptions, arrangements, editions. *Recreations:* photography, reading. *Address:* CH-3654, Gunten, Lake of Thun, Switzerland. *T:* (0)33–511867/ 513592.
Died 6 Aug. 1991.

ROSTRON, Sir Frank, Kt 1967; MBE 1954; FIEE; Director, Ferranti Ltd, Hollinwood, Lancs, 1958–68; *b* 11 Sept. 1900; *s* of late Samuel Ernest and Martha Rostron, Oldham; *m* 1929, Helen Jodrell Owen (*d* 1984); one *s* one *d. Educ:* Oldham High Sch.; Manchester Coll. of Tech. Ferranti Ltd, 1917–68. Served War of 1939–45: Electrical Engineer Officer, RAF Bomber Comd; released with rank of Squadron Leader. President, Manchester Chamber of Commerce, 1956 and 1957. Director: National Vulcan Boiler and General Insurance Co. Ltd, 1961–70; Aron Meters Ltd, 1961–68; McKechnie Brothers Ltd, 1966–71. Chairman: Cotton Board, 1963–67 (Independent Member, 1959); Cotton and Allied Textiles Industry Training Board, 1966–67 (Founder); Textile Council, 1967–68. *Address:* 17D Bowview Nursing Home, 4628 Montgomery Boulevard, NW, Calgary, Alberta T3B 0K7, Canada.
Died 25 Aug. 1991.

ROTHENSTEIN, Sir John (Knewstub Maurice), Kt 1952; CBE 1948; PhD (London 1931); writer; Director of the Tate Gallery, 1938–64; Hon. Fellow: Worcester College,

Oxford, 1963; University College London, 1976; Member: Architectural and Art Advisory Committee, Westminster Cathedral, since 1979 (of Advisory Committee on Decoration, 1953–79); Council, Friends of the Tate Gallery, since 1958; President: Friends of the Bradford City Art Gallery and Museums, since 1973; Friends of the Stanley Spencer Gallery, Cookham, since 1981; *b* London, 11 July 1901; *er s* of Sir William Rothenstein and Alice Mary, *e c* of Walter John Knewstub, Chelsea; *m* 1929, Elizabeth Kennard Whittington, 2nd *d* of Charles Judson Smith, Lexington, Kentucky; one *d. Educ:* Bedales School; Worcester College, Oxford (MA); University College, London (PhD). Assistant Professor: of Art History in the University of Kentucky, 1927–28; Department of Fine Arts, University of Pittsburgh, 1928–29; Director: City Art Gallery, Leeds, 1932–34; City Art Galleries and Ruskin Museum, Sheffield, 1933–38; Member: Executive Committee, Contemporary Art Society, 1938–65; British Council, 1938–64; Art Panel, Arts Council of Great Britain, 1943–56. Rector, University of St Andrews, 1964–67. Visiting Professor: Dept of Fine Arts, Fordham Univ., USA, 1967–68; of History of Art, Agnes Scott Coll., Ga, USA, 1969–70; Distinguished Prof., City Univ. of NY, at Brooklyn Coll., 1971, 1972; Regents' Lectr, Univ. of Calif at Irvine, 1973. Pres., Friends of the Stanley Spencer Gall., 1980–87. Editor, The Masters, 1965–67; Hon. Editor, Museums Jl, 1959–61. Hon. LLD (New Brunswick 1961; St Andrews 1964). KCStG 1977; Knight Commander, Mexican Order of the Aztec Eagle, 1953. *Television:* Churchill the Painter, COI, 1968; Collection and Recollection, BBC, 1968. *Publications:* The Portrait Drawings of William Rothenstein, 1889–1925, 1926; Eric Gill, 1927; The Artists of the 1890s, 1928; Morning Sorrow: a novel, 1930; (ed) Sixteen Letters from Oscar Wilde, 1930; British Artists and the War, 1931; Nineteenth Century Painting, 1932; An Introduction to English Painting, 1933; The Life and Death of Conder, 1938; Augustus John (Phaidon British Artists), 1944; Edward Burra (Penguin Modern Painters), 1945; Manet, 1945; Modern Foreign Pictures in the Tate Gallery, 1949; Turner, 1949; London's River, 1951 (with Father Vincent Turner, SJ); Modern English Painters, vol. I, Sickert to Smith, 1952, vol. II, Lewis to Moore, 1956, vol. III, Wood to Hockney, 1973, new enl. edn, as Modern English Painters: Sickert to Hockney, 1984; The Tate Gallery, 1958 (new edn 1962); Turner, 1960; British Art since 1900: an Anthology, 1962; Sickert, 1961; Paul Nash, 1961; Augustus John, 1962; Matthew Smith, 1962; Turner (with Martin Butlin), 1963; Francis Bacon (with Ronald Alley), 1964; Edward Burra, 1973; Victor Hammer: artist and craftsman, 1978; (ed) Stanley Spencer the Man: Correspondence and Reminiscences, 1979; John Nash, 1984; Stanley Spencer, 1989; *autobiography:* Summer's Lease (I), 1965; Brave Day, Hideous Night (II), 1966; Time's Thievish Progress (III), 1970; contribs to DNB. *Address:* Beauforest House, Newington, Dorchester-on-Thames, Oxon OX9 8AG. *Clubs:* Athenæum (Hon. Mem.), Chelsea Arts (Hon. Mem.).
Died 27 Feb. 1992.

ROTHENSTEIN, Michael, RA 1983 (ARA 1977); Hon. RE; painter and print-maker; *b* 1908; *yr s* of late Sir William Rothenstein and Alice Mary, *e c* of Walter John Knewstub, Chelea; *m* 1936, Betty Desmond Fitz-Gerald (marr. diss. 1957); one *s* one *d*; *m* 1958, Diana, 2nd *d* of late Comdr H. C. Arnold-Forster, CMG. Sen. Fellow, RCA, 1990. Hon. Dr Central England, 1993. *Works* acquired by: Museum of Modern Art, New York; Tate Gallery; British Museum; Victoria and Albert Museum; *exhibitions:* Ljubljana Biennale of Graphic Art; Albertina, Vienna; Tokyo Internat. Print Exhibn, and many others; *retrospective exhibitions:* Kunst-nernes Hus, Oslo, 1969; Stoke-on-Trent, 1989; *one-man shows:* The Early Years,

Redfern Gall., 1986; Prints of the '50s and '60s, Redfern Gall., 1987; Angela Flowers Gall., 1988; Rothenstein's Boxes, Royal Acad., Prints from the Seventies, Peter Nahum, Prints from the Sixties, Redfern Gall., New Paintings, Flowers East, 1992. *Publications:* Frontiers of Printmaking, 1966; Relief Printing, 1970; Suns and Moons, 1972; Seven Colours (with Edward Lucie Smith), 1975; Song of Songs (folio), 1979. *Address:* Columbia House, Stisted, Braintree, Essex CM7 8AW. *T:* Braintree (0376) 25444.   *Died 6 July 1993.*

ROTHMAN, Sydney; Chairman of Rothmans Tobacco (Holdings) Ltd, 1953–79 (Chairman and Managing Director, Rothmans Ltd, 1929–53); *b* 2 Dec. 1897; *s* of Louis and Jane Rothman; *m* 1929, Jeannette Tropp; one *s* one *d. Educ:* Highgate School. Joined L. Rothman & Company, 1919, Partner, 1923, Rothmans Ltd. Ministry of Supply, 1941–45. *Recreation:* golf.
                                    Died 19 June 1995.

ROUSE, Sir Anthony (Gerald Roderick), KCMG 1969 (CMG 1961); OBE 1945; HM Diplomatic Service, retired; *b* 9 April 1911; *s* of late Lt-Col Maxwell Rouse and Mrs Rouse, Eastbourne; *m* 1935, Beatrice Catherine Ellis. *Educ:* Harrow; Heidelberg Univ. Joined HAC 1935; RA (T) 1938; 2 Lt 1940; transf. to Intelligence Corps; served MEF and CMF on staff of 3rd Corps (commendation); Lt-Col 1944. Entered Foreign Service, 1946; First Secretary (Information), Athens, 1946; Foreign Office, 1949; British Embassy, Moscow, 1952–54; Counsellor, 1955; Office of UK High Commissioner, Canberra, 1955–57; HM Inspector of Foreign Service Establishments, 1957–59; Counsellor (Information) British Embassy, Bonn, 1959–62; British Deputy Commandant, Berlin, 1962–64; HM Minister, British Embassy, Rome, 1964–66; Consul-General, New York, 1966–71. *Address:* The Devonshire, 56 Carlisle Road, Eastbourne, E Sussex BN20 7TB.
                                    Died 8 Oct. 1994.

ROW, Hon. Sir John Alfred, Kt 1974; sugar cane farmer since 1926; Minister for Primary Industries, Queensland, Australia, 1963–72, retired; *b* Hamleigh, Ingham, Qld, Aust., 1 Jan. 1905; *s* of Charles Edward and Emily Harriet Row; *m* 1st, 1929, Gladys M. (decd), *d* of late H. E. Hollins; one *d*; 2nd, 1966, Irene, *d* of late F. C. Gough. *Educ:* Toowoomba Grammar Sch., Qld; Trebonne State Sch., Qld. Mem. for Hinchinbrook, Qld Legislative Assembly, 1960–72. Mem. Victoria Mill Suppliers Cttee and Herbert River Cane Growers Exec., 1932–60. Rep. Local Cane Prices Bd, 1948–60; Dir, Co-op Cane Growers Store, 1955–60; Councillor, Hinchinbrook Shire, and Rep. on Townsville Regional Electricity Bd, 1952–63; Life Mem.: Aust. Sugar Producers' Assoc.; Herbert River Pastoral and Agricultural Assoc. *Recreations:* bowls (past Pres. and Trustee of Ingham Bowls Club), gardening. *Address:* 10 Gort Street, Ingham, Queensland 4850, Australia. *T:* (77) 761671.   *Died 15 May 1993.*

ROWALLAN, 3rd Baron *cr* 1911; **Arthur Cameron Corbett;** *b* 17 Dec. 1919; *s* of 2nd Baron Rowallan, KT, KBE, MC, TD, and Gwyn Mervyn (*d* 1971), *d* of J. B. Grimond, St Andrews; *S* father, 1977; *m* 1st, 1945, Eleanor Mary (marr. diss. 1962), *o d* of late Captain George Boyle, The Royal Scots Fusiliers; one *s* three *d*; 2nd, 1963, April Ashley (marr. annulled, 1970). *Educ:* Eton; Balliol College, Oxford. Served War of 1939–45. Croix de Guerre (France), 1944. *Heir: s* Hon. John Polson Cameron Corbett [*b* 8 March 1947; *m* 1st, 1970, Susan Jane Dianne Green (marr. diss. 1983); one *s* one *d*; 2nd, 1984, Sandrew Filomena (separated 1991), *d* of William Bryson; one *s* one *d*]. *Address:* c/o Hon. John Corbett, Meiklemosside, Fenwick, Ayrshire KA3 6AY.
                                    Died 24 June 1993.

ROWE, Sir Henry (Peter), KCB 1978 (CB 1971); QC 1978; First Parliamentary Counsel, 1977–81; *b* 18 Aug. 1916; 3rd *s* of late Dr Richard Röhr and Olga Röhr, Vienna; *m* 1947, Patricia, *yr d* of R. W. King, London; two *s* one *d. Educ:* Vienna; Gonville and Caius Coll., Cambridge. War service, Pioneer Corps, RAC, Military Govt, British Troops, Berlin, 1941–46. Called to Bar, Gray's Inn, 1947. Joined Parliamentary Counsel Office, 1947; Jt Second Parly Counsel, 1973–76. Commonwealth Fund Travelling Fellowship in US, 1955; with Law Commn, 1966–68. *Recreations:* music, reading, walking. *Address:* 19 Paxton Gardens, Woking, Surrey GU21 5TR. *T:* Byfleet (0932) 343816.   *Died 13 Feb. 1992.*

ROWE, Norbert Edward, CBE 1944; FEng 1976; Hon. FRAeS; FIMechE; Vice-President, Engineering De Havilland Aircraft of Canada, 1962–66, retired; *b* 18 June 1898; *s* of Harold Arthur and Jane Rowe, Plymouth, Devon; *m* 1929, Cecilia Brown; two *s* two *d. Educ:* City and Guilds (Engineering) Coll. Whitworth Exhibition, 1921; BSc Eng London, 1st Cl. Hons, 1923; Associate of City and Guilds Institute, 1923; DIC 1924; Hon. FRAeS 1962 (FRAeS 1944). Royal Aircraft Establishment, Air Ministry, 1924, Junior Technical Officer, 1925; Technical Officer, Testing Establishment, 1926; Senior Technical Officer, 1937; Chief Technical Officer, Testing Establishment, 1937; Asst Director, Headquarters, 1938; Deputy Director, Research and Develt of Aircraft, Ministry of Aircraft Production Headquarters, 1940; Director of Technical Development, Ministry of Aircraft Production, 1941–45, Director-General of Technical Development, 1945–46; Controller of Research and Special Developments, British European Airways Corporation (on resignation from Civil Service), 1946–51; Technical Director Blackburn and General Aircraft Ltd, E Yorks, 1952–61; Joint Managing Director of the Blackburn Aircraft Company, 1960–61; Director, Hawker Siddeley Aviation, 1961–62. Member: Air Registration Bd, 1968; ARC, 1969–72. Fellow Inst. Aeronautical Sciences of Amer., 1953; FCGI 1954. President: Royal Aeronautical Society, 1955–56; Helicopter Assoc. of GB, 1959–60; Whitworth Soc., 1974–75. Hon. Fellow, Canadian Aeronautics and Space Inst. (formerly Canadian Aerospace Inst.), 1965. *Address:* Old Water Hall, Mirfield, West Yorks WF14 8AE.   *Died 5 Feb. 1995.*

ROWE, Norman Lester, CBE 1976; FRCS, FDSRCS; retired; Honorary Consultant in Oral and Maxillofacial Surgery to: Westminster Hospital; Plastic and Oral Surgery Centre, Queen Mary's Hospital, Roehampton; Institute of Dental Surgery, WC1; Emeritus Consultant to the Royal Navy and Retired Consultant to the Army; Recognised Teacher in Oral Surgery, University of London; *b* 15 Dec. 1915; *s* of late A. W. Rowe, OBE and of L. L. Rowe; *m* 1938, Cynthia Mary Freeman; one *s* one *d. Educ:* Malvern College; Guy's Hospital. LRCP, LMSSA; HDD RCSE. Gen. Practice, 1937–41; Captain RADC, 1941–46. Senior Registrar, Plastic and Jaw Injuries Unit, Hill End Hosp., St Albans, 1947; Consultant in Oral Surgery, Plastic and Oral Surgery Centre, Rooksdown House, Park Prewett, Basingstoke, 1948–59; formerly Mem., Army Med. Adv. Bd; Mem. Bd of Faculty of Dental Surgery, RCS, 1956–74, Vice-Dean, 1967, Colyer Gold Medal, 1981. Lectures: Webb-Johnson, RCS, 1969; Richardson Meml, Boston, 1975; President's, BAOS, 1975; William Guy Meml, RCSE, 1981; Wood Meml, RN Portsmouth, 1981; President's, Amer. Soc. Aesth. & Plastic Surg., LA, 1983; Roscoe Clarke Meml, Inst. Accident Surgery, Birmingham, 1983; Waldron Meml, Amer. Soc. Maxillofacial Surgs, LA, 1986; Evelyn Sprawson Meml, London, 1987; Mackenzie, Bolton, 1989. Formerly Examr, RCS, RCSE, RCPGlas and RCSI. Foundn Fellow, Brit. Assoc. of Oral and Maxillofacial Surgeons (formerly Brit. Assoc. of Oral Surgeons), Hon. Sec., 1962–68, Pres.,

1969–70, Hon. Fellow, 1981 (Down's Surgical Prize Medal, 1976); Foundn Mem., European Assoc. for Maxillofacial Surgery, Pres., 1974–76, Vice-Pres., 1977–82, Hon. Fellow 1982; Hon. Fellow Internat. Assoc. of Oral and Maxillofacial Surgeons, 1986 (Sec. Gen., 1968–71); Member: BMA; BDA (Tomes Medal, 1985); Fedn Dent. Internat.; Oral Surgery Club (GB); Hon. Member: Academia Nacional de Medicina de Buenos Aires, Argentina; Académie de Chirurgie Dentaire, Paris; Egyptian Dental Assoc.; Soc. of Amer. Oral Surgeons in Europe; Asociacion Mexicana de Cirugia Bucal; Amer. Soc. Maxillofacial Surgs; Canadian Assoc. of Oral and Maxillofacial Surgs; Inst. of Accident Surgery; N Californian Soc. of Oral and Maxillofacial Surgs; Academia de Odontologia da Bahia, Brasil, 1987; Sociedad Argentina de Cirugia y Traumatologia Buco-Maxilo-Facial; Emeritus Fellow, Colegio Brasileiro de Cirurgia e Traumatologia Buco-Maxilo-Facial (Le Fort Prize Medal, 1970); Hon. Fellow: Sociedad Venezolana de Cirurgia Bucal; Finnish Soc. of Oral Surgeons; Australian and New Zealand Soc. of Oral Surgeons; Assoc. Française des Chirurgiens Maxillofaciaux; Soc. Royale Belge de Stomatol. et de Chirurgie Maxillofaciale; Deutsche Gesellschaft für Mund-Kiefer und Gesichtschirurgie; Soc. of Maxillofacial and Oral Surgeons of S Africa; Polish Stomatological Soc.; Israel Soc. of Oral and Maxillofacial Surgery; Hon. FDSRCPSGlas; Hon. FFDRCSI; Hon. FRCSE; Hon. FDSRCSE; Hon. FRACDS (OMS); Hon. FIMFT. *Publications:* (jtly) Fractures of the Facial Skeleton, 1955, 2nd edn, 1968; (jtly) chapters in Plastic Surgery in Infancy and Childhood, 2nd edn, 1979; chapter in Maxillofacial Trauma, 1984; (jtly) Maxillofacial Injuries, 1985; various articles in British and foreign medical and dental jls. *Address:* Brackendale, Holly Bank Road, Hook Heath, Woking, Surrey GU22 0JP. *T:* Woking (0483) 760008. *Club:* Royal Naval Medical. *Died 4 Aug. 1991.*

ROWLAND, Herbert Grimley; *b* 10 Feb. 1905; *s* of Frank Rowland, MRCS, LRCP, and Josephine Mary (*née* Quirke); *m* 1938, Margaret Jane Elizabeth, *yr d* of Robert Crawford Higginson and Mary Higginson; one *d. Educ:* Nautical Coll., Pangbourne; Peterhouse, Cambridge. Called to Bar, 1928; admitted Solicitor, 1933; private practice, Solicitor, 1933–40; joined Office of Solicitor of Inland Revenue, 1940; Prin. Asst Solicitor of Inland Revenue, 1961–65; Acting Solicitor of Inland Revenue, 1961; Special Commissioner of Income Tax, 1965–70. Chm., S Middlesex Rent Tribunal, 1972–76. *Recreation:* golf. *Address:* 10 Hillcrest, Durlston Road, Swanage, Dorset BH19 2HS. *T:* Swanage (0929) 423256. *Clubs:* Bramley Golf (Surrey); Isle of Purbeck (Swanage). *Died 21 Dec. 1991.*

ROWLING, Rt Hon. Sir Wallace (Edward), KCMG 1983; PC 1974; President, New Zealand Institute of International Affairs, since 1990; *b* Motueka, 15 Nov. 1927; *s* of A. Rowling; *m* 1951, Glen Elna, *d* of Captain J. M. Reeves; two *s* one *d* (and two *d* decd). *Educ:* Nelson Coll.; Canterbury Univ. (MA). Fulbright Schol., 1955–56. Formerly Asst Dir of Educn, NZ Army. MP (Lab) for Buller (later for Tasman), NZ, 1962–84; Minister of Finance, 1972–74; Prime Minister of NZ, 1974–75; Leader of Opposition, 1975–83. Ambassador to USA, 1985–88. Chairman: Superannuation Investment Ltd, 1992–; Tasman Electric Power Trust, 1993–; Port Nelson Ltd, 1994–; Mutual Funds Ltd, 1994–. Governor for New Zealand, IMF. Rep. NZ at annual meeting of ADB, Kuala Lumpur, 1974. Pres., Asia Pacific Socialist Orgn, 1977–83. Chairman: Mus. of NZ, 1994–; Fifeshire Foundn, 1994–; NZ Orthopaedic Trust, 1994–. Col Comdt, NZ Army Educn Corps, 1977–82. Hon. LLD Canterbury, NZ, 1987. *Recreation:* golf. *Address:* PO Box 78, Motueka, Nelson, New Zealand. *Died 31 Oct. 1995.*

ROWNTREE, Sir Norman Andrew Forster, Kt 1970; CEng; FICE; retired; *b* 11 March 1912; *s* of Arthur Thomas Rowntree, London, and Ethel, *d* of Andrew Forster; *m* 1939, Betty, *d* of William Arthur Thomas; two *s* one *d. Educ:* Tottenham County Sch.; London Univ. (BSc(Eng)). Consulting Engineer, 1953–64; Mem. and Dir, Water Resources Bd, 1964–73; Prof. of Civil Engineering, UMIST, 1975–79; Consultant to Allott and Lomax, Consulting Engineers, 1979–80. Member: Adv. Council for Applied R&D, 1976–80; Meteorological Office Cttee, 1979–80; Commn for Commonwealth Scholarship, 1979–80; Scientific Council, Centre de Formation Internationale à la Gestion des Ressources en Eau (France), 1977–80, Hon. Vice-Pres., 1980–86; Expert Adv. Cttee, State of New Jersey Water Supply Master Plan, 1976–80. Pres., Inst. of Water Engineers, 1962–63. Vice-Pres., ICE, 1972–75, Pres. 1975–76. Vis. Prof., KCL, 1972–75; Lectures: Graham Clark, CEI, 1972; Hawksley, IMechE, 1976. Hon. DSc City Univ, 1974. Gold Medal, Soc. Chem. Ind., 1977. *Address:* 97 Quarry Lane, Kelsall, Tarporley, Cheshire CW6 0NJ. *T:* Kelsall (0829) 51195. *Died 22 July 1991.*

ROYALTON KISCH, Alastair; *see* Kisch.

RUCKER, Sir Arthur Nevil, KCMG 1942; CB 1941; CBE 1937; Chairman of Stevenage New Town Corporation, 1962–66 (Vice-Chairman, 1956–62); *b* 20 June 1895; *o s* of late Sir Arthur Rücker, FRS, and Lady (Thereza) Rücker, Everington House, nr Newbury; *m* 1922, Elsie Marion Broadbent (*d* 1991); two *s* two *d. Educ:* Marlborough; Trinity College, Cambridge. Served European War (12th Suffolk Regiment, Lieutenant), 1915–18; entered Civil Service as Assistant Principal, 1920; Private Secretary to successive Ministers of Health, 1928–36; Director of Establishments and Public Relations, Ministry of Health, 1937–39; Principal Private Secretary to Prime Minister, 1939–40; seconded for special duties, 1941, returned to Ministry of Health as Deputy Secretary, 1943; Deputy Director-General, IRO, 1948. Deputy Agent-General of the UN Korean Reconstruction Agency, 1951; Member Commonwealth War Graves Commission, 1956–69. Hon. LLD Wales, 1965. Korean Order of Diplomatic Merit, Heung-in Medal, 1974. *Club:* Athenæum. *Died 12 July 1991.*

RUDÉ, Prof. George Frederick Elliot; Professor of History, Concordia University, Montreal, 1970–87, Emeritus Professor, 1988; *b* 8 Feb. 1910; *s* of Jens Essendrop Rude, Norway, and Amy Geraldine Elliot Rude, England; *m* 1940, Doreen, *d* of J. W. De la Hoyde, Dublin; no *c. Educ:* Shrewsbury Sch.; Trinity Coll., Cambridge. Dr of Letters (Adelaide), 1967. Taught at: Stowe Sch., Bucks, 1931–35; St Paul's Sch., London, 1936–49; Sir Walter St John's Sch., London, 1950–54; Holloway Sch., London, 1954–59; Univ. of Adelaide: Sen. Lectr in History, 1960–63; Prof. of History, 1964–67; Prof. of History, Flinders Univ., SA, 1968–70; Leverhulme Vis. Prof., Univ. of Tokyo, Sept.-Nov. 1967; Vis. Prof., Univ. of Stirling, 1968; Vis. Prof. Fellow, Univ. of Sussex, 1979–82; Pinckney Harrison Vis. Prof., Coll. of William and Mary, Williamsburg, USA, 1980–81. Dir, Norway Mission, UNWRA, 1945. Mem., Australian Research Grants Cttee, 1969. Alexander Prize, Roy. Hist. Soc., 1955. FRHistS 1957; Fellow, Australian Acad. of Humanities, 1963. Kt of Mark Twain, 1986. *Publications:* The Crowd in the French Revolution, 1959; Wilkes and Liberty, 1962; Revolutionary Europe 1783–1815, 1964; The Crowd in History, 1964; (ed) The Eighteenth Century 1715–1815, 1965; (ed) Robespierre, 1967; (with E. J. Hobsbawm) Captain Swing, 1969; Paris and London in the 18th Century, 1970; Hanoverian London 1714–1808, 1971; Debate on Europe 1815–1850, 1972; Europe in the Eighteenth Century, 1972; Robespierre, 1975; Protest and

Punishment, 1978; Ideology and Popular Protest, 1980; Criminal and Victim: crime and society in early 19th century England, 1985; The French Revolution after 200 years, 1988; contribs to Eng. Hist. Review, Eng. Econ. Hist. Review, Revue Historique, Past and Present, etc. *Recreations:* swimming, reading, public speaking. *Address:* 24 Cadborough Cliff, Rye, Sussex TN31 7EB. *T:* Rye (0797) 223442. *Died 8 Jan. 1993.*

RUFF, William Willis, CBE 1973; DL; Clerk of the Surrey County Council, 1952–74; *b* 22 Sept. 1914; *s* of late William Ruff, Whitby, Yorks; *m* 1939, Agnes, *d* of late Howard Nankivell; two *s. Educ:* Durham School. Served War of 1939–45: Royal Signals, North Africa and India, 1940–45; Capt., 1942; Maj., 1943. Asst Solicitor: Scarborough Corp., 1937; Heston and Isleworth Corp., 1938; Surrey County Council: Asst Solicitor, 1939; Senior Asst Solicitor, 1947; Asst Clerk, 1948; Deputy Clerk, 1951. Chm., Soc. of Clerks of Peace and of Surrey of County Councils, 1969–72. Mem., Parly Boundary Commn for England, 1974–83. DL Surrey, 1964. *Recreations:* music, watching cricket. *Address:* 3 Brympton Close, Ridgeway Road, Dorking, Surrey RH4 3AU. *T:* Dorking (0306) 882406.

Died 23 May 1992.

RUMBOLD, Sir (Horace) Algernon (Fraser), KCMG 1960 (CMG 1953); CIE 1947; *b* 27 Feb. 1906; *s* of late Colonel William Edwin Rumbold, CMG and Elizabeth Gordon, *d* of Rev. R. Cameron, Burntisland; *m* 1946, Margaret Adél, *d* of late Arthur Joseph Hughes, OBE; two *d. Educ:* Wellington College; Christ Church, Oxford. Assistant Principal, India Office, 1929; Private Sec. to Parliamentary Under-Secretaries of State for India, 1930–33, and to Permanent Under-Secretary of State, 1933–34; Principal, 1934; Asst Sec., 1943; transferred to Commonwealth Relations Office, 1947; Deputy High Commissioner in the Union of South Africa, 1949–53; Asst Under Sec. of State, 1954–58; Dep. Under Sec. of State, 1958–66; retired, 1966. Chm. Cttee on Inter-Territorial Questions in Central Africa, 1963; Advr, Welsh Office, 1967. Dep. Chm., Air Transport Licensing Bd, 1971–72. Mem. Governing Body, SOAS, 1965–80, Hon. Fellow, 1981. Pres., Tibet Soc. of the UK, 1977–88. *Publication:* Watershed in India 1914–1922, 1979. *Address:* Shortwoods, West Clandon, Surrey GU4 7UB. *T:* Guildford (0483) 222757. *Club:* Travellers'.

Died 23 Oct. 1993.

RUNCORN, Prof. (Stanley) Keith, FRS 1965; Sydney Chapman Professor of Physical Science, University of Alaska, since 1988; Senior Research Fellow, Imperial College of Science, Technology and Medicine, since 1989; *b* 19 Nov. 1922; *s* of W. H. Runcorn, Southport, Lancs; unmarried. *Educ:* King George V Sch., Southport; Gonville and Caius Coll., Cambridge. ScD 1963. Radar Research and Develt Establishment, Min. of Supply, 1943–46; Asst Lecturer, 1946–48, and Lecturer, 1948–49, in Physics, Univ. of Manchester; Asst Dir of Research in Geophysics, Cambridge Univ., 1950–55; Research Geophysicist, Univ. of California at Los Angeles, 1952 and 1953; Fellow of Gonville and Caius Coll., Cambridge, 1948–55; Prof. of Physics, Univ. of Durham (King's Coll.), 1956–63, Univ. of Newcastle upon Tyne, 1963–88 (Head, Dept of Physics, 1956–88). Visiting Scientist, Dominion Observatory, Ottawa, 1955; Visiting Professor of Geophysics: CIT, 1957; Univ. of Miami, 1966; Pa State Univ., 1967; Florida State Univ., 1968; UCLA, 1975; Kiel Univ., 1992; Max Planck Inst., Mainz, 1994; J. Ellerton Becker Senior Visiting Fellow, Australian Academy of Science, 1963; Res. Associate, Mus. of N Arizona, 1957–72; Rutherford Memorial Lectr (Kenya, Tanzania and Uganda), 1970; du Toit Meml Lectr (S Africa), 1971; Halley Lectr, Oxford Univ., 1972–73; Hitchcock Foundn

Prof., Univ. of California, Berkeley, 1981; Vis. Scholar, Sydney Univ., 1991, 1993, 1995. Mem., NERC, 1965–69. Pres., Section A (Phys. and Maths), British Assoc., 1980–81. Member: Pontifical Acad. of Sciences, 1981; Academia Europæa, 1989; Hon. Member: Royal Netherlands Acad. of Arts and Sciences, 1970; Royal Norwegian Soc. of Sci. and Letters, 1985; Royal Soc., NSW, 1993; For. Mem., Indian Nat. Acad. of Science, 1980; Corresp. Mem., Bavarian Acad. of Sci., 1990. Napier Shaw Prize, Royal Met. Soc., 1959; Charles Chree Medal and Prize, Inst. of Physics, 1969; Vetlesen Prize, 1971; John Adams Fleming Medal, Amer. Geophysical Union, 1983; Gold Medal, Royal Astronomical Soc., 1984; Wegener Medal, European Union of Geoscis, 1987. Hon. DSc: Utrecht, 1969; Ghent, 1971; Paris, 1979; Bergen, 1980. *Publications:* scientific papers. *Recreations:* usual. *Address:* Blackett Laboratory, Imperial College, SW7 2BZ. *Clubs:* Athenæum; Union (Newcastle upon Tyne). *Died 5 Dec. 1995.*

RUSHBROOKE, Prof. G(eorge) Stanley, MA, PhD; FRS 1982; FRSE; Professor of Theoretical Physics, University of Newcastle upon Tyne, 1951–80; Head of Department of Theoretical Physics, 1965–80; Deputy Head, School of Physics, 1972–80; *b* 19 Jan. 1915; *s* of George Henry Rushbrooke and Frances Isobel Rushbrooke (*née* Wright), Willenhall, Staffs; *m* 1949, Thelma Barbara Cox (*d* 1977). *Educ:* Wolverhampton Grammar School; St John's College, Cambridge (Schol. 1933–37). Research Asst, Bristol Univ., 1938–39; Senior DSIR award and Carnegie Teaching Fellowship, 1939–44, UC Dundee, Univ. of St Andrews; Lectr in Mathematical Chemistry, Leeds Univ., 1944–48; Sen. Lectr in Theoretical Physics, Oxford, Univ. and Lecturer in Mathematics, University Coll., Oxford, 1948–51. Leverhulme Emeritus Fellow, 1981. Vis. Prof., Dept of Chemistry, Univ. of Oregon, USA, 1962–63; Vis. Prof. of Physics and Chemistry, Rice Univ., Houston, 1967. *Publications:* Introduction to Statistical Mechanics, 1949; research papers in scientific journals. *Recreations:* hillwalking, birdwatching. *Address:* 46 Belle Vue Avenue, Newcastle upon Tyne NE3 1AH.

Died 14 Dec. 1995.

RUSK, Dean, Hon. KBE 1976; appointed Professor of International Law, University of Georgia School of Law, Athens, Georgia, 1971, later Professor Emeritus; *b* 9 Feb. 1909; *s* of Robert Hugh Rusk and Frances Elizabeth Clotfelter; *m* 1937, Virginia Foisie; two *s* one *d. Educ:* Davidson College, North Carolina; St John's College, Oxford. Associate Prof. of Government and Dean of Faculty, Mills Coll., 1934–40; US Army, 1940–46; Special Asst to Secretary of War, 1946; US Dept of State, 1947–51; Asst Sec. of State for UN Affairs, 1949; Dep. Under Sec. of State, 1949–50; Asst Sec. of State for Far Eastern Affairs, 1950–51; President, The Rockefeller Foundation, 1952–61, Distinguished Fellow, 1969–; Sec. of State, 1961–69. Hon. Fellow, St John's Coll., Oxford, 1955. Hon. LLD: Mills Coll., Calif, 1948; Davidson Coll., 1950; Univ. of Calif, 1961; Emory Univ., Georgia, 1961; Princeton Univ., NJ, 1961; Louisiana State Univ. 1962; Amherst Coll., 1962; Columbia Univ., 1963; Harvard Univ., 1963; Rhode Island Univ., 1963; Valparaiso Univ., 1964; Williams Coll., 1964; Univ. of N Carolina, 1964; George Washington Univ., 1965; Oberlin Coll., 1965; Maryville Coll., 1965; Denver Univ., 1966; Erskine Coll., 1967; Hon. DCL Oxford, 1962; Hon. LHD: Westminster Coll., 1962; Hebrew Union Coll., 1963; Hardin-Simmons Univ., 1967. Cecil Peace Prize, 1933. Legion of Merit (Oak Leaf Cluster). *Publication:* As I Saw It: a Secretary of State's memoirs, 1991. *Address:* 1 Lafayette Square, 620 Hill Street, Athens, Ga 30606, USA.

Died 20 Dec. 1994.

RUSSELL, Sir Archibald (Edward), Kt 1972; CBE 1954; FRS 1970; FEng 1976; Joint Chairman, Concorde Executive Committee of Directors, 1965–69; Vice-Chairman, BAC-Sud Aviation Concorde Committee, 1969–70, retired; *b* 30 May 1904; *s* of Arthur Hallett Russell; *m* 1st, 1929, Lorna (*d* 1984), *d* of J. J. Mansfield; one *s* one *d*; 2nd, 1986, Judith, *d* of M. Humphrey. *Educ:* Fairfield Secondary Sch.; Bristol Univ. Joined Bristol Aeroplane Co. Ltd, 1926; Chief Technician, 1931; Technical Designer, 1938; Chief Engineer, 1944; Dir, 1951; Tech. Dir, 1960–66; Chm., British Aircraft Corporation, Filton Div., 1967–69 (Man. Dir, 1966–67). Wright Bros Memorial Lecture, Washington, 1949; 42nd Wilbur Wright Memorial Lecture, London, 1954; RAeS British Gold Medal, 1951; David Guggenheim Medal, 1971; Hon. DSc Bristol, 1951. FIAeS; Hon. FRAeS 1967. *Publications:* papers in R&M Series of Aeronautical Research Cttee and RAeS Journal. *Address:* Runnymead, 21 Riverside, Angarrack, Hayle, Cornwall TR27 5JD. *T:* Hayle (01736) 757208.   *Died 29 May 1995.*

RUSSELL, Brian Fitzgerald, MD, FRCP; Consulting Physician, Department of Dermatology, The London Hospital (Physician, 1951–69); Consulting Physician, St John's Hospital for Diseases of the Skin (Physician, 1947–69); Civilian Consultant in Dermatology to the Royal Navy, 1955–69; past Dean, Institute of Dermatology; *b* 1 Sept. 1904; *s* of Dr John Hutchinson Russell and Helen Margaret (*née* Collingwood); *m* 1932, Phyllis Daisy Woodward; three *s* one *d*. *Educ:* Merchant Taylors' School. MD (London) 1929; FRCP 1951; DPH (Eng.) 1943. Medical First Asst, London Hosp., 1930–32; general medical practice, 1933–45; Dermatologist, Prince of Wales's Hosp., Tottenham, 1946–51; Asst Physician, Dept of Dermatology, St Bartholomew's Hosp., 1946–51. President: St John's Hosp. Dermatological Soc., 1958–60; Dermatological Sect., RSM, 1968–69 (Hon. Mem., 1977); Corr. Mem.: American Dermatological Soc.; Danish Dermatological Soc. *Publications:* St John's Hospital for Diseases of the Skin, 1863–1963, 1963; (with Eric Wittkower) Emotional Factors in Skin Diseases, 1953; Section on Dermatology in Price's Medicine (ed by Bodley Scott), 1973. *Recreation:* rustication. *Address:* Arches, Hilltop Lane, Saffron Walden, Essex CB11 4AS.
                      Died 15 June 1994.

RUSSELL, Dilys, (Mrs Leonard Russell); *see* Powell, E. D.

RUSSELL, Edward Walter, CMG 1960; MA, PhD Cantab; Professor of Soil Science, Reading University, 1964–70, then Professor Emeritus; *b* Wye, Kent, 27 Oct. 1904; *e s* of late Sir (Edward) John Russell, OBE, FRS and Elnor, *y d* of late Walter Oldham, Manchester; *m* 1933, Margaret, *y d* of late Sir Hugh Calthrop Webster; one *s* two *d*. *Educ:* Oundle; Gonville and Caius College, Cambridge. Soil Physicist, Rothamsted Experimental Station, Harpenden, 1930–48; Reader in Soil Science, Oxford Univ., 1948–55; Director, East African Agriculture and Forestry Research Organisation, 1955–64. Member: Scientific Council for Africa, 1956–63; Agricultural Research Council of Central Africa, 1959–64. FInstP; FIBiol; FIAgrE. Hon. Member: British Soc. of Soil Science (Pres., 1968–70); Internat. Soc. of Soil Science. For. Corr. Mem., French Acad. of Agriculture, 1969. Hon. Councillor, Consejo Superior de Investigaciones Cientificas, Madrid, 1970. Hon DSc Univ. of East Africa, 1970. *Publications:* 8th, 9th and 10th Editions of Soil Conditions and Plant Growth; contrib. on physics and chemistry of soils to agricultural and soil science journals. *Address:* 592 Fox Hollies Road, Hall Green, Birmingham B28 9DX. *T:* 0121–777 3689.
                      Died 22 Oct. 1994.

RUSSELL, Sir Evelyn (Charles Sackville), Kt 1982; Chief Metropolitan Stipendiary Magistrate, 1978–82; *b* 2 Dec. 1912; *s* of late Henry Frederick Russell and Kathleen Isabel, *d* of Richard Morphy; *m* 1939, Joan (*d* 1990), *er d* of Harold Edward Jocelyn Camps; one *d. Educ:* Douai School; Château de Mesnières, Seine Maritime, France. Hon. Artillery Co., 1938. Served War of 1939–45, Royal Artillery, in UK, N Africa, Italy and Greece. Called to the Bar, Gray's Inn, 1945 (Hon. Bencher 1980); Metropolitan Stipendiary Magistrate, 1961. KCHS 1980 (KHS 1964). *Address:* The Gate House, Coopersale, Epping, Essex CM16 7QT. *T:* Epping (0992) 572568.
                      Died 14 Oct. 1992.

RUSSELL, Sir George Michael, 7th Bt, *cr* 1812; *b* 30 Sept. 1908; *s* of Sir Arthur Edward Ian Montagu Russell, 6th Bt, MBE and late Aileen Kerr, *y d* of Admiral Mark Robert Pechell; *S* father, 1964; *m* 1936, Joy Frances Bedford, *d* of late W. Mitchell, Irwin, Western Australia; two *d. Educ:* Radley, Berkshire, England. Heir: half-*b* Arthur Mervyn Russell [*b* 7 Feb. 1923; *m* 1945, Ruth, *d* of C. G. Holloway; one *s*].   *Died March 1993.*

RUSSELL, John Lawson; Commissioner for Local Administration in Scotland, 1978–82; *b* 29 May 1917; *er s* of late George William Russell and Joan Tait Russell; *m* 1946, Rachel Essington Howgate; three *s. Educ:* Central School and Anderson Inst., Lerwick; Edinburgh Univ. (BL). Enrolled Solicitor. Served Royal Scots, Royal Artillery, Gordon Highlanders and 30 Commando, 1939–46 (despatches). Assistant Secretary, Assoc. of County Councils in Scotland, 1946–49; Depute County Clerk: West Lothian, 1950–57; Caithness, 1957–58; County Clerk: Caithness, 1958–67; Aberdeen, 1967–75; Chief Executive, Grampian Region, 1974–77. Member, Countryside Commission for Scotland, 1978–82. *Recreations:* sailing, hill-walking, camping, photography. *Address:* 2A Montgomery Court, 110 Hepburn Gardens, St Andrews, Fife KY16 9LT. *T:* St Andrews (0334) 75727.   *Died 22 Aug. 1992.*

RUSSELL, William Robert; Vice-President, Australian British Trade Association, 1980–86 (Chairman, 1967–72 and 1975–77; Deputy Chairman, 1972–74 and 1977–80); *b* 6 Aug. 1913; *s* of William Andrew Russell and Mary Margaret Russell; *m* 1940, Muriel Faith Rolfe; one *s* one *d. Educ:* Wakefield Road Central, East Ham. Served War of 1939–45: Mine-Sweeping and Anti-Submarine vessels; commissioned, 1942; appointed to command, 1943. Joined Shaw Savill & Albion Co. Ltd, 1929; Director, 1958; Manager, 1959; Gen. Manager, 1961; Dep. Chm., 1966; Chm. and Man. Dir, 1968–73. Chm., London Bd, Bank of NZ, 1981–84 (Dir, 1968–84). Chairman: Council of European and Japanese Nat. Shipowners Assocs, 1969–71 and 1973–75; Aust. and NZ Adv. Cttee to BOTB, 1975–77 (Dep. Chm., 1977–79); NZ/UK Chamber of Commerce and Industry, 1979–84. Mem., Tandridge Dist Council, 1978–82. *Recreations:* gardening, golf, sailing. *Address:* Westland Cottage, 4 Peter Avenue, Oxted, Surrey RH8 9LG. *T:* Oxted (0883) 713080. *Clubs:* Naval; Royal Lymington Yacht.   *Died 11 April 1994.*

RUTTLE, His Honour Henry Samuel; a Circuit Judge (formerly Judge of County Courts), 1959–81; *b* 10 Nov. 1906; *yr s* of late Michael Ruttle, Portlaw, Co. Waterford, Ireland; *m* 1st, 1943, Joyce Mayo Moriarty (*d* 1968), *yr d* of late J. O. M. Moriarty, Plymouth; one *s* two *d*; 2nd, 1978, Mary Kathleen Scott, *d* of late F. T. Scott, Wimbledon. *Educ:* Wesley College, Dublin and Trinity College, Dublin. BA (Moderatorship in Legal and Political Science) and LLB, 1929; LLD 1933; MA 1950. Called to the Bar, Gray's Inn, 1933; practised in Common Law; London and Western Circuit; served War of 1939–45: RAFVR, 1940–45; Squadron Leader; Deputy Judge Advocate, Judge Advocate General's Office; resumed practice at Bar, 1945. Member of Church Assembly, 1948–55; Mem., General Council of the Bar, 1957–59;

Deputy Chairman Agricultural Land Tribunal (SW Area), 1958–59; Mem., County Court Rules Cttee, 1969–81 (Chm., 1978–81). Jt Editor, The County Court Practice, 1973–81. JP, Co. Surrey, 1961. *Recreations:* Rugby football (Leinster Inter-Provincial, 1927; Captain London Irish RFC, 1935–36; Middlesex County), fly-fishing. *Address:* 1 Rutland Lodge, Clifton Road, Wimbledon Common, SW19 4QZ. *Died 11 Sept. 1995.*

RYDEN, Kenneth, MC and Bar 1945; DL; *b* 15 Feb. 1917; *s* of Walter and Elizabeth Ryden; *m* 1950, Catherine Kershaw (*née* Wilkinson); two *s*. *Educ:* Queen Elizabeth's Grammar School, Blackburn. FRICS. Served War of 1939–45 (MC and Bar, despatches 1945): RE, attached Royal Bombay Sappers and Miners, India, Assam and Burma, 1940–46, retd (Captain). Articled pupil and prof. trng, 1936–39; Min. of Works: Estate Surveyor, 1946–47; attached UK High Commns, India and Pakistan, 1947–50; Sen. Estate Surveyor, Scotland, 1950–59; Founder and Sen. Partner, Kenneth Ryden & Partners (Chartered Surveyors), subseq. Ryden, Edinburgh, Glasgow and London (later also in Aberdeen and Prague), 1959–74, retd, Consultant 1974–80. Chm., Scottish Br., Chartered Auctioneers and Estate Agents' Institute, 1960–61; Member: Edinburgh Valuation Appeal Cttee, 1965–75, 1981– (Chm., 1987–90); Scottish Solicitors' Discipline Tribunal, 1985–93. Mem. Bd, Housing Corp., 1972–76. Master, Co. of Merchants of City of Edinburgh, 1976–78; Liveryman, Chartered Surveyors' Co. DL City of Edinburgh, 1978. FRCPE 1985. *Recreations:* fishing, golf, Scottish art. *Address:* 19 Belgrave Crescent, Edinburgh EH4 3AJ. *T:* 0131–332 5893. *Club:* New (Edinburgh).
Died 7 Oct. 1994.

RYDER, Peter Hugh Dudley, MBE 1944; Managing Director, Thomas Tilling Ltd, 1957–68; *b* 28 April 1913; *s* of Hon. Archibald Dudley Ryder (2nd *s* of 4th Earl of Harrowby) and Eleanor Frederica Fisher-Rowe; *m* 1940, Sarah Susannah Bowes-Lyon; two *s* one *d. Educ:* Oundle School. Provincial Newspapers Ltd, Hull and Leeds, 1930–33; Illustrated Newspapers Ltd, 1933–39; seconded from TA to Political Intell. Dept of FO, 1939–45 (Hon. Lt-Col 1944). Man. Dir, Contact Publications Ltd, 1945; Man. Dir, Daimler Hire Ltd, 1950; Commercial Dir, James A. Jobling & Co. Ltd, Sunderland, 1953; Chairman: James A. Jobling & Co. Ltd, 1957–62 and 1967–68; Heinemann Gp of Publishers Ltd, 1961–68; Director: District Bank Ltd, 1961–69; Cornhill Insce Co. Ltd, 1965–68. Mem. Council, BIM, 1966–69 (Mem. Bd of Fellows, 1968–69); Mem. Bd of Govs, Ashridge Management Coll., 1968. *Address:* Ardmore, 21 Riverbank Road, Ramsey, Isle of Man. *Died 17 Sept. 1993.*

RYDON, Prof. (Henry) Norman, DSc, PhD (London), DPhil (Oxon); FRSC; Professor of Chemistry, University of Exeter, 1957–77, then Emeritus; Deputy Vice-Chancellor, 1973–75; Public Orator, 1976–77; *b* 24 March 1912; *o s* of late Henry William Rydon and Elizabeth Mary Anne (*née* Salmon); *m* 1st, 1937, Eleanor Alice Tattersall (*d* 1968); one *d*; 2nd, 1968, Lovis Elna Hibbard (*née* Davies) (*d* 1983); 3rd, 1985, Clare Warfield Hill (*née* Kenner) (marr. diss.). *Educ:* Central Foundation Sch., London; Imperial Coll., London. BSc (London), 1931; PhD (London), 1933; DSc (London), 1938; DPhil (Oxon), 1939. Demonstrator in Organic Chemistry, Imperial College, London, 1933–37; Demonstrator in Chemistry, Birkbeck College, London, 1933–37; 1851 Exhibition Senior Student, Oxford University, 1937–40; Chemical

Defence Experimental Station, Porton, 1940–45; Member Scientific Staff, Medical Research Council, Lister Institute, 1945–47; Reader in Organic Chemistry, Birkbeck Coll., London, 1947–49; Asst Prof. and Reader in Organic Chemistry, Imperial Coll., London, 1949–52; Professor of Chemistry and Director of the Chemical Laboratories, Manchester College of Science and Technology, 1952–57. Member Council: Chem. Society, 1947–50, 1951–52, 1954–57, 1964–67; Roy. Inst. of Chemistry, 1955–58, 1959–62, 1963–66, 1971–73; Soc. of Chemical Industry, 1961–63; Regional Scientific Adviser for Civil Defence, Home Office, 1951–52, 1955–57. Member: Chemical Defence Adv. Bd, MoD, 1955–66; Scientific Adv. Council, MoD, 1960–63. Hon. DSc Exeter, 1981. Meldola Medal, Roy. Inst. of Chemistry, 1939; Harrison Memorial Prize, Chem. Soc., 1941. *Publications:* papers in Jl of Chem. Soc. and other scientific jls, 1933–. *Recreations:* travel, gardening, motoring. *Address:* Stadmans, Dunsford, Exeter EX6 7DD. *T:* Christow (0647) 52532; Hunting Hills, 5401 Ijamsville Road, Ijamsville, Md 21754, USA. *T:* (301) 662–2058. *Died 12 Sept. 1991.*

RYLAND, Judge John, CIE 1946; Royal Indian Navy (retired); Judge for British Columbia, 1969; retired; *b* 31 March 1900; *s* of late W. J. Ryland, Surbiton; *m* 1938, Lucy Lenore, *d* of J. W. Bryden, Victoria, BC; two *s*. *Educ:* King's College School; HMS Conway. *Address:* Royston, BC V0R 2V0, Canada.
Died 22 Aug. 1991.

RYLE, Kenneth Sherriff, CBE 1964; MC 1945; Secretary to the Church Commissioners for England, 1969–75; *b* 13 April 1912; *s* of Herbert Ryle, CVO, OBE and Mary, *d* of George Weir Wilson; *m* 1941, Jean Margaret Watt; one *s* one *d. Educ:* Cheltenham Coll. Chartered Accountant, 1936; Queen Anne's Bounty, 1936–48. Served in RA, 1940–45: India, Persia, Middle East, Sicily, Italy, Germany; Captain 1944. Church Commissioners, 1948–75 (Dep. Sec., 1964–69). *Recreation:* golf. *Address:* 47 Albyfield, Bickley, Kent BR1 2HY. *T:* 081–467 6319. *Club:* Chislehurst Golf. *Died 12 April 1993.*

RYMER-JONES, Brig. John Murray, CBE 1950 (OBE 1941); MC 1917, and Bar 1918; QPM 1959; Assistant Commissioner Metropolitan Police, 1950–59, retired; Secretary, Drinking Fountain Association, 1959–76; Committee Member, Royal Humane Society, 1957–77; *b* 12 July 1897; *s* of late John and Lilian Rymer-Jones; *m* 1930, Gertrude Alice Wobey; one *s* two *d. Educ:* Felsted School; RMA, Woolwich. Commissioned RFA, 1916; served European War: France and Flanders, 1916–18; Army of Rhine, 1919; Ireland, 1920–21 with KORR (Lancaster); Plebiscite, Upper Silesia, 1921; HQ British Army in Egypt, 1921–25; HQ Shanghai Defence Force, 1927–28; Company Commander and Instructor, RMA, Woolwich, 1929–33; retired as Captain, RA. Joined Metropolitan Police as Chief Inspector, 1934; Superintendent, 1935; Chief Constable, 1936; Inspector-General and Brigadier commanding Palestine Police, 1943–46; Commander Metropolitan Police, 1946–50. Area Comr, St John Ambulance, North Kent, 1963–66. Commander of St John of Jerusalem, 1952; Chevalier, Légion d'Honneur, 1950. Unpublished memoirs lodged with Imperial War Mus., 1987. *Recreations:* talking, music. *Address:* Lion House Lodge, High Halden, Kent TN26 3LS. *T:* High Halden (023385) 538.
Died 17 Dec. 1993.

S

SABBEN-CLARE, Ernest E., MA Oxon, BA London; Information Officer to University of Oxford, 1970–77; *b* 11 Aug. 1910; *s* of late Mr and Mrs J. W. Sabben-Clare; *m* 1938, Rosamond Dorothy Mary Scott; two *s* one *d. Educ:* Winchester Coll. (schol.); New College, Oxford (schol.). 1st cl. Mod. Hist., Oxford, 1932; 1st cl. French, London Univ. (external), 1954. Asst Master, Winchester Coll., 1932–34; Asst Dist Officer, Tanganyika, 1935–40; seconded Colonial Office, 1940–47; Lt, 10th Essex Bn Home Guard; Colonial Attaché, British Embassy, Washington, and Comr, Caribbean Commn, 1947–49; Nigerian Govt, 1950–55; Permanent Sec., Min. of Commerce, 1953–55; Asst Master, Marlborough Coll., 1955–60 (Under-Master, 1957–60); Headmaster, Bishop Wordsworth's School, Salisbury, 1960–63; Headmaster, Leeds Grammar Sch., 1963–70. Chairman of Governors: Bramcote Sch., Scarborough, 1970–80; Badminton Sch., 1981–85. Editor, Wilts Archæological and Natural History Magazine, 1956–62. *Publication:* (ed jtly) Health in Tropical Africa during the Colonial Period, 1980. *Recreations:* walking, gardening. *Address:* 4 Denham Close, Abbey Hill Road, Winchester SO23 7BL. *Club:* Athenæum. *Died 24 Jan. 1993.*

SABIN, Prof. Albert (Bruce); retired; Consultant to World Health Organization, 1969–86; Senior Expert Consultant, Fogarty International Center, National Institutes of Health, Bethesda, Md, 1984–86; *b* 26 Aug. 1906; *s* of Jacob Sabin and Tillie Krugman; *m* 1935, Sylvia Tregillus (*d* 1966); two *d*; *m* 1967, Jane Blach Warner (marr. diss. 1971); *m* 1972, Heloisa Dunshee de Abranches. *Educ:* New York Univ. (MD). Ho. Phys., Bellevue Hosp., NY, 1932–33; Nat. Research Council Fellow, Lister Inst., London, 1934; Rockefeller Inst. for Med. Research, NY, 1935–39; Associate Prof. of Research Pediatrics, Univ. of Cincinnati, 1939–43; active duty, US Army, 1943–46 (Legion of Merit, 1945); Prof. of Research Pediatrics, Univ. of Cincinnati Coll. of Medicine and The Children's Hosp. Research Foundn, 1946–60, Distinguished Service Prof., 1960–71, Emeritus, 1971–; Distinguished Res. Prof. of Biomedicine, Med. Univ. of SC, Charleston, 1974–82. Pres., Weizmann Inst. of Science, Israel, 1970–72. Fogarty Scholar, NIH, 1973. Mem. Nat. Acad. of Sciences of the USA; Fellow, Amer. Acad. of Arts and Sciences; Mem. and Hon. Mem. of various Amer. and foreign societies; Foreign Mem., USSR Acad. of Med. Scis, 1986; Hon. Member: Royal Acad. of Med. of Belgium; British Paediatric Association. Hon. degrees; awards include: Feltrinelli Prize ($40,000) of Accad. Naz. dei Lincei, Rome, 1964; Lasker ($10,000) Prize for Clinical Medicine Research, 1965. Gold Medal, Royal Soc. of Health, 1969; National Medal of Science (USA), 1970; Statesman in Medicine Award (USA), 1973; US Medal of Freedom, 1986; US Medal of Liberty, 1986; Order of Friendship Among Peoples, Presidium of Supreme Soviet, 1986; Carlos Finlay Medal (Cuba), 1987. Hon. FRSH. *Publications:* numerous papers on pneumococcus infection, poliomyelitis, encephalitis, virus diseases of nervous system, toxoplasmosis, sandfly fever, dengue, other topics relating to various infectious diseases and virus-cancer relationships. *Recreations:* reading, music, home. *Address:* Sutton Towers, Apt 1001, 3101 New Mexico Avenue NW, Washington, DC 20016–5902, USA. *Club:* Cosmos (Washington, DC). *Died 3 March 1993.*

SABINE, Neville Warde, CMG 1960; CBE 1957; *b* 6 April 1910; *s* of late John William Sabine; *m* 1954, Zoë Margherita Bargna; two *d. Educ:* Manchester Grammar School; Brasenose College, Oxford. BA Hons (Oxon) 1934. Colonial Service (Colonial Audit Dept) 1934; served Gold Coast, Malaya, Uganda, Leeward Islands, and N Borneo; served War of 1939–45: Gold Coast Regt, 1939–40; Singapore RA (V), 1940–42; British Military Administration, Malaya, 1945–46; Auditor-General, Ghana, 1954–64; Secretary, Central Bd of Finance of Church of England, 1964–75. Sec., Soc. of Sussex Downsmen, 1976–84. *Recreations:* bridge, walking. *Address:* 11 Windlesham Road, Brighton BN1 3AG. *T:* Brighton (0273) 732157. *Died 14 March 1994.*

SAINER, Leonard; *b* 12 Oct. 1909; *s* of late Archer and Sarah Sainer; *m* 1989, Wendy Harris. *Educ:* UCL. Solicitor, 1933; Consultant, Titmuss Sainer & Webb, Solicitors (Partner, 1938–78). Life President, Sears plc, 1985 (Chairman, 1978–85). Trustee: Clore Foundn, 1964–89. *Address:* (business) 40 Duke Street, W1; (home) 8 Farm Street, W1X 7RE. *Died 30 Sept. 1991.*

SAINSBURY, Richard Eric, CBE 1964; *b* 15 Sept. 1909; 2nd *s* of E. A. Sainsbury and F. W. Sainsbury (*née* Hill), Trowbridge, Wilts; *m* 1936, Margaret (*née* Horne); one *s. Educ:* Lewisham School, Weston-super-Mare; Bristol University. Grad. in Engineering, 1932. Time-study with J. Lucas, 1934; subseq. with various firms; Ministry of Aircraft Production, 1940, Deputy Director, 1943; Joint Services Staff College, 1947; Director Instrument and Radio Production, Ministry of Supply, 1950; Imperial Defence College, 1959; Director, Guided Weapons Production, 1960; Dir-Gen., Electronics and Weapons Prodn, Min. of Aviation, 1961–67, Min. of Technology, 1967–70, Min. of Aviation Supply, 1970–71; Dir Gen., Telecommunications, MoD, 1971–72. Dir, Aeromaritime Ltd, Hounslow, 1973–75. Coronation Medal, 1953. *Recreations:* walking, reading. *Address:* c/o Lloyds Bank, Summertown Road, Oxford. *Died 7 Sept. 1991.*

ST ALDWYN, 2nd Earl, *cr* 1915, of Coln St Aldwyns; **Michael John Hicks Beach,** GBE 1980 (KBE 1964); TD 1949; PC 1959; JP; Bt 1619; Viscount St Aldwyn, 1906; Viscount Quenington, 1915; Vice Lord-Lieutenant, Gloucestershire, 1981–87; *b* 9 Oct. 1912; *s* of Visc. Quenington, Royal Glos Hussars Yeo. (*d* 1916; *o s* of 1st Earl) and Marjorie (*d* 1916), *d* of late H. Dent Brocklehurst, Sudeley Castle, Glos; *S* grandfather, 1916 (his father having been killed in action a week previously); *m* 1948, Diana Mary Christian, DStJ (she *m* 1st, 1939, Major Richard Patrick Pilkington Smyly, MC; marriage annulled, 1942), *o d* of late Henry C. G. and Mrs Mills; two *s* (and one *s* decd). *Educ:* Eton; Christ Church, Oxford. Major Royal Glos Hussars Yeomanry, 1942. Parliamentary Secretary, Ministry of Agriculture and Fisheries, 1954–58; Captain of the Honourable Corps of Gentlemen-at-Arms and Govt Chief Whip, House of Lords, 1958–64 and 1970–74; Opposition Chief Whip, House of Lords, 1964–70 and 1974–78. DL 1950, JP 1952, Glos. GCStJ 1978; Chancellor, Order of St John, 1978–87 (Vice-Chancellor, 1969–78). *Heir: s* Viscount Quenington [*b* 7

Feb. 1950; *m* 1982, Gilda Maria, *o d* of Barão Saavedra, Rio de Janeiro; two *d*]. *Address:* Williamstrip Park, Cirencester, Gloucestershire GL7 5AT. *T:* Coln St Aldwyns (028575) 226; 13 Upper Belgrave Street, SW1X 8BA. *T:* 071–235 8464. *Clubs:* Carlton, Pratt's; Royal Yacht Squadron. *Died 29 Jan. 1992.*

ST CLAIR-FORD, Capt. Sir Aubrey, 6th Bt, *cr* 1793, of Ember Court, Surrey; DSO 1942; Royal Navy, retired; *b* 29 Feb. 1904; *e s* of late Anson (*g s* of 2nd Bt) and Isabel Maria Frances, (Elsie), St Clair-Ford; *S* kinsman, 1948; *m* 1945, Anne, *o d* of Harold Christopherson, Penerley Lodge, Beaulieu, Hants; one *s* one *d. Educ:* Stubbington House; RNC, Osborne and Dartmouth. Served War of 1939–45 (despatches, DSO and bar); Korean War of 1950–53 (despatches, Officer, Legion of Merit, US); retd 1955. *Heir: s* James Anson St Clair-Ford [*b* 16 March 1952; *m* 1st, 1977, Jennifer Margaret (marr. diss. 1984), *yr d* of Cdre Robin Grindle, RN; 2nd, 1987, Mary Anne, *er d* of late His Honour Nathaniel Robert Blaker]. *Address:* Corner House, Sandle Copse, Fordingbridge, Hants SP6 1DX. *Died 8 April 1991.*

ST DAVIDS, 2nd Viscount, *cr* 1918; **Jestyn Reginald Austen Plantagenet Philipps;** Baron Strange of Knokin, 1299; Baron Hungerford, 1426; Baron de Moleyns, 1445; Bt 1621; Baron St Davids, 1908; Founder and Patron, Pirate Club, Floating Youth Club for Boys and Girls; *b* 19 Feb. 1917; *s* of 1st Viscount and Elizabeth Frances (Baroness Strange of Knokin, Baroness Hungerford and Baroness de Moleyns), *d* of late Hon. Paulyn F. C. Rawdon-Hastings, The Manor House, Ashby-de-la-Zouch; *S* father, 1938, and to baronies of mother, 1974; *m* 1st, 1938, Doreen Guinness (marr. diss., 1954; she *d* 1956), *o d* of late Captain Arthur Jowett, Toorak, Australia; one *s* four *d*; 2nd, 1954, Elisabeth Joyce (marr. diss. 1959), *e d* of Dr E. A. Woolf, Hove, Sussex; 3rd, 1959, Evelyn Marjorie, *d* of late Dr J. E. G. Harris, Bray, Berks. *Educ:* Eton; Trinity Coll., Cambridge. *Heir: s* Hon. Colwyn Jestyn John Philipps [*b* 30 Jan. 1939; *m* 1965, Augusta Victoria Correa Larrain, *d* of late Don Estantislao Correa Ugarte; two *s*]. *Address:* 15 St Mark's Crescent, Regent's Park, NW1. *Died 10 June 1991.*

ST JOSEPH, Prof. John Kenneth Sinclair, CBE 1979 (OBE 1964); FBA 1978; Professor of Aerial Photographic Studies, University of Cambridge, 1973–80, then Professor Emeritus; Fellow of Selwyn College, Cambridge, since 1939 (Senior Fellow, since 1989, Professorial Fellow, 1973–80); *b* 13 Nov. 1912; *s* of late John D. St Joseph and Irma Robertson (*née* Marris); *m* 1945, Daphne Margaret, *d* of late H. March, Worcester; two *s* two *d. Educ:* Bromsgrove Sch.; Selwyn Coll., Cambridge (Scholar). BA 1934, PhD 1937, MA 1938, LittD 1976. Harkness Scholar, 1934; Goldsmiths' Company Senior Student, 1935–37; DSIR Sen. Research Award, 1936–37; Lectr in Natural Sciences, Selwyn Coll., and Dean, 1939–62; Tutor, 1945–62; Librarian, 1946–62; Vice Master, 1974–80; Univ. Demonstrator in Geology, 1937–45; Operational Research, Min. of Aircraft Production, 1942–45; Univ. Lectr in Geology, 1945–48; Leverhulme Research Fellow, 1948–49; Curator in Aerial Photography at Cambridge, 1948–62; Dir in Aerial Photography, 1962–80. Undertook aerial reconnaissance and photography, in aid of research, over the United Kingdom, Ireland, Denmark, the Netherlands, Northern France and Hungary. Governor, Stratton Sch., Biggleswade, 1952–64; Hon. Corresp. Mem., German Archæological Inst., 1964–; Member: Council for British Archaeology, 1944–; Ancient Monuments Bd (England), 1969–84; Royal Commn on Historical Monuments (England), 1972–81; Council, British Acad., 1980–83; Vice-Pres., Soc. for Promotion of Roman Studies, 1975–; Hon. Vice-Pres., Royal Archaeological Inst., 1982–. Lectures: Chatwin Meml,

Birmingham, 1969; David Murray, Glasgow Univ., 1973; Kroon, Amsterdam Univ., 1981. Cuthbert Peek Award, RGS, 1976; President's Award, Inst. of Incorporated Photographers, 1977. FGS 1937; FSAScot 1940; FSA 1944; Hon. ScD Trinity Coll., Dublin; Hon. LLD Dundee, 1971; Dr *hc* in Maths and Science, Amsterdam, 1982. *Publications:* The Pentameracea of the Oslo Region, 1939; chapters in The Roman Occupation of SW Scotland (ed S. N. Miller), 1945; Monastic Sites from the Air (with M. C. Knowles), 1952; Medieval England, an aerial survey (with M. W. Beresford), 1958, 2nd rev. edn, 1979; (ed) The Uses of Air Photography, 1966, 2nd rev. edn 1977; The Early Development of Irish Society (with E. R. Norman), 1970; Roman Britain from the Air (with S. S. Frere), 1983; chapters in Inchtuthil: the Roman legionary fortress (ed S. S. Frere), 1985; papers in learned jls on fossil Silurian Brachiopoda, and on aerial photography and archæology, especially of Roman Britain. *Recreations:* gardening, lumbering. *Address:* Selwyn College, Cambridge CB3 9DQ. *T:* Cambridge (0223) 335846; Histon Manor, Cambridge CB4 4JJ. *T:* Cambridge (0223) 232383. *Died 11 March 1994.*

SAKZEWSKI, Sir Albert, Kt 1973; FCA, FASA; chartered accountant; Founder, Sir Albert Sakzewski Foundation; Chairman: Avanis Pty Ltd; Blend Investments Pty Ltd; Commercial Finance Pty Ltd; Queensland Securities Pty Ltd; Southern Cross Products Pty Ltd; *b* Lowood, Qld, 12 Nov. 1905; *s* of O. T. Sakzewski, Lowood and Brisbane; *m* 1935, Winifred May (*d* 1972), *d* of W. P. Reade; two *s. Educ:* Ipswich High Sch., Qld. Founder and Sen. Partner, A. Sakzewski & Co./Court & Co., Chartered Accountants, 1929–76. Man. Dir, CON Pty Ltd, Brisbane, 1937–71; Dep. Chm., CON Hldgs Ltd, 1961–77. Chairman: Flinders House Pty Ltd, 1956–77; Qld Bd, Sun Insce Office Ltd, 1955–62 (Dir, 1947–62); Qld Bd of Advice, Custom Credit Corp. Ltd, 1964–78; Rover Mowers (Aust) Pty Ltd, 1966–77. Chm. and Govt Nominee, Totalisator Admin Bd of Qld, 1962–81. Dir, Nat. Heart Foundn (Queensland Div.), 1960–76 (Chm., Building Appeal, 1978). Past Pres., Australian Amateur Billiards Council; Member: Aust./Britain Soc.; Aust. Ballet Foundn; Qld Art Gall. Foundn. *Recreations:* horse racing and breeding (administrator (Tattersall's) 1935–56, owner 1941–), billiards (Australian Amateur Billiards Champion, 1932, with a then Australian Record break of 206; Qld Amateur Billiards Champion 6 times), snooker (Qld Amateur Snooker Champion 8 times), golf. *Address:* (home) Ilya Lodge, 1 Rossiter Parade, Hamilton, Qld 4007, Australia; (office) National Bank House, 255 Adelaide Street, Brisbane, Qld 4000, Australia; GPO Box 11, Brisbane, Qld 4001. *Clubs:* Commonwealth Trust; Brisbane, Tattersall's (Trustee; Life Mem.) (Brisbane); Queensland Turf, Tattersall's Racing (Life Mem.), Brisbane Amateur Turf (Life Mem.), Gold Coast Turf, Rockhampton Jockey (Life Mem.); Royal Queensland Golf, Southport Golf (Life Mem.). *Died 6 July 1991.*

SALAMAN, Myer Head, MD; Research Pathologist, Royal College of Surgeons, 1968–74; *b* 2 Aug. 1902; *e s* of Redcliffe N. Salaman, MD, FRS and Nina Salaman; *m* 1926, Esther Polianowsky; one *s* three *d. Educ:* Clifton College; Bedales School; Trinity College, Cambridge; London Hospital Medical College. Natural Science Tripos Pts I and II, Cambridge, 1921–25; MA 1926, MD 1936 Cantab; MRCS, LRCP, 1930; Dipl. Bact. London, 1936. London Hosp.: clinical training, 1927–30; house appts, 1931–32; research on viruses, 1932–34, and Lister Inst. (Junior Beit Mem. Fellow), 1935–38; cancer research, St Bartholomew's Hosp., 1939; Asst Pathologist, Emergency Public Health Service, 1940–42; cancer and virus research, Strangeways Lab., 1942–43; Temp. Major, RAMC, 1943–46; engaged in cancer research at the London Hospital, 1946–48; Dir, Dept of Cancer Research, London

Hosp. Med. Sch., 1948–67; engaged in cancer research at RCS, 1968–74. FRSocMed. *Publications:* papers on virus diseases, and on cancer, in Jl Pathology and Bacteriology, Proc. Roy. Soc. (B), Brit. Jl Cancer, etc. *Recreations:* reading, writing. *Address:* 23 Bisham Gardens, Highgate, N6 6DJ. *T:* 0181–340 1019.   *Died 31 Dec. 1994.*

SALES, William Henry, BSc (Econ) Hons London; Chairman, Yorkshire (late North East) Division of the National Coal Board, 1957–67, retired (Member, National Coal Board, 1953–57); *b* 26 April 1903. *Educ:* pit; Fircroft; London School of Economics. Miners' Welfare Scholarship. Varied career; pit; boys' clubs; WEA Lecturer; schoolmaster. Dep. Labour Director, East Midlands Division, NCB, 1947–51; Deputy Chairman, North-Western Division, 1951–53. Chm. Church of England Industrial Council, 1967–71. Hon. Fellow, LSE, 1960. *Publications:* various papers in economic and sociological journals. *Address:* Handley Cross, Cantley, Doncaster, S Yorks.   *Died 13 Feb. 1991.*

SALISBURY, Harrison Evans; *b* 14 Nov. 1908; *s* of Percy Pritchard Salisbury and Georgiana Evans Salisbury; *m* 1st, 1933, Mary Hollis (marr. diss.); two *s*; 2nd, 1964, Charlotte Young Rand. *Educ:* Univ. of Minnesota (AB). United Press, 1930: London Manager, 1943; Foreign Editor, 1945; New York Times: Moscow Corresp., 1949–54; National Editor, 1962; Asst Man. Editor, 1964–69; Associate Editor and Editor Opposite-Editorial Page, 1970–73. Pres., Amer. Acad. and Inst. of Arts and Letters, 1975–77; Mem., Amer. Acad. of Arts and Letters, 1986. Pres., Authors' League, 1980–85. Amer. Philosophical Soc. Pulitzer Prize, International Correspondence, 1955. Hon. doctorates. *Publications:* Russia on the Way, 1946; American in Russia, 1955; The Shook-up Generation, 1958; To Moscow—And Beyond, 1960; Moscow Journal, 1961; The Northern Palmyra Affair, 1962; A New Russia?, 1962; Russia, 1965; Orbit of China, 1967; Behind the Lines—Hanoi 1967; The Soviet Union—The 50 Years, 1967; The 900 Days, the Siege of Leningrad, 1969; The Coming War Between Russia and China, 1969; The Many Americas Shall Be One, 1971; The Eloquence of Protest: voices of the seventies, 1972; To Peking—and Beyond, 1973; The Gates of Hell, 1975; Black Night, White Snow: Russia's Revolutions 1905–1917, 1978; Russia in Revolution 1900–1930, 1978; The Unknown War, 1978; Without Fear or Favor: The New York Times and *its* times, 1980; A Journey for Our Times, 1983; China: 100 Years of Revolution, 1983; The Long March: the untold story, 1985; A Time of Change, 1988; The Great Black Dragon Fire: a Chinese inferno, 1989; Tiananmen Diary: thirteen days in June, 1989; Disturber of the Peace, 1989; The New Emperors: China in the era of Mao and Deng, 1992; Heroes of My Time, 1993. *Address:* Box 70, Taconic, Conn, USA. *Clubs:* Century Association (New York); National Press (Washington, DC).
                Died 5 July 1993.

SALK, Jonas Edward, BS, MD; Founding Director, since 1975, and Distinguished Professor in International Health Sciences, since 1984, Salk Institute for Biological Studies (Director, 1963–75; Fellow, 1963–84); Adjunct Professor of Health Sciences in Departments of Psychiatry, Community Medicine, and Medicine, University of California at San Diego, since 1970; *b* New York, 28 Oct. 1914; *s* of Daniel B. Salk and Dora Press; *m* 1st, 1939, Donna Lindsay (marr. diss. 1968); three *s*; 2nd, 1970, Françoise Gilot. *Educ:* NY University College of Medicine; Coll. of New York City (BS). Fellow, NY Univ. Coll. of Medicine, 1935–40; Intern, Mount Sinai Hosp., NYC, 1940–42; Nat. Research Council Fellow, Sch. of Public Health, Univ. of Michigan, 1942–43, Research Fellow in Epidemiology, 1943–44, Research Associate, 1944–46, Asst Professor, 1946–47; School of Medicine,

University of Pittsburgh: Associate Prof. of Bacteriology, 1947–49; Director of Virus Research Laboratory, 1947–63; Research Prof., 1949–54; Prof. of Preventive Medicine, and Chm. of Dept, 1954–57; Commonwealth Professor of Experimental Medicine, 1957–62. Vis. Prof.-at-Large, Pittsburgh, 1963. Consultant in epidemic diseases to Sec. of War, 1944–47, to Sec. of Army, 1947–54; specialist in polio research; developed antipoliomyelitis vaccine, 1955. Emeritus Member: Amer. Epidemiological Soc.; Amer. Soc. of Clinical Investigation; Assoc. of Amer. Physicians; Soc. for Exptl Biol. and Medicine; Sen. Mem., Inst. of Medicine, Nat. Acad. of Scis; mem. of other socs. Fellow: Amer. Public Health Assoc.; AAAS; Amer. Acad. of Arts and Scis; Hon. Fellow: Amer. Acad. of Pediatrics; Royal Soc. of Health. US Medal of Freedom, 1977. *Publications:* Man Unfolding, 1972; The Survival of the Wisest, 1973; (with Jonathan Salk) World Population and Human Values: a new reality, 1981; Anatomy of Reality: merging of intuition and reason, 1983. *Address:* The Salk Institute, PO Box 85800, San Diego, CA 92186–5800, USA. *T:* (619) 4534100.   *Died 23 June 1995.*

SALMON, Baron *cr* 1972 (Life Peer), of Sandwich, Kent; **Cyril Barnet Salmon,** Kt 1957; PC 1964; a Lord of Appeal in Ordinary, 1972–80; *b* 28 Dec. 1903; *s* of late Montagu Salmon; *m* 1st, 1929, Rencie (*d* 1942), *d* of late Sidney Gorton Vanderfelt, OBE; one *s* one *d*; 2nd, 1946, Jean, Lady Morris (*d* 1989), *d* of late Lt-Col D. Maitland-Makgill-Crichton. *Educ:* Mill Hill; Pembroke College, Cambridge. BA 1925. Called to Bar, Middle Temple, 1925 (Bencher, 1953; Treasurer, 1972); QC 1945; Recorder of Gravesend, 1947–57; Commissioner of Assize, Wales and Chester Circuit, 1955; Judge of High Court of Justice, Queen's Bench Division, 1957–64; a Lord Justice of Appeal, 1964–72. Chairman: Royal Commission on the Working of the Tribunals of Inquiry (Evidence) Act, 1921, 1966; Royal Commission on Standards of Conduct in Public Life, 1974–76. Commissioned Royal Artillery, 1940. 8th Army HQ Staff, 1943–44. JP (Kent), 1949. Captain of the Royal St George's, Sandwich, 1972–73. Commissary of Cambridge Univ., 1979–. Governor of Mill Hill School. Hon. Fellow, Pembroke College, Cambridge. Hon. DCL Kent, 1978; Hon. LLD Cambridge, 1982. *Recreations:* golf, fishing. *Address:* Eldon House, 1 Dorset Street, W1H 3FB. *T:* 071–487 3461.   *Died 7 Nov. 1991.*

SALT, Sir Anthony (Houlton), 6th Bt *cr* 1869, of Saltaire, Yorkshire; Associate, Williams de Broe Ltd (formerly Williams de Broe Hill Chaplin & Co.) (Stockbrokers), since 1987 (Chairman, 1981–84; Director, 1968–85); *b* 15 Sept. 1931; *s* of Sir John Salt, 4th Bt, and Stella Houlton Jackson (*d* 1974); *S* brother, 1978; *m* 1957, Prudence Meath Baker; four *d*. *Educ:* Stowe. Member of the Stock Exchange, 1957; Partner, Hill Chaplin & Co. (Stockbrokers), 1957. *Heir: b* Patrick MacDonnell Salt [*b* 25 Sept. 1932; *m* 1976, Ann Elizabeth Mary, *d* of late Dr T. K. MacLachlan and *widow* of Denys Kilham Roberts, OBE]. *Address:* Dellow House, Ugley Green, Bishop's Stortford, Herts CM22 6HN. *T:* Bishop's Stortford (0279) 813141. *Clubs:* City of London, City University, Oriental.   *Died 16 Jan. 1991.*

SALTZMAN, Charles Eskridge, DSM 1945 (US); Legion of Merit (US) 1943; Hon. OBE 1943; Partner, Goldman, Sachs & Co. (investment banking), 1956, Limited Partner since 1973; *b* 19 Sept. 1903; *s* of Maj.-Gen. Charles McKinley Saltzman and Mary Saltzman (*née* Eskridge); *m* 1st, 1931, Gertrude Lamont (marr. diss.); one *s*; 2nd, 1947, Cynthia Southall Myrick (marr. diss.); two *d* (one *s* decd); 3rd, 1978, Clotilde McCormick (*née* Knapp). *Educ:* Cornell Univ.; US Mil. Acad.; Magdalen College, Oxford University. BS (US Mil. Acad.); BA, MA (Rhodes Scholar)

(Oxford Univ.). Served as 2nd Lt, Corps of Engrs, US Army, 1925–30; commissioned 1st Lieut, NY National Guard, 1930; Lieutenant-Colonel 1940; on active duty in US Army, 1940–46, serving overseas, 1942–46; Brigadier-General 1945; relieved from active duty, 1946; Maj.-Gen. AUS (retd). With NY Telephone Co., 1930–35; with NY Stock Exchange, 1935–49 (Asst to Exec. Vice-Pres., later Sec. and Vice-Pres.); Asst Sec. of State, 1947–49; Partner Henry Sears & Co., 1949–56; Under-Sec. of State for Admin, 1954–55. Former Dir, Continental Can Co. and A. H. Robins Co., Inc. Pres., English-Speaking Union of the US, 1961–66 (latterly Hon. Director); Emeritus Pres., Assoc. of Graduates, US Mil. Academy, 1978 (Trustee, 1940–41, 1959–62, 1963–74; Pres., 1974–78); Mem. Pilgrims of the United States; Hon. Mem., Soc. of the Cincinnati. Member, Director, or Trustee of many boards, societies and religious, philanthropic and educational institutions. Hon. Dr Mil. Sci. Mil. Coll. of S Carolina, 1984. Foreign decorations. *Address:* (home) 30 E 62nd Street, New York, NY 10021, USA. *T:* (212) 7595655; (office) 85 Broad Street, New York, NY 10004, USA. *T:* (212) 9021000. *Clubs:* Century Association, Union, University (New York); Metropolitan (Washington).

Died 16 June 1994.

SAMMAN, Peter Derrick, MD, FRCP; Physician to Dermatological Department, Westminster Hospital, 1951–79, and St John's Hospital for Diseases of the Skin, 1959–79; Consultant Dermatologist, Orpington and Sevenoaks Hospitals, 1951–77; Dean, Institute of Dermatology, 1965–70; *b* 20 March 1914; *y* s of Herbert Frederick Samman and Emily Elizabeth Savage; *m* 1953, Judith Mary Kelly; three *d. Educ:* King William's Coll., IOM; Emmanual Coll., Cambridge; King's Coll. Hosp., London. BA (Nat. Scis Tripos), 1936; MB, BChir Cantab 1939; MRCP 1946; MA, MD Cantab 1948; FRCP 1963. House Surg., King's Coll. Hosp., 1939; Sqdn Ldr, RAFVR, 1940–45; House Phys. and Registrar, King's Coll. Hosp., 1946; Sen. Dermatological Registrar and Tutor in Dermatology, United Bristol Hosps, 1947–48; Sen. Registrar, St John's Hosp. for Diseases of the Skin, 1949–50. FRSocMed; Mem. Brit. Assoc. of Dermatology; Hon. Mem., Dermatological Soc. of S Africa. *Publications:* The Nails in Disease, 1965, 4th edn 1986; chapters in Textbook of Dermatology (ed Rook, Wilkinson and Ebling), 1968; (jtly) Tutorials in Postgraduate Medicine: Dermatology, 1977; A History of St John's Hospital for Diseases of the Skin 1963–1988, 1990; various articles in med. jls. *Recreation:* gardening. *Address:* 18 Sutherland Avenue, Orpington, Kent BR5 1QZ. *T:* Orpington (0689) 820839.

Died 1 Dec. 1992.

SANDBACH, Prof. (Francis) Henry, FBA 1968; Fellow of Trinity College, Cambridge, since 1927; *b* 23 Feb. 1903; *s* of late Prof. F. E. and Ethel Sandbach; *m* 1932, Mary Warburton Mathews (*d* 1990); one *s* one *d* (and one *s* decd). *Educ:* King Edward's Sch., Birmingham; Trinity Coll., Cambridge. Browne Schol., 1922; Craven Schol., 1923; Chancellor's Medallist, 1925; Charles Oldham Class. Schol., 1925. Asst Lectr, Manchester Univ., 1926–28; University of Cambridge: Lectr in Classics, 1929–67; Brereton Reader in Classics, 1951–67; Prof. of Classics, 1967–70; Junior Proctor, 1940–41; Trinity College: Lecturer in Classics, 1929–63; Tutor, 1945–52; Sen. Tutor, 1952–56. For. Mem., Kungl. Vetenskaps- och Vitterhets- Samhället i Göteborg. *Publications:* (some jointly): Plutarch's Moralia, vol. ix, 1961, vol. xi, 1965, vol. xv, 1969; Plutarchus Moralia, vol. vii, 1967; Menandri Reliquiae Selectae, 1972; Menander: a commentary, 1973; The Stoics, 1975; The Comic Theatre of Greece and Rome, 1977; Aristotle and the Stoics, 1985; articles in

class. jls. *Address:* 2 Hedgerley Close, Cambridge CB3 0EW. *T:* Cambridge (0223) 353152.

Died 18 Sept. 1991.

SANDERS, Christopher Cavania, RA 1961 (ARA 1953); RP 1968; ARCA 1928; artist-painter; *b* near Wakefield, 25 Dec. 1905; *s* of Alfred B. Sanders; *m* 1931, Barbara L. Stubbs (ARCA 1928) (*d* 1967), *d* of Francis F. Stubbs, Isleworth and Felpham; two *s* two *d. Educ:* Ossett Grammar Sch.; Wakefield Sch. of Art; Leeds Coll. of Art; Royal Coll. of Art. Gold Medallist, Paris Salon, 1955. *Address:* 2 Tudor Gardens, Slough, Berks SL1 6HJ.

Died 7 Aug. 1991.

SANDERSON, Sir (Frank Philip) Bryan, 2nd Bt, *cr* 1920, of Malling Deanery, South Malling, Sussex; Lieutenant-Commander, RNVR; *b* 18 Feb. 1910; *s* of Sir Frank Bernard Sanderson, 1st Bt, and Amy Edith (*d* 1949), *d* of David Wing, Scarborough; *S* father 1965; *m* 1933, Annette Irene Caroline (*d* 1967), *d* of late Col Korab Laskowski, Warsaw, and *g d* of General Count de Castellaz; two *s* one *d. Educ:* Stowe; Pembroke College, Oxford. Served War of 1939–45 with Fleet Air Arm. A Member of Lloyd's. Dir, Humber Fertilisers (formerly Humber Fishing and Fish Manure Co.), Hull, retd 1988 (Chm., 1965–80). *Recreation:* shooting. *Heir: s* Frank Linton Sanderson [*b* 21 Nov. 1933; *m* 1961, Margaret Ann, *o d* of John C. Maxwell; two *s* three *d*]. *Address:* Lychgate Cottage, Scaynes Hill, Haywards Heath, West Sussex RH17 7NH.

Died 4 Dec. 1992.

SANDERSON, Air Vice-Marshal Keith Fred, CB 1986; Planning Consultant, Ericsson Ltd, since 1989; *b* 25 Nov. 1932; *s* of late Arnold and Emily Sanderson; *m* 1957, Margaret Ward; two *d. Educ:* Hutton Grammar Sch., Lancs. RAF Navigator, 1950–74; Staff of CDS, 1974–75; Comd RAF Leconfield, 1976; RCDS, 1977; AOA RAF Germany, 1978–80; AOC Personnel Management Centre and Dir of Personnel (Air), 1980–83; AOA, HQ Strike Command, 1983–87. BDO Binder Hamlyn, 1987–89. *Recreations:* walking, golf. *Club:* Royal Air Force.

Died 7 April 1994.

SANDILANDS, Sir Francis (Edwin Prescott), Kt 1976; CBE 1967; Director, 1965–83 and Chairman, 1972–83, Commercial Union Assurance Co. Ltd; *b* 11 Dec. 1913; *s* of late Lieut-Col Prescott Sandilands, DSO, RM, and Gladys Baird Murton; *m* 1939, Susan Gillian Jackson; two *s. Educ:* Eton; Corpus Christi College, Cambridge (Hon. Fellow, 1975). MA 1938. Served War of 1939–45, Royal Scots Fusiliers and General Staff, UK and NW Europe (Lt-Col; despatches). Joined Ocean Accident and Guarantee Corporation Ltd, 1935, Manager, 1955; General Manager, then Chief General Manager, 1958–72, Vice-Chm., 1968–72, Commercial Union Assurance Co. Ltd; Chm., Royal Trust Company of Canada, 1974–84; Dir, Kleinwort, Benson, Lonsdale Ltd, 1979–86. Trustee: British Museum, 1977–85; Royal Opera House, 1974–86 (Chm. Trustees, 1980–84; Dir, 1975–85); Mem., Royal Fine Art Commn, 1980–85. Chairman: London Salvage Corps, 1962–63; British Insurance Assoc., 1965–67; Pres., Insurance Inst. of London, 1969–70. Chairman: Govt Cttee of Enquiry on Inflation and Company Accounts, 1974–75; Cttee on Invisible Exports, 1975–83; Member: BOTB, 1976–83; Adv. Cttee, Queen's Award to Industry, 1976–83. Treas., UCL, 1973–81 (Hon. Fellow, 1981). Commandeur de l'Ordre de la Couronne (Belgium), 1974. *Address:* 53 Cadogan Square, SW1X 0HY. *T:* 0171–235 6384. *Died 29 May 1995.*

SANDWICH, 10th Earl of; *see* Montagu, A. V. E. P.

SANGSTER, John Laing; *b* 21 Nov. 1922; *s* of Albert James Laing Sangster and Ottilie Elizabeth Ritzdorff; *m* 1952, Mary Louise Fitz-Alan Stuart; two *s. Educ:* Emanuel Sch., London; Emmanuel Coll., Cambridge (MA). Joined

Bank of England, 1949; Adviser, Foreign Exchange, 1965; Deputy Chief Cashier, 1975; Chief Adviser, 1979; Asst Dir, Foreign Exchange Div., 1980–82. Exco International: Dep. Chm., 1983–84; Chm., 1984–86; Chm., London Forfaiting Co. Ltd, 1984–86. *Recreations:* touring, walking, bird watching. *Clubs:* Bankers'; Thames Rowing; Leander (Henley on Thames). *Died 8 Sept. 1993.*

SANSBURY, Rt Rev. (Cyril) Kenneth, MA Cantab; Hon. DD (Trinity College, Wycliffe College, Toronto); retired; *b* 21 Jan. 1905; *s* of late Cyril J. Sansbury; *m* 1931, Ada Ethelreda Mary, *d* of late Captain P. B. Wamsley; one *s* two *d. Educ:* St Paul's School; Peterhouse, Cambridge; Westcott House, Cambridge. 2nd cl. Classical Tripos, 1926; 1st cl. Theological Tripos, Pt I 1927 and Pt II 1928. Deacon, 1928; priest, 1929; Curate of St Peter's, Dulwich Common, 1928–31 and Wimbledon, 1931–32; SPG Missionary, Numazu, Japan, 1932–34; Prof. at Central Theological Coll. and British Chaplain at St Andrew's, Tokyo, 1934–41; Chaplain to HM Embassy, Tokyo, 1938–41; Chaplain, RCAF, 1941–45; Warden, Lincoln Theological Coll., 1945–52; Canon and Prebendary of Asgarby in Lincoln Cathedral, 1948–53; Warden, St Augustine's College, Canterbury (Central College of the Anglican Communion), 1952–61; Hon. Canon, Canterbury Cathedral, 1953–61; Bishop of Singapore and Malaya, 1961–66; Asst Bishop, dio. London, 1966–73; Gen. Sec., British Council of Churches, 1966–73; Priest-in-Charge of St Mary in the Marsh, Norwich, 1973–83. *Publications:* Truth, Unity and Concord, 1967; Combating Racism, 1975. *Address:* 20 The Close, Norwich NR1 4DZ. *Club:* Royal Over-Seas League.
Died 25 Aug. 1993.

SANSOM, Andrew William, FCCA; Chief Executive and Secretary, Chartered Association of Certified Accountants, since 1988; *b* 1 Jan. 1937; *s* of Reginald Henry Charles Sansom and Marjorie Frances (*née* Pearce); *m* 1970, Rosanne Louise Best; one *s. Educ:* Sidcot School; Univ. of Wales (BA). FCCA 1975 (ACCA 1970). Served Welch Regt, 2nd Lieut, 1957–59. Joined HMOCS, 1959; Overseas Audit Service: Tanganyika, 1960–63; Bechuanaland (later Botswana), 1963–70; London Merchant Securities Ltd, 1971–73; Assoc. of Certified Accountants: Admin Sec., 1974–76; Dep. Sec., 1976–88. Dir, Accountancy Television Service Ltd, 1992–. Mem. Court, Univ. of Bath, 1991–. FRSA. *Publications:* articles on accountancy profession in nat. and professional press. *Recreations:* theatre, horticulture, swimming, Church of England matters. *Address:* 29 Lincoln's Inn Fields, WC2A 3EE. *T:* 071–242 6855; Spring Cottage, Sheep Street, Charlbury, Oxon OX7 3RR. *T:* Charlbury (0608) 810914. *Died 19 Nov. 1992.*

SARAJČIĆ, Ivo; elected Member, Council of the Republic, Croatia, 1983; President, Board for Foreign Policy and International Relations, National Assembly of Croatia, 1978–82, retired; *b* 10 March 1915; *s* of Ivan and Elizabeth Sarajčić; *m* 1944, Marija Godlar; three *s. Educ:* Univ. of Philosophy, Zagreb. Participated in War of Liberation from (beginning) 1941 (Partizan Remembrance Medal); held various prominent political positions; subsequently: Secretary, Presidium of Nat. Assembly of Croatia; Editor-in-Chief of Borba; Asst Minister of Educn; Dir of Information Office of Yugoslav Govt; MEC, Croatia; also Mem. Central Cttee of League of Communists of Croatia, Mem. Federal Assembly, Mem. Council for Foreign Affairs and Internat. Relations. Yugoslav Diplomatic Service, 1959; Ambassador to Austria, 1960–63; Asst Sec. of State for Foreign Affairs, 1963–66; Ambassador to London, 1966–70; Dir, Inst. for Developing Countries, Zagreb, 1970–78. *Died 12 Jan. 1994.*

SATTERTHWAITE, Lt-Col Richard George, LVO 1985; OBE 1961; Director and General Secretary, 1972–85,

Vice President, 1986, National Playing Fields Association; *b* 8 April 1920; *s* of R. E. Satterthwaite and A. M. Elers; *m* 1949, Rosemary Ann, *d* of Gen. Sir Frank Messervy, KCSI, KBE, CB, DSO; three *s* (one *d* decd). *Educ:* Rugby Sch.; RMC Sandhurst. 2nd Lieut, 19th King George V's Own Lancers, 1939; served India, Burma, Malaya; transf. to 17th/21st Lancers, 1949; comd 17th/21st Lancers, 1959–61; retd 1962. Vice Pres. and Chm. Management Cttee, British Sports Trust, 1988–. *Recreations:* cricket, golf. *Address:* Meadow Cottage, East Harting, Petersfield, Hants GU31 5LX. *T:* Harting (0730) 825516.
Died 14 March 1993.

SAUNDERS, Maj.-Gen. Kenneth, CB 1979; OBE 1970; Paymaster in Chief and Inspector of Army Pay Services, 1975–79, retired; *b* 1 Jan. 1920; *m* 1953, Ann Lawrence Addison; one *s. Educ:* Lancastrian Sch., Shrewsbury. Enlisted King's Shropshire LI, 1939; commnd Royal Welch Fus., 1940; served in France, Belgium, Holland and Germany (despatches 1945); various staff appts, NW Europe and Far East, 1945–52; transf. to RAPC, 1952; Staff Paymaster: WO 1962–63; HQ Div./Malaya, 1965–67; MoD, 1967–70; Chief Paymaster: MoD, 1970–71; 1 British Corps, 1971–72; Dep. Paymaster in Chief, 1972–75; Maj.-Gen. 1975; Col Comdt, RAPC, 1979–84. *Recreations:* fishing, travel. *Address:* 31 Prestonville Court, Dyke Road, Brighton BN1 3UG. *T:* Brighton (01273) 328866. *Died 23 Dec. 1994.*

SAUNDERS, Sir Owen (Alfred), Kt 1965; MA, DSc; FRS 1958; FEng; FInstP; FInstF; FRAeS; Emeritus Professor of Mechanical Engineering, University of London, Imperial College (Professor, 1946; Head of Department, 1946–65; Pro-Rector, 1964–67, Acting Rector, 1966–67); Vice-Chancellor, University of London, 1967–69; *b* 24 Sept. 1904; *s* of Alfred George Saunders and Margaret Ellen Jones; *m* 1st, 1935, Marion Isabel McKechney (*d* 1981); one *s* two *d*; 2nd, 1981, Mrs Daphne Holmes. *Educ:* Emanuel School; Birkbeck College, London; Trinity College, Cambridge (Senior Scholar). Scientific Officer, Dept of Scientific and Industrial Research, 1926; Lecturer in Applied Mathematical Physics, Imperial College, 1932; Clothworkers' Reader in Applied Thermodynamics, Univ. of London, 1937; on loan to Directorate of Turbine Engines, MAP, 1942–45. Dean, City and Guilds Coll., 1955–64. Past Pres., IMechE; Mem., ITA, 1964–69; President: British Flame Research Cttee; Section G, British Assoc., 1959. Founder Fellow, Fellowship of Engineering, 1976. Hon. FIMechE; Hon. FCGI; Honorary Member: Yugoslav Acad., 1959–; Japan Soc. of Mechanical Engrs, 1960–; ASME, 1961 (Life Mem.); For. Associate, Nat. Acad. of Engrg, USA, 1979. Hon. Fellow, RHC, 1983 (Chm. Council, 1971–85). Hon. DSc Strathclyde, 1964. Melchett medallist, Inst. of Fuel, 1962; Max Jakob Award, ASME, 1966. Hon. Mem., Mark Twain Soc., 1976. *Publications:* The Calculation of Heat Transmission, 1932; An Introduction to Heat Transfer, 1950; various scientific and technical papers in Proceedings of Royal Society, Phil. Mag., Physical Society, Engineering, and the Institutions. *Recreation:* music. *Address:* 28 Ashfields, Alma Road, Reigate, Surrey RH2 0DN. *Club:* Athenæum. *Died 10 Oct. 1993.*

SAUVÉ, Rt Hon. Jeanne Mathilde, CC 1984; CMM 1984; CD 1984; PC (Can.) 1972; Governor-General and Commander-in-Chief of Canada, 1984–89; Founder, and Honorary Chairman, Jeanne Sauvé Youth Foundation, since 1990; *b* 26 April 1922; *d* of Charles Albert Benoit and Anna Vaillant; *m* 1948, Hon. Maurice Sauvé (*d* 1992); one *s. Educ:* Notre-Dame du Rosaire Convent, Ottawa; Ottawa Univ.; Paris Univ. Journalist; Founder, Youth Movements Fedn, 1947; Asst to Dir of Youth Section, UNESCO, Paris, 1951; Union des Artistes, Montreal: Mem., Admin. Council, 1961–72; Deleg. to Film and TV

Writers Congress, Moscow, 1968; Vice-Pres., 1968–70; Sec. Gen., Fédération des Auteurs et des Artistes du Canada, 1966–72. MP (L) for Montreal Laval-les-Rapides (formerly Montreal-Ahuntsic), 1972–84; Minister of State for Science and Technol., 1972–74; Minister of the Environment, 1974–75; Minister of Communications, 1975–79; Advisor to Sec. of State for External Affairs for relations with the French-speaking world, 1978–79; Speaker of the House of Commons, 1980–84. Pres., Canadian Inst. of Public Affairs, 1964 (Vice-Pres., 1962–64); Founding Mem., Inst. of Political Res., 1972; Member: Centennial Commn, 1967; Admin. Council, YMCA, 1969–72; Internat. Adv. Council, Power Corp. of Canada, 1991. Hon. FRAIC 1974; Hon. FRSC 1991. Hon. DSc New Brunswick, 1974; Hon. LLD: Calgary, 1982; McGill, 1984; Toronto, 1984; Queen's, 1984; Carleton, 1986; Laurentian, 1987; Royal Mil. Coll., Kingston, 1987; Manitoba, 1988; Moncton, 1988; Royal Roads Mil. Coll., Victoria, 1989; Univ. of Regina, Saskatchewan, 1991; Hon. DHL: Mount St Vincent, 1983; St-Lawrence in Canton, NY, 1987; Hon. DU: Ottawa, 1984; Laval, 1984; Montreal, 1985; Hon. Dr in Political Science, Chulalongkorn, Bangkok, 1987. Médaille des Universités de Paris, 1988; Grand Montréalais Award, 1991. *Recreations:* cultivating flowers and plants, reading, tennis. *Address:* 3474 de la Montagne, Montréal, Qué H3G 2A6, Canada. *Died 26 Jan. 1993.*

SAVAGE, Albert Walter, CMG 1954; Director-General (retired), Colonial Civil Aviation Service; *b* 12 June 1898; *s* of William Albert Savage, Wheathampstead, Herts; *m* 1923, Lilian Marie Gertrude Storch; one *s* one *d. Educ:* Northern Polytechnic, Northampton Institute and Sheffield University. Apprentice, Grahame White Flying School, 1914–16. Served European War, 1914–18: RFC, 1916 to end of war. Aeronautical Inspection Directorate, Air Ministry, UK 1921–34, India, 1934–36; seconded to Egyptian Govt as Chief Technical Inspector, Civil Aviation Dept, Cairo, 1936–46; Colonial Civil Aviation Service, 1946: Director of Civil Aviation, W Africa, 1946–49; Director-General of Civil Aviation, Malaya/Borneo territories, 1949–54; Civil Aviation Adviser, Government of Jordan, 1954–55; Director of Civil Aviation, Leeward and Windward Islands, 1956–60; Director of Civil Aviation, Sierra Leone, 1961–62. *Recreations:* golf, tennis, squash. *Address:* 71 Eridge Road, Eastbourne BN21 2TS. *T:* Eastbourne (0323) 37905. *Died 6 Nov. 1993.*

SAYERS, Eric Colin, CBE 1981; FCA; Chairman, Duport Ltd, 1973–81; *b* 20 Sept. 1916; *s* of Alfred William and Emily Clara Sayers; *m* 1940, Winifred Bristow; two *d. Educ:* Acton County Grammar School. JDipMA, CBIM. Joined Duport Ltd, 1956; Director, 1962; Managing Director, 1966–75. Director: Ductile Steels PLC, 1973–82; International Timber Corp. PLC, 1977–83; Durapipe Internat. Ltd, 1979–81. Part-time Member, Midlands Electricity Board, 1973–81; Member: Council of CBI, 1975–81 (Chm. Energy Policy Cttee, 1975–81); Government's Advisory Council on Energy Conservation, 1977–79; Energy Commn, 1977–79; Birmingham Cttee of Inst. of Directors, 1974–84. Pres., Birmingham and W Midlands Soc. of Chartered Accountants, 1971–72; Inst. of Chartered Accountants in England and Wales: Council Member, 1966–83; Vice-Pres., 1976; Dep. Pres., 1977; Pres., 1978. Chm., Solihull County Scouts Council, 1983–88. Treas., Univ. of Aston in Birmingham, 1976–88. Hon. DSc Aston, 1985. *Recreations:* golf, fishing. *Address:* 73 Silhill Hall Road, Solihull, West Midlands B91 1JT. *T:* 021–705 3973. *Club:* Lansdowne. *Died 16 March 1991.*

SAYERS, Prof. James, MSc, PhD Cantab; Professor of Electron Physics, University of Birmingham, 1946–72; *b* 2 Sept. 1912; *s* of late J. Sayers; *m* 1943, Diana Ailsa Joan Montgomery; two *s* one *d. Educ:* Ballymena Academy; University of Belfast; St John's College, Cambridge. Fellow of St John's College, Cambridge, 1941–46. Research for Admiralty in Univ. of Birmingham, 1939–43, on micro-wave radar; Member of British Group of Atomic Scientists transferred to work on the US Manhattan Project, 1943–45. British delegate to Internat. Scientific Radio Union, Zürich, 1950. Life Fellow, Franklin Inst. of State of Pennsylvania. Award by the Royal Commission on Awards to Inventors, 1949; John Price Wetherill Medallist, for discovery in Physical Science, 1958. *Publications:* papers in Proc. Royal Soc., Proc. Phys. Soc., and in the reports of various internat. scientific conferences, on upper atmosphere physics and the physics of ionized gases. *Recreations:* gardening, photography. *Address:* Edgewood Gables, The Holloway, Alvechurch, Worcestershire. *T:* Redditch (0527) 64414. *Died 13 March 1993.*

SAYLES, Prof. George Osborne, LittD, DLitt, LLD; FBA 1962; MRIA; *b* 20 April 1901; *s* of Rev. L. P. Sayles and Margaret Brown, Glasgow; *m* 1936, Agnes, *d* of George Sutherland, Glasgow; one *d* (one *s* decd). *Educ:* Ilkeston Grammar Sch.; Glasgow Univ.; University Coll., London. Open Bursar, Ewing Gold Medallist, First Cl. Hons History, Glasgow Univ., 1923; Carnegie Res. Schol., University Coll., London, 1923–24. Asst, 1924, Lectr, 1925 and Sen. Lectr, 1934–45, in History, Glasgow Univ.; Leverhulme Res. Fellow, 1939; Professor of Modern History in the Queen's University, Belfast, 1945–53; Burnett-Fletcher Professor of History in the Univ. of Aberdeen, 1953–62; first Kenan Prof. of History, New York Univ., 1967; Vis. Prof., Louvain Univ., Belgium, 1951; Woodward Lectr, Yale Univ., USA, 1952; Fellow, Folger Library, Washington, 1960–61; Vis. Mem., Inst. for Advanced Study, Princeton, NJ, 1969; Corr. Fellow, American Soc. for Legal History, 1971; Hon. Fellow, Medieval Acad. of America, 1980; Hon. Mem., Selden Soc., London, 1985 (Vice-Pres., 1954–86). Chm. Advisory Cttee, Official War History of Northern Ireland, 1949; Member: Commission Internationale pour l'Histoire des Assemblées d'Etats; Advisory Historical Committee, Official Histories of War (Gt Brit.), 1950; Irish Manuscripts Commn, Dublin, 1949; Scottish Cttee on History of Scottish Parliament, 1937; Council of Stair Soc. (Scotland). Hon. LittD Trinity Coll. Dublin, 1965; Hon. LLD Glasgow, 1979. James Barr Ames Medal, Fac. of Law, Harvard Univ., 1958. Intelligence Officer (voluntary) to District Commissioner for Civil Defence SW Scotland, 1939–44; HG, Glasgow 12th Bn 1940. *Publications:* author, editor or joint editor of: The Early Statutes, 1934; Rotuli Parliamentorum Anglie Hactenus Inediti, 1935; Select Cases in Court of King's Bench: under Edward I (3 vols), 1936–39; Edward II (1 vol.), 1956; Edward III (2 vols), 1958, 1965; Richard II, Henry IV, Henry V (1 vol.), 1972; Select Cases in Procedure without Writ, 1943; Parliaments and Councils of Medieval Ireland, 1947; Medieval Foundations of England, 1948, 3rd edn 1964, American edn, 1950; Irish Parliament in the Middle Ages, 1952, 2nd edn 1964; The Irish Parliament in 1782, 1954; Fleta, vol. I, 1955, vol. II, 1972, vol. III, 1984; Parliaments and Great Councils in Medieval England, 1961; Governance of Medieval England, 1963; The Administration of Ireland, 1172–1377, 1964; Law and Legislation in Medieval England, 1966; The King's Parliament of England, 1974; Documents on the Affairs of Ireland before the King's Council, 1979; The English Parliament in the Middle Ages, 1981; Scripta Diversa, 1983; The Functions of the Medieval Parliament of England, 1988; articles and reviews in Eng. Hist. Review, Scot. Hist. Review, Law Quarterly Review, Proc. RIA, etc. *Recreations:* travel, motoring. *Address:* Warren Hill,

Crowborough, East Sussex TN6 1RA. *T:* Crowborough (0892) 661439. *Died 28 Feb. 1994.*

SCARLETT, Hon. John Leopold Campbell, CBE 1973; Deputy to Health Service Commissioner, 1973–76; *b* 18 Dec. 1916; 2nd *s* of 7th Baron Abinger and Marjorie, 2nd *d* of John McPhillamy, Bathurst, NSW; *m* 1947, Bridget Valerie, *d* of late H. B. Crook; two *s* one *d. Educ:* Eton; Magdalene Coll., Cambridge (MA). Served War of 1939–45, France, Madagascar, Burma (despatches); 2nd Lieut 1940; Major 1944, RA. House Governor, London Hosp., 1962–72. *Address:* Bramblewood, Castle Walk, Wadhurst, Sussex TN5 6DB. *T:* Wadhurst (01892) 782642. *Club:* Royal Automobile.
Died 19 Aug. 1994.

SCHILLER, Prof. Dr Karl; Member of Deutscher Bundestag, 1965–72; Professor of Political Economy, University of Hamburg, and Director of Institute for Foreign Trade and Overseas Economy, 1947–72; Member, Ford European Advisory Council, since 1976; *b* 24 April 1911; *s* of Carl and Maria Schiller; *m; one s. Educ:* Univs of Kiel, Frankfurt, Berlin, Heidelberg. Research Asst, Institut für Weltwirtschaft, Kiel, 1935–39; Lectr, Univ. of Kiel, 1945–46; Rector, Univ. of Hamburg, 1956–58. Senator for Economic Affairs and Transportation, Hamburg, 1948–53; Mem., Bürgerschaft Hamburg, 1949–57; Senator for Economics, West Berlin, 1961–65; Federal Minister of Economics, 1966–71, of Economics and Finance, 1971–72. Pres., Econ. Develt of Equatorial and Southern Africa, 1973–79. Hon. Senator, Univ. of Hamburg, 1983. Alexander Ruestow Plaque, Ruestow Soc., 1976; Ludwig Erhard Prize, Ludwig Erhard Foundn, Bonn, 1978; Burgermeister Stolten Medal, Senate of Hamburg, 1986; Bernhard Harms Medal, Inst. of World Economics, Kiel, 1989. Hon. Dr rer. pol. Münster Univ., 1991. *Publications:* Sozialismus und Wettbewerb, 1955; Neuere Entwicklungen in der Theorie der Wirtschaftspolitik, 1958; Zur Wachstumsproblematik der Entwicklungsländer, 1960; Der Ökonom und die Gesellschaft, 1964; Reden zur Wirtschaft und Finanzpolitik (10 vols), 1966–72; Betrachtungen zur Geld- und Konjunkturpolitik, 1984; Der schwierige Weg in die offene Gesellschaft, 1994, etc. *Address:* 22299 Hamburg, Leinpfad 71, Germany. *Died 26 Dec. 1994.*

SCHNYDER, Félix; Ambassador of Switzerland to the United States, 1966–75; *b* 5 March 1910; *s* of Maximilian Schnyder and Louise (*née* Steiner); *m* 1941, Sigrid Bucher; one *d. Educ:* University of Berne. Barrister, 1938; activities in private enterprise, 1938–40; joined Federal Political Dept, 1940; assigned to Swiss Legation in Moscow, 1947–49; Counsellor of Legation, Head of Swiss Delegation in Berlin, 1949–54; First Counsellor, Swiss Legation in Washington, 1954–57; Swiss Minister in Israel, 1957; Permanent Observer for Switzerland at UN in New York, 1958–61; Swiss Delegate to Technical Assistance Cttee; Swiss Delegate to Exec. Board of UNICEF (Chm. 1960); UN High Comr for Refugees, 1961–65. President: Swiss Nat. Cttee for UNESCO, 1976–80; Swiss Foreign Policy Assoc., 1976–84. *Address:* Via Navegna 25, 6648 Minusio-Locarno, Switzerland.
Died 8 Nov. 1992.

SCHOFIELD, Alfred, FCIB; Director, Leeds Permanent Building Society, 1970–86; *b* 18 Feb. 1913; *s* of James Henry and Alice Schofield; *m* 1939, Kathleen Risingham; one *d. Educ:* Queen Elizabeth's Grammar Sch., Wakefield. Apptd General Manager, Leeds Permanent Bldg Soc., 1967, retd, 1973; Pres., 1975–78. Consultant: Homeowners Friendly Soc., 1983–91; Springfield Trustees Ltd, 1987–91. *Recreation:* orchid growing. *Address:* 6 Tolls Close, Redhouse Farm, Whitley Bay, Tyne and Wear NE25 9XY. *T:* 0191–297 1390.
Died 16 Dec. 1994.

SCHOFIELD, Sidney; *b* March 1911; *m;* two *s. Educ:* Barnsley. Coal-face worker at Glass Houghton Colliery, near Castleford, for many years. Served War of 1939–45, in Mediterranean etc, with RE, 1940–46. MP (Lab) Barnsley, Nov. 1951–Jan. 1953. National Union of Mineworkers: Area Sec., Yorks, 1964; Vice-Pres., 1969–73. *Died Dec. 1992.*

SCHOLEFIELD, Charles Edward, QC 1959; *b* 15 July 1902; *e s* of Edward Scholefield, Castleford, Yorks; *m* 1966, Catherine Heléne (formerly Childs), *o d* of Reginald and Marguerite Blyth; one step *s* one step *d. Educ:* St Peter's School, York. Admitted a Solicitor, 1925; Barrister, Middle Temple, 1934; North Eastern Circuit. Served in Royal Army Pay Corps, 1940–45; Captain, 1943–45. Chm., Council of Professions supplementary to Medicine, 1966–73. Master of the Bench of the Middle Temple, 1966. *Publications:* (ed) 11th and 12th edns, Lumley's Public Health. *Recreations:* watching cricket and Rugby football, Sherlock Holmes Society of London, Society of Yorkshiremen in London (Past Chairman). *Address:* 4 Gray's Inn Square, WC1; Flat 12, Parkside Nursing Home, Park Road, Banstead, Surrey SM7 3BY. *T:* Burgh Heath (0737) 361334. *Died 23 Sept. 1993.*

SCHON, Baron *cr* 1976 (Life Peer), of Whitehaven, Cumbria; **Frank Schon,** Kt 1966; Chairman, National Research Development Corporation, 1969–79 (Member, 1967–79); *b* 18 May 1912; *o s* of Dr Frederick Schon and Henriette (*née* Nettel); *m* 1936, Gertrude Secher (*d* 1993); two *d. Educ:* Rainer Gymnasium, Vienna II; University of Prague; University of Vienna (studied law externally). Co-founder: Marchon Products Ltd, 1939; Solway Chemicals Ltd, 1943; Chm. and Man. Dir of both until May 1967; Dir, Albright & Wilson Ltd, 1956–67; Non-exec. Dir, Blue Circle Industries PLC (formerly Associated Portland Cement Manufacturers Ltd), 1967–82. Mem. Council, King's College, Durham, 1959–63; Mem. Council, 1963–66, Mem. Court, 1963–78, Univ. of Newcastle upon Tyne. Chm. Cumberland Development Council, 1964–68; Member: Northern Economic Planning Council, 1965–68; Industrial Reorganisation Corp., 1966–71; Adv. Council of Technology, 1968–70; part-time Mem., Northern Gas Bd, 1963–66. Hon. Freeman of Whitehaven, 1961. Hon. DCL Durham, 1961. *Recreations:* golf, reading. *Address:* Flat 82, Prince Albert Court, 33 Prince Albert Road, NW8 7LU. *T:* 0171–586 1461. *Died 7 Jan. 1995.*

SCHREIBER, Gaby, FCSD; general consultant designer for industry; specialist in colour consultancy and interiors; adviser on purchases of works of art; Chairman, Gaby Schreiber & Associates; *d* of Gunther George Peter Wolff; *m* 1st, Leopold Schreiber (marr. diss.; he *d* 1961); 2nd, 1953, William Fishbein (marr. diss.). *Educ:* studied art and stage and interior design in Vienna, Florence, Berlin and Paris. Interior Design Consultant to: William Clark & Sons Ltd, NI, 1981–84; National Westminster Bank Ltd; Westminster Foreign Bank, Brussels, 1972–73; Chm.'s offices, GHP Gp Ltd, 1974; Pres.'s offices, Gulf Oil-Eastern Hemisphere, 1973–74; Lythe Hill Hotel, Haslemere, Surrey; Anglo-Continental Investment & Finance Co. and Continental Bankers Agents, London; Myers & Co.; Peter Robinson Ltd; David Morgan, Cardiff; W Cumberland Hosp.; Newcastle Regnl Hosp. Bd; Fine Fare Ltd (Queensway Store, Crawley); Gen. Consultant and Designer to: Cunard Steamship Co. Ltd (QE2); Zarach Ltd; Marquess of Londonderry; Crown Agents; Allen and Hanbury (Surgical Engineering) Limited; BOAC (whole fleet of aeroplanes, 1957–63); Divs of Dunlop Rubber Gp; Bartrev Gp of Cos; Hawker Siddeley Aviation Ltd (for the Queen's Flight and RAF); Rank Organisation Ltd; Design Consultant on Plastics to Marks & Spencer Ltd; yachts: Sir Gerard d'Erlanger; Whitney Straight, and others; designed exhibn stands in Britain, Europe and USA.

Member CoID, 1960–62 (Mem. Design Awards Cttee, 1961); Judge on Indep. Panel, to select Duke of Edinburgh's Prize for Elegant Design, 1960 and 1961. Society of Industrial Artists and Designers: Fellow; Past Chm., Consultant Designers Gp and Internat. Relations Cttee; Mem. Council; UK delegate at Gen. Assembly of Internat. Council of Soc. of Ind. Design, Venice, 1961. Mem., Panel of Judges for newspaper and magazine competitions on ind. design. Broadcast and appeared on TV. *Publications:* her work appeared in internat. books and jls on design. *Recreations:* gardening, farming, golf, arts and crafts. *Address:* 26 Kylestrome House, Cundy Street, SW1W 9JT. *T:* 071–235 4656.
Died 3 July 1991.

SCHRODER, Ernest Melville, CMG 1970; retired 1980; *b* 23 Aug. 1901; *s* of Harold Schroder and Florence L. A. Schroder (*née* Stimson; *m* 1928, Winsome Dawson; two *s* one d. *Educ:* Newcastle (NSW) High Sch.; Newcastle Techn. College. Chief Chemist: Kandos Cement Co., Sydney, 1927–30; Australian Cement Ltd, Geelong, 1930–44; Man. Dir, Adelaide Cement Ltd, Adelaide, 1944–68, Chm., 1970–77; Dir, Quarry Industries Ltd, 1965–77. Pres., SA Chamber of Manufacturers, 1963–64, 1964–65; Vice-Pres., Assoc. Chamber of Manufrs of Aust., 1964–65; Pres., Cement and Concrete Assoc. of Aust., 1953–54, 1960–61; State Cttee Mem., CSIRO, 1954–71; Mem., CSIRO Adv. Council, 1955–61. FRACI; Associate IEAust. *Recreation:* gardening. *Address:* 23 Coreega Avenue, Springfield, SA 5062, Australia. *T:* (8) 3796452. *Died 15 Feb. 1993.*

SCHULTZ, Sir Joseph Leopold, (Sir Leo), Kt 1966; OBE 1945; Member, Kingston upon Hull District Council, 1973–83; *b* 4 Feb. 1900; *s* of Solomon Schultz; *m* 1928, Kate, *d* of George Pickersgill; one *s. Educ:* Hull. Alderman, City of Kingston upon Hull, 1962–74. Chm., Humberside Local Govt Reorganisation Jt Cttee, 1973; Mem., Humberside County Council, 1973–76. *Recreation:* cricket. *Address:* Grove House, Beverley Road, Hull HU5 1NA. *Died 22 July 1991.*

SCHWARZ, Rudolf, CBE 1973; Conductor Laureate, Northern Sinfonia of England (formerly Northern Sinfonia Orchestra, Newcastle upon Tyne), 1982–85 (Principal Guest Conductor, 1973–82); *b* Vienna, Austria, 29 April 1905; *s* of Josef Schwarz and Berth Roth; British subject, 1952; *m* 1950, Greta Ohlson (*d* 1984); one *s*, and one step *s* one step d. *Educ:* Vienna. Conductor, Opera House, Düsseldorf, 1923–27; Conductor, Opera House, Karlsruhe, 1927–33; Musical Director, Jewish Cultural Organisation, Berlin, 1936–41; Conductor, Bournemouth Municipal Orchestra, 1947–51; Conductor, City of Birmingham Symphony Orchestra, 1951–57; Chief Conductor of the BBC Symphony Orchestra, 1957–62; Principal Conductor, Northern Sinfonia Orchestra, Newcastle upon Tyne, 1964–73; Guest Conductor, Bergen Orchestra, Norway, 1964–71; Principal Guest Conductor, Bournemouth Symphony Orchestra, 1970–79. Hon. RAM; Hon. GSM; DMus (*hc*) Newcastle upon Tyne, 1972. *Address:* 24 Wildcroft Manor, SW15 3TS.
Died 30 Jan. 1994.

SCHWARZENBERGER, Prof. Georg; Professor of International Law in the University of London, 1962–75, then Emeritus; Dean, Faculty of Laws, University College, London, 1965–67 (Vice-Dean, 1949–55 and 1963–65); Director, London Institute of World Affairs since 1943; Barrister-at-Law, Gray's Inn, since 1955; *b* 20 May 1908; *o s* of Ludwig and Ferry Schwarzenberger; *m* 1931, Suse Schwarz; one *s. Educ:* Karls-Gymnasium, Heilbronn aN; Univs of Heidelberg, Frankfurt, Berlin, Tübingen, Paris and London. Dr Jur (Tübingen) 1930; PhD (London) 1936. Sec. London Inst. of World Affairs (formerly New Commonwealth Inst.), 1934–43; Lectr in Internat. Law

and Relations, University Coll., London, 1938–45; Sub-Dean and Tutor, Faculty of Laws, 1942–49; Reader in Internat. Law, 1945–62. Co-Editor (with G. W. Keeton) of: The Library of World Affairs, 1946–; The Year Book of World Affairs, 1947–84; Current Legal Problems, 1948–72. Member, Permanent Finnish-Netherlands Conciliation Commission. Hon. LLD Dalhousie, 1979. *Publications:* The League of Nations and World Order, 1936; Power Politics: A Study of World Society, 1941, 3rd edn 1964; International Law and Totalitarian Lawlessness, 1943; International Law as Applied by International Court and Tribunals, Vol. I, 1945, 3rd edn 1957, Vol. II, 1968, Vol. III, 1976, Vol. IV, 1986; A Manual of International Law, 1947, 6th edn (with E. D. Brown) 1976; The Fundamental Principles of International Law, Hague Academy of Internat. Law (Recueil, Vol. 87), 1955; The Legality of Nuclear Weapons, 1958; The Frontiers of International Law, 1962; The Inductive Approach to International Law, 1965; The Principles and Standards of International Economic Law, Hague Acad. of Internat. Law (Recueil, Vol. 117), 1966; Foreign Investments and International Law, 1969; International Law and Order, 1971; The Dynamics of International Law, 1976. *Recreations:* gardening, swimming. *Address:* 4 Bowers Way, Harpenden, Herts AL5 4EW. *T:* Harpenden (0582) 713497. *Died 20 Sept. 1991.*

SCHWEITZER, Pierre-Paul; Grand Croix de la Légion d'Honneur; Croix de Guerre (1939–45); Médaille de la Résistance avec rosette; Inspecteur Général des Finances Honoraire, 1974; *b* 29 May 1912; *s* of Paul Schweitzer and Emma Munch; *m* 1941, Catherine Hatt; one *s* one d. *Educ:* Univs of Strasbourg and Paris; Ecole Libre des Sciences Politiques. Joined French Treasury as Inspecteur des Finances, 1936; Dep. Dir for Internat. Finance, French Treasury, Paris, 1946; Alternate Exec. Dir, IMF, Washington, 1947; Sec.-Gen. for European Economic Cooperation in the French Administration, Paris, 1948; Financial Counsellor, French Embassy, Washington, 1949; Director, Treasury, Paris, 1953; Dep. Governor of the Banque de France, Paris, 1960–63; Inspecteur Général des Finances, 1963; Man. Dir and Chm. Exec. Bd, IMF, 1963–73. Chairman: Bank of America International, Luxembourg, 1974–77; Cie Monégasque de Banque, Monaco, 1978–88; Director: Banque Pétrofigaz, Paris, 1974–91 (Chm., 1974–79); Robeco Gp, Rotterdam, 1974–82; Compagnie de Participations et d'Investissements Holding SA, Luxembourg, 1975–87 (Chm., 1975–84); Société Financière Internationale de Participations, Paris, 1976–87 (Chm., 1976–84); Adv. Dir, Bank of America, NY, 1974–77, and Unilever NV, Rotterdam, 1974–84. Hon. LLD: Yale, 1966; Harvard, 1966; Leeds, 1968; New York, 1968; George Washington Univ., 1972; Wales, 1972; Williams, 1973. *Address:* 170 route de Mon Idée, 1253 Vandoeuvres, Switzerland. *T:* (022) 7501313. *Died 2 Jan. 1994.*

SCHWINGER, Prof. Julian Seymour, AB, PhD; University Professor, University of California at Los Angeles, since 1980 (Professor of Physics, 1972–80); *b* 12 Feb. 1918; *s* of Benjamin Schwinger and Belle Schwinger (*née* Rosenfeld); *m* 1947, Clarice Carrol. *Educ:* Columbia University. Nat. Research Council Fellow, 1939–40; Research Associate, University of California at Berkeley, 1940–41; Instructor, later Assistant Professor, Purdue University, 1941–43; Member Staff: Radiation Laboratory, MIT, 1943–46; Metallurgy Laboratory, University of Chicago, 1943; Associate Professor of Physics, Harvard University, 1945–47, Prof., 1947–72; Higgins Prof. of Physics, 1966–72. Writer and presenter of series Understanding Space and Time, BBC (jt Univ. of Calif and Open Univ. prodn). Member, Board of Sponsors, Bulletin of the Atomic Scientists. Member: Nat. Acad. of Scis; Amer. Acad. of Arts and Scis; Amer. Assoc.

for Advancement of Science; NY Acad. of Sciences; Bd of Sponsors, Amer. Fedn of Scientists; Civil Liberties Union. Guggenheim Fellow, 1970. Hon. DSc: Purdue, 1961; Harvard, 1962; Columbia, 1966; Brandeis, 1973; Gustavus Adolphus Coll., 1975; Nottingham, 1993; Hon. LLD City Univ. of NY, 1972; Hon. Dr Univ. of Paris, 1990. US Nat. Medal of Sci., 1964; Nobel Prize for Physics with R. Feynman and S. Tomonaga), 1965; Humboldt Prize, 1981; many other awards and medals. *Publications:* Quantum Electrodynamics (ed), 1958; (with D. Saxon) Discontinuities in Wave Guides, 1968; Particles and Sources, 1969; Quantum Kinematics and Dynamics, 1970; Particles, Sources and Fields, vol. I, 1970, vol. II, 1973, vol. III, 1989. *Recreations:* tennis, swimming, skiing, driving, being one of the world's worst pianists. *Address:* Department of Physics, University of California at Los Angeles, Calif 90024, USA; 10727 Stradella Court, Los Angeles, Calif 90077. 				*Died 16 July 1994.*

SCOONES, Maj.-Gen. Sir Reginald (Laurence), KBE 1955 (OBE 1941); CB 1951; DSO 1945; late Royal Armoured Corps; Director, The Brewers' Society, 1957–69; *b* 18 Dec. 1900; *s* of late Major Fitzmaurice Scoones, Royal Fusiliers; *m* 1933, Isabella Bowie, *d* of John Nisbet, Cumbrae Isles, Scotland; one *d. Educ:* Wellington College; RMC, Sandhurst. 2nd Lieut Royal Fusiliers, 1920; transferred Royal Tank Corps, 1923; attd Sudan Defence Force, 1926–34; Adjt 1 RTR, 1935; GSO3 Mobile Div., 1938; served War of 1939–45, Middle East and Burma: Brigade Major, Cavalry Brigade, Cairo, 1939; GSO2 Western Desert Corps, 1940; CO 42 RTR, 1941; GSO1 War Office, 1941; Brig. Dep. Dir Military Trng, 1942; Comdr, 254 Tank Brigade, Burma, 1943; Dep. Dir Military Trng, 1945; Asst Kaid, Sudan Defence Force, 1947–50; Maj.-Gen. 1950; Major-General Commanding British Troops Sudan and Commandant Sudan Defence Force, 1950–54. *Address:* Flat 51, 50 Sloane Street, SW1X 9SV. 				*Died 6 Oct. 1991.*

SCOTT, Prof. Alexander Whiteford, CBE 1960; Professor of Chemical Engineering, University of Strathclyde, Glasgow, 1955–71; Hon. Engineering Consultant to Ministry of Agriculture, Fisheries and Food, 1946–62; *b* 28 Jan. 1904; *s* of Alexander Scott, Glasgow; *m* 1933, Rowena Christianna (*d* 1970), *d* of John Craig, Glasgow; one *s. Educ:* Royal College of Science and Technology, Glasgow. BSc, PhD, ARCST. Pres., Instn of Engineers and Shipbuilders in Scotland, 1975–76 and 1976–77. FIMechE, FIChemE, Hon. FCIBS. Hon. LLD Strathclyde, 1980. *Address:* 9 Rowallan Road, Thornliebank, Glasgow G46 7EP. *T:* 041–638 2968. 			*Died 6 April 1993.*

SCOTT, Sir (Charles) Hilary, Kt 1967; Partner Slaughter & May, London, 1937–74; *b* Bradford, 27 March 1906; *s* of late Lieutenant-Colonel C. E. Scott and Mrs M. E. M. Scott, Bradford; *m* 1932, Beatrice Margery, *d* of late Reverend Canon Garrad; one *s* two *d. Educ:* Sedbergh Sch. Articled with Wade & Co., Bradford. Qual. as Solicitor (Class 2 Hons) 1930. Served in RNVR, 1940–45 (Lieut-Comdr). President of the Law Society, 1966–67 (Mem. Council, 1948–71; Vice-Pres. 1965–66); Member: Nat. Film Finance Corp., 1948–70 (Chm. 1964–69); Jenkins Cttee on Company Law, 1959–62; Panel of Judges of The Accountant Awards for company accounts, 1961–69; London Adv. Bd of Salvation Army, 1968–82; Noise Adv. Council, 1971–75; Council, Royal Sch. of Church Music, 1974–85; Chm., Cttee on Property Bonds and Equity-linked Life Assurance, 1971–73. Trustee, Glyndebourne Arts Trust, 1961–76. Director: Tarmac Ltd, 1968–76; Equity & Law Life Assurance Society Ltd, 1955–81; London Board, Bank of Scotland, 1966–76. FRSA. *Recreations:* travel, music. *Address:* Knowle House, Bishop's Walk, Addington, Surrey CR0 5BA. *T:* 081–654 3638. 				*Died 9 April 1991.*

SCOTT, Sir James (Walter), 2nd Bt, *cr* 1962, of Rotherfield Park, Alton, Hants; JP; Lord-Lieutenant of Hampshire, since 1982; Lieutenant, HM Body Guard, Honourable Corps of Gentlemen-at-Arms, since 1993 (Member, since 1977; Standard Bearer, 1990–93); *b* 26 Oct. 1924; *e s* of Col Sir Jervoise Bolitho Scott, 1st Bt, and Kathleen Isabel, *yr d* of late Godfrey Walter, Malshanger, Basingstoke; *S* father 1965; *m* 1951, Anne Constantia, *e d* of late Lt-Col Clive Austin, Roundwood, Micheldever, Hants and Lady Lilian Austin, *d* of late Brig. O. V. G. A. Lumley (3rd *s* of 9th Earl of Scarborough); three *s* one *d* (and one *d* decd). *Educ:* Eton. Lt-Col The Life Guards, formerly Grenadier Guards; served War of 1939–45: NW Europe, 1944–45; Palestine, 1945–46; ADC to Viceroy and Gov.-Gen. of India, 1946–48; Malaya, 1948–49; Cyprus, 1958, 1960, 1964; Malaysia, 1966; retd 1969. Hon. Colonel: 2nd Bn Wessex Regt (Volunteers), 1985–90; Hants and IoW ACF, 1990–. Underwriting Member of Lloyd's. Master, Mercers' Co., 1976. Chm. Hants Branch, Country Landowners' Assoc., 1981–84. Councillor, Hants CC, 1973–83. DL 1978, High Sheriff 1981–82, JP 1982, Hants. KStJ 1983. *Heir: s* James Jervoise Scott [*b* 12 Oct. 1952; *m* 1982, Mrs Judy Lyndon-Skeggs, *d* of Brian Trafford; one *s* one *d* and two step *d*]. *Address:* Rotherfield Park, Alton, Hampshire GU34 3QL. *T:* Tisted (042058) 204. *Clubs:* Cavalry and Guards, Farmers', Institute of Directors. 				*Died 2 Nov. 1993.*

SCOTT, Maj.-Gen. Michael Frederick, JP; farmer; *b* 25 Oct. 1911; *s* of Col F. W. Scott, Romsey, Hants; *m* 1961, Laila Wallis (*née* Tatchell). *Educ:* Harrow. Apprenticed as Mechanical Engr to John I. Thornycroft Co., Basingstoke, 1932–35; commnd Lieut, RAOC, 1935; transf. REME 1942; served: India, 1938–44; Palestine, 1947–48; Germany, 1951–54; Cyprus, 1955–58; Inspector, REME, 1960–63; Commandant Technical Group, REME, 1963–65 (retd); Col Comdt, REME, 1968–73. CEng; FIMechE. JP Somerset, 1967. *Recreations:* sailing, shooting, country pursuits. *Address:* Parsonage Farm, South Barrow, Yeovil, Somerset BA22 7LF. *T:* North Cadbury (01963) 440417. *Club:* Royal Ocean Racing. 				*Died 13 May 1995.*

SCOTT, Rev. Dr Percy; Warden of Hartley Hall, Manchester, 1973–77, retired; *b* 14 Nov. 1910; *s* of Herbert and Emma Scott; *m* 1937, Christa Schleining; one *s* two *d. Educ:* Lincoln City School; London and Marburg Universities. Richmond College, London, 1931–35; Marburg, 1935–37; Minister at: Exeter, 1937–39; Stockton-on-Tees, 1939–45; Leeds, 1945–47; Tutor in Systematic Theology at Hartley Victoria College, 1947–73; Member, Faculty of Theology, Manchester Univ., 1953–77; Principal, Hartley Victoria Coll., Manchester, 1959–73. *Publications:* John Wesley's Lehre von der Heiligung, 1938; (trans.) Day by Day we Magnify Thee (Luther), 1950; other translations from German; signed reviews in The Expository Times and London Quarterly; articles. *Recreation:* sport. *Address:* 53 Alexandra Road South, Manchester M16 8GH. *T:* 061–226 7311. *Club:* Rotarian (Manchester South).

				Died 25 Jan. 1991.

SCOTT, Maj.-Gen. Robert, CB 1989; FRCS; Commandant and Post-Graduate Dean, Royal Army Medical College, 1986–89; *b* 16 Aug. 1929; *s* of late Thomas Montgomery Scott and of Margaret Scott; *m* 1957, Rosemary Stott Sunderland; one *s* two *d. Educ:* Campbell College; University College, Oxford (MA, MCh); King's College Hospital. Joined RAMC 1956; Consultant surgeon, mil. hospitals at home and overseas, and BAOR, 1956–86. QHS 1987–89. FRSocMed. *Publications:* chapters and papers on military surgery. *Recreations:* golf, sailing,

bagpiping. *Address:* Aish Barton, Aish, Stoke Gabriel, South Devon. *T:* Stoke Gabriel (080428) 477.
Died 19 March 1991.

SCOTT, Sir Terence Charles Stuart M.; *see* Morrison-Scott.

SCOTT, Sir Walter, 4th Bt, *cr* 1907, of Beauclerc, Bywell St Andrew, Northumberland; DL; *b* 29 July 1918; *s* of Sir Walter Scott, 3rd Bt, and Nancie Margot, *d* of S. H. March; *S* father, 1967; *m* 1st, 1945, Diana Mary (*d* 1985), *d* of J. R. Owen; one *s* one *d*; 2nd, 1991, Anna-Louise, *d* of Aubrey Derwent Healing. *Educ:* Eton; Jesus College, Cambridge. Served 1st Royal Dragoons, 1939–46; Temp. Major, 1945. JP East Sussex, 1963; DL East Sussex, 1975. *Recreations:* field sports. *Heir:* *s* (Walter) John Scott [*b* 24 Feb. 1948; *m* 1st, 1969, Lowell Patria (marr. diss. 1971), *d* of late Pat Vaughan Goddard, Auckland, NZ; one *d*; 2nd, 1977, Mary Gavin, *d* of Alexander Fairly Anderson, Gartocharn, Dunbartonshire; one *s* one *d*]. *Address:* Newhouse Farm, Chalvington, Hailsham, Sussex.
Died 29 Nov. 1992.

SCOTT, Warwick; *see* Trevor, E.

SCOTT-HOPKINS, Major Sir James (Sidney Rawdon), Kt 1981; *b* 29 Nov. 1921; *s* of late Col R. Scott-Hopkins, DSO, MC and Mrs Scott-Hopkins; *m* 1946, Geraldine Elizabeth Mary Hargreaves, CBE; three *s* one *d*. *Educ:* Eton; Oxford. Army, 1939–50; farming, 1950–59. MP (C) North Cornwall, 1959–66, Derbyshire West, Nov. 1967–1979; Joint Parliamentary Secretary, Ministry of Agriculture, Fisheries and Food, 1962–64. MEP (C), 1973–94 (elected MEP, Hereford and Worcester, 1979–94); European Parliament: Dep. Leader Cons. Gp and Spokesman on Agric., 1973–79; Vice-Pres., 1976–79; Chm., European Democratic Gp, 1979–82. *Recreations:* riding, shooting. *Address:* 602 Nelson House, Dolphin Square, SW1V 3NZ; Bicknor House, English Bicknor, Coleford, Glos GL16 7PF. *Club:* Carlton.
Died 11 March 1995.

SCOTT-MILLER, Comdr Ronald, VRD 1942; RNVR (retired); *b* 1 Nov. 1904; *s* of late Colonel Walter Scott-Miller, DL; *m* 1932, Stella Louise Farquhar (*d* 1988), *d* of late Farquhar Deuchar, Shortridge Hall, Northumberland. *Educ:* Aldro School, Eastbourne; Uppingham. Joined London Division, RNVR, as Midshipman, 1924; War of 1939–45 (despatches): HMS Dunedin, Northern Patrol, 1939; HMS London, Atlantic, Russian Convoys, 1940–43; Combined Operations, Mediterranean, NW Europe, 1943–45; Commander, 1943; retired, 1946. MP (C) King's Lynn Division of Norfolk, 1951–59; Parliamentary Private Secretary: to Financial Secretary to Treasury, Dec. 1953–July 1954; to Minister of Transport, 1954–56; to Minister of Pensions and National Insurance, 1956–59. Trustee of Uppingham School, 1954–59. Freeman of the City of London, and Liveryman of Worshipful Company of Butchers, 1926. US Legion of Merit (Legionaire), 1943. *Recreations:* shooting, sailing. *Club:* Naval.
Died 10 March 1992.

SCRUTTON, (Thomas) Hugh, CBE 1967; *b* 8 June 1917; *s* of late Rev. Canon Tom Burton Scrutton and Lesley Hay; *m* 1st, 1941, Helen Greeves (marr. diss. 1952); one *d*; 2nd, 1960, Elizabeth Quayle. *Educ:* Charterhouse; King's Coll., Cambridge (MA). War Service, 1940–45, Army. Temporary Asst Keeper, Print Room, British Museum, 1946; Asst, 1947, and Director, 1948, Whitechapel Art Gallery; Director: Walker Art Gallery, Liverpool, 1952–70; Nat. Galls of Scotland, Edinburgh, 1971–77, retired; Penwith Galleries, St Ives, 1978–80. Pres., Museums Assoc., 1970–71. Hon. DLitt Liverpool, 1971. *Address:* 11 Upper Coltbridge Terrace, Edinburgh EH12 6AD. *T:* 031–337 2732. *Club:* New (Edinburgh).
Died 28 Aug. 1991.

SEABORN, Most Rev. Robert Lowder; Chancellor, University of Trinity College, Toronto, 1983–91; *b* 9 July 1911; *s* of Rev. Richard Seaborn and Muriel Kathleen Reid; *m* 1938, Mary Elizabeth Gilchrist; four *s* one *d*. *Educ:* Univ. of Toronto Schs; Trinity Coll., Univ. of Toronto (MA); Oxford Univ. Deacon, 1934; priest, 1935; Asst Curate, St Simon's, Toronto, 1934–36; Asst Curate, St James's Cathedral, Toronto, 1937–41; Rector, St Peter's, Cobourg, Ont, 1941–48; Chaplain, Canadian Army, 1942–45 (Padre Canadian Scottish Regt); Dean of Quebec and Rector of Parish of Quebec, 1948–57; Rector, St Mary's, Kerrisdale, Vancouver, BC, 1957–58; Asst Bishop of Newfoundland, 1958–65, Coadjutor, June-Dec. 1965; Bishop of Newfoundland, 1965–75, of Eastern Newfoundland and Labrador, 1975–80; Archbishop of Newfoundland and Metropolitan of Ecclesiastical Province of Canada, 1975–80; Bishop Ordinary (Anglican) to Canadian Forces, 1980–86. Croix de Guerre avec étoile de vermeil (French), 1945. DD (*jure dignitatis*), Trinity Coll., 1948; DCL (*hc*), Bishop's Univ., 1962; Hon. LLD Meml Univ. of Newfoundland, 1972; Hon. DD Montreal Diocesan Theological Coll., 1980. *Publication:* Faith in our Time, 1963. *Recreations:* camping, golf. *Address:* 247 Lake Street, Cobourg, Ont K9A 1R6, Canada.
Died 15 Feb. 1993.

SEABY, Wilfred Arthur; retired museum official; Director, Ulster Museum (previously Belfast Museum and Art Gallery), 1953–70, in charge of Numismatic Section, Department of Technology and Local History, 1970–73; *b* 16 Sept. 1910; *y* *s* of late Allen W. Seaby, sometime Prof. of Art, Univ. of Reading; *m* 1937, Nora, *d* of late A. E. Pecover, Reading; two *s* one *d*. *Educ:* Wycliffe College; Reading University, College of Art. Dip. Museums Assoc., 1939. Served War of 1939–45, Royal Air Force, 1940–46 (Flt-Lt). B. A. Seaby Ltd, 1927–30; Reading, Birmingham, and Taunton Museums, 1931–53. Volunteer Numismatist, Warwickshire Mus., 1974–. FSA 1948. Hon. MA QUB, 1971. *Publication:* Hiberno-Norse Coins in the Ulster Museum, 1984. *Recreation:* water colour painting. *Address:* 36 Ladbrook Road, Solihull, West Midlands.
Died 30 Oct. 1991.

SEAMAN, Reginald Jaspar, (Dick); Director of Information, Department of Employment, 1978–80; *b* 19 March 1923; *o* *s* of Jaspar and Flora Seaman, Wandsworth; *m* 1950, Marian, *o* *d* of Henry and Ethel Sarah Moser. *Educ:* West Hill Elem. Sch., Wandsworth, SW18. Served War, 1940–46, RAF aircrew. Entered Civil Service as Post Office Messenger, 1937; Clerical Officer, HM Treasury, 1950; Asst Inf. Officer, Treasury, 1959–61; Inf. Officer, MAFF, 1961–64; Sen. Inf. Officer, DEA, 1964–67; Principal Inf. Officer, 1967–69; Chief Press Officer, DEP, 1969–72; Chief Inf. Officer, Northern Ireland Office, 1972–78. Silver Jubilee Medal, 1977. *Recreations:* orchids, horticulture (Chm., Caterham Horticultural Soc.). *Address:* 9 Ninehams Road, Caterham, Surrey CR3 5LH. *Died 17 Dec. 1993.*

SEARLE, Rear-Adm. Malcolm Walter St Leger, CB 1955; CBE 1945; *b* Cape Colony, S Africa, 23 Dec. 1900; *e* *s* of late Sir Malcolm William Searle; *m* 1930, Betty Margaret, *d* of Dr H. R. Crampton; one *s* two *d*. *Educ:* accepted as Dominion cadet to enter RN by Gen. Jan Smuts, 1912; RN Colleges Osborne and Dartmouth, 1914–17. Served European War, 1914–19 (Grand Fleet and Baltic, 1917–19); specialised in Gunnery, 1927; Comdr 1936 (Anti-aircraft Comdr); served War of 1939–45: Fleet Gunnery Officer, Home Fleet, 1939–41; HMS Sheffield, Mediterranean and Arctic, 1941–43; Capt. 1943; CSO to Vice-Adm., E Fleet, 1943–44; COS to C-in-C East Indies Fleet, 1944–46; Dir of Plans (Q), Naval Staff, 1948–51; Commodore, RN Barracks, Portsmouth, 1951; Rear-Adm. 1952; Deputy Chief of Naval Personnel,

1953–55; retired, 1956. *Recreations:* formerly: small boat sailing, mountaineering, ski-ing. *Address:* Lindens, Kithurst Park, Storrington, Pulborough, West Sussex RH20 4JH. *Died 4 May 1994.*

SEARLE, Peter; Director-General, Mental Health Foundation, since 1990; *b* 5 Jan. 1941; *s* of Neville Searle and Edith Searle (*née* Hoyle); *m* 1964, (Margaret) Ann Parker; three *d* and one foster *d. Educ:* Manchester Grammar Sch.; Univ. of Bristol. Lewis's Ltd (retailers), 1961–67; Don Summers Evangelistic Assoc., 1968–70; Principal, St Brandon's Sch., Clevedon, 1971–78; Proprietor, Moxhull Hall, 1978–81; Exec. Dir, World Vision of Britain, 1981–89. Dep. Chm., Royal Commonwealth Soc. MInstD; MBIM. *Publications:* articles in professional jls. *Recreations:* sailing, talking, sleeping. *Address:* Mental Health Foundation, 8 Hallam Street, W1N 6DH. *T:* 071–580 0145. *Clubs:* Commonwealth Trust; Safari (Nairobi).
Died 10 Dec. 1991.

SEDDON, Dr John; aeronautical consultant; *b* 29 Sept. 1915; *m* 1940, Barbara Mary Mackintosh; one *s* two *d. Educ:* Leeds Modern Sch.; Univ. of Leeds. BSc 1937, PhD 1939; DSc Bristol, 1982. Scientific Officer, RAE, Farnborough, 1939–55; Harkness Fund Fellow, California Inst. of Technology, 1955–56; Head of Experimental Supersonics, RAE, Farnborough, 1957–59; Supt, Tunnels II Div., RAE, Bedford, 1959–66; Dir, Scientific Research (Air), Min. of Technology, 1966–68; Dir-Gen. Research, Aircraft, MoD, 1969–75. Consultant: Westland Helicopters, 1976–84; Rolls-Royce, 1985–86. Sen. Res. Fellow, Bristol Univ., 1976–82; Visiting Professor: Nanjing Aeronautical Inst., China, 1980 and 1984 (Hon. Prof., 1984); Middle East Technological Univ., Ankara, Turkey, 1985, 1986 and 1987. *Publications:* Intake Aerodynamics (with E. L. Goldsmith), 1985; Basic Helicopter Aerodynamics, 1990; papers on air intakes and other aerodynamic subjects, in ARC Reports and Memoranda Series and other scientific media. *Recreation:* music. *Address:* 7 Vicarage Hill, The Bourne, Farnham, Surrey GU9 8HG. *T:* Farnham (0252) 723680.
Died 13 July 1991.

SELBY, Sir Kenneth, Kt 1970; FCMA, FCCA, CBIM, FIQ; President, Bath & Portland Group plc, 1983–86; *b* 16 Feb. 1914; *s* of Thomas William Selby; *m* 1937, Elma Gertrude, *d* of Johnstone Sleator; two *s. Educ:* High School for Boys, Worthing. Bath & Portland Group Ltd: Managing Director, 1963–81; Chm., 1969–82. Governor, Wells Cathedral Sch., 1976–91; Mem., Ct and Council, 1975–, Chm. Council, 1975–84, Pro Chancellor, 1975–, Bath Univ. Chm., Air Travel Reserve Fund Agency, 1975–86. Hon. LLD Bath, 1985. *Address:* 21 Clan House, Sydney Road, Bath, Avon BA2 6NS. *T:* Bath (0225) 465445. *Club:* Reform. *Died 9 Nov. 1992.*

SELBY, Rear-Adm. William Halford, CB 1955; DSC 1942; *b* 29 April 1902; *s* of E. H. Selby; *m* 1926, Hilary Elizabeth Salter (*d* 1960); two *d; m* 1961, Mrs R. Milne. *Educ:* Royal Naval Colleges, Osborne and Dartmouth. Entered Royal Navy, 1916; Midshipman, HMS Royal Oak, Black Sea and Dardanelles, 1920; Sub-Lt HMS Vendetta and HMY Victoria and Albert, 1924; Destroyers, Mediterranean and China Station between 1927 and 1936; Naval Staff Coll., 1939; War of 1939–45: in comd HMS Wren, Mashona (despatches), Onslaught (despatches); Capt. 1943; Chief of Staff, Londonderry, 1944–45; Capt. 'D' Third Flotilla in comd HMS Saumarez, 1946–47; Dep. Dir Ops Div., Admty, 1948–50; Capt.-in-Charge, Simonstown, 1950–52; Rear-Adm. 1953; Head of British Naval Mission to Greece, 1953–55; retired, 1956. *Address:* The Old Cottage, Chittoe, Chippenham, Wilts SN15 2EN. *Died 3 July 1994.*

SELBY WRIGHT, Very Rev. Ronald (William Vernon); *see* Wright.

SELIGMAN, Henry, OBE 1958; PhD; President, EXEC AG, Basle, 1975–85; Scientific Consultant (part-time) to International Atomic Energy Agency, Vienna, since 1969; scientific adviser to various industries, since 1970; *b* Frankfurt am Main, 25 Feb. 1909; *s* of Milton Seligman and Marie (*née* Gans); *m* 1st, 1941, Lesley Bradley (marr. diss. 1992); two *s*; 2nd, 1992, Margaret de Takacsy. *Educ:* Liebigschule, Frankfurt; Sorbonne; Universities of Lausanne and Zürich. Staff, DSIR, Cavendish Lab., Cambridge, 1942–43; joined British-Canadian Research Project at Montreal, 1943, Chalk River, Ontario, 1944–46; Staff, Brit. Atomic Energy Project, 1946; Head of Isotope Div., Atomic Energy Research Establishment, Harwell, UK, 1947–58; Dep. Dir Gen., Dept of Research and Isotopes, Internat. Atomic Energy Agency, Vienna, 1958–69. Austrian Decoration for Science and Art, 1977; Austrian Commander's Cross, 2nd class, 1986. Editor-in-Chief: Scientific Jl; Internat. Jl of Applied Radiation and Isotopes, 1973–. *Publications:* papers on: physical constants necessary for reactor development; waste disposal; production and uses of radioisotopes; contrib. scientific journals. *Address:* Scherpegasse 8/6/3, A–1190 Vienna, Austria. *T:* Vienna 323225.
Died 3 March 1993.

SELKIRK, 10th Earl of, *cr* 1646; **George Nigel Douglas-Hamilton,** KT 1976; GCMG 1959; GBE 1963 (OBE 1941); AFC 1938; AE; PC 1955; QC (Scot.) 1959; late Group Captain, Auxiliary Air Force; Scottish Representative Peer, 1945–63; *b* Merly, Wimborne, Dorset, 4 Jan. 1906; 2nd *s* of 13th Duke of Hamilton and Brandon and Nina Mary Benita, *y d* of Major R. Poore, Salisbury; *S* to Earldom of father under terms of special remainder, 1940; *m* 1949, Audrey Durell, *o d* of late Maurice Drummond-Sale-Barker and Mrs H. S. Brooks. *Educ:* Eton; Balliol College, Oxford (MA); Edinburgh University (LLB); Univs of Bonn, Vienna and Paris (Sorbonne). Admitted to Faculty of Advocates, 1935. Captain, 44th Co., Boys' Brigade, 1932–38; commanded 603 Squadron AAF, 1934–38; served War of 1939–45 (OBE, despatches twice). Member of Edinburgh Town Council, 1935–40; Commisssioner of General Board of Control (Scotland), 1936–39; Commissioner for Special Areas in Scotland, 1937–39. A Lord-in-Waiting to the Queen, 1952–53 (to King George VI, 1951–52); Paymaster-General, Nov. 1953–Dec. 1955; Chancellor of the Duchy of Lancaster, Dec. 1955–Jan. 1957; First Lord of the Admiralty, 1957–Oct. 1959; UK Commissioner for Singapore and Comr Gen. for SE Asia, 1959–63; also UK Council Representative to SEATO, 1960–63; Chm., Cons. Commonwealth Council, 1965–72. Freeman of Hamilton, 1938. President: National Ski Fedn of Great Britain, 1964–68; Anglo-Swiss Society, 1965–74; Building Societies Assoc., 1965–82; Royal Soc. for Asian Affairs, 1966–76; Assoc. of Independent Unionist Peers, 1967–79. Chm., Victoria League, 1971–77. Hon. Chief, Saulteaux Indians, 1967. Hon. Citizen of the City of Winnipeg and of the Town of Selkirk in Manitoba. *Address:* Rose Lawn Coppice, Wimborne, Dorset BH21 3DB. *T:* Wimborne (01202) 883160; 60 Eaton Place, SW1X 8AT. *T:* 0171–235 6926. *Clubs:* Athenæum, Caledonian; New (Edinburgh).
Died 24 Nov. 1994.

SELLERS, His Honour Norman William Malin, VRD; DL; a Circuit Judge, 1974–90; *b* 29 Aug. 1919; *e s* of late Rt Hon. Sir Frederic Sellers, MC, and Grace (*née* Malin); *m* 1946, Angela Laurie, *er d* of Sidney Jukes, Barnet; four *d. Educ:* Merchant Taylors' Sch., Crosby; Silcoates Sch., Wakefield; Hertford Coll., Oxford (MA). Officer, RNVR, 1940–65 (despatches, HMS Nelson, 1942); Lt Comdr 1953, comd HMS Mersey. Called to Bar, Gray's Inn,

1947; Northern Circuit; Asst Recorder of Blackpool, 1962–71; Recorder of Crown Court, 1972–74. Contested (L) Crosby Div. of Lancs, 1964. DL Lancs, 1986. *Recreation:* sailing. *Address:* Hillside, Lower Road, Longridge, Preston PR3 2YN. *T:* Longridge (0772) 783222. *Clubs:* Bar Yacht, Ribble Cruising.
Died 28 Dec. 1993.

SELLS, Sir David (Perronet), Kt 1980; *b* 23 June 1918; *s* of late Edward Perronet Sells; *m* 1948, Beryl Cecilia, *er d* of late C. E. W. Charrington, MC; three *s. Educ:* Sandroyd Sch.; Repton Sch.; Christ Church, Oxford. Commissioned, Coldstream Guards, 1941; active service, N Africa and Italy. Called to Bar, Inner Temple, 1947. Chairman: Cambridgeshire Conservative and Unionist Assoc., 1962–67; Conservative Council for Europ. Constit. of Cambs, 1978–85; Mem. Executive Cttee, Nat. Union of Conservative and Unionist Assocs, 1965–81; Chairman, Conservative Central Council and Conservative Party Conf., 1977–78. *Recreations:* fishing, painting, shooting. *Address:* Garden House, Church Street, Guilden Morden, Royston, Herts SG8 0JD. *T:* Steeple Morden (0763) 853237. *Club:* Savile. *Died 29 Sept. 1993.*

SELVON, Samuel Dickson; author since 1954; *b* Trinidad, West Indies, 20 May 1923; *m* 1st, 1947, Draupadi Persaud; one *d*; 2nd, 1963, Althea Nesta Daroux; two *s* one *d. Educ:* Naparima College, Trinidad. Wireless Operator, 1940–45; Journalist, 1946–50; Civil Servant, 1950–53. Fellow, John Simon Guggenheim Memorial Foundn (USA), 1954 and 1968; Travelling Schol., Soc. of Authors (London), 1958; Trinidad Govt Schol., 1962. Hon. DLitt: Univ. of West Indies, 1985; Warwick, 1989. Humming Bird Medal (Trinidad), 1969. *Publications:* A Brighter Sun, 1952; An Island is a World, 1954; The Lonely Londoners, 1956; Ways of Sunlight, 1957; Turn Again Tiger, 1959; I Hear Thunder, 1963; The Housing Lark, 1965; The Plains of Caroni, 1970; Those Who Eat the Cascadura, 1972; Moses Ascending, 1975; Moses Migrating, 1983; Foreday Morning, 1989; Eldorado West One, 1989; contribs to London Magazine, New Statesman, Nation, Sunday Times, also Evergreen Review (USA). *Recreations:* tennis, swimming, gardening, cooking.
Died 16 April 1994.

SEMPILL, Lady (20th in line, of the Lordship *cr* 1489); **Ann Moira Sempill** (*née* Forbes-Sempill); *b* 19 March 1920; *d* of 19th Lord Sempill, AFC and 1st wife, Eileen Marion (*d* 1935), *e d* of Sir John Lavery, RA; *S* father, 1965; *m* 1st, 1941, Captain Eric Holt (marr. diss., 1945); one *d*; 2nd, 1948, Lt-Col Stuart Whitemore Chant (*d* 1991), OBE, MC (who assumed by decree of Lyon Court, 1966, the additional surname of Sempill); two *s. Educ:* Austrian, German and English Convents. Served War, 1939–42 (Petty Officer, WRNS). Mem. Cttee, Anglo Austrian Soc., 1966–. *Heir: s* Master of Sempill [*b* 25 Feb. 1949; *m* 1977, Josephine Ann Edith, *e d* of J. Norman Rees, Johannesburg; one *s* one *d*]. *Address:* East Lodge, Druminnor, Rhynie, Aberdeenshire AB5 4LT; 15 Onslow Court, Drayton Gardens, SW10 9RL.
Died 6 July 1995.

SEMPLE, (William) David (Crowe), CBE 1991; Director of Education, Lothian Region, 1974–93; *b* 11 June 1933; *s* of late George Crowe and Helen Davidson Semple (*née* Paterson); *m* 1958, Margaret Bain Donald; one *s* one *d. Educ:* Glasgow Univ.; Jordanhill Coll. of Educn; London Univ. BSc Hons, DipEd. FBIM. Educn Officer, Northern Rhodesia, 1958–64; Zambia: Dep. Chief Educn Officer, 1964–66; Chief Educn Officer, 1966–67; Actg Dir of Techn. Educn, 1967–68; Edinburgh: Asst Dir of Educn, 1968–72; Depute Dir of Educn, 1972–74. Gen. Sec., Assoc. of Dirs of Educn, Scotland, 1985–93; Member: Sec. of State (Scot.) Wkg Party on Educnl Catering, 1971–73; Council for Tertiary Educn in Scotland,

1979–83; STV Educn Adv. Cttee, 1979–85; UK Nat. Cttee for UNESCO, 1981–85; UGC, 1983–89; Sec. of State (Scot.) Cttee reviewing examinations in 5th and 6th years, 1990–92. *Publications:* contrib. various journals. *Recreations:* gardening, reading, gastronomy. *Address:* 15 Essex Park, Edinburgh EH4 6LH. *T:* 031–339 6157.
Died 31 March 1994.

SEN, Shri Binay Ranjan, Padmavibhusan 1970; CIE 1944; Director-General of the United Nations Food and Agriculture Organisation, Rome, 1956–67; *b* 1 Jan. 1898; *s* of Dr K. M. Sen; *m* 1931, Chiroprova Chatterjee; four *d. Educ:* Calcutta and Oxford Universities. Secretary to Govt of Bengal, Political and Appointment Departments, and Press Officer, 1931–34; District Magistrate, Midnapore, 1937–40; Revenue Secretary to Government of Bengal, 1940–43; Director of Civil Evacuation, Bengal, 1942–43; Relief Commissioner, 1942–43; Director-General of Food, Government of India, 1943–46; Sec. to Food Dept, Govt of India, 1946; Minister of the Embassy of India, at Washington, 1947–50; Indian Ambassador to: Italy and Yugoslavia, 1950–51; US and Mexico, 1951–52; Italy and Yugoslavia, 1952–55; Japan, 1955–56. Member Indian Delegation to General Assembly of United Nations, 1947; India's Rep. to United Nations Security Council, 1947; Agriculture Sec. to Govt of India, 1948; Head of Jt Mission of FAO and ECAFE (Economic Commn for Asia and the Far East) to study agricultural rehabilitation in China and SE Asian countries; Head of Ind. Delegn to: ECOSOC (Economic and Social Council of the UN), 1949 and 1953; Annual Conf. of FAO, 1949, and FAO Coun., 1950, 1951, 1953. Hon. Mem., Internat. Mark Twain Soc., 1976. Hon. Fellow, St Catherine's Coll., Oxford. Award, NFU of US, 1960. Several hon. degrees and decorations, incl. Kt Comdr Piani Ordinis, and Kt Grand Cross Ordinis Sancti Silvetri Papae. *Address:* 14/2 Palm Avenue, Calcutta 19, India. *Died 12 June 1993.*

SENIOR, Sir Edward (Walters), Kt 1970; CMG 1955; Chairman, Ransome Hoffman Pollard Ltd, 1953–72; Chairman, George Senior & Sons Ltd, since 1930 (Managing Director, 1929); *b* 29 March 1902; *s* of Albert Senior; *m* 1928, Stephanie Vera Heald (*d* 1990); one *s* one *d. Educ:* Repton School; Sheffield University. RA, TA, Major, 1938. General Director of Alloy and Special Steels, Iron and Steel Control, 1941; Director, Steel Division of Raw Materials Mission, Washington, DC, 1942; Controller of Ball and Roller Bearings, 1944; British Iron and Steel Federation: Commercial Dir, 1949–61; Dir, 1961–62; Dir-Gen., 1962–66; retd, Dec. 1966; Exec. Chm., Derbyshire Stone Ltd, 1967–68; Dep. Chm., Tarmac Derby Ltd, 1968–71. Master of Cutlers' Company of Hallamshire in County of York, 1947; Vice-President of the Sheffield Chamber of Commerce, 1948; Chairman of Steel Re-Armament Panel, 1951. Vice-Consul for Sweden, in Sheffield, 1930. FIMgt 1971. JP Sheffield, 1937–50. *Recreations:* normal country activities. *Address:* Hollies, Church Close, Brenchley, Tonbridge, Kent TN12 7AA. *T:* Brenchley (0189272) 2359. *Club:* Sheffield (Sheffield). *Died 18 June 1995.*

SENNA, Ayrton; racing driver; *b* São Paulo, 21 March 1960; *m* (marr. diss.). Started driving karts; first raced as Ayrton Senna da Silva; Formula Ford, 1982; first Formula Three win, Thruxton, 1983; Toleman Team, 1984; Lotus, 1985–87; McLaren, 1988–93; Renault-Williams, 1994–; first Grand Prix race, Brazil, 1984; first win, Portugal, 1985; World Champion, 1988, 1990, 1991; won 41 Grand Prix, to Nov. 1993. *Address:* c/o F J Associates, 3 Manchester Square, W1M 5RF. *T:* 071–935 5373.
Died 1 May 1994.

SERIES, Prof. George William, FRS 1971; Hon. Research Fellow, Clarendon Laboratory, Oxford, since 1983; Professor of Physics, University of Reading, 1968,

Emeritus 1982; *b* 22 Feb. 1920; *s* of William Series and Alice (*née* Crosthwaite); *m* 1948, Annette (*née* Pepper); three *s* one *d. Educ:* Reading Sch.; St John's Coll., Oxford (Open Schol., Oxford, 1938; MA 1946; 1st cl. hons Physics, 1947; DPhil 1950; DSc 1969). Served with Friends' Ambulance Unit, 1942–46. Nuffield Research Fellow, 1950; University Demonstrator, Oxford, 1951; St Edmund Hall, Oxford: Lectr, 1953; Fellow, 1954; Emeritus Fellow, 1969. William Evans Vis. Prof., Univ. of Otago, 1972; Raman Vis. Prof., Indian Acad. of Sci., 1982–83. Hon. Fellow, Indian Acad. of Science, 1984. Hon. Editor, Jl of Physics B (Atomic and Molecular Physics), 1975–79; Editor, Europ. Jl Physics, 1980–85. William F. Meggers Award, Optical Soc. Amer., 1982. *Publications:* Spectrum of Atomic Hydrogen, 1957; Laser Spectroscopy and other topics, 1985; Spectrum of Atomic Hydrogen: advances, 1988. *Recreation:* family. *Address:* Clarendon Laboratory, Oxford OX1 3PU. *T:* Oxford (0865) 272200.
Died 2 Jan. 1995.

SERJEANT, Robert Bertram, FBA 1986; Sir Thomas Adams's Professor of Arabic, 1970–82, and Director, Middle East Centre, 1965–82, University of Cambridge; *b* 23 March 1915; *er s* of R. T. R. and A. B. Serjeant; *m* Marion Keith (*née* Robertson), MB, ChB; one *s* one *d. Educ:* Edinburgh; Trinity Coll., Cambridge. Vans Dunlop Schol. 1935; visit to Syria, 1935; MA 1st Cl. Hons Semitic Langs, Edinburgh Univ., 1936; PhD Cambridge 1939. Tweedie Fellow Edinburgh, 1939; Studentship, SOAS, for research in S Arabia, 1940; Governor's Commn in Aden Protectorate Govt Guards, 1940–41 (attached Mission 106); Lectr, SOAS, 1941; seconded to BBC Eastern Service, 1942; Editor, Arabic Listener, 1943–45; Min. of Inf., Editor Arabic pubns, 1944; Colonial Research Fellow, in Hadramawt, 1947–48; Reader in Arabic, SOAS, 1948; Professor of Arabic, Middle East Department, SOAS, University of London, 1955–64; Lectr in Islamic History, ME Centre, Univ. of Cambridge, 1964–66, Reader in Arabic Studies, 1966–70. Research in S Arabia and Persian Gulf, 1953–54; in N Nigeria, Minister of Education's mission to examine instruction in Arabic, 1956; Sec. of State for Colonies' mission to examine Muslim Education in E Africa, 1957; Inter-University Council's Advisory Delegation on University of N Nigeria, 1961; Research in Trucial States, Yemen, Aden, 1963–64 and 1966; Member: ME Comd Expedition to Socotra, 1967; Cambridge expedn to San'ā' and N Yemen, 1972. Member: Royal Soc. for Asian Affairs; Royal Asiatic Soc.; Arab Acad., Cairo, 1976. Hon. DLitt Edinburgh, 1985. Lawrence of Arabia Meml Medal, RCAS, 1974; Sir Richard Burton Meml Medal, RAS, 1981. Co-editor, Arabian Studies, 1973–; Mem. Editl Bd, Cambridge History of Arabic Literature, 1983–. *Publications:* Catalogue of Arabic, Persian & Hindustani MSS in New College, Edinburgh, 1942; Materials for a History of Islamic Textiles, 1942–51; Prose and Poetry from Hadramawt, I, 1950; Saiyids of Hadramawt, 1957; Portuguese off the South Arabian Coast, 1961; The South Arabian Hunt, 1976; (ed) The Islamic City, 1980; Studies in Arabic History and Civilisation, 1981; (ed with R. Lewcock) San'ā': an Arabian Islamic city, 1983; Customary and Sharī'ah Law in Arabian Society, 1991; articles in Bull. SOAS, RAS, Le Muséon, Rivista d. Studi Orientali, Islamic Culture, etc. *Address:* Summerhill Cottage, Denhead, near St Andrews, Fife KY16 18PA. *Died 29 April 1993.*

SERKIN, Rudolf, Presidential Medal of Freedom, 1963; pianist; Director, Curtis Institute of Music, Philadelphia, Pa, 1968–76, Head of Piano Department, 1939–76; *b* 28 March 1903; *s* of Mordko Serkin and Augusta Schargl; *m* 1935, Irene Busch; two *s* four *d. Educ:* Vienna, Austria. Concert pianist: début, Vienna, 1915; USA, 1933–; New York Philharmonic with Arturo Toscanini, 1936. President and Artistic Director of Marlboro School of Music,

Marlboro, Vermont. Former Mem., Nat. Council on the Arts, Carnegie Commn Report. Fellow, Amer. Acad. of Arts and Scis; Hon. Member: Accademia Nationale di Santa Cecilia; Verein Beethoven Haus, Bonn; Philharmonic-Symphony Soc. of NY; Amer. Philosophical Soc.; Riemenschneider Bach Inst.; Konzertverein, Vienna; Neue Bachgesellschaft, Bonn. Dr *hc*: Curtis Inst., Philadelphia; Temple Univ., Philadelphia; Univ. of Vermont; Williams Coll., Williamstown, Mass; Oberlin Coll.; Rochester Univ.; Harvard; Marlboro Coll. Kennedy Center Honors, 1981; Ernst von Siemens Musikpreis; Nat. Medal of Arts, Washington, 1988. Grand Officiale del Ordina, Italy; Cross of Honor for Scis and Art, Austria; Commander's Cross, Icelandic Order of Falcon; Chevalier de l'Ordre National de la Legion d'Honneur; Orden pour le Mérite für Wissenschaften und Künste, W Germany, 1981. *Address:* RFD 3, Box 297, Brattleboro, Vermont 05301, USA. *Died 8 May 1991.*

SETON, Alice Ida, (Lady Seton), CBE 1949; Group Officer, Women's Royal Air Force, retired; *d* of late P. C. Hodge, Port Elizabeth, South Africa; *m* 1923, Capt. Sir John Hastings Seton, 10th Bt (marr. diss. 1950); (one *s* one *d* decd). Joined WAAF as Assistant Section Officer, 1939. *Address:* Collin House, 108 Ridgway, Wimbledon, SW19 4RD. *Died 28 July 1995.*

SETON, Sir Robert (James), 11th Bt, *cr* 1683 (NS), of Pitmedden, Aberdeenshire; *b* 20 April 1926; *s* of Captain Sir John Hastings Seton, 10th Bt and of Alice Ida Seton, CBE, *d* of Percy Hodge, Cape Civil Service; *S* father, 1956; unmarried. *Educ:* HMS Worcester (Thames Nautical Training College). Midshipman RNVR (invalided), 1943–44. Banker, with Hong Kong and Shanghai Banking Corpn, 1946–61 (retd). *Heir: kinsman* James Christall Seton [*b* 21 Jan. 1913; *m* 1939, Evelyn, *d* of Ray Hafer]. *Address:* 4B Morella Road, Balham, SW12 8UH.
Died 29 Oct. 1993.

SEXTON, Maj.-Gen. (Francis) Michael, CB 1980; OBE 1966; retired; Director of Military Survey and Chief of Geographic Section of General Staff, Ministry of Defence, 1977–80; *b* 15 July 1923; *s* of Timothy and Catherine Sexton; *m* 1947, Naomi, *d* of Bertram Alonzo and Dorothy May Middleton; one *s* one *d. Educ:* Wanstead County High Sch.; Birmingham Univ. Commnd into RE, Kirkee, India, 1943; Royal Bombay Sappers and Miners and 5th/16th Punjab Regt, India, Assam and Burma, 1943–46; RE units, UK, Egypt and Cyprus, 1946–53; Dept of Mines and Surveys, Canada, 1953–56; Asst Dir, MoD, 1964–65; Dep. Dir, Ordnance Survey, 1966–70; Chief Geographic Officer, SHAPE, Belgium, 1970–73; Brig. (Survey), 1973–77. Bursar and Fellow, St Peter's Coll., Oxford, 1980–85. Mem., Panel of Indep. Inspectors, 1980–93. MA Oxon, 1980. *Club:* MCC. *Died 19 June 1995.*

SHACKLE, Prof. George Lennox Sharman, FBA 1967; Brunner Professor of Economic Science in the University of Liverpool, 1951–69, then Professor Emeritus; *b* 14 July 1903; *s* of Robert Walker Shackle, MA (Cambridge) and Fanny Shackle (*née* Sharman); *m* 1st, 1939, Gertrude Courtney Susan Rowe (*d* 1978); two *s* one *d* (and one *d* decd); 2nd, 1979, Catherine Squarey Gibb (*née* Weldsmith). *Educ:* The Perse School, Cambridge; The London School of Economics; New College, Oxford. BA (London) 1931; Leverhulme Research Schol., 1934; PhD (Econ) (London), 1937; DPhil (Oxford), 1940. Oxford University Institute of Statistics, 1937; University of St Andrews, 1939; Admiralty and Cabinet Office; Sir Winston Churchill's Statistical Branch, 1939; Economic Section of Cabinet Secretariat, 1945; Reader in Economic Theory, Univ. of Leeds, 1950. F. de Vries Lecturer, Amsterdam, 1957; Visiting Professor: Columbia University, 1957–58; of Economics and Philosophy, Univ. of Pittsburgh, 1967; Keynes Lectr, British Acad., 1976.

Mem. Council, Royal Economic Society, 1955–69; Pres., Section F, BAAS, 1966. Fellow of Econometric Society, 1960; Distinguished Fellow, Amer. Hist. of Econs Soc., 1985. Hon. DSc NUU, 1974; Hon. DSocSc Birmingham, 1978; Hon. DLitt Strathclyde, 1988. *Publications:* Expectations, Investment, and Income, 1938, 2nd edn 1968; Expectation in Economics, 1949, 2nd edn 1952; Mathematics at the Fireside, 1952 (French edn 1967); Uncertainty in Economics and Other Reflections, 1955; Time in Economics, 1957; Economics for Pleasure, 1959, 2nd edn 1968 (also foreign editions); Decision, Order and Time in Human Affairs, 1961, 2nd edn 1969 (also foreign editions); A Scheme of Economic Theory, 1965 (also Portuguese edn); The Nature of Economic Thought, 1966 (also Spanish edn); The Years of High Theory, 1967 (Italian edn 1985); Expectation, Enterprise and Profit, 1970 (Spanish edn 1976); Epistemics and Economics, 1973 (Spanish edn 1976); An Economic Querist, 1973 (Spanish edn 1976); Keynesian Kaleidics, 1974; Imagination and the Nature of Choice, 1979; (ed and contrib.) Uncertainty and Business Decisions, 1954, 2nd edn, 1957; The Theory of General Static Equilibrium, 1957; A New Prospect of Economics, 1958; On the Nature of Business Success, 1968; Business, Time and Thought (essays), 1988; articles in Chambers's Encyclopædia, 1950, 1967, Internat. Encyclopedia of the Social Sciences, 1968, and in other books; seventy or more main articles in learned jls. *Address:* Rudloe, Alde House Drive, Aldeburgh, Suffolk IP15 5EE. *T:* Aldeburgh (072885) 2227 and 2003. *Died 3 March 1992.*

SHACKLETON, Baron *cr* 1958 (Life Peer), of Burley, Co. of Southampton; **Edward Arthur Alexander Shackleton,** KG 1974; OBE 1945; PC 1966; FRS 1989; *b* 15 July 1911; *s* of late Sir Ernest Shackleton, CVO, OBE and Emily Mary, 2nd *d* of Charles Dorman; *m* 1938, Betty Homan; one *d* (one *s* decd). *Educ:* Radley College; Magdalen College, Oxford (MA; Hon. Fellow, 1986). Surveyor, Oxford University Expedition to Sarawak, 1932; first ascent of Mt Mulu; Organiser and Surveyor, Oxford University Expedition to Ellesmereland, 1934–35; Lecture tours in Europe and America; BBC talks producer, MOI. Served War of 1939–45, 1940–45; RAF Station Intelligence Officer, St Eval; Anti-U-Boat Planner and Intelligence Officer, Coastal Command; Naval and Military Intelligence, Air Ministry; Wing Comdr (despatches twice, OBE). Contested (Lab) Epsom, General Election, and Bournemouth by-election, 1945; MP (Lab), Preston (by-election), 1946–50, Preston South, 1950–55. Parliamentary Private Secretary to Minister of Supply, 1949–50; Parliamentary Private Sec. to Foreign Sec., March-Oct. 1951 (to Lord President of the Council, 1950–51); Minister of Defence for the RAF, 1964–67; Mission to S Arabia, 1967; Minister Without Portfolio and Deputy Leader, House of Lords, 1967–68; Lord Privy Seal, Jan.-April, 1968; Paymaster-General, April-Oct. 1968; Leader of the House of Lords, April 1968–70; Lord Privy Seal, Oct. 1968–1970; Minister in charge, Civil Service Dept, Nov. 1968–1970; Opposition Leader, House of Lords, 1970–74. Chm., H of L Select Cttee on Sci. and Technol., 1988–89. Sen. Executive and Director, J. Lewis Partnership, 1955–64; Dir, Personnel and Admin, 1973–82, Dep. Chm., 1975–82, RTZ Corp. Ltd; Chairman: RTZ Develt Enterprises, 1973–83; Anglesey Aluminium Ltd, 1981–86. Chairman: Adv. Council on Oil Pollution, 1962–64; Political Honours Scrutiny Committee, 1976–92; East European Trade Council, 1977–86 (Hon. Pres., 1986–); Mem., BOTB, 1975–78. Member, Council: Industrial Soc., 1963–83; RIIA, 1980–86; President: British Assoc. of Industrial Editors, 1960–64; ASLIB, 1963–65; Royal Geographical Society, 1971–74 (formerly Vice-Pres.); Parly and Scientific Cttee, 1976–80 (formerly Vice-Pres.); British Standards Inst., 1977–80. Chm., Arctic

Club, 1960, 1979. Pro-Chancellor, Southampton Univ. Vice-Pres., YHA. Governor: London Chest Hosps, 1947–51; Imperial Coll. of Science, 1950–53. Mem. Council, SSAFA, 1951–55. Freedom of Stanley, Falkland Is, 1988. Hon. Elder Brother, Trinity Hse, 1980; Hon. Fellow, St Hugh's Coll., Oxford; Hon. Mem., RICS. CBIM. Hon. LLD Univ. of Newfoundland, 1970; Hon. DSc: Warwick, 1978; Southampton, 1986. Cuthbert Peek Award, 1933, Special Gold Medal, 1990, RGS; Ludwig Medallist, Munich Geog. Soc., 1938. Hon. AC 1990. *Publications:* Arctic Journeys; Nansen, the Explorer; (part-author) Borneo Jungle; Economic Survey of Falkland Islands, 1976, updated 1982; Review of UK Anti-Terrorist Legislation, 1978; articles, broadcasts, etc on geographical and political subjects and personnel and general administration. *Address:* Hurstly, Sandy Down, Boldre, Lymington, Hants SO41 8PN.

Died 22 Sept. 1994.

SHANKS, Ernest Pattison, CBE 1975; QC (Singapore) 1958; Deputy Bailiff of Guernsey, 1973–76; *b* 11 Jan. 1911; *e s* of late Hugh P. Shanks and Mary E. Shanks; *m* 1st, 1937, Audrey E. Moore; one *s*; 2nd, 1947, Betty Katherine Battersby (*d* 1991); two *s* one *d*. *Educ:* Mill Hill Sch.; Downing Coll., Cambridge (MA); Inner Temple; Staff Coll., Camberley. Called to the Bar, Inner Temple, 1936; N Eastern Circuit. SRO, Mddx Regt, 1939–44: Princess Louise's Kensington Regt, France (despatches); Sicily, Italy, 1944; Staff Coll., Camberley, 1944–46; Sen. Legal Officer, Schleswig-Holstein, Mil. Govt, Germany, 1946; Lt-Col RARO, 1946. Colonial Legal Service: Dist Judge, Trengganu, Malaya, 1946; Singapore: Dist Judge and First Magistrate, 1947; Crown Counsel and Solicitor-Gen.; Attorney-Gen. and Minister of Legal Affairs, 1957–59; HM Comptroller, Guernsey, 1960, HM Procureur, 1969. *Address:* Le Petit Mas, Clos des Fosses, St Martin's, Guernsey. *T:* Guernsey (0481) 38300. *Clubs:* Old Millhillians (Pres., 1979–80), Commonwealth Trust, Royal Over-Seas League; Royal Channel Islands Yacht, Royal Guernsey Golf. *Died 18 Jan. 1994.*

SHARMA, Vishnu Datt; President, Ealing Community Relations Council, since 1987 (Senior Supervisor, 1981–87); Member, Executive Committee, National Council for Civil Liberties, since 1982 (Race Relations Officer, 1979–80); *b* 19 Oct. 1921; *s* of late Pandit Girdhari Lal Kaushik and Shrimati Ganga Devi; *m* 1960, Krishna Sharma; one *d*. *Educ:* High Sch. in India. Came to UK from India, 1957; worked in factories until 1967; apptd Mem. Nat. Cttee for Commonwealth Immigrants (by the Prime Minister, Rt Hon. Harold Wilson); twice elected Gen. Sec. of Indian Workers' Assoc., Southall, 1961–63 and 1965–67, and once Pres., 1977–79; Nat. Organiser, Campaign Against Racial Discrimination (later Vice-Chm.); Chm., Jt Council for the Welfare of Immigrants (Gen. Sec., Exec. Sec. and again Gen. Sec., 1967–77); Vice-Chm., Steering Cttee, Anti-Nazi League. Member: Adv. Cttee BBC, Asian Magazine; Editl Bd, Sher-e-Punjab, 1987–; Chief Editor, Charcha (Punjabi journal). Attended five internat. confs on migrant workers and race relns. *Recreations:* cinema, watching television, sight-seeing, etc. *Address:* 43 Lady Margaret Road, Southall, Mddx UB1 2PJ. *T:* 081–843 0518.

Died 22 April 1992.

SHARP OF GRIMSDYKE, Baron *cr* 1989 (Life Peer), of Stanmore in the London Borough of Harrow; **Eric Sharp,** Kt 1984; CBE 1980; Chairman, 1980–90, and Chief Executive, 1981–90, Cable and Wireless PLC; *b* 17 Aug. 1916; *s* of Isaac and Martha Sharp; *m* 1950, Marion (*née* Freeman); one *s* one *d* (and one *d* decd). *Educ:* London School of Economics (BScEcon Hons; Hon. Fellow, 1986). CBIM. Served Army, 1940–46, Staff Captain SOIII Southern Comd, 1944. Principal, Min. of Power, 1948;

UK Delegate, Coal and Petroleum Cttees of OEEC, 1948–50; Vice-Chm., Electricity Cttee, OEEC, 1951–54; Sec. to Herbert Cttee of Inquiry into Electricity Supply Industry, 1955–56; British Nylon Spinners Ltd, 1957–64; Director, ICI Fibres Ltd, 1964–68; Mem. Board, Monsanto Europe, 1969; Resident USA, Mem. Management Bd, 1970–72; Dep. Chm., 1973–74, Chm., 1975–81, Monsanto Ltd; Chairman: Polyamide Intermediates Ltd, 1975–81; (non-exec.) Stanhope Properties, 1987–; non exec. Director: Morgan Grenfell Group, 1987–90; Carlton Communications, 1990–; Unifi Inc., 1991–. Chm., Chemical Industry Safety and Health Council, 1977–79; President: Chemical Industries Assoc., 1979–80; Sino-British Trade Council, 1985–90; part-time Mem., London Electricity Bd, 1969–78; Member: EDC for Chemical Industry, 1980–82; Central Electricity Generating Board, 1980–86. Freeman, City of London, 1982. Officer, Order of Merit (Cameroon). *Recreations:* family, food, music, conversation. *Address:* c/o House of Lords, SW1A 0PW. *Club:* Athenæum.   *Died 2 May 1994.*

SHARP, Sir Angus; *see* Sharp, Sir W. H. A.

SHARP, Margery; novelist and playwright; *b* 25 Jan. 1905; *m* 1938, Major Geoffrey L. Castle, RA (*d* 1990). *Educ:* Streatham Hill High School; London University. French Honours BA. *Publications:* Rhododendron Pie; Fanfare for Tin Trumpets; The Flowering Thorn; Four Gardens, 1935; The Nymph and the Nobleman; Sophy Cassmajor; Meeting at Night (play); The Nutmeg Tree, 1937 (play: USA 1940, England 1941, filmed as Julia Misbehaves, 1948); The Stone of Chastity, 1940; Cluny Brown, 1944 (filmed 1946); Britannia Mews, 1946 (filmed 1949); The Foolish Gentlewoman, 1948 (play, London, 1949); Lise Lillywhite, 1951; The Gipsy in the Parlour, 1953; The Tigress on the Hearth, 1955; The Eye of Love, 1957; Something Light, 1960; Martha in Paris, 1962; Martha, Eric and George, 1964; The Sun in Scorpio, 1965; In Pious Memory, 1968; Rosa, 1969; The Innocents, 1971; The Faithful Servants, 1975; *books for children:* The Rescuers, 1959; Miss Bianca, 1962; The Turret, 1964 (USA 1963); Miss Bianca in the Salt Mines, 1966; Lost at the Fair, 1967; Miss Bianca in the Orient, 1970; Miss Bianca in the Antarctic, 1971; Miss Bianca and the Bridesmaid, 1972; The Magical Cockatoo, 1974; The Children Next Door, 1974; Bernard the Brave, 1976; Summer Visits, 1977; *short stories:* The Lost Chapel Picnic, 1973. *Address:* c/o William Heinemann Ltd, Michelin House, 81 Fulham Road, SW3 6RB.

Died 14 March 1991.

SHARP, Sir (William Harold) Angus, KBE 1974; QPM 1969; *b* Auckland, 1915. *Educ:* Cathedral Grammar School, Christchurch. Graduated Imperial Defence College, 1966. Joined New Zealand Police Force, 1937; Commissioner of Police, 1970; retd NZ Police, 1975; Commissioner, Police and Prisons Dept, Western Samoa, 1977–78. *Address:* 23A Sumner Street, Rotorua, New Zealand.   *Died 21 April 1993.*

SHARPE, Sir Reginald (Taaffe), Kt 1947; QC; *b* 20 Nov. 1898; *o s* of late Herbert Sharpe, Lindfield, Sussex; *m* 1st, 1922, Phyllis Maude (marr. diss. 1929), *d* of late Major Edward Whinney, Haywards Heath, Sussex; one *d* (and one *d* decd); 2nd, 1930, Eileen Kate (*d* 1946), *d* of Thomas Howarth Usherwood, Christ's Hospital, Sussex; 3rd, 1947, Vivien Travers (*d* 1971), *d* of late Rev. Herbert Seddon Rowley, Wretham, Norfolk; 4th, 1976, Mary Millicent (*d* 1994), *d* of late Maj.-Gen. Patrick Barclay Sangster, CB, CMG, DSO, Roehampton. *Educ:* Westminster School. Served European War: enlisted in Army, 1916; 2nd Lieut Grenadier Guards (SR), Jan. 1917; Lt, 1918; served with 2nd Bn in France (wounded). Called to Bar at Gray's Inn, Easter, 1920. Went South-Eastern Circuit and Sussex Sessions. Judge of High Court, Rangoon, 1937–48;

Director of Supply, Burma (at Calcutta), 1942–44; Trustee of Rangoon University Endowment Fund, 1946–48; KC Feb. 1949; HM Comr of Assize: Western and Northern Circuits, 1949; Midland and Western Circuits, 1950; South-Eastern Circuit, 1952; North-Eastern Circuit, 1954; Birmingham October Assize, 1954; Midland Circuit, 1960. Deputy Chairman QS: E Sussex, 1949–69; W Kent, 1949–62; Kent, 1962–69; Mddx, 1963–65 (Asst Chm. 1951–63); Mddx area of Greater London, 1965–71; Asst Chm., W Sussex QS, 1950–70; Dep. Chm., Hailsham Petty Sessional Div., 1950–57 and 1959–70 (Chm., 1957–58); Mem. Standing Jt Cttee for E Sussex, 1958–65, for W Sussex, 1953–65. Special Comr for Divorce Causes, 1948–67. Chm., Nat. Health Service Tribunal for England and Wales, 1948–71; Mem., Nat. Arbitration Tribunal, 1951, and of Industrial Disputes Tribunal, 1951; Chairman, 1951–54, of Joint Council, and Independent Chairman, 1955–57, of Conciliation Board set up by Assoc. of Health and Pleasure Resorts and the Musicians' Union; Sole Commissioner to hold British Honduras Inquiry at Belize, March 1954; Chm., Departmental Cttee on Summary Trial of Minor Offences in Magistrates' Courts, 1954–55. Mem., Governing Body, Westminster Sch., 1955–83. JP East Sussex. *Address:* The Old Post Office, Rushlake Green, Sussex TN21 9QL. *T:* Rushlake Green (0435) 830253.   *Died 2 Aug. 1994.*

SHARPE, William James, CBE 1967 (OBE 1950); Director of Communications, Foreign and Commonwealth Office (formerly Foreign Office), 1965–69, retired; *b* 3 Jan. 1908; *s* of James Sharpe; *m* 1940, Doreen Winifred Cockell (*d* 1992); three *s*. *Educ:* Aldershot Grammar School. 1927–39: Merchant Navy; Marconi International; Marine Communications Company; commissioned Royal Corps of Signals, 1940; served in France and South East Asia; Lt-Col 1945. Diplomatic Wireless Service, 1947; Deputy Director of Communications, 1959. *Address:* The Mount, Tingewick, Buckingham MK18 4QN. *T:* Finmere (01280) 848291.   *Died 14 Nov. 1994.*

SHATTOCK, John Swithun Harvey, CMG 1952; OBE 1946; HM Diplomatic Service, 1947–67; *b* 21 Nov. 1907; *s* of late Rev. E. A. Shattock, Kingston St Mary, nr Taunton; unmarried. *Educ:* Westminster School; Christ Church, Oxford. Entered ICS, 1931; served in Bengal, 1931–36; Under Sec., Govt of India (Defence Dept), 1936–39; joined Indian Political Service, 1939; served in Kathiawar, Baroda, and Kashmir Residencies, 1939–44; Dep. Sec. to Crown Representative (Political Dept), New Delhi, 1944–46; Chief Minister, Chamba State, 1946–47; apptd HM Diplomatic Service, 1947; served in UK High Commission, New Delhi, 1947–49; Head of Far Eastern Dept, Foreign Office, London, 1950–51; Head of China and Korea Dept, FO 1951; FO Rep. at Imperial Defence Coll., London, 1952; Head of China and Korea Dept, FO, 1953; Counsellor, British Embassy, Belgrade, Dec. 1953–Nov. 1955; Political Representative, Middle East Forces, Cyprus, Jan. 1956–Nov. 1958. Deputy to UK Permanent Representative on North Atlantic Council, Paris, 1959–61; Minister, UK Delegation to Disarmament Conference, Geneva, 1961–63; FO, 1963–67. *Address:* St Mary's Cottage, Kingston St Mary, near Taunton, Somerset TA2 8HN; Grindlay's Bank, 13 St James's Square, SW1. *Club:* Travellers'.

Died 6 June 1993.

SHAW, James B.; *see* Byam Shaw.

SHAW, James John Sutherland, CB 1970; Chairman, Civil Service Appeal Board, 1973–77 (Deputy Chairman, 1972–73); *b* 5 Jan. 1912; *s* of Robert Shaw and Christina Macallum Sutherland; *m* 1947, Rosamond Chisholm Sharman. *Educ:* Ardrossan Academy, Ayrshire; Glasgow and London Universities. Glasgow University: MA 1st Class Hons History, 1932, PhD 1935. Served War with

RAF, 1940–45, Navigator, AC2 to Sqdn Leader (despatches). Lecturer in History, 1936–40, Senior Lecturer in History, 1945–46, Glasgow Univ.; HM Treasury, 1946–68: Principal, Asst Sec., Under-Sec.; Under-Sec., 1968–69, Dep. Sec., 1969–72, CSD. OECD Consultant on Greek CS, 1973; Chm., Internat. Commn on Reform, Sudan CS, 1973–74; consultant to Commn on Structure and Functions, Ghana CS, 1974, to States of Jersey on Jersey CS, 1975. *Recreations:* talking, walking, gardening. *Address:* North Field, Neaves Lane, Stradbroke, Eye, Suffolk IP21 5JP. *T:* Stradbroke (0379) 384535.   *Died 18 June 1994.*

SHAW, Richard John Gildroy; Chairman, since 1992, and Chief Executive, since 1979, Lowndes Lambert Group Holdings; Chairman and Chief Executive, Lowndes Lambert Group, since 1979; *b* 7 June 1936; *s* of Edward Philip Shaw and Mary Elizabeth Shaw (*née* Tanner); *m* 1973, Yvonne Kathleen Maskell; one *s. Educ:* Dragon Sch.; Eton. J. H. Minet & Co., 1957–66; H. J. Symons & Co., 1967–70; Dep. Chm., C. E. Heath & Co. (Insce Broking Ltd), 1970–79; Chm. and Managing Dir, C. E. Heath (Internat.), 1970–79; Chm., C. E. Heath (Latin America), 1970–79; Dep. Chm., Lowndes Lambert Gp Hldgs, 1979–92; Dir, Hill Samuel Gp, 1979–88. *Recreations:* golf, yachting, reading, cricket. *Address:* Lowndes Lambert Group, Lowndes Lambert House, Friary Court, Crutched Friars, EC3N 2NP. *T:* 0171–560 3000; 18 Phillimore Gardens, W8 7QE. *T:* 0171–937 2942. *Clubs:* Carlton, City of London, Portland, Clermont, St James's, Royal Thames Yacht; Lloyd's Golf, Lloyds Yacht, Sunningdale Golf.   *Died 23 Nov. 1995.*

SHAW, Sydney Herbert, CMG 1963; OBE 1958; *b* 6 Nov. 1903; 2nd *s* of John Beaumont and Gertrude Shaw; *m* 1930, Mary Louise, *e d* of Ernest Lewin Chapman; one *s* one *d. Educ:* King's College School; Royal School of Mines, London University. BSc Hons 1st cl. Mining Engineering, 1925 and Mining Geology, 1926; MSc (Birm.) 1937; PhD (Lond.) 1949. Geophysics prospecting, N and S Rhodesia, 1926–28; Imperial Geophys Experimental Survey, Aust., 1928–30; geophys prospecting, Cyprus, 1930; Demonstrator, Geology Dept, Roy. Sch. of Mines, 1931; Lectr in Geology, Birmingham Univ., 1932–37; Govt Geologist, Palestine, 1937–48 (seconded as Dep. Controller Heavy Industries, Palestine, 1942–45); Colonial (later Overseas) Geological Surveys, London, 1949, Deputy Director, 1950, Dir, 1959–65; Head, Overseas Div., Inst. of Geological Sciences, 1965–68. Geological Adviser, Colonial Office (subseq. Dept of Tech. Co-op., then Min. of Overseas Develt), 1959–68; retd, 1968. FIMM (Pres., 1968–69); FGS. *Publications:* scientific papers in various jls. *Recreation:* gardening. *Address:* Bisham Edge, Stoney Ware, Marlow, Bucks SL7 1RN. *T:* Marlow (06284) 484951.
Died 1 Nov. 1991.

SHAWE-TAYLOR, Desmond (Christopher), CBE 1965; music critic and journalist; *b* 29 May 1907; *s* of Frank Shawe-Taylor and Agnes Ussher. *Educ:* Shrewsbury Sch.; Oriel Coll., Oxford. Literary and occasional musical criticism, New Statesman, etc until 1939. Served War of 1939–45 with the Royal Artillery. Music Critic, New Statesman, 1945–58; Guest Music Critic, New Yorker, 1973–74; Chief Music Critic, The Sunday Times, 1958–83, thereafter frequent contributor on music and gramophone records. *Publications:* Covent Garden, 1948; (with Edward Sackville-West, later Lord Sackville) The Record Guide (with supplements and revisions, 1951–56). *Recreations:* travel, croquet, gramophone. *Address:* Long Crichel House, Wimborne, Dorset BH21 5JU. *T:* Tarrant Hinton (01258) 830250. *Clubs:* Brooks's, Groucho.
Died 1 Nov. 1995.

SHEARER, Thomas Hamilton, CB 1974; *b* 7 Nov. 1923; *o s* of late Thomas Appleby Shearer, OBE; *m* 1945, Sybil Mary Robinson, Stratford-on-Avon; one *s* one *d. Educ:* Haberdashers' Aske's, Hatcham; Emmanuel Coll., Cambridge (open exhibition in English). Served RAF, 1942–45 (despatches). Entered Air Ministry, as Asst Principal, 1948; Principal, 1951; Sec. to Grigg Cttee on Recruitment to Armed Forces, 1958; Asst Sec., 1959; transf. Min. of Public Building and Works, 1963; student, IDC, 1965; Under-Sec., 1967; Dir of Establishments, MPBW, 1967–70, DoE, 1970; Dir of Personnel Management, DoE, 1970–72; Dep. Chief Exec. II, PSA, DoE, 1972–73; Deputy Secretary, DoE, 1973–81. Chairman: Maplin Develt Authority, 1974–77; British Channel Tunnel Company, 1975–77; Location of Offices Bureau, 1980. A Controller, Royal Opera House Develt Land Trust, 1981–86. Dir, Sheltered Property Rental Ltd, 1989–94. *Recreations:* opera, claret. *Address:* 9 Denny Crescent, SE11 4UY. *T:* 0171–587 0921.
Died 3 July 1995.

SHELBOURNE, Sir Philip, Kt 1984; Chairman, Henry Ansbacher Holdings, 1988–91; Deputy Chairman, Panel on Take-overs and Mergers, 1987–91; *b* 15 June 1924; *s* of late Leslie John Shelbourne. *Educ:* Radley Coll.; Corpus Christi Coll., Oxford (MA); Harvard Law School. Called to Bar, Inner Temple, Hon. Bencher 1984. Barrister specialising in taxation, 1951–62; Partner, N. M. Rothschild & Sons, 1962–70; Chief Exec., Drayton Corp., 1971–72; Chm., Drayton Gp and Drayton Corp., 1973–74; Chm. and Chief Exec., Samuel Montagu & Co., 1974–80; Chm. and Chief Exec., BNOC, 1980–82; Chm., Britoil, 1982–88. Mem., SIB, 1987–88. *Recreation:* music. *Address:* Myles Place, 68 The Close, Salisbury, Wilts SP1 2EN. *Club:* Brooks's.   *Died 15 April 1993.*

SHELLEY, Charles William Evans; Charity Commissioner, 1968–74; *b* 15 Aug. 1912; *s* of George Shelley and Frances Mary Anne Shelley (*née* Dain); *m* 1939, Patricia May Dolby; three *d* (and one *d* decd). *Educ:* Alleyn's Sch., Dulwich; Fitzwilliam House, Cambridge. Called to Bar, Inner Temple, 1937; practised at the Bar, to 1940. Served in Army: first in RAPC and later in Dept of Judge Advocate-General, rank Major, 1940–47. Joined Charity Commn as Legal Asst, 1947; Sen. Legal Asst, 1958; Dep. Comr, 1964. *Recreations:* English literature, listening to music, mountaineering. *Address:* Pen y Bryn, Llansilin, Oswestry, Shropshire SY10 7QG. *T:* Llansilin (069170) 273.   *Died 3 March 1993.*

SHELLEY, Ursula, MD, FRCP; retired 1971; Physician to Royal Free Hospital's Children's Department, 1940–71 (Assistant Physician, 1935–40), to Princess Louise (Kensington) Hospital for Children, 1944–71 (Assistant Physician, 1937–44), and to Queen Elizabeth Hospital for Children, 1946–71; *b* 11 April 1906; *d* of Frederick Farey Shelley, FIC, and Rachel Hicks Shelley, MB, BS. *Educ:* St Paul's Girls' School; Royal Free Hospital School of Medicine. MB, BS Lond., Univ. Gold Medal, 1930; MD Lond., 1932; FRCP 1948. Examiner: Coll. of Physicians, 1960–70; Univ. of London, 1965–70. Vice-Pres., Nat. Assoc. of Family Life and Child Care (formerly Nat. Assoc. of Nursery Matrons), 1968– (Pres., 1960–65); Member: Medical Women's Fedn, 1936–; British Pædiatric Assoc., 1946–85. Liveryman, Worshipful Soc. of Apothecaries; Freeman of City of London, 1950. *Publications:* numerous articles in medical journals. *Recreations:* gardening, lion dogs. *Address:* 15 Hyde Park Gate, SW7 5DG. *T:* 071–584 7941; Threeways, 2 Mincing Lane, Chobham GU24 8RX.   *Died 6 Dec. 1993.*

SHENTON, Clive; QC (Scot.) 1990; barrister; *b* 7 Oct. 1946; *s* of John Shenton and Mary Louise Gutridge. *Educ:* Durban High Sch.; RMA, Sandhurst; Univ. of Edinburgh (LLB). Served: Black Watch, 1966–70; Parachute Regt

(T&AVR), 1971–77 (Captain 1973, Major 1975). Called to the Scots Bar, 1975; called to the Bar, Middle Temple, 1990. Standing Jun. Counsel to MoD (Army Dept) in Scotland, 1983–90; Temp. Sheriff, 1988–90, 1992–. Treasurer, Advocates' Criminal Law Gp, 1984–88. Contested (C) Dunfermline E, 1983, 1987. *Recreation:* cricket. *Address:* 8 Moray Place, Edinburgh EH3 6DS. *T:* 031–225 1118; 36 Essex Street, WC2R 3AS. *T:* 071–413 0353. *Clubs:* Army and Navy, MCC; New (Edinburgh).
Died 29 Aug. 1994.

SHEPHARD, George Clifford, CBE 1979; Board Member for Industrial Relations, National Coal Board, 1969–80, retired; Member, Paul Finet Foundation, since 1974; *b* 2 Aug. 1915; British; *m* 1942, Mollie Dorothy Mansfield; one *s* (one *d* decd). *Educ:* Chesterfield Grammar School. Bolsover Colliery Co. Ltd, Head Office, 1933–40. Served in Army, N Africa, various Comd HQs, 1940–45, commnd 1942. Official, National Union of Mineworkers, 1945–69. Director, 1969–80: Coal Products Div., NCB; Associated Heat Services Ltd; Compower Ltd; British Investment; former Dir, Inst. of Occupational Medicine. Member: CBI Cttees; ECSC. Jt Hon. Sec., Coal Industry Social Welfare Organisation; Chm., Mineworkers' Pension Scheme. Editor, various bulletins and tracts. FCIS, ACMA, CBIM. *Recreations:* golf, music. *Address:* c/o Queensgate Hotel, 398–402 North Promenade, Blackpool FY1 2LB.
Died 6 June 1994.

SHEPHERD, Eric William, CB 1967; *b* London, 17 May 1913; *s* of late Charles Thomas Shepherd; *m* 1938, Marie Noele Carpenter; two *d*. *Educ:* Hackney Downs School; The Polytechnic, Regent Street. BSc 1st Class Hons (Maths and Physics) London, 1932. Entered Post Office as Executive Officer, 1932; served War of 1939–45, with Royal Engineers (Postal Section), 1940–46; Principal, Post Office, 1948; Treasury, 1949–52; Asst Accountant General, Post Office, 1952; Dep. Comptroller and Accountant General, 1953; Assistant Secretary, 1956; Director of Finance and Accounts, 1960; Senior Director, 1967–73. *Recreations:* music, especially choral singing, golf. *Address:* 2 Arkley View, Arkley, Barnet, Herts EN5 3JP. *T:* 081–449 9316.   *Died 10 Oct. 1992.*

SHEPHERD, Geoffrey Thomas, CBE 1979; FIMechE, FIEE; engineering consultant, since 1982; *b* 1922; *s* of Thomas Henry and Louise Shepherd; *m* Irene Wilkes; one *d*. *Educ:* King Edward's Sch., Birmingham; Coll. of Technology, Birmingham. BSc (Hons). GEC Ltd; British Electricity Authority (several positions in management of power stations); Nuclear Ops Engr, CEGB, 1958–61; Regional Dir (Western Div.), 1962–65; Dir of Engrg, South of Scotland Electricity Bd, 1965–69; Dep. Chm., LEB, 1969–72; Chm., Midlands Electricity Bd, 1972–82; part-time Mem., CEGB, 1977–82. Pres., IEE, 1986–87. Hon. DSc Aston, 1986. *Recreations:* fair weather sailing, railways. *Address:* Tree Tops, Pensham Hill, Pershore, Worcs WR10 3HA. *T:* Pershore (0386) 553076.
Died 18 Oct. 1993.

SHEPPARD, Tan Sri Dato Mervyn Cecil ffranck, CMG 1957; MBE 1946; ED 1947; PSM 1969; DJPD 1967; SJJ 1992; DPMS 1982; DSNS 1988; JMN 1963; *b* 1905; *s* of late Canon J. W. ff. Sheppard; *m* 1940, Rosemary, *d* of late Major Edward Oakeley; one *d*. *Educ:* Marlborough; Magdalene Coll., Cambridge (MA). Cadet, Federated Malay States, 1928; interned by Japanese, 1942–45; Major, FMS Volunteer Force, retd 1946; Director of Public Relations, 1946; District Officer, Klang, 1947–50; British Adviser, Negeri Sembilan, 1952; Head of the Emergency Food Denial Organisation, Federation of Malaya, 1956; First Keeper of Public Records, 1957–62, and Director of Museums, 1958–63, Federation of Malaya; retired CS, 1963. Vice Pres. and Hon. Editor, Malaysian Br., RAS, 1971–; Co-Founder, Heritage of Malaysia Trust,

1983– (Vice-Pres., 1983–93). Hon. Curator, Nat. Museum, Kuala Lumpur. Hon. DLitt: Univ. of Science, Malaysia, 1984; Nat. Univ. of Malaysia, 1991. Biennial Award, Tun Abdul Razak Foundn, 1983. *Publications:* Taman Indera, Royal Pleasure Ground, 1972; Living Crafts of Malaysia, 1978; Memoirs of an Unorthodox Civil Servant, 1979; Tunku: a pictorial biography, part 1, 1903–1957, 1984, part 2, 1957–1987, 1987. *Address:* Apartment 7C, Crescent Court, Brickfields, 50470 Kuala Lumpur, Malaysia. *Clubs:* United Oxford & Cambridge University; Royal Selangor (Kuala Lumpur).   *Died 11 Sept. 1994.*

SHERWIN-WHITE, Adrian Nicholas, MA; FBA 1956; Reader in Ancient History, University of Oxford, 1966–79; Fellow and Tutor of St John's College, Oxford, 1936–79, Fellow Emeritus 1979; Keeper of the Groves, 1970; *b* 10 Aug. 1911; *s* of H. N. Sherwin-White, Solicitors' Dept of LCC. *Educ:* Merchant Taylors' School; St John's College, Oxford (Derby Scholar, 1935; Arnold Historical Essay Prize, 1935; MA, 1937). War Service in RN and Admiralty, 1942–45. Conington Prize, 1947. Sarum Lecturer, Oxford Univ., 1960–61; Gray Lecturer, Cambridge Univ., 1965–66; Special Lectr, Open Univ., 1973–81. Pres., Soc. for Promotion of Roman Studies, 1974–77. Corresp. Fellow, Bayerische Akademie der Wissenschaften, 1977. *Publications:* Roman Citizenship, 1939, enlarged edn 1973; Ancient Rome (Then and There Series), 1959; Roman Society and Roman Law in the New Testament, 1963; Historical Commentary on the Letters of Pliny the Younger, 1966; Racial Prejudice in Imperial Rome, 1967; Roman Foreign Policy in the East 167BC-AD1, 1983; (contrib.) Cambridge Ancient History, 1985; (ed) Geographical Handbook Series; contrib. Jl Roman Studies. *Recreations:* watching horses, growing hardy plants. *Address:* St John's College, Oxford OX1 3JP. *T:* Frilford Heath (0865) 390496.   *Died 1 Nov. 1993.*

SHIELDS, Maj.-Gen. Ronald Frederick, OBE 1943; BSc (Eng); CEng; FIEE; *b* 4 Nov. 1912; *s* of late John Benjamin Frederick Shields, Chichester; *m* 1944, Lorna, *d* of late Frederick Murgatroyd, Manchester; one *s* one *d*. *Educ:* Portsmouth Grammar School. Lieut RAOC, 1936; served War of 1939–45 in Middle East and NW Europe; transferred to REME, 1942; Staff College Camberley, 1945; MELF, 1948–51; AQMG, HQ Northern Comd, 1952–55; War Office, 1956–59; REME Training Centre, 1959–62; DEME, HQ, BAOR, 1962–65; Comdt, Technical Group, REME, 1965–68; retd 1968. Col, 1955; Brig. 1962; Maj.-Gen. 1965. Col Comdt, REME, 1968–73. *Address:* 12 Churchfield Court, Roebuck Close, Reigate, Surrey RH2 7RS.   *Died 5 May 1991.*

SHILLITO, Edward Alan, CB 1964; retired Civil Servant; *b* 13 May 1910; *s* of late Rev. Edward and Mrs Annie Shillito, Buckhurst Hill, Essex; *m* 1934, Dorothy Jean, *d* of late Robert J. Davies, Buckhurst Hill, Essex; two *s* three *d*. *Educ:* Chigwell School; Oriel College, Oxford (Exhibitioner). Lit.Hum. 2nd Class, 1933; MA 1985. Customs and Excise, 1934–36; HM Treas., 1936–57; Under-Secretary, 1951; Admiralty, and MoD, 1957–69; Dir, Greenwich Hosp., 1969–71; a Gen. Comr of Income Tax, 1972–82. Imperial Defence College course, 1953. *Recreations:* music, lacrosse (Oxford Univ., 1931–33). *Address:* 8 Baldwins Hill, Loughton, Essex IG10 1SD. *T:* 081–508 1988.   *Died 3 March 1991.*

SHINDLER, His Honour George (John); QC 1970; a Circuit Judge, 1980–92; Senior Resident Judge, Inner London Crown Court, 1987–92; *b* 27 Oct. 1922; named Hans Georg Schindler; *yr s* of late Dr Bruno and Mrs Alma Schindler; *m* 1955, Eva Muller; three *s*. *Educ:* Regent's Park Sch.; University Coll. Sch., Hampstead. Served in Royal Tank Regt, NW Europe, 1942–47. Called to Bar, Inner Temple, 1952; Bencher 1978. Standing Counsel to Inland Revenue at Central Criminal Court and

all London sessions, 1965–70; a Recorder of the Crown Court, 1972–80. Legal Mem., Mental Health Review Tribunal, 1983–87; Mem., Inner London Probation Cttee, 1987–92. Pres., Inner London Magistrates' Assoc., 1987–93. *Recreations:* theatre, music, reading, watching soccer and cricket, travel. *Address:* c/o Queen Elizabeth Building, Temple, EC4Y 9BS. *Club:* MCC.
Died 10 Dec. 1994.

SHIRER, William Lawrence; broadcaster, journalist, author; *b* Chicago, 23 Feb. 1904; *s* of Seward Smith Shirer; *m* 1931, Theresa Stiberitz (marr. diss. 1970); two *d*; *m* 1988, Irina Lugovskaya. *Educ:* Coe College (Hon. DLitt); Coll. de France. Légion d'Honneur. *Publications:* Berlin Diary, 1941; End of a Berlin Diary, 1947; The Traitor (novel), 1950; Mid-Century Journey, 1953; Stranger Come Home (novel), 1954; The Challenge of Scandinavia, 1955; The Consul's Wife (novel), 1956; The Rise and Fall of The Third Reich, 1960; The Rise and Fall of Adolf Hitler, 1961; The Sinking of the Bismarck, 1962; The Collapse of the Third Republic, 1970; 20th Century Journey: a memoir of a Life and the Times, vol. I, The Start 1904–1930, 1976, vol. II, The Nightmare Years 1930–1940, 1984, vol. III, A Native's Return 1945–1988, 1990; Gandhi, a Memoir, 1979. *Recreations:* walking, sailing. *Address:* Box 487, Lenox, Mass 01240, USA. *Club:* Century (New York). *Died 28 Dec. 1993.*

SHONE, Sir Robert Minshull, Kt 1955; CBE 1949; *b* 27 May 1906; *s* of Robert Harold Shone. *Educ:* Sedbergh School; Liverpool University (MEng); Chicago Univ. (MA Economics). Commonwealth Fellow, USA, 1932–34; Lecturer, London School of Economics, 1935–36; British Iron and Steel Federation, 1936–39; Iron and Steel Control, 1940–45, Gen. Dir, 1943–45; BISF, 1946–53, Director 1950–53; Executive Member, Iron and Steel Board, 1953–62; Joint Chairman, UK and ECSC Steel Committee, 1954–62; Dir-Gen., Nat. Economic Develt Council, 1962–66. Research Fellow, Nuffield Coll., Oxford, 1966–67; Special Prof., Nottingham Univ., 1971–73; Vis. Prof., City Univ., 1967–83. Director: M & G Gp, 1966–84; Rank Orgn, 1968–78; A. P. V. Holdings Ltd, 1969–75. Hon. Fellow, LSE. Pres., Soc. of Business Economists, 1963–68. *Publications:* Problems of Investment, 1971; Price and Investment Relationships, 1975; contributions to: Some Modern Business Problems, 1937; The Industrial Future of Great Britain, 1948; Large Scale Organisation, 1950; Models for Decision, 1965; Britain and the Common Market, 1967; Financial Management Handbook, 1978; articles in journals. *Recreation:* golf. *Address:* 7 Windmill Hill, Hampstead, NW3. *T:* 071–435 1930. *Died 13 Dec. 1992.*

SHOPPEE, Prof. Charles William, FRS 1956; FAA 1958; Emeritus Professor of Chemistry, University of Sydney; *b* London, 24 Feb. 1904; *er s* of J. W. and Elizabeth Shoppee, Totteridge; *m* 1929, Eileen Alice West; one *d*. *Educ:* Stationers' Company's Sch.; Univs of London and Leeds. PhD, DSc (London); MA, DPhil (Basle). Sen. Student of Royal Commn for Exhibition of 1851, 1926–28; Asst Lecturer and Lecturer in Organic Chemistry, Univ. of Leeds, 1929–39; Rockefeller Research Fellow, Univ. of Basle, 1939–45; Reader in Chemistry, Univ. of London, at Royal Cancer Hosp., 1945–48; Prof. of Chemistry, Univ. of Wales, at University Coll., Swansea, 1948–56; Prof. of Organic Chemistry, Univ. of Sydney, 1956–70; Foundation Welch Prof. of Chemistry, Texas Tech. Univ., 1970–75. Visiting Professor of Chemistry: Duke Univ., N Carolina, USA, 1963; Univ. of Georgia, USA, 1966; Univ. of Mississippi, USA, 1968; Hon. Professorial Fellow in Chem., Macquarie Univ., 1976–79; Hon. Vis. Prof. of Organic Chem., La Trobe Univ., 1980–. *Publications:* scientific papers in Jl Chem. Soc., Helvetica Chimica Acta and Aust. Jl Chem. *Recreations:* bowls, music, bridge.

Address: 80A Studley Park Road, Kew, Vic 3101, Australia. *T:* (3) 8535815. *Club:* Royal Automobile of Victoria. *Died 20 Oct. 1994.*

SHUCKBURGH, Sir (Charles Arthur) Evelyn, GCMG 1967 (KCMG 1959; CMG 1949); CB 1954; HM Diplomatic Service, retired; Chairman, Executive Committee, British Red Cross Society, 1970–80 (Chairman, Council, 1976–80, Vice-Chairman, 1980–81); Member, Standing Commission, International Red Cross, 1974–81 (Chairman, 1977–81); *b* 26 May 1909; *e s* of late Sir John Shuckburgh, KCMG, CB and Lilian Violet, *er d* of A. G. Peskett; *m* 1937, Nancy Brett, 2nd *d* of 3rd Viscount Esher, GBE; two *s* one *d*. *Educ:* Winchester; King's College, Cambridge. Entered Diplomatic Service, 1933; served at HM Embassy, Cairo, 1937–39; seconded for service on staff of UK High Comr in Ottawa, 1940; transferred to Buenos Aires, 1942; Chargé d'Affaires there in 1944; First Secretary at HM Embassy, Prague, 1945–47; Head of South American Department, FO, 1947–48; Western Dept, 1949–50; Western Organizations Dept, 1950–51; Principal Private Secretary to Secretary of State for Foreign Affairs, 1951–54; Assistant Under-Secretary, Foreign Office, 1954–56; Senior Civilian Instructor, IDC, 1956–58; Asst Sec.-Gen. (Polit.) of NATO, Paris, 1958–60; Dep. Under-Sec., FO, 1960–62; Perm. Brit. Rep. to N Atlantic Council, in Paris, 1962–66; Ambassador to Italy, 1966–69. Dir, Commercial Union Assurance, 1971–80. Chm., N Home Counties Regional Cttee, National Trust, 1975–79. *Publications:* Descent to Suez (Diaries, 1951–1956), 1986; (ed and trans.) The Memoirs of Madame Roland, 1989. *Address:* High Wood House, Watlington, Oxon OX9 5HG. *T:* Watlington (0149161) 2433. *Died 12 Dec. 1994.*

SIBBALD, Maj.-Gen. Peter Frank Aubrey, CB 1982; OBE 1972; consultant in defence industries; *b* 24 March 1928; *s* of Major Francis Victor Sibbald, MBE, MM, BEM, and Mrs Alice Emma Hawking, The Hoe, Plymouth; *m* 1st, 1957, Margaret Maureen Entwistle (*d* 1990); one *s* one *d*; 2nd, 1994, Sandra Lee Gardner. *Educ:* ISC, Haileybury. Commnd, 1948; served with 1 KOYLI, 1948–53; Malayan Emergency, 1948–51 (mentioned in despatches); Korea, 1953–54; Kenya Emergency, 1954–55; Instr, Sch. of Inf., 1955–57; psc 1961; Aden, 1965–66; Bde Maj., 151 Inf. Bde, 1962–64; jssc 1964; GSO2 HQ FARELF, 1966–68; CO 2 LI, 1968–71; Col GS HQ BAOR, 1972; Comdr 51 Inf. Bde, 1972–74; Div. Brig., Light Div., 1975–77; GOC NW District, 1977–80; Dir of Infantry, 1980–83. Dep. Col, Light Infantry (Yorks), 1977–80; Col Comdt, The Light Div., 1980–83. *Recreations:* game shooting, fishing, squash, swimming. *Club:* Army and Navy. *Died 5 July 1994.*

SICH, Sir Rupert (Leigh), Kt 1968; CB 1953; Registrar of Restrictive Trading Agreements, 1956–73; *b* 3 Aug. 1908; *s* of late A. E. Sich, Caterham, Surrey; *m* 1933, Elizabeth Mary (*d* 1991), *d* of late R. W. Hutchison, Gerrards Cross; one *s* two *d*. *Educ:* Radley College; Merton College, Oxford. Called to Bar, Inner Temple, 1930. Board of Trade Solicitor's Dept, 1932–48; Treasury Solicitor's Dept, 1948–56. *Recreations:* J. S. Bach, gardening. *Address:* Norfolk House, The Mall, Chiswick, W4 2PS. *T:* 0181–994 2133. *Clubs:* United Oxford & Cambridge University, MCC. *Died 14 Sept. 1995.*

SIDDIQUI, Prof. Salimuzzaman, MBE 1946; Tamgha-i-Pakistan 1958; Sitara-i-Imtiaz (Pakistan) 1962; Hilal-e-Imtiaz, 1980; DPhil Nat; FRS 1961; Professor/Director, H. E. J. Research Institute of Chemistry, University of Karachi, since 1966; *b* 19 Oct. 1897. *Educ:* Lucknow; Mohammedan Anglo-Oriental College, Aligarh, UP; University College, London; Univ. of Frankfurt-on-Main. Returned to India, 1928; planned and directed Research Inst. at Ayurvedic and Unani Tibbi Coll., Delhi, 1928–40;

joined Council of Scientific and Industrial Research (India): Asst Dir, later Dir, Chemical Laboratories, 1940–51; Director and Chairman of Pakistan Council of Scientific and Industrial Research, 1951–66. Chairman, Nat. Science Council, 1962–66; Pres., Pakistan Acad. of Sciences, 1967; Founding Fellow, Islamic Acad. of Scis, Saudi Arabia; Fellow: Pakistan Acad. of Med. Scis, 1987; Islamic Acad. of Scis, Jordan, 1988; Foreign Fellow, Indian Nat. Sci. Acad., 1989. A chemist, working on the chemistry of natural products; led the promotion of scientific and industrial research in Pakistan; rep. Pakistan at internat. scientific confs, etc. Elected Mem., Vatican Acad. of Sciences, and apptd Pontifical Academician, 1964. Hon. DMed Frankfurt-on-Main, 1958; Hon. DSc: Karachi, 1967; Leeds, 1967. Gold Medal, Russian Acad., 1958; President's Pride of Performance Medal (Pakistan), 1966; Prize of Islamic Medicine Orgn, Kuwait Foundn for Advancement of Scis, 1981; special prize, Council of Third World Acad. of Scis, for contribs to chemistry of Rauwolfia alkaloids, 1986. *Publications:* author of over 200 research papers. *Address:* Chair Professor, H. E. J. Research Institute of Chemistry, University of Karachi, Karachi, Pakistan. *T:* (21) 472780.

Died 14 April 1994.

SIKRI, Sarv Mittra; *b* 26 April 1908; *s* of late Dr Nihal Chand; *m* 1937, Leila Ali Khan; one *s*. *Educ:* Trinity Hall, Cambridge (BA). Barrister-at-Law, Lincoln's Inn; started practice in Lahore High Court, 1930; Asst Advocate Gen., Punjab, 1949; Advocate Gen., Punjab, 1951–64; Judge, Supreme Ct of India, 1964–71; Chief Justice of India, 1971–73. Chm., Railway Accidents Enquiry Cttee, 1978–80; Chm., Jammu and Kashmir Enquiry Cttee, 1979–80. Alternate rep., UN Cttee on Codification and Develt of Internat. Law, 1947; Legal Adviser to Min. of Irrigation and Power, Govt of India, 1949; Mem. Internat. Law Assoc. Cttee on Internat. Rivers, 1955; Mem., Indian Law Commn, 1955–58. Delegate to: Law of the Sea Conf., Geneva, 1958; World Peace Through Law Conf., Tokyo, 1961; Athens, 1963; Accra Assembly, Accra, 1962. Pres., Indian Br. of Internat. Law Assoc., 1971–73; Member: Indian Commn of Jurists; Univ. Grants Commn, 1979–82; Chm., Sir Ganga Ram Hosp. Trust; Hon. Mem., Acad. of Political Sci., NY; Vice-Pres., Delhi Public School Soc. *Recreations:* golf, tennis, bridge. *Address:* 3 Nizam-uddin East, New Delhi 110013, India. *T:* 692327. *Clubs:* Delhi Golf, Delhi Gymkhana (both in New Delhi).

Died 24 Sept. 1992.

SILVERWOOD-COPE, Maclachlan Alan Carl, CBE 1959; FCA 1960; ATII 1978; chartered accountant; HM Diplomatic Service, retired; *b* 15 Dec. 1915; *s* of late Alan Lachlan Silverwood-Cope and Elizabeth Masters; *m* 1st, 1940, Hilkka (*née* Halme) (marr. diss. 1970); one *s* one *d*; 2nd, 1971, Jane (*née* Monier-Williams); one *s* one *d*. *Educ:* Malvern College. ACA 1939. HM Forces, 1939–45 (Major, RA). Foreign (later Diplomatic) Service, 1939–71: served as 3rd Sec., Stockholm, 1945–50; 1st Sec., Washington, 1951 and 1956–57; Tokyo, 1952–55; Copenhagen, 1960–64; Counsellor, Buenos Aires, 1966–68; FCO, 1968–71. Finance appts with Aspro-Nicholas Ltd, 1971–78. Home Front Medal (Finland), 1940; Freedom Cross (Norway), 1945. *Recreations:* tennis, bridge, music. *Address:* Brock Hill, Winkfield Row, Berks RG12 6LS. *T:* Winkfield Row (0344) 882746. *Club:* Middlesex County Cricket.

Died 22 April 1993.

SIM, John Mackay, MBE (mil.) 1945; Deputy Chairman, Inchcape & Co. Ltd, 1975–82 (Deputy Chairman and Managing Director, 1965–75); *b* 4 Oct. 1917; *s* of William Aberdeen Mackay Sim and Zoe Sim; *m* 1st, Dora Cecilia Plumridge Levita (*d* 1951); two *d*; 2nd, Mrs Muriel Harvard, (Peggie), Norman. *Educ:* Glenalmond; Pembroke Coll., Cambridge (MA). Lieut RA, 1940, Captain 1942;

served NW Europe (despatches). Smith Mackenzie & Co. Ltd (East Africa), 1946–62, Chm. 1960–62; Dir, subseq. Man. Dir, Inchcape & Co. Ltd, 1962. *Recreation:* gardening. *Address:* 6 Bryanston Mews West, W1H 7FR. *T:* 071–262 7673.

Died 11 Sept. 1993.

SIMMONDS, Prof. Kenneth Royston; Emeritus Professor of International Law, University of London, since 1992 (Professor of International Law at Queen Mary College, later Queen Mary and Westfield College, 1976–92); Gresham Professor of Law, City of London, 1986–92; *b* 11 Nov. 1927; *s* of Frederick John Simmonds and Maude (*née* Coxhill); *m* 1958, Gloria Mary (*née* Tatchell); one *s* one *d*. *Educ:* Watford Grammar Sch.; Exeter Coll., Oxford. BA, MA, DPhil (Oxon). Amelia Jackson Sen. Fellow, Exeter Coll., Oxford, 1951–53; Lectr, UCW, 1953–58; Lectr, Univ. of Liverpool, 1958–61; Sen. Lectr, QUB, 1961–63; Prof. of Law, Univ. of. Kent, 1970–72; British Institute of International and Comparative Law: Asst Dir, 1963–65; Dir, 1965–76; Hon. Dir, 1976–82; Dean, Faculty of Law, QMC, 1980–84. Gen. Editor, International and Comparative Law Qly, 1966–86; Editor, Common Market Law Review, 1967–91; Gen. Editor, Encyclopedia of European Community Law, 1972–93; Member Editorial Committee: British Year Book of International Law, 1967–; The International Lawyer, 1986–; Dir, Simmonds and Hill Publishing Ltd. Visiting Professor: McGill Univ., 1963; Univ. of Wyoming, 1969; Free Univ. of Brussels, 1972 and 1973; Univ. of Amsterdam, annually, 1979–; Univ. of Kentucky, 1985; Univ. of Texas at Austin, 1986–87; The Hague Acad. of Internat. Law, 1989. Mem., Legal Adv. Cttee, British Council, 1966–86; Chm., UK Nat. Cttee of Comparative Law, 1973–76; Pres., Internat. Assoc. of Legal Science, 1975–76; Consultant, EEC, 1983–84. FRSA. Chevalier, l'Ordre de Mérite, 1973; Comdr's Cross of Order of Merit, Federal Republic of Germany, 1983; Officier de l'Ordre des Palmes Académiques, France, 1992. *Publications:* Resources of the Ocean Bed, 1970; New Directions in the Law of the Sea, 1972–81, 1983–; (ed) Legal Problems of an Enlarged European Community, 1972; (ed) Sweet and Maxwell's European Community Treaties, 1972, 4th edn 1980; Cases on the Law of the Sea, 1976–84, second series, 1990–; (ed, with C. M. Schmitthoff) International Economic and Trade Law, 1976; Legal Problems of Multinational Corporations, 1978; (ed, with R. M. Goode) Commercial Operations in Europe, 1978; Multinational Corporations Law, 1979–; The UN Convention on the Law of the Sea, 1982; (ed with B. H. W. Hill) Commercial Arbitration in Asia and the Pacific, 1987; (ed with B. H. W. Hill) GATT Law and Practice, 1987–; The European Community, the Soviet Union and Eastern Europe, 1991; The Antarctic Conventions, 1993; The International Maritime Organization, 1994; numerous articles in Internat. and Comparative Law Qly, Common Market Law Rev., Europarecht. *Recreations:* travel (espec. in the Americas), classical music, cats. *Address:* The Oast Barn, Bell's Forstal, Throwley, near Faversham, Kent ME13 0JS.

Died 29 April 1995.

SIMMONDS, Kenneth Willison, CMG 1956; FRSA; *b* Carmacoup, Douglas, Lanarkshire, 13 May 1912; *s* of late William Henry Simmonds, Civil Servant, and Ida, *d* of John Willison, Acharn, Killin, Perthshire; *m* 1st, 1939, Ruth Constance Sargant (marr. diss. 1974); two *s*; 2nd, 1974, Mrs Catherine Clare Lewis, *y d* of late Col F. J. Brakenridge, CMG, Chew Magna. *Educ:* Bedford Sch.; Humberstone Sch.; St Catharine's Coll., Cambridge (MA). District Officer, Colonial Administrative Service, Kenya, 1935–48; Deputy Financial Secretary, Uganda, 1948–51; Financial Secretary, Nyasaland Protectorate, 1951–57; Chief Secretary, Aden, 1957–63. Exhibited paintings: Southern Arts Open Field; Royal Acad.; Royal West of

England Acad.; Bladon, Andover; Westward Open; Royal Bath and West; group and collective exhibns. *Address:* 1 Fons George Road, Taunton, Somerset TA1 3JU. *T:* Taunton (0823) 333128. *Died 18 Nov. 1991.*

SIMMS, Most Rev. George Otto, DD; MRIA 1957; *b* 4 July 1910; 3rd *s* of John F. A. Simms, Crown Solicitor, County Tyrone, and Mrs Simms, Combermore, Lifford, County Donegal; *m* 1941, Mercy Felicia, *o d* of Brian James Gwynn, Temple Hill, Terenure, Dublin; three *s* two *d. Educ:* St Edmund's School, Hindhead; Cheltenham College; Trinity College, Dublin. Scholar, 1930; Moderator in Classics, and History and Political Science, 1932; Berkeley Medallist; Vice-Chancellor's Latin Medallist; Theological Exhibnr; MA 1935; BD 1936; PhD 1950; DD (*jure dignitatis,* Dublin), 1952; Hon. Fellow, 1978. Deacon, 1935; priest, 1936; Curate-asst, St Bartholomew's Church, Dublin, 1935–38; Chaplain Lincoln Theol Coll., 1938–39; Dean of Residence, Trinity Coll., Dublin, 1939–52; Asst Lectr to Archbishop King's Prof. of Divinity, Dublin Univ., 1939–52; Chaplain-Secretary, Church of Ireland Training Coll., 1943–52; Hon. Clerical Vicar, Christ Church Cathedral, Dublin, 1937–52; Dean of Cork, 1952; Bishop of Cork, Cloyne, and Ross, 1952–56; Archbishop of Dublin and Primate of Ireland, 1956–69; also Bishop of Glendalough and Bishop of Kildare; Archbishop of Armagh and Primate of All Ireland, 1969–80. Member Governing Body, University College, Cork, 1953–57; President: The Leprosy Mission, 1964–; APCK, 1983–. Hon. Life Mem., Royal Dublin Soc., 1984. DD *hc* Huron, 1963; Hon. DCL Kent, 1978; Hon. DLitt New Univ. of Ulster, 1981. *Publications:* For Better, for Worse, 1945; The Book of Kells: a short description, 1950; (ed with E. H. Alton and P. Meyer) The Book of Kells (facsimile edn), Berne, 1951; The Bible in Perspective, 1953; (contrib.) The Book of Durrow (fac. edn), 1960; Memoir of Michael Lloyd Ferrar, 1962; Christ within Me, 1975; (contrib.) Irish Life, by Sharon Gmelch, 1979; Irish Illuminated Manuscripts, 1980; In My Understanding, 1982; Tullow's Story, 1983; (contrib.) Ireland: a cultural encyclopaedia, ed B. de Breffny, 1983; (with R. G. F. Jenkins) Pioneers and Partners, 1985; (contrib.) Treasures of the Library of Trinity College Dublin, 1986; Angels and Saints, 1988; Exploring the Book of Kells, 1988; Brendan the Navigator, 1989; (contrib.) Faith in Place, by Adrian Hewson, 1990; articles in Hermathena, Theology, Dublin Magazine, JTS; contrib. to New Divinity, Booklore, Search, Newman Review. *Address:* 62 Cypress Grove Road, Dublin 6W. *T:* Dublin 905594. *Died 15 Nov. 1991.*

SIMON, 2nd Viscount, *cr* 1940, of Stackpole Elidor; **John Gilbert Simon,** CMG 1947; *b* 2 Sept. 1902; *o s* of 1st Viscount Simon, GCSI, GCVO, PC, and Ethel Mary (*d* 1902), *d* of Gilbert Venables; *S* father, 1954; *m* 1930, (James) Christie, *d* of William Stanley Hunt; one *s* one *d. Educ:* Winchester; Balliol College, Oxford (Scholar). With Ministry of War Transport, 1940–47. Man. Dir, 1947–58, Dep. Chm., 1951–58, Peninsular and Oriental Steam Navigation Co.; Chm., PLA, 1958–71; Mem., Nat. Ports Council, 1967–71. President: Chamber of Shipping of UK, 1957–58; Inst. of Marine Engineers, 1960–61; RINA, 1961–71; British Hydromechanics Res. Assoc., 1968–80. Officer Order of Orange Nassau, Netherlands. *Heir: s* Hon. Jan David Simon [*b* 20 July 1940; *m* 1969, Mary Elizabeth Burns, Sydney; one *d*]. *Address:* 2 Church Cottages, Abbotskerswell, Newton Abbot, Devon TQ12 5NY. *T:* Newton Abbot (0626) 65573. *Died 5 Dec. 1993.*

SIMPSON, Sir James (Joseph Trevor), KBE 1965 (CBE 1957); Director, James Simpson & Co. Ltd; Chairman, Uganda Development Corporation, Ltd, 1952–64, retired; *b* 9 Jan. 1908; forename James added by deed poll, 1965;

reverted to British nationality, 1988, after Uganda citizenship, 1962–88; 2nd *s* of late Lieut-Colonel Herbert Simpson, OBE, MC, and Mrs Henrietta Augusta Simpson; *m* 1940, Enid Florence (*née* Danzelman) (*d* 1979). *Educ:* Ardingly College, Sussex. Branch Manager, Vacuum Oil Co., Nakuru, Nairobi, Dar es Salaam, Mombasa, Kampala, 1932–46; General Manager, The Uganda Company Ltd, 1947–52; President, Uganda Chamber of Commerce, 1941, 1946–50. Member: Uganda Executive Council, 1952–55; Uganda Legislative Council, 1950–58 (Chm. Representative Members Organization, 1951–58); E African Legislative Assembly, 1957–60, 1962–63; E African Railways and Harbours, Transport Advisory Council, 1948–61; E African Industrial Council, 1947–61; Uganda Electricity Bd, 1955–60; East African Airways Corporation, 1958–73; Minister of Economic Affairs, Uganda, 1962–63. *Recreation:* bridge. *Address:* PO Box 48816, Nairobi, Kenya. *Club:* Muthaiga (Kenya). *Died 10 April 1994.*

SIMPSON, John Ferguson, FRCS; Consulting Surgeon to Ear, Nose and Throat Department, St Mary's Hospital, retired; formerly Civil Consultant, Ministry of Aviation; *b* 10 Oct. 1902; *s* of late Col P. J. Simpson, DSO, FRCVS, Maidenhead; *m* 1947, Winifred Beatrice Rood; one *s* one *d. Educ:* Reading Sch.; St Mary's Hosp. MRCS, LRCP 1926; FRCS 1929. Formerly: Lectr in Diseases of the Ear, Nose and Throat, Univ. of London; Specialist in Otorhino-laryngology, RAF; Hon. Surg. Royal Nat. Throat, Nose and Ear Hosp. FRSocMed (ex-President Section of Otology; Hon. Life Mem., Section of Laryngology); Hon. Life Mem., British Assoc. of Otolaryngologists. Liveryman, Farriers' Co. Sir W. Dalby Meml Prize in Otology (jtly), RSM, 1948. *Publications:* A Synopsis of Otorhinolaryngology (jointly), 1957; chapters: Operative Surgery, 1957; ENT Diseases, 1965. *Recreations:* entomology; formerly Rugby football. *Address:* Waverley Cottage, Upton Grey, Basingstoke, Hants RG25 2RA. *T:* Basingstoke (01256) 862433. *Died 12 Sept. 1995.*

SINCLAIR, (Ernest) Keith, CMG 1966; OBE 1946; DFC 1943; journalist-consultant; Commissioner, Australian Heritage Commission, 1976–81; Associate Commissioner, Industries Assistance Commission, 1974–81; *b* 13 Nov. 1914; 2nd *s* of Ernest and Florence Sinclair, Victoria, Australia; *m* 1949, Jill, *d* of John and Muriel Nelder, Pangbourne; one *s. Educ:* Melbourne High School, Australia. Served War of 1939–45, RAF, 1940–45 (despatches, 1944). Literary staff, The Age, 1932–38, Associate Editor, The Age, Melbourne, 1946–59, Editor, 1959–66. Consultant to Dept of Prime Minister and Cabinet, 1967–74 and 1977–81 (to Prime Minister of Australia, 1967–72). Dep. Chm., Australian Tourist Commn, 1969–75 (Mem. 1966). Director: Australian Associated Press, 1959–66 (Chm., 1965–66); Gen. Television Corp. (Melbourne), 1959–66; Australian Paper Manufacturers Ltd, 1966–85; Member: Australian Council, Internat. Press Inst., 1959–66; Schools Bd for the Humanities, Victoria Inst. of Colleges, 1969–72 (Chm.); Library Council of Victoria, 1966–78; Council, Royal Historical Soc. of Victoria, 1981–86 (Hon. Editor, Jl, 1982–86); Observer, Nat. Capital Planning Cttee, 1967–72; Dep. Chm., Library Council, and Trustee, Nat. Museum and Sci. Museum of Victoria, 1976–78. *Publication:* The Spreading Tree: a history of APM and AMCOR 1844–1989, 1991. *Recreations:* historical writing, gardening, reading. *Address:* 138 Toorak Road West, South Yarra, Victoria 3141, Australia. *T:* (3) 8671405. *Club:* Melbourne (Melbourne). *Died 27 March 1995.*

SINCLAIR, Rear-Adm. Erroll Norman, CB 1963; DSC 1944; retired; *b* 6 March 1909; *s* of late Col John Norman

Sinclair, RHA; *m* 1940, Frances Elinor Knox-Gore; two *s.* *Educ:* RNC Dartmouth. Served HMS Cumberland, 1934–35; HMS Cairo, 1936–38; HMS Gallant, 1938–40 (Dunkirk); in comd HMS Fortune, 1940, HMS Antelope, 1941–43, N African Landings; in comd HMS Eskimo, 10th Destroyer Flotilla, 1943–45 (DSC); First Lieut, RN Barracks, Chatham, 1946, Comdr 1946; Exec. Officer, RN Air Station, Eglinton, 1947; Staff Officer Ops to C-in-C, S Atlantic Station, Simonstown, and UK Liaison Officer to S African Naval Forces, until 1951; in comd HMS St Kitts, 5th Destroyer Sqdn, Home Fleet, 1951–53; Capt. 1952; Pres. Second Admiralty Interview Board, 1953–54; Naval Attaché at Ankara, Teheran and Tel Aviv, 1955; Capt. (D) 4th Destroyer Sqdn, HMS Agincourt, 1957–59; in comd HMS Sea Eagle and Sen. Naval Officer N Ireland, and Naval Director, Joint Anti-Submarine School, Londonderry, 1959–61; Flag Officer, Gibraltar, and Admiral Superintendent, HM Dockyard, Gibraltar, also NATO Commander of Gibraltar sub areas, 1962–64; retd list, 1964; Naval Regional Officer (North), 1964–68. *Club:* Rye Golf. *Died 29 Oct. 1993.*

SINCLAIR, Keith; *see* Sinclair, E. K.

SINCLAIR, Prof. Sir Keith, Kt 1985; CBE 1983; Professor of History, University of Auckland, 1963–87, then Emeritus; *b* 5 Dec. 1922; *s* of Ernest Duncan and Florence Sinclair; *m* 1st, 1947, Mary Edith Land; four *s*; 2nd, 1976, Raewyn Mary Dalziel. *Educ:* Mount Albert Grammar Sch.; Auckland University Coll. (MA, PhD (NZ); LittD (Auckland)); Univ. of London. War service, NZ Army, 1941–43; RNZNVR, in UK, 1944–45. Lectr in History, 1947, Senior Lectr, 1952, Associate Prof., 1960, Auckland University Coll. Carnegie Commonwealth Fellow, Inst. of Commonwealth Studies, London, 1954–55; Carnegie Travelling Grant, USA, 1955; Vis. Fellow, Inst. of Advanced Studies, ANU, 1967, 1978, 1983; Smuts Vis. Fellow, Cambridge, 1968–69. Labour candidate, Eden electorate, 1969 (elected for 3 weeks, defeated on postal ballot). Chm., NZ Authors' Fund Cttee, 1973–85; Trustee, NZ Nat. Library, 1981–90; Mem., NZ 1990 Commn (planning sesquicentenary), 1987–90. *Publications:* Maori Land League, 1950; Songs for a Summer, 1952; Strangers or Beasts, 1954; Imperial Federation, 1955; Origins of the Maori Wars, 1957; A History of New Zealand, 1959, rev. edn 1980; (ed) The Maori King, by J. E. Gorst, 1959; (with W. F. Mandle) The Bank of New South Wales in New Zealand, 1961; (ed) Distance Looks Our Way, 1961; A Time to Embrace, 1963; (ed with R. M. Chapman) Studies of a Small Democracy, 1963; William Pember Reeves, 1965; The Firewheel Tree, 1973; Walter Nash, 1977; The Reefs of Fire, 1977; (with Wendy Harrex) Looking Back: a photographic history of New Zealand, 1978; History of the University of Auckland, 1983; (with Judith Bassett and Marcia Stenson) The Story of New Zealand, 1985; A Destiny Apart: New Zealand's search for national identity, 1986; (ed) Tasman Relations: New Zealand and Australia 1788–1988, 1987; (ed) Oxford Illustrated History of New Zealand, 1990; Kinds of Peace: Maori people after the Wars 1870–85, 1991; Moontalk: poems new and selected, 1993; Half Way Round the Harbour (autobiog.), 1993; articles in learned jls. *Recreations:* fishing, gardening. *Address:* 13 Mariposa Crescent, Birkenhead, Auckland 10, New Zealand. *T:* (9) 4805057. *Died 20 June 1993.*

SINGER, Isaac Bashevis; writer; *b* Poland, 14 July 1904; *s* of Pinchos Menachem Singer and Bathsheba Singer (*née* Zylberman); *m* 1st, Rachel (marr. diss.); one *s*; 2nd, 1940, Alma Haimann. *Educ:* Tachkemoni Rabbinical Seminary, Warsaw. Worked for publishing firms, Poland, 1926–35; with Jewish Daily Forward, NY, 1935–. Fellow: Jewish Acad. of Arts and Scis; Amer. Acad. and Inst. of Arts and Letters, NY (Gold Medal, 1989); Mem., Amer. Acad. of Arts and Sciences, Boston. Nat. Book Award, 1970, 1974; Nobel Prize for Literature, 1978. DHL Hebrew Union Coll., Cincinnati, Ohio, 1963. *Publications:* The Family Moskat, 1950; Satan in Goray, 1955; Gimpel the Fool and Other Stories, 1957; The Magician of Lublin, 1959; The Spinoza of Market Street, 1961; The Slave, 1962; Short Friday, 1964; Zlateh the Goat and Other Stories, 1966; In My Father's Court, 1966; The Manor, 1967; The Seance, 1968; The Estate, 1969; A Friend of Kafka and Other Stories, 1970; A Day of Pleasure (for children), 1970; Enemies, A Love Story, 1972; Crown of Feathers, 1973; When Shlemiel Went to Warsaw and Other Stories, 1974; Passions, 1976; Shosha, 1979; Old Love, 1980; The Collected Stories of Isaac Bashevis Singer, 1982; The Penitent, 1984; Love and Exile (memoirs), 1985; The Image and Other Stories, 1986; Stories for Children, 1987; The Death of Methuselah and Other Stories, 1988; The King of the Fields, 1988; *posthumous publication:* Scum, 1991. *Address:* 9511 Collins Avenue 703, Surfside, Fla 33154, USA. *Died 24 July 1991.*

SINGH, Dinesh; Minister without portfolio, India, since 1995; Member (Congress (I)) Rajya Sabha, Haryana, since 1993; *b* 19 July 1925; *s* of Raja Avadhesh Singh and Rani Lakshmi Kumari; *m* 1944, Neelima Kumari; six *d. Educ:* Doon Sch., Dehradun; Colvin Coll., Lucknow; Univ. of Lucknow. Member of Parliament: Lok Sabha, 1957–77; Rajya Sabha, 1977–82; Lok Sabha, 1984–91. Ministry of External Affairs: Dep. Minister, 1962–66; Minister of State, 1966–67; Minister of: Commerce, 1967–69; Ext. Affairs, 1969–70 and 1993–95; Industrial Develt and Internal Trade, 1970–71; Water Resources, Feb.–June 1988; Commerce, 1988–89. Leader Indian delegation to: The Economic and Social Council, 1963 and 1967; UNCTAD II, 1969 (Pres., 1968–72); UN Gen. Assembly, 1969, 1993. *Publications:* Towards New Horizons, 1971; India and the Changing Asian Scene, 1973; articles in magazines and nat. newspapers. *Recreations:* photography, wild life. *Address:* 1 Thyagaraja Marg, New Delhi 110011, India. *T:* (11) 3011766/3792945. *Clubs:* Delhi Gymkhana, Delhi Golf (New Delhi); Cricket of India (Bombay). *Died 30 Nov. 1995.*

SINGH, Sardar Swaran; President, Indian Council of World Affairs; *b* 19 Aug. 1907; *m*; four *d. Educ:* Government College, Lahore; Lahore Law College. MSc (Physics) 1930; LLB 1932. Elected to Punjab Legislative Assembly, 1946; Punjab State Government: Minister for Development, Food and Civil Supplies, 1946–47; Member, Partition Committee, 1947; Minister: of Home, General Administration, Revenue, Irrigation and Electricity, 1947–49; of Capital Projects and Electricity, 1952; for Works, Housing and Supply, 1952–57, Govt of India; Member, Upper House of Indian Legislature, 1952–57; Member, Lower House of Indian Legislature, 1957; Minister: for Steel, Mines and Fuel, 1957–62; for Railways, 1962–63; for Food and Agriculture, 1963–64; for Industry and Supply, 1964; for External Affairs, 1964–66; Foreign Minister, 1970–74; Minister of Defence, 1966–70 and 1974–75. Led many Indian delegations to the United Nations, its agencies, foreign countries and international conferences; Mem., Commonwealth Cttee on Pretoria dialogue, 1985. *Address:* c/o Indian National Congress, 5 Dr Rajendra Prasad Road, New Dehli, India. *Died 30 Oct. 1994.*

SINGH, Giani Zail; President of India, 1982–87; *b* Faridkot, 5 May 1916; *s* of Kishan Singh and Ind Kaur; *m* Pardan Kaur; one *s* three *d.* Founded Faridkot State Congress, 1946; formed govt in Faridkot State, 1948; Pres., State Praja Mandal, 1946–48; Government of Patiala and E Punjab States Union: Revenue Minister, 1948–49; Minister for Public Works and Agric., 1951–52; Pres., Provincial Congress Cttee, 1955–56; Member: Rajya

Sabha, 1956–62; Punjab Assembly, 1962; Minister of State, and Pres. Punjab Provincial Congress Cttee, 1966–72; Chief Minister of Punjab, 1972–77; Minister of Home Affairs, 1980–82. *Address:* 4 Circular Road, Chanakyaduri, New Delhi 110023, India.

Died 25 Dec. 1994.

SINGLETON, Sir Edward (Henry Sibbald), (Tim), Kt 1975; arbitrator and solicitor; Member of Council, The Law Society, 1961–80 (Vice-President of the Society, 1973, President, 1974); *b* 7 April 1921; *s* of W. P. Singleton, Colwall, and Florence, *d* of Sir Francis Sibbald Scott, 5th Bt; *m* 1943, Margaret Vere Hutton; three *s* one *d*. *Educ:* Shrewsbury; BNC, Oxford. MA 1946. Served War, as Pilot, Fleet Air Arm, 1941–45. Solicitor, 1949; Partner in Macfarlanes, 1954, consultant 1977–86; FCIArb 1982; Companion, Instn of Civil Engrs, 1982. Chm. and Dir of various public and private cos; Dir, Abbey Nat. Bldg Soc., 1977–89. Member: Council for the Securities Industry, 1978–83; Council of Management, The White Ensign Assoc. Ltd, 1984; Trustee: Fleet Air Arm Museum; Temple Bar Trust; Westminster Hospital, 1978–84. *Recreation:* relaxing. *Address:* Flat 7, 62 Queen's Gate, SW7 5JP. *T:* 071–581 3616. *Died 6 Sept. 1992.*

SINKER, Rev. Canon Michael Roy; Canon Emeritus of Lincoln Cathedral, 1969; *b* 28 Sept. 1908; 3rd *s* of late Rev. Francis Sinker, sometime Vicar of Ilkley; *m* 1939, Edith Watt Applegate; one *s* two *d*. *Educ:* Haileybury; Clare College, Cambridge (MA); Cuddesdon College, Oxford. Deacon, 1932; priest, 1933; Curate of Dalston, Cumberland, 1932–34; Chaplain to South African Church Railway Mission, 1935–38; Curate of Bishop's Hatfield 1938–39; Vicar of Dalton-in-Furness, 1939–46; Vicar of Saffron Walden, 1946–63; Hon. Canon of Chelmsford Cathedral, 1955–63; Rural Dean of Saffron Walden, 1948–63; Archdeacon of Stow, 1963–67; Rector of St Matthew, Ipswich, 1967–77. *Address:* 4 Avebury Close, Westbury, Wilts BA13 3TE. *Died 8 March 1994.*

SINNAMON, Sir Hercules Vincent, Kt 1985; OBE 1980; *b* 13 Nov. 1899; *s* of James Sinnamon and Janie Sinnamon (*née* Jackson). *Educ:* Taringa State School; Stott's Business College, Brisbane. FCISA; FIBA; AASA. Joined National Mutual Life Association, 1914; Manager, Townsville, Sub Accountant, and other executive positions; retired as Executive Officer, 1965. Retirement was happily spent furthering community projects and breeding beef and dairy cattle. *Publication:* The Gentleman Farmer's Paradise, 1980. *Recreations:* outdoors, riding, surfing. *Address:* Glen Ross, 619 Rocks and Sinnamon Roads, Sinnamon Park, Qld 4073, Australia. *T:* (7) 3761540. *Club:* National Mutual Life 25 Years' and Retired Officers' (Brisbane). *Died Feb. 1994.*

SISSON, Sir (Eric) Roy, Kt 1980; CEng; Chairman, 1976–85, and Chief Executive, 1976–81, Smiths Industries Ltd; *b* 17 June 1914; *s* of Bernard Sisson and Violet (*née* Hagg); *m* 1943, Constance Mary Cutchey; two *s* two *d*. *Educ:* Regent Street Polytechnic. De Havilland Aircraft Co. Ltd, 1933–37; Flight Engineer and Station Engineer, BOAC, 1944–47; BOAC rep. at de Havilland Aircraft Co., 1948; Smiths Industries: joined, 1955; Divl Dir, 1964; Chief Exec., Aviation Div., 1966; Managing Dir, 1973. Pres., SBAC, 1973–74. Councillor, Wheathampstead Parish Council, 1987–91. FBIM. Hon. FRAeS 1985. *Recreations:* sailing, tennis. *Address:* Gustard Wood House, Gustard Wood, near Wheathampstead, Herts AL4 8RP. *Clubs:* Royal Air Force; Royal Dart Yacht.

Died 7 Feb. 1993.

SITWELL, Rev. (Francis) Gerard, MA; OSB; *b* 22 Dec. 1906; *s* of late Major Francis Sitwell and Margaret Elizabeth, *d* of late Matthew Culley, Coupland Castle, Northumberland. *Educ:* Ampleforth; St Benet's Hall,

Oxford. Received Benedictine Habit, 1924; professed, 1925; priest, 1933; Assistant Master at Ampleforth, 1933–39; Assistant Procurator at Ampleforth, 1939–47; Subprior of Ampleforth, 1946–47; Master of St Benet's Hall, Oxford, 1947–64; Priest of Our Lady and St Wilfrid, Warwick Bridge, Carlisle, 1966–69. *Publications:* Walter Hilton, Scale of Perfection (trans. and ed), 1953; St Odo of Cluny, 1958; Medieval Spirituality, 1959; articles in Ampleforth Journal, Downside Review, Clergy Review, Month, etc. *Address:* Ampleforth Abbey, York YO6 4EN. *Died 20 Dec. 1993.*

SIVEWRIGHT, Col Robert Charles Townsend, CB 1983; MC 1945; DL; Joint Principal (with Molly Sivewright) of the Talland School of Equitation, since 1959; *b* 7 Sept. 1923; *s* of late Captain R. H. V. Sivewright, DSC, RN and Sylvia Townsend (*née* Cobbold); *m* 1951, (Pamela) Molly Ryder-Richardson, FIH, FBHS (as Molly Sivewright, author of Thinking Riding); three *d*. *Educ:* Repton; Royal Agricultural Coll., Cirencester. Served Regular Army, 11th Hussars (PAO), 1943–52; TA, Royal Glos Hussars, 1959–67 (CO, 1964–67); Chm., Western Wessex TA&VRA, 1970–83; Vice-Chm., Council of TA&VRAs, 1979–83. DL 1965, High Sheriff 1977, Glos. *Recreation:* National Hunt racing. *Address:* Talland House, Clarks Hay, South Cerney, Cirencester, Glos GL7 5UA. *T:* Cirencester (0285) 860830. *Died 5 May 1994.*

SKAN, Peter Henry O.; *see* Ogle-Skan.

SKEFFINGTON-LODGE, Thomas Cecil; *b* 15 Jan. 1905; *s* of late Thomas Robert Lodge and Winifred Marian Skeffington; unmarried. *Educ:* privately; Giggleswick and Westminster Schools. For some years engaged in Advertising and Publicity both in London and the North of England; later did Public Relations and administrative work in the Coal Trade as Northern Area Organiser for the Coal Utilisation Council, in which he served Cttees of Coal Trade in North-East, North-West and Yorkshire; on the outbreak of war, became a Mines Dept official; then volunteered for the Navy; from early 1941 a Naval Officer. MP (Lab) Bedford, 1945–50; Mem., Parly Delegn, Nüremberg Trials. Lecture tour in USA under auspices of Anglo-American Parly Gp, 1949; Mem. of post-war Parly Delegns to Eire, Belgium, Luxembourg and USA; formerly Mem., Parly Ecclesiastical Cttee, and served on Parochial Church Council, St Margaret's, Westminster. Contested (Lab) York, 1951, Mid-Bedfordshire, 1955; Grantham, 1959; Brighton (Pavilion), March 1969; Personal Asst to Chm., Colonial Development Corp., 1950–52. Past-Pres. and Chm., Pudsey Divisional Labour Party; Pres., Brighton and Hove Fabian Soc.; Member: Labour Party many years; Socialist Christian Movement (Vice-Pres.); IPU; Exec. Cttee, Brighton and Hove Br. UNA; German-British Christian Fellowship (past Chm.); Union of Shop, Distributive and Allied Workers; Conservation Soc.; CPRE (Chm., Brighton Dist Cttee, Sussex Branch); RSPB; Georgian Group; Friends of the Lake District; Amnesty Internat.; British-Soviet Friendship Soc.; Anglo-German Assoc.; Anglo-Belgian Assoc.; former Chm., Socialist Christian League and Parly Socialist Christian Group. *Recreations:* travel, gardening, politics and associating Christianity with them, in the hope of erecting fairer national and international living conditions for mankind. *Address:* 5 Powis Grove, Brighton, East Sussex BN1 3HF. *T:* Brighton (0273) 25472. *Club:* Savile.

Died 23 Feb. 1994.

SKELTON, Rear-Adm. Peter, CB 1956; *b* 27 Dec. 1901; *s* of Peter John and Selina Frances Skelton; *m* 1928, Janice Brown Clark; two *d*. *Educ:* RN Colleges, Osborne and Dartmouth; Trinity Hall, Cambridge. Cadet, 1915; Midshipman, HMS Valiant, 1918; Commander, 1936; served War of 1939–45, as Staff Officer in HMS Aurora, later at Admiralty in Torpedo Division; Commander and

Actg Capt. in HMS Royal Sovereign, 1942; Capt. 1944; Director of Trade Div., Admiralty, 1944; Supt of Torpedo Experimental Establishment, 1946; Sen. Naval Officer, Persian Gulf, 1949; Captain of Dockyard, Portsmouth, 1951; Rear-Adm., 1953; Admiral Superintendent, Rosyth, 1953–56; retired. Bucks CC, 1958. *Recreations:* golf, tennis, shooting. *Address:* Craigie Barns, Kippen, Stirlingshire FK8 3DT.   *Died 29 Nov. 1994.*

SKEMP, Prof. Joseph Bright, MA Cantab, PhD Edinburgh; Emeritus Professor of Greek, in the University of Durham; *b* 10 May 1910; *s* of late Thomas William Widlake Skemp, solicitor and local government officer, and Caroline (*née* Southall); *m* 1941, Ruby James (*d* 1987); no *c. Educ:* Wolverhampton Grammar School; Gonville and Caius College, Cambridge. Unofficial Drosier Fellow, Gonville and Caius College, Cambridge, 1936–47; Warden of Refugee Club and Asst Sec. to Refugee Cttee, Cambridge, 1940–46; Sec., Soc. for the Protection of Science and Learning, 1944–46; Lecturer in Greek and Latin, Univ. of Manchester, 1946–49; Reader in Greek, Univ. of Durham (Newcastle Div.), 1949–50; Prof. of Greek, Univ. of Durham, 1950–73; Vis. Prof., Univ. of Alexandria, 1977. Editor, Durham University Journal, 1953–57; Joint Editor, Phronesis, 1955–64. *Publications:* The Theory of Motion in Plato's Later Dialogues, 1942 (enlarged 1967); Plato's Statesman, 1952, repr. with postscript, 1987; The Greeks and the Gospel, 1964; Plato (supplementary vol. periodical Greece and Rome), 1976. *Recreations:* walking, history of railways. *Address:* Flat 6, 7 Clarence Road North, Weston-super-Mare BS23 4AT. *T:* Weston-super-Mare (0934) 641200.   *Died 10 Oct. 1992.*

SKINNER, Prof. Andrew Forrester, MA, BSc, PhD (St Andrews); MA (Columbia); FEIS; Professor of Education, Ontario College of Education, University of Toronto, 1954–70, then Emeritus Professor; *b* 21 May 1902; *s* of Alexander H. and Jessie F. Skinner, Kingskettle, Scotland; *m* 1932, Elizabeth Balmer Lockhart (*d* 1983), Manchester. *Educ:* Bell-Baxter School, Cupar, Fife; University of St Andrews. MA, BSc, 1st Cl. Hons Maths and Phys Sci., 1925; Carnegie Research Fellow in Chemistry, PhD, 1928; Commonwealth Fund Fellow, Columbia, New York, 1929–31 (Educn MA). Teacher in various schools, 1931–37; Asst Dir of Education, Co. of Aberdeen, 1937–39; Principal Lecturer in Methods, Dundee Trg Coll., 1939–41; Prof. of Education, Univ. of St Andrews, and Principal, Dundee Trg Coll., 1941–54. Visiting Professor: Ontario Coll. of Educn, Univ. of Toronto, 1950 and 1954; E Tennessee State Coll., 1951; State Univ. of Iowa, 1951–52; Univ. of British Columbia, 1962; Univ. of Victoria, 1964; Queen's Univ., Kingston, 1971. Former Member: Scottish Council for Research in Education; Scottish Universities Entrance Bd; School Broadcasting Council for Scotland; Mem., Bd of Directors, Comparative Educn Soc. of USA; Mem. Exec., Comparative and Internat. Educn Soc. of Canada, Vice-Pres., 1968–69; Pres., 1969–70, Hon. Mem. *Publications:* (booklet) Scottish Education in Schools, 1942; (booklet) Introductory Course on Education in Scotland, 1944; Citizenship in the Training of Teachers, 1948; Teachers' Heritage: an introduction to the study of education, 1979; articles in Jl of Amer. Chem. Soc.; Trans Chem. Soc.; Scottish Educnl Jl; The Year Book of Education; Educnl Forum: Educational Record of Quebec; The American People's Encyclopedia; Canadian and International Education; Canadian Education and Research Digest. *Recreations:* golf, gardening, walking. *Address:* 296 Ferry Road, Edinburgh EH5 3NP. *T:* 0131–552 4907.
                              Died 13 Feb. 1995.

SKINNER, Martyn; *b* 24 Aug. 1906; *s* of late Sir Sydney Skinner and Emelie Madeline, *d* of Samuel Belling, Cornwall; *m* 1938, Pauline Giles (marr. diss. 1987); three

s one *d* (and one *s* one *d* decd). *Educ:* two well-known Public Schools; Magdalen College, Oxford (no degree taken). Hawthornden prize, 1943; Heinemann Award, 1947; Runner-up, Barley Championship, Brewers' Exhibition, 1949. *Publications:* Sir Elfadore and Mabyna, 1935; Letters to Malaya: I and II, 1941; III and IV, 1943; V, 1947; Two Colloquies, 1949; The Return of Arthur, 1966; Old Rectory (Prologue), 1970; Old Rectory (The Session), 1973; Old Rectory (Epilogue), 1977; (with R. C. Hutchinson) Two Men of Letters, 1979; Alms for Oblivion, 1983; Old Rectory (complete edn), 1984. *Address:* Fitzhead, Taunton, Somerset. *T:* Milverton (0823) 400337.   *Died 24 Oct. 1993.*

SKINNER, Maj.-Gen. Michael Timothy, CB 1986; Lay Canon, Chapter Clerk and Comptroller of Rochester Cathedral, since 1988; *b* 5 Aug. 1931; *s* of Wilfred Skinner, MBE, FCIS and Ethel Skinner (*née* Jones); *m* 1959, Anne Kathleen Perry; three *s. Educ:* Merchant Taylors' School; RMA Sandhurst; psc, ptsc. MA Univ. of Kent, 1991. Commissioned Royal Regt of Artillery, 1953; Malaya, 1955–58 (despatches); Parachute Brigade, UK, and Commando Brigade, Malta, 1958–62; RMCS and Staff Coll.; staff (weapon locating), RRE, 1967–68; GSO2 (future equipment), HQ Dir RA, 1971–72; CO 4th Regt RA, 1972–75, Germany and UK (despatches); MGO Secretariat, 1975–78; GS Op. Requirements and Dir, Heavy Weapons Projects, MoD, 1978–84; Vice Master-General of the Ordnance, 1984–86; Dir Gen. Weapons (Army), 1986–88. Hon. Col, 4th Regt RA, 1985–91. Chm., Kent SSAFA, 1990–. Chm., Bd of Govs, Fort Pitt Grammar Sch., 1990–. FBIM. *Recreations:* travel, opera, roses, campaign medals. *Address:* c/o Lloyds Bank, 18 Week Street, Maidstone, Kent ME14 1RW.
                              Died 16 March 1992.

SKINNER, Sir Thomas (Edward), KBE 1976; JP; Chairman, New Zealand Shipping Line, 1973–82; *b* 18 April 1909; *s* of Thomas Edward Skinner and Alice Skinner; *m* 1942, Mary Ethel Yardley; two *s* one *d. Educ:* Bayfield District Sch. Pres., NZ Fedn of Labour, 1963–79. Chairman: The Shipping Corp. of New Zealand Ltd, 1973–82; Container Terminals Ltd, 1975–82. Chm., St John Ambulance Trust Bd, Auckland, 1973–; KStJ 1970. JP New Zealand, 1943. *Recreations:* racing, boating, fishing. *Address:* 5 Dudley Road, Mission Bay, Auckland 5, New Zealand. *T:* 587–571. *Clubs:* Avondale Jockey (New Zealand); Auckland Branch, International Lions.
                              Died 11 Nov. 1991.

SKONE JAMES, Edmund Purcell; barrister; *b* 14 June 1927; *s* of Francis Edmund Skone James and Kate Eve Skone James; *m* 1952, Jean Norah Knight; one *s* one *d. Educ:* Westminster Sch.; New Coll., Oxford (MA). Served RASC, 2nd Lieut, 1946–48. Called to the Bar, Middle Temple, 1951; Bencher, Middle Temple, 1977. Mem., Whitford Cttee to Consider the Law on Copyright and Designs, 1973 (Report 1977). *Publication:* Copinger and Skone James on Copyright, 9th edn 1958–13th edn 1991. *Recreations:* gardening, walking, reading fiction. *Address:* 5 New Square, Lincoln's Inn, WC2A 3RJ. *T:* 071–404 0404.   *Died 23 June 1992.*

SLACK, Prof. Geoffrey Layton, CBE 1974 (OBE (mil.) 1944); TD 1946; Emeritus Professor, University of London, since 1977; Professor of Community Dental Health, 1976–77 (formerly Professor of Dental Surgery, 1959–76), The London Hospital Medical College; *b* 27 March 1912; *er s* of late Charles Garrett Slack and Gertrude Wild, Southport; *m* Doreen Percival Ball, *d* of late Walter Knight Ball and Mary Percival, Birkdale; two *d. Educ:* Preparatory school, Croxton and Terra Nova; Leys School, Cambridge. LDS (with distinction) Univ. of Liverpool, 1934; DDS Northwestern Univ., Chicago, 1947; FDSRCS, 1948; Nuffield Fellow, 1949; Dipl. in

Bacteriology, Manchester Univ. 1950; FFDRCSI 1978; FDSRCPSGlas 1979. TA, RASC, 1934–39; served in RASC, 1939–45; Major, DADST (T) Eastern Comd HQ, 1941–43; Lieut-Col ADST (T) HQ Second Army, 1943–44; Lieut-Col ADST (T) HQ 21 Army Gp, 1944–45. Private practice, 1934–39, 1945–46; Lectr in Preventive Dentistry, Univ. of Liverpool, 1948–51; Sen. Lectr, 1951–59; Head of Dept of Preventive and Children's Dentistry, 1948–59; Consultant Dental Surgeon, United Liverpool Hosps, 1948–59; Dean of Dental Studies, The London Hosp. Med. Coll. Dental Sch., 1965–69. Mem., Central Health Services Council, 1969–80; Mem., 1956–80, Chm., 1974–80, Standing Dental Adv. Cttee to DHSS; Mem. General Dental Council, 1974–79; Consultant Adviser, DHSS, 1974–77; Vice-Chm. Dental Health Cttee, British Dental Assoc., 1959. Hon. Dir, MRC Dental Epidemiology Unit, 1971–77; Hon. Consultant in Dental Surgery to the Army, 1975–77; Civilian Consultant in Community Dentistry to the RAF, 1975–83. Mem. Council, RCS, 1971–77; Mem. Board of Faculty of Dental Surgery, RCS, 1961–77 (Vice-Dean, 1968–69, Dean, 1971–74); Governor: The London Hosp. Med. Coll., 1963–69 (Fellow, 1986); The London Hospital, 1963–69. WHO Consultant, 1963–84. Fellow Amer. College of Dentists, 1963. RCS John Tomes Prize, 1960–62; RCS Charles Tomes Lectr, 1965. Hon. Dr of Odontology, Göteborg, 1974. *Publications:* (part-author) Dental Health, 1957; World Survey of Teaching Methods in Children's Dentistry, 1958; (with T. H. Melville) Bacteriology for Dental Students, 1960; (part-author) Demand and Need for Dental Care (Report to Nuffield Foundation), 1968; (part-author) Child Dental Health, 1969; (jt author) GSS Adult Dental Health in England and Wales in 1968, 1970; (ed) Dental Public Health, 1973, 2nd rev. edn, 1981; many contribs to medical and dental journals. *Recreations:* croquet, reflection on times past; formerly hockey (played Lancashire 1933–39, 1945–52 (57 Caps), North of England, 1935–39, 1945–52, England XI 1938–39). *Address:* 1 Treesdale Close, Birkdale, Southport PR8 2EL. *T:* Southport (0704) 64007. *Clubs:* Commonwealth Trust; Union (Pres., 1986) (Southport); Royal Birkdale Golf.

Died 5 June 1991.

SLATER, Gordon James Augustus; HM Diplomatic Service, retired; Secretary to Government, and Adviser to Foreign Affairs Department, Tuvalu, 1985–86; *b* 8 July 1922; *s* of William Augustus Slater and Edith Garden; *m* 1st, 1952, Beryl Ruth Oliver (marr. diss. 1968); one *s* one *d*; 2nd, 1976, Gina Michelle Lambert (marr. diss. 1988); one *d*; 3rd, 1993, Mrs Barbara Betty Buckley; one step *s*. *Educ:* Sydney, Australia. Foreign and Commonwealth Office (formerly Commonwealth Relations Office), 1958–82; High Comr, Honiara, Solomon Is, 1978–82. *Recreations:* sailing, diving, golf. *Address:* 69 Villiers Avenue, Surbiton KT5 8BE.   *Died 2 March 1995.*

SLEMON, Air Marshal (Charles) Roy, CB 1946; CBE 1943; retired from Royal Canadian Air Force, 1964; *b* Winnipeg, Manitoba, Canada, 7 Nov. 1904; *s* of Samuel Slemon and Mary Bonser; *m* 1935, Marion Pamela Slemon, Bowmanville, Ont; one *s* two *d*. *Educ:* University of Manitoba (BSc). Lieut COTC (Army), Canada, 1923; Cadet Royal Canadian Air Force, 1923; Royal Air Force Staff College Course, England, 1938; Senior Air Staff Officer at Western Air Command Headquarters, Canada, 1939–41; commanded Western Air Command, Canada, for 5 months in 1941; Director of Operations at RCAF HQ Ottawa, 1941–42; Senior Air Staff Officer, No 6 (RCAF) Bomber Group, England, 1942–44; Air Vice-Marshal, 1945; Deputy AOC-in-C, RCAF Overseas, March 1945; commanded Canadian Air Forces preparing for the Pacific, 1945; Air Council Member for Supply and Organization, 1946; Air Council Member for Operations and Training, 1947–48; AOC Trg Comd, RCAF, 1949–53;

Chief of the Air Staff, Canada, 1953–57; Dep. C-in-C, N American Defence Comd (Canada-USA), 1957–64, retd. Exec. Vice-Pres., US Air Force Acad. Foundn Inc., 1964–81. Hon. LLD (Univ. of Manitoba), 1953; Hon. DMSc (RMC), Kingston, Ont, 1965. USA Legion of Merit, 1946; French Legion of Honour and Croix de Guerre with Palm, 1947. *Recreations:* golf, swimming. *Address:* 8 Thayer Road, Broadmoor Heights, Colorado Springs, Colorado 80906, USA.

Died 12 Feb. 1992.

SLIGO, 10th Marquess of, *cr* 1800; **Denis Edward Browne; Baron Mount Eagle,** 1760; Viscount Westport, 1768; Earl of Altamont, 1771; Earl of Clanricarde, 1543 and 1800 (special remainder); Baron Monteagle (UK), 1806; *b* 13 Dec. 1908; *er s* of late Lt-Col Lord Alfred Eden Browne, DSO (5th *s* of 5th Marquess) and Cicely, *d* of Edward Wormald, 15 Berkeley Square, W; *S* uncle, 1952; *m* 1930, José Gauche; one *s*. *Educ:* Eton. *Heir:* *s* Earl of Altamont [*b* 4 June 1939; *m* 1961, Jennifer June, *d* of Major Derek Cooper, Co. Donegal; five *d*]. *Address:* c/o Messrs Trowers & Hamlins, 6 New Square, Lincoln's Inn, WC2.

Died 11 Sept. 1991.

SLIMMINGS, Sir William Kenneth MacLeod, Kt 1966; CBE 1960; *b* 15 Dec. 1912; *s* of George and Robina Slimmings; *m* 1943, Lilian Ellen Willis; one *s* one *d*. *Educ:* Dunfermline High School. Chartered Accountant. Partner in Thomson McLintock & Co., Chartered Accountants, London, etc, 1946–78. Member: Committee of Inquiry on the Cost of Housebuilding, 1947–53; Committee on Tax-paid Stocks, 1952–53; Committee on Cheque Endorsement, 1955–56; Performing Right Tribunal, 1963–77; Crown Agents Tribunal, 1978–82; Chairman: Board of Trade Advisory Committee, 1957–66; Review Bd for Govt Contracts, 1971–81; Accounting Standards Cttee, 1976–78. Member: Council, Inst. Chartered Accountants of Scotland, 1962–66 (Pres., 1969–70); Scottish Tourist Bd, 1969–76; Review Body on Doctors' and Dentists' Pay, 1976–83. Independent Chm., Cement Makers' Fedn, 1977–80. Hon. DLitt, Heriot-Watt, 1970. *Recreation:* gardening. *Address:* 62 The Avenue, Worcester Park, Surrey KT4 7HH. *T:* 0181–337 2579. *Club:* Caledonian.

Died 27 Jan. 1995.

SMALE, John Arthur, CBE 1953; AFC 1919; Technical Consultant, Marconi's Wireless Telegraph Co. Ltd, 1957–62, retired; *b* 16 Feb. 1895; *s* of Charles Blackwell and Ann Smale; *m* 1920, Hilda Marguerita Watts; one *d* (one *s* killed on active service, RAF, 1941). *Educ:* Wycliffe Coll., Stonehouse; Bristol Univ. (BSc). Apprentice British Thompson Houston, Rugby, 1914; served European War, 1914–18, in RNAS; RAF, 1918–19; Engineer, Marconi's Wireless Telegraph Co. Ltd, 1919–29; Cable & Wireless Ltd, 1929–57, retired (Asst Engineer-in-Chief, 1935–48; Engineer-in-Chief, 1948–57). Chairman Cyprus Inland Telecommunications Authority, 1955–60, retired. FIEE 1941; Chairman, Radio Section of IEE, 1953; FIEEE 1958. *Recreations:* sport, music. *Address:* Cotswold, 21 Ilex Way, Goring-By-Sea, W Sussex BN12 4UZ.

Died 17 April 1993.

SMALL, Very Rev. (Robert) Leonard, CBE 1975 (OBE 1958); DD; Minister of St Cuthbert's Parish Church, Edinburgh, 1956–75; Chaplain to the Queen in Scotland, 1967–75, Extra Chaplain since 1975; *b* N Berwick, 12 May 1905; *s* of Rev. Robert Small, MA, and Marion C. McEwen; *m* 1931, Jane Hay McGregor (*d* 1979); three *s* one *d*. *Educ:* N Berwick High Sch.; Edinburgh Univ.; New Coll., Edinburgh. MA 1st cl. hons Classics; Sen. Cunningham Fellowship; studied in Rome, Berlin and Zurich; DD 1957. Ordained, 1931, to St John's, Bathgate; W High Church, Kilmarnock, 1935–44; Cramond Church, Edinburgh 1944–56. Moderator of the General Assembly of the Church of Scotland, 1966–67. Convener: C of S Cttee on Huts and Canteens for HM Forces, 1946–58; Cttee on Temperance and Morals, 1958–63; Social and Moral Welfare Bd, 1963–64; Stewardship and Budget Cttee, 1964–69; Mem., Scottish Adv. Cttee on Treatment of Offenders; Regional Chaplain (Scotland), Air Trng Corps; Hon. Vice-Pres., Boys' Brigade; awarded Silver Wolf by Chief Scout, 1990. Warrack Lectr on Preaching, 1959. Guest Preacher: Knox Church, Dunedin, 1950; Fifth Ave, Presbyterian Church, NY, 1960; St Stephen's Presbyterian Church, Sydney, 1962, 1971, 1976, 1981, 1987; Scots Church, Melbourne, 1971, 1976, 1979; St Columba's C of S, London, 1983–84; St Andrew's, Canberra, 1985. First Chm., Scottish Parole Bd, 1967–73; Chm., Parkinson's Disease Soc., Edinburgh; Chm., Age Concern, Scotland, 1980–83 (Hon. Pres., 1989). TV Series, What I Believe, 1970. *Publications:* With Ardour and Accuracy (Warrack Lectures), 1959; No Uncertain Sound (Scholar as Preacher Series), 1964; No Other Name, 1966; contribs to The Expository Times. *Recreations:* boating, walking; formerly Association football (Edinburgh Univ. Blue, captained team, 1927–28; played as amateur for St Bernard's FC, 1928–29; capped *v* England (Amateur), 1929; Chaplain, Co-optimist RFC). *Address:* 5 Craighill Gardens, Edinburgh EH10 5PY. *T:* 031–447 4243. *Club:* Royal Over-Seas League.

Died 8 April 1994.

SMALLPEICE, Sir Basil, KCVO 1961; chartered accountant and air/sea transport executive, retired; *b* Rio de Janeiro, Brazil, 18 Sept. 1906; *s* of Herbert Charles Smallpeice, bank manager, and Georgina Ruth (*née* Rust); *m* 1931, Kathleen Ivey Singleton Brame (*d* 1973), *d* of late Edwin Singleton Brame; *m* 1973, Rita Burns, *yr d* of late Major William Burns, MBE. *Educ:* Shrewsbury. BComm London. Articled to Bullimore & Co., Chartered Accts, 1925–30; Accountant of Hoover Ltd, 1930–37; Chief Accountant and later Sec. of Doulton & Co. Ltd, 1937–48; Dir of Costs and Statistics, British Transport Commission, 1948–50; BOAC: Financial Comptroller, 1950–56; Member of Board, 1953–63; Deputy Chief Executive, 1954–56; Man. Dir, 1956–63; Chm., Nat. Jt Council for Civil Air Transport, 1960–61; Man. Dir, BOAC-Cunard Ltd, from its inception in 1962 till end of 1963; Chairman: Cunard Steam-Ship Co. Ltd, 1965–71 (Dir, 1964; a Dep. Chm., 1965); Cunard Line Ltd, 1965–71; Cunard-Brocklebank, 1967–70; Cunard Cargo Shipping, 1970–71; ACT (Australia)/Australian Nat. Line Co-ordinating Bd, 1969–79; Associated Container Transportation (Australia), 1971–79; a Dep. Chm., Lonrho Ltd, 1972–73; Director: Martins Bank Ltd, 1966–69; London Local Bd, Barclays Bank, 1969–74. Member Council: Inst. of Chartered Accountants, 1948–57; Inst. of Transport, 1958–61; Brit. Inst. of Management, 1959–64 and 1965–75 (Chm., 1970–72; a Vice-Pres., 1972–); Pres., Inst. of Freight Forwarders, 1977–78. Mem., Cttee for Exports to the US, 1964–66. Administrative Adviser in HM Household, 1964–80. Chairman: The English Speaking Union of the Commonwealth, 1965–68; Leatherhead New Theatre (Thorndike) Trust, 1966–74; Air League, 1971–74. President: Friends of Cobham Cottage Hosp., 1987–; Friends of St George's Church, Esher, 1987–. Companion, RAeS, 1960–75; Liveryman: Guild of Air Pilots and Air Navigators, 1960; Coachmakers and Coach Harness Makers' Co., 1961. Key to the City of San Francisco, 1959. Order of the Cedar, Lebanon, 1955. Pioneers Award for contribs to develt of containerization, Containerization Inst., NY, 1981. *Publications:* Of Comets and Queens (autobiog.), 1981; various articles in the 1940s on the development of industrial and management accounting. *Recreations:* gardening, golf. *Address:* Bridge House, 45 Leigh Hill Road, Cobham, Surrey KT11 2HU.

T: Cobham (0932) 865425. *Clubs:* Athenæum, Boodle's; Melbourne (Melbourne, Australia).

Died 12 July 1992.

SMEETON, Vice-Adm. Sir Richard Michael, KCB 1964 (CB 1961); MBE 1942; DL; FRAeS 1973; *b* 24 Sept. 1912; *s* of Edward Leaf Smeeton and Charlotte Mildred Leighton; *m* 1940, Maria Elizabeth Hawkins; no *c*. *Educ:* RNC, Dartmouth. 800 Squadron i/c HMS Ark Royal, 1940–41; Assistant Naval Attaché (Air), Washington, DC, 1941–43; staff of Admiral Nimitz, USN, 1943–44; Air Plans Officer, British Pacific Fleet, 1944–45; Captain (Air) Med., 1952–54; Imperial Defence College, 1955; Captain, HMS Albion, 1956–57; Director of Plans, Admiralty, 1958–59; Flag Officer Aircraft Carriers, 1960–62; NATO Deputy Supreme Allied Commander, Atlantic, 1962–64; Flag Officer, Naval Air Command, 1964–65. Rear-Admiral, 1959; Vice-Admiral, 1962; retired Nov. 1965, at own request. Dir and Chief Exec., Soc. of British Aerospace Cos, 1966–79; Sec., Defence Industries Council, 1970–79. Mem. Council, Inst. of Dirs. DL Surrey, 1976. *Address:* St Mary's Cottage, Shamley Green, Guildford, Surrey GU5 0SP. *T:* Guildford (0483) 893478. *Club:* Army and Navy. *Died 29 March 1992.*

SMIJTH-WINDHAM, Brig. William Russell, CBE 1946; DSO 1942; *b* 21 Oct. 1907; *s* of late Arthur Russell Smijth-Windham; *m* 1934, Helen Teresa, *d* of late Brig. H. Clementi Smith, DSO; one *s* three *d*. *Educ:* Wellington College; Royal Military Academy, Woolwich. Commissioned Royal Corps of Signals, 1927; Mount Everest Expedition, 1933 and 1936; Mohmand Ops, 1935; Army Revolver VIII, 1937–39; British Pistol VIII, 1939; served War of 1939–45, Greece and Crete, 1941; Western Desert and Tunisia, 1942–43; France and Germany, 1944–45 (despatches); British Mil. Mission to Greece during Greek Civil War, 1948–49; Chief Signal Officer, Eastern Command and UKLF, 1957–60, retd 1960; ADC to the Queen, 1957–60. FIEE. *Address:* Estate Corner, Pitney, Langport, Somerset TA10 9AF. *T:* Langport (01458) 250525. *Died 12 Nov. 1994.*

SMIRK, Sir (Frederick) Horace, KBE 1958; Emeritus Professor, University of Otago, Dunedin, New Zealand (Professor of Medicine, 1940–61); Director, Wellcome Research Institute, 1962–68, engaged in honororary research 1969–76; *b* 12 Dec. 1902; *s* of Thomas Smirk and Betsy Ann (*née* Cunliffe); *m* 1931, Aileen Winifrede (*d* 1988), *d* of Rev. Arthur Bamforth and Martha Bamforth; three *s* one *d*. *Educ:* Haslingden Gram. Sch.; Univ. of Manchester. Gaskill mathematical schol., 1919; MB, ChB 1st Cl. Hons 1925; MD Gold Medallist, 1927; FRCP 1940; FRACP (Hon.) 1940. Med. Registrar, Manchester Royal Infirmary, 1926–29; RMO 1929; Dickenson Travelling Scholar, University of Vienna, 1930; Beit Memorial Fellow, successively Asst Depts of Pharmacology, and Medicine, Univ. Coll. London, 1930–34; Prof. of Pharmacology and Physician Postgrad. Dept, Egyptian Univ., 1935–39. Visiting Prof., Brit. Postgrad. Med. Sch., London, 1949; McIlraith Visiting Prof., Roy. Prince Alfred Hosp., Sydney, 1953; Holme Lectr Univ. Coll. Hosp. Med. Sch., 1949; Alexander Gibson Lectr, Edinburgh Coll. of Physicians, 1956; Dr N. D. Patel Inaugural Lecture, Bombay, 1959. Royal Australasian College of Physicians: Member Board of Censors, later Senior Censor, 1940–58; Vice-President, 1958–60; Chairman Clinical Reseach Committee, 1942, Psychiatric Research Cttee, 1957–60; Mem. Council, Med. Research Council of NZ, 1944–60; Mem. Expert Cttee on Hypertension and Ischaemic Heart Disease, WHO; Life Member, New York Acad. of Science, 1961; formerly Councillor, International Society of Cardiology (Mem. Hypertension Research Sub-Cttee); Hon. overseas Mem. Assoc. of Physicians of GB, 1967. Hon. DSc: Hahneman

Coll., Pa, 1961; Otago, 1975. Gairdner Foundn International Award for Research in Medicine, 1965. *Publications:* Hypotensive Drugs, 1956; Arterial Hypertension, 1957; Antihypertensive Agents, 1967; jointly: Modern Trends in Geriatrics, 1956; Current Therapy, 1956; Annual Reviews of Medicine, 1955; contrib. to med. jls, mainly on disorders of the heart. *Recreations:* reading, writing, travel. *Address:* 68 Cannington Road, Maori Hill, Dunedin, New Zealand.
Died 17 May 1991.

SMITH; *see* Walker-Smith.

SMITH, Rt Hon. Alick (Laidlaw) B.; *see* Buchanan-Smith.

SMITH, Arnold Cantwell, OC 1985; CH 1975; *b* 18 Jan. 1915; *m* 1st, 1938, Evelyn Hardwick Stewart (*d* 1987); two *s* one *d*; 2nd, 1989, Frances McFarland Lee. *Educ:* Upper Canada Coll., Toronto; Lycée Champoléon, Grenoble; Univ. of Toronto; Christ Church, Oxford (Rhodes Scholar for Ont). BA Toronto, 1935; BA (Juris) Oxon 1937 (MA 1968); BCL 1938. Editor, The Baltic Times, Tallinn, Estonia, and Associate Prof. of Polit. Econ., Univ. of Tartu, Estonia, 1939–40; Attaché, British Legation, Tallinn, 1940; Attaché, British Embassy, Cairo, 1940–43; part-time Lectr in Polit. Sci. and Econs, Egyptian State Univ., Cairo, 1940–42; transf. to Canadian Diplomatic Service, 1943; Sec., Canadian Legation, Kuibyshev, USSR, 1943; Sec., Canadian Embassy, Moscow, 1943–45; Dept of External Affairs, Ottawa, 1946–47; Associate Dir, Nat. Def. Coll. of Canada, Kingston, Ont, 1947–49; Mem. Canadian Delegns to various UN Confs, 1947–51; Alternate Perm. Deleg. of Canada to UN Security Coun. and Atomic Energy Commn, 1949–50; Counsellor, Canadian Embassy, Brussels, and Head of Canadian Delegn to Inter-Allied Reparations Agency, 1950–53; Special Asst to Sec. of State for External Affairs, 1953–55; Internat. Truce Comr in Indochina, 1955–56; Canadian Minister to UK, 1956–58; Canadian Ambassador to UAR, 1958–61; Canadian Ambassador to USSR, 1961–63; Asst Under-Sec. of State for External Affairs, Ottawa, 1963–65; Secretary-General of the Commonwealth, 1965–75; Lester B. Pearson Prof. of Internat. Affairs, Carleton Univ., Ottawa, 1975–81. Montague Burton Lectr in Internat. Relations, Leeds Univ., 1982; 75th Anniv. Lectr, Univ. of Alberta, 1983. Chairman: North-South Inst.; Hudson Inst. of Canada; Internat. Peace Acad., NY; Hon. Pres., Canadian Mediterranean Inst., 1981–; Trustee: Hudson Inst., Croton, NJ, 1976–81; Cambridge Univ. Commonwealth Trust, 1982–; Governor, Newsconcern Internat. Foundn; Mem. Univ. College Cttee, Univ. of Toronto, 1982–; Life Vice-Pres., Royal Commonwealth Soc. Hon. Fellow, Lady Eaton Coll., Trent Univ. R. B. Bennett Commonwealth Prize, RSA, 1975. Hon. LLD: Ricker Coll., 1964; Queen's Univ., Kingston, Ont, 1966; Univ. of New Brunswick, 1968; Univ. of BC, 1969; Univ. of Toronto, 1969; Leeds Univ., 1975; Trent Univ., 1979; Hon. DCL: Michigan, 1966; Oxon, 1975; Bishop's Univ., 1978. Zimbabwe Independence Medal, 1980. *Publications:* Stitches in Time—the Commonwealth in World Politics, 1981; The We-They Frontier: from international relations to world politics, 1983; (with Arthur Lall) Multilateral Negotiation and Mediation—Instruments and Methods, 1985; Tisserands de l'Histoire, 1987; reports; articles in learned jls. *Recreations:* fishing, reading, travelling, farming in France. *Address:* 260 Metcalfe Street, Apt 4–B, Ottawa, Ont K2P 1R6, Canada. *T:* (613) 2353073; 120 Rosedale Valley Road, Apt 609, Toronto, Ont M4W 1P8; (summer) Aux Anjeaux, Gavaudun, 47150 Monflanquin, France. *T:* 53409414. *Clubs:* Athenæum; Rideau, National Press (Ottawa); University, Arts and Letters (Toronto).
Died 7 Feb. 1994.

SMITH, Basil Gerald P.; *see* Parsons-Smith.

SMITH, Basil Gerrard, TD 1950; *b* 29 Jan. 1911; *m* 1938, Marjorie Elizabeth Artz; one *s* two *d*. *Educ:* Epsom College, Surrey; Merton College, Oxford (MA). Solicitor, 1938; called to the Bar, Gray's Inn, 1950. War Service, 1939–46; Hon. Lt-Col. Colonial Legal Service, Malaya, 1946–60: District Judge: Pahang, 1946; Selangor, 1947; Perak, 1948; President, Sessions Court: Ipoh, 1949; Georgetown, Penang, 1950; Federal Counsel and Deputy Public Prosecutor, 1953; Asst Legal Draftsman, 1954; Actg Legal Draftsman, 1955; Judge, Supreme Court, Federation of Malaya, 1956–60; Attorney-General, Southern Cameroons, 1960–61; Legal Adviser to the UK Commissioner, Malta, 1962–64; Legal Asst, Solicitor's Dept, Post Office, 1964, Senior Legal Assistant, 1967–69; Treasury Solicitor's Office, 1969–77; Adjudicator, Immigration Act, 1977–81. Law Reviser, Kiribati and Tuvalu, 1970, 1976, 1980 and 1981. *Address:* 7 Langley Grove, New Malden, Surrey KT3 3AL. *T:* 081–949 4366.
Died 27 March 1993.

SMITH, Campbell Sherston, (Campbell Williams); retired; *b* 24 April 1906; *s* of Herbert Smith and Carlotta Amelia Smith (*née* Newbury); *m* 1st, 1936, Leonora Florence Beeney (marr. diss., 1948); one *s*; 2nd, 1948, Gwenllian Elizabeth Anne Williams (marr. diss., 1963); one *s*; 3rd, 1964, Barbara Irene Winstone. *Educ:* City of London School. Squadron Leader, RAF, 1939–45 (Defence Medal). General Departmental Manager, Keith Prowse & Co. Ltd, 1932, Director and General Manager, 1936; Assistant Managing Director, Keith Prowse & Co. Ltd, 1945, Managing Director, 1951–54; Managing Director: Mechanical Copyright Protection Soc., 1945–57; Campbell Williams Ltd, 1960–75; Director: Performing Right Society, 1951–54; MEEC Productions Ltd, 1953–62; Proprietor, Mayfair Hotel, Worthing, 1964–75. Chm., Execs Assoc. of GB, 1939–40. Administrator of the Arts Theatre Club, 1954–62: *principal productions:* Saint Joan, 1954; The Immoralist, 1954; South, 1955; Waiting for Godot, 1955; Waltz of the Toreadors, 1956; The Bald Prima Donna, 1956; No Laughing Matter, 1957; The Balcony, 1957; The Iceman Cometh, 1958; The Imperial Nightingale, 1958; Madame de ....., 1959; Traveller without Luggage, 1959; Ulysses in Nighttown, 1959; A Moon for the Misbegotten, 1959; The Caretaker, 1959; The Naked Island, 1960; Three, 1961; Stop It Whoever You Are, 1961; The Knacker's Yard, 1962; Everything in the Garden, 1962. *Recreation:* theatre. *Address:* 32 Wordsworth Road, Worthing, West Sussex BN11 3NJ. *Clubs:* Garrick, Arts Theatre.
Died 22 Oct. 1992.

SMITH, (Charles Edward) Gordon, CB 1970; MD, FRCP, FRCPath; Dean, London School of Hygiene and Tropical Medicine, 1971–89; *b* 12 May 1924; *s* of late John A. and Margaret Smith, Lundin Links, Fife; *m* 1948, Elsie, *d* of late S. S. McClellan, Lorton, Cumberland; one *s* two *d*. *Educ:* Forfar Academy; St Andrews University. MB, ChB (with commendation) 1947; MD (with hons and Singapore Gold Medal) 1956. House Surgeon and Physician, Cumberland Infirmary, Carlisle, 1947–48; HM Colonial Medical Service, 1948–57: clinical appts Malacca, Kuala Lumpur, 1949–51; Virologist, Inst. for Med. Research, Kuala Lumpur, 1952–57; Sen. Lectr in Bacteriology, London Sch. of Hygiene and Trop. Med., 1957–61; Reader in Virology, London Sch. of Hygiene and Trop. Med., 1961–64; Director, Microbiological Research Estab., MoD, 1964–70. Chairman: Public Health Lab. Service Bd, 1972–89; Independent Commn on the Onchocerciasis Control Programme, 1979–81. A Wellcome Trustee, 1972– (Dep. Chm., 1983–). President: Royal Soc. of Tropical Medicine and Hygiene, 1975–77; Assoc. of Schs of Public Health in the European Region, 1979–81 (Pres.-elect 1977–79); Assoc. European Schs and Insts of

Tropical Medicine, 1988–89; Vice-Pres., Zoological Soc. of London, 1974–76, 1978–82, 1985–86. Prime Warden, Goldsmiths' Co., 1991–92. Chalmers Medal, 1961, George Macdonald Medal, 1990, Royal Soc. of Trop. Med. and Hygiene; Stewart Prize, BMA, 1973; Tulloch Award, Dundee, 1982. Hon. DSc St Andrews, 1975. *Publications:* papers mainly on tropical diseases and third world development. *Recreations:* gardening, golf. *Address:* Wild Close, Woodgreen, Fordingbridge, Hants SP6 2QX. *Clubs:* Savile; Bramshaw Golf.   *Died 4 Aug. 1991.*

SMITH, Dr Charles Stuart, FEng 1985; FRINA; Head of Structures Research, Admiralty Research Establishment, since 1982; *b* 21 April 1936; *s* of Ebenezer and Mary Smith; *m* 1962, Colette Marie Claude Paulicand; one *s* three *d. Educ:* George Watson's College; Glasgow University (BSc, PhD, DSc). MIStructE. Joined Naval Construction Research Establishment, 1962; Head of Ship Structures Division, 1974. Gold Medal, 1976, Silver Medal, 1987, Bronze Medals, 1973, 1983, 1985, RINA; James Alfred Ewing Medal, ICE and Royal Society, 1989. *Publication:* Design of Marine Structures in Composite Materials, 1990. *Recreations:* squash, sailing, ski-ing. *Address:* Admiralty Research Establishment, St Leonard's Hill, Dunfermline, Fife KY11 5PW.

Died 13 July 1991.

SMITH, Cyril Robert, OBE 1945; consultant and lecturer; *b* 28 Dec. 1907; *s* of late Robert Smith and Rose Smith (*née* Sommerville); *m* 1933, Margaret Jane Kathleen Gwladys Hughes; two *s. Educ:* Whitgift; Queen Mary's Coll., Univ. of London. Served in Army, Europe, N Africa, 1939–45 (despatches, OBE; Col). Entered PO as Asst Traffic Supt Telephones, 1927; Asst Inspector, Telephone Traffic PO Headquarters, 1930; Asst Surveyor, Postal Services, 1935; Asst Principal, PO Headquarters, 1936; Asst Postal Controller, 1941; Instructor, PO Management Training Centre, 1954; Postal Controller, 1955; Asst Sec. i/c of Central Organisation and Methods Br., PO Headquarters, 1958; Director, Computer Development, 1965–67; Dir, National Data Processing, GPO, 1967–68. UN Advisor to Greek Govt on computers in public service, 1971–74. FBCS; FBIM. *Publications:* various papers on computer matters in Computer Jl, etc. *Address:* 64 Copse Avenue, West Wickham, Kent BR4 9NR. *T:* 081–777 1100.   *Died 20 April 1993.*

SMITH, Dan; *see* Smith, T. D.

SMITH, Maj.-Gen. Desmond; *see* Smith, Maj.-Gen. J. D. B.

SMITH, E(rnest) Lester, DSc; FRS 1957; formerly Consultant, Glaxo Laboratories, Greenford; *b* 7 Aug. 1904; *s* of Lester and Rose Smith; *m* 1931, Winifred R. Fitch (*d* 1989); no *c. Educ:* Wood Green County School; Chelsea Polytechnic. Joined Glaxo Laboratories, 1926, as first post after graduation; various posts in development, Fine Chemical Production (Head), then Biochemical Research; shared responsibility for production of penicillin during War of 1939–45; isolation of vitamin B_{12} accomplished, 1948. *Publications:* Vitamin B_{12} (in series of Biochemical Monographs), 1960, 3rd edn 1965; Intelligence Came First, 1975, 2nd edn 1990; Our Last Adventure, 1982; Inner Adventures, 1988; numerous research papers in various scientific journals, 1927–. *Recreations:* horticulture, classical music. *Address:* Tinkers, Kingshall Green, Bradfield St George, Suffolk IP30 0BA.   *Died 5 Nov. 1992.*

SMITH, Sir (Frank) Ewart, Kt 1946; MA; FRS 1957; FEng 1976; Hon. FIMechE; FIChemE; a past Technical Director and Deputy Chairman, Imperial Chemical Industries, Ltd; *b* 31 May 1897; *s* of late Richard Sidney Smith; *m* 1924, Kathleen Winifred (*d* 1978), *d* of late H. Rudd Dawes; one *d* (one *s* decd). *Educ:* Christ's Hospital; Sidney Sussex College, Cambridge (Scholar, 1st Class

Mech. Science Tripos, John Winbolt Prizeman). War service, 1916–19, RA. Various engineering and managerial posts, Billingham Works, ICI Ltd, 1923–42 (Chief Engineer, 1932–42); Chief Engineer and Supt of Armament Design, Ministry of Supply, 1942–45. Formerly Member: Advisory Council on Scientific Policy; Scientific Advisory Council of Ministry of Works and Ministry of Fuel and Power; British Productivity Council, Cttee on Scientific Manpower; Chairman, National Health Service Advisory Council for Management Efficiency (England and Wales), etc. Hon. Fellow Sidney Sussex College; Hon. Member, City and Guilds of London Institute; Hon. FIMS; Hon. Associate, Univ. of Aston. James Clayton Prize, IMechE. American Medal of Freedom with Palm, 1946. *Publications:* various technical papers. *Recreation:* gardening. *Address:* Parkhill Cottage, Sandy Lane, Watersfield, Pulborough, W Sussex RH20 1NF. *T:* Bury (01798) 831354.   *Died 14 June 1995.*

SMITH, Prof. George, MBE 1945; FRSE 1979; Chief of Surgery, Veterans' Administration Hospital, Fayetteville, North Carolina, 1982–89; Consultant Professor of Surgery, Duke University Medical Centre, since 1984; Regius Professor of Surgery, University of Aberdeen, 1962–82, then Emeritus; *b* 4 June 1919; *s* of late John Shand Smith and Lilimina Myles Mathers Smith; *m* 1951, Vivienne Marie Tuck, BA, Wooster, Ohio, USA, *d* of Rev. Robert Sidney Tuck, DD; two *s* one *d. Educ:* Grove Academy; Queen's College, Univ. of St Andrews. MB, ChB (St Andrews) 1942, MD (Hons) 1957, ChM (Hons) 1959; DSc (Glasgow) 1964; FRFPSG 1949; FRCSE 1949; FACS 1958; FACCP 1963; FInstBiol 1963. Commonwealth Fund Fellow, 1949–51 (Johns Hopkins, Columbia and Western Reserve Medical Schools); formerly Reader in Cardiovascular Surgery, Univ. of Glasgow; Dean of Medicine, Aberdeen Univ., 1974–76, Dir, Inst. of Environmental and Offshore Med., 1975–78. Chm., NE Region Med. Postgrad. Cttee; Civil Consultant in surgery to RN; Governor: Robert Gordon's Colleges; Amer. Coll. of Chest Physicians. Mason: Scottish Rite, 32°; York Rite; Knight Templar; Sudan Shrine. *Publications:* (ed jtly) Resuscitation and Cardiac Pacing, 1965; The Biology of Affluence, 1972; The Staphylococci, 1981; (ed) Proceedings, 6th International Congress on Hyperbaric Medicine, 1979; sections in books and some 300 papers, mainly on cardio-vascular, respiratory, bacteriological and educnl topics. *Recreations:* sailing, gardening, golf. *Address:* 110 Ann Street, Beaufort, NC 28516, USA. *T:* (919) 7287274. *Clubs:* Naval; RNVR (Glasgow); Fort Bragg Officers (Fayetteville).

Died 12 Sept. 1994.

SMITH, George; Director-General of Ordnance Factories (Finance), 1972–76; *b* 13 Dec. 1914; *s* of George Smith and Catherine Annie Smith (*née* Ashby); *m* 1939, Alice May Smith; two *s. Educ:* Alderman Newton's Sch., Leicester. FCCA. Various posts in industry, 1929–40; joined Min. of Supply, 1940; various posts in Royal Ordnance Factories, 1940–52; Asst Dir of Ordnance Factories (Accounts), 1952; Civil Asst, ROF Woolwich, 1958; Dir of Ordnance Factories (Accounts), 1962. *Recreations:* gardening, walking, bowls. *Address:* 14 Blenheim Gardens, Sanderstead, Surrey CR2 9AA. *T:* 0181–657 5826.   *Died 25 May 1994.*

SMITH, Gordon; *see* Smith, C. E. G.

SMITH, Hon. Sir James (Alfred), Kt 1979; CBE 1964; TD; President of Court of Appeal for Belize, 1984–89; Member of the Court of Appeal for Turks and Caicos Islands, 1981–89; *b* Llandyssul, Cardiganshire, 11 May 1913; *s* of late Charles Silas and Elizabeth Smith (*née* Williams), Timberdine, Lampeter, Cardiganshire. *Educ:* Christ Coll., Brecon. Solicitor of the Supreme Court, 1937;

called to the Bar, Lincoln's Inn, 1949. Served War of 1939–45: various Army Staff appointments; on staff of Supreme Allied Commander, South-East Asia, with rank of Major, 1944–45. Appointed to Colonial Legal Service, as Resident Magistrate, Nigeria, 1946; Chief Magistrate, 1951; Chief Registrar of the Supreme Court, Nigeria, 1953; Puisne Judge, Nigeria, 1955; Judge, High Court, Northern Nigeria, 1955; Senior Puisne Judge, High Court, N Nigeria, 1960–65; Puisne Judge, Supreme Court, Bahamas, 1965–75, Sen. Justice, 1975–78, Chief Justice, 1978–80; Justice of Appeal: for Bermuda, 1980–84; for Bahamas, 1981–83; for Belize, 1981–84. Pres., Commn of Inquiry into transshipment of drugs through Bahamas to USA, 1983–84. *Address:* PO Box CB 11508, Cable Beach, Nassau, Bahamas. *Clubs:* Naval and Military; Lyford Cay (Nassau).   *Died 3 June 1993.*

SMITH, Maj.-Gen. (James) Desmond (Blaise), CBE 1944; DSO 1944; CD 1948; Chairman: Blaise Investments Ltd; Desmond Smith Investments Ltd; Dashabel Properties and Interiors Ltd; Member, Commonwealth War Graves Commission, since 1986; *b* 7 Oct. 1911; *s* of William George Smith, Ottawa, Canada; *m* 1st, 1937, Miriam Irene Blackburn (*d* 1969); two *s*; 2nd, 1979, Mrs Belle Shenkman, Ottawa. *Educ:* Ottawa University, Canada; Royal Military College, Canada. Joined Canadian Army, Royal Canadian Dragoons, 1933; National Defence HQ, Ottawa, as Assistant Field Officer in Bde Waiting to Governor-General of Canada, 1939; served War of 1939–45, in England, Italy and NW Europe holding following commands and appts: CO Royal Canadian Dragoons; Comdr: 4th Cdn Armoured Bde; 5th Cdn Armoured Bde; 1st Cdn Inf. Bde; 5th Cdn Armoured Div.; 1st Cdn Inf. Div.; Chief of Staff, 1st Cdn Corps; Comdt Canadian Army Staff Coll., 1946; Imp. Defence Coll., 1947; Sec. Chiefs of Staff Cttee, 1948–50; Military Sec. Cdn Cabinet Defence Cttee, 1948–50; QMG, Canadian Army, 1951; Chairman, Canadian Joint Staff, London, 1951–54; Commandant, National Defence College of Canada, 1954–58; Adjutant-General of the Canadian Army, 1958–62. Colonel, HM Regt of Canadian Guards, 1961–66. Director, numerous cos; Chm. and Chief Exec. Officer, Pillar Engineering Ltd, 1966–82 (Queen's Award for Export Achievement, 1979); Dir, RTZ Pillar, 1973–82. Vice Pres., Engrg Assoc. of GB, 1974–77; Chairman: Nat. Export Cttee, EIA, 1977–81; Nat. Engrg Marketing Award Cttee, 1978–81; Sec. Gen., Canada Meml Foundn, 1988–90. Freedom, City of London, 1954. Croix de Guerre, 1944, Chevalier, Legion of Honour, 1944 (France); Comdr Military Order of Italy, 1944; Officer Legion of Merit (USA), 1944; Order of Valour (Greece), 1945. KStJ 1961 (CStJ 1952); KLJ 1985. *Recreations:* shooting, tennis, ski-ing, painting. *Address:* 50 Albert Court, SW7 2BH. *Clubs:* Mark's, Annabel's, Harry's Bar.
                                          Died 11 Oct. 1991.

SMITH, Rt Hon. John, PC 1978; QC (Scot.) 1983; MP (Lab) Monklands East, since 1983 (Lanarkshire North, 1970–83); Leader of the Labour Party, and Leader of the Opposition, since 1992; *b* 13 Sept. 1938; *s* of late Archibald Leitch Smith and of Sarah Cameron Smith; *m* 1967, Elizabeth Margaret Bennett; three *d*. *Educ:* Dunoon Grammar Sch.; Glasgow Univ. (MA, LLB). Advocate, Scottish Bar, 1967–. Contested Fife, 1961 by-election and 1964. PPS to Sec. of State for Scotland, Feb.-Oct. 1974; Parly Under-Sec. of State, 1974–75, Minister of State, 1975–76, Dept of Energy; Minister of State, Privy Council Office, 1976–78; Sec. of State for Trade, 1978–79; principal Opposition Spokesman on Trade, Prices and Consumer Protection, 1979–82, on Energy, 1982–83, on Employment, 1983–84, on Trade and Industry, 1984–87, on Treasury and Economic Affairs, 1987–92. Nat. Pres., Industrial Common Ownership Movement, 1988–; Vice-Pres., Socialist Internat., 1992–. Vice-Chm., Britain-

Russia Centre (formerly GB-USSR Assoc.), 1985–. Gov., Ditchley Foundn, 1987–. Hon. Bencher, Inner Temple, 1993. Winner, Observer Mace, Nat. Debating Tournament, 1962. *Recreations:* opera, hill-walking. *Address:* 21 Cluny Drive, Edinburgh EH10 6DW. *T:* 031–447 3667.
                                          Died 12 May 1994.

SMITH, Rev. John Sandwith B.; *see* Boys Smith.

SMITH, Sir John (Wilson), Kt 1990; CBE 1982; JP; DL; Chairman, Sports Council, 1985–89 (Member, 1980–89); *b* 6 Nov. 1920; *s* of Robert Henry Smith, JP and Edith (*née* Wilson); *m* 1946, Doris Mabel Parfitt; one *s*. *Educ:* Oulton High School, Liverpool. Director: Tetley Walker Ltd, 1966–77; First Castle Electronics plc, 1978–. Member: Football Trust, 1980–92; Football Assoc., 1981–86; Dir, Football League, 1981–86 (Mem., Restructuring Cttee, 1982); Chairman: Liverpool FC, 1973–90; Duke of Edinburgh's Merseyside Industrial Award Council, 1977–; Cttee of Inquiry into Lawn Tennis (report, 1980); Anfield Foundn, 1984–; Dep. Chm., Merseyside Develt Corp., 1985–89. JP Liverpool, 1971; DL Merseyside, 1983. Hon. LLD Liverpool, 1993. *Recreation:* golf. *Address:* Pine Close, Mill Lane, Gayton, Wirral, Merseyside L60 2TG. *T:* 0151–342 5362. *Club:* Reform.   *Died 1 Feb. 1995.*

SMITH, His Honour Mark Barnet; a Circuit Judge, 1972–87; *b* 11 Feb. 1917; *s* of David Smith and Sophie Smith (*née* Abrahams); *m* 1943, Edith Winifred Harrison (*d* 1991); two *d*. *Educ:* Freehold Council Sch., Oldham; Manchester Grammar Sch.; Sidney Sussex Coll., Cambridge. MA (Hons) (Natural Sci.). Asst Examr in HM Patent Office, 1939 (and promoted Examr in 1944, while on war service); served War, RA (Staff Sergt), 1940–46; returned to Patent Office, 1946; called to Bar, Middle Temple, 1948; left Patent Office, end of 1948; pupil at the Bar, 1949. Temp. Recorder of Folkestone, 1971; a Recorder of the Crown Court, Jan.-Apr. 1972. *Address:* 4 Elm Gardens, Claygate, Esher, Surrey KT10 0JS.
                                          Died 15 Sept. 1994.

SMITH, Prof. Michael Garfield; Crosby Professor of Human Environment, Department of Anthropology, Yale University, 1978–86, then Emeritus; Senior Research Fellow, Research Institute for the Study of Man, New York, since 1986; *b* 18 Aug. 1921; *m* 1947, Mary F. Morrison; three *s*. *Educ:* University College London. BA 1948, PhD 1951; Fellow, 1985. Research Fellow, Inst. of Social and Economic Research, University Coll. of the West Indies, 1952–56, Sen. Research Fellow, 1956–58; Sen. Research Fellow, Nigerian Inst. of Social and Economic Research, Ibadan, 1958–60; Sen. Lectr (Sociology), Univ. Coll. of the WI, 1960–61; Prof. of Anthropology: Univ. of California, Los Angeles, 1961–69; University Coll. London, 1969–75. Special Advr to Prime Minister of Jamaica, 1975–78. Hon. LLD McGill, 1976; Hon. DLitt Univ. of W Indies, 1989. Order of Merit (Jamaica), 1973. *Publications:* The Economy of Hausa Communities of Zaria, 1955; Labour Supply in Rural Jamaica, 1956; (with G. J. Kruijer) A Sociological Manual for Caribbean Extension Workers, 1957; Government in Zazzau, 1800–1950, 1960; Kinship and Community in Carriacou, 1962; West Indian Family Structure, 1962; Dark Puritan, 1963; The Plural Society in the British West Indies, 1965; Stratification in Grenada, 1965; (ed with Leo Kuper) Pluralism in Africa, 1969; Corporations and Society, 1974; The Affairs of Daura, 1978; Culture, Race and Class in the Commonwealth Caribbean, 1986; Poverty in Jamaica, 1989; Pluralism, Politics and Ideology in the Creole Caribbean, 1991.   *Died 5 Jan. 1993.*

SMITH, Ralph G.; *see* Gordon-Smith.

SMITH, Sir Reginald V.; *see* Verdon-Smith.

SMITH, Sir Richard Rathborne V.; *see* Vassar-Smith.

SMITH, Sir Richard Robert L.; *see* Law-Smith.

SMITH, Sydney M.; *see* Macdonald-Smith.

SMITH, T(homas) Dan; Founder, New Directions, projects to assist ex-offenders, 1978; *b* 11 May 1915; *m* 1939; one *s* two *d.* City Councillor, Newcastle upon Tyne, 1950–65 (Chairman, Finance Cttee); Chairman: Northern Economic Planning Council, 1965–70; Peterlee and Aycliffe Develt Corp., 1968–70. Member: Nat. Sports Council, 1965–69; Royal Commission on Local Government, 1966–69; Shakespeare Theatre Trust, 1968–. Researcher for Amber Films, 1982–85. Consultant on the develt of an internat. science and technology paper, Change, 1982–86; Mem., Save British Science, 1990–. Lecturer, broadcaster on constitutional reform and other subjects, 1987–88. Chairman: Mill House Tenants Assoc., 1987–; Spital Tongues Community Assoc., 1987–; Vice Chm., Northern Reg., Nat. Pensioners Convention, 1993–; Mem. Exec., Newcastle Tenants Fedn, 1990–. Hon. DCL Newcastle University, 1966. *Publications:* Essays in Local Government, 1965; (contrib.) Which Way, 1970; Education, Science and Technology (paper to British Assoc. for Advancement of Science), 1970; An Autobiography, 1971. *Recreations:* painting, music, writing, sport. *Address:* 92 Millhouse, 5 Hunters Road, Spital Tongues, Newcastle upon Tyne NE2 4AQ.
Died 27 July 1993.

SMITH, Sir William Reardon Reardon-, 3rd Bt, *cr* 1920, of Appledore, Devon; Major, Royal Artillery (TA); *b* 12 March 1911; *e s* of Sir Willie Reardon-Smith, 2nd Bt, and Elizabeth Ann (*d* 1986), *d* of John and Mary Wakely; *S* father, 1950; *m* 1st, 1935, Nesta (marr. diss., 1954; she *d* 1959), *d* of late Frederick J. Phillips; three *s* one *d*; 2nd, 1954, Beryl, *d* of William H. Powell; one *s* three *d. Educ:* Blundell's Sch., Tiverton. Served War of 1939–45. *Heir: s* (William) Antony (John) Reardon-Smith [*b* 20 June 1937; *m* 1962, Susan, *d* of H. W. Gibson, Cardiff; three *s* one *d*]. *Address:* Rhode Farm, Romansleigh, South Molton, Devon EX36 4JW. *T:* Bishops Nympton (01769) 550371. *Club:* Cardiff and County (Cardiff).
Died 13 June 1995.

SMITHERMAN, Frank, MBE 1951; HM Diplomatic Service, retired; *b* 13 Oct. 1913; *s* of Lt-Col H. C. Smitherman and Mildred E. Holten; *m* 1937, Frances Ellen Rivers Calvert; one *s* one *d. Educ:* Sir Joseph Williamson's Mathematical Sch., Rochester. Indian Police, Burma, 1933; served in: Yenangyaung; Rangoon; Myitkyina; Sagaing; Thayetmyo; Thaton; served War of 1939–45 (despatches, 1945), Burma Army Reserve of Officers; Major 1944; joined Civil Affairs Service; Foreign Office, 1949; subseq. service in: Amoy; Cairo; Rome; Khartoum; Miami; Consul-General, Bordeaux, 1967–69; Counsellor, Moscow, 1969–70; Ambassador to Togo and Dahomey, 1970–73. *Recreations:* fishing, gardening. *Address:* Grange Cottage, Grange Road, New Buckenham, Norfolk. *T:* Attleborough (0953) 860452.
Died 5 March 1993.

SMITHERS, Prof. Sir David (Waldron), Kt 1969; MD, FRCP, FRCS, FRCR; Professor of Radiotherapy in the University of London, 1943–73, then Emeritus; Director of the Radiotherapy Department at the Royal Marsden Hospital, 1943–73; *b* 17 Jan. 1908; *s* of late Sir Waldron Smithers, MP and Marjory Prudence, *d* of Rev. F. Page-Roberts; *m* 1933, Gwladys Margaret, (Marjorie) (*d* 1992), *d* of Harry Reeve Angel, Officer (1st class) Order of White Rose of Finland; one *s* one *d. Educ:* Boxgrove School, Guildford; Charterhouse; Clare College, Cambridge; St Thomas's Hospital. MRCS, LRCP 1933; MB, BChir (Cantab) 1934; MD (Cantab) 1937; DMR (London) 1937; MRCP 1946; FRCP 1952; FRCR (FFR 1953); FRCS

1963. Pres. British Inst. of Radiology, 1946–47. President, Faculty of Radiologists, 1959–61. Kt Comdr, Order of St John of Jerusalem, Kts of Malta, 1973. *Publications:* Dickens's Doctors, 1979; Castles in Kent, 1980; Jane Austen in Kent, 1981; Not a Moment to Lose: some reminiscences, 1989; This Idle Trade: on doctors who were writers, 1989; papers on cancer and radiotherapy. *Recreations:* growing roses, book collecting. *Address:* Ringfield, Knockholt, Kent TN14 7JE. *T:* Knockholt (01959) 532122.
Died 20 July 1995.

SMITHERS, Hon. Sir Reginald (Allfree), Kt 1980; Judge of Federal Court of Australia, 1977–86; Additional Judge, Supreme Court of ACT and Supreme Court of NT, 1964–80; *b* Echuca, 3 Feb. 1903; *s* of F. Smithers, Hove, Brighton, England; *m* 1932, Dorothy, *d* of J. Smalley, Bendigo; two *s* one *d. Educ:* Melbourne Grammar School; Melbourne Univ. (LLB 1924). Admitted to Victorian Bar, 1929; QC 1951. Served War, RAAF, 1942–45 (Sqdn Ldr); Censorship Liaison Officer to Gen. MacArthur, 1944–45, New Guinea and Philippines. Judge of Supreme Court of Papua and New Guinea, 1962–64; Judge, Australian Industrial Court, 1965–77; Dep. Pres., Administrative Appeals Tribunal, 1977–80. Chancellor, La Trobe Univ., 1972–80 (DUniv 1982); Pres., Australian Assoc. of Youth Clubs, 1967–. *Address:* 11 Florence Avenue, Kew, Victoria 3101, Australia.
Died 2 Jan. 1994.

SMYTH, Margaret Jane, CBE 1959 (OBE 1955); retired; *b* 23 Sept. 1897; *d* of late Colonel John Smyth, IMS. *Educ:* Uplands School (Church Education Corporation); Clifton High School. Trained at Univ. Settlement, Bristol; Health Visitors Certificate; Roy. Sanitary Inst., 1918; Central Midwives Board, SCM, 1920; Maternity and Child Welfare Certificate, RSI, 1921; SRN, 1925, trained in Nightingale Trng School, St Thomas Hosp. Sister, St Thomas Hosp., 1926–34; Matron, St Thomas Babies' Hostel, 1934–37; Warden, St Christopher's Nursery Trng Coll., 1937–39; Dep. Matron, St Thomas Hosp., 1939–45; Supt, Nightingale Trng School and Matron, St Thomas Hospital, 1945–55; Chairman of the General Nursing Council for England and Wales, 1955–60; President Royal College of Nursing, 1960–62; Chairman, South West Metropolitan Area, Nurse Training Cttee, 1952–64; Mem., Kingston and Long Grove Hosp. Management Cttee, 1967–69. *Address:* 9 Stockbridge Gardens, Chichester, West Sussex.
Died 17 Nov. 1991.

SNELL, Frederick Rowlandson, MA, BSc; *b* 18 Sept. 1903; *s* of Rev. C. D. Snell; *m* 1928, Margaret Lucy Sidebottom; one *s* three *d. Educ:* Winchester College (Scholar); Oriel College, Oxford (Scholar). BA, 1925; BSc, 1927. Lecturer in Chemistry, St John's College, Agra, UP, India, 1927–32; Senior Science Master, Eastbourne College, 1932–38; Rector of Michaelhouse, Natal, SA, 1939–52; Founder and first Rector of Peterhouse, Rhodesia, 1953–67; Treasurer, Anglican Church in Central Africa, 1968–82. *Recreations:* walking, music. *Address:* Borradaile Trust, P/Bag 3795, Marondera, Zimbabwe.
Died 19 April 1991.

SNELSON, Sir Edward Alec Abbott, KBE 1954 (OBE 1946); Justice, Supreme Restitution Court, Herford, German Federal Republic, 1962–81; Judge, Arbitral Tribunal for Agreement on German External Debts and Mixed Commission, Koblenz, 1969–77; *b* 31 Oct. 1904; *er s* of Thomas Edward and Alice Martha Snelson; *m* Greer Garson, Hon. CBE (marr. diss.); *m* 1956, Prof. Jean Johnston Mackay, MA, 3rd *d* of Donald and Isabella Mackay; two *s. Educ:* St Olave's; Gonville and Caius Coll., Cambridge. Called to Bar, Gray's Inn, 1929; entered ICS 1929; served in Central Provinces, District and Sessions Judge, 1936; Registrar, High Court, 1941; Legal Secretary, 1946; Joint Secretary, Govt of India, 1947; retired, 1947; Official Draftsman, Govt of Pakistan, 1948;

Sec. Min. of Law, Pakistan, 1951–61, also of Parliamentary Affairs, 1952–58. Mem. Exec. Cttee, Arts Council of Pakistan, 1953–61. *Publication:* Father Damien, 1938. *Recreations:* sailing, music, theatre. *Address:* The Forge House, Binstead, Alton, Hants GU34 4PB. *Clubs:* United Oxford & Cambridge University; Challoner.
Died 8 Dec. 1992.

SNOY ET d'OPPUERS, Comte Jean-Charles; Grand Officier de l'Ordre de Léopold, Belgium; Grand Officier de l'Ordre de la Couronne, Belgium; Hon. KBE 1975 (OBE 1948); Member of Belgian Parliament, 1968–71; Minister of Finance, Belgium, 1968–72; *b* 2 July 1907; *s* of 9th Baron and Claire de Beughem de Houtem; created Count, 1982; *m* 1935, Nathalie, Countess d'Alcantara; two *s* five *d. Educ:* Collège Saint-Pierre, Uccle; University of Louvain; Harvard Univ. Secretary Société Belge de Banque, 1932; Attaché to Cabinet Minister of Economic Affairs, 1934; Directeur Ministry Econ. Affairs, 1936; Secrétaire Général, Ministère des Affaires Economiques, 1939–60; Président du Conseil de l'Union Benelux, 1945–60. War Service: Services de Renseignements et d'Action, 1940–44. Chairman, Four Party Supply Cttee, Belgium, 1945; Président du Conseil, Organisation Européenne de Coopération Economique, 1948–50 (OEEC in English); Chm., Steering Board for Trade, OEEC, 1952–61; Chef de la délégation Belge pour la négociation des Traités de Rome, 1957; Président, Comité Intérimaire du Marché Commun et de l'Euratom, 1957–58; Representant Permanent de la Belgique, Communauté Economique Européenne, 1958–59; Administrateur-Délégué de la Compagnie Lambert pour l'Industrie et la Finance, Brussels, 1960–68. Several foreign decorations. *Publications:* La Commission des Douanes, 1932; L'Aristocratie de Demain, 1936; La Profession et l'Organisation de la Production, 1942; Revue Générale Belge; La Libre Belgique. *Recreations:* shooting, tennis. *Heir: s* Bernard, Baron Snoy, *b* 11 March 1945. *Address:* Château de Bois-Seigneur-Isaac, 1421 Braine l'Alleud, Belgium. *T:* Nivelles 21.22.27. *Club:* Fondation Universitaire (Brussels). *Died 17 May 1991.*

SOBELL, Sir Michael, Kt 1972; Chairman, GEC (Radio & Television) Ltd, since 1968; *b* 1 Nov. 1892; *s* of Lewis and Esther Sobell; *m* 1917, Anne Rakusen; two *d. Educ:* Central 7118London Foundation Sch. Freeman and Liveryman, Carmen Co. Hon. FRCPath, 1981; Hon. Fellow: Bar Ilan Univ.; Jews' Coll.; Hon. Dr Science and Technol., Technion Inst., Haifa, 1980; Hon. Dr Bar-Ilan Univ. *Recreations:* racing, charitable work. *Address:* Bakeham House, Englefield Green, Surrey TW20 9TX. *Clubs:* City Livery; Jockey (Newmarket).
Died 31 Aug. 1993.

SOLÉ-ROMEO, Dr Luis Alberto; Ambassador Extraordinary and Plenipotentiary of the Oriental Republic of Uruguay to the Court of St James's, since 1987; *b* 31 Aug. 1934; *m* 1st; three *d*; 2nd, 1984, Mrs Mónica de Assumpçao de Solé-Romeo. *Educ:* Univ. of Oriental Republic of Uruguay (Dr in Law and Soc. Scis). Attorney Counsellor of the Government Exchequer, 1973–84; Dir, Maritime and Fluvial Matters Office, Min. of Foreign Affairs, 1985–87; Legal Diplomatic Counsel, Min. of Foreign Affairs, 1985–. Pres., Nat. Assoc. of Broadcasters, 1971–75; Dir Gen., Internat. Assoc. of Broadcasting, 1974–87; Dir, Correo de los viernes (weekly), 1981–85; Co-Dir, El Día (daily newspaper), Montevideo, 1985–86. Mem., Exec. Cttee, World Press Freedom Cttee, Washington, DC, 1978–. Gold Medal, Ethics and Permanent Cttee, Inter-Amer. Assoc. of Broadcasters, for professional ethics and defence of freedom of expression 1975–77, 1977. *Publications:* Bases for an Educational Policy for Private Broadcasting in America, 1971, USA 1976; Uruguayan Laws and Regulations on Broadcasting,

2 vols, 1974; (with Gonzalo Aguirre Ramírez) Broadcasting Law: some basic concepts, 1974; Preventive Control of the Exchequer, 1976; Freedom, essential for a Cultural Broadcasting, 1977; The Sex of the Angels: sketches on freedom, 1978; articles and essays in newspapers and jls. *Recreations:* reading, travelling, music, gardening, shooting. *Address:* 1 Campden Hill, W8. *T:* 071–727 6557. *Clubs:* Athenæum, Travellers', Les Ambassadeurs; Six Continents; Golf del Uruguay (Montevideo, Uruguay). *Died 20 Feb. 1993.*

SOLOMONS, Hon. Sir Adrian; *see* Solomons, Hon. Sir L. A.

SOLOMONS, Prof. David; Professor of Accounting in the University of Pennsylvania (Wharton School), USA, 1959–83, then Professor Emeritus; Chairman of Accounting Department, 1969–75; designated Arthur Young Professor, 1974; *b* London, 11 Oct. 1912; *e s* of Louis Solomons and Hannah Solomons (*née* Isaacs); *m* 1945, Kate Miriam (*née* Goldschmidt); one *s* one *d. Educ:* Hackney Downs Sch., London, E8; London School of Economics. BCom (London) 1932; DSc (Econ) (London), 1966. Chartered accountant, 1936; engaged in professional accountancy until Sept. 1939; enlisted in ranks on outbreak of war; 2nd Lieut, RASC, 1941; Temp. Captain, 1942; Petrol Supply Officer, HQ 88 Area (Tobruk), 1942; prisoner-of-war in Italy and Germany, 1942–45; Lectr in Accounting, LSE, 1946; Reader in Accounting, Univ. of London, 1948–55; Prof. of Accounting, University of Bristol, 1955–59. Visiting Associate Prof., University of California, 1954; Prof. at Institut pour l'Etude des Méthodes de Direction de l'Entreprise, Lausanne, 1963–64; Visiting Professor: Univ. of Auckland, NZ, 1967, 1991; Nat. Univ. of Singapore, 1984; Graduate Inst. of Business Admin, Chulalongkorn Univ., Bangkok, 1985 and 1986; Vis. Erskine Fellow, Univ. of Canterbury, NZ, 1976; AAA Distinguished Internat. Lectr, 1984; Lee Kuan Yew Disting. Visitor, Nat. Univ. of Singapore, 1986. Mem., AICPA Study on Establishment of Accounting Principles, 1971–72; directed (UK) Adv. Bd of Accountancy Educn Long-range Enquiry into Educn and Trng for Accountancy Profession, 1972–74; Dir of Res., Amer. Accounting Assoc., 1968–70, Pres., 1977–78. Mem., Financial Accounting Standards Adv. Council, 1982–85. Hon. DHL Widener, 1986; Hon. DSc Buckingham, 1987. AICPA Award for Notable Contribution to Accounting Literature, 1969; Jl of Accountancy Literary Award, 1979; AAA Outstanding Accounting Educator Award, 1980; Walter Taplin Prize, Accounting and Business Research, 1984; Internat. Award, ICAEW, 1989. Inducted into the Accounting Hall of Fame, 1992. *Publications:* Divisional Performance: Measurement and Control, 1965; (ed and contrib.) Studies in Cost Analysis, 1968; Prospectus for a Profession, 1974; Collected Papers on Accounting and Accounting Education (2 vols), 1984; Making Accounting Policy: the Quest for Credibility in Financial Reporting, 1986; Guidelines for Financial Reporting Standards, 1989. *Address:* 205 Elm Avenue, Swarthmore, Pa 19081, USA. *T:* (610) 5448193. *Died 12 Feb. 1995.*

SOLOMONS, Hon. Sir (Louis) Adrian, Kt 1982; Member since 1969, and Deputy President and Chairman of Committees since 1988, Legislative Council of New South Wales; Consultant, Messrs Everingham, Solomons & Co., Solicitors, since 1986 (Senior Partner, 1975–86); *b* 9 June 1922; *s* of George Albert Solomons and Katie Isabel (*née* Rowland); *m* 1944 (whilst on War Service), Olwyn Ainslie Bishop; two *s. Educ:* New England University Coll.; Sydney Univ. (BA *in absentia* 1945, LLB 1949). Admitted solicitor, 1949. National Country Party of Australia (later National Party), NSW: Mem., Central Exec., 1964–67; Vice Chm., 1967–69; Chm., 1969–74; National Pres.,

1974–80. Mem., Bd of Governors, Law Foundn of NSW, 1984–. *Recreation:* deep sea fishing. *Address:* Fairview, 17 Campbell Road, Calala, Tamworth, NSW 2340, Australia. *T:* (067) 65–9899. *Clubs:* National Liberal, Lansdowne; Tattersall's (Sydney); Tamworth (NSW).
Died 20 Dec. 1991.

SOMERFIELD, Stafford William; editorial consultant, since 1970; *b* 9 Jan. 1911; *m* 1st, 1933, Gertrude Camfield (marr. diss. 1951); two *d*; 2nd, 1951, Elizabeth Montgomery (*d* 1977), 3rd, 1977, Ferelith Hamilton. *Educ:* Ashleigh Road School, Barnstaple. Exeter Express and Echo, Bristol Evening World, Daily Telegraph, 1934–39; News Chronicle, 1939, until outbreak of War; Rifleman, Queen's Westminsters, 1939–40; Major, Gloucestershire Regt, 1945; News of the World: Features Editor, Asst Editor, Northern Editor, Dep. Editor; Editor, 1960–70; Chm., Dog World, 1982–91. *Publications:* John George Haigh, 1950; Banner Headlines, 1979; The Boxer, 1985. *Recreation:* pedigree dogs. *Address:* Ivy Lodge, Ivychurch, Romney Marsh, Kent TN29 0AL. *T:* Brookland (01797) 344240.
Died 13 Jan. 1995.

SOMERS, 8th Baron *cr* 1784; **John Patrick Somers Cocks;** Bt 1772; *b* 30 April 1907; *o s* of 7th Baron and Mary Benita (*d* 1950), *d* of late Major Luther M. Sabin, United States Army; *S* father, 1953; *m* 1st, 1935, Barbara Marianne (*d* 1959), *d* of Charles Henry Southall, Norwich; 2nd, 1961, Dora Helen (*d* 1993), *d* of late John Mountfort. *Educ:* privately; Royal College of Music, London. 2nd Music Master, Westonbirt School, 1935–38; Director of Music, Epsom Coll., 1949–53; Prof. of Composition and Theory, RCM, 1967–77. BMus, ARCM. *Publications:* (as John Somers-Cocks): Three Sketches for Oboe and Piano; New Year's Eve (song); The Song of the Redeemed (for chorus and orchestra); Sonatina for Oboe and Piano; Four Psalms (for two-part choir); Organ Sonata. *Heir: cousin* Philip Sebastian Somers-Cocks, *b* 4 Jan. 1948. *Address:* Dulas Court, Dulas, Herefordshire HR2 0HL.
Died 15 Feb. 1995.

SOMERS-COCKS, John; *see* Somers, 8th Baron.

SOMERVILLE, Sir Robert, KCVO 1961 (CVO 1953); MA; FSA; FRHistS; Clerk of the Council of the Duchy of Lancaster, 1952–70; *b* 5 June 1906; *s* of late Robert Somerville, FRSE, Dunfermline; *m* 1st, 1932, Marie-Louise Cornelia Bergené (*d* 1976), Aachen; one *d*; 2nd, 1981, Mrs Jessie B. Warburton, Sydney. *Educ:* Fettes; St John's Coll., Cambridge (1st cl. Class. Tripos, 1929); Edinburgh Univ. Entered Duchy of Lancaster Office, 1930; Ministry of Shipping, 1940–44; Chief Clerk, Duchy of Lancaster, 1945. Hon. Research Asst, History of Medicine, UCL, 1935–38; Chairman: Council, British Records Assoc., 1957–67 (Hon. Secretary, 1947–56); London Record Soc., 1964–84; Member: Advisory Council on Public Records, 1959–64; Royal Commn on Historical MSS, 1966–88. Hon. DLitt Lancaster, 1990. Alexander Medallist, Royal Historical Society, 1940. *Publications:* History of the Duchy of Lancaster, 2 vols, 1953, 1970; The Savoy, 1960; Handlist of Record Publications, 1951; Duchy of Lancaster Office-Holders from 1603, 1972; (joint editor) John of Gaunt's Register, 1937; contribs to historical journals, etc. *Address:* 3 Hunt's Close, Morden Road, SE3 0AH.
Died 16 July 1992.

SOMERVILLE, Maj.-Gen. Ronald Macaulay, CB 1974; OBE 1963 (MBE 1945); *b* 2 July 1919; 2nd *s* of late Rev. David Somerville and Euphemia Somerville; *m* 1947, Jean McEwen Balderston; no *c*. *Educ:* George Watson's Coll., Edinburgh. Joined TA, 1939; commnd RA, 1940; regtl and Staff War Service in UK, NW Europe and Far East, 1939–45 (MBE, despatches, 1945); psc 1944; jssc 1956; comd Maiwand Battery, Cyprus Emergency, 1957–59

(despatches, 1958); Bt Lt-Col, 1960; CO 4th Light Regt RA, 1963–65; Borneo Emergency, 1965; CRA 51st (H) Div., 1965–66; idc 1967; DQMG, BAOR, 1968–70; GOC Yorks District, 1970–72; VQMG, MoD, 1972–74; Chm., Logistic Reorganisation Cttee, 1974–75; retd 1975. Gen. Manager, Scottish Special Housing Assoc., 1975–83; Chm. of Dirs, Bldgs Investigation Centre Ltd, 1985–89. Hon. Col, 3rd Bn Yorkshire Volunteers, 1972–77; Col Comdt, RA, 1974–79. Comr, Royal Hospital, Chelsea, 1972–74; Chairman: Officers Assoc., Scotland, 1988–; RA Council for Scotland, 1975–79; President: RA Assoc., Scotland, 1978–; Scottish Union Jack Assoc., 1982–. Chm., West End Community Council, Edinburgh, 1980–83; Pres., Glasgow Soc. of Sons of the Clergy, 1987–91; Mem., RBL Scotland Housing Assoc., 1989–. CBIM 1984. Hon. MIH 1987. Kt Officer, Order of Orange Nassau, with Swords (Netherlands), 1946. *Recreations:* painting, golf, gardening. *Address:* 6 Magdala Mews, Edinburgh EH12 5BX. *T:* 031–346 0371; Bynack Mhor, Boat of Garten, Inverness-shire PH24 3BP. *T:* Boat of Garten (047983) 245. *Club:* New (Edinburgh).
Died 25 Jan. 1991.

SOMES, Michael (George), CBE 1959; Principal Repetiteur, Royal Ballet, Covent Garden 1970–84; *b* 28 Sept. 1917; British; *m* 1st, 1956, Deirdre Annette Dixon (*d* 1959); 2nd, 1964, Antoinette Sibley (marr. diss. 1973); 3rd, Wendy Ellis. *Educ:* Huish's Grammar Sch., Taunton, Somerset. Started dancing at Sadler's Wells, 1934; first important rôle in Horoscope, 1938; Leading Male Dancer, Royal Ballet, Covent Garden, 1951–68; Asst Director, 1963–70. *Recreation:* music.
Died 19 Nov. 1994.

SOREF, Harold Benjamin; Chairman and Managing Director, Soref Brothers Ltd, 1955–88; *b* 18 Dec. 1916; *o s* of late Paul Soref and Zelma Soref (*née* Goodman), Hampstead. *Educ:* Hall Sch., Hampstead; St Paul's Sch.; Queen's Coll., Oxford. Served with Royal Scots and Intell. Corps, 1940–46. Editor, The Debater (Britain's first inter-public schs magazine), 1934–35; Co-Editor, Equator, 1945–46; Founder and Editor, The Jewish Monthly, 1947–51. Contested (C): Dudley, 1951; Rugby, 1955. MP (C) Lancashire, Ormskirk, 1970–Feb. 1974. Delegate, first all-British Africa Conf. held Bulawayo, 1938, to form Africa Defence Fedn; formerly Vice-Chm., Monday Club and Chm., Africa Cttee, Monday Club; Mem. Council, Anglo-Jewish Assoc.; Founder Mem., Conservative Commonwealth Council. *Publications:* (jtly) The War of 1939, 1940; (with Ian Greig) The Puppeteers, 1965; numerous articles in press and periodicals. *Recreations:* research, reading, writing. *Address:* 20 Meriden Court, Chelsea Manor Street, SW3 3TT. *T:* 071–352 0691.
Died 14 March 1993.

SOUKOP, Wilhelm Josef, RA 1969 (ARA 1963); RBA 1950; FRBS 1956; freelance sculptor; Master of Sculpture, Royal Academy Schools, 1969–82; *b* 5 Jan. 1907; *s* of Karl Soukop and Anna Soukop (*née* Vogel); *m* 1945, Simone (*née* Moser) (*d* 1993); one *s* one *d. Educ:* Vienna State School; apprenticed to an engraver; Academy of Fine Art, Vienna. Arrived in England, Dartington Hall, 1934; taught at Dartington Hall, Bryanston and Blundell's Schools, 1935–45; moved to London, 1945, and taught at Bromley Sch. of Art, 1945–46, Guildford Sch. of Art, 1945–47; sculpture teacher, Chelsea Sch. of Art, 1947–72. Examr for Scotland, 1959–62. Sculptures for new schools in Herts, Leics, Derbs, Staffs, LCC; work for housing estates. Sculptures in museums: USA; Cordova Mus., Boston; Chantry Bequest; Tate Gallery; Cheltenham Mus. and Gall.; Collection of LCC Educn Cttee; work in many private collections in England, America, Canada, Europe. Archibald McIndoe Award, 1964. *Recreation:* gardening. *Address:* 26 Greville Road, NW6 5JA. *T:* 0171–624 5987.
Died 8 Feb. 1995.

SOUTHBOROUGH, 4th Baron *cr* 1917, of Southborough, Co. of Kent; **Francis Michael Hopwood;** *b* 3 May 1922; *s* of 3rd Baron Southborough and of Audrey (Evelyn Dorothy), Baroness Southborough, *d* of late Edgar George Money; *S* father, 1982; *m* 1945, Moyna Kemp (*d* 1987), *d* of Robert John Kemp Chattey; one *d. Educ:* Wellington College; Christ Church, Oxford. An Underwriting Member of Lloyd's, 1949–; Dep. Chairman, Glanvill, Enthoven & Co. Ltd, 1977–80 (Director, 1954); Chairman, Robert Woodson Ltd, 1970–72 (Director, 1950). Served War of 1939–45 as Lieut, The Rifle Brigade. *Heir:* none. *Address:* 50A Eaton Square, SW1W 9BE. *Clubs:* Brooks's, City of London. *Died 15 June 1992 (ext).*

SOUTHESK, 11th Earl of *cr* 1633; **Charles Alexander Carnegie,** KCVO 1926; Major late Scots Guards; Baron Carnegie, 1616; Bt (NS) 1663; Baron Balinhard, 1869; *b* 23 Sept. 1893; *e s* of 10th Earl of Southesk and Ethel (*d* 1947), *o c* of Sir Alexander Bannerman, 9th Bt, Elsick; *S* father, 1941; *m* 1st, 1923, HH Princess Maud (*d* 1945), 2nd *d* of HRH Princess Louise, The Princess Royal and 1st Duke of Fife; one *s*; 2nd, 1952, Evelyn, *e d* of Lieut-Colonel A. P. Williams-Freeman, and *widow* of Major Ion E. F. Campbell, DCLI. *Educ:* Eton; Sandhurst. *Heir: s* Duke of Fife [*b* 23 Sept. 1929; *m* 1956, Hon. Caroline Cicely Dewar (marr. diss. 1966), *er d* of 3rd Baron Forteviot, MBE; one *s* one *d*]. *Address:* Kinnaird Castle, Brechin, Angus DD9 6TZ. *T:* Bridge of Dun (067481) 209. *Died 16 Feb. 1992.*

SPAGHT, Monroe Edward, MA, PhD; Director: Shell Oil Co., USA, 1953–80 (Chairman, 1965–70); Royal Dutch Petroleum Co., 1965–80; various Royal Dutch/Shell companies, 1965–80, retired; *b* Eureka, California, 9 Dec. 1909; *s* of Fred E. and Alpha L. Spaght; *m*; two *s* one *d. Educ:* Humboldt State Univ.; Stanford Univ.; University of Leipzig. AB 1929, MA 1930, PhD 1933, Stanford Univ. (Chemistry). Research scientist and technologist, Shell Oil Co., 1933–45; Vice-President, Shell Development Co., 1945–48, President, 1949–52; Exec. Vice-President, Shell Oil Co., 1953–60, President, 1961–65; Man. Dir, Royal Dutch/Shell Group, 1965–70. Director: Stanford Research Inst., 1953–70; Inst. of International Education, 1953– (Chm., 1971–74); American Petroleum Inst., 1953–; American Standard, 1972–82; Belden & Blake Cos, 1984–; Mem. Adv. Bd, The Boston Co., 1979–80 (Dir, 1971–79). Chm., Internat. Adv. Bd of Chemical Bank, 1977–80; Mem., Internat. Adv. Cttee, Wells Fargo Bank, 1977–84. Trustee, Stanford Univ., 1955–65. President, Economic Club of New York, 1964–65. Mem., Nat. Acad. of Engrg, USA, 1969. Hon. DSc: Rensselaer Polytechnic Inst., 1958; Drexel Inst. of Technology, 1962; Hon. LLD: Manchester, 1964; California State Colleges, 1965; Millikin Univ., Illinois, 1967; Wesleyan Univ., Middletown, Conn, 1968; Hon. DEng, Colorado Sch. of Mines, 1971. Order of Francisco de Miranda, Venezuela, 1968; Comdr, Order of Oranje–Nassau, Netherlands, 1970. *Publications:* The Bright Key, 1965; Minding My Own Business, 1971; Here's What I Said, 1977; The Multinational Corporation, its Manners, Methods and Myths, 1977; The Long Road from Eureka, 1986; contribs to scientific journals. *Address:* 2 Lyall Mews, Belgravia, SW1X 8DJ. *Clubs:* Athenæum; Blind Brook Country (New York). *Died 27 June 1993.*

SPARROW, John Hanbury Angus, OBE 1946; Warden of All Souls College, Oxford, 1952–77; *b* New Oxley, near Wolverhampton, 13 Nov. 1906; *e s* of I. S. Sparrow and Margaret Macgregor; unmarried. *Educ:* Winchester (Scholar); New Coll., Oxford (Scholar). 1st Class, Hon. Mods, 1927; 1st Class, Lit.Hum. 1929. Fellow of All Souls Coll., 1929 (re-elected 1937, 1946); Chancellor's Prize for Latin Verse, 1929; Eldon Scholar, 1929; called

to Bar, Middle Temple, 1931; practised in Chancery Division, 1931–39; enlisted in Oxford and Bucks LI, 1939; commnd Coldstream Guards, 1940; Military Asst to Lt-Gen. Sir H. C. B. Wemyss in War Office and on Military Mission in Washington, Feb.-Dec. 1941; rejoined regt in England, 1942; DAAG&AAG, War Office, 1942–45; resumed practice at Bar, 1946; ceased to practise on appointment as Warden of All Souls Coll., 1952; Hon. Bencher, Middle Temple, 1952; Fellow of Winchester Coll., 1951–81; Hon. Fellow, New Coll., Oxford, 1956. Hon. DLitt, Univ. of Warwick, 1967. *Publications:* various; mostly reviews and essays in periodicals, some of which were collected in Independent Essays, 1963, and Controversial Essays, 1966; Half-lines and Repetitions in Virgil, 1931; Sense and Poetry: essays on the place of meaning in contemporary verse, 1934; Mark Pattison and the Idea of a University (Clark Lectures), 1967; After the Assassination, 1968; Visible Words (Sandars Lectures), 1969; (with A. Perosa) Renaissance Latin Verse: an anthology, 1979; Grave Epigrams and Other Verses, 1981; Words on the Air, 1981; (ed with John Gere) Geoffrey Madan's Notebooks, 1981; Leaves from a Victorian Diary, 1985. *Address:* Beechwood House, Iffley Turn, Oxford. *Clubs:* Garrick, Reform, Beefsteak. *Died 24 Jan. 1992.*

SPENCER, 8th Earl *cr* 1765; **Edward John Spencer,** LVO 1954; DL; Baron and Viscount Spencer, 1761; Viscount Althorp, 1765; Viscount Althorp (UK), 1905; President, Northamptonshire Association of Boys' Clubs; Deputy President, National Association of Boys' Clubs, since 1980 (Chairman, 1962–80); *b* 24 Jan. 1924; *o s* of 7th Earl Spencer, TD, and Lady Cynthia Elinor Beatrix Hamilton, DCVO, OBE (*d* 1972), *d* of 3rd Duke of Abercorn; *S* father, 1975; *m* 1st, 1954, Hon. Frances Ruth Burke Roche (marr. diss. 1969), *yr d* of 4th Baron Fermoy; one *s* three *d* (and one *s* decd); 2nd, 1976, Raine, *d* of late Alexander George McCorquodale and of Dame Barbara Cartland, DBE, and former wife of 9th Earl of Dartmouth. *Educ:* Eton; RMC Sandhurst and RAC, Cirencester. ADC to Gov. of South Australia, 1947–50; Equerry to the Queen, 1952–54 (to King George VI, 1950–52). Formerly Capt. Royal Scots Greys; Hon. Col The Northamptonshire Regt (Territorials), T&AVR, 1967–71; a Dep. Hon. Col, The Royal Anglian Regt, 1971–79. Chairman: SGBI, 1962–; The Nene Foundn, 1978–. Trustee: King George's Jubilee Trust; Queen's Silver Jubilee Appeal; Mem. UK Council European Architectural Heritage Year, 1975. CC Northants, 1952–81; High Sheriff of Northants, 1959; DL Northants, 1961; JP Norfolk, 1970. *Publications:* photographs for The Spencers on Spas, by Countess Spencer, 1983; Japan and the East (book of photographs), 1986. *Heir: s* Viscount Althorp [*b* 20 May 1964; *m* 1989, Victoria, *d* of John Lockwood; one *d*]. *Address:* Althorp, Northampton NN7 4HG. *T:* (estate office) Northampton (0604) 770006. *Clubs:* Turf, Brooks's, MCC, Royal Over-Seas League. *Died 29 March 1992.*

SPENCER, Prof. Herbert, MD London, PhD; FRCP, FRCS, FRCPath; Professor of Morbid Anatomy, St Thomas's Hospital Medical School, 1965–80, then Emeritus Professor; *b* 8 Feb. 1915; *s* of Hubert and Edith Maude Spencer; *m* 1940, Eileen Mabel Morgan; one *s* three *d. Educ:* Highgate Sch.; St Mary's Hosp. Med. Sch. Served War of 1939–45: Specialist Pathologist, RAMC, 1942–47. Reader in Pathology, St Thomas's Hosp. Med. Sch., 1954–65. Visiting Associate Prof. of Pathology, Yale Univ. Sch. of Med., 1961. Erasmus Wilson Lectr, RCS. Mem., Histopathology Unit, RCS/ICRF. Examiner: RCS, 1958–70; Univ. of London, 1974–77; Univ. of Liverpool, 1972–76; RCP, 1973–. *Publications:* Pathology of the Lung, 1962, 4th edn 1985; Tropical Pathology, 1973; contribs to numerous British and foreign med. jls and books. *Recreation:* woodwork. *Address:* Uplands

Cottage, Barnet Road, Arkley, Barnet, Herts EN5 3ET. *T:* 081–449 7030.   *Died 1 June 1993.*

SPENCER, Air Vice-Marshal Ian James, CB 1963; DFC 1941 (Bar 1943); *b* 6 June 1916; *s* of late Percival James Spencer; *m* 1940, Kathleen Jeune Follis, *d* of late Canon Charles Follis; two *s.* Commissioned 1937; War of 1939–45: bomber sqdns of No 2 Gp (despatches); RAF Staff College, 1948; Air Attaché, Berne, 1950–53; CO, Univ. of London Air Sqdn, 1954–56; Director of Plans Second Allied TAF, 1956–59; commanded RAF Benson, 1959–61; AOA, Transport Command, 1961–64; Dir of Personnel, MoD, 1964–65; AOA, Far East Air Force, 1965–67; retired 1968. Member: CPRE; Franco-British Soc.; Anglo-Swiss Soc.; MIMgt. Croix de Guerre, 1944, Légion d'Honneur 1945, France. *Recreations:* internat. affairs, the countryside.   *Died 5 May 1994.*

SPENCER, Sir Kelvin (Tallent), Kt 1959; CBE 1950; MC 1918; Chief Scientist, Ministry of Power, 1954–59, retired; awaiting ecological recycling; *b* 7 July 1898; *s* of Charles Tallent and Edith Ælfrida Spencer; *m* 1927, Phœbe Mary Wills (*d* 1989); one *s.* *Educ:* University College School, Hampstead; City and Guilds Engineering Coll., London Univ. Founder Mem., Scientific and Medical Network. FCGI 1959. Formerly MICE, FRAeS. Hon. LLD Exeter, 1981. *Address:* Wootans, Branscombe, Seaton, Devon EX12 3DN. *T:* Branscombe (029780) 242; Honey Ditches House, Seaton Down Road, Seaton, Devon EX12 2JD.
                    Died 28 Feb. 1993.

SPENCER, Oscar Alan, CMG 1957; economic consultant; Economic Adviser to Government of Seychelles, 1976–83; *b* Eastleigh, Hants, 12 Dec. 1913; *m* 1952, Diana Mary, *d* of late Edmund Walker, Henley-on-Thames; two *s* one *d.* *Educ:* Mayfield Coll., Sussex; London Sch. of Economics. BCom (Hons) 1936. Premchand Prize in Banking and Currency, 1936; John Coleman Postgraduate Scholar in Business Administration, 1936–37. Served War of 1939–45, Lt-Col (despatches twice). HM Colonial Service, 1945–60: Economic Adviser and Development Comr, British Guiana, 1945; also Comr, Interior, 1949; Economic Sec., Malaya, 1950; Member, 1951, Minister, 1955, for Economic Affairs; Economic Adviser, and Head of Economic Secretariat, Fedn of Malaya, 1956–60; Chm., Central Electricity Board, Malaya, 1952–55, 1956–60; UN Technical Assistance Service, 1960–76: Econ. Adviser to Govt of Sudan, 1960–64; Sen. Regl Advr on Public Finance and Hd of Fiscal Section, UN Econ. Commn for Africa, 1964–66; Financial Advr to Govt of Ethiopia, 1966–76; Dep. Chm., Seychelles Nat. Investment Corp., 1979–81. British Guiana Delegate, Caribbean Commn, 1948; Malayan Adviser to Sec. of State, Commonwealth Finance Ministers' Conf., 1951; Leader of Malayan Reps, Internat. Rubber Study Gp, London, 1952, Copenhagen, 1953; Malayan Deleg., Internat. Tin Conf., Geneva, 1953; Adviser to Malayan Delegation, London Constitutional and Financial Confs, 1956 and 1957. Comdr, Order of St Agatha, San Marino, 1944; Knight of the Order of Defenders of the Realm (PMN), Malaya, 1958. *Publications:* The Finances of British Guiana, 1920–45, 1946; The Development Plan of British Guiana, 1947. *Recreations:* swimming, history, fine wines (Confrérie de Tastevin de Bourgogne). *Address:* Gatehurst, Pett, near Hastings, East Sussex TN35 4HG. *T:* Hastings (0424) 812197. *Club:* East India, Devonshire, Sports and Public Schools.   *Died 11 Sept. 1993.*

SPENCER CHURCHILL, John George; *see* Churchill.

SPENCER WILLS, Sir John; *see* Wills.

SPENDER, Sir Stephen (Harold), Kt 1983; CBE 1962; CLit 1977; FRSL; poet and critic; Professor of English, University College, London University, 1970–77, then Emeritus; *b* 28 Feb. 1909; *s* of Edward Harold Spender

and Violet Hilda Schuster; *m* 1st, 1936, Agnes Marie (Inez), *o d* of late William Henry Pearn; 2nd, 1941, Natasha Litvin; one *s* one *d.* *Educ:* University College Sch.; University College, Oxford (Hon. Fellow, 1973). Co-editor Horizon Magazine, 1939–41; Counsellor, Section of Letters, Unesco, 1947; Co-Editor, Encounter, 1953–67. Fireman in NFS, 1941–44. Elliston Chair of Poetry, Univ. of Cincinnati, 1953; Beckman Prof., Univ. of California, 1959; Visiting Professor: Univ. of Connecticut, 1969; Vanderbilt Univ., 1979; Emory Univ.; Visiting Lecturer, Northwestern Univ., Illinois, 1963; Consultant in Poetry in English, Library of Congress, Washington, 1965; Clark Lectures (Cambridge), 1966; Mellon Lectures, Washington, DC, 1968; Northcliffe Lectures (London Univ.), 1969. Pres., English Centre, PEN Internat., 1975; Vice-Pres., RSL, 1987–. Fellow, Inst. of Advanced Studies, Wesleyan Univ., 1967. Hon. Mem. Phi Beta Kappa (Harvard Univ.); Hon. Mem. Amer. Acad. of Arts and Letters and Nat. Inst. of Arts and Letters, 1969. Queen's Gold Medal for Poetry for 1971. Hon. DLitt: Montpellier Univ.; Cornell Coll.; Loyola Univ.; Macerata Univ. *Publications:* 20 Poems; Poems, the Destructive Element, 1934; Vienna, 1934; The Burning Cactus, 1936; Forward from Liberalism, 1937; Trial of a Judge (verse play), 1937; Poems for Spain, 1939; The Still Centre, 1939; Ruins and Visions, 1941; Life and the Poet, 1942; Citizens in War and After, 1945; Poems of Dedication, 1946; European Witness, 1946; The Edge of Being, 1949; essay, in The God that Failed, 1949; World Within World (autobiog.), 1951; Learning Laughter (travels in Israel), 1952; The Creative Element, 1953; Collected Poems, 1954; The Making of a Poem, 1955; Engaged in Writing (stories), 1958; Schiller's Mary Stuart (trans.), 1958 (staged at Old Vic, 1961); The Struggle of the Modern, 1963; Selected Poems, 1965; The Year of the Young Rebels, 1969; The Generous Days (poems), 1971; (ed) A Choice of Shelley's Verse, 1971; (ed) D. H. Lawrence: novelist, poet, prophet, 1973; Love-Hate Relations, 1974; T. S. Eliot, 1975; (ed) W. H. Auden: a tribute, 1975; The Thirties and After, 1978; (with David Hockney) China Diary, 1982; Oedipus Trilogy (trans.), 1983 (staged, Oxford Playhouse, 1983); Journals 1939–1983, 1985; Collected Poems 1930–1985, 1985; The Temple (novel), 1988; Dolphins (poems), 1994. *Address:* 15 Loudoun Road, NW8 0LS. *Clubs:* Savile, Beefsteak.   *Died 16 July 1995.*

SPENSLEY, Philip Calvert, DPhil; CChem, FRSC; Editor, Tropical Science, since 1984; Director, Tropical Products Institute, Overseas Development Administration, Foreign and Commonwealth Office, 1966–81; *b* 7 May 1920; *s* of late Kent and Mary Spensley, Ealing; *m* 1957, Sheila Ross Fraser, *d* of late Alexander and Annie Fraser, Forres, Scotland; one *s* three *d.* *Educ:* St Paul's Sch., London; Keble Coll., Oxford (MA, BSc). Technical Officer, Royal Ordnance Factories, Ministry of Supply, 1940–45; Research Chemist, Nat. Inst. for Medical Research, MRC, 1950–54; Scientific Secretary, Colonial Products Council, Colonial Office, 1954–58; Asst Director, Tropical Products Inst., DSIR, 1958–61, Dep. Director, 1961–66, Director, 1966. Freelance consultant in post-harvest sci. and technol. and orgn of R&D, 1981–84. Mem., Panel of Chairmen, Sci. Div., Civil Service Commn, 1982–86; Mem. Council, Royal Institution, 1985–88 (Chm., Cttee of Visitors, 1959). Member: FAO/WHO/Unicef Protein Adv. Gp, 1968–71; Cttee on Needs of Developing Countries, Internat. Union of Food Science and Technology, 1970–78; Food Science and Technol. Bd, MAFF/ARC/Dept of Agric. and Fisheries for Scotland Jt Consultative Organisation, 1973–79; UK Rep., CENTO Council for Scientific Educn and Research, 1970–78. Member: Internat. Cttee, RSC, 1982–87; British Nat. Cttee for Chemistry, Royal Soc., 1986–89. Hon. Treas., Keble

Assoc., 1987–93. Received MRC/NRDC Inventors Awards, 1963 and 1971. Freeman, City of London, 1951. *Publications:* Tropical Products Institute Crop and Product Digests, vol. 1, 1971; various research and review papers, particularly in the fields of chemotherapeutic substances, plant sources of drugs, aflatoxin (name coined 1962), food losses, and work of Tropical Products Inst.; patents on extraction of hecogenin from sisal. *Recreations:* house and garden design, DIY, travel. *Address:* Hardy House, 96 Laurel Way, Totteridge, N20 8HU. *T:* 081–445 7895. *Clubs:* Athenæum, Royal Automobile; Island Cruising (Salcombe).   *Died 22 May 1994.*

SPERRY, Prof. Roger Wolcott, PhD; Hixon Professor of Psychobiology, 1954–84, Trustee Professor Emeritus, since 1984, California Institute of Technology; *b* 20 Aug. 1913; *s* of Francis Bushnell Sperry and Florence Kraemer Sperry; *m* 1949, Norma Gay Deupree; one *s* one *d. Educ:* Oberlin Coll. (Amos C. Miller Schol.; AB English 1935; MA Psych. 1937; Univ. of Chicago (PhD Zoology 1941). Nat. Research Council Fellow, Harvard Univ., 1941–42; Biology Research Fellow, Harvard Univ. at Yerkes Labs of Primate Biology, 1942–46; Asst Prof., Dept of Anatomy, Univ. of Chicago, 1946–52; Section Chief, Neurolog. Diseases and Blindness, NIH, 1952–53; Associate Prof. of Psychology, Univ. of Chicago, 1952–53. Fellow: Amer. Psycholog. Assoc. (Distinguished Scientific Contribn Award, 1971); Amer. Assoc. for Advancement of Sci.; Member: Nat. Acad. of Scis, 1960–; Pontifical Acad. of Scis, 1978–; Amer. Philosophical Soc., 1974– (Karl Lashley Award, 1976); Amer. Acad. of Arts and Scis, 1963–; (Hon.) Amer. Neurolog. Assoc., 1974–; Internat. Neuropsychology Soc.; Amer. Assoc. for Anatomists; Soc. for Developmental Biology; Amer. Physiological Soc.; Psychonomic Soc.; Soc. for Neuroscience (Ralph Gerard Award, 1979); Internat. Brain Res. Org.; Internat. Soc. of Developmental Biologists; Soc. of Sigma XI; Amer. Assoc. of Univ. Profs; Foreign Member: Royal Soc., 1976; USSR Acad. of Sciences, 1988. Hon. Dr of Science: Cambridge, 1972; Chicago, 1976; Kenyon Coll., 1979; Rockefeller, 1980; Oberlin Coll., 1982; Howard Crosby Warren Medal, Soc. of Exper. Psychologists, 1969; Calif. Scientist of the Year Award, Calif. Mus. of Sci. and Industry, 1972; (jtly) William Thomson Wakeman Res. Award, Nat. Paraplegia Foundn, 1972; Passano Award in Med. Sci., 1973; Claude Bernard Science Journalism Award, 1975; (jtly) Wolf Prize in Medicine, 1979; Internat. Visual Literacy Assoc. Special Award, 1979; Albert Lasker Med. Res. Award, 1979; Golden Plate Award of Amer. Acad. of Achievement, 1980; (jtly) Nobel Prize in Physiology or Medicine, 1981; Realia Award, Inst. for Advanced Philosophic Res., 1985; Mentor Soc. Award, 1987; Nat. Medal of Science, USA, 1989. *Publications:* Science and Moral Priority, 1982; jl articles and book chapters on re-education after nerve-endorgan transplants, chemoaffinity and cell adhesion in growth of brain connections, single-cell coding for position information, subpial slicing of brain cortex, split-brain surgery and theory, brain laterality, mind-brain relation and the consciousness revolution. *Recreations:* paleontology, ceramics, sculpture, Baja camping/boating/fishing, tinkering. *Address:* 3625 Lombardy Road, Pasadena, California 91107, USA. *T:* (818) 7930117. *Club:* Athenæum of Pasadena (Calif).
                Died 17 April 1994.

SPICER, (Sir) Peter James, 4th Bt *cr* 1906 (but did not use the title), of Lancaster Gate, Paddington; retired; *b* 20 May 1921; *s* of Captain Sir Stewart Dykes Spicer, 3rd Bt, RN, and Margaret Grace (*née* Gillespie) (*d* 1967); *S* father, 1968; *m* 1949, Margaret, *e d* of late Sir Steuart Wilson and Ann Mary Grace (who *m* 2nd, Sir Adrian Boult, CH); one *s* three *d* (and one *d* decd). *Educ:* Winchester Coll. (Schol.); Trinity Coll., Cambridge (Exhibr); Christ Church,

Oxford (MA). Served War of 1939–45 (despatches, 1944); Royal Sussex Regt, then RN (Temp. Lieut, RNVR). Trinity Coll., Cambridge, 1939–40; Christ Church, Oxford, 1945–47. Member of publishing staff, Oxford University Press, 1947–81. Co-opted Member, Educn Cttee of Oxfordshire CC, 1959–74 (Chairman, Libraries Sub-Cttee, 1961–74). Congregational Rep., British Council of Churches, 1963–72; Chm., Educational Publishers' Council, 1976–78. Trustee, Mansfield Coll., Oxford, 1988–. *Recreations:* theology, gardening, walking, sailing, music, large family gatherings. *Heir: s* Dr Nicholas Adrian Albert Spicer [*b* 28 Oct. 1953; *m* 1992, Patricia Carol, *d* of Warwick Dye; one *s*]. *Address:* Salt Mill House, Mill Lane, Chichester PO19 3JN. *T:* Chichester (0243) 782825.   *Died 30 Sept. 1993.*

SPIERS, Prof. Frederick William, CBE 1962; Professor of Medical Physics, University of Leeds, 1950–72, then Emeritus; *b* 29 July 1907; *er s* of Charles Edward and Annie Spiers; *m* 1936, Kathleen M. Brown; one *d. Educ:* Prince Henry's Grammar Sch., Evesham; University of Birmingham. 1st Class Hons Physics, 1929; PhD 1932; DSc 1952. Anglo-German Exchange Scholar, Univ. of Munich, 1930. Demonstrator in Physics, University of Leeds, 1931; Senior Physicist, General Infirmary, Leeds, 1935; Vis. Lecturer, Washington Univ., St Louis, USA, 1950; Chief Regional Scientific Advr for Civil Defence, NE Region, 1952–77; Hon. Director: MRC Environmental Radiation Unit, 1959–72; MRC Regional Radiological Protection Service, Leeds, 1963–70; Consultant to the Dir, NRPB, 1972–87; Pt-time Dir, Bone Dosimetry Res., Univ. of Leeds, 1972–78; Vis. Scientist, Argonne Nat. Laboratory, Univ. of Chicago, 1979. President, British Inst. of Radiology, 1955–56; Chairman: Hospital Physicists Assoc., 1944–45; British Cttee on Radiation Units and Measurements, 1967–77; Home Defence Scientific Adv. Standing Conference, 1972–77; Hon. Mem., Royal Coll. of Radiologists; Member: MRC Protection Cttee; Radio-active Substances Adv. Cttee, 1960–70; Internat. Commn on Radiation Units and Measurements, 1969–73; Statutory Adv. Cttee to National Radiological Protection Bd; Adv. Council on Calibration and Measurement, 1973–77. Silvanus Thompson Meml Lectr, British Inst. Radiology, 1973; Douglas Lea Meml Lectr, Inst. of Physical Sciences in Medicine, 1987. Röntgen Prize, 1950; Barclay Medal, 1970; Silver Jubilee Medal, 1977. FInstP 1970. *Publications:* Radioisotopes in the Human Body, 1968; contribs in: British Practice in Radiotherapy, 1955; Radiation Dosimetry, 1956, 1969; Encyclopedia of Medical Radiology, 1968; Manual on Radiation Haematology, 1971; articles on radiation physics and radiobiology in scientific journals. *Recreations:* photography, music, gardening. *Address:* Lanesfield House, Old Lane, Bramhope, near Leeds LS16 9AZ. *T:* Leeds (0532) 842680.   *Died 8 April 1993.*

SPIRO, Sidney, MC 1945; Consultant, Hambros Bank Ltd, since 1985; Chairman, Landor Associates (Europe) Ltd, since 1985; *b* Kroon, 27 July 1914; *s* of Marcus and Clara Spiro; *m* 1949, Diana Susskind; two *d. Educ:* Grey Coll., Bloemfontein; Cape Town Univ. (Law degree). RA in Middle East, Italy, 1939–45. Joined Anglo American Corp., 1953, Exec. Dir 1961–77, International Banking Consultant, 1977–; Man. Dir, 1969–71, and Chm., 1971–76, Charter Consolidated; Dir, Hambros plc, 1977–84. Dir, De Beers Consolidated Mines Ltd, 1970–. Founder Mem., Nat. Bd, Scripps Clinic and Res. Foundn. FRSA. *Recreations:* shooting, golf, tennis, music. *Address:* 9 Cedar House, Marloes Road, W8. *Clubs:* White's; Swinley Forest Golf.   *Died 2 Dec. 1991.*

SPOFFORD, Charles Merville, DSM and Purple Heart (US), 1945; CBE (Hon.) 1945; lawyer (US); Trustee: Carnegie Corporation of New York; Juillard Musical

Foundation; Director Emeritus: Council on Foreign Relations; Metropolitan Opera Association (Chairman Executive Committee, 1956–71, Member since 1971, President, 1946–50); Vice-Chairman and Director Emeritus, Lincoln Center for the Performing Arts, Inc.; *b* 17 Nov. 1902; *s* of Charles W. and Beulah Merville Spofford; *m* 1st, 1930, Margaret Mercer Walker (marr. diss. 1960); two *s* two *d*; 2nd, 1960, Carolyn Storrs Andre (*d* 1970); 3rd, 1970, Sydney Brewster Luddy. *Educ:* Northwest Univ.; University of Grenoble; Yale Univ. (AB 1924; Hon. MA 1956); Harvard Law Sch. JD 1928. Instructor, European History, Yale Univ., 1924–25, and sometime Alumni Fellow; practised law, Chicago, 1929–30, New York (Davis Polk & Wardwell), 1930–40, member of firm, 1940–50 and 1952–; Deputy US Representative, North Atlantic Council, and Chairman, North Atlantic Council Deputies, 1950–52; Member European Co-ordinating Cttee (US); resigned 1952, to rejoin law firm. Lieut-Colonel 1942, AFHQ Algiers; advr on econ. and supply, French N Africa and French W Africa, 1942–43; Chief of Planning Staff (for Allied Mil. Govt Sicily and Italy); Dep. Chief Civil Affairs Officer for Sicily and S Italy, 1943–44; AFHQ, Asst Chief of Staff, (G-5) Med. Theatre, 1944–45; War Dept as Military Advr to State Dept, 1945; Colonel, 1943; Brig-General, 1944. Asst to President and Special Counsel to American National Red Cross, 1946–50; also other former civic activities. Formerly Director: American Univ. in Beirut, 1957–63; Nat. Council, English-Speaking Union, 1955–64; The Distillers Co. Ltd, 1952–76; subsid. CIBA Corp., 1957–71; Inst. for Defense Analyses, 1960–70. Member Exec. Cttee, American Branch, International Law Association; former Member Exec. Council, American Society International Law, etc.; Trustee, The Mutual Life Insurance Co. of New York. Carnegie Lectr, Hague Acad. of Internat. Law, 1964. Hon. LLD Northwestern Univ., 1959. Comdr, Order of Nishan Iftikhar, Tunisia, 1943; Croix de Guerre with palm, France, 1945; Commander, Order of SS Maurice and Lazarus, Italy, 1945; Commander, Legion of Honour, France, 1952; Commander with Star, Order of the Falcon, Iceland, 1953; Grand Officer, Order of the Crown, Belgium. *Recreation:* golf. *Publications:* articles in journals. *Address:* (business) 1 Chase Manhattan Plaza, New York, NY 10005, USA; (residence) PO Box XX, Windmill Lane, East Hampton, New York, NY 11937. *Clubs:* Century Association, Links (New York); Maidstone (East Hampton).

Died 23 March 1991.

SPOONER, Edward Tenney Casswell, CMG 1966; MD, MA; MRCS, LRCP, FRCP; *b* 22 May 1904; *s* of William Casswell Spooner, MB, and Edith Maud Spooner, Blandford, Dorset; *m* 1948, Colin Mary Stewart. *Educ:* Epsom Coll.; Clare Coll., Cambridge; St Bartholomew's Hospital. Foundation Scholar of Clare Coll., 1923; House Physician, St Bartholomew's Hospital, 1927–28; Commonwealth Fellow, Harvard Medical Sch., 1929–31; Fellow of Clare Coll., 1929–47; Tutor of Clare Coll., 1939–47; University Demonstrator and Lecturer, Dept of Pathology, University of Cambridge, 1931–46; Professor of Bacteriology and Immunology, London School of Hygiene and Tropical Medicine, 1947–60, Dean, 1960–70. Temporary Major, RAMC, in No 1 Medical Research Section, 1942–43; Director, Emergency Public Health Laboratory, Cambridge, 1943–44. Editor, Journal of Hygiene, 1949–55; Member Medical Research Council, 1953–57; Chm., Public Health Lab. Service Bd, 1963–72; Member Council Epsom Coll., 1955–65. *Publications:* papers on tetanus, certain virus diseases and wound infection. *Address:* Ellergarth, Dalditch Lane, Knowle, Budleigh Salterton, Devon EX9 7AH.

Died 30 Aug. 1995.

SPRECKLEY, Sir (John) Nicholas (Teague), KCVO 1989; CMG 1983; HM Diplomatic Service, retired; Chairman, Natural Resources (2000) Ltd, since 1992; *b* 6 Dec. 1934; *s* of late Air Marshal Sir Herbert Spreckley, KBE, CB, and Winifred Emery Teague; *m* 1958, Margaret Paula Jane, *er d* of late Prof. W. McC. Stewart; one *s* one *d. Educ:* Winchester Coll.; Magdalene Coll., Cambridge (BA). Tokyo, 1957–62; FO, 1962–66; Dakar, 1966–70; Paris, 1970–75; Head of Referendum Unit, FCO, 1975; Counsellor and Head of Chancery, Tokyo, 1976–78; Fellow, Center for Internat. Affairs, Harvard Univ., 1978–79; Head of European Communities Dept (Internal), FCO, 1979–83; Ambassador to Republic of Korea, 1983–86; High Comr to Malaysia, 1986–91. Dir, First Korean Small Cos Fund, 1991–. Dir. Assoc. for Prevention of Addiction, 1983–. *Address:* 9 Wellesley Road, Chiswick, W4 4BS. *T:* 0181–994 5031. *Club:* Army and Navy.

Died 3 Dec. 1994.

SPRINGER, Sir Hugh (Worrell), GCMG 1984 (KCMG 1971); GCVO 1985; KA 1984; CBE 1961 (OBE 1954); Governor-General, Barbados, 1984–90; barrister-at-law; *b* 22 June 1913; 2nd *s* of late Charles W. Springer, Barbados, and Florence Springer; *m* 1942, Dorothy Drinan, 3rd *d* of late Lionel Gittens, Barbados, and Cora Gittens; three *s* one *d. Educ:* Harrison Coll., Barbados; Hertford Coll., Oxford (Hon. Fellow 1974). BA 1936, MA 1944. Called to Bar, Inner Temple, 1938. Practice at the Bar, Barbados, 1938–47; MCP, 1940–47, MEC 1944–47, Barbados; Gen.-Sec., Barbados Lab. Party, 1940–47; Organiser and first Gen.-Sec., Workers' Union, 1940–47; Mem., West Indies Cttee of the Asquith Commn on Higher Educn, 1944; Mem., Provisional Council, University Coll. of the West Indies, 1947; first Registrar, Univ. Coll. of WI, 1947–63; John Simon Guggenheim Fellow and Fellow of Harvard Center for Internat. Affairs, 1961–62; first Dir, Univ. of WI Inst. of Educn, 1963–66; Actg Governor of Barbados, 1964; Commonwealth Asst Sec.-Gen., 1966–70; Sec.-Gen., ACU, 1970–80. Mem., Bermuda Civil Disorder Commn, 1968. Chm., Commonwealth Caribbean Med. Res. Council (formerly Brit. Caribbean Med. Research Cttee), 1965–84; Past Mem., Public Service and other Commns and Cttees in Barbados, Jamaica and W Indies. Sen. Vis. Fellow of All Souls Coll., Oxford, 1962–63 (Hon. Fellow 1988). Vice-Pres., British Caribbean Assoc., 1974–80; Trustee, Bernard Van Leer Foundn, 1967–78; Barbados Trustee, Commonwealth Foundn, 1967–80, and Chm., 1974–77; Member, Court of Governors: LSE, 1970–80; Exeter Univ., 1970–80; Hull Univ., 1970–80; London Sch. of Hygiene and Tropical Medicine, 1974–77; Inst. of Commonwealth Studies, 1974–80. Trustee, Harlow Campus, Meml Univ. of Newfoundland, 1975–79. Jt Sec., UK Commonwealth Scholarships Commn, 1970–80; Exec. Sec., Marshall Scholarships Commn, 1970–80; Sec., Kennedy Memorial Trust, 1970–80; Chm., Commonwealth Human Ecology Council, 1971–84 (Hon. Pres., 1984–); Member: Council, USPG, 1972–79; Adv. Cttee, Sci. Policy Foundn, 1977–; Bd of Dirs, United World Colleges, 1978–90; Bd of Trustees, Sir Ernest Cassel Educational Trust, 1978–81; Pres., Educn Section, British Assoc., 1974–75; Mem., President's Cttee, Campaign for Oxford, 1988–; Chm., Jt Commonwealth Socs Council, 1978–80. Hon. Prof. of Educn, Mauritius, 1981. Hon. DScSoc Laval, 1958; Hon. LLD: Victoria, BC, 1972; Univ. of WI, 1973; City, 1978; Manchester, 1979; York, Ontario, 1980; Zimbabwe, 1981; Bristol, 1982; Birmingham, 1983; Hon. DLitt: Warwick, 1974; Ulster, 1974; Heriot-Watt, 1976; Hong Kong, 1977; St Andrews, 1977; Hon. DCL: New Brunswick, 1980; Oxon, 1980; East Anglia, 1980. KStJ 1985. *Publications:* Reflections on the Failure of the First West Indian Federation, 1962 (USA); articles and lectures on West Indian and Commonwealth Educn and Development, in:

The Round Table, Commonwealth, RSA Jl, Caribbean Quarterly, Internat. Organisation, Jl of Negro History, etc. *Recreations:* walking, talking. *Address:* Gibbes, St Peter, Barbados. *T:* 4222591. *Clubs:* Athenæum, Commonwealth Trust.
Died 14 April 1994.

SPRY, Brig. Sir Charles Chambers Fowell, Kt 1964; CBE 1956; DSO 1943; Director-General, Australian Security Intelligence Organization, 1950–70, retired; *b* 26 June 1910; *s* of A. F. Spry, Brisbane; *m* 1939, Kathleen Edith Hull, *d* of Rev. Godfrey Smith; one *s* two *d. Educ:* Brisbane Grammar School. Graduated Royal Military College, Duntroon. Served War of 1939–45 as Col, Australian Imperial Force in SW Pacific (DSO) and Middle East; Director of Military Intelligence, 1946–50. Hon. ADC to Gov. Gen., 1946. *Recreation:* golf. *Address:* 2 Mandeville Crescent, Toorak, Victoria 3142, Australia. *Clubs:* Melbourne; Royal Melbourne Golf.
Died 29 May 1994.

SQUIBB, George Drewry, LVO 1982; QC 1956; Norfolk Herald Extraordinary since 1959; Earl Marshal's Lieutenant, Assessor and Surrogate in the Court of Chivalry, since 1976; *b* 1 Dec. 1906; *o s* of Reginald Augustus Hodder Squibb, Chester; *m* 1st, 1936, Bessie (*d* 1954), *d* of George Whittaker, Burley, Hants; one *d*; 2nd, 1955, Evelyn May (*d* 1992), *d* of Frederick Richard Higgins, Overleigh Manor, Chester. *Educ:* King's School, Chester; Queen's College, Oxford (BCL, MA). Barrister-at-Law, Inner Temple, 1930; Bencher, 1951; Reader, 1975; Treasurer, 1976. Army Officers' Emergency Reserve, 1938. Deputy Chairman Dorset Quarter Sessions, 1950–53, Chairman, 1953–71; Junior Counsel to the Crown in Peerage and Baronetcy Cases, 1954–56; Hon. Historical Adviser in Peerage Cases to the Attorney-General, 1965–; Pres., Transport Tribunal, 1962–81; Chief Commons Commissioner, 1971–85. Member: Cttee on Rating of Charities, 1958–59; Adv. Council on Public Records, 1964–81; Council, Selden Soc., 1961–90 (Vice-Pres., 1969–72). FSA 1946; FSG 1973; FRHistS 1978. Master, Scriveners' Co., 1979–80. JP Dorset, 1943. *Publications:* The Law of Arms in England, 1953; Wiltshire Visitation Pedigrees, 1623, 1955; Reports of Heraldic Cases in the Court of Chivalry, 1956; The High Court of Chivalry, 1959; Visitation Pedigrees and the Genealogist, 1964, 2nd edn 1978; Founders' Kin, 1972; Doctors' Commons, 1977; Visitation of Dorset 1677, 1977; Precedence in England and Wales, 1981; Munimenta Heraldica, 1985; Visitation of Nottinghamshire 1662–64, 1986; Dugdale's Nottinghamshire and Derbyshire Visitation Papers, 1987; Visitation of Derbyshire 1662–64, 1989; Visitation of Hampshire and the Isle of Wight 1686, 1991; Visitation of Somerset 1672, 1992; Visitation of Oxfordshire 1669 and 1675, 1993; papers in legal and antiquarian journals. *Recreation:* genealogical and heraldic research. *Address:* The Old House, Cerne Abbas, Dorset DT2 7JQ. *T:* Cerne Abbas (0300) 341272. *Clubs:* Athenæum, United Oxford & Cambridge University.
Died 3 Jan. 1994.

SQUIRE, Warwick Nevison, CBE 1982; FRAeS; aviation and defence consultant; *b* 19 July 1921; *s* of late Alfred Squire and Elizabeth Timms; *m* 1947, Adelheid Elli Behrendt; one *d. Educ:* Cheltenham Higher Technical Sch. Apprenticeship, H. H. Martyn, Cheltenham, 1936–40; Aircraft Components Ltd (subseq. Dowty Gp), 1940–42; HM Forces and German Control Commn, 1942–46; Dowty Group Plc: Gen. Management, 1946–75; Group Dir and Man. Dir, 1975–83 and Chm., 1983–84, Aerospace and Defence Div. FRAeS 1980; FRSA 1982. *Recreations:* gardening, golf, cricket. *Address:* Highlands, Daisy Bank Road, Leckhampton Hill, Cheltenham, Glos GL53 9QQ. *T:* Cheltenham (0242) 521038.
Died 5 Feb. 1992.

STACEY, Prof. Maurice, CBE 1966; FRS 1950; Mason Professor of Chemistry, 1956–74, then Emeritus, and Head of Department, 1956–74, University of Birmingham; Dean of Faculty of Science, 1963–66; Hon. Senior Research Fellow, 1974–76; *b* 8 April 1907; *s* of J. H. Stacey, Bromstead, Newport, Shropshire; *m* 1937, Constance Mary (decd), *d* of William Pugh, Birmingham; one *s* two *d* (and one *s* decd). *Educ:* Adam's School, Newport, Shropshire; Universities of Birmingham, London and Columbia (New York). BSc (Hons) 1929, PhD 1932, Birmingham Univ.; DSc London, 1939. Demonstrator, Chemistry, Birmingham Univ., 1929–32; Beit Memorial Fellow for Medical Research, School of Tropical Medicine, London Univ., 1933–37; Travelling Fellow, Columbia Univ., New York, 1937; Lecturer in Chemistry, Univ. of Birmingham, 1937–44, Reader in Biological Chemistry, 1944–46, Prof. of Chemistry, 1946–56. Tilden Lecturer of Chemical Society, 1946; P. F. Frankland Lectr, Roy. Inst. of Chemistry, 1955; Ivan Levinstein Lectr, 1956, Jubilee Meml Lectr, 1973, Soc. Chem. Industry; Vice-Pres. Chemical Society, 1950–53, 1955–58, 1960–63, 1968–71. Associate Editor, Advances in Carbohydrate Chem., 1950; Editor, Advances in Fluorine Chem., 1960–73; Founder Editor, European Polymer Jl. Chief Scientific Adviser for Civil Defence, Midland Region, 1957–78; Vice-Pres., Home Office Sci. Council, 1974– (Mem., 1963–74); Governor, National Vegetable Research Institute, 1961–73. Former Member, Court of Governors: Univ. of Keele; Univ. of Warwick; Univ. of Loughborough; Gov., Adam's Sch., 1956–74; Mem. Council, Edgbaston High Sch. for Girls, 1963–84 (Vice-Pres., 1984–). Meldola Medal, Inst. of Chemistry, 1933; Sugar Research Prize of National Academy of Science, New York, 1950; John Scott Medal and Award, 1969; Haworth Meml Medal, 1970. Captain, 2nd in Command Birmingham Home Guard, Chemical Warfare School, 1942–44. Defence Medal, 1945. Visiting Lecturer, Universities of Oslo, Stockholm, Uppsala and Lund, 1949, Helsinki, 1955. Holder of foreign hon. doctorate and medals. Hon. DSc Keele, 1977. *Publications:* (with S. A. Barker): Polysaccharides of Micro-organisms, 1961; Carbohydrates of Living Tissues, 1962; about 400 scientific contribs to Jl of Chem. Soc., Proc. Royal Soc., etc, on organic and biological chemistry subjects. *Recreations:* foreign travel, athletics (Life Mem. AAA), horticulture, science antiques. *Address:* 12 Bryony Road, Weoley Hill, Birmingham B29 4BU. *T:* 0121–475 2065; The University, Birmingham B15 2TT. *T:* 0121–414 4360. *Club:* Athenæum.
Died 9 Oct. 1994.

STACK, Air Chief Marshal Sir (Thomas) Neville, KCB 1972 (CB 1969); CVO 1963; CBE 1965; AFC 1957; Extra Gentleman Usher to the Queen, since 1989 (Gentleman Usher, 1978–89); *b* 19 Oct. 1919; *s* of T. Neville Stack, AFC, pioneer airman, and Edythe Mary (*née* Lyster); *m* 1955, Diana Virginia, *d* of late Oliver Stuart Todd, MBE; one *s* one *d. Educ:* St Edmund's College, Ware; RAF College, Cranwell. Served on flying boats, N Atlantic, 1939–45 (despatches); Coastal Command, 1945–52; Transport Support flying in Far East (Malaya Ops) and UK, 1954–59; Dep. Captain of The Queen's Flight, 1960–62; Transport Support in Far East (Borneo Ops), 1962–65; Comdt, RAF Coll., Cranwell, 1967–70; UK Perm. Mil. Deputy, CENTO, Ankara, 1970–72; AOC-in-C, RAF Trng Comd, 1973–75; Air Sec., 1976–78. Air ADC to the Queen, 1976–78. Dir-Gen., Asbestos Internat. Assoc., 1978–89. Mem. Council, CRC, 1978– (Mem. Exec. Cttee, 1978–88). Pres., Old Cranwellian Assoc., 1984–. Governor, Wellington Coll., 1978–90. Freeman, City of London; Liveryman, Guild of Air Pilots and Air Navigators. FRMetS, 1945–90; FBIM, 1970–88. *Recreations:* various outdoor sports, undergardening,

Address: 4 Perrymead Street, SW6 3SP. *Clubs:* Royal Air Force, Boodle's, Hurlingham.

Died 26 Jan. 1994.

STAFFORD, Frank Edmund, CMG 1951; CBE 1946 (OBE 1931); Malayan Civil Service, retired 1951; *b* 24 Aug. 1895; *s* of late Frank Stafford and Marie Stafford; *m* 1943, Ida Wadham (marr. diss., 1950), *d* of late Conway Burton-Durham; one *s*; *m* 1953, Catherine Rolfe (*d* 1984); *m* 1985, Mrs Doreen Voll. *Educ:* Royal Gram. School, Guildford. Served World War I, 1914–19, India and Mesopotamia, Queen's Royal West Surrey Regt. Joined staff of Civil Commissioner, Iraq, 1919; appointed to High Commission, Iraq, 1921; Financial Secretary, 1924; Financial Adviser, British Embassy, Baghdad, 1931; Colonial Service, Nigeria, 1936 (Asst Treasurer, Principal Asst Sec., Actg Financial Sec.); War of 1939–45, commissioned in Army (Lt-Col) for service with Occupied Enemy Territory Administration, 1941; Financial Adviser, Ethiopian Govt, 1942; attached LHQ Australia, 1944; Col, Military Administration, British Borneo, 1945; demobilized, 1946 (Brig.); seconded to Foreign Office, 1946; Member UK Delegn Italian Peace Conference and Council of Foreign Ministers; Head UK Delegn Four Power Commission, 1947; Member UK Delegn to UN, 1948, 1949, 1950, 1952; Foreign Office Adviser (Minister) to Chief Administrator, Eritrea, 1951–53; Adviser to Ethiopian Govt, 1953–60. Chm. Council, Royal Soc. of St George, 1978. FRAS, FRGS. Order of Star of Honour (Ethiopia), 1944, Grand Officer, 1955. *Publications:* contributions to Encyc. Britannica, Kipling Jl, and International Affairs. *Recreations:* horticulture, hagiology. *Address:* 3 Holbrook Park, Horsham, West Sussex RH12 5PW. *T:* Horsham (0403) 252497. *Club:* National Liberal.   *Died 19 April 1994.*

STAHL, Prof. Ernest Ludwig, DLitt Oxon; retired; Taylor Professor of the German Language and Literature and Fellow of The Queen's College, Oxford, 1959–69; Supernumerary Fellow, since 1969; Student Emeritus of Christ Church Oxford, since 1960 (Student, 1945–59); *b* Senekal, OFS, S Africa, 10 Dec. 1902; *s* of Philip and Theresa Stahl; *m* 1942, Kathleen Mary Hudson, MA Oxon, author. *Educ:* Univ. of Capetown (MA 1925); Heidelberg Univ.; Oxford Univ. (First Class Hons, 1927; DLitt 1980); Berne Univ. (PhD *magna cum laude* 1931). Assistant Lecturer in German, Birmingham, 1932–35; Lecturer in German, Oxford, 1935–45; Reader in German Literature, Oxford, 1945–59. Vis. Professor: Cornell, 1956; Princeton, 1958; Yale, 1964; Kansas, 1968; Calif (Davis), 1969–70. Gold Medal, Goethe Gesellschaft, 1966. *Publications:* Die religiöse und die philosophische Bildungsidee und die Entstehung des Bildungsromans, 1934; Hölderlin's Symbolism, 1944; The Dramas of Heinrich von Kleist, 1948 (revised edn, 1961); (trans. with Louis MacNeice) Goethe's Faust pts I and II (abridged), 1951; Schiller's Drama: Theory and Practice, 1954; Goethe's Iphigenie auf Tauris, 1962; (ed) Oxford Book of German Verse, 3rd edn 1967; (with W. E. Yuill) Introduction to German Literature, vol. III, 1970; The Faust Translation in Time Was Away: the world of Louis MacNeice, 1975; editions of Goethe's Werther, 1942 (new edn, 1972), Lessing's Emilia Galotti, 1946, Goethe's Torquato Tasso, 1962, and R. M. Rilke's Duino Elegies, 1965; articles in Modern Language Review, Germanic Review, German Life and Letters, Journal of English and Germanic Philology, Oxford German Studies, Yearbook of Comparative Criticism; contrib. to Festschrift for Ralph Farrell. *Address:* 43 Plantation Road, Oxford OX2 6JE. *T:* Oxford (0865) 515896.   *Died 14 Sept. 1992.*

STALLARD, Sir Peter (Hyla Gawne), KCMG 1961 (CMG 1960); CVO 1956; MBE 1945; Secretary to the Prime Minister of the Federation of Nigeria, 1958–61; *b* 6 March 1915; *y c* of Rev. L. B. Stallard and Eleanor, *e d* of Colonel J. M. Gawne; *m* 1941, Mary Elizabeth Kirke, CStJ; one *s* one *d*. *Educ:* Bromsgrove Sch.; Corpus Christi Coll., Oxford (MA). Cadet, Colonial Administrative Service, Northern Nigeria, 1937. Military Service, Nigeria, Gold Coast, Burma, 1939–45. Governor and Commander-in-Chief of British Honduras, 1961–66; Lt Governor of the Isle of Man, 1966–74. Pres., Devon and Cornwall Rent Assessment Panel, 1976–85. Pres., Somerset Assoc. of Boys Clubs, 1977–91; Chm., Dartmoor Steering Gp, 1978–89. KStJ 1961; Chapter-Gen., Order of St John, 1976–93. *Recreation:* golf. *Address:* 18 Henley Road, Taunton, Somerset TA1 5BJ. *T:* Taunton (01823) 331505. *Club:* Athenæum.   *Died 25 Oct. 1995.*

STALLIBRASS, Geoffrey Ward, CB 1972; OBE 1952; FRAeS; Controller, National Air Traffic Services (Civil Aviation Authority/Ministry of Defence), 1969–74 (Joint Field Commander, 1966–69); *b* 17 Dec. 1911; *s* of Thomas and Ivy Stallibrass, Midhurst; *m* 1940, Alison, *e d* of late James and Rita Scott, Norwich; two *s* three *d*. *Educ:* Wellingborough Sch. Air Service Training, Hamble (Commercial Pilot/Instrument Rating Course), 1948. Dep. Director, Civil Aviation Ops, Ministry of Civil Aviation, 1946; attached to BOAC, 1949; Dep. Director of Control and Navigation (Development), 1950; Director of Aerodromes (Tech.), Ministry of Transport and Civil Aviation, 1953; Director of Flight Safety, Min. of Aviation, 1962. *Publications:* articles on conservation subjects. *Recreations:* walking, birdwatching, conservation work, music. *Address:* Turkey Island Corner, East Harting, Petersfield, Hants GU31 5LT. *T:* Harting (01730) 825220.   *Died 20 Oct. 1994.*

STALLWORTHY, Sir John (Arthur), Kt 1972; Nuffield Professor of Obstetrics and Gynæcology, University of Oxford, 1967–73, then Emeritus; Fellow Emeritus, Oriel College, Oxford, 1973, Hon. Fellow, 1974; *b* 26 July 1906; *s* of Arthur John Stallworthy; *m* 1934, Margaret Wright Howie (*d* 1980); one *s* twin *d*. *Educ:* Auckland Grammar Sch.; Universities of Auckland and Otago, NZ. Distinction and gold medal in surgery, gynæcology and obstetrics, 1930; travelling med. schol., 1931; obstetrical travelling schol., 1932; postgrad. experience in Melbourne, London and Vienna. MRCOG 1935; FRCS 1936; FRCOG 1951. Joseph Price Orator, US, 1950; McIlrath Guest Prof., Sydney, 1952; Sommer Meml Lecturer, US, 1958; Hunterian Prof., RCS, 1963; Sims Black Prof. S Africa, 1964. Sometime Examiner in Obstetrics and Gynæcology for RCOG, RCS of S Africa, Universities of Oxford, Birmingham, Leeds, E Africa and Singapore. Hon. Cons., Royal Prince Alfred Hospital, Sydney, 1952; Associate Obstetrician, National Maternity Hospital, Dublin, 1959. Vice-Pres., RCOG, 1969; President: RSM, 1974–75, 1980–81 (Hon. Fellow, 1976; Chm. Appeal Cttee); Medical Protection Soc.; BMA, 1975 (Gold Medal, 1981; Chm. Working Party, The Medical Effects of Nuclear War, 1981–83). Hon. Fellow, Surgical, Obstetrical and Gynæcological Societies in US, Wales, Canada, S Africa, Spain and Turkey; Hon. FACS 1954; Hon. FCOG(SA) 1964; Hon. FACOG 1974; Hon. FRCSI 1976. Hon. DSc: Otago, 1975; Leeds, 1975. Victor Bonney Prize, RCS, 1970. Member, Honourable Order of Kentucky Colonels, 1968. *Publications:* (jointly) Problems of Fertility in General Practice, 1948; (contrib.) British Obstetric Practice, 3rd edn 1963; (contrib.) British Gynæcological Practice, 3rd edn 1963; (jointly) Recent Advances in Obstetrics and Gynæcology, 1966–79; (jointly) Bonney's Gynæcological Surgery, 8th edn; (ed jtly) The Medical Effects of Nuclear War, 1983; (contrib.) Cancer of the Uterine Cervix, 1984. *Recreations:* formerly Rugby football, tennis, swimming, driving fast cars; latterly gardening, writing, driving fast cars more slowly. *Address:* 8a College Green, Gloucester GL1 2LX. *T:* Gloucester (0452) 421243. *Died 19 Nov. 1993.*

STAMLER, Samuel Aaron, QC 1971; a Recorder of the Crown Court, 1974–89; *b* 3 Dec. 1925; *s* of late Herman Stamler and Bronia Stamler; *m* 1953, Honor, *d* of A. G. Brotman; two *s* one *d. Educ:* Berkhamsted; King's College, Cambridge. Called to Bar, Middle Temple, 1949, Bencher, 1979. *Recreations:* walking, grandchildren. *Address:* 1 Essex Court, Temple, EC4Y 9AR. *T:* 0171–583 2000. *Club:* Athenæum. *Died 12 Nov. 1994.*

STANFORD, Adm. Sir Peter (Maxwell), GCB 1986 (KCB 1983); LVO 1970; Commander-in-Chief, Naval Home Command, 1985–87; Director, BT (Marine) Ltd, since 1988; *b* 11 July 1929; *s* of late Brig. Henry Morrant Stanford, CBE, MC, and of Edith Hamilton Stanford; *m* 1957, Helen Ann Lingard; one *s* two *d. Educ:* Britannia Royal Naval College. Midshipman, W Indies Sqdn, 1947–48; HMS Kenya, Korea, 1950–51; HMS Welfare, 1952–54; French Interpreter, 1954; HMS Camberford, 1954–56; Long Signals Course, 1956–57; Staff of C-in-C Mediterranean, 1957–58; Signal Officer, 3rd Destroyer Sqdn, 1958–59; HM Signal Sch., 1960–62; i/c HMS Grafton, 1962–63; Signal Div., Naval Staff, 1963–65; i/c HMS Brighton, 1966–67; HM Signal Sch., 1967–68; HM Yacht Britannia, 1969–70; Asst Dir Naval Plans, 1970–72; RCDS 1973; i/c HMS Hermione and Captain (F) 5, 1974–75; Commodore 1975; Sec., Chiefs of Staff Cttee, 1975–78; Flag Officer, Second Flotilla, 1978–80; Asst Chief of Naval Staff (Op. Req.), 1980–82; VCNS, 1982–85. Flag ADC to the Queen, 1985–87. Trustee, Imperial War Museum, 1987–. *Publications:* papers, reviews, etc, for maritime jls. *Recreations:* field sports, ornithology. *Address:* c/o Lloyds Bank, Cox's & King's Branch, 7 Pall Mall, SW1Y 5NA. *Clubs:* Flyfishers', Naval. *Died 22 May 1991.*

STANIER, Brig. Sir Alexander Beville Gibbons, 2nd Bt, *cr* 1917, of Peplow Hall, Hodnet, Salop; DSO 1940 (and Bar, 1945); MC; JP; DL; *b* 31 Jan. 1899; *s* of Sir Beville Stanier, 1st Bt, MP and Constance (*d* 1948), *d* of late Rev. B. Gibbons; *S* father, 1921; *m* 1927, Dorothy Gladys (*d* 1973), *e d* of late Brig.-Gen. Alfred Douglas Miller, CBE, DSO; one *s* one *d. Educ:* Eton; RMC, Sandhurst. Served European War in France, 1918 (MC); Adjutant 1st Bn Welsh Guards, 1923–26; Military Secretary, Gibraltar, 1927–30; served War of 1939–45, in France 1940 and 1944 (despatches, DSO and Bar, American Silver Star, Comdr Order of Leopold of Belgium with palm, Belgian Croix de Guerre with palm): commanded 2nd Battalion Welsh Guards, 1939–40; temp. Brigadier, 1940–45; Lieut-Colonel Commanding Welsh Guards, 1945–48. CC Salop, 1950–58. High Sheriff of Shropshire, 1951. County President of the St John Ambulance Bde, 1950–60; CStJ. Comdr, Order of Legion of Honour (France), 1988. *Heir:* *s* Beville Douglas Stanier [*b* 20 April 1934; *m* 1963, Shelagh, *er d* of late Major and Mrs J. S. Sinnott, Tetbury, Glos; one *s* two *d*]. *Address:* Hill House, Shotover Park, Wheatley, Oxford OX33 1QN. *T:* Wheatley (01865) 872996; Park Cottage, Ludford, Ludlow SY8 1PP. *T:* Ludlow (01584) 872675. *Died 10 Jan. 1995.*

STANLEY, Henry Sydney Herbert Cloete, CMG 1968; HM Diplomatic Service, retired; British High Commissioner to Trinidad and Tobago and (non-resident) to Grenada, 1977–80; *b* 5 March 1920; *er s* of late Sir Herbert Stanley, GCMG and Reniera (*née* Cloete), DBE; *m* 1941, Margaret (*d* 1994), *d* of late Professor H. B. Dixon, CBE, FRS; three *s. Educ:* Eton; Balliol College, Oxford. Served with King's Royal Rifle Corps, 1940–46 (Capt.); N-W Europe, 1944–46, also HQ, CCG. Appointed to Commonwealth Relations Office, 1947. Served in Pakistan, 1950–52; Swaziland and South Africa, 1954–57;

USA, 1959–61; Tanganyika, 1961–63; Kenya, 1963–65; Inspector, HM Diplomatic Service, 1966–68, Chief Inspector, 1968–70; High Comr, Ghana, 1970–75; Asst Under Sec. of State, FCO, 1975–77; High Comr for the New Hebrides (non-resident), 1976–77. *Address:* 8 Birch Grove, W3 9SN. *Died 29 Dec. 1995.*

STANLEY, Hon. Pamela Margaret, (Hon. Lady Cunynghame); *b* 6 Sept. 1909; *d* of 5th Baron Stanley of Alderley and Margaret Evans Gordon; *m* 1941, Sir David Cunynghame, 11th Bt (*d* 1978); three *s. Educ:* Switzerland; France. Studied at Webber-Douglas School of Acting and Singing; first appearance Lyric, Hammersmith, 1932, in Derby Day; six months at Oxford Repertory, 1933; with Martin Harvey in The Bells, Savoy, 1933; Sydney Carroll's Open Air Theatre, 1934; Wendy in Peter Pan, 1934; Queen Victoria in Victoria Regina, Gate Theatre, 1935; went to USA with Leslie Howard in Hamlet, 1936; Queen Victoria in Victoria Regina, Lyric, 1937–38; Open Air Theatre, 1938; Queen Victoria in The Queen's Highland Servant, Savoy, 1968. *Address:* 83 Clarendon Street, Leamington Spa, Warwickshire. *Died 30 June 1991.*

STANNARD, John Anthony; His Honour Judge Stannard; a Circuit Judge, since 1983; nominated to conduct Official Referee's business on Northern Circuit, since 1984; Circuit Commercial Judge, Northern Circuit, since 1990; *b* 30 Sept. 1931; *s* of late Anthony Stannard and Joan Stannard (*née* Joslin); *m* 1956, Madeline Betty (*née* Limb); two *d. Educ:* Quarry Bank High School, Liverpool (state scholar); Trinity College, Cambridge (Major Scholar, 1951; Sen. Scholar, 1953; Whittaker Scholar, 1955; 1st Cl. History Tripos; Prizeman; MA). Called to the Bar, Lincoln's Inn, 1956 (Chomley Scholar, 1953; Cassels Scholar, 1954). Practised on Northern Circuit, 1956–83; a Recorder, 1980–83. Captain RARO. *Recreations:* walking, reading. *Address:* Robinswood, Glenrose Road, Woolton, Liverpool L25 5JT. *T:* 051–428 1187; Queen Elizabeth II Law Courts, Derby Square, Liverpool L2 1XA. *Club:* Athenæum (Liverpool). *Died 12 Feb. 1992.*

STANSFIELD, His Honour James Warden; a Circuit Judge (formerly County Court Judge), 1963–78, retired; *b* 7 April 1906; *s* of James Hampson Stansfield, Sunny Lea, Wilmslow, Cheshire; *m* 1937, Florence Evelyn, *d* of Arthur Harry Holdcroft, Congleton, Cheshire; two *s* one *d. Educ:* King's School, Macclesfield; Sidney Sussex College, University of Cambridge. Called to the Bar, Inner Temple, 1929; practised Northern Circuit. Contested (C) Platting Division of Manchester, 1935. Served War of 1939–45: Royal Air Force, Middle East, and Staff of Judge Advocate-General; formerly RAFVR (Squadron Leader). Chairman: Manchester Licensing Planning Cttee, 1955–63; Manchester Mental Health Review Tribunal, 1962; Warrington Licensed Premises Cttee, 1970. *Recreations:* golf, walking. *Address:* Oak Lea, Victoria Road, Wilmslow, Cheshire. *T:* Wilmslow (0625) 523915. *Died 30 Sept. 1991.*

STANTON-JONES, Richard, FEng 1984; engineering consultant since 1984; *b* 25 Sept. 1926; *s* of John C. Stanton Jones and Katharine Stanton; *m* 1949, Dorine Mary Watkins; one *s. Educ:* King's College, Cambridge (MA); Cranfield College of Aeronautics (MSc). CEng. Aerodynamicist, de Havilland, Saunders-Roe, Lockheed (USA), 1949–56; Chief Aerodynamicist, Saunders-Roe/ British Hovercraft Corp. (SRN series of hovercraft), 1959–66; British Hovercraft Corp.: Technical Dir, 1966–68; Managing Dir, 1968–82; Dep. Chm., 1982–84; established RSJ Engineering, 1984. Hon. DSc Exeter 1987. RAeS Silver Medal, 1965; Elmer A. Sperry Award (Transportation), 1968. *Publications:* numerous papers on hovercraft for tech. instns; author of 31 patents on hovercraft. *Recreations:* sailing, carpentry. *Address:*

Doubloon, Springvale, Seaview, Isle of Wight PO34 5AP. *T:* Isle of Wight (0983) 613363. *Clubs:* Naval and Military; Island Sailing (Cowes).

Died 23 Jan. 1991.

STAPLETON, Sir (Henry) Alfred, 10th Bt *cr* 1679, of The Leeward Islands; *b* 2 May 1913; *s* of Brig. Francis Harry Stapleton, CMG (*d* 1956) and Maud Ellen (*d* 1958), *d* of late Major Alfred Edward Wrottesley; *g g s* of Sir Francis Jarvis Stapleton, 7th Bt; *S* kinsman, 1977; *m* 1961, Rosslyne Murray, *d* of late Capt. H. S. Warren, RN. *Educ:* Marlborough; Christ Church, Oxford. Served War of 1939–45, Oxfordshire and Bucks Light Infantry. *Recreations:* cricket umpiring, gardening. *Heir:* none. *Address:* 13 Hillbrook Court, Sherborne, Dorset DT9 3NZ. *T:* Sherborne (01935) 812295. *Clubs:* Garrick, MCC. *Died 5 Jan. 1995 (ext).*

STARK, Dame Freya (Madeline), DBE 1972 (CBE 1953); *b* 31 Jan. 1893; *d* of late Robert Stark, sculptor, Ford Park, Chagford, Devon; *m* 1947, Stewart Perowne, OBE (*d* 1989). *Educ:* privately in Italy; Bedford College, London University; School of Oriental Studies, London. Engaged on Govt service in Middle East and elsewhere, 1939–45. Awarded Back Grant, 1933, for travel in Luristan; Triennial Burton Memorial Medal from Royal Asiatic Society, 1934; Mungo Park Medal from Royal Scottish Geographical Society, 1936; Founder's Medal from Royal Geographical Society, 1942; Percy Sykes Memorial Medal from Royal Central Asian Soc., 1951. Sister of the Order of St John of Jerusalem, 1949, Sister Comdr, 1981. Hon. LLD Glasgow Univ., 1951; Hon. DLitt Durham, 1971. *Publications:* Bagdad Sketches, 1933, enlarged edition, 1937; The Valleys of the Assassins, 1934; The Southern Gates of Arabia, 1936; Seen in the Hadhramaut, 1938; A Winter in Arabia, 1940; Letters from Syria, 1942; East is West, 1945; Perseus in the Wind, 1948; Traveller's Prelude, 1950, reissued 1989; Beyond Euphrates, 1951, reissued 1989; The Coast of Incense, 1953; Ionia: a Quest, 1954; The Lycian Shore, 1956, reissued 1989; Alexander's Path, 1958; Riding to the Tigris, 1959; Dust in the Lion's Paw, 1961; The Journey's Echo, 1963; Rome on the Euphrates, 1966; The Zodiac Arch, 1968; Space, Time and Movement in Landscape, 1969; The Minaret of Djam, 1970; Turkey: a sketch of Turkish History, 1971; A Peak in Darien, 1976; Rivers of Time, 1982; Letters (vols 1–6 ed Lucy Moorehead; vols 7–8 ed Caroline Moorehead): vol. 1, The Furnace and the Cup, 1914–1930, 1974; vol. 2, The Open Road, 1930–1935, 1975; vol. 3, The Growth of Danger, 1935–1939, 1976; vol. 4, The Bridge of the Levant, 1940–1943, 1977; vol. 5, New Worlds for Old, 1943–1946, 1978; vol. 6, The Broken Road, 1947–1952, 1981; vol. 7, Some Talk of Alexander, 1952–59, 1982; vol. 8, Traveller's Epilogue, 1960–80, 1982; (ed Caroline Moorehead) Over the Rim of the World: selected letters, 1988. *Recreations:* travel, mountaineering, embroidery. *Address:* Via Canova, Asolo (Treviso), Italy; c/o John Murray, 50 Albemarle Street, W1.

Died 9 May 1993.

STEEDMAN, Air Chief Marshal Sir Alexander McKay Sinclair, (Sir Alasdair), GCB 1980 (KCB 1976; CB 1973); CBE 1965; DFC 1944; Controller, Royal Air Force Benevolent Fund, 1981–88; *b* 29 Jan. 1922; *s* of late James Steedman, Hampton-on-Thames, Mddx, and Anna McKay Steedman (*née* Sinclair); *m* 1945, Dorothy Isobel (*d* 1983), *d* of late Col Walter Todd, Knockbrex, Kirkcudbright; one *s* two *d*. *Educ:* Hampton Grammar School. Entered RAF, Jan. 1941; reconnaissance ops, 1942–45; (241 and 2 Sqns) Air Ministry (DP2), 1945–48; comd 39 Sqdn, Khartoum, 1948–49; comd 8 Sqdn, Aden, 1949–50; CFS Course, 1951; Training Sqn Comdr 201 Advanced Flying Sch., 1951–53; Syndicate Leader Aircrew Selection Centre, Hornchurch, 1953–54; psa 1955; Chief Instructor, CFS

(B), 1955–57; Comdr Royal Ceylon Air Force, Katanayake, 1957–59; jssc 1959; Dir Staff, Jt Services Staff Coll., 1960–62; Comdr RAF Lyneham, 1962–65; CAS, Royal Malaysian Air Force, 1965–67; Dir of Defence Plans (Air), 1967–68; Dir Defence Operations Staff, 1968–69; ACAS (Policy), MoD, 1969–71; SASO, HQ Strike Comd, 1971–72; Comdt, RAF Staff Coll., 1972–75; Air Member of Air Force Bd for Supply and Organisation, 1976–77; UK Mil. Rep. to NATO, 1977–80; RAF retd, 1981. Mem., Security Commn, 1982–. Vice-Pres., Nat. Adv. Centre for Careers for Women, 1988–; Member of Council: ISCO, 1986–; GBA, 1988–. Governor: Hampton Sch., 1976– (Chm. of Govs, 1988–); Gordon Sch., 1987– (Mem. Foundn Cttee, 1981–). Patron, Central Flying Sch. Assoc., 1984–; Vice Patron: RAF Small Arms Assoc., 1978–; Internat. Air Tattoo, 1988– (Chm., 1981–88); Pres., British Pistol Club, 1986–. Liveryman, GAPAN, 1985 (Chm., Guild Benevolent Fund, 1990–). FRAeS 1981; CBIM 1979. Johan Mangku Negara (Malaysia), 1967; Commander, Order of Polonia Restituta (Poland), 1990. *Recreations:* defence, golf, reading. *Address:* Rutherford, St Chloe Lane, Amberley, Stroud, Glos GL5 5AS. *Club:* Royal Air Force. *Died 2 Jan. 1992.*

STEEGMULLER, Francis; writer; *b* New Haven, Conn, 3 July 1906; *s* of Joseph Francis Steegmuller and Bertha Tierney; *m* 1st, 1935, Beatrice Stein (decd); 2nd, 1963, Shirley Hazzard. *Educ:* Columbia University, New York. Office of War Information, 1942–43; Office of Strategic Services, 1944–45. Member, Nat. Inst. of Arts and Letters, 1966. Gold Medal for Biography, 1982. Chevalier de la Légion d'Honneur, 1957; Chevalier de l'Ordre des Arts et des Lettres, 1984. *Publications:* O Rare Ben Jonson (under pseudonym Byron Steel), 1928; Flaubert and Madame Bovary, 1939, reprinted 1947, 1958, 1968, 1993; States of Grace, 1947; Maupassant, 1950, repr. 1973; Blue Harpsichord (under pseudonym David Keith), 1950, repr. 1977 (under name Steegmuller); The Two Lives of James Jackson Jarves, 1953; (trans. and ed) The Selected Letters of Gustave Flaubert, 1954; La Grande Mademoiselle, 1955; The Christening Party, 1961; Le Hibou et la Poussiquette, 1961; Apollinaire, 1963, repr. 1986; Papillot, Clignot et Dodo (with Norbert Guterman), 1965; (trans.) Gustave Flaubert, Intimate Notebook, 1967; Cocteau, 1970, repr. 1986 (Nat. Book Award 1971); Stories and True Stories, 1972; (trans. and ed) Flaubert in Egypt, 1972, repr. 1982; (ed) Your Isadora, 1975; (trans. and ed) The Letters of Gustave Flaubert, 1830–1857, 1980 (American Book Award 1981), 2nd vol. 1983; A Woman, a Man, and Two Kingdoms: the story of Madame d'Épinay and the Abbé Galiani, 1991; (trans. with Barbara Bray) Gustave Flaubert-George Sand: the correspondence, 1992; works published abroad include a translation of Madame Bovary, 1957, Silence at Salerno (novel), 1979; many short stories and articles in The New Yorker. *Address:* 200 East 66th Street, New York, NY 10021, USA. *Clubs:* Century (New York); Circolo del Remo e della Vela "Italia" (Naples). *Died 20 Oct. 1994.*

STEEL, Byron; *see* Steegmuller, Francis.

STEEL, Brig. Charles Deane, CMG 1957; OBE 1941; *b* 29 May 1901; *s* of Dr Gerard Steel, JP, Leominster, Herefordshire; *m* 1932, Elizabeth Chenevix-Trench (*d* 1973); one *s* (and one *s* decd). *Educ:* Bedford; Royal Military Academy, Woolwich. Prize Cadetship, Woolwich, 1919; Armstrong Memorial Prize, 1921. Commissioned 2nd Lieut RE, 1921; served in India (Bengal Sappers and Miners), 1924–29; Staff College, Camberley, 1936–37; War of 1939–45: E Africa and Abyssinia, 1941; Western Desert, 1942; POW, 1942; Switzerland, 1943; Dep. Head, British Mil. Mission to Greece, 1945–49; Dep. Mil. Sec., 1949–52; retd Feb. 1952; Head of Conference and Supply Dept, Foreign

Office, 1952–64; Head of Accommodation Department Diplomatic Service, 1965–67. *Recreations:* formerly golf, gardening, latterly reading. *Address:* Little Hill, Nettlebed, Oxfordshire RG9 5BD. *T:* Nettlebed (0491) 641287.

Died 7 Feb. 1993.

STEEL, Major Sir (Fiennes) William Strang, 2nd Bt, *cr* 1938, of Philiphaugh, Selkirk; JP; DL; Major (retired), 17/21st Lancers; Forestry Commissioner, 1958–73; *b* 24 July 1912; *e s* of Sir Samuel Strang Steel, 1st Bt and Hon. Vere Mabel (*d* 1964), *d* of 1st Baron Cornwallis; *S* father, 1961; *m* 1941, Joan (*d* 1982), *d* of late Brig.-Gen. Sir Brodie Haldane Henderson, KCMG, CB, Braughing, Ware; two *s* (one *d* decd). *Educ:* Eton; RMC, Sandhurst. Joined 17/21st Lancers, 1933; Major, 1941; retired, 1947. Convener, Selkirk CC, 1967–75. DL Selkirkshire, 1955, JP 1965. *Heir: s* Major (Fiennes) Michael Strang Steel, DL, 17/21 Lancers [*b* 22 Feb. 1943; *m* 1977, Sarah Russell; two *s* one *d*]. *Address:* Philiphaugh, Selkirk. *T:* Selkirk (0750) 21216. *Club:* Cavalry and Guards.

Died 13 Dec. 1992.

STEEL, Sir James, Kt 1967; CBE 1964; Lord-Lieutenant of Tyne and Wear, 1974–84; Chairman, Furness Withy & Co. Ltd, 1975–79; *b* 19 May 1909; *s* of Alfred Steel and Katharine (*née* Meikle); *m* 1935, Margaret Jean MacLauchlan (*d* 1987); two *s* two *d. Educ:* Trent College. Mem., Commn on the Constitution, 1969–73. Trustee, Sir John Priestman Charity Trust. Chairman: British Productivity Council, 1966–67; Textile Council, 1968–72; Washington Develt Corp., 1964–77. Pres., TA for N of England, 1979–84; Vice-Pres., Wildfowl Trust. Liveryman, Worshipful Co. of Founders. JP Sunderland, 1964; Durham: DL 1969; Sheriff 1972–73. KStJ 1975. Hon. DCL Dunelm, 1978. *Publication:* Bird Quest, 1989. *Recreation:* ornithology. *Address:* Fawnlees Hall, Wolsingham, County Durham DL13 3LW. *T:* Weardale (01388) 527307. *Died 17 Nov. 1994.*

STEEL, Major Sir William Strang; *see* Steel, Major Sir F. W. S.

STEELE-PERKINS, Surg.-Vice-Adm. Sir Derek (Duncombe), KCB 1966 (CB 1963); KCVO 1964 (CVO 1954); FRCS; FRACS; *b* 19 June 1908; *s* of late Dr Duncombe Steele-Perkins, Honiton, Devon, and Sybil Mary Hill-Jones, Edinburgh; *m* 1937, Joan Boddan (*d* 1985), Birkdale, Lancashire; three *d. Educ:* Allhallows School, Rousdon; College of Surgeons (Edin.). Entered RN, 1932; RN Hosp., Haslar, 1932; HMS Mantis, China, 1934–36; HMS Ganges, Shotley, 1936–38; HMS Vindictive, 1938–39; RN Hospitals: Haslar, 1939–40; Chatham, 1940–44; Sydney, Australia, 1944–46; Malta, 1946–50; RY Gothic, 1951–52; Chatham, 1952–59; Senior Surgical Specialist, RN Hosp., Bighi, Malta, 1959–61; Medical Officer-in-Charge, Royal Naval Hospital, Haslar, 1961; Command MO to C-in-C, Portsmouth, 1962–63; Medical Director of the Navy, 1963–66. Royal Commonwealth Tours, 1953–66. QHS 1961. FRSocMed. CStJ. *Recreations:* sailing, fly-fishing, shooting. *Address:* c/o National Westminster Bank, Lymington, Hants SO41 8NR. *Club:* Royal Lymington Yacht (Cdre 1969–72).

Died 9 Dec. 1994.

STEER, William Reed Hornby, MA, LLM; barrister-at-law; Recorder of South Molton, 1936–51; Deputy Chairman, London County Council, 1948–49; Lieutenant-Colonel in the Army (released July 1945); *b* 5 April 1899; *s* of late Rev. W. H. Hornby Steer, TD, JP, MA; unmarried. *Educ:* Eton; Trinity College, Cambridge. Commissioned in Royal Field Artillery; served European War, France and Belgium. Called to Bar, Inner Temple, 1922; joined Western Circuit; Standing Counsel: to Commons, Open Spaces, and Footpaths Preservation Society; to Council for Preservation of Rural England; to National Smoke Abatement Society and to Pure Rivers Society; an Examiner in Law to Chartered Institute of Secretaries; Legal Member of Town Planning Inst.; Fellow of Royal Soc. of Health; Associate of Royal Institution of Chartered Surveyors; a representative for Hampstead on London County Council, 1931–52; a representative of London County Council on International Union of Local Authorities; Master of Worshipful Company of Turners, 1949–50; a Governor of Haberdashers' Aske's Schools and of Royal Free Hospital; a Governor and an Almoner of Christ's Hospital, Dep. Chm. Council of Almoners, 1970–75; Chairman Children's Hospital, Hampstead; Vice-Chairman London Old Age Pensions Committee; Treasurer, London Soc.; Kt of Justice, Order of St John; Joint Hon. Secretary of League of Mercy; Gold Staff Officer at Coronation of King George VI; Inspector of Metropolitan Special Constabulary. Army Officers Emergency Reserve, 1938; Extra Regimentally Employed, Military Dept, Judge Advocate-General's Office, 1939; Deputy Judge Advocate-General, Malta, 1941–43; graded Assistant Adjutant-General, War Office, 1944; Staff Officer (I), Control Commission for Germany, 1945; Captain, 1939; Major, 1941; Lt-Col 1943; Member of Territorial Army and Air Force Association of the County of London. *Publications:* Assistant Editor of Glen's Public Health Act, 1936; Steer's Law of Smoke Nuisances, 1938, 2nd edn 1948; contributions to Lord Macmillan's Local Government Law and Administration; articles on the law relating to highways. *Recreation:* sailing. *Address:* 71A Whitehall Court, SW1A 2EL. *T:* 071–930 3160. *Clubs:* United Oxford & Cambridge University, Carlton, Pratt's, MCC; Royal Corinthian Yacht (Burnham-on-Crouch).

Died 24 Feb. 1993.

STEINBERG, Jack; President, Steinberg Group, 1982–85 (Chairman, 1966–81); *b* 23 May 1913; *s* of Alexander and Sophie Steinberg; *m* 1938, Hannah Anne, *d* of late Solomon Wolfson, JP; two *d. Educ:* privately, London. Underwriting Member of Lloyd's. Chairman: Horrockes Fashions Ltd; Butte Knit (London) Ltd. Mem., NEDC, 1966–78; Vice-President: British Mantle Manufacturers' Assoc., 1968–; Clothing Export Council, 1974– (Chm., 1970–74); Chairman: KCH Res. Trust, 1977–; King's Medical Res. Trust, 1979–. Member of Plumbers' Livery Co.; Freeman, City of London. *Address:* 74 Portland Place, W1. *T:* 071–580 5908. *Clubs:* Brooks's, Portland, Carlton. *Died 14 July 1991.*

STEPHENS, Prof. Arthur Veryan, MA Cantab; CEng; FRAeS; Professor of Aeronautical Engineering, The Queen's University, Belfast, 1956–73, later Emeritus Professor; *b* 9 July 1908; *s* of Arthur John Stephens and Mildred, *d* of Robert Fowler Sturge; *m* 1st, 1938, Jane Dows, *d* of F. W. Lester; three *s* one *d*; 2nd, 1981, Marjorie Phyllis Irene Sprince (*d* 1986); 3rd, 1987, Sheila Joy Franglen (*d* 1991). *Educ:* Clifton Coll.; St John's Coll., Cambridge (Mechanical Sciences Tripos, John Bernard Seely Prize). Scientific Officer, Royal Aircraft Establishment, 1930–34; Fellow of St John's College, Cambridge, 1934–39; Lawrence Hargrave Professor of Aeronautics, 1939–56, Dean of the Faculty of Engineering, 1947–56, University of Sydney, NSW; Dean of Faculty of Applied Science and Technology, 1961–64, Vice-President (Buildings), 1964–67, QUB. Edward Busk Meml Prize of RAeS, 1934; Member: Australian Flying Personnel Research Cttee, 1940–45; Australian Council for Aeronautics, 1941–46; Chairman: Aeronautical Research Consultative Cttee, 1947–54; Australian Aeronautical Research Cttee, 1954–56; Member, Australian Defence Research and Development Policy Cttee, 1953–56; Chairman, Australian Division of Royal Aeronautical Society, 1947–56. *Publications:* numerous papers on applied aerodynamics published by Aeronautical Research Council, Australian Dept of Supply and in Jl of

RAeS. *Recreations:* golf, real tennis, antiquarian horology. *Address:* 2 St Mary's Gardens, Chichester, W Sussex PO19 1NW. *Club:* Athenæum.

Died 3 Sept. 1992.

STEPHENS, Cedric John; Chairman, Exford (Highcliffe) Ltd, since 1991; *b* 13 Feb. 1921; *s* of late Col J. E. Stephens, Truro, Cornwall. *Educ:* London University (BSc (Eng) Hons). CEng, FRAeS, FIEE. Entered Scientific Civil Service, 1951; Dir, Space Activities, Min. of Aviation, 1961; Mem. Coun., European Launcher Development Organisation, Paris, 1962; Chm. Technical Cttee, European Coun. on Satellite Communications, 1964; Imperial Defence Coll., 1965; Director, Signals Research and Develt Estabt, Min. of Technology, 1966–67; Chief Scientific Adviser, Home Office, 1968; Dir-Gen. of Research and Chief Scientist, Home Office, 1969–73 (Mem., Defence Scientific Adv. Council, 1970–72). Called to Bar, Gray's Inn, 1971. Mem., Electronics Div. Bd, IEE, 1972. *Recreation:* viola playing. *Address:* 6 Newlyn Road, Welling, Kent DA16 3LH. *Club:* Athenæum.

Died 14 Oct. 1994.

STEPHENS, Maj.-Gen. Keith Fielding, CB 1970; OBE 1957; Medical Officer, Department of Health and Social Security, 1970–85, retired; *b* Taplow, Bucks, 28 July 1910; *s* of late Edgar Percy and Mary Louise Stephens; *m* 1937, Margaret Ann, *d* of late Alexander MacGregor; two *s. Educ:* Eastbourne College; St Bartholomew's Hospital. MB, BS London 1934; FFARCS 1953; DA 1945. Commissioned into RAMC, 1937; served in India, 1937–43; France and Germany, 1944–46; Cyprus, 1954–56; Adviser in Anæsthetics to the Army, 1949–53 and 1957–66; Commandant and Director of Studies, Royal Army Medical College, 1966–68; DDMS, Southern Command, 1968–70, retired. QHS, 1964–70. FRSocMed (Pres., Sect. of Anæsthetics, 1970–71); Hon. Member, Assoc. of Anæsthetists of Gt Brit. and Ireland. Fellow, Med. Soc. of London. Hon. FFARCSI 1970; Hon. Col, 221 (Surrey) Field Ambulance RAMC(V), 1972–76. Mitchiner Medal, 1962. CStJ 1967. *Publications:* numerous articles in medical journals. *Address:* 3 Carnegie Place, Parkside, Wimbledon, SW19 5NG. *T:* 0181–946 0911. *Club:* Naval and Military.

Died 17 June 1995.

STEPHENS, Major Robert, CVO 1964; ERD 1947; Administrative Officer, Hillsborough Castle (formerly Government House), 1973–78; retired; *b* 19 Nov. 1909; *s* of late John Samuel Stephens; *m* 1939, Kathleen, *d* of late R. I. Trelford, Helen's Bay, Belfast. *Educ:* Campbell Coll., Belfast. Ulster Bank, 1929–39. Served War of 1939–45: RA, Middle East, 1941–45. Commercial Manager, Newforge Ltd, 1946–55; Private Secretary to the Governor of Northern Ireland, 1955–73; Comptroller to: Lord Wakehurst, 1955–64; Lord Erskine of Rerrick, 1964–68; Lord Grey of Naunton, 1968–73. Hon. Sec., SSAFA (NI), 1979. OStJ 1980. *Recreation:* golf. *Address:* c/o Alma House, Ballynahinch, Co. Down, Northern Ireland.

Died 10 March 1994.

STEPHENS, Sir Robert (Graham), Kt 1995; actor; *b* 14 July 1931; *s* of Rueben Stephens and Gladys (*née* Deverell); *m* 1st, Ann Simmonds (marr. diss.); one *s*; 2nd, Tarn Bassett; one *d*; 3rd, 1967, Maggie Smith (Dame Maggie Smith, DBE), (marr. diss. 1975); two *s*; 4th, 1995, Patricia Quinn. *Educ:* Bradford Civic Theatre School. Started with Caryl Jenner Mobile Theatre Co.; Mem. English Stage Co., Royal Court, 1956. *Stage:* The Crucible, Don Juan, The Death of Satan, Cards of Identity, The Good Woman of Setzuan and The Country Wife (also at Adelphi, 1957); The Apollo de Bellac, Yes-and After, The Making of Moo, How Can We Save Father?, The Waters of Babylon, Royal Court, 1957; The Entertainer, Palace, 1957; Epitaph for George Dillon, Royal Court, Comedy,

Golden (NY), 1958 and Henry Miller, 1959; Look After Lulu (also at New) and The Kitchen (also 1961), Royal Court, 1959; The Wrong Side of the Park, Cambridge, 1960; The Sponge Room, Squat Betty, Royal Court, 1962; Chichester and Edinburgh Festival, 1963; Design for Living (Los Angeles), 1971; Private Lives, Queen's, 1972; The Seagull, Chichester, 1973; Apropos The Falling Sleet (dir.), Open Space, 1973; Ghosts, The Seagull, Hamlet, Greenwich, 1974; Sherlock Holmes, NY and Canada, 1975; Murderer, Garrick, 1975; Zoo Story, 1975, Othello, 1976, Open Air, Regent's Park; Pygmalion, Los Angeles, 1979; Othello, Cape Town, SA, 1982; WCPC, Half Moon, 1982; Light Up the Sky, Old Vic, 1985; Falstaff in Henry IV, parts I and II (Olivier Best Actor Award), Julius Caesar, 1991, King Lear, 1993, RSC (Shakespeare Globe Classic Best Actor Award; Variety Club Stage Actor Award); *National Theatre Company:* Hamlet, St Joan, The Recruiting Officer, 1963; Andorra, Play, The Royal Hunt of the Sun (also Chichester Fest.), Hay Fever, 1964; Much Ado About Nothing, Armstrong's Last Goodnight, Trelawny of the Wells (also Chichester Fest.), 1965; A Bond Honoured, Black Comedy, 1966; The Dance of Death, The Three Sisters (at Los Angeles, 1968), As You Like It, Tartuffe, 1967; Most Unwarrantable Intrusion (also dir.), Home and Beauty, 1968; Macrune's Guevara (also co-dir), 1969; The Beaux' Stratagem (also Los Angeles), Hedda Gabler, 1970; The Cherry Orchard, Brand, The Double Dealer, Has "Washington" Legs?, 1978; A Midsummer Night's Dream, Inner Voices, Cinderella, 1983; Passion Plays. *Films:* A Taste of Honey, 1961; The Small World of Sammy Lee, 1962; Cleopatra, 1963; The Prime of Miss Jean Brodie, 1967; The Private Life of Sherlock Holmes, 1969; Travels with my Aunt, 1972; The Asphyx, 1972; Luther, 1972; QBVII, 1973; Alexander the Great, 1980; Ill Fares The Land, 1982; High Season, 1986; Comrades, 1987; Empire of the Sun, 1987; The Fruit Machine, 1988; Henry V, 1989; Chaplin, 1992; The Dualists; The Shout; Ada in the Jungle; Children; Wings of Fame; Bonfire of the Vanities; Ferdy Duke; The Pope Must Die; Searching For Bobby Fischer, 1992; Century, 1993; Secret Rapture, 1993. *Television* includes: Vienna 1900 (6 part series), 1973; Tribute to J. B. Priestley, 1974; Kean, 1978; Voyage of Charles Darwin, 1978; Office Story, 1978; Friends in Space, 1979; Suez, 1979; The Executioner, 1980; Adelaide Bartlett (series), 1980; Winter's Tale, 1980; The Double Dealer, 1980; The Trial of Madame Farnay, 1980; Holocaust (USA), 1980; Eden End, 1981; The Year of the French (RTE), 1981; Anyone for Denis?, 1982; Tales Out of School, 1982; Box of Delights, 1984; Puccini, 1984; By the Sword Divided (series), 1984; Hells Bells (series), 1985; War and Remembrance (film series), 1986; Fortunes of War (series), 1986; Lizzie's Pictures (series), 1986; Shostokovich, 1987; Adam Bede; L. P. Hartley Trilogy; An Actor's Life For Me; Down Where the Buffalo Go; American Roulette; Fine Romance; Stolen; Greek Myths; In my own Defence; Roger Casement. *Radio* plays include: The Light Shines in the Darkness (BBC), 1985; Timon of Athens (BBC), 1989. Variety Club Award for stage actor, 1965. *Posthumous publication:* (with Michael Goveney) Knight Errant: memoirs of a vagabond actor, 1995. *Recreations:* cooking, gymnastics, swimming. *Address:* c/o Michael Foster, ICM, Oxford House, 76 Oxford Street, W1N 0AX. *Died 12 Nov. 1995.*

STEPHENSON, Donald, CBE 1957 (OBE 1943); Controller, Overseas and Foreign Relations, BBC, 1966–71; *b* 18 May 1909; *yr s* of late J. V. G. Stephenson; *m* 1st, 1940, Alison (*d* 1965), *yr d* of late Wynn ap H. Thomas, OBE, LLB; three *d* (one *s* decd); 2nd, 1982, Francesca, *yr d* of late Captain Charles Francis Ward, RHA. *Educ:* Denstone College (Scholar); Paris; Baghdad. Banking business, 1925–31; permanent commission, RAF,

1932; Flt Lt, 1936; served France and Middle East, 1935–37; language specialist (interpreter, French and Arabic); Special Duty List, 1938; Arabic Editor, BBC, 1939; Director, BBC, New Delhi, 1944–45; Director, Eastern Services, 1946–47; Asst Controller in Overseas Div., 1948; Controller, North Region, 1948–56; Controller, Overseas Services, BBC, 1956–58; Chief Executive, Anglia Television Ltd, 1959; Head of Overseas and Foreign Relations, BBC, Dec. 1960. A Governor of Manchester Univ., 1950–58. A delegate to 5th Commonwealth Broadcasting Conf., Canada, 1963, to 7th Conf., NZ, 1968, and 8th Conf., Jamaica, 1970. *Recreation:* family life. *Address:* 14 Mill Street, Islip, Kidlington, Oxford OX5 2SY. *Died 2 Jan. 1993.*

STEPHENSON, Henry Shepherd, CEng, FIMinE; Chairman, Mining Qualifications Board, 1970–75; *b* 1 Oct. 1905; *m* 1934, Faith Estelle, 3rd *d* of Tom Edward Arnold, Bolton Old Hall, Bradford; two *d. Educ:* Whitehaven Grammar School; Armstrong College, Durham University (BSc). Articled apprentice Mining Engineer, Whitehaven Colliery Co., 1924–28; official posts, Whitehaven Colliery Co., 1928–35; HM Junior Inspector of Mines Northern Div., 1935–39; Mining Agent, Cumberland Coal Co., 1939–41; HM Junior Inspector of Mines and Quarries (Yorkshire), 1941–44; Senior Inspector (Scotland), 1944–47; Senior Dist Inspector (Durham), 1948–52; Senior Dist Inspector (West Midland), 1952–58; Divisional Inspector (East Midland), 1958–62; Deputy Chief Inspector, Jan. 1962; Chief Inspector, 1962–70. Hon. DSc Newcastle upon Tyne, 1971. *Address:* 4 St Margarets Court, Topsham, Devon EX3 0JL. *Died 10 Sept. 1993.*

STEPHENSON, Philip Robert, CMG 1962; OBE 1951; *b* 29 May 1914; *s* of late Robert Barnard Stephenson and Lilian Stephenson (*née* Sharp); *m* 1947, Marianne Hurst Wraith; two *s. Educ:* Berkhamsted School; Imperial College, London; Downing College, Cambridge; Imperial College of Tropical Agriculture, Trinidad. Colonial Agricultural Service, Entomologist, Uganda, 1938; Military Service, 1940–43; East African Anti-Locust Directorate, 1943–47, Director, Desert Locust Survey, 1948–62, HM Overseas Service. Member, British Advisory Mission on Tropical Agriculture in Bolivia, Dept of Technical Co-operation, 1963–64. *Address:* c/o Lloyds Bank, Berkhamsted, Herts HP4 1AP. *Club:* MCC.
Died 31 July 1994.

STERN, Prof. Joseph Peter Maria, PhD, LittD; FBA 1990; Professor of German, University of London, and Head of Department, University College, 1972–86, then Professor Emeritus; Research Fellow, University College London, since 1990; *b* 25 Dec. 1920; *s* of Gustav Stern and Louisa (*née* Bondy); *m* 1944, Sheila Frances, *d* of late Joseph Patrick and Frances McMullan; two *s* two *d. Educ:* Czech schs in Prague and Vienna; Barry County Sch. for Boys, Glam; St John's Coll., Cambridge (MA 1947, PhD 1949, LittD 1975; Hon. Fellow, 1990). Wartime service in Czech Army and RAF (VR). Asst Lectr, Bedford Coll., London, 1950–52; Asst Lectr, then Lectr, Cambridge Univ., 1952–72; Fellow, St John's Coll., Cambridge, 1954–72 (Tutor, 1963–70, 1972); Chm. of Bd, Germanic Languages and Literature, Univ. of London, 1978–79; Hon. Dir, Inst. of Germanic Studies, Univ. of London, 1981–85. Prof.-at-Large, Cornell Univ., Ithaca, NY, 1976–82. Vis. Professor: City Coll. of New York, 1958; Univ. of Calif at Berkeley, 1964 and 1967; State Univ. of NY at Buffalo, 1969; Univ. of Va, Charlottesville, 1971; Univ. of Calif at Irvine, 1988; Merton Prof., Univ. of Göttingen, 1965; Bernhard Vis. Prof., Williams Coll., Williamstown, Mass, 1986–87; Hochschule für angewandte Kunst, Vienna, 1988–89. Fellow, Center for Humanities, Wesleyan Univ., 1972. Lewis Fry Meml Lectr, Univ. of Bristol, 1973; British

Academy Master Mind Lectr, 1978. General Editor, Landmarks of World Literature, 1986–. Mem., Acad. of Sciences, Göttingen, 1988–. Goethe Medal, Goethe Inst., 1980; Alexander von Humboldt Research Prize, 1980. *Publications:* Ernst Jünger: a writer of our time, 1952; (trans.) R. W. Meyer, Leibnitz and the seventeenth-century revolution, 1952; (trans.) H.-E. Holthusen, R. M. Rilke: a study of his later poetry, 1952; G. C. Lichtenberg: a doctrine of scattered occasions, 1959; Re-Interpretations: seven studies in nineteenth-century German literature, 1964, repr. 1981; (ed) Arthur Schnitzler: Liebelei, Leutnant Gustl, and Die letzten Masken, 1966; Idylls and Realities: studies in nineteenth-century German literature, 1971; On Realism, 1973, rev. German version, 1982; Hitler: the Führer and the People, 1975 (3rd edn 1990, German version 1978, French trans. rev. by S. F. Stern, 1985, Czech version, 1987); Nietzsche (Fontana Modern Masters), 1978; A Study of Nietzsche, 1979, rev. German version, 1982; (with Michael Silk) Nietzsche on Tragedy, 1981 (J. G. Robertson Prize, 1988); (ed) The World of Franz Kafka, 1981; (ed) London German Studies II, 1984, III, 1986; (ed) Paths and Labyrinths: a Kafka symposium, 1985; contribs (incl. 42 Poems from the Czech, trans. with S. F. Stern) and articles in English and foreign jls and newspapers; *posthumous publication:* The Heart of Europe: essays on literature and ideology, 1992. *Address:* 83 Barton Road, Cambridge CB3 9LL. *T:* Cambridge (0223) 353078. *Died 18 Nov. 1991.*

STEVENS, (Arthur) Edwin, CBE 1979; *b* 17 Oct. 1905; *s* of Arthur Edwin Stevens and Bessie Annie (*née* Dowden); *m* 1933, Kathleen Alberta James; three *s. Educ:* West Monmouth Sch.; University Coll., Cardiff (BSc Hons 1927; Hon. Fellow 1981); Jesus Coll., Oxford (MA Hons 1929). Founder, Amplivox Ltd: Chm. and Man. Dir, 1935–75; designed world's first wearable electronic hearing aid, 1935; collector of world's most comprehensive exhibn of aids to hearing covering 400 yrs. Hon. Fellow, Jesus Coll., Oxford, 1973; financed building of Stevens Close, Jesus Coll. Hall of Residence opened by the Queen, 1976; New Assembly Hall, Jesus Coll., 1988; inaugurated Princess Alice Hospice, Esher, 1979; founded RSM Edwin Stevens Lectures for Laity, 1970. Hon. FRSM 1981. Hon. LLD Wales, 1984. *Address:* Oak Lawn, 1 Copsem Way, Esher, Surrey KT10 9ER. *T:* Esher (01372) 466767. *Died 29 Jan. 1995.*

STEVENS, Frank Leonard; formerly Editor, FBI Review and Publicity Officer, Federation of British Industries; *b* Mexborough, 8 Jan. 1898; *s* of late Frederick Thomas Stevens; *m* 1925, Winifred (*d* 1985), 2nd *d* of Alexander Bruce, JP; two *s. Educ:* Mexborough Grammar School; University College, London. After a year as teacher, three years in the Army (1916–19), entered journalism; South Yorkshire Times; Allied Newspapers, Manchester; Manchester Evening News; assistant editor, John O' London's Weekly; Daily News sub-editorial staff; associate editor, Everyman; joint editor, monthly Clarion. *Publications:* Through Merrie England, 1926; On Going to Press, 1928; Under London, 1939. *Recreations:* reading, sketching. *Address:* Barn Cottage, Singleton, Chichester, West Sussex PO18 0HD. *T:* Singleton (024363) 653.
Died 15 April 1991.

STEVENS, Philip Theodore; Professor of Greek in the University of London (Bedford College), 1950–74, then Emeritus; *b* 11 Nov. 1906; *s* of late Rev. Herbert Stevens, Vicar of Milwich; *m* 1939, Evelyn Grace (*d* 1990), 2nd *d* of late G. L. Crickmay, FRIBA, Oatlands Park, Weybridge, Surrey; one *s. Educ:* Wolverhampton Grammar School; New Coll., Oxford (Scholar; 1st Cl. Hon. Mods, 1927; 2nd Cl. Lit.Hum., 1929); PhD Aberdeen, 1939. Asst Master, Liverpool Institute, 1929–30; Tutor at Univ. Corresp. Coll., Cambridge, 1930–32; Asst Lecturer in

Greek, Univ. of Aberdeen, 1933–38; Lectr in Classics, Univ. of Cape Town, 1938–41; War Service, S African Mil. Intelligence, 1941–45; Lecturer in Latin and Greek, University of Liverpool, 1945–50. Trustee, Hellenic Soc., 1961–. *Publications:* Euripides, Andromache, 1971; Colloquial Expressions in Euripides, 1976; The Society for the Promotion of Hellenic Studies 1879–1979, 1979; contribs to English and foreign classical periodicals. *Recreation:* music. *Address:* The Old Prebendal House, Shipton-under-Wychwood, Oxon OX7 6BQ.

Died 17 Dec. 1992.

STEVENSON, Dr Alan Carruth; *b* 27 Jan. 1909; *s* of Allan Stevenson, CBE, and Christina Kennedy Lawson; *m* 1937, Annie Gordon Sheila Steven (*d* 1989); two *s* one *d. Educ:* Glasgow Academy; Glasgow University. BSc 1930, MB, ChB 1933, MD 1946, Glasgow; MRCP 1935; FRCP 1955. Appointments: Royal Infirmary, Glasgow; Highgate Hospital, London; London Hospital. Served RAMC, 1939–45 (despatches); hon. rank of Lieutenant-Colonel, 1946–48, retd. Professor of Social and Preventive Medicine, The Queen's University, Belfast, 1948–58; Reader in Public Health, London University; Dir, MRC Population Genetics Unit, Oxford, and Lectr in Human Genetics, Oxford Univ., 1958–74. *Publications:* Build your own Enlarger, 1943; Recent Advances in Social Medicine, 1948; Genetic Counselling, 1971; articles on tropical and preventive medicine and human genetics in appropriate scientific journals. *Recreation:* fishing. *Address:* 17 Little Dene Copse, Pennington, Lymington, Hants SO41 8EW. *T:* Lymington (01590) 76444.

Died 18 Sept. 1995.

STEVENSON, Robert Barron Kerr, CBE 1976; MA; FSA; Keeper, National Museum of Antiquities of Scotland, 1946–78, Trustee, 1975–78; *b* 16 July 1913; *s* of late Professor William B. Stevenson and Margaret Bell, *d* of David Kerr, Clonin; *m* 1950, Elizabeth M. Begg; twin *s. Educ:* Edinburgh Univ. Member: Ancient Monuments Board for Scotland, 1961–79; Cttees of Inquiry: Field Monuments, 1966–68; Provincial Museums, 1972–73. Pres., Soc. of Antiquaries of Scotland, 1975–78. Mem., Deutsches Archäologisches Institut, 1953–. Fellow, UCL, 1977. FMA, 1953–78. Hon. FRNS 1979; Hon. DLitt Edinburgh, 1981. *Address:* 51/1 Mortonhall Road, Edinburgh EH9 2HN. *T:* 031–662 0826.

Died 6 June 1992.

STEWARD, Prof. Frederick Campion, FRS 1957; Charles A. Alexander Professor of Biological Sciences and Director of Laboratory for Cell Physiology and Growth, Cornell University, Ithaca, NY, 1965–72, then Professor Emeritus (Professor of Botany, 1950–65); *b* 16 June 1904; *s* of Frederick Walter and Mary Daglish Steward; *m* 1929, Anne Temple Gordon, Richmond, Va, USA; one *s. Educ:* Heckmondwike Gram. Sch., Yorks; Leeds Univ. BSc 1924 (1st Class Hons); PhD 1926; DSc London 1937. Demonstrator in Botany, Leeds Univ., 1926; Rockefeller Fellow: Cornell Univ., 1927; Univ. of California, 1928; Asst Lecturer, Univ. of Leeds (Botany), 1929; Rockefeller Foundation Fellow, 1933–34; Reader in Botany, Univ. of London (Birkbeck Coll.), 1934; War Service with MAP (Dir of Aircraft Equipment), 1940–45; Prof. of Botany and Chm. of Dept, Univ. of Rochester, Rochester, NY, 1946–50. John Simon Guggenheim Fellow, 1963–64; Sir C. V. Raman Vis. Prof., Madras Univ., 1974. Fellow American Academy of Arts and Sciences, 1956. Merit Award, Botanical Society of America, 1961. Hon. DSc: Delhi, 1974; William and Mary, 1982; Guelph, 1983. *Publications:* Plants at Work, 1964; Growth and Organisation in Plants, 1968; Plants, Chemicals and Growth, 1971; (ed) Treatise on Plant Physiology, 6 vols and 11 tomes, 1959–72, Vols 7–9, 1983–86; papers in scientific journals and proceedings of learned societies.

Recreations: gardening, swimming. *Address:* 4947 Woodland Forrest Drive, Tuscaloosa, Ala 35405, USA.

Died 14 Sept. 1993.

STEWARD, Nigel Oliver Willoughby, OBE 1946; MA Oxon, BA Cantab; Consul-General, Haifa, 1955–59, retired; *b* 16 Oct. 1899; *s* of Arthur Bennett Steward, ICS, and Alice Willoughby; *m* 1933, Raquel Wyneken, Viña del Mar, Chile; three *d. Educ:* Winchester (Scholar); Trinity College, Oxford. Entered Consular Service, 1924; Vice-Consul at San Francisco, Valparaiso, Guatemala (Second Secretary), and Paris; Consul and First Secretary at Montevideo; Minister (local rank) to Paraguay; First Secretary, Bucharest, 1946; Deputy Consul-Gen., New York, 1946–48; Minister to Nicaragua, 1948–52; Consul-General, Nice and Monaco, 1952–55. *Address:* Church Cottage, 13 Gravel Walk, Cullompton, Devon EX15 1DA. *Club:* United Oxford & Cambridge University.

Died 13 May 1991.

STEWART, Andrew, CBE 1954; *b* 23 June 1907; *s* of James Stewart; *m* 1937, Agnes Isabella Burnet (*d* 1991), *d* of James McKechnie, JP. *Educ:* Glasgow University (MA). Hon LLD Glasgow, 1970. Joined BBC at Glasgow, 1926; Glasgow Representative, 1931–35; Scottish Programme Director, 1935–48 (Min. of Information, 1939–41); Controller (N Ire.), 1948–52; Controller (Home Service), 1953–57; Controller, Scotland, 1957–68. Director, Scottish Television, 1968–77. Chm., Scottish Music Archive, 1972–82; Chm., Films of Scotland Committee. Governor, National Film School, 1971–76. Hon. Pres., Scottish Radio Industries Club, 1972–89. *Recreations:* reading, the theatre, mountaineering. *Address:* 36 Sherbrooke Avenue, Glasgow G41 4EP.

Died 5 Nov. 1991.

STEWART, Sir David (Brodribb), 2nd Bt *cr* 1960, of Strathgarry, Perth; TD 1948; Managing Director, Francis Price (Fabrics) Ltd, Manchester, 1960–81; retired; *b* 20 Dec. 1913; *s* of Sir Kenneth Dugald Stewart, 1st Bt, GBE, and Noel (*d* 1946), *y d* of Kenric Brodribb, Melbourne; *S* father, 1972; *m* 1963, Barbara Dykes, *d* of late Harry Dykes Lloyd and *widow* of Donald Ian Stewart. *Educ:* Marlborough College; Manchester College of Technology (BSc (Tech), Textile Technology). Joined Stewart Thomson & Co. Ltd, Textile Merchant Converters, 1935; continuously employed in this company, except for six years war service, until absorbed into the Haighton & Dewhurst Group, 1958 (Francis Price (Fabrics) Ltd a subsidiary of this Group). Commissioned 8th Bn Lancashire Fusiliers (TA), 1934; war service, 1939–45; joined Duke of Lancaster's Own Yeomanry (TA) on re-formation of TA, 1947; in comd, 1952–56; retd with rank of Bt Col. *Recreation:* gardening. *Heir: b* Alastair Robin Stewart [*b* 26 Sept. 1925; *m* 1953, Patricia Helen, *d* of late J. A. Merrett; one *s* three *d*]. *Address:* Delamere, Heyes Lane, Alderley Edge, Cheshire SK9 7JY. *T:* Alderley Edge (0625) 582312.

Died 17 Oct. 1992.

STEWART, Rt Hon. Donald James, PC 1977; *b* 17 Oct. 1920; *m* 1955, Christina Macaulay. *Educ:* Nicolson Institute, Stornoway. Provost of Stornoway, 1958–64 and 1968–70; Hon. Sheriff, 1960. MP (SNP) Western Isles, 1970–87; Leader, Parly SNP, 1974–87; Pres., SNP, 1982–87. *Recreations:* fishing, photography, gardening. *Address:* Hillcrest, 41 Goathill Road, Stornoway, Isle of Lewis. *T:* Stornoway (0851) 2672.

Died 23 Aug. 1992.

STEWART, Sir Hugh Charlie Godfray, 6th Bt, *cr* 1803, of Athenree, Tyrone; DL; Major; High Sheriff, Co. Tyrone, 1955; *b* 13 April 1897; *s* of Colonel Sir George Powell Stewart, 5th Bt, and Florence Maria Georgina, *d* of Sir James Godfray; *S* father, 1945; *m* 1st, 1929, Rosemary Elinor Dorothy (marr. diss. 1942), *d* of Major

George Peacocke; one *s* one *d*; 2nd, 1948, Diana Margaret, *d* of late Capt. J. E. Hibbert, MC, DFC, and Mrs R. B. Bannon, Jersey; one *s* one *d*. *Educ:* Bradfield Coll., Berkshire; RMC, Sandhurst. Served War, Royal Inniskilling Fusiliers, 1916; Arras, 1917 (wounded); France, 1939–40. Foreign Service included India, Iraq, China, Malaya, South Africa and Syria; retired. DL Co. Tyrone, 1971. *Heir: s* David John Christopher Stewart [*b* 19 June 1935; *m* 1959, Bridget Anne, *er d* of late Patrick W. Sim and of Mrs Leslie Parkhouse; three *d*]. *Address:* Cottesbrook, Sandy Pluck Lane, Bentham, near Cheltenham, Glos GL51 5UB.

Died 31 July 1994.

STEWART, James Gill, CB 1958; CBE 1952; *b* 13 March 1907; *s* of John Stewart (builder) and Isabella Stewart, late of Edinburgh; *m* 1936, Jessie Dodd (*d* 1988); one *s* one *d*. *Educ:* George Watson's College, Edinburgh; Edinburgh University. Passed Home Civil Service Administrative Class Competition, 1929; entered Min. of Labour, Asst Principal, 1930; Private Sec. to Permanent Sec., 1934; Principal, 1936; Asst Sec., 1941; on loan to Min. of Works, 1941–43; on loan to UN (Bureau of Personnel), 1946–47; on loan to Cabinet Office, 1947–49; Industrial Relations Dept, 1950–53; Under-Sec., Employment Dept, 1953; Training Dept, 1960, retired, 1967. Hon. FITD. *Recreations:* choral singing, hill walking. *Address:* The Close, Burcot, Abingdon. *Died 3 July 1991.*

STEWART, James Lablache; *see* Granger, Stewart.

STEWART, John Anthony Benedict, CMG 1979; OBE 1973; HM Diplomatic Service, retired; Chairman, Civil Service Selection Board, since 1987; consultant; *b* 24 May 1927; *e s* of late Edward Vincent Stewart and Emily Veronica (*née* Jones); *m* 1960, Geraldine Margaret, *o d* of late Captain G. C. Clifton; one *s* one *d* (and one *s* decd). *Educ:* St Illtyd's Coll.; Univ. of Wales; Cambridge Univ.; Imperial Coll. of Science and Technology. RNVR Ordinary Seaman, later Midshipman, 1944–47. Colonial Geol. Survey Service, Somaliland Protectorate, 1952–56; Dist Officer, 1956–57; seconded to Anglo-Ethiopian Liaison Service, 1957–60 (Sen. Liaison Officer, 1960); transf. N Rhodesia as Dist Officer, 1960, Dist Comr, 1962–64; Resident Local Govt Officer, Barotseland, 1964–67; entered HM Diplomatic Service, 1968; served FCO, Barbados, Uganda; RCDS, 1974; Ambassador to Democratic Republic of Vietnam, 1975–76; Head of Hong Kong Dept, FCO, 1976–78; Ambassador: to Laos, 1978–80; to Mozambique, 1980–84; High Comr to Sri Lanka, 1984–87. Cox Gold medal for Geology, 1950. *Publications:* The Geology of the Mait Area, 1955; papers in geological jls. *Recreations:* shooting, fishing. *Club:* Commonwealth Trust. *Died 12 Sept. 1995.*

STEWART, John Innes Mackintosh; Reader in English Literature, Oxford University, 1969–73; Student of Christ Church, Oxford, 1949–73, then Emeritus; *b* 30 Sept. 1906; *s* of late John Stewart, Director of Education in the City of Edinburgh, and Eliza Jane, *d* of James Clark, Golford, Nairn; *m* 1932, Margaret Hardwick (*d* 1979); three *s* two *d*. *Educ:* Edinburgh Academy; Oriel College, Oxford. Bishop Fraser's Scholar, 1930; 1st class Eng. Lang. and Lit. 1928; Matthew Arnold Memorial Prize, 1929. Lectr in English in Univ. of Leeds, 1930–35; Jury Professor of English in Univ. of Adelaide, 1935–45; Lectr in Queen's Univ., Belfast, 1946–48; Walker-Ames Prof., Univ. of Washington, 1961. Hon. FRSE 1990. Hon. DLitt: New Brunswick, 1962; Leicester, 1979; St Andrews, 1980. *Publications:* Montaigne's Essays: John Florio's Translation, 1931; Character and Motive in Shakespeare, 1949; Eight Modern Writers, 1963; Rudyard Kipling, 1966; Joseph Conrad, 1968; Thomas Hardy, 1971; Shakespeare's Lofty Scene (Shakespeare Lectr, British Acad.), 1971; detective novels and broadcast scripts (under

pseudonym of Michael Innes): Death at the President's Lodging, 1936; Hamlet Revenge!, 1937; Lament for a Maker, 1938; Stop Press, 1939; There Came Both Mist and Snow, 1940; The Secret Vanguard, 1940; Appleby on Ararat, 1941; The Daffodil Affair, 1942; The Weight of the Evidence, 1944; Appleby's End, 1945; From London Far, 1946; What Happened at Hazelwood, 1947; A Night of Errors, 1948; The Hawk and the Handsaw, 1948; The Journeying Boy, 1949; Operation Pax, 1951; A Private View, 1952; Christmas at Candleshoe, 1953; Appleby Talking, 1954; The Man From the Sea, 1955; Old Hall, New Hall, 1956; Appleby Talks Again, 1956; Appleby Plays Chicken, 1956; The Long Farewell, 1958; Hare Sitting Up, 1959; The New Sonia Wayward, 1960; Silence Observed, 1961; A Connoisseur's Case, 1962; Money from Holme, 1964; The Bloody Wood, 1966; A Change of Heir, 1966; Appleby at Allington, 1968; A Family Affair, 1969; Death at the Chase, 1970; An Awkward Lie, 1971; The Open House, 1972; Appleby's Answer, 1973; Appleby's Other Story, 1974; The Mysterious Commission, 1974; The Appleby File, 1975; The Gay Phoenix, 1976; Honeybath's Haven, 1977; The Ampersand Papers, 1978; Going It Alone, 1980; Lord Mullion's Secret, 1981; Sheiks and Adders, 1982; Appleby and Honeybath, 1983; Carson's Conspiracy, 1984; Appleby and the Ospreys, 1986; novels (as J. I. M. Stewart): Mark Lambert's Supper, 1954; The Guardians, 1955; A Use of Riches, 1957; The Man Who Wrote Detective Stories, 1959; The Man Who Won the Pools, 1961; The Last Tresilians, 1963; An Acre of Grass, 1965; The Aylwins, 1966; Vanderlyn's Kingdom, 1967; Cucumber Sandwiches, 1969; Avery's Mission, 1971; A Palace of Art, 1972; Mungo's Dream, 1973; quintet, A Staircase in Surrey, 1974–78 (The Gaudy, 1974; Young Pattullo, 1975; A Memorial Service, 1976; The Madonna of the Astrolabe, 1977; Full Term, 1978); Our England is a Garden and other stories, 1979; Andrew and Tobias, 1981; The Bridge at Arta and other stories, 1981; A Villa in France, 1982; My Aunt Christina and Other Stories, 1983; An Open Prison, 1984; The Naylors, 1985; Parlour 4 and other stories, 1986; *autobiography:* Myself and Michael Innes, 1987. *Recreation:* walking. *Address:* c/o 79 South Hill Park, NW3 2SS.

Died 12 Nov. 1994.

STEWART, Sir Michael (Norman Francis), KCMG 1966 (CMG 1957); OBE 1948; HM Diplomatic Service, retired; Director, Sotheby's, since 1977; *b* 18 Jan. 1911; *s* of late Sir Francis Stewart, CIE, and Lady (Frances Henrietta) Stewart; *m* 1951, Katharine Damaris Houssemayne du Boulay; one *s* two *d*. *Educ:* Shrewsbury; Trinity College, Cambridge. Assistant Keeper, Victoria and Albert Museum, 1935–39; Ministry of Information, 1939–41; Press Attaché: HM Embassy, Lisbon, 1941–44; HM Embassy, Rome, 1944–48; employed in Foreign Office, 1948–51; Counsellor: Office of Comr-Gen. for UK in SE Asia, 1951–54; HM Embassy, Ankara, 1954–59; HM Chargé d'Affaires, Peking, 1959–62; Senior Civilian Instructor, IDC, 1962–64; HM Minister, British Embassy, Washington, 1964–67; Ambassador to Greece, 1967–71. Dir, Ditchley Foundn, 1971–76. *Recreation:* country life. *Address:* Combe, near Newbury, Berks RG15 0EH. *Club:* Buck's. *Died 25 Sept. 1994.*

STEWART, Richard, CBE 1976; JP; Leader of Council, Strathclyde Regional Council, 1974–86; *b* 27 May 1920; *s* of Richard Stewart and Agnes (*née* Cunningham); *m* 1942, Elizabeth Peat; one *d*. *Educ:* Harthill Sch., Harthill. Mem., Lanark CC for 15 years (Chm. several cttees, finally Chm., Social Work Cttee). Full-time Sec./Organiser, Labour Party, 1950–82; Agent for: Rt Hon. Miss Margaret Herbison for 20 years; Rt Hon. John Smith, MP, 1970–82. Mem., Bd of Dirs, Scottish Transport Group, 1975–88. Pres., Convention of Scottish Local

Authorities, 1984–86. Past Chairman: Scottish Council of Labour Party; Nat. Union of Labour Organisers. Dir, Scottish Exhibition Centre, 1983–86. JP Lanark, 1964. Hon. LLB Strathclyde Univ., 1986. *Recreations:* music, chess. *Address:* 28 Hawthorn Drive, Harthill, Shotts ML7 5SG. *T:* Harthill (0501) 51303.

Died 7 April 1991.

STEWART, Stanley Toft, CMG 1958; PJG 1962; *b* 13 June 1910; *s* of Charles Campbell Stewart and Jeanette Matilda Doral; *m* 1935, Therese Zelie de Souza; seven *d. Educ:* St Xavier's Instn, Penang; Raffles Coll., Singapore. Straits Settlements CS, 1934–46; Overseas Civil Service, 1946–55: District Officer, Butterworth, Province Wellesley, 1947–52; Dep. Chm., Rural Board, Singapore, 1952–54; Chm., Rural Board, Singapore, 1954; Dep. Sec., Ministry of Local Government, Lands and Housing, Singapore, 1955, Actg Permanent Sec., 1955; Actg Chief Sec., Singapore, Oct. 1957–Jan. 1958; Permanent Secretary: Home Affairs, 1959–63; to Prime Minister, 1961–66; Singapore High Comr in Australia, 1966–69; Permanent Sec., Min. of Foreign Affairs, Singapore, 1969–72; Exec. Sec., Nat. Stadium Corp., 1973. *Recreations:* tennis, gardening. *Clubs:* Singapore Recreation, Club 200 (Singapore).

Died 9 Feb. 1992.

STEWART, Stephen Malcolm, CBE 1986; QC 1979; Chairman, Common Law Institute of Intellectual Property, since 1981; *b* 22 April 1914; *s* of Dr Siegmund and Helen Strauss; *m* 1st, 1946, Marie Josephine (*née* Bere) (*d* 1990); two *s*; 2nd, 1992, Jane (*née* Taylor-Allen). *Educ:* Univ. of Vienna (LLD 1936); Ecole des Sciences Politiques, Paris (Diploma 1938); Univ. of London. Overseas Service, BBC, 1939; served Army, 1940–47; Captain, Liaison Officer, Free French Forces and Belgian Army, 1944–45; Major JAG's Branch, 21 Army Group, 1945; Chief Prosecuting Officer, War Crimes Trials, 1946–47; UN War Crimes Commn, 1947–48; called to the Bar, Inner Temple, 1948; practice at the Bar, 1948–61; Director General, IFPI, 1961–79. Mem., Gen. Council of the Bar, 1969–71; Vice-Chm., Bar Assoc. for Commerce, Finance and Industry, 1974–76, Chm., 1976–78; Member of Senate of the Inns of Court and Bar, 1976–81. Governor: Polytechnic of the South Bank, 1967–70; Sevenoaks School, 1968–83. Golden Cross of the Republic, Austria, 1983. *Publications:* The Clearinghouse System for Copyright Licences, 1966; 200 Years of English Copyright Law, 1976; International Copyright in the 1980s (Geiringer Meml Lecture, NY), 1980; International Copyright and Neighbouring Rights, 1983, 3rd edn 1993. *Recreations:* music, tennis. *Address:* Oakwood, Chittoe, Wilts SN15 2EW. *T:* Devizes (01380) 850066. *Club:* Reform.

Died 17 April 1995.

STIGLER, Prof. George Joseph, PhD; economist; Charles R. Walgreen Distinguished Service Professor Emeritus of American Institutions, University of Chicago, since 1981; *b* 17 Jan. 1911; *s* of Joseph Stigler and Elizabeth Stigler (*née* Hungler); *m* 1936, Margaret Mack (*d* 1970); three *s. Educ:* Seattle schools; Univ. of Washington (BBA); Northwestern Univ. (MBA); Univ. of Chicago (PhD 1938). Asst Prof., Iowa State Univ., 1936–38; Asst Prof., later Prof., Univ. of Minnesota, 1938–46 (war-time Mem., Stats Res. Group, Columbia Univ.); Professor: Brown Univ., 1946–47; Columbia Univ., 1947–58; Charles R. Walgreen Prof. of Amer. Instns, Graduate Sch. of Business, Univ. of Chicago, 1958, Dist. Service Prof., 1963; Founder, Center for Study of the Economy and the States, Univ. of Chicago, 1977. Member: Nat. Acad. of Sciences, 1975; Amer. Economic Assoc. (Pres., 1964); Guggenheim Fellow, 1955. Nobel Prize for Economic Science, 1982; Nat. Medal of Science, 1987. Editor, Jl of Political Economy, 1974–. *Publications:* Production and Distribution Theories, 1940; The Theory of Competitive Price, 1942; The Theory of Price, 1946 (numerous rev. edns); Trends in Employment in the Service Industries, 1956; The Intellectual and the Market Place, 1964, rev. edn 1984; Essays in the History of Economics, 1965; The Organization of Industry, 1968; The Citizen and the State, 1975; The Economist as Preacher, 1982; Memoirs of an Unregulated Economist (autobiog.), 1988; essays and articles for Nat. Bureau of Economic Research, Fortune, Jl of Political Economy (The Economics of Information, 1961), Jl of Business, Jl of Law and Economics, Bell Jl of Economics and Management Science, Antitrust Bulletin and other learned jls. *Recreations:* book collecting, golf, photography. *Address:* University of Chicago Graduate School of Business, 1101 East 58th Street, Chicago, Ill 60637, USA; 5825 Dorchester Avenue, Chicago, Ill 60637, USA.

Died 1 Dec. 1991.

STIRLING, Sir James (Frazer), Kt 1992; RA 1991 (ARA 1985); ARIBA 1950; architect; *b* 22 April 1926; *s* of Joseph Stirling and Louisa Frazer; *m* 1966, Mary, *d* of Morton Shand and Sybil Sissons; one *s* two *d. Educ:* Quarry Bank High Sch., Liverpool; Liverpool Sch. of Art, 1942. Served War of 1939–45: Lieut, Black Watch and Paratroops (D-Day Landing). Sch. of Architecture, Liverpool Univ., 1945–50. With Assoc. of Town Planning and Regional Research, London, 1950–52; worked for Lyons, Israel and Ellis, London, 1953–56; entered a series of architectural competitions, and Mem. ICA Indep. Gp, 1952–56; private practice, 1956– (Partners: James Gowan until 1963 and Michael Wilford, 1971–). Projects include: Flats at Ham Common, 1955–58; Churchill Coll. Comp., 1958; Selwyn Coll., Cambridge, 1959; Leicester Univ. Engrg Bldg, 1959–63 (USA Reynolds Award); Andrew Melville Hall, St Andrews Univ., 1964–68; Dorman Long Steel Co. HQ, 1965; Runcorn New Town Housing, 1968–; re-development plan of West Mid-Town Manhatten, for New York City Planning Commn, USA, 1968–69; Olivetti Trng Sch., Surrey, 1969–72; Siemens AG Computer Centre Munich, 1970; buildings in Iran, Berlin and Stuttgart, 1977; New State Art Gall., Stuttgart, 1977–83; mus. buildings for Harvard, Columbia, and Rice, Houston, Univs, 1979; Clore Gall., Tate, 1983–87. Visiting teacher at: Architectural Assoc., London, 1955; Regent Street Polytechnic, London, 1956–57; Cambridge Univ. Sch. of Architecture, 1958; Charles Davenport Visiting Prof., Yale Univ. Sch. of Architecture, USA, 1970; Master Class, Kunstakademie, Düsseldorf, 1977–. Invited UK Architect, in internat. limited competitions for Govt/United Nations low cost housing for Peru, 1969. Hon. Mem., Akademie der Kunst, Berlin, 1969; Hon. FAIA, 1976; Hon. Dr RCA, 1979. Exhibitions: "James Stirling—Three Buildings", at Museum of Modern Art, NY, USA, 1969; (drawings) RIBA Heinz Gall., 1974 (associated pubn, James Stirling, 1974); "Foster, Rogers and Stirling", RA, 1987. BBC/Arts Council film, James Stirling's Architecture, 1973. Brunner Award, USA, 1976; Aalto Medal, Finland, 1978; Royal Gold Medal, RIBA, 1980; Pritzker Prize, 1981. *Relevant publication:* James Stirling: Buildings and Projects, 1985. *Address:* 8 Fitzroy Square, W1P 5AH.

Died 25 June 1992.

STOBART, Patrick Desmond, CBE 1976 (MBE 1950); HM Diplomatic Service, retired; *b* 14 Feb. 1920; *s* of late Reginald and Eva Stobart; *m* 1st, 1951, Sheila (marr. diss. 1973), *d* of late A. W. Brown, Belfast; three *s* one *d*; 2nd, 1974, Erika Marie Witharn (marr. diss. 1975), *d* of late Carl Deuschle, Göppingen. *Educ:* Cathedral and Cleveland House Schools, Salisbury; St Edmund Hall, Oxford. Served Royal Artillery and Wilts Regiment, 1940–46. Tübingen University, 1946; Political Officer, Trucial Oman, 1947; Chancery, Bonn, 1951–53; FO, 1953–54; Consul, Benghazi, 1954–58; FO, 1958–60; Commercial Counsellor, British Embassy, Helsinki, 1960–64,

Copenhagen, 1964–66; Consul-General, Gothenburg, 1966–68; seconded to Aero-Engine Div., Rolls-Royce Ltd, 1968–69; Gwilym Gibbon Research Fellow, Nuffield College, Oxford, 1969–70; Head of Export Promotion Dept, FCO, 1970–71; Consul-Gen., Zürich, 1971–75; seconded to Commercial Relations and Exports Div., DoT, 1976–79. Mem. of Secretariat, Internat. Primary Aluminium Inst., 1979–86. *Publication:* (also ed) The Centenary Book of the Hall and Héroult Processes for the Production of Aluminium, 1986. *Recreation:* history.

Died 3 Dec. 1991.

STOCKWOOD, Rt Rev. (Arthur) Mervyn, DD; Hon. Assistant Bishop, Diocese of Bath and Wells; *b* 27 May 1913; *s* of late Arthur Stockwood, solicitor, and Beatrice Ethel Stockwood; unmarried. *Educ:* Kelly Coll., Tavistock; Christ's Coll., Cambridge (MA). Deacon, 1936; priest, 1937; Curate of St Matthew, Moorfields, Bristol, 1936–41; Missioner, Blundell's Sch., 1936–41; Vicar, St Matthew, Moorfields, Bristol, 1941–55; Hon. Canon of Bristol, 1952–55; Vicar of the University Church, Cambridge, 1955–59; Bishop of Southwark, 1959–80. Member: Bristol CC, 1946–55; Cambridge CC, 1956–59; House of Lords, 1963–80. Mem. Council, Bath Univ., 1980–. Freeman of City of London, 1976. DD Lambeth, 1959; Hon. DLitt Sussex, 1963; Hon. DD Bucharest, 1977. *Publications:* There is a Tide, 1946; Whom They Pierced, 1948; Christianity and Marxism, 1949; I Went to Moscow, 1955; The Faith To-day, 1959; Cambridge Sermons, 1959; Bishop's Journal, 1965; The Cross and the Sickle, 1978; From Strength to Strength, 1980; Chanctonbury Ring (autobiog.), 1982. *Address:* 15 Sydney Buildings, Bath, Avon BA2 6BZ. *T:* Bath (01225) 462788. *Died 13 Jan. 1995.*

STONE, Gilbert Seymour, FCA; Chairman, Manganese Bronze Holdings plc, since 1987 (Director, since 1976); *b* 4 Feb. 1915; *s* of J. Stone; *m* 1941, Josephine Tolhurst; one *s. Educ:* Clifton College. War service as Air Crew with RAF, 1939–45 (Sqdn-Ldr); with Industrial & Commercial Finance Corp. Ltd, 1945–59, latterly Asst Gen. Manager; Dir, Gresham Trust Ltd, 1959–61; practised on own account, 1961–72 and 1974–85; Dir, Industrial Develt Unit, DTI, 1972–74. Director: Babcock Internat. Gp plc (formerly FKI Babcock plc); Smith New Court plc; Household Mortgage Corp. plc. *Recreations:* golf, travel. *Address:* 2 Priory Close, Sunningdale, Berks SL5 9SE. *Clubs:* Garrick; Sunningdale Golf.

Died 18 April 1992.

STONE, Sir (John) Richard (Nicholas), Kt 1978; CBE 1946; ScD; FBA 1956; P. D. Leake Professor of Finance and Accounting, University of Cambridge, 1955–80, retired; Fellow of King's College, Cambridge, since 1945; *b* 30 Aug. 1913; *o c* of late Sir Gilbert Stone and Elsie Lawton Scott; *m* 1936, Winifred Jenkins (marr. diss. 1940); *m* 1941, Feodora Leontinoff (*d* 1956); one *d*; *m* 1960, Mrs Giovanna Croft-Murray, *d* of Count Aurelio Saffi. *Educ:* Westminster School (Hon. Fellow, 1989); Gonville and Caius College, Cambridge (Hon. Fellow, 1976). MA 1938; ScD 1957. With C. E. Heath and Co., Lloyd's Brokers, 1936–39; Ministry of Economic Warfare, 1939–40; Offices of the War Cabinet, Central Statistical Office, 1940–45; Dir Dept of Applied Economics, Cambridge, 1945–55. Mem., Internat. Statistical Inst. President: Econometric Soc., 1955; Royal Econ. Soc., 1978–80; Hon. Member: Soc. of Incorp. Accountants, 1954; Amer. Economic Assoc., 1976; For. Hon. Mem., Amer. Acad. of Arts and Sciences, 1968; For. Mem., Accad. dei Lincei, 1987. Hon. doctorates, Univs of Oslo and Brussels, 1965, Geneva, 1971, Warwick, 1975, Paris, 1977, Bristol, 1978. Lectures: Mattioli, 1986; Solari, 1987. Nobel Prize for Economics, 1984. *Publications:* National Income and Expenditure, 1st edn (with J. E. Meade), 1944,

10th edn (with G. Stone), 1977; The Role of Measurement in Economics, 1951; (with others) The Measurement of Consumers' Expenditure and Behaviour in the United Kingdom 1920–1938, vol. 1 1954, vol. 2 1966; Quantity and Price Indexes in National Accounts, 1956; Input-Output and National Accounts, 1961; Mathematics in the Social Sciences, and Other Essays, 1966; Mathematical Models of the Economy, and Other Essays, 1970; Demographic Accounting and Model Building, 1971; Aspects of Economic and Social Modelling, 1980; gen. editor and pt author series A Programme for Growth, 1962–74; numerous articles in learned journals, particularly on social accounting and econometrics, 1936–. *Recreation:* staying at home. *Address:* 13 Millington Road, Cambridge. *Died 6 Dec. 1991.*

STOODLEY, Peter Ernest William; County Treasurer of Kent, 1972–80; *b* 27 July 1925; *s* of Ernest and Esther Stoodley; *m* 1970, June (*née* Bennett). *Educ:* Weymouth Grammar Sch.; Administrative Staff Coll.; Inst. of Public Finance Accountants. Accountant with County Council of: Dorset, 1947–56; Staffordshire, 1956–61; Kent, 1961–65; Asst Co. Treasurer of Kent, 1965–69; Dep. Co. Treasurer of Kent, 1969–72. *Recreations:* ornithology, cricket. *Address:* Cranby, Horseshoe Lane, Leeds, Maidstone, Kent ME17 1SR. *T:* Maidstone (01622) 861287. *Died 2 March 1995.*

STOPS, Gervase Frank Ashworth J.; *see* Jackson-Stops.

STOREY, Christopher, MA, PhD; Headmaster, Culford School, Bury St Edmunds, 1951–71; *b* 23 July 1908; *s* of William Storey and Margaret T. B. Cowan, Newcastle upon Tyne; *m* 1937, Gertrude Appleby, Scarborough; four *s. Educ:* Rutherford Coll., Newcastle upon Tyne; King's Coll., Univ. of Durham (BA Hons French, cl. I); Univ. of Strasbourg (PhD). Modern Languages Master, Mundella Sch., Nottingham, 1931–34; French Master: Scarborough High Sch. for Boys, 1934–36; City of London Sch., 1936–42; Headmaster, Johnston Grammar Sch., Durham, 1942–51. Officier d'Académie, 1947. *Publications:* Etude critique de la Vie de St Alexis, 1934; Apprenons le mot juste!, 1939; (ed) La Vie de St Alexis, 1946, 2nd rev. edn, 1968; Sprechen und Schreiben (with C. E. Bond), 1950; A Guide to Alexis Studies, 1987; articles in Modern Language Review, French Studies, and Medium Aevum. *Address:* 13 The Paddox, Oxford OX2 7PN. *T:* Oxford (01865) 52328. *Died 27 Dec. 1994.*

STOTT, Prof. Peter Frank, CBE 1978; MA; FEng 1978; FICE, FIHT; Nash Professor of Civil Engineering, King's College, London University, 1983–89, then Professor Emeritus; *b* 8 Aug. 1927; *s* of late Clarence Stott and of Mabel Sutcliffe; *m* 1953, Vera Watkins; two *s. Educ:* Bradford Grammar Sch.; Clare Coll., Cambridge. Partner, G. Maunsell & Partners, Consulting Engineers, 1955–63; Deputy Chief Engineer (Roads) and later Chief Engineer, London County Council, 1963–65; Dir of Highways and Transportation, GLC, 1964–67; Traffic Comr and Dir of Transportation, GLC, 1967–69; Controller of Planning and Transportation, GLC, 1969–73; Dir-Gen., Nat. Water Council, 1973–83. Sec.-Gen., Internat. Water Supply Assoc., 1980–83. President: Reinforced Concrete Assoc., 1964; Concrete Soc., 1967; Instn of Highway Engineers, 1971–72; ICE, 1989–90 (Vice-Pres., 1987–89). Chm. Quality Scheme for Ready Mixed Concrete Ltd, 1984–; Dir, Mid Kent Hldgs, 1991–. *Recreations:* fine arts, pottery. *Address:* 7 Frank Dixon Way, SE21 7BB. *T:* 081–693 5121. *Club:* Athenæum.

Died 16 Aug. 1993.

STOURTON, Hon. John Joseph, TD; *b* 5 March 1899; *yr s* of 24th Baron Mowbray, Segrave and Stourton, and Mary, *o c* of Thomas Angus Constable, Yorks; *m* 1st, 1923, Kathleen Alice (marr. diss. 1933; she *d* 1986), *d* of late Robert Louis George Gunther, 8 Princes Gardens and Park Wood, Englefield Green, Surrey; two *s* two *d*; 2nd, 1934, Gladys Leila (marr. diss. 1947; she *d* 1953), *d* of late Col Sir William James Waldron. *Educ:* Downside School. MP (C) South Salford, 1931–45. Sec., Cons. Foreign Affairs Cttee, 1944–45. Served N Russian Relief Force at Archangel, 1919; and in War, 1939–43; late Lt 10th Royal Hussars; Major The Royal Norfolk Regiment. *Address:* 3 Rosebery Avenue, Hampden Park, Eastbourne, East Sussex.   *Died 2 Feb. 1992.*

STRACHAN, Graham Robert, CBE 1977; DL; FEng 1979; Director, Scott Lithgow Ltd, since 1984; *b* 1 Nov. 1931; *o c* of late George Strachan and Lily Elizabeth (*née* Ayres); *m* 1960, Catherine Nicol Liston, *o d* of late John and Eileen Vivian; two *s*. *Educ:* Trinity Coll., Glenalmond; Trinity Coll., Cambridge (MA, Mech. Scis Tripos). Apprentice Engineer: Alexander Stephen and Sons Ltd, 1950–52; John Brown & Co. (Clydebank) Ltd, 1952–55; National Service, RNVR, Temp. Sub-Lieut (E), 1955–57; John Brown & Co. (Clydebank) Ltd: Design Engr, 1957; Develt Engr, 1959; Engrg Dir, 1963; John Brown Engineering Ltd: Dir and Gen. Manager, 1966; Man. Dir, 1968; Gp Man. Dir, 1975; Dep. Chm., 1983–84; Director: British Smelter Constructions Ltd, 1968–73; CJB Offshore Ltd, 1975–80; John Brown & Co. (Overseas), 1976–84; Chairman: JBE Offshore Ltd, 1976–81 (Dep. Chm., 1974); JBE Gas Turbines, 1976–84; Stephens of Linthouse Ltd, 1982–84. Member: CBI Oil Steering Gp, 1975–79; Exec. Cttee, Scottish Engrg Employers' Assoc., 1966–82; Chm., Scottish Council Foundn, 1991–; Vice Pres., Scottish Council (Develt and Industry), 1983–; Mem. Council, Inst. of Engineers and Shipbuilders in Scotland, 1985–88. Dir, Glasgow Chamber of Commerce, 1978–. Mem. Court, Univ. of Strathclyde, 1979–83. DL Dumbarton, 1979. *Recreations:* skiing, golf, early jazz. *Address:* The Mill House, Strathblane, Glasgow G63 9EP. *T:* Blanefield (01360) 770220. *Clubs:* Caledonian, Royal Over-Seas League; Buchanan Castle Golf (Drymen).
   Died 1 Jan. 1995.

STRADLING THOMAS, Sir John, Kt 1985; MP (C) Monmouth, since 1970; farmer; *b* 10 June 1925; *s* of Thomas Roger Thomas and Catherine Thomas (*née* Delahay); *m* 1957, Freda Rhys Evans (marr. diss. 1982); one *s* two *d*. *Educ:* Rugby School. Contested (C) Aberavon, 1964; Cardigan, 1966. Asst Govt Whip, 1971–73; a Lord Comr, HM Treasury, 1973–74; an Opposition Whip, 1974–79; Treasurer of HM Household and Dep. Chief Whip, 1979–83; Minister of State, Welsh Office, 1983–85; Member: Select Cttee on the Civil List, 1971; Chairman's Panel. Pres., Fedn of Cons. Clubs, 1984. Mem., Gen. Adv. Council, BBC. Member Council, NFU, 1963–70. Trustee, Parly Pension Fund. Hon. Associate MRCVS, 1984; Hon. Mem., BVA. *Address:* House of Commons, SW1A 0AA. *Club:* White's.   *Died 29 March 1991.*

STRANG STEEL, Major Sir (Fiennes) William; *see* Steel.

STRATHSPEY, 5th Baron, *cr* 1884; **Donald Patrick Trevor Grant of Grant;** Bt (NS) 1625; 32nd Chief of Grant; Lieutenant-Colonel retired; *b* 18 March 1912; *s* of 4th Baron and Alice Louisa (*d* 1945), *d* of T. M. Hardy-Johnston, MICE (London), Christchurch, NZ; *S* father, 1948; *m* 1st, 1938, Alice (marr. diss. 1951), *o c* of late Francis Bowe, Timaru, NZ; one *s* two *d*; 2nd, 1951, Olive, *d* of W. H. Grant, Norwich; one *s* one *d*. *Educ:* Stowe Sch.; South Eastern Agricultural Coll. War Dept Land Agent and Valuer, Portsmouth, 1944–48; Command Land Agent, HQ Scottish Command, 1948–60; Asst Chief Land Agent and Valuer, War Office, 1960–63; Command Land Agent, HQ Cyprus District, 1963–64; Asst Director of Lands, NW Europe, 1964–66; Asst Chief Land Agent, MoD HQ, 1966–72. Associate, Land Agents' Soc. Fellow, Royal Institution of Chartered Surveyors, retd 1972.

Member: Standing Council of Scottish Chiefs; Highland Soc. of London; Pres., Clan Grant Socs of Australia, Canada, Nova Scotia, UK and USA. Hon. Mem., Los Angeles Saint Andrew's Soc.; Knight, Mark Twain Soc., Missouri; Patron: American Scottish Foundn; Soc. for Protection of Endangered Species. Defence Medal; Coronation Medal. *Publication:* A History of Clan Grant, 1983. *Recreations:* yachting, gardening, carpentry. *Heir:* *s* Hon. James Patrick Grant of Grant [*b* 9 Sept. 1943; *m* 1966, Linda (marr. diss. 1984), *d* of David Piggott; three *d*]. *Address:* Elms Cottage, Elms Ride, West Wittering, West Sussex. *Clubs:* Lancia Motor, House of Lords Motor, House of Lords Sailing, Civil Service Motoring Association (Pres.), West Wittering Sailing; West Wittering Horticultural and Produce Assoc.
   Died 27 Jan. 1992.

STRATTON, Andrew, MSc, FInstP, CEng, FIEE, FInstNav; navigation consultant; *b* 5 Sept. 1918; *m* 1949, Ruth Deutsch (*d* 1987); one *s* one *d*. *Educ:* Skinners' Company Sch., Tunbridge Wells; University Coll. of the South West, Exeter; Univ. of London (BSc 1st cl. Hons Physics). RAE Farnborough: Air Defence and Armament Depts, 1939–54; Supt, Instruments and Inertial Navigation Div., 1954–62; Head of Weapon Research and Assessment Group, 1962–66; Prof. and Head of Maths Dept, Coll. of Aeronautics, Cranfield, 1966–68; Dir, Defence Operational Analysis Estabt, 1968–76; Under Sec., MoD, on secondment as Consultant, 1977, Senior Consultant, 1978–81, ICI Ltd; Technical Dir, Terrafix Ltd, 1983–88. Pt-time Mem., CAA, 1980–83; Chm., Civil Aviation R&D Prog. Bd, 1981–84. Faraday Lecture, IEE, 1972–73. Former Chm. and Mem. of Cttees, Aeronautical and Electronics Research Councils; former Mem., Home Office Scientific Adv. Council. Pres., Inst. of Navigation, 1967–70; Chm. of Convocation, Univ. of Exeter, 1959–83. Hon. DSc Exeter, 1972. Hodgson Prize, RAeS, 1969; Bronze Medal, 1971 and 1975, Gold Medal, 1973, Royal Inst of Navigation. US Medal of Freedom with Bronze Palm, 1947. *Publications:* (contrib.) Unless Peace Comes, 1968; (contrib.) The Future of Aeronautics, 1970; (ed) Energy and Feedstocks in the Chemical Industry, 1983; papers on: aircraft instruments, navigation, air traffic, operational analysis in Jl IEE, Jl IMechE, Jl RAeS, Jl Inst. Navigation; energy, and chemical feedstock in Chem. and Ind., Omega, Process Econ. Internat. *Recreations:* painting, rambling. *Address:* Chartley, 39 Salisbury Road, Farnborough, Hants GU14 7AJ. *T:* Farnborough (01252) 542514.   *Died 13 Oct. 1994.*

STRATTON, Julius Adams, ScD; President Emeritus, Massachusetts Institute of Technology; *b* Seattle, 18 May 1901; *s* of Julius A. Stratton and Laura (*née* Adams); *m* 1935, Catherine N. Coffman; three *d*. *Educ:* Univ. of Washington; Mass Inst. of Technology (SB, SM); Eidgenössische Technische Hochschule, Zurich (ScD). Expert Consultant, Sec. of War, 1942–46. MIT: Res. Assistant, Elect. Engrg, 1924–26; Asst Prof., Electrical Engrg, 1928–30; Asst Prof., Physics, 1930–35; Associate Prof., Physics, 1935–41; Prof., Physics, 1941–51; Mem. Staff, Radiation Lab., 1940–45; Dir, Res. Lab. of Electronics, 1944–49; Provost, 1949–56; Vice-Pres., 1951–56; Chancellor, 1956–59; Actg Pres., 1957–59; Pres., 1959–66; Pres. Emer., 1966–. Trustee, Ford Foundn, 1955–71 (Chm. of Board, 1966–71). Chm., Commn on Marine Science, Engrg and Resources, 1967–69; Member: National Adv. Cttee on Oceans and Atmosphere, 1971–73; National Science Bd, 1956–62 and 1964–67; Naval Res. Adv. Cttee, 1954–59 (Chm., 1956–57). Life Mem. Corp., MIT; Life Trustee, Boston Museum of Science. Hon. Life FIEEE; FAAAS; Fellow: Amer. Acad. of Arts and Scis; Amer. Phys. Soc.; Founding Mem., National Acad. of Engrg; Member: Council on For. Relations; Amer. Philos. Soc.; Nat. Acad. of Scis (Vice-Pres., 1961–65); Sigma Xi;

Tau Beta Pi; Eminent Mem., Eta Kappa Nu. Hon. Fellow, Coll. of Science and Technology, Manchester, England, 1963; Hon. Mem. Senate, Technical Univ. of Berlin, 1966. Numerous hon. doctorates of Engrg, Humane Letters, Laws and Science incl. DSc: Leeds, 1967; Heriot-Watt, 1971; ScD Cantab 1972. Medal for Merit, 1946; Distinguished Public Service Award, US Navy, 1957; Medal of Honor, Inst. Radio Engrs, 1957; Faraday Medal, IEE, 1961; Boston Medal for Distinguished Achievement, 1966. Officer, Legion of Honour, France, 1961; Orden de Boyacá, Colombia, 1964; Kt Comdr, Order of Merit, Germany, 1966. *Publications:* Electromagnetic Theory, 1941; Science and the Educated Man, 1966; numerous papers in scientific and professional jls. *Address:* (home) 100 Memorial Drive, Cambridge, Mass 02142, USA; (office) Room 14N–112, Massachusetts Institute of Technology, Cambridge, Mass 02139–4307. *Clubs:* Century Association (New York); St Botolph (Boston).
Died 22 June 1994.

STRATTON, Monica Enid, (Mrs Roy Olin Stratton); *see* Dickens, M. E.

STRAUB, Marianne, OBE 1985; RDI 1972; textile designer, retired; *b* 23 Sept. 1909; *d* of Karl Straub and Cécile (*née* Kappeler). *Educ:* in Switzerland. Dip. Kunstgewerbeschule Zürich. Textile Designer: Rural Industries Bureau, 1934–37; Helios Ltd, Bolton, 1937–50; Warner & Sons Ltd, Braintree, 1950–69. Teaching posts: Central School of Art and Design, 1958–63; Hornsey College of Art, 1963–68; Royal College of Art, 1968–74. Hon. Fellow: RCA, 1981; Liverpool Polytechnic, 1991. Hon. FTI (Misha Black Meml Medal, 1994). *Publication:* Hand Weaving and Cloth Design, 1977. *Address:* Haus Stern, Neutal, 8267 Berlingen, Switzerland.
Died 8 Nov. 1994.

STRAUSS, Baron *cr* 1979 (Life Peer), of Vauxhall in the London Borough of Lambeth; **George Russell Strauss;** PC 1947; *b* 18 July 1901; *s* of Arthur Strauss, formerly MP (C) Camborne Div. of Cornwall and N Paddington, and Minna Cohen; *m* 1st, 1932, Patricia O'Flynn (*d* 1987); two *s* one *d*; 2nd, 1987, Benita Armstrong. *Educ:* Rugby. MP (Lab) Lambeth North, 1929–31 and 1934–50, Lambeth, Vauxhall, 1950–79; PPS to Minister of Transport, 1929–31, to Lord Privy Seal, and later Minister of Aircraft Production, 1942–45; Parly Sec., Min. of Transport, 1945–47; Minister of Supply, 1947–51 (introd Iron and Steel Nationalisation Bill, 1949); introduced Theatres Bill for the abolition of stage censorship, 1968. Father of the House of Commons, 1974. LCC Representative: N Lambeth, 1925–31; SE Southwark, 1932–46; LCC: Chm. Highways Cttee, 1934–37; Vice-Chm. Finance Cttee, 1934–37; Chm. Supplies Cttee, 1937–39; Mem. London and Home Counties Traffic Advisory Cttee, 1934–39. *Recreations:* painting, chess. *Address:* 1 Palace Green, W8 4QA. *T:* 071–937 1630; House of Lords, SW1A 0PW. *Died 5 June 1993.*

STREDDER, James Cecil; Headmaster, Wellington School, Somerset, 1957–73; *b* 22 Sept. 1912; 4th *s* of late Rev. J. Clifton Stredder and Mrs Stredder; *m* 1938, Catherine Jane, *er d* of late Rev. A. R. Price, RN (Retd), Paignton, Devon; one *d*. *Educ:* King Edward VI School, Stratford-on-Avon; Jesus College, Oxford. BA (Hons) Natural Science (Chemistry) Oxon 1935, MA 1943. Senior Chemistry Master at: Victoria College, Alexandria, Egypt, 1935; St Lawrence Coll., Ramsgate, 1936; Fettes Coll., Edinburgh, 1940; Tonbridge School, 1942–57. *Recreation:* walking. *Address:* 44 Bedford Street, Hitchin, Herts SG5 2JG. *Died 5 Nov. 1991.*

STRICKLAND-CONSTABLE, Sir Robert (Frederick), 11th Bt *cr* 1641, of Boynton, Yorkshire; *b* 22 Oct. 1903; 2nd *s* of Lt-Col Frederick Charles Strickland-Constable (*d*

1916) (*g g s* of 7th Bt) and Margaret Elizabeth (*d* 1961), *d* of late Rear-Adm. Hon. Thomas Alexander Pakenham; *S* brother, 1975; *m* 1936, Lettice, *y d* of late Major Frederick Strickland; two *s* two *d*. *Educ:* Magdalen Coll., Oxford (BA 1925, MA 1936, DPhil 1940). Served War of 1939–45, Lieut Comdr RNVR. Teaching Staff, Chem. Engineering Dept, Imperial Coll., Univ. of London, 1948–71, Readership 1963–71. Mem. Faraday Soc. *Publications:* Kinetics and Mechanism of Crystallization, 1968; approx. 50 contribs to scientific jls. *Recreations:* music, mountains, bird-watching. *Heir:* *s* Frederick Strickland-Constable [*b* 21 Oct. 1944; *m* 1981, Pauline Margaret Harding; one *s* one *d*].
Died 11 Dec. 1994.

STRUDWICK, John Philip, CBE 1970; CVO 1973; Assistant Secretary, Board of Inland Revenue, 1950–74, retired; *b* 30 May 1914; *s* of Philip Strudwick, FRICS and Marjorie Strudwick (*née* Clements); *m* 1942, Elizabeth Marion Stemson; two *s* three *d* (and one *d* decd). *Educ:* Eltham Coll.; St John's Coll., Cambridge. BA 1936, MA 1973. Asst Principal, Bd of Inland Revenue, 1937; Principal 1942. Sec., Millard Tucker Cttee on Taxation Treatment of Provisions for Retirement, 1951–53. KSG 1977. *Recreations:* music, gardening, voluntary social work (Chm. of Univ. of Sussex Catholic Chaplaincy Assoc., 1972–76 and Edenbridge Volunteer Bureau, 1978–82). *Address:* The Moat, Cowden, Edenbridge, Kent TN8 7DP. *T:* Cowden (0342) 850441.
Died 18 May 1994.

STUART, Charles Rowell, FRAeS, FCIT; Chairman, South Western Regional Health Authority, since 1990; *b* 20 May 1928; *s* of Charles Stuart and Agnes (*née* Spence); *m* 1951, Anne Grace Mingo; one *s* two *d*. *Educ:* St Olave's and St Saviour's Grammar Sch.; LSE (BSc Econ). FCIT 1964; FRAeS 1977. With British Rail, 1951–69; Marketing Dir and Mem. Bd, BEA, 1969–77; Hd of Commercial Develt and Exec. Bd Mem., British Airways, 1977–83; also Dir of travel cos, 1969–83; Chm. and Chief Exec., Brymon Airways, Plymouth City Airport, 1983–91. Director: SW Water plc, 1987–; Exeter and Devon Airport Ltd, 1991–. Governor: Plymouth Univ. (formerly Polytechnic SW), 1986–; E Devon Coll., 1986–. Trustee, Bishop Simeon CR Trust. Voluntary driver, Exe Valley Market Bus, 1988–. FInstD 1985. *Publications:* articles in professional jls. *Recreations:* running, reading. *Address:* c/o South Western Regional Health Authority, King Square House, Bristol BS2 8EF. *T:* Bristol (0272) 423271. *Clubs:* Oriental, Farmers', Royal Automobile.
Died 7 April 1993.

STUART, Malcolm Moncrieff, CIE 1947; OBE 1944; Indian Civil Service, retired; *b* 21 May 1903; *s* of George Malcolm Stuart and Mary Elizabeth Scott Moncrieff; *m* 1928, Grizel Graham Balfour Paul; one *s* one *d*. *Educ:* Sedbergh; St John's College, Cambridge; Queen's Coll., Oxford. Entered ICS 1927; served as Dist Magistrate of various districts and was on special duty for Govt Estates, 1938; during War of 1939–45 was mostly Dist Magistrate of Chittagong and also Comr there; served in Pakistan until 1950, as additional Member, Board of Revenue. Hon. MA Edinburgh, 1978. *Publications:* Bob Potts at Murshedabad (Bengal Past and Present), 1933; Handbook to Bengal Records, 1948; and other stories. *Recreations:* golf, shooting, bridge. *Address:* Smeaton Dower, 3 Smeaton Grove, Inveresk, Musselburgh EH21 7TW. *Clubs:* New (Edinburgh); Muirfield Golf.
Died 30 April 1991.

STUART-COLE, James; DL; Chairman, Merseyside Region, Co-operative Retail Services Ltd, 1974; *b* 6 March 1916; *s* of Charles Albert Stuart-Cole and Gertrude Mary Stuart-Cole; *m* 1937, Margaret Evelyn Robb; one *s* two *d*. *Educ:* Birley Street Central Sch., Manchester. Engr,

1930–55; Political Organiser, Labour Party, 1955–60; Political Sec., Co-operative Soc., 1960–81. Mem. Bd, Merseyside Development Corp, 1981. Merseyside County Council: Mem., 1973–86; Leader, 1981–82; Chm., 1983–84. DL Merseyside, 1983. *Recreations:* sport, grandchildren. *Address:* 85 Kylemore Drive, Pensby, Wirral, Merseyside L61 6XZ. *T:* 051–342 6180.
Died 1 June 1992.

STURGE, Harold Francis Ralph; Metropolitan Magistrate, 1947–68; *b* 15 May 1902; *y s* of Ernest Harold Sturge; *m* 1936, Doreen, *e d* of Sir Percy Greenaway, 1st Bt; two *s* (and one *s* decd). *Educ:* Highgate Sch.; Oriel Coll., Oxford, MA (Lit.Hum.). Called to Bar, Inner Temple, 1925; Midland Circuit. War of 1939–45, served on staff of Judge Advocate-General. Mem., Departmental Cttee on the Probation Service, 1959–62; President, Old Cholmelian Society, 1962–63. *Publications:* The Road Haulage Wages Act, 1938; (with T. D. Corpe, OBE) Road Haulage Law and Compensation, 1947; (with C. A. Reston, LLB) The Main Rules of Evidence in Criminal Cases, 1972. *Recreation:* painting. *Address:* 10 Tilney Court, Catherine Road, Surbiton, Surrey KT6 4HA.
Died 7 Sept. 1993.

SUDDARDS, His Honour (Henry) Gaunt; a Circuit Judge (formerly Judge of County Courts), 1963–80, retired; *b* 30 July 1910; *s* of Fred Suddards and Agnes Suddards (*née* Gaunt); unmarried. *Educ:* Cheltenham College; Trinity College, Cambridge (MA). Barrister, Inner Temple, 1932; joined NE Circuit, 1933. Served War of 1939–45: RAFVR, 1940–46. Recorder of Pontefract, 1960–61; Recorder of Middlesbrough, 1961–63; Dep. Chm., West Riding QS, 1961–71; Chairman, Agricultural Land Tribunal, Northern Area, 1961–63, Dep. Chairman 1960. *Recreations:* fishing, shooting, sailing. *Address:* Rockville, Frizinghall, Shipley, West Yorkshire BD18 3AA. *Club:* Bradford (Bradford).
Died 25 Nov. 1992.

SUDDARDS, Roger Whitley, CBE 1987; DL; Consultant, Hammond Suddards, solicitors, 1988–95; Chairman, Hammond Suddards Research Ltd, 1989–94; *b* 5 June 1930; *s* of John Whitley Suddards, OBE and Jean Suddards (*née* Rollitt); *m* 1963, Elizabeth Anne Rayner; two *d.* *Educ:* Bradford Grammar Sch. Admitted solicitor, 1952; Sen. Partner, Last Suddards, 1952–88; Dir, Yorkshire BS, 1985–95 (Chm., 1988–91). Vis. Lectr, Leeds Sch. of Town Planning, 1964–74; Planning Law Consultant: to UN, 1974–77; to Govt of Mauritius, 1981–82 and 1989–94. Former Chairman: Examinations Bd, ISVA; Adv. Cttee for Land Commn for Yorks and Humberside; Chm., Working Party on Future of Bradford Churches, 1978–79. Member: Law Society Bye-Laws Revision Cttee, 1984–87; Law Society Planning Law Cttee, 1964–81; Pres., Bradford Law Soc., 1969; Legal Mem., RTPI (Hon. Solr and Hon. Sec., 1991–95). Sec., Hand Knitting Assoc., 1958–75. Chm., Bradford Disaster Appeal Trust, 1985–89. Mem. Cttee, Nat. Mus. Photography, Film and TV, 1984–; Comr, English Heritage, 1992–95; Dir, Mus. Trng Inst. (Dep. Chm., 1987–93); Member: W Yorks Residuary Body, 1986–89; Civic Trust, 1988–. Chm., Educn Assets Bd, 1994–. Pro-Chancellor, 1987–93, and Chm. of Council, 1987–93, Bradford Univ. Mem. of Bd, 1979–86, Vice Chm. and Chm, 1985–88, Bradford Grammar Sch. Hon. FSVA. DL W Yorks, 1990. Hon. LLD Bradford, 1993. *Publications:* Town Planning Law of West Indies, 1974; History of Bradford Law Society, 1975; Listed Buildings, 1982, 3rd edn 1995; A Lawyer's Peregrination, 1984, 2nd edn 1987; Bradford Disaster Appeal, 1986; articles in Jl of Planning and Environmental Law, and Law Society Gazette. *Recreations:* theatre, music, reading, travel. *Address:* Low House, High Eldwick, Bingley, West

Yorks BD16 3AZ. *T:* Bradford (01274) 564832, 532233. *Clubs:* Arts; Bradford (Bradford).
Died 30 Dec. 1995.

SULLY, Leonard Thomas George, CBE 1963; Covent Garden Market Authority, 1967–80 (Assistant General Manager, 1967); Member, Industrial Tribunals Panel, 1976–80; *b* 25 June 1909; *s* of Thomas James Sully, Bristol; British; *m* 1935, Phyllis Emily Phipps, Bristol; one *d.* *Educ:* elementary schs; Fairfield Grammar Sch., Bristol. Public Health Dept, Bristol Corp., 1927; Assistance Officer, Unemployment Assistance Board, Bristol District, 1934; subseq. served in Bath, Weston-super-Mare, etc; Staff Officer, Air Ministry, London, 1943; Principal, and allocated to Air Ministry, 1949; Asst Sec., 1954; Dir of Contracts, 1960; Dir of Contracts (Air) MoD, 1964. *Recreation:* gardening. *Address:* Coppins, 20 Brackendale Close, Camberley, Surrey GU15 1HP. *T:* Camberley (0276) 63604.
Died 31 March 1994.

SULTAN, Syed Abdus; lawyer, Supreme Court of Bangladesh, Dacca, since 1976; *b* 1 Feb. 1917; Bengali Muslim; *m* 1938, Begum Kulsum Sultan; two *s* two *d.* *Educ:* Calcutta and Dacca Univs. Grad. Calcutta 1936, LLB Dacca 1949. Joined Dacca High Court Bar, 1949; Mem. Nat. Assembly of Pakistan, 1962; Delegate Inter-Parly Union Conf., Belgrade, 1963; toured Europe and Middle East; Mem. Pakistan Bar Council, 1967; Mem. Pakistan Nat. Assembly, 1970 with Sheikh Mujibur Rahman (Mem. Constitution Drafting Cttee); joined Bangladesh liberation movt, 1971; visited India, UK, USA and Canada to project cause of Bangladesh; Mem. Unofficial Delegn of Govt of Bangladesh to UN; Ambassador, later High Comr, for Bangladesh in UK, 1972–75. Member: Bangladesh Inst. of Law and Internat. Affairs; Bangla Academy. *Publications:* (in Bengali): Biography of M. A. Jinnah, 1948; Pancha Nadir Palimati, 1953; Ibne Sina, 1955; Man Over the Ages (history), 1969; Manirag (Belles Lettres), 1969; Byati Kramer Ek Adhyaya (One Chapter of Difference), 1981; Ar Rakta Nay (No more Blood), 1982; translations of short stories. *Recreations:* tennis, cricket, literature, literary and cultural activities. *Address:* Supreme Court Bar Association, Dacca, Bangladesh.
Died 11 March 1991.

SUMMERSON, Sir John (Newenham), CH 1987; Kt 1958; CBE 1952; BA (Arch.); FBA 1954; FSA; ARIBA; Curator of Sir John Soane's Museum, 1945–84; *b* 25 Nov. 1904; *o s* of late Samuel James Summerson, Darlington and Dorothea Worth Newenham; *m* 1938, Elizabeth Alison (*d* 1991), *d* of H. R. Hepworth, CBE, Leeds; three *s.* *Educ:* Harrow; University College, London. From 1926 worked in architects' offices, including those of late W. D. Caröe and Sir Giles Gilbert Scott, OM; Instructor in Sch. of Architecture, Edinburgh Coll. of Art, 1929–30; Asst Editor, Architect and Building News, 1934–41; Dep. Dir, National Buildings Record, 1941–45. Lectr in History of Architecture: Architectural Assoc., 1949–62; Birkbeck Coll., 1950–67; Slade Prof. of Fine Art, Oxford, 1958–59; Ferens Prof. of Fine Art, Hull, 1960–61 and 1970–71; Slade Prof. of Fine Art, Cambridge, 1966–67; Bampton Lectr, Columbia Univ., 1968; Page-Barbour Lectr, Virginia Univ., 1972; Banister Fletcher Prof., UCL, 1981. Member: Royal Fine Art Commn, 1947–54; Royal Commn on Historical Monuments (England), 1953–74; Historic Buildings Council, 1953–78; Arts Council Art Panel, 1953–56; Historical Manuscripts Commn, 1959–83; Listed Buildings Cttee, Min. of Housing and Local Govt, 1944–66 (Chm., 1960–62); Adv. Council on Public Records, 1968–74; Council, Architectural Assoc., 1940–45; Chairman, National Council for Diplomas in Art and Design, 1961–70; Trustee, National Portrait Gallery, 1966–73. Hon. Fellow, Trinity Hall, Cambridge, 1968; Fellow, UCL. Foreign Hon. Mem., Amer. Acad. of

Arts and Sciences, 1967; Hon. DLitt: Leicester, 1959; Oxford, 1963; Hull, 1971; Newcastle, 1973; Hon. DSc Edinburgh, 1968; Hon. Dr, RCA, 1975. Hon. RSA 1982. RIBA Silver Medal (Essay), 1937; RIBA Royal Gold Medal for Architecture, 1976. *Publications:* Architecture Here and Now (with C. Williams-Ellis), 1934; John Nash, Architect to George IV, 1935; The Bombed Buildings of Britain (with J. M. Richards), 1942 and 1945; Georgian London, 1946, rev. edn 1988; The Architectural Association (Centenary History), 1947; Ben Nicholson (Penguin Modern Painters), 1948; Heavenly Mansions (essays), 1949; Sir John Soane, 1952; Sir Christopher Wren, 1953; Architecture in Britain, 1530–1830 (Pelican History of Art), 1953, 8th edn 1991; New Description of Sir J. Soane's Museum, 1955; The Classical Language of Architecture, 1964, rev. edn 1980; The Book of John Thorpe (Walpole Soc., vol. 40), 1966; Inigo Jones, 1966; Victorian Architecture (four studies in evaluation), 1969; (ed) Concerning Architecture, 1969; The London Building World of the Eighteen-Sixties, 1974; (jt author) The History of the King's Works (ed H. M. Colvin), vol. 3, 1976, vol. 4, 1982; The Life and Work of John Nash, Architect, 1981; The Architecture of the Eighteenth Century, 1986; The Unromantic Castle (essays), 1990. *Address:* 1 Eton Villas, NW3 4SX. *T:* 071–722 6247. *Club:* Athenæum. *Died 10 Nov. 1992.*

SUMSION, Herbert Whitton, CBE 1961; FRCM, Hon. RAM, FRCO, FRSCM; Organist of Gloucester Cathedral, 1928–67; Director of Music, Ladies' College, Cheltenham, 1935–68; *b* Gloucester, 19 Jan. 1899; *s* of Charles H. Sumsion; *m* 1927, Alice Hartley Garlichs, BA; three *s*. *Educ:* Durham Univ. (MusB 1920). DMus Lambeth, 1947. Organist and Choirmaster at Christ Church, Lancaster Gate; Director of Music, Bishop's Stortford College; Asst Instructor in Music at Morley Coll., London; Teacher of Harmony and Counterpoint, Curtis Institute, Philadelphia, 1926–28; Conductor Three Choirs Fest., 1928, 1931, 1934, 1937, 1947, 1950, 1953, 1956, 1959, 1962, 1965. *Publications:* Introduction and Theme for Organ, 1935; Morning and Evening Service in G, 1935; Two pieces for Cello and Piano, 1939 (No 1 arranged for String Orchestra); Magnificat and Nunc Dimittis in G for Boys' Voices, 1953, for Men's Voices, 1953, for Boys' Voices in D, 1973; Cradle Song for Organ, 1953; Benedicite in B flat, 1955; Four Carol Preludes for Organ, 1956; Festival Benedicite in D, 1971; They That Go Down to the Sea in Ships (anthem), 1979; Transposition Exercises, 1980; Piano Technique, a Book of Exercises, 1980; There is a Green Hill Far Away (anthem), 1981; Two Anthems for Holy Communion, 1981; In Exile (By the Waters of Babylon) (anthem), 1981; A Unison Communion Service, 1991; (contrib.) Sing The Seasons, 1991; Cello Sonata, 1992. *Address:* Church End House, Frampton-on-Severn, Glos GL2 7EH. *T:* Gloucester (01452) 741074.
Died 11 Aug. 1995.

SUNDERLAND, Prof. Sir Sydney, Kt 1971; CMG 1961; FAA 1954; Professor of Experimental Neurology, 1961–75, then Emeritus Professor, and Dean of the Faculty of Medicine, 1953–71, University of Melbourne; *b* Brisbane, Aust., 31 Dec. 1910; *s* of Harry and Anne Sunderland; *m* 1939, Nina Gwendoline Johnston, LLB; one *s*. *Educ:* University of Melbourne. BM, BS 1935, DSc 1945, MD 1946, Melbourne. FRACP 1941; FRACS 1952. Sen. Lectr in Anatomy, Univ. of Melbourne, 1936–37; Demonstrator in Human Anatomy, Oxford, 1938–39; Prof. of Anatomy, Univ. of Melbourne, 1940–61. Visiting Specialist (Hon. Major) 115 Aust. Gen. Mil. Hosp., 1941–45. Mem. Zool Bd of Vic, 1944–65 (Chm. Scientific Cttee, 1958–62); Dep. Chm., Adv. Cttee to Mental Hygiene Dept, Vic, 1952–63; Mem. Nat. Health and MRC, 1953–69 (Chm., Med. Research Adv. Cttee, 1964–69). Visiting Prof. of Anatomy, Johns Hopkins Univ., 1953–54; Sec.,

Div. of Biol Sciences, Aust. Acad. Sci., 1955–58; Member: Nat. Radiation Adv. Cttee, 1957–64 (Chm. 1958–64); Defence Research and Development Policy Cttee, 1957–75; Med. Services Cttee, Dept of Defence, 1957–78; Council, AMA, Victorian Branch, 1960–68; Safety Review Cttee, Aust. Atomic Energy Commn, 1961–74 (Chm.); Aust. Univs Commn, 1962–76; Cttee of Management, Royal Melbourne Hosp., 1963–71; Protective Chemistry Research Adv. Cttee, Dept of Supply, 1964–73 (Chm.); Victorian Med. Adv. Cttee, 1962–71; Board of Walter and Eliza Hall Inst. of Med. Research, 1968–75. Governor, Ian Potter Foundn, 1964–. Trustee: National Museum, 1954–82; Van Cleef Foundn, 1971–. Fogarty Scholar in residence, Nat. Inst. of Health, Bethesda, USA, 1972–73. Foundn Fellow, Aust. Acad. of Science, 1954, and rep. on Pacific Science Council, 1957–69. Hon. MD: Tasmania, 1970; Queensland, 1975; Hon. LLD: Melbourne, 1975; Monash, 1977. *Publications:* Nerves and Nerve Injuries, 1968, 2nd edn 1978; Nerve Injuries and Their Repair: a critical appraisal, 1991; about 100 articles in scientific jls in Gt Britain, Europe, US and Australia. *Address:* 72 Kingstoun, 461 St Kilda Road, Melbourne, Victoria 3004, Australia. *T:* (3) 2665858. *Club:* Melbourne. *Died 27 Aug. 1993.*

SUTCLIFF, Rosemary, CBE 1992 (OBE 1975 (for services to children's literature)); FRSL 1982; writer of historical novels for adults and children; *b* 14 Dec. 1920; *d* of George Ernest Sutcliff and Elizabeth Sutcliff (*née* Lawton). *Educ:* privately. Carne Medal, 1959; The Other Award, 1978; Phoenix Award, 1985. *Publications:* Chronicles of Robin Hood, 1950; The Queen Elizabeth Story, 1950; The Armourer's House, 1951; Brother Dusty-feet, 1952; Simon, 1953; The Eagle of the Ninth, 1954; Outcast, 1955; Lady in Waiting, 1956; The Shield Ring, 1956; The Silver Branch, 1957; Warrior Scarlet, 1958; Rider of the White Horse, 1959; Lantern Bearers, 1959; Houses and History, 1960; Knights Fee, 1960; Rudyard Kipling, 1960; Beowulf, 1961; Dawn Wind, 1961; Sword at Sunset, 1963; The Hound of Ulster, 1963; The Mark of the Horse Lord, 1965; Heroes and History, 1965; The Chief's Daughter, 1967; The High Deeds of Finn McCool, 1967; A Circlet of Oak Leaves, 1968; The Flowers of Adonis, 1969; The Witches' Brat, 1970; Tristan and Iseult, 1971; The Capricorn Bracelet, 1973; The Changeling, 1974; Blood Feud, 1977; Sun Horse, Moon Horse, 1977; Shifting Sands, 1977; Song for a Dark Queen, 1978; The Light Beyond the Forest, 1979; Frontier Wolf, 1980; The Sword and the Circle: King Arthur and the Knights of the Round Table, 1981; Eagle's Egg, 1981; The Road to Camlann, 1981; Blue Remembered Hills (childhood memoir), 1982; Bonnie Dundee, 1983; Flame Coloured Taffeta, 1985; The Roundabout Horse, 1986; A Little Dog Like You, 1987; Blood and Sand, 1987; The Shining Company, 1990; *posthumous publications:* Black Ships Before Troy, 1993; The Minstrel and the Dragon Pup, 1993. *Recreations:* painting, needlework, dogs, travel. *Address:* Swallowshaw, Walberton, Arundel, West Sussex BN18 0PQ. *T:* Yapton (0243) 551316.
Died 23 July 1992.

SUTCLIFFE, His Honour Edward Davis, QC 1959; a Circuit Judge and Additional Judge of the Central Criminal Court, 1969–84; *b* 25 Aug. 1917; 3rd *s* of late Richard Joseph and Anne Sutcliffe; *m* 1939, Elsie Eileen Brooks; two *d*. *Educ:* University College School, Hampstead; Wadham College, Oxford (MA). Served Royal Artillery, 1939–46 (despatches). Called to Bar, Inner Temple, 1946; Bencher, 1966. Recorder of Canterbury, 1968–69, and Hon. Recorder, 1974–84. Mem., Criminal Injuries Compensation Board, 1964–69; Legal Assessor, GMC and GDC, 1967–69; Chm., Statutory Cttee, Pharmaceutical Soc., 1986–90. Governor: Bedford Coll., London, 1968–76; St Michael's Sch., Otford, 1973–83. Hon.

Freedom of Canterbury, 1983. Liveryman, Needlemakers' Co. *Address:* 39 Southwood Park, Southwood Lawn Road, Highgate, N6 5SG.   *Died 6 Jan. 1995.*

SUTCLIFFE, Kenneth Edward; Headmaster, Latymer Upper School, Hammersmith, W6, 1958–71; *b* 24 March 1911; *s* of late Rev. James Sutcliffe; *m* 1937, Nora, *d* of late Charles Herbert Burcham; two *d*. *Educ:* Manchester Grammar School; King's College, Cambridge (Scholar). BA Modern and Medieval Languages Tripos 1932; MA 1936. Assistant Master, Stockport Grammar School, 1933–38; Assistant Master, Liverpool Institute High School, 1938–46; Headmaster, Cockburn High School, Leeds, 1946–57. Served with Royal Armoured Corps and Intelligence Corps, 1940–46, Captain (General Staff). Lay Reader, dios of Ripon, Guildford, Bath and Wells, 1953–81. *Publications:* German Translation and Composition, 1948; French Translation and Composition, 1951; Fahrt ins Blaue (a German course for schools), 1960. *Address:* Hatherlow, Springfield Drive, Wedmore, Somerset BS28 4BT. *T:* Wedmore (0934) 712049.
            Died 8 Nov. 1991.

SUTCLIFFE, Prof. Reginald Cockcroft, CB 1961; OBE 1942; BSc, PhD Leeds; FRS 1957; Professor of Meteorology, Reading University, 1965–70, then Emeritus Professor; *b* 16 Nov. 1904; 2nd *s* of late O. G. Sutcliffe and Jessie Sutcliffe (*née* Cockcroft), Cleckheaton, Yorkshire; *m* 1929, Evelyn, *d* of late Rev. William Williams, Halkyn; two *d*. *Educ:* Whitcliffe Mount Grammar Sch., Cleckheaton; Leeds Univ.; University Coll., Bangor. Professional Asst, Meteorological Office, 1927; Meteorological Office appointments: Malta, 1928–32; Felixstowe, 1932–35; Air Ministry, 1935–37; Thorney Island, 1937–39; Squadron Leader RAFVR, France, 1939–40; Sen. Meteorological Officer, No 3 Bomber Group RAF, 1941–44; Group Capt., Chief Meteorological Officer AEAF, later BAFO, Germany, 1944–46; Research in Meteorological Office, 1946–65; Director of Research, 1957–65. President, Commission for Aerology of World Meteorological Organization, 1957–61; Mem. Adv. Cttee, World Meteorological Organization, 1964–68; Mem. Council, Royal Soc., 1968–70; Pres., Internat. Assoc. of Meteorology, 1967–71; Hon. Mem., Amer. Meteorological Soc., 1975–; Royal Meteorological Society: Pres., 1955–57; Hon. Mem., 1976; Editor, Quarterly Jl, 1970–73; Buchan Prize, 1950; Symons Gold Medal, 1955. Charles Chree Medal, Physical Soc., 1959; Internat. Meteorological Organization Prize, 1963. *Publications:* Meteorology for Aviators, 1938; Weather and Climate, 1966; meteorological papers in jls. *Address:* Pound Farm, Cadmore End, near High Wycombe, Bucks HP14 3PF. *T:* High Wycombe (0494) 883007.
            Died 28 May 1991.

SUTTON, Denys Miller, CBE 1985; Editor of Apollo, 1962–87; *b* 10 Aug. 1917; *s* of Edmund Sutton and Dulcie Laura Wheeler; *m* 1940, Sonja Kilbansky (marr. diss.); one *d*; *m* 1952, Gertrud Kœbke-Knudson (marr. diss.); one *s*; *m* 1960, Cynthia Sassoon. *Educ:* Uppingham School; Exeter Coll., Oxford (BA, BLitt). Foreign Office Research Dept, 1940–45; Sec., Internat. Commn for Restitution of Cultural Material, 1945; Fine Arts Specialist at UNESCO 1948; Visiting lectr at Yale Univ., 1949. Organiser of exhibitions: Bonnard Exhibition, Royal Acad., 1966; France in the 18th Century, Royal Acad., 1968; British Art, Columbus, Ohio, 1971; Venice Rediscovered, Wildenstein, London, 1972; Irish Art, Columbus, Ohio, 1974; Fragonard, Tokyo, 1980; Boucher, Tokyo, 1982; Phillips Collection, Tokyo, 1983; Fantin-Latour, Wildenstein, London, 1984; Constable, Tokyo, 1985; Whistler, Tokyo, 1987; Sargent, Tokyo, 1989; French Art, Yokohama, 1989; Detroit Treasures, Tokyo, 1989. Formerly: Art Critic to Country Life and to Financial

Times; Saleroom Correspondent of Daily Telegraph. Former Mem. Exec. Cttee, Nat. Art Collections Fund. Corresp. Membre de l'Institut. Chevalier, Légion d'Honneur. *Publications:* Watteau's Les Charmes de la Vie, 1946; Matisse, 1946; Picasso, Blue and Pink Periods, 1948; French Drawings of the 18th Century, 1949; American Painting, 1949; Flemish Painting, 1950; Bonnard, 1957; Christie's since the War, 1959; André Derain, 1959; Nicholas de Staël, 1960; Gaspard Dughet, 1962; Toulouse-Lautrec, 1962; Titian, 1963; Nocturne: The Art of Whistler, 1963; Sergio de Castro, 1965; Triumphant Satyr, 1966; Whistler: Paintings, Drawings, Etchings and Water-colours, 1966; Vélazquez, 1967; An Italian Sketchbook by Richard Wilson RA, 1968; Van Dongen, 1971; (ed and introd) Letters of Roger Fry, 1973; Manguin, 1974; Walter Sickert: a biography, 1976; Fads and Fancies, 1980; Delights of a Dilettante, 1980; R. L. Douglas, Connoisseur of Art and Life, 1980; The World of Sacheverell Sitwell, 1981; Early Italian Art and the English, 1985; Degas: man and work, 1986; Une Vie de Bohème: lettres du peintre Armand Sequin à Roderic O'Conor, 1989; *introductions:* Vlaminck, Dangerous Corner, 1961; R. A. M. Stevenson, Velasquez, 1962; *jointly:* Artists in 17th Century Rome (with Denis Mahon), 1955; Catalogue of French, Spanish and German schools in Fitzwilliam Museum, Cambridge (with J. W. Goodison), 1960; Painting in Florence and Siena (with St John Gore), 1965; Richard Ford in Spain (with Brinsley Ford), 1974; contribs to magazines, etc. *Recreation:* theatre. *Address:* 22 Chelsea Park Gardens, SW3 6AA. *T:* 071–352 5141. *Club:* Travellers'.   *Died 25 Jan. 1991.*

SUTTON, Prof. John, DSc, PhD; ARCS; FRS 1966; FGS; Senior Research Fellow, Centre for Environmental Technology, 1983–90, Professor of Geology, 1958–83, then Emeritus, Imperial College of Science and Technology, London; *b* 8 July 1919; *e s* of Gerald John Sutton; *m* 1st, 1949, Janet Vida Watson, FRS (*d* 1985); 2nd, 1985, Betty Middleton-Sandford. *Educ:* King's School, Worcester; Royal College of Science, London. Service with RAOC and REME, 1941–46. Imperial College: research, 1946–48; Lecturer in Geology, 1948; Reader in Geology, 1956; Head of Geol. Dept, 1964–74; Dean, Royal Sch. of Mines, 1965–68, 1974–77; Pro-Rector, External Develt, 1979–80, Pro-Rector, 1980–83; Fellow, 1985. A Trustee, BM (Nat. Hist.), 1976–81. Mem., NERC, 1977–79. Mem. Council, Univ. of Zimbabwe, 1980–83. President, Geologists' Association, 1966–68. A Vice-Pres., Royal Society, 1975–77; Pres., Remote Sensing Soc., 1977–84. For. Mem., Royal Netherlands Acad., 1978; Hon. For. Fellow, Geol Soc. of Amer. Bigsby Medal, Geological Society of London, 1965 (jointly with Janet Watson); Murchison Medal, 1975. *Publications:* papers dealing with the geology of the Scottish Highlands. *Recreation:* gardening. *Address:* Imperial College of Science, Technology and Medicine, SW7.   *Died 6 Sept. 1992.*

SUTTON, Leslie Ernest, MA, DPhil Oxon; FRS 1950; Fellow and Lecturer in Chemistry, Magdalen College, Oxford, 1936–73, Fellow Emeritus, 1973; Reader in Physical Chemistry, Oxford University, 1962–73 (University Demonstrator and Lecturer in Chemistry, 1945–62); *b* 22 June 1906; *o c* of Edgar William Sutton; *m* 1st, 1932, Catharine Virginia Stock (*d* 1962), *er d* of Wallace Teall Stock, Maplewood, NY, USA; two *s* one *d*; 2nd, 1963, Rachel Ann Long (*d* 1987), *er d* of Lt-Col J. F. Batten, Swyncombe, Henley-on-Thames; two *s*. *Educ:* Watford Gram. Sch.; Lincoln Coll., Oxford (Scholar). 1st Class Hon. School Chemistry, 1928. Research at Leipzig Univ., 1928–29, and at Oxford University; Fellow by Examination, Magdalen College, 1932–36; Rockefeller Fellow, California Inst. of Technology, 1933–34; Tilden Lectr, Chemical Soc., 1940; Visiting Prof., Heidelberg

Univ., 1960, 1964, 1967. Vice-Pres., Magdalen College, 1947–48. Hon. Sec., Chemical Soc., 1951–57, Vice-Pres., 1957–60. Chairman: Lawes Agricl Trust Cttee, Rothamsted Experimental Stn, 1982–89 (Treas., 1978–82); Dielectrics Soc., 1975–86. Hon. DSc Salford, 1973. Meldola Medal, RIC, 1932; Harrison Prize, Chemical Soc., 1935. *Publications:* (as scientific Editor) Tables of Interatomic Distances and Configuration in Molecules and Ions, 1958, 1964; Chemische Bindung und Molekülstruktur, 1961; papers in scientific jls. *Address:* 62 Osler Road, Headington, Oxford OX3 9BN. *T:* Oxford (0865) 66456. *Died 30 Oct. 1992.*

SUTTON, Sir Stafford William Powell F.; *see* Foster-Sutton.

SUTTON, Thomas Francis; Chairman, AE-International Inc., since 1981; Director and Executive Vice-President, J. Walter Thompson Co., New York, 1965–85; Executive Vice-President, JWT Group Inc., New York, 1982–86; *b* 9 Feb. 1923; *m* 1st, 1950, Anne Fleming (marr. diss. 1974); one *s* two *d*; 2nd, 1982, Maki Watanabe. *Educ:* King's School, Worcester; St Peter's College, Oxford. Research Officer, British Market Research Bureau Ltd, 1949–51; Advertising Manager, Pasolds Ltd, 1951–52; Managing Director, J. Walter Thompson GmbH, Frankfurt, Germany, 1952–59; Dir, J. Walter Thompson Co. Ltd, 1960–73, Man. Dir, 1960–66; Dir, internat. operations, J. Walter Thompson, NY, 1966–72; Man. Dir, J. Walter Thompson Co. Japan, Tokyo, 1972–80; Exec. Vice-Pres./Dir, J. Walter Thompson Asia/Pacific, 1980–81. Chm., E-A Advertising, NY, 1982–86; Dir, Lansdowneuro, 1982–85 (Chm., 1984). Part-time Lecturer in advertising and marketing: Rutger's Univ., NJ, 1968–71; Columbia Univ., NY, 1971–73; Sophia Univ., Tokyo, 1974–81. Chm., Internat. Support Gp, YMCA Japan, 1981–82. FIPA; FIS; FSS. Internat. Advertising Man of the Year Award, 1970. *Recreations:* chess, riding, Pudding Club. *Address:* Rushway House, Willington, Shipston-on-Stour, Warwicks CV36 5AS. *Clubs:* Princeton (New York); Probus (Shipston-on-Stour); Walton Hall Country (Warwickshire). *Died 9 Dec. 1994.*

SWALLOW, John Crossley, PhD; FRS 1968; physical oceanographer, Institute of Oceanographic Sciences (formerly National Institute of Oceanography), 1954–83; *b* 11 Oct. 1923; *s* of Alfred Swallow and Elizabeth (*née* Crossley); *m* 1958, Mary Morgan (*née* McKenzie); (one step *d* decd). *Educ:* Holme Valley Gram. Sch.; St John's Coll., Cambridge. Admty Signal Estabt, 1943–47; research in marine geophysics, at Cambridge and in HMS Challenger, 1948–54; work on ocean circulation, in RRS Discovery II, and in RRS Discovery, and other vessels, 1954–83. Rossby Fellow, Woods Hole Oceanographic Inst., 1973–74. Murchison Grant of RGS, 1965. Foreign Hon. Mem., Amer. Acad. of Arts and Sciences, 1975. Four American awards in oceanography. Commem. medal of Prince Albert I of Monaco, Inst Océanographique, Paris, 1982. *Publications:* papers on physical oceanography. *Address:* Heath Cottage, Station Road, Drakewalls, Gunnislake, Cornwall PL18 9DX. *T:* Tavistock (01822) 832100. *Died 3 Dec. 1994.*

SWAN, Maj.-Gen. Dennis Charles Tarrant, CB 1953; CBE 1948; *b* 2 Sept. 1900; *s* of late Lt-Col C. T. Swan, IA; *m* 1930, Patricia Ethel Mary Thorne (*d* 1960); one *d* (one *s* decd). *Educ:* Wellington Coll., Berks; Royal Military Academy, Woolwich. Commissioned as 2nd Lt RE, 1919; served War of 1939–45 (despatches twice): with BEF France, Feb.-May 1940; CRE 1 Burma Div., 1941; Comdt No 6 Mech. Eqpt Group, Indian Empire, 1944; Chief Engineer, 15 India Corps, 1945; District Chief Engineer, BAOR, 1946, Chief Engineer, 1948; Director of Fortification and Works, War Office, 1952–55, retired. Captain 1930; Adjutant, 36 (Mddx) AA Bn, 1935; Major,

1938; Lt-Col, 1945; Colonel 1947; Brig. 1948; Maj.-Gen., 1952. Pres., Instn of Royal Engineers, 1961–65. *Address:* Lordington Park, Chichester, West Sussex. *T:* Emsworth (0243) 378229; c/o Hindon House, 30 Havant Road, Emsworth, Hampshire PO10 7JE. *T:* Emsworth (0243) 372528. *Died 7 March 1992.*

SWANN, Sir Anthony (Charles Christopher), 3rd Bt *cr* 1906, of Prince's Gardens, Royal Borough of Kensington; CMG 1958; OBE 1950; Minister for Defence and Internal Security, Kenya, 1959–63; *b* 29 June 1913; *s* of Sir (Charles) Duncan Swann, 2nd Bt and Dorothy Margaret, *d* of Capt. Robert Harry Johnson; *m* 1940, Jean Margaret Niblock-Stuart; one *s*. *Educ:* Eton College; New College, Oxford. Joined Colonial Service, Kenya, 1936. Served, 1940–43, with King's African Rifles (Major). District Commissioner, Kenya, 1946–54; Provincial Commissioner, Kenya, 1955–59. Chairman East African Land Forces Organisation, 1959–60. *Recreations:* music, reading, fishing, shooting. *Heir: s* Michael Christopher Swann, TD [*b* 23 Sept. 1941; *m* 1965, Hon. Lydia Mary Hewitt (marr. diss. 1983), *e d* of 8th Viscount Lifford; two *s* one *d*; 2nd, 1988, Marilyn Ann Morse (*née* Tobitt)]. *Address:* 23 Montpelier Square, SW7. *Clubs:* Army and Navy, Pratt's. *Died 3 Feb. 1991.*

SWANN, Donald Ibrahim, MA; composer and performer, free-lance since 1948; *b* 30 Sept. 1923; *s* of late Dr Herbert William Swann, Richmond, Surrey and Naguimé Sultan; *m* 1st, 1955, Janet Mary (*née* Oxborrow) (marr. diss. 1983), Ipswich, Suffolk; two *d*; 2nd, 1993, Alison Smith. *Educ:* Westminster School; Christ Church, Oxford. Hons Degree Mod. Langs (Russian and Mod. Greek). Contributed music to London revues, including Airs on a Shoestring, 1953–54, as joint leader writer with Michael Flanders; Wild Thyme, musical play, with Philip Guard, 1955; in At the Drop of a Hat, 1957, appeared for first time (with Michael Flanders) as singer and accompanist of own songs (this show ran over 2 yrs in London; was part of Edinburgh Festival, 1959; Broadway, 1959–60; American and Canadian tour, 1960–61; tour of Great Britain and Ireland, 1962–63); At the Drop of Another Hat (with Michael Flanders), Haymarket, 1963–64, Globe, 1965 (Aust. and NZ tour, 1964; US Tour, 1966–67). Arranged concerts of own settings: Set by Swann; An Evening in Crete; Soundings by Swann; Between the Bars: an autobiography in music; A Crack in Time, a concert in search of peace. Musician in Residence, Quaker Study Center, Pendle Hill, USA, Jan.-June 1983; worked in song-writing and performing partnerships with Jeremy Taylor, Sydney Carter, Frank Topping, John Amis; solo entertainments in theatres and concert halls (Stand Clear for Wonders, with peace exploration songs); with Digby Fairweather and jazz group, Swann in Jazz, 1987; Swann's Way, synoptic concert series, Brighton Fest., 1988. Founded Albert House Press for special publications, 1974. *Compositions and publications include:* Lucy and the Hunter, musical play with Sydney Carter; satirical music to Third Programme series by Henry Reed, ghosting for Hilda Tablet; London Sketches with Sebastian Shaw, 1958; Festival Matins, 1962; Perelandra, music drama with David Marsh based on the novel of C. S. Lewis, 1961–62; Settings of John Betjeman Poems, 1964; Sing Round the Year (Book of New Carols for Children), 1965; The Road Goes Ever On, book of songs with J. R. R. Tolkien, 1968, rev. edn 1978; The Space Between the Bars: a book of reflections, 1968; Requiem for the Living, to words of C. Day Lewis, 1969; The Rope of Love: around the earth in song, 1973; Swann's Way Out: a posthumous adventure, 1974; (with Albert Friedlander) The Five Scrolls, 1975; Omnibus Flanders and Swann Songbook, 1977; Round the Piano with Donald Swann, 1979; (with Alec Davison) The Yeast Factory, music drama, 1979; South African Song Cycle, 1982;

Alphabetaphon: 26 essays A-Z (illus. by Natasha Etheridge and Robert Poulter), 1987, also trilogy of cassettes, 80 Songs A to Z in personal performance; (with Alison Smith) Art, Music and the Numinous (lectures), 1990; Beyond War: can the Arts mediate?, 1991; Swann's Way, an autobiography (as told to Lyn Smith), 1991; song cycles and settings of poems by Emily Dickinson, Edna St Vincent Millay, Rumi, Alun Lewis, Francis Thompson, Marina Tsvetaeva, Kapetanakis, Milton, 1991–93; *songs and operas:* The Song of Caedmon, 1971; Candle Tree, 1980; The Visitors (based on Tolstoy), 1984; Brendan A-hoy!, 1985; (with Evelyn Kirkhart and Mary Morgan) Mamahuhu (musical play), 1986; (with Richard Crane) Envy (musical play), 1986; Victorian Song Cycle, 1987; William Blake and John Clare Song Cycle, 1989; Swann's Way: a life in song, 1991; (with Arthur Scholey): Singalive, 1978; Wacky and his Fuddlejig (children's musical play), 1978; Baboushka (a Christmas cantata), 1980. *Recreations:* travelling in Greece, going to the launderette. *Address:* 13 Albert Bridge Road, SW11 4PX. *T:* 071–622 4281. *Died 23 March 1994.*

SWANN, (Frederick) Ralph (Holland), CBE 1974 (OBE (mil.) 1944); Life Vice President, Royal National Lifeboat Institution (Chairman, 1972–75); *b* 4 Oct. 1904; *s* of F. Holland Swann, JP, Steeple, Dorset; *m* 1940, Philippa Jocelyn Braithwaite (*d* 1968); no *c. Educ:* Eton; Trinity Coll., Cambridge (MA). Mem. London Stock Exchange, 1932–64; a Comr of Income Tax, City of London, 1964–76. Joined RNVSR, 1937; served in HMS Northern Gift, 1939–40 (despatches); comd HMS Sapphire, 1940–41; Senior Fighter Direction Officer, HMS Formidable, 1941–43; Comdr RNVR 1944, QO status, 1945; Exec. Officer, HMS Biter, 1944 and HMS Hunter, 1944–45 (in comd, 1945). Mem. Cttee of Management, RNLI, 1953, Dep. Chm. 1964–72. A Vice-Pres., Royal Humane Soc., 1973; Hon. Life Mem., Norwegian Soc. for Sea Rescue, 1975. *Recreations:* fishing, gardening. *Address:* Stratford Mill, Stratford-sub-Castle, Salisbury, Wilts SP1 3LJ. *T:* Salisbury (0722) 336563. *Clubs:* United Oxford & Cambridge University, Royal Cruising (Cdre 1966–72), Cruising Association (Hon. Mem.); Royal Corinthian Yacht. *Died 23 April 1992.*

SWAYNE, Sir Ronald (Oliver Carless), Kt 1979; MC 1945; Director: National Freight Company, later National Freight Consortium, 1973–85; Banque Nationale de Paris Ltd, since 1981; Member, Monopolies and Mergers Commission, 1982–86; *b* 11 May 1918; *s* of Col O. R. Swayne, DSO, and Brenda (*née* Butler); *m* 1941, Charmian (*d* 1984), *d* of Major W. E. P. Cairnes, Bollingham, Herefordshire; one *s* one *d. Educ:* Bromsgrove Sch., Worcester; University Coll., Oxford, 1936–39 and 1945–46 (MA). Served with Herefordshire Regt, 1939–40, No 1 Commando, 1940–45 (MC). Joined Ocean Steam Ship Co., 1946; became partner of Alfred Holt & Co. and Man. Dir of Ocean Steam Ship Co., 1955; Dir, 1965, Dep. Chm., 1969, Chm., 1973–82, Man. Dir, 1978–82, Overseas Containers Ltd. Vice-Chm., British Shipping Fedn, 1967; President: Cttee des Assocs d'Armateurs of EEC, 1974–75; Gen. Council of British Shipping, 1978–79; Inst. of Freight Forwarders, 1980. Industrial Adviser, Churchill Coll., Cambridge, 1974–82; Member: Design Council, 1975–78; Careers Res. Adv. Council, 1975–82; New Philharmonia Trust, 1968–82; Dir, ENO, 1980–86; Vice-Pres., British Maritime League, 1982–84. *Recreations:* fishing, shooting, music. *Address:* Puddle House, Chicksgrove, Tisbury, Salisbury SP3 6NA. *T:* Teffont (072276) 454; 32 Edith Road, W14. *T:* 071–602 4103. *Clubs:* Flyfishers'; Houghton (Stockbridge). *Died 29 Oct. 1991.*

SWAYTHLING, Dowager Lady; Jean Marcia Montagu, CBE 1943; Chief Controller and Director, Auxiliary Territorial Service, 1941–43 (as Mrs Jean Knox); *b* 14 Aug. 1908; *d* of G. G. Leith-Marshall; *m* Squadron Leader G. R. M. Knox; one *d*; *m* 1945, 3rd Baron Swaythling, OBE (*d* 1990). *Address:* Terwick Hill House, Rogate, Petersfield, Hants GU31 5EH. *T:* Rogate (0730) 821279. *Died 13 Dec. 1993.*

SWEETING, William Hart, CMG 1969; CBE 1961; Chairman, Board of Directors, Bank of London and Montreal, 1970–79; *b* 18 Dec. 1909; *s* of late Charles Cecil Sweeting, Nassau, Bahamas; *m* 1950, Isabel Jean (*née* Woodall). *Educ:* Queen's Coll., Nassau; London Univ. Entered Bahamas Public Service as Cadet, 1927; served in Colonial Secretary's Office, 1927–37; acted as Asst Colonial Sec. for short periods in 1928 and 1936; transferred to Treasury, 1937; Cashier, Public Treasury, 1941; Asst Treasurer and Receiver of Crown Dues, 1946; seconded as Financial Sec., Dominica, 1950–52; Receiver-Gen. and Treasurer, Bahamas, 1955; MLC, Bahamas, 1960–64; acted as Governor various periods 1959, 1964, 1965, 1966, 1968, 1969; acted as Colonial Secretary various periods, 1962–63; Chief Secretary, Bahamas 1964; Dep. Governor, Bahamas, 1969, retired 1970. Chairman: Bahamas Currency Comrs, 1955–63; Bahamas Broadcasting and Television Commn, 1957–62; Bahamas Public Disclosure Commn, 1978–84. Member: Bahamas Music Soc.; Trinity Coll. of Music Local Exams Cttee, 1961–86; United World Colleges Local Cttee, 1970–87. Elder, St Andrew's Presbyterian Church. *Recreations:* swimming, painting, music, bird watching. *Address:* PO Box N 573, Nassau, Bahamas. *T:* (39) 31518. *Club:* Corona. *Died 19 Dec. 1994.*

SWEETT, Cyril, CEng, AIStructE; FRICS; FCIArb; Founder Partner, Cyril Sweett & Partners, Chartered Quantity Surveyors, 1928; *b* 7 April 1903; *s* of William Thomas Sweett; *m* 1931, Barbara Mary, *d* of late Henry Thomas Loft, Canterbury and London; one *d. Educ:* Whitgift Sch.; Coll. of Estate Management. Artists Rifles, TA, 1923–27. Army Service: RE, 1939–43, France, N Africa and Italy; demob. as Lt-Col. Member: Council, RICS, 1959–61, 1970–72; Management Cttee, Royal Instn of GB, 1962–65 (Vice-Pres., 1964–65); Cttee, London Library, 1973–86; Chm., Nat. Jt Consultative Cttee of Architects, Quantity Surveyors and Builders, 1962–63. Master, Worshipful Co. of Painter Stainers, 1964–65, 1966–67; Sheriff of City of London, 1965–66. Jordanian Star, 1966; Silver Star of Honour, Austria, 1966. *Address:* 14 Princes Crescent, Hove, East Sussex BN3 4GS. *T:* Brighton (0273) 777292. *Clubs:* Garrick, MCC; Royal Thames Yacht, Royal Burnham Yacht (Cdre, 1963–65). *Died 18 Nov. 1991.*

SWIFT, Reginald Stanley, CB 1969; Under-Secretary, Ministry of Social Security, 1962–68, Department of Health and Social Security, 1968–76, retired; *b* 2 Nov. 1914; *e s* of Stanley John and Annie Swift; *m* 1940, Mildred Joan Easter; no *c. Educ:* Watford Grammar School; Christ's College, Cambridge. BA Cantab (1st Cl. Hons in Classics) 1936; MA Cantab 1940; BSc (Econ.) London 1944. Entered Civil Service as Asst Comr, National Savings Cttee, 1938; transferred to Min. of National Insurance as Principal, 1947; Principal Private Secretary to Minister, 1953–54; Assistant Secretary, 1954; Under-Secretary, 1962. *Recreations:* gardening, golf. *Address:* 16 Beechfield, Banstead, Surrey SM7 3RG. *T:* Burgh Heath (0737) 361773. *Club:* Kingswood Golf. *Died 13 Nov. 1993.*

SWINBURNE, Hon. Ivan Archie, CMG 1973; Member of Legislative Council of Victoria, Australia, 1946–76, retired; *b* 6 March 1908; *s* of George Arthur and Hilda Maud Swinburne; *m* 1950, Isabella Mary, *d* of James Alexander Moore; one *d. Educ:* Hurdle Creek West and Milawa State Schs; Wangaratta and Essendon High Schs. MLC, for NE Prov., Vic, 1946–76; Dep. Leader of Country

Party, 1954–69, Leader of Country Party in Legislative Council, 1969–76; Minister of Housing and Materials, 1950–52; Mem., Subordinate Legislation Cttee, 1961–67 and 1973. Councillor, Shire of Bright, 1940–47 (Pres., 1943–44). Mem., Bush Nursing Council of Victoria, 1948–84; Chm. Cttee of Management, Mount Buffalo National Park, 1963–84. *Recreation:* football administration. *Address:* PO Box 340, Myrtle Street, Myrtleford, Victoria 3737, Australia. *T:* (57) 521167. *Clubs:* Royal Automobile of Victoria (Melbourne); Wangaratta (Wangaratta). *Died 12 Aug. 1994.*

SWINDLEHURST, Rt Rev. Owen Francis; Bishop Auxiliary of Hexham and Newcastle, (RC), since 1977; Titular Bishop of Chester-le-Street; *b* 10 May 1928; *s* of Francis and Ellen Swindlehurst. *Educ:* Ushaw College, Durham; English College, Rome. PhL, STL, LCL (Gregorian Univ., Rome). Assistant Priest: St Matthew's, Ponteland, 1959–67; St Bede's, Denton Burn, Newcastle, 1967–72; Parish Priest at Holy Name, Jesmond, Newcastle, 1967–77. *Recreations:* walking, geriatric squash, reading. *Address:* Oaklea, Tunstall Road, Sunderland SR2 7JR. *T:* Sunderland (0191) 41158. *Died 28 Aug. 1995.*

SWYER, Dr Gerald Isaac Macdonald, FRCP; Consultant Endocrinologist, Department of Obstetrics and Gynæcology, University College Hospital, London, 1951–78, retired; Councillor, London Borough of Camden, 1982–86; *b* 17 Nov. 1917; *s* of Nathan Swyer; *m* 1945, Lynda Irene (*née* Nash); one *s* one *d*. *Educ:* St Paul's School; Magdalen College and St John's College, Oxford; University of California; Middlesex Hospital Medical School. Foundation Schol. and Leaving Exhib., St Paul's School, 1931–36; Open Exhib. and Casberd Schol., St John's Coll., Oxford, 1936–39; Welsh Memorial Prize, 1937; Theodore Williams Schol. in Anatomy, 1938; 1st Cl. Final Honour School of Animal Physiology, 1939; Senior Demy, Magdalen Coll., 1940; Rockefeller Medical Student, Univ. of Calif, 1941. MA, DPhil, BM Oxon 1943; MD Calif, 1943; DM Oxon 1948; MRCP 1945; FRCP 1964; FRCOG *ad eundem* 1975. Mem. of Scientific Staff, Nat. Inst. for Med. Res., 1946–47; Endocrinologist, UCH Med. Sch., 1947. 1st Sec., formerly Chm., Soc. for the Study of Fertility; formerly Mem. Council, Soc. for Endocrinology (Hon. Mem.); formerly Pres., Sect. of Endocrinology, Roy. Soc. Med.; formerly Sec.-Gen., Internat. Fedn of Fertility Societies and Mem. Exec. Sub-Cttee Internat. Endocrine Soc. *Publications:* Reproduction and Sex, 1954; papers in medical and scientific journals. *Recreations:* golf, music, making things. *Address:* Flat 4, 71 Fitzjohn's Avenue, NW3 6PD. *T:* 0171–435 4723. *Died 19 Sept. 1995.*

SYKES, Lt-Col Arthur Patrick, MBE 1945; JP; DL; *b* 1 Sept. 1906; *e s* of late Herbert R. Sykes, JP; *m* 1936, Prudence Margaret (marr. diss. 1966), *d* of late Maj.-Gen. D. E. Robertson, CB, DSO, Indian Army; one *s* one *d*; *m* 1968, Katharine Diana, *d* of Lt-Col. A. J. N. Bartlett, DSO, OBE. *Educ:* Eton; Magdalene College, Cambridge. 2nd Lt 60th Rifles, 1929; served India, Burma, Palestine; ADC to Governor of Bengal, 1933–35; War of 1939–45, Middle East (wounded); Lt-Col 1944. JP 1951, DL 1951, High Sheriff, 1961, Shropshire. *Address:* Lydham Manor, Bishop's Castle, Shropshire SY9 5HA. *T:* Bishop's Castle (0588) 638486. *Died 27 April 1994.*

SYKES, Dr John Bradbury; General Editor, English Dictionaries, Oxford University Press, 1992–94; *b* Folkestone, Kent, 26 Jan. 1929; *s* of late Stanley William Sykes and Eleanor Sykes Sykes (*née* Bradbury); *m* 1955, Avril Barbara Hart (marr. diss. 1988); one *s*. *Educ:* Wallasey Grammar Sch.; Rochdale High Sch.; St Lawrence Coll.; Wadham Coll., Oxford (BA Maths 1950); Balliol Coll., Oxford (Skynner Sen. Student); Merton Coll., Oxford (Harmsworth Sen. Schol., MA and DPhil

Astrophysics 1953). CPhys; FInstP. AERE, Harwell, 1953–71 (Head of Translations Office 1958, Principal Scientific Officer 1960); Member, Internat. Astronomical Union, 1958 (Pres., Commn for Documentation, 1967–73). Oxford University Press: Editor, Concise and Pocket Oxford Dictionaries, 1971–81; Hd of German Dictionaries, 1981–89; Gen. Editor, New Shorter OED, 1989–91. Mem. Bd, Translators' Guild, 1980–88 (Chm., 1984–88). Fellow: Inst. of Linguists, 1960–86 (Mem. Council, 1977–86; Editor, Incorporated Linguist, 1980–86); Inst. of Translation and Interpreting, 1988 (Chm. Council, 1986–91). FRSA. Hon. DLitt City, 1984. *Publications:* (with B. Davison) Neutron Transport Theory, 1957; (ed) Technical Translator's Manual, 1971; (ed) Concise Oxford Dictionary, 6th edn, 1976, 7th edn, 1982; (ed) Pocket Oxford Dictionary, 6th edn, 1978; (ed jtly) Oxford–Duden German Dictionary, 1990; translations of many Russian textbooks in physics and astronomy; contribs to Incorporated Linguist. *Recreation:* crossword-solving (National Champion 1958, 1972–75, 1977, 1980, 1983, 1985, 1989, 1990). *Address:* 68 Woodstock Close, Oxford OX2 8DD. *T:* Oxford (0865) 57532. *Club:* PEN. *Died 3 Sept. 1993.*

SYKES, Air Vice-Marshal William, OBE 1945; CEng; FRAeS; FIIM; FBIM; Royal Air Force, retired, 1975; General Manager, British Aerospace (Oman), 1976–85; *b* 14 March 1920; *s* of Edmund and Margaret Sykes, Appleby, Westmorland; *m* 1st, 1946, Jean Begg (*d* 1985), *d* of Alexander and Wilemena Harrold, Watten, Caithness; one *s* one *d*; 2nd, 1986, Suzanne Penelope Margaret Lane, *d* of Ronald Frederick and Sylvia Lane, Hempsted, Kent. *Educ:* Raley Sch. and Technical Coll., Barnsley, Yorks. HNC Mech. and Aero Eng. 1942; CEng, AFRAeS 1968, FRAeS 1974, FBIM (MBIM 1975), FIIM 1979. Joined RAF as Aircraft Apprentice, 1936; served War: No 51 (Bomber) Sqdn, 1939–41; various engrg specialist courses; commissioned, 1942; Coastal Command: Invergordon, Pembroke Dock, Gibraltar, Hamworthy, Reykjavik (Iceland) and Tain; after 1945: appts at Marine Aircraft Exptl Estabt, Felixstowe; HQ No 23 Gp; CSDE; RAE; 2nd TAF, Germany; Dept of ACAS (OR); Electrical Specialist Course, 1948; Staff Coll., 1953–54; jssc 1959–60; during period 1960–72: served a further tour with CSDE as OC Projects Wing; was OC Engrg Wing, Wyton; Station Comdr, No 8 of TT, Weeton; Comd Engrg Officer, FEAF; Dir of Mechanical Engrg (RAF), MoD (AFD); Air Officer Engrg, NEAF; attended IDC, 1967; Vice-Pres., Ordnance Board, 1972–74, Pres., 1974–75. *Recreation:* travel. *Address:* 5 Clifton Court, 297 Clifton Drive South, St Anne's-on-Sea, Lancs FY8 1HN. *T:* St Anne's (0253) 727689. *Club:* Royal Air Force. *Died 28 Jan. 1991.*

SYLVESTER, George Harold, CBE 1967; Chief Education Officer for Bristol, 1942–67, retired; *b* 26 May 1907; *s* of late George Henry and Martha Sylvester; *m* 1936, Elsie Emmett; one *s*. *Educ:* Stretford Grammar School; Manchester University. BA Manchester 1928; MA Bristol 1944. Teaching, Manchester, 1929–32; administrative posts (Education) in Wolverhampton and Bradford, 1932–39; Assistant Education Officer, Bristol, 1939–42; Chief Education Officer, Bristol, 1942–67. Hon. MEd Bristol, 1967. *Recreations:* golf, music. *Address:* 43 Hill View, Henleaze, Bristol BS9 4QE. *T:* Bristol (0272) 629287. *Died 18 Sept. 1994.*

SYMONS, Julian Gustave, FRSL; author; *b* 30 May 1912; *y s* of M. A. Symons and Minnie Louise Bull; *m* 1941, Kathleen Clark; one *s* (one *d* decd). Editor, Twentieth Century Verse, 1937–39. Sunday Times Reviewer, 1958–. Chairman: Crime Writers Association, 1958–59; Cttee of Management, Soc. of Authors, 1970–71. President: Detection Club, 1976–85; Conan Doyle Soc., 1989–93.

Mem. Council, Westfield Coll., Univ. of London, 1972–75. Grand Master: Swedish Acad. of Detection, 1977; Mystery Writers of America, 1982; Internat. Crime Writers, 1991. FRSL 1975. Cartier Diamond Dagger Award, CWA, 1990. *Publications:* Confusions About X, 1938; (ed) Anthology of War Poetry, 1942; The Second Man, 1944; A. J. A. Symons, 1950; Charles Dickens, 1951; Thomas Carlyle, 1952; Horatio Bottomley, 1955; The General Strike, 1957; A Reasonable Doubt, 1960; The Thirties, 1960, with additions, as The Thirties and the Nineties, 1990; The Detective Story in Britain, 1962; Buller's Campaign, 1963; England's Pride, 1965; Critical Occasions, 1966; A Picture History of Crime and Detection, 1966; (ed) Essays and Biographies by A. J. A. Symons, 1969; Bloody Murder: from the detective story to the crime novel, a history, 1972 (MWA Edgar Allan Poe Award), 3rd edn 1992; Notes from Another Country, 1972; Between the Wars, 1972; The Hungry Thirties, 1976; The Tell-Tale Heart, 1978; Conan Doyle, 1979; The Great Detectives, 1981; Critical Observations, 1981; The Tigers of Subtopia (short stories), 1982; (ed) New Poetry 9, 1983; (ed) The Penguin Classic Crime Omnibus, 1984; Dashiell Hammett, 1985; (ed) Tchekov's The Shooting Party, 1986; Makers of the New, 1987; (ed) The Essential Wyndham Lewis, 1989; Criminal Practices (criticism), 1994; author of 28 crime novels, including: The 31st of February, 1950; The Broken Penny, 1952; The Colour of Murder, 1957 (CWA Critics Award); The Progress of a Crime, 1960 (MWA Edgar Allan Poe Award); The End of Solomon Grundy, 1964; The Man Who Killed Himself, 1967; The Man Whose Dreams Came True, 1968; The Man Who Lost His Wife, 1970; The Players and the Game, 1972; A Three Pipe Problem, 1975; The Blackheath Poisonings, 1978; Sweet Adelaide, 1980; The Detling Murders, 1982; The Name of Annabel Lee, 1983; The Criminal Comedy of the Contented Couple, 1985; The Kentish Manor Murders, 1988; Death's Darkest Face, 1990; Portraits of the Missing, 1991; Something Like A Love Affair, 1992; Playing Happy Families, 1994; several plays for television. *Recreations:* watching cricket, snooker and Association football, wandering in cities. *Address:* Groton House, 330 Dover Road, Walmer, Deal, Kent CT14 7NX. *T:* Deal (01304) 365209.

Died 19 Nov. 1994.

SYMONS, Patrick Stewart, RA 1991 (ARA 1983); painter in oils; teacher, Chelsea School of Art, 1959–86; *b* 24 Oct 1925; *s* of Norman H. Symons and Nora Westlake. *Educ:* Bryanston Sch.; Camberwell Sch. of Arts and Crafts. One-man exhibitions: New Art Centre, 1960; William Darby Gall., 1975–76; Browse and Darby, 1982, 1989. *Address:* 20 Grove Hill Road, Camberwell, SE5 8DG. *T:* 071–274 2373.   *Died 30 Oct. 1993.*

SYNGE, John Lighton, FRS 1943; MA, ScD Dublin; MRIA; FRSC (Tory Medal, 1943); Senior Professor, School of Theoretical Physics, Dublin Institute for Advanced Studies, 1948–72, then Emeritus; *b* Dublin, 23 March 1897; *y s* of Edward Synge and Ellen (*née* Price); *m* 1918, Elizabeth Allen (*d* 1985); three *d*. *Educ:* St Andrew's Coll., Dublin; Trinity Coll., Dublin. Senior Moderator and Gold Medallist in Mathematics and Experimental Science, 1919; Lecturer in Mathematics, Trinity College, Dublin, 1920; Assistant Professor of Mathematics, University of Toronto, 1920–25; Fellow of Trinity College, Dublin, and University Professor of Natural Philosophy, 1925–30; Professor of Applied Mathematics, Univ. of Toronto, 1930–43; Professor of Mathematics and Chm. of Dept, Ohio State Univ., 1943–46; Prof. of Mathematics and Head of Dept, Carnegie Inst. of Technology, 1946–48. Visiting Lecturer, Princeton Univ., 1939; Vis. Prof.: Brown Univ., 1941–42; Inst. for Fluid Dynamics and Applied Maths, University of Maryland, 1951. Secretary to the International Mathematical Congress, Toronto, 1924; Treas., Royal Irish Academy, 1929–30, Sec., 1949–52, Pres., 1961–64. Ballistics Mathematician, United States Army Air Force, 1944–45. Hon. FTCD. Hon. LLD St Andrews, 1966; Hon. ScD: QUB, 1969; NUI, 1970. Boyle Medal, RDS, 1972. *Publications:* Sir W. R. Hamilton's Mathematical Papers, Vol. I (ed jtly), 1931; Geometrical Optics, 1937; (with B. A. Griffith) Principles of Mechanics, 1942; (with A. E. Schild) Tensor Calculus, 1949; Science: Sense and Nonsense, 1951; Geometrical Mechanics and de Broglie Waves, 1954; Relativity: the Special Theory, 1956; The Hypercircle in Mathematical Physics, 1957; The Relativistic Gas, 1957; Kandelman's Krim, 1957; Relativity: the General Theory, 1960; Talking about Relativity, 1970; papers on geometry and applied mathematics. *Address:* Newtonpark House, Newtonpark Avenue, Blackrock, Co. Dublin. *T:* Dublin 2881552.

Died 30 March 1995.

SYNGE, Richard Laurence Millington, FRS 1950; Hon. Professor of Biology, University of East Anglia, Norwich, 1968–84; *b* 28 Oct. 1914; *s* of late Laurence M. Synge and Katharine C. Synge (*née* Swan), Great Barrow, Chester; *m* 1943, Ann, *d* of late Adrian L. Stephen and Karin Stephen (*née* Costelloe), both of London; three *s* four *d*. *Educ:* Winchester College; Trinity College, Cambridge (Hon. Fellow, 1972). International Wool Secretariat Research Student, University of Cambridge, 1938; Biochemist: Wool Industries Research Assoc., Leeds, 1941; Lister Institute of Preventive Medicine, London, 1943; Rowett Research Inst., Bucksburn, Aberdeen, 1948; Food Research Inst., Norwich, 1967–76. Editorial Board, Biochemical Journal, 1949–55. Hon. MRIA 1972; Hon. DSc: East Anglia, 1977; Aberdeen, 1987; Hon. PhD Uppsala, 1980. (Jtly) Nobel Prize for Chemistry, 1952. *Publications:* papers in biochemical and chemical journals, etc, 1937–. *Address:* 19 Meadow Rise Road, Norwich NR2 3QE. *T:* Norwich (0603) 53503.

Died 18 Aug. 1994.

T

TALBOT, Maj.-Gen. Dennis Edmund Blaquière, CB 1960; CBE 1955; DSO 1945; MC 1944; DL; *b* 23 Sept. 1908; *s* of late Walter Blaquière Talbot, St John, Jersey and The White House, Hadlow, Kent; *m* 1939, Barbara Anne, *o d* of late Rev. R. B. Pyper, Rector of Pluckley, Kent; three *s* two *d. Educ:* Tonbridge; RMC Sandhurst. 2nd Lieut Roy. West Kent Regt, 1928; served India, 1928–37; served War of 1939–45 (despatches, DSO, MC); Brigade Major: 30th Infantry Bde, BEF; 141 Inf. Bde; GSO 2, HQ 1st Corps; GSO 2 and 1, Combined Ops; 2nd i/c 5th Bn Dorset Regt; in command, 7th Bn Hampshire Regt, NW Europe, 1944–45; i/c 2nd Bn Royal W Kent Regt, 1945–46; GSO 1, HQ, FARELF, 1947–48; Senior UK Army Liaison Officer, NZ, 1948–51; Lt-Col 1949; AAG (Col), War Office, 1951–53; Col 1952; i/c 18th Inf. Bde and 99th Gurkha Inf. Bde, Malaya, 1953–55; Brig. 1956; BGS, HQ, BAOR, 1957–58; Maj.-Gen. 1958; GOC, E Anglian Dist and 54th Inf. Div. (TA), 1958–61; Dep. Comdr, BAOR, and Comdr British Army Group Troops, 1961–63; Chief of Staff, BAOR, and GOC Rhine Army Troops, 1963–64, retired; Civil Service, 1964–73. Graduate of: Staff Coll., Camberley; RN Staff Coll., Greenwich; Joint Services Staff Coll., Latimer; Imperial Defence College, London; Civil Defence Staff Coll., Sunningdale. Col, The Queen's Own Royal West Kent Regt, 1959–61; Dep. Colonel, The Queen's Own Buffs, The Royal Kent Regt, 1961–65; Hon. Col, 8 Queen's Cadre (formerly 8 Bn The Queen's Regt (West Kent)), 1968–71. Chm., Kent Cttee, Army Benev. Fund, 1964–84. Pres., local horticultural soc., 1980–92; Vice-Pres., local br., Royal British Legion. DL Kent, 1964. Knight Commander 1962, Grand Cross 1965, Order of the Dannebrog (Denmark). *Recreations:* gardening, regimental history. *Address:* Oast Court, Barham, near Canterbury, Kent CT4 6PG.   *Died 27 June 1994.*

TALBOT, His Honour (Richard) Michael (Arthur) Chetwynd-; a Circuit Judge, 1972–83; *b* 28 Sept. 1911; 3rd *s* of late Rev. Prebendary A. H. Talbot and Mrs E. M. Talbot; unmarried. *Educ:* Harrow; Magdalene College, Cambridge (MA). Called to Bar by Middle Temple, 1936, Bencher, 1962. Mem. Bar Council, 1957–61. Dep. Chm., 1950–67, Chm., 1967–71, Shropshire QS; Recorder of Banbury, 1955–71, Hon. Recorder, 1972–. Served War of 1939–45, in Army; Major, King's Shropshire Light Infantry. *Address:* 7 St Leonard's Close, Bridgnorth, Salop WV16 4EJ. *T:* Bridgnorth (0746) 763619.
          Died 15 Jan. 1993.

TALBOT, Thomas George, CB 1960; QC 1954; *b* 21 Dec. 1904; *s* of late Rt Hon. Sir George John Talbot and Gertrude Harriet, *d* of late Albemarle Cator, Woodbastwick Hall, Norfolk; *m* 1933, Hon. Cynthia Edith Guest; one *s* three *d. Educ:* Winchester; New Coll., Oxford. Called to Bar, Inner Temple, 1929; Bencher, 1960. RE (TA), 1938; Scots Guards, 1940–44 (Hon. Captain). Assistant, subsequently Deputy, Parliamentary Counsel to Treasury, 1944–53; Counsel to Chm. of Cttees, H of L, 1953–77; Asst Counsel to Chm. of Cttees, H of L, 1977–82. *Address:* Falconhurst, Edenbridge, Kent. *T:* Cowden (034286) 850641. *Club:* Brooks's.
          Died 8 Feb. 1992.

TAME, William Charles, CB 1963; Deputy Secretary, Ministry of Agriculture, Fisheries and Food, 1967–71; *b* 25 June 1909; *s* of late Charles Henry Tame, Wimbledon, Surrey; *m* 1935, Alice Margaret, *o d* of late G. B. Forrest, Witherslack, Cumbria; one *d* (one *s* decd). *Educ:* King's College School, Wimbledon; Hertford College, Oxford. Entered Ministry of Agriculture as Assistant Principal, 1933. Chairman: International Whaling Commission, 1966–68; Fisheries R&D Bd, 1972–78. Member: Council, Royal Veterinary Coll., Univ. of London, 1972–80 (Vice-Chm., 1973–80); Governing Body, Animal Virus Res. Inst., 1972–76. *Recreation:* music.
          Died 27 Dec. 1995.

TANDY, Jessica Alice; actress, stage and screen; *b* London, 7 June 1909; *d* of Harry Tandy and Jessie Helen (*née* Horspool); *m* 1st, 1932, Jack Hawkins (marr. diss. 1940); one *d*; 2nd, 1942, Hume Cronyn; one *s* one *d. Educ:* Dame Owen's Girls' Sch.; Ben Greet Acad. of Acting. Birmingham Repertory Theatre, 1928; first London appearance, 1929; first New York appearance, 1930; subsequently alternated between London and New York. *London plays include:* The Rumour, 1929; Autumn Crocus, Lyric, 1931; Children in Uniform, Duchess, 1932; Hamlet, New, 1934; French without Tears, Criterion, 1936; Anthony and Anna, Whitehall, 1935; The Gin Game, Lyric, 1979; Open-Air Theatre, London, 1933 and 1939; Old Vic, 1937 and 1940, leading Shakespearian rôles, etc; *New York plays include:* The Matriarch, 1930; The Last Enemy, 1930; Time and the Conways, 1938; The White Steed, 1939; Geneva, 1940; Jupiter Laughs, 1940; Anne of England, 1941; Yesterday's Magic, 1942; A Streetcar Named Desire, 1947–49 (Antoinette Perry Award, 1948); Hilda Crane, 1950; The Fourposter, 1951–53 (Comœdia Matinee Club Bronze Medallion, 1952); Madame Will You Walk?, 1953; Face to Face, 1954; the Honeys, 1955; A Day by the Sea, 1955; The Man in the Dog Suit, 1957–58; Triple Play, 1959; Five Finger Exercise, 1959 (New York League's Delia Austria Medal, 1960); The Physicists, 1964; A Delicate Balance, 1966–67; Camino Real, 1970; Home, 1971; All Over, 1971; Happy Days, Not I (Samuel Beckett Festival), 1972 (Drama Desk Award, 1973); Rose, 1981; Foxfire, 1982–83 (Antoinette Perry, Drama Desk, Outer Critics Circle awards, 1983); Glass Menagerie, 1983; Salonika, 1985; The Petition, 1986; tours: Promenade All, 1972; Not I, 1973; Many Faces of Love, 1974, 1975 and 1976; Noel Coward in Two Keys, 1974, 1975; The Gin Game, 1977 (US and USSR Tour, 1978–79; Sarah Siddons Award, Chicago and Los Angeles Critics' Award); toured Canada, 1939; tour of US with husband, (poetry and prose readings), 1954; they also toured Summer Theatres (in plays), 1957. Opening Season of the Tyrone Guthrie Theatre Minneapolis, USA: Hamlet, Three Sisters, Death of A Salesman, 1963; The Way of the World, The Cherry Orchard, The Caucasian Chalk Circle, 1965; Foxfire, 1981; The Miser, Los Angeles, 1968; Heartbreak House, Shaw Festival, Niagara-on-the-Lake, Ontario, 1968; Tchin-Tchin, Chicago, 1969; Eve, The Way of the World and A Midsummer Night's Dream, Stratford, Ontario Festival, 1976; Long Day's Journey Into Night, London, Ontario, 1977, Stratford, Ont, 1980; The Gin Game, Long Wharf Theatre, New Haven, Conn, 1977 (Drama Desk Award, 1977–78; Antoinette Perry Award, 1978); Foxfire, Stratford, Ont, 1980; Ahmanson, LA, 1985–86. *Films include:* The Indiscretions of Eve, The Seventh Cross, The

Valley of Decision, Dragonwyck, The Green Years, A Woman's Vengeance, Forever Amber, September Affair, Rommel-Desert Fox, A Light in the Forest, Adventures of a Young Man, The Birds, Butley; Honky Tonk Freeway, 1980; Still of the Night, 1981; Garp, 1981; Best Friends, 1982; The Bostonians, 1984; Cocoon, 1985; The House on Carroll Street; Batteries Not Included; Cocoon: the return, 1988; Driving Miss Daisy, 1990 (Academy Award, 1990; BAFTA Award, 1991); Used People, 1991; Fried Green Tomatoes, 1991. *Television:* major American dramatic programs. Obie Award, 1972–73; Brandeis Theatre Arts Medal, 1978; elected to Theatre Hall of Fame, 1979; Commonwealth Award for distinguished service in dramatic arts, 1983; Honoree, Kennedy Center Honors, 1986; Nat. Medal of Arts, 1990. Hon. LLD Univ. of Western Ontario, 1974; Hon. DHL Fordham Univ., 1985. *Died 11 Sept. 1994.*

TANNER, Dr Bernice Alture, FRCGP; general practitioner in London W11 area, 1948–85, retired; *b* 23 Sept. 1917; *m* 1942, Prof. James M. Tanner, MD, DSc, FRCP; one *d* (one *s* decd). *Educ:* Cornell Univ., USA; New York Univ.; McGill Univ., Canada; Medical Coll. of Pennsylvania, USA. BA 1939; MD 1943 (Med. Coll., Pa); FRCGP 1980. Convenor, Educational Cttee, London NW Faculty RCGP; Course organizer, St Charles Hosp. Vocational Trng Scheme for Gen. Practice; Mem., AHA Cttee paediatric care, London NW Area. Mem., Supplementary Benefits Commn, 1976–79. *Publications:* (ed) Language and Communication in General Practice, 1976; Signposts for the Future of General Practice: health, human biology and primary care, 1991. *Recreations:* music, postgraduate medical education. *Address:* 127 Oakwood Court, Abbotsbury Road, W14. *T:* 071–603 7881.
Died 12 Dec. 1991.

TANSLEY, Sir Eric (Crawford), Kt 1953; CMG 1946; Chairman, Pacol, 1962–72; formerly Director: Bank of West Africa; Standard Bank Ltd; Standard & Chartered Banking Group Ltd; Gill & Duffus Ltd; *b* 25 May 1901; *o s* of William and Margaret Tansley; *m* 1931, Iris, *yr d* of Thomas Richards; one *s* one *d*. *Educ:* Mercers' Sch. Formerly: Mem., Colonial, later Commonwealth, Development Corporation, 1948–51, 1961–68; Chairman: London Cocoa Terminal Market Assoc., 1932; Cocoa Assoc. of London, 1936–37; Marketing Director, West African Produce Control Board (Colonial Office), 1940–47; retired, 1961 as Managing Director, Ghana Cocoa Marketing Co. and Adviser, Nigerian Produce Marketing Co. *Address:* 11 Cadogan Square, SW1. *T:* 071–235 2752. *Died 1 Sept. 1992.*

TAPP, Maj.-Gen. Sir Nigel (Prior Hanson), KBE 1960 (CBE 1954); CB 1956; DSO 1945; DL; *b* 11 June 1904; *y s* of late Lt-Col J. Hanson Tapp, DSO, and Mrs Hanson Tapp (*née* Molesworth), Duns, Berwickshire; *m* 1948, Dorothy (*d* 1978), *y d* of late Alexander Harvey. *Educ:* Cheltenham College; Royal Military Academy, Woolwich. 2nd Lieutenant RA, 1924; Sudan Defence Force, 1932–38; ADC to Governor-General, Sudan, 1935–36; Staff College, Camberley, 1939; GSO 3, 1 Corps BEF, 1940; GSO 2, War Office, 1940–41; GSO 1 Staff College, Camberley, 1941–42; CO, 7 Field Regt, RA, UK, Normandy, Belgium, and Holland, 1942–45; Comd RA 25 Div., SEAC, 1945; District Commander, Eritrea, 1946–47; Dep. Dir Land/Air Warfare, 1948; Dep. Dir RA, 1949; idc, 1950; Commander 1 Corps Royal Artillery, BAOR, 1951–53; General Officer Commanding 2 AA Group, 1954; Director of Military Training, War Office, 1955–57; GOC East Africa Command, 1957–60; retd 1961; Lieut-Governor and Sec., Royal Hosp., Chelsea, 1967–73. Col Comdt, Royal Regt of Artillery, 1963–68. Pres., Assoc. of Service Newspapers, 1974–86. Hon. Freeman, City of London, 1978. DL Greater London,

1973–82. *Recreations:* reading, fishing. *Address:* 9 Cadogan Square, SW1X 0HT. *Club:* Army and Navy.
Died 9 Feb. 1991.

TAPPER-JONES, Sydney, LLB (London); Town Clerk and Clerk of the Peace, Cardiff, 1942–70; *b* 12 March 1904; *s* of David and Frances Caroline Mary Jones; *m* 1947, Florence Mary, (Joan), Hellyer; one *d*. *Educ:* Pentre (Rhondda) Secondary School. Articled Cousins, Botsford & Co., Solicitors, Cardiff; LLB Lond. (External) (Hons), 1924; Solicitors' Final Exam. (Hons), 1925; admitted Solicitor, 1925. Managing Clerk with Allen Pratt & Geldard (with whom were amalgamated Vachell & Co.), Solicitors, Cardiff, 1925–27; Cardiff Corporation: Conveyancing Solicitor, 1927–29; Prosecuting Solicitor, 1929–33; Deputy Town Clerk and Deputy Clerk of the Peace, 1933–42; Commissioner for Oaths. Mem. Ct of Governors, UCW, 1960; Governor, Howell's Sch., Llandaff, 1963–85. Member of Convocation, 1925. Member, Order of St John, 1966. *Address:* Maes-y-Coed, 59 Heath Park Avenue, Cardiff CF4 3RG. *T:* Cardiff (0222) 751306. *Died 2 Feb. 1991.*

TATE, Ellalice; *see* Hibbert, Eleanor.

TATE, Lt-Col Sir Henry, 4th Bt, *cr* 1898, of Park Hill, Streatham; TD; DL; late Royal Welch Fusiliers TA; *b* 29 June 1902; *s* of Sir Ernest Tate, 3rd Bt and Mildred Mary, 2nd *d* of F. H. Gossage, Camp Hill, Woolton, Liverpool; *S* father, 1939; *m* 1st, 1927, Nairne (*d* 1984), *d* of late Saxon Gregson-Ellis, JP; two *s*; 2nd, 1988, Edna Stokes. Sometime Lt Grenadier Guards; Commanding 1st Bn Rutland Home Guard, 1954–57. Joint Master Cottesmore Hounds, 1946–58. Councillor Rutland CC, 1958–69, 1970–74; High Sheriff of Rutland, 1949–50; DL, Co. of Rutland, 1964. *Heir: s* (Henry) Saxon Tate [*b* 28 Nov. 1931; *m* 1st, 1953, Sheila Ann (marr. diss. 1975; she *d* 1987), *e d* of Duncan Robertson; four *s* (incl. twin *s*); 2nd, 1975, Virginia Sturm]. *Address:* Preston Lodge, Withcote, Oakham, Rutland, Leics LE15 8DP. *Club:* Buck's.
Died 11 March 1994.

TAUKALO, Sir (David) Dawea, Kt 1985; MBE 1970; Independence Medal, Solomon Islands, 1984; Doctor, retired 1975; *b* 24 Feb. 1920; *s* of J. Paiyom and H. Tevio; *m* 1951, Anne Kamamara; three *s* five *d* (and one *s* decd). *Educ:* Church School, The Solomons; Govt School, Fiji (Dip. in Medicine and Surgery; Cert. in Public Health). General practitioner, Central Hosp. sanitary and mosquito control inspection, Honiara Town, 1947; MO i/c Eastern District Hosp. and clinics, 1951; postgrad. course, Fiji, 1960; returned to Central Hosp., i/c medical patients; rural hosp., eastern Solomons, 1969, to advise Council and field med. workers that good health could not be achieved by building huge hosp. and employing numerous doctors, but by telling people to develop their lands and seas. Premier in Provincial Assembly until 1984. *Publication:* booklet on health of Solomon Islands. *Recreations:* soccer fan, farming, sailing. *Address:* Rocky Hill, Lata, Santa Cruz Temotu Province, Solomon Islands.
Died 5 Jan. 1993.

TAUNTON, Doidge Estcourt, CB 1951; DSO and bar 1945; DL; Secretary, Northamptonshire Territorial and Auxiliary Forces Association, 1952–68; *b* 9 Nov. 1902; *s* of late J. G. C. Taunton, Launceston, Cornwall; *m* 1st, 1930, Rhona Caroline Wetherall (*d* 1951); one *s* (and one *s* decd), *m* 2nd, 1956, Mary Finch. *Educ:* Cheltenham College; RMC Sandhurst. 2nd Lt Northamptonshire Regt, 1923; Lt 1925; Capt. 1935, and Adjt TA, 1932–36; Major 1940; Lt-Col 1941; Col 1948; Temp. Brig. 1945–47 and 1948–52. Served NWF India, 1936–38 (Medal and 2 clasps); War of 1939–45, India and Burma, 1936–45; French Indo-China and Netherlands East Indies, 1945–46 (Medal and clasp); Comd Somaliland Area, 1948–50;

Comd 2nd Inf. Brigade, 1950–51; retired pay, 1951. DL Northants, 1969. *Address:* Great Hayne, Duston, Northampton. *Died 16 Nov. 1991.*

TAYLER, Alan Breach, CBE 1993; DPhil; Director, Oxford University Centre for Industrial and Applied Mathematics, since 1989; Fellow, St Catherine's College, Oxford, since 1959; *b* 5 Sept. 1931; *s* of Edward Henry Tayler and Edith Nellie (*née* Fair); *m* 1955, June Earp; four *d. Educ:* King's College Sch., Wimbledon; Brasenose Coll., Oxford (MA, DPhil). Oxford University: Jun. Lectr in Maths, 1956–59; University Lectr, 1959–; St Catherine's College: Finance Bursar, 1978–85; Vice-Master, 1985–87; Res. Fellow, Harvard Univ., 1965–66. Pres., European Consortium for Maths in Industry, 1989. *Publications:* Inviscid Fluid Flows, 1983; Mathematical Models in Applied Mechanics, 1986. *Recreations:* gardening, travel, Rugby football. *Address:* Windrush Farmhouse, The Square, Ducklington, Oxford OX8 7UD. *T:* Witney (01993) 704983, (office) Oxford (01865) 270514. *Died 29 Jan. 1995.*

TAYLOR OF HADFIELD, Baron *cr* 1982 (Life Peer), of Hadfield in the County of Derbyshire; **Francis Taylor,** Kt 1974; Founder, 1921, and Life President, 1979, Taylor Woodrow Group (Managing Director, 1935–79; Chairman, 1937–74); *b* 7 Jan. 1905; *s* of late Francis Taylor and Sarah Ann Earnshaw; *m* 1st, 1929 (marr. diss.); two *d*; 2nd, 1956, Christine Enid Hughes; one *d*. Founded, 1921, Taylor Woodrow, Building, Civil & Mechanical Engineering Contractors, which became Public Company, in 1935. Member of Advisory Council to Minister of State, 1954–55; Chm. Export Group for Constructional Industries, 1954–55; President, Provident Institution of Builders' Foremen and Clerks of Works, 1950; Dir, Freedom Federal Savings and Loan Assoc., Worcester, Mass, 1972–82. Director: BOAC, 1958–60; Monarch Investments Ltd, Canada, 1954–84. Pres., Aims of Industry, 1990–. Governor, Queenswood School for Girls, 1948–77. Hon. DSc Salford, 1973. Fellow, Chartered Inst. of Building, Hon. Fellow 1979; Hon. FFB 1986; Hon. FICE 1987. *Recreations:* tennis, swimming, riding. *Clubs:* Royal Automobile, Queen's, Hurlingham, All England. *Died 15 Feb. 1995.*

TAYLOR OF MANSFIELD, Baron *cr* 1966 (Life Peer), of Mansfield, Co. of Nottingham; **Harry Bernard Taylor,** CBE 1966; *b* 18 Sept. 1895; *s* of Henry Taylor, Mansfield Woodhouse, and Mary Ann, *d* of George Wheat; *m* 1921, Clara (*d* 1983), *d* of John Ashley; one *s. Educ:* Council Schools. A Coal Miner. MP (Lab) Mansfield Div. of Nottinghamshire, 1941–66; Parliamentary Private Secretary: to Parliamentary Secretary, Ministry of Aircraft Production, 1942; to Minister of National Insurance, 1945; Parliamentary Secretary, Ministry of National Insurance, 1950–51. *Publication:* Uphill all the Way (autobiog.), 1973. *Address:* 47 Shakespeare Avenue, Mansfield Woodhouse, Nottinghamshire. *Died 11 April 1991.*

TAYLOR, Sir Alvin B.; *see* Burton-Taylor.

TAYLOR, Prof. Arthur John; Professor of Modern History, Leeds University, 1961–84, then Emeritus; University Archivist, Leeds, 1984–89; *b* 29 Aug. 1919; *s* of Victor Henry and Mary Lydia Taylor, Manchester; *m* 1955, Elizabeth Ann Jeffries; one *s* two *d. Educ:* Manchester Grammar School; Manchester University. Assistant Lecturer in History, University Coll. London, 1948; Lecturer, 1950. Pro-Vice-Chancellor, Leeds Univ., 1971–73. Chm., Jt Matriculation Bd, 1970–73. *Publications:* Laissez-faire and State Intervention in Nineteenth Century Britain, 1973; The Standard of Living in Britain in the Industrial Revolution, 1975; (with P. H. J. H. Gosden) Studies in the History of a University: Leeds 1874–1974, 1975; contrib. to books and learned journals.

Address: Redgarth, Leeds Road, Collingham, Wetherby, West Yorks LS22 5AA. *T:* Collingham Bridge (0937) 572930. *Died 18 Oct. 1992.*

TAYLOR, Arthur William Charles, CBE 1981; PhD; CChem, FRSC; Chairman, Heavy Organics (Petrochemical Division), Imperial Chemical Industries Ltd, 1972–75; *b* 4 Jan. 1913; *s* of Edward Charles Taylor and Alice (*née* Lucas); *m* 1936, Rosina Peggy (*née* Gardner); one *s* one *d. Educ:* Brighton Hove and Sussex Grammar Sch.; University Coll. London (BSc, PhD). FInstPet. Imperial Chemical Industries Ltd: Billingham Division: Research Chemist, 1935–45; Jt Research Manager, 1945–57; Plastics Division: Technical and Research Director, 1958–64; Heavy Organics (Petrochemical Division): Technical Dir, 1964–66; Dep. Chm., 1966–72. Chairman: British Ports Assoc., 1978–80; Tees and Hartlepool Port Authority, 1976–82 (Mem., 1974–83); Tees Pilotage Authority, 1978–83; Mem., Nat. Ports Council, 1978–80; Chm., NE Industrial Develt Bd, 1979–81. Chm. of Governors, Teesside Polytechnic, 1975–78. Fellow, University Coll. London, 1977; FRSA 1976. *Publications:* papers in Chemistry and Industry, particularly the Holroyd Meml Lecture, 1976. *Address:* 35 The Grove, Marton, Middlesbrough, Cleveland TS7 8AF. *T:* Middlesbrough (0642) 315639. *Died 12 Jan. 1992.*

TAYLOR, Desmond S.; *see* Shawe-Taylor.

TAYLOR, Eric Scollick, PhD; Presiding Bishop, Liberal Catholic Church, 1984–93; Clerk of Committee Records, House of Commons, 1975–83; *b* 16 April 1918; *s* of late Percy Scollick Taylor and Jessie Devlin. *Educ:* Durham Univ. (MA); Edinburgh Univ. (PhD 1942). Asst Clerk, House of Commons, 1942; Dep. Principal Clerk, 1962; Principal Clerk, 1972; Clerk to: Cttee of Privileges, 1949–57; Estimates Cttee, 1957–64; Cttee of Public Accounts, 1964–68; Clerk of the Journals, 1972–75. Ordained priest, Liberal Catholic Church, 1943; consecrated Bishop, 1977; Regionary Bishop, Great Britain and Ireland, 1985–93. *Publications:* The House of Commons at Work, 1951, 9th rev. edn 1979; The Liberal Catholic Church—what is it?, 1966, 2nd edn 1979 (also foreign trans.); The Houses of Parliament, 1976; contribs to Times Lit. Supp., etc. *Recreations:* walking, listening to music, preaching to the converted, worship. *Address:* 113 Beaufort Street, SW3 6BA. *T:* 0171–351 1765. *Died 4 June 1995.*

TAYLOR, Ernest Richard; Headmaster of Wolverhampton Grammar School, 1956–73; *b* Oldham, 9 Aug. 1910; *e s* of late Louis Whitfield Taylor and Annie Taylor; *m* 1936, Muriel Hardill; twin *s. Educ:* Hulme Grammar School, Oldham; Trinity College, Cambridge. Hist. Tripos, Class I, 1931; Sen. Schol. and Earl of Derby Research Student (Trinity), 1931–32; Thirlwall and Gladstone Prizes, 1933; MA 1935. War Service in RA and AEC, 1940–46. Asst Master, Culford School, 1932–36; Moseley Gram. Sch., Birmingham, 1936–39; Manchester Gram. Sch., 1939–47; Headmaster of Quarry Bank High School, Liverpool, 1947–56. Member, Schools Council for Curriculum and Examinations (formerly Secondary Schools Examinations Council), 1962–84. Walter Hines Page Scholar, HMC, 1964. Pres. Incorporated Assoc. of Head Masters, 1965; Chm. Central Exec., Jt Four Secondary Assocs, 1970–72. Member: President's Council of Methodist Church, 1976–79; Churches' Council for Covenanting, 1978–82. Hon. Life Mem., Secondary Heads Assoc., 1979. Hon. Fellow, Selly Oak Colls, Birmingham, 1989. *Publications:* Methodism and Politics, (1791–1851), 1935; Padre Brown of Gibraltar, 1955; Religious Education of pupils from 16 to 19 years, 1962. *Recreation:* golf. *Address:* Highcliff, Whitcliffe, Ludlow, Shropshire SY8 2HD. *T:* Ludlow (0584) 872093. *Died 10 April 1993.*

TAYLOR, Sir George, Kt 1962; DSc; FRS 1968, FRSE, FLS; Director, Royal Botanic Gardens, Kew, 1956–71; *b* 15 Feb. 1904; *o s* of George William Taylor and Jane Sloan; *m* 1st, 1929, Alice Helen Pendrich (marr. diss.; she *d* 1977); two *s*; 2nd, Norah English (*d* 1967); 3rd, 1969, Beryl, Lady Colwyn (*d* 1987); 4th, 1989, June Maitland. *Educ:* George Heriot's Sch., Edinburgh; Edinburgh Univ. BSc (1st class hons Botany), 1926; Vans Dunlop Scholar. Member of Botanical Expedition to South Africa and Rhodesia, 1927–28; Joint Leader of British Museum Expedition to Ruwenzori and mountains of East Africa, 1934–35; Expedition to SE Tibet and Bhutan, 1938. Principal in Air Ministry, 1940–45. Deputy Keeper of Botany, British Museum (Natural History), 1945–50, Keeper of Botany, 1950–56; Dir, 1970–89, Consultant, 1989–, Stanley Smith Horticultural Trust. Vis. Prof., Reading Univ., 1969. Botanical Sec. Linnean Soc., 1950–56; Vice-Pres. 1956. Percy Sladen Trustee, 1951–81. Royal Horticultural Soc.: Mem. Council, 1951–73, Vice-Pres., and Prof. of Botany, 1974–; Council Member National Trust (Chm. Gardens Cttee), 1961–72; RGS, 1957–61 (Vice-Pres. 1964); Mem. Min. of Transport Adv. Cttee on Landscaping Treatment of Trunk Roads, 1956–81 (Chm. 1969–81). Editor, Curtis's Botanical Magazine, 1962–71. Gen. Sec., Brit. Assoc. for the Advancement of Science, 1951–58. Hon. Botanical Adviser, Commonwealth War Graves Commn, 1956–77. President: Botanical Society of British Isles, 1955; Division of Botany, Internat. Union Biol Sci., 1964–69; Internat. Assoc. for Plant Taxonomy, 1969–72. Member Royal Society Science, Uppsala, 1956; Corr. Member Royal Botanical Soc. Netherlands; Hon. Mem., Botanical Soc. of S Africa; Hon. Mem., American Orchid Soc. Hon. FRHS 1948. Hon. Freeman, Worshipful Co. of Gardeners, 1967. Hon. LLD Dundee, 1972. VMH 1956; Veitch Gold Medal, Royal Horticultural Soc., 1963; Bradford Washburn Award, Museum of Science, Boston, USA, 1969; Scottish Horticultural Medal, Royal Caledonian Horticultural Soc., 1984. Hon. DrPhil Gothenburg, 1958. *Publications:* An Account of the Genus Meconopsis, 1934; contributions on flowering plants to various periodicals. *Recreations:* angling, gardening, music. *Address:* The Glen, Innerleithen, Peeblesshire EH44 6PX. *T:* Innerleithen (0896) 830579. *Clubs:* Athenæum; New (Edinburgh). *Died 13 Nov. 1993.*

TAYLOR, Prof. Gerard William, MS, FRCS; Hon. FACS; Professor of Surgery, University of London, 1960–84; formerly Surgeon and Director Surgical Professorial Unit, St Bartholomew's Hospital, London; Honorary Consultant in Vascular Surgery to the Army since 1962; *b* 23 Sept. 1920; *s* of William Ivan Taylor; *m* 1951, Olivia Gay; one *s* one *d. Educ:* Bemrose School, Derby; St Bartholomew's Hospital Medical College. Served War of 1939–45, Capt. RAMC, 1944–47. Fellow in Surgery, Asst Resident, Fulbright Schol., Stanford Univ. Hosp., San Francisco, Calif, 1950–51; Surgeon, St Bartholomew's Hosp., London, Reader in Surgery, Univ. of London, 1955. Prof. of Surgery, King Khalid Univ. Hosp., 1984. Hunterian Prof., RCS, 1962; Visiting Professor of Surgery: Univ. of Calif., Los Angeles, 1965; Univ. of Melbourne, 1969; Sir James Wattie Prof., NZ, 1972. Examiner in Surgery: Univ. of London, 1960; NUI, 1966; Univ. of Cambridge, 1966; Trinity Coll., Dublin, 1969; Univ. of Liverpool, 1974; Univ. of Birmingham, 1978. Governor, St Bartholomew's Hosp., 1971; Mem. Council, Epsom Coll., 1972. President: Vascular Surgical Soc. of GB and Ireland, 1975; Surgical Res. Soc., 1976; Assoc. of Surgeons of GB and Ireland, 1979. *Publications:* articles on general and arterial surgery in scientific journals. *Recreation:* motoring. *Address:* Maple Farm, Shantock Lane, Bovingdon, Herts HP3 0NN. *T:* Hemel Hempstead (01442) 833170. *Died 3 Jan. 1995.*

TAYLOR, Greville Laughton; company director; *b* 23 Oct. 1902; *s* of Rowland Henry and Edith Louise Taylor; *m* 1947, Mary Eileen Reece Mahon; one *s* one *d. Educ:* Lodge School, Barbados; St John's College, Oxford. Called to the Bar, Lincoln's Inn, 1927. Clerk to the House of Assembly, Barbados, 1930–36; Police Magistrate, Barbados, 1936–44; Army 1940–44 (UK, N Africa, Italy); Registrar, Barbados, 1944–46; Judge of the Assistant Court of Appeal, Barbados, 1947–57; Puisne Judge, Windward Islands and Leeward Islands, 1957–64. *Recreations:* reading, shooting, fishing. *Address:* Frangipani, No 9 Long Bay, St Philip, Barbados, West Indies. *T:* 207. *Club:* Barbados Yacht. *Died 16 Nov. 1993.*

TAYLOR, Harold Joseph, CBE 1966; Chief Director, Prison Department, Home Office, 1965–68, retired; *b* 7 May 1904; *s* of Herbert Taylor and Gertrude Mary Taylor; *m* 1940, Olive Alice Slade, *d* of Harry Slade, Honor Oak Park, SE; (one adopted *s* decd). *Educ:* Blandford Sec. Gram. Sch.; Southampton University. Teacher, Brighton Education Authority, 1924–28; Asst Housemaster, Prison Commission, HM Borstal, Portland, 1928; Housemaster, Portland Borstal, 1930; Superintendent, Borstal Training School, Thayetmyo, Burma, 1933–37; Governor, HM Borstal: Feltham, Middx, 1938–41; Lowdham Grange, 1941–46; Governor, HM Prison: Camp Hill, IoW, 1946–49; Sudbury, Derby, 1949–51; Asst Comr, HM Prison Commission, 1951–57; Comr and Director of Borstal Administration, 1958–65. *Recreations:* fishing, country lore, tinkering. *Address:* 45 Church Way, Pagham, Bognor Regis, West Sussex PO21 4QQ. *T:* Pagham (0243) 263750. *Died 29 May 1993.*

TAYLOR, Harold McCarter, CBE 1955; TD 1945; retired, 1967; *b* Dunedin, New Zealand, 13 May 1907; *s* of late James Taylor, and late Louisa Urquhart Taylor; *m* 1st, 1933, Joan (*d* 1965), *d* of late George Reginald Sills, Lincoln; two *s* two *d*; 2nd, 1966, Dorothy Judith, *d* of late Charles Samuel, Liverpool. *Educ:* Otago Boys' High School and Univ. of Otago, NZ; Clare Coll., Cambridge. MSc New Zealand, 1928; MA, PhD Cambridge, 1933. Allen Scholar and Smith's Prizeman, 1932. Fellow of Clare College, Cambridge, 1933–61; Hon. Fellow, 1961–; Lecturer in Mathematics, University of Cambridge, 1934–45; Treasurer of the University, 1945–53; Secretary General of the Faculties, 1953–61; Vice-Chancellor, University of Keele, 1962–67 (Principal, University College of North Staffordshire, 1961–62); Rede Lecturer, Cambridge University, 1966. Mem., Royal Commn on Historical Monuments (England), 1972–78. Pres., Royal Archaeol Inst., 1972–75; Vice-Pres., Soc. of Antiquaries of London, 1974–77 (Frend Medal, 1981). Hon. LLD Cambridge, 1967; Hon. DLitt: Keele, 1968; Birmingham, 1983. Commissioned in TA, NZ, 1925; served War of 1939–45 as Major and Lieut-Col RA; Instructor and Senior Instructor in Gunnery at School of Artillery, Larkhill; J. H. Lefroy Medal, RA, 1946. *Publications:* Anglo-Saxon Architecture, vols I and II (with Joan Taylor), 1965, vol. III, 1978; many articles in nat. and county archaeological jls. *Recreations:* mountaineering and ski-ing; Anglo-Saxon art and architecture; photography. *Address:* 192 Huntingdon Road, Cambridge CB3 0LB. *T:* Cambridge (01223) 276324. *Died 23 Oct. 1995.*

TAYLOR, Sir Henry Milton, Kt 1980; JP; Acting Governor-General, Commonwealth of the Bahamas, 1988–92; Editor of Hansard, Bahamas House of Assembly, since 1979; *b* 4 Nov. 1903; adopted *s* of Joseph and Evelyn Taylor; *m* 1962, Eula Mae Sisco; three step *c*; four *d* by previous marriage. *Educ:* Govt Grade Sch.; privately. Teacher; Headmaster, Public Sch. at Pompey Bay, Acklins Island, 1925–26. Elected Mem., House of Assembly,

1949; Co-founded and organized estabt of Progressive Liberal Party of Bahamas (first political party of Bahamas), 1953–64; Nat. Party Chm., 1953–64, Hon. Chm. for life, 1963; MP for 10 yrs; Leader of delegns to Westminster: to upgrade antiquated Acts of Parliament, 1956; in interest of Women's Suffrage, 1960. Temp. Dep. Governor-General of The Bahamas, July-Aug. and Nov. 1981, Aug.-Nov. 1982 and June 1984. Mem., Develt Bd (Tourist), 1960–62; successfully toured Britain, Eire, W Germany and Sweden in interests of tourism and financial investments; officially visited Nassau/Lahn. (First) Dir, Princess Margaret Hosp. Blood Bank, 1954–55. Organised Bahamas Soc. of Arms and Awards, 1984. Letters Patent for Armorial Bearing approved by Duke of Norfolk, 1981. JP Bahama Isles, 1984. *Publications:* (compiled and ed) United Bahamian Party Annual Handbook, 1967, 1968; My Political Memoirs, 1986. *Address:* PO Box N10846, Nassau, Bahamas; Lucaya at Brentwood, 221 NE 44 Street, Miami, Fla 33137, USA. *Club:* British Floridian (Miami). *Died 14 Feb. 1994.*

TAYLOR, Sir James, Kt 1966; MBE 1945; DSc, FRSC, Hon. FInstP, Hon. MIMinE; Director, Surrey Independent Hospital plc, 1981–86; Deputy Chairman, Royal Ordnance Factories Board, 1959–72 (Member, 1952–72); Chairman, Chloride Silent Power Ltd, 1974–81; *b* 16 Aug. 1902; *s* of James and Alice Taylor; *m* 1929, Margaret Lennox Stewart (*d* 1990); two *s* one *d. Educ:* Bede College, Sunderland; Rutherford College, Newcastle upon Tyne; Universities of Durham, Sorbonne, Utrecht, Cambridge. BSc (1st cl. Hons Physics) 1923; PhD 1925; Dr of Physics and Maths (*cum laude*) Utrecht, 1927; DSc Dunelm, 1931. FRSC (FRIC 1945); MIMinE 1947 (Hon. Member, 1960); FInstP 1948 (Hon. FInstP 1972). ICI Ltd: joined Nobel Div. 1928; Research Dir, 1946; Jt Man. Dir, 1951; Director, 1952–64; Chairman: Yorkshire Imperial Metals Ltd, 1958–64; Imperial Aluminium Co. Ltd, 1959–64; Imperial Metal Industries Ltd, 1962–64. Director: Nuclear Developments Ltd, 1961–64; European Plumbing Materials Ltd, 1962–64; BDH Group Ltd, 1965–67; Oldham & Son Ltd, 1965–69; Oldham (International) Ltd, 1969–72. Member: Adv. Coun. on Scientific Research and Tech. Develt, MoD, 1965–68; NPL Steering Committee, 1966; Adv. Coun. on Calibration and Measurement, 1966; Chairman: Glazebrook Cttee, NPL, 1966; Fulmer Res. Inst., 1976–78. Member: Court, Brunel Univ., 1967–82; Council, British Non-Ferrous Metals Research Assoc., 1954–67 (Vice-Chm. 1961–67); Council, City and Guilds of London, 1969–71; Court, RCA, 1969–71; Pres. Section B British Assoc. 1960, Council 1965; Pres. Inst. of Physics and Physical Society, 1966–68 (Hon. Treas. 1957–66). FRSA 1962 (Member Council 1964–86, Vice-Pres., 1969, Chm., 1969–71, Vice-Pres. Emeritus, 1988, Silver Medal, 1969); Hon. Pres., Research and Development Soc., 1970; Hon. Mem., Newcomen Soc. in N America, 1970. Mem., Inst. of Dirs, 1964–. Hon. DSc Bradford, 1968; Hon. DCL Newcastle, 1969. Medal, Society Chemical Industry, 1965; Silver Medal, Chem. Soc., 1972. *Publications:* On the Sparking Potentials of Electric Discharge Tubes, 1927; Detonation in Condensed Explosives, 1952; British Coal Mining Explosives, 1958; Solid Propellant and Exothermic Compositions, 1959; The Modern Chemical Industry in Great Britain (Cantor Lectures, Jl of RSA), 1961; Restrictive Practices (Soc. of Chem. Ind. Lecture), 1965; Monopolies and Restrictive Practices (RSA), 1967; The Scientist and The Technologist in Britain Today (Pres. Address, IPPS), 1967; Britain's Technological Future (Inst. of Phys Jubilee Address), 1968; Arts, Crafts and Technology (RSA), 1969; Cobalt, Madder and Computers (RSA), 1969; The Seventies and the Society (RSA), 1970; The American Dream and the RSA, 1971; New Horizons in Research and Development (RSA), 1971; The Scientific Community, 1973; numerous contribs to Proc. Roy. Soc.,

Phil. Mag., Trans Inst. Min. Eng, Advancement of Science, ICI Magazine. *Recreations:* gardening, cooking, writing. *Address:* Culvers, Seale, near Farnham, Surrey GU10 1JN. *T:* Farnham (01252) 782210. *Club:* RNVR Carrick (Hon.) (Glasgow). *Died 4 Oct. 1994.*

TAYLOR, His Honour John Barrington, MBE 1945; TD 1957; a Circuit Judge, 1977–89; *b* 3 Aug. 1914; *y s* of Robert Edward Taylor, Bath; *m* 1941, Constance Aleen (*d* 1991), *y d* of J. Barkly Macadam, Edinburgh and Suffolk; two *s* three *d* (and one *s* decd). *Educ:* King Edward's Sch., Bath. LLB (London). Admitted a Solicitor, 1936, and practised at Bath until 1960. Enlisted Somerset LI, 1939; overseas service 1942–46: DAAG, HQ 5 Corps, 1943; demobilised, Lieut-Col, 1946. HM Coroner, City of Bath, 1958–72; Registrar, Bath Gp of County Courts, 1960–77; a Recorder of the Crown Court, 1972–77. JP Somerset, 1962, Essex, 1978. *Recreation:* gardening. *Address:* Guelder Rose, Manley Lane, Tiverton, Devon EX16 4PZ. *Died 10 Sept. 1993.*

TAYLOR, John Ralph Carlisle, CIE 1943; Past Director, Davy-Ashmore International Co. Ltd; *b* Sydney, NSW, Australia, 18 Aug. 1902; *o s* of Charles Carlisle Taylor and Jean Sawers; *m* 1933, Nancy (Ann) Marguerite Sorel-Cameron (*d* 1972); (one *s* decd). *Educ:* Winchester. Shaw Wallace & Co., London, Calcutta, Karachi, 1921–28; Burmah-Shell, 1928–39 and 1945–54; General Manager in India, 1951–54; Chairman, Shell Group of Companies in Australia, 1955–60; retired from Shell, 1960. Service in RIASC (Lt-Col), 1941–42, GHQ India (Lt-Col) 1942; Petroleum Officer; *ex-officio* Dep. Sec., Defence Dept, Govt of India, 1942–45. *Recreations:* walking, reading, racing. *Address:* 166 Oakwood Court, W14 8JE. *Clubs:* Hurlingham, Oriental. *Died 28 June 1991.*

TAYLOR, Kenneth John; His Honour Judge Kenneth Taylor; a Circuit Judge, since 1977; *b* 29 March 1929; *s* of Hereford Phillips Taylor and Florence Gertrude Taylor; *m* 1953, Joan Cattermole; one *s* one *d. Educ:* William Hulme's Grammar Sch., Manchester; Manchester Univ. (LLB). Called to Bar, Middle Temple, 1951. A Recorder of the Crown Court, 1972–77. *Recreations:* reading, music. *Address:* 25 Mill Lane, off The Bank, Scholar Green, Stoke-on-Trent ST7 3LD. *Died 20 June 1995.*

TAYLOR, Leon Eric Manners; Research Analyst; *b* 28 Oct. 1917; *s* of late Leon Eric Taylor and Veronica Dalmahoy (*née* Rogers); *m* 1963, Margaret Betty Thompson; no *c. Educ:* Fettes Coll., Edinburgh; Oriel Coll., Oxford. Captain RA (Service, 1939–46). Called to Bar, Inner Temple, 1951. Asst Principal, 1945, Principal, 1948, in Bd of Trade until 1963; Attended Joint Services Staff College, 1952; First Sec., UK Delegn to the European Communities, 1963–66; Econ. Counsellor, British High Commn, Kuala Lumpur, 1966–70; Hon. Visiting Fellow, Centre for Contemporary European Studies, University of Sussex, 1970–71; Counsellor (Commercial), The Hague, 1971–72; Research Fellow, Univ. of Sussex, 1973–75. *Recreations:* walking, amateur theatre, golf. *Address:* Sam's Hill Cottage, 47 North Street, Middle Barton, Chipping Norton, Oxon OX7 7BH. *T:* Steeple Aston (01869) 47256. *Died 6 Dec. 1995.*

TAYLOR, Sir Michael (Goodiff), Kt 1989; CBE 1983; auctioneer and valuer; Chairman, Michael Taylor (Valuations) Ltd, since 1990; *b* 17 Oct. 1929; *s* of P. C. G. Taylor and K. M. Taylor (*née* Read); *m* 1957, Hazel Mary Gordon; two *s* one *d. Educ:* privately; Sutton Valence Sch., Kent. FSVA (Fellow, Inc. Soc. of Auctioneers and Land Property Agents, 1961). Joined: John D. Wood & Co., London, 1947; T. Bannister & Co., Haywards Heath, 1955; founded Taylor & Tester, East Grinstead, and branches, 1961; sold firm to Leeds Property (UK) Ltd,

1988. Joined Conservative party, 1947; Chairman: Sussex YCs, 1951; SE Area, 1982–86 (Treas., 1975–82); Member: Cons. Central Bd of Finance, 1975–82; Exec., Nat. Union of Cons. Assocs, 1973–83; Pres., Mid Sussex Cons. Assoc., 1982–. Mem., E Sussex CC, 1970–77. Mem., Country Landowners' Assoc.; Conservator, Ashdown Forest, 1974–85. President's Prize, Incorporated Soc. of Auctioneers, 1952. *Recreation:* small livestock breeding (dogs and rabbits). *Address:* Duckyls, near East Grinstead, West Sussex RH19 4LP. *T:* Sharpthorne (0342) 811017. *Club:* Carlton.   *Died 31 July 1991.*

TAYLOR, Robert Martin, OBE 1976; Editorial Director, The Croydon Advertiser Ltd, 1967–76; *b* 25 Nov. 1914; *s* of Ernest H. and Charlotte Taylor; *m* 1947, Ray Turney; one *s* one *d*. *Educ:* Simon Langton, Canterbury. Croydon Advertiser: Editor, 1950–58; Managing Editor, 1958–74; Dir, 1967–76. Mem., Nat. Council for the Training of Journalists, 1967–71; Pres., Guild of British Newspaper Editors, 1971–72, Hon. Vice-Pres., 1976; Mem., Press Council, 1974–76. Sec., Glenurquhart Community Council, 1982–86; Hon. Treasurer, Glenurquart Rural Community Assoc., 1984–86, Chm., 1988–91. Founded Glenurquart Newsletter, 1985. *Publications:* (editor and co-author) Essential Law for Journalists, 1954, 6th edn 1975; Glenurquhart Official Guide, 1980. *Address:* Glengarry, Milton, Drumnadrochit, Inverness-shire. *T:* Drumnadrochit (04562) 291.   *Died 16 July 1992.*

TAYLOR, Robert Richardson, QC (Scot.) 1959; MA, LLB, PhD; Sheriff-Principal of Tayside Central and Fife, 1975–90; *b* 16 Sept. 1919; *m* 1949, Märtha Birgitta Björkling; two *s* one *d*. *Educ:* Glasgow High School; Glasgow University. Called to Bar, Scotland, 1944; called to Bar, Middle Temple, 1948. Lectr in Internat. Private Law, Edinburgh Univ., 1947–69; Sheriff-Principal, Stirling, Dunbarton and Clackmannan, 1971–75. Chm., Sheriff Ct Rules Council, 1982–89. Contested (U and NL): Dundee East, 1955; Dundee West, 1959 and Nov. 1963. Chm., Central and Southern Region, Scottish Cons. Assoc., 1969–71. Chm., Northern Lighthouse Bd, 1985–86. *Recreations:* lapidary, mineral collecting. *Address:* 51 Northumberland Street, Edinburgh EH3 6JQ. *T:* 031–556 1722.   *Died 21 May 1993.*

TAYLOR, Most Rev. Robert Selby, CBE 1983; OGS; Archbishop Emeritus of Cape Town, 1987; *b* 1 March 1909; *s* of late Robert Taylor, Eden Bank, Wetheral, Cumberland; unmarried. *Educ:* Harrow; St Catharine's Coll., Cambridge; Cuddesdon Coll. Ordained deacon, 1932; priest, 1933; served as a curate at St Olave's, York; went out to Diocese of Northern Rhodesia in 1935 as a Mission priest; OGS, 1935–; Principal of Diocesan Theological Coll., 1939; Bishop of Northern Rhodesia, 1941–51; Bishop of Pretoria, 1951–59; Bishop of Grahamstown, 1959–64; Archbishop of Cape Town, 1964–74; Bishop of Central Zambia, 1979–84. Hon. Fellow, St Catharine's Coll., Cambridge, 1964. DD (Hon.) Rhodes Univ., 1966; DD Lambeth, 1991. *Address:* Braehead House, Auburn Road, Kenilworth 7700, South Africa. *T:* (21) 771440. *Clubs:* Commonwealth Trust; City and Civil Service (Cape Town).
                                            Died 23 April 1995.

TAYLOR, William Leonard, CBE 1982; JP; DL; solicitor, retired; *b* 21 Dec. 1916; *s* of Joseph and May Taylor; *m* 1943, Gladys Carling; one *s*. *Educ:* Whitehill School; Glasgow Univ. (BL). Chairman: Livingston Develt Corp., 1965–72; Scottish Water Adv. Cttee, 1969–72; Mem., Scottish Adv. Cttee on Civil Aviation, 1965–72; Chm., Panel of Assessors, River Clyde Planning Study, 1972–74. Chairman: Planning Exchange, 1972–; Scottish Adv. Council on Social Work, 1974–81; Vice-Chm., Commn for Local Authority Accounts in Scotland, 1974–83; Mem., Housing Corp., 1974–80; Chm. Scottish Special

Housing Assoc., 1978–81; Member: Scottish Economic Council, 1975–81; Extra-Parly Panel under Private Legislation Procedure (Scotland) Act 1936, 1971–86. Councillor, City of Glasgow, 1952–69; Magistrate, City of Glasgow, 1956–60; Sen. Magistrate, 1960–61; Leader, Labour Gp in Glasgow Corp., 1962–69; Leader of Council, 1962–68; Convener of Cttees: Planning, Glasgow Airport, Sports Centre, Parly Bills. Governor, Centre for Environmental Studies, 1966–79; Trustee, Scottish Civic Trust, 1967–; Chm., Glasgow Citizens' Theatre Ltd, 1970–; Mem., Nat. Executive (and Chm. Scottish Exec.), Town & Country Planning Assoc. Hon. Pres., Scotland-USSR Friendship Soc. Hon. FRTPI. JP 1953; DL Glasgow, 1971. Hon. LLD Glasgow, 1991. Knight, Order of Polonia Restituta (Poland), 1969. *Recreations:* fishing, theatre, reading. *Address:* Cruachan, 18 Bruce Road, Glasgow G41 5EF. *T:* 041–429 1776.   *Died 4 Aug. 1991.*

TEARE, Dr (Hugo) Douglas, CVO 1973; Physician Superintendent, King Edward VII Hospital, Midhurst, Sussex, 1971–77; *b* 20 April 1917; *s* of A. H. Teare, JP, and Margaret Green; *m* 1945, Evelyn Bertha Hider; three *s*. *Educ:* King William's Coll., Isle of Man; Gonville and Caius Coll., Cambridge; St George's Hospital, London. BA 1938; MRCS, LRCP 1941; MB, BChir 1942. House Physician and Casualty Officer, St George's Hospital, 1941; Resident Surgical Officer and Med. Registrar, Brompton Hospital, 1943; Dep. Med. Superintendent, King Edward VII Hospital (Sanatorium), Midhurst, 1946–70. MHK, 1981–84. OStJ. *Recreation:* reading. *Address:* Lismore, 6 St Olave's Close, Ramsey, Isle of Man. *T:* Ramsey (0624) 812065.
                                            Died 9 June 1991.

TEDDER, 2nd Baron, *cr* 1946, of Glenguin, Co. of Stirling; **John Michael Tedder,** MA, ScD, PhD, DSc; Purdie Professor of Chemistry, St Salvator's College, University of St Andrews, 1969–89, then Emeritus; *b* 4 July 1926; 2nd and *er* surv. *s* of 1st Baron Tedder, GCB, and Rosalinde (*née* Maclardy); *S* father, 1967; *m* 1952, Peggy Eileen Growcott; two *s* one *d*. *Educ:* Dauntsey's School, Wilts; Magdalene College, Cambridge (MA 1951; ScD 1965); University of Birmingham (PhD 1951; DSc 1961). Roscoe Professor of Chemistry, University of Dundee, 1964–69. Mem., Ct of Univ. of St Andrews, 1971–76. Vice-Pres., Perkin Div., RSC, 1980–83. FRSE; FRSC. *Publications:* Valence Theory, 1966; Basic Organic Chemistry, 1966; The Chemical Bond, 1978; Radicals, 1979; papers in Jl of RSC and other scientific jls. *Heir: s* Hon. Robin John Tedder [*b* 6 April 1955; *m* 1st, 1977, Jennifer Peggy (*d* 1978), *d* of John Mangan, NZ; 2nd, 1980, Rita Aristeia, *yr d* of John Frangidis, Sydney, NSW; two *s* one *d*]. *Address:* Little Rathmore, Kennedy Gardens, St Andrews, Fife KY16 9DJ. *T:* St Andrews (0334) 73546.   *Died 18 Feb. 1994.*

TEI ABAL, Sir, Kt 1976; CBE 1974; MHA, PNG; *b* 1932; *m*; six *c*. Became a tea-planter and trader in Papua New Guinea; a Leader of the Engi Clan in Western Highlands. Member for Wabag, open electorate, PNG; former Member (Ministerial) in 1st, 2nd and 3rd Houses of Assembly; Leader of the Opposition, UP, and later Minister of Public Utilities, 1979–80, in Somare Govt. *Address:* c/o PO Box 1828, Port Moresby, Papua New Guinea; Wabag, Papua New Guinea.   *Died 14 March 1995.*

TEMIN, Prof. Howard M(artin), PhD; Professor of Oncology, since 1969, Harry Steenbock Professor of Biological Science, since 1982, Harold P. Rusch Professor of Cancer Research, since 1980 and American Cancer Society Professor of Viral Oncology and Cell Biology, since 1974, University of Wisconsin-Madison; *b* 10 Dec. 1934; *s* of Henry Temin and Annette Lehman Temin; *m* 1962, Rayla Greenberg; two *d*. *Educ:* Swarthmore Coll., Swarthmore, Pa (BA 1955); Calif Inst. of Technol.,

Pasadena (PhD 1959). Postdoctoral Fellow, Calif Inst. of Technol., Pasadena, 1959–60; Asst Prof. of Oncology, Univ. of Wisconsin-Madison, 1960–64, Associate Prof. of Oncol., 1964–69, Wisconsin Alumni Res. Foundn Prof. of Cancer Res, 1971–80. Foreign Mem., Royal Soc., 1988. Hon. DSc: Swarthmore Coll., 1972; NY Med. Coll., 1972; Univ. of Pa, 1976; Hahnemann Med. Coll., 1976; Lawrence Univ., 1976; Temple Univ., 1979; Medical Coll., Wisconsin, 1981; Colorado State Univ., 1987; Univ. Paris V, 1988; Univ. Med. Dent., NJ, 1989. US Public Health Service Res. Career Develt Award, National Cancer Inst., 1964–74; (jtly) Nobel Prize for Physiology or Medicine, 1975; Nat. Medal of Sci., US, 1992. *Publications:* articles on viruses and cancer, on RNA-directed DNA synthesis, on evolution of viruses from cellular movable genetic elements, on retrovirus vectors, and on retrovirus genetics. *Address:* McArdle Laboratory, University of Wisconsin-Madison, Madison, Wis 53706, USA. *T:* (608) 2621209. *Died 9 Feb. 1994.*

TEMPLE, George Frederick James, CBE 1955; PhD, DSc, MA; FRS 1943; OSB; Sedleian Professor of Natural Philosophy, University of Oxford, 1953–68; then Professor Emeritus; Hon. Fellow of Queen's College, Oxford, 1970; *b* 2 Sept. 1901; *o s* of late James Temple, London; *m* 1930, Dorothy Lydia (*d* 1979), *e d* of late Thomas Ellis Carson, Liverpool. *Educ:* Ealing County School; Birkbeck College, University of London; Trinity College, Cambridge. Research Assistant and Demonstrator, Physics Dept, Birkbeck College, 1922–24; Assistant Lecturer, Maths Dept, City and Guilds (Eng.) College, 1924–28; Keddey Fletcher Warr Studentship, 1928; 1851 Exhibition Research Student, 1928–30; Assistant Professor in Maths Dept, Royal College of Science, 1930–32; Professor of Mathematics, University of London, King's College, 1932–53. Seconded to Royal Aircraft Establishment, Farnborough, 1939–45. Chairman, Aeronautical Research Council, 1961–64. Leverhulme Emeritus Fellowship, 1971–73. Professed as Benedictine monk, 1982. Hon. DSc: Dublin, 1961; Louvain, 1966; Reading, 1980; Hon. LLD W Ontario, 1969. Sylvester Medal (Royal Soc.), 1970. *Publications:* An Introduction to Quantum Theory, 1931; Rayleigh's Principle, 1933; General Principles of Quantum Theory, 1934; An Introduction to Fluid Dynamics, 1958; Cartesian Tensors, 1960; The Structure of Lebesgue Integration Theory, 1971; papers on mathematical physics, relativity, quantum theory, aerodynamics, distribution theory, history of mathematics. *Address:* Quarr Abbey, Ryde, Isle of Wight. *Died 30 Jan. 1992.*

TEMPLE, Sir John (Meredith), Kt 1983; JP; DL; *b* 9 June 1910; *m* 1942, Nancy Violet, *d* of late Brig.-Gen. Robert William Hare, CMG, DSO, DL, Cobh, Eire, and Norwich; one *s* one *d. Educ:* Charterhouse; Clare College, Cambridge (BA). Served War of 1939–45 (despatches); ADC to Governor of S Australia, 1941. MP (C) City of Chester, Nov. 1956–Feb. 1974. Pres., Ellesmere Port and Neston Cons. Assoc.; Vice-Pres., Chester Conservative Club; Vice-Chairman: British Group, IPU, 1973–74; Cons. Finance Cttee, 1966–68; Vice-President: Army Benevolent Fund (Chester Branch); Anglo-Colombian Society; Cerro Galan Expedn, Argentina, 1981; Salmon and Trout Assoc. JP Cheshire 1949, DL 1975; High Sheriff of Cheshire, 1980–81. Great Officer: Order of San Carlos, Colombia, 1973; Order of Boyacà, Colombia, 1974; Order of the Liberator, Venezuela, 1974. *Address:* Picton Gorse, Chester CH2 4JU. *T:* Mickle Trafford (01244) 300239. *Clubs:* Carlton; Racquet (Liverpool). *Died 10 Dec. 1994.*

TENNYSON, 4th Baron *cr* 1884; **Harold Christopher Tennyson;** *b* 25 March 1919; *e s* of 3rd Baron and Hon. Clarissa Tennant (*d* 1960), *o d* of 1st Baron Glenconner;

S father 1951. *Educ:* Eton; Trinity Coll., Cambridge. BA 1940. Employed War Office, 1939–46. Co-founder, Tennyson Research Centre, Lincoln. Hon. Freeman, City of Lincoln, 1964. *Heir: b* Hon. Mark Aubrey Tennyson, DSC 1943, RN retd [*b* 28 March 1920; *m* 1964, Deline Celeste Budler]. *Address:* 18 Rue Galilée, 75016 Paris, France. *Clubs:* White's, Royal Automobile; Royal and Ancient. *Died 19 Oct. 1991.*

TERRY, Sir George (Walter Roberts), Kt 1982; CBE 1976; QPM 1967; DL; Chief Constable of Sussex, 1973–83; *b* 29 May 1921; *s* of late Walter George Tygh Terry and Constance Elizabeth Terry; *m* 1942, Charlotte Elizabeth Kresina; one *s. Educ:* Peterborough, Northants. Served War, Northamptonshire Regt, in Italy, 1942–46 (Staff Captain). Chief Constable: Pembrokeshire, 1958–65; East Sussex, 1965–67; Dep. Chief Constable, Sussex, 1968–69; Chief Constable, Lincolnshire, 1970–73. Chm., Traffic Cttee, 1976–79, Pres., 1980–81, Assoc. of Chief Police Officers; Dir, Police Extended Interviews, 1977–83. Dir, Terrafix Ltd, 1984–. Trustee: Disabled Housing Trust, 1985–; Coll. of Driver Educn, 1989–. CStJ. DL E Sussex, 1983. *Recreations:* horticulture, motoring. *Address:* c/o National Westminster Bank, 173 High Street, Lewes, Sussex BN7 1XD.
Died 18 Aug. 1995.

TERRY, Sir John Elliott, Kt 1976; Consultant with Denton Hall & Burgin; Managing Director, National Film Finance Corporation, 1958–78; *b* 11 June 1913; *s* of Ernest Fairchild Terry, OBE, FRICS, and Zabelle Terry (*née* Costikyan), Pulborough, Sussex; *m* 1940, Joan Christine, *d* of Frank Alfred Ernest Howard Fell and Ethel Christine Fell (*née* Nilson), Stoke D'Abernon, Surrey; one *s* one *d. Educ:* Mill Hill School; Univ. of London (LLB). Articled with Denton Hall & Burgin, London; admitted solicitor, 1938. London Fire Service, 1939–40; Friends' Ambulance Unit, 1941–44; Nat. Council of Social Service, 1944–46; Film Producers' Guild, 1946–47; The Rank Organisation's Legal Dept, 1947–49; joined Nat. Film Finance Corp. as Solicitor, 1949, also Sec., 1956. Hon. Vice Pres., British Screen Adv. Council, 1993–. Governor: Nat. Film Sch., 1970–81; London Internat. Film Sch., 1982–90; Royal Nat. Coll. for the Blind, 1980–; Pres., Copinger Soc., 1981–83. *Address:* Still Point, Branscombe, Devon EX12 3DQ. *Club:* Savile. *Died 29 March 1995.*

TERRY, Walter Frederick; Political Editor, The Sun, 1978–83 (Member of Political Staff, 1976–78); *b* 18 Aug. 1924; *s* of Fred Terry and Helen MacKenzie Bruce; *m* 1950, Mavis Landen; one *s* one *d* (and one *s* decd). *Educ:* at school and later by experience. Entered journalism, Glossop Chronicle, 1943; Derby Evening Telegraph, 1947; Nottingham Journal, 1948; Daily Mail, Manchester, 1949; Daily Mail: Parliamentary Staff, 1955; Political Correspondent, 1959; Political Editor, 1965; Washington Correspondent, 1969; Dep.-Editor, 1970–71; Political Editor, 1971–73; Political Editor, Daily Express, 1973–75. Journalist of the Year (first awards), 1963. *Address:* St Germans House, Eliot Place, SE3 0QL. *T:* 081–852 2526; 8 Fort Rise, Newhaven Harbour, Sussex BN9 9DW. *T:* Newhaven (0273) 514347. *Died 25 Jan. 1991.*

TETLEY, Kenneth James; a Recorder of Crown and County Courts, since 1972; *b* Ashton-under-Lyne, Lancs, 17 Oct. 1921; *o s* of William Tetley, Dukinfield, Cheshire, and Annie Lees, Oldham; *m* 1945, Edna Rita, *e d* of Peter Charles Spurrin Gray and Annie Gray, Audenshaw, Manchester; one *s* three *d. Educ:* Ashton-under-Lyne Grammar Sch.; Manchester Univ. Served War of 1939–45: joined RN, 1941; Lieut RNVR (attached Combined Ops); discharged, 1945. Admitted Solicitor, 1947; Councillor, Ashton-under-Lyne Borough Council, 1955; Alderman, 1967. *Recreations:* Rugby Union football, fell-walking, photography. *Address:* 6 Pine Lodge, 28 London Road

South, Poynton, Stockport, Cheshire SK12 1NJ. *T:* (home) Poynton (0625) 859126; (office) 061–330 2865. *Clubs:* Rugby (Ashton-under-Lyne); Romiley Golf; Lancashire County RFU. *Died 4 Jan. 1993.*

THALMANN, Dr Ernesto; retired Swiss Ambassador; *b* 14 Jan. 1914; *s* of Friedrich Thalmann and Clara (*née* Good) *m* 1943, Paula Degen; two *s* one *d. Educ:* Gymnasium, Zürich; Univ. of Zürich (LLD). Entered Federal Dept of Public Economy, 1941; Federal Political Dept (Swiss Foreign Office), 1945; Minister/Counsellor and Dep. Head of Mission, Swiss Embassy, Washington, 1957–61; Permanent Observer to UN, New York (Ambassador Extraordinary and Plenipotentiary), 1961–66; Head of Internat. Organizations Div., Fed. Political Dept, Berne, 1966–71; Special Mission in Jerusalem, after 6–day war, as Personal Rep. of UN Secretary-General, U Thant, 1967; Secretary-General, Fed. Political Dept and Director of Political Affairs, 1971–75; Swiss Ambassador to the Court of St James's, 1976–79. Pres., Nat. Swiss Unesco Commn, 1981–85. *Address:* 8 Anshelmstrasse, 3005 Berne, Switzerland. *Died 12 Feb. 1993.*

THIESS, Sir Leslie Charles, Kt 1971; CBE 1968; Chairman of Directors: Thiess Watkins Group of Companies, 1982–88; Breakwater Island Ltd, since 1984; Governing Director, Drayton Investments Pty Ltd, since 1953; *b* 8 April 1909; *m* 1929, Christina Mary (*née* Erbacher) (decd); two *s* three *d. Educ:* Drayton, Queensland. Founded Thiess Bros as a private company, 1933; Managing Dir, Thiess Holdings Ltd when it was formed in 1950; also when firm became a public company, 1958; Chairman: Thiess Group of Cos, 1968–80; Thiess Consortium, 1981–82; Chm. of Dirs, 1971–86, Hon. Chm., 1986–, Thiess Toyota Pty Ltd; Chairman of Directors: Daihatsu Australia Pty Ltd, 1975–86; Queensland Metals Corp., 1983–87 (Dir, 1987–). FCIT (London), 1971. Total Community Development Award, 1982. Order of the Sacred Treasure (third class), Japan, 1972. *Publication:* Thiess Story. *Recreation:* deep sea fishing. *Address:* 121 King Arthur Terrace, Tennyson, Qld 4105, Australia. *Clubs:* Tattersall's, Royal Queensland Yacht (Brisbane); Huntington, NSW Sports (NSW). *Died 25 Nov. 1992.*

THOMAS, Brinley, CBE 1971 (OBE 1955); MA, PhD; FBA 1973; Professor of Economics, University College, Cardiff, 1946–73, then Emeritus; Director, Manpower Research Unit, 1974–76; *b* 6 Jan. 1906; *e s* of late Thomas Thomas and Anne Walters; *m* 1943, Cynthia, *d* of late Dr Charles T. Loram, New Haven, Connecticut; one *d. Educ:* Port Talbot County School; University College of Wales, Aberystwyth; London School of Economics. MA (Wales) (with distinction), 1928; Fellow of the University of Wales, 1929–31; Social Science Research Training Scholar, 1929–31; PhD (London), 1931; Hutchinson Silver Medal, London School of Economics, 1931; Acland Travelling Scholar in Germany and Sweden, 1932–34. Lecturer in Economics, London School of Economics, 1931–39; War Trade Department, British Embassy, Washington, 1941–42; Dir, Northern Section, Political Intelligence Dept of Foreign Office, 1942–45. Member: National Assistance Bd, 1948–53; Anderson Cttee on Grants to Students, 1958–60; Dept of Employment Retail Prices Index Advisory Cttee; Prince of Wales Cttee, 1969–76. Chairman: Welsh Advisory Cttee of British Council, 1966–74; Welsh Council, 1968–71; Assoc. of Univ. Teachers of Econs, 1965–68; Mem. Exec. Cttee, British Council, 1966–74; Pres., Atlantic Economic Soc. Nat. Science Foundn Fellow, 1971. University of California, Berkeley: Ford Vis. Res. Prof., 1976–77; Vis. Prof., 1978–79 and 1979–83; Visiting Professor: Queen's Univ., Canada, 1977–78; Univ. of California, Davis,

1984–86. Governor, Centre for Environmental Studies, 1972–74. *Publications:* Monetary Policy and Crises, A Study of Swedish Experience, 1936; Migration and Economic Growth, A Study of Great Britain and the Atlantic Economy, 1954, 2nd edn 1973; International Migration and Economic Development: A Trend Report and Bibliography, 1961; Migration and Urban Development, 1972; (ed) Economics of International Migration, 1958; (ed) The Welsh Economy: Studies in Expansion, 1962; The Industrial Revolution and the Atlantic Economy: selected essays, 1993; articles in various journals. *Address:* 44a Church Road, Whitchurch, Cardiff CF4 2EA. *T:* Cardiff (0222) 693835. *Died 31 Aug. 1994.*

THOMAS, Air Vice-Marshal Geoffrey Percy Sansom, CB 1970; OBE 1945; retired; *b* 24 April 1915; *s* of Reginald Ernest Sansom Thomas, New Malden; *m* 1940, Sally, *d* of Horace Biddle, Gainsborough; one *s* one *d. Educ:* King's College School, Wimbledon. Commissioned RAF, 1939; served India and Ceylon, 1942–45; on loan to Turkish Air Force, 1950–52; Group Captain, 1958; served with RAAF, 1960–62; Air Commodore, 1965; Director of Movements, 1965; Air Vice-Marshal, 1969; SASO, Maintenance Comd, 1969–71. *Address:* Elms Wood House, Elms Vale, Dover, Kent CT15 7AR. *T:* Dover (0304) 206375. *Died 7 April 1992.*

THOMAS, Maj.-Gen. George Arthur, CB 1960; CBE 1957; retired; *b* 2 May 1906; *s* of Colonel F. H. S. Thomas, CB, and Diana Thomas; *m* 1936, Diana Zaidee Browne; one *s* one *d. Educ:* Cheltenham College; Royal Military Academy, Woolwich. Commissioned, Royal Artillery, 1926; served in UK and Egypt; Staff College, 1940; CO 17 Field Regt, 1st Army, 1942–43; GSO1, 4 Division, 1943–44; BGS 8th Army, 1944–45; Commanding Officer, 1945–46: 138 Field Regt; 17 Medium Regt; 7 RHA; CRA 16 Airborne Div., 1947–48; Imperial Defence Coll., 1952; BGS, MELF, 1955–57; Chief of Staff, HQ Northern Command, 1958–60; Chief of Staff, GHQ Far ELF, 1960–62; retired, 1962. *Recreations:* games and sports of all kinds. *Address:* Fishing Cottage, Upper Clatford, Andover, Hants. *T:* Andover (0264) 52120. *Club:* Army and Navy. *Died 3 July 1992.*

THOMAS, Ivor B.; *see* Bulmer-Thomas.

THOMAS, Rt Rev. John James Absalom, DD Lambeth 1958; *b* 17 May 1908; *s* of William David and Martha Thomas; *m* 1941, Elizabeth Louise, *d* of Very Rev. H. L. James, DD, former Dean of Bangor; one *s. Educ:* University College of Wales, Aberystwyth; Keble College, Oxford. Deacon, 1931; priest, 1932; Curate of Llanguicke, 1931–34; Curate of Sketty, 1934–36; Bishop's Messenger and Examining Chaplain, 1936–40; Warden of Church Hostel, Bangor, and Lecturer in University Coll. of N Wales, 1940–44; Vicar of Swansea, 1945–58, also Chaplain to Bishop of Swansea and Brecon; Canon of Brecon Cathedral, 1946, Precentor, 1952; Rural Dean of Swansea, 1952–54; Archdeacon of Gower, 1954–58; Bishop of Swansea and Brecon, 1958–76. Chm. of Governors, Christ Coll., Brecon, 1961. Chaplain and Sub-Prelate, Order of St John of Jerusalem, 1965. *Address:* Woodbine Cottage, St Mary Street, Tenby, Dyfed SA70 7HN. *Died 27 Feb. 1995.*

THOMAS, Sir John S.; *see* Stradling Thomas.

THOMAS, Dr Roger Gareth; family medical practitioner, since 1952; *b* 14 Nov. 1925; *m* 1958, Indeg Thomas; one *s* one *d. Educ:* Amman Valley Grammar Sch.; London Hosp. Med. Coll. Captain, RAMC, 1949–52. MP (Lab) Carmarthen, 1979–87. *Recreation:* music. *Address:* Ffynnon Wén, Capel Hendre, Ammanford, Dyfed SA18 3SD. *T:* Cross Hands (0269) 843093. *Died 1 Sept. 1994.*

THOMAS, Trevor, BA; artist, author; retired; *b* Ynysddu, Gwent, 8 June 1907; 2nd *s* of William Thomas and Mary Richards; *m* 1947, Sheila Margaret, 2nd *d* of George William Pilkington and Florence Broadley, Tunstall, Lancs; two *s. Educ:* Sir Alfred Jones Scholar, University Coll. of Wales, Aberystwyth. Demonstrator, Dept of Geography and Anthropology, University Coll. of Wales, Aberystwyth, 1929–30; Secretary and Lecturer-Assistant, Department of Geography, Victoria University, Manchester, 1930–31; Cartographer to Geographical Association, Manchester, 1930–31; Keeper, Departments of Ethnology and Shipping, Liverpool Public Museums, 1931–40; Rockefeller Foundation Museums Fellow, USA, 1938–39; Director, Museum and Art Gallery, Leicester, 1940–46; Surveyor, Regional Guide to Works of Art, Arts Council of Great Britain, 1946–48; Designer of Exhibitions for the British Institute of Adult Education, 1946–48; Director, Crafts Centre of Great Britain, 1947–48; Programme Specialist for Education through the Arts, UNESCO, Paris, 1949–56; Visiting Prof. of Art Education, Teachers' Coll., Columbia Univ., NY, USA, 1956; Prof. of Art, State Univ. of New York, College for Teachers, Buffalo, 1957–58; Prof. of Art Hist., University of Buffalo, and Art Critic, Buffalo Evening News, 1959–60; Art Editor, Gordon Fraser Gall. Ltd, 1960–72. Exhibitions: The Gall., Wellingborough, Bowen-West Gall., Bedford, 1988; Primrose Hill Community Centre, London, 1991. Mem. Exec. Cttee, Campaign for Homosexual Equality, 1976–78, 1979–82; Hon. Sec., Gaydaid, 1980–87; Hon. Member: United Soc. of Artists, 1980–; Bedford Soc. of Artists, 1988–. *Publications:* Penny Plain Twopence Coloured: the Aesthetics of Museum Display (Museums Jl, April 1939); Education and Art: a Symposium (jt Editor with Edwin Ziegfield), Unesco, 1953; Creating with Paper: basic forms and variations (Foreword and associate writer with Pauline Johnson), 1958; Sylvia Plath: Last Encounters, 1989; contribs to: Museums Journal, Dec. 1933, April 1935, April 1939, Oct. 1941; Parnassus, Jan. and April 1940; Unesco Educn. Abstracts, Feb. 1953. *Recreations:* art, music, theatre, gardening. *Address:* 36 Pembroke Street, Bedford MK40 3RH. *T:* Bedford (0234) 358879. *Died 27 May 1993.*

THOMPSON, Charles, OBE 1989; HM Diplomatic Service, retired; High Commissioner to Kiribati, 1983–90; *b* 20 March 1930; *s* of Walter Thompson and Irene Thompson; *m* 1st, 1956, Claudia Hilpern; 2nd, 1977, Maria Anna Kalderimis. *Educ:* Harrison Jones School, Liverpool. GPO, 1944–55; entered Foreign (later Diplomatic) Service, 1955; served Rome, Washington, Tokyo, Leopoldville (later Kinshasa), 1956–68; FCO, 1968–71; Second Sec., Rangoon, 1972–74; Second Sec. (Commercial), Wellington, 1974–79; Second (later First) Sec., FCO, 1980–83. *Recreations:* music, reading, travel, real ale. *Address:* 6 Holmwood Avenue, Sanderstead, Surrey CR2 9HY. *Club:* Civil Service.
Died 28 Feb. 1991.

THOMPSON, David Richard, CB 1974; QC 1980; Master of the Crown Office and Queen's Coroner and Attorney, Registrar of Criminal Appeals and of the Courts Martial Appeal Court, 1965–85; *b* 11 Feb. 1916; *s* of William George Thompson; *m* 1952, Sally Jennifer Rowntree Thompson (*née* Stockton); one *s* three *d*, and one *s* one *d* from previous marriage. *Educ:* Alleyn's Sch., Dulwich; Jesus Coll., Oxford (BA Physics 1938). Royal Corps of Signals, 1939–46 (despatches). Called to Bar, Lincoln's Inn, 1946, Bencher, 1982; Office of DPP, 1948–54; Dep. Asst Registrar, then Asst Registrar, Court of Criminal Appeal, 1954–65. *Publications:* (with H. W. Wollaston) Court of Appeal Criminal Division, 1969; (with Morrish and McLean) Proceedings in the Criminal Division of the Court of Appeal, 1979. *Recreation:* personal computer

word processor. *Address:* 54 Highbury Grove, N5 2AG. *T:* 0171–226 6514. *Died 28 Sept. 1995.*

THOMPSON, Prof. Edward Arthur, FBA 1964; Professor of Classics, University of Nottingham, 1948–79; *b* 22 May 1914; *s* of late Robert J. Thompson and Margaret Thompson, Waterford; *m* 1945, Thelma Phelps (marr. diss. 1958); one *s* one *d*; *m* 1964, Hazel Casken; one *d*. *Educ:* Trinity Coll., Dublin. Lecturer in Classics: Dublin, 1939–41; Swansea, 1942–45; King's College, London, 1945–48. Vis. Bentley Prof. of History, Univ. of Michigan, 1969–71; H. F. Johnson Res. Prof., Univ. of Wisconsin (Madison), 1979–80. *Publications:* The Historical Work of Ammianus Marcellinus, 1947; A History of Attila and The Huns, 1948; A Roman Reformer and Inventor, 1952; The Early Germans, 1965; The Visigoths in the Time of Ulfila, 1966; The Goths in Spain, 1969; Romans and Barbarians, 1982; St Germanus of Auxerre and the End of Roman Britain, 1984; Who was St Patrick?, 1985. *Address:* 32A Mapperley Hall Drive, Mapperley Park, Nottingham NG3 5EY. *Died 1 Jan. 1994.*

THOMPSON, Sir Edward (Hugh Dudley), Kt 1967; MBE 1945; TD; DL; Director: Allied Breweries Ltd, 1961–78; P-E Consulting Group Ltd, 1968–73 (Chairman, 1971–73); *b* 12 May 1907; *s* of Neale Dudley Thompson and Mary Gwendoline Scutt; *m* 1st, 1931, Ruth Monica, 3rd *d* of Charles Henry Wainwright, JP; two *s*; 2nd, 1947, Doreen Maud (*d* 1990), *d* of George Tibbitt; one *s* one *d*; 3rd, 1991, Margaret, *widow* of Dr Leslie Jennings. *Educ:* Uppingham; Lincoln Coll., Oxford. Served War of 1939–45 (despatches twice, MBE); 1st Derbyshire Yeomanry, 1939–43, in N Africa; General Staff, 1943–45, in Italy and Germany. Solicitor, 1931–36; Asst Man. Dir, Ind Coope & Allsopp Ltd, 1936–39, Managing Director, 1939; Chairman: Ind Coope & Allsopp Ltd, Burton on Trent, 1955–62; Allied Breweries Ltd (formerly Ind Coope Tetley Ansell Ltd), 1961–68. Director: Sun Insurance Ltd, 1946–59; Sun Alliance & London Insurance Ltd, 1959–77. Chm., Brewers' Soc., 1959–61; Trustee, Civic Trust; Mem. Northumberland Foot and Mouth Cttee. Mem. Council, Nottingham Univ., 1969–87. Mem. Council, RASE, 1972–85 (Hon. Vice Pres., 1985–). High Sheriff of Derbyshire, 1964; DL Derbyshire, 1978. Hon. LLD Nottingham, 1984. *Recreations:* farming, sailing, ski-ing. *Address:* Culland Hall, Brailsford, Derby DE6 3BW. *T:* Ashbourne (0335) 60247. *Club:* Boodle's.
Died 20 May 1994.

THOMPSON, Edward Palmer, FBA 1992; free-lance writer, since 1971; *b* 3 Feb. 1924; *s* of Edward John Thompson and Theodosia Jessup; *m* 1948, Dorothy Towers; two *s* one *d*. *Educ:* Corpus Christi Coll., Cambridge (BA 1946; MA). Extra-Mural Dept, Leeds Univ., 1948–65; Reader in Social History, Warwick Univ., 1965–71. Foreign Hon. Fellow, Amer. Acad. of Arts and Scis. Hon. Fellow, Corpus Christi Coll., Cambridge. Hon. degrees from Hull, Loughborough and Open Univs. *Publications:* William Morris: romantic to revolutionary, 1955, 2nd edn 1977; The Making of the English Working Class, 1963, 2nd edn 1968; Whigs and Hunters, 1975; Poverty of Theory and Other Essays, 1978; Writing by Candlelight, 1980; Zero Option, 1982; Double Exposure, 1985; Heavy Dancers, 1985; Sykaos Papers, 1988; Customs in Common, 1991. *Recreation:* invalid gardening. *Address:* Wick Episcopi, Upper Wick, Worcester WR2 5SY. *T:* Worcester (0905) 423376.
Died 28 Aug. 1993.

THOMPSON, Air Cdre Frederick William, CBE 1957; DSO 1944; DFC 1942; AFC 1944; Director, Air Weapons, British Aerospace Dynamics Group, 1977–80, retired; *b* 9 July 1914; *s* of William Edward Thompson, Winster, Poulton-le-Fylde, Lancs; *m* 1941, Marian, *d* of William Bootyman, Hessle, E Yorks; two *d. Educ:* Baines's

Grammar School; Liverpool University. BSc 2nd Cl. Hons Maths; Advanced Diploma in General Hygiene (Hons). Joined RAF, 1935, invalided 1936; S Rhodesian Education Dept, 1936–39; served War of 1939–45 (despatches, DFC, AFC, DSO): S Rhodesian Air Force, 1940, Pilot Officer; seconded to RAFVR, 4 Gp Bomber Command, 1940; Flight Comdr 10 Sqdn Bombers, 1941; 1658 HCU, 1942; CO 44 Bomber Sqdn, 1944; Bomber Command Instructor's School, 1944; Station Commander, RAF Heany, 1945; HQ Mid Med., 1946–47; Min. of Defence, 1947–50; HQ CC, 1950–53; OC ASWDU, 1953; Group Capt., CO Luqa, 1954; Deputy Director Operational Requirements (1), Air Ministry, 1957–60; Air Cdre Imperial Defence Coll., 1960; Director of Guided Weapons (Trials), Ministry of Aviation, 1961; retired from RAF at own request to join de Havilland Aircraft Co. Ltd as Representative of the Company on the West Coast of America; Engrg Manager, Hawker Siddeley Dynamics Co. Ltd, 1964, Divisional Manager, Air Weapons Div., 1972–77. idc, jssc, psc, cfs. *Recreations:* tennis, swimming. *Address:* Westwick, Lye Green Road, Chesham, Bucks HP5 3NH. *T:* Chesham (0494) 785413. *Club:* Royal Air Force.   *Died 19 Feb. 1994.*

THOMPSON, Gerald Francis Michael Perronet; Chairman, Kleinwort Benson Ltd, 1971–75, retired (Director 1961, Vice-Chairman 1970); Member, Accepting Houses Committee, 1971–75; *b* 10 Oct. 1910; *s* of late Sir John Perronet Thompson, KCSI, KCIE, and Ada Lucia Tyrrell; *m* 1944, Margaret Mary Bodenham Smith; two *s* one *d. Educ:* Repton; King's Coll., Cambridge (Scholar, MA); London Sch. of Economics (post graduate). Served War, RAFVR, 1939–46 (despatches): in France, UK, and Middle East, Wing Comdr. Kleinwort Sons & Co., 1933; Director: Kleinwort Sons & Co., 1960; Kleinwort Benson Lonsdale Ltd, 1970–82. Lectures and broadcasts on monetary and internat. affairs, 1957–; lecture on merchant banking, RSA, 1966 (FRSA). Received into RC Church, 1939; Hon. Treasurer, Westminster Cathedral Appeal Fund, 1978–84; Trustee, Tablet Trust, 1977–. Governor, New Hall Sch., 1977–83. *Publication:* contrib. Festschrift presented to Fernand Collin, 1972. *Recreations:* travel, garden. *Address:* Whitewebs, Margaretting, Essex CM4 9HX. *T:* Ingatestone (0277) 352002. *Club:* United Oxford & Cambridge University.   *Died 10 March 1994.*

THOMPSON, Sir John, Kt 1961; Judge of the High Court of Justice, Queen's Bench Division, 1961–82; *b* Glasgow, 16 Dec. 1907; *e s* of Donald Cameron Thompson and Jeanie Dunn Thompson (*née* Nisbet); *m* 1934, Agnes Baird, (Nancy), *o d* of John and Jeanie Drummond, Glasgow; two *s. Educ:* Bellahouston Academy; Glasgow University; Oriel College, Oxford (Neale Schol.). Glasgow University: MA and Arthur Jones Memorial Prize, 1928; Ewing Gold Medal, 1929; Oxford University: BA, 1930; MA 1943. Called to the Bar, Middle Temple, 1933 (Powell Prize, 1933); Bencher, Middle Temple, 1961; Lent Reader, 1977; Dep. Treasurer, 1977; Treasurer, 1978. QC 1954. Vice-Chm., Gen. Council of the Bar, 1960–61 (Mem. 1958–61). Commissioner of Assize (Birmingham), 1961. *Publications:* (ed with H. R. Rogers) Redgrave's Factories, Truck and Shops Acts. *Recreation:* golf. *Address:* 73 Sevenoaks Road, Orpington, Kent BR6 9JN. *T:* Orpington (01689) 822339. *Clubs:* Royal & Ancient Golf (St Andrews); Sundridge Park Golf (Capt., 1958–59).
Died 11 July 1995.

THOMPSON, Air Cdre John Marlow, CBE 1954; DSO 1943; DFC 1940 (and Bar 1942); AFC 1952; RAF retired; *b* 16 Aug. 1914; *s* of late John Thompson and Florence Thompson (*née* Marlow); one *s* one *d* (and one *s* decd). *Educ:* Bristol Grammar School. Joined RAF 1934; comd 111 Sqdn,

Battle of Britain; Spitfire Wing, Malta, 1942–43; SASO 11 Group, 1952–54; comd RAF Leeming, 1956–57; Dir of Air Defence, Air Ministry, 1958–60; Graduate Imperial Defence Coll., 1961; AOC, Military Air Traffic Ops, 1962–65; Gen. Manager, Airwork Services, Saudi Arabia, 1966–68. Belgian MC 1st Class, 1942; Danish Order of Dannebrog, 1951. *Recreation:* golf. *Address:* Flat 3, 35 Adelaide Crescent, Hove, East Sussex BN3 2JJ. *Clubs:* Royal Air Force; Moor Park Golf; Monte Carlo Golf (Dir, 1973–83).   *Died 23 July 1994.*

THOMPSON, Major Lloyd H.; *see* Hall-Thompson.

THOMPSON, Oliver Frederic, OBE 1945; Pro-Chancellor of The City University, 1966–72; *b* 26 Jan. 1905; 3rd *s* of late W. Graham Thompson and Oliveria C. Prescott; *m* 1939, Frances Phyllida, *d* of late F. H. Bryant; one *s* three *d. Educ:* Tonbridge. Mem. Shell Gp of Cos, 1924–64: managerial posts in USA, Caribbean, London; Head of Oil Sect., Min. of Econ. Warfare, and Mem. War Cabinet Sub-Cttee on Oil, 1942–46. Rep. UK, Suez Canal Users Assoc.; rep. UK on various UN and OECD Cttees; Mem. Parly and Sci. Cttee, 1955–65. Past Master and Mem. Ct, Worshipful Co. of Skinners. Chm. Governing Body, Northampton Coll. of Advanced Technology, 1956–66 (became City University, 1966); Governor, Tonbridge Sch. FInstP (Past Mem. Council); Chm. Qualifications Cttee, British Computer Society, 1968 (Hon. Fellow, 1972). County Councillor, Surrey, 1965–77 (Majority Leader, 1970–73). Hon. DSc, City Univ., 1967. *Publications:* various papers on economics of energy and petroleum. *Recreation:* country pursuits. *Address:* 32 Park Road, Aldeburgh, Suffolk IP15 5EU. *T:* Aldeburgh (0728) 452424.   *Died 28 Feb. 1993.*

THOMPSON, Sir Ralph (Patrick), Kt 1980; Barrister and Solicitor of the High Court of New Zealand, since 1938; *b* 19 June 1916; *m* 1st, 1940, Dorothy Maud Simes (*d* 1982); one *s* two *d*; 2nd, 1988, Dorothy Maisie Collins. *Educ:* Napier Boys High Sch.; Dannevirke High Sch.; Canterbury Univ. (LLB 1937). Admitted barrister and solicitor, 1938; in practice in Christchurch. Former Chairman: United Building Soc; Waitaki NZ Refrigerating Ltd; M. O'Brien & Co. Ltd; Director: New Zealand Refining Co. Ltd, 1967–86; Waitaki International Ltd (formerly Waitaki NZ Ltd), 1975–86; Barclays Bank New Zealand Ltd (formerly New Zealand United Corp. Ltd), 1976–86. *Recreations:* reading, racing, walking. *Address:* 115 Heaton Street, Christchurch 5, New Zealand. *T:* 557490. *Clubs:* Canterbury, Canterbury University (Hon. Life Mem.), Canterbury Jockey; New Zealand Metropolitan Trotting (Christchurch).
Died 6 Aug. 1991.

THOMPSON, Reginald Harry; Chairman, National Dock Labour Board, 1983; *b* 26 Oct. 1925; *s* of late Ernest and Phyllis Thompson; *m* 1951, Winifred (*née* Hoyle); one *s* one *d. Educ:* Ecclesfield Grammar School, Sheffield. Thorncliffe Collieries, 1940; Yorkshire Mineworkers Assoc., 1941; RN, 1942; Admin. and Conciliation Officer, NUM (Yorks Area), 1946; National Coal Board: Labour Officer, S Barnsley Area, 1955; Area Industrial Relations Officer, N Barnsley Area, 1962, N Yorks Area, 1967; Dep. Area Dir, N Yorks Area, 1970; Dir of Wages, HQ, 1973; Dep. Dir Gen., 1974, Dir Gen., 1975–83, Ind. Relations. Member: Industrial Tribunals, 1983–; Solicitors Disciplinary Tribunal, 1985–. FBIM 1978. *Publications:* articles in technical jls. *Recreations:* local government affairs, golf. *Address:* Rowley Road, Priory Hill, St Neots, Huntingdon, Cambs PE19 1UF. *T:* Huntingdon (0480) 73691.   *Died 17 Sept. 1991.*

THOMPSON, (Reginald) Stanley; Headmaster of Bloxham School, 1952–65, retired; *b* 23 Sept. 1899; *s* of late Reverend Canon C. H. Thompson, formerly Vicar of

Eastleigh, Hants, and of Newport, Isle of Wight; *m* 1938, Phyllis Barbara, *y d* of Henry White, Solicitor, Winchester, Hants; one *s* two *d*. *Educ:* Hereford Cathedral School; Lancing College; Oriel College, Oxford. Assistant Master at Sherborne School, 1922–52 (Housemaster, 1936–52). *Recreations:* music, books, cricket. *Address:* Davenham, Graham Road, Malvern, Worcs WR14 2HY.

Died 28 Jan. 1994.

THOMPSON, Sir Robert Grainger Ker, KBE 1965; CMG 1961; DSO 1945; MC 1943; *b* 12 April 1916; *s* of late Canon W. G. Thompson; *m* 1950, Merryn Newboult; one *s* one *d*. *Educ:* Marlborough; Sidney Sussex College, Cambridge (MA). Served War of 1939–45 (MC, DSO), RAF, 1941–46. Cadet, Malayan Civil Service, 1938; Asst Commissioner of Labour, Perak, 1946; despatches 1948; jssc 1948–49; Staff Officer (Civil) to Director of Operations, 1950; Co-ordinating Officer, Security, 1955; Dep. Sec. for Def., Fedn of Malaya, 1957; Perm. Sec. for Def., 1959–61; Head, British Advisory Mission to Vietnam, 1961–65. Author and consultant. JMN 1958. *Publications:* Defeating Communist Insurgency, 1966; The Royal Flying Corps, 1968; No Exit from Vietnam, 1969; Revolutionary War in World Strategy, 1945–1969, 1970; Peace Is Not At Hand, 1974; (ed) War in Peace: an analysis of warfare since 1945, 1981; Make for the Hills, 1989. *Recreations:* all country pursuits. *Address:* Pitcott House, Winsford, Minehead, Som TA24 7JE.

Died 16 May 1992.

THOMPSON, Major Robert Lloyd H.; *see* Hall-Thompson.

THOMPSON, Stanley; *see* Thompson, R. S.

THOMPSON, Vernon Cecil, MB, BS London; FRCS; retired 1970 as Surgeon to Department of Thoracic Surgery, The London Hospital; Surgeon, London Chest Hospital; Hon. Consulting Thoracic Surgeon to: West London Hospital, Hammersmith; King Edward VII Hospital, Windsor; Harefield Hospital, Middlesex; Broomfield and Black Notley Hospitals, Essex; *b* 17 Sept. 1905; 2nd *s* of Dr C. C. B. Thompson, Tidenham, Glos; *m* 1942, Jean, *d* of late H. J. Hilary; one *s* one *d*. *Educ:* Monmouth School; St Bartholomew's Hospital. Resident House appointments followed by First Assistant to a Surgical Unit, St Bartholomew's Hospital, 1929–37. Dorothy Temple Cross Travelling Fellowship, Vienna, and University Hosp., Ann Arbor, Michigan, USA, 1937. President, Soc. of Thoracic Surgeons of Great Britain and Ireland, 1966; Hon. Mem. Amer. Soc. for Thoracic Surgery, 1967. *Publications:* contrib. on surgical diseases of the chest to jls and text books. *Recreations:* fishing, shooting, gardening. *Address:* 2 Elms Road, SW4 9EU.

Died 27 Nov. 1995.

THOMSON, Bryden; Orchestral Conductor; Artistic Director, since 1977, and Principal Conductor, 1977–85 (then Conductor Emeritus) Ulster Orchestra; Principal Conductor, RTE Symphony Orchestra, since 1984; *b* Ayr, Scotland, 26 July 1928; *m* 1st, 1955, Beth McKill; two *s*; 2nd, Mary Ellison. *Educ:* Ayr Academy; Royal Scottish Academy of Music; Staatliche Hochschule für Musik, Hamburg. BMus Dunelm; DipMusEd (Hons); RSAM; LRAM; ARCM; FRSAMD. Asst Conductor, BBC Scottish Orchestra, 1958; Conductor: Royal Ballet, 1962; Den Norske Opera, Oslo, 1964; Stora Teatern, Göteborg, Sweden, 1965; Royal Opera, Stockholm, 1966; NI Opera Trust, 1981 and 1982; Associate Conductor, Scottish National Orch., 1966; Principal Conductor: BBC Northern Symphony Orch., 1968–73; BBC Welsh Symphony Orch., 1978–83; Prin. Conductor and Music Dir, Scottish National Orch., subseq. Royal Scottish Orch., 1988–91. Guest Conducting: Norway; Sweden; Denmark; Canada; Germany; S Africa; France; Italy; Principal Guest

Conductor, Trondheim Symphony Orch., 1977. Recordings of many works by British and foreign composers. Hon. DLitt NUU, 1984. Award for services to contemporary Scottish music, Scottish Soc. of Composers, 1985. *Recreations:* golf, learning about music. *Address:* Garinish, 19a Greenfield Park, Donnybrook, Dublin 4.

Died 14 Nov. 1991.

THOMSON, Air Chief Marshal Sir (Charles) John, GCB 1994 (KCB 1991); CBE 1984; AFC 1979; Commander-in-Chief, Allied Forces Northwestern Europe, since 1994; *b* 7 June 1941; *e s* of Dr Charles Thomson and Elizabeth Susan (*née* McCaughey); *m* 1972, Jan Hart Bishop; two *d* (and one *d* decd). *Educ:* Campbell College; RAF College; psc, rcds. Commissioned 1962; flying and staff appts include: 43 Sqn, Aden; 2 Sqn, Germany; USAF 67 TRW, Texas; OC 41 Sqn, 1976–78; Personal Staff Officer to Chief of Air Staff, 1979–81; Station Comdr, RAF Brüggen, 1982–83; Dir, Defence Concepts Staff, 1985–86; AOC No 1 Gp, 1987–89; Asst Chief of Air Staff, 1989–91; AOC-in-C, RAF Support Comd, 1991–92; AOC-in-C, RAF Strike Command and C-in-C, UK Air Forces, 1992–94. Freeman, City of London, 1992; Liveryman, Turners' Co., 1993–. Cdre, RAF Sailing Assoc., 1988–. *Recreations:* sailing, shooting, ski-ing, reading. *Address:* c/o Royal Bank of Scotland, Drummonds Branch, 49 Charing Cross, SW1A 2DX. *Club:* Royal Air Force.

Died 10 July 1994.

THOMSON, David Kinnear, CBE 1972 (MBE 1945); TD 1945; JP, DL; Former President, Peter Thomson (Perth) Ltd, whisky blenders and exporters; Chairman, Tayside Health Board, 1973–77; *b* Perth, 26 March 1910; *s* of Peter Thomson, whisky blender, and Jessie Kinnear; unmarried. *Educ:* Perth Academy; Strathallan School. Mem., Perth Local Authority, 1949–72; Chm. Bd of Management, Perth Technical Coll., 1972–75; Mem., ITA (Scottish Br.), 1968–73; Mem., Scottish Economic Council, 1968–75; Director: Scottish Transport Gp, 1972–76; Scottish Opera, 1973–81; Chm., Perth Festival of the Arts, 1973–85 (Pres., 1985–90). Mem. Court, Dundee Univ., 1975–79. Chm., Scottish Licensed Trade, 1981–82. Lord Provost of Perth, 1966–72, and Hon. Sheriff of Perth; DL 1966–72, 1980–, JP 1955, Perth and Kinross; Freeman, Perth and Kinross District, 1982. CStJ 1984. *Recreations:* golf, walking, listening to music. *Address:* Fairhill, Oakbank Road, Perth PH1 1HD. *T:* Perth (0738) 26593. *Club:* Royal Perth Golfing Society.

Died 27 Dec. 1992.

THOMSON, Sir Evan (Rees Whitaker), Kt 1977; FRCS, FRACS, FACS; Hon. Consultant Surgeon, Princess Alexandra Hospital, Brisbane; *b* 14 July 1919; *s* of Frederick Thorpe Thomson and Ann Margaret Thomson (*née* Evans); *m* 1955, Mary Kennedy. *Educ:* Brisbane Boys' Coll.; Univ. of Queensland (MB BS). Full time staff, Brisbane General Hospital, 1942–48; RAAF Reserve, 1942–45; Visiting Surgeon: Brisbane General Hospital, 1950–56; Princess Alexandra Hospital, 1956–71; Clinical Lectr in Surgery, Univ. of Queensland, 1951–71. Qld Branch, Australian Medical Association: Councillor, 1966–78; Pres., 1967–68; a Vice-Pres., 1980–; Chm. of Council; Chm. of Ethics Cttee. Pres., 4th Aust. Med. Congress, 1971. Member: Med. Bd of Queensland; Wesley Hospital Bd, etc; Pres., Qld Council of Professions, 1970–72; Vice-Patron, Medico-Legal Soc. of Qld; Governor, Univ. of Qld Foundn; Life Governor, Aust. Postgrad. Fedn in Medicine. Patron, Aust. Nat. Flag Assoc. (Qld). Silver Jubilee Medal, 1977. *Publications:* Future Needs for Medical Education in Queensland (ed), 1981; (jtly) Ernest Sandford Jackson: the life and times of a pioneer Australian surgeon, 1987; papers in medical and allied jls. *Recreations:* golf, swimming. *Address:* 19/104 Station Road, Indooroopilly, Qld 4068, Australia. *Clubs:*

Queensland, University of Queensland Staff and Graduates (Life Mem.); Mooloolaba Yacht.

Died 14 Jan. 1993.

THOMSON, Sir Ivo Wilfrid Home, 2nd Bt, *cr* 1925, of Old Nunthorpe, Co. York; *b* 14 Oct. 1902; *s* of Sir Wilfrid Thomson, 1st Bt, and Ethel Henrietta, 2nd *d* of late Hon. Reginald Parker; *S* father, 1939; *m* 1st, 1933, Sybil Marguerite (marr. diss.), *yr d* of C. W. Thompson, The Red House, Escrick; one *s* (one *d* decd); 2nd, 1954, Viola Mabel (who *m* 1st, 1937, Keith Home Thomson (marr. diss.)), *d* of Roland Dudley, Linkenholt Manor, Andover. *Educ:* Eton. *Heir: s* Mark Wilfrid Home Thomson [*b* 29 Dec. 1939; *m* 1976, Lady Jacqueline Rufus Isaacs, *d* of 3rd Marquess of Reading, MBE, MC; three *s* one *d*]. *Address:* Barfield, Chapel Row, Bucklebury, Reading, Berks RG7 6PB. *T:* Woolhampton (0734) 712172.

Died 6 Jan. 1991.

THOMSON, Air Chief Marshal Sir John; *see* Thomson, Air Chief Marshal Sir C. J.

THOMSON, Peter; *b* 1914; *s* of John Thomson, SSC, and Martha Lindsay Miller; *m* 1939, Jean Laird Nicoll; two *s* one *d*. *Educ:* Royal High School, Edinburgh; Edinburgh University. Gordon Highlanders, 1941–46; Capt. 1944. Called to Scottish Bar, 1946. Founded Scottish Plebiscite Society, 1947. Sheriff Substitute of Caithness, Sutherland, Orkney and Zetland, 1955; Sheriff of South Strathclyde, Dumfries and Galloway (formerly Lanarkshire) at Hamilton, 1962–77. Dir, Inst. of Scotland, 1979–. *Recreations:* walking, golf. *Address:* Haughhead Farm House, Uddingston, Glasgow G71 7RR.

Died 23 April 1991.

THOMSON, Robert Norman; Executive Director, Royal Society of Medicine, 1982–93; Director, since 1984, Vice-President, since 1988, Royal Society of Medicine Foundation Inc., New York; *b* 14 Nov. 1935. *Educ:* Wells Cathedral School; Clare College, Cambridge (MA). Royal Society of Medicine: Assistant Executive Director, 1973; Deputy Executive Director, 1977; Hon. Fellow, 1993. Freedom, Apothecaries' Soc., 1991. *Recreations:* music, cooking. *Address:* 9 Downside Lodge, 29 Upper Park Road, NW3 2UY. *T:* 071–722 7176. *Clubs:* Athenæum; University (New York). *Died 2 March 1994.*

THORNE, Prof. Christopher Guy, DLitt; FBA 1982; Professor of International Relations, University of Sussex, since 1977; *b* 17 May 1934; *s* of Reginald Harry Thorne and late Alice Thorne (*née* Pickard); *m* 1958, Beryl Lloyd Jones; two *d*. *Educ:* King Edward VI Royal Grammar Sch., Guildford; St Edmund Hall, Oxford (Hon. Fellow 1989). BA 1958; MA 1962; DLitt 1980. Nat. Service, RN, 1953–55. Teacher, St Paul's Sch., London, 1958–61; Sen. Hist. Master, Charterhouse, 1961–66; Head of Further Educn, BBC Radio, 1966–68; Lectr in Internat. Relations, 1968, Reader, 1972, Univ. of Sussex. Resident Fellow, Netherlands Inst. for Advanced Study, 1979–80. Lectures: Lees-Knowles, Cambridge, 1977; Raleigh, British Acad., 1980; Phillips, British Acad., 1986; Becker, Cornell, 1988; Shaw, Johns Hopkins, 1991. *Publications:* Ideology and Power, 1965; Chartism, 1966; The Approach of War 1938–39, 1967; The Limits of Foreign Policy: the West, the League, and the Far Eastern Crisis of 1931–33, 1972; Allies of a Kind: the United States, Britain, and the war against Japan 1941–1945, 1978 (Bancroft Prize, 1979); Racial Aspects of the Far Eastern War of 1941–45, 1982; The Issue of War: states, societies and the Far Eastern conflict of 1941–45, 1985, repr. as The Far Eastern War, 1986; American Political Culture and the Asian Frontier 1943–1973, 1988; Border Crossings: studies in international history, 1988. *Recreations:* music, Crete. *Address:* School of English and American Studies,

University of Sussex, Brighton, Sussex BN1 9QN. *T:* Brighton (0273) 606755. *Died 20 April 1992.*

THORNEYCROFT, Baron *cr* 1967 (Life Peer), of Dunston; **George Edward Peter Thorneycroft,** CH 1980; PC 1951; barrister-at-law; late Royal Artillery; Chairman of the Conservative Party, 1975–81; President: Pirelli General plc (formerly Pirelli General Cable Works Ltd), since 1987 (Chairman, 1967–87); Pirelli plc, since 1987 (Chairman, 1969–87); Pirelli UK plc, since 1989 (Chairman, 1987–89); Forte plc (formerly Trusthouse Forte Ltd), 1982–92 (Chairman, 1969–81); *b* 26 July 1909; *s* of late Major George Edward Mervyn Thorneycroft, DSO, and Dorothy Hope, *d* of Sir W. Franklyn, KCB; *m* 1st, 1938, Sheila Wells Page (who obtained a divorce, 1949); one *s*; 2nd, 1949, Countess Carla Roberti; one *d*. *Educ:* Eton; Roy. Mil. Acad., Woolwich. Commissioned in Royal Artillery, 1930; resigned Commission, 1933; called to Bar, Inner Temple, 1935; practised Birmingham (Oxford Circuit); MP (C) Stafford, 1938–45, Monmouth, 1945–66. Parliamentary Secretary, Ministry of War Transport, 1945; President of the Board of Trade, 1951–57; Chancellor of the Exchequer, 1957–58, resigned; Minister of Aviation, 1960–62; Minister of Defence, 1962–64; Secretary of State for Defence, Apr.-Oct. 1964. Chairman: SITPRO, 1968–75; BOTB, 1972–75; Pye of Cambridge Ltd, 1967–79; British Reserve Insurance Co. Ltd, 1980–87; Gil, Carvajal & Partners Ltd, 1981–; Cinzano UK Ltd, 1982–85; Director: Riunione Adriatica di Sicurta, 1981–89; Banca Nazionale del Lavoro, 1984–. Exhibitions of paintings: Trafford Gallery, 1961, 1970; Café Royal, 1981, 1989; Mall Galls, 1984; Cadogan Gall., 1987. Mem., Royal Soc. of British Artists, 1978. *Publication:* The Amateur: a companion to watercolour, 1985. *Address:* House of Lords, SW1A 0PW; 42 Eaton Square, SW1W 9BD. *Club:* Army and Navy.

Died 4 June 1994.

THORNTON, Ernest, MBE 1951; JP; DL; *b* Burnley, Lancs, 18 May 1905; *s* of Charles Thornton and Margaret (*née* Whittaker); *m* 1930, Evelyn, *d* of Fred Ingham, Blacko, Nelson; one *s* (and one *s* decd). *Educ:* Walverden Council Sch., Nelson, Lancs. Cotton weaver, 1918–26; costing clerk, 1926–29. Asst Secretary, 1929–40, Secretary, 1940–70, Rochdale Weavers and Winders' Assoc.; President, Amalgamated Weavers' Assoc., 1960–65; Secretary, United Textile Factory Workers' Assoc., 1943–53. Member: Lord President's Advisory Council for Scientific and Industrial Research, 1943–48; Council of British Cotton Industry Research Assoc., 1948–53. MP (Lab) Farnworth, 1952–70; Joint Parliamentary Secretary, Min. of Labour, 1964–66. Member: UK Trade Mission to China, 1946; Anglo-American Cotton Textile Mission to Japan, 1950; Cotton Board's Mission to India, 1950. Mayor of County Borough of Rochdale, 1942–43. Comp/TI 1966. JP 1944, DL Manchester Metropolitan County (formerly Lancaster), 1970. *Address:* 31 Lynnwood Drive, Rochdale, Lancs. *T:* Rochdale (0706) 31954. *Died 5 Feb. 1992.*

THORPE, Sir Ronald Laurence G.; *see* Gardner-Thorpe.

THOYTS, Robert Francis Newman; solicitor, retired; Under Secretary, Department of Health and Social Security, 1971–78; *b* 13 March 1913; *o s* of late Lt-Comdr Robert Elmhirst Thoyts, RN, and Kathleen Olive Thoyts (*née* Hobbs); *m* 1938, Joyce Eliza Gillingham, *er d* of late Rev. William Samuel Probert and Evangeline Eliza Probert; one *s* four *d*. *Educ:* Bradfield Coll. Admitted Solicitor, 1936. Served War, RAF, 1941–45; Flt Lieut. Govt Legal Service, 1936–78; solicitor in private practice, 1978–88. Civil Service Legal Soc.: Gen. Sec. 1945–50; Chm. 1965–67. Mem. Salaried Solicitors' Cttee of Law Soc., 1948–78. Trustee, Thames Ditton Almshouse Charity. Civil Service Sports Council Award of Merit,

1990. *Recreations:* sailing (Civil Service Rep. Sailing Badge, 1966), amenity interests. *Address:* 37 Queen's Drive, Thames Ditton, Surrey KT7 0TJ. *T:* 081–398 0469. *Clubs:* Law Society; Civil Service Sailing Assoc. (Hon. Life Mem., 1974; Hon. Life Mem., Portsmouth Gp, 1987; Chm., 1959–74; Rear-Cdre, 1977–80; Trustee, 1980–; Heathcoat-Amory Cup, 1966, 1988); River Thames Soc. (Vice-Chm. 1971; Hon. Gen. Sec., 1978–86; Vice-Pres., 1986–; Hon. Life Mem., 1986); Littleton Sailing (Cdre, 1961–65; Hon. Life Mem., 1965); Frostbite Yacht Club of America (Hon. Cdre, 1966).

Died 14 June 1991.

THROCKMORTON, Sir Anthony (John Benedict), 12th Bt *cr* 1642, of Coughton, Warwickshire; *b* 9 Feb. 1916; *s* of Herbert Throckmorton (*d* 1941) (3rd *s* of 10th Bt) and Ethel (*d* 1929), *d* of late Frederick Stapleton-Bretherton; *S* cousin, 1989; *m* 1972, Violet Virginia, *d* of late Anders Anderson. *Educ:* Beaumont Coll., Old Windsor, Berks. Ordained 1943, dio. Northampton; served Bury St Edmunds, Cambridge, Oundle; archdio. Seattle, 1952; retired 1963. Univ. of Washington Mailing Services, 1966–82. *Heir:* none. *Address:* 2006 Oakes Avenue, Everett, Washington 98201, USA. *T:* (206) 2581394.

Died 17 Oct. 1994 (ext).

THURBURN, Gwynneth Loveday, OBE 1956; Hon. FCST; Principal, Central School of Speech and Drama, 1942–67; *b* 17 July 1899; *d* of Robert Augustus Thurburn and Bertha Loveday. *Educ:* Birklands, St Albans; Central School of Speech and Drama. Vice-Pres., Central Sch. of Speech and Drama. *Publication:* Voice and Speech. *Address:* Leiston Old Abbey, Leiston, Suffolk IP16 4RP.

Died 20 March 1993.

THURLOW, Very Rev. Alfred Gilbert Goddard, MA; Dean of Gloucester, 1972–82, then Dean Emeritus; *b* 6 April 1911; *s* of Rev. A. R. Thurlow; *m* 1955, Thelda Mary Hook; two *s. Educ:* Selwyn Coll., Cambridge; Cuddesdon Coll., Oxford. MA Cantab. 1936. Deacon, 1934; priest, 1935; Curate, All Saints, Wokingham, 1934–39; Precentor of Norwich Cathedral, 1939–55; Rector of St Clement, St George Colegate and St Edmund Norwich, 1943–52; Vicar of: St Andrew and St Michael at Plea, Norwich, 1952–55; St Nicholas, Great Yarmouth, 1955–64; Canon Residentiary of Norwich, 1964–72, Vice-Dean, 1969–72. FSA 1948; FRHistS 1962. *Publications:* Church Bells and Ringers of Norwich, 1947; St George Colegate Norwich, a Redundant Church, 1950; The Mediæval Painted Panels of Norwich Cathedral, 1959; Norwich Cathedral, 1962; Great Yarmouth Priory and Parish Church, 1963; Cathedrals at Work, 1966; City of Norwich, 1970; Cathedrals in Colour, 1971; Norwich Cathedral, 1972; Biblical Myths and Mysteries, 1974; Gloucester and Berkeley: Edward II, Martyr King, 1976; City of Gloucester, 1981; Cathedrals and Abbeys, 1986. *Recreations:* change ringing, travel, interpreting historic buildings. *Address:* 2 East Pallant, Chichester, West Sussex PO19 1TR. *T:* Chichester (0243) 783977. *Clubs:* Cambridge Union; Rotary. *Died 24 April 1991.*

THURSO, 2nd Viscount *cr* 1952, of Ulbster; **Robin Macdonald Sinclair;** JP; Bt 1786; Baron of Thurso; Lord-Lieutenant of Caithness, since 1973; Founder and first Chairman, Caithness Glass Ltd; Chairman: Sinclair Family Trust Ltd; Lochdhu Hotels Ltd; Thurso Fisheries Ltd; Director, Stephens (Plastics) Ltd; *b* 24 Dec. 1922; *s* of 1st Viscount Thurso, KT, CMG, PC, and Marigold (*d* 1975), *d* of late Col J. S. Forbes, DSO; *S* father, 1970; *m* 1952, Margaret Beaumont Brokensha, *d* of Col J. J. Robertson, DSO, TD, DL and *widow* of Lieut G. W. Brokensha, DSC, RN; two *s* one *d. Educ:* Eton; New College, Oxford; Edinburgh Univ. Served RAF, 1941–46; Flight Lieut 684 Sqdn, 540 Sqdn, commanded Edinburgh Univ. Air Sqdn, 1946; Captain of Boats, Edinburgh Univ. Boat Club,

1946–47, Green 1946, Blue, 1947. Caithness CC, 1949, 1952, 1955, 1958; Thurso Town Council, 1957, 1960, resigned 1961, re-elected 1965, 1968, 1971, Dean of Guild 1968, Baillie 1960, 1969, Police Judge 1971. President: North Country Cheviot Sheep Soc., 1951–54; Assoc. of Scottish Dist Salmon Fishery Bds (Chm., Caithness Dist Salmon Fishery Bd); Mem., Red Deer Commn, 1965–74. Chm. Caithness and Sutherland Youth Employment Cttee, 1957–75; Brigade Pres., Boys Brigade, 1985–93. Mem. Council, Royal Nat. Mission to Deep Sea Fishermen, 1983–84. Pres., Highland Soc. of London, 1980–82. Elder, Thurso West C of S. DL 1952, JP 1959, Vice-Lieutenant, 1964–73, Caithness. *Recreations:* fishing, shooting, amateur drama. *Heir: s* Hon. John Archibald Sinclair [*b* 10 Sept. 1953; *m* 1976, Marion Ticknor, *d* of Louis D. Sage, Connecticut, USA, and of Mrs A. R. Ward; two *s* one *d*]. *Address:* Thurso East Mains, Thurso, Caithness KW14 8HW. *T:* Thurso (01847) 62600. *Clubs:* Royal Air Force; New (Edinburgh). *Died 29 April 1995.*

THWAITES, Brig. Peter Trevenen; Chairman: Individual School Direction Ltd, since 1981; Hurlingham Polo Association, since 1982; *b* 30 July 1926; *yr* surv. *s* of late Lt-Col Norman Graham Thwaites, CBE, MVO, MC, and Eleanor Lucia Thwaites, Barley End, Tring, Herts; *m* 1st, 1950, Ellen Theresa King (marr. diss.; she *d* 1976); one *s* two *d* (and one *s* decd); 2nd, 1974, Jacqueline Ann Inchbald. *Educ:* Rugby. Commnd Grenadier Guards, 1944; served 1st, 2nd and 4th Bns in Germany, Egypt, British Cameroons, British Guiana; Mem., Sir William Penney's Scientific Party to UK Atomic Trials in S Australia, 1956; Bde Major, 2 Fed. Inf. Bde, Malaya, 1959–61; Staff Coll., JSSC, MoD, 1958–67; Aden, 1967; comd Muscat Regt, Sultan of Muscat's Armed Forces, 1967–70; AQMG London Dist, 1970–71; Comdr, British Army Staff, Singapore (Col) and Governor, Singapore Internat. Sch., 1971–73; Dep. Dir, Defence Operational Plans (Army), 1973–74; Brig. 1975; Head of MoD Logistics Survey Team to Saudi Arabia, 1976, retired 1977. Chm., Jt Staff, Sultan of Oman's Armed Forces, 1977–81. Sultan's Commendation, 1967; Sultan's Dist. Service Medal, 1969; Sultan's Bravery Medal, 1970. *Publications: plays:* (with Charles Ross) Love or Money, 1958; (with Charles Ross) Master of None, 1960; Roger's Last Stand, 1976; Caught in the Act, 1981; (with Charles Ross) Relative Strangers, 1984. *Recreations:* polo, shooting. *Address:* 32 Eccleston Square, SW1V 1PB; The Manor House, Ayot St Lawrence, Herts. *Clubs:* White's, Beefsteak, Cavalry and Guards.

Died 23 May 1991.

TIARKS, Henry Frederic, FRAS; *b* 8 Sept. 1900; *e s* of late Frank Cyril Tiarks, OBE and Emmy Maria Franziska Brodermann; *m* 1st, 1930, Lady Millicent Olivia Taylour (marr. diss. 1936), *d* of 4th Marquess of Headfort; (one *s* decd); 2nd, 1936, Joan (*d* 1989), *d* of Francis Marshman-Bell; one *d* (one *s* decd). *Educ:* Eton College. Served European War, 1914–19: Midshipman RNVR 1918; served War of 1939–45: Sqdn Ldr AAF, 1940; Wing Commander, 1942–43, retd (invalided). Mem., pre-war German Standstill Cttee (to negotiate repayment of German Debt); Negotiating Mem., British Banking Cttee for German Affairs, 1948–62. Former directorships: J. Henry Schroder & Co. (Partner 1926–57); J. Henry Schroder & Co. Ltd, 1957–62; J. Henry Schroder Wagg & Co. Ltd, 1962 (May to Sept.); Schroders Ltd, 1962–65; J. Henry Schroder Banking Corp., NY, 1945–62; Antofagasta (Chile) and Bolivia Railway Co. Ltd, 1926–67 (Chairman, 1966–67); Securicor Ltd (founder), 1939–68; Pressed Steel Co. Ltd, 1936–66; Joseph Lucas Ltd, 1946–68; Bank of London & South America Ltd, 1958–68; Bank of London & Montreal Ltd, Nassau, 1959–69; Anglo-Scottish Amalgamated Corp. Ltd, 1935–68. Member: Dollar Exports Council, 1952–60; Western

Hemisphere Exports Council, 1960–64; European League for Economic Co-operation (European Central Council); Internat. EFTA Action Cttee, 1967–75; Vice-Pres., European-Atlantic Gp. Mem., The Wildfowl Trust; Trustee, World Wildlife Fund (International), Morges, Switzerland, 1966–76; Founder Mem., WWF, Adena, Spain. Mem. Cttee of Managers, Royal Institution, 1960–62; Mem., British Astronomical Assoc.; Founder Mem., Sociedad Malagueña de Astronomia, Spain. Gran Oficial, Order of Merit, Chile. *Recreations:* golf, observational astronomy, photography, travel. *Address:* Casa Ina, Urbanización Las Torres, Carraterra Cadiz Km 178, 29600 Marbella (Málaga), Spain. *T:* (5) 2861872, *Fax:* (5) 2860049. *Clubs:* Overseas Member: White's, Royal Thames Yacht; Royal and Ancient Golf (St Andrews); Valderrama Golf (Sotogrande, Cadiz); Brook (New York); Lyford Cay (Nassau, Bahamas); Royal Bermuda Yacht. *Died 2 July 1995.*

TICKLE, Rt Rev. Gerard William; Titular Bishop of Bela; *b* 2 Nov. 1909; 2nd *s* of William Joseph Tickle and Rosanna Kelly. *Educ:* Douai School; Venerable English College, Rome. Priest, 1934. Curate at St Joseph's Church, Sale, 1935–41; Army Chaplain, 1941–46; Vice-Rector, 1946, Rector, 1952, Venerable English College, Rome; Bishop-in-Ordinary to HM Forces, 1963–78; Apostolic Administrator, 1978–79. Privy Chamberlain to Pope Pius XII, 1949; Domestic Prelate to Pope Pius XII, 1953. *Address:* Ty Mair, 115 Mwrog Street, Ruthin, Clwyd LL15 1LE. *Died 14 Sept. 1994.*

TIERNEY, Dom (Francis) Alphonsus, MA; OSB; parish priest since 1977; *b* 7 March 1910; *s* of James Francis Tierney and Alice Mary Claypoole. *Educ:* Douai; St Benet's Hall, Oxford. Headmaster of: Douai Junior School, Ditcham Park, 1948–52; Douai Sch., 1952–73; Prior of Douai Abbey, 1973–77. *Address:* St Gregory's Priory, 10 St James Square, Cheltenham, Glos GL50 3PR. *T:* Cheltenham (0242) 523737. *Died 28 Feb. 1992.*

TILEY, Arthur, CBE 1972; JP; retired as insurance broker and marine underwriter; *b* 17 Jan. 1910; *m* 1936, Mary, *d* of late Craven and Mary Tankard, Great Horton; one *s* one *d. Educ:* Grange High School, Bradford. Treasurer, Young Women's Christian Association, Bradford, 1934–50. Contested (C and NL) Bradford Central, 1951. MP (C and NL) Bradford West, 1955–66. Opposition front bench spokesman on pensions and national insurance, 1964–66. Served War of 1939–45 as Senior Company Officer, National Fire Service. Mem. Council, Churchill Memorial Trust, 1965–76. Hon. MA Bradford, 1981. JP Bradford, 1967. *Address:* 40 The Majestic, North Promenade, St Annes-on-Sea, Lancs FY8 2LZ.
Died 5 June 1994.

TILLARD, Maj.-Gen. Philip Blencowe, CBE 1973 (OBE 1966); Chairman, East Sussex British Field Sports Society, since 1988; *b* 2 Jan. 1923; *s* of late Brig. John Arthur Stuart Tillard, OBE, MC and of Margaret Penelope (*née* Blencowe); *m* 1953, Patricia Susan (*née* Robertson) (*d* 1988); three *s* one *d. Educ:* Winchester College. Commnd into 60th Rifles, 1942; served Syria, Italy and Greece, 1943–45; ADC to GOC 2 Div. and to Army Comdr Malaya, 1946; ADC to GOC N Midland Dist, 1947; transf. to 13th/18th Royal Hussars (QMO), 1947; served in Libya, Malaya (despatches, 1950) and Germany, comd Regt, 1964–66; psc 1956; jssc 1962; Comdr RAC 3rd Div., 1967–69; BGS (Army Trng), MoD, 1970–73 (produced: Tillard Report on RMA Sandhurst course for young officers; Suffield Report setting up Army tank trng area in Canada); ADC to the Queen, 1970–73; COS, BAOR, 1973–76. With Borough of Brighton, 1977–87. *Recreations:* normal family pursuits, shooting. *Address:*

Church House, Chailey Green, Lewes, East Sussex BN8 4DA. *T:* Newick (0825) 722759. *Clubs:* Farmers'; Sussex. *Died 3 April 1994.*

TILNEY, Sir John (Dudley Robert Tarleton), Kt 1973; TD; JP; *b* 19 Dec. 1907; *yr s* of late Col R. H. Tilney, DSO; *m* 1954, Dame Guinevere Tilney, DBE; one step *s. Educ:* Eton; Magdalen College, Oxford. Served during War of 1939–45 (despatches), with 59th (4th West Lancs) Medium Regt, RA, and 11th Medium Regt, RA; commanded 47/49 359 (4th West Lancs), Medium Regt RA TA; Hon. Col 470 (3 W Lancs), LAA Regt, 1957–61. MP (C) Wavertree, Liverpool, 1950–Feb. 1974; Parliamentary Private Sec. to: Sec. of State for War, 1951–55; Postmaster-General, 1957–59; Chm. Inter-Parly Union, Brit. Gp, 1959–62; Chm. Conservative Commonwealth Council W Africa Cttee, 1954–62; PPS to Minister of Transport, 1959–62; Parly Under-Sec. of State for Commonwealth Relations, 1962–64 and for the Colonies, 1963–64; Member: Select Cttee on Expenditure; Exec. Cttee, Nat. Union of Conservative and Unionist Assocs, 1965–73; Chm. Merseyside Conservative MPs, 1964–74 (Vice-Chm., NW Area Cttee); Treasurer, UK Branch, Commonwealth Parly Assoc., 1968–70; Mem., Exec. Cttee, Cons. Political Centre, 1972–81. Chairman: Liverpool Luncheon Club, 1948–49; Liverpool Branch, Royal Commonwealth Soc., 1955–60 (Pres., 1965); Sir Winston Churchill Meml Statue Cttee; Pres., Airey Neave Meml Trust, 1983–93 (Chm., 1979–83); Pres., Victoria Square Assoc. (Chm., 1959–83). Member: Liverpool Cathedral Gen. Council; Exec. Cttee, Westminster Soc., 1975–91; Council, Imperial Soc. of Knights Bachelor, 1978–90. Pres., Assoc. of Lancastrians in London, 1980–81. Trustee, Bluecoat Sch.; Governor, Liverpool Coll. JP Liverpool, 1946. Croix de Guerre with Gilt Star, 1945; Legion of Honour, 1960. *Recreations:* gardening, travel. *Address:* 3 Victoria Square, SW1W 0QZ. *T:* 071–828 8674. *Clubs:* Pratt's; Jesters; Liverpool Racquet. *Died 26 April 1994.*

TILSTON, Col Frederick Albert, VC 1945; CD; *b* Toronto, Ontario, 11 June 1906; *s* of late Fred Tilston, English birth, and Agnes Estelle Le May, Cdn birth; *m* 1946; one *s. Educ:* De La Salle Collegiate, Toronto; Ontario College of Pharmacy (graduated 1929). Salesman for Sterling Products Ltd, Windsor, Ont, manufacturers of nationally advertised drug products, 1930–36; Canadian Sales Manager for Sterling Products Ltd, 1937–40; Vice-Pres. in charge of sales, Sterling Products Ltd, Windsor, Ontario, 1946–57; Pres., Sterling Drug Ltd, 1957–70; retired 1971. Canadian Army, 1941–46: Essex Scottish Regt, the Hochwald, Germany, 1945 (VC). KStJ 1984. Hon. Dr Laws Windsor, 1977. *Recreations:* swimming, ice hockey, golf, amateur pianist. *Address:* 188 Douglas Avenue, Toronto, Ont M5M 1G6, Canada. *T:* (416) 482 6482. *Clubs:* New Windsor, Essex County Golf and Country (Windsor, Ont); Royal Canadian Military Institute (Toronto); Summitt Golf and Country (Oak Ridges). *Died 23 Sept. 1992.*

TINBERGEN, Dr Jan; Officer, Order of The Lion; Commander, Order of Orange Nassau; Professor Emeritus, Erasmus University, Rotterdam; *b* 12 April 1903; *s* of Dirk Cornelis Tinbergen and Jeannette Van Eek; *m* 1929, Tine Johanna De Wit; three *d* (and one *d* decd). *Educ:* Leiden University. On Staff, Central Bureau of Statistics, 1929–45; Prof., Netherlands Sch. of Economics, 1933–73 (became Erasmus Univ., 1973); Staff, League of Nations, 1936–38; Director, Central Planning Bureau (Dutch Government), 1945–55; Advisor to various governments and international organisations, 1955–; Chm., UN Develt Planning Cttee, 1965–72. Hon. Degrees from 20 Universities, 1954–. (Jointly) Nobel Prize for Economics, 1969. *Publications:* Economic Policy, Principles and

Design, 1956; Selected Papers, 1959; Shaping the World Economy, 1962; Income Distribution, 1975; (with D. Fischer) Warfare and Welfare, 1987; World Security and Equity, 1990; articles. *Recreations:* languages, drawing. *Address:* Haviklaan 31, 2566XD The Hague, Netherlands. *T:* (70) 3644630. *Died 9 June 1994.*

TINDALL, Rev. Canon Frederick Cryer, BD 1923; FKC 1950 (AKC 1922); Principal Emeritus of Salisbury Theological College since 1965; Canon and Prebendary Emeritus of Salisbury Cathedral since 1981; *b* 2 July 1900; *s* of late Frederick and Frances Tindall, Hove, Sussex; *m* 1942, Rosemary Phyllis, *d* of late Frank and Katharine Alice Newman, Woking; one *s* (one *d* decd). *Educ:* Brighton Grammar Sch.; King's Coll., London; Ely Theological College. Curate of S Cyprian, S Marylebone, 1924–28; Lecturer and Bursar, Chichester Theological College, 1928–30, Vice-Principal, 1930–36; Warden of Connaught Hall and Lecturer in Theology, Southampton Univ., 1936–39; Vicar of St Augustine, Brighton, 1939–50; Principal, Salisbury Theological Coll., 1950–65 (Sabbatical Year 1965–66). Proctor in Convocation for Diocese of Chichester, 1936–45, 1949–50; Examining Chaplain to Bishop of Chichester, 1941–50, Canon and Prebendary of Chichester Cathedral, 1948–50; Canon and Prebendary of Salisbury Cathedral, 1950–81; Proctor in Convocation for Diocese of Salisbury, 1950–75; Vice-Pres. and Chm. House of Clergy, Salisbury Diocesan Synod, 1970–76; Chm., Salisbury Diocesan Liturgical Cttee, 1973–81; Member: Commn for Revision of the Catechism, 1958; Church Assembly Standing Orders Cttee, 1963; Archbishop's Commn on London and SE England, 1965; Greater London Area Liaison Cttee, 1968; Pastoral Measure Appeal Tribunal, 1969–75; General Synod Standing Orders Cttee, 1970–75. Clerical Judge, Court of Arches, Canterbury, 1969–80. Pro-Prolocutor, Lower House of Convocation of Canterbury, 1959–75. Trustee, St John's Hosp., Heytesbury, 1968–83. *Publications:* England Expects, 1946; a History of S Augustine's Brighton, 1946; Christian Initiation, Anglican Principles and Practice, 1951; contributor to: History of Christian Thought, 1937; Encyclopædia Britannica Year Book, 1939; Baptism To-Day, 1949; Theology, Church Quarterly Review, Guardian, etc. *Recreations:* music, travelling, golf, gardening. *Address:* 16 The Close, Salisbury, Wilts SP1 2EB. *T:* Salisbury (01722) 322373. *Clubs:* Athenæum, Commonwealth Trust, Ski Club of Great Britain. *Died 4 Dec. 1995.*

TINSLEY, Charles Henry, FRICS; Deputy Chief Valuer, Inland Revenue Valuation Office, 1974–78; *b* 3 March 1914; *s* of Arthur William and Teresa Tinsley; *m* 1938, Solway Lees; two *s* one *d*. *Educ:* Ratcliffe Coll., Leicester. Served War: joined TA, 1939; commn in Royal Artillery, 1941; with Lanarkshire Yeomanry, RA, in ME, Sicily and Italy; GSOII, in ME Supply Centre, Tehran, 1945–46; re-joined TA, 1948, and retd as Lt-Col, 1955. Nottinghamshire and W Riding of Yorkshire County Valuation Depts, 1929–39; Co. Valuer, N Riding of Yorkshire, 1948; joined Inland Revenue Valuation Office, 1949; Suptg Valuer (Rating), Northern Region, 1949–68; Asst Chief Valuer, 1968. *Recreations:* the violin, travel, reading. *Address:* 44 Belgrave Manor, Brooklyn Road, Woking, Surrey GU22 7TW. *T:* Woking (01483) 767444. *Died 6 March 1995.*

TINSLEY, Rt Rev. (Ernest) John; *b* 22 March 1919; *s* of Ernest William and Esther Tinsley; *m* 1947, Marjorie Dixon (*d* 1977); two *d*. *Educ:* St John's Coll., Univ. of Durham (BA, MA, BD); Westcott House, Cambridge. Deacon, 1942; priest, 1943; Curate: S Mary-le-Bow, Durham, 1942–44; South Westoe, 1944–46; Lectr in Theology, University Coll. of Hull, 1946–61; Sen. Lectr and Head of Dept of Theology, Univ. of Hull, 1961–62;

Lectr of St Mary, Lowgate, Hull, 1955–62; Prof. of Theology, 1962–75, and Dean of Faculty of Arts, 1965–67, Univ. of Leeds; Bishop of Bristol, 1976–85; Special Lectr in Theology, Univ. of Bristol, 1976–84. Hulsean Preacher, Cambridge Univ., 1982; Bishop John Prideaux Lectr, Exeter Univ., 1982. Examining Chaplain: to Archbp of York, 1957–63; to Bp of Sheffield, 1963–75. Hon. Canon of Ripon Cath., 1966–75. Jt Chm., Gen. Synod's Bd of Educn and of Nat. Soc. for Promoting Religious Educn, 1979–82; Member: Doctrine Commn, 1967–69; Home Office Cttee on obscenity and film censorship, 1977–79. *Publications:* The Imitation of God in Christ, 1960; The Gospel according to Luke, 1965; (ed) Modern Theology, 1979; Tragedy, Irony and Faith, 1985; Tell it Slant, 1990; contributor to: The Church and the Arts, 1960; Vindications, 1966; A Dictionary of Christian Ethics, 1967; A Dictionary of Christian Theology, 1969; Art and Religion as Communication, 1974; Dictionary of Christian Spirituality, 1983; In Search of Christianity, 1986. *Recreations:* France, Romanesque art. *Address:* 100 Acre End Street, Eynsham, Oxford OX8 1PD. *T:* Oxford (0865) 880822. *Died 20 July 1992.*

TIZARD, Sir (John) Peter (Mills), Kt 1982; Professor of Pædiatrics, University of Oxford, 1972–83, then Professor Emeritus; Fellow of Jesus College, Oxford, 1972–83, Hon. Fellow 1983; Hon. Consultant Children's Physician, Oxfordshire Health Authority, 1972–83; *b* London, 1 April 1916; *e s* of late Sir Henry Thomas Tizard, GCB, AFC, FRS, and Lady (Kathleen Eleanor) Tizard; *m* 1945, Elisabeth Joy, *yr d* of late Clifford John Taylor, FRCSE; two *s* one *d*. *Educ:* Rugby Sch.; Oriel Coll., Oxford; Middlesex Hospital. BA Oxon 1938 (3rd cl. Hons Honour Sch. of Natural Science); Oxford and Cambridge Schol. (Biochemistry and Physiology), Middlesex Hospital, 1938; MA, BM, BCh Oxon 1941; MRCP 1944; FRCP 1958; DCH England 1947. Served War of 1939–45 with RAMC, 1942–46 (Temp. Major). Med. Registrar and Pathologist, Hospital for Sick Children, Great Ormond Street, 1947; Asst Director, Pædiatric Unit, St Mary's Hospital Medical Sch., 1949; Physician, Paddington Green Children's Hospital, 1949; Nuffield Foundation Medical Fellow, 1951; Research Fellow in Pediatrics, Harvard Univ., 1951; Reader in Child Health, 1954–64, Prof. of Pædiatrics, 1964–72, Inst. of Child Health, Royal Postgraduate Med. Sch., Univ. of London; Hon. Cons. Children's Physician, Hammersmith Hosp., 1954–72; Chm., Med. Cttee, Hammersmith Hosp., 1970–71. Mem., Oxford AHA, 1979–82; Chm., Exec. Cttee, British Pædiatric Surveillance Unit, 1985–89. McLaughlin Gallie Vis. Prof., Royal Coll. of Physicians and Surgs of Canada, 1984. Lectures: Blackfan Meml, Harvard Univ., 1963; Samuel Gee, RCP, 1972; Carl Fridericksen, Danish Paediatric Soc., 1972; Perlstein, Louisville Univ., 1973; Clausen Meml, Rochester Univ., NY, 1975; Choremis Meml, Hellenic Paediatric Soc., 1975; Croonian, RCP 1978; Woolmer Meml, Biol Engrg Soc., 1982; Orator, Reading Pathological Soc., 1973. Mem. Ct of Assistants, 1971–, Master, 1983–84, Soc. of Apothecaries of London. FRSocMed 1941 (Pres., Sect. of Paediatrics, 1980–81; Hon. Fellow, 1984); Second Vice-Pres., RCP, 1977–78; Member: British Pædiatric Assoc., 1953 (Pres. 1982–85; Hon. Mem., 1987); European Pædiatric Research Soc., 1959 (Pres., 1970–71); Neonatal Society, 1959–83 (Hon. Sec. 1964–66; Pres., 1975–78; Hon. Mem., 1983); Assoc. Physicians of Great Britain and Ireland, 1965; Assoc. British Neurologists, 1969; German Acad. of Scientists, Leopoldina, 1972; Harveian Soc., 1974– (Pres., 1977); British Pædiatric Neurol. Assoc., 1975– (Pres., 1979–82; Hon. Mem., 1991); Corresp. Member: Société française de Pédiatrie, 1969; Pædiatric Soc. of Chile, 1968; Austrian Paediatric Soc., 1972; Swiss Paediatric Soc., 1973; Hon. Member: Pædiatric Soc. of Concepcion, 1968;

Czechoslovak Med. Assoc. J. E. Purkyněi, 1971; Dutch Pædiatric Soc., 1971; Amer. Pediatric Soc., 1976; Hellenic Soc. Perinatal Medicine, 1979; Deutsche Ges. für Kinderheilkunde, 1984. Dawson Williams Meml Prize, BMA, 1982; James Spence Medal, BPA, 1986. *Publications:* Medical Care of Newborn Babies (jtly), 1972; papers in scientific and medical journals. *Address:* Holly Cottage, Court Drive, Hillingdon, Uxbridge, Mddx UB10 0BN. *T:* Uxbridge (0895) 811055; Jesus College, Oxford OX1 3DW. *Club:* Athenæum.

Died 27 Oct. 1993.

TODD, Ann; actress; *b* 24 Jan. 1909; *m* 1933, Victor Malcolm; one *s*; *m* 1939, Nigel Tangye; one *d*; *m* 1949, Sir David Lean, CBE (marr. diss. 1957; he *d* 1991). Stage plays and films include: *plays:* Peter, in Peter Pan, Winter Garden, 1942–43; Lottie, in Lottie Dundass, Vaudeville, 1943; Madeleine Smith, in The Rest is Silence, Prince of Wales, 1944; Francesca Cunningham in The Seventh Veil, Princes, 1951; Foreign Field, 1953; Old Vic Season, 1954–55: Macbeth; Love's Labour's Lost; Taming of the Shrew; Henry IV, Parts I and II; Jennifer Dubedat in The Doctor's Dilemma, Saville, 1956; Four Winds, New York, 1957; Duel of Angels, London, 1958; *films:* The Seventh Veil, 1945; Daybreak, 1948; The Paradine Case, 1948; So Evil My Love, 1948; The Passionate Friends, 1949; Madeleine, 1950; The Sound Barrier, 1952; The Green Scarf, 1954; Time Without Pity, 1956; Taste of Fear, 1960; Son of Captain Blood, 1961; 90 Degrees in the Shade, 1964; The Vortex, 1965; Beware my Brethren, 1970; The Fiend, 1971; The Human Factor, 1980; Persian Fairy Tale; produced, wrote and appeared in Diary Documentaries, 1964–76: Thunder in Heaven (Kathmandu); Thunder of the Gods (Delphi); Thunder of the Kings (Egypt); Free in the Sun (Australia); Thunder of Silence (Jordan); Thunder of Light (Scotland); Hebrides (Scotland). TV appearances include: The Last Target, BBC, 1972; Maelstrom (series), Norway, 1983; The McGuffin, 1985; frequent radio and television appearances both in USA and GB. Hon. DLitt Durham, 1989. *Publications:* two novels; The Eighth Veil (autobiog.), 1980. *Died 6 May 1993.*

TODD, John Arthur, FRS 1948; PhD; Emeritus Reader in Geometry in the University of Cambridge; Fellow of Downing College, 1958–73, Hon. Fellow 1973; *b* 23 Aug. 1908; *s* of John Arthur and Agnes Todd. *Educ:* Liverpool Collegiate School; Trinity Coll., Cambridge. Assistant Lecturer in Mathematics, University of Manchester, 1931–37; Lecturer in Mathematics in the University of Cambridge, 1937–60, Reader in Geometry 1960–73. *Publications:* Projective and Analytical Geometry, 1947; various mathematical papers. *Address:* 10 Reddington Close, Sanderstead, South Croydon, Surrey CR2 0QZ. *T:* 0181–657 4994. *Died 22 Dec. 1994.*

TOLLEY, Leslie John, CBE 1973; FEng 1977; Chairman, Excelsior Industrial Holdings Ltd (formerly Wheatfield Engineering Holdings), 1983–90, retired; *b* Oxford, 11 Nov. 1913; *s* of late Henry Edward Charles and Gertrude Eleanor Tolley; *m* 1939, Margaret Butterfield, *d* of late Walter Bishop and Nellie May Butterfield; one *s* one *d*. *Educ:* Oxford Sch. of Technology. FIEE; CIMgt. Gen. Manager, Nuffield Metal Products, 1941–52; Gen. Works Manager, 1952, Works Dir, 1954, Renold Chains Ltd; Gp Man. Dir, 1962, Chm., 1972–82, Renold Ltd; Chairman: Fodens Ltd, 1975–80; Francis Shaw & Co. Ltd, 1977–81; Dir, NW Regional Bd, Lloyds Bank Ltd, 1975–84. A Vice-Chm., 1973–78, Chm., 1978–80, BIM. *Recreation:* golf. *Address:* 5 The Redlands, Manor Road, Sidmouth, Devon EX10 8RT. *Died 14 July 1995.*

TOMKINS, Rt Rev. Oliver Stratford, MA, DD, LLD; *b* 9 June 1908; *s* of Rev. Leopold Charles Fellows Tomkins and Mary Katie (*née* Stratford); *m* 1939, Ursula Mary Dunn; one *s* three *d*. *Educ:* Trent Coll; Christ's Coll, Cambridge; Westcott House, Cambridge. Asst Gen. Sec., Student Christian Movement, 1933–40, and Editor, Student Movement Magazine, 1937–40. Deacon, 1935; priest, 1936; Vicar of Holy Trinity, Millhouses, Sheffield, 1940–45; an Associate Gen. Sec. World Council of Churches and Sec. of its Commission on Faith and Order, 1945–52; Warden of Lincoln Theological College (Scholae Cancellarii) and Canon and Prebend, Lincoln Cathedral, 1953–59; Bishop of Bristol, 1959–75. Mem. Central Cttee, World Council of Churches, 1968–75. DD (*hon. causa*) Edinburgh University, 1953; Hon. LLD Bristol, 1975. *Publications:* The Universal Church in God's Design (ed and contrib.), 1948; The Wholeness of the Church, 1949; The Church in the Purpose of God, 1950; Intercommunion, 1951; (ed) Faith and Order (Lund Conference Report), 1953; Life of E. S. Woods, Bishop of Lichfield, 1957; A Time for Unity, 1964; Guarded by Faith, 1971; Prayer for Unity, 1987. *Recreation:* simply being. *Address:* 23 St Paul's Road West, Dorking, Surrey RH4 2HT. *T:* Dorking (0306) 885536.

Died 29 Oct. 1992.

TOMKINSON, John Stanley, CBE 1981; FRCS; Hon. Secretary General, International Federation of Gynaecology and Obstetrics (Secretary General, 1976–85); Obstetric Surgeon, Queen Charlotte's Maternity Hospital, 1953–79; Obstetric and Gynæcological Surgeon, Guy's Hospital, 1953–79; Gynæcological Surgeon, Chelsea Hospital for Women, 1971–79; *b* 8 March 1916; *o s* of Harry Stanley and Katie Mills Tomkinson, Stafford; *m* 1954, Barbara Marie Pilkington; one *s* one *d* (and one *s* decd). *Educ:* Rydal Sch.; Birmingham University Medical Sch.; St Thomas' Hospital. MRCS, LRCP 1941; MB, ChB Birmingham 1941; FRCS 1949; MRCOG 1952; FRCOG 1967. Medal in Surgery and Priestley-Smith Prize, Birmingham. Surgeon Lieut, RNVR, 1942–46. Demonstrator of Anatomy, Birmingham Medical School, 1946; appointments in General Surgery, Obst. and Gynæcol., at Birmingham and Midland Hosp. for Women, Birmingham Maternity Hospital, and Queen Elizabeth Hospital, Birmingham, 1941–42 and 1947–52; Registrar, Professorial Unit in General Surgery and Professorial Unit in Obst. and Gynæcol., Birmingham; Chief Asst, Chelsea Hospital for Women, 1952–53; Resident Obstetrician and Tutor in Obstetrics (Postgrad. Inst. of Obst. and Gynæcol. of University of London), Queen Charlotte's Maternity Hospital, 1952–53. Travelling Fellow (Guy's Hospital), USA and Canada, 1954. Vis. Prof., Spanish Hospital, Mexico City, 1972. Consultant Advr in Obstetrics and Gynæcol., Min. of Health, later DHSS, 1966–81; Consultant, WHO, 1981–. Lectures: William Hawksworth Meml, 1969; Sir Winston Churchill Meml, Canterbury, 1970; Edward Sharp Meml, 1977; Foundn, Amer. Assoc. of Gynecol. and Obstetrics, 1978; Charter Day, Nat. Maternity Hosp., Dublin, 1979; John Figgis Jewett Meml, Mass Med. Soc., USA, 1988; Bert B. Hershenson Meml, Brigham and Women's Hosp., Boston, Mass, 1988. Examiner for: Univs of Oxford, Cambridge, London, Birmingham, QUB; Univs of Haile Selassie I in Ethiopia, East Africa in Uganda, El Fateh in Tripoli, Singapore; RCOG; Conjoint Examining Bd, Central Midwives Bd. FRSM. Member: Gynæcological Club of Great Britain; Birmingham and Midland Obst. and Gynæcol. Society; Central Midwives Board; Member Council: RCOG; RCS; section of Obstetrics and Gynæcology, RSM; Mem. Exec. Council, Internat. Fedn of Obstetrics and Gynaecology; Past Chm., Jt Study Working Gp of Internat. Confedn of Midwives and Internat. Fedn of Gynaecology and Obstetrics. Jt Editor, Report on Confidential Enquiries into Maternal Deaths in England and Wales, 1964–66, 1967–69, 1970–72, 1973–75, 1976–78. Foreign Member, Continental Gynecol. Society (of America). Hon. Fellow:

Soc. of Gynaecologists and Obstetricians of Colombia, 1972; Nigerian Soc. Obst. and Gynaecol., 1977; Italian Soc. Obst. and Gynaecol., 1978; Romanian Soc. Obst. and Gynaecol., 1978; South African Soc. Obst. and Gynaecol., 1980; Spanish Soc. Obst. and Gynaecol., 1981.; Polish Soc. Obst. and Gynaecol., 1984 (Hon. Mem. 1985); Canadian Soc. Obst. and Gynaecol., 1984; Brazilian Soc. Obst. and Gynaecol., 1985; Jordanian Soc. Obst. and Gynaecol., 1985; Korean Soc. Obst. and Gynaecol., 1986. Copernicus Medal, Copernicus Acad. of Medicine, Cracow, 1985; Medal of Polish Nation for Aid and Co-operation in Medicine, 1985. *Publications:* (ed) Queen Charlotte's Textbook of Midwifery; papers of general surgical, obstetric and gynæcological interest. *Recreations:* fly-fishing, painting, the arts generally. *Address:* Keats House, Guy's Hospital, SE1. *T:* 071–955 5000, ext. 5570; 3 Downside, St John's Avenue, SW15 2AE. *T:* 081–789 9422; Rose Cottage, Up Somborne, Hants SO20 6QY. *T:* Romsey (0794) 388837. *Clubs:* Athenæum, Flyfishers', MCC.

Died 11 April 1992.

TOMLINSON, Sir (Frank) Stanley, KCMG 1966 (CMG 1954); HM Diplomatic Service, retired; *b* 21 March 1912; *s* of J. D. Tomlinson, WR Yorks Constabulary and Mary Tomlinson; *m* 1959, Nancy, *d* of late E. Gleeson-White and Mrs Gleeson-White, Sydney, Australia. *Educ:* High Pavement Sch., Nottingham; University College, Nottingham. Entered Consular Service by competitive examination, 1935; served in Japan, 1935–41; Saigon, 1941–42; United States, 1943; Washington, 1945; Acting Consul-General, Manila, 1945, Chargé d'Affaires, 1946; Foreign Office, 1947; Washington, 1951; Imperial Defence Coll., 1954; Counsellor and Head, SE Asia Dept, 1955; Dep. Commandant, British Sector, Berlin, 1958; Minister, UK Permanent Delegation to NATO, 1961–64; Consul General, New York, 1964–66; British High Comr, Colombo, 1966–69; Dep. Under-Sec. of State, FCO, 1969–72. Hon. LLD Nottingham, 1970. *Recreations:* drinking, reading and talking about wine, reading, the company of old friends. *Address:* 32 Long Street, Devizes, Wilts SN10 1NT. *Club:* Oriental.

Died 10 Sept. 1994.

TOMPKINS, Prof. Frederick Clifford, FRS 1955; Professor in Physical Chemistry, Imperial College of Science and Technology, SW7, 1959–77, then Emeritus; Editor and Secretary of Faraday Division of The Chemical Society (formerly The Faraday Society), 1950–77, President, 1978; *b* 29 Aug. 1910; *m* 1936, Catherine Livingstone Macdougal; one *d. Educ:* Yeovil Sch.; Bristol Univ. Asst Lectr, King's Coll., Strand, 1934–37; Lectr and Senior Lectr, Natal Univ., Natal, S Africa, 1937–46; ICI Fellow, King's College, Strand, 1946–47; Reader in Physical Chemistry, Imperial College of Science and Technology, 1947; Hon. ARCS 1964. Hon. DSc Bradford, 1975. *Publications:* Chemisorption of Gases on Metals, 1978; contributions to Proc. Royal Society, Journal Chem. Soc., Trans Faraday Soc., Jl Chem. Physics, Zeitung Elektrochem. *Died 5 Nov. 1995.*

TOMPKINS, (Granville) Richard (Francis), CBE 1992; Founder, Chairman and Managing Director: Green Shield Trading Stamp Co. Ltd, since 1958; Argos Distributors Ltd, 1973–79; *b* 15 May 1918; *s* of late Richard and Ethel May Tompkins; *m* 1st, 1942, Valerie Margaret Try (marr. diss. 1970); two *d*; 2nd, 1970, Elizabeth Nancy Duke (Cross of Merit with Crown, Order Pro Merito Melitensi SMO Malta; Comdr, Order of Holy Cross of Jerusalem, Bailiwick of St Louis); one *d. Educ:* Pakeman St LCC Sch., London, N7. Engineering Draughtsman, Home Forces, 1939–46; founded several companies in printing and advertising, 1945. Patron: The Tompkins Foundn, 1980; Regimental Museum of the Buffs—the East Kent

Regt, 1985. Hon. DH Lewis Univ., Chicago, 1985. Hon. FRCP, 1985. KStJ 1991; Knight Grand Cross of Merit, Order Pro Merito Melitensi SMO Malta, 1984; Grand Cross, Order of Holy Cross of Jerusalem, Bailiwick of Saint Louis, 1985; Knight Grand Comdr, Noble Companions of the Swan, 1987. *Recreations:* travel, theatre, golf. *Address:* 7 Belgrave Square, SW1.

Died 6 Dec. 1992.

TONGE, Prof. (Cecil) Howard, TD; DDSc; FDSRCS; Professor of Oral Anatomy, 1964–81, Professor Emeritus 1981, and Dental Postgraduate Sub-Dean, 1968–82, University of Newcastle upon Tyne; *b* 16 Dec. 1915; *s* of Norman Cecil Tonge and Gladys Marian (*née* Avison); *m* 1946, Helen Wilson Currie. *Educ:* Univ. of Durham. DDSc, MB, BS, BDS (Dunelm); FDSRCS 1973. House Surg., later Asst Resident MO, Royal Victoria Inf., 1939; Demonstrator in Anatomy, Medical Sch., Newcastle upon Tyne, 1940; Lectr in Anatomy, 1944, Sen. Lectr, 1952, Reader in Oral Anatomy, 1956, Univ. of Durham. Lieut RAMC (TA), 1941; Lt-Col RAMC (TA) Comdg 151 (N) Field Ambulance, 1954–58; Hon. Col, Northumbrian Univ. OTC, 1974–82. Chairman, Council of Military Educn Cttees of Univs of UK, 1968–82; Pres., British Div. Internat. Assoc. for Dental Research, 1968–71; Northern Regional Adviser in Postgrad. Dental Educn of RCS, 1970–83; Chm., Dental Cttee, Council for Postgrad. Medical Educn, 1978–84; British Dental Association: Pres., 1981–82; (Life) Vice-Pres., 1983; Member: Representative Bd, 1970–; Council, 1970–82; Chm., Central Cttee for Univ. Teachers and Res. Workers, 1976–81. Member, Sunderland AHA, 1973–82; Vice-Chm., Sunderland DHA, 1982–87. Consultant to several commns estabd by FDI, 1976–89. *Publications:* chapters in: Scientific Foundations of Dentistry, 1976; Handbook of Microscopic Anatomy, vol. V/6: Teeth, 1989; papers in Dental Anatomy and Embryology; contribs to Brit. Jl of Nutrition, Jl of Anatomy, Jl of Dental Res., Jl of RCSE, Brit. Dental Jl, Dental Update, Nature, Internat. Dental Jl. *Recreation:* history. *Died 16 Sept. 1992.*

TONGE, Rev. David Theophilus; Chaplain to the Queen, since 1984; Vicar of St Godwald's, Finstall, Bromsgrove, 1976–92; *b* 15 Sept. 1930; *s* of late Robert and of Magdalene Tonge; *m* 1952, Christobelle Augusta Richards; three *d. Educ:* Johnson's Point Public School, Antigua; Teacher's Certificate (Leeward); General Ordination Certificate. Pupil teacher, 1944; uncertificated teacher, 1952; postman, 1956; postal and telegraph officer, 1960. Wells Theol. Coll., 1968; deacon 1970, priest 1971; Curate of Kidderminster, 1970–75; Asst C of E Chaplain, Brockhill Remand Centre, Redditch, 1983. *Recreations:* gardening, music. *Address:* 96 Hume Street, Kidderminster, Worcs DY11 6RB.

Died 16 Jan. 1995.

TONGE, Howard; *see* Tonge, C. H.

TOOKER, Hyde Charnock W.; *see* Whalley-Tooker.

TOPPING, Prof. James, CBE 1977; MSc, PhD, DIC; FInstP; FIMA; Vice-Chancellor, Brunel University, 1966–71; Emeritus Professor, 1971; *b* 9 Dec. 1904; 3rd *s* of James and Mary A. Topping, Ince, Lancashire; *m* 1934, Muriel Phyllis Hall (*d* 1963); one *s*; *m* 1965, Phyllis Iles. *Educ:* Univ. of Manchester; Imperial Coll. of Science and Technology. BSc (Manchester), 1924; PhD (London), 1926; Beit Scientific Research Fellow, 1926–28. Asst Lectr, Imperial Coll., 1928–30; Lectr Chelsea Polytechnic, 1930–32; Lectr, Coll. of Technology, Manchester, 1932–37; Head, Dept of Maths and Physics, Polytechnic, Regent St, 1937–53; Principal, Technical Coll., Guildford, 1953–54; Principal, Brunel College, W3, 1955–66. Vice-Pres., Inst. of Physics, 1951–54, 1960–63; Chairman: Nuffield Secondary Science Consultative Cttee, 1965–71;

Hillingdon Gp Hosp. Management Cttee, 1971–74; London Conf. on Overseas Students, 1971–81; Council, Roehampton Inst. of Higher Educn, 1975–78; Council, Polytechnic of the S Bank, 1975–81; Vis. Cttee, Cranfield Inst. of Technol., 1970–78; Member: Anderson Cttee on Student Grants, 1958–60; Nat. Council for Technological Awards, 1955–64; CNAA, 1964–70. Hon. DTech Brunel, 1967; Hon. DSc CNAA, 1969. *Publications:* Shorter Intermediate Mechanics (with D. Humphrey), 1949; Errors of Observation, 1955; The Beginnings of Brunel University, 1981; papers in scientific jls. *Address:* Forge Cottage, Forest Green, near Dorking, Surrey RH5 5SF. *T:* Forest Green (030670) 358. *Died 3 June 1994.*

TORLESSE, Rear-Adm. Arthur David, CB 1953; DSO 1946; retired; Regional Director of Civil Defence, North Midlands Region, 1955–67; *b* 24 Jan. 1902; *e s* of Captain A. W. Torlesse, Royal Navy, and H. M. Torlesse (*née* Jeans); *m* 1933, Sheila Mary Susan (*d* 1993), *d* of Lt-Col Duncan Darroch, Gourock; two *s* one *d. Educ:* Stanmore Park; Royal Naval Colleges, Osborne and Dartmouth. Served as midshipman, Grand Fleet, 1918; specialised as observer, Fleet Air Arm, 1926; Commander, 1935; staff appointments in HMS Hood and at Singapore and Bangkok (Naval Attaché), 1936–39; Executive Officer, HMS Suffolk, 1939–40; aviation staff appointments at Lee on Solent and Admiralty, 1940–44; Captain, 1942; commanded HMS Hunter, 1944–45; Director of Air Equipment, Admiralty, 1946–48; Imperial Defence College, 1949; commanded HMS Triumph, Far East, 1950, taking part in first 3 months of Korean War (despatches); Rear-Admiral, 1951; Flag Officer, Special Squadron and in command of Monte Bello atomic trial expedition, 1952; Flag Officer, Ground Training, 1953–54, retired Dec. 1954. Officer, US Legion of Merit, 1954. *Recreations:* formerly fishing, entomology. *Address:* 1 Sway Lodge, Sway, Lymington, Hants SO41 6EB. *T:* Lymington (01590) 682550. *Club:* Naval and Military. *Died 19 July 1995.*

TOUCH, Dr Arthur Gerald, CMG 1967; Chief Scientist, Government Communications Headquarters, 1961–71; *b* 5 July 1911; *s* of A. H. Touch, Northampton; *m* 1938, Phyllis Wallbank, Birmingham; one *s. Educ:* Oundle; Jesus College, Oxford. MA, DPhil 1937. Bawdsey Research Station, Air Ministry, 1936; Radio Dept, RAE, Farnborough, 1940; British Air Commn, Washington, DC, 1941; Supt, Blind Landing Experimental Unit, RAE, 1947; Director: Electronic R&D (Air), Min. of Supply, 1953; Electronic R&D (Ground), Min. of Supply, 1956–59; Imperial Defence College, 1957; Head, Radio Dept, RAE, 1959; Min. of Defence, 1960. *Recreations:* fly fishing, horticulture (orchids). *Address:* Yonder, Ideford, Newton Abbot, Devon TQ13 0BG. *T:* Chudleigh (01626) 852258. *Died 26 Nov. 1994.*

TOWNSEND, Group Captain Peter Wooldridge, CVO 1947; DSO 1941; DFC and Bar, 1940; *b* 22 Nov. 1914; *s* of late Lt-Col E. C. Townsend; *m* 1st, 1941, Rosemary (marr. diss.), *d* of Brig. Hanbury Pawle, CBE; two *s*; 2nd, 1959, Marie Luce, *d* of Franz Jamagne, Brussels, Belgium; one *s* two *d. Educ:* Haileybury; Royal Air Force Coll., Cranwell. Royal Air Force, 1933; served War of 1939–45, Wing Commander, 1941 (despatches, DFC and Bar, DSO); Equerry to King George VI, 1944–52; Deputy Master of HM Household, 1950; Equerry to the Queen, 1952–53; Air Attaché, Brussels, 1953–56. *Publications:* Earth, My Friend, 1959; Duel of Eagles, 1970; The Last Emperor, 1975; Time and Chance (autobiog.), 1978; The Smallest Pawns in the Game, 1979; The Girl in the White Ship, 1981; The Postman of Nagasaki, 1984; Duel in the Dark, 1986; Nostalgia Britannica, 1994. *Address:* La Mare aux Oiseaux, Route des Grands Coins, 78610 Saint Léger-en-Yvelines, France. *Died 19 June 1995.*

TRACY, Walter Valentine, RDI 1973; *b* 14 Feb. 1914; *s* of Walter and Anne Tracy; *m* 1942, Muriel Frances Campbell. *Educ:* Central Sch. of Arts and Crafts. Apprentice compositor, Wm Clowes Ltd, 1930–35; typographic studio, Baynard Press, 1935–38; Notley Advertising, 1938–46; freelance, 1946–47; on staff of (British) Linotype Co., editor Linotype Matrix, i/c typographic design, 1947–73; Linotype-Paul, 1973–78. In 1965, assisted Editor of The Times in re-designing the paper for news on front page, May 1966; designed newspaper types: Jubilee, 1953; Adsans, 1959; Maximus, 1967; Telegraph Modern, 1969; Times-Europa, 1972; Monitor, 1989; also designed: Hebrew types Gold, Silver, 1975 (under pseudonym David Silver); Arabic types Kufic Light, Med., Bold, 1979; Qadi, 1983; Oasis, 1985; Malik, Sharif and Medina, 1988. *Publications:* Letters of Credit: a view of type design, 1986; The Typographic Scene, 1988; contribs to Penrose Annual, Alphabet, Motif, Typographica, Bull. of Printing Histl Soc. *Address:* 2 Cedar Court, The Drive, Finchley Way, N3 1AE. *T:* 0181–349 3785. *Club:* Double Crown (Hon. Mem.). *Died 28 April 1995.*

TRAHERNE, Sir Cennydd (George), KG 1970; Kt 1964; TD 1950; MA; HM Lord-Lieutenant of Mid, South and West Glamorgan, 1974–85 (HM Lieutenant for Glamorgan, 1952–74); *b* 14 Dec. 1910; *er s* of late Comdr L. E. Traherne, RN, Coedarhydyglyn, near Cardiff, and Dorothy, *d* of G. F. S. Sinclair; *m* 1934, Olivera Rowena, OBE, JP, BA, DStJ (*d* 1986), *d* of late James Binney and Lady Marjory Binney, Pampisford Hall, Cambridgeshire. *Educ:* Wellington; Brasenose Coll., Oxford. Barrister, Inner Temple, 1938 (Hon. Bencher, 1983). 81st Field Regt RA (TA), 1934–43; 102 Provost Co., Corps of Military Police, 1943–45 (despatches); Dep. Asst Provost Marshal, Second British Army, 1945; 53rd Div. Provost Company, Royal Military Police, 1947–49, TA; Hon. Colonel: 53 Div. Signal Regt, 1953–58; 282 (Glamorgan Yeomanry) Field Regt RA (TA), 1958–61; 282 (Glam and Mon) Regt RA (TA), 1962–67; 37 (Wessex and Welsh) Signal Regt, T&AVR, 1971–75; Glamorgan ACF, 1982. DL 1946, JP 1946, Glamorgan; Deputy Chairman Glamorgan Quarter Sessions, 1949–52. President: Welsh College of Advanced Technology, 1957–65; Welsh Nat. Sch. of Medicine, 1970–83; Univ. of Wales Coll. of Medicine, 1983–87 (Hon. Fellow, 1989). Chairman, Rep. Body of the Church in Wales, 1965–77. Director: Cardiff Building Society, 1953–85 (Chm., 1964–85); Wales Gas Board, 1958–71; Commercial Bank of Wales, 1972–88; Chm., Wales Gas Consultative Council, 1958–71. Member, Gorsedd of the Bards of Wales. Honorary Freeman: Borough of Cowbridge, 1971; Borough of Vale of Glamorgan, 1984; City of Cardiff, 1985. Hon. LLD University of Wales. GCStJ 1991 (Sub Prior, Priory of Wales, 1978–90). *Address:* Coedarhydyglyn, near Cardiff, S Wales CF5 6SF. *T:* Peterston-super-Ely (01446) 760321. *Clubs:* Athenæum; Cardiff and County (Cardiff). *Died 26 Jan. 1995.*

TRANMIRE, Baron *cr* 1974 (Life Peer), of Upsall, North Yorkshire; **Robert Hugh Turton,** KBE 1971; MC 1942; PC 1955; JP; DL; *b* 8 Aug. 1903; *s* of late Major R. B. Turton, Kildale Hall, Kildale, Yorks; *m* 1928, Ruby Christian, *d* of late Robert T. Scott, Beechmont, Sevenoaks; two *s* one *d* (and one *s* decd). *Educ:* Eton; Balliol Coll., Oxford. Called to Bar, Inner Temple, 1926. Joined 4th Bn of Green Howards at outbreak of war, 1939; served as DAAG 50th (N) Division, AAG GHQ MEF. MP (C) Thirsk and Malton, 1929–Feb. 1974. Parly Sec., Min. of Nat. Insurance, 1951–53, Min. of Pensions and Nat. Insce, 1953–54; Joint Parly Under-Sec. of State for Foreign Affairs, Oct. 1954–Dec. 1955; Minister of Health, Dec. 1955–Jan. 1957; Chm., Select Cttee on Procedure, 1970–74. Chm., Commonwealth Industries Assoc.,

1963–74. JP 1936, DL 1962, N Riding, Co. York. Hon. Colonel, 4/5th Bn The Green Howards (TA), 1963–67. *Address:* Upsall Castle, Thirsk, N Yorks YO7 2QJ. *T:* Thirsk (0845) 537202; 15 Grey Coat Gardens, SW1P 2QA. *T:* 071–834 1535. *Died 17 Jan. 1994.*

TRANTER, Prof. Clement John, CBE 1967 (OBE 1953); Bashforth Professor of Mathematical Physics, Royal Military College of Science, Shrivenham, 1953–74, then Emeritus; *b* 16 Aug. 1909; *s* of late Archibald Tranter, and Mrs Tranter, Cirencester, Glos; *m* 1937, Joan Louise Hatton, *d* of late J. Hatton, MBE, and Mrs Hatton, Plumstead, SE18. *Educ:* Cirencester Grammar Sch.; Queen's Coll., Oxford (Open Math. Scholar; 1st Class Hons Mathematical Mods, 1929; 1st Class Hons Final Sch. of Maths, 1931; MA (Oxon) 1940; DSc (Oxon) 1953). Commissioned RA, TA, 1932; Captain, 1938. Junior Assistant Research Dept, Woolwich, 1931–34; Senior Lecturer, Gunnery and Mathematics Branch, Military College of Science, Woolwich, 1935–40; Asst Professor 1940–46; Associate Professor of Mathematics, Royal Military College of Science, Shrivenham, 1946–53. *Publications:* Integral Transforms in Mathematical Physics, 1951; Advanced Level Pure Mathematics, 1953; Techniques of Mathematical Analysis, 1957; (with C. G. Lambe) Differential Equations for Engineers and Scientists, 1961; Mathematics for Sixth Form Scientists, 1964; (with C. G. Lambe) Advanced Level Mathematics, 1966; Bessel Functions with some Physical Applications, 1968; mathematical papers in various journals. *Recreations:* painting, golf, fly-fishing. *Address:* Flagstones, Stanton Fitzwarren, near Swindon, Wilts SN6 7RZ. *T:* Swindon (0793) 762913.

Died 27 Oct. 1991.

TRAPP, Rt Rev. Eric Joseph; *b* 17 July 1910; *s* of late Archibald Edward Trapp and Agnes Trapp, Leicester and Coventry; *m* 1937, Edna Noreen Thornton, SRN; two *d*. *Educ:* Alderman Newton's Sch., Leicester; Leeds Univ.; College of the Resurrection, Mirfield. BA 1st Class, philosophy. Deacon, 1934; priest, 1935; Asst Curate, St Olave's, Mitcham, Surrey, 1934–37; Director, Masite Mission, Basutoland, 1937–40; Rector, St Augustine's Bethlehem, Orange Free State, 1940–43; Rector, St John's, Maseru and Director of Maseru Mission, Basutoland, 1943–47; Canon of Bloemfontein Cathedral, 1944–47; Bishop of Zululand, 1947–57; Sec., Soc. for the Propagation of the Gospel, 1957–64, United Soc. for the Propagation of the Gospel, 1965–70; Bishop of Bermuda, 1970–75; Hon. Asst Bishop, Dio. St Albans, 1976–final retirement in 1980. Hon. DD Trinity College, Toronto, 1967. *Address:* Flat 15, Manormead, Tilford Road, Hindhead, Surrey GU26 6RA. *T:* Hindhead (0428) 607301. *Died 8 Sept. 1993.*

TRAVANCORE, Rajpramukh of; Maj.-Gen. HH Sri Padmanabha Dasa Bala Rama Varma, GCSI 1946; GCIE 1935; *b* 7 Nov. 1912; *S* father as Maharajah of Travancore, 1924 (regency until aged 18). Appointed Rajpramukh (President) of Travancore-Cochin, 1949; Founder of Travancore University and sometime Chancellor. Formerly: Colonel-in-Chief of Travancore State Forces; Hon. Major-General in British Army. Introduced many reforms, incl. giving low-caste Hindus the right to enter temples, 1936. Hon. doctorates. *Address:* Kaudiar Palace, Trivandrum 3, Kerala State, S India. *Died 19 July 1991.*

TRAVERS, Rt Rev. Mgr Brendan; *b* 21 March 1931; *s* of Dr Charles Travers and Eileen Travers (*née* Gordon). *Educ:* Belmont Abbey Sch.; Venerable English College, Rome; Gregorian Univ., Rome. (STL, JCL, PhL). Ordained priest, 1955; Curate, Salford diocese, 1957–72; Bishop's Secretary, 1961–64; Chm., Manchester Catholic Marriage Adv. Council, 1966–71; Rector, Pontifical Beda College,

Rome, 1972–78; Parish Priest, All Souls, Salford, 1978–. *Recreation:* golf. *Address:* All Souls Presbytery, Liverpool Street, Weaste, Salford M5 2HQ. *Club:* Worsley Golf (Manchester). *Died 18 June 1992.*

TREMLETT, Rt Rev. Anthony Paul; *b* 14 May 1914; *s* of late Laurence and Nyda Tremlett; unmarried. *Educ:* King's Sch., Bruton; King's Coll., Cambridge; Cuddesdon Theological Coll. Ordained deacon, 1938; priest, 1939; Curate of St Barnabas, Northolt Park, Middx; Chaplain to the Forces (Emergency Commission), 1941–46 (despatches); Domestic Chaplain to the Bishop of Trinidad, BWI, 1946–49; Chaplain of Trinity Hall, Cambridge, 1949–58; Vicar of St Stephen with St John, Westminster, 1958–64; Bishop Suffragan of Dover, 1964–80. *Address:* Doctors Commons, The Square, Northleach, Gloucestershire. *T:* Cotswold (0451) 60426.

Died 22 Aug. 1992.

TRENDALL, Prof. Arthur Dale, AC 1976; CMG 1961; MA, LittD; FSA; FBA 1968; FAHA; Resident Fellow, Menzies College, La Trobe University, since 1969; Emeritus Professor, University of Sydney, 1954; *b* Auckland, NZ, 28 March 1909; *s* of late Arthur D. Trendall and late Iza W. Uttley-Todd; unmarried. *Educ:* King's College, Auckland; Univs. of Otago (MA 1929; LittD 1936); Cambridge Univ. (MA 1937; LittD 1968); DLitt La Trobe, 1991. FSA 1939. NZ Post-Graduate Scholar in Arts, 1931; Rome Scholar in Archæology, 1934–35; Fellow of Trinity Coll., Cambridge, 1936–40; Librarian, British School at Rome, 1936–38; University of Sydney: Professor of Greek, 1939–54; Dean, Faculty of Arts, 1947–50; Chairman, Professorial Board, 1949–50, 1952; Acting Vice-Chancellor, 1953; Australian National University: Master of Univ. House, 1954–69; Deputy Vice-Chancellor, 1958–64; Hon. Fellow, 1969. Hon. Curator, Greek and Roman Section, Nicholson Museum, 1954, and Hon. Consultant, National Gallery of Victoria, 1957; Mem. Royal Commn on Univ. of Tas., 1955. Geddes-Harrower Professor of Greek Art and Archæology, Aberdeen Univ., 1966–67; Guest Scholar, J. Paul Getty Mus., 1985. Chm. Aust. Humanities Research Council, 1957–59. Mem., Nat. Capital Planning Cttee, 1958–67; Mem. Australian Universities Commission, 1959–70. Member: Accademia dei Lincei, Rome, 1971; Athens Acad., 1973; Corresp. Mem., Pontifical Acad. of Archaeology, Rome, 1973; Life Mem., Nat. Gall. of Victoria, 1976; For. Mem., Royal Netherlands Acad., 1977; Hon. Member: Hellenic Soc., 1982; Archaeol Inst. of Amer., 1987. Hon. Fellow: Athens Archaeological Soc., 1975; British School at Rome, 1983. Hon. LittD: Melbourne, 1956; ANU 1970; Hon. DLitt: Adelaide, 1960; Sydney, 1972; Tasmania, 1979; Hon. Dott. in Lettere, Lecce, 1981. For. Galileo Galilei Prize for Archaeology, 1971; Cassano Gold Medal for Magna Graecia Studies, 1971; Britannica Award (Australia), 1973; Kenyon Medal, British Acad., 1983. KCSG, 1956; Commendatore, Ordine al Merito, Republic of Italy, 1965 (Cavaliere Ufficiale 1961). *Publications:* Paestan Pottery, 1936; Frühitaliotische Vasen, 1938; Guide to the Cast Collection of the Nicholson Museum, Sydney, 1941; The Shellal Mosaic, 1942, 4th edn 1973; Handbook to the Nicholson Museum (editor), 2nd edn 1948; Paestan Pottery, Supplement, 1952; Vasi Italioti del Vaticano, vol. i, 1953; vol. ii, 1955; The Felton Greek Vases, 1958; Phlyax Vases, 1959, 2nd edn 1967; Paestan Addenda, 1960; Apulian Vase Painters of the Plain Style (with A. Cambitoglou), 1962; South Italian Vase Painting (British Museum Guide), 1966, 2nd edn 1976; The Red-figured Vases of Lucania, Campania and Sicily, 1967, Supplement I, 1970, Supplement II, 1973, Supplement III, 1983; Greek Vases in the Felton Collection, 1968, 2nd edn 1978; Greek Vases in the Logie Collection, Christchurch, NZ, 1971; Illustrations of Greek Drama (with T. B. L. Webster),

1971; Early South Italian Vase-painting, 1974; Eine Gruppe Apulischer Grabvasen in Basel (with M. Schmidt and A. Cambitoglou), 1976; Vasi antichi dipinti del Vaticano—Collezione Astarita: (iii) Vasi italiòti, 1976; (with A. Cambitoglou) The Red-figured Vases of Apulia, 2 vols, 1978, 1982, Supplement I, 1983, Supplement II, 1991; (with Ian McPhee) Greek Red-figured Fish-plates, 1987; The Red-figured Vases of Paestum, 1987; Red-figure Vases of South Italy and Sicily, 1989, German edn 1991;ʾ (with Marit Jentoft Nilsen) Corpus Vasorum Antiquorum, Malibu, J. Paul Getty Museum, vol. 3, 1990, vol. 4, 1991, vol. 5, 1994; several articles in learned periodicals. *Address:* Menzies College, La Trobe University, Bundoora, Vic 3083, Australia.

Died 13 Nov. 1995.

TRETHOWAN, Prof. Sir William (Henry), Kt 1980; CBE 1975; FRCP, FRACP; Professor of Psychiatry, University of Birmingham, 1962–82, Emeritus since 1983; Hon. Consultant Psychiatrist: Hollymoor Hospital, 1964–82; Midland Centre for Neurosurgery, 1975–82; Central Birmingham Health District, since 1983; *b* 3 June 1917; *s* of William Henry Trethowan and Joan Durham Trethowan (*née* Hickson); *m* 1st, 1941, Pamela Waters (*d* 1985); one *s* two *d*; 2nd, 1988, Heather Dalton (*née* Gardiner). *Educ:* Oundle Sch.; Clare Coll., Cambridge; Guy's Hosp. Med. Sch. MA, MB, BChir (Cantab) 1943; MRCP 1948; FRACP 1961; FRCP 1963; FRCPsych 1971 (Hon. Fellow 1983). Served War, RAMC: Major, Med. Specialist, 1944–47. Psychiatric Registrar, Maudsley Hosp., 1948–50; Psychiatric Resident, Mass Gen. Hosp., and Hon. Teaching Fellow, Harvard, 1951; Lectr and Sen. Lectr in Psychiatry, Univ. of Manchester, 1951–56; Prof. of Psychiatry, Univ. of Sydney, and Hon. Consultant Psychiatrist, Royal Prince Alfred and Royal North Shore Hosps, Sydney, 1956–62. Mem. GMC, 1969–81 (Treasurer, 1978–81); Cons. Adviser in Psychiatry, DHSS, 1964–78; Dean, Univ. of Birmingham Med. Sch., 1968–74; Chm., Standing Mental Health Adv. Cttee, 1968–74; Mem., UGC Med. Subcttee, 1974–81. Member: Birmingham Reg. Hosp. Bd, 1964–74; Standing Med. Adv. Cttee, 1966–82 (Chm., 1976); Central Health Services Council, 1966–80 (Vice-Chm., 1976–80); W Midlands Regional Health Authority, 1974–76. Chm., Med. Acad. Adv. Cttee, Chinese Univ. of Hong Kong, 1976–86. FRSocMed; Hon. Fellow, Royal Aust. and NZ Coll. of Psychiatry (FRANZCP 1962); Corresp. Fellow, Amer. Psychiatric Assoc. Hon. DSc Chinese Univ. of Hong Kong, 1979. Hon. FRCPsych. *Publications:* Psychiatry, 2nd edn (with Prof. E. W. Anderson), 1967, 5th edn (with Prof. A. C. P. Sims), 1983; Uncommon Psychiatric Syndromes, 1967, 3rd edn (with M. D. Enoch), 1991; numerous scientific and other articles in various jls; book reviews, etc. *Recreations:* music, cooking, natural history. *Address:* 31 High Point, Richmond Hill Road, Birmingham B15 3RU. *Died 15 Dec. 1995.*

TREVOR, Elleston; author; *b* Bromley, Kent, 17 Feb. 1920; *m* 1st, 1947, Jonquil Burgess (*d* 1986); one *s*; 2nd, 1987, Chaille Anne Groom. *Educ:* Sevenoaks. Apprenticed as a racing driver upon leaving school, 1938. Served in Royal Air Force, War of 1939–45. Began writing professionally in 1945. Member: Writers' Guild of GB; Authors' Guild of America. Amer. Mystery Writers' award, 1965; French Grand Prix de Littérature Policière, 1965. *Plays:* Touch of Purple, Globe, London, 1972; Just Before Dawn, Murder by All Means, 1972. *Publications:* Chorus of Echoes, 1950 (filmed); Tiger Street, 1951; Redfern's Miracle, 1951; A Blaze of Roses, 1952; The Passion and the Pity, 1953; The Big Pick-up, 1955 (filmed); Squadron Airborne, 1955; The Killing-Ground, 1956; Gale Force, 1956 (filmed); The Pillars of Midnight, 1957 (filmed); The VIP, 1959 (filmed); The Billboard Madonna, 1961; The Burning Shore (The Pasang Run, USA), 1962; Flight of the Phœnix,

1964 (filmed); The Shoot, 1966; The Freebooters, 1967 (filmed); A Place for the Wicked, 1968; Bury Him Among Kings, 1970; The Theta Syndrome, 1977 (filmed); Blue Jay Summer, 1977; Deathwatch, 1985; The Sister, 1994; under pseudonym Warwick Scott: Image in the Dust, 1951; The Domesday Story, 1951; Naked Canvas, 1952; under pseudonym Simon Rattray: Knight Sinister, Queen in Danger, Bishop in Check, Dead Silence, Dead Circuit (all 1951–53); under pseudonym Adam Hall: Volcanoes of San Domingo, 1964; The Berlin Memorandum, 1964 (filmed as The Quiller Memorandum); The 9th Directive, 1966; The Striker Portfolio, 1969; The Warsaw Document, 1971; The Tango Briefing, 1973; The Mandarin Cypher, 1975; The Kobra Manifesto, 1976; The Sinkiang Executive, 1978; The Scorpion Signal, 1979; The Pekin Target, 1981; Northlight, 1985; Quiller's Run, 1988; Quiller KGB, 1989; Quiller Barracuda, 1991; Quiller Bamboo, 1991; Quiller Solitaire, 1992; Quiller Meridian, 1993; under pseudonym Caesar Smith: Heatwave, 1957 (filmed); under pseudonym Roger Fitzalan: A Blaze of Arms, 1967; under pseudonym Howard North: Expressway, 1973; The Paragon (Night Stop, USA), 1974; The Sibling, 1979; The Damocles Sword, 1981; The Penthouse, 1982; Deathwatch, 1986; under pseudonym Lesley Stone: Siren Song, 1985; Riviera Story, 1987. *Recreations:* astronomy, metaphysics; first degree black belt in Shotokan karate, 1984. *Address:* 6902 E Dynamite Boulevard, Cave Creek, AZ 85331, USA. *T:* (602) 5853686. *Died 21 July 1995.*

TRIGER, Prof. David Ronald, DPhil; FRCP; Professor of Medicine and Postgraduate Medical Dean, University of Sheffield, since 1992; *b* 14 Sept. 1941; *s* of late Kurt Triger and of Olga Triger; *m* 1972, Jennifer Ann; three *s* one *d*. *Educ:* Cheltenham Coll.; St John's Coll., Oxford (MA, BM, BCh, DPhil); Oxford Univ. Med. Sch. FRCP 1980. Mary Goodger Scholar, Univ. of Oxford, 1970–72; Lectr in Med., Univ. of Southampton, 1972–77; MRC Travelling Fellow, Univ. of S California, 1975–76; University of Sheffield: Sen Lectr in Medicine, 1977–84; Reader, 1984–91. *Publications:* Practical Management of Liver Disease, 1981; Clinical Immunology of the Liver and Gastrointestinal Tract, 1985; Liver Disease and Gallstones: the facts, 1987, 2nd edn 1992. *Recreations:* gardening, philately, Indian cooking. *Address:* University of Sheffield Medical School, Beech Hill Road, Sheffield S10 2RX. *Died 13 March 1993.*

TRILLO, Rt Rev. (Albert) John, MTh; *b* 4 July 1915; *s* of late Albert Chowns and Margaret Trillo; *m* 1942, Patricia Eva Williams; two *s* one *d*. *Educ:* The Quintin Sch.; King's Coll., University of London. Business career, 1931–36; University, 1936–38, BD (1st Class Hons) and AKC (1st Class Hons), 1938; MTh 1943. Deacon, 1938; priest, 1939; Asst Curate, Christ Church, Fulham, 1938–41; Asst Curate, St Gabriel's, Cricklewood (in charge of St Michael's), 1941–45; Secretary, SCM in Schools, 1945–50; Rector of Friern Barnet and Lecturer in New Testament Greek, King's Coll., London, 1950–55; Principal, Bishops' Coll., Cheshunt, 1955–63; Bishop Suffragan of Bedford, 1963–68; Bishop Suffragan of Hertford, 1968–71; Bishop of Chelmsford, 1971–85. Examining Chaplain to Bishop of St Edmundsbury and Ipswich, 1955–63, to Bishop of St Albans, 1963–71. Hon. Canon, Cathedral and Abbey Church at St Albans, 1958–63; Canon Residentiary, 1963–65; Proctor in Convocation for Dean and Chapter of St Albans, 1963–64; Proctor-in-Convocation for the Clergy, 1965. Governor: Aldenham Sch., 1963–71; Harper Trust Schs, Bedford, 1963–68; Queenswood Sch., 1969–71; Forest Sch., 1976–. Chairman: Church of England Youth Council, 1970–74; Exec. Cttee, British Council of Churches, 1974–77 (Chm., Fund for Ireland, 1978–); Church of England's Cttee on Roman Catholic Relations, 1975–85; Jt Chm., English

Anglican/Roman Catholic Commn. Fellow of King's Coll., London, 1959. *Recreations:* reading, walking. *Address:* Copperfield, Back Road, Wenhaston, Halesworth, Suffolk. *Died 2 Aug. 1992.*

TRINDER, Air Vice-Marshal Frank Noel, CB 1949; CBE 1944; psa; *b* 24 Dec. 1895; *s* of Alfred Probus Trinder, MRCS, LRCP, Parkstone, Dorset; *m* 1925, Marjorie Agnes Scott (*d* 1986), *d* of Archie Scott Blake, Melrose, Scotland; one *s. Educ:* Epsom College. Served European War, 1914–18: with North Staffordshire Regt, 1915–17; France, 1915 (wounded); Lieut, 1916; transferred to RFC, 1917; Egypt, 1917–20; Iraq, 1920; Air Ministry, 1921–28; Staff College, 1929; Headquarters, India, 1930–35; Wing Commander, 1937; War of 1939–45 (despatches, CBE): Group Captain, 1940; Headquarters, Far East, 1938–40; USA, 1940–43; Air Commodore, 1943; COSSAC Staff, 1943–44; SHAEF, 1944–45; Air Div. CCG, 1945–46; Senior Air Staff Officer, Headquarters Maintenance Command, 1947–49; Director-General of Equipment, Air Ministry, 1949–52; retired, 1952. *Address:* Quob Farm, Wickham, Hants PO17 5PG. *Clubs:* Royal Air Force Yacht; Tamesis Sailing. *Died 21 Aug. 1991.*

TRISTRAM, William John, CBE 1965; JP; FRPharmS; pharmaceutical chemist; Liverpool City Council, 1934–55 (Alderman, 1944–55; appointed Hon. Alderman, 1964); Lord Mayor of Liverpool, 1953–54 (Deputy Lord Mayor, 1954–55); *b* 6 Oct. 1896; *s* of late Rev. W. J. Tristram and Elizabeth Critchlow; *m* 1966, Philomena Mary Moylan (*d* 1986), Drogheda. *Educ:* Scarborough High Sch.; Leeds Central High Sch.; Liverpool College of Pharmacy. Member Council Pharmaceutical Society of Great Britain, 1944–67 (President, 1952–53, FPS 1966, Gold Medal, 1968); Hon. Treasurer and Member Executive National Pharmaceutical Union, 1936–68 (Chairman, 1943–44); Chairman, Joint Cttee for the Pharmaceutical Service, 1946–52; Member Central Health Services Council (Min. of Health), 1948–64; Vice-Chairman, Standing Pharmaceutical Advisory Cttee (Min. of Health), 1946–48 (Chairman, 1948–59); Chairman, Liverpool Licensing Cttee, 1965–70; Dep. Chairman, South Liverpool Hospitals Management Cttee, 1965–70; Mem., Liverpool Exec. Council (Min. of Health), 1948–70 (Chairman, 1960–64); Chairman, Liverpool Homœopathic Hospital, 1960–70. Pres., Heswall Br., Royal British Legion. JP Liverpool, 1938. *Recreations:* cricket-watching, walking. *Address:* Fairfield Nursing Home, 10 Quarry Road East, Heswall, Wirral, Merseyside L61 6XD. *T:* 051–342 7618. *Clubs:* National Liberal; Lyceum (Liverpool). *Died 8 Sept. 1992.*

TROUGHTON, Sir Charles (Hugh Willis), Kt 1977; CBE 1966; MC 1940; TD 1959; Director, Whitbread Investment Co. Ltd, since 1981; *b* 27 Aug. 1916; *o s* of late Charles Vivian and Constance Scylla Troughton; *m* 1947, Constance Gillean Mitford, DL, OStJ, *d* of Colonel Philip Mitford, Berryfield House, Lentran, Inverness-shire; three *s* one *d. Educ:* Haileybury Coll.; Trinity Coll., Cambridge. BA 1938. Joined TA, 38; served War of 1939–45, Oxford and Bucks Light Infantry; Prisoner of War, 1940–45. Called to the Bar, 1945. Dir, 1949–77 and Chm., 1972–77, W. H. Smith & Son (Holdings) Ltd; Dir, 1967–87 and Chm., 1977–80, Electric & General Investment Co.; former Dir, Equity & Law Life Assce Soc. Ltd; Director: Thomas Tilling Ltd, 1973–79; Barclays Bank UK Management Ltd, 1973–81; Barclays Bank Internat., 1977–82; Whitbread & Co. Ltd, 1978–85; Times Newspaper Hldgs Ltd, 1983–88; Wm Collins and Sons, 1977–89 (a Vice-Chm., 1984–85, Dep. Chm., 1985–89). President: British Council, 1985– (Chm., 1977–84); National Book League, 1985–. Member: Board of Management of NAAFI, 1953–73; Design Council, 1975–78; Council, RCA, 1977–79; Governor, LSE,

1975–90. Chm., Brit. Kidney Patient Assoc. Investment Trust, 1982–87. *Address:* Little Leckmelm House, by Garve, Lochbroom, Ross and Cromarty IV23 2RH; 104 Cranmer Court, Whiteheads Grove, SW3 3HJ. *Clubs:* Garrick, MCC. *Died 13 May 1991.*

TROUGHTON, Henry Lionel, BSc(Eng), CEng, FIMechE, MIEE; Deputy Director, Projects and Research, Military Vehicles and Engineering Establishment, Ministry of Defence, 1970–74; *b* 30 March 1914; *o s* of late Henry James Troughton; *m* 1940, Dorothy Janet Louie (*née* Webb); one *d. Educ:* Mill Hill Sch.; University Coll., London. War of 1939–45: commissioned REME (Major), 1940–47; Fighting Vehicles Research and Development Estabt, 1947 (subseq. Mil. Vehicles and Engineering Estabt); Asst Dir (Electrical), later Asst Dir (Power Plant), and Dep. Dir (Vehicles), 1960; retired 1974. *Recreations:* gardening, travel. *Address:* 3 Northcroft Court, South Warnborough, near Basingstoke, Hants RG25 1RW. *Died 26 Dec. 1993.*

TRYPANIS, Constantine Athanasius, MA (Oxon); DLitt (Oxon) 1970; DPhil (Athens); FRSL; Secretary-General, 1981–85, President, 1986, Academy of Athens; Minister of Culture and Science, Government of Greece, 1974–77; *b* Chios, 22 Jan. 1909; *s* of Athanasius and Maria Zolota; *m* 1942, Alice Macri; one *d. Educ:* Chios Gymnasium; Universities of Athens, Berlin and Munich. Classical Lecturer, Athens Univ., 1939–47; Bywater and Sotheby Professor of Byzantine and Modern Greek Language and Literature, and Fellow of Exeter Coll., Oxford, 1947–68; Emeritus Fellow, 1968–; Univ. Prof. of Classics, Chicago Univ., 1968–74, Emeritus Prof., 1974–. Gray Lectr, Cambridge Univ., 1947. Mem. Poetry Panel, Arts Council of GB, 1962–65. FRSL, 1958; Hon. FBA 1978; Life Fellow, International Institute of Arts and Letters, 1958; Member Institute for Advanced Study, Princeton, USA, 1959–60; Visiting Professor: Hunter Coll., New York, 1963; Harvard Univ., 1963, 1964; Univ. of Chicago, 1965–66; Univ. of Cape Town, 1969; Univ. of Vienna, 1971. Corresp. Mem., Inst. for Balkan Studies (Greece); Member: Athens Academy, 1974 (Corresp. Mem., 1971); Medieval Acad. of America; Accademia Tiburina, Rome, 1982. Hon. Fellow, Internat. Poetry Soc., 1977; Fellow: Greek Archaeol. Soc., 1985; Soc. for Promotion of Greek Letters, 1985; Hon. Mem., Soc. for Promotion of Hellenic Studies, 1979; Hon. MRIA 1988. Dr of Humane Letters *hc*: MacMurray Coll., USA, 1974; Assumption Coll., 1977. Gottfried von Herder Prize, Vienna Univ., 1983. Ordre des Arts et des Lettres; Ordre National du Mérite. Archon Megas Hieromnemon of the Oecumenical Patriarchate, 1972. *Publications:* Influence of Hesiod upon Homeric Hymn of Hermes, 1939; Influence of Hesiod upon Homeric Hymn on Apollo, 1940; Alexandrian Poetry, 1943; Tartessos, 1945; Medieval and Modern Greek Poetry, 1951; Pedasus, 1955; Callimachus, 1956; The Stones of Troy, 1956; The Cocks of Hades, 1958; (with P. Maas) Sancti Romani Melodi Cantica, 1963, vol. II, 1970; Pompeian Dog, 1964; The Elegies of a Glass Adonis, 1967; Fourteen Early Byzantine Cantica, 1968; (ed) The Penguin Book of Greek Verse, 1971; The Glass Adonis, 1973; The Homeric Epics, 1975; Greek Poetry: from Homer to Seferis, 1981; Atticism and the Greek Language Question, 1984; Skias Onar (poems in Greek), 1986; (trans.) Sophocles, Three Theban Plays, 1986; Katalepton (poems in Greek), 1990; articles in Enc. Brit., Oxford Classical Dictionary and in classical and literary periodicals. *Recreations:* walking, tennis, painting. *Address:* 3 Georgiou Nikolaou Kefisia, 14561 Athens, Greece. *Clubs:* Athenæum; Athens. *Died 18 Jan. 1993.*

TRYTHALL, Rear-Adm. John Douglas, CB 1970; OBE 1953; *b* 21 June 1914; *er s* of Alfonso Charles Trythall,

Camborne, and Hilda Elizabeth (*née* Monson); *m* 1943, Elizabeth Loveday (*née* Donald); two *s* two *d. Educ:* Stretford Grammar Sch. Cadet, 1931; appointments in Home Fleet, America and West Indies, East Indies; lent to RNZN, 1939; Battle of River Plate; Western Approaches; BJSM, Washington; Pacific; Hong Kong; Mediterranean; Secretary to: Second Sea Lord, C-in-C The Nore, and C-in-C Plymouth; Asst Director of Plans, 1960–62; Captain of the Fleet, Medit., 1964–65; Head of Personnel Panel, MoD, 1966–67; subseq. on MoD Cttee; Asst Chief, Personnel and Logistics, MoD, 1969–72. JSSC, 1953; IDC, 1963. Commander, 1949; Captain, 1959; Rear-Admiral, 1968; retired 1972. Admiralty Bd's Governor on RN Benevolent Trust, 1972–79 (Vice Patron, 1980–). Chm., Taunton Constituency Cons. Assoc., 1974–75. FCIS 1956. Commander and Commissioner, St John Ambulance in Somerset, 1975–82. KStJ 1982 (OStJ 1973, CStJ 1977). *Address:* The Old Vicarage, Corfe, Taunton, Som. *T:* Blagdon Hill (082342) 463. *Club:* MCC.

Died 24 Feb. 1991.

TUBBS, Oswald Sydney, FRCS; Consulting Surgeon: in Cardiothoracic Surgery, St Bartholomew's Hospital; to Brompton Hospital; *b* 21 March 1908; *s* of late Sydney Walter Tubbs, The Glebe, Hadley Common, Hertfordshire; *m* 1934, Marjorie Betty Wilkins (*d* 1976); one *s* one *d. Educ:* Shrewsbury School; Caius College, Cambridge; St Bartholomew's Hospital. MA, MB, BCh; FRCS 1935. Surgical training at St Bartholomew's Hosp. and Brompton Hosp. Dorothy Temple Cross Fellowship, spent as Surgical Fellow at Lahey Clinic, Boston, USA. Served War of 1939–45, in EMS. Consulting Chest Surgeon to Royal Navy, Papworth Village Settlement and to various Local Authorities. President: Soc. of Thoracic and Cardiovascular Surgeons of GB and Ireland, 1971–72; Thoracic Soc., 1973. *Publications:* papers on surgical subjects. *Recreations:* fishing, gardening. *Address:* The White Cottage, 136 Coast Road, West Mersea, Colchester, Essex CO5 8PA. *T:* Colchester (0206) 382355.

Died 12 Nov. 1993.

TUCKER, Rt Rev. Cyril James, CBE 1975; *b* 17 Nov. 1911; British; *s* of Henry Castledine and Lilian Beatrice Tucker; *m* 1936, Kathleen Mabel, *d* of Major Merry; one *s* two *d. Educ:* Highgate Sch.; St Catharine's Coll., Cambridge (MA; athletics blue, 1934); Ridley Hall, Cambridge. MA Oxford (by Incorporation), 1951. Deacon, 1935; priest, 1936; Curate, St Mark's, Dalston (in charge Highgate Sch. Mission), 1935; Curate, St Barnabas, Cambridge, 1937; Youth Sec., British and Foreign Bible Soc., 1938; Chaplain, RAFVR, 1939–46; Warden of Monmouth Sch., 1946; Chaplain, Wadham Coll., Oxford, and Chaplain of the Oxford Pastorate, 1949; Vicar of Holy Trinity, Cambridge, 1957–63; Rural Dean of Cambridge, 1959–63; Chaplain of the Cambridge Pastorate, 1957–63; Bishop in Argentina and Eastern S America, 1963–75; Bishop of the Falkland Islands, 1963–76. Hon. Exec. Dir, Argentine Dio. Assoc., 1976–83. *Publications:* contrib. Encyclopaedia Britannica. *Recreations:* walking, fishing. *Address:* 202 Gilbert Road, Cambridge CB4 3PB. *T:* Cambridge (0223) 358345. *Clubs:* Hawks (Cambridge); Hurlingham (Buenos Aires). *Died 3 Sept. 1992.*

TUCKER, Edward William, CB 1969; Head of Royal Naval Engineering Service, 1966–70; Director of Dockyards, Ministry of Defence, at Bath, 1967–70, retired; *b* 3 Nov. 1908; *s* of Henry Tucker, Plymouth; *m* 1935, Eva (*d* 1986), *d* of Arthur Banks, Plymouth; one *s* two *d. Educ:* Imperial Coll. of Science and Technology, London Univ.; Royal Naval Coll., Greenwich. BSc (Eng). Electrical Engineer in Admiralty service, at Plymouth, London, Hong Kong and Bath, 1935–64; General Manager of HM Dockyard, Chatham, 1964–66. *Recreation:* bridge.

Address: 18 Salt Quay Moorings, Embankment Road, Kingsbridge, Devon. *T:* Kingsbridge (01548) 856894.

Died 12 Sept. 1995.

TUCKER, Robert St John P.; *see* Pitts-Tucker.

TUCKER, William Eldon, CVO 1954; MBE 1944; TD 1951; FRCS; retired; formerly Honorary Orthopædic Surgeon, Royal London Homœopathic Hospital; Director and Surgeon, The Clinic, Park Street, 1936–80; *b* 6 Aug. 1903; *s* of late Dr W. E. Tucker, Hamilton, Bermuda; *m* 1931, Jean Stella (marr. diss. 1953), *d* of James Ferguson, Rudgwick, Sussex; two *s*; *m* 1956, Mary Beatrice Castle (*d* 1987). *Educ:* Sherborne; Gonville and Caius Coll., Cambridge. MA 1931; FRCS 1930; MB, BCh 1946. Lt RAMC, TA, 1930–34; Major RAMC, Orthopædic Specialist, 1939–45; Lt-Col, RAMC, TA, 1946–51; Col and Hon. Col 17th General Hospital, TA, 1951–63. St George's Hospital, 1925–34; Surgeon, St John's Hosp., Lewisham, 1931–37; Registrar, Royal Nat. Orthop. Hosp. 1933–34; Orthopædic Consultant, Horsham Hosp., 1945, Dorking Hosp., 1956. Hunterian Prof., RCS, Oct. 1958. Fellow, British Orthopædic Assoc.; Corresp. Mem., Amer. Orthopædic Assoc.; Emeritus Mem., Société Internationale de Chirurgie Orthopaedique et Traumatologie. Vice-Pres., Amateur Dancing Assoc.; Pres. and Patron, Blackheath Football Club. Past Master, Co. of Makers of Playing Cards. *Publications:* Active Alerted Posture, 1960; Home Treatment in Injury and Osteoarthritis, 1961, new edn, Home Treatment and Posture in Injury, Rheumatism and Osteoarthritis, 1969; (with J. R. Armstrong) Injury in Sport, 1964; (with Molly Castle) Sportsmen and their Injuries, 1978. *Recreations:* tennis, Rugby football exec. (formerly Cambridge XV, Captain 1925; England XV, 1926–30, 3 caps); ball-room dancing. *Address:* West Dunes, 44 South Road, Paget, Bermuda PG 04. *T:* (809) 236–4637. *Clubs:* Pilgrims, MCC (Hon. Life Mem.); Middlesex CC (Life Vice-Pres.), Surrey CC (Life Vice-Pres.); Royal Bermuda Yacht, Royal Hamilton Amateur Dinghy. *Died 4 Aug. 1991.*

TUDOR, Sir James Cameron, KCMG 1987 (CMG 1970); High Commissioner for Barbados in Canada, since 1990; *b* St Michael, Barbados, 18 Oct. 1919; *e s* of James A. Tudor, JP, St Michael, Barbados; unmarried. *Educ:* Roebuck Boys' Sch.; Combermere Sch.; Harrison Coll., Barbados; Lodge Sch.; (again) Harrison Coll.; Keble Coll., Oxford, 1939–43. BA Hons (Mod. Greats), 1943, MA 1948; Pres., Oxford Union, 1942. Broadcaster, BBC: Lobby Correspondent (Parliament); Overseas Service, 1942–44; Lectr, Extra-Mural Dept, Reading Univ., 1944–45; History Master, Combermere Sch., Barbados, 1946–48; Civics and History Master, Queen's Coll., British Guiana, 1948–51; Sixth Form Master, Modern High Sch., Barbados, 1952–61, also free-lance journalist, lectr, broadcaster, over the same period. Mem., Barbados Lab. Party, 1951–52; MLC, Barbados, 1954–72; Foundn Mem., Democratic Lab. Party, 1955 (Gen. Sec., 1955–63); Third Vice-Chm., 1964–65 and 1965–66). Minister of: Educn, 1961–67; of State for Caribbean and Latin American Affairs, 1967–71 (Leader of the House, 1965–71); of External Affairs, 1971–72 (Leader of the Senate, 1971–72); High Comr for Barbados in UK, 1972–75; Perm. Rep. of Barbados to UN, 1976–79; Minister of Foreign Affairs and Leader of the Senate, 1986–89. Mem. Council, Univ. of the West Indies, 1962–65; awarded US State Dept Foreign Leader Grant, to study US Educn Instns, 1962. Silver Star, Order of Christopher Columbus (Dominican Republic), 1969. *Recreations:* reading, lecturing; keen on Masonic and other fraternities. *Address:* Barbados High Commission, 368 Lisgar Road, Rockcliffe Park, Ont K1M 0E9, Canada; Lemon Grove, Westbury New Road, St Michael, Barbados. *Died 9 July 1995.*

TUKE, Comdr Seymour Charles, DSO 1940; Royal Navy; *b* 20 May 1903; 3rd *s* of late Rear-Adm. J. A. Tuke; *m* 1928, Marjorie Alice Moller (*d* 1985); one *s* one *d. Educ:* Stonyhurst; RNC, Osborne and Dartmouth. Midshipman, 1921; Lieutenant, 1926; Acting Commander, 1945; FAA, 1927–29; Local Fishery Naval Officer, English Channel, 1935–37; served War of 1939–45 (DSO, 1939–45 Medal, Atlantic Star, Italy Star, War Medal); in command of SS Hannah Boge (first prize of the war), 1939; Senior Officer Res. Fleet, Harwich, 1946; Maintenance Comdr to Senior Officer Res. Fleet, 1947–48; retired, 1948. *Address:* c/o National Westminster Bank, 32 Market Place, Cirencester, Glos GL7 2NW. *Died 11 Oct. 1994.*

TULLIS, Major Ramsey; Vice Lord-Lieutenant of Clackmannanshire, since 1974; farmer, retired 1987; *b* 16 June 1916; *s* of late Major J. Kennedy Tullis, Tullibody, Clackmannanshire; *m* 1943, Daphne Mabon, *d* of late Lt-Col H. L. Warden, CBE, DSO, Edinburgh; three *s. Educ:* Trinity Coll., Glenalmond; Worcester Coll., Oxford (BA). 2nd Lieut, Cameronians, 1936; served War, 1939–45: Cameronians, Parachute Regt; Major 1943; psc 1949; retired, 1958. Income Tax Comr, 1964–90. County Comr for Scouts, Clackmannanshire, 1958–73; Mem. Cttee, Council of Scout Assoc., 1967–72; Activities Comr, Scottish HQ, Scout Assoc., 1974. Chm. Visiting Cttee, Glenochil Young Offenders Instn and Detention Centre, 1974–83. Clackmannanshire: JP 1960, DL 1962. *Recreations:* golf, gardening. *Address:* Woodacre, Pool of Muckhart, by Dollar, Clackmannanshire FK14 7JW. *Club:* Senior Golfers' Society. *Died 9 Dec. 1991.*

TURNBULL, Sir George (Henry), Kt 1990; BSc (Hons); CEng, FIMechE, FIProdE; Chairman and Chief Executive, Inchcape PLC, 1986–91 (Group Managing Director, 1984–86; Group Chief Executive, 1985–86); *b* 17 Oct. 1926; *s* of Bartholomew and Pauline A. Turnbull; *m* 1950, Marion Wing; one *s* two *d. Educ:* King Henry VIII Sch., Coventry; Birmingham Univ. (BSc (Hons)). PA to Techn. Dir, Standard Motors, 1950–51; Liaison Officer between Standard Motors and Rolls Royce, 1951–53; Exec., i/c Experimental, 1954–55; Works Manager, Petters Ltd, 1955–56; Standard Motors: Divl Manager Cars, 1956–59; Gen. Man., 1959–62; Standard Triumph International: Dir and Gen. Man., 1962; Dep. Chm., 1969; British Leyland Motor Corporation Ltd: Dir, 1967; Dep. Man. Dir, 1968–73; Man. Dir, 1973; Man. Dir, BL Austin Morris Ltd, 1968–73; Chm., Truck & Bus Div., BL, 1972–73; Vice-Pres. and Dir, Hyundai Motors, Seoul, South Korea, 1974–77; Consultant Advr to Chm. and Man. Dir, Iran Nat. Motor Co., Tehran, 1977–78; Dep. Man. Dir, 1978–79; Chm., Talbot UK, 1979–84. Director: Bank in Liechtenstein (UK) Ltd, 1988–90; Kleinwort Benson Group plc, 1988–91; Westland Group plc, 1991. Pres., SMMT, 1982–84 (Dep. Pres., 1984–86); Chairman: Industrial Soc., 1987–90; Korea-Europe Fund Ltd, 1987–91; Dir, Euro-Asia Centre, 1987–91; Mem. Council, Birmingham Chamber of Commerce and Industry, 1972 (Vice-Pres., 1973); past Member: Careers Adv. Bd, Univ. of Warwick; Management Bd, Engineering Employers' Assoc.; Engineering Employers' Fedn; Engrg Industry Trng Bd. Governor, Bablake Sch., Coventry. FIMI; Fellow, Inst. of Directors. *Recreations:* golf, tennis, fishing. *Address:* c/o Inchcape plc, St James's House, 23 King Street, SW1Y 6QY. *T:* 071–321 0110; *Telex:* 885395; *Fax:* 071–321 0604. *Died 22 Dec. 1992.*

TURNBULL, Reginald March Graham; *b* 10 Jan. 1907; *s* of late Sir March and Lady (Gertrude) Turnbull; *m* twice; one *s. Educ:* Horton Sch.; Eton; Trinity Coll., Cambridge (MA). Family shipping firm, Turnbull, Scott & Co., 1928–77 (Chm.); Dep. Chm., Lloyd's Register of Shipping, 1961–77. *Recreations:* teaching golf, motoring,

New River, water mills. *Address:* Sarum, Church Lane, Worplesdon, Surrey GU3 3RU. *Died 17 April 1995.*

TURNER, Rt Hon. Sir Alexander (Kingcome), KBE 1973; Kt 1963; PC 1968; *b* Auckland, New Zealand, 18 Nov. 1901; *s* of J. H. Turner; *m* 1934, Dorothea F., *d* of Alan Mulgan; two *s* one *d. Educ:* Auckland Grammar Sch.; Auckland Univ. (Scholar). BA 1921; MA 1922; LLB 1923. Served War of 1939–45, National Military Reserve, New Zealand. Barrister and Solicitor, 1923; QC (NZ) 1952. Carnegie Travelling Fellowship, 1949. Judge of the Supreme Court of New Zealand, 1953–62; Senior Resident Judge at Auckland, 1958–62; Judge of Court of Appeal, 1962–71, Pres., 1972–73. President, Auckland University Students' Assoc., 1928; President, Auckland District Court of Convocation, 1933; Member, Auckland Univ. Council, 1935–51; Vice-President, Auckland Univ., 1950–51; a Governor, Massey Agricultural Coll., 1944–53. Hon. LLD Auckland, 1965. *Publications:* (with George Spencer Bower) The Law of Estoppel by Representation, 1966; Res Judicata, 1969; The Law of Actionable Misrepresentation, 1974. *Recreations:* gardening, golf, bush conservation, agriculture. *Address:* 14 St Michael's Crescent, Kelburn, Wellington 5, New Zealand. *T:* (4) 757768. *Clubs:* Wellington; Auckland. *Died 6 July 1993.*

TURNER, Adm. Sir (Arthur) Francis, KCB 1970 (CB 1966); DSC 1945; Chief of Fleet Support, Ministry of Defence, 1967–71; *b* 23 June 1912; *s* of Rear-Admiral A. W. J. Turner and Mrs A. M. Turner (*née* Lochrane); *m* 1963, Elizabeth Clare de Trafford; two *s. Educ:* Stonyhurst Coll. Entered RN, 1931; Commander, 1947; Captain, 1956; Rear-Admiral, 1964; Vice-Admiral, 1968; Admiral, 1970. Dir.-Gen. Aircraft (Navy), MoD, 1966–67. *Recreations:* cricket, golf. *Address:* Plantation House, East Horsley, Surrey. *Clubs:* Army and Navy; Union (Malta). *Died 26 Oct. 1991.*

TURNER, Air Cdre Clifford John, CB 1973; MBE 1953; *b* 21 Dec. 1918; *s* of J. E. Turner; *m* 1942, Isabel Emily Cormack; two *s. Educ:* Parkstone Grammar Sch.; RAF Techn. College. Engrg Apprentice, 1935–38; various RAF engrg appts, 1938–64; Group Dir, RAF Staff Coll., 1965–67; Stn Comdr, RAF Colerne, 1968–69; AO Engineering, Training Comd, 1969–73. *Address:* Garnet Drive, Vernon, RR4, BC V1T 6L7, Canada. *Died 30 July 1992.*

TURNER, Brig. Dame Evelyn Marguerite, (Brig. Dame Margot), DBE 1965 (MBE 1946); RRC 1956; Matron-in-Chief and Director Army Nursing Service, 1964–68; *b* 10 May 1910; *d* of late Thomas Frederick Turner and Molly Cecilia (*née* Bryan). *Educ:* Finchley County Sch., Middlesex. Trained at St Bartholomew's Hospital, London, 1931–35. Joined QAIMNS, 1937 (became QARANC, 1949); served in UK, India, Malaya, Hong Kong, Bermuda, Germany and Near East; POW Sumatra, Feb. 1942–Aug. 1945; Col Comdt, QARANC, 1969–74. CStJ 1966. *Relevant publication:* Will to Live: the story of Dame Margot Turner, by Sir John Smyth, 1970. *Recreations:* formerly: reading, photography, golf, tennis. *Address:* St Dunstan's, Pearson House, Abbey Road, Brighton BN2 1ES. *T:* Brighton (0273) 307811. *Died 24 Sept. 1993.*

TURNER, Sir Francis; *see* Turner, Sir A. F.

TURNER, Rev. Prof. Henry Ernest William, (Hugh), DD; Canon Residentiary, Durham Cathedral, 1950–73, then Canon Emeritus; Treasurer, 1956–73; Sub-Dean, 1959–73; Acting Dean, 1973; Van Mildert Professor of Divinity, Durham University, 1958–73, then Emeritus; *b* 14 Jan. 1907; *o s* of Henry Frederick Richard and Ethel Turner, Sheffield; *m* 1936, Constance Parker, *d* of Dr E.

P. Haythornthwaite, Rowrah, Cumberland; two *s*. *Educ:* King Edward VII Sch., Sheffield; St John's Coll., Oxford; Wycliffe Hall, Oxford. MA 1933; BD 1940; DD 1955. Deacon, 1931; priest, 1932; Curate, Christ Church, Cockermouth, 1931–34; Curate, Holy Trinity, Wavertree, 1934–35; Fellow, Chaplain and Tutor, Lincoln Coll., Oxford, 1935–50; Chaplain, RAFVR, 1940–45; Librarian, Lincoln Coll., 1945–48; Senior Tutor, Lincoln Coll., 1948–50; Lightfoot Prof. of Divinity, Durham Univ., 1950–58. Select Preacher, Oxford Univ., 1950–51; Bampton Lectr, Oxford, 1954. Member: Anglican delegation to Third Conference of World Council of Churches, Lund, 1952; Doctrine Commn of the Church of England, 1967–76; formerly Mem., Anglican-Presbyterian Conversations; Theological Consultant to Anglican Roman Catholic Conversations, 1970. *Publications:* The Life and Person of Jesus Christ, 1951; The Patristic Doctrine of Redemption, 1952; Jesus Master and Lord, 1953; The Pattern of Christian Truth (Bampton Lectures), 1955; Why Bishops?, 1955; The Meaning of the Cross, 1959; (jt author with H. Montefiore) Thomas and the Evangelists, 1962; Historicity and the Gospels, 1963; Jesus the Christ, 1976; contributions to the Guardian, Theology and Church Quarterly Review. *Address:* Realands, Eskdale, near Holmrook, Cumbria CA19 1TW. *T:* Eskdale (019467) 23321. *Died 14 Dec. 1995.*

TURNER, Brig. Dame Margot; *see* Turner, Brig. Dame E. M.

TURNER, Prof. Paul, CBE 1992; MD; FRCP, FFPM; Professor of Clinical Pharmacology, University of London and Consultant Physician, St Bartholomew's Hospital, 1972–93, then Emeritus Professor; *b* 16 April 1933; *s* of Leonard Percy and Florence Maud Turner; *m* 1st, 1954, Margaret Diana Doris Manton (marr. diss. 1967); one *d*; 2nd, 1968, Kathleen Weaver; one *d*. *Educ:* Roan Sch. for Boys, Blackheath; Middlesex Hosp. Med. Sch. (BSc Hons Anatomy, MB BS, MD). MRCP 1962, FRCP 1973; FFPM 1990; MRPharmS 1977. House Officer, Middlesex Hosp., 1959–60; Sen. House Officer, Royal Free Hosp., 1960–61; Med. Registrar, Edgware Gen. Hosp., 1961–62; St Bartholomew's Hospital: Lectr in Pharmacology and Clinical Pharmacology, 1963–64; Sen. Lectr, 1965–66; Reader in Clinical Pharmacology and Hon. Consultant Physician, 1967–72. Chairman: Cttee of Toxicity, DoH, 1976–91; Adv. Bd on Homoeopathic Registration, DoH, 1994–; Vice-Chm., British Pharmacopeia Commn, 1980–. Pres., Med. Soc. of London, 1991–92; Vice-Pres., 1992–94, Academic Dean, 1994–, RSocMed. Mem. Court, Soc. of Apothecaries, 1989–. *Publications:* Clinical Aspects of Autonomic Pharmacology, 1969; Clinical Pharmacology, 1974, 5th edn 1986; Drug Treatment in Psychiatry, 1974, 4th edn 1988; Recent Advances in Clinical Pharmacology, 1978, 4th edn 1989; Drugs Handbook, 1978, 13th edn 1994; General and Applied Toxicology, 1993; papers in internat. medical, clinical pharmacological and toxicological jls. *Recreations:* organ, piano, travel, reading, food and wine. *Address:* 2 Englemere Wood, Kings Ride, Ascot, Berks SL5 8DE. *T:* Bracknell (01344) 21541; 62 Defoe House, Barbican, EC2Y 8DN. *T:* 0171–638 5946. *Clubs:* Athenæum, Royal Society of Medicine. *Died 25 Dec. 1994.*

TURNER, Philip, CBE 1975; LLB (London); in private practice with Infields, Hampton Wick, Surrey, 1978–91; *b* 1 June 1913; *er s* of late George Francis and late Daisy Louise Turner (*née* Frayn), Alverstoke, Hants; *m* 1938, Hazel Edith, *d* of late Douglas Anton and late Edith Ada Benda; one *d* (and one *d* decd). *Educ:* Peter Symonds, Winchester. Admitted Solicitor, 1935. Entered General Post Office Solicitor's Dept, 1935. Served in Royal Navy, 1940–46 (Lt-Comdr). Asst Solicitor to General Post Office, 1953; Principal Asst Solicitor, 1962–72, Solicitor

to the Post Office, 1972–75; temp. mem. of legal staff, DoE, 1976–77. Chm., Civil Service Legal Soc., 1957–58; Chm., Internat. Bar Assoc.'s Cttee on Public Utility Law, 1972–77. FRSA 1955. *Recreations:* piano, golf. *Address:* 8 Walters Mead, Ashtead, Surrey KT21 2BP. *T:* Ashtead (01372) 273656. *Clubs:* Naval, Royal Automobile, Law Society; Hampshire County Cricket, Surrey County Cricket. *Died 14 Nov. 1995.*

TURNER, Raymond C.; *see* Clifford-Turner.

TURNER, Richard, CMG 1956; LRIBA; consultant architect, retired 1983; *b* 2 May 1909; *s* of Frederick Henry Turner; *m* 1933, Annie Elizabeth, *d* of late Rev. R. W. Gair; one *d*. *Educ:* Dame Alice Owen's School. Entered Office of Works, 1929; in charge of ME Office, 1938–47, centred in Istanbul and, later, Cairo; Asst Chief Architect, Min. of Works, 1951; Dir of Works (Overseas), 1960–65; Dir, Overseas Services, MPBW, 1965–69, retired. Mem., Esher UDC, 1969–72. *Address:* 2 Coburg Terrace, Sidmouth, Devon EX10 8NH. *T:* Sidmouth (0395) 513805. *Club:* Travellers'. *Died 2 July 1994.*

TURNER, Dr Richard Wainwright Duke, OBE 1945; Senior Research Fellow in Preventive Cardiology, University of Edinburgh, 1974–84, retired (Reader in Medicine, 1960–74); Senior Physician and Physician in Charge of the Cardiac Department, Western General Hospital, Edinburgh, 1946–74; *b* Purley, Surrey, 30 May 1909; *s* of Sydney Duke Turner, MD (General Practitioner), and Lilian Maude, *d* of Sir James Wainwright; *m* Paula, *d* of Henry Meulen, Wimbledon; three *s* one *d*. *Educ:* Epsom Coll.; Clare Coll., Cambridge; St Thomas' Hosp., London. 1st Class Hons Nat. Sci. Tripos, Cambridge, 1934; MA, MB, BChir Cantab 1934; MRCS, LRCP 1935; MRCP 1936; MD Cantab 1940; FRCP 1950; FRCPE 1952. Served in RAMC, 1939–45: UK, Egypt and Italy (Lt-Col); officer i/c Med. Div. 31st and 92nd British General Hospitals. Examiner in Medicine: Univs of Edinburgh and Leeds; RCP; RCPE. Chm., Coronary Prevention Group, 1978. Member: Assoc. Physicians of GB; British Cardiac Soc.; Hon. Member, Cardiol Socs of India and Pakistan. *Publications:* Diseases of Cardiovascular System in Davidson's Principles and Practice of Medicine, vols 1–11, 1952–65; Electrocardiography, 1963; Auscultation of the Heart, 1st edn 1963 to 6th edn 1984; contribs to British Heart Jl, Lancet, BMJ, Quarterly Jl of Med., American Heart Jl, etc. *Recreations:* travel, climbing, gardening, photography. *Address:* Cotterlings, Ditchling, Sussex BN6 8TS. *T:* Hassocks (07918) 3392; Cardiac Department, Western General Hospital, Edinburgh EH4 2XU. *T:* 031–332 2525. *Clubs:* Royal Over-Seas League; University Staff (Edinburgh). *Died 1 Sept. 1992.*

TURTON-HART, Sir Francis (Edmund), KBE 1963 (MBE 1942); *b* 29 May 1908; *s* of David Edwin Hart and Zoe Evelyn Turton; *m* 1947, Margaret Greaves; one *d*. *Educ:* Uppingham. Served with Royal Engineers, 1939–46 (Hon. Major, 1946). East Africa, 1924–38; Portugal, 1939; West Africa, 1946–65; Federal House of Representatives, Nigeria, 1956–60; President, Lagos Chamber of Commerce, 1960–63. *Recreations:* shooting, fishing, golf. *Address:* 28 Vincent Road, Kingsbridge, South Devon TQ7 1RP. *T:* Kingsbridge (0548) 2872. *Club:* Thurlestone Golf. *Died 6 Feb. 1993.*

TUSTIN, Arnold, MSc; FIEE; Professor Emeritus, retired; *b* 16 July 1899; *m* 1948, Frances Tustin; no *c*. *Educ:* King's Coll., Univ. of Durham. Subsequently Chief Asst Engineer, Metropolitan-Vickers Electrical Co., until 1945. Visiting Webster Prof., Massachusetts Inst. of Technology, 1953–54; Prof. of Electrical Engineering, Univ. of Birmingham, 1947–55; Prof. of Heavy Electrical

Engineering, Imperial Coll., Univ. of London, 1955–64. Chm. Measurement and Control Section, IEE, 1959–60; Chm. Research Adv. Council, Transport Commn, 1960. Hon. DTech Bradford, 1968. *Publications:* Direct Current Machines for Control Systems, 1952; The Mechanism of Economic Systems, 1953; (ed) Automatic and Manual Control, 1951. *Address:* 17 Orchard Lane, Amersham-on-the-Hill, Bucks HP6 5AA.			*Died 9 Jan. 1994.*

TWEEDIE, Jill Sheila; author, journalist, scriptwriter; *b* 22 May 1936; *d* of late Patrick Graeme Tweedie, CBE and of Sheila (*née* Whittall); *m* 1954, Count Bela Cziraky; one *s* one *d* (and one *s* decd); partner, 1963, Robert d'Ancona; one *s*; *m* 1973, Alan Brien. *Educ:* eight girls' schools, ranging from PNEU to GPDST and Switzerland. Columnist with the Guardian newspaper, 1969–88; freelance writer for Press, radio and television. Woman Journalist of the Year, IPC Nat. Press Awards, 1971; Granada TV Award, 1972. *Publications:* In The Name Of Love, 1979; It's Only Me, 1980; Letters from a Faint-hearted Feminist, 1982; More from Martha, 1983; Bliss (novel), 1984; Internal Affairs (novel), 1986; Eating Children (autobiog.), 1993. *Recreations:* getting out of London, getting back to London. *Address:* 15 Marlborough Yard, Marlborough Road, N19 4ND.
			Died 12 Nov. 1993.

TWEEDIE, Brig. John William, CBE 1958; DSO 1944; *b* 5 June 1907; *e s* of late Col William Tweedie, CMG, CBE and Violet Mary, *d* of Major T. Moore; *m* 1937, Sheila Mary, (*d* 1984), *d* of Brig.-Gen. Thomas Hudson, CB; one *s* one *d. Educ:* Ampleforth; Royal Military College, Sandhurst. 2/Lt Argyll and Sutherland Highldrs, 1926; Adjutant, 1935–39; OC 2nd Bn, 1942–44; Brigade Commander, 39 Inf. Bde, 1951–54; ADC to the Queen, 1959–61; retired 1961. DL Dumfries, 1975–84. Croix de Guerre, 1944. *Club:* Army and Navy.
			Died 27 July 1991.

TWISLETON-WYKEHAM-FIENNES, Sir Maurice (Alberic); *see* Fiennes.

TWISS, Adm. Sir Frank (Roddam), KCB 1965 (CB 1962); KCVO 1978; DSC 1945; Gentleman Usher of the Black Rod, House of Lords, 1970–78; Serjeant-at-Arms, House of Lords, and Secretary to the Lord Great Chamberlain, 1971–78; *b* 7 July 1910; *s* of Col E. K. Twiss, DSO; *m* 1st, 1936, Prudence Dorothy Hutchison (*d* 1974); two *s* one *d;* 2nd, 1978, Rosemary Maitland (*née* Howe), *widow* of Captain Denis Chilton, RN. *Educ:* RNC Dartmouth. Cadet 1924; Midshipman 1928; Lieut 1931; Comdr 1945; Captain 1950; Rear-Adm. 1960; Vice-Adm. 1963; Adm. 1967. Naval Sec., Admty, 1960–62; Flag Officer, Flotillas, Home Fleet, 1962–64; Comdr Far East Fleet, 1965–67; Second Sea Lord and Chief of Naval Personnel, 1967–70. Mem., Commonwealth War Graves Commn, 1970–79. *Recreations:* fishing, walking. *Address:* East Marsh Farm, Bratton, near Westbury, Wilts BA13 4RG. *Club:* Army and Navy.			*Died 26 Jan. 1994.*

TYLER, Cyril, DSc, PhD, FRSC; Professor of Physiology and Biochemistry, 1958–76, then Emeritus, and Deputy Vice-Chancellor, 1968–76, Reading University; *b* 26 Jan. 1911; *er s* of John and Annie Tyler; *m* 1st, 1939, Myra Eileen (*d* 1971), *d* of George and Rosa Batten; two *s* one *d;* 2nd, 1971, Rita Patricia, *d* of Sidney and Lilian Jones. *Educ:* Ossett Grammar Sch.; Univ. of Leeds (BSc 1st Class Hons 1933; PhD 1935; DSc 1959). Lectr in Agricultural Chemistry, RAC, Cirencester, 1935–39; University of Reading: Lecturer in Agricultural Chemistry, 1939–47; Professor, 1947–58; Dean of the Faculty of Agriculture, 1959–62. Playing Mem., Glos CCC, 1936–39. *Publications:* Organic Chemistry for Students of Agriculture, 1946; Animal Nutrition (2nd edn), 1964; Wilhelm von Nathusius 1821–1899 on Avian Eggshells,

1964; numerous papers on poultry metabolism and egg shells in scientific journals. *Recreations:* gardening, history of animal nutrition. *Address:* 22 Belle Avenue, Reading, Berks RG6 2BL.			*Died 25 Jan. 1995.*

TYLER, Maj.-Gen. Sir Leslie (Norman), KBE 1961 (OBE 1942); CB 1955; BScEng; CEng; FIMechE; *b* 26 April 1904; *s* of late Major Norman Tyler, Addiscombe, Surrey; *m* 1st, 1930, Louie Teresa Franklin (*d* 1950); one *s* one *d;* 2nd, 1953, Sheila, *d* of Eric Athelstane Field and *widow* of Maj.-Gen. L. H. Cox, CB, CBE, MC; two *s*, and two step *d. Educ:* Diocesan Coll., Rondebosch, SA; RN Colleges Osborne and Dartmouth; King's College, Univ. of London. Commissioned Lieut, RAOC, 1927; served War of 1939–45, Malta and NW Europe; transferred to REME, 1942; DDME, Second Army, 1945; Comdt REME Training Centre, 1945–47; AAG, War Office, 1948–49; DME, MELF, 1949–50; DDME, War Office, 1950–53; DME, MELF, 1953–55; Commandant, Headquarters Base Workshop Group, REME, 1956–57; Director of Electrical and Mechanical Engineering, War Office, 1957–60; retd 1960. Regional Dir, MPBW, Central Mediterranean Region, 1963–69. Chm., Royal Hosp. and Home for Incurables, Putney, 1971–76. Colonel Commandant, REME, 1962–67. Freeman, City of London; Liveryman, 1961, Master, 1982–83, Worshipful Company of Turners. FKC 1969. FRSA 1984. *Address:* 51 Chiltley Way, Liphook, Hants GU30 7HE. *T:* Liphook (0428) 722335. *Club:* Army and Navy.			*Died 6 Jan. 1992.*

TYRRELL, Gerald Fraser; former Buyer, Stewart Dry Goods Co., Louisville, USA, and London; retired 1974; *b* London, 7 March 1907; *s* of late Lt-Col G. E. Tyrrell, DSO, RA, and C. R. Tyrrell (*née* Fraser); *m* 1937, Virginia Lee Gettys, Louisville, Kentucky; three *s* one *d. Educ:* Eton; Magdalene Coll., Cambridge. Student Interpreter, China Consular Service, 1930; served in Tientsin, Chungking, Shanghai, Foochow, Canton; Vice-Consul at San Francisco, 1941; Vice-Consul, Boston, 1942, Acting Consul-General, 1944; 1st Secretary, Washington, 1945; Consul at Cincinnati, 1946; Acting Consul-General, New Orleans, 1947; Consul-General, Canton, 1948; Foreign Office, 1949, resigned, 1950. *Address:* 1201 Lyndon Lane, Louisville, KY 40222, USA.			*Died 27 July 1993.*

TYRRELL, Sir Murray (Louis), KCVO 1968 (CVO 1954); CBE 1959; JP; Official Secretary to Governor-General of Australia, 1947–73; *b* 1 Dec. 1913; *s* of late Thomas Michael and Florence Evelyn Tyrrell; *m* 1939, Ellen St Clair (*d* 1990), *d* of late E. W. St Clair Greig; one *s* two *d. Educ:* Orbost and Melbourne Boys' High Schools, Victoria. Central Office, Postmaster General's Department, Melbourne, 1929–39; Asst Private Secretary to Minister for Air and Civil Aviation, 1940; Private Secretary to Minister for Air, 1940, to Minister for Munitions, 1940; Personal Asst to Secretary, Min. of Munitions, 1942; Private Secretary to Commonwealth Treas. and Min. for Post-War Reconstruction, 1943, to Prime Minister and Treasurer, 1945; Official Secretary and Comptroller to Governor-General, 1947; resigned Comptrollership, 1953. Attached Royal Household, Buckingham Palace, May-Aug. 1962. Director: Nat. Heart Foundn of Australia, 1970–80; Canberra C of E Girls' Grammar Sch., 1952–65; Canberra Grammar Sch., 1954–65; Registrar, Order of St John of Jerusalem in Australia, 1976; Mem., Buildings and Grounds Cttee, ANU, 1974–80. Alderman, Queanbeyan CC, 1974–77; Mem., Southern Tablelands CC, 1974–77. KStJ (CStJ 1969). Australian of the Year, 1977. *Recreation:* fishing. *Address:* 136 Learmonth Drive, Kambah, ACT 2902, Australia.			*Died 13 July 1994.*

TYTLER, Christian Helen F.; *see* Fraser-Tytler.

TYTLER, Rt Rev. Donald Alexander; Bishop Suffragan of Middleton, since 1982; *b* 2 May 1925; *s* of Alexander and Cicely Tytler; *m* 1948, Jane Evelyn Hodgson (*d* 1990); two *d*. *Educ:* Eastbourne College; Christ's College, Cambridge (MA); Ridley Hall, Cambridge. Asst Curate of Yardley, Birmingham, 1949; SCM Chaplain, Univ. of Birmingham, 1952; Precentor, Birmingham Cathedral, 1955; Diocesan Director of Education, Birmingham, 1957; Vicar of St Mark, Londonderry and Rural Dean of Warley, dio. Birmingham, 1963; Canon Residentiary of Birmingham Cathedral, 1972; Archdeacon of Aston, 1977–82. *Publications:* Operation Think, 1963; (contrib.) Stirrings (essays), 1976. *Recreations:* music, gardening. *Address:* The Hollies, Manchester Road, Rochdale, Lancs OL11 3QY. *T:* Rochdale (0706) 358550.

Died 12 Nov. 1992.

U

UNDERHILL, Baron *cr* 1979 (Life Peer), of Leyton in Greater London; **Henry Reginall Underhill,** CBE 1976; *b* 8 May 1914; *s* of Henry James and Alice Maud Underhill; *m* 1937, Flora Janet Philbrick; two *s* one *d*. *Educ:* Norlington Road Elementary School; Tom Hood Central School, Leyton. Junior Clerk, C. A. Hardman & Sons Ltd, Lloyd's Underwriters, 1929; joined Labour Party, 1930; joined Labour Party Head Office as Junior Accounts Clerk, 1933; National Fire Service, 1939–45; Assistant to Mr Morgan Phillips, Labour Party Gen. Sec., 1945; Admin. Assistant to National Agent, 1945; Propaganda Officer, 1947; Regional Organiser, W Midlands, 1948; Assistant National Agent, 1960; National Agent, 1972–79. Vice-Chm. 1933, Hon. Sec. 1937–48, Leyton West Constituency Labour Party. House of Lords: Dep. Leader of the Opposition, 1982–89; Opposition front bench spokesman on transport, 1980–90, and on electoral affairs, 1983–. Pres., AMA, 1982–92. Member: APEX, 1931– (Life Mem. and Gold Badge); Nat. Union of Labour Organisers, 1945– (Hon. Mem.); Fire Bdes Union, 1939–45 (Br. Sec. and Chm., Dist, Div. and Area Cttees). Member: HO Electoral Adv. Cttee, 1970–79; Houghton Cttee on Financial Aid to Political Parties, 1975–76; Parly delegn to Zimbabwe, 1980 and to USSR, 1986; Kilbrandon Ind. Inquiry into New Ireland Forum, 1984. Hon. Sec., British Workers' Sports Assoc., 1935–37. *Recreations:* golf, life-long support of Leyton Orient FC, countryside rambling. *Address:* 94 Loughton Way, Buckhurst Hill, Essex IG9 6AH. *T:* 081–504 1910.

Died 12 March 1993.

UNDERWOOD, Michael; *see* Evelyn, J. M.

UPHAM, Captain Charles Hazlitt, VC 1941 and Bar, 1943; JP; sheep-farmer; *b* Christchurch, New Zealand, 21 Sept. 1908; *s* of John Hazlitt Upham, barrister, and Agatha Mary Upham, Christchurch, NZ; *m* 1945, Mary Eileen, *d* of James and Mary McTamney, Dunedin, New Zealand; three *d* (incl. twins). *Educ:* Waihi Prep. School, Winchester; Christ's Coll., Christchurch, NZ; Canterbury Agric. Coll., Lincoln, NZ (Diploma). Post-grad. course in valuation and farm management. Farm manager and musterer, 1930–36; govt valuer, 1937–39; farmer, 1945–. Served War of 1939–45 (VC and Bar, despatches): volunteered, Sept. 1939; 2nd NZEF (Sgt 1st echelon advance party); 2nd Lt; served Greece, Crete, W Desert (VC, Crete; Bar, Ruweisat); Captain; POW, released 1945. *Relevant publication:* Mark of the Lion: The Story of Captain Charles Upham, VC and Bar (by Kenneth Sandford), 1962. *Recreations:* rowing, Rugby (1st XV Lincoln Coll., NZ). *Address:* Lansdowne, Hundalee, North Canterbury, NZ. *Clubs:* Canterbury, Christchurch, RSA (all NZ). *Died 22 Nov. 1994.*

URQUHART, Donald John, CBE 1970; Director General, British Library Lending Services, 1973–74; *b* 27 Nov. 1909; *s* of late Roderick and Rose Catherine Urquhart, Whitley Bay; *m* 1939, Beatrice Winefride, *d* of late W. G. Parker, Sheffield; two *s*. *Educ:* Barnard Castle School; Sheffield University (BSc, PhD). Research Dept, English Steel Corp., 1934–37; Science Museum Library, 1938–39; Admiralty, 1939–40; Min. of Supply, 1940–45; Science Museum Library, 1945–48; DSIR Headquarters, 1948–61; Dir, Nat. Lending Library for Science and Technology, 1961–73. Hon. Lectr, Postgrad. Sch. of Librarianship and Information Science, Sheffield Univ., 1970; Vis. Prof., Loughborough Univ. Dept of Library and Information Studies, 1973–80. Chm., Standing Conf. of Nat. and Univ. Libraries, 1969–71. FLA, Pres., Library Assoc., 1972. Hon. DSc: Heriot-Watt, 1974; Sheffield, 1974; Salford, 1974. Hon. Citation, Amer. Library Assoc., 1978. *Publications:* The Principles of Librarianship, 1981; Mr Boston Spa, 1990; papers on library and scientific information questions. *Recreation:* gardening. *Address:* Wood Garth, First Avenue, Bardsey, Leeds LS17 9BE. *T:* Collingham Bridge (01937) 573228. *Club:* Athenæum.

Died 2 Dec. 1994.

USHER, Sir Robert (Edward), 6th Bt *cr* 1899, of Norton, Midlothian, and of Wells, Co. Roxburgh; *b* 18 April 1934; *yr s* of Sir (Robert) Stuart Usher, 4th Bt, and Gertrude Martha (*d* 1984), 2nd *d* of Lionel Barnard Sampson; *S* brother, 1990. *Heir: kinsman* (William) John Tevenar Usher [*b* 18 April 1940; *m* 1962, Rosemary Margaret, *d* of Col Sir Reginald Houldsworth, 4th Bt, OBE, TD; two *s* one *d*]. *Died 26 Sept. 1994.*

UTIGER, Ronald Ernest, CBE 1977; Director: British Alcan Aluminium, 1982–95; National Grid Co., since 1990; *b* 5 May 1926; *s* of Ernest Frederick Utiger and Kathleen Utiger (*née* Cram); *m* 1953, Barbara Anna von Mohl; one *s* one *d*. *Educ:* Shrewsbury Sch.; Worcester Coll., Oxford (2nd cl. Hons PPE 1950; MA). Economist, Courtaulds Ltd, 1950–61; British Aluminium Ltd: Financial Controller, 1961–64; Commercial Dir, 1965–68; Man. Dir, 1968–79; Chm., 1979–82; BNOC: Dir, 1976–80; Chm., 1979–80; Tube Investments, subseq. TI Group: Dir, 1979–89; Dep. Chm. and Gp Man. Dir, 1982–84; Man. Dir, 1984–86; Chm., 1984–89. Dir, Ultramar, 1983–91. Member: NEDC, 1981–84; BBC Gen. Adv. Council, 1987–91. Chm., Internat. Primary Aluminium Inst., 1976–78; Pres., European Primary Aluminium Assoc., 1976–77. Chm., CBI Economic and Financial Policy Cttee, 1980–83; Mem., British Library Bd, 1987–95; Governor, NIESR, 1983– (Pres., 1986–94). FRSA; CIMgt (CBIM 1975). *Recreations:* music, gardening. *Address:* 9 Ailsa Road, St Margaret's-on-Thames, Twickenham TW1 1QJ. *T:* 0181–892 5810.

Died 27 July 1995.

V

van BELLINGHEN, Jean-Paul; Grand Officer, Order of Leopold; Grand Officer, Order of the Crown; Grand Officer, Order of Leopold II; Belgian Ambassador to the Court of St James's, 1984–90, retired; *b* 21 Oct. 1925; *s* of Albert and Fernande van Bellinghen; *m* Martine Vander Elst (*d* 1991); one *s* one *d* (and one *s* decd). *Educ:* Catholic University of Leuven. Fellow, Centre for Internat. Affairs, Harvard Univ.; Lectr, Univ. of Grenoble. Joined Diplomatic Service, 1953; served Cairo, Washington, New York (UN), Min. of Foreign Affairs, Geneva, 1968–74; Chef de Cabinet to Minister of Foreign Affairs, 1974–77, to Minister of Foreign Trade, 1977–79; Ambassador in Kinshasa, 1980–83. Numerous foreign decorations. *Publications:* Servitude in the Sky (Harvard Centre for Internat. Affairs), 1967; (contrib.) Modern Belgium, 1991. *Recreations:* golf, ski-ing, filming. *Address:* 8 Avenue de l'Orée, 1050 Brussels, Belgium. *Club:* Royal Anglo-Belgian. *Died 5 Dec. 1993.*

VAN OSS, (Adam) Oliver, MA; FSA; Master of the London Charterhouse, 1973–84; *b* 28 March 1909; *s* of S. F. Van Oss, The Hague, newspaper proprietor; *m* 1945, Audrey (*d* 1960), widow of Capt. J. R. Allsopp; two *d,* and two step *s*. *Educ:* Dragon Sch., Oxford; Clifton; Magdalen Coll., Oxford. Housemaster and Head of Modern Language Dept, Eton Coll.; Lower Master, Eton Coll., 1959–64; Acting Headmaster, 1964; Headmaster of Charterhouse, 1965–73. Mem. Council, City Univ. Chevalier de la Légion d'Honneur. *Publications:* Eton Days, 1976; (ed jtly) Cassell's French Dictionary, 8th edn; articles on ceramics, travel and education. *Recreations:* all forms of art and sport. *Address:* 7 Park Lane, Woodstock OX7 1UD. *Clubs:* Pratt's, Beefsteak.

Died 14 Nov. 1992.

van PRAAG, Louis, CBE 1986; FCSD; Senior Partner, Design Resource, since 1989; Chairman, Sabre International Group, 1976–88; Director, Sabre Group, 1958–88; *b* 9 Aug. 1926; *s* of Barend van Praag and Rosalie (*née* Monnickendam); *m* 1st, 1947, Angela McCorquodale; two *s* one *d*; 2nd, 1964, Kathy Titelman; one *s* two *d*. *Educ:* Owen's Sch.; Univ. of Paris, Sorbonne (LèsL). Member: Nat Council for Diplomas in Art and Design, 1971–74; CNAA, 1974–83; Chm., Design Res. Cttee, 1976–79; Mem., Nat. Adv. Body, Art and Design Bd, 1981–83; Chairman: DTI Wkg Party on Management of Design, 1980–84; DTI Steering Gp for Management of Design, 1989–93; DoE Wkg Party, Industry Lead Body for Design, 1989–90; Member: Financial Times Design Management Awards Cttee, 1987–92; Adv. Bd, Music at Oxford, 1988–; Design Adv. Cttee, London Business Sch., 1989–; Corporate Adv. Cttee, Design Mus., 1989–92; Chm., Industry Lead Body for Design, 1990. Royal College of Art: Chm., RCA Enterprises, 1979–83; Member: Council, 1979–83; Court, 1980–; Hon. Fellow, 1980. Chm., Mus. of Modern Art, Oxford, 1984–88; Mem. Adv. Bd, Ashmolean Museum, 1988–92; Mem. Council, Ecole Nat. Sup. de Création Industrielle, Paris, 1986–92; Gov., Winchester Coll. of Art, 1976–79; Mem., OU Validations Cttee, 1993–. Hon. Dr Des CNAA, 1987. Bicentenary Medal, RSA, 1989. *Publications:* various papers and articles on management of design. *Recreations:* walking, ski-ing, listening to traditional and modern jazz, opera and, sometimes, Schoenberg. *Address:* 53 St John Street, Oxford OX1 2LQ. *Died 1 June 1993.*

VARAH, (Doris) Susan, OBE 1976; *b* 29 Oct. 1916; *d* of Harry W. and Matilda H. Whanslaw; *m* 1940, Rev. (Edward) Chad Varah, OBE; four *s* (three of them triplets) one *d*. *Educ:* Trinity Coll. of Music. Mothers' Union: Diocesan Pres., Southwark, 1956–64; Vice-Chm., Central Young Members' Cttee, 1962–64; Central Vice-Pres., 1962–70; Vice-Chm., Central Social Problems Cttee, 1965–67, Chm., 1970–76; Chm., Central Overseas Cttee, 1968–70, 1977–82; Central Pres., 1970–76. *Recreations:* music, gardening, reading. *Address:* 42 Hillersdon Avenue, SW13 0EF. *T:* 081–876 5720.

Died 22 July 1993.

VASSAR-SMITH, Major Sir Richard Rathborne, 3rd Bt, *cr* 1917, of Charlton Park, Charlton Kings, Co. of Gloucester; TD; late Royal Artillery; Partner at St Ronan's Preparatory School, since 1957; *b* 24 Nov. 1909; *s* of late Major Charles Martin Vassar-Smith (2nd *s* of 1st Bt) and Gladys Emmeline, *d* of Col William Hans Rathborne, RE; *S* uncle, 1942; *m* 1932, Mary Dawn, *d* of late Sir Raymond Woods, CBE; one *s* one *d*. *Educ:* Lancing; Pembroke College, Cambridge. Employed by Lloyds Bank Ltd, 1932–37; schoolmaster, 1938–39. War of 1939–45, Major, RA. *Recreation:* Association football (Cambridge, 1928–31). *Heir:* *s* John Rathborne Vassar-Smith [*b* 23 July 1936; *m* 1971, Roberta Elaine, *y d* of Wing Comdr N. Williamson; two *s*]. *Address:* Chestnut, Rye Road, Hawkhurst, Cranbrook, Kent TN18 4HD. *T:* Hawkhurst (01580) 752817. *Clubs:* Hawks (Cambridge); Kent County Cricket; Rye Golf. *Died 12 Aug. 1995.*

VAUGHAN, Sir (George) Edgar, KBE 1963 (CBE 1956; OBE 1937); HM Diplomatic Service, retired; *b* 24 Feb. 1907; *s* of late William John Vaughan, BSc, Cardiff, and Emma Kate Caudle; *m* 1st, 1933, Elsie Winifred Deubert (*d* 1982); one *s* two *d*; 2nd, 1987, Mrs Mary Sayers. *Educ:* Cheltenham Grammar Sch.; Jesus Coll., Oxford (Exhibitioner and later Hon. Scholar; Hon. Fellow, 1966). 1st Cl. Honour School of Mod. Hist., 1928; 1st Cl. Honour School of Philosophy, Politics and Economics, 1929; Laming Travelling Fellow of the Queen's College, Oxford, 1929–31. Entered Consular Service, 1930; Vice-Consul at: Hamburg, 1931; La Paz, 1932–35; Barcelona, 1935–38; Buenos Aires, 1938–44; Chargé d'Affaires, Monrovia, 1945–46; Consul at Seattle, Washington, 1946–49; Consul-General at Lourenço Marques, 1949–53; Amsterdam, 1953–56; Minister and Consul-General at Buenos Aires, 1956–60; Ambassador, 1960–63 and Consul-General, 1963, at Panama; Ambassador to Colombia, 1964–66. Univ. of Saskatchewan, Regina Campus: Special Lectr, 1966–67; Prof. of History, 1967–74; Dean of Arts and Science, 1969–73. FRHistS 1965. Order of Andrés Bello, First Class (Venezuela), 1990. *Publication:* Joseph Lancaster en Caracas 1824–1827 y sus relaciones con el Libertador Simón Bolívar, vol. 1 1987, vol. 2 1989. *Address:* 9 The Glade, Sandy Lane, Cheam, Surrey SM2 7NZ. *T:* 081–643 1958. *Club:* Royal Automobile. *Died 25 Jan. 1994.*

VAUGHAN, Henry William Campbell, JP; DL; Lord Provost and Lord Lieutenant of the City of Dundee, 1977–80; *b* 15 March 1919; *s* of Harry Skene Vaughan and Flora Lamont Campbell Blair; *m* 1947, Margaret Cowie Flett; one *s* one *d*. *Educ:* Dundee Training Coll.; Logie and Stobswell Secondary Schools. Apprentice

Stationer, Burns & Harris, 1934–39; RAF (Volunteer Reserve), 1939–46; Chief Buyer, Messrs Valentine & Son, Fine Art Publishers, Dundee, 1946–64; Group Purchasing Officer, Scott & Robertson (Tay Textiles Ltd), 1964–75; Stationery Manager, Burns & Harris Ltd, Dundee, 1975–78; Paper Sales Rep., James McNaughton Paper Gp Ltd, London, 1978–79. Mem., Inst. of Purchasing and Supply. JP Dundee, 1969; DL Dundee, 1980. Silver Jubilee Medal, 1977. *Recreations:* cine photography, fishing, water colour painting, sketching. *Address:* 15 Fraser Street, Dundee DD3 6RE. *T:* Dundee (0382) 826175.   *Died 11 March 1991.*

VAUGHAN, Dame Janet (Maria), DBE 1957 (OBE 1944); DM, FRCP; FRS 1979; Principal of Somerville College, Oxford, 1945–67, Hon. Fellow since 1967; *b* 18 Oct. 1899; *d* of William Wyamar Vaughan and Margaret Symonds; *m* 1930, David Gourlay (*d* 1963); two *d. Educ:* North Foreland Lodge; Somerville College, Oxford; University College Hospital (Goldsmith Entrance Scholar). Asst Clinical Pathologist, Univ. Coll. Hosp.; Rockefeller Fellowship, 1929–30; Beit Memorial Fellowship, 1930–33; Leverhulme Fellow, RCP, 1933–34; Asst in Clinical Pathology, British Post-Graduate Medical School, 1934–39; Mem. Inter-Departmental Cttee on Medical Schools, 1942; Nuffield Trustee, 1943; late Medical Officer in charge North-West London Blood Supply Depot for Medical Research Council. Mem., Royal Commn on Equal Pay, 1944; Chm., Oxford Regional Hosp. Board, 1950–51 (Vice-Chm. 1948); Member: Cttee on Economic and Financial Problems of Provision for Old Age, 1953–54; Medical Adv. Cttee of University Grants Cttee; University Grants Cttee on Libraries; Commonwealth Scholarship Commn in the UK. Fogarty Scholar, NIH, 1973. Hon. FRSM, 1980. Osler Meml Medal, Univ. of Oxford. Hon. Fellow: Wolfson Coll., Oxford, 1981; Girton Coll., Cambridge, 1986. Hon. DSc: Wales, 1960; Leeds, 1973; Hon. DCL: Oxford, 1967; London, 1968; Bristol, 1971. *Publications:* The Anæmias, 1934, 2nd edn 1936; The Physiology of Bone, 1969, 3rd edn 1981; The Effects of Irradiation on the Skeleton, 1973; numerous papers in scientific jls on blood diseases, blood transfusion and metabolism of strontium and plutonium isotopes; section on leukæmias, Brit. Ency. Med. Pract.; section on blood transfusion in British Surgical Practice, 1945. *Recreations:* travel, gardening. *Address:* 5 Fairlawn Flats, First Turn, Wolvercote, Oxford. *T:* Oxford (0865) 514069.   *Died 9 Jan. 1993.*

VAUGHAN-MORGAN, family name of **Baron Reigate.**

VEIRA, Sir Philip (Henry), KBE 1988 (OBE); merchant, since 1942; *b* 14 Aug. 1921; *s* of Benedict and Mary Veira; *m* 1943, Clara Lauretta; one *s* seven *d. Educ:* St Mary's Roman Catholic Sch., St Vincent. Knighted for public and philanthropic services. *Recreations:* fishing, reading. *Address:* Kingstown Park, St Vincent, West Indies.   *Died 17 May 1991.*

VERCORS, (Jean Marcel Bruller); Commandeur, Légion d'honneur; médaille de la Résistance; Commandeur des Arts et des Lettres; writer; designer-engraver (as Jean Bruller); *b* Paris, 26 Feb. 1902; *s* of Louis Bruller and E. Bourbon; *m* 1931, Jeanne Barusseaud (marr. diss.); three *s*; *m* 1956, Rita Barisse. *Educ:* Ecole Alsacienne, Paris. Dessinateur-graveur, 1926–; retrospective exhibitions: Vienna, 1970; Budapest, Cologne, 1971; exposition rétrospective de l'oeuvre graphique de Jean Bruller, Saint-Nazaire, 1989, Paris, 1990; designed set and costumes for Voltaire's L'Orphelin de la Chine, Comédie Française, 1965. *Plays produced include:* Zoo, Carcassonne, 1963, Paris, 1964, and other European countries and USA; Oedipe-Roi (adaptation), La Rochelle, 1967, Paris, 1970; Le Fer et le Velours, Nîmes, 1969; Hamlet (adaptation), Lyons, 1977; Macbeth (adaptation), Anjou, Paris and

Martinique, 1977. Founded Editions de Minuit clandestines, 1941, and began to publish under the name of Vercors. *Publications: as Jean Bruller:* albums: 21 Recettes de Mort Violente, 1926, repr. 1977; Hypothèses sur les Amateurs de Peinture, 1927; Un Homme Coupé en tranches, 1929; Nouvelle Clé des Songes, 1934; L'enfer, 1935; Visions intimes et rassurantes de la guerre, 1936; Silences, 1937; Les Relevés Trimestriels, planches dont l'ensemble (160 planches) forme La Danse des Vivants, 1932–38; nombreuses illustrations pour livres de luxe; *as Vercors:* Le Silence de la Mer, 1942; La Marche à l'Etoile, 1943; Le Songe, 1944; Le Sable du Temps, 1945; Les Armes de la Nuit, 1946; Les Yeux et la Lumière, 1948; Plus ou Moins Homme, 1950; La Puissance du jour, 1951; Les Animaux dénaturés (Borderline), 1952; Les Pas dans le Sable, 1954; Portrait d'une Amitié, 1954; Divagations d'un Français en Chine, 1956; Colères, 1956 (The Insurgents); PPC, 1957; Sur ce rivage (I Le Périple, 1958, II Monsieur Prousthe, 1958, III Liberté de Décembre, 1959); Sylva, 1961; Hamlet (trans. and illus.), 1965; (with P. Misraki) Les Chemins de L'Etre, 1965; (with M. Coronel) Quota ou les Pléthoriens, 1966; La Bataille du Silence, 1967; Le Radeau de la Méduse, 1969; Oedipe et Hamlet, 1970; Contes des Cataplasmes, 1971; Sillages, 1972; Sept Sentiers du Désert (short stories), 1972; Questions sur la vie à Messieurs les Biologistes (essay), 1973; Comme un Frère, 1973; Tendre Naufrage, 1974; Ce que je crois (essay), 1976; Je cuisine comme un chef (cook book), 1976; Les Chevaux du Temps, 1977; Collected Plays, vol. 1 (Zoo, Le Fer et le Velours, Le Silence de la Mer), 1978, Vol. 2, Pour Shakespeare (Hamlet, Macbeth), 1978; Sens et Non-sens de l'Histoire (essay), 1978; Camille ou l'Enfant double (children's story), 1978; Le Piège à Loup (novel), 1979; Assez Mentir! (essay, collab. O. Wormser-Migot), 1980; Cent ans d'histoire de France 1862–1962: vol. I, Moi Aristide Briand, 1981; vol. II, Les Occasions Perdues, 1982; vol. III, Les nouveaux jours, 1984; Anne Boleyn, 1985; Le Tigre d'Anvers, 1986; numerous articles in periodicals. *Address:* 58 Quai des Orfèvres, 75001 Paris, France. *Clubs:* PEN, section française; Comité National des Ecrivains (Hon. Pres.).   *Died 10 June 1991.*

VERDON-SMITH, Sir (William) Reginald, Kt 1953; DL; Pro-Chancellor, Bristol University, 1965–86; Vice Lord-Lieutenant, Avon, 1980–88; *b* 5 Nov. 1912; *s* of late Sir William George Verdon Smith, CBE, JP and Diana Florence, *er d* of M. Anders, Cheshire; *m* 1946, Jane Margaret, *d* of late V. W. J. Hobbs; one *s* one *d. Educ:* Repton School; Brasenose College, Oxford (Scholar). 1st class School of Jurisprudence, 1935; BCL 1936 and Vinerian Law Scholar; Barrister-at-law, Inner Temple. Bristol Aeroplane Co., 1938–68: Dir., 1942; Jt Asst Man. Dir., 1947; Jt Man. Dir., 1952; Chm. 1955; Vice-Chm., Rolls Royce Ltd, 1966–68; Chm., British Aircraft Corp. (Hldgs) Ltd, 1969–72; Dir, Lloyds Bank Ltd, 1951–83; Chairman: Lloyds Bank Internat., 1973–79; Lloyds Bank Bristol Region, 1976–83. Pres. SBAC, 1946–48; Chm., Fatstock and Meat Marketing Committee of Enquiry, 1962–64; Mem. of Council, Univ. of Bristol, 1945–86 (Chm., 1949–56). Mem. Cttee on the Working of the Monetary System (Radcliffe Cttee), 1957–59. Mem., Review Body on Remuneration of Doctors and Dentists, 1964–68. Master, Worshipful Co. of Coachmakers and Coach Harness Makers, 1960–61; Master, Soc. of Merchant Venturers, 1968–69. FRSA. DL Avon, 1974. Hon. LLD Bristol, 1959; Hon. DSc Cranfield Inst. of Technology, 1971; Hon. Fellow: Brasenose Coll., Oxford, 1965; Bristol Univ., 1986. *Recreations:* golf, sailing. *Address:* Flat 3, Spring Leigh, Church Road, Leigh Woods, Bristol BS8 3PG. *Clubs:* United Oxford & Cambridge University; Royal Cruising; Royal Yacht Squadron.   *Died 2 June 1992.*

VERNEY, Sir John, 2nd Bt, *cr* 1946, of Eaton Square, City of Westminster; MC 1944; TD 1970; painter, illustrator, author; *b* 30 Sept. 1913; *s* of Sir Ralph Verney, 1st Bt, CB, CIE, CVO (Speaker's Secretary, 1921–55), and Janette, *d* of Hon. J. T. Walker, Sydney, NSW; *S* father, 1959; *m* 1939, Lucinda, *d* of late Major Herbert Musgrave, DSO; one *s* five *d* (and one *s* decd). *Educ:* Eton; Christ Church, Oxford. Served War of 1939–45 with N. Somerset Yeomanry, RAC and SAS Regt in Palestine, Syria, Egypt, Italy, France and Germany (despatches twice, MC). Exhibitor: RBA; London Group; Leicester, Redfern, New Grafton Gall., etc. Légion d'Honneur, 1945. *Publications:* Verney Abroad, 1954; Going to the Wars, 1955; Friday's Tunnel, 1959; Look at Houses, 1959; February's Road, 1961; Every Advantage, 1961; The Mad King of Chichiboo, 1963; ismo, 1964; A Dinner of Herbs, 1966; Fine Day for a Picnic, 1968; Seven Sunflower Seeds, 1968; Samson's Hoard, 1973; A John Verney Collection, 1989; periodic contributor to Cornhill etc; annually, The Dodo Pad (the amusing telephone diary). *Heir: s* (John) Sebastian Verney, *b* 30 Aug. 1945. *Address:* The White House, Clare, Suffolk CO10 8NP. *T:* Clare (0787) 277494. *Died 2 Feb. 1993.*

VERNON, Prof. Magdalen Dorothea, MA (Cantab) 1926; ScD (Cantab) 1953; Professor of Psychology in the University of Reading, 1956–67; *b* 25 June 1901; *d* of Dr Horace Middleton Vernon and Katharine Dorothea Ewart. *Educ:* Oxford High Sch.; Newnham Coll., Cambridge. Asst Investigator to the Industrial Health Research Board, 1924–27; Research Investigator to the Medical Research Council, in the Psychological Laboratory, Cambridge, 1927–46; Lecturer in Psychology, 1946–51, Senior Lecturer in Psychology, 1951–55, Reader in Psychology, 1955–66, University of Reading. President, British Psychological Society, 1958 (Hon. Fellow, 1970); President, Psychology Section, British Assoc., 1959. *Publications:* The Experimental Study of Reading, 1931; Visual Perception, 1937; A Further Study of Visual Perception, 1952; Backwardness in Reading, 1957; The Psychology of Perception, 1962; Experiments in Visual Perception, 1966; Human Motivation, 1969; Perception through Experience, 1970; Reading and its Difficulties, 1971; numerous papers on perception, etc, in British Journal of Psychology and British Journal of Educational Psychology. *Recreations:* walking, gardening. *Address:* 50 Cressingham Road, Reading, Berks. *T:* Reading (0734) 871088. *Club:* University Women's. *Died 1 Dec. 1991.*

VICARS-HARRIS, Noël Hedley, CMG 1953; *b* 22 Nov. 1901; *o s* of late C. F. Harris and Evelyn C. Vicars, The Gate House, Rugby; *m* 1st, 1926, Maria Guimarães (marr. diss. 1939), São Paulo, Brazil; two *s*; 2nd, 1940, Joan Marguerite Francis; one *s*. *Educ:* Charterhouse; St John's Coll., Cambridge. BA Agric., 1924. Employed in Brazil by Brazil Plantations Syndicate Ltd, 1924–27; HM Colonial Service, Tanganyika, 1927–55; Official Member of Legislative and Executive Councils, Tanganyika, 1950–Nov. 1953; Member for Lands and Mines, Tanganyika, 1950–55. *Recreation:* gardening. *Address:* 3 Orchard Close, Sparkford, Somerset BA22 7JL. *T:* North Cadbury (0963) 40454. *Died 4 May 1991.*

VICKERS, Baroness *cr* 1974 (Life Peer), of Devonport; **Joan Helen Vickers,** DBE 1964 (MBE 1946); *b* 3 June 1907; *e d* of late Horace Cecil Vickers and Lilian Monro Lambert Grose. *Educ:* St Monica's Coll., Burgh Heath, Surrey. Member, LCC, Norwood Division of Lambeth, 1937–45. Contested (C) South Poplar, 1945. Served with British Red Cross in SE Asia (MBE); Colonial Service in Malaya, 1946–50. MP (C) Plymouth, Devonport, 1955–Feb. 1974; UK Delegate (C), Council of Europe and WEU, 1967–74. Chairman, Anglo-Indonesian Society;

UK Delegate, UK Status of Women Commn, 1960–64; President: Status of Women Cttee; Internat. Friendship League; Inst. of Qualified Private Secretaries; Europe China Assoc. Chm., National Centre for Cued Speech. Netherlands Red Cross Medal. *Address:* The Manor House, East Chisenbury, Pewsey, Wilts. *Died 23 May 1994.*

VIDLER, Rev. Alexander Roper, LittD; Dean of King's College, Cambridge, 1956–66; Fellow of King's College, 1956–67, Hon. Fellow since 1972; *b* 1899; *s* of late Leopold Amon Vidler, JP, Rye, Sussex; unmarried. *Educ:* Sutton Valence Sch.; Selwyn Coll., Cambridge; Wells Theological Coll. BA 2nd Class Theol. Tripos, 1921; MA 1925; Norrisian Prize, 1933; BD 1938; LittD 1957; University of Edinburgh, DD, 1946; Hon. DD: University of Toronto, 1961; College of Emmanuel and St Chad, Saskatoon, 1966. Deacon, 1922; priest, 1923; Curate of St Philip's, Newcastle upon Tyne, 1922–24; of St Aidan's, Birmingham, 1925–31; on staff of the Oratory House, Cambridge, 1931–38; Warden of St Deiniol's Library, Hawarden, 1939–48; Hon. Canon of Derby Cathedral, 1946–48; Canon of St George's Chapel, Windsor, 1948–56; licensed by Cambridge Univ. to preach throughout England, 1957; University Lecturer in Divinity, 1959–67. Commissary for Bishop of New Guinea, 1936–62. Hale Lecturer (USA), 1947; Birkbeck Lecturer (Trinity Coll., Cambridge), 1953; Firth Lecturer (Nottingham Univ.), 1955; Robertson Lecturer (Glasgow Univ.), 1964; Sarum Lecturer (Oxford Univ.), 1968–69. Sec., Christian Frontier Council, 1949–56. Mayor of Rye, 1972–74. Acting Principal, Chichester Theological Coll., 1981. Editor, Theology, 1939–64; Co-editor of The Frontier, 1950–52. *Publications:* Magic and Religion, 1930; Sex, Marriage and Religion, 1932; The Modernist Movement in the Roman Church, 1934; A Plain Man's Guide to Christianity, 1936; God's Demand and Man's Response, 1938; God's Judgement on Europe, 1940; Secular Despair and Christian Faith, 1941; Christ's Strange Work, 1944; The Orb and the Cross, 1945; Good News for Mankind, 1947; The Theology of F. D. Maurice, 1949; Christian Belief, 1950; Prophecy and Papacy, 1954; Christian Belief and This World, 1956; Essays in Liberality, 1957; Windsor Sermons, 1958; The Church in an Age of Revolution, 1961; A Century of Social Catholicism, 1964; 20th Century Defenders of the Faith, 1965; F. D. Maurice and Company, 1966; A Variety of Catholic Modernists, 1970; Scenes from a Clerical Life (autobiog.), 1977; Read, Mark, Learn, 1980; (jointly): The Development of Modern Catholicism, 1933; The Gospel of God and the Authority of the Church, 1937; Natural Law, 1946; Editor, Soundings: Essays concerning Christian Understanding, 1962; Objections to Christian Belief, 1963; (with Malcolm Muggeridge) Paul: envoy extraordinary, 1972. *Address:* Acacia House, Ashford Road, St Michael's, Tenterden, Kent TN30 6QA. *Died 25 July 1991.*

VILLIERS, Sir Charles (Hyde), Kt 1975; MC 1945; Director, W. C. Norris Institute, Minneapolis, since 1989; Chairman, Theatre Royal, Windsor; *b* 14 Aug. 1912; *s* of Algernon Hyde Villiers (killed in action, 1917) and Beatrix Paul (who *m* 2nd, 4th Baron Aldenham) (Dowager Lady Aldenham) (*d* 1978); *m* 1st, 1938, Pamela Constance Flower (*d* 1943); one *s*; 2nd, 1946, Marie José, *d* of Count Henri de la Barre d'Erquelinnes, Jurbise, Belgium; two *d*. *Educ:* Eton; New Coll., Oxford. Grenadier Guards (SRO), 1936; served at Dunkirk, 1940 (wounded, 1942); Special Ops Exec., London and Italy, 1943–45; parachuted into Yugoslavia and Austria, 1944; Lt-Col and Comd 6 Special Force Staff Section, 1945 (MC). Asst to Rev. P. B. Clayton, of Toc H, 1931; Glyn Mills, Bankers, 1932; a Man. Dir, Helbert Wagg, 1948, and J. Henry Schroder Wagg, 1960–68; Managing Director, Industrial

Reorganisation Corporation, 1968–71; Chm., Guinness Mahon & Co. Ltd, 1971–76; Exec. Dep. Chm., Guinness Peat Gp, 1973–76; Chairman: British Steel Corp., 1976–80; BSC (Industry), 1977–89. Formerly Director: Bass Charrington; Courtaulds; Sun Life Assurance; Banque Belge; Financor SA; Darling & Co. (Pty); European Industrial Equity Co. SA, 1986–; W. C. Norris Inst., Minneapolis; formerly Chm., Ashdown Trans-Europe and Trans-Australian Investment Trusts. Chairman: Federal Trust Gp on European Monetary Integration, 1972; Northern Ireland Finance Corp., 1972–73. Chm., 13th Internat. Small Business Congress, 1986–87; Co-Chairman: Europalia Festival, 1973; British-American Project, 1990–. Member: Inst. Internat. d'Etudes Bancaires, 1959–76 (Pres. 1964); Minister of Labour's Resettlement Cttee for London and SE, 1958 (Chm. 1961–68); Review Body for N Ireland Economic Develt, 1971; NEDC, 1976–80. Lubbock Meml Lectr, Oxford, 1971. Mem., Chelsea Borough Council, 1950–53. Order of the People, Yugoslavia, 1970; Grand Officier de l'Ordre de Léopold II (Belgium), 1974; Gold Medal of Inst. for Reconstruction of Industry, Italy, 1975. *Publication:* Start again, Britain, 1984. *Recreation:* gardening. *Address:* Blacknest House, Sunninghill, Berks SL5 0PS. *T:* Ascot (0344) 22137.   *Died 22 Jan. 1992.*

VINCENT, Ivor Francis Sutherland, CMG 1966; MBE 1945; HM Diplomatic Service, retired; Hon. Secretary, The Andean Project, since 1983; *b* 14 Oct. 1916; *s* of late Lt-Col Frank Lloyd Vincent and Gladys Clarke; *m* 1949, Patricia Mayne; three *d* (and one *d* decd). *Educ:* St Peter's Coll., Radley; Christ Church, Oxford. Served Indian Army, Royal Garhwal Rifles, 1941–46. Entered HM Foreign Service, 1946; Second Secretary, Foreign Office, 1946–48; First Sec., Buenos Aires, 1948–51; UK Delegn, NATO, Paris, 1951–53; FO, 1954–57; Rabat, 1957–59; Geneva (Disarmt Delegn), 1960; Paris (UK Delegn to OECD), 1960–62; Counsellor, FO, 1962–66; Baghdad, Jan.-June, 1967; Caracas, Oct. 1967–1970; Ambassador to Nicaragua, 1970–73; Consul-Gen., Melbourne, 1973–76, retired. Dir, Fairbridge Soc. (Inc.), 1978–83. *Recreations:* music, walking. *Address:* c/o Lloyds Bank plc, Waterloo Place, Pall Mall, SW1Y 5NJ. *Club:* Lansdowne.   *Died 5 May 1994.*

VINCENT-JONES, Captain Desmond, DSC; Royal Navy; retired 1964; *b* 13 Feb. 1912; *s* of late Sir Vincent Jones, KBE and Mary, *d* of Col Joscelyn Fitzroy Bagot; *m* 1944, Jacqueline, *e d* of Col A. J. H. Sloggett, CBE, DSO; two *d. Educ:* Beacon School, Crowborough; Royal Naval College, Dartmouth. Served in Royal Navy, 1929–64; War of 1939–45, in aircraft carrier operations in Atlantic and Mediterranean (DSC and Bar); served in Air Staff appointments and in command of HM Ships, 1946–64: Director: Naval Air Warfare, 1960–61; Naval Air Div., 1961–64. Graduate of US Armed Forces and British Services Staff Colleges. Naval and Military Attaché to Buenos Aires and Montevideo, 1958–60. On retirement from RN joined Marine Consortiums as consultant. *Recreations:* golf, tennis, fishing, cruising. *Address:* 8 High Street, Chobham, Surrey. *T:* Chobham (0276) 857274. *Clubs:* Free Foresters; Sunningdale Golf.
                              Died 9 Feb 1992.

VINCZE, Paul, FRBS, FRNS; *b* Hungary, 15 Aug. 1907; *s* of Lajos Vincze; British subject, 1948; *m* 1958, Emilienne Chauzeix. *Educ:* High School of Arts and Crafts, Budapest, later under E. Telcs. Won a travelling scholarship to Rome, 1935–37; came to England, 1938. *Exhibited:* Royal Academy, Rome, Budapest, Paris, etc; *works represented in:* British Museum, London; Museum of Fine Arts, Budapest; Ashmolean Museum, Oxford; Swedish Historical Museum; Danish Nat. Museum; Museum of Amer. Numismatic Soc.; Smithsonian Instn, Washington;

Cabinet des Médailles, Paris, etc. *Works include:* Aga Khan Platinum Jubilee Portrait; Sir Bernard Pares Memorial Tablet, Senate House, London Univ.; President Truman, portrait medallion; Pope Paul VI, portrait medallion; official medal to commemorate 400th Anniversary of birth of William Shakespeare; medal to commemorate Independence of Ghana; official seal of Ghana Govt; Smithsonian Instn Award Medal, 1965; Nat. Commemorative Society (USA) Winston Churchill Medal; Florence Nightingale Medal for Société Commemorative de Femmes Célèbres; E. and J. De Rothschild Medal for inauguration of Knesset, 1966; Yehudi Menuhin 50th Birthday Medal, 1966; Prince Karim Aga Khan 10th Anniversary Medal, 1968; Cassandra Memorial Tablet for Internat. Publishing Corp. Bldg, 1968; Shakespeare-Garrick Medal, 1969; Medal to commemorate 100th Anniversary of birth of Sir Henry J. Wood, 1969; Dickens 100th Anniversary Medal for Dickens Fellowship, 1970; Medal to commemorate J. B. Priestley's 80th birthday, 1974; Internat. Shakespeare Assoc. Congress Medal, USA, 1976; Self-portrait Medal to commemorate 70th birthday, 1978; Wall Panel illustrating all Shakespeare's plays for new Shakespeare Centre, Stratford-upon-Avon, 1981; Archie F. Carr award medal for Conservation for Florida State Museum, USA; Amer. Numismatic Assoc. 90th Anniversary Medal, 1981; Karim Aga Khan Silver Jubilee Medal, 1983; portrait-tablets: Harry Guy Bartholomew, Cecil H. King, Lord Cudlipp, for the Mirror's headquarters, 1985. *Coin designs:* obverse and reverses, Libya, 1951; obverses, Guatemala, 1954; reverses, threepence, sixpence and shilling, Cen. African Fedn, 1955; obverses, Ghana, 1958; reverses, Guernsey, 1957; threepence and florin, Nigeria, 1960; guinea, obverse and reverses, Malawi, 1964; reverse, Uganda crown, 1968; Bustamante Portrait for obverse of Jamaican dollar, 1969; reverses for decimal coins, Guernsey, 1970, etc. Awarded Premio Especial, Internat. Exhib., Madrid, 1951; Silver Medal, Paris Salon, 1964; first gold Medal of Amer. Numismatic Assoc., 1966. *Address:* Villa La Méridienne, 81 avenue de la Bastide, 06520 Magagnosc, France. *T:* 93364754.
                              Died 5 March 1994.

VINE, Philip Mesban, CBE 1981; DL; Member, since 1976, Chairman, 1977–90, New Towns Staff Commission; Member, New Towns Commission, since 1978; *b* 26 Oct. 1919; *s* of late Major George H. M. Vine and Elsie Mary (*née* Shephard), London; *m* 1944, Paulina, JP, *d* of late Arthur Oyler, Great Hormead Hall, Herts; one *s* one *d. Educ:* Sherborne Sch.; Taft Sch., USA; Sidney Sussex Coll., Cambridge (MA, LLM); Nottingham Univ. (MPhil 1981, PhD 1987). Served in Royal Artillery, 1939–45; Adjutant 90th Field Regt, RA. Articled to W. H. Bentley, Town Clerk of Paddington; admitted Solicitor, 1948; Asst Solicitor, Paddington, 1948–50; Chief Asst Solicitor, Birkenhead, 1950–53; Deputy Town Clerk: Wallasey, 1953–59; Southend-on-Sea, 1959–62; Town Clerk, Cambridge, 1963–66; Town Clerk and Chief Exec. Officer, Nottingham, 1966–74. Chairman: Notts Local Valuation Panel, 1974–85; London Housing Staff Commn, 1979–86; Mem., Local Radio Council for BBC Radio Nottingham, 1970–76; Indep. Chm., Home Sec.'s Adv. Cttee, Wireless and Telegraphy Act 1949, 1975–89; Member: Panel of Asst Comrs of Local Govt Boundary Commn, 1974–89; Panel of Indep. Inspectors, DoE, 1974–89; Bd, Telford (New Town) Develt Corp., 1975–89; Police Complaints Bd, 1977–80; Ind. Review of the Radio Spectrum (30–960 MHz), 1982–83. Gen. Comr of Income Tax, 1975–. Mem., Bd, English Sinfonia, 1980–. Gov., Derbyshire Coll. of Higher Educn, 1985–89; Mem. Court, Nottingham Univ., 1966–74. Liveryman, Clockmakers' Co. (Mem. Court, 1981; Master, 1988). DL Notts, 1974. *Publication:* The Neolithic and Bronze Age Cultures of the Middle and Upper Trent Basin (British Archaeological Reports, British

Series 105), 1982. *Recreations:* fishing, archaeology, enjoyment of music. *Address:* 42 Magdala Road, Mapperley Park, Nottingham NG3 5DF. *T:* Nottingham (0602) 621269. *Clubs:* Army and Navy; United Services (Nottingham). *Died 5 Feb. 1992.*

VIVENOT, Baroness de; Hermine Hallam Hipwell, OBE 1967; freelance writer; *b* Buenos Aires, 23 April 1907; *d* of late Humphrey Hallam Hipwell and Gertrude Hermine Isebrée-Moens tot Bloois; *m* 1931, Baron Raoul de Vivenot (*d* 1973), *e s* of Baron de Vivenot and Countess Kuenburg, Vienna; one *s*. *Educ:* Northlands, Buenos Aires. Staff of Buenos Aires Herald, 1928–31. Joined Min. of Information, 1941; transferred Foreign Office, 1946; appointed to Foreign (subseq. Diplomatic) Service, Jan. 1947; Vice-Consul, Bordeaux, 1949–52, Nantes, 1952–53; Foreign Office, 1953–55; First Secretary (Information), HM Embassy, Brussels, 1955–59; Foreign Office, 1959–62; First Secretary (Information), HM Embassy, The Hague, 1962–66; retired 1967. External Examiner in Spanish, Univ. of London. *Publications:* The Niñas of Balcarce, a novel, 1935; Younger Argentine Painters; Argentine Art Notes; Buenos Aires Vignettes; articles in La Nación and Buenos Aires Herald. *Recreations:* whippet racing and coursing, gardening, grandchildren. *Address:* The Flat, Aughton House, Collingbourne Kingston, Marlborough, Wilts SN8 3SA. *T:* Collingbourne Ducis (026485) 0682.
Died 25 Feb. 1992.

VIVIAN, 5th Baron, *cr* 1841; **Anthony Crespigny Claude Vivian;** Bt 1828; *b* 4 March 1906; *e s* of 4th Baron and Barbara, *d* of William A. Fanning; *S* father, 1940; *m* 1930, Victoria (*d* 1985), *er d* of late Captain H. G. L. Oliphant, DSO, MVO; two *s* one *d*. *Educ:* Eton. Served RA. *Heir: s* Brig. Hon. Nicholas Crespigny Laurence Vivian, 16/5 Lancers [*b* 11 Dec. 1935; *m* 1st, 1960, Catherine Joyce (marr. diss. 1972), *y d* of late James Kenneth Hope, CBE; one *s* one *d*; 2nd, 1972, Carol, *d* of F. Alan Martineau; two *d*]. *Address:* 154 Coleherne Court, Redcliffe Gardens, SW5 0DX. *Died 24 June 1991.*

VOYSEY, Reginald George, FIMechE; consultant; Deputy Director, National Physical Laboratory, 1970–77; *b* 26 May 1916; *s* of Richard Voysey and Anne Paul; *m* 1943, Laidley Mary Elizabeth Barley (*d* 1987); one *s* three *d* (and one *s* decd). *Educ:* Royal Dockyard Sch., Portsmouth; Imperial Coll. of Science. ACGI, DIC, WhSch. Dep. Develt Manager, Power Jets Ltd, 1940–45; Gas Turbine Dept Manager, C. A. Parsons & Co., 1945–48; Engineering Asst to Chief Scientist, Min. of Fuel and Power, 1948–66; IDC 1963; Scientific Counsellor, British Embassy, and Dir, UK Sci. Mission to Washington, 1966–69. *Publications:* patents and articles in jls. *Recreations:* swimming, sailing, painting. *Address:* 16 Beauchamp Road, East Molesey, Surrey KT8 0PA. *T:* 081–979 3762.
Died 7 May 1993.

VYSE, Lt-Gen. Sir Edward Dacre H.; *see* Howard-Vyse.

VYVYAN, Sir John (Stanley), 12th Bt *cr* 1645; owner of Trelowarren Estate, since 1950 (property acquired by marriage in 1427); *b* 20 Jan. 1916; *s* of Major-General Ralph Ernest Vyvyan, CBE, MC (*d* 1971) and Vera Grace (*d* 1956), *d* of Robert Arthur Alexander; *S* cousin, 1978; *m* 1958, Jonet Noël, *d* of Lt-Col Alexander Hubert Barclay, DSO, MC; one *s* one *d* (and one *d* (decd) of former marriage). *Educ:* Charterhouse; and British-American Tobacco Co. Ltd, who sent him to London School of Oriental Studies. With British-American Tobacco Co. Ltd in England and China until War. Commissioned RCS in India, 1940 and served, 1940–46, in Arakan, Bangalore, etc; Temp. Major; GSO II Signals, Southern Army, 1944. *Recreations:* gardening, photography and books; travel when possible. *Heir: s* Ralph Ferrers Alexander Vyvyan [*b* 21 Aug. 1960; *m* 1986, Victoria, *y d* of M. B. Ogle, Skerraton, Buckfastleigh, Devon; four *s*]. *Address:* Trelowarren Mill, Mawgan, Helston, Cornwall TR12 6AE. *T:* Mawgan (01326) 221505. *Clubs:* Army and Navy; Royal Cornwall Yacht (Falmouth).
Died 6 Oct. 1995.

W

WADDINGTON, Very Rev. John Albert Henry, MBE 1945; TD 1951; MA (Lambeth) 1959; Provost of Bury St Edmunds, 1958–76, then Provost Emeritus; a Church Commissioner, 1972–76; *b* 10 Feb. 1910; *s* of H. Waddington, Tooting Graveney, Surrey; *m* 1938, Marguerite Elisabeth (*d* 1986), *d* of F. Day, Wallington, Surrey; two *d. Educ:* Wandsworth Sch.; London Univ.; London College of Divinity. BCom London Univ., 1929. Deacon, 1933; priest, 1934; Curate of St Andrew's, Streatham, 1933–35; Curate of St Paul's, Furzedown, 1935–38; Rector of Great Bircham, 1938–45; Vicar of St Peter Mancroft, Norwich, 1945; Chaplain to High Sheriff of Norfolk, 1950; Proctor in Convocation of Canterbury, 1950; Hon. Canon of Norwich, 1951. Chaplain to Forces (TA) 1935–58; Staff Chaplain, Eighth Army, 1943 (despatches twice); DACG XIII Corps, 1945, Eastern Command TA, 1951. *Recreations:* travel, theatre and cinema, religious journalism. *Address:* The Chantry, 67 Churchgate Street, Bury St Edmunds, Suffolk IP33 1RL. *T:* Bury St Edmunds (01284) 754494.

Died 23 Nov. 1994.

WADSWORTH, Vivian Michael, DSc; former chairman of several public and private companies, retired 1986; *b* 12 April 1921; *s* of Frank Wadsworth and Tillie Wadsworth (*née* Widdop); *m* 1943, Ethel Mary Rigby; three *s* four *d. Educ:* Univs of Reading (BScAgric), Bristol, Leeds, and Natal, S Africa (MA, DSc). Economics Lectr, Bristol, Leeds and Natal Univs, 1942–49; Economic Adviser to Govt of S Rhodesia, 1949–55; Under Secretary for Agriculture, Fedn of Rhodesia and Nyasaland, 1955–61; Asst Sec. to Industrial Division, and Principal Economic Adviser, Distillers Co., 1961–63; Man. Dir, Fabrica Nacional de Margerina (SARL), Lisbon, Portugal (food company and former Distillers subsidiary), 1963–68; Tanganyika Concessions: Dir, Chief Exec. and Chm. of all UK subsidiaries, of which Elbar Group Industrial Holding Co. was the principal, 1968–83; Dir, Benguela Railway, Angola, 1974–83; Chm., Harland and Wolff Ltd, Belfast, 1981–83. CBIM. *Recreations:* gardening, travel, walking. *Address:* High Walls, Houndscroft, near Stroud, Glos GL5 5DG. *T:* Amberley (045387) 2434.

Died 15 Feb. 1992.

WAGNER, Sir Anthony (Richard), KCB 1978; KCVO 1961 (CVO 1953); DLitt, MA, Oxon; FSA; Clarenceux King of Arms, since 1978; Director, Heralds' Museum, Tower of London, 1978–83; Knight Principal, Imperial Society of Knights Bachelor, 1962–83; Secretary of Order of the Garter, 1952–61; Joint Register of Court of Chivalry, since 1954; General Editor, Society of Antiquaries' Dictionary of British Arms, since 1940 (first volume published, 1992); *b* 6 Sept. 1908; *o s* of late Orlando Henry Wagner, 90 Queen's Gate, SW7, and Monica, *d* of late Rev. G. E. Bell, Henley in Arden; *m* 1953, Gillian Mary Millicent Graham, (Dame Gillian Wagner, DBE); two *s* one *d. Educ:* Eton (King's Scholar); Balliol Coll., Oxford (Robin Hollway Scholar; Hon. Fellow, 1979). Portcullis Pursuivant, 1931–43; Richmond Herald, 1943–61; Garter Principal King of Arms, 1961–78; Registrar of College of Arms, 1953–60; Genealogist: the Order of the Bath, 1961–72; the Order of St John, 1961–75; Inspector of Regtl Colours, 1961–77. Served in WO, 1939–43; Ministry of Town and Country Planning, 1943–46: Private Secretary to Minister, 1944–45;

Secretary, 1945–46, Member, 1947–66, Advisory Cttee on Buildings of special architectural or historic interest. President: Chelsea Soc., 1967–73; Aldeburgh Soc., 1970–83. Mem. Council, Nat. Trust, 1953–74; Trustee, Nat. Portrait Gallery, 1973–80; Chm. of Trustees, Marc Fitch Fund, 1971–77. Master, Vintners' Co., 1973–74. Hon. Fellow, Heraldry Soc. of Canada, 1976. KStJ. *Publications:* Catalogue of the Heralds' Commemorative Exhibition (compiler), 1934; Historic Heraldry of Britain, 1939, repr. 1972; Heralds and Heraldry in the Middle Ages, 1939; Heraldry in England, 1946; Catalogue of English Mediæval Rolls of Arms, 1950; The Records and Collections of the College of Arms, 1952; English Genealogy, 1960, 2nd edn 1983; English Ancestry, 1961; Heralds of England, 1967; Pedigree and Progress, 1975; Heralds and Ancestors, 1978; Stephen Martin Leake's Heraldo-Memoriale (Roxburghe Club), 1982; (jtly) The Wagners of Brighton, 1983; How Lord Birkenhead Saved the Heralds, 1986; A Herald's World, 1988; (with A. L. Rowse) John Austis, Garter King of Arms, 1992; genealogical and heraldic articles, incl. in Chambers's Encyclopædia. *Address:* College of Arms, Queen Victoria Street, EC4V 4BT. *T:* 0171–248 4300; 10 Physic Place, Royal Hospital Road, SW3 4HQ. *T:* 0171–352 0934; Wyndham Cottage, Aldeburgh, Suffolk IP15 5DL. *T:* Aldeburgh (01728) 452596. *Clubs:* Athenæum, Garrick, Beefsteak.

Died 5 May 1995.

WAGSTAFF, Col Henry Wynter, CSI 1945; MC 1917; FCIT; Royal Engineers (retired); *b* 19 July 1890; *s* of Edward Wynter Wagstaff and Flora de Smidt; *m* 1st, 1918, Jean, MB, BS (decd), *d* of George Frederick Mathieson; two *s*; 2nd, 1967, Margaret, *o d* of late Sir John Hubert Marshall, CIE. *Educ:* Woodbridge; RMA, Woolwich. Commissioned RE 1910; served in India and Mesopotamia in European War, 1914–18 (despatches, MC); Captain, 1916; seconded Indian State Railways, 1921; Major, 1927; 1929–46, employed on problems connected with labour in general and railway labour in particular; Lieut-Colonel, 1934; Colonel, 1940; Member, Railway Board, Government of India, New Delhi, 1942–46; retired, 1948. *Publication:* Operation of Indian Railways in Recent Years, 1931. *Recreations:* reading, writing. *Address:* c/o Lloyds Bank, 7 Pall Mall, SW1.

Died 13 Sept. 1992.

WAIN, John Barrington, CBE 1984; author; Professor of Poetry, University of Oxford, 1973–78; *b* 14 March 1925; *e* surv. *s* of Arnold A. Wain and Anne Wain, Stoke-on-Trent; *m* 1st, 1947, Marianne Urmstone (marr. diss. 1956); 2nd, 1960, Eirian (*d* 1988), *o d* of late T. E. James; three *s*; 3rd, 1989, Patricia, *o d* of R. F. Dunn. *Educ:* The High Sch., Newcastle-under-Lyme; St John's Coll., Oxford (Hon. Fellow, 1985). Fereday Fellow, St John's Coll., Oxford, 1946–49; Lecturer in English Literature, University of Reading, 1947–55; resigned to become freelance author and critic. Churchill Visiting Prof., University of Bristol, 1967; Vis. Prof., Centre Universitaire Expérimentale de Vincennes, Paris, 1969. First Fellow in creative arts, Brasenose College, Oxford, 1971–72, Supernumerary Fellow, 1973–. Pres., Johnson Soc. of Lichfield, 1976–77. FRSL 1960, resigned 1961. Hon. DLitt: Keele, 1985; Loughborough, 1985. Radio plays: You Wouldn't Remember, 1978; Frank, 1983; Good Morning Blues, 1986; (with Laszlo Solymar)

Mathematical Triangle (trilogy), 1991. *Publications include: fiction:* Hurry On Down, 1953, repr. 1978; Living in the Present, 1955; The Contenders, 1958; A Travelling Woman, 1959; Nuncle and other stories, 1960; Strike the Father Dead, 1962; The Young Visitors, 1965; Death of the Hind Legs and other stories, 1966; The Smaller Sky, 1967; A Winter in the Hills, 1970; The Life Guard and Other Stories, 1971; The Pardoner's Tale, 1978; Lizzie's Floating Shop, 1981; Young Shoulders, 1982 (Whitbread Prize) (televised, BBC, 1984); Where the Rivers Meet, 1988; Comedies, 1990; *plays:* Harry in the Night, 1975; *poetry:* A Word Carved on a Sill, 1956; Weep Before God, 1961; Wildtrack, 1965; Letters to Five Artists, 1969; Feng, 1975; Poems 1949–79, 1981; Open Country, 1987; *criticism:* Preliminary Essays, 1957; Essays on Literature and Ideas, 1963; The Living World of Shakespeare, 1964, new edn 1979; A House for the Truth, 1972; Professing Poetry, 1977; *biography:* Samuel Johnson, 1974, new edn 1980 (James Tait Black Meml Prize; Heinemann Award, 1975); *autobiography:* Sprightly Running, 1962; Dear Shadows: portraits from memory, 1986; much work as editor, anthologist, reviewer, broadcaster, etc. *Recreations:* wet country walks, travelling by train, especially in France. *Address:* c/o Curtis Brown Ltd, 164–168 Regent Street, W1R 5TB. *Died 24 May 1994.*

WAINWRIGHT, Rear-Adm. Rupert Charles Purchas, CB 1966; DSC 1943; Vice Naval Deputy to Supreme Allied Commander Europe, 1965–67, retired; with Redditch Development Corporation, 1968–77; *b* 16 Oct. 1913; *s* of late Lieut Comdr O. J. Wainwright and Mrs S. Wainwright; *m* 1937, Patricia Mary Helen, *d* of late Col F. H. Blackwood, DSO and Mrs Blackwood; two *s* two *d*. *Educ:* Royal Naval College, Dartmouth. Commanded HM Ships Actaeon, Tintagel Castle, Zephyr, 1952–54; Captain HMS Cambridge, 1955–57; Chief of Staff, S Atlantic and S America Station, 1958–60; Director Naval Recruiting, 1960–62; Commodore Naval Drafting, 1962–64. Comdr 1949; Capt. 1955; Rear-Adm. 1965. ADC to the Queen, 1964. Mem. Council, Missions to Seamen. Member: Stratford-on-Avon DC, 1973–86 (Vice-Chm., 1983–84; Chm., 1984–85); Assoc. District Councils, 1976–83. Vice-Pres., Stratford-upon-Avon Soc. Mem., Waste Management Adv. Council, 1978–81. *Publications:* two Prize Essays, RUSI Jl. *Recreations:* hockey (Combined Services; a Vice-Pres., England Hockey Assoc.), swimming (Royal Navy), tennis. *Address:* Regency Cottage, 30 Maidenhead Road, Stratford-upon-Avon, Warwicks CV37 6XS. *Club:* Royal Navy.
Died 15 Aug. 1991.

WAKEHURST, Dowager Lady; Dame Margaret Wakehurst, DBE 1965; *b* 4 Nov. 1899; *d* of Sir Charles Tennant, 1st Bt and 2nd wife, Marguerite (*née* Miles); *m* 1920, John de Vere Loder (later 2nd Baron Wakehurst, KG, KCMG) (*d* 1970); three *s* one *d*. Founder, Northern Ireland Assoc. for Mental Health; Founder Mem., National Schizophrenia Fellowship (Pres., 1984–86); Vice-Pres., Royal College of Nursing, 1958–78. Hon. LLD Queen's Univ., Belfast; Hon. DLitt New Univ. of Ulster, 1973. DStJ 1959; GCStJ 1970. *Address:* 31 Lennox Gardens, SW1X 0DE. *T:* 071–589 0956.

Died 19 Aug. 1994.

WAKELY, Leonard John Dean, CMG 1965; OBE 1945; Ambassador to Burma, 1965–67; *b* 18 June 1909; *s* of Sir Leonard Wakely, KCIE, CB and Florence Dean, *d* of William Titley; *m* 1938, Margaret Houssemayne Tinson; two *s*. *Educ:* Westminster School; Christ Church, Oxford; School of Oriental Studies, London. Indian Civil Service, 1932–47: served in the Punjab and in the Defence Co-ordination, Defence and Legislative Departments of the Government of India; appointed to Commonwealth Relations Office, 1947; Office of UK High Commissioner

in the Union of South Africa, 1950–52; Dep. High Comr in India (Madras), 1953–57; Asst Sec., 1955; Dep. High Comr in Ghana, 1957–60; Dep. High Comr in Canada, 1962–65. *Address:* Long Meadow, Forest Road, East Horsley, Surrey KT24 5BL. *Died 24 June 1994.*

WAKEMAN, Sir (Offley) David, 5th Bt *cr* 1828, of Perdiswell Hall, Worcestershire; *b* 6 March 1922; *s* of Sir Offley Wakeman, 4th Bt, CBE, and 1st wife, Winifred (*d* 1924), 2nd *d* of late Col C. R. Prideaux-Brune; *S* father, 1975; *m* 1946, Pamela Rose Arabella, *d* of late Lt-Col C. Hunter Little, DSO, MBE. *Educ:* Canford School. *Heir: half-brother* Edward Offley Bertram Wakeman, *b* 31 July 1934. *Address:* Peverey House, Bomere Heath, Shrewsbury, Salop. *T:* Shrewsbury (0743) 850561. *Club:* Lansdowne. *Died 24 Feb. 1991.*

WALDEGRAVE, 12th Earl, *cr* 1729; **Geoffrey Noel Waldegrave,** KG 1971; GCVO 1976; TD; DL; Bt 1643; Baron Waldegrave, 1685; Viscount Chewton, 1729; Member of the Prince's Council of the Duchy of Cornwall, 1951–58 and 1965–76, Lord Warden of the Stannaries, 1965–76; *b* 21 Nov. 1905; *o s* of 11th Earl and Anne Katharine (*d* 1962), *d* of late Rev. W. P. Bastard, Buckland Court and Kitley, Devon; *S* father, 1936; *m* 1930, Mary Hermione, *d* of Lt-Col A. M. Grenfell, DSO; two *s* five *d*. *Educ:* Winchester; Trinity Coll., Cambridge (BA). Served War of 1939–45, Major RA (TA). Chm., Som AEC, 1948–51; Liaison Officer to Min. of Agriculture, Fisheries and Food (formerly Min. of Agriculture and Fisheries), for Som, Wilts and Glos, 1952–57; Jt Parly Sec., Min. of Agriculture, Fisheries and Food, 1958–62; Chairman: Forestry Commn, 1963–65; Adv. Cttee on Meat Research, 1969–73. Director: Lloyds Bank Ltd, 1964–76 (Chm., Bristol Regional Bd, 1966–76); Bristol Waterworks Co., 1938–58 and 1963–78. Pres., Somerset Trust for Nature Conservation, 1964–80. Mem., BBC Gen. Adv. Council, 1963–66. Mem. Council and Trustee, Royal Bath and West and Southern Counties Soc. (Pres., 1974); Trustee, Partis Coll., Bath, 1935–88; formerly Mem. Court and Council, and Chm. Agricl Cttee, Bristol Univ. Chm., Friends of Wells Cathedral, 1970–84. Hon. LLD Bristol, 1976. Former Governor: Wells Cathedral Sch.; Nat. Fruit and Cider Inst., Long Ashton. Mem. Som CC, 1937–58; CA, 1949–58; DL Somerset, 1951; Vice-Lieutenant Somerset, 1955–60. Officer, Legion of Merit, USA. *Heir: s* Viscount Chewton [*b* 8 Dec. 1940; *m* 1986, Mary Alison Anthea, *d* of late Sir Robert Furness, KBE, CMG, two *s*]. *Address:* House of Lords, SW1A 0PW. *Club:* Travellers'. *Died 23 May 1995.*

WALDRON, Brig. John Graham Claverhouse, CBE 1958 (OBE 1944); DSO 1945; *b* 15 Nov. 1909; *s* of William Slade Olver, Falmouth; *m* 1933, Marjorie, *d* of Arthur Waldron, Newbury; one *s* one *d*. *Educ:* Marlborough; RMC, Sandhurst. jssc, psc. 2nd Lieut, Gloucestershire Regt, 1929; served War of 1939–45 (OBE, DSO): 5 British Division and 1st Bn Green Howards, in India, Middle East, Italy, NW Europe; Lt-Col, 10th Gurkha Rifles, 1951; Brigadier, 1958; ADC to the Queen, 1960–61; retired, 1961. *Address:* c/o Lloyds Bank, Cox's and Kings Branch, 6 Pall Mall, SW1Y 5NL. *Club:* Army and Navy. *Died 25 Dec. 1993.*

WALEY, (Andrew) Felix, VRD 1960 and Clasp 1970; QC 1973; DL; **His Honour Judge Waley;** a Circuit Judge, since 1982; Resident Judge, County of Kent, since 1985; Judge Advocate of the Fleet, since 1986; *b* 14 April 1926; *s* of Guy Felix Waley and Anne Elizabeth (*née* Dickson); *m* 1955, Petica Mary, *d* of Sir Philip Rose, 3rd Bt; one *s* three *d* (and one *d* decd). *Educ:* Charterhouse; Worcester Coll., Oxford (MA). RN, 1944–48; RNR, 1951–71, retd as Comdr. Oxford, 1948–51; called to the Bar, Middle Temple, 1953, Bencher, 1981; a Recorder of the Crown Court, 1974–82. Pres., Council of HM Circuit Judges,

1994. Conservative Councillor, Paddington, 1956–59. Contested (C) Dagenham, 1959. DL Kent, 1992. *Recreations:* gardens, boats, birds. *Address:* c/o The Law Courts, Barker Road, Maidstone, Kent ME16 8EQ. *Clubs:* Garrick, Naval; Royal Naval Sailing Association.
Died 16 April 1995.

WALEY-COHEN, Sir Bernard (Nathaniel), 1st Bt *cr* 1961, of Honeymead, Co. Somerset; Kt 1957; Director: Lloyds Bank Ltd Central London Region, 1962–84; Matthews Wrightson Pulbrook Ltd, 1971–84; Kleeman Industrial Holdings Ltd, since 1957 and other companies; *b* 29 May 1914; *er s* of late Sir Robert Waley Cohen, KBE and Alice Violet, *d* of Henry Edward Beddington, London and Newmarket; *m* 1943, Hon. Joyce Constance Ina Nathan; two *s* two *d. Educ:* HMS Britannia (RNC Dartmouth); Clifton College; Magdalene Coll., Cambridge (MA). Mem. of staff, Duke of York's Camp, Southwold, 1932–36; Gunner, HAC, 1937–38. Mem. of Public School Empire Tour, New Zealand, 1932–33. Liveryman, Clothworkers' Company, 1936, Court 1966, Chm., Finance Cttee, 1971–79, Master, 1975. Underwriting Member of Lloyd's 1939; Principal, Ministry of Fuel and Power 1940–47. Alderman, City of London Portsoken Ward, 1949–84; Sheriff, City of London, 1955–56; Lord Mayor of London, 1960–61; one of HM Lieutenants, City of London, 1949–. Mem. Council and Board of Governors, Clifton Coll., 1952–81; Mem., College Cttee, University College London, 1953–80, Treasurer 1962–70, Vice-Chm. 1970, Chm., 1971–80; Mem. Senate, 1962–78, Court, 1966–78, London Univ.; Governor, Wellesley House Prep. Sch., 1965, Chm., 1965–77. Hon. Sec. and Treasurer, Devon and Somerset Staghounds, 1940, Chm. 1953–85, Pres, 1985–; Mem. Finance and General Purposes Cttee, British Field Sports Soc., 1957, Treasurer 1965–78, Trustee, 1979, Dep. Pres., 1980; President: Bath and West and Southern Counties Show, 1963; Devon Cattle Breeders' Soc., 1963; W of England Hound Show, Honiton, 1974. Mem., Marshall Aid Commemoration Commn, 1957–60; Member: Jewish Cttee, HM Forces, 1947, Vice-Pres., 1980; Jewish Meml Council, 1947; Treasurer, Jewish Welfare Board, 1948–53; Vice-President: United Synagogue, 1952–61; Anglo-Jewish Assoc., 1962; Trades Adv. Council, 1963, Pres., 1981–84; Pres., Jewish Museum, 1964; Vice-Chairman: Palestine Corp., 1947–53; Union Bank of Israel Ltd, 1950–53; Chm., Simo Securities Trust Ltd, 1955–70; Mem., Nat. Corporation for Care of Old People, 1965–78; Mem., Executive Cttee and Central Council, Probation and After Care Cttees, 1965–69; Mem., Club Facilities Cttee, MCC, 1965–77; Trustee, Coll. of Arms Trust, 1970; Mem., Exec. Cttee, St Paul's Cathedral Appeal, 1970–72. Comr and Dep. Chm., Public Works Loan Board, 1971–72, Chm. 1972–79. Governor, Hon. Irish Soc., 1973–76. Mem. Foundn Cttee, Cambridge Soc., 1975, Exec. Cttee and Council 1976, Vice-Pres., 1980. Hon. Liveryman of Farmers' Company, 1961. Assoc. KStJ 1961. Hon. LLD London, 1961. *Recreations:* hunting, racing, shooting. *Heir: s* Stephen Harry Waley-Cohen [*b* 22 June 1946; *m* 1st, 1972, Pamela Elizabeth Doniger (marr. diss.); two *s* one *d*; 2nd, 1986, Josephine Burnett Spencer, *yr d* of late Duncan M. Spencer and Josephine Spencer; two *d*]. *Address:* Honeymead, Simonsbath, Minehead, Somerset TA24 7JX. *T:* Exford (064383) 242. *Clubs:* Boodle's, Pratts, MCC, Harlequins Rugby Football, City Livery; Jockey Club Rooms (Newmarket); University Pitt (Cambridge). *Died 3 July 1991.*

WALKER, Sir Allan (Grierson), Kt 1968; QC (Scot.); Sheriff Principal of Lanarkshire, 1963–74; *b* 1 May 1907; *er s* of late Joseph Walker, merchant, London, and Mary Grierson; *m* 1935, Audrey Margaret, *o d* of late Dr T. A. Glover, Doncaster; one *s. Educ:* Whitgift Sch., Croydon; Edinburgh Univ. Practised at Scottish Bar, 1931–39;

Sheriff-Substitute of Roxburgh, Berwick, and Selkirk at Selkirk and of the County of Peebles, 1942–45; Sheriff-Substitute of Stirling, Dumbarton and Clackmannan at Dumbarton, 1945–50; Sheriff-Substitute of Lanarkshire at Glasgow, 1950–63. Member, Law Reform Cttee for Scotland, 1964–70; Chm., Sheriff Court Rules Council, 1972–74. Hon. LLD Glasgow, 1967. *Publications:* The Law of Evidence in Scotland (joint author); Purves' Scottish Licensing Laws (7th, 8th edns). *Recreations:* walking, gardening.   *Died 22 May 1994.*

WALKER, Major David Harry, CM 1987; MBE 1946; author; *b* 9 Feb. 1911; *s* of Harry Giles Walker and Elizabeth Bewley (*née* Newsom); *m* 1939, Willa Magee, Montreal; four *s* (and one *s* decd). *Educ:* Shrewsbury; Sandhurst. The Black Watch, 1931–47 (retired); ADC to Gov.-Gen. of Canada, 1938–39; Comptroller to Viceroy of India, 1946–47. Member: Queen's Body Guard for Scotland; Canada Council, 1957–61; Chm., Roosevelt-Campobello Internat. Park Commn, 1970–72 (Canadian Comr, 1965). Hon. DLitt, Univ. of New Brunswick, 1955. FRSL. *Publications: novels:* The Storm and the Silence, 1950 (USA 1949); Geordie, 1950 (filmed 1955); The Pillar, 1952; Digby, 1953; Harry Black, 1956 (filmed, 1957); Sandy was a Soldier's Boy, 1957; Where the High Winds Blow, 1960; Storms of Our Journey and Other Stories, 1962; Dragon Hill (for children), 1962; Winter of Madness, 1964; Mallabec, 1965; Come Back, Geordie, 1966; Devil's Plunge (USA, Cab-Intersec), 1968; Pirate Rock, 1969; Big Ben (for children), 1970; The Lord's Pink Ocean, 1972; Black Dougal, 1973 (USA 1974); Ash, 1976; Pot of Gold, 1977; *non-fiction:* Lean, Wind, Lean: a few times remembered (memoirs), 1984. *Address:* Strathcroix, St Andrews, NB E0G 2X0, Canada. *Club:* Royal and Ancient.   *Died 5 March 1992.*

WALKER, Geoffrey Basil W.; *see* Woodd Walker.

WALKER, Prof. James, CBE 1971; BSc, MD, FRCPGlas, FRCOG; Professor of Obstetrics and Gynæcology, University of Dundee, 1967–81 (University of St Andrews, 1956–67); *b* 8 March 1916; *s* of James Walker, FEIS; *m* 1940, Catherine Clark Johnston, *d* of George R. A. Johnston; one *s* two *d. Educ:* High Schs of Falkirk and Stirling; Univ. of Glasgow. BSc 1935; MB, ChB (Hons) 1938; Brunton Memorial Prize; MRCOG 1947; MD (Hons) 1954; FRCOG 1957; MRCPGlas 1963, FRCPGlas 1968. Served War of 1939–45, RAFVR, UK and India, 1941–46. Hon. Surgeon to Out Patients, Royal Infirmary, Glasgow, Hall Tutor in Midwifery, Univ. Glasgow, 1946; Sen. Lectr in Midwifery and Gynæcology, Univ. of Aberdeen, Consultant NE Regional Hospital Board (Scotland), 1948; Reader in Obst. and Gynæcology, Univ. of London, Consultant, Hammersmith Hospital, 1955. Consultant, Eastern Regional Hosp. Bd, Scotland, 1956–81; Chm., Nat. Medical Consultative Cttee, Scotland, 1979–81; Chm., Cttee on Annual Reports Records and Definition of Terms in Human Reproduction, Internat. Fedn of Gynæcology and Obstetrics, 1976–88. Visiting Professor: New York State, 1957, 1970; Florida, 1965, 1970; McGill, 1967; Alexandria, 1979; Malaysia, 1981, 1984; Duke (USA), 1981; Stellenbosch, 1986; Prof. in Obst. and Gyn., Univ. Kebangsaan Malaysia, 1982–83. Blair Bell Memorial Lectr, Royal Coll. Obstetrics and Gynæcology, 1953. *Publications:* senior editor, Combined Textbook of Obstetrics and Gynæcology, 9th edn, 1976; contrib. on Obstetrics and Gynæcology to textbooks and learned jls. *Address:* 31 Ravenscraig Gardens, West Ferry, Dundee DD5 1LT. *T:* Dundee (01382) 779238. *Club:* Royal Air Force.   *Died 27 June 1995.*

WALKER, John; Director, National Gallery of Art, Washington, DC, 1956–69, then Director Emeritus; *b* 24 Dec. 1906; *s* of Hay Walker and Rebekah Jane Friend; *m* 1937, Lady Margaret Gwendolen Mary Drummond (*d*

1987); one *d* (one *s* decd). *Educ:* Harvard Univ. (AB). Associate in charge Dept Fine Arts American Acad., Rome, 1935–39 (later Trustee); Chief Curator, National Gall., Washington DC, 1939–56. Connected with protection and preservation of artistic and historic monuments; John Harvard Fellow, Harvard Univ., 1930–31; American Federation of Arts; Board of Advisers, Dumbarton Oaks; Trustee: Andrew W. Mellon Educational and Charitable Trust; American Federation of Arts; Wallace Foundation, NY; National Trust for Historic Preservation; Mem., Art Adv. Panel, National Trust (UK); Member Advisory Council: Univ. of Notre Dame; New York Univ.; Hon. Dr Fine Arts: Tufts Univ., 1958; Brown Univ., 1959; La Salle Coll., 1962; LittD: Notre Dame, 1959, Washington and Jefferson Univs, 1960; LHD: Catholic Univ. of America, 1964; Univ. of New York, 1965; Maryland Inst.; Georgetown Univ., 1966; William and Mary Univ., 1967. Holder of foreign decorations. *Publications:* (with Macgill James) Great American Paintings from Smibert to Bellows, 1943; (with Huntington Cairns) Masterpieces of Painting from National Gallery of Art, 1944; Paintings from America, 1951; (with Huntington Cairns) Great Paintings from the National Gallery of Art, 1952; National Gallery of Art, Washington, 1956; Bellini and Titian at Ferrara, 1957; Treasures from the National Gallery of Art, 1963; The National Gallery of Art, Washington, DC, 1964; (with H. Cairns) Pageant of Painting, 1966; Self-Portrait with Donors, 1974; National Gallery of Art, 1976; Turner, 1976; Constable, 1978; Whistler, 1987. *Address:* Easter Barton, Amberley, near Arundel, Sussex BN18 9NE; 214 South Beach Road, Jupiter Island, Hobe Sound, FL 33435, USA. *Clubs:* Turf, Dilettanti, Pilgrims'; Century Association (New York City); Chevy Chase, Metropolitan (Washington, DC).
Died 16 Oct. 1995.

WALKER, (Richard) Sebastian (Maynard); Chairman, Walker Books Ltd, since 1978; *b* 11 Dec. 1942; *s* of Richard and Christine Walker. *Educ:* Rugby Sch.; New Coll., Oxford (BA French Lang. and Lit.). Family engrg co., until 1970; Jonathan Cape, Chatto & Windus, 1970–75; Marshall Cavendish Ltd, 1975–77; Dir, Chatto & Windus, 1977–79; founded Walker Books, the children's book publisher, 1978. Dir, Rambert Dance Co., 1987–; Trustee, Music in Country Churches, 1989–. *Recreations:* piano, 20th century British art. *Address:* Walker Books Ltd, 87 Vauxhall Walk, SE11 5HJ. *T:* 071–793 0909.   *Died 16 June 1991.*

WALKER, Robert Scott, FRICS; City Surveyor, City of London Corporation, 1955–75; *b* 13 June 1913; *s* of Harold and Mary Walker; *m* 1946, Anne Armstrong; no *c*. *Educ:* West Buckland Sch., North Devon. War Service, 1939–45, Major RA. Assistant City Surveyor, Manchester, 1946–55. *Address:* 10 Woodcote Close, Epsom, Surrey KT18 7QJ. *T:* Epsom (01372) 721220.
Died 12 April 1995.

WALKER, Sebastian; *see* Walker, R. S. M.

WALKER, Stanley Kenneth; Director and Chief General Manager, Leeds Permanent Building Society, 1978–82; *b* 18 Feb. 1916; *s* of Robert and Gertrude Walker; *m* 1956, Diana, *d* of Fred Broadhead; one *s*. *Educ:* Cockburn Sch., Leeds. FCIS, FCBSI. Served War of 1939–45, Middle East (despatches, 1944). Leeds Permanent Building Society: Branch Manager, Newcastle upon Tyne, 1960–62; Asst Sec., 1962–66; Asst Gen. Manager, 1967–77; Gen. Manager, 1977–78. Mem. Council, Building Societies Assoc., 1978–81; Vice-Pres., Leeds Centre, Chartered Building Socs Inst., 1983. *Recreations:* tennis, walking, theatre. *Club:* Royal Automobile.
Died 11 Sept. 1993.

WALKER, Dame Susan (Armour), DBE 1972 (CBE 1963); Vice-Chairman, 1970–74, Deputy Chairman, 1974–77, Women's Royal Voluntary Service; *b* 15 April 1906; *d* of James Walker, Bowmont, Dunbar; unmarried. *Educ:* Grammar School, Dunbar. Conservative Central Office Agent, Yorkshire, 1950–56; Deputy Chief Organisation Officer, Conservative Central Office, 1956–64; Vice-Chm., Cons. Party Organisation, 1964–68, retired 1968. *Recreations:* golf, walking. *Address:* The Glebe House, Hownam, Kelso, Roxburghshire TD5 8AL. *T:* Morebattle (05734) 277.   *Died 11 July 1993.*

WALKER-SMITH, family name of **Baron Broxbourne.**

WALL, Hon. Sir Gerard (Aloysius), Kt 1987; medical practitioner; *b* 24 Jan. 1920; *m* 1951, Uru Raupo (*née* Cameron); two *s* three *d*. *Educ:* St Bede's College, Christchurch; Canterbury Univ.; Otago Univ. MB ChB; FRCSE. House Surgeon, Christchurch Public Hosp., 1948–49; GP, Denniston, 1949–53; Mem., Buller Hosp. Bd, 1949–50; House Surgeon, Postgraduate Hosp., London, 1953; Royal Nat. Orthopaedic Hosp., London, 1955; Res. Surgical Officer, Hitchin Hosp., 1954–55; Sen. Plastic Surgical Registrar: Birmingham Accident Hosp., 1956–57; Norwich Hosp., 1957–59; Surgeon Dep. Supt, Wairau Hosp., 1960–69; Mem., Marlborough Hosp. Bd, 1965–68; Porirua Hosp., 1968–69. MP (Lab) Porirua, 1969–85; Speaker, House of Reps, NZ, 1984–85. Mem. Govt Select Committees: Maori Affairs, Health and Social Services, Local Govt, Statutes Revision, Foreign Affairs; Chm., Parly Service Comm, 1985. Mem., Blenheim Borough Council, 1962–68. *Recreations:* woodworking, building. *Address:* 39 Tangare Drive, Elsdon, Porirua, New Zealand. *T:* (04) 375015.
Died 22 Nov. 1992.

WALL, Ronald George Robert, CB 1961; *b* 25 Jan. 1910; *s* of George Thomas and Sophia Jane Wall; *m* 1st, 1936, Winifred Evans (marr. diss., 1950); one *s*; 2nd, 1960, Mrs Muriel Sorrell (*née* Page). *Educ:* Alleyn's School, Dulwich; St John's College, Oxford (MA). Administrative Civil Service; entered Ministry of Agriculture and Fisheries, 1933; Gwilym Gibbon Research Fellow, Nuffield College, Oxford, 1951–52; Fisheries Sec., 1952–59; President of Permanent Commission under Internat. Fisheries Convention of 1946, 1953–56; Chairman of the International Whaling Commission, 1958–60; Dep. Sec., Min. of Agriculture, Fisheries and Food, 1961–70. Chm., Sugar Bd, 1970–77. *Recreations:* theatre, music, gardening, travel. *Address:* 201 London Road, Twickenham, Mddx. *T:* 081–892 7086. *Clubs:* United Oxford & Cambridge University, Arts Theatre.
Died 8 Sept. 1991.

WALLACE, David Mitchell, CBE 1978 (OBE 1942); MS, FRCS; retired, 1978; Professor of Urology, Riyadh Medical College, Saudi Arabia, 1974–78; *b* 8 May 1913; *s* of F. David Wallace and M. I. F. Wallace; *m* 1940, Noel Wilson; one *s* three *d*. *Educ:* Mill Hill; University Coll., London. BSc 1934; MB, BS 1938; FRCS 1939; MS 1948. Served War of 1939–45, Wing Comdr, RAF (despatches). Hunterian Prof., Royal Coll. of Surgeons, London, 1956, 1978. Formerly: Surgeon, St Peter's Hospital; Urologist, Royal Marsden Hospital, Chelsea Hospital for Women, and Manor House Hospitals; Lecturer, Institute of Urology; Adviser on Cancer to WHO. Mem., Amer. Radium Soc., 1968. *Publications:* Tumours of the Bladder, 1957; contrib. to Cancer, British Jl of Urology, Proc. Royal Soc. Med. *Recreations:* cine photography, pistol shooting. *Address:* 45 Fort Picklecombe, Tor Point, Cornwall PL10 1JB.
Died 11 Jan. 1992.

WALLACE, Robert, CBE 1970; JP; BL; Chairman, Highland Health Board, 1973–81; *b* 20 May 1911; *s* of late John Wallace, Glespin, Lanarkshire, and Elizabeth

Brydson; *m* 1st, 1940, Jane Maxwell (decd), *d* of late John Smith Rankin, Waulkmill, Thornhill, Dumfriesshire and Jane Maxwell; no *c*; 2nd, 1987, Mary Isobel, *d* of late Hector M. Macdonald, Conon Bridge, Ross-shire, and Catherine Ross. *Educ:* Sanquhar Sch.; Glasgow University. Solicitor 1932; BL (Dist.) 1933. Private legal practice, 1932–40; Depute Town Clerk, Ayr Burgh, 1940–44; Civil Defence Controller, Ayr Burgh, 1941–44; Depute County Clerk and Treas., Co. Inverness, 1944–48; County Clerk, Treasurer and Collector of the County of Inverness, 1948–73; Temp. Sheriff, Grampian, Highland and Islands, 1976–84. Hon. Sheriff at Inverness, 1967. JP Co. Inverness, 1951. *Recreations:* bowling, fishing, gardening. *Address:* Eildon, School Road, Conon Bridge, Ross-shire IV7 8AE. *T:* Dingwall (01349) 863592.
Died 16 Aug. 1995.

WALLACE, Walter Ian James, CMG 1957; OBE 1943; retired; *b* 18 Dec. 1905; *e s* of late David Wallace, Sandgate, Kent; *m* 1940, Olive Mary (*d* 1973), 4th *d* of late Col Charles William Spriggs, Southsea; no *c*. *Educ:* Bedford Modern School; St Catharine's College, Cambridge. Entered ICS 1928, posted to Burma; Dep. Commissioner, 1933; Settlement Officer, 1934–38; Dep. Commissioner, 1939–42; Defence Secretary, 1942–44; Military Administration of Burma (Col and Dep. Director Civil Affairs), 1944–45 (despatches); Commissioner, 1946; Chief Secretary, 1946–47; joined Colonial Office, 1947, Asst Sec., 1949–62; Asst Under-Sec. of State, 1962–66, retired. *Publication:* Revision Settlement Operations in the Minbu District of Upper Burma, 1939. *Recreation:* local history. *Club:* East India, Devonshire, Sports and Public Schools. *Died 17 Dec. 1993.*

WALLER, Sir (John) Keith, Kt 1968; CBE 1961 (OBE 1957); Secretary, Department of Foreign Affairs, Canberra, 1970–74, retired; *b* 19 Feb. 1914; *s* of late A. J. Waller, Melbourne; *m* 1943, Alison Irwin Dent; two *d*. *Educ:* Scotch Coll., Melbourne; Melbourne Univ. Entered Dept of External Affairs, Australia, 1936; Private Sec. to Rt Hon. W. M. Hughes, 1937–40; Second Sec., Australian Legation, Chungking, 1941; Sec.-Gen., Australian Delegn, San Francisco Conf., 1945; First Sec., Australian Legation, Rio de Janeiro, 1945; Chargé d'Affaires, 1946; First Sec., Washington, 1947; Consul-Gen., Manila, 1948; Officer-in-Charge, Political Intelligence Div., Canberra, 1950; External Affairs Officer, London, 1951; Asst Sec., Dept of External Affairs, Canberra, 1953–57; Ambassador to Thailand, 1957–60; Ambassador to USSR, 1960–62; First Asst Sec., Dept of External Affairs, 1963–64; Ambassador to US, 1964–70. Member: Australian Council for the Arts, 1973; Interim Film Board, 1974. Chm., Radio Australia Inquiry, 1975. *Address:* 17 Canterbury Crescent, Deakin, ACT 2600, Australia. *Club:* Commonwealth (Canberra).
Died 14 Nov. 1992.

WALLER, Sir John Stanier, 7th Bt, *cr* 1815, of Braywick Lodge, Berkshire; author, poet, and journalist; *b* 27 July 1917; *s* of Capt. Stanier Edmund William Waller (*d* 1923), and Alice Amy (who *m* 2nd, 1940, Gerald H. Holiday; she *d* 1959), *d* of J. W. Harris, Oxford; *S* kinsman, Sir Edmund Waller, 6th Bt, 1954; *m* 1974, Anne Eileen Mileham (marr. diss.). *Educ:* Weymouth Coll.; Worcester Coll., Oxford (Exhibnr in History, 1936; BA in Eng. Lang. and Lit., 1939; DipEd (Teaching), 1940). Founder-Editor of quarterly, Kingdom Come, first new literary magazine of war, 1939–41; served 1940–46 with RASC (in Middle East, 1941–46); Adjt RASC, HQ, Cairo Area; Capt. 1942; Features Editor, Brit. Min. of Inf., Middle East, 1943–45; Chief Press Officer, Brit. Embassy, Bagdad, 1945; News and Features Editor, Min. of Inf., ME, Cairo, 1945–46; Dramatic Critic Cairo Weekly, The Sphinx, 1943–46; Founder-Mem. Salamander Soc. of Poets, Cairo, 1942; lectured in Pantheon Theatre, Athens, 1945; Lectr and

Tutor in English and Eng. Lit. at Carlisle and Gregson (Jimmy's), Ltd, 1953–54; Asst Master, London Nautical Sch., May-June 1954; Information Officer, Overseas Press Services Div., Central Office of Information, 1954–59. Director: Literature Ltd, 1940–42; Richard Congreve Ltd, 1948–50; Export Trade Ships Ltd, 1956; Bristol Stone and Concrete Ltd, 1974; Mercantile Land and Marine Ltd, 1979. Greenwood Award for Poetry, 1947; Keats Prize, 1974; FRSL 1948. *Publications:* The Confessions of Peter Pan, 1941; Fortunate Hamlet, 1941; Spring Legend, 1942; The Merry Ghosts, 1946; Middle East Anthology (editor), 1946; Crusade, 1946; The Kiss of Stars, 1948; The Collected Poems of Keith Douglas (editor), 1951 and 1966; Shaggy Dog, 1953; Alamein to Zem Zem by Keith Douglas (editor), 1966; Goldenhair and the Two Black Hawks, 1971; Return to Oasis (co-editor), 1980; contrib. to numerous anthologies and periodicals at home and abroad. *Recreations:* portrait photography, teaching. *Heir:* none. *Address:* Winchcombe, 37A Madeira Road, Ventnor, Isle of Wight PO38 1TQ. *T:* Isle of Wight (01983) 854443. *Died 22 Jan. 1995 (ext).*

WALLER, Sir Keith; *see* Waller, Sir J. K.

WALLIS, Col Hugh Macdonell, OC 1969; DSO 1919; OBE 1945; MC; VD 1930, CD 1967; *b* 7 Dec. 1893; *s* of John McCall Wallis, Peterborough, Ont, and Gertrude Thornton, *d* of Lt-Col Samuel Smith Macdonell, QC, LLD, DCL, Windsor, Ont; *m* 1st, 1935, Leslie (marr. diss., 1953), *d* of late Mr and Mrs K. K. Carson, London; 2nd, 1969, Corinne de Boucherville (*d* 1981), *widow* of Hon. Jean Desy. *Educ:* Lakefield Preparatory Sch.; Toronto Univ. Enlisted 1st CEF, Sept. 1914; served France, Belgium, Germany, 1915–19; Bde Major 4th Can. Inf. Bde, 1918 (DSO, MC, despatches twice); Colonel Comdg The Black Watch, Royal Highlanders of Canada, then Permanent Active Militia, 1930; R of O, 1931; Hon. ADC to Earl of Bessborough, Gov.-Gen. of Canada, 1931–35; Active Service, Canadian Forces, 1940–45; Colonel Asst DAG Nat. Defence HQ (OBE); Hon. Lt-Col 3rd Bn The Black Watch of Canada, 1961–68. Chartered Accountant, with McDonald, Currie & Co., 1923; Man. Dir and Pres., Mount Royal Rice Mills Ltd, Montreal, 1924–53. Past President: Canadian Citizenship Council, St Andrews Soc. of Montreal, Canadian Club of Montreal, Montreal Museum of Fine Arts. Governor: Council for Canadian Unity; Lakefield College Sch.; Montreal General Hosp.; Montreal Children's Hosp. (Past Chm. of Exec.); l'Hôpital Marie Enfant; Chm., Adv. Bd, Canadian Centenary (1967) Council (past Chm. Org. and Exec. Cttees). Hon. Sponsor, Trent Univ., Ont, 1963; Associate, McGill Univ. and l'Univ. de Montréal. FRSA 1959. KCLJ. Outstanding Citizen Award, Montreal Citizenship Council, 1967. Canada Centennial Medal, 1967; Jubilee Medal, 1977. *Recreations:* travel, fine arts, Canadiana books and history. *Address:* c/o Hugh Parker Wallis, 139 New Erin Road, Huntingdon, Qué J0S IH0, Canada. *Clubs:* Canadian, United Services (Montreal).
Died 21 March 1991.

WALSER, Ven. David; Archdeacon of Ely, and Hon. Canon, 1981–93, then Emeritus; *b* 12 March 1923; *s* of William and Nora Walser; *m* 1975, Dr Elizabeth Enid Shillito. *Educ:* Claysmore School; St Edmund Hall, Oxford (MA, DipTh); St Stephen's House, Oxford. Served RA and Royal Indian Mountain Artillery, 1942–46. Deacon 1950, priest 1951; Asst Curate, St Gregory the Great, Horfield, 1950–54; Vice-Principal, St Stephen's House, 1954–60; Asst Chaplain, Exeter Coll., Oxford, 1956–57; Junior Chaplain, Merton Coll., Oxford, 1957–60; Minor Canon, Ely Cathedral and Chaplain of King's School, 1961–71; Vicar of Linton, dio. Ely, 1971–81; Rector of Bartlow, 1973–81; RD of Linton, 1976–81; Rector of St Botolph's, Cambridge, 1981–89;

Priest-in-Charge, St Clement's, Cambridge, 1985–89. *Recreations:* hill walking, music, reading, caravanning, crosswords, hymn writing for local use. *Address:* 27 Tavistock Road, Cambridge CB4 3NB. *T:* Cambridge (0223) 62750. *Died 1 Oct. 1993.*

WALSH, Surg. Rear-Adm. Dermot Francis, CB 1960; OBE 1952; FRCSE; *b* 21 Jan. 1901; *s* of Dr J. A. Walsh. *Educ:* Belvedere Coll., Dublin; Trinity Coll., Dublin. BA 1927; MB, BCh, BAO, 1928; FRCSE 1943. Joined RN Medical Service, 1929; MO i/c RN Hosp., Malta and Med. Advr to C-in-C Allied Forces, Mediterranean, 1958–61. QHS 1958–61. Naval Rep., BMA Council, 1961–66. CStJ 1958. *Recreations:* golf, gardening, music. *Address:* 20 Hazelwood, Shankill, Co. Dublin, Eire. *T:* Dublin 2823653. *Died 22 Oct. 1992.*

WALSH, Dr John James; Consultant to Paddocks Private Clinic, Aylesbury Road, Princes Risborough; *b* 4 July 1917; *s* of Dr Thomas Walsh and Margaret (*née* O'Sullivan); *m* 1946, Joan Mary (decd), *d* of Henry Teasdale and Nita Birks; three *s* and *d. Educ:* Mungret Coll.; University Coll., Cork. MB, BCh 1940; MD 1963; MRCP 1968, FRCP 1975; FRCS 1969. Various hospital appointments, including Medical Officer, Spinal Injuries Centre, Stoke Mandeville Hospital, Aylesbury, 1947; Deputy Director, National Spinal Injuries Centre, Stoke Mandeville Hospital, 1957–66, Dir, 1966–77. *Publications:* Understanding Paraplegia, 1964; a number of publications on subjects pertaining to paraplegia in medical journals. *Recreation:* shooting. *Address:* Alena, Bridge Street, Great Kimble, Aylesbury, Bucks HP17 9TN. *T:* Princes Risborough (08444) 3347.

Died 31 Dec. 1992.

WALSHAM, Rear-Adm. Sir John Scarlett Warren, 4th Bt, *cr* 1831, of Knill Court, Herefordshire; CB 1963; OBE 1944; Royal Navy, retired; Admiral Superintendent HM Dockyard, Portsmouth, 1961–64; *b* 29 Nov. 1910; *s* of Sir John S. Walsham, 3rd Bt, and Bessie Geraldine Gundreda (*d* 1941), *e d* of late Vice-Admiral John B. Warren; *S* father, 1940; *m* 1936, Sheila Christina, *o d* of Comdr Bertrand Bannerman, DSO; one *s* two *d.* Rear-Admiral, 1961. *Heir: s* Timothy John Walsham, *b* 26 April 1939. *Address:* Priory Cottage, Middle Coombe, Shaftesbury, Dorset. *Died 22 Oct. 1992.*

WALSTON, Baron *cr* 1961 (Life Peer), of Newton, Co. of Cambridge; **Henry David Leonard George Walston,** CVO 1976; JP; farmer; *b* 16 June 1912; *o s* of late Sir Charles Walston, LittD, LHD, PhD, and Florence, *d* of David Einstein; *m* 1st, 1935, Catherine Macdonald (*d* 1978), *d* of late D. H. Crompton and Mrs Charles Tobey; three *s* two *d* (and one *s* decd); 2nd, 1979, Elizabeth Scott, *d* of late Robert Bissett-Robinson. *Educ:* Eton; King's Coll., Cambridge (MA). Research Fellow in Bacteriology, Harvard, USA, 1934–35; Mem., Hunts War Agricultural Cttee, 1939–45; Dir of Agriculture, British Zone of Germany, 1946–47; Agricultural Adviser for Germany to FO, 1947–48; Counsellor, Duchy of Lancaster, 1948–54. Contested: (L) Hunts, 1945; (Lab) Cambridgeshire, 1951 and 1955; (Lab) Gainsborough, 1957 (by-election), and 1959. Parly Under-Sec. of State, FO, 1964–67; Parly Sec., BoT, Jan.-Aug. 1967; Member: UK Delegn to Council of Europe and WEU, 1970–75; European Parlt, 1975–77; joined SDP, 1981; SDP Chief Whip, House of Lords, 1988–89. HM Special Ambassador to inauguration of Presidents of Mexico, 1964, of Columbia, 1966, and of Liberia, 1968. Crown Estate Comr, 1968–76; Chm., Inst. of Race Relations, 1968–71; Mem., Commonwealth Development Corp., 1975–83 (Dep. Chm., 1981–83). Minister of Agriculture's Liaison Officer, 1969–70; Chairman: East Anglia Regional Planning Council, 1969–79; GB/East Europe Centre, 1974–86; Centre of E Anglian Studies, 1975–79; Harwich Harbour Conservancy Bd, 1975–79; Member: Cambs Agricultural Cttee, 1948–50; Home Office Cttee on Experiments on Animals, 1961–62. Chm., Harlow Group Hosp. Management Cttee, 1962–64; Dep. Chm., Council, Royal Commonwealth Soc., 1963–64 (Vice-Pres., 1970–); Vice-Pres., VSO, 1981–; Trustee, Rural Industries Bureau, 1959–64; Governor, Guy's Hosp., 1944–47. Hon. DCL East Anglia. JP Cambridge, 1944. *Publications:* From Forces to Farming, 1944; Our Daily Bread, 1952; No More Bread, 1954; Life on the Land, 1954; (with John Mackie) Land Nationalisation, for and against, 1958; Agriculture under Communism, 1961; The Farmer and Europe, 1962; The Farm Gate to Europe, 1970; Dealing with Hunger, 1976; contribs to Proc. of Experimental Biology and Medicine, Jl of Hygiene, Observer, Economist, New Statesman, Spectator. *Recreations:* shooting, sailing. *Address:* Selwood Manor, Frome, Somerset BA11 3NL. *Clubs:* Brooks's, MCC; House of Lords Yacht.

Died 29 May 1991.

WALTERS, Peter (Hugh Bennetts) Ensor, OBE 1957; public relations and fund raising consultant since 1959; *b* 18 July 1912; *yr s* of late Rev. C. Ensor Walters, a President of the Methodist Conference, and Muriel Havergal, *d* of late Alderman J. H. Bennetts, JP, Penzance; *m* 1936, (Ella) Marcia, *er d* of Percival Burdle Hayter; no *c. Educ:* Manor House Sch.; St Peter's Coll., Oxford. On staff of late Rt Hon. David Lloyd George, 1935–39; enlisted as volunteer in Army, 1940; commissioned in Royal Army Pay Corps, 1942; National Organizer, National Liberal Organization, 1944–51; General Sec., National Liberal Organization, Hon. Sec. and Treas., National Liberal Party Council, and Dir, National Liberal Forum, 1951–58. Vice-Chm., Nat. Liberal Club, 1972–74. Pres., Worthing Central Cons. Assoc., 1984–89. *Recreation:* travel. *Address:* 2 Hopedene Court, Wordsworth Road, Worthing, W Sussex BN11 1TB. *T:* Worthing (0903) 205678. *Club:* Union Society (Oxford).

Died 14 Jan. 1994.

WALTON, Ernest Thomas Sinton, MA, MSc, PhD; Fellow of Trinity College, Dublin, 1934–74 (Fellow Emeritus 1974), and Erasmus Smith's Professor of Natural and Experimental Philosophy 1947–74; *b* 6 Oct. 1903; *s* of Rev. J. A. Walton, MA and Anne Elizabeth (*née* Sinton); *m* 1934, Winifred Isabel Wilson (*d* 1983); two *s* two *d. Educ:* Methodist College, Belfast; Trinity College, Dublin; Cambridge University. 1851 Overseas Research Scholarship, 1927–30; Senior Research Award of Dept of Scientific and Industrial Research, 1930–34; Clerk Maxwell Scholar, 1932–34. Hon. Life Mem., RDS, 1981. Hon. FIEI 1985; Hon. FInstP 1988. Hon. DSc: QUB, 1959; Gustavus Adolphus Coll., Minn, USA, 1975; Ulster, 1988; Hon. PhD Dublin City Univ., 1991. Awarded Hughes Medal by Royal Society, 1938; (with Sir John Cockcroft) Nobel Prize for Physics, 1951. *Publications:* papers on hydrodynamics, nuclear physics and microwaves. *Address:* 37 Deramore Park South, Belfast BT9 5JY. *T:* Belfast (01232) 681554.

Died 25 June 1995.

WALWYN, Fulke Thomas Tyndall, CVO 1983; racehorse trainer, retired 1990; *b* 8 Nov. 1910; *s* of Col Fulke Walwyn, DSO and Norah Walwyn; *m* 1st, 1937, Diana Carlos Clarke (*d* 1949); 2nd, 1952, Catherine de Trafford; one *d. Educ:* Malvern; RMA Sandhurst. 9th Lancers, 1930–36; leading amateur rider 3 times; turned professional jockey, 1936; rode Reynoldstown to Grand National win, 1936; started to train, 1939, to train for HM the Queen Mother, 1973; trained over 2,000 winners; Leading Trainer 5 times. *Address:* Saxon House Stables, Lambourn, Berks RG16 7QL. *T:* Lambourn (0488) 71555. *Died 18 Feb. 1991.*

WANAMAKER, Sam, Hon. CBE 1993; actor, director, producer; *b* Chicago, 14 June 1919; *s* of Morris Wanamaker and Molly (*née* Bobele); *m* 1940, Charlotte Holland; three *d. Educ:* Drake University, Iowa, USA. Studied for the stage at Goodman Theatre, Chicago. Appeared in summer theatres, Chicago (acting and directing), 1936–39; joined Globe Shakespearian Theatre Group; first New York Appearance, Café Crown, 1941; Counter Attack, 1942; served in United States Armed Forces, 1943–46; in several parts on New York stage, 1946–49; appeared in This, Too, Shall Pass, 1946; directed and played in: Joan of Lorraine, 1946–47; Goodbye My Fancy, 1948–49; directed: Caeser and Cleopatra, 1950; The Soldier and the Lady, 1954; created Festival Repertory Theatre, New York, 1950; first performance (also producer) on London stage as Bernie Dodd, in Winter Journey, St James's, 1952; presented and appeared in The Shrike, Prince's, 1953; produced: Purple Dust, Glasgow, 1953; Foreign Field, Birmingham, 1954; directed and appeared in One More River, Cat on a Hot Tin Roof, and The Potting Shed, 1957; in Liverpool, 1957, created New Shakespeare Theatre Cultural Center, where produced (appearing in some): Tea and Sympathy, A View from the Bridge, 1957; The Rose Tattoo, Finian's Rainbow, Bus Stop, The Rainmaker, and Reclining Figure (all in 1958). *Presented, produced and appeared in:* The Big Knife, Duke of York's 1954; The Lovers, Winter Garden, 1955; The Rainmaker, St Martin's, 1956; A Hatful of Rain, Prince's, 1957; The Rose Tattoo, New, 1959; Iago, Stratford-on-Avon, 1959; Dr Breuer, in A Far Country, New York, 1961; The Watergate Tapes, Royal Court, 1974; *produced:* The World of Sholom Aleichem, Embassy, 1955; King Priam, Coventry Theatre and Royal Opera House, Covent Garden, 1962, 1967, and 1972; Verdi's La Forza del Destino, Royal Opera House, Covent Garden, 1962; John Player season, Globe, 1972–73; Southwark Summer Festival, 1974; Shakespeare Birthday Celebrations, 1974; *directed:* Children from their Games, New York, 1963; A Case of Libel, New York, 1963; A Murder Among Us, New York, 1964; Defenders, 1964; War and Peace (première), Sydney Opera House, 1973; The Ice Break, Royal Opera House, Covent Garden, 1977; Chicago Lyric Opera Gala, 1979; Stravinsky's Oedipus, Boston Symphony Orch., Tanglewood, 1982; *acted and directed* Macbeth, Goodman Theater, Chicago, 1964; *directed and wrote* This Wooden O, Carnegie Hall, Pittsburgh, 1983; *acted (films):* Give Us This Day; Taras Bulba; Those Magnificent Men in Their Flying Machines, 1964; The Winston Affair, 1964; The Spy Who Came in from the Cold, 1964; Warning Shot; The Law, 1974; Spiral Staircase, 1974; The Sell-Out, 1975; The Voyage of the Damned, 1975; Billy Jack goes to Washington, 1976; From Hell to Victory, 1978; Private Benjamin, 1980; The Competition, 1980; Irreconcilable Differences, 1983; The Aviator, 1983; (film for TV) Embassy, 1985; Raw Deal, 1985; Superman IV, 1986; Judgement in Berlin, 1987; Secret Ingredient, 1987; Baby Boom, 1988; Guilty By Suspicion, 1989; Pure Luck, 1990; Fear No Evil, 1990; *films directed:* Hawk, 1965; Lancer, 1966; Custer, 1967; File of the Golden Goose, 1968; The Executioner, 1969; Catlow, 1970; Sinbad and the Eye of the Tiger, 1975; The Killing of Randy Webster, 1981; *directed (opera):* Aida, San Francisco, 1981; Tosca, San Diego, 1987; *directed (television):* Colombo, 1977; Hawaii 5–0, 1978; Dark Side of Love, Man Undercover, Mrs Columbo, Hart to Hart, 1979; Grand Deception (Columbo series), 1989; *acted and directed (TV):* The Holocaust, 1977; The Return of the Saint, 1978; *acted (TV):* Blind Love, 1976; Charlie Muffin, 1979; The Family Business, 1981; The Ghost Writer, 1982; The Berrengers, 1984; Heartsounds, 1984; The Ferret, 1984; Two Mrs Grenvilles, 1986; Baby Boom (series), 1988. Founder and Executive Vice-Chairman: Globe Playhouse Trust Ltd, 1971; Internat. Shakespeare Globe Centre (formerly World Centre for Shakespeare Studies Ltd). Fellow QMW, 1992. Hon. LLD New Brunswick, 1989; Hon. DFA Roosevelt, 1990. Benjamin Franklin Medal, RSA, 1989. *Address:* Bear Gardens, SE1 9ED.
Died 18 Dec. 1993.

WARD, Gen. Sir (Alfred) Dudley, GCB 1959 (KCB 1957; CB 1945); KBE 1953 (CBE 1945); DSO 1944; *b* 27 Jan. 1905; *s* of L. H. Ward, Wimborne, Dorset; *m* 1st, 1933, Beatrice Constance (*d* 1962), *d* of Rev. T. F. Griffith, The Bourne, Farnham, Surrey; one *d*; 2nd, 1963, Joan Elspeth de Pechell, *d* of late Colonel D. C. Scott, CBE, Netherbury, Dorset. *Educ:* Wimborne Grammar Sch.; Royal Military Coll., Sandhurst. 2nd Lieut, Dorset Regt, 1929; Captain, The King's Regt, 1937; served War of 1939–45 (DSO, CBE, CB); Director of Military Operations, War Office, 1947–48; Commandant, Staff Coll., Camberley, 1948–51; Commander of the 1st Corps, 1951–52; Deputy Chief of Imperial General Staff, 1953–56; Commander, Northern Army Group and Commander-in-Chief, British Army of the Rhine, 1957–Dec. 1959; Comdr in Chief, British Forces, Near East, 1960–62; Governor and Commander in Chief of Gibraltar, 1962–65. Colonel, King's Regt, 1947–57; Colonel Commandant, REME, 1958–63; ADC General to the Queen, 1959–61. DL Suffolk, 1968–84. Order of Suvorov, USSR, 1944; Legion of Merit, USA, 1946. *Recreation:* golf. *Address:* Wynney's Farmhouse, Dennington, Woodbridge, Suffolk. *T:* Badingham (072875) 663. *Club:* Army and Navy.
Died 28 Dec. 1991.

WARD, Sir Arthur (Hugh), KBE 1979 (OBE 1962); ACA; FNZIAS; Chancellor, Massey University, 1975–81 (Pro-Chancellor, 1970–75); *b* 25 March 1906; *s* of Arthur Ward and Ada Elizabeth Ward; *m* 1936, Jean Bannatyne Mueller; one *s* three *d. Educ:* Middlesbrough High Sch., Yorks. ACA (NZ); FNZIAS 1969. Sec., NZ Co-op. Herd Testing Assoc., 1929–36; Dir, Herd Improvement, NZ Dairy Bd, 1945–54; Gen. Man., Dairy Bd, 1954–70. Chm., W. M. Angus & Co., 1970–75; Dep. Chm., Ivon Watkins Dow, 1971–76. Member: NZ Monetary and Econ. Council, 1970–79; Remuneration Authority, 1971–72; National Res. Adv. Council, 1970–72 (Chm., 1971–72); Council, Massey Univ., 1967–81. Hon. DSc Massey, 1991. Marsden Medal for services to science, 1975; Queen's Silver Jubilee Medal, 1977. *Publications:* A Command of Co-operatives, 1975; articles on dairy cattle husbandry and dairy cattle breeding. *Recreations:* writing, reading, gardening, golf. *Address:* 4 Pukeko Street, Woodlands, Waikanae, New Zealand. *T:* (2) 2936466; PO Box 56, Waikanae.
Died 1 Nov. 1993.

WARD, Rev. Canon Charles Leslie; Canon Treasurer of Wells and Prebendary of Warminster in Wells Cathedral, 1978–85, then Canon Emeritus; Hon. Assistant, St Mary's, Charlton Kings, Cheltenham, since 1993; *b* 11 June 1916; *s* of Amos Ward and Maude Hazeldine Ballard; *m* 1943, Barbara, *d* of George and Alice Stoneman; two *s. Educ:* Mexborough Grammar Sch.; Lichfield Theological Coll. (Potter-Selwyn Exhibnr). Underground Surveyor, Cadeby Colliery, S Yorks, 1933–36; deacon, 1939; priest, 1940; Assistant Curate: Parkgate, 1939; Rossington, 1940; Taunton, 1942; Bishop of Blackburn's Youth Chaplain and Succentor of Blackburn Cathedral, 1945; Vicar: St Michael, Ashton on Ribble, 1948; St Peter, Cheltenham, 1951; Northleach, Stowell, Hampnett, Yanworth and Eastington, 1960; Holy Trinity, Yeovil, 1964; Minehead, 1967; pastoral care for Elmore and Longney, Gloucester, 1990–93. Fellow, St Paul's and St Mary's Colls, Cheltenham, 1954–. *Recreations:* church spotting, driving motor cars, listening to music. *Address:* 25 Withyholt Court, Charlton Kings, Cheltenham GL53 9BQ. *T:* Cheltenham (0242) 252348.
Died 22 March 1994.

WARD, Gen. Sir Dudley; *see* Ward, Gen. Sir A. D.

WARD, Edward; *see* Bangor, 7th Viscount.

WARD, Air Cdre Ellacott Lyne Stephens, CB 1954; DFC 1939; Royal Air Force, retired; *b* 22 Aug. 1905; *s* of late Lt-Col E. L. Ward, CBE, IMS and Charlotte Lyne, *d* of W. E. L. Veale, RN; *m* 1929, Sylvia Winifred Constance Etheridge (*d* 1974), *d* of late Lt-Col F. Etheridge, DSO, IA, and Mrs Etheridge; one *s* one *d*. *Educ:* Bradfield; Cranwell. No 20 Sqdn, India, 1926–30; Engineering Course, and Engineering duties, UK, 1930–34; Instr, Sch. of Army Co-operation, RAF Old Sarum, 1934–36; student, Army Staff Coll., Quetta, 1936–37; comd No 28 Sqdn, RAF, 1938–39; MAP, 1940–42; Instructor, RAF Staff Coll., 1942–43; commanded stns in 5 Gp, Bomber Comd, 1943–45; Dep. Head, RAF Mission to Chinese Air Force Staff Coll., Chengtu, China, 1945–46; SASO, Burma, 1946–47; Air Ministry, 1947–49; Flying Training Comd, 1949–52; Head of British Services Mission to Burma, 1952–54; AOC No 64 (N) Group, Royal Air Force, 1954–57. Order of Cloud and Banner (China), 1946; Air Force Order of Ch'len Yuan (China), 1946. *Recreation:* (retired from) bookbinding. *Address:* Carousel, 37 Brownsea Road, Sandbanks, Poole, Dorset BH13 7QW. *T:* Canford Cliffs (0202) 709455.

Died 2 Oct. 1991.

WARD, Frank; *see* Ward, W. E. F.

WARD, Sir John (Guthrie), GCMG 1967 (KCMG 1956; CMG 1947); HM Diplomatic Service, retired; *b* 3 March 1909; *o s* of late Herbert John Ward and Alice Ward (*née* Guthrie); *m* 1st, 1933, Bettine (*d* 1941), *d* of late Col Sydney Hankey; one *s* one *d*; 2nd, 1942, Daphne (*d* 1983), *d* of late Captain Hon. Andrew Mulholland (*e s* of 2nd Baron Dunleath) and Joan, Countess of Cavan; two *d*. *Educ:* Wellington Coll.; Pembroke Coll., Cambridge (History Schol.). BA 1929, Hon. Fellow 1976; Member of University Air Squadron. Entered Diplomatic Service, 1931; served Foreign Office, and British Embassies, Baghdad, 1932–34 and Cairo, 1938–40; British Representative on League of Nations Cttee for settlement of Assyrians, 1935–37; Second Sec., 1936; First Sec., 1941; Mem. of UK Delegns to Moscow confs, 1943–44–45 and Potsdam conf., 1945; Counsellor and Head of UN Dept, Foreign Office, 1946; Counsellor, British Embassy, Rome, 1946–49; Civilian Member of Directing Staff of Imperial Defence Coll., London, 1950; Dep. UK High Comr in Germany, 1951–54; Dep. Under-Sec. of State, Foreign Office, 1954–56; British Ambassador to Argentina, 1957–61; British Ambassador to Italy, 1962–66; retired 1967. Chairman, British-Italian Soc., 1967–74. Mem. Council, RSPCA, 1970–75; Pres., ISPA. *Recreations:* history, gardening. *Address:* Lenox, St Margarets Bay, near Dover. *Club:* Royal Automobile.

Died 12 Jan. 1991.

WARD, Martyn Eric; Hon. Mr Justice Ward; Judge of the Supreme Court of Bermuda, since 1987; *b* 10 Oct. 1927; 3rd *s* of Arthur George Ward, DSM and Dorothy Ward (*née* Perkins); *m* 1st, 1957, Rosaleen Iona Soloman; one *d*; 2nd, 1966, Rosanna Maria Giubarelli; two *s*. Royal Navy, 1945–48. Called to Bar, Lincoln's Inn, 1955. A Circuit Judge, 1972–87. *Recreations:* ski-ing, tennis, swimming. *Address:* c/o Supreme Court, 21 Parliament Street, Hamilton HL12, Bermuda.

Died 27 Nov. 1991.

WARD, Sir Terence George, Kt 1971; CBE 1961 (MBE 1945); Dean of the Faculty of Dental Surgery, Royal College of Surgeons, 1965–68; *b* 16 Jan. 1906; *m* 1931, Elizabeth Ambrose Wilson (*d* 1981); one *s* one *d*; *m* 1982, Sheila Elizabeth Lawry. *Educ:* Edinburgh. LRCP, LRCSE 1928; LRFPS(G) 1930; LDS (Edinburgh) 1928; FDSRCS 1948; FRCS 1970. Mem., SE Metropolitan Regional

Hosp. Bd; Exmr, DSRCSE, FDRCSI. Pres., Internat. Assoc. Oral Surgeons; Past Pres., British Association of Oral Surgeons; Consulting Oral Surgeon to the Royal Navy; Consulting Dental Surgeon: to the British Army, 1954–71, Emeritus 1971; to the Royal Air Force; to Dept of Health and Social Security; to the Queen Victoria Hospital, East Grinstead. FACD 1959; FACDS; FFDRCSI, 1964; Hon. FDSRCSE, 1966; Hon. FRCCD, 1966. DDSc, Melbourne, 1963; Dr Odontology, Lund Univ. Mem., SA Dental Assoc.; Hon. Member: Amer. Soc. Oral Surgeons; Dutch Soc. Oral Surgeons; Hon. Fellow: Scandinavian Assoc. Oral Surgeons; Spanish Assoc. Oral Surgeons. *Publication:* The Dental Treatment of Maxillo-facial Injuries, 1956. *Recreation:* golf. *Address:* 22 Marina Court Avenue, Bexhill-on-Sea, East Sussex. *T:* Bexhill-on-Sea (0424) 4760.

Died 30 Sept. 1991.

WARD, (William Ernest) Frank, CMG 1945; *b* 24 Dec. 1900; *s* of W. H. Ward, Borough Treasurer, Battersea; *m* 1926, Sylvia Grace (*d* 1992), *d* of Arthur Clayton Vallance, Mansfield, Notts; no *c*. *Educ:* LCC elementary school; Mercers' Sch.; Dulwich Coll.; Lincoln Coll., Oxford (BLitt, MA); Ridley Hall, Cambridge (Diploma in Education). Master, Achimota Coll., Gold Coast, 1924; Director of Education, Mauritius, 1940; Deputy Educational Adviser, Colonial Office, 1945–56. Editor, Oversea Education, 1946–63. Member of UK delegation to seven general conferences of UNESCO and many other international meetings on education. *Publications:* History of the Gold Coast, 1948, new edn as History of Ghana, 1967; Educating Young Nations, 1959; Fraser of Trinity and Achimota, 1965; The Royal Navy and the Slavers, 1969; My Africa, 1991; various historical works and educational textbooks. *Recreations:* music, walking. *Address:* Roseacre, Holly Hill Drive, Banstead, Surrey SM7 2BD. *T:* Burgh Heath (0737) 353547.

Died 9 July 1994.

WARD-JACKSON, Adrian Alexander, CBE 1991; Member, since 1989, Chairman, Dance Panel, since 1990, Arts Council; Chairman and Director, Adrian Ward-Jackson Ltd, since 1975; *b* 6 June 1950; 3rd *s* of William Ward-Jackson and Catherine Elizabeth Ward-Jackson (*née* Trew). *Educ:* Westminster; Vienna. Drawings Dept, Christie's, London, 1970–71; Dir, P. & D. Colnaghi & Co., 1971–75. Chairman: Ballet Rambert, 1984–90; Mercury Theatre Trust, 1984–90; Governor, Royal Ballet, 1985–; Bd Mem., Ballet Bd, Royal Opera House, 1985–90; Dir, Royal Opera House Trust, 1987–90; Chm., Contemporary Art Soc., 1990–; Dir, Contemporary Arts Soc. Projects Ltd, 1988–; Dir, Soc. of British Theatre Designers, 1989–; Member: Theatre Mus. Cttee., V&A, 1990–; Steering Gp on the structure of Arts funding, Office of Arts and Libraries, 1990–. Dep. Chm., Creative Dance Artists' Trust, 1985–90; Trustee: Aphrodisias Trust, 1985–; Dancers' Resettlement Fund, 1987–; Silver Trust, 1988–; Dancers' Pension Fund, 1989–; Dame Margot Fonteyn Scholarship Fund, 1990–. Dep. Chm., Council, AIDS Crisis Trust, 1987–. *Recreations:* performing arts, contemporary art, ski-ing, fishing. *Address:* (office) 120 Mount Street, W1Y 5HB. *T:* 071–493 8768; 37 Great Cumberland Place, W1H 7LG. *T:* 071–262 3558. *Club:* Turf.

Died 23 Aug. 1991.

WARDS, Brig. George Thexton, CMG 1943; OBE 1935; late Indian Army; Historian, Cabinet Office, 1951–69; *b* 17 June 1897; *e s* of late Capt. J. Wards. *Educ:* Heversham Sch., Westmorland. Served European War, 1914–18, with 7 London Regt, France and Belgium, 1917–18; 2nd Lieut, Indian Army, 1918; attached to HM Embassy, Tokyo, 1923–28; NW Frontier of India, 1930; Bt Major, 1933; Staff Officer to British Troops in North China, 1932–36; Lt-Col and Asst Military Attaché, Tokyo, 1937–41; Brig., Military Attaché, Tokyo, 1941; GSO1, GHQ India, 1942;

Commandant Intelligence Sch., India, 1943–45; Commandant Intelligence Corps, Training Centre, India, 1945–47. Lt-Col, 1944; Col, 1945. Official Interpreter in Japanese to Govt of India, 1928–32, 1936, and 1944–47. Information Officer, Min. of Food, 1949; Chief Enforcement Officer, Min. of Food, 1950. Chm., Nat. Anti-Vivisection Soc., 1954–57; Mem. Council, RSPCA, 1956–67; Official visit to Japan, 1966. *Publication:* (joint author) Official History, The War against Japan, Vol. I 1955, Vol. II 1958, Vol. III 1962, Vol. IV 1965, Vol. V 1969. *Club:* Army and Navy.   *Died 14 Dec. 1991.*

WARMAN, Ven. Francis Frederic Guy; Archdeacon of Aston, 1965–77, Emeritus since 1977; Canon Residentiary of Birmingham, 1965–77, Emeritus since 1977; *b* 1 Dec. 1904; *er s* of Frederic Sumpter Guy Warman, one time Bishop of Manchester, and Gertrude Warman (*née* Earle); *m* 1932, Kathleen Olive, *d* of O. C. Phillips; one *s* one *d*. *Educ:* Weymouth Coll.; Worcester Coll., Oxford; Ridley Hall, Cambridge. Ordained as deacon, 1927, priest, 1928; Curate of Radford, Coventry, 1927; Curate of Chilvers Coton, Nuneaton, 1930; Vicar of: St James, Selby, 1932; Beeston, Leeds, 1936; Ward End, Birmingham, 1943; Aston-juxta-Birmingham, 1946. Rural Dean of East Birmingham, 1944–46; Proctor in Convocation, 1945–75; Hon. Canon of Birmingham, 1948–65. *Recreations:* music, golf. *Address:* 76 Winterbourne Close, Lewes, Sussex BN7 1JZ. *T:* Lewes (0273) 472440.

Died 25 July 1991.

WARMINGTON, Lt-Comdr Sir Marshall George Clitheroe, 3rd Bt, *cr* 1908, of Pembridge Square, Royal Borough of Kensington; Royal Navy, retired; *b* 26 May 1910; *o s* of Sir Marshall Denham Warmington, 2nd Bt, and 1st wife, Alice Daisy Ing (*d* 1913); *S* father, 1935; *m* 1st, 1933, Mollie (marr. diss. 1941), *er d* of late Capt. M. A. Kennard, RN (retired); one *s* one *d*; 2nd, 1942, Eileen Mary (*d* 1969), *o d* of late P. J. Howes; two *s*; 3rd, 1972, Sheila (marr. diss. 1977; she *d* 1988), *d* of Stanley Brotherhood, Peterborough, and *widow* of Adm. Hon. Sir Cyril Douglas-Pennant, KCB, CBE, DSO, DSC. *Educ:* Charterhouse. *Heir: s* Marshall Denham Malcolm Warmington, *b* 5 Jan. 1934. *Address:* Swallowfield Park, near Reading, Berks RG7 1TG. *T:* Reading (01734) 882210. *Club:* MCC.   *Died 5 Feb. 1995.*

WARNER, Sir Frederick Archibald, (Sir Fred), GCVO 1975; KCMG 1972 (CMG 1963); HM Diplomatic Service, retired; consultant; Director, Globalstar Telecommunications Ltd; *b* 2 May 1918; *s* of Frederick A. Warner, Chaguanas, Trinidad, and Marjorie Miller Winants, New Jersey, USA; *m* 1971, Mrs Simone Georgina de Ferranti, *d* of late Col Hubert Jocelyn Nangle; two *s*, and one step *d*. *Educ:* Wixenford; RNC Dartmouth; Magdalen Coll., Oxford; Sheffield Univ. Served War of 1939–45. Asst Principal, Foreign Office, Feb. 1946; Member of Foreign Service, April 1946; promoted 2nd Sec., May 1946; promoted 1st Sec., and transferred to Moscow, 1950; Foreign Office, Dec. 1951; Rangoon, 1956 (acted as Chargé d'Affaires, 1956); transferred to Athens, 1958; Head of South-East Asia Dept, Foreign Office, 1960; Imperial Defence College, 1964; Ambassador to Laos, 1965–67; Minister, NATO, 1968; Under-Secretary of State, FCO, 1969; Ambassador and Dep. Permanent UK Rep. to UN, 1969–72; Ambassador to Japan, 1972–75. Mem. (C) Somerset, European Parlt, 1979–84. Formerly Director: Mercantile and General Reinsurance Co. Ltd; Chloride Gp Ltd; Guinness Peat Gp; Loral Internat. Inc.; Vicarello SpA. Chairman: Overseas Cttee, CBI, 1985–88; Wessex Region of National Trust, 1976–78. Order of the Rising Sun, 1st class (Japan). *Publication:* Anglo-Japanese Financial Relations, 1991. *Address:* Inkpen House, Newbury, Berks RG15 0DS. *T:* Inkpen (01488) 668266; 3 Kelvin Court, Kensington Park Road, W11 2BT. *Clubs:* Beefsteak, Turf; Puffin's (Edinburgh).   *Died 30 Sept. 1995.*

WARNER, Dr Michael Henry Charles; author, engaged on historical research; *b* 21 May 1927; *s* of Captain Herbert H. M. Warner, MA, RGA, and Mrs Jessie R. H. Warner; *m* 1971, Gillian Margaret (*née* Easby); one *s* by previous *m*. *Educ:* Monkton Combe Sch., Bath; Queens' Coll., Cambridge (BA 1951, MA 1955); King's Coll., London (PhD 1973). Served RAF, 1945–48. Government Communications HQ: Exec. Officer, 1952; Higher Exec. Officer, 1956; Deptl Specialist Officer, 1957; Principal, 1965, Asst Sec., 1974, MoD; Counsellor, FCO, 1979; Dep. Leader, UK Delegn to Comprehensive Test Ban Treaty Negotiations, Geneva, 1979–80; Hd ER3 Div., MoD, 1981–84. Leverhulme Fellow, 1971–72. *Publications:* contrib. Thomas Hardy Yearbook, Anglo-Welsh Rev., Envoi, Dorset County Magazine, and BBC 2. *Recreation:* bridge. *Address:* 62 Poulett Gardens, Twickenham, Mddx TW1 4QR. *T:* 0181–892 1456.

Died 6 Nov. 1994.

WARNOCK, Sir Geoffrey (James), Kt 1986; Principal, Hertford College, Oxford, 1971–88, Hon. Fellow, 1988; Vice-Chancellor, University of Oxford, 1981–85; *b* 16 Aug. 1923; *s* of James Warnock, OBE, MD; *m* 1949, Helen Mary Wilson (Baroness Warnock, DBE); two *s* three *d*. *Educ:* Winchester Coll.; New Coll., Oxford (Hon. Fellow, 1973). Served War of 1939–45: Irish Guards, 1942–45 (Captain). Fellow by Examination, Magdalen Coll., 1949; Fellow and Tutor, Brasenose Coll., 1950–53; Fellow and Tutor in Philosophy, Magdalen Coll., 1953–71, Emeritus Fellow, 1972, Hon. Fellow, 1980. Visiting Lectr, Univ. of Illinois, 1957; Visiting Professor: Princeton Univ., 1962; Univ. of Wisconsin, 1966. Hon. DH Univ. of Hartford, 1986. *Publications:* Berkeley, 1953; English Philosophy since 1900, 1958, 2nd edn 1969; Contemporary Moral Philosophy, 1967; (ed with J. O. Urmson) J. L. Austin: Philosophical Papers, 2nd edn, 1970; The Object of Morality, 1971; Morality and Language, 1983; J. L. Austin, 1989; articles in: Mind, Proc. Aristotelian Soc., etc. *Address:* Brick House, Axford, Marlborough, Wilts SN8 2EX.   *Died 8 Oct. 1995.*

WARREN, Douglas Ernest, CMG 1973; *b* 8 June 1918; *s* of late Samuel Henry Warren; *m* 1945, Constance Vera (*née* Nix); two *d*. *Educ:* High Storrs Grammar Sch., Sheffield; Sheffield Univ. (BSc). FRICS. Royal Corps of Signals, 1940–46 (Captain): POW Thailand, 1942–45. Joined Colonial Service (later HMOCS), Tanganyika, as Surveyor, 1946: Supt of Surveys, 1955; transf. to Kenya as Asst Dir of Surveys, 1957; Dir of Survey of Kenya, 1961–65; retd from HMOCS, 1965; joined UK Civil Service as Dep. to Dir of Overseas Surveys, Min. of Overseas Develt, 1965; Dir of Overseas Surveys and Survey Adviser, 1968–80. Member: Land Surveyors Council, RICS, 1965–72; Council, RGS, 1968–71; various Royal Society cttees; Pres., Photogrammetric Soc., 1969–71. Patron's Medal, RGS, 1982. *Recreations:* travel, golf. *Address:* Flat 2, 19 St John's Road, Eastbourne, East Sussex BN20 7NQ. *T:* Eastbourne (0323) 639320. *Club:* Royal Eastbourne Golf.   *Died 22 Sept. 1993.*

WARREN, Dr Wilfrid, FRCP, FRCPsych; Physician, Bethlem Royal Hospital and the Maudsley Hospital, 1948–75, then Emeritus; *b* 11 Oct. 1910; *s* of Frank Warren, JP, FSA, and Maud Warren; *m* 1938, Elizabeth Margaret Park; one *s* one *d*. *Educ:* Sherborne Sch.; Sidney Sussex Coll., Cambridge (MA; MD 1948); St Bartholomew's Hosp., London. DPM 1946. FRCP 1972; FRCPsych 1971. Served War, 1939–45: Surgeon Lt Comdr, RNVR. Consultant Adviser, Child and Adolescent Psychiatry, DHSS (formerly Min. of Health), 1961–76; Hon. Consultant in Child Psych. to Army, 1969–75.

President: Sect. of Mental Health, Soc. of Med. Officers of Health, 1962–63; Sect. of Psych., RSM, 1970–71. Treasurer, Royal Coll. of Psychiatrists (formerly Royal Medico-Psychol Soc.), 1962–79 (Vice-Pres., 1974–76). Distinguished Hon. Fellow, Amer. Psychiatric Assoc., 1968; Hon. FRCPsych, 1979. *Publications:* articles in learned jls on child and adolescent psychiatry. *Recreations:* gardening, literature, music. *Address:* 54 Vincent Drive, Westminster Park, Chester CH4 7RL.
Died 8 Jan. 1991.

WARSOP, Rear-Adm. John Charles, CB 1984; CEng, FIMechE; Flag Officer Portsmouth and Naval Base Commander Portsmouth, 1983–85; RN retired, 1986; *b* 9 May 1927; *s* of John Charles Warsop and Elsie Lily Warsop; *m* 1958, Josephine Franklin Cotterell; two *d*. *Educ:* Gateway Sch., Leicester; RN Coll., Eaton Hall, Chester; RN Engineering Coll., Keyham, Plymouth, 1945–48. CEng 1981; FIMechE 1983. HM Ships Theseus and Gambia, 1949–50; RNC Greenwich, 1950–52; HMS Superb, 1952–54; Staff, RNEC, 1954–56; Min. of Defence, 1956–59; Sen. Engr, HMS Ark Royal, 1959–61; MoD, 1961–65; British Defence Staff, Washington, USA, 1965–68; MoD, 1968–70; Engr Officer, HMS Blake, 1970–72; MoD, 1972–75; CO, HMS Fisgard, 1975–78; MoD, 1979–81; Rear-Adm. 1981; Port Adm., Rosyth, 1981–83. Hon. Engrg Adviser, HMS Warrior (1860), 1986–. Chm., Soc. of Friends, RN Mus. and HMS Victory, 1989–. *Publications:* papers for Instn of Marine Engineers. *Recreations:* offshore cruising, Rugby. *Club:* Royal Naval Sailing Association.
Died 13 July 1995.

WARTIOVAARA, Otso Uolevi, Hon. GCVO; Ambassador of Finland to the Court of St James's, 1968–74; retired; *b* Helsinki, 16 Nov. 1908; *s* of J. V. Wartiovaara, Dir-Gen. of Finnish Govt Accounting Office, and Siiri Nystén; *m* 1936, Maine Alanen; three *s*. *Educ:* Helsinki Univ. Master of Law, 1932; Asst Judge, 1934. Entered Foreign Service, 1934; Attaché, Paris, 1936–39; Sec. and Head of Section, Min. for For. Affairs, 1939–42; Counsellor, Stockholm, 1942–44; Consul, Haaparanta, Sweden, 1944–45; Head of Section, Min. for For. Affairs, 1945–49; Counsellor, Washington, 1949–52; Head of Admin. Dept, Min. for For. Affairs, 1952–54; Envoy and Minister, 1954; Head of Legal Dept, Min. for For. Affairs, 1954–56; Minister, Belgrade and Athens, 1956–58; Ambassador, Belgrade, and Minister to Athens, 1958–61; Ambassador to Vienna, 1961–68, and to Holy See, 1966–68, also Perm. Rep. to Internat. Atomic Energy Organization, 1961–68. Grand Cross, Order of Lion of Finland; Kt Comdr, Order of White Rose of Finland; Cross of Freedom; Silver Cross of Sport, Finland. Grand Gold Cross of Austria; Grand Cross, Orders of Phœnix (Greece); Pius IX, Flag (Yugoslavia); Comdr, Orders of Northern Star (Sweden); St Olav (Norway) and Vasa (Sweden). *Recreations:* golf, shooting. *Address:* Lutherinkatn 6. A, 00100 Helsinki 10, Finland.
Died 27 March 1991.

WARWICK, Prof. Roger; retired; Professor Emeritus, University of London; *b* 27 Dec. 1912; *m* 1942, Nina Seaford (later Dr Nina Murray) (marr. diss. 1952); one *d*; *m,* 1962, Carolyn Rigby (*d* 1985). *Educ:* Altrincham Grammar Sch. (*Victor Ludorum*, 1930, 1931 and 1932; prizes in Greek, Latin and English); Victoria University of Manchester (BSc 1935; MB, ChB 1937 (Sydney Renshaw Prize in Physiology, 1937); MD (Gold Medal), 1952; PhD, 1955). House Physician and House Surgeon, Professorial Unit, Manchester Royal Infirmary, 1938–39; Surgeon Lieut, RNVR, 1939–45; Demonstrator and Lectr in Anatomy, Univ. of Manchester, 1945–55; Prof. of Anatomy and Dir of Dept of Anatomy, Guy's Hosp. Med. Sch., London Univ., 1955–85. Arris and Gale Lectr, RCS, 1960; Fison Lectr, Guy's Hosp., 1986. Member: Anatomical Society of Great Britain (Symington Memorial

Prize, 1953); Anatomical Socs of Brazil, India, China and SA; Scientific Fellow of Zoological Society. Hon. Sec., Internat. Anat. Nomenclature Cttee. Hallett Prize, RCS. *Publications:* Gray's Anatomy (co-ed), 35th–37th edns, 1973–89; (ed) Wolff's Anatomy of the Eye and Orbit, 7th edn, 1977; (ed) Nomina Anatomica, 4th–6th edns, 1972–90, and other books; contributions to Brain, Journal Anat., Journal Comp. Neurol., etc. *Recreations:* Natural history, especially *Lepidoptera*, archæology. *Address:* c/o Department of Anatomy, Guy's Hospital Medical School, SE1 9RT; 55 Hall Drive, Sydenham, SE26 6XL.
Died 14 Sept. 1991.

WASSERSTEIN, Prof. Abraham; Professor of Greek, Hebrew University of Jerusalem, 1969–89, then Emeritus; *b* Frankfurt/Main, Germany, 5 Oct. 1921; *s* of late Berl Bernhard Wasserstein and Czarna Cilla (*née* Laub); *m* 1942, Margaret Eva (*née* Ecker); two *s* one *d*. *Educ:* schools in Berlin and Rome; privately in Palestine; Birkbeck Coll., London Univ. BA 1949, PhD 1951. Assistant in Greek, 1951–52, Lecturer in Greek, 1952–60, Glasgow Univ.; Prof. of Classics, Leicester Univ., 1960–69, and Dean of Faculty of Arts, 1966–69. Visiting Fellow: Centre for Postgraduate Hebrew Studies, Oriental Inst., Univ. of Oxford, 1973–74; Wolfson Coll., Oxford, 1986; Vis. Professor: Hochschule für Jüdische Studien, Heidelberg, 1980–81; Univ. of Heidelberg, 1983. Mem. Inst. for Advanced Study, Princeton, 1975–76 and 1985–86. Fellow, Annenberg Res. Inst., Philadelphia, 1988. FRAS 1961; Pres., Classical Assoc. of Israel, 1971–74. *Publications:* Flavius Josephus, 1974; Galen, On Airs, Waters, Places (critical edn, with trans. and notes), 1982; contrib. to learned journals. *Recreations:* theatre, travel. *Address:* Department of Classics, The Hebrew University, Jerusalem, Israel.
Died 20 July 1995.

WATERS, Garth Rodney; Under-Secretary, Land Use, Conservation and Countryside, Ministry of Agriculture, Fisheries and Food, since 1990; *b* 2 March 1944; *s* of Edmund Claude and Bertha May Waters; *m* 1st, 1967, Malin Essen-Möller (marr. diss. 1975); two *s*; 2nd, 1976, Ann Margaret Evans; one *s* one *d*. *Educ:* Perse Sch., Cambridge; Oriel Coll., Oxford (MA Modern History). Teacher of English, British Centre, Sweden, 1966–67; joined MAFF, 1968; Private Sec. to Minister of State, 1971–73; Head of Pesticides Branch, 1973; Durham Office, 1974–75; Milk, 1975–78; Principal Private Sec. to Minister of Agriculture, 1979–80; Head, Beef Div., 1980; Head, Marine Envmt Protection Div., 1984; joined Glaxo Holdings as Head, Corporate Policy Unit, 1987; Dir, Glaxo Europe, 1989–90; rejoined MAFF, 1990, as Head, Agric. Resources Policy Div; Under Sec., 1990. *Recreations:* swimming, reading, being very silly (*sic*). *Address:* Ministry of Agriculture, Fisheries and Food, Nobel House, 17 Smith Square, SW1P 3JR. *T:* 0171–238 5684. *Club:* Royal Automobile.
Died 17 Feb. 1995.

WATKINS-PITCHFORD, Dr John, CB 1968; Chief Medical Adviser, Department of Health and Social Security (formerly Ministry of Social Security and Ministry of Pensions and National Insurance), 1965–73; retired 1973; *b* 20 April 1912; *s* of Wilfred Watkins Pitchford, FRCS, first Director of South African Institute of Medical Research, and Olive Mary (*née* Nichol); *m* 1945, Elizabeth Patricia Wright; one *s*. *Educ:* Shrewsbury School; St Thomas' Hospital. MRCS, LRCP 1937; MB, BS 1939 (London); MD 1946 (London); DPH 1946; DIH 1949. Various hosp. appts War of 1939–45: served RAFVR, Sqdn Ldr. Med. Inspector of Factories, 1947–50; Sen. Med. Off., Min. of Nat. Insce, 1950. Mem., Industrial Injuries Adv. Council, 1975–84. QHP 1971–74. *Publications:* articles on occupational medicine.

Recreation: gardening. *Address:* Hill House, Farley Lane, Westerham, Kent TN16 1UD. *T:* Westerham (0959) 64448. *Died 18 April 1994.*

WATKINSON, 1st Viscount *cr* 1964, of Woking; **Harold Arthur Watkinson,** CH 1962; PC 1955; President, Confederation of British Industry, 1976–77; Chairman of Cadbury Schweppes Ltd, 1969–74 (Group Managing Director, Schweppes Ltd, 1963–68); Director: British Insulated Callender's Cables, 1968–77; Midland Bank Ltd, 1970–83; *b* 25 Jan. 1910; *e s* of A. G. Watkinson, Walton-on-Thames; *m* 1939, Vera, *y d* of John Langmead, West Sussex; two *d. Educ:* Queen's College, Taunton; King's College, London. Family business, 1929–35; technical and engineering journalism, 1935–39. Served War of 1939–45, active service, Lieut-Comdr RNVR. Chairman Production Efficiency Panel for S England, Machine Tool Trades Association, 1948; Chairman (first) Dorking Div. Conservative Assoc., 1948–49. MP (C) Woking Division of Surrey, 1950–64; Parliamentary Private Secretary to the Minister of Transport and Civil Aviation, 1951–52; Parliamentary Secretary to Ministry of Labour and National Service, 1952–55; Minister of Transport and Civil Aviation, Dec. 1955–59; Minister of Defence, 1959–62; Cabinet Minister, 1957–62. Mem., Brit. Nat. Export Council 1964–70; Chairman: Cttee for Exports to the United States, 1964–67; Nat. Advisory Cttee on the Employment of Older Men and Women, 1952–55; Companies Cttee, CBI, 1972–; a Vice-Pres., Council, BIM, 1970–73, Pres., 1973–78 (Chm., 1968–70). President: Grocers' Inst., 1970–71; Inst. of Grocery Distribution, 1972–73; Member: Council, RSA, 1972–77; NEDC, 1976–77; Falkland Islands Review Cttee, 1982–83. President: RNVR Officers' Assoc., 1973–76; Weald and Downland Museum, 1982–88. Chairman: Council, Cranleigh and Bramley Schools, 1973–87; Recruitment Working Party, Duke of Edinburgh's 1974 Study Conf., 1972–74. *Publications:* Blueprint for Industrial Survival, 1976; Turning Points, 1986; The Mountain, 1988; Jewels and Old Shoes, 1990. *Recreations:* mountaineering, walking, sailing. *Heir:* none. *Address:* Tyma House, Bosham, near Chichester, Sussex PO18 8HZ. *Clubs:* Naval; Royal Southern Yacht (Southampton). *Died 19 Dec. 1995 (ext).*

WATKISS, Ronald Frederick, CBE 1981; company director; Leader, Conservative Party, Cardiff City Council, since 1973; Lord Mayor of Cardiff, 1981–82; *b* 21 May 1920; *o s* of Bertie Miles Watkiss and Isabella Watkiss; *m* 1941, Marion Preston; one *d* (one *s* decd). *Educ:* Howard Gardens High Sch., Cardiff. Served War, TA, 1939, Royal Corps of Signals, 1939–46; Burma, 1944–46 (1939–45 star, Burma star, Territorial medal). Elected to Cardiff City Council, 1960; Alderman, 1967–74; re-elected Councillor, 1973; Leader, 1976–79, 1983–87; Chairman: Planning Cttee, 1969–74, 1976–79; Policy Cttee, 1976–79, 1983–. Vice Chm., Assoc. District Councils, 1989–(Mem., 1976–79, 1983–); Member: Land Authority for Wales, 1984–; Cardiff Bay Develt Corp., 1987–. Pres., Cardiff North (formerly NW) Conservative Constituency Assoc., 1983–89 (Chm., 1978–81). President: Cardiff Credit Traders Assoc., 1953–54 and 1963–64; S Wales Dist Council Credit Traders, 1957–58. Hon. Fellow, University Coll. Cardiff, 1985. Queen's Silver Jubilee Medal, 1977. *Recreations:* Rugby and cricket (regret only as spectator latterly); relaxing at caravan whenever possible. *Address:* 69 King George V Drive, Heath, Cardiff CF4 4EF. *T:* Cardiff (0222) 752716. *Club:* Victory Services. *Died 21 April 1991.*

WATSON, Sir Francis (John Bagott), KCVO 1973 (CVO 1965; MVO 1959); BA Cantab; Hon. MA Oxon 1969; FBA 1969; FSA; Director, Wallace Collection, 1963–74; Surveyor of The Queen's Works of Art, 1963–72, retired; Advisor for Works of Art, since 1972; *b* 24 Aug. 1907; *s* of Hugh Watson, Blakedown, and Helen Marian Bagott, Dudley; *m* 1941, Mary Rosalie Gray (*d* 1969), *d* of George Strong, Bognor; one adopted *s. Educ:* Shrewsbury School; St John's College, Cambridge. Registrar, Courtauld Inst. of Art, 1934–38; Asst Keeper (later Dep. Dir), Wallace Collection, 1938–63; Deputy Surveyor of The Queen's (until 1952 The King's) Works of Art, 1947–63; Trustee, Whitechapel Art Gallery, 1949–74; Chairman: Furniture History Society, 1966–74; Walpole Society, 1970–76. Slade Prof. of Fine Art, Oxford, 1969–70; Wrightsman Prof., NY Univ., 1970–71; Vis. Lectr, Univ. of California, 1970; Kress Prof., National Gallery, Washington DC, 1975–76; Regent Fellow, Smithsonian Instn, 1982–84. Ufficiale del Ordine al Merito della Repubblica Italiana, 1961. New York University Gold Medal, 1966. *Publications:* Canaletto, 1949 (rev. 2nd edn, 1954); (jtly) Southill, A Regency House, 1951; Wallace Collection: Catalogue of Furniture, 1956; Louis XVI Furniture, 1959 (rev. French edn, 1963); The Choiseul Gold Box (Charlton Lecture), 1963; (jtly) Great Family Collections, 1965; The Guardi Family of Painters (Fred Cook Memorial Lecture), 1966; (jtly) Eighteenth Century Gold Boxes, 1966, 3rd rev. edn 1990; The Wrightsman Collection Catalogue, Vols 1 and 2: Furniture, 1966, Vols 3 and 4: Furniture, Goldsmith's Work and Ceramics, 1970, Vol. 5: Paintings and Sculpture, 1974; Giambattista Tiepolo, 1966; Fragonard, 1967; Chinese Porcelains in European Mounts, 1980; (jtly) Catalogue of the Mounted Oriental Porcelains in the J. Paul Getty Museum, 1983; (contrib.) Vergoldete Bronzen-Die Bronzearbeiten des Spätbarok zu Klassizmus: Einfurung, 1985; Oriental Porcelains in European Mounts, 1986; Systematic Catalogue of Seventeenth and Eighteenth Century French Furniture, National Gallery, Washington, 1992; numerous contribs to learned journals, in Europe, America and Asia. *Recreations:* sinology, Western Americana. *Address:* West Farm House, Corton, Wilts BA12 0SY. *Club:* Beefsteak. *Died 27 Sept. 1992.*

WATSON, Rear-Adm. John Garth, CB 1965; BSc(Eng); CEng, FICE, FIEE; Secretary, Institution of Civil Engineers, 1967–79; *b* 20 Feb. 1914; *er s* of Alexander Henry St Croix Watson and Gladys Margaret Watson (*née* Payne); *m* 1943, Barbara Elizabeth Falloon; two *s* one *d. Educ:* Univ. Coll. School, Hampstead; Northampton Engineering Coll., Univ. of London. BSc (Eng). 1st Bn Herts Regt (TA), 1932; resigned on joining Admiralty, 1939; HMS Vernon, 1939; Development of Magnetic Minesweepers, Dec. 1939; Warship Electrical Supt, London and SE Area, 1943; BJSM, Washington, DC, 1945; Admlty, 1948; transf. to Naval Elec. Branch, 1949; served in Destroyers and on Staff of Flag Officer, Flot., Home Fleet, 1950; Admlty, 1952; HM Dockyard Devonport, 1953; promoted Capt. 1955; Staff of C-in-C Home Fleet, Fleet Elec. Officer, 1955; Suptg Elec. Engr, HM Dockyard Gibraltar, 1957; Sen. Officers' War Course, 1960; Asst Dir of Elec. Engineering, Admlty, Nov. 1961; promoted Rear Adm. 1963; Adm. Superintendent, Rosyth, 1963–66. ADC to the Queen, 1962. Mem., Smeatonian Soc. of Civil Engineers, 1968 (Pres., 1987). Hon. Mem., Soc. of Civil Engrg Technicians, 1979. Chm., Queen's Jubilee Scholarship Trust, ICE, 1980–86; Vice-Chm., Civil Engineers' Club, 1980–86. Liveryman: Engineers' Co., 1986–; Guild of Freemen, 1986–. FInstD 1977; FRSA 1988. Hon DSc City Univ., 1984. *Publications:* A Short History: Institution of Civil Engineers, 1982; The Civils, 1987; The Smeatonians, 1989; contrib. 15th edn Encyc. Britannica, 1974. *Recreations:* sailing, light gardening. *Address:* Little Hall Court, Shedfield, near Southampton SO3 2HL. *T:* Wickham (0329) 833216. *Clubs:* Athenæum, Royal Thames Yacht; Royal Naval and Royal Albert Yacht (Portsmouth). *Died 31 March 1992.*

WATSON, Rev. John T., BA (London); LTCL; General Secretary, British and Foreign Bible Society, 1960–69, retired; *b* 13 Jan. 1904; *s* of late F. Watson, Sutton Bridge, Lincs; *m* 1933, Gertrude Emily Crossley (*d* 1982), Farsley, Leeds; two *s* one *d. Educ:* Moulton Grammar School; Westminster Training College, London; Didsbury Training College, Manchester. School-master, 1924–26; missionary (under Methodist Missionary Soc.) in Dahomey, W Africa, 1929–34; Methodist Minister: Plymouth, 1935–38; Golders Green, 1938–46; Bible Society: Secretary for Schools and Colleges, 1946–49; Asst Home Sec., 1949–54; Asst Gen. Sec., 1954–60. Hon. DD, West Virginia Wesleyan Coll., 1966. *Publications:* Seen and Heard in Dahomey, 1934; Daily Prayers for the Methodist Church, 1951. *Recreation:* music. *Address:* 16 Beverington Road, Eastbourne, East Sussex BN21 2SD. *T:* Eastbourne (0323) 29838.　　　　*Died 2 Oct. 1992.*

WATSON, Joseph Stanley, MBE 1946; QC 1955; Social Security (formerly National Insurance) Commissioner, 1965–85, retired; *b* 13 Sept. 1910; *er s* of late Joseph Watson and Gertrude Ethel (*née* Catton); *m* 1951, Elizabeth Elliston, *d* of late Col G. Elliston Allen, TD; four *d. Educ:* Rossall Sch.; Jesus Coll., Cambridge (MA). Barrister, Inner Temple, 1933. Served War of 1939–45 (MBE): RA (Field), UK, MEF, Force 281, Dodecanese in Unit and on Gen. Staff (Greek Military Cross), rank of Major; CSO on surrender of Gen. Wagener, Comdr German Forces E Aegen, VE day. No 7 (NW) Legal Aid Area Cttee, 1949–55. Mem. Gen. Council of the Bar, 1959–64; Master of the Bench, Inner Temple, 1961; Recorder of Blackpool, 1961–65. Recorded on tape at their request his experiences in Dodecanese for Imp. War Museum. *Address:* The Old Dairy, Mickleham, Surrey. *T:* Leatherhead (0372) 374387.　　　　*Died 30 May 1991.*

WATSON, Air Cdre Michael, CB 1952; CBE 1945 (OBE 1942); *b* 12 Aug. 1909; *s* of late William Watson, Kew; *m* 1st, 1939, Maria Mazankova, Czechoslovakia; 2nd, 1960, Ramona Gloria (marr. diss.), *d* of E. Ridling, Big Bear Lake, Calif. *Educ:* St Paul's Prep. School; Saffron Walden School. Joined RAF 1929, and qualified as Pilot; trained as Signals Officer, 1933; served War of 1939–45 (despatches twice); Air Min. Combined Ops Signals Plans 1942; HQ, AEAF, 1943; SHAEF 1944; HQ Middle East, 1946; Air Ministry, 1947; Comdg RAF Welford, 1949; HQ, Fighter Comd, 1950–53; Director of Signals, Air Ministry, 1953–54; retired from RAF at own request, 1954. Rolls Royce Representative with N American Aviation Inc., Calif, 1956–60; Asst Gen. Man., Sales and Service, Rolls Royce, Ltd, 1961–62; Space Div., N American Rockwell Inc., Calif, 1964–71, retired. Chevalier de la Légion d'Honneur, 1944; Officer US Legion of Merit, 1945. *Recreations:* fishing, sailing. *Address:* Box 5321, Big Bear Lake, Calif 92315, USA.
　　　　Died 22 March 1991.

WATSON, Roderick Anthony, QC 1967; *b* 1920; *o s* of late O. C. Watson, CBE and Peggy (*née* Donnelly); *m* Ann, *o d* of late W. L. Wilson; three *s* one *d. Educ:* Christian Brothers, Beulah Hill; King's Coll., Univ. of London. Served War of 1939–45, Captain RASC. Called to the Bar, Lincoln's Inn, 1949, Bencher, 1975. Dir, Standard Chartered Bank (IOM) Ltd, 1977–90; Dep. Chm., Isle of Man Financial Supervision Commn, 1983–. *Address:* Merton House, 11 The Promenade, Castletown, Isle of Man. *Clubs:* Army and Navy, Garrick.
　　　　Died 11 July 1993.

WATSON, Sydney, OBE 1970; MA, DMus; FRCO, FRCM; Student, Organist and Lecturer in Music, Christ Church, Oxford, 1955–70; Professor, Royal College of Music, 1946–71; Examiner, Royal Schools of Music, 1943–83; *b* Denton, Lancashire, 3 Sept. 1903; *s* of W. T. Watson; unmarried. *Educ:* Warwick Sch.; Royal College of Music;

Keble Coll., Oxford (Organ Scholar). Assistant music master, Stowe School, 1925–28; Precentor of Radley Coll., 1929–33; Conductor of Abingdon Madrigal Society, 1931–36; Organist of New Coll., Oxford, 1933–38; Organist of Sheldonian Theatre, Conductor of Oxford Harmonic Society, 1933–38; Oxford Orchestral Society, 1936–38; Director of Concerts, Balliol Coll., 1933–38, 1962–69; Choragus to Oxford Univ., 1963–68; Master of Music, Winchester Coll., and Conductor Winchester Music Club, 1938–45; Precentor and Director of Music, Eton Coll., 1946–55; Conductor: Petersfield Festival, 1946–64; Slough Philharmonic Society, 1946–55; Windsor and Eton Choral Society, 1949–55; Oxford Bach Choir, 1955–70; Oxford Orchestral Society, 1956–70. *Publications:* church music. *Address:* Aynhoe Park, Aynho, Banbury, Oxon OX17 3BQ. *Club:* Athenæum.
　　　　Died 17 Feb. 1991.

WATSON, Thomas Frederick, FCA, FCIS; Governor, National Society for Epilepsy, 1971–81 (Chairman, 1974–78); *b* 18 April 1906; *s* of late Frederick Watson and Jane Lucy (*née* Britton); *m* 1932, Eveline Dorothy Strang; one *d. Educ:* Tiffins Sch., Kingston-on-Thames. FCIS 1957; FCA 1960. With Deloitte Co., Chartered Accountants, 1925–45; qual. as Chartered Sec., 1930; Incorporated Accountant, 1945. Chm. and Chief Exec., Exchange Telegraph Co. Ltd, 1961–68, retired. Mem. Council, Commonwealth Press Union, 1959–68. *Recreations:* gardening, bridge, theatre, charity work.
　　　　Died 1 July 1994.

WATT, Richard Lorimer, CA; CBIM; retired; Vice-Chairman, EMI Group, 1978–81; *b* 20 June 1921; *s* of George Lorimer Watt and Sophia Fordyce Watt; *m* 1952, Elizabeth (*née* Hancock); one *s. Educ:* George Watson's Boys' Coll., Edinburgh; Edinburgh Univ. Brush Group (subseq. part of Hawker Siddeley Group): various finance responsibilities, 1948–55; Planning Dir, 1955–57, Dir and Gen. Man., 1957–60, Mirrlees, Bickerton & Day Ltd; Dir and Gen. Man., National Gas Oil Engines Ltd, 1958–60; Booker Group: Exec. Dir, latterly Chm., Booker Industrial Holdings Ltd, 1960–70; Exec. Dir, latterly Dep. Chm., Booker Engineering Holdings Ltd, 1964–70; EMI Group: Gp Financial Controller, 1970–71; Gp Finance Dir, 1971–75; Asst Man. Dir, 1975–77; Gp Man. Dir, 1977–78; Dir, Trusthouses Forte Leisure, later First Leisure Corp., 1981–86. Director: Capitol Industries-EMI Inc., 1971–81; South Bank Theatre Bd, 1977–82. *Recreations:* music, ballet, swimming, various charity committees. *Address:* Flat 40, 75 Crawford Street, W1H 1HS. *T:* 071–723 8355. *Club:* Caledonian.　　　　*Died 27 June 1991.*

WATTS, Ronald George Henry, CBE 1962; HM Diplomatic Service, retired; *b* 15 May 1914; *s* of Frederick Thomas Watts; *m* 1940, Ruth Hansen (*d* 1970); one *s* two *d*; *m* 1972, Margit Tester. *Educ:* Latymer Sch., Edmonton; St John's Coll., Cambridge. Entered Foreign Service, 1937; appointed Counsellor, Foreign Office, 1958; Consul-Gen., Osaka-Kobe, 1958–63; Head of Consular Dept, FO, 1963–65; Consul-Gen., Paris, 1966–67; FCO, 1967–69, retired. *Recreation:* church organist.
　　　　Died 2 March 1993.

WATTS, Sir Roy, Kt 1992; CBE 1978; Chairman: Thames Water Authority, since 1983; Frank Graham Group Ltd, since 1991; IBC Plc, since 1991; Frank Graham Group Ltd, since 1991; *b* 17 Aug. 1925; *m* 1951, Jean Rosaline; one *s* two *d. Educ:* Doncaster Grammar Sch.; Edinburgh Univ. (MA). FRAeS, FCIT, IPFA. Army, 1943–47: commnd Sandhurst; 8th RTR. Accountant in local govt until 1955; joined BEA, 1955: Head of Systems Study Section (O & M Br.); Chief Internal Auditor; Area Man., Sweden and Finland; Fleet Planning Man.; Regional Gen. Man., North and East Europe; Dir, S1–11 Div; Chief Exec. BEA British Airways, 1972–74 (Chm., Jan.-March

1974); Chief Exec., European Div., British Airways, 1974–77; Dir, Commercial Operations, British Airways, 1977, Dir, Finance and Planning, 1978–79, Chief Exec., 1979–82; Group Man. Dir, 1982–83; Jt Dep. Chm., BA Bd, 1980–83 (Mem., 1974–83); Chairman: WaterAid, 1984–88; Armstrong Equipment plc, 1986–89; Lowndes Lambert Gp Hldgs, 1988–92. Chm., Assoc. of European Airlines, 1982. Hon. DBA Internat. Management Centre, Buckingham, 1987. *Recreations:* walking, cricket. *Address:* 14 Cavendish Place, W1M 9DJ. *T:* 071–636 8686. *Died April 1993.*

WAUD, Christopher Denis George Pierre; barrister-at-law; a Recorder of the Crown Court, since Dec. 1974; full-time Chairman of Industrial Tribunals, since 1982 (part-time, 1977–82); *b* 5 Dec. 1928; *s* of late Christopher William Henry Pierre Waud and Vera Constance Maria Waud; *m* 1954, Rosemary Paynter Bradshaw Moorhead; one *s* four *d* (and one *s* decd). *Educ:* Charterhouse; Christ Church, Oxford. Called to Bar, Middle Temple, 1956. *Publications:* Redundancy and Unfair Dismissal, annually 1981–84; Employment Law (formerly Guide to Employment Law), annually, 1985–. *Recreations:* sailing, walking. *Address:* 19/29 Woburn Place, WC1H 0LU. *Clubs:* Old Carthusian Yacht, Bar Yacht.

Died 25 June 1995.

WEBBER, Fernley Douglas, CMG 1959; MC 1942; TD 1954; HM Diplomatic Service, retired; Secretary, Committee for Environmental Conservation, 1975–77; *b* 12 March 1918; *s* of Herbert Webber; *m* 1947, Veronica Elizabeth Ann, *d* of Major F. B. Hitchcock, MC; two *s* two *d. Educ:* Cotham School, Bristol; Jesus College, Cambridge. Served War of 1939–45, Burma, 1940–45; Comd 624 LAA Regt RA (RF) TA, 1952–54, Bt-Col, 1954. Entered Colonial Office after open competition, 1939; Principal, CO, 1946; Asst Sec. 1950; Establishment Officer, 1952–58; Head of E Afr. Dept, 1958–63; idc 1964; joined HM Diplomatic Service, 1965; Deputy High Commissioner in Eastern Malaysia during part of 1965; High Commissioner in Brunei, 1965–67; Asst Under-Sec. of State, FCO, 1967; Minister, British High Commn in Canberra, 1967–68; FCO, 1969–70. *Address:* 6 Mills Lane, Rodbridge Corner, Long Melford, Suffolk.

Died 13 May 1991.

WEBSTER, Prof. John Roger, OBE 1988; MA, PhD; Professor of Education, and Dean of Faculty of Education, University College of Wales, Aberystwyth, 1978–91, then Emeritus; *b* 24 June 1926; *s* of Samuel and Jessie Webster; *m* 1963, Ivy Mary Garlick; one *s* one *d. Educ:* Llangefni Secondary Sch.; University College of Wales, Aberystwyth. Lectr, Trinity Coll., Carmarthen, 1948; Lectr in Educn, University Coll., Swansea, 1951; Director for Wales, Arts Council of GB, 1961–66; Prof. of Educn, University Coll. of North Wales, Bangor, 1966–78. Member: Lloyd Cttee on Nat. Film Sch., 1965–66; James Cttee on Teacher Educn and Trng, 1971; Venables Cttee on Continuing Educn, 1974–76; Council, Open Univ. (Chm., Educnl Studies Adv. Cttee), 1969–78; Chm., Standing Conf. on Studies in Educn, 1972–76; Member: CNAA, 1976–79; British Council Welsh Adv. Cttee, 1982–91; Post Office Users Nat. Council, 1981–88 (Chm., Wales, 1981–88); Chm., Wales Telecommunications Adv. Cttee, 1984–88. Governor, Commonwealth Inst., 1984–91. *Publications:* Ceri Richards, 1961; Joseph Herman, 1962; School and Community in Rural Wales, 1991; contribs on educn and the arts to collective works and learned jls. *Address:* Bron y Glyn, Rhydyfelin, Aberystwyth, Dyfed SY23 4QD. *Died 30 March 1995.*

WEEKS, Sir Hugh (Thomas), Kt 1966; CMG 1946; Chairman: Leopold Joseph Holdings Ltd, 1966–78; London American Finance Corporation Ltd, 1970–78; Electrical Industrial Securities, 1971–77; *b* 27 April 1904;

s of R. M. Weeks; *m* 1st, 1929, Jessamine, *d* of Alger and Edith Petts; one *d* (one *s* decd); 2nd, 1949, Constance Tomkinson; one *d. Educ:* Hendon Secondary and Kilburn Grammar Schools; Emmanuel College, Cambridge (MA). Research and Statistical Manager, Cadbury Bros, till 1939; Director of Statistics, Min. of Supply, 1939–42; Director-General of Statistics and Programmes and Member of Supply Council, 1942–43; Head of Programmes and Planning Division, Ministry of Production, 1943–45. Represented Ministries of Supply and Production on various Missions to N America, 1941–45; Director J. S. Fry & Sons, 1945–47; Mem. Economic Planning Bd, 1947–48, 1959–61; Joint Controller of Colonial Development Corporation, 1948–51; Chm., NIESR, 1970–74. Deputy Chairman: Truscon, 1951–60; Richard Thomas & Baldwins, 1965–68; Director: Finance Corp. for Industry, 1956–74; Industrial and Commercial Finance Corp., 1960–74; S Wales and Strip Mill Bds, BSC, 1968–72. UK Representative, UN Cttee for Industrial Development, 1961–63. Chairman: EDC for Distributive Trades, 1964–70; Econ. Cttees, FBI and CBI, 1957–72. Pres., British Export Houses Assoc., 1972–74. Medal of Freedom with Silver Palm (US). *Publications:* Market Research (with Paul Redmayne); various articles. *Address:* 14 St John's Street, Chichester, W Sussex PO19 1UU. *T:* Chichester (0243) 788631. *Died 13 July 1992.*

WEEVERS, Theodoor, Officier in de Orde van Oranje-Nassau; LitD (Leyden); Professor of Dutch Language and Literature, University of London, 1945–71; *b* Amersfoort, 3 June 1904; *e s* of Prof. Theodorus Weevers and Cornelia Jeannette, *d* of J. de Graaff; *m* 1933, Sybil Doreen, 2nd *d* of Alfred Jervis; two *s. Educ:* Gymnasia at Amersfoort and Groningen; Universities of Groningen and Leyden. Lecturer in Dutch at University College and Bedford College, London, 1931–36; Reader in Dutch Language and Literature in University of London, 1937–45; Lecturer in Dutch at Birkbeck College (Univ. of London), 1942–45. During War of 1939–45 Language Supervisor and Announcer-Translator in European News Service of BBC (Dutch Section), 1940–44. Corr. mem. Koninklijke Nederlandse Akademie van Wetenschappen te Amsterdam; hon. mem. Koninklijke Academie voor Nederlandse Taal en Letterkunde, Gent; mem. Maatschappij der Nederlandse Letterkunde. *Publications:* Coornhert's Dolinghe van Ulysse, 1934; De Dolinge van Ulysse door Dierick Volckertsz Coornhert, 1939; The Idea of Holland in Dutch Poetry, 1948; Poetry of the Netherlands in its European Context, 1170–1930, 1960; Mythe en Vorm in de gedichten van Albert Verwey, 1965; Albert Verwey's Portrayal of the Growth of the Poetic Imagination, in Essays in German and Dutch Literature, 1973; Droom en Beeld: De Poëzie van Albert Verwey, 1978; Vision and Form in the Poetry of Albert Verwey, 1986; articles and reviews in Modern Language Review, Mededelingen Kon. Nederlandse Akademie van Wetenschappen, Tijdschrift v. Nederl. Taal en Letterkunde, De Nieuwe Taalgids, Neophilologus, Journal of English and Germanic Philology, German Life and Letters, Spiegel der Letteren, Publications of the English Goethe Society, English Studies. *Recreations:* music, walking. *Address:* Warnscale, 42 Pasture Lane, Clayton, Bradford, W Yorks BD14 6LN.

Died 11 Jan. 1992.

WEIR, Rev. Cecil James Mullo, MA, DD, DPhil; Professor of Hebrew and Semitic Languages, University of Glasgow, 1937–68 (Dean, Faculty of Divinity, 1951–54); *b* Edinburgh, 4 Dec. 1897; *e s* of late James Mullo Weir, SSC, FSAScot, Solicitor, Edinburgh; unmarried. *Educ:* Royal High School, Edinburgh; Universities of Edinburgh, Marburg, Paris and Leipzig; Jesus College, Oxford. MA Edinburgh with 1st Class Honours in Classics, 1923; 1st Class Honours in Semitic Languages, 1925; BD

Edinburgh, 1926; DPhil Oxford, 1930. Served World War I, 1917–19, with Expeditionary Force in France, Belgium and Germany. Tutor in Hebrew, University of Edinburgh, 1921–22; Minister of Orwell, Kinross-shire, 1932–34; Rankin Lecturer and Head of Department of Hebrew and Ancient Semitic Languages, University of Liverpool, 1934–37; Lecturer in the Institute of Archæology, Liverpool, 1934–37. President, Glasgow Archæological Soc., 1945–48. Hon. DD (Edinburgh), 1959; FRAS, FSAScot. *Publications:* A Lexicon of Accadian Prayers in the Rituals of Expiation, 1934; contributed to: A Companion to the Bible (ed Manson), 1939; Fortuna Domus, 1952; Documents from Old Testament Times (ed Thomas), 1958; Hastings's Dictionary of the Bible, 1963; A Companion to the Bible (ed Rowley), 1963; Archæology and Old Testament Study (ed Thomas), 1967; edited Transactions of Glasgow University Oriental Soc., Studia Semitica et Orientalia, Transactions of Glasgow Archæological Soc.; articles and reviews of books. *Recreations:* golf, travel. *Address:* 4/17 Gillsland Road, Edinburgh EH10 5BW. *T:* 0131–228 6965.

Died 4 March 1995.

WELCH, Anthony Edward, CB 1957; CMG 1949; Under-Secretary, Board of Trade, 1946–66 (Ministry of Materials, 1951–54); *b* 17 July 1906; *s* of late Francis Bertram Welch; *m* 1946, Margaret Eileen Strudwick (*d* 1978); no *c. Educ:* Cheltenham College; New College, Oxford. *Address:* Marlborough House, Southwold, Suffolk IP18 6LR. *T:* Southwold (0502) 724643.

Died 23 Feb. 1993.

WELCH, Air Vice-Marshal Edward Lawrence C.; *see* Colbeck-Welch.

WELD, Col Sir Joseph William, Kt 1973; OBE 1946; TD 1947 (two Bars); JP; DL; Lord-Lieutenant of Dorset, 1964–84; Chairman, Wessex Regional Health Authority (formerly Wessex Regional Hospital Board), 1972–75; *b* 22 Sept. 1909; *s* of Wilfrid Joseph Weld, Avon Dassett, Warwickshire; *m* 1933, Elizabeth (*d* 1991), *d* of E. J. Bellord; one *s* four *d* (and two *d* decd). *Educ:* Stonyhurst; Balliol College, Oxford. Served with Dorset Regt, TA, 1932–41; Staff College, Camberley, 1941; GSO2, General Headquarters Home Forces, 1942; Instructor, Staff College, Camberley, 1942–43; GSO1, Headquarters SEAC, 1943–46; commanded 4th Battalion Dorset Regt, 1947–51; Colonel, 1951. Hon. Colonel, 4th Battalion Dorset Regiment (TA). Chairman of Dorset Branch, County Landowners' Assoc., 1949–60; Chm. S Dorset Conservative Assoc., 1952–55 (Pres., 1955–59). Privy Chamberlain of Sword and Cape to Pope Pius XII. JP 1938, High Sheriff 1951, DL 1952, CC 1961, Dorset. KStJ 1967. *Address:* Lulworth Manor, East Lulworth, Dorset. *T:* West Lulworth (092941) 2352. *Club:* Royal Dorset Yacht. *Died 14 Aug. 1992.*

WELENSKY, Rt Hon. Sir Roland, (Sir Roy), KCMG 1959 (CMG 1946); Kt 1953; PC 1960; *b* Salisbury, Southern Rhodesia, 20 Jan. 1907; named Raphael; *s* of Michael and Leah Welensky; *m* 1st, 1928, Elizabeth Henderson (*d* 1969); one *s* one *d*; 2nd, 1972, Valerie Scott; two *d. Educ:* Salisbury, S Rhodesia. Joined Railway service, 1924; Member National Council of the Railway Workers Union; Director of Manpower, Northern Rhodesia, 1941–46; formed N Rhodesia Labour Party, 1941; Member of Sir John Forster's commission to investigate the 1940 riots in Copperbelt; Chairman of various conciliation Boards and member of the Strauss (1943) and Grant (1946) Railway Arbitration Tribunals; Member of delegn to London to discuss Mineral Royalties (1949) and Constitution (1950 and 1951); Member of Northern Rhodesia delegation to Closer Association Conference at Victoria Falls, 1951. MLC, N Rhodesia, 1938, MEC 1940–53. Chm. Unofficial Members Assoc.

1946–53. Federation of Rhodesia and Nyasaland: Minister of Transport, Communications and Posts, 1953–56; Leader of the House and Deputy Prime Minister, 1955–56; Prime Minister and Minister of External Affairs, 1956–63 (also Minister of Defence, 1956–59). Heavy-weight boxing champion of the Rhodesias, 1926–28. *Publication:* Welensky's 4000 Days, The Life and Death of the Federation of Rhodesia and Nyasaland, 1964; *relevant publications:* The Rhodesian, by Don Taylor; Welensky's Story, by Garry Allighan; The Welensky Papers, by Dr J. R. T. Wood. *Recreation:* gardening. *Address:* Shaftesbury House, Milldown Road, Blandford Forum, Dorset DT11 7DE. *Club:* Farmers'. *Died 5 Dec. 1991.*

WELLS, Lt-Col Herbert James, CBE 1958; MC 1918; JP; DL; FCA 1934; *b* 27 March 1897; *s* of late James J. Wells, NSW; *m* 1926, Rose Hamilton (*d* 1983), *d* of late H. D. Brown, Bournemouth; no *c. Educ:* NSW. Chartered Accountant; Consultant (formerly Sen. Partner), Amsdon Cossart & Wells. Surrey CC: Alderman, 1960; Vice-Chm., 1959–62; Chm., 1962–65. JP Surrey 1952 (Chm., Magistrates' Ct, Wallington, 1960–70); DL 1962, High Sheriff 1965, Surrey. A General Comr for Income Tax. Freeman, City of London. Former Pres. Brit. Red Cross, Carshalton and Sutton Division; former Member, Surrey T&AFA, retired 1968; Chairman, Queen Mary's Hospital for Children, Carshalton, 1958–60; Member, Carshalton UDC, 1945–62 (Chm. 1950–52 and 1955–56). Served European War, 1914–18 with Aust. Inf. and Aust. Flying Corps in Egypt and France (MC); served War of 1939–45. DUniv Surrey, 1975. *Recreations:* football, hockey, tennis, squash, latterly golf. *Address:* 17 Oakhurst Rise, Carshalton Beeches, Surrey SM5 4AG. *T:* 081–643 4125. *Club:* Royal Automobile. *Died 12 May 1993.*

WELLS-PESTELL, Baron *cr* 1965 (Life Peer), of Combs in the County of Suffolk; **Reginald Alfred Wells-Pestell,** CBE 1988; JP; MA, LLD, FPhS; sociologist; Deputy Speaker, House of Lords and Deputy Chairman of Committees, since 1981; *b* 27 Jan. 1910; *o s* of Robert Pestell and Mary (*née* Manning); surname amended to Wells-Pestell, 1960; *m* 1935, Irene (*d* 1991), *y d* of late Arthur Wells; two *s. Educ:* elementary and grammar schs; Univ. of London (Dip. in Econ. and Social Sciences). Formerly London Probation Service; Vice-Pres., Nat. Assoc. of Probation Officers, 1974–79. A Founder, Nat. Marriage Guidance Council (latterly a Vice-Pres.). JP London, 1946; a Chm., Chelsea and E London Matrimonial Courts. Mem. LCC, 1946–52; Stoke Newington Borough, 1945–49 (Leader of Council, 1946; Mayor 1947–49); Mem. E Suffolk County Council, 1964–67. Contested (Lab) Taunton, 1955 and 1956, Hornsey, 1950 and 1951. Lord in Waiting (a Govt Whip), 1974–79; Spokesman in House of Lords for DHSS, 1974–79; Parly Under-Sec. of State, DHSS, 1979; Dep. Chief Opposition Whip, 1979–81. Member: Church of England Council for Social Aid (Vice-Chm.); Bridgehead Cttee (appointed by Home Office); Cttee and Council of Outcasts (providing help for the socially inadequate), and Chm. of Trustees; Wireless for the Bedridden (former Chm.); Pres., Handcrafts Adv. Assoc. for the Disabled; Pres. or Patron, other voluntary organisations; delegations to Far East, Africa and Israel, and to 5th Commonwealth Med. Conf., NZ, 1977. Captain KRRC, 9th Bn City of London HG, 1940–45. Freeman, City of London, 1952. *Publications:* articles and pamphlets on marriage and family life, delinquency and social problems for press and jls. *Recreations:* music, opera. *Address:* 22 Vicarage Close, Oxford OX4 4PL. *T:* Oxford (0865) 771142. *Died 17 Jan. 1991.*

WESSEL, Robert Leslie, OBE 1969; Chairman, N. Corah & Sons Ltd, 1957–69, retired; *b* 21 Oct. 1912; *s* of late H. L. Wessel, Copenhagen, Denmark; *m* 1936, Dora Elizabeth, *d* of G. C. G. Gee, Rothley, Leics; two *s* two *d.*

Educ: Malvern College. Entered N. Corah & Sons Ltd, 1932. Served War of 1939–45, 44th Searchlight Regt RA (TA), 1939–41. Chairman: Nat. Youth Bureau, 1972–76; Youth Service Information Centre, 1968–72; Nat. Coll. for Training Youth Leaders, 1960–70. Member: Council of Industrial Soc. (Chm., 1969–72); Cttee of Management, RNLI, 1974–82. Group Chairman, Duke of Edinburgh's Conference, 1956. Mem., N and E Midlands Regional Bd, Lloyds Bank Ltd, 1962–78; Dir, Loughborough Consultants Ltd, 1970–78. Pro-Chancellor, Loughborough University of Technology, 1969–78. FIMgt; FIWM. Mem., Worshipful Co. of Framework Knitters (Master, 1969–70). Hon. DTech Loughborough, 1978. *Recreations:* painting, photography, music, travel. *Address:* 12 St Elmo Court, Sandhills Road, Salcombe, South Devon TQ8 8JP. *T:* Salcombe (01548) 842456.

Died 21 Feb. 1995.

WEST, Christopher Robin; Chief Executive, Portsmouth and South East Hampshire Health Commission, since 1992; Member, Audit Commission, since 1990; *b* 26 April 1944; *s* of George Edward Harry West and Queenie (*née* Rickwood); *m* 1970, Lesley Jane Dadd; two *s. Educ:* Sir James Smith's Grammar Sch., Camelford, Cornwall; Durham Univ. (MSc). AHSM. Health Service appointments: Bristol, 1965–66; Torquay, 1966–67; Sunderland, 1967–68; Asst Hosp. Sec., Westminster Hosp., 1968–72; Asst Clerk, Bd of Govs, Guy's Hosp., 1972–75; Regl Management Services Officer and Head of Strategic Planning, Oxford RHA, 1975–78; Area Administrator, Wilts AHA, 1978–82; Dist Administrator, 1982–84, Dist Gen. Manager, 1984–92, Portsmouth and SE Hants HA. Chm., NHS Health Commn Cttee on Open Govt; Mem., NHS Cttee on Corporate Governance; Special Advr, Select Cttee on Health. Member: Bd of Governors, Portsmouth Univ. (formerly Portsmouth Poly), 1991–; Bd, Portsmouth Business Sch., 1990–. Associate Ed., Quality in Health Care. *Publications:* Education for Senior NHS Management, 1975 (Chm., Business Graduates Assoc. Report); (jtly) Industrial Relations: in search for a system, 1979; (jtly) Health Care in the United Kingdom, 1982; (jtly) Walk, don't run, 1987; (jtly) Day Care, Surgery, Anaesthesia and Management, 1989; (jtly) Policy Issues in Nursing, 1992; (jtly) NHS Trusts in Practice, 1993; articles in various jls. *Recreations:* sailing, photography, cricket, ornithology, reading, gardening, an interest in all things related to Cornwall. *Address:* (office) Finchdean House, Milton Road, Portsmouth PO3 6DP. *T:* Portsmouth (0705) 838340. *Clubs:* Newport Sailing; Cornwall Rugby Football. *Died 28 Dec. 1994.*

WEST, Prof. William Dixon, CIE 1947; ScD, FGS, FNA (Geol.); Emeritus Professor of Applied Geology, University of Saugar; *b* 1901; *s* of Arthur Joseph West. *Educ:* King's Sch., Canterbury; St John's Coll., Cambridge (BA, ScD). Former Director, Geological Survey of India; former Vice-Chancellor, Univ. of Saugar. Lyell Medal, Geological Soc. of London, 1950; Wadia Medal, Indian Nat. Science Acad., 1983. *Address:* Department of Applied Geology, Doctor Harisingh Gour Vishwavidyalaya, Sagar, Madhya Pradesh 470003, India.

Died 23 July 1994.

WESTALL, Robert Atkinson; freelance author; *b* 7 Oct. 1929; *s* of Robert Atkinson Westall and Maggie Alexandra Leggett; *m* 1958, Jean Underhill; (one *s* decd). *Educ:* Tynemouth High Sch.; Durham Univ. (1st Cl. Hons Fine Art); London Univ. (Slade Dip.). National Service, L-Corp. Royal Signals, Egypt, 1953–55. Art Master: Erdington Hall Sec. Mod. Sch., 1957–58; Keighley Boys Grammar Sch., 1958–60; Hd of Art, Hd of Careers, Sir John Deane's GS, later Coll., Cheshire, 1960–85; antique dealer, 1985–86. Dir, Telephone Samaritans of Mid-Cheshire, 1966–75. Member: Soc. of Authors; PEN

America. Carnegie Medal, 1975, 1980; Horn Book Award (American), 1976, 1981; Preis der Leseratten (German), 1988, 1989, 1991; Smarties Prize, 1990; Guardian Award, 1991. *Publications: for children:* The Machine-Gunners, 1975; The Wind Eye, 1976; The Watch House, 1977; The Devil on the Road, 1978; Fathom Five, 1979; Scarecrows, 1980; Break of Dark, 1981; The Haunting of Chas McGill, 1982; Futuretrack Five, 1983; The Cats of Seroster, 1984; Rachel and the Angel, 1986; Urn Burial, 1986; Ghosts and Journeys, 1986; The Creature in the Dark, 1987; Ghost Abbey, 1988; Blitzcat, 1989; Old Man on a Horse, 1989; The Call and Other Stories, 1989; Echoes of War, 1989; A Walk on the Wild Side, 1989; The Kingdom by the Sea, 1990; The Promise, 1990; Stormsearch, 1990; If Cats Could Fly, 1990; Yaxley's Cat, 1991; The Christmas Cat, 1991; The Stones of Muncaster Cathedral 1991; Gulf, 1992; The Fearful Lovers, 1992; The Christmas Ghost, 1992; The Wheatstone Pond, 1993; *for adults:* Antique Dust, 1989; *non-fiction:* The Children of the Blitz, 1985. *Recreations:* cats, Gothic architecture, local history, film, still a practising sculptor, religion and the supernatural. *Address:* c/o Macmillan Publishers, 4 Little Essex Street, WC2R 3LF. *Died 15 April 1993.*

WESTALL, Rupert Vyvyan Hawksley, MA Cantab; Lieutenant Commander Royal Navy (retired); Head Master, Kelly College, Tavistock, Devon, 1939–59; *b* 27 July 1899; *s* of late Rev. William Hawksley Westall and Adela Clara Pope; *m* 1925, Sylvia G. D. Page (*d* 1979); two *s* three *d. Educ:* RN Colleges Osborne and Dartmouth; Queens' College, Cambridge (Exhibitioner and schol.; MA 1926, 1st division first part, 2nd class 2nd part History Tripos). Royal Navy, 1912–22; served European War, 1914–18; served in HMS Goliath, HMS Canada, HMS Ure and four years in The Submarine Service; Service on East African Station and Gallipoli, 1914–15, Jutland, China Station; Queens' College, Cambridge, 1922–26; Training College for Schoolmasters, Cambridge, 1925–26; VI form and Careers Master, Blundell's School, 1926–34; Head Master West Buckland School, 1934–38. *Address:* Penrose, 9 Kimberley Place, Falmouth, Cornwall TR11 3QL. *T:* Falmouth (0326) 313238.

Died 22 June 1992.

WESTLAKE, Prof. Henry Dickinson; Hulme Professor of Greek in the University of Manchester, 1949–72, then Professor Emeritus; *b* 4 Sept. 1906; *s* of C. A. Westlake and Charlotte M. Westlake (*née* Manlove); *m* 1940, Mary Helen Sayers; one *s* one *d. Educ:* Uppingham School; St John's College, Cambridge (Scholar). Strathcona Student, 1929; Assistant Lecturer, University College, Swansea, 1930–32; Fellow of St John's College, Cambridge, 1932–35; Assistant Lecturer, University of Bristol, 1936–37; Lecturer, King's College, Newcastle, 1937–46; Administrative Assistant, Ministry of Home Security, 1941–44; Reader in Greek, University of Durham, 1946–49; Dean of the Faculty of Arts, Univ. of Manchester, 1960–61; Pro-Vice-Chancellor, 1965–68. *Publications:* Thessaly in the Fourth Century BC, 1935; Timoleon and his relations with tyrants, 1952; Individuals in Thucydides, 1968; Essays on the Greek Historians and Greek History, 1969; Studies in Thucydides and Greek History, 1989; articles and reviews in learned periodicals. *Address:* West Lodge, Manor Farm Road, Waresley, Sandy, Bedfordshire SG19 3BX. *T:* Gamlingay (0767) 50877.

Died 23 July 1992.

WESTMORLAND, 15th Earl of *cr* 1624; **David Anthony Thomas Fane,** GCVO 1991 (KCVO 1970); DL; Baron Burghersh, 1624; late Royal Horse Guards; a Permanent Lord in Waiting to the Queen, since 1991; Director: Sotheby Parke Bernet Group, since 1965 (Deputy Chairman, 1979, Chairman, 1980–82); Sotheby Holdings Inc., since 1983; Sotheby Advisory Board, since 1987; *b*

31 March 1924; *e s* of 14th Earl of Westmorland and Hon. Diana Lister (*d* 1983), *y d* of 4th Baron Ribblesdale, and *widow* of Capt. Arthur Edward Capel, CBE; *S* father 1948; *m* 1950, Jane, *d* of Lt-Col Sir Roland Lewis Findlay, 3rd Bt, and Barbara Joan, *d* of late Maj. H. S. Garrard; two *s* one *d*. Served War of 1939–45 (wounded); resigned from RHG with hon. rank of Captain, 1950. A Lord in Waiting to the Queen, 1955–78; Master of the Horse, 1978–91. DL Glos, 1991. *Heir: s* Lord Burghersh [*b* 1 Aug. 1951; *m* 1985, Caroline Eldred, *d* of Keon Hughes; one *d*]. *Address:* Kingsmead, Didmarton, Badminton, Avon; 26 Laxford House, Cundy Street, SW1. *Clubs:* Buck's, White's.   *Died 8 Sept. 1993.*

WESTOLL, Prof. Thomas Stanley, BSc, PhD Dunelm; DSc Aberdeen; FRS 1952; FRSE, FGS, FLS; J. B. Simpson Professor of Geology, University of Newcastle upon Tyne (formerly King's College, Newcastle upon Tyne, University of Durham), 1948–77, then Emeritus; Chairman of Convocation, Newcastle upon Tyne University, 1979–89; *b* W Hartlepool, Durham, 3 July 1912; *e s* of Horace Stanley Raine Westoll; *m* 1st, 1939, Dorothy Cecil Isobel Wood (marr. diss. 1951); one *s*; 2nd, 1952, Barbara Swanson McAdie. *Educ:* West Hartlepool Grammar School; Armstrong (later King's) Coll., Univ. of Durham; University College, London. Senior Research Award, DSIR, 1934–37; Lecturer in Geology, Univ. of Aberdeen, 1937–48. Leverhulme Emeritus Res. Fellow, 1977–79. Alexander Agassiz Visiting Professor of Vertebrate Paleontology, Harvard University, 1952; Huxley Lectr, Univ. of Birmingham, 1967. J. B. Tyrell Fund, 1937, and Daniel Pidgeon Fund, 1939, Geological Soc. of London. President: Palæontological Assoc., 1966–68; Section C, British Assoc. for Advancement of Science, Durham, 1970; Geological Soc., 1972–74; Mem. Council, Royal Soc., 1966–68. Corr. Mem., Amer. Museum of Natural History; Hon. Life Mem., Soc. of Vertebrate Paleontology, USA, 1976. Hon. LLD Aberdeen, 1979. Murchison Medal, Geol Soc. London, 1967; Clough Medal, Geol Soc. of Edinburgh, 1977; Linnean Gold Medal (Zool.), 1978. *Publications:* (ed) Studies on Fossil Vertebrates, 1958; (ed, with D. G. Murchison) Coal and Coal-bearing Strata, 1968; (ed, with N. Rast) Geology of the USSR, by D. V. Nalivkin, 1973; numerous papers and monographs on vertebrate anatomy and palæontology and geological topics, in several journals. *Recreations:* photography, numismatics. *Address:* 21 Osborne Avenue, Newcastle upon Tyne NE2 1JQ. *T:* 0191–281 1622.   *Died 19 Sept. 1995.*

WESTON, Rear-Adm. William Kenneth, CB 1956; OBE 1945; Royal Navy, retired; *b* 8 Nov. 1904; *s* of late William Weston; *m* 1934, Mary Ursula Shine; one *s* two *d*. *Educ:* RNC Osborne and Dartmouth; RNEC Keyham; RNC Greenwich. Served on staff of Flag Officer Destroyers, Pacific, 1945–46; Admiralty District Engineer Overseer, NW District, 1951–54; Staff of C-in-C Plymouth, 1954–58; retired, 1958. Court of Assistants of the Worshipful Company of Salters, 1959, Master, 1963, resigned 1989. *Address:* Brackleyways, Hartley Wintney, Hants. *T:* Hartley Wintney (025126) 2546. *Club:* Naval and Military.   *Died 10 March 1992.*

WESTWOOD, 2nd Baron, *cr* 1944, of Gosforth; **William Westwood**, JP; company director; *b* 25 Dec. 1907; *s* of 1st Baron and Margaret Taylor Young (*d* 1916); *S* father 1953; *m* 1937, Marjorie, *o c* of Arthur Bonwick, Newcastle upon Tyne; two *s*. *Educ:* Glasgow. Dir of several private companies. Hon. Vice-Pres., Football Association, 1981 (Vice-Pres., 1974–81); Life Mem., Football League, 1981. JP Newcastle upon Tyne, 1949. FRSA; FCIS. *Heir: s* Hon. William Gavin Westwood [*b* 30 Jan. 1944; *m* 1969, Penelope, *er d* of Dr C. E. Shafto, Newcastle upon Tyne;

two *s*]. *Address:* 55 Moor Court, Westfield, Gosforth, Newcastle upon Tyne NE3 4YD.
                                    Died 8 Nov. 1991.

WHALLEY-TOOKER, Hyde Charnock, MA, LLM (Cantab), MA (Oxon); Emeritus Fellow of Downing College, Cambridge (Fellow, 1927–67, and Senior Tutor, 1931–47); University Lecturer in Law, 1931–67; *b* 1 Sept. 1900; *o s* of Edward Whalley-Tooker; *m* 1935, Frances (*d* 1987), *er d* of late Thomas Halsted; one *d*. *Educ:* Eton; Trinity Hall, Cambridge; Balliol College, Oxford. Law Tripos Part I, Class I, 1921; Part II, Class I, 1922. *Address:* 5 Wilberforce Road, Cambridge. *T:* Cambridge (0223) 350073.   *Died 16 Jan. 1992.*

WHEATLEY, Sir (George) Andrew, Kt 1967; CBE 1960; MA; BCL; Clerk of the Peace and Clerk of Hampshire County Council, 1946–67; *b* 1908; *s* of late Robert Albert Wheatley; *m* 1937, Mary Vera Hunt (*d* 1988); three *s* two *d*. *Educ:* Rugby; Exeter Coll., Oxford. Asst Solicitor: Pembrokeshire CC, 1932–34; East Suffolk CC, 1934–36; N Riding, Yorks, 1936–39; Dep. Clerk of the Peace and Dep. Clerk of Cumberland CC, 1939–42; Clerk of the Peace and Clerk of the Cumberland CC, 1942–46. Hon. Sec., Society of Clerks of the Peace of Counties and of Clerks of County Councils, 1961; former Member: Local Government Advisory Panel, Dept of Technical Co-operation; Home Office Adv. Council on Child Care; Central Training Council in Child Care; Min. of Housing and Local Govt Departmental Cttee on Management in Local Govt; Royal Commn on Assizes and Quarter Sessions; Mem., English Local Govt Boundary Commn 1971–78. DL Hants, 1967–70. *Address:* 9 St Thomas Park, Lymington, Hants SO41 9NF.
                                    Died 21 May 1991.

WHEELDON, Rt Rev. Philip William, OBE 1946; *b* 20 May 1913; *e s* of late Alfred Leonard Wheeldon and Margaret Proctor Wheeldon (*née* Smith); *m* 1966, Margaret Redfearn. *Educ:* Clifton Coll., Bristol; Downing Coll., Cambridge; Westcott House Theological Coll. BA 1935, MA 1942. Deacon, 1937; priest, 1938; Farnham Parish Church, Dio. Guildford, 1937–39; Chaplain to the Forces, 1939–46; Chaplain, 1st Bn Coldstream Guards, 1939–42; Senior Chaplain, 79th Armoured Div., 1942–43; Dep. Asst Chaplain-Gen. 12th Corps, 1943–45, 8th Corps, 1945–46; Hon. Chaplain to the Forces, 1946; Domestic Chaplain to Archbishop of York, 1946–49, Hon. Chaplain, 1950–54; General Sec., CACTM, 1949–54; Prebendary of Wedmore II in Wells Cathedral, 1952–54; Suffragan Bishop of Whitby, 1954–61; Bishop of Kimberley and Kuruman, 1961–65; resigned, 1965; an Asst Bishop, Dio. Worcester, 1965–68; Bishop of Kimberley and Kuruman, 1968–76. Hon. Asst Bishop, Diocese of Worcester 1976–77, Diocese of Wakefield 1977–85. *Recreations:* music, gardening. *Address:* 11 Toothill Avenue, Brighouse, West Yorks HD6 3SA.
                                    Died 6 March 1992.

WHEELER, Michael Mortimer, TD 1961; QC 1961; *b* Westminster, 8 Jan. 1915; *o s* of late Sir Mortimer Wheeler, CH, CIE, MC, TD, and Tessa Verney Wheeler, FSA; *m* 1939, Sheila, *e d* of late M. S. Mayou, FRCS; two *d*. *Educ:* Dragon School, Oxford; Rugby School; Christ Church, Oxford. Barrister: Gray's Inn, 1938; Lincoln's Inn, 1946 (Bencher 1967; Treasurer, 1986); Dep. High Court Judge (Chancery Div.), 1972–89. Served throughout War of 1939–45, with RA (TA) in UK and Italy (Lt-Col 1945; despatches). *Address:* 114 Hallam Street, W1N 5LW. *T:* 071–580 7284. *Clubs:* Garrick, MCC.
                                    Died 7 Aug. 1992.

WHEELER, Maj.-Gen. Richard Henry Littleton, CB 1960; CBE 1953; *b* 2 Nov. 1906; *s* of Maj. Henry Littleton Wheeler, CB, DSO, and Vera Gillum Webb; *m* 1941, Iris

Letitia Hope; one d. *Educ:* Uppingham; RMA, Woolwich. 2nd Lt RA, 1926; served War of 1939–45, 50th Division; Lt-Col 1942; Brigadier 1950; HQ Northern Army Group, 1958–61; Maj.-Gen. 1959. Col Comdt RA, 1963–71. *Recreations:* riding, music. *Address:* Manor Farm, Knighton, Sherborne, Dorset DT9 6QU. *Club:* Army and Navy. *Died 28 Aug. 1994.*

WHEWELL, Prof. Charles Smalley, PhD; Professor of Textile Industries, University of Leeds, 1963–77; Emeritus Professor 1977 (Professor of Textile Technology, 1954–63, Head of Department, 1963–75); b 26 April 1912; m 1937, Emma Stott, PhD; one s. *Educ:* Grammar School, Darwen, Lancs; University of Leeds (BSc, PhD). Research Chemist, Wool Industries Research Association, 1935–37; University of Leeds, 1937–77: Lecturer in Textile Chemistry; Lecturer in Textile Finishing; Senior Lecturer in Textile Chemistry; Reader in Textile Finishing; Pro-Vice-Chancellor, 1973–75. Pres., Textile Inst., 1977–79. Hon. Liveryman, Clothworkers' Company, 1970. Hon. Fellow: Huddersfield Polytechnic, 1977; Textile Inst., 1979 (Hon. Life Mem., 1987). Textile Institute Medal, 1954; Warner Memorial Medal, 1960; Textile Institute Service Medal, 1971; Distinguished Service Award, Indian Inst. of Technol., Delhi, 1985. *Publications:* contrib. to: Waterproofing and Water-repellency, 1963; Chemistry of Natural Protein Fibers, ed R. S. Asquith, 1977; Oxford History of Technology, ed Williams; Chambers's Encyclopædia; Encyclopædia Britannica; British Wool Manual; Jl Soc. of Dyers and Colourists; Jl Textile Inst. *Recreations:* music, travel. *Address:* 8 Weetwood Avenue, Leeds LS16 5NF. *T:* Leeds (0113) 275 1654. *Died 31 May 1995.*

WHISTLER, Maj.-Gen. Alwyne Michael Webster, CB 1963; CBE 1959; retired, 1965; b 30 Dec. 1909; s of Rev. W. W. Whistler and Lilian Whistler (née Meade), Elsted, Sussex; m 1936, Margaret Louise Michelette (d 1986), d of Brig.-Gen. Malcolm Welch, CB, CMG, JP, Stedham, Sussex; one s two d. *Educ:* Gresham's Sch., Holt; RMA Woolwich. 2nd Lt Royal Signals, 1929; served in India, 1932–44; War of 1939–45: Staff Coll., Camberley, 1944; Burma Campaign, 19 and 25 Indian Divs and XII Army, 1944–45 (despatches twice); Asst Dir PR, Berlin, 1946; GSO1 (Military Adviser), Military Governor of Germany, 1946–48; AQMG, War Office, 1949–50; JSSC 1950; Comdg Royal Signals, 3 Div., 1951–54; Col GS, War Office, 1955–57; Col Q FARELF, 1957–58; Comdr Corps Royal Signals, 1 (British) Corps, BAOR, 1959–60; Signal Officer-in-Chief, War Office, 1960–62; Chairman, British Joint Communications Board, Ministry of Defence, 1962–64; Assistant Chief of the Defence Staff (Signals), 1964–65. Hon. Col Princess Louise's Kensington Regt (41st Signals) TA, 1963–66; Col Commandant, Royal Corps of Signals, 1964–68; Hon. Col 32nd (Scottish) Signal Regiment (V), 1967–72. Princess Mary Medal, Royal Signals Instn, 1978. Master of Fox Hounds, Nerbudda Vale Hunt, 1938–40. *T:* Wareham (092955) 2605. *Died 30 Sept. 1993.*

WHITBREAD, William Henry, TD; MA Cantab; President, Whitbread and Company, Ltd, 1972–79 (Chairman, 1944–71, Managing Director, 1927–68); Chairman, Whitbread Investment Co. Ltd, 1956–77; Vice-President: Brewers' Society (Chairman, 1952–53); Institute of Brewing; Past-Master, Brewers' Company; b 22 Dec. 1900; s of late Henry William Whitbread, Norton Bavant, Wiltshire; m 1st, 1927, Ann Joscelyne (d 1936), d of late Samuel Howard Whitbread, CB, Southill, Beds; one s one d (and one s decd); 2nd, 1941, Betty Parr, d of Samuel Russell, ICS; one s two d. *Educ:* Eton; Corpus Christi College, Cambridge. Lovat Scouts, 1920–41; served War of 1939–45: Lovat Scouts, 1939–41; Reconnaissance Corps, 1941–45; parachutist. Chairman:

Parliamentary Cttee, Brewers' Society, 1948–52; Res. Cttee, Inst. of Brewing, 1948–52. Director: Barclays Bank Ltd, 1958–73; Eagle Star Insurance Co., 1958–74. Member Governing Body, Aldenham School, 1929–61 (Chairman, 1948–58). President: BSJA, 1966–68; Shire Horse Soc., 1971–72; Member: National Hunt Committee, 1956–68; Jockey Club, 1968–; Hurlingham Club Polo Committee, 1932–45; Master, Trinity Foot Beagles, 1921–23. *Recreations:* shooting, fishing, sailing. *Address:* Hazelhurst, Bunch Lane, Haslemere, Surrey GU27 1AJ; Farleaze, near Malmesbury, Wilts SN16 0LB. *Clubs:* Brooks's, Pratt's, Royal Thames Yacht; Royal Yacht Squadron. *Died 23 Nov. 1994.*

WHITE OF HULL, Baron cr 1991 (Life Peer), of Hull in the County of Humberside; **Vincent Gordon Lindsay White,** KBE 1979; Chairman, Hanson Industries, since 1983; b 11 May 1923; s of late Charles White and Lily May (née Wilson); m 1st, 1958, Elisabeth Kalen (marr. diss. 1968); two d; 2nd, 1974, Virginia Anne North (marr. diss. 1979); one s; 3rd, 1992, Victoria Ann Tucker. *Educ:* De Aston Sch., Lincs. Served War, 1940–46: SOE, Force 136, Captain. Chairman, family publishing business, Welbecson Ltd, 1947–65; Dep. Chm., Hanson Trust Ltd, 1965–73; Special Commn to open Hanson Trust's opportunities overseas, 1973–83. Mem. Bd and Chm., Internat. Cttee, Congressional Award, 1984–92; Chm., Zoological Soc. of London Develt Trust, 1989–91; Member: Bd of Dirs, Shakespeare Theatre, Folger Library, Washington, 1985–92; Council, City of Technology Colls Trust Ltd, 1987–. Bd Mem., British Airways, 1989–93. Governor, BFI, 1982–84. Hon. Fellow, St Peter's Coll., Oxford, 1984. Hon. DSc(Econ), Hull, 1988. Nat. Voluntary Leadership Award, Congressional Award 1984; (with Lord Hanson) Aims of Industry Free Enterprise Award, 1985; People to People Internat. Award, 1986. *Recreations:* flying (holder of helicopter licence), riding, skiing, tennis. *Address:* 410 Park Avenue, New York, NY 10022, USA. *T:* (212) 7598477. *Clubs:* Special Forces; Brook, Explorers' (New York).

Died 23 Aug. 1995.

WHITE, Adrian Nicholas S.; *see* Sherwin-White.

WHITE, Prof. Alan Richard, BA, PhD; Ferens Professor of Philosophy in the University of Hull, 1961–89; b Toronto, Canada, 9 Oct. 1922; s of late George Albert White and Jean Gabriel Kingston; m 1st, 1948, Eileen Anne Jarvis; one s two d; 2nd, 1979, Enid Elizabeth Alderson. *Educ:* Midleton College and Presentation College, Cork; Trinity College, Dublin. Dublin: Schol. and 1st class Moderator in Classics, 1st class Moderator in Mental and Moral Science; Boxing Pink; President of the 'Phil'. Univ. Student in Classics and Dep. Lecturer in Logic, TCD, 1945–46; Asst Lecturer, Lecturer, Sen. Lecturer in Philosophy, Univ. of Hull, 1946–61, Dean of Arts, 1969–71, Pro-Vice-Chancellor, 1976–79. Visiting Professor: Univ. of Maryland, 1967–68; 1980; Temple Univ., 1974; Simon Fraser Univ., 1983; Univ. of Delaware, 1986; Bowling Green State Univ., Ohio, 1988; Special Prof., Univ. of Nottingham, 1986–. Secretary, Mind Assoc., 1960–69, Pres., 1972. Pres., Aristotelian Soc., 1979–80. 42nd Dublin Rifles (LDF), 1941–45. *Publications:* G. E. Moore: A Critical Exposition, 1958; Attention, 1964; The Philosophy of Mind, 1967; (ed) The Philosophy of Action, 1968; Truth, 1970; Modal Thinking, 1975; The Nature of Knowledge, 1982; Rights, 1984; Grounds of Liability, 1985; Methods of Metaphysics, 1987; The Language of Imagination, 1990; Misleading Cases, 1991; articles in philosophical journals. *Recreations:* dilettantism, odd-jobbery. *Address:* 77 Newfield Road, Sherwood, Nottingham NG5 1HF. *T:* Nottingham (0602) 605078. *Died 23 Feb. 1992.*

WHITE, Arthur John Stanley, CMG 1947; OBE 1932; *b* 28 Aug. 1896; *s* of A. R. White, OBE, DL, and Minnie B. White, OBE (*née* Beauchamp); *m* 1932, Joan, *d* of R. O. Davies and *niece* of 1st and last Baron Waring; four *s* one *d. Educ:* Marlborough College; Clare College, Cambridge (Scholar). MA 1930. Served European War, Wiltshire Regt, 1915–20, France and Ireland; Indian Civil Service, Burma, 1922; Under-Secretary, Home and Political Dept, 1924; Deputy Commissioner, 1928 (Burma Rebellion 1931–32, OBE); Secretary to Government of Burma, 1934; appointed to British Council as Dep. Sec.-Gen., 1937, Sec.-Gen. 1940–47, Controller, 1947–62; retired 1962. Director, OPOS (Office for placing overseas boys and girls in British Schs), 1964–67. *Recreations:* hockey (International Trials, 1921 and 1922), cricket, tennis, shooting. *Address:* The Red House, Mere, Warminster, Wilts. *T:* Mere (0747) 860551. *Club:* East India, Devonshire, Sports and Public Schools.
Died 8 Feb. 1991.

WHITE, Prof. Cedric Masey, DSc(Eng), PhD; Professor Emeritus, University of London, 1966; consultant for river and coastal projects; *b* 19 Oct. 1898; *s* of Joseph Masey White, Nottingham; *m* 1st, 1921, Dorothy F. Lowe; 2nd, 1946, Josephine M. Ramage (*d* 1991); one *d. Educ:* privately; University College, Nottingham. Served European War, in Tank Corps, 1917–19. Lecturer in Civil Engineering, Univ. of London, King's Coll., 1927–33; Reader in Civil Engineering, and Asst Prof. in Imperial Coll. of Science and Technology, 1933–45; responsible for work of Hawksley Hydraulic Lab., 1933–66; Professor of Fluid Mechanics and Hydraulic Engineering, 1946–66. Completed various investigations for Admiralty, WO, MAP, etc, during War of 1939–45, and investigations of proposed river-structures for Hydro-Power here and abroad, 1946–56. Founder Member, Hydraulic Research Bd, 1946–51, 1959–67; sometime member of Research Committees of Instn of Civil Engineers; delegation on Hydrology to Internat. Union of Geodesy and Geophysics, 1939, 1948, 1951; Member: Council of British Hydromechanics Research Assoc., 1949–59; Internat. Assoc. for Hydraulic Research, 1947–59. Hon. ACGI, 1951. *Publications:* various engineering reports and scientific papers, chiefly on the motion of air and water. *Address:* Marsh Hill Farm, RR4, Stirling, Ont K0K 3E0, Canada. *Died 27 Dec. 1993.*

WHITE, Sir Dick (Goldsmith), KCMG 1960; KBE 1955 (CBE 1950; OBE 1942); formerly attached to Foreign and Commonwealth Office, retired 1972; *b* 20 Dec. 1906; *s* of Percy Hall White and Gertrude White (*née* Farthing); *m* 1945, Kathleen Bellamy; two *s. Educ:* Bishops Stortford Coll.; Christ Church, Oxford (Hon. Student, 1981); Universities of Michigan and California, USA. US Legion of Merit; Croix de Guerre (France). *Club:* Garrick.
[Sir Dick was Director-General of MI5, 1953–56, and of MI6, 1956–72.] *Died 20 Feb. 1993.*

WHITE, Erica, FRBS (retired); sculptor and painter; *b* 13 June 1904; *d* of Frederic Charles White, solicitor and Mildred S. Hutchings. *Educ:* St George's School, Harpenden; Slade School of Art (Sculpture Scholarship two years and Painting Prize); gained London University Diploma in Fine Arts; studied at Central School of Arts and Crafts; gained British Institution Scholarship in Sculpture; studied at Royal Acad. Schools (Silver and Bronze Medallist); awarded Feodora Gleichen Memorial Fund Grant. Exhibited at Royal Academy and at Glasgow, Brighton, Bournemouth and other art galleries. *Recreations:* outdoor sports, music. *Address:* South Cliff Cottage, 3 South Cliff, Bexhill-on-Sea, Sussex TN39 3EJ. *T:* Bexhill (0424) 211013. *Died 5 Feb. 1991.*

WHITE, Sir Frederick William George, KBE 1962 (CBE 1954); PhD; FAA 1960; FRS 1966; Chairman, Commonwealth Scientific and Industrial Research Organization, 1959–70 (Deputy Chairman, 1957–59; Chief Executive Officer, 1949–57); *b* 26 May 1905; *s* of late William Henry White; *m* 1932, Elizabeth Cooper; one *s* one *d. Educ:* Wellington College, New Zealand; Victoria University College, Univ. of New Zealand (MSc 1928); Cambridge Univ. (PhD 1932). Postgrad. Schol. in Science, Univ. of NZ and Strathcona Schol., St John's Coll., Cambridge; Research in Physics, Cavendish Laboratory, 1929–31; Asst Lecturer in Physics, King's Coll., Univ. of London, 1931–36; Professor of Physics, Canterbury University Coll., NZ, 1937–41; Radio Research Cttee, DSIR NZ, 1937; Advisor to NZ Govt on radar research, 1939; seconded to Aust. CSIR, 1941; Chm., Radiophysics Adv. Bd, 1941; Chief, Div. of Radiophysics, 1942–44; Exec. Officer, 1945–49, Mem., Exec. Cttee, 1946, CSIR Aust. Member: Radio Research Bd, 1942; Scientific Adv. Cttee, Aust. Atomic Energy Commn, 1953. Member, British Empire Cancer Campaign Soc., Canterbury Branch Cttee, 1938. FInstP; Fellow Aust. Instn of Radio Engrs. Hon. DSc: Monash Univ.; ANU; Univ. of Papua and New Guinea. *Publications:* Electromagnetic Waves, 1934; scientific papers on nature of ionosphere over NZ, on propagation of radio waves, and on songs of Australian birds (1985–87). *Address:* Sheridan Hall, 10 Marion Street, Brighton, Vic 3186, Australia.
Died 17 Aug. 1994.

WHITE, Sir Harold (Leslie), Kt 1970; CBE 1962; MA; FLAA; FAHA; FASSA; National Librarian, National Library of Australia, Canberra, 1947–70; Commonwealth Parliamentary Librarian, 1947–67; *b* Numurkah, Vic, 14 June 1905; *s* of late James White, Canterbury, Vic; *m* 1930, Elizabeth (MBE), *d* of Richard Wilson; two *s* two *d. Educ:* Wesley College, Melbourne; Queen's College, University of Melbourne (Fellow, 1988–). Commonwealth Parliamentary Library, 1923–67. Visited US as Carnegie Scholar, 1939, and as first Australian under "Leaders and Specialists programme" of Smith Mundt Act, 1950. Represented Australia at various overseas Conferences, 1939–69. Chairman, Standing Cttee, Aust. Advisory Council on Bibliographical Services, 1960–70; Member: various Aust. cttees for UNESCO; Aust. Nat. Film Bd; UNESCO Internat. Cttee on Bibliography, Documentation and Terminology, 1961–64; Nat. Meml Cttee, 1975–; Chm., Adv. Cttee, Australian Encyclopaedia, 1970–87; Governor, Australian Film Inst., 1958–77; Hon. Vice Pres., Library Assoc. of UK, 1970–. H. C. L. Anderson Award, Library Assoc. of Australia, 1983. *Publications:* (ed) Canberra: A Nation's Capital; contribs to various jls. *Address:* 27 Mugga Way, Canberra, ACT 2603, Australia. *Died 31 Aug. 1992.*

WHITE, James, CA; Chairman, Aerospace Composite Technologies, since 1993; *b* 22 Oct. 1937; *s* of John and Helen White; *m* 1961, Mary Jardine; two *d. Educ:* Wishaw High Sen. Secondary Sch. CA (Scotland) 1961. Operations Dir (UK), SKF, 1961–70; Main Bd Dir, Lex Service PLC, 1970–79; Chief Exec., 1980–90, Chm., 1989–90, Bunzl PLC. Chm., Ashley Gp, 1988–94; Director: Lucas Industries plc, 1985–; Redland PLC, 1986–94; Beecham Group plc, 1986–89; Smithkline Beecham PLC, 1989–; Perry Gp, 1992–; Bowater Inc., 1993–; Miller Insurance Gp, 1993–. *Recreations:* golf, athletics, gardening. *Address:* Aerospace Composite Technologies, London Luton Airport, Luton, Beds. *Club:* St Stephen's Constitutional. *Died 24 June 1994.*

WHITE, John Alan; Deputy Chairman, Associated Book Publishers Ltd, 1963–68 (Managing Director, 1946–62); former Director: British Publishers Guild Ltd; Eyre & Spottiswoode Ltd; Chapman & Hall Ltd; Book Centre Ltd; *b* 20 June 1905; *e s* of Percy Hall White and Gertrude (*née* Farthing); *m* 1st, Marjorie Lovelace Vincent (*d* 1958);

two s; 2nd, Vivienne Rosalie Musgrave. *Educ:* Bishops Stortford College. President, Publishers' Association, 1955–57; Chairman, National Book League, 1963–65. *Recreations:* reading, gardening. *Address:* Hayfield House, College Road, Cork, Ireland. *T:* Cork 271519. *Club:* Garrick. *Died 19 Nov. 1991.*

WHITE, Captain Richard Taylor, DSO 1940 (Bars 1941 and 1942); RN retired; *b* 29 Jan. 1908; *s* of Sir Archibald White, 4th Bt and Gladys Becher, *d* of Rev. E. A. B. Pitman; *heir-pres.* to Sir Thomas White, 5th Bt; *m* 1936, Gabrielle Ursula Style; three *s* two *d. Educ:* RN College, Dartmouth. Served War of 1939–45 (DSO and two Bars); retired 1955. *Address:* Lavender, Lavender Road, West Malling, Kent ME19 6HP. *T:* West Malling (01732) 873969. *Died 3 March 1995.*

WHITE, Terence de Vere, FRSL; *b* 29 April 1912; *s* of Frederick S. de Vere White, LLD, and Ethel (*née* Perry); *m* 1st, 1941, Mary O'Farrell (marr. diss. 1982); two *s* one *d*; one *d* by Dervla Murphy; 2nd, 1982, Hon. Victoria Glendinning. *Educ:* St Stephen's Green Sch., Dublin: Trinity Coll., Dublin (BA, LLB). Admitted solicitor, 1933. Mem. Council, Incorporated Law Society, retd 1961. Literary Editor, The Irish Times, 1961–77. Vice-Chm., Board of Governors, National Gallery of Ireland; Trustee: National Library, 1946–79; Chester Beatty Library, 1959–80; Dir, Gate Theatre, 1969–81. Mem., Irish Academy of Letters, 1968; Hon. RHA 1968; Hon. Prof. of Literature, RHA, 1973; FRSL 1981; Mem., Aosdána, 1989. *Publications:* The Road of Excess, 1945; Kevin O'Higgins, 1948; The Story of the Royal Dublin Society, 1955; A Fretful Midge, 1957; A Leaf from the Yellow Book, 1958; An Affair with the Moon, 1959; Prenez Garde, 1962; The Remainder Man, 1963; Lucifer Falling, 1965; The Parents of Oscar Wilde, 1967; Tara, 1967; Leinster, 1968; Ireland, 1968; The Lambert Mile, 1969; The March Hare, 1970; Mr Stephen, 1971; The Anglo-Irish, 1972; The Distance and the Dark, 1973; The Radish Memoirs, 1974; Big Fleas and Little Fleas, 1976; Chimes at Midnight, 1977; Tom Moore, 1977; My Name is Norval, 1978; Birds of Prey, 1980; Johnnie Cross, 1983; Chat Show, 1987; contribs to 19th Century, Cambridge Review, Horizon, The Spectator, NY Times, Sunday Telegraph. *Recreation:* formerly riding. *Address:* Davis Cottage, Torriano Cottages, NW5 2TA. *Club:* Garrick. *Died 17 June 1994.*

WHITE, Wilfrid H.; *see* Hyde White.

WHITFIELD, Prof. John Humphreys; Serena Professor of Italian Language and Literature in the University of Birmingham, 1946–74; *b* 2 Oct. 1906; *s* of J. A. Whitfield; *m* 1936, Joan Herrin (*d* 1995), ARCA, Lectr in Design Sch., RCA, 1928–36; two *s. Educ:* Handsworth Grammar School; Magdalen College, Oxford. William Doncaster Scholar, Magdalen Coll., 1925–29; Double First Class Hons in Mod. Langs, 1928, 1929; Paget Toynbee Prizeman, 1933. Asst Master, King Edward VII School, Sheffield, 1930–36; University Lecturer in Italian, Oxford University, 1936–46. Part-time Temporary Assistant Civil Officer, Naval Intelligence Department, 1943. Chairman, Society for Italian Studies, 1962–74; Senior Editor of Italian Studies, 1967–74. President: Dante Alighieri Society (Comitato di Birmingham), 1957–75; Assoc. of Teachers of Italian, 1976–77. Awarder to Oxford and Cambridge Schools Examination Bd, 1940–68. Hon. Fellow, Inst. for Advanced Res. in the Humanities, Univ. of Birmingham, 1984–87. Barlow Lecturer on Dante, University College, London, 1958–59, Barlow Centenary Lecture, 1977; Donald Dudley Meml Lecture, Birmingham, 1980. Edmund G. Gardner Memorial Prize, 1959; Amedeo Maiuri Prize (Rome), 1965; Serena Medal for Italian Studies, British Acad., 1984. Commendatore, Ordine al Merito della Repubblica Italiana, 1972 (Cavaliere

Ufficiale, 1960). *Publications:* Petrarch and the Renascence, 1943 (NY, 1966); Machiavelli, 1947 (NY, 1966); Petrarca e il Rinascimento (trans. V. Capocci, Laterza), 1949; Dante and Virgil, 1949; Giacomo Leopardi, 1954 (Italian trans. 1964); A Short History of Italian Literature, 1960, 5th edn 1980; The Barlow Lectures on Dante, 1960; Leopardi's Canti, trans. into English Verse, 1962; Leopardi's Canti, ed with Introduction and notes, 1967, rev. edn 1978; Discourses on Machiavelli, 1969; The Charlecote Manuscript of Machiavelli's Prince, facsimile edn with an Essay on the Prince, 1969; Castiglione: The Courtier, ed with introduction, 1974; Guarini: Il Pastor Fido, ed bilingual edn with introduction, 1976; Painting in Naples from Caravaggio to Giordano (trans. of Italian texts), 1982; articles and reviews contrib. to Modern Language Review, Italian Studies, History, Medium Aevum, Comparative Literature, Problemi della Pedagogia, Le parole e le Idee, Encyclopædia Britannica, Chambers's Encyclopædia, Hutchinson's Encyclopædia, Concise Encyclopædia of the Italian Renaissance, Apollo, etc; *festschrift:* Essays in Honour of John Humphreys Whitfield, 1975. *Address:* 2 Woodbourne Road, Edgbaston, Birmingham B15 3QH. *T:* 0121–454 1035.
Died 20 Feb. 1995.

WHITTEMORE, Ernest William, MM 1944 and Bar 1945; Under-Secretary, Department of Health and Social Security, 1973–76; *b* 31 Aug. 1916; *s* of late Ernest William Whittemore and Hilda Whittemore; *m* 1942, Irene Mollie Hudson; two *d. Educ:* Raine's Sch., Stepney; King's Coll., London (BA Hons English). Receiver's Office, New Scotland Yard, 1934–35; Min. of Health, 1935–45; Royal Artillery, 1942–46; Min. of Nat. Insce (and successor depts), 1945–76. *Recreations:* bibliomania, travel, sweet peas. *Address:* 39 Montalt Road, Woodford Green, Essex IG8 9RS. *T:* 0181–504 7028.
Died 31 Dec. 1995.

WHITTERIDGE, Prof. David, FRS 1953; FRSE 1951; Waynflete Professor of Physiology, University of Oxford, 1968–79, then Emeritus Professor; *b* 22 June 1912; 2nd *s* of Walter and Jeanne Whitteridge; *m* 1938, Gweneth (*d* 1993), Hon. FRCP, *d* of S. Hutchings; three *d. Educ:* Whitgift School, Croydon; Magdalen College, Oxford (1st cl. Physiology Finals, 1934); King's College Hospital. BSc 1936; BM, BCh 1937; DM 1945; FRCP 1966. Beit Memorial Fellowship, 1940; Schorstein Research Fellow, 1944; Fellow by Special Election, Magdalen College, Oxford, 1945–50; University Demonstrator in Physiology, Univ. of Oxford, 1944–50; Prof. of Physiology, Univ. of Edinburgh, 1950–68. Fellow of Magdalen Coll., Oxford, 1968–79, Hon. Fellow, 1979. Leverhulme Vis. Prof., Univ. Delhi, 1967 and 1973; Lectures: Sherrington, RSM, 1972; Victor Horsley Meml, BMA, 1972; Bowman, OSUK, 1977; Bayliss Starling, Physiol Soc., 1979; G. Parr Meml, EEG Soc., 1980; K. N. Seneviratue Meml Oration, Physiol Soc. of Sri Lanka, 1987. Mem. Bd of Trustees, Nat. Liby of Scotland, 1966–70. Physiological Society: Sec., 1947–51; Foreign Sec., 1980–86; Hon. Mem., 1982. Vice-Pres., RSE, 1956–59. Hon. Mem., Assoc. of British Neurologists, 1984; Foreign FNA, 1982. Hon. DSc Edinburgh, 1993. Feldberg Prize, Feldberg Foundn, 1962. *Publications:* One hundred years of Congresses of Physiology, 1989; papers on physiological topics in Jl Physiol., Brain, etc. *Address:* Winterslow, Lincombe Lane, Boar's Hill, Oxford OX1 5DZ. *T:* Oxford (0865) 735211. *Died 15 June 1994.*

WHITTERIDGE, Sir Gordon (Coligny), KCMG 1964 (CMG 1956); OBE 1946; FSA; HM Diplomatic Service, retired; *b* 6 Nov. 1908; *s* of late Walter Randall and Jeanne Whitteridge, Croydon; *m* 1st, 1938, Margaret Lungley (*d* 1942; one *s* one *d* decd 1942); 2nd, 1951, Jane (*d* 1979), twin *d* of Frederick J. Driscoll, Brookline, Mass, USA;

one *s*; 3rd, 1983, Mrs Jill Stanley (*née* Belcham). *Educ:* Whitgift School, Croydon; Fitzwilliam Coll., Cambridge. FSA 1991. Joined Consular Service, 1932; one of HM Vice-Consuls, Siam, 1933; Vice-Consul, Batavia, 1936; Acting Consul, Batavia, 1937, 1938, and 1939; Acting Consul, Medan, Sept. 1941–Feb. 1942; employed at Foreign Office from June, 1942; promoted Consul (Grade II), Foreign Office, 1944, Consul, 1945; 1st Secretary, Moscow, 1948–49; Consul-General Stuttgart, 1949–51; Counsellor/Consul-Gen., 1950; Counsellor, Bangkok, 1951–56 (Chargé d'Affaires in 1952, 1953, 1954, 1955); Consul-Gen., Seattle, Wash, 1956–60; HM Consul-General, Istanbul, 1960–62; Ambassador: to Burma, 1962–65; to Afghanistan, 1965–68; retired, 1968. Chm., Anglo-Thai Soc., 1971–76; Hon. Treasurer: Soc. for Afghan Studies, 1972–83; Soc. for S Asian Studies, 1983–85. (Lay) Mem., Immigration Appeal Tribunal, 1970–81. *Publication:* Charles Masson of Afghanistan, 1986. *Recreations:* music, history. *Address:* Stonebank, Blighton Lane, The Sands, near Farnham, Surrey GU10 1PU. *Club:* Travellers'. *Died 11 Jan. 1995.*

WHITTINGTON, Charles Richard, MC 1944; Chamberlain of London, 1964–73; *b* 8 March 1908; *er s* of late Charles Henry Whittington, Stock Exchange, and Vera Whittington; *m* 1938, Helen Irene Minnie (*d* 1990), *d* of late Lieutenant-Colonel J. E. Hance, RHA; one *s* four *d. Educ:* Uppingham School. Served War of 1939–45. Member of The Stock Exchange, London, 1931–64. Liveryman Mercers' Company, 1931; Mem. of Court of Common Council for Ward of Broad Street, 1939–64; one of HM Lieutenants, City of London, 1964–73. *Recreation:* gardening. *Address:* Wood Cottage, Brampton Bryan, Bucknell, Salop SY7 0DH. *T:* Bucknell (05474) 291.
Died 11 Aug. 1992.

WHITTINGTON, Joseph Basil, OBE 1981; HM Diplomatic Service, retired; Consul-General, Rotterdam, 1977–80; *b* 24 Oct. 1921; *s* of Joseph and Margaret Whittington; *m* 1947, Hazel Joan Rushton (*d* 1992); two *s* one *d. Educ:* Cotton Coll., North Staffs; St Philip's Grammar Sch., Birmingham. Served Army, 1940–46; Captain, Royal Artillery. Post Office, 1938–48; Regional Boards for Industry, 1948–52; Bd of Trade, 1952–64: Asst Trade Commissioner, Jamaica, 1953–55; Bahamas and Bermuda, 1955–57 and Jamaica, 1957–58; Trade Commissioner, Johannesburg, 1958–62 and Toronto, 1963–67; transf. to Diplomatic Service, 1964; Head of Chancery, First Sec. (Commercial) and Consul, Liberia, 1968–70; First Sec. (Economic/Commercial), Zambia, 1970–73 and Malta, 1974–77. *Recreations:* gardening, golf, walking. *Address:* Heathcote, Darlington Road, Bath BA2 6NL. *T:* Bath (01225) 461697.
Died 22 Feb. 1995.

WHITTON, Cuthbert Henry; *b* 18 Feb. 1905; *s* of Henry and Eleanor Whitton; *m* 1938, Iris Elva Moody; one *d. Educ:* St Andrew's College, Dublin; Dublin University. Called to the Bar, Gray's Inn, 1939. Malayan Civil Service, 1929; Colonial Legal Service, 1939; Puisne Judge, Federation of Malaya, 1951; Puisne Judge, Supreme Court, Singapore, 1954; Foreign Compensation Commn, Legal Dept, 1959–71. *Recreations:* golf, gardening. *Address:* 5 Marsham Lodge, Marsham Lane, Gerrards Cross, Bucks SL9 7AB. *T:* Gerrards Cross (01753) 885608. *Clubs:* Commonwealth Trust; Kildare Street and University (Dublin). *Died 27 Aug. 1995.*

WHITWORTH, Group Captain Frank, QC 1965; a Recorder of the Crown Court, 1972–82; *b* 13 May 1910; *o s* of late Daniel Arthur Whitworth, Didsbury, Manchester; *m* 1st, 1939, Mary Lucy (*d* 1979), *o d* of late Sir John Holdsworth Robinson, JP, Bingley, Yorks; no *c*; 2nd, 1980, Mrs Irene Lannon (*d* 1991). *Educ:* Shrewsbury Sch.; Trinity Hall, Cambridge. Served with RAFVR

(Special Duties), 1940–45, retired. Called to Bar, Gray's Inn, 1934. Judge of Courts of Appeal of Jersey and Guernsey, 1971–80. Member of Dorking and Horley RDC, 1939–68. Contested (C) St Helens, 1945. Master, Clockmakers' Co., 1962 and 1971. Trustee, Whiteley Village Homes, 1963–93. *Publications:* miscellaneous verse and articles. *Recreation:* farming. *Address:* Little Manor House, Westcott, near Dorking, Surrey RH4 3NJ. *T:* Dorking (01306) 889966; 13 King's Bench Walk, Temple, EC4. *T:* 0171–353 7204. *Club:* United Oxford & Cambridge University. *Died 2 March 1995.*

WIBBERLEY, Prof. Gerald Percy, CBE 1972; Ernest Cook Professor of Countryside Planning in the University of London, University College/Wye College, 1969–82; *b* 15 April 1915; *m* 1st, 1943, Helen Yeomans (*d* 1963); one *d*; 2nd, 1972, Peggy Samways. *Educ:* King Henry VIII Grammar Sch., Abergavenny; Univs of Wales, Oxford, and Illinois, USA. BSc, MS, PhD. Asst Lectr, Univ. of Manchester, 1940–41; E Sussex Agricultural Cttee: Dist Officer, 1941–43; Asst Exec. Officer, 1943–44; Min. of Agriculture: Asst Rural Land Utilisation Officer, 1944–49; Research Officer, Land Use, 1949–54; Univ. of London, Wye Coll.: Head of Dept of Economics, 1954–69, also Reader in Agricultural Economics, 1958–62; Prof. of Rural Economy, 1963–69; Fellow 1985. Dir, CoSIRA, 1968–86; Mem., Nature Conservancy Council, 1973–80; Pres., British Agricl Econs Soc., 1975–76. Chm., Rural Planning Services Ltd, 1972–82. Hon. Associate Mem. TPI, 1949–67; Hon. Mem., RTPI, 1967–. Hon. DSc Bradford, 1982. *Publications:* Agriculture and Urban Growth, 1959; (part author): The Agricultural Significance of the Hills, 1956; Land Use in an Urban Environment, 1960; Outdoor Recreation in the British Countryside, 1963; An Agricultural Land Budget for Britain 1965–2000, 1970; The Nature and Distribution of Second Homes in England and Wales, 1973; (jtly) Planning and the Rural Environment, 1976; Countryside Planning: a personal evaluation, 1982; Gipsy Sites — the present position, 1986; contributor to Jls of: Agricl Economics, Land Economics, Town and Country Planning. *Recreations:* music, altering old houses, arguing about rural affairs. *Address:* Vicarage Cottage, 7 Upper Bridge Street, Wye, near Ashford, Kent TN25 5AW. *T:* Wye (0233) 812377. *Club:* Farmers'. *Died 8 Nov. 1993.*

WICKHAM, Rt Rev. Edward Ralph; Assistant Bishop, Diocese of Manchester, since 1982; *b* 3 Nov. 1911; *s* of Edward Wickham, London; *m* 1944, Dorothy Helen Neville Moss, *d* of Prof. Kenneth Neville Moss, Birmingham; one *s* two *d. Educ:* University of London (BD); St Stephen's House, Oxford. Deacon, 1938; priest, 1939; Curate, Christ Church, Shieldfield, Newcastle upon Tyne, 1938–41; Chaplain, Royal Ordnance Factory, Swynnerton, 1941–44; Curate-in-charge, Swynnerton, 1943–44; Diocesan Missioner to Industry, Sheffield, 1944–59; Hon. Chaplain to Bishop of Sheffield, 1950–59; Canon Residentiary, Sheffield, 1951–59; Bishop Suffragan of Middleton, 1959–82. Sir H. Stephenson Fellow, Sheffield University, 1955–57. Chm. Working Party, Gen. Synod Industrial Cttee, 1977 (report: Understanding Closed Shops); Chairman: Bd for Social Responsibility Working Party on The Future of Work, 1980; Royal Soc. of Arts Industry Year 1986 Churches' Cttee, 1985–86. Chm. Council, and Pro-Chancellor, Salford Univ., 1975–83. FRSA 1986. Hon. DLitt Salford, 1973. *Publications:* Church and People in an Industrial City, 1957; Encounter with Modern Society, 1964; Growth & Inflation, 1975; Growth, Justice and Work, 1985; contributions to: Theology, The Ecumenical Review, Industrial Welfare, etc. *Recreations:* mountaineering, rock-climbing. *Address:* 12 Westminster Road, Eccles, Manchester M30 9HF. *T:* 0161–789 3144.
Died 29 Sept. 1994.

WIESNER, Dr Jerome Bert; President Emeritus, since 1980, and Institute Professor Emeritus, since 1985, Massachusetts Institute of Technology (Dean of Science, 1964–66; Provost, 1966–71; President, 1971–80; Institute Professor, 1980–85); *b* 30 May 1915; *s* of Joseph and Ida Friedman Wiesner; *m* 1940, Laya Wainger; three *s* one *d. Educ:* University of Michigan, Ann Arbor, Michigan. PhD in electrical engineering, 1950. Staff, University of Michigan, 1937–40; Chief Engineer, Library of Congress, 1940–42; Staff, MIT Radiation Lab., 1942–45; Staff, Univ. of Calif Los Alamos Lab., 1945–46; Massachusetts Institute of Technology: Asst Prof. of Electrical Engrg, 1946; Associate Prof. of Electrical Engrg, 1947; Prof. of Electrical Engrg, 1950–64; Dir, Res. Lab. of Electronics, 1952–61. Special Assistant to the President of the USA, for Science and Technology, The White House, 1961–64; Director, Office of Science and Technology, Exec. Office of the President, 1962–64; Chm., Tech. Assessment Adv. Council, Office of Tech. Assessment, US Congress, 1976–78. Member, Board of Directors: Faxon Co.; MacArthur Foundn; Consultants for Management, Inc.; Mem., Bd of Overseers, Harvard Univ. *Publications:* Where Science and Politics Meet, 1965; contrib.: Modern Physics for the Engineer, 1954; Arms Control, Disarmament and National Security, 1960; Arms Control, issues for the Public, 1961; Lectures on Modern Communications, 1961; technical papers in Science, Physical Rev., Applied Physics, Scientific American, Proc. Inst. Radio Engineers, etc. *Recreations:* photography, boating. *Address:* Massachusetts Institute of Technology, Building E15–207, Cambridge, Mass 02139, USA. *T:* (617) 2532800. *Clubs:* Cosmos (Washington, DC); St Botolph's (Boston); Harvard (New York City).

Died 21 Oct. 1994.

WIGGIN, Sir John (Henry), 4th Bt *cr* 1892, of Metchley Grange, Harborne, Staffs; MC 1946; DL; Major, Grenadier Guards, retired; *b* 3 March 1921; *s* of Sir Charles Richard Henry Wiggin, 3rd Bt, TD, and Mabel Violet Mary (*d* 1961), *d* of Sir William Jaffray, 2nd Bt; *S* father, 1972; *m* 1st, 1947, Lady Cecilia Evelyn Anson (marr. diss. 1961; she *d* 1963), *yr d* of 4th Earl of Lichfield; two *s*; 2nd, 1963, Sarah, *d* of Brigadier Stewart Forster; two *s. Educ:* Eton; Trinity College, Cambridge. Served War of 1939–45 (prisoner-of-war). High Sheriff, 1976, DL 1985, Warwicks. *Heir: s* Charles Rupert John Wiggin, Major, Grenadier Guards [*b* 2 July 1949; *m* 1979, Mrs Mary Burnett-Hitchcock; one *s* one *d*]. *Address:* Honington Hall, Shipston-on-Stour, Warwicks CV36 5AA. *T:* Shipston-on-Stour (0608) 61434.

Died 1 Jan. 1992.

WIGGLESWORTH, Sir Vincent (Brian), Kt 1964; CBE 1951; MA, MD, BCh Cantab; FRS 1939; FRES; Director, Agricultural Research Council Unit of Insect Physiology, 1943–67, retired; Quick Professor of Biology, University of Cambridge, 1952–66; Fellow of Gonville and Caius College; *b* 17 April 1899; *s* of late Sidney Wigglesworth, MRCS; *m* 1928, Mabel Katherine (*d* 1986), *d* of late Col Sir David Semple, IMS; three *s* one *d. Educ:* Repton; Caius Coll., Cambridge (Scholar); St Thomas' Hosp. 2nd Lt RFA, 1917–18, served in France. Frank Smart Student of Caius College, 1922–24; Lecturer in Medical Entomology in London School of Hygiene and Tropical Medicine, 1926; Reader in Entomology in University of London, 1936–44; Reader in Entomology, in University of Cambridge, 1945–52. Fellow, Imperial College, London, 1977. Hon. Member: Royal Entomological Soc.; Physiological Soc.; Soc. Experimental Biology; Assoc. Applied Biology; International Confs of Entomology; Soc. of European Endocrinologists; Royal Danish Academy of Science; Amer. Philosophical Soc.; US Nat. Academy of Sciences; American Academy of Arts and Sciences; Kaiserliche Deutsche Akademie der Naturforscher,

Leopoldina; Deutsche Entomologische Gesellschaft; Amer. Soc. of Zoologists; American Entomol Soc.; USSR Acad. of Sciences; All-Union Entomol Soc.; Entomol Soc. of India; Société Zoologique de France; Société Entomologique de France, Société Entomologique d'Egypte; Entomological Society of the Netherlands; Schweizerische Entomologische Gesellschaft; Indian Academy of Zoology; Corresponding Member: Accademia delle Scienze dell' Istituto di Bologna; Société de Pathologie Exotique; Entomological Soc. of Finland. Dunham Lecturer, Harvard, 1945; Woodward Lecturer, Yale, 1945; Croonian Lecturer, Royal Society, 1948; Messenger Lecturer, Cornell, 1958; Tercentenary Lecturer, Royal Society, 1960. Hon. FRCP 1989. DPhil (*hc*) University, Berne; DSc (*hc*): Paris, Newcastle and Cambridge. Royal Medal, Royal Society, 1955; Swammerdam Medal, Soc. Med. Chir., Amsterdam, 1966; Gregor Mendel Gold Medal, Czechoslovak Acad. of Science, 1967; Frink Medal, Zoological Soc., 1979; Wigglesworth Medal, Royal Entomological Soc., 1981. *Publications:* Insect Physiology, 1934; The Principles of Insect Physiology, 1939; The Physiology of Insect Metamorphosis, 1954; The Life of Insects, 1964; Insect Hormones, 1970; Insects and the Life of Man, 1976; numerous papers on comparative physiology. *Address:* 14 Shilling Street, Lavenham, Suffolk CO10 9RH. *T:* Lavenham (0787) 247293. *Died 11 Feb. 1994.*

WIGHT, James Alfred, OBE 1979; FRCVS; practising veterinary surgeon, 1939–90; author, since 1970; *b* 3 Oct. 1916; *s* of James Henry and Hannah Wight; *m* 1941, Joan Catherine Danbury; one *s* one *d. Educ:* Hillhead High Sch.; Glasgow Veterinary Coll. FRCVS 1982. Started in general veterinary practice in Thirsk, Yorks, 1940, and there ever since with the exception of war-time service with the RAF; began to write at the ripe age of 50 and quite unexpectedly became a best-selling author of books on his veterinary experiences which have been translated into all European languages and many others, incl. Japanese. Hon. Member: British Vet. Assoc., 1975; British Small Animal Vet. Assoc., 1989. Hon. DLitt Heriot-Watt, 1979; Hon. DVSc Liverpool, 1983. *Publications:* (as James Herriot): If Only They Could Talk, 1970; It Shouldn't Happen to a Vet, 1972; All Creatures Great and Small, (USA) 1972; Let Sleeping Vets Lie, 1973; All Things Bright and Beautiful, (USA) 1973; Vet in Harness, 1974; Vets Might Fly, 1976; Vet in a Spin, 1977; James Herriot's Yorkshire, 1979; The Lord God Made Them All, 1981; The Best of James Herriot, 1982; James Herriot's Dog Stories, 1985; Blossom Comes Home, 1988; The Market Square Dog, 1989; Every Living Thing, 1992; *for children:* Moses the Kitten, 1984; Only One Woof, 1985; The Christmas Day Kitten, 1986; Bonny's Big Day, 1987. *Recreations:* music, dog-walking. *Address:* Mire Beck, Thirlby, Thirsk, Yorks YO7 2DJ.

Died 23 Feb. 1995.

WIGNER, Prof. Eugene P(aul); Thomas D. Jones Professor of Mathematical Physics of Princeton University, 1938–71, retired; *b* 17 Nov. 1902; *s* of Anthony and Elizabeth Wigner; *m* 1st, 1936, Amelia Z. Frank (*d* 1937); 2nd, 1941, Mary Annette Wheeler (*d* 1977); one *s* one *d;* 3rd, 1979, Eileen C. P. Hamilton. *Educ:* Technische Hochschule, Berlin. Dr ing 1925. Asst and concurrently Extraordinary Prof., Technische Hochschule, Berlin, 1926–35; Lectr, Princeton Univ., 1930, half-time Prof. of Mathematical Physics, 1931–36; Prof. of Physics, Univ. of Wisconsin, 1936–38. Metallurgical Lab., Univ. of Chicago, 1942–45. Member: Gen. Adv. Cttee to US Atomic Energy Commn, 1952–57, 1959–64; Bd of Advrs, Federal Emergency Management Agency, 1982–91; Director: Nat. Acad. of Sciences Harbor Project for Civil Defense, 1963; Civil Defense Project, Oak Ridge Nat. Lab., 1964–65. Pres., Amer. Physical Soc., 1956 (Vice-

Pres., 1955); Member: Amer. Physical Soc.; Amer. Assoc. of Physics Teachers; Amer. Math. Soc.; Amer. Nuclear Soc.; Amer. Assoc. for Advancement of Sci.; Sigma Xi; Franklin Inst.; German Physical Soc.; Royal Netherlands Acad. of Science and Letters, 1960; Austrian Acad. Sciences, 1968; Nat. Acad. Sci. (US); Amer. Philos. Soc.; Amer. Acad. of Arts and Scis; Foreign Mem., Royal Soc., 1970; Corresp. Mem. Acad. of Science, Göttingen, 1951; Hon. Mem., Eötvös Lorand Soc., Hungary, 1976. Numerous hon. doctorates. Citation, NJ Sci. Teachers' Assoc., 1951. US Government Medal for Merit, 1946; Franklin Medal, 1950; Fermi Award, 1958; Atoms for Peace Award, 1960; Max Planck Medal of German Phys. Soc., 1961; Nobel Prize for Physics, 1963; George Washington Award, Amer. Hungarian Studies Assoc., 1964; Semmelweiss Medal, Amer. Hungarian Med. Assoc., 1965; US Nat. Medal for Science, 1969; Pfizer Award, 1971; Albert Einstein Award, 1972; Wigner Medal, 1978; Eugene P. Wigner Award, Amer. Nuclear Soc., 1990; Leo Szilárd Medal, Hungarian Nuclear Soc., 1994. Order of the Banner (Republic of Hungary), 1990; Order of Merit (Republic of Hungary), 1994. *Publications:* Nuclear Structure (with L. Eisenbud), 1958; The Physical Theory of Neutron Chain Reactors (with A. M. Weinberg), 1958; Group Theory (orig. in German, 1931), English trans., NY, 1959 (trans. Hungarian, Russian, 1979); Symmetries and Reflections, 1967 (trans. Hungarian, Russian, 1971); Survival and the Bomb, 1969. *Address:* 8 Ober Road, Princeton, NJ 08540, USA. *T:* (609) 9241189. *Club:* Cosmos (Washington, DC).

Died 1 Jan. 1995.

WILD, Rt Rev. Eric; Bishop Suffragan of Reading, 1972–82; an Assistant Bishop, Diocese of Oxford, since 1982; *b* 6 Nov. 1914; *s* of R. E. and E. S. Wild; *m* 1946, Frances Moyra, *d* of late Archibald and Alice Reynolds; one *s* one *d*. *Educ:* Manchester Grammar School; Keble College, Oxford. Ordained deacon 1937, priest 1938, Liverpool Cathedral; Curate, St Anne, Stanley, 1937–40; Curate, St James, Haydock, 1940–42; Chaplain, RNVR, 1942–46; Vicar, St George, Wigan, 1946–52; Vicar, All Saints, Hindley, 1952–59; Director of Religious Education, Dio. Peterborough, 1959–62; Rector, Cranford with Grafton Underwood, 1959–62; Canon of Peterborough, 1961, Emeritus, 1962; Gen. Sec. of National Society and Secretary of C of E Schools Council, 1962–67; Rector of Milton, 1967–72; Archdeacon of Berks, 1967–73. *Publications:* articles in periodicals; reviews, etc. *Recreations:* gardening, walking. *Address:* 2 Speen Place, Speen, Newbury, Berks RG13 1RX. *T:* Newbury (0635) 45572. *Club:* Army and Navy.

Died 10 Aug. 1991.

WILD, Very Rev. John Herbert Severn, MA Oxon; Hon. DD Durham, 1958; Dean of Durham, 1951–73, Dean Emeritus, since 1973; *b* 22 Dec. 1904; *e s* of Right Rev. Herbert Louis Wild and Helen Christian, *d* of Walter Severn; *m* 1945, Margaret Elizabeth Everard, *d* of G. B. Wainwright, OBE, MB. *Educ:* Clifton Coll.; Brasenose College, Oxford (Scholar); Westcott House, Cambridge. Represented Oxford against Cambridge at Three Miles, 1927. Deacon, 1929; priest, 1930; Curate of St Aidan, Newcastle upon Tyne, 1929–33; Chaplain-Fellow of University College, Oxford, 1933–45, Master, 1945–51, Hon. Fellow, 1951–; Select Preacher, Univ. of Oxford, 1948–49. Church Comr, 1958–73. ChStJ, 1966–. *Recreations:* fishing, walking. *Address:* Deacons Farmhouse, Rapps, Ilminster, Somerset TA19 9LG. *T:* Ilminster (0460) 53398. *Club:* United Oxford & Cambridge University.   *Died 15 Aug. 1992.*

WILDE, Derek Edward, CBE 1978; Vice Chairman, 1972–77, and Director, 1969–83, Barclays Bank Ltd; Deputy Chairman, Charterhouse Group, 1980–83; *b* 6

May 1912; *s* of late William Henry Wilde and Ethel May Wilde; *m* 1940, Helen (*d* 1992), *d* of William Harrison; (one *d* decd). *Educ:* King Edward VII School, Sheffield. Entered Barclays Bank Ltd, Sheffield, 1929; General Manager, 1961; Sen. General Manager, 1966–72. Dir, Yorkshire Bank Ltd, 1972–80; Chairman: Keyser Ullmann Holdings, 1975–81; Charterhouse Japhet, 1980–81. Governor, Midhurst Med. Res. Inst., 1970–85. Fellow, Inst. of Bankers (Hon. Fellow 1975). Hon. DLitt Loughborough, 1980. *Recreation:* gardening.

Died 3 Oct. 1993.

WILKES, His Honour Lyall; a Circuit Judge (formerly Judge of the County Courts), 1964–82; *b* 19 May 1914; *e s* of George Wilkes, MBE and Doris Wilkes, Newcastle upon Tyne; *m* 1946, Margaret Tait, *er d* of Fred and Mabel Tait, Gateshead; four *d*. *Educ:* Newcastle Grammar School; Balliol Coll., Oxford (MA). Secretary Oxford Union Society, 1937. Joined Middlesex Regiment 1940; served one year in the ranks; active service North Africa, Italy and German-occupied Greece, attached Force 133; Major, 1944 (despatches). Called to Bar, Middle Temple, 1947; practised North-Eastern Circuit; Dep. Chm., County of Durham QS, 1961–64; Asst Recorder, Sheffield and Newcastle upon Tyne, 1960–62. MP (Lab) Newcastle Central, 1945–51, when did not stand for re-election. Jt Pres., HM Council of Circuit Judges, 1981. Pres., Friends of Laing Art Gall., Newcastle upon Tyne, 1981–. FSA 1987. *Publications:* (with Gordon Dodds) Tyneside Classical: the Newcastle of Grainger, Dobson and Clayton, 1964; Tyneside Portraits: studies in Art and Life, 1971; Old Jesmond and other poems (limited edn), 1975; John Dobson: Architect and Landscape Gardener, 1980; (contrib.) Shell Book of English Villages, 1980; (contrib.) The Oxford Book of Death, 1983; South and North and other poems, 1983; The Aesthetic Obsession: a portrait of Sir William Eden, Bt, 1985; (contrib.) Everyman Anthology of 2nd World War Poetry, Vol. I 1985, Vol. II 1989; Festing—Field Marshal; a study of "Front line Frankie" Festing, 1990. *Recreation:* regretting the 20th century and avoiding its architecture. *Club:* Northern Counties (Newcastle-upon-Tyne).

Died 28 March 1991.

WILKINS, Lt-Gen. Sir Michael (Compton Lockwood), KCB 1985; OBE 1975; Lieutenant-Governor and Commander-in-Chief, Guernsey, since 1990; *b* 4 Jan. 1933; *s* of Eric Wilkins and Lucy (*née* Lockwood); *m* 1960, Anne Catherine (*née* Skivington); one *s* two *d*. *Educ:* Mill Hill School. Joined Royal Marines, 2nd Lieut, 1951; 40 Commando RM, 1954–56; Special Boat Sqdn, 1957–61; 41 Commando RM, 1961–62; RM Eastney, 1962–64; sc 1965; GSO2 (Ops) 17 Division, 1966–67; Plans Division, Naval Staff, 1968–69; Bde Major 3 Commando Bde, 1970–71; Directing Staff, Army Staff Coll., 1972–73; CO 40 Commando RM, 1974–75; NATO Defence Coll., 1976; Director of Drafting and Records, 1977–78; Comdr 3 Commando Bde, 1979–80; COS to Comdt Gen. RM, 1981–82; Maj.-Gen. Commando Forces RM, 1982–84; Comdt Gen., RM, 1984–87, retd. Hon. Col, Exeter Univ. OTC, 1990. KStJ 1990. *Recreations:* sailing, country pursuits. *Clubs:* Army and Navy; Royal Yacht Squadron (Cowes).   *Died 25 April 1994.*

WILKINSON, Prof. Andrew Wood, CBE 1979; ChM (Edinburgh); FRCSE; FRCS; Emeritus Professor of Pædiatric Surgery, University of London; Surgeon, Hospital for Sick Children, Great Ormond Street, since 1958; Hon. Consultant Pædiatric Surgeon, Postgraduate Medical School, Hammersmith, and Queen Elizabeth Hospital for Children; Civilian Consultant in Pediatric Surgery to the Royal Navy; *b* 19 April 1914; *s* of Andrew W. and Caroline G. Wilkinson; *m* 1941, Joan Longair Sharp (*d* 1994); two *s* two *d*. *Educ:* Univ. of Edinburgh.

MB, ChB, Edin., 1937; ChM (1st cl. hons and gold medal for thesis), 1949; FRCSE 1940; FRCS 1959. Surg. specialist, Lt-Col RAMC, 1942–46. Syme Surgical Fellowship, Univ. of Edinburgh, 1946–49; Senior University Clinical Tutor in Surgery, 1946–51; Lecturer in Surgery, University of Edinburgh and Assistant Surgeon, Deaconess Hosp., Edinburgh, 1951–53; Sen. Lectr in Surgery, Univ. of Aberd. and Asst Surg., Roy. Inf. and Roy. Aberd. Hosp. for Sick Children, 1953–58; Nuffield Prof. of Paediatric Surgery, Inst. of Child Health, Univ. of London, 1958–79. Dir, Internat. Sch. of Med. Scis, Ettore Majorana Foundn, 1970–. Royal College of Surgeons of Edinburgh: Mem. Council, 1964–73; Vice-Pres., 1973–76; Pres., 1976–79; Founder and Mem., Appeal Cttee, 1978–. Member: Armed Forces Med. Adv. Bd; Nat. Med. Consultative Cttee. Examr Primary and Final FRCSE; Past Examiner: Univ. Glasgow, DCH London; Primary FRCS. Lectures: Tisdall, Canadian Med. Assoc., 1966; Mason Brown Meml, 1972; Forshall, 1979; Simpson Smith Meml, 1980; Tan Sri Datu Ismail Oration, Kuala Lumpur, 1980. Hunterian Prof., RCS, 1965. Visiting Prof. Univ. of Alexandria, 1965, Albert Einstein Coll. of Medicine, 1967. Member: Bd of Governors, Hosp. for Sick Children, 1972–80; Cttee of Management, Inst. of Child Health, 1959–79. Founder Mem., Scottish Surgical Pædiatric Soc.; Hon. Mem., and Past Pres., British Assoc. of Pediatric Surgeons, 1970–72 (Denis Browne Gold Medal, 1981). FRSocMed (Pres. Open Section, 1974–76). Hon. FRCSI; Hon. FRACS; Hon. FCPS (Pak); Hon. FCPS (S Africa); Hon. Fellow: Brasilian Soc. Pædiatric Surgery; Yugoslavian Pediatric Surgical Soc.; Greek Pædiatric Surgical Soc.; Amer. Acad. Pediatrics; Italian Pediatric Surgical Soc.; Pediatric Surgical Soc. of Ecuador; Hong Kong Surgical Soc.; Amer. Coll. Surgeons; Hon. Member: Neonatal Soc.; BPA; Peruvian Socs Pediatrics and Pædiatric Surgery; Hellenic Surgical Soc.; Assoc. of Surgeons of India; Corresp. Member: Scandinavian Pediatric Surgical Assoc.; Sicilian Calabrian Soc. of Pædiatric Surgery. *Publications:* Body Fluids in Surgery, 1955, 4th edn 1973 (Japanese edn, 1978); Recent Advances in Pædiatric Surgery, 1963, 3rd edn 1974 (Spanish edn, 1977); (jtly) Research in Burns, 1966; Parenteral Feeding, 1972; (ed jtly) Metabolism and the Response to Injury, 1976; Early Nutrition and Later Development, 1976; (jtly) Placental Transport, 1978; Inflammatory Bowel Disease, 1980; Investigation of Brain Function, 1981; Immunology of Breast Feeding, 1981; chapters, articles and reviews in various books, and surgical and other jls. *Recreations:* fishing, gardening, cooking, eating. *Address:* Auchenbrae, Rockcliffe, Dalbeattie, Kirkcudbrightshire DG5 4QF. *Club:* New (Edinburgh). *Died 18 Aug. 1995.*

WILKINSON, Rev. Canon Raymond Stewart; Rector of Solihull, 1971–87; Chaplain to the Queen, 1982–89; Hon. Canon of Birmingham, since 1976; *b* 5 June 1919; *s* of Sidney Ewart and Florence Miriam Wilkinson; *m* 1945, Dorothy Elinor Church; four *s. Educ:* Luton Grammar Sch.; King's Coll., London (AKC); Bishop's Coll., Cheshunt. Curate of Croxley Green, 1943–45; Vicar: St Oswald's, Croxley Green, 1945–50; Abbot's Langley, 1950–61; Rector of Woodchurch, 1961–71; Proctor in Convocation and Mem., Church Assembly, 1964–71. Member, various educnl governing bodies. *Publications:* To the More Edifying, 1952; The Church and Parish of Abbot's Langley, 1955; My Confirmation Search Book, 1962, 10th edn 1982; An Adult Confirmation Candidate's Handbook, 1964, 6th edn 1984; Gospel Sermons for Alternative Service Book, 1983; Learning about Vestments and Altar Serving, 1984; A Pocket Guide for Servers, 1985; The Essence of Anglicanism, 1986. *Recreations:* producing, acting in and conducting Gilbert and Sullivan operas; church architecture, organising youth holidays. *Address:* 42 Coten End, Warwick, CV34 4NP. *T:* Warwick

(01926) 493510. *Clubs:* Commonwealth Trust, Royal Society of Arts. *Died 30 Oct. 1995.*

WILLAN, Prof. Thomas Stuart, MA, BLitt, DPhil; FBA 1991; Professor of Economic History, University of Manchester, 1961–73, then Emeritus; *b* 3 Jan. 1910; 3rd *s* of Matthew Willan and Jane (*née* Stuart); unmarried. *Educ:* Queen Elizabeth's Sch., Kirkby Lonsdale; The Queen's Coll., Oxford. Asst Lecturer, School of Economics and Commerce, Dundee, 1934–35; University of Manchester: Asst Lecturer in History, 1935–45; Lecturer in History, 1945–47; Senior Lecturer in History, 1947–49; Reader in History, 1949–61. *Publications:* River Navigation in England, 1600–1750, 1936; The English Coasting Trade, 1600–1750, 1938; (ed with E. W. Crossley) Three Seventeenth-century Yorkshire Surveys, 1941; The Navigation of the Great Ouse between St Ives and Bedford in the Seventeenth Century, 1946; The Navigation of the River Weaver in the Eighteenth Century, 1951; The Muscovy Merchants of 1555, 1953; The Early History of the Russia Company, 1553–1603, 1956; Studies in Elizabethan Foreign Trade, 1959; (ed) A Tudor Book of Rates, 1962; The Early History of the Don Navigation, 1965; An Eighteenth-Century Shopkeeper, Abraham Dent of Kirkby Stephen, 1970; The Inland Trade, 1976; Elizabethan Manchester, 1980; articles in English Historical Review, Economic History Review, etc. *Address:* 3 Raynham Avenue, Didsbury, Manchester M20 6BW. *T:* 061–445 4771. *Club:* Penn.

Died 4 June 1994.

WILLETT, Archibald Anthony; Investment Chairman, Cable & Wireless Pension Funds, 1984–92; *b* 27 Jan. 1924; *s* of Reginald Beckett Willett and Mabel Alice (*née* Plaister); *m* 1948, Doris Marjorie Peat; one *d* (one *s* decd). *Educ:* Oswestry High Sch.; Southall Grammar School. Lloyds Bank Ltd, 1940; Great Western Railway Co., 1941–42 and 1947–48; RAF (Signals Branch), 1942–47; Cable & Wireless Ltd, 1948–77: Dir, 1967–77; Dep. Man. Dir, 1971–72; Man. Dir, 1973–77. Bursar and Fellow, St Antony's Coll., Oxford, 1977–84, Fellow Emeritus 1984. MA Oxon 1977; FCIS 1963. *Address:* St Antony's College, Oxford OX2 6JF. *Clubs:* Royal Automobile; Exiles' (Twickenham). *Died 4 Oct. 1992.*

WILLETT, Prof. Frederick John, AO 1984; DSC 1944; consultant in education administration; *b* 26 Feb. 1922; *s* of E. Willett; *m* 1949, Jane Cunningham Westwater; one *s* two *d. Educ:* Fitzwilliam House, Cambridge. MA (Cambridge), MBA (Melb.). Observer, Fleet Air Arm, Atlantic, Mediterranean, Indian and Pacific theatres, 1939–46; served with British Naval Liaison Mission, Washington, 1942–43. Asst Director of Research in Industrial Management, Univ. of Cambridge, 1957–62; Sidney Myer Prof. of Commerce and Business Administration, 1962–72, then Emeritus, and Pro Vice-Chancellor, 1966–72, University of Melbourne; Vice-Chancellor, Griffith Univ., Qld, 1972–84; Academic Dir, Graduate Sch., Bangkok Univ., 1986–89. Mem., Aust.-China Council, 1979–82; Chm., Indonesian Social Sciences Project, 1983–86. Hon. LLD Melbourne, 1973; Hon. DEcon Qld, 1983; DUniv Griffith, 1983. *Publications:* many articles and papers. *Address:* 2 Yallaroo Drive, Blackmans Bay, Tas 7052, Australia. *Club:* Tasmanian (Hobart). *Died 3 Sept. 1993.*

WILLETTS, Bernard Frederick, PhD; CEng, FIMechE; CIMgt; Deputy Chairman and Managing Director, International Development Corporation Ltd, since 1988; Non-Executive Director, Trinity International Holdings, 1976–91; *b* 24 March 1927; *s* of James Frederick Willetts and Effie Hurst; *m* 1952, Norah Elizabeth Law; two *s. Educ:* Birmingham Central Grammar Sch.; Birmingham Univ. (BSc); Durham Univ. (MSc, PhD). Section Leader, Vickers-Armstrong (Engineers) Ltd, 1954–58; Massey-

Ferguson (UK) Ltd: Chief Engineer, 1959; Director, Engineering, 1962; Director, Manufacturing, 1965; Dep. Managing Director, 1967; Plessey Co. Ltd: Group Managing Director, Telecommunications, 1968; Main Board Director, 1969; Dep. Chief Exec., 1975–78; Vickers Ltd: Asst Managing Director, 1978; Man. Dir, 1980–81; Dep. Chief Exec., Dubai Aluminium Co. Ltd, 1981–88. Vice-Pres., Instn of Production Engineers, 1979–82. *Recreations:* gardening, golf, stamp collecting. *Address:* Suna Court, Pearson Road, Sonning-on-Thames, Berkshire. *T:* Reading (0734) 695050. *Clubs:* Lansdowne; Parkstone Yacht. *Died 22 June 1993.*

WILLIAMS, Prof. Alan Frederick, PhD; FRS 1990; Director, Medical Research Council Cellular Immunology Unit, since 1977; Professor of Immunology, and Fellow of Brasenose College, University of Oxford, since 1990; *b* 25 May 1945; *s* of late Walter Alan and of Mary Elizabeth Williams; *m* 1967, Rosalind Margaret Wright; one *s* one *d. Educ:* Box Hill High Sch., Melbourne; Melbourne Univ. (BAgrSc); Adelaide Univ. (PhD Biochem). Departmental Demonstrator, Biochemistry Dept, Oxford Univ., 1970–72; Jun. Research Fellow, Linacre Coll., Oxford, 1970–72; Staff Member, MRC Immunochemistry Unit, Oxford, 1972–77. Mem., Eur. Molecular Biology Orgn, 1984–. Hon. Member: Amer. Assoc. of Immunologists, 1989; Scandinavian Soc. of Immunology, 1990. *Publications:* contribs to biochemistry and immunology scientific jls. *Recreations:* gardening, modern art. *Address:* Sir William Dunn School of Pathology, University of Oxford, Oxford OX1 3RE. *T:* Oxford (0865) 275595. *Died 9 April 1992.*

WILLIAMS, Arthur Vivian, CBE 1969; General Manager and Solicitor, Peterlee (New Town) Development Corporation, 1948–74, and of Aycliffe (New Town) Development Corporation, 1954–74; *b* 2 Jan. 1909; *s* of N. T. and Gwendolen Williams; *m* 1937, Charlotte Moyra (*d* 1985), *d* of Dr E. H. M. Milligan; three *s* one *d. Educ:* William Hulme's Grammar Sch., Manchester; Jesus Coll., Oxford. MA (Oxon). Admitted as Solicitor, 1936; Dep. Town Clerk of Finchley, 1938–41; Town Clerk of Bilston, 1941–46; Town Clerk and Clerk of the Peace, Dudley, 1946–48. *Address:* 7 Majestic Court, Spring Grove, Harrogate HG1 2HT. *T:* Harrogate (0423) 568451. *Died 15 Nov. 1993.*

WILLIAMS, Basil Hugh G.; *see* Garnons Williams.

WILLIAMS, Campbell Sherston; *see* Smith, C. S.

WILLIAMS, Dr Cicely Delphine, CMG 1968; retired (except on demand); *b* 2 Dec. 1893; *d* of James Rowland Williams (Dir of Educn, Jamaica), Kew Park, Jamaica, and Margaret E. C. Williams (*née* Farewell). *Educ:* Bath High Sch. for Girls; Somerville Coll., Oxford (Hon. Fellow, 1979); King's Coll. Hosp. DM, FRCP, DTM&H. Colonial Med. Service: appts, 1929–48; WHO Advr in Maternal and Child Health, 1948–51; research on vomiting sickness, 1951–53; Sen. Lectr in Nutrition, London, 1953–55; consulting visits to various countries, 1955–59; Visiting Professor: of Maternal and Child Health, Amer. Univ. of Beirut, 1959–64; Tulane Sch. of Public Health, New Orleans, 1971 (Emer. Prof. of Maternal and Child Health, Nursing and Nutrition, 1974). Advr in Trng Progrs, Family Planning Assoc., 1964–67. Lectures: Milroy, RCP, 1958; Blackfan, Harvard Med. Sch., 1973; Balgopal Oration, Paediatric Soc., Katmandu, Nepal, 1981; Speaker, Pakistan Paediatric Assoc., 1982. Hon. FRSM 1976; Hon. Fellow: King's Coll. Hosp. Medical Sch, 1978; Green Coll., Oxford, 1985. Hon. DSc: Univ. of WI; Univ. of Maryland; Univ. of Tulane; Smith Coll., Northampton, Mass. James Spence Meml Medal, British Paed. Assoc., 1965; Goldberger Award in Clin. Nutrition, Amer. Med. Assoc., 1967; (jt) Dawson-Williams Award in Paediatrics,

BMA, 1973; Galen Medal, Worshipful Soc. of Apothecaries, London, 1984. Order of Merit, Jamaica, 1975. *Publications:* (with D. B. Jelliffe) Mother and Child Health: delivering the services, 1972; chapters in: Diseases of Children in the Tropics, 1954; Sick Children, 1956; The Matrix of Medicine, 1958; contrib. to: The Lancet, Archives of Diseases in Childhood (which reissued, 1982, as 'perhaps the most important ever published in the Archives', her paper A Nutritional Disease of Childhood, 1933), Tropical Pediatrics, etc. *Recreations:* people, solitude. *Address:* Highfield, The Common, Marlborough, Wilts SN8 1DL. *T:* Marlborough (0672) 52671. *Club:* Commonwealth Trust. *Died 13 July 1992.*

WILLIAMS, Cyril Robert, CBE 1945; *b* 11 May 1895; *s* of Rev. F. J. Williams, MA; *m* 1928, Ethel Winifred Wise (*d* 1989); two *d. Educ:* Wellington College, Berks; New College, Oxford. Dist Loco. Supt, Khartoum, Sudan Rlys, 1923; Asst Mech. Engineer (Outdoor), 1924; Loco. Running Supt, 1927; Works Manager, 1932; Asst Chief Mech. Engineer, 1936; Deputy General Manager, 1939; General Manager, 1941. JP Somerset, 1947–69. *Recreation:* philately. *Address:* Ballacree, Somerton, Somerset TA11 6RW. *T:* Somerton (0458) 72408. *Died 23 Dec. 1991.*

WILLIAMS, Rear-Adm. David Apthorp, CB 1965; DSC 1942; *b* 27 Jan. 1911; *s* of Thomas Pettit Williams and Vera Frederica Dudley Williams (*née* Apthorp); *m* 1951, Susan Eastlake (*d* 1987), 3rd *d* of late Dr W. H. Lamplough and *widow* of Surg. Comdr H. de B. Kempthorne, RN; one *s*, two step *d. Educ:* Cheltenham College; Royal Naval Engineering College, Keyham. Joined RN, 1929; served War, Engineer Officer, HMS Hasty, 1939–42 (DSC, despatches four times): 2nd Destroyer Flotilla, Med. Fleet, S Atlantic Stn, Home Fleet, E Med. Fleet; Sen. Engineer, HMS Implacable, 1942–45: Home Fleet, and 1st Aircraft Carrier Sqdn, British Pacific Fleet; Comdr (E) 1945; Capt. 1955; Rear-Adm. 1963; Dir Gen. Aircraft, Admiralty, 1962–64; Dir Gen., Aircraft (Naval), Ministry of Defence, 1964–65; retired list, 1965. CEng, MIMechE. *Recreations:* various. *Address:* 3 Ellachie Gardens, Alverstoke, Hants PO12 2DS. *T:* Gosport (01705) 583375. *Club:* Army and Navy. *Died 20 March 1995.*

WILLIAMS, David Barry, TD 1964; QC 1975; **His Honour Judge Williams;** a Circuit Judge, since 1979; Deputy Senior Judge (non-resident), 1983–95, Acting Senior Judge, since 1995, Sovereign Base Areas, Cyprus; *b* 20 Feb. 1931; *s* of Dr W. B. Williams and Mrs G. Williams, Garndiffaith, Mon; *m* 1961, Angela Joy Davies; three *s* one *d. Educ:* Cardiff High Sch. for Boys; Wellington Sch., Somerset; Exeter Coll., Oxford (MA). Served with South Wales Borderers, 1949–51, 2nd Bn Monmouthshire Regt (TA), 1951–67, retired (Major). Called to Bar, Gray's Inn, 1955; Wales and Chester Circuit, 1957. A Recorder of the Crown Court, 1972–79; Asst Comr, Local Govt Boundary Commn for Wales, 1976–79; Comr for trial of Local Govt election petitions, 1978–79; Liaison Judge for W Glamorgan, 1983–87; Designated Resident Judge, Swansea Crown Court, 1984–93. A Pres., Mental Health Review Tribunals, 1983–; Mem., Parole Bd for England and Wales, 1988–91. Chm., Legal Affairs Cttee, Welsh Centre for Internat. Affairs, 1980–89; Mem., Court and Council, Univ. of Wales Coll. of Cardiff, 1889– (Mem., Court, University Coll., Cardiff, 1980–89); Vice-Pres., UWIST, 1985–89 (Mem. Court and Council, 1981–89; Vice-Chm. Council, 1983–89). *Recreations:* mountain walking, Rugby football. *Address:* 52 Cyncoed Road, Cardiff CF2 6BH. *Clubs:* Army and Navy; Cardiff and County (Cardiff). *Died 15 July 1995.*

WILLIAMS, David Carlton, PhD; retired; President and Vice-Chancellor, University of Western Ontario, 1967–77; *b* 7 July 1912; *s* of John Andrew Williams and Anna (*née*

Carlton); *m* 1943, Margaret Ashwell Carson; one *s* one *d. Educ:* Gordon Bell and Kelvin High Schs; Univ. of Manitoba, Winnipeg (BA); Univ. of Toronto (MA, PhD, Psych.). Special Lectr in Psychology, Univ. of Toronto, 1946; Associate Prof. of Psychology, Univ. of Manitoba, 1947; Prof. and Head, Dept of Psychology, Univ. of Manitoba, 1948; Prof. of Psychology, Univ. of Toronto, 1949–58 (Cons. to Toronto Juvenile Ct Clinic, 1951–58); Dir of Univ. Extension, Univ. of Toronto, 1958; Vice-Pres., Univ. of Toronto, for Scarborough and Erindale Colls, 1963–67; Principal of Scarborough Coll., Univ. of Toronto, 1963; Principal of Erindale Coll., Univ. of Toronto, 1965. A Dir, John Howard Soc., Toronto, 1956–67; Mem., Royal Commn on Govt Organization, 1961; Chm., Ontario Commn on Freedom of Information and Individual Privacy, 1977. Dir, Assoc. of Univs and Colls of Canada, 1970–; Chairman: Council of Ontario Univs, 1970–73; Bd, University Hosp., London, Ont, 1984–86; London Teaching Hosps Council, 1990–. Mem., Ontario Press Council, 1990–. Hon. LLD: Univ. of Manitoba, 1969; Univ. Windsor, 1977; Univ. of Western Ontario, 1977; Toronto Univ., 1977. *Publications:* The Arts as Communication, 1963; University Television, 1965. *Recreations:* photography, music, swimming, fishing. *Address:* Apt 407, 1201 Richmond Street, London, Ontario N6A 3L6, Canada. *T:* (519) 4331436. *Clubs:* University, London Hunt and Country (London, Ont); York (Toronto). *Died 6 April 1994.*

WILLIAMS, Dr David Iorwerth, FRCP, FKC; Dean, King's College Hospital Medical School, 1966–77, then Dean Emeritus and Fellow; formerly: Consultant in Dermatology, King's College Hospital; Consultant to Kuwait Health Office, London; *b* 7 May 1913; *s* of William Tom Williams and Mabel Williams (*née* Edwards); *m* 1939, Ethel Margaret Wiseman; one *s* (one *d* decd). *Educ:* Dulwich Coll. (Jun. and Sen. Scholar); King's College Hosp. Med. Sch. Warneford and Raymond Gooch Scholar; MB, BS 1938; FRCP 1953; AKC 1934; FKC 1977. RAMC, 1940–46, Lt-Col. Member: BMA; Brit. Assoc. of Dermatology (Past Pres. and Past Sec., Hon. Mem. 1979); Royal Soc. of Med. (Past Pres. Dermatology Section); West Kent Medico-Chirurgical Soc. (Past Pres.); Hon. (or Foreign) Member: American, Austrian, Danish, French and S African Dermatological Socs. Gold Medal of Brit. Assoc. of Dermatology, 1965. *Publications:* articles in various med. jls over 40 yrs. *Recreations:* my stroke, music. *Address:* 28 South Row, SE3 0RY. *T:* 0181–852 7060. *Died 6 Nov. 1994.*

WILLIAMS, Sir Edgar (Trevor), Kt 1973; CB 1946; CBE 1944; DSO 1943; DL; Emeritus Fellow, Balliol College, Oxford, since 1980; a Radcliffe Trustee, since 1960; a Freeman of Chester; *b* 20 Nov. 1912; *e s* of late Rev. J. E. Williams; *m* 1938, Monica (marr. diss. 1945), *d* of late Prof. P. W. Robertson; one *d*; *m* 1946, Gillian, *yr d* of late Major-General M. D. Gambier-Parry, MC; one *s* one *d. Educ:* Tettenhall College; King Edward VII Sch., Sheffield; Merton College, Oxford (Chambers Postmaster, 1931–34; First Class, Modern History, 1934; Harmsworth Senior Scholar, 1934–35; Junior Research Fellow, 1937–39; MA 1938; Hon. Fellow, 1964). FRHistS 1947. Asst Lectr, Univ. of Liverpool, 1936. Served War of 1939–45 (despatches thrice); 2nd Lieut (SRO), 1st King's Dragoon Guards, 1939; Western Desert, 1941; GHQ MEF, 1941–42; GSO1, Eighth Army, North Africa, 1942–43; Sicily and Italy, 1943; Brig., Gen. Staff I, 21st Army Gp, 1944–45; Rhine Army, 1945–46; UN Security Council Secretariat, 1946–47. Fellow, Balliol Coll., Oxford, 1945–80; Warden, Rhodes House, Univ. of Oxford, 1952–80, Sec., Rhodes Trust, 1959–80; a Pro-Vice-Chancellor, Oxford Univ., 1968–80. Editor, DNB, 1949–80. Mem., Devlin Nyasaland Commn, 1959; UK Observer, Rhodesian elections, 1980. Mem., DSAC,

1966–78. Trustee, Nuffield Provincial Hosps Trust, 1963–91 (Chm., 1966–88); Gov., St Edward's Sch., Oxford, 1960–95. DL Oxfordshire, 1964. President, OUCC, 1966–68 (Sen. Treasurer, 1949–61). Hon. Fellow: Queen Elizabeth House, Oxford, 1975; Wolfson Coll., Oxford, 1981. Hon. LLD: Waynesburg Coll., Pa, 1947; Univ. of Windsor, Ontario, 1969; Hon. LHD, Williams Coll., Mass, 1965; Hon. PdD, Franklin and Marshall Coll., Pa, 1966; Hon. DLitt: Warwick, 1967; Hull, 1970; Mt Allison, NB, 1980; Liverpool, 1982; Hon. LittD: Swarthmore Coll., Pa, 1969; Sheffield, 1981. Officer, US Legion of Merit, 1945. *Festschrift:* Oxford and the Idea of Commonwealth (ed A. F. Madden and D. K. Fieldhouse), 1982. *Address:* 94 Lonsdale Road, Oxford OX2 7ER. *T:* Oxford (01865) 515199. *Clubs:* Athenæum, Savile, MCC, I Zingari, Free Foresters; Vincent's (Oxford).
Died 26 June 1995.

WILLIAMS, Maj.-Gen. Edward Alexander Wilmot, CB 1962; CBE 1958; MC 1940; DL; *b* 8 June 1910; *s* of late Captain B. C. W. Williams, JP, DL, Herringston, Dorchester and Hon. Mrs Winifred Mary Williams (MBE 1920), *er d* of 2nd Baron Addington; *m* 1943, Sybilla Margaret, *er d* of late Colonel O. A. Archdale, MBE, late The Rifle Brigade, West Knighton House, Dorchester; one *s* three *d. Educ:* Eton; Royal Military College. 2nd Lieut 60th Rifles, 1930; Adjutant, 2nd Battalion (Calais), 1938–39; served War of 1939–45; commanded 1st Bn 60th Rifles, 1944; mentioned in despatches, 1945; US Armed Forces Staff Coll. (course 1), 1947; Bt Lieut-Col, 1950; Directing Staff, Joint Services Staff College, 1950–52; commanded 2nd Bn 60th Rifles, 1954–55; Comdr 2nd Infantry Brigade, 1956–57; Imperial Defence College, 1958; Brigadier Author, War Office, 1959; GOC 2nd Div. BAOR, 1960–62: Chief of Staff, GHQ Far East Land Forces, May-Nov. 1962; General Officer Commanding Singapore Base District, 1962–63; Chairman, Vehicle Cttee, Min. of Defence, 1964; retired 1965. Colonel Commandant, 2nd Bn The Royal Green Jackets (The King's Royal Rifle Corps), 1965–70. DL Dorset, 1965; High Sheriff of Dorset, 1970–71. *Recreations:* fishing, shooting. *Address:* Herringston, Dorchester, Dorset DT2 9PU. *T:* Dorchester (01305) 264122. *Clubs:* Army and Navy, Pratt's, Lansdowne; Royal Dorset Yacht. *Died 9 Nov. 1994.*

WILLIAMS, Sir Francis (John Watkin), 8th Bt *cr* 1798, of Bodelwyddan, Flintshire; QC 1952; *b* Anglesey, 24 Jan. 1905; *s* of Col Lawrence Williams, OBE, JP, DL (*d* 1958) (*gs* of 1st Bt), and 1st wife, Catherine Elizabeth Anne (*d* 1905), *d* of 2nd Baron Addington; *S* brother, 1971; *m* 1932, Brenda, *d* of Sir John Jarvis, 1st Bt; four *d. Educ:* Malvern College; Trinity Hall, Cambridge. Barrister of Middle Temple, 1928. Served War of 1939–45; Wing Comdr, RAFVR. Recorder of Birkenhead, 1950–58; Recorder of Chester, 1958–71; Chm., Anglesey QS, 1960–71 (Dep. Chm., 1949–60); Chm., Flint QS, 1961–71 (Dep Chm., 1953–61); Dep. Chm., Cheshire QS, 1952–71; a Recorder of the Crown Court, 1972–74. Hon. Mem., Wales and Chester Circuit, 1986. Chm. Medical Appeal Tribunal for N Wales Areas, 1954–57; Chancellor, Diocese of St Asaph, 1966–83. JP Denbighshire, 1951–74; High Sheriff: of Denbighshire, 1957, of Anglesey, 1963. Freeman of City of Chester, 1960. *Heir: half-b* Lawrence Hugh Williams [*b* 25 Aug. 1929; *m* 1952, Sara Margaret Helen, 3rd *d* of Sir Harry Platt, 1st Bt; two *d*]. *Address:* Llys, Middle Lane, Denbigh, Clwyd LL16 3UW. *T:* Denbigh (0174581) 2984. *Club:* United Oxford & Cambridge University. *Died 3 Jan. 1995.*

WILLIAMS, George W.; *see* Wynn-Williams.

WILLIAMS, Rev. Dr Glen Garfield; General Secretary, Conference of European Churches, 1968–87, retired 1988; *b* 14 Sept. 1923; *s* of John Archibald Douglas Williams

and Violet May (*née* Tucker); *m* 1945, Velia Cristina (*née* Baglio). *Educ:* Newport High Sch.; Universities of Wales (Cardiff), London, Tübingen. Military Service, 1943–47. Univ. studies, 1947–55. Minister, Dagnall Street Baptist Church, St Albans, 1955–59; European Area Secretary, World Council of Churches, Geneva, 1959–68. Vis. Prof. of Church History, Presbyterian Theological Seminary, Austin, Texas, 1987. Hon. DTh Budapest, 1975; Hon. DD Bucharest, 1981. Order of St Vladimir, 1976, and St Sergius, 1979, Russian Orthodox Church; Order of St Mary Magdalene, Polish Orthodox Church, 1980; Order of St Augustine, C of E, 1986; Order of SS Cyril and Methodius, Bulgarian Orthodox Church, 1987. *Publications:* contrib. to Handbook on Western Europe, 1967, etc; numerous articles, mainly in Continental journals. *Recreations:* travel, reading, archæology. *Address:* 139 Rue de Lausanne, 1202 Geneva, Switzerland. *T:* (22) 7313016. *Club:* Athenæum.
Died 28 March 1994.

WILLIAMS, Air Vice-Marshal Harold Guy L.; *see* Leonard-Williams.

WILLIAMS, Rev. Dr (Henry) Howard; Minister, Bloomsbury Central Baptist Church, 1958–86, then Minister Emeritus; Moderator, Free Church Federal Council, 1984–85; *b* 30 April 1918; *s* of Rev. Henry James Williams and Edith Gwenllian Williams; *m* 1950, Athena Mary (*née* Maurice); three *s* one *d*. *Educ:* Mountain Ash Grammar Sch.; Rawdon Coll.; Leeds Univ. BA, BD, PhD. Minister: Blenheim Baptist Church, Leeds, 1943–53; Beechen Grove, Watford, 1953–58. Member: Baptist Union Council, 1954–91; Central Religious Advisory Council, BBC, 1962–65; Religious Advisory Panel, ITA, 1965–70. Pres., Baptist Union of Great Britain and Ireland, 1965; Dir, Baptist Times Ltd. Hon. Life Mem., Central YMCA, London (former Dir). Mem. Editorial Bd, New Christian, 1965–70. *Publications:* Down to Earth, 1964; Noughts and Crosses, 1965; Old Memories and New Ways, 1965; The Song of the Devil, 1972; My Word, 1973; contributor to Expository Times. *Recreations:* latterly reduced to viewing the activity of others. *Address:* 12 Radyr Court Rise, Llandaff, Cardiff CF5 2QH. *T:* Cardiff (0222) 553128.   *Died 27 Feb. 1991.*

WILLIAMS, (James) Vaughan, DSO 1942; OBE 1959; TD 1947; JP; Lord-Lieutenant for the County of West Glamorgan, 1985–88; *b* 25 Oct. 1912; *s* of James Vaughan Williams, Merthyr Tydfil; *m* 1938, Mary Edith Jones (*d* 1972), *d* of G. Bryn Jones, OBE, JP, Merthyr Tydfil; two *d*. Local Govt Service, 1930–39. Commnd RE (TA), 1934; served War of 1939–45, BEF, France, Egypt, Italy, Berlin (despatches 1942 and 1943); psc 1946; Lt-Col TA, 1947–59; Hon. Col 53rd (W) Div. RE, 1959–67; Mem. Wales TA&VRA, 1968; Vice-Chm. Glam TA&VRA Cttee, 1968. Pres., Dunkirk Veteran Assoc.; Past President, Swansea Branch, Royal British Legion; Scout Council West Glamorgan; West Glam Council St John of Jerusalem; West Glam SSAFA; Royal Engrs Assoc. Past Chm., S Wales Assoc. ICE. DL Glam, 1959; HM Lieut, W Glam, 1974–85; JP Glamorgan, 1975. KStJ 1979. *Recreations:* travel, gardening. *Address:* 5 The Grove, Mumbles, Swansea, West Glamorgan SA3 4AP. *T:* Swansea (0792) 368551. *Club:* Bristol Channel Yacht.
Died 11 April 1994.

WILLIAMS, Sir (John) Leslie, Kt 1974; CBE 1970; Chairman, Civil Service Appeal Board, 1977–78 (Deputy Chairman, 1973–77); Secretary General, Civil Service National Whitley Council (Staff Side), 1966–73; *b* 1 Aug. 1913; *s* of Thomas Oliver Williams and Mary Ellen Williams; *m* 1937, Florrie Read Jones (*d* 1992); one *s*. *Educ:* Grove Park Grammar Sch., Wrexham, N Wales. Civil Servant, 1931–46. Society of Civil Servants: Asst Secretary, 1947–49; Dep. General Secretary, 1949–56;

General Secretary, 1956–66. Royal Institute of Public Administration: Executive Council Member, 1955–74; Chairman, 1968; Vice-Pres., 1974–84. Member Board of Governors: Nat. Hospitals for Nervous Diseases, 1962–82 (Chm., 1974–82); Hospital for Sick Children, 1976–81; Member: NW Metropolitan Regional Hospital Board, 1963–65; (part-time) UKAEA, 1970–80; Adv. Council, Civil Service Coll., 1970–76; (part-time) Pay Bd, 1974; Royal Commn on Standards of Conduct in Public Life, 1974–76; Armed Forces Pay Review Body, 1975–80; (part-time) Independent Chm., Conciliation Cttees, Nat. Jt Council for Civil Air Transport, 1974–77; Standing Commn on Pay Comparability, 1979–80; London Adv. Gp on NHS, 1980–81. *Recreations:* cricket, gardening, music. *Address:* 73 Millside, Stalham, Norwich NR12 9PB. *T:* Stalham (0692) 582557.
Died 18 Oct. 1993.

WILLIAMS, Leslie Henry; Deputy Chairman, Imperial Chemical Industries Ltd, 1960–67; Chairman, ICI Fibres Ltd, 1965–67; *b* 26 Jan. 1903; *s* of late Edward Henry Williams; *m* 1930, Alice (*d* 1986), *d* of late Henry Oliver Harrison; one *s*. *Educ:* Highbury County Sch.; London Univ. (BSc). Joined ICI Ltd, Paints Division, 1929; appointed Director, 1943; Managing Director, 1946; Chairman, 1949; Director of ICI Main Board, 1957, Dep. Chm., 1960; Director, British Nylon Spinners Ltd, 1957–64; Director Ilford Ltd, 1958–67. FRIC 1945; President, Royal Institute of Chemistry, 1967–70. Member, Monopolies Commission, 1967–73. Hon. FRSC 1978. Hon. DSc Salford, 1972. *Recreations:* gardening, music. *Address:* Apartment 18, Albury Park, Albury, Guildford, Surrey GU5 9BB. *T:* Shere (048641) 3373. *Club:* Royal Automobile.   *Died 1 May 1991.*

WILLIAMS, Peter H.; *see* Havard-Williams.

WILLIAMS, Peter Lancelot, OBE 1971; editor, writer on dance, designer; chairman of committees on dance; *b* 12 June 1914; *s* of Col G. T. Williams and Awdrie Elkington. *Educ:* Harrow Sch.; Central Sch. of Art and Design, London. Dress designer with own business, 1934–39; Transport Officer, Civil Defence (Falmouth Div.), 1939–45; Head Designer, Jantzen Ltd, 1945–47; stage designer, 1947–. Arts Council of Great Britain, 1965–80: served on most panels with connections with ballet and music; resp. for ballet sect. on Opera and Ballet Enquiry, 1966–69 (led to devolt of dance theatre throughout GB); Chm., Dance Advisory Cttee (formerly Dance Theatre Cttee), 1973–80. Chairman: Brit. Council's Drama Adv. Cttee, 1976–81; (also Founder), Dancers Pensions and Resettlement Fund, 1975–92; Creative Dance Artists Ltd, 1979–; Royal Ballet Benevolent Fund 1984–; Gov., Royal Ballet, 1986–; Mem., most cttees concerned with dance: Royal Acad. of Dancing; Cecchetti Soc. Asst Editor, Ballet, 1949–50; Founder Editor/Art Dir, Dance and Dancers, 1950–80; Ballet Critic, Daily Mail, 1950–53; Dance Critic, The Observer, 1982–83 (Deputy, 1970). *Publications:* Masterpieces of Ballet Design, 1981; contrib. articles, mainly on dance and theatre, to newspapers and magazines in GB and internationally. *Address:* Tredrea, Perranarworthal, Truro, Cornwall TR3 7QG; 47A Limerston Street, SW10 0BL.
Died 10 Aug. 1995.

WILLIAMS, Vaughan; *see* Williams, J. V.

WILLIAMS, William Thomas, OBE 1980; ARCS; PhD, DSc (London); DIC; FIBiol; FLS; FAA 1978; with Australian Institute of Marine Science, Cape Ferguson, Townsville, 1980–85; pianoforte teacher (LMus Australia), since 1973; *b* 18 April 1913; *o s* of William Thomas and Clara Williams. *Educ:* Stationers' Company's School, London; Imperial College of Science and Technology. Demonstrator in Botany, Imperial College,

1933–36; Lecturer in Biology, Sir John Cass' College, 1936–40. Served War, 1940–46; RA (Sjt), RAOC (2/Lt), REME (T/Major). Lecturer in Botany, Bedford College, London, 1946–51; Professor of Botany, University of Southampton, 1951–65; CSIRO Division of Computing Research, Canberra, Australia, 1966–68; Div. of Tropical Pastures, Brisbane, 1968–73; Chief Res. Scientist, CSIRO, 1970–73; with Townsville Lab., CSIRO, 1973–80. Sometime Secretary of Society for Experimental Biology, and of Sherlock Holmes Society of London. Past Editor, Journal of Experimental Botany. Hon. DSc Queensland, 1973. *Publications:* The Four Prisons of Man, 1971; (ed) Pattern Analysis in Agricultural Science, 1976; over 150 papers on plant physiology, numerical taxonomy and statistical ecology in scientific journals. *Recreations:* music, drinking beer. *Address:* 10 Surrey Street, Hyde Park, Townsville, Qld 4812, Australia. *T:* (77) 794596.
Died 15 Oct. 1995.

WILLIAMS, Yvonne Lovat; Secretary, Monopolies and Mergers Commission, 1974–79, retired; *b* 23 Feb. 1920; *d* of late Wendros Williams, CBE and Vera Lovat Williams. *Educ:* Queenswood Sch., Hatfield; Newnham Coll., Cambridge. BA History 1941, MA 1946. Temp. Civil Servant, BoT, 1941–46; Asst Principal, BoT, 1946–48, Principal 1948–56; Treasury, 1956–58; BoT, 1958–63; Asst Sec., BoT, Min. of Technol., DTI, 1963–73. *Recreations:* visiting friends, theatres and old places. *Address:* Flat 16, The Limes, 34–36 Linden Gardens, W2 4ET. *T:* 071–727 9851. *Died 29 March 1994.*

WILLIAMS-BULKELEY, Sir Richard Harry David, 13th Bt, *cr* 1661, of Penrhyn, Caernarvonshire; TD; JP; Lord Lieutenant of Gwynedd, 1974–83 (HM Lieutenant for the County of Anglesey, 1947–74); Member, Anglesey County Council, 1946–74 (Chairman, 1955–57); Mayor of Beaumaris, 1949–51; *b* 5 Oct. 1911; *s* of late Maj. R. G. W. Williams-Bulkeley, MC (*o s* of 12th Bt) and Mrs V. Williams-Bulkeley; *S* grandfather, 1942; *m* 1938, Renée Arundell, *yr d* of Sir Thomas L. H. Neave, 5th Bt; two *s. Educ:* Eton. Served with 9th and 8th Bns Royal Welch Fusiliers, 1939–44, 2nd in Command of both Battalions and with Allied Land Forces South East Asia; specially employed, 1944–Sept. 1945; Lt-Col Comdt, Anglesey and Caernarvonshire Army Cadet Force, 1946–47 (resigned on appointment as HM Lieut). CStJ. *Recreations:* shooting, golf, hunting. *Heir: s* Richard Thomas Williams-Bulkeley [*b* 25 May 1939; *m* 1964, Sarah Susan, *er d* of Rt Hon. Sir Henry Josceline Phillimore, OBE; twin *s* one *d*]. *Address:* Plâs Meigan, Beaumaris, Gwynedd. *T:* Beaumaris (0248) 810345. *Club:* Army and Navy. *Died 3 Feb. 1992.*

WILLIAMSON, David Theodore Nelson, FRS 1968; Group Director of Engineering, Rank Xerox Ltd, 1974–76; Director, Xerox Research (UK) Ltd, 1975–76; retired; *b* 15 Feb. 1923; *s* of David Williamson and Ellie (*née* Nelson); *m* 1951, Alexandra Janet Smith Neilson; two *s* two *d. Educ:* George Heriot's Sch., Edinburgh; Univ. of Edinburgh. MO Valve Co. Ltd, 1943–46; Ferranti Ltd, Edinburgh, 1946–61; pioneered numerical control of machine tools, 1951; Manager, Machine Tool Control Div., 1959–61; work on sound reproduction: Williamson amplifier, 1947, Ferranti pickup, 1949; collab. with P. J. Walker in develt of first wide-range electrostatic loud-speaker, 1951–56; Dir of Res. and Develt, Molins Ltd, 1961–74. Member: NEL Metrology and Noise Control Sub cttee, 1954–57; NEL Cttee on Automatic Design and Machine Tool Control, 1964–66; Min. of Technology Working Party on Computer-Aided Design, 1967; Penny Cttee on Computer-Aided Design, 1967–69; Steering Cttee, IAMTACT, 1967–69; SRC Mech. and Prod. Engrg Cttee, 1965–69; SRC Control Panel, 1966–69; Mech. Engrg EDC, 1968–74; SRC Engrg Bd, 1969–75; Adv.

Cttee for Mech. Engrg, 1969–71; Court, Cranfield Inst. of Technology, 1970–79; Council and Exec. Cttee, British Hydrodynamics Research Assoc., 1970–73; Design Council (formerly CoID) Engrg Design Adv. Cttee, 1971–75; Council for Scientific Policy, 1972–73; Science Mus. Adv. Cttee, 1972–79; SRC Manufrg Technology Cttee, 1972–75 (Chm.); Mech. Engrg and Machine Tool Requirements Bd, DTI subseq. DoI, 1973–76; Council, Royal Soc., 1977–78. James Clayton Lecture, IMechE, 1968. Hon. DSc: Heriot-Watt, 1971; Edinburgh, 1985. *Publications:* contrib. to: Electronic Engineers' Reference Book, 1959; Progress in Automation, 1960; Numerical Control Handbook, 1968; NEDO Discussion Paper No 1, 1971; papers and articles on engrg subjects. *Recreations:* music, photography. *Address:* Villa Belvedere, La Cima 10, Tuoro-sul-Trasimeno, 06069 Pg, Umbria, Italy. *T:* (075) 826285. *Died 10 May 1992.*

WILLIS, Baron, *cr* 1963 (Life Peer), of Chislehurst, Co. of Kent; **Edward Henry Willis,** FRTS; FRSA; playwright (as Ted Willis); Director: World Wide Pictures, since 1967; Vitalcall Ltd, since 1983; *b* London, 13 Jan. 1918; *s* of Alfred John and Maria Harriet Willis; *m* 1944, Audrey Hale; one *s* one *d. Educ:* Tottenham Central School. *Plays include:* Hot Summer Night, New, 1957 (filmed as Flame in the Streets, 1961); God Bless the Guv'nor, Unity, 1959; A Slow Roll of Drums, 1964; Queenie, 1967; Mr Polly, 1977; Doctor on the Boil, 1978; Stardust, 1983; Cat and Mouse, 1985; Old Flames, 1986; Tommy Boy, 1988; Intent to Kill, 1990; The Killing Edge, 1991; A Home for Animals, 1991; *television scripts:* Dixon of Dock Green Series, 1953–75; Sergeant Cork, 1963–67; Knock on any Door, 1964; Crime of Passion, 1970; Hunter's Walk, 1973; Black Beauty, 1979; Buckingham Palace Connection, 1981; Eine Heim für Tiere (Germany), 1984; Racecourse, 1987; *films include:* Woman in a Dressing Gown, 1958 (Berlin Award; play, 1962); Bitter Harvest, 1963; A Long Way to Shiloh, 1969; Maneater, 1979; The Iron Man, 1983; Mrs Harris MP, 1984; Mrs Harris Goes to New York, 1985; The Left-Handed Sleeper, 1986; Mrs Harris Goes to Moscow, 1986; Mrs Harris Goes to Monte Carlo, 1987; Mrs Harris Goes to Majorca, 1990. President, Writers Guild of GB, 1958–68, 1976–79, Life Pres., 1988; Mem., Sports Council, 1971–73. Awards include: Writers' Guild Zita, 1966, 1974; Internat. Writers' Guild Distinguished Writing, 1972; Variety Club of GB for Distinguished Service, 1974; Pye TV for Outstanding Service, 1983; RSA Silver Medal, 1966. *Publications:* Woman in a Dressing Gown and other TV plays, 1959; Whatever Happened to Tom Mix? (autobiog.), 1970; Evening All (autobiog.), 1991; *novels:* Death May Surprise Us, 1974; The Left-Handed Sleeper, 1975; Man-eater, 1976; The Churchill Commando, 1977; The Buckingham Palace Connection, 1978 (Current Crime Cup); The Lions of Judah, 1979; The Naked Sun, 1980; The Most Beautiful Girl in the World, 1981; Spring at the Winged Horse, 1983; A Problem for Mother Christmas (children's novel), 1986; The Green Leaves of Summer, 1987; The Bells of Autumn, 1990. *Recreations:* tennis, Association football. *Address:* 5 Shepherds Green, Chislehurst, Kent BR7 6PB. *Club:* Garrick. *Died 22 Dec. 1992.*

WILLIS, Ted; *see* Willis, Baron.

WILLOUGHBY, Maj.-Gen. Sir John (Edward Francis), KBE 1967 (CBE 1963; OBE 1953); CB 1966; *b* 18 June 1913; *s* of Major N. E. G. Willoughby, The Middlesex Regt, and Mrs B. A. M. Willoughby, Heytesbury, Wiltshire; *m* 1938, Muriel Alexandra Rosamund Scott; three *d.* Commissioned, Middlesex Regt, 1933; served War of 1939–45 with Middlesex Regt, BEF, 1940; OC 2 Middlesex Regt, 1943; GSO 1 220 Military Mission, USA, Pacific, Burma and UK, 1943–44; OC 1 Dorsets Regt, NW Europe, 1944; served with Middlesex Regt,

FARELF, Korea, 1950–51; GSO1, 3 Inf. Div., UK and MELF, 1951–53; OC 1 Middlesex Regt, British Troops Austria, UK and MELF, 1954–56; Colonel, The Middlesex Regt, 1959–65; Chief of Staff, Land Forces, Hong Kong, 1961; GOC, 48 Inf. Div. (TA) and W Midland District, 1963–65; GOC Land Forces ME Comd, Inspector-Gen. of Federal Regular Army of S Arabia and Security Comdr Aden State, 1965–67; Adviser on Defence to Fedn of Arab Emirates, 1968–71.   *Died 23 Feb. 1991.*

WILLS, Sir John Spencer, Kt 1969; FCIT; Chairman, British Electric Traction Co. Ltd, 1966–82 (Director, 1939–82, Managing Director, 1946–73, Deputy Chairman, 1951–66); Director and Chairman: National Electric Construction Co. Ltd, since 1945; Birmingham and District Investment Trust Ltd, since 1946; Electrical & Industrial Investment Co. Ltd, since 1946; *b* 10 Aug. 1904; *s* of Cedric Spencer Wills and Cécile Charlotte; *m* 1936, Elizabeth Drusilla Alice Clare Garcke; two *s*. *Educ:* Cleobury Mortimer Coll., Shropshire; Merchant Taylors' Sch., London. Asst to Secs, British Traction Co. Ltd and British Automobile Traction Ltd, 1922–23; Sec., Wrexham and Dist Transport Co. Ltd, 1924–26; Gen. Manager, E Yorks Motor Services Ltd, 1926–31, Dir and Chm., 1931–65; Chm., Birmingham & Midland Motor Omnibus Co. Ltd, 1946–68; Dir, 1947–73, Dep. Chm., 1953–71, Monotype Corp. Ltd; Man. Dir, 1947–67, Chm., 1947–78, Broadcast Relay Service Ltd, later Rediffusion Ltd; Chm., Associated-Rediffusion Ltd, later Rediffusion Television Ltd, 1954–78; Director and Chairman: E Midland Motor Services Ltd, 1931–44; Yorks Woollen Dist Transport Co. Ltd, 1931–43; Hebble Motor Services Ltd, 1932–45; Yorks Traction Co. Ltd, 1932–46; Mexborough & Swinton Traction Co. Ltd, 1933–47; Western Welsh Omnibus Co. Ltd, 1933–60; Crosville Motor Services Ltd, 1933–41; Ribble Motor Services Ltd, 1942–47; N Western Road Car Co. Ltd, 1943–45; S Wales Transport Co. Ltd, Swansea Improvements & Tramways Co. Ltd, 1943–46; Devon Gen. Omnibus and Touring Co. Ltd, 1946–47; Man. Dir, British and Foreign Aviation Ltd and Great Western and Southern Air Lines Ltd, 1938–42; Director: Olley Air Service Ltd, Channel Air Ferries Ltd, West Coast Air Services Ltd, Air Booking Co. Ltd, 1938–42; Air Commerce Ltd, 1939–42; Yorks Electric Power Co., 1942–48; Wembley Stadium Ltd, 1960–82 (Chm., 1965–82). Chm., Hull and Grimsby Sect., Incorp. Secs' Assoc., 1929–31; Member of Council: BET Fedn, 1933 (Pres., 1946–79); Public Road Transport Assoc. (formerly Public Transport Assoc.), 1943–68 (Chm., 1945–46; Hon. Mem., 1969), subseq. Confedn of British Road Passenger Transport Ltd (Hon. Mem., 1975); Chairman: Omnibus Owners' Assoc., 1943–44; Nat. Council for Omnibus Industry, 1944–45 (Mem. 1940–66); Standing Cttee, Air Transport Sect., London Chamber of Commerce, 1953–65 (Mem. 1943; Dep. Chm. 1949). FCIT (Henry Spurrier Meml Lectr, 1946, Pres., 1950–51). Governor, Royal Shakespeare Theatre, Stratford upon Avon, 1946–74; Mem. Council, Royal Opera House Soc., 1962–74; Trustee, LSO Trust, 1962–68; Vice-Patron, Theatre Royal Windsor Trust, 1965–. Member, UK Council, European Movement, 1966–. *Recreations:* complete idleness; formerly: flying, swimming, ski-ing, tennis, riding, shooting; continued occupations: forestry, farming. *Address:* Beech Farm, Battle, East Sussex. *T:* Battle (04246) 2950. *Clubs:* Naval and Military, East India, Devonshire, Sports and Public Schools.
       Died 28 Oct. 1991.

WILLSON, Douglas James, CBE 1953; TD; *b* 30 Oct. 1906; *s* of late Ernest Victor Willson and Mary Willson; *m* 1942, Morna Josephine, *d* of Stanley Hine; one *d. Educ:* Bishop's Stortford Coll., Herts. Admitted Solicitor, 1928; joined Customs and Excise, 1928; Solicitor for Bd of Customs and Excise, 1963–71. Served War, 1939–45,

Lieut-Colonel, RA. *Publications:* Titles Purchase Tax and Excise in Halsbury's Encyclopædia of Laws of England, 3rd edn; Willson & Mainprice on Value Added Tax. *Recreations:* gardening, bird watching. *Address:* Dove Cottage, West Farleigh, Kent. *T:* Maidstone (0622) 812203.   *Died 8 June 1993.*

WILMOT, Sir John Assheton E.; *see* Eardley-Wilmot.

WILSON OF RIEVAULX, Baron *cr* 1983 (Life Peer), of Kirklees in the County of West Yorkshire; **James Harold Wilson,** KG 1976; OBE 1945; PC 1947; FRS 1969; *b* 11 March 1916; *s* of late James Herbert and Ethel Wilson, Huddersfield, Yorks (formerly of Manchester); *m* 1940, (Gladys) Mary, *d* of Rev. D. Baldwin, The Manse, Duxford, Cambridge; two *s. Educ:* Milnsbridge Council Sch. and Royds Hall Sch., Huddersfield; Wirral Grammar Sch., Bebington, Cheshire; Jesus Coll., Oxford (Gladstone Memorial Prize, Webb Medley Economics Scholarship, First Class Hons Philosophy, Politics and Economics). Lecturer in Economics, New Coll., Oxford, 1937; Fellow of University Coll., 1938–45, Praelector in Economics and Domestic Bursar, 1945. Dir of Econs and Stats, Min. of Fuel and Power, 1943–44. MP (Lab) Ormskirk, 1945–50, Huyton, Lancs, 1950–83; Parly Sec. to Ministry of Works, 1945–March 1947; Sec. for Overseas Trade, March-Oct. 1947; Pres., BoT, Oct. 1947–April 1951; Chairman: Labour Party Exec. Cttee, 1961–62; Public Accounts Cttee, 1959–63; Leader, Labour Party, 1963–76; Prime Minister and First Lord of the Treasury, 1964–70, 1974–76; Leader of the Opposition, 1963–64, 1970–74. Chairman: Cttee to Review the Functioning of Financial Instns, 1976–80; British Screen Adv. Council, 1985–87. Pres., Royal Statistical Soc., 1972–73. An Elder Brother of Trinity House, 1968. Hon. Fellow, Jesus and University Colleges, Oxford, 1963. Hon. Freeman, City of London, 1975. Hon. Pres., Great Britain-USSR Assoc., 1976. Pres., Royal Shakespeare Theatre Co., 1976–85. Chancellor, Bradford Univ., 1966–85. Hon. LLD: Lancaster, 1964; Liverpool, 1965; Nottingham, 1966; Sussex, 1966; Hon. DCL, Oxford, 1965; Hon. DTech Bradford, 1966; DUniv: Essex, 1967; Open, 1974. *Publications:* New Deal for Coal, 1945; In Place of Dollars, 1952; The War on World Poverty, 1953; The Relevance of British Socialism, 1964; Purpose in Politics, 1964; The New Britain, 1964; Purpose in Power, 1966; The Labour Government 1964–70, 1971; The Governance of Britain, 1976; A Prime Minister on Prime Ministers, 1977; Final Term: the Labour Government 1974–76, 1979; The Chariot of Israel, 1981; Harold Wilson Memoirs 1916–64, 1986. *Address:* House of Lords, SW1A 0PW.   *Died 24 May 1995.*

WILSON, Sir Alan (Herries), Kt 1961; FRS 1942; Chairman, Glaxo Group Ltd, 1963–73; *b* 2 July 1906; *o s* of H. and A. Wilson; *m* 1934, Margaret Constance Monks (*d* 1961); two *s. Educ:* Wallasey Gram. Sch.; Emmanuel College, Cambridge. Smith's Prize, 1928; Adams Prize, 1931–32. Fellow of Emmanuel College, Cambridge, 1929–33; Fellow and Lecturer of Trinity College, Cambridge, 1933–45; University Lecturer in Mathematics in the University of Cambridge, 1933–45; joined Courtaulds Ltd, 1945; Man. Dir, 1954; Dep. Chm., 1957–62. Dir, Internat. Computers (Hldgs) Ltd, 1962–72. Chairman: Committee on Coal Derivatives, 1959–60; Committee on Noise, 1960–63; Nuclear Safety Adv. Committee, 1965–66; Central Adv. Water Cttee, 1969–74; Dep. Chm. and pt-time Mem., Electricity Council, 1966–76; Member: Iron and Steel Board, 1960–67; UGC, 1964–66; President: Inst. of Physics and Physical Soc., 1963–64; Nat. Society for Clean Air, 1965–66; Aslib, 1971–73. Chm. Governing Body, Nat. Inst. of Agricultural Engrg, 1971–76; Chm., Bd of Governors, Bethlem Royal and Maudsley Hosps, 1973–80. Prime Warden, Goldsmiths' Co., 1969–70. Hon. Fellow: Emmanuel

College, Cambridge; St Catherine's College, Oxford; UMIST. Hon. FIChemE; Hon. FInstP; Hon. FIMA. Hon. DSc: Oxford; Edinburgh. *Publications:* The Theory of Metals, 1936, 2nd edition 1953; Semi-conductors and Metals, 1939; Thermo-dynamics and Statistical Mechanics, 1957; many papers on atomic physics. *Address:* 65 Oakleigh Park South, Whetstone, N20 9JL. *T:* 0181–445 3030. *Club:* Athenæum.

Died 30 Sept. 1995.

WILSON, Prof. Allan Charles, FRS 1986; Professor of Biochemistry and Molecular Biology (formerly Professor of Biochemistry), University of California, Berkeley, since 1964; *b* 18 Oct. 1934; *s* of Charles and Eunice Boyce Wilson; *m* 1958, Leona Greenbaum; one *s* one *d. Educ:* King's College, NZ; Otago Univ. (BSc 1955); Washington State Univ. (MS 1957); Univ. of California (PhD 1961). Postdoctoral Fellow, Brandeis Univ., 1961–64; Asst Prof., 1964–68, Associate Prof., 1968–72, Prof., 1972–, Univ. of California. Guggenheim Fellow: Weizmann Inst. and Nairobi Univ., 1972–73; Harvard Univ., 1979–80; MacArthur Fellow, John D. and Catherine T. MacArthur Foundn, 1986–91. Mem., Amer. Acad. of Arts and Sciences, 1983. Hon. DSc Otago, 1989. Distinguished Achievement Award, Washington State Univ., 1990; 3M Life Scis Award, Fedn of Amer. Socs of Exptl Biology and Medicine, 1991. *Publications:* author and co-author of numerous papers in sci. jls. *Address:* 1004 Park Hills Road, Berkeley, Calif 94708, USA. *T:* (415) 848–1784.

Died 21 July 1991.

WILSON, Sir Angus (Frank Johnstone), Kt 1980; CBE 1968; CLit 1972; FRSL 1958; author; Professor of English Literature, University of East Anglia, 1966–78, then Emeritus; *b* 11 Aug. 1913; *s* of William Johnstone-Wilson, Dumfriesshire, and Maude (*née* Caney), Durban, Natal, South Africa. *Educ:* Westminster School (Hon. Fellow, 1991); Merton College, Oxford. Foreign Office, 1942–46. Deputy to Superintendent of Reading Room, British Museum, 1949–55. Lectr, Sch. of Eng. Studies, E Anglia Univ., 1963–66. Began to write in 1946. Lectr, Internat. Assoc. of Professors of English, Lausanne, 1959; Ewing Lectr, Los Angeles, 1960; Bergen Lectr, Yale Univ., 1960; Wm Vaughan Moody Lectr, Chicago, 1960; Northcliffe Lectrs, Lond., 1961; Leslie Stephen Lectr, Cambridge, 1962–63; Beckman Prof., Univ. of California, Berkeley, 1967; John Hinkley Vis. Prof., Johns Hopkins Univ., Baltimore, 1974; Visiting Professor: Univ. of Delaware, 1977, 1980,1983; Univ. of Iowa, 1978; Georgia State Univ., 1979; Univ. of Michigan, 1979; Univ. of Minnesota, 1980; Univ. of Missouri, 1982; Andrew Mellon Vis. Prof., Univ. of Pittsburgh, 1981; Univ. of Arizona, 1984. Mem. Cttee, Royal Literary Fund, 1966. Mem. Arts Council, 1967–69; Chm., NBL, 1971–74. President: Powys Soc., 1970–80; Dickens Fellowship, 1974–75; Kipling Soc., 1981–88; RSL, 1982–88. Foreign Hon. Mem., Amer. Acad. and Inst. of Arts and Letters, 1980. Hon. DLitt: Leicester, 1977; East Anglia, 1979; Sussex, 1981; Hon. LittD Liverpool, 1979; Hon. Dr Sorbonne, 1983. Chevalier de l'Ordre des Arts et des Lettres, 1972. TV plays: After the Show (perf. 1959); The Stranger (perf. 1960); The Invasion (perf. 1963). *Publications:* (short stories, novels, etc): The Wrong Set, 1949; Such Darling Dodos, 1950; Emile Zola, 1950; Hemlock and After (novel), 1952; For Whom The Cloche Tolls, 1953, 2nd edn, 1973; The Mulberry Bush (play), 1956 (prod Bristol, 1955, Royal Court Theatre, London, 1956); Anglo-Saxon Attitudes (novel), 1956; A Bit off the Map, 1957; The Middle Age of Mrs Eliot (novel), 1958 (James Tait Black Meml Prize; Prix du Meilleur Roman Etranger, Paris); The Old Men at the Zoo (novel), 1961; The Wild Garden, 1963; Late Call (novel), 1964 (adapted for TV, 1975); No Laughing Matter (novel), 1967; The World of Charles Dickens, 1970 (Yorkshire Post Book of the Year, 1970); (with Edwin

Smith and Olive Cook) England, 1971; As If By Magic (novel), 1973; The Naughty Nineties, 1976; The Strange Ride of Rudyard Kipling, 1977; Setting the World on Fire (novel), 1980; (with Tony Garrett) East Anglia in Verse, 1982; Diversity and Depth in Fiction, 1983; (ed) The Viking Portable Dickens, 1983; Reflections in a Writer's Eye, 1986; The Collected Stories of Angus Wilson, 1987. *Recreations:* gardening, travel. *Address:* Pinford End Nursing Home, Hawstead, Bury St Edmunds, Suffolk. *Club:* Athenæum.

Died 31 May 1991.

WILSON, Prof. Arthur James Cochran, FRS 1963; Professor of Crystallography, Department of Physics, Birmingham University, 1965–82, then Emeritus; *b* 28 Nov. 1914; *o s* of Arthur A. C. Wilson and Hildegarde Gretchen (*née* Geldert), Springhill, Nova Scotia, Canada; *m* 1946, Harriett Charlotte, BSc, PhD (*née* Friedeberg), sociologist; two *s* one *d. Educ:* King's Collegiate School, Windsor, Nova Scotia, Canada; Dalhousie University, Halifax, Canada (MSc); Massachusetts Institute of Technology (PhD); Cambridge University (PhD). 1851 Exhibition Scholar, 1937–40; Res. Asst, Cavendish Lab., Cambridge, 1940–45; Lecturer, 1945, and Senior Lecturer, 1946, in Physics, University College, Cardiff; Professor of Physics, University College, Cardiff, 1954–65. Visiting Professor: Georgia Inst. of Technology, 1965, 1968, 1971; Univ. of Tokyo, 1972. Editor of Structure Reports, 1948–59; Editor of Acta Crystallographica, 1960–77; Associate Editor, Proc. Royal Society, 1978–83; Editor of International Tables for Crystallography, 1982–. Member: Exec. Cttee, Internat. Union of Crystallography, 1954–60 and 1978–81 (Vice-Pres., 1978–81); ICSU Abstracting Bd (later Internat. Council for Scientific and Technical Information), 1971–77, 1980–86 (Vice-Pres.). Hon. LLD Dalhousie, 1991. *Publications:* X-ray Optics, 1949, 2nd edn 1962 (Russian edn1951); Mathematical Theory of X-ray Powder Diffractometry, 1963 (French edn 1964, German edn 1965); Elements of X-ray Crystallography, 1970; (with L. V. Azároff and others) X-ray Diffraction, 1974; (ed jtly) Crystallographic Statistics: Progress and Problems, 1982; (ed) Structure and Statistics in Crystallography, 1985; (ed jtly) Direct Methods, Macromolecular Methods and Crystallographic Statistics, 1987; (ed and contrib.) International Tables for Crystallography, Vol. C, 1992, repr. with corrections and additions, 1995; numerous papers in Proc. Phys. Soc., Proc. Roy. Soc., Acta Cryst., etc. *Address:* 25 Kings Road, Cambridge CB3 9DY.

Died 1 July 1995.

WILSON, Prof. Charles Henry, CBE 1981; LittD; FBA 1966; Emeritus Fellow of Jesus College, Cambridge, since 1979 (Fellow, 1938); Professor of Modern History, Cambridge University, 1965–79; *b* 16 April 1914; *s* of Joseph Edwin Wilson and Louisa Wilson; *m* 1st, 1939, Angela (marr. diss. 1972), *d* of John Marshman; one *d*; 2nd, 1972, Alena, *d* of Dr Vladimir Kouril, Ostrava, Czechoslovakia. *Educ:* De Aston Grammar Sch., Lincs; Jesus Coll., Cambridge. DLitt Cambridge, 1976. Pres., Cambridge Univ. Music Club, 1936–37. Studied in Holland and Germany, 1937–38. Served in RNVR and Admiralty, 1940–45. Univ. Lecturer in History, 1945–64, Reader in Modern Economic History, 1964–65, Cambridge Univ.; Prof. of History and Civilization, European Univ. Inst., Florence (seconded from Cambridge), 1976–79, Vis. Prof. 1980–81. Bursar of Jesus Coll., 1945–55. Ford Lecturer in English History, Oxford Univ., for 1968–69. Vis. Prof., Univ. of Tokyo, 1974. Member: Lord Chancellor's Adv. Council on Public Records, 1972–77; Adv. Council, Business History Unit (LSE), 1981. Governor, British Inst. of Florence, 1980–; British Acad. deleg. to European Science Foundn, 1980. British Govt Representative, Anglo-Netherlands Cultural Commn, 1956–72. Mem., William and Mary Tercentenary Trust, 1987– (Chm., Historical Cttee, 1987–). Corres.

Fellow: Royal Danish Acad. of Arts and Science, 1970; Royal Belgian Acad., 1973. Manager, Istituto Datini, Prato, 1971 (Mem., Cttee of Honour, 1988). Hon. Vice-Pres., RHistS, 1981. LittD (*hc*): Univ. of Groningen, 1964; Univ. of Louvain, 1977. Comdr, Order of Oranje-Nassau (Netherlands), 1974. Jt Ed., Econ. Hist. Review, 1960–67; Mem. Editorial Cttee, Jl of European Econ. Hist. (Rome), 1975–. *Publications:* Anglo-Dutch Commerce and Finance in 18th Century, 1940; Holland and Britain, 1945; History of Unilever, 1954; Profit and Power, 1957; Mercantilism, 1958, 5th edn, 1971; (with William Reader) Men and Machines, 1958; A Memoir of Sir Ellis Hunter, 1962; A Man and His Times, 1962; England's Apprenticeship 1603–1763, 1965, 2nd edn 1985; Unilever, 1945–65, 1968; The Dutch Republic and the Civilization of the Seventeenth Century, 1968; Economic History and the Historian, 1969; Queen Elizabeth and the Revolt of the Netherlands, 1970; Parliaments, Peoples and Mass Media, 1970; The Relevance of History, (Brussels) 1975; (chapter) Colonialism in Africa, Vol. 4 1975; The Transformation of Europe, 1976; (ed with N. G. Parker) The Sources of European Economic History, 1977; Il Cammino verso l'industrializzone, (Bologna) 1979; Oxford, China and Italy: writings in honour of Sir Harold Acton (ed by E. Chaney and N. Ritchie), 1984; (ed and contrib.) Geoffrey Heyworth, A Memoir, 1985; First With the News: a history of W. H. Smith 1792–1972, 1985; Australia 1788–1988: the creation of a nation, 1987; The Dutch Connection: the founding of the Fitzwilliam Museum, 1988; (contrib.) Mirror of Empire: Dutch marine art of the seventeenth century (ed by George Keyes), 1990; Cambridge Economic History of Europe: (ed jtly with Prof. E. E. Rich, and contrib.) Vol. IV 1967, Vol. V 1977; New Cambridge Modern History: (chapters on economic history) Vol. VII 1957, Vol. XI 1962; numerous articles. *Recreation:* music. *Address:* 1211 East Point Tower, Edgecliff, Sydney, NSW 2027, Australia; Jesus College, Cambridge. *Club:* University Pitt (Cambridge).
Died 1 Aug. 1991.

WILSON, Dr Douglas George, CB 1984; Chief Government Medical Officer, Queensland, 1968–84, retired 1984; Senior Lecturer in Forensic Medicine, University of Queensland, since 1968; *b* 21 Jan. 1924; *s* of William John Wilson and Mary Catherine Mitchell; *m* 1951, Heloise, *d* of J. J. McCormack; one *s*. *Educ:* St Joseph's College, Nudgee, Qld. MB BS Qld 1952; DPH Sydney 1965; Dip. Med. Jurisp., Soc. of Apothecaries of London, 1975. War service, 2nd AIF, 1942–44; RAAMC, 1953. Resident MO, Brisbane Gen. Hosp., 1952–53; private practice, Caloundra, 1954–65; Dep. MOH, NSW Dept of Public Health, 1965–67. Founder Dep. Chm., Qld Road Safety Council Res. Cttee, 1975–; Mem., Traffic Adv. Cttee, 1968–84; Dep. Chm. Med. Div. and Mem. Internat. Med. Commn, XII Commonwealth Games, Brisbane, 1982. Nat. Health and MRC Travelling Fellowship in Forensic Medicine, 1975; Fulbright Sen. Schol. in Traffic Medicine, Central Missouri State Univ., 1978. Member: British Acad. of Forensic Scis; Forensic Sci. Soc.; Internat. Assoc. for Accident and Traffic Medicine; Aust. and Pacific Area Police Med. Officers' Assoc. Foundation Chairman: Sunshine Coast Br., Arthritis Foundn of Aust., 1985; Qld Estuarine Res. Gp, 1985. Gold Medal, Internat. Assoc. for Accident and Traffic Medicine, 1985. SBStJ 1978. *Publications:* Rationale of the Determination of Blood Alcohol Concentration by Breath Analysis (Training Manual), 1968; numerous papers on alcohol, drugs and traffic safety, forensic subjects in learned jls. *Recreations:* swimming, boating, golf, tropical fruit farming. *Address:* 3 Alfred Street, Caloundra, Qld 4551, Australia. *T:* (071) 91 1610. *Clubs:* University of Queensland (Brisbane);

Caloundra Golf, Caloundra Power Boat, Caloundra Returned Services. *Died 24 Oct. 1991.*

WILSON, Gilbert; *b* 2 March 1908; *s* of J. E. Wilson and Emily Bracken (*née* Hamerton); *m* 1934, Janet Joy Turner; two *d*. *Educ:* Auckland Grammar School. Served with 2nd NZEF, Middle East, 1940–43. Joined National Bank of New Zealand, 1924; joined Reserve Bank of New Zealand, 1935; Dep. Chief Cashier, 1948–53; Chief Cashier, 1953–56; Dep. Governor, 1956–62; Governor, 1962–67; also Alternate Governor for New Zealand of International Monetary Fund, 1962–67. *Address:* 41 Mere Road, Taupo, New Zealand. *Died 29 March 1994.*

WILSON, Graeme McDonald, CMG 1975; British Civil Aviation Representative (Far East), 1964–81, retired; *b* 9 May 1919; *s* of Robert Linton McDonald Wilson and Sophie Hamilton Wilson (*née* Milner); *m* 1968, Yabu Masae; three *s*. *Educ:* Rendcomb Coll., Glos; Schloss Schule Salem, Germany; Lincoln Coll., Oxford; Gray's Inn, London. Served in Fleet Air Arm, 1939–46. Joined Home Civil Service, 1946; Private Sec. to Parly Sec., Min. of Civil Aviation, 1946–49; Planning 1, 1949–53; Dep. UK Rep. on Council of ICAO, 1953–56; Lt-Comdr (A) (O) (Ph) (q) RCNR, 1954; Internat. Relations 1, Min. of Transport and Civil Aviation, 1956–61; Asst Sec. Interdependence, Exports and Electronics, Min. of Aviation, 1961–64; seconded to Foreign Service as Counsellor and Civil Air Attaché, at twelve Far Eastern posts, 1964. Ford Foundn Fellow, Nat. Translation Center, Austin, Texas, 1968–69. UN Expert on Air Services Agreements, 1984. *Publications:* Face At The Bottom Of The World: translations of the modern Japanese poetry of Hagiwara Sakutaro, 1969; (trans., with Ito Aiko) I Am a Cat, 1971; (trans., with Atsumi Ikuko) Three Contemporary Japanese Poets, 1972; (trans., with Ito Aiko) Ten Nights of Dream, 1973; Nihon no Kindaishi to Gendaishi no Dai Yon-sho: Hagiwara Sakutaro, 1974; (trans., with Ito Aiko) I Am a Cat II, 1979; (trans., with Ito Aiko) I Am a Cat III, 1985; From the Morning of the World (trans. of selected Japanese poems from the Manyōshū of 759), 1991; articles on East Asian literature and poems (mostly Japanese, Chinese, Vietnamese and Korean trans). *Address:* 42 Cranford Avenue, Exmouth, Devon. *T:* Exmouth (0395) 264786. *Clubs:* Naval; PEN of Japan (Tokyo). *Died 2 Sept. 1992.*

WILSON, Henry Moir, CB 1969; CMG 1965; MBE 1946; PhD, BSc, FRAeS; *b* 3 Sept. 1910; 3rd *s* of late Charles Wilson, Belfast; *m* 1937, Susan Eveline Wilson; one *s* three *d*. *Educ:* Royal Belfast Academical Institution; Queen's Univ., Belfast. Apprentice in Mech. Eng, Combe Barbour, Belfast, 1927–31; QUB, 1927–31 (part-time) and 1931–34 (full-time); BSc with 1st Class Hons in Elect. Eng, 1932; PhD 1934 (Thesis on High Voltage Transients on Power Transmission Lines); College Apprentice, Metropolitan-Vickers, Manchester, 1934–35. Joined RAF Educational Service, 1935; commissioned RAFVR, 1939; Senior Tutor, RAF Advanced Armament Course, Ft Halstead, 1943–46; Senior Educn Officer, Empire Air Armament School, Manby (Acting Wing Comdr), 1946–47. Joined Ministry of Supply, 1947, as Senior Principal Sci. Officer, Supt Servo Div., Guided Projectile Estab., Westcott, 1947; Supt Guidance and Control Div. Guided Weapons Dept, RAE, 1947–49; Head of Armament Dept, RAE, 1949–56; Dep. Chief Sci. Officer, 1952; Chief Scientific Officer, 1956; Director-General, Aircraft Equipment Research and Develt, Ministry of Aviation, 1956–62; Head, Defence Research and Development Staff, British Embassy, Washington, DC, 1962–65; Dep. Chief Scientist (Army), 1965–66, Chief Scientist (Army), 1967–70; Dir, SHAPE Tech. Centre, 1970–75. Hon. DSc QUB, 1971. *Recreations:* golf, gardening. *Address:* 7 Carlinwark Drive, Camberley, Surrey GU15 3TX. *Died 18 June 1992.*

WILSON, Air Vice-Marshal James Stewart, CBE 1959; Hon. Civil Consultant in Preventive Medicine to the Royal Air Force, since 1983; *b* 4 Sept. 1909; *s* of late J. Wilson, Broughty Ferry, Angus, and Helen Fyffe Wilson; *m* 1937, Elizabeth Elias; one *s* (and one *s* decd). *Educ:* Dundee High Sch.; St Andrews Univ. (MB, ChB). DPH (London) 1948; FFCM RCP 1974. House Surgeon, Dundee Royal Infirmary, 1933; House Surgeon, Arbroath Infirmary, 1934; commissioned Royal Air Force, 1935; served North Africa, 1942–45; Director Hygiene and Research, Air Ministry, London, 1956–59; Principal Medical Officer, Flying Training Command, 1959–61; Director-General of Medical Services, Royal Australian Air Force, 1961–63; QHP 1961–65; Principal Medical Officer, Bomber Command, 1963–65, retired. Special Adviser in Epidemiology and Applied Entomology, Inst. of Community Medicine, RAF Halton, 1965–83. *Publications:* articles (jointly) on respiratory virus infections, in medical journals. *Recreations:* golf, fishing, shooting. *Address:* Orgreave Hall, Alrewas, Burton-upon-Trent, Staffs DE13 7DG. *Club:* Royal Air Force.
Died 30 April 1994.

WILSON, John Anthony Burgess; *see* Burgess, A.

WILSON, Sir John Gardiner, Kt 1982; CBE 1972; Chairman, Australian Paper Manufacturers Ltd, 1978–84; *b* 13 July 1913; *s* of J. S. Wilson; *m* 1944, Margaret Louise De Ravin; three *d*. *Educ:* Melbourne Grammar Sch.; Clare Coll., Cambridge (MA 1935). Served RAE, AIF, 1939–46, Col. With J. S. Wilson & Co., actuaries and sharebrokers, 1934–39; Mem., Melbourne Stock Exchange, 1935–47; joined Australian Paper Manufacturers, 1947: Dep. Man. Dir, 1953–59; Man. Dir, 1959–78. Former Director: Vickers Australia; Vickers Cockatoo Dockyard Pty. *Address:* 6 Woorigoleen Road, Toorak, Vic 3142, Australia. *Clubs:* Melbourne, Australian, Royal Melbourne Golf (Melbourne).
Died 22 Aug. 1994.

WILSON, Sir John (Martindale), KCB 1974 (CB 1960); a Vice-President, Civil Service Retirement Fellowship, since 1982; *b* 3 Sept. 1915; *e s* of late John and Kate Wilson; *m* 1941, Penelope Beatrice, *e d* of late Francis A. Bolton, JP, Oakamoor, Staffs; one *s* one *d*. *Educ:* Bradfield Coll.; Gonville and Caius Coll., Cambridge. BA (Cantab), 1st Class Law Trip., 1937; MA 1946. Asst Principal, Dept of Agriculture for Scotland, 1938; Ministry of Supply, 1939; served War, 1939–46 (despatches) with Royal Artillery in India and Burma; Private Sec. to Minister of Supply, 1946–50; Asst Sec., 1950; Under-Sec., 1954; Cabinet Office, 1955–58; MoD, 1958–60; Dep. Sec., Min. of Aviation, 1961–65; Dep. Under-Sec. of State, MoD, 1965–72; Second Permanent Under-Sec. of State (Admin), MoD, 1972–75. Chairman: Crown Housing Assoc., 1975–78; CS Appeal Bd, 1978–81 (Dep. Chm., 1975–78); Civil Service Retirement Fellowship, 1978–82. *Recreation:* gardening. *Address:* Bourne Close, Bourne Lane, Twyford, near Winchester, Hants SO21 1NX. *T:* Twyford (0962) 713488. *Club:* Civil Service.
Died 26 July 1993.

WILSON, John Spark, CBE 1979 (OBE 1969); Assistant Commissioner, Traffic and Technical Support Department, Metropolitan Police, 1977–82, retired; Director, Security and Investigation Service, T. Miller & Co., 1982–87; *b* 9 May 1922; *s* of John Wilson and Elizabeth Kidd Wilson; *m* 1948, Marguerite Chisholm Wilson; two *s* one *d*. *Educ:* Logie Central Sch., Dundee. Joined Metropolitan Police, 1946; Special Branch, 1948–67; Detective Chief Supt, 1968; Comdr, 1969; went to Wales re Investiture of Prince

of Wales, 1969; Dep. Asst Comr (CID), 1972; Asst Comr (Crime), 1975. *Recreations:* football, Rugby, boxing.
Died 15 Sept. 1993.

WILSON, (John) Tuzo, CC 1974 (OC 1970); OBE 1946; FRS 1968; FRSC 1949; Chancellor, York University, Toronto, 1983–86; Professor of Geophysics, University of Toronto, 1946–74, Emeritus Professor, 1977; Director-General, Ontario Science Centre, 1974–85; *b* Ottawa, 24 Oct. 1908; *s* of John Armitstead Wilson, CBE, and Henrietta L. Tuzo; *m* 1938, Isabel Jean Dickson; two *d*. *Educ:* Ottawa; Universities of Toronto (Governor-General's medal, Trinity Coll., 1930; Massey Fellow, 1930), Cambridge (ScD), and Princeton (PhD). Asst Geologist, Geological Survey of Canada, 1936–46; Principal, Erindale Coll., Univ. of Toronto, 1967–74. Regimental service and staff appointments, Royal Canadian Engrs, UK and Sicily, 1939–43; Director, Opl Research, Nat. Defence HQ, Ottawa (Colonel), 1944–46. President, International Union of Geodesy and Geophysics, 1957–60. Visiting Professor: Australian Nat. Univ., 1950 and 1965; Ohio State Univ., 1968; California Inst. of Technology, 1976. Member Nat. Research Council of Canada, 1957–63; Member Defence Res. Board, 1958–64. Canadian Delegation to Gen. Ass., UNESCO, 1962, 1964, 1966. President: Royal Society of Canada, 1972–73; Amer. Geophysical Union, 1980–82. Overseas Fellow, Churchill Coll., Cambridge, 1965; Trustee, Nat. Museums of Canada, 1967–74. Hon. Fellow: Trinity Coll., University of Toronto, 1962; St John's Coll., Cambridge, 1981; Hon. FRSE 1986. Foreign Associate, Nat. Acad. of Sciences, USA, 1968; Foreign Hon. Mem., Amer. Acad. of Arts and Sciences; For. Mem., Royal Swedish Acad. of Sciences, 1981; Associé, Académie Royale de Belgique, 1981. Hon. doctorates and hon. or foreign memberships and medals, etc, in Canada and abroad. Vetlesen Prize, Columbia Univ., 1978; Britannica Award, 1986. *Publications:* One Chinese Moon, 1959; Physics and Geology (with J. A. Jacobs and R. D. Russell), 1959; IGY: Year of the New Moons, 1961; (ed) Continents Adrift, 1972; Unglazed China, 1973; (ed) Continents Adrift and Continents Aground, 1976; scientific papers. *Recreation:* travel. *Address:* 27 Pricefield Road, Toronto, Ont M4W 1Z8, Canada. *T:* 923–4244. *Clubs:* Arts and Letters, York (Toronto). *Died 15 April 1993.*

WILSON, Rev. Canon Leslie Rule; Hon. Canon of Holy Cross Cathedral, Geraldton, since 1966; *b* 19 July 1909; *y s* of late Rev. John and Mary Adelaide Wilson; *m* 1st (wife *d* 1980); 2nd, 1984, Mrs Margaret Nunns, *widow* of R. C. Nunns, Stocksfield. *Educ:* Royal Grammar Sch., Newcastle upon Tyne; University College, Durham; Edinburgh Theological College. Asst Priest, Old St Paul's, Edinburgh, 1934–36; Rector of Fort William, 1936–42, with Nether Lochaber and Portree, 1938–42; Canon of Argyll and The Isles, 1940–42; Education Officer, 1942–45; Welfare Officer, SEAC (Toc H), 1945–46; Vicar of Malacca, Malaya, 1946–50; Principal Probation Officer, Federation of Malaya, 1950–52; Vicar of Kuching, Sarawak, 1952–55; Provost and Canon of St Thomas' Cathedral, Kuching, 1955–59; Rector of Geraldton, W Australia, 1960–64; Dean of Geraldton, 1964–66 (Administrator, Diocese of NW Australia, 1966); Archdeacon of Carpentaria, 1966–67; Rector of Winterbourne Stickland with Turnworth and Winterbourne Houghton, 1967–69; Vicar of Holmside, 1969–74; retired 1974; permission to officiate, Diocese of Durham, 1975–. Commissary for Bp of NW Australia, 1966–83. Founder and Chairman, Parson Woodforde Society, 1968–75 (Hon. Life Pres., 1975). *Recreations:* reading, genealogy. *Address:* 11 Norwich Close, Great Lumley, Chester-le-Street, Co. Durham DH3 4QL. *T:* Durham (091) 3892366. *Died 29 Dec. 1991.*

WILSON, Sir (Mathew) Martin, 5th Bt, *cr* 1874, of Eshton Hall, Co. York; *b* 2 July 1906; *s* of Lieut-Colonel Sir Mathew Richard Henry Wilson, 4th Bt, and Hon. Barbara Lister (*d* 1943), *d* of 4th Baron Ribblesdale; *S* father, 1958. *Educ:* Eton. *Heir: nephew* Brig. Mathew John Anthony Wilson, OBE, MC [*b* 2 Oct. 1935; *m* 1962, Janet Mary, *e d* of late E. W. Mowll, JP; one *s* one *d*]. *Address:* 1 Sandgate Esplanade, Folkestone, Kent.
Died 20 March 1991.

WILSON, Sir Michael M.; *see* McNair-Wilson.

WILSON, Norman George, CMG 1966; grazier, since 1973; company director; *b* 20 Oct. 1911; *s* of Percy Wilson; *m* 1939, Dorothy Gwen, *d* of late Sir (William) Lennon Raws; one *s* two *d*. *Educ:* Melbourne University (BCE). Joined ICI Australia Ltd, 1935: Exec. positions, 1936–48; General Manager, Dyes and Plastics Group, 1949–54; Director, 1959–73; Man. Dir, Dulux Pty Ltd, 1954–62; Man. Dir, 1962–72, Dep. Chm., 1972–73, Fibremakers Ltd; Commercial Dir, ICI of Australia Ltd, 1972–73. Business Adviser to Dept of Air, and Dep. Chm. Defence Business Board, Commonwealth Government, 1957–76; Chairman Production Board, Dept of Manufacturing Industries, Commonwealth Government, 1960–76. Member: Export Develt Council, Dept of Trade and Industry, Commonwealth Govt, 1966–72; Australia/Japan Business Co-operation Cttee, 1970–73; Pacific Basin Econ. Co-operation Council, 1966–73. Mem. Bd, Victorian Railways, 1973–83; Dep. Chm., Victorian Conservation Trust, 1973–83; Foundn Pres., Australia/Britain Soc., Vic, 1971–76. FInstD, FAIM, FRACI. *Recreations:* farming, landscape paintings. *Address:* The Highlands, Kerrie, Romsey, Vic 3434, Australia. *T:* 054 270232. *Clubs:* Australian (Melbourne); Melbourne Cricket, Victoria Racing.
Died 4 Sept. 1992.

WILSON, Prof. Raymond; Professor of Education, 1968–89, then Emeritus, and Chairman of School of Education, 1969–76 and 1980–89, University of Reading; *b* 20 Dec. 1925; *s* of John William Wilson and Edith (*née* Walker); *m* 1950, Gertrude Mary Russell; two *s* one *d*. *Educ:* London Univ. (BA English, 1st Cl.). Teacher, secondary schs, 1950–57; English Master, subseq. Chief English Master, Dulwich Coll., 1957–65; Lectr, Southampton Univ., 1965–68. Mem. Adv. Bd, World Book Encyclopedia (Internat.), 1988–92. *Publications:* numerous textbooks and anthologies; papers on English language and literature, philosophy of education, and the humanities; occasional poet and writer of fiction. *Recreations:* walking, natural history. *Address:* 7 Northfield Court, Northfield Close, Henley-on-Thames, Oxon RG9 2LH. *T:* Henley (01491) 575395. *Club:* Phyllis Court (Henley).
Died 21 March 1995.

WILSON, Prof. Roger Cowan; Professor of Education, University of Bristol, 1951–71, Emeritus 1971; Visiting Professor: University of Malawi, 1966; Harvard University, 1968; *b* 3 Aug. 1906; 2nd *s* of Alexander Cowan Wilson and Edith Jane Brayshaw; *m* 1931, Margery Lilian, *y d* of late Rev. C. W. Emmet, Fellow of University College, Oxford, and Gertrude (*née* Weir); one *s* one *d*. *Educ:* Manchester Grammar School; The Queen's College, Oxford (Exhibitioner); Manchester College of Technology. Chairman, OU Labour Club, 1927; President, Oxford Union, 1929; First Cl. in Philosophy, Politics and Economics, 1929. Apprentice in cotton industry, 1929–35; Talks Staff of BBC, 1935–40; dismissed from BBC as conscientious objector; General Secretary, Friends Relief Service, 1940–46; head of Dept of Social Studies, University College, Hull, 1946–51. Mem., Colonial Office and Min. of Overseas Develt adv. cttees and consultative missions, 1957–71. Senior Adviser on Social Affairs, United Nations Operation in the Congo, 1961–62. Chairman: Bd of Visitors, Shepton Mallet Prison,

1966–70; Council for Voluntary Action, South Lakeland, 1974–79; Cumbria Council on Alcoholism, 1979–81; Pres., Friends Historical Society, 1988; Clerk, London Yearly Meeting of Society of Friends, 1975–78. JP Bristol, 1954–67. Médaille de la Reconnaisance Française, 1948. *Publications:* Frank Lenwood, a biography, 1936; Authority, Leadership and Concern, a study of motive and administration in Quaker relief work, 1948; Quaker Relief, 1940–48, 1952; The Teacher: instructor or educator, 1952; (with Kuenstler and others) Social Group Work in Great Britain, 1955; Difficult Housing Estates, 1963; (jtly) Social Aspects of Urban Development, 1966; Jesus the Liberator, 1981; Manchester, Manchester and Manchester Again, 1990. *Recreations:* walking, Quaker history. *Address:* Peter Hill House, Yealand Conyers, near Carnforth, Lancs LA5 9SG. *T:* Carnforth (0524) 733519.
Died 31 July 1991.

WILSON, Tuzo; *see* Wilson, J. T.

WILSON, Prof. William Adam; Lord President Reid Professor of Law, University of Edinburgh, since 1972; *b* 28 July 1928; *s* of Hugh Wilson and Anne Adam. *Educ:* Hillhead High Sch., Glasgow; Glasgow Univ. MA 1948, LLB 1951. Solicitor, 1951. Lectr in Scots Law, Edinburgh Univ., 1960, Sen. Lectr 1965. Dep. Chm., Consumer Protection Adv. Cttee, 1974–82. FRSE 1991. *Publications:* (with A. G. M. Duncan) Law of Trusts, Trustees and Executors, 1975; Introductory Essays on Scots Law, 1978, 2nd edn 1984; Law of Debt, 1981, 2nd edn 1991; articles in legal jls. *Address:* 2 Great Stuart Street, Edinburgh EH3 6AW. *T:* 031–225 4958.
Died 14 March 1994.

WILSON, William Lawrence, CB 1967; OBE 1954; retired as Deputy Secretary, Department of the Environment, latterly Consultant; *b* 11 Sept. 1912; *s* of Joseph Osmond and Ann Wilson;—1936, Doris Irene Goddard; two *s*; *m* 1964, Constance V. Richards. *Educ:* Stockton on Tees Secondary School; Constantine College, Middlesbrough. BSc (London), FIMechE, Whitworth Prizeman. Apprentice, ICI Billingham 1928–33; Technical Asst, ICI, 1933–36; Assistant Engineer, HM Office of Works, 1937; subsequently Engineer, 1939; Superintending Engineer, Min. of Works, 1945; Assistant Chief Engineer, 1954; Chief Engineer, 1962; Deputy Secretary, MPBW, later DoE, 1969–73. Pres., Assoc. of Supervising Electrical Engineers. FRSA; Hon. FCIBSE. Coronation Medal. *Publications:* papers on radioactive wastes; contrib. to World Power Conference, USSR and USA. *Recreations:* cricket, fishing, watching all forms of sport. *Address:* Oakwood, Chestnut Avenue, Rickmansworth, Herts WD3 4HB. *T:* Rickmansworth (0923) 774419.
Died 29 Aug. 1993.

WILTSHIRE, Sir Frederick Munro, Kt 1976; CBE 1970 (OBE 1966); FTS 1976; Managing Director: Wiltshire File Co. Pty Ltd, Australia, 1938–77; Wiltshire Cutlery Co. Pty Ltd, 1959–77; Director: Repco Ltd, 1966–81; Australian Paper Manufacturers Ltd, 1966–83; *b* 5 June 1911; *m* 1938, Jennie L., *d* of F. M. Frencham; one *d*. Chm., Dept of Trade and Industry Adv. Cttee on Small Businesses, 1968; Chm., Cttees of Inquiry, etc. Mem., Executive, CSIRO, 1974–78. Past Pres., Aust. Industries Develt Assoc.; Member, Manufacturing Industries Adv. Council, 1957–77 (Vice-Pres. 1972); Industrial Member, Science and Industry Forum of Aust. Acad. of Science, 1967–80; FAIM (Councillor, 1955–59). *Address:* 38 Rockley Road, South Yarra, Vic 3141, Australia. *Clubs:* Athenæum (Melbourne); Kingston Heath Golf (Aust.).
Died 1 Feb. 1994.

WIMBORNE, 3rd Viscount, *cr* 1918; **Ivor Fox-Strangways Guest;** Baron Wimborne, 1880; Baron Ashby St Ledgers, 1910; Bt 1838; Chairman, Harris and Dixon Holdings Ltd, since 1976; *b* 2 Dec. 1939; *s* of 2nd Viscount and of Dowager Viscountess Wimborne, (Mabel Edith), *d* of 6th Earl of Ilchester; *S* father, 1967; *m* 1st, 1966, Victoria Ann (marr. diss. 1981), *o d* of late Col Mervyn Vigors, DSO, MC; one *s*; 2nd, 1983, Mrs Venetia Margaret Barker, *er d* of Richard Quarry; one *d. Educ:* Eton. Chairman: Harris & Dixon Ltd, 1972–76 (Man. Dir, 1967–71); Harris & Dixon Group of Cos, 1977–; Dep. Chm., Ermitage Group. Jt Master, Pytchley Hounds, 1968–76. *Heir: s* Hon. Ivor Mervyn Vigors Guest, *b* 19 Sept. 1968. *Clubs:* Travellers', Cercle Interalliée, Polo (Paris). *Died 17 Dec. 1993.*

WIMBUSH, Rt Rev. Richard Knyvet; an Assistant Bishop, Diocese of York, since 1977; *b* 18 March 1909; *s* of late Rev. Canon J. S. Wimbush, Terrington, Yorks, and Judith Isabel Wimbush, *d* of Sir Douglas Fox; *m* 1937, Mary Margaret (*d* 1989), *d* of Rev. E. H. Smith; three *s* one *d. Educ:* Haileybury Coll.; Oriel Coll., Oxford; Cuddesdon Coll. 2nd cl. Classical Mods 1930; BA 1st cl. Theol. 1932; MA 1935. Deacon, 1934; priest, 1935; Chaplain, Cuddesdon Coll., Oxon, 1934–37; Curate: Pocklington, Yorks, 1937–39; St Wilfrid, Harrogate, 1939–42; Rector, Melsonby, Yorks, 1942–48; Principal, Edinburgh Theological Coll., 1948–63; Bishop of Argyll and the Isles, 1963–77; Primus of the Episcopal Church in Scotland, 1974–77; Priest-in-charge of Etton with Dalton Holme, dio. York, 1977–83. Canon of St Mary's Cathedral, Edinburgh, 1948–63; Exam. Chap. to Bp of Edinburgh, 1949–62; Select Preacher, Oxford Univ., 1971. *Recreations:* gardening, walking. *Address:* 5 Tower Place, York YO1 1RZ. *T:* York (0904) 641971.
Died 4 Jan. 1994.

WINCHESTER, Ian Sinclair, CMG 1982; HM Diplomatic Service, retired; *b* 14 March 1931; *s* of late Dr Alexander Hugh Winchester, FRCSEd, and Mary Stewart (*née* Duguid); *m* 1957, Shirley Louise Milner; three *s. Educ:* Lewes County Grammar Sch., Sussex; Magdalen Coll., Oxford. Foreign Office, 1953; Third Sec. (Oriental), Cairo, 1955–56; FO, 1956–60; Asst Political Agent, Dubai, 1960–62; Actg Political Agent, Doha, 1962; First Sec. (Inf.), Vienna, 1962–65; First Sec. (Commercial), Damascus, 1965–67; FO (later FCO), 1967–70; Counsellor, Jedda, 1970–72; Counsellor (Commercial), Brussels, 1973–76; FCO, 1976–81; Minister, Jedda, 1982–83; Asst Under-Sec. of State (Dir of Communications and Technical Services), FCO, 1985–89. *Address:* 134 College Road, SE19 1XD.
Died 20 Feb. 1994.

WINDEYER, Sir Brian (Wellingham), Kt 1961; FRCP, FRCS, FRCSE, FRSM, FRCR, DMRE; retired; Vice-Chancellor, University of London, 1969–72; Professor of Radiology (Therapeutic), Middlesex Hospital Medical School, University of London, 1942–69; Dean, Middlesex Hospital Medical School, 1954–67; formerly Director: Meyerstein Institute of Radiotherapy, Middlesex Hospital; Radiotherapy Department, Mount Vernon Hospital; Consultant Adviser in Radiotherapy to Ministry of Health, 1948–72; *b* 7 Feb. 1904; *s* of Richard Windeyer, KC, Sydney, Australia, and Mabel Fuller Windeyer; *m* 1st, 1928, Joyce Ziele, *d* of Harry Russell, Sydney; one *s* one *d*; 2nd, 1948, Elspeth Anne, *d* of H. Bowrey, Singapore; one *s* two *d. Educ:* Sydney C of E Grammar Sch.; St Andrew's Coll., Univ. of Sydney. Sydney Univ. Rugby Team, 1922–27; combined Australian and NZ Univs Rugby Team, 1923; coll. crew, 1922–26. MB, BS Sydney, 1927; FRCSE 1930; DMRE Cambridge, 1933; FRCR (FFR 1940); FRCS (*ad eundem*) 1948; MRCP 1957. Formerly House Physician, House Surgeon and Radium Registrar, Royal Prince Alfred Hosp., Sydney; Asst, Fondation Curie, Paris, 1929–30; Middlesex Hospital: Radium Officer, 1931; MO i/c Radiotherapy Dept, 1936; Medical Comdt, 1940–45; Dir, EMS Radiotherapy Dept,

Mt Vernon Hosp., 1940–46; Dean, Faculty of Medicine, Univ. of London, 1964–68. Skinner Lectr, Faculty of Radiologists, 1943 (Pres. of Faculty, 1949–52); Hunterian Prof., RCS, 1951. Pres., Radiology Section, RSM, 1958–59. Chairman: Radio-active Substances Adv. Cttee, 1961–70; Nat. Radiological Protection Bd, 1970–78; Academic Council, Univ. of London, 1967–69; Matilda and Terence Kennedy Inst. of Rheumatology, 1970–77; Inst. of Educn, Univ. of London, 1974–83; Council, RSA, 1973–78. Member: Royal Commn on Med. Educn; Grand Council and Exec. Cttee, British Empire Cancer Campaign; British Inst. of Radiology (late Mem. Council); Med. Soc. of London; MRC, 1958–62 and 1968–71; Clinical Research Bd, 1954–62 (Chm., 1968); a Vice Pres., Royal Surgical Aid Soc. (formerly Chm.). Co-opted Mem. Council, RCS, to rep. radiology, 1948–53. Former Chm., Throgmorton Club. Mem. Court, 1963–78, Master, 1972–73, Apothecaries' Soc. Hon. Mem., Amer. Radium Soc., 1948. Hon. FRACS, 1951; Hon. FRACR (Hon. FCRA 1955); Hon. FACR 1966. Hon. DSc: British Columbia, 1952; Wales, 1965; Cantab, 1971; Hon. LLD Glasgow, 1968; Hon. MD Sydney, 1979. *Publications:* various articles on cancer and radiotherapy. *Recreation:* gardening. *Address:* 49 Trinity Street, Oxford OX1 1TY. *T:* Oxford (01865) 250265. *Died 26 Oct. 1994.*

WINDHAM, Brig. William Russell S.; *see* Smijth-Windham.

WINNER, Prof. Harold Ivor, MA, MD, FRCP, FRCPath; Professor of Medical Microbiology, University of London, at Charing Cross Hospital Medical School, 1965–83, then Emeritus; Consulting Microbiologist, Charing Cross Hospital, (Consultant Microbiologist, 1954–83); *b* 1 June 1918; *y s* of late Jacob Davis and Janet Winner; *m* 1945, Nina (*d* 1986), *e d* of Jacques and Lily Katz; two *s. Educ:* St Paul's Sch.; Downing Coll., Cambridge (Maj. Schol.); University College Hospital Medical School. 1st class hons, Nat. Scis Tripos Cambridge, 1939. House Surgeon, Addenbrooke's Hospital, Cambridge, 1942; served RAMC, 1942–44; Asst Pathologist, EMS, 1945–48 and NW Group Laboratory, Hampstead, 1948–50; Lecturer, Sen. Lecturer, and Reader in Bacteriology, Charing Cross Hospital Medical Sch., 1950–64. Mem. School Council, 1967–69 and 1977–83. Member: Univs' Cttee on Safety, 1981; Adv. Cttee on Dangerous Pathogens, 1981–84. Examiner: Examining Board in England, 1962–77; Royal Coll. of Surgeons, 1971–76; Royal Coll. of Pathologists, 1975–; universities at home and overseas. Founder Fellow and Archivist, RCPath; formerly Pres. and Hon. Editor, Section of Pathology, and Vice-Pres., Sect. of Comparative Medicine, RSM; Chm., Med. Scis Historical Soc., 1982–83; Vis. Prof., Guest Lectr and Corresp. Mem., various univs and medical insts at home and overseas. *Publications:* Candida albicans (jointly), 1964; Symposium on Candida Infections (jointly), 1966; Microbiology in Modern Nursing, 1969; Microbiology in Patient Care, 1973, 2nd edn 1978; Louis Pasteur and Microbiology, 1974; chapters in medical books; papers in medical, scientific and nursing journals. *Recreations:* listening to music, looking at pictures and buildings, gardening, travel. *Address:* 48 Lyndale Avenue, NW2 2QA. *T:* 071–435 5959. *Died 18 Dec. 1992.*

WINNIFRITH, Sir (Alfred) John (Digby), KCB 1959 (CB 1950); *b* 16 Oct. 1908; *s* of Rev. B. T. Winnifrith; *m* 1935, Lesbia Margaret (*d* 1981), *d* of late Sir Arthur Cochrane, KCVO; two *s* one *d. Educ:* Westminster School; Christ Church, Oxford. Entered Board of Trade, 1932; transferred to HM Treasury, 1934; Asst Sec., War Cabinet Office and Civil Sec., Combined Operations HQ, 1942–44, till return to HM Treasury; Third Secretary, HM Treasury, 1951–59; Permanent Secretary, Ministry of Agriculture, Fisheries and Food, 1959–67; Dir-Gen., National Trust, 1968–70.

Trustee, British Museum (Natural History), 1967–72; Member: Royal Commn on Environmental Pollution, 1970–73; Commonwealth War Graves Commn, 1970–83; Hops Marketing Board, 1970–78. Hon. ARCVS 1974. *Address:* Hallhouse Farm, Appledore, Kent. *T:* Appledore (023383) 264. *Died 1 Jan. 1993.*

WINNINGTON-INGRAM, Prof. Reginald Pepys, FBA 1958; Professor of Greek Language and Literature in the University of London (King's College), 1953–71, then Professor Emeritus; Fellow of King's College, since 1969; *b* 22 Jan. 1904; *s* of late Rear-Admiral and Mrs C. W. Winnington-Ingram; *m* 1938, Mary (*d* 1992), *d* of late Thomas Cousins. *Educ:* Clifton Coll., Trinity Coll., Cambridge. BA 1925; MA 1929; Scholar of Trinity Coll., 1922, Fellow, 1928–32; 1st Class Classical Tripos, Part I, 1923; Waddington Schol., 1924; 1st Class Classical Tripos, Part II, 1925; Charles Oldham Classical Schol., 1926. Asst Lecturer and Lecturer, University of Manchester, 1928, 1930 and 1933; Reader in Classics, University of London (Birkbeck College), 1934–48; Temp. Civil Servant, Ministry of Labour and National Service, 1940–45 (Asst Secretary, 1944); Professor of Classics in the University of London (Westfield Coll.), 1948–53; Director, University of London Inst. of Classical Studies, 1964–67. J. H. Gray Lectures, Cambridge Univ., 1956. Vis. Prof., Univ. of Texas at Austin, 1971, 1973; Vis. Aurelio Prof., Boston Univ., 1975. President, Society for the Promotion of Hellenic Studies, 1959–62 (Hon. Secretary, 1963–82, Hon. Mem., 1983). Hon. DLitt: Glasgow, 1969; London, 1985. *Publications:* Mode in Ancient Greek Music, 1936; Euripides and Dionysus, 1948; (ed) Aristides Quintilianus, *De Musica,* 1963; Sophocles: an interpretation, 1980; Studies in Aeschylus, 1983; contribs to classical and musical journals, dictionaries, etc. *Recreation:* music. *Address:* 12 Greenhill, NW3 5UB. *T:* 071–435 6843. *Club:* Athenæum.
Died 3 Jan. 1993.

WINSTANLEY, Baron *cr* 1975 (Life Peer), of Urmston in Greater Manchester; **Michael Platt Winstanley;** television and radio broadcaster, author, journalist, columnist, medical practitioner; Chairman, Countryside Commission, 1978–80; *b* Nantwich, Cheshire, 27 Aug. 1918; *e s* of late Dr Sydney A. Winstanley; *m* 1st, 1945, Nancy Penney (marr. diss. 1952); one *s*; 2nd, 1955, Joyce M. Woodhouse; one *s* one *d. Educ:* Manchester Grammar Sch.; Manchester Univ. President, Manchester Univ. Union, 1940–41; Captain, Manchester Univ. Cricket Club, 1940–42; Captain Combined English Univs Cricket Team, 1941; Ed. University magazine, 1941–42. MRCS, LRCP 1944. Resident Surgical Officer, Wigan Infirmary, 1945; Surgical Specialist, RAMC, 1946; GP, Urmston, Manchester, 1948–66; MO, Royal Ordnance Factory, Patricroft, 1950–66; Treasury MO and Admiralty Surgeon and Agent, 1953–66; Member Lancs Local Med. Cttee, 1954–66; Member Lancs Exec. Council, 1956–65. Spokesman for Manchester Div. of BMA, 1957–65. Member Liberal Party Council, 1962–66. Contested (L) Stretford, 1964; MP (L) Cheadle, 1966–70; MP (L) Hazel Grove, Feb.-Sept. 1974. Chairman Liberal Party Health Cttee, 1965–66; Liberal Party Spokesman on health, Post Office and broadcasting. TV and radio broadcaster, 1957– (own series on Indep. TV and BBC); cricket columnist, Manchester Evening News, 1964–65; weekly personal column, Manchester Evening News, 1970–76. Member: BBC Gen. Adv. Council, 1967–70; Post Office Bd, 1978–80; Water Space Amenity Commn, 1980–82. President: Fluoridation Soc., 1984–; Gingerbread, 1984–; Birth Control Campaign, 1984–; Chm., Groundwork Trust, 1980–. A Dep. Pro-Chancellor, Univ. of Lancaster, 1986–. *Publications:* Home Truths for Home Doctors, 1963; The Anatomy of First-Aid, 1966; The British Ombudsman, 1970; Tell Me, Doctor, 1972; Know Your Rights, 1975;

articles on current affairs, health, etc. *Recreations:* cricket, golf, playing the bagpipes. *Address:* Hare Hall, Dunnerdale, Broughton-in-Furness, Cumbria. *Clubs:* National Liberal, Authors'. *Died 18 July 1993.*

WINSTONE, (Frank) Reece, FRPS; self employed, since 1925; illustrative photographer, since 1937; book designer, publisher and distributor, since 1957; *b* Bristol, 3 Sept. 1909; *s* of John Ephraim Winstone and Lillian Kate (*née* Reece); *m* 1937, Dorothy Agnes Attrill; one *s. Educ:* Bristol Cathedral Sch. FRPS 1976. Partner, father's menswear business, 1925–36. RAF Photographer, 1940–45. *Publications:* Bristol As It Was 1939–1914, 1957 (5th edn 1978); Bristol As It Was 1914–1900, 1957 (3rd edn 1972); Bristol Today, 1958 (4th edn 1971); Bristol in the 1890s, 1960 (3rd edn 1973); Bristol in the 1940s, 1961 (2nd edn 1970); Bristol in the 1880s, 1962 (2nd edn 1978); Bristol As It Was 1950–1953, 1964 (2nd edn 1970); Bristol As It Was 1879–1874, 1965 (3rd edn 1984); Bristol As It Was 1874–1866, 1966 (2nd edn 1971); Bristol As It Was 1866–1860, 1967 (2nd edn 1972); Bristol Fashion, 1968; Bristol in the 1850s, 1968 (2nd edn 1978); Bristol As It Was 1953–1956, 1969, (2nd edn 1979); Bristol's Earliest Photographs, 1970 (2nd edn 1975); Bristol Tradition, 1970; Bristol in the 1920s, 1971 (2nd edn 1977); Bristol As It Was 1956–1959, 1972 (2nd edn 1986); Bristol Blitzed, 1973 (2nd edn 1976); Bristol's Trams, 1974; Bristol As It Was 1913–1921, 1976; Bristol's Suburbs in the 1920s and 1930s, 1977; Bristol As It Was 1928–1933, 1979; Bath As It Was, 1980; Bristol As It Was 1960–1962, 1981; Bristol As It Was 1845–1900, 1983; Bristol's Suburbs Long Ago, 1985; Bristol As It Was 1934–1936, 1986; Bristol As It Was 1937–1939, 1987; Changes in the Face of Bristol, 1987; Bristol As It Was 1940–1960, 1988; (ed) Bristol's History: Vol. 1, 1966 (3rd edn 1980); Vol. 2, 1975; (ed) Miss Ann Green of Clifton, 1974; (ed) History of Bristol's Suburbs, 1977. *Recreations:* local preservation societies, motoring, the gramophone, serious broadcast programmes, reading. *Address:* Ilex House, Front Street, Churchill, Bristol BS19 5LZ. *T:* Churchill (0934) 852132.
Died 30 May 1991.

WINT, Dr Arthur Stanley, OJ 1989; CD 1973; MBE 1954; FRCS; private medical practitioner, retired; Doctor and Surgeon in charge, Linstead General Hospital, Jamaica, 1978–85; *b* 25 May 1920; *s* of John Samuel Wint and Hilda Wint; *m* 1949, Norma Wint (*née* Marsh); three *d. Educ:* Calabar High School; Excelsior College, Jamaica; St Bartholomew's Medical School. MB BS; FRCS 1962; FICS 1972; DMJ (Clin), 1975. Served RAF, 1942–47; Medical School, 1947–53. Participated in international athletics, 1936–53; Olympics 1948: Gold medal, 400 m; Silver medal, 800 m; Olympics 1952: Gold medal, 4x400 m Relay; Silver medal, 800 m. Medical practitioner, 1953–73; Jamaican High Comr in the UK, 1974–78. Hon. DLitt Loughborough, 1982. *Recreations:* badminton, swimming, walking. *Address:* 21 King Street, Linstead, St Catherine, Jamaica, WI. *Club:* Polytechnic Harriers.
Died 19 Oct. 1992.

WINTERBOTTOM, Baron, *cr* 1965 (Life Peer), of Clopton in the county of Northampton; **Ian Winterbottom;** former Chairman: Dynavest Ltd; Anglo Global Limited; *b* 6 April 1913; *s* of G. H. Winterbottom, Horton House, Northants, and Georgina MacLeod; *m* 1st, 1939, Rosemary Mills (marr. diss. 1944); one *d*; 2nd, 1944, Irene Eva, (Ira), Munk; two *s* one *d. Educ:* Charterhouse; Clare Coll., Cambridge. Worked in textile and engineering trades in Manchester, Derby, and Bamberg and Cologne, Germany. Captain Royal Horse Guards; served War of 1939–45, NW European Campaign; ADC and subsequently Personal Assistant to Regional Commissioner, Hamburg, 1946–49. MP (Lab) Nottingham Central, 1950–55; Parly Under Sec.

of State, Royal Navy, MoD, 1966–67; Parly Sec., MPBW, 1967–68; Parly Under-Sec. of State, RAF, MoD, 1968–70; opposition spokesman on defence, 1970–74; a Lord in Waiting (Govt Whip), 1974–78; spokesman on: defence, 1974–78; trade and industry, 1976–78; resigned from Govt, 1978; Founder Mem., SDP; latterly a Conservative. Deleg., UN Trusteeship Council, 1974; Founder Mem., House of Lords All-Party Defence Study Gp; Member: Parly and Scientific Cttee; CPA; Anglo-Nigerian Soc. Director: Winterbottom Bookcloth Co., 1955–57; Venesta Internat., 1957–66, 1970–74 (Chm., 1972–74); Chairman: Centurion Housing Association, 1980–; Collins Aircraft Co., 1980–; Consultant, C. Z. Scientific Instruments Ltd, 1980–. *Recreations:* birdwatching, music. *Address:* Lower Farm, Fossbury, Marlborough, Wilts SN8 3NJ. *T:* Oxenwood (026489) 269. *Club:* Athenæum.

Died 4 July 1992.

WINTERTON, 7th Earl, *cr* 1766 (Ire.); **Robert Chad Turnour;** Baron Winterton 1761 (Ire.); Viscount Turnour, 1766 (Ire.); Royal Canadian Air Force; *b* 13 Sept. 1915; *s* of Cecil Turnour (*g g s* of Adolphus Augustus Turnour (brother of 3rd Earl)) (*d* 1953), Saskatoon, Sask, and Effie Annie (*d* 1956), *d* of Robert McMillan, London, Ont; *S* kinsman, 1962; *m* 1st, 1941, Kathleen Ella (*d* 1969), *d* of D. B. Whyte; 2nd, 1971, Marion Eleanor, *d* of late Arthur Phillips. *Educ:* Nutana Coll., Canada. Joined RCAF, 1940; with Canadian NATO Force Sqdn, Sardinia, 1957–58. *Heir:* nephew Donald David Turnour [*b* 13 Oct. 1943; *m* 1968, Jill Pauline, *d* of late J. G. Esplen; two *d*]. *Address:* 1326 55th Street, Delta, BC V4M 3K3, Canada.

Died 2 June 1991.

WISDOM, Prof. Arthur John Terence Dibben, MA; Professor of Philosophy, University of Oregon, 1968–72; Fellow of Trinity College, Cambridge; *b* 1904; *s* of Rev. H. C. Wisdom and Edith S. Wisdom; *m* Pamela Strain (*d* 1989); one *s* from previous marriage. *Educ:* Aldeburgh Lodge School; Fitzwilliam House (subseq. College), Cambridge (Hon. Fellow, Fitzwilliam Coll., 1978). BA 1924; MA 1934. Lecturer in Moral Sciences, Trinity Coll., Cambridge; Prof. of Philosophy, Cambridge Univ., 1952–68. DU Essex, 1978. *Publications:* Other Minds, 1952; Philosophy and Psycho-Analysis, 1952; Paradox and Discovery, 1966; Proof and Explanation, 1990; contributions to Mind and to Proceedings of the Aristotelian Society. *Address:* 154 Stanley Road, Cambridge CB5 8LB. *Died 9 Dec. 1993.*

WITHERS, Rupert Alfred; Director, Dalgety Ltd, 1969–83 (Deputy Chairman and Managing Director, 1969–71; Chairman, 1972–77); *b* 29 Oct. 1913; *o s* of late Herbert Withers, FRAM and Marguerite (*née* Elzy); *m* Betty (*d* 1985); two *d* and one step *d*. *Educ:* University College School. Fellow Institute of Chartered Accountants, 1938. Secretary and Chief Accountant, Gloster Aircraft Co. Ltd, 1940–44; a Senior Partner of Urwick Orr & Partners Ltd until 1959; Man. Dir, Ilford Ltd, 1959–64, Chm. and Chief Executive, 1964–68. *Recreations:* music, books, theatre. *Address:* 11K Stuart Tower, Maida Vale, W9 1UH. *T:* 0171–286 8706. *Clubs:* Savile, Buck's.

Died 11 Dec. 1995.

WITTE, Prof. William, FRSE; Professor of German in the University of Aberdeen, 1951–77; *b* 18 Feb. 1907; *o s* of W. G. J. and E. O. Witte; *m* 1937, Edith Mary Stenhouse Melvin; one *s* one *d*. *Educ:* Universities of Breslau, Munich, Berlin. MA, DLit (London); PhD (Aberdeen); FRSE 1978. Assistant, Department of German: Aberdeen, 1931–36; Edinburgh, 1936–37; Lecturer, Department of German, Aberdeen, 1937; Head of Dept, 1945; Reader in German, 1947. Gold Medal, Goethe Inst., 1971. Cross of the Order of Merit (Federal Republic of Germany), 1974. *Publications:* Modern German Prose Usage, 1937; Schiller, 1949; (ed) Schiller's Wallenstein, 1952; (ed) Two

Stories by Thomas Mann, 1957; Schiller and Burns, and Other Essays, 1959; (ed) Schiller's Wallensteins Tod, 1962; (ed) Schiller's Maria Stuart, 1965; (ed) Goethe's Clavigo, 1973; contributions to collective works; articles in Modern Language Review, German Life and Letters, Oxford German Studies, Publications of the English Goethe Society, Publications of the Carlyle Soc., Aberdeen Univ. Rev., Wisconsin Monatshefte, Schiller-Jahrbuch, Forum for Modern Language Studies, Encyclopædia Britannica, etc. *Recreation:* gardening. *Address:* 41 Beechgrove Terrace, Aberdeen AB2 4DS. *T:* Aberdeen (0224) 643799. *Died 22 Sept. 1992.*

WITTON-DAVIES, Ven. Carlyle; Archdeacon Emeritus of Oxford, since 1985; *b* 10 June 1913; *s* of late Prof. T. Witton Davies, DD, and Hilda Mabel Witton Davies (*née* Everett); *m* 1941, Mary Rees, BA, *o d* of late Canon W. J. Rees, St Asaph, Clwyd; three *s* four *d*. *Educ:* Friars School, Bangor; University College of N Wales, Bangor; Exeter College, Oxford; Cuddesdon College, Oxford; Hebrew University, Jerusalem. Exhib., University Coll. of N Wales, Bangor, 1930–34; BA (Wales), 1st Cl. Hons Hebrew, 1934; BA (Oxon), 2nd Cl. Hons Theology, 1937; Junior Hall Houghton Septuagint Prize, Oxford, 1938, Senior, 1939; MA (Oxon), 1940. Deacon, 1937, priest, 1938, St Asaph; Assistant Curate, Buckley, 1937–40; Subwarden, St Michael's College, Llandaff, 1940–44; Examining Chaplain to Bishop of Monmouth, 1940–44; Adviser on Judaica to Anglican Bishop in Jerusalem, 1944–49; Examining Chaplain to Bishop in Jerusalem, 1945–49; Canon Residentiary of Nazareth in St George's Collegiate Church, Jerusalem, 1947–49; Dean and Precentor of St David's Cathedral, 1949–57; Examining Chaplain to Bishop of St David's, 1950–57; Chaplain, Order of St John of Jerusalem, 1954–; Archdeacon of Oxford and Canon of Christ Church, Oxford, 1957–82, Sub Dean, 1972–82 (Student Emeritus of Christ Church, 1982–); Examining Chaplain to Bishop of Oxford, 1965–82. Chairman, Council of Christians and Jews, 1957–78 (Vice-Pres., 1978–); Mem., Archbishops' Commn on Crown Appointments, 1962–64; Censor Theologiae, Christ Church, 1972–75, 1978–80; Member, Convocation of Canterbury, and Church Assembly/General Synod of C of E, 1957–75, 1978–80. First recipient, Sir Sigmund Sternberg Award, 1979. *Publications:* (part translated) Martin Buber's Hasidism, 1948; (translated) Martin Buber's The Prophetic Faith, 1949; (contrib.) Oxford Dictionary of the Christian Church, 1957; Journey of a Lifetime, 1962; (contrib.) The Mission of Israel, 1963. *Recreations:* music, lawn tennis, swimming, travel. *Address:* 199 Divinity Road, Oxford OX4 1LS. *T:* Oxford (0865) 247301.

Died 25 March 1993.

WOLFSON, Sir Isaac, 1st Bt *cr* 1962, of St Marylebone, Co. of London; FRS 1963; Hon. Fellow: Weizmann Institute of Science, Israel; St Edmund Hall, Oxford; Jews' College; Lady Margaret Hall, Oxford; Founder Fellow, Wolfson College, Oxford; Hon. Life President, The Great Universal Stores Ltd, since 1987 (formerly Joint Chairman); *b* 17 Sept. 1897; *s* of Solomon Wolfson, JP, Glasgow, and Naelia Williamovsky; *m* 1926, Edith Specterman (*d* 1981); one *s*. *Educ:* Queen's Park School, Glasgow. Joined The Great Universal Stores Ltd, 1932. Member, Worshipful Company of Pattenmakers; Member, Grand Council, Cancer Research Campaign; Hon. Pres., Weizmann Institute of Science Foundation; Trustee, Religious Centre, Jerusalem; Patron, Royal College of Surgeons; Founder, and Pres., 1975– (formerly Chm.), and Trustee, Wolfson Foundation which was created in 1955 for the advancement of health, education and youth activities. Fellow, Royal Postgrad. Med. Sch., 1972; Hon. FRCP 1959; Hon. FRCS 1969; Hon. FRCPSGlas. Hon. DCL Oxford, 1963; Hon. LLD: London, 1958; Glasgow,

1963; Cambridge, 1966; Manchester, 1967; Strathclyde, 1969; Brandeis Univ., US 1969; Nottingham, 1971; Hon. PhD Jerusalem, 1970. Einstein Award, US, 1967; Herbert Lehmann Award, US, 1968. Freeman, City of Glasgow, 1971. *Heir: s* Baron Wolfson (Life Peer) [*b* 11 Nov. 1927; *m* 1949, Ruth, *d* of Ernest A. Sterling; four *d*].
Died 20 June 1991.

WOLSELEY, Sir Garnet, 12th Bt, *cr* 1745 (Ire.), of Mount Wolseley, Co. Carlow; emigrated to Ontario, Canada, 1951; *b* 27 May 1915; *s* of late Richard Bingham Wolseley and 2nd wife, Mary Alexandra, *d* of John Edward Read; *S* kinsman (Rev. Sir William Augustus Wolseley), 1950; *m* 1950, Lillian Mary, *d* of late William Bertram Ellison, Wallasey. *Educ:* New Brighton Secondary Sch. Served War of 1939–45, Northants Regt, Madagascar, Sicily, Italy and Germany. Boot Repairer Manager, 1946. *Heir: kinsman* James Douglas Wolseley [*b* 17 Sept. 1937; *m* 1st, 1965, Patricia Lynn (marr. diss. 1971), *d* of William R. Hunter; 2nd, 1984, Mary Anne, *d* of Thomas G. Brown]. *Address:* 73 Dorothy Street, Brantford, Ontario, Canada. *T:* 753–7957.
Died 3 Oct. 1991.

WOLTERS, Very Rev. Conrad Clifton; Chaplain to the Society of St Margaret, 1976–85; Provost Emeritus of Newcastle, since 1976; *b* 3 April 1909; *e s* of Frederick Charles and Gertrude Elizabeth Wolters; *m* 1937, Joyce Cunnold; one *s. Educ:* privately; London College of Divinity; St John's College, Durham. ALCD 1932; LTh 1932; BA 1933; MA 1936. Deacon, 1933; priest, 1934; Curate: Christ Church, Gipsy Hill, SE19, 1933–37; Christ Church, Beckenham, 1937–41; Vicar, St Luke's, Wimbledon Park, 1941–49; Rector, Sanderstead, Surrey, 1949–59; Canon of Newcastle, 1959–62; Vicar of Newcastle and Provost of the Cathedral, 1962–76. *Publications:* (ed) Cloud of Unknowing, 1960; (ed) Revelations of Divine Love, 1966; (ed) The Fire of Love, 1971; (ed) The Cloud of Unknowing and Other Works, 1978; (ed) A Study of Wisdom, 1980. *Address:* Flat 1, 7 Chatsworth Gardens, Eastbourne, Sussex BN20 7JP. *T:* Eastbourne (0323) 648871.
Died 7 Feb. 1991.

WONTNER, Sir Hugh (Walter Kingwell), GBE 1974; Kt 1972; CVO 1969 (MVO 1950); President, The Savoy Hotel plc, since 1990; Chairman: Claridge's and the Berkeley Hotels, London, since 1948; Lancaster Hotel, Paris, since 1973; Chairman and Managing Director, The Savoy Theatre, since 1948; Director, Forest Mere, since 1977; Clerk of the Royal Kitchens, since 1953, and a Catering Adviser in the Royal Household, since 1938; Underwriting Member of Lloyd's, since 1937; *b* 22 Oct. 1908; *er s* of Arthur Wontner, actor-manager, and Rosecleer Alice Amelia Blanche Kingwell; *m* 1936, Catherine, *o d* of Lieut T. W. Irvin, Gordon Highlanders (*d* of wounds, France, 1916); two *s* one *d. Educ:* Oundle and in France. On staff of London Chamber of Commerce, 1927–33; Asst Sec., Home Cttee, Associated Chambers of Commerce of India and Ceylon, 1930–31; Sec., London Cttee, Burma Chamber of Commerce, 1931; Gen. Sec., Hotels and Restaurants Assoc. of Great Britain, 1933–38; Asst to Sir George Reeves-Smith at The Savoy, 1938–41; Director, The Savoy Hotel Ltd, 1940–88, Man. Dir, 1941–79, Chm., 1948–84. Chm., Eurocard International, 1964–78. Sec., Coronation Accommodation Cttee, 1936–37, Chm., 1953; a British delegate, Internat. Hotel Alliance, 1933–38; Pres., Internat. Hotel Assoc., 1961–64, Mem. of Honour, 1965–. Chairman: Exec. Cttee, British Hotels and Restaurants Assoc., 1957–60 (Vice-Chm., 1952–57); Vice-Chm. of Council, 1961–68; Chm., London Div., 1949–51); Chm. of Council, British Hotels, Restaurants and Caterers Assoc., 1969–73; London Hotels Information Service, 1952–56; Working Party, Owners of Historic Houses open to the public, 1965–66; Historic Houses Cttee, BTA, 1966–77. Member: Historic Buildings

Council, 1968–73; British Heritage Cttee, 1977–; Heritage of London Trust, 1980–; Barbican Centre Cttee, 1979–84; Board of BTA, 1950–69; LCC Consultative Cttee, Hotel and Restaurant Technical School, 1933–38; Court of Assistants, Irish Soc., 1967–68, 1971–73; Vis. Cttee, Holloway Prison, 1963–68. Governor: University Coll. Hosp., 1945–53 (Chm., Nutrition Cttee, 1945–52); Christ's Hosp., 1963. Trustee: College of Arms Trust; Southwark Cathedral Develt Trust; D'Oyly Carte Opera Trust; Morden Coll., Blackheath; Chm., Temple Bar Trustees; Vice Pres., The Pilgrims. Liveryman: Worshipful Co. of Feltmakers, 1934– (Master, 1962–63 and 1973–74); Clockmakers' Co., 1967– (Warden, 1971–; Master, 1975–76); Hon. Liveryman: Worshipful Co. of Launderers, 1970; Plaisterers, 1975; Chancellor, The City Univ., 1973–74; one of HM Lieuts and a JP for the City of London, 1963–80, Chief Magistrate, 1973–74; Freeman of the City, 1934; Alderman for Broad Street Ward, 1963–79; Sheriff, 1970–71; Lord Mayor of London, 1973–74. Hon. Citizen, St Emilion, 1974; Freeman of the Seychelles, 1974. Order of Cisneros, Spain, 1964; Officer, L'Etoile Equatoriale (Gabon), 1970; Médaille de Vermeil, City of Paris, 1972; Ordre de l'Etoile Civique, 1972; Officier du Mérite Agricole (France), 1973; Comdr, Nat. Order of the Leopard, Zaire, 1974; Knight Comdr, Order of the Dannebrog (Denmark), 1974; Order of the Crown of Malaysia, 1974; Knight Comdr, Royal Swedish Order of the Polar Star, 1980. KStJ 1973 (OStJ 1971). Hon. DLitt 1973. *Recreations:* genealogy, acting. *Address:* 1 Savoy Hill, WC2. *T:* 071–836 1533. *Clubs:* Garrick, City Livery.
Died 25 Nov. 1992.

WOOD, Alfred Arden, CBE 1988; TD 1960; FRIBA, FRTPI; architect and town planner; *b* 8 Sept. 1926; *s* of late Henry Arden Wood, AMIMechE, and Victoria Wood (*née* Holt); *m* 1957, Dorinda Rae (*née* Hartley) (*d* 1990); one *s* one *d. Educ:* Ashville Coll., Harrogate; Harrogate Grammar Sch.; Hertford Coll., Oxford; Leeds Schs of Architecture and Town Planning. Dip. and Dip. with Dist. Served 8th Royal Tank Regt, Leeds Rifles TA and Westminster Dragoons TA, 1944–62. Architect, Stockholm CC, Harlow New Town, W Riding CC, Leeds CC, Glasgow Corp., partner in private practice, 1951–65; City Planning Officer, Norwich, 1965–72; County Planner, Hereford and Worcester CC, 1972–73; County Architect and Planner, W Midlands CC, 1973–84; Head of Area Conservation, English Heritage, 1984–87. Buildings and other works include: housing in Harlow, Leeds and Glasgow, 1953–65; conservation, 1965–72, and first pedestrianisation in UK, Norwich, 1967; conservation, Jewellry Quarter, Birmingham, 1980–84; Birmingham Internat. Airport, 1984. Member: Historic Buildings Council for England, 1969–84; RTPI Council, 1969–75; UK Exec. European Architectural Heritage Year, 1975 (Chm., Heritage Grants Cttee); Preservation Policy Gp, 1967–70; Environmental Bd, 1975–78; Bd, Sheffield Develt Corp., 1990–94 (Chm., Design Panel, 1989–94); Comr, Indep. Transport Commn, 1972–74. Prof., Centre for the Conservation of Historic Towns and Bldgs, Katholieke Univ., Leuven, Belgium, ex Coll. of Europe, Bruges, 1976–86; External Examiner at several univs; adviser, at various times, Council of Europe, Strasbourg, and OECD, Paris; various lecture tours and conf. addresses in Europe and N America. Civic Trust awards, 1969, 1971. *Publications:* contributions to jls of learned societies. *Recreations:* cities, buildings, travel, trams, trains, music, many wines. *Address:* The Hall Barn, Dunley, near Stourport-on-Severn, Worcestershire DY13 0TX.
Died 8 Dec. 1995.

WOOD, Prof. Edward James; Professor of Latin, University of Leeds, 1938–67, Professor Emeritus, 1967; Pro-Vice-Chancellor, University of Leeds, 1957–59; *b* 3 Sept. 1902; *s* of James M. A. Wood, Advocate in

Aberdeen; *m* 1933, Marion Grace Chorley; one *s* one *d*.
Educ: Aberdeen Grammar School; Aberdeen University;
Trinity College, Cambridge. Lectr in Classics, Manchester
University, 1928; Professor of Latin, Aberystwyth, 1932.
Publications: contributions to: Classical Review, Gnomon.
Address: The Towans, Berrow Road, Burnham-on-Sea,
Somerset TA8 2EZ. *T:* Burnham-on-Sea (0278) 782762.
Died 6 May 1993.

WOOD, Sir Henry (Peart), Kt 1967; CBE 1960; Principal,
Jordanhill College of Education, Glasgow, 1949–71,
retired; *b* 30 Nov. 1908; *s* of T. M. Wood, Bedlington,
Northumberland; *m* 1937, Isobel Mary, *d* of W. F. Stamp,
Carbis Bay, Cornwall; one *s* two *d. Educ:* Morpeth
Grammar Sch.; Durham University. BSc 1930, MSc 1934,
Durham; MA 1938, MEd 1941, Manchester. Lecturer,
Manchester University, 1937–44; Jordanhill College of
Education: Principal Lecturer, 1944–46; Vice-Principal,
1947–49. Part-time Lectr, Glasgow Univ., 1972–78;
Assessor in Educn, Strathclyde Univ., 1972–82; Vis. Prof.
in Educn, Strathclyde Univ., 1978–84. Hon. LLD:
Glasgow, 1972; Strathclyde, 1982. *Address:* 15a
Hughenden Court, Hughenden Road, Glasgow G12 9XP.
T: 041–334 3647.   *Died 22 March 1994.*

WOOD, Robert Eric, CBE 1972; Director, City of Leicester
Polytechnic, 1969–73; *b* 6 May 1909; *e s* of Robert and
Emma Wood; *m* 1935, Beatrice May Skinner (*d* 1983);
one *s* one *d. Educ:* Birkenhead Inst.; Liverpool Univ. BSc
1st cl. hons, MSc; FInstP. Lectr and Demonstrator,
Liverpool Univ., 1930; Lecturer: Borough Road Trng
Coll., 1931; Kingston Techn. Coll., 1934; Woolwich
Polytechnic, 1939; Head of Physics Dept, Wigan Techn.
Coll., 1942; Principal: Grimsby Techn. Coll., 1947;
Leicester Regional Coll. of Technology, 1953. Assoc. of
Principals of Technical Instns: Hon. Sec., 1960–65; Pres.,
1965–66; Chm., Interim Cttee of Polytechnic Directors,
1969–70; Mem. Council, CNAA, 1964–70; Mem., Council
for Techn. Educn and Trng in Overseas Countries,
1962–66; Vice-Chm., Nat. Adv. Council on Educn for
Industry and Commerce, 1967–72. Hon. FCFI.
Died 31 Aug. 1995.

WOOD, Sam, MSc; Director of Statistics and Business
Research, Post Office, 1965–72, retired; *b* 10 Oct. 1911;
m 1940, Lucy Greenhalgh Whittaker; two *d. Educ:*
Glossop Grammar School, Derbyshire; University of
Manchester. Gaskell Open Scholarship, Derbyshire Major
Scholarship, 1929; BSc (1st cl. Hons) Maths; Bishop
Harvey Goodwin Research Scholarship, 1932; MSc 1933.
Civil Service: GPO, 1933–34; National Assistance Board,
1934–43; Min. of Aircraft Production, 1943–46; Treasury,
1946–50; GPO: Statistician, 1950; Chief Statistician,
1954. *Publications:* articles in Jl of Inst. of Statisticians,
British Jl of Industrial Relations. *Address:* Flat 1, The
Rookery, East Avenue, Benton, Newcastle upon Tyne
NE12 9PH.   *Died 29 Jan. 1992.*

WOODCOCK, Dr George, FRGS; Editor, Canadian
Literature, 1959–77; author; *b* 8 May 1912; *s* of Samuel
Arthur Woodcock and Margaret Gertrude Woodcock (*née*
Lewis); *m* 1949, Ingeborg Hedwig Elisabeth Linzer. *Educ:*
Sir William Borlase's Sch., Marlow. Editor, Now, London,
1940–47; freelance writer, 1947–54; Lectr in English,
Univ. of Washington, 1954–56; Lectr, Asst Prof. and
finally Associate Prof. of English, Univ. of British
Columbia, 1956–63; Lectr in Asian Studies, Univ. of
British Columbia, 1966–67. At the same time continued
writing books and talks; also plays and documentaries for
Canadian Broadcasting Corporation (prepared a series of
nine documentary films on South Pacific, 1972–73).
Freeman, City of Vancouver, 1994. Hon. LLD: Victoria,
1967; Winnipeg, 1975; Hon. DLitt: Sir George Williams
Univ., 1970; Univ. of Ottawa, 1974; Univ. of British
Columbia, 1977. John Simon Guggenheim Fellow, 1950;

Canadian Govt Overseas Fellow, 1957; Canada Council:
Killam Fellow, 1970; Senior Arts Fellow, 1975. Governor-
General's Award for Non-Fiction, 1967; Molson Prize,
1973; UBC Medal for Popular Biography, 1973 and 1976.
FRSC 1968, FRGS 1971. *Publications:* William Godwin,
1946; The Anarchist Prince, 1950; Proudhon, 1956; To
the City of the Dead, 1956; Selected Poems, 1967;
Anarchism, 1962; Faces of India, 1964; The Greeks in
India, 1966; The Crystal Spirit: a study of George Orwell,
1966; Canada and the Canadians, 1970; Dawn and the
Darkest Hour, 1971; Gandhi, 1971; Rejection of Politics,
1972; Herbert Read, 1972; Who Killed the British Empire?,
1974; Gabriel Dumont, 1975; Notes on Visitations, 1975;
South Sea Journey, 1976; Peoples of the Coast, 1977;
Thomas Merton, Monk and Poet, 1978; Two Plays, 1978;
The Canadians, 1980; The World of Canadian Writing,
1980; The George Woodcock Reader, 1980; The Mountain
Road, 1981; Confederation Betrayed, 1981; Taking It to
the Letter, 1981; Letter to the Past, 1982; Collected Poems,
1983; British Columbia: a celebration, 1983; Orwell's
Message, 1984; Strange Bedfellows, 1985; The Walls of
India, 1985; The University of British Columbia, 1986;
Northern Spring, 1987; Beyond the Blue Mountains, 1987;
The Social History of Canada, 1988; The Caves in the
Desert, 1988; The Marvellous Century, 1988; Powers of
Observation, 1989; A History of British Columbia, 1990;
Tolstoy at Yasnaya Polyana, 1991; The Monk and his
Message, 1992; Anarchism and Anarchists, 1992; Letter
from the Khyber Pass, 1993; George Woodcock on
Canadian Poetry, 1993; George Woodcock on Canadian
Fiction, 1993; The Cherry Tree on Cherry Street (poems),
1994; Walking in the Valley, 1994; also many articles.
Recreation: travel. *Address:* 6429 McCleery Street,
Vancouver, BC V6N 1G5, Canada. *T:* (604) 2669393.
Club: Faculty (Vancouver).   *Died 28 Jan. 1995.*

WOODD WALKER, Geoffrey Basil, FRCS; retired as a
Consultant Surgeon (West London Hospital, 1930–65); *b*
9 June 1900; *s* of Basil Woodd Walker, MD, and Margaret
Jane Routledge; *m* 1932, Ulla Troili; two *s. Educ:* Rugby
Sch.; King's Coll., Cambridge; St Mary's Hospital. MA
Cambridge; MB, BCh; MRCS, LRCP; FRCS 1928.
Recreation: zoology (FZS). *Address:* 33 Lexden Road,
Colchester, Essex CO3 3PX. *Club:* Athenæum.
Died 28 May 1991.

**WOODFORD, Colin Godwin Patrick; His Honour Judge
Woodford;** a Circuit Judge, since 1991; *b* 30 Jan. 1934; *s*
of late Reginald Godwin Woodford and of Cecilia Mary
Agnes (*née* Green); *m* 1st, 1955, Julia Mary Howe (marr.
diss. 1976); two *s* one *d*; 2nd, 1978, Jane Ellen Woolston;
one *d. Educ:* St Joseph's Coll., Beulah Hill, W Norwood;
St Joseph's Coll., Ipswich; University Coll. London
(LLB). Baker and confectioner, 1949–52; RAF, 1952–54;
local govt Treasurer's Dept, 1954; Constable to Chief
Inspector, Essex Constabulary, 1954–72; called to the Bar,
Middle Temple, 1972; Barrister, London and E Anglia,
1972–91. *Recreations:* computer studies, sailing, reading.
Address: The Law Courts, Bishopsgate, Norwich NR3
1CR.   *Died 1 Oct. 1993.*

WOODHAMS, Ven. Brian Watson; Archdeacon of
Newark, 1965–79, Archdeacon Emeritus since 1980; Hon.
Canon of Southwell Minister, 1960–79; Rector of Staunton
with Flawborough and Kilvington, 1971–79; *b* 16 Jan.
1911; *s* of Herbert and Florence Osmond Woodhams; *m*
1941, Vera Charlotte White; one *s. Educ:* Dover Coll.;
Oak Hill Theological Coll.; St John's Coll., University of
Durham. LTh 1934, BA 1936, Durham. Deacon, 1936;
priest, 1937; Curate: St Mary Magdalene, Holloway,
1936–39; St James-the-Less, Bethnal Green, 1939–41;
Christ Church, New Malden, i/c of St John, New Malden,
1941–43; Vicar: St Mark, Poplar, 1943–45; St James-the-
Less, Bethnal Green, 1945–50; St Jude's, Mapperley,

Nottingham, 1950–65; Farndon with Thorpe-by-Newark, 1965–71. Proctor in York Convocation, 1955–65. Chairman, Southwell Diocesan Board of Women's Work, 1966–79. Bishop's Hon. Chaplain to Retired Clergy, dio. of Southwell, 1980–. *Recreations:* children's and refugee work, joys and problems of retirement, interested in sport (local FA football referee). *Address:* 2 Lunn Lane, Collingham, Newark, Notts NG23 7LP. *T:* Newark (0636) 892207.   *Died 25 Aug. 1992.*

WOODHEAD, (Susan) Jane, (Mrs D. C. Woodhead); Building Societies Ombudsman, since 1991; *b* 6 March 1954; *d* of John Darroll Angus and Greta Geraldine Angus; *m* 1978, Donald Christopher Woodhead; two *d* (one *s* decd). *Educ:* Beaconsfield Girls' High Sch.; Bristol Univ. (LLB). Admitted as solicitor, 1978. Asst solicitor, private practice, 1980–82; Legal Asst, Insurance Ombudsman Bureau, 1983–89; Sen. Legal Officer, Office of Building Socs Ombudsman, 1989–91. *Publications:* contrib. legal periodicals. *Recreations:* reading, France. *Address:* Grosvenor Gardens House, 35–37 Grosvenor Gardens, SW1X 7AW. *T:* 071–931 0044.
                    Died 21 May 1993.

WOODHOUSE, Ven. Samuel Mostyn Forbes; Archdeacon of London and Canon Residentiary of St Paul's, 1967–78, Archdeacon Emeritus and Canon Emeritus, 1978; Archdeacon to: Retired Clergy, Bath and Wells, since 1978; Retired Clergy Association, since 1980; *b* 28 April 1912; *s* of Rev. Major James D. F. Woodhouse, DSO, and Elsie Noel Woodhouse, Water, Manaton, Devon; *m* 1939, Patricia Daniel; two *s* one *d. Educ:* Shrewsbury; Christ Church, Oxford; Wells Theological Coll. BA 1934; MA 1942. Deacon, 1936, Priest, 1937, Diocese of Blackburn; Curate, Lancaster Priory, 1936–39. Chaplain to the Forces (Army), 1939–45 (despatches thrice). Vicar, Holy Trinity, South Shore, Blackpool, 1945–49; Vicar of Leominster, 1949–57; Rural Dean of Leominster, 1956–57; Rector of Bristol City Parish Church (St Stephen's), 1957–67. *Recreations:* painting, architecture. *Address:* Under Copse Cottage, Redhill, Wrington, Bristol BS18 7SH. *T:* Wrington (01934) 862711. *Clubs:* Leander; Vincent's (Oxford).
                    Died 13 Oct. 1995.

WOODRUFF, Prof. Alan Waller, CMG 1978; OBE 1989; Professor of Medicine, University of Juba, Sudan, since 1981; Wellcome Professor of Clinical Tropical Medicine, London School of Hygiene and Tropical Medicine, 1952–81; Hon. Consultant in Tropical Diseases to: the Army, 1956–81; British Airways, 1962–89; *b* 27 June 1916; *s* of late William Henry Woodruff, Sunderland, and Mary Margaret Woodruff; *m* 1946, Mercia Helen, *d* of late Leonard Frederick Arnold, Dorking, and Amy Elizabeth Arnold; two *s* one *d. Educ:* Bede Collegiate Sch., Sunderland; Durham Univ. MB, BS 1939, MD 1941, Durham; DTM&H England, 1946; PhD London, 1952; FRCP 1953; FRCPE 1960. House Physician and House Surgeon, Royal Victoria Infirmary, Newcastle upon Tyne, 1939–40; MO and Med. Specialist, RAFVR, 1940–46; Med. Registrar, Royal Victoria Infirmary, Newcastle upon Tyne, 1946–48; Sen. Lectr in Clinical Tropical Medicine, London Sch. of Hygiene and Trop. Medicine, 1948–52; First Asst, 1948–52, Physician, 1952–81, Hosp. for Tropical Diseases, University Coll. Hosp., London; Lectr in Tropical Medicine, Royal Free Hosp. Sch. of Medicine, 1952–81; William Julius Mickle Fellow, Univ. of London, 1959. Lectures: Goulstonian, RCP, 1954; Lettsomian, Med. Soc. of London, 1969; Watson-Smith, RCP, 1970; Halliburton Hume, Newcastle-upon-Tyne, 1981. Orator, Reading Pathological Soc., 1976. Member: WHO Expert Adv. Panel on Parasitic Diseases, 1963–88; Med. Cttee of Overseas Develt Administration. Visiting Professor at Universities: Alexandria, 1963; Ain Shams, Cairo, 1964;

Baghdad, 1966, 1968, 1971, 1974; Mosul, 1977–79; Basrah, 1973–74; Makerere, 1973; Khartoum, 1974, 1978; Benghazi, 1976–80. Mem., Assoc. of Physicians of GB and Ireland; President: Durham Univ. Soc., 1963–73; Royal Soc. of Tropical Medicine and Hygiene, 1973–75; Medical Soc. of London, 1975–76; Section of History of Medicine, Royal Soc. Med., 1977–79. Hon. Mem., Burma Med. Assoc., 1966; Hon. Mem., Société de Pathologie Exotique, Paris; Hon. Associate Mem., Soc. Belge de Médecine Tropicale, 1965; Hon. Mem., Brazilian Soc. of Tropical Medicine; Hon. Fellow, Canadian Soc. of Tropical Medicine and International Health, 1976. Katherine Bishop Harman Prize, BMA, 1951; Cullen Prize, RCPE, 1982. Hon. RE 1979. Gold Medal of Univ. of Pernambuco, Brazil, 1980. *Publications:* (with S. Bell) A Synopsis of Infectious and Tropical Diseases, 1968, (with S. G. Wright) 3rd edn 1987; (ed) Alimentary and Haematological Aspects of Tropical Disease, 1970; (ed) Medicine in the Tropics, 1974, 2nd edn 1984; sections in: Paediatrics for the Practitioner (ed Gaisford and Lightwood); Price's Textbook of Medicine; contribs to BMJ, Lancet, Trans Royal Soc. Trop. Medicine and Hygiene, W African Med. Jl, E African Med. Jl, Newcastle Med. Jl, Practitioner, Clinical Science, Proc. Nutrition Soc., etc. *Recreation:* engraving. *Address:* 122 Ferndene Road, SE24 0BA. *T:* 071–274 3578; University of Juba, PO Box 82, Juba, Sudan. *Clubs:* Athenæum; Sunderland (Sunderland).   *Died 12 Oct. 1992.*

WOODS, Most Rev. Frank, KBE 1972; Archbishop of Melbourne, 1957–77; Primate of Australia, 1971–77; *b* 6 April 1907; *s* of late Rt Rev. E. S. Woods, DD, Bishop of Lichfield; *m* 1936, Jean Margaret Sprules; two *s* two *d. Educ:* Marlborough; Trinity Coll., Cambridge. Deacon, 1931; priest, 1932; Curate of Portsea Parish Church, 1932–33; Chaplain, Trinity Coll., Cambridge, 1933–36; Vice-Principal, Wells Theological Coll., 1936–39; Chaplain to the Forces, 1939–45; Vicar of Huddersfield, 1945–52; Suffragan Bishop of Middleton, 1952–57. Proctor in Convocation, 1946–51; Chaplain to the King, 1951–52; Chaplain, Victoria Order of St John, 1962. Hon. Fellow, Trinity Coll., Melbourne, 1981. Hon. DD Lambeth, 1957; Hon. LLD Monash, 1979. *Recreation:* walking. *Address:* 18 Victoria Road, Camberwell, Vic 3124, Australia. *Clubs:* Melbourne, Australian (Melbourne).   *Died 29 Nov. 1992.*

WOODWARD, Geoffrey Royston; Under-Secretary, Ministry of Agriculture, Fisheries and Food, 1970–81; *b* 26 June 1921; *o s* of James Edward Woodward and Gwendolen May (*née* Dodridge); *m* 1st, 1947, Marjorie Beatrice Bishop (marr. diss. 1974); three *s*; 2nd, 1974, Doreen Parker, MBE. *Educ:* Bradford Grammar Sch. Entered Civil Service, 1938; joined Min. of Agriculture and Fisheries, 1948. Served RAFVR, 1941–46 (Flt-Lt, despatches). *Recreation:* armchair archaeology. *Address:* 1 Long Down, Petersfield, Hants GU31 4PD. *Club:* Reform.   *Died 7 Sept. 1991.*

WOOTTON, Gordon Henry; His Honour Judge Wootton; a Circuit Judge, since 1980; *b* 23 April 1927; *s* of William Henry Wootton and Winifred Beatrice Wootton; *m* 1st, 1953, Camilla Bowes (marr. diss. 1979); two *s*; 2nd, 1979, Eileen Mary North. *Educ:* Queen's Univ., Belfast (LLB Hons). Captain, RE, 1947. Called to the Bar, Middle Temple, 1952; Resident Magistrate, Uganda, 1954–62; a Recorder of the Crown Court, 1975–80. *Address:* Beech-Hurst, Abbotswood, Greenhill, Evesham, Worcs WR11 4NS.   *Died 29 Oct. 1991.*

WORKMAN, Robert Little, CB 1974; Under-Secretary, HM Treasury, 1967–74; *b* 30 Oct. 1914; *s* of late Robert Workman and Jesse Little; *m* 1940, Gladys Munroe Foord; two *d. Educ:* Sedbergh Sch.; Clare Coll., Cambridge. Economist, Export Credits Guarantee Dept, 1938–49; HM

Treasury: Principal, 1949–59; Asst Secretary, 1959–66. Member, St Pancras Borough Council, 1945–49. *Recreations:* building, the visual arts. *Address:* Flatts Farm, Hawstead, Bury St Edmunds, Suffolk IP29 5NW. *T:* Sicklesmere (0284) 386497.
Died 12 March 1994.

WORMALD, Maj.-Gen. Derrick Bruce, DSO 1944; MC 1940, Bar 1945; Director-General of Fighting Vehicles and Engineer Equipment, Ministry of Defence, 1966–70, retired; *b* 28 April 1916; 2nd *s* of late Arthur and Veronica Wormald; *m* 1953, Betty Craddock (*d* 1993); two *d. Educ:* Bryanston Sch.; RMA Sandhurst. Commnd into 13/18 Royal Hussars (QMO), 1936; served in India, 1936–38, BEF, 1939–40 and BLA, 1944–45; Comd, 25th Dragoons, India, 1945–47; Staff Coll., Quetta, 1947; War Office, 1948–50; Comdr, 1st Armoured Car Regt of Arab Legion, 1951–52; Comdr Arab Legion Armoured Corps, 1953–54; jssc 1955; GSO1, 11th Armoured Div., 1956; Comd, 3rd The King's Own Hussars, 1956, and The Queen's Own Hussars, 1958; Comdr, Aden Protectorate Levies, 1959–61; Comdr, Salisbury Plain Sub District, 1962–65. Col, 13th/18th Royal Hussars (QMO), 1974–79. Order of El Istiqlal (Jordan), 1953. *Recreations:* shooting, fishing, sailing. *Address:* Ballards, Wickham Bishops, Essex CM8 3JJ. *T:* Maldon (0621) 891218. *Club:* Cavalry and Guards.
Died 27 March 1994.

WORMALD, Dame Ethel (May), DBE 1968; DL; *b* 19 Nov. 1901; *d* of late John Robert Robinson, journalist, Newcastle upon Tyne; *m* 1923, Stanley Wormald, MA, MEd, BSc (*d* 1951); two *s. Educ:* Whitley Bay High Sch.; Leeds Univ. (BA, DipEd). Liverpool City Councillor, 1953–67; Lord Mayor of Liverpool, 1967–68. President, Assoc. of Education Cttees, 1961–62; Chairman, Liverpool Education Cttee, 1955–61, and 1963–67. JP Liverpool, 1948–71; DL Lancaster, 1970, Merseyside, 1974. *Address:* 17 Rhes James, Bethesda, Gwynedd LL57 3RA. *T:* Bethesda (0248) 601800.
Died 23 Feb. 1993.

WÖRNER, Dr Manfred; Secretary-General of NATO, since 1988; *b* Stuttgart, 24 Sept. 1934; *s* of Carl Wörner; *m* 1982, Elfriede (*née* Reinsch); one *s* of previous marriage. *Educ:* Univ. of Heidelberg; Univ. of Paris; Univ. of Munich (Dr jur). Lawyer, 1957. Joined CDU, 1956; CDU State Parly Advr, Baden Württemberg, 1962–64; Mem., Bundestag, 1965–88; Minister of Defence, FRG, 1982–88. Dep. Chm., CDU Parly Gp, 1969–71; CDU/CSU Bundestag Parliamentary Party: Chm., Defence Working Gp, 1972–76; Dep. Chm., 1980–82; Chm., Bundestag Defence Cttee, 1976–80. *Address:* NATO Headquarters, Brussels 1110, Belgium.
Died 13 Aug. 1994.

WORRALL, Alfred Stanley, CBE 1983 (OBE 1975); *b* 28 Jan. 1912; *s* of Rev. Sidney A. Worrall and Margaret Worrall (*née* White); *m* 1936, Mary Frances Marshall; one *s* two *d* (and one *s* decd). *Educ:* King Edward's Sch., Bath; St Catharine's Coll., Cambridge (Schol.; MA); BD London. Teaching posts at St George's Sch., Bristol, 1935–38, Leeds Grammar Sch., 1938–49; war service in Non-combatant Corps (bomb disposal) and coal mining, 1941–46; Headmaster: Rock Ferry High Sch., 1949–57; Sir Thomas Rich's Sch., 1957–61; Methodist Coll., Belfast, 1961–74, retired. Member, Methodist Conference, 1955, 1959, 1961–64, also of the Conf. in Ireland, 1966–83. Pres., Ulster Headmasters' Assoc., 1966–68; Chairman: BBC Religious Adv. Council, N Ireland, 1968–73; Arts Council of N Ire., 1974–82; New Ulster Movement, 1974–79; Chm. of Governors, Stranmillis Coll. of Educn, 1974–83; Mem., Radio Telefis Eireann Authority, Dublin, 1979–83; Chm., Liby and Inf. Services Council, NI, 1982–83. Hon. Life Mem., SHA, 1980. Hon. LLD QUB, 1974. *Publications:* (with Cahal B. Daly) Ballymascanlon: a venture in Irish inter-church dialogue,

1978; (with Eric Gallagher) Christians in Ulster 1968–80, 1982; (trans.) Origène, by H. Crouzel, 1989. *Recreations:* travel, enjoyment of the arts. *Address:* 27 Selly Park Road, Birmingham B29 7PH. *T:* 021–471 5140.
Died 15 Nov. 1991.

WORTH, George Arthur, MBE; JP; farmer and landowner; *b* 3 May 1907; *s* of late Arthur Hovendon Worth and Lizzie, *d* of George Thompson, Long Sutton, Lincs; *m* 1935, Janet Maitland, *d* of late Air Chief Marshal Sir A. M. Longmore, GCB, DSO; two *s* two *d. Educ:* Marlborough Coll.; Sidney Sussex Coll., Cambridge. Served War of 1939–45, RAF. JP Parts of Holland, Lincs, 1939; High Sheriff of Lincolnshire, 1948–49; DL Lincs, 1950–73. *Address:* 5 Church Lane, Manton, Oakham, Leics LE15 8SP.
Died 25 Aug. 1994.

WORTHINGTON, Air Vice-Marshal Sir Geoffrey (Luis), KBE 1960 (CBE 1945); CB 1957; idc; psa; Director-General of Equipment, Air Ministry, 1958–61, retired; *b* 26 April 1903; *s* of late Commander H. E. F. Worthington, RN; *m* 1931, Margaret Joan (*d* 1989), *d* of late Maj.-Gen. A. G. Stevenson, CB, CMG, DSO; two *s* one *d. Educ:* HMS Conway; Eastbourne Coll.; RAF Coll., Cranwell, 1921. BA Open 1988. Joined RAF, 1922; resigned 1924; re-joined, 1926, in Stores Branch; RAF Staff Coll., 1934; served War of 1939–45 (despatches, CBE): HQ Maintenance Comd, 1939–43; Air Cdre, 1943; HQ AEAF, 1944; SHAEF, 1944–45; Air Comd, Far East, 1945–47; Director of Equipment B, Air Ministry, 1948–49; idc 1950; Director of Equipment D, Air Ministry, 1951–53; AOC No 42 Group, Maintenance Comd, 1954–55; Air Vice-Marshal, 1956; AOC No 40 Group, 1955–58. Comdr US Legion of Merit, 1955. *Address:* 30 Brickwall Close, Burnham-on-Crouch, Essex CM0 8HB. *T:* Maldon (0621) 782388. *Clubs:* Royal Air Force; Royal Burnham Yacht.
Died 28 April 1992.

WRAY, Martin Osterfield, CMG 1956; OBE 1954; *b* 14 June 1912; *s* of late C. N. O. Wray; *m* 1938, Lilian Joyce, *d* of late R. W. Playfair, Nairobi, Kenya; one *s* two *d. Educ:* St George's Sch., Harpenden; Wadham Coll., Oxford. Colonial Administrative Service in Uganda, 1935; Administrative Secretary, Zanzibar, 1949; Administrative Secretary to High Commissioner for Basutoland, the Bechuanaland Protectorate and Swaziland, 1952; Resident Commissioner, Bechuanaland Protectorate, 1955–59; Chief Secretary, Northern Rhodesia, 1959–62. *Address:* 4 Fairlane, The Sycamores, Shaftesbury, Dorset SP7 8RT. *Club:* Commonwealth Trust.
Died 2 Sept. 1991.

WREY, Sir (Castel Richard) Bourchier, 14th Bt, *cr* 1628, of Trebitch, Cornwall; *b* 27 March 1903; *s* of late Edward Castel Wrey (7th *s* of Sir Henry Bourchier Toke Wrey, 10th Bt) and Katharine Joan, *d* of Rev. John Dene; *S* uncle, 1948; *m* 1946, Alice Sybil, *d* of Dr George Lubke, Durban, S Africa; two *s. Educ:* Oundle. Served War of 1939–45: 2nd Lieut, RASC (Supp. Res.), France, 1939–40 (invalided); joined RN as ordinary seaman, 1940; Lieut, RNVR, 1942. *Heir: s* George Richard Bourchier Wrey [*b* 2 Oct. 1948; *m* 1981, Lady Caroline Lindesay-Bethune, *d* of 15th Earl of Lindsay; two *s* one *d*]. *Address:* Hollamoor Farm, Tawstock, Barnstaple, N Devon; 511 Currie Road, Durban, South Africa.
Died 16 Oct. 1991.

WRIGHT, Billy; *see* Wright, W. A.

WRIGHT, (Edmund) Kenneth, MA, FCA; chartered accountant; Partner in Dearden, Farrow, 1940–76; *b* 10 Dec. 1909; *s* of late William Ameers Wright and Martha Wright; *m* 1942, Daisy, *d* of late Rev. T. W. Thornton and Mrs Thornton; one *s* one *d. Educ:* preparatory schs in Southern Africa; Leighton Park Sch.; St Catharine's Coll., Cambridge (Engl. and Economics Triposes). ACA 1937, FCA 1945. London Ambulance Service, 1940–45. Chm., London and Dist Soc. of Chartered Accountants, 1957–58;

Mem. Council, Inst. of Chartered Accountants, 1959–76 (Dep. Pres., 1972, Pres., 1973). Governor, Leighton Park Sch., 1949–84. *Publications:* numerous books and papers on fiscal and accountancy subjects in national and professional press, including: The Development of an Accounting Practice, 1965; Professional Goodwill and Partnership Annuities, 1967; (with Andrew Tappin) Financial Planning for Individuals, 1970, 3rd edn 1979; (with Malcolm Penney and Derek Robinson) Capital Transfer Tax Planning, 1975, 4th edn 1984; studies in the postal history of Rhodesia incl. (with Alan Drysdall) The Oates Correspondence: postal history of Frank Oates' travels in Matabeleland and Zambesia 1873–1875, 1988. *Recreations:* gardening, philately, writing, walking. *Address:* Old Orchard, Sevenoaks Road, Ightham, Kent TN15 9AE. *T:* Borough Green (0732) 882374. *Club:* Reform. *Died 17 Feb. 1991.*

WRIGHT, Adm. Jerauld, DSM (US) (twice); Silver and Bronze Star Medals; Legion of Merit (US); USN retired; US Ambassador to Nationalist China, 1963–65; *b* Amherst, Mass, 4 June 1898; *s* of Gen. William Mason Wright and Marjorie R. (Jerauld) Wright; *m* 1938, Phyllis B. Thompson; one *s* one *d. Educ:* US Naval Academy. Ensign, USN, 1917; promoted through grades to Admiral, 1954; Executive Staff of US Naval Academy; operational staff appointments for N African, Sicilian and Italian landings; Mem., Gen. Mark Clark's Expedition to North Africa, 1942; Comd British Sub. HMS Seraph in evacuation of Gen. Henri Giraud from S France to Gibraltar, 1942; Staff Advr to Sir Andrew B. Cunningham, RN, in N African invasion, 1942; Staff Comdr, 8th Fleet in Sicily and Salerno landings, 1943; Comdr, USS Santa Fe, Pacific, 1943–44; Comdr Amphibious Group Five, 1944–45; Comdr Cruiser Div. Six, 1945; Asst Chief of Naval Operations for Fleet Readiness, 1945–48; Comdr Amphibious Force, US Atlantic Fleet, 1949–51; US Rep. NATO Standing Group, Washington, 1951–52; C-in-C US Naval Forces, E Atlantic and Medit., 1952–54; Supreme Allied Commander, Atlantic, and C-in-C Western Atlantic Area, NATO, 1954–60; C-in-C Atlantic (US Unified Command), and C-in-C Atlantic Fleet, 1954–60. Pres. US Naval Inst., 1959. Hon. doctorates in Laws and Science. Awarded foreign decorations. *Address:* (home) 4101 Cathedral Avenue NW, Apt 1001, Washington, DC 20016, USA. *Clubs:* Metropolitan, Alibi, Chevy Chase (Washington); Knickerbocker, Brook (New York). *Died 27 April 1995.*

WRIGHT, John Keith; JP; economic and financial consultant; Under Secretary, Overseas Development Administration, Foreign and Commonwealth Office (formerly Ministry of Overseas Development), 1971–84; *b* 30 May 1928; *s* of late James Wright and Elsie Wright, Walton-on-Thames, Surrey; *m* 1958, Thérèse Marie Claire, *er d* of René Aubenas, Paris. *Educ:* Tiffins' Sch.; King's Coll., Cambridge (Schol. 1949; MA Hist., 1950; Dipl. in Economics, 1954; Gladstone Memorial Prize, 1954); Yale Univ. OEEC, Paris: Economics and Statistics Directorate, 1951–52; Agriculture and Food Directorate, 1954–56; UK Atomic Energy Authority, 1956–61; Chief Scientific Adviser's staff, MoD, 1961–66 (UK Delegn to 18 Nation Disarmament Conf., 1962–64); Sen. Econ. Adviser, CRO, 1966–68; Head of Economists Dept and subseq. Dir (Economic), FCO, 1968–71. Chm., Economists' Panel, First Division Assoc., 1973–75. Dir, Sadlers Wells (Trading) Ltd, 1983–86. Mem., Social Security Appeals Tribunal, Central London, 1985–. Member: Court of Governors, London Sch. of Hygiene and Tropical Medicine, 1979–81; Councils, Queen Elizabeth Coll., 1982–85, King's Coll., 1984–93, Univ. of London (FKC 1992); Bd of Visitors, Canterbury Prison, 1987–. Trustee, Thomson Foundn, 1985–. JP Dover and East Kent, 1983. Exhibited at Royal Academy. *Publications:* articles on

economic subjects and on nuclear strategy. *Recreations:* economic and military history, music, amateur radio (G4IOL). *Address:* Laurie House, Airlie Gardens, W8 7AW; Bowling Corner, Sandwich, Kent CT13 9EX. *Clubs:* Athenæum, Beefsteak.

Died 24 Dec. 1994.

WRIGHT, Kenneth; *see* Wright, E. K.

WRIGHT, Very Rev. Ronald (William Vernon) Selby, CVO 1968; TD; DD; FRSE; FSA Scotland; JP; Minister Emeritus of the Canongate (The Kirk of Holyroodhouse), Edinburgh, and of Edinburgh Castle (Minister, 1936–77); Extra Chaplain to the Queen in Scotland, 1961–63 and since 1978 (Chaplain, 1963–78); Chaplain to The Queen's Body Guard for Scotland, Royal Company of Archers, 1973–93, Hon. Member, since 1994; *b* 12 June 1908; *s* of late Vernon O. Wright, ARCM, and late Anna Gilberta, *d* of Major R. E. Selby; unmarried. *Educ:* Edinburgh Academy; Melville Coll.; Edinburgh Univ. (MA; Hon. DD 1956); New Coll. Edinburgh. Warden, St Giles' Cathedral Boys' Club, 1927–36, and Canongate Boys' Club (formerly St Giles'), 1937–78. Cadet Officer, The Royal Scots, 1927–31; Student-Asst at St Giles' Cathedral, 1929–36; Asst Minister of Glasgow Cathedral, 1936; Warden of first Scottish Public Schools' and Clubs' Camp, 1938; Chaplain to 7th/9th (Highlanders) Bn The Royal Scots, 1938–42 (France, 1940), 1947–49; Senior Chaplain to the Forces: 52nd (Lowland) Div., 1942–43; Edinburgh Garrison, 1943; Middle East Forces, 1943–44; NE London, 1944; 10th Indian Div., CMF, 1944–45 (despatches); Hon. SCF, 1945–. Special Preacher, Oxford Univ., 1944; Select Preacher, Cambridge Univ., 1947; Visiting Preacher: Aberdeen Univ., 1946, 1953, 1965, 1973; St Andrews Univ., 1951, 1956, 1967, 1973; Glasgow Univ., 1955, 1973; Edinburgh Univ., 1959; Birmingham Univ., 1959; Hull Univ., 1967; Dundee Univ., 1973. Chaplain to, the Lord High Comr, 1959, and 1960. Conducted numerous series of religious broadcasts for BBC as Radio Padre, toured for War Office and BBC all Home Comds in 1942 and 1943 and MEF, 1943–44; toured transit camps etc in Italy, Austria, S Germany, etc, 1945; toured, for Church of Scotland: India, 1972; for HM Forces: Hong Kong 1973; Singapore, 1973. Moderator, Presbytery of Edinburgh, 1963; Moderator, Gen. Assembly of the Church of Scotland, 1972–73. Chm., Edinburgh and Leith Old People's Welfare Council, 1956–69; Extraordinary Dir, The Edinburgh Academy, 1973–; Hon. Church of Scotland Chaplain to: Fettes Coll., 1957–60, 1979–93 (Hon. Mem., 1994); Loretto Sch., 1960–84 (Hon. Old Lorettonian, 1976); Edinburgh Acad., 1966–73; Hon. Mem. Cargilfield Sch., 1985; Chaplain to: Governor of Edinburgh Castle, 1937–91; Merchant Co. of Edinburgh, 1973–82; ChStJ 1976; President: Scottish Church Soc., 1971–74; Scottish Assoc. of Boys Clubs; Vice-Pres., Old Edinburgh Club; Hon. Pres. Scottish Churches FA; Patron, Lothian Amateur FA. Mem. Edinburgh Educn Cttee, 1960–70. JP Edinburgh, 1963. Cross of St Mark, 1970. *Publications:* Asking Why (with A. W. Loos), 1939; The Average Man, 1942; Let's Ask the Padre, 1943; The Greater Victory, 1943; The Padre Presents, 1944; Small Talks, 1945; Whatever the Years, 1947; What Worries Me, 1950; Great Men, 1951; They Looked to Him, 1954; Our Club, 1954; The Kirk in the Canongate, 1956; The Selfsame Miracles, 1957; Our Club and Panmure House, 1958; Roses in December, 1960; The Seven Words, 1964; An Illustrated Guide to the Canongate, 1965; Take up God's Armour, 1967; The Seven Dwarfs, 1968; Haply I May Remember, 1970; In Christ We Are All One, 1972; Seven Sevens, 1977; Another Home, 1980; The Shadow on the Wall, 1992; *edited and contributed to:* Asking Them Questions, 1936; A Scottish Camper's Prayer Book, 1936; I Attack, 1937; Asking Them Questions-Second Series, 1938; Front Line Religion, 1941; Soldiers Also

Asked, 1943; Asking Them Questions-Third Series, 1950; Asking Them Questions (a Selection), 1953; The Beloved Captain: Essays by Donald Hankey, 1956; (with L. Menzies and R. A. Knox) St Margaret, Queen of Scotland, 1957; A Manual of Church Doctrine (with T. F. Torrance), 1960; Fathers of the Kirk, 1960; Asking Them Questions, a new series, 1972, 1973; The Wind on the Heath, 1994; contrib. to Chambers's Encyclopædia, DNB, etc. Editor, Scottish Forces' Magazine (quarterly), 1941–76. *Recreation:* after trying to run Boys' Clubs and Camps, 1927–78 and a busy parish, enjoying a busy retirement. *Address:* The Queen's House, 36 Moray Place, Edinburgh EH3 6BX. *T:* 0131–226 5566. *Clubs:* Athenæum; New (Hon. Mem.) (Edinburgh). *Died 24 Oct. 1995.*

WRIGHT, Sir Rowland (Sydney), Kt 1976; CBE 1970; Director: Hawker Siddeley Group, since 1979; Blue Circle Industries PLC, 1978–86 (Chairman 1978–83); Chairman, Blue Circle Trust, since 1983; Chancellor, Queen's University, Belfast, since 1984; *b* 4 Oct. 1915; *s* of late Sydney Henry Wright and Elsie May; *m* 1940, Kathleen Mary Hodgkinson, BA; two *s* one *d. Educ:* High Pavement Sch., Nottingham; UC Nottingham. BSc London; CChem; FRSC. Joined ICI Ltd, Dyestuffs Div., 1937; Production Dir, Imperial Chemical (Pharmaceuticals) Ltd, 1955–57; Production Dir, Dyestuffs Div., 1957–58; Research Dir, 1958–61; Jt Man. Dir, ICI Ltd Agricultural Div., 1961–63, Chm. 1964–65; Personnel Dir, ICI Ltd, 1966–70; Dep. Chm., ICI Ltd, 1971–75, Chm., 1975–78; Director: AE&CI Ltd, 1970–75 (Dep. Chm., 1971–75); Royal Insurance Co., 1973–79; Barclays Bank Ltd, 1977–84; Shell Transport & Trading Co. Ltd, 1981–86. Chm., Reorganisation Commn for Eggs, 1967–68; Past Mem. Council, Foundn for Management Educn; Mem. Council, Chemical Industries Assoc., 1968–73; Pres. Inst. of Manpower Studies, 1971–77, Hon. Pres., 1977–; Vice-Pres., Soc. of Chemical Industry, 1971–74; Mem., British Shippers' Council, 1975–78; Trustee: Civic Trust, 1975–78; Westminster Abbey Trust, 1984–90. Mem. Court, Univ. of Sussex, 1983–. Governor, London Graduate School of Business Studies, 1975–78. FRSA 1970–; CBIM 1975; FIChemE; Mem., Royal Instn, 1971–. Hon. LLD: St Andrews, 1977; Belfast, 1978; Nottingham, 1978; Hon. DSc QUB, 1985. *Recreations:* gardening, photography. *Address:* Hawker Siddeley Group, 18 St James's Square, SW1Y 4LJ. *Club:* Athenæum.
Died 14 June 1991.

WRIGHT, Roy William, CBE 1970; MIEE; Director, 1957–85, Deputy Chairman and Deputy Chief Executive, 1965–75, The Rio Tinto-Zinc Corporation; Director: Davy Corporation Ltd, 1976–85; A. P. V. Holdings Ltd, 1976–85; Transportation Systems and Market Research, 1978–85; *b* 10 Sept. 1914; *s* of late Arthur William Wright; *m* 1939, Mary Letitia, *d* of late Llewelyn Davies; two *d. Educ:* King Edward VI Sch., Chelmsford; Faraday House Coll., London. Served War of 1939–45, S African Navy and RN in S Atlantic, N Atlantic and Arctic; Lt-Comdr 1944. Joined Rio Tinto Co. Ltd, 1952; Man. Dir, Rio Tinto Canada, 1956; Chm. of Palabora and Lornex mines during financing and start up phases (largest mines in Africa and Canada respectively); Director: Rio Tinto Co. Ltd, 1957; Lornex Mining Co., Vancouver, 1970–79; Rio Algom Ltd, Toronto, 1960–80; Palabora Mining Co., Johannesburg, 1963–80; Rio Tinto South Africa Ltd, Johannesburg, 1960–79. Chairman: Process Plant Expert Cttee, Min. of Technology, 1968; Econ. Develt Cttee for Electronics Industry, NEDO, 1971–76. *Address:* Cobbers, Forest Row, East Sussex RH18 5JZ. *T:* Forest Row (01342) 822009. *Clubs:* Athenæum, Royal Automobile; Toronto (Toronto). *Died 23 Nov. 1994.*

WRIGHT, William Ambrose, (Billy), CBE 1959; Consultant, Central Independent Television Ltd, 1985–89

(Controller of Sport, 1982–85; Head of Sport and Outside Broadcasts, ATV Network Ltd, 1966–81); *b* 6 Feb. 1924; *m* 1958, Joy Beverley; two *d*, and one step *s. Educ:* Madeley Secondary Modern Sch. Professional Footballer; became Captain, Wolverhampton Wanderers Football Club; played for England 105 times; Captain of England 90 times; Manager of Arsenal Football Club, 1962–66. FA Cup Winners medal; 3 Football League Winners Medals. Director: Wolverhampton Wanderers FC; Midlands Cable Ltd; Telford Telecommunications Ltd. *Publications:* Captain of England, 1950; The World's my Football Pitch, 1956. *Recreations:* golf, cricket. *Address:* 26 Farnham Close, Whetstone, N20 9PU.
Died 3 Sept. 1994.

WRIGLEY, Michael Harold, OBE 1971; HM Diplomatic Service, retired; *b* 30 July 1924; *e s* of Edward Whittaker Wrigley and Audrey Margaret Wrigley; *m* 1950, Anne Phillida Brewis; two *s* two *d. Educ:* Harrow; Worcester Coll., Oxford. Served War of 1939–45: Rifle Brigade, 1943–47. HM Diplomatic Service, 1950; served HM Embassies: Brussels, 1952–54; Bangkok, 1956–59; Office of Commissioner-Gen. for South-East Asia, Singapore, 1959–60; HM Embassy, Bangkok, 1961–64 and 1966–71; Counsellor, Kuala Lumpur, 1971–74; Counsellor, FCO, 1974–76. Mem., North Yorkshire CC, 1977–85. *Recreations:* shooting, racing. *Address:* Ganton Hall, Scarborough, N Yorks YO12 4NT. *T:* Sherburn (01944) 70223. *Clubs:* White's, Turf, Jockey; Royal Bangkok Sports (Bangkok). *Died 13 Jan. 1995.*

WROTH, Prof. (Charles) Peter, MA, PhD, DSc; FEng 1982; MICE; FGS; Master of Emmanuel College, Cambridge, since 1990; *b* 2 June 1929; *s* of late Charles Wroth and Violet Beynon Wroth (*née* Jenour); *m* 1st, 1954, Mary Parlane Weller (*d* 1988); two *s* twin *d*; 2nd, 1989, Rachel Anne Britton. *Educ:* Marlborough Coll.; Emmanuel Coll., Cambridge (MA, PhD). Schoolmaster, Felsted Sch., 1953–54; Research Student, Univ. of Cambridge, 1954–58; Engineer, G. Maunsell & Partners, London, 1958–61; University of Cambridge: Lectr in Engineering, 1961–75; Reader in Soil Mechanics, 1975–79; Fellow of Churchill Coll., 1963–79; University of Oxford: Prof. of Engrg Science, 1979–90; Fellow of Brasenose Coll., 1979–90. Chairman: British Geotechnical Soc., 1979, 1980, 1981; Géotechnique Adv. Panel, 1979, 1980, 1981. *Publications:* (with A. N. Schofield) Critical State Soil Mechanics, 1968; contribs to learned jls on soil mechanics and foundation engineering. *Recreations:* golf, Real tennis, crosswords. *Address:* Master's Lodge, Emmanuel College, Cambridge CB2 3AP. *Clubs:* MCC; Hawks (Cambridge); Jesters. *Died 3 Feb. 1991.*

WYKEHAM, Air Marshal Sir Peter (Guy), KCB 1965 (CB 1961); DSO 1943 and Bar 1944; OBE 1949; DFC 1940 and Bar 1941; AFC 1951; technical consultant, since 1969; *b* 13 Sept. 1915; *s* of Guy Vane and Audrey Irene Wykeham-Barnes; family changed name by Deed Poll, 1955, from Wykeham-Barnes to Wykeham; *m* 1949, Barbara Priestley, RIBA, AA Dip., *d* of late J. B. Priestley, OM; two *s* one *d. Educ:* RAF Halton. Commissioned, 1937; served with fighter sqns, 1937–43 (commanded Nos 73, 257 and 23 sqns); commanded fighter sectors and wings, 1943–45; Air Ministry, 1946–48; Test Pilot, 1948–51; seconded to US Air Force, Korea, 1950; commanded fighter stations, 1951–53; NATO, 1953–56; staff appointments, 1956–59; AOC No 38 Gp, RAF, 1960–62; Dir, Jt Warfare Staff, Min. of Defence, 1962–64; Comdr, FEAF, 1964–66; Dep. Chief of Air Staff, 1967–69. Chm., Wykehams Ltd; Partner, Anglo-European Liaison. FRAeS 1968; FIMgt. Chevalier, Order of Dannebrog, 1945; US Air Medal, 1950. *Publications:* Fighter Command, 1960; Santos-Dumont, 1962. *Recreations:*

sailing, writing. *Address:* Green Place, Stockbridge, Hampshire SO20 6HN. *Club:* Royal Automobile.
Died 23 Feb. 1995.

WYKES, James Cochrane, MA (Cantab); *b* 19 Oct. 1913; *m* 1938, Cecile Winifred Graham, *e d* of J. Graham Rankin; one *s* one *d. Educ:* Oundle Sch.; Clare Coll., Cambridge (Open Exhibn in Classics). Asst Master, Loretto Sch., 1935–51; Headmaster, St Bees Sch., 1951–63; Head of Educational Broadcasting, ATV Network, 1963–66; Inner London Education Authority: Dir of Television, 1966–75; Television Adviser, 1975–78. Chm., Nat. Educnl Closed Circuit Television Assoc., 1970–72. Served War of 1939–45: Black Watch (RHR), 1940–44. *Publication:* Caesar at Alexandria, 1951. *Recreations:* walking, fishing, ornithology, music. *Address:* 36 Crimple Meadows, Pannal, Harrogate, N Yorks HG3 1EN. *T:* Harrogate (0423) 870307. *Club:* New (Edinburgh). *Died 19 Oct. 1992.*

WYLIE, Sir Campbell, Kt 1963; ED 1946; *b* NZ, 14 May 1905; *s* of William James Wylie and Edith Grace Stagg; *m* 1933, Leita Caroline Clark (*d* 1984); no *c. Educ:* Dannevirke High Sch.; Auckland Grammar Sch.; Univ. of New Zealand. LLM 1st Class hons (Univ. of New Zealand), 1928; Barrister and Solicitor (New Zealand), 1928; Barrister-at-law, Inner Temple, 1950. Was in private practice, New Zealand, until 1940. War service, 1940–46 (despatches). Crown Counsel, Malaya, 1946; Senior Federal Counsel, 1950; Attorney-General: Barbados, 1951; British Guiana, 1955; The West Indies, 1956; Federal Justice, Supreme Court of The West Indies, 1959–62; Chief Justice, Unified Judiciary of Sarawak, N Borneo and Brunei, 1962–63; Chief Justice, High Court in Borneo, 1963–66; Law Revision Commissioner, Tonga, 1966–67; Chief Justice, Seychelles, 1967–69; Comr for Law Revision and Reform, Seychelles, 1970–71. QC 1952 (Barbados), 1955 (British Guiana). *Address:* Remuera Life Care Centre, 28/10 Gerard Way, Meadowbank, Auckland 5, New Zealand. *T:* (9) 5213082.
Died 2 Aug. 1992.

WYLLIE, Robert Lyon, CBE 1960; JP; DL; FCA; *b* 4 March 1897; *s* of Rev. Robert Howie Wyllie, MA, Dundee; *m* 1924, Anne, *d* of Thomas Rutherford, Harrington, Cumberland; two *d. Educ:* Hermitage Sch., Helensburgh; Queen's Park Sch., Glasgow. Served European War, 1914–18, with Lothians and Border Horse (France). Chartered Accountant, 1920; FCA 1949. Dir, Ashley and Rock Ltd, 1966–90. Life Vice-President, Cumberland Development Council Ltd. Formerly: Chairman: W Cumberland Industrial Develt Co. Ltd; W Cumberland Silk Mills Ltd; Cumberland Develt Council Ltd; Whitehaven & Dist Disablement Advisory Cttee, and Youth Employment Cttee; Vice-Chm. W Cumberland Hosp. Management Cttee; Hon. Treas., NW Div., YMCA. JP 1951; DL Cumbria (formerly Cumberland), 1957–84. OStJ 1976. *Recreation:* fishing. *Address:* Millfield Residential Home, Penrith Road, Keswick CA12 4HB.
Died 26 July 1995.

WYMAN, John Bernard, MBE 1945; FRCS; FFARCS; Consultant Anaesthetist, Westminster Hospital, 1948–81; Dean, Westminster Medical School, 1964–81 (Sub-Dean, 1959–64); *b* 24 May 1916; *s* of Louis Wyman and Bertha Wyman; *m* 1948, Joan Dorothea Beighton; three *s* one *d. Educ:* Davenant Foundn Sch., London; King's Coll., London (Fellow 1980); Westminster Med. Sch. MRCS, LRCP 1941; DA 1945; FFARCS 1953; FRCS 1981. Military Service, 1942–46: Major RAMC; N Africa, Italy and India. Cons. Anaesthetist, Woolwich War Memorial Hospital Hosp., 1946–64; formerly Hon. Anaesthetist, Italian Hosp. Hunterian Prof., RCS, 1953. Member: Bd of Governors, Westminster Hosp., 1959–74; Sch. Council, Westminster Med. Sch., 1959–81; Croydon AHA,

1974–75; Kensington and Chelsea and Westminster AHA, 1975–81. *Publications:* chapters in med. text books and papers in gen. and specialist jls on anaesthesia and med. educn. *Recreation:* gardening. *Address:* Chilling Street Cottage, Sharpthorne, Sussex RH19 4HZ. *T:* Sharpthorne (0342) 810281. *Club:* Savage.
Died 22 Sept. 1994.

WYNN-WILLIAMS, George, MB, BS London; FRCS; FRCOG; Surgeon, Chelsea Hospital for Women; Consulting Obstetrician to City of Westminster; Consulting Gynæcologist, Chelsea Hospital for Women; Consulting Obstetric Surgeon, Queen Charlotte's Hospital; Consulting Gynæcologist to the Civil Service; Teacher in Gynæcology and Obstetrics, London University; *b* 10 Aug. 1911; *er s* of William Wynn-Williams, MRCS, LRCP, and Jane Anderson Brymer, Caernarvon, N Wales; *m* 1943, Penelope, *o d* of 1st and last Earl Jowitt, PC, and Lesley McIntyre; two *s* one *d. Educ:* Rossall; King's Coll.; Westminster Hospital. MRCS, LRCP 1937; MB, BS (London) 1937; MRCOG 1941; FRCS 1943; FRCOG 1967. Alfred Hughes Anatomy Prize, King's Coll.; Chadwick Prize in Clinical Surgery, Forensic Medicine and Public Health Prizes, Westminster Hospital. Various appointments 1937–41; Chief Asst and Surgical Registrar and Grade I Surgeon, EMS, 1941–45; Acting Obst. and Gynæcol Registrar, Westminster Hosp., 1941–46; Surgeon-in-Charge, Mobile Surg. Team to Portsmouth and Southampton, June-Oct. 1944; Chief Asst, Chelsea Hosp. for Women, 1946–47; Obst. Registrar, Queen Charlotte's Hosp., 1946–50; Cons. Obstetrician, Borough of Tottenham; Cons. Gynæcologist, Weir Hosp. Surgical Tutor, Westminster Hosp., 1941–46; Obst. and Gynæcol Tutor, Westminster Hosp., 1941–48; Lectr and Demonstrator to Postgrad. Students, Queen Charlotte's Hosp., 1946–50; Lectr to Postgrad. Students, Chelsea Women's Hosp., 1946–; Examiner, Central Midwives' Board; Recognized Lectr of London Univ.; Associate Examiner in Obst. and Gynæcol., Worshipful Co. of Apothecaries. Woodhull Lectr, Royal Instn, 1978. Member: BMA; Soc. for Study of Fertility; The Pilgrims. FRSM. *Publications:* (jtly) Queen Charlotte's Text Book of Obstetrics, 1968; contributions to medical journals, including Human Artificial Insemination, in Hospital Medicine, 1973; Infertile Patients with Positive Immune Fluorescent Serum, 1976; Spermatazoal Antibodies treated with Condom Coitus, 1976; The Woodhull Lecture on Infertility and its Control, 1978. *Recreations:* tennis, shooting, fishing. *Address:* 48 Wimpole Street, W1M 7DG. *T:* 071–487 4866; 39 Hurlingham Court, SW6; The Hall, Wittersham, Isle of Oxney, Kent. *Clubs:* Hurlingham, Chelsea Arts, English-Speaking Union, Oriental; Rye Golf. *Died 3 April 1993.*

WYNNE MASON, Walter, CMG 1967; MC 1941; *b* 21 March 1910; *y s* of late George and Eva Mason, Wellington, NZ; *m* 1945, Freda Miller, *d* of late Frederick and Lilian Miller, Woodford, Essex; two *s* one *d. Educ:* Scots Coll., NZ; Victoria University College, NZ (MA). NZ Govt Education Service 1934–39; served 2nd NZEF in War of 1939–45, UK, Greece, Crete, Libya; NZ War Histories, 1946–48; NZ Diplomatic Service, Paris and London, 1949–54; Commonwealth War Graves Commission: Chief, Middle East, 1954–56; Dep. Dir-Gen., 1956–70; Mem., Sec. of State for Environment's panel of independent Inspectors, 1972–77; retired 1978. *Publications:* Prisoners of War, 1954; (with Philip Longworth and Edmund Blunden) The Unending Vigil: a history of the Commonwealth War Graves Commission, 1967. *Recreations:* lawn tennis, theatre, music. *Address:* Keene House, 10 Hillier Road, Guildford, Surrey GU1 2JQ. *T:* Guildford (0483) 572601.
Died 30 Dec. 1992.

Y

YARBOROUGH, 7th Earl of, *cr* 1837; **John Edward Pelham;** Baron Yarborough, 1794; Baron Worsley, 1837; JP; Major Grenadier Guards, retired 1952; Vice Lord-Lieutenant (formerly Vice-Lieutenant), Lincolnshire, since 1964; *b* 2 June 1920; *s* of 6th Earl of Yarborough; *S* father, 1966; *m* 1957, Mrs Ann Duffin, *d* of late John Herbert Upton, Ingmire Hall, Yorkshire; one *s* three *d. Educ:* Eton; Trinity College, Cambridge. Contested (C) Grimsby, 1955. Pres., Royal Forestry Soc. for England, Wales and NI, 1987–89. President: Midland Area, British Legion, 1959–60, East Midland Area, 1960–62; Nat. Exec. Council, British Legion, 1962–73; Patron, E Midlands Area, 1974–. Hon. Col, 440 Light AD Regt, RA (TA), 1965–69, Humber Regt, RA T&AVR, 1969–71; Dep. Hon. Col, 2nd Bn, Yorkshire Volunteers, 1971–72. High Sheriff of Lincolnshire, 1964; JP, Parts of Lindsey, 1965. *Recreations:* shooting, sailing. *Heir: s* Lord Worsley [*b* 5 Nov. 1963; *m* 1990, Anna-Karin Zecevic, *d* of George Zecevic; one *s*]. *Address:* Brocklesby Park, Habrough, South Humberside DN37 8PL. *T:* Roxton (0469) 60242. *Clubs:* Cavalry and Guards, Boodle's; Royal Yacht Squadron. *Died 21 March 1991.*

YATES, Frank, CBE 1963; ScD; FRS 1948; Honorary Scientist, Rothamsted Experimental Station, since 1968 (formerly Head of Statistics Department and Agricultural Research Statistical Service, and Deputy Director); *b* 12 May 1902; *s* of Percy and Edith Yates, Didsbury, Manchester; *m* 1939, Pauline (*d* 1976), *d* of Vladimir Shoubersky; *m* 1981, Ruth, *d* of William James Hunt, Manchester. *Educ:* Clifton; St John's Coll., Cambridge. Research Officer and Mathematical Adviser, Gold Coast Geodetic Survey, 1927–31; Rothamsted Experimental Station, 1931; Dept of Statistics, 1933; Agric. Res. Statistical Service, 1947, Dep. Dir, 1958. Wing Comdr (Hon.) RAF, 1943–45. Scientific Adviser to various Mins, UNO, FAO, 1939–; Mem. UN Sub-Commn on Statistical Sampling, 1947–52. Sen. Res. Fellow, Imperial Coll., 1969–74; Sen. Vis. Fellow, Imperial Coll., 1974–77. Pres., British Computer Society, 1960–61; Pres., Royal Statistical Society, 1967–68. Royal Medal of the Royal Society, 1966. Hon. DSc London, 1982. *Publications:* Design and Analysis of Factorial Experiments, 1937; (with R. A. Fisher) Statistical Tables for Biological, Medical and Agricultural Research, 1938 (6th edn 1963); Sampling Methods for Censuses and Surveys, 1949 (4th edn 1981); Experimental Design: Selected Papers, 1970; numerous scientific papers. *Recreation:* mountaineering. *Address:* Stackyard, Rothamsted, Harpenden, Herts AL5 2BQ. *T:* Harpenden (0582) 712732. *Died 17 June 1994.*

YATES-BELL, John Geoffrey, FRCS; retired; Consultant Urologist to King's College Hospital; *b* 6 Dec. 1902; *s* of John Bell, FRCVS, and Matilda Bell, London; *m* 1932, Winifred Frances Hordern (*née* Perryman) (*d* 1979); one *s* one *d. Educ:* St Dunstan's College; King's College, London. MB, BS London 1926; FRCS 1930. King's College Hospital: House Surgeon, 1926–28; Surgical Registrar, 1928–29; Junior Urological Surgeon, 1930; Hon. Urological Surgeon, 1937. Emeritus Urological Surgeon, Epsom and Leatherhead Hosps. President, Urological Section, RSM, 1952 (Vice-Pres. 1939); Fellow Internat. Soc. of Urology, 1934; Founder Member, British Assoc. of Urological Surgeons (Hon. Treas., 1954–56). *Publications:* Kidney and Ureter Stone, in British Surgical Practice, 1950; Mythology of Greece and Rome, 1980; articles in British Jl of Urology, Jl of Urology, Medical Press, Lancet, etc. *Recreation:* lawn tennis. *Address:* The Oaks, Manor Park, Chislehurst, Kent BR7 5QE. *Died 29 April 1991.*

YEATES, W(illiam) Keith, MD, MS; FRCS; FRCSEd (without examination); Honorary Consultant Urologist, Newcastle Health Authority, since 1985 (Consultant Urologist, 1951–85); Hon. Senior Lecturer, Institute of Urology, University of London, since 1981; Chairman, Intercollegiate Board in Urology, 1984–88; *b* 10 March 1920; *s* of William Ravensbourne Yeates and Winifred (*née* Scott); *m* 1946, Jozy McIntyre Fairweather; one *s* one *d. Educ:* Glasgow Academy; Whitley Bay Grammar Sch.; King's Coll., Newcastle, Univ. of Durham. Consultant Advr in Urology, DHSS, 1978–84. Chm., Specialist Adv. Cttee in Urology, Jt Cttee on Higher Surgical Trng, RCS, 1984–86. Visiting Professor: Universities of: Baghdad, 1974, 1978; California, LA, 1976; Texas, Dallas, 1976; Delhi, 1977; Cairo, 1978; Kuwait, 1980; Guest Prof., New York section, Amer. Urolog. Assoc., 1977, 1985; Principal Guest Lectr, Urolog. Soc. of Australasia, 1977; Guest Lecturer: Italian Urolog. Assoc., 1978; Yugoslavian Urolog. Assoc., 1980; Vis. Lectr, Rio de Janeiro, 1975. Senior Member: Internat. Soc. of Urology, 1986– (Mem., 1958–86); European Assoc. of Urology, 1986– (Foundn Mem., 1974–86); Hon. Member: Urolog. Soc. of Australasia, 1977–; Canadian Urological Assoc., 1981–; British Assoc. of Urolog. Surgeons, 1985–. President: N of England Surgical Soc., 1971–72; British Assoc. of Urological Surgeons, 1980–82 (Vice-Pres., 1978–80, St Peter's Medal, 1983). British Journal of Urology: Editor, 1973–78; Chm., Editorial Cttee, 1978–84; Consulting Editor, 1985–90. *Publications:* various papers, chapters in text books on urology, particularly on bladder dysfunction and male infertility. *Address:* 22 Castleton Grove, Jesmond, Newcastle upon Tyne NE2 2HD. *T:* 091–2814030; 71 King Henry's Road, NW3 3QU. *T:* 071–586 7633. *Died 26 July 1992.*

YEEND, Sir Geoffrey (John), AC 1986; Kt 1979; CBE 1976; FAIM; consultant; Chancellor, Australian National University, since 1990; Director: Coca Cola AMATIL (formerly AMATIL) Ltd, since 1986; ALCAN Australia Ltd, since 1986; Menzies Memorial Trust, since 1986; Mercantile Mutual Holdings Ltd, since 1988; Australian Capital Television Ltd, since 1989; *b* 1 May 1927; *s* of Herbert Yeend; *m* 1952, Laurel, *d* of L. G. Mahoney; one *s* one *d. Educ:* Canberra High Sch.; Melbourne Univ. (Canberra University Coll.) (BCom). Served RAE, AIF, 1945–46. Dept of Post War Reconstruction, 1947–49; Prime Minister's Dept, 1950–86, incl.: Private Sec. to Prime Minister (Sir Robert Menzies), 1952–55; Asst Sec., Aust. High Commn, London, 1958–61; Dep. Sec., 1972–77; Head of Dept and Sec. to Cabinet, 1978–86; Mem., Defence Cttee, 1978–86. Mem. and leader of Aust. delegns to internat. confs. Dir, Canberra Advance Bank, 1986–92. Mem., Adv. Council on Aust. Archives, 1985–87. Nat. Vice Pres., and Pres., ACT, Multiple Sclerosis Soc. of Aust., 1989–. Pro-Chancellor, ANU, 1988–90. Mem. Bd of Govs, Australian Nat. Gall. Foundn, 1992–. Aust. Eisenhower Fellow, 1971. International Hockey Federation: Councillor, 1959–66; Vice-Pres., 1967–76; Member of Honour, 1979; Trustee, 1988–; Life

Mem., Australian and ACT Hockey Assocs. Patron, Woden Valley Choir, 1980–; Vice-Patron, Volleyball Australia, 1989–. *Recreations:* golf, fishing. *Address:* 1 Loftus Street, Yarralumla, ACT 2600, Australia. *T:* (6) 2813266. *Clubs:* Commonwealth (Canberra); Royal Canberra Golf. *Died 6 Oct. 1994.*

YEMM, Prof. Edmund William, BA, MA, DPhil Oxon; FLS; Melville Wills Professor of Botany, University of Bristol, 1955–74, Emeritus Professor 1974; *b* 16 July 1909; *s* of William H. Yemm and Annie L. Brett; *m* 1935, Marie Solari; one *s* three *d. Educ:* Wyggeston School, Leicester; Queen's College, Oxford. Foundation, Schol., Queen's Coll., 1928; Christopher Welch Schol., 1931. Major, REME, 1942–45. Research Fellow, Queen's Coll., 1935–38; Lecturer, Univ. of Bristol, 1939–49; Reader in Botany, Univ. of Bristol, 1950–55; Pro-Vice-Chancellor, Bristol Univ., 1970–73. Fellowship, Rockefeller Foundation, 1954; Vis. Prof., Western Reserve Univ., 1966–67. *Publications:* scientific papers in Proc. Royal Soc., New Phytologist, Biochemical Jl, Jl of Ecology, Jl of Experimental Botany. *Recreations:* cricket, gardening; formerly football (Oxford Univ. Assoc. Football Blue, 1929–31). *Address:* The Wycke, 61 Long Ashton Road, Bristol BS18 9HW. *T:* Long Ashton (0272) 392258. *Died 22 Nov. 1993.*

YERBY, Frank Garvin; novelist; *b* 5 Sept. 1916; *s* of Rufus Garvin Yerby and Wilhelmina Smythe; *m* 1st, 1941, Flora Helen Claire Williams (marr. diss.); two *s* two *d*; 2nd, 1956, Blanca Calle Pérez. *Educ:* Haines Institute; Paine College; Fisk Univ.; Univ. of Chicago. Teacher, Florida Agricultural and Mechanical Coll., 1939; Southern Univ. (Baton Rouge, Louisiana), 1940–41; War work: laboratory technician, Ford Motor Company, Detroit, 1941–44; Ranger Aircraft, New York, 1944–45; writer, 1944–. O. Henry Award for short story, 1944. *Publications:* The Foxes of Harrow, 1946; The Vixens, 1947; The Golden Hawk, 1948; Pride's Castle, 1949; Floodtide, 1950; A Woman Called Fancy, 1951; The Saracen Blade, 1952; The Devil's Laughter, 1953; Benton's Row, 1954; The Treasure of Pleasant Valley, 1955; Captain Rebel, 1956; Fairoaks, 1957; The Serpent and the Staff, 1958; Jarrett's Jade, 1959; Gillian, 1960; The Garfield Honor, 1961; Griffin's Way, 1962; The Old Gods Laugh, 1964; An Odor of Sanctity, 1965; Goat Song, 1967; Judas, My Brother, 1968; Speak Now, 1969; The Man from Dahomey, 1970; The Girl from Storyville, 1972; The Voyage Unplanned, 1974; Tobias and the Angel, 1975; A Rose for Ana María, 1976; Hail the Conquering Hero, 1977; A Darkness at Ingraham's Crest, 1978; Western, 1983; Devilseed, 1984; McKenzie's Hundred, 1985. *Recreations:* photography, painting. *Address:* c/o Wm Morris Agency, 1350 Avenue of the Americas, New York, NY 10019, USA. *Clubs:* Authors Guild (New York); Real Sociedad Hipica Española (Madrid). *Died 29 Nov. 1991.*

YIN, Leslie Charles Bowyer; *see* Charteris, L.

YOFFEY, Joseph Mendel, DSc, MD, FRCS; Visiting Professor, Hebrew University of Jerusalem, since 1969; Professor of Anatomy, University of Bristol, 1942–67, then Professor Emeritus; *b* 10 July 1902; *s* of Rabbi Israel Jacob Yoffey and Pere Jaffe; *m* 1940, Betty Gillis, LLB; three *d. Educ:* Manchester Grammar School; Univ. of Manchester. Leech Research Fellow, University of Manchester, 1926–27; Research Scholar, BMA, 1928–29; House Surgeon, Manchester Royal Infirmary, 1929–30; Asst Lectr in Anatomy, Univ. of Manchester, 1930; Senior Lectr in Anatomy, University College of South Wales and Monmouthshire, Cardiff. Hunterian Prof., RCS, 1933 and 1940; Fellow of Rockefeller Foundn, 1937–39. Visiting Professor: Univ. of Washington, 1958; Univ. of Calif, San Francisco, 1967–68; John Curtin Sch. of Medical

Research, ANU, 1968–69. Hon. Life Mem., Reticulendotheliol Soc., 1978; Hon. Mem., Amer. Assoc. of Anatomists, 1980. John Hunter Triennial Medal, RCS, 1968. Hon. LLD Manchester, 1973. Knight First Class of the Order of the Dannebrog (Denmark), 1959. *Publications:* Quantitative Cellular Hæmatology, 1960; Bone Marrow Reactions, 1966; (with Dr F. C. Courtice) Lymphatics, Lymph and the Lymphomyeloid Complex, 1970; Bone Marrow in Hypoxia and Rebound, 1973; (with M. Tavassoli) Bone Marrow: structure and function, 1983; numerous scientific papers. *Recreations:* music, walking, modern Hebrew. *Address:* 4 Rehov Pick, Kiryat Moshe, Jerusalem 96105, Israel. *T:* Jerusalem (2) 513050. *Died 16 March 1994.*

YONGE, Dame (Ida) Felicity (Ann), DBE 1982 (MBE 1958); Special Adviser in Government Chief Whip's Office, 1979–83; *b* 28 Feb. 1921; *d* of Comdr W. H. N. Yonge, RN, and Kathleen Yonge. *Educ:* Convent of the Holy Child, St Leonard's-on-Sea. Served WRNS (2nd Officer), 1940–46. Purser's Office, P&OSN Co., 1947–50; Private Secretary: to Chairman of the Conservative Party, 1951–64; to Leader of the Opposition, 1964–65; to Opposition Chief Whip, 1965–70 and 1974–79; to Leader of House of Commons, 1970–74. *Recreations:* gardening, bridge. *Address:* 58 Leopold Road, Wimbledon, SW19 7JF. *Died 1 April 1995.*

YORKE, Richard Michael, QC 1971; a Recorder of the Crown Court, 1972–83; *b* 13 July 1930; *e s* of Gilbert Victor Yorke, Civil Engineer. *Educ:* Solihull Sch., Warwickshire; Balliol Coll., Oxford (MA). Commissioned 2nd Lt, RA, July 1949 (Prize of Honour, Best Officer Cadet); Lieut, Honourable Artillery Company, 1951; Captain, 1953. Asst to Sec., British Road Services, 1953–56. Called to Bar, Gray's Inn, 1956 (Lee Prizeman), Bencher 1981; Inner Temple, *ad eund.*, 1968; Barrister, Supreme Court of NSW and High Court of Australia, 1972; QC NSW 1974. Consultant, Bodington & Yturbe, Paris, 1973–82. Contested (C): Durham, 1966; Loughborough, Feb. and Oct. 1974. Pres., Civil Aviation Review Bd, 1972–75. Vice-Chm., Senate/Law Soc. Jt Working Party on Banking Law, 1975–83; Member: Special Panel, Transport Tribunal, 1976–85; Panel of Arbitrators, Amer. Arbitrators Assoc., 1983–; Mem., LMAA, 1984–; Mem., CIArb, 1985–. Voluntary Governor, Bart's Hospital, 1974; Governor, Sadler's Wells Trust, 1985–. *Recreations:* ski-ing, sailing, tennis. *Address:* 4 and 5 Gray's Inn Square, Gray's Inn, WC1R 5AY. *T:* 071–404 5252, *Telex:* 895 3743 Gralaw, *Fax:* 071–242 7803 and 071–831 0202; 5 Cliveden Place, SW1W 8LA. *T:* 071–730 6054, *Fax:* 071–823 6068; Eden Roc, Rue de Ransou, 1936 Verbier, Switzerland. *T:* (26) 313504, *Fax:* (26) 315154; La Mandragore, Tourrettes sur Loup, AM, France. *T:* (93) 24 18 08. *Clubs:* Royal Ocean Racing, Hurlingham; Island Sailing (Cowes). *Died 12 April 1991.*

YOUELL, Rev. Canon George; *b* 23 Dec. 1910; *s* of late Herbert Youell, Beccles; *m* 1st, 1936, Gertrude Barron (*d* 1982), *d* of late J. Irvine, West Hartlepool; two *s* three *d*; 2nd, 1983, Mary Nina, *d* of late Rev. H. G. Phillipson. *Educ:* Beccles; St Michaels; Hartley Coll., Manchester; St Stephen's House, Oxford; Univ. of Keele (MA 1969). Ordained deacon 1933, priest 1934; Curate, St John's, Chester, 1933; Clerical Dir of Industrial Christian Fellowship, 1937; Chaplain attached to 2nd Bn Grenadier Guards (BEF and Guards Armoured Div.), 1939; Sen. Chaplain to Forces: Nigeria, 1942; Woolwich and SE London, 1944; Nigeria and Gold Coast, 1945; Rector of Ightfield with Calverhall, Salop, 1947; Rural Dean of Leek, 1952–56; Vicar of Leek, 1952–61; Archdeacon of Stoke-upon-Trent, 1956–70; Vicar of Horton, Leek, 1968–70; Chaplain, Univ. of Keele, 1961–68; Hon. Canon,

Lichfield Cathedral, 1967–70; Canon Residentiary of Ely Cathedral, 1970–81, Vice-Dean and Treas., 1973–81. *Publications:* Africa Marches, 1949; contributor on colonial and sociological affairs to the Guardian, 1947–51. *Recreations:* fell walking, gardening. *Address:* 6 St Mary's Court, Ely, Cambs CB7 4HQ.

Died 21 Jan. 1995.

YOUENS, Ven. John Ross, CB 1970; OBE 1959; MC 1946; Chaplain to the Queen 1969–84; Senior Treasurer, Corporation of the Sons of the Clergy, 1982–84; *b* 29 Sept. 1914; *e s* of late Canon F. A. C. Youens and Dorothy Mary, *o d* of William and Annie Ross, Blackpool; *m* 1940, Pamela Gordon Lincoln (*née* Chandler); one *s* (two *d* decd). *Educ:* Buxton Coll.; Kelham Theological Coll. Deacon, 1939; priest, 1940; Curate of Warsop, Notts, 1939–40; commissioned RA Chaplains' Dept, 1940; Aldershot and SE Comd, 1940–42; Sen. Chaplain: 59 Inf. Div., 1942; Chatham, 1943; 2nd Army Troops, June 1944; Guards Armd Div., Nov. 1944–1945; 3rd Inf. Div. in Egypt and Palestine, 1945–48; 7th Armd Div. in Germany, 1948–50; Aldershot, 1950–51; DACG, Egypt, 1951–53, Tripoli, 1953–54; Sen. Chaplain, RMA Sandhurst, 1955–58; DACG, Gibraltar, 1958–60; ACG War Office, 1960–61, Rhine Army, 1961–66; Chaplain General to the Forces, 1966–74; Archdeacon Emeritus, 1974. Dep. Chairman, Keston Coll., Centre for the Study of Religion and Communism (Mem. Council, 1975–84). *Address:* King Edward VII Convalescent Home, Osborne House, East Cowes, Isle of Wight PO32 6JY. *Clubs:* Cavalry and Guards (Hon. Mem.), MCC. *Died 24 Aug. 1993.*

YOUNG, Air Vice-Marshal Brian Pashley, CB 1972; CBE 1960 (OBE 1944); Commandant General, Royal Air Force Regiment, 1968–73; *b* 5 May 1918; *s* of Kenneth Noel Young and Flora Elizabeth Young, Natal, S Africa; *m* 1942, Patricia Josephine, *d* of Thomas Edward Cole, Bedford; three *s* two *d. Educ:* Michaelhouse, Natal, SA; RAF Coll., Cranwell. Fighter Comd, UK and France, 1938–40 (wounded); hosp., 1941–42; Coastal Comd, N Ire. and Western Isles, 1942–43; Aden and Persian Gulf, 1944; Staff Coll., Haifa, 1945; Middle East, 1946–47; Air Min., 1948–50; Bomber Comd HQ No 1 Gp, Hemswell/Gaydon, 1951–57; HQ Bomber Comd, 1958–60; Asst Chief of Staff, Intelligence, NATO, Fontainebleau, 1960–62; IDC 1963; AOC, Central Reconnaisance Estabt, 1964–67. Planning Inspector, DoE, 1973–83. Rep. RAF: athletics, 1939, Rugby, 1947–48. *Address:* Chapel Walk House, The Street, Didmarton, Glos. *Club:* Royal Air Force. *Died 26 July 1992.*

YOUNG, Air Vice-Marshal Gordon, CBE 1963; retired; *b* 29 May 1919; *s* of late Robert Young, MBE, and Emily Florence Young, Doncaster; *m* 1943, Pamela Doris Weatherstone-Smith; two *d. Educ:* Maltby Grammar School; Sheffield Univ. Served War of 1939–45, Flying Boat Ops S Atlantic and Western Approaches (despatches); Air Min., 1945–47; Asst Air Attaché, Moscow, 1949–52; OC No 204 Sqdn, 1954–55; RAF Staff Coll., 1956; OC Flying Wing, RAF St Mawgan, 1958–60; Asst Chief, Comdrs-in-Chief Mission to Soviet Forces in Germany, 1960–63; OC RAF Wyton, 1963–65; Air Attaché, Bonn, 1966–68; SASO Coastal Command, 1968–69; COS No 18 (M) Gp, 1969–71. *Recreation:* bird-watching (MBOU 1969). *Address:* PO Box 24, Bath, Ont K0H 1G0, Canada. *T:* 613-352-3498. *Club:* Royal Air Force.

Died 7 Dec. 1993.

YOUNG, Leslie, DSc (London), PhD; FRSC; Professor of Biochemistry in the University of London, and Head of the Department of Biochemistry, St Thomas's Hospital Medical School, London, SE1, 1948–76, then Professor Emeritus; Hon. Consultant, St Thomas' Hospital; *b* 27 Feb. 1911; *o c* of John and Ethel Young; *m* 1939, Ruth Elliott; one *s. Educ:* Sir Joseph Williamson's Mathematical

Sch., Rochester; Royal College of Science, London; University College, London. Sir Edward Frankland Prize and Medal of Royal Institute of Chemistry, 1932. Bayliss-Starling Memorial Scholar in Physiology, University Coll., London, 1933–34; Asst Lectr in Biochemistry, University College, London, 1934–35; Commonwealth Fund Fellow in Biochemistry at Washington Univ. Medical School and Yale Univ., USA, 1935–37; Lectr in Biochemistry, University Coll., London, 1937–39; Associate Prof. of Biochemistry, Univ. of Toronto, 1939–44; chemical warfare research for the Dept of Nat. Defence, Canada, 1940–46; Prof. of Biochemistry, Univ. of Toronto, 1944–47; Reader in Biochemistry, University Coll., London, 1947–48. Hon. Sec., The Biochemical Soc., 1950–53; Vice-Pres., The Royal Institute of Chemistry, 1964–66; Mem., Bd of Governors, St Thomas' Hosp., 1970–74; Chm. of Council, Queen Elizabeth Coll., London Univ., 1975–80, Hon. Fellow, 1980. FKC 1980. *Publications:* (with G. A. Maw) The Metabolism of Sulphur Compounds, 1958; papers on chem. and biochem. subjects in various scientific journals. *Address:* 23 Oaklands Avenue, Esher, Surrey KT10 8HX. *T:* 081–398 1262. *Died 26 Dec. 1992.*

YOUNG, Mark; General Secretary, British Air Line Pilots' Association, since 1974; *b* 7 June 1929; *s* of Arnold Young and Florence May (*née* Lambert) *m* 1st, 1952, Charlotte Maria (*née* Rigol) (*d* 1978); two *s* two *d*; 2nd, 1979, Marie-Thérèse, (Mollie) (*née* Craig); one *s. Educ:* Pendower Technical Sch., Newcastle upon Tyne. Electrician, 1944–61; Head of Res., ETU, 1961; National Officer, ETU, 1963–73. *Recreations:* flying, ballooning. *Address:* (office) 81 New Road, Harlington, Hayes, Mddx UB3 5BG. *Died 15 Aug. 1991.*

YOUNG-HERRIES, Sir Michael Alexander Robert; *see* Herries.

YOUNGER, Charles Frank Johnston, DSO 1944; TD 1952; *b* 11 Dec. 1908; *s* of late Major Charles Arthur Johnston Younger, King's Dragoon Guards; *m* 1935, Joanna, *e d* of late Rev. John Kyrle Chatfield, BD, MA, LLB; one *d. Educ:* Royal Naval Coll., Dartmouth. Served Royal Navy, 1926–37; resigned commn to enter William Younger & Co. Ltd, Brewers, Edinburgh, 1937; served War of 1939–45 (despatches, DSO): RA (Field), 15th Scottish Division, 1939–41; 17th Indian Light Div., Burma, 1942–45; commanded 129th Lowland Field Regt, RA, 1942–45 and 278th Lowland Field Regt RA (TA), 1946–52 (Lt-Col). Director: William Younger & Co. Ltd, 1945–73; Scottish & Newcastle Breweries Ltd, 1946–73; Bank of Scotland, 1960–79. Vice Pres., Brewers' Soc., 1964– (Chm., 1963–64; Chairman: Parly Cttee, 1961–63; Survey Cttee, 1967–75). Chm., Scottish Union & National Insurance Co., 1954–57, 1966–68, Dep. Chm., 1968–79; Dir, Norwich Union and Associated Cos, 1966–79, Vice-Chm., 1976–79. Chm., Scottish Adv. Bd, 1976–80. UK deleg. to EFTA Brewing Ind. Council, 1964–73; Mem. Council, CBI, 1965–73. Mem., Worshipful Company of Brewers. Mem., Royal Company of Archers (Queen's Body Guard for Scotland). Freeman of the City of London. *Recreations:* country pursuits. *Address:* Painsthorpe Hall, Kirby Underdale, York YO4 1RQ. *T:* Bishop Wilton (01759) 368342. *Club:* Boodle's.

Died 6 June 1995.

YOUNGER, Sir William McEwan, 1st Bt, *cr* 1964, of Fountainbridge, in the City of Edinburgh; DSO 1942; DL; Chairman: Scottish & Newcastle Breweries Ltd, 1960–69 (Managing Director, 1960–67); The Second Scottish Investment Trust Company Ltd, 1965–75; *b* 6 Sept. 1905; *y s* of late William Younger (brother of 1st Viscount Younger of Leckie), Ravenswood, Melrose, and Katharine Theodora, *d* of Comdr A. A. D. Dundas of Dundas, RN; *m* 1st, 1936, Nora Elizabeth Balfour (marr. diss., 1967);

one d; 2nd, 1983, June Peck. *Educ:* Winchester; Balliol Coll., Oxford (Hon. Fellow 1984). Served War of 1939–45 (despatches, DSO); Western Desert, 1941–43; Italy, 1943–45; Lt-Col, RA. Hon. Sec., Scottish Unionist Assoc., 1955–64; Chm., Conservative Party in Scotland, 1971–74. Mem., Royal Co. of Archers, Queen's Body Guard for Scotland. Director: British Linen Bank, 1955–71; Scottish Television, 1964–71; Chm., Highland Tourist (Cairngorm Development) Ltd, 1966–78. DL Midlothian, later City of Edinburgh, 1956–84. *Recreations:* mountaineering, fishing. *Heir:* none. *Address:* Little Hill Cottage, Harpsden, Henley-on-Thames, Oxon RG9 4HR. *T:* Henley-on-Thames (0491) 574339; 27 Moray Place, Edinburgh EH3 6DA. *T:* 031–225 8173. *Clubs:* Carlton, Alpine; New (Edinburgh).   *Died 15 April 1992 (ext).*

YUDKIN, John, MA, PhD, MD, BCh (Cambridge); BSc (London); FRCP, FRSC, FIBiol; Professor of Nutrition, University of London, at Queen Elizabeth College, 1954–71, Emeritus Professor, since 1971; *b* 8 Aug. 1910; 3rd *s* of Louis and Sarah Yudkin, London; *m* 1933, Emily Himmelweit; three *s*. *Educ:* Hackney Downs (formerly Grocers' Company) School, London; Chelsea Polytechnic; Christ's Coll., Cambridge; London Hospital. Research in Biochemical Laboratory, Cambridge, 1931–36; research in Nutritional Laboratory, Cambridge, 1938–43; Benn Levy Research Student, 1933–35; Grocers' Company Research Scholar, 1938–39; Sir Halley Stewart Research Fellow, 1940–43; Dir of Medical Studies, Christ's Coll., Cambridge, 1940–43; Prof. of Physiology, Queen Elizabeth Coll., Univ. of London, 1945–54; FKC (Fellow, Queen Elizabeth Coll., London, 1976). William Julius Mickle Fellow for Medical Res., London Univ., 1961–62; Leverhulme Emeritus Res. Fellow, 1982–83. Responsible for introd. first comprehensive univ. courses leading to Bachelor and Master degrees in nutrition, 1953. Chm., Food Gp, SCI. Mem., Bd of Govs, Hebrew Univ., Jerusalem (Hon. Fellow, 1993). *Publications:* This Slimming Business, 1958; The Complete Slimmer, 1964; Changing Food Habits, 1964; Our Changing Fare, 1966; Pure, White and Deadly, 1972, 2nd edn 1986; This Nutrition Business, 1976; A-Z of Slimming, 1977; Penguin Encyclopaedia of Nutrition, 1985; The Sensible Person's Guide to Weight Control, 1990; more than 300 articles on biochemistry and nutrition in scientific and medical journals. *Address:* 20 Wellington Court, Wellington Road, St John's Wood, NW8 9TA. *T:* 0171–586 5586.

Died 12 July 1995.

Z

ZAIDI, Syed Bashir Husain, CIE 1941; Padma Vibhushan 1976; director of several industrial concerns; *b* 1898; *s* of Syed Shaukat Husain Zaidi; *m* 1937, Qudsia Abdullah (*d* 1960); two *s* one *d*. *Educ:* St Stephen's College, Delhi; Cambridge University. Called to Bar, Lincoln's Inn, 1923; served Aligarh Univ., 1923–30; entered Rampur State Service, 1930; Chief Minister Rampur State, UP, 1936–49; Member: Indian Constituent Assembly, 1947–49, Indian Parliament, 1950–52; Indian Delegation to Gen. Assembly of UN, 1951; Indian Parliament (Lok Sabha), 1952–57; (Rajya Sabha) 1964–70; Govt of India's Commn of Inquiry on Communal Disturbances, 1967–69. Chm., Associated Journals Ltd, 1952–77. Vice-Chancellor, Aligarh Muslim University, 1956–62. Leader, Good Will Mission to 9 Afro-Asian countries, 1964; Leader, Cultural Delegn to participate in Afghan Independence Week celebrations, 1965. Trustee: HEH the Nizam's Trusts, 1962–; Youth Hostels Assoc. of India, 1970–. Member: Governing Body, Dr Zakir Husain Coll., New Delhi, 1974–; Ct, Aligarh Muslim Univ., 1983–. DLitt *hc* Aligarh 1964; Kanpur, 1974. *Address:* Zaidi Villa, Jamianagar, New Delhi, India. *T:* 631648.

Died 29 March 1992.

ZETTERLING, Mai Elizabeth; actress, films and stage; film director; writer; *b* 24 May 1925; *d* of Joel and Lina Zetterling; *m* 1st, 1944, Tutte Lemkow; one *s* one *d*; 2nd, 1958, David John Hughes (marr. diss. 1977). *Educ:* Stockholm, Sweden. Graduate of Royal Theatre School of Drama, Stockholm. First appeared as Cecilia in Midsummer Dream in the Workhouse, Blanche Theatre, Stockholm, Oct. 1941; stage successes (all at Royal Theatre, Stockholm) include: Janet in St Mark's Eve; Agnes in The Beautiful People; Brigid in Shadow and Substance; Maria in Twelfth Night; Nerissa in Merchant of Venice; Electra in Les Mouches; Adela in House of Bernarda; first appearance in London, as Hedwig in The Wild Duck, St Martin's, Nov. 1948; subsequently Nina in The Seagull, Lyric, Hammersmith, and St James's, 1949; Eurydice in Point of Departure, Lyric, Hammersmith and Duke of York's, 1950; Karen in The Trap, Duke of York's, 1952; Nora Helmer in A Doll's House, Lyric, Hammersmith, 1953; Poppy in The Count of Clérambard, Garrick, 1955; Thérèse Tard in Restless Heart, St James's, 1957; Tekla in Creditors, Lyric, Hammersmith, 1959, etc. *Swedish films* include: Frenzy, Iris, Rain Follows Dew, Music in the Dark, A Doll's House, Swinging on a Rainbow. *English films* include: Frieda, The Bad Lord Byron, Quartet, Portrait from Life, Lost People, Blackmailed, Hell is Sold Out, Tall Headlines, Desperate Moment, Faces in the Dark, Offbeat, The Main Attraction, Only Two Can Play, Hidden Agenda. *United States films* include: Knock on Wood, Prize of Gold, and Seven Waves Away. Director of documentary films for BBC; Dir and Prod and co-writer with David Hughes of short film The War Game; 1st Award at Venice for Narrative Shorts, 1963; Director: Swedish full-length films, Alskande Par, (Eng.) Loving Couples, 1965; Night Games, 1966; Dr Glas, 1968; Flickorna, (Eng.) The Girls, 1968; Sunday Pursuit, 1992; Writer and Director: Visions of Eight (Olympics film), USA, 1972; Vincent the Dutchman, (award 1973); We Have Many Names (and actress), Sweden, 1975; The Moon is a Green Cheese, Sweden, 1976; The Native Squatter (for Canadian TV), Sweden,

1977; Lady Policeman (Granada TV documentary), 1979; Of Seals and Men (with Greenland trade dept), 1979; Love, Canada, 1980; Love and Marriage (Canadian TV documentary); (dir and co-writer) Scrubbers, 1981 (feature film, England); Amorosa (feature film, Sweden), 1989; The Stuff of Madness, 1991; starred in film, The Witches, 1990. Dir and Deviser, Playthings, Vienna English Theatre, New Half Moon Theatre, 1980. *Publications:* The Cat's Tale (with David Hughes), 1965; Night Games (novel), 1966; Shadow of the Sun (short stories), 1975; Bird of Passage (novel), 1976; Rains Hat (children's book), 1979; Ice Island (novel), 1979; All Those Tomorrows (autobiog.), 1985. *Recreations:* gardening, cooking, philosophical, alchemy. *Address:* c/o Joyce Edwards, 275 Kennington Road, SE11 6BY.

Died 17 March 1994.

ZSÖGÖD, Géza Benjamin G.; *see* Grosschmid-Zsögöd.

ZUCKERMAN, Baron *cr* 1971 (Life Peer), of Burnham Thorpe, Norfolk; **Solly Zuckerman,** OM 1968; KCB 1964 (CB 1946); Kt 1956; MA, MD, DSc; MRCS, FRCP; FRS 1943, FIBiol; Hon. FRCS, Hon. FPS; President, British Industrial Biological Research Association, since 1974; *b* Cape Town, 30 May 1904; *s* of Moses Zuckerman; *m* 1939, Lady Joan Rufus Isaacs, *er d* of 2nd Marquess of Reading; one *s* (one *d* decd). *Educ:* S African College Sch.; Univ. of Cape Town (Libermann Scholar); University Coll. Hosp., London (Goldsmid Exhibnr). Demonstrator of Anatomy, Univ. of Cape Town, 1923–25; Union Res. Scholar, 1925; Res. Anatomist to Zoological Soc. of London and Demonstrator of Anatomy, UCL, 1928–32; Res. Associate and Rockefeller Res. Fellow, Yale Univ., 1933–34; Beit Meml Res. Fellow, 1934–37, Univ. Demonstrator and Lectr in Human Anatomy, 1934–45, Oxford Univ.; William Julius Mickle Fellow, Univ. of London, 1935; Hunterian Prof., Royal Coll. of Surgeons, 1937; Sands Cox Prof. of Anatomy, Univ. of Birmingham, 1943–68, then Prof. Emeritus; Professor-at-Large, Univ. of E Anglia, 1969–74, then Prof. Emeritus. Visitor, Bedford Coll., 1968–85 (Hon. Fellow, 1989). Scientific Adviser, Combined Operations HQ; Scientific Advr on planning, AEAF, MAAF, SHAEF, 1939–46 (Gp Capt. (Hon.) RAF, 1943–46). Member: Min. of Works Sci. Cttee, 1945–47; Cttee on Future Sci. Policy (Barlow Cttee), 1946–48; Min. of Fuel and Power Sci. Adv. Cttee, 1948–55; Associate Mem., Ordnance Bd, 1947–69 (latterly Associate Mem. Emeritus); Dep. Chm., Adv. Council on Sci. Policy, 1948–64; Mem., Agricl Res. Council, 1949–59; Chairman: Cttee on Sci. Manpower, 1950–64; Natural Resources (Technical) Cttee, 1951–64; UK Delegate, NATO Science Cttee, 1957–66; Mem., BBC Gen. Adv. Council, 1957–62; Chairman: Cttee on Management and Control of Research and Develt, 1958–61; Defence Research Policy Cttee, 1960–64; Chief Scientific Adviser: to Sec. of State for Defence, 1960–66; to HM Govt, 1964–71; Chm., Central Adv. Cttee for Science and Technology, 1965–70; UK Delegate on UN disarmament working gps, 1966–71; Trustee, British Museum (Natural History), 1967–77; Chm., Hosp. Sci. and Tech. Services Cttee, 1967–68; Mem., Royal Commn on Environmental Pollution, 1970–74; Chm., Commn on Mining and the Environment, 1971–72; Mem., WHO Adv. Cttee on Med. Research, 1973–77. President: Parly and Sci. Cttee, 1973–76; Assoc., of Learned and Professional

Soc. Publishers, 1973–77; Fauna Preservation Soc., 1974–81; Zoological Soc. of London, 1977–84 (Hon. Sec., 1955–77; Hon. Fellow, 1984); Bath Inst. of Med. Engrg, 1980–. Lectures: Gregynog, UC Wales, 1956; Mason, Univ. of Birmingham, 1957; Caltech Commencement, 1959; Lees Knowles, Cambridge, 1965; Maurice Lubbock, Oxford, 1967; Maurice Bloch, Glasgow, 1969; Trueman Wood, RSA, 1969; Compton, MIT, 1972; Edwin Stevens, RSocMed, 1974; Romanes, Oxford, 1975; Rhodes, S Africa, 1975; Jubilee, Imperial Coll., 1982; E. A. Lane, Clare Coll., Cambridge, 1983; Keith Morden Meml, Portland State Univ., 1985. Fellow, University College, London; Fellow Commoner, Christ's College, Cambridge. Hon. Member: Academia das Ciencias, Lisboa; Anatomical Soc.; Physiological Soc.; Soc. for Endocrinology; Foreign Member: Amer. Philosophical Soc., Amer. Acad. of Arts and Sciences. Dr *hc* Bordeaux, 1961; Hon. DSc: Sussex, 1963; Jacksonville, USA, 1964; Bradford, 1966; Hull, 1977; Columbia, USA, 1977; East Anglia, 1980; Reading, 1984; Hon. LLD: Birmingham, 1970; St Andrews, 1980. Gold Medal, Zoological Soc. of London, 1971. Medal of Freedom with Silver Palm (USA); Chevalier de la Lègion d'Honneur. *Publications:* The Social Life of Monkeys and Apes, 1932, 2nd edn 1981; Functional Affinities of Man, Monkeys and Apes, 1933; (ed, anonymous) Science in War, 1940; A New System of Anatomy, 1961, 2nd edn, 1981; (ed) The Ovary, 2 vols, 1962, 2nd edn 1977; Scientists and War, 1966; Beyond the Ivory Tower, 1970; (ed) Great Zoos of the World, 1980; Science Advisers, Scientific Advisers and Nuclear Weapons, 1980; Nuclear Illusion and Reality, 1982; Star Wars in a Nuclear World, 1986; *autobiography:* From Apes to Warlords, 1978; Monkeys, Men and Missiles, 1988; Six Men out of the Ordinary, 1992; contribs to scientific jls since 1925. *Address:* University of East Anglia, Norwich NR4 7TJ. *Clubs:* Beefsteak, Brooks's.

Died 1 April 1993.

ZUNTZ, Prof. Günther, DrPhil (Marburg); FBA 1956; Emeritus Professor, Manchester University; Professor of Hellenistic Greek, 1963–69; *b* 28 Jan. 1902; *s* of Dr Leo Zuntz and Edith (*née* Bähring); *m* 1947, Mary Alyson Garratt; two *s* one *d*, and one *s* two *d* by previous marriage. *Educ:* Bismarck-Gymnasium, Berlin-Wilmersdorf; Berlin,

Marburg, Göttingen and Graz Universities. Teacher, Odenwaldschule, 1924–26; Teacher, Marburg Gymnasium and Kassel Gymnasium, 1926–32; worked for Monumenta Musicae Byzantinae, in Copenhagen, 1935–39, in Oxford, 1939–47; Librarian, Mansfield College, Oxford, 1944–47; Senior Lecturer, Manchester University, 1947–55 (Reader, 1955–63). Corresponding Member: Oesterreich. Akad. der Wissenschaften, 1974; Heidelberger Akademie der Wissenschaften, 1985. Dr phil *hc* Tübingen, 1983. *Publications:* Hölderlins Pindar-Übersetzung, 1928; (with C. Höeg) Prophetologium, i-vi, 1939–71; The Ancestry of the Harklean New Testament, 1945; The Text of the Epistles, 1953; The Political Plays of Euripides, 1955, corrected repr., 1963; The Transmission of the Plays of Euripides, 1965; Persephone, 1971; Opuscula Selecta, 1972; Ein griechischer Lehrgang, 3 vols, 1983, rev. edn 1991 (trans. A Greek Course, 1992); Drei Kapitel zur Griechischen Metrik, 1984; Aion, Gott des Römerreichs, 1989; articles in many learned journals. *Recreation:* music. *Address:* 1 Humberstone Road, Cambridge CB4 1JD. *T:* Cambridge (0223) 357789.

Died 3 April 1992.

ZURENUO, Rt Rev. Sir Zurewe (Kamong), Kt 1981; OBE 1971; Head Bishop of Evangelical Lutheran Church of Papua New Guinea, 1973–82; *b* 5 July 1920; *s* of Zurenuo and Kbasung (previously the people took only one name and were known by none other); *m* 1941, Eleju; two *s* three *d* (and one *s* decd). *Educ:* Lutheran Mission schools (8 years in formal schools and 2 years teacher trng). Began teaching in Lutheran Schools, 1939, interrupted by illness, 1946; also did pastoral work; became Church Secretary of Sattelberg Circuit of Lutheran Church, 1953, and was elected General Secretary of Evangelical Lutheran Church of New Guinea, 1962; ordained, 1966; instrumental in leading the church from mission status to indigenous church status; played a leading role in writing the constitution of the church; active in community affairs and inter-church relations; Chairman, Melanesian Council of Churches, 1970–73; established Lae City Christian Council, 1972 (Chm., 1972–82). *Address:* Evangelical Lutheran Church of Papua New Guinea, PO Box 80, Lae, Papua New Guinea.

Died 20 Aug. 1994.